UPFRONT

Colour pages giving you
information about this guide and
how to get the best out of it.

PLACES TO STAY

Hotels and guesthouses
listed alphabetically by
town within England's
12 tourist regions.

INFORMATION PAGES

Lots of useful information to help
you choose the right place to stay.

INDEXES

KEY TO SYMBOLS

The fold-out back cover gives a
convenient key to all the symbols
used in this guide.

1

WELCOME TO THE GUIDE

THIS 'WHERE TO STAY' GUIDE *is designed to give you all the information you need to help you find accommodation in England in the right place, at the right price and with the facilities and services that are right for you.*

WHATEVER YOUR REASON *for staying away from home — holiday, shopping trip, visiting friends or relatives — you're sure to find in this guide accommodation that suits you best.*

AND TO HELP *in your selection, most of the accommodation entries in this guide show their national Crown ratings awarded by the Tourist Board (see pages 4-5).*

A UNIQUE *and helpful feature of this 'Where to Stay' guide is that all the essential information you need is presented in a straightforward and easy-to-read style, along with a brief description of the establishment.*

SYMBOLS *are used only to give you all the very detailed — but perhaps necessary — information about additional services and facilities. But there's no need to flick back and forth between pages to find out what all the symbols mean — just fold out the back cover and you can check them as you go.*

THIS GUIDE ALSO CONTAINS *full-colour maps (towards the back), which not only pinpoint all those cities, towns and villages with accommodation*

listings, but are also useful as route maps. They show major towns, motorways, main 'A' roads, airports, towns with BR InterCity stations, main ferry routes, and much, much more.

ALSO AT THE BACK *is a comprehensive town index to make it easy for you to check out what accommodation is available in a particular place.*

AND THERE'S MORE! *Each of the 12 regional sections features an introduction and map to the region, suggests places to visit and gives details of major events through the year. Throughout the guide you'll also find thumbnail town descriptions to give you a quick picture of each place.*

TO COMPLETE *the 'Where to Stay' package you'll find the Information Pages (starting on page 529) full of useful advice on such things as booking, cancellation, accommodation for physically disabled people, complaints, etc.*

'WHERE TO STAY' IS A SERIES OF FOUR GUIDES, ALL AVAILABLE FROM YOUR LOCAL BOOKSHOP: HOTELS & GUESTHOUSES IN ENGLAND £7.95 BED & BREAKFAST, FARMHOUSES, INNS & HOSTELS IN ENGLAND £6.95 SELF-CATERING HOLIDAY HOMES IN ENGLAND £4.95 CAMPING AND CARAVAN PARKS IN BRITAIN £5.50

SURE SIGN OF WHERE TO STAY

WHEN YOU SEE *the Crown or 'Listed' sign at a hotel, guesthouse, farmhouse, inn or B&B or in their advertising you can be confident that the establishment has been inspected and found to meet Tourist Board standards for facilities and services.*

OVER 17,000 PLACES *throughout England, Scotland and Wales now offer the reassurance of a national Crown rating — and the number grows daily.*

TO HELP YOU FIND *accommodation that offers even higher standards than those required for a simple Crown rating, the Tourist Boards have introduced three levels of quality grading, using the terms* **APPROVED, COMMENDED** *and* **HIGHLY COMMENDED.** *Establishments that apply for a quality grading are subject to a more rigorous inspection, which takes into account such important aspects as warmth of welcome, atmosphere and efficiency of service as well as the quality of furnishings, fitments and equipment. If no grade is shown, you can still expect high standards of cleanliness and service.*

Listed
Clean and comfortable accommodation, but the range of facilities and services may be limited.

 Accommodation with additional facilities, including washbasins and chairs in all bedrooms and use of a telephone.

  A wider range of facilities and services, including morning tea and calls, bedside lights, colour TV in lounge or bedrooms, assistance with luggage.

   At least one-third of the bedrooms with ensuite WC and bath or shower, plus easy chair and full-length mirror. Shoe cleaning facilities and hairdryers available. Hot evening meals available.

    At least three-quarters of the bedrooms with ensuite WC and bath or shower, plus colour TV, radio and telephone. 24-hour access, lounge service until midnight and last orders for evening meals 20.30hrs or later.

     All bedrooms with ensuite WC, bath and shower. A wide range of facilities and services, including room service, all-night lounge service and laundry service. Restaurant open for breakfast, lunch and dinner.

A MORE DETAILED EXPLANATION OF THE NATIONAL CROWN SCHEME IS GIVEN ON PAGE 536.

A LOOK AT SOME OF THE BEST

THE FOLLOWING *hotels and guesthouses, included in this 'Where to Stay' guide, have achieved the distinction of a* **HIGHLY COMMENDED** *grade for the exceptionally high quality standard of the facilities and services they provide.*

USE THE TOWN INDEX *on page 577 to find page numbers for the full entries.*

Albright Hussey Hotel & Restaurant, Shrewsbury, Shropshire

Audley House, Bath, Avon

Bank House, Castle Bytham, Lincolnshire

The Bel Alp House Country Hotel, Haytor, Devon

Birchley, Biddenden, Kent

Boscundle Manor, St. Austell, Cornwall

Broadview, Crewkerne, Somerset

Brockencote Hall, Kidderminster, Hereford & Worcester

BUCKLAND MANOR

Brookfield on Longhill, Buxton, Derbyshire

Buckland Manor, Buckland, Gloucestershire

Burgoyne Hotel, Reeth, N. Yorkshire

Buxted Park, Uckfield, E. Sussex

Castle Hotel, Taunton, Somerset

Chester Grosvenor, Chester, Cheshire

The Churchill, London W1 (Central London 1)

Combe Grove Manor Hotel & Country Club, Bath, Avon

CASTLE HOTEL

Coniston Lodge, Coniston, Cumbria

Cotswold House Hotel & Restaurant, Chipping Campden, Gloucestershire

Crit Hall, Benenden, Kent

Devonshire Arms Country House Hotel, Bolton Abbey, N. Yorkshire

Ettington Park Hotel, Stratford-upon-Avon, Warwickshire

Garden Hotel & Restaurant, Faversham, Kent

Gilpin Lodge Country House Hotel & Restaurant, Windermere, Cumbria

Goodwood Park Hotel, Golf & Country Club, Goodwood, W. Sussex

Grange Hotel, York, N. Yorkshire

Haleys Hotel & Restaurant, Leeds, W. Yorkshire

Hall House, Hertford, Hertfordshire

Hanbury Manor, Ware, Hertfordshire

Hartwell House, Aylesbury, Buckinghamshire

Hipping Hall, Kirkby Lonsdale, Cumbria

Holly Lodge, Bath, Avon

Linden Hall Hotel, Longhorsley, Northumberland

London Hilton on Park Lane, London W1 (Central London 1)

Manor House, Castle Combe, Wiltshire

Merewood Country House Hotel, Windermere, Cumbria

Newbridge House, Bath, Avon

Norfolk Royale Hotel, Bournemouth, Dorset

The Old Plough, Retford, Nottinghamshire

The Old Rectory, Broadway, Hereford & Worcester

Old Vicarage Hotel, Bridgnorth, Shropshire

Parkside House, Hastings, E. Sussex

Pickett Howe, Buttermere, Cumbria

Pontlands Park Country Hotel & Restaurant, Great Baddow, Essex

Pool Court Restaurant, Pool, W. Yorkshire

The Priory Hotel, Wareham, Dorset

Redworth Hall, Newton Aycliffe, Co. Durham

Hotel Riviera, Sidmouth, Devon

Royal Crescent Hotel, Bath, Avon

Severn Lodge, Ironbridge, Shropshire

Stakis Keswick Lodore Swiss Hotel, Keswick, Cumbria

The Steppes, Ullingswick, Hereford & Worcester

Stock Hill House Hotel & Restaurant, Gillingham, Dorset

Swinside Lodge, Keswick, Cumbria

Tavern House, Tetbury, Gloucestershire

Waren House Hotel, Bamburgh, Northumberland

Wharton Lodge Country House Hotel & Restaurant, Ross-on-Wye, Hereford & Worcester

Whites Hotel, London W2 (Central London 4)

Winteringham Fields, Winteringham, Humberside

Withenfield, Leominster, Hereford & Worcester

Wood Hall Hotel, Wetherby, W. Yorkshire

CHESTER GROSVENOR

WAREN HOUSE HOTEL

7

FINDING A PLACE TO STAY

THIS 'WHERE TO STAY' GUIDE *will make it easy for you to find accommodation to suit your mood and your pocket. The content has been structured to enable you to find a place to stay even if you have only a general idea of the area you are planning to visit. Just follow the notes below and you'll soon find accommodation that's right for you.*

THE MAIN BODY OF THIS GUIDE *is divided into 12 sections corresponding to England's tourist regions. Each regional section begins with a location map and an introduction with details of attractions and events.*

THE REGION'S *cities, towns and villages with their accommodation are then listed alphabetically. Accompanying each place name is a map reference which refers to the colour maps towards the back of the guide. This enables you to pinpoint the exact location.*

KINGSTON-UPON-HULL

Humberside
Map ref 4D1

Busy seaport with a modern city centre and deep-sea fishing base at junction of the Rivers Hull and Humber founded by Cistercian monks in 12th C. Maritime traditions in the town, docks and the museum, and the home of William Wilberforce, the slavery abolitionist, whose house is now a museum. The world's longest single span suspension bridge crosses the Humber 5 miles west.
Tourist Information Centre
☎ *(0482) 223344, 223559 & 702118*

THERE IS A COMPLETE *town index at the back which lists all the places with accommodation featured in the guide.*

IF YOU ALREADY KNOW *the name of the town in which you wish to stay, simply use the town index to find the* relevant page number. If you are touring or only know the general area in which you wish to stay, look at the colour maps (which pinpoint all the places with accommodation listed in the guide) to find place names in the area and then refer to the town index for page numbers.

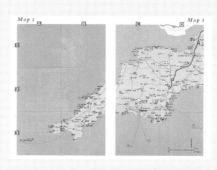

ACCOMMODATION INFORMATION has been provided by the proprietors of the establishments. Some information is represented by symbols and you will find a key to these inside the back cover flap.

CHANGES may have occurred since the guide went to press or may occur during 1992 — so please check any aspects which are important to you before booking. We also advise you to read the Information Pages towards the back of the guide, particularly the section on cancellations.

ENQUIRY COUPONS are included at the back of the guide. One type will help you when contacting establishments about accommodation; the other can be used to request information from advertisers.

THE TOURIST REGIONS

ENGLAND IS DIVIDED *into 12 tourist regions, each of which has its own section in this guide. The regions are shown on the map and also listed opposite together with an index which identifies the region in which each county is located.*

COLOUR MAPS *showing all the places with accommodation listed in this guide and an index to the place names can be found towards the back.*

NORTHUMBRIA

CUMBRIA

YORKSHIRE & HUMBERSIDE

NORTH WEST

EAST MIDLANDS

HEART OF ENGLAND

EAST ANGLIA

THAMES & CHILTERNS

LONDON

SOUTH OF ENGLAND

SOUTH EAST ENGLAND

WEST COUNTRY

COUNTY INDEX

USE YOUR *i*'S

WHEN IT COMES to your next English break, the first stage of your journey could be closer than you think. You've probably got a Tourist Information Centre nearby. But you might not

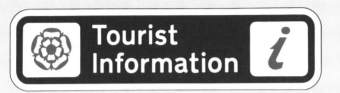

have realised that it's there to serve the local community — as well as visitors.

SO MAKE US your first stop. We'll be happy to help you, wherever you're heading.

MANY INFORMATION CENTRES can provide you with maps and guides, helping you plan well in advance. And sometimes it's even  possible for us to book your accommodation, too.

A VISIT to your nearest Information Centre can pay off in other ways as well. We can point you in the right direction when it comes to finding out about all the special events which are happening in the local region.

IN FACT, we can give you details of places to visit within easy reach...and perhaps tempt you to plan a day trip or weekend

away.

ACROSS THE COUNTRY, there are more than 600 Information Centres to choose from. So you're never far away. You'll find the address of your nearest Tourist Information Centre in your local Phone Book.

SURE SIGNS

OF WHERE TO STAY

Throughout Britain, the tourist boards now inspect over 30,000 places to stay, every year, to help you find the ones that suit you best.

 Looking for a hotel, guesthouse, inn, B&B or farmhouse? Look for the **CROWN**. The classifications: 'Listed', and then **ONE to FIVE CROWN,** tell you the range of facilities and services you can expect. The more Crowns, the wider the range.

Looking for a self-catering holiday home? Look for the **KEY**. The classifications: **ONE to FIVE KEY,** tell you the range of facilities and equipment you can expect. The more Keys, the wider the range.

THE GRADES: **APPROVED, COMMENDED or HIGHLY COMMENDED**, whether alongside the **CROWNS** or the **KEYS**, indicate the quality standard of what is provided. If no grade is shown, you can still expect a high standard of cleanliness.

Looking for a holiday caravan, chalet or camping park? Look for the **Q** symbol. The more ✓s in the Q (from one to five), the higher the quality standard of what is provided.

English Tourist Board

We've checked them out before you check in!

More detailed information on the **CROWNS**, the **KEYS** and the **Q** is given in free *SURE SIGN* leaflets, available at any Tourist Information Centre

13

A RICH MIX *of pageantry, history, culture and tradition — plus the variety and vitality of a modern capital city. Top shops in the West End, restaurants catering for every taste and an electric nightlife of theatres, cinemas, pubs and clubs. There are museums, galleries and parks galore plus the new visitor attractions — such as the Covent Garden area, revitalised Docklands and the Barbican. Don't forget, also, the outer "villages": Richmond, Greenwich, Hampstead to name but a few. London: always changing, always something new and always worth a visit at any time of the year.*

WHERE TO GO, WHAT TO SEE

HMS Belfast
Morgans Lane, Tooley Street,
London SE1 2JH
☎ 071-407 6434
11,500-tonne World War II cruiser, now a floating naval museum, with 7 decks to explore. Many naval exhibits.

British Museum
Great Russell Street, London
WC1B 3DG
☎ 071-636 1555
One of the greatest museums in the world, showing the works of man from all over the world from prehistoric to comparatively modern times.

Cabinet War Rooms
Clive Steps, King Charles
Street, London SW1A 2AQ
☎ 071-930 6961
Suite of 21 historic rooms, including Cabinet room, transatlantic telephone room, map room and Prime Minister's room. Were in operational use 1939–1945.

Design Museum
Butler's Wharf, Shad Thames,
London SE1 2YD
☎ 071-403 6933

World's first museum to analyse the past, present and future of mass-produced consumer goods and how design contributes to the quality of life.

Dickens House
48 Doughty Street, London
WC1N 2LF
☎ 071-405 2127
Letters, pictures, first editions, furniture, memorabilia, restored rooms.

Guinness World of Records
The Trocadero, Piccadilly,
London W1V 7FD
☎ 071-439 7331

Exhibition using models, videos, computers and electronic displays to bring to life the Guinness Book of Records.

Imperial War Museum
Lambeth Road, London
SE1 6HZ
☎ 071-416 5000
Illustrates and records all aspects of World Wars I and II and other conflicts involving Britain and the Commonwealth since 1914. Blitz Experience, Operation Jericho.

**Kensington Palace
State Apartments**
Kensington Gardens, London
W8 4PX
☎ 071-937 9561
Furniture from the Stuart-Hanoverian periods, 3 rooms from the Victorian era. Works of art from the royal collection, court dress collection.

**Kenwood House
(Iveagh Bequest)**
Hampstead Lane, London
NW3 7JR
☎ 081-348 1286
Collection of English and foreign paintings. Works by Vermeer, Rembrandt, Gainsborough and Reynolds. Hull Grundy collection of jewellery.

Kew Bridge Steam Museum
Green Dragon Lane, Brentford,
Middlesex TW8 0EN
☎ 081-568 4757
Victorian waterworks housing massive steam-powered pumping engines. Steam railway, water history. Tea room, shop.

London Dungeon
28–34 Tooley Street, London
SE1 2SZ
☎ 071-403 0606
World's first medieval horror museum. Two major shows — "The Great Fire of London" and "The Theatre of the Guillotine".

14

London Planetarium

Marylebone Road, London
NW1 5LR
☎ 071-486 1121
*Space Trail and Star Shows. No
children under 5 please.*

London Toy and Model Museum

21 – 23 Craven Hill, London
W2 3EN
☎ 071-262 9450/7905
*One of the most extensive
collections of commercially-
made toys and models in
Europe, dating from 1850
onwards – including trains,
cars, planes, nursery toys.
Bookshop.*

Discover the secrets behind the making of Spitting Image

London Transport Museum

The Piazza, Covent Garden,
London WC2E 7BB
☎ 071-379 6344
*Horse buses, motor buses,
trolleybuses, trams and
underground trains. Unique
working displays, video
programmes and museum shop.*

William Morris Gallery

Lloyd Park, Forest Road,
Walthamstow, London E17 4PP
☎ 081-527 3782
*Mid-18th C house, home of
William Morris. Collection of
decorative art by Morris & Co
and The Century Guild.
Paintings and drawings by
pre-Raphaelites and
F. Brangwyn.*

Museum of London

150 London Wall, London
EC2Y 5HN
☎ 071-600 3699
*Galleries illustrating over 2,000
years of London's social history,
from prehistoric times to the
20th C.*

Museum of the Moving Image

South Bank, London SE1 8XT
☎ 071-928 3535
*Celebration of cinema and
television. 50 exhibition areas,
offering plenty of hands-on
participation, and a cast of
actors to tell visitors more.*

National Army Museum

Royal Hospital Road, Chelsea,
London SW3 4HT
☎ 071-730 0717
*The history of the British army
through 5 centuries from 1485,
the Indian army up to
independence in 1947 and
colonial land forces.*

National Maritime Museum

Romney Road, Greenwich,
London SE10 9NF
☎ 081-858 4422
*Britain's maritime heritage
illustrated through actual and
model ships, paintings, uniforms,
navigation and astronomy
instruments, archives and
photographs.*

Royal Air Force Museum

Grahame Park Way, Hendon,
London NW9 5LL
☎ 081-205 2266
*3 halls displaying almost 70
full-size aircraft. "Battle of
Britain Experience", flight
simulator, free film shows. Shop
and restaurant.*

Science Museum

Exhibition Road, South
Kensington, London SW7 2DD
☎ 071-938 8000
*National museum of science and
industry. Full-size replica of
Apollo II Lunar Lander, launch
pad. Wellcome Museum of the
History of Medicine.*

Spitting Image Rubberworks

Cubitts Yard, James Street,
Covent Garden, London
WC2E 8PA
☎ 071-240 0838
*12-minute show with Mrs
Thatcher, the Queen, etc, in the
form of a TV-style panel game.
Extensive talk with videos about
the making of Spitting Image.*

Joan Collins (right) with her wax portrait — on display in Superstars at Madame Tussauds

Thames Barrier Visitor Centre
Unity Way, Woolwich, London SE18 5NJ
☎ 081-854 1373
Two audio-visual exhibitions about the construction of the barrier and why it was needed to prevent flooding.

Tower Bridge
London SE1 2UP
☎ 071-403 3761
Video film of raising of bridge, museum with original steam-powered engines and walkway with panoramic views of London. Exhibition on history of bridge. Gift shop.

Tower Hill Pageant
1 Tower Hill Terrace, London EC3N 4EE
☎ 071-709 0081
Automatic vehicles transport visitors past tableaux depicting the history of the City and its port. Display of archaeological finds. Shop and restaurant.

Tower of London
Tower Hill, London EC3N 4AB
☎ 071-709 0765
Building spans 900 years of British history. Crown Jewels, regalia and coronation robes. Home of the Beefeaters and ravens.

Madame Tussauds
Marylebone Road, London NW1 5LR
☎ 071-935 6861
The Garden Party, 200 years of Madame Tussauds, Superstars, Grand Hall, Chamber of Horrors, café and gift shop.

Victoria and Albert Museum
Cromwell Road, South Kensington, London SW7 2RL
☎ 071-938 8500
Magnificent Victorian building. Fine and decorative arts from 15th – 20th C, jewellery, silver, textiles, fashions, ceramics.

Wimbledon Lawn Tennis Museum
All England Club, Church Road, Wimbledon, London SW19
☎ 081-946 6131
Exhibits include Victorian parlour, racket maker's workshop, costumes, trophies, equipment. Films of matches, shop.

MAKE A DATE FOR...

London International Boat Show
Earl's Court Exhibition Centre, Warwick Road, London SW5
2 – 12 January

Daily Mail Ideal Home Exhibition
Earl's Court Exhibition Centre, Warwick Road, London SW5
12 March – 5 April

London Marathon
Greenwich Park, London SE10, to Westminster Bridge, London SW1
12 April

Football Association Challenge Cup Final
Wembley Stadium, Wembley, Middlesex
9 May

Chelsea Flower Show
Royal Hospital, Chelsea, London SW3
19 – 22 May (Members only 19 – 20 May)

Trooping the Colour – the Queen's Official Birthday Parade
Horse Guards Parade, Whitehall, London SW1
13 June

Lawn Tennis Championships
All England Lawn Tennis and Croquet Club, Wimbledon, London SW19
22 June – 5 July

BBC Henry Wood Promenade Concerts
Royal Albert Hall, Kensington Gore, London SW7
17 July – 12 September

Lord Mayor's Procession and Show
The City, London EC2
14 November

Royal Smithfield Show and Agricultural Machinery Exhibition
Earl's Court Exhibition Centre, Warwick Road, London SW5
7 – 10 December

FIND OUT MORE

Further information about holidays and attractions in the London region is available from:
London Tourist Board and Convention Bureau
26 Grosvenor Gardens, London SW1W 0DU
☎ 071-730 3488

TOURIST INFORMATION

Tourist and leisure information can be obtained from Tourist Information Centres throughout England. Details of centres and other information services in Greater London are given below. The symbol 🛏 means that an accommodation booking service is provided.

TOURIST INFORMATION CENTRES

CENTRAL LONDON

Victoria Station, Forecourt, SW1 🛏
Monday – Saturday 0800 – 1900. Sunday 0800 – 1600.
The information centre on the station forecourt provides a London and Britain tourist information service, offers a hotel accommodation booking service, stocks free and saleable publications on Britain and London and sells theatre tickets, tourist tickets for bus and underground and tickets for sightseeing tours.

Liverpool Street Underground Station, EC2 🛏
Monday – Saturday 0900 – 1630. Sunday 0830 – 1530 (extended according to season).
The information centre at the main entrance from the station to the underground provides a London and Britain information service, offers a hotel accommodation booking service, stocks free and saleable publications on Britain and London and sells theatre tickets and tour and transport tickets.

British Travel Centre 🛏
12 Regent Street, Piccadilly Circus, SW1Y 4PQ
Monday – Friday 0900 – 1830. Saturday 0900 – 1700. Sunday 1000 – 1600. Reduced opening hours in winter.
Information on travel, accommodation, events and entertainment in England, Scotland, Wales and Ireland.

Booking service for rail, air, coach and car travel, sightseeing tours, theatre tickets and accommodation. Bureau de change, bookshop and gift shop.

Bloomsbury Tourist Information Centre 🛏
35 – 36 Woburn Place, WC1H 0JR
☎ 071-580 4599
Daily 0730 – 1930.
Information on the London area, free literature on London and England, tickets for sightseeing tours and an accommodation booking service.

Clerkenwell Heritage Centre 🛏
35 St. John's Square, EC1M 4DN
☎ 071-250 1039
Monday – Friday 1000 – 1730.
This centre offers information on Clerkenwell and the London Borough of Islington and provides an accommodation booking service.

Selfridges 🛏
Oxford Street, W1 (Basement Services Arcade) and
Harrods 🛏
Knightsbridge, SW1 (Basement Banking Hall)
Open during normal store hours, these centres supply tourist information, leaflets, useful publications, tourist tickets for bus and underground and sightseeing tours and provide an accommodation booking service.

GREATER LONDON

Heathrow Terminals 1, 2, 3 Underground Station Concourse (Heathrow Airport) 🛏
Daily 0830 – 1830.
This centre provides tourist information on London and Britain, offers a hotel accommodation booking service, stocks free and saleable publications and sells theatre tickets.

Croydon Tourist Information Centre
Katharine Street, Croydon, Surrey CR9 1ET
☎ 081-760 5630
Monday 0930 – 1900.
Tuesday – Friday 0930 – 1800.
Saturday 0900 – 1700.

Greenwich Tourist Information Centre 🚁
46 Greenwich Church Street, SE10 9BL
☎ 081-858 6376
Daily 1000 – 1300 and 1400 – 1700.

Harrow Tourist Information Centre
Civic Centre, Station Road, Harrow, Middlesex HA1 2UH
☎ 081-424 1103
Monday – Friday 0900 – 1700.

Hillingdon Tourist Information Centre
Central Library, High Street, Uxbridge, Middlesex
☎ Uxbridge (0895) 50706
Monday – Friday 0930 – 2000.
Saturday 0930 – 1700.

Hounslow Tourist Information Centre
Library Centre, The Treaty Centre, Hounslow High Street, Hounslow, Middlesex
☎ 081-570 0622
Monday, Wednesday 0930 – 1730. Tuesday, Thursday – Saturday 0930 – 2000.

Kingston upon Thames Tourist Information Centre
Heritage Centre, Fairfield West, Kingston upon Thames, Surrey KT1 2PS
☎ 081-546 5386
Monday, Thursday – Saturday 1000 – 1700.
Tuesday 1000 – 1900.

Lewisham Tourist Information Centre
Lewisham Library, Lewisham High Street, SE13 6LG
☎ 081-690 8325
Saturday, Monday 0930 – 1700. Tuesday, Thursday 0930 – 2000.
Friday 0930 – 1300.

Redbridge Tourist Information Centre
Town Hall, High Road, Ilford, Essex IG1 1DD
☎ 081-478 3020
Monday – Friday 0830 – 1700.

Richmond Tourist Information Centre 🚁
Old Town Hall, Whittaker Avenue, Richmond upon Thames, Surrey
☎ 081-940 9125
Monday – Friday 1000 – 1800.
Saturday 1000 – 1700.
Telephone for Sunday and Bank Holiday opening hours.

Tower Hamlets Tourist Information Centre
Mayfield House, Cambridge Heath Road, E2 9LJ
☎ 081-980 4831 ext. 5313/5
Monday – Friday 0900 – 1700.

Twickenham Tourist Information Centre
Civic Centre, York Street, Twickenham, Middlesex TW1 3BZ
☎ 081-891 1411
Monday – Friday 0900 – 1700.

TELEPHONE INFORMATION SERVICE

A telephone information service on Greater London is provided from Monday to Friday, 0900 – 1800, on 071-730 3488 (an automatic queueing system is in operation). A Riverboat Information Service operates on 071-730 4812.

HOTEL ACCOMMODATION SERVICE

The London Tourist Board and Convention Bureau helps visitors to find and book accommodation at a wide range of prices in hotels and guesthouses, including budget accommodation, throughout the Greater London area. Reservations are made with hotels which are members of LTB denoted in this guide with the symbol **M** by their name.

Reservations can be made by credit card holders via the telephone accommodation reservations service on 071-824 8844 by simply giving the reservations clerk your card details (Access or Visa) and room requirements. LTB takes an administrative booking fee. The service operates Monday – Friday 0900 – 1800.

Alternatively, LTB accepts reservation requests by post. Please write to the Accommodation Services Department at LTB's head office at 26 Grosvenor Gardens, London SW1W 0DU stating your requirements.

Reservations on arrival are handled at the Tourist Information Centres operated by LTB at Victoria Station forecourt, Heathrow Terminals 1, 2, 3 Underground Station Concourse, Liverpool Street Station, Harrods and Selfridges. Go to any of them on the day when you need accommodation. A communication charge and a refundable deposit are payable when making a reservation.

WHICH PART OF LONDON?

The majority of tourist accommodation is situated in Central London and is therefore very convenient for most of the city's attractions and night life.

However, there are many hotels in Outer London which provide other advantages, such as easier parking. In the 'Places to Stay' pages which follow, you will find accommodation listed under 5 Central London areas and 5 Outer London areas, as shown below. See also colour maps 6 and 7 at the back of this guide.

CENTRAL 1
(see page 22)
Covering West End, Piccadilly, Soho, Regent Street, Mayfair, Park Lane, Westminster, Victoria, Elephant and Castle, Whitehall.

CENTRAL 2
(see page 25)
Covering Knightsbridge, South Kensington, Chelsea, Earl's Court, Fulham.

CENTRAL 3
(see page 27)
Covering High Street Kensington, West Kensington, Holland Park, Notting Hill, Olympia, Hammersmith.

CENTRAL 4
(see page 29)
Covering Bayswater, Paddington, Maida Vale.

CENTRAL 5
(see page 32)
Covering King's Cross, St. Pancras, Euston, Bloomsbury, Kingsway, Marylebone, Regents Park, Leicester Square, Strand, Charing Cross, Fleet Street, Holborn, City.

EAST LONDON
(see page 34)
Covering the London boroughs of Barking, Hackney, Havering, Newham, Redbridge, Tower Hamlets, Waltham Forest.

NORTH LONDON
(see page 35)
Covering the London boroughs of Barnet, Brent, Camden, Enfield, Haringey, Harrow, Islington.

SOUTH EAST LONDON
(see page 38)
Covering the London boroughs of Bexley, Bromley, Croydon, Greenwich, Lewisham, Southwark.

SOUTH WEST LONDON
(see page 39)
Covering the London boroughs of Kingston upon Thames, Lambeth, Merton, Richmond upon Thames, Sutton, Wandsworth.

WEST LONDON
(see page 40)
Covering the London boroughs of Ealing, Hammersmith, Hillingdon, Hounslow, also London Airport (Heathrow).

London index

IF YOU ARE LOOKING *for accommodation in a particular establishment in London and you know its name, this index will give you the page number of the full entry in the guide.*

Use a coupon

When enquiring about accommodation you may find it helpful to use the booking enquiry coupons which can be found towards the end of the guide. These should be cut out and mailed direct to the establishments in which you are interested. Do remember to include your name and address.

I'M LOOKING FOR **STATUS** SYMBOLS

WHERE TO STAY

Key to symbols

Information about many of the services and facilities at establishments listed in this guide is given in the form of symbols. The key to these symbols is inside the back cover flap. You may find it helpful to keep the flap open when referring to the entry listings.

Places to stay

ACCOMMODATION ENTRIES in this regional section are listed under 5 Central London areas and 5 Outer London areas — shown on colour maps 6 and 7 towards the end of the guide. If you want to look up a particular establishment, use the index to establishments (pages 20 – 21) to find the page number.

THE SYMBOLS at the end of each accommodation entry give information about services and facilities. A 'key' to these symbols is inside the back cover flap, which can be kept open for easy reference.

CENTRAL LONDON 1

Covering West End, Piccadilly, Soho, Regent Street, Mayfair, Park Lane, Westminster, Victoria, Elephant and Castle, Whitehall. See colour map 6.

Alexander House Hotel
Listed
32 Hugh St., London
SW1 1RT
☎ 071-834 5320
Guesthouse with TV in bedrooms. Full English breakfast.
Bedrooms: 2 single, 3 double & 2 twin, 2 family rooms.
Bathrooms: 2 public.
Bed & breakfast: £18-£23 single, £26-£32 double.
⬛ symbols

Athenaeum Hotel ♨
116 Piccadilly, London
W1V 0BJ
☎ 071-499 3464 Telex 261589
⬛ Rank
On Piccadilly overlooking Green Park, well placed for the fashionable shopping areas of Knightsbridge and Bond Street.
Bedrooms: 16 single, 22 double & 52 twin, 22 family rooms.
Bathrooms: 112 private.
Bed & breakfast: £187.50-£205.85 single, £217.50-£238.70 double.
Lunch available.

> *The enquiry coupons at the back will help you when contacting proprietors.*

Evening meal 6pm (l.o. 10.30pm).
Credit: Access, Visa, C.Bl., Diners, Amex.
⬛ symbols

Bentinck House Hotel ♨
20 Bentinck St., London
W1M 5RL
☎ 071-935 9141
Fax 071-224 5903
Telex 8954111
Family-run bed and breakfast hotel in the heart of London's fashionable West End, close to Bond Street underground and Oxford Street.
Bedrooms: 8 single, 1 double & 5 twin, 3 family rooms.
Bathrooms: 9 private, 4 public.
Bed & breakfast: £33-£49 single, £55-£65 double.
Half board: £43-£59 daily.
Credit: Access, Visa, C.Bl., Diners, Amex.
⬛ symbols

Blandford Hotel
80 Chiltern St., London
W1M 1PS
☎ 071-486 3103 Telex 262594
Centrally located hotel, close to Baker Street underground station and Madame Tussauds. Harley Street and Oxford Street within walking distance.
Bedrooms: 9 single, 6 double & 13 twin, 5 family rooms.
Bathrooms: 33 private.
Bed & breakfast: from £60 single, from £77 double.
Credit: Access, Visa, Diners, Amex.
⬛ symbols

Britannia Inter-Continental Hotel ♨
Grosvenor Sq., London
W1A 3AN
☎ 071-629 9400 &
(Fax:) 071-629 7736
Telex 23941
In Grosvenor Square, Mayfair. The elegance of the Georgian facade is reflected in the stylish rooms and public areas.
Bedrooms: 29 single, 211 double & 70 twin, 16 family rooms.
Bathrooms: 326 private.
Bed & breakfast: £215-£250 single, £225-£260 double.
Half board: £230-£270 daily.
Lunch available.
Evening meal 6.30pm (l.o. 11.30pm).
Parking for 200.
Credit: Access, Visa, C.Bl., Diners, Amex.
⬛ symbols

Caswell Hotel
Listed
25 Gloucester St., London
SW1V 2DB
☎ 071-834 6345
Pleasant, family-run hotel, near Victoria coach and rail stations, yet in a quiet location.
Bedrooms: 1 single, 6 double & 6 twin, 5 family rooms.
Bathrooms: 7 private, 5 public.
Bed & breakfast: £24-£34 single, £33-£62 double.
⬛ symbols

Chesham House Hotel ♨
Listed
64-66 Ebury St., London
SW1W 9QD
☎ 071-730 8513 &
(Fax:) 071-730 3267
Telex 946797 PRONTO G CSP
Cheerful simplicity is the hallmark of this hotel, which is not far from Victoria.
Bedrooms: 5 single, 7 double & 8 twin, 3 family rooms.
Bathrooms: 6 public.
Bed & breakfast: £28-£30 single, £43-£45 double.
Credit: Access, Visa, Diners, Amex.
⬛ symbols

Chester House ♨
Listed
134 Ebury St., London
SW1W 9QQ
☎ 071-730 3632 & 071-824 8444 Fax: 071-824 8446
Small, friendly bed and breakfast close to Sloane Square and 10 minutes' walk from Harrods. Convenient for public transport.
Bedrooms: 3 single, 4 double & 5 twin, 2 family rooms.
Bathrooms: 4 private, 2 public.
Bed & breakfast: £27-£36 single, £40-£44 double.
Credit: Access, Visa, C.Bl., Diners, Amex.
⬛ symbols

> *Individual proprietors have supplied all details of accommodation. Although we do check for accuracy, we advise you to confirm prices and other information at the time of booking.*

The Churchill ♨

HIGHLY COMMENDED

30 Portman Sq., London
W1A 4ZX
☎ 071-486 5800 &
(Fax:) 071-935 0431
Telex 264831 CHURCH G
*Hotel in the heart of the West
End, specialising in providing a
highly personalised service.*
Bedrooms: 452 double.
Bathrooms: 452 private.
Bed & breakfast: from
£227.13 single, from £254.50
double.
Lunch available.
Evening meal 7pm (l.o.
12.45am).
Parking for 60.
Credit: Access, Visa, C.Bl.,
Diners, Amex.

Clifton Ford Hotel

Welbeck St., London
W1M 8DN
☎ 071-486 6600 Telex 22569
*Centrally located hotel in a
quiet Georgian street, offering
comfort and service.*
Bedrooms: 65 single,
81 double & 65 twin, 4 family
rooms.
Bathrooms: 215 private.
Bed & breakfast: £151.75-
£216.37 single, £180.12-
£227.12 double.
Half board: £111.56-£144.06
daily.
Lunch available.
Evening meal 6pm (l.o.
10pm).
Parking for 20.
Credit: Access, Visa, Diners,
Amex.

Collin House ♨

COMMENDED

104 Ebury St., London
SW1W 9QD
☎ 071-730 8031
*Convenient for Victoria rail,
underground and coach
stations. Ideal base for visiting
London and the surrounding
places of interest.*
Bedrooms: 3 single, 3 double
& 3 twin, 4 family rooms.
Bathrooms: 8 private,
3 public.
Bed & breakfast: £32-£34
single, £44-£54 double.

Ebury Court Hotel

COMMENDED

28 Ebury St., London
SW1W 0LU
☎ 071-730 8147

*Charming country house hotel
in Belgravia with restaurant.
Family owned and run for 54
years. Victoria station close by.*
Bedrooms: 20 single,
14 double & 12 twin, 3 family
rooms.
Bathrooms: 22 private,
10 public; 2 private showers.
Bed & breakfast: £70-£75
single, £120-£150 double.
Half board: £85-£120 daily.
Lunch available.
Evening meal 7pm (l.o.
11pm).
Credit: Access, Visa, Diners.

Eccleston Hotel ♨

Eccleston Sq., London
SW1V 1PS
☎ 071-834 8042
Telex 8955775
Ⓡ Friendly
*Centrally located within
minutes of Victoria railway
and coach stations. Conference
and banqueting facilities
available.*
Bedrooms: 43 single,
21 double & 45 twin, 6 family
rooms.
Bathrooms: 115 private,
5 public.
Bed & breakfast: £59.25-
£71.95 single, £77.50-£92.65
double.
Lunch available.
Evening meal 6pm (l.o.
9.45pm).
Credit: Access, Visa, Diners,
Amex.

Edward House Hotel

5 St. George's Drive, London
SW1V 4DP
☎ 071-834 5207 & 071-828
8456
Fax: 071-976 5428
*Near the National Express
coach station, 2 minutes from
Victoria underground and
mainline station. All rooms
have full central heating, TV,
tea making facilities and direct
dial telephone.*
Bedrooms: 2 single, 6 double
& 3 twin, 9 family rooms.
Bathrooms: 6 private,
3 public; 8 private showers.
Bed & breakfast: £25-£30
single, £32-£42 double.
Credit: Access, Visa, Amex.

The Edward Lear Hotel ♨

30 Seymour St., London
W1H 5WD
☎ 071-402 5401 &
(Fax:) 071-706 3766

*Family-run Georgian town
residence, with informal but
efficient atmosphere, in a
central location. 1 minute from
Oxford Street and Marble
Arch.*
Bedrooms: 14 single, 5 double
& 9 twin, 4 family rooms.
Bathrooms: 4 private,
7 public; 8 private showers.
Bed & breakfast: £37.50-£55
single, £49.50-£62.50 double.
Credit: Access, Visa.

Elizabeth Hotel ♨

37 Eccleston Sq., London
SW1V 1PB
☎ 071-828 6812
*Friendly, quiet hotel
overlooking lovely gardens of
stately residential square (circa
1835), close to Belgravia and
within 5 minutes' walk of
Victoria.*
Bedrooms: 8 single, 14 double
& 4 twin, 15 family rooms.
Bathrooms: 14 private,
6 public; 4 private showers.
Bed & breakfast: £33-£55
single, £51-£75 double.

⊕ Display advertisement
appears on page 44.

Georgian House Hotel ♨

87 Gloucester Pl., London
W1H 3PG
☎ 071-935 2211 &
(Fax:) 071-486 7535
Telex 266079 GLAD G
*Small comfortable hotel
providing personal service.
Newly refurbished rooms with
private facilities. Ideally
situated.*
Bedrooms: 4 single, 6 double
& 5 twin, 4 family rooms.
Bathrooms: 15 private;
4 private showers.
Bed & breakfast: £45-£50
single, £60-£65 double.
Credit: Access, Visa, Amex.

The Goring Hotel ♨

COMMENDED

15 Beeston Pl., Grosvenor
Gdns., London SW1W 0JW
☎ 071-834 8211 Telex 919166
*Family-owned hotel with
private garden, near
Buckingham Palace and royal
parks.*
Bedrooms: 35 single,
19 double & 20 twin, 10 family
rooms.
Bathrooms: 84 private.

Bed & breakfast: £125-£133
single, from £180 double.
Half board: from £150 daily.
Lunch available.
Evening meal 6pm (l.o.
10pm).
Parking for 7.
Credit: Access, Visa, C.Bl.,
Diners, Amex.

Hallam Hotel ♨

12 Hallam St., Portland Pl.,
London W1N 5LJ
☎ 071-580 1166 &
(Fax:) 071-323 4527
*Quiet, family-run hotel in the
heart of London's West End.
Close to shops, theatres and
main tourist attractions.*
Bedrooms: 13 single, 10 twin.
Bathrooms: 23 private.
Bed & breakfast: £55-£65
single, £78-£85 double.
Credit: Access, Visa, Diners,
Amex.

Hamilton House Hotel ♨

60 Warwick Way, London
SW1V 1SA
☎ 071-821 7113 & Fax
071-630 0806 Telex 28604 Ref
1502
*Hotel close to Victoria station
and the West End. Warm and
friendly atmosphere. Modern
decor. Satellite TV.
Comfortable family restaurant.*
Bedrooms: 20 double &
21 twin, 2 family rooms.
Bathrooms: 29 private,
8 public.
Bed & breakfast: £48-£58
single, £58-£70 double.
Lunch available.
Evening meal 5pm (l.o.
10pm).
Credit: Access, Visa.

Holly House Hotel ♨

Listed

20 Hugh St., Victoria,
London SW1V 1RP
☎ 071-834 5671
*Small private bed and
breakfast establishment with
colour TV in rooms. In the
heart of London, 2 minutes
from Victoria station.*
Bedrooms: 7 single, 6 double
& 8 twin, 5 family rooms.
Bathrooms: 1 private,
5 public.
Bed & breakfast: £22-£25
single, £32-£35 double.
Credit: Access, Visa, Diners,
Amex.

CENTRAL LONDON 1

Continued

Kenwood House Hotel ♨

114 Gloucester Pl., London
W1H 3DB
☎ 071-935 3473 & 9455 &
071-486 5007
Fax: 071-224 0582
Friendly, family-run hotel in a central location, with budget prices.
Bedrooms: 4 single, 2 double & 5 twin, 5 family rooms.
Bathrooms: 3 private,
4 public; 2 private showers.
Bed & breakfast: £20-£26 single, £35-£48 double.
Credit: Visa, Amex.
🅱 ⚿ ⬚ ⌂ 💺 📺 ◉ ▥ ✈ ♨ ♠

Kirness Hotel ♨

29 Belgrave Rd., Victoria,
London SW1V 1RB
☎ 071-834 0030
Small friendly guesthouse. All main European languages spoken. Suitable for students.
Bedrooms: 2 single, 1 double & 1 twin, 2 family rooms.
Bathrooms: 1 public;
6 private showers.
Bed & breakfast: £20-£25 single, £30-£35 double.
📺8 ⚿ ▮ ▥ ✈ ♠ ♨ SP Ⓣ

Knightsbridge Green Hotel ♨

♨♨ COMMENDED

159 Knightsbridge, London
SW1X 7PD
☎ 071-584 6274 & Fax
071-225 1635
Small family-owned and run hotel close to Harrods.
Bedrooms: 4 single, 6 double, 14 family rooms.
Bathrooms: 24 private.
Bed & breakfast: max. £91 single, max. £106 double.
Credit: Access, Visa, Amex.
🅱 ⚿ ⬚ ⚿ ▮ ▥ 💺 ▥ ✈ ♨ ♠

Lincoln House Hotel ♨

Listed APPROVED

33 Gloucester Pl., London
W1H 3PD
☎ 071-935 6238 & Fax
071-486 0166
Newly refurbished Georgian hotel, offering budget accommodation in the heart of London's West End. Close to theatres, nightlife and Oxford Street shops.
Bedrooms: 4 single, 9 double & 5 twin, 4 family rooms.
Bathrooms: 18 private,
2 public.
Bed & breakfast: £35-£45 single, £49-£59 double.

Evening meal 3.30pm (l.o.
11.30pm).
Credit: Access, Visa, Amex.
🅱 ▥ ⌂ 💺 ⚿ ▮ ⌂ 📺 ◉ ▥ ✈ ♨ ♨ SP ♨ 📺

London Hilton on Park Lane ♨

♨♨♨♨ HIGHLY COMMENDED

22 Park Lane, London
W1A 2HH
☎ 071-493 8000 Telex 24873
LONHIT G
Ⓒ Hilton
In the heart of Mayfair overlooking Hyde Park, Green Park and St James's Park. Convenient for Knightsbridge shops and theatreland. An ETB "5 Gold Crown" award hotel.
Bedrooms: 38 single,
197 double & 121 twin,
92 family rooms.
Bathrooms: 448 private.
Bed & breakfast: £203.28-£222.08 single, £284.35-£320.78 double.
Lunch available.
Evening meal 7pm (l.o.
midnight).
Parking for 350.
Credit: Access, Visa, C.Bl.,
Diners, Amex.
🅱 ⚿ ⬚ ▥ ⌂ ◉ ▥ ▥
▮ ⏻ ⚿ Ⓤ SP Ⓣ

London Mews Hilton ♨

Stanhope Row, Park Lane,
London W1Y 7HE
☎ 071-493 7222 Telex 24665
Ⓒ Hilton
Mayfair location, just off Park Lane. Near Oxford Street and Knightsbridge. Direct underground from Hyde Park Corner to Heathrow.
Bedrooms: 12 single,
30 double & 30 twin.
Bathrooms: 72 private.
Bed & breakfast: £138-£148 single, £164-£174 double.
Parking for 15.
Credit: Access, Visa, C.Bl.,
Diners, Amex.
🅱 ⚿ ⬚ ▥ ⚿ ▥ ✈ ⚿
◉ ▤ ▥ ▮ ⏻ ♨ SP Ⓣ

Luna House Hotel ♨

Listed

47 Belgrave Rd., London
SW1V 2BB
☎ 071-834 5897
Friendly, good value, bed and breakfast hotel. Within easy walking distance of Victoria rail, underground and coach stations. Opposite bus stop.
Bedrooms: 2 single, 7 double & 5 twin, 3 family rooms.
Bathrooms: 8 private,
2 public; 1 private shower.
Bed & breakfast: £17-£22 single, £28-£44 double.
🅱 ▥ ▥ ▥ 📺 ◉ ▥ ▤ ▮ ✈
OAP ♨ SP

Melita House Hotel ♨

♨♨

35 Charlwood St., London
SW1V 2DU
☎ 071-828 0471 & 071-834 1387
Fax: 071-630 8905
Family-run, budget bed and breakfast establishment with homely atmosphere. Centrally situated close to Victoria station.
Bedrooms: 3 single, 6 double & 5 twin, 2 family rooms.
Bathrooms: 10 private,
2 public; 4 private showers.
Bed & breakfast: £22-£30 single, £32-£45 double.
🅱 ⬚ ▥ ▥ 📺 ▥ ▤ ✈ ♨ ♨
Ⓣ

Palace Hotel ♨

31 Great Cumberland Pl.,
Marble Arch, London
W1H 7LF
☎ 071-262 5585 &
(Fax:) 071-706 2427
Telex 297989 PALACE G
Elegant hotel in Great Cumberland Place, one minute from Marble Arch, Hyde Park and Oxford Street.
Bedrooms: 10 double &
12 twin, 6 family rooms.
Bathrooms: 21 private,
3 public; 5 private showers.
Bed & breakfast: from £45 single, from £65 double.
Credit: Access, Visa, Diners, Amex.
🅱 ⚿ ⚿ ⬚ ▥ ⌂ 📺 ◉ ▮
▤ ▮ ✈ OAP ♨ SP Ⓣ

Prince Regent Hotel ♨

♨ APPROVED

37 Nottingham Pl., London
W1M 3FF
☎ 071-487 5153 & 071-935 4276
Fax: 071-224 1582
In the heart of London's West End yet in a dignified quiet position. Ideal for people coming to Harley Street hospitals and clinics. Near Regents Park and Baker Street underground stations.
Bedrooms: 4 single, 3 double & 4 twin, 9 family rooms.
Bathrooms: 20 private,
2 public.
Bed & breakfast: £40-£45 single, £60-£70 double.
Credit: Visa, Amex.
🅱 ⚿ ⚿ ⬚ ⚿ ▥ ✈ 📺 ◉
▮ ▤ ▮ ✈ ✈ OAP ♨ SP
♨ Ⓣ

Regency Hotel ♨

♨♨♨♨

19 Nottingham Pl., London
W1M 3FF
☎ 071-486 5347 &
(Fax:) 071-224 6057

Budget priced hotel with fully furnished and en-suite accommodation, in the heart of London's West End.
Bedrooms: 9 single, 7 double & 2 twin, 2 family rooms.
Bathrooms: 20 private.
Bed & breakfast: £40-£55 single, £55-£75 double.
Half board: £50-£65 daily.
Lunch available.
Evening meal 6pm (l.o.
8.30pm).
Credit: Access, Visa, Diners, Amex.
🅱 ⚿ ⚿ ⬚ ⬚ ▥ Ⓤ ▮ ▥
✈ ⌂ 📺 ◉ ▥ ▤ ▮ ✈ OAP
♨ SP Ⓣ

Richmond House Hotel

Listed

38b Charlwood St., Victoria,
London SW1V 2DX
☎ 071-834 4577
Small, family-run bed and breakfast guesthouse.
Bedrooms: 2 single, 2 double & 3 twin, 5 family rooms.
Bathrooms: 3 public.
Bed & breakfast: £22-£24 single, £36-£38 double.
Open February-November.
🅱 ⚿ ⬚ ⚿ Ⓤ ▥ ✈ ♨ 📺

Rubens Hotel ♨

39-41 Buckingham Palace
Rd., London SW1W 0PS
☎ 071-834 6600 Telex 916577
Traditional hotel opposite the Royal Mews of Buckingham Palace. Ideally placed for West End and Victoria.
Bedrooms: 32 single,
64 double & 83 twin, 9 family rooms.
Bathrooms: 188 private.
Bed & breakfast: £105.95-£123.95 single, £140.90-£155.90 double.
Lunch available.
Evening meal 6pm (l.o. 8pm).
Credit: Access, Visa, Diners, Amex.
🅱 ⚿ ⬚ ▥ ⚿ ▥ Ⓤ ✈ ▥
◉ ▤ ▥ ▮ ▮ ✈ ♨ SP Ⓣ

Scandic Crown Hotel ♨

♨♨♨♨

2 Bridge Pl., Victoria,
London SW1V 1QA
☎ 071-834 8123
Conveniently located in central London, this fully air-conditioned hotel has all modern amenities, including the intimate Gourmet restaurant, a coffee house, 3 bars and the Scandic Health and Leisure Centre. Conference facilities for up to 200.
Bedrooms: 22 single,
58 double & 125 twin,
5 family rooms.
Bathrooms: 210 private.
Bed & breakfast: £85-£123.50 single, £100-£154 double.

Lunch available.
Evening meal 6pm (l.o. 10.30pm).
Credit: Access, Visa, Diners, Amex.

🛇 📞 ⌨ 🖵 � 🅸 Ⓥ ✗ ●
✠ 🎴 🛏 🍽 🐾 🗙 💈 🎇 SP
Ⓣ

Sheraton Park Tower M
😊😊😊😊😊 COMMENDED

101 Knightsbridge, London
SW1X 7RN
☎ 071-235 8050 Telex 917222
Conveniently situated in the elite shopping area of Knightsbridge, 4 minutes from Harrods and opposite Hyde Park.
Bedrooms: 120 double & 175 twin.
Bathrooms: 295 private.
Bed & breakfast: £164.50-£270.50 single.
Lunch available.
Evening meal 6.30pm (l.o. 11.30pm).
Parking for 100.
Credit: Access, Visa, C.Bl., Diners, Amex.

🛇 📞 ⌨ 🖵 🅸 Ⓥ ✗ ● ✠
🎇 🛏 🍽 🗙 DAP 💈 SP
Ⓣ

Stakis London St. Ermin's Hotel M
😊😊😊

Caxton St., London
SW1H 0QW
☎ 071-222 7888 &
(Fax:) 071-222 6914
Telex 917731
Ⓒ Ⓡ Stakis
An elegant Edwardian property. Traditional furnishings add charm in a relaxing atmosphere. The terraced facade hides an efficient, recently refurbished hotel. Adjacent to St. James's Park underground. Half board rate based on a minimum 2 night stay.
Bedrooms: 83 single, 30 double & 125 twin, 52 family rooms.
Bathrooms: 290 private.
Bed & breakfast: £135-£165 single, £180-£215 double.
Half board: from £49 daily.
Lunch available.
Evening meal 6pm (l.o. 9.30pm).
Parking for 22.
Credit: Access, Visa, C.Bl., Diners, Amex.

🛇 📞 📞 ⌨ 🖵 🅸 Ⓥ ⊟
Ⓣ ● 📞 🎇 🛏 🍽 💈 DAP SP
🐾 Ⓣ

Wilbraham Hotel M
😊😊😊 APPROVED

1 Wilbraham Pl., Sloane St., London SW1X 9AE
☎ 071-730 8296 &
(Fax:) 071-730 6815

Victorian building in Belgravia. Excellent location for visitors to London.
Bedrooms: 13 single, 16 double & 23 twin, 6 family rooms.
Bathrooms: 38 private, 4 public.
Bed & breakfast: £48-£68 single, £68-£90 double.
Half board: £60-£80 daily.
Lunch available.
Evening meal 6pm (l.o. 9.45pm).

🛇 📞 📞 🅸 ♦ Ⓣ ● ⊟ 🎇
🛏 🗙 🎴

Windermere Hotel M
😊😊😊 COMMENDED

142-144 Warwick Way, Victoria, London SW1V 4JE
☎ 071-834 5163 & 5480 &
(Fax:) 071-630 8831
Telex 94017182 WIREG
Well-maintained small hotel with nicely equipped bedrooms and pretty breakfast room. Hospitable proprietors create a welcoming atmosphere.
Bedrooms: 2 single, 11 double & 6 twin, 5 family rooms.
Bathrooms: 20 private, 2 public.
Bed & breakfast: £38-£45 single, £39-£60 double.
Half board: £26-£41 daily.
Lunch available.
Evening meal 6pm (l.o. 9pm).

🛇 📞 📞 🖵 🅸 ♦ Ⓣ Ⓥ ● 🖵
🛏 🗙 DAP SP Ⓣ

Wyndham Hotel
Listed

30 Wyndham St., London
W1H 1DD
☎ 071-723 7204 & 9400
Small family-run bed and breakfast close to Baker Street and Marylebone stations. Well within walking distance of Oxford Street.
Bedrooms: 6 single, 2 double & 3 twin.
Bathrooms: 1 public; 10 private showers.
Bed & breakfast: £24-£26 single, £34-£36 double.

🛇 📞 🖵 ♦ UL CB 🛏 🛏 🗙
🎴 Ⓣ

CENTRAL LONDON 2

Covering Knightsbridge, South Kensington, Chelsea, Earl's Court, Fulham. See colour map 6.

Abcone Hotel M
😊😊😊 APPROVED

10 Ashburn Gdns., London, SW7 4DG
☎ 071-370 3383/4/5
Telex 926054 ABCONE G

Close to Gloucester Road underground and convenient for High Street Kensington, Knightsbridge, Olympia, Earl's Court, museums and Hyde Park.
Bedrooms: 11 single, 14 double & 8 twin, 3 family rooms.
Bathrooms: 27 private, 3 public.
Bed & breakfast: £35-£49 single, £48-£78 double.
Credit: Access, Visa, Diners, Amex.

🛇 📞 📞 ⌨ 🖵 UL CB 🛏 🛏
● 🎇 🛏 🍽 🗙 🎴 Ⓣ

Alexander Hotel
😊😊😊

9 Sumner Pl., London
SW7 3EE
☎ 071-581 1591 Telex 917133
Ⓒ Ⓡ Best Western
Small, Victorian terrace hotel ideally located in South Kensington for easy access to Knightsbridge, Hyde Park etc. Added attraction of small private conservatory.
Bedrooms: 5 single, 16 double & 15 twin, 1 family room.
Bathrooms: 37 private.
Bed & breakfast: from £77 single, £99-£143 double.
Lunch available.
Credit: Access, Visa, Diners, Amex.

🛇 📞 ⌨ 🖵 ♦ UL Ⓥ 🛏 ●
⊟ 🎇 🛏 DAP SP 🎴 Ⓣ

Amsterdam Hotel M
😊😊😊

7 Trebovir Rd., London
SW5 9LS
☎ 071-370 5084 &
(Fax:) 071-244 7608
Comfortable, attractively furnished rooms all with private bathroom, colour TV and direct dial telephone.
Bedrooms: 4 single, 8 double & 4 twin, 4 family rooms.
Bathrooms: 20 private, 1 public.
Bed & breakfast: £40-£42 single, £52-£54 double.
Credit: Access, Visa, Amex.

🛇 📞 📞 ⌨ 🖵 UL CB 🛏 ⊟
🎇 🛏 🗙 🛏 🐾 Ⓣ

Beaver Hotel M
57-59 Philbeach Gdns., London SW5 9ED
☎ 071-373 4553
In a quiet, tree-lined crescent of late Victorian terraced houses, close to Earl's Court Exhibition Centre and 10 minutes from the West End.
Bedrooms: 19 single, 7 double & 9 twin, 4 family rooms.
Bathrooms: 20 private, 9 public.

Bed & breakfast: £26-£44 single, £36-£55 double.
Parking for 23.
Credit: Access, Visa, Amex.

🛇 📞 📞 ⌨ 🖵 Ⓣ 🎇 🛏 Ⓣ

Blair House Hotel M
😊😊😊 APPROVED

34 Draycott Pl., London
SW3 2SA
☎ 071-581 2323/4/5 &
(Fax:) 071-823 7752
In a quiet elegant street close to Harrods and museums.
Bedrooms: 5 single, 2 double & 4 twin, 6 family rooms.
Bathrooms: 9 private, 5 public; 1 private shower.
Bed & breakfast: £38-£60 single, £55-£70 double.
Credit: Access, Visa, Diners, Amex.

🛇 📞 📞 ⌨ 🖵 ♦ UL 🅸 🛏
Ⓣ 🎇 🛏 DAP SP Ⓣ

Brompton Hotel
30-32 Old Brompton Rd., London SW7 3DL
☎ 071-584 4517
Recently refurbished hotel, close to South Kensington underground station. Location is ideal for both holidays and business.
Bedrooms: 2 single, 10 double & 2 twin, 2 family rooms.
Bathrooms: 16 private.
Bed & breakfast: £40-£46 single, £60-£69 double.
Credit: Access, Visa.

🛇 📞 ⌨ 🖵 ♦ UL CB 🛏 ●
🎇 🛏 🐾

The Burns Park Hotel M
😊😊😊😊 COMMENDED

18-26 Barkston Gdns., Kensington, London
SW5 0EN
☎ 071-373 3151 &
(Fax:) 071-370 4090
Telex 27885
Ⓒ Ⓡ Park Hotels
Recently refurbished, elegant hotel offering the attention to detail and service that a discerning traveller would expect. Close to the West End, Knightsbridge, Earl's Court and Olympia.
Bedrooms: 38 single, 15 double & 45 twin, 8 family rooms.
Bathrooms: 106 private.
Bed & breakfast: £35-£97.50 single, £70-£125 double.
Half board: £42-£111.50 daily.
Evening meal 6.30pm (l.o. 10pm).
Credit: Access, Visa, Diners, Amex.

🛇 📞 📞 ⌨ 🖵 🅸 Ⓥ ●
⊟ 🎇 🛏 🍽 🐾 SP Ⓣ

Concord Hotel M

155-157 Cromwell Rd.,
London SW5 0TQ
☎ 071-370 4151
*Centrally placed on direct line
to Heathrow Airport.
Comfortable rooms, friendly
24-hour service.*
Bedrooms: 14 single, 9 double
& 12 twin, 5 family rooms.
Bathrooms: 12 private,
6 public; 5 private showers.
Bed & breakfast: £30.35-
£36.50 single, £42.75-£58.75
double.
Credit: Access, Visa, Amex.

Fenja Hotel M
COMMENDED

69 Cadogan Gdns., London
SW3 2RB
☎ 071-589 7333 &
(Fax:) 071-581 4958
Telex 934272
Small Luxury Hotels
*Edwardian town house,
meticulously restored,
overlooking Cadogan Gardens
in Knightsbridge. Individually
designed bedrooms, well
appointed and furnished with
antiques.*
Bedrooms: 1 single, 3 double
& 9 twin.
Bathrooms: 13 private.
Bed & breakfast: from
£112.85 single, £148.85-
£220.70 double.
Lunch available.
Evening meal 7pm (l.o. 8pm).
Credit: Access, Visa, Diners,
Amex.

Five Sumner Place Hotel

5 Sumner Pl., South
Kensington, London
SW7 3EE
☎ 071-584 7586 &
(Fax:) 071-823 9962
*Victorian terrace hotel close to
South Kensington station.
Small rear garden with
Victorian conservatory where
breakfast is provided.*
Bedrooms: 3 single, 6 double
& 4 twin.
Bathrooms: 13 private.
Bed & breakfast: £60-£69
single, £80-£89 double.
Credit: Access, Visa, Amex.

*Please check prices
and other details at
the time of booking.*

Hotel George M
APPROVED

Templeton Pl., Earl's Court,
London SW5 9NB
☎ 071-370 1092
Telex 8814825
*Victorian hotel with large
garden and free car park.
Close to Kensington,
Knightsbridge and Earl's Court
and Olympia exhibition halls.*
Bedrooms: 8 single, 36 double
& 75 twin, 36 family rooms.
Bathrooms: 155 private.
Bed & breakfast: £73.25-
£81.25 single, £93.50-£97.50
double.
Lunch available.
Evening meal 6pm (l.o.
9.45pm).
Parking for 20.
Credit: Access, Visa, Amex.

The Gloucester Hotel M

4-18 Harrington Gdns.,
London SW7 4LH
☎ 071-373 6030 &
(Fax:) 071-835 1854
Telex 917505
Rank
*In a quiet location just 2
minutes' walk from Gloucester
Road underground station,
making Knightsbridge and the
West End only minutes away.*
Bedrooms: 15 single,
223 double & 273 twin,
39 family rooms.
Bathrooms: 550 private.
Bed & breakfast: £146.70-
£169.50 single, £175.40-£201
double.
Lunch available.
Evening meal 5pm (l.o.
11.30pm).
Parking for 112.
Credit: Access, Visa, C.Bl.,
Diners, Amex.

Half Moon Hotel M
Listed **APPROVED**

10 Earl's Court Sq., London
SW5 9DP
☎ 071-373 9956 & 2900 &
(Fax:) 071-244 6610
Telex 949631 DELTA G
*In a central position 2 minutes'
walk from the underground
station and with easy access to
the M4 and Heathrow Airport.*
Bedrooms: 11 single, 7 double
& 6 twin, 3 family rooms.
Bathrooms: 9 private,
6 public; 2 private showers.
Bed & breakfast: £19-£22
single, £29-£30 double.

Henley House Hotel M

30 Barkston Gdns., Earl's
Court, London SW5 0EN
☎ 071-370 4111
*Overlooking a beautiful garden
square, within minutes of the
West End, the hotel offers
elegant accommodation in a
friendly atmosphere.*
Bedrooms: 5 single, 8 double
& 5 twin, 2 family rooms.
Bathrooms: 15 private;
5 private showers.
Bed & breakfast: £32-£47
single, £49-£58 double.
Credit: Access, Visa, Amex.

The Knightsbridge M

10 Beaufort Gdns., London
SW3 1PT
☎ 071-589 9271 &
(Fax:) 071-823 9692
*Ideally located in a quiet tree-
lined square in the heart of
Knightsbridge, moments away
from Harrods. Friendly
atmosphere, peaceful
surroundings, personal
attention.*
Bedrooms: 9 single, 1 double
& 8 twin, 2 family rooms.
Bathrooms: 9 private,
3 public; 4 private showers.
Bed & breakfast: £40-£60
single, £60-£90 double.
Credit: Access, Visa, Amex.

Majestic Hotel

160 Cromwell Rd., London
SW5 0TL
☎ 071-373 3083 &
(Fax:) 071-373 9101
Telex 8811844
*Victorian building with friendly
atmosphere. Bar, restaurant,
conservatory-style coffee shop.
Women-only health and beauty
centre.*
Bedrooms: 12 single,
18 double & 46 twin, 7 family
rooms.
Bathrooms: 83 private.
Bed & breakfast: £55-£60
single, £70-£75 double.
Half board: £65-£75 daily.
Lunch available.
Evening meal 5pm (l.o.
10pm).
Credit: Access, Visa, Diners,
Amex.

Manor Hotel M
Listed **APPROVED**

23 Nevern Pl., London
SW5 9NR
☎ 071-370 6018 & 4164 &
(Fax:) 071-244 6610
Telex 949631 DELTA

*Centrally located, a few
minutes' walk from Earl's
Court underground station.
Pleasant atmosphere. Easy
access to Heathrow via M4.*
Bedrooms: 6 single, 10 double
& 8 twin, 3 family rooms.
Bathrooms: 13 private,
4 public; 2 private showers.
Bed & breakfast: £19-£22
single, £24-£30 double.

Mayflower Hotel

26-28 Trebovir Rd., London
SW5
☎ 071-370 0991
*Family-run centrally located
hotel. Easy access to shops and
theatres.*
Bedrooms: 10 single,
17 double & 11 twin, 9 family
rooms.
Bathrooms: 45 private,
1 public.
Bed & breakfast: £30-£35
single, £40-£45 double.
Credit: Access, Visa, Diners,
Amex.

Merlyn Court Hotel M

2 Barkston Gdns., London
SW5 0EN
☎ 071-370 1640
*Well-established, family-run
hotel in quiet Edwardian
square, close to Earl's Court
and Olympia, with direct
underground link to Heathrow,
the West End and most rail
stations.*
Bedrooms: 4 single, 4 double
& 4 twin, 5 family rooms.
Bathrooms: 6 public;
2 private showers.
Bed & breakfast: £22-£30
single, £30-£50 double.
Credit: Access, Visa.

Nevern Hotel M

29-31 Nevern Pl., London
SW5 9NP
☎ 071-244 8366/7
*Small hotel located in a quiet
residential area. Convenient for
Earl's Court, Olympia and
within easy reach of West End.*
Bedrooms: 8 single, 6 double
& 8 twin, 14 family rooms.
Bathrooms: 14 private,
7 public.
Bed & breakfast: £24-£40
single, £32-£52 double.
Credit: Access, Visa, Amex.

Hotel Number Sixteen ᴍ
😊😊 COMMENDED
16 Sumner Pl., London SW7 3EG
☎ 071-589 5232 &
(Fax:) 071-584 8615
Telex 266638
With atmosphere of a comfortable town house (in 4 Victorian houses) in very attractive street.
Bedrooms: 9 single, 27 double.
Bathrooms: 34 private; 1 private shower.
Bed & breakfast: £60-£100 single, £125-£170 double.
Credit: Access, Visa, Diners, Amex.
🎱12 📶 📞 ⬛ CB 🛏 🎇 💷 ▥ ♿ 💢 🅟 T

The Park International Hotel ᴍ
😊😊😊 COMMENDED
117-125 Cromwell Rd., London SW7 4DS
☎ 071-370 5711 Telex 296822
CR Park Hotels
Elegant, well-appointed hotel close to Knightsbridge and the West End. 1 minute's walk from Gloucester Road underground station with direct links to the City, West End and Heathrow.
Bedrooms: 26 single, 29 double & 57 twin, 5 family rooms.
Bathrooms: 117 private.
Bed & breakfast: £35-£97.50 single, £70-£125 double.
Half board: £42-£111.50 daily.
Evening meal 6.30pm (l.o. 10pm).
Credit: Access, Visa, Diners, Amex.
🎱 📶 📞 ⬛ 🛏 ♿ 🧍 V 🛏
● 💷 💢 ⬛ 🍴 🐾 SP 🅟 T

Prince Hotel
6 Sumner Pl., London SW7 3EE
☎ 071-589 6488 Telex 917133
Small, Victorian terrace hotel, ideally located in South Kensington for easy access to Knightsbridge, Hyde Park etc.
Bedrooms: 5 single, 7 double & 8 twin.
Bathrooms: 12 private; 7 private showers.
Bed & breakfast: £35-£40 single, £50-£60 double.
Credit: Access, Visa, C.Bl., Diners, Amex.
🎱 📞 ⬛ 🛏 💢 UL V 🛏 ●
💷 ▥ T

We advise you to confirm your booking in writing.

Rasool Court Hotel ᴍ
APPROVED
19-21 Penywern Rd., Earl's Court, London SW5 9TT
☎ 071-373 8900 & 4893 &
(Fax:) 071-244 6835
Located near Earl's Court underground station. Few minutes' tube journey to the West End and direct route to Heathrow Airport.
Bedrooms: 27 single, 17 double & 8 twin, 5 family rooms.
Bathrooms: 4 private, 5 public; 23 private showers.
Bed & breakfast: £15-£18 single, £22-£30 double.
Credit: Access, Visa.
🎱 💢 ⬛ UL CB 🛏 ● 💷 ▥ ✈

Regency Hotel ᴍ
😊😊😊 COMMENDED
100 Queen's Gate, Kensington, London SW7 5AG
☎ 071-370 4595 Telex 267594
Privately owned Regency hotel offering traditional personal service and attention. A short walk from Harrods.
Bedrooms: 25 single, 58 double & 116 twin, 11 family rooms.
Bathrooms: 210 private.
Bed & breakfast: from £111 single, from £131 double.
Half board: from £130 daily.
Lunch available.
Evening meal 5.30pm (l.o. 10.30pm).
Credit: Access, Visa, C.Bl., Diners, Amex.
🎱 💢 ⬛ 🛏 🧍 V 🛏
● 💷 ▥ 💢 🍴 🐾 ✈ DAP 🐾
SP T

Rushmore Hotel ᴍ
11 Trebovir Rd., London SW5 9LS
☎ 071-370 3839 & 6505 &
(Fax:) 071-370 0274
Telex 297761 ref. 1933
Each room stylishly and individually-themed, making the hotel unique in its category. All rooms have colour TV and direct-dial telephone. Within a minute's walk from both Earl's Court underground station and exhibition centre.
Bedrooms: 2 single, 8 double & 7 twin, 5 family rooms.
Bathrooms: 22 private.
Bed & breakfast: £35-£45 single, £45-£55 double.
Parking for 5.
Credit: Access, Visa, Diners, Amex.
🎱 💢 🛏 📞 ⬛ 🛏 UL CB ✂
TV ● ▥ 💢 🐾 SP T

Swallow International Hotel ᴍ
Cromwell Rd., London SW5 0TH
☎ 071-973 1000 &
(Fax:) 071-244 8194
Telex 27260
CR Swallow
Bright modern hotel offering an exclusive leisure club. Near Earl's Court and Olympia Exhibition Halls, fashionable Knightsbridge and Kensington's parks and museums.
Bedrooms: 78 single, 81 double & 210 twin, 48 family rooms.
Bathrooms: 417 private.
Bed & breakfast: £100-£107 single, £124-£131 double.
Lunch available.
Evening meal 6pm (l.o. midnight).
Parking for 70.
Credit: Access, Visa, Diners, Amex.
🎱 📞 ⬛ 🛏 🧍 V ✂ ●
💷 ▥ 💢 🍴 🐾 🐾 🐾 SP 🅟 T

Windsor House ᴍ
Listed
12 Penywern Rd., London SW5 9ST
☎ 071-373 9087
Budget-priced bed and breakfast establishment in Earl's Court. Easily reached from airports and motorway. The West End is minutes away by underground.
Bedrooms: 2 single, 5 double & 3 twin, 5 family rooms.
Bathrooms: 1 private, 5 public; 5 private showers.
Bed & breakfast: £22-£30 single, £28-£40 double.
Parking for 10.
Credit: Access, Visa, C.Bl., Diners, Amex.
🎱 💢 ⬛ UL TV ● ▥ 💷 💢 DAP
🐾 SP T

York House Hotel ᴍ
28 Philbeach Gdns., London SW5 9EA
☎ 071-373 7519 & 7579
Bed and breakfast hotel, conveniently located close to the Earl's Court and Olympia Exhibition Centres and the West End.
Bedrooms: 20 single, 9 double & 3 twin, 6 family rooms.
Bathrooms: 1 private, 8 public.
Bed & breakfast: £22-£24 single, £35.25-£36.50 double.
Credit: Access, Visa, Amex.
🎱 💢 ⬛ 🛏 TV ✈ SP T

CENTRAL LONDON 3
Covering High Street Kensington, West Kensington, Holland Park, Notting Hill, Olympia, Hammersmith. See colour map 6.

Hotel Apollo
18-22 Lexham Gdns., London W8 5JE
☎ 071-835 1133 &
(Fax:) 071-370 4853
Telex 264189
Modernised Victorian building near museums, Albert Hall, Hyde Park, antique shops and markets, Olympia and Earl's Court exhibition centres.
Bedrooms: 28 single, 3 double & 24 twin, 4 family rooms.
Bathrooms: 50 private, 8 public.
Bed & breakfast: £30-£46 single, £44-£56 double.
Credit: Access, Visa, C.Bl., Diners, Amex.
🎱 💢 📞 ⬛ 🛏 ✈ 💢 T

Hotel Atlas
24-30 Lexham Gdns., London W8 5JE
☎ 071-835 1155 &
(Fax:) 071-370 4853
Telex 264189
Modernised Victorian building close to High Street Kensington, Earl's Court and Gloucester Road underground stations. Airbus to Heathrow nearby.
Bedrooms: 35 single, 4 double & 19 twin, 6 family rooms.
Bathrooms: 45 private, 6 public.
Bed & breakfast: £30-£46 single, £44-£56 double.
Credit: Access, Visa, C.Bl., Diners, Amex.
🎱 💢 📞 ⬛ 🛏 TV ● 💷
▥ 💢 🍴 ✈ 💢 T

Avonmore Hotel ᴍ
😊😊 COMMENDED
66 Avonmore Rd., Kensington, London W14 8RS
☎ 071-603 3121 & 4296 &
(Fax:) 071-603 4035
Telex 945922 Gladex G(Att AV32)
Privately owned, with a friendly atmosphere. 3 minutes' walk from West Kensington underground station, Olympia Exhibition Centre and Earl's Court.
Bedrooms: 1 single, 2 double & 3 twin, 3 family rooms.
Continued ▶

CENTRAL LONDON 3

Continued

Bathrooms: 7 private,
1 public.
Bed & breakfast: £37-£47.80
single, £49-£57 double.

[symbols]

B & B Flatlets ♏

64 Holland Rd., London W14
☎ 071-229 9233 &
(Fax:) 071-221 1077
*Clean, family-run guesthouse
offering budget rates. Centrally
located, very close to public
transport. All rooms have
cooking facilities and full
English breakfast is served in
room. Also at 72, Holland
Park Avenue London W11.*
Bedrooms: 2 single, 2 twin,
4 family rooms.
Bathrooms: 4 public.
Bed & breakfast: £22.50-
£23.50 single, £31.50-£39
double.
Credit: Access, Visa.

[symbols]

B & B Flatlets ♏

72 Holland Park Ave.,
London W11 3QZ
☎ 071-229 9233 &
(Fax:) 071-221 1077
*Clean, friendly, family-run
guesthouse offering budget
accommodation. Full English
breakfast served to rooms. All
rooms have their own complete
cooking facilities. Near public
transport. Also at 64 Holland
Road, London W14.*
Bedrooms: 3 twin, 2 family
rooms.
Bathrooms: 1 private,
2 public.
Bed & breakfast: £22.50-
£23.50 single, £31.50-£39
double.
Credit: Access, Visa.

[symbols]

Clearlake Hotel

18-19 Prince of Wales Ter.,
Kensington, London W8 5PQ
☎ 071-937 3274
*Comfortable rooms in a hotel
in a quiet cul-de-sac, with view
of Hyde Park. Self-catering
apartments also available.
Close to shops and transport.*
Bedrooms: 1 single, 5 double
& 2 twin, 9 family rooms.
Bathrooms: 17 private.
Bed & breakfast: £31.05-
£36.50 single, £50-£68 double.
Credit: Access, Visa, Diners,
Amex.

[symbols]

Copthorne Tara Hotel ♏

[symbols] **COMMENDED**

Scarsdale Pl., Kensington,
London W8 5SR
☎ 071-937 7211 &
(Fax:) 071-937 7100
Telex 918834
*Large modern hotel convenient
for the West End, the city and
major motorways. Wide choice
of bars and restaurants.*
Bedrooms: 204 double &
627 twin.
Bathrooms: 831 private.
Bed & breakfast: £105.40-
£134.15 single, £126.80-
£158.30 double.
Lunch available.
Evening meal 5.30pm (l.o.
1.30am).
Parking for 90.
Credit: Access, Visa, C.Bl.,
Diners, Amex.

[symbols]

De Vere Park Hotel

[symbols] **APPROVED**

60 Hyde Park Gate, London
W8 5AS
☎ 071-584 0051
Telex 8953644
*Overlooking Kensington Palace
and gardens and with easy
access to the West End.*
Bedrooms: 17 single,
60 double, 18 family rooms.
Bathrooms: 95 private.
Bed & breakfast: £85-£95
single, £95-£120 double.
Lunch available.
Evening meal 5.30pm (l.o.
9.30pm).
Credit: Access, Visa, Diners,
Amex.

[symbols]

Demetriou Guest House ♏

Listed **APPROVED**

9 Strathmore Gdns., London
W8 4RZ
☎ 071-229 6709
*Small privately-owned
guesthouse, close to Kensington
Gardens and Kensington High
Street. Convenient for Notting
Hill Gate underground.*
Bedrooms: 1 single, 3 double
& 3 twin, 2 family rooms.
Bathrooms: 3 public.
Bed & breakfast: from £25
single, from £40 double.

[symbols]

The Gate Hotel ♏

6 Portobello Rd., London
W11 3DG
☎ 071-221 2403

*Bed and breakfast hotel near
Notting Hill underground
station in the famous
Portobello Road. Close to all
the antique shops.*
Bedrooms: 2 single, 4 double,
2 family rooms.
Bathrooms: 3 private,
1 public; 2 private showers.
Bed & breakfast: £30-£36
single, £40-£65 double.
Credit: Access, Visa.

[symbols]

Gillett Hotel

120 Shepherds Bush Rd.,
London W6 7PD
☎ 071-603 0784 & 2811
*Family-run hotel close to
Hammersmith and Shepherds
Bush. Convenient for Olympia,
Earl's Court and West End.*
Bedrooms: 1 single, 1 double
& 5 twin, 4 family rooms.
Bathrooms: 3 public.
Bed & breakfast: £23.50-
£25.85 single, £28.20-£30.50
double.
Credit: Amex.

[symbols]

Halcyon Hotel ♏

[symbols] **COMMENDED**

81-82 Holland Park, London
W11 3RZ
☎ 071-727 7288 Telex 266721
*Elegant hotel. All rooms
individually designed and
decorated with marble
bathrooms. Air-conditioning,
satellite TV, mini-bars.*
Bedrooms: 3 single, 33 double
& 8 twin.
Bathrooms: 44 private.
Bed & breakfast: £133-£163
single, £165-£250 double.
Lunch available.
Evening meal 7.30pm (l.o.
11.30pm).
Credit: Access, Visa, C.Bl.,
Diners, Amex.

[symbols]

Hotel Lexham ♏

[symbols] **APPROVED**

32-38 Lexham Gdns., London
W8 5JU
☎ 071-373 6471 &
(Fax:) 071-244 7827
Telex 268141
METMAK/HOTLEX
*Long-established, owner-run
hotel, with a pleasant outlook
over a garden square.
Conveniently central and close
to the museums.*
Bedrooms: 23 single, 8 double
& 22 twin, 13 family rooms.
Bathrooms: 48 private,
9 public.
Bed & breakfast: £34-£48.50
single, £45-£69.50 double.

Half board: £31.25-£57.25
daily, £206-£373 weekly.
Lunch available.
Evening meal 6.45pm (l.o.
8pm).
Credit: Access, Visa.

[symbols]

London Olympia Hilton ♏

380 Kensington High St.,
London W14 8NL
☎ 071-603 3333 &
(Fax:) 071-603 4846
Telex 22229
🄷 Hilton
*Convenient for Kensington
shops and the West End. Close
to Olympia and Kensington
Exhibition Centre.*
Bedrooms: 93 single,
109 double & 186 twin,
18 family rooms.
Bathrooms: 406 private.
Bed & breakfast: £105-£155
single, £115-£180 double.
Lunch available.
Evening meal 5pm (l.o.
11pm).
Credit: Access, Visa, Diners,
Amex.

[symbols]

Observatory House Hotel ♏

[symbols]

37 Hornton St., London
W8 7NR
☎ 071-937 1577 & 6353
Telex 914972 OBSERV
*Delightful hotel in an attractive
residential area near High
Street Kensington station. All
rooms with private facilities,
TV, tea/coffee making and
telephones.*
Bedrooms: 5 single, 9 double
& 5 twin, 6 family rooms.
Bathrooms: 25 private,
1 public.
Bed & breakfast: £59.90-
£61.20 single, £79.90-£82.40
double.
Lunch available.
Credit: Access, Visa, Diners,
Amex.

[symbols]

Premier West Hotel ♏

[symbols]

28-34 Glenthorne Rd.,
Hammersmith, London
W6 0LS
☎ 081-748 6181 &
(Fax:) 081-748 2195
*Friendly hotel with affordable
prices, conveniently situated for
West End, Earl's Court and
Olympia exhibition centres and
Heathrow Airport.*

Bedrooms: 10 single, 4 double & 17 twin, 18 family rooms. Bathrooms: 41 private, 4 public.
Bed & breakfast: £32.50-£65 single, £45-£75 double. Lunch available. Evening meal 6pm (l.o. 9pm). Parking for 6. Credit: Access, Visa, Diners, Amex.

⌖ ⌖ ⌖ ⌖ ⌖ ⌖ ⌖ ⌖ ⌖
⌖ ⌖ ⌖ ⌖ ⌖ ⌖ ⌖ ⌖

Royal Garden Hotel ⋈

Kensington High St., London W8 4PT
☎ 071-937 8000 Telex 263151
Ⓖ Rank
Modern hotel overlooking Hyde Park and Kensington Gardens and adjacent to Kensington Palace. Preferential car parking rates are available to residents.
Bedrooms: 99 single, 105 double & 165 twin, 21 family rooms.
Bathrooms: 390 private.
Bed & breakfast: £157.95-£199.95 single, £212.90-£231.90 double.
Lunch available. Evening meal 5pm (l.o. 11.30pm). Parking for 160. Credit: Access, Visa, C.Bl., Diners, Amex.

⌖ ⌖ ⌖ ⌖ ⌖ ⌖ ⌖ ⌖ ⌖
⌖ ⌖ ⌖ ⌖ ⌖ ⌖ ⌖ ⌖

Vicarage Private Hotel ⌖

10 Vicarage Gate, Kensington, London W8 4AG
☎ 071-229 4030
Family-run hotel.
Bedrooms: 9 single, 2 double & 5 twin, 3 family rooms.
Bathrooms: 5 public.
Bed & breakfast: £26 single, £48 double.

⌖4 ⌖ ⌖ ⌖ ⌖ ⌖ ⌖ ⌖ ⌖
⌖

CENTRAL LONDON 4

Covering Bayswater, Paddington, Maida Vale. See colour map 6.

The Abbey Court

⌖ ⌖ ⌖ **COMMENDED**
20 Pembridge Gdns., London W2 4DU
☎ 071-221 7518 &
(Fax:) 071-792 0858
Telex 262167 ABBYCT
Listed Victorian building. All bedrooms individually designed. Italian marble bathrooms with whirlpool baths and showers. Close to shops,

restaurants and antique markets. Conservatory bar/lounge.
Bedrooms: 6 single, 10 double & 6 twin.
Bathrooms: 22 private.
Bed & breakfast: £70 single, £99-£143 double.
Half board: £70 daily.
Credit: Access, Visa, Diners, Amex.

⌖12 ⌖ ⌖ ⌖ ⌖ ⌖ ⌖
⌖ ⌖ ⌖ ⌖ ⌖ ⌖

Abbey Court Hotel ⋈

174 Sussex Gdns., London W2 1TP
☎ 071-402 0704
Central London hotel, reasonable prices. Within walking distance of Lancaster Gate, Paddington station and Hyde Park.
Bedrooms: 1 single, 16 double & 20 twin, 8 family rooms.
Bathrooms: 8 private, 3 public; 20 private showers.
Bed & breakfast: £18-£29 single, £25-£35 double.
Parking for 12.
Credit: Access, Visa, C.Bl., Diners, Amex.

⌖ ⌖ ⌖ ⌖ ⌖ ⌖ ⌖ ⌖
⌖ ⌖ ⌖ ⌖ ⌖ ⌖ ⌖ ⌖
➌ Display advertisement appears on page 43.

Albro House Hotel ⋈

⌖
155 Sussex Gdns., London W2 2RY
☎ 071-724 2931
Ideal location for sightseeing and shopping. Pleasant atmosphere. Nice rooms, English breakfast. Friendly and safe, ideal for families and couples. Small groups welcome.
Bedrooms: 2 single, 3 double & 6 twin, 5 family rooms.
Bathrooms: 7 private, 3 public; 1 private shower.
Bed & breakfast: £26-£36 single, £34-£48 double.
Credit: Access, Visa, Diners, Amex.

⌖ ⌖ ⌖ ⌖ ⌖ ⌖ ⌖ ⌖
⌖ ⌖ ⌖ ⌖ ⌖ ⌖

Allandale Hotel

3 Devonshire Ter., Lancaster Gate, London W2 3DN
☎ 071-723 8311 & 7807
Small, select, well-cared for family hotel, close to Hyde Park, West End and Lancaster Gate and Paddington stations. English breakfast.
Bedrooms: 1 single, 11 double & 4 twin, 4 family rooms.
Bathrooms: 14 private, 1 public; 2 private showers.

Bed & breakfast: £28.75-£35 single, £38-£43 double.
Credit: Access, Visa, Diners.

⌖ ⌖ ⌖ ⌖ ⌖ ⌖ ⌖ ⌖ ⌖
⌖ ⌖ ⌖ ⌖ ⌖ ⌖

Andrews Hotel ⋈

Listed
12 Westbourne St., Hyde Park, London W2 2TZ
☎ 071-723 5365 & 4514
Within walking distance of Oxford Street and all tourist attractions, 2 minutes from Lancaster Gate and Paddington underground stations, also the Airbus to Heathrow. Hebrew and other languages spoken.
Bedrooms: 1 single, 6 double & 4 twin, 6 family rooms.
Bathrooms: 1 private, 3 public; 9 private showers.
Bed & breakfast: £20-£25 single, £28-£35 double.
Credit: Access, Visa, C.Bl., Diners.

⌖ ⌖ ⌖ ⌖ ⌖ ⌖ ⌖ ⌖ ⌖
⌖ ⌖ ⌖ ⌖ ⌖

Ashley Hotel

Listed
15 Norfolk Sq., London W2 1RU
☎ 071-723 3375
19th C town house hotel in a quiet garden square, very convenient for sightseeing and shopping. Tube and buses nearby.
Bedrooms: 4 single, 7 double & 4 twin, 1 family room.
Bathrooms: 6 private, 2 public; 2 private showers.
Bed & breakfast: £22-£24 single, £40-£46 double.

⌖ ⌖ ⌖ ⌖ ⌖ ⌖ ⌖ ⌖ ⌖
⌖ ⌖ ⌖ ⌖

Averard Hotel

10 Lancaster Gate, Hyde Park, London W2 3LH
☎ 071-723 8877
Opposite Hyde Park and close to Paddington and Lancaster Gate underground. Victorian-style public rooms, comfortable bedrooms and friendly staff.
Bedrooms: 19 single, 5 double & 22 twin, 15 family rooms.
Bathrooms: 61 private.
Bed & breakfast: £45-£55 single, £55-£65 double.
Credit: Access, Visa, Diners, Amex.

⌖ ⌖ ⌖ ⌖ ⌖ ⌖ ⌖ ⌖
⌖ ⌖ ⌖ ⌖ ⌖ ⌖

Barry House Hotel ⋈

Listed **APPROVED**
12 Sussex Pl., London W2 2TP
☎ 071-723 7340 & 0994
Fax: 071-723 9775

Family-run bed and breakfast hotel, 4 minutes' walking distance from Paddington station. Hyde Park, Marble Arch and Oxford Street close by.
Bedrooms: 3 single, 2 double & 6 twin, 7 family rooms.
Bathrooms: 14 private, 2 public.
Bed & breakfast: £28-£38 single, £44-£54 double.
Credit: Access, Visa, Amex.

⌖ ⌖ ⌖ ⌖ ⌖ ⌖ ⌖ ⌖ ⌖
⌖ ⌖ ⌖ ⌖ ⌖ ⌖ ⌖ ⌖
⌖ ⌖
➌ Display advertisement appears on page 44.

Beverley House Hotel ⋈

⌖ ⌖ ⌖
142 Sussex Gdns., London W2 1UB
☎ 071-723 3380 &
(Fax:) 071-402 3292
Opened in July 1990, a bed and breakfast hotel offering high standards at low prices. Close to Paddington station, Hyde Park and museums.
Bedrooms: 6 single, 5 double & 6 twin, 6 family rooms.
Bathrooms: 23 private.
Bed & breakfast: £35-£45 single, £40-£56 double.
Parking for 2.
Credit: Access, Visa, C.Bl., Diners, Amex.

⌖ ⌖ ⌖ ⌖ ⌖ ⌖ ⌖ ⌖ ⌖
⌖ ⌖ ⌖

The Blakemore Hotel ⋈

30 Leinster Gdns., London W2 3AU
☎ 071-262 4591 Telex 291634
LENTOW G
Close to Queensway, convenient for shopping in West End, near Hyde Park and Kensington Gardens. Elegant bar, coffee lounge and restaurant. Banqueting facilities available.
Bedrooms: 59 single, 22 double & 66 twin, 23 family rooms.
Bathrooms: 170 private.
Bed & breakfast: £60-£70 single, £75-£85 double.
Half board: £42.50-£70 daily.
Evening meal 6pm.
Credit: Access, Visa, C.Bl., Diners, Amex.

⌖ ⌖ ⌖ ⌖ ⌖ ⌖ ⌖ ⌖ ⌖
⌖ ⌖ ⌖ ⌖ ⌖ ⌖ ⌖ ⌖

Brides and McCormacks Hotels

1 Devonshire Ter., London W2 3DN
☎ 071-724 2557
Continued ▶

CENTRAL LONDON 4

Continued

Comfortable rooms, most en-suite. Large continental breakfast. Close to Paddington station. Personal, attentive service.
Bedrooms: 16 single, 15 double, 10 family rooms.
Bathrooms: 20 private, 4 public; 12 private showers.
Bed & breakfast: £22–£27 single, £30–£40 double.
Credit: Access, Visa.

Camelot Hotel M
COMMENDED
45-47 Norfolk Sq., Paddington, London W2 1RX
☎ 071-262 1980 & 071-723 9118 Telex 268312 WESCOM G CENTRAL
Beautifully restored town house, now a bed and breakfast hotel offering charming, stylish accommodation in central London.
Bedrooms: 13 single, 12 double & 12 twin, 7 family rooms.
Bathrooms: 36 private, 1 public; 4 private showers.
Bed & breakfast: £36–£53 single, £72 double.
Credit: Access, Visa.

Chrysos Hotel M
25 Norfolk Sq., London W2 1RX
☎ 071-262 2417 & (Fax:) 071-402 4142
Central London hotel with lift to all floors and double glazing. All rooms en-suite, with colour TV and telephone. English breakfast.
Bedrooms: 3 single, 3 double & 9 twin, 5 family rooms.
Bathrooms: 20 private.
Bed & breakfast: £35–£40 single, £45–£55 double.

Coburg Hotel
COMMENDED
129 Bayswater Rd., London W2 4RJ
☎ 071-221 2217 Telex 268235
Best Western
Newly refurbished Edwardian hotel conveniently located overlooking Kensington Gardens, ideal for tourists and business travellers.
Bedrooms: 29 single, 46 double & 57 twin.
Bathrooms: 132 private.

Bed & breakfast: from £79.50 single, £109.50–£129.50 double.
Lunch available.
Credit: Access, Visa, Diners, Amex.

The Delmere Hotel M
COMMENDED
130 Sussex Gdns., Hyde Park, London W2 1UB
☎ 071-706 3344 & (Fax:) 071-262 1863
Telex 8953857
Recently refurbished hotel. Winner of a "Certificate of Distinction" in the British Tourist Authority's London Bed and Breakfast Awards 1990.
Bedrooms: 11 single, 13 double & 13 twin, 1 family room.
Bathrooms: 36 private, 1 public; 1 private shower.
Bed & breakfast: £53.50–£71 single, £75.50–£87 double.
Evening meal 6pm (l.o. 9.30pm).
Credit: Access, Visa, Diners, Amex.

Duke of Leinster M
APPROVED
34 Queen's Gdns., London W2 3AA
☎ 071-258 0079 & 1839
Telex 264266
Listed building near Hyde Park. Former residence of the Duke of Leinster.
Bedrooms: 2 single, 11 double & 21 twin, 8 family rooms.
Bathrooms: 42 private.
Bed & breakfast: £35–£45 single, £50–£60 double.
Credit: Access, Visa, Diners, Amex.

Eden Park Hotel
Inverness Ter., London W2
☎ 071-221 2220 Telex 263260
Park Hotels
Recently refurbished, close to beautiful Kensington Gardens and Hyde Park. Queensway and Bayswater underground stations nearby.
Bedrooms: 55 single, 18 double & 56 twin, 8 family rooms.
Bathrooms: 55 private.
Bed & breakfast: £35–£93.50 single, £70–£111 double.
Half board: £42–£107.50 daily.
Lunch available.

Evening meal 7pm (l.o. 9.30pm).
Credit: Access, Visa, C.Bl., Diners, Amex.

Europa House Hotel M
APPROVED
151 Sussex Gdns., London W2 2RY
☎ 071-723 7343 & 071-402 1923
Fax: 071-224 9331
Close to Hyde Park, and convenient for the Heathrow Airbus link. All rooms with en-suite facilities, tea and coffee making facilities, colour TV. English breakfast included.
Bedrooms: 2 single, 1 double & 8 twin, 7 family rooms.
Bathrooms: 18 private, 1 public.
Bed & breakfast: £30–£32 single, £40–£45 double.
Evening meal 6pm (l.o. 11pm).
Parking for 1.
Credit: Access, Visa, Amex.

Garden Court Hotel M
APPROVED
30-31 Kensington Gardens Sq., London W2 4BG
☎ 071-229 2553 & (Fax:) 071-727 2749
Small friendly hotel in a quiet Victorian garden square in central London. Convenient for all transport.
Bedrooms: 15 single, 6 double & 10 twin, 6 family rooms.
Bathrooms: 12 private, 6 public.
Bed & breakfast: £26–£38 single, £38–£50 double.
Credit: Access, Visa, Amex.

Henry VIII Hotel M
APPROVED
19 Leinster Gdns., London W2 3AN
☎ 071-262 0117 Telex 261365
Convenient for Queensway and Bayswater underground stations, with Hyde Park nearby. Banqueting accommodation for up to 100 persons.
Bedrooms: 29 single, 12 double & 59 twin, 7 family rooms.
Bathrooms: 107 private.
Bed & breakfast: from £85 single, from £100 double.
Lunch available.
Evening meal 6pm (l.o. 10pm).

Credit: Access, Visa, C.Bl., Diners, Amex.

The Hyde Park Towers Hotel
Inverness Ter., London W2 3JN
☎ 071-221 8484 Telex 263260
Park Hotels
Recently refurbished, business class hotel close to Hyde Park, convenient for Queensway and Bayswater underground stations.
Bedrooms: 35 single, 22 double & 54 twin, 4 family rooms.
Bathrooms: 115 private.
Bed & breakfast: £35–£93.50 single, £70–£111 double.
Half board: £42–£107.50 daily.
Lunch available.
Evening meal 7pm (l.o. 9.30pm).
Credit: Access, Visa, C.Bl., Diners, Amex.

The Julius Caesar Hotel M
26-33 Queen's Gdns., Hyde Park, London W2 3BD
☎ 071-262 0022 Telex 24442 CAESAR G
Park Hotels
Centrally-located hotel, ideal for the tourist. Close to Hyde Park and convenient for Queensway and Bayswater underground stations.
Bedrooms: 16 single, 14 double & 54 twin, 27 family rooms.
Bathrooms: 111 private, 1 public.
Bed & breakfast: from £55 single, from £70 double.
Lunch available.
Evening meal 6pm (l.o. 9pm).
Credit: Access, Visa, Diners, Amex.

Kingsway Hotel M
COMMENDED
27 Norfolk Sq., Hyde Park, London W2 1RX
☎ 071-723 5569 & 7784 & (Fax:) 071-723 7317
Telex 885299
In a quiet square, close to Paddington underground and Hyde Park. High standard hotel, with lift and en-suite facilities.
Bedrooms: 11 single, 10 double & 6 twin, 7 family rooms.
Bathrooms: 30 private, 2 public.

Bed & breakfast: £28-£44 single, £42-£58 double.
Credit: Access, Visa, Diners, Amex.

⛄ 👤 📞 🖥 ⓤ🔒 ⛐ 📺 ◐
⊞ 🖩 🛏 ✕ ᴰᴬᶠ ⚐ SP 🏨 Ⓣ

Linden House Hotel ⋒
Listed **APPROVED**
4-6 Sussex Pl., London
W2 2TP
☎ 071-723 9853 & 071-262
0804
Fax: 071-724 1454
*Regency-style building close to
Hyde Park, with a friendly
family atmosphere.*
Bedrooms: 5 single, 3 double
& 11 twin, 11 family rooms.
Bathrooms: 20 private,
5 public.
Bed & breakfast: £18-£40
single, £30-£55 double.

⛄ 👤 📞 ⚡ 🚽 ⓘ V ⛐ 🛏
⊙ Ⓣ

London House Hotel ⋒
80 Kensington Gardens Sq.,
London W2 4DJ
☎ 071-727 0696 Telex 24923
*Friendly, comfortable budget
hotel, convenient for shops,
theatres and sightseeing.
Public transport close by.*
Bedrooms: 3 single, 13 double
& 11 twin, 19 family rooms.
Bathrooms: 7 public;
13 private showers.
Bed & breakfast: from £33
single, from £41 double.

⛄ ⓤ🔒 🇨🇧 ⛐ 📺 ◐ 🖩 ✕ Ⓣ

Mitre House Hotel ⋒
⛉⛉⛉⛉ **APPROVED**
178-180 Sussex Gdns., Hyde
Park, London, W2 1TU
☎ 071-723 8040 & 071-402
5695
Fax: 071-402 0990
*A family-run hotel, recently
refurbished.*
Bedrooms: 9 single, 18 double
& 26 twin, 17 family rooms.
Bathrooms: 67 private,
3 public.
Bed & breakfast: £55-£60
single, £65-£70 double.
Parking for 20.
Credit: Access, Visa, Diners,
Amex.

⛄ 👤 📞 ⓘ 🚽 V ⛱ ⛐ 📺
◐ ⊞ 🖩 🛏 ♿ ✕ 🏨 Ⓣ

Mornington Hotel ⋒
12 Lancaster Gate, London
W2 3LG
☎ 071-262 7361 &
(Fax:) 071-706 1028
Telex 24281
ⒸⓇ Best Western
*Modernised hotel in a quiet
residential street opposite Hyde
Park.*
Bedrooms: 34 single, 9 double
& 23 twin, 2 family rooms.
Bathrooms: 68 private.

Bed & breakfast: from £75
single, £86-£103 double.
Credit: Access, Visa, C.Bl.,
Diners, Amex.

⛄ 👤 📞 ⓘ 🚽 ⛐ ◐ ⊞ 🖩
🛏 ⛉ 🏨 Ⓣ

Nayland Hotel ⋒
⛉⛉⛉⛉ **COMMENDED**
132-134 Sussex Gdns., London
W2 1UB
☎ 071-723 4615 &
(Fax:) 071-402 3292
Telex 268312
*Centrally located, close to
many amenities and within
walking distance of Hyde Park
and Oxford Street. Quality
you can afford.*
Bedrooms: 11 single, 8 double
& 17 twin, 5 family rooms.
Bathrooms: 41 private.
Bed & breakfast: £39-£49
single, £46-£59 double.
Parking for 5.
Credit: Access, Visa, C.Bl.,
Diners, Amex.

⛄ 👤 📞 ⓘ 🚽 ⛐ ◐ ⊞ 🖩
🛏 ♿ 🏨 Ⓣ

Norfolk Towers Hotel ⋒
⛉⛉⛉⛉ **APPROVED**
34 Norfolk Pl., London
W2 1QW
☎ 071-262 3123 Telex 268583
NORTOW
*Elegant hotel, completely
renovated and refurbished, with
cocktail bar, restaurant and
wine bar. Close to city centre
and West End.*
Bedrooms: 14 single,
22 double & 46 twin, 3 family
rooms.
Bathrooms: 85 private.
Bed & breakfast: from £69
single, from £82 double.
Lunch available.
Evening meal 6pm (l.o.
9.30pm).
Credit: Access, Visa, C.Bl.,
Diners, Amex.

⛄ 👤 📞 ⓘ 🚽 ⓘ V ⛐ 📺
◐ ⊞ 🖩 🛏 ♿ ✕ 🏨 Ⓣ

Parkwood Hotel ⋒
⛉⛉⛉ **COMMENDED**
4 Stanhope Pl., London
W2 2HB
☎ 071-402 2241
Fax: 071-402 1574
*Smart town house convenient
for Hyde Park and Oxford
Street. Comfortable bedrooms
and friendly atmosphere.*
Bedrooms: 4 single, 3 double
& 7 twin, 4 family rooms.
Bathrooms: 12 private,
2 public.
Bed & breakfast: £39.75-£55
single, £54.50-£64.50 double.
Credit: Access, Visa.

⛄ 👤 📞 ⓘ 🚽 ⚡ ⓤ🔒 V ⛱ ⛐
📺 ◐ 🖩 🛏 ✕ 🅿 ᴰᴬᶠ ⚐ SP
Ⓣ

Pembridge Court
Hotel ⋒
⛉⛉⛉⛉
34 Pembridge Gdns., London
W2 4DX
☎ 071-229 9977 Telex 298363
*Small privately-owned town
house hotel located in quiet
tree-lined gardens. Easy access
to West End shops and
theatres.*
Bedrooms: 10 single, 9 double
& 6 twin.
Bathrooms: 25 private.
Bed & breakfast: £76-£103.50
single, £99-£130 double.
Evening meal 6pm (l.o.
11.15pm).
Parking for 2.
Credit: Access, Visa, Diners,
Amex.

⛄ 👤 📞 ⓘ 🚽 ⛐ ◐ ⊞ 🖩
🛏 ⛱ ᴰᴬᶠ SP 🏨 Ⓣ

Picton House Hotel
122 Sussex Gdns., London
W2 1UB
☎ 071-723 5498
*Small, privately-owned hotel in
desirable location near Oxford
Street and Hyde Park and
convenient for Madame
Tussauds. High standard of
personal service.*
Bedrooms: 2 single, 6 double
& 6 twin, 1 family room.
Bathrooms: 5 private,
2 public; 3 private showers.
Bed & breakfast: £25-£30
single, £35-£45 double.
Parking for 1.
Credit: Access, Visa, Diners,
Amex.

⛄ 👤 📞 ⚡ 🚽 V ⛱ 📺 🖩 ✕
🏨

Plaza on Hyde Park ⋒
Lancaster Gate, London
W2 3NA
☎ 071-262 5022
Telex 8954372
ⒸⓇ Hilton
*Immediately opposite Hyde
Park, 2 minutes from
Lancaster Gate underground
station. Bar and restaurants.
New Plaza executive wing built
1990, with separate lift and
many extras in the rooms.*
Bedrooms: 109 single,
130 double & 119 twin,
44 family rooms.
Bathrooms: 402 private.
Bed & breakfast: £80-£190
single, £115-£210 double.
Lunch available.
Evening meal 6pm (l.o.
10.30pm).
Credit: Access, Visa, C.Bl.,
Diners, Amex.

⛄ 👤 📞 ⓘ 🚽 ⚡ ⓘ V ⛱
⛐ ◐ ⊞ 🖩 🛏 ⛱ ✕ 🏨 Ⓣ

Queensway Hotel ⋒
⛉⛉⛉
147-149 Sussex Gdns., Hyde
Park, London W2 2RY
☎ 071-723 7749 &
(Fax:) 071-262 5707
*Family-run hotel, close to
Paddington and within easy
reach of the West End.*
Bedrooms: 10 single, 8 double
& 18 twin, 7 family rooms.
Bathrooms: 43 private.
Bed & breakfast: £40-£56
single, £55-£70 double.
Credit: Access, Visa, Diners,
Amex.

⛄ 👤 📞 ⓘ 🚽 ⚡ ⓤ🔒 ⛐ ◐
⊞ 🖩 🛏 SP 🏨 Ⓣ

Royal Lancaster
Hotel ⋒
Lancaster Ter., London
W2 2TY
☎ 071-262 6737 &
(Fax:) 071-724 3191
Telex 24822
ⒸⓇ Rank
*Modern hotel overlooking
Hyde Park and close to
Marble Arch and Oxford
Street. 4 conference suites,
largest seating 1,000.
Restaurant, cafe and bar.*
Bedrooms: 24 single,
166 double & 208 twin,
20 family rooms.
Bathrooms: 418 private.
Bed & breakfast: £157-£180
single, £186-£212 double.
Lunch available.
Evening meal 6pm (l.o.
10.45pm).
Parking for 130.
Credit: Access, Visa, C.Bl.,
Diners, Amex.

⛄ 📞 ⓘ 🚽 ⓘ V ⛱ ⛐ ◐
⊞ 🖩 🛏 ⛱ ✕ ⚐ SP Ⓣ

Royal Park Hotel ⋒
⛉⛉⛉
2-5 Westbourne Ter., London
W2 3UL
☎ 071-402 6187 &
(Fax:) 071-224 9426
*Modernised hotel built in 1854.
Comfortable and well-equipped
for bus and underground to the
West End. Free car parking
available.*
Bedrooms: 8 single, 10 double
& 35 twin, 8 family rooms.
Bathrooms: 61 private.
Bed & breakfast: max. £57
single, max. £70 double.
Evening meal 6pm (l.o.
10pm).
Parking for 15.
Credit: Access, Visa, Amex.

⛄ 👤 📞 ⓘ 🚽 ⚡ ⛐ ◐ ⊞
🖩 🛏 ⛱ ✕ 🏨 Ⓣ

St. Charles Hotel
66 Queensborough Ter.,
London W2 3SH
☎ 071-221 0022

Continued ▶

Well-appointed small hotel, 2 minutes' walk from Kensington Gardens and within easy reach of the West End.
Bedrooms: 5 single, 3 double & 5 twin, 3 family rooms.
Bathrooms: 4 private; 12 private showers.
Bed & breakfast: £23-£28 single, £34-£40 double.
≿ ♨ Ⓤ ⊨ ⒯ Ⅷ ⚹ ⅹ ⌗ Ⓣ

Sass House Hotel ⋒
10 & 11 Craven Ter., London W2 3QD
☎ 071-262 2325
Budget accommodation, convenient for central London, Hyde Park and the West End. Paddington and Lancaster Gate underground stations nearby. Easy access to tourist attractions.
Bedrooms: 4 single, 6 double & 2 twin, 6 family rooms.
Bathrooms: 3 public.
Bed & breakfast: £15-£22 single, £18-£30 double.
Parking for 4.
Credit: Access, Visa, Diners, Amex.
≿ Ⓓ Ⓤ 🛉 ⊨ ⒯ Ⅷ ⚹ ⅹ
ⒹⒶⓅ ⚶ SP Ⓣ
⚫ Display advertisement appears on page 43.

Springfield Hotel
Listed APPROVED
154 Sussex Gdns., London W2 1UD
☎ 071-723 9898
Small hotel close to Hyde Park and Marble Arch.
Bedrooms: 3 single, 5 double & 5 twin, 4 family rooms.
Bathrooms: 15 private, 3 public.
Bed & breakfast: £22-£25 single, £36-£40 double.
Parking for 2.
Credit: Access, Visa.
≿ ♨ ℂ Ⓓ ⊡ ♥ Ⓤ ⊨ ⒯
Ⅷ ⚹ ⅒ ⅹ ⌗ ⚶ SP

Strutton Park Hotel ⋒
Listed
45 Palace Ct., London W2 4LS
☎ 071-727 5074 & 071-229 6330 & 3098 Telex 896559
GECOMS G STRUTTON
Attractive Victorian building in quiet Bayswater area close to Hyde Park, museums and antique markets. Direct transport to most places including airport.
Bedrooms: 8 single, 7 double & 10 twin, 2 family rooms.
Bathrooms: 2 public; 24 private showers.

Bed & breakfast: £30-£40 single, £45-£50 double.
Credit: Access, Visa, Diners, Amex.
≿ ♨ ℂ Ⓓ ⊡ Ⓤ ⚫ ⅒ ⌗
ⅹ ⒹⒶⓅ SP Ⓣ

Tregaron Hotel
17 Norfolk Sq., Paddington, London W2 1RU
☎ 071-723 9966
Quiet, small, central townhouse hotel, family-owned for 23 years, situated in an attractive Victorian garden square.
Bedrooms: 4 single, 6 double & 4 twin, 3 family rooms.
Bathrooms: 7 private, 3 public; 2 private showers.
Bed & breakfast: £22-£26 single, £40-£46 double.
≿ ♨ Ⓓ ⊡ ♥ Ⓤ ⊨ ⒯ Ⓘ
⚹ ⅹ ⌗

West Two Hotel ⋒
22-23 Kensington Gardens Sq., London W2 4BG
☎ 071-229 4288 Telex 24923
In a quiet garden square, close to bustling Queensway and convenient for central London.
Bedrooms: 7 single, 6 twin, 17 family rooms.
Bathrooms: 7 public.
Bed & breakfast: from £33 single, from £41 double.
≿ ♨ ⊨ ⒯ Ⅷ ⚫ ⅒ ⅹ
Ⓣ

Westland Hotel
⚜ ⚜ ⚜ ⚜ APPROVED
154 Bayswater Rd., London W2 4HP
☎ 071-229 9191
Telex 94016297 WEST G
Small, friendly hotel. Well located for West End shopping, touring or relaxing in a beautiful park. Your home-from-home.
Bedrooms: 2 single, 5 double & 19 twin, 4 family rooms.
Bathrooms: 30 private.
Bed & breakfast: £47-£55 single, £57.25-£67.50 double.
Half board: £37-£42.25 daily.
Evening meal 6.30pm (l.o. 10.30pm).
Parking for 9.
Credit: Access, Visa, C.Bl., Diners, Amex.
≿ ♨ ℂ Ⓓ ⊡ ♥ ⊨ ⚫ ⅒
Ⅷ ⚹ Ⓣ

The Westminster ⋒
16 Leinster Sq., London W2 4PR
☎ 071-286 5294 Telex 24923
Convenient for major shopping centres and places of historical interest.
Bedrooms: 30 single, 12 double & 52 twin, 8 family rooms.

Bathrooms: 102 private.
Bed & breakfast: £85-£100 single, £100-£120 double.
Evening meal 6pm (l.o. 10pm).
Credit: Access, Visa, C.Bl., Diners, Amex.
≿ ♨ ℂ Ⓓ ⊡ ♥ ⅒ ⌗ ⅹ
⅒ Ⅷ ⚹ ⅹ SP Ⓣ

Westpoint Hotel ⋒
170-172 Sussex Gdns., London W2 1TP
☎ 071-402 0281
Inexpensive accommodation in central London. Close to Paddington and Lancaster Gate underground stations. Easy access to tourist attractions and Hyde Park.
Bedrooms: 5 single, 7 double & 8 twin, 5 family rooms.
Bathrooms: 19 private, 3 public.
Bed & breakfast: £16-£25 single, £22-£35 double.
Parking for 8.
Credit: Access, Visa, C.Bl., Diners, Amex.
≿ ♨ Ⓓ Ⓤ ⊨ ⅒ ⒯ ⚫
Ⅷ ⚹ ⅹ ⌗ ⚶ SP Ⓣ
⚫ Display advertisement appears on page 43.

Whites Hotel ⋒
⚜ ⚜ ⚜ ⚜ HIGHLY COMMENDED
90-92 Lancaster Gate, London W2 3NR
☎ 071-262 2711 &
(Fax:) 071-262 2147
Telex 24771
In the style of a Victorian country mansion, the hotel overlooks Royal Kensington Gardens and Hyde Park. Within easy reach of the City and the West End.
Bedrooms: 19 single, 21 double & 14 twin.
Bathrooms: 54 private.
Bed & breakfast: max. £150 single, max. £195 double.
Half board: from £166 daily.
Lunch available.
Evening meal 6.30pm (l.o. 10.30pm).
Parking for 25.
Credit: Access, Visa, C.Bl., Diners, Amex.
≿ ♨ ℂ Ⓓ ⊡ 🛉 Ⓥ ⅒ ⊨
⚫ ⅒ Ⅷ ⚹ ⅒ ⅹ ⌗ ⚶ SP
Ⓣ

National Crown ratings were correct at the time of going to press but are subject to change. Please check at the time of booking.

Covering King's Cross, St. Pancras, Euston, Bloomsbury, Kingsway, Marylebone, Regent's Park, Leicester Square, The Strand, Charing Cross, Fleet Street, Holborn, City. See colour map 6.

Academy Hotel ⋒
⚜ ⚜ ⚜ COMMENDED
17-21 Gower St., London WC1E 6HG
☎ 071-631 4115 &
(Fax:) 071-636 3442
Telex 24364 ASTOR HG
Newly refurbished Georgian hotel in Bloomsbury. Fine restaurant and bar. Library, patio garden for afternoon tea.
Bedrooms: 9 single, 14 double & 7 twin, 2 family rooms.
Bathrooms: 26 private, 4 public.
Bed & breakfast: £68-£84 single, £80-£99 double.
Half board: £80-£97 daily.
Lunch available.
Evening meal 7pm (l.o. midnight).
Credit: Access, Visa, Diners, Amex.
≿ ♨ ℂ Ⓓ ⊡ ♥ ⊨ ⚫ Ⅷ
⅒ ⚹ ⅹ ⌗ ⚶ SP ⅏ Ⓣ

Acorns Hotel
Listed
42 Tavistock Pl., London WC1H 9RE
☎ 071-837 3077 & 2723
Grade II listed Victorian house, well-placed between West End and the City, ideal for business or pleasure. Minutes' walk to Russell Square, Euston and King's Cross.
Bedrooms: 2 single, 6 double & 4 twin, 2 family rooms.
Bathrooms: 4 public.
Bed & breakfast: £20-£25 single, £30-£36 double.
Credit: Access, Visa, C.Bl., Diners, Amex.
≿ 6 Ⓓ ⊡ ♥ Ⓤ ⅒ ⊨ ⚫ Ⅷ
⅒ ⅹ ⒹⒶⓅ SP ⌗

Bonnington Hotel ⋒
⚜ ⚜ ⚜ ⚜ COMMENDED
92 Southampton Row, London WC1B 4BH
☎ 071-242 2828 Telex 261591
Between the City and West End. Close to mainline stations and on the underground from Heathrow Airport.
Bedrooms: 109 single, 44 double & 45 twin, 17 family rooms.
Bathrooms: 215 private.
Bed & breakfast: £55-£92 single, £90-£116 double.
Half board: £70-£107 daily.

Lunch available.
Evening meal 6pm (l.o. 11pm).
Credit: Access, Visa, Diners, Amex.

🛏 📠 🖂 🖵 ♥ 🛈 Ⓥ ⌖ 🛏
● 🎦 ♨ 🔳 ♟ ♿ SP Ⓣ

County Hotel M
☎

Upper Woburn Pl., London, WC1H 0JW
☎ 071-387 5544 & 071-278 7871 Telex 263951 or 21822
Close to Euston and King's Cross railway stations. Modest, comfortable rooms. Popular bar and restaurant. Underground parking at adjacent garage.
Bedrooms: 127 single, 13 double & 35 twin.
Bathrooms: 42 public; 175 private showers.
Bed & breakfast: £30.50 single, £42 double.
Half board: £28.75-£38.25 daily.
Lunch available.
Evening meal 6pm (l.o. 7.30pm).
Parking for 150.
Credit: Access, Visa, C.Bl., Diners, Amex.

🛏 📠 Ⓥ 🛏 📺 ● 🎦 🖩 ♨
♟ ♿ SP Ⓣ

Crescent Hotel M
Listed

49-50 Cartwright Gdns., London WC1H 9EL
☎ 071-387 1515
Comfortable family-run hotel in a quiet Georgian crescent, with private gardens and tennis courts. All rooms have colour TV.
Bedrooms: 10 single, 4 double & 6 twin, 8 family rooms.
Bathrooms: 6 private, 6 public; 2 private showers.
Bed & breakfast: £30-£33 single, £44-£57.50 double.
Credit: Access, Visa.

🛏 📠 🖵 ♥ Ⓤ 🛏 📺 🖩 ♨
🔎 ❋ ♟ 🖩 SP

Euro & George Hotels

51-53 Cartwright Gdns., London WC1H 9EL
☎ 071-387 8666 & 8777 & (Fax:) 071-383 5044
Centrally located hotel close to the West End and British Museum. Bright, spacious rooms with TV, radio, direct-dial telephone, tea/coffee facilities, video films, satellite channel.
Bedrooms: 8 single, 2 double & 11 twin, 14 family rooms.
Bathrooms: 12 public.

Bed & breakfast: £29.50-£42 single, £43-£52.50 double.
Credit: Access, Visa.

🛏 📠 ♥ 🖵 🖩 ♨ Ⓤ 🛏 📺
● 🎦 🖩 ♨ ❋ ♟ OAP ♿ SP 🖩
Ⓣ

Euston Square Hotel
152-156 North Gower St., London NW1 2ND
☎ 071-388 0099 & (Fax:) 071-383 7165
Telex 264503
Well-appointed city centre hotel, close to Oxford Street and Euston station.
Bedrooms: 15 single, 29 double & 22 twin, 13 family rooms.
Bathrooms: 79 private.
Bed & breakfast: from £40 single, from £58 double.
Evening meal 7pm (l.o. 9pm).
Credit: Access, Visa, Diners, Amex.

🛏 📠 ♥ 🖵 ♥ 🛈 Ⓥ ⌖
🛏 📺 ● 🎦 🖩 ♨ ❋ SP Ⓣ

Gower House Hotel M
☎

57 Gower St., London WC1E 6HJ
☎ 071-636 4685
Friendly bed and breakfast hotel, close to Goodge Street underground station, and within easy walking distance of British Museum, shops, theatres and restaurants.
Bedrooms: 4 single, 2 double & 6 twin, 4 family rooms.
Bathrooms: 3 private, 3 public.
Bed & breakfast: £28-£30 single, £38-£40 double.
Credit: Access, Visa.

🛏 📠 Ⓤ 🛏 📺 🖩 ♨ ❋

Grange House Hotel M
☎

5 Endsleigh St., London WC1H 0DS
☎ 071-380 0616 & (Fax:) 071-380 0492
Family-run, centrally located hotel. Refurbished Georgian building. 15 per cent reduction for weekly B & B.
Bedrooms: 9 single, 4 double, 2 family rooms.
Bathrooms: 5 private; 10 private showers.
Bed & breakfast: max. £37.50 single, max. £57 double.
Credit: Access, Visa, Diners, Amex.

🛏 3 📠 🖵 ♥ Ⓤ CB ● 🖩 ❋
♿ SP Ⓣ

The symbols are explained on the flap inside the back cover.

Imperial Hotel M
🏰🏰🏰🏰

Russell Sq., London WC1B 5BB
☎ 071-837 3655 & (Fax:) 071-837 4653
Telex 263951
Central London hotel near mainline stations and underground direct to Heathrow Airport. Grill/bar open until 2 am. Extensive conference facilities. Underground parking. Rooms with colour TV and satellite channels.
Bedrooms: 233 single, 15 double & 187 twin, 12 family rooms.
Bathrooms: 447 private.
Bed & breakfast: £63 single, £75.60 double.
Half board: £46.20-£72 daily.
Lunch available.
Evening meal 6pm (l.o. 10pm).
Parking for 130.
Credit: Access, Visa, C.Bl., Diners, Amex.

🛏 ♥ 📠 🖵 🛈 Ⓥ 🛏 📺 ●
🎦 🖩 ♨ ❋ ♿ SP Ⓣ

Lonsdale Hotel M
☎

9-10 Bedford Pl., Bloomsbury, London WC1B 5JA
☎ 071-636 1812 & 071-580 9902 Telex 296012
Established bed and breakfast hotel of character, in a central yet quiet location close to the British Museum.
Bedrooms: 5 single, 6 double & 20 twin, 2 family rooms.
Bathrooms: 2 private, 8 public; 1 private shower.
Bed & breakfast: £35-£39 single, £51-£67 double.
Credit: Access, Visa.

🛏 2 📠 🖵 ♥ Ⓤ 🛏 📺 🖩 ♨
❋ 🖩 SP Ⓣ

Montague Park Hotel M
🏰🏰🏰 **COMMENDED**

12-20 Montague St., Bloomsbury, London WC1B 5BJ
☎ 071-637 1001 Telex 23307 MONTGU G
This lovely Georgian hotel has recently undergone a £7.5m restoration. Centrally situated for theatreland and Oxford Street and with bedrooms overlooking private gardens.
Bedrooms: 36 single, 53 double & 18 twin, 2 family rooms.
Bathrooms: 109 private.
Bed & breakfast: £96.50-£100 single, £129.50-£132 double.
Half board: £113-£116.50 daily.

Lunch available.
Evening meal 6pm (l.o. 10.30pm).
Credit: Access, Visa, Diners, Amex.

🛏 📠 🛏 ♥ 🖵 ♥ Ⓥ ⌖
🛏 ● 🎦 🖩 ♨ ♟ ♿ ⊘ U
OAP ♿ SP Ⓣ

Pastoria Hotel M
3-6 St. Martin's St., Leicester Square, London WC2H 7HL
☎ 071-930 8641 Telex 25538
Small friendly hotel in central London between Leicester Square and Trafalgar Square. Ideal for businessmen and visitors alike. Prices do not include breakfast.
Bedrooms: 11 single, 15 double & 32 twin.
Bathrooms: 58 private.
Bed & breakfast: £95-£99 single, £115-£119 double.
Lunch available.
Evening meal midday (l.o. 10pm).
Credit: Access, Visa, Diners, Amex.

🛏 📠 🖵 🖩 🛈 ⌖ 🛏 ● 🖩
🖩 ♟ ❋ OAP ♿ SP Ⓣ

The Portland Bloomsbury Hotel and Restaurant M
🏰🏰🏰🏰 **COMMENDED**

7 Montague St., London WC1B 5BP
☎ 071-323 1717
Country house-style hotel located in Bloomsbury.
Bedrooms: 5 single, 10 double & 10 twin, 2 family rooms.
Bathrooms: 27 private.
Bed & breakfast: £75-£85 single, £80-£120 double.
Half board: £87-£97 daily, £575-£650 weekly.
Lunch available.
Evening meal 7pm (l.o. 10.30pm).
Credit: Access, Visa, Diners, Amex.

🛏 📠 🛏 ♥ 🖵 🛈 Ⓥ 🛏
● 🎦 🖩 ♨ 🖩 ♟ ❋ ♿ SP Ⓣ

Hotel President M
🏰🏰🏰

Russell Sq., London WC1N 1DB
☎ 071-837 8844 & (Fax:) 071-837 4653
Telex 263951
Centrally located hotel. Direct access by underground to Heathrow Airport. All rooms have private facilities. Colour TV with satellite channel. Underground parking.
Bedrooms: 141 single, 170 double & 136 twin.
Bathrooms: 447 private.
Bed & breakfast: £51.50 single, £64 double.
Continued ▶

Half board: £40.45-£59.85
daily.
Lunch available.
Evening meal 6pm (l.o. 10pm).
Parking for 120.
Credit: Access, Visa, C.Bl.,
Diners, Amex.

Royal Adelphi Hotel ₥
⌣⌣⌣ APPROVED
21 Villiers St., London
WC2N 6ND
☎ 071-930 8764 &
(Fax:) 071-930 8765
Telex 262433 RAH
*Centrally located, near
Embankment and Charing
Cross underground. All rooms
with colour TV, hair-dryer,
tea/coffee facilities. Discount
on group rates and English
breakfast supplement. Evening
meal available.*
Bedrooms: 26 single, 9 double
& 16 twin.
Bathrooms: 23 private,
8 public.
Bed & breakfast: £32-£45
single, £47-£58 double.
Credit: Access, Visa, Diners,
Amex.

St. Giles Hotel ₥
Bedford Ave., London
WC1B 3AS
☎ 071-636 8616 Telex 22683
*Close to Oxford Street, and 2
minutes' walk from British
Museum. Parking available at
extra cost.*
Bedrooms: 234 single,
222 double & 132 twin,
12 family rooms.
Bathrooms: 600 private,
47 public.
Bed & breakfast: £60-£63
single, £94-£102 double.
Half board: £57-£61 daily.
Lunch available.
Evening meal 6pm (l.o.
10.30pm).
Parking for 150.
Credit: Access, Visa, Diners,
Amex.

Somerset House Hotel ₥
6 Dorset Sq., London
NW1 6QA
☎ 071-723 0741 &
(Fax:) 071-723 6081
*Spacious rooms with colour TV.
Bridal suites available. Cooked
breakfast. Located close to
Baker Street station. All rooms
with en-suite bathroom.*

Bedrooms: 8 single, 8 double
& 8 twin, 4 family rooms.
Bathrooms: 28 private.
Bed & breakfast: £29.50-
£39.50 single, £45-£55 double.
Half board: £39.50-£49.50
daily.
Evening meal 6pm (l.o.
10pm).
Credit: Access, Visa, Diners,
Amex.

Thanet Hotel
⌣⌣⌣ COMMENDED
8 Bedford Pl., London
WC1B 5JA
☎ 071-636 2869 & 071-580
3377
*Comfortable, family-run hotel,
with colour TV in all rooms.
Full English breakfast.*
Bedrooms: 2 single, 2 double
& 4 twin, 4 family rooms.
Bathrooms: 4 private,
4 public; 1 private shower.
Bed & breakfast: £33-£35
single, £48-£60 double.
Credit: Access, Visa.

The White House ₥
Regents Park, London
NW1 3UP
☎ 071-387 1200 & 071-388
0091 Telex 24111
⊕ Rank
*Near Regents Park, the zoo
and Madame Tussauds. A few
minutes from Euston Station
and about 10 minutes' walk
from Oxford Circus. There are
3 underground stations within
walking distance.*
Bedrooms: 71 single,
103 double & 309 twin,
93 family rooms.
Bathrooms: 576 private.
Bed & breakfast: £126.75-
£143.75 single, £155.50-
£174.50 double.
Lunch available.
Evening meal 6.30pm (l.o.
11.30pm).
Credit: Access, Visa, C.Bl.,
Diners, Amex.

Covering the boroughs of
Barking, Hackney,
Havering, Newham,
Redbridge, Tower
Hamlets, Waltham Forest.
See colour map 7.

Balfour Hotel
⌣⌣
31 Balfour Rd., Ilford, Essex
IG1 4HP
☎ 081-514 3238

*Small friendly hotel close to
Ilford station, the M11 and
M25. Colour TV in rooms.*
Bedrooms: 2 single, 1 twin,
2 family rooms.
Bathrooms: 2 public.
Bed & breakfast: £20-£25
single, £34-£38 double.
Parking for 3.

Forest View Hotel ₥
⌣⌣⌣ APPROVED
227 Romford Rd., Forest
Gate, London E7 9HL
☎ 081-534 4844 &
(Fax:) 081-534 8959
*Fully-equipped hotel, catering
for business and tourist
clientele. Close to London's
Docklands.*
Bedrooms: 8 single, 5 double
& 2 twin, 5 family rooms.
Bathrooms: 7 private,
3 public.
Bed & breakfast: £32.20
single, £46-£55.20 double.
Half board: £37.20-£41.20
daily.
Evening meal 6.30pm (l.o.
9pm).
Parking for 15.
Credit: Access, Visa.

Grangewood Lodge Hotel ₥
Listed
104 Clova Rd., Forest Gate,
London E7 9AF
☎ 081-534 0637
*Comfortable budget
accommodation in a quiet road,
pleasant garden. Easy access
to central London, Docklands
and M11. 12 minutes to
Liverpool Street station.*
Bedrooms: 10 single, 6 twin,
4 family rooms.
Bathrooms: 3 public;
1 private shower.
Bed & breakfast: £15-£17
single, £24-£32 double.
Credit: Access, Visa.

Grove Hill Hotel
38 Grove Hill, South
Woodford, London E18 2JG
☎ 081-989 3344
*Just off the A11/M11 and
A406; convenient for
underground station, cinemas,
shops and restaurants. Lounge
bar and lock-up garaging. Half
minute walk from town centre.*
Bedrooms: 8 single, 9 double
& 2 twin, 2 family rooms.
Bathrooms: 5 private,
3 public.

Bed & breakfast: £25-£37
single, £44-£54 double.
Parking for 13.
Credit: Access, Visa, Amex.

Hilton National ₥
⌣⌣⌣⌣ COMMENDED
Southend Arterial Rd.,
Hornchurch, Essex
RM11 3UJ
☎ (040 23) 46789
Telex 897315
⊕ Hilton
*Easy access to central London
from this modern hotel. Stylish
restaurant and bar, extensive
conference facilities.*
Bedrooms: 60 double &
73 twin, 4 family rooms.
Bathrooms: 137 private.
Bed & breakfast: £92.43-
£147.36 single, £113.36-
£157.36 double.
Lunch available.
Evening meal 7pm (l.o.
10.30pm).
Parking for 300.
Credit: Access, Visa, Diners,
Amex.

Manor House Hotel
235 Romford Rd., Forest
Gate, London E7 9HL
☎ 081-519 5432 &
(Fax:) 081-519 8395
*Family-run hotel close to
Central Line station at
Stratford. Near city and
Docklands, easy access to
M11, M25 and North Circular
road. Comfortable rooms and
friendly service.*
Bedrooms: 8 single, 4 double
& 2 twin.
Bathrooms: 14 private.
Bed & breakfast: £25-£29
single, £35-£39 double.
Parking for 12.
Credit: Access, Visa, Amex.

Packfords Hotel
⌣⌣⌣ COMMENDED
16 Snakes Lane (West),
Woodford Green, Essex
IG8 0BS
☎ 081-504 2642 & 9317 &
081-505 5508
Fax: 081-505 5778
*Small hotel with individually
designed rooms. Banqueting
and conference facilities
available.*
Bedrooms: 1 single, 6 double,
4 family rooms.
Bathrooms: 11 private.
Bed & breakfast: max. £50
single, max. £65 double.
Half board: max. £60 daily,
max. £315 weekly.

Evening meal 6.30pm (l.o. 8.30pm).
Parking for 15.
Credit: Access, Visa, Amex.

⅃ ♨ ℂ ▯ ♦ ▮ Ⓥ ⊟ ⊡
▦ ⌧ ⏚ ❄ ⋈ SP

Repton Private Hotel
18 Repton Dr., Gidea Park,
Romford, Essex RM2 5LP
☎ Romford (0708) 45253
*Small family-run hotel in quiet
residential area. Central
London easily accessible.*
Bedrooms: 4 single, 2 double
& 2 twin, 1 family room.
Bathrooms: 1 private,
2 public.
Bed & breakfast: from £20
single, from £32 double.

⅃ ♨ ▯ ♦ ⓊⓁ ⊟ ⊡ ▦ ⌧

Sans Souci House
11 Chelmsford Rd.,
Leytonstone, London
E11 1BT
☎ 081-539 1367 &
(Fax:) 081-558 9189
*Comfortable accommodation
with all amenities, in a quiet
road near Leytonstone
underground station. 20
minutes from central London.
Easy access to M11 and M25.*
Bedrooms: 2 single, 6 twin.
Bathrooms: 2 public.
Bed & breakfast: £18.40-
£23.50 single, £32.20-£41.13
double.
Parking for 4.
Credit: Access, Visa, Amex.

⅃ ⚂ ♨ ⓑ ▯ ⓊⓁ ▮ ●
▦ ⌧ ⋈ ❄ ⚄ SP ⊡

NORTH LONDON

Covering the boroughs of
Barnet, Brent, Camden,
Enfield, Haringey,
Harrow, Islington. See
colour map 7.

Angrada
21 Hawthorne Ave., Harrow,
Middlesex HA3 8AG
☎ 081-907 4237
*Convenient for Wembley and
the West End.*
Bedrooms: 1 single, 1 double
& 1 twin.
Bathrooms: 1 public.
Bed & breakfast: £15-£17
single, £26 double.

⚂ ⓊⓁ Ⓥ ▦ ⌧ ⋈ ❄

Brookland Guest House
220 Golders Green Rd.,
London NW11 9AT
☎ 081-455 6678
*In a residential area, close to
Brent Cross underground
station, 20 minutes from the
West End. Free parking.*
Bedrooms: 4 single, 7 twin,
1 family room.

Bathrooms: 3 private,
2 public.
Bed & breakfast: £20-£25
single, £30-£36 double.
Parking for 6.

⅃ ♨ ▯ ⓑ CB ≭ ♦ ⊟ ▦
⌧ Ⓣ ⋈ ⓓⒶⓅ ⚄ SP Ⓣ

Brookside Hotel ⋔
💤 APPROVED
32 Brook Ave., Wembley
Pk., Middlesex HA9 8PH
☎ 081-904 0019 & 081-908
5336
*20 minutes from central
London, a stone's throw from
Wembley Stadium and
Conference Centre.*
Bedrooms: 4 single, 4 double
& 3 twin, 2 family rooms.
Bathrooms: 3 private,
2 public.
Bed & breakfast: £20-£30
single, £38-£45 double.
Half board: £25-£35 daily,
£175-£200 weekly.
Lunch available.
Evening meal 6pm (l.o.
7.30pm).
Parking for 6.
Credit: Access, Visa.

⅃ ⚂ ♨ ⓑ CB ▮ Ⓥ ⊟ ⊡
● ▦ ⌧ ⏚ ❄ ⋈ ⚄ SP

Byron Villa
138 Bayham St., Camden
Town, London NW1 0BA
☎ 081-888 1278
*Edwardian terraced house
convenient for shops,
restaurants and pubs. Close to
undergound and centre of
London. Conservatory dining
room.*
Bedrooms: 2 single, 2 double
& 1 twin, 2 family rooms.
Bathrooms: 2 public.
Bed & breakfast: £22-£25
single, £32-£34 double.

⅃ ♨ ⓊⓁ ⊟ ⊡ ● ▦ ⌧
❄ ⋈ ⚄ SP

Cavendish Guest House
24 Cavendish Rd., London
NW6 7XP
☎ 081-451 3249
*In a quiet residential street, 5
minutes' walk from Kilburn
underground station, 20
minutes travelling time to the
West End.*
Bedrooms: 4 single, 3 double
& 1 twin.
Bathrooms: 3 public.
Bed & breakfast: max. £20
single, max. £33 double.
Parking for 3.

⅃ ⚂ ⓑ ♦ ⓊⓁ ▦ ⌧ ⋈ ❄

Central Hotel ⋔
Listed APPROVED
35 Hoop Lane, Golders
Green, London NW11 8BS
☎ 081-458 5636 &
(Fax:) 081-455 4792

*In a quiet residential area, 5
minutes' walk from Golders
Green underground station.*
Bedrooms: 9 single, 6 double
& 16 twin, 4 family rooms.
Bathrooms: 17 private,
6 public.
Bed & breakfast: £30-£45
single, £40-£65 double.
Parking for 8.
Credit: Access, Visa, Diners,
Amex.

⅃ ♨ ℂ ⓑ ⓊⓁ ▮ ⊟ ▦
⌧ ⋈ ⚄ SP Ⓣ

Charles Bernard Hotel
👑👑👑 COMMENDED
5 Frognal Rd., Hampstead,
London NW3 6AL
☎ 071-794 0101 Telex 23560
*Purpose built hotel (1971),
approximately 4 miles from
Oxford Circus, offering a
happy, friendly atmosphere.*
Bedrooms: 9 double &
48 twin.
Bathrooms: 57 private.
Bed & breakfast: £47.50-£69
single, £57.50-£85 double.
Half board: £57-£86 daily.
Lunch available.
Evening meal 6.30pm (l.o.
9.30pm).
Parking for 18.
Credit: Access, Visa, C.Bl.,
Diners, Amex.

⅃ ♨ ℂ ⓑ ▯ ♦ Ⓥ ⊟ ⊡
● ⚅ ▦ ⌧ ⏚ ⋈ ❄ ⓓⒶⓅ ⚄ SP
Ⓣ

Charlotte Guest House & Restaurant ⋔
Listed APPROVED
221 West End Lane, West
Hampstead, London
NW6 1XJ
☎ 071-794 6476 &
(Fax:) 071-431 3584
*Rooms with private facilities.
Restaurant and coffee lounge
available. French and German
spoken. Direct trains to
Gatwick, Luton and City
Airports.*
Bedrooms: 9 single, 12 double
& 6 twin, 3 family rooms.
Bathrooms: 9 private,
4 public; 3 private showers.
Bed & breakfast: £16-£25
single, £25-£35 double.
Half board: £21-£30 daily.
Lunch available.
Evening meal 6pm (l.o.
10pm).

⅃ ♨ ▯ ♦ ▮ Ⓥ ⊟ ▦ ⋈
⊡ ⓓⒶⓅ SP Ⓣ

Chumleigh Lodge Hotel ⋔
👑👑
226-228 Nether St., Finchley,
London N3 1HU
☎ 081-346 1614

*Comfortable, clean and
pleasant rooms. Easy access to
M1, A1, North Circular, West
End, Alexandra Palace and
Wembley. Residential bar and
full English breakfast.*
Bedrooms: 8 single, 5 double
& 3 twin, 4 family rooms.
Bathrooms: 6 private,
3 public; 2 private showers.
Bed & breakfast: £25-£30
single, £33-£40 double.
Half board: £26-£45 daily,
£168-£287 weekly.
Parking for 11.
Credit: Access, Visa, Diners.

⅃ ♨ ▯ ♦ Ⓥ ⊟ ⊡ ▦ ⌧
⋈ ⓓⒶⓅ ⚄ SP Ⓣ

Claremont Hotel ⋔
👑👑👑
154 High St., Wealdstone,
Harrow, Middlesex
HA3 7AT
☎ 081-427 2738 &
(Fax:) 081-427 0181
*Small friendly hotel with easy
access to central London and
Wembley Conference Centre.
Licensed bar, satellite TV, off-
street parking.*
Bedrooms: 1 single, 7 double
& 4 twin, 1 family room.
Bathrooms: 6 private,
2 public; 4 private showers.
Bed & breakfast: £28-£40
single, £38-£45 double.
Half board: £23-£45 daily,
£137-£261 weekly.
Evening meal 7.30pm (l.o.
9.30pm).
Parking for 14.
Credit: Access, Visa, Amex.

⅃ ♨ ℂ ▯ ♦ ▮ Ⓥ ⊟
⊡ ⌧ ⏚ ⋈ ⓓⒶⓅ SP ⊞
Ⓣ

Clive Hotel at Hampstead ⋔
Primrose Hill Rd.,
Hampstead, London
NW3 3NA
☎ 071-586 2233 Telex 22759
Ⓒⓗ Hilton
*Near Primrose Hill, the hotel
offers a relaxed atmosphere.
Popular restaurant and bar.*
Bedrooms: 10 single,
27 double & 54 twin, 5 family
rooms.
Bathrooms: 96 private.
Bed & breakfast: £50-£91
single, £100-£125 double.
Lunch available.
Evening meal 7pm (l.o.
9.45pm).
Parking for 12.
Credit: Access, Visa, Diners,
Amex.

⅃ ℂ ⓑ ▯ ♦ ▮ Ⓥ ≭ ⊟
⊡ ● ⚄ ⚅ ⏚ ▦ ⌧ ⓓⒶⓅ ⚄ SP
Ⓣ

Costello Palace Hotel

374 Seven Sisters Rd.,
Finsbury Pk., London
N4 2PG
☎ 081-802 6551
*Attractive, family-run hotel
opposite park and on the main
road. Close to Finsbury Park
and Manor House
undergrounds. Convenient for
all amenities. Full English
breakfast.*
Bedrooms: 9 single, 16 double
& 15 twin, 4 family rooms.
Bathrooms: 18 private,
6 public; 8 private showers.
Bed & breakfast: £25-£30
single, £32-£42 double.
Parking for 30.
Credit: Access, Visa.

Crescent Lodge Hotel ⋀
🏶🏶🏶 COMMENDED

58-60 Welldon Cres., Harrow,
Middlesex HA1 1QR
☎ 081-863 5491 & 5163 &
(0836) 779203
Fax: 081-427 5965
*In a quiet residential area, 10
minutes' walk from Harrow
and Wealdstone BR station
and 5 minutes from
underground. Convenient for
Wembley Conference Centre,
West End and M1.*
Bedrooms: 9 single, 3 double
& 7 twin, 2 family rooms.
Bathrooms: 12 private,
4 public.
Bed & breakfast: £32-£45
single, £48-£60 double.
Half board: £44-£57 daily,
£308-£380 weekly.
Lunch available.
Evening meal 7pm (l.o.
8.30pm).
Parking for 7.
Credit: Access, Visa, Diners.

Elm Hotel ⋀
🏶🏶 COMMENDED

1-7 Elm Rd., Wembley,
Middlesex HA9 7JA
☎ 081-902 1764
*Ten minutes' walk (1200
yards) from Wembley Stadium
and Conference Centre. 150
yards from Wembley Central
underground and mainline
station.*
Bedrooms: 8 single, 8 double
& 9 twin, 5 family rooms.
Bathrooms: 20 private,
5 public.

Bed & breakfast: £32-£45
single, £42-£57 double.
Parking for 6.

Forty Towers Hotel

4 Forty Lane, Wembley,
Middlesex HA9 9EB
☎ 081-904 5629 & 081-908
6694
*Close to Wembley Stadium
and Wembley Park
underground, 15 minutes from
West End. Attractive decor.
Bar and lounge.*
Bedrooms: 1 single, 3 double
& 2 twin, 2 family rooms.
Bathrooms: 3 public.
Bed & breakfast: £18-£22
single, £35-£45 double.
Parking for 8.

Hilton National Wembley ⋀

Empire Way, Wembley,
Middlesex HA9 8DS
☎ 081-902 8839 &
(Fax:) 081-900 2201
Telex 24837
🅒🅡 Hilton
*Adjacent to the Wembley
complex, this is the
headquarters hotel for the
conference centre. Within easy
reach of major motorways and
20 minutes on the underground
from central London.*
Bedrooms: 4 single, 82 double
& 188 twin, 26 family rooms.
Bathrooms: 300 private.
Bed & breakfast: £101-£108
single, £140-£150 double.
Lunch available.
Evening meal 6.45pm (l.o.
10pm).
Parking for 300.
Credit: Access, Visa, Diners,
Amex.

Hindes Hotel
🏶🏶

8 Hindes Rd., Harrow,
Middlesex HA1 1SJ
☎ 081-427 7468
*Homely owner-run bed and
breakfast hotel near the M1.
West End 15 minutes by
underground. Convenient for
Wembley Stadium complex.*
Bedrooms: 3 single, 1 double
& 7 twin, 2 family rooms.
Bathrooms: 1 private,
3 public.
Bed & breakfast: £28-£38
single, £39-£49 double.
Parking for 5.
Credit: Access, Visa.

J and T Guest House

98 Park Ave., North,
Willesden Green, London
NW10 1JY
☎ 081-452 4085 &
(Fax:) 081-450 2503
*Small guesthouse in north west
London close to underground.
Easy access to Wembley
Stadium complex. 5 minutes
from M1.*
Bedrooms: 1 single, 1 twin,
1 family room.
Bathrooms: 1 private,
2 public.
Bed & breakfast: £15-£25
single, £30-£36 double.
Parking for 2.

Kandara Guest House

68 Ockendon Rd., London
N1 3NW
☎ 071-226 5721 & 3379
*Small family-run guesthouse
near the Angel, Islington. Free
street parking and good public
transport to West End and
City.*
Bedrooms: 4 single, 1 double,
3 family rooms.
Bathrooms: 2 public.
Bed & breakfast: £17.50-
£18.50 single, £24-£26 double.

Kempsford House Hotel

21-23 St. John's Rd., Harrow,
Middlesex HA1 2EE
☎ 081-427 4983 & 0390
*Comfortable, family-run hotel
in central Harrow. Convenient
for shops, the station and
Heathrow Airport.*
Bedrooms: 15 single, 7 double
& 7 twin, 3 family rooms.
Bathrooms: 10 private,
4 public; 8 private showers.
Bed & breakfast: £26-£43
single, £39-£53 double.
Parking for 20.
Credit: Access, Visa.

Keren Hotel ⋀
🏶

14 Highbury New Pk.,
Islington, London N5 2DB
☎ 071-226 1035
*Friendly hotel 12 minutes from
Oxford Circus. Full English
breakfast, TV lounge.*
Bedrooms: 13 single, 3 double
& 3 twin, 1 family room.
Bathrooms: 4 public.
Bed & breakfast: £20-£24
single, £36-£42 double.
Parking for 8.

Mr and Mrs Kim's Private Guest House
Listed

85 Station Rd., Finchley,
London N3 2SH
☎ 081-346 4413 &
(0707) 56436
*Close to Finchley Central
underground and near shops.
15 minutes to central London,
access to M1 and M25.
German spoken.*
Bedrooms: 2 single, 1 double
& 1 twin.
Bathrooms: 1 public.
Bed & breakfast: £16-£18
single, £30-£34 double.
Parking for 2.

La Gaffe ⋀
🏶🏶🏶 COMMENDED

107-111 Heath St.,
Hampstead, London
NW3 6SS
☎ 071-435 4941 & 8965 &
(Fax:) 071-794 7592
*On Hampstead Heath, 200
yards from the underground
and 12 minutes from the West
End.*
Bedrooms: 4 single, 6 double
& 4 twin.
Bathrooms: 14 private.
Bed & breakfast: £42.50-
£52.50 single, £65-£75 double.
Lunch available.
Evening meal 6.30pm (l.o.
11.15pm).
Credit: Access, Visa, Diners,
Amex.

The Langorf Hotel ⋀
🏶🏶🏶🏶 COMMENDED

20 Frognal, Hampstead,
London NW3 6AG
☎ 071-794 4483
*Three minutes' walk from
Finchley Road underground,
this elegant Edwardian
residence in Hampstead boasts
attractive bedrooms with full
facilities.*
Bedrooms: 4 single, 20 double
& 8 twin.
Bathrooms: 32 private.
Bed & breakfast: £35-£69
single, £50-£89 double.
Lunch available.
Evening meal 6pm (l.o.
11pm).
Parking for 5.
Credit: Access, Visa, Diners,
Amex.

Lindal Hotel M

COMMENDED

2 Hindes Rd., Harrow,
Middlesex HA1 1SJ
☎ 081-863 3164
*Close to busy town centre with
extensive shopping facilities,
restaurants and cinemas. Easy
reach motorways, central
London and Wembley.*
Bedrooms: 10 single, 3 double
& 7 twin, 1 family room.
Bathrooms: 18 private,
1 public.
Bed & breakfast: £34-£44.50
single, £46-£54.50 double.
Half board: max. £64 daily.
Evening meal 7pm (l.o.
8.45pm).
Parking for 20.
Credit: Access, Visa.

Mullane Guest House

Listed

66 Wembley Hill Rd.,
Wembley, Middlesex
HA9 8EA
☎ 081-902 9211 & 8066
*Less than 5 minutes from
Wembley complex.*
Bedrooms: 3 single, 2 double
& 6 twin, 1 family room.
Bathrooms: 2 private,
2 public.
Bed & breakfast: £13-£14
single, from £26 double.
Parking for 8.
Credit: Visa.

Oak Lodge Hotel

COMMENDED

80 Village Rd., Bush Hill
Park, Enfield, Middlesex
EN1 2EU
☎ 081-360 7082 &
(Fax:) 081-364 0040
*"Director's choice" country
house with beautiful gardens.
Small executive conference
suite. Concessionary
weekend/national tariff. 30
minutes to Stansted, central
London and close to M25.*
Bedrooms: 2 single, 2 double.
Bathrooms: 4 private,
1 public.
Bed & breakfast: £45-£65
single, £55-£75 double.
Lunch available.
Evening meal 7.30pm (l.o.
8.30pm).
Parking for 4.
Credit: Access, Visa, C.Bl.,
Diners, Amex.

Parkside Hotel

384 Seven Sisters Rd.,
Finsbury Park, London
N4 2PQ
☎ 081-800 8888
*Established hotel overlooking
Finsbury Park. A few minutes
from Manor House
underground station with direct
routes to Heathrow Airport,
West End and City.*
Bedrooms: 38 single,
20 double & 26 twin, 15 family
rooms.
Bathrooms: 44 private,
11 public.
Bed & breakfast: £17.50-£28
single, £30-£38 double.
Evening meal 6pm (l.o. 8pm).
Parking for 50.
Credit: Access, Visa.

Queens Hotel M

5-7 Queens Ave., Muswell
Hill, London N10 3PE
☎ 081-883 4384 & 0722 &
(Fax:) 081-883 4384
*Small hotel near Alexandra
Palace and Park.*
Bedrooms: 18 single,
14 double & 9 twin, 4 family
rooms.
Bathrooms: 16 private,
3 public; 19 private showers.
Bed & breakfast: £25-£40
single, £38-£50 double.
Evening meal 7pm (l.o. 9pm).
Parking for 10.
Credit: Access, Visa, Diners,
Amex.

Redland Hotel M

418 Seven Sisters Rd.,
London N4 2LX
☎ 081-800 1826 & 9961 &
(Fax:) 081-802 7080
Telex 265218 SPRING G
*Next to Manor House
underground station offering
easy access to West End, City
and Heathrow Airport and
close to Alexandra Palace.*
Bedrooms: 8 single, 8 double
& 4 twin, 4 family rooms.
Bathrooms: 6 public;
2 private showers.
Bed & breakfast: £35 single,
£45 double.
Parking for 12.
Credit: Access, Visa, Diners,
Amex.

Rilux House M

1 Lodge Rd., London
NW4 4DD
☎ 081-203 0933 &
(Fax:) 081-203 6446

*High standard establishment
for 2/3 people, with own
shower, WC, kitchen, tea
facilities and video. Separate
entry and garden. Few
minutes' walk from Hendon
Central underground and
buses.*
Bedrooms: 1 family room.
Bathrooms: 1 private.
Bed & breakfast: £19-£27
single, £30-£50 double.
Parking for 1.

Royal Chace Hotel M

COMMENDED

162 The Ridgeway, Enfield,
Middlesex EN2 3AR
☎ 081-366 6500 Telex 266628
R CHACE
*Pleasant hotel of character, set
in Green Belt, with access to
London and motorway. Ideal
for businessmen and tourists.*
Bedrooms: 43 double &
47 twin, 3 family rooms.
Bathrooms: 93 private.
Bed & breakfast: £45-£69
single, £55-£84 double.
Half board: £43.45-£84.95
daily.
Lunch available.
Evening meal 7pm (l.o.
10pm).
Parking for 300.
Credit: Access, Visa, Diners,
Amex.

Seaford Lodge M

2 Fellows Rd., Hampstead,
London NW3 3LP
☎ 071-722 5032
*Small family-run hotel
convenient for central London
and the City. Hotel has 2
bedrooms that have wheelchair
access and are equipped with
rails in the bathrooms, etc.*
Bedrooms: 2 single, 5 double
& 7 twin, 1 family room.
Bathrooms: 15 private.
Bed & breakfast: £40-£50
single, £60-£75 double.
Parking for 6.
Credit: Access, Visa, Diners.

Spring Park Hotel M

400 Seven Sisters Rd., London
N4 2LX
☎ 081-800 6030 &
(Fax:) 081-802 5652
Telex 265218 SPRING G
*Overlooking Finsbury Park,
next to Manor House
underground station for
Piccadilly line direct to the
West End and Heathrow
Airport.*

Bedrooms: 7 single, 21 double
& 13 twin.
Bathrooms: 19 private,
8 public.
Bed & breakfast: £45-£55
single, £55-£63 double.
Lunch available.
Evening meal 6pm (l.o.
10.45pm).
Parking for 50.
Credit: Access, Visa, C.Bl.,
Diners, Amex.

Tudor Lodge Hotel

50 Field End Rd., Eastcote,
Pinner, Middlesex HA5 2QN
☎ 081-429 0585 & 081-866
6027
*16th C hotel, with character
and taste, offering all modern
amenities. Convenient for
London airports, motorways
and many golf-courses. 25
minutes from town.*
Bedrooms: 10 single, 9 double
& 6 twin, 8 family rooms.
Bathrooms: 27 private,
5 public.
Bed & breakfast: £25-£62
single, £35-£72 double.
Parking for 40.
Credit: Access, Visa, Amex.

West Lodge Park

COMMENDED

Cockfosters Rd., Hadley
Wood, Near Barnet,
Hertfordshire EN4 0PY
☎ 081-440 8311 Telex 24734
*White-painted Georgian
country house set in 35 acres of
grounds in rolling countryside.*
Bedrooms: 20 single,
20 double & 10 twin.
Bathrooms: 50 private.
Bed & breakfast: £79.50-
£89.50 single, £107.50-£132.50
double.
Lunch available.
Evening meal 7.15pm (l.o.
9.45pm).
Parking for 100.
Credit: Access, Visa, Amex.

White Lodge Hotel M

1 Church Lane, Hornsey,
London N8 7BU
☎ 081-348 9765
*Small, friendly, family hotel
offering personal service.
Extended and refurbished in
1989. Easy access to all
transport.*
Bedrooms: 6 single, 6 double
& 2 twin, 3 family rooms.
Bathrooms: 6 private,
3 public.

Continued ▶

NORTH LONDON

Continued

Bed & breakfast: £20-£22 single, £30-£38 double.
Evening meal 6pm (l.o. 7pm).
Credit: Access, Visa.

SOUTH EAST LONDON

Covering the boroughs of Bexley, Bromley, Croydon, Greenwich, Lewisham, Southwark. See colour map 7.

Bailey's

77 Belmont Hill, London SE13 5AX
☎ 081-852 7373
Extensively restored old house in good position near Greenwich. 15 minutes by train from central London and 5 minutes from station and local shops.
Bedrooms: 2 twin, 1 family room.
Bathrooms: 1 public.
Bed & breakfast: £15-£20 single, £25-£30 double.
Half board: £20-£25 daily.
Parking for 1.

Be My Guest ♠

79 Venner Rd., Sydenham, London SE26 5HU
☎ 081-659 5413 & 071-233 0201 Fax: 081-776 8151
Spacious Victorian residence, 20 minutes to central London from nearby stations. Free travel in London with reservations of 3 days or more. Car and driver service by arrangement.
Bedrooms: 1 double, 2 family rooms.
Bathrooms: 1 private, 1 public.
Bed & breakfast: £40-£46 single, £45-£55 double.
Half board: £32.50-£56 daily.
Evening meal 7pm (l.o. 11pm).
Parking for 2.
Credit: Access, Visa.

Bedknobs

Listed APPROVED
58 Glengarry Rd., East Dulwich, London SE22 8QD
☎ 081-299 2004
Victorian family-run house, carefully restored providing modern-day comforts and a friendly service. Easy access to City and West End.

Bedrooms: 1 single, 1 double & 2 twin, 1 family room.
Bathrooms: 2 public.
Bed & breakfast: £19-£22.50 single, £34-£38 double.

Briarley Hotel

8 Outram Rd., Croydon, Surrey CR0 6XE
☎ 081-654 1000 & (Fax:) 081-656 6084
Victorian exterior with a modern 1990s interior and facilities. Friendly atmosphere. Bar, restaurant, garden, parking. Good public transport.
Bedrooms: 20 single, 8 double & 8 twin, 2 family rooms.
Bathrooms: 38 private.
Bed & breakfast: from £59.50 single, from £69.50 double.
Evening meal 6.30pm (l.o. 10pm).
Parking for 25.
Credit: Access, Visa, Diners, Amex.

Buxted Lodge

40 Parkhurst Rd., Bexley, Kent DA5 1AS
☎ Crayford (0322) 54010
Victorian lodge retaining many of the original features, with beautiful grounds. 30 minutes to central London by British Rail.
Bedrooms: 3 single, 3 double & 6 twin, 2 family rooms.
Bathrooms: 2 private, 4 public.
Bed & breakfast: £18-£25 single, £35-£45 double.
Half board: £30-£35 daily, £180-£210 weekly.
Evening meal 6.30pm (l.o. 8pm).
Parking for 14.

Clarendon Hotel ♠

APPROVED
8-16 Montpelier Row, Blackheath, London SE3 0RW
☎ 081-318 4321 & (Fax:) 081-318 4378
Telex 896367 CLADN G
Facing the heath and 22 minutes by train from central London. 10 minutes' walk from Greenwich, 5 minutes' walk from Greenwich Royal Park.
Bedrooms: 47 single, 81 double & 64 twin, 5 family rooms.
Bathrooms: 170 private, 18 public.
Bed & breakfast: £41.25-£45 single, £67-£76 double.

Half board: £53.75-£57.50 daily.
Lunch available.
Evening meal 6.30pm (l.o. 9.45pm).
Parking for 80.
Credit: Access, Visa, Diners, Amex.

Crystal Palace Tower Hotel

114 Church Rd., Crystal Palace, London SE19 2UB
☎ 081-653 0176
Family-run hotel converted from a large Victorian house, 40 minutes from the centre of London.
Bedrooms: 2 single, 1 double & 3 twin, 5 family rooms.
Bathrooms: 4 private, 2 public; 1 private shower.
Bed & breakfast: £21-£25 single, £32-£36 double.
Parking for 10.

Diana Hotel

88 Thurlow Park Rd., London SE21 8HY
☎ 081-670 3250
Small friendly family-run hotel in a pleasant suburb of Dulwich, 10 minutes from central London.
Bedrooms: 2 single, 4 double & 3 twin, 4 family rooms.
Bathrooms: 2 private, 2 public; 1 private shower.
Bed & breakfast: £30-£38 single, £35-£45 double.
Evening meal 6pm (l.o. 7.30pm).
Parking for 3.

The Dome Hotel

51-53 Camberwell Church St., London SE5 8TR
☎ 071-703 5262 & (Fax:) 071-252 7457
On the main road to Dover, convenient for Kings College, Dulwich and Maudsley hospitals. Oval underground station allows access to central London.
Bedrooms: 3 single, 6 double & 10 twin, 11 family rooms.
Bathrooms: 4 private, 1 public; 18 private showers.
Bed & breakfast: £25-£45 single, £35-£55 double.
Half board: £35-£55 daily.
Evening meal 6pm (l.o. 9pm).
Credit: Access, Visa, Diners, Amex.

Glendevon House Hotel

80 Southborough Rd., Bickley, Kent BR1 2EN
☎ 081-467 2183
Small hotel with private car park. Convenient for central London. Caters for tourists and businessmen.
Bedrooms: 5 single, 3 double & 2 twin, 1 family room.
Bathrooms: 3 public; 3 private showers.
Bed & breakfast: £19.75-£28.75 single, £35.75-£41 double.
Parking for 6.
Credit: Access, Visa.

Kirkdale Hotel

COMMENDED
22 St. Peter's Rd., Croydon, Surrey CR0 1HD
☎ 081-688 5898 & (Fax:) 081-667 0817
Large detached corner house close to Croydon shopping and business centre, on bus route and with easy commuting to London. Maintained by owner family.
Bedrooms: 11 single, 7 twin.
Bathrooms: 7 private, 2 public.
Bed & breakfast: £23-£35 single, £37-£50 double.
Evening meal 6pm (l.o. 7.30pm).
Parking for 12.
Credit: Access, Visa.

Markington Hotel

9 Haling Park Rd., South Croydon, Surrey CR2 6NG
☎ 081-681 6494 & (Fax:) 081-688 6530
Family-run Victorian property fitted out to modern standards, in a quiet road overlooking woodland. Bus stop 100 yards away.
Bedrooms: 9 single, 6 double & 4 twin, 1 family room.
Bathrooms: 20 private, 2 public.
Bed & breakfast: £30-£52 single, £48-£65 double.
Evening meal 6.30pm (l.o. 8.30pm).
Parking for 17.
Credit: Access, Visa, Amex.

Meadow Croft Lodge ♠

APPROVED
96-98 Southwood Rd., New Eltham, London SE9 3QS
☎ 081-859 1488

Between A2 and A20, near New Eltham station with easy access to London. Warm and friendly atmosphere. TV in rooms. British Tourist Authority London B&B award 1990.
Bedrooms: 4 single, 3 double & 9 twin, 1 family room.
Bathrooms: 1 private, 4 public; 10 private showers.
Bed & breakfast: £21-£26 single, £37-£45 double.
Parking for 9.
Credit: Access, Visa.

Mrs. M. Noonan
| Listed |

13 Wellmeadow Rd., Hither Green, Lewisham, London SE13 6SY
☎ 081-697 1398
Family home offering bed and breakfast.
Bedrooms: 1 single, 2 double, 1 family room.
Bathrooms: 2 public.
Bed & breakfast: £15 single, £26 double.
Half board: £18 daily, £126 weekly.

Norfolk Court Hotel
♛♛♛

315 Beulah Hill, Upper Norwood, London SE19 3HW
☎ 081-670 3744 &
(Fax:) 081-761 9246
Telex 264503 ESHG
A small hotel catering for both businessmen and tourists. Easy access to central London.
Bedrooms: 2 single, 5 double & 8 twin, 4 family rooms.
Bathrooms: 15 private, 3 public.
Bed & breakfast: from £45 single, from £55 double.
Evening meal 7pm (l.o. 9.30pm).
Parking for 25.
Credit: Access, Visa, Diners, Amex.

Norfolk House Hotel ♨
♛♛♛♛

587 London Rd., Thornton Heath, Croydon, Surrey CR4 6AY
☎ 081-689 8989 &
(Fax:) 081-689 0335
Hotel with wide range of facilities. Discounts for weekend group bookings.
Bedrooms: 33 single, 25 double & 40 twin, 4 family rooms.
Bathrooms: 102 private.

Bed & breakfast: £35-£72 single, £58-£90 double.
Half board: £40.95-£56.95 daily, £370.65 weekly.
Lunch available.
Evening meal 6.30pm (l.o. 10pm).
Parking for 100.
Credit: Access, Visa, Diners, Amex.

Norwood Lodge Hotel
♛♛♛

17-19 South Norwood Hill, London SE25 6AA
☎ 081-653 3962 &
(Fax:) 081-653 0332
Comfortable small hotel with a friendly atmosphere. All rooms with en-suite facilities, colour TV, trouser press, direct-dial telephone and tea/coffee making facilities.
Bedrooms: 6 single, 5 double & 8 twin, 1 family room.
Bathrooms: 20 private, 1 public.
Bed & breakfast: £35-£45 single, £45-£55 double.
Lunch available.
Evening meal 6pm (l.o. 8pm).
Parking for 15.
Credit: Access, Visa, Diners, Amex.

Selsdon Park Hotel ♨
♛♛♛♛♛ | COMMENDED |

Sanderstead, South Croydon, Surrey CR2 8YA
☎ 081-657 8811 Telex 945003
Country house hotel, 10 minutes from the M25, 30 minutes from London and Gatwick. Set in 200 acres of parkland. Special weekend rates.
Bedrooms: 40 single, 50 double & 80 twin.
Bathrooms: 170 private.
Bed & breakfast: £111.50-£126.50 single, £143-£175 double.
Half board: £95.50-£150.50 daily.
Lunch available.
Evening meal 7.30pm (l.o. 9.15pm).
Parking for 265.
Credit: Access, Visa, Diners, Amex.

Traditional Bed and Breakfast
34 Devonshire Dr., Greenwich, London SE10 8JZ
☎ 081-691 1918

Small Victorian guesthouse in historic Greenwich. Period decor, full breakfasts, 24-hour access to rooms on separate guest floor.
Bedrooms: 1 single, 1 double & 1 twin.
Bathrooms: 1 public.
Bed & breakfast: £18-£19 single, £32-£38 double.

Wellesley Hotel, Wellesley Centre ♨
1 Lansdowne Rd., Croydon, Surrey CR0 2BX
☎ 081-760 9885
In the heart of Croydon, close to shopping centre, concert hall and theatre and 5 minutes' walk from East Croydon station. Conference facilities, sports and leisure complex.
Bedrooms: 10 single, 12 double & 18 twin, 2 family rooms.
Bathrooms: 42 private, 10 public.
Bed & breakfast: max. £49 single, max. £61 double.
Lunch available.
Evening meal 5pm (l.o. 9.30pm).
Credit: Access, Visa, Amex.

Weston House
♛♛♛ | APPROVED |

8 Eltham Green, Eltham, London SE9 5LB
☎ 081-850 5191
An early Victorian villa with modern comforts in outer London, close to the two major Channel Port roads.
Bedrooms: 3 single, 2 double & 3 twin, 1 family room.
Bathrooms: 3 private, 1 public; 4 private showers.
Bed & breakfast: £30-£35 single, £40-£45 double.
Evening meal 7pm.
Parking for 6.
Credit: Access, Visa.

The White House
| Listed |

242 Norwood Rd., West Norwood, London SE27 9AW
☎ 081-670 3607 & 081-761 8892
Listed Georgian house with forecourt parking, on main road. Buses and Southern Region trains to the city. Close to the Crystal Palace National Sports Centre.
Bedrooms: 3 single, 1 family room.

Bathrooms: 1 private, 2 public.
Bed & breakfast: £9-£11 single, £20-£22 double.
Parking for 3.

SOUTH WEST LONDON

Covering the boroughs of Kingston upon Thames, Lambeth, Merton, Richmond, Sutton, Wandsworth. See colour map 7.

Hotel Antoinette of Kingston ♨
26 Beaufort Rd., Kingston upon Thames, Surrey KT1 2TQ
☎ 081-546 1044
Fax: 081-547 2595
Telex 928180
Tourist hotel close to Kew, Windsor and Hampton Court. Easy access to Central London by road or public transport.
Bedrooms: 36 single, 19 double & 34 twin, 25 family rooms.
Bathrooms: 114 private.
Bed & breakfast: £40-£45 single, £45-£50 double.
Evening meal 6.30pm (l.o. 9.15pm).
Parking for 80.
Credit: Access, Visa, Amex.

Bremic Guest House
♛♛ | COMMENDED |

10 Russell Rd., Twickenham, Middlesex
☎ 081-892 9664
Small family-run guesthouse conveniently located, 30 minutes from central London and 20 minutes from Heathrow.
Bedrooms: 3 single, 2 twin, 1 family room.
Bathrooms: 2 private, 1 public.
Bed & breakfast: £25-£30 single, £37-£45 double.
Parking for 5.

Bushy Park Lodge Hotel
| Listed |

6 Sandy Lane, Teddington, Middlesex TW11 0DR
☎ 081-943 5428 & 081-943 1917
Close to Kingston Bridge and Hampton Court. Purpose-built in 1989. No restaurant.
Bedrooms: 5 double & 1 twin.
Bathrooms: 6 private.
Continued ▶

SOUTH WEST LONDON

Continued

Bed & breakfast: £45 single, £55-£60 double.
Parking for 8.
Credit: Access, Visa, Diners, Amex.

Chase Lodge
🏆🏆 COMMENDED

10 Park Rd., Hampton Wick, Kingston upon Thames, Surrey KT1 4AS
☎ 081-943 1862
In conservation area and next to Hampton Court, Bushy Park and River Thames. 20 minutes from centre of London.
Bedrooms: 1 single, 2 double & 2 twin, 1 family room.
Bathrooms: 3 private, 1 public.
Bed & breakfast: £26-£42 single, £40-£51 double.
Half board: £35.95-£51.95 daily.
Credit: Access, Visa, Amex.

Compton Guest House
Listed

65 Compton Rd., Wimbledon, London SW19 7QA
☎ 081-947 4488 & 081-879 3245
Family-run guesthouse of a high standard, in a pleasant and peaceful area. 5 minutes from Wimbledon station (British Rail and District Line), offering quick and easy access to the West End and central London.
Bedrooms: 2 single, 1 double & 2 twin, 3 family rooms.
Bathrooms: 2 public.
Bed & breakfast: £30-£35 single, £40-£45 double.
Parking for 2.

The Dittons Hotel

47 Lovelace Rd., Long Ditton, Surrey KT6 6NA
☎ 081-399 7482
Small country house hotel with a large garden surrounded by trees. Convenient for Hampton Court, Wimbledon, Sandown Park and Richmond. 16 minutes to Waterloo by train.
Bedrooms: 4 single, 3 double & 3 twin, 1 family room.
Bathrooms: 3 public.
Bed & breakfast: £35.25 single, £47 double.
Lunch available.

Evening meal 8pm (l.o. 10pm).
Parking for 8.
Credit: Amex.

The Petersham Hotel

Nightingale Lane, Richmond upon Thames, Surrey TW10 6UZ
☎ 081-940 7471 Telex 928556
Built in 1865, this mansion commands famous views over the River Thames from its four poster bedrooms and restaurant. Richmond's antique shops and traditional pubs within walking distance. Easy access to London and main motorways.
Bedrooms: 28 single, 12 double & 14 twin, 2 family rooms.
Bathrooms: 56 private.
Bed & breakfast: £90-£100 single, £110-£145 double.
Lunch available.
Evening meal 7pm (l.o. 9.45pm).
Parking for 50.
Credit: Access, Visa, C.Bl., Diners, Amex.

Riverside Hotel
🏆🏆

23 Petersham Rd., Richmond, Surrey TW10 6UH
☎ 081-940 1339
Elegant Victorian house overlooking the Thames, close to Richmond Bridge. En-suite rooms, colour TVs, tea and coffee facilities.
Bedrooms: 5 single, 4 double & 3 twin, 1 family room.
Bathrooms: 11 private, 1 public; 2 private showers.
Bed & breakfast: £38-£50 single, £55-£60 double.
Credit: Access, Visa, Amex.

Surbiton Lodge

4 Cranes Park Ave., Surbiton, Surrey KT5 8BX
☎ 081-399 5848
Comfortable, friendly guesthouse in quiet residential locality. Close to restaurants, shops, trains and buses. Within 20 minutes of Heathrow, Hampton Court, Kew Gardens and London.
Bedrooms: 4 single, 1 double, 1 family room.
Bathrooms: 3 public.
Bed & breakfast: £22.50-£25.50 single, £29.50-£32.50 double.
Parking for 3.

Thatched House Hotel
🏆🏆🏆 COMMENDED

135 Cheam Rd., Sutton, Surrey SM1 2BN
☎ 081-642 3131
An old cottage-style detached thatched hotel. Completely modernised. A few minutes from Sutton station and 20 minutes from central London.
Bedrooms: 6 single, 13 double & 8 twin.
Bathrooms: 18 private, 4 public; 1 private shower.
Bed & breakfast: £37.50-£52.50 single, £49.50-£65 double.
Half board: £49-£65 daily.
Evening meal 7pm (l.o. 8.45pm).
Parking for 20.
Credit: Access, Visa, C.Bl.

Warwick Guest House

321 Ewell Rd., Surbiton, Surrey KT6 7BX
☎ 081-399 2405 & 5837
Comfortable family-run guesthouse, close to Kingston town centre, Hampton Court and both the London airports. About 10 miles from London, with a fast train service to the West End. Ideal for tourists and business people.
Bedrooms: 1 single, 4 double & 2 twin, 2 family rooms.
Bathrooms: 1 private, 2 public; 3 private showers.
Bed & breakfast: £28-£34 single, £40-£46 double.
Evening meal 6.30pm (l.o. 4pm).
Parking for 8.
Credit: Access, Visa.

White Walls Guest House
🏆🏆

12 Lingfield Ave., Kingston upon Thames, Surrey KT1 2TN
☎ 081-546 2719
Small friendly guesthouse convenient for London, Hampton Court, Windsor Castle, Heathrow and Gatwick Airports.
Bedrooms: 3 single, 2 twin, 3 family rooms.
Bathrooms: 3 private, 1 public; 2 private showers.
Bed & breakfast: from £35.25 single, £47-£54.05 double.
Parking for 4.

Wimbledon Hotel
🏆🏆

78 Worple Rd., Wimbledon, London SW19 4HZ
☎ 081-946 9265 & 081-946 1581
Small hotel offering a high standard of service and video security for your peace of mind. Within easy reach of London, Hampton Court and Kingston, and close to plenty of local restaurants.
Bedrooms: 2 single, 2 double & 3 twin, 7 family rooms.
Bathrooms: 5 private, 2 public; 6 private showers.
Bed & breakfast: £45-£48 single, £51-£58 double.
Parking for 9.
Credit: Access, Visa.

WEST LONDON

Covering the boroughs of Ealing, Hammersmith, Hillingdon, Hounslow, also London Airport (Heathrow). See colour map 7.

Acton Park Hotel 🅼
🏆🏆🏆 COMMENDED

116 The Vale, Acton, London W3 7JT
☎ 081-743 9417 &
(Fax:) 081-743 9417
Telex 919412
Small, friendly, family-run hotel, just off the North Circular Road, between Heathrow and the West End, overlooking parkland. Ample parking.
Bedrooms: 7 single, 4 double & 8 twin, 2 family rooms.
Bathrooms: 21 private.
Bed & breakfast: £36.50-£42.50 single, £44.60-£53 double.
Half board: £214-£280 weekly.
Lunch available.
Evening meal 6pm (l.o. 9.30pm).
Parking for 20.
Credit: Access, Visa, C.Bl., Diners, Amex.

The Cedars
Listed

59 Grange Rd., Ealing, London W5 5BU
☎ 081-579 1070
Privately-run bed and breakfast within easy access of Heathrow Airport and central London.
Bedrooms: 1 single, 1 double & 2 twin, 2 family rooms.

Bathrooms: 6 private.
Bed & breakfast: £28-£30 single, £38-£40 double.
Parking for 7.

⚒ ♨ ❏ ♦ ⑪ ▥ 🗙 💺

Mrs. Josephine Clements M

♨♨ **COMMENDED**

17 Madeley Rd., London
W5 2LA
☎ 081-998 5222 &
(Fax:) 081-994 9144
Telex 933859
Beautifully renovated detached house with spacious rooms. Easy access to A4, M4, M40, central London's attractions, Heathrow Airport, Hampton Court and Kew Gardens.
Bedrooms: 1 single, 1 double & 1 twin, 1 family room.
Bathrooms: 2 private, 1 public.
Bed & breakfast: £36-£40 single, £40-£60 double.
Parking for 3.

⚒ ▥ Ⓥ ▤ ⑪ ▥ ▴ ❋ 🐾
🗙 🖤 ⒹⒶⓅ

🆎 Display advertisement appears on page 44.

Dalmacia Hotel M

Listed

71 Shepherds Bush Rd., Hammersmith, London
W6 7LS
☎ 071-603 2887 &
(0831) 309692
Fax: 071-602 9226
Family-run bed and breakfast within easy reach of the West End.
Bedrooms: 3 single, 6 double & 2 twin, 3 family rooms.
Bathrooms: 6 private; 8 private showers.
Bed & breakfast: £23-£25 single, £32-£42 double.
Half board: £30-£32 daily.
Evening meal 6.30pm (l.o. 9pm).
Credit: Access, Visa, Diners, Amex.

⚒5 ▴ ⚒ ❏ ⑪ ⓛ Ⓥ ▤ ▥
▴ 🗙 ⒹⒶⓅ ⚒ 🖤

Grange Lodge

♨♨

48-50 Grange Rd., Ealing, London W5 5BX
☎ 081-567 1049 Telex 269571
Quiet, comfortable hotel within a few hundred yards of the underground station. Midway between central London and Heathrow.
Bedrooms: 7 single, 1 double & 2 twin, 4 family rooms.
Bathrooms: 4 private, 2 public.

Bed & breakfast: £21-£31 single, £31-£41 double.
Parking for 10.
Credit: Access, Visa.

⚒ ▴ ❏ ⓛ Ⓥ ▤ ⑪ ▥ ▴
ⒹⒶⓅ 🖤 Ⓣ

Gresham Hotel M

♨♨

10 Hanger Lane, Ealing, London W5 3HH
☎ 081-992 0801 &
(Fax:) 081-993 7468
Conveniently located family-run bed and breakfast, ideal for London Airport and city centre. Colour TV with Sky movies, tea/coffee facilities in all rooms.
Bedrooms: 4 single, 2 double & 4 twin, 3 family rooms.
Bathrooms: 6 private, 7 public; 2 private showers.
Bed & breakfast: £27-£50 single, £43-£65 double.
Half board: £37-£60 daily, £222-£360 weekly.
Evening meal 6pm (l.o. 8.30pm).
Parking for 14.
Credit: Access, Visa, C.Bl., Diners, Amex.

⚒ ▴ ⚒ ❏ ♦ ⓛ ⚒ ▤ ⑪
◐ ▥ ▴ 🍴 ⒹⒶⓅ 🖤 ⚒

Kenton House Hotel M

5 Hillcrest Rd., Ealing, London W5 2JL
☎ 081-997 8436
Telex 8812544
Family-run hotel in a quiet location opposite a park. Convenient for access to central London.
Bedrooms: 36 single, 3 double & 5 twin, 7 family rooms.
Bathrooms: 51 private.
Bed & breakfast: £58.75-£68.75 single, £66.75-£76.75 double.
Evening meal 6.30pm (l.o. 10pm).
Parking for 27.
Credit: Access, Visa, Diners, Amex.

⚒ ▴ ⚒ Ⓡ ❏ ▤ ⑪ ◐ ▥
▴ ⚒ ⚒ Ⓣ

The Lancers Hotel

34 Barrowgate Rd., London
W4 4QY
☎ 081-994 5306 & 9985
Small family-run hotel close to Chiswick Park and Kew Gardens.
Bedrooms: 4 single, 9 twin, 2 family rooms.
Bathrooms: 9 private, 2 public.
Bed & breakfast: £25-£39 single, £44-£49 double.

Evening meal 6pm (l.o. 11pm).
Parking for 6.
Credit: Access, Visa.

⚒ ▴ ⚒ ❏ ▤ ⑪ ▥ ▴ 🐾
▥ ⚒

Mrs H.E. Miles

37 Brewster Gdns., London
W10 6AQ
☎ 081-969 7024
Pleasant room in a family house, on the bus route to the West End. Close to shops and White City underground station on the Central Line.
Bedrooms: 1 family room.
Bathrooms: 1 public.
Bed & breakfast: £7 single, £14 double.

⚒ ▥ ⓛ ⒸⒷ ▴ 🗙 🖤

Royal Crimea Hotel

Listed

354 Uxbridge Rd., Acton, London W3 9SL
☎ 081-992 3853 & 1068
2 minutes' walk from Ealing Common underground station, offering quick links to Heathrow and the West End.
Bedrooms: 4 single, 7 double & 4 twin.
Bathrooms: 9 private, 3 public.
Bed & breakfast: £23-£30 single, £32-£40 double.
Evening meal 6pm (l.o. 7pm).
Parking for 10.

⚒ ▴ ❏ ▤ ⑪ ▥ ▴ 🗙 ⒹⒶⓅ
🖤 ⚒ Ⓣ

Shalimar Hotel M

♨♨

215-221 Staines Rd., Hounslow, Middlesex
TW3 3JJ
☎ 081-572 2816 & 081-577 7070 Fax: 081-569 6789
Family-run hotel, close to Heathrow, M4, M25, underground and shopping centre. Residents' bar, evening meals, dining room and lounge.
Bedrooms: 6 single, 4 double & 14 twin, 7 family rooms.
Bathrooms: 21 private; 10 private showers.
Bed & breakfast: £34-£38 single, £44-£48 double.
Lunch available.
Evening meal 6pm (l.o. 8pm).
Parking for 7.
Credit: Access, Visa, Diners, Amex.

⚒ ▴ ⚒ ❏ ♦ ▤ ⑪ ⑪ ◐
▥ ▴ 🍴 ⚒ ❋ 🗙 ▥ ⚒
Ⓣ

Shepiston Lodge

♨ **APPROVED**

31 Shepiston Lane, Hayes, Middlesex UB3 1LJ
☎ 081-573 0266 &
(Fax:) 081-569 2279

Homely guesthouse 10 minutes from Heathrow Airport.
Bedrooms: 3 single, 7 twin, 3 family rooms.
Bathrooms: 3 public; 7 private showers.
Bed & breakfast: from £26 single, from £39.50 double.
Parking for 13.
Credit: Access, Visa, Amex.

⚒8 ▴ ❏ ⓛ ▥ ⑪ ▥ ▴ 🗙
▥

Shiva Hotel M

♨♨ **COMMENDED**

4 Tring Ave., Ealing Common, London W5 3HH
☎ 081-992 0016 &
(Fax:) 081-993 7468
Friendly family-run hotel close to all amenities. Convenient for Heathrow Airport and the West End.
Bedrooms: 9 single, 2 double & 3 twin, 3 family rooms.
Bathrooms: 4 private, 4 public; 3 private showers.
Bed & breakfast: £32-£50 single, £45-£65 double.
Half board: £42-£60 daily, £252-£360 weekly.
Evening meal 6pm (l.o. 8.30pm).
Parking for 6.
Credit: Access, Visa, C.Bl., Diners, Amex.

⚒ ▴ ⚒ ❏ ▤ ⓛ Ⓥ ▥ ▤
⑪ ◐ ▥ ▴ 🍴 ⒹⒶⓅ ▥ ⚒

Stewart Guest House

Listed

178 Southfield Rd., Chiswick, London W4 5LD
☎ 081-995 3564
Family-run guesthouse.
Bedrooms: 4 single, 2 twin, 2 family rooms.
Bathrooms: 2 public.
Bed & breakfast: max. £17 single, max. £30 double.

⚒ ⚒ ▴ ❏ ♦ ⓛ ▥ ⑪ ▴
🗙

National Crown ratings were correct at the time of going to press but are subject to change. Please check at the time of booking.

The national Crown scheme is explained in full on pages 536 – 539.

Please mention this guide when making a booking.

43

THE CROWN IS YOUR SURE SIGN OF WHERE TO STAY

HOTELS, GUESTHOUSES, INNS, B&Bs & FARMHOUSES

Throughout Britain, the tourist boards now inspect over 17,000 hotels, guesthouses, inns, B&Bs and farmhouses, every year, to help you find the ones that suit you best.

THE CLASSIFICATIONS: '**Listed**', and then **ONE to FIVE CROWN,** tell you the range of facilities and services you can expect. The more Crowns, the wider the range.

THE GRADES: **APPROVED, COMMENDED and HIGHLY COMMENDED,** where they appear, indicate the quality standard provided. If no grade is shown, you can still expect a high standard of cleanliness.

Every classified place to stay has a Fire Certificate, where this is required under the Fire Precautions Act, and all carry Public Liability Insurance.

'**Listed**': Clean and comfortable accommodation, but the range of facilities and services may be limited.

ONE CROWN: Accommodation with additional facilities, including washbasins in all bedrooms, a lounge and use of a phone.

TWO CROWN: A wider range of facilities and services, including morning tea and calls, bedside lights, colour TV in lounge or bedrooms, assistance with luggage.

THREE CROWN: At least one-third of the bedrooms with ensuite WC and bath or shower, plus easy chair, full length mirror. Shoe cleaning facilities and hairdryers available. Hot evening meals available.

FOUR CROWN: At least three-quarters of the bedrooms with ensuite WC and bath/shower plus colour TV, radio and phone, 24-hour access and lounge service until midnight. Last orders for meals 8.30 pm or later.

FIVE CROWN: All bedrooms having WC, bath and shower ensuite, plus a wide range of facilities and services, including room service, all-night lounge service and laundry service. Restaurant open for breakfast, lunch and dinner.

Every Crown classified place to stay is likely to provide some of the facilities and services of a higher classification. More information available from any Tourist Information Centre.

We've checked them out before you check in!

CUMBRIA

A REGION OF BREATHTAKING BEAUTY *and dramatic scenery — impressive peaks and plunging valleys, rugged fells and crags, quiet lakes and tarns, tumbling rivers. Best known for the English Lakes, a collection of water "playgrounds". It's great walking and motoring country and great sporting country, full of*

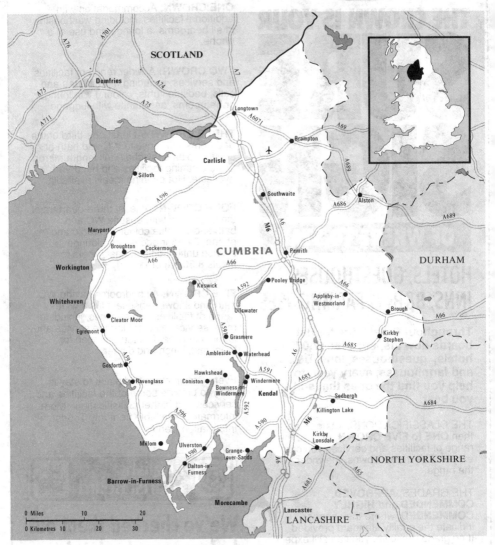

PLEASE REFER TO THE COLOUR MAPS AT THE BACK OF THIS GUIDE FOR ALL PLACES WITH ACCOMMODATION LISTINGS.

fascinating towns and villages. Away from the Lakes there's the unspoilt coast stretching from the Solway Firth down to Morecambe Bay — with quiet resorts and pretty coastal villages — while to the north there's Hadrian's Wall and Carlisle, both resounding to the echoes of past troubled times.

WHERE TO GO, WHAT TO SEE

Abbot Hall Art Gallery
Abbot Hall, Kendal, Cumbria
LA9 5AL
☎ Kendal (0539) 722464
18th C mansion house. Paintings by Romney, Ruskin and Turner. Furniture by Gillows. Changing exhibitions.

Appleby Castle Conservation Centre
Appleby-in-Westmorland,
Cumbria CA16 6XH
☎ Appleby (076 83) 51402
Norman keep. Great Hall of house with Clifford family triptych. Large collection of waterfowl, owls, pheasants, rare breeds of farm animals.

Brockhole — Lake District National Park Visitor Centre
Windermere, Cumbria
LA23 1LJ
☎ Windermere (053 94) 46601
Exhibition of National Park story, slide shows, films, shop, gardens, adventure playground, drystone walling area, trails, events.

Cumberland Pencil Museum
Southey Works, Greta Bridge,
Keswick, Cumbria CA12 5NG
☎ Keswick (076 87) 73626
The story of pencils from the discovery of graphite to present methods. Video presentation of operations inside pencil factory, use of watercolour pencils and mines exhibition.

Cumberland Toy and Model Museum
Banks Court, Market Place,
Cockermouth, Cumbria
CA13 9NG
☎ Cockermouth (0900) 827606

The restored 1951 Clyde tug, *Flying Buzzard*

100 years of toys with visitor-operated exhibits. Free family toy quiz.

Dove Cottage and Wordsworth Museum
Town End, Grasmere, Cumbria
LA22 9SH
☎ Grasmere (053 94) 35544
Wordsworth's home 1799 – 1808. Museum, poet's possessions, manuscripts, paintings and drawings, farmhouse reconstruction.

Eskdale Corn Mill
Boot, Holmrook, Cumbria
CA19 1TG
☎ Eskdale (094 03) 335
Historic water-powered corn mill near Dalegarth Station, approached via packhorse bridge. Early wooden machinery, milling and farming exhibition, waterfalls.

Flying Buzzard
Elizabeth Dock, South Quay,
Maryport, Cumbria CA15 8AB
☎ Maryport (0900) 815954
Restored 1951 Clyde tug. Guided tours of ship including engine room.

Furness Abbey
Barrow-in-Furness, Cumbria
LA13 0TJ
☎ Barrow-in-Furness (0229) 23420
Ruins of 12th C Cistercian abbey. Extensive remains include transepts, choir and west tower of church, canopied seats, arches.

Holehird Gardens
Holehird Trust Estate,
Patterdale Road, Troutbeck,
Windermere, Cumbria
☎ Windermere (053 94) 46008
Formal gardens with extensive ▶

Holker Hall and Gardens

▶ views of Lakeland peaks. Many rare plants and shrubs, woodland and tarn walks.

Holker Hall and Gardens
Cark-in-Cartmel, Grange-over-Sands, Cumbria LA11 7PL
☎ Flookburgh (053 95) 58328
Victorian new wing, formal and woodland garden, deer park, motor museum, adventure playground, gift shop, craft and countryside exhibition, patch and quilt display and demonstration.

Hutton-in-the-Forest
Skelton, Penrith, Cumbria CA11 9TH
☎ Skelton (085 34) 449
14th C pele tower with later additions. Tapestries, furniture, paintings, china, armour. Formal gardens, dovecote, lake, woods with specimen trees.

Lanercost Priory
Lanercost, Brampton, Cumbria CA8 2HQ
☎ Brampton (069 77) 3030
Impressive red sandstone priory made of stones from Hadrian's Wall. Founded in 1166 for Augustinian canons. Ruined nave restored in 18th C as parish church.

Lingholm Gardens
Lingholm, Keswick, Cumbria CA12 5UA
☎ Keswick (076 87) 72003
Formal and woodland gardens. Azaleas, rhododendrons, plant centre. Views of Borrowdale and Skiddaw.

Muncaster Castle and Gardens
Ravenglass, Cumbria CA18 1RQ
☎ Ravenglass (0229) 717614
14th C pele tower with 15th and 19th C additions. Gardens with exceptional collection of rhododendrons and azaleas. Extensive collection of owls.

Naworth Castle
Brampton, Cumbria
☎ Brampton (069 77) 3666
Historic Border fortress, built in 1335 and renovated in 1602. Great hall, Gobelin tapestries, Pre-Raphaelite library, 14th C dungeons.

Penrith Steam Museum
Castlegate Foundry, Penrith, Cumbria CA11 7JB
☎ Penrith (0768) 62154
Steam traction engines, vintage farm machinery, working

blacksmith's shop, pattern shop, steam models, furnished Victorian cottage.

Ponsonby Farm Park
Ponsonby, Nr. Calderbridge, Cumbria CA20 1BX
☎ Beckermet (0946) 841426
Working farm with rare breeds of farm animals, old and modern buildings, farm walks.

Ravenglass and Eskdale Railway
Ravenglass, Cumbria CA18 1SW
☎ Ravenglass (0229) 717171
England's oldest narrow-gauge railway runs for 7 miles through glorious scenery to the foot of England's highest hills. Most trains steam hauled.

Senhouse Roman Museum
The Battery, Sea Brows, Maryport, Cumbria CA15 6JD
☎ Maryport (0900) 816168
Oldest archaeological collection in UK. Large collection of Roman altars and inscriptions.

Sizergh Castle
Kendal, Cumbria LA8 8AE
☎ Sedgwick (053 95) 60070
14th C pele tower, 15th C great hall, 16th C wings. Stuart connections. Rock garden and rose garden.

South Tynedale Railway
Railway Station, Alston, Cumbria CA9 3JB
☎ Alston (0434) 381696
2ft gauge railway following part of the route of the former Alston to Haltwhistle branch line through South Tynedale.

Steam Yacht Gondola
Pier Cottage, Coniston, Cumbria LA21 8AJ
☎ Coniston (053 94) 41288
Launched in 1859, completely renovated, with opulently upholstered saloon. Steam powered. Carries 86 passengers. Piers at Coniston and Park-a-Moor.

Stott Park Bobbin Mill
Finsthwaite, Nr. Ulverston, Cumbria LA12 8AX

☎ Newby Bridge (053 95)
31087
*Restored 19th C bobbin mill
with working turning machinery.*

Tullie House
Castle Street, Carlisle, Cumbria
CA3 8TP
☎ Carlisle (0228) 34781
*Major tourist complex housing
museum, art gallery, theatre,
shops, restaurant, bars.*

**Windermere Iron
Steamboat Company**
Lakeside Pier, Newby Bridge,
Ulverston, Cumbria LA12 8AS
☎ Newby Bridge (053 95)
31188
*3 vessels sailing on Lake
Windermere. Booking offices at
Lakeside, Bowness and
Ambleside.*

MAKE A DATE FOR...

Carlisle Races
Carlisle Racecourse, Durdar,
Carlisle, Cumbria
7 – 8 May

Coniston Water Festival
Coniston Sailing Club,
Coniston Old Hall, Coniston,
Cumbria
22 – 31 May

**Great Garden and
Countryside Festival**
Holker Hall and Gardens,
Cark-in-Cartmel, Grange-over-
Sands, Cumbria
5 – 7 June

**Cumberland
Agricultural Show**
Bitts Park, Carlisle, Cumbria
23 July

**Lake District
Summer Music Festival**
Charlotte Mason College,
Rydal Road, Ambleside,
Cumbria
1 – 15 August

**Skelton Horticultural
and Agricultural Show**
Hutton-in-the-Forest, Skelton,
Penrith, Cumbria
15 August

Steam Yacht Gondola on Coniston Water

Patterdale Sheepdog Trials
Playing Fields, Patterdale,
Cumbria
29 August

Egremont Crab Fair
Baybarrow, Egremont,
Cumbria
19 September

Wasdale Agricultural Show
Wasdale Head, Seascale,
Cumbria
10 October

**Biggest Liar in
the World Competition**
Santon Bridge Inn, Holmrook,
Cumbria
19 November

FIND OUT MORE

Further information about
holidays and attractions in the
Cumbria region is available
from:
Cumbria Tourist Board
Ashleigh, Holly Road,
Windermere, Cumbria
LA23 2AQ
☎ (053 94) 44444

These publications are available
from the Cumbria Tourist
Board (post free):

*Cumbria English Lake District
Touring Map* (including tourist
information and touring caravan
and camping parks) £1.95

*Places to Visit and Things to Do
in Cumbria The Lake District*
(over 200 ideas for a great day
out) 85p

*Short Walks – Good for
Families* (route descriptions,
maps and information for 14
walks in the lesser-known areas
of Cumbria) 95p

Places to stay

ACCOMMODATION ENTRIES in this regional section are listed in alphabetical order of place name, and then in alphabetical order of establishment.

THE MAP REFERENCES refer to the colour maps towards the end of the guide. The first figure is the map number; the letter and figure which follow indicate the grid reference on the map.

THE SYMBOLS at the end of each accommodation entry give information about services and facilities. A 'key' to these symbols is inside the back cover flap, which can be kept open for easy reference.

ALLONBY

Cumbria
Map ref 5A2

5m NE. Maryport
Small village on Solway Firth with good sandy beaches.

Sandpiper Hotel M
😊😊 APPROVED
Allonby, Maryport,
CA15 6PE
☎ (090 084) 398
Modern hotel facing sea, with beach very close. Convenient for North Lakes, Carlisle and Workington.
Bedrooms: 6 double & 3 twin.
Bathrooms: 4 private,
2 public.
Bed & breakfast: £16-£17.50 single, £30-£33 double.
Half board: £20-£26 daily, from £135 weekly.
Lunch available.
Evening meal 6pm (l.o. 9pm).
Parking for 18.
Credit: Access, Visa.
🌣🖵👌🖊️🔌 V 🖵 📺 🎞 ⬜
🛎 🅿 DAP 🐾 SP

Individual proprietors have supplied all details of accommodation. Although we do check for accuracy, we advise you to confirm prices and other information at the time of booking.

ALSTON

Cumbria
Map ref 5B2

Market town amongst the highest fells of the Pennines and close to the Pennine Way in an area of outstanding natural beauty.

Hillcrest Hotel M
Townfoot, Alston, CA9 3RN
☎ (0434) 381251
Fine country house hotel in a magnificent setting. Warm welcome, relaxed atmosphere and varied food. A perfect break.
Bedrooms: 1 single, 3 double & 3 twin, 2 family rooms.
Bathrooms: 3 private,
4 public.
Bed & breakfast: £23-£25 single, £43-£55 double.
Lunch available.
Evening meal 7pm (l.o. 8.30pm).
Parking for 25.
Credit: Access, Visa, Amex.
🌣 🖊️ V 🖊️ 🔌 📺 🎞 🍴 ∪
🅿 ❀ 🐾 SP 🅵🅱

Lovelady Shield Country House Hotel M
😊😊😊 COMMENDED
Nenthead Rd., Nr Alston,
CA9 3LF
☎ (0434) 381203
Fax (0434) 381515
Attractive Georgian-style country house standing in its own grounds. Idyllic and peaceful location in beautiful Pennine countryside. Noted for cuisine.
Bedrooms: 2 single, 6 double & 4 twin.
Bathrooms: 12 private.

Bed & breakfast: from £37.50 single, £76-£97 double.
Half board: £57-£69 daily.
Lunch available.
Evening meal 7.30pm (l.o. 8.30pm).
Parking for 25.
Open February-December.
Credit: Access, Visa, Diners, Amex.
🌣 🖼️ 📞 🔌 🖵 👌 🖊️ V 🖊️
🖵 🎞 🛎 🍴 🅿 ❀ 🐾 ⬜ SP
🅃

Lowbyer Manor Hotel M
😊😊😊 APPROVED
Alston, CA9 3JX
☎ Alston (0434) 381230
Traditional 17th C stone-built manor house in its own gardens and grounds. Quiet and friendly atmosphere. Restaurant with traditional a la carte menu. Old world bar. Elegant drawing room.
Bedrooms: 1 single, 6 double & 4 twin.
Bathrooms: 11 private.
Bed & breakfast: from £30 single, £55-£75 double.
Lunch available.
Evening meal 7pm (l.o. 8.30pm).
Parking for 14.
Credit: Access, Visa, Diners, Amex.
🌣8🛎 📞 🔌 🖵 👌 🖊️ V 🖵
🎞 🛎 🍴 ∪ 🅿 ❀ 🐾 SP 🅱
🅃

Half board prices shown are per person but in some cases may be based on double/twin occupancy.

AMBLESIDE

Cumbria
Map ref 5A3

4m NW. Windermere
At the head of Lake Windermere and surrounded by fells. Good centre for touring, walking and sailing.

Betty Fold Guest House M
😊😊😊 COMMENDED
Hawkshead Hill, Ambleside,
LA22 0PS
☎ Hawkshead (096 66) 611
In the heart of Lakeland, the house and garden offer peace and panoramic views. Hawkshead, Coniston and Ambleside are only a short distance away.
Bedrooms: 1 double & 1 twin, 1 family room.
Bathrooms: 3 private.
Bed & breakfast: £20-£25 single, £38-£45 double.
Half board: £30-£35 daily, £200-£240 weekly.
Evening meal 7pm (l.o. 9am).
Parking for 10.
🌣🖵👌🖊️ V 🖵 🎞 🛎 ❀
🖭 🐾 SP 🅱

Borrans Park Hotel M
😊😊😊😊 COMMENDED
Borrans Rd., Ambleside,
LA22 0EN
☎ (053 94) 33454
Recently converted Georgian house in a secluded position between the village and the lake. We offer candlelit dinners, four-posters and 120 fine wines.
Bedrooms: 1 single, 10 double & 3 twin.

50

Bathrooms: 13 private,
1 public.
Bed & breakfast: £30-£50
single, £60-£72 double.
Half board: £44-£64 daily,
£295-£335 weekly.
Evening meal 7pm (l.o.
7.30pm).
Parking for 20.
Credit: Access, Visa.

Brantholme Guest House **M**
☰☰☰ COMMENDED
Millans Park, Ambleside,
LA22 9AG
☎ (053 94) 32034
*In a quiet part of Ambleside, 3
minutes' walk from the village,
with commanding views of
Loughrigg Fell and Fairfield.
Patio and garden with
barbecue. Honeymoon suite
with four-poster bed available.*
Bedrooms: 1 single, 3 double
& 2 twin, 2 family rooms.
Bathrooms: 8 private.
Bed & breakfast: £18 single,
£38-£42 double.
Half board: £18-£29 daily,
£203-£220 weekly.
Parking for 7.

Cherry Garth Hotel **M**
☰☰☰ COMMENDED
Old Lake Rd., Ambleside,
LA22 0DH
☎ (053 94) 33128
*Ideally located accommodation
between Lake and village.
Family-run hotel overlooking
beautiful landscaped gardens
and spectacular Lakeland
views.*
Bedrooms: 7 double & 2 twin,
1 family room.
Bathrooms: 8 private,
1 public.
Bed & breakfast: £19-£35
single, £38-£70 double.
Half board: £29-£45 daily,
£195-£280 weekly.
Evening meal 7pm (l.o. 8pm).
Parking for 15.
Credit: Access, Visa.

Claremont House **M**
☰☰
Compston Rd., Ambleside,
LA22 9DJ
☎ (053 94) 33448
*All rooms have TV, tea/coffee
makers. Most rooms en-suite.
Chef/proprietor was once head
chef at two of Lakeland's
leading hotels.*
Bedrooms: 1 single, 4 double
& 1 twin, 1 family room.
Bathrooms: 4 private,
1 public.

Bed & breakfast: £12-£15
single, £24-£36 double.
Half board: £22-£28 daily.
Evening meal 6.30pm (l.o.
6.30pm).
Parking for 3.

Compston House Hotel **M**
☰☰ APPROVED
Compston Rd., Ambleside,
LA22 9DJ
☎ (053 94) 32305
*Lakeland-stone hotel in
Ambleside village, with lovely
views of surrounding fells. All
rooms en-suite with colour TV
and teamakers.*
Bedrooms: 6 double & 1 twin,
1 family room.
Bathrooms: 8 private.
Bed & breakfast: £29-£49
double.
Half board: £23-£33 daily,
£156-£226 weekly.
Evening meal 7pm (l.o. 5pm).

Crow How Hotel **M**
☰☰☰ APPROVED
Rydal Rd., Ambleside,
LA22 9PN
☎ (053 94) 32193
*Victorian country house in a
quiet location, with 2 acres of
grounds. Only 1 mile from the
centre of Ambleside.*
Bedrooms: 6 double & 1 twin,
2 family rooms.
Bathrooms: 8 private;
1 private shower.
Bed & breakfast: £22.50-
£23.50 single, £45-£56 double.
Half board: £33.50-£39 daily,
£211-£345.50 weekly.
Evening meal 7.30pm (l.o.
7.30pm).
Parking for 12.

The Dower House
☰☰ COMMENDED
Wray Castle, Ambleside,
LA22 0JA
☎ (053 94) 33211
*The house overlooks Lake
Windermere, 3 miles from
Ambleside. Through the main
gates of Wray Castle and up
the drive.*
Bedrooms: 2 double & 1 twin.
Bathrooms: 2 public.
Bed & breakfast: £17 single,
£32-£34 double.
Half board: £24.50-£25.50
daily, £172.50 weekly.
Evening meal 7pm (l.o.
7.30pm).
Parking for 14.

Elder Grove Hotel **M**
☰☰☰ COMMENDED
Lake Rd., Ambleside,
LA22 0DB
☎ (053 94) 32504
*Elegant Victorian family-run
hotel in central position.
Unique Lakeland stone dining
room, imaginative cooking,
relaxing bar and pretty
bedrooms.*
Bedrooms: 2 single, 7 double
& 2 twin, 1 family room.
Bathrooms: 12 private.
Bed & breakfast: from £25
single, from £50 double.
Half board: £34-£38 daily,
£236-£250 weekly.
Evening meal 7.30pm (l.o.
7.30pm).
Parking for 14.
Open March-November.
Credit: Access, Visa.

Eltermere Country House Hotel **M**
☰☰☰ COMMENDED
Elterwater, Ambleside,
LA22 9HY
☎ Langdale (096 67) 207
*Friendly country house hotel in
a quiet rural setting in the
heart of the Langdale Valley.
Personally run by the owners.*
Bedrooms: 3 single, 8 double
& 7 twin.
Bathrooms: 15 private,
3 public.
Bed & breakfast: £27.50-
£31.50 single, £55-£63 double.
Half board: £38.75-£42.50
daily, £260-£285 weekly.
Evening meal 7pm (l.o. 8pm).
Parking for 20.

Fisherbeck Farmhouse **M**
☰☰
Old Lake Rd., Ambleside,
LA22 0DH
☎ (053 94) 32523
*Off the main road, a few
minutes' level walk from the
centre of Ambleside. Not a
working farm.*
Bedrooms: 2 double & 1 twin.
Bathrooms: 1 public.
Bed & breakfast: £14-£16.50
single, £28-£33 double.
Parking for 3.
Open March-November.

Fisherbeck Hotel **M**
☰☰☰ COMMENDED
Lake Rd., Ambleside,
LA22 0DH
☎ (053 94) 33215

Family-run hotel
*Family-run hotel ideally
situated for touring and all
Lakeland activities,
overlooking Loughrigg Fell.
Reputation for food and
comfort.*
Bedrooms: 1 single, 14 double
& 2 twin, 3 family rooms.
Bathrooms: 17 private,
2 public; 1 private shower.
Bed & breakfast: £29-£53.50
single, £50-£66.40 double.
Half board: £34.50-£43.95
daily, £236-£295 weekly.
Lunch available.
Evening meal 7pm (l.o. 8pm).
Parking for 20.
Credit: Access, Visa.

The Gables Hotel **M**
☰☰☰ APPROVED
Compston Rd., Ambleside,
LA22 9DJ
☎ (053 94) 33272
*In a quiet residential area
overlooking the park, tennis
courts, bowling green and
Loughrigg Fell. Convenient for
the shops, walking and water
sport.*
Bedrooms: 3 single, 6 double,
4 family rooms.
Bathrooms: 13 private.
Bed & breakfast: £18.25-£22
single, £36.50-£44 double.
Half board: £29-£32.75 daily,
from £203 weekly.
Evening meal 7pm (l.o. 5pm).
Parking for 7.
Open January-November.

Grey Friar Lodge Country House Hotel **M**
☰☰☰ COMMENDED
Brathay, Ambleside,
LA22 9NE
☎ (053 94) 33158
*Lovely, traditional Lakeland
stone country house
overlooking the River Brathay
valley. Noted for food and
hospitality.*
Bedrooms: 5 double & 2 twin,
1 family room.
Bathrooms: 8 private.
Half board: £34-£43 daily,
£217-£280 weekly.
Evening meal 7pm (l.o.
7.30pm).
Parking for 12.
Open March-October.

Hillsdale Hotel **M**
☰☰
Church St., Ambleside,
LA22 0BT
☎ (053 94) 33174
Continued ▶

Family-run hotel in centre of village. 10 minutes' walk from lake. Central for touring all lakes and near bowling green, tennis courts and putting green.
Bedrooms: 1 single, 6 double & 1 twin.
Bathrooms: 1 private, 1 public; 4 private showers.
Bed & breakfast: £20-£25 single, £32-£38 double.

Holker House M

Compston Rd., Ambleside, LA22 9DJ
☎ (053 94) 33365
Centrally situated in picturesque Ambleside, close to all amenities. Local facilities include tennis, putting green and children's adventure playground.
Bedrooms: 2 single, 1 double, 2 family rooms.
Bathrooms: 2 private, 1 public; 1 private shower.
Bed & breakfast: £14.50-£16.50 single, £32-£36 double.
Half board: £22-£26 daily, £150-£170 weekly.
Evening meal 6.30pm (l.o. 7pm).
Parking for 1.

Kirkstone Foot Country House Hotel M
COMMENDED

Kirkstone Pass Rd., Ambleside, LA22 9EH
☎ (053 94) 32232
Secluded 17th C manor house in its own grounds, with adjoining self-contained apartments and cottages.
Bedrooms: 1 single, 9 double & 4 twin, 2 family rooms.
Bathrooms: 16 private.
Half board: £37.50-£52 daily, £271.50-£336 weekly.
Evening meal 8pm (l.o. 8.30pm).
Parking for 30.
Open February-December.
Credit: Access, Visa, Diners, Amex.

Lattendale Hotel M

Compston Rd., Ambleside, LA22 9DJ
☎ (053 94) 32368

Traditional Lakeland hotel, in the heart of the town. A good base for many pursuits, offering interesting food and wines in a comfortable and relaxed atmosphere.
Bedrooms: 2 single, 2 double & 2 twin, 1 family room.
Bathrooms: 5 private, 1 public.
Bed & breakfast: £12-£15 single, £30-£36 double.
Half board: £22-£28 daily, £150-£180 weekly.
Evening meal 6.30pm (l.o. 5pm).
Open February-December.
Credit: Access, Visa.

Laurel Villa Hotel M
COMMENDED

Lake Rd., Ambleside, LA22 0DB
☎ (053 94) 33240 & (053 94) 32744 (Guests)
Victorian house, personally run by resident proprietors. Spacious en-suite bedrooms decorated in William Morris style. Overlooking the fells.
Bedrooms: 7 double & 2 twin.
Bathrooms: 9 private.
Bed & breakfast: £40 single, £55 double.
Evening meal 7pm (l.o. 5pm).
Parking for 14.
Credit: Access, Visa.

Loughrigg Brow M

Ambleside, LA22 9SA
☎ (053 94) 3229
Telex 667047
Large country house beautifully positioned amongst some of the finest mountain scenery to be found in the British Isles.
Bedrooms: 6 single, 14 twin, 6 family rooms.
Bathrooms: 10 public.
Bed & breakfast: £13.25-£20.25 single, £22-£36 double.
Half board: £20.25-£28.25 daily, £130-£220 weekly.
Lunch available.
Evening meal 7pm.
Parking for 20.

Lyndhurst Hotel M
COMMENDED

Wansfell Rd., Ambleside, Cumbria. LA22 0EG
☎ (053 94) 32421
Attractive Victorian Lakeland stone hotel, with private car park. In quiet position. Friendly service, all en-suite. Four-poster bed.
Bedrooms: 5 double & 2 twin, 1 family room.

Bathrooms: 8 private.
Bed & breakfast: £18-£25 double.
Half board: £27-£35 daily, £185-£235 weekly.
Evening meal 6.30pm (l.o. 8pm).
Parking for 8.
Open February-December.

Meadowbank

Rydal Rd., Ambleside, LA22 9BA
☎ (053 94) 32710
Old house in private garden overlooking open meadows and fells. Ideal as walking base.
Bedrooms: 1 single, 2 double & 2 twin, 2 family rooms.
Bathrooms: 3 private, 2 public.
Bed & breakfast: £15-£17 single, £30-£36 double.
Parking for 10.

Melrose Guest House M

Church St., Ambleside, LA22 0BT
☎ (053 94) 32500
Typical stone, terraced Victorian Lakeland house on four floors.
Bedrooms: 1 single, 1 twin, 3 family rooms.
Bathrooms: 3 private, 1 public.
Bed & breakfast: £12-£14 single, £24-£34 double.

Nanny Brow Country House Hotel M
COMMENDED

Clappersgate, Ambleside, LA22 9NF
☎ (053 94) 32036
Country house in 5 acres of secluded gardens with magnificent views. Lying below Loughrigg Fell, 2 miles from Ambleside.
Bedrooms: 1 single, 10 double & 5 twin, 3 family rooms.
Bathrooms: 17 private.
Bed & breakfast: £63-£83 single, £86-£162 double.
Half board: £50-£89 daily, £315-£560 weekly.
Evening meal 7.30pm (l.o. 8.30pm).
Parking for 22.
Credit: Access, Visa, Amex.

The Old Vicarage M

Vicarage Rd., Ambleside, LA22 9DH
☎ (053 94) 33364
Fax (053 94) 34734
Traditional Lakeland-stone house, pleasantly situated in own grounds in heart of village. Quality accommodation. All en-suite.
Bedrooms: 6 double & 1 twin, 3 family rooms.
Bathrooms: 10 private.
Bed & breakfast: £17-£23 single, £34-£46 double.
Parking for 12.
Credit: Access, Visa.

Queens Hotel M
APPROVED

Market Place, Ambleside, LA22 9BU
☎ (053 94) 32206
Fax (053 94) 32721
In the heart of the Lakes and convenient for walking, climbing and other leisure activities. 2 fully licensed bars, meals and snacks available all day.
Bedrooms: 4 single, 15 double & 2 twin, 3 family rooms.
Bathrooms: 24 private.
Bed & breakfast: £19-£34 single, £38-£68 double.
Lunch available.
Evening meal 7pm (l.o. 10pm).
Parking for 12.
Credit: Access, Visa, Diners, Amex.

Riverside Hotel M
COMMENDED

Under Loughrigg, Nr. Rothay Bridge, Ambleside, LA22 9LJ
☎ (053 94) 32395
Small country hotel in a peaceful setting overlooking the river, with extensive grounds and direct access on to the fells.
Bedrooms: 6 double & 2 twin, 2 family rooms.
Bathrooms: 10 private.
Bed & breakfast: £60-£70 double.
Half board: £39.75-£43 daily, £245.70-£267.40 weekly.
Evening meal 7pm (l.o. 8pm).
Parking for 20.
Open February-November.
Credit: Access, Visa, Amex.

Riverside Lodge Country House M
COMMENDED
Nr. Rothay Bridge,
Ambleside, LA22 OEH
☎ (053 94) 34208
Georgian country house of character with 2 acres of grounds through which the River Rothay flows. 500 yards from the centre of Ambleside.
Bedrooms: 4 double, 1 family room.
Bathrooms: 5 private.
Bed & breakfast: £40-£55 double.
Parking for 20.
Credit: Access, Visa.
☼↻ ♨ ✆ ⊡ �’ ⚗ ⅋
⇥ ▥ ♨ ♪ ❀ ⚘ ➘ ❦ SP
▥

Rothay Garth Hotel M
COMMENDED
Rothay Rd., Ambleside,
LA22 OEE
☎ (053 94) 32217
Fax (053 94) 34400
Comfortable, warm, distinctive hotel in central Lakeland. Elegant Loughrigg restaurant overlooks lovely gardens and nearby mountains. Close to village centre and Lake Windermere. All-season breaks.
Bedrooms: 2 single, 9 double & 2 twin, 3 family rooms.
Bathrooms: 14 private, 2 public.
Bed & breakfast: £32-£40 single, £64-£80 double.
Half board: £44-£54 daily, £177.50-£320 weekly.
Lunch available.
Evening meal 7pm (l.o. 8pm).
Parking for 17.
Credit: Access, Visa, Diners, Amex.
☼↻ ♨ ✆ ⊡ ➘ ⚗ ✚ ⊻ ⅋
⇥ ▥ ♨ ➘ ☂ ⅃ ✣ ❂ ❀ ⚘
SP ▥ Ⓣ
⦿ Display advertisement appears on page 86.

Rothay Manor Hotel M
COMMENDED
Rothay Bridge, Ambleside,
LA22 OEH
☎ (053 94) 33605
Elegant Regency country house hotel with a well-known restaurant. Balcony rooms overlook the garden. Suites for families and disabled guests. Free use of nearby leisure club.
Bedrooms: 2 single, 6 double & 3 twin, 7 family rooms.
Bathrooms: 18 private.
Bed & breakfast: £63-£69 single, £98-£108 double.
Half board: £72-£77 daily.
Lunch available.
Evening meal 8pm (l.o. 9pm).
Parking for 40.

Open February-December.
Credit: Access, Visa, Diners, Amex.
☼↻ ♨ ✆ ⊡ ➘ ⚗ ✚ ⚗ ⅋
⇥ ▥ ♨ ⅃ ⚘ ❀ ❦ ❦ ▥ ⧓
SP ▥

Rowanfield Country Guesthouse M
COMMENDED
Kirkstone Rd., Ambleside
LA22 9ET
☎ (053 94) 33686
Idyllic setting, panoramic lake and mountain view. Laura Ashley style decor. Scrumptious food created by proprietor/chef. Special break prices.
Bedrooms: 5 double & 1 twin, 1 family room.
Bathrooms: 7 private.
Bed & breakfast: £31-£36 single, £42-£52 double.
Half board: £37.50-£40.50 daily, £212-£233 weekly.
Evening meal 7pm (l.o. 7.30pm).
Parking for 8.
Open March-December.
Credit: Access, Visa.
☼↻5 ♨ ⊡ ➘ ⅓ ⊻ ⅋ ▥
♨ ❀ ⚘ ➘ ❦ SP ▥

The Rysdale Hotel M
COMMENDED
Rothay Rd., Ambleside,
LA22 OEE
☎ (053 94) 32140
Enjoy the friendly atmosphere of our family-run hotel, with magnificent views of the Lakeland fells. En-suite and family rooms available.
Bedrooms: 1 single, 5 double & 1 twin, 2 family rooms.
Bathrooms: 6 private, 2 public.
Bed & breakfast: £16.50-£20.50 single, £33-£48 double.
Half board: £25.50-£33 daily, £170-£220 weekly.
Evening meal 7pm.
Parking for 2.
Credit: Access, Visa.
☼↻8 ⊡ ➘ ⚗ ⅋ ⊻ ⅋ ▥
♨ ❦ ⚘ ➘ SP ▥

The Salutation Hotel M
⚘⚘⚘
Lake Road, Ambleside,
LA22 9BX
☎ (053 94) 32244
Fax: (053 94) 34157
Traditional hotel overlooking central Ambleside, with well-appointed, comfortable rooms, where a warm and friendly welcome is assured.
Bedrooms: 17 double & 8 twin, 4 family rooms.
Bathrooms: 29 private.
Bed & breakfast: £26-£37 single, £52-£74 double.
Half board: £38-£50 daily.

Lunch available.
Evening meal 7pm (l.o. 9pm).
Parking for 40.
Credit: Access, Visa.

Smallwood House Hotel M
⚘⚘
Compston Rd., Ambleside,
LA22 9DJ
☎ (053 94) 32330
Family-run hotel in central position, offering warm and friendly service, good home cooking and value-for-money quality and standards.
Bedrooms: 3 single, 6 double & 2 twin, 3 family rooms.
Bathrooms: 4 private, 3 public.
Bed & breakfast: £18-£26 single, £36-£40 double.
Half board: £28-£36 daily, £170-£182 weekly.
Evening meal 7pm (l.o. 5pm).
Parking for 11.
☼↻ ♨ ⊡ ➘ ⚗ ✚ ⊻ ⅋ ▥
♨ ⚗ ➘ ❦ SP

Thorneyfield Guest House M
APPROVED
Compston Rd., Ambleside,
LA22 9DJ
☎ (053 94) 32464
Cosy family-run guesthouse in the town centre with friendly and helpful service. Close to the park, miniature golf, tennis and lake.
Bedrooms: 1 single, 2 double, 3 family rooms.
Bathrooms: 2 public.
Bed & breakfast: £14-£16 single, £28-£32 double.
Parking for 3.
☼↻5 ⊡ ➘ ⅃ ⚗ ✚ ⊻ ⅋ ▥
⚗ SP

Wanslea Guest House M
APPROVED
Lake Rd., Ambleside,
LA22 0DB
☎ (053 94) 33884
Spacious, comfortable, family-run Victorian guesthouse. English cooking a speciality. Superb views. Easy walk to lake and village. Packed lunches available.
Bedrooms: 1 single, 3 double & 1 twin, 3 family rooms.
Bathrooms: 2 private, 3 public.
Bed & breakfast: £17.50-£22.50 single, £35-£47 double.
Half board: £27.50-£32.50 daily, £160-£175 weekly.
Evening meal 6.45pm (l.o. 3pm).
☼↻ ⚗ ➘ ⚗ ✚ ⊻ ⅋ ▥ ⧓ ♨ ❦
⚗ ➘ SP

Wateredge Hotel M
⚘⚘⚘ **COMMENDED**
Waterhead Bay, Ambleside,
LA22 0EP
☎ (053 94) 32332
Delightful location with gardens extending to lake's edge. Private jetty. Relaxed, friendly atmosphere. Log fires.
Bedrooms: 3 single, 11 double & 8 twin, 1 family room.
Bathrooms: 23 private.
Bed & breakfast: £46.50-£58.50 single, £78-£140 double.
Half board: £47-£78 daily, £330-£527 weekly.
Lunch available.
Evening meal 7pm (l.o. 8.30pm).
Parking for 25.
Open February-December.
Credit: Access, Visa, Amex.
☼↻7 ♨ ✆ ⊡ ➘ ⚗ ⊻ ⅋
⊺ ▥ ♨ ⅃ ✣ ❀ ❦ SP ▥
⦿ Display advertisement appears on page 86.

Waterhead Hotel M
⚘⚘⚘ **APPROVED**
Ambleside, LA22 0ER
☎ (053 94) 32566
Fax (053 94) 34275
Telex 65273 WATERHEAD
On the edge of Lake Windermere, an ideal central base for touring the lovely English Lakes.
Bedrooms: 3 single, 10 double & 12 twin, 1 family room.
Bathrooms: 26 private.
Bed & breakfast: £36-£45 single, £72-£90 double.
Half board: from £43 daily, from £294 weekly.
Lunch available.
Evening meal 7pm (l.o. 8.30pm).
Parking for 50.
Credit: Access, Visa, Diners, Amex.
☼↻ ♨ ✆ ⊡ ➘ ⚗ ✚ ⊻ ⅋
▥ ♨ ⅃ ⚗ ♪ ➘ ❀ ❦ SP
▥

National Crown ratings were correct at the time of going to press but are subject to change. Please check at the time of booking.

The national Crown scheme is explained in full on pages 536–539.

APPLEBY-IN-WESTMORLAND

Cumbria
Map ref 5B3

Former county town of Westmorland, at the foot of the Pennines in the Eden Valley. The castle was rebuilt in the 17th C, except for its Norman keep and the ditches and ramparts. It now houses a Rare Breeds Survival Trust Centre. Good centre for walking and exploring the Eden Valley.
Tourist Information Centre ☎ *(076 83) 51177*

Appleby Manor Country House Hotel ⚊
⚘⚘⚘ COMMENDED
Roman Rd., Appleby-in-Westmorland, CA16 6JD
☎ (076 83) 51571
⊕ Best Western
Country house hotel with fine timber features, in wooded grounds overlooking Appleby Castle. Panoramic views of the Pennines and the Lakeland fells. Indoor leisure club.
Bedrooms: 11 double & 11 twin, 8 family rooms.
Bathrooms: 30 private.
Bed & breakfast: £47.25-£57 single, £72.50-£92 double.
Half board: £45-£73 daily, £285-£427 weekly.
Lunch available.
Evening meal 7pm (l.o. 9pm).
Parking for 48.
Credit: Access, Visa, Diners, Amex.
⌇ ⊞ ⊞ ☎ ▣ ♨ ⚑ Ⓥ
✕ ⚑ ▥ ⚷ ⏧ ⚘ ⚘ ⊠
⟲ ▸ ⚙ ⅋ ⟲ SP ⚏

Bongate House ⚊
⚘⚘⚘ APPROVED
Appleby-in-Westmorland, CA16 6UE
☎ (076 83) 51245
Family-run Georgian guesthouse on the outskirts of a small market town. Large garden. Relaxed friendly atmosphere, good home cooking.
Bedrooms: 1 single, 1 double & 2 twin, 4 family rooms.
Bathrooms: 5 private, 1 public.
Bed & breakfast: £15 single, £30-£36 double.
Half board: £22-£25 daily, £140-£160 weekly.
Evening meal 7pm (l.o. 6pm).
Parking for 10.
⌇⟲ ♨ ⚑ Ⓥ ⚑ ⏧ ▥ ⚑ ⅋
⟲ ▸ ⚙ ⚏ DAP SP ⚏

New Inn
Brampton, Appleby-in-Westmorland, CA16 6JS
☎ (076 83) 51231
Small family-run inn of character, circa 1730. In the Vale of Eden, midway between the dales and Lake District.
Bedrooms: 1 double & 1 twin, 1 family room.
Bathrooms: 2 public.
Bed & breakfast: £18-£20 single, £36-£40 double.
Lunch available.
Evening meal 7pm (l.o. 9pm).
Parking for 30.
⌇ ⊞ ♨ ⚑ Ⓥ ⏧ ⟲ Ⓤ ▸
✓ ⚑ ⚏

BARROW-IN-FURNESS

Cumbria
Map ref 5A3

Modern shipbuilding and industrial centre on a peninsula in Morecambe Bay. Ruins of 12th C Cistercian Furness Abbey. Sandy beaches and a nature reserve on Walney Island.
Tourist Information Centre ☎ *(0229) 870156*

Abbey House Hotel ⚊
⚘⚘⚘⚘
Abbey Rd., Barrow-in-Furness, LA13 0PA
☎ Barrow (0229) 838282
Fax (0229) 820403
Friendly country house hotel, in idyllic location for that romantic weekend and an excellent base for touring the Lake District.
Bedrooms: 3 single, 11 double & 5 twin, 8 family rooms.
Bathrooms: 27 private.
Bed & breakfast: £42-£79.50 single, £62-£104.50 double.
Half board: £56.50-£86.45 daily.
Evening meal 7pm (l.o. 10pm).
Parking for 60.
Credit: Access, Visa, Diners, Amex.
⌇ ⚑ ⊞ ☎ ♨ ▣ Ⓥ
⚑ ⊕ ⚑ ⏧ ⚑ ⅋ ⚊ ⚘
SP ⚏ ⏧

Arlington House Hotel and Restaurant ⚊
⚘⚘⚘⚘ COMMENDED
200/202 Abbey Rd., Barrow-in-Furness, LA14 5LD
☎ (0229) 31976
A relaxed hotel with an elegant restaurant. In the town, yet not far away from the Lakes and sea.
Bedrooms: 8 double.
Bathrooms: 8 private.

Bed & breakfast: £45-£49.50
single, £61.50-£67 double.
Half board: from £63.50 daily.
Evening meal 7.30pm (l.o. 9pm).
Parking for 32.
Credit: Access, Visa.
⌇ ⚑ ⊞ ☎ ♨ ⏧ Ⓥ ⚑ ⊞
⚑ ⅋ ⚷ ⚘ ⚑ ⚏

Chetwynde Hotel
⚘⚘⚘
369 Abbey Rd., Barrow-in-Furness, LA13 9JS
☎ (0229) 811011
Quiet hotel with restaurant for residents. All rooms en-suite. Family room available. Pleasant beaches and beautiful countryside.
Bedrooms: 1 single, 4 double & 6 twin, 1 family room.
Bathrooms: 12 private.
Bed & breakfast: £55-£65 single, £70-£80 double.
Lunch available.
Evening meal 7pm (l.o. 9pm).
Parking for 30.
Credit: Access, Visa, Amex.
⌇ ⚑ ☎ ♨ ⏧ Ⓥ ⚑ ⏧
⊕ ⚑ ⚑ ⅋ ⚑ ⚑ ⚏ ⏧

East Mount Hotel
55, East Mount, Barrow-in-Furness, LA13 9AD
☎ (0229) 825242
Easy access to amenities, close to bus route. Some en-suite rooms available, TV, tea/coffee facilities in all rooms. Home cooking.
Bedrooms: 4 single, 3 double & 3 twin, 2 family rooms.
Bathrooms: 5 private, 2 public; 1 private shower.
Bed & breakfast: £17-£28 single, £30-£38 double.
Evening meal 6pm (l.o. 4pm).
Parking for 12.
Credit: Access, Visa.
⌇ ⚑ ♨ ⚑ Ⓥ ⚑ ⏧ ⚑
⅋ DAP ⚑ SP ⏧

The Gables
⚘
197 Abbey Rd., Barrow-in-Furness, LA14 5JP
☎ (0229) 825497
Friendly family-run hotel. All bedrooms with TV and tea-making facilities. Restaurant and licensed bar.
Bedrooms: 7 single, 2 double & 2 twin, 3 family rooms.
Bathrooms: 1 private, 2 public; 2 private showers.
Bed & breakfast: £12-£17 single, £28-£36 double.
Half board: £15.95-£20.95 daily.
Evening meal 7pm (l.o. 9pm).
Parking for 6.
⌇ ⚑ ☎ ♨ ⚑ Ⓥ ⚑ ⏧
⚑ ⚑ ⅋ ⚷ ⚑ SP

Victoria Park Hotel ⚊
⚘⚘⚘⚘ APPROVED
Victoria Rd., Barrow-in-Furness, LA14 5JS
☎ (0229) 821159
Fax: (0229) 870303
⊕ Consort
Near the coast and only 30 minutes from the heart of the Lake District. Ideally located for the businessman or tourist visiting Barrow and South Cumbria. Function rooms, cocktail bar.
Bedrooms: 12 single, 10 double & 16 twin, 2 family rooms.
Bathrooms: 35 private, 3 public.
Bed & breakfast: £35-£45 single, £40-£55 double.
Half board: £40-£50 daily, £245-£280 weekly.
Lunch available.
Evening meal 7pm (l.o. 9.30pm).
Parking for 60.
Credit: Access, Visa, Amex.
⌇ ☎ ⊞ ♨ ⚑ Ⓥ ⚑ ⚑ ◑
⚏ ⚑ ⅋ DAP ⚏ SP ⚏

BASSENTHWAITE

Cumbria
Map ref 5A2

Village near the north end of Bassenthwaite Lake. The area is visited by many varieties of migrating birds.

Armathwaite Hall ⚊
Bassenthwaite, Keswick, CA12 4RE
☎ (076 87) 76551
Telex 64319
Family-owned and run country house, with oak panelling, log fires, and all modern amenities. Amidst 450 acres of parkland with lake frontage.
Bedrooms: 3 single, 14 double & 19 twin, 6 family rooms.
Bathrooms: 42 private.
Bed & breakfast: £50-£90 single, £100-£180 double.
Lunch available.
Evening meal 7.30pm (l.o. 9.30pm).
Parking for 100.
Credit: Access, Visa, Diners, Amex.
⌇ ⚑ ⚑ ☎ ♨ ⚑ ⚑ Ⓥ
⚑ ◑ ⅋ ⚑ ⚑ ⏧ ⚷ ⚏ ⚏
⅋ ⟲ ⅋ ▸ ⚙ ⚏ SP ⚏ ⏧

Overwater Hall ⚊
Bassenthwaite, Nr. Ireby, CA15 1HH
☎ (076 87) 76566

Country house in 18 acres of woodland and gardens. Offering high standards of comfort, cleanliness and personal service.
Bedrooms: 1 single, 6 double & 3 twin, 3 family rooms.
Bathrooms: 13 private.
Half board: from £40 daily, from £260 weekly.
Evening meal 7pm (l.o. 8.30pm).
Parking for 25.
Open February-December.
Credit: Access, Visa.
🔥 ⚓ ⓒ ▯ ✿ ▮ Ⓥ ⌇ 🃏 ▥ ▲ ♣ ❄ 🗡 SP 🏵

Pheasant Inn ⚘
♛♛♛
Bassenthwaite Lake, Nr. Cockermouth, CA13 9YE
☎ (076 87) 76234
Fax (076 87) 76002
Peacefully situated just off the A66 at the northern end of Bassenthwaite Lake. A 16th C farmhouse with all the charm and character of that age.
Bedrooms: 4 single, 9 double & 7 twin.
Bathrooms: 20 private.
Bed & breakfast: max. £47 single.
Half board: max. £59 daily, max. £375 weekly.
Lunch available.
Evening meal 7pm (l.o. 8.30pm).
Parking for 80.
🔥 ⚓ ▮ Ⓥ ⌇ 🃏 ▥ ▲ ❉ 👁 ▮ ☘ ❄ 🗡 ▥ SP 🏵

Ravenstone Hotel ⚘
♛♛♛ COMMENDED
Bassenthwaite, Nr. Keswick, CA12 4QG
☎ (076 87) 76240
Charming dower house offering comfort and relaxation in beautiful surroundings. Hospitable bar, full-size snooker table, games room. Personal service.
Bedrooms: 1 single, 9 double & 3 twin, 1 family room.
Bathrooms: 14 private, 1 public.
Bed & breakfast: £26-£28 single, £52-£56 double.
Half board: £33-£35 daily, £224-£238 weekly.
Evening meal 7pm (l.o. 7.30pm).
Parking for 20.
Open March-October.
🔥 ⚓ ▯ ✿ ▮ Ⓥ ▥ ▥ ▲ ♣ ❄ 🗡

> *The symbols are explained on the flap inside the back cover.*

BORROWDALE
Cumbria
Map ref 5A3

Lying south of Derwentwater in the heart of the Lake District, the valley is backed by towering fells and mountains. Good centre for walking and climbing.

Derwent House ⚘
♛♛♛ COMMENDED
Grange-in-Borrowdale, Borrowdale, CA12 5UY
☎ (076 87) 77658
Victorian, family-run guesthouse in the lovely Borrowdale Valley. All rooms enjoy beautiful views of surrounding fells.
Bedrooms: 5 double & 4 twin, 1 family room.
Bathrooms: 6 private, 1 public.
Bed & breakfast: £22-£26 single, £34-£42 double.
Half board: £27-£31 daily, £189-£217 weekly.
Evening meal 7pm (l.o. 7pm).
Parking for 10.
Open February-December.
Credit: Diners.
🔥 ⚓ ▯ ▮ ⌇ 🃏 ▥ ▥ ▲ ❄ 🗡 🏵 ⒪AP SP Ⓣ

Hazel Bank Hotel ⚘
♛♛♛ COMMENDED
Rosthwaite, Borrowdale, Nr. Keswick, CA12 5XB
☎ (076 87) 77248
Victorian country house in 4 acres of parkland with views of the Lakeland mountains. Elegant lounge and bar with log fires.
Bedrooms: 1 single, 4 double & 4 twin.
Bathrooms: 8 private, 2 public.
Half board: £34-£36 daily, £219-£230 weekly.
Evening meal 7pm.
Parking for 12.
Open March-November.
🔥6 ⚓ ▮ ✿ ▮ Ⓣ ▥ ▲ ❄ 🗡 🏵

Royal Oak Hotel ⚘
♛♛♛ COMMENDED
Rosthwaite, Borrowdale, Nr. Keswick, CA12 5XB
☎ (076 87) 77214
Small family-run, traditional Lakeland hotel 6 miles south of Keswick. Cosy atmosphere, home cooking and friendly service.
Bedrooms: 2 single, 4 double & 2 twin, 4 family rooms.
Bathrooms: 8 private, 3 public.

Half board: £22-£34 daily, £161-£210 weekly.
Evening meal 7pm (l.o. 7pm).
Parking for 12.
Open January-November.
Credit: Access.
🔥 ⚓ ✿ ▮ ▥ Ⓣ ▥ ▲ 🗡 SP

BRAITHWAITE
Cumbria
Map ref 5A3

At the entry to Whinlatter Pass, the starting point for climbing Grisedale Pike.

Coledale Inn ⚘
♛♛♛ COMMENDED
Braithwaite, Keswick, CA12 5TN
☎ (076 87) 78272
Victorian country house hotel and Georgian inn, in a peaceful hillside position away from traffic, with superb mountain views.
Bedrooms: 1 single, 2 double & 1 twin, 4 family rooms.
Bathrooms: 8 private.
Bed & breakfast: £16.50-£20.50 single, £41-£49 double.
Lunch available.
Evening meal 6.30pm (l.o. 9pm).
Parking for 15.
Credit: Access, Visa.
🔥 ☎ ⓒ ▯ ✿ ▮ Ⓥ ⌇ 🃏 ▥ ▲ ▮ ❄ 🗡 ▥ SP 🏵

Ivy House Hotel ⚘
♛♛♛ COMMENDED
Braithwaite, Keswick, CA12 5SY
☎ (076 87) 78338
Oak-beamed house with log fires, in a small village among the fells. Elegant restaurant offers traditional English and French dishes. Restaurant is non-smoking.
Bedrooms: 2 single, 8 double & 2 twin.
Bathrooms: 12 private.
Bed & breakfast: £29-£31 single, £58-£62 double.
Half board: £39-£49 daily, £259-£322 weekly.
Evening meal 7pm (l.o. 7.30pm).
Parking for 20.
Open February-December.
Credit: Access, Visa, Diners, Amex.
⚓ ▮ ☎ ▯ ✿ ▮ Ⓥ 🃏 ▥ ▲ 🗡 ▥ SP Ⓣ

Maple Bank ⚘
♛♛♛
Braithwaite, Keswick, CA12 5RY
☎ Braithwaite (076 87) 78229

Delightfully friendly country guesthouse with magnificent views of Skiddaw and surrounding countryside. Home cooking. Open four seasons.
Bedrooms: 6 double & 1 twin.
Bathrooms: 4 private, 2 public.
Bed & breakfast: £40-£46 double.
Half board: £28-£31.50 daily, £186.20-£209.47 weekly.
Evening meal 6.30pm (l.o. 4pm).
Parking for 10.
🔥8 ▯ ✿ ▮ Ⓥ ⌇ 🃏 ▥ ▲ ❄ 🗡 🃏 ◣ SP

Thelmlea ⚘
♛♛♛
Braithwaite, Nr. Keswick, Cumbria. CA12 5TD
☎ (076 87) 78305
Country house in 1.75 acre grounds. Friendly relaxed atmosphere, log fire, home cooking. Superb views. Ideal base for walkers or touring. Within easy reach of all Lakes, coast and Carlisle (30/40 minute drive).
Bedrooms: 1 double & 1 twin, 2 family rooms.
Bathrooms: 3 private, 1 public.
Bed & breakfast: £27-£36 double.
Half board: £22-£26.50 daily, £140-£175 weekly.
Lunch available.
Evening meal 6.30pm (l.o. 7pm).
Parking for 9.
🔥 ▯ ✿ Ⓤ ▮ Ⓥ 🃏 Ⓣ ▥ ▲ ❄ 🗡 ⒪AP SP

BRAMPTON
Cumbria
Map ref 5B2

9m NE. Carlisle
Pleasant market town and a good centre from which to explore Hadrian's Wall. Lanercost Priory is 2 miles away.

Blacksmiths Arms Hotel ⚘
Listed COMMENDED
Talkin Village, Brampton, CA8 1LE
☎ (069 77) 3452
Country pub in scenic countryside half a mile from Talkin Tarn with walking, golf, pony trekking, sailing, windsurfing, fishing, Hadrian's Wall and the Lake District within easy reach.
Bedrooms: 2 double & 3 twin.
Bathrooms: 5 private.

Continued ▶

BRAMPTON

Continued

Bed & breakfast: £25-£28 single, £38-£42 double.
Half board: £25-£38 daily.
Lunch available.
Evening meal 7pm (l.o. 9.30pm).
Parking for 10.
Credit: Access, Visa.

Hullerbank ⋔
`COMMENDED`

Talkin, Brampton, CA8 1LB
☎ Hallbankgate
(069 77) 46668
14-acre mixed farm. Georgian farmhouse guesthouse, part dated 1635 and 1751, near Talkin Village. 9 miles from M6 junction 43 and 3 miles from Brampton.
Bedrooms: 1 double & 2 twin.
Bathrooms: 3 private.
Bed & breakfast: £18-£20 single, £32-£33 double.
Half board: £25-£25.50 daily, £160-£165 weekly.
Evening meal 6.30pm (l.o. 6pm).
Parking for 6.

Kirby Moor Country House Hotel ⋔
`COMMENDED`

Longtown Rd., Brampton, Nr. Carlisle, CA8 2AB
☎ (069 77) 3893
Detached Victorian house on the A6071 well back from the road with ample parking and extensive views. 6 miles from Hadrian's Wall. Set in 2.5 acres of grounds.
Bedrooms: 1 single, 3 double & 1 twin, 1 family room.
Bathrooms: 6 private, 1 public.
Bed & breakfast: £26.50-£28.50 single, £38-£40 double.
Half board: from £30 daily, from £192.50 weekly.
Lunch available.
Evening meal 7pm (l.o. 9.30pm).
Parking for 30.
Credit: Access, Visa.

The enquiry coupons at the back will help you when contacting proprietors.

BROUGHTON-IN-FURNESS

Cumbria
Map ref 5A3

Old market village whose historic charter is still proclaimed every year on the first day of August in the market square, when coins are distributed. Good centre for touring the Duddon Valley.

Cobblers Cottage ⋔
`APPROVED`

Griffin St., Broughton-in-Furness, LA20 6HH
☎ (0229) 716413
17th C cottage with original oak beams and fireplace, offering interesting food in a relaxed and informal atmosphere. Ideally situated for exploring South Lakes and beautiful Duddon Valley.
Bedrooms: 2 double & 1 twin.
Bathrooms: 1 public.
Bed & breakfast: £14.50-£20 single, £29-£34 double.
Half board: £24-£29.50 daily, £161-£178.50 weekly.
Evening meal 7pm (l.o. 5pm).

The Garner Guest House ⋔

Church St., Broughton-in-Furness, LA20 6HJ
☎ (0229) 716462
Comfortable Victorian family house of character, with a sunny walled garden. On the outskirts of this old market town.
Bedrooms: 2 double & 1 twin.
Bathrooms: 1 private, 1 public.
Bed & breakfast: £16.50 single, £27-£30 double.
Half board: £24-£25.50 daily.
Evening meal 7pm.

Please check prices and other details at the time of booking.

Individual proprietors have supplied all details of accommodation. Although we do check for accuracy, we advise you to confirm prices and other information at the time of booking.

BUTTERMERE

Cumbria
Map ref 5A3

Halfway between the north end of Buttermere Lake and Crummock Water, this village is an ideal centre for walking and climbing the nearby peaks.

Bridge Hotel ⋔

Buttermere, CA13 9UZ
☎ (059 685) 252/266
Historic Lakeland hotel with modern comforts and facilities, in an area of outstanding beauty which is superb walking country.
Bedrooms: 2 single, 8 double & 12 twin.
Bathrooms: 22 private.
Half board: £39-£48 daily, £246-£303 weekly.
Lunch available.
Evening meal 7pm (l.o. 8.30pm).
Parking for 30.

Pickett Howe ⋔
`HIGHLY COMMENDED`

Brackenthwaite, Buttermere Valley, Cockermouth, Cumbria. CA13 9UY
☎ Lorton (0900) 85444
Well-appointed 17th C longhouse, peacefully situated between Crummock and Loweswater Lakes off the B5289, 4 miles from Buttermere. Renowned for creative cooking and relaxing atmosphere.
Bedrooms: 3 double & 1 twin.
Bathrooms: 4 private.
Bed & breakfast: £42-£65 double.
Half board: £36-£49 daily, £252-£315 weekly.
Evening meal 7.15pm (l.o. 7pm).
Parking for 4.
Open February-November.
Credit: Access, Visa, Amex.

CALDBECK

Cumbria
Map ref 5A2

Quaint limestone village lying at the northern edge of the Lake District National Park. John Peel, the famous huntsman who is immortalised in song, is buried in the churchyard.

High Greenrigg House ⋔
`APPROVED`

Caldbeck, Wigton, CA7 8HD
☎ Caldbeck (069 98) 430
Converted 17th C farmhouse in the remote northern fells of the Lake District National Park. Home cooking and a warm welcome.
Bedrooms: 2 single, 3 double & 2 twin, 1 family room.
Bathrooms: 6 private, 1 public.
Bed & breakfast: £19.50-£25 single, £39 double.
Half board: £32-£37.50 daily.
Evening meal 7pm (l.o. 4pm).
Parking for 8.
Open March-October.

CARLISLE

Cumbria
Map ref 5A2

Near the border with Scotland, this cathedral city suffered years of strife through the centuries, often changing hands between England and Scotland. The red sandstone cathedral with its beautiful east window is the second smallest cathedral in England. The castle was founded in 1092 and later enlarged. The keep now houses a museum of the history of the Border Regiment. *Tourist Information Centre* ☎ *(0228) 512444*

Aidan View Guesthouse
`Listed`

154 Warwick Rd., Carlisle, CA1 1LG
☎ (0228) 32353
Comfortable guesthouse, near parks and golf course. 3 minutes junction 43 off M6, 5 minutes to town centre, rail and coach station. Evening meals available.
Bedrooms: 1 twin, 2 family rooms.
Bathrooms: 1 public.

Bed & breakfast: £12-£13 single, £24-£25 double.
Half board: £18 daily.
⌣ ⊙ ▢ ♥ 🅤 🛉 🆅 🛏 🎬 🍽 🗙 🛏 🅼

Avondale ▲
♔
3 St. Aidan's Road, Carlisle, CA1 1LT
☎ (0228) 23012
Attractive Edwardian house in quiet situation close to city centre. Private parking. Comfortable rooms with TV. Warm welcome. M6 junction 43.
Bedrooms: 1 double & 2 twin.
Bathrooms: 1 private, 1 public.
Bed & breakfast: £15-£16 double.
Half board: £21-£22 daily.
Evening meal 6.30pm (l.o. midday).
Parking for 3.
⌣ ⊙ ▢ ♥ 🅤 🛉 🆅 🛏 🎬 🍽 ▲ 🗙 🛏 🅳🅰🅵 🆂🅿

Calreena Guest House ▲
123 Warwick Road, Carlisle, CA1 1JZ
☎ Carlisle (0228) 25020
Comfortable friendly guesthouse. Central heating. Home cooking. Colour TV and tea making facilities in all rooms. 2 minutes from city centre, railway and bus stations. 2 minutes from M6 junction 43.
Bedrooms: 1 single, 1 double & 1 twin, 1 family room.
Bathrooms: 2 public.
Bed & breakfast: £12 single, £24 double.
Half board: £15 daily.
Evening meal 5pm (l.o. 8pm).
⌣ ▢ ♥ 🅤 🛉 🆅 🛏 🎬 ▲ 🛏 🆂🅿

Central Plaza Hotel
♔♔♔
Victoria Viaduct, Carlisle, CA3 8AL
☎ (0228) 20256
Fax (0228) 514657
🆎 Inter
Elegant hotel with modern comforts in traditional surroundings. Conference facilities for 200. Group theme/entertainment breaks a speciality. Close to many attractions.
Bedrooms: 19 single, 36 double & 25 twin, 4 family rooms.
Bathrooms: 84 private.
Bed & breakfast: £62-£73 single, £72-£83 double.
Half board: from £76.50 daily, from £280 weekly.
Lunch available.
Evening meal 7pm (l.o. 9pm).

Parking for 25.
Credit: Access, Visa, Diners, Amex.
⌣ 🏚 🕿 ⊙ ▢ ♥ 🛉 🆅 🛏 🎬 ● 🎦 🛏 ▲ 🍽 🅳🅰🅵 🖋 🆂🅿 🛏 🆃

County Hotel ▲
♔♔♔♔ COMMENDED
Botchergate, Carlisle, CA1 1QS
☎ (0228) 31316
Fax (0228) 515456
Telex 64370
Built in 1853 and extensively refurbished with every modern convenience. City centre location, adjacent to railway station.
Bedrooms: 30 single, 35 double & 15 twin, 4 family rooms.
Bathrooms: 84 private.
Bed & breakfast: £29-£34 single, £48-£56 double.
Half board: £35-£40 daily.
Lunch available.
Evening meal 7pm (l.o. 10pm).
Parking for 70.
Credit: Access, Visa, Diners, Amex.
⌣ 🏚 🕿 ⊙ ▢ ♥ 🛉 🆅 🛏 🎬 ● 🎦 🛏 ▲ 🍽 🅳🅰🅵 🆂🅿 🛏 🆃

Craighead ▲
♔♔
6 Hartington Place, Carlisle, CA1 1HL
☎ (0228) 27443
Attractive Victorian town house with spacious rooms and original features. Minutes' walk to city centre, bus and rail stations. Friendly and comfortable. Fresh farm food.
Bedrooms: 1 single, 1 double & 1 twin, 1 family room.
Bathrooms: 2 public.
Bed & breakfast: £13-£15 single, £24-£28 double.

Crossroads House ▲
♔♔ COMMENDED
Brisco, Carlisle, CA4 0QZ
☎ (0228) 28994
Detached house built in 1810. 3 miles from Carlisle city centre and three quarters of a mile from the M6 junction 42 Dalston turn off. Roman well inside house. Panoramic views from every room. A warm welcome awaits.
Bedrooms: 1 single, 1 double & 2 twin, 1 family room.
Bathrooms: 2 public.
Bed & breakfast: £16.50-£22 single, £30-£33 double.

Half board: £23-£25 daily.
Evening meal 6pm (l.o. 10am).
Parking for 7.
⌣ 🛉 🆅 🛏 🎬 🛏 ▲ 🛏 🏯

Cumbria Park Hotel
♔♔♔♔ COMMENDED
32 Scotland Rd., Carlisle, CA3 9DG
☎ (0228) 22887
Fax (0228) 514796
One mile from the city centre, in its own ornamental gardens. A part of Hadrian's Wall (the only part on display in Carlisle) is in our car park.
Bedrooms: 7 single, 17 double & 23 twin, 4 family rooms.
Bathrooms: 51 private.
Bed & breakfast: £52-£72 single, £64-£97 double.
Half board: from £67.50 daily.
Lunch available.
Evening meal 6.30pm (l.o. 9pm).
Parking for 40.
Credit: Access, Visa, Amex.
⌣ 🏚 🕿 🕿 ⊙ ▢ ♥ 🛉 🆅 🛏 ● 🎦 🛏 ▲ 🍽 ♿ 🖋 🆂🅿 🏯 🆃

Cumbrian Hotel ▲
Court Square, Carlisle, CA1 1QY
☎ (0228) 31951 Telex 64287
This building dates from 1852, was used by Queen Victoria and overlooks the Crown Court and the old city.
Bedrooms: 26 single, 36 double & 30 twin, 4 family rooms.
Bed & breakfast: from £69 single, from £91 double.
Lunch available.
Evening meal 7pm (l.o. 10pm).
Parking for 30.
Credit: Access, Visa, C.Bl., Diners, Amex.
⌣ 🏚 🕿 ⊙ ▢ ♥ 🛉 🆅 ● 🎦 🛏 ▲ 🍽 🖋 🆂🅿 🏯 🆃

Howard House ▲
♔♔ COMMENDED
27 Howard Place, Carlisle, CA1 1HR
☎ (0228) 29159
Victorian house in quiet location 2 minutes from city centre. A warm welcome awaits from Lawrence and Sandra. Family historians welcome.
Bedrooms: 1 single, 1 double & 1 twin, 2 family rooms.
Bathrooms: 2 private, 2 public.
Bed & breakfast: £12-£15 single, £24-£32 double.

Half board: £17-£21 daily, £110-£140 weekly.
Evening meal 6pm (l.o. 10am).
⌣ 🏚 ⊙ ▢ ♥ 🅤 🛉 🆅 🛏 🎬 🛏 ▲ 🛏 🆂🅿 🆃

Howard Lodge Guesthouse
90 Warwick Rd., Carlisle, CA1 1JW
☎ (0228) 29842
Victorian townhouse on main road 400 metres from city centre. Tastefully decorated and offering modern facilities.
Bedrooms: 1 double & 1 twin, 1 family room.
Bathrooms: 1 private, 2 public.
Bed & breakfast: £15-£20 single, £28-£33 double.
Evening meal 6pm (l.o. 2pm).
Parking for 2.
⌣ ▢ ♥ 🅤 🛉 🛏 ▲ 🛏 🏯

Kingstown Hotel
246/248 Kingstown Rd., Carlisle, CA3 0DE
☎ (0228) 515292
Convenient touring base for Lakes, Scotland or overnight stops. Near M6 junction 44. Licensed a la carte restaurant.
Bedrooms: 1 single, 3 double & 2 twin, 1 family room.
Bathrooms: 2 private, 2 public; 2 private showers.
Bed & breakfast: £20-£27.50 single, £30-£40 double.
Half board: £28-£35.50 daily.
Evening meal 7pm (l.o. 9.30pm).
Parking for 12.
Credit: Access, Visa.
⌣ 🏚 ⊙ ▢ ♥ 🛉 🆅 🛏 ▲ 🍽 ♿ ❋

Langleigh House ▲
♔♔ COMMENDED
6 Howard Place, Carlisle
☎ (0228) 30440
Beautifully restored late Victorian house. Ten minutes' walk from city centre. Friendly atmosphere.
Bedrooms: 3 family rooms.
Bathrooms: 3 private.
Bed & breakfast: £16 single, £30 double.
Parking for 10.
⌣ 🏚 ▢ ♥ 🅤 ● 🛏 ▲ 🛏 🗙 🅳🅰🅵 🆂🅿

Montrose Guest House
▨ Listed
24 London Rd., Carlisle, CA1 2EL
☎ (0228) 28696
Family-run guesthouse, close to city centre, central for Scotland/Lakes, on main thoroughfare. 5 minutes' walking distance from station.
Continued ▶

CARLISLE

Continued

Bedrooms: 3 single, 3 double & 6 twin, 5 family rooms.
Bathrooms: 6 public.
Bed & breakfast: £15-£20 single, £25-£30 double.
Evening meal 6pm (l.o. 7pm).

Park View

38 Aglionby St., Carlisle, CA1 1JA
☎ (0228) 33599/35109
Comfortable accommodation near city centre. Easy access rail/coach stations and M6. Centrally heated, h & c in all bedrooms. Pleasant atmosphere.
Bedrooms: 4 single, 3 double & 1 twin, 1 family room.
Bathrooms: 3 public.
Bed & breakfast: £11-£12 single, £22-£24 double.

Parkland Guest House M
COMMENDED

136 Petteril Street, Carlisle
☎ (0228) 48331
Run by friendly young couple. 5 minutes' walk from city centre and close to all amenities.
Bedrooms: 1 double & 1 twin, 1 family room.
Bathrooms: 1 public; 2 private showers.
Bed & breakfast: £13.50-£15 single, £23-£25 double.
Half board: from £17.50 daily.
Parking for 3.

Redruth House M

46 Victoria Place, Carlisle, CA1 1EX
☎ (0228) 21631
Well-appointed central guesthouse, close to city amenities. Convenient for the Borders, Roman Wall and Lakes. Easy access M6 junction 43.
Bedrooms: 1 single, 3 twin, 2 family rooms.
Bathrooms: 1 public; 2 private showers.
Bed & breakfast: £12.50-£15 single, £25-£30 double.
Half board: £17.50-£20 daily, £122.50-£140 weekly.
Evening meal 6pm (l.o. 9pm).

Riverston Guest House M
Listed

68 St. James Rd., Denton Holme, Carlisle, CA2 5PD
☎ (0228) 20825 & (0228) 818060
Large Victorian house on the west side of city in quiet residential area. Close to River Caldew, park, bowling greens, shopping area.
Bedrooms: 2 single, 2 double & 1 twin, 1 family room.
Bathrooms: 2 public.
Bed & breakfast: £14.50-£16 single, £27-£29 double.
Evening meal 6pm (l.o. 8pm).
Parking for 3.

Royal Hotel M

9 Lowther St., Carlisle, CA3 8ES
☎ (0228) 22103
Family-run hotel. All bedrooms have colour TV. Breakfast, bar lunches and evening meals served.
Bedrooms: 8 single, 4 double & 8 twin, 3 family rooms.
Bathrooms: 15 private, 5 public.
Bed & breakfast: £17-£26.50 single, £28.50-£38 double.
Half board: £23-£36.90 daily, £161-£252 weekly.
Lunch available.
Evening meal 6.30pm (l.o. 8.30pm).
Credit: Access, Visa, Amex.

String of Horses Inn & Restaurant M
COMMENDED

Faugh, Heads Nook, Carlisle, CA4 9EG
☎ (0228) 70297 or 702509
17th C English country inn with log fires, antique furnishings, solarium, indoor whirlpool spa and outside heated pool.
Bedrooms: 12 double & 2 twin.
Bathrooms: 14 private.
Bed & breakfast: £58-£72 single, £65-£95 double.
Lunch available.
Evening meal 7.30pm (l.o. 10pm).
Parking for 50.
Credit: Access, Visa, C.Bl., Diners, Amex.

Swallow Hilltop Hotel M
COMMENDED

London Rd., Carlisle, CA1 2PQ
☎ (0228) 29255 Telex 64292
Ⓒ Swallow
Modern comfortable hotel with leisure facilities. Ideal touring base for the Border, Lakes, Roman Wall and the Solway Coast. Special cabaret weekends. Winner of English Tourist Board's "England Entertains" best promotion award.
Bedrooms: 2 single, 25 double & 56 twin, 9 family rooms.
Bathrooms: 92 private.
Bed & breakfast: £70-£75 single, £80-£85 double.
Half board: £96.90-£98 daily.
Lunch available.
Evening meal 7pm (l.o. 10pm).
Parking for 351.
Credit: Access, Visa, Diners, Amex.

Vallum House Garden Hotel M
APPROVED

Burgh Rd., Carlisle, CA2 7NB
☎ (0228) 21860
In a select residential area on the west side of the city, en route to the Solway coast. Close to Stoneyholm Golf Course and Edward I monument. Bar meals available lunchtime and evening plus a la carte.
Bedrooms: 6 single, 3 twin.
Bathrooms: 5 private, 2 public.
Bed & breakfast: £25-£30 single, £35-£45 double.
Half board: £34-£41 daily.
Lunch available.
Evening meal 6pm (l.o. 9pm).
Parking for 50.
Credit: Access.

Wallfoot Hotel & Restaurant M
COMMENDED

Park Broom, Carlisle, CA6 4QH
☎ (0228) 73696
Warm welcome and good food in family-run hotel. Located in beautiful countryside on route of Hadrian's Wall, yet only 3 minutes from exit 44 M6 (follow airport signs) and 10 minutes from Carlisle city centre. Ideal for Border break or overnight stop en-route for Scotland.

Bedrooms: 3 single, 2 double & 2 twin, 3 family rooms.
Bathrooms: 6 private, 1 public.
Bed & breakfast: £18-£30 single, £36-£50 double.
Lunch available.
Evening meal 6pm (l.o. 10pm).
Parking for 30.
Credit: Access, Visa.

Warren Guesthouse
APPROVED

368 Warwick Road, Carlisle, CA1 2RU
☎ (0228) 33663 & (0228) 512916
Near Hadrian's Wall. Good base for Scotland and Lake District. Very comfortable, friendly. Half a mile from M6. Evening meals by request. No smoking in bedrooms. Exclusive chamber pot collection.
Bedrooms: 1 single, 2 double & 1 twin, 2 family rooms.
Bathrooms: 4 private, 2 public.
Bed & breakfast: £14-£20 single, £28-£32 double.
Half board: £19.50-£21 daily, £128-£135 weekly.
Evening meal 6pm (l.o. 8pm).
Parking for 4.

White Lea Guest House

191 Warwick Rd., Carlisle, CA1 1LP
☎ (0228) 33139
Take the M6 junction 43, straight on to the Warwick road and into Carlisle. Located 10 minutes' walk from the city centre. Municipal golf-course, park and shops are close by.
Bedrooms: 1 single, 2 double & 1 twin, 1 family room.
Bathrooms: 2 public.
Bed & breakfast: £12.50-£14.50 single, £25-£29 double.
Half board: £19.50-£22.50 daily.
Evening meal 6pm.
Parking for 5.

> *National Crown ratings were correct at the time of going to press but are subject to change. Please check at the time of booking.*

CARTMEL

Cumbria
Map ref 5A3

Picturesque conserved village based on a 12th C priory with a well-preserved church and gatehouse. Just over 3 miles north of Morecambe Bay and 8 miles from the south tip of Lake Windermere. A peaceful base for fell-walking, with historic houses and beautiful scenery.

Aynsome Manor Hotel M

Cartmel, Grange-over-Sands, LA11 6HH
☎ (053 95) 36653
Lovely old manor house, nestling in the vale of Cartmel. Good food, attentive service, a log fire and comfort. Lunches served on Sundays. No smoking in restaurant.
Bedrooms: 1 single, 6 double & 4 twin, 2 family rooms.
Bathrooms: 12 private, 2 public.
Half board: £36.50-£49 daily.
Evening meal 7pm (l.o. 8.15pm).
Parking for 20.
Open February-December.
Credit: Access, Visa, Amex.

Cavendish Arms Hotel

Cavendish St., Cartmel, Grange-over-Sands, LA11 6QA
☎ (053 95) 36240
The oldest country inn in Cartmel with open fires and a cosy candlelit dining room, serving guaranteed Aberdeen Angus steaks.
Bedrooms: 3 double & 2 twin.
Bathrooms: 5 private.
Bed & breakfast: £18-£28 single, £36-£70 double.
Lunch available.
Evening meal 6pm (l.o. 9.30pm).
Parking for 20.
Credit: Access, Visa.

The Grammar Hotel M
COMMENDED

Cartmel, Grange-over-Sands, LA11 7SG
☎ (053 95) 36367

17th C country hotel in beautiful Vale of Cartmel. All rooms en-suite, with colour TV and tea making facilities. Peace and tranquillity guaranteed.
Bedrooms: 4 double & 4 twin, 2 family rooms.
Bathrooms: 10 private.
Bed & breakfast: £25-£33 single, £50-£64 double.
Half board: £35-£45 daily, £220-£270 weekly.
Lunch available.
Evening meal 6.30pm (l.o. 8.30pm).
Parking for 30.
Open March-December.
Credit: Access, Visa.

CLEATOR

Cumbria
Map ref 5A3

6 miles from the Georgian port of Whitehaven and with easy access to the western fells.

The Ennerdale Country House Hotel M

Cleator, CA23 3DT
☎ (0946) 813907
16th C country house hotel set in 6 acres of gardens, on the A5086 Cockermouth to Egremont road. Easy access to the Solway Coast, Lakes and fells.
Bedrooms: 4 single, 10 double & 6 twin.
Bathrooms: 20 private.
Bed & breakfast: £30-£65 single, £39.95-£80 double.
Lunch available.
Evening meal 7pm (l.o. 9.30pm).
Parking for 80.
Credit: Access, Visa, C.Bl., Diners, Amex.

Grove Court M
COMMENDED

Cleator Gate, Cleator, CA23 3DT
☎ (0946) 810503
Family-run hotel with reputation for food. Convenient for Lake District and Solway coast.
Bedrooms: 4 single, 4 double & 2 twin, 1 family room.
Bathrooms: 11 private.
Bed & breakfast: £35-£40 single, £50-£60 double.
Lunch available.
Evening meal 7pm (l.o. 8pm).

Parking for 100.
Credit: Access, Visa, Amex.

COCKERMOUTH

Cumbria
Map ref 5A2

Market town at the confluence of the Rivers Cocker and Derwent, and the birthplace of William Wordsworth, the Lakeland poet, in 1770. The house where he was born stands at one end of the town's broad, tree-lined main street and is now owned by the National Trust. Good base for motoring tours into the Lake District.
Tourist Information Centre ☎ (0900) 822634

The Grecian Villa's Hotel M
COMMENDED

Crown Street, Cockermouth, CA13 OEH
☎ (0900) 827575
Fax (0900) 827772
Hotel providing all en-suite facilities and modern conveniences. Within easy walking distance of Wordsworth's house.
Bedrooms: 1 single, 8 double & 3 twin, 1 family room.
Bathrooms: 13 private.
Bed & breakfast: from £45 single, from £59 double.
Half board: from £45 daily, from £375 weekly.
Lunch available.
Evening meal 7pm (l.o. 9.30pm).
Parking for 25.
Credit: Access, Visa, Diners, Amex.

Low Hall Country Guesthouse M
COMMENDED

Brandlingill, Cockermouth, CA13 ORE
☎ Cockermouth (0900) 826654
Secluded 17th C former farmhouse overlooking Lorton Fells, near Wordsworth's birthplace and the quiet fells and lakes.
Bedrooms: 5 double & 1 twin.
Bathrooms: 6 private.
Bed & breakfast: £46-£49 double.
Half board: £36-£37.50 daily, £238-£248 weekly.

Evening meal 7pm (l.o. 7.30pm).
Parking for 10.
Open March-November.
Credit: Access, Visa.

Rose Cottage Guest House
COMMENDED

Lorton Rd., Cockermouth, CA13 9DX
☎ (0900) 822189
In a pleasant position, this guesthouse is within easy reach of the Lakes and the coast.
Bedrooms: 2 single, 4 double & 2 twin, 2 family rooms.
Bathrooms: 2 private, 3 public.
Bed & breakfast: £18.50-£21 single, £33-£36 double.
Half board: £28.50-£31 daily.
Evening meal 6.30pm (l.o. 4.30pm).
Parking for 10.

Wordsworth Hotel

Main St., Cockermouth, CA13 9JS
☎ (0900) 822757
17th C coaching inn close to the birthplace of William Wordsworth.
Bedrooms: 3 single, 12 double & 2 twin, 1 family room.
Bathrooms: 12 private, 1 public; 1 private shower.
Bed & breakfast: £20-£33 single, £37-£44 double.
Half board: £22.50-£27 daily.
Lunch available.
Evening meal 7pm (l.o. 9.30pm).
Parking for 30.
Credit: Access, Visa, Diners, Amex.

Individual proprietors have supplied all details of accommodation. Although we do check for accuracy, we advise you to confirm prices and other information at the time of booking.

CONISTON

Cumbria
Map ref 5A3

Village lying at the north end of Coniston Water. To the north-west of the village run the Coniston Fells, dominated by Coniston Old Man. Fine centre for walkers. John Ruskin, the Victorian critic, is buried beneath a splendidly-carved cross in the churchyard.

Arrowfield

Little Arrow, Coniston, Cumbria. LA21 8AU
☎ (053 94) 41741
Elegant 19th C Lakeland house in beautiful rural setting. Adjacent to Coniston/Torver road (A593). 2 miles from Coniston village.
Bedrooms: 1 single, 3 twin, 1 family room.
Bathrooms: 2 private, 1 public.
Bed & breakfast: £15-£17 single, £30-£36 double.
Half board: £25-£28 daily, £165-£186 weekly.
Evening meal 7pm (l.o. midday).
Parking for 6.
Open March-November.

Brocklebank Ground Country Guest House ♨
🏵🏵 APPROVED
Broughton Road, Torver, Coniston, LA21 8BS
☎ (053 94) 41449
Comfortable, traditional Georgian guesthouse in secluded woodland. Easy access to Coniston Lake. Home comforts a speciality.
Bedrooms: 2 double & 2 twin, 1 family room.
Bathrooms: 3 private, 1 public.
Bed & breakfast: £17.50-£20 single, £35-£40 double.
Half board: £25.50-£28 daily.
Evening meal 6.30pm (l.o. 8pm).
Parking for 6.
Credit: Access, Visa.

Coniston Lodge ♨
🏵🏵 HIGHLY COMMENDED
Sunny Brow, Coniston, LA21 8HH
☎ (053 94) 41201
Small family-run hotel offering accommodation and food to a high standard in beautiful surroundings. Non-smokers only please.
Bedrooms: 3 double & 3 twin.
Bathrooms: 6 private.
Bed & breakfast: £27-£39 single, £54-£70 double.
Half board: £40.50-£49 daily.
Evening meal 7pm (l.o. 7.30pm).
Parking for 9.
Credit: Access, Visa.

Crown Hotel ♨
🏵🏵 APPROVED
Coniston, LA21 8EA
☎ (053 94) 41243
At the foot of Coniston Old Man, 10 minutes' walk to the lake where Donald Campbell attempted to break the world water speed record.
Bedrooms: 1 single, 2 double & 1 twin, 3 family rooms.
Bathrooms: 2 public.
Bed & breakfast: £17-£19 single, £32-£36 double.
Half board: £25-£30 daily.
Lunch available.
Evening meal 7pm (l.o. 9pm).
Parking for 30.
Credit: Access, Visa, Diners, Amex.

Old Rectory House Hotel ♨
🏵🏵🏵 COMMENDED
Torver, Coniston, LA21 8AY
☎ (053 94) 41353
Converted rectory in rural setting 2 miles south of Coniston. Set in 3 acres of garden, close to lake shore.
Bedrooms: 4 double & 2 twin, 1 family room.
Bathrooms: 7 private.
Bed & breakfast: £44-£60 double.
Half board: £30-£42.50 daily, £200-£279 weekly.
Evening meal 7.30pm (l.o. 7.30pm).
Parking for 10.

Sun Hotel Coniston ♨
🏵🏵🏵 COMMENDED
Coniston, LA21 8HQ
☎ (053 94) 41248
Country house hotel and 16th C inn, in spectacular mountain setting on the fringe of the village and at the foot of the Coniston Old Man.
Bedrooms: 1 single, 6 double & 4 twin.
Bathrooms: 10 private.
Bed & breakfast: £30-£38 single, £60-£75 double.
Lunch available.
Evening meal 7pm (l.o. 8.30pm).
Parking for 20.
Credit: Access, Visa.

Wheelgate Hotel ♨
🏵🏵🏵 COMMENDED
Little Arrow, Torver, Coniston, LA21 8AU
☎ (053 94) 41418
Well positioned and an ideal touring base, with pretty bedrooms and lovely views. Cosy bar, home cooking, selected wines and personal supervision.
Bedrooms: 5 double & 2 twin.
Bathrooms: 5 private, 2 public.
Bed & breakfast: £30-£40 single, £36-£52 double.
Half board: £32-£40 daily.
Evening meal 7.30pm (l.o. 7.30pm).
Parking for 8.
Open March-November.

Yewdale Hotel ♨
🏵🏵🏵 COMMENDED
Yewdale Rd., Coniston, LA21 8LU
☎ (053 94) 41280
Built of local materials in 1896 as a bank, now a modern hotel skilfully refurbished throughout. Reduced rate breaks available.
Bedrooms: 5 double & 2 twin, 3 family rooms.
Bathrooms: 8 private, 2 public.
Bed & breakfast: £21-£30 single, £42-£60 double.
Half board: £31.50-£39 daily, £165-£228 weekly.
Lunch available.
Evening meal (l.o. 9pm).
Parking for 6.
Credit: Access, Visa.

CROOKLANDS

Cumbria
Map ref 5B3

6m SE. Kendal
Village set amid the rolling fields, hedges and hills of England's largest drumlin belt.

Crooklands Hotel ♨
🏵🏵🏵🏵 COMMENDED
Crooklands, Nr. Milnthorpe, LA7 7NW
☎ (044 87) 432
Telex 94017303
ⓒⓡ Best Western
Ideal for Windermere and South Lakes, rurally located but minutes from the motorway. Strategically placed for business meetings, conferences, tourists and travellers to Scotland. Renowned for friendly attitude and flexible approach to looking after guests' needs. Carvery, French restaurant, refurbished public lounges and bars.
Bedrooms: 7 double & 24 twin.
Bathrooms: 31 private.
Bed & breakfast: £55-£65 single, £70-£80 double.
Half board: £80-£90 daily, from £250 weekly.
Lunch available.
Evening meal 7pm (l.o. 9.30pm).
Parking for 120.
Credit: Access, Visa, Diners, Amex.

CROSBY-ON-EDEN

Cumbria
Map ref 5A2

3.5 miles north-east of Carlisle, Crosby stands by the River Eden and is a small village comprising attractive old and new dwellings.

Crosby Lodge Hotel ♨
🏵🏵🏵 COMMENDED
High Crosby, Crosby-on-Eden, Carlisle, CA6 4QZ
☎ (0228) 573618
Fax (0228) 573428
18th C country mansion overlooking parkland and the river. Chef-proprietor provides a varied English and continental menu. Full afternoon teas available on request.
Bedrooms: 1 single, 5 double & 4 twin, 1 family room.
Bathrooms: 11 private.

---

*The symbol **ⓒⓡ** and the name of a hotel group or consortium after a hotel address means that bookings can be made through a central reservations office. These are listed on page 540.*

Bed & breakfast: £65-£68 single, £85-£95 double.
Half board: £67.50-£90 daily.
Lunch available.
Evening meal 7.30pm (l.o. 9pm).
Parking for 40.
Open February-December.
Credit: Access, Visa, Amex.
⌂ ♨ 📞 ⊙ ♦ ▯ ¶ ⚑ 🖾
🛏 ⚓ ⚓ ✿ 🅗 SP 🔥

Cumbria
Map ref 5A3

Crosthwaite House ♨
☻☻ COMMENDED
Crosthwaite, Nr. Kendal, LA8 8BP
☎ (044 88) 264
Mid-18th C building with unspoilt views of the Lyth and Winster valleys, 5 miles from Bowness and Kendal. Family atmosphere and home cooking. Self-catering cottages available.
Bedrooms: 1 single, 3 double & 2 twin.
Bathrooms: 6 private.
Bed & breakfast: £20-£22 single, £40-£44 double.
Half board: £30-£33 daily, £200-£215 weekly.
Evening meal 7pm (l.o. 7pm).
Parking for 10.
Open March-November.
⌂ ♨ ¶ ▯ ⊙ 📺 🖾 ⚓ ✿ 🅗
🔥

Cumbria
Map ref 5A3

Old capital of the Furness district until the Dissolution. A restored 14th C pele tower stands in the market-place. Birthplace of George Romney, the portrait-painter, in 1734.

Chequers Motel & Restaurant
10 Abbey Rd., Dalton-in-Furness, LA15 8LF
☎ (0229) 62124
Converted school building providing quality en-suite accommodation with all modern facilities. Home-cooked meals served every lunchtime and evening. Weekend rates.
Bedrooms: 1 single, 6 double & 6 twin.
Bathrooms: 10 private, 1 public.
Bed & breakfast: £30-£40 single, £40-£55 double.
Half board: £35-£45 daily.

Lunch available.
Evening meal 6.30pm (l.o. 10pm).
Parking for 25.
Credit: Access, Visa.
⌂ ♨ 🅗 ⊙ ▯ ⊙ ♦ ¶ ▯ 🅥 ⚑
🖾 ⚓ 🅣 ⚓ 🌟 ✿ 🅗 DAF SP
🔥

Cumbria
Map ref 5B3

Picturesque village with narrow cobbled streets lying in the valley of the River Dee in the Yorkshire Dales National Park.

George & Dragon Hotel ♨
☻☻ APPROVED
Main St., Dent, Cumbria.
LA10 5QL
☎ (058 75) 256
Excellent centre for exploring the Yorkshire Dales National Park. Ideal for family holidays or the overnight traveller.
Bedrooms: 4 double & 3 twin, 2 family rooms.
Bathrooms: 3 private, 2 public.
Bed & breakfast: £20-£24 single, £32-£37 double.
Half board: £23.50-£26 daily, £155-£170 weekly.
Lunch available.
Evening meal 7pm (l.o. 10pm).
Parking for 14.
Credit: Access, Visa.
⌂ ▯ ⊙ ♦ ¶ 🅥 ⚑ 🖾 ⚓ 🅣
⊙ 🅗 DAF 🗝 SP 🔥

Cumbria
Map ref 5A3

Small town with the ruins of a Norman castle.
Tourist Information Centre ☎ (0946) 820693

Old Vicarage Guest House
Nr. Thornhill, Egremont, CA22 2NX
☎ Beckermet (0946) 841577
Imposing 19th C vicarage of character in attractive grounds. Within easy reach of sea and mountains.
Bedrooms: 2 twin, 1 family room.
Bathrooms: 2 public.
Bed & breakfast: £12-£15 single, £24-£30 double.
Parking for 6.
⌂ ♨ ⊙ ⚓ UL 🅥 ⚑ 📺 🖾 ⚓
✿ 🅗

Cumbria
Map ref 5A3

Several minor roads lead to the west end of this beautiful valley. The approach from the east is over the extremely steep Hardknott Pass. The Scafell peaks and Bow Fell lie to the north. A miniature railway links the Eskdale Valley with Ravenglass on the coast.

Brook House Hotel and Restaurant ♨
☻☻☻ COMMENDED
Boot, Eskdale, CA19 1TG
☎ (094 67) 23288
Small family-run hotel in the beautiful unspoilt valley of Eskdale. Magnificent views from all bedrooms. Home cooking.
Bedrooms: 1 single, 1 double & 4 twin, 2 family rooms.
Bathrooms: 5 private, 2 public; 3 private showers.
Bed & breakfast: £18-£21.50 single, £36-£43 double.
Half board: £26.50-£30 daily, £160-£185 weekly.
Lunch available.
Evening meal 7pm (l.o. 8.30pm).
Parking for 15.
Credit: Access, Visa.
⌂ ▯ ⊙ ♦ 🅥 ⚑ 🖾 ⚓ 🍴
🅗 🅣

Stanley Ghyll House ♨
Boot, Holmrook, CA19 1TF
☎ (094 67) 23327
Telex 667047
A centre for walking holidays in one of the valleys of Cumbria. Ideal for touring Scafell and Wasdale.
Bedrooms: 5 single, 7 twin, 13 family rooms.
Bathrooms: 11 public.
Bed & breakfast: £12.25-£18.25 single, £20-£32 double.
Half board: £17-£26.25 daily, £130-£192.50 weekly.
Lunch available.
Evening meal 7pm.
Parking for 20.
Open March-September.
⌂ ♨2 UL ▯ ♦ 🅥 ⚑ 🖾 ⚓ ♦ 🍴
🅗 DAF 🗝 SP

Half board prices shown are per person but in some cases may be based on double/twin occupancy.

Cumbria
Map ref 5A3

Sheltered seaside resort overlooking Morecambe Bay. Pleasant seafront walks and beautiful gardens. The bay attracts many species of wading birds. Large seawater swimming pool.

Clare House
☻☻☻ COMMENDED
Park Rd., Grange-over-Sands, LA11 7HQ
☎ (053 95) 33026
Charming hotel with well-appointed bedrooms and pleasant lounges set in grounds with magnificent bay views.
Bedrooms: 3 single, 2 double & 11 twin, 1 family room.
Bathrooms: 16 private, 2 public.
Bed & breakfast: £25-£27 single, £50-£54 double.
Half board: £35-£38 daily, £200-£230 weekly.
Lunch available.
Evening meal 6.45pm.
Parking for 16.
Open April-October.
⌂ ♨ ⚓ 📞 ⊙ ⚑ 🖾 🖾 ⚓
✿ 🅗 🅗 SP

Craiglands Hotel ♨
☻☻ APPROVED
Methven Terrace, Kents Bank Rd., Grange-over-Sands, LA11 7DP
☎ (053 95) 32348
Family-run hotel with traditional home cooking. Some rooms with sea view. Sun lounge and patios. Open all year round.
Bedrooms: 4 double & 3 twin, 8 family rooms.
Bathrooms: 8 private, 2 public.
Bed & breakfast: £24.50-£28.50 single, £39-£47 double.
Half board: £28-£32 daily, £186-£210 weekly.
Evening meal 6.30pm (l.o. 4.30pm).
Parking for 7.
Credit: Access, Visa.
⌂ ♨2 ♨ ⊙ ▯ ⊙ ¶ ✂ ⚑ 📺
🖾 ⚓ DAF 🗝 SP

Elton Hotel ♨
☻☻☻ COMMENDED
2/3 Windermere Rd., Grange-over-Sands, LA11 6EQ
☎ (053 95) 32838
A warm, generous welcome, good food and superior accommodation. An ideal base for exploring the impressive Lakeland scenery.

Continued ▶

Continued

Bedrooms: 1 single, 4 double
& 2 twin.
Bathrooms: 5 private;
2 private showers.
Bed & breakfast: £23-£25
single, £36-£44 double.
Half board: £28-£32 daily,
£182-£210 weekly.
Evening meal 7.30pm (l.o.
4pm).

Graythwaite Manor Hotel M

Fernhill Rd., Grange-over-
Sands, LA11 7JE
☎ (053 95) 32001 &
(053 95) 33755
*Beautiful family-run country
house in extensive gardens
overlooking estuary and hills.
Generous bedrooms, spacious
lounges, log fires. Good cuisine
and wine cellar.*
Bedrooms: 5 single, 3 double
& 12 twin, 2 family rooms.
Bathrooms: 20 private,
4 public.
Bed & breakfast: £35-£45
single, £70-£90 double.
Half board: £45-£60 daily,
£262.50-£385 weekly.
Lunch available.
Evening meal 7pm (l.o.
8.30pm).
Parking for 35.
Credit: Access, Visa.

Hampsfell House Hotel M

☺☺☺ COMMENDED

Hampsfell Rd., Grange-over-
Sands, LA11 6BG
☎ (053 95) 32567
*Peaceful country setting in own
grounds. Fresh and
imaginatively prepared food.
Extensive wine list. Ample safe
parking.*
Bedrooms: 4 double & 4 twin,
1 family room.
Bathrooms: 7 private,
1 public.
Bed & breakfast: £22.50-
£27.50 single, £39-£45 double.
Half board: £30.50-£36 daily,
£205-£230 weekly.
Lunch available.
Evening meal 6.30pm (l.o.
8.30pm).
Parking for 20.
Open March-November.
Credit: Access, Visa.

Holme Lea Guest House M

☺☺☺

90 Kentsford Rd., Kents
Bank, Grange-over-Sands,
LA11 7BB
☎ (053 95) 32545
*Quiet position overlooking bay.
Plentiful varied home-made
food. Large lounge with colour
TV and log fire. Well
furnished bedrooms. Packed
lunches available.*
Bedrooms: 1 single, 2 double
& 1 twin, 2 family rooms.
Bathrooms: 2 public.
Bed & breakfast: from £13
single, from £26 double.
Half board: from £19 daily,
from £126 weekly.
Evening meal 6.30pm (l.o.
5pm).
Parking for 7.
Open March-October.

Kents Bank Hotel M

☺☺☺

Kentsford Rd., Kents Bank,
Grange-over-Sands,
LA11 7BB
☎ (053 95) 32054
*A small hotel in a residential
area, overlooking Morecambe
Bay and close to the Lake
District. Licensed bar,
beautiful views.*
Bedrooms: 2 double & 2 twin,
1 family room.
Bathrooms: 5 private,
1 public.
Bed & breakfast: £23-£28
single, £42-£51 double.
Half board: £28-£33 daily,
£162.80-£195 weekly.
Lunch available.
Evening meal 6pm (l.o. 9pm).
Parking for 30.

Lyndene Guest House M

86 Kentsford Rd., Kents
Bank, Grange-over-Sands,
LA11 7BB
☎ (053 95) 33189
*Homely guesthouse, personally
supervised and providing home
cooking. Pleasant garden, deck
chairs and sea views.*
Bedrooms: 2 single, 2 double,
2 family rooms.
Bathrooms: 2 public.
Bed & breakfast: max. £12
single, max. £24 double.
Half board: max. £16 daily,
max. £105 weekly.
Evening meal 6.30pm (l.o.
4pm).
Parking for 3.
Open February-October.

Milton House

Fell Rd., Grange-over-Sands,
LA11 6DH
☎ (053 95) 33398
*Small well-established
guesthouse with extensive sea
views and home cooking. Ideal
for hikers and tourists with
comfort and cleanliness
assured.*
Bedrooms: 1 double & 1 twin,
1 family room.
Bathrooms: 1 public.
Bed & breakfast: £14-£16
single, £28-£32 double.
Half board: £20-£22 daily,
£133-£147 weekly.
Evening meal 6.30pm.
Parking for 3.
Open May-August.

Netherwood Hotel M

☺☺☺☺

Grange-over-Sands,
LA11 6ET
☎ (053 95) 32552 &
(044 84) 2230
*Built in 1893 and a building of
high architectural and historic
interest.*
Bedrooms: 4 single, 10 double
& 10 twin, 8 family rooms.
Bathrooms: 29 private,
3 public.
Bed & breakfast: £37.75-
£44.75 single, £68.50-£89.50
double.
Half board: £51.25-£58.25
daily, £353.75-£402.75
weekly.
Lunch available.
Evening meal 7pm (l.o.
8.30pm).
Parking for 160.

Prospect House Hotel M

☺☺ APPROVED

Kents Bank Rd., Grange-
over-Sands, LA11 7DJ
☎ (053 95) 32116
*Our best advertisement is the
many return visits we receive
every year. Imaginative meals
and a friendly welcome are
guaranteed.*
Bedrooms: 5 double & 2 twin.
Bathrooms: 6 private,
1 public.
Bed & breakfast: £18.50-
£23.50 single, £32.50-£39
double.
Half board: £26-£30 daily,
£170-£185 weekly.
Evening meal 6.45pm (l.o.
3.30pm).
Parking for 5.

Cumbria
Map ref 5A3

Described by William
Wordsworth as 'the
loveliest spot that man
hath ever found', this
village is in a beautiful
setting by-passed by the
main road and
overlooked by Helm Crag.
Wordsworth lived at Dove
Cottage for 9 years and
the cottage and museum
are now open to the
public. Grasmere
gingerbread is made in
the old school to a
traditional village recipe.
Good centre for touring
and walking.

Beck Allans

College Street, Grasmere,
Cumbria. LA22 9SZ
☎ (053 94) 35563
*A new but traditional
Lakeland house, hidden in the
delightful well timbered
grounds of Beck Allans
Holiday Apartments. Centre of
village, adjacent River Rothay,
super views. Accommodation
includes two-bedroom family
suite.*
Bedrooms: 1 single, 3 twin.
Bathrooms: 3 private;
1 private shower.
Bed & breakfast: £17.50-
£30.75 single, £35-£41 double.
Parking for 14.
Credit: Access, Visa.

2 Ben Place M

Grasmere, Ambleside,
LA22 9RL
☎ (053 94) 35581
*In a very quiet area near the
village, with a secluded garden
and lovely views from all the
rooms.*
Bedrooms: 1 single, 1 twin,
1 family room.
Bathrooms: 3 private
showers.
Bed & breakfast: £18-£21
single, £36-£38 double.
Parking for 6.
Open January-October.

Bramriggs

Listed APPROVED

Grasmere, Nr. Ambleside,
LA22 9RU
☎ (053 94) 35360

Small country house with garden bordering footpath to Helvellyn. Tranquil setting, spectacular views of almost entire valley. 1 mile north of Grasmere Village. Lovely walking country.
Bedrooms: 1 single, 1 twin, 2 family rooms.
Bathrooms: 1 public.
Bed & breakfast: £15-£16 single, £30-£32 double.
Parking for 7.

⌖ Ⓜ □ ⊕ ⌷ ▮ Ⓥ ⊤Ⓥ ❋ ⋈ ⊤

Bridge House Hotel ⋔
😃😃😃 COMMENDED
Stock Lane, Grasmere, LA22 9SN
☎ (053 94) 35425
Family-run hotel close to the village centre, in 2 acres of garden. Relaxing atmosphere, home cooking and ample parking. Room available for special occasions such as honeymoon and anniversary.
Bedrooms: 2 single, 5 double & 5 twin.
Bathrooms: 10 private, 1 public.
Bed & breakfast: £21-£33 single, £42-£66 double.
Half board: £30-£42 daily, £205-£265 weekly.
Evening meal 7pm (l.o. 7.30pm).
Parking for 20.
Open March-November.
Credit: Access, Visa.

⌖5 ♨ □ ⊕ ⌿ ⊞ ▥ ❋ ⋈ ⋈ 〓 SP

Chestnut Villa ⋔
😃😃😃😃
Keswick Rd., Grasmere, LA22 9RE
☎ (053 94) 35218
On the A591 close to the village and surrounded by Lakeland fells. Ideal for fell walking and boating.
Bedrooms: 2 single, 3 double, 2 family rooms.
Bathrooms: 2 private, 3 public.
Bed & breakfast: £15-£16 single, £30-£32 double.
Parking for 10.

⌖ ⊕ Ⓤ ▮ ⌷ ⊤Ⓥ ▥ 〓 ⋈

The Grasmere Hotel ⋔
😃😃😃😃
Grasmere, LA22 9TA
☎ (053 94) 35277
In the midst of beautiful mountain scenery with the restaurant overlooking a large garden, the river and surrounding hills.
Bedrooms: 1 single, 8 double & 3 twin.
Bathrooms: 12 private, 1 public.

Bed & breakfast: £35-£45 single, £60-£88 double.
Half board: £35-£48 daily, £224-£315 weekly.
Evening meal 7.30pm (l.o. 8pm).
Parking for 14.
Open February-December.
Credit: Access, Visa.

⌖6 ♨ ♥ ⌧ ⊕ □ ⊕ ▮ Ⓥ ⋈ ▥ 〓 ⌶ ❋ ⋈ DAP ⋈ SP ⊤

Harwood Hotel ⋔
😃😃😃 APPROVED
Red Lion Square, Grasmere, LA22 9SP
☎ (053 94) 35248
Family-run hotel in the heart of Grasmere. Comfortable rooms and good home cooking. Ideal for exploring the Lake District.
Bedrooms: 1 single, 4 double & 1 twin, 1 family room.
Bathrooms: 7 private.
Bed & breakfast: £19.50-£23 single, £39-£46 double.
Half board: £29.25-£32.50 daily, £190-£210 weekly.
Lunch available.
Evening meal 7pm (l.o. 7.30pm).
Parking for 8.
Open January-November.
Credit: Access, Visa.

⌖ ⊕ ⌷ ▥ Ⓥ ⌿ ⋈ ⊤Ⓥ ▥ 〓 ⌶ ❋ ⋈ 〓 SP

Lake View Guest House ⋔
😃😃😃 COMMENDED
Lake View Drive, Grasmere, LA22 9TD
☎ (053 94) 35384
In private grounds overlooking the lake and with private access. Located in the village but off the main road.
Bedrooms: 1 single, 3 double & 1 twin.
Bathrooms: 2 private, 1 public.
Bed & breakfast: £21-£25 single, £42-£50 double.
Half board: £31-£35 daily, £207-£226 weekly.
Evening meal 6.30pm (l.o. midday).
Parking for 10.
Open March-November.

⌖12 ⊕ ⌷ ▮ Ⓥ ⋈ ⊤Ⓥ 〓 ⋈ ❋ ⋈ 〓 SP

Lancrigg Vegetarian Country House Hotel ⋔
Easedale, Grasmere, LA22 9QN
☎ (053 94) 35317

| Please mention this guide when making a booking. |

Historic listed building in 27 acres, in peaceful Easedale, 10 minutes' walk from Grasmere village. Good walking, views, log fires and vegetarian wholefood.
Bedrooms: 1 single, 9 double & 3 twin, 2 family rooms.
Bathrooms: 11 private, 2 public.
Half board: £39.50-£75 daily, £215-£450 weekly.
Lunch available.
Evening meal 7pm (l.o. 8pm).
Parking for 16.
Credit: Access, Visa.

⌖ ♨ ⌧ ♥ ⊕ □ ⊕ ▮ Ⓥ ⋿ ⋈ 〓 ⌶ ❋ ⋈ ⋈ DAP ⋈ SP 〓

Moss Grove Hotel ⋔
😃😃😃 APPROVED
Grasmere, Nr. Ambleside, LA22 9SW
☎ (053 94) 35251
Fax (053 94) 35691
Ⓡ Minotels
Elegant recently refurbished Lakeland hotel. Four-poster bedrooms with south-facing balconies. Cosy bar, sauna and use of adjacent indoor swimming pool.
Bedrooms: 2 single, 7 double & 3 twin, 2 family rooms.
Bathrooms: 13 private, 2 public.
Bed & breakfast: £23.50-£39 single, £53-£64.25 double.
Half board: £31.95-£43.25 daily, £223.65-£303.50 weekly.
Lunch available.
Evening meal 7.30pm (l.o. 8.30pm).
Parking for 16.
Open February-December.
Credit: Access, Visa.

⌖ ⌧ ♥ □ ⊕ ▮ Ⓥ ⋈ ▥ 〓 ⌶ ⋈ ❋ ⋈ SP ⊤

Oak Bank Hotel ⋔
Broadgate, Grasmere, LA22 9TA
☎ (053 94) 35217
Traditionally built 100 years ago in Lakeland stone and now modernised throughout. Cordon bleu cuisine, good cellar - pamper yourself!
Bedrooms: 1 single, 9 double & 3 twin, 1 family room.
Bathrooms: 14 private.
Bed & breakfast: £25-£36 single, £50-£72 double.
Half board: £30-£45 daily, £210-£300 weekly.
Evening meal 7pm (l.o. 8pm).
Parking for 14.
Open February-December.
Credit: Access, Visa.

⌖ ♨ ♥ □ ⊕ ⊕ ▮ Ⓥ ⋈ ⊤Ⓥ ▥ 〓 ⌶ ❋ ⋈ SP ⊤

Red Lion ⋔
😃😃😃😃
Red Lion Square, Grasmere, LA22 9SS
☎ Grasmere (053 94) 35456
Fax (053 94) 34157
Ⓡ Consort
200-year-old coaching inn, in the centre of Wordsworth country. Ideal for a relaxing holiday.
Bedrooms: 4 single, 15 double & 13 twin, 3 family rooms.
Bathrooms: 35 private.
Bed & breakfast: £30-£39 single, £60-£78 double.
Half board: £43-£54 daily.
Lunch available.
Evening meal 7pm (l.o. 9pm).
Parking for 28.
Credit: Access, Visa, Diners, Amex.

⌖ ♥ □ ⊕ ▮ Ⓥ ⋈ 〓 ▥ 〓 ⌶ ⋈ SP 〓 ⊤

Roundhill ⋔
Easedale, Grasmere, LA22 9QT
☎ (053 94) 35233
Enjoy true Lakeland atmosphere in our traditional stone-built family house; peacefully situated with stunning, elevated views. Vegetarian and English breakfasts.
Bedrooms: 1 double & 1 twin, 1 family room.
Bathrooms: 1 public.
Bed & breakfast: £17.50-£20 single, £32-£40 double.
Parking for 4.
Open February-October.

⌖3 ⊕ Ⓤ Ⓥ ⋈ ⊤Ⓥ ▥ ❋ ⋈ 〓 〓 ⊤

Wordsworth Hotel ⋔
Grasmere, LA22 9SW
☎ (053 94) 35592
Telex 65329
Fax: (053 94) 35765
Traditional style hotel with amenities for both business and leisure including the stylish Prelude Restaurant, jacuzzi, mini-gym, pool, sauna and solarium.
Bedrooms: 1 single, 17 double & 15 twin, 4 family rooms.
Bathrooms: 37 private.
Bed & breakfast: £48-£64 single, £88-£130 double.
Lunch available.
Evening meal 7pm (l.o. 8pm).
Parking for 54.
Credit: Access, Visa, Diners, Amex.

⌖ ♨ ⌧ ♥ □ ⊕ ▮ Ⓥ ⋈ 〓 ▥ 〓 ⌶ ⋈ 〓 ⋈ ⋈ ❋ ⋈ ⋈ SP 〓 ⊤

| We advise you to confirm your booking in writing. |

Cumbria
Map ref 5A2

Gretna, the first settlement in Scotland, is renowned for its many 'marriage booths' in history, including a blacksmith's shop. It still has an air of romance today.

The Gretna Chase Hotel M

👑👑👑 COMMENDED

Gretna, Carlisle, CA6 5JB
☎ (0461) 37517
Tastefully modernised Victorian house set in 2.5 acres of beautiful, award-winning gardens. Full-colour brochure available.
Bedrooms: 2 single, 5 double & 2 twin.
Bathrooms: 6 private; 3 private showers.
Bed & breakfast: £35-£45 single, £48-£80 double.
Lunch available.
Evening meal 5.30pm (l.o. 10pm).
Parking for 40.
Open February-December.
Credit: Access, Visa, Diners, Amex.
🛇 🖰 🗗 🌢 🛉 🗓 🖂 🛍 🛳
🍽 🌣 🖾 🖾 T

Hunters Lodge Hotel

👑👑 COMMENDED

Annan Road, Gretna, Carlisle, CA6 5DL
☎ (0461) 38214
In the heart of Gretna, "The Gateway to Scotland", close to famous Registry office and offering a warm and friendly atmosphere.
Bedrooms: 1 single, 4 double & 1 twin, 2 family rooms.
Bathrooms: 5 private, 1 public.
Bed & breakfast: £27-£30 single, £33-£45 double.
Evening meal 7pm (l.o. 8pm).
Parking for 20.
🛇 🖰 🗗 🌢 🛉 🗓 🖂 🕂 🛍
🛳 🍽 🌣 🖾 🖾

The symbols are explained on the flap inside the back cover.

Map references apply to the colour maps towards the end of this guide.

Cumbria
Map ref 5A3

Set in the Levens Valley south-west of Newby Bridge. Headquarters of the Lakeside and Haverthwaite Railway Company. Many craft workshops.

Broad Oaks M

👑👑 COMMENDED

Haverthwaite, Nr. Ulverston, LA12 8AL
☎ Newby Bridge
(053 95) 31756
An unusual modern building in a woodland setting. Elevated residents' lounge and dining room giving views at tree-top level.
Bedrooms: 1 double & 1 twin.
Bathrooms: 2 private.
Bed & breakfast: £16-£20 single, £32-£40 double.
Half board: £25-£29 daily, £150-£160 weekly.
Evening meal 7pm.
Parking for 4.
Open March-November.
🛇 🗗5 🛳 🗗 🌢 🗓 🖂 🗓
🌣 🍽 🖾 DAP SP

Cumbria
Map ref 5A3

Lying near Esthwaite Water, this village has great charm and character. Its small squares are linked by flagged or cobbled alleys and the main square is dominated by the market house or Shambles where the butchers had their stalls in days gone by.

Greenbank Country House Hotel M

Hawkshead, Ambleside, LA22 0NS
☎ (096 66) 497
Well-appointed country house hotel in this picturesque village. Central for all activities. Good home cooking.
Bedrooms: 3 single, 4 double & 2 twin, 1 family room.
Bathrooms: 4 private, 2 public.
Bed & breakfast: £16.50-£18.50 single, £33-£41 double.
Half board: £24.50-£30 daily, £162-£185 weekly.
Evening meal 6.30pm (l.o. 4pm).
Parking for 12.
🛇 🛳 🗗 🛉 🗓 🗶 🖂 🗓 🛍
🛳 🖾 DAP SP

Highfield House Hotel M

👑👑👑 COMMENDED

Hawkshead Hill, Nr. Ambleside, LA22 0PN
☎ (096 66) 344
Traditional Lakeland country house with extensive views, in 2.5 acres of grounds. An ideal centre for walking and touring.
Bedrooms: 2 single, 5 double & 3 twin, 1 family room.
Bathrooms: 10 private, 2 public.
Bed & breakfast: £22.50-£31.50 single, £45-£65 double.
Half board: £36.50-£45.50 daily, £224-£282 weekly.
Lunch available.
Evening meal 7pm (l.o. 8pm).
Parking for 12.
🛇 🖰 🗗 🌢 🗓 🖂 🛍 🛳
🌣 SP

Ivy House Hotel M

👑👑

Main St., Hawkshead, LA22 0NS
☎ (096 66) 204
Attractive Georgian house and Grade II listed building located in the centre of village. Family-run hotel providing English food in a friendly and relaxed atmosphere.
Bedrooms: 6 double & 3 twin, 2 family rooms.
Bathrooms: 6 private, 2 public.
Bed & breakfast: £19.50-£24 single, £39-£48 double.
Half board: £28-£32.50 daily, £175-£206.50 weekly.
Evening meal 7pm (l.o. 4pm).
Parking for 15.
Open March-November.
🛇 🛳 🌢 🗓 🖂 🛍 🛳 🗗
🖾 SP 🖾

Queens Head Hotel

👑👑👑 APPROVED

Hawkshead, LA22 0NS
☎ (096 66) 271
Located between Lakes Windermere and Coniston. The home of Beatrix Potter, Wordsworth's grammar school and Ann Tyson's cottage. Amenities include mountain bikes and a bowling green.
Bedrooms: 9 double & 2 twin, 2 family rooms.
Bathrooms: 9 private, 2 public.
Bed & breakfast: £28-£36 single, £44-£51 double.
Lunch available.
Evening meal 6.15pm (l.o. 9.30pm).
Credit: Access, Visa, Amex.
🛇8 🛳 📞 🖰 🗗 🌢 🛉 🗓
🖾 🛍 🛳 🖰 🕂 🖾 🗞 🖾 🖾

Silverholme M

Graythwaite, Hawkshead, LA12 8AZ
☎ Newby Bridge
(053 95) 31332
Set in its own grounds, overlooking Lake Windermere, this small mansion house provides a quiet, comfortable, relaxed atmosphere. Home cooking.
Bedrooms: 1 single, 3 double.
Bathrooms: 2 public.
Bed & breakfast: £16.50-£19.50 single, £33-£39 double.
Half board: £25-£28 daily, £170-£190 weekly.
Evening meal 7pm (l.o. 5pm).
Parking for 6.
🛇 🌢 UL 🛉 🗓 🗶 🖂 🗓 🛍
🛳 🌣 🖾 SP 🖾

Tarn Hows Hotel M

👑👑👑👑

Hawkshead, Nr. Ambleside, LA22 0PR
☎ (096 66) 330
Fax (096 66) 294
Refurbished quiet country house hotel in 25 acres of garden and parkland, overlooking Hawkshead and Esthwaite.
Bedrooms: 2 single, 12 double & 8 twin.
Bathrooms: 22 private.
Bed & breakfast: £45-£65 single, £90-£110 double.
Half board: £55-£75 daily, £330-£520 weekly.
Lunch available.
Evening meal 7pm (l.o. 8.30pm).
Parking for 40.
Credit: Access, Visa, Diners, Amex.
🛇 🖰 📞 🖰 🗗 🌢 🛉 🗶
🗶 🗓 🛳 🖰 🍽 🖾 🗞 🌣 🖾
SP T

Cumbria
Map ref 5B3

6m S. Penrith
'A place on the side of a hill', Helton nestles in a quiet, undisturbed corner of the Lakes yet has easy access to Penrith and junction 40 of the M6.

Beckfoot Country House M

👑👑👑 COMMENDED

Helton, Penrith, CA10 2QB
☎ Bampton (093 13) 241
Beautiful country house in an unspoilt corner of the National Park. Exit 39 on the M6 from the south and exit 40 from the north.

Bedrooms: 1 single, 3 double & 2 twin.
Bathrooms: 6 private.
Bed & breakfast: £25-£28 single, £45-£50 double.
Evening meal 7pm (l.o. 7pm).
Parking for 12.
Open April-November.
🛇 ♥ 🛊 Ⓥ 🏳 📺 🕸 ▲ 🏋
❄ 🎮 SP 🏮

HEVERSHAM

Cumbria
Map ref 5B3

6m SW. Kendal
This attractive village is set on a hill, and has a grammar school founded in 1613.

The Blue Bell at Heversham 🅜
😃😃😃😃 APPROVED
Princes Way, Heversham, Milnthorpe, LA7 7EE
☎ Milnthorpe (053 95) 62018
Country hotel in a rural haven – an ideal touring centre.
Bedrooms: 4 single, 10 double & 7 twin.
Bathrooms: 21 private, 2 public.
Bed & breakfast: £41-£50 single, £62-£75 double.
Half board: £49-£55 daily.
Lunch available.
Evening meal 7pm (l.o. 9pm).
Parking for 100.
Credit: Access, Visa, Amex.
🛇 📞 🐫 🏳 🛇 🛊 Ⓥ 🏳 📺
🕸 ▲ 🏋 🖾 🎮 🐾 SP 🏮

Individual proprietors have supplied all details of accommodation. Although we do check for accuracy, we advise you to confirm prices and other information at the time of booking.

National Crown ratings were correct at the time of going to press but are subject to change. Please check at the time of booking.

KENDAL

Cumbria
Map ref 5B3

The 'Auld Grey Town', so called because of its many grey limestone buildings, lies in the valley of the River Kent with a backcloth of limestone fells on 3 sides. Situated just outside the Lake District National Park, a good centre from which to tour the Lakes and surrounding countryside. The ruined Norman castle was the birthplace of Catherine Parr, Henry VIII's 6th wife.
Tourist Information Centre ☎ (0539) 725758

Beech House 🅜
40 Greenside, Kendal, LA9 4LD
☎ (0539) 720385
Charming small hotel offering comfort and hospitality. 2 minutes from town centre. Overlooking green. Ideal touring base. Traditional Lakeland fare. Mountain activity holidays arranged.
Bedrooms: 1 single, 2 double & 2 twin, 1 family room.
Bathrooms: 2 public.
Bed & breakfast: £16-£18 single, £28-£30 double.
Half board: £22-£24 daily, £126-£138 weekly.
Evening meal 6.30pm (l.o. 3pm).
Parking for 6.
🛇 🐫 🛇 🛊 Ⓥ 🏳 📺 🕸 ▲
🏮 DAP 🐾 SP

Brantholme 🅜
7 Sedbergh Rd., Kendal, LA9 6AD
☎ (0539) 722340
Family-run guesthouse in own grounds. All rooms with private facilities. Good meals from fresh local produce.
Bedrooms: 3 twin.
Bathrooms: 3 private.
Bed & breakfast: £20-£25 single, £30-£35 double.
Half board: £20-£26 daily, £126-£168 weekly.
Evening meal 6.30pm (l.o. 5.30pm).
Parking for 6.
Open March-October.
🛇 🅄 🛊 Ⓥ 📺 🕸 ❄ 🎮 DAP
SP 🏮

Burrow Hall Country Guesthouse 🅜
😃😃😃 COMMENDED
Plantation Bridge, Kendal, LA8 9JR
☎ Staveley (0539) 821711

Beautifully furnished, 17th C Lakeland house with two residents' lounges. Sits peacefully in idyllic south Lakeland countryside between Kendal and Windermere.
Bedrooms: 1 double & 2 twin.
Bathrooms: 3 private.
Bed & breakfast: £35-£45 double.
Half board: £28.75-£33.75 daily, £188.75-£218.75 weekly.
Evening meal 8pm (l.o. 7pm).
Parking for 8.
Credit: Access, Visa.
Ⓒ 🛊 🏳 📺 🕸 ▲ ❄ 🏋 🖾
🐾 SP

Garden House 🅜
😃😃😃😃 COMMENDED
Fowling Lane, Kendal, LA9 6PH
☎ (0539) 731131
Fax (0539) 740064
On the outskirts of Kendal with its own large, pretty gardens and individually designed homely bedrooms. Ideal Lakes/dales touring base.
Bedrooms: 2 single, 3 double & 3 twin, 2 family rooms.
Bathrooms: 10 private.
Bed & breakfast: £45-£55 single, £65-£75 double.
Half board: from £60 daily.
Lunch available.
Evening meal 7pm (l.o. 9pm).
Parking for 15.
Credit: Access, Visa, Amex.
🛇 1 🔥 🎿 📞 🛇 🛊 Ⓥ
🏐 🏳 ⦿ 🖾 ▲ 🏋 ❄ 🎮 SP
🏮 🇹

Gateway Hotel & Inn
Crook Rd., Plumgarth, Kendal, LA8 8LX
☎ (0539) 720605 & 724187
A Victorian house in its own grounds, with ornate ceilings and large picture windows. At the gateway to the Lakes with panoramic views, yet just off the main A591 road. Ideal for Lakes, dales and Morecambe Bay.
Bedrooms: 2 single, 3 double & 2 twin, 2 family rooms.
Bathrooms: 4 private, 2 public.
Bed & breakfast: £20-£35 single, £35-£55 double.
Lunch available.
Evening meal 7pm (l.o. 9.30pm).
Parking for 32.
Credit: Access, Visa.
🛇 🏳 🏐 🛊 🏳 🖾 ▲ 🏋
🏁 ❄ 🏋 DAP

Headlands Hotel 🅜
😃😃😃 COMMENDED
53 Milnthorpe Rd., Kendal, LA9 5QG
☎ (0539) 720424

Small family hotel, 10 minutes' walk from the town centre. Central for touring the Lakes, Yorkshire Dales and the coast.
Bedrooms: 1 single, 2 double & 2 twin, 2 family rooms.
Bathrooms: 4 private, 1 public.
Bed & breakfast: £14-£20 single, £28-£40 double.
Half board: £23-£30 daily.
Evening meal 7pm (l.o. 5pm).
Parking for 8.
🛇 📞 🏐 🛇 🛊 Ⓥ 🏳 📺
🖾 ▲ 🏋

Heaves Hotel 🅜
😃😃
Nr. Kendal, LA8 8EF
☎ Sedgwick (053 95) 60269 & 60396
Georgian mansion in 10 acres, 4 miles from M6 junction 36 and Kendal.
Bedrooms: 5 single, 4 double & 4 twin, 2 family rooms.
Bathrooms: 11 private, 3 public.
Bed & breakfast: £20-£25 single, £38-£45 double.
Half board: £29-£34 daily, £182-£212 weekly.
Lunch available.
Evening meal 7pm (l.o. 8pm).
Parking for 24.
Credit: Access, Visa, Diners, Amex.
🛇 ♥ 🛊 Ⓥ 🏳 📺 ▲ 🏋 ♠
❄ SP 🏮 🇹

High Laverock House Hotel 🅜
😃😃😃 APPROVED
Meal Bank, Kendal, LA8 9DJ
☎ (0539) 723082
Family-run hotel.
Bedrooms: 1 single, 5 double & 2 twin, 1 family room.
Bathrooms: 9 private.
Bed & breakfast: from £35 single, from £48 double.
Lunch available.
Evening meal 6pm (l.o. 9pm).
Parking for 80.
Credit: Access, Visa.
🛇 📞 🏐 🛇 🛊 Ⓥ 🏳 🕸
▲ 🏋 🝙 ❄ 🎮 SP

Higher House Farm 🅜
😃😃😃
Oxenholme Lane, Natland, Kendal, LA9 7QH
☎ Sedgwick (053 95) 61177
17th C beamed farmhouse in tranquil village south of Kendal, overlooking Lakeland fells. Near M6 and Oxenholme Station. Home cooking. Four poster bed.
Continued ▶

KENDAL
Continued

Bedrooms: 2 double & 1 twin.
Bathrooms: 2 private,
1 public.
Bed & breakfast: £16.50-
£21.50 single, £27-£43 double.
Half board: £23.50-£31.50
daily, £150-£200 weekly.
Evening meal 7pm (l.o.
9.30pm).
Parking for 9.

Hillside Guest House
COMMENDED

4 Beast Banks, Kendal,
LA9 4JW
☎ (0539) 722836
*Small guesthouse near the
shops and town facilities,
convenient for the Lakes,
Yorkshire Dales and
Morecambe Bay.*
Bedrooms: 2 single, 3 double
& 1 twin.
Bathrooms: 4 private,
2 public.
Bed & breakfast: £14-£17
single, £28-£34 double.
Parking for 2.

Lane Head House Country Hotel M
COMMENDED

Helsington, Kendal, LA9 5RJ
☎ (0539) 731283
*Country hotel of character
enjoying magnificent
panoramic views of surrounding
fells. On the southern boundary
of Kendal, half a mile off the
A6 Milnthorpe road.*
Bedrooms: 4 double & 3 twin.
Bathrooms: 7 private.
Bed & breakfast: £35-£40
single, £50-£60 double.
Half board: £40-£45 daily.
Evening meal 7pm (l.o. 5pm).
Parking for 10.
Credit: Access, Visa.

Rainbow Hotel
APPROVED

32 Highgate, Kendal,
LA9 4SX
☎ (0539) 724178
*Old town centre coaching
house, opposite the town hall
and market square. Open oak
beams, dining room and
residents' lounge.*
Bedrooms: 3 double & 2 twin,
1 family room.
Bathrooms: 6 private.
Bed & breakfast: £25-£34
single, £34-£50 double.

Lunch available.
Parking for 30.
Open January-October,
December.
Credit: Access, Visa.

Riverside Hotel & Restaurant M
COMMENDED

Stramongate Bridge, Kendal,
LA9 4BZ
☎ (0539) 724707
*A converted 17th C tannery
fully modernised with 2
restaurants, conference and
banqueting facilities for up to
200 persons.*
Bedrooms: 37 double &
2 twin, 8 family rooms.
Bathrooms: 47 private.
Bed & breakfast: max. £56
single, max. £75 double.
Half board: £44-£70.90 daily,
max. £323 weekly.
Lunch available.
Evening meal 6pm (l.o.
10pm).
Credit: Access, Visa, Diners,
Amex.

Riversleigh M

49 Milnthorpe Rd., Kendal,
LA9 5QG
☎ (0539) 726392
*Charming Victorian
guesthouse, 10 minutes' walk
from the town centre. Central
for the Lakes and Yorkshire
Dales.*
Bedrooms: 1 single, 3 double.
Bathrooms: 1 public.
Bed & breakfast: £14.50-
£16.50 single, £28-£32 double.
Parking for 6.

Woolpack Hotel M

Stricklandgate, Kendal,
LA9 4ND
☎ (0539) 723852
Fax (0539) 728608
*Quickly reached by M6
motorway. A 17th C coaching
inn, tastefully modernised but
retaining its old world charm.
Warm hospitality.*
Bedrooms: 3 single, 12 double
& 35 twin, 4 family rooms.
Bathrooms: 54 private.
Bed & breakfast: £45-£65
single, £65-£85 double.
Half board: £40-£75 daily.
Lunch available.
Evening meal 7pm (l.o.
9.30pm).

Parking for 60.
Credit: Access, Visa, Diners,
Amex.

KESWICK

Cumbria
Map ref 5A3

Attractive town in a
beautiful position beside
Derwentwater and below
the mountains of Skiddaw
and Saddleback. A
natural convergence of
roads makes it a good
base for touring. Motor-
launches operate on
Derwentwater and motor
boats and rowing boats
can be hired.
*Tourist Information
Centre ☎ (076 87) 72645*

Acorn House Hotel M
COMMENDED

Ambleside Rd., Keswick,
CA12 4DL
☎ (076 87) 72553
*Detached Georgian house with
newly refurbished rooms, set in
own garden. Quiet location
close to town centre and 10
minutes from Derwentwater.*
Bedrooms: 5 double & 2 twin,
3 family rooms.
Bathrooms: 9 private,
1 public.
Bed & breakfast: from £20
single, £36-£50 double.
Parking for 10.
Open February-November.
Credit: Access, Visa.

Anworth House M
Listed

27 Eskin St., Keswick,
CA12 4DQ
☎ (076 87) 72923
*Friendly and comfortable
guesthouse within easy walking
distance of the town, lake and
parks.*
Bedrooms: 3 double & 1 twin,
1 family room.
Bathrooms: 5 private.
Bed & breakfast: £30-£33
double.
Half board: £22.50-£24 daily,
£150-£160 weekly.
Evening meal 6pm (l.o. 3pm).

Applethwaite Country House Hotel M
COMMENDED

Applethwaite,
Underskiddaw, Keswick,
CA12 4PL
☎ (076 87) 72413

*Just over a mile from Keswick
on the slopes of Skiddaw with
views of Derwentwater and the
surrounding mountains.
Family-run with home cooking
and fresh farm foods.*
Bedrooms: 1 single, 5 double
& 4 twin, 3 family rooms.
Bathrooms: 12 private,
1 public.
Bed & breakfast: max. £27
single, max. £54 double.
Half board: max. £42.50
daily, max. £266 weekly.
Evening meal 7pm (l.o. 6pm).
Parking for 12.
Open April-October.
Credit: Access, Visa.

Beckside M

5 Wordsworth St., Keswick,
CA12 4HU
☎ (076 87) 73093
*A small, comfortable
guesthouse under the personal
supervision of the proprietor,
central for the shops, park and
lake.*
Bedrooms: 2 double & 1 twin.
Bathrooms: 1 public.
Bed & breakfast: £32 double.
Half board: £24 daily, £160
weekly.
Open March-November.

Berkeley Guest House M

The Heads, Keswick,
CA12 5ER
☎ (076 87) 74222
*On a quiet road overlooking
the mini golf-course, with
splendid views from each
comfortable room. Close to the
town centre and lake.*
Bedrooms: 1 single, 4 double
& 1 twin.
Bathrooms: 1 public;
2 private showers.
Bed & breakfast: £25-£34
double.
Evening meal 6.30pm (l.o.
2pm).
Parking for 3.
Open February-December.

Bonshaw Guest House M
Listed

20 Eskin St., Keswick,
CA12 4DG
☎ (076 87) 73084
*Small, friendly, comfortable
guesthouse, providing home
cooking. Convenient for town
centre and all amenities.*
Bedrooms: 2 single, 2 double
& 1 twin, 1 family room.
Bathrooms: 1 public.

Bed & breakfast: £12 single, £24 double.
Half board: £17 daily, £116 weekly.
Evening meal 6.30pm (l.o. 4pm).
Parking for 6.

Brienz Guesthouse
Listed COMMENDED
3, Greta Street, Keswick, CA12 4HS
☎ (076 87) 71049
Small, friendly guesthouse offering a high standard of comfort. Imaginative home cooking, choice of menu. Non-smoking.
Bedrooms: 2 double & 1 twin.
Bathrooms: 1 public;
2 private showers.
Bed & breakfast: £25-£27 double.
Half board: £20-£22 daily, £130-£145 weekly.
Evening meal 7pm (l.o. 4pm).

Brierholme Guest House M
21 Bank St., Keswick, CA12 5JZ
☎ (076 87) 72938
Friendly guesthouse in town centre. Private parking. Close to park, leisure pool and lake. Choice of en-suite or standard rooms with mountain views.
Bedrooms: 5 double, 1 family room.
Bathrooms: 5 private;
1 private shower.
Bed & breakfast: £30-£38 double.
Half board: £48.50-£56.50 daily.
Parking for 6.

Charnwood M
COMMENDED
6 Eskin St., Keswick, CA12 4DH
☎ (076 87) 74111
Victorian house in quiet position but near town centre. Home cooking, friendly service. Spacious, comfortable rooms, all facilities.
Bedrooms: 4 double & 1 twin, 1 family room.
Bathrooms: 6 private, 1 public.
Bed & breakfast: £34-£35 double.
Half board: £24.50-£25.50 daily, £165-£170 weekly.
Evening meal 6.35pm (l.o. 3pm).
Open March-November.

Chaucer House Hotel M
COMMENDED
Ambleside Rd., Keswick, CA12 4DR
☎ (076 87) 72318/73223
Quiet, informal, comfortable, licensed family-run hotel overlooking Skiddaw, Grisedale and Derwentwater. Fresh home-cooked food our speciality.
Bedrooms: 10 single, 13 double & 7 twin, 6 family rooms.
Bathrooms: 23 private, 4 public.
Bed & breakfast: £22.90-£29.50 single, £37.50-£55 double.
Half board: £29-£38.50 daily, £184.50-£244.50 weekly.
Evening meal 6.30pm (l.o. 7.30pm).
Parking for 25.
Open March-October.
Credit: Access, Visa, Diners, Amex.

Claremont House
COMMENDED
Chestnut Hill, Keswick, CA12 4LT
☎ (076 87) 72089
Comfortable, homely guesthouse offering pretty bedrooms with en-suite facilities. Food is our priority, with a reputation over the years for consistently high quality. Vegetarians very welcome.
Bedrooms: 1 single, 4 double.
Bathrooms: 3 private.
Bed & breakfast: £20-£22.50 single, £45-£53 double.
Half board: £34-£36.50 daily, £232-£270 weekly.
Evening meal 7pm (l.o. 4pm).
Parking for 6.

Clarence House M
COMMENDED
14 Eskin St., Keswick, CA12 4DQ
☎ (076 87) 73186
Friendly, well-appointed establishment offering home cooking. 5 minutes' walk from the lakeside, parks and shops. Non-smokers only please.
Bedrooms: 2 single, 4 double & 2 twin, 1 family room.
Bathrooms: 7 private, 1 public.
Bed & breakfast: from £14.50 single, from £34 double.
Half board: £21.50-£24 daily, £145-£163 weekly.

Evening meal 6.30pm (l.o. 3pm).
Credit: Access, Visa.

Crow Park Hotel M
The Heads, Keswick, CA12 5ER
☎ (076 87) 72208
Quiet but central, between the lake and the town centre. Magnificent views all round of the Lakeland fells.
Bedrooms: 4 single, 14 double & 7 twin, 1 family room.
Bathrooms: 26 private.
Bed & breakfast: £19-£29 single, £38-£58 double.
Half board: £28.50-£43 daily, £199-£290 weekly.
Evening meal 6.45pm (l.o. 8pm).
Parking for 26.
Credit: Access, Visa.

Cumbria Hotel M
COMMENDED
1 Derwentwater Place, Keswick, CA12 4DR
☎ (076 87) 73171
Early Victorian house, close to the centre of Keswick and within easy walking distance of the lake. Lovely views from most bedrooms.
Bedrooms: 3 single, 4 double, 2 family rooms.
Bathrooms: 4 private, 2 public.
Bed & breakfast: £15-£15.50 single, £30-£36 double.
Half board: £23-£26 daily, £147-£165 weekly.
Evening meal 6.45pm (l.o. 6.45pm).
Parking for 8.
Open February-October.
Credit: Access, Visa.

Dalegarth House Country Hotel M
COMMENDED
Portinscale, Keswick, CA12 5RQ
☎ (076 87) 72817
Edwardian house 1 mile from Keswick, with views of Skiddaw and Derwentwater. Licensed bar, 2 lounges and 5-course evening meal. Non-smokers only please.
Bedrooms: 4 double & 2 twin.
Bathrooms: 6 private.
Bed & breakfast: £22.50-£24 single, £45-£48 double.
Half board: £32.80-£35 daily, £215-£230 weekly.

Evening meal 7pm (l.o. 5.30pm).
Parking for 8.
Credit: Access, Visa.

Derwent Cottage
Portinscale, Nr. Keswick, CA12 5RF
☎ (076 87) 74838
Elegant, large roomed Lakeland house in 0.75 acres of secluded ground, in a quiet village one mile from Keswick.
Bedrooms: 1 single, 5 double.
Bathrooms: 6 private.
Bed & breakfast: £20 single, £50-£60 double.
Half board: £32-£42 daily, £196-£238 weekly.
Evening meal 7pm (l.o. 7pm).
Parking for 10.
Open March-November.

Derwentwater Hotel and Tower Annexe M
COMMENDED
Portinscale, Keswick, CA12 5RE
☎ (076 87) 72538
Fax (076 87) 71002
Consort
Well-positioned on the shore of Lake Derwentwater in 16 acres of grounds, offering comfortable accommodation. Half board price is based on a minimum 2 night stay.
Bedrooms: 7 single, 26 double & 39 twin, 12 family rooms.
Bathrooms: 84 private.
Bed & breakfast: £53.50-£54 single, £84-£90 double.
Half board: £39.75-£53 daily, £210-£320 weekly.
Lunch available.
Evening meal 7pm (l.o. 9.30pm).
Parking for 140.
Credit: Access, Visa, Diners, Amex.

Display advertisement appears on page 85.

Dollywaggon M
17 Helvellyn St., Keswick, CA12 4EN
☎ (076 87) 73593
"Home from home", family-run, no-smoking guesthouse. Quietly situated, within 5 minutes' walk of town centre. Ample on-street parking.
Bedrooms: 4 double & 1 twin, 1 family room.
Bathrooms: 6 private.
Bed & breakfast: £27-£31 double.

Continued ▶

KESWICK

Continued

Half board: £20.50-£22.50 daily, £143.50 weekly. Evening meal 6.30pm (l.o. 9am).

♨7🛆🖵♥🛉🗡🛏🖿🍴♨📶

Edwardene Guest House
24-26 Southey St., Keswick, CA12 4EF
☎ (076 87) 73586
Family-run guesthouse, close to town centre. Spacious rooms, 2 lounges, one with TV. Home cooking and relaxed atmosphere.
Bedrooms: 2 single, 5 double & 3 twin, 1 family room.
Bathrooms: 3 private, 2 public.
Bed & breakfast: £15-£19 single, £30-£38 double.
Half board: £25-£29 daily, £160-£190 weekly.
Evening meal 7pm (l.o. 4pm). Credit: Access, Visa.

♨5🛉▥♥🖿📺🍴♨✦ ⬛📶

Fell House
COMMENDED
28 Stanger St., Keswick, CA12 5JU
☎ (076 87) 72669
Spacious, centrally situated Victorian house with comfortable accommodation and informal hospitality. Mountain views. Colour TV in all bedrooms (not metered).
Bedrooms: 1 single, 3 double & 1 twin, 1 family room.
Bathrooms: 2 private, 1 public.
Bed & breakfast: £13-£14.25 single, £24-£32.50 double.
Evening meal 6.30pm (l.o. 10am).
Parking for 4.

♨🖵♥▥▥📺🍴♨ ✦♨📶

Foye House
Listed APPROVED
23 Eskin St., Keswick, CA12 4DQ
☎ (076 87) 73288
Friendly, comfortable, well-established guesthouse offering home cooking. Situated in quiet residential area, 4 minutes' walk from town.
Bedrooms: 3 single, 2 double & 1 twin, 1 family room.
Bathrooms: 2 public.
Bed & breakfast: £12-£15 single, £24-£30 double.
Half board: £19-£23 daily, £130-£140 weekly.
Evening meal 7pm (l.o. 4pm).

♨🖵♥▥▥🗡🍴♨✦ ♨📶

Glaramara
Seatoller, Keswick, CA12 5XQ
☎ Borrowdale (076 87) 77222
Telex 667047
Ideal for walkers, Glaramara offers warmth, comfort and good food after a day's walking. Many single rooms at no supplement.
Bedrooms: 19 single, 14 twin.
Bathrooms: 14 public.
Bed & breakfast: £13.25-£20.25 single, £22-£36 double.
Half board: £20.25-£28.25 daily, £130-£220 weekly.
Lunch available.
Evening meal 7pm.
Parking for 30.

♨2🛆▥▦♥▥🖿📶🍴♨📶

Glaramara Guest House
9 Acorn St., Keswick, CA12 4EA
☎ (076 87) 73216
Comfortable family-run guesthouse, home-cooked food. 4 minutes' easy walk to lake centre and lake. Rooms with showers.
Bedrooms: 1 single, 2 double & 1 twin, 1 family room.
Bathrooms: 1 public; 2 private showers.
Bed & breakfast: £11-£12.50 single, £22-£25 double.
Half board: £17.50-£18.50 daily.
Evening meal 6.30pm (l.o. 4pm).
Parking for 3.

♨♥🛉▥🖿📺🍴♨

Goodwin House
29 Southey St., Keswick, CA12 4EE
☎ (076 87) 74634
Warm, friendly, comfortable guesthouse with home cooking. In a quiet area, with access to shops, Lakes and fells. Own keys, open all year.
Bedrooms: 1 single, 1 double & 1 twin, 3 family rooms.
Bathrooms: 3 private, 1 public.
Bed & breakfast: £12-£17 single, £24-£34 double.
Half board: £19.50-£24.50 daily.
Evening meal 6.30pm.

♨🖵♥▥▥🛉📺🍴♨ 📶🍴

The Grange Country House Hotel
COMMENDED
Manor Brow, Ambleside Rd., Keswick, CA12 4BA
☎ (076 87) 72500

A building of charm, fully restored and refurbished, with many antiques. Quiet, overlooking Keswick with panoramic mountain views. Log fires, freshly prepared food and attractive bedrooms.
Bedrooms: 7 double & 3 twin.
Bathrooms: 10 private, 1 public.
Bed & breakfast: £60-£68.50 double.
Half board: £39.25-£43.25 daily, £253.75-£272.50 weekly.
Lunch available.
Evening meal 7pm (l.o. 8.30pm).
Parking for 13.
Open March-November, Christmas/New Year.
Credit: Access, Visa.

♨5🖵🔑📱🖵🛉▥🗡 ♨🍴♨⚓♡♨✦▦♨📶 ♨

Greystones
COMMENDED
Ambleside Rd., Keswick, CA12 4DP
☎ (076 87) 73108
Friendly hotel with a fine reputation and personal service. Ideally located for town, lake and fells.
Bedrooms: 5 double & 2 twin, 1 family room.
Bathrooms: 8 private, 1 public.
Bed & breakfast: £19-£20 single, £35-£37 double.
Half board: £29-£30 daily, £183-£190 weekly.
Evening meal 6.30pm (l.o. 2pm).
Parking for 9.
Open February-November.

♨8🖵♥🛉📺🖿🍴♨ 🍴🖿✦♨📶🍴

Hazeldene Hotel
The Heads, Keswick, CA12 5ER
☎ (076 87) 72106
Beautiful and central with open views over Derwentwater to Borrowdale and the Newlands Valley. Close to the town centre and shops.
Bedrooms: 5 single, 8 double & 4 twin, 5 family rooms.
Bathrooms: 18 private, 3 public.
Bed & breakfast: £19-£24 single, £38-£48 double.
Half board: £32-£37 daily, £218-£251 weekly.
Evening meal 6.30pm (l.o. 4pm).
Parking for 18.
Open March-November.

♨🔑🖵♥🛉📺🗡📺🍴♨ ♨♡▦

Hazelgrove
COMMENDED
4 Ratcliffe Place, Keswick, CA12 4DZ
☎ (076 87) 73391
Warm friendly guesthouse with home cooking, convenient for shops, parks and lake. Under supervision of owner.
Bedrooms: 2 double & 1 twin, 1 family room.
Bathrooms: 3 private, 1 public.
Bed & breakfast: £10 single, £12-£15 double.
Half board: £19-£22 daily, £125-£154 weekly.
Evening meal 6.30pm (l.o. 6.30pm).
Open March-October.

♨♥🖿🖵♥▥📱▥🗡📺

Hazelmere
Listed
Crosthwaite Rd., Keswick, CA12 5PG
☎ (076 87) 72445
Large Victorian house, 5 minutes' walk from town centre. Good private parking. Walkers welcome.
Bedrooms: 3 double, 3 family rooms.
Bathrooms: 3 private, 1 public.
Bed & breakfast: £13-£17 single, £26-£34 double.
Parking for 6.

♨🖵♥▥▥▥📺🖿♨ ✦♨📶

Highfield Hotel
COMMENDED
The Heads, Keswick, CA12 5ER
☎ (076 87) 72508
Small hotel near the town and the lakeside. Peaceful situation with superb views. Home-made bread.
Bedrooms: 5 single, 7 double & 4 twin, 3 family rooms.
Bathrooms: 15 private, 1 public.
Bed & breakfast: £16.65-£24.90 single, £40.80-£49.80 double.
Half board: £26.65-£34.90 daily, £177-£232 weekly.
Evening meal 6.30pm (l.o. 6pm).
Parking for 19.
Open April-October.

♨5♥🛉▥🗡📺🖿♨⚓✦

The Keswick Hotel
Station Rd., Keswick, CA12 4NQ
☎ (076 87) 72020
🆎 Principal

Family hotel offering a friendly atmosphere. Set in acres of gardens with magnificent views from all bedrooms.
Bedrooms: 11 single, 14 double & 41 twin.
Bathrooms: 66 private.
Bed & breakfast: from £60 single, from £72 double.
Half board: from £53 daily.
Lunch available.
Evening meal 7pm (l.o. 9pm).
Parking for 50.
Credit: Access, Visa, C.Bl., Diners, Amex.

King's Arms Hotel M
🏵🏵🏵

Main St., Keswick,
CA12 5BL
☎ (076 87) 72083
18th C coaching inn. Central. All bedrooms en-suite. Restaurant offers big "help yourself" salad bar, traditional home cooking and speciality dishes. Also Pizzeria and Video Bar.
Bedrooms: 6 double & 5 twin, 2 family rooms.
Bathrooms: 13 private.
Bed & breakfast: £29-£35 single, £42-£48 double.
Half board: £25-£29 daily, £192-£261 weekly.
Lunch available.
Evening meal 6pm (l.o. 10.30pm).
Credit: Access, Visa.

Ladstock Country House Hotel M
🏵🏵🏵 COMMENDED

Thornthwaite, Keswick,
CA12 5RZ
☎ Braithwaite (076 87) 78210
18th C country house hotel 3 miles from Keswick, set in own grounds. Panoramic views. Rooms with four-poster beds. 3 day breaks. Weddings and conferences.
Bedrooms: 2 single, 13 double & 6 twin, 2 family rooms.
Bathrooms: 13 private, 2 public; 7 private showers.
Bed & breakfast: £25-£36 single, £36-£62 double.
Half board: £35-£45 daily, £190-£385 weekly.
Lunch available.
Evening meal 7pm (l.o. 9pm).
Parking for 60.
Open February-December.
Credit: Access, Visa.

Lincoln House
23 Stanger St., Keswick,
CA12 5JX
☎ (076 87) 72597
Large semi-detached house facing south in a quiet cul-de-sac. 100 yards from main street.
Bedrooms: 1 single, 3 double & 1 twin, 1 family room.
Bathrooms: 2 public; 2 private showers.
Bed & breakfast: £13-£15 single, £26-£28 double.
Evening meal 6.30pm (l.o. 4pm).
Parking for 5.

Linnett Hill Hotel M
🏵🏵🏵 COMMENDED

4 Penrith Rd., Keswick,
CA12 4HF
☎ (076 87) 73109
Charming 1812 hotel overlooking Skiddaw and Latrigg Hills. Opposite parks, gardens and river. Fresh home-cooked food, including a la carte menus with quality wines. No smoking allowed in bedrooms.
Bedrooms: 1 single, 6 double & 2 twin.
Bathrooms: 9 private.
Bed & breakfast: from £21.50 single, from £39 double.
Half board: £29.50-£34 daily, £192.50-£225 weekly.
Lunch available.
Evening meal 7pm (l.o. 6.30pm).
Parking for 12.
Credit: Access, Visa.

Littletown Farm M
Newlands, Keswick,
CA12 5TU
☎ Braithwaite (076 87) 78353
150-acre mixed farm. In the beautiful, unspoilt Newlands Valley. En-suite bedrooms. Comfortable residents' lounge, dining room and cosy bar. Traditional 4-course dinner 6 nights a week.
Bedrooms: 1 single, 4 double & 2 twin, 2 family rooms.
Bathrooms: 6 private, 2 public.
Bed & breakfast: £20-£25 single, £40-£50 double.
Half board: £28-£34 daily, £190-£215 weekly.
Evening meal 7pm.
Parking for 10.
Open March-December.

Lonnin Garth Country Guest House
Lonnin Garth, Portinscale, Keswick, CA12 5RS
☎ Keswick (076 87) 74095
Country house in own mature grounds at the end of a private lane off A66 road just outside Portinscale. No smoking in dining room and bedrooms.
Bedrooms: 3 double & 1 twin.
Bathrooms: 2 private, 1 public.
Bed & breakfast: £32-£36 double.
Half board: £26-£28 daily.
Evening meal 7pm.
Parking for 7.

Lyzzick Hall Hotel M
🏵🏵🏵 COMMENDED

Underskiddaw, Nr. Keswick,
CA12 4PY
☎ (076 87) 72277
Peaceful country house hotel in its own grounds, with excellent views, varied food and a friendly, relaxed atmosphere.
Bedrooms: 3 single, 10 double & 5 twin, 2 family rooms.
Bathrooms: 20 private, 1 public.
Bed & breakfast: £28-£31 single, £56-£62 double.
Half board: £38-£40 daily, £240-£252 weekly.
Lunch available.
Evening meal 7pm (l.o. 9.30pm).
Parking for 30.
Open January, March-December.
Credit: Access, Visa, Diners, Amex.

Mary Mount M
🏵🏵

Keswick, CA12 5UU
☎ Borrowdale (076 87) 77223
Fax: (076 87) 77343
Small and quiet, catering for those looking for peace and tranquillity and making the most of the surrounding lake, mountain and woodland scenery.
Bedrooms: 1 single, 3 double & 8 twin, 1 family room.
Bathrooms: 13 private.
Bed & breakfast: £27-£33 single, £54-£64 double.
Lunch available.
Evening meal 6.30pm (l.o. 8.45pm).
Parking for 40.
Open April-November.
Credit: Access, Visa, Diners, Amex.

Melbreak House
29 Church St., Keswick,
CA12 4DX
☎ (076 87) 73398
A large guesthouse, well-equipped for family holidays and with facilities for larger groups.
Bedrooms: 1 single, 6 double & 1 twin, 4 family rooms.
Bathrooms: 5 private, 3 public.
Bed & breakfast: £11-£12.50 single, £25-£29 double.
Evening meal 6pm (l.o. 4pm).

Middle Ruddings Hotel M
🏵🏵🏵 COMMENDED

Braithwaite, Keswick,
CA12 5RY
☎ (076 87) 78436
Lakeland country hotel in 2 acres facing Skiddaw, with magnificent views all round. Tennis and bowls free for residents.
Bedrooms: 1 single, 8 double & 4 twin.
Bathrooms: 13 private, 1 public.
Bed & breakfast: from £39 single, £70-£76 double.
Half board: £47-£51 daily, £294-£309 weekly.
Lunch available.
Evening meal 7pm (l.o. 8.45pm).
Parking for 21.
Credit: Access, Visa.

Monkstones
62 Blencathra St., Keswick,
CA12 4HX
☎ (076 87) 74098
We pride ourselves on making guests feel as comfortable as possible. A friendly home-from-home.
Bedrooms: 1 single, 1 double & 1 twin, 2 family rooms.
Bathrooms: 2 public.
Bed & breakfast: £10 single, £20 double.
Half board: £16 daily, £112 weekly.
Evening meal 6pm (l.o. 7pm).
Parking for 3.

Pinehill
7, Leonard St., Keswick,
CA12 4EJ
☎ (076 87) 75029
Small, friendly guesthouse, clean and tastefully decorated with comfort in mind, close to town centre and amenities.
Continued ▶

Bedrooms: 1 single, 1 double,
1 family room.
Bathrooms: 2 private,
1 public.
Bed & breakfast: £14-£16
single, £28-£32 double.
Half board: £22-£24 daily,
£150-£185 weekly.

Queen's Hotel ⚑

Main St., Keswick,
CA12 5JF
☎ (076 87) 73333
*In the centre of Keswick, well
placed for both the shops and
countryside.*
Bedrooms: 8 single, 8 double
& 2 twin, 18 family rooms.
Bathrooms: 36 private.
Bed & breakfast: £32-£36
single, £56-£64 double.
Half board: £227-£250
weekly.
Lunch available.
Evening meal 6.30pm (l.o.
8.30pm).
Parking for 16.
Credit: Access, Visa, Diners,
Amex.

Ravensworth Hotel ⚑
COMMENDED

Station St., Keswick,
CA12 5HH
☎ (076 87) 72476
*Pleasant, family-run licensed
hotel where you can be at your
ease, adjacent to Fitz Park
and the town centre.*
Bedrooms: 8 double.
Bathrooms: 8 private.
Bed & breakfast: £27.50-£31
single, £34-£44 double.
Half board: £24.30-£31 daily,
£170-£217 weekly.
Evening meal 7pm (l.o. 7pm).
Parking for 5.
Open March-November.
Credit: Access, Visa.

Red House Hotel ⚑

Underskiddaw Keswick,
CA12 4QA
☎ (076 87) 72211
*Country house hotel in
extensive wooded grounds with
superb mountain views.
Reputation for tempting food.
Dogs particularly welcome.*
Bedrooms: 2 single, 7 double
& 9 twin, 4 family rooms.
Bathrooms: 22 private.
Bed & breakfast: £30-£35
single, £55-£65 double.

Half board: £42-£48 daily,
£280-£320 weekly.
Lunch available.
Evening meal 7pm (l.o.
8.30pm).
Parking for 25.
Credit: Access, Visa, Amex.

Rickerby Grange ⚑
COMMENDED

Portinscale, Keswick,
CA12 5RH
☎ (076 87) 72344
*Detached country hotel in its
own gardens, in a quiet village
on the outskirts of Keswick.
Provides imaginative cooking,
a bar and TV lounge. Ground
floor bedrooms available.*
Bedrooms: 2 single, 8 double
& 1 twin, 3 family rooms.
Bathrooms: 11 private,
1 public; 1 private shower.
Bed & breakfast: £21-£24.50
single, £42-£49 double.
Half board: £31.50-£35 daily,
£208-£230 weekly.
Evening meal 7pm (l.o. 6pm).
Parking for 14.

Rooking House ⚑
COMMENDED

Portinscale, Keswick,
CA12 5RD
☎ (076 87) 72506
*Enjoy the friendly atmosphere
and cuisine in this fine
Edwardian house with superb
views of the hills and lake.*
Bedrooms: 3 double & 3 twin.
Bathrooms: 6 private.
Bed & breakfast: £37-£41
double.
Half board: £29-£35 daily,
£183-£195 weekly.
Evening meal 7.30pm (l.o.
6pm).
Parking for 6.
Open February-December.

Sandon ⚑

13 Southey St., Keswick,
CA12 4EG
☎ (076 87) 73648
*Family-run guesthouse offering
good accommodation and fare.
Within minutes' walk of all
amenities. A pleasurable stay is
assured.*
Bedrooms: 2 single, 3 double,
1 family room.
Bathrooms: 2 private,
1 public.
Bed & breakfast: £12-£15.50
single, £24-£30 double.
Half board: £18.50-£21 daily,
£101-£113.40 weekly.

Lunch available.
Evening meal 6.30pm (l.o.
4pm).

Seven Oaks Guest House ⚑

7 Acorn St., Keswick,
CA12 4EA
☎ (076 87) 72088
*Small terraced guesthouse in a
quiet, residential area within
easy walking distance of town
centre, parks and lake.
Comfortable rooms, cleanliness
guaranteed.*
Bedrooms: 1 single, 2 double,
3 family rooms.
Bathrooms: 1 public;
5 private showers.
Bed & breakfast: £12.50-£13
single, £25-£26 double.
Half board: £18-£18.50 daily.
Evening meal 6.30pm (l.o.
6.30pm).
Parking for 2.
Open February-November.

Seymour House ⚑
Listed

36 Lake Road, Keswick,
CA12 5DQ
☎ (076 87) 72764
*Traditionl Lakeland house with
magnificnt views, midway
between Derwentwater Lake
and Keswick town centre.*
Bedrooms: 7 double & 1 twin,
2 family rooms.
Bathrooms: 4 private,
3 public.
Bed & breakfast: £15-£20
single, £30-£42 double.
Half board: £24-£30 daily,
£160-£202 weekly.
Evening meal 6.30pm (l.o.
2pm).
Credit: Access, Visa.

Skiddaw Grove Hotel ⚑

Vicarage Hill, Keswick,
CA12 5QB
☎ (076 87) 73324
*Detached Victorian hotel with
magnificent views of Skiddaw
and offering a high standard of
accommodation.*
Bedrooms: 1 single, 6 double
& 2 twin, 1 family room.
Bathrooms: 9 private,
1 public.
Bed & breakfast: £15-£16
single, £34-£36 double.
Half board: £26.50-£27.50
daily, £185.50-£192.50
weekly.
Evening meal 7pm (l.o. 5pm).
Parking for 13.

Skiddaw Hotel ⚑
COMMENDED

Main St., Keswick,
CA12 5BN
☎ (076 87) 72071
Fax (076 87) 74850
*Family-owned and supervised
hotel in the town centre.
Saunas, solarium, midweek
golf and squash.*
Bedrooms: 10 single,
11 double & 11 twin, 8 family
rooms.
Bathrooms: 40 private.
Bed & breakfast: £27.50-£29
single, £48-£51 double.
Lunch available.
Evening meal 6.30pm (l.o.
9pm).
Parking for 20.
Credit: Access, Visa, Amex.

Squirrel Lodge
Listed

43 Eskin St., Keswick,
CA12 4DG
☎ (076 87) 73091
*Colour TV and tea/coffee
facilities in all rooms. Optional
dinner menu. Non-smokers
only, please. Bargain breaks
from November-May.*
Bedrooms: 3 single, 4 double
& 1 twin.
Bathrooms: 2 public.
Bed & breakfast: £12-£13
single, £24-£26 double.
Evening meal 7pm (l.o.
4.30pm).
Parking for 2.
Credit: Access, Visa, Amex.

Stakis Keswick Lodore Swiss Hotel ⚑
HIGHLY COMMENDED

Keswick, CA12 5UX
☎ Borrowdale (076 87) 77285
Telex 64305
ⓒⓡ Stakis
*The original part of the local
stone building dates back to
1660 and the main building is
19th C. Famous Lodore Falls
are within the grounds.
Extensive indoor and outdoor
leisure facilities. Half board is
based on a minimum 2 night
stay.*
Bedrooms: 10 single,
15 double & 44 twin, 1 family
room.
Bathrooms: 70 private,
1 public.
Bed & breakfast: from £69
single, from £116 double.
Half board: from £53 daily.
Lunch available.
Evening meal 7.30pm (l.o.
9.30pm).
Parking for 143.

Open February-December.
Credit: Access, Visa, Diners,
Amex.

Swinside Lodge **M**
HIGHLY COMMENDED
Newlands, Keswick,
CA12 5UE
☎ (076 87) 72948
*Well-appointed, secluded and
informal Victorian house
beneath Cat Bells. High
standard of food, service and
accommodation. Comfortable
and tranquil surroundings.*
Bedrooms: 7 double & 2 twin.
Bathrooms: 8 private,
1 public.
Bed & breakfast: £34-£42
single, £57-£62 double.
Half board: £52-£60 daily.
Evening meal 7.30pm (l.o.
8pm).
Parking for 12.
Open February-November.

Thornleigh Guest House **M**
COMMENDED
23 Bank St., Keswick,
CA12 5JZ
☎ (076 87) 72863
*Located in centre of Keswick,
yet with breathtaking views of
Skiddaw and Cat Bells, only
10 minutes' walk from
Lakeside.*
Bedrooms: 6 double.
Bathrooms: 6 private.
Bed & breakfast: £36-£40
double.
Half board: £28-£30 daily.
Evening meal 7pm (l.o. 4pm).
Parking for 3.
Credit: Access, Visa.

Whitehouse Guest House **M**
COMMENDED
15 Ambleside Rd., Keswick,
CA12 4DL
☎ (076 87) 73176
*Fully refurbished small,
friendly guesthouse 5 minutes'
walk from the town centre.
Colour TV, electric blankets,
tea/coffee, most rooms with en-
suite facilities.*
Bedrooms: 4 double.
Bathrooms: 3 private,
1 public.
Bed & breakfast: £26-£32
double.
Parking for 3.
Open April-October.

Winchester House **M**
58 Blencathra St., Keswick,
CA12 4HT
☎ (076 87) 73664
*Comfortable, well-appointed
and quietly situated spacious
guesthouse with good views
from most rooms and friendly
atmosphere. Substantial full
English breakfast. Non-
smokers only please.*
Bedrooms: 2 double & 1 twin,
2 family rooms.
Bathrooms: 2 public.
Bed & breakfast: £12.50-£14
single, £25-£28 double.
Half board: £17.50-£19.50
daily, £110-£128 weekly.
Evening meal 6.30pm (l.o.
4pm).

KIRKBY LONSDALE
Cumbria
Map ref 5B3

Charming old town of
narrow streets and
Georgian buildings. The
Devil's Bridge over the
River Lune is probably
13th C.
*Tourist Information
Centre* ☎ *(052 42) 71437*

The Copper Kettle
Listed **APPROVED**
3 & 5 Market St., Kirkby
Lonsdale, Via Carnforth,
Lancashire LA6 2AU
☎ (052 42) 71714
*Part of an old manor house,
built in 1610, on the border
between the Yorkshire Dales
and the Lakes.*
Bedrooms: 2 double & 2 twin.
Bathrooms: 3 public.
Bed & breakfast: £17 single,
£26 double.
Half board: £23-£30 daily,
£160-£200 weekly.
Lunch available.
Evening meal 6pm (l.o. 9pm).
Credit: Access, Visa, Diners,
Amex.

Hipping Hall **M**
HIGHLY COMMENDED
Cowan Bridge, Nr. Kirkby
Lonsdale, Lancashire LA6 2JJ
☎ (052 42) 71187
Fax (052 42) 72452
*17th C country estate in 4
acres of walled gardens near
Kirkby Lonsdale. Ideal for the
Lakes and dales.*
Bedrooms: 5 double & 2 twin.
Bathrooms: 7 private.
Bed & breakfast: £69 double.
Half board: £53 daily, £318
weekly.

Evening meal 8pm (l.o.
8.30pm).
Parking for 13.
Open March-December.
Credit: Access, Visa.

Pheasant Inn **M**
COMMENDED
Casterton, Kirkby Lonsdale,
Via Carnforth, Lancashire
LA6 2RX
☎ (052 42) 71230
*An old world country inn
specialising in food and service,
ideal for touring the Lakes,
dales and coast. Situated
amidst the peaceful Lunesdale
Fells.*
Bedrooms: 3 single, 5 double
& 2 twin.
Bathrooms: 10 private.
Bed & breakfast: £37.50-£40
single, £52.50-£55 double.
Lunch available.
Evening meal 7pm (l.o.
9.15pm).
Parking for 60.
Open February-December.
Credit: Access, Visa.

Whoop Hall Inn **M**
COMMENDED
Burrow with Burrow, Kirkby
Lonsdale, Carnforth,
Lancashire LA6 2HP
☎ (052 42) 71284
Fax (052 42) 72154
*17th C coaching inn, now fully
refurbished with all home
comforts and noted for its food.
Between Lakes and dales, 6
miles from M6 junction 36.*
Bedrooms: 4 single, 5 double
& 5 twin, 2 family rooms.
Bathrooms: 16 private.
Bed & breakfast: from £35
single, from £55 double.
Lunch available.
Evening meal 6pm (l.o.
10pm).
Parking for 120.
Credit: Access, Visa.

*The symbols are
explained on the
flap inside the
back cover.*

*The national Crown
scheme is explained
in full on pages
536 - 539.*

KIRKBY STEPHEN
Cumbria
Map ref 5B3

Picturesque old market
town on the River Eden.
Good centre for exploring
the Eden Valley.
*Tourist Information
Centre* ☎ *(076 83) 71199*

The George Hotel
Main St., Brough, Kirkby
Stephen, CA17 4AY
☎ (076 83) 41357
*300-year-old former coaching
inn. Bar meals, restaurant,
function room, games room.*
Bedrooms: 2 single, 1 double,
1 family room.
Bathrooms: 2 public.
Bed & breakfast: £12.50-
£13.50 single, £25-£27 double.
Lunch available.
Evening meal 5.30pm (l.o.
8pm).
Parking for 50.

Ing Hill **M**
COMMENDED
Mallerstang, Kirkby Stephen,
CA17 4JT
☎ (076 83) 71153
*Delightful Georgian country
house in Mallerstang Valley
with glorious views. Peace,
quiet, open fires, home cooking
and a warm welcome.*
Bedrooms: 1 single, 2 double
& 1 twin.
Bathrooms: 3 private,
1 public.
Bed & breakfast: £22 single,
£44 double.
Evening meal 7.30pm (l.o.
8pm).
Parking for 5.

Kings Arms Hotel **M**
APPROVED
Kirkby Stephen, CA17 4QN
☎ (076 83) 71378
*17th C former posting inn, in
the centre of market town,
providing home-made food,
local game and fresh garden
produce.*
Bedrooms: 2 single, 4 double
& 4 twin, 1 family room.
Bathrooms: 5 private,
3 public.
Bed & breakfast: £26.50-£32
single, £45-£50 double.
Lunch available.
Evening meal 6.45pm (l.o.
9pm).
Parking for 12.
Credit: Access, Visa.

KIRKBY STEPHEN

Continued

The Thrang Country Hotel ⋔
👑👑👑 COMMENDED

Mallerstang, Kirkby Stephen, CA17 4JX
☎ (0763) 71889
Comfortable Victorian rectory set in the breathtaking scenery of Mallerstang, the upper Eden Valley. 6 miles south of Kirkby Stephen on B6259.
Bedrooms: 1 single, 3 double & 1 twin, 1 family room.
Bathrooms: 5 private, 1 public; 1 private shower.
Bed & breakfast: from £22.50 single.
Half board: from £35.50 daily.
Lunch available.
Evening meal 7.30pm (l.o. 6pm).
Parking for 8.
Credit: Access, Visa.
➤ 🅱 ⊘ 🛉 Ⓥ ⊬ Ⓣ ◑ ▥
🖂 🍴 🛎 ☽ ✳ 🖾 ᴅᴀᴘ ↘ SP
🎠

LAKESIDE
Cumbria
Map ref 5A3

10m NE. Ulverston
There is a pier at Lakeside for the lake steamer service on Windermere and steam trains run from here along the 3-mile track to Haverthwaite during the summer.

The Knoll Country Guest House ⋔
👑👑👑

Lakeside, Newby Bridge, LA12 8AU
☎ Newby Bridge (053 95) 31347
Victorian detached residence in quiet grounds backing on to Grizedale Forest. 3 minutes' walk from the steamer pier and lakeside.
Bedrooms: 2 single, 3 double & 1 twin, 3 family rooms.
Bathrooms: 6 private, 1 public.
Bed & breakfast: £14.50-£23.50 single, £33-£37 double.
Half board: £25-£29 daily, £170-£200 weekly.
Evening meal 7pm (l.o. 4.30pm).
Parking for 16.
➤ ⊘ 🛉 Ⓥ ⊬ Ⓣ ▥ ▱ ✳
🖂 ↘ SP 🎠

Landing Cottage ⋔
👑👑👑

Lakeside, Newby Bridge, Ulverston, LA12 8AS
☎ (053 95) 31719
19th C Lakeland-stone cottage, 100 yards from the shores of Lake Windermere, close to the steamer boat terminal and the Lakeside/Haverthwaite pleasure steam train.
Bedrooms: 3 double, 2 family rooms.
Bathrooms: 2 private, 2 public.
Bed & breakfast: £16-£20 single, £28-£33 double.
Half board: £22.50-£25 daily, £150-£160 weekly.
Evening meal 7pm (l.o. 4.30pm).
Parking for 6.
➤ 🛉 🍴 Ⓥ ⊬ Ⓣ ▥ ▱ ☽ ✕
🖂 SP

LANERCOST
Cumbria
Map ref 5B2

In this locality stand the remains of an interesting medieval priory, whose buildings are 12th C.

Abbey Bridge Inn ⋔
👑👑👑

Lanercost, Brampton, Nr. Carlisle, CA8 2HG
☎ Brampton (069 77) 2224
Peaceful riverside setting on a B road 2 miles from Brampton. Incorporates Blacksmith's restaurant, which dates back to 1690. Good food, real ale. Ideal for touring Hadrian's Wall and Lakes.
Bedrooms: 2 single, 3 double & 2 twin.
Bathrooms: 4 private, 2 public.
Bed & breakfast: £19-£25 single, £38-£44 double.
Lunch available.
Evening meal 7pm (l.o. 8.45pm).
Parking for 20.
Credit: Access, Visa.
➤ 🛁 ⊘ 🛉 Ⓥ ⊬ Ⓣ ▥ ▱
🖂 🎠 ⊤

Map references apply to the colour maps towards the end of this guide.

Please mention this guide when making a booking.

LANGDALE
Cumbria
Map ref 5A3

The 2 Langdale valleys (Great Langdale and Little Langdale) lie in the heart of beautiful mountain scenery. The craggy Langdale Pikes are almost 2500 ft high. An ideal walking and climbing area.

Britannia Inn ⋔
👑👑👑 COMMENDED

Elterwater, Nr. Ambleside, LA22 9HP
☎ Langdale (096 67) 210 & 382
A 400-year-old traditional Lake District inn on a village green in the beautiful Langdale Valley. A warm welcome to all. TV available in bedrooms.
Bedrooms: 7 double & 2 twin.
Bathrooms: 6 private, 2 public.
Bed & breakfast: £36-£46 single, £42-£58 double.
Half board: £38.50-£44.50 daily, £245-£299.25 weekly.
Lunch available.
Evening meal 7.30pm (l.o. 7.30pm).
Parking for 10.
Credit: Access, Visa.
➤ ➘ 🛀 ⊘ 🛉 Ⓥ ⊬ ▥ ▱
🖂 🎠 ⊤

LITTLE CLIFTON
Cumbria
Map ref 5A2

5m SW. Cockermouth
Very small village between Cockermouth and Workington, with an interesting 19th C church.

Crossbarrow Motel ⋔
Little Clifton, Workington, CA14 1XS
☎ Workington (0900) 61443
Fax: (0900) 61443 Ext 222
Situated in a quiet corner of West Cumbria between the Lake District National Park and the sea with superb views of the Lakeland fells.
Bedrooms: 10 double & 16 twin, 1 family room.
Bathrooms: 27 private.
Bed & breakfast: £37-£38 single, £55-£56 double.
Half board: £35-£48 daily.
Lunch available.
Evening meal 7pm (l.o. 9.30pm).
Parking for 50.
Credit: Access, Visa, Amex.
➤ 🛁 🛀 📞 🅱 ▢ ⊘ 🛉 Ⓥ ⊬
▥ 🍴 ☽ ✳ SP

LONGTOWN
Cumbria
Map ref 5A2

The last town in England. Once important for the Scottish drovers and now enjoyed by those touring the Border country. Hadrian's Wall is close by.
Tourist Information Centre ☎ (0228) 791876

Craigburn ⋔
👑👑👑 COMMENDED

Penton, Longtown, Carlisle, CA6 5QP
☎ Nicholforest (022 877) 214
250-acre mixed farm. Near the Scottish border. We provide comfort and farmhouse cooking for weekend breaks, longer stays or a stopover to or from Scotland.
Bedrooms: 2 double & 2 twin, 2 family rooms.
Bathrooms: 6 private.
Bed & breakfast: £21-£23 single, £32-£36 double.
Half board: £26-£28 daily, £163.80-£176.40 weekly.
Evening meal 6pm (l.o. 2pm).
Parking for 20.
➤ ⊘ 🛉 Ⓥ ⊬ Ⓣ ▥ ▱
🍴 🞿 ✳ ↘ SP ⊤

Sportsmans Restaurant, Marchbank Hotel
👑👑👑 COMMENDED

Scotsdyke, Nr. Longtown, Carlisle, CA6 5XP
☎ (0228) 791325
Charming small country hotel serving good food and using local produce cooked by the chef patron. Specialising in game and wild salmon.
Bedrooms: 1 single, 1 double & 3 twin.
Bathrooms: 3 private, 1 public; 2 private showers.
Bed & breakfast: £20-£33 single, £44-£54 double.
Half board: £33-£44 daily.
Lunch available.
Evening meal 6pm (l.o. 9pm).
Parking for 20.
Credit: Access, Visa, Amex.
➤ 🛀 ▢ ⊘ 🛉 Ⓥ ⊬ ▥ ▱
🎣 ✳ 🖾 🎠

National Crown ratings were correct at the time of going to press but are subject to change. Please check at the time of booking.

LOWESWATER

Cumbria
Map ref 5A3

This village lies between Loweswater, one of the smaller lakes of the Lake District, and Crummock Water. Several mountains lie beyond the village.

Grange Country House Hotel

Loweswater, Water-End, Nr. Cockermouth, CA13 0SU
☎ Lamplugh (0946) 861211
Peaceful 17th C manor house and modern annexe in an attractive garden overlooking the lake and fells, with log fires and colour TV. 2 four-poster suites available.
Bedrooms: 1 single, 4 double & 5 twin, 1 family room.
Bathrooms: 9 private, 3 public; 1 private shower.
Bed & breakfast: £28-£30 single, £56-£60 double.
Half board: £40-£42 daily, £266-£280 weekly.
Lunch available.
Evening meal 7pm (l.o. 8pm).
Parking for 32.
Open March-December.
⛄ ⬛ 🏠 🛏 🍴 🖤 ▥ 🖥 📺
🅿 ⬛ 🍴 ❄ 🎿 🐾 SP 🅵

MEALSGATE

Cumbria
Map ref 5A2

6m SW. Wigton
Scattered village between Cockermouth and Wigton, the birthplace of the 19th C philanthropist, George Moore.

Pink House Hotel

😊😊😊 COMMENDED
Mealsgate, Nr. Wigton, Carlisle, CA5 1JP
☎ Low Ireby (096 57) 229
A small Victorian country house hotel set amongst lovely trees and gardens. Beautifully appointed rooms and open fires. Warm, friendly atmosphere.
Bedrooms: 1 single, 2 double & 1 twin, 2 family rooms.
Bathrooms: 6 private.
Bed & breakfast: £36 single, £50 double.
Lunch available.
Evening meal 6.30pm (l.o. 8.45pm).
Parking for 30.
Credit: Access, Visa, Diners.
⛄ 📞 🖤 🛏 ▥ 🖥 📺 🖤
🍴 🚶 ❄ 🅵 SP

MUNGRISDALE

Cumbria
Map ref 5A2

The simple, white church in this hamlet has a 3-decker pulpit and box pews.

Near Howe Farm Hotel

😊😊😊 COMMENDED
Mungrisdale, Penrith, CA11 0SH
☎ (076 87) 79678
350-acre mixed farm. Farmhouse in quiet surroundings 1 mile from Mungrisdale, half a mile from the A66 and within easy reach of all the lakes.
Bedrooms: 3 double & 1 twin, 3 family rooms.
Bathrooms: 5 private, 1 public.
Bed & breakfast: £14-£17 single.
Half board: £22-£25 daily, £154-£175 weekly.
Evening meal 7pm (l.o. 5pm).
Parking for 12.
Open April-October.
⛄ 🛏 🍴 ▥ 🖥 📺 ⬛ 🐾
❄ 🚶

NEWBY BRIDGE

Cumbria
Map ref 5A3

At the southern end of Windermere on the River Leven, this village has an unusual stone bridge with arches of unequal size. The Lakeside and Haverthwaite Railway has a stop here, and steamer cruises on Lake Windermere leave from Lakeside.

Swan Hotel

😊😊😊😊 COMMENDED
Newby Bridge, Nr. Ulverston, LA12 8NB
☎ (053 95) 31681
Fax (053 95) 31917
Telex 65108
CR Inter
Privately-owned hotel enjoying a beautiful site at the foot of Lake Windermere. We offer facilities appreciated by both holiday and business visitors.
Bedrooms: 7 single, 13 double & 10 twin, 6 family rooms.
Bathrooms: 36 private.
Bed & breakfast: £50-£75 single, £84-£125 double.
Half board: £54-£70 daily, £360-£500 weekly.
Lunch available.
Evening meal 7pm (l.o. 9.30pm).

Parking for 106.
Credit: Access, Visa, Diners, Amex.
⛄ 📞 ⬛ 🛏 🍴 🖤 ▥ 🖥 📺
● ▥ 🍴 🚶 ❄ 🎿 🐾 🐾
SP 🅵 🅣

Whitewater Hotel 🅜

😊😊😊😊😊
The Lakeland Village, Backbarrow, Newby Bridge, Nr. Ulverston, LA12 8PX
☎ (053 95) 31133
Fax (053 95) 31881
Old mill built of Lakeland stone, now converted into a hotel with all facilities, including a leisure centre in the grounds.
Bedrooms: 4 single, 14 double & 7 twin, 10 family rooms.
Bathrooms: 35 private.
Bed & breakfast: max. £66.50 single, max. £97 double.
Half board: max. £60 daily.
Lunch available.
Evening meal 7.15pm (l.o. 9pm).
Parking for 50.
Credit: Access, Visa, Diners, Amex.
⛄ 🛏 🖤 📞 ⬛ 🛏 🍴 🖤 ▥
🖥 ● 🎿 ▥ 🍴 🐾 🐾 🅣
🐾 🚶 🕐 🚶 ❄ 🐾 SP 🅣

PENRITH

Cumbria
Map ref 5B2

This ancient and historic market town is the northern gateway to the Lake District. Penrith Castle was built as a defence against the Scots. Its ruins, open to the public, stand in the public park. High above the town is the famous Penrith Beacon.
Tourist Information Centre ☎ (0768) 67466

Brackenrigg Hotel

Watermillock, Penrith, CA11 0LP
☎ Pooley Bridge (076 84) 86206
18th C coaching inn overlooking Ullswater with 11 bedrooms and 3 self-catering cottages recently converted from old stables. Bar, games room and breakfast room/dining room. Open to non-residents.
Bedrooms: 6 double & 2 twin, 3 family rooms.
Bathrooms: 2 public.
Bed & breakfast: from £20 single, from £31 double.
Lunch available.

Evening meal 6.30pm (l.o. 9.30pm).
Parking for 50.
Open March-December.
⛄ 🛏 ▥ 🖥 📺 🍴 🐾 🚶 SP

Brantwood Country House Hotel 🅜

😊😊😊
Stainton, Penrith, CA11 0EP
☎ (0768) 62748
Family-owned and run. Standing in secluded gardens in rural location, 1.5 miles from M6 junction 40 and 3 miles from Ullswater.
Bedrooms: 2 single, 7 double & 2 twin.
Bathrooms: 11 private, 1 public.
Bed & breakfast: £30-£33 single, £46-£60 double.
Half board: £30-£44 daily, £200-£300 weekly.
Lunch available.
Evening meal 6.30pm (l.o. 9pm).
Parking for 40.
Credit: Access, Visa.
⛄ 🖤 🛏 ⬛ 🛏 🖤 🛏 ▥ 🖤
🍴 ▥ ⬛ 🍴 ❄ 🚶 🐾 DAP SP 🅵

George Hotel 🅜

😊😊😊 APPROVED
Penrith, CA11 7SU
☎ (0768) 62696
Fax (0768) 68223
300-year-old, famous coaching inn providing modern facilities, in the centre of Penrith. Privately owned and managed.
Bedrooms: 12 single, 10 double & 9 twin.
Bathrooms: 30 private, 1 public.
Bed & breakfast: from £37 single, from £51 double.
Half board: from £48.50 daily, from £339.50 weekly.
Lunch available.
Evening meal 7pm (l.o. 8.30pm).
Parking for 30.
Credit: Access, Visa.
⛄ 📞 ⬛ 🛏 🖤 🛏 ▥ ● ▥
🍴 SP 🅣

Norcroft Guesthouse

😊😊😊 COMMENDED
Graham St., Penrith, CA11 9LQ
☎ (0768) 62365
Spacious Victorian house with large comfortable rooms. In a quiet residential area near the town centre.
Bedrooms: 2 double & 4 twin, 2 family rooms.
Bathrooms: 5 private, 1 public.
Bed & breakfast: £14.50-£22.50 single, £30-£37.50 double.

Continued ▶

PENRITH
Continued

Half board: £22.50-£30.50 daily, £154-£175 weekly. Evening meal 7.30pm (l.o. 4.30pm). Parking for 8.

⌨ 🔥 🖥 ♦ 🛡 📖 ⟊ 📺 ▥ ➘
🕸 🎪 🍴 ⚑ 🔌 📶

Old Victoria Hotel ♨
APPROVED
46 Castlegate, Penrith, CA11 7HY
☎ (0768) 62467
Family-run hotel with public bar, bar lunches and evening meals. Home-cooked specialities.
Bedrooms: 4 double & 3 twin.
Bathrooms: 2 private, 1 public; 5 private showers.
Bed & breakfast: £25-£33 single, £40-£45 double.
Half board: £30-£38 daily, £190-£230 weekly.
Lunch available.
Evening meal 7.30pm (l.o. 9pm).
Parking for 12.

⌨ 🖥 ♦ 🛡 ▥ ➘ 🍴 🔌 📖
📶 📶 🛡 Ⓣ

The Pategill Hotel
Carlton Rd., Penrith, CA11 8JW
☎ (0768) 63153
Hotel with friendly service, 5 minutes from town centre. A la carte menu, children's menu, also lunches available. Parking area.
Bedrooms: 2 single, 1 twin, 8 family rooms.
Bathrooms: 2 public.
Bed & breakfast: £18.50-£19.50 single, £34.50-£36.50 double.
Half board: £23-£31.50 daily.
Lunch available.
Evening meal 6pm (l.o. 9pm).
Parking for 14.

⌨ ♦ 🛡 ▣ 🔌 📺 ▥ 🍴 ∪
📖 📶 📶

The White House ♨
COMMENDED
Clifton, Penrith, CA10 2EL
☎ (0768) 65115
Built in 1790, converted farmhouse set in attractive gardens, double-glazed and centrally heated throughout. Non-smokers only please.
Bedrooms: 2 single, 1 double & 1 twin, 1 family room.
Bathrooms: 2 private, 2 public.
Bed & breakfast: £14 single, £30-£34 double.
Half board: £24-£26 daily, £161-£175 weekly.

Evening meal 7pm (l.o. midday).
Parking for 8.
Open January-October.

⌨ 🔥 🍴 ♦ 🛡 ▣ 🔌 ⚑ 📺 ▥
➘ 🎪 🍴 📶 🍴

Woodland House Hotel ♨
COMMENDED
Wordsworth St., Penrith, CA11 7QY
☎ (0768) 64177
Elegant red sandstone house with a library of books and maps for walkers, nature lovers and sightseers. Most bedrooms en-suite. No smoking in hotel.
Bedrooms: 3 single, 2 double & 2 twin, 1 family room.
Bathrooms: 6 private, 1 public.
Bed & breakfast: £16-£19 single, £31-£35 double.
Half board: £23.95-£26.95 daily.
Evening meal 6.45pm (l.o. 5pm).
Parking for 13.

⌨ 🖥 ♦ 🛡 ▣ ⚑ 📺 ▥ ➘
🍴 🔌 📶 📶

RAVENGLASS
Cumbria
Map ref 5A3

Coastal village on the River Esk Estuary. The Romans established a supply base here, and a well-preserved bath house just south of the village can be seen. A miniature railway runs from Ravenglass to Boot in the Eskdale Valley. Muncaster Castle, open to the public, is 1 mile east of the village.

Muncaster Country Guesthouse
Muncaster, Ravenglass, CA18 1RD
☎ (0229) 717693
Licensed country guesthouse, originally the village school, conveniently situated opposite Muncaster Castle gardens. Friendly, cosy atmosphere. Ideal for exploring western Lakeland. Pleasant garden. Outdoor holidays and fell walking organised.
Bedrooms: 1 single, 3 double & 2 twin, 1 family room.
Bathrooms: 2 private, 3 public.
Bed & breakfast: £16.50-£18 single, £30-£38 double.
Half board: £27-£30 daily, £189-£210 weekly.

Evening meal 6.30pm (l.o. 7.30pm).
Parking for 20.

⌨ 🔥 🍴 ♦ 🛡 ▣ 🔌 📺 ▥ ➘
🍴 🕴 ∪ 🎪 🍴 📶 📶

Rosegarth ♨
Main St., Ravenglass, CA18 1SQ
☎ (0229) 717275
In a rural seaside village with views across the village green to the Irish Sea.
Bedrooms: 1 single, 3 double & 1 twin.
Bathrooms: 1 private, 2 public.
Bed & breakfast: £13.50-£14.50 single, £27-£29 double.
Parking for 3.

⌨ 🔥 ♦ 🛡 ▣ 🔌 📺 ▥
➘ 🎪 🍴 📶 📶

RAVENSTONEDALE
Cumbria
Map ref 5B3

Set below Ash Fell, this village has a fine church with an unusual interior where sections of the congregation sit facing each other. There is a 3-decker pulpit.

The Black Swan Hotel ♨
COMMENDED
Ravenstonedale, Kirkby Stephen, CA17 4NG
☎ Newbiggin-on-Lune (058 73) 204
A delightful family-run hotel, set amidst beautiful countryside in a picturesque village. Renowned for food, comfort and hospitality.
Bedrooms: 1 single, 8 double & 4 twin, 1 family room.
Bathrooms: 14 private, 1 public.
Bed & breakfast: £41-£43 single, £57-£61 double.
Half board: £59-£61 daily, £265-£350 weekly.
Lunch available.
Evening meal 7pm (l.o. 9.30pm).
Parking for 20.
Credit: Access, Visa, Amex.

⌨ 🔥 ☎ 🔌 ♦ 🛡 ▣ 🔌
📺 ➘ 🍴 🕴 🍷 ∪ 🍴 ▶
🎪 📶 📶 Ⓣ

RYDAL
Cumbria
Map ref 5A3

Hamlet at the east end of Rydal Water, a small, beautiful lake sheltered by Rydal Fell. A good centre for touring and walking.

The Glen Rothay Hotel ♨
COMMENDED
Rydal, Nr. Ambleside, LA22 9LR
☎ Ambleside (053 94) 32524
Fax (053 94) 31079
17th C historic inn with Wordsworth associations, in a beautiful setting facing Rydal Water.
Bedrooms: 2 single, 7 double & 1 twin, 1 family room.
Bathrooms: 11 private, 1 public.
Bed & breakfast: £32-£37 single, £64-£130 double.
Half board: £42-£75 daily, £273-£490 weekly.
Lunch available.
Evening meal 7.30pm (l.o. 8pm).
Parking for 40.
Open February-December.
Credit: Access, Visa, Amex.

⌨ 🔌 ☎ 🔌 ⌨ ♦ 🛡 ▣ ⚑
🔌 📺 ▥ ➘ 🍴 🎪 📶 🍴 📶
📶

Nab Cottage Guest House
Nab Cottage, Rydal, Ambleside, LA22 9SD
☎ (053 94) 35311
17th C cottage nestling near the lakeshore, surrounded by fells. Many literary connections and a cosy, friendly atmosphere.
Bedrooms: 1 single, 4 double & 2 twin.
Bathrooms: 2 private, 2 public.
Bed & breakfast: from £16.50 single, from £37 double.
Half board: £28-£30 daily.
Evening meal 7pm (l.o. 5pm).
Parking for 10.

⌨ ♦ 🛡 ▣ ⚑ 🔌 📺 ▥ ➘
∪ 🍴 🎪 🍴 📶

Individual proprietors have supplied all details of accommodation. Although we do check for accuracy, we advise you to confirm prices and other information at the time of booking.

ST BEES

Cumbria
Map ref 5A3

Small coastal resort with a good beach. The cliffs at nearby St. Bees Head are a sanctuary for nesting sea birds and have superb clifftop walks. Home of a public school which was founded in the 16th C.

Queen's Hotel M

Main St., St. Bees,
CA27 0DE
☎ Egremont (0946) 822287
17th C coaching inn on Cumbrian coast close to the western lakes. Restaurant, garden bar and large gymnasium.
Bedrooms: 5 single, 5 double & 5 twin.
Bathrooms: 12 private,
1 public.
Bed & breakfast: £25 single, £40 double.
Lunch available.
Evening meal 7.30pm (l.o. 9.30pm).
Parking for 8.
Credit: Access, Visa.
🏧 ☐ 🅰 🛡 ▦ 🍴 ∪ ❄
SP ▦

Seacote Hotel M
☆☆☆ APPROVED

Beach Rd., St. Bees,
CA27 0ES
☎ (0946) 822777
Overlooking St. Bees Beach and St. Bees Head. Excellent walking area, bird sanctuary, golf-course. Conference and function facilities for up to 250. Ideal base for touring the Lakes.
Bedrooms: 7 single, 12 double & 11 twin, 2 family rooms.
Bathrooms: 32 private,
1 public.
Bed & breakfast: £30-£35 single, £48-£52 double.
Half board: from £40.50 daily, from £280 weekly.
Lunch available.
Evening meal 6.30pm (l.o. 9.30pm).
Parking for 60.
Credit: Access, Visa, Amex.
🏧 📞 🅰 ☐ 🅰 🛡 ▦ 🍴 ⊟
▦ 🅰 🍴 🛒 ∪ ❄ 🅰 🍴
SP T

The enquiry coupons at the back will help you when contacting proprietors.

SATTERTHWAITE

Cumbria
Map ref 5A3

4m S. Hawkshead
Secluded village set in the heart of the Grizedale Forest with visitors' centre. Forest trails and pretty waterfalls nearby.

Pepper House M
☆☆☆ COMMENDED

Satterthwaite, LA12 8LS
☎ Satterthwaite
(0229) 860206
Peace and comfort in beautiful Grizedale Valley. Traditional English food, vegetarians and special diets catered for. Bar. Near Hawkshead.
Bedrooms: 1 single, 7 double & 4 twin.
Bathrooms: 12 private.
Bed & breakfast: £18.50-£19.50 single, £37-£39 double.
Half board: £25.50-£29.50 daily, £171.50-£185 weekly.
Evening meal 7pm (l.o. 10.30pm).
Parking for 14.
🏧 🅰 ☐ 🅰 🛡 ▦ ⋉ 🅰
TV ▦ 🅰 🛒 ∪ ❄ 🅰 🍴 SP
▦ T

SAWREY

Cumbria
Map ref 5A3

Far Sawrey and Near Sawrey lie near Esthwaite Water. Both villages are small but Near Sawrey is famous for Hill Top Farm, home of Beatrix Potter, now owned by the National Trust and open to the public.

Ees Wyke Country House M
☆☆☆ COMMENDED

Nr. Sawrey, Ambleside,
LA22 0JZ
☎ Hawkshead (096 66) 393
Charming Georgian country house overlooking the peaceful and beautiful Esthwaite Water. Fine views of the lake, mountains and fells.
Bedrooms: 4 double & 2 twin.
Bathrooms: 6 private,
1 public.
Bed & breakfast: £56-£64 double.
Half board: £40-£44 daily.
Lunch available.
Evening meal 7pm (l.o. 7.30pm).
Parking for 10.
🏧 🅰 ☐ 🅰 🛡 ▦ ⋉ 🅰 ▦
🅰 🍴 ∪ 🛒 ❄ 🅰 🍴 SP ▦
T

Sawrey Hotel M
☆☆☆

Far Sawrey, Nr. Ambleside,
LA22 0LQ
☎ Windermere
(053 94) 43425
Country inn on the quieter side of Windermere, 1 mile from the car ferry on the B5285 to Hawkshead. The bar is in the old stables and has log fires.
Bedrooms: 4 single, 6 double & 4 twin, 3 family rooms.
Bathrooms: 13 private,
1 public.
Bed & breakfast: £21.50-£26.50 single, £43-£53 double.
Half board: £29-£35 daily, £185-£199 weekly.
Lunch available.
Evening meal 7pm (l.o. 8.45pm).
Parking for 30.
Credit: Access, Visa.
🏧 🅰 📞 ☐ 🛡 🅰 ▦ 🅰 🅰
🍴 🛒 ∪ ❄ 🅰 🍴 SP ▦

Sawrey House Country Hotel M

Near Sawrey, Nr. Ambleside,
LA22 0LF
☎ Hawkshead (096 66) 387
Near Sawrey (home of Beatrix Potter). Warm friendly atmosphere, comfortable accommodation, good food, magnificent views, 3 acres and large car park.
Bedrooms: 2 single, 3 double & 2 twin, 3 family rooms.
Bathrooms: 7 private,
2 public.
Bed & breakfast: £22.50-£26 single, £45-£52 double.
Half board: £33-£36.50 daily, £217-£241 weekly.
Evening meal 7pm (l.o. midday).
Parking for 15.
Open March-October.
🏧 🅰 🅰 🛡 ▦ 🅰 TV ▦ 🅰
🍴 🅰 ❄ 🅰 SP

West Vale Country Guest House M
☆☆☆ COMMENDED

Far Sawrey, Nr. Hawkshead,
Ambleside, LA22 0LQ
☎ Windermere
(053 94) 42817
Warm welcome awaits you at this peaceful family-run guesthouse, with home cooking, log fire and fine views.
Bedrooms: 5 double & 1 twin, 2 family rooms.
Bathrooms: 7 private,
1 public.
Bed & breakfast: £16-£19 single, £32-£38 double.
Half board: £25-£28 daily, £161-£182 weekly.

Lunch available.
Evening meal 7pm (l.o. 4pm).
🏧 7 🅰 🛡 ▦ 🅰 ⊟ TV ▦ 🅰 ∪
🅰 🅰 ▦

SEASCALE

Cumbria
Map ref 5A3

Small seaside resort with good sands and a golf-course.

Calder House Hotel M
☆☆☆ APPROVED

The Banks, Seascale,
CA20 1QP
☎ (094 67) 28538
Family-run private hotel, overlooking beach, offering bed, breakfast and evening meal. Also golf weekend breaks.
Bedrooms: 8 single, 10 twin, 1 family room.
Bathrooms: 6 private,
6 public.
Bed & breakfast: £19-£22 single, £35-£39 double.
Half board: £25-£28 daily, £160-£180 weekly.
Evening meal 7pm (l.o. midday).
Parking for 25.
🏧 🅰 📞 🅰 🛡 🅰 ⋉
🅰 TV ▦ 🅰 🍴 🅰 🍴 ❄ 🅰
▦ 🅰

SHAP

Cumbria
Map ref 5B3

Village lying nearly 1000 ft above sea-level. Shap Abbey, open to the public, is hidden in a valley nearby. Most of the ruins date from the early 13th C, but the tower is 16th C.

Brookfield

Shap, Penrith, CA10 3PZ
☎ (093 16) 397
Only 2 minutes' drive from the M6 junction 39. Offering home cooking, a large dining room, well-appointed bedrooms with remote-control colour TV and tea/coffee facilities. Renowned for food, comfort and personal attention. Sorry, no pets.
Bedrooms: 1 single, 4 double & 3 twin, 2 family rooms.
Bathrooms: 1 public.
Bed & breakfast: from £15 single, £28-£30 double.
Half board: £28-£30 daily.
Evening meal 7.30pm (l.o. 7pm).
Parking for 30.
Open March-December.
🏧 ☐ 🅰 🛡 ▦ 🅰 🅰 TV ▦ 🅰
🍴 🅰 🅰

SHAP
Continued

Kings Arms Hotel M
Main St., Shap, Penrith,
CA10 3NU
☎ (093 16) 277
*Comfortable friendly
accommodation on the fringe of
the Lake District near M6
junction 39. Directly on the
"Coast to Coast" walk.*
Bedrooms: 2 double & 2 twin,
2 family rooms.
Bathrooms: 2 public.
Bed & breakfast: max. £16
single, max. £32 double.
Lunch available.
Evening meal 7pm (l.o.
10pm).
Parking for 15.
Credit: Access.

Shap Wells Hotel M
Shap, Nr. Penrith,
CA10 3QU
☎ (093 16) 628 & 744
Fax (093 16) 377
*In a secluded valley in the
Shap Fells. Ideal for exploring
the Lakes, dales and Border
country. Half board price is
based on a minimum 2 night
stay.*
Bedrooms: 10 single,
32 double & 41 twin, 7 family
rooms.
Bathrooms: 88 private,
2 public.
Bed & breakfast: £36-£48
single, £55-£70 double.
Half board: £30-£60.50 daily.
Lunch available.
Evening meal 7pm (l.o.
8.30pm).
Parking for 100.
Open February-December.
Credit: Access, Visa, Diners,
Amex.

TEBAY
Cumbria
Map ref 5B3

Village among high fells
at the north end of the
Lune Gorge.

Carmel House
COMMENDED
Mount Pleasant, Tebay,
CA10 3TH
☎ (058 74) 651
*Colour TV, tea and coffee
facilities. All rooms en-suite.
Quarter of a mile from junction
38 of M6.*

Bedrooms: 2 single, 2 double
& 1 twin.
Bathrooms: 5 private.
Bed & breakfast: £15.50-£18
single, £31-£36 double.
Parking for 5.
Credit: Access, Visa.

Tebay Mountain Lodge Hotel M
Orton, Penrith, CA10 3SB
☎ (058 74) 351
Fax (058 74) 354
*Modern hotel set on the open
Cumbrian fells at the mouth of
Lune Gorge. Ideal for touring
Lakes and Yorkshire Dales.
Access 1 mile north of M6
junction 38.*
Bedrooms: 9 double &
14 twin, 7 family rooms.
Bathrooms: 30 private.
Bed & breakfast: £34.75-£38
single, £40-£48 double.
Half board: from £31.50
daily.
Evening meal 7pm (l.o. 9pm).
Parking for 40.
Credit: Access, Visa, Diners,
Amex.

TEMPLE SOWERBY
Cumbria
Map ref 5B3

Pleasant village with a
green, an old church and
a 4-arch bridge. On the
outskirts is Acorn Bank, a
red sandstone house. Its
walled rose and herb
gardens are open to the
public.

Kings Arms Hotel
Temple Sowerby, Penrith,
CA10 1SB
☎ Kirkby Thore
(076 83) 61211
*Hotel with public bars and
catering for residents and non-
residents. Bar meals and
evening meals available
(reservations only).*
Bedrooms: 3 single, 3 double
& 5 twin.
Bathrooms: 1 private,
3 public; 4 private showers.
Bed & breakfast: from £24
single, £31-£40 double.
Half board: from £35 daily.
Lunch available.
Evening meal 7pm (l.o. 9pm).
Parking for 12.

THORNTHWAITE
Cumbria
Map ref 5A3

3m NW. Keswick
Small village, west of
Keswick, at the southern
tip of Bassenthwaite
Lake. Forest trails in
Thornthwaite Forest.

Swan Hotel M
Thornthwaite, Keswick,
CA12 5SQ
☎ Braithwaite (076 87) 78256
*Set amidst magnificent
Lakeland scenery, in a quiet,
elevated postion overlooking
Skiddaw and the Derwent
Valley.*
Bedrooms: 2 single, 8 double
& 4 twin.
Bathrooms: 8 private,
2 public.
Bed & breakfast: £22.80-
£30.75 single, £45.60-£61.50
double.
Half board: £34-£41.95 daily,
£226-£279 weekly.
Lunch available.
Evening meal 6.45pm (l.o.
8.30pm).
Parking for 63.
Open April-November.
Credit: Access, Visa, Amex.

Thwaite Howe Hotel M
COMMENDED
Thornthwaite, Keswick,
CA12 5SA
☎ Braithwaite (076 87) 78281
*Country house hotel in its own
grounds of 2.5 acres, with
spectacular views of Skiddaw.
Close to Bassenthwaite Lake.*
Bedrooms: 4 double & 4 twin.
Bathrooms: 8 private.
Bed & breakfast: £48-£52
double.
Half board: £34-£36 daily,
£217 weekly.
Evening meal 7pm (l.o. 7pm).
Parking for 12.
Open March-November.

---

*National Crown
ratings were correct
at the time of going
to press but are
subject to change.
Please check at the
time of booking.*

TROUTBECK WINDERMERE
Cumbria
Map ref 5A3

Most of the houses in this
quiet and picturesque
village are 17th C and
some retain their spinning
galleries and oak-
mullioned windows. At
the southern end of the
village is Townend,
owned by the National
Trust and open to the
public. It is an excellently
preserved example of a
yeoman farmer's or
statesman's house.

Mortal Man Hotel M
COMMENDED
Troutbeck, Windermere,
LA23 1PL
☎ (053 94) 33193
*Ideal centre for walking,
touring or for a very quiet and
restful holiday. Beautiful
location with homely charm.*
Bedrooms: 2 single, 4 double
& 6 twin.
Bathrooms: 12 private.
Half board: £45-£50 daily,
£275-£300 weekly.
Evening meal 7.30pm (l.o.
8pm).
Parking for 30.
Open February-November.

ULLSWATER
Cumbria
Map ref 5A3

This beautiful lake, which
is over 7 miles long, runs
from Patterdale to Pooley
Bridge. Lofty peaks
ranging round the lake
make an impressive
background. A steamer
service operates along
the lake between Pooley
Bridge and Glenridding in
the summer.

Cragside Cottage M
APPROVED
Thackthwaite, Ullswater,
Penrith, CA11 0ND
☎ Pooley Bridge
(076 84) 86385
*Mountainside location, 3 miles
north of Ullswater. All rooms
have toilet, shower and
washbasin, tea making
facilities, TV. Reserved
parking space. Meals served in
room. Brochure available.*
Bedrooms: 2 double, 3 family
rooms.
Bathrooms: 5 private.
Bed & breakfast: £29 double.

Evening meal 7pm (l.o. 4pm).
Parking for 5.
Open March-October.
Credit: Access, Visa.
📞2 🅿 ➡ 🅄 🎞 ⬛ 🐾

Glenridding Hotel ⋒
Glenridding, Penrith,
CA11 0PB
☎ Glenridding
(076 84) 82228
Fax (076 84) 82555
🅲🅡 Best Western
*Old established family hotel,
adjacent to the lake and
surrounded by mountains. We
offer value breaks, log fires
and traditional food.*
Bedrooms: 6 single, 17 double
& 16 twin, 5 family rooms.
Bathrooms: 44 private.
Bed & breakfast: from £45
single, from £72 double.
Half board: from £64 daily,
from £320 weekly.
Lunch available.
Evening meal 7pm (l.o.
8.30pm).
Parking for 30.
Open February-December.
Credit: Access, Visa, Diners,
Amex.
📞 🕯 🗄 🕻 🖾 🖵 ➡ 🍴 🔲
🍴 🎞 ⬛ 🍴 🕱 🖵 🆂🅿 🅃

Knotts Mill Country Lodge ⋒
🍃🍃 COMMENDED
Watermillock, Ullswater,
Penrith, CA11 0JN
☎ Pooley Bridge
(076 84) 86472
Fax (076 84) 86699
*Rural location with superb
views. Bedrooms (three on
ground floor) are well-fitted
and there is a comfortable
lounge. Licensed restaurant. 10
minutes from M6, junction 40.*
Bedrooms: 4 double & 1 twin,
3 family rooms.
Bathrooms: 5 private,
1 public.
Bed & breakfast: £19-£25
single, £28-£46 double.
Half board: £22-£31 daily.
Evening meal 7.30pm (l.o.
9pm).
Parking for 12.
Credit: Access, Visa.
📞 🕯 🖵 🍴 🔲 🖵 ➡ ⬛
🕭 ☀ 🕱 🖾 🆂🅿

Moss Crag
Glenridding, Penrith,
CA11 0PA
☎ Glenridding
(076 84) 82500
*By Glenridding Beck, 200
yards from the lake, with views
of Place Fell and Ullswater.
Post office and general store
nearby.*
Bedrooms: 1 single, 4 double
& 1 twin, 1 family room.

Bathrooms: 3 private,
1 public.
Bed & breakfast: £14.50-
£15.50 single, £29-£37 double.
Half board: £25.50-£29.50
daily, £175-£203 weekly.
Evening meal 7.30pm (l.o.
7.30pm).
Parking for 4.
📞5 🖵 🍴 🅄 🔲 ▨ ⅄ ➡ 🎞
🕱 🖾 🅾🅿

Patterdale Hotel ⋒
🍃🍃🍃
Patterdale, Lake Ullswater,
Nr. Penrith, CA11 0NN
☎ Glenridding
(076 84) 82231
*Family-run hotel, within the
same family for 65 years. All
rooms with private facilities,
colour TV and telephone.*
Bedrooms: 14 single,
16 double & 23 twin, 4 family
rooms.
Bathrooms: 57 private,
10 public.
Bed & breakfast: £28-£30
single, £56-£60 double.
Half board: £40-£44 daily,
£250-£280 weekly.
Lunch available.
Evening meal 7pm (l.o. 8pm).
Parking for 100.
Open March-November.
Credit: Access, Visa.
📞 🕯 🕻 🖵 🍴 🔲 ▨ ➡ 🎞
🎞 ⬛ 🍴 ☀ ☀ ☼

Rampsbeck Hotel ⋒
🍃🍃🍃
Watermillock, Ullswater,
CA11 0LP
☎ Pooley Bridge
(076 84) 86442/86671
*Country house hotel in 17 acres
of grounds on the shores of
Lake Ullswater. Superb
location, award-winning
restaurant. All rooms en-suite.*
Bedrooms: 3 single, 11 double
& 3 twin, 2 family rooms.
Bathrooms: 18 private.
Bed & breakfast: £35-£55
single, £60-£120 double.
Half board: £45-£80 daily,
from £300 weekly.
Lunch available.
Evening meal 7pm (l.o. 9pm).
Parking for 40.
Open February-December.
Credit: Access, Visa.
📞5 🅄 ⬛ 🖵 🍴 🔲 ▨ ➡ 🎞 ⬛
🍴 ☼ ☀ 🕱 🖾 🆂🅿 🅃

Swiss Chalet Inn ⋒
🍃🍃🍃 APPROVED
Pooley Bridge, Penrith,
CA10 2NN
☎ (076 84) 86215

---

*Set in charming village on
shores of beautiful Ullswater, 5
miles from M6. All rooms en-
suite.
Swiss/Continental/English
cuisine.*
Bedrooms: 6 double & 1 twin,
2 family rooms.
Bathrooms: 9 private.
Bed & breakfast: £25-£30
single, £40-£48 double.
Lunch available.
Evening meal 6pm (l.o.
9.45pm).
Parking for 40.
Open February-December.
Credit: Access, Visa.
📞 🗄 🅲🅡 🖵 🔲 ▨ 🎞 ⬛
🍴 🕱 🅃

Ullswater Hotel ⋒
🍃🍃🍃🍃 COMMENDED
Lake Ullswater, Glenridding,
Penrith, CA11 0PA
☎ Glenridding
(076 84) 82444 Telex 58164
Fax (076 84) 82303
*Standing in 20 acres on the
lakeshore, the Ullswater enjoys
the peace and beauty of the
Lake District.*
Bedrooms: 6 single, 12 double
& 21 twin, 9 family rooms.
Bathrooms: 48 private.
Bed & breakfast: £44-£55
single, £88-£110 double.
Half board: £55-£65 daily,
£350-£420 weekly.
Lunch available.
Evening meal 7pm (l.o.
9.30pm).
Parking for 180.
Credit: Access, Visa, Diners,
Amex.
📞 🕯 🗄 🕻 🖾 🖵 🍴 ⬛
➡ 🎞 🖲 🖾 🎞 ⬛ 🍴 🕯 🕭
🖾 ♩ ➤ ☀ 🅾🅿 ☼ 🆂🅿 🅃

Wreay Farm Guest House ⋒
Listed COMMENDED
Watermillock, Ullswater,
CA11 0LT
☎ (076 84) 86296
*Comfortable guesthouse in
beautiful area, overlooking
Lake Ullswater. Home cooking
by proprietor.*
Bedrooms: 7 double, 3 family
rooms.
Bathrooms: 5 private,
2 public.
Half board: £24.10-£33.50
daily, £168.70-£218.40 weekly.
Evening meal 7.30pm.
Parking for 12.
Open March-November.
📞 🕯 🖵 🔲 🍴 ▨ ➡ 🎞 🎞
🕭 🖾

> *The enquiry coupons at the back will
> help you when contacting proprietors.*

Market town lying
between green fells and
the sea. The lighthouse
on the Hoad is a
monument to Sir John
Barrow, founder of the
Royal Geographical
Society.
*Tourist Information
Centre ☎ (0229) 57120*

Hill Foot Hotel
Hill Foot, Ulverston,
LA12 7ES
☎ (0229) 52166
*Victorian country house in
lovely gardens. All rooms en-
suite. Bar and steakhouse
restaurant.*
Bedrooms: 2 single, 6 double
& 1 twin, 1 family room.
Bathrooms: 10 private.
Bed & breakfast: £30-£40
single, £39-£60 double.
Lunch available.
Evening meal 7pm (l.o.
9.15pm).
Parking for 70.
Credit: Access, Visa, Diners.
📞 🕯 🗄 🕻 🖵 🔲 🍴 ▨ 🎞
🎞 ⬛ 🍴 🕭 🕯 ☀ ☼ 🕱 🅾🅿 ▨
🆂🅿 🖾

Lonsdale House Hotel ⋒
🍃🍃🍃
Daltongate, Ulverston,
LA12 7BD
☎ (0229) 52598
Fax (0229) 581260
*Located in beautiful walled
garden. All rooms with
bathroom, TV, video, tea/coffee
facilities, trouser press and
telephone.*
Bedrooms: 8 single, 6 double
& 5 twin, 1 family room.
Bathrooms: 20 private.
Bed & breakfast: £25-£40
single, £46-£60 double.
Half board: £37.50-£52.50
daily.
Lunch available.
Evening meal 7pm (l.o. 9pm).
Parking for 2.
Credit: Access, Visa, Diners,
Amex.
📞 🕯 🕻 🖵 🔲 🍴 ▨ 🎞 ➡
🎞 ⬛ 🍴 🕭 ☀ ▨ 🆂🅿 🖾 🅃

Trinity House Hotel
🍃🍃🍃 COMMENDED
Prince's St., Ulverston,
LA12 7NB
☎ (0229) 57639
*Former Georgian rectory,
elegant licensed restaurant
with local food. En-suite
bedrooms are spacious and
stylishly decorated.*

Continued ▶

ULVERSTON
Continued

Bedrooms: 1 single, 4 double, 1 family room.
Bathrooms: 6 private.
Bed & breakfast: £35-£45 single, £48-£60 double.
Half board: £36-£42 daily, £225-£265 weekly.
Evening meal 7pm (l.o. 9pm).
Parking for 7.
Open February-December.
Credit: Access, Visa, Amex.

WASDALE
Cumbria
Map ref 5A3

In the valley lies Wastwater, the deepest English lake. A road leads along its north-west side as far as Wasdale Head, a starting point for ascending the majestic Scafell peaks and other mountains.

Burnthwaite
Wasdale Head, Seascale, CA20 1EX
☎ (069 74) 26242
In the Valley of Wasdale at the bottom of Great Gable, ideal for walking and climbing.
Bedrooms: 2 single, 3 double & 2 twin, 1 family room.
Bathrooms: 2 public.
Bed & breakfast: from £13.50 single, from £27 double.
Half board: from £18.50 daily.
Evening meal 7pm.
Parking for 10.

Low Wood Hall Hotel M
😃😃 COMMENDED
Nether Wasdale, Wasdale, CA20 1ET
☎ Wasdale (094 67) 26289
Gracious Victorian country house with fine views across Wasdale. Close to Scafell, Wastwater and sea. Bar, billiard room. Extensive dinner menu.
Bedrooms: 6 double & 7 twin.
Bathrooms: 13 private.
Bed & breakfast: £30-£34 single, £48-£53 double.
Half board: £32-£36 daily, £196-£220 weekly.
Evening meal 6.30pm (l.o. 8.45pm).
Parking for 24.
Credit: Access, Visa.

Wasdale Head Inn M
Wasdale Head, Nr. Gosforth, CA20 1EX
☎ Wasdale (094 67) 26229
Fax (094 67) 26334
Traditional mountain inn with modern facilities and secluded setting, at the head of one of Lakeland's remote and unspoilt valleys. Birthplace of rock climbing in Great Britain.
Bedrooms: 2 single, 4 double & 2 twin, 2 family rooms.
Bathrooms: 10 private.
Half board: £49.50-£51.50 daily, £325-£339.50 weekly.
Lunch available.
Evening meal 7.30pm (l.o. 7.30pm).
Parking for 50.
Open March-November.
Credit: Access, Visa.

WHITEHAVEN
Cumbria
Map ref 5A3

Small port on the west coast. The town was developed in the 17th C and many of the fine buildings of that period have been preserved.
Tourist Information Centre ☎ *(0946) 695678*

Corkickle Guest House
1, Corkickle, Whitehaven, CA28 8AA
☎ (0946) 692073
Small homely guesthouse offering high standards of comfort. Within easy walking distance of town centre.
Bedrooms: 3 single, 1 double & 2 twin.
Bathrooms: 2 private, 1 public; 3 private showers.
Bed & breakfast: £19-£23 single, £33-£36 double.
Parking for 2.

Howgate Hotel M
Howgate, Whitehaven, CA28 6PL
☎ (0946) 66286
Family-owned and run hotel 2 miles from Whitehaven. Easy access to Lake District and West Cumbria.
Bedrooms: 4 single, 3 double & 12 twin, 1 family room.
Bathrooms: 20 private.
Bed & breakfast: £42-£52 single, £56-£66 double.
Half board: £57-£67 daily, £319-£469 weekly.
Lunch available.
Evening meal 7pm (l.o. 9.30pm).

Parking for 100.
Credit: Access, Visa, Diners, Amex.

WINDERMERE
Cumbria
Map ref 5A3

This tourist centre was a tiny hamlet before the introduction of the railway in 1847. The town adjoins Bowness which is on the lakeside. It is an inland water centre for sailing and boating. A scenic way of seeing the lake is to take a trip on a passenger steamer. Windermere Steamboat Museum has a fine collection of old steamboats.
Tourist Information Centre ☎ *(053 94) 46499*

Aaron Slack M
😃😃
48 Ellerthwaite Road, Windermere, LA23 2BS
☎ (053 94) 44649
Small friendly guesthouse in a quiet part of Windermere, close to all amenities and concentrating on personal service.
Bedrooms: 2 double & 1 twin.
Bathrooms: 3 private.
Bed & breakfast: £18-£19 single, £30-£32 double.
Evening meal 7pm (l.o. 7pm).
Credit: Access, Visa.

Almeria House M
😃😃
17 Broad St., Windermere, LA23 2AB
☎ (053 94) 43026
Homely accommodation with a pleasant atmosphere, close to all amenities.
Bedrooms: 4 double, 1 family room.
Bathrooms: 3 private, 1 public.
Bed & breakfast: £11-£17 single, £21-£35 double.
Half board: £17-£24.50 daily, £118-£170 weekly.
Evening meal 6pm (l.o. 4pm).
Open February-October.

Applegarth Hotel M
College Rd., Windermere, LA23 2AE
☎ (053 94) 43206

Elegant Victorian mansion house with individually designed bedrooms and four-poster suites with lake and fell views.
Bedrooms: 4 single, 6 double & 1 twin, 5 family rooms.
Bathrooms: 16 private.
Bed & breakfast: £20-£30 single, £32-£70 double.
Parking for 25.
Credit: Access, Visa, Amex.

The Archway M
😃😃 COMMENDED
13 College Rd., Windermere, LA23 1BY
☎ (053 94) 45613
Impeccable Victorian stone house, beautifully furnished throughout. Antiques, interesting paintings, fresh flowers, mountain views, gourmet home cooking.
Bedrooms: 1 single, 2 double & 2 twin.
Bathrooms: 4 private, 1 public.
Bed & breakfast: £16-£23 single, £36-£48 double.
Half board: £26.50-£34.50 daily.
Evening meal 6.45pm (l.o. 4pm).
Parking for 3.

Belmont Manor Hotel M
Windermere, LA23 1LN
☎ (053 94) 33316
New hotel in 7 acres of beautiful grounds. Whirlpools in every bathroom. Emphasis on food and service. 10% discount on weekly bookings.
Bedrooms: 10 double & 4 twin.
Bathrooms: 14 private.
Bed & breakfast: from £48 single, from £75 double.
Half board: from £50 daily.
Lunch available.
Evening meal 7.30pm.

Belsfield Guest House M
😃😃 COMMENDED
4 Belsfield Terrace, Kendal Rd., Bowness-on-Windermere, LA23 3EQ
☎ Windermere (053 94) 45823
Family-run guesthouse in the heart of Bowness, 2 minutes' walk from the lake front.
Bedrooms: 2 single, 2 double & 1 twin, 4 family rooms.

Bathrooms: 9 private.
Bed & breakfast: £20-£25.50
single, £36-£43 double.
🛏🛁📺🆙🔊📼🍴🖲🅿
♿ ✕ SP

Birch House ♨

11 Birch St., Windermere,
LA23 1EG
☎ (053 94) 45070
*Small family-run guesthouse in
quiet street, near to shops,
restaurants and station.*
Bedrooms: 4 double.
Bathrooms: 4 private.
Bed & breakfast: £12-£20
single, £24-£36 double.
🛏10📺🖲🆙 🔊📼🖲✕
🖲 OAP 🔌 SP T

Biskey Howe Villa Hotel ♨
🏵🏵🏵

Craig Walk, Bowness-on-
Windermere, LA23 3AX
☎ (053 94) 43988
Fax (053 94) 88379
*In a peaceful spot above Lake
Windermere, commanding
beautiful views of the lake and
surrounding mountains. Close
to Bowness Bay.*
Bedrooms: 6 double & 2 twin,
3 family rooms.
Bathrooms: 10 private,
1 public.
Bed & breakfast: £25-£30
single, £45-£55 double.
Half board: £35-£42 daily.
Evening meal 6.30pm (l.o.
7.30pm).
Parking for 11.
🛏🕯📀📺🖲🆙🔊🛏📼
📺🖲🏋🕈✕🔌 SP T

Bordriggs Country House Hotel ♨
🏵🏵🏵

Longtail Hill, Bowness on
Windermere, Windermere,
LA23 3LD
☎ (053 94) 43567
Fax (053 94) 46949
*Charming country house in
beautiful gardens, with pool.
Graciously appointed, elegant
lounge, pretty bedrooms. Lake
and golf-course nearby.*
Bedrooms: 1 single, 6 double
& 2 twin, 2 family rooms.
Bathrooms: 11 private.
Bed & breakfast: from £27.50
single, from £50 double.
Half board: from £40 daily,
from £266 weekly.
Evening meal 7pm (l.o.
8.30pm).
Parking for 20.
🛏10🛁📺🕯📀📺 🖲
🛏🖲🏊♿🕈🏋🕈✕✕🖲
SP T

Bowfell Cottage ♨
🏵🏵

Middle Entrance Drive,
Storrs Park, Bowness-on-
Windermere, LA23 3JY
☎ Windermere
(053 94) 44835
*Cottage in a delightful setting,
about 1 mile south of Bowness
just off the A5074, offering
traditional Lakeland
hospitality.*
Bedrooms: 1 double & 1 twin,
1 family room.
Bathrooms: 1 public.
Bed & breakfast: £16.50-
£17.50 single, £30-£32 double.
Half board: £22.50-£23.50
daily, £150-£155 weekly.
Evening meal 6pm (l.o. 8pm).
Parking for 2.
🛏🅱📺🕯🆙🔊 🛏📼🖲
🖲🕈🏋☀🔊 OAP🔌 SP T

Braemount House Hotel ♨
🏵🏵🏵 COMMENDED

Sunny Bank Rd.,
Windermere, LA23 2EN
☎ (053 94) 45967
*Small, comfortable family-run
hotel with a friendly
atmosphere, offering the finest
in cuisine, good wines and a
cheerful welcome.*
Bedrooms: 4 double & 1 twin,
1 family room.
Bathrooms: 6 private.
Bed & breakfast: max. £34.50
single, £49-£64 double.
Half board: £38-£45.50 daily,
£255.25-£305.25 weekly.
Evening meal 8.30pm.
Parking for 6.
Credit: Access, Visa.
🛏🕯📀📺🖲🆙🔊 🖲📼🛏
🖲🛏✕🔌 SP T

Broadlands Guest House ♨
Listed COMMENDED

19 Broad St., Windermere,
LA23 2AB
☎ (053 94) 46532
*Small, friendly traditional
Lakeland guesthouse.
Comfortable accommodation
and good breakfasts.
Convenient for lake, stations,
tours, shops, restaurants,
walking and parking.*
Bedrooms: 4 double & 1 twin,
1 family room.
Bathrooms: 3 private,
1 public.
Bed & breakfast: £24-£36
double.
Credit: Access, Visa.
🛏📺🆙🔊📼🖲✕🛏📼
🖲🛏✕ SP

Brooklands ♨
🏵🏵 COMMENDED

Ferry View, Windermere,
LA23 3JB
☎ (053 94) 42344
*Comfortable guesthouse on the
outskirts of Bowness village,
with fine lake and mountain
views. Accent on food and
hospitality.*
Bedrooms: 1 single, 1 double
& 1 twin, 3 family rooms.
Bathrooms: 3 private,
1 public.
Bed & breakfast: £18-£20
single, £32-£38 double.
Parking for 6.
🛏📺🕯 OAP🔊 🔊🖲📼🖲
🖲 OAP🔌 SP

The Burn How Garden House Hotel & Motel ♨
🏵🏵🏵🏵 COMMENDED

Back Belsfield Rd.,
Windermere, LA23 3HH
☎ (053 94) 46226
*Unique combination of
Victorian houses and private
chalets in secluded gardens in
the heart of a picturesque
village. Full facilities. Four-
poster beds available.*
Bedrooms: 2 single, 8 double
& 8 twin, 8 family rooms.
Bathrooms: 26 private.
Bed & breakfast: £39-£46
single, £58-£72 double.
Half board: £43-£59 daily,
£190-£320 weekly.
Lunch available.
Evening meal 7pm (l.o.
9.15pm).
Parking for 30.
Credit: Access, Visa, Amex.
🛏🛁🖲🕯🅱📺🖲 🖲
🖲🛏🕈📼🕈♿☀✕
🔊 SP T

Cedar Manor Hotel ♨
🏵🏵🏵🏵 COMMENDED

Ambleside Rd., Windermere,
LA23 1AX
☎ (053 94) 43192
*Traditional Lakeland house
with interesting architectural
features. Elegantly furnished
and in a country garden
setting. Some rooms have lake
views.*
Bedrooms: 7 double & 3 twin,
2 family rooms.
Bathrooms: 12 private.
Bed & breakfast: £27-£43
single, £54-£66 double.
Half board: £35-£43 daily,
£203-£259 weekly.
Evening meal 7.30pm (l.o.
8.30pm).
Parking for 20.
Credit: Access, Visa.
🛏🛁🖲🕯🅱📺🖲 🖲
🛏🖲🅱🖲🕈♪☀🔊 SP
🖲 T

Clifton Guest House ♨
🏵🏵 COMMENDED

28 Ellerthwaite Rd.,
Windermere, LA23 2AH
☎ (053 94) 44968
*Small friendly guesthouse in a
very quiet part of the village,
about 4 minutes' walk from the
shops and restaurants.*
Bedrooms: 2 single, 3 double,
1 family room.
Bathrooms: 1 private,
1 public; 4 private showers.
Bed & breakfast: £12-£16
single, £25-£32 double.
Parking for 4.
🛏📺🆙🔊🛏📼🖲🖲
✕ 🖲

Crag Brow Cottage Hotel ♨
🏵🏵🏵🏵 COMMENDED

Helm Rd., Bowness-on-
Windermere, LA23 3BU
☎ Windermere
(053 94) 44080
*In heart of Bowness, 2 minutes
to lake. High standard en-suite
rooms, a la carte and table
d'hote restaurant. Ample
parking.*
Bedrooms: 10 double, 1 family
room.
Bathrooms: 11 private.
Bed & breakfast: £45-£60
single, £55-£69 double.
Half board: £45-£55 daily,
£275-£325 weekly.
Lunch available.
Evening meal 6.30pm (l.o.
9.30pm).
Parking for 30.
Credit: Access, Visa.
🛏🕯📀📺🖲🆙 🔊📼🖲
🖲🕈☀✕✕ SP 🖲

Cranleigh Hotel ♨
🏵🏵🏵 COMMENDED

Kendal Rd., Bowness-on-
Windermere, LA23 3EW
☎ Windermere
(053 94) 43293
*Comfortable, quiet hotel with
private parking, yet only two
minutes from the lake and the
village shops and restaurants.*
Bedrooms: 2 single, 9 double
& 3 twin, 1 family room.
Bathrooms: 15 private.
Bed & breakfast: £46-£50
double.
Half board: £36-£38 daily.
Evening meal 7pm (l.o. 9pm).
Parking for 15.
Open March-November.
Credit: Access, Visa, Amex.
🛏5🛁📺🖲🕯✕🛏📼🖲
🖲🛏✕🛏🖲 SP T

Dene Crest ♨

13 Woodland Rd.,
Windermere, LA23 2AE
☎ (053 94) 44979

Continued ▶

WINDERMERE
Continued

Small and friendly guesthouse which has been modernised throughout, offering home cooking and a choice on all menus.
Bedrooms: 3 double, 2 family rooms.
Bathrooms: 5 private.
Bed & breakfast: £15-£20 single, £25-£36 double.
Half board: £19.50-£25 daily, £115-£170 weekly.
Evening meal 7pm (l.o. 4pm).
ら32 ﾛ♥ â ▨ ⅵ ⼌ ⼀ ⼀
â ☐ ⼌ SP ☐

Denehurst ⋀
♛♛
40 Queens Drive, Windermere, LA23 3EL
☎ (053 94) 44710
Breakfasts are our business. Different one each day. Good beds, hot showers, warm welcome. Book now. Enjoy your stay.
Bedrooms: 4 double & 1 twin, 1 family room.
Bathrooms: 4 private, 1 public.
Bed & breakfast: £28-£34 double.
ら �ﾛ ♥ UL â ⅵ ⼌ TV
▥ â ▶ ▨ SP

Eastbourne Hotel ⋀
♛♛
Biskey Howe Rd., Bowness-on-Windermere, LA23 2JR
☎ Windermere
(053 94) 43525
Small family-run hotel offering private facilities and a friendly welcome. Located in a quiet position close to Lake Windermere, an ideal central touring base.
Bedrooms: 2 single, 4 double, 2 family rooms.
Bathrooms: 6 private, 1 public; 1 private shower.
Bed & breakfast: £14.50-£21 single, £29-£42 double.
Half board: £25.50-£32 daily, £173-£216 weekly.
Evening meal 6.30pm.
Parking for 3.
ら ⼀ ♥ â ⅵ ⼀ ▥ â ∪
⼀ ▨ ☐ ⼌ SP

Elim Bank Hotel ⋀
Lake Rd., Bowness-on-Windermere, LA23 2JJ
☎ (053 94) 44810
Outstanding Victorian slate-built house, close to all amenities. Noted for its friendly atmosphere, comfort and cuisine.
Bedrooms: 1 single, 5 double, 3 family rooms.

Bathrooms: 7 private, 1 public.
Bed & breakfast: £20-£22 single, £36-£45 double.
Half board: £28-£32.50 daily, £182-£213.50 weekly.
Lunch available.
Evening meal 6.30pm (l.o. 9.30pm).
Parking for 12.
Credit: Access, Visa.

Fairfield Country House Hotel ⋀
♛♛ APPROVED
Brantfell Rd., Bowness-on-Windermere, LA23 3AE
☎ Windermere
(053 94) 46565
Small, friendly 200-year-old country house with half an acre of peaceful secluded gardens. 2 minutes' walk from Lake Windermere and village.
Bedrooms: 1 single, 3 double & 1 twin, 3 family rooms.
Bathrooms: 7 private, 1 public.
Bed & breakfast: £35-£37 single, £48-£54 double.
Lunch available.
Parking for 14.
Credit: Access, Visa.

Fayrer Holme Country House ⋀
Upper Storrs Rd., Bowness-on-Windermere, LA23 3JP
☎ Windermere
(053 94) 88195
Claims to be "the best B&B in the world - or nearly!"
Beautiful, well-appointed country house in splendid grounds overlooking Lake Windermere.
Bedrooms: 5 double & 1 twin, 1 family room.
Bathrooms: 7 private.
Bed & breakfast: £25-£42.50 single, £50-£65 double.
Parking for 12.
Credit: Access, Visa.
ら â ⼀ ♥ ⅵ ⼀ ⼌ ⼀
▥ â ♪ ∪ ▶ ⼌ ▨ SP

Gilpin Lodge Country House Hotel & Restaurant ⋀
♛♛♛ HIGHLY COMMENDED
Crook Rd., Windermere, LA23 3NE
☎ (053 94) 88818
Elegant and tranquil family-run hotel in rural setting, 2 miles from Windermere. Sumptuous bedrooms. Lovingly prepared food. Telephone 0800 269460 (toll free).
Bedrooms: 7 double & 1 twin, 1 family room.

Bathrooms: 9 private.
Bed & breakfast: £45-£59 single, £70-£108 double.
Half board: £45-£69 daily, £209-£375 weekly.
Lunch available.
Evening meal 7pm (l.o. 9pm).
Parking for 40.
Credit: Access, Visa, Diners, Amex.
ら9 â ⼀ ⼉ ⼀ ☐ ⼌ â ⅵ
⼌ â ∪ ⼀ ⼌ ☐ ⼌ SP ☐

Glenburn ⋀
♛♛♛ COMMENDED
New Rd., Windermere, LA23 2EE
☎ (053 94) 42649
Newly refurbished hotel offering a high standard of comfort, cleanliness and service. Ideal location between Windermere and the lake.
Bedrooms: 3 single, 8 double & 1 twin, 4 family rooms.
Bathrooms: 16 private, 1 public.
Bed & breakfast: £42-£56 double.
Half board: £33.50-£40 daily, £219-£259 weekly.
Evening meal 7pm (l.o. 4pm).
Parking for 17.
Credit: Access, Visa, Amex.
ら5 â ⼀ ⼉ ⼀ ☐ ⼌ â ⅵ ⼌
⼀ TV â ⼀ ⼀ ▨ SP ☐

Glencree Hotel ⋀
♛♛
Lake Rd., Windermere, LA23 2EQ
☎ (053 94) 45822
A delightful, elegantly furnished and decorated house. Lovely woodland outlook. Convenient location, warm hospitality.
Bedrooms: 4 double & 1 twin.
Bathrooms: 5 private.
Bed & breakfast: £42-£60 double.
Half board: £38.50-£47.50 daily.
Evening meal 7pm.
Parking for 9.
Open February-November.
Credit: Access, Visa.
ら14 ⼀ ♥ ⅵ ⼀ ▥ â ⼀
▥

Glenville ⋀
♛♛♛
Lake Rd., Windermere, LA23 2EQ
☎ (053 94) 43371
Midway between Windermere and Bowness and perfectly positioned for access to all amenities. The lake is an easy 10 minute walk.
Bedrooms: 1 single, 6 double & 1 twin, 1 family room.
Bathrooms: 9 private.

Bed & breakfast: £17.50-£22 single, £35-£44 double.
Evening meal 6.30pm (l.o. 2pm).
Parking for 12.
Open February-November.
ら ⼀ ♥ â ⅵ ⼌ ⼀ ▥
â ⼀ ▨ SP ☐

Hawksmoor ⋀
♛♛♛ COMMENDED
Lake Rd., Windermere, LA23 2EQ
☎ (059 34) 42110
Ivy-covered house with a large garden to the side and woodlands to the rear. Private car park.
Bedrooms: 7 double, 3 family rooms.
Bathrooms: 10 private.
Bed & breakfast: £25-£30 single, £37-£55 double.
Half board: £28.50-£37.50 daily, £180-£240 weekly.
Evening meal 6.30pm (l.o. 5.30pm).
Parking for 12.
Open February-November.
ら6 â ⼀ ⼌ ⼀ ⼌ ⼀ ▥
â

Heatherbank Guest House ⋀
♛♛♛ COMMENDED
13 Birch St., Windermere, LA23 1EG
☎ (053 94) 46503
Family-run Victorian guesthouse, quiet and comfortable. Convenient for local amenities and beauty spots. Ideal for sightseers and walkers alike. Residential licensed bar.
Bedrooms: 3 double & 1 twin, 1 family room.
Bathrooms: 5 private.
Bed & breakfast: £26-£40 double.
Half board: £25-£32 daily.
Evening meal 7pm (l.o. midday).
Parking for 4.
Credit: Access, Visa.
ら â ⼀ ♥ UL â ⼌ ⼀ TV
▥ â ⼀ ▨ ⼌ SP ☐

Hideaway Hotel ⋀
♛♛♛ COMMENDED
Phoenix Way, Windermere, LA23 1DB
☎ (053 94) 43070
Friendly, small hotel away from the main road, with a pleasant garden, well-trained chefs, open fires and well-equipped, comfortable bedrooms.
Bedrooms: 2 single, 10 double & 1 twin, 3 family rooms.
Bathrooms: 15 private.
Bed & breakfast: £31-£44 single, £62-£90 double.

Half board: £36-£50 daily,
£217-£308 weekly.
Evening meal 7.30pm.
Parking for 16.
Credit: Access, Visa.
♿ 🅿 ⚑ 🛏 🔌 ☎ ‖ V ✂
♨ ▥ ⌂ ↻ 🐾 🐕 SP T
🅰 Display advertisement
appears on page 560.

Hilton House Hotel M
😊😊

New Rd., Windermere,
LA23 2EE
☎ (053 94) 43934
*Large Lakeland residence in a
woodland setting. Colour TV
in all rooms. Golf, riding,
boating nearby. Non-smoking
rooms available.*
Bedrooms: 1 single, 4 double,
1 family room.
Bathrooms: 4 private,
1 public.
Bed & breakfast: £15-£17
single, £34-£40 double.
Parking for 14.
Open March-October,
December.
♿ 🅿 🔌 ✂ ♨ TV ▥ ⌂ ❉
🐕 T

Holbeck Ghyll Country House Hotel M
😊😊😊 COMMENDED

Holbeck Lane, Windermere,
LA23 1LU
☎ Ambleside (053 94) 32375
Fax (053 94) 34743
*Magnificent 19th C country
house overlooking Lake
Windermere. Set in own
peaceful grounds. Spacious
lounges, log fires.*
Bedrooms: 10 double &
3 twin, 1 family room.
Bathrooms: 14 private.
Half board: £45-£70 daily.
Evening meal 7pm (l.o. 9pm).
Parking for 22.
Open February-December.
Credit: Access, Visa.
♿ 🅿 ☎ ‖ 🔌 🏵 ⚑ V ✂
♨ ▥ ⌂ ♈ 🍴 ☀ ↻ ♪ ♭ ❉
🐕 🐾 SP 🏠

Holly Lodge M
😊 APPROVED

6 College Rd., Windermere,
LA23 1BX
☎ (053 94) 43873
*Traditional Lakeland stone
guesthouse, built in 1854. In a
quiet area off the main road,
close to the village centre,
buses, railway station and all
amenities.*
Bedrooms: 1 single, 5 double
& 2 twin, 3 family rooms.
Bathrooms: 3 private,
3 public.
Bed & breakfast: £15-£20
single, £30-£40 double.

Half board: £23.50-£28.50
daily, £164.50-£199.50
weekly.
Evening meal 7pm (l.o.
10am).
Parking for 7.
♿ 🅿 ⚑ 🛏 ‖ V ⌂ ▥ ⚑ 🍴
🐕 🐾 T

Holly Park House M
😊😊 COMMENDED

1 Park Rd., Windermere,
LA23 2AW
☎ (053 94) 42107
*Handsome stone-built
Victorian guesthouse with
spacious rooms. Quiet area,
convenient for village shops
and coach/rail services.*
Bedrooms: 6 double.
Bathrooms: 6 private.
Bed & breakfast: £20-£27.50
single, £29-£40 double.
Parking for 3.
Open March-October.
♿ 🅿 🔌 UL V ✂ ⚑ ⌂ ⚑
🐾 🐕 SP

Holly-Wood Guest House M
Holly Rd., Windermere,
LA23 2AF
☎ (053 94) 42219
*Family-run guesthouse in a
quiet, central position. Within
walking distance of rail and
bus terminus. Convenient for
all amenities.*
Bedrooms: 1 single, 2 double
& 2 twin, 2 family rooms.
Bathrooms: 2 private,
2 public.
Bed & breakfast: £12.50-£14
single, £25-£29 double.
Open March-November.
♿ 🅿 🔌 🏵 ‖ ✂ ⚑ TV ▥
🐾 🐕 SP

Kirkwood Guest House M
😊😊

Prince's Rd., Windermere,
LA23 2DD
☎ (053 94) 43907
*Traditional Lakeland-stone
house on a quiet corner,
between Windermere and
Bowness. Convenient for all
Lakeland activities and
amenities.*
Bedrooms: 1 double, 6 family
rooms.
Bathrooms: 4 private,
1 public.
Bed & breakfast: £28-£40
double.
Parking for 1.
Credit: Access, Visa.
♿ 🅿 🔌 🏵 UL ‖ V ✂ ⚑
▥ ⌂ 🐕 SP

Knoll Hotel M
😊😊

Lake Rd., Windermere,
LA23 2JF
☎ (053 94) 43756
*In quiet grounds, with
magnificent views overlooking
Lake Windermere and the
mountains. Free use of
Parklands leisure club.*
Bedrooms: 4 single, 3 double
& 1 twin, 4 family rooms.
Bathrooms: 9 private,
1 public.
Bed & breakfast: £22-£27
single, £54 double.
Half board: £34.50-£49.50
daily, £235-£475 weekly.
Evening meal 7pm (l.o.
7.30pm).
Parking for 15.
Open March-October.
Credit: Access, Visa.
♿ 3 ☎ 🔌 🏵 ‖ V ⚑ TV
▥ ⌂ ❉ 🐕 🐾 DAP SP 🏠 T

Lakes Hotel M
😊😊

1 High St., Windermere,
LA23 1AF
☎ (053 94) 42751 & 88133 &
Fax (053 94) 46026
*Superb Victorian building of
local stone. All rooms with
colour TV. 150 yards from
rail/bus stations and close to
shops. "Los Angeles Times"
recommended. Local mini-
coach tours available.*
Bedrooms: 1 single, 5 double
& 2 twin, 1 family room.
Bathrooms: 8 private;
1 private shower.
Bed & breakfast: £22.50-£25
single, £38-£44 double.
Evening meal 6.30pm (l.o.
8pm).
Parking for 10.
Credit: Access, Visa.
♿ 🅿 🔌 🏵 ‖ V ⚑ TV ▥
⌂ 🐾 DAP SP 🏠 T

Lakeside Hotel on Windermere M
😊😊😊😊 COMMENDED

Newby Bridge, LA12 8AT
☎ (053 95) 31207
Telex 65149
🅒🅡 Consort
*Traditional Victorian hotel, by
steamer jetty and Lakeside-to-
Haverthwaite steam train.
Boat launching and moorings
available. Summer terrace,
refurbished rooms, restaurant
and lounges have magnificent
views over the lake. New
conservatory.*
Bedrooms: 2 single, 31 double
& 37 twin, 4 family rooms.
Bathrooms: 74 private.
Bed & breakfast: £40-£62
single, £90-£124 double.
Half board: £50-£85 daily,
from £300 weekly.
Lunch available.

Evening meal 6pm (l.o.
9.30pm).
Parking for 100.
Credit: Access, Visa, Diners,
Amex.
♿ 🅿 🔌 🏵 ☎ 🔌 🏵 ‖ V
⚑ ⦿ ▥ ⌂ 🍴 ♨ ↻ ↻ ♪
⚑ ❉ 🐾 DAP SP 🏠 T

Langdale Chase Hotel M
😊😊😊😊

Windermere, LA23 1LW
☎ Ambleside (053 94) 32201
*Country house hotel in
landscaped gardens on the
edge of Lake Windermere.*
Bedrooms: 7 single, 13 double
& 10 twin, 1 family room.
Bathrooms: 30 private,
2 public.
Bed & breakfast: £47-£58
single, £94-£120 double.
Lunch available.
Evening meal 7pm (l.o.
8.45pm).
Parking for 50.
Credit: Access, Visa, Diners,
Amex.
♿ 🅿 🔌 ☎ ⚑ 🔌 🏵 ‖ V
⚑ ⦿ ▥ ⌂ 🍴 ♔ ❉ 🐕 🐾
SP

Laurieston Guesthouse M
😊😊 APPROVED

40 Oak St., Windermere,
LA23 1EN
☎ (053 94) 44253
*Traditional stone-built house,
offering en-suite facilities in a
warm, friendly atmosphere.
Non-smokers only please.*
Bedrooms: 3 double & 1 twin,
1 family room.
Bathrooms: 2 private,
1 public.
Bed & breakfast: £15-£25
single, £30-£36 double.
Half board: £24-£27 daily,
£160-£180 weekly.
Evening meal 7pm (l.o. 8pm).
♿ 🅿 🔌 ☎ 🔌 🏵 ‖ V ▥ ⌂
🐕 🐾 SP

Lindeth Fell Country House Hotel M
😊😊😊😊 COMMENDED

Windermere, LA23 3JP
☎ (053 94) 43286 & 44287
*Beautifully situated in
magnificent private grounds on
the hill above Lake
Windermere, Lindeth Fell
offers brilliant views, cooking
to Cordon Bleu standards and
elegant surroundings. All
bedrooms have full facilities.*
Bedrooms: 2 single, 3 double
& 5 twin, 2 family rooms.
Bathrooms: 14 private.
Half board: £45-£55 daily,
£300-£365 weekly.
Evening meal 7.30pm (l.o.
8.30pm).

Continued ▶

WINDERMERE

Continued

Parking for 20.
Open March-November.
Credit: Access, Visa.

Linthwaite House Hotel. M
COMMENDED

Crook Rd., Bowness-on-
Windermere, LA23 3JA
☎ Windermere
(053 94) 88600 & Fax
(053 94) 88601
*Peaceful location in 14 acres of
gardens, 1 mile south of village
and with panoramic views over
the lake.*
Bedrooms: 1 single, 10 double
& 7 twin.
Bathrooms: 18 private.
Bed & breakfast: £35-£80
single, £59-£99 double.
Half board: £49-£57 daily,
£295-£390 weekly.
Lunch available.
Evening meal 7.15pm (l.o.
9pm).
Parking for 30.
Credit: Access, Visa, Diners,
Amex.

Little Beck House M
APPROVED

3 Park Avenue, Windermere,
LA23 2AR
☎ (053 94) 88014
*Warm, friendly family-run
guesthouse, quietly situated a
few minutes from Windermere
town centre. Colour TV in all
rooms.*
Bedrooms: 1 single, 4 double.
Bathrooms: 2 public.
Bed & breakfast: £15-£18
single, £28-£32 double.
Half board: £22-£25 daily,
£140-£165 weekly.
Evening meal (l.o. 9pm).
Open March-December.
Credit: Access, Visa.

Lonsdale Hotel M
APPROVED

Lake Rd., Bowness-on-
Windermere, LA23 2JJ
☎ Windermere
(053 94) 43348
*In Bowness on the main road
from Windermere. Within easy
walking distance of the shops,
buses and lake shore.*
Bedrooms: 2 double, 7 family
rooms.
Bathrooms: 9 private.

Bed & breakfast: £19.50-£35
single, £39-£50 double.
Parking for 10.
Open February-October.
Credit: Access, Visa.

Low Spring Wood Hotel M
COMMENDED

Thornbarrow Rd.,
Windermere, LA23 2DF
☎ (053 94) 46383
*Secluded hotel in its own
grounds with lovely lake and
fell views, midway between
Bowness and Windermere.
Dogs welcome.*
Bedrooms: 1 single, 4 double
& 1 twin, 1 family room.
Bathrooms: 7 private.
Bed & breakfast: £22-£26
single, £40-£52 double.
Half board: £30-£38 daily,
£210-£266 weekly.
Evening meal 7.30pm (l.o.
8pm).
Parking for 12.
Open March-December.

Low Wood Hotel M
COMMENDED

Windermere, LA23 1LP
☎ Ambleside (053 94) 33338
Fax (053 94) 34072
Telex 65273
*Almost a mile of lake frontage.
Boat launching, water ski
tuition and superb lake and
mountain views. Also leisure
centre, indoor heated swimming
pool, bubble beds, sauna room,
health and beauty centre,
gymnasium, conference centre
for 300, syndicate rooms, video
and computer link-up. Half
board price based on a
minimum 2 night stay.*
Bedrooms: 16 single,
38 double & 30 twin, 15 family
rooms.
Bathrooms: 99 private,
2 public.
Bed & breakfast: £59.25-£120
single, £118.50-£159 double.
Half board: £61.50-£130
daily, £408-£620 weekly.
Lunch available.
Evening meal 6.30pm (l.o.
10pm).
Parking for 200.
Credit: Access, Visa, Diners,
Amex.

Meadfoot M
COMMENDED

New Rd., Windermere,
LA23 2LA
☎ (053 94) 42610
*Modern detached house on the
edge of the town. It has a
beautiful garden for guests to
enjoy.*
Bedrooms: 1 single, 5 double
& 1 twin, 1 family room.
Bathrooms: 4 private,
1 public; 1 private shower.
Bed & breakfast: £15-£20
single, £30-£40 double.
Parking for 9.
Open February-November.

Merewood Country House Hotel M
HIGHLY COMMENDED

Ecclerigg, Windermere,
LA23 1LH
☎ (053 94) 46484 & 44974
*Victorian country house hotel
set in 20 acres of parkland,
overlooking Lake Windermere.
Laura Ashley decorations.*
Bedrooms: 18 double &
2 twin.
Bathrooms: 20 private.
Bed & breakfast: £45-£75
single, £90-£150 double.
Half board: £55-£85 daily.
Lunch available.
Evening meal 7.30pm (l.o.
9pm).
Parking for 70.
Credit: Access, Visa, Diners,
Amex.

Mountain Ash Hotel M

Ambleside Rd., Windermere,
LA23 1AT
☎ (053 94) 43715 & 46527
*Lakeland stone hotel
refurbished to provide four-
poster water-beds and spa
baths. Open log fire, cocktail
bar, lake views.*
Bedrooms: 4 single,
15 double, 1 family room.
Bathrooms: 20 private.
Bed & breakfast: £24.50-£55
single, £49-£110 double.
Half board: £37-£67.50 daily,
£255-£465 weekly.
Lunch available.
Evening meal 7pm (l.o. 9pm).
Parking for 30.
Credit: Access, Visa.

Mylne Bridge House M
Listed APPROVED

Brookside, Lake Rd.,
Windermere, LA23 2BX
☎ (053 94) 43314
*Comfortable, traditional
Lakeland stone guesthouse
with a warm, friendly
atmosphere. Between village
and the lake.*
Bedrooms: 2 single, 6 double
& 1 twin, 1 family room.
Bathrooms: 7 private,
1 public.
Bed & breakfast: £14.50-£18
single, £29-£37 double.
Parking for 12.
Open March-November.

Oldfield House M
COMMENDED

Oldfield Rd., Windermere,
LA23 2BY
☎ (053 94) 88445
*Friendly, informal atmosphere
within a traditionally-built
Lakeland residence. Quiet
central location, free use of
swimming and leisure club.*
Bedrooms: 2 single, 3 double
& 1 twin, 1 family room.
Bathrooms: 4 private,
2 public.
Bed & breakfast: £15-£21
single, £30-£40 double.
Parking for 7.
Credit: Access, Visa.

Osborne Guest House

3 High St., Windermere,
LA23 1AF
☎ (053 94) 46452
*Traditional Lakeland house,
central for all transport, tours
and walks. Clean, comfortable
accommodation. Full
breakfast. Developed by
present owners since 1982.*
Bedrooms: 1 double, 2 family
rooms.
Bathrooms: 3 private,
1 public.
Bed & breakfast: £20-£22
single, £26-£28 double.

Parson Wyke Country House

Glebe Rd., Bowness-on-
Windermere
☎ Windermere
(053 94) 42837
*Former rectory, Grade II
listed, in beautiful and peaceful
lakeside situation in 2 acres of
grounds. Only 5 minutes' walk
to Bowness.*
Bedrooms: 1 single, 2 double,
1 family room.
Bathrooms: 4 private.

---

*The symbols are explained on the flap
inside the back cover.*

Bed & breakfast: £30-£35 single, £45-£60 double.
Parking for 8.
♿ ⌷ ⌾ Ⓤ Ⓥ ⊨ �📺 ⠿ ▱
✿ ✗ ⌸ ⌑

The Poplars ⋀
⎰⎰ **APPROVED**
Lake Rd., Windermere,
LA23 2EQ
☎ (053 94) 42325 & 46690
Small family-run guesthouse on the main lake road offering every home comfort. A limited number of non-residents catered for. Advance booking essential for evening meal.
Bedrooms: 1 single, 3 double & 2 twin, 1 family room.
Bathrooms: 3 private, 2 public.
Bed & breakfast: £16-£19.50 single, £32-£39 double.
Half board: £26-£29.50 daily, £175-£196 weekly.
Evening meal 6.30pm (l.o. 7pm).
Parking for 7.
♿ ⌕ ⌷ ⌾ ⓘ Ⓥ ⊨ 📺 ⠿
▱ ▶ ⌸ SP

Ravensworth Hotel ⋀
⎰⎰⎰⎰
Ambleside Rd., Windermere,
LA23 1BA
☎ (053 94) 43747
Close to the village centre, lake and fells. Providing English and continental cooking. Variety of accommodation available.
Bedrooms: 2 single, 9 double & 2 twin, 1 family room.
Bathrooms: 14 private.
Bed & breakfast: from £33.50 single, £62-£78 double.
Half board: £43.25-£52.25 daily, £245-£276.50 weekly.
Evening meal 7pm (l.o. 8pm).
Parking for 16.
Credit: Access, Visa.
♿ ⌕ ⌷ ⌾ ⓘ Ⓥ
⊬ ⊨ ⠿ ▱ ⌑ ⍾ ⌣ ▶ ⌸
⍉ SP Ⓣ

Rockside
⎰⎰
Ambleside Rd., Windermere,
LA23 1AQ
☎ (053 94) 45343
100 yards from Windermere village and its amenities. Tours and walks arranged if required. Railway and bus station 250 yards. Large car park.
Bedrooms: 2 single, 4 double & 7 twin, 1 family room.
Bathrooms: 10 private, 2 public.

Bed & breakfast: £15.50-£19.50 single, £31-£46 double.
Parking for 12.
Credit: Access, Visa.
♿ ⌕ ⌾ ⓛ ⍉ ⌷ Ⓤ ⓘ Ⓥ ⊨
⠿ ▱ ⌑ ✗ ⍾ SP Ⓣ

Rosemount Private Hotel ⋀
⎰⎰ **COMMENDED**
Lake Rd., Windermere,
LA23 2EQ
☎ (053 94) 43739
Small well-appointed hotel, tastefully decorated and furnished, just a short stroll from Lake Windermere and Bowness. Non-smokers only please.
Bedrooms: 2 single, 5 double & 1 twin.
Bathrooms: 8 private.
Bed & breakfast: £18.50-£24 single, £37-£48 double.
Parking for 8.
Credit: Access, Visa.
♿ ⌕ ⌷ ⌾ ⓘ Ⓥ ⊬ ▱ ⠿
▱ ✗ ⍾ ⌑ SP

Royal Hotel ⋀
⎰⎰⎰ **APPROVED**
Queens Square, Bowness-on-Windermere, LA23 3DB
☎ Windermere
(053 94) 43045 & 45267 &
Fax (053 94) 42498
Telex 65464
One of Lakeland's oldest hotels, offering modern amenities and only 100 yards from the lake. Most rooms have lake and mountain views. Free leisure facilities.
Bedrooms: 6 single, 11 double & 7 twin, 5 family rooms.
Bathrooms: 29 private.
Bed & breakfast: £32.50-£39.50 single, £65-£79 double.
Half board: £42.50-£49.50 daily, £245-£294 weekly.
Lunch available.
Evening meal 6pm (l.o. 10pm).
Parking for 21.
Credit: Access, Visa, Diners, Amex.
♿ ⌕ ⌾ ⌦ ⓛ ⌷ ⌾ ⓘ Ⓥ ⊬
⊨ ⠿ ▱ ⌑ ⌣ Ů ▶ ✿ ⍉
SP ⌸ Ⓣ

St. John's Lodge ⋀
⎰⎰⎰ **COMMENDED**
Lake Rd., Windermere,
LA23 2EQ
☎ (053 94) 43078
Small private hotel midway between Windermere and the lake, managed by the chef/proprietor and convenient for all amenities and services. Facilities of local sports and leisure club available to guests.
Bedrooms: 10 double & 2 twin, 2 family rooms.
Bathrooms: 14 private.

Bed & breakfast: £16.50-£25 single, £33-£45 double.
Half board: £26.50-£33 daily, £178-£210 weekly.
Evening meal 7pm (l.o. 6pm).
Parking for 11.
♿⌕2⌷⌾ ⓘ Ⓥ ⊬ ▱
◖ ⠿ ▱ ✗ ⌸ ⍉ DAP SP Ⓣ

South View ⋀
⎰⎰⎰
Cross St., Windermere,
LA23 1AE
☎ (053 94) 42951
Small Georgian hotel in a quiet position, central for attractions and transport. Accent on good food and friendliness. Indoor swimming pool.
Bedrooms: 1 single, 4 double & 2 twin.
Bathrooms: 5 private, 2 public.
Bed & breakfast: £18-£22 single, £40-£52 double.
Half board: £30-£36 daily, £200-£250 weekly.
Evening meal 6.30pm (l.o. 4pm).
Parking for 5.
♿ ⌕ ⌷ ⌾ ⌾ Ⓤ ▱ Ⓥ ⊬ ⊨
📺 ⠿ ▱ ⌣ ⍾ ⌸ ⍉ SP Ⓣ

Sun Hotel
⎰⎰⎰ **COMMENDED**
Troutbeck Bridge,
Windermere, LA23 1HH
☎ (053 94) 43274
220-year-old coaching inn. Private lake frontage. Sky movies. A la carte restaurant. Bar meals available.
Bedrooms: 5 double & 1 twin, 5 family rooms.
Bathrooms: 5 private, 2 public; 2 private showers.
Bed & breakfast: £18.50-£29.50 single, £35-£50 double.
Half board: £23.50-£34.50 daily.
Lunch available.
Evening meal 6pm (l.o. 9pm).
Credit: Access, Visa, C.Bl., Diners, Amex.
♿ ⌷ ⌾ ⓘ Ⓥ ⊨ 📺 ⠿
▱ ⌣ ⍷ ⌣ ⍾ SP

Thornbank Private Hotel ⋀
⎰⎰ **APPROVED**
4, Thornbarrow Road,.
Windermere, LA23 2EW
☎ (053 94) 43724
Small family-run hotel offering comfortable accommodation and home-cooked English food. Convenient for shops and lake.
Bedrooms: 1 single, 4 double & 2 twin, 2 family rooms.
Bathrooms: 4 private, 2 public.
Bed & breakfast: £15-£21.50 single, £26-£39 double.
Half board: £22.50-£29 daily, £154-£185.50 weekly.

Evening meal 6.45pm (l.o. 4pm).
Parking for 11.
Credit: Access, Visa.
♿ ⌕ ⌷ ⌾ ⓘ Ⓥ ⊬
▱ 📺 ⠿ ▱ ▶ ⌸ DAP ⍾ SP
Ⓣ

Westlake ⋀
⎰⎰⎰ **COMMENDED**
Lake Rd., Windermere,
LA23 2EQ
☎ (053 94) 43020
Family-run, private hotel between Windermere and the lake. All rooms en-suite, with colour TV and tea-making facilities. Brochure available.
Bedrooms: 5 double & 1 twin, 2 family rooms.
Bathrooms: 8 private.
Bed & breakfast: £17-£21 single, £34-£42 double.
Half board: £27-£31 daily, £185-£205 weekly.
Evening meal 6.30pm (l.o. 3.30pm).
Parking for 8.
♿ ⌕ ⌷ ⌷ ⌾ ⓘ Ⓥ ⊨ ▱
⠿ ▱ ✗ ⌸ ⌸ SP

Wild Boar Hotel ⋀
⎰⎰⎰ **COMMENDED**
Crook, Nr. Windermere,
LA23 3NF
☎ (053 94) 45225
Fax (053 94) 42498
Telex 65464
Former 17th C inn, renowned for its food. In the Gilpin Valley, on the B5284, 3 miles from the lake.
Bedrooms: 1 single, 16 double & 16 twin, 3 family rooms.
Bathrooms: 36 private.
Bed & breakfast: £47.50-£70 single, £95-£110 double.
Half board: £68-£75.50 daily, £340-£410 weekly.
Lunch available.
Evening meal 7pm (l.o. 8.45pm).
Parking for 80.
Credit: Access, Visa, Diners, Amex.
♿ ⌕ ⌷ ⌣ ⌾ ⌷ ⌾ ⓘ Ⓥ
⊨ ⠿ ⌑ ⌣ Ů ▶ ✿ ⍾ SP
Ⓣ

The Willowsmere Hotel ⋀
⎰⎰⎰
Ambleside Rd., Windermere,
LA23 1ES
☎ (053 94) 43575
Offers a comfortable and friendly atmosphere. Run by the fifth generation of local hoteliers. Varied food using fresh local produce.
Bedrooms: 2 single, 3 double & 1 twin, 7 family rooms.
Bathrooms: 13 private.
Continued ▶

WINDERMERE

Continued

Bed & breakfast: £24-£26 single, £48-£52 double.
Half board: £38-£40 daily, £150-£230 weekly.
Evening meal 7pm (l.o. 7pm).
Parking for 40.
Open March-November.
Credit: Access, Visa, Diners, Amex.
⛥ ♨ ♥ ▮ Ⅴ ⊬ ⊨ ⅋ ⃢ ▦
▣ ✿ ✕ SP

Winbrook House ⋔
30 Ellerthwaite Rd., Windermere, LA23 2AH
☎ (053 94) 44932
Modern guesthouse with a friendly atmosphere, offering English cooking. Access to rooms at all times. Private parking.
Bedrooms: 1 single, 4 double & 1 twin.
Bathrooms: 3 private; 3 private showers.
Bed & breakfast: £14-£20 single, £26.50-£36 double.
Lunch available.
Parking for 7.
Open March-December.
⛥5 ⊡ ♥ ⓤⓛ ▮ Ⅴ ⊨ ⅋ ⃢ ▦ ✕ SP

Yorkshire House ⋔
⛥⛥ APPROVED
1 Upper Oak St., Windermere, LA23 2LB
☎ (053 94) 44689
Situated in secluded cul-de-sac close to town centre. Bright rooms, plentiful home-cooked food served in a warm, friendly atmosphere. Licensed.
Bedrooms: 2 double, 3 family rooms.
Bathrooms: 1 private, 2 public.

Bed & breakfast: £12-£17.50 single, £24-£35 double.
Half board: £20-£25.50 daily, £135-£155 weekly.
Evening meal 6.30pm (l.o. 11am).
Parking for 5.
⛥ ♥ ▮ Ⅴ ⊨ ⓣⓥ ⃢ ▣ ✕
✕ SP

WITHERSLACK

Cumbria
Map ref 5A3

Quiet wooded valley, famous for its damsons and with its own garden centre.

The Old Vicarage Country House Hotel ⋔
⛥⛥⛥⛥ COMMENDED
Church Rd., Witherslack, Grange-over-Sands, LA11 6RS
☎ (044 852) 381
Fax (044 852) 373
Secluded Georgian country vicarage sheltered by gentle Lakeland fells. Near Lake Windermere and M6 junction 36. Dine by candlelight on fresh local produce.
Bedrooms: 10 double & 4 twin.
Bathrooms: 14 private.
Bed & breakfast: £46-£98 single, £65-£123 double.
Half board: £72-£124 daily, £412-£523 weekly.
Evening meal 8pm (l.o. 7.30pm).
Parking for 25.
Credit: Access, Visa, Diners, Amex.
⛥12 ♨ ⊡ ℂ ⑩ ⊡ ♥
Ⅴ ⊬ ⊨ ⃢ ▣ ☎ ♪ ✿ ✕ SP
▥ ⓣ

WORKINGTON

Cumbria
Map ref 5A2

A deep-water port on the Solway Firth. There are the ruins of the 14th C Workington Hall, where Mary Queen of Scots stayed in 1568.
Tourist Information Centre ☎ *(0900) 602923*

Hall Park Hotel
Ramson Brow, Workington, CA14 4BX
☎ Workington (0900) 602968
Small family-run establishment which provides a warm and friendly atmosphere as well as catering for the needs of businessmen.
Bedrooms: 2 single, 2 double & 4 twin, 1 family room.
Bathrooms: 6 private, 3 public.
Bed & breakfast: £22.50-£38.50 single, £35-£49.50 double.
Lunch available.
Evening meal 7pm (l.o. 10pm).
Credit: Access, Visa, Amex.
⛥ ℂ ⑩ ⊡ ♥ ▮ Ⅴ ⊨ ⓣⓥ
⃢ ▣ ⓣ ✕ ▦ ✕ SP

Morven Guest House ⋔
⛥⛥⛥
Siddick Rd., Siddick, Workington, CA14 1LE
☎ Workington (0900) 602118
Detached house north-west of Workington. Ideal base for touring the Lake District and West Cumbria. Large car park.
Bedrooms: 2 single, 1 double & 2 twin, 1 family room.
Bathrooms: 5 private, 1 public.
Bed & breakfast: £18-£30 single, £30-£40 double.
Lunch available.
Evening meal 6pm (l.o. 4pm).
Parking for 20.
⛥ ♨ ⊡ ♥ ▮ ⊬ ⊨ ⓣⓥ ⃢
▣ ♣ ✿ ▦

Key to symbols

Information about many of the services and facilities at establishments listed in this guide is given in the form of symbols. The key to these symbols is inside the back cover flap. You may find it helpful to keep the flap open when referring to the entry listings.

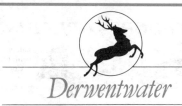

THE CROWN IS YOUR SURE SIGN
OF WHERE TO STAY

HOTELS, GUESTHOUSES, INNS, B&Bs & FARMHOUSES

Throughout Britain, the tourist boards now inspect over 17,000 hotels, guesthouses, inns, B&Bs and farmhouses, every year, to help you find the ones that suit you best.

THE CLASSIFICATIONS: '**Listed**', and then **ONE to FIVE CROWN,** tell you the range of facilities and services you can expect. The more Crowns, the wider the range.

THE GRADES: **APPROVED, COMMENDED and HIGHLY COMMENDED,** where they appear, indicate the quality standard provided. If no grade is shown, you can still expect a high standard of cleanliness.

Every classified place to stay has a Fire Certificate, where this is required under the Fire Precautions Act, and all carry Public Liability Insurance.

'**Listed**': Clean and comfortable accommodation, but the range of facilities and services may be limited.

ONE CROWN: Accommodation with additional facilities, including washbasins in all bedrooms, a lounge and use of a phone.

TWO CROWN: A wider range of facilities and services, including morning tea and calls, bedside lights, colour TV in lounge or bedrooms, assistance with luggage.

THREE CROWN: At least one-third of the bedrooms with ensuite WC and bath or shower, plus easy chair, full length mirror. Shoe cleaning facilities and hairdryers available. Hot evening meals available.

FOUR CROWN: At least three-quarters of the bedrooms with ensuite WC and bath/shower plus colour TV, radio and phone, 24-hour access and lounge service until midnight. Last orders for meals 8.30 pm or later.

FIVE CROWN: All bedrooms having WC, bath and shower ensuite, plus a wide range of facilities and services, including room service, all-night lounge service and laundry service. Restaurant open for breakfast, lunch and dinner.

Every Crown classified place to stay is likely to provide some of the facilities and services of a higher classification. More information available from any Tourist Information Centre.

We've checked them out before you check in!

NORTHUMBRIA

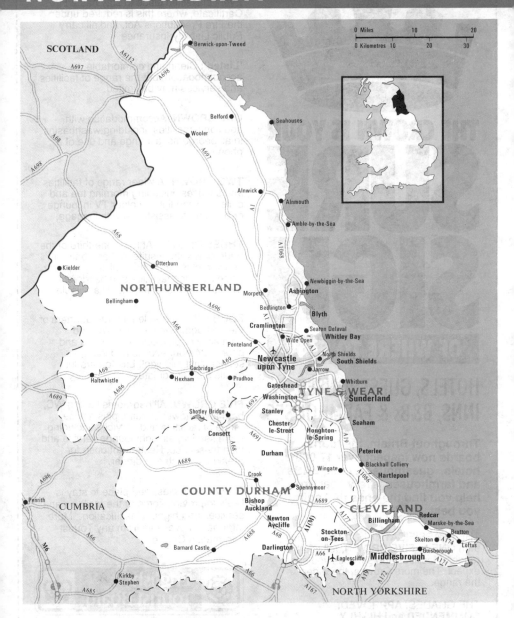

PLEASE REFER TO THE COLOUR MAPS AT THE BACK OF THIS GUIDE FOR
ALL PLACES WITH ACCOMMODATION LISTINGS.

KNOWN AS THE "KINGDOM OF NORTHUMBRIA" — *and for no uncertain reason. This northernmost region of England has seen its fair share of battles and is replete with castles, border strongholds and fortifications, including the magnificent Hadrian's Wall. Wild, rugged, empty and yet romantic. The quietness of the national park and the dramatic scenery of the Cheviots contrast with the bustling nightlife of the region's "capital", Newcastle upon Tyne. And there's history everywhere you step, including leisure trails dedicated to local celebrities Captain Cook and Catherine Cookson.*

WHERE TO GO, WHAT TO SEE

Alnwick Castle
Alnwick, Northumberland
NE66 1NQ
☎ Alnwick (0665) 510777
*Home of the Duke of
Northumberland. Magnificent
border fortress dating back to
the 11th C. Main restoration
done by Salvin in the 19th C.*

Bamburgh Castle
Bamburgh, Northumberland
NE69 7DE
☎ Bamburgh (066 84) 208
*Magnificent coastal castle
completely restored in 1900.
Collections of china, porcelain,
furniture, paintings, arms and
armour.*

**Beamish — The North of
England Open Air Museum**
Beamish, Co. Durham
DH9 0RG
☎ Stanley (0207) 231811
*Open air museum of northern
life around the turn of the
century. Buildings re-erected to
form a town with shops and
houses. Colliery village, station
and working farm.*

The Bowes Museum
Barnard Castle, Co. Durham
DL12 8NP
☎ Teesdale (0833) 690606
*Fine and decorative 15th and
19th C art collections. Paintings,
furniture, ceramics and textiles
from Britain and western Europe.*

**Captain Cook
Birthplace Museum**
Stewart Park, Marton,
Middlesbrough, Cleveland
TS7 6AS
☎ Middlesbrough (0642)
311211
*Early life and voyages of
Captain Cook. Temporary
exhibitions changing monthly.*

**Cragside House
and Country Park**
Cragside, Rothbury, Morpeth,
Northumberland NE65 7PX

☎ Rothbury (0669) 20333
*House built 1864—95 for the
first Lord Armstrong, Tyneside
industrialist. First house to be lit
by electricity generated by water
power.*

Durham Castle
Palace Green, Durham City,
Co. Durham DH1 3RW
☎ 091-374 3800
*Castle founded in 1072. Norman
chapel dating from 1080,
kitchens and great hall dated
1499 and 1284 respectively.*

Cheese-making in the dairy at Home Farm, Beamish

Durham Cathedral seen from the west

Hancock Museum

The University, Newcastle upon Tyne, Tyne & Wear NE2 4PT
☎ 091-222 7418
Zoology and geology galleries, bird room. Displays for children: Abel's Ark and Bewick Shrine.

Housesteads Roman Fort

Haydon Bridge, Hexham, Northumberland NE47 6NN
☎ Hexham (0434) 344363
Best preserved and most impressive of the Roman forts. Vercovicium was 5-acre fort for 100 infantry, surrounded by extensive civil settlement.

Killhope Leadmining Centre

Cowshill, Upper Weardale, Co. Durham DL13 1AR
☎ Weardale (0388) 537505
Most complete lead mining site in Great Britain. Includes crushing mill with 34-ft water wheel, reconstruction of Victorian machinery, railway system and miners' accommodation.

Durham Cathedral

Durham City, Co. Durham DH1 3EQ
☎ 091-386 2367
Widely considered to be the finest example of Norman church architecture in England. Tombs of St. Cuthbert and the Venerable Bede.

Farne Islands

off Northumberland Coast
Small group of islands which during the summer provide a home for 18 different species of seabirds. Large colony of grey seals.

Gibside Chapel and Grounds

Gibside, Burnopfield, Newcastle upon Tyne, Tyne & Wear NE16 6BG
☎ Consett (0207) 542255
The mausoleum of 5 members of the Bowes family, built to a design by James Paine between 1760 and 1812. Restored in 1965. Avenue of Turkey Oak trees.

Gisborough Priory

Guisborough, Cleveland TS14 6HL
☎ Guisborough (0287) 638301
Remains of 12th C Augustinian priory founded by Robert de Brus, in the grounds of Gisborough Hall. 12th C gatehouse, 14th C church.

Green Dragon Museum

Theatre Yard, Stockton-on-Tees, Cleveland TS18 1AT
☎ Stockton (0642) 674308

Local history museum recording development of Stockton. Dawn of the "railway age" is displayed in an exciting audio-visual show.

Lindisfarne Castle

Holy Island, Berwick-upon-Tweed, Northumberland
☎ Berwick-upon-Tweed (0289) 89244
Built about 1550. Sir Edwin Lutyens' inspired restoration (1903) provided a comfortable home totally in character.

Metroland

39 Garden Walk, MetroCentre, Gateshead, Tyne & Wear NE11 9YZ
☎ 091-493 2048
Europe's only indoor theme park within a large shopping complex. Rollercoaster, dodgems, swinging chairs, electronic games, lasers. Creche facilities.

Morpeth Chantry Bagpipe Museum
The Chantry, Bridge Street, Morpeth, Northumberland NE61 1PJ
☎ Morpeth (0670) 519466
The Chantry is in use as a craft centre, Tourist Information Centre and museum. Extensive collection of bagpipes, including Northumberland, Scottish, Irish and Border half-longs.

Ormesby Hall
Ormesby, Middlesbrough, Cleveland TS7 9AS
☎ Middlesbrough (0642) 324188
Mid 18th C house with fine decorative plasterwork, Jacobean doorway, stable block, attributed to Carr of York.

Preston Park Museum
Yarm Road, Stockton-on-Tees, Cleveland TS18 3RH
☎ Stockton (0642) 781184
Social history museum with period street and rooms, working craftsmen, arms, armour, costume and toys. Set in 116 acres of beautiful parkland. Aviary, pitch and putt.

Raby Castle
Staindrop, Darlington, Co. Durham DL2 3AH
☎ Staindrop (0833) 60202
Medieval castle in 200-acre park. 600-year-old kitchen and carriage collection. Walled gardens and deer park.

Souter Point Lighthouse
Coast Road, Whitburn, South Shields, Tyne & Wear SR6 7NH
☎ 091-529 3061
The lighthouse and associated buildings were constructed in 1871 and contained the most advanced lighthouse technology of the day.

Vindolanda
Haltwhistle, Northumberland NE47 7JN
☎ Haltwhistle (0434) 344277
Visitors may wander through the excavations to the superb museum set in ornamental gardens. Replica section of Hadrian's Wall.

The Wildfowl and Wetlands Trust
District 15, Washington, Tyne & Wear NE38 8LE
☎ 091-416 5454
Collection of 1,250 wildfowl of 108 varieties. Viewing gallery, picnic areas, hides and winter wild bird feeding station. Bird food available.

MAKE A DATE FOR...

Riding the Bounds of Berwick-upon-Tweed
Town Hall, Marygate, Berwick-upon-Tweed, Northumberland
1 May

North Shields Fishquay Festival
North Shields, Tyne & Wear
2 – 4 May

Newcastle Hoppings
Town Moor, Grandstand Road, Newcastle upon Tyne, Tyne & Wear
19 – 27 June

Alnwick Fair
Market Place, Alnwick, Northumberland
28 June – 4 July

Durham Miners' Gala
Racecourse, Durham, Co. Durham
11 July

Durham County Agricultural Show
Lambton Park Garden Centre, Lambton Park, Chester-le-Street, Co. Durham
11 – 12 July

Billingham International Folklore Festival
Forum Theatre, Town Centre, Billingham, Cleveland
15 – 22 August

Sunderland Illuminations
Roker and Seaburn, Sunderland, Tyne & Wear
28 August – 5 November

Great North Run
Newcastle upon Tyne to South Shields
20 September

Allendale Baal Festival
Market Square, Allendale, Northumberland
31 December

FIND OUT MORE

Further information about holidays and attractions in the Northumbria region is available from:
Northumbria Tourist Board
Aykley Heads, Durham DH1 5UX
☎ 091-384 6905

The following publications are available free from the Northumbria Tourist Board:
Northumbria Holiday Guide 1992
Bed & Breakfast map – Northumbria and Cumbria
Places to Visit, Things to Do (map)
Caravan and Camping Guide – North-east England
Educational brochure
Farm Holidays
Places to Visit in Winter

Also available is (price includes postage and packing):
Northumbria touring map and guide £4.30

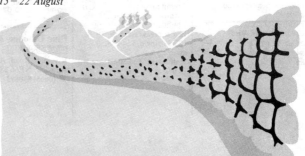

The magnificent Hadrian's Wall

Places to stay

ACCOMMODATION ENTRIES *in this regional section are listed in alphabetical order of place name, and then in alphabetical order of establishment.*

THE MAP REFERENCES *refer to the colour maps towards the end of the guide. The first figure is the map number; the letter and figure which follow indicate the grid reference on the map.*

THE SYMBOLS *at the end of each accommodation entry give information about services and facilities. A 'key' to these symbols is inside the back cover flap, which can be kept open for easy reference.*

ALLENDALE

Northumberland
Map ref 5B2

10m SW. Hexham
Attractive small town set amongst moors, 10 miles south-west of Hexham and claimed to be the geographical centre of Britain. Surrounded by unspoilt walking country, with many well-signposted walks along the East and West Allen Rivers. On New Year's Eve the Allendale Fire Festival is a spectacular traditional event.

Bishopfield Country House Hotel & Restaurant M
COMMENDED
Allendale, Hexham,
NE47 9EJ
☎ (0434) 683248
Family-run 17th C hotel and restaurant in an area of outstanding natural beauty.
Bedrooms: 1 single, 3 double & 4 twin, 3 family rooms.
Bathrooms: 11 private.
Bed & breakfast: £37-£47 single, £74-£78 double.
Half board: £51-£55 daily.
Lunch available.
Evening meal 7pm (l.o. 8.30pm).
Parking for 15.
Credit: Access, Visa.

Heatherlea Hotel M
APPROVED
Allendale, Hexham,
NE47 9BJ
☎ (0434) 683236
Family-run hotel, noted for home cooking and baking. Facilities include snooker and table tennis. The garden has a putting green, bowls, swings and sun lounge.
Bedrooms: 4 single, 5 double & 5 twin, 3 family rooms.
Bathrooms: 8 private, 3 public.
Bed & breakfast: £22-£27 single, £40-£50 double.
Half board: £28-£33 daily, £168-£198 weekly.
Lunch available.
Evening meal 7pm (l.o. 8pm).
Parking for 10.
Open May-October, December.

Hotspur Hotel M
Allendale, Hexham,
NE47 9BW
☎ (0434) 683 355
Family-run country hotel offering a homely atmosphere, good home cooking and comfortable accommodation. Some recreation facilities at hotel, others nearby.
Bedrooms: 3 double & 2 twin, 2 family rooms.
Bathrooms: 2 private, 2 public.
Bed & breakfast: £19.50-£23.50 single, £34-£38.50 double.
Half board: £24.50-£31 daily.
Lunch available.

Evening meal 7pm (l.o. 9.30pm).
Parking for 6.

The Old Hostel M
1 Allen View, Catton, Nr. Allendale, Hexham,
NE47 9QQ
☎ (0434) 683 780
3-storey house with lovely views from all rooms. First house on left coming out of Catton, towards Allendale. Run by June and Eric Dobbing.
Bedrooms: 2 single, 2 double, 1 family room.
Bathrooms: 2 public.
Bed & breakfast: £12.50-£14.50 single, £25-£28 double.
Parking for 4.

ALNMOUTH

Northumberland
Map ref 5C1

4m SE. Alnwick
Quiet village with pleasant old buildings, at the mouth of the River Aln where extensive dunes and sands stretch along Alnmouth Bay. 18th C granaries, some converted to dwellings, still stand.

Blue Dolphins M
COMMENDED
Riverside Road, Alnwick, Alnmouth, NE66 2SD
☎ (0665) 830893

Beautifully situated, well-furnished Edwardian house with uninterrupted views over mouth of River Aln and North Sea. All rooms en-suite.
Bedrooms: 4 double & 1 twin.
Bathrooms: 5 private.
Bed & breakfast: £20-£22 single, £40-£44 double.
Parking for 5.

Glendower Guest House M
23 Argyle Street, Alnmouth, NE66 2SB
☎ (0665) 830262
Near the river and sea, with rail and bus links. Chef/proprietor. Licensed, good food, warm welcome.
Bedrooms: 2 single, 1 double & 1 twin, 1 family room.
Bathrooms: 2 public.
Bed & breakfast: £18-£19 single, £36-£38 double.
Half board: from £29 daily, £190-£205 weekly.
Credit: Access, Visa.

Marine House Private Hotel M
COMMENDED
1 Marine Road, Alnmouth, Alnwick, NE66 2RW
☎ (0665) 830349
200-year-old converted granary overlooking golf links and the sea. Offering cocktail bar and home cooking.
Bedrooms: 3 double & 4 twin, 3 family rooms.
Bathrooms: 10 private, 1 public.
Bed & breakfast: £46-£50 double.

Half board: £33-£37 daily,
£231-£256 weekly.
Evening meal 7pm.
Parking for 12.

🐾 ♨ 🅟 Ⓥ ⇔ 📺 ▥ ▵ 🔊 ♨
🅟 🖨 ⒹⒶⓅ ⓈⓅ ▥

Schooner Hotel M
♨♨♨

Northumberland Street,
Alnmouth, Alnwick,
NE66 2RS
☎ (0665) 830216
Fax (0665) 830216 Ext 201
*17th C coaching inn, ideally
situated 1 minute from beach,
golf-courses and lovely walks.
Real ale bars. Choice of
restaurants.*
Bedrooms: 3 single, 7 double
& 13 twin, 4 family rooms.
Bathrooms: 27 private,
1 public.
Bed & breakfast: £30-£50
single, £50-£85 double.
Half board: £39-£62 daily.
Lunch available.
Evening meal 7pm (l.o.
10.30pm).
Parking for 50.
Credit: Access, Visa, Diners,
Amex.

🐾 ☎ Ⓡ 🖨 ♨ ♨ Ⓥ ⇔ 📺
● ▥ ▵ 🍴 🏹 ∪ 🅟 ⒹⒶⓅ ➤
ⓈⓅ 🖨 Ⓣ

Northumberland
Map ref 5C1

17m N. Morpeth
Ancient and historic
market town, entered
through the Hotspur
Tower, an original gate in
the town walls. The
medieval castle, the
second biggest in
England and still the seat
of the Dukes of
Northumberland, was
restored from ruin in the
18th C. The castle has 7
acres of grounds
landscaped by Capability
Brown and its Italianate
interiors contrast with the
powerful exterior. Fishing
enthusiasts will enjoy the
House of Hardy Museum.
*Tourist Information
Centre ☎ (0665) 510665*

Bondgate House
Hotel M
♨♨♨ APPROVED

20 Bondgate Without,
Alnwick, NE66 1PN
☎ (0665) 602025
Fax (0665) 602554
*A small family-run hotel near
the medieval town gateway and
interesting local shops. Well-
placed for touring.*

Bedrooms: 3 double & 2 twin,
3 family rooms.
Bathrooms: 3 private,
2 public.
Bed & breakfast: £18-£25
single, £30-£36 double.
Half board: £26-£33 daily.
Evening meal 6.30pm (l.o.
4.30pm).
Parking for 8.

🐾 🖵 ✦ 🎁 Ⓥ ⇔ 📺 ▥ ▵
🍴 🏹 ⓈⓅ 🖨

Crosshills House
♨♨ COMMENDED

40 Blakelaw Road, Alnwick,
NE66 1BA
☎ (0665) 602518
*Detached house on quiet road
with open views.*
Bedrooms: 1 double & 1 twin.
Bathrooms: 2 private.
Bed & breakfast: £34-£36
double.
Parking for 2.
Open April-September.

🖵 ✦ ⓊⓁ 📺 ▥ 🏹 🖨

Hotspur Hotel M
♨♨♨

Bondgate Without, Alnwick,
NE66 1PR
☎ (0665) 510101
Fax (0665) 605033
*Originally a coaching inn,
offering old-style friendly
hospitality with up-to-date
standards of comfort and
Northumbrian food.*
Bedrooms: 4 single, 8 double
& 14 twin, 1 family room.
Bathrooms: 21 private,
3 public.
Bed & breakfast: £30-£35
single, £45-£55 double.
Half board: £35-£38 daily.
Lunch available.
Evening meal 7pm (l.o. 9pm).
Parking for 20.
Credit: Access, Visa, Diners,
Amex.

🐾 ☎ Ⓡ 🖵 ✦ 🎁 Ⓥ ⇔ 📺
▥ ▵ 🍴 ⓈⓅ 🖨

Masons Arms M
♨♨♨ COMMENDED

Stamford Cott, Nr.
Rennington, Alnwick,
NE66 3RX
☎ (0665) 577 275
*Country inn offering real ale
and good food. En-suite
bedrooms. 3.5 miles from A1
towards coast and beaches on
B1340.*
Bedrooms: 2 single, 2 double
& 2 twin, 2 family rooms.
Bathrooms: 4 private,
1 public.
Bed & breakfast: £19.50
single, £35-£44 double.
Half board: from £22.50
daily.
Lunch available.

Evening meal 6.30pm (l.o.
9.30pm).
Parking for 20.

🐾 14 ♨ ✦ 🎁 Ⓥ ⇔ 📺 ▥
▵ 🅟 🖨 ⓈⓅ

New Moor House
♨♨

Edlingham, Alnwick,
NE66 2BT
☎ Whittingham
(066 574) 638
*6-acre smallholding. Old stone-
built house with lots of
character, oak beams,
comfortable bedrooms and
good food. Centrally situated
for exploring Northumberland.*
Bedrooms: 1 single, 1 double
& 2 twin.
Bathrooms: 1 private,
2 public.
Bed & breakfast: £14.50-
£15.50 single, £29-£31 double.
Half board: £23-£24.50 daily,
£146-£154 weekly.
Evening meal 7pm (l.o. 7pm).
Parking for 8.
Open March-November.

🐾 ✦ ♨ ⓊⓁ Ⓥ ⇔ 📺 ▥ 🖨

The Oaks Hotel M
♨♨♨ APPROVED

South Road, Alnwick,
NE66 2PN
☎ (0665) 510014
Fax (0665) 603219
*A stone-built property (part
circa 1800) comprising recently
refurbished cocktail bar, dining
room and bedrooms.*
Bedrooms: 1 single, 8 double
& 3 twin, 1 family room.
Bathrooms: 13 private.
Bed & breakfast: £35-£49
single, £45-£65 double.
Half board: £50-£64 daily,
£315-£385 weekly.
Lunch available.
Evening meal 7pm (l.o. 9pm).
Parking for 25.
Credit: Access, Visa, Diners,
Amex.

🐾 ♨ ☎ Ⓡ 🖵 ✦ 🎁 Ⓥ ⇔
▥ ▵ 🍴 🅟 🖨

Queens Head Hotel M
♨♨

Market Street, Alnwick,
NE66 1SS
☎ (0665) 602442
*Traditional old coaching inn
near market place, with off-
street parking. Bars open all
day. A la carte dining room.*
Bedrooms: 2 single, 1 double
& 1 twin, 1 family room.
Bathrooms: 1 public.
Bed & breakfast: £16-£18
single, £32-£36 double.
Lunch available.
Evening meal 7pm (l.o. 9pm).
Parking for 15.

🐾 🖵 ✦ 🎁 Ⓥ ⇔ ▥ ▵ 🍴 🏹

Northumberland
Map ref 5C1

Village with a spectacular
red sandstone castle
standing 150 ft above the
sea. On the village green
the magnificent Norman
church stands opposite a
museum containing
mementoes of the
heroine Grace Darling.
Wide sandy beach.

Lord Crewe Arms
Hotel M
♨♨♨

Front Street, Bamburgh,
NE69 7BL
☎ (066 84) 243 & 393
*Cosy village hotel offering
modern comfort and old world
charm, with oak beams and
open fires, featuring a
restaurant and buttery. Near
Bamburgh Castle.*
Bedrooms: 1 single, 10 double
& 13 twin, 1 family room.
Bathrooms: 20 private,
3 public.
Bed & breakfast: £32-£42
single, £55-£60 double.
Half board: £44-£48 daily,
£270-£285 weekly.
Lunch available.
Evening meal 7pm (l.o. 9pm).
Parking for 34.
Open March-October.
Credit: Access, Visa.

🐾 5 ♨ 🖵 ✦ Ⓥ ✂ ⇔ ▥ ▵
🖨 ⓈⓅ 🖨

Mizen Head Hotel M
♨♨

Lucker Road, Bamburgh,
NE69 7BS
☎ (066 84) 254
*Privately-owned, family-run
hotel in its own grounds, with
accent on food and service.
Convenient for beaches, castle
and golf.*
Bedrooms: 2 single, 5 double
& 5 twin, 3 family rooms.
Bathrooms: 7 private,
3 public.
Bed & breakfast: £18-£27.50
single, £29-£49 double.
Half board: £22.50-£38.50
daily, £166-£245 weekly.
Lunch available.
Evening meal 6.30pm (l.o.
8.30pm).
Parking for 35.
Credit: Access, Visa.

🐾 🖵 ✦ 🎁 Ⓥ ⇔ 📺 🍴 ❋
ⒹⒶⓅ 🐾 ⓈⓅ

BAMBURGH

Continued

Waren House Hotel M

HIGHLY COMMENDED

Waren Mill, Belford,
NE70 7EE
☎ (066 84) 581
Fax (066 84) 484
*18th C manor house hotel in 6
acres of grounds within bird
sanctuary. Log fires, accent on
food and wine.*
Bedrooms: 5 double & 2 twin.
Bathrooms: 7 private.
Bed & breakfast: £72.50-£75
single, £105-£125 double.
Half board: £70-£80 daily.
Evening meal 7pm (l.o.
8.30pm).
Parking for 25.
Credit: Access, Visa, Diners,
Amex.

BARDON MILL

Northumberland
Map ref 5B2

Small hamlet midway
between Haydon Bridge
and Haltwhistle, within
easy walking distance of
Vindolanda, an excavated
Roman settlement, and
near the best stretches of
Hadrian's Wall.

Vallum Lodge Hotel M

COMMENDED

Military Road, Twice Brewed,
Bardon Mill, NE47 7AN
☎ (0434) 344248
*Small, quiet, comfortable hotel
on the B6318, in the
Northumberland National
Park. Close to the most
spectacular part of Hadrian's
Wall and the Pennine Way.
Good choice of freshly cooked
food.*
Bedrooms: 1 single, 3 double
& 3 twin.
Bathrooms: 3 private,
2 public.
Bed & breakfast: £19-£20
single, £17-£23 double.
Half board: £28-£34 daily,
£196-£217 weekly.
Lunch available.
Evening meal 7pm (l.o.
8.30pm).
Parking for 25.
Open February-November.

BARNARD CASTLE

Co. Durham
Map ref 5B3

On the Tees, a thriving
market town with a busy
market square. Bernard
Baliol's 12th C castle
(now ruins) stands
nearby. The Bowes
Museum, housed in a
grand 19th C French
chateau, holds fine
paintings and furniture.
Nearby are the
magnificent Raby Castle,
Boose Castle, Rokeby
Hall and Egglestone
Abbey.
*Tourist Information
Centre ☎ (0833) 690909*

Fox and Hounds Country Inn & Restaurant M

COMMENDED

Cotherstone, Nr. Barnard
Castle, DL12 9PF
☎ (0833) 50241/50811
*Old coaching inn set back from
the B6277 on the village green
amidst picturesque scenery.
Heavily beamed throughout,
peaceful atmosphere.*
Bedrooms: 2 double & 1 twin.
Bathrooms: 3 private.
Bed & breakfast: £35-£38
single, £45-£48 double.
Half board: £32.50-£37.50
daily.
Lunch available.
Evening meal 7pm (l.o. 9pm).
Parking for 20.
Credit: Access, Visa.

Marwood View M

COMMENDED

98 Galgate, Barnard Castle
☎ Teesdale (0833) 37493
*Victorian end-of-terrace house
set back from the main road,
with gardens front and rear.
Sauna available.*
Bedrooms: 2 single, 2 double.
Bathrooms: 4 private.
Bed & breakfast: £15-£17
single, £27-£33 double.
Half board: £22-£23.50 daily,
£144-£175 weekly.
Evening meal 6.30pm (l.o.
7.30pm).
Parking for 4.

The Redwell Inn M

Harmire Road, Barnard
Castle, DL12 8QJ
☎ (0833) 37002/38023

*Family-run inn central for
touring Lakes and moors.
Good local leisure facilities and
golf. Fishing, walking. Home-
cooked food.*
Bedrooms: 3 single, 2 double
& 1 twin, 1 family room.
Bathrooms: 7 private.
Bed & breakfast: £30-£38
single, £40-£49.50 double.
Half board: £40-£48 daily,
£225-£300 weekly.
Lunch available.
Evening meal 7pm (l.o.
9.30pm).
Parking for 50.
Credit: Access, Visa.

BARRASFORD

Northumberland
Map ref 5B2

6m N. Hexham
Lovely village on the
North Tyne River which is
overlooked by the
restored 14th C Haughton
Castle on the opposite
bank of the river.

Barrasford Arms M

APPROVED

Barrasford, Hexham,
NE48 4AA
☎ Humshaugh (0434) 681237
*Small country hotel in this
lovely hamlet, only 8 miles
from Hexham and 4 miles to
the Roman Wall. An ideal
centre for touring
Northumberland.*
Bedrooms: 4 twin, 1 family
room.
Bathrooms: 2 private,
1 public; 2 private showers.
Bed & breakfast: £16-£20
single, £28-£37 double.
Half board: £21-£45 daily.
Evening meal 7.30pm (l.o.
9.15pm).
Parking for 45.
Open February-October.

BELLINGHAM

Northumberland
Map ref 5B2

Set in the beautiful valley
of the North Tyne, small
border town close to the
Kielder Forest, Kielder
Water and lonely
moorland below the
Cheviots. The church,
which stands close to the
river and to St. Cuthbert's
Well, has an ancient
stone wagon roof fortified
in the 18th C with
buttresses.
*Tourist Information
Centre ☎ (0434) 220616*

Eals Lodge M

COMMENDED

Tarset, Bellingham,
NE48 1LF
☎ (0434) 240269
*A small, rural, family-run
guesthouse. 4 miles from
Bellingham on the road to
Kielder Water. Personal
service our priority.*
Bedrooms: 2 double & 1 twin.
Bathrooms: 3 private.
Bed & breakfast: max. £26
single, max. £43 double.
Half board: £32-£36.50 daily,
£224-£255.50 weekly.
Lunch available.
Evening meal 7.30pm (l.o.
7pm).
Parking for 15.

Riverdale Hall Hotel M

COMMENDED

Bellingham, Hexham,
NE48 2JT
☎ (0434) 220254
*Spacious country hall in large
grounds. Indoor swimming
pool, sauna, fishing, cricket
field and golf opposite. Award-
winning restaurant in
hospitable family-run hotel.*
Bedrooms: 3 single, 4 double
& 9 twin, 4 family rooms.
Bathrooms: 20 private.
Bed & breakfast: £32-£37.50
single, £54-£65 double.
Half board: £44-£49 daily,
£259-£279 weekly.
Lunch available.
Evening meal 7pm (l.o.
10pm).
Parking for 60.
Credit: Access, Visa, Diners,
Amex.

BERWICK-UPON-TWEED

Northumberland
Map ref 5B1

Guarding the mouth of the Tweed, England's northernmost town with the best 16th C city walls in Europe. The handsome Guildhall and barracks date from the 18th C. The church, unusually, was completed by the Puritans. 3 bridges cross to Tweedmouth, the oldest built in 1634. The Barracks hold the regimental museum, town museum and part of the Burrell Art Collection.
Tourist Information Centre ☎ (0289) 330733

Harvone House M
APPROVED

18 Main Street, Spittal, Berwick-upon-Tweed, TD15 1QY
☎ (0289) 302580
Family-run guesthouse offering value for money with comfortable surroundings and friendly atmosphere. Two minutes' walk from River Tweed and sandy Spittal beach.
Bedrooms: 2 double & 1 twin, 1 family room.
Bathrooms: 1 private, 1 public.
Bed & breakfast: £14-£17 single, £28-£36 double.
Half board: £20-£23 daily, £126-£145 weekly.
Evening meal 6.30pm (l.o. 8pm).
ᄎ ≐ 🗋 ♥ 🗎 Ⓥ ⊨ 🎟 ✕ 🏢

Kings Arms Hotel M
COMMENDED

Hide Hill, Berwick-upon-Tweed, TD15 1EJ
☎ (0289) 307454
Well-known Georgian coaching inn with a walled garden, an ideal centre for touring the Borders and the coast.
Bedrooms: 10 single, 10 double & 13 twin, 3 family rooms.
Bathrooms: 36 private.
Bed & breakfast: £46-£55 single, max. £70 double.
Half board: £48-£67.50 daily.
Lunch available.
Evening meal 6pm (l.o. 10pm).
Credit: Access, Visa, Diners, Amex.
ᄎ 🏢 ✆ 🖉 🗋 ♥ 🗎 Ⓥ ⊨
● 🎟 ⚓ Ⓣ ♡ ☼ ⚘ ⛅ SP
🏢 Ⓣ

Meadow Hill Guest House M
COMMENDED

Duns Road, Berwick-upon-Tweed, TD15 1UB
☎ (0289) 306325
Attractive 150-year-old house with panoramic views of the River Tweed and Cheviot Hills.
Bedrooms: 1 double, 4 family rooms.
Bathrooms: 1 private, 2 public.
Bed & breakfast: £13.50-£20 single, £27-£40 double.
Half board: £20-£27 daily.
Evening meal 7.30pm (l.o. 9am).
Parking for 10.
ᄎ ≐ 🗋 ♥ 🖉 🗎 🎟 🖩 ⚓
🏢 🏢 🏢

Ness Gate Hotel M

1 Palace Street East, Berwick-upon-Tweed, TD15 1HT
☎ (0289) 307123
Family-run hotel in an early 19th C listed building, close to the old town walls and the sea. Convenient for the shops, cinema and theatre.
Bedrooms: 6 single, 7 double & 4 twin, 4 family rooms.
Bathrooms: 7 private, 4 public; 4 private showers.
Bed & breakfast: £16.50-£23.50 single, £33-£47 double.
Half board: £23-£30 daily, £138-£180 weekly.
Lunch available.
Evening meal 6.15pm (l.o. 7.30pm).
Credit: Access, Visa, Diners.
ᄎ ≐ 🗋 ♥ 🗎 Ⓥ ⊨ 🎟 🖩
Ⓣ 🖟 OAP 🏢 Ⓣ

The Old Vicarage Guest House M
COMMENDED

24, Church Road, Tweedmouth, Berwick-upon Tweed, TD15 2AN
☎ (0289) 306909
Spacious, detached 19th C vicarage, recently refurbished to a high standard. 10 minutes' walk from town centre and beautiful beaches.
Bedrooms: 1 single, 2 double & 1 twin, 3 family rooms.
Bathrooms: 4 private, 1 public.
Bed & breakfast: £13-£15 single, £26-£38 double.
ᄎ ≐ 🗋 ♥ ⓤ Ⓥ ⊨ 🖩 ⚓
OAP SP

We advise you to confirm your booking in writing.

Queens Head Hotel M

Sandgate, Berwick-upon-Tweed, TD15 1EP
☎ (0289) 307852 & 306442
Near the town centre, opposite the swimming baths and adjacent to the historic town walls.
Bedrooms: 1 single, 2 twin, 3 family rooms.
Bathrooms: 6 private, 1 public.
Bed & breakfast: from £25 single, from £49.50 double.
Half board: from £30 daily.
Lunch available.
Evening meal 6.30pm (l.o. 9pm).
Credit: Access, Visa.
ᄎ ✆ 🖉 🗋 ♥ 🗎 Ⓥ ✕ ⊨
🎟 🖩 Ⓣ 🏢 Ⓣ

Turret House Hotel M
COMMENDED

Etal Road, Tweedmouth, Berwick-upon-Tweed, TD15 2EG
☎ (0289) 330808
Fax (0289) 330467
Ⓒ Inter
Privately owned and run, the hotel is quietly set in 2 acres of grounds very near the town centre.
Bedrooms: 2 single, 7 double & 3 twin, 1 family room.
Bathrooms: 13 private.
Bed & breakfast: £46.50-£49.50 single, £63-£68 double.
Lunch available.
Evening meal 7.30pm (l.o. 9pm).
Parking for 100.
Credit: Access, Visa, Diners, Amex.
ᄎ ≐ ✆ 🖉 🗋 ♥ Ⓥ ⊨
🖩 ⚓ Ⓣ ⚘ 🖟 OAP SP 🏢
Ⓣ

The Walls Guest House
COMMENDED

8 Quay Walls, Berwick-upon-Tweed, TD15 1HB
☎ (0289) 330140
Listed Georgian house offering tastefully modernised accommodation on the ancient town walls overlooking quay, river, swans, net fishing and old bridge.
Bedrooms: 1 single, 2 double & 1 twin, 1 family room.
Bathrooms: 5 private, 1 public.
Half board: £33-£40 daily, £205-£258 weekly.
Evening meal 7pm (l.o. 7.15pm).
Credit: Access, Visa.
ᄎ ≐ 🗋 ♥ 🗎 Ⓥ ⊨ 🖩 ⚓
Ⓣ ⚓ Ⓟ ✕ 🏢 🏢

BILLINGHAM

Cleveland
Map ref 5C3

A Teesside boom-town of the early 20th C, originally a 10th C settlement, with echoes of the 'Anglo-Saxon' in its church. The town centre has an ambitious modern complex providing shopping, culture, entertainment and sporting facilities. The town holds an annual international folk festival.

Billingham Arms Hotel M
COMMENDED

The Causeway, Billingham, TS23 2HD
☎ Stockton (0642) 553661
Telex 587746
Fax (0642) 552104
In the town square, this modern hotel is perfectly placed for station and airport and for touring Captain Cook country.
Bedrooms: 16 single, 41 double & 3 twin, 9 family rooms.
Bathrooms: 69 private, 5 public.
Bed & breakfast: £25.50-£52 single, £51-£70 double.
Lunch available.
Evening meal 6pm (l.o. 11pm).
Parking for 200.
Credit: Access, Visa, C.Bl., Diners, Amex.
ᄎ 🏢 ✆ 🖉 🗋 ♥ Ⓥ ✕
⊨ ● 🖟 🖩 ⚓ Ⓣ ⚘ ⚘
SP Ⓣ

BISHOP AUCKLAND

Co. Durham
Map ref 5C2

Busy market town on the bank of the Wear. The Palace, a castellated Norman manor house altered in the 18th C, stands in beautiful gardens. Open to the public and entered from the market square by a handsome 18th C gatehouse, the park is a peaceful retreat of trees and streams.

Albion Cottage Guest House
Listed

Albion Terrace, Bishop Auckland, DL14 6EL
☎ (0388) 602217
Continued ▶

BISHOP AUCKLAND

Continued

Detached early Victorian house with front and rear gardens, close to the shops, station and national bus routes.
Bedrooms: 2 single, 1 double & 1 twin.
Bathrooms: 1 public.
Bed & breakfast: £12.50 single, £25 double.
Parking for 10.
♨ ♿ �㉿ ⓘ ▯ 🅥 ⌷ ⓣⓥ ▥ ☎
❄ ✠ 🐾 🐴

BLANCHLAND

Northumberland
Map ref 5B2

Beautiful medieval village rebuilt in the 18th C with stone from its ruined abbey, for lead miners working on the surrounding wild moors. The village is approached over a stone bridge across the Derwent or, from the north, through the ancient gatehouse.

Lord Crewe Arms Hotel ⋀

Blanchland, Consett, Co. Durham DH8 9SP
☎ (0434) 675251
Fax (0434) 675337
Originally Blanchland Abbey (built in 13th C), now a hotel, reputedly with a delightful ghost. Set in the Derwent Valley and surrounded by Northumberland moors.
Bedrooms: 10 double & 5 twin, 3 family rooms.
Bathrooms: 18 private.
Bed & breakfast: from £71.50 single, from £96 double.
Lunch available.
Evening meal 7pm (l.o. 9.15pm).
Credit: Access, Visa, Diners, Amex.
♨ ♨ ⌷ ☎ ℝ ▯ ⓥ ✠ ⓘ ▯
⌷ ▥ ☎ 🍴 ❄ 🐾 🆂🅿 🐴 ⓣ

Individual proprietors have supplied all details of accommodation. Although we do check for accuracy, we advise you to confirm prices and other information at the time of booking.

CHOLLERFORD

Northumberland
Map ref 5B2

At the crossing of the military road and Hadrian's Wall over the North Tyne River and close to an important fort. Chesters Roman fort with the remains of its bridge, its living quarters and its bath houses stands in the park of an 18th C mansion.

George Hotel ⋀

🏰🏰🏰🏰 COMMENDED
Chollerford, Hexham, NE46 4EW
☎ (0434) 681611 Telex 53168
Ⓒ Swallow
In a lovely riverside setting close to Hadrian's Wall and Chesters Fort, 5 miles from Hexham. Many bedrooms and the restaurant overlook the attractive gardens and the river. Leisure centre.
Bedrooms: 9 single, 15 double & 30 twin.
Bathrooms: 54 private.
Bed & breakfast: max. £90 single, max. £95 double.
Half board: max. £86.50 daily.
Lunch available.
Evening meal 7pm (l.o. 9.30pm).
Parking for 100.
Credit: Access, Visa, Diners, Amex.
♨ ♨ ☎ ⌷ ℝ ♿ ⓘ ▯
⌷ ▥ ⓘ ♨ 🍴 ♿ 🐾 ⓘ ♪
❄ ⒹⒶⓅ ❧ 🆂🅿 🐴 ⓣ

CONSETT

Co. Durham
Map ref 5B2

Former steel town on the edge of rolling moors. Modern development includes the shopping centre and a handsome Roman Catholic church, designed by a local architect. To the west, the Derwent Reservoir provides water sports and pleasant walks.

Bee Cottage Farm ⋀

Listed COMMENDED
Castleside, Consett, DH8 9HW
☎ (0207) 508224
46-acre livestock farm. 1.5 miles west of the A68, between Castleside and Tow Law. Unspoilt views. Ideally located for Beamish Museum and Durham. No smoking in main farmhouse.

Bedrooms: 1 single, 5 double & 5 twin, 3 family rooms.
Bathrooms: 1 private, 5 public.
Bed & breakfast: £16-£30 single, £32-£60 double.
Half board: £25.50-£39.50 daily, £178.50-£276.50 weekly.
Lunch available.
Evening meal 5pm (l.o. 9.30pm).
Parking for 20.
♨ ❄ ♿ ⌷ ⓘ ▯ ⓥ ✠ ♨ ⓣⓥ
▥ ☎ ♨ 🐾

CORBRIDGE

Northumberland
Map ref 5B2

Small town on the River Tyne. Close by are extensive remains of the Roman military town Corstopitum, with a museum housing important discoveries from excavations. The town itself is attractive with shady trees, a 17th C bridge and interesting old buildings, notably a 14th C fortified vicarage and a pele tower house about 200 years older.

Clive House

Appletree Lane, Corbridge, NE45 5DN
☎ (0434) 632617
Old village school (1840) converted to dwelling house; tasteful decor throughout; exposed beams, gallery, and a log fire in breakfast room. Good eating places nearby.
Bedrooms: 2 double & 1 twin.
Bathrooms: 3 private.
Bed & breakfast: £28-£30 single, £36-£40 double.
Parking for 3.
Credit: Access, Visa.
♨ 12 ☎ ⌷ ☎ ♿ ⓘ ▯
♨ ⓣⓥ ▥ ♨ ✠ 🐴 🆂🅿 🐴

Fellcroft ⋀

🏰🏰 COMMENDED
Station Road, Corbridge, NE45 5AY
☎ (0434) 632384
Well-appointed stone-built Edwardian house with full private facilities and colour TV in all bedrooms. Quiet road in country setting, half a mile south of market square. Excellent choice of eating places nearby. Non-smokers only please.
Bedrooms: 2 twin.
Bathrooms: 2 private.

Bed & breakfast: £16-£18 single, £28-£30 double.
Parking for 2.
Open March-October.
Ⓡ ⌷ ♿ �㉿ ✠ ♨ ⓣⓥ ▥ ♨
Ⓤ ✠ 🐴

Fox & Hounds Hotel ⋀

Stagshaw Bank, Corbridge, NE45 5QW
☎ (0434) 633024
On the A68, just north of historic Corbridge. Extensive a la carte, bar snacks, Sunday lunches, barbecue facilities. 10 minutes from Hexham, 20 minutes from Newcastle. Next to Hadrian's Wall.
Bedrooms: 4 double & 3 twin, 1 family room.
Bathrooms: 8 private.
Bed & breakfast: £25-£30 single, £40-£50 double.
Half board: £31-£47 daily, £217-£329 weekly.
Lunch available.
Evening meal 7pm (l.o. 9.30pm).
Parking for 65.
Credit: Access, Visa.
♨ ☎ ♨ ⌷ ⓘ ▯ ⓥ ▥ ♨ 🐾 ♦
❄ 🐴 ⒹⒶⓅ 🆂🅿

The Hayes Guest House ⋀

🏰🏰
Newcastle Road, Corbridge, NE45 5LP
☎ (0434) 632010
Large house set amidst 7.5 acres of woodland and gardens with delightful views. Self-catering flat, caravan and cottages also available.
Bedrooms: 2 single, 1 double & 2 twin, 1 family room.
Bathrooms: 2 public; 2 private showers.
Bed & breakfast: £14.50-£15 single, £29-£30 double.
Half board: £21-£21.50 daily, £140 weekly.
Evening meal 7pm (l.o. 4pm).
Parking for 14.
Open January-November.
Credit: Amex.
♨ ⌷ ⓘ ▯ ⓥ ♨ ⓣⓥ ▤ ▥ ♨ ♦
♿ Ⓤ ❄ 🐴 ⒹⒶⓅ 🆂🅿 🐴 ⓣ

The symbol Ⓒⓡ and the name of a hotel group or consortium after a hotel address means that bookings can be made through a central reservations office. These are listed on page 540.

CRASTER

Northumberland
Map ref 5C1

Small fishing village with
a fine northward view of
Dunstanburgh Castle.
Fishing cobles in the tiny
harbour, stone cottages
at the water's edge and a
kippering shed where
Craster's famous delicacy
is produced give the
village its unspoilt charm.

Cottage Inn

Dunstan Village, Craster,
Alnwick, NE66 3ZS
☎ Embleton (066 576) 658
*Old stone building with walled
garden, half a mile from the
sea. Winter weekend breaks
are available from October to
March.*
Bedrooms: 2 double &
14 twin, 1 family room.
Bathrooms: 10 private,
2 public.
Bed & breakfast: max. £35
single, max. £55 double.
Half board: max. £40 daily,
max. £250 weekly.
Lunch available.
Evening meal 6pm (l.o.
9.30pm).
Parking for 30.
Credit: Access, Visa.
➤ ✿ ☼ 🅿 📶 ▥ ☎ 📺 ▥ ▤
🍴 ✿ ❋ ✗ ◈ SP

CROOK

Co. Durham
Map ref 5C2

5m NW. Bishop Auckland
Pleasant market town
sometimes referred to as
'the gateway to
Weardale'. The town's
shopping centre
surrounds a large, open
green, attractively laid out
with lawns and
flowerbeds around the
Devil's Stone, a relic from
the Ice Age.

Greenhead Country House Hotel ⋒
☺☺☺ COMMENDED

Fir Tree, Crook, DL15 8BL
☎ Bishop Auckland
(0388) 763143
*Superbly located in
countryside, 10 miles from
Durham. Comfortable well
appointed hotel. Overlooks
secluded fields and wooded
area. Lounge with sandstone
arches, log fire and oak beams.*
Bedrooms: 1 single, 4 double
& 1 twin.
Bathrooms: 6 private.

Bed & breakfast: £30-£35
single, £40-£45 double.
Half board: £30-£40 daily.
Evening meal 6pm (l.o. 5pm).
Parking for 15.
Credit: Access, Visa.
➤ 13 ✿ 🅿 📺 ▢ 🐾 ☼ 🍴 ▢ 🛏
📺 ▥ ▤ 🍴 Ŭ 🅿 ❋ ✗ ◈
SP 📶 T
🅰 Display advertisement
appears on page 110.

Helme Park Hall Country House Hotel ⋒
☺☺☺ COMMENDED

Fir Tree, Crook, DL13 4NW
☎ Bishop Auckland
(0388) 730970
*Comfortable, fully-refurbished
hotel with open fires and warm
welcoming atmosphere, in 5
acres of grounds and with
spectacular views over the
dales. A haven of peace and
tranquillity.*
Bedrooms: 1 single, 6 double
& 1 twin, 2 family rooms.
Bathrooms: 10 private.
Bed & breakfast: £48.95-
£65.60 single, £67-£95.60
double.
Lunch available.
Evening meal 7pm (l.o.
10pm).
Parking for 70.
Credit: Access, Visa, Amex.
➤ 🅿 ☎ 📺 ▢ 🐾 ☎ 🛏
📺 ▥ ▤ 🍴 ❋ ✗ ◈ ◈ SP
📶
🅰 Display advertisement
appears on page 110.

Kensington Hall Hotel ⋒
☺☺☺ COMMENDED

Kensington Terrace,
Willington, Crook, DL15 0PJ
☎ (0388) 745071
*Comfortable family-run hotel
with lounge bar and restaurant.
Meals available daily. 8 miles
from Durham on A690 to
Crook.*
Bedrooms: 1 double & 4 twin.
Bathrooms: 5 private.
Bed & breakfast: £24-£25
single, £40-£41 double.
Evening meal (l.o. 9.45pm).
Parking for 40.
Credit: Access, Visa.
▢ 🐾 ☎ ▥ ▤ Ŭ ✗ ◈

---

*National Crown
ratings were correct
at the time of going
to press but are
subject to change.
Please check at the
time of booking.*

CROOKHAM

Northumberland
Map ref 5B1

*3.5m S. Cornhill-on-
Tweed*
Pretty hamlet taking its
name from the winding
course of the River Till
which flows in the shape
of a shepherd's crook. 3
castles - Etal, Duddo and
Ford - can be seen, and
nearby the restored
Heatherslaw Mill is of
great interest.

The Coach House ⋒
☺☺☺ COMMENDED

Crookham, Cornhill-on-
Tweed, TD12 4TD
☎ (089 082) 293
*Spacious rooms, arranged
around a courtyard, in rolling
country near the Scottish
Border. Home-cooked, quality
fresh food. We have rooms
specially equipped for our
disabled guests.*
Bedrooms: 2 single, 2 double
& 5 twin.
Bathrooms: 7 private,
2 public.
Bed & breakfast: £19-£28
single, £38-£56 double.
Half board: £31.50-£40.50
daily.
Evening meal 7.30pm (l.o.
7.30pm).
Parking for 12.
Open March-November.
➤ ✿ ☼ ▢ ▥ 🅿 📺 ▥ ▤ ☎ ⅙
✿ ❋ ✗ 📶

DARLINGTON

Co. Durham
Map ref 5C3

Industrial town on the
River Skerne, home of
the earliest passenger
railway which first ran to
Stockton in 1825. Now
the home of a railway
museum. Originally a
prosperous market town
occupying the site of an
Anglo-Saxon settlement,
it still holds an open
market in the square.
*Tourist Information
Centre* ☎ *(0325) 382698*

George Hotel ⋒
☺☺☺

Cliffe, Piercebridge,
Richmond, N. Yorkshire
DL2 3SW
☎ Darlington (0325) 374576
& Fax (0325) 374577

---

*Old coaching inn on the
Yorkshire bank of the River
Tees, 5 miles west of
Darlington. Recently
refurbished bedrooms are set in
the converted stables, some of
which overlook the riverside
gardens.*
Bedrooms: 2 single, 27 double
& 4 twin, 2 family rooms.
Bathrooms: 35 private.
Bed & breakfast: £40 single,
£50 double.
Half board: £52.50 daily,
£315 weekly.
Lunch available.
Evening meal 6pm (l.o.
10pm).
Parking for 200.
Credit: Access, Visa, Amex.
➤ ✿ ☼ 🅿 ☎ ▢ 🐾 ☎ 🍴 V
🍴 ▥ ▤ ☎ 🍴 ⅙ ☎ ❋ ✗ ◈ ▨
SP 📶

Grange Guest House

171 Grange Road,
Darlington, DL1 5NT
☎ (0325) 380727
*Stylish Victorian town house
easy to locate near rail and bus
terminals, but near southern
edge of town, close to parks
and golf-courses.*
Bedrooms: 2 twin, 1 family
room.
Bathrooms: 2 public.
Bed & breakfast: £14-£20
single, £28-£36 double.
Half board: £19-£25 daily,
£105-£180 weekly.
Evening meal 7pm (l.o.
midday).
➤ 8 ✿ ☼ ▢ 🅿 ⅙ 🍴 📺 ▥ ▤ ▤
✗ 📶 SP 📶

Grange Hotel

South End, Coniscliffe Road,
Darlington, DL3 7HZ
☎ (0325) 464555
*Imposing stately mansion built
1804, once the home of Joseph
Pease, first Quaker MP and
promoter of early railways.*
Bedrooms: 2 single, 2 double
& 6 twin, 1 family room.
Bathrooms: 11 private,
1 public.
Bed & breakfast: from £28
single, from £40 double.
Evening meal 5pm (l.o. 6pm).
Parking for 50.
➤ ✿ ☎ ▢ 🐾 📺 V ⅙ 🍴 📺
▥ ▤ ☎ 🍴 ❋ SP 📶 T

Swallow King's Head Hotel ⋒
☺☺☺☺

Priestgate, Darlington,
DL1 1NW
☎ (0325) 380222
Telex 587112
CR Swallow
Continued ▶

DARLINGTON

Continued

A comfortable hotel, in the town centre close to shops and entertainments, with restaurant, coffee shop and bar.
Bedrooms: 30 single, 11 double & 19 twin.
Bathrooms: 60 private.
Bed & breakfast: £50-£75 single, £70-£85 double.
Half board: from £45 daily.
Lunch available.
Evening meal 7pm (l.o. 9.30pm).
Parking for 26.
Credit: Access, Visa, Diners, Amex.

DURHAM CITY

Co. Durham
Map ref 5C2

Ancient city with its Norman castle and cathedral set on a bluff high over the Wear. A market and university town and regional centre, spreading beyond the market-place on both banks of the river. July Miners' Gala is a celebrated Durham tradition.
Tourist Information Centre ☎ 091-384 3720

Bay Horse Inn M
APPROVED
Brandon Village, Durham City, DH7 8ST.
☎ 091-378 0498
3 miles from Durham city centre. Stone-built chalets all with shower, toilet, TV, tea and coffee facilities and telephone. Ample car parking.
Bedrooms: 4 twin.
Bathrooms: 4 private.
Bed & breakfast: £26 single, £35 double.
Lunch available.
Evening meal 7pm (l.o. 10pm).
Parking for 15.
Credit: Access.

Bowburn Hall Hotel M
Bowburn, Durham City, DH6 5NH
☎ 091-377 0311
Telex 537681
Large country house set in 5 acres of private grounds, 3 miles from Durham City.
Bedrooms: 5 single, 7 double & 8 twin.

Bathrooms: 19 private.
Bed & breakfast: £40-£50 single, £52-£62 double.
Evening meal 6.30pm (l.o. 10pm).
Parking for 100.
Credit: Access, Visa, C.Bl., Diners, Amex.

Castle View Guest House M
4 Crossgate, Durham City, DH1 4PS
☎ 091-386 8852
250-year-old, listed building in the heart of the old city with woodland and riverside walks, and a magnificent view of the cathedral and castle.
Bedrooms: 1 single, 2 double & 2 twin, 1 family room.
Bathrooms: 3 private, 1 public; 1 private shower.
Bed & breakfast: £20-£30 single, £35-£45 double.

Country View Guest House M
Listed
40 Claypath, Durham City, DH1 1QS
☎ 091-386 1436
Family-run guesthouse in city centre with splendid views over open countryside. 5 minutes' walk castle and cathedral, close to A1.
Bedrooms: 1 single, 3 double & 2 twin, 5 family rooms.
Bathrooms: 4 private, 3 public.
Half board: £21-£38 daily.
Evening meal 6pm.

Crossways Hotel M
Dunelm Road, Thornley, Durham City, DH6 3HT
☎ Wellfield (0429) 821248
Fax No. 0429 820034
Well-appointed private hotel, all rooms en-suite, satellite TV. Solarium, 3 bars, ballroom and a la carte restaurant. Entertainment certain nights. Durham Cathedral 6 miles.
Bedrooms: 5 single, 6 double & 11 twin, 1 family room.
Bathrooms: 23 private.
Bed & breakfast: £45-£70 single, £59-£95 double.
Lunch available.
Evening meal 7pm (l.o. 9.45pm).
Parking for 100.
Credit: Access, Visa, Diners, Amex.

Drumforke
25 Crossgate Peth, Durham City, DH1 4PZ
☎ 091-384 2966
Near the city centre and providing a useful base for touring the beautiful dales of Weardale and Teesdale.
Bedrooms: 2 twin, 1 family room.
Bathrooms: 1 public.
Bed & breakfast: from £15 single, from £30 double.
Parking for 4.

The Georgian Town House M
10 Crossgate, Durham City, DH1 4PS
☎ 091-386 8070
Georgian town house overlooking the cathedral and castle. 2 minutes' walk from city centre and close to riverside walks.
Bedrooms: 3 double & 3 twin.
Bathrooms: 6 private.
Bed & breakfast: £35-£40 single, £40-£45 double.

Hallgarth Manor Hotel M
Pittington, Durham City, DH6 1AB
☎ 091-372 1188 Telex 537023
Best Western
Country house hotel in own four acres of grounds. Facilities include two bars, lounge and restaurant.
Bedrooms: 6 single, 11 double & 6 twin.
Bathrooms: 23 private.
Bed & breakfast: £60-£70 single, £72-£80 double.
Half board: £75-£85 daily, £315-£350 weekly.
Lunch available.
Evening meal 7pm (l.o. 9.15pm).
Parking for 101.
Credit: Access, Visa, Diners, Amex.

Hill Rise Guest House
13 Durham Road, Bowburn, Durham City, DH6 5AU
☎ 091-377 0302
200 yards on left hand side from the A1(M) towards Durham. Convenient for local amenities, touring or onward travel. Friendly, relaxed atmosphere.

Bedrooms: 1 single, 2 double & 1 twin, 1 family room.
Bathrooms: 1 private, 3 public.
Bed & breakfast: £15-£20 single, £30-£40 double.
Half board: £20-£25 daily, £140-£175 weekly.
Evening meal 6.50pm (l.o. 7pm).
Parking for 4.

Nevilles Cross Hotel
Listed
Nevilles Cross, Darlington Road, Durham City, DH1 4JX
☎ 091-384 3872
Small, comfortable and friendly hotel with Tudor-style restaurant. At the crossroads of the A167 and A690, 1 mile from Durham City. Personally supervised by the proprietors, Bryan and Beryl Holland.
Bedrooms: 1 double & 3 twin, 1 family room.
Bathrooms: 2 public.
Bed & breakfast: from £27.50 single, from £35 double.
Half board: from £34 daily.
Lunch available.
Evening meal 7pm (l.o. 9.30pm).
Parking for 10.
Credit: Access, Visa, Diners, Amex.

Ramside Hall Hotel M
Carrville, Durham City, DH1 1TD
☎ 091-386 5282 Telex 537681
Attractive en-suite bedrooms, 3 eating areas, entertainment nightly. Set in 240 acres of farm and parkland, 3 miles from Durham.
Bedrooms: 2 single, 48 double & 32 twin.
Bathrooms: 82 private.
Bed & breakfast: £74-£90 single, £96-£200 double.
Half board: from £67 daily.
Lunch available.
Evening meal 7pm (l.o. 10.30pm).
Parking for 500.
Credit: Access, Visa, Diners, Amex.

Redhills Hotel M
Redhills Lane, Crossgate Moor, Durham City, DH1 4AW
☎ 091-386 4331

*Small, quiet family hotel with
well-appointed bedrooms, only
two minutes from Durham City
centre.*
Bedrooms: 5 single, 1 double.
Bathrooms: 2 public.
Bed & breakfast: from £35
single, from £50 double.
Lunch available.
Evening meal 7pm (l.o.
10pm).
Parking for 80.
Credit: Access, Visa, Diners,
Amex.

Royal County Hotel M
COMMENDED
Old Elvet, Durham City,
DH1 3JN
☎ 091-386 6821 Telex 538238
CR Swallow
*In the heart of historic
cathedral city, this well-
appointed hotel contains
antique furniture and has a
fascinating history.*
Bedrooms: 38 single,
39 double & 63 twin, 10 family
rooms.
Bathrooms: 150 private.
Bed & breakfast: £80-£88
single, £95-£105 double.
Half board: £93.50-£98.25
daily.
Lunch available.
Evening meal 7pm (l.o.
10.15pm).
Parking for 300.
Credit: Access, Visa, Diners,
Amex.

St. Aidan's College M
Listed
Windmill Hill, Durham City,
DH1 3LJ
☎ 091-374 3269
*Comfortable, modern college
designed by the late Sir Basil
Spence, in beautiful landscaped
gardens overlooking the
cathedral. Free tennis and
croquet. Adjacent to golf-
course.*
Bedrooms: 213 single,
52 twin.
Bathrooms: 2 private,
48 public.
Bed & breakfast: £15-£16.50
single, £30-£33 double.
Half board: £22.50-£24 daily,
£142 weekly.
Lunch available.
Evening meal 6.30pm (l.o.
7pm).
Parking for 50.
Open January, March-April,
July-September, December.

Three Tuns Hotel M
New Elvet, Durham City,
DH1 3AQ
☎ 091-386 4326 Telex 538238
CR Swallow
*Originally a coaching inn, the
hotel has been tastefully
modernised to provide first-
class facilities. Within easy
walking distance of the
magnificent Norman cathedral.*
Bedrooms: 14 single,
11 double & 20 twin, 2 family
rooms.
Bathrooms: 47 private.
Bed & breakfast: max. £75
single, max. £90 double.
Half board: max. £88 daily.
Lunch available.
Evening meal 7pm (l.o.
9.30pm).
Parking for 60.
Credit: Access, Visa, Diners,
Amex.

Trevelyan College M
Elvet Hill Road, Durham
City, DH1 3LN
☎ 091-374 3765/8
Fax 091-374 3789
*In parkland within 1 mile of
Durham City centre.
Comfortable Cloister Bar and
lounges. Conference facilities.*
Bedrooms: 253 single,
27 twin.
Bathrooms: 50 private,
47 public.
Bed & breakfast: £15.60-
£22.50 single, £31.20-£45
double.
Half board: from £23.55
daily, £152.25 weekly.
Lunch available.
Evening meal 6.30pm (l.o.
10.30pm).
Parking for 100.
Open March-April, June-
September.

Wharton Park Bed &
Breakfast M
Listed COMMENDED
2 Victoria Terrace, North
Road, Durham City,
DH1 4RW
☎ 091-386 5973
*Family-run Victorian town
house in the city opposite
Wharton Park with tennis and
putting. Near to railway and
bus stations.*
Bedrooms: 1 double & 2 twin,
1 family room.
Bathrooms: 1 private,
1 public.
Bed & breakfast: £14-£16
single, £33-£38 double.

EAGLESCLIFFE
Cleveland
Map ref 5C3

Railway suburb of
Stockton-on-Tees on the
road to Yarm. Preston
Hall Park has a zoo,
riverside walks, fishing
and picnicking places.

Sunnyside Hotel
APPROVED
580-582 Yarm Road,
Eaglescliffe, Stockton-on-
Tees, TS16 0DF
☎ (0642) 780075
*Friendly family hotel, ideal for
touring Cleveland and North
Yorkshire, with easy access to
all main roads, the station and
airport.*
Bedrooms: 17 single, 4 double
& 2 twin, 2 family rooms.
Bathrooms: 10 private,
4 public.
Bed & breakfast: £21-£29
single, £32-£42 double.
Half board: £28-£40 daily.
Evening meal 6.45pm (l.o.
8pm).
Parking for 22.

EBCHESTER
Co. Durham
Map ref 5B2

Old village standing on
the 4-acre Roman fort
Vindomara close to the
place where the Roman
road Dere Street crossed
the River Derwent.

The Raven Hotel M
COMMENDED
Broomhill, Ebchester,
DH8 6RY
☎ (0207) 560367/560082
Fax (0207) 560262
*Stone-built, traditionally
decorated hotel with views of
Derwent Valley from
conservatory and all rooms. On
B6309 Ebchester to Leadgate
road, only 15 minutes either
way to the Gateshead
MetroCentre on A694 or
historic Durham City on A691.*
Bedrooms: 3 single, 1 double
& 17 twin, 7 family rooms.
Bathrooms: 28 private.
Bed & breakfast: £45-£59
single, £65-£78 double.
Half board: £67-£73 daily,
£468 weekly.
Lunch available.
Evening meal 7pm (l.o.
10pm).

Parking for 100.
Credit: Access, Visa, Amex.
❶ Display advertisement
appears on page 110.

FALSTONE
Northumberland
Map ref 5B2

Remote village on the
edge of Kielder Forest
where it spreads beneath
the heathery slopes of the
south-west Cheviots
along the valley of the
North Tyne. Just 1 mile
west lies Kielder Water, a
vast man-made lake
which adds boating and
fishing to forest
recreations.

The Pheasant Inn, (by
Kielder Water) M
APPROVED
Stannersburn, Falstone,
Hexham, NE48 1DD
☎ (0434) 240382
*Historic inn with beamed
ceilings and open fires. Home
cooking. Fishing, riding and all
water sports nearby. Close to
Kielder Water, Hadrian's Wall
and the Scottish border.*
Bedrooms: 4 single, 2 double
& 3 twin, 1 family room.
Bathrooms: 5 private,
1 public.
Bed & breakfast: £20-£30
single, £38-£54 double.
Half board: £32.50-£42.50
daily, £213-£276.50 weekly.
Lunch available.
Evening meal 7pm (l.o. 9pm).
Parking for 30.

GAINFORD
Co. Durham
Map ref 5C3

Interesting and beautiful
village hidden from the
main road beside the
River Tees. Darlington
merchants built the
Georgian and Regency
residences facing the
large, sloping green,
where curving High Row
with its walled back
gardens has a charming
mixture of fine houses
and humbler cottages.

Headlam Hall Hotel M
COMMENDED
Headlam, Nr. Gainford,
Darlington, DL2 3HA
☎ (0325) 730238

Continued ▶

GAINFORD

Continued

Charming old country house in own secluded farmland and beautiful gardens. Residential and catering facilities for holidays, business accommodation, conferences and weddings.
Bedrooms: 12 double & 8 twin, 2 family rooms.
Bathrooms: 22 private.
Bed & breakfast: £47-£60 single, £59-£72 double.
Half board: £43.50-£61 daily.
Lunch available.
Evening meal 7.30pm (l.o. 10pm).
Parking for 60.
Credit: Access, Visa, Amex.

GATESHEAD

Tyne & Wear
Map ref 5C2

Facing Newcastle across the Tyne, a busy industrial centre which grew rapidly early this century. Now it is a town of glass, steel and concrete buildings with an ancient church almost entirely rebuilt after the devastating fire of 1854. Home of one of Europe's largest indoor shopping and leisure complex, the MetroCentre.
Tourist Information Centre 091-477 3478 or 460 6345

The Angel Guest House M
APPROVED
6 Front Street, Swalwell, Gateshead, NE16 3DW
☎ 091-496 0186
Fully licensed Victorianised 17th C coaching inn, within easy distance of MetroCentre and Newcastle Business Park. Good base for touring in Northumberland and Durham. Just off the A1.
Bedrooms: 2 single, 2 twin.
Bathrooms: 2 private, 1 public.
Bed & breakfast: £18.50-£22.50 single, £39.50-£45 double.
Half board: £27-£32 daily.
Evening meal 6.45pm (l.o. 8pm).
Parking for 2.
Credit: Access, Visa.

Barrington House
3 Barrington Place, Gateshead, NE8 1XA
☎ 091-477 4359
Listed Georgian house situated in quiet area with easy access to Tyneside and MetroCentre.
Bedrooms: 1 single, 2 twin, 1 family room.
Bathrooms: 1 private, 1 public.
Bed & breakfast: £15 single, £30 double.
Half board: £20 daily, £100 weekly.
Evening meal 6pm (l.o. 7pm).
Parking for 4.

Bewick Lodge
Listed
93 Bewick Road, Gateshead, NE8 1RR
☎ 091-477 3401
Situated in a mixed commercial/residential area. Close to all amenities. With ample parking in front road.
Bedrooms: 4 single, 5 twin.
Bathrooms: 2 public; 4 private showers.
Bed & breakfast: £12.50-£15 single, £25-£30 double.
Half board: £15-£17 daily, £90-£100 weekly.
Evening meal 5pm (l.o. 6.30pm).

Dunster Lodge
Earls Drive, Low Fell, Gateshead, NE9 6AB
☎ 091-487 9078 & 091-285 2911
Detached property with third of an acre of private gardens in pleasant, quiet situation. German spoken.
Bedrooms: 2 double, 1 family room.
Bathrooms: 1 private, 1 public.
Bed & breakfast: £14-£18 single, £28-£32 double.
Half board: £19-£21 daily, £100-£125 weekly.
Evening meal 7pm (l.o. 8pm).
Parking for 8.

Hedgefield County Hotel and Lodge M
APPROVED
Stella Bank, Main Hexham Road, Ryton, Gateshead, NE40 4LU
☎ 091-413 2921
Family-run hotel close to A1, MetroCentre and Newcastle. An ideal base for touring Northumbria.

Bedrooms: 7 single, 5 double & 8 twin, 1 family room.
Bathrooms: 21 private.
Bed & breakfast: £28-£44 single, £40-£56 double.
Lunch available.
Evening meal 6.30pm (l.o. 9.30pm).
Parking for 40.
Credit: Access, Visa, Amex.

Shaftesbury House M
245 Prince Consort Road, Gateshead, NE8 4DT
☎ 091-478 2544
Charming Victorian small family hotel, very central and convenient for the MetroCentre, stadium, restaurants, nightlife, Newcastle, Beamish and beaches.
Bedrooms: 2 single, 2 double & 4 twin, 2 family rooms.
Bathrooms: 2 private, 3 public.
Bed & breakfast: £20-£30 single, £30-£40 double.
Half board: £29-£39 daily.
Evening meal 5pm (l.o. 6.30pm).
Parking for 8.

Swallow Hotel M
High West Street, Gateshead, NE8 1PE
☎ 091-477 1105 Telex 53534
Swallow
A modern hotel 1 mile from Newcastle city centre just south of the River Tyne. Leisure complex incorporating pool, sauna, solarium and mini-gym. Well placed for visiting the MetroCentre.
Bedrooms: 28 single, 37 double & 31 twin, 7 family rooms.
Bathrooms: 103 private.
Bed & breakfast: £70-£75 single, £82-£87 double.
Half board: £80-£85 daily.
Lunch available.
Evening meal 6.30pm (l.o. 10pm).
Parking for 140.
Credit: Access, Visa, Diners, Amex.

HAMSTERLEY FOREST

Co. Durham

See Barnard Castle, Bishop Auckland, Crook, Tow Law.

HARTLEPOOL

Cleveland
Map ref 5C2

Major industrial port north of Tees Bay. Occupying an ancient site, the town's buildings are predominantly modern. Local history can be followed in the Gray Museum and Art Gallery and there is a good maritime museum.
Tourist Information Centre ☎ *(0429) 869706*

Grand Hotel M
Swainson Street, Hartlepool, TS24 8AA
☎ (0429) 266345
Traditional 19th C city centre hotel close to modern enclosed shopping centre. Extensively refurbished and an excellent base for visiting North Yorks Moors and Durham Cathedral.
Bedrooms: 22 single, 9 double & 17 twin.
Bathrooms: 40 private, 7 public.
Bed & breakfast: £24.75-£55 single, £46.75-£79.75 double.
Lunch available.
Evening meal 7.30pm (l.o. 10pm).
Parking for 5.
Credit: Access, Visa, C.Bl., Diners, Amex.

HAYDON BRIDGE

Northumberland
Map ref 5B2

Small town on the banks of the South Tyne with an ancient church, built of stone from sites along the Roman Wall just north. Ideally situated for exploring Hadrian's Wall and the Border country.

Anchor Hotel M
John Martin Street, Haydon Bridge, Hexham, NE47 6AB
☎ (0434) 684227
Riverside inn, in a village close to the Roman Wall. Ideal centre for touring the North Pennines and Northumberland National Park.
Bedrooms: 1 single, 5 double & 4 twin, 2 family rooms.
Bathrooms: 10 private, 1 public.
Bed & breakfast: £30-£38 single, £40-£48 double.
Lunch available.

Evening meal 7pm (l.o. 8.30pm).
Parking for 20.
Credit: Access, Visa, Diners, Amex.

ঙ ৬ & ⬚ ▢ ⬚ ᵻ ▣ ⬛
⊡ ⬛ ⛾ ⚓ ◔ ⚘ ⅄ ► ⬛
ᴰᴬ ⛫ ⬛ ⊤

Northumberland
Map ref 5B2

Old coaching and market town near Hadrian's Wall. Lively social and commercial centre for the fertile Tyne Valley. Since pre-Norman times a weekly market has been held in the centre with its market-place and abbey park, and the richly-furnished 12th C abbey church has a superb Anglo-Saxon crypt. There is a racecourse at High Yarridge.
Tourist Information Centre ☎ *(0434) 605255*

Beaumont Hotel M

⛫⛫⛫⛫ COMMENDED

Beaumont Street, Hexham, NE46 3LT
☎ (0434) 602331
Attractive refurbished hotel overlooking the lovely park and abbey. 2 comfortable bars and an a la carte restaurant. Lunch/dinner, morning coffee and afternoon teas served daily. Lift to all floors.
Bedrooms: 6 single, 10 double & 6 twin, 1 family room.
Bathrooms: 23 private.
Bed & breakfast: from £47 single, from £75 double.
Lunch available.
Evening meal 7pm (l.o. 9.45pm).
Parking for 6.
Credit: Access, Visa, Diners, Amex.

ঙ ⬚ ⛾ & ⬚ ▢ ⬚ ᵻ ▣ ⌇
⇥ ◉ ⬚ ⬛ ⚓ ⛾ ⩍ ⬛ ⛫
⊤

County Hotel M

⛫⛫⛫⛫ COMMENDED

Priestpopple, Hexham, NE46 1PS
☎ (0434) 602030
Warm and comfortable hotel in the town centre. Ideal for touring the Roman Wall and border country. Kielder Water and Forest.
Bedrooms: 2 single, 4 double & 3 twin.
Bathrooms: 9 private, 1 public.
Bed & breakfast: max. £43 single, max. £55 double.
Lunch available.

Evening meal 7pm (l.o. 9.30pm).
Parking for 2.
Credit: Access, Visa, Amex.

ঙ ⛾ ⬚ ▢ ⬚ ᵻ ▣ ⅄ ◉
⬛ ⬛ ⛾ ⛫ ⊤

High Reins
Leazes Lane, Hexham, NE46 3AT
☎ (0434) 603590
Large detached, stone-built house in quiet residential area. Close to open countryside and golf-course. Two-bedroomed family suite now available.
Bedrooms: 1 single, 2 double & 1 twin.
Bathrooms: 4 private.
Bed & breakfast: £19-£24 single, £33-£40 double.
Evening meal 6.30pm (l.o. 7pm).
Parking for 10.

ঙ & ⬚ ▢ ⛾ ⬚ ᵻ ▣ ⅄ ⊡
⬛ ⬛ ⛾ ⚓ ► ⚘ ⩍ ⬛ ᴰᴬ
⛫

Mariners Cottage Hotel
Fallowfield Dene Road, Acomb, Hexham, NE46 4RP
☎ Hexham (0434) 603666
In a country setting with splendid views over Tynedale. 3 miles from the market town of Hexham and near the Roman Wall.
Bedrooms: 2 single, 1 double & 2 twin, 1 family room.
Bathrooms: 2 private, 2 public.
Bed & breakfast: £16-£20 single, £28-£38 double.
Lunch available.
Evening meal 7.30pm (l.o. 9pm).
Parking for 60.

ঙ ⬚ ⛾ ᵻ ⬛ ⛾ ᵻ ⬛

Queens Arms Hotel M

⛫⛫

Main Street, Acomb, Hexham, NE46 4PT
☎ (0434) 602176
Traditional village inn, 2 miles north of Hexham in Tynedale's beautiful countryside. Easy access to A68 and A69 (half a mile).
Bedrooms: 1 single, 4 double & 2 twin.
Bathrooms: 5 private, 2 public.
Bed & breakfast: £15-£25 single, £30-£40 double.
Lunch available.
Evening meal 7pm (l.o. 9pm).
Parking for 12.

ঙ ⬚ ▢ ⛾ ᵻ ▣ ⅄ ⬛ ⬛ ⛾ ᵻ
⚓ ► ᴰᴬ ⬛

Queensgate House

⛫⛫ COMMENDED

Cockshaw, Hexham, NE46 3QU
☎ (0434) 605592

Family-run, converted Victorian house within 300 yards of the abbey and market square.
Bedrooms: 2 single, 1 double & 1 twin, 1 family room.
Bathrooms: 3 private, 1 public.
Bed & breakfast: £18-£25 single, £35-£37.50 double.
Half board: £24-£31 daily, £150-£195 weekly.
Evening meal 6pm (l.o. 8pm).
Parking for 5.
Credit: Amex.

ঙ & ⬚ ▢ ⬚ ᵻ ▣ ⅄ ⊡ ⬛
⬛ ⬛

Royal Hotel M

⛫⛫⛫⛫ APPROVED

22-26 Priestpopple, Hexham, NE46 1PQ
☎ (0434) 602270 Telex 57515 ATTN.115
CR Consort
Former coaching inn offering modern comfort in traditional surroundings. A la carte restaurant and cocktail bar. Private car park.
Bedrooms: 5 single, 7 double & 9 twin, 3 family rooms.
Bathrooms: 24 private.
Bed & breakfast: £40-£43 single, £62-£65 double.
Half board: £40-£55 daily, £280-£350 weekly.
Lunch available.
Evening meal 7pm (l.o. 9.30pm).
Parking for 20.
Credit: Access, Visa, Diners, Amex.

ঙ ⛾ ⬚ ▢ ⛾ ᵻ ▣ ⅄ ⊡
⬛ ⬛ ᵻ ◉ ► ⛫ ⬛ ⊤

Northumberland
Map ref 5B1

Still an idyllic retreat, tiny island and fishing village and cradle of northern Christianity. It is approached from the mainland at low water by a causeway. The clifftop castle (National Trust) was restored by Sir Edwin Lutyens.

Manor House Hotel M
Holy Island, Berwick-upon-Tweed, TD15 2RX
☎ Berwick-upon-Tweed (0289) 89207
Family-run hotel set in its own grounds with uninterrupted views of Farne Islands, Lindisfarne Castle and Priory.
Bedrooms: 1 single, 4 double, 4 family rooms.
Bathrooms: 7 private, 1 public.

Bed & breakfast: £27.50-£40 single, £40-£60 double.
Half board: £37.50-£50 daily, £180-£240 weekly.
Lunch available.
Evening meal 6.30pm (l.o. 8pm).
Parking for 5.
Credit: Access, Visa.

ঙ ⛾ ⬚ ⛾ ᵻ ▣ ⬛ ⬛ ᵻ
❄ ⩍ ⬛ ⛫ ⬛

Northumberland

See Bellingham, Falstone.

Northumberland
Map ref 5B2

Small village set in hilly countryside near the River Wansbeck. The church, which stands apart from the stone cottages across a field, has been much altered since the 13th C. Southward stretches a moorland area of rivers and small loughs or reservoirs. Near to the birthplace of Capability Brown.

Knowesgate Hotel M
Knowesgate, Kirkwhelpington, NE19 2SH
☎ (0830) 40261 & (0830) 40367
Small modern stone-built hotel, privately owned, in mid-Northumberland. An ideal base for touring, walking and fishing.
Bedrooms: 8 double & 8 twin.
Bathrooms: 16 private.
Bed & breakfast: £38 single, £52 double.
Half board: £40 daily.
Lunch available.
Evening meal 6pm (l.o. 9pm).
Parking for 60.
Credit: Access, Visa, Amex.

ঙ & ⛾ ⬚ ▢ ⛾ ᵻ ▣ ⅄
⬛ ⬛ ⛾ ᵻ ⚓ ◔ ► ᴰᴬ
⛫ ⊤

> *The symbols are explained on the flap inside the back cover.*

> *The national Crown scheme is explained in full on pages 536–539.*

Northumberland
Map ref 5B2

Small hamlet by a tiny lake, set in beautiful countryside south of Haydon Bridge and the River South Tyne. The road from Haydon Bridge to Langley winds through woodland and past the Derwentwater Memorial and Langley Castle.

Langley Castle M
COMMENDED

Langley-on-Tyne, Hexham, NE47 5LU
☎ Haydon Bridge (0434) 688888
14th C castle restored to a magnificent and comfortable hotel. 2 miles south west of Haydon Bridge, 30 minutes from Newcastle and 40 minutes from Newcastle Airport. Near A69-A686 junction.
Bedrooms: 6 double & 2 twin.
Bathrooms: 8 private.
Bed & breakfast: £42-£85 single, £58-£98 double.
Lunch available.
Evening meal 7.30pm (l.o. 9pm).
Parking for 100.
Credit: Access, Visa, Diners, Amex.

Northumberland
Map ref 5C1

Village set between the hills and the sea, close to Longdike Beck. A battlemented tower here is thought to date from the 16th C. 3 miles north-westward at Brinkburn on the River Coquet a beautiful Augustinian priory, restored in the 19th C, stands in idyllic surroundings near a ruined water-mill.

Linden Hall Hotel M
HIGHLY COMMENDED

Longhorsley, Morpeth, NE65 8XF
☎ (0670) 516611
Telex 538224
Small Luxury Hotels
Country house hotel set in 300-acre estate with wide range of leisure and sporting facilities.
Bedrooms: 2 single, 21 double & 18 twin, 4 family rooms.
Bathrooms: 45 private.

Bed & breakfast: £89.50-£92.50 single, £110-£120 double.
Half board: £65-£70 daily, £455-£525 weekly.
Lunch available.
Evening meal 7pm (l.o. 9.30pm).
Parking for 340.
Credit: Access, Visa, C.Bl., Diners, Amex.

Cleveland
Map ref 5C3

Boom-town of the mid 19th C, today's Teesside industrial and conference town has a modern shopping complex and predominantly modern buildings. An engineering miracle of the early 20th C is the Transporter Bridge which replaced an old ferry. Middlesbrough's ancient history is told in the Dorman Museum near Albert Park. The Captain Cook Birthplace Museum in Stewart Park traces the explorer's exciting life.
Tourist Information Centre ☎ (0642) 243425 or 245432

Highfield Hotel M
358, Marton Road, Middlesbrough, TS4 2PA
☎ (0642) 817638
Large former family house, built in early 1900s, set in its own gardens. Conveniently placed for the shopping centre.
Bedrooms: 4 single, 11 double & 8 twin.
Bathrooms: 23 private.
Bed & breakfast: £43-£49 single, £56 double.
Lunch available.
Evening meal 6pm (l.o. 10.30pm).
Parking for 104.
Credit: Access, Visa, Diners, Amex.

National Crown ratings were correct at the time of going to press but are subject to change. Please check at the time of booking.

Co. Durham
Map ref 5B3

Small stone town of hillside terraces overlooking the river, developed by the London Lead Company in the 18th C. There is a handsome Victorian fountain and the company headquarters is now a shooting lodge. 5 miles up-river is the spectacular 70-ft waterfall, High Force.
Tourist Information Centre ☎ (0833) 40400

Brunswick House M
55 Market Place, Middleton-in-Teesdale, DL12 0QH
☎ (0833) 40393
18th C listed stone-built guesthouse retaining much character and many original features. Comfort, friendly service and home cooking are assured.
Bedrooms: 2 double & 1 twin, 1 family room.
Bathrooms: 2 private, 1 public.
Bed & breakfast: £25-£28 single, £37-£39 double.
Half board: £22-£29.50 daily, £172-£180 weekly.
Lunch available.
Evening meal 7.30pm (l.o. 7.30pm).
Parking for 4.

Teesdale Hotel M
APPROVED

Middleton-in-Teesdale, Barnard Castle, DL12 0QG
☎ Teesdale (0833) 40264
Tastefully modernised family-run 18th C coaching inn serving home cooking and fine wines. All rooms with telephone, radio and TV. Also 4 comfortable holiday cottages in a courtyard.
Bedrooms: 2 single, 7 double & 3 twin, 1 family room.
Bathrooms: 10 private, 1 public.
Bed & breakfast: £36-£38 single, £62.50-£66 double.
Half board: £51.95-£53.95 daily.
Lunch available.
Evening meal 7.30pm (l.o. 8.30pm).
Parking for 24.
Credit: Access, Visa.

Tyne & Wear
Map ref 5C2

Commercial and cultural centre of the North East, with a large indoor shopping centre, Quayside market, museums and theatres which offer an annual 6 week season by the Royal Shakespeare Company. The Norman castle keep and the town's medieval alleys are near the river with its 6 bridges, old Guildhall and timbered merchants' houses.
Tourist Information Centre ☎ 091-261 0691 ext 231

Airport Moat House, Newcastle M
Woolsington, Newcastle upon Tyne, NE13 8DJ
☎ (0661) 24911 Telex 537121
CR Queens Moat Houses
300 yards from Newcastle Airport terminal building, with splendid conference and banqueting facilities.
Bedrooms: 16 double & 84 twin.
Bathrooms: 100 private.
Bed & breakfast: £45-£67.50 single, £55-£78.50 double.
Half board: £37.50-£81 daily, from £262.50 weekly.
Lunch available.
Evening meal 6.30pm (l.o. 10pm).
Parking for 150.
Credit: Access, Visa, Diners, Amex.

Alexandra Villa
10 Heaton Park View, Heaton, Newcastle upon Tyne, NE6 5AH
☎ 091-265 9371
Large Victorian house originally built for the Sheriff of Newcastle. Set in gardens with delightful views. Newly decorated in Victorian style.
Bedrooms: 2 twin.
Bathrooms: 1 public.
Bed & breakfast: £28 double.
Evening meal 6pm (l.o. midday).
Parking for 2.

Please check prices and other details at the time of booking.

Chirton House Hotel

COMMENDED

46 Clifton Road, Off Grainger Park Road, Newcastle upon Tyne, NE4 6XH
☎ 091-273 0407
Comfortable, privately-owned hotel in its own grounds, with a friendly, country-house atmosphere. Close to the city centre, A1M and A69.
Bedrooms: 3 single, 2 double & 3 twin, 3 family rooms.
Bathrooms: 5 private, 2 public.
Bed & breakfast: £22-£32 single, £36-£45 double.
Half board: £29.50-£39.50 daily, £150-£250 weekly.
Evening meal 6.30pm (l.o. 5.30pm).
Parking for 12.
Credit: Access, Visa.

The Copthorne, Newcastle M

COMMENDED

The Close, Quayside, Newcastle upon Tyne, NE1 3RT
☎ 091-222 0333
International standard hotel with leisure and conference facilities. River views from all rooms.
Bedrooms: 122 double & 24 twin, 10 family rooms.
Bathrooms: 156 private.
Bed & breakfast: £59-£120 single, £99-£130 double.
Half board: £74-£134 daily.
Lunch available.
Evening meal 6.30pm (l.o. 10.20pm).
Parking for 180.
Credit: Access, Visa, C.Bl., Diners, Amex.

Dene Hotel M

40-42 Grosvenor Road, Jesmond, Newcastle upon Tyne, NE2 2RP
☎ 091-281 1502
Fax 091-281 8110
In a quiet residential area close to beautiful Jesmond Dene with its small children's zoo. Within easy reach of the city centre.
Bedrooms: 10 single, 4 twin, 3 family rooms.
Bathrooms: 3 public; 14 private showers.
Bed & breakfast: £18.50-£19.50 single, £36-£39 double.
Half board: £23.50-£28.50 daily.
Lunch available.

Evening meal 5.30pm (l.o. 6pm).
Parking for 9.
Credit: Access, Visa, Diners, Amex.

Grosvenor Hotel M

APPROVED

24-28 Grosvenor Road, Jesmond, Newcastle upon Tyne, NE2 2RR
☎ 091-281 0543
Fax 091-281 9217
Friendly hotel in quiet residential suburb, offering a wide range of facilities. Close to city centre.
Bedrooms: 19 single, 11 double & 13 twin, 1 family room.
Bathrooms: 30 private, 5 public.
Bed & breakfast: £16-£40 single, £35-£60 double.
Half board: £25-£50 daily.
Lunch available.
Evening meal 6.30pm (l.o. 9.30pm).
Parking for 30.
Credit: Access, Visa, Diners, Amex.

Grove Hotel M

APPROVED

134 Brighton Grove, Newcastle upon Tyne, NE4 5NT
☎ 091-273 8248
Fax 091-272 5609
Situated near a park, central and convenient. All rooms have baby listening, TV, telephone, tea-making facilities. Most en-suite.
Bedrooms: 11 single, 8 double & 6 twin, 2 family rooms.
Bathrooms: 16 private, 3 public.
Bed & breakfast: £22-£34 single, £38-£52 double.
Lunch available.
Evening meal 7pm (l.o. 8.30pm).
Parking for 13.
Credit: Access, Visa.

Imperial Swallow Hotel M

Jesmond Road, Newcastle upon Tyne, NE2 1PR
☎ 091-281 5511 Telex 537972
Swallow
Modern hotel 10 minutes' walk from the city centre, near Jesmond Metro station, with leisure facilities and popular bars with a friendly atmosphere. Leisure club.

Bedrooms: 56 single, 26 double & 40 twin, 7 family rooms.
Bathrooms: 127 private.
Bed & breakfast: £35-£70 single, £50-£85 double.
Half board: £45-£85 daily.
Lunch available.
Evening meal 7pm (l.o. 10pm).
Parking for 140.
Credit: Access, Visa, C.Bl., Diners, Amex.

Jesmond Park Hotel M

74-76 Queens Road, Jesmond, Newcastle upon Tyne, NE2 2PR
☎ 091-281 2821
Clean and friendly hotel offering good English breakfast, in a quiet area close to city centre.
Bedrooms: 7 single, 3 double & 3 twin, 3 family rooms.
Bathrooms: 3 private, 3 public; 5 private showers.
Bed & breakfast: £19-£25 single, £32-£40 double.
Parking for 14.

Kenilworth Hotel M

COMMENDED

44 Osborne Road, Jesmond, Newcastle upon Tyne, NE2 2AL
☎ 091-281 8111
Exclusive family-run hotel, offering friendly personal attention to travellers and business persons. In Newcastle's main hotel area.
Bedrooms: 3 single, 3 double & 3 twin, 1 family room.
Bathrooms: 8 private, 1 public.
Bed & breakfast: £29-£42 single, £38-£55 double.
Half board: £35-£48 daily.
Evening meal 6pm (l.o. 8.30pm).
Parking for 10.

New Kent Hotel M

COMMENDED

Osborne Road, Jesmond, Newcastle upon Tyne, NE2 2TB
☎ 091-281 1083
Best Western
Family-run hotel in a quiet suburban area, with accent on food and warm, personal service. Congenial atmosphere. Established 20 years ago.
Bedrooms: 16 single, 6 double & 6 twin, 4 family rooms.
Bathrooms: 32 private.

Bed & breakfast: £35-£65 single, £56-£75 double.
Evening meal 6pm (l.o. 10pm).
Parking for 15.
Credit: Access, Visa, C.Bl., Diners, Amex.

Osborne Hotel M

Osborne Road, Jesmond, Newcastle upon Tyne, NE2 2AE
☎ 091-281 3385
Well-appointed owner-managed hotel, with emphasis on personal attention. Convenient for city centre, near Metro and bus services.
Bedrooms: 19 single, 2 double & 3 twin.
Bathrooms: 12 private, 4 public.
Bed & breakfast: £20-£40 single, £40-£60 double.
Half board: £27-£47 daily, £378-£518 weekly.
Evening meal 7pm (l.o. 8.30pm).
Parking for 6.
Credit: Access, Visa.

The Rise, Newcastle Airport M

Main Road, Woolsington, Newcastle upon Tyne, NE13 8BN
☎ 091-286 4963
Attractive detached house standing in 1 acre of beautiful gardens. In a rural setting within half a mile of Newcastle Airport on the A696 to Scotland.
Bedrooms: 2 single, 2 twin.
Bathrooms: 2 private, 1 public.
Bed & breakfast: £20-£30 single, £30-£40 double.
Parking for 8.

Surtees Hotel Ltd. M

12/16 Dean Street, Newcastle upon Tyne, NE1 1PG
☎ 091-261 7771
In the historic Quayside area. Favoured by television, theatre and recording personalities. Ideal for business and pleasure. Satellite television, fax. Supervised parking.
Bedrooms: 12 single, 6 double & 5 twin, 4 family rooms.
Bathrooms: 27 private.
Bed & breakfast: £67.50-£77.50 single, £77.50-£87.50 double.
Half board: £75-£85 daily.
Lunch available.

Continued ▶

NEWCASTLE UPON TYNE

Continued

Evening meal 6pm (l.o. 11pm).
Parking for 30.
Credit: Access, Visa, Diners, Amex.

Swallow Gosforth Park Hotel 𝕄

High Gosforth Park,
Newcastle upon Tyne,
NE3 5HN
☎ 091-236 4111 Telex 53655
🄶🄱 Swallow
Hotel set in 60 acres of woodland. 5 miles north of city centre. Facilities include restaurants, 3 bars, a leisure complex and conference facilities.
Bedrooms: 11 single,
76 double & 86 twin, 5 family rooms.
Bathrooms: 178 private.
Bed & breakfast: £98-£103 single, £119-£124 double.
Lunch available.
Evening meal 6pm (l.o. 10.30pm).
Parking for 300.
Credit: Access, Visa, C.Bl., Diners, Amex.

West Parade Hotel

West Parade, Newcastle upon Tyne, NE4 7LB
☎ 091-273 3034
Purpose-built hotel in its own grounds, half a mile from the Central Station and the Redheugh Bridge ring road.
Bedrooms: 25 single, 6 double & 31 twin, 3 family rooms.
Bathrooms: 30 private, 4 public.
Bed & breakfast: £21-£29.90 single, £29-£39 double.
Lunch available.
Evening meal 6pm (l.o. 9.30pm).
Parking for 56.
Credit: Access, Visa, Diners, Amex.

Western House Hotel

1 West Avenue, Gosforth,
Newcastle upon Tyne,
NE3 4ES
☎ 091-285 6812
Early Victorian end-of-terrace house offering personal service. Close to golf-course, racecourse and tennis courts, 2 miles from the city centre.

Bedrooms: 5 single, 4 double & 2 twin, 3 family rooms.
Bathrooms: 5 public.
Bed & breakfast: £16-£22 single, £31-£45 double.
Half board: £22.50-£29 daily, £137.50-£183 weekly.
Evening meal 7pm (l.o. 7pm).
Credit: Visa.

Whites Hotel 𝕄

⬚⬚⬚ **APPROVED**
38-42 Osoborne Road,
Jesmond, Newcastle upon Tyne, NE2 2AL
☎ 091-281 5126
Well-furnished comfortable hotel run by resident owners. Suburban but convenient for the city centre, near the Metro and bus services.
Bedrooms: 11 single,
18 double & 8 twin, 2 family rooms.
Bathrooms: 24 private, 4 public; 6 private showers.
Bed & breakfast: £30-£47 single, £41-£52 double.
Half board: £38.95-£55.95 daily.
Lunch available.
Evening meal 6pm (l.o. 9.30pm).
Parking for 40.
Credit: Access, Visa, Diners, Amex.

NEWTON AYCLIFFE

Co. Durham
Map ref 5C3

Northern England's first New Town growing from 60 persons in 1947 to over 27,000 today. Leisure centres in the town centre and at Spennymoor offer a wide range of facilities.

Redworth Hall 𝕄

⬚⬚⬚⬚ **HIGHLY COMMENDED**
Redworth, Newton Aycliffe,
DL5 6NL
☎ Bishop Auckland
(0388) 772442
Set in beautiful grounds, offering all amenities to the discerning guest. Ideal for holidays, breaks and conferences. Excellent leisure facilities.
Bedrooms: 3 single, 47 double & 46 twin, 3 family rooms.
Bathrooms: 99 private.
Bed & breakfast: £79.50-£94.50 single, £94.50-£109.50 double.
Lunch available.
Evening meal 7pm (l.o. 10pm).
Parking for 200.

Credit: Access, Visa, Diners, Amex.

NORTH SHIELDS

Tyne & Wear
Map ref 5C2

Bay Hotel 𝕄

⬚⬚⬚
Front Street, Cullercoats,
North Shields, NE30 4QB
☎ 091-252 3150
On the seafront overlooking Cullercoats Bay, this comfortable family hotel was the home of Winslow Homer for 2 years last century. His "Sponge Boats", painted in Cullercoats, was sold at Christies, New York, a few years ago for £307,288.
Bedrooms: 7 single, 8 double & 3 twin.
Bathrooms: 9 private, 4 public.
Bed & breakfast: £17-£27 single, £34-£52 double.
Lunch available.
Evening meal 7pm (l.o. 9pm).
Parking for 20.
Credit: Access, Visa, Diners, Amex.

OTTERBURN

Northumberland
Map ref 5B1

Small village set at the meeting of the River Rede with Otter Burn, the site of the Battle of Otterburn in 1388. A peaceful tradition continues in the sale of Otterburn tweeds in this beautiful region, which is ideal for exploring the Border country and the Cheviots.

The Butterchurn 𝕄

⬚⬚⬚ **APPROVED**
Main Street, Otterburn,
Newcastle upon Tyne, Tyne & Wear NE19 1TP
☎ (0830) 20585
In village centre, on the River Rede. Central for Roman Wall and forts. Within easy reach of Northumberland coast. Fishing permits available.
Bedrooms: 2 double & 1 twin, 5 family rooms.
Bathrooms: 8 private.
Bed & breakfast: £15-£18 single, £24-£30 double.
Half board: £21-£24 daily.
Lunch available.

Evening meal 7pm (l.o. 8.30pm).
Parking for 10.

Redesdale Arms Hotel 𝕄

⬚⬚⬚
Rochester, Otterburn,
Newcastle upon Tyne, Tyne & Wear NE19 1TA
☎ (0830) 20668/20530
Family-run old coaching inn with log fires. Central for Hadrian's Wall and the Kielder Forest.
Bedrooms: 3 single, 5 double & 3 twin, 1 family room.
Bathrooms: 4 private, 2 public; 1 private shower.
Bed & breakfast: £16.50-£33 single, £33-£46.50 double.
Lunch available.
Evening meal 7pm (l.o. 10pm).
Parking for 34.
Credit: Access, Visa, Diners.

OVINGTON

Northumberland
Map ref 5B2

Quiet village on the north bank of the River Tyne linked to the adjacent village of Ovingham which has a 17th C packhorse bridge and was the birthplace of the famous artist and engraver Thomas Bewick.

The Highlander Inn 𝕄

⬚⬚⬚
Ovington, Prudhoe,
NE42 6DH
☎ Prudhoe (0661) 32016
Country inn, dating from 1640, features open log fires and a French restaurant. Only 12 miles west of Newcastle, overlooking the River Tyne Valley.
Bedrooms: 1 single, 3 double & 1 twin.
Bathrooms: 2 private, 1 public.
Bed & breakfast: £19.50-£33 single, £30-£43 double.
Half board: £24-£45.95 daily, £150-£286 weekly.
Lunch available.
Evening meal 7pm (l.o. 9.30pm).
Parking for 20.
Credit: Access, Visa, Amex.

REDCAR

Cleveland
Map ref 5C3

Lively holiday resort near Teesside with broad sandy beaches, a fine racecourse, a large indoor funfair at Coatham and other seaside amusements. Britain's oldest existing lifeboat can be seen at the Zetland Museum.
Tourist Information Centre ☎ *(0642) 471921*

Falcon Hotel ♠

☺☺ APPROVED

13 Station Road, Redcar, TS10 1AH
☎ (0642) 484300
Small licensed hotel in centre of town providing home cooking and a warm welcome. Within easy reach of the Cleveland Hills and surrounding countryside.
Bedrooms: 4 single, 3 twin, 5 family rooms.
Bathrooms: 4 private, 3 public.
Bed & breakfast: from £16 single, £26-£32 double.
Half board: from £21 daily.
Evening meal 5pm (l.o. 7pm).
[icons]

Park Hotel ♠

☺☺☺ COMMENDED

Granville Terrace, Redcar, TS10 3AR
☎ (0642) 490888
The hotel is a small family-run business catering for the discerning client who wishes to eat and reside in comfortable surroundings.
Bedrooms: 3 single, 13 double & 9 twin.
Bathrooms: 25 private.
Bed & breakfast: £35-£62 single, £42-£72 double.
Half board: £27.75-£79.70 daily.
Lunch available.
Evening meal 7pm (l.o. 9.30pm).
Parking for 40.
Credit: Access, Visa, Diners, Amex.
[icons]

Red Barns

☺☺☺

31 Kirkleatham Street, Redcar, TS10 1QH
☎ (0642) 477622/489909
Half a mile from the beach and town centre.
Bedrooms: 5 single, 2 double & 6 twin, 1 family room.
Bathrooms: 14 private.

Bed & breakfast: £28-£33 single, £38-£48 double.
Half board: £35.95-£40.95 daily, £271.65 weekly.
Lunch available.
Evening meal 6.30pm (l.o. 10pm).
Parking for 54.
Credit: Access, Visa, Diners, Amex.
[icons]

Sans Souci

36 Newcomen Terrace, Redcar, TS10 1DB
☎ (0642) 489430
On seafront within a few minutes' walk of leisure centre and town for shops, buses and trains.
Bedrooms: 1 single, 1 twin, 1 family room.
Bathrooms: 1 public.
Bed & breakfast: max. £13 single, from £25 double.
Half board: from £16.50 daily.
Evening meal 6pm.
[icons]

Waterside House ♠

☺ APPROVED

35 Newcomen Terrace, Redcar, TS10 1DB
☎ (0642) 481062
Large terraced property overlooking the sea. Close to town centre and leisure centre. Warm friendly atmosphere with true Yorkshire hospitality.
Bedrooms: 2 single, 4 family rooms.
Bathrooms: 2 public.
Bed & breakfast: from £14 single, from £24 double.
Half board: from £19 daily.
Evening meal 5pm (l.o. 7pm).
[icons]

Willow House ♠

☺ APPROVED

8 Newcomen Terrace, Redcar
☎ (0642) 485330
Large, terraced property overlooking the sea and close to the town centre. Warm, friendly atmosphere with home cooking.
Bedrooms: 1 single, 5 family rooms.
Bathrooms: 3 public.
Bed & breakfast: from £14 single, from £24 double.
Half board: from £19 daily.
Evening meal 5pm (l.o. 7pm).
[icons]

ROTHBURY

Northumberland
Map ref 5B1

Old market town on the River Coquet near the Simonside Hills. With its leafy, sloping main street, attractive green and lovely views of river and hills it makes an ideal centre for walking and fishing or for exploring all this beautiful area from the coast to the Cheviots. Cragside House and Gardens (National Trust) are open to the public.

Orchard Guest House ♠

☺☺☺ COMMENDED

High Street, Rothbury, Morpeth, NE65 7TL
☎ (0669) 20684
Charming guesthouse in the middle of a lovely village, an ideal centre for visiting all Northumbria's attractions. Comfortable surroundings.
Bedrooms: 2 double & 1 twin, 3 family rooms.
Bathrooms: 4 private, 3 public.
Bed & breakfast: £36.50-£39 double.
Half board: £29.50-£31.50 daily, £199.50-£213.50 weekly.
Evening meal 7pm (l.o. 7pm).
Open March-October.
[icons]

RUSHYFORD

Co. Durham
Map ref 5C2

Small village on the old Great North Road.

Eden Arms Swallow ♠

☺☺☺☺

Rushyford, DL17 0LL
☎ Bishop Auckland
(0388) 720541 Telex 53168
Ⓖ Swallow
17th C coaching inn full of character, ideal for visiting Durham Cathedral, Bowes Museum and the beautiful Tees Valley.
Bedrooms: 15 single, 12 double & 14 twin, 5 family rooms.
Bathrooms: 46 private, 1 public.
Bed & breakfast: £45-£65 single, £60-£85 double.
Lunch available.
Evening meal 7pm (l.o. 9.30pm).
Parking for 150.

Credit: Access, Visa, Diners, Amex.
[icons]

SALTBURN-BY-SEA

Cleveland
Map ref 5C3

Set on fine cliffs just north of the Cleveland Hills, a gracious Victorian resort with later developments and wide, firm sands. Lively annual Victorian festival. Further west lies Teesside and a fascinating high coastline stretches south-eastward to Whitby. A handsome Jacobean mansion at Marske can be reached along the sands.
Tourist Information Centre ☎ *(0287) 622422*

Rushpool Hall Hotel ♠

Saltburn Lane, Saltburn-by-Sea, TS12 1HD
☎ Guisborough
(0287) 624111
Fax (0287) 624111
Warm welcome and an old fashioned atmosphere assured in this Victorian country house, set in 90 acres of woodland.
Bedrooms: 2 single, 12 double & 2 twin, 4 family rooms.
Bathrooms: 20 private.
Bed & breakfast: £65-£85 single, £85-£95 double.
Half board: £75-£95 daily, £495-£525 weekly.
Lunch available.
Evening meal 7pm (l.o. 9.30pm).
Parking for 150.
Credit: Access, Visa, Diners, Amex.
[icons]

Individual proprietors have supplied all details of accommodation. Although we do check for accuracy, we advise you to confirm prices and other information at the time of booking.

SEAHOUSES

Northumberland
Map ref 5C1

Small modern resort developed around a 19th C herring port. Just offshore, and reached by boat from here, are the rocky Farne Islands (National Trust) where there is an important bird reserve. The bird observatory occupies a medieval pele tower.

Beach House Hotel M
� � � COMMENDED

Sea Front, Seahouses,
NE68 7SR
☎ (0665) 720337
Fax (0665) 720103
Quiet, comfortable and friendly, family-run hotel overlooking the Farne Islands. Specialising in imaginative home cooking and baking.
Bedrooms: 2 single, 4 double & 6 twin, 2 family rooms.
Bathrooms: 14 private,
2 public.
Bed & breakfast: £25.50-£36 single, £51-£65 double.
Half board: £39-£44 daily,
£235-£271 weekly.
Evening meal 6.30pm (l.o.
7.30pm).
Parking for 16.
Open March-November.
Credit: Access, Visa.

Links Hotel M
⌖ ⌖ APPROVED

8 King Street, Seahouses,
NE68 7XP
☎ (0665) 720062
All rooms with colour TV and tea making facilities. Lounge, bar and dining room. 2 minutes from harbour.
Bedrooms: 3 double & 3 twin,
3 family rooms.
Bathrooms: 4 private,
2 public.
Bed & breakfast: £35-£49 double.
Half board: £25-£33 daily,
£157.50-£208 weekly.
Lunch available.
Evening meal 7pm (l.o. 7pm).
Parking for 16.
Credit: Access, Visa.

Olde Ship Hotel M
⌖ ⌖ ⌖ APPROVED

Seahouses, NE68 7RD
☎ (0665) 720200
Hotel with a long-established reputation for food and drink in comfortably relaxing old-fashioned surroundings.

Bedrooms: 2 single, 7 double & 6 twin, 1 family room.
Bathrooms: 16 private,
2 public.
Bed & breakfast: £27-£32 single, £54-£64 double.
Half board: £38-£44 daily,
£255-£300 weekly.
Lunch available.
Evening meal 7pm (l.o.
8.30pm).
Parking for 12.
Open February-November.
Credit: Access, Visa.

The St. Aidan Hotel and Restaurant M
⌖ ⌖

Seafront, Seahouses,
NE68 7SR
☎ (0665) 720355
On the seafront, overlooking the Farne Islands. The food is prepared and presented by the internationally trained chef/proprietor.
Bedrooms: 1 single, 2 double & 5 twin, 2 family rooms.
Bathrooms: 6 private,
1 public; 1 private shower.
Bed & breakfast: £20-£35 single, £40-£50 double.
Half board: £30-£45 daily,
£200-£280 weekly.
Evening meal 6.30pm (l.o.
8.30pm).
Parking for 15.
Open February-November.
Credit: Access, Visa, Diners.

SEATON CAREW

Cleveland
Map ref 5C2

Small resort with long golden sands and a seaside golf-course, just north of Tees Bay. Burn Valley Gardens have a 'Floral Mile'.

Old Lifeboat Guest House
9 Southend, Seaton Carew,
Hartlepool, TS25 1DB
☎ (0429) 231420
Historic house (185 years old) on Seaton front. Adjacent golf club.
Bedrooms: 3 single, 2 twin,
1 family room.
Bathrooms: 3 public.
Bed & breakfast: from £11 single, from £22 double.
Half board: from £15 daily.
Parking for 5.

SEDGEFIELD

Co. Durham
Map ref 5C2

Ancient market town, a centre for hunting and steeplechasing, with a racecourse nearby. Handsome 18th C buildings include the town council's former Georgian mansion and the rectory. The church with its magnificent spire has 17th C wood-carvings by a local craftsman. Nearby is Hardwick Hall country park.

Crosshill Hotel & Restaurant M
⌖ ⌖ ⌖ APPROVED

1 The Square, Sedgefield,
Stockton-on-Tees, Cleveland
TS21 2AB
☎ (0740) 20153 & 21206
In a conservation area overlooking the village green and the 13th C church, in the heart of historic County Durham.
Bedrooms: 1 single, 5 double,
2 family rooms.
Bathrooms: 8 private.
Bed & breakfast: £47-£50 single, £58-£62 double.
Half board: £52-£66 daily.
Lunch available.
Evening meal 7.30pm (l.o.
10.30pm).
Parking for 7.
Credit: Access, Visa, Amex.

The Hardwick Arms Hotel
1 North End, Sedgefield,
Stockton-on-Tees, Cleveland
TS21 2AZ
☎ (0740) 20218
Located in the centre of village, a Grade II coaching inn, used as a staging post on the York to Edinburgh route.
Bedrooms: 2 single, 6 double & 2 twin, 1 family room.
Bathrooms: 11 private.
Bed & breakfast: £35 single,
£45 double.
Lunch available.
Evening meal 7pm (l.o.
10pm).
Parking for 20.
Credit: Access, Visa.

The enquiry coupons at the back will help you when contacting proprietors.

SOUTH SHIELDS

Tyne & Wear
Map ref 5C2

At the mouth of the Tyne, shipbuilding and industrial centre developed around a 19th C coalport and occupying the site of an important Roman fort and granary port. The seafront has sands, gardens and parks. The town's museum has mementoes of the earliest self-righting lifeboat, built here in 1789.
Tourist Information Centre ☎ 091-454 6612

Chalyns Guest House
Listed

81 Ocean Road, South
Shields, NE33 2JJ
☎ 091-456 3262
Ideal for beach and town centre. Clean, modern, comfortable accommodation with full English breakfast.
Bedrooms: 1 single, 2 twin,
2 family rooms.
Bathrooms: 2 public.
Bed & breakfast: £14-£15 single, £24-£25 double.

Dunlin Guest House M
⌖

11 Urfa Terrace, South
Shields, NE33 2ES
☎ 091-456 7442
Family-run guesthouse near to parks, beach and town centre.
Bedrooms: 1 single, 1 double,
1 family room.
Bathrooms: 2 public.
Bed & breakfast: £14 single,
£24-£28 double.
Half board: £16-£18 daily,
£105-£130 weekly.
Evening meal 5pm (l.o. 7pm).

Julian House
58 Julian Avenue, South
Shields, NE33 2EW
☎ 091-455 1748
Clean and comfortable guesthouse, 2 minutes from the park, town centre, fairground, beach and amusements.
Bedrooms: 2 double & 1 twin,
1 family room.
Bathrooms: 2 public.
Bed & breakfast: £12.50-£15 single, £25-£30 double.
Half board: £16.50-£19 daily,
£110-£125 weekly.
Evening meal 6pm (l.o.
midday).
Parking for 3.

Marina Guest House

32 Seaview Terrace, South Shields, NE33 2NW
☎ 091-4561998
In pleasant position with panoramic sea views from most rooms.
Bedrooms: 1 single, 1 twin, 2 family rooms.
Bathrooms: 2 public.
Bed & breakfast: £16-£17 single, £28-£30 double.
Parking for 1.

Parkside Guest House

6 Seafield Terrace, South Shields, NE33 2NP
☎ 091-455 1621
Quiet central position opposite Marine Gardens and seafront. Ample street parking. Warm welcome.
Bedrooms: 1 single, 2 double & 1 twin, 1 family room.
Bathrooms: 1 public; 3 private showers.
Bed & breakfast: £13.50-£15.50 single, £27-£31 double.

Sea Crest
34 Lawe Road, South Shields, NE33 2EU
☎ 091-427 1447
Well-appointed house with magnificent views over sea and harbour. Entrance to parks and all amenities within walking distance.
Bedrooms: 3 single, 1 twin, 3 family rooms.
Bathrooms: 2 public.
Bed & breakfast: £16-£18 single, £26-£28 double.

Sea Hotel

Sea Road, South Shields, NE33 2LD
☎ 091-427 0999 Telex 53533
On the seafront in the heart of Catherine Cookson country. Popular restaurant offering French and English cooking.
Bedrooms: 18 single, 6 double & 6 twin, 3 family rooms.
Bathrooms: 33 private.
Bed & breakfast: £58-£60 single, £65-£75 double.
Half board: £44-£68 daily.
Lunch available.
Evening meal 7pm (l.o. 9.30pm).
Parking for 65.
Credit: Access, Visa, Diners, Amex.

Sir William Fox Hotel
Westoe Village, South Shields, NE33 3DZ
☎ 091-564 554
18th C building, fully licensed, in residential area of South Tyneside. Easy access to Newcastle, Sunderland and Durham.
Bedrooms: 8 single, 3 double & 2 twin, 1 family room.
Bathrooms: 14 private, 2 public.
Bed & breakfast: max. £30.55 single, max. £44.65 double.
Half board: max. £42.30 daily.
Evening meal 6.30pm (l.o. 8pm).
Parking for 14.
Credit: Access, Visa.

Stay the Voyage
111 Beach Road, South Shields, NE33 2LZ
☎ 091-4560517
Family guesthouse close to parks, beaches and town centre. Good food and a warm welcome are assured.
Bedrooms: 2 double & 2 twin, 1 family room.
Bathrooms: 1 public.
Bed & breakfast: £15-£16 single, £23-£24 double.
Half board: £15.45-£20.25 daily.
Evening meal 6pm (l.o. 8pm).
Parking for 2.

SPENNYMOOR

Co. Durham
Map ref 5C2

Booming coal and iron town from the 18th C until early in the present century when traditional industry gave way to lighter manufacturing and trading estates were built. On the moors south of the town there are fine views of the Wear Valley.

Idsley House
APPROVED
4 Green Lane, Spennymoor, DL16 6HD
☎ Bishop Auckland (0388) 814237
Long-established Victorian guesthouse on A167/A688 run by local family. Ideal for Durham City. Colour TV in bedrooms. Brochure on request.
Bedrooms: 1 single, 3 twin, 1 family room.
Bathrooms: 4 private, 1 public.
Bed & breakfast: from £15 single, from £30 double.
Parking for 8.

STOCKTON-ON-TEES

Cleveland
Map ref 5C3

Industrial complex on Teesside, first developed in the 19th C around the ancient market town with its broad main street and stately 18th C Town Hall. The street has been the site of a regular market since 1310. Green Dragon Yard has a Georgian theatre and old inn among other heritage buildings.
Tourist Information Centre ☎ (0642) 615080

Parkmore Hotel

636 Yarm Road, Eaglescliffe, Stockton-on-Tees, TS16 0DH
☎ (0642) 786815 Telex 58298
CR Best Western
Warm, friendly hotel with leisure club opposite golf-course near Yarm. Ideal for visiting North York Moors, the dales, Durham and York.
Bedrooms: 18 single, 18 double & 16 twin, 3 family rooms.
Bathrooms: 55 private.
Bed & breakfast: £40-£60 single, £52-£80 double.
Lunch available.
Evening meal 6.45pm (l.o. 9.30pm).
Parking for 100.
Credit: Access, Visa, Diners, Amex.

Stockton Arms Hotel
APPROVED
Darlington Road, Hartburn, Stockton-on-Tees, TS18 5BH
☎ (0642) 580104
Traditional English public house with letting bedrooms in traditional English setting. Within easy reach of North York Moors National Park, heritage coast and Yorkshire Dales.
Bedrooms: 1 single, 2 double & 1 twin.
Bathrooms: 2 private, 2 public; 2 private showers.
Bed & breakfast: from £22.50 single, from £30 double.
Lunch available.
Evening meal 7pm (l.o. 9.30pm).
Parking for 50.
Credit: Access, Visa, Amex.

SUNDERLAND

Tyne & Wear
Map ref 5C2

Town and seaport at the mouth of the River Wear, which has successfully made the transition from mining and shipbuilding to light engineering and tourism. Beaches at nearby Whitburn, Seaburn and Roker. North across the Wear, Monkwearmouth has a historic church with an Anglo-Saxon tower and a grand Victorian railway station preserved as a museum.
Tourist Information Centre ☎ 091-565 0960 or 565 0990

Bed & Breakfast Stop
Listed COMMENDED
183 Newcastle Road, Fulwell, Sunderland, SR5 1NR
☎ 091-548 2291
Tudor-style semi-detached house on the A1018 Newcastle to Sunderland road, 5 minutes to the railway station and 10 minutes to the seafront.
Bedrooms: 1 single, 1 twin, 1 family room.
Bathrooms: 1 public.
Bed & breakfast: £12-£13 single, £22-£24 double.
Half board: £16-£16.50 daily, £105-£112 weekly.
Evening meal 6pm (l.o. midday).
Parking for 3.

Braeside Guest House

26 Western Hill, Near Polytechnic, Sunderland, SR2 7PH
☎ 091-565 4801

Continued ▶

SUNDERLAND

Continued

Situated in Sunderland town centre. Attractive Victorian lounge, theme bedrooms, central heating throughout. Weekly golf and tennis arranged at top venues.
Bedrooms: 1 double & 2 twin.
Bathrooms: 1 private, 1 public.
Bed & breakfast: £15 single, £25-£36 double.
Parking for 2.

Felicitations M

94 Ewesley Road, High Barnes, Sunderland, SR4 7RJ
☎ 091-5220960/5289062
Private guesthouse and china-painting workshop. Hand-painted products on display. Near main bus route, polytechnic, Empire Theatre and Crowtree Leisure Centre.
Bedrooms: 1 single, 1 double, 1 family room.
Bathrooms: 1 public.
Bed & breakfast: £15-£18 single, £25-£28 double.
Half board: £20-£25 daily, £133-£147 weekly.
Evening meal 6pm (l.o. 6.30pm).
Parking for 1.

Friendly Hotel M

Junction A19/A184, Witney Way, Boldon, NE35 9PE
☎ 091-519 1999
CR Friendly
Purpose-built hotel and leisure centre with conference facilities for 220 and several smaller meeting rooms. Opened June 1990.
Bedrooms: 43 double & 27 twin, 12 family rooms.
Bathrooms: 82 private.
Bed & breakfast: £56.75-£69.45 single, £77.50-£92.65 double.
Lunch available.
Evening meal 7pm (l.o. 9.45pm).
Parking for 150.
Credit: Access, Visa, Diners, Amex.

Roker Hotel M

Roker Terrace, Roker, Sunderland, SR6 0PH
☎ 091-567 1786

Hotel taking its name from popular nearby seaside resort. Situated almost on the beach, within easy reach of the town centre.
Bedrooms: 20 single, 8 double & 9 twin, 8 family rooms.
Bathrooms: 45 private.
Bed & breakfast: £44-£51 single, £56 double.
Lunch available.
Evening meal 6pm (l.o. 10.30pm).
Parking for 200.
Credit: Access, Visa, Diners, Amex.

Swallow Hotel M

Queens Parade, Seaburn, Sunderland, SR6 8DB
☎ 091-529 2041 Telex 53168
CR Swallow
Re-opened in 1991 after rebuilding, with all modern amenities including leisure club. Fine views of the coastline from many of the suite-style rooms.
Bedrooms: 5 single, 27 double & 31 twin, 3 family rooms.
Bathrooms: 66 private.
Bed & breakfast: £75-£90 single, £90-£130 double.
Half board: from £92.50 daily.
Lunch available.
Evening meal 7pm (l.o. 9.30pm).
Parking for 100.
Credit: Access, Visa, Diners, Amex.

TOW LAW

Co. Durham
Map ref 5B2

The North Point Hotel M
APPROVED

1 High Street, Tow Law, Bishop Auckland, DL13 4DL
☎ (0388) 731087
Tow Law, main A68 trunk road. Close to Durham Dales, MetroCentre and Metroland. Offering warm hospitality and modern comforts. Fully licensed.
Bedrooms: 1 double & 4 twin.
Bathrooms: 5 private.
Bed & breakfast: £22-£25 single, £44-£48 double.
Half board: £28-£30 daily, £196-£210 weekly.
Evening meal 6pm (l.o. 7pm).
Parking for 12.
Credit: Access, Visa.

TYNEMOUTH

Tyne & Wear
Map ref 5C2

At the mouth of the Tyne, old Tyneside resort adjoining North Shields with its fish quay and market. The pier is overlooked by the gaunt ruins of a Benedictine priory and a castle. Splendid sands, amusement centre and park.

Grand Hotel M

Grand Parade, Tynemouth, NE30 4ER
☎ 091-257 2106
Fax 091-258 1919
CR Consort
High on the cliffs overlooking beautiful Long Sands beach, this imposing Victorian building was the seaside home of the Duchess of Northumberland. Building is now completely modernised to offer every comfort.
Bedrooms: 18 single, 10 double & 12 twin, 4 family rooms.
Bathrooms: 42 private, 3 public.
Bed & breakfast: £35-£45 single, £40-£55 double.
Half board: £40-£50 daily, £210-£224 weekly.
Lunch available.
Evening meal 7pm (l.o. 9.30pm).
Parking for 28.
Credit: Access, Visa, Diners, Amex.

Hope House M
COMMENDED

47 Percy Gardens, Tynemouth, NE30 4HH
☎ 091-257 1989
Double-fronted Victorian house with superb coastal views from most rooms. Period furnishing and large bedrooms.
Bedrooms: 2 double & 1 twin.
Bathrooms: 3 private, 1 public.
Bed & breakfast: £35-£50 double.
Half board: £30-£72.50 daily.
Lunch available.
Evening meal 6pm (l.o. 9pm).
Parking for 5.
Credit: Amex.

Park Hotel M

Grand Parade, Tynemouth, NE30 4JQ
☎ 091-257 1406
Fax 091-257 1716
Large, recently modernised hotel in an elevated position with an attractive bar overlooking the sea. The beach is only 1 minute's walk away.
Bedrooms: 11 single, 16 double & 17 twin, 5 family rooms.
Bathrooms: 43 private, 2 public.
Bed & breakfast: £35-£65 single, £60-£85 double.
Half board: £50-£90 daily.
Lunch available.
Evening meal 7pm (l.o. 9.30pm).
Parking for 400.
Credit: Access, Visa, Diners, Amex.

WASHINGTON

Tyne & Wear
Map ref 5C2

New Town based on an old coal-mining village close to Sunderland and Tyneside. The original pit-head buildings and mining apparatus now serve as a museum. The Old Hall (National Trust), seat of George Washington's ancestors, was rescued from its dilapidated state in the 1930s, restored and furnished. Washington Waterfowl Park is open all year.

The Sheiling M
APPROVED

Biddick Lane, Washington, NE38 7DT
☎ 091-416 0877
Comfort and good food are priorities. Easy access to all amenities/attractions. Please ring for brochure.
Bedrooms: 2 double & 3 twin, 1 family room.
Bathrooms: 2 private, 1 public; 1 private shower.
Bed & breakfast: £16-£25 single, £30-£38 double.
Half board: £23-£32 daily, £161-£224 weekly.
Evening meal 6pm (l.o. 7pm).
Parking for 8.

WHITLEY BAY

Tyne & Wear
Map ref 5C2

Seaside resort just north of Tyneside. A wide variety of diversions include a large golf-course, amusement parks and an ice-rink. The town is edged with wide sands which stretch northward toward a more rugged coastline. St. Mary's Island, which can be reached at low tide, has a redundant lighthouse.
Tourist Information Centre ☎ *091-252 4494*

The Cara M

9 The Links, Whitley Bay, NE26 1PS
☎ 091-253 0172
Overlooking the links and seashore and central for all holiday facilities.
Bedrooms: 3 single, 2 double & 1 twin, 3 family rooms.
Bathrooms: 3 public.
Bed & breakfast: from £12 single, from £24 double.

Marlborough Hotel M

20-21 East Parade, The Promenade, Whitley Bay, NE26 1AP
☎ 091-251 3628
Traditional seaside hotel in the centre of the promenade, with fine sea views.
Bedrooms: 4 single, 2 double & 3 twin, 5 family rooms.
Bathrooms: 8 private, 2 public; 2 private showers.
Bed & breakfast: from £20 single, £38-£40 double.
Half board: £27.50-£32.50 daily.
Evening meal 6pm (l.o. 6.30pm).
Parking for 7.
Credit: Access, Visa.

Park Lodge Hotel M
COMMENDED
162-164 Park Avenue, Whitley Bay, NE26 1AU
☎ 091-252 6879 & 091-253 0288 Fax No. 091 297 1006
Small and friendly hotel in a good position near the beach and entertainments.
Bedrooms: 8 single, 4 double & 4 twin, 1 family room.
Bathrooms: 12 private, 1 public; 2 private showers.
Bed & breakfast: £25-£40 single, £55-£64 double.
Half board: £39-£54 daily.
Evening meal 6pm (l.o. 9pm).

Parking for 8.
Credit: Access, Visa, Diners, Amex.

Hotel Valmar

1-3 Esplanade Avenue, Whitley Bay, NE26 2AD
☎ 091-252 3888
Small, friendly, family-run establishment near the seafront with numerous day and night time entertainments nearby.
Bedrooms: 5 single, 4 double & 1 twin, 2 family rooms.
Bathrooms: 4 public.
Bed & breakfast: £12.50-£14 single, £25-£28 double.
Evening meal 7pm (l.o. 8pm).
Parking for 5.

Waverley Hotel

44 South Parade, Whitley Bay, NE26 2RQ
☎ 091-251 3803
Small, modern hotel with public bar. Situated between town centre and the beach.
Bedrooms: 4 single, 3 double & 2 twin, 2 family rooms.
Bathrooms: 3 public.
Bed & breakfast: from £18.50 single, from £30 double.
Half board: from £24 daily.
Parking for 6.

White-Surf Guest House
APPROVED
8 South Parade, Whitley Bay, NE26 2RG
☎ 091-253 0103
A family-run guesthouse at the gateway to Northumbria. Central for all amenities, 2 minutes from beach and Metro transport.
Bedrooms: 3 single, 1 double & 3 twin, 2 family rooms.
Bathrooms: 2 public.
Bed & breakfast: £14.50-£16.50 single, £29-£33 double.
Half board: £20.50-£22.50 daily.
Evening meal 6pm (l.o. 5.30pm).
Parking for 9.

Windsor Hotel M
COMMENDED
35-45 South Parade, Whitley Bay, NE25 8UT
☎ 091-252 3317 Telex 537388
Private hotel close to the seafront and amusement park. An ice rink, roller rink and excellent leisure pool are nearby.
Bedrooms: 3 single, 12 double & 20 twin, 10 family rooms.

Bathrooms: 45 private, 1 public.
Bed & breakfast: £33-£52.50 single, £48-£58 double.
Evening meal 6pm (l.o. 9.30pm).
Parking for 22.
Credit: Access, Visa, Diners, Amex.

York House Hotel M
COMMENDED
30 Park Parade, Whitley Bay, NE26 1DX
☎ 091-252 8313
Established over 20 years. All rooms en-suite with TV/radio, tea/coffee facilities. Menu choice for both breakfast and dinner. Direct-dial telephone.
Bedrooms: 1 single, 4 double & 1 twin, 2 family rooms.
Bathrooms: 7 private; 1 private shower.
Bed & breakfast: £21.50-£23.50 single, £33-£35 double.
Half board: £28-£30 daily, £185-£200 weekly.
Evening meal 7pm (l.o. 7.30pm).
Parking for 2.
Credit: Access, Visa, Diners, Amex.

WOOLER

Northumberland
Map ref 5B1

Old grey-stone town, market-place for foresters and hill farmers, set at the edge of the north-east Cheviots. This makes a good base for excursions to Northumberland's loveliest coastline, or for angling and walking in the Borderlands.
Tourist Information Centre ☎ *(0668) 81602*

Loreto Guest House M

1 Ryecroft Way, Wooler, NE71 6BW
☎ (0668) 81350
Family-run early Georgian house with spacious grounds, in the lovely Cheviot village of Wooler. Central for touring and walking and close to coastline.
Bedrooms: 1 single, 2 double & 2 twin, 1 family room.
Bathrooms: 6 private, 2 public.
Bed & breakfast: from £15 single, from £28 double.
Half board: from £19.50 daily, from £135 weekly.

Evening meal 6.30pm (l.o. 7pm).
Parking for 12.

Red Lion M

1 High Street, Wooler, NE71 6LD
☎ (0668) 81629
17th C former coaching inn, located in the town of Wooler in Northumberland.
Bedrooms: 2 double & 3 twin, 1 family room.
Bathrooms: 4 private, 1 public.
Bed & breakfast: £28-£36 double.
Lunch available.
Evening meal 7pm (l.o. 8.45pm).
Parking for 6.
Credit: Access, Visa, Diners.

WYLAM-ON-TYNE

Northumberland
Map ref 5B2

Well-kept village on the River Tyne, famous as the birthplace of the railway pioneer, George Stephenson. The cottage in which he was born is open to the public, and the Wylam Railway Museum also commemorates William Hedley and Timothy Hackworth.

Laburnum House Restaurant

Wylam-on-Tyne, NE41 8AJ
☎ (0661) 852185
Individually decorated, large double rooms. A la carte restaurant with over 40 covers.
Bedrooms: 4 double.
Bathrooms: 4 private.
Bed & breakfast: from £40 single, from £50 double.
Evening meal 6.30pm (l.o. 9.30pm).
Parking for 4.
Credit: Access, Visa, Diners, Amex.

National Crown ratings were correct at the time of going to press but are subject to change. Please check at the time of booking.

The Greenhead Country House Hotel

Firtree, Crook, Co. Durham DL15 8BL. ☎ 0388 763143
One of the most prestigious new developments created for touring the Prince Bishops Countryside. Located at the Foot of the lovely Weardale Valley. The Hotel has complete en-suite accommodation together with colour T.V., tea & coffee facilities, radio alarms in each individually colour co-ordinated bedroom. Superb residents' lounge complemented with fully licensed facilities. Lovely rural location. B&B Booking rates:

£42 double/twin room en-suite
£35 single room en-suite
Evening meals available on request.
Contact Paul & Anne Birbeck.

AA Selected Q Q Q Q
RAC Highly Acclaimed

Northumbria TOURIST BOARD
MEMBER

Helme Park Hall Country House Hotel

Completely refurbished to an exceptional standard. All rooms have en-suite facilities A la Carte Restaurant and Bar Meals available. The Hotel is set in 5 acres of beautiful wooded gardens with the finest panoramic views over the Dales, an area of Outstanding Natural Beauty. Excellent road network for touring; Lake District, Scottish Borders and York only 1 hour. Historic Durham, Hadrians Wall and a myriad of Castles within ½ an hour. The warmest welcome in Northern England from resident owner, Chris Close.
👑👑👑 Commended AA ★★★ RAC ★★★

**Nr. Firtree, Bishop Auckland,
Co. Durham DL13 4NW**

A68. Midway Darlington/Corbridge.
1 mile north of Fir Tree. ☎ 0388 730970

The Raven Hotel

**Broomhill, Ebchester, County Durham DH8 6RY.
Tel (0207) 560367/560082 Fax (0207) 560262**

👑👑👑 Commended AA ★★★ RAC ★★★

Derwentside's newest and largest hotel is centrally situated with traffic free access to Durham City (15 mins), Beamish Museum (15 mins) or the Gateshead Metro Centre (20 mins).
Fine stone building of traditional design. Conservatory, restaurant and 28 en-suite bedrooms. Every room in the hotel enjoys a spectacular rural view.
Disabled facilities available. Also 4 poster bed.
Please telephone for brochure and tariffs.

Use a coupon

When requesting further information from advertisers in this guide, you may find it helpful to use the advertisement enquiry coupons which can be found towards the end of the guide. These should be cut out and mailed direct to the companies in which you are interested. Do remember to include your name and address.

THE CROWN IS YOUR SURE SIGN OF WHERE TO STAY

HOTELS, GUESTHOUSES, INNS, B&Bs & FARMHOUSES

Throughout Britain, the tourist boards now inspect over 17,000 hotels, guesthouses, inns, B&Bs and farmhouses, every year, to help you find the ones that suit you best.

THE CLASSIFICATIONS: **'Listed'**, and then **ONE to FIVE CROWN,** tell you the range of facilities and services you can expect. The more Crowns, the wider the range.

THE GRADES: **APPROVED, COMMENDED and HIGHLY COMMENDED,** where they appear, indicate the quality standard provided. If no grade is shown, you can still expect a high standard of cleanliness.

Every classified place to stay has a Fire Certificate, where this is required under the Fire Precautions Act, and all carry Public Liability Insurance.

'Listed': Clean and comfortable accommodation, but the range of facilities and services may be limited.

ONE CROWN: Accommodation with additional facilities, including washbasins in all bedrooms, a lounge and use of a phone.

TWO CROWN: A wider range of facilities and services, including morning tea and calls, bedside lights, colour TV in lounge or bedrooms, assistance with luggage.

THREE CROWN: At least one-third of the bedrooms with ensuite WC and bath or shower, plus easy chair, full length mirror. Shoe cleaning facilities and hairdryers available. Hot evening meals available.

FOUR CROWN: At least three-quarters of the bedrooms with ensuite WC and bath/shower plus colour TV, radio and phone, 24-hour access and lounge service until midnight. Last orders for meals 8.30 pm or later.

FIVE CROWN: All bedrooms having WC, bath and shower ensuite, plus a wide range of facilities and services, including room service, all-night lounge service and laundry service. Restaurant open for breakfast, lunch and dinner.

Every Crown classified place to stay is likely to provide some of the facilities and services of a higher classification. More information available from any Tourist Information Centre.

We've checked them out before you check in!

PLEASE REFER TO THE COLOUR MAPS AT THE BACK OF THIS GUIDE FOR ALL PLACES WITH ACCOMMODATION LISTINGS.

ON THE COAST – *miles of sand with the resorts to match, including serene Southport, lovely Lytham, marvellous Morecambe and the jewel in the crown, brilliant Blackpool. And inland – the rich Cheshire plain with its half-timbered black and white houses, the quiet Forest of Bowland, the beautiful Ribble Valley, the wooded Lune Valley and the rugged Pennines. And then there are the cities – Liverpool, with its Beatles "industry" and the new galleries and museums, Manchester, a great industrial and commercial centre, and Chester, with its medieval buildings and Roman remains.*

WHERE TO GO, WHAT TO SEE

Alice in Wonderland Tours
Daresbury Village, Warrington, Cheshire
☎ Comberbach (0606) 891303
Memorial marking site of parsonage where Lewis Carroll was born. Church with Alice window, Wonderland weather vane, font in which Carroll was christened.

Arley Hall and Gardens
Northwich, Cheshire CW9 6NA
☎ Arley (0565) 777353
Early Victorian hall set in 12 acres of magnificent gardens. 15th C tithe barn. Unique collection of watercolours of the area. Woodland walk. Shop and craftsmen.

Beeston Castle
Beeston, Tarporley, Cheshire
☎ Bunbury (0829) 260464
Ruined 13th C castle in dramatic situation on top of Peckforton Hills. Dramatic views of surrounding countryside. Exhibition on history of castle.

Blackpool Pleasure Beach
South Shore, Blackpool, Lancashire FY4 1EZ
☎ Blackpool (0253) 41033
Europe's greatest amusement park. Avalanche bobsleigh ride, Big Dipper, twin-track roller coaster, Revolution, Funshineland for children. Summer season ice show,

cabaret in the Horseshoe Bar. New Tourist Information Centre with hotel bed database.

Butterfly World
Queens Park, Chorley New Road, Bolton, Gtr. Manchester
☎ Bolton (0204) 22311
Butterflies and moths in free flight, goldfish, Koi carp, insects.

Camelot Adventure Theme Park
Park Hall Road, Charnock Richard, Chorley, Nr. Preston

Lancashire PR7 5LP
☎ Eccleston (0257) 453044
Family theme park based on participation. 80 rides (mostly under cover), jousting, falcony, marionettes.

Capesthorne Hall
Siddington, Macclesfield, Cheshire SK11 9JY
☎ Chelford (0625) 861221
Sculpture, paintings, furniture, Greek vases, family muniments. Georgian chapel, tea rooms, gardens, lakes, nature walks.

Europe's greatest amusement park, Blackpool Pleasure Beach

Part of the 20-piece model fairground at the Museum of Childhood

Chester Zoo
Upton-by-Chester, Chester,
Cheshire CH2 1LH
☎ Chester (0244) 380280
*Penguin pool with underwater
views, tropical house,
spectacular displays of spring
and summer bedding plants.
Chimpanzee house and outdoor
enclosure.*

**Croxteth Hall
and Country Park**
Off Muirhead Avenue East,
Liverpool, Merseyside L12 0HB
☎ 051-228 5311
*500-acre country park and hall
with displays and furnished
rooms. Walled garden, farm
with rare breeds, miniature
railway, gift shop, picnic areas,
riding centre.*

East Lancashire Railway
Bolton Street Station, Bury,
Gtr. Manchester BL9 0EY
☎ 061-764 7790
*Four mile long preserved railway
operated principally by steam
traction. Transport museum
nearby.*

Healey Dell Nature Reserve
The Visitor Centre, Healey Hall
Mills, Shawclough, Rochdale,
Gtr. Manchester OL12 6BG
☎ Rochdale (0706) 350459
*Nature reserve, information
centre and field study centre.*

Helmshore Textile Museum
Higher Mill, Holcombe Road,
Helmshore, Haslingden,
Lancashire BB4 6RE
☎ Rossendale (0706) 226459
*Textile machinery, water wheel
and many working exhibits,
especially carding engines and
cotton spinning mules.*

**Hollingworth Lake
Country Park**
Rakewood Road,
Littleborough, Gtr. Manchester
OL15 0AQ
☎ Littleborough (0706) 73421
*Permanent and temporary
exhibitions, slide show, 30ft
mural by Walter Kershaw.*

Knowsley Safari Park
Prescot, Merseyside L34 4AN
☎ 051-430 9009

*Five-mile drive through game
reserves, set in 400 acres of
parkland containing lions, tigers,
elephants, rhinos, etc. Large
picnic areas and children's
amusement park.*

Lyme Park
Disley, Stockport, Cheshire
SK12 2NX
☎ Disley (0663) 62023
*State rooms, period furniture,
tapestry. Grinling Gibbons
carvings in hall, clock collection.
Nature trails, herds of red and
fallow deer.*

Manchester Jewish Museum
190 Cheetham Hill Road,
Manchester, Gtr. Manchester
M8 8LW
☎ 061-834 9879
*Restored former Spanish and
Portuguese synagogue (1874).
Grade II listed building. History of
Manchester's Jewish community.*

Museum of Childhood
Church Street, Ribchester,
Lancashire PR3 3YE
☎ Ribchester (0254) 878520

Large building containing childhood toys, dolls, over 50 dolls' houses, 20-piece model fairground, Tom Thumb replica, collectors' toy shop.

Museum of Science and Industry
Liverpool Road, Castlefield, Manchester, Gtr. Manchester M3 4JP
☎ 061-832 2244
Europe's largest industrial museum based on the site of the oldest railway station in the world. Exhibitions include the Power Hall and Air and Space Gallery.

Norton Priory Museum and Gardens
Tudor Road, Manor Park, Runcorn, Cheshire WA7 1SX
☎ Runcorn (0928) 569895
Excavated Augustinian priory, remains of church, cloister, chapter house. Later site of Tudor mansion and Georgian house. Display of site history.

Pleasureland
Marine Drive, Southport, Merseyside PR8 1RX
☎ Southport (0704) 32717
Traditional amusement park on the sands with more than 50 thrilling rides, including new Log Flume.

Port Sunlight Heritage Centre
Greendale Road, Port Sunlight, Wirral, Merseyside L62 4ZP
☎ 051-644 6466
In listed building, display showing creation of village, with photos, drawings, models, Victorian model house.

Salford Museum and Art Gallery
Peel Park, The Crescent, Salford, Gtr. Manchester M5 4WU
☎ 061-736 2649
Reconstructed period street: "Lark Hill Place". Largest publicly owned collection of works of L.S. Lowry. Temporary art exhibitions.

Samlesbury Hall
Preston New Road, Samlesbury, Preston, Lancashire PR5 0UP
☎ Mellor (025 481) 2010
Historic hall and buildings, antiques, collectors' items. Changing exhibitions and craftsmen and women at work.

Stapeley Water Gardens and the Palms Tropical Oasis
London Road, Stapeley, Nantwich, Cheshire CW5 7LH
☎ Nantwich (0270) 623868
Exotic birds, rare plants, sharks, piranhas, tropical and coldwater fish, trees and shrubs. Pool and garden equipment.

Steamtown Railway Museum
Warton Road, Carnforth, Lancashire LA5 9HX
☎ Carnforth (0524) 732100
Former BR engine shed housing over 30 mainline and industrial locomotives. Signal box, turntable, coaling plant, model railway and gift shop.

Wycoller Country Park
Wycoller, Colne, Lancashire
☎ Colne (0282) 863627
Country park and conservation area enclosing hamlet of Wycoller. Scenic, historic and literary interest. Brontë associations. Information centre.

MAKE A DATE FOR...

Horse racing – Grand National Meeting
Aintree Racecourse, Liverpool, Merseyside
2 – 4 April

Golf – Lytham Trophy
Royal Lytham and St. Anne's Golf Course, Links Gate, Lytham St. Anne's, Lancashire
2 – 3 May

Manchester Air Show
Barton Aerodrome, Eccles, Gtr. Manchester
24 May

Morecambe Illuminations
Promenade, Morecambe, Lancashire
5 August – 1 November

Southport Flower Show
Victoria Park, Southport, Merseyside
20 – 22 August

Preston Guild '92
Various venues, Preston, Lancashire
29 August – 5 September

Castlefield Carnival
Liverpool Road, Manchester, Gtr. Manchester
1 – 30 September

Blackpool Illuminations
Promenade, Blackpool, Lancashire
4 September – 8 November

FIND OUT MORE

Further information about holidays and attractions in the North West region is available from:

North West Tourist Board
Swan House, Swan Meadow Road, Wigan Pier, Wigan WN3 5BB
☎ (0942) 821222

These publications are available free from the North West Tourist Board:

North West Welcome Pack

Discover England's North West (map)

Conference brochure

Overseas brochure

Group Visits

Bed & Breakfast map

Farmhouse brochure

Places to Visit in Winter

Places to stay

ACCOMMODATION ENTRIES *in this regional section are listed in alphabetical order of place name, and then in alphabetical order of establishment.*

THE MAP REFERENCES *refer to the colour maps towards the end of the guide. The first figure is the map number; the letter and figure which follow indicate the grid reference on the map.*

THE SYMBOLS *at the end of each accommodation entry give information about services and facilities. A 'key' to these symbols is inside the back cover flap, which can be kept open for easy reference.*

ACCRINGTON

Lancashire
Map ref 4A1

5m E. Blackburn
Victorian town noted for its red bricks which were extensively used in public buildings throughout Britain. Famous for textiles and general engineering. The Haworth Art Gallery contains collections of Early English watercolours and Tiffany glass.
Tourist Information Centre ☎ *(0254) 386807*

Dunkenhalgh Hotel M
😊😊😊😊😊
Blackburn Road, Clayton-le-Moors, Accrington, BB5 5JP
☎ (0254) 398021 Telex 63282
🅒🅡 Rank
Gothic-fronted mansion house with Georgian interior, set in 17 acres of parkland, at exit 7 of the M65. Many fine public rooms and conference facilities for up to 400. Sauna and indoor heated swimming pool.
Bedrooms: 6 single, 33 double & 31 twin, 10 family rooms.
Bathrooms: 80 private.
Bed & breakfast: £51-£74 single, £72-£89 double.
Lunch available.
Evening meal 7pm (l.o. 9.45pm).
Parking for 250.
Credit: Access, Visa, Diners, Amex.
➤ 📷 🏠 📞 🗣 🅓 🖵 🛇 🏋 📺
🖃 🔘 🏧 🏮 📍 🆚 🔇 🔌 ❄️ 🅱 🅤
📍 ✿ 🐾 SP 🅿 🆃

Kendall's Hotel M
Listed
163 Blackburn Road, Accrington, BB5 0AA
☎ (0254) 232851
Warm and comfortable with relaxed atmosphere, designed to make the guest feel at home.
Bedrooms: 6 single, 1 double & 1 twin, 1 family room.
Bathrooms: 1 public.
Bed & breakfast: £11.50-£18 single, £19-£25 double.
Half board: £17-£25 daily.
Evening meal 6pm (l.o. 4pm).
Credit: Access, Visa, Diners, Amex.
➤ 📷 🆚 🍽 📺 🏮 🚪 🎿 🏮
🆃

ALDERLEY EDGE

Cheshire
Map ref 4B2

5m S. Manchester Airport
Residential town taking its name from the hill which rises to a height of 600 ft from the Cheshire Plain. The Edge is a well-known beauty spot with superb views. Many historic buildings including Chorley Old Hall (the oldest surviving manor house in Cheshire).

The Alderley Edge Hotel M
😊😊😊😊 COMMENDED
Macclesfield Road, Alderley Edge, SK9 7BJ
☎ (0625) 583033

Converted country mansion built originally for one of the Manchester cotton barons. Close to the Edge beauty spot and near the village of Alderley, Jodrell Bank and Gawsworth Hall.
Bedrooms: 32 double.
Bathrooms: 32 private.
Bed & breakfast: £40-£105 single, £74-£128 double.
Half board: £62.50-£127.50 daily.
Lunch available.
Evening meal 7pm (l.o. 10.30pm).
Parking for 70.
Credit: Access, Visa, Diners, Amex.
➤ 🔔 🏠 📞 🅓 🖵 🛇 🏋 🆚
🍽 🔘 🏧 🏮 📍 🎿 📍 ❄️ 🆚 SP
🅱 🆃

Milverton House Hotel M
😊😊😊
Wilmslow Road, Alderley Edge, SK9 7QL
☎ (0625) 583615 & 585555
Well-appointed Victorian villa on main road with open country views. Home cooking.
Bedrooms: 2 single, 7 double & 3 twin, 1 family room.
Bathrooms: 8 private, 4 public; 2 private showers.
Bed & breakfast: £30-£50 single, £45-£66 double.
Half board: £40-£58 daily, £185-£250 weekly.
Evening meal 6.30pm.
Parking for 16.
Credit: Access, Visa.
➤ 🏧 🖵 🔔 🅓 📺 🏮 🏠 🚪 👍
🏮 ✿ 🆃

ALTRINCHAM

Gtr. Manchester
Map ref 4A2

8m SW. Manchester
On the edge of the Cheshire Plain, close to Manchester. Once a thriving textile town, Altrincham is now mainly residential. Good centre for local beauty spots including 18th C Dunham Massey Hall (National Trust) with its deer park.
Tourist Information Centre ☎ *061-941 7337*

Beech Mount Hotel M
😊😊 APPROVED
46 Barrington Road, Altrincham, WA14 1HN
☎ 061-928 4523
Family-run hotel with restaurant, within easy reach of Manchester Airport and city centre. Convenient for public transport and shopping centre.
Bedrooms: 12 single, 8 double & 10 twin, 4 family rooms.
Bathrooms: 34 private, 1 public.
Bed & breakfast: £27.80-£29.80 single, max. £48.50 double.
Half board: £35.80-£37.80 daily.
Evening meal 6.30pm (l.o. 8.30pm).
Parking for 32.
Credit: Access, Visa.
➤ 🏧 🅓 🖵 🛇 🔔 📺 🏮 🏮
🎿 🚪 🏮

Please mention this guide when making a booking.

Belvedere Guest House
Listed APPROVED

58 Barrington Road,
Altrincham, WA14 1HY
☎ 061-941 5996
*10 minutes from Manchester
Airport; free taxi service.
Close to city centre, convenient
for buses and trains. All rooms
have satellite TV.*
Bedrooms: 1 single, 1 double
& 1 twin, 1 family room.
Bathrooms: 3 private,
1 public.
Bed & breakfast: £16-£25
single, £32-£40 double.
Half board: £20-£30 daily,
£120-£150 weekly.
Evening meal 6pm (l.o. 8pm).
Parking for 6.
Credit: Access, Visa.

Bowdon Hotel M
COMMENDED

Langham Road, Bowdon,
Altrincham, WA14 2HT
☎ 061-928 7121 & 8825
Telex 668208
*Victorian house incorporating
modern extension and
facilities. Set in rural suburbs
at the gateway to the lovely
Cheshire countryside.*
Bedrooms: 26 single,
11 double & 43 twin, 2 family
rooms.
Bathrooms: 82 private.
Bed & breakfast: £33-£58
single, £49-£69 double.
Half board: £37.50-£48.50
daily.
Lunch available.
Evening meal 7pm (l.o.
10pm).
Parking for 170.
Credit: Access, Visa, Diners,
Amex.

---

*National Crown
ratings were correct
at the time of going
to press but are
subject to change.
Please check at the
time of booking.*

---

*The enquiry
coupons at the
back will help you
when contacting
proprietors.*

Gtr. Manchester
Map ref 4B1

6m E. Manchester
Now part of the borough
of Tameside, this old
market town lies on the
north bank of the River
Tame. The Assheton
family, who owned the
manor of Ashton from the
14th C, are portrayed in
the stained glass
windows of St. Michael's
Church.

Welbeck House Hotel
COMMENDED

324 Katherine Street, Ashton-
Under-Lyne, OL6 7BD
☎ 061-344 0751 & Fax. 061-
343 4278
*Small exclusive hotel offering
personal service and run
entirely by the owners.*
Bedrooms: 6 single, 2 family
rooms.
Bathrooms: 8 private.
Bed & breakfast: £42-£48
single, £50-£55 double.
Evening meal 4pm (l.o. 8pm).
Parking for 20.
Credit: Access, Visa, Diners,
Amex.

York House Hotel M
COMMENDED

York Place, Off Richmond
Street, Ashton-under-Lyne,
OL6 7TT
☎ 061-330 5899 & Fax 061-
343 1613
*Recently refurbished hotel with
restaurant. Emphasis on food
and fine wines. Garden,
function room. Ideal base for
touring the north of England.*
Bedrooms: 8 single, 19 double
& 5 twin, 2 family rooms.
Bathrooms: 34 private.
Bed & breakfast: £46-£58.50
single, £66-£71 double.
Lunch available.
Evening meal 7pm (l.o.
9.30pm).
Parking for 36.
Credit: Access, Visa, C.Bl.,
Diners, Amex.

---

*The symbol **CR** and the name of a hotel
group or consortium after a hotel address
means that bookings can be made through
a central reservations office. These are
listed on page 540.*

Merseyside
Map ref 4A2

3m S. Birkenhead
Town on the Wirral
Peninsula, the mainstay
of which is the Unilever
complex of chemical,
soap, detergent and food
companies. Port Sunlight
model village, built for
Unilever employees,
houses a fine collection
of paintings and sculpture
in the Lady Lever Art
Gallery.

The Bebington Hotel
24 Town Lane, Bebington,
Wirral, L63 5JG
☎ 051-645 0608
*Well-appointed private hotel,
ideally located for tourists or
business people visiting
Merseyside, Liverpool, Chester
and Wales.*
Bedrooms: 4 single, 3 double
& 1 twin, 3 family rooms.
Bathrooms: 11 private,
2 public.
Bed & breakfast: £19.50-
£28.50 single, £35-£39.50
double.
Half board: £25-£34 daily.
Evening meal 7pm (l.o. 9pm).
Parking for 20.
Credit: Access, Visa.

The Bridge Inn Hotel M
APPROVED

Bolton Road, Port Sunlight
Village, Bebington, L62 4UQ
☎ 051-645 8441
*Unique, charming, historic
hotel in famous village. Chester
20 minutes' drive, Liverpool 15
minutes' drive. Ideal for
exploring Wirral.*
Bedrooms: 10 single, 1 double
& 3 twin, 2 family rooms.
Bathrooms: 11 private,
2 public; 5 private showers.
Bed & breakfast: £29.50-
£45.50 single, £52.50-£57.50
double.
Half board: £38-£54 daily.
Lunch available.
Evening meal 7pm (l.o.
10pm).
Parking for 60.
Credit: Access, Visa, Amex.

Cheshire
Map ref 4A2

11m SE. Chester
Hamlet below the
Peckforton Hills which
rise from the Cheshire
Plain to 740 ft. Medieval
Beeston Castle (English
Heritage) overlies a
prehistoric hill fort.

Wild Boar Hotel M
COMMENDED

Whitchurch Road, Nr.
Beeston, Tarporley,
CW6 9NW
☎ Bunbury (0829) 260309 &
Fax (0829) 261081
Telex 61222
CR Rank
*18th C black and white
building of character, in typical
style of Cheshire. 13 miles
from Chester and ideally
located for exploring the
Cheshire countryside.*
Bedrooms: 15 double &
3 twin, 19 family rooms.
Bathrooms: 37 private.
Bed & breakfast: £51-£74
single, £72-£89 double.
Lunch available.
Evening meal 7pm (l.o.
10pm).
Parking for 100.
Credit: Access, Visa, C.Bl.,
Diners, Amex.

Merseyside
Map ref 4A2

Shipbuilding, docks and
later the Mersey Tunnel
turned Birkenhead into a
busy town. Good
Victorian architecture in
Hamilton Square and
Town Hall. Williamson Art
Gallery contains English
watercolours, pottery and
porcelain.
*Tourist Information
Centre* ☎ *051-647 6780*

Ashgrove M
14 Ashville Road, Claughton,
Birkenhead, L43 8SA
☎ 051-653 3794
*Friendly, family-run
establishment overlooking
Birkenhead Park. 10 minutes'
walk to train and 2 stops to
Liverpool station. Excellent
shopping facilities nearby,
numerous sports facilities.
Resident folk singer (owner).*
Continued ▶

BIRKENHEAD

Continued

Bedrooms: 2 single, 2 double
& 3 twin, 1 family room.
Bathrooms: 2 private,
3 public.
Bed & breakfast: £12-£16
single, £22-£32 double.
Half board: £15-£20 daily,
£100-£130 weekly.
Lunch available.
Evening meal 6pm (l.o. 4pm).
Parking for 10.

Lincluden Lodge Hotel
114 Storeton Road, Prenton,
Birkenhead, Wirral,
L42 8NA
☎ 051-608 3732
*For discerning guests looking
for a warm welcome and value
for money. Convenient for
Chester, Liverpool, the Lakes
and North Wales. 1 mile along
the B5151 from the M53
junction 4.*
Bedrooms: 6 single, 6 double
& 6 twin, 1 family room.
Bathrooms: 5 private,
3 public.
Bed & breakfast: £18-£26
single, £30-£36 double.
Half board: £23-£31 daily,
£147-£203 weekly.
Lunch available.
Evening meal 6pm (l.o.
7.30pm).
Parking for 18.
Credit: Access, Visa.

Shrewsbury Guest House
31 Shrewsbury Road, Oxton,
Birkenhead, L43 2JF
☎ 051-652 4029
*Friendly guesthouse offering
good home cooking. Colour TV
in all rooms. Free tea and
coffee facilities always
available. Relaxed atmosphere.
Restaurant and licensed bar.
Further 10-bedroom extension
for 1992 season.*
Bedrooms: 3 double & 5 twin.
Bathrooms: 5 private,
2 public; 1 private shower.
Bed & breakfast: £15-£20
single, £24-£30 double.
Half board: £18.50-£25 daily,
£129.50-£175 weekly.
Evening meal 5pm (l.o. 8pm).
Parking for 10.

*We advise you to confirm your booking
in writing.*

Yew Tree Hotel
58 Rock Lane West, Rock
Ferry, Birkenhead, L42 4PA
☎ 051-645 4112
*Warm, comfortable
accommodation in friendly,
elegant, Georgian house, all
rooms with Sky satellite TV.
Quiet situation, convenient for
motorways, Birkenhead tunnel,
public transport, Irish and
Manx ferries.*
Bedrooms: 8 single, 1 double
& 4 twin, 1 family room.
Bathrooms: 5 private,
3 public; 2 private showers.
Bed & breakfast: £21-£31
single, £25-£40 daily.
Half board: £25-£40 daily.
Evening meal 7pm (l.o. 8pm).
Parking for 20.
Credit: Access, Visa, Amex.

BLACKBURN

Lancashire
Map ref 4A1

Once a thriving cotton
town. Models of the old
machinery may be seen in
Lewis Textile Museum.
Relics of the Roman
occupation in Blackburn
Museum. 19th C
cathedral, Victorian
landscaped Corporation
Park.
*Tourist Information
Centre* ☎ *(0254) 53277 or
55201 ext 214*

Northcote Manor Hotel ⚑
😊😊😊😊 COMMENDED
Northcote Road, Old Langho,
Nr. Blackburn, BB6 8BE
☎ (0254) 240555 &
Fax (0254) 246568
*Pleasant country house hotel in
true English style. Warm and
friendly atmosphere in an ideal
location for business and
pleasure.*
Bedrooms: 1 single, 4 double
& 1 twin.
Bathrooms: 6 private.
Bed & breakfast: £60-£65
single, £70-£75 double.
Half board: £80-£100 daily.
Lunch available.
Evening meal 7pm (l.o.
9.30pm).
Parking for 50.
Credit: Access, Visa, Diners,
Amex.

BLACKPOOL

Lancashire
Map ref 4A1

Largest fun resort in the
North with every
entertainment including
amusement parks, piers,
tram-rides along the
promenade, sandy
beaches and the famous
Tower. Among its annual
events are the 'Milk
Race', the Veteran Car
Run and the spectacular
autumn illuminations.
*Tourist Information
Centre* ☎ *(0253) 21623 or
21891 or 403223 or
(weekdays only) 25212*

Adelphi Private Hotel
😊😊
44 King Edward Avenue,
Blackpool, FY2 9TA
☎ (0253) 52932
*Family-owned and run hotel,
off North Promenade, close to
Gynn Gardens and North
Shore Golf Club.*
Bedrooms: 5 single, 1 double,
3 family rooms.
Bathrooms: 5 private,
1 public.
Bed & breakfast: £14.50-
£18.50 single, £29-£37 double.
Half board: £17.50-£22 daily,
£110-£145 weekly.
Evening meal 5pm (l.o. 3pm).

Alberts Ramsden Arms Hotel ⚑
Listed
204 Talbot Road, Blackpool,
FY1 3AZ
☎ (0253) 23215
*Classic country-style inn close
to beach, town centre, theatres,
stations.*
Bedrooms: 3 twin.
Bathrooms: 1 private,
2 public.
Bed & breakfast: £15-£20
single, £25-£35 double.
Parking for 10.

Alderley Hotel ⚑
😊😊😊 APPROVED
581 South Promenade,
Blackpool, FY4 1NG
☎ (0253) 42173
*Quiet seafront licensed hotel,
with en-suite and ground-floor
bedrooms. Main course choice
of 10 dishes.*
Bedrooms: 6 double, 4 family
rooms.
Bathrooms: 10 private.
Bed & breakfast: £30-£40
single, £40-£50 double.
Lunch available.

Evening meal 6pm (l.o. 6pm).
Parking for 8.
Credit: Access, Visa, Amex.

Arncliffe Hotel
24 Osborne Road, Blackpool
S.S., FY4 1HJ
☎ (0253) 45209
*Small, homely family-run hotel
1 minute from Sandcastle,
Pleasure Beach and sea.*
Bedrooms: 1 single, 6 double
& 1 twin, 3 family rooms.
Bathrooms: 2 public.
Bed & breakfast: £10-£15
single, £20-£30 double.
Half board: £13-£18 daily,
£85-£102 weekly.
Evening meal 5pm (l.o.
midday).
Open March-November.

Ash Lodge
131 Hornby Road, Blackpool,
FY1 4JG
☎ (0253) 27637
*Small, private licensed hotel
with a warm friendly welcome
and home cooking. Centrally
located with ample car
parking.*
Bedrooms: 7 double & 2 twin,
3 family rooms.
Bathrooms: 5 private,
3 public.
Bed & breakfast: £12.50-£15
single, £25-£30 double.
Half board: £16-£20 daily,
£105-£133 weekly.
Evening meal 5pm (l.o.
6.30pm).
Parking for 15.

Ashbeian Hotel
😊😊😊
49 High Street, Blackpool
N.S., FY1 2BN
☎ (0253) 26301
*In central yet quiet location.
You choose time for breakfast
and dinner - all meals offer
choice from menus.*
Bedrooms: 1 single, 1 double
& 1 twin, 2 family rooms.
Bathrooms: 5 private.
Bed & breakfast: £13-£19
single, £20-£36 double.
Half board: £17.50-£23.50
daily, £85-£125 weekly.
Evening meal 5pm (l.o.
7.30pm).
Credit: Access, Visa.

Ashcroft Hotel ⚑
Listed COMMENDED
42 King Edward Avenue,
Blackpool, FY2 9TA
☎ (0253) 51538

Small friendly hotel off Queens Promenade, 2 minutes from sea and Gynn Gardens, offering personal service. Cleanliness assured.
Bedrooms: 3 single, 2 double & 2 twin, 3 family rooms.
Bathrooms: 2 public.
Bed & breakfast: £15-£17 single, £30-£34 double.
Half board: £19-£23 daily, £123-£151 weekly.
Evening meal 5pm (l.o. 2pm).
Parking for 3.

The Avon Guest House
2 Bute Avenue, Blackpool, FY1 2HR
☎ (0253) 294715
Friendly family-run guesthouse with spacious bedrooms, adjacent to promenade and amenities. Home cooking and comfort assured.
Bedrooms: 1 single, 3 double & 1 twin, 3 family rooms.
Bathrooms: 1 public.
Bed & breakfast: £11-£13.50 single, £22-£27 double.
Half board: £14-£16.50 daily, £80-£84 weekly.
Evening meal 5.15pm.
Open April-October.

The Hotel Bambi M
COMMENDED
27 Bright Street, Blackpool S.S., FY4 1BS
☎ (0253) 43756
Friendly, family-run guesthouse with good facilities.
Bedrooms: 1 single, 3 double, 1 family room.
Bathrooms: 5 private.
Bed & breakfast: £12.50-£13 single, £25-£26 double.
Half board: £16-£16.50 daily, £112-£115.50 weekly.
Evening meal 5pm.
Parking for 2.
Credit: Access, Visa, Amex.

Baron Hotel M
APPROVED
296 North Promenade, Blackpool, FY1 2EY
☎ (0253) 22729
Small, friendly hotel offering good food and personal service. Prominent position on the promenade, within easy reach of all amenities. All rooms en-suite.
Bedrooms: 10 double & 10 twin, 2 family rooms.
Bathrooms: 22 private.
Bed & breakfast: £20-£22 single, £36-£40 double.
Half board: £22-£26 daily.

Evening meal 5pm (l.o. 5.30pm).
Parking for 17.

Bedford Hotel
298-300 North Promenade, Blackpool, FY1 2EY
☎ (0253) 23475
Fax (0253) 23475
Well-managed family-run hotel on the seafront, indoor swimming pool and large comfortable bedrooms. Choice of menu at all meals.
Bedrooms: 21 double & 5 twin, 16 family rooms.
Bathrooms: 42 private.
Bed & breakfast: £25-£50 single, £40-£60 double.
Half board: £25-£55 daily, £150-£250 weekly.
Lunch available.
Evening meal 6pm (l.o. 6.30pm).
Parking for 24.
Credit: Access, Visa, Amex.

Belmont Private Hotel M
Listed
9 Napier Avenue, Blackpool S.S., FY4 1PA
☎ (0253) 42383
Comfortable, family-run, relaxing hotel with friendly atmosphere. All bedrooms tastefully furnished. Well-stocked bar, personal and caring service. Close to promenade, Pleasure Beach and Sandcastle.
Bedrooms: 4 single, 3 double & 1 twin, 1 family room.
Bathrooms: 1 public.
Bed & breakfast: £13-£16 single, £26-£32 double.
Half board: £15-£18 daily, £70-£105 weekly.
Evening meal 5pm.
Parking for 4.

Berwyn Hotel
COMMENDED
1 Finchley Road, Gynn Square, Blackpool, FY1 2LP
☎ (0253) 52896
Residential licensed hotel overlooking the lovely Gynn Gardens and promenade. Our standards are high and our aim is to please.
Bedrooms: 1 single, 11 double & 5 twin, 3 family rooms.
Bathrooms: 20 private.
Bed & breakfast: £20-£25 single, £40-£50 double.

Half board: £25-£30 daily, £150-£180 weekly.
Evening meal 6pm (l.o. 6pm).
Parking for 3.

Birch's Palace Apart Hotel
453-459 Promenade, Blackpool, FY4 1AR
☎ (0253) 46172
Seafront position on South Promenade. Restaurant, licensed, all en-suite. Self-catering rooms also available.
Bedrooms: 7 double & 1 twin.
Bathrooms: 8 private.
Bed & breakfast: £16.95-£29 single, £31-£49 double.
Half board: £22-£34 daily, £150-£210 weekly.
Lunch available.
Evening meal 5pm (l.o. 7pm).
Parking for 18.
Credit: Access.

Brabyns Hotel M
1 Shaftesbury Avenue, Blackpool, FY2 9QQ
☎ (0253) 54263
Fax (0253) 52915
CD Minotels
Family-run hotel with modern and well-equipped bedrooms. Special attention is paid to cooking, service and cleanliness.
Bedrooms: 6 single, 8 double & 11 twin.
Bathrooms: 25 private.
Bed & breakfast: £30-£35 single, £54-£62 double.
Lunch available.
Evening meal 6pm (l.o. 7.30pm).
Parking for 12.
Credit: Access, Visa, Diners.

Claremont House Hotel M
COMMENDED
14 Gynn Avenue, Blackpool N.S., FY1 2LD
☎ (0253) 51783
Licensed private hotel with home cooking. Close to town centre and theatres, on quiet North Shore. Family owned and managed.
Bedrooms: 2 single, 3 double & 2 twin, 3 family rooms.
Bathrooms: 1 private, 2 public.
Bed & breakfast: £12.50-£25 single, £25-£40 double.

Half board: £15.50-£23 daily, £75-£125 weekly.
Evening meal 5pm (l.o. 5.30pm).

Cliff Head Hotel M
APPROVED
174 Queens Promenade, Bispham, Blackpool, FY2 9JN
☎ (0253) 591086
Family-run hotel, excellent corner position on the promenade. Overlooking the sea and with views to Cumbrian mountains.
Bedrooms: 1 single, 3 double & 2 twin, 1 family room.
Bathrooms: 7 private.
Bed & breakfast: £14.50-£17.50 single, £29-£35 double.
Half board: £18.50-£24.50 daily, £97.50-£135 weekly.
Evening meal 5pm (l.o. 7pm).
Parking for 4.

Cliffs Hotel M
Queens Promenade, Blackpool, FY2 9SG
☎ (0253) 52388
Fax (0253) 50039
Telex 67191 CLIFFS
Impressive 1930's style building. Seafront hotel with sauna, swimming pool and squash court. Entertainment nightly June-October. Kids Club.
Bedrooms: 1 single, 77 double & 70 twin, 13 family rooms.
Bathrooms: 161 private.
Bed & breakfast: £30-£70 single, £60-£85 double.
Half board: £41-£60 daily, £205-£300 weekly.
Lunch available.
Evening meal 6.30pm (l.o. 9pm).
Parking for 70.
Credit: Access, Visa, Amex.

Collingwood Hotel M
8-10 Holmfield Road, Blackpool N.S., FY2 9SL
☎ (0253) 52929
In a select area just off Queens Promenade and Gynn Gardens. Good reputation for service, home cooking, cleanliness and value for money. All rooms en-suite.
Bedrooms: 2 single, 9 double & 2 twin, 4 family rooms.
Bathrooms: 17 private.
Bed & breakfast: £18-£21 single, £36-£42 double.

Continued ▶

BLACKPOOL
Continued

Half board: £21-£26 daily, £105-£140 weekly.
Lunch available.
Evening meal 5pm.
Parking for 13.
Credit: Access, Visa.

Colris Hotel ♨
♛♛♛

209 Central Promenade, Blackpool, FY1 5DL
☎ (0253) 25461
Redesigned and newly appointed, giving the comfort of a continental hotel. Minutes from the town centre and shows.
Bedrooms: 2 single, 13 double & 11 twin, 4 family rooms.
Bathrooms: 30 private.
Bed & breakfast: £22-£27.50 single, £40-£46 double.
Half board: £27.50-£33 daily, £170-£192.50 weekly.
Lunch available.
Evening meal 5pm (l.o. 6pm).

Dorchester Hotel
28 Queens Promenade, Blackpool N.S., FY2 9RN
☎ (0253) 52508
Splendid seafront location in prestigious North Shore. Close to Tower, entertainment, shops, golf-course, Gynn Gardens, children's boating and fun pool. Coaches and groups welcome.
Bedrooms: 16 double & 2 twin, 14 family rooms.
Bathrooms: 24 private, 3 public.
Bed & breakfast: £15-£30 single, £30-£60 double.
Half board: £17.50-£32.50 daily, £122.50-£160 weekly.
Lunch available.
Evening meal 6pm (l.o. 5pm).
Parking for 6.
Credit: Access, Visa.

Elgin Hotel ♨
♛♛♛ APPROVED

40-42 Queens Promenade, Blackpool, FY2 9RW
☎ (0253) 51433
Friendly, family-run hotel offering entertainment, fun and varied food. High standard of service in beautiful surroundings.
Bedrooms: 1 single, 9 double & 14 twin, 17 family rooms.
Bathrooms: 40 private, 1 public.
Bed & breakfast: £18.90-£45 single, £37.80-£83.40 double.

Half board: £24.40-£50 daily, £163.80-£322 weekly.
Evening meal 5.45pm (l.o. 5.45pm).
Parking for 8.
Credit: Access, Visa.

Fairway Hotel
34-36 Hull Road, Blackpool, FY1 4QB
☎ (0253) 23777 & 27751
Family-run hotel in the heart of Blackpool close to the Tower Theatre, Winter Gardens, shops and promenade. Guide dogs welcome.
Bedrooms: 4 single, 9 double & 5 twin, 5 family rooms.
Bathrooms: 8 private, 2 public; 1 private shower.
Bed & breakfast: £15.24-£17.24 single, £24.48-£28.48 double.
Half board: £17.24-£19.24 daily, £102.31-£120.32 weekly.
Evening meal 5pm (l.o. 2pm).

Fern Royd Hotel
♛♛ APPROVED

35 Holmfield Road, Blackpool N.S., FY2 9TE
☎ (0253) 51066
Friendly family-run hotel, offering good home cooking using fresh produce and personal attention at all times. Whirl-spa bath available.
Bedrooms: 2 single, 7 double & 2 twin, 2 family rooms.
Bathrooms: 4 private, 2 public.
Bed & breakfast: £14-£20 single, £28-£40 double.
Half board: £18-£24 daily, £120-£162 weekly.
Evening meal 5pm (l.o. 5pm).
Parking for 8.

Harwood Private Hotel ♨
46 Osborne Road, Blackpool S.S., FY4 1HQ
☎ (0253) 42241
Family-run private hotel with friendly atmosphere and home cooking. Adjacent to Pleasure Beach, promenade, Sandcastle and South Pier.
Bedrooms: 1 single, 4 double & 2 twin, 1 family room.
Bathrooms: 8 private.
Bed & breakfast: £12-£20 single, £22-£40 double.
Half board: £15-£24 daily, £85-£130 weekly.
Lunch available.
Evening meal 5pm (l.o. 3pm).

Iona Guest House ♨
7 Bright Street, Blackpool S.S., FY4 1BS
☎ (0253) 41608
Small, family-run guesthouse with unrestricted access, close to South Pier and Pleasure Beach. All rooms have central heating and tea/coffee facilities.
Bedrooms: 1 single, 1 double & 2 twin, 2 family rooms.
Bathrooms: 1 public.
Bed & breakfast: £10-£15 single, £20-£30 double.
Half board: £13.50-£18.50 daily, £90-£125 weekly.
Evening meal 5pm (l.o. 10pm).
Parking for 2.
Credit: Access, Visa.

The Kingsbury Private Hotel
♛♛♛

579 New South Promenade, Blackpool, FY4 1NG
☎ (0253) 44279
Panoramic sea views, friendly atmosphere, choice of menu, parking. Close to Pleasure Beach and Sandcastle. All bedrooms recently refurbished. Comfort assured. Special break terms available.
Bedrooms: 1 single, 5 double & 1 twin, 4 family rooms.
Bathrooms: 7 private, 2 public.
Bed & breakfast: £13-£17 single, £26-£34 double.
Half board: £17.50-£23 daily, £115-£137.50 weekly.
Evening meal 5.30pm (l.o. 10am).
Parking for 4.
Credit: Access, Visa, Diners.

Langwood Hotel ♨
♛♛♛

250 Queens Promenade, Bispham, Blackpool, FY2 9HA
☎ (0253) 51370
Small family-run hotel, catering mainly for families and senior citizens. Small pets made welcome. Most rooms have sea view.
Bedrooms: 6 single, 9 double & 10 twin, 3 family rooms.
Bathrooms: 16 private, 3 public.
Half board: £21-£24 daily, £140-£150 weekly.
Evening meal 6pm (l.o. 7pm).
Parking for 14.
Open April-December.

Llanryan House
37 Reads Avenue, Blackpool, FY1 4DD
☎ (0253) 28446
Ideal for town centre, theatres and working men's clubs.
Bedrooms: 1 single, 5 double, 4 family rooms.
Bathrooms: 1 public.
Bed & breakfast: £10-£13 single, £20-£26 double.
Half board: £12.50-£16 daily, £75-£85 weekly.
Evening meal 5pm (l.o. 5pm).
Credit: Access, Visa.

Mains Hall Country House Hotel ♨
♛♛♛♛ COMMENDED

Mains Lane, (A585), Poulton-le-Fylde, FY6 7LE
☎ (0253) 885130
16th C manor house steeped in history on the banks of the River Wyre, close to Blackpool and the Lake District.
Bedrooms: 4 double & 4 twin, 1 family room.
Bathrooms: 9 private.
Bed & breakfast: £45-£65 single, £65-£120 double.
Half board: £55-£82.50 daily.
Evening meal 7pm (l.o. 9pm).
Parking for 62.
Credit: Access, Visa.

Manor Royd Hotel
♛♛♛

96-98 Albert Road, Blackpool C., FY1 4PR
☎ (0253) 23175 & 26437
Central hotel, close to Winter Gardens, Tower, promenade and all holiday and shopping amenities.
Bedrooms: 3 single, 19 double & 1 twin, 10 family rooms.
Bathrooms: 26 private, 2 public.
Bed & breakfast: £22-£33 single, £30-£78 double.
Half board: £20-£39 daily, £125-£158 weekly.
Evening meal 5pm (l.o. 5.30pm).
Parking for 9.

Newlyn Rex Hotel
♛♛♛

56-58 Central Drive, Blackpool, FY1 5QB
☎ (0253) 25444
Located centrally for promenade, theatres, clubs, discos and shopping centre. Opposite car park for 800 cars.

Bedrooms: 6 single, 18 double
& 3 twin, 7 family rooms.
Bathrooms: 16 private,
3 public.
Bed & breakfast: £17.50-
£19.50 single, £31-£35 double.
Half board: £21-£23 daily,
£147-£161 weekly.
Evening meal 5pm.
Parking for 3.

Normandy Private Hotel

278 Queens Promenade,
Bispham, Blackpool,
FY2 9AX
☎ (0253) 52160
*Small hotel situated on the
promenade with panoramic sea
views and private parking.*
Bedrooms: 6 double & 3 twin.
Bathrooms: 9 private.
Bed & breakfast: £20-£22
single, £40-£44 double.
Half board: £24-£26 daily,
£168-£182 weekly.
Evening meal 5pm (l.o. 3pm).
Parking for 9.

Park House Hotel **M**

308 North Promenade,
Blackpool, FY1 2HA
☎ (0253) 20081
*Beautifully situated on
promenade within easy reach of
Winter Gardens, piers, golf-
courses, town centre and
Stanley Park.*
Bedrooms: 21 single,
32 double & 36 twin,
17 family rooms.
Bathrooms: 88 private,
3 public.
Bed & breakfast: £24-£30.50
single, £43-£56 double.
Half board: £27.50-£34 daily,
£175-£228 weekly.
Lunch available.
Evening meal 6pm (l.o.
8.30pm).
Parking for 52.
Credit: Access, Visa, Amex.

Pembroke Private Hotel **M**

11 King Edward Avenue,
Blackpool, FY2 9TD
☎ (0253) 51306
*Warm welcome assured to all
at our small beautifully
decorated hotel, which offers a
quiet relaxed atmosphere.*
Bedrooms: 2 single, 6 double
& 1 twin, 2 family rooms.
Bathrooms: 8 private,
1 public.
Bed & breakfast: £15-£21
single, £30-£42 double.

Half board: £17-£23 daily,
£112-£152 weekly.
Evening meal 5.30pm (l.o.
6.30pm).
Parking for 8.

Richmond House

270 Central Drive,
Blackpool, FY1 5JB
☎ (0253) 48100
*Small, friendly, licensed
establishment close to town
centre, promenade and leisure
facilities.*
Bedrooms: 1 single, 2 double
& 1 twin, 4 family rooms.
Bathrooms: 2 private,
2 public.
Bed & breakfast: £10-£16
single, £20-£32 double.
Half board: £13-£19 daily,
£80-£130 weekly.
Evening meal 5.30pm (l.o.
3pm).
Parking for 2.

Roblyn Court **M**

Listed

7 Clevedon Road, Blackpool
N.S., FY1 2NX
☎ (0253) 21012
*In a quiet road, 4 minutes from
seafront and 10 minutes from
town centre. Clean, modern
and cheerful accommodation.
Close to working men's clubs.*
Bedrooms: 2 double & 1 twin,
1 family room.
Bathrooms: 1 public.
Bed & breakfast: £10-£11
single, £20-£22 double.
Half board: £12-£14 daily,
£77-£90 weekly.
Evening meal 5pm (l.o. 6pm).
Parking for 1.

Rock Dene Guest House

50 St. Chads Road,
Blackpool, FY1 6BP
☎ (0253) 45810
*Good home cooking on
premises. Clean comfortable
rooms, clients' individual needs
catered for. Close to
promenade and entertainments.*
Bedrooms: 2 single, 6 double,
3 family rooms.
Bathrooms: 5 private,
2 public; 1 private shower.
Bed & breakfast: £12-£15
single, £24-£30 double.
Half board: £14-£18 daily,
£90-£105 weekly.
Evening meal 5pm.
Parking for 2.

Royal York Hotel

APPROVED

242 North Promenade,
Blackpool, FY1 1RZ
☎ (0253) 752424
*All rooms en-suite with colour
TV, tea-making facilities,
telephone. Choice of menu,
entertainment nightly. Lift to
all floors.*
Bedrooms: 6 single, 33 double
& 5 twin, 23 family rooms.
Bathrooms: 67 private.
Bed & breakfast: £21.96-
£39.33 single, £43.92-£78.60
double.
Evening meal 6pm (l.o. 7pm).
Parking for 25.
Credit: Access, Visa.

Ruskin Hotel **M**

COMMENDED

55-61 Albert Road, Blackpool,
FY1 4PW
☎ (0253) 24063 &
Fax. (0253) 23571
*One of the town's premier
hotels, totally refurbished and
providing a central haven of
excellence. The Tower, Winter
Gardens and theatres all within
400 yards.*
Bedrooms: 7 single, 30 double
& 28 twin, 15 family rooms.
Bathrooms: 80 private.
Bed & breakfast: £36-£60
single, £53-£70 double.
Half board: £35-£45 daily.
Lunch available.
Evening meal 6pm (l.o.
8.30pm).
Parking for 16.
Credit: Access, Visa.

Sal-Mar Guest House

Listed **APPROVED**

138 Albert Road, Blackpool,
FY1 4PL
☎ (0253) 23183
*Small, central hotel, convenient
for all Blackpool has to offer
the visitor.*
Bedrooms: 3 single, 2 double,
2 family rooms.
Bathrooms: 1 public.
Bed & breakfast: £12.50-
£13.50 single, £25-£27 double.
Half board: £13.50-£14.50
daily, £91-£98 weekly.
Lunch available.
Evening meal 5pm (l.o. 6pm).
Parking for 4.

Savoy Hotel

COMMENDED

Queens Promenade,
Blackpool, FY2 9SJ
☎ (0253) 52561 &
Fax. (0253) 500735
*In prime position on refined
North Shore. Short tram ride
from town centre, major
attractions and nightlife.*
Bedrooms: 46 single,
63 double & 28 twin, 10 family
rooms.
Bathrooms: 147 private.
Bed & breakfast: £35-£65
single, £55-£95 double.
Half board: £45.50-£75.50
daily.
Lunch available.
Evening meal 6.30pm (l.o.
10.30pm).
Parking for 55.
Credit: Access, Visa, Diners,
Amex.

Sherwood Private Hotel **M**

414 North Promenade,
Blackpool, FY1 2LB
☎ (0253) 51898
*Friendly hotel, occupying one
of the finest positions on the
promenade overlooking the sea.
The aim is to provide that
extra personal touch with
quality, at prices you can
afford.*
Bedrooms: 3 single, 14 double
& 3 twin, 11 family rooms.
Bathrooms: 20 private,
2 public.
Bed & breakfast: £14.50-
£19.50 single, £29-£39 double.
Half board: £17.50-£22.50
daily.
Lunch available.
Evening meal 5pm (l.o.
10pm).
Parking for 3.
Credit: Access, Visa.

Sunray Hotel **M**

COMMENDED

42 Knowle Avenue,
Blackpool, FY2 9TQ
☎ (0253) 51937
*All-round service and care at
modest prices, especially in low
season and for senior citizens.*
Bedrooms: 3 single, 2 double
& 2 twin, 2 family rooms.
Bathrooms: 9 private,
1 public.
Bed & breakfast: £20-£28
single, £40-£56 double.
Half board: £28-£39 daily,
£175-£224 weekly.

Continued ▶

Evening meal 5pm (l.o. 3pm).
Parking for 6.
Open January-November.
⊠ ⅃ ⌕ ⊡ ⊡ ✧ ⓤ ⌑ ⅁ ⊡
▥ ▴ ⩗ ⒹⒶ⒫ ⓈⓅ ⊤

Warwick Hotel **M**
⛉⛉⛉⛉ APPROVED
603-609 New South
Promenade, Blackpool,
FY4 1NG
☎ (0253) 42192 Telex 677334
Ⓒ Best Western
*Modern seafront hotel with
heated swimming pool, 2 bars,
solarium and comfortable
lounges.*
Bedrooms: 9 single, 12 double
& 4 twin, 27 family rooms.
Bathrooms: 52 private.
Bed & breakfast: £34.20-
£39.20 single, £57.70-£66.70
double.
Half board: £38.30-£47.90
daily, £254.69-£318.53 weekly.
Lunch available.
Evening meal 7pm (l.o.
8.30pm).
Parking for 32.
Credit: Access, Visa, Diners,
Amex.
⊠ ⅃ ⌕ ⊡ ⌑ ⩗ ⓘ ⅁ ◑
▥ ▴ ⅂ ⊡Ⓐ⒫ ✧ ⓈⓅ ⊤

Waverley Hotel
⛉⛉⛉ APPROVED
95 Reads Avenue, Blackpool,
FY1 4DG
☎ (0253) 21633
*Family-run licensed hotel
where a warm and friendly
welcome awaits you. Central
for all amenities, close to
Tower, Winter Gardens,
shopping precinct and
promenade. Traditional
English breakfasts. Private
parking available.*
Bedrooms: 1 single, 10 double
& 1 twin, 2 family rooms.
Bathrooms: 8 private,
1 public.
Bed & breakfast: £12-£20
single, £24-£40 double.
Half board: £16-£25 daily,
£110-£175 weekly.
Evening meal 5pm (l.o. 6pm).
Parking for 5.
Open January-November.
⊠ ⅃ ⌕ ⓘ ⅁ ⌑ ⅁ ⊡ ▥ ▴
⒟Ⓐ⒫ ✧ ⓈⓅ

Westdean Hotel
⛉⛉
59 Dean Street, Blackpool,
FY3 1BP
☎ (0253) 42904
*Comfortable family-run hotel
close to South Pier, promenade
and pleasure beach. Tastefully-
furnished rooms, choice of
menu, well-stocked bar.*

Bedrooms: 1 single, 5 double
& 2 twin, 4 family rooms.
Bathrooms: 3 private,
2 public.
Bed & breakfast: £12-£22
single, £24-£44 double.
Half board: £16-£26 daily,
£84-£104 weekly.
Evening meal 5pm (l.o. 6pm).
Parking for 2.
⊠ ✧ ⌑ ⅁ ⊡ ▥ ▴ ⅂ ⒟Ⓐ⒫
✎ ⓈⓅ

*3m NE. Macclesfield.
Small town in hilly
countryside on the
Cheshire border with the
Peak District National
Park. Residential and
industrial.*

Lukic - Belgrade
Country House Hotel **M**
⛉⛉⛉
Jackson Lane, Kerridge,
Bollington, Nr. Macclesfield,
SK10 5BG
☎ (0625) 573246
Fax (0625) 574791
Telex 667554
*Country house hotel with
classically English restaurant,
comprehensive wine list and
well-appointed cocktail bar. 20
minutes from Manchester
Airport. Easy motorway access
north and south.*
Bedrooms: 22 double &
30 twin, 2 family rooms.
Bathrooms: 54 private.
Bed & breakfast: £30-£55
single, £40-£62 double.
Half board: £33.25-£68.25
daily.
Lunch available.
Evening meal 7pm (l.o.
10.30pm).
Parking for 150.
Credit: Access, Visa, Diners,
Amex.
⊠ ⅃ ⊡ ⌑ ✧ ⓘ ◑ ▥
▴ ⅂ ∪ ⅀ ✧ ✎ ⓈⓅ ⍟ ⊤

Turners Arms Hotel
⛉⛉⛉
1 Ingersley Road, Bollington,
Nr. Macclesfield, SK10 5RE
☎ (0625) 573864
*Traditional stone-built inn with
lounge bar and games room.
Set in delightful village in the
Cheshire Peaks and plains.*
Bedrooms: 2 single, 4 double
& 1 twin, 1 family room.
Bathrooms: 3 private,
1 public.
Bed & breakfast: £19-£40
single, £38-£50 double.
Half board: £26-£46 daily,
£154-£300 weekly.
Lunch available.

Evening meal 7.30pm (l.o.
9.30pm).
Parking for 5.
Credit: Access, Visa.
⊠ ⅃ ✧ ⓘ ⅁ ⌑ ⅁ ▥ ▴
⅂ ▰ ⒟Ⓐ⒫ ⓈⓅ ⊤

*Once a prosperous
cotton town with Civil War
connections, now has
one of the finest shopping
centres in the region.
Attractions include Hall i'
th' Wood, Smithill's Hall,
Central Museum, Art
Gallery and Octagon
Theatre.*
*Tourist Information
Centre ☎ (0204) 364333
or 384174*

Commercial Royal
Hotel **M**
⛉⛉⛉ COMMENDED
13-15 Bolton Road, Moses
Gate, Farnworth, Bolton,
BL4 7JN
☎ (0204) 73661 & Fax (0204)
74147
*New hotel offering a high
standard of service and decor.
Restaurant serves English
cuisine, with choice of menu for
evening meal.*
Bedrooms: 5 single, 4 double
& 1 twin.
Bathrooms: 5 private,
2 public.
Bed & breakfast: £20-£39
single, £30-£49 double.
Half board: £25-£44 daily.
Evening meal 6.30pm (l.o.
10pm).
Parking for 15.
Credit: Access, Visa.
⊠ ⅃ ▰ ⅁ ⓘ ⅁ ⌑ ⅁ ⓘ ⅁
∠ ⅁ ⊡ ◑ ▥ ▴ ⅂ ⅂ ⒟Ⓐ⒫
✎ ⓈⓅ

Egerton House Hotel **M**
⛉⛉⛉ COMMENDED
Blackburn Road, Egerton,
Bolton, BL7 9PL
☎ (0204) 57171 & Fax (0204)
593030
Ⓒ Rank
*Dating back to the 17th C, this
small country house hotel, set
in 4.5 acres of landscaped
gardens, offers the elegance of
years gone by enhanced with
20th C facilities.*
Bedrooms: 8 single, 17 double
& 1 twin, 8 family rooms.
Bathrooms: 34 private.
Bed & breakfast: £51-£76
single, £72-£91 double.
Lunch available.
Evening meal 7pm (l.o.
9.30pm).
Parking for 150.

Credit: Access, Visa, Diners,
Amex.
⊠ ▴ ⅁ ⅂ ⊡ ⅁ ✧ ⓘ ▥ ⅁
◑ ▥ ▴ ⅂ ∪ ⅁ ✧ ⒟Ⓐ⒫ ⓈⓅ
⊤

Georgian House
Restaurant & Hotel **M**
⛉⛉⛉⛉
Manchester Road, Blackrod,
Bolton, BL6 5RU
☎ Westhoughton
(0942) 814598
*Georgian house with added
extension and all modern
facilities. Set in semi rural
location with views of
Rivington Pike and Winter Hill.*
Bedrooms: 15 single,
56 double & 26 twin, 4 family
rooms.
Bathrooms: 101 private.
Bed & breakfast: £56.50-£82
single, £82-£96 double.
Lunch available.
Evening meal 7pm (l.o. 9pm).
Parking for 200.
Credit: Access, Visa, C.Bl.,
Diners, Amex.
⊠ ▴ ⅁ ⅃ ⊡ ⅁ ✧ ⓘ ⅁
∠ ⅁ ⊡ ◑ ▥ ▴ ⅂ ⅃ ⅁
⅁ ⅁ ⅁ ⅂ ✧ ⓈⓅ ⍟

Ivy Grange Guest House
Listed
Albert Place, 75 Market
Street, Little Lever, Nr.
Bolton, BL3 1HH
☎ (0204) 75482 & 75428
*On the outskirts of Bolton
convenient for Bolton and Bury
town centres. Easy access to
M62 and M61. Bus stop 50yds
from front door for
Manchester, Bolton and Bury
buses.*
Bedrooms: 3 single, 1 double
& 2 twin, 1 family room.
Bathrooms: 3 public.
Bed & breakfast: from £15
single, from £24 double.
Half board: from £20 daily.
Evening meal 7pm (l.o. 9pm).
Parking for 12.
⊠ ▴ ⅁ ⌑ ⓤ ⅁ ⅀ ∠ ⅁ ⊡
▥ ▴ ✎ ⅁ ⒟Ⓐ⒫

Last Drop Village
Hotel **M**
⛉⛉⛉⛉
Hospital Road, Bromley
Cross, Bolton, BL7 9PZ
☎ (0204) 591131
Telex 635322
Ⓒ Rank
*A collection of 18th C farm
buildings transformed into a
"living village", with 2
restaurants, tea shop, leisure
club and hotel.*
Bedrooms: 40 double &
6 twin, 37 family rooms.
Bathrooms: 83 private.
Bed & breakfast: £56-£76
single, £77-£91 double.

Lunch available.
Evening meal 7pm (l.o.
10.30pm).
Parking for 400.
Credit: Access, Visa, Diners,
Amex.

[symbols]

Morden Grange Guest House

15 Chadwick Street, Haulgh,
Bolton, BL2 1JN
☎ (0204) 22000
*Attractive double fronted
detached residence with several
stained glass windows and
antique pine staircase. Situated
5 minutes' walking distance
from the town centre.*
Bedrooms: 1 single, 1 double
& 1 twin, 4 family rooms.
Bathrooms: 1 public.
Bed & breakfast: £14-£15
single, £26-£28 double.
Half board: £18.50-£19.50
daily.
Evening meal 6pm.

[symbols]

BOLTON-BY-BOWLAND

Lancashire
Map ref 4A1

*6m NE. Clitheroe
Unspoilt village near the
Ribble with 2 greens, one
with stump of 13th C
market cross and stocks.
Whitewashed and
greystone cottages.*

Harrop Fold Country Farmhouse Hotel ♏

☺☺☺ COMMENDED

Harrop Fold, Bolton-by-
Bowland, Clitheroe, BB7 4PJ
☎ (020 07) 600 Telex 635562
Grifin
*280-acre hill farm. Well-
appointed hotel with your
comfort and care at heart, 3
miles from Bolton-by-Bowland
in the hamlet of Harrop Fold.
A beautiful, peaceful setting.*
Bedrooms: 6 double & 2 twin.
Bathrooms: 8 private.
Bed & breakfast: £44.50-£50
single, £64-£70 double.
Half board: £44.50-£57 daily.
Evening meal 7pm (l.o.
10pm).
Parking for 14.
Credit: Access, Visa.

[symbols]

---

*Half board prices
shown are per
person but in some
cases may be based
on double/twin
occupancy.*

BROMBOROUGH

Merseyside
Map ref 4A2

Residential town in
beautiful Wirral
countryside, yet within
easy reach of
Birkenhead, Liverpool
and Chester.

Cromwell Hotel ♏

☺☺☺ COMMENDED

High Street, Bromborough,
Wirral, L62 7HZ
☎ 051-334 2917 & Fax 051-
346 1175 Telex 628225
Ⓖ Lansbury
*A new hotel, convenient for the
bustling city of Liverpool and
the countryside of North Wales
and the Wirral.*
Bedrooms: 3 single, 7 double
& 18 twin, 3 family rooms.
Bathrooms: 31 private.
Bed & breakfast: £23-£65
single, £46-£77 double.
Half board: £35-£80 daily.
Lunch available.
Evening meal 7pm (l.o.
10pm).
Parking for 102.
Credit: Access, Visa, Diners,
Amex.

[symbols]

Dresden Hotel

☺☺☺ COMMENDED

866 New Chester Road,
Bromborough, L62 7HF
☎ 051-334 1331 & 1353
*Owned and managed by a
Swiss family on continental
lines and with the Swiss
tradition of personal service.*
Bedrooms: 4 single, 1 double
& 1 twin.
Bathrooms: 2 private,
1 public.
Bed & breakfast: from £25
single, £33.50-£41.50 double.
Half board: from £30 daily.
Lunch available.
Evening meal 7pm (l.o. 9pm).
Parking for 20.

[symbols]

---

*The symbols are explained on the flap
inside the back cover.*

BURNLEY

Lancashire
Map ref 4B1

Once the largest cotton-
weaving centre in the
world but now dominated
by engineering. 14th C
Towneley Hall has fine
period rooms and the
entrance hall houses an
art gallery and museum.
The Kay-Shuttleworth
collection of lace and
embroidery can be seen
at Gawthorpe Hall
(National Trust).
*Tourist Information
Centre ☎ (0282) 30055*

Alexander Hotel

☺☺☺ COMMENDED

2 Tarleton Avenue,
Todmorden Road, Burnley,
BB11 3ET
☎ (0282) 22684
*Family-run hotel with accent
on personal service. Near the
town centre, in quiet residential
area.*
Bedrooms: 8 single, 5 double
& 4 twin, 2 family rooms.
Bathrooms: 15 private,
1 public; 1 private shower.
Bed & breakfast: £22-£40
single, £39-£49 double.
Half board: £27-£45 daily.
Evening meal 6.15pm (l.o.
8.45pm).
Parking for 16.
Credit: Access, Visa.

[symbols]

Higher Trapp Country House Hotel ♏

☺☺☺ COMMENDED

Trapp Lane, Simonstone, Nr.
Burnley, BB12 7QW
☎ (0282) 72781
*Country house hotel with
terraced gardens set in 4.5
acres. Take the M65 junction 8
turn-off, follow the A6068
Clitheroe road, turn left at
second set of lights, first right,
1.5 miles on left.*
Bedrooms: 4 single, 13 double
& 3 twin.
Bathrooms: 20 private.
Bed & breakfast: £35-£45
single, £45-£60 double.
Lunch available.
Evening meal 7pm (l.o.
10pm).
Parking for 70.
Credit: Access, Visa.

[symbols]

Keirby Hotel ♏

☺☺☺☺ APPROVED

Keirby Walk, Burnley,
BB11 2DH
☎ (0282) 27611 Telex 63119
Ⓖ Friendly
*Modern town centre hotel with
banqueting and conference
facilities for 300.*
Bedrooms: 10 single,
28 double & 8 twin, 3 family
rooms.
Bathrooms: 49 private.
Bed & breakfast: £53.50-
£66.20 single, £66.75-£81.90
double.
Evening meal 7pm (l.o.
9.30pm).
Parking for 45.
Credit: Access, Visa, Diners,
Amex.

[symbols]

Ormerod Private Hotel

Listed

121-123 Ormerod Road,
Burnley, BB11 3QW
☎ (0282) 23255
*Small bed and breakfast hotel
in quiet, pleasant surroundings,
facing local parks. Recently
refurbished, all en-suite
facilities. 5 minutes from town
centre.*
Bedrooms: 5 single, 2 double
& 1 twin, 2 family rooms.
Bathrooms: 10 private.
Bed & breakfast: £16-£20
single, £30-£32 double.
Half board: £21-£25 daily.
Parking for 7.

[symbols]

BURY

Gtr. Manchester
Map ref 4B1

Birthplace of Sir Robert
Peel, Prime Minister and
founder of police force,
commemorated by statue
in market-place. The East
Lancashire Railway
operates from Bury and
items connected with
steam railways are found
at the Transport Museum.
*Tourist Information
Centre ☎ 061-705 5111*

The Bolholt Hotel & Restaurant ♏

☺☺☺☺ COMMENDED

off Walshaw Road, Bury,
BL8 1PS
☎ 061-764 5239 & 3888
*Large family-run hotel and
conference centre in a historic
and picturesque setting. Home-
cooked fresh food our
speciality.*

Continued ▶

BURY

Continued

Bedrooms: 11 single,
26 double & 8 twin, 2 family
rooms.
Bathrooms: 43 private,
3 public.
Bed & breakfast: £44-£48
single, £58 double.
Lunch available.
Evening meal 7pm (l.o. 9pm).
Parking for 150.
Credit: Access, Visa, Diners,
Amex.

Normandie Hotel M

COMMENDED

Elbut Lane, Birtle, Bury,
BL9 6UT
☎ 061-764 3869 Telex 635091
*Modern comfortable hotel,
noted locally for the
preparation and presentation of
traditional French cooking.*
Bedrooms: 7 single, 10 double
& 7 twin.
Bathrooms: 24 private.
Bed & breakfast: £59-£69
single, £69-£79 double.
Lunch available.
Evening meal 7pm (l.o.
9.30pm).
Parking for 60.
Credit: Access, Visa, Diners,
Amex.

The Old Mill Hotel & Restaurant M

COMMENDED

Springwood, Ramsbottom,
Nr. Bury, BL0 9DS
☎ (0706) 822991
Fax (0706) 822291
*Converted old mill with old
world appearance but very
modern bedrooms. Standing in
its own grounds, close to city
and country life. Full leisure
centre, swimming pool, sauna,
whirlpool, solarium and
gymnasium.*
Bedrooms: 12 single,
12 double & 12 twin.
Bathrooms: 36 private.
Bed & breakfast: £30.50-
£44.50 single, £39.50-£56
double.
Half board: £43-£57.50 daily,
£360 weekly.
Lunch available.
Evening meal 6.30pm (l.o.
10.30pm).
Parking for 100.
Credit: Access, Visa, Diners,
Amex.

Red Hall Hotel & Restaurant M

COMMENDED

Manchester Road,
Walmersley, Bury, BL9 5NA
☎ Ramsbottom
(0706) 822476
Fax (0706) 828086
*A small family-run hotel and
restaurant offering friendly
service in a comfortable
atmosphere.*
Bedrooms: 10 single, 6 double
& 4 twin.
Bathrooms: 20 private.
Bed & breakfast: £34-£48
single, £47-£60 double.
Half board: £45-£59 daily.
Lunch available.
Evening meal 7pm (l.o.
9.30pm).
Parking for 50.
Credit: Access, Visa, Diners,
Amex.

Rostrevor Hotel M

148 Manchester Road, Bury,
BL9 OTL
☎ 061-764 3944
*Small, family hotel close to
Bury town centre, convenient
for M66 and M62 motorways.
Home cooking and friendly
atmosphere.*
Bedrooms: 6 single, 3 double
& 6 twin, 1 family room.
Bathrooms: 4 private,
2 public.
Bed & breakfast: £24-£31
single, £38-£46 double.
Half board: £28-£40 daily.
Lunch available.
Evening meal 6pm (l.o. 8pm).
Parking for 14.
Credit: Access, Visa, Amex.

CARNFORTH

Lancashire
Map ref 5B3

Permanent home of the
'Flying Scotsman' in
Steamtown Railway
Museum. Nearby are
Borwick Hall, an
Elizabethan manor house,
and Leighton House
which has good paintings
and early furniture and is
open to the public.

The Pine Lake Hotel M

Pine Lake Resort, Carnforth,
LA6 1JZ
☎ (0524) 736191
*Set amidst the 100 acres of
Pine Lake Resort, just off the
M6 at junction 35.*

Bedrooms: 7 double &
13 twin, 3 family rooms.
Bathrooms: 23 private.
Bed & breakfast: £45 single,
£60 double.
Lunch available.
Evening meal 6pm (l.o.
9.30pm).
Parking for 75.
Credit: Access, Visa, Diners,
Amex.

Royal Station Hotel M

APPROVED

Market Street, Carnforth,
LA5 9BT
☎ (0524) 732033
*Refurbished, comfortable,
friendly hotel in centre of this
historic market town
surrounded by the beautiful
countryside of Lonsdale.
English Lakes 20 minutes, 1
mile M6 junction 35. English,
French and Italian cooking.*
Bedrooms: 2 single, 5 double
& 4 twin, 1 family room.
Bathrooms: 12 private,
4 public.
Bed & breakfast: £26-£28
single, £44 double.
Lunch available.
Evening meal 6pm (l.o.
8.30pm).
Parking for 18.
Credit: Access, Visa, Diners,
Amex.

CATON

Lancashire
Map ref 5B3

*5m NE. Lancaster exit 34
M6 to A683*
Village on a curve of the
River Lune made famous
by Turner who painted its
celebrated Crook O'Lune.

Scarthwaite Hotel M

Crook O'Lune, Caton,
Lancaster, LA2 9HR
☎ (0524) 770267
*Large Victorian house on an
extensive wooded estate facing
the River Lune. Ideal for
fishing.*
Bedrooms: 1 single, 6 double
& 1 twin, 2 family rooms.
Bathrooms: 10 private.
Bed & breakfast: £33-£38
single, £48-£55 double.
Lunch available.
Evening meal 6pm (l.o.
9.30pm).
Parking for 80.
Credit: Access, Visa, Amex.

CHEADLE HULME

Gtr. Manchester
Map ref 4B2

2m SW. Stockport
Residential area near
Manchester with some
older buildings dating
from 19th C once
occupied by merchants
and industrialists from
surrounding towns,
including red-brick Gothic
Town Hall. Several fine
timber-framed houses
notably Tudor Bramall
Hall.
*Tourist Information
Centre* ☎ 061-486 0283

Spring Cottage Guest House M

Listed COMMENDED

60 Hulme Hall Road,
Cheadle Hulme, Stockport,
Cheshire SK8 6JZ
☎ 061-485 1037
*Beautifully furnished Victorian
house in historic part of
Cheadle Hulme. Convenient
for airport, rail station and
variety of local restaurants.*
Bedrooms: 1 single, 1 double
& 3 twin, 1 family room.
Bathrooms: 3 private,
1 public.
Bed & breakfast: £17-£18.50
single, £29.50-£36 double.
Parking for 6.
Credit: Access, Visa.

CHESTER

Cheshire
Map ref 4A2

Interesting Roman and
medieval walled city rich
in architectural and
archaeological treasures.
Fine timber-framed and
plaster buildings.
Shopping in the Rows
(galleried arcades
reached by steps from
the street). Grosvenor
Museum (Roman
remains), 14th C
cathedral, castle and zoo.
*Tourist Information
Centre* ☎ (0244) 313126
or 351609

Abbots Well Hotel and Leisure Club M

APPROVED

Whitchurch Road,
Christleton, Chester,
CH3 5QL
☎ (0244) 332121
Fax (0244) 335287
Telex 61561

Located 1.5 miles from Chester with extensive gardens adjoining open Green Belt. Modern comfortable bedrooms, pleasant atmosphere and popular bar. Leisure facilities.
Bedrooms: 25 single, 16 double & 85 twin, 1 family room.
Bathrooms: 127 private.
Bed & breakfast: £75-£89.50 single, £89.50-£99.50 double.
Half board: £75-£128.50 daily.
Lunch available.
Evening meal 7pm (l.o. 10pm).
Parking for 250.
Credit: Access, Visa, Diners, Amex.

Allenby Lodge
11 Newton Lane, Hoole, Chester, CH2 3RB
☎ (0244) 318367
Small, family-run guesthouse. Large Victorian building, 50 yards off main A56 road, one mile to town and motorway, two minutes to local amenities. On local bus route.
Bedrooms: 2 single, 2 double, 2 family rooms.
Bathrooms: 6 private.
Bed & breakfast: £12-£20 single, £24-£30 double.
Parking for 6.
Credit: Visa.

Bawn Park Hotel M
10 Hoole Road, Hoole, Chester, CH2 3NH
☎ (0244) 324971
Small family-run hotel in own grounds with large private car park, one mile to M53, half mile from city centre.
Bedrooms: 3 double & 2 twin, 2 family rooms.
Bathrooms: 7 private, 1 public.
Bed & breakfast: £25-£38 double.
Parking for 12.
Credit: Access, Visa.

Brookside Hotel M
⊛⊛⊛ COMMENDED
Brook Lane, Chester, CH2 2AN
☎ (0244) 381943
Fax (0244) 379701
Recently refurbished family-run hotel in residential area, off the A5116 Liverpool road near Northgate Arena. 7 minutes' walk from the city.
Bedrooms: 8 single, 5 double & 6 twin, 6 family rooms.

Bathrooms: 25 private, 3 public.
Bed & breakfast: £29.50-£32.50 single, £46-£50.50 double.
Half board: £28-£37.50 daily.
Evening meal 7pm (l.o. 9.30pm).
Parking for 12.
Credit: Access, Visa.
⊛ Display advertisement appears on page 144.

Chester Grosvenor M
⊛⊛⊛⊛⊛ HIGHLY COMMENDED
Eastgate Street, Chester, CH1 1LT
☎ (0244) 324024 Telex 61240
Owned by and named after one of England's oldest aristocratic families. The hotel completed a £12 million refurbishment in spring 1988. An ETB "5 Gold Crown" award hotel.
Bedrooms: 86 double.
Bathrooms: 86 private.
Bed & breakfast: £124.40-£144.38 single, £194.75-£218.25 double.
Lunch available.
Evening meal 6pm (l.o. 11pm).
Parking for 600.
Credit: Access, Visa, C.Bl., Diners, Amex.

Chester International Hotel M
⊛⊛⊛⊛ COMMENDED
Trinity Street, Chester, CH1 2BD
☎ (0244) 322330 Telex 61251
⊕ Queens Moat Houses
Modern city centre hotel, within ancient city walls. Close to racecourse and with views over North Wales.
Bedrooms: 29 single, 40 double & 83 twin.
Bathrooms: 152 private.
Bed & breakfast: £50.52-£98.70 single, £90-£141 double.
Half board: £55-£120 daily.
Lunch available.
Evening meal 6pm (l.o. 10.30pm).
Parking for 70.
Credit: Access, Visa, Diners, Amex.

Cheyney Lodge Hotel
77-79 Cheyney Road, Chester, CH1 4BS
☎ (0244) 381925

Small, friendly hotel of unusual design, featuring indoor garden and fish pond. 7 minutes' walk from city centre and on main bus route. Personally supervised with emphasis on good food.
Bedrooms: 5 double & 2 twin, 1 family room.
Bathrooms: 7 private, 2 public.
Bed & breakfast: £17-£28 single, £29-£38 double.
Half board: £23-£26.50 daily.
Lunch available.
Evening meal 6pm (l.o. 9pm).
Parking for 2.
Credit: Access, Visa.

Cromwell Court Hotel
5-7 St. Martins Way, Chester, CH1 2NR
☎ (0244) 349202
Well-appointed hotel suites within Georgian facade in city centre, each offering built-in microwave and refrigerator.
Bedrooms: 5 double & 6 twin.
Bathrooms: 11 private.
Bed & breakfast: from £36 single, from £46 double.
Parking for 10.
Credit: Access, Visa, Amex.

Curzon Hotel M
⊛⊛⊛
52-54 Hough Green, Chester, CH4 8JQ
☎ (0244) 678581
Fax (0244) 680866
Large Victorian house set well back in its own grounds. Close to golf, River Dee, racecourse, leisure centre and all amenities.
Bedrooms: 6 single, 7 double & 1 twin, 2 family rooms.
Bathrooms: 16 private.
Bed & breakfast: from £35 single, from £45 double.
Half board: from £50 daily, from £200 weekly.
Evening meal 7pm (l.o. 9pm).
Parking for 24.
Credit: Access, Visa, Diners, Amex.

Dene Hotel M
⊛⊛⊛⊛ APPROVED
Hoole Road, Chester, CH2 3ND
☎ (0244) 321165
Family-owned hotel conveniently situated on A56 approach to city centre. Adjacent to Alexandra Park.
Bedrooms: 11 single, 21 double & 13 twin, 4 family rooms.

Bathrooms: 47 private, 2 public.
Bed & breakfast: £39-£43 single, £51-£56 double.
Half board: £215.25-£228 weekly.
Evening meal 7pm (l.o. 8.30pm).
Parking for 50.
Credit: Access, Visa.

Derry Raghan Guest House M
⊛⊛⊛ COMMENDED
54 Hoole Road, Chester, CH2 3NL
☎ (0244) 318740
Friendly, spacious Victorian guesthouse 1 mile from historic city centre, 2 miles from Chester Zoo. Close to M56 and M53.
Bedrooms: 1 single, 2 double & 2 twin, 1 family room.
Bathrooms: 6 private.
Bed & breakfast: £16-£19 single, £32-£34 double.
Parking for 6.

Eaton Hotel M
⊛⊛⊛ APPROVED
29-31 City Road, Chester, CH1 3AE
☎ (0244) 320840
⊕ Minotels
Welcoming and relaxing hotel, convenient for station and 5 minutes' walk from the famous shopping centre, Roman walls and river. Bargain breaks available all year.
Bedrooms: 2 single, 8 double & 9 twin, 3 family rooms.
Bathrooms: 13 private; 9 private showers.
Bed & breakfast: £28-£38 single, £42-£54 double.
Half board: £33-£49 daily, £203-£301 weekly.
Lunch available.
Evening meal 6.30pm (l.o. 8pm).
Parking for 10.
Credit: Access, Visa, Diners, Amex.

Edwards House Hotel M
⊛⊛⊛ COMMENDED
61-63 Hoole Road, Chester, CH2 3NJ
☎ (0244) 318055
Early Victorian hotel with well proportioned bedrooms, all en-suite and fitted to a high standard.
Bedrooms: 4 double, 4 family rooms.
Bathrooms: 8 private.

Continued ▶

CHESTER
Continued

Bed & breakfast: £27-£28
single, £38 double.
Evening meal 6.30pm (l.o.
7.30pm).
Parking for 8.
Credit: Access, Visa.

Gables Guest House M
Listed APPROVED
5 Vicarage Road, Off Hoole
Road, Chester, CH2 3HZ
☎ (0244) 323969
*Guesthouse in quiet road 1 mile
from city centre. Park and
tennis courts nearby. Easy
access to motorways.*
Bedrooms: 1 double & 1 twin,
4 family rooms.
Bathrooms: 2 public.
Bed & breakfast: £14-£18
single, £24-£27 double.
Parking for 7.

Glann Hotel M
COMMENDED
2 Stone Place, Hoole,
Chester, CH2 3NR
☎ (0244) 344800
*Family-owned hotel in a quiet
location, with a friendly,
relaxed atmosphere.
Comfortable lounge with bar,
large private car park.*
Bedrooms: 2 single, 2 double
& 1 twin, 1 family room.
Bathrooms: 5 private,
1 public.
Bed & breakfast: £21-£24
single, £45-£48 double.
Half board: £30-£33 daily,
£200-£220 weekly.
Evening meal 6.30pm (l.o.
8pm).
Parking for 15.
Credit: Access, Visa.

Glen Garth Guest House
59 Hoole Road, Chester,
CH2 3NJ
☎ (0244) 310260
*Family-run guesthouse under
the personal supervision of the
owners. Large Victorian
building completely refurbished
within the last three years.*
Bedrooms: 2 double & 1 twin,
3 family rooms.
Bathrooms: 1 private,
2 public.
Bed & breakfast: £20-£22
single, £28-£36 double.
Parking for 7.

Green Bough Hotel M
COMMENDED
60 Hoole Road, Chester,
CH2 3NL
☎ (0244) 326241
Fax (0244) 326265
*Comfortable, family-run hotel
with friendly, relaxed
atmosphere. Tastefully
decorated with many antique
furnishings. Restaurant
renowned for good English
cooking.*
Bedrooms: 10 double &
2 twin, 5 family rooms.
Bathrooms: 17 private.
Bed & breakfast: £40-£44
single, £50.50-£55.50 double.
Half board: £50.45-£55.50
daily.
Lunch available.
Evening meal 7pm (l.o.
8.30pm).
Parking for 21.
Credit: Access, Visa.

Green Gables Guest
House M
COMMENDED
11 Eversley Park, Chester,
CH2 2AJ
☎ (0244) 372243
*Family-run guesthouse
decorated to a high standard,
situated just under 1 mile from
town centre. All amenities
available.*
Bedrooms: 2 double & 1 twin,
1 family room.
Bathrooms: 3 private,
1 public.
Bed & breakfast: £20-£25
single, from £33 double.
Parking for 8.

Kent House
147 Boughton, Chester,
CH3 5BH
☎ (0244) 324171
*Small, family-run guesthouse,
10 minutes' walk from city
centre, on bus route. A warm
welcome guaranteed by
Chrissie and Mike Turner.*
Bedrooms: 1 double & 1 twin,
1 family room.
Bathrooms: 3 private.
Bed & breakfast: max. £20
single, £25-£28 double.

Latymer House M
82 Hough Green, Chester,
CH4 8JW
☎ (0244) 675074

*Charming, comfortable house
set in its own gardens. All
bedrooms en-suite. Residential
licence. Large car park.
Emphasis on cooking to guests'
tastes.*
Bedrooms: 3 single, 3 double
& 4 twin, 1 family room.
Bathrooms: 11 private,
1 public.
Bed & breakfast: £20.50-£25
single, £33-£37 double.
Half board: £25-£33.50 daily,
£175-£234.50 weekly.
Evening meal 7pm (l.o. 5pm).
Parking for 20.

The Limes Hotel M
COMMENDED
12 Hoole Road, Chester,
CH2 3NJ
☎ (0244) 328239
*Family-run licensed Victorian
hotel within one mile of city
centre. Furnished to a high
standard and offering food and
hospitality.*
Bedrooms: 1 single, 2 double
& 2 twin, 3 family rooms.
Bathrooms: 8 private.
Bed & breakfast: £30-£33
single, £43-£45 double.
Half board: £31-£40 daily.
Evening meal 7pm (l.o. 8pm).
Parking for 10.
Credit: Access, Visa, Amex.

Lloyd's Guest House M
108 Brook Street, Chester,
CH3 1DU
☎ (0244) 325838 & 317491
*Friendly, family-run
guesthouse very near rail
station, and only 10 minutes'
walk from city centre. We
serve a good English breakfast.*
Bedrooms: 2 single, 3 double
& 3 twin, 6 family rooms.
Bathrooms: 6 private,
2 public.
Bed & breakfast: £13-£15
single, £32-£36 double.

Malvern Guest House
21 Victoria Road, Chester,
CH2 2AX
☎ (0244) 380865
*Victorian terraced town house
comprising 2 storeys, within 8
minutes' walk of the cathedral
and adjacent to a leisure
centre.*
Bedrooms: 1 single, 1 double
& 2 twin, 2 family rooms.
Bathrooms: 2 public.
Bed & breakfast: £12-£14
single, £24-£28 double.

Half board: £15.50-£17.50
daily, £100-£125 weekly.
Evening meal 6pm (l.o. 5pm).

Plantation Quality
Inn M
Liverpool Road, Chester,
CH2 1AG
☎ (0244) 374100 Telex 61263
*Ideally situated close to the
medieval city centre, the hotel
is the perfect base for exploring
North Wales and the Welsh
Borderlands.*
Bedrooms: 22 single,
16 double & 34 twin, 6 family
rooms.
Bathrooms: 78 private.
Bed & breakfast: £50-£75
single, £65-£95 double.
Lunch available.
Evening meal 7pm (l.o.
10.30pm).
Parking for 150.
Credit: Access, Visa, C.Bl.,
Diners, Amex.

Queen Hotel M
APPROVED
City Road, Chester,
CH1 3AH
☎ (0244) 328341
Telex 617101
*Fully modernised hotel that
still retains an elegant
Victorian air. It is close to the
station and all amenities.*
Bedrooms: 12 single,
19 double & 56 twin, 3 family
rooms.
Bathrooms: 90 private.
Bed & breakfast: £50-£65
single, £70-£90 double.
Half board: £40-£50 daily.
Lunch available.
Evening meal 6.30pm (l.o.
9.30pm).
Parking for 130.
Credit: Access, Visa, C.Bl.,
Diners, Amex.

Redland Private
Hotel M
64 Hough Green, Chester,
CH4 8JY
☎ (0244) 671024
*Victorian mansion, spacious
and comfortable, with many
unique features. 1 mile from
cathedral city centre, on Welsh
border with coast and
Snowdonia 1 hour's drive
away.*
Bedrooms: 2 single, 7 double
& 3 twin, 1 family room.
Bathrooms: 13 private,
1 public.

Bed & breakfast: £40 single,
£45-£60 double.
Parking for 12.
Credit: Access, Visa.

Rowton Hall Hotel **M**
Rowton Lane, Whitchurch
Road, Rowton, Chester,
CH3 6AD
☎ (0244) 335262
Fax (0244) 335464
Telex 61172
CR Consort
*Country house hotel set in 8
acres of garden, 2 miles from
Chester. Restaurant and bar
open to non-residents. Heated
indoor swimming pool.*
Bedrooms: 1 single, 24 double
& 14 twin, 3 family rooms.
Bathrooms: 42 private.
Bed & breakfast: £70-£80
single, £86-£92 double.
Lunch available.
Evening meal 7pm (l.o.
9.30pm).
Parking for 206.
Credit: Access, Visa, Diners,
Amex.

Stafford Hotel **M**
City Road, Chester,
CH1 3AE
☎ (0244) 326052
*Comfortable, friendly, family-
run hotel within easy walking
distance of city centre.
Overnight street parking.*
Bedrooms: 4 single, 11 double
& 7 twin, 2 family rooms.
Bathrooms: 23 private,
3 public.
Bed & breakfast: £25-£35
single, £45-£49 double.
Half board: £31-£34.45 daily.
Evening meal 6.30pm (l.o.
9pm).
Credit: Access, Visa, Amex.

Westminster Hotel **M**
City Road, Chester,
CH1 3AF
☎ (0244) 317341
*Adjacent to railway station
and 2 minutes' walk from city
centre. Entertainment most
evenings.*
Bedrooms: 13 single,
15 double & 35 twin,
10 family rooms.
Bathrooms: 73 private.
Bed & breakfast: £33-£41
single, £49.50-£58 double.
Half board: £32-£42 daily,
£189-£231 weekly.
Lunch available.

Evening meal 6.30pm (l.o.
9pm).
Credit: Access, Visa.

Woodhey Hotel
Berwick Road, Little Sutton,
Nr. Chester, L66 4PS
☎ 051-339 5121
CR Consort
*Friendly hotel in scenic country
location. Excellent touring base
for Chester, North Wales and
Wirral. 1 mile from M53
junction 5.*
Bedrooms: 2 single, 22 double
& 21 twin, 8 family rooms.
Bathrooms: 53 private.
Bed & breakfast: £35-£75
single, £55-£95 double.
Half board: £40-£75 daily,
£180-£255 weekly.
Lunch available.
Evening meal 7pm (l.o.
10pm).
Parking for 150.
Credit: Access, Visa, Diners,
Amex.

Gibbon Bridge Country House Hotel **M**
COMMENDED
Moss Lane, Chipping, Nr.
Preston, PR3 2TQ
☎ (0995) 61456 & Fax (0995)
61277
*Delightful country house in the
heart of the Ribble Valley.
Privately owned and run, with
health and gym facilities,
beauty salon, tennis court and
conference facilities.*
Bedrooms: 3 single, 8 double
& 15 twin, 4 family rooms.
Bathrooms: 30 private.
Bed & breakfast: £55-£90
single, £65-£150 double.
Half board: £75-£110 daily,
from £245 weekly.
Lunch available.
Evening meal 7pm (l.o. 8pm).
Parking for 150.
Credit: Access, Visa.

*Half board prices
shown are per
person but in some
cases may be based
on double/twin
occupancy.*

10m NW. Bolton
Despite its cotton-
weaving background,
Chorley has a busy
market town atmosphere.
Jacobean Astley Hall, set
in extensive parkland, has
fine furniture and long
gallery with shovel-board
table.

Astley House Hotel
COMMENDED
3 Southport Road, Chorley,
PR7 1LB
☎ (0257) 272315
*An elegant Victorian house
with 20th C comforts. Just a
few minutes' walk from
Chorley town centre and park.*
Bedrooms: 4 single, 2 twin.
Bathrooms: 3 private,
1 public.
Bed & breakfast: £15-£20
single, £42 double.
Evening meal 6pm.
Parking for 6.
Credit: Access, Visa, Amex.

10m NE. Blackburn
Intriguing town with the
castle as its chief
attraction. The castle and
keep house a museum
with special features
including an exhibition
relating to the Salthill
Geology Trail. The
Edisford Recreation Area
with pitch and putt, picnic
area and Ribblesdale
Pool, and the unique Civic
Hall cinema, a period
piece which still houses
the grand piano used in
the days of silent movies,
are further attractions.
Country market on
Tuesdays and Saturdays.
*Tourist Information
Centre ☎ (0200) 25566*

Brooklyn **M**
COMMENDED
32 Pimlico Road, Clitheroe,
BB7 2AH
☎ (0200) 28268
*Elegant Victorian townhouse
and annexe, close to the town
centre, offering quality
accommodation. Evening meals
in licensed dining room.*
Bedrooms: 4 single, 4 twin.
Bathrooms: 6 private,
1 public.

Bed & breakfast: £18-£19
single, £34-£37 double.
Half board: £26.50-£28.50
daily, £178.50-£192.50 weekly.
Evening meal 6.30pm (l.o.
7.30pm).
Credit: Access, Visa.

Calf's Head Hotel **M**
COMMENDED
Worston, Clitheroe, BB7 1QA
☎ Clitheroe (0200) 41218
*Nestling at the foot of Pendle
Hill, relaxing hotel and
restaurant offering discerning
guests speciality dishes or
traditional fare. Restaurant
open daily for lunch and
dinner.*
Bedrooms: 3 double & 2 twin,
1 family room.
Bathrooms: 6 private,
1 public.
Bed & breakfast: £40-£45
single, £50-£60 double.
Half board: £55-£65 daily.
Lunch available.
Evening meal 7pm (l.o.
9.30pm).
Parking for 100.
Credit: Access, Visa, Diners,
Amex.

Shireburn Arms Hotel **M**
COMMENDED
Whalley Road, Hurst Green,
Nr. Blackburn, BB6 9QJ
☎ Stonyhurst (025 486) 518
*17th C listed building close to
Stonyhurst College with
delightful views over Ribble
Valley. Extensive a la carte
menu.*
Bedrooms: 2 single, 6 double
& 5 twin, 2 family rooms.
Bathrooms: 15 private,
1 public.
Bed & breakfast: £41-£45
single, £64.50-£82.50 double.
Half board: £44.75-£57.75
daily, £285-£375 weekly.
Lunch available.
Evening meal 7pm (l.o. 9pm).
Parking for 80.
Credit: Access, Visa, Amex.

*National Crown
ratings were correct
at the time of going
to press but are
subject to change.
Please check at the
time of booking.*

COLNE

Lancashire
Map ref 4B1

Old market town with mixed industries bordering the moorland Bronte country. Nearby are the ruins of Wycoller House, featured in Charlotte Bronte's 'Jane Eyre' as Ferndean Manor.

Ashville House
Listed

75 Albert Road, Colne, BB8 0BP
☎ (0282) 869008
Family-run old Victorian small hotel, fully centrally heated. Bar/lounge. Vegetarian meals on request.
Bedrooms: 2 single, 3 double & 1 twin, 1 family room.
Bathrooms: 2 public.
Bed & breakfast: £15-£20 single, £30 double.
Half board: £20-£25 daily, £120-£140 weekly.
Lunch available.
Evening meal 5.30pm.
Parking for 6.
Credit: Access, Visa, Diners, Amex.
🔲🔲🔲🔲🔲🔲🔲🔲🔲
🔲🔲🔲🔲

CONGLETON

Cheshire
Map ref 4B2

Important cattle market and silk town on the River Dane, now concerned with general textiles. Nearby are Little Moreton Hall, a Tudor house surrounded by a moat, the Bridestones, a chambered tomb, and Mow Cop, topped by a folly.
Tourist Information Centre ☎ (0260) 271095

Lion & Swan Hotel M
😊😊😊😊 **COMMENDED**

Swan Bank, Congleton, CW12 1JR
☎ (0260) 273115
Oak-beamed 16th C coaching inn, refurbished in late 1989. High standards create an ideal base for business and leisure.
Bedrooms: 3 single, 15 double & 2 twin, 1 family room.
Bathrooms: 21 private.
Bed & breakfast: £40-£56.50 single, £50-£75 double.
Half board: from £35 daily.
Lunch available.
Evening meal 7pm (l.o. 9.30pm).
Parking for 73.

Credit: Access, Visa, Diners, Amex.
🔲🔲🔲🔲🔲🔲🔲🔲🔲🔲🔲🔲🔲🔲🔲🔲🔲🔲🔲

CREWE

Cheshire
Map ref 4A2

Famous for its railway junction. The railway reached Crewe in 1837 when the Warrington to Birmingham line passed through, transforming this small market town into the first great railway town.
Tourist Information Centre ☎ (0270) 537730

Hunters Lodge Hotel M
😊😊😊😊

Sydney Road, Crewe, CW1 1LU
☎ (0270) 583440 & 588216
Family-run country-style hotel set in 14 acres of land with wide open views. 1 mile from Crewe and 6 miles from M6.
Bedrooms: 7 single, 31 double & 3 twin, 1 family room.
Bathrooms: 42 private.
Bed & breakfast: £40-£53 single, £53-£65 double.
Half board: from £52 daily.
Lunch available.
Evening meal 7pm (l.o. 10pm).
Parking for 250.
Credit: Access, Visa, Amex.
🔲🔲🔲🔲🔲🔲🔲🔲🔲🔲🔲🔲🔲🔲🔲🔲🔲🔲🔲🔲

FRODSHAM

Cheshire
Map ref 4A2

3m S. Runcorn
Spacious, tree-lined main street flanked by 17th, 18th and 19th C buildings. Near Delamere Forest and Sandstone Trail.

Forest Hills Hotel M
😊😊😊😊 **COMMENDED**

Belle Monte Road, Overton Hill, Frodsham, WA6 6HH
☎ Runcorn (0928) 35255 & Fax (0928) 35517
Modern hotel with leisure complex, situated on top of Overton Hill with panoramic views over the Cheshire countryside.
Bedrooms: 24 double & 30 twin, 4 family rooms.
Bathrooms: 58 private.
Bed & breakfast: £44-£76 single, £64-£94 double.

Half board: £45-£91 daily, £301 weekly.
Lunch available.
Evening meal 7pm (l.o. 9.45pm).
Parking for 250.
Credit: Access, Visa, Diners, Amex.
🔲🔲🔲🔲🔲🔲🔲🔲🔲🔲🔲🔲🔲🔲🔲🔲🔲🔲🔲🔲🔲

Old Hall Hotel M

Main Street, Frodsham, WA6 7AB
☎ (0928) 32052 & 31452
Telex 629794
15th C town centre hotel beautifully and sympathetically modernised under the direction of the resident owners.
Bedrooms: 8 single, 10 double & 2 twin, 1 family room.
Bathrooms: 21 private.
Bed & breakfast: £35-£60 single, £45-£70 double.
Lunch available.
Evening meal 7pm (l.o. 10pm).
Parking for 30.
Credit: Access, Visa, Diners, Amex.
🔲🔲🔲🔲🔲🔲🔲🔲🔲🔲🔲🔲🔲🔲🔲🔲

GARSTANG

Lancashire
Map ref 4A1

10m N. Preston
Picturesque country market town in the east of the borough. Regarded as the gateway to the fells, it stands on the Lancaster Canal and is popular as a cruising centre. Close by are the remains of Greenhalgh Castle and the Bleasdale Circle. Discovery Centre.
Tourist Information Centre ☎ (0995) 602125

Crofters Hotel M
😊😊😊😊

A6, Cabus, Garstang, PR3 1PH
☎ (0995) 604128
CR Consort
Family owned and managed hotel with all modern facilities, situated midway between Preston and Lancaster.
Bedrooms: 1 single, 4 double & 12 twin, 3 family rooms.
Bathrooms: 20 private.
Bed & breakfast: £42-£60 single, £47-£66 double.
Lunch available.
Evening meal 7pm (l.o. 10pm).

Parking for 200.
Credit: Access, Visa, Diners, Amex.
🔲🔲🔲🔲🔲🔲🔲🔲🔲🔲🔲🔲🔲🔲🔲🔲

GISBURN

Lancashire
Map ref 4B1

8m NE. Clitheroe
This village on the A59 has an ancient church and houses and cottages that illustrate its long history. Weekly cattle auction. Annual steeplechase on the first Saturday in May.

Stirk House Hotel M
😊😊😊😊

Gisburn, Nr. Clitheroe, BB7 4LJ
☎ (0200) 445581
Fax (0200) 445744
Telex 635238
CR Consort
Original country house hotel, with modern facilities, within 20 minutes' drive of several large Pennine towns.
Bedrooms: 14 single, 8 double & 24 twin, 2 family rooms.
Bathrooms: 48 private.
Bed & breakfast: £35-£55 single, £50-£66 double.
Half board: £51.50-£71.50 daily.
Lunch available.
Evening meal 7.30pm (l.o. 9.30pm).
Parking for 100.
Credit: Access, Visa, Diners, Amex.
🔲🔲🔲🔲🔲🔲🔲🔲🔲🔲🔲🔲🔲🔲🔲🔲🔲🔲🔲

GREAT HARWOOD

Lancashire
Map ref 4A1

Royal Hotel
😊😊

Station Road, Great Harwood, BB6 7BA
☎ (0254) 883541
Recently restored and modernised Victorian public house. Access to the Ribble Valley and Pennine Hills.
Bedrooms: 2 single, 2 twin.
Bathrooms: 3 private, 1 public.
Bed & breakfast: £20-£35 single, £40-£70 double.
Lunch available.
Evening meal 7pm (l.o. 10pm).
Parking for 6.
🔲🔲🔲🔲🔲🔲🔲🔲🔲🔲🔲🔲🔲🔲🔲

HASLINGDEN

Lancashire
Map ref 4A1

Bank House Hotel
Bank Street, Off
Deardengate, Haslingden,
Rossendale, BB4 5PS
☎ (0706) 217641
*Charming family-run hotel
offering spacious modern en-
suite rooms, home cooking and
a central location. Convenient
for shops and buses.*
Bedrooms: 2 single, 2 double
& 3 twin.
Bathrooms: 7 private.
Bed & breakfast: £20-£23
single, £30-£35 double.
Half board: £27.95-£30.95
daily, from £130 weekly.
Evening meal 6.30pm (l.o.
7.30pm).
Parking for 10.
Credit: Access, Visa.
🖳 📺 🏧 🐾 🅿 🛏 🎹 ⚓ 🍽
🧵 🚲

HELSBY

Cheshire
Map ref 4A2

*8m NE. Chester
Residential village with its
own industries. Helsby
Hill rises to 460 ft with
fine views over the
Helsby Estuary. Attractive
hilly countryside to the
south.*

Poplars Guest House
130 Chester Road, Helsby,
Via Warrington, WA6 9NN
☎ (0928) 723433
*Victorian building set in half
an acre of garden.*
Bedrooms: 3 single, 1 double,
2 family rooms.
Bathrooms: 2 public.
Bed & breakfast: £17-£18
single, £30-£31 double.
Parking for 6.
🖳 📺 🆄 🅿 💷 📺 🎹 ✳ 🚲

HOLMES CHAPEL

Cheshire
Map ref 4A2

*4m E. Middlewich
Large village with some
interesting 18th C
buildings and St. Luke's
Church encased in brick
hiding the 15th C original.*

Holly Lodge Hotel
😃😃😃
70 London Road, Holmes
Chapel, CW4 7AS
☎ (0477) 37033
Fax (0477) 35823

*Charming Victorian country
hotel, professionally managed
and family-owned. Friendly
and efficient service. Close to
junction 18 of M6. Modern
bedrooms with all facilities.
A la carte restaurant,
conference and meeting rooms.*
Bedrooms: 6 single, 16 double
& 10 twin, 2 family rooms.
Bathrooms: 34 private.
Bed & breakfast: £29-£58
single, £46-£70 double.
Half board: £43-£65 daily.
Lunch available.
Evening meal 7.30pm (l.o.
9.45pm).
Parking for 80.
Credit: Access, Visa, Diners,
Amex.
🖳 📺 🏧 🐾 📞 🖨 💻 🅿 ☎ 🎹 🅥
🚫 🛏 💷 ⚓ 🍽 🔥 ✳ 🆂🅿 🆃

HOYLAKE

Merseyside
Map ref 4A2

*7m W. Birkenhead
Once a major port, this
residential resort has
good beaches, a 4-mile
promenade and, nearby,
the Royal Liverpool Golf
Club. Variety of bird life
on small offshore Hillbre
Islands.*

Kings Gap Court Hotel
😃😃
Valentia Road, Hoylake,
Wirral, L47 2AN
☎ 051-632 2073
*Old established family hotel
close to seafront and many
championship golf-courses.
Ideal centre for Wales, Chester
and Liverpool.*
Bedrooms: 4 single, 22 twin,
1 family room.
Bathrooms: 17 private,
5 public.
Bed & breakfast: £23.50-£30
single, £36 double.
Half board: £30-£36 daily,
£164-£199 weekly.
Lunch available.
Evening meal 6.30pm (l.o.
2.30pm).
Parking for 89.
Credit: Visa, Amex.
🖳 📺 🏧 🐾 📞 🅥 🚫 🖨 📺
⚫ 💻 ⚓ 🍽 ✳ 🚲 🐕 🆂🅿

---

*National Crown
ratings were correct
at the time of going
to press but are
subject to change.
Please check at the
time of booking.*

KNUTSFORD

Cheshire
Map ref 4A2

*6m W. Wilmslow
Derives its name from
Canute, King of the
Danes, said to have
forded the local stream.
Ancient and colourful May
Day celebrations. Nearby
is the Georgian mansion
of Tatton Park.*
*Tourist Information
Centre* ☎ *(0565) 632611
or 632210*

Laburnum Cottage
Guest House M
Listed COMMENDED
Knutsford Road, Mobberley,
Nr. Knutsford, WA16 7PU
☎ (0565) 872464
*Small country house set amidst
Cheshire countryside on B5085
close to Tatton Park, 4 miles
from Manchester Airport, 4
miles from Wilmslow, 2 miles
from M6 exit 19 and 2 miles
from M56. Pretty garden and
log fires, taxi service to airport.
Non-smokers only please.*
Bedrooms: 2 single, 1 double
& 2 twin.
Bathrooms: 4 private,
1 public.
Bed & breakfast: £21-£30
single, £38-£44 double.
Parking for 6.
🖳 ⚫ 📺 🆄 🏧 📞 🅥 🚫 🖨 📺
💻 ✳ 🚲 🅼 🆂🅿 🆃

Longview Hotel and
Restaurant M
😃😃😃 COMMENDED
Manchester Road, Knutsford,
WA16 0LX
☎ (0565) 632119 &
Fax (0565) 652402
*Period Victorian hotel with
many antiques and a relaxed
comfortable atmosphere,
overlooking town common.
Varied food. Close to exit 19
of M6 and airport.*
Bedrooms: 6 single, 8 double
& 7 twin, 2 family rooms.
Bathrooms: 23 private.
Bed & breakfast: £31-£50
single, £54-£65 double.
Half board: £44.75-£63.75
daily.
Evening meal 7pm (l.o. 9pm).
Parking for 17.
🖳 📺 📞 ⚫ 🖨 🐾 🅿 🎹 🅥 🖨
💻 ⚓ 🍽

Royal George Hotel M
King Street, Knutsford,
WA16 6EE
☎ (0565) 634151
Fax (0565) 634955

*In the historic town of
Knutsford, close to the M6 and
5 miles south of Manchester.
Built in the 14th C, one of the
oldest hostelries in Cheshire.
"Royal" because of Princess
Victoria's visit. Mrs Gaskell
wrote "Cranford" here.*
Bedrooms: 13 single,
12 double & 5 twin, 1 family
room.
Bathrooms: 31 private.
Bed & breakfast: £62-£67
single, £76 double.
Lunch available.
Evening meal 6pm (l.o.
11pm).
Parking for 50.
Credit: Access, Visa, Diners,
Amex.
🖳 📺 🏧 🐾 📞 🖨 🅿 🎹 🅥
🚫 🖨 ⚫ ✳ 💻 ⚓ 🍽 🔥 🅥
🐾 🆂🅿 🎹

The Toft M
Toft Road, Knutsford,
WA16 9EH
☎ (0565) 3470 & 4443
Telex 667441
*Small family-run hotel and
vegetarian restaurant. Close to
M6, three-quarters of a mile
south of Knutsford on the A50.
Non-smokers only please.*
Bedrooms: 2 single, 8 double
& 2 twin.
Bathrooms: 12 private,
1 public.
Bed & breakfast: £23-£39
single, £39-£51 double.
Evening meal 7.30pm (l.o.
9pm).
Parking for 30.
Credit: Access, Visa.
🖳 10 📺 🅥 🚫 🖨 📺 💻 ⚓
🍽 🐕 🚲 🆂🅿 🎹

LANCASTER

Lancashire
Map ref 4A1

*Interesting old county
town on the River Lune
with history dating back
to Roman times. Norman
castle, St. Mary's Church,
Customs House, City and
Maritime Museums,
Ashton Memorial and
Butterfly House are
among many places of
note. Good centre for
touring the Lake District.*
*Tourist Information
Centre* ☎ *(0524) 32878*

The Old Mill House
Waggon Road, Lower
Dolphinholme, Nr.
Lancaster, LA2 9AX
☎ Forton (0524) 791855
Continued ▶

LANCASTER
Continued

17th C mill house with extensive landscaped gardens on River Wyre. Private woodland and ponds, adjacent to Forest of Bowland. 5 minutes from junction 33 of M6.
Bedrooms: 2 double & 1 twin.
Bathrooms: 1 private, 1 public.
Bed & breakfast: £20-£30 single, £30-£40 double.
Half board: £29.50-£40 daily, £180-£252 weekly.
Evening meal 7pm (l.o. midday).
Parking for 5.

Royal Kings Arms Hotel M
75 Market Street, Lancaster, LA1 1HP
☎ (0524) 32451 & Fax (0524) 841698
🅒🅡 Principal
At the centre of historic Lancaster, close to shops and with easy access to Lake District. Comfortable rooms.
Bedrooms: 12 single, 20 double & 21 twin, 2 family rooms.
Bathrooms: 55 private.
Bed & breakfast: from £61 single, from £78 double.
Half board: from £42 daily.
Lunch available.
Evening meal 7pm (l.o. 9.30pm).
Parking for 25.
Credit: Access, Visa, Diners, Amex.

LANGHO
Lancashire
Map ref 4A1

This parish can trace its history back to Saxon times when in 798 AD a battle was fought at Billangohoh from which the names of Billington and Langho were derived. A flourishing community of mainly cattle farms, near both the River Ribble and the River Calder.

Mytton Fold Farm Hotel M
😃😃😃 COMMENDED
Whalley Road, Langho, Nr. Blackburn, BB6 8AB
☎ Blackburn (0254) 240662 & Fax (0254) 248119

---

10 miles from the M6 exit 31. Peacefully secluded, yet only 300 yards from the A59. Ideal centre for walking, fishing and golf.
Bedrooms: 13 double & 14 twin.
Bathrooms: 27 private.
Bed & breakfast: £32-£47 single, £51.25-£61.50 double.
Lunch available.
Evening meal 6.30pm (l.o. 9.30pm).
Parking for 100.
Credit: Access, Visa.

LITTLEBOROUGH
Gtr. Manchester
Map ref 4B1

3m NE. Rochdale Exit 21 M62
Industrial town near Hollingworth Lake and the Pennine Way. Rakewood viaduct and country park.

Dearnley Cottage Hotel
😃😃😃 COMMENDED
New Road, Littleborough, Nr. Rochdale, OL15 8PL
☎ (0706) 79670 & Fax (0706) 41891
Old world hotel, near country park, moorland walks, sailing, fishing, golfing and Pennine Way.
Bedrooms: 1 single, 7 double & 2 twin.
Bathrooms: 10 private.
Bed & breakfast: £27-£36 single, £40-£50 double.
Half board: £45-£56 daily, £240-£300 weekly.
Lunch available.
Evening meal 6.30pm (l.o. 9.45pm).
Parking for 50.
Credit: Access, Visa.

Individual proprietors have supplied all details of accommodation. Although we do check for accuracy, we advise you to confirm prices and other information at the time of booking.

LIVERPOOL
Merseyside
Map ref 4A2

Shipping and the sugar and slave trades transformed Liverpool into a major port in the 18th C. Landmarks include 2 cathedrals (Anglican and Roman Catholic), Town Hall, Walker Art Gallery and the Albert Dock complex containing the Beatles Story and the Merseyside Maritime Museum. Excellent shopping centre, entertainment and sports facilities (Aintree Racecourse). Speke Hall (National Trust).
Tourist Information Centre ☎ 051-709 3631 or 708 8854

Aachen Hotel M
89-91 Mount Pleasant, Liverpool, L3 5TB
☎ 051-709 3477 & 1126 & Fax 051-709 1126
Listed building in conservation area, in city centre close to theatres, shops, cinemas, boat/rail/coach stations. Albert Dock and Maritime Museum close by.
Bedrooms: 2 single, 4 double & 5 twin, 6 family rooms.
Bathrooms: 6 private, 2 public; 6 private showers.
Bed & breakfast: £18-£28 single, £34-£42 double.
Half board: £46-£56 daily, £168-£238 weekly.
Evening meal 6.30pm (l.o. 8.30pm).
Parking for 2.
Credit: Access, Visa, Diners, Amex.

Antrim Hotel M
😃😃😃
73 Mount Pleasant, Liverpool, L3 5TB
☎ 051-709 5239 & 9212 & Fax 051-709 7169
Friendly, family-run city centre hotel, convenient for shops, railway and bus stations, Albert Dock, and 20 minutes from the airport.
Bedrooms: 6 single, 4 double & 8 twin, 2 family rooms.
Bathrooms: 7 private, 1 public; 9 private showers.
Bed & breakfast: £22-£38 single, £35-£50 double.
Half board: £30-£46 daily, £210-£322 weekly.
Evening meal 6pm (l.o. 8pm).

Parking for 2.
Credit: Access, Visa, Diners, Amex.

Aplin House Hotel M
😃😃😃
35 Clarendon Road, Garston, Liverpool, L19 6PJ
☎ 051-427 5047
Detached Victorian residence facing park. Airport 2.5 miles (bus route). City centre 10 minutes by frequent trains. Roadside parking.
Bedrooms: 3 twin, 2 family rooms.
Bathrooms: 1 public; 1 private shower.
Bed & breakfast: £20-£24 single, £32-£40 double.
Half board: £25-£32 daily, £180-£190 weekly.
Evening meal 6.30pm (l.o. 9am).

Blundellsands Hotel
😃😃😃😃 COMMENDED
The Serpentine, Blundellsands, Crosby, Liverpool, L23 6TN
☎ 051-924 6515 & Fax 051-931 5364 Telex 626270
🅒🅡 Lansbury
Magnificent red brick building in a quiet suburb of Crosby. Within easy reach of Aintree, Royal Birkdale and the new Albert Dock complex.
Bedrooms: 21 single, 9 double & 5 twin, 7 family rooms.
Bathrooms: 42 private.
Bed & breakfast: £22-£62 single, £44-£74 double.
Half board: £34-£77 daily.
Lunch available.
Evening meal 7pm (l.o. 9.30pm).
Parking for 250.
Credit: Access, Visa, C.Bl., Diners, Amex.

Gateacre Hall Hotel
😃😃😃😃 COMMENDED
The Nook, Halewood Road, Liverpool, L25 5PG
☎ 051-428 6322 & Fax. 051-428 4302
Originally built in 1652 and under a preservation order. Extension specially designed to blend in with the existing structure.
Bedrooms: 2 single, 24 double & 8 twin.
Bathrooms: 34 private.
Bed & breakfast: £36-£52 single, £50.50-£72 double.
Lunch available.
Evening meal 6.30pm (l.o. 10.30pm).

Parking for 170.
Credit: Access, Visa, Diners, Amex.

Green Park Hotel M

4-6 Green Bank Drive, Liverpool, L17 1AN
☎ 051-733 3382
Two miles from city centre and three miles from Liverpool Airport.
Bedrooms: 2 single, 7 double & 7 twin, 7 family rooms.
Bathrooms: 16 private, 5 public.
Bed & breakfast: £28-£35 single, £36-£45 double.
Half board: £34-£52 daily.
Lunch available.
Evening meal 6.30pm (l.o. 9pm).
Parking for 25.
Credit: Access, Visa, Diners, Amex.

Rockland Hotel M

View Road, Rainhill, Prescot, Nr. Liverpool, L35 0LG
☎ 051-426 4603
Georgian hotel set in own grounds in quiet suburban location. Easy access to motorway (1 mile) and 10 miles from Liverpool city centre.
Bedrooms: 9 single, 3 double & 1 twin, 4 family rooms.
Bathrooms: 16 private, 1 public.
Bed & breakfast: £26-£36.50 single, £35-£55 double.
Lunch available.
Evening meal 6.30pm (l.o. 8.30pm).
Parking for 30.
Credit: Access, Visa.

Ullet Lodge M
Listed

77 Ullet Road, Liverpool, L17 2AA
☎ 051-733 1680
Large Victorian family home overlooking Sefton Park. Convenient for city centre, airport and M62. Spacious, comfortable rooms. Central heating throughout.
Bedrooms: 2 double & 2 twin, 4 family rooms.
Bathrooms: 2 public.
Bed & breakfast: from £15 single, from £25 double.
Parking for 3.

Woodlands Guest House
APPROVED

10 Haigh Road, Waterloo, Liverpool, L22 3XP
☎ 051-920 5373
In quiet residential area of Waterloo Park. A few minutes' walking distance from railway station, local shops and amenities.
Bedrooms: 8 twin.
Bathrooms: 7 private, 1 public.
Bed & breakfast: £23-£25 single, £36-£40 double.
Parking for 10.

LONGRIDGE
Lancashire
Map ref 4A1

Exit 32 M6
Comprises the parishes of Alston and Dilworth and serves as the shopping and social centre for the surrounding farming districts.

Brickhouse Country Hotel & Restaurant M
COMMENDED

Chipping, Nr. Preston, PR3 2QH
☎ (0995) 61316 & Fax (0995) 61085
18th C former farmhouse, now a tastefully modernised hotel. Spectacular views from intimate restaurant, providing home-cooked food.
Bedrooms: 2 double & 2 twin, 1 family room.
Bathrooms: 5 private.
Bed & breakfast: max. £36.50 single, max. £49.50 double.
Half board: £37.25-£56 daily, £234-£350 weekly.
Lunch available.
Evening meal 6pm (l.o. 9.30pm).
Parking for 100.
Credit: Access, Visa.

LYMM
Cheshire
Map ref 4A2

Pleasant country town with old market cross and distinctive lake.

Dingle Hotel M
COMMENDED

Rectory Lane, Lymm, WA13 0AH
☎ (092 575) 2297 & Fax (092 575) 2267

Family-run hotel situated in Roman village of Lymm. Set in own grounds surrounded by woodlands with nearby picturesque lake.
Bedrooms: 12 single, 13 double & 6 twin.
Bathrooms: 31 private.
Bed & breakfast: £40-£71.50 single, £49.50-£82.50 double.
Half board: £52.50-£84 daily, £368-£588 weekly.
Lunch available.
Evening meal 7pm (l.o. 9.30pm).
Parking for 113.
Credit: Access, Visa, Diners, Amex.

LYTHAM ST. ANNES
Lancashire
Map ref 4A1

12m W. Preston
Pleasant resort famous for its championship golf-courses, notably the Royal Lytham and St. Annes. Fine sands and attractive gardens. Some half-timbered buildings and an old windmill recently restored.
Tourist Information Centre ☎ (0253) 721222 or 725610

Chadwick Hotel M
COMMENDED

South Promenade, Lytham St. Annes, FY8 1NP
☎ (0253) 720061
Modern family-run hotel and leisure complex. Accent on food, comfort and personal service.
Bedrooms: 10 single, 11 double & 30 twin, 21 family rooms.
Bathrooms: 72 private.
Bed & breakfast: £30.50-£35 single, £42-£46 double.
Half board: £32.70-£37 daily, £228.90-£259 weekly.
Lunch available.
Evening meal 7pm (l.o. 8.30pm).
Parking for 40.
Credit: Access, Visa, Diners, Amex.

✎ Display advertisement appears on page 144.

Please mention this guide when making a booking.

Clifton Arms Hotel M

West Beach, Lytham St. Annes, FY8 5QJ
☎ (0253) 739898
Fax (0253) 730657
Telex 677463
© Lansbury
In the lovely old town of Lytham, overlooking the famous Green and the River Ribble.
Bedrooms: 10 single, 16 double & 13 twin, 2 family rooms.
Bathrooms: 41 private.
Bed & breakfast: £37-£85 single, £74-£97 double.
Half board: £49-£100 daily.
Lunch available.
Evening meal 7pm (l.o. 9.45pm).
Parking for 67.
Credit: Access, Visa, Diners, Amex.

Craigavon Hotel M

299-301 Clifton Drive South, Lytham St. Annes, FY8 1HN
☎ (0253) 721735 & 725801
Double-fronted hotel with sun lounge. Near shops, beach and many other facilities. Function licence for 100 people. Special winter weekend breaks.
Bedrooms: 6 single, 15 double & 6 twin, 2 family rooms.
Bathrooms: 24 private, 3 public.
Bed & breakfast: £22-£26 single, £42-£50 double.
Half board: £29.50-£33.50 daily, £200-£230 weekly.
Evening meal 6pm (l.o. midday).
Parking for 18.
Credit: Access, Visa.

Cullerne Hotel

55 Lightburne Avenue, Lytham St. Annes, FY8 1JE
☎ (0253) 721753
Located just off the promenade, offering comfortable accommodation with colour TV in all rooms.
Bedrooms: 1 single, 1 double & 1 twin, 2 family rooms.
Bathrooms: 1 public.
Bed & breakfast: £13 single, £26 double.
Half board: £17 daily, £104 weekly.
Evening meal 5.30pm.
Parking for 4.

LYTHAM ST. ANNES

Continued

Dalmeny Hotel M
▱▱▱▱ **COMMENDED**
19-27 South Promenade,
Lytham St.Annes, FY8 1LX
☎ (0253) 712236
Room-only rate on application.
Choose any of the 4
restaurants or use the small
kitchen in the suites specially
designed for families with
babies and small children.
Bedrooms: 1 single, 27 double,
76 family rooms.
Bathrooms: 104 private.
Bed & breakfast: £30-£60
single, £50-£80 double.
Half board: £43-£72 daily.
Lunch available.
Evening meal 5pm (l.o.
10.30pm).
Parking for 95.
Credit: Access, Visa.

Langcliffe Hotel
69-71 South Promenade,
Lytham St. Annes, FY8 1LZ
☎ (0253) 724454
Comfortable hotel to suit
business and holiday trade.
You are assured of a friendly
northern welcome.
Bedrooms: 3 single, 13 double
& 10 twin, 9 family rooms.
Bathrooms: 20 private,
4 public.
Bed & breakfast: from £19.50
single, from £39 double.
Half board: from £28 daily,
from £56 weekly.
Lunch available.
Evening meal 6pm (l.o. 7pm).
Parking for 20.
Credit: Access, Visa.

Lindum Hotel M
▱▱▱ **APPROVED**
63-67 South Promenade,
Lytham St. Annes, FY8 1LZ
☎ (0253) 721534 & 722516 &
Fax (0253) 721364
Family-run, seafront hotel with
good reputation for cooking
and comfortable
accommodation. Close to fine
shops and championship golf
courses.
Bedrooms: 6 single, 33 double
& 15 twin, 26 family rooms.
Bathrooms: 80 private,
2 public.
Bed & breakfast: £26-£30
single, £39-£42 double.
Half board: £28-£30 daily.
Lunch available.

Evening meal 6pm (l.o. 7pm).
Parking for 25.
Credit: Access, Visa, Amex.

MACCLESFIELD

Cheshire
Map ref 4B2

Former silk-
manufacturing town with
cobbled streets and
picturesque cottages
overlooking Bollin Valley.
West Park Museum and
Art Gallery and
Gawsworth Hall are
places of interest.
Tourist Information
Centre ☎ (0625) 500500

Chadwick House M
▱▱▱ **COMMENDED**
55 Beech Lane, Macclesfield,
SK10 2DS
☎ (0625) 615558
Tastefully refurbished large
town house, close to town
centre and stations. Licensed
bar, restaurant sauna, solarium
and gym available. Sky TV in
all rooms.
Bedrooms: 5 single, 5 double
& 2 twin.
Bathrooms: 8 private,
2 public.
Bed & breakfast: £23-£40
single, £44-£65 double.
Half board: £30-£47 daily.
Evening meal 7.30pm.
Parking for 10.
Credit: Access, Visa.

Moorhayes House Hotel M
▱▱▱
27 Manchester Road,
Tytherington, Macclesfield,
SK10 2JJ
☎ (0625) 433228
Modern, comfortable house in
secluded position half a mile
from town centre. 5 minutes
from Peak District National
Park, 20 minutes from
Manchester Airport.
Bedrooms: 2 single, 5 double
& 2 twin.
Bathrooms: 5 private,
2 public.
Bed & breakfast: £26-£38
single, £40-£50 double.
Evening meal 6pm.
Parking for 14.

Shrigley Hall Hotel, Golf and Country Club
▱▱▱▱▱
Shrigley Park, Pott Shrigley,
Nr. Macclesfield, SK10 5SB
☎ (0625) 575757
Fax (0625) 573323
Country house hotel built in
1825 in the 262-acre estate of
Shrigley Park. Overlooks the
Cheshire plain and Peak
District. 18-hole golf-course
and full leisure club.
Bedrooms: 10 single,
121 double & 20 twin,
7 family rooms.
Bathrooms: 158 private.
Bed & breakfast: £60-£80
single, £70-£125 double.
Half board: £49-£70 daily.
Lunch available.
Evening meal 7pm (l.o.
9.45pm).
Parking for 500.
Credit: Access, Visa, Diners,
Amex.

MANCHESTER

Gtr. Manchester
Map ref 4B1

The industrial capital of
the North, second only to
London as a commercial,
financial, banking and
newspaper centre.
Victorian architecture,
many churches,
museums, art galleries,
libraries, 15th C cathedral
and the exciting Granada
Studio Tours
development. Superb
shopping centre.
Tourist Information
Centre ☎ 061-234 3157
or 3158

Albany Guest House M
21 Albany Road, Chorlton-
cum-Hardy, Manchester,
M21 1AY
☎ 061-881 6774
Recently renovated Victorian
guesthouse, convenient for city
centre, airport and leisure
activities. Family-run with
warm atmosphere. Colour TV,
clock radio and hairdryer in all
rooms.
Bedrooms: 5 single, 4 double
& 6 twin, 4 family rooms.
Bathrooms: 12 private,
3 public; 7 private showers.
Bed & breakfast: £24.75-
£31.50 single, £39-£42.50
double.
Half board: £30-£37 daily,
£171-£230 weekly.

Evening meal 6pm (l.o.
9.30pm).
Parking for 8.

Ashdene Hotel M
▱▱▱
48 Wellington Road, Eccles,
Manchester, M30 9QW
☎ 061-789 4762 & Fax. 061-
787 8394
Centrally located in the Eccles
area, just off exit 2 of the
M602. 4.5 miles from
Manchester city centre. Ideal
for business, convenient for
Manchester Airport.
Bedrooms: 3 single, 1 double
& 2 twin, 1 family room.
Bathrooms: 7 private.
Bed & breakfast: £37-£41
single, £41-£53 double.
Half board: £45-£46 daily.
Lunch available.
Evening meal 7pm (l.o. 9pm).
Parking for 7.
Credit: Access, Visa.

Baron Hotel M
▱▱▱
116 Palatine Road, West
Didsbury, Manchester,
M20 9ZA
☎ 061-445 3877
Newly opened hotel, all rooms
with en-suite facilities. 3 miles
from Manchester Airport and
city centre. Half a mile from
the motorway network.
Bedrooms: 10 single, 5 twin,
1 family room.
Bathrooms: 16 private.
Bed & breakfast: £20-£27
single, £30-£40 double.
Half board: £30-£38 daily.
Evening meal 7pm (l.o.
8.30pm).
Parking for 25.
Credit: Access, Visa, Diners.

Britannia Hotel
Portland Street, Manchester,
M1 3LA
☎ 061-228 2288 Telex 665007
Well-appointed city centre
hotel. Two restaurants, bistro,
pub, nightclub and health club
facilities. Prices quoted are for
room only.
Bedrooms: 101 single,
133 double & 77 twin,
51 family rooms.
Bathrooms: 362 private.
Bed & breakfast: £30-£40
single, £60-£70 double.
Lunch available.
Evening meal 7pm (l.o.
10.30pm).

Credit: Access, Visa, Diners, Amex.

ॐ ♨ ℄ ▣ ⌷ ♥ 🛈 ▣
🖅 ⧖ ● ☒ ▥ ☎ ⌾ ⎕ ⚲ ℟
ᴅᴀᴘ ⚒ SP ஐ ⊤

The Copthorne Manchester ₥
▩▩▩▩▩ COMMENDED

Clipper Quay, Salford Quays, Manchester, M5 3DL
☎ 061-873 7321 & Fax 061-873 7318 Telex 669090
COPMAN
Waterfront location, close to city centre. Local attractions include Old Trafford, Granada TV studio tours, G-Mex Centre and China Town.
Bedrooms: 111 double & 55 twin.
Bathrooms: 166 private.
Bed & breakfast: £87-£98 single, £97-£108 double.
Half board: £70.70-£78.70 daily.
Lunch available.
Evening meal 7pm (l.o. 10.45pm).
Parking for 103.
Credit: Access, Visa, Diners, Amex.

ॐ ♨ ℄ ▣ ⌷ ♥ 🛈 ▣ ✂
🖅 ⧖ ● ☒ ▥ ☎ ⌾ ⎕ ⚲ ℟
✗ SP ⊤

Crescent Gate Hotel ₥
▩▩▩ COMMENDED

Park Crescent, Victoria Park, Manchester, M14 5RE
☎ 061-224 0672 & Fax 061-257 2822
2 miles from city centre, in quiet residential crescent, convenient for airport. One of Manchester's popular independent hotels.
Bedrooms: 21 single, 2 double & 2 twin, 1 family room.
Bathrooms: 18 private, 2 public.
Bed & breakfast: £28-£35 single, £48 double.
Half board: £36-£43 daily.
Lunch available.
Evening meal 7pm (l.o. 8pm).
Parking for 18.
Credit: Access, Visa, Diners, Amex.

ॐ ♨ ℄ ▣ ⌷ ♥ 🛈 ▣ 🖅
⧖ ● ▥ ☎ ⌾ ⎕ ⚲
⊕ Display advertisement appears on page 145.

Ebor Hotel ₥
▩▩

402 Wilbraham Road, Chorlton-cum-Hardy, Manchester, M21 1UH
☎ 061-881 1911 & 4855
Hotel offering comfortable accommodation and friendly service, within easy reach of airport, Manchester city centre and motorway network.

Bedrooms: 6 single, 3 double & 4 twin, 3 family rooms.
Bathrooms: 1 private, 3 public; 3 private showers.
Bed & breakfast: £22-£28 single, £33-£38 double.
Half board: £27.50-£33.50 daily, £190-£230 weekly.
Evening meal 6.30pm (l.o. 5pm).
Parking for 20.

ॐ ♨ ⌷ ♥ ▣ ⧖ ▥ ☎ ⚲ ✗ SP
⊤
⊕ Display advertisement appears on page 145.

Elm Grange Hotel ₥
▩▩

559-561 Wilmslow Road, Withington, Manchester, M20 9GJ
☎ 061-445 3336
On main bus routes and near city centre and airport. Cleanliness, service, value for money. Warm welcome assured. Convenient for theatres, shops, restaurants, hospitals and university.
Bedrooms: 17 single, 4 double & 11 twin.
Bathrooms: 15 private, 3 public.
Bed & breakfast: £22.91-£35.25 single, £41.13-£49.94 double.
Half board: £29-£42 daily, £140.37-£225.75 weekly.
Evening meal 6pm (l.o. 8pm).
Parking for 41.
Credit: Access, Visa.

ॐ ♨ ℄ ▣ ⌷ ♥ 🛈 ▣ ✂
🖅 ⎕ ☎ ⚲ ⊤

Four Seasons Hotel, Manchester Airport ₥

Hale Road, Hale Barns, Nr. Altrincham, Cheshire
WA15 8XW
☎ 061-904 0301 Telex 665492
A civilised oasis in the business world of Greater Manchester. Only 5 minutes from Manchester Airport and the motorway network.
Bedrooms: 42 double & 40 twin, 12 family rooms.
Bathrooms: 94 private.
Bed & breakfast: £46.50-£97.50 single, £61.50-£108.50 double.
Lunch available.
Evening meal 6pm (l.o. 11pm).
Parking for 360.
Credit: Access, Visa, Diners, Amex.

ॐ ♨ ℄ ▣ ⌷ ♥ 🛈 ▣
🖅 ● ☒ ▥ ☎ ⌾ ⎕ ᴅᴀᴘ ⚒ SP
ஐ ⊤

The symbols are explained on the flap inside the back cover.

Gardens Hotel ₥
▩▩▩▩ COMMENDED

55 Piccadilly, Manchester, M1 2AP
☎ 061-236 5155
ⓒⓡ Best Western
Situated in the heart of the city, overlooking Piccadilly Gardens. This hotel is furnished to modern standards.
Bedrooms: 12 single, 42 double & 47 twin.
Bathrooms: 101 private.
Bed & breakfast: £43-£100 single, £62-£120 double.
Lunch available.
Evening meal 6.30pm (l.o. 10pm).
Credit: Access, Visa, Diners, Amex.

ॐ ♨ ℄ ▣ ⌷ ♥ 🛈 ▣ ✂
🖅 ⧖ ▥ ☎ ⚲ SP ⊤

Granada Hotel ₥

404 Wilmslow Road, Withington, Manchester, M20 9BM
☎ 061-445 5908 & Fax 061-445 4902
Comfortable hotel close to Manchester city centre and airport. En-suite rooms, colour TV, telephone, hair-dryer. Lounge, bar and restaurant. Parking.
Bedrooms: 3 single, 2 double & 3 twin, 2 family rooms.
Bathrooms: 10 private.
Bed & breakfast: £28-£38 single, £39-£49 double.
Evening meal 6pm (l.o. 11.30pm).
Parking for 20.
Credit: Access, Visa, Diners, Amex.

ॐ ♨ ℄ ▣ ⌷ ♥ 🛈 ▣ 🖅
☒ ▥ ☎ ⚲ ᴅᴀᴘ ⚒ SP

Green Gables Guest House ₥

152 Barlow Moor Road, West Didsbury, Manchester, M20 8UT
☎ 061-445 5365
Refurbished guesthouse with relaxed, warm and friendly atmosphere. Next to M56 and M63, 5 minutes from airport, city centre and G-Mex centre.
Bedrooms: 7 single, 3 double & 2 twin, 3 family rooms.
Bathrooms: 1 private, 4 public.
Bed & breakfast: £13.50-£17.50 single, £26-£32 double.
Half board: £17.45-£22.20 daily, £99-£135 weekly.
Evening meal 6pm (l.o. 7pm).
Parking for 9.

ॐ ♨ ⌷ ♥ ⊍ 🛈 ▣ 🖅 ☎ ▥ ⚲
✗ ᴅᴀᴘ ⚒ SP ⊤

Horizon Hotel ₥
Listed APPROVED

69 Palatine Road, Didsbury, Manchester, M20 9LJ
☎ 061-445 4705
Small, well-appointed hotel convenient for airport and town centre. Large car park, bar and restaurant.
Bedrooms: 8 single, 6 double & 3 twin, 1 family room.
Bathrooms: 11 private; 7 private showers.
Bed & breakfast: £24-£27 single, £36-£42 double.
Half board: £32-£34 daily.
Evening meal 6.30pm (l.o. 8.30pm).
Parking for 30.
Credit: Access, Visa.

ॐ ♨ ℄ ▣ ⌷ ♥ 🛈 ▣ ✂ 🖅
☒ ● ▥ ☎ ⌾ ⚲ ✗ ᴅᴀᴘ
SP ⊤

Imperial Hotel ₥
▩▩▩

157 Hathersage Road, Manchester, M13 0HY
☎ 061-225 6500
Recently modernised and refurbished hotel. 1.25 miles south of city centre, in the vicinity of university and teaching hospitals.
Bedrooms: 13 single, 5 double & 9 twin.
Bathrooms: 21 private, 3 public.
Bed & breakfast: £27-£32 single, £38-£40 double.
Half board: from £35 daily.
Evening meal 6.30pm (l.o. 8.30pm).
Parking for 30.
Credit: Access, Visa, Diners, Amex.

ॐ ♨ ⌷ ♥ 🛈 ▣ 🖅 ☒ ●
▥ ☎ ⌾ ⚲ SP ⊤

New White Lion Hotel ₥
▩▩

27 Middleton Old Road, Blackley, Manchester, M9 3DS
☎ 061-720 7218
Old world public house/inn, 3 miles from city centre and 2 miles from M62.
Bedrooms: 2 double & 1 twin, 2 family rooms.
Bathrooms: 5 private.
Bed & breakfast: £20-£25 single, £35-£55 double.
Lunch available.
Parking for 25.
Credit: Access, Visa.

℄ ⌷ ♥ ⧖ ☒ ▥ ☎ ⚲ ℟
✗ ᴅᴀᴘ SP

Parkside Guest House ₥

58 Cromwell Road, Stretford, Manchester, M32 8QJ
☎ 061-865 2860
Continued ▶

MANCHESTER

Continued

Clean, friendly service in a quiet residential area, convenient for Old Trafford football and cricket ground, city centre M63 exit 7. Children over 7 welcome. Family rooms available.
Bedrooms: 1 single, 1 double & 2 twin, 1 family room.
Bathrooms: 3 private, 1 public.
Bed & breakfast: £16-£18 single, £29-£31 double.
Parking for 3.

Hotel Piccadilly **M**
⚜⚜⚜⚜ COMMENDED
P.O. Box 107, Piccadilly, Manchester, M60 1QR
☎ 061-236 8414 Telex 668765
Situated in the heart of Manchester, minutes away from the shopping areas, the hotel has every facility, including a health and leisure club.
Bedrooms: 150 single, 61 double & 60 twin.
Bathrooms: 271 private.
Bed & breakfast: £34.50-£38 single, £69-£76 double.
Half board: £53-£58 daily.
Lunch available.
Evening meal 6.30pm (l.o. 10pm).
Parking for 280.
Credit: Access, Visa, C.Bl., Diners, Amex.

Ramada Renaissance Hotel **M**
Deansgate, Blackfriars Street, Manchester, M3 2EQ
☎ 061-835 2555 Telex 669699 RAMMAN
Excellent city centre location. Car porterage. 24-hour room service. Theatre booking and short break package available.
Bedrooms: 5 single, 46 double & 154 twin.
Bathrooms: 205 private.
Bed & breakfast: £61.25-£106.25 single, £70.50-£131.10 double.
Half board: £76.20-£121.25 daily.
Lunch available.
Evening meal 7.30pm (l.o. 11pm).
Parking for 80.
Credit: Access, Visa, C.Bl., Diners, Amex.

The Royals Hotel **M**
⚜⚜⚜⚜ APPROVED
Altrincham Road, Wythenshawe, Manchester, M22 4BJ
☎ 061-998 9011 & Fax 061-998 4641
© Consort
Large mock Tudor inn beside M56 Sharston/Altrincham exit, near to M63 and 2 miles from Manchester Airport.
Bedrooms: 10 single, 9 double & 11 twin, 4 family rooms.
Bathrooms: 34 private.
Bed & breakfast: from £46 single, from £62 double.
Lunch available.
Evening meal 7pm (l.o. 9.45pm).
Parking for 100.
Credit: Access, Visa, Diners, Amex.

Thistlewood Hotel
203 Urmston Lane, Stretford, M32 9DD
☎ 061-865 3611
Small friendly hotel in town 4 miles south of Manchester, close to M63 and convenient for airport. Town is home of Manchester United FC and Lancashire County CC.
Bedrooms: 5 single, 2 double & 6 twin, 1 family room.
Bathrooms: 9 private, 1 public.
Bed & breakfast: £24.50-£32 single, £39.50-£54 double.
Half board: £29.50-£39.50 daily, £175-£245 weekly.
Evening meal 6.30pm (l.o. 7.30pm).
Parking for 12.
Credit: Access, Visa, Diners, Amex.

West Lynne Hotel **M**
⚜⚜⚜
16 Middleton Lane, Crumpsall, Manchester, M8 6DS
☎ 061-721 4922 & 4866
Quarter of a mile from M62 junction 15 and four miles from city centre.
Bedrooms: 5 single, 2 double & 5 twin, 2 family rooms.
Bathrooms: 14 private.
Bed & breakfast: £30-£47 single, £40-£50 double.
Half board: £37.50-£54.50 daily.
Evening meal 6pm (l.o. 7.30pm).
Parking for 12.
Credit: Access, Visa, Diners, Amex.

Willow Bank Hotel **M**
⚜⚜⚜⚜ COMMENDED
340 Wilmslow Road, Fallowfield, Manchester, M14 6AF
☎ 061-224 0461 & Fax. 061-257 2561 Telex 668222
International restaurant. Easy access to Manchester Airport, the M6, M56, M62 and M63, city centre, and conference and exhibition sites. Weekend rates available.
Bedrooms: 60 single, 27 double & 29 twin, 2 family rooms.
Bathrooms: 118 private.
Bed & breakfast: £30-£48 single, £38-£65 double.
Half board: £40-£58 daily.
Lunch available.
Evening meal 7pm (l.o. 10.15pm).
Parking for 110.
Credit: Access, Visa, Diners, Amex.

Wilmslow Hotel
356 Wilmslow Road, Fallowfield, Manchester, M14 6AB
☎ 061-225 3030
Fax 061-257 2854
Comfortable hotel close to city centre, shops and nightlife. On direct bus route for Manchester Airport.
Bedrooms: 16 single, 17 double & 9 twin, 10 family rooms.
Bathrooms: 24 private, 5 public; 9 private showers.
Bed & breakfast: £19.95-£33.65 single, £34.30-£41.50 double.
Half board: £25.90-£40.60 daily, £121-£182 weekly.
Evening meal 6.30pm (l.o. 9pm).
Parking for 35.
Credit: Access, Visa, Amex.

MANCHESTER AIRPORT

Map ref 4B2

See also Alderley Edge, Altrincham, Cheadle Hulme, Knutsford, Manchester, Sale, Salford, Stockport, Stretford, Wilmslow. Tourist Information Centre ☎ 061-436 3344

Etrop Grange **M**
⚜⚜⚜⚜
Outwood Lane, Ringway, Manchester M22 5NR
☎ 061-499 0500

Family-run Georgian country house hotel in its own secluded grounds, next to Manchester Airport.
Bedrooms: 3 single, 33 double & 4 twin, 1 family room.
Bathrooms: 41 private.
Bed & breakfast: from £85 single, from £95 double.
Half board: from £120 daily.
Lunch available.
Evening meal 7pm (l.o. 10pm).
Parking for 90.
Credit: Access, Visa, Diners, Amex.

Wilmslow Moat House **M**
Altrincham Road, Wilmslow, Cheshire SK9 4LR
☎ (0625) 529201
Telex 666401
© Queens Moat Houses
Tyrolean-style hotel near Manchester Airport and Wilmslow on the fringe of Styal Country Park. Country Club offering jacuzzi, saunas, gymnasium, steamroom, squash courts, sunbeds and snooker room. Special weekend rates.
Bedrooms: 13 single, 76 double & 36 twin.
Bathrooms: 125 private.
Bed & breakfast: £47.20-£52.50 single, £64.40-£70 double.
Half board: £60.20-£67.50 daily.
Lunch available.
Evening meal 7pm (l.o. 10pm).
Parking for 400.
Credit: Access, Visa, Diners, Amex.

National Crown ratings were correct at the time of going to press but are subject to change. Please check at the time of booking.

Map references apply to the colour maps towards the end of this guide.

MORECAMBE

Lancashire
Map ref 5A3

3m NW. Lancaster
Famous for its shrimps,
Morecambe is a
traditional resort on a
wide bay with spacious
beaches, entertainments
and seafront
illuminations. Bubbles
Leisure Park. Carnforth
Railway Museum nearby.
*Tourist Information
Centre* ☎ *(0524) 414110*

Carnbrea Hotel
17 Clarendon Road,
Morecambe, LA4 4HR
☎ (0524) 417878
*Family-run hotel just
two streets from promenade
and seafront and 3 minutes
from Frontierland, Bubbles
leisure pool and the Dome.
Close to Regent Park with its
putting, tennis and bowls.
Personal service, home
cooking.*
Bedrooms: 4 single, 3 double
& 1 twin, 1 family room.
Bathrooms: 1 public.
Bed & breakfast: £10-£12.50
single, £20-£25 double.
Half board: £13-£15 daily,
£75-£85 weekly.
Evening meal 5pm (l.o. 6pm).
⌂ ⌷ ⏻ ⓘ Ⓥ ⏟ ⏢ 🖻 ♣
⊁ ⒹⒶ⒫ Ⓢⓟ

Clarendon Hotel ⋔
≌≌≌≌ APPROVED
76 Marine Road West,
Morecambe, LA4 4EP
☎ (0524) 410180
*On the promenade and close to
entertainment. Panoramic
views of the Lakeland hills.*
Bedrooms: 5 single, 6 double
& 17 twin, 3 family rooms.
Bathrooms: 29 private,
4 public; 1 private showers.
Bed & breakfast: £25-£29
single, £40-£45 double.
Half board: from £34.25
daily, from £235 weekly.
Lunch available.
Evening meal 7pm (l.o. 9pm).
Parking for 2.
Credit: Access, Visa, Diners,
Amex.
⌂ ⌇ ⏻ ⒹⓆ ⏟ ⓘ Ⓥ ⏟ ⏢
⏢ ⊞ ⎚ ⏢ ⎗ ⏢ ♣ ⒹⒶ⒫ Ⓢⓟ
Ⓣ

Silverwell Christian Hotel ⋔
20 West End Road,
Morecambe, LA4 4DL
☎ (0524) 410532
*Family-run hotel, 100 yards
from promenade, offering good
food and fellowship. Non-
smoking establishment.
Unlicensed.*
Bedrooms: 1 single, 8 double
& 3 twin, 4 family rooms.
Bathrooms: 3 public.
Half board: from £16 daily,
£75-£105 weekly.
Evening meal 6pm.
Credit: Access, Visa.
⌂ ⏻ ⏟ ⓤⓛ Ⓥ ⏟ 🖻 ⏢ ⏢
⊁ ⊁ Ⓝ Ⓢⓟ

Uppington Licensed Private Hotel
≌
15 Thornton Road,
Morecambe, LA4 5PD
☎ (0524) 410887
*Small, friendly hotel, adjacent
to promenade. Pleasant and
relaxed atmosphere. Children
and pets welcome.*
Bedrooms: 2 single, 6 double
& 2 twin, 3 family rooms.
Bathrooms: 6 private,
3 public.
Bed & breakfast: £11-£14
single, £22-£28 double.
Half board: £15-£18 daily,
£80-£100 weekly.
Evening meal 6pm (l.o. 4pm).
Parking for 2.
Open April-October.
⌂ ⏟ ⒹⓆ ⏻ ⓘ Ⓥ ⏟ ⏢
ⒹⒶ⒫ ⊁ Ⓢⓟ

Westleigh Hotel
≌≌≌
9 Marine Road, Morecambe,
LA3 1BS
☎ (0524) 418352
*Comfortable family-run hotel
on the promenade, overlooking
gardens, Morecambe Bay and
Lakeland hills. Close to all
tourist amenities. Stair lift.
Colour TVs in all bedrooms.*
Bedrooms: 1 single, 3 double
& 6 twin, 2 family rooms.
Bathrooms: 9 private,
1 public.
Bed & breakfast: £12-£14.50
single, £24-£29 double.
Half board: £18-£20.50 daily,
£98-£110 weekly.
Evening meal 5pm (l.o. 6pm).
Credit: Access, Visa.
⌂ ⏟ ⒹⓆ ⏻ ⓘ Ⓥ ⏟ ⏢ ⎚
⏢ ⒹⒶ⒫ ⊁ Ⓢⓟ Ⓣ

MORETON

Merseyside
Map ref 4A2

Leasowe Castle Hotel & Conference Centre ⋔
≌≌≌≌
Leasowe Road, Moreton,
L46 3RF
☎ 051-606 9191
Fax 051-678 5551
*16th C building converted to a
hotel. All rooms with direct-
dial telephone, trouser press
and hairdryer. 3 bars, health
club, a la carte restaurant.
Golf-course adjacent.*
Bedrooms: 25 double &
25 twin.
Bathrooms: 50 private.
Bed & breakfast: £33-£51.51
single, £36.50-£66.07 double.
Half board: £44.25-£62.76
daily, £238.23-£265.64
weekly.
Evening meal 7pm (l.o.
10pm).
Parking for 200.
Credit: Access, Visa, Diners,
Amex.
⌂ ⏟ ⌇ ⒹⓆ ⏻ ⓘ Ⓥ ⏟
⏢ Ⓣ ⎚ ⏢ ⏢ 🖻 ♣
⏻ ⏢ ⊁ ⊁ ⒹⒶ⒫ Ⓢⓟ ⏢ Ⓣ

NANTWICH

Cheshire
Map ref 4A2

Pleasant old market town
on the River Weaver
made prosperous in
Roman times by salt
springs. Fire destroyed
the town in 1583 and
many fine buildings were
rebuilt in Elizabethan
style. Churche's Mansion
(open to the public)
survived the fire.
Surrounding agricultural
area produces Cheshire
cheese.
*Tourist Information
Centre* ☎ *(0270) 623914*

Alvaston Hall Hotel ⋔
Middlewich Road,
Nantwich, CW5 6PD
☎ (0270) 624341 Telex 36311
⏚ Rank
*18th C country house set in 14
acres of grounds. Silver Cloud
restaurant. Facilities include
full leisure complex, golf
driving range.*
Bedrooms: 17 single,
46 double & 17 twin, 8 family
rooms.
Bathrooms: 88 private,
2 public.
Bed & breakfast: £49-£76
single, £67-£91 double.
Lunch available.

Evening meal 7pm (l.o.
9.30pm).
Parking for 250.
Credit: Access, Visa, Diners,
Amex.
⌂ ⏟ ⌇ ⒹⓆ ⏻ ⓘ Ⓥ ⏟
⏟ ⏢ ⎚ ⏢ Ⓣ ⏢ ⏢ ⏢ ⏢
⏢ ⏢ ⊁ ⒹⒶ⒫ ⊁ Ⓢⓟ ⏢ Ⓣ

Lamb Hotel ⋔
Hospital Street, Nantwich,
CW5 5RH
☎ (0270) 625286
*200-year-old coaching inn with
restaurant, in the centre of
historic Nantwich. We have a
popular lounge bar and offer a
wide selection of cold and hot
food, 7 days a week.*
Bedrooms: 4 single, 3 double
& 7 twin, 2 family rooms.
Bathrooms: 13 private,
2 public.
Bed & breakfast: £23.50-£34
single, £47-£51 double.
Lunch available.
Evening meal 7pm (l.o.
9.30pm).
Parking for 35.
Credit: Access, Visa.
⌂ ⏟ ⏻ Ⓥ ⏟ 🖻 ⏢ ⏢ Ⓣ
⊁ Ⓢⓟ

NELSON

Lancashire
Map ref 4B1

4m N. Burnley
The name of this textile
town was taken from the
'Nelson Inn', called after
the famous admiral and
around which the town
grew in 19th C. Bronze
Age and Roman artefacts
have been found in the
area.
*Tourist Information
Centre* ☎ *(0282) 692890
or 67731 ext 267*

The Groves Hotel
144 Manchester Road,
Nelson, BB9 7AH
☎ (0282) 65948/68228
*Victorian Gothic mansion,
approximately half mile from
Nelson town centre, a few miles
from Pendle Hill, home of the
Lancashire Witches.*
Bedrooms: 8 single, 12 double
& 3 twin, 1 family room.
Bathrooms: 24 private.
Bed & breakfast: from £35
single, from £45 double.
Lunch available.
Evening meal 7pm (l.o.
9.30pm).
Parking for 100.
Credit: Access, Visa, Diners,
Amex.
⌂ ⏟ ⌇ ⒹⓆ ⏻ ⓘ Ⓥ ⏟
⏟ Ⓣ ⎚ ⏢ ⏢ Ⓣ ⏻ ⊁ ⏢
⊁ Ⓢⓟ

---

*Half board prices shown are per person
but in some cases may be based on
double/twin occupancy.*

NELSON

Continued

Wintersfield Hotel M
♨♨

230-236 Manchester Road, Nelson, BB9 7DE
☎ (0282) 65379
Modern family-run hotel, clean and friendly, adjacent to exit 12 of the M65. Easy access to many local beauty spots and places of interest.
Bedrooms: 7 single, 3 double & 8 twin, 1 family room.
Bathrooms: 1 private, 3 public.
Bed & breakfast: £14-£20 single, £26-£35 double.
Half board: £19.25-£25.25 daily, £119-£161 weekly.
Evening meal 6.15pm.
Parking for 16.
🛎 🐕 🎍 💺 Ⓥ ☎ 🖥 💻 🖤 🍽

NEWTON-LE-WILLOWS

Merseyside
Map ref 4A2

5m E. St. Helens
Small industrial town with some 17th C cottages and Elizabethan farmhouses.

Kirkfield Hotel M
♨♨♨ APPROVED

4 Church Street, Newton-le-Willows, WA12 9SU
☎ (092 52) 28196
Family hotel with bar and function facilities. Easy access to M6 and M62, close to Haydock Park racecourse.
Bedrooms: 6 single, 5 double & 4 twin, 1 family room.
Bathrooms: 13 private, 1 public.
Bed & breakfast: £26-£36 single, £40-£48 double.
Lunch available.
Evening meal 7pm (l.o. 8.30pm).
Parking for 50.
Credit: Access, Visa.
🛎 📞 🖵 💺 Ⓥ 🍽 ☎ 🖥 💻 🍽 🍴 ✳ 🎿 🖤 🍽

The enquiry coupons at the back will help you when contacting proprietors.

Please mention this guide when making a booking.

NORTHWICH

Cheshire
Map ref 4A2

An important salt-producing town since Roman times, Northwich has been replanned with a modern shopping centre and a number of black and white buildings. Unique Anderton boat-lift on northern outskirts of town.

Ayrshire Guest House
♨♨ COMMENDED

31 Winnington Lane, Northwich, CW8 4DE
☎ (0606) 74871
Close to Northwich market town, this comfortable, friendly guesthouse is convenient for motorways and all parts of the north west.
Bedrooms: 3 single, 2 double & 2 twin.
Bathrooms: 3 private, 1 public.
Bed & breakfast: £15.50-£20 single, £30-£34 double.
Parking for 6.
🛎 🎍 💺 Ⓤ 💺 🍽 ☎ 💻 ☎ 🖤

Friendly Floatel M
♨♨♨ COMMENDED

London Road, Northwich, CW9 5HD
☎ (0606) 44443 & Fax (0606) 42596
Ⓒ Friendly
The first "hotel at water", constructed on the meeting point of the Weaver and Dane rivers.
Bedrooms: 21 single, 19 double & 20 twin, 2 family rooms.
Bathrooms: 62 private.
Bed & breakfast: £53.50-£66.20 single, £66.75-£81.90 double.
Lunch available.
Evening meal 7pm (l.o. 10pm).
Parking for 60.
Credit: Access, Visa, C.Bl., Diners, Amex.
🛎 🎍 📞 💺 Ⓡ 🖵 💺 Ⓥ 🍽 🍽 ☎ ● 🖥 💻 🍽 🍴 🎿 🖤 🍴 ✳ 🎿 Ⓓ SP 🍽 Ⓣ

Springfield Guest House M
♨♨ COMMENDED

Chester Road, Oakmere, Northwich, CW8 2HB
☎ Sandiway (0606) 882538

Family guesthouse erected in 1863. On A556 close to Delamere Forest, midway between Chester and M6 motorway junction 19. Manchester Airport 25 minutes' drive.
Bedrooms: 4 single, 1 double & 1 twin, 1 family room.
Bathrooms: 2 private, 1 public.
Bed & breakfast: £19.50 single, £34 double.
Half board: £24 daily.
Evening meal 6pm (l.o. 8pm).
Parking for 10.
🛎 🎍 Ⓡ 💺 Ⓤ 🍽 🍽 ☎ 💻 ✳ 🎿 🖤 🍽

Wincham Hall M
♨♨♨ COMMENDED

Hall Lane, Wincham, Northwich, CW9 6DG
☎ (0606) 43453
Family-run, country hotel with personal attention and friendly atmosphere. Set in 4 acres of grounds A la carte restaurant.
Bedrooms: 2 single, 2 double & 5 twin, 1 family room.
Bathrooms: 1 public.
Bed & breakfast: £25-£42.50 single, £42-£56 double.
Half board: £32-£66 daily.
Lunch available.
Evening meal 5.30pm (l.o. 9.30pm).
Parking for 200.
Credit: Access, Visa.
🛎 🎍 📞 💺 Ⓥ 🍽 ☎ 💻 🍽 🍴 Ⓤ ✳

OLDHAM

Gtr. Manchester
Map ref 4B1

Large important textile town, boosted in 19th C by Arkwright's spinning-frame and Watt's steam engine. Outstanding watercolours in Art Gallery and impressive neo-classical Town Hall.
Tourist Information Centre ☎ 061-678 4654

Avant Hotel M
♨♨♨♨ COMMENDED

Windsor Road, Manchester Street, Oldham, OL8 4AS
☎ 061-627 5500 Telex 668264 AVANTI G
Located just 5 miles from Manchester city centre and 4 miles from the M62 connecting east and west.
Bedrooms: 3 single, 30 double & 66 twin, 4 family rooms.
Bathrooms: 103 private.
Bed & breakfast: from £63 single, from £70 double.
Half board: from £41 daily.
Lunch available.

Evening meal 7pm (l.o. 10pm).
Parking for 152.
Credit: Access, Visa, Diners, Amex.
🛎 📞 Ⓡ 🖵 💺 🎍 Ⓥ 🍴 🍽 ● 🖥 🍽 🍴 🎿 🖤 ✳ SP Ⓣ

High Point Hotel M
♨♨♨ COMMENDED

Napier Street East, Oldham, OL8 1TR
☎ 061-624 4130 & Fax. 061-627 2757
Warm, friendly family-run hotel with a la carte restaurant. Only 2 minutes from M62 link road.
Bedrooms: 6 single, 6 double & 4 twin, 2 family rooms.
Bathrooms: 16 private, 1 public.
Bed & breakfast: £30-£40 single, £40-£55 double.
Half board: £39.95-£49.95 daily.
Lunch available.
Evening meal 7.15pm (l.o. 9.30pm).
Parking for 30.
Credit: Access, Visa, Diners, Amex.
🛎 🍽 📞 Ⓡ 🖵 💺 🎍 Ⓥ 🍽 ● 🖥 🍴 🍴 Ⓤ SP Ⓣ

Periquito Hotel M
♨♨♨ COMMENDED

Manchester Street, Oldham, OL8 1UZ
☎ 061-624 0555 & Fax. 061-627 2031
Modern town centre hotel, fully refurbished in 1990 with bright welcoming decor. 5 minutes from British Rail and M62 junction 20.
Bedrooms: 80 double, 50 family rooms.
Bathrooms: 130 private.
Bed & breakfast: £41-£59.50 single, £44.50-£63 double.
Evening meal 6pm (l.o. 10.30pm).
Parking for 270.
Credit: Access, Visa, Diners, Amex.
🛎 📞 Ⓡ 🖵 💺 🎍 Ⓥ 🍽 ● 🖥 🍴 🍴 🎿 🖤 ✳ SP Ⓣ

Individual proprietors have supplied all details of accommodation. Although we do check for accuracy, we advise you to confirm prices and other information at the time of booking.

PARKGATE

Cheshire
Map ref 4A2

1m NW. Neston
Once a busy port on the
Dee Estuary, Parkgate
was the scene of
Handel's departure for
the great performance of
'Messiah' in Dublin in
1741. The George Inn
where he stayed is now
Mostyn House School.

Parkgate Hotel M
Boathouse Lane, Parkgate,
L64 6RD
☎ 051-336 5001 & Fax 051-
336 8504 Telex 629469
Pagdte G
Ⓒ Lansbury
*Rural Wirral hotel on the edge
of the unspoilt Dee Marshes
conservation area, set in
landscaped gardens. Just 20
minutes' drive from Chester.*
Bedrooms: 1 single, 6 double
& 16 twin, 4 family rooms.
Bathrooms: 27 private.
Bed & breakfast: £22-£60
single, £44-£72 double.
Half board: £34-£75 daily.
Lunch available.
Evening meal 7pm (l.o.
10.30pm).
Parking for 125.
Credit: Access, Visa, Diners,
Amex.
⛟ 🏠 📞 ⓓ 🖵 🛏 🍴 🖵 🆅 ✂
🖂 ● 🖿 ☎ 🍴 🆂🅿 🆃

PRESTON

Lancashire
Map ref 4A1

Scene of decisive
Royalist defeat by
Cromwell in the Civil War
and later of riots in the
Industrial Revolution.
Local history exhibited in
Harris Museum.
*Tourist Information
Centre* ☎ *(0772) 53731*

Ashfield House M
Lea Road, Lea, Preston,
PR4 ORA
☎ (0772) 720201
*Detached property set in 2
acres of grounds. 3 miles from
the M6 and M55, 7 minutes'
drive from Preston centre.*
Bedrooms: 1 double & 1 twin,
1 family room.
Bathrooms: 1 private,
1 public.
Bed & breakfast: £17.50-£23
single, £30-£35 double.

Evening meal 6pm (l.o. 8pm).
Parking for 8.
Credit: Access, Visa.
⛟ 🖵 🛏 🍴 🆅 🖾 📺 🖿 ⚓
✿ ✈ 🖾 �androDAP

Birley Arms
Bryning Lane, Warton,
Preston, PR4 1TN
☎ (0772) 679988
Fax (0772) 679435
*Rural motel with pub and
restaurant adjoining. Good
location between Preston and
Lytham St. Annes.*
Bedrooms: 1 single, 15 twin.
Bathrooms: 16 private.
Bed & breakfast: £27-£37
single, £35-£46.50 double.
Lunch available.
Evening meal 6.30pm (l.o.
9pm).
Parking for 150.
Credit: Access, Visa, Diners,
Amex.
⛟ 📞 🖵 🛏 🍴 🖿 ∪ ✈ ⚲
🆂🅿 🆃

Brook House Guest House M
🏆🏆 COMMENDED
544 Blackpool Road, Ashton,
Preston, PR2 1HY
☎ (0772) 728684
*Detached property 10 minutes
from town centre and on bus
route. TV lounge, car park.*
Bedrooms: 2 single, 1 double
& 1 twin.
Bathrooms: 1 private,
1 public.
Bed & breakfast: £16.50-
£27.50 single, £33-£41.25
double.
Half board: £24.50-£35.50
daily.
Evening meal 6pm (l.o. 6pm).
Parking for 6.
⛟ 🏠 🖵 🖾 ✂ 🖿 📺 🖿
🖾 ✈ 🖾 🆂🅿

Brook House Hotel M
🏆🏆🏆
662 Preston Road, Clayton-
le-Woods, Nr. Chorley,
PR6 7EH
☎ (0772) 36403
Fax (0772) 36403
*Set in half an acre and
personally supervised by the
resident owners, this licensed
hotel offers the businessman
and tourist comfortable rooms
with a high standard of
facilities, at sensible prices.*
Bedrooms: 3 single, 11 double
& 4 twin, 2 family rooms.
Bathrooms: 15 private,
2 public.
Bed & breakfast: £22-£30
single, £34-£42 double.

Evening meal 7pm (l.o.
8.30pm).
Parking for 28.
Credit: Access, Visa.
⛟ 🏠 📞 ⓓ 🖵 🛏 🍴 🆅 🖾
🖿 🖾 🍴 ✿ ✈ 🖾 🆃

Carleton Hotel M
Listed
1 Stanley Place, Fishergate
Hill, Preston, PR1 8NA
☎ (0772) 51146
*Close to railway station and
town centre.*
Bedrooms: 2 single, 3 double
& 5 twin.
Bathrooms: 2 public;
8 private showers.
Bed & breakfast: £16.50-£35
single, £33-£35 double.
Parking for 10.
⛟ 🖵 🛏 ✂ 🖾 🖾 🍴

Claremont Hotel
🏆🏆 COMMENDED
516 Blackpool Road, Ashton,
Preston, PR2 1HY
☎ (0772) 729738
Fax (0772) 726274
*Large Victorian house in own
grounds. Homely atmosphere
and friendly service.*
Bedrooms: 6 single, 5 double
& 2 twin, 1 family room.
Bathrooms: 12 private,
2 public.
Bed & breakfast: £30-£36
single, £38-£49 double.
Half board: £28.50-£32.50
daily.
Evening meal 7pm (l.o.
8.30pm).
Parking for 25.
Credit: Access, Visa.
⛟ 📞 🖵 ✂ 🛏 🍴 🆅 🖾 📺 🖿
🖾 🍴 ✿ ✈ 🖾

County Hotel M
🏆🏆
Fishergate Hill, Preston,
PR1 8UL
☎ (0772) 53188
*Warm and friendly older-type
hotel, close to the railway
station.*
Bedrooms: 6 single, 4 double
& 3 twin, 1 family room.
Bathrooms: 5 private,
2 public; 2 private showers.
Bed & breakfast: £18-£22.50
single, £31-£36 double.
Parking for 6.
⛟ 🖵 ✂ 🖾 📺 🖿 🖾 🍴

Dean Court Hotel M
🏆🏆🏆 COMMENDED
Brownedge Lane, Bamber
Bridge, Preston, PR5 6TB
☎ (0772) 35114

*Family-run licensed hotel and
restaurant specialising in fresh,
traditional English dishes and
Lancashire hospitality. New
stables bar for bar meals.
Four-poster bedrooms, bridal-
suites.*
Bedrooms: 1 single, 6 double
& 2 twin.
Bathrooms: 9 private,
1 public.
Bed & breakfast: £27.50-
£47.50 single, £40-£65 double.
Half board: £37.50-£50 daily.
Lunch available.
Evening meal 6.30pm (l.o.
9.30pm).
Parking for 40.
Credit: Access, Visa.
⛟ 10 🏠 📞 ⓓ 🖵 ✂ 🛏 🆅
🖿 📺 🖿 🖾 🍴 ✿ ✈ 🆂🅿

Olde Duncombe House M
🏆🏆 COMMENDED
Garstang Road, Bilsborrow,
Nr. Preston, PR3 ORE
☎ (0995) 40336
*In the beautiful Ribble Valley
next to the Lancaster canal,
convenient for canal boat
enthusiasts. 4 miles north of
the M6 junction 32.*
Bedrooms: 1 single, 5 double
& 2 twin, 2 family rooms.
Bathrooms: 10 private.
Bed & breakfast: £29.50-£35
single, £39.50-£49.50 double.
Lunch available.
Evening meal 6pm (l.o.
8.30pm).
Parking for 12.
Credit: Access, Visa.
⛟ 🏠 📞 ⓓ 🖵 ✂ 🛏 🆅 🖿
🖿 🖾 ✈ 🖾 🆃

Stanley House Hotel M
Listed APPROVED
6 Stanley Terrace, (Off
Fishergate Hill), Preston,
PR1 8LQ
☎ (0772) 54486
*Budget, family-run
accommodation in a quiet
location near the town centre.*
Bedrooms: 3 single, 2 twin,
2 family rooms.
Bathrooms: 2 public;
4 private showers.
Bed & breakfast: £14-£16.50
single, £26-£32 double.
Parking for 4.
⛟ 🏠 🖵 ✂ 🖾 🆅 🖿 🖾 DAP
🆂🅿 🚲

Tickled Trout Hotel M
🏆🏆🏆 COMMENDED
Preston New Road,
Samlesbury, Preston,
PR5 0UJ
☎ (0772) 877671
Telex 677625
Ⓒ Rank

Continued ▶

---

*The symbols are explained on the flap
inside the back cover.*

PRESTON
Continued

Magnificent views from all bedrooms of this hotel situated on the banks of the River Ribble. Located at exit 31 of the M6, halfway between London and Glasgow.
Bedrooms: 2 single, 17 double & 1 twin, 52 family rooms.
Bathrooms: 72 private.
Bed & breakfast: £49-£74 single, £67-£89 double.
Lunch available.
Evening meal 7pm (l.o. 9.45pm).
Parking for 170.
Credit: Access, Visa, Diners, Amex.

Tulketh Hotel M
COMMENDED
209 Tulketh Road, Ashton, Preston, PR2 1ES
☎ (0772) 728096 & 726250
Hotel of fine quality and with personal service, in a quiet residential area. A la carte menu. 5 minutes from town centre, 10 minutes from M6 motorway.
Bedrooms: 5 single, 2 double & 5 twin.
Bathrooms: 11 private, 1 public.
Bed & breakfast: £29-£37.50 single, £40-£48 double.
Evening meal 6.30pm (l.o. 7.30pm).
Parking for 12.
Credit: Access, Visa.

RADCLIFFE
Gtr. Manchester
Map ref 4A1

2m SW. Bury
Radcliffe has a local history museum containing exhibits about the district from prehistoric times and the remains of Radcliffe Tower.

Hawthorn Hotel M
139-143 Stand Lane, Radcliffe, M26 9JR
☎ 061-723 2706
Comfortable family hotel convenient for M62 junction 17, motorway network and close to Bury, Bolton and Manchester. Offers home cooking.
Bedrooms: 7 single, 3 double & 4 twin, 2 family rooms.

Bathrooms: 11 private, 2 public; 1 private shower.
Bed & breakfast: £21.74-£32.90 single, £45.83 double.
Half board: £31.73-£42.89 daily, £200-£250 weekly.
Evening meal 6pm (l.o. 7pm).
Parking for 9.
Credit: Access, Visa.

RIBBLE VALLEY

See Clitheroe, Langho, Slaidburn.

ROCHDALE
Gtr. Manchester
Map ref 4B1

Old Pennine mill town made prosperous by wool and later cotton-spinning, famous for the Co-operative Movement started in 1844 by a group of Rochdale working men. Birthplace of John Bright (Corn Law opponent) and more recently Gracie Fields. Roman and Bronze Age antiquities in museum.
Tourist Information Centre ☎ *(0706) 356592*

Norton Grange Hotel M
COMMENDED
Manchester Road, Castleton, Rochdale, OL11 2XZ
☎ (0706) 30788 & Fax (0706) 49313
Ⓡ Rank
19th C character hotel located just 5 minutes' drive from the M62 exit 20 and 15 minutes' drive from Manchester. Facilities include newly refurbished bedrooms, the Pickwick Bar and an a la carte restaurant serving international cuisine.
Bedrooms: 6 single, 12 double & 4 twin, 28 family rooms.
Bathrooms: 50 private.
Bed & breakfast: £39-£70 single, £57-£85 double.
Lunch available.
Evening meal 7pm (l.o. 10pm).
Parking for 120.
Credit: Access, Visa, C.Bl., Diners, Amex.

ROSSENDALE
Lancashire
Map ref 4B1

Sykeside Country House Hotel M
COMMENDED
Rawtenstall Road End, Haslingden, Rossendale, BB4 6QE
☎ (0706) 831163
Fax (0706) 830090
Listed country house hotel offering traditional English cooking. Personal service from the owners. Easy motorway access.
Bedrooms: 4 single, 3 double & 3 twin.
Bathrooms: 10 private.
Bed & breakfast: £55-£85 single, £70-£100 double.
Evening meal 7pm (l.o. 9pm).
Parking for 25.
Credit: Access, Visa, Diners, Amex.

SADDLEWORTH
Gtr. Manchester
Map ref 4B1

6m E. Oldham
Area of outstanding countryside and expanse of moorland.
Tourist Information Centre ☎ *(045 787) 4093 or 0336*

Bobbin House Hotel M
COMMENDED
The Square, High Street, Uppermill, Saddleworth, OL3 6BD
☎ (0457) 870800
Friendly owner-run hotel in heritage village at foot of Pennines 10 minutes from M62 junction 21/22, 40 minutes from Manchester Airport and Leeds.
Bedrooms: 2 double & 2 twin, 2 family rooms.
Bathrooms: 6 private.
Bed & breakfast: £35-£39.50 single, £40-£46.50 double.
Lunch available.
Evening meal 6pm (l.o. 8.30pm).
Parking for 8.
Credit: Access, Visa, Amex.

SALE
Gtr. Manchester
Map ref 4A2

Residential district of Manchester which developed as a result of the opening in 1849 of the railway between Altrincham and Manchester.

Belmore Hotel M
143 Brooklands Road, Sale, M33 3QU
☎ 061-973 2538
Victorian residence of character set in mature gardens, comfortably decorated and furnished. Personal service.
Bedrooms: 12 single, 6 double & 2 twin.
Bathrooms: 18 private; 2 private showers.
Bed & breakfast: from £47 single, £55-£60 double.
Half board: from £48.50 daily, from £305.55 weekly.
Evening meal 6.30pm (l.o. 8pm).
Parking for 25.
Credit: Access, Visa.

Holly Bank Hotel M
Holly Bank, Off Derbyshire Road, Sale, M33 3EJ
☎ 061-973 2002
Fax 061-962 5050
19th C Victorian-style building overlooking parkland and convenient for Manchester Airport, motorway system and Manchester. Close to local shops and sports complex.
Bedrooms: 8 single, 4 double & 3 twin.
Bathrooms: 15 private.
Bed & breakfast: £27.50-£43.50 single, £40.50-£57 double.
Evening meal 6pm (l.o. 9pm).
Parking for 35.
Credit: Access, Visa, Amex.

The symbols are explained on the flap inside the back cover.

National Crown ratings were correct at the time of going to press but are subject to change. Please check at the time of booking.

Map references apply to the colour maps towards the end of this guide.

SALFORD

Gtr. Manchester
Map ref 4B1

Industrial city close to Manchester with Roman Catholic cathedral and university. Lowry often painted Salford's industrial architecture and much of his work is in the local art gallery.

Beaucliffe Hotel M
♛♛♛

254 Eccles Old Road, Salford, M6 8ES
☎ 061-789 5092
Warm, welcoming hotel with friendly bar and restaurant and resident proprietors. Easy access to Manchester centre, Salford Quays, G-Mex, airport and motorways.
Bedrooms: 10 single, 2 double & 8 twin, 1 family room.
Bathrooms: 17 private, 1 public.
Bed & breakfast: £30-£39 single, £40-£52 double.
Half board: £38-£54 daily.
Lunch available.
Evening meal 6.45pm (l.o. 8.45pm).
Parking for 32.
Credit: Access, Visa, Diners, Amex.
⌖6♿⌨☎➡♻ ▮ Ⅴ ⌨ ⊕
▦ ➡ ℐ ✗ ℝ SP T

The Egerton Arms
♛

2 Gore Street, Salford, M33 5FP
☎ 061-834 3182
Central for Deansgate, shopping centre, train and bus stations. Full facilities in all rooms. Friendly atmosphere. Restaurant with all home-cooked food.
Bedrooms: 4 single, 1 twin.
Bathrooms: 2 public.
Bed & breakfast: from £18 single, from £34 double.
Evening meal 6pm (l.o. 10pm).
⌖➡♻ ▮ Ⅴ ⌨ ⊕ ▦ ➡

White Lodge Private Hotel
♛♛

87-89 Great Cheetham Street West, Broughton, Salford, M7 9JA.
☎ 061-792 3047
Small, family-run hotel, close to city centre amenities.
Bedrooms: 3 single, 3 double & 3 twin.

Bathrooms: 2 public.
Bed & breakfast: from £20 single, from £32 double.
Parking for 6.
⌖2 Ⅴ ⌨ ⊕ ▦ ➡ ✗ ℝ

SANDBACH

Cheshire
Map ref 4A2

5m NE. Crewe
Small industrial town, originally important for salt production. Contains narrow, winding streets, timbered houses and a cobbled market-place. Town square has 2 Anglo-Saxon crosses placed there 1300 years ago to commemorate the conversion to Christianity of the son of the King of Mercia.
Tourist Information Centre ☎ *(0270) 760460 or 761879*

Chimney House Hotel M
♛♛♛

Congleton Road, Sandbach, CW11 0ST
☎ Crewe (0270) 764141 & Fax (0270) 768916
Telex 367323
CR Lansbury
Set in 7.5 acres, 500 yards from the M6 exit 17. Convenient for interrupting your journey north or south, or for your business appointment in the north west.
Bedrooms: 18 single, 22 double & 8 twin, 2 family rooms.
Bathrooms: 50 private.
Bed & breakfast: £26-£75 single, £52-£87 double.
Half board: £38-£90 daily.
Lunch available.
Evening meal 7pm (l.o. 10pm).
Parking for 110.
Credit: Access, Visa, Diners, Amex.
⌖♿ ✆ ⊕ ➡ ♻ ▮ Ⅴ ✂
⌨ ⊕ ▦ ➡ ℐ ♿ ✿ ✗
❧ SP T

Poplar Mount Guest House M
♛♛ COMMENDED

2 Station Road, Elworth, Sandbach, CW11 9JG
☎ (0270) 761268
Family-run guesthouse, convenient for M6, railway station and Manchester Airport.
Bedrooms: 2 single, 1 double & 1 twin, 1 family room.
Bathrooms: 2 private, 1 public.
Bed & breakfast: from £15 single, from £32 double.

Half board: from £22 daily.
Lunch available.
Evening meal 6.30pm (l.o. 8pm).
Parking for 6.
Credit: Access, Visa.
⌖♿ ♻ UL ▮ ⌨ ⊕ ▦ ➡ ℝ
CAP

Saxon Cross Hotel M
♛♛♛♛ COMMENDED

M6 Exit 17, Sandbach, CW11 9SE
☎ Crewe (0270) 763281 & Fax. (0270) 768723
Telex 367169
Adjacent to the M6 exit 17, in a quiet rural setting 1 mile from Sandbach.
Bedrooms: 10 single, 10 double & 18 twin, 14 family rooms.
Bathrooms: 52 private.
Bed & breakfast: £33-£54 single, £45-£68 double.
Half board: £44.50-£71 daily.
Lunch available.
Evening meal 7pm (l.o. 10pm).
Parking for 200.
Credit: Access, Visa, Diners, Amex.
⌖♿ ✆ ⊕ ➡ ♻ ▮ Ⅴ ⌨
⊕ ▦ ➡ ℐ ♿ ✿ SP T

SANDIWAY

Cheshire
Map ref 4A2

4m SW. Northwich

Nunsmere Hall Country House Hotel M
Tarporley Road (A49), Sandiway, CW8 2ES
☎ (0606) 889100 & Fax (0606) 889055
Privately-owned country house hotel set in 10 acres of woodland and completely surrounded by a 60-acre lake. Well-appointed rooms. Specialising in cuisine naturelle, using only the very finest, freshest ingredients. Half board price is based on a minimum 2 night stay (must include Saturday).
Bedrooms: 7 double & 26 twin.
Bathrooms: 33 private.
Bed & breakfast: £90-£110 single, £110-£200 double.
Half board: from £75 daily.
Lunch available.
Evening meal 7.30pm (l.o. 9.30pm).
Parking for 75.
Credit: Access, Visa, Amex.
⌖12 ♿ ✆ ⊕ ➡ ♻ ▮ Ⅴ
⌨ ⊕ ▦ ➡ ℐ ♿ ∪ ♉
✎ ✿ ✗ ℝ ❧ SP ⊞ T

SILVERDALE

Lancashire
Map ref 5A3

4m NW. Carnforth
On the shores of Morecambe Bay, this picturesque village is in the centre of a designated area of outstanding natural beauty.

Lindeth House
♛♛♛ COMMENDED

Lindeth Road, Silverdale, Nr. Carnforth, LA5 0TX
☎ (0524) 701238
Pleasant country house with licensed dining room offering fine English cooking. Ideal for a restful break or as base for touring Lake District.
Bedrooms: 1 double & 2 twin.
Bathrooms: 3 private.
Bed & breakfast: £25-£30 single, £36-£40 double.
Half board: £33.50-£40.50 daily.
Evening meal 7pm (l.o. 9pm).
Parking for 15.
Open February-December.
⌖♿ ⊕ ➡ ♻ ▮ Ⅴ ✂ ⌨
➡ ℐ ✿ ✗ ℝ

Silverdale Hotel
♛♛♛ COMMENDED

Shore Road, Silverdale, LA5 0TP
☎ (0524) 701206
Grade II listed building with lots of beams and brasses, overlooking fells and bay in an area of outstanding natural beauty.
Bedrooms: 1 single, 4 double & 4 twin, 1 family room.
Bathrooms: 5 private, 2 public.
Bed & breakfast: £19.50-£24.50 single, £30-£35.50 double.
Lunch available.
Evening meal 6.30pm (l.o. 9.30pm).
Parking for 40.
Credit: Access, Visa.
⌖ ✆ ⊕ ➡ ♻ ▮ Ⅴ ⌨
▦ ➡ ℐ ♨ SP ⊞

The symbol **CR** *and the name of a hotel group or consortium after a hotel address means that bookings can be made through a central reservations office. These are listed on page 540.*

SLAIDBURN

Lancashire
Map ref 4A1

7m N. Clitheroe
Picturesque grey-stone village set in moorland region of the Forest of Bowland, with 13th C church, old grammar school, village green and war memorial.

Gold Hill Farmhouse Hotel ♨
🏆🏆🏆 COMMENDED
Woodhouse Lane, Slaidburn, Clitheroe, BB7 3AH
☎ (020 06) 202
150-acre beef and sheep farm. Family-run 17th C country house with log fires, minstrels' gallery and accent on cooking. Breathtaking views and sporting rights. 1 mile from Slaidburn.
Bedrooms: 1 double & 1 twin, 1 family room.
Bathrooms: 3 private.
Bed & breakfast: £20 single, £40 double.
Half board: from £30 daily.
Lunch available.
Evening meal 7pm.
Parking for 20.
Credit: Access, Visa.
🛇🖵🗇🐾 UL ⓘ Ⅴ �㎒ ⓉⓋ
▥ 🕿 ☯ ✓ ❀ ♨ 🎿 ꝺꜰ ꝓ SP
🎠

Parrock Head Hotel ♨
🏆🏆🏆 COMMENDED
Woodhouse Lane, Slaidburn, Nr. Clitheroe, BB7 3AH
☎ (020 06) 614
Tastefully converted 17th C farmhouse with all modern facilities, in remote and beautiful countryside. Country house atmosphere.
Bedrooms: 4 double & 4 twin, 1 family room.
Bathrooms: 9 private.
Bed & breakfast: £35-£40 single, £55-£60 double.
Half board: £41-£45 daily.
Lunch available.
Evening meal 7pm (l.o. 9pm).
Parking for 20.
Credit: Access, Visa, Amex.
🛇🖵🗇🐾 ⓘ Ⅴ �㎒
▥ 🕿 🎿 ⚻ ❀ ꝺ ⅍ SP 🎠

National Crown ratings were correct at the time of going to press but are subject to change. Please check at the time of booking.

SOUTHPORT

Merseyside
Map ref 4A1

Pleasant resort noted for its gardens, long sandy beach and many golf-courses, particularly Royal Birkdale. Southport Flower Show is an annual event. Lord Street is a tree-lined boulevard with fine shops. Atkinson Art Gallery and Steamport Transport Museum are attractions.
Tourist Information Centre ☎ *(0704) 533333*

Allendale Hotel ♨
21 Avondale Road, Southport, PR9 0EP
☎ (0704) 530032
Small friendly, private hotel, between Lord Street and the promenade. Home-cooked food. Value for money.
Bedrooms: 1 single, 2 double & 1 twin, 2 family rooms.
Bathrooms: 1 public.
Bed & breakfast: from £12 single, from £23 double.
Half board: from £16.50 daily.
Evening meal 6pm (l.o. 3pm).
Parking for 6.
🛇5 🐾 ☯ ㎒ ⓉⓋ ▥ 🕿 ꝺꜰ SP

Ambassador Private Hotel
🏆🏆 COMMENDED
13 Bath Street, Southport, PR9 0DP
☎ (0704) 530459 & 543998
Delightful small hotel, 200 yards from promenade and conference centre.
Bedrooms: 1 single, 2 double & 3 twin, 2 family rooms.
Bathrooms: 8 private, 2 public.
Bed & breakfast: £30-£33 single, £50-£56 double.
Half board: £35-£40 daily, £175 weekly.
Lunch available.
Evening meal 6pm (l.o. 6.30pm).
Parking for 6.
Credit: Access, Visa.
🛇4 🐾 🖸 🖵 🗇 ⓘ Ⅴ ꝺ ㎒
▥ 🕿 🎿 ꝓ ⓉⒸ

Balmoral Lodge ♨
🏆🏆🏆 COMMENDED
41 Queens Road, Southport, PR9 9EX
☎ (0704) 544298 & 530751 & Fax (0704) 501224
High standard accommodation, close to town centre. All rooms en-suite, with attractive garden wing balcony rooms available. Free sauna. Bargain breaks.

Bedrooms: 4 single, 3 double & 7 twin, 1 family room.
Bathrooms: 15 private, 1 public.
Bed & breakfast: £28-£55 single, £55-£66 double.
Half board: from £60 daily, £242-£275 weekly.
Lunch available.
Evening meal 6.30pm (l.o. 8.30pm).
Parking for 10.
Credit: Access, Visa.
🛇2 🐾 ㎒ ⓘ 🕿 🖵 🗇 ⓘ ꝺ
ⓉⓋ ▥ 🕿 ☯ 🎿 ❀ ✕ ꝺ Ⓣ

Derby House Hotel
6 Knowsley Road, Southport, PR9 0HG
☎ (0704) 530103
Friendly, family, licensed hotel with heated indoor swimming pool. Under new management.
Bedrooms: 2 single, 1 double & 3 twin, 6 family rooms.
Bathrooms: 6 private, 2 public.
Bed & breakfast: £17-£21 single, £34-£38 double.
Half board: £22-£26 daily.
Evening meal 6pm (l.o. 6pm).
Parking for 10.
🛇🖵🗇🐾 ⓘ Ⅴ ꝺ ⓉⓋ ▥ 🎿
🕿 Ü ꝺꜰ ꝓ SP

Dukes Folly Hotel ♨
🏆🏆🏆
11 Duke Street, Southport, PR8 1LS
☎ (0704) 533355
Licensed family-run hotel noted for its high standards and friendly atmosphere. On the corner of Duke Street and Lord Street and within easy reach of all local amenities.
Bedrooms: 5 single, 4 double & 9 twin, 1 family room.
Bathrooms: 19 private.
Bed & breakfast: £30-£38.50 single, £48-£56 double.
Half board: £37.50-£51.50 daily, £240-£260 weekly.
Evening meal 6pm (l.o. 10pm).
Parking for 12.
Credit: Access, Visa, Amex.
🛇🖵🗇🐾 🕿 🖸 🖵 🗇 ⓘ Ⅴ
⅍ ꝺ ⓉⓋ ▥ 🕿 🎿 ꝓ Ⓣ

Leicester Hotel
🏆🏆
24 Leicester Street, Southport, PR9 0EZ
☎ (0704) 530049
Family-run hotel with personal attention, clean and comfortable, close to all amenities. Car park. Licensed bar.
Bedrooms: 2 single, 4 double & 2 twin.
Bathrooms: 1 private, 2 public.
Bed & breakfast: from £15 single, from £28 double.

Half board: from £20 daily.
Evening meal 6pm.
Parking for 6.
Credit: Access, Visa.
🛇🖵🗇🐾 ⓘ Ⅴ ꝺ ⓉⓋ ▥ 🐾
🕿 ▥ ꝺꜰ SP

Lockerbie House Hotel ♨
🏆🏆🏆
11 Trafalgar Road, Birkdale, Southport, PR8 2EA
☎ (0704) 65298
Large detached hotel, comfortably furnished, in a quiet location close to Royal Birkdale and Hillside Golf Clubs. Full-size snooker table available.
Bedrooms: 4 single, 2 double & 7 twin, 1 family room.
Bathrooms: 14 private.
Bed & breakfast: from £24 single, from £44 double.
Half board: from £33 daily.
Evening meal 7pm (l.o. 8pm).
Parking for 16.
Credit: Access, Visa, Diners, Amex.
🛇🖵🗇🐾 ⓘ Ⅴ ꝺ ⓉⓋ ▥
🐾 🕿 ꝺꜰ SP

Metropole Hotel ♨
🏆🏆🏆
3 Portland Street, Southport, PR8 1LL
☎ (0704) 536836
Family hotel with resident proprietors. Centrally located with 6 golf-courses nearby. Full-size snooker table. Full licence.
Bedrooms: 14 single, 3 double & 5 twin, 3 family rooms.
Bathrooms: 18 private, 4 public.
Bed & breakfast: £24.50-£33.50 single, £44.50-£59.50 double.
Half board: £35-£44 daily, £229-£285 weekly.
Lunch available.
Evening meal 7pm (l.o. 8.30pm).
Parking for 12.
Credit: Access, Visa, Amex.
🛇🕿 🖸 🖵 🗇 ⓘ Ⅴ ꝺ ⓉⓋ
▥ 🐾 ꝓ SP

Rosedale Hotel ♨
🏆🏆🏆 APPROVED
11 Talbot Street, Southport, PR8 1HP
☎ (0704) 530604
Well-established, centrally situated private hotel with licensed bar and reading room. All bedrooms have colour TV with satellite link.
Bedrooms: 3 single, 3 double & 2 twin, 2 family rooms.
Bathrooms: 6 private, 1 public.
Bed & breakfast: £18-£22 single, £36-£44 double.

Half board: £25-£29 daily, £144-£170 weekly.
Evening meal 6pm (l.o. 4pm).
Parking for 10.

Scarisbrick Hotel M
☺☺☺ COMMENDED

239 Lord Street, Southport, PR8 1NZ
☎ (0704) 543000
Fax (0704) 533335
Consort
Prominent town-centre traditional hotel. A la carte and table d'hote restaurant, several bars, function rooms and conference suites.
Bedrooms: 7 single, 28 double & 26 twin, 5 family rooms.
Bathrooms: 66 private.
Bed & breakfast: £60-£75 single, £75-£130 double.
Half board: from £37 daily, from £252 weekly.
Lunch available.
Evening meal 7pm (l.o. 9.30pm).
Parking for 55.
Credit: Access, Visa, Diners, Amex.

Sidbrook Hotel
☺☺☺

14 Talbot Street, Southport, PR8 1HP
☎ (0704) 530608 & 531491 & Fax (0704) 531198
Detached Victorian house in quiet street, yet centrally located. Sauna, sunbed, pool table and free in-room Sky satellite TV. Secluded garden.
Bedrooms: 4 single, 4 double & 1 twin.
Bathrooms: 8 private, 1 public.
Bed & breakfast: £18-£28 single, £30-£50 double.
Half board: £26-£36 daily, £182-£231 weekly.
Lunch available.
Evening meal 7pm (l.o. 8.30pm).
Parking for 10.
Credit: Access, Visa, Amex.

Stutelea Hotel, and Leisure Club M
☺☺☺☺ COMMENDED

Alexandra Road, Southport, PR9 0NB
☎ (0704) 544220 & Fax (0704) 500232

Charming, licensed hotel, in pleasant gardens with heated indoor swimming pool, sauna, jacuzzi, gymnasium, solarium and games room. Convenient for promenade, marina, golf-courses and shopping centre. Also self-catering apartments.
Bedrooms: 1 single, 9 double & 7 twin, 3 family rooms.
Bathrooms: 20 private, 4 public.
Bed & breakfast: £40 single, £60-£65 double.
Half board: £69-£75 daily.
Lunch available.
Evening meal 7pm (l.o. 8.30pm).
Parking for 16.
Credit: Access, Visa, Diners, Amex.

Sunningdale Hotel M
☺☺☺ APPROVED

85 Leyland Road, Southport, PR9 0NJ
☎ (0704) 538673
Private hotel at the quiet northern end of Southport town centre. Supervised by the resident proprietors.
Bedrooms: 4 single, 1 double & 5 twin, 4 family rooms.
Bathrooms: 12 private, 1 public.
Bed & breakfast: £21-£23 single, £44 double.
Half board: £29-£31 daily, £196-£210 weekly.
Evening meal 5.30pm (l.o. 4pm).
Parking for 10.
Credit: Access, Visa.

Talbot Hotel M
☺☺☺

23-25 Portland Street, Southport, PR8 1LR
☎ (0704) 533975 & 530126
Detached, medium-sized family-run hotel, in a central, quiet position near main shopping areas, entertainments and services.
Bedrooms: 2 single, 5 double & 15 twin, 2 family rooms.
Bathrooms: 18 private, 2 public.
Bed & breakfast: £28-£37 single, £46-£54 double.
Half board: £38-£52 daily.
Lunch available.
Evening meal 6pm (l.o. 8pm).
Parking for 30.
Open January-November.
Credit: Access, Visa, Amex.

Victorian Hotel M
☺☺☺

52 Avondale Road, Southport, PR9 0NE
☎ (0704) 530755
The hotel provides a bar/restaurant of distinctive character with authentic Victorian furnishings. Good cooking, clean comfortable rooms, beautiful gardens.
Bedrooms: 1 single, 2 double & 2 twin, 3 family rooms.
Bathrooms: 3 private, 1 public.
Bed & breakfast: £16-£18 single, £32-£36 double.
Half board: £22-£24 daily, £100-£130 weekly.
Evening meal 5pm (l.o. 10pm).
Parking for 4.
Credit: Access, Visa.

STOCKPORT
Gtr. Manchester
Map ref 4B2

This former market town on the River Mersey, built by Cheshire gentry, became an important cotton-spinning and railway centre. Town has an impressive railway viaduct and a shopping precinct covering the Mersey, and an ancient grammar school. Lyme Hall and Vernon Park Museum nearby.
Tourist Information Centre ☎ 061-474 3320

Ascot House Hotel
☺☺☺

195 Wellington Road North, Heaton Norris, Stockport, SK4 2PB
☎ 061-432 2380 Telex 666514 Tortec G
Convenient for Manchester Airport, city centre and the Peak District. 2 minutes from the M63.
Bedrooms: 6 single, 7 double & 5 twin.
Bathrooms: 12 private, 3 public; 4 private showers.
Bed & breakfast: £20-£40 single, £35-£45 double.
Evening meal 5.30pm (l.o. 7.15pm).
Parking for 21.
Credit: Access, Visa, Amex.

Brackley House Hotel M
☺☺ COMMENDED

292 Wellington Road North, Heaton Chapel, Stockport, SK4 2QS
☎ 061-432 1684
Family-owned hotel with en-suite facilities, on main Manchester to Stockport bus and rail routes. 12 minutes to airport, 5 minutes to station.
Bedrooms: 4 single, 2 double, 1 family room.
Bathrooms: 5 private, 1 public.
Bed & breakfast: £18-£22 single, £36-£44 double.
Half board: from £27 daily.
Evening meal 6.30pm (l.o. 6.30pm).
Parking for 10.

Heathville Guest House
24 Broomfield Road, Heaton Moor, Stockport, SK4 4ND
☎ 061-431 7531
Edwardian house in a quiet, leafy area. Good standard rooms. Convenient for Manchester, Stockport, motorway, airport. Pleasant pubs and restaurants nearby.
Bedrooms: 1 double & 1 twin, 1 family room.
Bathrooms: 1 private, 1 public.
Bed & breakfast: £17-£24 single, £29-£36 double.
Half board: £19.50-£30 daily, £122-£189 weekly.
Parking for 3.
Credit: Access, Visa.

Pymgate Lodge Hotel M
☺☺ COMMENDED

147 Styal Road, Gatley, Stockport, SK8 3TG
☎ 061-436 4103 & Fax 061-499 9171
Within 1 mile of Manchester Airport, every bedroom overlooks garden or open fields. Courtesy transport to airport inclusive. Decorated and furnished to a high standard. Licensed a la carte restaurant. Courtesy tray in each room.
Bedrooms: 3 double & 3 twin, 2 family rooms.
Bathrooms: 6 private, 1 public.
Bed & breakfast: £40-£46 single, £46-£50 double.
Half board: £48.50-£55 daily.
Lunch available.

Continued ▶

Please mention this guide when making a booking.

STOCKPORT

Continued

Evening meal 6pm (l.o. 9.30pm).
Parking for 14.
Credit: Access, Visa, Amex.

Saxonholme Hotel M
APPROVED

230 Wellington Road North, Stockport, SK4 2QN
☎ 061-432 2335
Refurbished Edwardian hotel with a la carte restaurant and bar. Easy access to Stockport, Manchester and the airport.
Bedrooms: 2 single, 4 double & 24 twin, 5 family rooms.
Bathrooms: 30 private, 1 public.
Bed & breakfast: £49.50-£55.50 single, £59.50-£65.50 double.
Half board: £62.45-£75 daily.
Lunch available.
Evening meal 7pm (l.o. 9.15pm).
Parking for 31.
Credit: Access, Visa.

STRETFORD

Gtr. Manchester
Map ref 4B2

Famous as home of Manchester United Football Club and Lancashire County Cricket Club at Old Trafford, Stretford developed with the opening of the Manchester Ship Canal in 1894.

Greatstone Hotel

845 Chester Road, Stretford, M32 0RN
☎ 061-865 1640
Family-run hotel a few miles from Manchester city centre. Most rooms have tea and coffee making facilities. Close to Old Trafford and Manchester United Football Club and Sports Centre.
Bedrooms: 12 single, 5 double & 10 twin, 2 family rooms.
Bathrooms: 7 private, 3 public; 10 private showers.
Bed & breakfast: £20-£22 single, £38-£40 double.
Half board: £26-£28 daily.
Lunch available.
Evening meal 6pm (l.o. 9pm).
Parking for 74.
Credit: Access.

THORNTON HOUGH

Merseyside
Map ref 4A2

2m NE. Neston
Traditional, picturesque village in the heart of beautiful Wirral countryside, boasting a collection of splendidly maintained houses, a neo-Norman church and a smithy alongside its village green.

Thornton Hall Hotel M
COMMENDED

Neston Road, Thornton Hough, Wirral, L63 1JF
☎ 051-336 3938 Telex 628678
An imposing building set in the heart of the Wirral countryside, yet only 20 minutes' drive to Liverpool or Chester.
Bedrooms: 33 double & 37 twin.
Bathrooms: 70 private.
Bed & breakfast: £50-£90 single, £65-£90 double.
Half board: from £62 daily.
Lunch available.
Evening meal 7pm (l.o. 9.30pm).
Parking for 200.
Credit: Access, Visa, C.Bl., Diners, Amex.

WALLASEY

Merseyside
Map ref 4A2

Resort and residential area on the north east corner of the Wirral peninsula overlooking the Mersey Estuary and linked to Liverpool by a short ferry crossing. Pleasant seafront promenade from Wallasey to New Brighton with sandy beach continuing to Hoylake.

Sea Level Hotel

126 Victoria Road, New Brighton, Wallasey, L45 9LD
☎ 051-639 3408
Homely, family-run hotel offering a warm welcome and wholesome food. Light meals available until 11.00 p.m.
Bedrooms: 8 single, 4 double & 2 twin, 1 family room.
Bathrooms: 1 private, 3 public; 2 private showers.

Bed & breakfast: £14.95-£19.50 single, £27.90-£39 double.
Half board: £21.40-£27.95 daily, £125-£170 weekly.
Evening meal 6.30pm (l.o. 7pm).
Parking for 10.
Credit: Access, Visa.

WARRINGTON

Cheshire
Map ref 4A2

16m SW. Manchester
Has prehistoric and Roman origins. Once the 'beer capital of Britain' because so much beer was brewed here. Developed in the 18th and 19th C as a commercial and industrial town. Municipal Museum and Art Gallery contain local history.
Tourist Information Centre ☎ (0925) 36501

Fir Grove Hotel M
COMMENDED

Knutsford Old Road, Warrington, WA4 2LD
☎ (0925) 67471 & Fax (0925) 601092 Telex 628117
Situated in residential area, on A50 2 miles from exit 20 of M6.
Bedrooms: 22 single, 8 double & 10 twin.
Bathrooms: 40 private.
Bed & breakfast: £20-£60 single, £40-£70 double.
Lunch available.
Evening meal 7pm (l.o. 9.45pm).
Parking for 100.
Credit: Access, Visa, Diners, Amex.

Holiday Inn Garden Court M
COMMENDED

1 Woolston Grange Avenue, Woolston, Warrington, WA1 4PX
☎ Padgate (0925) 838779 & 831158 Reservations
Fax (0925) 838859
CR Holiday Inn
Holiday Inn Garden Court hotels are very competitively priced, offering intimate reception area, informal restaurant and bar, and fitness room.
Bedrooms: 86 double, 14 family rooms.
Bathrooms: 100 private.
Bed & breakfast: £45-£65 single, £45-£65 double.

Half board: £35-£50 daily.
Evening meal 6.30pm (l.o. 9.45pm).
Parking for 108.
Credit: Access, Visa, C.Bl., Diners, Amex.

Kenilworth Hotel M

2 Victoria Road, A50 Knutsford Road, Grappenhall, Warrington, WA4 2EN
☎ (0925) 262323
Small family-run hotel, offering a high standard of accommodation at competitive rates. 2 miles from M6/M56. Manchester airport 15 minutes away.
Bedrooms: 10 single, 3 double & 3 twin, 1 family room.
Bathrooms: 17 private, 1 public.
Bed & breakfast: £24-£34 single, £36-£45 double.
Evening meal 7pm (l.o. 8.30pm).
Parking for 18.
Credit: Access, Visa.

Rockfield Hotel
COMMENDED

Alexandra Road, Grappenhall, Warrington, WA4 2EL
☎ (0925) 62898
Elegant Edwardian hotel in quiet surroundings, 2.5 miles from exit 20. Good facilities and a la carte restaurant.
Bedrooms: 6 single, 5 double & 2 twin.
Bathrooms: 11 private, 1 public.
Bed & breakfast: £35-£45 single, £40-£55 double.
Half board: £33-£58 daily.
Evening meal 6.30pm (l.o. 9pm).
Parking for 30.
Credit: Access, Visa, Diners.

The symbol **CR** *and the name of a hotel group or consortium after a hotel address means that bookings can be made through a central reservations office. These are listed on page 540.*

WIDNES
Cheshire
Map ref 4A2

5m E. Liverpool Airport
A collection of small villages with a ferry across the Mersey until 1845 when the world's first railway, canal and dock complex was completed there by the Runcorn Gap and St. Helens Railway Company. Introduction of coal and salt formed basis of thriving alkali industry.
Tourist Information Centre ☎ 051-424 2061

Kingsway Hotel
66-70 Victoria Road, Widnes, WA8 7RA
☎ 051-423 2747
Town centre hotel with easy access to M6, M56 and M62 motorways. Liverpool Airport 10 minutes and Manchester Airport 30 minutes.
Bedrooms: 4 single, 3 double & 13 twin, 1 family room.
Bathrooms: 1 private, 4 public; 10 private showers.
Bed & breakfast: £26.95-£28.95 single, £38.95-£44.95 double.
Half board: £34.45-£36.45 daily.
Lunch available.
Evening meal 7pm (l.o. 9.50pm).
Parking for 8.
Credit: Access, Visa, Diners, Amex.
➲ ⦿ ▭ ✿ 🛈 ▣ ⊭ 📺 ◑ ▥ ◭ 🍴 ✗

WIGAN
Gtr. Manchester
Map ref 4A1

Although a major industrial town, Wigan is an ancient settlement which received a royal charter in 1246. Famous for its pier distinguished in Orwell's 'Road to Wigan Pier'. The pier has now been developed as a major tourist attraction and reinstated to its former working condition.
Tourist Information Centre ☎ (0942) 825677

Charles Dickens Hotel ⋒
14 Upper Dicconson Street, Wigan, WN1 2AD
☎ (0942) 323263
Residential town centre hotel with large public bar, restaurant and car park.

Bedrooms: 9 single, 1 double & 3 twin, 3 family rooms.
Bathrooms: 16 private.
Bed & breakfast: £21 single, £30 double.
Half board: £21-£28 daily.
Lunch available.
Evening meal 6pm (l.o. 9pm).
Parking for 7.
Credit: Access, Visa, Diners, Amex.
➲ ▭ 🛈 ⦿ ▥ ◭ 🍴 ✗ ▣

Kilhey Court Hotel ⋒
Chorley Road, Worthington, Wigan, WN1 2XN
☎ Standish (0257) 472100
Telex 67460
Ⓑ Best Western
Country house hotel with superb indoor leisure club set in 10 acres of gardens, fringed by Worthington lakes and nature reserve.
Bedrooms: 28 double & 25 twin.
Bathrooms: 53 private.
Bed & breakfast: £45-£95 single, £60-£110 double.
Half board: £61.50-£111.50 daily.
Lunch available.
Evening meal 7pm (l.o. 9.45pm).
Parking for 210.
Credit: Access, Visa, Diners, Amex.
➲ ⦿ ▭ ✿ 🛈 ▣ ⊭ ◭ 📺 ⦿ ▥ ▤ ◑ 🍴 ▦ & 🖉 ◭ ◑ ♪ ✿ ▣ ▥ ◻

WILMSLOW
Cheshire
Map ref 4B2

4m SE. Manchester Airport
This residential suburb of Manchester is on the River Bollin and bordered on 3 sides by open country.

Dean Bank Hotel ⋒
Adlington Road, Wilmslow, SK9 2BT
☎ (0625) 524268
Easily accessible from M6, M56, M63 and Manchester Airport. Family-run hotel set in lawned gardens and surrounded by fields. 2 miles from centre of Wilmslow. Ideal base for many interesting outings.
Bedrooms: 1 single, 6 double & 6 twin, 4 family rooms.
Bathrooms: 14 private, 1 public.
Bed & breakfast: £25-£33 single, £35-£45 double.
Half board: from £32 daily.

Evening meal 6.30pm (l.o. 2pm).
Parking for 18.
Credit: Access, Visa.
➲ ♨ ⦿ ▭ ◭ ▥ ▥ ◻ ◭ & ◑ ✿ ✗ ◭ ▣ ◻

Fern Bank Guest House
👑👑 COMMENDED
188 Wilmslow Road, Handforth, Wilmslow SK9 3JX
☎ (0625) 523729
Detached Victorian house, built 1881, standing in its own grounds. Tastefully furnished with antiques and large south facing conservatory. Manchester Airport 10 minutes by car. Long stay car parking next door.
Bedrooms: 2 double & 1 twin, 1 family room.
Bathrooms: 4 private, 1 public.
Bed & breakfast: £27.50-£33 single, £38.50-£44 double.
Parking for 7.
➲ ⦿ ▭ ✿ ▥ ⊬ ◭ 📺 ▥ ◭ ◻ ◻

Lisieux ⋒
👑👑👑 COMMENDED
199 Wilmslow Road, Handforth, Wilmslow, SK9 3JX
☎ (0625) 522113
Homely and offering a high standard of accommodation. Extensive breakfast menu available at whatever time required by guests. Manchester Airport 3 miles.
Bedrooms: 1 single, 1 double & 1 twin.
Bathrooms: 2 private, 1 public.
Bed & breakfast: £26 single, £36.50 double.
Half board: £41.50-£52 daily, £290.50-£364 weekly.
Evening meal 6pm (l.o. 7pm).
Parking for 5.
➲ ♨ ⦿ ▭ ✿ ▥ 🛈 ▣ ◭ 📺 ▥ ◭ ✿ ◭

WIRRAL
See Bebington, Birkenhead, Bromborough, Hoylake, Moreton, Parkgate, Wallasey.

YEALAND CONYERS
Lancashire
Map ref 5B3

The Bower
Yealand Conyers, Carnforth, LA5 9SF
☎ (0524) 734585
Comfortable Georgian country house in area of outstanding natural beauty. Convenient for Lakes, dales and stopovers to Scotland. Non-smokers only please.
Bedrooms: 1 double, 1 family room.
Bathrooms: 2 private.
Bed & breakfast: £27.50-£31.50 single, £40-£48 double.
Half board: £33.50-£45 daily, £219.50-£294.50 weekly.
Evening meal 6pm (l.o. 9pm).
Parking for 4.
➲ ▣12 ⦿ ▭ ✿ ▥ 🛈 ▣ ⊬ ◭ 📺 ▥ ◭ ✿ ◭ ▣ ▦

THE CROWN IS YOUR
SURE
SIGN
OF WHERE TO STAY

National Crown ratings were correct at the time of going to press but are subject to change. Please check at the time of booking.

Individual proprietors have supplied all details of accommodation. Although we do check for accuracy, we advise you to confirm prices and other information at the time of booking.

May — Dene Private Hotel
(LICENSED)

10 Dean Street, South Shore, Blackpool FY4 1AU

A well recommended friendly family Hotel, in a Sun-Trap Area, close to the Prom South Pier Sandcastle & Pleasure Beach.
★ Good Food ★ Full Central Heating ★ Open All Year ★ Car Park
Bed & Breakfast: £10-£13 (single)   £20-£26 (double)
Half Board: £12.50-£17.50 daily   £80-£105 weekly
Discounts for OAPs and children
Write or Phone for Brochure. (0253) 43464

EBOR HOTEL

402, Wilbraham Road, Chorlton-cum-Hardy, Manchester M21 1UH

061-881 1911   **061-881 4855**
(Reservations)   **(Guests)**

RESIDENTIAL LICENSED HOTEL
• 16 bedrooms   • Central heating throughout
• Tea & coffee making facilities   • T.V. in bedrooms
• Attractive bar lounge   • Evening meals   • Car park
• Close to airport and motorways
• 3 miles from city centre

YOUR COMFORT IS OUR CONCERN

RAC ★ ★
AA ★ ★
ETB COMMENDED

CRESCENT GATE HOTEL

Park Crescent, Victoria Park, Manchester M14 5RE
TEL: 061·224·0672
FAX: 061·257·2822

A 26 bedroom hotel ideally situated in a tree-lined crescent only 2 miles from the city centre. Most rooms with en-suite bathrooms, and all have colour TV, direct dial telephones and tea makers. Private car park.

ONE OF MANCHESTERS MOST POPULAR INDEPENDENT HOTELS

Please write or telephone for further details and brochure.

Use a coupon

When requesting further information from advertisers in this guide, you may find it helpful to use the advertisement enquiry coupons which can be found towards the end of the guide. These should be cut out and mailed direct to the companies in which you are interested. Do remember to include your name and address.

YORKSHIRE & HUMBERSIDE

DESERVEDLY *a location for so many books, plays and films — from the literary works of the three sisters, Charlotte, Emily and Anne Brontë, to the more recent television series, including Emmerdale Farm, Last of the Summer Wine, All Creatures Great and Small and Brideshead Revisited. For country lovers there are*

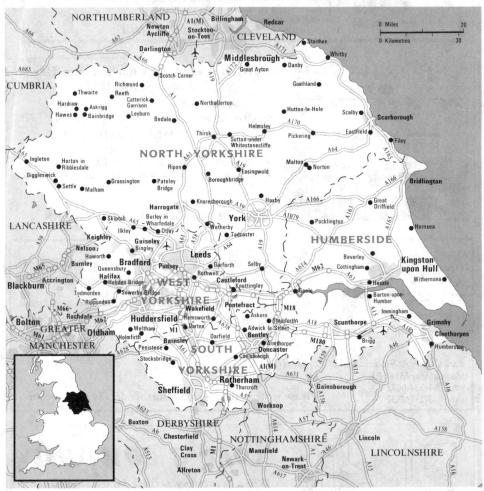

PLEASE REFER TO THE COLOUR MAPS AT THE BACK OF THIS GUIDE FOR ALL PLACES WITH ACCOMMODATION LISTINGS.

the North York Moors, the Yorkshire Dales and the Wolds. For those seeking sea and sand, there's the coastline with its holiday resorts of Bridlington, Filey, Scarborough and Cleethorpes. "City" people will appreciate the treasure trove of York and the Victorian virtues of Leeds and Bradford, Halifax and Sheffield.

WHERE TO GO, WHAT TO SEE

Abbeydale Industrial Hamlet
Abbeydale Road South,
Sheffield, S. Yorkshire S7 2QW
☎ Sheffield (0742) 367731
Working museum. Water powered scythe works, steel furnaces and workers' furnished houses.

Bolton Priory
Bolton Abbey, Skipton,
N. Yorkshire BD23 6EX
☎ Bolton Abbey (0756) 710533
Ruins of 12th C priory in park setting by River Wharfe. Tea shops, nature trails, fishing, fell walking and picturesque countryside.

Bridlington Leisure World
The Promenade, Bridlington,
Humberside YO15 2QQ
☎ Bridlington (0262) 606715
Wave pool, adult and junior pools. Multi-purpose hall with indoor bowling area. Entertainment centre, club, disco, dance and sporting events.

Cannon Hall Country Park
Cawthorne, Barnsley,
S. Yorkshire S75 4AT
☎ Barnsley (0226) 733272
18th C landscaped parkland with lakes stocked with ornamental and indigenous waterfowl. Museum, garden centre, open farm.

Castle Howard
Malton, N. Yorkshire YO6 7DA
☎ Coneysthorpe (065 384) 333
Set in 1,000 acres of magnificent parkland with nature walks, scenic lake and stunning rose gardens. Important furniture and works of art.

The Temple of the Four Winds at Castle Howard

Clifford's Tower
Tower Street, York,
N. Yorkshire YO1 1SA
☎ York (0904) 646940
13th C keep of York Castle, built by Henry III to replace William the Conqueror's wooden tower. Roger de Clifford executed and hung in chains in 1322. Used as prison in 19th C.

Dalby Forest Drive and Visitor Centre
Low Dalby, Pickering,
N. Yorkshire YO18 7LS
☎ Pickering (0751) 60295
9-mile scenic drive with car parks, picnic areas, waymarked walks (2 – 7 miles). Visitor centre with forestry exhibition.

Eden Camp
Malton, N. Yorkshire
YO17 0SD
☎ Malton (0653) 697777
Modern history theme museum depicting civilian way of life in Britain during World War II. Based in a genuine ex-PoW camp with original buildings.

Flamingo Land Zoo and Funpark
Kirby Misperton, Malton,
N. Yorkshire YO17 0UX
☎ Kirby Misperton (065 386) 287
One-price family funpark, with over 100 free attractions including 8 shows and Europe's largest privately-owned zoo. Large lake, children's and thrill rides.

Fountains Abbey and Studley Royal Park
Ripon, N. Yorkshire HG4 3DZ
☎ Sawley (0765) 620333
Largest monastic ruin in Britain, founded by Cistercian monks in 1132. Landscaped garden laid out 1720−40 with lake, formal watergarden and temples, deer park.

Harewood House
Harewood, Leeds, W. Yorkshire LS17 9LQ
☎ Harewood (0532) 886225
18th C Carr/Adam house, Capability Brown landscape. Fine Sevres and Chinese porcelain, English and Italian paintings, Chippendale furniture. Exotic bird garden.

Hornsea Pottery
Hornsea, Humberside HU18 1UD
☎ Hornsea (0964) 532161
Pottery factory in landscaped parkland. Shops, playground and fort, birds of prey, butterfly farm, model village, Yorkshire car collection.

Hull and East Riding Museum
High Street, Hull, Humberside
☎ Hull (0482) 222737
Humberside archaeology. Iron Age Hasholme boat and chariot burials, magnificent display of Romano-British mosaics.

Jorvik Viking Centre
Coppergate, York, N. Yorkshire YO1 1NT
☎ York (0904) 643211
Visitors travel in electric cars down a time tunnel to a re-creation of Viking York. Excavated remains of Viking houses and a display of objects found.

Leeds City Art Gallery and Henry Moore Centre
The Headrow, Leeds, W. Yorkshire LS1 3AA
☎ Leeds (0532) 462495
19th and 20th C paintings, sculptures, prints and drawings. Permanent collection of 20th C sculpture in Henry Moore Centre.

Museum of Army Transport
Flemingate, Beverley, Humberside HU17 0NG
☎ Hull (0482) 860445
Two acres of army road, rail, sea and air exhibits excitingly displayed in 2 exhibition halls, plus the huge last remaining Blackburn Beverley aircraft. Gulf exhibition.

National Fishing Heritage Centre
Alexandra Dock, Grimsby, Humberside DN31 1UF
☎ Grimsby (0472) 344867
Spectacular 1950s steam trawler experience. See, hear, smell and touch a series of re-created environments. Museum displays, aquarium, shop.

National Museum of Photography, Film and Television
Prince's View, Bradford, W. Yorkshire BD5 0TR
☎ Bradford (0274) 727488
The largest cinema screen (Imax) in Britain. Kodak Museum. Fly on a magic carpet, operate TV camera, become a newsreader for a day.

National Railway Museum
Leeman Road, York, N. Yorkshire YO2 4XJ
☎ York (0904) 621261
Collection of locomotives and carriages with displays depicting the technical, social and economic development of Britain's railway heritage.

Normanby Hall Country Park
Normanby, Nr. Scunthorpe, Humberside DN15 9HU
☎ Scunthorpe (0724) 720588
Regency mansion by Sir Robert Smirke, architect of the British Museum. Furnished and decorated in period, with costume displays. Country park of 350 acres with farming museum, deer park, miniature railway.

North Yorkshire Moors Railway
Pickering Station, Pickering, N. Yorkshire YO18 7AJ
☎ Pickering (0751) 72508
18-mile railway through National Park. Steam and diesel trains.

Piece Hall
Halifax, W. Yorkshire HX1 1RE
☎ Halifax (0422) 358087
Historic colonnaded cloth hall, surrounding open-air courtyard and comprising 50 shops, art gallery, museum.

Rother Valley Country Park
Mansfield Road, Wales Bar, Sheffield, S. Yorkshire S31 8PE
☎ Sheffield (0742) 471452
Country park with canoes, sailboards, rowing boats and sailing dinghies for hire. Nature reserve, visitor and craft centres, fishing, ski slope.

Sheffield City Museum
Weston Park, Sheffield, S. Yorkshire S10 2TP
☎ Sheffield (0742) 768588

A steam train on the 18-mile North Yorkshire Moors Railway

World-famous cutlery, old Sheffield plate, ceramics, glass, clocks, archaeology, wildlife.

Skipton Castle

Skipton, N. Yorkshire
BD23 1AQ
☎ Skipton (0756) 792442
One of the most complete and best preserved medieval castles in England. Conduit Court with famous yew.

Thrybergh Country Park

Doncaster Road, Thrybergh, Rotherham, S. Yorkshire
S65 4NU
☎ Rotherham (0709) 850353
63-acre country park, including 35-acre lake. Fly fishing, sailing, windsurfing, canoeing, picnic area.

Tropical World

Canal Gardens, Roundhay Park, Leeds, W. Yorkshire LS8 1DF
☎ Leeds (0532) 661850
Greenhouses, temperate house, butterfly house, tropical house, Jungle Experience, aquaria, insects, fish, streams, waterfalls.

York Castle Museum

The Eye of York, York, N. Yorkshire YO1 1RY
☎ York (0904) 653611
Museum of everyday life with reconstructed streets and period rooms. Edwardian park, costume and jewellery, arms and armour, craft workshops.

York Minster

Deangate, York, N. Yorkshire
YO1 2JA
☎ York (0904) 624426

Impressive Gothic cathedral with unrivalled Norman tower. Treasury, museum of Saxon/ Norman remains, crypt, chapter house.

Yorkshire Mining Museum

Caphouse Colliery, New Road, Overton, Wakefield, W. Yorkshire WF4 4RH
☎ Wakefield (0924) 848806
Exciting award-winning museum of the Yorkshire coalfield, including guided underground tour of authentic old workings.

MAKE A DATE FOR...

Haxey Hood Game

Various venues, Haxey, Humberside
6 January

Jorvik Viking Festival

Various venues, York, N. Yorkshire
14 – 29 February

Harrogate International Youth Music Festival

Various venues, Harrogate, N. Yorkshire
15 – 22 April

World Coal Carrying Championship

Gawthorpe, Ossett, W. Yorkshire
20 April

Harrogate Spring Flower Show

Valley Gardens, Harrogate, N. Yorkshire
23 – 25 April

York Festival and Mystery Plays

Various venues, York, N. Yorkshire
13 June – 5 July

Great Yorkshire Show

Great Yorkshire Showground, Wetherby Road, Harrogate, N. Yorkshire
14 – 16 July

Masham Steam Engine and Fair Organ Rally

Low Burton Hall, Masham, N. Yorkshire
18 – 19 July

Harrogate International Festival

Various venues, Harrogate, N. Yorkshire
30 July – 13 August

Great Autumn Flower Show

Exhibition Centre, Ripon Road, Harrogate, N. Yorkshire
18 – 19 September

FIND OUT MORE

Further information about holidays and attractions in the Yorkshire & Humberside region is available from:
Yorkshire & Humberside Tourist Board
312 Tadcaster Road, York, North Yorkshire YO2 2HF
☎ (0904) 707961
Fax: (0904) 701414

Please contact the board for details of publications available.

Places to stay

ACCOMMODATION ENTRIES *in this regional section are listed in alphabetical order of place name, and then in alphabetical order of establishment.*

THE MAP REFERENCES *refer to the colour maps towards the end of the guide. The first figure is the map number; the letter and figure which follow indicate the grid reference on the map.*

THE SYMBOLS *at the end of each accommodation entry give information about services and facilities. A 'key' to these symbols is inside the back cover flap, which can be kept open for easy reference.*

ACASTER MALBIS

N. Yorkshire
Map ref 4C1

5m S. York

Manor Country Guest House Ⓜ
Acaster Malbis, York,
YO2 1UL
☎ York (0904) 706723
Peaceful, modernised 18th C house in 6 acres of landscaped woodland gardens by the River Ouse, 4.5 miles from York centre.
Bedrooms: 4 single, 2 double & 4 twin, 2 family rooms.
Bathrooms: 5 private,
2 public.
Bed & breakfast: £18-£22.50 single, £30-£45 double.
Half board: £25-£29.50 daily, £149-£199 weekly.
Evening meal 6pm (l.o. 6.30pm).
Parking for 16.
ⓈⒶ Ⓥ UK Ⓘ Ⓥ ⮑ TV ☒
▦ ❀ SP

ALLERSTON

N. Yorkshire
Map ref 5D3

5m NE. Pickering

Cayley Arms Hotel Ⓜ
♨♨♨ **COMMENDED**
Allerston, Pickering,
YO18 7PJ
☎ Scarborough
(0723) 859338
Refurbished to high standard. Ideally situated for North York Moors and coast. Trout stream flows through gardens.

Bedrooms: 5 double & 1 twin, 1 family room.
Bathrooms: 7 private.
Bed & breakfast: £25-£28 double.
Evening meal 7pm (l.o. 9.30pm).
Parking for 50.
Credit: Access, Visa.
ⓈⒹ♥Ⓘ Ⓥ ▦ ▲ Ⓜ ☒
SP

APPLETON-LE-MOORS

N. Yorkshire
Map ref 5C3

5m NW. Pickering
Small village on the edge of the North York Moors, with spired Victorian church.

Dweldapilton Hall Hotel Ⓜ
♨♨♨
Appleton-le-Moors, York,
YO6 6TF
☎ Lastingham (075 15) 227
A mellowed, early Victorian villa with fine Italian plasterwork. Enhanced by mature specimen trees in a pleasant 2-acre setting.
Bedrooms: 2 single, 5 double & 3 twin.
Bathrooms: 10 private.
Bed & breakfast: £38.50 single, £77-£87 double.
Half board: £58 daily, £359.50-£393.50 weekly.
Lunch available.
Evening meal 7pm (l.o. 8pm).
Parking for 20.
Credit: Access, Visa, Amex.
Ⓛ ⊡ Ⓣ ♥ Ⓘ Ⓥ ⮑ TV ☒
▦ ▲ Ⓣ ❀ Ⓜ ☒ SP ▦ Ⓣ

ARKENGARTHDALE

N. Yorkshire
Map ref 5B3

Picturesque Yorkshire dale, once an important and prosperous lead-mining valley developed by Charles Bathurst in the 18th C. A tributary of the River Swale.

The White House Ⓜ
♨♨♨ **COMMENDED**
Arkle Town, Arkengarthdale,
Richmond, DL11 6RB
☎ Richmond (0748) 84203
Former old farmhouse, standing above the road with superb views of the dale. A good centre for walking and touring in Herriot country.
Bedrooms: 2 double & 1 twin.
Bathrooms: 1 private,
1 public.
Bed & breakfast: £28-£33 double.
Half board: £23-£25.50 daily, £154-£171.50 weekly.
Evening meal 6pm (l.o. 6.30pm).
Parking for 3.
Open January-November.
Ⓢ8♥ UK Ⓘ Ⓥ ⤢ TV ▦
▲ ⤬ Ⓜ SP

ARNCLIFFE

N. Yorkshire
Map ref 5B3

On the River Skirfare in Littondale, Arncliffe is an attractive dales village with a green and 17th C stone cottages and houses.

Amerdale House Hotel Ⓜ
Arncliffe, Littondale,
Skipton, BD23 5QE
☎ (0756) 770250
Country house hotel with beautiful open views of Littondale. Offering comfortable, elegant accommodation, with emphasis on food and friendly, caring hospitality.
Bedrooms: 6 double & 4 twin, 2 family rooms.
Bathrooms: 1 te,
1 public.
Half board: £4 £50.50 daily.
Evening meal 7pm (l.o. 8.30pm).
Parking for 20.
Open March-November.
Credit: Access, Visa.
Ⓢ ▲ ▦ ⊡ ♥ Ⓘ Ⓥ ⤢ ⮑
▲ Ⓣ ♿ ❀ Ⓜ ▦

> *Individual proprietors have supplied all details of accommodation. Although we do check for accuracy, we advise you to confirm prices and other information at the time of booking.*

ARRATHORNE

N. Yorkshire
Map ref 5C3

5m NW. Bedale

Elmfield House
COMMENDED

Arrathorne, Bedale,
DL8 1NE
☎ Bedale (0677) 50558
*Country house in its own
grounds with open views of the
countryside. Special emphasis
on standards and home
cooking. Solarium.*
Bedrooms: 4 double & 3 twin,
2 family rooms.
Bathrooms: 9 private,
1 public.
Bed & breakfast: £25-£27
single, £36-£40 double.
Half board: £28-£35 daily,
£189-£238 weekly.
Evening meal 7pm.
Parking for 10.

ASKRIGG

N. Yorkshire
Map ref 5B3

4m NW. Aysgarth
The name of this Dales
village means 'ash tree
ridge'. It is centred on a
steep main street of high,
narrow 3-storey houses
and thrived on cotton and
later wool in 18th C. A TV
location for James Herriot
series. Once famous for
its clock making.

Kings Arms Hotel &
Restaurant **M**
APPROVED

Market Place, Askrigg,
Leyburn (Wensleydale),
DL8 3HQ
☎ (0969) 50258
CR Minotels
*Old coaching inn of great
character, featured as the
Drovers Arms in BBC's James
Herriot series, in the heart of
the Yorkshire Dales National
Park.*
Bedrooms: 10 double &
6 twin, 2 family rooms.
Bathrooms: 18 private.
Bed & breakfast: £40-£60
single, £60-£85 double.
Half board: £56.50-£76.50
daily, £285-£345 weekly.
Lunch available.
Evening meal 6.30pm (l.o.
8.45pm).
Parking for 7.
Credit: Access, Visa.

AUSTWICK

N. Yorkshire
Map ref 5B3

4m NW. Settle
Picturesque dales village
with pleasant cottages, a
green, an old cross and
an Elizabethan Hall.

The Traddock **M**

Austwick, Lancaster,
Lancashire LA2 8BY
☎ Clapham (046 85) 224
*Elegant, family-run, early
Georgian country house in a
delightful unspoilt village in the
Yorkshire Dales National
Park. Ideal for the Three
Peaks, dales, lakes, Bronte and
Herriot country. Emphasis on
food and wines.*
Bedrooms: 2 single, 3 double
& 3 twin, 4 family rooms.
Bathrooms: 11 private,
1 public.
Bed & breakfast: £28-£40
single, £45-£58 double.
Half board: £38-£54 daily,
£245-£300 weekly.
Evening meal 7.30pm (l.o.
9pm).
Parking for 30.
Credit: Access, Visa.

AYSGARTH

N. Yorkshire
Map ref 5B3

Famous for its beautiful
Falls - a series of 3
cascades extending for
half a mile on the River
Ure in Wensleydale.
There is a coach and
carriage museum with a
crafts centre at Old Yore
Mill and a National Park
Centre.

Stow House Hotel **M**

Aysgarth Falls, Wensleydale,
Leyburn, DL8 3SR
☎ (0969) 663635
*Converted Victorian vicarage
in 2 acres, with panoramic
views, on the A684 near
Aysgarth Falls. Excellent
location for holidays in the
Yorkshire Dales National
Park. Croquet lawn and tennis
court in season.*
Bedrooms: 6 double & 3 twin.
Bathrooms: 9 private.
Bed & breakfast: £35-£40
single, £50-£70 double.
Half board: £37-£47 daily,
£238-£308 weekly.

Evening meal 5.30pm (l.o.
8pm).
Parking for 10.
Credit: Access, Visa.

BAINBRIDGE

N. Yorkshire
Map ref 5B3

This Wensleydale grey-
stone village, with fine
views of the River Bain,
reputedly England's
shortest river, was once a
Roman settlement, some
of it still visible. Boating
and water-skiing on
nearby Semerwater.
Ancient foresters' custom
of hornblowing still
continues.

Riverdale House
Country Hotel **M**
APPROVED

Bainbridge, Leyburn,
DL8 3EW
☎ Wensleydale (0969) 50311
*Tastefully-appointed,
comfortable house, with special
emphasis on food. In the centre
of a lovely village in Upper
Wensleydale, the area used for
the filming of the James
Herriot stories.*
Bedrooms: 8 double & 4 twin,
2 family rooms.
Bathrooms: 10 private,
4 public.
Bed & breakfast: £20-£30.50
single, £40-£61 double.
Evening meal 7.30pm.
Parking for 4.

Rose & Crown Hotel **M**
APPROVED

Bainbridge, Leyburn
(Wensleydale), DL8 3EE
☎ Wensleydale (0969) 50225
*Comfort, specialist cooking and
a warm welcome are hallmarks
of this 15th C coaching inn.
Overlooking the beautiful
greens of one of Herriot's
favourite dales villages.
Fishing available.*
Bedrooms: 9 double & 2 twin,
1 family room.
Bathrooms: 12 private,
1 public.
Bed & breakfast: from £43
single, from £68 double.
Half board: from £47 daily,
from £297 weekly.
Lunch available.
Evening meal 7pm (l.o.
9.30pm).
Parking for 60.
Credit: Access, Visa.

BARNSLEY

S. Yorkshire
Map ref 4B1

12m N. Sheffield
Barnsley became rich
through coal and glass. It
has Norman origins and
ruins of Monk Bretton
Priory include 13th C
chapter house and
church. Attractions are
Cooper Art Gallery,
Cannon Hall (country
house museum) and
Worsbrough Mill (working
museum with country
park and corn mills).
*Tourist Information
Centre* ☎ (0226) 206757

Brooklands Restaurants
Ltd. & Motel Chalets **M**

Barnsley Rd., Dodworth,
Barnsley, S. Yorkshire
S75 3JT
☎ Barnsley (0226) 299571 &
Fax (0226) 249465
Telex 54623
*Located 500 yards west of the
M1, junction 37. All rooms
contain a double and a three-
quarter bed and can be used as
a single, twin or family.*
Bedrooms: 56 twin.
Bathrooms: 56 private.
Bed & breakfast: £39.50-£45
single, £39.50-£49.50 double.
Half board: £52-£57.50 daily,
£364-£402.50 weekly.
Lunch available.
Evening meal 6.30pm (l.o.
9.30pm).
Parking for 300.
Open January-November.
Credit: Access, Visa, C.Bl.,
Diners, Amex.

Periquito Hotel **M**
COMMENDED

Regent St., Barnsley,
S70 2HQ
☎ (0226) 731010
Fax (0226) 248791
*Listed Victorian town centre
hotel, fully refurbished in 1990
with bright welcoming decor
which enhances original
features. 5 minutes from M1
junction 37.*
Bedrooms: 28 single,
10 double & 9 twin, 4 family
rooms.
Bathrooms: 51 private.
Bed & breakfast: £43-£57.50
single, £48.50-£65 double.
Lunch available.
Evening meal 7pm (l.o.
10pm).
Credit: Access, Visa, Diners,
Amex.

BARROW UPON HUMBER

Humberside
Map ref 4C1

3m E. Barton-upon-Humber

Haven Inn ♨
APPROVED
Ferry Rd., Barrow Haven,
Barrow upon Humber,
S. Humberside DN19 7EX
☎ (0469) 30247
Fax (0469) 30625
Old coaching inn, built in 1730, with beams and log fires. In rural position, 2 miles from the Humber Bridge.
Bedrooms: 3 double & 5 twin, 1 family room.
Bathrooms: 9 private, 2 public.
Bed & breakfast: £36 single, £45 double.
Evening meal 7pm (l.o. 10pm).
Parking for 200.
Credit: Access, Visa, Diners, Amex.

BATLEY

W. Yorkshire
Map ref 4B1

New industries are replacing heavy woollen goods made at Batley for centuries. All Saints Church, partly 15th C, has fine carved screen. 40-acre Wilton Park has lakes, walks and Bagshaw Museum containing local history and archaeology. Nearby is Oakwell Hall and Country Park.

Alder House Hotel ♨
COMMENDED
Towngate Rd., Batley,
WF17 7HR
☎ (0924) 444777
Fax (0924) 442644
Handsome, tastefully converted Georgian house dating from around 1730. Recently built new wing with 7 bedrooms and function suite. Approached via Healey Lane.
Bedrooms: 7 single, 9 double & 4 twin, 1 family room.
Bathrooms: 21 private.
Bed & breakfast: £43-£55 single, £65-£70 double.
Lunch available.
Evening meal 7pm (l.o. 9pm).
Parking for 29.
Credit: Access, Visa, Amex.

BAWTRY

S. Yorkshire
Map ref 4C2

Market town, once the gateway to Yorkshire on the Great North Road through which many Kings and Queens of England passed on their way north.

Bawtry Lodge Hotel ♨
20 High St., Bawtry,
Doncaster, DN10 6JE
☎ Doncaster (0302) 710252
On the borders of three counties: Yorkshire, Nottinghamshire and Lincolnshire. In the centre of a market town on the crossroads of the A631, A614 and A638. Evening meal by arrangement.
Bedrooms: 3 double, 2 family rooms.
Bathrooms: 5 private.
Bed & breakfast: £28-£32 single, £38-£45 double.
Lunch available.
Parking for 6.
Credit: Access, Visa, Amex.

BEVERLEY

Humberside
Map ref 4C1

Beverley's most famous landmark is its beautiful medieval Minster with Percy family tomb. Many attractive squares and streets, notably Wednesday and Saturday Market, North Bar Gateway and the Museum of Army Transport, Flemingate. Famous racecourse.
Tourist Information Centre ☎ *(0482) 867430 or 867813*

Eastgate Guest House ♨
7 Eastgate, Beverley,
N. Humberside HU17 0DR
☎ Hull (0482) 868464
Family-run Victorian guesthouse, established and run by the same proprietor for 23 years. Close to the town centre, Beverley Minster, Museum of Army Transport and railway station.
Bedrooms: 5 single, 5 double & 4 twin, 4 family rooms.
Bathrooms: 5 private, 3 public.
Bed & breakfast: £16-£30 single, £26-£40 double.

Pinewood
COMMENDED
45 North Bar Without,
Beverley, N. Humberside
HU17 7AG
☎ (0482) 861366
Grade II listed, Victorian mock-Tudor town house in a row of beautiful, historic houses. Close to town centre.
Bedrooms: 3 double.
Bathrooms: 1 public; 1 private shower.
Bed & breakfast: £23 single, £38 double.
Parking for 6.

Tickton Grange Hotel & Restaurant ♨
Tickton Grange, Tickton,
Beverley, N. Humberside
HU17 9SH
☎ Hornsea (0964) 543666
Fax (0964) 542556
Family-run Georgian country house set in rose gardens, 2 miles from historic Beverley. Country house cooking.
Bedrooms: 3 single, 10 double & 2 twin, 1 family room.
Bathrooms: 16 private.
Bed & breakfast: £38-£65 single, £53.50-£80.50 double.
Lunch available.
Evening meal 7pm (l.o. 9.30pm).
Parking for 65.
Credit: Access, Visa, Diners, Amex.

BINGLEY

W. Yorkshire
Map ref 4B1

Bingley Five-Rise is an impressive group of locks on the Leeds and Liverpool Canal. Town claims to have first bred the Airedale terrier originally used for otter hunting. Among fine Georgian houses is Myrtle Grove where John Wesley stayed. East Riddlesden Hall, a 17th C manor house, is nearby.

The Croft Hotel & Restaurant ♨
COMMENDED
Otley Rd., High Eldwick,
Bingley, BD16 3BE
☎ Bradford (0274) 567789

17th C farmhouse on the edge of Ilkley Moor with panoramic views of the Aire Valley. Drawing room with a double open fire and an intimate restaurant with open fire and beamed ceiling. Furnishings, paintings and antiques help create an elegant old world ambience.
Bedrooms: 1 single, 1 double & 3 twin.
Bathrooms: 5 private.
Bed & breakfast: £38.50 single, £52 double.
Lunch available.
Evening meal 7.30pm (l.o. 9.30pm).
Parking for 20.
Credit: Access, Visa.

BOLTON ABBEY

N. Yorkshire
Map ref 4B1

This hamlet is best known for its priory situated near a bend in the River Wharfe. It was founded in 1151 by Alicia de Romilly and before that was site of Anglo-Saxon manor. Popular with painters, amongst them Landseer.

Devonshire Arms Country House Hotel ♨
HIGHLY COMMENDED
Bolton Abbey, Skipton,
BD23 6AJ
☎ (0756) 710441 Telex 51218
Ⓡ Best Western
Traditional country house hotel in the Yorkshire Dales. Open log fires in handsome lounges furnished with antiques from the Duke and Duchess of Devonshire's home, Chatsworth. International cuisine with local game in season.
Bedrooms: 21 double & 19 twin.
Bathrooms: 40 private.
Bed & breakfast: £78-£83 single, £98-£112 double.
Lunch available.
Evening meal 7pm (l.o. 9.45pm).
Parking for 150.
Credit: Access, Visa, C.Bl., Diners, Amex.

The symbols are explained on the flap inside the back cover.

BOROUGHBRIDGE

N. Yorkshire
Map ref 5C3

On the River Ure, Boroughbridge was once an important coaching centre with 22 inns and in the 18th C a port for Knaresborough's linens. It has fine old houses, many trees, a cobbled square with market cross, also fishing and boating. Nearby stand 3 megaliths known as the Devil's Arrows.

Farndale Town House Hotel M

Horsefair, Boroughbridge, York, YO5 9AH
☎ (0423) 323463
Family-run guesthouse offering home cooking and a friendly atmosphere. Ideal for touring the dales and moors, and within easy reach of York, Harrogate and Ripon.
Bedrooms: 3 single, 4 double & 4 twin, 1 family room.
Bathrooms: 4 private, 3 public.
Bed & breakfast: £18-£30 single, £32-£45 double.
Half board: £25-£30 daily.
Lunch available.
Evening meal 6pm (l.o. 8pm).
Parking for 10.
Credit: Access, Visa, C.Bl., Diners, Amex.

BOSTON SPA

W. Yorkshire
Map ref 4B1

Largest of a cluster of villages on the lower Wharfe built of limestone from Tadcaster quarries. Saline waters were discovered in 1774 and the town developed as a spa with fine Georgian houses until superseded by Harrogate.

Royal Hotel
COMMENDED
182 High St., Boston Spa, Wetherby, LS23 7AY
☎ Wetherby (0937) 842142
Originally a coaching inn dating back to 1771, now a comfortable family hotel with a friendly atmosphere.
Bedrooms: 4 single, 7 double & 2 twin.
Bathrooms: 13 private.
Bed & breakfast: £39-£44 single, £52 double.

Lunch available.
Evening meal 7pm (l.o. 10.30pm).
Parking for 65.
Credit: Access, Visa, Diners, Amex.

BRADFORD

W. Yorkshire
Map ref 4B1

City founded on wool, with fine Victorian and modern buildings. Attractions include the cathedral, city hall, Cartwright Hall, Lister Park, Moorside Mills Industrial Museum and National Museum of Photography, Film and Television.
Tourist Information Centre ☎ (0274) 753678

Balmoral Hotel M
8 Blenheim Mount, Manningham La., Bradford, BD8 7NE
☎ (0274) 491310
Family-run establishment providing a home-from-home service. Of special interest to steam railway enthusiasts.
Lunch is available on request.
Bedrooms: 5 single, 6 double & 3 twin, 3 family rooms.
Bathrooms: 15 private, 2 public.
Bed & breakfast: £13.50-£23.65 single, £35-£43 double.
Evening meal 6pm (l.o. 9pm).
Parking for 10.

Diplomat Hotel M
APPROVED
144 Sunbridge Rd., Bradford, BD1 2HA
☎ (0274) 723918
Family-run, city centre hotel wih full en-suite accommodation. 5 minutes from all services. Traditional hand-pulled beers, genuine home-cooked cuisine.
Bedrooms: 5 single, 5 twin.
Bathrooms: 10 private.
Bed & breakfast: max. £28 single, max. £48 double.
Lunch available.
Evening meal 7pm (l.o. 9.30pm).
Parking for 4.
Credit: Access, Visa, Diners, Amex.

Farcliffe Guest House M
1 Farcliffe Terrace, Bradford, BD8 8QE
☎ (0274) 547813
Large, sandstone house on the corner of a terrace with an attractive garden and fish pond. Lounge, TV room and dining room. Close to Listers Mill, Cartwright Hall and Listers Park.
Bedrooms: 2 single, 2 twin, 2 family rooms.
Bathrooms: 3 public.
Bed & breakfast: £12-£14 single, £22-£24 double.
Parking for 4.

Guide Post Hotel M
Common Rd., Low Moor, Bradford, BD12 0ST
☎ (0274) 607866
Fax (0274) 671085
Telex 517635 GUIDE P.
Well-appointed hotel with an open restaurant and bar. Within easy reach of the M606, M62 and M1 motorways.
Bedrooms: 3 single, 25 double & 12 twin, 3 family rooms.
Bathrooms: 43 private, 2 public.
Bed & breakfast: £50-£70 single, £60-£80 double.
Lunch available.
Evening meal 7pm (l.o. 10pm).
Parking for 20.
Credit: Access, Visa, Diners, Amex.

New Beehive Inn M
171 Westgate, Bradford, BD1 3AA
☎ (0274) 721784
Prominent, large, detached city centre inn offering a warm atmosphere in spacious surroundings.
Bedrooms: 2 single, 2 double & 1 twin, 2 family rooms.
Bathrooms: 7 private.
Bed & breakfast: £22-£26 single, £38-£42 double.
Half board: £27-£31 daily, £180 weekly.
Lunch available.
Evening meal 7pm (l.o. 7pm).
Parking for 22.
Credit: Visa.

We advise you to confirm your booking in writing.

Park Drive Hotel M
COMMENDED
12 Park Drive, Heaton, Bradford, BD9 4DR
☎ (0274) 480194
Former Victorian residence, now a beautifully appointed hotel peacefully situated amongst trees in a conservation area. Convenient for the city and surrounding areas.
Bedrooms: 5 single, 3 double & 2 twin, 1 family room.
Bathrooms: 11 private.
Bed & breakfast: £39-£48 single, £49-£58 double.
Half board: from £36 daily, from £245 weekly.
Evening meal 7pm (l.o. 8pm).
Parking for 9.
Credit: Access, Visa, Amex.

Park Grove Hotel M
28 Park Grove, Frizinghall, Bradford, BD9 4JY
☎ (0274) 543444
Fax (0274) 495619
Victorian establishment in a secluded preserved area of Bradford, 1.5 miles from the city centre. Gateway to the dales.
Bedrooms: 5 single, 3 double & 1 twin, 2 family rooms.
Bathrooms: 11 private.
Bed & breakfast: £40-£44 single, £50-£54 double.
Half board: £50-£54 daily, £300-£350 weekly.
Evening meal 7.30pm (l.o. 9pm).
Parking for 8.
Credit: Access, Visa, Amex.

Park Hotel M
APPROVED
6 Oak Avenue, Manningham, Bradford, BD8 7AQ
☎ (0274) 546262
Fax (0274) 482207
Large, family-run hotel recently completely refurbished. 1 mile from the city centre, just off the A650 with easy access to motorways and the airport. Large gardens, lounges and 3 bars.
Bedrooms: 11 single, 6 twin, 3 family rooms.
Bathrooms: 20 private.
Bed & breakfast: £28-£35 single, £56-£64 double.
Lunch available.
Evening meal 5pm (l.o. 9pm).
Parking for 20.
Credit: Access, Visa, Diners.

BRADFORD

Continued

Stakis Bradford Norfolk Gardens Hotel ⚑
⚜⚜⚜
Hall Ings, Bradford,
BD1 5SH
☎ (0274) 734734
Telex 517573
ⒼⒷ Stakis
In the city centre, adjacent to train and coach terminals, with easy access to the airport and motorways. Half board rate based on a minimum 2 night stay.
Bedrooms: 52 double & 70 twin, 4 family rooms.
Bathrooms: 126 private.
Bed & breakfast: £91-£101 single, £120-£130 double.
Half board: from £40 daily.
Lunch available.
Evening meal 7pm (l.o. 10pm).
Credit: Access, Visa, Diners, Amex.
⛵ 📞 ▥ 🖵 🛗 ⟟ ▣ 🗝 🚫 ⊟ ▦ 🛏 🍽 ◻◻ ⟨SP⟩ Ⓣ

Westleigh Hotel
30 Easby Rd., Bradford,
BD7 1QX
☎ (0274) 727089
Pleasant hotel with a friendly atmosphere. Centrally located, 5 minutes' walk from town centre, theatres and museums.
Bedrooms: 12 single, 6 double & 14 twin, 3 family rooms.
Bathrooms: 12 private, 4 public.
Bed & breakfast: £25-£31 single, £42-£48 double.
Lunch available.
Parking for 27.
Credit: Access, Visa.
⛵ ♨ 📞 ▥ 🖵 🛗 ▣ ⊟ 🛏 ▣ ▦ 🛏 🍽 ⟨SP⟩

National Crown ratings were correct at the time of going to press but are subject to change. Please check at the time of booking.

Half board prices shown are per person but in some cases may be based on double/twin occupancy.

BRANDESBURTON

Humberside
Map ref 4D1

6m W. Hornsea
The village church retains work from the Norman period through to the 15thC, and the shaft of a medieval cross stands on the village green.

Burton Lodge Hotel ⚑
⚜⚜ COMMENDED
Brandesburton, Driffield,
N. Humberside YO25 8RU
☎ Hornsea (0964) 542847
Country house situated in own grounds adjoining 18-hole parkland golf course. 7 miles from Beverley on the A165.
Bedrooms: 1 single, 1 double & 4 twin.
Bathrooms: 5 private; 1 private shower.
Bed & breakfast: £25-£30 single, £40-£45 double.
Half board: £35-£42 daily, £200-£220 weekly.
Evening meal 7pm (l.o. 9pm).
Parking for 13.
Credit: Access, Visa.
⛵ 📞 ▥ 🖵 🛗 ▣ 🛏 ❋ 🛏 ▦ ⟨SP⟩

BRIDLINGTON

Humberside
Map ref 5D3

Lively seaside resort with long sandy beaches, Leisureworld and busy harbour with fishing trips in cobles. Priory church of St. Mary whose Bayle Gate is now a museum. Mementoes of flying pioneer, Amy Johnson, in Sewerby Hall. Harbour Museum and Aquarium.
Tourist Information Centre ☎ (0262) 673474 or 679626 or 606383

Badsworth House
78 Marshall Avenue,
Bridlington, N. Humberside
YO15 2DS
☎ (0262) 674996
Warm, friendly, clean and comfortable guesthouse.
Bedrooms: 2 single, 2 double & 1 twin, 3 family rooms.
Bathrooms: 2 public.
Bed & breakfast: from £11 single, from £22 double.
Half board: £13-£14 daily, £80-£85 weekly.
Evening meal 5pm (l.o. 5pm).
Open April-September.
⛵ 🛗 ▣ ▥ ▦ ▣ 🛏 ❋ ◻◻

Bay Ridge Hotel ⚑
⚜⚜⚜ COMMENDED
11-13 Summerfield Rd.,
Bridlington, N. Humberside
YO15 3LF
☎ (0262) 673425
Friendly, comfortable and caring family-run hotel near the South Beach and Spa Complex. Good value for money.
Bedrooms: 2 single, 6 double & 2 twin, 4 family rooms.
Bathrooms: 12 private, 1 public; 2 private showers.
Bed & breakfast: £16.50-£17.50 single, £33-£35 double.
Half board: £19.50-£21.50 daily, £128-£135 weekly.
Lunch available.
Evening meal 5.45pm (l.o. 6.15pm).
Parking for 7.
Credit: Visa.
⛵ 🖵 🛗 ▣ ▥ 🚫 🛏 ▣ ▥▥
🛏 🍽 ⟨OAP⟩ 🚫 ⟨SP⟩ Ⓣ

Central Guest House ⚑
Listed
1 Springfield Avenue,
Bridlington, N. Humberside
YO15 3AA
☎ (0262) 400266
Family guesthouse close to the town centre attractions, harbour, coach and railway stations.
Bedrooms: 1 double, 2 family rooms.
Bathrooms: 1 public.
Bed & breakfast: £12.50-£14 single, £25-£28 double.
Half board: £17.50-£19 daily, £105-£114 weekly.
Evening meal 5.30pm.
⛵ 🖵 🛗 🛗 🛏 ▣ ▣ 🛏 ❋ ▦ ⟨SP⟩

Expanse Hotel ⚑
⚜⚜⚜⚜ COMMENDED
North Marine Drive,
Bridlington, N. Humberside
YO15 2LS
☎ (0262) 675347
In a unique position overlooking the beach and sea, with panoramic views of the bay and Heritage Coast.
Bedrooms: 12 single, 12 double & 20 twin, 4 family rooms.
Bathrooms: 48 private.
Bed & breakfast: £40.75-£48 single, £65.50-£73.50 double.
Half board: £72-£98 daily.
Lunch available.
Evening meal 6.30pm (l.o. 9pm).
Parking for 32.
Credit: Access, Visa, Diners, Amex.
⛵ ♨ 📞 🖵 🛗 ▣ ▥ 🛏
▣ 🚫 ▦ 🛏 ▣ 🍽 🛏 🚫 ⟨SP⟩ Ⓣ

Flaneburg Hotel ⚑
⚜⚜⚜
North Marine Rd.,
Flamborough, Bridlington,
N. Humberside YO15 1LF
☎ Bridlington (0262) 850284
Family-owned, purpose-built hotel in a heritage coastal fishing village. An ornithologist's, geologist's and rambler's paradise. Minimum 2 day stay; in spring and autumn 10% reduction on room and breakfast tariff. 4.5 miles from Bridlington.
Bedrooms: 4 single, 6 double & 2 twin, 2 family rooms.
Bathrooms: 8 private, 2 public.
Bed & breakfast: £17-£25 single, £34-£40 double.
Half board: £25.50-£33.50 daily, £149-£169 weekly.
Evening meal 7pm (l.o. 10pm).
Parking for 20.
Open March-December.
⛵ 🖵 🛗 ▣ ▥ 🛏 ▣ ▦ 🛏 ▣
🛏 ▦ 🛏 ⟨OAP⟩ ⟨SP⟩

Glen Alan Hotel ⚑
⚜⚜ APPROVED
21 Flamborough Rd.,
Bridlington, N. Humberside
YO15 2HU
☎ (0262) 674650
Family-run hotel in pleasant residential area, ideal for beach, "Leisure World" and town centre. Warm welcome guaranteed.
Bedrooms: 5 single, 4 double & 1 twin, 2 family rooms.
Bathrooms: 2 private, 3 public.
Bed & breakfast: £14-£16 single, £28-£32 double.
Half board: £19-£22 daily, £125-£140 weekly.
Evening meal 5.30pm (l.o. 5.30pm).
Open March-November.
Credit: Access, Visa.
⛵ 🛗 ▥ 🛏 ▣ ▦ 🛏 ▣ 🍽 ⟨OAP⟩
⟨SP⟩

Kelowna Hotel
11 Shaftesbury Rd.,
Bridlington, N. Humberside
YO15 3NW
☎ (0262) 675231
Licensed hotel, 50 yards from Bridlington's south beach. Some en-suite rooms available. Close to the Spa Theatre complex. Colour TV and tea and coffee in all rooms.
Bedrooms: 1 single, 3 double, 4 family rooms.
Bathrooms: 3 private, 1 public.
Bed & breakfast: £29-£33.50 double.

Half board: £22.50-£24.75 daily, £150-£160 weekly. Evening meal 6pm (l.o. 7pm). Parking for 3.

London Hotel
1 Royal Crescent, York Rd., Bridlington, N. Humberside YO15 2PF
☎ (0262) 675377
Close to a new indoor resort. All rooms with sea views, some en-suite. Lift to all floors.
Bedrooms: 4 single, 2 double & 4 twin, 2 family rooms.
Bathrooms: 6 private, 4 public.
Bed & breakfast: £19 single, £38 double.
Half board: £23 daily, £161 weekly.
Evening meal 5.30pm (l.o. 3.30pm).

Manor Court Hotel & Restaurant M
APPROVED
53 Main St., Carnaby, Bridlington, N. Humberside YO16 4UJ
☎ Bridlington (0262) 606468 & Fax (0262) 400217
Award-winning, family-run hotel, 3 miles from Bridlington, incorporating the Wishing Well Inn, popular for bar meals.
Bedrooms: 1 single, 3 double & 1 twin, 2 family rooms.
Bathrooms: 7 private.
Bed & breakfast: £40-£50 single, £55-£65 double.
Lunch available.
Evening meal 7pm (l.o. 10pm).
Parking for 60.
Credit: Access, Visa, Amex.

Monarch Hotel M
APPROVED
South Marine Drive, Bridlington, N. Humberside YO15 3JJ
☎ (0262) 674447 Telex 57515 ATTN. 24
Consort
Large seafront hotel, convenient for the harbour and town. Ideally placed as a touring centre.
Bedrooms: 8 single, 10 double & 17 twin, 5 family rooms.
Bathrooms: 36 private, 3 public.
Bed & breakfast: £35-£45 single, £51.50-£67 double.
Half board: £47-£57 daily, £294-£325 weekly.
Lunch available.
Evening meal 6pm (l.o. 8.30pm).

Parking for 10.
Credit: Access, Visa, Diners, Amex.

Northcote Inn & Hotel M
8 Trinity Rd., Bridlington, N. Humberside YO15 2EY
☎ (0262) 675764 & 678888
Close to the sea, parks and shops. En-suite bedrooms with colour TV, some four-poster beds. Fully licensed bar.
Bedrooms: 3 single, 5 double & 2 twin, 2 family rooms.
Bathrooms: 12 private, 1 public.
Bed & breakfast: £19-£21 single, £34-£38 double.
Half board: £23-£25 daily, £135-£150 weekly.
Lunch available.
Evening meal 5.30pm.
Credit: Access, Visa.

Park View Licensed Family Hotel M
9-11 Tennyson Avenue, Bridlington, N. Humberside YO15 2EU
☎ (0262) 672140
Small, family-run hotel 250 yards from the beach and close to all amenities including the new Leisure World indoor leisure centre.
Bedrooms: 5 single, 4 double & 4 twin, 4 family rooms.
Bathrooms: 4 public.
Bed & breakfast: £12-£15 single, £24-£30 double.
Half board: £16-£21 daily, £110-£140 weekly.
Evening meal 5pm (l.o. 5pm).

Popinjays Guest House M
58 Wellington Rd., Bridlington, N. Humberside YO15 2AZ
☎ (0262) 606409
Small, friendly, family guesthouse in a quiet area of town, a few minutes' walk from the centre and all amenities - coach and rail stations, bowling greens and tennis courts.
Bedrooms: 1 single, 1 double & 2 twin, 2 family rooms.
Bathrooms: 2 public.
Bed & breakfast: £12 single, £24 double.

Half board: £15 daily, £95 weekly.
Evening meal 5.30pm (l.o. 6pm).

South Bay Hotel
APPROVED
11 Roundhay Rd., Bridlington, N. Humberside YO15 3LA
☎ (0262) 674944
Small family-run hotel, specialising in good quality, courtesy and service.
Bedrooms: 1 single, 3 double & 2 twin, 4 family rooms.
Bathrooms: 3 private, 2 public.
Bed & breakfast: £16-£19 single, £32-£38 double.
Half board: £21.50-£28 daily, £105-£160 weekly.
Evening meal 5.30pm.
Parking for 5.
Open March-December.
Credit: Access, Visa.

Spa Hotel M
South Marine Drive, Bridlington, N. Humberside YO15 3JJ
☎ (0262) 674225
Seafront hotel near to the harbour, golf and entertainments. Choice of English cooking. Colour TV available in bedrooms on request.
Bedrooms: 7 single, 9 double & 9 twin, 9 family rooms.
Bathrooms: 14 private, 5 public.
Bed & breakfast: £20-£28 single, £40-£56 double.
Half board: £27-£35 daily, £170-£215 weekly.
Lunch available.
Evening meal 6pm (l.o. 7pm).
Parking for 5.
Open March-October, December.
Credit: Access, Visa.

The Tennyson M
COMMENDED
19 Tennyson Avenue, Bridlington, N. Humberside YO15 2EU
☎ (0262) 604382
Hotel offers fine cuisine in attractive surroundings, close to sea and Leisure World. Special diets catered for. Free newspapers.
Bedrooms: 3 double & 2 twin, 1 family room.
Bathrooms: 6 private.
Bed & breakfast: £16-£22 single, £32-£34 double.

Evening meal 6pm (l.o. 8.30pm).
Parking for 3.
Credit: Access, Visa.

White Rose Guest House M
123 Cardigan Rd., Bridlington, N. Humberside YO15 3LP
☎ (0262) 673245
Personal attention with warm, friendly hospitality and emphasis on food. No hidden extras. Near the South Beach, spa and golf course.
Bedrooms: 2 single, 3 double & 1 twin, 1 family room.
Bathrooms: 3 private, 1 public; 1 private shower.
Bed & breakfast: £14.50-£17.50 single, £29-£35 double.
Half board: £18.50-£21.50 daily, £120-£130 weekly.
Evening meal 5.30pm (l.o. 6pm).
Parking for 2.

BRIGG
Humberside
Map ref 4C1

Small town at an ancient crossing of the River Ancholme, granted a weekly Thursday market and annual horsefair by Henry III in 1235.

Exchange Coach House Inn M
Bigby St., Brigg, S. Humberside DN20 8EJ
☎ (0652) 57633
Fax (0652) 57636
Telex 527073
Grade II listed building restored to a mixture of Edwardian and Victorian splendour. Offering facilities for weddings, discos and conferences. 5 miles from Humberside Airport and only a half-hour journey from Hull and Lincoln.*
Bedrooms: 8 single, 8 double, 1 family room.
Bathrooms: 17 private.
Bed & breakfast: £47.50-£53 single, £55-£65 double.
Half board: £65-£75 daily.
Lunch available.
Evening meal 6pm (l.o. 10.30pm).
Parking for 28.
Credit: Access, Visa, Amex.

BRIGHOUSE

W. Yorkshire
Map ref 4B1

One of several small, woollen textile communities in Calder Valley. In the 18th C, Brighouse became an important canal port with opening of Calder and Hebble Canal. Later cotton and silk were spun there.

Grove Inn Motel **M**
APPROVED

Elland Rd., Brook Foot, Brighouse, HD6 2RG
☎ Huddersfield
(0484) 713049 & 715855
Old coaching inn overlooking lakes, the Calder Valley, Hebble Waterways and adjacent to Brough Woods. 3 miles from the M62 (exits 24/25).
Bedrooms: 3 single, 7 double & 1 twin, 1 family room.
Bathrooms: 10 private, 1 public.
Bed & breakfast: £17-£32.50 single, £45-£50 double.
Half board: £25-£40.50 daily.
Lunch available.
Evening meal 6.30pm (l.o. 10pm).
Parking for 50.
Credit: Access, Visa, Diners.

BROUGH

Humberside
Map ref 4C1

Hemingford House

Church St., Welton, Brough, N. Humberside HU15 1NH
☎ Hull (0482) 668405/668097
Georgian-style house in a very pretty conservation village with a friendly local inn. Within easy reach of Humber Bridge, Hull, Beverley. 20 miles from York and Lincoln.
Bedrooms: 3 single, 2 double & 1 twin.
Bathrooms: 6 private.
Bed & breakfast: £22-£26 single, £32-£36 double.
Parking for 8.

The enquiry coupons at the back will help you when contacting proprietors.

BROUGHTON

Humberside
Map ref 4C1

3m NW. Brigg

Briggate Lodge Inn **M**
COMMENDED

Ermine St., Broughton, Brigg, S. Humberside DN20 0NQ
☎ Brigg (0652) 650770 &
Fax (0652) 650495
Built 1988 in 5 acres of mature woodland. 200 yards from M180 junction 4, on crossroads of A18 and A15. 20 miles from Lincoln, 10 miles from Humber Bridge and Humberside Airport. 5 18-hole golf-courses within 6 miles. Most rooms overlook Ancholme Valley.
Bedrooms: 8 double & 13 twin.
Bathrooms: 21 private.
Bed & breakfast: from £57 single, from £68 double.
Lunch available.
Evening meal 7pm (l.o. 10pm).
Parking for 125.
Credit: Access, Visa, Amex.

BURYTHORPE

N. Yorkshire
Map ref 5D3

Surrounded by gently undulating countryside between the Vale of York and the Yorkshire Wolds. The deserted medieval village of Wharram Percy lies a short distance away.

Burythorpe House Hotel & Restaurant **M**
COMMENDED

Burythorpe, Malton, YO17 9LB
☎ (065 385) 200
Family-owned and managed Georgian country house with leisure facilities. Set in rural heart of Ryedale, 15 miles north of York.
Bedrooms: 8 double & 2 twin.
Bathrooms: 10 private, 3 public.
Bed & breakfast: £50-£120 double.
Lunch available.
Evening meal 6.30pm (l.o. 9.30pm).
Parking for 50.
Open February-December.
Credit: Access, Visa.

CARPERBY

N. Yorkshire
Map ref 5B3

Charming Wensleydale street village over a mile long.

The Grayford **M**
COMMENDED

Carperby, Leyburn, DL8 4DW
☎ Wensleydale
(0969) 663517
Private hotel with a licensed restaurant open to non-residents. Small parties catered for. In heart of Herriot country.
Bedrooms: 4 double.
Bathrooms: 1 private, 2 public.
Bed & breakfast: £40-£55 double.
Evening meal 7pm (l.o. 9pm).
Parking for 12.
Credit: Access, Visa.

CATTERICK

N. Yorkshire
Map ref 5C3

A military camp since Roman times, known then as Cataractonium, Catterick used to be a major coaching stop on Great North Road. Crowds once gathered to watch cock-fighting where nowadays they come to Catterick Bridge for horse-racing.

Rose Cottage Guest House, Tea Room & Shop **M**
APPROVED

26 High St., Catterick Village, Richmond, DL10 7LJ
☎ Richmond (0748) 811164
Family-run establishment, close to A1 and midway between London and Edinburgh. Convenient for Yorkshire Dales, Coast-to-Coast Walk and the racecourse.
Bedrooms: 1 double & 2 twin.
Bathrooms: 2 private, 1 public.
Bed & breakfast: from £22.50 single, £37-£43 double.
Half board: £25-£32.50 daily, £140-£175 weekly.
Lunch available.
Evening meal 7.30pm (l.o. 8.30pm).
Parking for 3.

CAWOOD

N. Yorkshire
Map ref 4C1

Attractive village on the River Ouse, with swing bridge, winding streets and rows of boats. Cawood Castle was once the palace of Archbishops of York. Cardinal Wolsey tried to rival Hampton Court with Cawood and was arrested here in 1530; his downfall is commemorated in the nursery rhyme 'Humpty Dumpty'. Gatehouse only remains.

Burleigh House Hotel **M**

Market Pl., Cawood, Selby, YO8 0SR
☎ (0757) 268281 & 268026
Family-run Georgian hotel of considerable charm in the historic village of Cawood. Ideal for visiting York and the Yorkshire area.
Bedrooms: 4 single, 3 double & 3 twin, 2 family rooms.
Bathrooms: 3 private, 2 public.
Bed & breakfast: £15-£17 single, £30-£32 double.
Half board: £20-£22 daily, £140-£154 weekly.
Lunch available.
Evening meal 6pm (l.o. 9.30pm).
Parking for 8.

CLAPHAM

N. Yorkshire
Map ref 5B3

Neat village of grey-stone houses and whitewashed cottages; a pot-holing centre. Upstream are Ingleborough Cave and Gaping Gill with its huge underground chamber. National Park Centre.

Arbutus House **M**

Riverside, Clapham, Lancaster, Lancashire LA2 8DS
☎ (052 42) 51240
Family-run guesthouse offering home cooking and a friendly atmosphere. Ideal for touring, walking and relaxing.
Bedrooms: 2 double & 2 twin, 1 family room.
Bathrooms: 3 private, 1 public.
Bed & breakfast: £32-£38.50 double.

Half board: £24.75-£28.50 daily, £170-£195 weekly.
Evening meal 6.30pm (l.o. midday).
Parking for 6.
Open February-November.
🛇🖵♿🖵 ⓊⓁ ⓘ Ⓥ 🖃 🖿 ▶ ✗ 🍴

New Inn Hotel M
⚜⚜⚜ COMMENDED
Clapham, Lancaster,
Lancashire LA2 8HH
☎ (052 42) 51203
Fax (052 42) 51496
18th C coaching inn in a picturesque Yorkshire Dales village 6 miles north-west of Settle, in dramatic river, waterfall and fell country.
Bedrooms: 9 double & 4 twin.
Bathrooms: 13 private.
Bed & breakfast: £35 single, £48 double.
Half board: £39.50-£50.50 daily.
Lunch available.
Evening meal 7pm (l.o. 9.30pm).
Parking for 50.
Credit: Access, Visa, Amex.
🛇⊡🖵♿ Ⓥ 🖃 ⓉⓋ 🖿
⛴ 🍴 🕯 Ⓤ 🖊 ⑆ ⚲ Ⓢ🅟 🎣

CLECKHEATON
W. Yorkshire
Map ref 4B1

Prospect Hall Hotel M
⚜⚜⚜ COMMENDED
Prospect Rd., Cleckheaton,
BD19 3HD
☎ Bradford (0274) 873022
Telex 517429 PHH
Hall, converted to provide a well-appointed hotel, close to the M62, Bronte country, the dales and Peak District.
Bedrooms: 7 single, 30 double & 3 twin.
Bathrooms: 40 private.
Bed & breakfast: £31-£41 single, £46.50-£56.50 double.
Half board: £49.95-£52.95 daily.
Lunch available.
Evening meal 7pm (l.o. 9.30pm).
Parking for 200.
Credit: Access, Visa, Diners, Amex.
🛇♿🕻 ⊡🖵♿ ⓘ Ⓥ ✂
Ⓞ 🖿 ⛴ 🍴 🕯 ✗

CLEETHORPES
Humberside
Map ref 4D1

Once a little fishing village, now a thriving holiday resort attracting many visitors to its 3 miles of sands, boating lake, Tropical Garden, promenade and pier. Attractive views of Humberside coast with Spurn Head light.
Tourist Information Centre ☎ *(0472) 200220*

Blundell Park Hotel
140 Grimsby Rd.,
Cleethorpes, S. Humberside
DN35 7DL
☎ (0472) 691970
Well-established hotel in a prime position on the main road between Grimsby and Cleethorpes and about 1 mile from seafront. Easy access to the Humber Bank industrial area and Humberside Airport. Restaurant specialises in steak dishes.
Bedrooms: 10 single, 4 double & 4 twin.
Bathrooms: 15 private, 1 public.
Bed & breakfast: £18.50-£38.50 single, £32.50-£49.50 double.
Lunch available.
Evening meal 7pm (l.o. 10pm).
Parking for 15.
Credit: Access, Visa, Diners, Amex.
🛇🕻 Ⓛ⊡🖵♿ ⓘ Ⓥ Ⓞ 🖿
⛴ ✗ 🅟 Ⓣ

Wellesley Court M
⚜⚜⚜ COMMENDED
40 Bradford Avenue,
Cleethorpes, S. Humberside
DN35 0BD
☎ (0472) 693014
Stylishly elegant house in quiet avenue near seafront. Deep sofas, log fires. Restaurant uses only fresh produce. 4-poster, spa baths.
Bedrooms: 2 single, 2 double & 1 twin, 1 family room.
Bathrooms: 6 private.
Bed & breakfast: £30-£60 single, £45-£70 double.
Parking for 12.
Credit: Access, Visa.
🛇♿🕻 Ⓛ🖵♿ ⓘ Ⓥ 🖃 🖿
🖿 ⛴ 🍴 ✗ 🅟 Ⓣ

CRATHORNE
N. Yorkshire
Map ref 5C3

4m S. Yarm
Off the A19 near the River Leven and the Northumbria border. Crathorne Mill, Hall and Church are unspoilt. Sir William Crathorne defended northern England when the Black Prince was at Crecy.

Crathorne Hall Hotel M
⚜⚜⚜⚜ COMMENDED
Crathorne, Yarm, Cleveland
TS15 0AR
☎ Stokesley (0642) 700398
Telex 587426
An Edwardian house promising a warm welcome, relaxing atmosphere and the splendour of by-gone days.
Bedrooms: 6 single, 29 double & 2 twin.
Bathrooms: 37 private.
Bed & breakfast: max. £90 single, max. £105 double.
Half board: max. £50 daily.
Lunch available.
Evening meal 7pm (l.o. 10pm).
Parking for 100.
Credit: Access, Visa, Diners, Amex.
🛇♿🕻 ⊡🖵 ⓘ Ⓥ 🖃
Ⓞ 🖿 ⛴ 🍴 Ⓤ 🖊 ▶ ✿
⚲ 🅟 🎣 Ⓣ

DEWSBURY
W. Yorkshire
Map ref 4B1

Although this town is most famous for its woollen products, its history stretches back to Saxon times. Robin Hood is reputed to have died and been buried in the Cistercian convent in Kirklees Park nearby.

Heath Cottage Hotel & Restaurant
⚜⚜⚜ COMMENDED
Wakefield Rd., Dewsbury,
WF12 8ET
☎ (0924) 465399
Fax (0924) 459405
Impressive Victorian house in well-kept gardens. On the A638, 2.5 miles from M1 junction 40.
Bedrooms: 9 single, 8 double & 1 twin, 2 family rooms.
Bathrooms: 20 private, 1 public.
Bed & breakfast: £47.50 single, £65 double.
Half board: from £57.50 daily.

Lunch available.
Evening meal 6.30pm (l.o. 9.30pm).
Parking for 40.
🛇♿🕻 Ⓞ🖵♿ ⓘ Ⓥ ✂
🖿 ⓉⓋ 🖿 ⛴ 🍴 ♿ ⚲ ✿ ✗

DONCASTER
S. Yorkshire
Map ref 4C1

Ancient Roman town famous for its railway works, heavy industries, butterscotch and racecourse (St. Leger), also centre of agricultural area. Attractions include 18th C Mansion House, Cusworth Hall Museum, Doncaster Museum of Roman and Saxon relics, St. George's Church, the Dome and Doncaster Leisure Park.
Tourist Information Centre ☎ *(0302) 734309*

Almel Hotel M
⚜⚜ APPROVED
20 Christchurch Rd.,
Doncaster, DN1 2QL
☎ (0302) 365230
Fax (0302) 341434
Licensed hotel in the town centre, close to the racecourse and leisure park. Coach parties welcome.
Bedrooms: 12 single, 1 double & 13 twin, 1 family room.
Bathrooms: 9 private, 5 public; 10 private showers.
Bed & breakfast: £18.50-£26 single, £32-£38 double.
Half board: £19.50-£30 daily, £120-£200 weekly.
Lunch available.
Evening meal 5pm (l.o. 7.30pm).
Parking for 8.
Credit: Access, Visa, Amex.
🛇♿🕻 ⊡🖵 ⓘ Ⓥ 🖃 ⓉⓋ
Ⓞ 🖿 ⛴ 🍴 Ⓤ

Bay Horse Hotel
Cooke St., Bentley,
Doncaster, DN5 0DE
☎ (0302) 874414
Small, family-run hotel with emphasis on personal attention, 5 minutes from the railway and bus stations.
Bedrooms: 2 single, 1 double & 5 twin.
Bathrooms: 3 public.
Bed & breakfast: £16-£20 single, £32-£52 double.
Half board: £20-£30 daily, £98-£156 weekly.
Lunch available.
Evening meal 6pm (l.o. 9pm).
Parking for 20.
🛇⊡🖵♿ ⓘ Ⓥ ✗ 🖃 ⓉⓋ
🖿 ⛴ 🍴 ⚲ 🎣

DONCASTER

Continued

C & A Bed & Breakfast M
☗

25 Windsor Rd., Town Moor,
Doncaster, DN2 5BS
☎ (0302) 327006
*Beautiful old house 10 minutes
from the town centre and
racecourse. Evening meals by
arrangement.*
Bedrooms: 1 single, 1 double
& 2 twin.
Bathrooms: 2 private,
2 public.
Bed & breakfast: £12.50-
£14.50 single, £23.50-£27
double.
Half board: £16.50-£18.50
daily, £108.50-£121.50
weekly.
Evening meal 6.20pm.
Parking for 2.
⛵ ⌑ ⚲ Ⓤ ☖ Ⅲ ♨ ㍻ ⃝ᴰᴬᴾ

Canda M
⚜⚜ COMMENDED

Hampole Balk La., 5 Lane
Ends, Skellow, Doncaster,
DN6 8LF
☎ Doncaster (0302) 724028
*Charming guesthouse with 6
ground floor bedrooms.
Situated close to A1 and ideal
for those travelling north/south.
Non-smokers only please.*
Bedrooms: 2 single, 3 double
& 2 twin, 1 family room.
Bathrooms: 4 private,
2 public.
Bed & breakfast: £20-£25
single, £32-£36 double.
Parking for 6.
Credit: Access, Visa.
⛵9 ⚱ ⚲ Ⓤ Ⅴ ⅏ ☒ ♨
⊟ ㍻ ▦

Danum Swallow Hotel M
High St., Doncaster,
DN1 1DN
☎ (0302) 342261
Telex 547533
ⒸⒹ Swallow
*Town centre hotel built in
1908, now fully modernised but
retaining the majestic
atmosphere of the past. Free
car parking available.*
Bedrooms: 22 single,
14 double & 28 twin, 2 family
rooms.
Bathrooms: 66 private.
Bed & breakfast: max. £67
single, max. £86 double.
Lunch available.
Evening meal 7pm (l.o.
9.45pm).
Parking for 78.
Credit: Access, Visa, Diners,
Amex.
⛵ ⚱ ☏ ⓑ ⌑ ⚲ Ⅴ ⅏
㊃ ⃝ ⊞ Ⅲ ♨ ⏋ & ⓓᴬᴾ ⚐
SP ⓣ

Mount Pleasant Hotel M
Great North Rd., Rossington,
Doncaster, DN11 0HP
☎ Doncaster (0302) 868219
& 868696 Fax 0302 865130
*Local eating house specialising
in accommodation for business
executives, conferences, small
business meetings and parties
for all occasions. In Pilgrim
Father country, and a good
touring base for the whole
area.*
Bedrooms: 19 single,
14 double & 4 twin.
Bathrooms: 33 private,
1 public.
Bed & breakfast: £49-£54
single, £59-£64 double.
Half board: from £63.95
daily.
Lunch available.
Evening meal 7pm (l.o.
9.30pm).
Parking for 102.
Credit: Access, Visa, Diners,
Amex.
⛵ ⚱ ⚲ ☏ ⓑ ⌑ ⚲ ⓘ Ⅴ
⅏ ⃝ Ⅲ ♨ ㊀ ❊ SP ㍻ ⓣ

Nelson's M
Cleveland St., Doncaster,
DN1 1TR
☎ (0302) 344550
*Recently refurbished
fashionable bar and hotel in the
centre of the town, close to
every amenity.*
Bedrooms: 2 single, 3 twin,
1 family room.
Bathrooms: 2 public.
Bed & breakfast: £15.99-
£19.50 single, max. £32
double.
⛵ ⌑ ⚲ ⓘ Ⅴ ⃝ Ⅲ ♨ ✈

Regent Hotel M
⚜⚜⚜

Regent Square, Doncaster,
DN1 2DS
☎ (0302) 364180 & 364336
Telex 54480 Fax: 0302
322331
*A home-from-home to all our
visitors. Bar, restaurant and
function facilities to suit every
occasion.*
Bedrooms: 21 single, 9 double
& 15 twin, 5 family rooms.
Bathrooms: 50 private.
Bed & breakfast: £42-£55
single, £45-£65 double.
Half board: £52-£65 daily.
Lunch available.
Evening meal 6pm (l.o.
10pm).
Parking for 26.
Credit: Access, Visa, Diners,
Amex.
⛵ ⚱ ⚱ ☏ ⓑ ⌑ ⚲ ⓘ Ⅴ
Ⅳ ⃝ ⊞ Ⅲ ♨ ㊀ & ⚲ ⓤ
SP

DRIFFIELD

Humberside
Map ref 4C1

Lively market town on
edge of Wolds with fine
Early English church, All
Saints. Popular with
anglers for its trout
streams which flow into
the River Hull. Its 18th C
canal is lined with barges
and houseboats.

Wold House Country Hotel M
⚜⚜⚜

Wold Rd., Nafferton,
Driffield, N. Humberside
YO25 0LD
☎ Driffield (0377) 44242
*Family-owned and managed
private hotel with home
cooking, log fires and personal
attention. Panoramic views,
close to York and the coast.*
Bedrooms: 2 single, 1 double
& 5 twin, 4 family rooms.
Bathrooms: 8 private,
2 public.
Bed & breakfast: £25-£37
single, £45-£55 double.
Half board: £37-£47 daily,
£200-£230 weekly.
Lunch available.
Evening meal 7.30pm (l.o.
8.45pm).
Parking for 40.
Credit: Access, Visa.
⛵ ⚱ ⌑ ⚲ ⓘ Ⅴ ⅏ ㊉ ♨
㊀ ⚲ ⓤ ⓟ ❊ SP ㍻ ⓣ

DRIGHLINGTON

W. Yorkshire
Map ref 4B1

3m W. Morley

Mullions Hotel
207A Moorside Rd.,
Drighlington, Bradford,
BD11 1JH
☎ Leeds
(0532) 852451/854423
*Small, exclusive private hotel
offering rooms with and
without en-suite facilities.
Parking within grounds.
Adjacent to junction 27 on the
M62.*
Bedrooms: 6 single, 2 double
& 4 twin.
Bathrooms: 6 private,
1 public.
Bed & breakfast: £30-£41
single, £44-£55 double.
Half board: £38-£49 daily.
Parking for 10.
Credit: Access, Visa.
⛵ ⚱ ⌑ ⚲ Ⓤ Ⅴ ⅏ ⃝
Ⅲ ♨ ⓤ ✈ ㍻ SP

DRIFFIELD

EASINGWOLD

N. Yorkshire
Map ref 5C3

Market town of charm
and character with a
cobbled square and many
fine Georgian buildings.

Old Farmhouse Country Hotel & Restaurant M
⚜⚜⚜ COMMENDED

Raskelf, York, YO6 3LF
☎ Easingwold (0347) 21971
*Former farmhouse converted to
a comfortable country hotel,
offering home cooking, log fires
and a warm welcome. In
Herriot country, 3 miles from
Easingwold and 15 miles from
York.*
Bedrooms: 6 double & 2 twin,
2 family rooms.
Bathrooms: 10 private.
Half board: £35-£41 daily,
£245-£266 weekly.
Evening meal 7pm (l.o.
8.30pm).
Parking for 12.
Open February-December.
⛵ ⚱ ⓘ Ⅴ ⅏ Ⅳ Ⅲ ♨ ⚱
SP

EBBERSTON

N. Yorkshire
Map ref 5D3

6m E. Pickering
Picturesque village with a
Norman church and hall,
overlooking the Vale of
Pickering.

Foxholm Hotel M
⚜⚜⚜

Ebberston, Scarborough,
YO13 9NJ
☎ Scarborough
(0723) 859550
*Small, family-run country hotel
in a peaceful, rural setting
within easy reach of the moors,
dales, sea and York.*
Bedrooms: 2 single, 2 double
& 4 twin, 1 family room.
Bathrooms: 6 private,
3 public; 2 private showers.
Bed & breakfast: £24-£26
single, £46-£50 double.
Half board: £32-£34 daily,
£218-£232 weekly.
Evening meal 7.30pm (l.o.
7pm).
Parking for 14.
Open March-October,
December.
⛵ ⚱ ⚲ ⚲ ⓘ Ⅴ ⅏ Ⅳ Ⅲ
❊ ㍻ SP

---

*Please mention this
guide when making
a booking.*

ELLERBY

N. Yorkshire
Map ref 5C3

3m S. Staithes

Ellerby Hotel **M**
COMMENDED
Ellerby, Saltburn-by-the-Sea,
Cleveland TS13 5LP
☎ Whitby (0947) 840342
*Residential country inn within
the North Yorkshire Moors
National Park, 9 miles north of
Whitby, 1 mile inland from
Runswick Bay.*
Bedrooms: 8 double, 2 family
rooms.
Bathrooms: 9 private,
1 public.
Bed & breakfast: £20-£28
single, £30-£42 double.
Lunch available.
Evening meal 7pm (l.o.
10pm).
Parking for 60.
Credit: Access, Visa.

ELSLACK

N. Yorkshire
Map ref 4B1

4m W. Skipton

Tempest Arms Hotel & Restaurant **M**
COMMENDED
Elslack, Skipton, BD23 3AY
☎ Earby (0282) 842450 &
Fax (0282) 843331
*18th C stone-built inn on the
A56 between Earby and
Skipton. Surrounded by green
fields and edged with a stream,
giving character to this
traditional Yorkshire pub.*
Bedrooms: 6 double & 2 twin,
2 family rooms.
Bathrooms: 10 private.
Bed & breakfast: £39.50-£42
single, £47-£49 double.
Half board: £45-£55 daily.
Lunch available.
Evening meal 6.30pm (l.o.
9.30pm).
Parking for 80.
Credit: Access, Visa, Amex.

EPWORTH

Humberside
Map ref 4C1

9m N. Gainsborough

Hillcrest Hotel **M**
High St., Epworth,
Doncaster, S. Yorkshire
DN9 1EP
☎ (0427) 873094

*Comfortable private hotel in
the centre of Epworth offering
quality cooking and comfort.
Easy access to M180, M18,
M62. Non-smoking
establishment.*
Bedrooms: 2 double & 3 twin.
Bathrooms: 2 private,
1 public.
Bed & breakfast: from £23
single, from £38 double.
Half board: from £30 daily.
Lunch available.
Evening meal 6pm (l.o. 9pm).
Parking for 8.

FILEY

N. Yorkshire
Map ref 5D3

Resort with elegant
Regency buildings along
the front and 6 miles of
sandy beaches bounded
by natural breakwater,
Filey Brigg. Starting point
of the Cleveland Way.

Abbot's Leigh Guest House **M**
COMMENDED
7 Rutland St., Filey,
YO14 9JA
☎ Scarborough
(0723) 513334
*Family-run guesthouse
providing comfortable facilities
and generous portions of home-
cooked food, including
vegetarian. Close to town
centre and beach.*
Bedrooms: 2 double & 1 twin,
2 family rooms.
Bathrooms: 5 private.
Bed & breakfast: £18-£26
single, £30 double.
Half board: £22-£33 daily,
£139-£208 weekly.
Evening meal 5.30pm (l.o.
2pm).
Parking for 4.
Open January-November.
Credit: Access, Visa.

Sea Brink Hotel
COMMENDED
The Beach, Filey, YO14 9LA
☎ Scarborough
(0723) 513257
*Seafront hotel overlooking the
beach. Magnificent views,
delightful en-suite rooms,
licensed restaurant, satellite
TV, jacuzzi.*
Bedrooms: 1 single, 2 double
& 2 twin, 4 family rooms.
Bathrooms: 7 private,
1 public.
Bed & breakfast: £17.50-
£20.50 single, £35-£41 double.

Half board: £23.50-£26.50
daily, £163.50-£175.50 weekly.
Lunch available.
Evening meal 6pm.
Credit: Access, Visa, Diners,
Amex.

GARGRAVE

N. Yorkshire
Map ref 4B1

Unspoilt Dales village in
the Aire gap, where the
River Aire meanders by
the roadside. Interesting
church and the most
northerly section of the
Leeds and Liverpool
Canal.

Kirk Syke Hotel **M**
APPROVED
19 High St., Gargrave,
Skipton, BD23 3RA
☎ Skipton (0756) 749356
*Small family-run hotel in the
heart of the Yorkshire Dales.
Regret, no animals accepted.*
Bedrooms: 1 single, 5 double
& 5 twin, 1 family room.
Bathrooms: 9 private,
1 public.
Bed & breakfast: £25-£27
single, £40-£42 double.
Half board: £36-£38 daily.
Evening meal 7pm (l.o.
10am).
Parking for 12.
Open February-December.

GIGGLESWICK

N. Yorkshire
Map ref 5B3

Picturesque Pennine
village of period stone
cottages with ancient
market cross, stocks and
tithe barn. Parish church
is dedicated to St. Alkeda,
an Anglo-Saxon saint
martyred by the Danes
and has a lychgate,
market cross, Roman and
Bronze Age relics and a
ebbing and flowing well.
During restoration work
the tomb of a 15th C
knight with his horse was
discovered.

Black Horse Hotel **M**
Church St., Giggleswick,
Settle, BD24 0BJ
☎ Settle (0729) 822506
*Secluded, friendly hotel, within
easy reach of the Yorkshire
Dales and the Lake District.
Bar meals/dining room.*
Bedrooms: 2 double & 1 twin.

Bathrooms: 3 private.
Bed & breakfast: £25-£27
single, £40-£44 double.
Half board: £25.70-£29.45
daily, £126-£140 weekly.
Lunch available.
Evening meal 7pm (l.o. 9pm).
Parking for 20.
Credit: Access, Diners.

Mount View
Belle Hill, Giggleswick,
Settle, BD24 0BA
☎ Settle (0729) 82 2953
*Attractive accommodation in
the Yorkshire Dales. Both
rooms en-suite with TV and
tea/coffee making facilities.
Homely atmosphere.*
Bedrooms: 1 double & 1 twin.
Bathrooms: 2 private.
Bed & breakfast: from £14
single.
Parking for 3.

GILLING WEST

N. Yorkshire
Map ref 5C3

Hartforth Hall Hotel **M**
Hartforth Lane, Gilling
West, Richmond, DL10 5JU
☎ Richmond (0748) 825715
& 825781
*Tastefully refurbished mansion
in a magnificent setting at the
gateway to the dales, 3 miles
from Scotch Corner and one
mile south of the A66.
Convenient for Bowes Museum
and Richmond Theatre.*
Bedrooms: 2 single, 2 double
& 2 twin, 2 family rooms.
Bathrooms: 7 private.
Bed & breakfast: £35-£55
single, £55-£80 double.
Lunch available.
Evening meal 7pm (l.o. 9pm).
Parking for 50.

*Individual
proprietors have
supplied all details
of accommodation.
Although we do
check for accuracy,
we advise you to
confirm prices and
other information
at the time of
booking.*

GOATHLAND

N. Yorkshire
Map ref 5D3

Spacious village has several large greens grazed by sheep and is an ideal centre for walking North York Moors. Nearby are several waterfalls, among them Mallyan Spout. Plough Monday celebrations held in January.

Fairhaven Country Hotel M
≝≝≝
The Common, Goathland, Whitby, YO22 5AN
☎ Whitby (0947) 86361
Edwardian country house in the centre of Goathland village, superb moorland setting. Relaxed atmosphere with warm hospitality. Log fires.
Bedrooms: 1 single, 4 double & 2 twin, 2 family rooms.
Bathrooms: 4 private, 3 public.
Bed & breakfast: £16.50-£20.50 single, £33-£41 double.
Half board: £25.50-£29.50 daily, £170-£195 weekly.
Evening meal 7pm (l.o. 5pm).
Parking for 10.

Inn on the Moor M
≝≝≝ COMMENDED
Goathland, Whitby, YO22 5LZ
☎ Whitby (0947) 86410 & Fax (0947) 86296
Country house hotel overlooking the Yorkshire Moors. A warm welcome, pleasant service, English food, fresh air and peace. All rooms have colour TV, 5 with four-poster beds, a family suite with 2 singles and a double bedroom. Hairdressing salon.
Bedrooms: 12 double & 10 twin, 2 family rooms.
Bathrooms: 24 private, 2 public.
Bed & breakfast: £30-£50 single, £60-£80 double.
Half board: £35-£60 daily.
Lunch available.
Evening meal 7pm (l.o. 8.30pm).
Parking for 30.
Credit: Access, Visa, Amex.

Mallyan Spout Hotel M
≝≝≝≝ COMMENDED
Goathland, Whitby, YO22 5AN
☎ Whitby (0947) 86206
Comfortable hotel with old-fashioned comforts, welcoming log fires and good dining facilities. An ideal centre for walking the North York Moors.
Bedrooms: 2 single, 12 double & 8 twin, 3 family rooms.
Bathrooms: 24 private.
Bed & breakfast: £45-£55 single, £60-£110 double.
Half board: £47.50-£60 daily.
Lunch available.
Evening meal 7pm (l.o. 9pm).
Parking for 100.
Credit: Access, Visa, Diners, Amex.

Whitfield House Hotel M
≝≝≝ COMMENDED
Darnholm, Goathland, Whitby, YO22 5LA
☎ Whitby (0947) 86215
Former 17th C farmhouse in quiet backwater, friendly atmosphere. Residential licence. All rooms en-suite with radio, tea/coffee making facilities, hair-dryers.
Bedrooms: 2 single, 5 double & 1 twin, 1 family room.
Bathrooms: 8 private, 1 public.
Bed & breakfast: max. £20 single, max. £40 double.
Half board: max. £29.50 daily, max. £199.50 weekly.
Evening meal 7pm (l.o. 5.30pm).
Parking for 10.
Open February-November.

Half board prices shown are per person but in some cases may be based on double/twin occupancy.

Please check prices and other details at the time of booking.

GOOLE

Humberside
Map ref 4C1

This busy port on the River Ouse developed with the opening of the Aire and Calder Canal in 1826 and is reminiscent of the Netherlands with its red brick buildings and flat, watery landscape. Goole Museum houses Garside Local History Collection.
Tourist Information Centre ☎ (0405) 762187

Clifton Hotel
≝≝
1 Clifton Gardens, Boothferry Rd., Goole, N. Humberside DN14 6AR
☎ (0405) 761336
Fax (0405) 762350
Family-run, small, but comfortable, commercial hotel, convenient for Humberside, East Yorkshire and Lincolnshire.
Bedrooms: 6 single, 3 double & 1 twin.
Bathrooms: 8 private, 1 public; 1 private shower.
Bed & breakfast: £32-£36 single, £40-£44 double.
Half board: £40-£44 daily.
Lunch available.
Evening meal 7pm (l.o. 9pm).
Parking for 8.
Credit: Access, Visa, Diners, Amex.

GRASSINGTON

N. Yorkshire
Map ref 5B3

Tourists visit this former lead-mining village to see its 'smiddy', antique and craft shops and Upper Wharfedale Museum of Country Trades. Popular with fishermen and walkers. Numerous prehistoric sites. Grassington Feast in October. National Park Centre.

Ashfield House Hotel
Grassington, Skipton, BD23 5AE
☎ (0756) 752584
Quiet and secluded 17th C hotel near the village square. Open fires and creative home cooking using only fresh foods.
Bedrooms: 5 double & 2 twin.
Bathrooms: 5 private, 1 public.

Half board: £33-£37 daily, £209-£235 weekly.
Evening meal 7pm (l.o. 7pm).
Parking for 7.
Open February-November.

Grassington House Hotel M
≝≝ COMMENDED
5 The Square, Grassington, Skipton, BD23 5AQ
☎ (0756) 752406
Fax (0756) 752135
Grade II listed, 18th C family-run hotel in the Yorkshire Dales. Parties catered for. Open to non-residents.
Bedrooms: 2 single, 4 double & 2 twin, 2 family rooms.
Bathrooms: 10 private.
Bed & breakfast: from £28 single, £56-£76 double.
Half board: £40-£50 daily.
Lunch available.
Evening meal 7pm (l.o. 9.30pm).
Parking for 24.
Credit: Access, Visa.

Greenways Guest House M
≝≝ COMMENDED
Wharfeside Avenue, Threshfield, Skipton, BD23 5BS
☎ Skipton (0756) 752598
Overlooking a most spectacular reach of the River Wharfe. An excellent centre for touring the dales and within walking distance of Grassington.
Bedrooms: 1 single, 4 twin.
Bathrooms: 2 public.
Bed & breakfast: £19-£24 single, £38 double.
Half board: £30-£34 daily, £189-£214 weekly.
Evening meal 7.30pm (l.o. 7.30pm).
Parking for 8.
Open April-October.

New Laithe House
Wood Lane, Grassington, Skipton, BD23 5LU
☎ (0756) 752764
Large detached house, converted from a barn, on the edge of the village. Magnificent views of the River Wharfe.
Bedrooms: 3 double & 2 twin, 2 family rooms.
Bathrooms: 3 private, 1 public; 2 private showers.

The symbols are explained on the flap inside the back cover.

Bed & breakfast: £30-£36 double.
Parking for 8.
Open March-November.

🏠 ⚘ 🖵 ♿ 🅄🅻 🏚 V 🅸 ⚓
🍴 👥 ✕ 🎠 🅳🅰🅿 🆂🅿

Townhead Guest House ⋒
🦀🦀 COMMENDED

1 Low La., Grassington,
Skipton, BD23 5AU
☎ (0756) 752811
Small, modern guesthouse in the heart of beautiful countryside. Ideal centre for walking and touring the dales.
Bedrooms: 3 double & 1 twin,
1 family room.
Bathrooms: 3 private,
1 public.
Bed & breakfast: £28-£34 double.
Half board: £22-£25 daily.
Evening meal 6.30pm (l.o. 5pm).
Parking for 5.

🏠5⚘🖵♿ 🅸 V 🚗🅸🏚
✕ 👥

GREEN HAMMERTON
N. Yorkshire
Map ref 4C1

Bay Horse Inn ⋒
🦀 COMMENDED

York Rd., Green Hammerton,
York, YO5 8BN
☎ Boroughbridge
(0423) 330338 & 331113
Fax (0423) 331279
Village inn 10 miles from York and Harrogate on the A59 and 3 miles off the A1.
Bedrooms: 1 single, 3 double
& 5 twin, 1 family room.
Bathrooms: 10 private.
Bed & breakfast: £25-£35 single, £35-£50 double.
Lunch available.
Evening meal 7pm (l.o. 10pm).
Parking for 40.
Credit: Access, Visa, Diners.

🏠⚘📞📱🖵♿ 🅸 V 🅸
🅳🅰🅿 🆂🅿 🆃

Individual proprietors have supplied all details of accommodation. Although we do check for accuracy, we advise you to confirm prices and other information at the time of booking.

GRIMSBY
Humberside
Map ref 4D1

Founded 1000 years ago by a Danish fisherman named Grim, Grimsby is today a major fishing port and docks. It has modern shopping precincts and Welholme Galleries Fishing and Maritime Museum.
Tourist Information Centre ☎ (0472) 240410

County Hotel
Brighowgate, Grimsby,
S. Humberside DN32 0QU
☎ (0472) 354422
Completely modernised hotel with a large lounge bar and friendly atmosphere, next to the coach and railway stations.
Bedrooms: 3 single, 3 double
& 3 twin.
Bathrooms: 9 private.
Bed & breakfast: £26-£35 single, £37.50-£50 double.
Half board: £23-£41.50 daily.
Lunch available.
Evening meal 5.30pm (l.o. 10pm).
Parking for 12.
Credit: Access, Visa, Amex.

🏠📞🖵♿ 🅸 V 🚗🅸
🅸 ⚓ 🆂🅿

Millfields ⋒
🦀🦀🦀🦀 COMMENDED

53 Bargate, Grimsby,
S. Humberside DN34 5AD
☎ (0472) 356068
Fax (0472) 250286
Built in 1879, an exclusive residential hotel and leisure club, close to the centre of Grimsby and surrounded by its own grounds.
Bedrooms: 7 double & 7 twin.
Bathrooms: 14 private.
Bed & breakfast: £35-£50 single, £45-£65 double.
Lunch available.
Evening meal 6.30pm (l.o. 9pm).
Parking for 50.
Credit: Access, Visa, Diners, Amex. *

🏠⚘📞🖵♿ 🅸 V 🚗
🅸⚓🍴👥✕🆂🅿🅸🆃

Yarborough Hotel
🦀🦀🦀

Bethlehem St., Grimsby,
S. Humberside DN3 1LY
☎ (0472) 242266
Fax (0472) 242266
In the very heart of the town, offering well-appointed, en-suite bedrooms with every modern facility, an 80-seater a la carte restaurant, 2 large banqueting rooms, a public bar and a cocktail lounge.

Bedrooms: 18 single,
24 double & 5 twin, 3 family rooms.
Bathrooms: 50 private.
Bed & breakfast: £40-£57.50 single, £50-£67.50 double.
Half board: £52-£69.50 daily.
Lunch available.
Evening meal 7pm (l.o. 9.30pm).
Parking for 12.
Credit: Access, Visa, Diners, Amex.

🏠📞🖵♿ 🅸 V 🚙 ⚫
🅸 🅸 ⚓ 🍴 🆂🅿 🅸 🆃

HALIFAX
W. Yorkshire
Map ref 4B1

Founded on the cloth trade, and famous for its building society, textiles, carpets and toffee. Most notable landmark is Piece Hall where wool merchants traded, now restored to house shops, museums and art gallery.
Tourist Information Centre ☎ (0422) 386725

Collyers Hotel
🦀🦀🦀 COMMENDED

Burnley Rd., Luddenden Foot, Halifax, HX2 6AH
☎ Halifax (0422) 882624
Small personal hotel, with elegant restaurant, lounge bar and individually styled bedrooms, overlooking Calder valley and the Rochdale Canal and just a few minutes from Halifax.
Bedrooms: 2 single, 2 double
& 2 twin.
Bathrooms: 4 private,
1 public.
Bed & breakfast: £20-£36.50 single, £45-£52.50 double.
Half board: from £30 daily.
Lunch available.
Evening meal 7pm (l.o. 9pm).
Parking for 15.
Credit: Access, Visa, Diners.

🏠📞🖵♿ 🅸 V 🚗
⚓🍴👤✳🎠🅳🅰🅿🆂🅿

Cottage Hotels
Listed APPROVED

15 Well St., Holywell Green,
Halifax, HX4 9BB
☎ (0422) 371476 & Bookings (0831) 206606
Fax (0422) 377374
Character stone cottages, in the heart of a rural Yorkshire village, let as hotel rooms or suites.
Bedrooms: 6 double, 4 family rooms.
Bathrooms: 5 private,
4 public.
Bed & breakfast: from £40 single, £45-£75 double.

Half board: £50-£90 daily.
Lunch available.
Evening meal 7.45pm (l.o. 7.45pm).
Parking for 12.
Credit: Access, Visa.

🏠🐾📞🖵♿ 🅄🅻 V 🥢
🚗🆃🆅⚫⚓🍴🔱🅸
🐾🅸

Holdsworth House ⋒
🦀🦀🦀🦀 COMMENDED

Holdsworth, Holmfield,
Halifax, HX2 9TG
☎ (0422) 240024
Telex 51574. Fax (0422) 245174
Converted country house, renovated and stylishly restored. Dining room is 350 years old. Emphasis on service and carefully prepared food. Civic Trust award for bedroom extension (1985).
Bedrooms: 20 single,
18 double & 2 twin.
Bathrooms: 40 private.
Bed & breakfast: £70-£75 single, £88-£100 double.
Lunch available.
Evening meal 7pm (l.o. 10pm).
Parking for 61.
Credit: Access, Visa, C.Bl., Diners, Amex.

🏠⚘📞📞🖵♿ 🅸 V 🥢
🚗🆃🆅⚫⚓🍴♿🎈❄
🆂🅿🅸🆃

Tower House Hotel ⋒
Master La.,(off Upper Washer La.,) Pye Nest,
Halifax, HX2 7DX
☎ (0422) 362481
Fax (0422) 320875
Family-run hotel. All bedrooms en-suite, colour TV and tea making facilities. Good restaurant and bar snacks. Ample, safe parking.
Bedrooms: 6 single, 5 double
& 2 twin, 3 family rooms.
Bathrooms: 16 private.
Bed & breakfast: £29.50-£42.75 single, £39.50-£51 double.
Half board: £43.50-£56.75 daily, £250-£330 weekly.
Lunch available.
Evening meal 7pm (l.o. 10pm).
Parking for 60.
Credit: Access, Visa.

🏠⚘📞🖵♿ 🅸 V 🚗
🆆🅸⚓🍴♿✕🐾🆂🅿🅸

Victoria Hotel ⋒
Listed APPROVED

31-35 Horton St., Halifax,
HX1 1QE
☎ (0422) 351209 & 358392

Continued ▶

HALIFAX

Continued

Close to tourist attractions, town centre, rail and motorway links. Most bedrooms en-suite. Restaurant and bars. Weekend entertainment with music and dancing.
Bedrooms: 4 single, 6 double & 7 twin, 6 family rooms.
Bathrooms: 12 private, 3 public; 11 private showers.
Bed & breakfast: £17-£35 single, £34-£50 double.
Half board: £24.50-£42.50 daily, £171.50-£297.50 weekly.
Lunch available.
Evening meal 5pm (l.o. 8pm).
Credit: Access, Visa, Amex.

White Swan Hotel M
✿✿✿✿ APPROVED
Princess St., Halifax, HX1 1TS
☎ (0422) 355541
Telex 518126
Listed building in the heart of Halifax.
Bedrooms: 26 single, 14 double & 12 twin, 5 family rooms.
Bathrooms: 57 private.
Bed & breakfast: from £60 single, from £70 double.
Half board: from £72 daily.
Lunch available.
Evening meal 6.30pm (l.o. 10pm).
Credit: Access, Visa, Diners, Amex.

HARROGATE

N. Yorkshire
Map ref 4B1

A major conference, exhibition and shopping centre, renowned for its spa heritage and award winning floral displays. Beautiful Victorian architecture complemented by spacious parks and gardens. Famous for antiques, toffee, fine shopping and excellent tea shops, also its Royal Pump Rooms and Baths. Nearby is Ripley Castle.
Tourist Information Centre ☎ (0423) 525666

Abbey Lodge M
✿✿✿ APPROVED
19-21 Ripon Rd., Harrogate, HG1 2JL
☎ (0423) 569712

Beautifully restored and ideally situated for the dales and moors, offering a combination of well-appointed accommodation and a relaxed atmosphere.
Bedrooms: 4 single, 8 double & 5 twin, 2 family rooms.
Bathrooms: 14 private, 2 public.
Bed & breakfast: £20.50-£23.50 single, £39-£45 double.
Half board: £30.45-£33.45 daily, £206.15-£234 weekly.
Evening meal 7pm (l.o. 8.30pm).
Parking for 18.
Credit: Access, Visa.

Acacia Lodge
21 Ripon Rd., Harrogate, HG1 2JL
☎ (0423) 560752
Beautifully appointed and furnished Victorian house with en-suite rooms. Select area of town centre. Pretty gardens. Good private parking.
Bedrooms: 1 single, 1 double & 2 twin, 1 family room.
Bathrooms: 5 private, 1 public.
Bed & breakfast: max. £25 single, max. £42 double.
Parking for 6.

Alamah M
✿✿✿ COMMENDED
88 Kings Rd., Harrogate, HG1 5JX
☎ (0423) 502187
Good base for touring the Yorkshire Dales. Close to the Valley Gardens, swimming pool, theatre and shops. 100 metres from the conference centre. Garages/parking.
Bedrooms: 2 single, 2 double & 2 twin, 1 family room.
Bathrooms: 3 private, 1 public; 3 private showers.
Bed & breakfast: £17-£20 single, £32-£40 double.
Half board: £27-£30 daily.
Evening meal 6.30pm (l.o. 4.30pm).
Parking for 8.

Alexa House Hotel and Stable Cottages M
✿✿
26 Ripon Rd., Harrogate, HG1 2JJ
☎ (0423) 501988
Small hotel, built for Baron de Ferrier in 1830. Maintains the old and gracious traditions of personal service and true Yorkshire hospitality.

Bedrooms: 3 single, 3 double & 6 twin, 1 family room.
Bathrooms: 11 private, 1 public; 1 private shower.
Bed & breakfast: £21-£25 single, £42-£50 double.
Parking for 9.
Credit: Access, Visa.

Alexander
✿✿
88 Franklin Rd., Harrogate, HG1 5EN
☎ (0423) 503348
Friendly family-run elegant Victorian guesthouse with en-suite facilities. Ideal for conference centre and Harrogate town. Good touring centre for dales.
Bedrooms: 1 single, 1 twin, 2 family rooms.
Bathrooms: 1 private, 2 public.
Bed & breakfast: £14 single, £28-£36 double.
Parking for 2.

Arden House Hotel M
✿✿ COMMENDED
69-71 Franklin Rd., Harrogate, HG1 5EH
☎ (0423) 509224
Family-run hotel with a warm, friendly atmosphere and real home cooking. Close to the town centre. Trouser press and hair-dryer in all rooms.
Bedrooms: 4 single, 5 double & 4 twin, 1 family room.
Bathrooms: 14 private.
Bed & breakfast: £19.50-£22 single, £39-£44 double.
Half board: £30.50-£33 daily, from £186 weekly.
Evening meal 7pm (l.o. 8pm).
Parking for 10.
Credit: Access, Visa.

Ascot House Hotel M
✿✿
53 Kings Rd., Harrogate, HG1 5HJ
☎ (0423) 531005
Fax (0423) 503523
Ⓜ Minotels
Delightful, family-run hotel near town and conference centres. Impressive Victorian decorative features, well-equipped bedrooms. Ring for colour brochure.
Bedrooms: 13 single, 4 double & 6 twin, 1 family room.
Bathrooms: 15 private; 9 private showers.
Bed & breakfast: £39.50-£54.50 single, £61.50-£84 double.

Half board: £38.25-£42.50 daily.
Evening meal 7pm (l.o. 9pm).
Parking for 14.
Credit: Access, Visa, Diners, Amex.

Ashley House Hotel M
✿✿ COMMENDED
36-40 Franklin Rd., Harrogate, HG1 5EE
☎ (0423) 507474 & 560858
Alan and Carole welcome you to their beautifully decorated home. An elegant residence in a quiet tree-lined road minutes from town centre, conference centre and Valley Gardens.
Bedrooms: 5 single, 6 double & 4 twin, 2 family rooms.
Bathrooms: 11 private, 3 public.
Bed & breakfast: £21.50-£30 single, £46-£56 double.
Half board: from £35 daily.
Evening meal 6.15pm (l.o. 6.30pm).
Parking for 7.
Credit: Access, Visa.

Ashwood House
✿✿ COMMENDED
7 Spring Grove, Harrogate, HG1 2HS
☎ (0423) 560081
Edwardian, double-fronted guesthouse in a quiet cul-de-sac. 5 minutes from the town centre and local amenities. Four-poster bedroom available.
Bedrooms: 2 single, 3 double & 3 twin, 2 family rooms.
Bathrooms: 8 private, 1 public.
Bed & breakfast: £20-£27 single, £40-£46 double.
Parking for 5.

Balmoral Hotel & Restaurant M
✿✿✿✿ COMMENDED
16-18 Franklin Mount, Harrogate, HG1 5EJ
☎ (0423) 508208
Fax (0423) 530652
Well-appointed, pleasant hotel with tastefully furnished rooms and a tranquil ambience. Eight four-poster rooms. Traditional English menu. Solarium. Special weekend rates.
Bedrooms: 4 single, 8 double & 5 twin, 3 family rooms.
Bathrooms: 20 private, 2 public.
Bed & breakfast: £64.50-£70 single, £87-£90 double.

Evening meal 7pm (l.o. 9.30pm).
Parking for 10.
Credit: Access, Visa, Amex.

🛇 ♨ ⌨ 🕻 ◉ ⌷ 🗘 🛈 Ⓥ
🛏 🏳 🅰 🍴 ☎ OAP SP T

The Belfry
Listed

27 Belmont Rd., Harrogate, HG2 0LR
☎ (0423) 522783
Friendly, family guesthouse within easy walking distance of the town centre and all tourist amenities. A wide choice of cooked breakfast is offered.
Bedrooms: 2 single, 1 double & 1 twin.
Bathrooms: 1 public.
Bed & breakfast: from £14 single, from £28 double.

🛇 🖵 🗘 UL Ⓥ 🖩 🛏 🏳

Berronton Hotel
♨ ♨

30 Ripon Rd., Harrogate, HG1 2JJ
☎ (0423) 569582
Detached, Victorian house on the A61, a short walk to the town and conference centre. Close to 4 golf-courses and other leisure amenities.
Bedrooms: 4 single, 1 double & 6 twin, 2 family rooms.
Bathrooms: 3 private, 3 public.
Bed & breakfast: £17.50-£18.50 single, £30-£38 double.
Parking for 8.

🛇 ♨ 🗘 Ⓥ 🖵 TV 🖩 📠
🏳

Brandsby Guest House
♨ ♨

10 Studley Rd., Harrogate, HG1 5JU
☎ (0423) 501592
Tastefully furnished Victorian terraced house with modern facilities, close to the town centre. Personal service from the owner.
Bedrooms: 1 double & 1 twin.
Bathrooms: 2 public.
Bed & breakfast: £15 single, £30 double.
Half board: £20-£23 daily.

🛇 ◉ 🖵 🗘 UL Ⓥ 🖵 TV 🖩
📠 🏳

Caesars Hotel M
♨ ♨ ♨ COMMENDED

51 Valley Drive, Harrogate, HG2 0JH
☎ (0423) 565818

Map references apply to the colour maps towards the end of this guide.

Victorian family home overlooks delightful Valley Gardens. Comfortable base for touring Yorkshire Dales and Bronte country. Local produce a regular feature of the popular restaurant. Families with young children especially welcome.
Bedrooms: 2 single, 1 double & 3 twin, 3 family rooms.
Bathrooms: 9 private.
Bed & breakfast: £42.50-£50 single, £60-£65 double.
Half board: £40-£44.50 daily.
Evening meal 7.30pm (l.o. 8.30pm).
Credit: Access, Visa.

🛇 🕻 🗘 🖵 Ⓥ 🖵 TV 🖩 📠
🍴 🐾 🛏 SP

Daryl House Hotel M
📠

42 Dragon Parade, Harrogate, HG1 5DA
☎ (0423) 502775
Small hotel offering a wide range of amenities and personal, friendly service from the proprietor. Close to the town centre, stations and exhibition hall. Evening meal by arrangement only.
Bedrooms: 2 single, 2 twin, 2 family rooms.
Bathrooms: 2 public.
Bed & breakfast: £13-£14 single, £26-£28 double.
Half board: £20-£21 daily, £130-£140 weekly.

🛇 🖵 🗘 UL Ⓥ 🖵 📠
🍴

Eton House
♨ ♨

3 Eton Terrace, Knaresborough Rd., Harrogate, HG2 7SU
☎ (0423) 886850
Homely guesthouse with spacious, comfortable rooms. On the main A59, on the edge of parkland close to the town.
Bedrooms: 1 single, 1 twin, 5 family rooms.
Bathrooms: 2 private, 2 public.
Bed & breakfast: £15-£18 single, £30-£36 double.
Parking for 10.

🛇 🗘 UL 🖵 TV 🖩

Franklin Lodge M
Listed

6 Franklin Rd., Harrogate, HG1 5EE
☎ (0423) 563599
Within 150 yards of the Harrogate International Centre and town centre. We offer standards of service and facilities usually associated with larger establishments.
Bedrooms: 3 single, 2 twin, 2 family rooms.

Bathrooms: 2 private, 1 public; 3 private showers.
Bed & breakfast: £12.50-£14.50 single, £25-£29 double.
Half board: £20.50-£22.50 daily, £140-£150 weekly.
Evening meal 6pm (l.o. 7.30pm).

🛇 🛈 🖵 🗘 TV 🖩 📠 🍴 🐾
🛏 OAP SP T

Garden House Hotel M
♨ ♨ ♨ COMMENDED

14 Harlow Moor Drive, Harrogate, HG2 0JX
☎ (0423) 503059
Small, family-run, Victorian hotel overlooking Valley Gardens, in a quiet location with unrestricted parking. Home cooking using fresh produce only.
Bedrooms: 3 single, 1 double & 3 twin.
Bathrooms: 5 private; 2 private showers.
Bed & breakfast: £21-£23 single, £40-£44 double.
Half board: £29.50-£32.50 daily, £206.50-£227.50 weekly.
Evening meal 7pm (l.o. midday).

🛇 ◉ 🖵 🗘 🛈 Ⓥ 🖵 🖩 📠
🛏 SP

Gibsons M

103-105 Valley Drive, Harrogate, HG2 0JP
☎ (0423) 522246
Fax (0423) 505522
Well-appointed hotel overlooking the Valley Gardens. Close to the town, conference and exhibition centre. 2 minutes to professional golf-course.
Bedrooms: 8 single, 5 double & 7 twin, 1 family room.
Bathrooms: 21 private.
Bed & breakfast: max. £32 single, max. £59 double.
Evening meal 7pm (l.o. 10pm).
Parking for 10.
Credit: Access, Visa, Diners, Amex.

🛇 🕻 🖵 🗘 🛈 Ⓥ 🖵
TV ◉ 🖩 📠 🍴 ▶ SP

Glenayr Hotel M
♨ ♨

19 Franklin Mount, Harrogate, HG1 5EJ
☎ (0423) 504259
Quietly situated, spacious Victorian house within 5 minutes' walk of all amenities. Home cooking and a comfortable, relaxing atmosphere.
Bedrooms: 2 single, 1 double & 3 twin.
Bathrooms: 4 private, 1 public.
Bed & breakfast: £16.50-£17.50 single, £40-£44 double.

Half board: £26.50-£32 daily, £175-£210 weekly.
Evening meal 6.30pm (l.o. 4pm).
Parking for 4.
Credit: Access, Visa, Amex.

🛇 ◉ 🖵 🗘 🛈 Ⓥ 🖵 🖩 📠
🛏 🏳 OAP 🐾 SP

Granby Hotel M
♨ ♨ ♨

Granby Rd., Harrogate, HG1 4SR
☎ (0423) 506151
Fax (0423) 531002 Telex 57423
Overlooking 200 acres of beautiful parkland known as the Harrogate Stray and a few minutes from the town centre. 2 restaurants: the informal "Garden Gate" and the elegant a la carte "Lillies".
Bedrooms: 20 single, 10 double & 63 twin.
Bathrooms: 93 private.
Bed & breakfast: max. £30 single, max. £60 double.
Half board: max. £40 daily.
Lunch available.
Evening meal 6.30pm (l.o. 9.30pm).
Parking for 300.
Credit: Access, Visa, Diners, Amex.

🛇 ♨ 🕻 ◉ 🖵 🗘 🛈 Ⓥ ⌇
🖵 ◉ 🖩 📠 🍴 ▶ 🌸 OAP
🐾 SP 🏳 T

Harrogate Brasserie with Rooms M

28-30 Cheltenham Parade, Harrogate, HG1 1DB
☎ (0423) 505041
Fax (0423) 530920
Comfortable, well-appointed, fully licensed brasserie and all day bar. Every room has been individually designed to reflect different periods between 1750-1990.
Bedrooms: 3 single, 6 double & 2 twin, 2 family rooms.
Bathrooms: 13 private.
Bed & breakfast: £35-£55 single, £55-£70 double.
Half board: £45-£90 daily.
Lunch available.
Evening meal 6.30pm (l.o. 11pm).
Parking for 10.
Credit: Access, Visa.

🛇 4 🕻 ◉ 🖵 🗘 🛈 Ⓥ ⌇ 🖵
TV 🖩 📠 🍴 🛏 🏳 SP

Imperial Hotel M

Prospect Place, Harrogate, HG1 1LA
☎ (0423) 565071 Telex 57606 PRS HTLIG
Ⓒ Principal
Situated at the heart of this famous spa town and offering a high standard of service. Enjoy a game of snooker in the Chesterfield Room.

Continued ▶

HARROGATE

Continued

Bedrooms: 12 single,
18 double & 55 twin.
Bathrooms: 85 private.
Bed & breakfast: from £78
single, from £99.50 double.
Half board: from £53 daily.
Lunch available.
Evening meal 7.30pm (l.o.
9.30pm).
Parking for 60.
Credit: Access, Visa, Diners,
Amex.

Lamont House ⋔
COMMENDED
12 St. Mary's Walk,
Harrogate, HG2 0LW
☎ (0423) 567143
*Built at the turn of this century
in a peaceful location, yet close
to Valley Gardens, shops and
conference centre.*
Bedrooms: 2 single, 3 double
& 1 twin, 3 family rooms.
Bathrooms: 2 private,
2 public.
Bed & breakfast: £18-£30
single, £30-£50 double.

Langham Hotel ⋔
21-27 Valley Drive,
Harrogate, HG2 0JL
☎ (0423) 502179
*Beautiful, family-owned hotel
in the heart of Harrogate
overlooking Valley Gardens.
Fine restaurant.*
Bedrooms: 16 single,
19 double & 13 twin, 2 family
rooms.
Bathrooms: 50 private.
Bed & breakfast: £41.50-
£57.75 single, £68.25-£78.25
double.
Half board: £41.50-£47.25
daily, £261-£297.50 weekly.
Lunch available.
Evening meal 7pm (l.o.
10pm).
Credit: Access, Visa, Diners,
Amex.

Lynton House ⋔
APPROVED
42 Studley Rd., Harrogate,
HG1 5JU
☎ (0423) 504715
*In a central, quiet tree-lined
avenue, 100 yards from the
exhibition halls and swimming
pool, and close to the Valley
Gardens. Personal supervision.
Own keys. Non-smokers only
please.*
Bedrooms: 2 single, 2 double
& 1 twin.

Bathrooms: 1 public.
Bed & breakfast: £14.50-
£16.50 single, £29-£30 double.

Lynwood Guest House ⋔
5 East Park Rd., Harrogate,
HG1 5QT
☎ (0423) 566101
*In a quiet urban position,
within easy walking distance of
the town centre and conference
centre.*
Bedrooms: 5 single.
Bathrooms: 2 public.
Bed & breakfast: £14-£16
single, from £25 double.
Parking for 4.

Manor Hotel ⋔
COMMENDED
3 Clarence Drive, Harrogate,
HG1 2QE
☎ (0423) 503916
*Recently modernised hotel, in a
secluded part of Harrogate
close to the famous Valley
Gardens and conference/
exhibition centre.*
Bedrooms: 4 single, 6 double
& 6 twin, 1 family room.
Bathrooms: 17 private.
Bed & breakfast: £42-£52
single, £62-£78 double.
Half board: £58-£70 daily.
Lunch available.
Evening meal 6.30pm (l.o.
9pm).
Parking for 12.
Credit: Access, Visa.

Norman Hotel ⋔
41 Valley Drive, Harrogate,
HG2 0JH
☎ (0423) 502171
*Small hotel overlooking the
Valley Gardens, specialising in
quality food and a friendly,
relaxed atmosphere.*
Bedrooms: 6 single, 2 double
& 3 twin, 2 family rooms.
Bathrooms: 6 private,
3 public.
Bed & breakfast: £22-£24
single, £38-£50 double.
Half board: £26.50-£32.50
daily.
Evening meal 6pm (l.o.
7.30pm).
Credit: Access, Visa.

Number Twenty Six ⋔
COMMENDED
26 Harlow Moor Drive,
Harrogate, HG2 0JY
☎ (0423) 524729

*Victorian house of elegant
proportions with original
fireplaces and architectural
features. Overlooking Valley
Gardens and close to town
centre. Non-smoking
establishment. 2 rooms are en-
suite with steam showers and
the third has a private
bathroom.*
Bedrooms: 3 double.
Bathrooms: 3 private.
Bed & breakfast: £35-£45
double.
Half board: £27-£45 daily,
£160-£300 weekly.
Evening meal 7pm (l.o. 4pm).
Parking for 3.

Roan
90 Kings Rd., Harrogate,
HG1 5JX
☎ (0423) 503087
*In a central position, 3 minutes
from the conference centre and
near Valley Gardens, town, bus
and rail stations. Ideal for
touring the dales. Home
cooking.*
Bedrooms: 3 single, 2 double
& 1 twin, 1 family room.
Bathrooms: 3 private,
1 public.
Bed & breakfast: from £17
single, from £32 double.
Half board: from £25 daily.
Evening meal 6.15pm (l.o.
4.30pm).

The Rosedale ⋔
COMMENDED
86 Kings Rd., Harrogate,
HG1 5JX
☎ (0423) 566630 & 524129
*Well-appointed hotel with a
private car park. All bedrooms
have colour TV and hair-dryer,
tea/coffee and en-suite
facilities.*
Bedrooms: 3 single, 1 double
& 3 twin, 1 family room.
Bathrooms: 7 private;
1 private shower.
Bed & breakfast: £24-£28.50
single, £42-£50 double.
Half board: £37-£41.50 daily.
Evening meal 6.30pm (l.o.
midday).
Parking for 8.
Credit: Access, Visa.

Russell Hotel ⋔
COMMENDED
Valley Drive, Harrogate,
HG2 0JN
☎ (0423) 509866

*Overlooking Valley Gardens.
Elegant restaurant in which to
enjoy cuisine of high standard,
well-equipped bedrooms.
Special 2-day rates available.*
Bedrooms: 7 single, 7 double
& 20 twin.
Bathrooms: 34 private.
Bed & breakfast: from £49.50
single, £64.95-£75 double.
Half board: from £65.45
daily.
Lunch available.
Evening meal 7pm (l.o.
10pm).
Credit: Access, Visa, C.Bl.,
Diners, Amex.

Hotel St. George Swallow ⋔
Ripon Rd., Harrogate,
HG1 2SY
☎ (0423) 561431
Fax (0423) 530037
Telex 57995
ⒸⒷ Swallow
*Traditional hotel, tastefully
restored with leisure complex,
pool, sauna, solarium, spa bath
and exercise gym. Close to the
Valley Gardens and other
historic attractions.*
Bedrooms: 25 single,
21 double & 32 twin, 15 family
rooms.
Bathrooms: 93 private.
Bed & breakfast: from £80
single, from £99 double.
Lunch available.
Evening meal 7pm (l.o.
9.30pm).
Parking for 50.
Credit: Access, Visa, Diners,
Amex.

Shannon Court Hotel ⋔
COMMENDED
65 Dragon Avenue,
Harrogate, HG1 5DS
☎ (0423) 509858
*Charming Victorian house
retaining many original
features, offering modern
facilities and a warm friendly
atmosphere.*
Bedrooms: 2 single, 3 double
& 1 twin, 2 family rooms.
Bathrooms: 8 private.
Bed & breakfast: £19.50-£25
single, £37-£50 double.
Half board: £30.50-£36 daily,
from £179 weekly.
Evening meal 7pm (l.o.
midday).
Parking for 3.

Stoney Lea Guest House M

COMMENDED

13 Spring Grove, Harrogate, HG1 2HS
☎ (0423) 501524
Small guesthouse in a quiet cul-de-sac. Centrally located within walking distance of all the town's tourist and business facilities.
Bedrooms: 2 single, 2 double & 3 twin.
Bathrooms: 7 private.
Bed & breakfast: £22-£25 single, £38 double.
Parking for 3.
🖬5 ⑩ 🖵 ♥ Ⓤ 🚪 ⓉⓋ ▥ ♨ ✕ 🚗

Studley Hotel M

COMMENDED

Swan Rd., Harrogate, HG1 2SE
☎ (0423) 560425 Telex 57506
Small hotel with an intimate French restaurant and genuine charcoal grill. Near the Valley Gardens and within easy reach of the shopping centre. All bedrooms have trouser press, hair-dryer, colour TV, Sky satellite TV and tea-making facilities.
Bedrooms: 16 single, 10 double & 10 twin.
Bathrooms: 36 private.
Bed & breakfast: £65-£80 single, £80-£90 double.
Lunch available.
Evening meal 7.30pm (l.o. 10pm).
Parking for 14.
Credit: Access, Visa, Diners, Amex.
🖬8 ✆ ⑩ 🖵 ♥ ⓘ Ⓥ 🚪 ⓉⓋ
◉ ▥ 🍴 ♨ & 𝐒𝐏
❺ Display advertisement appears on page 204.

Valley Hotel M

APPROVED

93-95 Valley Drive, Harrogate, HG2 0JP
☎ (0423) 504868
Fax (0423) 531940
Hotel overlooking the Valley Gardens, offering a warm welcome to both tourists and business people. Licensed restaurant.
Bedrooms: 2 double & 5 twin, 6 family rooms.
Bathrooms: 13 private.
Bed & breakfast: £35-£45 single, £46-£56 double.
Half board: £33-£38 daily.
Lunch available.
Evening meal 6pm (l.o. 9.30pm).
Parking for 4.
Credit: Access, Visa.
🖬 ✆ ⑩ 🖵 ♥ ⓘ Ⓥ 🚪 ⓉⓋ
▤ ▥ ◢ 🍴 𝐒𝐏

Welford Hotel M

27 Franklin Rd., Harrogate, HG1 5ED
☎ (0423) 566041
Small, private hotel run entirely by the owners. Emphasis on food and comfortable accommodation. Close to the town centre and conference halls.
Bedrooms: 3 single, 1 double & 2 twin.
Bathrooms: 4 private, 1 public.
Bed & breakfast: £16-£19.50 single, £36 double.
Half board: £24.50-£28 daily, £171.50-£196 weekly.
Evening meal 7pm (l.o. 4pm).
Parking for 2.
🖬 ⑩ 🖵 ♥ Ⓤ ⓘ Ⓥ ▥
▢ ♨ Ⓣ

West Park Hotel

19 West Park, Harrogate, HG1 1BL
☎ (0423) 524471
Town centre, family-run hotel with a la carte restaurant, two bars. Conference facilities. Friendly and professional atmosphere.
Bedrooms: 2 single, 3 double & 10 twin, 2 family rooms.
Bathrooms: 16 private, 2 public.
Bed & breakfast: £35-£45 single, £50-£60 double.
Half board: £45-£55 daily, £300-£375 weekly.
Lunch available.
Evening meal 6pm (l.o. 10.30pm).
Parking for 10.
Credit: Access, Visa.
🖬 ✆ ⑩ 🖵 ♥ ⓘ Ⓥ 🚪 ⓉⓋ
▥ ▢ 🍴 𝐒𝐏

Youngs Hotel M

APPROVED

15 York Rd., (Off Swan Rd.), Harrogate, HG1 2QL
☎ (0423) 567336 & 521231
Family-run hotel with large attractive gardens in a quiet residential area, within walking distance of the town.
Bedrooms: 5 single, 5 double & 4 twin, 2 family rooms.
Bathrooms: 16 private, 1 public.
Bed & breakfast: from £35 single, from £56 double.
Half board: from £40 daily, from £220 weekly.
Evening meal 7pm (l.o. 7pm).
Parking for 19.
Credit: Access, Visa.
🖬 ✆ ⑩ 🖵 ♥ ⓘ 🚪
▥ ▢ 🍴 ❀ ⒹⒶⒻ 𝐒𝐏

N. Yorkshire
Map ref 5B3

The capital of Upper Wensleydale on the famous Pennine Way, renowned for great cheeses. Popular with walkers. Dales National Park Information Centre and Folk Museum. Nearby is spectacular Hardraw Force Waterfall. *Tourist Information Centre ☎ (0969) 667450*

Brandymires Guest House

COMMENDED

Muker Rd., Hawes, DL8 3PR
☎ Wensleydale (0969) 667482
Comfortable, 3-storey stone house in a tranquil setting, offering magnificent views of Wensleydale. Home cooking. Non-smokers only please.
Bedrooms: 3 double & 1 twin.
Bathrooms: 2 public.
Bed & breakfast: £23.50 single, £31 double.
Half board: from £25 daily.
Evening meal 7pm (l.o. 7pm).
Parking for 6.
Open April-October.
▤ ⓘ ✕ ▥ ♨

Cocketts Hotel M

COMMENDED

Market Place, Hawes, DL8 3RD
☎ (0969) 667312
17th C stone-built hotel in the market place. Ideally situated for touring the dales. English and French cuisine.
Bedrooms: 6 double & 2 twin.
Bathrooms: 6 private, 1 public.
Bed & breakfast: £26-£30 single, £40-£60 double.
Half board: £34.50-£46 daily.
Lunch available.
Evening meal 7.30pm (l.o. 9.30pm).
Credit: Access, Visa.
🖬8 ♨ 🍴 ✆ ⑩ 🖵 ♥ Ⓥ
✕ 🚪 ▥ ▢ ⓤ ✕ ♨ ⓉⓋ 𝐒𝐏
♨

Crosby Guest House M

Burtersett Rd., Hawes, DL8 3NP
☎ Wensleydale (0969) 667322
Small guesthouse with spacious rooms and parking at the rear. For quiet relaxation and exploring the dales.
Bedrooms: 1 double & 1 twin, 1 family room.

Bathrooms: 1 private, 2 public.
Bed & breakfast: £13-£16 single, £24-£32 double.
Parking for 3.
Open April-October.
🖬 ⑩ 🖵 Ⓤ ⓘ Ⓥ 🚪 ⓉⓋ
▥ ♨

Ebor Guest House M

Burtersett Rd., Hawes, DL8 3NT
☎ Wensleydale (0969) 667337
Small, family-run guesthouse, double-glazed and centrally-heated throughout. Walkers are particularly welcome. Clothes washing and drying facilities available.
Bedrooms: 1 single, 2 double & 1 twin.
Bathrooms: 1 private, 1 public.
Bed & breakfast: £13-£15 single, £30-£32 double.
Parking for 5.
🖬 ⑩ 🖵 Ⓤ ⓘ 🚪 ⓉⓋ ▥ ♨
♨ ⒹⒶⒻ

Rookhurst Georgian Country Hotel M

West End, Gayle, Hawes, DL8 3RT
☎ Wensleydale (0969) 667454
Personal service and a varied menu with home-made specialities using fresh food. Peace and quiet in unique period surroundings. Antique furnishings and bridal suite.
Bedrooms: 4 double & 1 twin.
Bathrooms: 5 private.
Bed & breakfast: £25-£40 single, £60-£80 double.
Half board: £42-£56 daily.
Evening meal 7.30pm (l.o. 6.30pm).
Parking for 10.
Open February-December.
Credit: Access, Visa.
▤ ⑩ 🖵 ♥ ⓘ Ⓥ ✕ 🚪 ▥
▢ 🍴 ❀ ✕ ♨ 𝐒𝐏 🈁

Simonstone Hall M

COMMENDED

Hawes, DL8 3LY
☎ Wensleydale (0969) 667255
Fax (0969) 667741
Family-run 18th C country house hotel in a glorious Wensleydale setting with panoramic views. Tawny Owl bar and extensive cellar. Dogs welcome. Special breaks available.
Bedrooms: 7 double & 3 twin.
Bathrooms: 10 private.
Bed & breakfast: £98-£122 double.
Half board: £60-£72 daily, £378-£455 weekly.

Continued ▶

HAWES

Continued

Lunch available.
Evening meal 7pm (l.o. 8.30pm).
Parking for 22.
Credit: Access, Visa.
ॐ ⊞ ▢ ♥ 🛗 Ⓥ 🖾 ◑ ▥
🖾 🍴 ✻ 🖾 🆊 SP 🏠 Ⓣ

Stone House Hotel ⋀
😊😊😊 COMMENDED
Sedbusk, Hawes, DL8 3PT
☎ Wensleydale
(0969) 667571
Fine old country house hotel in a beautiful old English garden with panoramic views of Upper Wensleydale.
Bedrooms: 2 single, 8 double & 3 twin, 2 family rooms.
Bathrooms: 14 private, 1 public.
Bed & breakfast: £27-£39 single, £43-£65 double.
Half board: £35.45-£46.45 daily.
Evening meal 7pm (l.o. 8pm).
Parking for 15.
Credit: Access, Visa.
ॐ 🚵 ⊞ 📞 ▢ ♥ 🛗 Ⓥ 🖾
▥ 🍴 🍷 ❍ ♨ ✻ 🆊 SP
🏠 Ⓣ

White Hart Inn
😊😊
Main St., Hawes, DL8 3QL
☎ Wensleydale
(0969) 667259
Small country inn with a friendly welcome, offering home-cooked meals using local produce. An ideal centre for exploring the Yorkshire Dales.
Bedrooms: 1 single, 4 double & 2 twin.
Bathrooms: 2 public.
Bed & breakfast: £16.50-£17.50 single, £29-£30 double.
Lunch available.
Evening meal 7pm (l.o. 8.30pm).
Parking for 7.
Open February-November.
ॐ ♥ 🛗 ▥ Ⓣ 🍴 SP 🏠

Individual proprietors have supplied all details of accommodation. Although we do check for accuracy, we advise you to confirm prices and other information at the time of booking.

HAWORTH

W. Yorkshire
Map ref 4B1

This small Pennine town is famous as home of the Bronte family. The parsonage is now a Bronte Museum where furniture and possessions of the family are displayed. Moors and Bronte waterfalls nearby and steam trains on the Keighley and Worth Valley Railway pass through the town.
Tourist Information Centre ☎ (0535) 642329 or 645864

Bridge House Private Hotel ⋀
Bridgehouse Lane, Haworth, Keighley, BD22 8PA
☎ (0535) 642372
Small family-run licensed hotel built as mill owner's Georgian residence. In the famous tourist village of Haworth, home of the Bronte sisters, close to the Keighley and Worth Valley Railway. Bar meals available. Car park.
Bedrooms: 2 single, 1 double & 2 twin.
Bathrooms: 3 private, 1 public.
Bed & breakfast: £14.50-£17 single, £36 double.
Parking for 12.
ॐ 3 🦢 ▢ ♥ 🛗 Ⓥ 🖾 ▥ 🍴
✻ 🆊 🖾 ᴰᴬᴾ SP 🏠

Ferncliffe
😊😊😊 COMMENDED
Hebden Rd., Haworth, Keighley, BD22 8RS
☎ (0535) 43405
Well-appointed, private hotel with panoramic views overlooking Haworth and the Worth Valley Steam Railway.
Bedrooms: 2 single, 2 double & 1 twin, 1 family room.
Bathrooms: 6 private.
Bed & breakfast: £21-£25 single, £42-£50 double.
Half board: £30-£34 daily, £210-£238 weekly.
Lunch available.
Evening meal 7pm (l.o. 9pm).
Parking for 12.
Credit: Visa.
ॐ ⑧ ▢ ♥ 🛗 Ⓥ 🖾 Ⓣ 🛗
🖾 🍴 ᴰᴬᴾ SP

Moorfield Guest House ⋀
80 West La., Haworth, Keighley, BD22 8EN
☎ (0535) 43689

Victorian house between the moors and village, with superb views over Bronte land. Garden terrace overlooks the cricket field.
Bedrooms: 1 single, 2 double & 2 twin, 1 family room..
Bathrooms: 5 private, 1 public.
Bed & breakfast: £15-£20 single, £30-£35 double.
Half board: £28-£35 daily.
Evening meal 7.15pm (l.o. 4.30pm).
Parking for 6.
Credit: Access, Visa.
ॐ ▢ ♥ 🛗 Ⓥ 🖾 ▥ ▥ 🖾
🖾 🏠

Newsholme Manor Hotel & Restaurant
Slaymaker Lane, Slack Lane, Oakworth, Keighley, BD22 0RQ
☎ Haworth (0535) 42964
Delightful country residence enjoying panoramic views, close to Bronte land. Free-house run by the Sexton family. A la carte menu, Italian food or bar snacks available. Close to golf and horse riding.
Bedrooms: 3 double & 1 twin, 1 family room.
Bathrooms: 3 private, 1 public.
Bed & breakfast: £15.50-£19.50 single, £25-£32.50 double.
Half board: £22-£26 daily, £154-£182 weekly.
Lunch available.
Evening meal 5pm (l.o. 9pm).
Parking for 50.
Credit: Access, Visa.
ॐ ▢ 🛗 Ⓥ 🖾 🖾 Ⓣ ▥ ▥
🍴 ❍ ✻ 🖾 🆊 SP Ⓣ

Old White Lion Hotel ⋀
😊😊😊😊 COMMENDED
Haworth, Keighley, BD22 8DU
☎ (0535) 642313
Family-run, centuries old coaching inn. Candlelit restaurant using local fresh produce cooked to order and featured in food guides. Old world bars serving extensive range of bar snacks and real ales.
Bedrooms: 3 single, 6 double & 2 twin, 3 family rooms.
Bathrooms: 14 private.
Bed & breakfast: from £33 single, from £48 double.
Lunch available.
Evening meal 7pm (l.o. 10pm).
Parking for 10.
Credit: Access, Visa, Diners, Amex.
ॐ 📞 ⑧ ▢ ♥ 🛗 Ⓥ 🖾 Ⓣ
▥ 🍴 🖾 🆊 SP 🏠

Springfield Guest House ⋀
Listed
Springfield, Shaw La., Oxenhope, Keighley, BD22 9QL
☎ Haworth (0535) 643951
Elegant Victorian house in beautiful Bronte country, 1 mile pleasant walk from Haworth. Good food and comfortable rooms with TV.
Bedrooms: 1 double & 1 twin, 1 family room.
Bathrooms: 1 public.
Bed & breakfast: £15-£18 single, £28-£30 double.
Half board: £20.50 daily, £120 weekly.
Evening meal 6pm (l.o. 5pm).
Parking for 9.
ॐ ♥ �ᴜᴸ 🛗 Ⓥ 🖾 Ⓣ ◑ 🛗
🖾 🍴 🆊 SP

Woodlands Grange Guest House
😊😊 COMMENDED
Woodlands Grange, Belle Isle, Haworth, Keighley, BD22 8PB
☎ (0535) 46814
Secluded, detached property 100 yards from the railway station. Emphasis on comfort and service.
Bedrooms: 2 double & 1 twin, 1 family room.
Bathrooms: 4 private.
Bed & breakfast: £20 single, £30 double.
Half board: £24 daily.
Parking for 10.
ॐ 🚵 ⑧ ▢ ♥ �ᴜᴸ 🖾 Ⓣ 🛗
🖾 🖾 SP

HEBDEN BRIDGE

W. Yorkshire
Map ref 4B1

Originally a small town on packhorse route, Hebden Bridge grew into a booming mill town in 18th C with rows of 'up-and-down' houses of several storeys built against hillsides. Ancient 'pace-egg play' custom held on Good Friday.
Tourist Information Centre ☎ (0422) 843831

Carlton Hotel ⋀
😊😊😊 COMMENDED
Albert St., Hebden Bridge, HX7 8ES
☎ (0422) 844400
ⓒⓡ Consort
In the centre of Hebden Bridge, close to the shops and railway station. All bedrooms with every modern facility. Special rates available.

Bedrooms: 6 single, 4 double & 8 twin.
Bathrooms: 18 private.
Bed & breakfast: £45-£55 single, £64-£74 double.
Half board: £42.50-£45 daily.
Lunch available.
Evening meal 7.30pm (l.o. 9.30pm).
Credit: Access, Visa, Amex.

Redacre Mill M
☳☳☳ COMMENDED
Redacre, Mytholmroyd, Hebden Bridge, HX7 5DQ
☎ Halifax (0422) 885563
Small country hotel featured on "Wish You Were Here". Peaceful canal side location, convenient for Bronte country, South Pennines and the Yorkshire Dales.
Bedrooms: 3 double & 2 twin, 1 public.
Bed & breakfast: £30-£35 single, £45-£55 double.
Half board: £30-£45 daily, £200-£250 weekly.
Evening meal 6pm (l.o. 8pm).
Parking for 8.
Open February-November.
Credit: Access, Visa.

HELMSLEY
N. Yorkshire
Map ref 5C3

Pretty town on the River Rye at the entrance to Ryedale and the North York Moors, with large cobbled square and remains of 12th C castle, several inns, notably the 16th C 'Black Swan', and All Saints' Church.

Crown Hotel M
☳☳ COMMENDED
Market Place, Helmsley, York, YO6 5BJ
☎ (0439) 70297
16th C inn with a Jacobean dining room offering traditional country cooking using fresh local produce whenever possible. All rooms en-suite and with colour TV and direct dial telephones. Special breaks October to May. Dogs welcome.
Bedrooms: 5 single, 4 double & 4 twin, 1 family room.
Bathrooms: 12 private, 1 public.
Bed & breakfast: £26.60-£28.60 single, max. £57.20 double.
Half board: £39.90-£41.90 daily, £265-£280 weekly.

Lunch available.
Evening meal 7.15pm (l.o. 8pm).
Parking for 15.
Credit: Access, Visa.

Feversham Arms Hotel M
☳☳☳ COMMENDED
1 High St., Helmsley, York, YO6 5AG
☎ (0439) 70766
Fax (0439) 70346
⊕ Best Western
Warm, elegant, family-run, historic inn in the North York Moors National Park. Wide variety of food and wines. 5 four-poster rooms, 6 ground floor rooms, 1 suite. Bonanza breaks all year.
Bedrooms: 1 single, 7 double & 7 twin, 3 family rooms.
Bathrooms: 18 private.
Bed & breakfast: £55-£65 single, £76-£86 double.
Lunch available.
Evening meal 7pm (l.o. 9pm).
Parking for 30.
Credit: Access, Visa, Diners, Amex.

Pheasant Hotel M
☳☳
Harome, Helmsley, YO6 5JG
☎ Helmsley (0439) 71241
In a quiet rural village, with a terrace and gardens overlooking the village pond. Oak-beamed bar in a former blacksmith's shop, English food and log fires. Children over 12 years are welcome.
Bedrooms: 5 double & 6 twin, 1 family room.
Bathrooms: 12 private.
Half board: £40-£56 daily.
Lunch available.
Evening meal 7.30pm (l.o. 8pm).
Parking for 20.
Open March-December.

National Crown ratings were correct at the time of going to press but are subject to change. Please check at the time of booking.

HOLMFIRTH
W. Yorkshire
Map ref 4B1

5m S. Huddersfield
This village has become famous as the location for the filming of the TV series 'Last of the Summer Wine'. It has a postcard museum and is on the edge of the Peak District National Park.
Tourist Information Centre ☎ (0484) 684992 or 687603

Old Bridge Hotel M
☳☳☳ COMMENDED
Norridge Bottom, Holmfirth, Huddersfield, HD7 1DA
☎ Huddersfield (0484) 681212
Fax (0484) 687978
Well-appointed hotel in the heart of "Summer Wine" country. Pub food and a restaurant providing attentive service.
Bedrooms: 7 single, 7 double & 2 twin, 4 family rooms.
Bathrooms: 20 private.
Bed & breakfast: £48.50-£50 single, £60-£70 double.
Half board: £60-£75 daily, £400-£500 weekly.
Lunch available.
Evening meal 7pm (l.o. 8pm).
Parking for 23.
Credit: Access, Visa, Amex.

HOOTON ROBERTS
S. Yorkshire
Map ref 4C2

4m NE. Rotherham

Earl of Strafford
☳☳☳☳ APPROVED
Doncaster Rd., Hooton Roberts, Rotherham, S65 4PF
☎ Rotherham (0709) 852737
& Fax (0709) 851903
Former dower house for Lady Strafford converted into an hotel with a 42-seater restaurant, function room and 2 public bars.
Bedrooms: 4 single, 14 double & 6 twin, 3 family rooms.
Bathrooms: 27 private.
Bed & breakfast: £62-£82 single, £77-£97 double.
Half board: £75-£102 daily.
Lunch available.
Evening meal 7pm (l.o. 9.30pm).
Parking for 60.

Credit: Access, Visa, Diners, Amex.

HORNSEA
Humberside
Map ref 4D1

Small holiday town situated on strip of land between beach bordering North Sea and Hornsea Mere, a large natural freshwater lake. Some sailing and fishing permitted on protected nature reserve. Hornsea Pottery attracts many visitors.

Ashburnham Guest House
☳☳
1 Victoria Avenue, Hornsea, N. Humberside HU18 1NH
☎ (0964) 535118
Guesthouse with excellent sea views, close to the RSPB reserves. Welcome trays, home cooking and a guests' lounge with TV. Weekly and off-season discounts. Colour TV in all rooms. Children and pets welcome.
Bedrooms: 1 single, 1 double & 2 twin, 2 family rooms.
Bathrooms: 2 public.
Bed & breakfast: £13 single, £26 double.
Parking for 4.
Credit: Access, Visa.

HORTON-IN-RIBBLESDALE
N. Yorkshire
Map ref 5B3

5m N. Settle
On the River Ribble and an ideal centre for pot-holing. The Pennine Way runs eastward over Pen-y-ghent, one of the famous 'Three Peaks'.
Tourist Information Centre ☎ (072 96) 333

Crown Hotel M
☳☳ APPROVED
Horton-in-Ribblesdale, Settle, BD24 0HF
☎ (072 96) 209
Small family-run country inn offering a warm welcome and friendly hospitality, in the heart of the dales.
Bedrooms: 3 single, 3 double, 4 family rooms.
Bathrooms: 1 private, 2 public; 6 private showers.
Continued ▶

HORTON-IN-RIBBLESDALE

Continued

Bed & breakfast: £17.75-£24.20 single, £35.50-£48.40 double.
Half board: £27.40-£33.85 daily, £186.70-£206.80 weekly.
Lunch available.
Evening meal 6.30pm (l.o. 7pm).
Parking for 15.
Credit: Diners.
⌖ 🛆 📺 🖃 ▦ 🍴 🎀 ✎
SP

Wagis Guest House M

APPROVED

Townend Cottage, Horton-in-Ribblesdale, Settle, BD24 0EX
☎ (072 96) 320
Farm and barn (dated 1735) conversion in a beautiful limestone area close to the Three Peaks, Pennine Way, Settle/Carlisle Railway and Yorkshire Dales National Park.
Bedrooms: 1 double & 1 twin, 1 family room.
Bathrooms: 2 private, 1 public.
Bed & breakfast: £30-£40 double.
Half board: £22-£27 daily.
Evening meal 6.30pm (l.o. 6.30pm).
Parking for 6.
⌖ 🛆 ✿ 🖃 📺 ▦ ❄ 🎀 ✎ SP 📮

HOWDEN

Humberside
Map ref 4C1

Small town near the River Ouse, dominated by partly-ruined medieval church of St. Peter's which has ancient origins but was rebuilt with a range of architectural styles over the centuries.

Wellington Hotel M

APPROVED

Bridgegate, Howden, Goole, N. Humberside DN14 7JG
☎ (0430) 430258
Fax (0430) 432139
16th C coaching inn with modern facilities in historic market town. Popular restaurant, bars and beer garden. Ideal for business or pleasure.
Bedrooms: 3 single, 2 double & 3 twin, 1 family room.
Bathrooms: 9 private.
Bed & breakfast: £28-£30 single, £39.50-£42 double.

Half board: from £35 daily.
Lunch available.
Evening meal 6pm (l.o. 10pm).
Parking for 60.
Credit: Access, Visa.
⌖ ⌕ 📺 ✿ 🛆 🖃 ▦ ⌂
🍴 ✎ SP 📮
☎ Display advertisement appears on page 204.

HUDDERSFIELD

W. Yorkshire
Map ref 4B1

Founded on wool and cloth, has a famous choral society. Town centre redeveloped, but several good Victorian buildings remain, including railway station, St. Peter's Church, Tolson Memorial Museum, art gallery and nearby Colne Valley Museum. Castle Hill overlooks the town.
Tourist Information Centre ☎ (0484) 430808

Elm Crest Guest House M

🏵🏵

2 Queens Rd., Edgerton, Huddersfield, HD2 2AG
☎ (0484) 530990
Fax (0484) 516227
Victorian residence with Victorian charm and quality, 1 mile from the town centre and 2 miles from the M62.
Bedrooms: 3 single, 3 twin, 2 family rooms.
Bathrooms: 3 private, 2 public.
Bed & breakfast: £22-£32 single, £41-£57 double.
Half board: £32-£42 daily.
Parking for 12.
Credit: Access, Visa, Amex.
⌖3 🖃 UL 🛆 ✂ 🖃 ▦ 🛆
✕ 🎀 ✎ T

Flying Horse Country Hotel M

Nettleton Hill Rd., Scapegoat Hill, Huddersfield, HD7 4NY
☎ (0484) 642368
Fax (0484) 642866
Country hotel within walking distance of the moors, 2 miles from the M62, exit 23.
Bedrooms: 1 single, 32 twin.
Bathrooms: 33 private.
Bed & breakfast: £25-£42.50 single, £30-£50 double.
Half board: £36-£53.50 daily.
Lunch available.
Evening meal 6pm (l.o. 10pm).
Parking for 60.

Credit: Access, Visa, Diners, Amex.
⌖ 🛆 📺 ⌕ 🖃 📺 ✿ 🛆 👤 V
🖃 📺 ● ▦ 🛆 🍴 ⌖ 👤 ✎
▶ ❄ DAP ✎ SP T

The George Hotel M

St. George's Square, Huddersfield, HD1 1JA
☎ (0484) 515444
Fax (0484) 435056
℗ Principal
This elegant town centre hotel has undergone a complete refurbishment. Located close to shops and within easy reach of Peak District.
Bedrooms: 34 single, 12 double & 11 twin, 2 family rooms.
Bathrooms: 59 private.
Bed & breakfast: from £73 single, from £89 double.
Half board: from £42 daily.
Lunch available.
Evening meal 7pm (l.o. 9.45pm).
Parking for 12.
Credit: Access, Visa, C.Bl., Diners, Amex.
⌖ 🛆 ⌕ ⌂ ⌖ 🖃 V 🖃
🖃 ▦ 🛆 🍴 DAP ✎ 📮 T

Holmcliffe M

🏵🏵

16 Mountjoy Rd., Edgerton, Huddersfield, HD1 5PZ
☎ (0484) 429598
Half a mile from town centre and 2 miles from junction 24 of M62. A warm and friendly welcome awaits you.
Bedrooms: 1 single, 1 double & 3 twin, 1 family room.
Bathrooms: 2 public.
Bed & breakfast: £18-£20 single, £27-£30 double.
Parking for 6.
⌖ 🛆 ✿ 🖃 UL 🛆 V 🖃
📺 ▦ 🛆 ✕ 🎀 ✎ SP

Huddersfield Hotel & Rosemary Lane Bistro M

🏵🏵🏵 **APPROVED**

33-47 Kirkgate, Huddersfield, HD1 1QT
☎ (0484) 512111 Telex 51575 HUDHOT G
Conference facilities, night club, jacuzzi, sauna, solarium and 4 public bars. 150 car spaces within 150 metres.
Bedrooms: 21 single, 10 double & 3 twin, 5 family rooms.
Bathrooms: 39 private.
Bed & breakfast: £26-£42 single, £36-£56 double.
Half board: £35-£52 daily.
Evening meal 6pm (l.o. midnight).
Parking for 60.

Credit: Access, Visa, C.Bl., Diners, Amex.
⌖ 🛆 ⌕ ⌕ 🖃 📺 ✿ 👤 V
🖃 📺 ● ⌂ ⌖ ▦ 🛆 🍴 🛆 🎀
🖃 ❄ ✎ SP 📮

The Lodge Hotel

🏵🏵🏵🏵 **COMMENDED**

48 Birkby Lodge Rd., Birkby, Huddersfield, HD2 2BG
☎ (0484) 431001
Fax (0484) 421590
Victorian residence, restored and converted to a hotel, 2 minutes from the town centre and the M62. 50-cover restaurant and billiard room.
Bedrooms: 4 single, 3 double & 2 twin, 2 family rooms.
Bathrooms: 11 private.
Bed & breakfast: £50-£60 single, £60-£75 double.
Half board: £65-£75 daily.
Lunch available.
Evening meal 7.30pm (l.o. 9.45pm).
Parking for 42.
Credit: Access, Visa, Amex.
⌖ 🛆 ⌕ ⌂ ⌖ 🖃 ✿ 👤 V
🖃 📺 🛆 🍴 🛆 🎀 ❄ SP
📮

Pennine Hilton National M

COMMENDED

M62, Exit 24, Ainley Top, Huddersfield, HD3 3RH
☎ Elland (0422) 375431
Telex 517346
℗ Hilton
Imposing modern hotel, surrounded by the rugged Pennines and ideal for business or pleasure. Close to Haworth (Bronte country) and Holmfirth (Summer Wine country).
Bedrooms: 52 double & 63 twin, 3 family rooms.
Bathrooms: 118 private.
Bed & breakfast: £86-£102.25 single, £98-£114.50 double.
Lunch available.
Evening meal 7pm (l.o. 10pm).
Parking for 250.
Credit: Access, Visa, Diners, Amex.

HULL

See Kingston-upon-Hull.

Half board prices shown are per person but in some cases may be based on double/twin occupancy.

HUTTON-LE-HOLE

N. Yorkshire
Map ref 5C3

2m N. Kirkbymoorside
Listed in Domesday
Book, this pretty village of
red-tiled stone cottages
situated around Hutton
Beck became a refuge for
persecuted Quakers in
17th C. Ryedale Folk
Museum.

Barn Hotel and Tea Room M
COMMENDED
Hutton-le-Hole, York,
YO6 6UA
☎ Lastingham (075 15) 311
*Stone walls and an inner
courtyard are part of the
character of this extended
barn. Centrally situated in
delightful village.*
Bedrooms: 2 single, 4 double
& 2 twin.
Bathrooms: 3 private,
2 public.
Bed & breakfast: £18 single,
£35-£42 double.
Half board: £30-£33 daily.
Lunch available.
Evening meal 7pm.
Parking for 15.
Open March-December.
Credit: Access, Visa.
♡ ⓘ ⇥ ⓣⓥ ▱ 🖾 SP

ILKLEY

W. Yorkshire
Map ref 4B1

This moorland spa town,
famous for its ballad, is a
lively tourist centre with
many hotels and shops.
16th C manor house, now
a museum, displays local
prehistoric and Roman
relics. Popular walk leads
up Heber's Ghyll to Ilkley
Moor, with the mysterious
Swastika Stone and
White Wells, 18th C
plunge baths.
*Tourist Information
Centre* ☎ *(0943) 602319*

Cow and Calf Hotel M
COMMENDED
Moor Top, Ilkley, LS29 8BT
☎ (0943) 607335
*Hotel of charm and character
on Ilkley Moor, commanding
unrivalled views of the
Yorkshire Dales. Bargain
breaks available.*
Bedrooms: 5 single, 7 double
& 7 twin, 1 family room.
Bathrooms: 20 private.
Bed & breakfast: £55-£65
single, £65-£75 double.

Lunch available.
Evening meal 7.15pm (l.o.
9.30pm).
Parking for 102.
Credit: Access, Visa, C.Bl.,
Diners, Amex.
♡ ⬛ ⬛ ⬛ ☏ ⬛ ⬛ ⓘ ⓥ
⇥ ▱ ⬛ ⬛ ※ 🖾 SP 🖾
ⓣ

Crescent Hotel M
APPROVED
Brook St., Ilkley, LS29 8DG
☎ (0943) 600012 & 600062
*Fully modernised hotel with
family rooms and self-catering
suites. In a central position in
town. Convenient for the dales.*
Bedrooms: 1 single, 4 double
& 12 twin, 4 family rooms.
Bathrooms: 21 private.
Bed & breakfast: £45-£49.50
single, £60-£72 double.
Half board: £55.50-£59.50
daily.
Lunch available.
Evening meal 6.30pm (l.o.
8.45pm).
Parking for 25.
Credit: Access, Visa, Amex.
♡ ⬛ ☏ ⬛ ⓘ ⓥ ✂ ⇥ ⬛
⬛ ▱ ⬛ ⬛ ※ 🖾 ⬛ SP
🖾 ⓣ

Grove Hotel M
COMMENDED
The Grove, Ilkley, LS29 9PA
☎ (0943) 600298
*Small friendly, private hotel
offering well-appointed
accommodation. Convenient for
Ilkley town centre, shops and
gardens.*
Bedrooms: 1 single, 1 double
& 2 twin, 2 family rooms.
Bathrooms: 6 private,
1 public.
Bed & breakfast: £37-£40
single, £48-£50 double.
Half board: £45-£52 daily.
Lunch available.
Evening meal 7pm (l.o.
8.30pm).
Parking for 5.
Credit: Access, Visa.
♡ 5 ▱ ♡ ⓘ ⓥ ⇥ ⓣⓥ ▱ ▱
🖾

Moorview Guest House
⬛⬛
104 Skipton Rd., Ilkley,
LS29 9HE
☎ (0943) 600156
*Imposing Victorian villa on
bank of River Wharfe, at start
of the Dales Way. Ideal
touring centre for dales and
Bronte country. Ample
parking.*
Bedrooms: 2 single, 3 double
& 2 twin, 5 family rooms.
Bathrooms: 9 private,
3 public.
Bed & breakfast: £25-£35
single, £32-£48 double.

Evening meal 6.30pm (l.o.
6.30pm).
Parking for 14.
♡ ▱ ♡ ⓘ ⓥ ⇥ ⓣⓥ ▱ ▱
🏊 ※ ✻ 🖾 🖾 ⓓⓐⓟ ⓣ

Summerhill Guest House
⬛⬛
24 Crossbeck Rd., Ilkley,
LS29 9TN
☎ (0943) 607067
*On the edge of Ilkley Moor
with lovely views and within
easy walking distance of the
town.*
Bedrooms: 1 single, 1 double
& 5 twin.
Bathrooms: 2 private,
1 public.
Bed & breakfast: £13-£15
single, £26-£30 double.
Half board: £19-£21 daily.
Evening meal 6.30pm (l.o.
6.30pm).
Parking for 5.
♡ ⓘ ⓥ ⇥ ⓣⓥ ▱ ▱ 🖾

INGLETON

N. Yorkshire
Map ref 5B3

Ingleton is a thriving
tourist centre for fell-
walkers, climbers and
pot-holers. Popular walks
up beautiful Twiss Valley
to Ingleborough Summit,
Whernside, White Scar
Caves and waterfalls.

Bridge End Guest House
⬛⬛
Mill Lane, Ingleton,
Carnforth, Lancashire
LA6 3EP
☎ (052 42) 41413
*Former mill house retaining
many Georgian features.
Vegetarians welcome. In a
pleasant location adjacent to
the entrance to the waterfalls
in the Yorkshire Dales
National Park. Within easy
reach of the Lake District.*
Bedrooms: 1 single, 1 double,
1 family room.
Bathrooms: 1 private,
1 public.
Bed & breakfast: £16-£20
single, £26-£32 double.
Half board: £20-£25 daily,
£133-£167 weekly.
Lunch available.
Evening meal 6.30pm (l.o.
9am).
Parking for 10.
♡ ▱ ♡ ⓤⓛ ⓘ ⓥ ⇥ ⓣⓥ ▱
▱ 🖾 ⓓⓐⓟ 🖾 SP 🖾

---

*We advise you to
confirm your
booking in writing.*

Langber Country Guest House
⬛⬛
Ingleton, Carnforth,
Lancashire LA6 3DT
☎ (052 42) 41587
*Detached country house in
hilltop position and with
panoramic views. Good touring
centre for dales and coast.
Comfortable accommodation,
home cooking and baking.*
Bedrooms: 1 single, 2 double
& 1 twin, 3 family rooms.
Bathrooms: 3 private,
2 public.
Bed & breakfast: from £13.50
single, from £26 double.
Half board: from £17.50
daily, from £115 weekly.
Evening meal 6.30pm (l.o.
5pm).
Parking for 6.
♡ ♡ ⓤⓛ ⓘ ⓥ ⇥ ⓣⓥ ▱ ▱
⬛ ※ ⓓⓐⓟ SP

Moorgarth Hall Country House Hotel M
COMMENDED
New Rd., Ingleton,
Carnforth, Lancashire
LA6 3HL
☎ (052 42) 41946
*Delightful Victorian country
house in wooded grounds.
Family-run. All rooms en-suite
with colour TV and central
heating. Log fires. Ideal for
Lakes and dales.*
Bedrooms: 1 single, 5 double
& 2 twin.
Bathrooms: 8 private.
Bed & breakfast: £28-£30
single, £50-£56 double.
Half board: £38-£40 daily,
£227-£253 weekly.
Evening meal 7.30pm (l.o.
8.30pm).
Parking for 12.
Open February-December.
Credit: Access, Visa.
♡ 🖾 ☏ ▱ ♡ ⓘ ⓥ ⇥ ▱
▱ 🖾 🖾 SP

Springfield Private Hotel M
APPROVED
Main St., Ingleton,
Carnforth, Lancashire
LA6 3HJ
☎ (052 42) 41280
*Detached Victorian villa in its
own small grounds with a
fountain and conservatory.*
Bedrooms: 1 double & 1 twin,
3 family rooms.
Bathrooms: 5 private,
1 public.
Bed & breakfast: £16-£18
single, £32-£36 double.
Half board: £23.50-£25.50
daily, £155-£170 weekly.

Continued ▶

INGLETON

Continued

Evening meal 6.30pm (l.o. 5pm).
Parking for 12.
Open January-October.

KEIGHLEY

W. Yorkshire
Map ref 4B1

Pleasant Victorian town where Charlotte Bronte used to shop. Cliffe Castle is an art gallery and museum with large collection of Victorian bygones. 17th C East Riddlesden Hall (National Trust) has fine medieval tithe barn. Trips on Keighley and Worth Valley Railway.

Dalesgate Hotel M

406 Skipton Rd., Utley, Keighley, BD20 6HP
☎ Keighley (0535) 664930
Charming, family-run hotel near the town. Ideal tourist area for the dales, Haworth, York and the steam railways.
Bedrooms: 8 single, 8 double & 4 twin, 1 family room.
Bathrooms: 21 private.
Bed & breakfast: £25.50-£38.50 single, £40-£48 double.
Half board: £30-£48.50 daily.
Evening meal 7pm (l.o. 11pm).
Parking for 22.
Credit: Access, Visa, Diners, Amex.

KEXBY

N. Yorkshire
Map ref 4C1

6m E. York

Kexby Bridge Hotel M
COMMENDED

Hull Rd., Kexby, York, YO5 5LD
☎ Wilberfoss (075 95) 8223
Fax 07595 8822
In 8 acres of landscaped gardens with private fishing and golf driving range. Leisure complex due to open in 1992. Guide dogs accepted. On A1079 York-Hull road.
Bedrooms: 26 double & 6 twin.
Bathrooms: 32 private.

Bed & breakfast: £50 single, £75 double.
Lunch available.
Evening meal 7pm (l.o. 9pm).
Parking for 60.
Credit: Access, Visa.

KILNSEY

N. Yorkshire
Map ref 5B3

4m NW. Grassington
The Manor of Kilnsey with Conistone once belonged to Fountains Abbey. Kilnsey Crag is an outstanding landmark in Upper Wharfedale and makes an impressive background for the Kilnsey Show and Crag Race held around August Bank Holiday each year.

Tennant Arms Hotel M
APPROVED

Kilnsey, Skipton, BD23 5PS
☎ Grassington (0756) 752301
17th C coaching inn nestling alongside Kilnsey Crag offering comfortable, attractive accommodation for those wishing to experience the beauty of Wharfedale.
Bedrooms: 4 double & 4 twin, 2 family rooms.
Bathrooms: 10 private.
Bed & breakfast: £46-£55 double.
Half board: £32.50-£35.75 daily, £210-£239 weekly.
Lunch available.
Evening meal 7pm (l.o. 9.30pm).
Parking for 40.
Credit: Access, Visa.

National Crown ratings were correct at the time of going to press but are subject to change. Please check at the time of booking.

Half board prices shown are per person but in some cases may be based on double/twin occupancy.

KINGSTON-UPON-HULL

Humberside
Map ref 4D1

Busy seaport with a modern city centre and excellent shopping facilities. Deep-sea fishing base at junction of the Rivers Hull and Humber, founded by Cistercian monks in 12th C. Maritime traditions in the town, docks and the museum, and the home of William Wilberforce, the slavery abolitionist, whose house is now a museum. The world's longest single-span suspension bridge crosses the Humber 5 miles west.
Tourist Information Centre ☎ (0482) 223344 or 223559 or 702118

Gledholt Hotel
APPROVED

13 Eldon Grove, Beverley Rd., Kingston-upon-Hull, N. Humberside HU5 2TJ
☎ (0482) 447024
Small, family-run hotel in carefully refurbished Victorian building of superb character. Victorian-style conservatory. In a conservation area.
Bedrooms: 1 single, 2 double & 1 twin, 3 family rooms.
Bathrooms: 3 private, 1 public.
Bed & breakfast: £20-£26 single, £32-£38 double.
Evening meal 6.30pm (l.o. 7.30pm).
Parking for 3.

Hastings Hotel
925 Spring Bank West, Kingston-upon-Hull, N. Humberside HU5 5BE
☎ (0482) 505645 & 51486
Public house with 2 pool tables and a dart board.
Bedrooms: 1 single, 1 double & 2 twin, 1 family room.
Bathrooms: 1 public.
Bed & breakfast: £13 single, £22 double.
Lunch available.
Parking for 20.

Hesslewood Hall Hotel M

Ferriby Rd., Hessle, N. Humberside HU13 OJB
☎ (0482) 641990
Fax (0482) 640990

English country mansion in 20 acres of private grounds. Magnificent views of the Humber and Humber Bridge. 6 minutes' drive from the city centre.
Bedrooms: 8 single, 13 double, 10 family rooms.
Bathrooms: 31 private.
Bed & breakfast: £37-£76.50 single, £64-£104 double.
Half board: £49-£88.50 daily, £88-£128 weekly.
Lunch available.
Evening meal 6pm (l.o. 10.30pm).
Parking for 300.
Credit: Access, Visa.

Hollies Hotel M

96 Park Avenue, Kingston-upon-Hull, N. Humberside HU5 3ET
☎ (0482) 41487
Family-run hotel in a quiet area, with licensed bar and private lock-up car park.
Bedrooms: 8 single, 1 double & 1 twin, 1 family room.
Bathrooms: 2 private, 3 public.
Bed & breakfast: £18.80-£27.60 single, £30.55-£38.77 double.
Half board: £25.85-£34.66 daily.
Evening meal 6.30pm (l.o. 4pm).
Parking for 8.

Kingstown Hotel M
COMMENDED

Hull Rd., Hedon, Kingston-upon-Hull, N. Humberside HU12 9DJ
☎ (0482) 890461
Fax (0482) 890713
New, family-run hotel where an "at home" atmosphere is encouraged without detriment to the high standards achieved.
Bedrooms: 11 single, 20 double & 4 twin.
Bathrooms: 35 private.
Bed & breakfast: £57-£72 single, £60-£85 double.
Lunch available.
Evening meal 7pm (l.o. 10pm).
Parking for 96.
Credit: Access, Visa.

The Mayfair M

333-335 Beverley Rd., Kingston-upon-Hull, N. Humberside HU5 1LD
☎ (0482) 42402 & 441196

Clean and comfortable family-run establishment providing home-cooked food. Restaurant and residential licence, ideal for weddings and small functions.
Bedrooms: 8 single, 4 double & 4 twin, 4 family rooms.
Bathrooms: 4 public.
Bed & breakfast: £13.50 single, £26 double.
Half board: £16.25-£18.50 daily, £113.75-£129.50 weekly.
Evening meal 6pm (l.o. 11pm).
Parking for 12.
☎ ♦ 🛉 ⭕ 📺 ⭕ 🏧 ♨ 👍

Paragon Hotel
Paragon St., Kingston-upon-Hull, N. Humberside
HU1 3PJ
☎ (0482) 26462 Telex 592431
Modern city centre hotel with conference and banqueting facilities for up to 240. Convenient for all public transport.
Bedrooms: 28 single, 30 double & 66 twin, 1 family room.
Bathrooms: 125 private.
Bed & breakfast: £25-£62 single, £50-£74 double.
Half board: £36-£83.90 daily.
Lunch available.
Evening meal 7pm (l.o. 9.45pm).
Credit: Access, Visa, Diners, Amex.
☎ ♦ ⭕ 🖥 ♦ 🛉 Ⓥ ✂ 🍴
⭕ 🖥 🏧 ♨ 👍 OAP SP 👍 Ⓣ

Pearson Park Hotel ♈
🌸🌸🌸🌸 APPROVED
Pearson Park, Kingston-upon-Hull, N. Humberside
HU5 2TQ
☎ (0482) 43043
Fax (0482) 447679
Tastefully converted Victorian villas just outside central area in a delightful park with bowling greens and conservatory. Under same ownership for 25 years.
Bedrooms: 14 single, 11 double & 8 twin, 2 family rooms.
Bathrooms: 29 private, 1 public; 4 private showers.
Bed & breakfast: £30-£45 single, £45-£60 double.
Half board: £39.50-£54.50 daily.
Lunch available.
Evening meal 6.30pm (l.o. 9pm).
Parking for 30.
Credit: Access, Visa, Diners, Amex.
☎ 🌸 🖥 🔔 ⭕ 🖥 ♦ 🛉 Ⓥ
🍴 ⭕ 🏧 ♨ 👍 SP 👍 Ⓣ

Valiant House Hotel ♈
Anlaby Rd., Kingston-upon-Hull, N. Humberside
HU1 2PJ
☎ (0482) 23299
Fax (0482) 214730
Newly renovated city centre hotel, with easy access to the M1, M62 and Humber Bridge. Ideal for touring Humberside and Yorkshire.
Bedrooms: 4 single, 35 double & 18 twin, 2 family rooms.
Bathrooms: 59 private.
Bed & breakfast: £37.50-£52.50 single, £47.50-£65 double.
Half board: £47.50-£66 daily.
Lunch available.
Evening meal 7pm (l.o. 9.30pm).
Parking for 9.
Credit: Access, Visa, Diners, Amex.
☎ 🔔 ⭕ 🖥 ♦ 🛉 Ⓥ 🍴 ⭕
🖥 🏧 🏧 ♨ 👍 ✗ SP Ⓣ

4m SE. Huddersfield

Springfield Park Hotel
🌸🌸🌸🌸 COMMENDED
Penistone Rd., Kirkburton, Huddersfield, HD8 0PE
☎ Huddersfield
(0484) 607788
Fax (0484) 607961
On the main Penistone road (A629) 15 minutes from the M62 junction 23 or 10 minutes from the M1, junction 38. Unique range of business facilities and a relaxing atmosphere.
Bedrooms: 27 double.
Bathrooms: 27 private.
Bed & breakfast: £62.50-£110 single, £70.50-£130 double.
Half board: £40-£65 daily, £280-£455 weekly.
Lunch available.
Evening meal 6pm (l.o. 11.30pm).
Parking for 150.
Credit: Access, Visa, Amex.

Attractive market town with remains of Norman castle. Good centre for exploring moors. Nearby are wild daffodils of Farndale.

George & Dragon Hotel
Market Place, Kirkbymoorside, York, YO6 6AA
☎ (0751) 31637
13th C inn of character at the foot of the Yorkshire Moors. Extensively modernised bedrooms, all with colour TV.
Bedrooms: 3 single, 14 double & 5 twin, 2 family rooms.
Bathrooms: 22 private, 1 public.
Bed & breakfast: from £27.50 single, £55-£75 double.
Half board: £44.40-£55 daily, £250-£300 weekly.
Lunch available.
Evening meal 7pm (l.o. 9.30pm).
Parking for 20.
Credit: Access, Visa.
☎ 🌸 🔔 ⭕ 🖥 ♦ 🛉 Ⓥ ⭕ 🖥
🏧 ♨ 👍 ➤ ✗ 👍 SP 🏧

Lion Inn ♈
Blakey Ridge, Kirkbymoorside, York, YO6 6LQ
☎ Lastingham (075 15) 320
13th C freehouse in the centre of the North York Moors, with breathtaking views.
Bedrooms: 6 double & 2 twin, 1 family room.
Bathrooms: 4 private, 1 public; 2 private showers.
Bed & breakfast: £15.50-£23 single, £40-£55 double.
Lunch available.
Evening meal (l.o. 10.30pm).
Parking for 100.
Credit: Access, Visa.
☎ 🌸 🔔 ⭕ 🖥 ♦ 🛉 Ⓥ ⭕ 🖥
🏧 ♨ 👍 ➤ ✳ ❄ 🏧

Individual proprietors have supplied all details of accommodation. Although we do check for accuracy, we advise you to confirm prices and other information at the time of booking.

Please mention this guide when making a booking.

Picturesque market town on the River Nidd, famous for its 11th C castle ruins, overlooking town and river gorge. Attractions include oldest chemist's shop in country, prophetess Mother Shipton's cave, Dropping Well and Court House Museum. Boating on river.

Ebor Mount ♈
🌸🌸
18 York Place, Knaresborough, HG5 0AA
☎ Harrogate (0423) 863315
250-year-old coaching house with comfortable, refurbished, en-suite rooms. Ideal touring centre.
Bedrooms: 1 single, 3 double & 2 twin, 2 family rooms.
Bathrooms: 7 private, 1 public.
Bed & breakfast: £16-£21 single, £32-£42 double.
Parking for 10.
Credit: Access, Visa.
☎ 🌸 ⭕ 🖥 ♦ Ⓤ 🏧 ♨ 🏧
OAP SP 🏧

Newton House Hotel ♈
🌸🌸 COMMENDED
York Place, Knaresborough, HG5 0AD
☎ Harrogate (0423) 863539
Beautifully converted Georgian town house of special historic interest, 2 minutes' walk from the market square, castle and river. 20 minutes from York, 30 minutes from the dales.
Bedrooms: 1 single, 7 double & 4 twin.
Bathrooms: 12 private.
Bed & breakfast: £30-£35 single, £50-£60 double.
Parking for 9.
Credit: Access, Visa, Amex.
☎ 🌸 🔔 🔔 ⭕ 🖥 ♦ Ⓥ 🏧
📺 🖥 🏧 ♨ 👍 ➤ ✳ OAP ❄ SP
🏧

Yorkshire Lass ♈
🌸🌸🌸 APPROVED
High Bridge, Harrogate Rd., Knaresborough, HG5 8DA
☎ Harrogate (0423) 862962
Detached inn on main Harrogate/York road, with attractive bedrooms overlooking River Nidd. Real ales, wines, large selection of whiskies. Specialising in traditional Yorkshire dishes.
Bedrooms: 1 single, 2 double & 2 twin, 1 family room.
Bathrooms: 6 private.

Continued ▶

KNARESBOROUGH

Continued

Bed & breakfast: £30-£40 single, £40-£50 double.
Half board: £32.50-£37.50 daily, £210-£230 weekly.
Lunch available.
Evening meal 5pm (l.o. 10pm).
Parking for 34.
Credit: Access, Visa, Amex.
❄ 📞 🅭 🖵 ♻ 🖐 Ⓥ ▥ ⚊
🍴 ▶ 🛏 🔨 🦴 SP ⊤

LACEBY

Humberside
Map ref 4D1

4m SW. Grimsby
Village close to the
Humberside/Lincolnshire
border, just east of the
Wolds.

Oaklands Hotel
☺☺☺

Barton St., Laceby, Grimsby,
S. Humberside DN37 7LF
☎ Grimsby (0472) 72248
Fax (0472) 78143
Ⓒ Best Western
*Country house hotel with
private grounds 22 miles from
the Humber Bridge.
Pub/carvery, a la carte
restaurant, leisure centre,
children's garden and golf
driving range.*
Bedrooms: 23 single, 9 double
& 13 twin, 1 family room.
Bathrooms: 46 private.
Bed & breakfast: £56-£63.60
single, £70-£76 double.
Lunch available.
Evening meal 7pm (l.o.
9.30pm).
Parking for 250.
Credit: Access, Visa, Diners,
Amex.
❄ 🔔 ♿ 📞 🅭 🖵 ♻ 🖐 Ⓥ
🗡 🛏 🅾 ▥ ⚊ 🍴 🐟 🔨 ❄
SP 🦴 ⊤

LANGTOFT

Humberside
Map ref 5D3

Old Mill Hotel & Restaurant M
☺☺☺☺ COMMENDED

Mill Lane, Langtoft, Driffield,
N. Humberside YO25 0BQ
☎ Driffield (0377) 87284
*Historic hotel on the Yorkshire
Wolds, set back off the
Scarborough to Bridlington
road.*
Bedrooms: 5 double & 4 twin.
Bathrooms: 9 private.
Bed & breakfast: £40-£50
single, £60-£70 double.

Lunch available.
Evening meal 6.30pm (l.o.
10pm).
Parking for 30.
Credit: Access, Visa.
📞 🅭 🖵 ♻ 🖐 Ⓥ 🗡 🛏 ⚊
▥ ⚊ 🍴 🔨 🦴 SP 🦴

LEEDS

W. Yorkshire
Map ref 4B1

Large city with excellent
modern shopping centre
and much splendid
Victorian architecture.
Notable buildings include
the Town Hall with its
225-ft clock tower, Civic
Hall built of white
Portland stone,
Mechanics Institute and
the oval-shaped Corn
Exchange. Museums and
galleries including Temple
Newsam House (the
Hampton Court of the
North) and Home of Opera
North and a new
playhouse.
*Tourist Information
Centre* ☎ *(0532) 462454
or 462455*

Aintree Hotel M
☺☺

38 Cardigan Rd.,
Headingley, Leeds, LS6 3AG
☎ (0532) 758290
*Small semi-detached family
hotel on a tree-lined road,
overlooking Headingley
Cricket Ground. Close to the
Arndale Shopping Centre.
Evening meal by arrangement
only.*
Bedrooms: 4 single, 2 double
& 2 twin.
Bathrooms: 4 private,
2 public.
Bed & breakfast: £20-£22
single, £30-£35 double.
Half board: £30-£33 daily.
Evening meal 6pm (l.o.
10am).
Parking for 11.
❄ 🖵 ♻ 🛏 ▥ ⚊ 🗡

Aragon Hotel M
☺☺☺

250 Stainbeck La., Leeds,
LS7 2PS
☎ (0532) 759306 & 757166
*Converted, late Victorian house
in quiet, wooded surroundings,
2 miles from the city centre.
Tea/coffee making facilities in
all bedrooms.*
Bedrooms: 4 single, 6 double
& 3 twin, 1 family room.
Bathrooms: 9 private,
2 public.

Bed & breakfast: £25.08-
£36.42 single, £37.82-£47.46
double.
Half board: £19.91-£46.32
daily.
Evening meal 7pm (l.o. 6pm).
Parking for 25.
Credit: Access, Visa, Diners,
Amex.
❄ ♿ 📞 🖵 ♻ 🖐 ▥ ⚊
🍴 ❄ 🔨 ⊤

Beegee's Guest House

18 Moor Allerton Drive, Off
Street La. Moortown, Leeds,
LS17 6RZ
☎ (0532) 666221
Fax (0532) 753300
*Small family-run guesthouse,
convenient for Harewood
House, 9 golf courses and
Leeds town centre. Elegant
bedrooms. Access to house at
all times. Breakfast in new
conservatory, overlooking
gardens. 5 minutes' walk from
Roundhay Park.*
Bedrooms: 1 single, 1 double
& 2 twin, 2 family rooms.
Bathrooms: 1 public;
1 private shower.
Bed & breakfast: £18-£22
single, £26-£29 double.
Parking for 5.
❄ ♿ 🖵 ♻ 🆄 ▥ 🖐 ⚊
⚊ ❄ 🔨 🔨 DAP 🦴 SP ⊤

Boundary Hotel

42 Cardigan Rd.,
Headingley, Leeds, LS6 3AG
☎ (0532) 757700 & 751523
*Small, family-run hotel 2 miles
from city centre and
overlooking the famous
Headingley Cricket Ground.
Specialising in home-cooked
food and a friendly welcome.
Good local facilities.*
Bedrooms: 5 single, 4 double
& 1 twin, 3 family rooms.
Bathrooms: 1 private,
3 public.
Bed & breakfast: £22-£35
single, £32-£48 double.
Evening meal 6.30pm (l.o.
9.30pm).
Parking for 15.
❄ 🖵 ♻ 🖐 Ⓥ 🛏 ⚊ ▥
⚊ 🍴

Broomhurst Hotel M
☺☺ COMMENDED

Chapel La., Headingley,
Leeds, LS6 3BW
☎ (0532) 786836
*Small, comfortable, owner-run
hotel in a quiet, pleasantly
wooded conservation area, 1.5
miles from the city centre.
Convenient for Yorkshire
County Cricket Ground and
university.*
Bedrooms: 5 single, 2 double
& 3 twin, 1 family room.
Bathrooms: 2 private,
2 public; 1 private shower.

Bed & breakfast: £20.80-
£32.70 single, £34.85-£42.70
double.
Half board: £29.80-£41.70
daily.
Evening meal 6pm (l.o. 9am).
Parking for 5.
❄6 ♿ 🖵 ♻ 🛏 ▥ ⚊ 🗡
🔨 SP

Cresta

381 Street Lane, Moortown,
Leeds, LS17 6SE
☎ (0532) 661706
*Small private hotel providing a
friendly, personal service.
Pleasant north Leeds suburb
with easy access to Harrogate,
York and the North Yorkshire
countryside.*
Bedrooms: 4 single, 2 twin,
2 family rooms.
Bathrooms: 2 public.
Bed & breakfast: £16 single,
£28 double.
Parking for 6.
❄ ♻ 🆄 🛏 ▥ ⚊ 🗡 🔨

Eagle Tavern M
Listed

North St., Leeds, LS7 1AF
☎ (0532) 457146
*Traditional pub in a
commercial district of Leeds,
offering friendly service at
reasonable prices. Close to the
city centre. Colour TV in all
rooms. Voted CAMRA pub of
the year 1989 and 1990.*
Bedrooms: 1 single, 6 twin,
2 family rooms.
Bathrooms: 2 public.
Bed & breakfast: from £18
single, from £36 double.
Evening meal 5.30pm (l.o.
7pm).
Parking for 12.
❄ 🖵 Ⓥ ▥ 🍴 🗡 🔨 🦴

Haleys Hotel and Restaurant M
☺☺☺☺ HIGHLY COMMENDED

Shire Oak Rd., Headingley,
Leeds, LS6 2DE
☎ (0532) 784446
Fax (0532) 753342
*Elegant Victorian town house
hotel in conservation area, 2
miles from city centre off
A660, Otley Road. Modern
English cooking.*
Bedrooms: 8 single, 10 double
& 4 twin.
Bathrooms: 22 private.
Bed & breakfast: from £85
single, from £98 double.
Evening meal 7.15pm (l.o.
9.45pm).
Parking for 16.
Credit: Access, Visa, Amex.
❄ 📞 🖵 ♻ 🖐 Ⓥ 🛏 ◐
▥ ⚊ 🍴 🗡 🔨 🦴 SP ⊤

Harewood Arms Hotel M
⚜⚜⚜⚜ COMMENDED

Harewood Rd., Harewood,
Leeds, LS17 9LH
☎ (0532) 886566
Fax (0532) 886064
*Stone-built hotel and
restaurant of character with a
rural aspect, 8 miles from
Harrogate and Leeds.
Opposite Harewood House and
close to all amenities, including
golf and racing.*
Bedrooms: 2 single, 10 double
& 12 twin.
Bathrooms: 24 private.
Bed & breakfast: £49-£65
single.
Half board: £65-£80 daily.
Lunch available.
Evening meal 7pm (l.o.
10pm).
Parking for 60.
Credit: Access, Visa, Diners,
Amex.
🖇🕭📞🐾🛏️👁️ⅤⅩ📠
⊙🆑🏨🍴✿ SP 🏠 Ⓣ

Hilton National M
Wakefield Rd., Garforth,
Leeds, LS25 1LH
☎ Leeds (0532) 866556
Telex 556324
ⒸⓇ Hilton
*Features Dukes Piano Bar and
Restaurant. Leisure centre with
pool, gym and sauna.*
Bedrooms: 44 single,
19 double & 54 twin, 26 family
rooms.
Bathrooms: 143 private.
Bed & breakfast: £53-£89.75
single, £65-£110.75 double.
Half board: £71-£105 daily.
Lunch available.
Evening meal 7pm (l.o.
10pm).
Parking for 300.
Credit: Access, Visa, C.Bl.,
Diners, Amex.
🖇🕭📞🐾🛏️👁️ⅤⅩ
📠⊙🆑🍴🐾🐕❉
SP Ⓣ

Holiday Inn Leeds M
Wellington St., Leeds,
LS1 4DL
☎ (0532) 442200
ⒸⓇ Holiday Inn
*City centre hotel with executive
bedrooms, suites, Lady
Executive and study rooms.*
Bedrooms: 125 double.
Bathrooms: 125 private.
Bed & breakfast: £48-£139
single, £96-£155 double.
Half board: £59-£159 daily.
Lunch available.
Evening meal 7pm (l.o.
10.30pm).
Parking for 120.
Credit: Access, Visa, C.Bl.,
Diners, Amex.
🖇📞🆑🏨🐾👁️ⅤⅩ⊙
🎷🆑🍴🍴🐕🐾 SP Ⓣ

Leeds Hilton M
Neville St., Leeds, LS1 4BX
☎ (0532) 442000
Telex 557143 Fax 0532
433577
ⒸⓇ Hilton
*City centre hotel offering 2
restaurants, a bar and a
continental-style coffee bar.*
Bedrooms: 110 double &
100 twin.
Bathrooms: 210 private.
Bed & breakfast: £75-£150
single, £85-£170 double.
Lunch available.
Evening meal 7pm (l.o.
10pm).
Parking for 71.
Credit: Access, Visa, Diners,
Amex.
🖇🕭🏨🐾🛏️👁️ ⅤⅩ📠
⊙🆑🏨🍴🐾🍴 SP Ⓣ

Manxdene Private Hotel M
⚜⚜

154 Woodsley Rd., Leeds,
LS2 9LZ
☎ (0532) 432586
*Large, Victorian, terraced,
family-run hotel adjacent to
the university and half a mile
from the city centre. Unlimited
street parking. Close to bus
services.*
Bedrooms: 6 single, 1 double
& 2 twin, 1 family rooms.
Bathrooms: 3 public.
Bed & breakfast: £20-£22
single, £30-£32 double.
Evening meal 6.15pm (l.o.
6.15pm).
🖇5🏨🐾👁️ Ⅴ📠Ⓣ🍴🐾
✈ SP

Nordic Residential Hotel M
⚜⚜

18 Kelso Rd., Leeds,
LS2 9PR
☎ (0532) 452357 & 448261
*Small family-run hotel in a
quiet location close to the city
centre. Tea and coffee making
facilities and colour TV in all
rooms. En-suite rooms
available.*
Bedrooms: 10 single, 3 twin,
3 family rooms.
Bathrooms: 3 private,
3 public.
Bed & breakfast: from £23
single, from £30 double.
Evening meal 6.15pm (l.o.
9pm).
Parking for 11.
🖇8🏨🐾👁️ Ⅴ📠Ⓣ🍴🐾✈
🐕

*The symbols are
explained on the
flap inside the
back cover.*

Parkway Hotel M
⚜⚜⚜ COMMENDED

Otley Rd., Bramhope, Leeds,
LS16 8AG
☎ Leeds (0532) 672551
Telex 556614
*Mock Tudor building in 2.5
acres of grounds, in suburb of
Leeds, 7 miles from city centre
on A660 road. Special
weekend rates.*
Bedrooms: 66 single,
13 double & 24 twin.
Bathrooms: 103 private.
Bed & breakfast: £33.75-
£97.50 single, £71.50-£111
double.
Lunch available.
Evening meal 7pm (l.o.
10pm).
Parking for 350.
Credit: Access, Visa, Diners,
Amex.
🖇🕭📞🏨🐾🛏️👁️ Ⅴ
📠⊙🆑🏨🍴🐾🐕🐾
Ⓣ🔎🐾✿ OAP 🐾 SP Ⓣ

Pinewood Private Hotel M
⚜⚜⚜

78 Potternewton La., Leeds,
LS7 3LW
☎ (0532) 622561 & 628485
*Friendly hotel with resident
proprietors and emphasis on
cleanliness.*
Bedrooms: 4 single, 1 double
& 3 twin, 2 family rooms.
Bathrooms: 6 private,
1 public; 2 private showers.
Bed & breakfast: £27-£33
single, £41-£49 double.
Half board: £36-£42 daily.
Evening meal 6.30pm (l.o.
10am).
Credit: Access, Visa.
🖇🕭🏨🐾👁️ Ⅴ📠Ⓣ🍴
🐾✈🐕🏨

St. Michael's Tower Hotel M
5 St. Michael's Villas,
Cardigan Rd., Headingley,
Leeds, LS6 3AF
☎ (0532) 755557
*Licensed, private hotel with
easy access to Leeds city
centre (2 miles) and close to
both the university and
Yorkshire Cricket Ground.*
Bedrooms: 5 single, 4 double
& 6 twin, 1 family room.
Bathrooms: 5 private,
4 public.
Bed & breakfast: £17-£25
single, £28-£32 double.
Half board: £23-£31 daily.
Parking for 16.
🖇🏨🐾👁️ Ⅴ📠Ⓣ🍴🐾
🍴✈ SP Ⓣ

Stakis Leeds Windmill Hotel M
⚜⚜⚜

Ring Rd., Seacroft, Leeds,
LS14 5QP
☎ (0532) 732323 Telex 55452
ⒸⓇ Stakis
*Ideal for both business and
holiday makers. On the main
Leeds to York road with easy
access to the airport and
motorways. Half board rate
based on a minimum 2 night
stay.*
Bedrooms: 22 single, 6 double
& 60 twin, 11 family rooms.
Bathrooms: 99 private.
Bed & breakfast: £87-£97
single, £108-£118 double.
Half board: from £40 daily.
Lunch available.
Evening meal 7pm (l.o.
10pm).
Parking for 120.
Credit: Access, Visa, Diners,
Amex.
🖇🕭📞🏨🐾👁️ ⅤⅩ📺
⊙🆑🏨🍴🐾 OAP 🐾 SP Ⓣ

**LEEDS/BRADFORD
AIRPORT**

*See Bingley, Bradford,
Leeds, Otley, Pool.*

LEEMING BAR

N. Yorkshire
Map ref 5C3

White Rose Hotel M
⚜⚜⚜⚜ APPROVED

Leeming Bar, Northallerton,
DL7 9AY
☎ Bedale (0677) 422707 &
424941 & 423235
Fax (0677) 425123
*Family-run private hotel and
restaurant ideally situated in
village half a mile from A1
motorway. Central for
Yorkshire Dales and coastal
resorts. Pets welcome.*
Bedrooms: 9 single, 1 double
& 6 twin, 2 family rooms.
Bathrooms: 18 private.
Bed & breakfast: from £28
single, from £42 double.
Half board: £32.95-£38.50
daily.
Lunch available.
Evening meal 7.30pm (l.o.
9.30pm).
Parking for 40.
Credit: Access, Visa, Diners,
Amex.
🖇🕭📞🏨🐾👁️ Ⅴ📠
🍴🐾🍴🐕🐾 SP Ⓣ

*Map references apply to the colour maps
towards the end of this guide.*

LEYBURN

N. Yorkshire
Map ref 5B3

Attractive dales market town where Mary Queen of Scots was reputedly captured after her escape from Bolton Castle. Fine views over Wensleydale from nearby.
Tourist Information Centre ☎ *(0969) 23069 or 22773*

Golden Lion Hotel & Licensed Restaurant M
⚜ ⚜ ⚜ APPROVED
Market Place, Leyburn, DL8 5AS
☎ Wensleydale (0969) 22161
Small family-run hotel in the market place of a busy dales town. A good base for touring the surrounding countryside.
Bedrooms: 4 single, 4 double & 3 twin, 4 family rooms.
Bathrooms: 12 private, 2 public.
Bed & breakfast: £20-£28 single, £40-£56 double.
Half board: £32-£40 daily.
Lunch available.
Evening meal 7pm (l.o. 9pm).
Parking for 12.
Credit: Access, Visa, Diners.
❧ ☎ ▥ ◻ ╚ ⅋ ▮ Ⅴ ◢ £
▥ ♠ ⚓ ☾ � ▸ ☒ ☒ SP
▥ T

Grove Hotel M
8 Grove Square, Leyburn, DL8 5AE
☎ Wensleydale (0969) 22569
Recently renovated listed building with a wealth of panelling and beams, in the oldest of Leyburn's 3 squares.
Bedrooms: 1 single, 3 double & 2 twin, 3 family rooms.
Bathrooms: 6 private, 1 public.
Bed & breakfast: £15-£18 single, £30-£36 double.
Lunch available.
Evening meal 5.30pm (l.o. 9pm).
Parking for 10.
Credit: Access, Visa.
❧ ♨ ◻ ╚ ▥ ◢ ▥ ⅄ ▥
❧ SP ▥

Secret Garden House M
⚜ ⚜ ⚜ COMMENDED
Grove Square, Leyburn, DL8 5AE
☎ Wensleydale (0969) 23589
Georgian house with secluded walled garden and conservatory, in market town, the heart of James Herriot country. Free off-street parking.
Bedrooms: 1 single, 2 double & 2 twin, 2 family rooms.

Bathrooms: 5 private, 1 public.
Bed & breakfast: £17-£25 single, £37-£45 double.
Half board: £29-£37 daily, £195-£255 weekly.
Evening meal 7.30pm (l.o. 8.30pm).
Parking for 10.
Credit: Access, Visa.
❧ 5 ♨ ◻ ╚ ▥ ⅄ ◢ ▥ ▥
▥ ♠ ▸ ☾ ▥ ▥ DAP ❧ SP ▥

Sunnyholme
8 St. Mary's Mount, Leyburn, DL8 5JB
☎ Wensleydale (0969) 23352
Well-situated family guesthouse.
Bedrooms: 1 double & 1 twin, 1 family room.
Bathrooms: 1 public.
Bed & breakfast: £12 single, £24 double.
Evening meal 6.30pm.
Parking for 2.
❧ ♨ ▥ UL Ⅴ ◢ ▥ ▥ ▥
DAP SP

White Swan Hotel M
Market Place, Middleham, Leyburn, DL8 4PE
☎ Wensleydale (0969) 22093
Country inn near the castle, offering comfort and friendly service. Home-cooked food. In the heart of the Yorkshire Dales, an ideal base for touring.
Bedrooms: 1 single, 2 double & 2 twin, 2 family rooms.
Bathrooms: 3 private, 2 public.
Bed & breakfast: £15-£22 single, £25-£36 double.
Half board: £34-£46 daily, £135-£285 weekly.
Lunch available.
Evening meal 6.30pm (l.o. 8.30pm).
Parking for 6.
Credit: Access, Visa.
❧ ◻ ╚ ▮ Ⅴ ▥ ◢ ▥ ⅄
SP ▥

LIVERSEDGE

W. Yorkshire
Map ref 4B1

3m NW. Dewsbury

Geordie Pride Lodge
112 Roberttown Lane, Roberttown, Liversedge, WF15 7LZ
☎ Wakefield (0924) 402069/410136
Two miles from M62, adjacent to city centre. Perfectly placed for both "Summer Wine" country and Yorkshire Dales. 7 miles from Leeds, Huddersfield and Bradford.
Bedrooms: 1 single, 7 double.
Bathrooms: 8 private.

Bed & breakfast: £30-£40 single, £38-£48 double.
Half board: £40.75-£50.75 daily, max. £250 weekly.
Lunch available.
Evening meal 6.30pm (l.o. 10.30pm).
Parking for 10.
Credit: Access, Visa.
❧ ♨ ◻ ╚ ⅋ ▮ Ⅴ ▥ ▥
▥ ✕ ▥

Healds Hall Hotel M
⚜ ⚜ ⚜
Leeds Rd., Liversedge, WF15 6JA
☎ Liversedge (0924) 409112
Family-run hotel with restaurant, in large gardens on A62 road near M1 and M62 motorways.
Bedrooms: 5 single, 12 double & 4 twin, 5 family rooms.
Bathrooms: 26 private.
Bed & breakfast: £30-£45 single, £40-£65 double.
Lunch available.
Evening meal 7pm (l.o. 9pm).
Parking for 49.
Credit: Access, Visa, Amex.
❧ ♨ ╚ ◻ ╚ ⅋ ▮ Ⅴ ▥
▥ ▥ ▥ ♠ ▸ ☾ ▥ SP ▥ ▥ T

MALHAM

N. Yorkshire
Map ref 5B3

11m NW. Skipton
Hamlet of stone cottages amid magnificent rugged limestone scenery in the Yorkshire Dales National Park. Malham Cove is a curving, sheer white cliff 240 ft high. Malham Tarn, one of Yorkshire's few natural lakes, belongs to the National Trust.
National Park Centre.

Beck Hall Guest House
Malham, Skipton, BD23 4DJ
☎ Airton (072 93) 332
Family-run guesthouse set in a spacious riverside garden. Homely atmosphere, four-poster beds, log fires and home cooking.
Bedrooms: 1 single, 8 double & 3 twin, 3 family rooms.
Bathrooms: 11 private, 3 public.
Bed & breakfast: £15-£20 single, £27-£34.50 double.
Half board: £20.50-£24.25 daily.
Lunch available.
Evening meal 7pm (l.o. 8pm).
Parking for 30.
Open January-November.
❧ 4 ♨ ▥ ▮ Ⅴ ▥ ◢ ▥ ⅋ ☾

MALTON

N. Yorkshire
Map ref 5D3

A thriving farming town on the River Derwent with large livestock market. Famous for race horse training. The local museum has Roman remains and many World War II relics from the 'Eden' prisoner of war camp on site in the town. Castle Howard within easy reach.

Crown Hotel M
Wheelgate, Malton, YO17 0HP
☎ (0653) 692038
Family-owned hotel which has been in the same family for over 100 years. Malton Brewery at rear of hotel.
Bedrooms: 2 single, 2 double & 4 twin, 2 family rooms.
Bathrooms: 1 private, 2 public.
Bed & breakfast: £16-£22 single, £30-£36 double.
Half board: £21-£35 daily.
Lunch available.
Evening meal 6.45pm (l.o. 8.15pm).
Parking for 14.
❧ ♨ ▮ Ⅴ ▥ ◢ ▥ ▥ ▥ ◢ ⅋
▥ ▥

Newstead Grange Country House Hotel
⚜ ⚜ ⚜ COMMENDED
Newstead Grange, Norton, Malton, YO17 9PJ
☎ (0653) 692502
Elegant Georgian country house in 2.5 acres, 1.5 miles from Malton on the Beverley road. Antique furniture. Non-smoking establishment. Children 12 years and over are welcome.
Bedrooms: 3 double & 3 twin.
Bathrooms: 6 private.
Bed & breakfast: £28-£35 single, £42-£62 double.
Half board: £31-£48 daily, £190-£285 weekly.
Evening meal 7.30pm.
Parking for 1.
▥ ◻ ╚ ⅄ ▥ ◢ ▥ ☾ ✕ ▥
SP ▥

Oakdene Country House Hotel M
⚜ ⚜ ⚜ COMMENDED
29 Middlecave Rd., Malton, YO17 ONE
☎ (0653) 693363

Elegant Victorian residence in its own grounds, in a select residential area of this beautiful market town in the heart of Ryedale. Home-grown vegetables in season and traditional home cooking.
Bedrooms: 4 double & 2 twin.
Bathrooms: 6 private.
Bed & breakfast: £20-£30 double.
Evening meal 7pm (l.o. 7.30pm).
Parking for 6.

Wentworth Arms Hotel M

Town St., Old Malton, Malton, YO17 0HD
☎ (0653) 692618
Former coaching inn, built early 1700s and run by the same family for 100 years. 20 miles from York. An excellent base for touring the Yorkshire Dales, North York Moors and the East Coast.
Bedrooms: 3 double & 2 twin.
Bathrooms: 4 private,
1 public.
Bed & breakfast: £20-£21 single, £40-£42 double.
Lunch available.
Evening meal 6pm (l.o. 8.45pm).
Parking for 30.
Credit: Access, Visa.

MARKET WEIGHTON

Humberside
Map ref 4C1

Small town on the western side of the Yorkshire Wolds. A tablet in the parish church records the death of William Bradley in 1820 at which time he was 7ft 9in tall and weighed 27 stone!

Londesborough Arms Hotel M

44 High St., Market Weighton, York,
N. Yorkshire YO4 3AH
☎ (0430) 872219 & 872214
Fine 3-storey Georgian hotel, fully restored to its original beauty. Contains Giant Bradley's chair - built for the tallest ever British man.
Bedrooms: 4 double & 12 twin.
Bathrooms: 16 private.
Bed & breakfast: £53.50-£56.50 single, £87-£138 double.

Lunch available.
Evening meal 6pm (l.o. 10.30pm).
Parking for 51.
Credit: Access, Visa, Diners, Amex.

MARSDEN

W. Yorkshire
Map ref 4B1

Hemmed in by its hills where rail and canal face the 3 miles of Standedge tunnel, a trifling matter for trains but once an unmitigated horror for canal barges.

Hey Green Hotel M
COMMENDED

Waters Rd., Marsden, Huddersfield, HD7 6NG
☎ Huddersfield (0484) 844235
Fax (0484) 847605
Country house hotel situated in 7 acres of beautiful woodland with own trout lake, nestling at the foot of the Colne Valley amidst delightful Pennine moorlands and dales.
Bedrooms: 3 double & 7 twin.
Bathrooms: 10 private.
Bed & breakfast: £55-£60 single, £70-£78 double.
Half board: £71.50-£78 daily.
Lunch available.
Evening meal 7pm (l.o. 9.50pm).
Parking for 70.
Credit: Access, Visa, Diners, Amex.

MASHAM

N. Yorkshire
Map ref 5C3

Famous market town on the River Ure, with a large market square. St. Mary's Church has Norman tower and 13th C spire. Theakston's 'Old Peculier' ale is brewed here.

Jervaulx Hall
COMMENDED

Jervaulx, Ripon, HG4 4PH
☎ Bedale (0677) 60235
Regency hotel in a picturesque setting with many wild flowers and adjoining Jervaulx Abbey ruins. Emphasis on food.
Bedrooms: 5 double & 5 twin.
Bathrooms: 10 private.
Bed & breakfast: £60 single, £75-£85 double.

Half board: £50-£59 daily, £330-£350 weekly.
Evening meal 8pm (l.o. 8pm).
Parking for 20.
Open March-November.

MIDDLEHAM

N. Yorkshire
Map ref 5C3

Town famous for racehorse training, with cobbled squares and houses of local stone. Norman castle, once principal residence of Warwick the Kingmaker and later Richard III. Ruins of Jervaulx Abbey nearby.

Black Swan Hotel M
APPROVED

Market Place, Middleham, Leyburn, DL8 4NP
☎ Wensleydale (0969) 22221
Unspoilt 17th C inn, with open fires and beamed ceilings, allied to 20th C comforts. Emphasis on food.
Bedrooms: 1 single, 4 double & 1 twin, 1 family room.
Bathrooms: 7 private.
Bed & breakfast: £23-£28 single, £36-£45 double.
Half board: £23-£28 daily.
Lunch available.
Evening meal 7pm (l.o. 9pm).
Credit: Access, Visa.

Miller's House Hotel M
COMMENDED

Market Place, Middleham, Leyburn, DL8 4NR
☎ Wensleydale (0969) 22630
Elegant Georgian country house in peaceful village of Middleham, heart of Herriot's Yorkshire Dales. Charming en-suite rooms and four-poster, colour TV, telephone, tea/coffee facilities. 20 minutes from A1.
Bedrooms: 1 single, 3 double & 3 twin.
Bathrooms: 7 private.
Bed & breakfast: £30-£33.50 single, from £60 double.
Half board: £44-£53 daily, £308-£343 weekly.
Evening meal 7.30pm (l.o. 8.30pm).
Parking for 8.
Open February-December.
Credit: Access, Visa.

Richard III Hotel

Market Place, Middleham, Leyburn, DL8 4NP
☎ Wensleydale (0969) 23240
Old hostelry, all rooms en-suite with trouser press, colour TV, hair-dryer. Delicious bar and dining room meals lunch and evening - freshly home-cooked.
Bedrooms: 4 double & 2 twin.
Bathrooms: 6 private.
Bed & breakfast: from £24.50 single, £39-£51 double.
Half board: £197-£231 weekly.
Lunch available.
Evening meal 6pm (l.o. 9pm).
Parking for 50.
Credit: Access, Visa, Amex.

MORLEY

W. Yorkshire
Map ref 4B1

On the outskirts of Leeds, just off the M62 and close to the M1, the Town Hall dominates the town.

Old Vicarage Guest House M
COMMENDED

Bruntcliffe Rd., Morley, Leeds, LS27 0JZ
☎ Leeds (0532) 532174
Within minutes of motorways, providing a Yorkshire welcome with home comforts in an authentic Victorian setting. Weekend rates available.
Bedrooms: 16 single, 5 double & 2 twin.
Bathrooms: 23 private.
Bed & breakfast: £32-£47 single, £53-£62 double.
Half board: £41-£56 daily.
Evening meal 6pm (l.o. 7pm).
Parking for 15.
Credit: Access, Visa.

MURTON

N. Yorkshire
Map ref 4C1

3m E. York

Dray Lodge Hotel M
COMMENDED

Moor La., Murton, York, YO1 3UH
☎ York (0904) 489591
Fax (0904) 488587
19th C horse carriage works, converted to a country hotel. On the east side of York, 3 miles from city centre.
Continued ▶

175

MURTON
Continued

Bedrooms: 3 single, 3 double
& 2 twin, 1 family room.
Bathrooms: 9 private.
Bed & breakfast: max. £27.05
single, £42.30-£47 double.
Half board: £28.50-£35.50
daily.
Evening meal 6.30pm (l.o.
8pm).
Parking for 12.
Credit: Access, Visa, Amex.

NEWBIGGIN
N. Yorkshire
Map ref 5B3

2m S. Aysgarth
Village in Bishopdale with
footpaths to the summit
of Noughtberry Hill and
Buckden Pike.

Bishop Garth ♨
COMMENDED
Newbiggin (Bishopdale),
Leyburn, DL8 3TD
☎ Wensleydale
(0969) 663429
*Comfortably-furnished,
modernised, old stone cottage
of the traditional dales type,
off the B6160. On a "no
through road" in a peaceful
village. Home-cooked food.
Packed lunches on request. En-
suite available. No young
children please.*
Bedrooms: 1 single, 2 double
& 1 twin.
Bathrooms: 1 private,
1 public.
Bed & breakfast: £14-£15
single, £28-£36 double.
Half board: £23-£28 daily,
£145-£175 weekly.
Evening meal 7pm.
Parking for 6.

NORTH DALTON
Humberside
Map ref 4C1

6m SW. Great Driffield
Pretty village in the
Yorkshire Wolds, midway
between Pocklington and
Driffield.

Old School Tearooms, Licensed Restaurant
North Dalton, Driffield,
N. Humberside YO25 9UX
☎ Middleton-on-the-Wolds
(037 781) 618

*Former old school house, still
retaining its original character
and charm. The former school
is now used as a soft furnishing
workroom, with showroom and
tearoom, tea garden. Dining
room is in one of the former
classrooms and contains
railway and other memorabilia.*
Bedrooms: 1 single, 1 double
& 2 twin.
Bathrooms: 2 public.
Bed & breakfast: £17.50
single, £35 double.
Half board: £25 daily, £150
weekly.
Lunch available.
Evening meal 5.30pm (l.o.
9pm).
Parking for 2.

NORTHALLERTON
N. Yorkshire
Map ref 5C3

Formerly a staging post
on coaching route to the
North and later a railway
town. Today a lively
market town and
administrative capital of
North Yorkshire. Parish
church of All Saints dates
from 1200.

Alverton Guest House
♨
26 South Parade,
Northallerton, DL7 8SG
☎ (0609) 776207
*Family-run guesthouse
convenient for many town
facilities and ideal for touring
the dales, moors and coastal
areas.*
Bedrooms: 2 single, 1 double
& 1 twin, 1 family room.
Bathrooms: 3 private,
1 public.
Bed & breakfast: £14.50-£17
single, £29-£35 double.
Half board: £24-£26 daily,
£152-£175 weekly.
Evening meal 7pm (l.o. 7pm).
Parking for 5.

Otterington Shorthorn Inn
South Otterington,
Northallerton, DL7 9HP
☎ Northallerton
(0609) 773816
*Early 19th C inn with an open
fire and oak beams, serving
traditional ales and offering a
warm welcome. Pool table,
juke box and darts.*
Bedrooms: 1 single, 3 double
& 1 twin.
Bathrooms: 1 public.

Bed & breakfast: £14-£18
single, £30-£36 double.
Half board: £19-£24 daily,
£120-£150 weekly.
Lunch available.
Evening meal 7pm (l.o.
9.30pm).
Parking for 12.

Porch House ♨
68 High St., Northallerton,
DL7 8EG
☎ (0609) 779831
*Small family house, 16th and
18th C Grade II listed,
associated with Charles I.
Parish church opposite.*
Bedrooms: 1 double & 4 twin.
Bathrooms: 5 private.
Bed & breakfast: from £30
single, from £42 double.
Half board: £31.50-£40.50
daily, £205-£263 weekly.
Evening meal 7.30pm (l.o.
5pm).
Parking for 5.
Credit: Access, Visa.

Sundial Hotel ♨
COMMENDED
Darlington Rd.,
Northallerton, DL6 2XF
☎ (0609) 780525
Fax (0609) 780525
*Newly-built, elegantly-
appointed hotel for
businessmen and tourists alike.
Fireside cocktail lounge and
restaurant, conference facilities
for up to 100. Facilities for the
disabled.*
Bedrooms: 3 double &
25 twin.
Bathrooms: 28 private.
Bed & breakfast: £45-£65
single, £60-£85 double.
Half board: £54-£75 daily,
£315 weekly.
Lunch available.
Evening meal 5.30pm (l.o.
10pm).
Parking for 100.
Credit: Access, Visa, Diners,
Amex.

Windsor Guest House
COMMENDED
56 South Parade,
Northallerton, DL7 8SL
☎ (0609) 774100
*Victorian house in a tree-lined
road near the town centre,
main-line railway station,
County Hall and Records
Office. Closed 24 December -
2 January.*
Bedrooms: 2 double & 3 twin,
1 family room.

Bathrooms: 3 private,
1 public.
Bed & breakfast: £19-£26
single, £29-£36 double.
Half board: £23-£34.50 daily.
Evening meal 6pm (l.o. 4pm).
Credit: Access, Visa.

OAKWORTH
W. Yorkshire
Map ref 4B1

2m SW. Keighley
This village lies on the
route of the Worth Valley
Railway which was the
location of the film 'The
Railway Children', and is
only 1 mile north of
Haworth.

Railway Cottage
59 Station Rd., Oakworth,
Keighley, BD22 0DZ
☎ Haworth (0535) 642693
*Small guesthouse adjacent to
Oakworth station on the
Keighley and Worth Valley
Railway. Ground floor
accommodation suitable for
disabled visitors.*
Bedrooms: 2 single, 3 double.
Bathrooms: 5 private.
Bed & breakfast: £14-£20
single, £24-£35 double.
Parking for 5.

OSMOTHERLEY
N. Yorkshire
Map ref 5C3

6m NE. Northallerton
The famous 'Lyke Wake
Walk', across the
Cleveland Hills to
Ravenscar 40 miles away,
starts here in this ancient
village. Attached to the
village cross is a large
stone table used as a
'pulpit' by John Wesley.

Queen Catherine Hotel
7 West End, Osmotherley,
Northallerton, DL6 3AG
☎ (060 983) 209
*18th C Grade II listed, stone-
built hotel of charm and
character. Within the North
York Moors National Park at
the centre of a picturesque
village backing on to the
church. Traditional home of
the Lyke Wake Walk.*
Bedrooms: 1 single, 1 double
& 3 twin.
Bathrooms: 1 public.
Bed & breakfast: from £16.50
single, from £33 double.
Lunch available.

Evening meal 7pm (l.o. 9pm).
Parking for 9.
Credit: Access, Visa.

W. Yorkshire
Map ref 4B1

Small town lying just off
the M1 west of
Dewsbury. Noted for its
textiles, engineering and
coal mining. World coal-
carrying championship
takes place every Easter
Monday.

Dimple Well Lodge Hotel M

COMMENDED

The Green, Ossett, WF5 8JX
☎ (0924) 264352
Fax (0924) 262958
*Family-run, Georgian house
hotel in own picturesque
gardens offering charm and
character. Close to the M1
junction 40 and M62.*
Bedrooms: 4 single, 4 double,
2 family rooms.
Bathrooms: 10 private.
Bed & breakfast: £33-£43
single, £45-£55 double.
Lunch available.
Evening meal 7pm (l.o. 7pm).
Parking for 14.
Credit: Access, Visa.

W. Yorkshire
Map ref 4B1

Market and
manufacturing town in
Lower Wharfedale, the
birthplace of Thomas
Chippendale. Has a
Maypole, several old inns,
rebuilt medieval bridge
and a local history
museum. All Saints
Church dates from
Norman times.
*Tourist Information
Centre* ☎ (0943) 465151

Chevin Lodge Country Park Hotel M

COMMENDED

Yorkgate, Otley, LS21 3NU
☎ (0943) 467818 Telex 51538
CHEVLOG
*Country park hotel set in 50
acres of peaceful woodland.
Convenient for nearby cities,
the airport and the dales. Also
Detached holiday lodges also
available.*

Bedrooms: 14 single,
27 double & 7 twin, 4 family
rooms.
Bathrooms: 52 private.
Bed & breakfast: £55-£85
single, £65-£96.50 double.
Lunch available.
Evening meal 7.30pm (l.o.
7.30pm).
Parking for 100.
Credit: Access, Visa, Amex.

Riverdale Guest House

1 Riverdale Rd., Otley,
LS21 1AS
☎ (0943) 461387
*Victorian, stone-built house in
a quiet location near the River
Wharfe and close to the town
centre. Coal fires and home
cooking.*
Bedrooms: 2 double & 2 twin,
1 family room.
Bathrooms: 1 public.
Bed & breakfast: from £20
single, from £32 double.
Half board: £23.50-£27.50
daily.
Evening meal 6.30pm.

W. Yorkshire
Map ref 4B1

4m W. Huddersfield

Old Golf House Hotel M

COMMENDED

New Hey Rd., Outlane,
Huddersfield, HD3 3YP
☎ Elland (0422) 379311 &
Fax (0422) 372694
Telex 51324
Lansbury
*Stone-built hotel with
conference facilities, set in 3
acres of gardens adjacent to
the M62.*
Bedrooms: 3 single, 30 double
& 13 twin, 4 family rooms.
Bathrooms: 50 private.
Bed & breakfast: £26-£69
single, £52-£81 double.
Half board: £40-£83 daily.
Lunch available.
Evening meal 7pm (l.o.
10pm).
Parking for 70.
Credit: Access, Visa, Diners,
Amex.

*Please mention this
guide when making
a booking.*

N. Yorkshire
Map ref 5C3

Small market town at
centre of Upper
Nidderdale. Flax and linen
industries once flourished
in this remote and
beautiful setting.

Grassfields Country House Hotel M

COMMENDED

Wath Rd., Pateley Bridge,
Harrogate, HG3 5HL
☎ Harrogate (0423) 711412
*Georgian building in 2 acres of
lawns and trees, within walking
distance of Pateley Bridge. 5-
bedroomed holiday cottage
also available.*
Bedrooms: 1 single, 2 double
& 4 twin, 2 family rooms.
Bathrooms: 9 private,
1 public.
Bed & breakfast: £30-£32
single, £50-£54 double.
Half board: £36-£38 daily.
Evening meal 7pm (l.o.
6.45pm).
Parking for 15.
Open February-November.
Credit: Amex.

Middlesmoor Crown Hotel M

APPROVED

Middlesmoor, Pateley Bridge,
Harrogate, HG3 5ST
☎ Harrogate (0423) 755296
& 755204
*Family-run hotel at the head of
Nidderdale with panoramic
views, 8 miles from Pateley
Bridge. Restaurant and bar
meals.*
Bedrooms: 1 single, 2 double
& 2 twin, 1 family rooms.
Bathrooms: 1 private,
2 public.
Bed & breakfast: £18.50-
£21.50 single, £29-£34 double.
Lunch available.
Evening meal 7pm (l.o. 9pm).
Parking for 20.
Credit: Access, Visa.

Talbot Hotel M

COMMENDED

High St., Pateley Bridge,
Harrogate, HG3 5AL
☎ Harrogate (0423) 711597
*Family owned and run small
hotel in the centre of Pateley
Bridge, in beautiful
Nidderdale. Ideal for touring
the dales.*
Bedrooms: 1 single, 5 double
& 1 twin, 1 family room.

Bathrooms: 6 private,
1 public.
Bed & breakfast: £19.50-
£21.50 single, £35-£37 double.
Half board: £28-£30 daily.
Evening meal 7pm (l.o. 6pm).
Parking for 9.
Open February-October.

Yorke Arms Hotel M

Ramsgill, Harrogate,
HG3 5RL
☎ Harrogate (0423) 755243
*18th C hostelry on village
green. In the heart of unspoilt
Nidderdale at the head of
Gouthwaite Reservoir Nature
Reserve.*
Bedrooms: 3 single, 3 double
& 5 twin, 2 family rooms.
Bathrooms: 13 private.
Bed & breakfast: £50-£55
single, £75-£85 double.
Half board: £35-£70 daily.
Lunch available.
Evening meal 7.30pm (l.o.
9pm).
Parking for 50.
Credit: Access, Visa.

N. Yorkshire
Map ref 5D3

Market town and tourist
centre on edge of North
York Moors. Parish
church has complete set
of 15th C wall paintings
depicting lives of saints.
Part of 12th C castle still
stands. Beck Isle
Museum. The North
Yorkshire Moors Railway
begins here.
*Tourist Information
Centre* ☎ (0751) 73791.

Beansheaf Restaurant Hotel M

COMMENDED

Malton Rd., Kirby Misperton,
Malton, YO17 0UE
☎ (065 386) 614 & 488
*Modern hotel with wine bar
and coffee shop surrounded by
fields and near Flamingo Zoo.
Pickering 2 miles, York 20
minutes, central for
Scarborough and Whitby.*
Bedrooms: 7 single, 7 double
& 4 twin, 2 family rooms.
Bathrooms: 20 private,
1 public.
Bed & breakfast: £28-£30
single, £46-£50 double.
Half board: £34-£36 daily,
£238-£252 weekly.
Lunch available.

Continued ▶

PICKERING

Continued

Evening meal 7pm (l.o. 9.30pm).
Parking for 50.
Credit: Access, Visa.

> ☎ 🏐 🖤 ① 📞 🛏 ⓥ
> ⚡ ⌨ 📺 🏧 ⚓ 🍴 🛆 ⚄ ✿
> ⚘ ⚬ 🅿 🎝

Burgate House Hotel & Restaurant ⋀

👑👑👑

17 Burgate, Pickering,
YO18 7AU
☎ (0751) 73463
Georgian residence with parts dating from the 16th century. 100 yards from Pickering Castle.
Bedrooms: 5 double & 1 twin, 1 family room.
Bathrooms: 2 private, 2 public; 2 private showers.
Bed & breakfast: £22-£32 single, £34-£55 double.
Half board: £33-£41 daily.
Lunch available.
Evening meal 7pm (l.o. 9pm).
Parking for 8.
Credit: Access, Visa.

> ☎ 📞 🏐 ① 📺 🛏 📺
> 🏧 ⚓ 🍴 ✕ 🌿 ⚘ 🅿 🎝

Cottage Leas Country Hotel ⋀

👑👑👑 COMMENDED

Nova, Middleton, Pickering,
YO18 8PN
☎ Pickering (0751) 72129
Secluded and peaceful 18th C country hotel, with fine restaurant, comfortable rooms, gardens, tennis court. Resident proprietors.
Bedrooms: 9 double & 1 twin, 2 family rooms.
Bathrooms: 12 private.
Bed & breakfast: £35-£38 single, £65-£67 double.
Half board: £45-£51 daily, £258-£266 weekly.
Lunch available.
Evening meal 7pm (l.o. 9.30pm).
Parking for 35.
Credit: Access, Visa.

> ☎ 🏐 🖤 📞 ① 🏐 🛏 ⓥ
> 🛏 🏧 ⚓ 🍴 ♪ 🔎 ⚘ ✿ 🎝 ⚘
> 🌿 🅿

Crossways Hotel ⋀

👑👑👑 COMMENDED

134 Eastgate, Pickering,
YO18 7DW
☎ (0751) 72804
Hotel with a restaurant, bar, delightful bedrooms, all with en-suite facilities, car park and private walled garden.
Bedrooms: 2 single, 3 double & 2 twin, 3 family rooms.

Bathrooms: 10 private, 2 public.
Bed & breakfast: £22-£28 single, £44-£56 double.
Half board: £30-£36 daily, £180-£216 weekly.
Lunch available.
Evening meal 7pm (l.o. 9pm).
Parking for 24.
Credit: Access, Visa.

> ☎ 🏐 🖤 ① ⓥ 🛏 📺 🏐 ⚓
> 🍴 ⚘ 🅿

Forest & Vale Hotel ⋀

👑👑👑👑 COMMENDED

Malton Rd., Pickering,
YO18 7DL
☎ (0751) 72722 Telex 57515
CONSRT G
Ⓒ Consort
Yorkshire stone manor house, comfortable yet elegant. Specialising in imaginative cuisine. Central for moors, coast and York.
Bedrooms: 2 single, 9 double & 3 twin, 3 family rooms.
Bathrooms: 17 private, 3 public.
Bed & breakfast: £42-£64 single, £68-£88 double.
Half board: £43-£73 daily, £271-£460 weekly.
Lunch available.
Evening meal 7pm (l.o. 9.30pm).
Parking for 75.
Credit: Access, Visa, Diners, Amex.

> ☎ 🏐 🖤 📞 ① 📺 🛏 ①
> 📺 🏧 ⚓ 🍴 ✕ 🌿 ✿ 🅿 🎝 ①

Lodge Country House Hotel ⋀

👑👑👑

Middleton Rd., Pickering,
YO18 8NQ
☎ (0751) 72976
Peaceful Victorian lodge set in 3 acres of lawns and terraces. Tastefully furbished throughout. Elegant restaurant and delightful bar.
Bedrooms: 1 single, 5 double & 3 twin, 1 family room.
Bathrooms: 10 private.
Bed & breakfast: £26-£34 single, £52-£68 double.
Half board: £38.50-£46.50 daily, £242.50-£293 weekly.
Lunch available.
Evening meal 6.30pm (l.o. 9.30pm).
Parking for 14.
Credit: Access, Visa, Amex.

> ☎ ⚄5 🏐 📞 🖤 ① 🛏 ⓥ ⚡
> 🛏 🏧 ⚓ 🍴 ✿ ✕ 🌿 🅿 🎝

PONTEFRACT

W. Yorkshire
Map ref 4C1

Close to the A1, this town has a long history, being one of the oldest boroughs in the country. Famous for its castle and locally-processed liquorice, used for sweets and medicines. Also well-known for its racecourse.

Kings Croft Hotel

Wakefield Rd., Pontefract,
WF8 4HA
☎ (0977) 703419 & 600550
Fax: 0977 704488
Georgian building on the outskirts of the town, in a quiet parkland area. Ample parking facilities.
Bedrooms: 5 single, 7 double & 7 twin.
Bathrooms: 19 private.
Bed & breakfast: £35-£42 single, £42-£60 double.
Half board: £45-£52 daily, £270-£310 weekly.
Lunch available.
Evening meal 6.30pm (l.o. 10pm).
Parking for 200.
Credit: Access, Visa, Amex.

> ☎ 🏐 ① ⓥ 🛏 📺 🏐 ⚓ 🍴 ✿
> ⚘ 🅿 🎝

Red Lion Hotel

Market Place, Pontefract,
WF8 1BN
☎ (0977) 702039 & 702379
17th C town centre former coaching inn, now a warm and friendly, family-run hotel. Public bars, lively fun bar with a disco and a DJ, a pool table, videos and darts. Open until 2am weekends.
Bedrooms: 8 single, 8 double & 5 twin, 1 family room.
Bathrooms: 4 public.
Bed & breakfast: from £13.95 single, £25 double.
Half board: from £17.90 daily, from £125 weekly.
Evening meal 6pm (l.o. 7.30pm).
Parking for 12.

> ☎ 🏐 ① 🖤 ⓥ ⚡ 🛏 📺 🏧
> ⚓ 🍴 ♪ ⚘ ⚬ 🅿 🎝

The symbols are explained on the flap inside the back cover.

Half board prices shown are per person but in some cases may be based on double/twin occupancy.

POOL

W. Yorkshire
Map ref 4B1

3m E. Otley

Pool Court Restaurant ⋀

👑👑👑👑 HIGHLY COMMENDED

Pool Bank, Pool
(Wharfedale), Otley,
LS21 1EH
☎ Leeds (0532) 842288
Fax (0532) 843115
A fine Georgian mansion 9 miles from Harrogate, Leeds and Bradford. Exceptionally warm welcome and renowned cuisine.
Bedrooms: 1 single, 3 double & 2 twin.
Bathrooms: 6 private.
Bed & breakfast: £70-£95 single, £95-£120 double.
Evening meal 7pm (l.o. 9.30pm).
Parking for 65.
Credit: Access, Visa, Diners, Amex.

> ☎ 🏐 📞 ① 🛏 ⓥ 🛏 📺 ⚓
> 🍴 ✿ ✕ 🌿 🎝 🅿 🎝

REETH

N. Yorkshire
Map ref 5B3

Once a market town and lead-mining centre, Reeth today serves holiday-makers in Swaledale with its folk museum and 18th C shops and inns lining the green at High Row.

Burgoyne Hotel ⋀

👑👑👑 HIGHLY COMMENDED

Reeth, Richmond, DL11 6SN
☎ Richmond (0748) 84292
Small Georgian hotel with south-facing panoramic views in the heart of Swaledale. Friendly and courteous service. Home cooking.
Bedrooms: 5 double & 2 twin, 1 family room.
Bathrooms: 8 private.
Bed & breakfast: £52.50 single, £60 double.
Half board: £47.50-£70 daily.
Evening meal 7.30pm (l.o. 8.30pm).
Parking for 6.
Credit: Access, Visa.

> ☎ ① 🏐 🖤 ① 🛏 ⓥ ⚡ 🛏 🏧
> ⚓ 🍴 ✿ 🌿 ⚘ 🅿 🎝

Kings Arms Hotel

Listed APPROVED

High Row, Reeth,
Richmond, DL11 6SY
☎ Richmond (0748) 84259

Family-run hotel dating from 1736, in a pleasant setting overlooking the village green with wonderful views of Swaledale.
Bedrooms: 1 double & 1 twin, 2 family rooms.
Bathrooms: 4 private showers.
Bed & breakfast: £13.50-£17.50 single, £24-£32 double.
Lunch available.
Evening meal 6.30pm (l.o. 9.30pm).

RICHMOND

N. Yorkshire
Map ref 5C3

Pleasant market town on edge of Swaledale with 11th C castle and Georgian and Victorian buildings surrounding large, cobbled market-place. Green Howards' Museum is in the former Holy Trinity Church. Attractions include the Georgian Theatre, Richmondshire Museum and Easby Abbey.
Tourist Information Centre ☎ (0748) 850252

Black Lion Hotel **M**
12 Finkle St., Richmond, DL10 4QB
☎ (0748) 823121
Old coaching inn with 3 bars, bar meals, wine cellar and restaurant.
Bedrooms: 4 single, 6 double & 3 twin, 1 family room.
Bathrooms: 5 public.
Bed & breakfast: from £18.60 single, from £34 double.
Lunch available.
Evening meal 6.30pm (l.o. 9.30pm).
Parking for 12.

King's Head Hotel **M**
🏆🏆🏆🏆 COMMENDED
Market Place, Richmond, DL10 4HS
☎ (0748) 850220
Fax (0748) 850635
CB Consort
Beautiful Georgian hotel ideal for touring Herriot country and the Yorkshire Dales. High standard of accommodation and service. Freshly prepared cuisine, extensive wine list.
Bedrooms: 8 single, 12 double & 7 twin, 1 family room.
Bathrooms: 28 private.
Bed & breakfast: £52 single, £76.50-£90 double.

Half board: £58-£115.50 daily, £340-£378 weekly.
Lunch available.
Evening meal 7pm (l.o. 9.30pm).
Parking for 25.
Credit: Access, Visa, Diners, Amex.

Old Brewery Guest House **M**
🏆🏆🏆
29 The Green, Richmond, DL10 4RG
☎ (0748) 822460
Owner-run, listed building with fine views of Richmond Castle, overlooking the green and 2 minutes from riverside walks. Policed car park nearby. Art courses and weekend/midweek winter breaks available.
Bedrooms: 2 double & 1 twin.
Bathrooms: 3 private.
Bed & breakfast: £29 single, £38-£46 double.
Lunch available.
Evening meal 7.30pm (l.o. 5.30pm).

Ridgeway Guest House
🏆🏆🏆 COMMENDED
47 Darlington Rd., Richmond, DL10 7BG
☎ (0748) 823801
Charming detached 1920's house with private parking. Convenient A1 and town. Comfortable rooms, imaginative home cooking and personal service. Pets welcome. Non-smokers only please.
Bedrooms: 3 double & 2 twin.
Bathrooms: 5 private.
Bed & breakfast: from £34 double.
Half board: from £26.50 daily.
Evening meal 6pm (l.o. 4pm).
Parking for 6.
Open February-October.

West End Guest House
🏆🏆🏆 COMMENDED
45 Reeth Rd., Richmond, DL10 4EX
☎ (0748) 824783
Peaceful 19th C house within a large garden, close to town and river. Home cooking a speciality. Ample parking. Dogs welcome.
Bedrooms: 1 single, 2 double & 1 twin, 1 family room.
Bathrooms: 4 private, 1 public.
Bed & breakfast: from £15 single, £30-£36 double.

Half board: from £25 daily.
Evening meal 7pm (l.o. 5pm).
Parking for 12.

RIPLEY

N. Yorkshire
Map ref 4B1

Boar's Head Hotel **M**
🏆🏆🏆 COMMENDED
Ripley, Harrogate, HG3 3AY
☎ Harrogate (0423) 771888
& Fax (0423) 771509
In a lovely setting in the centre of Ripley village, only 100 yards from the gates of the castle.
Bedrooms: 5 double & 20 twin.
Bathrooms: 25 private.
Bed & breakfast: £75-£80 single, £92-£100 double.
Half board: £68-£74 daily, £476-£518 weekly.
Lunch available.
Evening meal 7pm (l.o. 9.30pm).
Parking for 40.
Credit: Access, Visa, Amex.

RIPON

N. Yorkshire
Map ref 5C3

Small, ancient city with impressive cathedral containing Saxon crypt which houses church treasures from all over Yorkshire. 'Setting the Watch' tradition kept nightly by horn-blower in Market Square. Fountains Abbey nearby.

Bridge Hotel **M**
🏆🏆🏆 COMMENDED
Magdalen Rd., Ripon, HG4 1HX
☎ (0765) 603687
Carefully restored Victorian property with a terrace and a charming garden. Interesting and comfortable accommodation with emphasis on food.
Bedrooms: 1 single, 6 double & 3 twin, 5 family rooms.
Bathrooms: 15 private.
Bed & breakfast: £48-£56 single, £60-£70 double.
Half board: £40-£45 daily.
Lunch available.
Evening meal 7pm (l.o. 9.30pm).
Parking for 15.

Credit: Access, Visa, Diners, Amex.

Crescent Lodge **M**
🏆🏆
42-42a North St., Ripon, HG4 1EN
☎ (0765) 602331
Reputedly the former Archbishop of York's town residence. Early Georgian house within easy walking distance of the city centre. Ample street parking. Special rates for children.
Bedrooms: 1 single, 4 double & 1 twin, 4 family rooms.
Bathrooms: 3 private, 3 public.
Bed & breakfast: £15 single, £24-£36 double.

ROSEDALE ABBEY

N. Yorkshire
Map ref 5C3

Sturdy hamlet built around Cistercian nunnery in the reign of Henry II, in the middle of Rosedale, largest of the moorland valleys.

Blacksmiths Arms Hotel **M**
🏆🏆🏆🏆 COMMENDED
Hartoft End, Rosedale Abbey, Pickering, YO18 8EN
☎ Lastingham (075 15) 331
Family-owned and managed country hotel in a beautiful forest and moorland setting. Tastefully decorated restaurant with special emphasis on traditional English food and good wine.
Bedrooms: 10 double & 4 twin.
Bathrooms: 14 private.
Half board: £39.95-£55 daily.
Lunch available.
Evening meal 7pm (l.o. 9.30pm).
Parking for 150.
Credit: Access, Visa, Diners.

Milburn Arms Hotel **M**
🏆🏆🏆 COMMENDED
Rosedale Abbey, Pickering, YO18 8RA
☎ Lastingham (075 15) 312
& Fax (075 15) 312
Historic inn, in a picturesque conservation area village, central to the national park and 15 miles from the Yorkshire Heritage Coast.

Continued ▶

ROSEDALE ABBEY
Continued

Bedrooms: 9 double & 2 twin.
Bathrooms: 11 private.
Bed & breakfast: £42-£48 single, £69-£75 double.
Half board: £48-£56 daily, £300-£360 weekly.
Lunch available.
Evening meal 7pm (l.o. 9.30pm).
Parking for 30.
Credit: Access, Visa.

White Horse Farm Hotel M
♛♛♛ COMMENDED
Rosedale Abbey, Pickering, YO18 8SE
☎ Lastingham (075 15) 239
㊛ Minotels
Charming Georgian country inn with magnificent views over Rosedale. Ideal base for a walking or touring holiday.
Bedrooms: 11 double & 3 twin, 1 family room.
Bathrooms: 15 private, 1 public.
Bed & breakfast: £30-£40 single, £60-£70 double.
Half board: £41-£48 daily.
Lunch available.
Evening meal 7pm (l.o. 8.45pm).
Parking for 50.
Credit: Access, Visa, Diners, Amex.

ROTHERHAM
S. Yorkshire
Map ref 4B2

In the Don Valley, Rotherham became an important industrial town in 19th C with discovery of coal and development of iron and steel industry by Joshua Walker who built Clifton House, now the town's museum. Magnificent 15th C All Saints Church is town's showpiece.
Tourist Information Centre ☎ *(0709) 823611*

Beeches Hotel & Leisure Complex M
♛♛♛♛ COMMENDED
(M1, Junction 33) West Bawtry Rd., Rotherham, S60 4HN
☎ (0709) 830630
Fax (0709) 548252

Modern, 4-storey building with extensive conference and banqueting facilities and leisure complex. Easy access from junction 33 of M1.
Bedrooms: 71 double & 30 twin, 10 family rooms.
Bathrooms: 111 private.
Bed & breakfast: from £35 single, from £60 double.
Half board: from £40 daily, from £195 weekly.
Lunch available.
Evening meal (l.o. 9.45pm).
Parking for 263.
Credit: Access, Visa, C.Bl., Diners, Amex.

Brentwood Hotel M
♛♛♛♛ COMMENDED
Moorgate Rd., Rotherham, S60 2TY
☎ (0709) 382772 & 820289
Telex 547291
Family-run Victorian mansion in its own gardens. Speciality restaurant and a fine wine cellar.
Bedrooms: 18 single, 19 double & 6 twin.
Bathrooms: 43 private.
Bed & breakfast: £20-£50 single, £35-£68 double.
Half board: £35.50-£65.50 daily.
Lunch available.
Evening meal 7pm (l.o. 9.30pm).
Parking for 65.
Credit: Access, Visa, Diners, Amex.

Consort Hotel, Banqueting & Conference Suite M
♛♛♛♛ COMMENDED
Brampton Rd., Thurcroft, Rotherham, S66 9JA
☎ Rotherham (0709) 530022
Fax 0709 531529
On the junction of the M1 and M18, access exits 1 on the M18 and 31 and 33 on the M1.
Bedrooms: 10 double & 8 twin.
Bathrooms: 18 private.
Bed & breakfast: £28-£60 single, £44-£70 double.
Half board: £37-£73 daily.
Lunch available.
Evening meal 6pm (l.o. 9.30pm).
Parking for 96.
Credit: Access, Visa, Amex.

Elton Hotel M
♛♛♛ COMMENDED
Main St., Bramley, Rotherham, S66 0SF
☎ (0709) 545681
Fax (0709) 549100
200-year-old, stone-built, Yorkshire house with a modern extension and a well known restaurant. Half a mile from junction 1 of M18, 2 miles from M1.
Bedrooms: 9 single, 12 double & 4 twin, 4 family rooms.
Bathrooms: 29 private.
Bed & breakfast: £30-£59 single, £55-£70 double.
Half board: £46-£75 daily.
Lunch available.
Evening meal 7pm (l.o. 9.30pm).
Parking for 50.
Credit: Access, Visa, Diners, Amex.

Regis Hotel
♛♛
1 Hall Rd., Moorgate, Rotherham, S60 2BP
☎ (0709) 376666 & 382564
Large stone-built hotel in its own grounds with a private car park. 2 minutes to Rotherham centre and 4 minutes to the M1 exit 33.
Bedrooms: 3 single, 2 double & 7 twin.
Bathrooms: 4 private, 2 public.
Bed & breakfast: £21.50-£30 single, £30-£40 double.
Parking for 10.
Credit: Access, Visa, Diners, Amex.

Rotherham Moat House
♛♛♛♛
Moorgate Rd., Rotherham, S60 2BG
☎ (0709) 364902
Fax (0709) 368960
Telex 547810
㊛ Queens Moat Houses
Modern hotel with conference facilities, a restaurant and theme bar. In a residential area, close to the M1 motorway.
Bedrooms: 40 single, 14 double & 27 twin.
Bathrooms: 81 private.
Bed & breakfast: £34.75-£70.75 single, £49.50-£85.50 double.
Half board: £47.25-£83.25 daily.
Lunch available.
Evening meal 7.30pm (l.o. 9.45pm).
Parking for 122.

Credit: Access, Visa, Diners, Amex.

RUNSWICK BAY
N. Yorkshire
Map ref 5D3

Cliffemount Hotel M
♛♛♛ APPROVED
Runswick Bay, Saltburn-by-the-Sea, Cleveland
TS13 5HU
☎ Whitby (0947) 840103
Relaxing hotel on the clifftop with panoramic views of Runswick Bay. 9 miles north of Whitby.
Bedrooms: 4 double & 1 twin, 1 family room.
Bathrooms: 4 private, 2 public.
Bed & breakfast: £14-£29 single, £35-£45 double.
Half board: £24-£49 daily.
Lunch available.
Evening meal 7pm (l.o. 9.30pm).
Parking for 30.

SCARBOROUGH
N. Yorkshire
Map ref 5D3

Large, popular east coast seaside resort, formerly a spa town. Beautiful gardens and splendid sandy beaches in North and South Bays. Castle ruins date from 1100, fine Georgian and Victorian houses in old town. September angling, theatres, cricket festivals and seasonal entertainment.
Tourist Information Centre ☎ *(0723) 373333*

Alton Hotel M
♛♛
16-17 Blenheim Terrace, North Bay, Scarborough, YO12 7HF
☎ (0723) 501015
Family-run hotel in superb location offering magnificent views of bay and castle. Licensed bar, comfortable lounges, warm and friendly atmosphere. Lift available.
Bedrooms: 13 single, 11 double & 20 twin, 6 family rooms.
Bathrooms: 16 private, 6 public.
Bed & breakfast: £18-£24 single, £36-£48 double.
Half board: £23-£29 daily.

Evening meal 6.30pm (l.o. 6.30pm).
Open April-October.
Credit: Visa.

Alver Hotel 🏨
Listed
8 Blenheim Terrace, Queen's Parade, Scarborough, YO12 7HF
☎ (0723) 373256
In an unrivalled position overlooking the North Bay and within easy walking distance of most amenities.
Bedrooms: 6 double & 2 twin, 5 family rooms.
Bathrooms: 3 public.
Bed & breakfast: £17.50-£20 single, £35-£40 double.
Half board: £22-£24 daily, £135-£163 weekly.
Evening meal 5pm (l.o. midday).
Parking for 3.
Open April-October.

Amber Lodge Guest House
17 Trinity Rd., South Cliff, Scarborough, YO11 2TD
☎ (0723) 369088
Elegant guesthouse with en-suite rooms. Close to South Bay and Spa. Vegetarian food our speciality. No smoking.
Bedrooms: 2 single, 3 double & 1 twin, 1 family room.
Bathrooms: 4 private, 1 public.
Bed & breakfast: £14 single, £28-£32 double.
Evening meal 6pm (l.o. 10am).
Parking for 6.
Open April-October.
Credit: Access, Visa.

Ash-Lea Private Hotel 🏨
119 Columbus Ravine, Scarborough, YO12 7QU
☎ (0723) 361874
Near Peasholm Park, Alexandra Bowls, Kinderland, Water Splash, North Beach, Sea Life Centre, town centre.
Bedrooms: 1 single, 1 double & 3 twin, 2 family rooms.
Bathrooms: 1 public.
Bed & breakfast: from £13 single, from £26 double.
Half board: from £16 daily.
Evening meal 5.30pm (l.o. 6.30pm).
Credit: Access, Visa.

Avoncroft Hotel 🏨
5, 6 & 7 Crown Terrace, South Cliff, Scarborough, YO11 2BL
☎ (0723) 372737
Listed Georgian terrace overlooking Crown Gardens. Close to spa and sports facilities. Convenient for town centre and all entertainments.
Bedrooms: 7 single, 10 double & 5 twin, 12 family rooms.
Bathrooms: 20 private, 5 public.
Bed & breakfast: £17.40-£19.40 single, £34.80-£38.80 double.
Half board: £23-£25 daily, £150-£163 weekly.
Lunch available.
Evening meal 5.30pm (l.o. 6.15pm).

Boundary Hotel 🏨
124-126 North Marine Rd., Scarborough, YO12 7HZ
☎ (0723) 376737
Comfortable family-run hotel on the north side of Scarborough. Overlooking cricket ground, close to town centre and all amenities.
Bedrooms: 2 single, 2 double & 1 twin, 7 family rooms.
Bathrooms: 12 private, 1 public.
Bed & breakfast: £16-£18 single, £32-£36 double.
Half board: £20-£22 daily.
Evening meal 5.30pm (l.o. 6pm).
Credit: Access, Visa.

Cairn Cleveleys 🏨
133-135 Castle Rd., Scarborough, YO11 1HX
☎ (0723) 374853
One of the few hotels in the resort to have panoramic views of the sea and coastline from all bedrooms. Full English breakfast.
Bedrooms: 3 single, 10 double & 3 twin, 4 family rooms.
Bathrooms: 3 private, 6 public; 1 private shower.
Bed & breakfast: £14 single, £28 double.
Half board: £14 daily, £95 weekly.
Evening meal 6pm.
Parking for 3.
Open March-October.

Central Guest House
6 & 7 Bell Vue Parade, Scarborough, YO11 1SU
☎ (0723) 372810
Close to the rail and bus stations, small family guesthouse offering home cooking. Tea making facilities, TV lounge and games room.
Bedrooms: 1 single, 4 double & 1 twin, 5 family rooms.
Bathrooms: 2 public.
Bed & breakfast: £9-£11 single, £18-£22 double.
Half board: £12.50-£14 daily, £85-£95 weekly.
Evening meal 5pm (l.o. 3pm).

Central Hotel & Restaurant 🏨
APPROVED
1-3 The Crescent, Scarborough, YO11 2PW
☎ (0723) 365766
Property of historic interest in a beautiful Georgian crescent. Central for all amenities, shops, sea and spa. Car park. Restaurant and wine bar with bar menu. Family owned and managed.
Bedrooms: 9 single, 13 double & 14 twin, 3 family rooms.
Bathrooms: 21 private, 5 public.
Bed & breakfast: £28.75-£33.25 single, £50.50-£59.50 double.
Half board: £36.50-£41 daily, £226-£253 weekly.
Lunch available.
Evening meal 6pm (l.o. 9.30pm).
Parking for 15.
Credit: Access, Visa, Diners, Amex.

Collingham Hotel 🏨
74 North Marine Rd., Scarborough, YO12 7PE
☎ (0723) 366184
Family-run, licensed hotel close to all amenities. Baby listening service, satellite TV, home cooking. School and coach parties welcome.
Bedrooms: 1 single, 4 double & 2 twin, 4 family rooms.
Bathrooms: 2 public.
Bed & breakfast: £14.50-£15.50 single, £29-£31 double.
Half board: £17.50-£19 daily, £122.50-£133 weekly.
Lunch available.
Evening meal 5pm (l.o. 5pm).

Hotel Diana
31 New Queen St., Scarborough, YO12 7HJ
☎ (0723) 372874
Family-run, licensed hotel overlooking the North Bay. Spacious guest and public rooms with full gas central heating. En-suite rooms available.
Bedrooms: 1 single, 2 double & 1 twin, 8 family rooms.
Bathrooms: 4 private, 3 public.
Bed & breakfast: £15 single, £30 double.
Half board: £18 daily, £126 weekly.
Evening meal 5.30pm.
Parking for 3.
Open April-October.

Dunvegan Manor Hotel
43 Northstead Manor Drive, Scarborough, YO12 6AF
☎ (0723) 372256
Detached hotel with all bedrooms on one floor. Overlooking Peasholm Park and a few minutes' walk to the beach and all North Bay amenities.
Bedrooms: 1 single, 4 double & 2 twin, 1 family room.
Bathrooms: 2 public.
Bed & breakfast: £15-£16 single, £30-£32 double.
Half board: £17-£20 daily, £112-£125 weekly.
Evening meal 5.45pm.
Open March-October.

Earlsmere Hotel
COMMENDED
5 Belvedere Rd., South Cliff, Scarborough, YO11 2UU
☎ (0723) 361340
Elegant Edwardian building of character retaining most of the original features. 2 minutes from the Esplanade. Choice of menus.
Bedrooms: 1 single, 3 double & 3 twin.
Bathrooms: 4 private, 1 public.
Bed & breakfast: £18-£22 single, £38-£42 double.
Half board: £24-£31 daily, £170-£190 weekly.
Lunch available.
Evening meal 6.30pm (l.o. 7pm).
Parking for 2.
Credit: Access, Visa.

Please mention this guide when making a booking.

181

SCARBOROUGH
Continued

East Ayton Lodge Country Hotel & Restaurant M

♛♛♛♛

Moor Lane, East Ayton,
Scarborough, YO13 9EW
☎ Scarborough
(0723) 864227
Fax (0723) 862680
*Country hotel and restaurant
in a beautiful 3-acre setting by
the River Derwent, in the
North York Moors National
Park only 3 miles from
Scarborough.*
Bedrooms: 8 double & 5 twin,
4 family rooms.
Bathrooms: 17 private.
Bed & breakfast: £35-£45
single, £45-£80 double.
Half board: £40-£62.50 daily,
£220-£325 weekly.
Lunch available.
Evening meal 6pm (l.o. 9pm).
Parking for 50.
Credit: Access, Visa, Amex.

Esplanade Hotel M

♛♛♛♛

Belmont Rd., Scarborough,
YO11 2AA
☎ (0723) 360382
*Welcoming period-style hotel
in good position on
Scarborough's South Cliff.
Close to beach, spa and town
centre. Landau restaurant,
parlour bar and roof terrace.*
Bedrooms: 18 single,
17 double & 28 twin,
10 family rooms.
Bathrooms: 73 private,
7 public.
Bed & breakfast: £33.75-£35
single, £61.30-£65 double.
Half board: £38.33-£48 daily,
£243.18-£259 weekly.
Lunch available.
Evening meal 6.30pm (l.o.
9pm).
Parking for 24.
Credit: Access, Visa, Diners,
Amex.

Excelsior Private Hotel M

Listed APPROVED

1 Marlborough St.,
Scarborough, YO12 7HG
☎ (0723) 360716
*Centrally situated on corner of
North Bay seafront. Personal
service, fresh produce, home-
made bread, soups and sweets.
No smoking in lounge and
dining room.*

Bedrooms: 3 single, 2 double
& 1 twin, 3 family rooms.
Bathrooms: 2 public.
Bed & breakfast: £13-£16
single, £26-£32 double.
Half board: £16-£20 daily,
£90-£115 weekly.
Evening meal 5.30pm.
Open April-October.

Green Gables Private Hotel M

Listed

West Bank, Scarborough,
YO12 4DX
☎ (0723) 361005
*Originally a late Victorian
hydropathic establishment, now
a family-owned hotel
particularly suited to family
holidays. Children very
welcome.*
Bedrooms: 2 twin, 21 family
rooms.
Bathrooms: 16 private,
6 public.
Bed & breakfast: £13-£15.55
single, £26-£31.10 double.
Half board: £18.50-£21.05
daily.
Evening meal 6pm (l.o. 6pm).
Parking for 26.
Open April-October.

Gridleys Crescent Hotel M

♛♛♛♛

The Crescent, Scarborough,
YO11 2PP
☎ (0723) 360929
Fax (0723) 354126
*Centrally situated, overlooking
Crescent Gardens and close to
all amenities. Carvery,
restaurant. Car park adjacent.*
Bedrooms: 3 single, 10 double
& 7 twin.
Bathrooms: 20 private.
Bed & breakfast: from £37.50
single, £65-£75 double.
Half board: £47-£52 daily.
Lunch available.
Evening meal 5pm (l.o.
10pm).
Credit: Access, Visa.

Highbank Hotel M

Listed COMMENDED

5 Givendale Rd.,
Scarborough, YO12 6LE
☎ (0723) 365265
*Small hotel in quiet, pleasant
setting. Friendly service
assured. Convenient for all
North Bay attractions. Safe
parking.*
Bedrooms: 2 single, 6 double
& 2 twin.

Bathrooms: 3 private,
2 public.
Bed & breakfast: £13-£14
single, £26-£28 double.
Half board: £17-£18 daily.
Evening meal 5.30pm (l.o.
6pm).
Parking for 9.
Open March-December.

Holmelea Guest House M

Listed APPROVED

8 Belle Vue Parade,
Scarborough, YO11 1SU
☎ (0723) 360139
*Family-run guesthouse. Rooms
centrally heated with divans,
duvets, tea/coffee making,
colour TV with satellite/video
link, radio alarms and razor
points.*
Bedrooms: 2 single, 2 double
& 1 twin, 1 family room.
Bathrooms: 1 public.
Bed & breakfast: £11-£13
single, £22-£24 double.
Half board: £14-£15 daily,
£94-£101 weekly.
Evening meal 5.30pm.

Invergarry M

Listed

4 St. Martin's Square, South
Cliff, Scarborough,
YO11 2DQ
☎ (0723) 372013
*Quiet, family-run guesthouse in
a pleasant square, within 2
minutes' walk of the seafront
and South Cliff Gardens.*
Bedrooms: 3 single, 6 double
& 1 twin.
Bathrooms: 2 public.
Bed & breakfast: £11-£11.50
single, £22-£23 double.
Half board: £14-£14.50 daily.
Evening meal 5.30pm.
Open January-October.

Manor Heath Hotel M

♛♛♛

67 Northstead Manor Drive,
Scarborough, YO12 6AF
☎ (0723) 365720
*Detached hotel with pleasant
gardens and a private car park,
overlooking Peasholm Park
and the sea. Close to all North
Bay attractions.*
Bedrooms: 3 single, 9 double,
4 family rooms.
Bathrooms: 11 private,
2 public.
Bed & breakfast: £15.50-£20
single, £31-£40 double.

Half board: £19.50-£24 daily,
£133-£165 weekly.
Evening meal 6pm.
Parking for 12.

Melbourne M

APPROVED

57 Moorland Rd.,
Scarborough, YO12 7RD
☎ (0723) 371172
*Small, comfortable, family-run
guesthouse close to all North
Bay amenities and the town
centre.*
Bedrooms: 2 single, 1 double
& 1 twin, 1 family room.
Bathrooms: 1 public.
Bed & breakfast: £12-£12.50
single, £23-£24 double.
Half board: £15.70-£16.70
daily, £102.90-£109.90
weekly.
Evening meal 6pm (l.o. 1pm).

Moseley Lodge Private Hotel M

♛♛♛

26 Avenue Victoria, South
Cliff, Scarborough,
YO11 2QT
☎ (0723) 360564
*Elegant Victorian licensed
hotel close to esplanade, spa,
gardens and town. Relaxed
atmosphere, comfortable
surroundings. Vegetarian and
special diets catered for.*
Bedrooms: 1 single, 5 double
& 3 twin.
Bathrooms: 5 private,
2 public.
Bed & breakfast: £17 single,
£34-£50 double.
Half board: £20-£26 daily,
£135-£162 weekly.
Evening meal 6pm (l.o. 6pm).

Northcote M

♛♛♛

114 Columbus Ravine,
Scarborough, YO12 7QZ
☎ (0723) 367758
*Modern, semi-detached private
hotel with bedrooms on 2 floors
only. Special offers available
for senior citizens. All rooms
en-suite and with colour TV.
Non-smokers only please.
Families welcome.*
Bedrooms: 1 single, 4 double
& 2 twin, 2 family rooms.
Bathrooms: 9 private,
1 public.
Bed & breakfast: £15-£16
single, £30-£32 double.
Half board: £20-£21 daily,
£125-£140 weekly.

Evening meal 5.30pm.
Parking for 5.
Open May-October.

Palm Court Hotel ⋈
🏵🏵🏵🏵 COMMENDED

St. Nicholas Cliff,
Scarborough, YO11 2ES
☎ (0723) 368161
Fax (0723) 371547
Telex 527579
Centrally situated yet only minutes from the beach. Ideal for conferences, seminars and private functions.
Complimentary car parking available.
Bedrooms: 14 single,
15 double & 10 twin, 11 family rooms.
Bathrooms: 50 private,
3 public.
Bed & breakfast: £34 single,
£58-£68 double.
Half board: £39.75-£44.75 daily, £250-£285 weekly.
Lunch available.
Evening meal 7pm (l.o. 9pm).
Parking for 86.
Credit: Access, Visa, Diners, Amex.

Paragon Hotel
🏵🏵🏵 COMMENDED

123 Queen's Parade,
Scarborough, YO12 7HU
☎ (0723) 372676
Modern, comfortable, superbly situated seafront hotel offering a choice and varied menu in pleasant surroundings.
Bedrooms: 2 single, 9 double & 2 twin, 3 family rooms.
Bathrooms: 16 private,
1 public.
Bed & breakfast: £25-£27 single, £36-£40 double.
Half board: £25-£27 daily.
Evening meal 6pm (l.o. 6.30pm).
Credit: Access, Visa, Diners.

Parmelia Hotel ⋈
🏵🏵🏵 COMMENDED

17 West St., Southcliff,
Scarborough, YO11 2QN
☎ (0723) 361914
Spacious, licensed hotel with emphasis on comfort, quality and home cooking. On the South Cliff near the Esplanade Gardens, the cliff lift to the spa and the beach.
Bedrooms: 2 single, 4 double & 6 twin, 3 family rooms.
Bathrooms: 11 private,
2 public.
Bed & breakfast: £16.50-£19 single, £33-£38 double.

Half board: £21.50-£24 daily.
Evening meal 6pm (l.o. 5pm).
Open April-October.

Philamon ⋈
🏵🏵

108 North Marine Rd.,
Scarborough, YO12 7JA
☎ (0723) 373107
North side family-run guesthouse overlooking the cricket ground at the rear. Home cooking and comfortable rooms with tea making facilities.
Bedrooms: 2 single, 3 double & 1 twin, 2 family rooms.
Bathrooms: 3 private,
1 public.
Bed & breakfast: from £12 single, from £24 double.
Half board: from £15.50 daily, from £108.50 weekly.
Evening meal 5.30pm (l.o. 5.30pm).

Pickwick Inn ⋈
🏵🏵🏵 COMMENDED

Huntriss Row, Scarborough,
YO11 2ED
☎ (0723) 375787
Recently fully-refurbished hotel with bars and restaurants, central for the beach and all other amenities.
Bedrooms: 2 single, 7 double & 2 twin.
Bathrooms: 11 private.
Bed & breakfast: £27-£32 single, £44-£55 double.
Half board: £36.50-£41.50 daily, £199.50-£220.50 weekly.
Lunch available.
Evening meal 7pm (l.o. 10.15pm).
Credit: Access, Visa, Diners, Amex.

Premier Hotel ⋈
🏵🏵

66 Esplanade, Scarborough,
YO11 2UZ
☎ (0723) 501038 & 501062
Lovely Victorian seafront hotel. Peace, tranquillity, wonderful sea views, lift to all floors and private parking.
Bedrooms: 6 single, 5 double & 5 twin, 3 family rooms.
Bathrooms: 19 private.
Bed & breakfast: £30-£35 single, £56-£70 double.
Half board: £34-£42 daily, £224-£259 weekly.
Evening meal 6pm (l.o. 6pm).
Parking for 7.
Open March-November.

Red Lea Hotel ⋈
🏵🏵🏵🏵 COMMENDED

Prince of Wales Terrace,
Scarborough, YO11 2AJ
☎ (0723) 362431
Traditional hotel with sea views, close to the Spa Centre. Restaurant, bar, lounges, lift and colour TVs. Solarium and indoor heated swimming pool.
Bedrooms: 19 single,
12 double & 37 twin.
Bathrooms: 68 private.
Bed & breakfast: £28-£30 single, £56-£60 double.
Half board: £39-£41 daily, £275-£280 weekly.
Lunch available.
Evening meal 6.30pm (l.o. 8pm).
Credit: Access, Visa.

Riga Hotel ⋈
🏵🏵 APPROVED

10 Crown Crescent,
Scarborough, YO11 2BJ
☎ (0723) 363994
Family-run, licensed hotel on the South Cliff, overlooking the Crown Gardens. Choice of menu. Children under 3 free.
Bedrooms: 3 single, 2 double & 4 twin, 4 family rooms.
Bathrooms: 1 private,
3 public.
Bed & breakfast: £12.50-£14.50 single, £28-£29 double.
Half board: £16-£18.50 daily, £108.50-£122.50 weekly.
Evening meal 6pm (l.o. 3.30pm).

Riviera Hotel ⋈
🏵🏵🏵 COMMENDED

St. Nicholas Cliff,
Scarborough, YO11 2ES
☎ (0723) 372277
Ideal central location within yards of beach, spa, town centre and theatres. All bedrooms with full facilities for maximum comfort.
Bedrooms: 5 single, 6 double & 2 twin, 7 family rooms.
Bathrooms: 20 private.
Bed & breakfast: £26-£30 single, £52-£60 double.
Half board: £37-£41 daily, £240-£260 weekly.
Evening meal 6pm (l.o. 7pm).
Credit: Access, Visa.

Ryndle Court Private Hotel
⋈

47 Northstead Manor Drive,
Scarborough, YO12 6AF
☎ (0723) 375188

Imposing detached hotel with bedrooms on 2 floors, in quiet surroundings overlooking Peasholm Park. Close to all amenities. Lunch available on request. TV and hair-dryer in all bedrooms.
Bedrooms: 2 single, 4 double & 7 twin, 2 family rooms.
Bathrooms: 8 private,
2 public.
Bed & breakfast: £20-£25 single, £40-£50 double.
Half board: £23-£29 daily, £145-£180 weekly.
Evening meal 5.30pm (l.o. 5pm).
Parking for 10.

Hotel St. Nicholas ⋈
🏵🏵🏵🏵 COMMENDED

St. Nicholas Cliff,
Scarborough, YO11 2EU
☎ (0723) 364101 Telex 52351
Ⓖ Principal
Overlooking the south bay of this popular resort. Facilities include a snooker room, leisure centre with indoor swimming pool. For children, the Junior Fun Club operates throughout the school holidays.
Bedrooms: 40 single,
26 double & 57 twin, 17 family rooms.
Bathrooms: 140 private.
Bed & breakfast: from £67 single, from £93 double.
Half board: from £50 daily.
Lunch available.
Evening meal 7pm (l.o. 9.15pm).
Parking for 22.
Credit: Access, Visa, Diners, Amex.

Southlands Hotel ⋈
🏵🏵🏵🏵 COMMENDED

West St., South Cliff,
Scarborough, YO11 2QW
☎ (0723) 361461
Fax (0723) 376035
Telex 57515/28
Ⓖ Consort
Spacious, comfortable, owner-run hotel with emphasis on food and personal attention. All modern facilities and a large, private car park. Close to beach, shops, golf, fishing, sports centre. Dogs by arrangement.
Bedrooms: 7 single, 20 double & 22 twin, 9 family rooms.
Bathrooms: 58 private,
2 public.
Bed & breakfast: £20-£35 single, £35-£65 double.
Half board: £30-£40 daily, £150-£240 weekly.

Continued ▶

YORKSHIRE & HUMBERSIDE

SCARBOROUGH

Continued

Lunch available.
Evening meal 6.30pm (l.o. 8.30pm).
Parking for 40.
Open March-November.
Credit: Access, Visa, Diners, Amex.

🌣 📞 🔄 ⌨ 💺 Ⅴ ⅄ ⊟
📺 ◐ ⚑ ▥ ⬛ ➔ ↑ ∪ ➤ ⌷
⚑ SP Ⓣ

Stewart Hotel ⋒
St. Nicholas Cliff,
Scarborough, YO11 2ES
☎ (0723) 361095
In an ideal position with sea views overlooking the South Bay and close to the beach and shopping centre.
Bedrooms: 2 single, 4 double & 2 twin, 9 family rooms.
Bathrooms: 6 private, 2 public.
Bed & breakfast: £17-£22 single, £34-£44 double.
Half board: £25-£30 daily, £160-£195 weekly.
Evening meal 5.30pm (l.o. 6.30pm).
Credit: Access, Visa.

🌣 ❐ 🔄 🅸 Ⅴ ⊟ ⬛ ➔ ✕
⚑ ⚑ SP ⊞

Sunningdale Private Hotel ⋒
👑👑👑
105 Peasholm Drive,
Scarborough, YO12 7NB
☎ (0723) 372041
Modern, detached hotel facing Peasholm Park and close to all north side attractions.
Bedrooms: 2 single, 4 double, 5 family rooms.
Bathrooms: 11 private, 1 public.
Bed & breakfast: £19-£21 single, £38-£42 double.
Half board: £23-£25 daily, £161-£175 weekly.
Evening meal 5.30pm.
Credit: Access, Visa.

🌣 ❐ ❐ 🔄 🅸 Ⅴ ⊟ ⬛
✕ ⚑ ⌷ ⚑ ⊞

Villa Marina Hotel ⋒
👑👑👑
59 Northstead Manor Drive,
Scarborough, YO12 6AF
☎ (0723) 361088
Modern, detached hotel in a beautiful location overlooking Peasholm Park and North Bay holiday attractions.
Bedrooms: 2 single, 4 double & 2 twin, 5 family rooms.
Bathrooms: 5 private, 2 public.
Bed & breakfast: £31-£33 double.
Half board: £37-£42 daily.

Evening meal 5.30pm (l.o. 5.30pm).
Parking for 9.
Open April-October.

🌣 ❐ 🔄 ⌨ Ⅵ Ⅴ ⅄ ⊟ 📺 ➔
✕ ⚑ ⌷

Wharncliffe Hotel ⋒
Listed
26 Blenheim Terrace,
Scarborough, YO12 7HD
☎ (0723) 374635
Overlooking the beautiful North Bay, this family hotel puts the emphasis on a homely atmosphere, friendly service, cleanliness and food. Close to the town and its amenities.
Bedrooms: 7 double & 2 twin, 4 family rooms.
Bathrooms: 8 private, 1 public.
Bed & breakfast: £32-£46 double.
Half board: £23-£28 daily, £147-£182 weekly.
Evening meal 6pm (l.o. midday).
Open January-October.

🌣 ❐ 🔄 🅸 Ⅴ ⊟ 📺 ⬛ ➔
↑ ✕ ⌷ ⚑

Wrea Head Country Hotel ⋒
Barmoor La., Wrea Head,
Scalby, Scarborough,
YO13 0PB
☎ Scarborough (0723) 378211
Charming and characterful country house in tranquil setting, in 14 acres bordering National Park. Well-appointed refurbished rooms with all facilities.
Bedrooms: 4 single, 4 double & 10 twin, 3 family rooms.
Bathrooms: 21 private.
Bed & breakfast: £45-£65 single, £90-£130 double.
Half board: £67.50-£97.50 daily.
Lunch available.
Evening meal 7pm (l.o. 9.15pm).
Parking for 101.
Credit: Access, Visa, Amex.

🌣 ❐ 🔄 📞 ⌨ ❐ 🅸 Ⅴ ⊟
◐ ⬛ ➔ ↑ ∪ ✿ ✕ ⚑ SP
⌷ ⊞

SCOTCH CORNER

N. Yorkshire
Map ref 5C3

Famous milestone at the junction of the A1 and A66 near Richmond.

Hunters End ⋒
APPROVED
Morris Grange, Scotch Corner, Richmond,
DL10 6PA
☎ Richmond (0748) 822895

A warm welcome with home cooking near England's most famous crossroads. Ideal base for touring dales, moors and historic sites of North Yorkshire.
Bedrooms: 1 double & 1 twin, 1 family room.
Bathrooms: 3 private, 2 public.
Bed & breakfast: £25-£27.50 single, £35-£39 double.
Half board: £26.50-£32 daily, £170-£195 weekly.
Evening meal 6pm (l.o. 7.30pm).
Parking for 7.
Credit: Access, Visa.

🌣 ❐ 🔄 🅸 Ⅴ ⊟ 📺 ⬛ ➔
✿ ✕ ⌷ ⚑ SP

Scotch Corner Hotel ⋒
COMMENDED
Scotch Corner, Richmond,
DL10 6NR
☎ Richmond (0748) 850900
Telex 587447
On the A1 midway between London and Glasgow, offering a welcoming, comfortable atmosphere for the tourist or businessman covering the North of England. 3 suites.
Bedrooms: 16 single, 20 double & 48 twin, 6 family rooms.
Bathrooms: 90 private.
Bed & breakfast: from £69 single, from £91 double.
Lunch available.
Evening meal 7pm (l.o. 10pm).
Parking for 208.
Credit: Access, Visa, Diners, Amex.

🌣 ❐ 📞 ⌨ ❐ 🔄 🅸 Ⅴ ⊟
◐ ⚑ ⬛ ➔ ↑ ⚷ ⌷ SP ⊞

Vintage Hotel ⋒
COMMENDED
Scotch Corner, Richmond,
DL10 6NP
☎ Richmond (0748) 824424 & 822961
Extremely convenient for a meal or overnight stay, or a good base for touring the Yorkshire Dales. Richmond is only 3 miles away.
Bedrooms: 3 single, 3 double & 2 twin.
Bathrooms: 5 private, 1 public.
Bed & breakfast: £27.50-£35 single, £40-£47 double.
Half board: £32.50-£50 daily, £195-£340 weekly.
Lunch available.
Evening meal 6.30pm (l.o. 9.30pm).
Parking for 50.
Credit: Access, Visa.

🌣 📞 ❐ 🔄 🅸 ⊟ 📺 ⬛ ➔
✕ ⚑ ⊞

SCUNTHORPE

Humberside
Map ref 4C1

Consisted of 5 small villages until 1860 when extensive ironstone beds were discovered. Today an industrial 'garden town' with some interesting modern buildings. Nearby Normanby Hall contains fine examples of Regency furniture.
Tourist Information Centre ☎ (0724) 860161

Beverley Hotel
👑👑👑 **APPROVED**
55 Old Brumby St.,
Scunthorpe, S. Humberside
DN16 2AJ
☎ (0724) 282212
In the pleasant, quiet residential district of Old Brumby off the A18, close to Scunthorpe town centre.
Bedrooms: 5 single, 3 double & 5 twin, 2 family rooms.
Bathrooms: 15 private.
Bed & breakfast: £35-£40 single, £45-£50 double.
Half board: £40.75-£52 daily, from £285.25 weekly.
Lunch available.
Evening meal 6pm (l.o. 8pm).
Parking for 15.
Credit: Access, Visa.

🌣 ⚷ ❐ 🔄 🅸 Ⅴ ⅄ ⊟ 📺
◐ ⬛ ➔ ↑ ⚷ ✿ ⊟ 📺

The Downs Guest House
Listed
33 Deyne Avenue,
Scunthorpe, S. Humberside
DN15 7PZ
☎ (0724) 850710
Clean and friendly, family-run guesthouse.
Bedrooms: 3 single, 2 double & 2 twin, 1 family room.
Bathrooms: 2 public.
Bed & breakfast: from £12.50 single, from £25 double.
Evening meal 6pm.
Parking for 4.

🌣 ✕ ⚷ ❐ ⌨ 🅸 Ⅴ 📺 ⬛
⬛ ✕ ⚑

Larchwood Hotel ⋒
1-5 Shelford St., Scunthorpe,
S. Humberside DN15 6NU
☎ (0724) 864712/847517
Private family-run hotel, in central position close to railway and bus station. Satellite TV in all rooms, residents' lounge/bar.
Bedrooms: 3 single, 3 double & 4 twin, 1 family room.
Bathrooms: 4 public.

184

Bed & breakfast: £21-£28 single, £31-£38 double.
Parking for 6.
Credit: Access, Visa.
♒2♨☐♿🐕 Ⓥ ⌀ ⇥ TV
● 🖩 🛋 ♿ SP

SELBY

N. Yorkshire
Map ref 4C1

Small market town on the River Ouse, believed to have been birthplace of Henry I, with a magnificent abbey containing much fine Norman and Early English architecture.
Tourist Information Centre ☎ (0757) 703263

Park View Hotel & Licensed Restaurant ▲
😊😊😊 APPROVED

20 Main St., Riccall, York, YO4 6PX
☎ (0757) 248458
Attractive country house hotel and a la carte restaurant. 4 miles from Selby and 9 miles from York, off the A19.
Bedrooms: 5 double & 1 twin, 1 family room.
Bathrooms: 7 private.
Bed & breakfast: from £38 single, from £47 double.
Lunch available.
Evening meal 7pm (l.o. 9.30pm).
Parking for 20.
Credit: Access, Visa.
♒☐♿🐕 Ⓥ ⇥ TV 🖩 🛋
🐾 ✿ ✕ ⊠ SP

SETTLE

N. Yorkshire
Map ref 5B3

Town of narrow streets and Georgian houses in an area of great limestone hills and crags. Panoramic view from Castleberg Crag which stands 300 ft above town.
Tourist Information Centre ☎ (072 92) 5192.

Falcon Manor Hotel ▲
😊😊😊 APPROVED

Skipton Rd., Settle, BD24 9BD
☎ (0729) 823814
Fax (0729) 822087
Family-owned country house hotel in the dales market town of Settle. Ideal for walking, motoring and the Settle to Carlisle Railway.
Bedrooms: 10 double & 6 twin, 3 family rooms.
Bathrooms: 19 private.

Bed & breakfast: £49-£65 single, £70-£100 double.
Half board: £45-£59 daily.
Lunch available.
Evening meal 7pm (l.o. 10pm).
Parking for 80.
Credit: Access, Visa, Diners.
♒♿🐕 ☎ ☐♿ 🐕 Ⓥ
⇥ 🖩 🛋 🍴♿ ⴷ ✿ ⊠ SP
⊞ T

Halsteads ▲
COMMENDED

3 Halsteads Terrace, Duke St., Settle, BD24 9AP
☎ (0729) 822823
With magnificent views and ideally situated near the town centre, this elegant Victorian house is the perfect base for exploring the dales or the Settle-Carlisle Railway. Generous discounts for longer holidays or off-peak breaks. Tourist information available.
Bedrooms: 2 double & 2 twin.
Bathrooms: 2 private, 1 public.
Bed & breakfast: £32-£39 double.
Parking for 3.
♒7♿ ⇥ Ⓤ🐕 î Ⓥ ⇥ Ⓥ
🖩 🛋 ∪ ⴷ 🍴 î DAP SP

Whitefriars ▲

Church St., Settle, BD24 9JD
☎ (0729) 823753
Comfortable family-run guesthouse set in spacious gardens in centre of Settle. Central for exploring Yorkshire Dales, Settle/Carlisle Railway. Non-smokers only please.
Bedrooms: 1 single, 3 double & 2 twin, 3 family rooms.
Bathrooms: 3 private, 2 public.
Bed & breakfast: £15.50-£16 single, £31-£38 double.
Half board: £24-£28 daily, £151.20-£176.40 weekly.
Evening meal 7pm (l.o. 8pm).
Parking for 9.
♒♿ î Ⓥ ⌀ ⇥ TV 🖩 🛋
🍴 ✿ ✕ ⊠ ⴷ SP ⊞

Individual proprietors have supplied all details of accommodation. Although we do check for accuracy, we advise you to confirm prices and other information at the time of booking.

SHEFFIELD

S. Yorkshire
Map ref 4B2

Local iron ore and coal gave Sheffield its prosperous steel and cutlery industries. The modern city centre retains many interesting buildings - cathedral, Cutlers' Hall, Crucible Theatre, Graves and Mappin Art Galleries - and has an excellent shopping centre.
Tourist Information Centre ☎ (0742) 734671 or 734672

Beauchief Hotel ▲
😊😊😊😊 COMMENDED

161 Abbeydale Road South, Sheffield, S7 2QW
☎ (0742) 620500 & 350197
Telex 54164
CR Lansbury
Hotel near city of Sheffield but only 3 miles from the Peak District.
Bedrooms: 28 double & 13 twin.
Bathrooms: 41 private.
Bed & breakfast: £33-£80 single, £66-£92 double.
Half board: £46-£96 daily.
Lunch available.
Evening meal 7pm (l.o. 10pm).
Parking for 200.
Credit: Access, Visa, Diners, Amex.
♒♿♿ ☎ ☐ ☐♿ î Ⓥ
⌀ ⇥ ● 🖩 🛋 🍴 ⴷ SP
⊞

Charnwood Hotel ▲

10 Sharrow La., Sheffield, S11 8AA
☎ (0742) 589411
Charming Georgian residence extended to form a well-appointed country house hotel within the heart of the city.
Bedrooms: 9 single, 5 double & 7 twin.
Bathrooms: 21 private.
Bed & breakfast: £65-£75 single, £78-£88 double.
Lunch available.
Evening meal 7pm (l.o. 10pm).
Parking for 22.
Credit: Access, Visa, Diners, Amex.
♒♿ ☎ ☐ ☐♿ î Ⓥ ⇥
● 🖩 🛋 🍴 ✕ ⊠ SP ⊞ T

Critchleys ▲
😊😊

6 Causeway Head Rd., Dore, Sheffield, S17 3DT
☎ Sheffield (0742) 364328

Modern property, well-furnished and appointed with good-sized rooms. Near the Peak District National Park, city centre and all facilities.
Bedrooms: 1 single, 2 double & 1 twin.
Bathrooms: 1 private, 2 public.
Bed & breakfast: £14-£18 single, £28-£32 double.
Parking for 4.
☐♿ Ⓤ 🛋 🛋 ✕

Etruria House Hotel ▲
😊😊😊 APPROVED

91 Crookes Rd., Broomhill, Sheffield, S10 5BD
☎ (0742) 662241 & 670853
Family-run hotel in elegant Victorian house, close to all amenities and city centre. Ideal base for Peak District.
Bedrooms: 5 single, 3 double & 2 twin, 1 family room.
Bathrooms: 7 private, 2 public.
Bed & breakfast: £23-£28 single, £36-£42 double.
Half board: £28-£36 daily.
Evening meal 6pm (l.o. midday).
Parking for 13.
Credit: Access, Visa.
♒♿● ☐♿ Ⓤ Ⓥ ⇥ TV
🖩 🛋 ✕ ⊞

Ivory House Hotel ▲

34 Wostenholm Rd., Sheffield, S7 1LJ
☎ (0742) 551853
Within easy reach of both the city centre and countryside. Personal service from the family management. Tea and coffee facilities in all rooms.
Bedrooms: 5 single, 1 twin, 2 family rooms.
Bathrooms: 3 public.
Bed & breakfast: £20-£24 single, £34-£38 double.
Parking for 11.
♒☐♿ î Ⓥ TV 🖩 🐾 ✕
DAP SP

Lindum Hotel
😊😊

91 Montgomery Rd., Nether Edge, Sheffield, S7 1LP
☎ (0742) 552356
On a quiet, tree-lined boulevard 1 mile from the city centre, on the route to Derbyshire and the Peak District.
Bedrooms: 5 single, 1 double & 5 twin.
Bathrooms: 1 private, 2 public.
Bed & breakfast: £16-£22.50 single, £36-£42 double.
Lunch available.

Continued ▶

SHEFFIELD

Continued

Evening meal 6pm (l.o. 7.30pm).
Parking for 4.

⟨symbols⟩

Rutland Hotel ♨
⟨symbols⟩
Glossop Rd., Sheffield,
S10 2PY
☎ (0742) 664411
Fax (0742) 670348
Telex 547500
*Fully modernised old hotel,
5 minutes from the city centre
and open countryside. Ideal as
a touring centre or conference
venue.*
Bedrooms: 50 single,
16 double & 15 twin, 9 family
rooms.
Bathrooms: 87 private,
3 public.
Bed & breakfast: £60-£64
single, £70-£76 double.
Half board: £70.50-£74.50
daily.
Lunch available.
Evening meal 6.30pm (l.o.
9.30pm).
Parking for 80.
Credit: Access, Visa, Diners,
Amex.

⟨symbols⟩

Sharrow View Hotel ♨
Sharrow View, Nether Edge,
Sheffield, S7 1ND
☎ (0742) 551542 & 557854
*Small private hotel in quiet
residential area near city
centre and Derbyshire border.
Friendly service, good food,
bar service. Non-smokers only,
please.*
Bedrooms: 14 single, 4 double
& 1 twin, 2 family rooms.
Bathrooms: 4 public.
Bed & breakfast: £24-£26
single, £35-£37 double.
Half board: £33-£35 daily.
Lunch available.
Evening meal 7pm (l.o.
8.30pm).
Parking for 25.

⟨symbols⟩

Staindrop Lodge Hotel & Restaurant ♨
⟨symbols⟩ COMMENDED
Lane End, Chapeltown,
Sheffield, S30 4UH
☎ (0742) 846727
Fax (0742) 846783
*Country-type, recently
refurbished hotel with special
emphasis on standards and
cuisine. 1 mile from the M1
junction 35.*
Bedrooms: 1 single, 8 double
& 3 twin, 1 family room.
Bathrooms: 13 private.
Bed & breakfast: from £60
single, from £75 double.
Half board: from £56 daily.
Lunch available.
Evening meal 7pm (l.o.
9.30pm).
Parking for 56.
Credit: Access, Visa, Diners,
Amex.

⟨symbols⟩

Swallow Hotel ♨
⟨symbols⟩ COMMENDED
Kenwood Rd., Sheffield,
S7 1NQ
☎ (0742) 583811
Telex 547030
⟨symbol⟩ Swallow
*Set in beautifully landscaped
private grounds of nearly 11
acres. An ideal centre for
business or pleasure.*
Bedrooms: 72 single,
32 double & 37 twin.
Bathrooms: 141 private.
Bed & breakfast: £45-£78
single, £70-£92 double.
Half board: from £60 daily.
Lunch available.
Evening meal 7pm (l.o.
10pm).
Parking for 200.
Credit: Access, Visa, Diners,
Amex.

⟨symbols⟩

Whitley Hall Hotel Ltd. ♨
Elliott Lane, Whitley,
Grenoside, Sheffield,
S30 3NR
☎ (0742) 454444
Fax (0742) 455414
*Elizabethan mansion with 30
acres of gardens and
woodlands, only a few miles
from the centres of Sheffield,
Rotherham and Barnsley.
Food a speciality with full a la
carte and table d'hote menus.*
Bedrooms: 2 single, 3 double
& 10 twin.
Bathrooms: 15 private.
Bed & breakfast: £55-£70
single, £70-£95 double.
Lunch available.
Evening meal 7pm (l.o.
9.30pm).

Parking for 100.
Credit: Access, Visa, Diners,
Amex.

⟨symbols⟩

SHIPTON-BY-BENINGBROUGH

N. Yorkshire
Map ref 4C1

5m NW. York
Village on the A19 north
of York. Beningbrough
Hall (National Trust)
nearby.

Redworth House ♨
⟨symbols⟩ APPROVED
Main St., Shipton-by-
Beningbrough, York,
YO6 1AA
☎ York (0904) 470694
*Family-run guesthouse 5 miles
north of York on the A19, close
to the Yorkshire Dales.
Ground floor rooms available
with all facilities.*
Bedrooms: 1 single, 2 double,
2 family rooms.
Bathrooms: 5 private.
Bed & breakfast: £18-£20
single, £32-£36 double.
Parking for 11.

⟨symbols⟩

SKIPTON

N. Yorkshire
Map ref 4B1

Pleasant market town
with farming community
atmosphere, at gateway
to Dales with a Palladian
Town Hall, parish church
and fully roofed castle at
the top of High Street.
*Tourist Information
Centre* ☎ (0756) 792809

Airedale View
26 Belle Vue Terrace,
Skipton, BD23 1RU
☎ (0756) 791195
*Small, family-run
establishment with a reputation
for a warm welcome.*
Bedrooms: 1 single, 1 twin,
2 family rooms.
Bathrooms: 2 public.
Bed & breakfast: £14-£14.50
single, £28-£29 double.
Lunch available.
Evening meal 5.30pm (l.o.
8.30pm).
Parking for 2.

⟨symbols⟩

Highfield Hotel ♨
⟨symbols⟩
58 Keighley Rd., Skipton,
BD23 2NB
☎ (0756) 793182 & 798834
*Friendly, family-run hotel
noted for home cooking. All
rooms with private facilities.
5 minutes from bus and rail
stations.*
Bedrooms: 2 single, 5 double
& 1 twin, 2 family rooms.
Bathrooms: 9 private,
1 public.
Bed & breakfast: £18-£19
single, £36-£38 double.
Half board: £28-£29 daily.
Evening meal 7.30pm (l.o.
5.30pm).
Open February-December.
Credit: Access, Visa.

⟨symbols⟩

Randells Hotel, Conference & Leisure Centre ♨
⟨symbols⟩ COMMENDED
Keighley Rd., Snaygill,
Skipton, BD23 2TA
☎ (0756) 700100
Fax (0756) 700107
*Newly-built independent hotel
on the edge of Skipton,
gateway to the dales.
Individually designed rooms
and suites, 2 restaurants and
conference facilities for 4 to
400 persons. Leisure centre
with squash and indoor pool.*
Bedrooms: 33 double &
20 twin, 8 family rooms.
Bathrooms: 61 private.
Bed & breakfast: £62-£85
single, £81-£159 double.
Half board: from £50 daily,
from £269 weekly.
Lunch available.
Parking for 150.
Credit: Access, Visa, Diners,
Amex.

⟨symbols⟩

Tudor Guest House
Bell Busk, Skipton,
BD23 4DT
☎ Airton (072 93) 301
*Unique, Tudor-style, small,
family-run country house with
magnificent views of
Malhamdale. Gardens and a
games room. Just north of
Skipton.*
Bedrooms: 1 single, 3 double
& 1 twin, 1 family room.
Bathrooms: 1 private,
2 public; 1 private shower.
Bed & breakfast: from £15
single, £27-£32 double.
Half board: £22.50-£25 daily,
£148-£163 weekly.

Evening meal 7pm.
Parking for 6.
Open March-December.
⌂5 ⊙ ♥ 🛁 Ⓥ ⊬ Ⓣ ⊞ 🍴 ☎
♨ ❋ 🗙 🍴 SP 🏮

Handsome market town
midway between the
North Yorkshire Moors
and the Cleveland border.
Famous for its annual
show in September.

Wainstones Hotel ⋔
😊😊😊😊 COMMENDED

High St., Great Broughton,
Middlesbrough, Cleveland
TS9 7EW
☎ Wainstones (0642) 712268
Fax (0642) 711560
*Stone-built hotel with a unique
restaurant and alcoves for
private parties and a large
character bar, which serves bar
meals.*
Bedrooms: 2 single, 4 double
& 10 twin.
Bathrooms: 16 private.
Bed & breakfast: £38.95-
£42.50 single, £49.50-£56
double.
Half board: £46.50-£54.95
daily.
Lunch available.
Evening meal 7pm (l.o.
9.45pm).
Parking for 48.
Credit: Access, Visa.

⌂ ▲ ⊟ ✆ ⊙ 🖵 ♥ 🛁 Ⓥ
⊬ ⋔ ⊞ ▲ 🍴 ❋ 🗙 ⊠ SP
Ⓣ

Through the village
meadows and cornfields
the River Derwent winds
towards the Ouse. The
attractive church stands
among trees; there is an
interesting village hall and
a nearby 2-arched stone
bridge carrying the road
to Elvington.

Old Rectory Hotel
😊😊😊 COMMENDED

Sutton upon Derwent, York,
N. Yorkshire YO4 5BN
☎ York (0904) 608548
*Georgian house of character,
furnished to a high standard.
In a pleasant village 7 miles
from York.*
Bedrooms: 1 single, 2 double
& 2 twin, 1 family room.

Bathrooms: 2 private,
1 public; 4 private showers.
Bed & breakfast: £30-£35
single, £48-£50 double.
Evening meal 6pm (l.o. 8pm).
Parking for 20.
Credit: Access, Visa.

⌂ 🖵 ♥ 🛁 Ⓥ ⊬ ⊞ ▲ 🍴
❋ SP 🏮

9m SW. York
Known for its breweries
which have been
established here since
18th C. Wharfe Bridge
has 7 arches. Above it
stands the 'virgin viaduct'
built for the railway which
never arrived.

Shann House Hotel
😊😊

47 Kirkgate, Tadcaster,
LS24 9AQ
☎ (0937) 833931
*Protected historic building,
tastefully restored in the
traditional manner. In peaceful
seclusion, in the centre of the
town and only minutes away
from the A1.*
Bedrooms: 2 single, 5 twin,
1 family room.
Bathrooms: 8 private.
Bed & breakfast: £20.50-£23
single, £31-£36 double.
Evening meal 5.30pm (l.o.
7pm).
Parking for 12.
Credit: Access, Visa.

⌂ ▲ 🖵 ♥ Ⓥ ⊬ ⊞ ▲ 🍴
🗙 SP 🏮

Thriving market town with
cobbled square
surrounded by old shops
and inns and also with a
local museum. St. Mary's
Church is probably the
best example of
Perpendicular work in
Yorkshire.

Doxford House ⋔
😊😊

Front St., Sowerby, Thirsk,
YO7 1JP
☎ (0845) 523238
*Handsome, Georgian house
with attractive gardens and
paddock with animals,
overlooking the greens of
Sowerby.*
Bedrooms: 1 double & 1 twin,
2 family rooms.
Bathrooms: 4 private.

Bed & breakfast: £13-£18
single, £26-£28 double.
Half board: £20-£21 daily,
£134-£140 weekly.
Evening meal 6.30pm.
Parking for 4.

⌂ ▲ ♥ Ⓤ ⊬ Ⓣ ⊞ ▲ &
☎ ❋ 🍴 🏮

Fourways Guest
House ⋔
😊😊 APPROVED

Town End, Thirsk, YO7 1PY
☎ (0845) 522601
*Guesthouse close to the town
centre, 2 minutes' walk from
the surgery of the famous vet
and author James Herriot.
Centrally located for touring
the North York Moors and the
Yorkshire Dales.*
Bedrooms: 1 single, 2 double
& 2 twin, 1 family room.
Bathrooms: 3 private,
1 public.
Bed & breakfast: £13-£15
single, £26-£30 double.
Half board: £18-£20 daily,
£126-£140 weekly.
Evening meal 6.30pm (l.o.
7.30pm).
Parking for 9.

⌂ 🖵 ♥ Ⓤ ⊞ ▲ 🍴 SP

Golden Fleece ⋔
😊😊

Market Place, Thirsk,
YO7 1LL
☎ (0845) 523108
Ⓒ Principal
*Situated in the market place
within easy reach of the
Yorkshire Dales and Moors.
This old coaching inn retains a
friendly and relaxing
atmosphere.*
Bedrooms: 8 single, 10 double
& 4 twin.
Bathrooms: 6 private,
5 public.
Bed & breakfast: £54-£65
single, £65-£81 double.
Half board: £38-£53 daily.
Lunch available.
Evening meal 7pm (l.o. 9pm).
Parking for 50.
Credit: Access, Visa, C.Bl.,
Diners, Amex.

⌂ ⊟ ✆ ⊙ 🖵 ♥ 🛁 Ⓥ ⊬
⊬ ⊞ ▲ 🍴 ♨ 🗙 ⊠ SP 🏮
Ⓣ

Old Red House ⋔
😊😊 APPROVED

Station Rd., Thirsk,
YO7 4LT
☎ (0845) 524383
*2-storey Georgian building,
with a bar lounge and open
fire.*
Bedrooms: 6 double & 6 twin.
Bathrooms: 12 private.
Bed & breakfast: £17-£21
single, £28 double.

Half board: £21-£28 daily,
£125-£140 weekly.
Lunch available.
Evening meal 7pm (l.o.
9.30pm).
Parking for 30.
Credit: Visa, Diners, Amex.

⌂ ▲ ✆ 🖵 ♥ 🛁 Ⓥ ⊞ ▲
🍴 ☎ 🗙 DAP ⊠ 🏮

Sheppard's Hotel &
Restaurant ⋔
😊😊😊 COMMENDED

Front Street, Sowerby,
Thirsk, YO7 1JF
☎ Thirsk (0845) 523655
*17th C building on the village
green. Carefully developed,
giving every comfort whilst
maintaining its rural
atmosphere. An ideal centre for
touring Herriot's Yorkshire.*
Bedrooms: 7 double, 1 family
room.
Bathrooms: 8 private.
Bed & breakfast: £50-£55
single, £65-£75 double.
Lunch available.
Evening meal 7pm (l.o.
9.30pm).
Parking for 35.
Credit: Access, Visa.

⌂ ✆ ✆ 🖵 ♥ 🛁 Ⓥ ⊬ ⊬
⊞ ▲ 🍴 🗙 ⊞ SP Ⓣ

Shires Court Hotel ⋔
😊😊😊 COMMENDED

Knayton, Thirsk, YO7 4BS
☎ Thirsk (0845) 537210
*Clean and comfortable
accommodation amidst peace
and tranquillity, beneath the
Hambleton Hills.*
Bedrooms: 2 single, 13 family
rooms.
Bathrooms: 15 private.
Bed & breakfast: £29-£32
single, £44-£54 double.
Half board: £39-£42 daily.
Evening meal 7pm (l.o.
8.30pm).
Parking for 20.
Open March-October.

⌂ ▲ 🖵 ♥ 🛁 Ⓥ ⊬ ⊞ ▲
& ♨ ❋ ⊠ SP 🏮

Market and mining town
near Doncaster with a
church of Norman origin.

Belmont Hotel ⋔
😊😊😊 COMMENDED

Horsefair Green, Thorne,
Doncaster, DN8 5EE
☎ (0405) 812320 Telex 54480
Continued ▶

THORNE

Continued

Ideal overnight stop for business people and tourists. Just 1 mile from junction 6 of M18. Convenient for York, Lincoln, Scunthorpe and Doncaster. Supervised by the proprietors.
Bedrooms: 8 single, 6 double & 6 twin, 3 family rooms.
Bathrooms: 23 private.
Bed & breakfast: £44.60-£47.60 single, £50-£59.60 double.
Half board: £54.35-£57.35 daily.
Lunch available.
Evening meal 7pm (l.o. 9.30pm).
Parking for 20.
Credit: Access, Visa.

⬛📶🏨📞⬛🖲✆🅰️ V
🅰️⬛🍴⬛🝙🕙 🅿️ ⓄⒶⓅ
🝙 SP T

THORNTON DALE

N. Yorkshire
Map ref 5D3

Picturesque village with Thorntondale Beck, traversed by tiny stone footbridges.

Bridgefoot Guest House ♠
👑👑👑

Thornton Dale, Pickering, YO18 7RR
☎ Pickering (0751) 74749
17th C house of character, near a trout beck in beautiful village of Thornton Dale. Emphasis on comfort. All bedrooms have electric blankets, tea and coffee facilities, colour TV.
Bedrooms: 1 single, 2 double & 3 twin, 2 family rooms.
Bathrooms: 5 private, 2 public.
Bed & breakfast: £14.50-£20 single, £29-£33 double.
Half board: £23.50-£25.50 daily, £164-£178 weekly.
Evening meal 6.30pm (l.o. 6pm).
Parking for 6.
Open April-October.
⬛📶⬗✆ 🝙 V 🝙 TV 🝙
🝙 Ö 🚻 ⬛ 🝙

Easthill ♠
👑👑👑 COMMENDED

Thornton Dale, Pickering, YO18 7QP
☎ Pickering (0751) 74561
Large, detached, friendly, family house with magnificent views and private woodland. Located in a picturesque village on the edge of the North York Moors.

Bedrooms: 2 single, 2 double & 2 twin, 2 family rooms.
Bathrooms: 8 private, 1 public.
Bed & breakfast: £20 single, £34-£40 double.
Half board: £25-£28 daily, £168-£189 weekly.
Evening meal 6.30pm (l.o. 6.30pm).
Parking for 10.
⬛🖲🝙 V 🝙 TV 🝙 🍴
🝙 ✆ Ö ❀ 🝙 🝙 🝙 SP

New Inn
The Square, Thornton Dale, Pickering, YO18 7LF
☎ Pickering (0751) 74226
Friendly, family-run coaching inn dating back to 1607, in the beautiful Yorkshire Dales. Specialising in traditional home-made Yorkshire fare. Children sharing - half price or under according to age.
Bedrooms: 2 double & 3 twin, 1 family room.
Bathrooms: 2 public.
Bed & breakfast: £19.50 single, £36 double.
Half board: £40-£55 daily.
Lunch available.
Evening meal 7pm (l.o. 8.30pm).
Parking for 10.
Open March-November.
⬛⬗🝙 V 🝙 TV 🝙 🍴 Ö
🝙 🝙 🝙

Warrington Guest House ♠
Whitbygate, Thornton Dale, Pickering, YO18 7RY
☎ Pickering (0751) 75028
Family-run guesthouse in the centre of a picturesque tourist village. All rooms have colour TV and tea making facilities.
Bedrooms: 1 single, 3 double & 1 twin, 1 family room.
Bathrooms: 1 public.
Bed & breakfast: £13-£16 single, £26-£32 double.
Credit: Access, Visa.
⬛🖲⬗ ⓊⓁ 🝙 V 🝙 🝙 SP

THORNTON WATLASS

N. Yorkshire
Map ref 5C3

3m SW. Bedale

The Buck Inn ♠
👑👑👑 COMMENDED

Thornton Watlass, Ripon, HG4 4AH
☎ Bedale (0677) 422461
Friendly village inn overlooking the delightful cricket green in a small village, 3 miles from Bedale on the Masham road, and close to the A1. In James Herriot country. Ideal for walking.

Bedrooms: 1 single, 1 double & 2 twin, 1 family room.
Bathrooms: 5 private.
Bed & breakfast: £25-£28 single, £40-£45 double.
Half board: from £25 daily.
Lunch available.
Evening meal 6.30pm (l.o. 9.30pm).
Parking for 40.
Credit: Access, Visa, Amex.
⬛🖲⬗🝙🖲🖲🝙 V 🝙 TV
🝙 ⬛ 🍴 🝙 🝙 ❀ 🝙 SP

THWAITE

N. Yorkshire
Map ref 5B3

10m N. Hawes
Quiet village, ideal for walking the almost untrodden fells of Great Shunner, Kisdon, High Seat, Rogan's Seat and Lovely Seat. Magnificent scenery.

Kearton Guest House ♠
👑

Thwaite, Richmond, DL11 6DR
☎ Richmond (0748) 86277
In the charming village of Thwaite in Swaledale, within easy reach of York, the Lake District, Herriot country and the Yorkshire Dales.
Bedrooms: 1 single, 4 double, 8 family rooms.
Bathrooms: 4 public; 3 private showers.
Bed & breakfast: £16 single, £32 double.
Half board: £22-£23.50 daily.
Lunch available.
Evening meal 6.30pm.
Parking for 20.
Open March-December.
⬛⬗🝙 V 🝙 🝙 🍴 Ö 🝙
🝙

TODMORDEN

W. Yorkshire
Map ref 4B1

8m NE. Rochdale
In beautiful scenery on the edge of the Pennines at junction of 3 sweeping valleys. Until 1888 the county boundary between Yorkshire and Lancashire cut this old cotton town in half, running through the middle of the Town Hall.
Tourist Information Centre ☎ *(0706) 818181*

The Berghof Brandstatter ♠
👑👑👑 COMMENDED

Cross Stone Rd., Todmorden, Lancashire OL14 8RQ
☎ (0706) 812966

Austrian-style hotel/restaurant standing in an elevated position overlooking the Calder Valley.
Bedrooms: 6 double & 1 twin.
Bathrooms: 7 private.
Bed & breakfast: £33-£75 single, £44-£90 double.
Lunch available.
Evening meal 7pm (l.o. 10pm).
Parking for 40.
Credit: Access, Visa, Diners.
⬛🖲✆🖲⬛🝙 V 🝙
🝙 ⬛ 🍴 🝙 🝙 SP 🝙

TODWICK

S. Yorkshire
Map ref 4C2

South Yorkshire village near the M1.

Red Lion Hotel ♠
👑👑👑👑

Worksop Rd., Todwick, Sheffield, S31 ODJ
☎ Worksop (0909) 771654 & 773704 Telex 54120
ⒸⓇ Lansbury
Recently built hotel close to the M1, ideal for visiting Sherwood Forest or shopping in the popular city of Sheffield.
Bedrooms: 10 double & 19 twin.
Bathrooms: 29 private.
Bed & breakfast: £30-£76 single, £60-£88 double.
Half board: £43-£90 daily.
Lunch available.
Evening meal 7pm (l.o. 10pm).
Parking for 90.
Credit: Access, Visa, Diners, Amex.
⬛🖲🏨✆🖲⬛🝙 V
🝙🝙 ⬛ 🍴 🝙 🝙 ✈
🝙 SP T

TOPCLIFFE

N. Yorkshire
Map ref 5C3

Angel Inn ♠
👑👑👑 COMMENDED

Long St., Topcliffe, Thirsk, YO7 3RW
☎ Thirsk (0845) 577237
Fax (0845) 578000
Large attractive village inn with a warm, traditional atmosphere. Restaurant, bar meals with an interesting selection of grills and featuring the chef's home-made specials. In Herriot country, a great centre for touring, sightseeing and fishing.
Bedrooms: 2 single, 7 double & 4 twin, 2 family rooms.
Bathrooms: 15 private.
Bed & breakfast: £30-£38 single, £46-£52 double.
Lunch available.

Evening meal 7pm (l.o. 9.30pm).
Parking for 100.
Credit: Access, Visa.
⌚2 📞 ⊡ ❑ ✿ 🛆 🛱 📺 ⠿ 🛆 ⛴ 🍴 🎣 ❄ 🌂 🏥 SP

W. Yorkshire
Map ref 4B1

Wool trade important here for 700 years from Norman Conquest, now its economy based on North Yorkshire coalfield. Cathedral church of All Saints has 247-ft spire. Old Bridge, a 9-arched structure, has fine medieval chantry chapels of St. Mary's. Fine Georgian architecture and good shopping centre (the Ridings), Yorkshire Mining Museum nearby.
Tourist Information Centre ☎ *(0924) 295000/1*

Bank House Hotel M
⌚⌚⌚

11 Bank St., Westgate, Wakefield, WF1 1EH
☎ (0924) 368248
City centre licensed hotel run by young people who care about service. All rooms have satellite TV, hair-dryer, kettle.
Bedrooms: 4 twin, 2 family rooms.
Bathrooms: 2 private, 2 public; 1 private shower.
Bed & breakfast: £22-£34 single, £30.75-£36.90 double.
Half board: £23.85-£57.85 daily, £166.95-£404.95 weekly.
Lunch available.
Evening meal (l.o. 9pm).
Parking for 2.
Credit: Access, Visa.
⌚ 📞 ⊡ ❑ ✿ 🛆 🛱 📺 ◗ ⠿ 🛆 🍴 SP

Cedar Court Hotel M
⌚⌚⌚⌚

Denby Dale Rd., Calder Grove, Wakefield, WF4 3QZ
☎ (0924) 276310
Telex 557647
International hotel, designed and built to high specifications. Close to the M1 and M62 motorways, halfway between London and Scotland. Suitable for business people, conferences, private functions and holidaymakers.
Bedrooms: 119 double & 23 twin, 9 family rooms.
Bathrooms: 151 private.
Bed & breakfast: £56.25-£91.50 single, £67.95-£107.25 double.

Lunch available.
Evening meal 6.30pm (l.o. 11pm).
Parking for 240.
Credit: Access, Visa, Diners, Amex.
⌚ 🛆 📞 ⊡ ❑ ✿ 🛆 🛱 ⠿ 🍴 📺 ◗ ❄ ⠿ 🛆 🍴 🛠 ❄ SP 🎱

The Harlequin Private Hotel M
⌚⌚

165 Westgate, Wakefield, WF2 9SA
☎ (0924) 372500 & 370026
Friendly, clean and comfortable, family-run hotel, specialising in English home-cooked meals, particularly breakfast. Within walking distance of Westgate InterCity station and town centre, 2 miles from M1 junctions 39, 40, 41.
Bedrooms: 6 single, 4 double & 2 twin, 2 family rooms.
Bathrooms: 5 private, 2 public.
Bed & breakfast: £20-£30 single, £33-£40 double.
Lunch available.
Evening meal 5pm (l.o. 8pm).
Parking for 2.
Credit: Access, Visa.
⌚ 🛆 ✿ ⊔ 🛆 📺 🛱 ⠿ 🛆 ❄

Parklands Hotel M
⌚⌚⌚⌚

143 Horbury Rd., Wakefield, WF2 8TY
☎ (0924) 377407
Elegant Victorian former vicarage overlooking 680 acres of beautiful parkland. Family-run for over 25 years, providing a high standard of service and cuisine and well-appointed en-suite bedrooms.
Bedrooms: 8 single, 2 double & 2 twin, 1 family room.
Bathrooms: 10 private; 3 private showers.
Bed & breakfast: £30-£40 single, £45-£53.50 double.
Evening meal 6.45pm (l.o. 6pm).
Parking for 20.
Credit: Access, Visa, Diners, Amex.
⌚ 📞 ⊡ ❑ ✿ 🛆 🛱 📺 ◗ ⠿ 🛆 🍴 🍴 ❄ SP 🏥 📺

The Poplars M
⌚⌚⌚

Bradford Rd., Wrenthorpe, Wakefield, WF2 0QL
☎ (0924) 375682
Tastefully restored, 200-year-old house with open beams. Country location close to Wakefield (A650), M1 exit 41 and M62 exit 29.
Bedrooms: 4 twin.

Bathrooms: 2 private, 1 public.
Bed & breakfast: £32-£35 single, £40-£43 double.
Parking for 6.
⊡ ✿ ⠿ 🛆 🛱 📺 🛆 ⛴ ❄ 🍴 🏥 🎱

Hotel St. Pierre
733 Barnsley Rd., Newmillerdam, Wakefield, WF2
☎ Wakefield (0924) 250441 & 263394
Detached property, five minutes' drive from Wakefield city centre on Barnsley road. Five minutes from exit 39 on M1 motorway.
Bedrooms: 32 double & 10 twin, 2 family rooms.
Bathrooms: 44 private.
Bed & breakfast: from £47.50 single, from £55 double.
Evening meal 6pm (l.o. 11pm).
Parking for 70.
Credit: Access, Visa, Diners, Amex.
⌚ 🛆 📞 ⊡ ❑ ✿ 🛆 🛱 📺 ◗ 🛠 ⠿ 🛆 🍴 🛠 ❄ SP 📺

Swallow Hotel M
⌚⌚⌚⌚ **COMMENDED**

Queens St., Wakefield, WF1 1JU
☎ (0924) 372111
Telex 557464
🆑 Swallow
Modern city centre hotel adjacent to Ridings shopping centre. Easy access from M1 and M62, 400 yards from railway station.
Bedrooms: 36 single, 8 double & 20 twin.
Bathrooms: 64 private.
Bed & breakfast: from £72 single, from £92 double.
Half board: from £88 daily.
Lunch available.
Evening meal 7pm (l.o. 9.15pm).
Parking for 50.
Credit: Access, Visa, Diners, Amex.
⌚ 📞 ⊡ ❑ ✿ 🛆 🛱 📺 🛆 ◗ ❄ ⠿ 🛆 🍴 🛠 ❄ SP 📺

Waterton Park Hotel M
⌚⌚⌚⌚ **COMMENDED**

Walton Hall, Walton, Wakefield, WF2 6PW
☎ Wakefield (0924) 257911
Fax 0924 240082
🆑 Consort
Georgian mansion, situated on an island, surrounded by a 26-acre lake, providing well-equipped bedrooms, swimming pool, jacuzzi, steamroom, sauna, solarium, fly-fishing.
Bedrooms: 5 single, 17 double & 9 twin.
Bathrooms: 31 private.

Bed & breakfast: £55-£75 single, £77-£95 double.
Half board: £70-£91 daily.
Lunch available.
Evening meal 7pm (l.o. 9.30pm).
Parking for 100.
Credit: Access, Visa, Diners, Amex.
⌚ 🛆 ⛳ 📞 ⊡ ❑ ✿ 🛆 📺 🛱 ◗ 🛆 🍴 ⛴ 🎣 🎱 🛠 ❄ ❄ 🛠 SP 🏥 📺

N. Yorkshire
Map ref 5B3

Popular Wensleydale village, where the burning of 'Owd Barle', effigy of an 18th C pig rustler, is held in August.

Ivydene Guest House
⌚⌚ **COMMENDED**

Main St., West Witton, Leyburn, DL8 4LP
☎ Wensleydale (0969) 22785
17th C licensed guesthouse in heart of Herriot country. Ideal for walking, riding, fishing, golf and touring.
Bedrooms: 1 single, 2 double & 2 twin, 1 family room.
Bathrooms: 3 private, 1 public.
Bed & breakfast: £16-£18 single, £30-£40 double.
Half board: £24.50-£29.50 daily, £162.90-£196 weekly.
Evening meal 7pm (l.o. 5pm).
Parking for 8.
Credit: Amex.
⌚⛳ ✿ 🛆 🛱 📺 ⠿ 🛆 ⛴ 🍴 ❄ SP 🏥

The Old Star
⌚⌚

West Witton, Leyburn, DL8 4LU
☎ Wensleydale (0969) 22949
17th C stone-built former coaching inn, in a farming community, with uninterrupted views of Wensleydale. Home cooking and a friendly atmosphere.
Bedrooms: 3 double & 1 twin, 2 family rooms.
Bathrooms: 4 private, 1 public.
Bed & breakfast: £12-£15 single, £24-£30 double.
Half board: £20-£23 daily, £133-£154 weekly.
Evening meal 6.30pm (l.o. 7.30pm).
Parking for 20.
⌚ 🛆 ✿ 🛆 🛱 📺 ⠿ 🛆 🍴 ❄ 🛠 SP 🏥

WEST WITTON

Continued

Wensleydale Heifer M
COMMENDED
Main St., West Witton,
Wensleydale, DL8 4LS
☎ Wensleydale (0969) 22322
& Fax (0969) 24183
Telex 57515 Attn. 80
Consort
*17th C inn in the heart of
James Herriot's Yorkshire
Dales. Exposed beams and log
fires in winter.*
Bedrooms: 12 double &
6 twin, 1 family room.
Bathrooms: 19 private.
Bed & breakfast: £45 single,
£62 double.
Lunch available.
Evening meal 7pm (l.o.
9.30pm).
Parking for 20.
Credit: Access, Visa, Diners,
Amex.
⚁ ⬟ ▦ ☏ ⊡ ▢ ♿ ▮ Ⓥ ⊟
▦ ▱ ♨ ♪ ♪ ▶ ⚒ SP ▦ Ⓣ

WETHERBY

W. Yorkshire
Map ref 4B1

Prosperous market town
on the River Wharfe
noted for horse-racing.
*Tourist Information
Centre* ☎ *(0937) 62706*

Number Fifty M
Listed COMMENDED
50 Westgate, Wetherby,
LS22 4NJ
☎ (0937) 583106
*Elegant early Victorian town
house with a large garden and
within easy walking distance of
market square, restaurants and
pleasant riverside.*
Bedrooms: 1 double & 2 twin.
Bathrooms: 1 public.
Bed & breakfast: from £18
single, from £28 double.
Parking for 4.
⚁ ⊡ ♿ Ⓤ Ⓥ ≯ ⊟ Ⓣ ▦
▱ ✕ ▦

Prospect House M
Listed
8 Caxton St., Wetherby,
LS22 4RU
☎ (0937) 582428
*Established for over 30 years,
with easy access to Harrogate,
York, the dales and James
Herriot country. Colour TV.
Pets welcome.*
Bedrooms: 1 single, 2 double
& 2 twin, 1 family room.
Bathrooms: 1 public.
Bed & breakfast: £15-£15.50
single, £30-£31 double.
Parking for 6.
⚁ Ⓤ ▮ Ⓥ ⊟ Ⓣ ▦ ▱

Wood Hall Hotel M
HIGHLY COMMENDED
Trip Lane, Linton, Wetherby,
LS22 4JA
☎ Wetherby (0937) 587271
Fax 0937 584353
*Georgian mansion with
extensive grounds, converted
into a country house hotel. In
an officially designated area of
outstanding natural beauty.*
Bedrooms: 5 double &
17 twin.
Bathrooms: 22 private.
Bed & breakfast: £98-£133
single, £108-£143 double.
Lunch available.
Evening meal 7.30pm (l.o.
9.30pm).
Parking for 50.
Credit: Access, Visa, Diners,
Amex.
⚁ ⬟ ▦ ☏ ⊡ ▢ ▮ Ⓥ ⊟
◉ ▦ ▱ ✕ ⚒ ▲ ♨ ⌖ ♪ ▶
⟋ ✼ ▦ ▱ SP ▦ Ⓣ

WHITBY

N. Yorkshire
Map ref 5D3

Quaint holiday town with
narrow streets and steep
alleys at the mouth of the
River Esk. Captain James
Cook, the famous
navigator, lived in Grape
Lane. 199 steps lead to
St. Mary's Church and St.
Hilda's Abbey overlooking
harbour. Connections
with Dracula, who is
reputed to have landed
here, are traced at the
"Dracula Experience".
Sandy beach.
*Tourist Information
Centre* ☎ *(0947) 602674*

Abbey House M
East Cliff, Whitby,
YO22 4JT
☎ (0947) 600557
*A fine mansion on Whitby's
East Cliff, next to the ancient
Abbey. A warm Yorkshire
welcome awaits.*
Bedrooms: 6 single, 19 twin,
6 family rooms.
Bathrooms: 11 public.
Bed & breakfast: £13.25-
£20.25 single, £22-£36 double.
Half board: £20.25-£28.25
daily, £130-£220 weekly.
Lunch available.
Evening meal 7pm.
Parking for 25.
Open March-December.
⚁ ⚁ ♿ ▦ ☏ ▱ ▶ ▲ ♨
✼ ✕ DAP ▦ SP ▦ Ⓣ

Arundel House Hotel &
Restaurant
Bagdale, Whitby, YO21 1QJ
☎ (0947) 603645

*Georgian manor house with
attractive restaurant, within
easy reach of the town centre.*
Bedrooms: 2 single, 3 double
& 2 twin, 2 family rooms.
Bathrooms: 3 private,
1 public; 3 private showers.
Bed & breakfast: £30-£40
single, £32-£40 double.
Half board: £157-£182
weekly.
Evening meal 7pm (l.o. 9pm).
Parking for 6.
Open March-December.
Credit: Access, Visa.
⚁ ▱ ♨ ▮ Ⓥ ≯ ⊟ ▦ ⌖
▦ ▱ SP ▦

Corra Lynn Private
Hotel M
APPROVED
28 Crescent Avenue, Whitby,
YO21 3EW
☎ (0947) 602214
*All rooms have private
facilities, colour TV and
hospitality tray. Private
parking. Convenient for coast,
country and local amenities.
Warm welcome assured.*
Bedrooms: 1 single, 1 double
& 2 twin, 2 family rooms.
Bathrooms: 6 private.
Bed & breakfast: £17.50-£22
single, £35-£44 double.
Evening meal 6pm (l.o. 3pm).
Parking for 4.
Open March-November.
⚁ ▱ ♿ ▮ ⊟ Ⓣ Ⓥ ▦ ▱ ▦
SP

Dunsley Hall M
COMMENDED
Dunsley, Whitby, YO21 3TL
☎ (0947) 83437
*Peaceful, elegant country hall
in 4 acres of secluded grounds
within North York Moors
National Park. Relaxing and
friendly atmosphere. Oak-
panelling, carved billiard room
with stained-glass windows.
Indoor heated swimming pool,
fitness room, tennis, croquet
and putting green.*
Bedrooms: 5 double & 2 twin.
Bathrooms: 7 private.
Bed & breakfast: £40-£50
single, £30-£34 double.
Half board: £44-£48 daily.
Evening meal 7.30pm (l.o.
6pm).
Parking for 10.
Credit: Access, Visa.
⚁ ⬟ ♿ ⊡ ▱ ♨ ≯ ⊟
▦ ▱ ⌖ ▲ ⚒ ♪ ▶ ✼ SP
Ⓣ

Esklet Guest House M
QQ
22 Crescent Avenue, West
Cliff, Whitby, YO21 3ED
☎ (0947) 605663

*Edwardian guesthouse with a
comfortable lounge and colour
TV. Home-cooked food served
in a pleasant dining room.*
Bedrooms: 1 single, 2 double
& 1 twin, 2 family rooms.
Bathrooms: 2 public.
Bed & breakfast: £12.50-
£14.50 single, £25-£29 double.
Half board: £17.50-£19.50
daily, £117-£131 weekly.
Evening meal 6pm (l.o. 4pm).
Parking for 1.
⚁ ♿ Ⓤ ▮ Ⓥ ≯ ⊟ Ⓣ ▦
▮ ▦

Haven Crest Hotel M
QQ
137 Upgang Lane, Whitby,
YO21 3JW
☎ (0947) 602726
*Small, family-run, licensed
hotel with home cooking. On
the outskirts of the town
overlooking the golf-course and
close to the beach. Full English
breakfast and early morning
tea. Home-baked bread.*
Bedrooms: 1 single, 4 double
& 2 twin.
Bathrooms: 3 private,
1 public.
Bed & breakfast: £12.50-
£13.50 single, £25-£32 double.
Half board: £19-£23 daily.
Evening meal 6.30pm.
Parking for 7.
Open March-October.
⚁ ⬟ ▮ Ⓥ ⊟ Ⓣ ▦ ▱ ▦

Kom Binne Guest
House M
5 Broomfield Terrace,
Whitby, YO21 1QP
☎ (0947) 602752
*Comfortable, tastefully
furnished guesthouse offering a
personal, friendly service,
where children are welcome.
Close to the harbour and the
main bus and rail stations.*
Bedrooms: 2 double & 1 twin,
3 family rooms.
Bathrooms: 2 public.
Bed & breakfast: £13-£14
single, £26-£28 double.
Half board: £19 daily, £130
weekly.
Evening meal 6pm (l.o. 6pm).
Parking for 2.
Open March-November.
⚁ ⬟ ♿ Ⓤ ▮ ⊟ Ⓣ ▦ ▱
DAP

Netherby M
QQQ APPROVED
90 Coach Rd., Sleights,
Whitby, YO22 5EQ
☎ Whitby (0947) 810211
*Well-situated Victorian villa
with 2 acres of garden
overlooking the Esk Valley.
Family-run, home cooking
using local and home-grown
produce. Village is 3 miles
from Whitby.*

Bedrooms: 1 single, 3 double & 2 twin, 1 family room.
Bathrooms: 7 private, 1 public.
Bed & breakfast: £18-£24 single, £36-£48 double.
Half board: £26-£34 daily, £182-£238 weekly.
Lunch available.
Evening meal 7.30pm (l.o. 9.30pm).
Parking for 11.
Credit: Access, Visa.

Old Hall Hotel

High St., Ruswarp, Whitby, YO21 1NH
☎ Whitby (0947) 602801
Elegant Jacobean hall with its own grounds, in a village setting. Built 1603, of exceptional historic, architectural and artistic interest. Offering charm, comfort and personal attention.
Bedrooms: 4 single, 9 double & 5 twin, 2 family rooms.
Bathrooms: 7 private, 3 public.
Bed & breakfast: £20-£24 single, £40-£48 double.
Evening meal 6.30pm (l.o. 6pm).
Parking for 20.
Open April-October.

Riviera Hotel

COMMENDED

4 Crescent Terrace, West Cliff, Whitby, YO21 3EL
☎ (0947) 602533
Family-run hotel overlooking the sea and only a few minutes' walk from the harbour and all amenities.
Bedrooms: 3 single, 4 double & 3 twin, 4 family rooms.
Bathrooms: 14 private, 1 public.
Bed & breakfast: £30-£40 single, £44 double.
Half board: £31-£32 daily.
Evening meal 6pm.
Open March-October.

Royal Hotel

West Cliff, Whitby, YO21 3HA
☎ (0947) 602234
Telex 820355
In a cliff-top location overlooking the harbour, beach and abbey.
Bedrooms: 19 single, 29 double & 51 twin, 24 family rooms.
Bathrooms: 94 private, 16 public.
Bed & breakfast: £36-£44 single, £56-£72 double.

Half board: £45-£53 daily, £165-£285 weekly.
Lunch available.
Evening meal 6.30pm (l.o. 9pm).
Parking for 80.
Credit: Access, Visa, Diners, Amex.

Saxonville Hotel M

COMMENDED

Ladysmith Avenue, Whitby, YO21 3HX
☎ (0947) 602631
Family-owned hotel, in operation since 1946, proud of its cuisine and friendly atmosphere.
Bedrooms: 2 single, 11 double & 7 twin, 4 family rooms.
Bathrooms: 24 private.
Bed & breakfast: £30-£33 single, £60-£66 double.
Half board: £40-£44 daily.
Lunch available.
Evening meal 7pm (l.o. 8.30pm).
Parking for 20.
Open April-October.
Credit: Access, Visa, Amex.

Seacliffe Hotel

COMMENDED

12 North Promenade, West Cliff, Whitby, YO21 3JX
☎ (0947) 603139
Small, friendly hotel with a restaurant offering an a la carte menu. In a prime position on the seafront.
Bedrooms: 1 single, 13 double & 2 twin, 4 family rooms.
Bathrooms: 19 private, 1 public.
Bed & breakfast: £31-£45 single, £53-£56 double.
Evening meal 6pm (l.o. 9pm).
Parking for 8.
Credit: Access, Visa, Diners, Amex.

Stakesby Manor M

COMMENDED

High Stakesby, Whitby, YO21 1HL
☎ (0947) 602773 & 602140
Georgian house dating back to 1710, in its own grounds, on the outskirts of Whitby in the North York Moors National Park. Facing south with views of the moors.
Bedrooms: 6 double & 2 twin.
Bathrooms: 8 private.
Bed & breakfast: max. £38 single, £56-£58 double.
Half board: £34-£39 daily, £238-£273 weekly.
Lunch available.

Evening meal 7pm (l.o. 9.30pm).
Parking for 30.
Credit: Access, Visa, Amex.

Wentworth House M

27 Hudson St., West Cliff, Whitby, YO21 3EP
☎ (0947) 602433
Spacious Victorian house offering comfortable accommodation, some en-suite. Traditional and vegetarian food. Free-range eggs. Close to all amenities. Non-smokers only please.
Bedrooms: 4 single, 2 double & 2 twin, 1 family room.
Bathrooms: 3 private, 2 public.
Bed & breakfast: from £13 single, from £26 double.
Half board: from £21 daily, from £147 weekly.
Evening meal 6.30pm.

WHITWELL-ON-THE-HILL

N. Yorkshire
Map ref 5C3

5m SW. Malton
Pretty village on the Howardian Hills with magnificent views overlooking the Vale of York and the lands of Castle Howard above. The houses, set about with parkland, line the approach to the Hall.

Whitwell Hall Country House Hotel M

COMMENDED

Whitwell-on-the-Hill, York, YO6 7JJ
☎ (065 381) 551
Fax (065 381) 554
Telex 57697 YORVEX G
Genuine country house hotel with a galleried hall, in 18 acres of gardens and woodlands overlooking York. Good sized indoor swimming pool.
Bedrooms: 4 single, 11 double & 8 twin.
Bathrooms: 23 private, 1 public.
Bed & breakfast: £50-£60 single, £60-£106 double.
Lunch available.
Evening meal 7.30pm (l.o. 8.30pm).

Parking for 56.
Credit: Access, Visa, Amex.

WILLERBY

Humberside
Map ref 4C1

5m NW. Hull
A suburb of Hull lying east of the Wolds and north of the Humber.

Grange Park Hotel M

COMMENDED

Main St., Willerby, Kingston-upon-Hull, N. Humberside HU10 6EA
☎ Hull (0482) 656488
Fax (0482) 655848
Telex 592773
Best Western
In its own 12 acres of grounds, very close to the centre of Hull.
Bedrooms: 4 single, 42 double & 59 twin, 4 family rooms.
Bathrooms: 109 private.
Bed & breakfast: £64.50-£97.50 single, £95-£117 double.
Lunch available.
Evening meal 6.30pm (l.o. 10.30pm).
Parking for 600.
Credit: Access, Visa, C.Bl., Diners, Amex.

Willerby Manor Hotel M

COMMENDED

Well Lane, Willerby, Hull, N. Humberside HU10 6ER
☎ Hull (0482) 652616
Fax (0482) 653901
Telex 592629
In 3 acres of landscaped gardens, in suburb of Hull, 5 miles from city centre. Fine restaurant serving modern French cuisine. Everglades bar is open at lunch-time for hot and cold snacks and Raffaele's Pasta and Pizza Bar is open each evening except Tuesday.
Bedrooms: 4 single, 22 double & 10 twin.
Bathrooms: 36 private.
Bed & breakfast: £55-£66.25 single, £68-£81.75 double.
Half board: from £78.75 daily.
Lunch available.
Evening meal 6.45pm (l.o. 9.30pm).
Parking for 200.
Credit: Access, Visa, Amex.

WINTERINGHAM

Humberside
Map ref 4C1

7m N. Scunthorpe

Winteringham Fields M
☰☰☰☰ HIGHLY COMMENDED

Lower Burgage
Winteringham, Scunthorpe,
S. Humberside DN15 9PF
☎ Scunthorpe (0724) 733096
Fax (0724) 733898
*16th C manor house with ships'
timbers and log fires, decorated
in authentic Victorian-style.
40-seater restaurant offering
French/Swiss cuisine and
specialising in local game. 2
full suites.*
Bedrooms: 3 double & 3 twin.
Bathrooms: 6 private.
Bed & breakfast: £60-£75
single, £75-£95 double.
Lunch available.
Evening meal 7pm (l.o.
9.30pm).
Parking for 20.
Credit: Access, Visa.
📺 ⓛ ☐ ▮ Ⓥ ⊁ ◿ ▥ 𝍤
☺ ► ⚸ ✗ 🐕 🏠

WYKEHAM

N. Yorkshire
Map ref 5D3

This alluring village in
Pickering Vale has an old
church of St. Helen and a
spring. There is little left
of the ruins of Wykeham
Abbey, but its setting is in
magnificent parkland with
fine trees.

Downe Arms Hotel M
☰☰☰ COMMENDED

Pickering Rd., Wykeham,
Scarborough, YO13 9QB
☎ Scarborough
(0723) 862471 Telex 527192
*Small hotel, 5 miles from
Scarborough. Well-furnished
accommodation and good
cuisine. Ideal for exploring
North York Moors and coast.*
Bedrooms: 1 single, 2 double
& 5 twin, 2 family rooms.
Bathrooms: 10 private.
Bed & breakfast: from £25.75
single, from £51.50 double.
Half board: from £38.50
daily.
Lunch available.
Evening meal 7.30pm (l.o.
9.30pm).
Parking for 152.
Credit: Access, Visa, Diners,
Amex.
☺ ☐ ⓛ ▮ Ⓥ ◿ ⓣ 🖵 ▱
🍴 ♪ ► ✒ ⚸ ✗ 🏠 🏠

YORK

N. Yorkshire
Map ref 4C1

Roman walled city nearly
2000 years old containing
many well-preserved
medieval buildings (the
Shambles, Stonegate). Its
Minster has over 100
stained glass windows
spanning 800 years.
Castle Museum contains
city's history and there is
the National Railway
Museum, Railway Show
and famous racecourse.
Many attractions
including a Wax Museum,
Jorvik Viking Centre and
York Dungeon.
*Tourist Information
Centre* ☎ *(0904) 621756
or 643700 or 620557*

Abacus Guest House M
Listed

5 Wenlock Terrace, Fulford
Rd., York, YO1 4DU
☎ (0904) 632301
*Friendly, informal guesthouse,
half a mile from the city walls
and three quarters of a mile
from the town centre, opposite
the police headquarters.*
Bedrooms: 1 single, 2 double
& 1 twin, 4 family rooms.
Bathrooms: 1 private,
2 public.
Bed & breakfast: £15-£20
single, £26-£32 double.
Half board: £22-£27 daily,
£140-£154 weekly.
Lunch available.
Evening meal 6pm (l.o. 4pm).
Parking for 4.
☺ ☐ ♦ ⓤ ⓛ ▮ Ⓥ ◿ ▥
▱ 🍴 🄰 ⓢⓟ ⓣ

Abbey Guest House M

14 Earlsborough Terrace,
Marygate, York, YO3 7BQ
☎ (0904) 627782
*Small family-run guesthouse on
the banks of the River Ouse,
450 yards from the city centre.*
Bedrooms: 2 single, 3 double
& 1 twin, 1 family room.
Bathrooms: 2 public.
Bed & breakfast: £15-£17.50
single, £28-£32 double.
Evening meal 6.30pm (l.o.
1pm).
Parking for 7.
Credit: Access, Visa.
☺ ▱ ⓒ ♦ ⓤ ◿ 🖵 ▱ ▮
🏠 ⓢⓟ

Abbots Mews Hotel M
☰☰☰☰ APPROVED

6 Marygate La., Bootham,
York, YO3 7DE
☎ (0904) 634866 & 622395
Telex 57777

---

*Converted Victorian
coachmen's cottages, quietly
located in a mews, with easy
access to the city centre.*
Bedrooms: 1 single, 23 double
& 18 twin, 8 family rooms.
Bathrooms: 50 private.
Bed & breakfast: £38-£42
single, £66-£70 double.
Half board: £45-£48 daily.
Lunch available.
Evening meal 7pm (l.o.
9.30pm).
Parking for 30.
Credit: Access, Visa, Diners,
Amex.
☺ 🄰 ⓛ ⓒ ☐ ♦ ▮ Ⓥ ◿
🖵 🄰 🍴 ✗ 🐕 ⓢⓟ 🏠 ⓣ

Aberford House Hotel M
☰☰

35-36 East Mount Rd., York,
YO2 2BD
☎ (0904) 622694
*Centrally situated, privately-
owned small hotel. Colour TV
in all bedrooms. Cellar bar.
Brochure on request.*
Bedrooms: 2 single, 5 double
& 4 twin, 1 family room.
Bathrooms: 2 private,
3 public; 2 private showers.
Bed & breakfast: £17-£21
single, £32-£46 double.
Parking for 7.
Credit: Access, Visa, Amex.
☺ 🄰 ▱ ☐ ♦ ▮ Ⓥ ◿ 🖵
🄰 ✗ 🄰 ⓢⓟ ⓣ

Acer House Hotel M
☰☰☰ APPROVED

52 Scarcroft Hill, The Mount,
York, YO2 1DE
☎ (0904) 653839
*Small Victorian hotel in a quiet
residential area adjoining the
Knavesmire and racecourse.
Half a mile from the city
centre.*
Bedrooms: 2 double & 2 twin,
2 family rooms.
Bathrooms: 6 private.
Bed & breakfast: max. £25
single, max. £40 double.
Half board: £35-£40 daily.
Lunch available.
Evening meal 6pm (l.o. 8pm).
Parking for 4.
Credit: Access, Visa, Amex.
☺ 🄰 ⓛ ☐ ♦ ▮ Ⓥ ◿
ⓣ 🖵 🄰 🄰 ⓢⓟ 🏠
🄰 Display advertisement
appears on page 202.

Acorn Guest House M
☰☰ APPROVED

1 Southlands Rd., York,
YO2 1NP
☎ (0904) 620081

---

*Victorian town house,
5 minutes' walk from city
walls, close to racecourse and
other main attractions.
Traditional food, most diets
catered for.*
Bedrooms: 1 single, 2 double
& 1 twin, 2 family rooms.
Bathrooms: 2 private,
1 public.
Bed & breakfast: £12-£15
single, £22-£30 double.
Half board: £17.50-£21.50
daily.
Lunch available.
Evening meal 6pm (l.o.
10am).
☺ 5 ☐ ♦ ⓤ ⓛ ▮ Ⓥ ◿ ⓣ 🖵
🄰 ⚸ ⓢⓟ ⓣ

Airden House
☰☰ COMMENDED

No. 1 St. Mary's, Bootham,
York, YO3 7DD
☎ (0904) 638915
*In a quiet city centre cul-de-
sac, within walking distance of
the station and all places of
interest.*
Bedrooms: 4 double & 2 twin,
2 family rooms.
Bathrooms: 2 private,
2 public.
Bed & breakfast: £28-£38
double.
Parking for 2.
☺ ♦ ⓤ ⓛ ◿ ⓣ 🖵 ✗ 🏠

Alcuin Lodge
Listed

15 Sycamore Place, Bootham,
York, YO3 7DW
☎ (0904) 632222
*Three-storey, Edwardian house
overlooking a bowling green, 10
minutes' walk from York
Minster.*
Bedrooms: 1 single, 3 double
& 1 twin, 1 family room.
Bathrooms: 2 private,
2 public.
Bed & breakfast: £12-£17
single, £25-£36 double.
Parking for 3.
Open February-November.
☺ 3 ☐ ♦ ⓤ ⓛ 🖵 ✗ 🏠

Alemar Guest House
Listed

19 Queen Anne's Rd.,
Bootham, York, YO3 7AA
☎ (0904) 652367
*Small, Victorian guesthouse in
a central conservation area.
Friendly welcome and family
atmosphere.*
Bedrooms: 1 single, 2 double
& 1 twin.
Bathrooms: 1 public.
Bed & breakfast: £12-£15.50
single, £24-£31 double.
☺ ☐ ♦ ⓤ ⓛ 🖵 ✗ 🏠

Alexander's Hotel ⚊
♛♛♛♛

18 Boroughbridge Rd., York,
YO2 5RU
☎ (0904) 795334
Fax (0904) 781389
*A good quality hotel with bar,
restaurant and car park, within
walking distance of the historic
city centre. Well-appointed
accommodation at economical
rates. Several ground floor
rooms.*
Bedrooms: 1 single, 5 double
& 4 twin, 4 family rooms.
Bathrooms: 14 private.
Bed & breakfast: £30-£42
single, £42-£55 double.
Half board: £29-£48 daily,
£175-£240 weekly.
Lunch available.
Evening meal 6.30pm (l.o.
8.30pm).
Parking for 12.
Credit: Access, Visa, Diners,
Amex.

⊱ ♨ ℄ ⊚ ⎅ ❖ ▮ Ⅴ ⅄
⊨ ▥ ♨ ⚘ ❦ ⒹⒶ⒫ ⅍ ⑤Ⓟ Ⓣ

Alfreda Guest House ⚊
♛♛♛ COMMENDED

61 Heslington Lane, Fulford,
York, YO1 4HN
☎ (0904) 631698
*Double-fronted, Edwardian
residence in 2.5 acres, close to
Fulford Golf Course and York
University. Large parking area
with security lighting.*
Bedrooms: 3 double & 3 twin,
4 family rooms.
Bathrooms: 8 private,
1 public.
Bed & breakfast: £18-£35
single, £25-£45 double.
Parking for 20.
Credit: Access, Visa.

⊱ ♨ ⌸ ❖ ⓊⓁ Ⅴ ⊨ ⒯Ⅴ
▥ ❄ ♨ ⒹⒶ⒫ ⅍ Ⓢ Ⓟ ⒻⒷ

Alhambra Court Hotel ⚊
♛♛♛♛ APPROVED

31 St Mary's, Bootham,
York, YO3 7DD
☎ (0904) 628474
*Early Georgian town house in
a quiet cul-de-sac near the city
centre. Family-run hotel with
bar, restaurant, open to non-
residents. Lift and parking.*
Bedrooms: 3 single, 7 double
& 10 twin, 5 family rooms.
Bathrooms: 25 private.
Bed & breakfast: £31.50-£37
single, £49-£57 double.
Half board: £35-£39 daily,
£203-£255.50 weekly.
Evening meal 6pm (l.o. 9pm).
Parking for 20.
Credit: Access, Visa.

⊱ ♨ ⌸ ℄ ⊚ ⎅ ❖ ▮ Ⅴ
▥ ⒯Ⅴ ⬛ ⛉ ♨ ⒹⒶ⒫ ⅍ Ⓢ Ⓟ ⒻⒷ
Ⓣ

Ambleside Guest House
♛♛♛

62 Bootham Crescent,
Bootham, York, YO3 7AH
☎ (0904) 637165
*Warm, friendly service, with
access to rooms at all times.
Only minutes from the city
centre.*
Bedrooms: 5 double & 2 twin,
1 family room.
Bathrooms: 4 private,
2 public.
Bed & breakfast: from £26
double.

⊱ ▯10 ⎅ ❖ ⓊⓁ Ⅴ ⊨ ⒯Ⅴ ▥
⋈ ⒹⒶ⒫

Annjoa House ⚊
♛♛

34 Millfield Rd., Scarcroft
Rd., York, YO2 1NQ
☎ (0904) 653731
*Quiet family-run hotel, close to
the city centre and racecourse.
Offering a friendly atmosphere
and home cooking.*
Bedrooms: 3 single, 5 double
& 2 twin, 2 family rooms.
Bathrooms: 6 private,
2 public.
Bed & breakfast: £12.50-
£14.50 single, £24-£35 double.
Half board: £20-£25.50 daily.
Evening meal 6pm (l.o.
midday).
Credit: Access, Visa.

⊱ ⎅ ❖ ▮ Ⅴ ⊨ ⒯Ⅴ ▥ ♨
⅍ Ⓢ Ⓟ

Arndale Hotel ⚊
♛♛♛ COMMENDED

290 Tadcaster Rd., York,
YO2 2ET
☎ (0904) 702424
*Welcoming, traditionally
furnished Victorian
gentleman's residence. Most
rooms have four-poster or half-
tester beds. Whirlpool baths.
Overlooking racecourse and
close to city centre.*
Bedrooms: 6 double & 2 twin,
1 family room.
Bathrooms: 9 private.
Bed & breakfast: £25-£40
single, £39-£57 double.
Half board: £32.75-£41.75
daily.
Evening meal 7pm (l.o.
midday).
Parking for 15.

⊱ ▯8 ♨ ⌸ ⊚ ⎅ ❖ ⊨ ▥ ♨
❄ ♨ Ⓢ Ⓟ ⒻⒷ Ⓣ

Ashbourne House
Hotel ⚊
♛♛♛

139 Fulford Road, York,
YO1 4HG
☎ (0904) 639912

*Charming, comfortable family-
owned and run licensed private
hotel. On main route into York
from the South. Walking
distance to city centre.*
Bedrooms: 3 double & 2 twin,
1 family room.
Bathrooms: 6 private,
1 public.
Bed & breakfast: from £20
single, £35-£45 double.
Parking for 7.
Credit: Access, Visa.

⊱ ⎅ ❖ ▮ Ⅴ ⊨ ⒯Ⅴ ▥ ♨
♟ ♨ ⒹⒶ⒫ ⅍ Ⓢ Ⓟ

Ashcroft Hotel ⚊
♛♛♛ APPROVED

294 Bishopthorpe Rd., York,
YO2 1LH
☎ (0904) 659286
Fax (0904) 640107
ⒸⓇ Minotels
*Former Victorian mansion in
2.5 acres of wooded grounds
overlooking the River Ouse,
only 1 mile from the city
centre. All bedrooms have
colour TV, radio, mini-bar,
telephone, coffee and tea
making facilities, hair-dryer
and trouser press.*
Bedrooms: 1 single, 6 double
& 5 twin, 3 family rooms.
Bathrooms: 15 private.
Bed & breakfast: from £36
single, from £62 double.
Half board: from £34.50
daily, from £241.50 weekly.
Lunch available.
Evening meal 6.30pm (l.o.
7.30pm).
Parking for 40.
Credit: Access, Visa, Diners,
Amex.

⊱ ♨ ℄ ⊚ ⎅ ❖ ▯ Ⅴ ⊨
⒯Ⅴ ▥ ♨ ♟ ❄ ⒹⒶ⒫ ⅍ Ⓢ Ⓟ Ⓣ

Avondale ⚊
Listed APPROVED

61 Bishopthorpe Rd., York,
YO2 1NX
☎ (0904) 633989
*Small, friendly guesthouse,
close to city centre, en-suite
facilities available.*
Bedrooms: 2 double & 2 twin.
Bathrooms: 4 private,
1 public.
Bed & breakfast: £32-£36
double.
Half board: £40-£48 daily.
Evening meal 6pm.

⊱ ⎅ ❖ ▥ ⊨ ⒯Ⅴ ▥ ♨ ▥
⅍

Barbican Hotel ⚊
♛♛ COMMENDED

20 Barbican Rd., York,
YO1 5AA
☎ (0904) 627617

*Small, friendly family-run
Victorian residence of charm
and character overlooking
medieval bar walls. 7 minutes'
walk to tourist attractions.*
Bedrooms: 4 double & 1 twin,
1 family room.
Bathrooms: 6 private,
1 public.
Bed & breakfast: £34-£50
double.
Half board: £27.50-£35.50
daily.
Evening meal 6.30pm.
Parking for 7.
Credit: Access, Visa.

⊱ ♨ ⌸ ℄ ⊚ ⎅ ❖ ⊨ ▥
♨ ⋈ ⋈ Ⓢ Ⓟ

Bedford Hotel ⚊
♛♛♛

108-110 Bootham, York,
YO3 7DG
☎ (0904) 624412
*Family-run hotel, 5 minutes'
walk along historic Bootham to
the famous York Minster and
city centre.*
Bedrooms: 2 single, 7 double
& 2 twin, 3 family rooms.
Bathrooms: 14 private.
Bed & breakfast: £26-£40
single, £38-£50 double.
Half board: £27.50-£48.50
daily, £192.50-£330.50
weekly.
Evening meal 6.30pm (l.o.
midday).
Parking for 14.
Credit: Access, Visa.

⊱ ⎅ ❖ ⊨ ⒯Ⅴ ▥ ♨ ⋈ ⋈
⅍ Ⓢ ⒻⒷ

Beech House ⚊
♛♛♛

6-7 Longfield Terrace,
Bootham, York, YO3 7DJ
☎ (0904) 634581
*Small, family-run guesthouse
with a warm welcome and a
relaxing atmosphere only
5 minutes' walk from York
Minster.*
Bedrooms: 1 single, 6 double
& 1 twin.
Bathrooms: 8 private.
Bed & breakfast: £18-£25
single, £34-£46 double.
Evening meal 6pm.
Parking for 5.

℄ ⊚ ⎅ ❖ ⓊⓁ ⊨ ▥ ♨ ⋈
⅍ Ⓢ

Beechwood Close
Hotel ⚊
♛♛♛♛ COMMENDED

19 Shipton Rd., Clifton,
York, YO3 6RE
☎ (0904) 658378
Fax (0904) 647124
ⒸⓇ Minotels

Continued ▶

---

*Please check prices and other details at
the time of booking.*

Spacious, detached, family-run house set among trees, located on the A19, 1 mile north of the city centre. Restaurant, bar, lounge, car park and a 9-hole putting green.
Bedrooms: 3 single, 4 double & 2 twin, 5 family rooms.
Bathrooms: 14 private.
Bed & breakfast: £36.30-£39.90 single, £59.50-£65 double.
Half board: £36.55-£50.85 daily, £255.85-£355.95 weekly.
Lunch available.
Evening meal 7pm (l.o. 9pm).
Parking for 36.
Credit: Access, Visa, Diners, Amex.
⑤ ✆ ◎ ➩ ♦ ⓘ Ⓥ ◢ ▥
◣ ♍ ⊁ ⋈ ㎡ SP Ⓣ

The Bentley Ⓜ
25 Grosvenor Terrace,
Bootham, York, YO3 7AG
☎ (0904) 644313
Fine house in Victorian terrace, with views of the minster. Close to city centre. Friendly service, care and comfort guaranteed.
Bedrooms: 4 double, 2 family rooms.
Bathrooms: 3 private, 2 public.
Bed & breakfast: £30-£42 double.
Half board: £23.50-£30 daily.
Evening meal 6pm (l.o. 4pm).
Open February-November.
⑤5◎➩ Ⓤ ⓘ ▥ ◣ ⊁ ⋈
DAP SP

Bishopgarth Guest House Ⓜ
♛♛
3 Southlands Rd.,
Bishopthorpe Rd., York,
YO2 1NP
☎ (0904) 635220
Victorian town house offering spacious and homely accommodation, close to the city centre.
Bedrooms: 1 single, 2 double & 2 twin, 1 family room.
Bathrooms: 1 private, 2 public.
Bed & breakfast: £12-£14 single, £22-£28 double.
Half board: £16-£20 daily, £112-£140 weekly.
Evening meal 5pm (l.o. midday).
⑤➩♦ Ⓤ Ⓥ ⊁◢ Ⓣ ▥
◣⊁ DAP SP

Blue Bridge Hotel Ⓜ
♛♛♛♛
Fishergate, York, YO1 4AP
☎ (0904) 621193

Friendly, private hotel, reputation for food, relaxed atmosphere and a warm welcome. Short riverside walk to city. Private car park.
Bedrooms: 2 single, 6 double & 3 twin, 5 family rooms.
Bathrooms: 14 private, 1 public.
Bed & breakfast: £40-£48 single, £58-£62 double.
Half board: £44-£60 daily.
Evening meal 6.30pm (l.o. 9.30pm).
Parking for 20.
Credit: Access, Visa.
⑤♙✆◎➩♦ ⓘ Ⓥ◢
Ⓣ▥◣♦ DAP ♌ SP Ⓣ

Bootham Bar Hotel Ⓜ
Listed APPROVED
4 High Petergate, York,
YO1 2EH
☎ (0904) 658516
Hotel garden is bordered by the city walls, 150 yards from York Minster. Luggage lift.
Bedrooms: 4 double & 3 twin, 2 family rooms.
Bathrooms: 9 private.
Bed & breakfast: £48-£60 double.
Lunch available.
Credit: Access, Visa.
⑤◎➩♦ Ⓤ Ⓥ◢▥⊁
⋈ ㎡
⓭ *Display advertisement appears on page 203.*

Bootham Park Hotel Ⓜ
♛♛♛
9 Grosvenor Terrace,
Bootham, York, YO3 7AG
☎ (0904) 644262
Elegant Victorian house 5 minutes' walk from York Minster and tourist attractions. En-suite rooms, with hair-dryer, alarm clock, colour TV and drinks tray.
Bedrooms: 2 double & 2 twin, 2 family rooms.
Bathrooms: 6 private.
Bed & breakfast: from £34 double.
Half board: from £27 daily.
Evening meal 6.30pm (l.o. 7.45pm).
Parking for 6.
Credit: Access, Visa.
⑤➩♦ ⓘ Ⓥ◢ Ⓣ▥◣
⊁ DAP SP

Bowen House Ⓜ
♛♛
4 Gladstone St., Huntington
Rd., York YO3 7RF
☎ (0904) 636881
Victorian townhouse, carefully restored using antique and period furniture. Very close to city centre, restaurants and tourist attractions. No smoking throughout.
Bedrooms: 1 single, 2 double & 1 twin, 1 family room.

Bathrooms: 2 private,
1 public; 1 private shower.
Bed & breakfast: £16-£18 single, £28-£40 double.
Parking for 4.
⑤◎➩♦ Ⓤ ⓘ Ⓥ⊁◢
Ⓣ▥◣♦ DAP SP ㎡ Ⓣ

Briar Lea Guest House Ⓜ
♛♛♛
8 Longfield Terrace,
Bootham, York, YO3 7DJ
☎ (0904) 635061
Victorian house with some rooms en-suite, 5 minutes' walk from the city centre and railway station.
Bedrooms: 1 single, 2 double & 1 twin, 1 family room.
Bathrooms: 2 private, 1 public.
Bed & breakfast: £12-£16 single, £24-£35 double.
Parking for 1.
⑤5➩♦ Ⓤ Ⓥ◢ Ⓣ▥
◣ ♙⊁⋈ DAP SP

Bronte House Ⓜ
♛♛♛
22 Grosvenor Terrace,
Bootham, York, YO3 7AG
☎ (0904) 621066
Bright, clean Victorian house close to the city centre, in view of York Minster.
Bedrooms: 1 single, 2 double & 1 twin, 2 family rooms.
Bathrooms: 4 private, 1 public.
Bed & breakfast: £10-£16 single, £20-£36 double.
Parking for 3.
Credit: Access, Visa, Amex.
⑤➩♦ Ⓤ Ⓥ◢ Ⓣ▥
⊁ ⋈ DAP Ⓣ

Carlton House Hotel Ⓜ
♛♛ **APPROVED**
134 The Mount, York,
YO2 2AS
☎ (0904) 622265
Family-run hotel, a short walk from the city centre, railway station and racecourse.
Bedrooms: 1 single, 7 double & 3 twin, 4 family rooms.
Bathrooms: 6 private, 3 public; 1 private shower.
Bed & breakfast: £18.50-£24 single, £35-£42 double.
Parking for 7.
⑤◎➩♦◢▥◣⊁ ㎡

Carousel Guest House Ⓜ
Listed APPROVED
83 Eldon St., Haxby Rd.,
York, YO3 7NH
☎ (0904) 646709
Warm, friendly licensed guesthouse in central location. All rooms en-suite with tea and coffee making facilities.

Bedrooms: 2 single, 4 double & 1 twin, 2 family rooms.
Bathrooms: 9 private.
Bed & breakfast: £15-£17.50 single, £30-£35 double.
Evening meal 5.30pm (l.o. 10am).
Parking for 15.
⑤♙◢◣Ⓣ▥◣⊁ ⋈ DAP
SP

Cavalier Private Hotel Ⓜ
Listed APPROVED
39 Monkgate, York,
YO3 7PB
☎ (0904) 636615
Small family-run hotel close to the city centre, only yards from the ancient Bar Walls and many of York's famous historic landmarks.
Bedrooms: 2 single, 4 double, 4 family rooms.
Bathrooms: 7 private, 3 public.
Bed & breakfast: £17-£18.50 single, £37-£40 double.
Evening meal 6pm (l.o. 3.30pm).
⑤➩♦ ⓘ Ⓥ◢ Ⓣ▥◣
♙⊁⋈

Chantry Hotel Ⓜ
130 The Mount, York,
YO2 2AS
☎ (0904) 659150
Elegant Georgian listed residence, built in 1830 and tastefully restored. Near the station and Micklegate Bar, an ancient entrance to the old city.
Bedrooms: 2 single, 3 double, 1 family room.
Bathrooms: 4 private, 1 public.
Bed & breakfast: £27-£35 single, £50-£60 double.
Half board: £37-£47 daily, £245-£320 weekly.
Evening meal 6.30pm (l.o. 8.30pm).
Parking for 2.
Credit: Access, Visa.
⑤2✆◎➩♦ ⓘ Ⓥ◢ Ⓣ
◉▥◣⋈ SP ㎡

City Guest House Ⓜ
♛♛
68 Monkgate, York,
YO3 7PF
☎ (0904) 622483
Cosy guesthouse 3 minutes from York Minster. En-suite rooms and car parking. Non-smokers only please.
Bedrooms: 1 single, 2 double & 2 twin, 1 family room.
Bathrooms: 3 private; 3 private showers.
Bed & breakfast: £12-£20 single, £28-£40 double.
Parking for 5.
⑤2➩♦ Ⓤ ⓘ ⊁◢ Ⓣ▥
◣⊁ SP

Clarence Gardens Hotel & Squash Courts M
♛♛♛

Haxby Rd., York, YO3 7JS
☎ (0904) 624252
Comfortable accommodation with emphasis on service. Use of squash courts free of charge to residents. 10 minutes' walk to the city centre.
Bedrooms: 4 double & 8 twin, 1 family room.
Bathrooms: 13 private.
Bed & breakfast: £32-£37 single, £44-£52 double.
Evening meal 5.30pm (l.o. 7pm).
Parking for 60.
Credit: Access, Visa, Amex.
🛏🖿📞🖢🕭●🎱🍴🔥
✕🔥

Clifton Bridge Hotel M
♛♛♛ COMMENDED

Water End, Clifton, York, YO3 6LL
☎ (0904) 610510
Fax (0904) 640208
On the north side of the city between the A19 and A59. Adjacent to a delightful riverside walk into the city centre and opposite a very pleasant park.
Bedrooms: 2 single, 2 double & 9 twin, 1 family room.
Bathrooms: 14 private.
Bed & breakfast: £35-£40 single, £50-£60 double.
Half board: £34.50-£43 daily, £220-£280 weekly.
Lunch available.
Evening meal 6.30pm (l.o. 7.45pm).
Parking for 14.
Credit: Access, Visa, Amex.
🛏🖿📞🖢🖥🕭🔥
🎱🍴🔥 OAP SP T

Clifton Guest House M
♛♛♛ APPROVED

127 Clifton, York, YO3 6BL
☎ (0904) 634031
Small family-run guesthouse with bedrooms on the ground and first floors. Less than a mile from York Minster.
Bedrooms: 1 single, 1 double & 2 twin, 1 family rooms.
Bathrooms: 3 private, 2 public.
Bed & breakfast: £15 single, £26-£30 double.
Half board: £21-£23 daily.
Evening meal 6pm (l.o. 9am).
Parking for 6.
🛏🖿🖿🖢🖥🔥🎱🍴🔥
✕🔥 SP

Clifton View Guest House M
♛♛

118 Clifton, York, YO3 6BQ
☎ (0904) 625047

Family-run guesthouse with private parking, 15 minutes' walk from the city centre. All rooms have colour TV.
Bedrooms: 4 double & 2 twin, 4 family rooms.
Bathrooms: 2 public; 8 private showers.
Bed & breakfast: £24-£29 double.
Half board: £18-£21.50 daily.
Evening meal 6pm (l.o. 10.30am).
Parking for 6.
🛏🖿🖿🖢🖥🔥🎱🍴🔥
OAP SP

Collingwood Hotel M
♛♛♛

163 Holgate Rd., York, YO2 4DF
☎ (0904) 783333
Georgian building with adequate parking within its own grounds. Dining room, lounge and lounge bar.
Bedrooms: 4 double & 3 twin, 3 family rooms.
Bathrooms: 10 private.
Bed & breakfast: £40-£48 double.
Parking for 10.
Credit: Access, Visa, Diners, Amex.
🛏5🖥🖿🖢🔥🖥🎱🍴
🔥

Copper's Lodge
Listed

15 Alma Terrace, Fulford Rd., York, YO1 4DQ
☎ (0904) 639871
Family-run guesthouse offering personal service. In a quiet location with a river walk close by and only 5 minutes' walk to the city centre.
Bedrooms: 1 single, 1 double & 1 twin, 4 family rooms.
Bathrooms: 3 public.
Bed & breakfast: £15-£18 single, £24-£26 double.
Half board: £18.50-£20 daily, £129.50-£140 weekly.
Evening meal 6pm (l.o. 6pm).
Parking for 7.
🛏🖥🖿🖢🖥🔥🍴🔥🖥
🎱 OAP SP T

Cornerways Guest House
♛♛

16 Murton Way, Osbaldwick, York, YO1 3UN
☎ (0904) 621888 & 413366
Detached house in a village location, yet only 5 minutes from the city and close to York's outer ring road, convenient for the coast.
Bedrooms: 1 single, 1 double & 1 twin.
Bathrooms: 2 private, 1 public.

Bed & breakfast: £12-£15 single, £30-£36 double.
Parking for 4.
🛏🖥🖿🖢🖥💡🖥🔥🔥
🖥🎱🍴🔥

Cottage Hotel M
♛♛♛♛ APPROVED

1 Clifton Green, York, YO3 6LH
☎ (0904) 643711
Family-run hotel within 15 minutes' walking distance of the city centre, overlooking the beautiful Clifton Green.
Bedrooms: 2 single, 10 double & 5 twin, 3 family rooms.
Bathrooms: 20 private.
Bed & breakfast: £35-£45 single, £50-£70 double.
Half board: £35-£43 daily.
Evening meal 7pm (l.o. 9pm).
Parking for 18.
Credit: Access, Visa, Diners, Amex.
🛏🖿📞🖥🖿🖢🖥🔥🎱
🎱🍴 SP

Crescent Guest House
♛♛♛ APPROVED

77 Bootham, York, YO3 7DQ
☎ (0904) 623216
Yorkshire family-run establishment close to the city centre and an ideal base for visiting the surrounding countryside and coast. Interesting Georgian, part-beamed building.
Bedrooms: 1 single, 6 double & 3 twin.
Bathrooms: 10 private, 1 public.
Bed & breakfast: £17.50-£25 single, £34-£45 double.
Half board: £27-£32 daily, £170-£205 weekly.
Evening meal 6pm (l.o. 10am).
Parking for 4.
Credit: Access, Visa, Diners, Amex.
🛏📞🖿🖢🖥🔥🎱🍴🔥
OAP SP

Crossways Guest House
Listed

23 Wigginton Rd., York, YO3 7HJ
☎ (0904) 637250
Comfortable Edwardian guesthouse, close to park and bowling green. 10 minutes' walk from city centre.
Bedrooms: 5 double & 1 twin.
Bathrooms: 6 private.
Bed & breakfast: £15-£18 single, £28-£34 double.
Half board: £25-£28 daily.
Evening meal 5.30pm (l.o. 5.30pm).
Parking for 2.
🛏🖿🖿🖢🖥🎱🍴✕🔥

Curzon Lodge and Stable Cottages M
♛♛ COMMENDED

23 Tadcaster Rd., Dringhouses, York, YO2 2QG
☎ (0904) 703157
Delightful 17th C listed house and former stables in pretty conservation area overlooking the racecourse, once a home of the Terry "chocolate" family. All en-suite, some four posters. Many antiques. Large enclosed car park.
Bedrooms: 1 single, 4 double & 3 twin, 2 family rooms.
Bathrooms: 10 private.
Bed & breakfast: £30-£36 single, £44-£54 double.
Parking for 16.
🛏8🖿🖥🖿📞🖢🖥🖥🔥
🖥🎱✕🔥🔥 OAP SP FB

Dean Court Hotel M
♛♛♛ COMMENDED

Duncombe Place, York, YO1 2EF
☎ (0904) 625082 Telex 57584
🆑 Best Western
Modernised Victorian building adjacent to York Minster in the centre of the city with a car park nearby. Lift, coffee shop and 2 comfortable bars.
Bedrooms: 17 single, 6 double & 17 twin.
Bathrooms: 40 private.
Bed & breakfast: £65-£75 single, £97-£125 double.
Lunch available.
Evening meal 6.30pm (l.o. 9.30pm).
Parking for 30.
Credit: Access, Visa, C.Bl., Diners, Amex.
🛏📞🖥🖿🖢💡🖥🔥🎱
🖥🎱🍴✕🔥 SP FB T

Deerthorpe Lodge M
Listed COMMENDED

77 Nunthorpe Rd., Off Scarcroft Rd., York, YO2 1BQ
☎ (0904) 626396
Small, homely guesthouse just outside the city walls and 5 minutes' walk from the town centre and racecourse.
Bedrooms: 1 single, 1 double & 2 twin, 1 family room.
Bathrooms: 3 private, 1 public.
Bed & breakfast: £13.50-£15 single, £27-£36 double.
Half board: £20-£24 daily.
Parking for 4.
🛏🖿🖿🖢🖥💡🖥🔥
🎱🍴✕🔥 OAP SP

Please mention this guide when making a booking.

Fairfax House, University of York ⚹

99 Heslington Rd., York, YO1 5BJ
☎ (0904) 432095
Student residence in quiet, spacious grounds within walking distance of the city centre. Colour TV and car park. Reduced rates for children under 12.
Bedrooms: 91 single.
Bathrooms: 14 public.
Bed & breakfast: £12.25-£15.30 single.
Parking for 40.
Open July-September.

Fairfield Manor Hotel ⚹

Shipton Rd., Skelton, York, YO3 6XW
☎ York (0904) 625621
Telex 57476 ATT FM
Georgian mansion in attractive country setting, three miles north of York. Recently refurbished. Four poster bedrooms and suites available.
Bedrooms: 12 single, 28 double & 30 twin, 20 family rooms.
Bathrooms: 90 private.
Bed & breakfast: £65-£75 single, £90-£100 double.
Half board: £52.50-£60 daily.
Lunch available.
Evening meal 6.30pm (l.o. 9.30pm).
Parking for 200.
Credit: Access, Visa, Diners, Amex.

Hotel Fairmount ⚹
APPROVED

230 Tadcaster Rd., Mount Vale, YO2 2ES
☎ (0904) 638298
Telex 557720 APO/G
Large, tastefully furnished, Victorian villa dated 1881, with open views over the racecourse and within walking distance of medieval York. All rooms have colour TV, tea making facilities and hair-dryer. Rooms for disabled people available.
Bedrooms: 2 single, 6 double & 1 twin, 3 family rooms.
Bathrooms: 12 private.
Bed & breakfast: £27-£35 single, £55-£62 double.
Half board: £42.50-£46 daily, £270-£290 weekly.
Lunch available.

Evening meal 7pm (l.o. 9pm).
Parking for 7.
Credit: Access, Visa.

Farthings Hotel ⚹

5 Nunthorpe Avenue, York, YO2 1PF
☎ (0904) 653545
Lovingly renovated Victorian residence with a friendly, informal atmosphere. In a quiet cul-de-sac approximately 10 minutes' walk from the city centre.
Bedrooms: 6 double & 1 twin, 2 family rooms.
Bathrooms: 3 private, 2 public.
Bed & breakfast: £28-£36 double.
Open March-November.

Feversham Lodge Hotel ⚹

Feversham Crescent, Wigginton Rd., York, YO3 7HQ
☎ (0904) 623882
Small family-run hotel within 10 minutes' walk of city centre, handy for moors and dales as well as local amenities.
Bedrooms: 1 single, 5 double & 3 twin, 1 family room.
Bathrooms: 6 private, 1 public.
Bed & breakfast: £14-£16 single, £32-£36 double.
Parking for 8.

Four Seasons Hotel ⚹

7 St. Peter's Grove, Clifton, York, YO3 6AQ
☎ (0904) 622621
Fax (0904) 430565
Licensed Victorian residence with modern facilities. Private car park, English breakfast. In quiet area, only 5 minutes' walk from York Minster.
Bedrooms: 2 double & 1 twin, 2 family rooms.
Bathrooms: 3 private, 1 public; 1 private shower.
Bed & breakfast: £21.50-£25.50 single, £33-£40.50 double.
Parking for 6.
Credit: Access, Visa.

Fourposter Lodge ⚹

68-70 Heslington Rd., York, YO1 5AU
☎ (0904) 651170

Victorian villa lovingly restored and furnished, 10 minutes' walk from historic York and all its fascinations.
Bedrooms: 1 single, 6 double & 1 twin, 2 family rooms.
Bathrooms: 8 private, 1 public; 1 private shower.
Bed & breakfast: £40-£56 double.
Half board: £31.50-£40 daily, £215-£266 weekly.
Evening meal 6.30pm (l.o. 8am).
Parking for 8.
Credit: Visa.

Freshneys Hotel ⚹
COMMENDED

54 Low Petergate, York, YO1 2HZ
☎ (0904) 622478
Georgian brick building of character, with views of the rose window of York Minster from some rooms. Owner managed.
Bedrooms: 2 single, 5 double & 3 twin, 1 family room.
Bathrooms: 5 private, 2 public.
Bed & breakfast: £20-£25 single, £30-£58 double.
Lunch available.
Evening meal 6pm (l.o. 10pm).
Credit: Access, Visa.

Gleneagles Lodge Guest House ⚹

27 Nunthorpe Avenue, York, YO2 1PF
☎ (0904) 637000
In a cul-de-sac close to the station, city centre and museums. Within easy walking distance of the racecourse.
Bedrooms: 2 double & 2 twin, 2 family rooms.
Bathrooms: 3 private, 2 public.
Bed & breakfast: £14-£20 single, £26-£32 double.
Parking for 2.

Glenville Guest House ⚹

132 East Parade, Heworth, York, YO3 7YG
☎ (0904) 425370
Warm, friendly accommodation in a quiet area 10 minutes' walk from York Minster and city centre. Special emphasis on English breakfast with evening meal available by arrangement. Unrestricted street parking.
Bedrooms: 2 single, 1 double & 1 twin, 1 family room.

Bathrooms: 1 public.
Bed & breakfast: £14-£15.50 single, £26-£31 double.
Half board: £19-£21 daily, £133-£147 weekly.
Parking for 2.

Grange Hotel ⚹
HIGHLY COMMENDED

Clifton, York, YO3 6AA
☎ (0904) 644744 Telex 57210
Fax 0904 612453
Classical, Regency town house hotel with all bedrooms individually decorated with antiques and English chintz. Within easy walking distance of York Minster.
Bedrooms: 3 single, 9 double & 17 twin.
Bathrooms: 29 private.
Bed & breakfast: £82 single, £98-£125 double.
Lunch available.
Evening meal 6.30pm (l.o. 11pm).
Parking for 26.
Credit: Access, Visa, Diners, Amex.

Grange Lodge ⚹
Listed

52 Bootham Crescent, Bootham, York, YO3 7AH
☎ (0904) 621137
Attractive, tastefully furnished Victorian town house with a friendly atmosphere. Special emphasis is given to food, cleanliness and hospitality. Basic and en-suite rooms available. Evening meal by arrangement.
Bedrooms: 1 single, 3 double & 1 twin, 2 family rooms.
Bathrooms: 4 private, 1 public.
Bed & breakfast: £13-£16 single, £24-£36 double.
Half board: £19-£25 daily, £133-£175 weekly.
Evening meal 6pm.

Greenside ⚹

124 Clifton, York, YO3 6BQ
☎ (0904) 623631
Owner-run guesthouse, fronting Clifton Green, ideally situated for all York's attractions. Offers many facilities and a homely atmosphere.
Bedrooms: 1 single, 3 double & 2 twin, 2 family rooms.
Bathrooms: 3 private, 2 public.
Bed & breakfast: from £13 single, from £20 double.

Half board: from £21.50 daily.
Evening meal 6pm (l.o. 6pm).
Parking for 6.

Hazelmere Guest House M

Listed

65 Monkgate, York,
YO3 7PA
☎ (0904) 655947
Georgian cottages, tastefully linked to retain their original character.
Bedrooms: 3 single, 5 double.
Bathrooms: 2 public.
Bed & breakfast: £14-£15 single, £28-£30 double.
Parking for 7.

The Hazelwood M

COMMENDED

24/25 Portland St., Gillygate,
York, YO3 7EH
☎ (0904) 626548
Fax (0904) 628032
Care and comfort in a quiet city centre location off Gillygate. Close to all of York's major attractions and many restaurants.
Bedrooms: 2 single, 8 double & 5 twin.
Bathrooms: 11 private, 3 public.
Bed & breakfast: £17-£20 single, £29-£48 double.
Parking for 9.
Credit: Access, Visa.

Hedley House M

APPROVED

3-4 Bootham Terrace, York,
YO3 7DH
☎ (0904) 637404
Family-run guesthouse close to the city centre. 1 ground floor bedroom. All rooms en-suite. Home cooking, special diets catered for.
Bedrooms: 2 single, 5 double & 5 twin, 3 family rooms.
Bathrooms: 15 private.
Bed & breakfast: from £18 single, £34-£48 double.
Half board: £27-£33 daily.
Lunch available.
Evening meal 6.30pm (l.o. 6.30pm).
Parking for 12.
Credit: Access, Visa, Amex.

We advise you to confirm your booking in writing.

Heworth Court Hotel M

COMMENDED

76-78 Heworth Green, York,
YO3 7TQ
☎ (0904) 425156
Fax (0904) 415290
Telex 57571
On the A1036 east side of York. Privately-owned, family-run hotel with emphasis on food and service.
Bedrooms: 3 single, 12 double & 6 twin, 6 family rooms.
Bathrooms: 27 private.
Bed & breakfast: £40.50-£44 single, £58-£64 double.
Half board: £38.50-£45.75 daily, £269.50-£297 weekly.
Lunch available.
Evening meal 6.30pm (l.o. 9.30pm).
Parking for 25.
Credit: Access, Visa, Diners, Amex.

Heworth Guest House M

Listed

126 East Parade, Heworth,
York, YO3 7YG
☎ (0904) 426384
Family-run hotel in a quiet conservation area, with easy parking, 15 minutes' walk from city centre. Excitingly different menus are the house speciality - vegetarian and vegan dishes always available.
Bedrooms: 3 single, 1 double & 2 twin.
Bathrooms: 2 public.
Bed & breakfast: £12.50-£15 single, £25-£30 double.
Evening meal 6pm (l.o. 9am).
Parking for 2.
Credit: Access, Visa.

Hillcrest Guest House M

110 Bishopthorpe Rd., York,
YO2 1JX
☎ (0904) 653160
2 elegant Victorian terraced houses converted into a guesthouse, close to the city centre, racecourse and station. Emphasis on offering personal attention and value for money.
Bedrooms: 3 single, 4 double & 1 twin, 4 family rooms.
Bathrooms: 3 public; 1 private shower.
Bed & breakfast: £13-£18 single, £24-£34 double.
Half board: £19.50-£24.50 daily.
Evening meal 6pm.
Parking for 8.

Holgate Bridge Hotel M

APPROVED

106-108 Holgate Rd., York,
YO2 4BB
☎ (0904) 635971 & 647288
Early Victorian town houses, converted into a small friendly, family-run hotel. On the A59, within easy walking distance of the city centre. Own car park and restaurant.
Bedrooms: 2 single, 7 double & 1 twin, 4 family rooms.
Bathrooms: 11 private, 1 public.
Bed & breakfast: £22-£36 single, £35-£52 double.
Half board: £28-£36 daily.
Lunch available.
Evening meal 6.30pm (l.o. 9pm).
Parking for 11.
Credit: Access, Visa, Amex.

Holgate Hill Hotel M

APPROVED

124 Holgate Rd., York,
YO2 4BB
☎ (0904) 653786
Fax (0904) 643223
Family hotel where home cooking is a speciality. Close to the city centre, points of historic interest and the racecourse.
Bedrooms: 6 single, 15 double & 7 twin, 5 family rooms.
Bathrooms: 33 private, 2 public.
Bed & breakfast: from £29 single, from £48 double.
Half board: from £34 daily.
Lunch available.
Evening meal 7pm (l.o. 8.30pm).
Parking for 14.
Credit: Access, Visa, Diners, Amex.

Holiday Inn York M

Tower St., York, YO1 1SB
☎ (0904) 648111 Telex 57566
Holiday Inn
Modern hotel on 4 floors in a city centre location overlooking Clifford's Tower. Restaurant, cocktail bar, lounge bar and informal restaurant. Conference facilities for up to 200. Business services available.
Bedrooms: 84 double & 44 twin.
Bathrooms: 128 private.
Bed & breakfast: £48-£50 single, £96-£100 double.
Half board: £58-£60 daily.
Lunch available.
Evening meal 7pm (l.o. 9.30pm).

Parking for 45.
Credit: Access, Visa, C.Bl., Diners, Amex.

The Hollies M

APPROVED

141 Fulford Rd., York,
YO1 4HG
☎ (0904) 634279
Comfortable family-run guesthouse, close to university and golf-course and with easy access to city centre. Tea/coffee facilities, colour TV in all rooms, some en-suite. Car parking. Evening meal in low season by arrangement.
Bedrooms: 1 single, 2 double, 2 family rooms.
Bathrooms: 2 private, 1 public.
Bed & breakfast: £18-£27 single, £26-£45 double.
Half board: £19-£28.50 daily.
Evening meal 6.30pm.
Parking for 5.
Credit: Access, Visa.

Holly Lodge M

APPROVED

206 Fulford Rd., York,
YO1 4DD
☎ (0904) 646005
Listed Georgian building on the A19, convenient for both the north and south and within walking distance of the city centre. Quiet rooms and private car park.
Bedrooms: 2 double & 2 twin, 1 family room.
Bathrooms: 5 private.
Bed & breakfast: £25-£28 single, £34-£45 double.
Parking for 5.
Open January-October.
Credit: Access, Visa.

Holme Lea Manor Guest House

18 St. Peter's Grove,
Bootham, York, YO3 6AQ
☎ (0904) 623529
Elegant Victorian house, providing spacious accommodation with a nice garden. An easy walk away from York city centre. Family-managed. French, Spanish and Italian are spoken.
Bedrooms: 4 double & 2 twin.
Bathrooms: 6 private.
Bed & breakfast: £36-£40 single, £40-£50 double.

Continued ▶

YORK

Continued

Half board: £27-£43 daily,
£180-£300 weekly.
Parking for 8.

Holmwood House Hotel M
⌂⌂⌂ COMMENDED
112-114 Holgate Rd., York,
YO2 4BB
☎ (0904) 626183
*Listed Victorian townhouse, 10
minutes from city walls,
redecorated and furnished with
antiques. Offers elegant
comfort in 10 attractive en-
suite rooms.*
Bedrooms: 7 double & 2 twin,
1 family room.
Bathrooms: 10 private.
Bed & breakfast: £38-£40
single, £48-£55 double.
Half board: £35-£38 daily.
Evening meal 7.30pm (l.o.
7.30pm).
Parking for 10.
Credit: Access, Visa.

Hudson's Hotel M
⌂⌂⌂
60 Bootham, York, YO3 7BZ
☎ (0904) 621267
Fax (0904) 654719
*Within easy walking distance
of the city, minster and Jorvik
Viking Centre. Victorian-style
restaurant and bar.*
Bedrooms: 1 single, 15 double
& 11 twin, 3 family rooms.
Bathrooms: 30 private.
Bed & breakfast: £39-£45
single, £69-£75 double.
Half board: £53-£59 daily,
£287-£322 weekly.
Lunch available.
Evening meal 6.30pm (l.o.
9.30pm).
Parking for 34.
Credit: Access, Visa, Diners,
Amex.

Jorvik Hotel M
⌂⌂⌂ APPROVED
Marygate, Bootham, York,
YO3 7BH
☎ (0904) 653511
*Small well-appointed family
hotel overlooking the gates of
Saint Mary's Abbey and the
Museum Gardens. Close to the
River Ouse.*
Bedrooms: 1 single, 11 double
& 8 twin, 2 family rooms.
Bathrooms: 22 private.
Bed & breakfast: £23-£26
single, £40-£50 double.

Half board: £30-£60 daily.
Evening meal 6.30pm (l.o.
8pm).
Parking for 6.
Credit: Access, Visa.

Judges Lodging M
⌂⌂⌂⌂ COMMENDED
9 Lendal, York, YO1 2AQ
☎ (0904) 623587 & 638733
Telex 57200
*Georgian town house of
exceptional historic importance,
set in the centre of this ancient
city. Lavishly decorated and
furnished.*
Bedrooms: 3 single, 6 double
& 4 twin.
Bathrooms: 13 private.
Bed & breakfast: £45-£65
single, £80-£110 double.
Half board: £50-£75 daily.
Lunch available.
Evening meal 7.30pm (l.o.
9.30pm).
Parking for 16.
Credit: Access, Visa, Diners,
Amex.

Keys House M
Listed COMMENDED
137 Fulford Rd., York,
YO1 4HG
☎ (0904) 658488
*Comfortable Edwardian house
providing spacious bedrooms
with showers and WCs. Own
key provided. Reductions for 3
or more nights.*
Bedrooms: 2 double & 2 twin,
1 family room.
Bathrooms: 5 private.
Bed & breakfast: £18-£32
single, £28-£40 double.
Parking for 5.

Kilima Hotel M
⌂⌂⌂⌂ COMMENDED
129 Holgate Rd., York,
YO2 4DE
☎ (0904) 625787 Fax
(0904) 612083 Telex 57928
⌂ Inter
*Extensively refurbished, 19th C
building with a fine restaurant
– a la carte and table d'hote.*
Bedrooms: 4 single, 7 double
& 3 twin, 1 family room.
Bathrooms: 15 private.
Bed & breakfast: £41-£51
single, £63.40-£73.40 double.
Half board: £47-£52 daily.
Lunch available.
Evening meal 6.30pm (l.o.
9.30pm).
Parking for 20.
Credit: Access, Visa, Diners,
Amex.

Kismet Guest House
Listed
147 Haxby Rd., York,
YO3 7JW
☎ (0904) 621056
18th C terraced house.
Bedrooms: 1 single, 2 double
& 1 twin, 1 family room.
Bathrooms: 1 private,
1 public; 4 private showers.
Bed & breakfast: £14-£16
single, £12-£30 double.
Parking for 5.
Open March-November.

Knavesmire Manor Hotel M
⌂⌂⌂
302 Tadcaster Rd., York,
YO2 2HE
☎ (0904) 702941
Fax (0904) 709274
*Built in 1833, this magnificent
house stands elevated,
commanding uninterrupted
views across the Knavesmire
and parkland site of York's
famous racecourse. Tropical
pool and spa.*
Bedrooms: 3 single, 10 double
& 6 twin, 3 family rooms.
Bathrooms: 18 private,
1 public; 1 private shower.
Bed & breakfast: £29.50-£52
single, £45-£69 double.
Evening meal 7pm (l.o.
10pm).
Parking for 27.
Credit: Access, Visa, Diners,
Amex.

Lady Anne Middleton's Hotel M
⌂⌂⌂ APPROVED
Skeldergate, York, YO1 1DS
☎ (0904) 632257 & 630456 &
611570
Fax (0904) 613043
*Historic buildings in English
gardens in the centre of York,
near the river. Jacuzzi, sauna,
health and fitness centre, car
parking.*
Bedrooms: 4 single, 29 double
& 21 twin, 3 family rooms.
Bathrooms: 57 private.
Bed & breakfast: £52 single,
£65 double.
Half board: £45-£64.50 daily.
Evening meal 6pm (l.o. 9pm).
Parking for 50.
Credit: Access, Visa, Amex.

The Limes M
Listed APPROVED
135 Fulford Rd., York,
YO1 4HE
☎ (0904) 624548

*Small, family-run hotel, 10
minutes from the city centre.
Licensed bar, colour TV in all
rooms. Family rooms available.*
Bedrooms: 5 double & 3 twin,
2 family rooms.
Bathrooms: 9 private,
1 public.
Bed & breakfast: £18-£50
single, £28-£55 double.
Evening meal 6.30pm (l.o.
7.30pm).
Parking for 14.
Credit: Access, Visa.

Linden Lodge M
⌂⌂
6 Nunthorpe Avenue,
Scarcroft Rd., York,
YO2 1PF
☎ (0904) 620107
*Victorian town house in a quiet
cul-de-sac, 10 minutes' walk
from racecourse, rail station
and city centre.*
Bedrooms: 2 single, 6 double
& 2 twin, 2 family rooms.
Bathrooms: 3 private,
3 public.
Bed & breakfast: £16-£25
single, £28-£40 double.
Open January-November.
Credit: Visa.

Lynton Guest House M
Listed
81-85 Main St., Fulford,
York, YO1 4PN
☎ (0904) 635367
*Family run guesthouse with
comfortable rooms, good food
and friendly atmosphere. Close
to the city centre, river and
country walks, the university
and Fulford golf club. Four
poster beds for the romantics.*
Bedrooms: 2 single, 6 double
& 1 twin, 1 family room.
Bathrooms: 2 private,
2 public.
Bed & breakfast: £15-£17.50
single, £30-£35 double.
Parking for 14.
Credit: Access, Visa, Amex.

Martin's Guest House M
Listed
5 Longfield Terrace,
Bootham, York, YO3 7DJ
☎ (0904) 634551
*Small, family-run guesthouse
with well-appointed bedrooms
and emphasis on standards.
Evening meal served on
request. 5 minutes' walk from
city centre and 10 minutes
from railway station.*

Bedrooms: 1 single, 2 double & 1 twin, 1 family room.
Bathrooms: 1 public.
Bed & breakfast: £13.50-£16 single, £26-£31 double.
Half board: £21.50-£24 daily, £145-£165 weekly.
Evening meal 6pm.
Parking for 1.
Open January-November.

Middlethorpe Hall M
Bishopthorpe Rd.,
Middlethorpe, York,
YO2 1QB
☎ (0904) 641241 & 620176
Telex CXL
A handsomely appointed and beautifully furnished Queen Anne country house with a fine kitchen and carefully chosen wine list. In 27 acres of green gardens bordering the racecourse, 1.5 miles from the centre of York.
Bedrooms: 6 single, 11 double & 12 twin, 1 family room.
Bathrooms: 30 private.
Bed & breakfast: from £99.50 single, £130-£208 double.
Half board: from £96 daily.
Lunch available.
Evening meal 7.30pm (l.o. 9.45pm).
Parking for 70.
Credit: Access, Visa, Diners, Amex.

Midway House Hotel M
COMMENDED
145 Fulford Rd., York,
YO1 4HG
☎ (0904) 659272
Modernised Victorian villa offering spacious and comfortable bedrooms, lounge and grounds. Near city centre, university and golf-course.
Bedrooms: 7 double & 3 twin, 2 family rooms.
Bathrooms: 11 private, 1 public.
Bed & breakfast: £20-£40 single, £36-£48 double.
Half board: £30-£50 daily, £180-£300 weekly.
Evening meal 6pm (l.o. 7pm).
Parking for 14.
Credit: Access, Visa, Amex.

Minster View Guest House
Listed
2 Grosvenor Terrace,
Bootham, York, YO3 7AG
☎ (0904) 655034

Restored Victorian residence with parkland views of the cathedral, 5 minutes' walk from the city centre. Family-run with emphasis on food.
Bedrooms: 2 single, 1 double, 6 family rooms.
Bathrooms: 4 private, 2 public.
Bed & breakfast: £12-£16 single, £24-£30 double.
Half board: £21-£33 daily.
Evening meal 6.30pm (l.o. midday).
Parking for 6.

Monkbar Hotel M
St. Maurice's Rd., York,
YO3 7JA
☎ (0904) 638086
A short walk from York Minster and all tourist attractions. Attractive bedrooms, four-poster room, jacuzzi.
Bedrooms: 34 double & 11 twin, 2 family rooms.
Bathrooms: 47 private.
Bed & breakfast: £64-£79 single, £84-£95 double.
Half board: £57-£94 daily.
Lunch available.
Evening meal 6pm (l.o. 10pm).
Parking for 30.
Credit: Access, Visa, C.Bl., Diners, Amex.

Mont-Clare Guest House M
32 Claremont Terrace,
Gillygate, York, YO3 7EJ
☎ (0904) 627054
City centre family-run guesthouse, situated in a quiet cul-de-sac. Priorities are cleanliness and friendliness. Reduced rates for weekly stay.
Bedrooms: 4 double & 1 twin, 1 family room.
Bathrooms: 2 private, 2 public.
Bed & breakfast: £20-£25 single, £30-£40 double.
Half board: £20-£25 daily.
Parking for 5.
Credit: Access, Visa.

Mulberry Guest House M
COMMENDED
124 East Parade, Heworth,
York, YO3 7YG
☎ (0904) 423468

Beautifully appointed Victorian town house, a short walk from city centre. Lovingly furnished throughout. Warm welcome assured. Non-smokers only please.
Bedrooms: 1 single, 1 double & 1 twin.
Bathrooms: 3 private showers.
Bed & breakfast: £15-£18 single, £30-£36 double.
Parking for 2.

Newington Hotel M
147-157 Mount Vale, York,
YO2 2DJ
☎ (0904) 625173 & 623090
Telex 65430 BURNS G
Hotel in a fine Georgian terrace, next to a large open area, within walking distance of the city centre. Large car park, solarium.
Bedrooms: 4 single, 16 double & 13 twin, 7 family rooms.
Bathrooms: 40 private, 1 public.
Bed & breakfast: £30-£42 single, £52-£62 double.
Half board: £36-£41 daily, £259 weekly.
Lunch available.
Evening meal 6pm (l.o. 9.15pm).
Parking for 32.
Credit: Access, Visa, Diners, Amex.

Newton Guest House
Neville St., Haxby Rd.,
York, YO3 7NP
☎ (0904) 635627
Large, end-of-terrace, Victorian house 10 minutes' walk from the centre of York. Private car parking. Bowling park close by.
Bedrooms: 1 single, 3 double & 1 twin.
Bathrooms: 1 private, 2 public; 3 private showers.
Bed & breakfast: £15-£16 single, £26-£34 double.
Parking for 5.
Open February-October.

Novotel York M
Fishergate, York, YO1 4AD
☎ (0904) 611660 Telex 57556
Fax 0904 610925
Novotel
Newly-built hotel on the riverside with terrace and indoor pool, 5 minutes' walk from the city centre. Special packages available for children sharing parents' room.

Bedrooms: 124 double, 124 family rooms.
Bathrooms: 124 private.
Bed & breakfast: £44-£54 single, £68-£88 double.
Half board: £45-£55 daily.
Lunch available.
Evening meal 6pm (l.o. midnight).
Parking for 150.
Credit: Access, Visa, Diners, Amex.

Orchard Court Hotel M
4 St. Peter's Grove, Bootham,
York, YO3 6AQ
☎ (0904) 653964
Small, Victorian hotel in a quiet location within easy walking distance of all places of interest.
Bedrooms: 3 single, 4 double & 2 twin, 2 family rooms.
Bathrooms: 8 private, 1 public.
Bed & breakfast: £20-£25 single, £44-£54 double.
Lunch available.
Evening meal 6pm (l.o. 8pm).
Parking for 11.
Credit: Access, Visa.

Palm Court Hotel M
Listed
17 Huntington Rd., York,
YO3 7RB
☎ (0904) 639387
Recently restored house 5 minutes from the city centre. Decorated and furnished with emphasis on standards. All bedrooms contain a double and a single bed.
Bedrooms: 3 double & 3 twin, 4 family rooms.
Bathrooms: 7 private, 1 public.
Bed & breakfast: £26-£36 double.
Half board: £21.50-£28 daily, £150.50-£164.50 weekly.
Evening meal 6pm (l.o. 8pm).
Parking for 10.
Open March-October.

Papillon Hotel M
43 Gillygate, York, YO3 7EA
☎ (0904) 636505
City centre hotel furnished with emphasis on standards. Personal attention at all times. 300 yards from York Minster.
Bedrooms: 2 single, 1 double & 2 twin, 3 family rooms.
Bathrooms: 3 private, 2 public.

Continued ▶

YORK

Continued

Bed & breakfast: £15-£25 single, £30-£45 double.
Parking for 7.

Pauleda House Hotel M
123 Clifton, York, YO3 6BL
☎ (0904) 634745
Family-run hotel with well-decorated, spacious rooms. Less than 1 mile from the city centre on the A19 north.
Bedrooms: 1 single, 5 double & 2 twin.
Bathrooms: 8 private.
Bed & breakfast: £15-£25 single, £30-£50 double.
Half board: £20-£30 daily.
Evening meal 6.30pm (l.o. midday).
Parking for 12.
Credit: Access, Visa.

Priory Hotel M
126-128 Fulford Rd., York, YO1 4BE
☎ (0904) 625280
Family hotel in a residential area with an adjacent riverside walk to the city centre.
Bedrooms: 1 single, 9 double & 6 twin, 4 family rooms.
Bathrooms: 20 private.
Bed & breakfast: £25-£30 single, £45-£50 double.
Evening meal 6.30pm (l.o. 9.30pm).
Parking for 24.
Credit: Access, Visa, Diners, Amex.

Regency House M
Listed
7 South Parade, Blossom St., York, YO2 2BA
☎ (0904) 633053
Fine example of Georgian architecture set on a private cobbled road, 5 minutes' walk from the station and 3 minutes from the Bar Walls.
Bedrooms: 1 single, 3 double & 2 twin, 1 family room.
Bathrooms: 2 private, 2 public.
Bed & breakfast: £13-£17 single, £26-£35 double.
Parking for 3.
Open January-November.

Riverside Walk Hotel M
APPROVED
9 Earlsborough Terrace, Marygate, York, YO3 7BQ
☎ (0904) 620769 & 646249

Family-run hotel, a 450-yard riverside walk from the city centre. Close to all amenities and the railway station.
Bedrooms: 2 single, 4 double & 2 twin, 2 family rooms.
Bathrooms: 10 private.
Bed & breakfast: £24-£27.50 single, £42-£48 double.
Lunch available.
Evening meal 7pm (l.o. 1pm).
Parking for 14.
Credit: Access, Visa.

Romley Guest House
APPROVED
2 Millfield Rd., Scarcroft Rd., York, YO2 1NQ
☎ (0904) 652822
Comfortable friendly family-run guesthouse offering a licensed bar and a variety of other facilities. 10 minutes from city centre.
Bedrooms: 3 single, 1 double & 1 twin, 2 family rooms.
Bathrooms: 1 public; 2 private showers.
Bed & breakfast: £12-£15 single, £24-£30 double.

Royal York Hotel M
Station Rd., York, YO2 2AA
☎ (0904) 653681
Telex 57912
Fax (0904) 623503
CR Principal
Grand Victorian building with all the comforts of a modern hotel. All major attractions within short walking distance.
Bedrooms: 24 single, 23 double & 96 twin, 5 family rooms.
Bathrooms: 133 private, 5 public; 15 private showers.
Bed & breakfast: £70-£90 single, £95-£180 double.
Half board: £47-£120 daily, £282-£402 weekly.
Lunch available.
Evening meal 7pm (l.o. 9.45pm).
Parking for 120.
Credit: Access, Visa, C.Bl., Diners, Amex.

St. Denys Hotel M
APPROVED
51 St. Denys Rd., York, YO1 1QD
☎ (0904) 622207
Old rectory opposite St. Denys Church, 2 minutes' walk from the Jorvik Viking Centre.
Bedrooms: 1 single, 5 double & 3 twin, 1 family room.
Bathrooms: 10 private, 1 public.

Bed & breakfast: £32-£42 single, £40-£48 double.
Half board: £40.50-£50.50 daily.
Evening meal 6pm.
Parking for 9.
Credit: Access, Visa.

St. Georges House Hotel M
APPROVED
6 St. George's Place, Tadcaster Rd., York, YO2 2DR
☎ (0904) 625056
Small family-run hotel in a quiet cul-de-sac near the racecourse and convenient for the city centre. Good car parking facilities.
Bedrooms: 4 double & 2 twin, 4 family rooms.
Bathrooms: 7 private, 1 public.
Bed & breakfast: £20-£25 single, £38-£42 double.
Evening meal 7pm (l.o. 8.30pm).
Parking for 9.
Credit: Access, Visa.

Savages Hotel M
APPROVED
15 St. Peter's Grove, Clifton, York, YO3 6AQ
☎ (0904) 610818
Fax (0904) 627729
Detached house and garden in a quiet cul-de-sac close to the city centre and historic attractions.
Bedrooms: 3 single, 6 double & 7 twin, 2 family rooms.
Bathrooms: 18 private.
Bed & breakfast: £30-£38 single, £56-£68 double.
Half board: £41.50-£49.50 daily.
Lunch available.
Evening meal 6pm (l.o. 9pm).
Parking for 14.
Credit: Access, Visa, Diners, Amex.

Saxon Hotel M
APPROVED
73 Fulford Rd., York, YO1 4BD
☎ (0904) 622106
Small, friendly Victorian hotel, minutes' walk from city walls and all tourist attractions. Resident proprietors look forward to welcoming guests.
Bedrooms: 2 single, 5 double & 3 twin, 4 family rooms.
Bathrooms: 9 private, 1 public.

Bed & breakfast: £18-£25 single, £36-£46 double.
Evening meal 6.30pm (l.o. 7.30pm).
Parking for 12.
Credit: Access, Visa.

Scarcroft Hotel M
COMMENDED
61 Wentworth Rd., York, YO2 1DG
☎ (0904) 633386
Warm welcome assured at this friendly Tudor-style hotel overlooking Knavesmire and the racecourse. Just 10 minutes' walk from the city centre.
Bedrooms: 3 single, 5 double, 2 family rooms.
Bathrooms: 10 private.
Bed & breakfast: £22-£25 single, £45-£66 double.
Credit: Access, Visa.

Staymor Guest House M
COMMENDED
2 Southlands Rd., York, YO2 1NP
☎ (0904) 626935
Hospitality, comfort and food at its best in a traditional guesthouse, quietly situated just 10 minutes' walk from the city centre.
Bedrooms: 1 single, 2 double & 1 twin, 2 family rooms.
Bathrooms: 3 private, 1 public.
Bed & breakfast: £11-£14 single, £20-£32 double.
Half board: £17.50-£23 daily.
Evening meal 6pm (l.o. 9.30pm).
Open February-November.

Swallow Hotel M
Tadcaster Rd., York, YO2 2QQ
☎ (0904) 701000 Telex 57582
CR Swallow
Set on the edge of York's beautiful racecourse on the Knavesmire. A traditional hotel with the extensive range of facilities of a Swallow Leisure Club, attractive bedrooms and a restaurant overlooking the hotel grounds.
Bedrooms: 8 single, 47 double & 47 twin, 10 family rooms.
Bathrooms: 112 private.
Bed & breakfast: from £78 single, £99-£160 double.
Half board: £70-£95 daily, from £112.20 weekly.
Lunch available.

Evening meal 7pm (l.o. 10pm).
Parking for 200.
Credit: Access, Visa, Diners, Amex.

🔣 🔣 🔣 🔣 🔣 🔣 🔣 🔣
🔣 🔣 🔣 🔣 🔣 🔣 🔣 🔣
🔣 🔣 🔣 SP T

Tower Guest House
🔣🔣🔣 COMMENDED

2 Feversham Crescent, Wigginton Rd., York, YO3 7HQ
☎ (0904) 655571 & 635924
Within easy walking distance of York Minster and the city centre. All en-suite, colour satellite TV and car park.
Bedrooms: 1 double & 2 twin, 3 family rooms.
Bathrooms: 6 private.
Bed & breakfast: £30-£38 double.
Evening meal 6.30pm (l.o. 7pm).
Parking for 6.
Open February-December.
Credit: Access, Visa.

🔣 🔣 🔣 🔣 🔣 🔣 🔣 🔣 🔣
🔣 🔣 OAP T

Town House Hotel M
🔣🔣🔣🔣

98-104 Holgate Rd., York, YO2 4BB
☎ (0904) 636171
Fax (0904) 623044
Personally-supervised, friendly hotel on the A59 just 15 minutes' walk from the city. All bedrooms have colour TV with a video film nightly and mini-bars. Grapevine Restaurant and pleasant conservatory. Large car park.

Bedrooms: 4 single, 11 double & 5 twin, 3 family rooms.
Bathrooms: 21 private, 1 public.
Bed & breakfast: £28-£40 single, £55-£70 double.
Half board: £39-£51 daily.
Lunch available.
Evening meal 6.30pm (l.o. 9.30pm).
Parking for 21.
Credit: Access, Visa.

🔣 🔣 🔣 🔣 🔣 🔣 🔣 🔣
🔣 SP 🔣 T

Tyburn House M
11 Albemarle Rd., York, YO2 1EN
☎ (0904) 655069
Family-owned and run guesthouse overlooking the racecourse. In a quiet and beautiful area, close to the city centre and railway station.
Bedrooms: 2 single, 4 double & 1 twin, 5 family rooms.
Bathrooms: 6 private, 2 public; 1 private shower.
Bed & breakfast: £16-£20 single, £32-£50 double.

🔣 🔣 🔣 🔣 🔣 🔣 🔣 🔣 🔣
🔣 🔣 OAP 🔣 SP

Victoria Villa
Listed

72 Heslington Rd., York, YO1 5AU
☎ (0904) 631647
Victorian town house, close to city centre. Offering clean and friendly accommodation and a full English breakfast.
Bedrooms: 1 single, 2 double & 1 twin, 2 family rooms.
Bathrooms: 2 public.
Bed & breakfast: £13-£17 single, £26-£30 double.
Parking for 2.

🔣 🔣 🔣 🔣 🔣 🔣 🔣 🔣 🔣
SP

Viking Hotel M
🔣🔣🔣🔣

North St., York, YO1 1JF
☎ (0904) 659822 Telex 57937
⊕ Queens Moat Houses
Beautifully situated on the riverside, within the old stone walls of York.
Bedrooms: 5 single, 45 double & 128 twin, 10 family rooms.
Bathrooms: 188 private.
Bed & breakfast: £78-£88 single, £95-£105 double.
Lunch available.
Evening meal 7pm (l.o. 9.45pm).
Parking for 78.
Credit: Access, Visa, C.Bl., Diners, Amex.

🔣 🔣 🔣 🔣 🔣 🔣 🔣 🔣 🔣
🔣 🔣 🔣 🔣 🔣 🔣 🔣 SP T

Westpark M
65 Acomb Rd., York, YO2 4EP
☎ (0904) 798449
Georgian house, built 1804, in one fifth of an acre of walled gardens, within walking distance of city centre.
Bedrooms: 2 single, 3 double & 1 twin, 2 family rooms.
Bathrooms: 3 private, 2 public.
Bed & breakfast: from £14 single, £24-£32 double.
Parking for 4.

🔣 🔣 🔣 🔣 🔣 🔣 🔣 🔣 🔣
🔣 🔣 OAP 🔣 SP 🔣 T

Winston House M
🔣🔣

4 Nunthorpe Drive, Bishopthorpe Rd., York, YO2 1DY
☎ (0904) 653171
Close to racecourse and 10 minutes' walk to city centre, railway station. All amenities.
Bedrooms: 1 double.
Bathrooms: 1 private.
Bed & breakfast: from £11 single, £24-£26 double.
Evening meal 6pm (l.o. 8pm).
Parking for 6.

🔣 🔣 🔣 🔣 🔣 🔣 🔣 🔣 🔣
OAP 🔣 SP

York Pavilion Hotel M
🔣🔣🔣🔣 COMMENDED

45 Main St., Fulford, York, YO1 4PJ
☎ (0904) 622099
⊕ Best Western
Georgian country house 1.5 miles from the city centre. Bedrooms of individual character, en-suite with all facilities. Private car park.
Bedrooms: 1 single, 9 double & 11 twin.
Bathrooms: 21 private.
Bed & breakfast: from £70 single, from £93 double.
Lunch available.
Evening meal 6.30pm (l.o. 9.30pm).
Parking for 45.
Credit: Access, Visa, Diners, Amex.

🔣 🔣 🔣 🔣 🔣 🔣 🔣 🔣 🔣
🔣 🔣 🔣 🔣 🔣 🔣 🔣 🔣 🔣
OAP 🔣 SP 🔣

I'M LOOKING FOR STATUS SYMBOLS

WHERE TO STAY

Key to symbols

Information about many of the services and facilities at establishments listed in this guide is given in the form of symbols. The key to these symbols is inside the back cover flap. You may find it helpful to keep the flap open when referring to the entry listings.

Bootham Bar Hotel

4 High Petergate
York YO1 2EH
Tel. (0904) 658516

One of the best locations in York. This 18th century building is situated only 100 yards from York Minster, adjacent to the city walls.

All York's other tourist attractions, shopping streets, restaurants and the theatre are within easy walking distance.

All our bedrooms are very comfortably furnished. Each room has private facilities, colour TV, radio with alarm and tea making facilities.

Our Victorian tearoom is open from Monday to Saturday for light refreshments
10-30 a.m. — 5-30 p.m.

Telephone or write to the resident proprietors: Mr. & Mrs. J. Dearnley for further details.

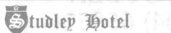

THE CROWN IS YOUR SURE SIGN
OF WHERE TO STAY

HOTELS, GUESTHOUSES, INNS, B&Bs & FARMHOUSES

Throughout Britain, the tourist boards now inspect over 17,000 hotels, guesthouses, inns, B&Bs and farmhouses, every year, to help you find the ones that suit you best.

THE CLASSIFICATIONS: '**Listed**', and then **ONE to FIVE CROWN,** tell you the range of facilities and services you can expect. The more Crowns, the wider the range.

THE GRADES: **APPROVED, COMMENDED and HIGHLY COMMENDED,** where they appear, indicate the quality standard provided. If no grade is shown, you can still expect a high standard of cleanliness.

Every classified place to stay has a Fire Certificate, where this is required under the Fire Precautions Act, and all carry Public Liability Insurance.

'**Listed**': Clean and comfortable accommodation, but the range of facilities and services may be limited.

ONE CROWN: Accommodation with additional facilities, including washbasins in all bedrooms, a lounge and use of a phone.

TWO CROWN: A wider range of facilities and services, including morning tea and calls, bedside lights, colour TV in lounge or bedrooms, assistance with luggage.

THREE CROWN: At least one-third of the bedrooms with ensuite WC and bath or shower, plus easy chair, full length mirror. Shoe cleaning facilities and hairdryers available. Hot evening meals available.

FOUR CROWN: At least three-quarters of the bedrooms with ensuite WC and bath/shower plus colour TV, radio and phone, 24-hour access and lounge service until midnight. Last orders for meals 8.30 pm or later.

FIVE CROWN: All bedrooms having WC, bath and shower ensuite, plus a wide range of facilities and services, including room service, all-night lounge service and laundry service. Restaurant open for breakfast, lunch and dinner.

Every Crown classified place to stay is likely to provide some of the facilities and services of a higher classification. More information available from any Tourist Information Centre.

We've checked them out before you check in!

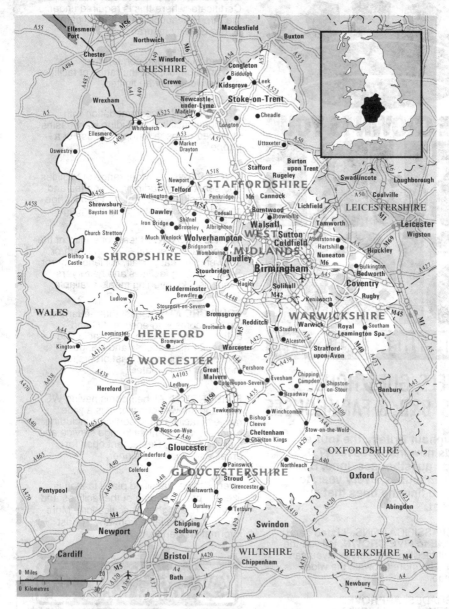

PLEASE REFER TO THE COLOUR MAPS AT THE BACK OF THIS
GUIDE FOR ALL PLACES WITH ACCOMMODATION LISTINGS.

A COSMOPOLITAN REGION, *embracing the "big heart" of industrial England — Birmingham — the wild Marches on the Welsh border to the west, Shakespeare Country to the south-east, the Potteries to the north and the limestone Cotswold villages to the south. There's the "cradle" of the Industrial Revolution at Ironbridge in Shropshire, contrasting with the cider apple orchards of Hereford and the fruit-growing Vale of Evesham. Cathedral cities such as Coventry, Worcester and Lichfield vie for attention with the elegant spa towns of Cheltenham, Malvern and Leamington.*

WHERE TO GO, WHAT TO SEE

Acton Scott Historic Working Farm
Wenlock Lodge, Acton Scott, Church Stretton, Shropshire SY6 6QN
☎ Marshbrook (069 46) 306
Historic working farm demonstrating agriculture at the turn of the century. Working Shire horses, rare animals, butter-making.

Almonry Museum
Abbey Gate, Evesham, Worcestershire WR11 4BG
☎ Evesham (0386) 446944
Romano-British, Anglo-Saxon, medieval and monastic remains. Agricultural implements and general exhibits of local historic interest.

Alton Towers Leisure Park
Alton, Staffordshire ST10 4DB
☎ Oakamoor (0538) 702200
Europe's premier leisure park. Over 100 attractions in magnificent setting. Corkscrew, Black Hole, Grand Canyon Rapids, Skyride, Beast, Mouse.

Arbury Hall
Nuneaton, Warwickshire CV10 7PT
☎ Nuneaton (0203) 382804
Elizabethan building "Gothicised" by Sir Roger Newdigate during second half of 18th C. Magnificent ceilings in Georgian plaster, landscaped garden.

Working Shire horses at Acton Scott Historic Working Farm

Ashorne Hall
Ashorne Hill, Nr. Warwick, Warwickshire CV33 9QN
☎ Barford (0926) 651444
Britain's only nickelodeon with unique presentation of automatic musical instruments. Vintage Kinema showing silent films with organ accompaniment.

Bass Museum, Visitor Centre and Shire Horse Stables
Horninglow Street, Burton upon Trent, Staffordshire DE14 1JZ
☎ Burton upon Trent (0283) 42031
First major museum of brewing industry. Story of different methods of transporting beer since the early 1800s.

Berkeley Castle
Berkeley, Gloucestershire GL13 9BQ
☎ Dursley (0453) 810332
Perfectly preserved 800-year-old castle, scene of Edward II's murder. 14th C great hall, keep, dungeon, kitchen, tapestries, furniture. Ornamental gardens.

Blists Hill Open Air Museum
Ironbridge, Shropshire TF8 7AW
☎ Ironbridge (0952) 433522
One of several museums and attractions at Ironbridge, this working Victorian town of 50 acres includes a wrought-iron works and reconstructed shops and offices.

Mazes, The Amazing Puzzle Shop, World of Butterflies, Wye Valley Visitor Centre, Sheep Shop.

Mappa Mundi Exhibition
Hereford Cathedral, 5 The Cloisters, Hereford, Herefordshire HR1 2NG
☎ Hereford (0432) 59880
Unique Mappa Mundi − recording how scholars interpreted the world − drawn in about 1290.

Cadbury World
Linden Road, Bournville, Birmingham, W. Midlands B30 2LD
☎ 021-433 4334
Story of chocolate from Aztec times to present day, including chocolate making demonstration.

Cider Museum and King Offa Distillery
Pomona Place, Whitecross Road, Hereford, Herefordshire HR4 0LW
☎ Hereford (0432) 354207
Displays on cider-making, cellars, 1920s cider factory, cooper's shop, huge vats from Napoleonic era.

The Commandery
Sidbury, Worcester, Worcestershire WR1 2HU
☎ Worcester (0905) 355071
15th C timber-framed building with great hall and panelled rooms. Civil War audio-visual show and exhibition. Displays on Worcester's working past.

Elgar's Birthplace
Crown East Lane, Lower Broadheath, Worcester, Worcestershire WR2 6RH
☎ Cotheridge (090 566) 224
Cottage in which Edward Elgar was born, now housing a museum of photographs, musical scores, letters and records associated with the composer.

James Gilbert Rugby Football Museum
5 St. Matthew's Street, Rugby, Warwickshire CV21 3BY
☎ Rugby (0788) 536500
Intriguing collection of rugby football memorabilia, housed in the shop in which Gilberts have made their world-famous rugby balls since 1842.

Gloucester Docks
Southgate Street, Gloucester, Gloucestershire GL1 2ER
☎ Gloucester (0452) 311190
Spectacular collection of Victorian warehouses, beautifully restored. National Waterways Museum, Robert Opie Collection, antique centre.

Hergest Croft Gardens
Ridgebourne, Kington, Herefordshire HR5 3EG
☎ Kington (0544) 230160
Spring bulbs, rhododendrons, azaleas, roses, herbaceous borders and spectacular autumn colour.

Jewellery Quarter Discovery Centre
77−79 Vyse Street, Hockley, Birmingham, W. Midlands B18 6HA
☎ 021-554 3598
The story of jewellery making in Birmingham, with a visit to a "time capsule" jewellery works.

The Jubilee Park
Symonds Yat (West), Ross-on-Wye, Herefordshire HR9 6DA
☎ Symonds Yat (0600) 890360
Jubilee Maze, a traditional hedge maze with carved stone temple centrepiece, created to celebrate Queen Elizabeth II's Jubilee in 1977. Museum of

Museum of British Road Transport
St. Agnes Lane, Hales Street, Coventry, W. Midlands CV1 1NN
☎ Coventry (0203) 832425
160 cars and commercial vehicles from 1896 to date; 200 bicycles from 1818 and 50 motorcycles from 1920.

Painswick Rococo Garden Trust
The Stables, Painswick House, Painswick, Gloucestershire GL6 6TH
☎ Painswick (0452) 813204
18th C rococo garden, set in a hidden combe.

Severn Valley Railway
The Railway Station, Bewdley, Worcestershire DY12 1BG
☎ Bewdley (0299) 403816
Preserved standard gauge steam railway running 16 miles between Kidderminster, Bewdley and Bridgnorth. Collection of locomotives, passenger coaches, etc.

Shugborough
Milford, Nr. Stafford, Staffordshire ST17 0XB
☎ Little Haywood (0889) 881388
18th C mansion house with fine

The Cheltenham Gold Cup Meeting − 10−12 March

Doll and Teddy Bear Festival
National Motorcycle Museum, Bickenhill, Solihull, W. Midlands
26−27 September

Shugborough Christmas Craft Show
Shugborough, Milford, Stafford, Staffordshire
17−18 October

British International Motor Show
National Exhibition Centre, Birmingham, W. Midlands
20 October−1 November

FIND OUT MORE

Further information about holidays and attractions in the Heart of England region is available from:
Heart of England Tourist Board
Woodside, Larkhill, Worcester WR5 2EQ
☎ (0905) 763436

These publications are available free from the Heart of England Tourist Board:

Bed & Breakfast Touring Map

Shakespeare's Country, Cotswolds and Heart of England

Short Breaks Guides, including:

The Cotswolds

Peak and Potteries

The Marches (where England and Wales meet)

Area accommodation guides *(Shropshire, Hereford & Worcester, Staffordshire, The Black Country and Birmingham, Gloucestershire and Warwickshire)*

Events List

Fact Sheets

Also available are:

Places to Visit in the Heart of England £2.50

Heart of England map £1.95

Cotwold/Wyedean map £2.60

Shropshire/Staffordshire map £2.40

---

collection of furniture and restored servants' quarters. Gardens and park contain beautiful neo-classical monuments.

Singing Cavern
High Street, Tipton, Dudley, W. Midlands DY4 8HH
☎ 021-520 5321
Underground boat trip into cavern, with sound and light display, demonstrations on echoes and talk on mining history.

Stone House Cottage Gardens and Nursery
Stone, Nr. Kidderminster, Worcestershire
☎ Kidderminster (0562) 69902
Attractive old walled garden with rare wall shrubs and climbers, herbaceous plants, nursery with plants for sale.

Warwick Castle
Warwick, Warwickshire CV34 4QU
☎ Warwick (0926) 495421
State rooms, armoury, dungeon, torture chamber, clock tower, barbican, towers. Madame Tussaud's "Royal Weekend Party 1898". 60 acres of grounds.

Wernlas Collection
Green Lane, Onibury, Ludlow, Shropshire SY7 9BL
☎ Bromfield (058 477) 318

The most extensive collection of large fowl in the UK, and rare farm animals, displayed in spectacular countryside.

MAKE A DATE FOR...

Crufts Dog Show
National Exhibition Centre, Birmingham, W. Midlands
9−12 January

Horse racing − Cheltenham Gold Cup Meeting
Cheltenham Racecourse, Prestbury, Cheltenham, Gloucestershire
10−12 March

Burton upon Trent Competitive Festival of Music and Drama
Town Hall, King Edward's Place, Burton upon Trent, Staffordshire
23−25 April

Edgbaston Tennis Tournament
Edgbaston Priory Club, Edgbaston, Birmingham, W. Midlands
8−14 June

Royal International Agricultural Show
National Agricultural Centre, Stoneleigh, Kenilworth, Warwickshire
6−9 July

Places to stay

ACCOMMODATION ENTRIES *in this regional section are listed in alphabetical order of place name, and then in alphabetical order of establishment.*

THE MAP REFERENCES *refer to the colour maps towards the end of the guide. The first figure is the map number; the letter and figure which follow indicate the grid reference on the map.*

THE SYMBOLS *at the end of each accommodation entry give information about services and facilities. A 'key' to these symbols is inside the back cover flap, which can be kept open for easy reference.*

ACOCKS GREEN

W. Midlands
Map ref 4B3

4m SE. Birmingham

Ennerdale Hotel
990 Warwick Rd., Acocks Green, Birmingham, B27 6QB
☎ 021-707 8778
Happy, friendly hotel with a variety of amenities including a full size snooker table.
Bedrooms: 4 single, 2 double & 6 twin, 2 family rooms.
Bathrooms: 12 private, 2 public; 1 private shower.
Bed & breakfast: £17.50-£28 single, £35-£40 double.
Evening meal 6pm (l.o. 9pm).
Parking for 24.
⌖🖪📺🛋🖵📺▥
🏠🍴✿✕🅿🔒🗝️⚙️ SP

Greswolde Park Hotel
980 Warwick Rd., Acocks Green, Birmingham, B27 6QG
☎ 021-706 4068
Family-run hotel offering high standard of accommodation combined with efficient, friendly and personal service. Near National Exhibition Centre and Birmingham Conference Centre.
Bedrooms: 2 single, 1 double & 6 twin.
Bathrooms: 6 private, 1 public.
Bed & breakfast: £15-£25 single, £30-£40 double.
Half board: £20-£35 daily.

Evening meal 6.30pm (l.o. 8pm).
Parking for 13.
Credit: Access, Visa.
⌖🖪📺🛋🖵📺▥
▦🗝️⚙️ SP

ALCESTER

Warwickshire
Map ref 2B1

7m W. Stratford-upon-Avon
Town has Roman origins and many old buildings around the High Street. It is close to Ragley Hall, the 18th C Palladian mansion with its magnificent baroque Great Hall.

Icknield House M
🏨🏨
54 Birmingham Rd., Alcester, B49 5EG
☎ (0789) 763287 & 763681
Comfortable, well-furnished Victorian house of character, on the main A435. Close to Warwick and the Cotswolds. 10 minutes from Stratford-upon-Avon. Excellent touring centre.
Bedrooms: 2 single, 2 double & 2 twin.
Bathrooms: 2 private, 1 public; 2 private showers.
Bed & breakfast: £16-£17.50 single, £30-£35 double.
Half board: £22.50-£23.50 daily, £142.50-£160 weekly.
Evening meal 6.30pm (l.o. 7.30pm).
Parking for 8.
⌖🖪📺🛋▥
● ▦ 🗝️⚙️ SP

Kings Court Hotel M
🏨🏨🏨🏨 COMMENDED
Kings Coughton, Nr.
Alcester, B49 5QQ
☎ (0789) 763111
Fax (0789) 400242
Comfortable chalet bedrooms set around the main part of the hotel, which is a listed Tudor building with modern extensions housing the bars, restaurant and function room.
Bedrooms: 6 single, 11 double & 1 twin, 1 family room.
Bathrooms: 19 private.
Bed & breakfast: from £47 single, from £58 double.
Lunch available.
Evening meal 7pm (l.o. 10pm).
Parking for 100.
Credit: Access, Visa, Amex.
⌖🖪📺🛋🔒🛋📺🖵📺
🍴✿✕ SP

Individual proprietors have supplied all details of accommodation. Although we do check for accuracy, we advise you to confirm prices and other information at the time of booking.

Please mention this guide when making a booking.

ALTON

Staffordshire
Map ref 4B2

4m E. Cheadle
Alton Castle, an impressive 19th C building now a school, dominates the village which is set in spectacular scenery. Nearby is Alton Towers, a romantic 19th C ruin with innumerable tourist attractions in its 800 acres of magnificent gardens.

The Admiral Jervis Inn and Restaurant M
🏨🏨🏨
Mill Rd., Oakamoor, Stoke-on-Trent, ST10 3AG
☎ (0538) 702187
Old riverside restaurant and inn with chef/proprietor. Peaceful and picturesque setting. 2 miles from Alton Towers and 9 miles from the Potteries.
Bedrooms: 1 double & 1 twin, 4 family rooms.
Bathrooms: 6 private.
Bed & breakfast: from £22.50 double.
Evening meal 7.30pm (l.o. 9.30pm).
Parking for 10.
Credit: Access, Visa, Amex.
⌖🖪📺🛋▥📺▦
🍴✕🖼️🏠

Bridge House Hotel M
🏨🏨🏨 COMMENDED
Station Road, Alton, Stoke-on-Trent, ST10 4BX
☎ Oakamoor (0538) 702338

Family-run 17th C riverside hotel, half a mile from Alton Towers in the beautiful Churnet Valley. Reputation for cuisine, service and friendliness.
Bedrooms: 5 double.
Bathrooms: 2 private,
1 public; 2 private showers.
Bed & breakfast: £25-£35 single, £36-£50 double.
Lunch available.
Evening meal 7pm (l.o. 10pm).
Parking for 30.
Credit: Access, Visa.

Wild Duck Inn
Listed
New Rd., Alton, Stoke-on-Trent, ST10 4AF
☎ Oakamoor (0538) 702218
Large country inn, near Alton Towers Leisure Park. Comfortable bedrooms, restaurant, bar and family lounge.
Bedrooms: 7 family rooms.
Bathrooms: 1 private,
1 public.
Bed & breakfast: £23.50-£34.50 double.
Evening meal 7pm (l.o. 8.30pm).
Parking for 50.
Open March-November.
Credit: Access, Visa.

ALVECHURCH

Hereford & Worcester
Map ref 4B3

3m N. Redditch
Close to industrial Redditch, Alvechurch has grown rapidly from village to town in recent years, but retains much of its old world charm. A centre for canal boat hire.

Westmead Hotel & Restaurant
Redditch Rd., Hopwood, Alvechurch, Birmingham, W Midlands B48 7AL
☎ 021-445 1202 Telex 335956
FAX 021-445 6163
⊕ Lansbury
Hotel located off junction 2 of the M42. Recently opened and within easy reach of Birmingham, Redditch and the National Exhibition Centre.
Bedrooms: 4 single, 18 double & 38 twin.
Bathrooms: 60 private.
Bed & breakfast: £22-£72 single, £44-£84 double.
Half board: £34-£87 daily.

Lunch available.
Evening meal 7pm (l.o. 10pm).
Parking for 250.
Credit: Access, Visa, Diners, Amex.

AMPNEY CRUCIS

Gloucestershire
Map ref 2B1

3m E. Cirencester
This is one of the 4 Ampney villages and is situated in pleasant countryside. Its church has Saxon features. The very attractive gardens at nearby Barnsley House are open Monday to Friday 10am - 6pm and offer plants for sale.

Crown of Crucis ⋒
COMMENDED
Ampney Crucis, Cirencester, GL7 5RS
☎ Cirencester (0285) 851806
& (0285) 851806
Fax (0285) 851735
Privately owned Cotswold hotel, 2.5 miles east of Cirencester on A417. 16th C building with bar and restaurant.
Bedrooms: 8 double & 16 twin, 2 family rooms.
Bathrooms: 26 private.
Bed & breakfast: £47-£49 single, £58-£60 double.
Half board: £59-£61 daily.
Lunch available.
Evening meal 6pm (l.o. 10pm).
Parking for 80.
Credit: Access, Visa, Amex.

APPERLEY

Gloucestershire
Map ref 2B1

7m NW. Cheltenham
Village in flat riverside country, near the Regency spa town of Cheltenham. The Romanesque church, in brick with pink terracotta dressings, dates from 1856 with later additions.

Tyms Holm Country Guest House ⋒
Upper Apperley, Gloucester, GL19 4DW
☎ Tirley (0452) 780386

Secluded, peaceful, country guesthouse in village near Tewkesbury. Lawn and tree landscaped garden covering 1 acre, with open views of the surrounding countryside.
Bedrooms: 1 single, 2 double & 2 twin.
Bathrooms: 2 private,
2 public.
Bed & breakfast: £17 single, £34-£38 double.
Half board: £24-£26 daily, £150-£170 weekly.
Lunch available.
Evening meal 6pm (l.o. 9pm).
Parking for 8.

ATHERSTONE

Warwickshire
Map ref 4B3

Pleasant market town with some 18th C houses and interesting old inns. Every Shrove Tuesday a game of football is played in the streets, a tradition which dates from the 13th C. Twycross Zoo is nearby with an extensive collection of reptiles and butterflies.

Chapel House Guest House and Restaurant
Friars Gate, Market Sq., Atherstone, CV9 1EY
☎ (0827) 718949
Fine example of an 18th C gentleman's house, with Victorian additions, on the borders of Warwickshire, Leicestershire and Staffordshire. Now a small hotel with modern comforts but preserving original elegance and style. Noted for food.
Bedrooms: 6 single, 4 double & 3 twin.
Bathrooms: 11 private,
2 public; 2 private showers.
Bed & breakfast: £37.50-£45 single, £49.50-£60 double.
Half board: £51.45-£61.95 daily.
Evening meal 7.30pm (l.o. 8.30pm).
Credit: Access, Visa, Diners.

National Crown ratings were correct at the time of going to press but are subject to change. Please check at the time of booking.

BALSALL COMMON

W. Midlands
Map ref 4B3

6m NW. Kenilworth
Close to Kenilworth and within easy reach of Coventry.

Haigs Hotel ⋒
COMMENDED
Kenilworth Rd., Balsall Common, Nr. Coventry, CV7 7EL
☎ Berkswell (0676) 32142
Fax 0676 34572
Family-run hotel within easy reach of Kenilworth, Warwick and the Warwickshire countryside, yet only 5 minutes from Birmingham Airport and the M6.
Bedrooms: 8 single, 5 twin.
Bathrooms: 12 private,
1 public; 1 private shower.
Bed & breakfast: £26.50-£48.50 single, £42.50-£69.50 double.
Half board: £41.50-£63.50 daily.
Evening meal 7.30pm (l.o. 9pm).
Parking for 25.
Credit: Access, Visa.

BERKELEY

Gloucestershire
Map ref 2B1

Town dominated by the castle where Edward II was murdered. Dating from Norman times, it is still the home of the Berkeley family and is open to the public. Slimbridge Wildfowl Trust is nearby.

The Old Schoolhouse ⋒
APPROVED
Canonbury St., Berkeley, GL13 9BG
☎ Dursley (0453) 811711
Family-run hotel next to Berkeley Castle, with restaurant which seats 32 and a fine cellar. Health and beauty clinic.
Bedrooms: 5 double & 2 twin.
Bathrooms: 7 private.
Bed & breakfast: £40-£43 single, £55-£58 double.
Lunch available.
Evening meal 7.30pm (l.o. 8.45pm).
Parking for 15.
Credit: Access, Visa.

BERKELEY

Continued

The Pillars ⚑

[APPROVED]

Berkeley Road, Berkeley,
GL13 9EZ
☎ Dursley (0453) 810636
*Just off A38, halfway between
junction 13 and 14 of M5.
Close to Wildfowl Trust, Bath,
South Cotswolds and Forest of
Dean. All rooms have colour
TV. Afternoon teas and
breakfasts served to non-
residents.*
Bedrooms: 1 double & 1 twin,
2 family rooms.
Bathrooms: 1 public.
Bed & breakfast: from £15
single, from £30 double.
Half board: from £19.90
daily.
Evening meal 7pm (l.o. 9pm).
Parking for 6.

Prince of Wales Hotel

Berkeley Road, Berkeley,
GL13 9HD
☎ Dursley (0453) 810474
*Exceptional location offering
easy access to Bristol and
Gloucester, combined with a
beautiful rural setting near
Berkeley Castle and
Slimbridge.*
Bedrooms: 22 double &
16 twin, 3 family rooms.
Bathrooms: 41 private.
Bed & breakfast: £40-£50
single, £45-£55 double.
Half board: £52.50-£62.50
daily.
Lunch available.
Evening meal 7pm (l.o.
9.30pm).
Parking for 150.
Credit: Access, Visa, Diners,
Amex.

---

*National Crown
ratings were correct
at the time of going
to press but are
subject to change.
Please check at the
time of booking.*

---

*The national Crown
scheme is explained
in full on pages
536 – 539.*

BERKSWELL

W. Midlands
Map ref 4B3

6m W. Coventry
Pretty village with an
unusual set of 5-holed
stocks on the green. It
has some fine houses,
cottages, a 16th C inn
and a windmill open to
the public every Sunday
from May until the end of
September (2.30 - 5.30).
The Norman church is
one of the finest in the
area, with many
interesting features.

Nailcote Hall Hotel and Restaurant ⚑

⚜⚜⚜⚜

Nailcote Lane, Berkswell,
Coventry, CV7 7DE
☎ Coventry (0203) 466174
Fax 0203 470720
*A historic country house hotel
and restaurant. Ideally located
for Heart of England visitors.
Situated along the B4101
Knowle to Coventry road.*
Bedrooms: 1 single, 6 double
& 13 twin.
Bathrooms: 20 private.
Bed & breakfast: £95-£110
single, £115-£120 double.
Lunch available.
Evening meal 7pm (l.o.
9.30pm).
Parking for 50.
Credit: Access, Visa, Diners,
Amex.

BEWDLEY

Hereford & Worcester
Map ref 4A3

Attractive hillside town
above the River Severn
and approached by a
bridge designed by
Telford. The town has
many elegant buildings
and an interesting
museum. It is the
southern terminus of the
Severn Valley Steam
Railway.
*Tourist Information
Centre* ☎ *(0299) 404740*

The Heath Hotel

Habberley Rd., Wribbenhall,
Bewdley, Worcestershire
DY12 1LJ
☎ (0299) 400900 Fax 0299
400921

---

*Extended Victorian building
set in 20 acres, 1 mile from
Severn Valley Steam Railway.
West Midland Safari Park is
5 minutes' walk away.*
Bedrooms: 4 single, 9 double
& 26 twin, 4 family rooms.
Bathrooms: 43 private.
Bed & breakfast: £63.50-
£74.75 single, £81.56-£88.27
double.
Half board: £78.30-£89.60
daily.
Lunch available.
Evening meal 7pm (l.o.
10pm).
Parking for 300.
Credit: Access, Visa, Diners,
Amex.

BIBURY

Gloucestershire
Map ref 2B1

Village on the River Coln
with stone houses and
the famous 17th C
Arlington Row, former
weavers' cottages.
Arlington Mill is now a
folk museum with a trout
farm nearby which is
open to the public.

Bibury Court Hotel ⚑

⚜⚜⚜ [COMMENDED]

Bibury, Cirencester,
GL7 5NT
☎ (028 574) 337 Fax 028 574
660
*Jacobean manor house in 6
acres of grounds by River
Coln. Family-run with informal
country house atmosphere.*
Bedrooms: 3 single, 10 double
& 4 twin, 1 family room.
Bathrooms: 18 private.
Bed & breakfast: £50-£60
single, £68-£90 double.
Half board: from £73 daily.
Lunch available.
Evening meal 7.30pm (l.o.
9pm).
Parking for 100.
Credit: Access, Visa.

Cotteswold House

⚜⚜

Arlington, Bibury,
Cirencester, GL7 5ND
☎ (0285) 74609
*Extensively refurbished
Regency-style house in the
Cotswold village of Bibury,
offers purpose-built facilities in
a friendly family atmosphere.*
Bedrooms: 2 double & 1 twin.
Bathrooms: 3 private.

Bed & breakfast: £20 single,
£35 double.
Parking for 4.
Credit: Access, Visa.

BIDFORD-ON-AVON

Warwickshire
Map ref 2B1

Attractive village with an
ancient 8-arched bridge
and a main street with
some interesting 15th C
houses.

Broom Hall Inn ⚑

⚜⚜⚜ [APPROVED]

Bidford Rd., Broom,
Alcester, B50 4HE
☎ (0789) 773757
*Family-owned country inn with
carvery restaurant and
extensive range of bar meals.
Close to Stratford-upon-Avon
and Cotswolds.*
Bedrooms: 4 single, 4 double
& 4 twin.
Bathrooms: 12 private.
Bed & breakfast: £32.50-£35
single, £50-£55 double.
Half board: £31-£35.50 daily.
Lunch available.
Evening meal 7pm (l.o.
10pm).
Parking for 80.
Credit: Access, Visa, Diners,
Amex.

BIRDLIP

Gloucestershire
Map ref 2B1

7m SE. Gloucester
Hamlet at the top of a
very steep descent down
to the Gloucester Vale
and close to the Crickley
Hill Country Park.

Royal George Hotel ⚑

⚜⚜⚜ [COMMENDED]

Birdlip, Gloucester, GL4 8JH
☎ (0452) 862506
Telex 437238 Fax 0452 862277
Ⓖ Lansbury
*Built around a Cotswold-stone
building, dating back to 17th
C. Ideal centre for touring,
Cheltenham, Gloucester and
Cirencester nearby.*
Bedrooms: 2 single, 23 double
& 7 twin, 4 family rooms.
Bathrooms: 36 private.
Bed & breakfast: £28-£68
single, £56-£80 double.
Half board: £40-£83 daily.
Lunch available.
Evening meal 7pm (l.o.
10pm).
Parking for 90.

Credit: Access, Visa, Diners, Amex.

༻ ♨ ⌱ ╲ ⊡ ⏢ ♻ ⅰ V
⅄ ⊨ ◉ ▥ ♠ ⊺ ⊟ ✣ ⃞
♫ SP ⊞ T

BIRMINGHAM

W. Midlands
Map ref 4B3

Britain's second city, with many attractions including the City Art Gallery, Barber Institute of Fine Arts, 17th C Aston Hall, a science museum, railway museum, 2 cathedrals and the 10-acre Botanical Gardens. It is well placed for exploring Shakespeare country.
Tourist Information Centre ☎ 021-780 4321 or 643 2514

Arden Hotel and Leisure Club ⋒
⚛⚛⚛ COMMENDED
Coventry Rd., Bickenhill, Birmingham, B92 0EH
☎ Hampton-in-Arden (067 55) 3226 Telex 334913 Arden G
Adjacent to the National Exhibition Centre, railway station and M42, and close to Birmingham Airport. Privately owned and managed. Guests have full use of leisure facilities.
Bedrooms: 4 single, 13 double & 57 twin, 2 family rooms.
Bathrooms: 76 private.
Bed & breakfast: £62-£72 single, £76.50-£86.50 double.
Lunch available.
Evening meal 6pm (l.o. 10pm).
Parking for 150.
Credit: Access, Visa, Diners, Amex.

༻ ♨ ╲ ⊡ ⌱ ♻ ⅰ V ⊨
⏢ ◉ ⊟ ▥ ♠ ⊺ ⅙ ⊟ ⚘
⎘ ✣ SP T

Asquith House
⚛⚛⚛ COMMENDED
19 Portland Rd., Edgbaston, Birmingham, B16 9UN
☎ 021-454 5282/6699
Fax 021-456 4668
Listed building (1854) of architectural interest, recently converted into a licensed private hotel. Well suited for mini-conferences and business meetings. Weddings are our speciality.
Bedrooms: 3 single, 1 double & 5 twin, 1 family room.
Bathrooms: 10 private, 2 public.

Bed & breakfast: £50.60-£56.22 single, from £61.80 double.
Half board: £68.70-£74.32 daily.
Evening meal 7.30pm (l.o. 9.30pm).
Credit: Access, Visa, Amex.
༻3 ╲ ⊡ ♻ ⅰ V ⊨ ⊤
▥ ♠ ⊺ ⊞ SP ⊞ T

Atholl Lodge
⚛⚛⚛
16 Elmdon Rd., Acocks Green, Birmingham, West Midlands B27 6LH
☎ 021-707 4417
Friendly guesthouse in a quiet location on the south side of Birmingham. The National Exhibition Centre, airport and town centre are all within easy reach.
Bedrooms: 4 single, 1 double & 4 twin, 1 family room.
Bathrooms: 1 private, 3 public.
Bed & breakfast: £16-£20 single, £32-£40 double.
Half board: £21-£25 daily.
Lunch available.
Evening meal 5pm (l.o. 9pm).
Parking for 10.
༻ ♨ ♻ ▦ V ⊨ ⊤ ▥
♠ SP

Awentsbury Hotel ⋒
⚛⚛⚛
21 Serpentine Rd., Selly Park, Birmingham, B29 7HU
☎ 021-472 1258 & 021-472 7634 Fax 021-428 1527
Victorian country house set in its own large garden. Close to buses, trains, Birmingham University, BBC Pebble Mill, Queen Elizabeth Hospital, Selly Oak Hospital. Only 2 miles from the city centre.
Bedrooms: 6 single, 2 double & 6 twin, 2 family rooms.
Bathrooms: 5 private, 2 public; 6 private showers.
Bed & breakfast: £24-£34 single, £38-£47 double.
Half board: £31-£41 daily.
Evening meal 7pm (l.o. 7.30pm).
Parking for 12.
Credit: Access, Visa, Amex.
༻ ♨ ╲ ⊡ ♻ ▦ ⅰ V ⊨
⊤ ▥ ♠ ⊺ ⅙ ✣ ⃞ ♫ SP
T

Bearwood Court Hotel
360-366 Bearwood Rd., Bearwood, Warley, B66 4ET
☎ 021-429 9731
Family-run establishment with personal service, convenient to Birmingham city centre and West Bromwich. 2 miles to junction 1 of M5.
Bedrooms: 9 single, 6 double & 7 twin, 2 family rooms.

Bathrooms: 13 private, 3 public; 7 private showers.
Bed & breakfast: £22-£28 single, £35-£42 double.
Half board: £32-£38 daily.
Evening meal 7pm (l.o. 8pm).
Parking for 20.
Credit: Access, Visa.
༻ ╲ ⊡ ♻ ⅰ V ⊨ ⊤
▥ ♠ ⊺ ✣ ♨

Beech House Hotel
⚛⚛⚛
21 Gravelly Hill North, Erdington, Birmingham, B23 6BT
☎ 021-373 0620
Edwardian Tudor-style house set well back from the road behind beautiful large beech trees.
Bedrooms: 4 single, 3 twin, 2 family rooms.
Bathrooms: 3 private, 1 public.
Bed & breakfast: £26-£33 single, £40-£47 double.
Half board: £40-£47 daily, £280-£329 weekly.
Evening meal 6pm (l.o. 7pm).
Parking for 10.
Credit: Access, Visa.
༻5 ♻ ▦ V ⅄ ⊨ ▥ ♠
⊺ ✣ ♨ ⊞

Beechwood Hotel ⋒
⚛⚛
201 Bristol Rd., Edgbaston, Birmingham, B5 7UB
☎ 021-440 2133 Fax 021 446 4549
Georgian property only 1 mile from city centre on A38, set in 2.5 acres of water gardens. Ample parking.
Bedrooms: 6 single, 6 double & 2 twin, 4 family rooms.
Bathrooms: 16 private, 1 public.
Bed & breakfast: £28-£35 single, £45-£55 double.
Half board: £36-£50 daily.
Lunch available.
Evening meal 6pm (l.o. 10pm).
Parking for 40.
Credit: Access, Visa, Diners.
༻ ♨ ╲ ⊡ ♻ ⅰ V ⊨ ⊤
▥ ♠ ⊺ ⚘ ✣ ⊟ SP T

Bilthoven ⋒
⚛⚛
1253 Stratford Road, Hall Green, Birmingham, B28 9AJ
☎ 021-777 3324
Detached house on main A3400, 4 miles to city centre and International Conference Centre, 8 miles to National Exhibition Centre. Main European languages spoken.
Bedrooms: 1 single, 1 double & 1 twin.
Bathrooms: 1 public.

Bed & breakfast: £18-£20 single, £34-£38 double.
Evening meal 7pm.
Parking for 8.
༻5 ♻ ⊨ ⊤ ◉ ▥ ♠ ⌤
⊀ ⊞ ♨

Birmingham Copthorne Hotel ⋒
⚛⚛⚛⚛⚛ COMMENDED
Paradise Circus, Birmingham, B3 3HJ
☎ 021-200 2727 Telex 339026
Hotel built to international standards, with restaurant, bar, leisure club and conference facilities.
Bedrooms: 3 single, 148 double & 50 twin, 11 family rooms.
Bathrooms: 212 private.
Bed & breakfast: £105-£116 single, £130-£141 double.
Half board: £121.50-£132.50 daily.
Lunch available.
Evening meal 6pm (l.o. 8.30pm).
Parking for 40.
Credit: Access, Visa, C.Bl., Diners, Amex.
༻ ╲ ⊡ ♻ ♨ ⅰ V ⅄ ♨
◉ ⊟ ▥ ♠ ⊺ ⅙ ⊟ ⎘ SP
T

Bridge House Hotel ⋒
⚛⚛⚛ COMMENDED
49 Sherbourne Rd., Acocks Green, Birmingham, West Midlands B27 6DX
☎ Bookings only 021-706 5900 & Guests 021-706 5395/7976 Fax 021 706 5900
Comfortably appointed private hotel with a range of facilities including pleasant dining room with a la carte menu, 2 licensed residential bars, TV lounge, patio and garden.
Bedrooms: 12 single, 6 double & 8 twin, 1 family room.
Bathrooms: 27 private, 1 public; 2 private showers.
Bed & breakfast: max. £28.20 single, max. £43.47 double.
Evening meal 7pm (l.o. 9pm).
Parking for 50.
Credit: Access, Visa, Amex.
༻ ♨ ╲ ⊡ ♻ ⅰ V ⅄
⊨ ⊤ ◉ ▥ ♠ ⊺

Cherrywood Guest House
721 Chester Rd., Erdington, Birmingham, B24 0BY
☎ 021-373 1644
Privately run guesthouse, conveniently located for Birmingham city centre, the National Exhibition Centre, motorway network and the Belfry Golf Course.
Bedrooms: 6 single, 9 double & 9 twin, 2 family rooms.
Continued ▶

BIRMINGHAM
Continued

Bathrooms: 3 public.
Bed & breakfast: from £12 single, from £20 double.
Parking for 18.

Edgbaston Park Hotel
410-412 Bristol Rd., Edgbaston Birmingham, B5 7SN
☎ 021-472 1098 Fax 021 472 1098
Hotel opposite Birmingham University catering for all types of visitor, business or pleasure. 5 minutes from the city centre, bus no 61, 62, or 63.
Bedrooms: 7 single, 4 double & 5 twin, 2 family rooms.
Bathrooms: 3 public; 18 private showers.
Bed & breakfast: from £16 single, from £32 double.
Parking for 20.
Credit: Access, Visa.

Fairlawns Hotel
302 Hagley Rd., Edgbaston, Birmingham, B17 8DJ
☎ 021-420 2303
Privately-owned hotel 2 miles from city centre. Licensed bar/restaurant. Conference facilities. August special - double/twin for single price.
Bedrooms: 11 single, 4 double, 9 family rooms.
Bathrooms: 7 private, 4 public; 4 private showers.
Bed & breakfast: £20-£32 single, £40-£48 double.
Evening meal 6.30pm (l.o. 10pm).
Parking for 12.
Credit: Access, Visa.

The Garden Croft
🌸🌸🌸 COMMENDED
2 Sherbourne Drive (off Sherbourne Rd), Acocks Green, Birmingham, B37 6DY
☎ (021) 706 5557
Stylish, country-style hotel with a reputation for good breakfasts and fine dinners. Lovely bedrooms all have garden views.
Bedrooms: 3 twin.
Bathrooms: 3 private.
Bed & breakfast: £35-£38 single, £50-£55 double.
Half board: £43-£50 daily.
Lunch available.

Evening meal 6pm (l.o. 10.30pm).
Parking for 8.
Credit: Access, Visa.

Great Barr Hotel and Conference Centre M
🌸🌸🌸 COMMENDED
Pear Tree Dr., Newton Rd., Great Barr, Birmingham, B43 6HS
☎ 021-357 1141
Telex 336406.
Fax 021-357 7557
Situated in a quiet suburb, 5 miles from Birmingham centre. Perfect for the busy executive or for exploring the Heart of England.
Bedrooms: 98 single, 12 double & 4 twin.
Bathrooms: 114 private.
Bed & breakfast: £62-£65 single, £72-£75 double.
Half board: £74-£80 daily.
Lunch available.
Evening meal 7pm (l.o. 9.45pm).
Parking for 250.
Credit: Access, Visa, Diners, Amex.

Greenway House Hotel
978 Warwick Rd., Acocks Green, Birmingham, B27 6QG
☎ 021-706 1361
A small, comfortable, privately-run hotel, close to the city centre, airport and National Exhibition Centre. Traditional English cooking, personal service and friendly atmosphere.
Bedrooms: 5 single, 4 double & 4 twin, 1 family room.
Bathrooms: 6 private, 2 public; 1 private shower.
Bed & breakfast: £18.80-£26 single, £29-£36 double.
Half board: £26.30-£33.50 daily.
Lunch available.
Evening meal 6.30pm (l.o. 7.30pm).
Parking for 14.

Grove Hotel
409-411 Hagley Rd., Edgbaston, Birmingham, B17 8BL
☎ 021-429 2502
Family-run hotel with easy access to city centre, train station, bus station and the M5/M6.
Bedrooms: 4 single, 17 double, 6 family rooms.
Bathrooms: 8 private, 4 public; 6 private showers.

Bed & breakfast: £23-£25 single, £28-£35 double.
Half board: £27.50-£32 daily.
Evening meal 6pm (l.o. 7pm).
Parking for 40.
Credit: Access, Visa.

The Guest House
106 Vivian Rd., Harborne, Birmingham B17 0DJ
☎ 021-426 5638
Large detached Victorian-style house, recently refurbished, with a large garden. Ideally situated for the centre of Birmingham, National Exhibition Centre and many other places of interest.
Bedrooms: 2 single, 4 twin.
Bathrooms: 1 private, 1 public; 3 private showers.
Bed & breakfast: from £15 single, from £30 double.
Parking for 4.

Hagley Court Hotel M
🌸🌸🌸🌸 APPROVED
229 Hagley Rd., Edgbaston, Birmingham, B16 9RP
☎ 021-454 6514 Fax 021 456 2722
A private hotel and restaurant, all rooms en-suite with TV, telephone. Rates include English breakfast. 1.5 miles from city centre.
Bedrooms: 9 single, 16 double & 3 twin.
Bathrooms: 28 private.
Bed & breakfast: £27-£48 single, £38-£66 double.
Evening meal 6pm (l.o. 10pm).
Parking for 27.
Credit: Access, Visa, Diners, Amex.

Heath Lodge Hotel M
🌸🌸🌸
Coleshill Rd., Marston Green, Birmingham, B37 7HT
☎ 021-779 2218
Licensed family-run hotel, quietly situated yet just 1.5 miles from the NEC and Birmingham Airport. Courtesy car to airport.
Bedrooms: 7 single, 3 double & 6 twin.
Bathrooms: 10 private, 1 public.
Bed & breakfast: £27.50-£39 single, £38-£49 double.
Lunch available.
Evening meal 6.30pm (l.o. 8.30pm).
Parking for 24.
Credit: Access, Visa, Amex.

Lambert Court Hotel
334-336 Hagley Rd., Edgbaston, Birmingham, B17 8BH
☎ 021-429 2201
Privately owned, set in 2 acres of gardens 3 miles from city centre. Easy access to motorways. Shops nearby.
Bedrooms: 23 single, 6 double & 4 twin, 1 family room.
Bathrooms: 14 private, 3 public.
Bed & breakfast: max. £65 single.
Lunch available.
Evening meal 7pm (l.o. 9.30pm).
Parking for 85.
Credit: Access, Visa.

Lyndhurst Hotel M
🌸🌸🌸
135 Kingsbury Rd., Erdington, Birmingham, B24 8QT
☎ 021-373 5695
Within half a mile of M6 (junction 6) and within easy reach of the city and National Exhibition Centre. Comfortable bedrooms, spacious restaurant. Personal service in a quiet friendly atmosphere.
Bedrooms: 10 single, 1 double, 3 family rooms.
Bathrooms: 12 private, 1 public.
Bed & breakfast: £29.50-£35 single, £48.50-£51.50 double.
Half board: £39-£46 daily.
Evening meal 6pm (l.o. 8pm).
Parking for 12.
Credit: Access, Visa, Diners, Amex.

Meadow Court Hotel
397 Hagley Rd., Edgbaston, Birmingham, B17 8BL
☎ 021-429 2377 & 021-420 3437 Fax 021 434 3140
Privately owned hotel recently refurbished throughout. All rooms en-suite. 5 minutes city/convention centre, 20 minutes National Exhibition Centre.
Bedrooms: 2 single, 5 double & 5 twin.
Bathrooms: 12 private.
Bed & breakfast: £39.50-£47 single, £49.50-£58 double.
Half board: £52.45-£59.95 daily.
Lunch available.
Evening meal 6pm (l.o. 8.30pm).

Parking for 18.
Credit: Access, Visa, Diners,
Amex.

New Cobden Hotel M
👑👑👑👑

166-174 Hagley Rd.,
Edgbaston, Birmingham,
B16 9NZ
☎ 021-454 6621 Telex 333851
ⓒⓡ Friendly
*Set in its own beautiful
gardens, 2 miles west of the
city centre and New Street
Station, on the A456. Indoor
leisure centre.*
Bedrooms: 117 single,
35 double & 70 twin, 8 family
rooms.
Bathrooms: 230 private.
Bed & breakfast: £53.50-
£66.20 single, £66.75-£81.90
double.
Lunch available.
Evening meal 7pm (l.o.
10pm).
Parking for 160.
Credit: Access, Visa, Diners,
Amex.

Norfolk Hotel M
👑👑👑

257-267 Hagley Rd.,
Edgbaston, Birmingham,
B16 9NA
☎ 021-454 8071 Telex 339715
ⓒⓡ Friendly
*Set in its own gardens, 2 miles
west of the city centre and New
Street Station, on the A456.
Ample free parking.*
Bedrooms: 102 single,
21 double & 49 twin,
18 family rooms.
Bathrooms: 169 private,
33 public.
Bed & breakfast: £53.50-
£66.20 single, £66.75-£81.90
double.
Lunch available.
Evening meal 6pm (l.o.
10pm).
Parking for 103.
Credit: Access, Visa, Diners,
Amex.

Old Farm Hotel and
Peaches Restaurant

108 Linden Rd., Bournville,
Birmingham, B30 1LA
☎ 021-458 3146 & 021-458
5108
*Private hotel in the unique
district of Bournville, 5 miles
from the city centre.*

Bedrooms: 10 single, 3 double
& 1 twin.
Bathrooms: 4 private,
3 public; 8 private showers.
Bed & breakfast: £27.60-
£40.90 single, £46-£51.10
double.
Evening meal 7pm (l.o.
10pm).
Parking for 15.
Credit: Access, Visa, Diners,
Amex.

The Park International
Hotel M
👑👑👑👑

New St., Birmingham,
B2 4RX
☎ 021-631 3331 Telex 338331
ⓒⓡ Park Hotels
*City centre hotel opposite New
Street Station, and well located
for National Exhibition Centre.*
Bedrooms: 57 single,
80 double & 50 twin, 4 family
rooms.
Bathrooms: 191 private.
Bed & breakfast: £22-£83.50
single, £44-£101 double.
Half board: £32-£90 daily.
Lunch available.
Evening meal 7pm (l.o.
10pm).
Credit: Access, Visa, Diners,
Amex.

Rollason Wood Hotel
👑👑

130 Wood End Rd.,
Erdington, Birmingham,
B24 8BJ
☎ 021-373 1230
*Friendly family-run hotel,
1 mile from M6 exit 6. Ideal
for National Exhibition Centre.
Bar, a la carte restaurant.*
Bedrooms: 19 single, 3 double
& 8 twin, 5 family rooms.
Bathrooms: 11 private,
5 public; 6 private showers.
Bed & breakfast: £17.77-
£36.03 single, £29.70-£52.25
double.
Evening meal 6pm (l.o. 9pm).
Parking for 43.
Credit: Access, Visa, Diners,
Amex.

Swiss Cottage Hotel
👑👑

475 Gillott Rd., Edgbaston,
Birmingham B16 9LJ
☎ 021-454 0371
*Privately-run hotel giving
personal service and English
and continental food. Situated
1 mile from the city centre.*
Bedrooms: 8 single, 1 double
& 4 twin, 1 family room.

Bathrooms: 1 private,
3 public.
Bed & breakfast: £17-£18
single, £33-£34 double.
Half board: £22-£23 daily.
Evening meal 6pm (l.o. 7pm).
Parking for 14.

Villanova Hotel
APPROVED

2 Grove Hill Rd.,
Handsworth Wood,
Birmingham, B21 9PA
☎ 021-523 7787 & 021-551
1139
*Our tastes are simple and we
insist on the best. We promise
you a thoroughly enjoyable
stay.*
Bedrooms: 7 single, 3 double
& 5 twin, 2 family rooms.
Bathrooms: 1 private,
4 public; 5 private showers.
Bed & breakfast: £25-£35
single, £45-£60 double.
Half board: £35-£45 daily.
Lunch available.
Evening meal 6pm (l.o. 9pm).
Parking for 20.

Westbourne Lodge
Hotel M
APPROVED

27-29 Fountain Rd.,
Edgbaston, Birmingham,
B17 8NJ
☎ 021-429 1003
Fax 021-429 7436
*Family-run hotel close to city,
motorways, National
Exhibition Centre and
International Convention
Centre. All rooms en-suite.*
Bedrooms: 8 single, 1 double
& 7 twin, 3 family rooms.
Bathrooms: 19 private.
Bed & breakfast: max. £40
single, max. £56 double.
Half board: max. £54 daily.
Lunch available.
Evening meal 6pm (l.o.
7.45pm).
Parking for 12.
Credit: Access, Visa.

Willow Tree Hotel M
👑👑👑

759 Chester Rd., Erdington,
Birmingham, B24 0BY
☎ 021-373 6388
*Convenient for city centre,
National Exhibition Centre,
airport, motorway, shops, taxis
and trains. All rooms have
hair-dryer, trouser press,
ironing board and iron.*
Bedrooms: 1 single, 2 double
& 4 twin.

Bathrooms: 5 private,
1 public.
Bed & breakfast: £26-£36
single, £49.35-£55 double.
Lunch available.
Evening meal 5pm (l.o. 8pm).
Parking for 8.
Credit: Access, Visa.

Woodlands Hotel M
👑👑

379-381 Hagley Rd.,
Edgbaston, Birmingham,
B17 8DL
☎ 021-420 2341 Fax 021-429
3935
*Family-run hotel, close to city
centre, Birmingham University,
convention centre, etc.*
Bedrooms: 3 single, 7 double
& 10 twin, 1 family room.
Bathrooms: 16 private,
2 public; 5 private showers.
Bed & breakfast: £26-£36
single, £38.50-£48 double.
Half board: £38-£48 daily.
Evening meal 6pm (l.o. 8pm).
Parking for 25.
Credit: Access, Visa, Diners,
Amex.

BIRMINGHAM AIRPORT

*See Acocks Green,
Balsall Common,
Berkswell, Birmingham,
Coleshill, Coventry,
Hampton-in-Arden,
Knowle, Meriden, Solihull.*

BISHOP'S CASTLE
Shropshire
Map ref 4A3

A 12th C Planned Town
with a castle site at the
top of the hill and a
church at the bottom of
the mainstreet. Many
interesting buildings with
original timber frames
hidden behind present
day houses. On the
Welsh border close to the
Clun Forest in quiet,
unspoilt countryside. An
excellent centre for
exploring Offa's Dyke and
the Shropshire
countryside.

The Boars Head M
👑👑👑

Church St., Bishop's Castle,
SY9 5AE
☎ (0588) 638521

Continued ▶

215

BISHOP'S CASTLE
Continued

Old world inn, with en-suite accommodation in original stables. Comfortable dining area serves wide choice from bar snacks to a la carte meals.
Bedrooms: 1 double & 2 twin, 1 family room.
Bathrooms: 4 private.
Bed & breakfast: £21.50-£26 single, £35-£42 double.
Lunch available.
Evening meal 7pm (l.o. 9pm).
Parking for 20.
Credit: Access, Visa.

BISHOP'S CLEEVE
Gloucestershire
Map ref 2B1

3m N. Cheltenham
Village close to Sudeley Castle and the Cotswolds.

Cleeveway House Restaurant
🏠🏠🏠

22 Evesham Rd., Bishops Cleeve, Cheltenham, GL52 4SA
☎ (0242) 672585
17th C Cotswold house with Regency style restaurant serving French and English dishes. Lovely gardens.
Bedrooms: 1 double & 2 twin.
Bathrooms: 3 private.
Bed & breakfast: £32 single, £54 double.
Lunch available.
Evening meal 7pm (l.o. 9.30pm).
Parking for 45.
Credit: Access, Visa.

The Old Manor House 🅜
🏠🏠

Station Rd., Bishops Cleeve, Cheltenham, GL52 4HH
☎ (0242) 674127
Original manor house, with walled garden, in old part of Bishop's Cleeve village. Close to Cheltenham.
Bedrooms: 2 single, 2 double & 1 twin, 1 family room.
Bathrooms: 1 public.
Bed & breakfast: £15.50-£18.50 single, from £29 double.
Parking for 8.

BLAKENEY
Gloucestershire
Map ref 2B1

4m NE. Lydney
Village near the Forest of Dean and the Severn Estuary in wooded hills. It is close to Lydney where the Norchard Steam Centre has full size railway engines, a museum and steam days.

Lower Viney Country Guesthouse 🅜
🏠🏠 COMMENDED

Viney Hill, Blakeney, GL15 4LT
☎ Dean (0594) 516000
Detached period farmhouse set in delightful gardens of approximately half an acre. Lovely rural setting with extensive views of surrounding countryside.
Bedrooms: 1 single, 3 double & 3 twin.
Bathrooms: 7 private.
Bed & breakfast: £20-£25 single, £35-£40 double.
Half board: £29-£37 daily.
Evening meal 7pm (l.o. 5pm).
Parking for 7.
Credit: Access, Visa.

BLORE
Staffordshire
Map ref 4B2

3m NW. Ashbourne
On the limestone uplands above Dovedale and commanding good views into the valley. The church dates from the 15th C, its tower a century earlier. Nearby Blore Hall is now a farm, but medieval windows and traces of its moat survive.

Blore Hall 🅜
🏠🏠🏠 COMMENDED

Blore, Ashbourne, Derbyshire DE6 2BS
☎ Thorpe Cloud (033 529) 525
Heated indoor pool, sauna, restaurant and bar complement beautiful rooms and cottages in the Peak District National Park, 8 miles from Alton Towers.
Bedrooms: 1 double, 1 family room.
Bathrooms: 2 private, 1 public.
Bed & breakfast: £22.50-£30 single, £45-£60 double.
Evening meal 6pm (l.o. 9pm).

Parking for 22.
Credit: Access, Visa.

BOURTON-ON-THE-WATER
Gloucestershire
Map ref 2B1

The River Windrush flows through this famous Cotswold village which has a green, and cottages and houses of Cotswold stone. Its many attractions include a model village, Birdland and a Motor Museum.

Chester House Hotel & Motel 🅜
🏠🏠🏠 APPROVED

Victoria St., Bourton-on-the-Water, Cheltenham, GL54 2BU
☎ Cotswold (0451) 20286
Fax 0451 20471
🅖🅡 Minotels
Ideal centre for touring the Cotswolds. All rooms have bathroom, colour TV, radio, central heating, tea/coffee facilities.
Bedrooms: 1 single, 6 double & 9 twin, 7 family rooms.
Bathrooms: 23 private, 1 public.
Bed & breakfast: £40-£44.25 single, £61-£77 double.
Half board: £47.30-£55.30 daily, £298-£348.40 weekly.
Lunch available.
Evening meal 7pm (l.o. 9.30pm).
Parking for 22.
Open February-December.
Credit: Access, Visa, C.Bl., Diners, Amex.
🅰 Display advertisement appears on page 262.

Coombe House 🅜

Rissington Rd., Bourton-on-the-Water, Cheltenham, GL54 2DL
☎ Cotswold (0451) 21966
Bright, fresh, comfortable, family-run "hotel garni". All en-suite facilities. Pretty garden, ample parking. Restaurants within walking distance. Non-smokers only please.
Bedrooms: 3 double & 2 twin, 2 family rooms.
Bathrooms: 7 private.

Bed & breakfast: £31-£35 single, £46-£51 double.
Parking for 10.

Dial House 🅜
🏠🏠🏠 COMMENDED

The Chestnuts, High St., Bourton-on-the-Water, Cheltenham, GL54 2AN
☎ Cotswold (0451) 22244
17th C Cotswold hotel providing every comfort. Tranquil situation in village centre. 1.5 acre walled garden. Four posters, log fires.
Bedrooms: 1 single, 6 double & 3 twin.
Bathrooms: 10 private.
Bed & breakfast: £35.75 single, £59.30-£75.60 double.
Half board: £41.40-£48.75 daily, £289-£342 weekly.
Lunch available.
Evening meal 7.30pm (l.o. 9pm).
Parking for 18.
Credit: Access, Visa.

Old New Inn 🅜
🏠🏠🏠 APPROVED

Bourton-on-the-Water, Cheltenham, GL54 2AF
☎ Cotswold (0451) 20467
Run by the same family for over 50 years. Traditional cooking and service. Log fires in winter. Large gardens. Ideal centre for touring.
Bedrooms: 7 single, 9 double & 5 twin, 1 family room.
Bathrooms: 3 public.
Bed & breakfast: £28-£35 single, £56-£70 double.
Half board: £40-£50 daily.
Lunch available.
Evening meal 7.30pm (l.o. 8.30pm).
Parking for 32.
Credit: Access, Visa.

BREDWARDINE
Hereford & Worcester
Map ref 2A1

Peaceful village on the River Wye, crossed by an 18th C brick bridge in an attractive rural setting. An excellent base for walking and fishing close to the Welsh border.

Red Lion Hotel

Bredwardine, Hereford, Herefordshire HR3 6BU
☎ Moccas (098 17) 303 & 215

17th C country hotel set in the peace of the middle Wye Valley. Ideal for touring Herefordshire and mid Wales.
Bedrooms: 1 single, 3 double & 3 twin, 3 family rooms.
Bathrooms: 10 private.
Bed & breakfast: £25-£38 single, £48-£60 double.
Half board: £29.50-£45 daily.
Evening meal 7pm (l.o. 8.30pm).
Parking for 33.
Open March-October.
Credit: Access, Visa, Diners, Amex.

Bed & breakfast: £42.50-£49 single, £45-£52.50 double.
Half board: £35-£42.50 daily.
Lunch available.
Evening meal 7.30pm (l.o. 9.30pm).
Parking for 11.
Credit: Access, Visa.

Old Vicarage Hotel M
HIGHLY COMMENDED
Worfield, Bridgnorth, WV15 5JZ
☎ Worfield (074 64) 497
Telex 35438 G Telcom
Country house hotel in a quiet peaceful location, ideal for business or pleasure, close to Ironbridge Gorge and Severn Valley Railway.
Bedrooms: 8 double & 5 twin, 1 family room.
Bathrooms: 14 private.
Bed & breakfast: £61.50-£72.50 single, £76.50-£84.50 double.
Half board: £46-£52 daily, £300-£350 weekly.
Lunch available.
Evening meal 7.30pm (l.o. 9.30pm).
Parking for 30.
Credit: Access, Visa, Diners, Amex.

Parlors Hall Hotel M
COMMENDED
Mill St., Low Town, Bridgnorth, WV15 5AL
☎ (0746) 761931 Fax 0746 767058
15th C residence of the Parlor family, built in 1419, with fine carved wood fireplaces and 18th C panelled lounge.
Bedrooms: 3 single, 9 double & 1 twin, 2 family rooms.
Bathrooms: 15 private.
Bed & breakfast: £43.50 single, £52 double.
Lunch available.
Evening meal 7pm (l.o. 10pm).
Parking for 26.
Credit: Access, Visa.

Severn Arms Hotel M
COMMENDED
Underhill St., Bridgnorth, WV16 4BB
☎ (0746) 764616
Listed building overlooking the River Severn, within walking distance of Severn Valley Railway and close to the famous Ironbridge Gorge Museums.

BRIDGNORTH
Shropshire
Map ref 4A3

Interesting red sandstone town in 2 parts - High and Low - linked by a cliff railway. It has much of interest including a ruined Norman keep, half-timbered 16th C houses, Midland Motor Museum and Severn Valley Railway.
Tourist Information Centre ☎ (0746) 763358

The Croft Hotel M
APPROVED
St. Mary's St., Bridgnorth, WV16 4DW
☎ (0746) 762416 & (0746) 767155
Listed building with a wealth of oak beams in an old street. Family-run and an ideal centre for exploring the delightful Shropshire countryside.
Bedrooms: 2 single, 5 double & 3 twin, 2 family rooms.
Bathrooms: 10 private, 1 public.
Bed & breakfast: £23.50-£39.50 single, £48 double.
Half board: £33.50-£38.50 daily.
Lunch available.
Evening meal 6pm (l.o. 8.30pm).
Credit: Access, Visa, Amex.

Cross Lane House Hotel
COMMENDED
Astley Abbotts, Bridgnorth, WV16 4SJ
☎ (0746) 764 887
Georgian farmhouse of great charm and character. Family owned and run, set in 2 acres of garden.
Bedrooms: 2 single, 4 double & 2 twin.
Bathrooms: 8 private.

Bedrooms: 2 single, 1 double & 4 twin, 3 family rooms.
Bathrooms: 6 private, 2 public.
Bed & breakfast: £23-£34.50 single, £37-£44 double.
Half board: £27.50-£44 daily.
Evening meal 6.30pm (l.o. 8pm).
Credit: Access, Visa, Amex.

BRIMFIELD
Hereford & Worcester
Map ref 4A3

5m S. Ludlow
Village of thatched and timbered houses near the River Teme, close to Ludlow and looking out towards the Clee Hills of Shropshire.

Roebuck Inn and Poppies Restaurant
COMMENDED
Brimfield, Ludlow, Shropshire SY8 4LN
☎ (058 472) 230
Situated 7 miles north of Leominster and 4 miles south of Ludlow, just off the main A49.
Bedrooms: 2 double & 1 twin.
Bathrooms: 3 private.
Bed & breakfast: £35 single, £60 double.
Lunch available.
Evening meal 6.30pm (l.o. 10pm).
Parking for 30.
Credit: Access, Visa.

BROADWAY
Hereford & Worcester
Map ref 2B1

Beautiful Cotswold village called the 'Show village of England', with 16th C stone houses and cottages. Near the village is Broadway Tower with magnificent views over 12 counties and a country park with nature trails and adventure playground.

Broadway Hotel M
The Green, Broadway, Worcestershire WR12 7AA
☎ (0386) 852401
Overlooking the village green, the hotel combines old world character and modern facilities. Courtyard and secluded garden.
Bedrooms: 3 single, 9 double & 9 twin, 2 family rooms.

Bathrooms: 21 private.
Bed & breakfast: £56-£58 single, £81-£87 double.
Half board: £48-£50 daily.
Lunch available.
Evening meal 7pm (l.o. 9.30pm).
Parking for 30.
Credit: Access, Visa, Diners, Amex.

Eastbank M
Station Drive, Broadway, Worcestershire WR12 7DF
☎ (0386) 852659
Quiet location, half mile from village. All rooms fully en-suite (bath and shower), with colour TV and beverage facilities. Homely atmosphere. Free brochure.
Bedrooms: 2 double & 2 twin, 2 family rooms.
Bathrooms: 6 private.
Bed & breakfast: £20-£30 single, £33-£44 double.
Half board: £28-£33.50 daily.
Evening meal 7pm (l.o. 10am).
Parking for 6.

Leasow House M
COMMENDED
Laverton Meadow, Broadway, Worcestershire WR12 7NA
☎ Stanton (038 673) 526
17th C Cotswold stone farmhouse tranquilly set in open countryside close to Broadway village.
Bedrooms: 4 double & 3 twin, 2 family rooms.
Bathrooms: 9 private.
Bed & breakfast: £38-£50 single, £48-£55 double.
Parking for 14.
Credit: Access, Visa, Amex.

Milestone House Hotel M
122 High St., Broadway, Worcestershire WR12 7AJ
☎ (0386) 853432
17th C listed building in beautiful area, run by Luigi and Pauline Bellorini. Victorian-style conservatory, Luigi's Backyard Restaurant, overlooking quiet garden. Licensed bar.
Bedrooms: 2 double & 2 twin.
Bathrooms: 4 private.
Bed & breakfast: max. £49.50 double.
Half board: max. £82.50 daily.

Continued ▶

217

BROADWAY

Continued

Evening meal 7.30pm (l.o.
9.30pm).
Parking for 6.
Open February-December.
Credit: Access, Visa, Amex.

The Old Rectory M
HIGHLY COMMENDED

Church St., Willersey,
Broadway, Worcestershire
WR12 7PN
☎ (0386) 853729
*A combination of the standards
of a good hotel with the
warmth of a private home - the
ultimate in B & B.*
Bedrooms: 4 double & 2 twin.
Bathrooms: 6 private.
Bed & breakfast: £49-£59
single, £59-£75 double.
Parking for 10.
Credit: Access, Visa.

Olive Branch Guest House M

78 High St., Broadway,
Worcestershire WR12 7AJ
☎ (0386) 853440
*Old house with modern
amenities close to centre of
village. Traditional English
breakfast served. Reduced
rates for 3 nights or more.*
Bedrooms: 3 single, 2 double
& 3 twin, 2 family rooms.
Bathrooms: 7 private,
2 public.
Bed & breakfast: £16.50-
£17.50 single, £36-£39 double.
Half board: £22-£27.50 daily.
Evening meal 7pm (l.o. 8pm).
Parking for 8.
Credit: Amex.

Pathlow House M
Listed

82 High St., Broadway,
Worcestershire WR12 7AJ
☎ (0386) 853444
*Comfortable period house,
central for village amenities.*
Bedrooms: 4 double & 2 twin.
Bathrooms: 6 private,
1 public.
Bed & breakfast: £35-£40
double.
Parking for 6.

Small Talk Lodge M
COMMENDED

Keil Close, High Street,
Broadway, Worcestershire
WR12 7DP
☎ (0386) 858953
*Cotswold stone lodge quietly
situated in centre of village.
Restaurant-style dinners using
fresh local produce.*
Bedrooms: 4 double & 3 twin,
1 family room.
Bathrooms: 6 private,
1 public.
Bed & breakfast: £34-£50
double.
Evening meal 7pm (l.o.
8.30pm).
Parking for 9.
Credit: Access, Visa.

Southwold House M
COMMENDED

Station Rd., Broadway,
Worcestershire WR12 7DE
☎ (0386) 853681
*Warm welcome, friendly
service and traditional cooking
at this large Edwardian house,
only 4 minutes' walk from
village centre. Reductions for 2
or more nights.*
Bedrooms: 1 single, 5 double
& 2 twin.
Bathrooms: 5 private,
2 public.
Bed & breakfast: from £16
single, £32-£40 double.
Parking for 8.
Open February-December.
Credit: Access, Visa.

White Acres Guesthouse M
COMMENDED

Station Rd., Broadway,
Worcestershire WR12 7DE
☎ (0386) 852320
*All rooms have private
showers, WCs, teasmades, and
remote-control colour TV. A
separate guests' lounge is
available. 4-course English
breakfast served. Ideal centre
for tourist areas.*
Bedrooms: 5 double & 1 twin.
Bathrooms: 6 private.
Bed & breakfast: £38-£40
double.
Parking for 6.
Open March-October.

Windrush House M
Listed COMMENDED

Station Rd., Broadway,
Worcestershire WR12 7DE
☎ (0386) 853577
*Edwardian guesthouse on the
A44, half a mile from the
village centre, offering personal
service. Evening meals with
choice of menu. 3 day break at
Christmas.*
Bedrooms: 3 double & 1 twin.
Bathrooms: 4 private.
Bed & breakfast: £25 single,
£36-£40 double.
Half board: £29.50-£31.50
daily, £193.90-£206.50 weekly.
Evening meal 7pm.
Parking for 5.
Credit: Access, Visa.

BROMSGROVE

Hereford & Worcester
Map ref 4B3

This market town in the
Lickey Hills has an
interesting 14th C church
with fine tombs and a
Carillon tower. The
Avoncroft Museum of
Buildings is nearby where
many old buildings have
been re-assembled,
having been saved from
destruction.
*Tourist Information
Centre ☎ (0527) 31809*

Stakis Country Court Hotel M

Birmingham Rd.,
Bromsgrove, Worcestershire
B61 0JB
☎ 021-447 7979
Telex 336976
Fax 021-447 7273
CB Stakis
*Attractive 2-storey hotel built
around a central landscaped
courtyard, with purpose-built
conference centre and leisure
club. Half board rate based on
a minimum 2 night stay.*
Bedrooms: 100 double &
31 twin, 10 family rooms.
Bathrooms: 141 private.
Bed & breakfast: from £90
single, from £108 double.
Half board: from £46 daily.
Lunch available.
Evening meal 7pm (l.o.
10pm).
Parking for 100.
Credit: Access, Visa, C.Bl.,
Diners, Amex.

Victoria Guest House

31 Victoria Rd., Bromsgrove,
Worcestershire B61 0DW
☎ (0527) 75777
*Homely, family-run guesthouse
near Bromsgrove town centre,
M5 and M42. Convenient for
the NEC/ICC and touring the
Cotswolds and Midlands.
Interest holidays and courses.*
Bedrooms: 3 single, 1 family
room.
Bathrooms: 1 public.
Bed & breakfast: £14.50-
£20.50 single, £26 double.
Half board: £18.50-£24.50
daily, £125.50-£167.50
weekly.
Evening meal 6pm (l.o. 5pm).
Parking for 3.

BUCKLAND

Gloucestershire
Map ref 2B1

1m S. Broadway
Village full of a church full
of interesting features
including a 15th C glass
east window. The rectory,
also 15th C, is one of the
oldest in England. Nearby
is Snowshill Manor,
owned by the National
Trust.

Buckland Manor M
HIGHLY COMMENDED

Buckland, Broadway,
Worcestershire WR12 7LY
☎ Broadway (0386) 852626
Fax 0386 853557
*13th C Cotswold manor in 10
acres, in idyllic secluded valley.
Log fires, central heating.
Tennis, riding, and complete
tranquillity. Under the new
ownership of Roy and Daphne
Vaughan.*
Bedrooms: 6 double & 5 twin.
Bathrooms: 11 private.
Bed & breakfast: £135-£230
single, £145-£240 double.
Lunch available.
Evening meal 7.30pm (l.o.
8.45pm).
Parking for 30.
Credit: Access, Visa.

> *Half board prices
> shown are per
> person but in some
> cases may be based
> on double/twin
> occupancy.*

> *The symbols are explained on the flap
> inside the back cover.*

BURTON UPON TRENT

Staffordshire
Map ref 4B3

An important brewing town with the Bass Museum of Brewing, where the Bass shire horses are stabled. There are 3 bridges with views over the river and some interesting public buildings including the 18th C St. Modwen's Church.
Tourist Information Centre ☎ *(0283) 45454*

The Delter Hotel
😊😊 COMMENDED

5 Derby Rd., Burton upon Trent, DE14 1RU
☎ (0283) 35115
Conveniently situated hotel, with resident proprietors. Comfortable en-suite bedrooms, private licensed dining room, cosy cellar bar and friendly atmosphere.
Bedrooms: 1 single, 1 double & 3 twin.
Bathrooms: 5 private.
Bed & breakfast: £28 single, £38 double.
Evening meal 6.30pm (l.o. 10pm).
Parking for 8.
Credit: Access, Visa.
🕭 🖵 🖭 💈 🗓 🅅 🖈 📺 ▥ ▮
🗙 🖻

Dovecliff Hall ▥
😊😊😊 COMMENDED

Dovecliff Rd., Stretton, Burton upon Trent, DE13 0DJ
☎ (0283) 31818 Fax 0283 516546
Magnificent Georgian house, with breathtaking views, overlooking the River Dove and set in 7 acres of landscaped gardens in open countryside. Half a mile from A38.
Bedrooms: 4 double & 2 twin.
Bathrooms: 6 private.
Bed & breakfast: £60-£80 single, £85-£95 double.
Lunch available.
Evening meal 7pm (l.o. 9.30pm).
Parking for 40.
Credit: Access, Visa.
🕭 🕻 🖭 🗓 💈 🅅 🖈 ▥ ▮
🏌 🏊 🗙 🖻 🖻

Edgecote Hotel ▥
😊😊

179 Ashby Rd., Burton upon Trent, DE15 0LB
☎ (0283) 68966

Family-run Victorian hotel with friendly atmosphere. 5 minutes from town centre. Attractive intimate restaurant. Small parties/functions catered for.
Bedrooms: 6 single, 2 double & 2 twin, 2 family rooms.
Bathrooms: 1 private, 3 public; 2 private showers.
Bed & breakfast: £18.50-£30 single, £32-£42 double.
Half board: from £24 daily.
Evening meal 7pm (l.o. 8.15pm).
Parking for 10.
Credit: Access, Visa.
🕭 🖵 💈 🗓 🅅 🖈 🖈 ▥
▥ ▮ 🗓 SP

The Queens Hotel

Bridge St., Burton upon Trent, DE14 1SY
☎ (0283) 64993
A newly created hotel within Burton's oldest licensed house. A choice of restaurants, bars and extensive conference and meeting facilities.
Bedrooms: 10 single, 11 double & 3 twin.
Bathrooms: 24 private.
Bed & breakfast: £35-£75 single, £39.50-£79.50 double.
Lunch available.
Evening meal 7pm (l.o. 10.30pm).
Parking for 52.
Credit: Access, Visa, Amex.
🕭 🖭 🕻 🖭 🖵 💈 🗓 🅅 🖈
🖲 ▥ ▮ 🗓 🗙 🖈 SP 🖻 ⊺

CANNOCK

Staffordshire
Map ref 4B3

Industrial town with Cannock Chase to the north, a former hunting forest now heath and woodlands with picnic areas and forest trails. It is ideal for walking and riding.
Tourist Information Centre ☎ *(0543) 578762*

Oak Farm Hotel ▥
Listed

Watling St., Hatherton, Cannock, WS11 1SF
☎ (0543) 462045
18th C farm situated in Green Belt, on A5, one mile from M6 motorway, junction 12.
Bedrooms: 1 single, 3 double & 2 twin.
Bathrooms: 6 private.
Bed & breakfast: £28.50-£39.50 single, £38.50-£49.50 double.

Evening meal 7.30pm (l.o. 8.30pm).
Parking for 25.
Credit: Access, Visa, Amex.
🕭 🖭 🖵 🕻 🖭 🖵 🖈 ▥ ▥
▮ 🗙 🖻 🖻

CHEADLE

Staffordshire
Map ref 4B2

Market town dominated by the 19th C Roman Catholic Church with its 200-ft spire. To the east of the town lie 300 acres of Hawksmoor Nature Reserve with many different birds and trees. Alton Towers is nearby.

High Gables Guesthouse
😊😊 COMMENDED

Totmonslow, Draycott Rd., Upper Tean, Nr. Cheadle, Stoke-on-Trent, ST10 4JJ
☎ (0538) 722638
Small country residence with all the comforts of home.
Bedrooms: 1 single, 1 double & 1 twin, 1 family room.
Bathrooms: 1 public.
Bed & breakfast: £15-£18 single, £25-£28 double.
Parking for 8.
Open February-October.
🕭 💈 🗓 📺 ▥ ▮ 🗙 🖻 DAP
SP

The Manor

Watt Pl., Cheadle, Stoke-on-Trent ST10 1NZ
☎ (0538) 753450
Georgian house, a former rectory, built in 1758.
Bedrooms: 2 double, 12 family rooms.
Bathrooms: 10 private, 1 public.
Bed & breakfast: £25-£27 single, £34.75-£35.50 double.
Half board: from £24.75 daily.
Lunch available.
Evening meal 6pm (l.o. 8pm).
Parking for 25.
🕭 🖭 🖵 🖈 💈 🅅 ▥ ▮ 🗓
✿ 🖻

Wheatsheaf Hotel

High St., Cheadle, Stoke-on-Trent, ST10 1AR
☎ (0538) 752797/753174
Coaching inn of character, with lively atmosphere, entertainment, functions and restaurant. Within 20 miles of Peaks, Potteries, Festival Park, pony trekking, fell walking, Alton Towers and Uttoxeter racing. Half board price is based on a minimum 2 night special break.

Bedrooms: 3 double & 3 twin, 4 family rooms.
Bathrooms: 4 private, 3 public; 1 private shower.
Bed & breakfast: £23.50-£31 single, £32-£48 double.
Half board: from £45 daily.
Lunch available.
Evening meal 6pm (l.o. 9.30pm).
Parking for 50.
Credit: Access, Visa, Amex.
🕭 🖭 🕻 🖭 🖵 🖈 💈 🅅 🖈
🖈 ▥ ▮ 🗓 🗙 SP 🖻

Woodhouse Farm Guest House ▥
🖵

Lockwood Rd., Cheadle, Stoke-on-Trent, ST10 4QU
☎ (0538) 754250 Fax 0538 754470
Old barns, renovated and modernised, situated in the peace and quiet of the Churnet Valley, 4 miles from Alton Towers, and close to the Peak District and the Potteries.
Bedrooms: 7 double & 3 twin, 4 family rooms.
Bathrooms: 9 private, 2 public.
Bed & breakfast: £16-£21 single, £28-£36 double.
Half board: £22.50-£26.50 daily.
Evening meal 6.30pm.
Parking for 20.
Credit: Access, Visa.
🕭 🖭 🖈 💈 🗓 🖈 ▥ ▮ 🖻 ✿
🗙 DAP 🖻

CHEDDLETON

Staffordshire
Map ref 4B2

3m S. Leek

Hillcrest

74 Folly Lane, Cheddleton, Leek, ST13 7DA
☎ Wetley Rocks
(0782) 550483
Country house pleasantly situated half a mile off the A520 to Leek. Convenient for Alton Towers, Peak District and the Potteries.
Bedrooms: 1 single, 1 double & 1 twin.
Bathrooms: 2 public.
Bed & breakfast: £12.50 single, £25 double.
Evening meal 7pm (l.o. 6pm).
Parking for 4.
Open April-October.
🕭 🖾 🆄 🖈 📺 ▥ ▮ 🖻 DAP

Map references apply to the colour maps towards the end of this guide.

CHELMARSH

Shropshire
Map ref 4A3

4m SE. Bridgnorth
An unspoilt village near
the River Severn, with old
timbered cottages and an
imposing 14th C church.

Bulls Head Inn ᴍ
⚬⚬⚬ COMMENDED

Chelmarsh, Bridgnorth,
WV16 6BA
☎ Highley (0746) 861469
*17th C village inn with warm
friendly atmosphere. All rooms
en-suite. TV lounge, jacuzzi,
solarium. Magnificent views.*
Bedrooms: 1 single, 2 double
& 2 twin, 1 family room.
Bathrooms: 6 private,
1 public.
Bed & breakfast: from £23
single, from £39 double.
Half board: £27-£32 daily.
Lunch available.
Evening meal 7pm (l.o.
9.30pm).
Parking for 50.
🛇 🛆 🖤 🖵 🕸 🗓 Ⓥ ⅋ ⅲ 🖚
🍽 🚾

CHELTENHAM

Gloucestershire
Map ref 2B1

Cheltenham was
developed as a spa town
in the 18th C and has
some beautiful Regency
architecture, in particular
the Pittville Pump Room.
It holds international
music and literature
festivals and is also
famous for its race
meetings and cricket.
*Tourist Information
Centre ☎ (0242) 522878*

The Abbey Hotel ᴍ
⚬⚬⚬ COMMENDED

14-16 Bath Parade,
Cheltenham, GL53 7HN
☎ (0242) 516053
Telex LANSDO G 437369
Fax (0242) 227765
*Recently completely
refurbished with most rooms
en-suite. Comfortable, clean
accommodation with all
facilities.*
Bedrooms: 5 single, 3 double
& 2 twin, 1 family room.
Bathrooms: 6 private,
1 public; 5 private showers.
Bed & breakfast: £25-£32
single, £45-£50 double.
Evening meal 7pm (l.o. 9pm).
Credit: Access, Visa, Diners.
🛇 🛆 🖤 🖵 🕸 🛉 Ⓥ ⅋
ⅲ 🖚 🍽 ᴅᴀᴘ 🕸 ꜱᴘ

Allards Hotel ᴍ
⚬⚬⚬

Shurdington Rd.,
Shurdington, Cheltenham,
GL51 5XA
☎ (0242) 862498
*On the A46, surrounded by
hills and fields. All rooms have
modern facilities, providing
comfort and convenience.*
Bedrooms: 1 single, 5 double
& 4 twin, 2 family rooms.
Bathrooms: 12 private,
1 public.
Bed & breakfast: £24-£28
single, £44-£48 double.
Evening meal 6.30pm (l.o.
9pm).
Parking for 27.
Credit: Access, Visa.
🛇 🛆 🖤 🖵 🕸 Ⓥ ⅋ ⅲ 🖚
🍽 ❊ 🛏 ᴅᴀᴘ 🕸 ꜱᴘ 🖚 🗓

Battledown Hotel
⚬⚬ COMMENDED

125 Hales Rd., Cheltenham,
GL52 6ST
☎ (0242) 233881
*Grade II listed, detached
Victorian house in French
Colonial style, within walking
distance of town centre. Colour
TV, parking.*
Bedrooms: 2 single, 2 twin.
Bathrooms: 4 private,
1 public.
Bed & breakfast: £16-£24
single, £40-£44 double.
Half board: £26-£36 daily.
Evening meal 6.30pm.
Parking for 6.
🛇 🖵 🕸 ᵁᴸ 🛉 Ⓥ ⅋ Ⓣᴠ ⅲ 🖚
🛏 🖚 🖚

Beaumont House Hotel ᴍ
⚬⚬⚬ COMMENDED

56 Shurdington Rd.,
Cheltenham, GL53 0JE
☎ (0242) 245986
*Gracious, detached, listed
Victorian building set in
pleasant gardens. On the A46,
minutes from town centre, with
ample private parking on
premises.*
Bedrooms: 4 single, 5 double
& 6 twin, 3 family rooms.
Bathrooms: 14 private,
1 public; 3 private showers.
Bed & breakfast: £17.50-£40
single, £45-£55 double.
Half board: £28.45-£53.95
daily.
Lunch available.
Evening meal 6.30pm (l.o.
2pm).
Parking for 21.
Credit: Access, Visa, Amex.
🛇 🛆 🖤 🖵 🕸 🛉 Ⓥ ⅋
⅋ Ⓣᴠ ⅲ 🖚 🍽 🕆 ❊ ᴅᴀᴘ 🕸
ꜱᴘ 🖚 🗓

Beechworth Lawn Hotel ᴍ
⚬⚬⚬ COMMENDED

133 Hales Rd., Cheltenham,
GL52 6ST
☎ (0242) 522583
*Carefully modernised and well-
appointed, detached Victorian
hotel, set in conifer and shrub
gardens. Convenient for
shopping centre and
racecourse.*
Bedrooms: 2 single, 1 double
& 2 twin, 2 family rooms.
Bathrooms: 4 private,
1 public.
Bed & breakfast: £17-£25
single, £32-£42 double.
Half board: £25-£33 daily.
Evening meal 6pm (l.o. 2pm).
Parking for 12.
🛇 🖵 🕸 ᵁᴸ 🛉 ⅋ Ⓣᴠ ⅲ 🖚
🚾

Bentons ᴍ
Listed

71 Bath Rd., Cheltenham,
GL53 7LH
☎ (0242) 517417
*Guesthouse supplying bed and
breakfast.*
Bedrooms: 2 single, 1 double
& 3 twin, 1 family room.
Bathrooms: 1 private,
1 public.
Bed & breakfast: £15-£18
single, £30-£36 double.
🛆 🖵 🕸 ᵁᴸ 🛏 🚾

Brent House Hotel ᴍ
⚬⚬⚬

382 Gloucester Rd.,
Cheltenham, GL51 7AY
☎ (0242) 514151
*Attractive detached Victorian
house on A40. Comfortable,
well-equipped bedrooms.
Garden with pool for guests'
use.*
Bedrooms: 1 single, 2 double
& 2 twin, 3 family rooms.
Bathrooms: 6 private,
1 public.
Bed & breakfast: £20-£32
single, £30-£45 double.
Half board: £30-£42 daily,
£120-£180 weekly.
Evening meal 6.30pm (l.o.
7.30pm).
Parking for 9.
Credit: Access, Visa, Diners,
Amex.
🛇 🛆 🖤 🖵 🕸 🛉 Ⓥ ⅋
ⅲ 🖚 🍽 ❊ 🛏 ᴅᴀᴘ ꜱᴘ

Carlton Hotel ᴍ
⚬⚬⚬⚬ APPROVED

Parabola Rd., Cheltenham,
GL50 3AQ
☎ (0242) 514453 Telex 43310
Fax 0242 226487

*The hotel is quietly and
conveniently placed in Regency
Cheltenham, an ideal base for
the town, Cotswolds and
surroundings.*
Bedrooms: 20 single,
15 double & 40 twin.
Bathrooms: 75 private.
Bed & breakfast: £50-£61
single, £74.50-£79.50 double.
Half board: £37-£45 daily,
£280.50-£315 weekly.
Lunch available.
Evening meal 7pm (l.o.
9.30pm).
Parking for 50.
Credit: Access, Visa, Diners,
Amex.
🛇 🛆 🖤 🖵 🕸 🛉 Ⓥ
⅋ 🖤 🖪 ⅲ 🖚 🍽 ᴅᴀᴘ 🕸 ꜱᴘ
🖚 🗓

Central Hotel ᴍ
⚬⚬

7-9 Portland St., Cheltenham,
GL52 2NZ
☎ (0242) 582172 & 524789
*Family-run hotel close to town
centre, shops, coach station,
racecourse, cinema and theatre.
Fully-licensed bar and
restaurant.*
Bedrooms: 3 single, 5 double
& 7 twin, 2 family rooms.
Bathrooms: 8 private,
2 public; 2 private showers.
Bed & breakfast: £22-£31
single, £39-£46 double.
Half board: £31-£40 daily,
£210-£270 weekly.
Lunch available.
Evening meal 6pm (l.o. 9pm).
Parking for 5.
Credit: Access, Visa, Diners,
Amex.
🛇 🛆 🖤 🖵 🕸 🛉 Ⓥ ⅋
Ⓣᴠ 🖚 🍽 ᴅᴀᴘ 🕸 ꜱᴘ 🖚

Charlton Kings Hotel ᴍ
⚬⚬⚬ COMMENDED

London Rd., Charlton Kings,
Cheltenham, GL52 6UU
☎ (0242) 231061
*2.5 miles from town centre in
an area of outstanding beauty.
Friendly staff, interesting
menus and quality
accommodation.*
Bedrooms: 6 single, 5 double
& 2 twin, 1 family room.
Bathrooms: 14 private.
Bed & breakfast: £50-£70
single, £65-£85 double.
Evening meal 7pm (l.o. 9pm).
Parking for 26.
Credit: Access, Visa.
🛇 🛆 🖤 🖵 🕸 🛉 Ⓥ ⅋
ⅲ 🖚 🍽 ❊ 🛏 🕸 ꜱᴘ 🗓

---

*The symbols are
explained on the
flap inside the
back cover.*

The Cheltenham Park Hotel M
♛♛♛♛

Cirencester Rd., Charlton Kings, Cheltenham, GL53 8EA
☎ (0242) 222021
Telex 437364 G
ᗰ Park Hotels
Beautifully renovated country house hotel, on the Cirencester Road in Charlton Kings, adjacent to the Lillybrok Golf Course. 2.5 miles from the centre of Cheltenham Spa.
Bedrooms: 13 single, 70 double & 70 twin, 1 family room.
Bathrooms: 154 private.
Bed & breakfast: £38-£96 single, £78-£134 double.
Half board: £48-£110 daily.
Lunch available.
Evening meal 7.30pm (l.o. 9.45pm).
Parking for 350.
Credit: Access, Visa, Diners, Amex.
🖨 🖇 ♨ ⌨ 🖥 🗣 🛎 🅟 Ⓥ
🖨 ⊙ 🎴 🛎 🍴 🏌 🌣 ✾ 🏹
SP 🎴 🏠
⊕ Display advertisement appears on page 262.

Crossways Guest House
⛰ APPROVED

Oriel Place, 57 Bath Rd., Cheltenham, GL53 7LH
☎ (0242) 527683
Fine Regency building, right in the heart of Cheltenham. Friendly and informal atmosphere with emphasis on quality food and service.
Bedrooms: 1 single, 1 double & 2 twin, 2 family rooms.
Bathrooms: 3 private, 1 public.
Bed & breakfast: £16-£27 single, £32-£40 double.
Credit: Access, Visa.
🖨 🖇 🗣 ♨ ⓊⓁ 🛎 Ⓥ 🖥
ⒹⒶⒻ SP 🏠

George Hotel M
♛♛♛♛ COMMENDED

41-49 St Georges Rd., Cheltenham, GL50 3DZ
☎ (0242) 235751
Telex 437304-GEORGE G
Fax 0242 224359
Regency building, centrally situated. Close to Promenade and Montpellier shops.
Bedrooms: 8 single, 26 double & 6 twin.
Bathrooms: 40 private.
Bed & breakfast: £45-£56 single, £52-£66 double.
Half board: £35-£68 daily.
Lunch available.
Evening meal 7pm (l.o. 9.15pm).

Parking for 28.
Credit: Access, Visa, Diners, Amex.
🖨 🖇 🗣 ⌨ 🖥 ♨ 🛎 Ⓥ Ⓞ
🖨 🛎 🍴 ⒹⒶⒻ 🏹 SP 🏠 Ⓣ

Hallery House M
♛♛♛

48 Shurdington Rd., Cheltenham, GL53 0JE
☎ (0242) 578450
Beautiful Grade II listed house, offering a warm and friendly atmosphere. Varied food. Colour and satellite TV all rooms. Close to town centre.
Bedrooms: 7 single, 4 double & 4 twin, 1 family room.
Bathrooms: 10 private, 1 public.
Bed & breakfast: £20-£35 single, £35-£60 double.
Half board: £30-£48 daily.
Lunch available.
Evening meal 7pm (l.o. 9.30pm).
Parking for 20.
Credit: Access, Visa, Amex.
🖇 🗣 ⌨ ♨ 🛎 Ⓥ ✂ 🖨
Ⓣ 🖥 🛎 🍴 ♨ ✾ ⒹⒶⒻ SP
🏠 Ⓣ

Hanover House M
♛♛♛

65 St George's Rd., Cheltenham, GL50 3DU
☎ (0242) 529867
Well-appointed and spacious accommodation in elegant, listed Victorian Cotswold-stone house. Close to theatre, town hall, gardens and shopping facilities.
Bedrooms: 2 single, 2 double & 1 twin, 1 family room.
Bathrooms: 2 private, 2 public.
Bed & breakfast: £18-£35 single, £40-£48 double.
Half board: max. £28 daily.
Evening meal 6.30pm (l.o. 9am).
Parking for 4.
Credit: Amex.
🖇 5 ⌨ 🗣 ♨ Ⓥ 🖨 🖥 🛎
🍴 ✾ 🏌 🏹 SP 🏠

Hilden Lodge Hotel M
♛♛♛ APPROVED

271 London Rd., Charlton Kings, Cheltenham, GL52 6YL
☎ (0242) 583242
Small, friendly family-run Regency hotel, 1.5 miles from Cheltenham, on the edge of the Cotswolds and adjacent to many miles of country walks. Large dining room to seat 40. Parties of any kind and weddings catered for.
Bedrooms: 1 single, 2 double & 5 twin, 2 family rooms.

Bathrooms: 10 private, 2 public.
Bed & breakfast: £25-£30 single, £35-£40 double.
Half board: £30-£40 daily.
Lunch available.
Evening meal 6pm (l.o. 10pm).
Parking for 12.
Credit: Access, Visa, Amex.
🖇 🖇 ♨ ♨ 🛎 Ⓥ ✂ 🖨 Ⓣ
🖥 🛎 🍴 ✾

Hollington House Hotel M
♛♛♛ COMMENDED

115 Hales Road., Cheltenham, GL52 6ST
☎ (0242) 519718 Fax 0242 570280
Detached Victorian house with ample parking, 1 mile from centre. En-suite bedrooms, colour TV, in-room beverages. Breakfast and dinner with menu choices. A warm welcome is assured.
Bedrooms: 2 single, 2 double & 4 twin, 1 family room.
Bathrooms: 9 private, 1 public.
Bed & breakfast: £22-£40 single, £40-£60 double.
Half board: £30-£50 daily.
Evening meal 7pm (l.o. 7.30pm).
Parking for 12.
Credit: Access, Visa, Amex.
🖇 3 🖇 ♨ 🗣 🛎 Ⓥ ✂ 🖨
🖥 🛎 🍴 ✾ 🏌 🏹 SP

Lonsdale House M
♛♛

Montpellier Drive, Cheltenham, GL50 1TX
☎ (0242) 232379
Regency house situated 5 minutes' walk from the Town Hall, promenade, shopping centre, parks and theatre. Easy access to all main routes.
Bedrooms: 5 single, 1 double & 2 twin, 3 family rooms.
Bathrooms: 4 public.
Bed & breakfast: £15.50-£18.50 single, £31-£35 double.
Parking for 6.
Credit: Access, Visa, Amex.
🖇 3 ⌨ 🗣 ♨ ⓊⓁ 🖨 🖥 🖨 Ⓣ 🖥
🛎 🏌 🏠 🏠

Micklinton Hotel
♛♛

12 Montpellier Dr., Cheltenham, GL50 1TX
☎ (0242) 520000
Family-run private hotel, 5 minutes' walk to town hall, theatres and shopping arcade. Ideal for touring the Cotswolds.
Bedrooms: 2 single, 1 double & 2 twin, 2 family rooms.
Bathrooms: 2 public; 2 private showers.

Bed & breakfast: £16-£25 single, £30-£45 double.
Half board: £25-£34 daily.
Evening meal 6.30pm (l.o. 8pm).
Parking for 6.
Credit: Access, Visa.
🖇 🖇 🖥 ♨ ⓊⓁ 🛎 Ⓥ ✂ 🖨
Ⓣ ⊙ 🛎 🖇 ⒹⒶⒻ 🏹 SP Ⓣ

Milton House M
♛♛♛

12 Royal Pde., Bayshill Rd., Cheltenham, GL50 3AY
☎ (0242) 582601 & 573631
Beautiful Regency listed building with freshly-decorated spacious bedrooms, set among tree-lined avenues, only 4 minutes' stroll from the promenade.
Bedrooms: 4 single, 2 double & 1 twin, 2 family rooms.
Bathrooms: 9 private.
Bed & breakfast: £33-£48 single, £46-£60 double.
Evening meal 7.30pm (l.o. 9pm).
Parking for 5.
Credit: Access, Visa, Amex.
🖇 🖇 🗣 ♨ 🖥 Ⓥ ✂ 🖨
Ⓣ 🖥 🛎 🏌 🏠 🏠

North Hall Hotel M
♛♛♛ APPROVED

Pittville Circus Rd., Cheltenham, GL52 2PZ
☎ Cheltenham (0242) 520589
Early Victorian town house situated in a wide tree-lined road near Pittville Park and town centre.
Bedrooms: 8 single, 6 double & 5 twin, 1 family room.
Bathrooms: 13 private, 5 public.
Bed & breakfast: £19.75-£29.75 single, £33-£46 double.
Half board: £30.25-£40.25 daily.
Lunch available.
Evening meal 6.30pm (l.o. 7.30pm).
Parking for 20.
Credit: Access, Visa.
🖇 🗣 ♨ 🖥 Ⓥ 🖨 Ⓣ 🖥
🛎 🍴 SP 🏠 Ⓣ

Old Rectory M
♛♛ APPROVED

Woolstone, Cheltenham, GL52 4RG
☎ Bishops Cleeve (024 267) 3766
Beautiful Victorian rectory in peaceful hamlet, 4 miles north of the Regency town of Cheltenham. Tranquil spot with lovely views.
Bedrooms: 1 double & 1 twin, 1 family room.
Bathrooms: 3 private.
Continued ▶

CHELTENHAM
Continued

Bed & breakfast: £20 single,
£35-£37 double.
Parking for 6.
Open March-November.

On the Park M
COMMENDED
Evesham Rd., Cheltenham,
GL52 2AH
☎ (0242) 518898 Fax 0242
511526
*Overlooking Pittville Park, this
delightful Regency villa offers
individual accommodation and
high standard dining facilities.
5 minutes' walk from the town
centre.*
Bedrooms: 2 single, 6 double
& 6 twin.
Bathrooms: 14 private.
Bed & breakfast: £54.50-
£82.50 single, £69-£97 double.
Half board: £64.50-£84.50
daily.
Lunch available.
Evening meal 7pm (l.o.
9.30pm).
Parking for 10.
Credit: Access, Visa, Diners,
Amex.

Prestbury House Hotel M
COMMENDED
The Burgage, Prestbury,
Cheltenham, GL52 3DN
☎ (0242) 529533 & 230106
Fax 0242 227076
*300-year-old Georgian country
manor house, set in 2 acres of
secluded gardens, beneath
Cleeve Hill.*
Bedrooms: 1 single, 4 double
& 9 twin, 3 family rooms.
Bathrooms: 17 private.
Bed & breakfast: £59 single,
£69 double.
Half board: £75-£85 daily.
Lunch available.
Evening meal 7pm (l.o. 9pm).
Parking for 50.
Credit: Access, Visa.

Regency House Hotel M
COMMENDED
50 Clarence Sq., Pittville,
Cheltenham, GL50 4JR
☎ (0242) 582718
*Restored Regency house in a
quiet Georgian square. Near a
beautiful park but only
minutes' walk from town
centre.*

Bedrooms: 2 single, 2 double
& 3 twin, 1 family room.
Bathrooms: 7 private;
1 private shower.
Bed & breakfast: £30-£35
single, £45-£50 double.
Half board: £32.50-£40 daily.
Evening meal 6pm.
Credit: Access, Visa.

Stretton Lodge M
Western Rd., Cheltenham,
GL50 3RN
☎ (0242) 528724 & 570771
*Carefully restored, early
Victorian house with warm and
comfortable relaxing
atmosphere. Spacious well-
appointed rooms. Quiet central
location. Brochure available.*
Bedrooms: 1 single, 3 double
& 3 twin, 2 family rooms.
Bathrooms: 9 private.
Bed & breakfast: £32.50-
£47.50 single, £50-£60 double.
Half board: £40-£60 daily.
Evening meal 6.30pm.
Parking for 5.
Credit: Access, Visa, Amex.

Wellesley Court Hotel M
Clarence Sq., Pittville,
Cheltenham, GL50 4JR
☎ Cheltenham (0242) 580411
Fax (0242) 224609
CR Minotels
*Listed Regency hotel in a quiet
Georgian square close to the
town centre, racecourse, leisure
complex, parks and cultural
venues.*
Bedrooms: 6 single, 3 double
& 4 twin, 5 family rooms.
Bathrooms: 11 private,
2 public; 2 private showers.
Bed & breakfast: £24.75-£45
single, £44-£66 double.
Half board: £31.75-£58 daily,
£178.50-£350 weekly.
Lunch available.
Evening meal 6.30pm (l.o.
9.30pm).
Parking for 18.
Credit: Access, Visa, Diners,
Amex.

Willoughby Hotel M
APPROVED
1 Suffolk Sq., Cheltenham,
GL50 2DR
☎ (0242) 522798
*Large Regency house of
architectural interest. Double
glazed throughout. In quiet
square overlooking garden and
bowling green.*
Bedrooms: 3 single, 3 double
& 3 twin, 1 family room.

Bathrooms: 5 private,
2 public.
Bed & breakfast: £23-£35
single, £42.50-£50 double.
Evening meal 6.30pm (l.o.
4pm).
Parking for 10.

Wishmoor Guest House M
COMMENDED
147 Hales Rd., Cheltenham,
GL52 6TD
☎ (0242) 238504
*Friendly family guesthouse
with parking off the road, 1
mile from the town centre and
convenient for the countryside.*
Bedrooms: 4 single, 2 double
& 2 twin, 2 family rooms.
Bathrooms: 4 private,
3 public.
Bed & breakfast: £17-£28
single, £32-£45 double.
Half board: £26-£35 daily.
Evening meal 6pm (l.o.
midday).
Parking for 8.
Credit: Access, Visa.

Wyastone Hotel M
Parabola Rd., Cheltenham,
GL50 3BG
☎ (0242) 245549/516654
Fax (0242) 522659
*Victorian building in well-
favoured Montpellier district,
which has beautiful gardens
and excellent shops.*
Bedrooms: 5 single, 3 double
& 5 twin, 1 family room.
Bathrooms: 14 private.
Bed & breakfast: £53 single,
£75 double.
Half board: from £69.50
daily.
Lunch available.
Evening meal 7pm (l.o. 9pm).
Parking for 20.
Credit: Access, Visa, Diners,
Amex.

---

*The symbol **CR**
and the name of a
hotel group or
consortium after a
hotel address means
that bookings can
be made through a
central reservations
office. These are
listed on page 540.*

CHIPPING CAMPDEN

Gloucestershire
Map ref 2B1

Outstanding Cotswold
wool town with many old
stone gabled houses, a
splendid church and 17th
C almshouses. There is a
collection of historic
sports cars and nearby
are Kiftsgate Court
Gardens and Hidcote
Manor Gardens (National
Trust).
*Tourist Information
Centre* ☎ (0386) 840101

Cotswold House Hotel and Restaurant M
HIGHLY COMMENDED
The Square, Chipping
Campden, GL55 6AN
☎ Evesham (0386) 840330
Fax 0386 840310
*Comfort, elegance, food and
friendly, personal service - all
to be found at this recently
refurbished historic country
town house hotel.*
Bedrooms: 3 single, 7 double
& 5 twin.
Bathrooms: 15 private.
Bed & breakfast: £60.50-£75
single, £92-£145 double.
Half board: £89.50-£100
daily.
Lunch available.
Evening meal 7.15pm (l.o.
9.30pm).
Parking for 14.
Credit: Access, Visa, Diners,
Amex.

The Malt House M
COMMENDED
Broad Campden, Chipping
Campden, GL55 6UU
☎ Evesham (0386) 840295
*Historic house of 16th C origin,
with traditional English
garden.*
Bedrooms: 1 double & 2 twin.
Bathrooms: 3 private,
1 public.
Bed & breakfast: £24 single,
£65-£90 double.
Evening meal 7.30pm.
Parking for 5.
Credit: Access, Visa.

Park House M
Park Rd., Chipping
Campden, GL55 6EB
☎ Evesham (0386) 841127

Cotswold-stone house offering elegantly furnished rooms, one with four-poster bed. Quiet position in this beautiful old wool town. Ideal base for touring Cotswolds and Shakespeare country.
Bedrooms: 1 double & 1 twin, 1 family room.
Bathrooms: 2 public.
Bed & breakfast: £32-£35 double.
Parking for 4.

🐾5 🛗 🖤 💺 UL V ⌷ TV 🎅
🔺 ❄ 🎿 🏵

CHURCH STRETTON

Shropshire
Map ref 4A3

Church Stretton lies under the eastern slope of the Longmynd surrounded by hills. It is ideal for walkers, with marvellous views, golf and gliding. The town has a small puppet theatre and Wenlock Edge is not far away.

Belvedere Guest House M
APPROVED
Burway Rd., Church Stretton, SY6 6DP
☎ (0694) 722232
Quiet detached house set in its own grounds, convenient for Church Stretton town centre and Longmynd Hills. Adequate parking.
Bedrooms: 3 single, 3 double & 2 twin, 4 family rooms.
Bathrooms: 6 private, 3 public.
Bed & breakfast: £18-£20 single, £36-£40 double.
Half board: £26-£28 daily, £163.80-£176.40 weekly.
Evening meal 7pm (l.o. 6pm).
Parking for 8.
Credit: Access, Visa.
🐾 🖤 💺 V ⌷ TV 🎅 🔺 🍴
🅿 🎿

Brookfields Guesthouse M
Watling St. North, Church Stretton, SY6 7AR
☎ (0694) 722314
Large Edwardian house set in three-quarters of an acre, ideally situated on the A49 in the heart of Church Stretton. Dinner available with extensive menu for around £12.50.
Bedrooms: 3 double & 1 twin.
Bathrooms: 5 private.
Bed & breakfast: from £20.50 single, £39-£45 double.

Evening meal 7pm (l.o. 9.30pm).
Parking for 6.
🚿 🛗 ⌷ 💺 UL 🛗 V ⌷ 🎅
🔺 ❄ 🎿 🎿

Longmynd Hotel M
🏵🏵🏵
Cunnery Rd., Church Stretton, SY6 6AG
☎ (0694) 722244
CR Inter
Family-run country hotel commanding panoramic views of the south Shropshire highlands. Situated in an area of outstanding natural beauty. Self-catering lodges available.
Bedrooms: 5 single, 25 double & 18 twin, 2 family rooms.
Bathrooms: 50 private, 4 public.
Bed & breakfast: max. £42 single, max. £69 double.
Half board: max. £34.50 daily, max. £220 weekly.
Lunch available.
Evening meal 7pm (l.o. 9.30pm).
Parking for 150.
Credit: Access, Visa, Diners, Amex.
🚿 🛗 📞 ⌷ 💺 🛗 V ⌷
🛗 🎅 🔺 🍴 🎿 💺 🎿 🎅 🎿 🍴 U
🅿 ❄ 🎿 SP 🎿

Mynd House Hotel M
🏵🏵🏵🏵 **COMMENDED**
Little Stretton, Church Stretton, SY6 6RB
☎ Church Stretton (0694) 722212
Fax (0694) 724180
Small Edwardian house hotel and restaurant. 2 suites available. Dine a la carte or table d'hote.
Bedrooms: 1 single, 3 double & 2 twin, 2 family rooms.
Bathrooms: 8 private.
Bed & breakfast: £35-£42 single, £51-£85 double.
Half board: £36-£55 daily, £260-£375 weekly.
Lunch available.
Evening meal 7.30pm (l.o. 9.15pm).
Parking for 16.
Open March-December.
Credit: Access, Visa, Amex.
🚿 🛗 ⌷ 💺 🛗 V 🎅 🔺
🛗 🔺 🍴 ❄ 🎿 SP

Paddock Lodge Luxury Guest House M
🏵🏵🏵
Shrewsbury Rd., All Stretton, Church Stretton, SY6 6HG
☎ (0694) 723702
Peacefully situated in south Shropshire hill country, which provides superb riding and walking. Local produce used extensively, including home-grown vegetables.

Bedrooms: 1 double & 1 twin, 1 family room.
Bathrooms: 3 private, 1 public.
Bed & breakfast: from £20 single, £34-£36 double.
Half board: £54-£56 daily.
Evening meal 7pm (l.o. 7.30pm).
Parking for 15.
🚿 🛗 ⌷ 💺 UL 🛗 V 🎅 TV
🛗 🔺 U ❄ 🎿

Stretton Hall Hotel
All Stretton, Church Stretton, SY6 6HG
☎ (0694) 723224
Country house hotel set amidst the Shropshire Hills in unspoilt countryside. Relaxing atmosphere, all rooms peaceful and quiet.
Bedrooms: 2 single, 8 double & 3 twin, 1 family room.
Bathrooms: 14 private.
Bed & breakfast: from £40 single, from £58 double.
Half board: from £78 daily.
Lunch available.
Evening meal 7pm (l.o. 9.30pm).
Parking for 60.
Credit: Access, Visa, Diners, Amex.
🚿 🔺 🛗 📞 ⌷ 🛗 💺 🛗 V
🎿 🎅 🔺 🍴 U 🎿 ❄ 🎿
🎿 SP

Travellers Rest Inn M
🏵🏵 **APPROVED**
Upper Affcot, Church Stretton, SY6 6RL
☎ Marshbrook (0694) 781275
Traditional inn between Craven Arms and Church Stretton in beautiful countryside, with good real ale, food and accommodation and good company.
Bedrooms: 2 single, 3 double & 2 twin, 3 family rooms.
Bathrooms: 4 private, 1 public.
Bed & breakfast: £19-£30 single, £38-£45 double.
Lunch available.
Evening meal 5.30pm (l.o. 9.30pm).
Parking for 80.
Credit: Access, Visa, Amex.
🚿 🛗 ⌷ 💺 🛗 V 🎅 🎅 🛗 🔺
🔺 ❄ 🎿 SP T

National Crown ratings were correct at the time of going to press but are subject to change. Please check at the time of booking.

CIRENCESTER

Gloucestershire
Map ref 2B1

'Capital of the Cotswolds', Cirencester was Britain's second most important Roman town with many finds housed in the Corinium Museum. It has a very fine Perpendicular church and old houses around the market place. Cirencester Park is open to the public with polo in summer.
Tourist Information Centre ☎ (0285) 654180

2 Cove House M
🏵🏵🏵
Ashton Keynes, Wiltshire SN6 6NS
☎ (0285) 861221
Original part of historic Cotswold 17th C manor house, set in a beautiful garden. Well placed for visiting Bath, Oxford and the Cotswold countryside. At White Hart, Ashton Keynes, turn east. Entrance 100 yards on left.
Bedrooms: 1 double & 1 twin, 1 family room.
Bathrooms: 3 private, 1 public.
Bed & breakfast: £26-£32 single, £36-£46 double.
Evening meal 7pm (l.o. 8pm).
Parking for 7.
Open January-November.
🚿 💺 UL 🎅 TV 🛗 🔺 U ❄
🎿 🎿

Eliot Arms Hotel Free House M
🏵🏵 **COMMENDED**
Clarks Hay, South Cerney, Cirencester, GL7 5UA
☎ (0285) 860215
Typical Cotswold freehouse hotel dating from the 16th C.
Bedrooms: 2 single, 2 double & 5 twin.
Bathrooms: 9 private.
Bed & breakfast: £28-£35 single, £40-£45 double.
Lunch available.
Evening meal 6.30pm (l.o. 10pm).
Parking for 25.
Credit: Access, Visa.
🚿 📞 ⌷ 💺 🛗 🎅 🛗 🔺
🍴 U 🎿 🎿 ❄ 🎿 DAP SP

Fleece Hotel M
🏵🏵🏵🏵 **COMMENDED**
Market Pl., Cirencester, GL7 2NZ
☎ (0285) 658507 Fax 0285 651017
CR Resort

Continued ▶

CIRENCESTER

Continued

Tudor coaching inn with individually styled bedrooms. Ideally located for exploring the Cotswolds. Bistro-style restaurant available.
Bedrooms: 4 single, 12 double & 7 twin, 2 family rooms.
Bathrooms: 21 private; 4 private showers.
Bed & breakfast: £32.50-£84.50 single, £65-£102 double.
Lunch available.
Evening meal 7.30pm (l.o. 9.30pm).
Parking for 10.
Credit: Access, Visa, Diners, Amex.

King's Head Hotel M

Market Pl., Cirencester, GL7 2NR
☎ (0285) 653322 Telex 43470
Fax 0285 655103
Ⓡ Best Western
Formerly an historic coaching inn, the hotel now combines old world charm with modern comfort. In 1642 the first blood of the Civil War was shed outside.
Bedrooms: 18 single, 22 double & 26 twin, 4 family rooms.
Bathrooms: 70 private.
Bed & breakfast: £50-£65 single, £70-£85 double.
Half board: £44-£52 daily, £264-£300 weekly.
Lunch available.
Evening meal 7pm (l.o. 9pm).
Parking for 20.
Credit: Access, Visa, C.Bl., Diners, Amex.

La Ronde Hotel M
52-54 Ashcroft Rd., Cirencester, GL7 1QX
☎ (0285) 654611
A large Cotswold-stone house in town centre. Ideal for touring the Cotswold area. Close to museum, church and Cirencester Park.
Bedrooms: 3 double & 5 twin, 2 family rooms.
Bathrooms: 10 private.
Bed & breakfast: £30-£43.50 single, £43.50-£48.50 double.
Half board: £39.75-£53.25 daily.
Lunch available.

Evening meal 7pm (l.o. 9pm).
Parking for 9.
Credit: Access, Visa.

Raydon House Hotel and Restaurant M
3 The Avenue, Cirencester, GL7 1EH
☎ (0285) 653485 & (0285) 650625
19th C Victorian detached residence in a tree-lined avenue close to the centre of the town.
Bedrooms: 2 single, 5 double & 2 twin, 2 family rooms.
Bathrooms: 11 private.
Bed & breakfast: £35-£45 single, £45-£65 double.
Half board: £35-£57 daily, £240-£390 weekly.
Evening meal 7pm (l.o. 8.30pm).
Parking for 5.
Credit: Access, Visa, Amex.

Stratton House Hotel M
Gloucester Rd., Cirencester, GL7 2LE
☎ (0285) 651761
Fax (0285) 640024
Ⓡ Forestdale
Part Jacobean/Georgian mansion furnished with antiques and paintings. Personal service and consideration.
Bedrooms: 4 single, 9 double & 11 twin, 1 family room.
Bathrooms: 25 private.
Bed & breakfast: from £57.50 single, £72.50-£82.50 double.
Lunch available.
Evening meal 7pm (l.o. 9.45pm).
Parking for 102.
Credit: Access, Visa, Diners, Amex.

Warwick Cottage Guest House M
COMMENDED
75 Victoria Rd., Cirencester, GL7 1ES
☎ (0285) 656279
Attractive Victorian townhouse, 5 minutes from the town centre. Good base for touring the Cotswolds. Family rooms available as doubles or twins.
Bedrooms: 2 double, 2 family rooms.
Bathrooms: 4 private, 1 public.
Bed & breakfast: £27-£31 double.

Half board: £18.50-£22 daily, £122.50-£142.50 weekly.
Evening meal 6.30pm.
Parking for 4.

Wimborne House M
APPROVED
91 Victoria Rd., Cirencester, GL7 1ES
☎ (0285) 653890
Cotswold-stone house, built in 1886, with a warm and friendly atmosphere and spacious rooms. Non-smokers only please.
Bedrooms: 4 double & 1 twin.
Bathrooms: 5 private.
Bed & breakfast: £25-£30 single, £28-£35 double.
Evening meal 6.30pm (l.o. 5.30pm).
Parking for 6.

CLEEVE HILL

Gloucestershire
Map ref 2B1

4m NE. Cheltenham Settlement with wonderful all round views above Cheltenham on the road to Winchcombe and Broadway.

Rising Sun Hotel M
Cleeve Hill, Cheltenham, GL52 3PX
☎ Cheltenham (0242) 676281
Telex 437410 Fax 0242 673069
Ⓡ Lansbury
Spectacular hilltop location with panoramic Cotswolds views, close to racecourse and golf-course. Ideal for exploring the Cotswolds.
Bedrooms: 3 single, 15 double & 6 twin.
Bathrooms: 24 private.
Bed & breakfast: £28-£62 single, £56-£74 double.
Half board: £40-£77 daily.
Lunch available.
Evening meal 7pm (l.o. 10.30pm).
Parking for 70.
Credit: Access, Visa, Diners, Amex.

The enquiry coupons at the back will help you when contacting proprietors.

CLEOBURY MORTIMER

Shropshire
Map ref 4A3

Village with attractive timbered and Georgian houses and a church with a wooden spire. It is close to the Clee Hills with marvellous views and Clee Hill Garden with over 400 birds and animals.

The Redfern Hotel M
APPROVED
Cleobury Mortimer, Kidderminster, Worcestershire DY14 8AA
☎ Cleobury Mortimer (0299) 270395 Telex 335176.
Fax 0299 271011
Ⓡ Minotels
18th C stone-built hotel in old market town. Attractive bathrooms. 4-poster available.
Bedrooms: 5 double & 5 twin, 1 family room.
Bathrooms: 11 private.
Bed & breakfast: £40-£50 single, £58-£73 double.
Half board: £38.50-£65 daily, £240-£300 weekly.
Lunch available.
Evening meal 7.30pm (l.o. 10pm).
Parking for 20.
Credit: Access, Visa, Diners, Amex.

CODSALL

Staffordshire
Map ref 4B3

Expanding residential village a few miles from Wolverhampton.

Moors Farm and Country Restaurant M
Chillington La., Codsall, Wolverhampton, WV8 1QF
☎ (0902) 842330
100-acre mixed farm. 200-year-old farmhouse, 1 mile from pretty village. All home produce used. Many local walks and places of interest.
Bedrooms: 1 double & 2 twin, 3 family rooms.
Bathrooms: 2 private, 2 public.
Bed & breakfast: £21-£26 single, £36-£44 double.
Half board: £29-£35 daily, £175-£235 weekly.
Lunch available.

Evening meal 6.30pm (l.o. 7pm).
Parking for 20.

📺4 ⊕ 🗄 � 🛡 Ⅴ ⊨ 🖥
🍴 ✕ ❋ 🏃 🛇 🚿 SP 🏠 T

Gloucestershire
Map ref 2A1

Small town in the Forest of Dean with the ancient iron mines at Clearwell Caves nearby, where mining equipment and geological samples are displayed. There are several forest trails in the area.
Tourist Information Centre ☎ *(0594) 36307*

Forest House Hotel ♨
♨♨

Cinder Hill, Coleford,
GL16 8HQ
☎ Dean (0594) 32424
changing to (0594) 832424
Gracious listed building with spacious, well-furnished rooms, 2 minutes' walk from town centre.
Bedrooms: 2 single, 3 double & 2 twin.
Bathrooms: 1 private, 2 public.
Bed & breakfast: £15-£16 single, £30-£38 double.
Half board: £23.50-£27.50 daily.
Evening meal 7pm (l.o. 8.30pm).
Parking for 10.

📺3 ⊕ 🗄 ½ ⊨ 📺 🖥 ✕ 🏃 🛇 🏠

The Lambsquay House Hotel ♨
♨♨♨♨

Royal Forest of Dean,
Coleford, GL16 8QB
☎ Dean (0594) 33127 (also Fax), changing to (0594) 833127
Georgian country house in the Royal Forest of Dean, surrounded by garden and fields. Well-equipped, comfortable accommodation. Fully licensed, varied food and wine. Open to non-residents.
Bedrooms: 1 single, 5 double & 2 twin, 1 family room.
Bathrooms: 9 private.
Bed & breakfast: £28-£37 single, £45-£58 double.
Half board: £32-£38 daily, £212-£252 weekly.
Lunch available.
Evening meal 7pm (l.o. 8.30pm).
Parking for 30.

Open February-December.
Credit: Access, Visa, Diners, Amex.

📺 ⊕ 🗄 ♥ 🛡 Ⅴ ⊨ 🖥
🍴 ❋ 🏃 DAP 🛇 SP 🏠

Poolway House Hotel & Restaurant ♨
♨♨♨

Gloucester Rd., Coleford,
GL16 8BN
☎ Dean (0594) 33937/33144
changing to (0594) 833937/833144
16th C oak-beamed manor. Comfortable restaurant, imaginative cuisine, cosy bedrooms. Reputed to have sheltered King Charles I (1642). Ideal base for exploring forest's natural splendour.
Bedrooms: 4 single, 3 double & 3 twin, 1 family room.
Bathrooms: 11 private.
Bed & breakfast: from £35 single, from £45 double.
Half board: from £33 daily, from £224 weekly.
Lunch available.
Evening meal 7pm (l.o. 9.15pm).
Parking for 22.
Credit: Access, Visa.

📺 🗄 ☎ ⊕ 🗄 ♥ 🛡 Ⅴ ⊨
🖥 🍴 ⊙ 🏃 ❋ 🏃 🛇 SP
🏠

Warwickshire
Map ref 4B3

9m E. Birmingham
Close to Birmingham's many attractions including the 17th C Aston Hall with its plasterwork and furnishings, the Railway Museum and Sarehole Mill, an 18th C water-powered mill restored to working order.

Coleshill Hotel
♨♨♨ COMMENDED

152 High St., Coleshill,
Birmingham, W. Midlands
B46 3BG
☎ (0675) 465527
Telex 333868 FAX 0675 464013
🅐 Lansbury
In traditional coaching inn style with restaurant, lounge bar and function/conference facilities. 5 minutes' drive from the National Exhibition Centre.
Bedrooms: 2 single, 11 double & 10 twin.
Bathrooms: 23 private.
Bed & breakfast: £22-£65 single, £44-£77 double.

Half board: £34-£80 daily.
Lunch available.
Evening meal 7pm (l.o. 10pm).
Parking for 48.
Credit: Access, Visa, Diners, Amex.

📺 🗄 ☎ ⊕ 🗄 ♥ 🛡 Ⅴ ½
⊙ 🖥 🍴 🏃 ► SP T

Gloucestershire
Map ref 2B1

Village close to Fairford with an unrivalled series of 15th C stained glass windows in its church.

New Inn
♨♨♨ ⊟ COMMENDED

Main St., Coln St Aldwyns,
Cirencester, GL7 5AN
☎ Coln St Aldwyns (0285) 75651 Fax 0285 75657
Between Fairford and Bibury in the picturesque Coln Valley. Extensively renovated. Comfortable bedrooms, haute cuisine, charm and a warm welcome.
Bedrooms: 9 double & 2 twin, 1 family room.
Bathrooms: 12 private.
Bed & breakfast: £30-£50 single, £50-£80 double.
Half board: £30-£57.50 daily.
Lunch available.
Evening meal 7.30pm (l.o. 9.30pm).
Parking for 30.
Credit: Access, Visa, Amex.

📺 🗄 ☎ ⊕ 🗄 ♥ 🛡 Ⅴ 🖥
🏃 ⊙ ♪ 🏃 🛇 SP 🏠

See Ampney Crucis, Apperley, Berkeley, Bibury, Birdlip, Blakeney, Bourton-on-the-Water, Broadway, Buckland, Cheltenham, Chipping Campden, Cirencester, Cleeve Hill, Coleford, Gloucester, Guiting Power, Lechlade, Mickleton, Minchinhampton, Moreton-in-Marsh, Nailsworth, North Nibley, Northleach, Nympsfield, Painswick, Slimbridge, Stow-on-the-Wold, Stroud, Tetbury, Tewkesbury, Winchcombe, Withington, Wotton-under-Edge.

Map references apply to the colour maps towards the end of this guide.

W. Midlands
Map ref 4B3

Modern city with a long history. It has many places of interest including the post-war and ruined medieval cathedrals, art gallery and museums, some 16th C almshouses, St. Mary's Guildhall, Lunt Roman fort and the Belgrade Theatre.
Tourist Information Centre ☎ *(0203) 832303*

Acorn Lodge Private Guest House, Pond Farm ♨
♨♨

Upper Eastern Green La.,
Coventry, CV5 7DP
☎ (0203) 465182
300-year-old beamed house of character in secluded position 100 yards off the road, with fields at the rear. Free tea or coffee always available.
Bedrooms: 2 single, 2 double & 1 twin.
Bathrooms: 1 private, 2 public.
Bed & breakfast: £14-£20 single, £28-£32 double.
Parking for 6.

📺10 ♨ ⓤ 🗄 ⊨ 📺 🖥 ►
❋ 🏃 🏃 SP 🏠

Ansty Hall ♨

Ansty, Coventry, CV7 9HZ
☎ Shilton (0203) 612222
Red brick country house hotel built in 1678 nestling in 8 acres of formal and informal gardens. Just outside Coventry in Ansty village.
Bedrooms: 15 double & 15 twin.
Bathrooms: 30 private.
Bed & breakfast: from £95 single, from £124 double.
Lunch available.
Evening meal 7pm (l.o. 9.45pm).
Parking for 50.
Credit: Access, Visa, Diners, Amex.

📺 ☎ ⊕ 🗄 ♥ 🛡 Ⅴ ½ ⊨
🖥 🏃 🍴 ❋ 🏃 🛇 SP 🏠 T

Arlon Guest House

25 St. Patricks Rd.,
Coventry, CV1 2LP
☎ (0203) 225942
Detached comfortable accommodation in a homely and friendly atmosphere. Close to railway station and central for all other amenities. Near National Exhibition Centre and National Agricultural Centre.

Continued ▶

COVENTRY
Continued

Bedrooms: 1 single, 2 twin,
1 family room.
Bathrooms: 2 private,
1 public.
Bed & breakfast: £15-£16
single, £28-£36 double.
Parking for 5.

Ashleigh House
Listed
17 Park Rd., Coventry,
CV1 2LH
☎ (0203) 223804
*Newly renovated guesthouse
only 100 yards from the
railway station. All city
amenities within 5 minutes'
walk.*
Bedrooms: 3 single, 2 twin,
5 family rooms.
Bathrooms: 8 private,
1 public.
Bed & breakfast: £18-£23
single, £28-£32 double.
Evening meal 5pm (l.o. 7pm).
Parking for 12.

Avalon Guest House ⋒
Listed **APPROVED**
28 Friars Rd., Coventry,
CV1 2LL
☎ (0203) 251839 Fax 0203
632737
*Well-appointed guesthouse
3 minutes' walk from the city
centre and rail station. All
rooms have colour TV,
tea/coffee facilities and full
central heating.*
Bedrooms: 3 single, 2 twin,
3 family rooms.
Bathrooms: 4 private,
1 public; 1 private shower.
Bed & breakfast: £18 single,
£30-£36 double.
Parking for 6.

Brooklands Grange
Hotel and Restaurant ⋒
COMMENDED
Holyhead Rd., Coventry,
CV5 8HX
☎ (0203) 601601 Fax 0203
601277
*Originally a Jacobean
farmhouse now a prestigious
privately owned hotel with
restaurant. Ideally situated for
touring the historic attractions
in the county of Warwickshire.*
Bedrooms: 4 single, 18 double
& 8 twin.
Bathrooms: 30 private.
Bed & breakfast: £80-£90
single, £90-£95 double.
Lunch available.

Evening meal 7pm (l.o.
9.30pm).
Parking for 54.
Credit: Access, Visa, Diners,
Amex.

Brymar Guest House
39a St Patricks Rd.,
Cheylesmore, Coventry,
CV1 2LP
☎ (0203) 225969
*Central guesthouse close to all
amenities and National
Exhibition Centre. Quality
accommodation offering value
for money. Take exit 5 off
Ring Road.*
Bedrooms: 2 single, 1 twin,
1 family room.
Bathrooms: 2 public;
2 private showers.
Bed & breakfast: £16-£20
single, £30-£36 double.

Coventry Knight Hotel
A45 London Rd., Ryton-on-
Dunsmore, Coventry,
CV8 3DY
☎ Coventry (0203) 301585
*Comfortable, modern hotel
with friendly atmosphere on the
main A45 just a couple of miles
from Coventry. Good touring
base for the Midlands.*
Bedrooms: 1 single, 12 double
& 32 twin, 4 family rooms.
Bathrooms: 49 private.
Bed & breakfast: £68-£74
single, £80-£100 double.
Lunch available.
Evening meal 7pm (l.o.
10pm).
Parking for 200.
Credit: Access, Visa, Diners,
Amex.

Crest Guest House
39 Friars Rd., Coventry,
CV1 2LJ
☎ (0203) 227822
*Near town centre, between
railway station and coach
station. 15 minutes by train to
National Exhibition Centre
and Birmingham Airport.*
Bedrooms: 2 single, 2 twin.
Bathrooms: 2 private,
1 public.
Bed & breakfast: £18-£20
single, £30-£40 double.
Parking for 6.

Fairlight Guest House
14 Regent St., off Queen's
Rd., Coventry, CV1 3EP
☎ (0203) 224215
*3-storey, double-fronted
Victorian house, half a mile
from the city centre and
cathedral, quarter of a mile
from the station.*
Bedrooms: 6 single, 1 double
& 4 twin, 1 family room.
Bathrooms: 1 private,
3 public.
Bed & breakfast: £14-£15
single, £28-£34 double.
Parking for 6.

Hotel Leofric
COMMENDED
Broadgate, Coventry,
CV1 1LZ
☎ (0203) 221371
Telex 311193
*Hotel with restaurant, coffee
shop and 3 bars. Overlooking
Coventry Cathedral.
Convenient for Kenilworth and
Warwick Castle.*
Bedrooms: 40 single,
10 double & 36 twin, 5 family
rooms.
Bathrooms: 91 private,
1 public.
Bed & breakfast: from £86
single, from £102 double.
Lunch available.
Evening meal 7pm (l.o.
9.45pm).
Credit: Access, Visa, C.Bl.,
Diners, Amex.

Merrick Lodge Hotel ⋒
COMMENDED
80-82 St. Nicholas St.,
Coventry, CV1 4BP
☎ (0203) 553940 Fax 0203
550112
*Former manor house,
5 minutes' walk from city
centre. Fully licensed, table
d'hote and a la carte
restaurant, 3 bars. Private
parties catered for.*
Bedrooms: 4 single, 6 double
& 10 twin, 6 family rooms.
Bathrooms: 21 private;
5 private showers.
Bed & breakfast: £40-£50
single, £57.50-£65 double.
Half board: £38.75-£60 daily,
£271.25-£540 weekly.
Lunch available.
Evening meal 6.30pm (l.o.
11pm).
Parking for 60.
Credit: Access, Visa, Amex.

Mount Guest House ⋒
Listed
9 Coundon Rd., Coventry,
CV1 4AR
☎ (0203) 225998
*Family guesthouse within
walking distance of city and
cathedral. Easy reach of the
National Exhibition Centre
and the Royal Showground.
Snacks available.*
Bedrooms: 2 single, 6 twin,
2 family rooms.
Bathrooms: 2 public.
Bed & breakfast: £13-£20
single, £26 double.

Northanger House ⋒
35 Westminster Rd.,
Coventry, CV1 3GB
☎ (0203) 226780
*Friendly home 5 minutes from
the city centre. Close to
railway and bus stations.
Convenient for all amenities.*
Bedrooms: 2 single, 2 double
& 3 twin, 2 family rooms.
Bathrooms: 3 public.
Bed & breakfast: £16-£17
single, £26-£30 double.
Parking for 1.

The Old Mill Hotel ⋒
COMMENDED
Mill Hill, Baginton, Coventry,
CV8 2BS
☎ (0203) 307070 Fax 0203
307070
*Hotel retaining many
interesting features preserved
from its working days as a
mill. The hotel's 5 acres of
gardens run down to the banks
of the River Sowe.*
Bedrooms: 11 double &
4 twin, 5 family rooms.
Bathrooms: 20 private.
Bed & breakfast: from £61
single, from £74 double.
Lunch available.
Evening meal 7pm (l.o.
9.30pm).
Parking for 200.
Credit: Access, Visa, Diners,
Amex.

---

*National Crown
ratings were correct
at the time of going
to press but are
subject to change.
Please check at the
time of booking.*

CROPTHORNE

Hereford & Worcester
Map ref 2B1

3m W. Evesham
Pretty village of mainly black and white cottages overlooking the River Avon.

Cedars Guest House M

Evesham Rd., Cropthorne, Pershore, Worcestershire WR10 3JU
☎ Evesham (0386) 860219
Friendly guesthouse in own grounds. Private parking. Ideal for touring Cotswolds, Vale of Evesham, Malverns, Stratford. Licensed bar.
Bedrooms: 1 single, 1 double & 2 twin, 2 family rooms.
Bathrooms: 2 private, 2 public.
Bed & breakfast: £15-£22 single, £30-£45 double.
Half board: £21-£28 daily.
Evening meal 7pm (l.o. 6pm).
Parking for 5.
Credit: Access, Visa.

DIDDLEBURY

Shropshire
Map ref 4A3

7m N. Ludlow
Village close to the beautiful countryside of Wenlock Edge and the Longmynd.

Glebe Farm M
COMMENDED
Diddlebury, Craven Arms, SY7 9DH
☎ Munslow (058 476) 221
123-acre beef & sheep farm. Listed 16th C farmhouse, an idyllic retreat, set in an old-fashioned garden by a stream amid the rolling hills of south Shropshire. Country-style cooking, joint runner up Best Breakfast 1991.
Bedrooms: 1 single, 3 double & 2 twin.
Bathrooms: 4 private, 2 public.
Bed & breakfast: £20-£24 single, £40-£52 double.
Half board: £33.50-£39.50 daily.
Evening meal 7.45pm (l.o. 6pm).
Parking for 12.
Open March-November.

DROITWICH

Hereford & Worcester
Map ref 2B1

Old town with natural brine springs, developed as a spa town at the beginning of the 19th C. It has some interesting churches, in particular the Church of the Sacred Heart with splendid mosaics. There are several fine parks and a Heritage Centre.
Tourist Information Centre ☎ (0905) 774312

Chateau Impney Hotel M

Droitwich, Worcestershire WR9 0BN
☎ (0905) 774411
Telex 336673
Reproduction chateau built by John Corbett, set in its own parkland. Centrally located, 1 mile from the M5 exit 5. Extensive conference and banqueting facilities.
Bedrooms: 22 single, 46 double & 39 twin, 9 family rooms.
Bathrooms: 116 private.
Bed & breakfast: £49.90-£99.90 single, £69.85-£119.85 double.
Lunch available.
Evening meal 7pm (l.o. 10pm).
Parking for 600.
Credit: Access, Visa, Diners, Amex.

Raven Hotel M

Droitwich, Worcestershire WR9 8DU
☎ (0905) 772224
Telex 336673
Traditional black and white half-timbered hotel. Centrally located, 1.5 miles from the M5 exit 5. Extensive conference and banqueting facilities.
Bedrooms: 31 single, 30 double & 10 twin, 1 family room.
Bathrooms: 72 private.
Bed & breakfast: £49.90-£99.90 single, £69.85-£119.85 double.
Lunch available.
Evening meal 7pm (l.o. 10pm).
Parking for 200.
Credit: Access, Visa, Diners, Amex.

Richmond Guest House M
Listed
3 Ombersley St. West, Droitwich, Worcestershire WR9 8HZ
☎ (0905) 775722
Victorian-built guesthouse in the town centre, 5 minutes from railway station and bus route. English breakfast. 30 minutes from National Exhibition Centre via M5/M42.
Bedrooms: 6 single, 1 double & 4 twin, 3 family rooms.
Bathrooms: 2 public.
Bed & breakfast: £15 single, £26 double.
Parking for 12.

ECCLESHALL

Staffordshire
Map ref 4B3

Small market town has long associations with the Bishops of Lichfield, 6 of whom are buried in the large 12th C parish church. The ruined castle was formerly the residence of these bishops.

King's Arms Hotel
Stafford St., Eccleshall, Stafford, ST21 6BL
☎ Stafford (0785) 850294
16th C coaching inn.
Bedrooms: 1 single, 2 double & 1 twin, 1 family room.
Bathrooms: 2 public.
Bed & breakfast: £19-£21 single, £35-£39.50 double.
Lunch available.
Evening meal 7pm (l.o. 10pm).
Parking for 50.
Credit: Access, Visa.

The St. George Hotel M
COMMENDED
Castle St., Eccleshall, Stafford, ST21 6DF
☎ (0785) 850300 Fax 0785 851452
Beautiful Georgian inn combining modern facilities with old fashioned comfort. In the centre of Eccleshall, 6 miles from M6 junction 14.
Bedrooms: 4 single, 5 double & 1 twin, 1 family room.
Bathrooms: 11 private.
Bed & breakfast: £25-£45 single, £50-£70 double.
Half board: £33-£60 daily.
Lunch available.
Evening meal 7pm (l.o. 9.30pm).

Parking for 20.
Credit: Access, Visa, Diners, Amex.

EVESHAM

Hereford & Worcester
Map ref 2B1

Evesham is a market town in the centre of a fruit-growing area. There are pleasant walks along the River Avon and many old houses and inns. A fine 16th C bell tower stands between 2 churches.
Tourist Information Centre ☎ (0386) 446944

Chequers Inn M
APPROVED
Fladbury, Pershore, Worcestershire WR10 2PZ
☎ Evesham (0386) 860276 & 860527
14th C inn between Evesham and Pershore, on the edge of the Cotswolds. Off B4084 and A44, in a quiet village location, 17 miles from Stratford-upon-Avon.
Bedrooms: 3 double & 4 twin, 1 family room.
Bathrooms: 8 private.
Bed & breakfast: £38.50-£41.25 single, from £61.50 double.
Lunch available.
Evening meal 6.30pm (l.o. 9.30pm).
Parking for 30.
Credit: Access, Visa.

Evesham Hotel M
COMMENDED
Cooper's La., off Waterside, Evesham, Worcestershire WR11 6DA
☎ (0386) 765566
Family-run Tudor mansion in 2.5-acre garden, offering unusual food and wine and all modern facilities. Ideal touring centre. New indoor pool.
Bedrooms: 6 single, 22 double & 11 twin, 1 family room.
Bathrooms: 40 private.
Bed & breakfast: £54-£66 single, £78-£90 double.
Half board: £40-£60 daily.
Lunch available.
Evening meal 7pm (l.o. 9.30pm).
Parking for 45.
Credit: Access, Visa, Diners, Amex.

The Mill at Harvington ₥
꧁꧁꧁꧁ COMMENDED

Anchor Lane, Harvington,
Evesham, Worcestershire
WR11 5NR
☎ (0386) 870688
*Peaceful, riverside hotel
tastefully converted from
beautiful house and mill. In
acres of gardens, quarter of a
mile from Evesham to
Stratford road.*
Bedrooms: 12 double &
3 twin.
Bathrooms: 15 private.
Bed & breakfast: £54 single,
£78 double.
Half board: £44.50-£49.50
daily.
Lunch available.
Evening meal 7pm (l.o.
8.45pm).
Parking for 25.
Credit: Access, Visa.
ॐ❿ ᕤ ↺ ☏ ⌥ ♦ ⓥ
⇲ ⌂ ⌷ ✿ ✗
⍩ SP ⊞ T

Nightingale Hotel ₥
꧁꧁꧁ COMMENDED

Bishampton, Pershore,
Worcestershire WR10 2NH
☎ (038 682) 521 &
(038 682) 384
*200-acre beef and arable farm.
Near Evesham and within easy
reach of Stratford, Cotswolds
and Malvern. Golfing, riding
and sports centre close by. A
friendly atmosphere awaits you.*
Bedrooms: 1 single, 1 double
& 1 twin, 1 family room.
Bathrooms: 4 private.
Bed & breakfast: £32 single,
£45 double.
Half board: £47 daily.
Evening meal 7.30pm (l.o.
9pm).
Parking for 24.
Credit: Access, Visa.
ॐ❿ ⊡ ⌷ ⓥ ✗ ⌂ ⍩ T̄ᵛ ⠿
⌂ ↺ ↻ ⌿ ✿ ✗ ⍩ ⌷ SP

Park View Hotel ₥
꧁꧁ APPROVED

Waterside, Evesham,
Worcestershire WR11 6BS
☎ (0386) 442639
*Riverside hotel offering
personal attention. Traditional
English breakfast included,
evening meal available. Base
for touring Cotswolds and
Shakespeare Country.*
Bedrooms: 13 single, 3 double
& 11 twin, 2 family rooms.
Bathrooms: 6 public.
Bed & breakfast: £17.75-
£19.75 single, £34-£38 double.
Half board: £27.50-£29.50
daily.

Lunch available.
Evening meal 6pm (l.o. 7pm).
Parking for 50.
Credit: Access, Visa, Amex.
ॐ ⓘ ⇲ T̄ᵛ ⌂ ⍩

Riverside Hotel ₥
꧁꧁꧁ COMMENDED

The Parks, Offenham Rd.,
Evesham, Worcestershire
WR11 5JP
☎ (0386) 446200 Fax 0386
40021
*Small country house hotel
offering panoramic views
across the Avon.*
Bedrooms: 3 double & 4 twin.
Bathrooms: 7 private.
Bed & breakfast: £50-£60
single, £70-£80 double.
Half board: £46-£56 daily.
Lunch available.
Evening meal 7.30pm (l.o.
9pm).
Parking for 45.
Credit: Access, Visa.
ॐ ⇲ ⌂ ↺ ✿ ✗ ⍩ SP ⊞ T

The Waterside Hotel ₥
꧁꧁꧁ COMMENDED

56 Waterside, Evesham,
Worcestershire WR11 6JZ
☎ (0386) 442420
*Proprietor-run hotel, with
happy relaxed atmosphere,
within walking distance of town
centre. Co-ordinated designer
bedrooms. Themed restaurant
and lounge. Riverside garden
overlooking park.*
Bedrooms: 9 double & 2 twin,
2 family rooms.
Bathrooms: 10 private,
1 public.
Bed & breakfast: £23.58-
£45.62 single, £39-£57.20
double.
Lunch available.
Evening meal 6.30pm (l.o.
9.30pm).
Parking for 30.
Credit: Access, Visa, Amex.
ॐ ⛪ ↺ ⊡ ⌷ ⍩ ⓥ ✗
⇲ T̄ᵛ ⌂ ⌷ ✿ ⌷ OAP ⍩
SP T

FOWNHOPE
Hereford & Worcester
Map ref 2A1

6m SE. Hereford
Attractive village close to
the River Wye with black
and white cottages and
other interesting houses.
It has a large church with
a Norman tower and a
14th C spire.

Green Man Inn ₥
꧁꧁꧁꧁ COMMENDED

Fownhope, Hereford,
Herefordshire HR1 4PE
☎ (0432) 860243

*15th C black and white
coaching inn, midway between
Ross-on-Wye and Hereford, in
the picturesque village of
Fownhope. On the B4224,
close to the River Wye and set
in the beautiful Wye Valley.
Self-catering cottage also
available.*
Bedrooms: 1 single, 13 double
& 1 twin, 4 family rooms.
Bathrooms: 19 private.
Bed & breakfast: £31.75-
£33.50 single, £44.50-£47
double.
Half board: £34.50-£35.50
daily, £224-£228 weekly.
Lunch available.
Evening meal 7.15pm (l.o.
9pm).
Parking for 80.
Credit: Access, Visa, Amex.
ॐ ⛪ ⇲ ↺ ⊡ ⌷ ⌿ ⓘ ⓥ
✗ ⇲ T̄ᵛ ⌂ ⌷ ⌷ ✿ ⍩
SP ⊞

GLOUCESTER
Gloucestershire
Map ref 2B1

A Roman city and inland
port on the Severn, its
cathedral is one of the
most beautiful in Britain.
Gloucester's many
attractions include
museums, old buildings
and inns and the house of
Beatrix Potter's 'Tailor of
Gloucester'.
*Tourist Information
Centre* ☎ *(0452) 421188*

Bowden Hall Resort Hotel ₥

Bondend Lane, Upton St.
Leonards, Gloucester,
GL4 8ED
☎ (0452) 614121 Fax 0452
611885
Ⓡ Resort
*Set in 13 acres of private
grounds, 8 miles from
Cheltenham. Excellent touring
base, close to Gloucester.
Conference facilities available.*
Bedrooms: 46 double &
7 twin, 20 family rooms.
Bathrooms: 73 private.
Bed & breakfast: £32.50-
£84.50 single, £65-£102
double.
Lunch available.
Evening meal 7pm (l.o.
9.30pm).
Parking for 150.
Credit: Access, Visa, Diners,
Amex.
ॐ ⛪ ↺ ⊡ ⌷ ⌿ ⓘ ⓥ ✗
⇲ T̄ᵛ ⌂ ⌷ ⌷ ⌷ ⍩
✿ SP ⊞ T

Claremont ₥
Listed

135 Stroud Rd., Gloucester,
GL1 5JL
☎ (0452) 29540 & 29270
*Small, family-run guesthouse,
within walking distance of city
centre, historic docks and
leisure centre.*
Bedrooms: 2 single, 1 double
& 1 twin, 3 family rooms.
Bathrooms: 2 public.
Bed & breakfast: £12-£15.50
single, £24-£29 double.
Parking for 6.
ॐ ⇲ ⓥ ⌂ T̄ᵛ ⍩ ✗ ⍩

Denmark Hotel ₥
꧁꧁꧁ APPROVED

36 Denmark Road
Gloucester, GL1 3JQ
☎ Gloucester (0452) 303808
*Small family hotel close to city
centre.*
Bedrooms: 7 single, 2 double,
1 family room.
Bathrooms: 5 private,
2 public.
Bed & breakfast: £16-£22
single, £28-£35 double.
Half board: £21.50-£27.50
daily.
Evening meal 6pm (l.o.
7.30pm).
Parking for 17.
ॐ ⛪ ⊡ ⌷ ⌷ UL ⓘ ⓥ ⇲
T̄ᵛ ⍩ ⌂ ✗ ⍩

Gloucester Hotel & Country Club ₥

Matson Lane, Robinswood
Hill, Gloucester, GL4 9EA
☎ (0452) 25653 Telex 43571
*Hotel and country club
specialising in conference and
leisure facilities, within the
boundaries of the Roman city
of Gloucester. Convenient for
touring the Cotswolds and the
Wye Valley.*
Bedrooms: 9 single, 34 double
& 57 twin, 7 family rooms.
Bathrooms: 107 private,
8 public.
Bed & breakfast: from £94.65
single, from £104.65 double.
Lunch available.
Evening meal 7.30pm (l.o.
10pm).
Parking for 400.
Credit: Access, Visa, Diners,
Amex.
ॐ ⛪ ↺ ⊡ ⌷ ⌷ ⓘ ⓥ ✗
⇲ T̄ᵛ ⓥ ⍩ ⌂ ⌷ ⍩ ♦ ⌿
✗ ↻ ↺ ✿ ⍩ SP ⊞ T

Hatton Court ₥
꧁꧁꧁꧁꧁

Upton Hill, Upton St.
Leonards, Gloucester,
GL4 8DE
☎ (0452) 617412
Telex 437334 HATCRT G

17th C Cotswold-stone country house set in 7 acres of gardens and 30 acres of pastures, 600 feet above Gloucester, with panoramic views of Severn Valley and Malvern Hills.
Bedrooms: 24 double & 22 twin.
Bathrooms: 46 private.
Bed & breakfast: £78-£88 single, £98-£118 double.
Half board: £99-£109 daily, £275-£325 weekly.
Lunch available.
Evening meal 7.30pm (l.o. 10pm).
Parking for 70.
Credit: Access, Visa, Diners, Amex.

The Limes
[APPROVED]
Stroud Rd., Brookthorpe, Gloucester, GL4 0UQ
☎ Painswick (0452) 812645
Charming Georgian 3-storey house on the A4173 between Gloucester and Stroud, set in the Cotswold Escarpment.
Bedrooms: 4 single, 1 double & 2 twin, 2 family rooms.
Bathrooms: 3 private, 3 public.
Bed & breakfast: £18-£22 single, £30-£36 double.
Half board: from £24 daily, £105-£144 weekly.
Lunch available.
Evening meal 6pm (l.o. 8pm).
Parking for 10.
Credit: Access, Visa.

Nicki's Hotel & Taverna
105-107 Westgate St., Gloucester, GL1 2PG
☎ (0452) 301359
Restaurant with full a la carte menu, English and Greek food. Refurbished in 1989. Near city centre, cathedral and docks.
Bedrooms: 3 single, 3 double & 4 twin, 4 family rooms.
Bathrooms: 13 private, 2 public; 1 private shower.
Bed & breakfast: £18-£23 single, £35-£40 double.
Half board: £25-£28 daily, £175-£200 weekly.
Lunch available.
Evening meal 5pm (l.o. 11pm).
Credit: Access, Visa, Amex.

Pembury Guest House
9 Pembury Rd., St. Barnabas, Gloucester, GL4 9UE
☎ (0452) 21856
Large, light, airy and interesting old house, full of charm and style. Lawned and wooded grounds.
Bedrooms: 2 single, 4 double & 4 twin, 1 family room.
Bathrooms: 5 private, 1 public; 3 private showers.
Bed & breakfast: £16-£26 single, £28-£37 double.
Evening meal 7.30pm (l.o. 9pm).
Parking for 8.
Credit: Access, Visa.

The Retreat
116 Bristol Rd., Quedgeley, Gloucester, GL2 6NA
☎ (0452) 728296
Large double-fronted detached house.
Bedrooms: 1 single, 1 double & 6 twin, 3 family rooms.
Bathrooms: 1 private, 6 public; 3 private showers.
Bed & breakfast: £16-£26 single, £28-£37 double.
Parking for 10.

Rotherfield House Hotel
5 Horton Rd., Gloucester, GL1 3PX
☎ (0452) 410500
Elegant Victorian detached property in quiet side road location, 1 mile from city centre. Family business. Choice of freshly-cooked dishes.
Bedrooms: 8 single, 1 double & 2 twin, 2 family rooms.
Bathrooms: 8 private, 2 public.
Bed & breakfast: £18.45-£27.75 single, max. £37.75 double.
Half board: £26.90-£36.20 daily, £178.88-£240.73 weekly.
Evening meal 6.45pm (l.o. 7.15pm).
Parking for 9.
Credit: Access, Visa, Diners, Amex.

Twigworth Lodge Hotel & Restaurant
Tewkesbury Rd., Twigworth, Gloucester, GL2 9PG
☎ (0452) 730266 Fax 0452 730099
Grade II listed building, well-known for good food, bar snacks and friendly atmosphere. Heated indoor pool, free car parking.
Bedrooms: 4 single, 19 double & 4 twin, 2 family rooms.
Bathrooms: 29 private, 1 public.
Bed & breakfast: £25-£60 single, £48-£74 double.
Half board: £35-£70 daily.
Lunch available.
Evening meal 7pm (l.o. 9.30pm).
Parking for 40.
Credit: Access, Visa, Diners, Amex.

Hundred House Hotel
[COMMENDED]
Great Witley, Worcester, Worcestershire WR6 6HS
☎ (0299) 896888 Fax 0299 896588
Family owned country hotel, on A443 Worcester to Tenbury road . Only 40 minutes from NEC, yet close to the Welsh border.
Bedrooms: 2 single, 6 double & 8 twin, 2 family rooms.
Bathrooms: 18 private.
Bed & breakfast: £41-£45 single, £56.50-£60 double.
Lunch available.
Evening meal 7pm (l.o. 9.45pm).
Parking for 120.
Credit: Access, Visa.

The symbols are explained on the flap inside the back cover.

5m SE. Winchcombe
Unspoilt village with stone cottages and a green. The Cotswold Farm Park, with a collection of rare breeds, an adventure playground and farm trail, is nearby.

Guiting Guesthouse
[COMMENDED]
Post Office Lane, Guiting Power, Cheltenham, GL54 5TZ
☎ (0451) 850470
Cotswold-stone farmhouse with inglenooks and four-posters. In centre of delightful village, convenient for Straford-upon-Avon, Cheltenham, Oxford, Stow, etc.
Bedrooms: 2 double & 1 twin.
Bathrooms: 3 private; 1 private shower.
Bed & breakfast: £16-£22 single, £32-£40 double.
Half board: £26-£36 daily.
Evening meal 6.45pm.
Parking for 4.

The Hollies
[Listed]
Kenilworth Rd., Hampton-in-Arden, Solihull, B92 0LW
☎ (067 55) 2941 & 2681
On the A452, ideally located for many major attractions of the Midlands, including the National Agricultural Centre, Warwick Castle and Stratford-upon-Avon. Only 5 minutes to National Motorcycle Museum and the National Exhibition Centre.
Bedrooms: 1 single, 2 double & 4 twin.
Bathrooms: 5 private, 1 public.
Bed & breakfast: £18-£20 single, £38-£40 double.
Parking for 10.

Individual proprietors have supplied all details of accommodation. Although we do check for accuracy, we advise you to confirm prices and other information at the time of booking.

The symbols are explained on the flap inside the back cover.

HENLEY-IN-ARDEN

Warwickshire
Map ref 2B1

Old market town which in Tudor times stood in the Forest of Arden. It has many ancient inns, a 15th C Guildhall and parish church. Coughton Court with its Gunpowder Plot connections is nearby.

Ashleigh House M
COMMENDED

Whitley Hill, Henley-in-Arden, Solihull, W. Midlands B95 5DL
☎ (0564) 792315 Fax 0564 794133
Spacious period house in own grounds with fine views, and furnished with antiques. On B4095 Warwick Road. Convenient for Stratford-upon-Avon, Shakespeare country and the National Exhibition Centre.
Bedrooms: 6 double & 4 twin.
Bathrooms: 10 private, 2 public.
Bed & breakfast: £35-£39 single, £45-£49 double.
Lunch available.
Evening meal 7pm (l.o. 9pm).
Parking for 12.
Credit: Access, Visa.

Henley Hotel

Tanworth Lane, Henley-in-Arden, Solihull, B95 5HR
☎ (0564) 794551
In delightful situation on banks of River Alne. Easy access to Stratford-upon-Avon, Warwick, Birmingham and NEC, only 10 minutes on M40/42. Riverside restaurant, function and conference suite.
Bedrooms: 4 single, 16 double & 1 twin, 4 family rooms.
Bathrooms: 25 private.
Bed & breakfast: £30-£35 single, £45-£55 double.
Half board: £37-£45 daily.
Lunch available.
Evening meal 7pm (l.o. 9pm).
Parking for 37.
Credit: Access, Visa, Diners, Amex.

Half board prices shown are per person but in some cases may be based on double/twin occupancy.

HEREFORD

Hereford & Worcester
Map ref 2A1

Agricultural county town, its cathedral containing much Norman work and a large chained library. The city's varied attractions include the Bulmer Railway Centre and several museums including a cider museum.
Tourist Information Centre ☎ (0432) 268430

The Ancient Camp Inn M
COMMENDED

Ruckhall, Eaton Bishop, Hereford, Herefordshire HR2 9QX
☎ Golden Valley (0981) 250449
This inn is on the site of an Iron Age fort dating from the 4th-5th C BC. Spectacular views of the River Wye. Restaurant and bar food a speciality.
Bedrooms: 4 double & 1 twin.
Bathrooms: 5 private.
Bed & breakfast: £35-£45 single, £50-£60 double.
Lunch available.
Evening meal 7pm (l.o. 9.30pm).
Parking for 45.
Credit: Access, Visa.

Aylestone Court Hotel M
COMMENDED

Aylestone Hill, Hereford, Herefordshire
☎ (0432) 341891
Three-storey Georgian building, tastefully renovated throughout. Spacious, comfortable public rooms and en-suite bedrooms. Lawns and gardens. 4 minutes' walk to city centre.
Bedrooms: 1 single, 5 double & 4 twin.
Bathrooms: 9 private.
Bed & breakfast: £20-£38 single, £40-£58 double.
Half board: £32-£50 daily, £195-£250 weekly.
Evening meal 6.30pm (l.o. 8.30pm).
Parking for 15.
Credit: Access, Visa, Amex.

Broughton House Guest House
Listed

32 Ledbury Rd, Hereford, Herefordshire HR1 1ZY
☎ (0432) 277984
Bed and breakfast guesthouse.

Bedrooms: 2 twin.
Bathrooms: 2 public.
Bed & breakfast: from £20 double.
Half board: from £13 daily.
Evening meal 5.30pm.
Parking for 6.

Castle Pool Hotel M
APPROVED

Castle St., Hereford, Herefordshire HR1 2NR
☎ (0432) 356321
The hotel garden is part of the old castle moat. Located minutes from the cathedral, river and sports facilities.
Bedrooms: 9 single, 8 double & 8 twin, 2 family rooms.
Bathrooms: 27 private.
Bed & breakfast: from £49 single, £68-£80 double.
Half board: £50.50-£65.50 daily, £311.50-£399 weekly.
Lunch available.
Evening meal 7.30pm (l.o. 9.30pm).
Parking for 14.
Credit: Access, Visa, Diners, Amex.

Cedar Tree Guest House M

123 Whitecross Rd., Whitecross, Hereford, Herefordshire HR4 0LS
☎ (0432) 267235
Situated on touring route, approximately 1 mile from Hereford, this Georgian family guesthouse has private parking.
Bedrooms: 1 twin, 3 family rooms.
Bathrooms: 1 public.
Bed & breakfast: £15-£16 single, £24-£26 double.
Parking for 10.

Chesley House M
COMMENDED

9 Southbank Rd., Hereford, Herefordshire HR1 2TJ
☎ (0432) 274800
Comfortable, family-run detached Victorian guesthouse, in a quiet part of the city near the centre, bus and train stations. Spacious gardens.
Bedrooms: 1 single, 1 double & 1 twin, 1 family room.
Bathrooms: 4 private, 1 public.
Bed & breakfast: £15-£20 single, £34-£40 double.
Half board: £25-£30 daily, £168-£200 weekly.

Lunch available.
Evening meal 6pm (l.o. 1pm).
Parking for 6.

Collins House Hotel and Restaurant M
COMMENDED

19 St Owens St., Hereford, Herefordshire HR1 2JB
☎ (0432) 272416 Fax 0432 341867
Unique Georgian city hotel. Elegant dining room, with cuisine and service to the highest standard.
Bedrooms: 3 double & 1 twin.
Bathrooms: 4 private.
Bed & breakfast: from £65 single, from £90 double.
Half board: from £70 daily.
Lunch available.
Evening meal 7pm (l.o. 9.30pm).
Parking for 4.
Credit: Access, Visa, Diners, Amex.

Hopbine Hotel M

The Hopbine, Roman Rd., Hereford, Herefordshire HR1 1LE
☎ (0432) 268722
Licensed hotel in extensive grounds. All rooms with colour TV, tea/coffee facilities. 1 mile from town centre, racecourse, golf and leisure centre.
Bedrooms: 3 single, 4 double & 2 twin, 1 family room.
Bathrooms: 3 private, 4 public.
Bed & breakfast: £19-£23 single, £30-£35 double.
Half board: £39-£44 daily.
Evening meal 7pm (l.o. 5pm).
Parking for 16.

Merton Hotel M
COMMENDED

Commercial Rd., Hereford, Herefordshire HR1 2BD
☎ (0432) 265925 Fax 0432 354983
Minotels
Of Georgian origin, this charming town house hotel has been modernised to provide comfortable, well-appointed accommodation with elegant "Governor's" restaurant.
Bedrooms: 8 single, 7 double & 3 twin, 1 family room.
Bathrooms: 19 private.
Bed & breakfast: £46.75-£52.25 single, £72-£78 double.
Half board: £63.75-£69.25 daily, £414-£449 weekly.
Lunch available.

Evening meal 6.30pm (l.o. 9.30pm).
Parking for 6.
Credit: Access, Visa, Diners, Amex.

Munstone House Country Hotel & Vinery Restaurant M
😊😊😊

Munstone, Hereford, Herefordshire HR1 3AH
☎ (0432) 267122
Spacious country house set in over 2 acres with splendid views of surrounding countryside and only 2 miles from Hereford city centre.
Bedrooms: 1 single, 3 double & 1 twin, 1 family room.
Bathrooms: 6 private.
Bed & breakfast: £21-£26 single, £38-£43 double.
Half board: £28.50-£33.50 daily.
Lunch available.
Evening meal 7pm (l.o. 9.15pm).
Parking for 30.
Credit: Access, Visa, C.Bl., Diners, Amex.

The New Priory Hotel M
😊😊😊

Stretton Sugwas, Hereford, Herefordshire HR4 7AR
☎ (0432) 760264
Set in pleasant peaceful surroundings, 2 miles from the centre of Hereford, with real ale and real atmosphere.
Bedrooms: 2 single, 5 double & 2 twin, 1 family room.
Bathrooms: 9 private, 1 public.
Bed & breakfast: £25-£35 single, £45-£55 double.
Half board: £35-£45 daily, £230-£250 weekly.
Lunch available.
Evening meal 7pm (l.o. 9.45pm).
Parking for 60.
Credit: Access, Visa.

Somerville Hotel M
😊😊😊 COMMENDED

Bodenham Rd., Hereford, Herefordshire HR1 2TS
☎ (0432) 273991
Quiet, family-run licensed hotel convenient for city centre and station. Lovely rooms and ample parking. Children welcome.

Bedrooms: 4 single, 4 double & 1 twin, 1 family room.
Bathrooms: 6 private, 3 public.
Bed & breakfast: £24.50-£30.50 single, £42-£50 double.
Half board: £31.75-£40.25 daily, £178-£225 weekly.
Lunch available.
Evening meal 7pm (l.o. 8pm).
Parking for 12.
Credit: Access, Visa, Amex.

HIMLEY

Staffordshire
Map ref 4B3

5m S. Wolverhampton
Village to the south of Dudley whose Himley Hall Park is open to the public. The grounds of the Hall were landscaped by Capability Brown and there are pools with trout and coarse fishing facilities. Dudley Show is held here in August.

Himley House Hotel
Himley, Dudley, W. Midlands DY3 4LD
☎ Wombourne
(0902) 892468 Fax 0902 892604
Striking old building originating from late 17th C. Wealth of period features, set in 3 acres of grounds, surrounded by pleasant countryside and just 15 minutes from Birmingham.
Bedrooms: 6 single, 8 double & 8 twin, 2 family rooms.
Bathrooms: 24 private.
Bed & breakfast: £52 single, £72 double.
Lunch available.
Evening meal 6pm (l.o. 10.30pm).
Parking for 120.
Credit: Access, Visa, Diners, Amex.

Individual proprietors have supplied all details of accommodation. Although we do check for accuracy, we advise you to confirm prices and other information at the time of booking.

HOCKLEY HEATH

W. Midlands
Map ref 4B3

Village near the National Trust property of Packwood House, with its well-known yew garden, and Kenilworth.

Nuthurst Grange Country House Hotel & Restaurant M
😊😊😊 COMMENDED

Nuthurst Grange La., Hockley Heath, B94 5NL
☎ Lapworth (056 478) 3972
Fax 056478 3919
Located close to motorway network in a rural setting of 7.5 acres. Relaxed country house atmosphere with acclaimed restaurant. Bedrooms en-suite with whirlpool baths.
Bedrooms: 5 double & 10 twin.
Bathrooms: 15 private.
Bed & breakfast: from £85 single, £99-£145 double.
Half board: £104.95-£120.50 daily.
Lunch available.
Evening meal 7pm (l.o. 9.30pm).
Parking for 46.
Credit: Access, Visa, Diners, Amex.

IRONBRIDGE

Shropshire
Map ref 4A3

Small town on the Severn where the Industrial Revolution began. It has the world's first iron bridge built in 1774. The Ironbridge Gorge Museum contains several industrial sites and museums spread over 2 miles and is exceptionally interesting.
Tourist Information Centre ☎ (0952) 432166

Bridge House M
😊😊 COMMENDED

Buildwas, Telford, TF8 7BN
☎ Ironbridge (0952) 432105
Half-timbered country residence on the banks of the River Severn, immediately opposite Buildwas Abbey. On the B3480, 2 miles from Ironbridge. Many interesting features and friendly atmosphere.

Bedrooms: 2 double & 1 twin, 1 family room.
Bathrooms: 1 private, 2 public; 1 private shower.
Bed & breakfast: £17-£19 single, £42-£45 double.
Parking for 12.

Broseley Guest House M
😊😊😊

The Square, Broseley, TF12 5EW
☎ Telford (0952) 882043
Well-appointed spacious accommodation in the centre of Broseley, close to Ironbridge and convenient for Telford business centres.
Bedrooms: 1 single, 3 double & 2 twin.
Bathrooms: 6 private.
Bed & breakfast: £24-£32 single, £44-£48 double.
Evening meal (l.o. 7pm).
Credit: Access, Visa.

Buckatree Hall Hotel M
😊😊😊😊

The Wrekin, Wellington, Telford, TF6 5AL
☎ (0952) 641821 Telex 35701 BCKTRE Fax 0952 47540
CR Best Western
Modern hotel nestling in woodlands on the slopes of the Wrekin Hill. Most rooms have balconies overlooking either the lake or hotel gardens. Satellite TV. 1 mile from exit 7 of the M54, 3 miles from Ironbridge.
Bedrooms: 6 single, 38 double & 18 twin, 2 family rooms.
Bathrooms: 64 private.
Bed & breakfast: from £69 single, from £79 double.
Half board: from £79 daily.
Lunch available.
Evening meal 7.30pm (l.o. 10pm).
Parking for 120.
Credit: Access, Visa, Diners, Amex.

Cradle Meadow Hotel M
😊😊😊

Prince St., Madeley, Telford, TF7 4EB
☎ (0952) 587753
Situated on the marked tourist route for Ironbridge museums, 15 minutes' walk to Blists Hill.
Bedrooms: 1 double & 4 twin, 2 family rooms.
Bathrooms: 7 private.
Bed & breakfast: £20-£25 single, £32-£37 double.
Continued ▶

IRONBRIDGE
Continued

Half board: £27.50-£32.50 daily, £180-£205 weekly.
Lunch available.
Evening meal 5pm (l.o. 6.45pm).
Parking for 6.
Credit: Access, Visa.

ॐ M ⬤ ℂ ▢ ♥ 🅿 🚗
⊞ ✗ 🅩 SP

Hundred House Hotel M
Bridgnorth Rd., A442., Norton, Shifnal, TF11 9EE
☎ (095 271) 353 Fax 095 271 355
Character, charm and a warm atmosphere in a family-run country inn. Patchwork theme bedrooms with antique furniture and all facilities. On the A442 at Norton between Bridgnorth and Ironbridge.
Bedrooms: 1 single, 2 double & 1 twin, 5 family rooms.
Bathrooms: 9 private.
Bed & breakfast: £59-£69 single, £69-£79 double.
Half board: £43-£70 daily.
Lunch available.
Evening meal 6pm (l.o. 10pm).
Parking for 30.
Credit: Access, Visa, Amex.

ॐ 🅟 ℂ ▢ ♥ 🅿 V ▪ ▱
🍴 ♦ ⌖ ✿ 🅩 ⚄ SP 🎭 ⊤

The Library House M
☖☖ COMMENDED
11 Severn Bank, Ironbridge, Telford, TF8 7AN
☎ (0952) 432299
Fascinating 18th C house near the Ironbridge where you are assured of a friendly, personal welcome, comfortable rooms and home cooking.
Bedrooms: 2 double, 1 family room.
Bathrooms: 3 private.
Bed & breakfast: £25-£28 single, £40-£42 double.
Half board: £31-£32 daily.
Evening meal 7pm.

ॐ ▢ 🅿 ⓦ V ⅍ 🚗 📺
⊞ ▪ 🅰 OAP SP 🎭

Severn Lodge M
☖☖ HIGHLY COMMENDED
New Rd., Ironbridge, Telford, TF8 7AX
☎ (0952) 432148
Georgian house set in a lovely garden and situated a few yards from the famous Ironbridge and River Severn.
Bedrooms: 2 double & 1 twin.
Bathrooms: 3 private.
Bed & breakfast: from £40 double.
Parking for 22.

ॐ ▢ 🅿 ⓦ V ⅍ 🚗 📺
⊞ ✿ ✗ 🅩 🎭

KENILWORTH
Warwickshire
Map ref 4B3

The main feature of the town is the ruined 12th C castle. It has many royal associations but was damaged by Cromwell. A good base for visiting Coventry, Leamington Spa and Warwick.
Tourist Information Centre ☎ (0926) 52595

Abbey Guest House M
☖☖ APPROVED
41 Station Road, Kenilworth, CV8 1JD
☎ (0926) 512707
Beautiful Victorian house full of charm and character. Tastefully presented, cosy bedrooms, all with colour TV.
Bedrooms: 1 single, 2 double & 3 twin, 1 family room.
Bathrooms: 2 private, 1 public; 1 private shower.
Bed & breakfast: £19.50 single, £34-£40 double.
Half board: £25-£28 daily.
Evening meal 7pm (l.o. 2pm).
Parking for 3.

ॐ ▢ ♥ 🅿 V 🚗 📺 ⊞ 🅰
✗ 🅩

Chesford Grange Hotel & Conference Centre M
☖☖☖
Chesford Bridge, Kenilworth, CV8 2LD
☎ (0926) 59331 Telex 311918
Set in 17 acres of grounds on the River Avon. Restaurant open every day except Saturday lunch.
Bedrooms: 1 single, 79 double & 47 twin, 3 family rooms.
Bathrooms: 130 private.
Bed & breakfast: £40-£82.50 single, £50-£135 double.
Half board: £35-£97.50 daily.
Lunch available.
Evening meal 7.15pm (l.o. 10.15pm).
Parking for 500.
Credit: Access, Visa, C.Bl., Diners, Amex.

ॐ 🅿 ℂ ▢ ♥ 🅿 🅰 V 🚗
◑ ⊞ 🅰 🍴 ♦ ✿ ⚄ SP
⊤

Clarendon House Hotel M
☖☖☖ APPROVED
Old High St., Kenilworth, CV8 1LZ
☎ (0926) 57668 Telex 311240
Hotel G
Ⓡ Inter

Unique and historic inn dating from 1430 and still supported by the old oak tree around which the former "Castle Tavern" was built. Own 16th C well. Antique brass, copper, silver, china and maps.
Bedrooms: 16 single, 9 double & 5 twin, 1 family room.
Bathrooms: 31 private.
Bed & breakfast: from £60 single, £80-£85 double.
Half board: from £72.50 daily.
Lunch available.
Evening meal 7pm (l.o. 9.30pm).
Parking for 34.
Credit: Access, Visa.

ॐ 🅿 🅟 ℂ ▢ ♥ 🅿 V
🚗 ⊞ 🅰 🍴 🅩 SP 🎭 ⊤

The Cottage Inn M
☖☖ APPROVED
36 Stoneleigh Rd., Kenilworth, CV8 2GD
☎ (0926) 53900
Traditional English pub located centrally for Warwick, Leamington, Stratford-upon-Avon, Coventry, Birmingham Airport, the National Exhibition Centre and the Royal Agricultural Showground at Stoneleigh. Bunkers Bistro now open.
Bedrooms: 2 double & 2 twin.
Bathrooms: 4 private.
Bed & breakfast: from £29 single, from £40 double.
Lunch available.
Evening meal 6pm (l.o. 9.30pm).
Parking for 12.
Credit: Access, Visa.

◑ ▢ ♥ 🅿 V 🚗 🅰 🍴 ∪
✗ 🅩 SP ⊤

Enderley Guest House M
☖☖ APPROVED
20 Queens Rd., Kenilworth, CV8 1JQ
☎ (0926) 55388
Family-run guesthouse, quietly situated near town centre and convenient for Warwick, Stratford-upon-Avon, Stoneleigh, Warwick University and the National Exhibition Centre.
Bedrooms: 1 single, 1 double & 2 twin, 1 family room.
Bathrooms: 5 private.
Bed & breakfast: £23-£29 single, £34-£40 double.
Parking for 2.

ॐ ♥ 🅿 🚗 🚗 📺 ⊞ 🅰 ✗
🅩

Ferndale Guest House M
☖☖
45 Priory Rd., Kenilworth, CV8 1LL
☎ (0926) 53214

Delightfully modernised Victorian house in a tree-lined avenue. Attractive bedrooms with colour TV. Ideal for National Exhibition Centre and the National Agricultural Centre at Stoneleigh.
Bedrooms: 2 single, 2 double & 2 twin, 1 family room.
Bathrooms: 8 private.
Bed & breakfast: £17-£18 single, £34-£36 double.
Parking for 8.

ॐ 🅿 ▢ ♥ 🚗 📺 ⊞ 🅰 ⅄
🅩

Hollyhurst Guest House M
☖☖ COMMENDED
47 Priory Rd., Kenilworth, CV8 1LL
☎ (0926) 53882
Comfortable family-run guesthouse in quiet location close to town centre, ideally situated for easy access to National Showground and tourist areas of Stratford-upon-Avon, Warwick and Coventry.
Bedrooms: 2 single, 1 double & 3 twin, 2 family rooms.
Bathrooms: 3 private, 2 public.
Bed & breakfast: £15-£18 single, £28-£32 double.
Half board: £18.50-£28.50 daily, £115-£185 weekly.
Lunch available.
Evening meal 6.45pm (l.o. 9.30pm).
Parking for 9.

ॐ 🅟 ▢ 🚗 V ⅄ 🚗 📺
🅰 🅩 OAP

Honiley Court Hotel
☖☖☖
Honiley, Kenilworth, CV8 1NP
☎ (0926) 484234
Telex 311306 Fax 0926 484474
Ⓡ Lansbury
Period-style hotel built around an original 16th C inn. Tastefully furnished with every modern comfort.
Bedrooms: 1 single, 9 double & 53 twin.
Bathrooms: 63 private.
Bed & breakfast: £20-£70 single, £40-£82 double.
Half board: £32-£85 daily.
Lunch available.
Evening meal 7pm (l.o. 10pm).
Parking for 110.
Credit: Access, Visa, Diners, Amex.

ॐ 🅿 ℂ ▢ ♥ 🅿 V ⅄
🚗 ◑ 🄴 ⊞ 🅰 🍴 ♦ ✗ SP
🎭 ⊤

KIDDERMINSTER

Hereford & Worcester
Map ref 4B3

The town is the centre for carpet manufacturing. It has a medieval church with good monuments and a statue of Sir Rowland Hill, a native of the town and founder of the penny post. West Midlands Safari Park is nearby.

Brockencote Hall M
HIGHLY COMMENDED

Chaddesley Corbett, Kidderminster, Worcestershire DY10 4PY
☎ (0562) 777876 Fax 0562 777872
Country house hotel set in 70 acres of parkland, offering traditional French cooking in an elegant and relaxed atmosphere.
Bedrooms: 6 double & 2 twin.
Bathrooms: 8 private.
Bed & breakfast: £60-£95 single, £90-£120 double.
Lunch available.
Evening meal 7.30pm (l.o. 9.30pm).
Parking for 50.
Credit: Access, Visa, Diners, Amex.

Cedars Hotel M
APPROVED

Mason Road, Kidderminster, Worcestershire DY11 6AL
☎ (0562) 515595 Fax 0562 751103
CR Minotels
Charming conversion of a Georgian building close to the River Severn, Severn Valley Railway and Worcestershire countryside. 15 minutes from the M5.
Bedrooms: 1 single, 7 double & 7 twin, 5 family rooms.
Bathrooms: 20 private.
Bed & breakfast: £34.50-£50 single, £47-£60.80 double.
Half board: £56-£63 daily.
Parking for 21.
Credit: Access, Visa, Diners, Amex.

Gainsborough House Hotel M

Bewdley Hill, Kidderminster, Worcestershire DY11 6BS
☎ (0562) 820041
Telex 333058
CR Consort

Traditional hotel close to River Severn. The Severn Valley Railway, West Midlands Safari Park and Worcestershire countryside are all close at hand. 15 minutes from M5.
Bedrooms: 1 single, 12 double & 24 twin, 5 family rooms.
Bathrooms: 42 private.
Bed & breakfast: £60-£71 single, £77-£90 double.
Lunch available.
Evening meal 7pm (l.o. 10pm).
Parking for 127.
Credit: Access, Visa, Diners, Amex.

The Granary Hotel and Restaurant M
COMMENDED

Shenstone, Kidderminster, Worcestershire DY10 4BS
☎ Chaddesley Corbett (0562) 777535
Family-owned restaurant and hotel renowned for food. Quiet rural location off A450 near Kidderminster. Close to motorways and railway stations.
Bedrooms: 5 double & 13 twin.
Bathrooms: 18 private.
Bed & breakfast: £35-£48 single, £40-£55 double.
Half board: £43-£60 daily.
Lunch available.
Evening meal 6.30pm (l.o. 9.30pm).
Parking for 60.
Credit: Access, Visa, C.Bl., Diners, Amex.

Individual proprietors have supplied all details of accommodation. Although we do check for accuracy, we advise you to confirm prices and other information at the time of booking.

Map references apply to the colour maps towards the end of this guide.

KINGTON

Hereford & Worcester
Map ref 2A1

Village on the Welsh border, with Offa's Dyke close by. The Hergest Croft Gardens are well-known for their beautiful displays of azaleas and rhododendrons during May and June.

Burton Hotel M
APPROVED

Mill St., Kington, Herefordshire HR5 3BQ
☎ (0544) 230323
Attractively modernised, authentic coaching inn, in centre of small market town near Welsh border and Offa's Dyke footpath.
Bedrooms: 2 single, 4 double & 5 twin, 4 family rooms.
Bathrooms: 15 private.
Bed & breakfast: from £40 single, from £53 double.
Half board: £40.50-£54 daily, £255.50-£346.50 weekly.
Lunch available.
Evening meal 7.30pm (l.o. 9.30pm).
Parking for 47.
Credit: Access, Visa, Diners, Amex.

KNOWLE

W. Midlands
Map ref 4B3

Knowle lies on the outskirts of Solihull and although there is much modern building, the centre still has some old buildings, including the medieval Chester House, which is now a library. Kenilworth Castle and Packwood House (National Trust) are nearby.

Ivy House
APPROVED

Warwick Rd., Heronfield, Knowle, Solihull, B93 0EB
☎ (0564) 770247
Set in 6 acres of its own land overlooking fields. Approximately 5 miles from the NEC and airport, 20 minutes from the ICC.
Bedrooms: 4 single, 2 double & 2 twin.
Bathrooms: 8 private.
Bed & breakfast: £18-£25 single, £36-£40 double.
Parking for 20.

LEAMINGTON SPA

Warwickshire
Map ref 4B3

18th C spa town with many fine Georgian and Regency houses. Tea can be taken in the 19th C Pump Room. The attractive Jephson Gardens are laid out alongside the river and there is a museum and art gallery.
Tourist Information Centre ☎ *(0926) 311470*

Adams Hotel

22 Avenue Rd., Leamington Spa, CV31 3PQ
☎ (0926) 450742 & 422758
Fax (0926) 313110
Privately owned 17th C listed hotel, with modern bedrooms, standing back from the road in a typical Regency setting.
Bedrooms: 6 single, 4 double & 4 twin.
Bathrooms: 14 private.
Bed & breakfast: £39.60-£50 single, £58.50-£62 double.
Half board: £57.60-£68 daily.
Evening meal 6pm (l.o. 8pm).
Parking for 10.
Credit: Access, Visa, Diners, Amex.

Beech Lodge Hotel M

28 Warwick New Rd., Leamington Spa, CV32 5JJ
☎ (0926) 422227
Elegant Regency building with spacious lounge, dining room and residents' bar. All bedrooms with colour TV, radio, telephone and tea/coffee-making facilities.
Bedrooms: 7 single, 4 double & 1 twin.
Bathrooms: 9 private, 2 public; 1 private shower.
Bed & breakfast: £28-£39 single, £44-£55 double.
Half board: £33-£47 daily, £240-£343 weekly.
Lunch available.
Evening meal 7pm (l.o. 9pm).
Parking for 14.
Credit: Access, Visa, Amex.

Half board prices shown are per person but in some cases may be based on double/twin occupancy.

Continued

Blackdown Hotel and Licensed Restaurant M
⌒⌒⌒

Sandy La., Leamington Spa,
CV32 6RD
☎ (0926) 424761 & 421998
Fax 0926 421998
Jacobean-style house built of local stone about 1873, standing in 9 acres of landscaped gardens. Convenient for National Exhibition Centre and National Agricultural Centre.
Bedrooms: 1 single, 2 double & 8 twin.
Bathrooms: 11 private.
Bed & breakfast: £69 single, £85 double.
Half board: from £85 daily, from £117 weekly.
Lunch available.
Evening meal 7.30pm (l.o. 10pm).
Parking for 200.
Credit: Access, Visa, Diners, Amex.

Buckland Lodge Hotel M
⌒⌒

35 Avenue Rd., Leamington Spa, CV31 3PG
☎ (0926) 423843
Central for rail and bus depots, shops, parks and the town's beautiful gardens.
Bedrooms: 3 single, 2 double & 3 twin, 2 family rooms.
Bathrooms: 6 private, 2 public.
Bed & breakfast: £18-£35 single, £34-£45 double.
Half board: £28-£45 daily.
Evening meal 6.30pm (l.o. 2.30pm).
Parking for 12.
Credit: Access, Visa, Diners, Amex.

Flowerdale House Hotel M
⌒⌒⌒

58 Warwick New Rd., Leamington Spa, CV32 6AA
☎ (0926) 426002
Tastefully modernised Victorian house with conservatory, overlooking a small garden. All bedrooms with private facilities and colour TV. Reduced rates for more than 1 night.

Bedrooms: 1 single, 2 double & 3 twin.
Bathrooms: 6 private.
Bed & breakfast: £19-£24 single, £33-£39 double.
Evening meal 7pm (l.o. 9pm).
Parking for 6.
Credit: Access, Visa.

Holiday Inn Garden Court M
⌒⌒⌒

Olympus Avenue, Tachbrook Park, Leamington Spa, CV34 6RJ
☎ (0926) 881313 & (0926) 425522 Fax 0926 881322
Ⓡ Holiday Inn
Country setting, offering a high standard of bedroom accommodation together with a comfortable and relaxed atmosphere. Beautiful views of Warwick Castle.
Bedrooms: 86 double & 12 twin, 2 family rooms.
Bathrooms: 100 private.
Bed & breakfast: £42.50-£63.75 single, £49.50-£71 double.
Half board: £55.50-£76.75 daily.
Lunch available.
Evening meal 6.30pm (l.o. 10pm).
Parking for 108.
Credit: Access, Visa, C.Bl., Diners, Amex.

Regent Hotel M
⌒⌒⌒ APPROVED

The Parade, Leamington Spa, CV32 4AX
☎ Leamington Spa (0926) 427231 Telex 311715
Ⓡ Best Western
Elegant Regency hotel, featured in the 'Guinness Book of Records' as the world's largest hotel in 1819. Old fashioned service proliferates. We clean shoes.
Bedrooms: 24 single, 14 double & 36 twin, 6 family rooms.
Bathrooms: 80 private.
Bed & breakfast: £61.50-£82 single, £84.50-£94.50 double.
Half board: from £54.25 daily.
Lunch available.
Evening meal 6.45pm (l.o. 10.45pm).
Parking for 100.
Credit: Access, Visa, Diners, Amex.

York House Hotel
⌒⌒⌒ COMMENDED

9 York Rd., Leamington Spa, CV31 3PR
☎ (0926) 424671
Victorian house overlooking River Leam and Royal Pump Room Gardens, over 100 years old and having many Victorian features.
Bedrooms: 2 single, 4 twin, 2 family rooms.
Bathrooms: 4 private, 1 public.
Bed & breakfast: £17-£38.50 single, £32-£50.50 double.
Half board: £27.50-£50.50 daily, £182.50-£343.50 weekly.
Evening meal 6.30pm (l.o. 7.30pm).
Parking for 3.
Credit: Access, Visa, Amex.

Gloucestershire
Map ref 2B1

Attractive village on the River Thames and a popular spot for boating. It has a number of fine Georgian houses and a 15th C church. Nearby is Kelmscott Manor, with its William Morris furnishings, and 18th C Buscot House (National Trust).

Red Lion
⌒

High St., Lechlade, GL7 3AD
☎ (0367) 52373
5 minutes from Thames fishing. Boating facilities close by. Popular restaurant with comprehensive menu including grills, foreign food and fish dishes, all at reasonable prices.
Bedrooms: 1 twin, 1 family room.
Bathrooms: 1 public.
Bed & breakfast: £22-£25 single, £29-£39 double.
Lunch available.
Evening meal 6.30pm (l.o. 9.30pm).
Parking for 20.

National Crown ratings were correct at the time of going to press but are subject to change. Please check at the time of booking.

Hereford & Worcester
Map ref 2B1

Town with cobbled streets and many black and white timbered houses, including the 17th C market house and old inns. Nearby is Eastnor Castle with an interesting collection of tapestries and armour.
Tourist Information Centre ☎ *(0531) 6147*

The Barn House M
⌒⌒ COMMENDED

New St., Ledbury, Herefordshire HR8 2DX
☎ (0531) 2825
17th C house of great character in the centre of the old market town of Ledbury, close to the Malverns.
Bedrooms: 2 double & 1 twin.
Bathrooms: 1 private, 1 public.
Bed & breakfast: £34-£41 double.
Parking for 4.
Open March-December.

Feathers Hotel M
⌒⌒⌒⌒ COMMENDED

High St., Ledbury, Herefordshire HR8 1DS
☎ (0531) 2600 & 5266
Fax (0531) 2001
Traditional Elizabethan coaching inn, situated in the centre of a small market town nestling under the Malvern Hills.
Bedrooms: 4 double & 4 twin, 3 family rooms.
Bathrooms: 11 private.
Bed & breakfast: £59.50-£69.50 single, £79.50-£100 double.
Half board: £74.50-£85.50 daily.
Lunch available.
Evening meal 6.30pm (l.o. 9.30pm).
Parking for 40.
Credit: Access, Visa, Diners, Amex.

The Royal Oak Hotel M
⌒⌒

The Southend, Ledbury, Herefordshire HR8 2EY
☎ (0531) 2110
Fax (0531) 4761

Family-owned historic coaching inn/hotel (15th C) with spacious bedrooms. Free house, bar meals and restaurant (14th C). At the foot of the Malvern Hills.
Bedrooms: 8 single, 3 double & 4 twin, 2 family rooms.
Bathrooms: 7 private,
1 public.
Bed & breakfast: £18.75-£29.75 single, £39.50 double.
Half board: from £29.50 daily.
Lunch available.
Evening meal 6.45pm (l.o. 9pm).
Parking for 28.
Credit: Access, Visa.

LEEK

Staffordshire
Map ref 4B2

Old silk and textile town, with some interesting buildings and a number of inns dating from the 17th C. Its art gallery has displays of embroidery. Brindley Mill, designed by James Brindley, has been restored as a museum.
Tourist Information Centre ☎ *(0538) 381000*

Three Horseshoes Inn ♨
🛏🛏 APPROVED
Blackshaw Moor, Leek, ST13 8TW
☎ Blackshaw (053 834) 296
Log fire, slate floor, oak and pine beams, good food and wines. Cottage-style rooms. Convenient for Peak District National Park and Alton Towers.
Bedrooms: 1 single, 3 double & 1 twin, 1 family room.
Bathrooms: 6 private,
2 public.
Bed & breakfast: £40-£55 single, £48-£60 double.
Half board: £35-£45 daily, £256-£275 weekly.
Lunch available.
Evening meal 7pm (l.o. 9.30pm).
Parking for 100.
Credit: Access, Visa, Diners, Amex.

Half board prices shown are per person but in some cases may be based on double/twin occupancy.

LEINTWARDINE

Hereford & Worcester
Map ref 4A3

7m W. Ludlow
Attractive border village where the Rivers Teme and Clun meet. It has some black and white cottages, old inns and an impressive church. It is near Hopton Castle and the beautiful scenery around Clun.

Lower House ♨
🛏🛏
Adforton, Leintwardine, Craven Arms, Shropshire SY7 0NF
☎ Wigmore (056 886) 223
Well-furnished 16th C former farmhouse with exposed beams. Open fires and feature inglenook in dining room. Home cooking.
Bedrooms: 2 double & 2 twin.
Bathrooms: 4 private.
Bed & breakfast: £20-£24 single, £40-£48 double.
Half board: £29-£35 daily, £195-£220 weekly.
Evening meal 7pm (l.o. 7.30pm).
Parking for 10.
Open March-October.

LEOMINSTER

Hereford & Worcester
Map ref 2A1

The town owed its prosperity to wool and has many interesting buildings, notably the timber-framed Grange Court, a former town hall. The impressive Norman priory church has 3 naves and a ducking stool. Berrington Hall (National Trust) is nearby.
Tourist Information Centre ☎ *(0568) 6460*

Highfield ♨
🛏🛏 COMMENDED
Ivington Rd., Newtown, Leominster, Herefordshire HR6 8QD
☎ (0568) 613216
Elegant Edwardian house in large garden, outside town. Cosy fire in TV lounge. Comfortable and peaceful. Home cooking.
Bedrooms: 1 double & 2 twin.
Bathrooms: 1 private,
2 public.
Bed & breakfast: £36-£39 double.

Half board: £27-£28.50 daily, £182-£192.50 weekly.
Lunch available.
Evening meal 6.30pm (l.o. 4pm).
Parking for 3.

Royal Oak Hotel ♨
🛏🛏 APPROVED
South St., Leominster, Herefordshire HR6 8JA
☎ (0568) 612610 Fax 0568 2710
CR Minotels
Town-centre Georgian coaching house dating from 1723, with log fires in winter, real ales and a reputation for home-made food.
Bedrooms: 2 single, 9 double & 5 twin, 2 family rooms.
Bathrooms: 18 private.
Bed & breakfast: £28.50 single, £45 double.
Lunch available.
Evening meal 6.30pm (l.o. 9.30pm).
Parking for 24.
Credit: Access, Visa, Diners, Amex.

Talbot Hotel ♨
🛏🛏🛏
West St., Leominster, Herefordshire HR6 8EP
☎ (0568) 616347 Telex 35332 ATTN. TALBOT
CR Best Western
15th C black and white coaching inn specialising in the preparation of menus from local produce.
Bedrooms: 3 single, 9 double & 10 twin, 3 family rooms.
Bathrooms: 23 private.
Bed & breakfast: £47-£54 single, £78-£92 double.
Lunch available.
Evening meal 7pm (l.o. 9.30pm).
Parking for 25.
Credit: Access, Visa, Diners, Amex.

Withenfield ♨
🛏🛏🛏 HIGHLY COMMENDED
South Street, Leominster, Herefordshire HR6 8JN
☎ (0568) 612011
Elegantly furnished Georgian house with modern facilities and conservatory overlooking garden. Conveniently situated for touring countryside, castles, black and white villages.
Bedrooms: 1 single, 2 double & 1 twin.
Bathrooms: 4 private.

Bed & breakfast: from £39 single, £56-£62 double.
Half board: £45.50-£56.50 daily.
Lunch available.
Evening meal 6.30pm.
Parking for 5.
Credit: Access, Visa.

LICHFIELD

Staffordshire
Map ref 4B3

Lichfield is Dr. Samuel Johnson's birthplace and commemorates him with a museum and statue. The 13th C cathedral has 3 spires and the west front is full of statues. There is a regimental museum and Heritage Centre.
Tourist Information Centre ☎ *(0543) 252109*

Fradley Arms Hotel ♨
🛏🛏 APPROVED
Rykneld St., Fradley, Nr. Lichfield, WS13 8RD
☎ Burton upon Trent (0283) 790186 & 790473 Fax (0283) 791464
A small, family-run, 18th C Georgian hotel with oak beams and log fires. Ideal for visiting Alton Towers, Lichfield Cathedral, Birmingham and West Midlands, Potteries, National Exhibition Centre.
Bedrooms: 2 single, 3 double & 1 twin, 1 family room.
Bathrooms: 6 private.
Bed & breakfast: from £38 single, from £52 double.
Lunch available.
Evening meal 7pm (l.o. 9.30pm).
Parking for 200.
Credit: Access, Visa, Diners, Amex.

Little Barrow Hotel ♨
🛏🛏🛏 COMMENDED
Beacon St., Lichfield, WS13 7AR
☎ (0543) 414500 Fax 0543 415734
Modern hotel offering old world charm, situated near Lichfield's famous cathedral and Dr. Johnson's house.
Bedrooms: 2 single, 6 double & 16 twin.
Bathrooms: 24 private.
Bed & breakfast: from £60 single, from £70 double.
Half board: from £70.50 daily.

Continued ▶

LICHFIELD
Continued

Lunch available.
Evening meal 7pm (l.o. 9.30pm).
Parking for 70.
Credit: Access, Visa, Diners, Amex.

LUDLOW

Shropshire
Map ref 4A3

Outstandingly interesting border town with a magnificent castle high above the River Teme, 2 half-timbered old inns and an impressive 15th C church. The Reader's House, with its 3-storey Jacobean porch, should also be seen.
Tourist Information Centre ☎ *(0584) 875053*

Cecil Guest House ⚑
😑😑 APPROVED

Sheet Rd., Ludlow, SY8 1LR
☎ (0584) 872442
Quietly located modern guesthouse under personal supervision in historic Ludlow.
Bedrooms: 3 single, 1 double & 5 twin, 1 family room.
Bathrooms: 3 private, 2 public.
Bed & breakfast: £15.75-£18.50 single, £31.50-£37 double.
Half board: £24.50-£27.25 daily, £158-£178 weekly.
Evening meal 7pm (l.o. 9am).
Parking for 11.
Credit: Access, Visa, Amex.

Cliffe Hotel ⚑
😑😑😑 APPROVED

Dinham, Ludlow, SY8 2JE
☎ (0584) 872063
Hotel facing Ludlow Castle next to the River Teme, with a panoramic view of the Shropshire countryside.
Bedrooms: 3 single, 2 double & 4 twin, 1 family room.
Bathrooms: 7 private, 1 public.
Bed & breakfast: from £25 single, from £42 double.
Half board: £28-£32 daily.
Lunch available.
Evening meal 7pm (l.o. 9.30pm).
Parking for 50.
Credit: Access, Visa, Amex.

Dinham Hall Hotel, By the Castle ⚑
😑😑😑😑

Ludlow, SY8 1EJ
☎ (0584) 876464 Fax 0584 876019
Splendid Georgian residence situated opposite Ludlow Castle and with open views of the countryside from all rooms. 2 minutes from town centre.
Bedrooms: 3 single, 4 double & 5 twin, 2 family rooms.
Bathrooms: 14 private.
Bed & breakfast: £49.50-£60.50 single, £76-£97.50 double.
Half board: £67 daily.
Lunch available.
Evening meal 7.30pm (l.o. 9.30pm).
Parking for 14.
Credit: Access, Visa, Diners, Amex.

Dinham Weir Hotel and Restaurant ⚑
😑😑😑 COMMENDED

Dinham Bridge, Ludlow, SY8 1EH
☎ (0584) 874431
Beautifully situated on the banks of River Teme. All bedrooms with riverside views. Intimate candelit restaurant.
Bedrooms: 4 double & 2 twin.
Bathrooms: 6 private.
Bed & breakfast: £40-£45 single, £55-£60 double.
Half board: £40-£45 daily, £248-£272 weekly.
Lunch available.
Evening meal 7pm (l.o. 8.30pm).
Parking for 8.
Credit: Access, Visa, Diners, Amex.

The Feathers at Ludlow ⚑
😑😑😑😑 COMMENDED

Bull Ring, Ludlow, SY8 1AA
☎ (0584) 875261 Fax 0584 876030
Historic inn with Jacobean interior and exterior, sited within the medieval walls of Ludlow, historic capital of the English/Welsh Marches.
Bedrooms: 11 single, 14 double & 12 twin, 3 family rooms.
Bathrooms: 40 private.
Bed & breakfast: £62-£75 single, £88-£104 double.
Half board: £300-£400 weekly.
Lunch available.

Evening meal 7pm (l.o. 9pm).
Parking for 40.
Credit: Access, Visa, C.Bl., Diners, Amex.

28 Lower Broad St. ⚑
😑😑😑 COMMENDED

Ludlow, SY8 1PQ
☎ (0584) 876996
Listed town house of charm and character. Secluded walled garden. Emphasis on good food and wines, warm hospitality and quiet relaxed atmosphere.
Bedrooms: 1 double & 1 twin.
Bathrooms: 2 private.
Bed & breakfast: £23-£26 single, £40-£46 double.
Half board: £32-£38 daily, £195-£250 weekly.
Evening meal 7.30pm (l.o. 8.30pm).
Credit: Access, Visa.

Number Eleven ⚑
😑😑😑 COMMENDED

Dinham, Ludlow, SY8 1EJ
☎ (0584) 878584
Fine Georgian townhouse in the centre of Ludlow overlooking the castle and gardens, offering good quality accommodation in elegant surroundings.
Bedrooms: 1 double & 4 twin.
Bathrooms: 5 private.
Bed & breakfast: £22-£25 single, £44-£56 double.
Half board: £32.50-£38.50 daily.
Evening meal 7.30pm (l.o. 7.30pm).
Parking for 2.
Credit: Access, Visa.

Overton Grange Hotel ⚑
😑😑😑😑 COMMENDED

Ludlow, SY8 4AD
☎ (0584) 873500
A country house hotel in its own grounds, with commanding views over the Shropshire countryside.
Bedrooms: 2 single, 8 double & 4 twin, 2 family rooms.
Bathrooms: 14 private, 3 public.
Bed & breakfast: £52-£55 single, £72-£95 double.
Half board: £44-£65 daily, £304-£325 weekly.
Lunch available.
Evening meal 7pm (l.o. 9.30pm).

Parking for 80.
Credit: Access, Visa, Diners, Amex.

MALVERN

Hereford & Worcester
Map ref 2B1

Spa town in Victorian times, its water is today bottled and sold worldwide. 6 resorts, set on the slopes of the Hills, form part of Malvern. Great Malvern Priory has splendid 15th C windows. It is an excellent walking centre with fine views from the Worcestershire Beacon.
Tourist Information Centre ☎ *(0684) 892289*

Colwall Park Hotel ⚑
😑😑😑😑 COMMENDED

Colwall, Malvern, Worcestershire WR13 6QG
☎ Colwall (0684) 40206
Telex 335626
Ⓒ Inter
Family-run hotel with new bedrooms. English menus. Quiet gardens leading to Malvern Hills. Ideal for walking, touring and exploring.
Bedrooms: 4 single, 8 double & 6 twin, 2 family rooms.
Bathrooms: 20 private.
Bed & breakfast: £52.50-£56.50 single, £70 double.
Half board: £68-£74 daily, £297.50-£320 weekly.
Lunch available.
Evening meal 7.30pm (l.o. 9pm).
Parking for 40.
Credit: Access, Visa, Amex.

Cottage in the Wood Hotel ⚑
😑😑😑😑 COMMENDED

Holywell Rd., Malvern Wells, Malvern, Worcestershire WR14 4LG
☎ (0684) 573487 Fax 0684 560662
Ⓒ Consort
Country house in 7 acres high on the Malvern Hills, with stunning 30-mile views. All bedrooms en-suite. Half board prices basd on minium 2 night stay.
Bedrooms: 2 single, 14 double & 4 twin.
Bathrooms: 20 private, 1 public.
Bed & breakfast: £62 single, £85-£120 double.
Half board: £40-£70 daily.
Lunch available.

Evening meal 7pm (l.o. 9pm).
Parking for 40.
Credit: Access, Visa, Amex.
🌊 ⛾ 🛂 📞 ⊡ 🖵 ♥ ▥ Ⅴ
🗂 🎞 ♨ 🍴 ♖ ✿ 🗡 ↘ SP
🅰 🆃

Deacon's Hotel and Restaurant
😊😊😊

34 Worcester Rd., Malvern,
Worcestershire WR14 4AA
☎ (0684) 566990 & 575323
*Attractive Georgian building
with magnificent views,
situated close to shops, railway
station and the Malvern Hills.*
Bedrooms: 2 single, 3 double
& 2 twin, 2 family rooms.
Bathrooms: 9 private,
1 public.
Bed & breakfast: £28–£30
single, £40–£47.50 double.
Evening meal 6.30pm (l.o.
7pm).
Parking for 10.
Credit: Access, Visa.
🌊 📞 ⊡ 🖵 ♥ ▥ Ⅴ ⅍ 🗖
🆃 🎞 ♨ 🍴 ✿ ↘ SP 🅰

Elm Bank ♨
😊😊😊 APPROVED

52 Worcester Rd., Malvern,
Worcestershire WR14 4AB
☎ (0684) 566051
*Elegant late Regency house,
quiet bedrooms enjoying
breathtaking views. 5 minutes'
walk from town centre. Free
admission to leisure pool.*
Bedrooms: 3 double & 2 twin,
1 family room.
Bathrooms: 4 private,
1 public.
Bed & breakfast: £25–£28
single, £42–£46 double.
Evening meal 6.30pm (l.o.
9am).
Parking for 9.
Credit: Amex.
🌊 🖵 ♥ ▥ Ⅴ ⅍ 🗖 ♨
✿ ♖ 🅳 ↘ SP 🅰

Harcourt Cottage ♨
😊

252 West Malvern Rd., West
Malvern, Malvern,
Worcestershire WR14 4DQ
☎ (0684) 574561
*Nestling on the west side of the
Malvern Hills, well placed for
walking holidays or as a base
for touring. English and
French cooking.*
Bedrooms: 1 double & 1 twin,
1 family room.
Bathrooms: 1 public;
2 private showers.
Bed & breakfast: £15–£20
single, £30 double.
Half board: £22–£27 daily,
£139–£170 weekly.

Evening meal 6.45pm (l.o.
6pm).
Parking for 3.
🌊 ⛾ ♥ 🍴 ▥ 🗖 📺 🎞 ♨
✖ ♖ SP

Holdfast Cottage Hotel ♨
😊😊😊😊 COMMENDED

Marlbank Rd., Welland,
Malvern, Worcestershire
WR13 6NA
☎ Hanley Swan
(0684) 310288
*Small oak-beamed country
house set in 2 acres of gardens
amid orchard and farmland at
the foot of the Malvern Hills.*
Bedrooms: 1 single, 5 double
& 2 twin.
Bathrooms: 8 private,
1 public.
Bed & breakfast: £34–£36
single, £64–£72 double.
Half board: £42–£48 daily,
£266–£292 weekly.
Evening meal 7pm (l.o. 9pm).
Parking for 20.
Credit: Access, Visa.
🌊 📞 ⊡ 🖵 ♥ ▥ Ⅴ 🗖
🍴 ✿ ♖ ↘ SP 🅰

Malvern Hills Hotel ♨
😊😊😊

British Camp, Wynd's Point,
Malvern, Worcestershire
WR13 6DW
☎ Colwall (0684) 40237 &
40191 Fax 0684 40327
*Entrancing hotel setting atop
the Malvern Hills on the
Hereford/Worcester border.
Magnificent views. Prettily
decorated guest rooms. Fine
local produce used where
possible. Friendly and efficient
staff.*
Bedrooms: 2 single, 6 double
& 6 twin, 2 family rooms.
Bathrooms: 15 private,
1 public.
Bed & breakfast: £42.50–£45
single, £67.50–£70 double.
Half board: £45–£48 daily,
£300–£350 weekly.
Lunch available.
Evening meal 7pm (l.o.
9.30pm).
Parking for 30.
Credit: Access, Visa.
🌊 ⛾ 🛂 🖵 ♥ ▥ Ⅴ
🗖 📺 🎞 ♨ 🍴 ✿ ↘ SP 🅰

Mount Pleasant Hotel ♨
😊😊😊

Belle Vue Ter., Malvern,
Worcestershire WR14 4PZ
☎ (0684) 561837
*Georgian building with
orangery in 1.5 acres of
garden with beautiful views.
Close to theatre and shops and
with direct access to Malvern
Hills.*

Bedrooms: 3 single, 6 double
& 5 twin, 1 family room.
Bathrooms: 14 private,
1 public.
Bed & breakfast: £41–£52
single, £54–£63 double.
Half board: £38–£63 daily,
£242.50–£325 weekly.
Lunch available.
Evening meal 7pm (l.o.
9.30pm).
Parking for 20.
Credit: Access, Visa, Diners,
Amex.
🌊7 📞 ⊡ 🖵 ♥ ▥ Ⅴ 🗖 🗖
♨ 🍴 ✿ ✖ ♖ SP 🅰 🆃

The Nupend ♨
😊😊😊

Cradley, Malvern,
Worcestershire WR13 5NP
☎ Ridgeway Cross
(0886) 880881
*Elegant Georgian farmhouse
set in grounds of 2 acres and
enjoying glorious views of
Malvern Hills. Ideal for
walkers, bird-watchers,
painters or as a touring base.
Peacefully situated off A4103.
French/German spoken. Non-
smokers only please.*
Bedrooms: 2 double & 2 twin.
Bathrooms: 4 private.
Bed & breakfast: £28–£38
single, £40–£48 double.
Evening meal 6pm (l.o.
7.30pm).
Parking for 10.
🖵 ♥ UL ♥ ▥ Ⅴ 🗖 🗖 ♨
✿ ✖ ♖ 🅳 SP 🅰

Oakwood ♨
😊😊😊 COMMENDED

Blackheath Way, West
Malvern, Malvern,
Worcestershire WR14 4DR
☎ Malvern (0684) 575508
*A quiet and peaceful house
enjoying splendid views over 3
counties and with easy access
to the Malvern Hills. 8 miles
from the M5 and M50. Non-
smokers only please.*
Bedrooms: 1 single, 2 double
& 1 twin.
Bathrooms: 3 private,
1 public.
Bed & breakfast: £20–£22.50
single, £32–£39 double.
Half board: £27.50–£34 daily,
£177.50–£223 weekly.
Lunch available.
Evening meal 6pm (l.o. 8pm).
Parking for 5.
🌊 🖵 ♥ UL ♥ ▥ Ⅴ ⅍ 🗖 🎞
♨ 🍴 ✿ ✖ ♖ 🅳 SP 🅰

Oriel Hotel ♨
😊😊😊

46 Worcester Rd., Malvern,
Worcestershire WR14 4AA
☎ (0684) 892832

*Family-run hotel providing
Arabic/Mediterranean cuisine,
or traditional English food.
Children's menu available. All
rooms en-suite with satellite
colour TV and video.*
Bedrooms: 1 single, 6 double
& 2 twin, 2 family rooms.
Bathrooms: 11 private.
Bed & breakfast: £35–£42
single, £48–£58 double.
Half board: £40–£45 daily,
£270–£280 weekly.
Lunch available.
Evening meal 7.23pm (l.o.
10pm).
Parking for 14.
Credit: Access, Visa, Diners,
Amex.
🌊 📞 ⊡ 🖵 ♥ 🍴 ▥ Ⅴ ⅍ 🗖
⊙ 🎞 ♨ 🍴 ✿ ✖ ♖ ↘ SP
🅰 🆃

Priory Holme
😊😊😊

18 Avenue Rd., Malvern,
Worcestershire WR14 3AR
☎ (0684) 568455
*Elegantly furnished large
Victorian house in a tree-lined
avenue. Well situated for all
local amenities.*
Bedrooms: 1 single, 1 double
& 1 twin, 1 family room.
Bathrooms: 1 private,
2 public.
Bed & breakfast: from £16
single, £32–£40 double.
Half board: £26–£30 daily,
£182–£210 weekly.
Evening meal 7pm (l.o. 8pm).
Parking for 5.
🌊 ⛾ UL ♥ ▥ Ⅴ 🗖 📺 🎞 ♨ ✿
♖

Priory Park Hotel ♨
😊😊😊😊 COMMENDED

4 Avenue Rd., Malvern,
Worcestershire WR14 3AG
☎ (0684) 893603 Fax 0684
893603
*Family home on the fringe of
Great Malvern's Priory Park,
close to the town centre yet in
a beautiful and quiet position.
Theatre and leisure activities
all close by. German and
French spoken.*
Bedrooms: 1 single, 2 double
& 1 twin, 2 family rooms.
Bathrooms: 6 private.
Bed & breakfast: £40–£58
single, £68–£78 double.
Half board: £54–£76 daily,
£200–£250 weekly.
Lunch available.
Evening meal 6pm (l.o.
10pm).
Parking for 9.
Credit: Access, Visa.
🌊 ⛾ 📞 ⊡ 🖵 ♥ ▥ Ⅴ ⅍
🗖 📺 ⊙ 🎞 ♨ 🍴 ⚘ ⛟ ▶
✿ 🅳 ↘ SP 🅰 🆃

MALVERN

Continued

Rock House ⋔
☖☖ COMMENDED

144 West Malvern Rd.,
Malvern, Worcestershire
WR14 4NJ
☎ Malvern (0684) 574536
*Late Georgian house on
Malvern Hills with large
garden and wonderful views.
Ideal for rambling and touring.
Groups and active elderly
welcome. Pretty self-catering
cottage also available.*
Bedrooms: 5 double & 4 twin,
2 family rooms.
Bathrooms: 1 private,
3 public.
Bed & breakfast: £22-£26
single, £31-£37 double.
Half board: £25.50-£28.50
daily.
Evening meal 6.30pm.
Parking for 10.
Open February-October.
☖3 ⬚ Ⓥ ⚡ ⌦ ⓣ ⧈ ▲ ❊
🐾 SP

Royal Malvern Hotel ⋔
☖☖☖ COMMENDED

Graham Rd., Malvern,
Worcestershire WR14 2HN
☎ (0684) 563411 Fax 0684
560514
Ⓜ Minotels
*Small hotel in the centre of
Malvern close to the Winter
Gardens, with all amenities.
Run by the proprietors.*
Bedrooms: 1 single, 8 double
& 5 twin.
Bathrooms: 12 private,
1 public.
Bed & breakfast: £30-£50
single, £44-£65 double.
Lunch available.
Evening meal 6.15pm (l.o.
9pm).
Parking for 9.
Credit: Access, Visa, Diners,
Amex.
☖ ⓵ ⬚ ▤ ⓥ ⚡ ⓥ ⌦ ⧈
⧈ ▲ ⓣ ▶ SP ⓣ

Sidney House ⋔
☖☖☖ COMMENDED

40 Worcester Rd., Malvern,
Worcestershire WR14 4AA
☎ (0684) 574994
*Small, attractive Georgian
hotel with personal and
friendly service. Magnificent
views over the Worcestershire
countryside. Close to town
centre and hills.*
Bedrooms: 1 single, 3 double
& 2 twin, 1 family rooms.
Bathrooms: 4 private,
1 public; 1 private shower.
Bed & breakfast: £20-£35
single, £39-£49 double.
Half board: £35-£50 daily.

Evening meal 7pm (l.o. 3pm).
Parking for 10.
Credit: Access, Visa, Amex.
☖ ▲ ⬚ ⌦ ⓵ ⓥ ⚡ ▤ ⓣ
⧈ ▲ ⧉ ⓙ ❊ ⧈ SP ⧈ ⓣ

Spa Guest House ⋔
☖

16 Manby Rd., Malvern,
Worcestershire WR14 3BB
☎ (0684) 561178
*Pleasant Victorian house with
hill views. Very convenient for
the shopping facilities of
Malvern and 2 minutes from
the station.*
Bedrooms: 1 single, 2 double
& 1 twin, 1 family room.
Bathrooms: 2 public.
Bed & breakfast: £17 single,
£34 double.
Half board: £24 daily.
Evening meal 6.30pm (l.o.
8pm).
Parking for 10.
☖ ⬚ ⓥ ⓵ ⌦ ⓣ ⧈ ▲ ⧈

Walmer Lodge Hotel ⋔
☖☖☖ APPROVED

49 Abbey Rd., Malvern,
Worcestershire WR14 3HH
☎ (0684) 574139
*Friendly, family-run hotel in
quiet location, convenient for
town centre. Special terms for
short breaks and extended
stays.*
Bedrooms: 4 double & 3 twin,
2 family rooms.
Bathrooms: 9 private.
Bed & breakfast: max. £25.50
single, max. £44.50 double.
Half board: from £209
weekly.
Evening meal 7pm (l.o.
8.30pm).
Parking for 6.
Credit: Access, Visa.
⧈ ⬚ ▤ ⬚ ⓥ ⚡ ⌦ ⓥ
⧈ ▲ ⓣ ❊ ⧈ ⧈ SP

MARKET DRAYTON
Shropshire
Map ref 4A2

Old market town with
black and white buildings
and 17th C houses.
Hodnet Hall is in the
vicinity with its beautiful
landscaped gardens
covering 60 acres.

Corbet Arms ⋔
☖☖☖ COMMENDED

High St., Market Drayton,
TF9 1PY
☎ (0630) 652037
*Traditional 16th C coaching
inn, in town centre position,
with ample car parking and
own bowling green. Golfing and
fishing by arrangement.*
Bedrooms: 3 single, 5 double
& 2 twin, 1 family room.

Bathrooms: 11 private,
1 public.
Bed & breakfast: £38-£48
single, £46-£58 double.
Lunch available.
Evening meal 7pm (l.o. 9pm).
Parking for 62.
Credit: Access, Visa, Diners,
Amex.
☖ ⓵ ⬚ ⌦ ⓥ ⓵ ⓥ ⌦ ⓣ
⧈ ▲ ⓣ ▶ ⧈ ⧈ SP ⧈ ⓣ

Rosehill Manor ⋔
☖☖☖ APPROVED

Tern Hill, Market Drayton,
TF9 2JF
☎ Tern Hill (063 083) 532
*Country house in 1.5 acres
with chef/proprietor. Log fires
in winter. Convenient for
Ironbridge, the Potteries and
Wales.*
Bedrooms: 3 single, 2 double,
1 family room.
Bathrooms: 4 private,
2 public.
Bed & breakfast: £24-£46
single, £37-£60 double.
Half board: £39-£65 daily.
Lunch available.
Evening meal 6.30pm (l.o.
8.30pm).
Parking for 20.
Credit: Access, Visa.
☖ ⓵ ⬚ ⌦ ⓥ ⓵ ⓥ ⌦ ⓞ
⧈ ▲ ❊ ⧉ ⧈ ⧈ SP

MERIDEN
W. Midlands
Map ref 4B3

Village halfway between
Coventry and
Birmingham. Said to be
the centre of England,
marked by a cross on the
green.

Strawberry Bank
Restaurant & Hotel ⋔

Main Rd., Meriden,
Coventry CV7 7NF
☎ (0676) 22117 Fax 0676
23804
*200-year-old country house set
in 2 acres of landscaped
gardens, between Coventry and
Birmingham. 3 miles from
Birmingham Airport,
Birmingham International
station and National
Exhibition Centre.*
Bedrooms: 3 single, 3 twin.
Bathrooms: 6 private.
Bed & breakfast: max. £40
single, max. £60 double.
Lunch available.
Evening meal 6.45pm (l.o.
10pm).
Parking for 60.
Credit: Access, Visa, Amex.
☖ ⓵ ⓵ ⬚ ⌦ ⓥ ⧈ ▲
⧉ ❊ ⧈

Woodlands Farm
House ⋔
☖☖ APPROVED

Back Lane, Meriden,
Coventry, CV7 7LD
☎ (0676) 22317
*12-acre farm. Oak-beamed,
comfortable farmhouse in old
Warwickshire countryside.
Ideal for touring Kenilworth,
Warwick and Stratford-upon-
Avon. Central for theatre,
concert and sports facilities.
Access to major road network,
airport, rail and the National
Exhibition Centre.*
Bedrooms: 2 twin.
Bathrooms: 2 private.
Bed & breakfast: £20-£22
single, £33-£36 double.
Parking for 10.
☖5 ▲ ⓤ ⓵ ⓥ ⌦ ⓣ ⧈ ▲
ⓣ ❊ ⧉ ⧈

MICKLETON
Gloucestershire
Map ref 2B1

Mickleton lies in the Vale
of Evesham and is close
to Hidcote Manor
Gardens (National Trust)
and to the beautiful
Cotswold town of
Chipping Campden.

Three Ways Hotel ⋔
☖☖☖☖

Chapel La., Mickleton,
Chipping Campden,
GL55 6SB
☎ (0386) 438429/438231
Telex 337242, Fax (0386)
438858
*Family-run country village
hotel famous for its Pudding
Club. Convenient for Stratford-
upon-Avon and the Cotswolds.*
Bedrooms: 3 single, 14 double
& 19 twin, 4 family rooms.
Bathrooms: 40 private.
Bed & breakfast: £40-£50
single, £63-£73 double.
Half board: £47-£52 daily,
£283.50-£313.50 weekly.
Lunch available.
Evening meal 7pm (l.o. 9pm).
Parking for 40.
Credit: Access, Visa, Diners,
Amex.
☖ ▲ ⓵ ⬚ ⌦ ⓥ ⓵ ⓥ ⌦
⧉ ⧈ ▲ ⓣ ⧉ ⧈ SP ⧈

---

*National Crown
ratings were correct
at the time of going
to press but are
subject to change.
Please check at the
time of booking.*

MINCHINHAMPTON

Gloucestershire
Map ref 2B1

4m SE. Stroud
A stone-built town, with many 17th/18th C buildings, owing its existence to the wool and cloth trades. A 17th C pillared market house may be found in the town square, near which is the Norman and 14th C church.

The Ragged Cot Inn M
😃😃😃

Hyde, Chalford, Stroud, GL6 8PE
☎ Brimscombe
(0453) 884643 & 731333
Half a mile from Gatcombe Park and adjacent to 600 acres of National Trust commonland. Cheltenham 15 miles, Bath 20 miles and Stroud 5 miles.
Bedrooms: 2 double & 8 twin.
Bathrooms: 10 private.
Bed & breakfast: £50-£55 single, £60-£80 double.
Half board: £60-£65 daily.
Lunch available.
Evening meal 7pm (l.o. 9.30pm).
Parking for 55.
Credit: Access, Visa, Amex.
⛐12🅿🔥 ⛗🏠💷☎ 🔌 Ⓥ
✗ ▥ 🔺 🍴 👤 ▶ ❄ ✗
🏠 DAP ⚲ SP 🏤

MINSTERLEY

Shropshire
Map ref 4A3

9m SW. Shrewsbury
Village with a curious little church of 1692 and a fine old black and white hall. The lofty ridge known as the Stiperstones is 4 miles to the south.

Cricklewood Cottage M
Listed COMMENDED

Plox Green, Minsterley, Shrewsbury, SY5 0HT
☎ Shrewsbury (0743) 791229
Delightful 18th C cottage with countryside views, at foot of Stiperstones Hills. Exposed beams, inglenook fireplace, traditional furnishings. Lovely cottage garden. Wholesome food.
Bedrooms: 2 double & 1 twin.
Bathrooms: 1 private, 1 public.
Bed & breakfast: £13-£19.50 single, £26-£34 double.

Half board: £21-£25 daily, £137.90-£163.10 weekly.
Evening meal 6pm (l.o. 5pm).
Parking for 6.
🔥 ⚲ ⛗ ⓊⓁ 🔌 Ⓥ ✗ 🏠 ⒯⒱ ▥
🔺 👤 ♨ ⚲ SP 🏤

MORETON-IN-MARSH

Gloucestershire
Map ref 2B1

Attractive town of Cotswold stone with 17th C houses, an ideal base for touring the Cotswolds. Some of the local attractions include Batsford Park Arboretum, the Jacobean Chastleton House and Sezincote Garden.

Manor House Hotel M
😃😃😃😃 COMMENDED

High St., Moreton-in-Marsh, GL56 0LJ
☎ (0608) 50501 Telex 837151
16th C privately-owned manor house with original features. Some four-poster beds, indoor pool and walled garden. All-weather tennis court.
Bedrooms: 5 single, 21 double & 12 twin.
Bathrooms: 38 private.
Bed & breakfast: £63.50-£70 single, £80-£98 double.
Half board: £56.50-£66.50 daily.
Lunch available.
Evening meal 7.15pm (l.o. 9.30pm).
Parking for 30.
Credit: Access, Visa, Diners, Amex.
⛐8🏠 ⛗ ☎ 🔌 💷 ▥ 🔌 Ⓥ 🏠
◉ 🈂 🔺 🍴 👤 🚗 ❄
✗ ⚲ SP 🏤 ⒯

Moreton House M
😃😃 APPROVED

Moreton-in-Marsh, GL56 0LQ
☎ (0608) 50747
Family-run guesthouse providing full English breakfast and optional evening meal. Tea shop, open 6 days a week, lounge bar with restaurant. Ideal for touring the Cotswolds. Children and dogs welcome.
Bedrooms: 3 single, 6 double & 3 twin.
Bathrooms: 5 private, 2 public.
Bed & breakfast: £19-£21 single, £34-£50 double.
Lunch available.

Evening meal 6pm (l.o. 8.30pm).
Parking for 5.
Credit: Access, Visa.
⚲ 🖵 🛡 🔌 Ⓥ ✗ 🏠 ⒯⒱ ◉
▥ 🔺 🏠 DAP ⚲

MUCH BIRCH

Hereford & Worcester
Map ref 2A1

6m S. Hereford
Village on the road between Ross-on-Wye and Hereford, with splendid views towards the Black Mountains.

Pilgrim Hotel M
😃😃😃 COMMENDED

Hereford, Herefordshire HR2 8HJ
☎ Golden Valley (0981) 540742 Telex 35332, Attn Pilgrim Hotel
🄶🄳 Inter
Country house hotel combining modern facilities with old world charm. Popular with country lovers and golfers. Set in 4 acres of grounds.
Bedrooms: 1 single, 9 double & 10 twin.
Bathrooms: 20 private.
Bed & breakfast: £41-£65 single, £62-£77 double.
Half board: £49.50-£59.50 daily, £278-£365 weekly.
Lunch available.
Evening meal 7pm (l.o. 10pm).
Parking for 40.
Credit: Access, Visa, Diners, Amex.
⚲ 🔥 ⛗ ☎ ◉ 🖵 🛡 Ⓥ
✗ 🔌 ▥ 🔺 🍴 👤 ▶ ❄
🏠 ⚲ SP ⒯

MUCH WENLOCK

Shropshire
Map ref 4A3

Small town close to Wenlock Edge in beautiful scenery and full of interest. In particular there are the remains of an 11th C priory with fine carving and the black and white 16th C Guildhall.

Bourton Manor M
😃😃😃😃 COMMENDED

Bourton, Much Wenlock, TF13 6QE
☎ Brockton (074 636) 531
Fax 074636 632
Beautiful English country house overlooking Corve Dale. Convenient for Ironbridge, Shrewsbury, Ludlow. Spacious bedrooms, comfortable panelled public rooms. Meals served to non-residents.

Bedrooms: 6 double & 1 twin, 1 family room.
Bathrooms: 8 private, 1 public.
Bed & breakfast: £50-£85 single, £60-£95 double.
Half board: £62-£105 daily, £275-£431 weekly.
Lunch available.
Evening meal 7pm (l.o. 10pm).
Parking for 150.
Credit: Access, Visa, Diners, Amex.
⚲ 🔥 🔌 ☎ 🖵 ⚲ 🛡 Ⓥ 🔌
⒯⒱ ▥ 🔺 🍴 👤 ♨ DAP ⚲ SP
🏤 ⒯

Gaskell Arms Hotel M
😃😃

Much Wenlock, TF13 6HF
☎ Telford (0952) 727212
17th C coaching inn built of stone and brick, with beamed ceilings. Family-run freehouse. Own private car park.
Bedrooms: 1 single, 6 double & 3 twin, 1 family room.
Bathrooms: 6 private, 2 public.
Bed & breakfast: £26-£38 single, £42-£58 double.
Half board: £30-£50 daily.
Lunch available.
Evening meal 7pm (l.o. 10pm).
Parking for 30.
Credit: Access, Visa, Amex.
⚲ 🔥 🖵 ☎ 🛡 Ⓥ 🔌 ▥ 🏠
🍴 ❄ ✗ DAP SP 🏤

NAILSWORTH

Gloucestershire
Map ref 2B1

Ancient wool town with several elegant Jacobean and Georgian houses, surrounded by wooded hillsides with fine views.

Apple Orchard House M
😃😃 APPROVED

Orchard Close, Springhill, Nailsworth, Stroud, GL6 0LX
☎ (0453) 832503
Fax (0453) 833544
Elegant and spacious Cotswold house in pretty 1 acre garden. Panoramic views from bedrooms of picturesque Cotswold hills. Excellent touring centre.
Bedrooms: 1 double & 1 twin, 1 family room.
Bathrooms: 3 private.
Bed & breakfast: £14-£18 single, £27-£28 double.
Half board: £22-£22.50 daily, £139-£142 weekly.
Evening meal 6pm (l.o. 10am).

Continued ▶

239

NAILSWORTH
Continued

Parking for 3.
Credit: Access, Visa.

North Farm M
COMMENDED
Nympsfield Rd., Nailsworth,
GL6 0ET
☎ (045 383) 3598
*Modernised former farmhouse,
3 large bedrooms, all with
bathroom en-suite. Panoramic
views of surrounding
countryside.*
Bedrooms: 1 double & 2 twin.
Bathrooms: 3 private.
Bed & breakfast: £15-£18
single, £28-£30 double.
Half board: £21-£26.50 daily.
Evening meal 6.30pm (l.o.
8pm).
Parking for 4.

NEWCASTLE-UNDER-LYME
Staffordshire
Map ref 4B2

Industrial town whose
museum and art gallery
give evidence of its past.
The Guildhall was built in
the 18th C and there is
the modern university of
Keele.
*Tourist Information
Centre ☎ (0782) 711964*

Borough Arms Hotel M
APPROVED
King St., Newcastle-under-
Lyme, ST5 1HX
☎ Stoke-on-Trent
(0782) 629421 Fax 0782
712388
*Former coaching inn close to
town centre with easy access to
all Potteries towns and Alton
Towers. Lounge bar and a la
carte restaurant.*
Bedrooms: 27 single, 6 double
& 12 twin.
Bathrooms: 45 private.
Bed & breakfast: £35.75-£46
single, £50.60-£60.25 double.
Half board: £45-£55 daily,
£315-£385 weekly.
Lunch available.
Evening meal 7pm (l.o.
10pm).
Parking for 45.
Credit: Access, Visa, Diners,
Amex.

Durlston Guest House M
Kimberley Rd., Newcastle-
under-Lyme, ST5 9EG
☎ (0782) 611708
*Small family-run guesthouse on
A34. Convenient for M6
junction 15/16, the Potteries,
the Peak District and Alton
Towers.*
Bedrooms: 3 single, 1 double
& 1 twin, 2 family rooms.
Bathrooms: 2 public.
Bed & breakfast: £16.50-
£17.50 single, £31-£32 double.
Parking for 10.
Credit: Access, Visa.

The Gables M
Listed
570-572 Etruria Rd.,
Newcastle-under-Lyme,
ST5 0SU
☎ (0782) 619748
*Gracious Edwardian hotel with
extensive grounds. On the A53
with easy access to the M6.
Adjacent to the New Victoria
Theatre. Well placed for
visitors to Stoke-on-Trent's
pottery factories and Alton
Towers.*
Bedrooms: 5 double & 2 twin,
6 family rooms.
Bathrooms: 3 public;
10 private showers.
Bed & breakfast: £15-£21
single, £25-£34 double.
Half board: £24-£30 daily.
Evening meal 6pm (l.o. 9pm).
Parking for 18.

Thomas Forshaw Hotel M
Liverpool Rd., Cross Heath,
Newcastle-under-Lyme,
ST5 9DX
☎ (0782) 717000
CR Friendly
*Modern hotel with all facilities,
located on A34 between
junctions 15 and 16 on the M6.*
Bedrooms: 29 double &
42 twin, 3 family rooms.
Bathrooms: 74 private.
Bed & breakfast: £53.50-
£66.20 single, £66.75-£81.90
double.
Lunch available.
Evening meal 7pm (l.o.
9.45pm).
Parking for 125.
Credit: Access, Visa, C.Bl.,
Diners, Amex.

NEWPORT
Shropshire
Map ref 4A3

Small market town on the
Shropshire Union Canal
has a wide High Street
and a church with some
interesting monuments.
Newport is close to
Aqualate Mere which is
the largest lake in
Staffordshire.
*Tourist Information
Centre ☎ (0952) 814109*

Adams House Hotel and Restaurant M
High St., Newport,
TF10 7AR
☎ Telford (0952) 820085
*Small, family-hotel offering en-
suite and budget
accommodation. Full bar and
restaurant facilities also
catering for wedding parties,
etc.*
Bedrooms: 2 single, 1 double
& 2 twin, 3 family rooms.
Bathrooms: 3 private,
2 public.
Bed & breakfast: £28-£40
single, £35-£54 double.
Half board: £35-£45 daily,
from £200 weekly.
Lunch available.
Evening meal 7pm (l.o.
10.30pm).
Parking for 10.
Credit: Access, Visa.

Bridge Inn
APPROVED
Chetwynd End, Newport,
TF10 7JB
☎ (0952) 811785
*Small, family-run
establishment, serving a wide
range of home-cooked food.
Parts of the building date from
1664.*
Bedrooms: 2 single, 1 double
& 2 twin.
Bathrooms: 2 private,
1 public.
Bed & breakfast: £17-£27.50
single, £34-£38 double.
Lunch available.
Evening meal 7pm (l.o.
10pm).
Parking for 40.
Credit: Access, Visa, C.Bl.,
Diners, Amex.

Norwood House Hotel and Restaurant M
Pave La., Newport,
TF10 9LQ
☎ (0952) 825896
*Hotel of character just off the
A41 Whitchurch to
Wolverhampton road, close to
Lilleshall National Sports
Centre.*
Bedrooms: 1 single, 3 double
& 2 twin.
Bathrooms: 6 private.
Bed & breakfast: £25-£30
single, £35-£39 double.
Lunch available.
Evening meal 7pm (l.o.
10.30pm).
Parking for 26.
Credit: Access, Visa, Amex.

NORTH NIBLEY
Gloucestershire
Map ref 2B2

2m SW. Dursley
Pleasant little village near
Dursley dominated by the
Tyndale Monument, a
tapering stone tower
erected in 1966 in
memory of the translator
of the New Testament.

Burrows Court Hotel M
APPROVED
Nibley Green, North Nibley,
Dursley, GL11 6AZ
☎ Dursley (0453) 546230
*Converted stone-built weaving
mill with many exposed beams,
commanding beautiful views of
Cotswolds escarpment.
Peaceful and homely
atmosphere.*
Bedrooms: 1 single, 7 double
& 2 twin.
Bathrooms: 10 private.
Bed & breakfast: max. £37
single, max. £51 double.
Half board: £39-£51 daily,
£205-£295 weekly.
Evening meal 7pm (l.o.
8.30pm).
Parking for 10.
Credit: Access, Visa, Amex.

---

*National Crown ratings were correct at
the time of going to press but are subject
to change. Please check at the time of
booking.*

NORTHLEACH

Gloucestershire
Map ref 2B1

Village famous for its beautiful 15th C wool church with its lovely porch and interesting interior. There are also some fine houses including 16th C almshouses, a 17th C manor house and a collection of agricultural instruments in the former prison.

Bank Villas Guesthouse M
♨♨

West-end, Northleach, Cheltenham, GL54 3HG
☎ Cotswold (0451) 60464
Semi-detached house in centre of Northleach, 12 miles from Cheltenham. Telephone for free brochure.
Bedrooms: 2 single, 1 double & 1 twin, 1 family room.
Bathrooms: 1 private, 2 public.
Bed & breakfast: from £14 single, from £25 double.
⚅ ♨ ⌂ ⮵ ☒ ⟮ 𝓣𝓥 ⬚ ▦ ⌕ & ✕ ⍟

Cotteswold House M
Listed COMMENDED
Market Pl., Northleach, Cheltenham, GL54 3EG
☎ Cotswold (0451) 60493
A traditional Cotswold-stone house with many interesting architectural features and modernised to a high standard. Ideal base from which to tour, or rest.
Bedrooms: 1 double & 2 twin, 1 family room.
Bathrooms: 3 public.
Bed & breakfast: £16-£18 single, £30-£33 double.
⚅10 ⚒ ☒ ⌂ 𝓣𝓥 ▦ ⌕ ✕ ⍟ ▦

Northfield Bed & Breakfast M
♨♨♨ APPROVED
Cirencester Rd., Northleach, Cheltenham, GL54 3JL
☎ Cotswold (0451) 60427
Detached family house in the country with large gardens and home-grown produce. Excellent centre for visiting the Cotswolds and close to local services.
Bedrooms: 1 double & 1 twin, 1 family room.
Bathrooms: 3 private, 1 public.
Bed & breakfast: £18-£20 single, £26-£36 double.
Half board: £30-£40 daily.

Lunch available.
Evening meal 7pm (l.o. 8pm).
Parking for 10.
⚅ ♨ ⌂ ☒ ⌂ ⮵ ⓘ ⟮ ✂ ⮮
𝓣𝓥 ▦ ⌕ ❋ ✕ ▦ SP

Wheatsheaf Hotel M
♨♨♨

Northleach, Cheltenham, GL54 3EZ
☎ Cotswold (0451) 60244
Period inn, an excellent centre for visiting lovely Cotswold countryside. Own garden produce.
Bedrooms: 5 double & 3 twin.
Bathrooms: 8 private, 1 public.
Bed & breakfast: from £35 single, £45-£65 double.
Lunch available.
Evening meal 7pm (l.o. 9.30pm).
Parking for 15.
Credit: Access, Visa.
⚅ ⌕ ⌂ ☒ ⮵ ⓘ ⟮ ▦ ⬚
❋ ✕ SP ▦

NUNEATON

Warwickshire
Map ref 4B3

Busy town with an art gallery and museum which has a permanent exhibition of the work of George Eliot. The library also has an interesting collection of material. Arbury Hall, a fine example of Gothic architecture, is nearby.
Tourist Information Centre ☎ (0203) 384027

Drachenfels Hotel M
♨♨

25 Attleborough Rd., Nuneaton, CV11 4HZ
☎ (0203) 383030
Built in early 20th C by a German nobleman along the lines of a German castle. Colour TV in all bedrooms. Cocktail bar. Overlooks playing fields.
Bedrooms: 2 single, 2 double & 3 twin, 1 family room.
Bathrooms: 2 private, 3 public.
Bed & breakfast: £19.50-£23.50 single, £29.50-£35.50 double.
Lunch available.
Evening meal 6pm (l.o. 9.30pm).
Parking for 8.
Credit: Access, Visa.
⚅ ⌂ ⌂ ⮵ ⓘ ⟮ ⌂ ▦ ⬚
⍟ SP ▦

Millers Hotel & Restaurant M
♨♨

Main Rd., Sibson, Nuneaton, CV13 6LB
☎ Tamworth (0827) 880223
Fax 0827 880223 EXT 222
Converted mill and bakery with wealth of beams. Working mill wheel and stream in lounge bar. 25 minutes from Birmingham National Exhibition Centre.
Bedrooms: 11 single, 15 double & 14 twin.
Bathrooms: 40 private.
Bed & breakfast: £16-£51 single, £32-£61 double.
Half board: £25-£62 daily, £301 weekly.
Lunch available.
Evening meal 6.30pm (l.o. 9.45pm).
Parking for 100.
Credit: Access, Visa, Diners, Amex.
⚅ ♨ ⌕ ⌂ ⮵ ⓘ ⟮
⌂ 𝓣𝓥 ◉ ▦ ⌂ ✆ ⌕ & ❋
DAP ⬚ SP ▦ ⓣ

Triple 'A' Lodge Guest House
Listed APPROVED
94-96 Coleshill Rd., Chapel End, Nuneaton, CU10 0PH
☎ Coventry (0203) 394515
Family-run guesthouse on the outskirts of Nuneaton, in the pleasant village of Chapel End. Tea/coffee facilities and colour TV all rooms. Evening meals available.
Bedrooms: 3 double & 3 twin.
Bathrooms: 2 public.
Bed & breakfast: £12-£15 single, £24-£30 double.
Evening meal 6pm (l.o. 9.30pm).
Parking for 12.
Credit: Diners, Amex.
⚅2 ⚒ ⌂ ⮵ ⟮ ⓘ ⌂ 𝓣𝓥
✕ ▦ DAP

NYMPSFIELD

Gloucestershire
Map ref 2B1

3m W. Nailsworth
Pretty village high up in the Cotswolds, with a simple mid-Victorian church and a prehistoric long barrow nearby.

Rose and Crown Inn M
Listed APPROVED
Nympsfield, Stonehouse, GL10 3TU
☎ Dursley (0453) 860240
300-year-old inn, in quiet Cotswold village, close to Cotswold Way and Nympsfield Gliding Club. Easy access to M4/M5.

Bedrooms: 1 double, 3 family rooms.
Bathrooms: 1 private, 1 public.
Bed & breakfast: £22 single, £30 double.
Half board: £18.50-£28 daily, £135-£196 weekly.
Lunch available.
Evening meal 6.30pm (l.o. 9.30pm).
Parking for 30.
Credit: Access, Visa.
⚅ ⌂ ⌂ ⮵ ⓘ ⟮ ▦ ⌂ ✕ ▦
DAP ⬚ SP

OMBERSLEY

Hereford & Worcester
Map ref 2B1

4m W. Droitwich
A particularly fine village full of black and white houses including the 17th C Dower House and some old inns. The church contains the original box pews.

The Crown and Sandys Arms M
♨♨ COMMENDED
Ombersley, Droitwich, Worcestershire WR9 0EW
☎ Worcester (0905) 620252
Freehouse with comfortable bedrooms, draught beers and open fires. Home-cooked meals available lunch and evenings, 7 days a week.
Bedrooms: 1 single, 5 double & 1 twin.
Bathrooms: 5 private, 1 public.
Bed & breakfast: £21-£30 single, £42-£47 double.
Lunch available.
Evening meal 6pm (l.o. 10pm).
Parking for 100.
Credit: Access, Visa.
⚅ ⌂ ⌂ ⮵ ⓘ ⟮ ✕ ▦ ⌂
⌂ ⓤ ❋ ✕ ▦ ⓣ

ONNELEY

Staffordshire
Map ref 4A2

6m SW. Newcastle-under-Lyme

The Wheatsheaf Inn at Onneley M
♨♨♨♨ COMMENDED
Bar Hill Rd., Onneley, CW3 9QF
☎ Stoke-on-Trent (0782) 751581 Fax 0782 751499

Continued ▶

ONNELEY

Continued

18th C country inn with bars, restaurant, conference and function facilities. On the A525, 3 miles from Bridgemere and Keele University, 7 miles from Newcastle-under-Lyme.
Bedrooms: 4 double & 1 twin.
Bathrooms: 5 private.
Bed & breakfast: £37-£42 single, £42-£52 double.
Half board: £52-£57 daily.
Lunch available.
Evening meal 6pm (l.o. 10pm).
Parking for 150.
Credit: Access, Visa, Amex.

OSWESTRY

Shropshire
Map ref 4A3

Town close to the Welsh border, the scene of many battles. To the north are the remains of a large Iron Age hill fort. An excellent centre for exploring Shropshire and Offa's Dyke.
Tourist Information Centre ☎ (0691) 662488 or 662753

Frankton Manor ⚊

🏆 COMMENDED

Welsh Frankton, Whittington, Oswestry, SY11 4NX
☎ Ellesmere (0691) 622454
Charming Victorian country house in small village near Oswestry. Beautifully decorated and furnished, spacious bedrooms. Large landscaped garden with lovely south-facing views.
Bedrooms: 1 single, 1 double, 1 family room.
Bathrooms: 1 public.
Bed & breakfast: £15.50-£17 single, £31-£34 double.
Half board: £24-£25.50 daily, £149-£159 weekly.
Evening meal 7pm (l.o. 11am).
Parking for 20.
Open March-October.

Pen-y-Dyffryn Hall Hotel ⚊

Rhyd-y-Croesau, Oswestry, SY10 7DT
☎ (0691) 653700
Charming stone-built Georgian rectory in 5 acres of grounds in Shropshire/Welsh border hill country. Fully licensed, extensive a la carte menu. Quiet and relaxed atmosphere. Shrewsbury 20 minutes.

Bedrooms: 1 single, 2 double & 3 twin, 1 family room.
Bathrooms: 7 private.
Bed & breakfast: £37-£42 single, £58-£63 double.
Half board: £39-£43 daily, £245-£265 weekly.
Lunch available.
Evening meal 7pm (l.o. 9pm).
Parking for 38.
Credit: Access, Visa, Amex.

The Wynnstay ⚊

🏆🏆🏆🏆 COMMENDED

Church St., Oswestry, SY11 2SZ
☎ Oswestry (0691) 655261
Fax 0691 670606
Attractively refurbished Georgian country house hotel near town centre, with crown bowling green and walled gardens. Close to Chester and Shrewsbury.
Bedrooms: 2 single, 12 double & 11 twin, 2 family rooms.
Bathrooms: 27 private.
Bed & breakfast: from £35 single, from £50 double.
Lunch available.
Evening meal 7pm (l.o. 11.30pm).
Parking for 70.
Credit: Access, Visa, C.Bl., Diners, Amex.

OXHILL

Warwickshire
Map ref 2C1

6m SE. Stratford-upon-Avon
Village in the Vale of Red Horse not far from the battlefield of Edgehill. Its church retains much that is Norman.

Nolands Farm and Country Restaurant ⚊

🏆🏆🏆

Oxhill, Warwick, CV35 0RJ
☎ Kineton (0926) 640309
300-acre arable farm. In a tranquil valley surrounded by fields. All rooms in converted barn annexe. Peaceful and quiet, overlooking old stable yard. Stocked lake, woods, walks and wildlife. Elegant four-poster bedrooms. Licensed restaurant with fresh country produce.
Bedrooms: 5 double & 1 twin, 3 family rooms.
Bathrooms: 9 private, 1 public.
Bed & breakfast: from £25 single, from £30 double.

Evening meal 6.30pm (l.o. 6.30pm).
Parking for 11.
Credit: Access.

PAINSWICK

Gloucestershire
Map ref 2B1

Picturesque wool town with inns and houses dating from the 14th C. Painswick House is a Palladian mansion with Chinese wallpaper. The churchyard is famous for its yew trees.
Tourist Information Centre ☎ (0452) 813552

Thorne ⚊

🏆🏆

Friday St., Painswick, Stroud, GL6 6QJ
☎ (0452) 812476
Thorne is the second oldest house in Painswick, a perfect example of Cotswold secular architecture. Part has market hall pillars "in situ". Outside used for filming "Poldark" television film. Situated on Cotswold Way Walk. Guide service available by Blue Badge Guide.
Bedrooms: 2 twin.
Bathrooms: 2 private.
Bed & breakfast: £18-£22 single, £30-£46 double.

REDDITCH

Hereford & Worcester
Map ref 4B3

Town has remains of a Cistercian Abbey which have been excavated to reveal the Abbey's history. Forge Mill is close by with a restored water wheel and Wynyates Craft Centre.
Tourist Information Centre ☎ (0527) 60806

Hotel Montville ⚊

🏆🏆

101 Mount Pleasant, Redditch, Worcestershire B97 4JE
☎ (0527) 544411/544341
Refurbished hotel convenient for the town centre, with a friendly, family atmosphere. A la carte "Granny's" Restaurant. Fully licensed.
Bedrooms: 9 single, 3 double & 2 twin, 2 family rooms.

Bathrooms: 13 private; 3 private showers.
Bed & breakfast: £35-£50 single, £45-£66 double.
Lunch available.
Evening meal 6.30pm (l.o. 9pm).
Parking for 18.
Credit: Access, Visa.

Southcrest Hotel ⚊

🏆🏆🏆🏆

Pool Bank, Southcrest, Redditch, Worcestershire B97 4JG
☎ (0527) 541511
Telex 338455
Country house hotel with French restaurant, set in 26 acres of landscaped gardens and woods.
Bedrooms: 10 single, 21 double & 27 twin.
Bathrooms: 58 private.
Bed & breakfast: £65-£75 single, £75-£85 double.
Half board: £78-£88 daily.
Lunch available.
Evening meal 7pm (l.o. 9.15pm).
Parking for 100.
Credit: Access, Visa, Diners, Amex.

ROLLESTON-ON-DOVE

Staffordshire
Map ref 4B3

3m NW. Burton upon Trent
Village close to Repton and Sudbury Hall, a National Trust property with a Museum of Childhood. The village church has a Saxon crypt.

The Brookhouse Inn ⚊

🏆🏆🏆🏆 COMMENDED

Brookside, Rolleston-on-Dove, Burton upon Trent, DE13 9AA
☎ Burton upon Trent (0283) 814188
Individually designed bedrooms with antique furniture and en-suite bathrooms. Intimate romantic restaurant. Also has a conservatory with relaxing atmosphere.
Bedrooms: 8 single, 10 double & 1 twin.
Bathrooms: 19 private.
Bed & breakfast: £59-£65 single, £75-£79 double.
Lunch available.
Evening meal 7.30pm (l.o. 10pm).

Parking for 40.
Credit: Access, Visa, Diners, Amex.

[icons]

ROSS-ON-WYE

Hereford & Worcester
Map ref 2A1

Attractive market town with a 17th C market hall, set above the River Wye. There are lovely views over the surrounding countryside from the Prospect and the town is close to Goodrich Castle and the Welsh border.
Tourist Information Centre ☎ *(1989) 62768*

The Arches Country House M

Walford Rd., Ross-on-Wye, Herefordshire HR9 5TP
☎ (0989) 63348
Family-run hotel set in half an acre of lawns, half a mile from the town centre. All bedrooms are furnished to a high standard and have views of the lawned garden. Warm, friendly atmosphere and personal service.
Bedrooms: 1 single, 2 double & 3 twin, 1 family room.
Bathrooms: 3 private, 2 public.
Bed & breakfast: from £17.50 single, £30-£40 double.
Half board: £25-£30 daily.
Evening meal 7pm (l.o. 5pm).
Parking for 8.

[icons]

Bridge House Hotel M
COMMENDED
Wilton, Ross-on-Wye, Herefordshire HR9 6AA
☎ (0989) 62655
Small riverside hotel with panoramic views from the gardens and pride in its comfort and cuisine. All rooms en-suite. Break terms available.
Bedrooms: 4 double & 3 twin.
Bathrooms: 7 private, 1 public.
Bed & breakfast: £31.50-£33 single, £53-£56 double.
Half board: £38-£40 daily, £230-£250 weekly.
Evening meal 7pm (l.o. 9pm).
Parking for 12.
Credit: Access, Visa.

[icons]

Chasedale Hotel M

Walford Rd., Ross-on-Wye, Herefordshire HR9 5PQ
☎ (0989) 62423 & 65801
Family-run country house hotel half a mile from Ross-on-Wye town centre, set in an English rose garden.
Bedrooms: 3 single, 4 double & 1 twin, 3 family rooms.
Bathrooms: 9 private, 1 public.
Bed & breakfast: £32-£34 single, £51-£55 double.
Half board: £35-£45 daily, £227-£275 weekly.
Lunch available.
Evening meal 7pm (l.o. 9pm).
Parking for 25.
Credit: Access, Visa, Diners.

[icons]

Edde Cross House M
COMMENDED
Edde Cross St., Ross-on-Wye, Herefordshire HR9 7BZ
☎ (0989) 65088
Georgian town house overlooking river, close to town centre. Bedrooms decorated and furnished to a high standard, with colour TV and tea/coffee facilities. Some en-suite rooms. Non-smokers only please.
Bedrooms: 1 single, 3 double & 1 twin.
Bathrooms: 2 private, 1 public.
Bed & breakfast: £17-£18 single, £32-£34 double.
Open February-November.

[icons]

Glewstone Court Hotel M
COMMENDED
Glewstone, Ross-on-Wye, Herefordshire HR9 6AW
☎ Llangarron (098 984) 367
Fax (098 984) 282
Elegant, listed, Georgian country house set in 4 acres of gardens overlooking the Wye Valley. Emphasis on informal comfort and hospitality coupled with good food and fine wine.
Bedrooms: 3 double & 2 twin, 2 family rooms.
Bathrooms: 7 private, 2 public.
Bed & breakfast: £50-£60 single, £74-£88 double.
Half board: £57-£80 daily, £360-£475 weekly.
Lunch available.
Evening meal 7pm (l.o. 10pm).

Parking for 20.
Credit: Access, Visa, Amex.

[icons]

New Inn
COMMENDED
St. Owens Cross, Hereford, Herefordshire HR2 8LQ
☎ Harewood End (098 987) 274
16th C coaching inn on the Symonds Yat to Hereford road. Half-timbered, with log fires and antique furniture. Comprehensive bar menu and full a la carte.
Bedrooms: 2 double.
Bathrooms: 2 private.
Bed & breakfast: £30-£45 single, £50-£80 double.
Lunch available.
Evening meal 7pm (l.o. 9.45pm).
Parking for 50.
Credit: Access, Visa.

[icons]

Orles Barn Hotel & Restaurant M
COMMENDED
Wilton, Ross-on-Wye, Herefordshire HR9 6AE
☎ (0989) 62155
Country house hotel set in 1.5 acres of gardens, with south-facing rooms. Home cooking by proprietors using fresh local produce.
Bedrooms: 1 single, 5 double & 2 twin, 1 family room.
Bathrooms: 9 private.
Bed & breakfast: £30-£45 single, £50-£70 double.
Half board: £40-£50 daily, £210-£250 weekly.
Lunch available.
Evening meal 7pm (l.o. 9.30pm).
Parking for 20.
Credit: Access, Visa, Diners, Amex.

[icons]

Pencraig Court Hotel M

Pencraig, Ross-on-Wye, Herefordshire HR9 6HR
☎ (098 984) 306
Georgian country house hotel, privately owned, providing both English and French cooking. Large attractive garden overlooking the River Wye.
Bedrooms: 2 single, 4 double & 4 twin.
Bathrooms: 10 private.
Bed & breakfast: £39-£44 single, £56-£66 double.
Half board: £41-£56 daily, £287-£364 weekly.

Evening meal 7pm (l.o. 9.30pm).
Parking for 20.
Open March-October.
Credit: Access, Visa, Diners, Amex.

[icons]

Pengethley Manor

Nr. Ross-on-Wye, Herefordshire HR9 6LL
☎ Harewood End (098 987) 211
Fax (098 987) 238
Best Western
Elegant Georgian country house in superb gardens with magnificent views over Herefordshire countryside. Restaurant has list of over 200 wines.
Bedrooms: 2 single, 10 double & 9 twin, 3 family rooms.
Bathrooms: 24 private.
Bed & breakfast: £67-£115 single, £100-£154 double.
Half board: £62-£87 daily, from £350 weekly.
Lunch available.
Evening meal 6.45pm (l.o. 9.30pm).
Parking for 72.
Credit: Access, Visa, Diners, Amex.

[icons]

Peterstow Country House

Peterstow, Ross-on-Wye, Herefordshire HR9 6LB
☎ (0989) 62826
Charming country house hotel and restaurant set in 25 acres. 3 miles on the A49, Ross-on-Wye to Hereford road. Only the freshest of produce is used in our cooking.
Bedrooms: 5 double & 4 twin.
Bathrooms: 9 private.
Bed & breakfast: £38.50-£69 single, £50-£90 double.
Half board: £45-£65 daily, £315-£455 weekly.
Lunch available.
Evening meal 7.30pm (l.o. 9pm).
Parking for 45.
Credit: Access, Visa, Diners, Amex.

[icons]

Ryefield House Hotel M
APPROVED
Gloucester Rd., Ross-on-Wye, Herefordshire HR9 5NA
☎ (0989) 63030

Continued ▶

ROSS-ON-WYE
Continued

Small private hotel in residential area. Attractive garden, large rooms and personal service. Colour TV in all bedrooms. Parking in grounds.
Bedrooms: 1 single, 2 double & 1 twin, 4 family rooms.
Bathrooms: 5 private, 1 public.
Bed & breakfast: £19-£21 single, £37-£52 double.
Half board: £28.50-£36 daily, £186-£233 weekly.
Evening meal 7pm (l.o. 5pm).
Parking for 10.
⛵ 📞 ♿ 🅿 🛇 🗘 🗑 🖥 🎖 🖫 🎃 🛇 SP

Sunnymount Hotel M
⚜⚜⚜ COMMENDED
Ryefield Rd., Ross-on-Wye, Herefordshire HR9 5LU
☎ (0989) 63880
Warm, comfortable hotel in quiet location on edge of town, offering French and English cooking with home-grown and local produce freshly cooked for each meal.
Bedrooms: 2 single, 3 double & 4 twin.
Bathrooms: 6 private, 1 public.
Bed & breakfast: £21-£32 single, £36-£48 double.
Half board: £30-£36 daily, £196-£220 weekly.
Evening meal 7pm (l.o. 5.30pm).
Parking for 7.
Credit: Access, Visa.
⛵ ♿ 🅿 🛇 🗑 🖥 🎖 🖫 🎃 ◼ DAP SP T

The symbols are explained on the flap inside the back cover.

Map references apply to the colour maps towards the end of this guide.

National Crown ratings were correct at the time of going to press but are subject to change. Please check at the time of booking.

Wharton Lodge Country House Hotel & Restaurant M
⚜⚜⚜ HIGHLY COMMENDED
Weston-under-Penyard, Ross-on-Wye, Herefordshire HR9 7JX
☎ Lea (098 981) 795 Fax 098 981 700
Elegant Georgian home with attractive en-suite bedrooms. Situated in 15 acres of parkland with beautiful terraces and walled gardens.
Bedrooms: 6 double & 3 twin.
Bathrooms: 9 private.
Bed & breakfast: from £90 single, £115-£130 double.
Half board: £82.50-£90 daily.
Lunch available.
Evening meal 7pm (l.o. 9.30pm).
Parking for 31.
Credit: Access, Visa, Diners, Amex.
⛵7 🔲 📞 ◖ 🗑 🅿 🗄 🖥 🎖 ◼ 🎃 🖫 🎃 ♿ 🎖 🕯 🗘 🗡 ◢ 🔆 🛇 🖩
🛇 SP T

Wilton Court Hotel M
Wilton, Ross-on-Wye, Herefordshire HR9 6AQ
☎ (0989) 62569
16th C hotel on the banks of the Wye set in own delightful gardens. Restaurant and bar meals available.
Bedrooms: 2 single, 7 double & 2 twin, 1 family room.
Bathrooms: 10 private, 1 public.
Bed & breakfast: £33-£35 single, £46-£60 double.
Half board: £38-£43 daily, from £240 weekly.
Lunch available.
Evening meal 7pm (l.o. 9.30pm).
Parking for 25.
Credit: Access, Visa, Amex.
⛵ ⊗ 🔲 🗘 ◖ 🗑 🅿 🗄 ◼ 🎖 🕯 🎃 DAP 🛇 SP 🖩

Ye Hostelrie Hotel
Goodrich, Ross-on-Wye, Herefordshire HR9 6HX
☎ Symonds Yat (0600) 890241
Listed building of pseudo-Gothic architecture, in a peaceful village near the renowned Goodrich Castle, overlooking the River Wye. The original building dates from the 17th C.
Bedrooms: 1 single, 4 double & 3 twin.
Bathrooms: 7 private, 2 public.
Bed & breakfast: £22-£30 single, £40 double.
Half board: £32-£42 daily.

Evening meal 7.30pm (l.o. 9pm).
Parking for 25.
⛵ 🔲 🗘 ◖ 🗑 V 🗄 🖥 🖫 ◼ 🎃 🖭 🖩

RUGBY
Warwickshire
Map ref 4C3

Town famous for its public school which gave its name to Rugby Union football and which featured in 'Tom Brown's Schooldays'.
Tourist Information Centre ☎ *(0788) 535348*

Avondale Guest House M
⚜⚜ APPROVED
16 Elsee Rd., Rugby, CV21 3BA
☎ (0788) 578639
Victorian town residence close to Rugby School, convenient for Warwick Castle, Coventry Cathedral, Leamington Spa, National Exhibition Centre and Birmingham.
Bedrooms: 3 twin, 1 family room.
Bathrooms: 1 private, 2 public; 1 private shower.
Bed & breakfast: max. £32 double.
Evening meal 6pm (l.o. 3pm).
Parking for 8.
⛵ 🗘 UL ◖ 🗑 🖥 🖫 ◼ ◢ ▶

Brownsover Hall Hotel M
⚜⚜⚜⚜
Brownsover Lane, Old Brownsover, Rugby, CV21 1HU
☎ (0788) 546 100
Telex 31658 BHHG-G
Fax (0788) 579241
CR Rank
Dating back to the 18th C and originally designed by Sir Gilbert Scott, the hotel is set in 7 acres of parkland, just minutes away from exit 1 of the M6. Table d'hote and a la carte menus, lounge bar and conference facilities.
Bedrooms: 9 single, 15 double & 5 twin, 2 family rooms.
Bathrooms: 31 private.
Bed & breakfast: £41-£80 single, £62-£95 double.
Lunch available.
Evening meal 7.30pm (l.o. 9.30pm).
Parking for 120.
Credit: Access, Visa, Diners, Amex.
⛵ 📞 🗑 🔲 🗘 ◖ V 🗄 🕯 🖫 ◼ 🎖 🔎 ▶ ◢ 🔆 🛇 SP 🖩 T

Hillmorton Manor Hotel M
⚜⚜⚜⚜ COMMENDED
78 High St., Hillmorton, Rugby, CV21 4EE
☎ (0788) 565533 or 72403
Hotel with a la carte restaurant, in a pleasant area of town.
Bedrooms: 5 single, 3 double & 2 twin, 1 family room.
Bathrooms: 11 private.
Bed & breakfast: £35-£45 single, £45-£58 double.
Lunch available.
Evening meal 7pm (l.o. 10pm).
Parking for 45.
Credit: Access, Visa, Amex.
⛵ 📞 🗑 🔲 🗘 ◖ 🗄 🖫 ◼ 🎖 🕯 🔆 ◢

School House Guest House M
⚜⚜⚜ COMMENDED
Bourton-on-Dunsmore, Rugby, CV23 9QY
☎ Marton (0926) 632959
Converted Victorian school, in a village setting. Comfortable and friendly atmosphere. 2 double bedrooms, study/TV lounge, dining and reception rooms.
Bedrooms: 1 double & 1 twin.
Bathrooms: 1 private, 1 public.
Bed & breakfast: from £19 single, from £31 double.
Half board: from £26 daily, from £156 weekly.
Evening meal 6pm (l.o. 7pm).
Parking for 3.
🎃 ⛵ 📞 🗑 🔲 🗘 UL ◖ V 🗄 🖥 🎖 ◢ 🔆 🖫 SP 🖩

RUGELEY
Staffordshire
Map ref 4B3

Town close to Cannock Chase which has over 2000 acres of heath and woodlands with forest trails and picnic sites. Nearby is Shugborough Hall (National Trust) with a fine collection of 18th C furniture and interesting monuments in the grounds.

Cedar Tree Hotel M
⚜⚜
Main Rd., Brereton, Rugeley, WS15 1DY
☎ (0889) 584241
Historic building only 5 miles from Lichfield, on the edge of the beautiful Cannock Chase. Solarium, four squash courts and attractive restaurant.
Bedrooms: 12 single, 6 double & 11 twin, 1 family room.

Bathrooms: 21 private,
4 public.
Bed & breakfast: £25-£29
single, £44-£50 double.
Half board: £35-£40 daily.
Lunch available.
Evening meal 7pm (l.o.
10pm).
Parking for 200.
Credit: Access, Visa, Diners,
Amex.

ST BRIAVELS

Gloucestershire
Map ref 2A1

Village with remains of a
13th C castle, set above
the Wye Valley in the
Forest of Dean. Tintern,
with its magnificent abbey
ruins, is nearby.

Cinderhill House M
Listed APPROVED

St. Briavels, Lydney,
GL15 6RH
☎ Dean (0594) 530393
*Lovely country house
commanding a magnificent
position high over the River
Wye, on the edge of an historic
village. Comfortable
accommodation and good food.
Excellent for walking, touring
and relaxing.*
Bedrooms: 2 double & 3 twin,
1 family room.
Bathrooms: 6 private,
1 public.
Bed & breakfast: from £21
single, £24-£30 double.
Half board: £39-£45 daily,
£250-£420 weekly.
Evening meal 7pm (l.o. 9pm).
Parking for 8.

*The symbol CR
and the name of a
hotel group or
consortium after a
hotel address means
that bookings can
be made through a
central reservations
office. These are
listed on page 540.*

*Please mention this
guide when making
a booking.*

SHIFNAL

Shropshire
Map ref 4A3

Small market town, once
an important staging
centre for coaches on the
Holyhead road. Where
industrialism has not
prevailed, the
predominating
architectural impression
is Georgian, though some
timber-framed houses
survived the Great Fire of
1591. Within easy reach
of the Ironbridge Gorge
Museum.

Park House Hotel M
APPROVED

Park St., Shifnal, TF11 9BA
☎ Telford (0952) 460128
Telex 35438
CR Rank
*Magnificent character hotel
converted from 2 17th C
country houses. Located just a
few minutes' drive from exit 4
of the M54. 40 minutes from
Birmingham. Leisure facilities.*
Bedrooms: 5 single, 27 double
& 19 twin, 3 family rooms.
Bathrooms: 54 private.
Bed & breakfast: £56-£82
single, £82-£97 double.
Lunch available.
Evening meal 6.30pm (l.o.
10pm).
Parking for 150.
Credit: Access, Visa, Diners,
Amex.

Village Farm Lodge M

Sheriffhales, Shifnal,
TF11 8RD
☎ Telford (0952) 462763
*Tastefully converted farm
buildings in Sheriffhales
village, situated on the B4379
off the A5. Minutes from
Telford and Ironbridge Gorge.*
Bedrooms: 1 single, 1 double
& 4 twin, 2 family rooms.
Bathrooms: 8 private.
Bed & breakfast: £25-£28.50
single, £35-£39.50 double.
Lunch available.
Evening meal 6.30pm (l.o.
8.30pm).
Parking for 8.
Credit: Access, Visa, Amex.

SHIPSTON ON STOUR

Warwickshire
Map ref 2B1

Old market town with
many Georgian houses
and inns. Honington Hall,
a small Carolean house,
is nearby and Stratford,
the Cotswolds, Chipping
Campden and Hidcote
Manor Gardens can be
easily reached.

The Old Mill Hotel & Restaurant

Shipston on Stour,
CV36 4AW
☎ (0608) 61880
*Converted water mill, on the
banks of the River Stour, with
comfortable bar, restaurant
and en-suite bedrooms. Off the
Banbury Road (B4035)
heading out of Shipston on
Stour.*
Bedrooms: 3 double & 2 twin.
Bathrooms: 5 private.
Bed & breakfast: max. £35
single, max. £46 double.
Lunch available.
Evening meal 7pm (l.o. 9pm).
Parking for 5.
Credit: Access, Visa, Diners,
Amex.

SHRAWLEY

Hereford & Worcester
Map ref 2B1

7m NW. Worcester
Scattered village along
the pleasant switch-back
road from Holt to
Stourport, with a hilltop
Norman church and the
mound of a castle once
belonging to Warwick the
Kingmaker.

Lenchford Hotel M
APPROVED

Shrawley, Worcester
Worcestershire WR6 6TB
☎ Worcester (0905) 620229
*Late Georgian house with
modern additions and
amenities in beautiful
countryside on bank of the
Severn. On B4196 Worcester
to Stourport road.*
Bedrooms: 4 single, 7 double
& 4 twin, 1 family room.
Bathrooms: 16 private,
1 public.
Bed & breakfast: £43.50-£47
single, £61.50 double.
Half board: £50-£60 daily.
Lunch available.

Evening meal 7pm (l.o.
9.30pm).
Parking for 75.
Credit: Access, Visa, Diners,
Amex.

SHREWSBURY

Shropshire
Map ref 4A3

Beautiful historic town on
the River Severn retaining
many fine old timber-
framed houses. Its
attractions include
Rowley's Museum with
Roman finds, remains of
a castle, Clive House
Museum, St. Chad's 18th
C round church and
rowing on the river.
*Tourist Information
Centre ☎ (0743) 350761
or 350762*

Abbey Lodge Guest House M
Listed APPROVED

68 Abbey Foregate,
Shrewsbury, SY2 6BE
☎ (0743) 235832
*Friendly family-run business
close to town centre. Evening
meals available, parking at
rear. Children welcome.*
Bedrooms: 4 single, 3 double
& 2 twin, 2 family rooms.
Bathrooms: 2 private,
2 public; 4 private showers.
Bed & breakfast: £13 single,
£15-£18 double.
Half board: £17.25-£22.50
daily.
Evening meal 6pm (l.o.
8.30am).
Parking for 10.
Credit: Visa.

Abbot's Mead Hotel M
APPROVED

9-10 St. Julian Friars,
Shrewsbury, SY1 1XL
☎ (0743) 235281
*Georgian town house between
town centre and the River
Severn. All bedrooms have
private facilities, colour TV
and tea/coffee makers. Car
parking.*
Bedrooms: 10 double &
4 twin.
Bathrooms: 14 private,
1 public.
Bed & breakfast: from £31
single, from £45 double.
Half board: £32-£39 daily.
Lunch available.
Evening meal 6pm (l.o.
9.30pm).

Continued ▶

245

Continued

Parking for 8.
Credit: Access, Visa, C.Bl., Diners, Amex.

Albright Hussey Hotel and Restaurant M
HIGHLY COMMENDED

Ellesmere Rd., Shrewsbury, SY4 3AF
☎ Bomere Heath
(0939) 290571 & (0939) 290523
Fax 0939 291143
Historic 16th C Shropshire manor, with moat, pretty gardens and assorted wildlife including mandarin ducks and black swans. 2 miles from Shrewsbury town centre.
Bedrooms: 3 double & 2 twin.
Bathrooms: 5 private.
Bed & breakfast: £60-£85 single, £65-£110 double.
Half board: £76-£86 daily.
Lunch available.
Evening meal 7pm (l.o. 10pm).
Parking for 60.
Credit: Access, Visa, C.Bl., Amex.

Albrighton Hall Hotel M
COMMENDED

Albrighton, Shrewsbury, SY4 3AG
☎ Bomere Heath
(0939) 291000 Telex 35726 ALBHAL G
Rank
Just 2 miles from Shrewsbury town centre, set in 15 acres of landscaped gardens with ornamental lake. Full leisure facilities. 39 bedrooms, many four-posters.
Bedrooms: 5 single, 27 double & 7 twin.
Bathrooms: 39 private.
Bed & breakfast: £56-£87 single, £76-£102 double.
Lunch available.
Evening meal 7pm (l.o. 10pm).
Parking for 200.
Credit: Access, Visa, Diners, Amex.

The Bancroft M
Listed

17 Coton Cres., Shrewsbury, SY1 2NY
☎ (0743) 231746

Bed and breakfast accommodation close to Shrewsbury centre and railway station. All rooms have TV, tea/coffee making facilities and wash basin.
Bedrooms: 1 single, 1 twin, 1 family room.
Bathrooms: 1 public.
Bed & breakfast: £15-£17 single, £28-£32 double.
Half board: from £21 daily.
Evening meal 6.30pm.
Parking for 3.
Credit: Access, Visa.

Hawkstone Park Hotel M

Weston-under-Redcastle, Shrewsbury, SY4 5UY
☎ Lee Brockhurst
(093 924) 611 Telex 35793
Fax (093 924) 311
Best Western
Busy golfing country hotel in 300-acre Shropshire estate with famous antiquities. 2 18-hole golf-courses. Sandy Lyle learned his game here. Non-residents welcome. Restaurants, bars and extensive conference/banqueting facilities. 14 miles north of Shrewsbury, off A49 Whitchurch road.
Bedrooms: 5 single, 2 double & 48 twin, 4 family rooms.
Bathrooms: 59 private.
Bed & breakfast: £68-£77 single, £100-£136 double.
Lunch available.
Evening meal 7.30pm (l.o. 9.45pm).
Parking for 300.
Credit: Access, Visa, Diners, Amex.

Pengwern Hotel M

Longden Rd., Shrewsbury, SY3 7JE
☎ (0743) 343871 Fax 0743 365387
Hotel close to town centre and with lively atmosphere, specialising in sports and special interest groups. All roooms are en-suite and have colour TV.
Bedrooms: 2 single, 4 double & 4 twin, 2 family rooms.
Bathrooms: 11 private; 1 private shower.
Bed & breakfast: £29-£45 single, £38-£59 double.
Half board: £31-£42 daily.
Lunch available.

Evening meal 7pm (l.o. 11.59pm).
Parking for 75.
Credit: Access, Visa, Diners.

Radbrook Hall Hotel M

Radbrook Rd., Shrewsbury, SY3 9BQ
☎ (0743) 236676 Fax 0743 59194
Country house with a colourful history, set in 5 acres of grounds just outside Shrewsbury, with squash courts, games room, sunbed, jacuzzi and sauna. Just off A5 on A488 to Bishop's Castle.
Bedrooms: 3 single, 14 double & 8 twin, 3 family rooms.
Bathrooms: 28 private.
Bed & breakfast: £51-£58 single, £65 double.
Lunch available.
Evening meal 6pm (l.o. 10.30pm).
Parking for 250.
Credit: Access, Visa, Diners, Amex.

Rowton Castle M
COMMENDED

Shrewsbury, SY5 9EP
☎ (0743) 884044
Fax (0743) 884949
Rowton Castle has been tastefully converted into a hotel, set in 20 acres yet only 10 minutes from historic Shrewsbury.
Bedrooms: 2 single, 17 double.
Bathrooms: 19 private.
Bed & breakfast: £62-£66 single, £72-£82 double.
Half board: £79.50-£83.50 daily.
Lunch available.
Evening meal 7pm (l.o. 10.30pm).
Parking for 120.
Credit: Access, Visa, Amex.

Sandford House Hotel
COMMENDED

St. Julian Friars, Shrewsbury, SY1 1XL
☎ (0743) 3829
Close to the river, with pleasant walks and access to good fishing. Easy parking and within a few minutes of the town centre.
Bedrooms: 2 single, 4 double & 2 twin, 2 family rooms.
Bathrooms: 5 private, 1 public; 2 private showers.

Bed & breakfast: £21-£21.50 single, £35-£42 double.
Parking for 3.

Sunbeams Guest House
Listed

1 Bishop St., Cherry Orchard, Shrewsbury, SY2 5HA
☎ (0743) 357495
Corner house on main road, near shops. Town centre 15 minutes' walking distance.
Bedrooms: 1 single, 2 double & 1 twin, 1 family room.
Bathrooms: 1 public.
Bed & breakfast: from £11.50 single, from £23 double.
Half board: from £17 daily, from £119 weekly.
Evening meal 6.30pm.

Sydney House Hotel M
APPROVED

Coton Cres., Coton Hill, Shrewsbury, SY1 2LJ
☎ (0743) 354681
Edwardian town house with period features, 10 minutes' walk from town centre and railway station. Some rooms en-suite. All with direct dial telephones, colour TV, hot drink facilities and hair-dryers.
Bedrooms: 2 single, 2 double & 2 twin, 1 family room.
Bathrooms: 3 private, 2 public.
Bed & breakfast: £27-£40 single, £40-£52 double.
Half board: £27.50-£36.50 daily, £170-£228 weekly.
Evening meal 7.30pm (l.o. 9pm).
Parking for 8.
Credit: Access, Visa.

Talbot House Hotel
COMMENDED

Cross Hill, Shrewsbury, SY1 1JH
☎ (0743) 368889
17th C Grade II listed building in quiet, town centre position, close to river. Tastefully redesigned and refurbished. Spacious bedrooms with many extra facilities. "Our aim is your comfort - your wish our command".
Bedrooms: 2 double & 1 twin.
Bathrooms: 3 private, 1 public.
Bed & breakfast: from £28 single, from £38 double.
Half board: £29-£38 daily, £203-£266 weekly.
Evening meal 6pm (l.o. midday).

SLIMBRIDGE

Gloucestershire
Map ref 2B1

The Wildfowl Trust was
founded by Sir Peter
Scott and has the world's
largest collection of
wildfowl. Of special
interest are the wild
swans and the geese
which wander around the
grounds.

Tudor Arms Lodge
☺☺☺

Shepherds Patch, Slimbridge,
Gloucester, GL2 7BP
☎ Dursley (0453) 890306
*Newly-built lodge adjoining an
18th C freehouse, alongside
Gloucester and Sharpness
Canal. Renowned Slimbridge
Wildfowl Trust only 800 yards
away.*
Bedrooms: 2 double & 8 twin,
2 family rooms.
Bathrooms: 12 private.
Bed & breakfast: £33-£43
single, £48-£54 double.
Lunch available.
Evening meal 7pm (l.o.
10pm).
Parking for 70.
Credit: Access, Visa.
☐☐☐☐☐☐☐☐☐
☐☐☐☐

SOLIHULL

W. Midlands
Map ref 4B3

On the outskirts of
Birmingham. Some Tudor
houses and a 13th C
church remain amongst
the new public buildings
and shopping centre. The
16th C Malvern Hall is
now a school and the
15th C Chester House at
Knowle is now a library.
*Tourist Information
Centre* ☎ *021-704 6130*

Cedarwood House ⚏
☺☺

347 Lyndon Road, Solihull,
B92 7QT
☎ 021-743 5844
*Private guesthouse, all
bedrooms elegantly furnished,
en-suite bathrooms. Within 2
miles of the National
Exhibition Centre, airport,
station and Solihull centre.*
Bedrooms: 3 single, 1 double
& 1 twin.
Bathrooms: 5 private.
Bed & breakfast: £30-£45
single, £40-£55 double.
Parking for 6.
☐3☐☐☐☐☐☐☐☐☐☐
☐☐☐

The Forest Hotel
☺☺☺ COMMENDED

Station Approach, Dorridge,
Solihull, B93 8JA
☎ Knowle (0564) 772120
*Attractive black and white
village hotel, with bus and rail
services adjacent, close to
National Exhibition Centre.*
Bedrooms: 2 double & 9 twin,
1 family room.
Bathrooms: 12 private.
Bed & breakfast: £55 single,
£65-£75 double.
Half board: £67-£70 daily,
£89-£95 weekly.
Lunch available.
Evening meal 7pm (l.o.
10pm).
Parking for 58.
Credit: Access, Visa, Diners,
Amex.
☐☐☐☐☐☐☐☐☐
☐☐☐☐

Richmond House
Hotel ⚏

47 Richmond Rd., Olton,
Solihull, B92 7RP
☎ 021-707 9746
*Modern small hotel with
cocktail bar, elegant
restaurant, banqueting and
conference facilities. Just 10
minutes' drive to Birmingham
Airport, NEC and city centre.*
Bedrooms: 4 single, 4 double
& 7 twin.
Bathrooms: 15 private.
Bed & breakfast: from £50
single, from £63 double.
Half board: from £65 daily,
from £400 weekly.
Lunch available.
Evening meal 6.30pm (l.o.
10.30pm).
Parking for 40.
Credit: Access, Visa, C.Bl.,
Diners, Amex.
☐☐☐☐☐☐☐☐☐
☐☐☐☐☐☐☐☐☐
☐☐☐☐

St. Johns Swallow Hotel
☺☺☺

651 Warwick Rd., Solihull,
B91 1AT
☎ 021-711 3000 Telex 339352
⊕ Swallow
*Well-appointed, modern hotel
close to Solihull town centre. A
good touring base for
Stratford, Warwick and
Coventry.*
Bedrooms: 61 single,
14 double & 123 twin,
8 family rooms.
Bathrooms: 206 private.
Bed & breakfast: from £86
single, from £105 double.
Lunch available.
Evening meal 7pm (l.o.
10pm).
Parking for 380.

Credit: Access, Visa, C.Bl.,
Diners, Amex.
☐☐☐☐☐☐☐☐☐
☐☐☐☐☐☐☐☐☐
☐☐☐☐

Solihull Moat House ⚏
☺☺☺☺

Homer Rd., Solihull,
B91 3QD
☎ 021-711 4700 Telex 333355
Fax 021 711 2696
⊕ Queens Moat Houses
*Mordern hotel, tastefully
furnished in traditional English
style, set in mature grounds
featuring a lake and fountain.*
Bedrooms: 67 double &
48 twin.
Bathrooms: 115 private.
Bed & breakfast: £33-£108
single, £55-£130 double.
Half board: £48-£80.50 daily.
Lunch available.
Evening meal 7pm (l.o.
10.30pm).
Parking for 161.
Credit: Access, Visa, C.Bl.,
Diners, Amex.
☐☐☐☐☐☐☐☐☐
☐☐☐☐☐☐☐☐☐
☐☐☐☐

STAFFORD

Staffordshire
Map ref 4B3

The town has a long
history and some half-
timbered buildings still
remain, notably the 16th
C High House. There are
several museums in the
town and Shugborough
Hall and the famous
angler Izaak Walton's
cottage, now a museum,
are nearby.
*Tourist Information
Centre* ☎ *(0785) 40204*

Fairfield Guest House ⚏

70 Lichfield Rd., Stafford,
ST17 4LW
☎ (0785) 52854
*All rooms have colour TV with
video and sky movies, hot and
cold water, radio alarm, tea
and coffee making facilities.*
Bedrooms: 4 single, 3 double
& 1 twin, 1 family room.
Bathrooms: 2 public;
2 private showers.
Bed & breakfast: £12-£15
single, £20-£22 double.
Half board: £14-£19 daily,
£70-£118 weekly.
Evening meal 6.30pm (l.o.
5.30pm).
Parking for 9.
☐☐☐☐☐☐☐☐☐
☐☐☐☐☐☐

The Old Parsonage
Coach House ⚏
☺☺☺

The Old Parsonage, High
Offley, Woodseaves,
Stafford, ST20 0NE
☎ Woodseaves (0785) 284446
*The Coach House at the Old
Parsonage, off the A519
Eccleshall to Newport road,
offers en-suite bedrooms and a
dining room with views to the
Welsh Hills.*
Bedrooms: 4 double.
Bathrooms: 4 private.
Bed & breakfast: £35 single,
£35 double.
Lunch available.
Evening meal 7.30pm (l.o.
10pm).
Parking for 13.
Credit: Access, Visa, Diners,
Amex.
☐☐☐☐☐☐☐☐☐
☐☐☐☐☐☐☐☐

Swan Hotel ⚏

Greengate St., Stafford,
ST16 2JA
☎ (0785) 58142 Fax 0785
223372
*Handsome 400-year-old former
coaching inn in a central
position, retaining many of its
original oak beams, with a
hidden priest hole and
Jacobean-style reception area.
Some of the oak panelling was
once in Stafford Castle.*
Bedrooms: 12 single,
11 double & 4 twin, 5 family
rooms.
Bathrooms: 32 private.
Bed & breakfast: £45-£49
single, £66 double.
Lunch available.
Evening meal 6pm (l.o.
10pm).
Parking for 50.
Credit: Access, Visa, Diners,
Amex.
☐☐☐☐☐☐☐☐☐
☐☐☐☐☐☐☐☐☐

STAVERTON

Gloucestershire
Map ref 2B1

4m W. Cheltenham

Hope Orchard Motel
☺

Gloucester Rd., Staverton,
Cheltenham GL51 0TF
☎ (0452) 855556
*Situated on B4063 midway
between Cheltenham and
Gloucester, ideally located for
excursions to Cotswold villages
and the Forest of Dean.*
Bedrooms: 1 single, 2 double
& 1 twin.

Continued ▶

STAVERTON
Continued

Bathrooms: 4 private.
Bed & breakfast: £15-£17.50
single, £25-£27.50 double.
Parking for 6.

STOKE-ON-TRENT

Staffordshire
Map ref 4B2

Famous for its pottery.
Factories of several
famous makers, including
Josiah Wedgwood, can
be visited. The City
Museum has one of the
finest pottery and
porcelain collections in
the world.
*Tourist Information
Centre* ☎ *(0782) 411222*

Central Hotel
86-96 Wellesley St., Shelton,
Stoke-on-Trent, ST1 4NW
☎ (0782) 272380 Fax 0782
285296
*Centrally located in the heart
of the 6 towns that form the
city of Stoke-on-Trent,
convenient for factory shops,
museums and Alton Towers.
Recently refurbished to
complement the turn-of-the-
century architecture.*
Bedrooms: 14 single,
12 double & 10 twin, 2 family
rooms.
Bathrooms: 38 private.
Bed & breakfast: £30-£37
single, £40-£47 double.
Half board: £36-£43 daily.
Lunch available.
Evening meal 6.30pm (l.o.
9pm).
Parking for 25.
Credit: Access, Visa, Diners,
Amex.

The Corrie Guest House M
13 Newton St., Basford,
Stoke-on-Trent, ST4 6JN
☎ (0782) 614838
*Owner-run guesthouse in quiet
residential area, close to public
transport and local amenities.
Within walking distance of the
New Victoria Theatre and
midway between Hanley and
Newcastle-under-Lyme.*
Bedrooms: 3 single, 1 double
& 2 twin, 1 family room.
Bathrooms: 1 private,
3 public.
Bed & breakfast: £15-£21
single, £30-£35 double.

Half board: £22-£28 daily.
Evening meal 6pm (l.o.
4.30pm).
Parking for 9.

The Crown Hotel M
Times Sq., Longton, Stoke-
on-Trent, ST3 1HD
☎ Stoke-on-Trent
(0782) 599343 Fax 0782
598062
*Completely refurbished town
centre hotel, with easy access
to all Potteries towns and
Alton Towers. Bar and a la
carte restaurant.*
Bedrooms: 21 single,
12 double & 7 twin.
Bathrooms: 40 private.
Bed & breakfast: £31.90-
£40.50 single, £46-£52.15
double.
Half board: £42.55-£51.15
daily, £297.85-£358 weekly.
Lunch available.
Evening meal 7pm (l.o.
10pm).
Parking for 45.
Credit: Access, Visa, Diners,
Amex.

Hanchurch Manor M
Hanchurch, Stoke-on-Trent,
ST4 8SD
☎ (0782) 643030
Fax (0782) 643035
*Early 19th C Grade II listed
building, set in 9 acres of
landscaped garden.*
Bedrooms: 4 single, 7 double
& 1 twin.
Bathrooms: 12 private.
Bed & breakfast: £75-£85
single, £95-£125 double.
Half board: £68.50-£91.50
daily.
Lunch available.
Evening meal 7pm (l.o.
9.30pm).
Parking for 40.
Credit: Access, Visa, Diners,
Amex.

The Hollies
Clay Lake, Endon, Stoke-on-
Trent, ST9 9DD
☎ Stoke-on-Trent
(0782) 503252
*Delightful, Victorian house in a
quiet country setting off
B5051. Convenient for M6, the
Potteries and Alton Towers.
Non-smokers only, please.*
Bedrooms: 2 double & 1 twin,
2 family rooms.
Bathrooms: 3 private,
1 public.

Bed & breakfast: £16-£25
single, £28-£36 double.
Parking for 5.

Rhodes Hotel M
Listed
42 Leek Rd., Stoke-on-Trent,
ST4 2AR
☎ (0782) 416320
*Family hotel offering bed and
breakfast. Our guests' comfort
is our pleasure. City centre,
easy access to M6, British
Rail, bus service to Alton
Towers and Potteries.*
Bedrooms: 2 double & 4 twin,
1 family room.
Bathrooms: 2 public;
2 private showers.
Bed & breakfast: £18-£20
single, £30-£32 double.

Sneyd Arms Hotel M
Tower Square, Tunstall,
Stoke-on-Trent, ST6 5AA
☎ (0782) 826722
*Residential town centre hotel,
restaurant and public house
with function suite, gym, sauna
and sunbeds. En-suite and
budget accommodation
available.*
Bedrooms: 5 single, 4 double
& 4 twin, 2 family rooms.
Bathrooms: 8 private,
2 public.
Bed & breakfast: £22-£33
single, £38-£45 double.
Lunch available.
Parking for 2.
Credit: Access, Visa, Diners,
Amex.

Stakis Stoke-on-Trent Grand Hotel M
COMMENDED
Trinity St., Hanley, Stoke-on-
Trent, ST1 5NB
☎ (0782) 202361
Telex 367264
CR Stakis
*In the centre of Hanley, the
commercial hub of the city of
Stoke-on-Trent. Late Victorian
building, recently renovated
and refurbished. Facilities for
conference and social
occasions. Indoor swimming
pool and leisure club. Half
board rate based on a
minimum 2 night stay.*
Bedrooms: 30 single,
61 double & 30 twin, 7 family
rooms.
Bathrooms: 128 private.
Bed & breakfast: £89-£99
single, £110-£120 double.
Half board: from £36 daily,
from £196 weekly.
Lunch available.

Evening meal 6.30pm (l.o.
10pm).
Parking for 170.
Credit: Access, Visa, Diners,
Amex.

Verdon Guest House
Listed
44 Charles St., Hanley,
Stoke-on-Trent, ST1 3JY
☎ (0782) 264244
*Large, friendly guesthouse
almost in town centre and close
to bus station. Convenient for
all pottery factory visits,
museum and Festival Park.
Alton Towers 20 minutes, M6
10 minutes.*
Bedrooms: 3 single, 3 double
& 3 twin, 3 family rooms.
Bathrooms: 4 public.
Bed & breakfast: £14-£16
single, £26-£30 double.
Parking for 7.

White Gables Hotel M
Trentham Rd., Blurton,
Stoke-on-Trent, ST3 3DT
☎ (0782) 324882
*Elegant, peaceful country
house style hotel in own
grounds. Beautifully
maintained with good facilities
for discerning businessmen and
families alike. Owner run. 1
mile from Wedgwood, 10 miles
from Alton Towers.*
Bedrooms: 1 single, 2 double
& 4 twin, 2 family rooms.
Bathrooms: 3 private,
2 public.
Bed & breakfast: £25-£50
single, £40-£60 double.
Half board: £25-£40 daily.
Evening meal 5pm (l.o. 7pm).
Parking for 11.
Credit: Access, Visa, Amex.

White House Hotel M
94 Stone Rd., Trent Vale,
Stoke-on-Trent, ST4 6SP
☎ (0782) 642460 & 657189
*A warm, friendly early
Victorian house. 1 mile from
M6 motorway, junction 15.
Ideal access to the world-
famous Potteries and local
tourist attractions.*
Bedrooms: 5 single, 2 double
& 1 twin, 2 family rooms.
Bathrooms: 2 private,
2 public.
Bed & breakfast: £21-£33
single, £26-£44 double.
Half board: £28.50-£40.50
daily, £190-£280 weekly.

Evening meal 6.30pm (l.o.
5.30pm).
Parking for 10.
Credit: Access, Visa, Amex.
🛏 🕹 📞 🖥 ⚡ 🛈 V ⛘ TV
🅿 ♨ ✕ 🌂 SP T

STONE

Staffordshire
Map ref 4B2

Town on the River Trent
with the remains of a 12th
C Augustinian priory. It is
surrounded by pleasant
countryside. Trentham
Gardens with 500 acres
of parklands and
recreational facilities is
within easy reach.

Stone House Hotel M
🍴🍴🍴 COMMENDED
Stone, ST15 0BQ
☎ (0785) 815531
Telex 367404 Fax 0785 814764
ⓒⓡ Lansbury
*Elegant building, set in its own
delightful grounds, offers
extensive leisure facilities,
including tennis courts and
swimming pool.*
Bedrooms: 20 single,
21 double & 8 twin, 1 family
room.
Bathrooms: 50 private.
Bed & breakfast: £28-£78
single, £56-£90 double.
Half board: £40-£93 daily.
Lunch available.
Evening meal 7pm (l.o.
10pm).
Parking for 100.
Credit: Access, Visa, Diners,
Amex.
🛏 🕹 📞 🖥 ⚡ 🛈 V
⚡ ⛘ TV ● 🍴 ♨ 🌂 ♿ ♨
🔲 ♒ ✕ SP T

STOURBRIDGE

W. Midlands
Map ref 4B3

Town on the River Stour,
famous for its
glassworks. Several of
the factories can be
visited and glassware
purchased at the factory
shops.

The Limes Hotel M
🍴🍴
260 Hagley Rd., Pedmore,
Stourbridge, DY9 0RW
☎ Hagley (0562) 882689
*Private hotel based on a
Victorian house run by the
owners and in half an acre of
grounds.*
Bedrooms: 6 single, 1 double
& 4 twin.
Bathrooms: 5 private,
2 public.

Bed & breakfast: £28.25-
£30.50 single, £35.25-£40.50
double.
Half board: £35.15-£37.40
daily, £225.35-£241.10
weekly.
Evening meal 6pm (l.o.
7.30pm).
Parking for 12.
Credit: Access, Visa.
🛏 🕹 📞 ⚡ 🛈 ⛘ TV 🅿
🅿 🍴 ♨ 🌂

STOW-ON-THE-WOLD

Gloucestershire
Map ref 2B1

Attractive Cotswold wool
town with a large market-
place and some fine
houses, especially the old
grammar school. There is
an interesting church
dating from Norman
times. Stow-on-the-Wold
is surrounded by lovely
countryside and Cotswold
villages.
*Tourist Information
Centre* ☎ *(0451) 31082*

Auld Stocks Hotel M
🍴🍴🍴
The Square, Stow-on-the-
Wold, Cheltenham,
GL54 1AF
☎ Cotswold (0451) 30666
Fax 0451 870014
*17th C hotel refurbished to
combine modern-day comforts
with original charm and
character. Facing quiet village
green on which original stocks
still stand. Exposed stone
walls, oak timbers and roaring
log fires.*
Bedrooms: 1 single, 13 double
& 2 twin, 1 family room.
Bathrooms: 17 private.
Bed & breakfast: £30-£35
single, £60-£70 double.
Half board: £36.50-£42.50
daily, £225-£297 weekly.
Lunch available.
Evening meal 7pm (l.o.
9.30pm).
Parking for 14.
Credit: Access, Visa, Diners,
Amex.
🛏 🕹 📞 ⚡ 🖥 ⚡ 🛈 V ⛘
TV 🅿 🅿 🍴 🕐 ♨ ♿ SP 🌂
T

Grapevine Hotel M
🍴🍴🍴🍴 COMMENDED
Sheep St., Stow-on-the-Wold,
Cheltenham, GL54 1AU
☎ Cotswold (0451) 30344
Fax 0451 32278
ⓒⓡ Best Western

*Exceptional small hotel in
antique centre of Cotswolds.
Accent on food and hospitality.
Lovely furnishings complement
the romantic, vine-clad
conservatory restaurant.*
Bedrooms: 15 double &
5 twin, 3 family rooms.
Bathrooms: 23 private.
Bed & breakfast: £92-£114
double.
Half board: £50.50-£93 daily.
Lunch available.
Evening meal 7pm (l.o.
9.30pm).
Parking for 23.
Credit: Access, Visa, Diners,
Amex.
🛏 🕹 🖥 📞 ⚡ 🖥 ⚡ 🛈 V
⚡ ⛘ 🅿 🅿 ✕ 🌂 SP 🌂
🌂

Old Farmhouse Hotel M
🍴🍴🍴 APPROVED
Lower Swell, Stow-on-the-
Wold, Cheltenham,
GL54 1LF
☎ Cotswold (0451) 30232
*Sympathetically converted 16th
C Cotswold stone farmhouse in
a quiet hamlet, 1 mile west of
Stow-on-the-Wold. Offers
warm and informal hospitality.*
Bedrooms: 11 double &
3 twin, 1 family room.
Bathrooms: 12 private,
1 public.
Bed & breakfast: £21.40-
£59.20 single, £42.80-£88.80
double.
Half board: £35.85-£58.85
daily, £250-£411 weekly.
Lunch available.
Evening meal 7pm (l.o. 9pm).
Parking for 25.
Credit: Access, Visa.
🛏 🕹 🖥 📞 ⚡ 🖥 ⚡ 🛈 V
⚡ ⛘ 🅿 🍴 ♨ 🌂 SP
🌂

Stow Lodge Hotel M
🍴🍴🍴 COMMENDED
The Square, Stow-on-the-
Wold, Cheltenham,
GL54 1AB
☎ Cotswold (0451) 30485
*Cotswold-stone manor house in
gardens overlooking market
square. Log fires in bar and
lounge.*
Bedrooms: 1 single, 12 double
& 9 twin.
Bathrooms: 20 private,
1 public.
Bed & breakfast: £38-£60
single, £50-£90 double.
Evening meal 7pm (l.o. 9pm).
Parking for 30.
Credit: Diners, Amex.
🛏 5 🖥 📞 ⚡ 🛈 ⛘ ● 🖥
♨ ✕ 🌂 SP 🌂

STRATFORD-UPON-AVON

Warwickshire
Map ref 2B1

Famous as
Shakespeare's home
town, Stratford's many
attractions include his
birthplace, New Place
where he died, the Royal
Shakespeare Theatre and
Gallery, 'The World of
Shakespeare' audio-
visual theatre, Hall's Croft
(his daughter's house)
and Holy Trinity Church
where he was buried.
*Tourist Information
Centre* ☎ *(0789) 293127*

Aberfoyle Guest House M
🍴🍴 APPROVED
3 Evesham Place, Stratford-
upon-Avon, CV37 6HT
☎ (0789) 295703
*Charming bijou Edwardian
residence with spacious
bedrooms, near town centre.
English breakfast. Garage.
Non-smokers only please.*
Bedrooms: 1 double & 1 twin.
Bathrooms: 1 private,
1 public.
Bed & breakfast: £27-£34
double.
Parking for 3.
🛏 7 📞 ⚡ UL 🛈 V ⛘ 🅿 DAP

Ambleside Guest House M
🍴🍴
41 Grove Rd., Stratford-
upon-Avon, CV37 6PB
☎ (0789) 297239/295670
*Small friendly guesthouse close
to town centre. One room has
pretty four-poster bed. Local
proprietors, established 1961.*
Bedrooms: 1 single, 1 double
& 1 twin, 3 family rooms.
Bathrooms: 3 private,
1 public.
Bed & breakfast: £15-£17
single, £30-£40 double.
Parking for 21.
Credit: Access, Visa.
🛏 🖥 📞 ⚡ UL V ⛘ TV 🅿
🅿 SP

Ashley Court Guest House M
🍴🍴
55 Shipston Rd., Stratford-
upon-Avon, CV37 7LN
☎ (0789) 297278
*In three-quarters of an acre of
grounds and within short
walking distance of town centre
and theatre.*
Bedrooms: 2 double & 1 twin,
3 family rooms.

Continued ▶

STRATFORD-UPON-AVON
Continued

Bathrooms: 6 private.
Bed & breakfast: £32-£38 double.
Parking for 10.

Avon View Hotel ᴍ

121 Shipston Rd., Stratford-upon-Avon, CV37 7LW
☎ (0789) 297542
Small family-run hotel within easy walking distance of the town, offering a warm welcome.
Bedrooms: 2 single, 5 double & 1 twin, 1 family room.
Bathrooms: 9 private.
Bed & breakfast: £22-£32 single, £40-£50 double.
Half board: £25-£50 daily.
Evening meal 5pm (l.o. 4pm).
Parking for 16.
Credit: Access, Visa, Diners, Amex.

Barbette ᴍ

165 Evesham Rd., Stratford-upon-Avon, CV37 9BP
☎ (0789) 297822
Approximately 10 minutes' walk from the town centre, with access all day and ample parking. Guests have use of the garden.
Bedrooms: 2 single, 1 double, 2 family rooms.
Bathrooms: 1 private, 1 public; 1 private shower.
Bed & breakfast: £15-£18 single, £29-£38 double.
Parking for 5.

Bradbourne Guest House ᴍ

44 Shipston Rd., Stratford-upon-Avon, CV37 7LP
☎ (0789) 204178
Detached Tudor-style property, 7 minutes' walk from the town and theatre. All rooms recently refurbished, ground floor bedrooms available.
Bedrooms: 1 single, 2 double & 2 twin, 1 family room.
Bathrooms: 2 private, 2 public; 2 private showers.
Bed & breakfast: £13-£16 single, £23-£40 double.
Parking for 8.

Brett House ᴍ

8 Broad Walk, Stratford-upon-Avon, CV37 6HS
☎ (0789) 266374
Mature house with spacious rooms, within easy walking distance of the theatre and town centre. Ample parking.
Bedrooms: 1 single, 1 double, 2 family rooms.
Bathrooms: 1 private, 1 public.
Bed & breakfast: £14-£15 single, £28-£31 double.
Parking for 3.

Brook Lodge ᴍ
COMMENDED

192 Alcester Rd., Stratford-upon-Avon, CV37 9DR
☎ (0789) 295988
Large detached family-run guesthouse, well-appointed and with a friendly atmosphere. Most rooms en-suite. Ample car parking.
Bedrooms: 4 double & 1 twin, 2 family rooms.
Bathrooms: 5 private, 1 public; 2 private showers.
Bed & breakfast: £32-£38 double.
Parking for 13.
Credit: Access, Visa, Amex.

Charlecote Pheasant Country Hotel ᴍ
COMMENDED

Charlecote, Warwick, CV35 9EW
☎ (0789) 470333 Fax 0789 470222
Ⓖ Queens Moat Houses
18th C farmhouse converted into a comfortable hotel, opposite Charlecote Park. Set in beautiful Warwickshire countryside, 4 miles from Stratford-upon-Avon.
Bedrooms: 5 single, 47 double & 6 twin, 2 family rooms.
Bathrooms: 60 private.
Bed & breakfast: £69.50-£78.50 single, £85-£100 double.
Half board: £47.50-£62.95 daily, from £332.50 weekly.
Lunch available.
Evening meal 7pm (l.o. 10pm).
Parking for 130.
Credit: Access, Visa, Diners, Amex.
⊕ Display advertisement appears on page 263.

Clomendy Guest House ᴍ

157 Evesham Rd., Stratford-upon-Avon, CV37 9BP
☎ (0789) 266957
Small, detached, mock-Tudor family-run guesthouse, convenient for town centre, Anne Hathaway's cottage and theatres. Stratford-in-Bloom commendation winner.
Bedrooms: 1 single, 1 double & 1 twin.
Bathrooms: 1 public; 1 private shower.
Bed & breakfast: £13-£17 single, £24-£33 double.
Parking for 4.

The Coach House Hotel ᴍ

17 Warwick Rd., Stratford-upon-Avon, CV37 6YW
☎ (0789) 204109 & 299468
Regency-style family-run hotel within 6 minutes' walk of town centre. Adjacent to sports centre and golf-courses. Cellar restaurant.
Bedrooms: 3 single, 11 double & 6 twin, 3 family rooms.
Bathrooms: 18 private, 2 public.
Bed & breakfast: £21-£37.50 single, £38-£85 double.
Half board: £31-£47.50 daily, £217-£427.50 weekly.
Lunch available.
Evening meal 5.30pm (l.o. 10.30pm).
Parking for 32.
Credit: Access, Visa, Amex.

Compton House ᴍ
Listed

22 Shipston Rd., Stratford-upon-Avon, CV37 7LP
☎ (0789) 205646
Small family guesthouse, extending a warm and homely welcome to all our guests. 5 minutes' walk from the theatre and town centre. Private parking.
Bedrooms: 1 single, 1 double, 3 family rooms.
Bathrooms: 1 public.
Bed & breakfast: £15-£17.50 single, £25-£30 double.
Parking for 6.

Courtland Hotel ᴍ
APPROVED

12 Guild St., Stratford-upon-Avon, CV37 6RE
☎ (0789) 292401

Elegant Georgian house in town centre at rear of Shakespeare's birthplace. Antique furniture. 3-4 minutes from theatre, close to coach terminal.
Bedrooms: 1 single, 4 double & 1 twin, 1 family room.
Bathrooms: 2 private, 2 public.
Bed & breakfast: £14.50-£15.50 single, £28-£40 double.
Parking for 3.
Credit: Amex.

Craig Cleeve House ᴍ

67-69 Shipston Rd., Stratford-upon-Avon, CV37 7LW
☎ (0789) 296573
Fax (0789) 299452
Small family hotel close to the town centre and theatre. Fax machine available.
Bedrooms: 1 single, 6 double & 4 twin, 3 family rooms.
Bathrooms: 9 private, 4 public.
Bed & breakfast: £17.50-£33 single, £36-£47 double.
Half board: £27.50-£43 daily.
Evening meal 6pm (l.o. 6pm).
Parking for 15.
Credit: Access, Visa, Diners, Amex.

Dukes Hotel ᴍ
COMMENDED

Payton St., Stratford-upon-Avon, CV37 6UA
☎ (0789) 269300 & 297921
Telex 31430 Fax 0789 414700
A quiet garden setting, alongside the Stratford canal and within 2 minutes' walk of the town centre and Shakespeare's birthplace. Large private car park.
Bedrooms: 4 single, 10 double & 8 twin.
Bathrooms: 22 private.
Bed & breakfast: £45-£55 single, £65-£100 double.
Lunch available.
Evening meal 6pm (l.o. 9.30pm).
Parking for 30.
Credit: Access, Visa, Diners, Amex.

Eastnor House Hotel ᴍ
COMMENDED

Shipston Rd., Stratford-upon-Avon, CV37 7LN
☎ (0789) 268115

Quiet comfortable private hotel, oak panelled and tastefully furnished. Spacious bedrooms with private bathrooms. Centrally located, River Avon 125 metres, theatre 300 metres.
Bedrooms: 3 double & 2 twin, 4 family rooms.
Bathrooms: 9 private.
Bed & breakfast: £33-£46 single, £44-£57 double.
Parking for 9.
Credit: Access, Visa, Amex.

Emsley ⋒
♨♨

4 Arden St., Stratford-upon-Avon, CV37 6PA
☎ (0789) 299557
Victorian building with large spacious and comfortable rooms. Full English breakfast. Close to town centre, railway, theatre, Shakespearean properties and many places of interest.
Bedrooms: 2 double & 1 twin, 2 family rooms.
Bathrooms: 4 private; 1 private shower.
Bed & breakfast: £20-£25 single, £35-£40 double.
Parking for 1.

Ettington Park Hotel ⋒
♨♨♨♨ HIGHLY COMMENDED

Alderminster, Stratford-upon-Avon, CV37 8BS
☎ (0789) 740740 Fax 0789 450472
Set in 40 acres of parkland, 5 miles from Stratford-upon-Avon, offering a combination of country house comfort and modern leisure facilities.
Bedrooms: 20 double & 15 twin, 13 family rooms.
Bathrooms: 48 private.
Bed & breakfast: from £115 single, from £145 double.
Lunch available.
Evening meal 7pm (l.o. 9.30pm).
Parking for 120.
Credit: Access, Visa, Diners, Amex.

Graveside Barn ⋒
♨♨ COMMENDED

Binton, Stratford-upon-Avon, CV37 9TU
☎ (0789) 750502/297000
Fax (0789) 298056
A peaceful converted barn, set on a hill in farmland. Magnificent views, great breakfasts. Easy access to

motorways and Stratford-upon-Avon.
Bedrooms: 2 double & 2 twin.
Bathrooms: 4 private.
Bed & breakfast: £35-£40 single, £50-£60 double.
Parking for 6.
Credit: Access, Visa.

Grosvenor House Hotel ⋒
♨♨♨♨

Warwick Rd., Stratford-upon-Avon, CV37 6YT
☎ (0789) 269213 &
(0789) 269213 Telex 311699
Fax 0789 266087
Ⓖ Best Western
Friendly hotel with restaurant overlooking gardens. Many refurbished bedrooms, 5 minutes' walk from town centre and theatre. Ample free parking.
Bedrooms: 14 single, 13 double & 22 twin, 2 family rooms.
Bathrooms: 51 private.
Bed & breakfast: £55-£65 single, £78-£88 double.
Half board: £45-£55 daily.
Lunch available.
Evening meal 6pm (l.o. 8.45pm).
Parking for 50.
Credit: Access, Visa, Diners, Amex.

Hardwick House ⋒
♨♨

1 Avenue Rd., Stratford-upon-Avon, CV37 6UY
☎ (0789) 204307 Fax 0789 296760
Family-run Victorian guesthouse in a quiet area, a short walking distance from town, theatre, swimming pool and other amenities.
Bedrooms: 2 single, 6 double & 4 twin, 2 family rooms.
Bathrooms: 7 private, 4 public.
Bed & breakfast: £16-£20 single, £32-£52 double.
Parking for 12.
Credit: Access, Visa, Amex.

Houndshill House ⋒
♨♨ APPROVED

Banbury Rd., Ettington, Stratford-upon-Avon, CV37 7NS
☎ (0789) 740267
Large, family-run country house with restaurant. 4 miles from Stratford-upon-Avon. Informal and friendly atmosphere.

Bedrooms: 2 single, 3 double & 2 twin, 1 family room.
Bathrooms: 8 private.
Bed & breakfast: from £32 single, from £52 double.
Lunch available.
Evening meal 7pm (l.o. 10pm).
Parking for 50.
Credit: Access, Visa.

King's Lodge ⋒
♨♨ COMMENDED

Long Marston, Stratford-upon-Avon, CV37 8RL
☎ (0789) 720705
Historic country house set in 4.5 acres of garden and parkland. Within easy reach of Stratford-upon-Avon and the Cotswolds, and near the National Exhibition Centre, Birmingham.
Bedrooms: 2 double & 1 twin.
Bathrooms: 1 private, 2 public.
Bed & breakfast: £17 single, £33-£46 double.
Half board: £25.50-£32 daily.
Evening meal 7pm.
Parking for 11.
Open February-November.

Melita Private Hotel ⋒
♨♨ COMMENDED

37 Shipston Rd., Stratford-upon-Avon, CV37 7LN
☎ (0789) 292432
Small, well-appointed family hotel, close to theatre and Shakespearean attractions. Convenient for touring the Cotswolds, NEC and National Agricultural Centre. Lounge bar.
Bedrooms: 3 single, 3 double & 3 twin, 3 family rooms.
Bathrooms: 12 private.
Bed & breakfast: £29-£40 single, £45-£57 double.
Parking for 12.
Credit: Access, Visa, Amex.

Moonraker House ⋒
♨♨ COMMENDED

40 Alcester Rd., Stratford-upon-Avon, CV37 9DB
☎ (0789) 299346 &
(0789) 67115
Ⓖ Minotels
Family-run, near town centre. Beautifully co-ordinated decor throughout. Some rooms with four-poster beds and garden terrace available for non-smokers.
Bedrooms: 15 double & 3 twin, 2 family rooms.
Bathrooms: 20 private.

Bed & breakfast: £28-£32 single, £36-£54 double.
Half board: £36-£46 daily, £245-£280 weekly.
Evening meal 5.30pm (l.o. 7pm).
Parking for 20.

Nando's ⋒
♨♨

18-19 Evesham Pl., Stratford-upon-Avon, CV37 6HT
☎ (0789) 204907
A warm welcome awaits from Pat and Peter. Convenient for theatre, town centre and Shakespeare properties. Full English breakfast.
Bedrooms: 5 single, 5 double & 6 twin, 5 family rooms.
Bathrooms: 7 private, 5 public.
Bed & breakfast: £14-£16 single, £22-£40 double.
Half board: £17.50-£26.50 daily.
Lunch available.
Evening meal 6pm.
Parking for 8.
Credit: Access, Visa, Amex.

Oxstalls Farm
♨♨ COMMENDED

Warwick Rd., Stratford-upon-Avon, CV37 0NS
☎ (0789) 205277
60-acre stud farm. Beautifully situated overlooking the Welcome Hills and golf-course. 1 mile from Stratford-upon-Avon.
Bedrooms: 2 single, 7 double & 4 twin, 7 family rooms.
Bathrooms: 11 private, 2 public; 3 private showers.
Bed & breakfast: £13-£20 single, £28-£45 double.
Parking for 20.

Parkfield ⋒
♨♨ APPROVED

3 Broad Walk, Stratford-upon-Avon, CV37 6HS
☎ (0789) 293313
Delightful Victorian house. Quiet location, 5 minutes' walk from theatre and town. En-suite available. Colour TV, tea and coffee facilities and parking.
Bedrooms: 1 single, 2 double & 2 twin, 2 family rooms.
Bathrooms: 4 private, 1 public.
Bed & breakfast: £15-£17 single, £30-£40 double.
Parking for 9.
Credit: Access, Visa.

Peartree Cottage M
⚜⚜ COMMENDED

7 Church Rd., Wilmcote,
Stratford-upon-Avon,
CV37 9UX
☎ Stratford-upon-Avon
(0789) 205889
*Elizabethan house, furnished
with antiques, set in beautiful
garden overlooking Mary
Arden's house. Pub and
restaurant within walking
distance.*
Bedrooms: 4 double & 2 twin,
1 family room.
Bathrooms: 7 private.
Bed & breakfast: £26-£28
single, £36-£38 double.
Parking for 6.
⮤ ♨ ☐ ⵜ ⮾ 🛉 ≒ ▣ ⓣ
▥ ▵ ᕦ ✿ ⺈ ꝑ

Penryn Guesthouse M
⚜⚜

126 Alcester Rd., Stratford-
upon-Avon, CV37 9DP
☎ (0789) 293718
*On the A422, 5 minutes from
the centre of Stratford and
Ann Hathaway's cottage.
Ample parking space.*
Bedrooms: 1 single, 4 double,
3 family rooms.
Bathrooms: 6 private,
1 public.
Bed & breakfast: £18.50-£35
single, £30-£40 double.
Parking for 9.
Credit: Access, Visa, Amex.
⮤ ♨ ☐ ⵜ ⮾ 🛉 ≒ ▥ ▵
🍴 SP

Quilt and Croissants M
Listed

33 Evesham Place, Stratford-
upon-Avon, CV37 6HT
☎ (0789) 267629 &
(0789) 267671
*Young, family-run business in
Victorian premises in the heart
of Stratford-upon-Avon.*
Bedrooms: 1 single, 3 double
& 1 twin, 3 family rooms.
Bathrooms: 4 private,
1 public.
Bed & breakfast: £15-£19
single, £30-£40 double.
Parking for 2.
⮤ ♨ ☐ ⵜ ⮾ 🛉 ▣ ▥ ▵
⺈ DAP

Ravenhurst M
⚜⚜ APPROVED

2 Broad Walk, Stratford-
upon-Avon, CV37 6HS
☎ (0789) 292515

*Quietly situated, a few minutes'
walk from the town centre and
places of historic interest.
Comfortable home, with
substantial breakfast provided.*
Bedrooms: 3 double & 2 twin,
2 family rooms.
Bathrooms: 3 private,
2 public.
Bed & breakfast: £17-£28
single, £30-£40 double.
Credit: Access, Visa, Diners,
Amex.
⮤ ☐ ⮾ ⵜ ⮾ ▣ ≒ ▵ ⺈ ꝑ

Salamander Guest
House M
⚜⚜

40 Grove Rd., Stratford-
upon-Avon, CV37 6PB
☎ (0789) 205728 & 297843
*5 minutes' walk from the town
centre, the Royal Shakespeare
Theatre and many historic
houses. Close to railway and
bus stations.*
Bedrooms: 3 single, 3 double,
1 family room.
Bathrooms: 2 private,
2 public; 1 private shower.
Bed & breakfast: £12.50-£16
single, £25-£36 double.
Half board: £18-£24 daily.
Evening meal 6pm (l.o. 6pm).
Parking for 7.
⮤ ⵜ ⮾ 🛉 ▣ ▥ ⓣ ▥ ▵
SP ⓣ

Sequoia House M
⚜⚜⚜

51-53 Shipston Rd.,
Stratford-upon-Avon,
CV37 7LN
☎ (0789) 268852 & 294940 &
(0789) 204805
Fax (0789) 414559
*Beautifully-appointed private
hotel with large car park and
delightful garden walk to the
theatre, riverside gardens and
Shakespeare properties. Fully
air-conditioned dining room.*
Bedrooms: 2 single, 9 double
& 8 twin, 6 family rooms.
Bathrooms: 19 private,
3 public; 2 private showers.
Bed & breakfast: £30-£55
single, £37-£72 double.
Half board: £31-£50 daily.
Lunch available.
Evening meal 6pm (l.o.
7.30pm).
Parking for 33.
Credit: Access, Visa, Diners,
Amex.
⮤ 5 ♨ ⵜ ☐ ⮾ 🛉 ▣ ⼅ ≒
▥ ▵ 🍴 ⅋ ✿ ⺈ SP ⓣ

Stratford House
Hotel M
⚜⚜⚜ COMMENDED

Sheep St., Stratford-upon-
Avon, CV37 6EF
☎ (0789) 268288 Fax 0789
295 580

*Privately-owned hotel, with
fine restaurant, 100 yards from
The Royal Shakespeare
Theatre. Theatre booking
service.*
Bedrooms: 1 single, 4 double
& 4 twin, 1 family room.
Bathrooms: 10 private.
Bed & breakfast: £60-£66
single, £57.50-£82 double.
Lunch available.
Evening meal 5.45pm (l.o.
9.30pm).
Credit: Access, Visa, Diners,
Amex.
⮤ 5 ♨ ☎ ⓢ ☐ ⮾ ▣ ≒ ▥
🍴 ⺈ ꝑ SP ᕦ ⓣ

Stratheden Hotel M
⚜⚜ COMMENDED

5 Chapel St., Stratford-
upon-Avon, CV37 6EP
☎ (0789) 297119
*Built in 1673 and located in
one of the most historic parts of
Stratford-upon-Avon. 2
minutes' walk from the theatre
and town centre.*
Bedrooms: 5 double & 3 twin,
1 family room.
Bathrooms: 8 private,
1 public.
Bed & breakfast: £25-£35
single, £36-£52 double.
Parking for 5.
Credit: Access, Visa.
⮤ ♨ ☐ ⵜ ⮾ 🛉 ▣ ≒ ▵
⺈ ᕦ ꝑ

Stretton House M
⚜ COMMENDED

38 Grove Rd., Stratford-
Avon, CV37 6PB
☎ (0789) 268647
*Convenient for theatre and
town centre. All rooms have
tea and coffee facilities, colour
TV, some have own shower.
Full English breakfast.
Parking.*
Bedrooms: 1 single, 1 double
& 2 twin, 2 family rooms.
Bathrooms: 3 private,
2 public.
Bed & breakfast: £14-£20
single, £25-£40 double.
Half board: £20.50-£26.50
daily, £140-£185.50 weekly.
Evening meal 5pm (l.o. 4pm).
Parking for 3.
⮤ ♨ ☐ ⵜ ⮾ 🛉 ▣ ▥ ⓣ
▥ ▵ 🍴 DAP SP

Swan House Hotel M
⚜⚜⚜ APPROVED

The Green, Wilmcote,
Stratford-upon-Avon,
CV37 9XJ
☎ Stratford-upon-Avon
(0789) 267030 Fax 0789
204875
*Friendly hotel, part 18th C inn,
100 yards from Mary Arden's
house. Ideal for exploring
Shakespeare Country, 3 miles
from Stratford. Varied menu.*

Bedrooms: 1 single, 5 double
& 4 twin, 2 family rooms.
Bathrooms: 12 private.
Bed & breakfast: £36-£40
single, £56-£60 double.
Lunch available.
Evening meal 7.30pm (l.o.
9.30pm).
Parking for 35.
Credit: Access, Visa, Amex.
⮤ ♨ ⓢ ☐ ⮾ 🛉 ▣ ▥ ▥
▵ 🍴 ⺈ SP ᕦ ⓣ

Twelfth Night M
⚜⚜⚜ COMMENDED

Evesham Place, Stratford-
upon-Avon, CV37 6HT
☎ (0789) 414595
*Gracious, centrally-located
Victorian villa, formerly owned
by The Royal Shakespeare
Theatre for 21 years for
accommodating actors.
Tastefully refurbished for your
comfort. Non-smokers only
please.*
Bedrooms: 1 single, 2 double
& 3 twin, 1 family room.
Bathrooms: 5 private,
1 public; 1 private shower.
Bed & breakfast: £17-£30
single, £34-£48 double.
Parking for 6.
⮤ 5 ☐ ⮾ ⵜ ⮾ ▣ ▥ ⼅ ≒
▵ ⺈ ᕦ ⓣ

Windmill Park Hotel
and Country Club M
⚜⚜⚜⚜

Warwick Road, Stratford-
upon-Avon, CV37 0PY
☎ (0789) 731173 Fax 0789
731131
CB Best Western
*A warm welcome awaits you at
this privately owned hotel, set
in over 20 acres of rolling
Warwickshire countryside.*
Bedrooms: 38 double &
62 twin.
Bathrooms: 100 private.
Bed & breakfast: £75-£85
single, £90-£100 double.
Half board: £48-£56 daily.
Lunch available.
Evening meal 7pm (l.o.
10pm).
Parking for 220.
Credit: Access, Visa, Diners,
Amex.
⮤ ♨ ☐ ⓢ ☎ ⓢ ☐ ⮾ ▣
≒ ⬤ ✥ ▵ ⺈ 🍴 ⟡ ⅋ ℞
𝄞 ✿ ꞁ SP ⓣ

---

*National Crown
ratings were correct
at the time of going
to press but are
subject to change.
Please check at the
time of booking.*

STROUD

Gloucestershire
Map ref 2B1

This old town has been producing broadcloth for centuries and the local museum has an interesting display on the subject. It is surrounded by attractive hilly country.
*Tourist Information
Centre ☎ (0453) 765768*

Ashleigh House M
♨♨♨

Bussage, Stroud, GL6 8AZ
☎ Brimscombe
(0453) 883944
Ideal Cotswold touring centre in beautiful village setting, providing cleanliness and comfort. All rooms en-suite.
Bedrooms: 3 double & 3 twin, 3 family rooms.
Bathrooms: 9 private.
Bed & breakfast: from £31.50 single, from £48.30 double.
Half board: £30-£44 daily, £162.75-£245 weekly.
Evening meal 6.30pm (l.o. 7pm).
Parking for 10.
Open April-October.
Credit: Access, Visa.
♨5 ♨ ⊡ ⊡ ♨ ⊟ ⊞ ▲ ✕
☒ SP

Bell Hotel & Restaurant M
♨♨♨ APPROVED

Wallbridge, Stroud, GL5 3JA
☎ (0453) 763556
Friendly, family-run hotel. All rooms en-suite with TV, tea/coffee facilities and telephone. Bridal suite. A la carte restaurant. Garden and bar on canal.
Bedrooms: 1 single, 4 double & 5 twin, 2 family rooms.
Bathrooms: 10 private, 1 public.
Bed & breakfast: £42-£70 single, £55-£85 double.
Half board: from £52 daily.
Lunch available.
Evening meal 7pm (l.o. 9.30pm).
Parking for 12.
Credit: Access, Visa, Diners, Amex.
♨ ⊞ ⓒ ⊡ ⊡ ♨ ⓘ ⊡ ⊟
⊡ ⊞ ▲ ⚏ ∪ ✻ ☒ ⚏ SP
⊞ ⊡

Burleigh Court Hotel
Minchinhampton, Stroud, GL5 2PF
☎ Brimscombe
(0453) 883804 & 883430
Fax (0453) 886870

18th C country house of character and atmosphere with superb views. Log fires. Listed Grade II building, with landscaped garden by Clough Williams-Ellis.
Bedrooms: 12 double & 4 twin, 1 family room.
Bathrooms: 17 private.
Bed & breakfast: £59-£64 single, £76-£96 double.
Lunch available.
Evening meal 7.30pm (l.o. 8.45pm).
Parking for 42.
Credit: Access, Visa, Diners, Amex.
♨ ♨ ⓒ ⊡ ⊡ ♨ ⓘ ⊡ ⊟
⊞ ⊡ ▲ ⚏ ⚏ ⚏ ✻ ✕ ☒
SP ⊞

The Crown Inn and Hotel
Frampton Mansell, Stroud, GL6 8JG
☎ (028 576) 601
Built approximately 600 years ago, and a listed building. The bedrooms are new, with bath/shower and WC en-suite, colour TV and telephones.
Bathrooms: 12 private.
Bedrooms: 4 double & 8 twin.
Bed & breakfast: from £40 single, from £50 double.
Lunch available.
Evening meal 7pm (l.o. 10pm).
Parking for 100.
Credit: Access, Visa.
♨ ⓒ ⊡ ⊡ ♨ ⓘ ⊡ ⊟ ⊞
▲ ⚏ ✻ ⚏ ☒ SP ⊞

Hawthorns
♨♨

Lower Littleworth, Amberley, Stroud, GL5 5AW
☎ Amberley (0453) 873535
Early 18th C house in National Trust setting and with glorious views. Walking. Half a mile west of Bear Inn, Rodborough along lane signposted "Houndscroft". Wild badgers feed on floodlit terrace at nightfall.
Bedrooms: 2 double & 1 twin.
Bathrooms: 2 private, 1 public.
Bed & breakfast: £20-£35 single, £30-£42 double.
Parking for 3.
♨ ⊡ ⓘ ⊡ ⊟ ⊞ ⊡ ▲ ∪
⚏ ✻ ☒ ⓒ SP ⊞

Imperial Hotel M
♨♨♨ COMMENDED

Station Rd., Stroud, GL5 3AP
☎ (0453) 764077
Fax (0453) 751314
Covered in ivy and over 150 years old, the hotel was originally a coaching and railway inn. Recently refurbished to a high standard.

Bedrooms: 3 single, 8 double & 12 twin, 2 family rooms.
Bathrooms: 25 private.
Bed & breakfast: £44-£48 single, £61 double.
Lunch available.
Evening meal 6pm (l.o. 10.30pm).
Parking for 15.
Credit: Access, Visa, Diners, Amex.
♨ ⊞ ⓒ ⊡ ⊡ ♨ ⓘ ⊡ ⊟ ⊞
▲ ✕ SP ⊞

London Hotel and Restaurant M
♨♨♨ COMMENDED

30-31 London Rd., Stroud, GL5 2AJ
☎ (0453) 759992
Attractive ivy clad, Georgian town centre hotel. Conveniently situated for touring the Cotswolds. Extensive menu available in candlelit restaurant.
Bedrooms: 2 single, 5 double & 3 twin.
Bathrooms: 8 private, 2 public.
Bed & breakfast: £26-£45 single, £39-£59 double.
Half board: £38.50-£62 daily, £210-£300 weekly.
Lunch available.
Evening meal 7pm (l.o. 9.30pm).
Parking for 10.
Credit: Access, Visa, Diners, Amex.
♨2 ⓒ ⊡ ⊡ ♨ ⓘ ⊡ ⊟ ⊟
⊡ ⊞ ▲ ⚏ ✕ ☒ SP

SUTTON COLDFIELD

W. Midlands
Map ref 4B3

Old market town now part of the conurbation of Birmingham. The 2400-acre Sutton Park has facilities for golf, fishing and riding, with walks around the woodlands and lakes.

The Berni Royal Hotel M

High St., Sutton Coldfield, B72 1UD
☎ 021-355 8222 Fax 021-355 1837
Located right in the heart of this busy Midlands town, this hotel is an attractive Georgian building which has undergone sympathetic refurbishment.
Bedrooms: 3 single, 9 double & 7 twin, 3 family rooms.
Bathrooms: 22 private.
Bed & breakfast: £50-£56 single, £67 double.
Lunch available.

Evening meal 6pm (l.o. 10pm).
Parking for 80.
Credit: Access, Visa, Diners, Amex.
♨ ⓒ ⊡ ♨ ♨ ⊟ ⊡ ⚏ ⓘ ⊞
▲ ⚏ ✕ SP ⊞

Lady Windsor Hotel M
♨♨♨ APPROVED

17 Anchorage Rd., Sutton Coldfield, B74 2PJ
☎ 021-354 5181
Small family-run hotel close to Wyndley Leisure Centre with all sporting facilities, and to 2800-acre Sutton Park with boating and golf. Close to railway station and town centre.
Bedrooms: 10 single, 5 double & 7 twin.
Bathrooms: 22 private.
Bed & breakfast: £43-£49 single, £53-£59 double.
Half board: £53-£59 daily.
Lunch available.
Evening meal 6.30pm (l.o. 10pm).
Parking for 32.
Credit: Access, Visa, Amex.
♨ ♨ ⓒ ⊡ ♨ ⓘ ⊡ ⊟
⊡ ⊞ ▲ ⓣ ⚏ ✻ ✕ ⚏ ⊞
⊡

Sutton Court Hotel & Court Yard Restaurant M
♨♨♨ APPROVED

60-66 Lichfield Rd., Sutton Coldfield, B74 2NA
☎ 021-355 6071 Telex 334175
SUTTON G
Ⓒ Consort
Half a mile walking distance from the town centre, this hotel retains its Victorian elegance combined with the best of modern facilities and old fashioned hospitality.
Bedrooms: 17 single, 20 double & 26 twin, 1 family room.
Bathrooms: 64 private.
Bed & breakfast: £41-£79 single, £53-£92 double.
Half board: £57-£95 daily, max. £551 weekly.
Lunch available.
Evening meal 7pm (l.o. 10pm).
Parking for 80.
Credit: Access, Visa, Diners, Amex.
♨ ⊞ ⓒ ⊡ ⊡ ♨ ⓘ ⊡ ⊟
⊟ ⊡ ⊙ ▲ ⚏ ⚏ SP ⊡

The enquiry coupons at the back will help you when contacting proprietors.

SWINSCOE

Staffordshire
Map ref 4B2

4m NW. Ashbourne
Hamlet close to Alton
Towers with its many
attractions and to the
beautiful scenery of
Dovedale.

Dog & Partridge Inn M
♛♛♛♛

Swinscoe, Ashbourne,
Derbyshire DE6 2HS
☎ Ashbourne (0335) 43183
*A warm welcome from Mary
and Martin at this 17th C inn.
Close to the Peak District,
Ashbourne and Alton Towers.
Vegetarian and special diets
catered for. Children and pets
welcome.*
Bedrooms: 6 double & 2 twin,
17 family rooms.
Bathrooms: 25 private.
Bed & breakfast: £35-£45
single, £45-£55 double.
Half board: £35-£45 daily,
£200-£245 weekly.
Lunch available.
Evening meal 5.30pm (l.o.
10.30pm).
Parking for 82.
Credit: Access, Visa, Diners,
Amex.
➷ ♨ ♨ ♗ ⦾ ⌷ ♥ 🛉 Ⓥ
⦿ Ⅲ ⚓ 🍴 ㄑ ♧ ✿ ◖ⅆⅽ⦖ ♨
⟦SP⟧ ⟦₧⟧ Ⓣ

SWYNNERTON

Staffordshire
Map ref 4B2

Village with thatched
cottages, a 17th C inn
and an interesting
Norman church.

Home Farm Hotel
⟦Listed⟧

Swynnerton, Stone,
ST15 0RA
☎ (078 135) 241
*Traditional, rural, small
family-run hotel which
welcomes children and senior
citizens. Special rates on
request. Near Alton Towers.*
Bedrooms: 3 single, 2 double
& 1 twin, 2 family rooms.
Bathrooms: 3 private,
2 public.
Bed & breakfast: £15-£17.50
single, £26-£30 double.
Half board: £20-£22.50 daily.
Parking for 33.
Credit: Access, Visa.
➷ ♨ ⌷ ♥ 🛉 Ⓥ ⚓ 📺 Ⅲ
⚓ ⟦₧⟧ ⦖ⅆⅽ⦖ ⟦SP⟧ ⟦₧⟧

SYMONDS YAT EAST

Hereford & Worcester
Map ref 2A1

Well-known beauty spot
where the River Wye
loops back on itself in a
narrow gorge. It is close
to the ruins of Goodrich
Castle, the Forest of
Dean and the Welsh
border.

Forest View Hotel M
♛♛♛ ⟦COMMENDED⟧

Symonds Yat East, Ross-on-
Wye, Herefordshire HR9 6JL
☎ Symonds Yat
(0600) 890210
*Set deep in the Wye Valley, a
small family hotel on the banks
of the River Wye.*
Bedrooms: 5 double & 2 twin.
Bathrooms: 7 private.
Half board: £40 daily, £225
weekly.
Evening meal 7.30pm (l.o.
7.30pm).
Parking for 10.
Open March-November.
♨ ♗ ⦾ ⌷ ♥ 🛉 Ⓥ ⚓ ⟦SP⟧
⚓ 🍴 ♩ ✿ 🍴 ⟦₧⟧ ♨ ⟦SP⟧

SYMONDS YAT ROCK

Gloucestershire
Map ref 2A1

Symonds Yat Rock Motel
⟦Listed⟧

Hillersland, Coleford,
GL16 7NY
☎ Dean (0594) 36191
*Small family-run motel with
personal attention, in a quiet
forest setting. Ideal centre for
touring. A new holiday home
has been added as extra
bedroom accommodation to the
motel or is available on a self-
catering basis. Dogs welcome.*
Bedrooms: 2 double & 2 twin,
1 family room.
Bathrooms: 5 private.
Bed & breakfast: £23-£24
single, £31-£32 double.
Lunch available.
Evening meal 6pm (l.o. 8pm).
Parking for 28.
Open January-November.
➷ ⌷ ♥ 🛉 Ⓥ ⚓ Ⅲ ♨
♧ ∪ ⟦₧⟧ ⟦SP⟧

*The symbols are
explained on the
flap inside the
back cover.*

SYMONDS YAT WEST

Hereford & Worcester
Map ref 2A1

Jubilee Maze and
Exhibition was created
here in 1977 to
commemorate Queen
Elizabeth II's Jubilee. The
area of Symonds Yat is a
world-renowned beauty
spot.

Old Court Hotel M
♛♛♛

Symonds Yat West, Ross-on-
Wye, Herefordshire
HR9 6DA
☎ Symonds Yat
(0600) 890367 Fax 0600
890964
*15th C manor house set in 2
acres of grounds opposite the
Wye Valley visitor centre.*
Bedrooms: 17 double &
3 twin.
Bathrooms: 14 private,
2 public.
Bed & breakfast: £35-£45
single, £50-£70 double.
Half board: £43-£45 daily.
Evening meal 7.30pm (l.o.
9.30pm).
Parking for 50.
Credit: Access, Visa, Diners,
Amex.
♨ ♗ ⦾ ⌷ ♥ 🛉 Ⓥ ⚓ Ⅲ
⚓ 🍴 ♩ ∪ ✿ ⟦ⅆⅽ⟧ ♨ ⟦SP⟧ ⟦₧⟧
Ⓣ

Riversdale Lodge Hotel
♛♛ ⟦COMMENDED⟧

Symonds Yat West, Ross-on-
Wye, Herefordshire HR9 6BL
☎ Symonds Yat
(0600) 890445
*High standard accommodation,
set in 2 acres on the banks of
the River Wye. Spectacular
views of the Ironbridge Gorge.
Traditional food.*
Bedrooms: 5 double.
Bathrooms: 5 private.
Bed & breakfast: £21-£23
single, £39-£45 double.
Half board: £33-£34 daily,
£231-£238 weekly.
Evening meal 7pm (l.o. 1pm).
Parking for 11.
➷ ⌷ ♥ Ⓥ ⚓ 📺 Ⅲ ♨
🍴 ♨ ㄑ ♩ ✿ ♨ Ⓣ

Woodlea Hotel M
♛♛♛

Symonds Yat West, Ross-on-
Wye, Herefordshire
HR9 6BL
☎ Symonds Yat
(0600) 890206

*Family-run Victorian country
house hotel in a quiet position
amid glorious scenery.
Imaginative home cooking and
friendly service.*
Bedrooms: 1 single, 4 double
& 2 twin, 2 family rooms.
Bathrooms: 6 private,
2 public.
Bed & breakfast: from £21.50
single, £43-£52 double.
Half board: £32-£36 daily,
£195-£225 weekly.
Evening meal 7pm (l.o. 7pm).
Parking for 9.
Open February-November.
Credit: Access, Visa, Amex.
➷ ♨ ⦾ ♥ Ⓥ ⚓ 📺 Ⅲ ♨ ♨ ㄑ
⟦₧⟧ ⟦SP⟧

TAMWORTH

Staffordshire
Map ref 4B3

Town with a Norman
castle which has a Tudor
banqueting hall, and a
museum with coins
minted at Tamworth in
Saxon times when it was
an important royal town.
The church has a
magnificent tower.
*Tourist Information
Centre* ☎ *(0827) 311222*

Buxton Hotel M

65 Coleshill St., Fazeley,
Tamworth, B78 3RG
☎ (0827) 284842 & 285805
*Close to Drayton Manor Park,
Kingsbury Water Park and
within easy driving distance of
Belfry National Golf Centre,
National Exhibition Centre
and Birmingham Airport.*
Bedrooms: 5 single, 3 double
& 3 twin, 4 family rooms.
Bathrooms: 12 private,
1 public.
Bed & breakfast: £23-£32
single, £32-£42 double.
Half board: £30-£45 daily.
Evening meal 6pm (l.o.
8.45pm).
Parking for 16.
Credit: Access, Visa.
➷ ♗ ⌷ ♥ 🛉 ♨ 📺 Ⅲ
⚓ 🍴 ♨ Ⓣ

Castle Hotel

Ladybank, Tamworth,
B79 7NB
☎ (0827) 57181 Fax 0827
54303
🄬 Rank
*Dating back to the 17th C, this
hotel is situated in the shadow
of Tamworth Castle in the
historic area of Ladybank.
Facilities include real ale pub
and sophisticated nightclub.*
Bedrooms: 5 single, 14 double
& 4 twin, 10 family rooms.

Bathrooms: 33 private.
Bed & breakfast: £36-£62
single, £57-£77 double.
Lunch available.
Evening meal 7pm (l.o.
10pm).
Parking for 6.
Credit: Access, Visa, Diners,
Amex.

TELFORD

Shropshire
Map ref 4A3

New Town named after
Thomas Telford, the
famous engineer who
designed many of the
country's canals, bridges
and viaducts. It is close to
Ironbridge with its
monuments and
museums to the Industrial
Revolution, including
restored 18th C buildings.
*Tourist Information
Centre* ☎ (0952) 291370

Arleston Inn Hotel
COMMENDED

Arleston Lane, Nr Lawley,
Wellington, Telford TF1 2LA
☎ Telford (0952) 501881
*Tudor-style building with many
exposed beamed ceilings. M54,
5 minutes from junction 6. A la
carte and bar menus.*
Bedrooms: 3 single, 4 double.
Bathrooms: 7 private.
Bed & breakfast: £25-£35
single, £36-£46 double.
Half board: £30-£45 daily.
Lunch available.
Evening meal 7pm (l.o.
10pm).
Parking for 40.
Credit: Access, Visa.

Caledonia Hotel
Listed

Lion St., Oakengates,
Telford, TF2 6AQ
☎ (0952) 613946
*Small, clean, family-run hotel
in the middle of Telford and
close to Ironbridge. Home-
made food.*
Bedrooms: 2 single, 1 double
& 3 twin.
Bathrooms: 6 private
showers.
Bed & breakfast: £20 single,
£40 double.
Half board: £28 daily.
Lunch available.
Evening meal 7.30pm (l.o.
7pm).
Parking for 20.

Falcon Hotel
COMMENDED

Holyhead Rd., Wellington,
Telford, TF1 2DD
☎ (0952) 255011
*Small, family-run 18th C
coaching hotel. 10 miles from
Shrewsbury, 4 miles from
Ironbridge, 18 miles from the
M6 at the end of the M54 exit
7.*
Bedrooms: 3 single, 5 double
& 4 twin, 1 family room.
Bathrooms: 6 private,
3 public.
Bed & breakfast: £30-£41
single, £40-£50 double.
Lunch available.
Evening meal 7pm (l.o. 9pm).
Parking for 30.
Credit: Access, Visa.

Glenmore House

1 Manse Rd., Hadley,
Telford, TF1 4NH
☎ (0952) 641460
*Family-run establishment.
Central for all major roads and
tourist attractions. Courtesy
and advice freely given.
Proprietor available 24 hours.*
Bedrooms: 1 double & 1 twin,
1 family room.
Bathrooms: 3 private.
Bed & breakfast: £15-£20
single, £30-£34 double.
Half board: £20-£22 daily,
£140-£154 weekly.
Lunch available.
Evening meal 6.30pm (l.o.
7.30pm).
Parking for 8.
Credit: Access, Visa.

The Granville Hotel

Wrockwardine Wood,
Telford, TF2 7AB
☎ (0952) 618563
*A former hostelry dating from
1734 with beamed dining room.
Provides comfortable
accommodation with all
modern facilities, run by the
resident proprietors.*
Bedrooms: 2 single, 4 double
& 3 twin, 1 family room.
Bathrooms: 10 private.
Bed & breakfast: max. £39.50
single, max. £48 double.
Lunch available.
Evening meal 7pm (l.o. 9pm).
Parking for 30.
Credit: Access, Visa, Amex.

*Please mention this
guide when making
a booking.*

Hazeldene Guest
House
Listed

13 Southall Rd., Dawley,
Telford, TF4 3NA
☎ (0952) 660212
*A small comfortable
guesthouse, on main B4373
Dawley to Ironbridge road,
within easy reach of all
Telford's amenities.*
Bedrooms: 4 twin.
Bathrooms: 2 public.
Bed & breakfast: £16.50
single, £25 double.
Half board: £16.50-£20.50
daily, £115.50-£143.50
weekly.
Evening meal 6.30pm (l.o.
7.30pm).
Parking for 6.

Telford Moat House
COMMENDED

Forgegate, Telford Centre,
Telford, TF3 4NA
☎ (0952) 291291 Telex 35588
CR Queens Moat Houses
*Modern conference hotel with
extensive leisure facilities in
the centre of Telford and close
to all major attractions in the
area.*
Bedrooms: 54 double &
86 twin, 8 family rooms.
Bathrooms: 148 private.
Bed & breakfast: £74.25-
£84.15 single, £78.65-£104.50
double.
Lunch available.
Evening meal 7pm (l.o.
10pm).
Parking for 350.
Credit: Access, Visa, Diners,
Amex.

Valley Hotel

Ironbridge, Telford,
TF8 7DW
☎ (0952) 432247/433280
Fax (0952) 432308
CR Inter
*Georgian listed building
situated in World Heritage
Site of Ironbridge. Recently
refurbished to high standards.*
Bedrooms: 9 single,
25 double, 2 family rooms.
Bathrooms: 36 private.
Bed & breakfast: £55-£60
single, £65-£70 double.
Half board: £68-£73 daily,
£546-£581 weekly.
Lunch available.
Evening meal 7pm (l.o.
10pm).

Parking for 100.
Credit: Access, Visa, Amex.

❹ Display advertisement
appears on page 263.

White House Hotel
COMMENDED

Wellington Rd., Donnington,
Muxton, Telford, TF2 8NG
☎ (0952) 604276
*Country house hotel set in 1
acre of lawns and gardens,
close to Lilleshall National
Sports Centre and Ironbridge.*
Bedrooms: 10 single, 6 double
& 6 twin, 8 family rooms.
Bathrooms: 30 private,
2 public.
Bed & breakfast: £40-£50
single, £50-£60 double.
Half board: £32.50-£62.50
daily.
Lunch available.
Evening meal 7pm (l.o.
10pm).
Parking for 100.
Credit: Access, Visa, Amex.

TENBURY WELLS

Hereford & Worcester
Map ref 4A3

Small market town on the
Teme possessing many
fine black and white
buildings. In 1839 mineral
springs were found here
and there were hopes of
a spa centre developing.
The waters never became
fashionable and today
only the old Pump Room
remains, a curious iron
structure which has a
wistful attraction. Nearby
Burford House Gardens
contain many rare plants
and trees.

Cadmore Lodge Country
Hotel

Berrington Green, Tenbury
Wells, Worcestershire
WR15 8TQ
☎ (0584) 810044
*Family-run lakeside hotel and
licensed restaurant. Private
golf, trout fishing, nature
reserve and Domesday mill on
50-acre estate.*
Bedrooms: 1 single, 2 double
& 1 twin.
Bathrooms: 2 private,
1 public.
Bed & breakfast: £20-£34.50
single, £25-£28.75 double.
Half board: £32.50-£46.50
daily, £220-£300 weekly.

Continued ▶

TENBURY WELLS
Continued

Lunch available.
Evening meal 7.30pm (l.o.
9pm).
Parking for 50.
Credit: Access, Visa.

TETBURY

Gloucestershire
Map ref 2B2

Small market town with
18th C houses and an
attractive 17th C Town
Hall. It is a good touring
centre with many places
of interest nearby
including Badminton
House and Westonbirt
Arboretum.

Hare and Hounds Hotel M

Westonbirt, Tetbury,
GL8 8QL
☎ Westonbirt (066 688) 233
Fax (066 688) 241
Ⓒ Best Western
*Family-run, Cotswold-stone
hotel in 10 acres of garden and
woodland.*
Bedrooms: 4 single, 12 double
& 12 twin, 2 family rooms.
Bathrooms: 30 private.
Bed & breakfast: £57-£67
single, £79-£88 double.
Half board: £57.25-£84.75
daily, £371-£490 weekly.
Lunch available.
Evening meal 7.30pm (l.o.
9pm).
Parking for 89.
Credit: Access, Visa, Amex.

Hunters Hall Inn M

Kingscote, Tetbury,
GL8 8XZ
☎ Dursley (0453) 860393
*16th C coaching inn with open
fireplaces and beamed ceilings,
separate restaurant and large
gardens. On the A4135
between Tetbury and Dursley.*
Bedrooms: 5 double & 6 twin,
1 family room.
Bathrooms: 12 private.
Bed & breakfast: £41-£45
single, £54-£58 double.
Half board: £35-£45 daily.
Lunch available.
Evening meal 7pm (l.o.
9.45pm).
Parking for 100.

Credit: Access, Visa, Diners,
Amex.

Snooty Fox Hotel M
COMMENDED

Market Place, Tetbury,
GL8 8DD
☎ (0666) 502 436
Telex 437334 ATT SNOOTY
*16th C inn in centre of market
town with a combination of
modern facilities and
traditional charm.*
Bedrooms: 1 single, 7 double
& 2 twin, 2 family rooms.
Bathrooms: 12 private.
Bed & breakfast: £66-£85
single, £86-£105 double.
Half board: £84.50-£103.50
daily, £275-£325 weekly.
Lunch available.
Evening meal 7.30pm (l.o.
10pm).
Credit: Access, Visa, Diners,
Amex.

Tavern House M
HIGHLY COMMENDED

Willesley, Tetbury, GL8 8QU
☎ (0666) 880444
*A Grade II listed Cotswold
stone house (formerly a staging
post) on the A433 Bath road, 1
mile from the Westonbirt
Arboretum and 4 miles from
Tetbury.*
Bedrooms: 3 double & 1 twin.
Bathrooms: 4 private.
Bed & breakfast: £27.50-£35
single, £43.50-£60 double.
Parking for 4.
Credit: Access, Visa.

TEWKESBURY

Gloucestershire
Map ref 2B1

Tewkesbury's
outstanding possession is
its magnificent church,
built as an abbey, with a
great Norman tower and
beautiful 14th C interior.
The town stands at the
confluence of the Severn
and Avon and has many
old houses, inns and
several museums.
*Tourist Information
Centre ☎ (0684) 295027*

The Abbey Hotel M
Listed

67 Church St., Tewkesbury,
GL20 5RX
☎ (0684) 294247 & 294097

*Family-run hotel offering
private and business
accommodation. En-suite
facilities with telephone and
TV. Restaurant. Special
weekend breaks.*
Bedrooms: 2 single, 4 double
& 4 twin, 4 family rooms.
Bathrooms: 12 private,
2 public.
Bed & breakfast: £30-£40
single, £40-£50 double.
Half board: £40-£55 daily,
£200-£385 weekly.
Evening meal 6pm (l.o.
9.30pm).
Parking for 11.
Credit: Access, Visa, Amex.

Bell Hotel M

52 Church St., Tewkesbury,
GL20 5SA
☎ (0684) 293293 Telex 43535
Ⓒ Best Western
*Historic black and white Tudor
hotel full of charm and
character and run on a highly
personalised basis. Log fires
when chilly.*
Bedrooms: 5 single, 15 double
& 5 twin.
Bathrooms: 25 private.
Bed & breakfast: £60-£80
single, £70-£110 double.
Half board: £46-£56 daily,
£300-£350 weekly.
Lunch available.
Evening meal 6.30pm (l.o.
9.30pm).
Parking for 50.
Credit: Access, Visa, Diners,
Amex.

Jessop House Hotel
COMMENDED

65 Church St., Tewkesbury,
GL20 5RZ
☎ (0684) 292017
*Georgian house facing the
abbey and medieval cottages,
peacefully overlooking
Tewkesbury's "Ham".*
Bedrooms: 3 double & 5 twin.
Bathrooms: 8 private.
Bed & breakfast: max. £55
single, max. £68 double.
Evening meal 7.30pm (l.o.
8.30pm).
Parking for 4.
Credit: Access, Visa.

Lampitt House M
COMMENDED

Lampitt Lane, Bredon's
Norton, Tewkesbury,
GL20 7HB
☎ Bredon (0684) 72295

*Large house set in 1.5-acre
garden in picturesque Cotswold
village at the foot of Bredon
Hill. Extensive views.
Tewkesbury 4 miles. Beautiful
hill and riverside walks.*
Bedrooms: 1 double & 2 twin.
Bathrooms: 3 private.
Bed & breakfast: £18-£26
single, £30-£32 double.
Half board: from £24 daily,
from £150 weekly.
Parking for 6.

Puckrup Hall Hotel M
COMMENDED

Puckrup, Tewkesbury,
GL20 6EL
☎ (0684) 296200
Fax (0684) 850788
*Elegant Regency manor house
in over 100 acres of parkland,
close to the M50/M5
intersection.*
Bedrooms: 12 double &
3 twin, 1 family room.
Bathrooms: 16 private.
Bed & breakfast: £82.50-£99
single, £99-£140 double.
Half board: £55-£69 daily.
Lunch available.
Evening meal 7pm (l.o.
9.30pm).
Parking for 120.
Credit: Access, Visa, Diners,
Amex.

Tudor House Hotel

High St., Tewkesbury,
GL20 5BH
☎ (0684) 297755
Ⓒ Resort
*In the market town of
Tewkesbury, offering attractive
bedrooms and a new brasserie-
style restaurant.*
Bedrooms: 5 single, 12 double
& 1 twin, 1 family room.
Bathrooms: 15 private,
2 public.
Bed & breakfast: £22.50-£51
single, £45-£66 double.
Lunch available.
Evening meal 7pm (l.o.
10pm).
Parking for 20.
Credit: Access, Visa, Diners,
Amex.

Upper Court M
COMMENDED

Kemerton, Tewkesbury,
GL20 7HY
☎ Overbury (038 689) 351

Small family-run Georgian manor with four-poster beds, antiques, beautiful grounds, personal service. Home grown produce.
Bedrooms: 2 double & 1 twin.
Bathrooms: 3 private, 1 public.
Bed & breakfast: £45-£50 single, £60-£75 double.
Half board: £62-£67 daily.
Parking for 10.
Credit: Access, Visa, Amex.

TUTBURY

Staffordshire
Map ref 4B3

Small town on the River Dove with an attractive High Street, old houses and the remains of a castle where Mary Queen of Scots was imprisoned.

Ye Olde Dog & Partridge Hotel M

High St., Tutbury, Burton upon Trent, DE13 9LS
☎ Burton upon Trent (0283) 813030 Fax 0283 813178
Coaching inn with wealth of beams and history. Carvery with grand piano played in the evenings. Beautiful gardens.
Bedrooms: 2 single, 7 double & 7 twin, 1 family room.
Bathrooms: 17 private.
Bed & breakfast: £52-£58 single, £60-£65 double.
Lunch available.
Evening meal 6.30pm (l.o. 9.45pm).
Parking for 100.
Credit: Access, Visa, Amex.

ULLINGSWICK

Hereford & Worcester
Map ref 2A1

6m SW. Bromyard
Village close to Hereford with its many attractions including the cathedral and the cider museum.

The Steppes M
HIGHLY COMMENDED

Ullingswick, Hereford, Herefordshire HR1 3JG
☎ Hereford (0432) 820424
17th C listed building with oak beams, log fires and inglenook fireplaces. Cordon bleu cuisine. Intimate atmosphere.

Bedrooms: 3 double & 2 twin.
Bathrooms: 5 private, 1 public.
Bed & breakfast: £20-£30 single, £40-£60 double.
Half board: £37.50-£47.50 daily, £245-£315 weekly.
Evening meal 7.30pm.
Parking for 8.
Credit: Access, Visa, Amex.

UPTON-UPON-SEVERN

Hereford & Worcester
Map ref 2B1

Attractive country town on the banks of the Severn and a good river cruising centre. It has many pleasant old houses and inns.

Pool House Riverside Country House Hotel M
COMMENDED

Hanley Rd., Upton-upon-Severn, Worcester, Worcestershire WR8 0PA
☎ (0684) 592151
Fine Queen Anne country house in large picturesque garden running down to the River Severn. Quiet, comfortable accommodation.
Bedrooms: 3 double & 4 twin, 2 family rooms.
Bathrooms: 6 private, 1 public.
Bed & breakfast: £20.50-£35.50 single, £33-£57 double.
Parking for 20.
Open February-November.
Credit: Access, Visa.

White Lion Hotel M
COMMENDED

Upton-upon-Severn, Worcester, Worcestershire WR8 0HJ
☎ (0684) 592551 Fax 0684 592551
Ⓒ Minotels
Former 16th C coaching inn with Georgian facade, in the historic town of Upton-upon-Severn. Tudor dining room with full a la carte menu.
Bedrooms: 2 single, 4 double & 4 twin.
Bathrooms: 10 private, 2 public.
Bed & breakfast: from £49.50 single, from £67.75 double.
Half board: from £43 daily, from £300 weekly.
Lunch available.
Evening meal 7pm (l.o. 9.30pm).

Parking for 21.
Credit: Access, Visa, Diners, Amex.

WALSALL

W. Midlands
Map ref 4B3

Industrial town with a magnificent collection of pictures and antiquities in its museum and art gallery. It has a fine arboretum with lakes and walks and illuminations each September.

Abberley Hotel M

Bescot Road, Walsall, WS2 9AD
☎ (0922) 27413
Fax (0922) 720933
Private hotel run by proprietors. A change from the larger hotel, without being intrusive. Ideally situated for motorway networks, quarter of a mile from M6 junction 9.
Bedrooms: 18 single, 6 double & 3 twin, 1 family room.
Bathrooms: 28 private.
Bed & breakfast: £39-£44 single, £52-£60 double.
Half board: £48-£52 daily, £286-£310 weekly.
Lunch available.
Evening meal 6.30pm (l.o. 8pm).
Parking for 30.
Credit: Access, Visa, Amex.

Fairlawns Hotel and Restaurant M

Little Aston Rd., Aldridge, Walsall, WS9 0NU
☎ Aldridge (0922) 55122
Telex 339873
Ⓒ Consort
Modern hotel in its own grounds, in a quiet, rural location, 20 minutes from Birmingham and 30 minutes from the National Exhibition Centre.
Bedrooms: 6 single, 19 double & 5 twin, 6 family rooms.
Bathrooms: 36 private.
Bed & breakfast: £35-£75 single, £45-£95 double.
Half board: £55-£110 daily, £455-£805 weekly.
Lunch available.
Evening meal 7pm (l.o. 10pm).
Parking for 82.
Credit: Access, Visa, Diners, Amex.

Friendly Hotel M

20 Wolverhampton Rd. West, Bentley, Walsall, WS2 0BS
☎ (0922) 724444
Telex 334854
Ⓒ Friendly
Hotel offering wide range of conference facilities for up to 200 persons. Carvery and a la carte menus. Own leisure complex. Direct access to M6 from the hotel's location at junction 10.
Bedrooms: 30 single, 20 double & 70 twin, 5 family rooms.
Bathrooms: 125 private.
Bed & breakfast: £56.75-£69.45 single, £77.50-£92.65 double.
Lunch available.
Evening meal 7pm (l.o. 10pm).
Parking for 135.
Credit: Access, Visa, Diners, Amex.

WARWICK

Warwickshire
Map ref 2B1

Warwick is outstanding for its castle rising above the River Avon and for the 15th C Beauchamp Chapel attached to St. Mary's Church. The medieval Lord Leycester's Hospital almshouses and several museums are amongst the other attractions.
Tourist Information Centre ☎ (0926) 492212

Austin House M
APPROVED

96 Emscote Rd., Warwick, CV34 5QJ
☎ (0926) 493583
Black and white Edwardian house situated half a mile from Warwick Castle, 1 mile from Royal Leamington Spa and 6 miles from Stratford-upon-Avon.
Bedrooms: 1 single, 1 double & 2 twin, 3 family rooms.
Bathrooms: 5 private, 1 public.
Bed & breakfast: £13.50-£16.50 single, £27-£33 double.
Parking for 8.
Credit: Amex.

Avon Guest House M
APPROVED
7 Emscote Rd., Warwick,
CV34 4PH
☎ (0926) 491367
*Family-run guesthouse with a
friendly atmosphere, in
pleasant surroundings near
town centre.*
Bedrooms: 3 single, 2 double
& 2 twin, 3 family rooms.
Bathrooms: 2 public;
4 private showers.
Bed & breakfast: £14 single,
£28 double.
Half board: £20 daily, £140
weekly.
Evening meal 6pm (l.o.
7.30pm).
Parking for 7.

Chesterfield M
APPROVED
84 Emscote Rd., Warwick,
CV34 5QJ
☎ (0926) 492396
Fax (0926) 494059
*Family-run guesthouse with
pleasant decor throughout and
colour TV in all rooms. Most
rooms have private showers
and king-size beds.*
Bedrooms: 2 single, 2 double
& 1 twin, 3 family rooms.
Bathrooms: 1 public;
5 private showers.
Bed & breakfast: £15-£22
single, £26-£32 double.
Parking for 10.
Credit: Access, Visa, Amex.

The Croft M
COMMENDED
Haseley Knob, Warwick,
CV35 7NL
☎ Haseley Knob
(0926) 484447
*4-acre smallholding with
friendly family atmosphere in
picturesque rural setting. On
A4177 between Balsall
Common and Warwick,
convenient for the NEC,
National Agricultural Centre,
Stratford and Coventry. 15
minutes from Birmingham
Airport.*
Bedrooms: 1 double & 1 twin,
1 family room.
Bathrooms: 2 private,
2 public.
Bed & breakfast: £16-£19.50
single, £32-£38 double.
Half board: £24-£30 daily.
Evening meal 6pm (l.o. 8pm).
Parking for 10.

Hilton National
A46, Stratford Rd., Warwick,
CV34 6RE
☎ (0926) 499555
Telex 312468
ⓒ Hilton
*Well-situated for business or
pleasure and offering modern
facilities. Set in own grounds
and with a large car park.*
Bedrooms: 18 single,
75 double & 78 twin, 10 family
rooms.
Bathrooms: 181 private.
Bed & breakfast: £40-£60
single, £52-£72 double.
Lunch available.
Evening meal 7pm (l.o.
10pm).
Parking for 220.
Credit: Access, Visa, Diners,
Amex.

Lord Leycester M
17 Jury Street, Warwick,
CV34 4EJ
☎ (0926) 491481 Telex 41363
ⓒ Calotels
*Georgian hotel close to
Warwick Castle, 8 miles from
Stratford, 2 miles from
Leamington Spa.*
Bedrooms: 13 single,
13 double & 21 twin, 5 family
rooms.
Bathrooms: 52 private.
Bed & breakfast: £27-£52
single, £54-£72 double.
Lunch available.
Evening meal 7pm (l.o.
8.30pm).
Parking for 50.
Credit: Access, Visa, Diners,
Amex.

Northleigh House M
COMMENDED
Five Ways Rd., Hatton,
Warwick, CV35 7HZ
☎ Warwick (0926) 484203
*Comfortable, peaceful country
house where the elegant rooms
are individually designed and
have en-suite bathroom, fridge,
kettle and colour TV.*
Bedrooms: 1 single, 4 double
& 1 twin.
Bathrooms: 6 private.
Bed & breakfast: £27-£36
single, £40-£52 double.
Half board: £32.50-£46.50
daily.
Parking for 8.
Open January-November.

The Old Fourpenny Shop Hotel M
COMMENDED
27-29 Crompton St.,
Warwick, CV34 6HJ
☎ (0926) 491360
Fax (0926) 491360
*Recently refurbished, offering
real ale and real food. Very
close to Warwick Castle, race
and golf courses and town
centre.*
Bedrooms: 2 single, 3 double
& 2 twin.
Bathrooms: 7 private.
Bed & breakfast: £30-£38
single, £47.50-£55 double.
Half board: £40-£48 daily.
Lunch available.
Evening meal 7pm (l.o.
10pm).
Parking for 7.
Credit: Access, Visa, Diners,
Amex.

Old Rectory
Vicarage Lane, Sherbourne,
Warwick, CV35 8AB
☎ Barford (0926) 624562
*Georgian country house with
beams and inglenook
fireplaces, furnished with
antiques. Well-appointed
bedrooms, many with brass
beds, all with en-suite facilities
and colour TV. Hearty
breakfast. Situated half a mile
from M40 junction 15.*
Bedrooms: 4 single, 6 double
& 2 twin, 2 family rooms.
Bathrooms: 14 private.
Bed & breakfast: £27.50-£38
single, £39-£48 double.
Parking for 14.

Penderrick Hotel M
36 Coten End, Warwick,
CV34 4NP
☎ (0926) 499399/497252
*Early Victorian family-run
hotel near castle, convenient for
National Agricultural Centre,
National Exhibition Centre,
Stratford, Cotswolds. Tea-
making facilities, TV,
telephone, comfortable en-suite
bedrooms. Residents' bar.*
Bedrooms: 2 single, 1 double
& 2 twin, 1 family rooms.
Bathrooms: 4 private,
1 public; 2 private showers.
Bed & breakfast: £26-£29.50
single, £45-£49.50 double.
Half board: £38.50-£42.50
daily.
Evening meal 7pm (l.o. 8pm).

Parking for 9.
Credit: Access, Visa, Diners,
Amex.

Tudor House Inn M
90-92 West St., Warwick,
CV34 6AW
☎ (0926) 495447 Fax 0926
492948
*Inn of character dating from
1472 with a wealth of beams.
One of the few buildings to
survive the great fire of
Warwick in 1694. Opposite
Warwick Castle and close to
Warwick racecourse.*
Bedrooms: 3 single, 5 double
& 2 twin, 1 family room.
Bathrooms: 6 private,
1 public; 2 private showers.
Bed & breakfast: £24-£42
single, £54-£59 double.
Half board: £34-£39 daily.
Lunch available.
Evening meal 6pm (l.o.
11pm).
Parking for 6.
Credit: Access, Visa, Diners,
Amex.

8m SE. Leek
Village in the valley of the
River Hamps, once the
terminus of the Leek and
Manifold Light Railway, 8
miles of which is now a
macadamised walkers'
path.

Croft House Farm Guest House M
COMMENDED
Waterfall, Waterhouses,
Stoke-on-Trent, ST10 3HZ
☎ (0538) 308553
*17th C farmhouse in Waterfall,
between Ashbourne and Leek,
surrounded by beautiful
countryside. Offers warm,
friendly hospitality and home
cooking. Reduction for
children.*
Bedrooms: 2 double & 2 twin,
2 family rooms.
Bathrooms: 2 public.
Bed & breakfast: from £22
single, from £34 double.
Half board: from £26 daily,
from £179.50 weekly.
Lunch available.
Evening meal 7pm (l.o. 8pm).
Parking for 15.

Old Beams Restaurant with Rooms M

♨♨♨

Leek Rd., Waterhouses,
ST10 3HW
☎ (0538) 308254
*Attractive 18th C house with
log fires and an abundance of
flowers. Good cuisine prepared
by chef/patron Nigel Wallis.
Beautiful bedrooms.*
Bedrooms: 6 double.
Bathrooms: 6 private.
Bed & breakfast: £52-£72.50
single, £67.50-£87 double.
Lunch available.
Evening meal 7pm (l.o.
10pm).
Parking for 22.
Credit: Access, Visa, Diners,
Amex.

WELLESBOURNE

Warwickshire
Map ref 2B1

Picturesque village with
several noteworthy inns.
The River Dene, which
divides the place in two,
once separated
Wellesbourne Hastings
from Wellesbourne
Mountford, but now both
parts are regarded as one
village.

Chadley House M

♨♨♨ COMMENDED

Loxley Road, Wellesbourne,
Warwick, CV35 9JL
☎ Stratford-upon-Avon
(0789) 840994
*Georgian farmhouse set in 6.5
acres, with small restaurant.
En-suite facilities in all rooms.
Close to Stratford-upon-Avon
and Cotswolds.*
Bedrooms: 1 single, 4 double
& 4 twin.
Bathrooms: 9 private.
Bed & breakfast: £35-£50
single, £60-£70 double.
Evening meal 7.30pm (l.o.
9.30pm).
Parking for 23.
Credit: Access, Visa.

---

*Please check prices
and other details at
the time of booking.*

---

*Half board prices shown are per person
but in some cases may be based on
double/twin occupancy.*

WEM

Shropshire
Map ref 4A3

Small town connected
with Judge Jeffreys who
lived in Lowe Hall. Well-
known for its ales.

Soulton Hall M

♨♨♨

Wem, Shrewsbury, SY4 5RS
☎ (0939) 32786
*560-acre mixed farm. Tudor
manor house with moated
Domesday site in grounds,
offering relaxing holiday.
Private riverside and woodland
walks.*
Bedrooms: 2 single, 1 double
& 1 twin, 1 family room.
Bathrooms: 4 private;
1 private shower.
Bed & breakfast: £24.25-
£34.50 single, £47.50-£56
double.
Half board: £37.25-£42.50
daily, £235-£268 weekly.
Evening meal 7pm (l.o.
8.30pm).
Parking for 12.
Credit: Access, Visa.

WINCHCOMBE

Gloucestershire
Map ref 2B1

Ancient town with a folk
museum and railway
museum. To the south
lies Sudeley Castle with
its fine collection of
paintings and toys and an
Elizabethan garden.

Pilgrims Bistro M

♨♨♨ COMMENDED

6 North St., Winchcombe,
Cheltenham, GL54 5LH
☎ (0242) 603544
*Busy bistro in centre of town,
offering highly individual style
of cooking. Building dates
back 300 years.*
Bedrooms: 2 double & 1 twin.
Bathrooms: 3 private.
Bed & breakfast: £25-£28
single, £46-£62 double.
Half board: from £33 daily.
Lunch available.
Evening meal 7pm (l.o.
9.30pm).
Credit: Access, Visa.

WITHINGTON

Gloucestershire
Map ref 2B1

8m SE. Cheltenham
Village near Chedworth
Roman Villa which is one
of the best preserved in
England.

Halewell Close M

♨♨♨ COMMENDED

Withington, Cheltenham,
GL54 4BN
☎ (024 289) 238
*Monastic, 15th C building with
hammer beam roof and gallery,
oak panelled dining room and
log fires in winter.*
Bedrooms: 4 double & 2 twin.
Bathrooms: 6 private.
Bed & breakfast: £49-£51
single, £78-£80 double.
Half board: £56.50-£68.50
daily.
Evening meal 8pm (l.o. 8pm).
Parking for 6.
Credit: Access, Visa, Amex.

WOLVERHAMPTON

W. Midlands
Map ref 4B3

Modern industrial town
with a long history, a fine
parish church and an
excellent art gallery.
There are several places
of interest in the vicinity
including Moseley Old
Hall and Wightwick Manor
with its William Morris
influence.
*Tourist Information
Centre ☎ (0902) 312051*

Ely House M

♨♨♨ COMMENDED

53 Tettenhall Rd.,
Wolverhampton, WV3 9NB
☎ (0902) 311311 Fax 0902
21098
*Fine imposing Georgian
building, fully restored, and in
a good central position,
adjacent to motorway network.
Ideal base for touring
throughout the West Midlands.*
Bedrooms: 6 single, 6 double
& 7 twin.
Bathrooms: 19 private.
Bed & breakfast: £48-£55
single, £60-£72 double.
Lunch available.
Evening meal 7pm (l.o.
10pm).
Parking for 16.
Credit: Access, Visa, Amex.

Fox Hotel M

♨♨♨

School St., Wolverhampton,
WV3 0NR
☎ (0902) 21680 &
(0902) 21719
*Town centre, free parking,
nearby shopping. All rooms en-
suite, satellite TV, direct dial
telephones. Bar and restaurant.*
Bedrooms: 27 single, 3 double
& 3 twin.
Bathrooms: 33 private.
Bed & breakfast: £24.50-
£34.50 single, £34.50-£44.50
double.
Lunch available.
Evening meal 7.30pm (l.o.
9pm).
Parking for 20.
Credit: Access, Visa, Diners,
Amex.

Patshull Park Hotel M

Patshull Park, Pattingham,
Wolverhampton, WV6 7HR
☎ Pattingham (0902) 700100
Telex 334849 Fax 0902
700874
*Modern, attractive country
hotel set in picturesque estate
with own golf-course and
fishing lakes. Health and
fitness complex includes sauna,
indoor pool and solarium. 3
miles from junction 3 of M54.*
Bedrooms: 6 double &
38 twin, 4 family rooms.
Bathrooms: 48 private,
4 public.
Bed & breakfast: £60-£72.50
single, £70-£95 double.
Half board: from £70 daily.
Lunch available.
Evening meal 7.30pm (l.o.
9.30pm).
Parking for 200.
Credit: Access, Visa.

⊕ Display advertisement
appears on page 262.

Rank Motor Lodge M

Hilton Park Services,
M6 Motorway, Between exits
10a & 11, Wolverhampton,
WV11 2DR
☎ (0922) 414100 Fax 0922
418762
*Modern bedrooms, close to all
the Midland tourist and
business destinations. Self-
service restaurant open 24
hours.*
Bedrooms: 6 double &
36 twin, 22 family rooms.
Bathrooms: 64 private.
Bed & breakfast: from £29.75
single, from £37.75 double.
Lunch available.
Evening meal (l.o. 10pm).

Continued ▶

WOLVERHAMPTON

Continued

Parking for 60.
Credit: Access, Visa, Diners, Amex.

Victoria Park Hotel M
Lichfield St.,
Wolverhampton, WV1 4DB
☎ (0902) 29922 Telex 338083
CR Park Hotels
Restored high standard international hotel, well located for visits to the National Exhibition Centre.
Bedrooms: 33 single,
40 double & 43 twin, 1 family room.
Bathrooms: 117 private.
Bed & breakfast: £22-£78 single, £44-£96 double.
Half board: £32-£92 daily.
Lunch available.
Evening meal 6pm (l.o. 11pm).
Credit: Access, Visa, C.Bl., Diners, Amex.

Wulfrun Hotel
37 Pipers Row,
Wolverhampton, WV1 3BJ
☎ (0902) 24017
Small homely hotel in the town centre, near railway, bus and coach stations.
Bedrooms: 3 single, 5 double & 5 twin, 1 family room.
Bathrooms: 3 public.
Bed & breakfast: from £22 single, from £36 double.
Half board: £26-£30 daily, £132-£180 weekly.
Lunch available.
Evening meal 4pm (l.o. 11.30pm).
Credit: Access, Visa.

> *National Crown ratings were correct at the time of going to press but are subject to change. Please check at the time of booking.*

> *The national Crown scheme is explained in full on pages 536 – 539.*

WORCESTER

Hereford & Worcester
Map ref 2B1

Lovely city which is dominated by its Norman and Early English cathedral, King John's burial place. The city has many old buildings including the 15th C Commandery and the 18th C Guildhall. There are several museums and the Royal Worcester porcelain factory.
Tourist Information Centre ☎ (0905) 726311

Abbeydore Guest House
APPROVED
34 Barbourne Rd.,
Worcester, Worcestershire
WR1 1HU
☎ (0905) 26731
Family-run guesthouse within walking distance of the city centre, shops, cathedral, racecourse and sports facilities.
Bedrooms: 2 single, 1 double & 1 twin, 3 family rooms.
Bathrooms: 2 public.
Bed & breakfast: £14-£16 single, £28-£30 double.
Credit: Access, Visa.

Abbott Accommodation
Listed
85 Bromyard Rd., Worcester, Worcestershire WR2 5BZ
☎ (0905) 425271
Quiet and homely guesthouse on the west side of St. John's, 10 minutes from the cathedral.
Bedrooms: 4 double & 1 twin, 1 family room.
Bathrooms: 1 private,
1 public; 2 private showers.
Bed & breakfast: £16-£20 single, £32-£36 double.
Half board: £23-£27 daily.
Evening meal (l.o. 10pm).
Parking for 8.

Bank House Hotel M
COMMENDED
Bransford, Worcester, Worcestershire WR6 5JD
☎ (0886) 33551 Fax 0886 32461
Sympathetically-converted country house hotel, located in beautiful countryside on A4103 Worcester to Hereford road, close to many local attractions.
Bedrooms: 20 single, 8 double & 12 twin, 2 family rooms.
Bathrooms: 42 private.
Bed & breakfast: £49.50-£75 single, £55-£95 double.
Lunch available.

Evening meal 7pm (l.o. 9.30pm).
Parking for 200.
Credit: Access, Visa, Diners, Amex.

11 Battenhall Rd., M
Listed **COMMENDED**
Worcester, Worcestershire
WR5 2BJ
☎ (0905) 350158
Edwardian residence very close to M5 and within easy walking distance of Worcester city centre, cathedral and Civil War Centre.
Bedrooms: 1 double & 1 twin.
Bathrooms: 1 public.
Bed & breakfast: from £16 single, from £26 double.
Parking for 2.
Credit: Access, Visa.

Belmont Hotel M
COMMENDED
22 Droitwich Road,
Worcester, Worcestershire
WR3 7LJ
☎ (0905) 22016
A comfortable old family house on the outskirts of the city centre. Racecourse, sports facilities and park within walking distance.
Bedrooms: 1 single, 1 double & 2 twin, 2 family rooms.
Bathrooms: 4 private,
1 public.
Bed & breakfast: £16-£26 single, £28-£32 double.
Parking for 6.

Croft Guest House M
Bransford, Worcester, Worcestershire WR6 5JD
☎ Leigh Sinton (0886) 32227
16th/18th C house in countryside, with views to Malvern Hills. Family-run, with comfortable surroundings and family jacuzzi. 10 minutes from M5, Worcester and Malvern, on A4103.
Bedrooms: 1 single, 2 double & 1 twin, 1 family room.
Bathrooms: 3 private,
2 public.
Bed & breakfast: £17-£23 single, £32-£40 double.
Half board: £22.50-£31.50 daily, £146-£176 weekly.
Evening meal 7pm (l.o. 6.30pm).
Parking for 8.

Dilmore House Hotel M
COMMENDED
Droitwich Rd., Fernhill Heath, Worcester, Worcestershire WR3 7UL
☎ (0905) 51543
Warm, comfortable, friendly hotel offering a high standard of facilities, midway between Worcester and Droitwich Spa. All rooms en-suite with colour TV.
Bedrooms: 2 single, 2 double & 1 twin.
Bathrooms: 5 private,
1 public.
Bed & breakfast: £27-£29 single, £39-£41 double.
Half board: £35-£39 daily.
Parking for 9.
Credit: Access, Visa.

Loch Ryan Hotel M
119 Sidbury, Worcester, Worcestershire WR5 2DH
☎ (0905) 351143
Historic hotel very close to the cathedral, Royal Worcester Porcelain factory and Commandery. Attractive terraced garden.
Bedrooms: 2 single, 4 double & 3 twin, 1 family room.
Bathrooms: 10 private,
2 public.
Bed & breakfast: £25-£40 single, £40-£60 double.
Half board: £30-£53.50 daily.
Lunch available.
Evening meal 6pm (l.o. 8pm).
Credit: Access, Visa, Diners, Amex.

The Maximillian Hotel M
APPROVED
Cromwell St., Shrub Hill, Worcester, Worcestershire, WR4 9EF
☎ (0905) 23867 & (0905) 21694
Family-run Georgian hotel situated just outside city centre, with ample car parking and easy access to Shrub Hill railway station and M5 junction 7.
Bedrooms: 6 single, 4 double & 5 twin, 2 family rooms.
Bathrooms: 13 private,
1 public.
Bed & breakfast: £39 single, £51.50 double.
Half board: £51.50 daily, £360.50 weekly.
Lunch available.

Evening meal 7pm (l.o. 10pm).
Parking for 15.
Credit: Access, Visa, Amex.
🛇 📞 🖃 🖵 💱 🔒 ☓ 🔛 📺 🌑 🛏 🍴 🛋 ☓ 🗺 SP 📻 Ⓣ

Shrubbery Guest House ⚏

38 Barbourne Rd.,
Worcester, Worcestershire
WR1 1HU
☎ (0905) 24871
*Large Victorian house within
15 minutes' walking distance of
Worcester Cathedral, city
centre and Royal Worcester
factory.*
Bedrooms: 3 double & 2 twin,
1 family room.
Bathrooms: 3 private,
2 public; 2 private showers.
Bed & breakfast: from £14
single, from £28 double.
🛇 🛋 🖵 🔛 🗺 📺 🌑 🛏 ☓

Wyatt Guest House ⚏
⚏

40 Barbourne Rd.,
Worcester, Worcestershire
WR1 1HU
☎ (0905) 26311
*Small, family-run guesthouse
close to city centre, parks, river
and racecourse.*
Bedrooms: 1 single, 1 double
& 2 twin, 4 family rooms.
Bathrooms: 4 private,
1 public; 1 private shower.
Bed & breakfast: £16-£18
single, £26-£30 double.
Half board: £20-£22 daily.
Evening meal 6pm (l.o. 7pm).
🛇 🛋 🖵 💱 🔛 🔒 🛏 📺 🌑
🛋

Ye Olde Talbot Hotel ⚏
⚏ ⚏ ⚏

Friar St., Worcester,
Worcestershire WR1 2NA
☎ (0905) 23573 Telex 333315
Fax 0905 612760

🅖🅡 Lansbury
*Originally an old courtroom,
located close to the town centre
and the cathedral, to which it
once belonged.*
Bedrooms: 10 single,
15 double & 4 twin.
Bathrooms: 29 private.
Bed & breakfast: £24-£62
single, £48-£74 double.
Half board: £36-£77 daily.
Lunch available.
Evening meal 7pm (l.o.
10.30pm).
Parking for 8.
Credit: Access, Visa, Diners,
Amex.
🛇 🛋 🔛 📞 🖃 🖵 💱 🔒 Ⓥ
☓ 🛏 🌑 🖩 🛋 🍴 SP 📻 Ⓣ

WOTTON-UNDER-EDGE
Gloucestershire Map ref 2B2

9m SW. Stroud
Small Cotswold town with
a replica of the Orpheus
Pavement, a Roman
mosaic, in the Tabernacle
Church. Berkeley Castle
is within easy reach.

Swan Hotel & Restaurant
14-16 Market St., Wotton-
Under-Edge, GL12 7AE
☎ Dursley (0453) 842329

*Late 15th C building which has
been modernised. Restaurant,
grill and a la carte menus. In
the centre of the town with
easy access to M5 junction 14.*
Bedrooms: 2 single, 8 double
& 6 twin.
Bathrooms: 16 private.
Bed & breakfast: £45-£56
single, £55-£72 double.
Half board: £40-£75 daily,
£280-£450 weekly.
Lunch available.
Evening meal 7pm (l.o.
10.15pm).
Parking for 6.
Credit: Access, Visa, Diners,
Amex.
🛇 📞 🖵 🔒 🛏 🖩 🍴 🔌 SP
📻 Ⓣ

WYE VALLEY

*See Hereford, Much
Birch, Ross-on-Wye,
Symonds Yat East,
Symonds Yat West.*

Key to symbols

*Information about many of the services
and facilities at establishments listed in
this guide is given in the form of
symbols. The key to these symbols is
inside the back cover flap. You may find
it helpful to keep the flap open when
referring to the entry listings.*

Check the maps

*The place you wish to visit may not
have accommodation entirely suited
to your needs, but there could be
somewhere ideal quite close by. Check
the colour maps towards the end of
this guide to identify nearby towns
and villages with accommodation
listed in the guide, and then use the
town index to find page numbers.*

The Charlecote Pheasant

THE CHARLECOTE PHEASANT HOTEL

The Charlecote Pheasant is set in the Warwickshire countryside at Charlecote, with easy access from nearby major roads (M1, M40, M6) and air/rail networks.

All 67 rooms including 8 four posters, offer private facilities, colour TV with satellite channels, radio, direct dial telephone, trouser press, hair dryer and tea & coffee making facilities.

Recreation includes solarium, steam room, pool table, fitness room with multi gym, and outdoor-heated swimming pool (seasonal), tennis and croquet.

Special weekend rates available from £47.50 per person inclusive of dinner, bed, breakfast and VAT, minimum 2 nights.

Restaurant and bar open to non residents, reservations required for Friday and Saturday Dinner and Sunday Lunch.

Please write or telephone for further details:-
Charlecote Pheasant Hotel
Charlecote, Warwickshire CV35 9EW
Telephone 0789 470333   Fax: 0789 470222

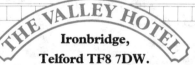

THE VALLEY HOTEL

Ironbridge,
Telford TF8 7DW.
Tel: (0952) 432247.   Fax: (0952) 432308.

👑👑👑   AA ★★★

The Valley Hotel is a beautifully refurbished listed Georgian building in its own spacious and secluded grounds within the World Heritage site of Ironbridge in the stunning Severn Gorge. The hotel is less than 10 minutes drive from Telford town centre and within easy reach of Birmingham city centre, the National Exhibition Centre, Wolverhampton and Shrewsbury.

All bedrooms, tastefully furnished in antique pine, have en-suite bathroom, colour TV, free satellite reception, in-house video service and direct dial telephone. Our conference suite, seating 220+, provides an ideal business or social venue and the licensed restaurant offers extensive and varied menus.

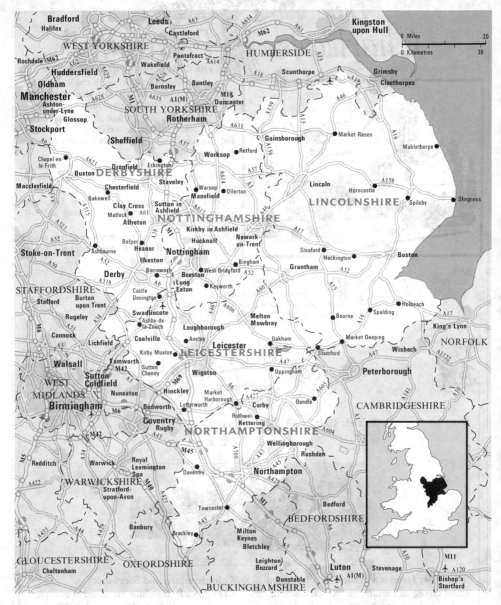

PLEASE REFER TO THE COLOUR MAPS AT THE BACK OF THIS GUIDE FOR ALL PLACES WITH ACCOMMODATION LISTINGS.

ALSO KNOWN AS "THE SHIRES OF MIDDLE ENGLAND", *this is a region where you can mix'n'match the peace of the countryside, the pulse of the city and the pleasure of the seaside. Enjoy the safe, sandy beaches of Skegness and Mablethorpe. Explore the forests of Sherwood, Rockingham and Charnwood. Trek through the unspoilt beauty of the Peak District — or, if that's too energetic, meander through the flat Fens or the gentle Lincolnshire Wolds. Take in Nottingham for its fine shopping, Lincoln for its history — and Bakewell for its renowned Pudding!*

WHERE TO GO, WHAT TO SEE

The American Adventure
Ilkeston, Derbyshire DE7 5SX
☎ Langley Mill (0773) 531521
American theme park with over 100 rides. Great Niagara Rapids Ride, the Missile, Cherokee Falls Log Flume. Shoot-out and shows daily.

Belton House
Grantham, Lincolnshire
NG32 2LS
☎ Grantham (0476) 66116
The crowning achievement of Restoration country house architecture, built in 1685 – 88 for Sir John Brownlow. Alterations by James Wyatt in 1777.

Billing Aquadrome
Little Billing, Northampton,
Northamptonshire NN3 4DA
☎ Northampton (0604) 408181
Boating, fishing, pleasure park, amusements, swimming pool and children's paddling pool.

Bosworth Battlefield Visitor Centre and Country Park
Sutton Cheney, Market Bosworth, Leicestershire CV13 0AD
☎ Market Bosworth (0455) 290429
Site of Battle of Bosworth Field in 1485. Battlefield visitor centre with models, flags, armour, film theatre. Battle trails to King Richard's well and field.

Butlins Funcoast World
Roman Bank, Skegness,
Lincolnshire PE25 1NJ
☎ Skegness (0754) 2311
Funsplash water world, amusement park, entertainment, funfair, monorail, boating, sports, cinema and shops.

Buxton Micrarium
The Crescent, Buxton,
Derbyshire SK17 6BQ
☎ Buxton (0298) 78662
Unique exhibition of the natural world under the microscope, using special push-button projection microscopes operated by visitors.

The Canal Museum
Canal Street, Nottingham,
Nottinghamshire NG1 7EH
☎ Nottingham (0602) 598835
Former canal warehouse with landing areas and wharves. Displays on history of the River Trent, canal and river transport, bridges, floods, natural history.

Discover the history of the River Trent at the Canal Museum

Busy open-top trams at The National Tramway Museum

Central Museum and Art Gallery
Guildhall Road, Northampton,
Northamptonshire NN1 1DP
☎ Northampton (0604) 39415
Displays on Northampton's history from earliest times to present, using objects, sound and film. Footwear through the ages, ceramics.

Church of All Saints
Church Street, Brixworth,
Northampton,
Northamptonshire
☎ Northampton (0604) 880286
One of the finest Anglo-Saxon churches in the country. Mostly original 7th C work, with much Roman material. Tower and stair turret added in 10th C.

Clumber
Worksop, Nottinghamshire
S80 3AZ
☎ Worksop (0909) 476592
Over 3,800 acres of 18th C landscape, with lake, "Duke's Drive" double avenue of lime trees, nature walks, fishing, cycle hire. Victorian Gothic chapel, 1886.

Derby City Museum and Art Gallery
The Strand, Derby, Derbyshire
DE1 1BS
☎ Derby (0332) 255586
Joseph Wright paintings, Derby porcelain, antiquities, natural history, archaeology and militaria.

Haddon Hall
Bakewell, Derbyshire DE4 1LA
☎ Bakewell (0629) 812855
Medieval manorial home built during 14th and 15th C. Banqueting hall, long gallery, chapel frescos. Terraced rose gardens.

Heckington Windmill
Hale Road, Heckington,
Lincolnshire NG34 0JW
☎ Sleaford (0529) 60765
Unique 8-sailed tower mill, built in 1830 and restored. Milling at weekends, weather permitting. Wholemeal flour for sale.

Kirby Hall
Deene, Nr. Corby,
Northamptonshire NN17 3EN
☎ Corby (0536) 203230
Elizabethan hall built in 1570 by Sir Humphrey Stafford, with 17th C alterations by Inigo Jones. Abandoned late 18th C.

Long Sutton Butterfly Park
Long Sutton, Spalding,
Lincolnshire PE12 9LE
☎ Holbeach (0406) 363833
Large walk-through tropical butterfly house, insectarium, adventure playground, farm animals, pets' corner.

Museum of Lincolnshire Life
Burton Road, Lincoln,
Lincolnshire LN1 3LY
☎ Lincoln (0522) 528448
Agricultural, industrial and social history of Lincolnshire

from 1800. Edwardian room setting, display of craftwork in progress and World War I tank.

The National Tramway Museum
Crich, Matlock, Derbyshire
DE4 5DP
☎ Ambergate (0773) 852565
Collection of 40 tramcars from Britain and overseas, built 1873 – 1953. Tram rides, tramway period street scene, depots, power station, workshops.

Newstead Abbey
Linby, Nottingham,
Nottinghamshire NG15 8GE
☎ Mansfield (0623) 793557
800-year-old remains of priory church, converted into country house in 16th C. Home of Lord Byron. Park, gardens, lake.

Old Dairy Farm Centre
Upper Stowe, Nr. Weedon,
Northamptonshire NN7 4SH
☎ Weedon (0327) 40525
Wood turning, picture framing and various craft workshops.

Our Little Farm
Lodge Farm, Harby Lane,
Plungar, Nottingham,
Nottinghamshire NG13 0JH
☎ Harby (0949) 60349
Traditional farmyard with pond, canalside nature trail, livestock, pets' corner, picnic areas, tearoom and gift shop.

Rutland Water
Sykes Lane, Empingham,
Oakham, Leicestershire
LE15 8PX
☎ Empingham (078 086) 321
Largest man-made lake in western Europe, 3,100 acres. Water and land based recreational facilities, pleasure cruiser, museum.

St. Botolph's Church
Market Place, Boston,
Lincolnshire
☎ Boston (0205) 362864
Large parish church, dating from 1309, with 272ft tower (the "Boston Stump") completed in 1470. Embossed roof, carved 14th C misericords.

Southwell Minster

Southwell, Nottinghamshire
☎ Southwell (0636) 812649
Building started in c 1108.
Saxon tympanum, Norman nave
and crossing, Early English
choir. Oustanding foliage
carving in chapter house.
Archbishop's palace ruins.

Stanford Hall and Motor Cycle Museum

Lutterworth, Leicestershire
LE17 6DH
☎ Rugby (0788) 860250
William and Mary house on
River Avon. Family costumes,
furniture, pictures. Replica 1898
flying machine. Motorcycle
museum, rose garden, nature
trail.

Sulgrave Manor

Sulgrave, Nr. Banbury,
Oxfordshire OX17 2SD
☎ Sulgrave (029 576) 205
Small manor house of
Shakespeare's time, with
furniture of period. Fine kitchen.
Early English home of ancestors
of George Washington.

The Tales of Robin Hood

30 – 38 Maid Marian Way,
Nottingham, Nottinghamshire
NG1 6GF
☎ Nottingham (0602) 414414
Join the world's greatest
medieval adventure and hide out
in the Sheriff's eerie cave. Ride
through the magical greenwood
and play the Silver Arrow game.

Whatton Gardens

Whatton House, Long
Whatton, Nr. Loughborough,
Leicestershire LE12 5BG
☎ Loughborough (0509) 842302
25-acre garden containing
formal and wilderness areas,
including rock pools with fish
and unusual plants.

White Post Modern Farm Centre

Farnsfield, Nr. Newark,
Nottinghamshire NG22 8HL
☎ Mansfield (0623) 882977
Working farm with llama,
ostriches, egg incubator,
free-range hens, lakes, picnic
areas, tea gardens.

Motor Cycle Museum at Stanford Hall

Wygston's House Museum of Costume

Applegate, Leicester,
Leicestershire
☎ Leicester (0533) 554100
Late medieval building with later
additions. Displays on costume
and accessories. 1920s draper's
and shoe shops. Symington
corsetry collection.

MAKE A DATE FOR...

Spalding Flower Festival and Parade

Spalding, Lincolnshire
2 – 4 May

Medieval Jousting Tournament

Belvoir Castle, Belvoir,
Leicestershire
24 – 25 May, 30 – 31 August

Tennyson Exhibition

Usher Gallery, Lindum Road,
Lincoln, Lincolnshire
4 July – 14 September*

Buxton International Festival

Various venues, Buxton,
Derbyshire
11 July – 9 August

Robin Hood Festival

Sherwood Forest Visitor
Centre, Edwinstowe,
Nottinghamshire
20 – 27 July

Bakewell Show

The Showground, Coombe
Road, Bakewell, Derbyshire
5 – 6 August

350th Commemoration of the English Civil War

Various venues, Nottingham
and Newark, Nottinghamshire
22 – 31 August

Nottingham Goose Fair

Forest Recreation Ground,
Nottingham, Nottinghamshire
1 – 3 October

World Conker Championship

Village Green, Ashton,
Nr. Oundle, Northamptonshire
11 October

Lincoln Christmas Market

Bailgate and Castle Square,
Lincoln, Lincolnshire
10 – 13 December

* Provisional dates only

FIND OUT MORE

Further information about
holidays and attractions in the
Shires of Middle England is
available from:
East Midlands Tourist Board
Exchequergate, Lincoln
LN2 1PZ ☎ (0522) 531521

These publications are available
free from the East Midlands
Tourist Board:

The Shires of Middle England
(including places to visit)

The Peak District 1992

Events List (please send large
stamped and addressed envelope)

Also available is (price includes
postage and packing):

*Shires of Middle England Leisure
Map* £2.50

Places to stay

ACCOMMODATION ENTRIES in this regional section are listed in alphabetical order of place name, and then in alphabetical order of establishment.

THE MAP REFERENCES refer to the colour maps towards the end of the guide. The first figure is the map number; the letter and figure which follow indicate the grid reference on the map.

THE SYMBOLS at the end of each accommodation entry give information about services and facilities. A 'key' to these symbols is inside the back cover flap, which can be kept open for easy reference.

ALDWARK

Derbyshire
Map ref 4B2

5m SW. Matlock

Tithe Farm ⚑
😊😊 **COMMENDED**
Grange Mill, Aldwark, Via
Derby, DE4 4HX
☎ Carsington (062 985) 263
*Peacefully situated, within 10
miles of Matlock, Bakewell,
Ashbourne, the dales and
historic houses. Fresh produce
and home baking are a
speciality.*
Bedrooms: 3 twin.
Bathrooms: 1 public.
Bed & breakfast: £29 double.
Half board: £23.50 daily,
£141 weekly.
Evening meal 7pm (l.o. 6pm).
Parking for 6.
Open April-October.

ANSTEY

Leicestershire
Map ref 4C3

4m NW. Leicester
Village on the edge of
Charnwood Forest, close
to the attractive ruins
of Lady Jane Grey's home
in Bradgate Park, noted
for its deer and fine
views.

Leys Guest House ⚑
67 Leicester Road, Anstey,
Leicester, LE7 7AT
☎ (0533) 365929

---

*A former telephone exchange,
2 miles from Leicester city
centre and 1.5 miles from
Bradgate Park beauty spot.*
Bedrooms: 1 single, 3 twin.
Bathrooms: 2 public.
Bed & breakfast: £12.50-£15
single, £25-£30 double.
Parking for 7.

ASHBOURNE

Derbyshire
Map ref 4B2

Market town on the edge
of the Peak District
National Park and an
excellent centre for
walking. Its impressive
church with 212-ft spire
stands in an untouched
old street. Ashbourne is
well-known for
gingerbread and its
Shrovetide football
match.
*Tourist Information
Centre ☎ (0335) 43666*

Bentley Brook ⚑
😊😊😊 **COMMENDED**
Fenny Bentley, Nr.
Ashbourne, DE6 1LF
☎ Thorpe Cloud
(033 529) 278
*A traditional owner-operated
country inn in the Peak
District National Park, close to
Dovedale, Alton Towers and
Chatsworth.*
Bedrooms: 1 single, 5 double
& 2 twin, 1 family room.
Bathrooms: 5 private,
1 public.

Bed & breakfast: £32.50-£38
single, £47.50-£55 double.
Half board: £36.25-£40 daily,
£190-£205 weekly.
Lunch available.
Evening meal 7pm (l.o.
9.30pm).
Parking for 60.
Credit: Access, Visa.

**Callow Hall Country
House Hotel &
Restaurant** ⚑
😊😊😊😊 **COMMENDED**
Mappleton, Ashbourne,
DE6 2AA
☎ (0335) 43164/42412
*Half a mile from the centre of
Ashbourne and set in an
elevated position in unspoilt
countryside, surrounded by its
own woodland and overlooking
the valleys of the Bentley
Brook and the River Dove.*
Bedrooms: 8 double & 4 twin.
Bathrooms: 12 private.
Bed & breakfast: £63-£78
single, £85-£115 double.
Half board: £66-£80 daily.
Evening meal 7.30pm (l.o.
9.30pm).
Parking for 50.
Credit: Access, Visa, Diners,
Amex.

> *The enquiry
> coupons at the
> back will help you
> when contacting
> proprietors.*

Stone Cottage ⚑
Listed COMMENDED
Green Lane, Clifton,
Ashbourne, DE6 2BL
☎ Ashbourne (0335) 43377
*Charming 19th C cottage in
the Derbyshire Dales. All
bedrooms have colour TV and
tea-making facilities. Near
Dovedale, Chatsworth,
Haddon Hall and Alton
Towers.*
Bedrooms: 2 double, 1 family
room.
Bathrooms: 1 private,
1 public.
Bed & breakfast: £15-£18
single, £27-£36 double.
Half board: £20.50-£25 daily,
£120-£140 weekly.
Evening meal 6pm (l.o.
7.30pm).
Parking for 4.

ASHBY-DE-LA-
ZOUCH

Leicestershire
Map ref 4B3

Lovely market town with
late 15th C church,
impressive ruined 15th C
castle, an interesting
small museum and a
wide, sloping main street
with Georgian buildings.
Twycross Zoo is nearby.
*Tourist Information
Centre ☎ (0530) 411767*

The Cedars ⚑
😊😊 **APPROVED**
60 Burton Road, Ashby-de-la-
Zouch, LE6 5LN
☎ (0530) 412017

A substantial Victorian house with a pleasant garden and large rooms, within walking distance of the town centre, castle, good pubs and restaurants.
Bedrooms: 4 single, 2 twin, 4 family rooms.
Bathrooms: 5 private, 2 public.
Bed & breakfast: £14-£20 single, £28-£36 double.
Parking for 12.

Holywell House Hotel
♨♨

58 Burton Road, Ashby-de-la-Zouch, LE6 5LN
☎ (0530) 412005
Spacious Victorian building with attractive gardens and within easy walking distance of town centre. Close to M1 and M42 junctons.
Bedrooms: 1 double & 3 twin, 4 family rooms.
Bathrooms: 6 private, 1 public.
Bed & breakfast: £12-£16 single, £24-£34 double.
Parking for 10.

ASHFORD-IN-THE-WATER
Derbyshire
Map ref 4B2

2m NW. Bakewell
Limestone village in attractive surroundings of the Peak District approached by 3 bridges over the River Wye. There is an annual well-dressing ceremony and the village was well-known in the 18th C for its black marble quarries.

Chy-an-Dour **M**
♨♨

Hillcross, Ashford-in-the-Water, Nr. Bakewell, DE4 1QL
☎ Bakewell (062 981) 3162
Bungalow overlooking a pretty village and offering a friendly welcome. An ideal base for visiting the nearby stately homes and Derbyshire Dales.
Bedrooms: 2 double & 1 twin.
Bathrooms: 3 private.
Bed & breakfast: £36-£40 double.
Parking for 3.

Riverside Country House Hotel **M**
♨♨ COMMENDED

Fennel Street, Ashford-in-the-Water, Nr. Bakewell, DE4 1QF
☎ Bakewell (0629) 814275
This 17th C manor house has its own river frontage and an acre of garden which supplies home produce. Inside is a panelled bar, antiques, four-poster beds and an inglenook fireplace with log fires.
Bedrooms: 2 single, 6 double & 7 twin.
Bathrooms: 15 private.
Bed & breakfast: £77 single, £80-£92.50 double.
Half board: £68.75-£74.25 daily, £465-£519.75 weekly.
Lunch available.
Evening meal 7pm (l.o. 9.30pm).
Parking for 25.
Credit: Access, Visa, Amex.

BAKEWELL
Derbyshire
Map ref 4B2

Pleasant market town, famous for its pudding. It is set in beautiful countryside on the River Wye and is an excellent centre for exploring the Derbyshire Dales, the Peak District National Park, Chatsworth and Haddon Hall.
Tourist Information Centre ☎ *(0629) 813227*

Castle Cliffe Private Hotel **M**
♨♨

Monsal Head, Bakewell, DE4 1NL
☎ Great Longstone (0629) 87258/640258
A stone house with views of Monsal Dale and its viaduct. Follow signs to Monsal Head from Ashford on the A6.
Bedrooms: 3 double & 4 twin, 2 family rooms.
Bathrooms: 2 private, 2 public; 6 private showers.
Bed & breakfast: £36-£40 double.
Half board: £27-£29 daily, £180-£200 weekly.
Lunch available.
Evening meal 7pm (l.o. 5pm).
Parking for 15.
Credit: Access, Visa.

The Croft Country House Hotel **M**
♨♨♨ COMMENDED

Main Street, Great Longstone, Bakewell, DE4 1TF
☎ Great Longstone (0629) 640278
An interesting Victorian country house in 4 acres in this beautiful Peak village. Freshly-cooked food with traditional hospitality.
Bedrooms: 1 single, 6 double & 2 twin.
Bathrooms: 7 private, 1 public.
Bed & breakfast: £50-£55 single, £62-£82 double.
Half board: £68.50-£73.50 daily, £310-£350 weekly.
Evening meal 7.30pm (l.o. 7pm).
Parking for 30.
Open March-December.
Credit: Access, Visa.

Merlin House
♨♨ COMMENDED

Ashford Lane, Monsal Head, Bakewell, DE4 1NL
☎ Great Longstone (0629) 87475/640475
Small private hotel set in its own attractive garden amid outstanding scenery, in the heart of the Peak District National Park. Close to Bakewell, Chatsworth and Haddon Hall.
Bedrooms: 1 single, 4 double & 1 twin.
Bathrooms: 6 private.
Bed & breakfast: £23-£26 single, £41-£48 double.
Parking for 6.
Open March-October.

Milford House Hotel **M**
♨♨♨

Mill Street, Bakewell, DE4 1DA
☎ (0629) 812130
Once owned by Robert Cross, the water engineer for the 4 Arkwright cotton mills, the house retains much of his work.
Bedrooms: 2 single, 5 double & 5 twin.
Bathrooms: 12 private, 1 public.
Bed & breakfast: £33-£35 single, £64-£70 double.
Half board: £45-£47 daily, from £294.35 weekly.
Lunch available.
Evening meal 7pm (l.o. 7.30pm).
Parking for 24.
Open March-November.

Rutland Arms Hotel **M**
♨♨♨♨ COMMENDED

The Square, Bakewell, DE4 1BT
☎ (0629) 812309
Ⓒ Best Western
This is the hotel in which the famous Bakewell Pudding was accidentally created and Jane Austen is reputed to have stayed.
Bedrooms: 9 single, 15 double & 11 twin, 1 family room.
Bathrooms: 36 private.
Bed & breakfast: £42-£51 single, £59-£69 double.
Half board: £42-£55 daily, £285-£330 weekly.
Lunch available.
Evening meal 7pm (l.o. 9.30pm).
Parking for 37.
Credit: Access, Visa, Diners, Amex.

✪ Display advertisement appears on page 294.

BAMFORD
Derbyshire
Map ref 4B2

12m NE. Buxton
Village in the Peak District near the Upper Derwent Reservoirs of Ladybower, Derwent and Howden. An excellent centre for walking.

The Snake Pass Inn
♨♨♨ APPROVED

Ashopton Woodlands, Bamford, Via Sheffield, S30 2BJ
☎ Hope Valley (0433) 51480
Ⓒ Consort
18th C coaching house set in the beautiful Ashopton Woodlands of the Peak District. All bedrooms en-suite. Satellite TV.
Bedrooms: 4 double & 2 twin, 1 family room.
Bathrooms: 7 private.
Bed & breakfast: £25-£28.50 single, £45-£50 double.
Lunch available.
Evening meal 6pm (l.o. 9pm).
Parking for 35.
Credit: Access, Visa.

> *Half board prices shown are per person but in some cases may be based on double/twin occupancy.*

BARNBY MOOR

Nottinghamshire
Map ref 4C2

4m NW. Retford
Village on the former
Great North Road, within
easy reach of Clumber
Park, Sherwood Forest
and Pilgrim Father
Country.

Ye Olde Bell ♨
Barnby Moor, Retford,
DN22 8QS
☎ Retford (0777) 705121
CR Principal
*In the heart of Robin Hood
country, this ancient coaching
inn offers comfortable
accommodation and a relaxing
and friendly atmosphere.*
Bedrooms: 19 single,
22 double & 14 twin.
Bathrooms: 55 private.
Bed & breakfast: from £71.50
single, from £89 double.
Half board: from £49 daily.
Lunch available.
Evening meal 7pm (l.o.
9.45pm).
Parking for 250.
Credit: Access, Visa, Diners,
Amex.
➳ ♨ ╚ ⊗ ⟶ ♉ ⓘ Ⅴ ⅏
♒ ● Ⅲ ♨ ♈ ❋ ♌ ♏ Ⓣ

BASLOW

Derbyshire
Map ref 4B2

Small village on the River
Derwent with a stone-built
toll-house and a
packhorse bridge.
Chatsworth, home of the
Duke of Devonshire, is
nearby.

Cavendish Hotel ♨
♕♕♕♕
Baslow, DE4 1SP
☎ (0246) 582311
Telex 547150 CAVTEL G
*Set on the Chatsworth Estate
in the heart of the Peak
District National Park, this
famous 18th C fishing inn -
formerly the Peacock - has
been extensively renovated.*
Bedrooms: 11 double &
12 twin, 1 family room.
Bathrooms: 24 private.
Bed & breakfast: £79-£89
single, £103-£113 double.
Lunch available.
Evening meal 7pm (l.o.
11pm).
Parking for 40.
Credit: Access, Visa, Diners,
Amex.
➳ ♨ ♨ ╚ ⊗ ⟶ ♉ ⓘ Ⅴ
⅏ ♒ ● Ⅲ ♨ ♈ ♌ ♏
♌ SP Ⓣ

BELTON

Lincolnshire
Map ref 3A1

3m NE. Grantham
Attractive village close to
17th C Belton House and
Park, owned by the
National Trust.

Belton Woods Hotel and Country Club ♨
♕♕♕♕ COMMENDED
Belton, Nr. Grantham,
NG32 2LN
☎ Grantham (0476) 593200
Telex 378508
*Country house hotel in 480-
acre parkland estate. 2
restaurants, leisure club, 3 golf-
courses, driving range, tennis
courts.*
Bedrooms: 32 double &
64 twin.
Bathrooms: 96 private.
Bed & breakfast: £92-£112
single, £112-£132 double.
Half board: £56-£76 daily,
from £335 weekly.
Lunch available.
Evening meal 6.30pm (l.o.
9.30pm).
Parking for 366.
Credit: Access, Visa, C.Bl.,
Diners, Amex.
➳ ♨ ♨ ╚ ⊗ ⟶ ♉ ⓘ Ⅴ ⅏
♒ ● Ⅲ ♨ ♈ ♉ ♌ ♏ ♋
♐ ♑ ♒ ⟶ ♈ ♌ ♏ Ⓡ
♌ SP
Ⓣ

BLAKESLEY

Northamptonshire
Map ref 2C1

4m NW. Towcester

Bartholomew Arms
30 High Street, Blakesley,
Towcester, NN12 8RE
☎ (0327) 860292
*An old village inn offering real
ale and furnished with many
interesting antiques, close to
Silverstone circuit.*
Bedrooms: 1 single, 1 double
& 3 twin.
Bathrooms: 1 private,
1 public.
Bed & breakfast: £18-£20
single, £35-£45 double.
Lunch available.
Evening meal 6pm (l.o.
8.30pm).
Parking for 6.
➳ ⟶ ♉ ⓘ Ⅴ Ⅲ ♨ ♏

*The enquiry
coupons at the
back will help you
when contacting
proprietors.*

BLYTH

Nottinghamshire
Map ref 4C2

Village on the old Great
North Road. A busy
staging post in Georgian
times with many
examples of Georgian
Gothic architecture. The
remains of a Norman
Benedictine priory survive
as the parish church.

The Charnwood Hotel ♨
Sheffield Road, Blyth, Nr.
Worksop, S81 8HF
☎ Worksop (0909) 591610
*On the A634 Sheffield road
between the village of Blyth
and Oldcotes, standing in 3
acres of landscaped gardens
with a natural wildlife pond.*
Bedrooms: 3 single, 10 double
& 6 twin, 1 family room.
Bathrooms: 20 private.
Bed & breakfast: £30-£60
single, £40-£60 double.
Half board: £43.75-£73.75
daily.
Lunch available.
Evening meal 7pm (l.o.
9.45pm).
Parking for 75.
Credit: Access, Visa, Diners,
Amex.
➳ 8♨ ╚ ⊗ ⟶ ♉ ⓘ Ⅴ ♒
Ⅲ ♨ ♈ ❋ ♌ Ⅲ SP Ⓣ

BOURNE

Lincolnshire
Map ref 3A1

Market town with remains
of a Norman abbey
incorporated into the
parish church. The
birthplace of Lord
Burghley.

Angel Hotel ♨
♕♕ COMMENDED
Market Place, Bourne,
PE10 9AE
☎ (0778) 422346
*This 16th C coaching inn in the
heart of a market town was
once the office of the Collector
of Taxes. Good centre for golf,
fishing, wildlife and flower
gardens.*
Bedrooms: 4 single, 6 double
& 4 twin.
Bathrooms: 14 private.
Bed & breakfast: £20-£36
single, £36-£54 double.
Half board: £30-£37 daily.
Lunch available.
Evening meal 7pm (l.o.
9.30pm).
Credit: Access, Visa, Amex.
➳ ♨ ╚ ⊗ ⟶ ♉ ⓘ Ⅴ Ⅲ
♨ ♈ ♏ ♌ SP ♏ Ⓣ

BRETBY

Derbyshire
Map ref 4B3

9m SW. Derby

Stanhope Hotel
Ashby Road East, Bretby,
Burton-on-Trent,
Staffordshire DE14 0PU
☎ Burton-on-Trent
(0283) 217954 Telex 347185
CR Lansbury
*Traditional coaching inn, fully-
equipped with modern
conveniences to enhance the
character and add to the
comfort. Guide dogs only,
please.*
Bedrooms: 4 single, 15 double
& 9 twin.
Bathrooms: 28 private.
Bed & breakfast: £22-£63
single, £44-£75 double.
Half board: £34-£78 daily.
Lunch available.
Evening meal 7pm (l.o.
10pm).
Parking for 200.
Credit: Access, Visa, Diners,
Amex.
➳ ♨ ╚ ⊗ ⟶ ♉ ⓘ Ⅴ ⅏
♒ ● Ⅲ ♨ ♈ ♉ ❋ ♌ SP
Ⓣ

*The symbol CR
and the name of a
hotel group or
consortium after a
hotel address means
that bookings can
be made through a
central reservations
office. These are
listed on page 540.*

*Half board prices
shown are per
person but in some
cases may be based
on double/twin
occupancy.*

*We advise you to
confirm your
booking in writing.*

*Please mention this
guide when making
a booking.*

BUXTON

Derbyshire
Map ref 4B2

The highest market town in England and one of the oldest spas, with an elegant Crescent, Micrarium, Poole's Cavern, Opera House and attractive Pavilion Gardens. An excellent centre for exploring the Peak District.
Tourist Information Centre ☎ (0298) 25106

Alison Park Hotel ⋒
ಆಆಆ

3 Temple Road, Buxton,
SK17 9BA
☎ (0298) 22473
Owner managed hotel set in its own grounds near all amenities. Facilities for disabled, en-suite bedrooms, TV, telephones.
Bedrooms: 6 single, 5 double & 6 twin, 3 family rooms.
Bathrooms: 14 private, 3 public.
Bed & breakfast: £24-£27 single, £48-£54 double.
Half board: £34.50-£37.50 daily, £224.70-£243.60 weekly.
Lunch available.
Evening meal 6.45pm (l.o. 8pm).
Parking for 20.
Credit: Access, Visa.
ಠ ♨ ⅃ ♡ 🛗 👁 ⅤⅤ ꝋ ⅏ ⅏ 🖿 ♨ ⅃ ⅊ 📼 ⊞ ⅏ ◻ ⅊ SP

National Crown ratings were correct at the time of going to press but are subject to change. Please check at the time of booking.

Individual proprietors have supplied all details of accommodation. Although we do check for accuracy, we advise you to confirm prices and other information at the time of booking.

Brookfield on Longhill
ಆಆಆ HIGHLY COMMENDED

Brookfield Hall, Long Hill,
Buxton, SK17 6SU
☎ (0298) 24151
Attractive country retreat, providing a peaceful and tranquil setting. Each room has its own distinctive character rich with fine furniture and exquisite drapes.
Bedrooms: 3 double & 1 twin.
Bathrooms: 4 private.
Bed & breakfast: £41-£45 single, £61.50-£70 double.
Half board: £45-£60 daily.
Lunch available.
Evening meal 6pm (l.o. 10pm).
Parking for 20.
Credit: Access, Visa, Amex.
ಠ ⅃ ♡ 🛗 👁 ⅤⅤ ⅊ ꝋ ⅏ ♨ ♡ ⅊ 👁 ꝋ ⊞

Brunswick Guest House ⋒
ಆಆ APPROVED

31 St. John's Road, Buxton,
SK17 6XG
☎ (0298) 71727
Overlooking the Serpentine Gardens and the River Wye, 2 minutes from the Opera House, Pavilion Gardens and a swimming pool. Ideal base for walking in the Peak District.
Bedrooms: 1 double & 1 twin, 1 family room.
Bathrooms: 2 private, 1 public; 1 private shower.
Bed & breakfast: £34 double.
Parking for 5.
Open April-October.
ಠ ◻ ♡ ⅏ 👁 ⅤⅤ ⅊ 📼 🖿 ♨ ⅏ ⅏ ⅊ ꝋ SP

Buckingham Hotel ⋒
ಆಆಆಆ COMMENDED

1 Burlington Road, Buxton,
SK17 9AS
☎ (0298) 70481
Ⓒ Consort
Long-established, owner-managed, traditional hotel on a broad, tree-lined avenue overlooking the Pavilion Gardens.
Bedrooms: 4 single, 10 double & 13 twin, 3 family rooms.
Bathrooms: 30 private.
Bed & breakfast: from £50 single, from £70 double.
Half board: from £50 daily, from £295 weekly.
Lunch available.
Evening meal 7.30pm (l.o. 9.30pm).
Parking for 20.
Credit: Access, Visa, Diners, Amex.
ಠ ⅃ ⅏ ◻ ♡ 👁 ⅤⅤ ⅊ 📼 ⊞ 🖿 ⅏ ♨ ⅊ ⅏ ⅏ SP ⅂

Buxton View ⋒
ಆಆಆ COMMENDED

74 Corbar Road, Buxton,
SK17 6RJ
☎ (0298) 79222
Guesthouse built from local stone, offering a friendly and relaxed atmosphere. In a quiet area with a commanding view over the town and surrounding hills, only a few minutes' walk from the town's amenities.
Bedrooms: 1 single, 1 double & 2 twin, 1 family room.
Bathrooms: 5 private.
Bed & breakfast: from £20 single, from £35 double.
Half board: £26.50-£29 daily, £173-£189 weekly.
Evening meal 7pm (l.o. 8pm).
Parking for 7.
Open March-November.
ಠ ⅏ ◻ ♡ 🛗 👁 ⅊ ꝋ 📼 🖿 ♨ ⅏ SP

Buxton Wheelhouse Hotel
19 College Road, Buxton,
SK17 9DZ
☎ (0298) 24869
Cosy, warm Victorian hotel, in an area of outstanding natural beauty, within easy walking distance of local amenities.
Bedrooms: 1 single, 3 double & 1 twin, 4 family rooms.
Bathrooms: 9 private.
Bed & breakfast: £22-£26 single, £34-£40 double.
Half board: £27.50-£30 daily, £180-£195 weekly.
Evening meal 6.30pm (l.o. 6.30pm).
Parking for 9.
ಠ ⅏ ◻ ♡ 👁 ⅤⅤ ⅊ ꝋ 🖿 ♨ ⅃

Coningsby ⋒
ಆಆ COMMENDED

6 Macclesfield Road, Buxton,
SK17 9AH
☎ (0298) 26735
Comfortable detached Victorian house of character in a pleasant area, close to the Pavilion Gardens and the many other attractions of this splendid spa resort. Non-smokers only please.
Bedrooms: 2 double & 1 twin.
Bathrooms: 3 private.
Bed & breakfast: from £30 single, from £35 double.
Evening meal 7pm (l.o. 4pm).
Parking for 6.
Open January-November.
⅏ ◻ ♡ 🛗 👁 ⅤⅤ ⅊ ꝋ 🖿 ♨ ⅏ ⅏ ⅊ SP

The national Crown scheme is explained in full on pages 536 – 539.

Edge Lee Guest House
ಆಆ COMMENDED

Edge Lee, Bishops Lane,
Burbage, Buxton, SK17 6UW
☎ (0298) 22870
Offering accommodation to non-smokers, this guesthouse overlooks open farmland and a golf-course. 400 yards off the Buxton to Macclesfield road, near the Duke of York Inn.
Bedrooms: 2 double, 1 family room.
Bathrooms: 3 private.
Bed & breakfast: £22-£25 single, £29-£35 double.
Parking for 6.
Open April-October.
Credit: Access, Visa.
ಠ5 ♨ ⅏ ◻ ♡ ⅏ 👁 ⅊ ꝋ 🖿 ♨ ⅏ ⅏ ⅂

Fairhaven ⋒
Listed APPROVED

1 Dale Terrace, Buxton,
SK17 6LU
☎ (0298) 24481
Centrally placed with ample roadside parking, offering English home cooking in a warm and friendly atmosphere.
Bedrooms: 1 single, 1 double & 1 twin, 3 family rooms.
Bathrooms: 1 public.
Bed & breakfast: £15.50-£18 single, £26-£31 double.
Half board: £17.75-£19 daily, £117.25-£126 weekly.
Evening meal 6pm (l.o. 4pm).
Credit: Access, Visa.
ಠ ◻ ♡ ⅏ 👁 🖿 ♨ ⅊

Griff Guest House ⋒
Listed

2 Compton Road, Buxton,
SK17 9DN
☎ (0298) 23628
Close to town centre, Buxton Opera House, and other amenities, and ideally situated for exploring the beautiful surrounding countryside.
Bedrooms: 1 single, 3 twin, 1 family room.
Bathrooms: 2 public.
Bed & breakfast: £12-£13.50 single, £24-£27 double.
Half board: £17-£19 daily.
Evening meal 6pm (l.o. 4.30pm).
Parking for 5.
ಠ ◻ ♡ ⅏ ⅤⅤ ⅊ 📼 🖿 ♨ ⅏ ⅊

The Grosvenor House Hotel and Coffee Shop ⋒
ಆಆ COMMENDED

1 Broad Walk, Buxton,
SK17 6JE
☎ (0298) 72439
Continued ▶

BUXTON

Continued

Family-run licensed hotel superbly situated overlooking the Pavilion Gardens and Opera House. Central yet quiet location. Home-cooked cuisine.
Bedrooms: 5 double & 1 twin, 2 family rooms.
Bathrooms: 8 private.
Bed & breakfast: £45-£50 single, £55-£76 double.
Half board: £41.50-£69 daily, £250-£380 weekly.
Lunch available.
Evening meal 7.30pm (l.o. 7.30pm).
Parking for 4.
Credit: Access, Visa.

Hawthorn Farm Guest House
👑👑 COMMENDED
Fairfield Road, Buxton, SK17 7ED
☎ (0298) 23230
A 400-year-old ex-farmhouse which has been in the family for 10 generations. Full English breakfast.
Bedrooms: 3 single, 4 double & 3 twin, 2 family rooms.
Bathrooms: 2 public.
Bed & breakfast: £15.50-£16.50 single, £31-£38 double.
Parking for 15.
Open April-October.

Lakenham Guest House M
👑👑👑 COMMENDED
11 Burlington Road, Buxton, SK17 9AL
☎ (0298) 79209
Elegant Victorian house in own grounds overlooking Pavilion Gardens. Furnished in Victorian manner and offering personal service in a friendly relaxed atmosphere.
Bedrooms: 3 double & 3 twin, 3 family rooms.
Bathrooms: 7 private, 2 public.
Bed & breakfast: from £23.50 single, from £36.50 double.
Half board: from £22 daily.
Evening meal 6pm (l.o. midday).
Parking for 10.
Credit: Access, Visa.

> *We advise you to confirm your booking in writing.*

Lee Wood Hotel M
👑👑👑 COMMENDED
The Park, Buxton, SK17 6TQ
☎ (0298) 23002 or 70421
Telex 669848 LEWOOD
Ⓒ Best Western
Georgian building facing due south in its own grounds. Although fully modernised, retains its original charm.
Bedrooms: 6 single, 16 double & 12 twin, 2 family rooms.
Bathrooms: 36 private.
Bed & breakfast: £56-£72 single, £64-£86 double.
Half board: £48-£56 daily.
Lunch available.
Evening meal 7.15pm (l.o. 9.30pm).
Parking for 50.
Credit: Access, Visa, Diners, Amex.

Old Hall Hotel M
👑👑👑 COMMENDED
The Square, Buxton, SK17 6BD
☎ (0298) 22841
This historic hotel, restaurant and wine bar is run by the proprietors and offers warm and friendly service. Located opposite the restored Opera House and 23 acres of parkland.
Bedrooms: 9 single, 17 double & 12 twin.
Bathrooms: 32 private, 2 public.
Bed & breakfast: £35-£50 single, £45-£65 double.
Half board: £40-£46 daily.
Lunch available.
Evening meal 6pm (l.o. 11pm).
Parking for 10.
Credit: Access, Visa, Amex.

Portland Hotel and Park Restaurant M
👑👑👑👑
32 St. John's Road, Buxton, SK17 6XQ
☎ (0298) 71493/72453
Comfortable, family-run, Peak District hotel, with conservatory restaurant. Opposite Buxton's Pavilion Gardens and swimming pool.
Bedrooms: 3 single, 11 double & 11 twin.
Bathrooms: 25 private.
Bed & breakfast: £52.80-£57.60 single, £61.60-£67.20 double.
Half board: £69.30-£74.10 daily.
Lunch available.

Evening meal 6.45pm (l.o. 9pm).
Parking for 17.
Credit: Access, Visa, Diners, Amex.

Quarnford Lodge
👑👑👑
Quarnford, Buxton, SK17 0TL
☎ Buxton (0298) 25565
Country house hotel of character, with restaurant, 4 miles from Buxton, 8 miles from Leek on A53. In the Peak District National Park, with lovely views.
Bedrooms: 3 double & 2 twin.
Bathrooms: 2 private, 2 public.
Bed & breakfast: £40-£50 double.
Half board: £34-£39 daily.
Lunch available.
Evening meal 7pm (l.o. 9pm).
Parking for 18.
Credit: Access, Visa, Amex.

Roseleigh Private Hotel
19 Broad Walk, Buxton, SK17 6JR
☎ (0298) 24904
Quiet, family-run hotel offering traditional home cooking and overlooking the Pavilion Gardens and lake. The town centre and Opera House are only minutes away.
Bedrooms: 3 single, 5 double & 5 twin.
Bathrooms: 9 private, 3 public.
Bed & breakfast: £16 single, £38-£40 double.
Half board: £27-£28 daily, max. £185 weekly.
Evening meal 6.30pm (l.o. 5pm).
Parking for 12.
Open February-December.

Thorn Heyes Private Hotel M
👑👑👑 APPROVED
137 London Road, Buxton, SK17 9NW
☎ (0298) 23539
A detached Victorian residence built of local stone and set in beautiful gardens, offering every facility for your comfort.
Bedrooms: 2 single, 3 double & 2 twin, 4 family rooms.
Bathrooms: 10 private; 1 private shower.
Bed & breakfast: £20-£30 single, £40 double.
Half board: from £31.25 daily, from £200 weekly.

Evening meal 6.30pm (l.o. 7pm).
Parking for 12.

Westminster Hotel M
21 Broad Walk, Buxton, SK17 6JR
☎ (0298) 23929
Private, family hotel overlooking the Pavilion Gardens and close to the town, shops and Opera House. Personal service and a varied menu. Ideal base for exploring the Peak District.
Bedrooms: 7 double & 5 twin.
Bathrooms: 12 private.
Bed & breakfast: from £24 single, £38-£42 double.
Half board: £27-£29 daily, £180-£194 weekly.
Evening meal 6.30pm (l.o. 3pm).
Parking for 14.
Open February-December.
Credit: Access, Visa, Amex.

CASTLE ASHBY

Northamptonshire
Map ref 2C1

6m E. Northampton
Castle Ashby is a fine Elizabethan mansion open for special events, product launches and conferences and set in landscaped grounds which are open to the public in summer. The church has many monuments to the Compton family.

Falcon Inn M
👑👑 COMMENDED
Castle Ashby, Northampton, NN7 1LF
☎ Yardley Hastings (060 129) 200 or 201
Telex 312207
On the Marquess of Northampton's estate and lakes and in 2 acres of gardens, this 16th C hotel serves restaurant and bar meals 7 days a week.
Bedrooms: 4 single, 9 double & 1 twin.
Bathrooms: 13 private, 1 public.
Bed & breakfast: £60 single, £75 double.
Lunch available.
Evening meal 7.30pm (l.o. 9.30pm).
Parking for 60.
Credit: Access, Visa, Amex.

CASTLE BYTHAM

Lincolnshire
Map ref 3A1

8m N. Stamford
Attractive village with
castle earthworks dating
from Saxon times and a
parish church, churchyard
and several houses of
interest. It also has a
duck pond and stream.

Bank House
HIGHLY COMMENDED
Cumberland Gardens, Castle
Bytham, Nr. Grantham,
NG33 4SQ
☎ Stamford (0780) 410523
*High standard accommodation
in a modern private house.
Restful garden with panoramic
views, on the edge of historic
conservation village. 3 miles off
the A1, north of Stamford.
Evening meals by arrangement.*
Bedrooms: 2 twin.
Bathrooms: 2 private.
Bed & breakfast: £22.50-
£27.50 single, £45-£55 double.
Half board: £30-£40 daily.
Evening meal 7pm (l.o. 8pm).
Parking for 4.
Open April-October.
⊞ ▥ ▤ ▮ Ⅴ ⮐ ⊡ ▥ ▦ ▲ ∪
▶ ✿ ✕ ♘

CASTLE DONINGTON

Leicestershire
Map ref 4C3

A Norman castle once
stood here. The world's
largest collection of
single-seater racing cars
is displayed at Donington
Park alongside the racing
circuit, and an Aeropark
Visitor Centre can be
seen at nearby East
Midlands International
Airport.

Delven Hotel ⋔
▤
12 Delven Lane, Castle
Donington, Derby DE7 2LJ
☎ Derby
(0332) 810153/850507
*Small, family-run hotel, 1 mile
from Donington race track and
2 miles from East Midlands
Airport.*
Bedrooms: 2 double & 4 twin,
1 family room.
Bathrooms: 3 public;
3 private showers.
Bed & breakfast: £15-£16.50
single, £30-£34 double.
Half board: £20-£25 daily.

Evening meal 5pm (l.o. 9pm).
Parking for 5.
Credit: Access, Visa.
▤ ▥ ☐ ▮ ▥ Ⅴ ⮐ ⊙ ▥
Ⓣ

The Lady in Grey
♛♛♛
Wilne Lane, Shardlow,
Derbyshire DE7 2HA
☎ Derby (0332) 792331
*Delightful 200-year-old
mansion in quiet surroundings
just off the A6. Convenient for
East Midlands International
Airport and junction 24 of M1.*
Bedrooms: 3 single, 5 double
& 1 twin.
Bathrooms: 9 private.
Bed & breakfast: £29.50-£42
single, £35-£52 double.
Lunch available.
Evening meal 7pm (l.o.
10pm).
Parking for 40.
Credit: Access, Visa, Diners,
Amex.
▤ ▥ ☏ ☐ ☐ ♵ ▮ Ⅴ ⮐
▥ ▲ ✿ ✕ ▥ ✂ ⓢⓟ ▦

Morton House Hotel ⋔
♛♛
78 Bondgate, Castle
Donington, Derby DE7 2NR
☎ Derby (0332) 812415
*Family-run private hotel with a
friendly atmosphere and a
lounge bar, only 1.5 miles from
both the M1, junction 24, and
from East Midlands
International Airport and 1
mile from Donington Park race
circuit.*
Bedrooms: 1 single, 2 double
& 4 twin, 3 family rooms.
Bathrooms: 2 private,
2 public.
Bed & breakfast: £19-£23
single, £30-£34 double.
Half board: from £25 daily.
Evening meal 6pm (l.o.
8.30pm).
Parking for 10.
Credit: Access, Visa, Diners,
Amex.
▤ ∪ ☐ ♵ ▮ Ⅴ ⮐ ⓽ ▥ ▲
✕ ▦ Ⓣ

Park Farmhouse Hotel ⋔
♛♛♛
Melbourne Road, Isley
Walton, Castle Donington,
Derby DE7 2RN
☎ Derby (0332) 862409
*40-acre mixed farm. Half-
timbered 17th C farmhouse, in
its own grounds. Spacious
rooms, farmhouse suppers.
Located at competitors'
entrance to Donington Park.*
Bedrooms: 1 single, 2 double
& 3 twin, 2 family rooms.
Bathrooms: 6 private,
2 public.

Bed & breakfast: £32.50-£45
single, £42.50-£55 double.
Evening meal 6pm (l.o. 8pm).
Parking for 15.
Credit: Access, Visa, Diners,
Amex.
▤ ▥ ☏ ☐ ☐ ♵ ▮ Ⅴ ⮐
▥ ▲ ✿ ⓢⓟ ▦ Ⓣ

Priest House Hotel ⋔
Kings Mills, Castle
Donington, Derby, DE7 2RR
☎ Derby (0332) 810649
Telex 341995
*Former watermill in peaceful
setting on River Trent. Log
fires, real ales, good food, only
3 miles M1 and airport.*
Bedrooms: 2 single, 13 double
& 17 twin, 2 family rooms.
Bathrooms: 34 private.
Bed & breakfast: £60-£70
single, £70-£90 double.
Lunch available.
Evening meal 7pm (l.o.
9.30pm).
Parking for 150.
Credit: Access, Visa, Diners,
Amex.
▤ ▥ ☏ ☐ ☐ ▮ Ⅴ
✕ ⮐ ▥ ▲ ▮ ⅃ ▲ ✂ ✿
✕ ⓢⓟ ▦ Ⓣ

CASTLETON

Derbyshire
Map ref 4B2

5m W. Hathersage
Large village in a
spectacular Peak District
setting with ruined Peveril
castle and 4 great show
caverns, where the Blue
John stone and lead were
mined. One cavern offers a
mile-long underground
boat journey.

Kelsey's Swiss House ⋔
♛♛♛ **COMMENDED**
How Lane, Castleton, Via
Sheffield, S30 2WJ
☎ Hope Valley (0433) 21098
*Small, family-run hotel
completely refurbished. All
rooms en-suite with colour TV,
tea/coffee facilities. Parking.
Popular licensed restaurant.
Hospitality assured.*
Bedrooms: 1 single, 6 double
& 2 twin, 1 family room.
Bathrooms: 10 private.
Bed & breakfast: £22.50-£23
single, £36-£39 double.
Half board: £27.75-£30 daily,
£174.83-£200 weekly.
Evening meal 6.30pm (l.o.
8.30pm).
Parking for 15.
▤ ∪ ☐ ♵ ▮ Ⅴ ⮐ ▥ ▲ ▮
∪ ✕ ✂ ⓢⓟ

Ye Olde Cheshire Cheese Inn
How Lane, Castleton, Via
Sheffield, S. Yorkshire
S30 2WJ
☎ Hope Valley (0433) 20330
*17th C inn providing home-
cooked food, set in the heart of
the Peak District.*
Bedrooms: 1 single, 3 double
& 2 twin.
Bathrooms: 6 private.
Bed & breakfast: £22.50
single, £37-£45 double.
Lunch available.
Evening meal 6pm (l.o.
10.50pm).
Parking for 100.
Credit: Access, Visa.
▤ ☐ ♵ ▮ Ⅴ ▥ ▲ ▮ ♘
∪ ✕ ▦ ▥

Ye Olde Nags Head ⋔
♛♛♛♛ **COMMENDED**
Castleton, Via Sheffield,
S. Yorkshire, S30 2WH
☎ Hope Valley (0433) 20248
*Old world hotel in the beautiful
countryside of the Peak
District National Park, near
the famous caverns and ancient
Peveril Castle.*
Bedrooms: 6 double & 2 twin.
Bathrooms: 8 private.
Bed & breakfast: £44-£63
single, £55-£85 double.
Lunch available.
Evening meal 7pm (l.o.
10pm).
Parking for 16.
Credit: Access, Visa, Diners,
Amex.
▤ ▥ ☏ ☐ ☐ ♵ ▮ Ⅴ ⮐
▥ ▲ ▮ ∪ ✕ ⓢⓟ ▦

CHAPEL-EN-LE-FRITH

Derbyshire
Map ref 4B2

Small market town and a
good base for climbing
and walking. Close to the
show caverns at
Castleton.

Kings Arms Hotel
Market Place, Chapel-en-le-
Frith, Via Stockport,
Cheshire SK12 6EN
☎ (0298) 812105
*17th C hotel offering
hospitality, comfort, a good
table and a friendly English
welcome. Some rooms have en-
suite, all have central heating,
colour TV and tea/coffee-
making facilities.*
Bedrooms: 4 single, 2 double
& 3 twin, 2 family rooms.
Bathrooms: 5 private,
2 public.
Bed & breakfast: £16-£27.50
single, £30-£47.50 double.
Continued ▶

CHAPEL-EN-LE-FRITH

Continued

Half board: £21-£40 daily.
Lunch available.
Evening meal 8pm (l.o.
9.30pm).
Parking for 8.
Credit: Access, Visa.
🛏🖵🎈♿🅿🅥🎯🍴♻☺ SP
🏠 Ⓣ

CHESTERFIELD

Derbyshire
Map ref 4B2

Famous for the twisted spire of its parish church, Chesterfield has some fine modern buildings and excellent shopping facilities, including a large, traditional open-air market. Hardwick Hall and Bolsover Castle are nearby.
Tourist Information Centre ☎ *(0246) 207777*

Abbey Dale Hotel M
😊😊😊 **COMMENDED**
1 Cobden Road, Chesterfield,
S40 4TD
☎ (0246) 277849
Ⓖ Minotels
Run by resident proprietors. In a quiet location within walking distance of town centre, close to Peak District and Chatsworth House.
Bedrooms: 5 single, 2 double & 3 twin, 1 family room.
Bathrooms: 9 private, 1 public.
Bed & breakfast: £28-£44 single, £51 double.
Half board: £35.60-£54 daily, £230-£340 weekly.
Evening meal 6.30pm (l.o. 8pm).
Parking for 12.
Credit: Access, Visa, Diners, Amex.
🛏🖵♿📞🅿🅥🎈♿🅥🍴♻🎯 SP

Acorn Guest House
😊😊
17 Fairfield Road,
Chesterfield, S40 4TR
☎ (0246) 211427
Comfortable guesthouse offering home-cooked food and a warm welcome. Within walking distance of the town.
Bedrooms: 2 single, 1 double & 1 twin.
Bathrooms: 1 public.
Bed & breakfast: £11-£12 single, £20-£22 double.
Half board: £15.50-£16 daily.

Lunch available.
Evening meal 5pm (l.o. 7.30pm).
🛏🖵♿🆒🅿🎈🅥🍴🅿🎯
🆙

Chesterfield Hotel M
Malkin Street, Chesterfield,
S41 7UA
☎ (0246) 271141
Telex 547492 CHCH
Ⓖ Best Western
Centrally located hotel with a friendly, comfortable atmosphere close to historic buildings, museums and theatre. Ideal family base for touring Peak District National Park and Sherwood Forest. Full leisure facilities including large pool.
Bedrooms: 16 single, 34 double & 22 twin, 1 family room.
Bathrooms: 73 private.
Bed & breakfast: £58-£70 single, £72-£82 double.
Lunch available.
Evening meal 7pm (l.o. 10pm).
Parking for 160.
Credit: Access, Visa, Amex.
🛏♿📞🅿♿🎈🅥🍴📺
🎯🗞🅿🍴♻🎱♿♻
SP Ⓣ

The Red Lion M
Listed
261 Chatsworth Road,
Chesterfield, S40 2BL
☎ (0246) 207869
A small hotel on the A619 Chesterfield to Buxton road, 1 mile from the town centre.
Bedrooms: 1 single, 2 double & 3 twin, 1 family room.
Bathrooms: 7 private, 1 public.
Bed & breakfast: £15-£20 single, £25-£35 double.
Half board: £18-£25 daily.
Lunch available.
Evening meal 6pm (l.o. 9pm).
Parking for 20.
Credit: Access, Visa.
🛏🆒🖵♿🎈🅥🍴📺🗞
🅿🍴🎯🎈

Sarnia House
62 Brockwell Lane,
Chesterfield, S40 4EE
☎ (0246) 279391
A small, private guesthouse with guests' own garden and patio. Convenient for the town centre. Within a short drive of the Derbyshire countryside.
Bedrooms: 2 single, 2 double & 1 twin.
Bathrooms: 5 private.
Bed & breakfast: £15.50-£17.50 single, £31 double.
Half board: £21-£23 daily.

Evening meal 6.30pm (l.o. 6pm).
Parking for 3.
🛏🆒🖵♿🆙🅥♿🎈🅥🍴
🗞🎈🎯

COALVILLE

Leicestershire
Map ref 4B3

North-west Leicestershire town, a few miles from Twycross Zoo and the Charnwood Forest area.
Tourist Information Centre ☎ *(0530) 35951 or 35952*

Hermitage Park Hotel M
Whitwick Road, Coalville,
LE6 3FA
☎ (0530) 814814
A new, purpose built hotel with a health centre, bars and a restaurant contained in a 150 foot long glazed atrium.
Bedrooms: 21 double & 4 twin.
Bathrooms: 25 private.
Bed & breakfast: £35-£65 single, £39.50-£79.50 double.
Lunch available.
Evening meal 7pm (l.o. 10.30pm).
Parking for 48.
Credit: Access, Visa, Amex.
🛏♿📞📺🖵♿🎈🅥🎯
🗞♿🍴🎈🍴♻🎱🎯 SP
Ⓣ

CORBY

Northamptonshire
Map ref 3A1

New Town with modern shopping, sports and recreational facilities. On the outskirts is the 100-acre East Carlton Park with rural craft workshops. Rockingham Castle and the partly-roofed Kirby Hall with 17th C gardens are nearby.
Tourist Information Centre ☎ *(0536) 402551*

Macallan Guest House
18-20 Lundy Avenue, Corby,
NN18 8BU
☎ (0356) 61848
Close to the town centre, bus and rail stations. Easy access to the A1, M1 and M6.
Bedrooms: 2 single, 2 twin.
Bathrooms: 2 public.
Bed & breakfast: £12.50-£15 single, £24-£30 double.
Half board: £17.50-£20 daily, £120-£140 weekly.
Parking for 6.
🖵♿🆙♿🎈🍴🗞📺🎈
🎯

DAVENTRY

Northamptonshire
Map ref 2C1

Ancient market town with an Iron Age camp on Borough Hill, from which 7 counties can be seen. The town still retains some Georgian buildings and 2 old inns and there is a country park.
Tourist Information Centre ☎ *(0327) 300277*

Kingsthorpe Guest House
18 Badby Road, Daventry,
NN11 4AW
☎ (0327) 702752
Licensed guesthouse close to the town centre, the M1 and M40.
Bedrooms: 3 single, 6 double & 3 twin, 2 family rooms.
Bathrooms: 4 private, 6 public.
Bed & breakfast: £15-£20 single, £30-£40 double.
Half board: £20-£25 daily.
Evening meal 6.30pm (l.o. 7.30pm).
Parking for 11.
Credit: Access, Visa.
🛏♿🖵♿🎈🅥📺♿🖵
🍴🎯🎈 SP

Staverton Park Hotel and Golf Complex M
😊😊😊 **COMMENDED**
Staverton, Nr. Daventry,
NN11 6JT
☎ Daventry (0327) 705911
A modern, comfortable hotel in 150 acres (including 18-hole golf-course) in rural Northamptonshire. Convenient for the M1, junctions 16 and 18. 1 mile west of Daventry on the A425.
Bedrooms: 2 single, 14 double & 34 twin.
Bathrooms: 50 private.
Bed & breakfast: from £95 single, from £115 double.
Lunch available.
Evening meal 6pm (l.o. 9.30pm).
Parking for 200.
Credit: Access, Visa, Amex.
🛏♿🆒🅥📞🖵♿🎈🅥🍴
🗞♿🍴🎈🍴🎯🎱🍴
♻ SP Ⓣ

Windsor Lodge Hotel M
😊😊 **APPROVED**
5 New Street, Daventry,
NN11 4BT
☎ (0327) 76533
Town centre hotel close to the market square and within easy reach of free parking. Comfortable accommodation and good food in delightful restaurant.

Bedrooms: 1 single, 1 double
& 3 twin, 1 family room.
Bathrooms: 1 private,
1 public; 3 private showers.
Bed & breakfast: £30.64-
£36.30 single, £40.70-£49.50
double.
Lunch available.
Evening meal 7.30pm (l.o.
9.30pm).
Credit: Access, Visa.

Derbyshire
Map ref 4B2

Modern industrial city but
with ancient origins.
There is a wide range of
attractions including
several museums (notably
Royal Crown Derby), a
theatre, a concert hall, the
cathedral with fine
ironwork and Bess of
Hardwick's tomb, and
Elvaston Castle Country
Park.
*Tourist Information
Centre* ☎ *(0332) 255802*

Braemar Guest House M
1061 London Road,
Alvaston, Derby, DE2 8PZ
☎ (0332) 572522
*Family-run guesthouse near
the city centre, Donington
Park, M1, airport, Alton
Towers, BMX track and Moor
Ways Sports Centre.*
Bedrooms: 6 single, 2 double
& 2 twin, 4 family rooms.
Bathrooms: 3 private,
5 public; 5 private showers.
Bed & breakfast: £16-£17
single, £30-£32 double.
Evening meal 6.30pm (l.o.
5.30pm).
Parking for 10.

Dalby House Hotel
Listed
100 Radbourne Street, (Off
Windmill Hill Lane), Derby,
DE3 3BU
☎ (0332) 42353
*Large, detached, Georgian-
style house in a very quiet
residential area. Convenient for
both the town centre and
countryside.*
Bedrooms: 4 single, 1 double
& 2 twin, 2 family rooms.
Bathrooms: 2 public.
Bed & breakfast: £17.50-£19
single, £33-£36 double.

Evening meal 6.30pm (l.o.
6pm).
Parking for 11.

Georgian House Hotel M
32-34 Ashbourne Road,
Derby, DE3 3AD
☎ (0332) 49806
*Listed building in a
conservation area half a mile
north of the city centre and
Assembly Rooms.*
Bedrooms: 10 single, 3 double
& 3 twin, 5 family rooms.
Bathrooms: 15 private,
2 public.
Bed & breakfast: £23-£40
single, £37-£52 double.
Half board: £33.75-£50.75
daily.
Lunch available.
Evening meal 6.30pm (l.o.
9.30pm).
Parking for 20.

International Hotel & Restaurant M
COMMENDED
Burton Road (A5250), Derby,
DE3 6AD
☎ (0332) 369321
Telex 377759
CR Consort
*Privately-owned modern hotel
with a continental atmosphere,
close to the city centre.*
Bedrooms: 11 single,
32 double & 15 twin, 4 family
rooms.
Bathrooms: 62 private.
Bed & breakfast: £25-£76
single, £35-£82 double.
Lunch available.
Evening meal 7.30pm (l.o.
10.30pm).
Parking for 70.
Credit: Access, Visa, Diners,
Amex.

Midland Hotel M
COMMENDED
Midland Road, Derby,
DE1 2SQ
☎ (0332) 45894 Telex 378373
*City centre hotel, built 1841.
Fine example of elegant
Victorian character, reflected
by its spacious public and
private areas. Set in beautiful
tree-lined garden. Friendly,
personal, yet unobtrusive
service.*
Bedrooms: 23 single, 7 double
& 19 twin.
Bathrooms: 49 private.
Bed & breakfast: £66-£71.50
single, £86-£91.50 double.

Lunch available.
Evening meal 7pm (l.o.
10pm).
Parking for 95.
Credit: Access, Visa, Diners,
Amex.

Periquito Hotel M
COMMENDED
119 London Road, Derby,
DE1 2QR
☎ (0332) 40633
*Converted Victorian vicarage,
5 minutes from city centre.
Fully refurbished in 1991 and
with bright welcoming decor.
10 miles from M1 junction 24.
Car park with video
surveillance.*
Bedrooms: 21 single,
40 double & 38 twin, 2 family
rooms.
Bathrooms: 101 private.
Bed & breakfast: £42-£53.50
single, £46.50-£69 double.
Lunch available.
Evening meal 6pm (l.o.
9.45pm).
Parking for 90.
Credit: Access, Visa, Amex.

Rangemoor Hotel
☷
67 Macklin Street, Derby,
DE1 1LF
☎ (0332) 47252
*Family-run city centre hotel
within walking distance of all
amenities and with a large
lock-up car park. En-suite
rooms for 1992.*
Bedrooms: 12 single, 5 double
& 4 twin, 3 family rooms.
Bathrooms: 6 public.
Bed & breakfast: £22-£24
single, £34-£36 double.
Parking for 28.

Tudor Court Hotel M
COMMENDED
Gypsy Lane, Draycott, Nr.
Derby, DE7 3PB
☎ Draycott (033 17) 4581
CR Best Western
*Modern hotel with conference
and entertainment complex, set
in 6 acres of woodlands. Easy
access from the M1 junction
25.*
Bedrooms: 4 single, 4 double
& 14 twin, 8 family rooms.
Bathrooms: 30 private.
Bed & breakfast: £25-£60
single, £50-£75 double.
Half board: £39.50-£79.50
daily.
Lunch available.
Evening meal 7pm (l.o.
10pm).

Parking for 500.
Credit: Access, Visa, C.Bl.,
Diners, Amex.

Leicestershire
Map ref 4C3

6m NW. Loughborough

Little Chimneys Guest House
COMMENDED
19 The Green, Diseworth,
Derby DE7 2QN
☎ Derby (0332) 812458
*Modern building in the
pleasant village of Diseworth
close to the M1, East
Midlands International Airport
and Donington race track.*
Bedrooms: 4 twin, 1 family
room.
Bathrooms: 5 private.
Bed & breakfast: £22.50
single, £32.50 double.
Parking for 7.
Credit: Access, Visa.

Derbyshire
Map ref 4B2

Charnwood Hotel
23 Cecil Road, Dronfield,
Via Sheffield, S. Yorkshire
S18 6GW
☎ (0246) 413217
*Hotel with a friendly
atmosphere in a quiet area, off
the main road. Easy access to
both the Peak District and
Sheffield.*
Bedrooms: 3 single, 1 double
& 1 twin, 2 family rooms.
Bathrooms: 1 private,
1 public.
Bed & breakfast: £14.50-£20
single, £29-£44 double.
Half board: £19.50-£25 daily,
from £136.50 weekly.
Evening meal 6.30pm (l.o.
6.30pm).
Parking for 5.
Credit: Access, Visa, Amex.

Derbyshire
Map ref 4B2

Stonecroft Hotel M
Listed COMMENDED
Grindsbrook, Edale, Via
Sheffield S30 2ZA
☎ Hope Valley
(0433) 670262

Continued ▶

EDALE
Continued

Small family-run hotel with lovely views. Specialists in walking holidays and vegetarian meals. No smoking anywhere in house and no pets please.
Bedrooms: 2 double & 1 twin.
Bathrooms: 3 public.
Bed & breakfast: £16-£19.50 single, £32-£33 double.
Half board: £26-£29.50 daily, £182-£206.50 weekly.
Evening meal 7.30pm (l.o. 8pm).
Parking for 5.
Credit: Access, Visa.

FARTHINGSTONE
Northamptonshire
Map ref 2C1

5m SE. Daventry

Farthingstone Hotel, Golf and Leisure Centre

Farthingstone, Nr. Towcester, NN12 8HA
☎ (0327) 36291/36560
In glorious wooded countryside, Farthingstone offers comfortable accommodation, a carvery restaurant, a real ale bar, a snooker room and an informal atmosphere.
Bedrooms: 12 twin, 4 family rooms.
Bathrooms: 16 private, 2 public.
Bed & breakfast: £35-£39.50 single, £48.50-£50 double.
Lunch available.
Evening meal 7.30pm (l.o. 9.30pm).
Parking for 100.
Credit: Access, Visa, Diners, Amex.

FINEDON
Northamptonshire
Map ref 3A2

Large ironstone village with interesting Victorian houses and cottages and an ironstone 14th C church. The inn claims to be the oldest in England.

Tudor Gate Hotel

35 High Street, Finedon, Nr. Wellingborough, NN9 5JN
☎ Wellingborough (0933) 680408

Converted from a 16th C farmhouse with 3 four-poster beds, conference facilities and a good range of restaurant facilities. Close to the new A1/M1 link.
Bedrooms: 4 single, 11 double & 1 twin.
Bathrooms: 16 private.
Bed & breakfast: £57.50-£63 single, £67.50-£74.50 double.
Lunch available.
Evening meal 7pm (l.o. 9.45pm).
Parking for 25.
Credit: Access, Visa, Diners, Amex.

FLORE
Northamptonshire
Map ref 2C1

Heyford Manor Hotel

COMMENDED
High Street, Flore, NN7 4LP
☎ Weedon (0327) 349022
Telex 312437
Lansbury
A recently opened modern hotel in a rural setting, only 1 mile from junction 16 of the M1.
Bedrooms: 25 double & 29 twin.
Bathrooms: 54 private.
Bed & breakfast: £29-£78 single, £58-£90 double.
Half board: £42-£94 daily.
Lunch available.
Evening meal 7pm (l.o. 9.30pm).
Parking for 100.
Credit: Access, Visa, Diners, Amex.

GAINSBOROUGH
Lincolnshire
Map ref 4C2

Hickman-Hill Hotel and Restaurant

COMMENDED
Cox's Hill, Gainsborough, DN21 1HH
☎ (0427) 613639
A 16th C grammar school, now a family-run hotel, offering a good selection of freshly cooked food with a wide-ranging wine list. Golfing, gliding, horse-riding and parachuting are all close by.
Bedrooms: 1 single, 3 double & 3 twin, 1 family room.
Bathrooms: 6 private, 1 public; 2 private showers.

Bed & breakfast: max. £38 single, max. £50 double.
Half board: max. £48.50 daily.
Lunch available.
Evening meal 7.30pm (l.o. 9.30pm).
Parking for 25.
Credit: Access, Visa.

GLOSSOP
Derbyshire
Map ref 4B2

Town in dramatic moorland surroundings with views over the High Peak. The settlement can be traced back to Roman times but expanded during the Industrial Revolution.
Tourist Information Centre ☎ (0457) 855920

Wind in the Willows Hotel

COMMENDED
Derbyshire Level, off Sheffield Road, (A57), Glossop, SK13 9PT
☎ (0457) 868001
Friendly country house hotel with open fires, offering home cooking, peace and relaxation. Views over the magnificent Peak District National Park. Adjacent to golf-course in excellent walking country.
Bedrooms: 5 double & 2 twin, 1 family room.
Bathrooms: 8 private.
Bed & breakfast: £57-£77 single, £69-£98 double.
Evening meal 7.30pm (l.o. 4pm).
Parking for 12.
Credit: Access, Visa, Amex.

National Crown ratings were correct at the time of going to press but are subject to change. Please check at the time of booking.

GRANTHAM
Lincolnshire
Map ref 3A1

On the road from London to York, Grantham has several old inns and its splendid parish church has a fine spire and chained library. Sir Isaac Newton was educated here and his statue stands in front of the museum which includes displays on Newton and other famous local people.
Tourist Information Centre ☎ (0476) 66444

Hawthornes Guest House

51 Cambridge Street, Grantham, NG31 6EZ
☎ (0476) 73644
A spacious, comfortable, family-run guesthouse with a warm and friendly atmosphere. Centrally located and within easy reach of amenities. Situated on the main A1 north-south route.
Bedrooms: 1 double & 2 twin.
Bathrooms: 1 public.
Bed & breakfast: £16-£18 single, £30 double.
Evening meal 6pm (l.o. 3pm).

Lanchester Guest House

84 Harrowby Road, Grantham, NG31 9DS
☎ (0476) 74169
Well established and run professionally to high standards but retaining its warm and friendly atmosphere. All rooms can be let as singles. Light suppers can be served until 9.00 pm.
Bedrooms: 1 twin, 1 family room.
Bathrooms: 1 private, 1 public.
Bed & breakfast: £15-£25 single, £28-£40 double.
Half board: £25-£35 daily.
Evening meal 6pm (l.o. midday).
Parking for 3.

Individual proprietors have supplied all details of accommodation. Although we do check for accuracy, we advise you to confirm prices and other information at the time of booking.

Sycamore Farm
⌂

Bassingthorpe, Grantham
☎ Ingoldsby (047 685) 274
*450-acre mixed farm.
Spacious, peaceful Victorian
farmhouse just 4.5 miles off A1
yet within easy reach of
Grantham, Lincoln, Stamford.
All bedrooms have modern
amenities and lovely views.
Home-cooked evening meal by
arrangement.*
Bedrooms: 2 twin, 1 family
room.
Bathrooms: 1 public.
Bed & breakfast: £12-£14
single, £24-£28 double.
Half board: £19.50-£21.50
daily.
Evening meal 7pm (l.o.
midday).
Parking for 6.
Open April-October.
☎⑥🅰♥ ⓤ ▯ Ⓥ ✕ ⓣⓥ ▥
☎ 🏦

Northamptonshire
Map ref 3A1

6m NE. Corby
Village with a medieval
cross, a 12th C church,
an inn and old manor
house. The 82 arches of
the 19th C Welland
railway viaduct dominate
the valley, which forms
the Northamptonshire/
Leicestershire border.

The White Swan M
🅰🅰🅰 COMMENDED

Seaton Road, Harringworth,
Nr. Corby, NN17 3AF
☎ Morcott (057 287) 543
*15th C coaching inn offering
en-suite accommodation, in a
delightful village, close to
many historic sites. Home-
cooked food and real ales.*
Bedrooms: 1 single, 4 double
& 1 twin.
Bathrooms: 6 private.
Bed & breakfast: from £37.50
single, from £50 double.
Lunch available.
Evening meal 7pm (l.o.
10pm).
Parking for 15.
Credit: Access, Visa.
☎⑩▯♥ ▯ Ⓥ ▥ ☎ ✕
🏦 SP 🏦 T

> *Half board prices
> shown are per
> person but in some
> cases may be based
> on double/twin
> occupancy.*

Derbyshire
Map ref 4B2

Village with a large
market-place set in fine
surroundings near the
River Dove, well-known
for its fishing and Izaak
Walton, author of 'The
Compleat Angler'.

Manifold Valley Hotel
🅰🅰🅰 APPROVED

Hulme End, Hartington,
Buxton, SK17 0EX
☎ (0298) 84537
*Freehouse on the banks of the
River Manifold, in countryside
noted for walking and cycling.
Ideal centre for exploring the
Peak District and the
Staffordshire Moorlands.*
Bedrooms: 1 single, 3 double
& 1 twin.
Bathrooms: 5 private.
Bed & breakfast: £30-£50
single, £42-£60 double.
Lunch available.
Evening meal 7pm (l.o.
9.30pm).
Parking for 40.
Credit: Access, Visa.
☎ 🅰🏦 ▯ ♥ ▯ Ⓥ ▥ ▥
☎ ♿ ✕ 🏦 SP

Derbyshire
Map ref 4B2

Hillside village in the Peak
District, dominated by the
church with many good
brasses and monuments
to the Eyre family which
provide a link with
Charlotte Bronte. Little
John, friend of Robin
Hood, is said to be buried
here.

George Hotel M
🅰🅰🅰🅰

Main Road, Hathersage,
S30 1BB
☎ Hope Valley (0433) 50436
Telex 547196
🆁 Lansbury
*16th C coaching inn located at
the focal point of the Hope
Valley. Easy access to the
Derbyshire Peak District.*
Bedrooms: 10 double &
5 twin, 3 family rooms.
Bathrooms: 18 private.
Bed & breakfast: max. £72
single, max. £84 double.
Half board: £48-£88 daily.
Lunch available.
Evening meal 7pm (l.o.
10pm).
Parking for 50.

Credit: Access, Visa, Diners,
Amex.
☎ 🅰🏦 ♥ ⑩▯ ♥ ▯ Ⓥ ✕
▥ ▥ ☎ ▯ ♿ ► ♦ SP 🏦
T

Hathersage Inn M

Main Road, Hathersage,
S30 1BB
☎ Hope Valley (0433) 50259
🆁 Best Western
*18th C village inn, completely
refurbished, with an intimate
candlelit restaurant and log
fires in the locals' bar in
winter. All bedrooms have en-
suite bathrooms and colour
TV.*
Bedrooms: 12 double &
2 twin, 1 family room.
Bathrooms: 15 private.
Bed & breakfast: £55-£60
single, £75-£80 double.
Lunch available.
Evening meal 7pm (l.o.
9.30pm).
Parking for 20.
Credit: Access, Visa, Diners,
Amex.
☎ 🅰🏦 ♥ ⑩▯ ♥ ▯ Ⓥ ✕
▥ ⓣⓥ ▥ ☎ ▯ ♿ ✕ SP 🏦
T

Derbyshire
Map ref 4B2

9m N. Buxton
Village set in spectacular
scenery at the highest
point of the Peak District
with the best approach to
the Kinder Scout plateau
via the Kinder Downfall.
An excellent centre for
walking. Three reservoirs
close by.

Bridge End Guest House and Restaurant

7 Church Street, Hayfield,
Via Stockport, SK12 5JE
☎ New Mills (0663) 747321
*In the picturesque conservation
area of Hayfield, adjoining
Kinder Scout and extensive
moorlands. Accessible to all
parts of the Peak District
National Park.*
Bedrooms: 4 double & 1 twin,
1 family room.
Bathrooms: 6 private.
Bed & breakfast: £23-£25
single, £35-£39 double.
Half board: from £35 daily.
Lunch available.
Evening meal 7pm (l.o.
10pm).
Parking for 6.
Credit: Access, Visa.
☎ ⑩▯ ♥ ▯ Ⓥ ▥ ☎ ▯
✕ 🏦 ▯ ♦ SP

Leicestershire
Map ref 4B3

The town has an
excellent leisure centre.
Bosworth Battlefield, with
its Visitor Centre and
Battle Trail, is 5 miles
away.
*Tourist Information
Centre* ☎ (0455) 230852
or 635106

Ambion Court M
🅰🅰🅰🅰 COMMENDED

The Green, Dadlington, Via
Nuneaton, Warwickshire
CV13 6JB
☎ Hinckley (0455) 212292
*Charming, modernised
farmhouse hotel overlooking
tranquil village green, 2 miles
north of Hinckley.
Conveniently located for M1,
M6, M69, NEC and
Birmingham Airport.*
Bedrooms: 1 single, 3 double
& 3 twin.
Bathrooms: 7 private.
Bed & breakfast: £30-£45
single, £40-£60 double.
Half board: £43-£58 daily,
£250-£350 weekly.
Evening meal 7pm (l.o.
8.30pm).
Parking for 8.
Credit: Access, Visa.
☎⑤🅰 ♥ ⑩▯ ♥ ▯ Ⓥ ▥
ⓣⓥ ▥ ☎ ▯ 🏦 ⒹⒶ⒫ SP T

Hollycroft Private Hotel
🅰🅰

24 Hollycroft, Hinckley,
LE10 0HG
☎ (0455) 637356
*Spacious, tastefully decorated,
detached residence near town
centre and opposite a park,
convenient for all motorways
and NEC.*
Bedrooms: 3 double & 2 twin.
Bathrooms: 5 private,
1 public.
Bed & breakfast: from £17.50
single, from £30 double.
Evening meal 6pm (l.o.
6.30pm).
Parking for 6.
☎ 🅰▯ ♥ ⓤ ▯ Ⓥ ▥ ⓣⓥ
▥ ☎ ▯ ♿

Kings Hotel & Restaurant
🅰🅰🅰

13-19 Mount Road, Hinckley,
LE10 1AD
☎ Hinckley (0455) 637193
*Hotel with lawns and gardens
to the front and rear, in the
centre of town yet in a quiet,
residential area.*
Bedrooms: 4 single, 3 double.
Bathrooms: 7 private.

Continued ►

HINCKLEY
Continued

Bed & breakfast: £45-£65 single, £55-£75 double.
Half board: £55-£75 daily.
Lunch available.
Evening meal 7pm (l.o. 10pm).
Parking for 23.
Credit: Access, Visa, Diners, Amex.

Woodside Farm Guest House ⚤
COMMENDED

Ashby Road, Stapleton, LE9 8JE
☎ Market Bosworth (0455) 291929
16-acre horse/arable farm. Close to the Battle of Bosworth site and Kirkby Mallory race track. 3 miles to North Hinckley on A447.
Bedrooms: 1 single, 2 double & 2 twin, 2 family rooms.
Bathrooms: 2 private, 2 public; 2 private showers.
Bed & breakfast: £18-£25 single, £33-£50 double.
Lunch available.
Evening meal 6.30pm (l.o. 9.30pm).
Parking for 17.
Credit: Access, Visa.

HOLBEACH
Lincolnshire
Map ref 3A1

Small town, mentioned in the Domesday Book, has a splendid 14th C church with a fine tower and spire. The surrounding villages also have interesting churches, and the area is well-known for its bulbfields.

Chequers Hotel
COMMENDED

15 High Street, Holbeach, Spalding, PE12 7DU
☎ (0406) 26767
A revamped hotel, owned and run by the resident proprietors. Car park.
Bedrooms: 5 double & 5 twin.
Bathrooms: 10 private.
Bed & breakfast: from £36 single, £45-£60 double.
Half board: £40-£50 daily.
Lunch available.
Evening meal 7pm (l.o. 10pm).

Parking for 34.
Credit: Access, Visa, Diners, Amex.

Pipwell Manor
Listed COMMENDED

Washway Road, Saracens Head, Holbeach, PE12 8AL
☎ (0406) 23119
Elegant Georgian manor house with extensive gardens and paddocks in the centre of a small, quiet, Fenland village. Just off the A17. Non-smokers only please.
Bedrooms: 1 single, 2 double & 1 twin.
Bathrooms: 1 private, 2 public.
Bed & breakfast: £16-£18 single, £30-£34 double.
Parking for 6.

HOPE
Derbyshire
Map ref 4B2

Village in the Hope Valley which is an excellent base for walking in the Peak District and for fishing and shooting. There is a well-dressing ceremony each June and its August sheep dog trials are well-known. Castleton Caves are nearby.

Moor Gate
Edale Rd., Hope, Via Sheffield, S. Yorkshire S30 2RF
☎ Hope Valley (0433) 21219
Newly refurbished country house in the heart of the Peak District. En-suite facilities now available.
Bedrooms: 9 single, 4 double & 16 twin.
Bathrooms: 12 private, 8 public.
Bed & breakfast: £15-£25 single, £25-£46 double.
Half board: £19.50-£34 daily, £143-£220 weekly.
Lunch available.
Evening meal 7pm.
Parking for 20.

Underleigh House ⚤
COMMENDED

Off Edale Road, Hope, S30 2RG
☎ Hope Valley (0433) 621372

A farmhouse-style home, 1.5 miles from the village of Hope on a private lane. Magnificent views over river valley to the moors beyond. Majority of rooms with en-suite facilities and colour TV.
Bedrooms: 3 double & 2 twin.
Bathrooms: 5 private.
Bed & breakfast: £15-£29 single, £36-£44 double.
Half board: £26-£33 daily.
Evening meal 7.30pm.
Parking for 8.

KEGWORTH
Leicestershire
Map ref 4C3

Village on the River Soar close to East Midlands Airport and Donington Park racing circuit. It has a 14th C church with a fine nave and chantry roof. The nearby churches of Staunton Harold, Melbourne and Breedon-on-the-Hill are of exceptional interest.

Yew Lodge Hotel ⚤
COMMENDED

33 Packington Hill, Kegworth, Derby DE7 2DF
☎ (0509) 672518
Telex 341995 Ref 211
Privately-owned hotel with restaurant offering English and continental cooking. 1 minute from the M1 junction 24. 5 minutes from East Midlands International Airport.
Bedrooms: 28 single, 9 double & 17 twin.
Bathrooms: 54 private.
Bed & breakfast: £57.50-£65.50 single, £69.50-£76.50 double.
Half board: £69.30-£77.30 daily.
Lunch available.
Evening meal 6.30pm (l.o. 10pm).
Parking for 120.
Credit: Access, Visa, Diners, Amex.

KERSALL
Nottinghamshire
Map ref 4C2

5m SE. Ollerton

Hill Farm Guest House
COMMENDED

Kersall, Newark, NG22 0BJ
☎ Caunton (063 686) 274

17th C farm cottage with splendid views over the countryside, a beamed dining room and a comfortable lounge with an open log fire. Southwell Minster, Newark and the Sherwood Forest Visitor Centre are all nearby.
Bedrooms: 1 double & 1 twin.
Bathrooms: 1 private, 1 public.
Bed & breakfast: £15-£18 single, £26-£29 double.
Parking for 6.
Open May-September.

KETTERING
Northamptonshire
Map ref 3A2

Ancient industrial town based on shoe-making. Wicksteed Park to the south has many children's amusements. The splendid 17th C ducal mansion of Boughton House is to the north.
Tourist Information Centre ☎ (0536) 410266 or 410333 ext 212

George Hotel ⚤
APPROVED

Sheep Street, Kettering, NN16 0AN
☎ (0536) 518620 Telex 341013
Coaching inn, dating from at least 1636, on the main approach road from Northampton. Within easy reach of many stately homes, Rutland Water, and Wicksteed Leisure Park.
Bedrooms: 21 single, 25 double & 5 twin, 1 family room.
Bathrooms: 33 private, 6 public; 2 private showers.
Bed & breakfast: £25-£59 single, £40-£65 double.
Half board: £31-£45 daily, £212-£233 weekly.
Lunch available.
Evening meal 7pm (l.o. 10pm).
Parking for 24.
Credit: Access, Visa, C.Bl., Diners, Amex.

Periquito Hotel ⚤
COMMENDED

Market Square, Kettering, NN16 8ST
☎ (0536) 520732
17th C coaching inn, fully refurbished in 1990 with bright welcoming decor that enhances original features. Opposite busy market. 15 minutes' drive from M1 junction 15.

Bedrooms: 16 single,
15 double & 6 twin, 2 family
rooms.
Bathrooms: 38 private,
1 public.
Bed & breakfast: £43-£65
single, £48.50-£73.50 double.
Lunch available.
Evening meal 7pm (l.o.
10.30pm).
Parking for 59.
Credit: Access, Visa, Diners,
Amex.

KETTON

Leicestershire
Map ref 3A1

3m SW. Stamford

The Priory M

Church Road, Ketton,
Stamford, Lincolnshire
PE9 3RD
☎ Stamford (0780) 720215
*A large, recently restored, 16th
C house with delightful
gardens and a large
conservatory. En-suite rooms
with TV, separate residents'
lounge and dining room.*
Bedrooms: 2 double & 1 twin.
Bathrooms: 2 private,
1 public.
Bed & breakfast: £20-£30
single, £30-£50 double.
Half board: £30-£35 daily.
Lunch available.
Evening meal 7pm (l.o. 9pm).
Parking for 10.
Credit: Access, Visa.

KNIPTON

Leicestershire
Map ref 4C2

7m SW. Grantham
Leicestershire Wolds
village close to Belvoir
Castle, where medieval
jousting tournaments and
other special events add
to the attractions in
summer.

Red House Inn
APPROVED

Knipton, Grantham,
Lincolnshire NG32 1RH
☎ Grantham (0476) 870352
*In the beautiful Vale of
Belvoir, within 1 mile of the
castle, this listed building was
a hunting lodge for
approximately 200 years.*
Bedrooms: 2 single, 2 double
& 4 twin.
Bathrooms: 3 private,
2 public.

Bed & breakfast: £18.50-£27
single, £29.50-£39.50 double.
Half board: £26.50-£45 daily.
Lunch available.
Evening meal 7pm (l.o.
9.30pm).
Parking for 60.
Credit: Access, Visa.

LANEHAM

Nottinghamshire
Map ref 4C2

8m SE. Retford

The Old Cottage

Main Street, Laneham,
Retford, DN22 0NA
☎ Dunham-on-Trent
(0777) 228555
*Small family-run licensed hotel
quietly situated in centre of
village near River Trent.
Convenient for Lincoln,
Newark and Sherwood Forest.*
Bedrooms: 2 single, 1 twin,
1 family room.
Bathrooms: 3 private,
1 public.
Bed & breakfast: £20-£22
single, £30-£33 double.
Lunch available.
Evening meal 7pm (l.o.
7.30pm).
Parking for 18.
Credit: Access, Visa.

LANGLEY MILL

Derbyshire
Map ref 4C2

8m NW. Nottingham

Stoneyford Lodge

Boat Lane, Jacksdale,
Stoneyford, (Nr. Langley
Mill) Nottingham,
Nottinghamshire NG16 5PR
☎ (0773) 713460
*Old world inn with oak beams,
a log fire in winter, a carvery
restaurant and a motel annexe,
in a rural location off the A610
at Aldecar Church.*
Bedrooms: 1 single, 4 double
& 1 twin.
Bathrooms: 1 public.
Bed & breakfast: from £25
single, from £35 double.
Half board: £35-£45 daily,
£210-£245 weekly.
Lunch available.
Evening meal 7.30pm (l.o.
10pm).
Parking for 150.
Credit: Access, Visa, Diners,
Amex.

LEICESTER

Leicestershire
Map ref 4C3

Modern industrial city
with a wide variety of
attractions including
Roman remains, ancient
churches, Georgian
houses and a Victorian
clock tower. There are
pedestrianised shopping
precincts, an excellent
market, several
museums, theatres,
concert hall and sports
and leisure centres.
*Tourist Information
Centre* ☎ *(0533) 511300
or 511301*

Belmont House Hotel M

De Montfort Street,
Leicester, LE1 7GR
☎ (0533) 544773 Telex 34619
Best Western
*This family-owned hotel is in a
peaceful Victorian conservation
area convenient for the city
centre.*
Bedrooms: 23 single,
26 double & 16 twin, 3 family
rooms.
Bathrooms: 68 private.
Bed & breakfast: £68-£78
single, £80-£95 double.
Lunch available.
Evening meal 7pm (l.o.
10pm).
Parking for 60.
Credit: Access, Visa, Diners,
Amex.

Burlington Hotel

Elmfield Avenue, Stoneygate,
Leicester, LE2 1RB
☎ (0533) 705112
*The hotel is in a quiet but
central position with a warm,
homely and comfortable
atmosphere.*
Bedrooms: 9 single, 4 double
& 2 twin, 1 family room.
Bathrooms: 11 private,
1 public; 4 private showers.
Bed & breakfast: £20-£30
single, £33-£38 double.
Half board: £27.50-£29.50
daily.
Evening meal 6.30pm (l.o.
8pm).
Parking for 18.
Credit: Access, Visa.

Craigleigh Hotel

17-19 Westleigh Road,
Leicester, LE3 0HH
☎ (0533) 546875

*A small family-run hotel 1 mile
from the city centre, with easy
access to the M1 and M69.
Close to sporting venues.*
Bedrooms: 3 single, 2 double
& 5 twin.
Bathrooms: 2 public.
Bed & breakfast: £20-£22
single, £37-£40 double.
Half board: £28-£31.75 daily.
Evening meal 6.30pm (l.o.
4pm).

Croft Hotel

3 Stanley Road, Leicester,
LE2 1RF
☎ (0533) 703220
*Built around 1900, the hotel
can be found in Stanley Road
just off London Road (A6) by
Victoria Park.*
Bedrooms: 16 single, 4 double
& 5 twin, 1 family room.
Bathrooms: 6 private,
4 public; 5 private showers.
Bed & breakfast: £22-£32
single, £30-£36 double.
Half board: £28-£38 daily.
Evening meal 6pm (l.o. 7pm).
Parking for 16.
Credit: Access, Visa.

Gables Hotel M

368 London Road, Leicester,
LE2 2PN
☎ (0533) 706969
*A comfortable hotel, offering a
traditional atmosphere with
modern facilities and a high
standard of cooking and
service.*
Bedrooms: 3 single, 11 double
& 8 twin, 9 family rooms.
Bathrooms: 31 private.
Bed & breakfast: £36-£40
single, £54-£63 double.
Half board: £45-£49 daily.
Lunch available.
Evening meal 7pm (l.o.
9.30pm).
Parking for 31.
Credit: Access, Visa, Diners.

Leicestershire Moat
House M

Wigston Road (B582),
Oadby, Leicester, LE2 5QE
☎ (0533) 719441
Queens Moat Houses
*This modern hotel prides itself
on its service and high
standard of facilities. 3 miles
from the city centre and 5
miles from the M1, it is an
excellent base for Leicester.*
Bedrooms: 8 single, 16 double
& 30 twin, 3 family rooms.
Continued ▶

LEICESTER
Continued

Bathrooms: 57 private.
Bed & breakfast: £29.50-£69.25 single, £44-£86.50 double.
Half board: £32-£81.35 daily.
Lunch available.
Evening meal 7pm (l.o. 9.45pm).
Parking for 160.
Credit: Access, Visa, Diners, Amex.

Park Hotel
125 London Road, Leicester, LE2 0QT
☎ (0533) 554329
Comfortable, friendly hotel under personal supervision. Convenient for the railway station, university, De Montfort Hall and the city centre.
Bedrooms: 8 single, 5 double & 4 twin, 4 family rooms.
Bathrooms: 1 private, 3 public; 5 private showers.
Bed & breakfast: £22-£28 single, £32-£40 double.
Parking for 4.
Credit: Access, Visa.

The Park International Hotel M
ఆఆఆ APPROVED
Humberstone Road, Leicester, LE5 3AT
☎ (0533) 620471
Telex 341460
CR Park Hotels
A city centre hotel, adjacent to the exhibition centre, with banqueting accommodation for up to 500.
Bedrooms: 122 single, 45 double & 39 twin, 3 family rooms.
Bathrooms: 209 private.
Bed & breakfast: £22-£64 single, £44-£81 double.
Half board: £32-£76 daily.
Lunch available.
Evening meal 6pm (l.o. 9.30pm).
Parking for 25.
Credit: Access, Visa, Diners, Amex.

The Red Cow
ఆఆఆ COMMENDED
Hinckley Road, Leicester Forest East, Leicester, LE3 3PG
☎ (0533) 387878
On the A47, 4 miles from Leicester city centre and 3 miles from the interchange of the M1 and M69.

Bedrooms: 27 double & 4 twin.
Bathrooms: 31 private.
Bed & breakfast: £29-£42 single, £34.50-£49.50 double.
Lunch available.
Evening meal 6pm (l.o. 10pm).
Parking for 90.
Credit: Access, Visa, Diners, Amex.

Regency Hotel
ఆఆఆ COMMENDED
360 London Road, Leicester, LE2 2PL
☎ (0533) 709634
A small friendly hotel with a restaurant which offers an a la carte menu and chef's specials, and has an extensive wine list.
Bedrooms: 28 single, 6 double & 1 twin, 2 family rooms.
Bathrooms: 37 private.
Bed & breakfast: £27-£45 single, £42-£50 double.
Half board: £39-£55 daily.
Lunch available.
Evening meal 6pm (l.o. 10pm).
Parking for 50.
Credit: Access, Visa, Diners, Amex.

Spindle Lodge Hotel
ఆఆ COMMENDED
2 West Walk, Leicester, LE1 7NA
☎ (0533) 551380
This Victorian house has a friendly atmosphere and is within easy walking distance of city centre, university, station, civic and entertainment centres.
Bedrooms: 5 single, 3 double & 3 twin, 2 family rooms.
Bathrooms: 5 private, 4 public.
Bed & breakfast: £23.50-£32.50 single, £43.50-£52.50 double.
Half board: £30-£44.50 daily.
Evening meal 6.30pm (l.o. 5.50pm).
Parking for 7.
Credit: Access, Visa.

Squash Leicester Hotel
ఆఆఆ
The Racecourse, Oadby, Leicester, LE2 3QH
☎ (0533) 703920
A purpose built, privately owned hotel and leisure complex on the south side of Leicester within 5 minutes of the M1 and the M69.
Bedrooms: 6 twin, 4 family rooms.

Bathrooms: 10 private, 12 public.
Bed & breakfast: £18-£33 single, £33-£48 double.
Lunch available.
Evening meal 5pm (l.o. 8pm).
Parking for 250.
Credit: Access, Visa, Amex.

The Stage Hotel M
ఆఆఆ
299 Leicester Road (A50), Wigston Fields, Leicester, LE8 1JW
☎ (0533) 886161
Establishment offers professional conference facilities for delegates, business meetings or seminars, and wedding receptions. Up to 200 persons can be seated for meals.
Bedrooms: 20 double & 59 twin.
Bathrooms: 79 private.
Bed & breakfast: £52-£62 single, £62-£72 double.
Half board: £60-£70 daily, £360-£400 weekly.
Lunch available.
Evening meal 7pm (l.o. 10pm).
Parking for 180.
Credit: Access, Visa, C.Bl., Diners, Amex.

Stakis Country Court Hotel
Junction 21 Approach, Braunstone, Leicester, LE3 2WQ
☎ Leicester (0533) 630066
Telex 34429
CR Stakis
Attractive 2-storey hotel built around a central landscaped courtyard. Purpose built conference and leisure club. Half board rate based on a minimum 2 night stay.
Bedrooms: 92 double & 39 twin, 10 family rooms.
Bathrooms: 141 private.
Bed & breakfast: from £89 single, from £99 double.
Half board: from £46 daily.
Lunch available.
Evening meal 7pm (l.o. 10pm).
Parking for 160.
Credit: Access, Visa, Diners, Amex.

Stanfre' House Hotel
ఆఆ
265 London Road, Leicester, LE2 3BE
☎ (0533) 704294
Family-run hotel on the A6, 1 mile from the city centre and close to the railway station, university, racecourse and De Montfort Hall.
Bedrooms: 3 single, 1 double & 6 twin, 1 family room.
Bathrooms: 2 public.
Bed & breakfast: £19 single, £30 double.
Parking for 6.

Time Out Hotel & Leisure
ఆఆఆ
15 Enderby Road, Blaby, Leicester, LE8 3GD
☎ (0533) 778746 & 771154
Family-run hotel with extensive leisure facilities - please see the symbols - plus snooker. Frequently changed table d'hote menu offers fresh local produce whenever possible and food is available in both the restaurant and brasserie.
Bedrooms: 9 single, 13 double & 2 twin.
Bathrooms: 24 private.
Bed & breakfast: £49.50-£60 single, £75-£85 double.
Half board: £65.45-£75.95 daily.
Lunch available.
Evening meal 7pm (l.o. 10pm).
Parking for 70.
Credit: Access, Visa, Diners, Amex.

Waltham House M
ఆఆ APPROVED
500 Narborough Road, Leicester, LE3 2FU
☎ (0533) 891129
Victorian detached house.
Bedrooms: 1 single, 2 twin.
Bathrooms: 1 public.
Bed & breakfast: £16-£18 single, £26-£28 double.
Half board: £24-£26 daily.
Evening meal 6pm.
Parking for 4.

Half board prices shown are per person but in some cases may be based on double/twin occupancy.

LINCOLN
Lincolnshire
Map ref 4C2

Ancient city dominated by the magnificent 11th C cathedral with its triple towers. A Roman gateway is still used and there are medieval houses lining narrow, cobbled streets. Other attractions include the Norman castle, several museums and the Usher Gallery.
Tourist Information Centre ☎ (0522) 529828 or 512971

Alder Hotel ⋔
2 Hamilton Road, St. Catherine's, Lincoln, LN5 8ED
☎ (0522) 528243
Small family-run Victorian hotel with modern amenities and a comfortable atmosphere, just over 1 mile to the south of the city centre.
Bedrooms: 1 single, 1 double & 4 twin, 2 family rooms.
Bathrooms: 2 public; 3 private showers.
Bed & breakfast: £14-£16.90 single, £25.40-£28 double.
Parking for 8.
Credit: Access, Visa, Amex.
⛱ 🖵 ⌨ ⓘ Ⓥ ⌹ ⓉⓋ ▥ 🅐
ⒹⒶⓅ ⓈⓅ Ⓣ

Avon Guest House ⋔
9 Ashlin Grove, Off West Parade, Lincoln, LN1 1LE
☎ (0522) 520674
In a quiet cul-de-sac, only 10 minutes from the city centre and the cathedral. Friendly atmosphere.
Bedrooms: 1 double & 3 twin, 2 family rooms.
Bathrooms: 2 public.
Bed & breakfast: from £20 single, from £26 double.
Parking for 6.
⛱ ⓐ 🖵 ⌨ ⓘ Ⓥ ⌹ ⓉⓋ ▥
🅐 ⓢ

Brierley House Hotel ⋔
54 South Park, Lincoln, LN5 8ER
☎ (0522) 526945
Victorian family-run hotel in quiet cul-de-sac, adjacent to the south common with its municipal golf-course.
Bedrooms: 4 single, 2 double & 5 twin.
Bathrooms: 6 private, 2 public.
Bed & breakfast: £19-£26 single, £38-£40 double.
Half board: £26-£27 daily.
Evening meal 7pm.
⛱ ⅓ ⓐ 🖵 ⌨ ⓘ Ⓥ ⌹ ⓉⓋ
▥ ⓐ 🅿 ✗ ▦ 🅗 ⓈⓅ

Castle Hotel ⋔
Westgate, Lincoln, LN1 3AS
☎ (0522) 538801
Fax (0522) 510291
Centrally located for all historic sights. All rooms overlook either cathedral or castle. 2 spacious car parks.
Bedrooms: 4 single, 11 double & 4 twin.
Bathrooms: 19 private, 1 public.
Bed & breakfast: £38-£45 single, £45-£55 double.
Half board: £49.50-£56.50 daily.
Lunch available.
Evening meal 7pm (l.o. 9.30pm).
Parking for 25.
Credit: Access, Visa.
⛱ ⅓ ⌨ 🖵 ⌨ ⓘ Ⓥ ⌹ ⓐ
🅐 ⒹⒶⓅ ⓢ ⓈⓅ Ⓣ

D'Isney Place Hotel ⋔
Eastgate, Lincoln, LN2 4AA
☎ (0522) 538881
Small family-run hotel near the cathedral, with individually styled bedrooms and an emphasis on comfort and privacy.
Bedrooms: 2 single, 10 double & 4 twin, 2 family rooms.
Bathrooms: 18 private.
Bed & breakfast: from £39 single, from £61 double.
Parking for 12.
Credit: Access, Visa, Diners, Amex.
⛱ ⅓ ⌨ ⌨ ⓒ 🖵 ⌨ Ⓤ ⓘ
Ⓥ ⌹ ▥ ⓐ ⅄ ⏚ ✿ 🅐 ⒹⒶⓅ
ⓈⓅ 🅗

Eardleys Hotel
⛶⛶
21 Cross O'Cliff Hill, Lincoln LN5 8PN
☎ (0522) 523050
Elegant, small hotel, just half a mile from city centre. Licensed bar, full restaurant. Some rooms with shower.
Bedrooms: 5 double.
Bathrooms: 1 public; 2 private showers.
Bed & breakfast: from £17 single, from £30 double.
Half board: £20.70-£24.70 daily.
Lunch available.
Evening meal 7pm (l.o. 10pm).
Parking for 12.
Credit: Access, Visa.
⛱ 🖵 ⌨ ⓘ Ⓥ ⌹ ⓉⓋ ▥
ⓐ 🅿 ✗ ▦ 🅗 ⓈⓅ

Fittock Cottage ⋔
⛶⛶ **COMMENDED**
Silver Street, Branston, Lincoln, LN4 1LR
☎ (0522) 791444

Comfortable stone cottage retaining old world charm, in a delightful country village only 4 miles from Lincoln. Parking.
Bedrooms: 1 single, 1 double & 1 twin.
Bathrooms: 1 public; 1 private shower.
Bed & breakfast: max. £16 single, max. £32 double.
Half board: max. £25.50 daily, max. £178.50 weekly.
Evening meal 7pm (l.o. 9pm).
Parking for 3.
Ⓐ Ⓤ ⓘ ⌹ ⓉⓋ ▥ ⓐ ✗ 🅗

Grand Hotel ⋔
⛶⛶⛶ **APPROVED**
St. Mary's Street, Lincoln, LN5 7EP
☎ (0522) 524211 Telex 56401 GRANDH G
Family-owned hotel, in the centre of the beautiful historic city of Lincoln. Breakaway weekends all year.
Bedrooms: 19 single, 15 double & 13 twin, 1 family room.
Bathrooms: 48 private.
Bed & breakfast: £45-£56.50 single, £55-£61.50 double.
Half board: £32.50-£46 daily.
Lunch available.
Evening meal 7pm (l.o. 9pm).
Parking for 30.
Credit: Access, Visa, Diners, Amex.
⛱ ⅓ ⌨ ⓒ 🖵 ⌨ ⓘ Ⓥ ⅄ ⌹
● ▥ ⓐ 🅿 ⅄ ⓈⓅ Ⓣ

Hillcrest Hotel ⋔
⛶⛶⛶ **COMMENDED**
15 Lindum Terrace, Lincoln, LN2 5RT
☎ (0522) 510182
Victorian rectory overlooking gardens and the arboretum. A peaceful location within 5 minutes' walk of the cathedral and the city centre.
Bedrooms: 6 single, 5 double & 2 twin, 4 family rooms.
Bathrooms: 17 private.
Bed & breakfast: £41.50 single, £56 double.
Half board: £40-£50 daily.
Lunch available.
Evening meal 7pm (l.o. 9pm).
Parking for 7.
Credit: Access, Visa, Amex.
⛱ ⅓ ⌨ ⓒ 🖵 ⌨ ⓘ Ⓥ ⌹
▥ ⓐ 🅿 ⓈⓅ Ⓣ

Loudor Hotel
37 Newark Road, North Hykeham, Lincoln, LN6 8RB
☎ (0522) 680333
Small family-run hotel, 3.5 miles south of the city centre on the Lincoln to Newark road. A friendly and comfortable atmosphere, and a warm welcome from the resident proprietors.

Bedrooms: 4 single, 3 double & 2 twin, 1 family room.
Bathrooms: 10 private.
Bed & breakfast: £28-£34 single, £40-£43 double.
Lunch available.
Evening meal 7pm (l.o. 8.30pm).
Parking for 14.
Credit: Access, Visa, Diners, Amex.
⛱ ⅓ ⌨ ⓒ 🖵 ⌨ ⓘ Ⓥ ⌹
▥ ⓐ 🅿 ▦ 🅗 ⓈⓅ

Mayfield Guest House
⛶⛶ **APPROVED**
213 Yarborough Road, Lincoln, LN1 3NQ
☎ (0522) 533732
Small homely guesthouse with views of the Trent Valley, a short level walk from the cathedral. Private enclosed car park.
Bedrooms: 1 single, 1 double & 1 twin, 2 family rooms.
Bathrooms: 3 private, 1 public.
Bed & breakfast: £13-£15 single, £26-£28 double.
Parking for 4.
Credit: Visa.
⛱ ⌨ ⓒ 🖵 ⌨ Ⓤ ⓘ Ⓥ ⅄ ⌹
ⓉⓋ ▥ ⓐ ✗ ▦ Ⓣ

Moor Lodge Hotel ⋔
⛶⛶⛶ **COMMENDED**
Branston, Nr. Lincoln, LN4 1HU
☎ (0522) 791366
Ⓒ⒭ Consort
Owner-managed hotel in the attractive village of Branston, 3 miles south-east of historic Lincoln on the B1188.
Bedrooms: 4 single, 4 double & 13 twin, 4 family rooms.
Bathrooms: 25 private.
Bed & breakfast: £62-£69.50 single, £76.50-£87.50 double.
Half board: £53-£62 daily, from £330 weekly.
Lunch available.
Evening meal 7pm (l.o. 9.15pm).
Parking for 150.
Credit: Access, Visa, Diners, Amex.
⛱ ⅓ ⌨ ⓒ 🖵 ⌨ ⓘ Ⓥ ⌹ ⓉⓋ
▥ ⓐ 🅿 ⏚ ⅄ ⓈⓅ Ⓣ

Tennyson Hotel ⋔
⛶⛶⛶ **APPROVED**
7 South Park Avenue, Lincoln, LN5 8EN
☎ (0522) 521624/513684
Hotel with a comfortable atmosphere, overlooking the South Park, 1 mile from the city centre. Personally supervised. Wide choice of food. Leisure breaks available.
Bedrooms: 2 single, 3 double & 2 twin, 1 family room.
Bathrooms: 8 private.

Continued ▶

LINCOLN

Continued

Bed & breakfast: £25-£28 single, £37-£41 double.
Half board: £37-£40 daily, £190-£200 weekly.
Evening meal 6.30pm (l.o. 8pm).
Parking for 8.
Credit: Access, Visa, Amex.

Washingborough Hall Country House Hotel ⋒
COMMENDED

Church Hill, Washingborough, Nr. Lincoln, LN4 1BE
☎ (0522) 790340
Minotels
Stone-built, former manor house in grounds of 3 acres, in a pleasant village 2.5 miles from the historic cathedral city of Lincoln.
Bedrooms: 2 single, 6 double & 6 twin.
Bathrooms: 14 private, 1 public.
Bed & breakfast: £47-£60 single, £65-£82 double.
Half board: from £36 daily.
Evening meal 7pm (l.o. 9pm).
Parking for 50.
Credit: Access, Visa, Diners, Amex.

LOCKINGTON

Leicestershire
Map ref 4C3

2km E Castle Donington

Hilton National

East Midlands Airport, Derby Road, Lockington, DE7 2RH
☎ Loughborough (0509) 674000
Hilton
Modern purpose-built hotel. Ideally located close to the M1 and East Midlands International Airport. Full leisure facilities.
Bedrooms: 80 double & 65 twin, 6 family rooms.
Bathrooms: 151 private.
Bed & breakfast: £96-£125 single, £125-£145 double.
Lunch available.
Evening meal 10pm (l.o. 9.45pm).
Parking for 240.
Credit: Access, Visa, Diners, Amex.

LOUGHBOROUGH

Leicestershire
Map ref 4C3

Industrial town famous for its bell foundry and 47-bell Carillon Tower. The Great Central Railway operates steam railway rides of over 7 miles through the attractive scenery of Charnwood Forest.
Tourist Information Centre ☎ (0509) 230131

Bridgeway Guest House
Listed

19a Bridge Street, Loughborough, LE11 1NQ
☎ (0509) 266678
Large Victorian, semi-detached house close to the town centre and bus station.
Bedrooms: 1 single, 2 double & 2 twin, 1 family room.
Bathrooms: 2 public.
Bed & breakfast: from £12 single, from £24 double.
Half board: from £16.50 daily, from £99 weekly.
Evening meal 6pm (l.o. 8pm).
Parking for 5.

De Montfort Hotel
APPROVED

88 Leicester Road, Loughborough, LE11 2AQ
☎ (0509) 216061
Comfortable, family-run hotel within easy walking distance of the town centre, opposite a park.
Bedrooms: 1 single, 1 double & 6 twin, 1 family room.
Bathrooms: 3 public.
Bed & breakfast: from £19 single, from £32 double.
Half board: from £26 daily.
Evening meal 6pm (l.o. 4pm).
Credit: Access, Visa.

Forest Rise Hotel
COMMENDED

55 Forest Road, Loughborough, LE11 3NW
☎ (0509) 215928
Friendly family-run hotel, fully modernised, on the Charnwood Forest side of town, with its own garden. Weddings and parties catered for.
Bedrooms: 9 single, 9 double & 2 twin, 4 family rooms.
Bathrooms: 16 private; 8 private showers.
Bed & breakfast: £31-£38 single, £44-£49 double.
Half board: £41-£48 daily, £246-£288 weekly.

Evening meal 6.30pm (l.o. 7.50pm).
Parking for 25.
Credit: Access, Visa.

Garendon Lodge Guest House
COMMENDED

136 Leicester Road, Loughborough, LE11 2AQ
☎ (0509) 211120
Spacious Victorian guesthouse, completely refurbished. In quiet surroundings but within 5 minutes of the town centre and nearby Charnwood Forest.
Bedrooms: 2 single, 1 double & 1 twin.
Bathrooms: 4 private.
Bed & breakfast: from £25 single, from £40 double.
Half board: £29-£34 daily, £203-£238 weekly.
Evening meal 6pm (l.o. 8pm).
Parking for 5.
Credit: Visa.

Garendon Park Hotel
APPROVED

92 Leicester Road, Loughborough, LE11 2AQ
☎ (0509) 236557
A Victorian building retaining many original features, now a new hotel run by owning family. Close to university and town centre.
Bedrooms: 1 single, 1 double & 5 twin, 2 family rooms.
Bathrooms: 4 public; 3 private showers.
Bed & breakfast: £18-£20.50 single, £31-£36 double.
Half board: £23-£29.50 daily, £161-£206.50 weekly.
Evening meal 7pm (l.o. 8.30pm).
Credit: Access, Visa.

The Mountsorrel Hotel
Listed

217 Loughborough Road, Mountsorrel, Loughborough, LE12 7AR
☎ Quorn (0509) 412627 & 416105
Small, friendly, family-run hotel in secluded grounds, off the main A6 midway between Leicester and Loughborough. Bradgate Park and Charnwood Forest are nearby.
Bedrooms: 5 single, 4 double.
Bathrooms: 3 private, 1 public; 2 private showers.
Bed & breakfast: £22-£26 single, £31-£36 double.
Half board: £29.95-£37.50 daily, £162-£190 weekly.

Evening meal 6.30pm (l.o. 8pm).
Parking for 10.
Credit: Access, Visa.

Peachnook ⋒

154 Ashby Road, Loughborough, LE11 3AG
☎ (0509) 264390
Small friendly guesthouse built around 1890. Near all amenities. Open all year.
Bedrooms: 1 single, 3 twin.
Bathrooms: 1 public.
Bed & breakfast: £10-£15 single, from £22 double.

The Poplars ⋒
Listed APPROVED

Watling Street, Mountsorrel, Loughborough, LE12 7BD
☎ Leicester (0533) 302102
Victorian house with a wooded secluded garden, on a hill overlooking the Soar Valley.
Bedrooms: 5 single, 1 double & 3 twin.
Bathrooms: 3 public.
Bed & breakfast: from £15 single, from £27.50 double.
Parking for 15.

Quorn Country Hotel ⋒

66 Leicester Road, Quorn, Loughborough, LE12 8BB
☎ (0509) 415050
Telex 347166
This privately-owned country hotel is set in 4 acres of garden and overlooks the River Soar. The bedrooms have been decorated and equipped to provide a high degree of comfort.
Bedrooms: 5 double & 11 twin, 3 family rooms.
Bathrooms: 19 private.
Bed & breakfast: £65-£85 single, £91-£111 double.
Half board: max. £102.95 daily.
Lunch available.
Evening meal 7pm (l.o. 10pm).
Parking for 100.
Credit: Access, Visa, Diners, Amex.

The enquiry coupons at the back will help you when contacting proprietors.

LYDDINGTON

Leicestershire
Map ref 3A1

2m SE. Uppingham

Marquess of Exeter Hotel M

52 Main Street, Lyddington,
Nr. Uppingham, LE15 9LT
☎ Uppingham (0572) 822477
Ⓒ Best Western
*16th C coaching inn with low
beams and an inglenook
fireplace, between Corby and
Uppingham, off the A6003.*
Bedrooms: 10 double &
7 twin.
Bathrooms: 16 private;
1 private shower.
Bed & breakfast: from £55
single, from £70 double.
Half board: from £62.50
daily.
Lunch available.
Evening meal 7.30pm (l.o.
9.45pm).
Parking for 60.
Credit: Access, Visa, Diners,
Amex.

MACKWORTH

Derbyshire
Map ref 4B2

Mundy Arms Hotel
COMMENDED

Ashbourne Road,
Mackworth, DE3 4LZ
☎ Derby
(0332) 824254/824664
Fax (0332) 824519
*Recently refurbished hotel on
A52, 1 mile north of Derby.
A la carte restaurant and
extensive hot and cold carvery.
Private function room.*
Bedrooms: 15 double &
14 twin, 1 family room.
Bathrooms: 29 private,
1 public.
Bed & breakfast: £36.50-£56
single, £40.50-£72 double.
Half board: £46.50-£66 daily.
Lunch available.
Evening meal 7pm (l.o.
10pm).
Parking for 98.
Credit: Access, Visa.

MANSFIELD

Nottinghamshire
Map ref 4C2

Ancient town, now an
industrial and shopping
centre, with a popular
market, in the heart of
Robin Hood country.
There is an impressive
19th C railway viaduct, 2
interesting churches, an
18th C Moot Hall and a
museum and art gallery.

Dalestorth Guest House M
Listed

Skegby Lane, Skegby,
Sutton-in-Ashfield,
NG17 3DH
☎ Mansfield (0623) 551110
*18th C ancestral house,
modernised to a high standard.
Clean, comfortable and
friendly. 5 miles junction 28 of
M1 and central for
Nottinghamshire and
Derbyshire.*
Bedrooms: 8 single, 3 double
& 1 twin.
Bathrooms: 7 public.
Bed & breakfast: max. £20
single, max. £35 double.
Half board: max. £25 daily,
max. £168 weekly.
Evening meal 7pm (l.o.
5.30pm).
Parking for 12.

Parkhurst Guest House M

28 Woodhouse Road,
Mansfield, NG18 2AF
☎ (0623) 27324
*A family-run guesthouse in
pleasant surroundings in the
heart of Robin Hood country.
Easy access to M1 and A1.*
Bedrooms: 3 single, 2 double
& 2 twin, 4 family rooms.
Bathrooms: 3 public.
Bed & breakfast: max. £17
single, max. £30 double.
Evening meal 5pm (l.o.
7.30pm).
Parking for 9.

MARKET BOSWORTH

Leicestershire
Map ref 4B3

Attractive small town,
close to Bosworth
Battlefield where a Visitor
Centre and Battlefield
Trails trace the course of
events in 1485 when
Richard III died.

Bosworth Hall Hotel M

The Park, Market Bosworth,
Near Nuneaton,
Warwickshire CV13 0LP
☎ (0455) 291919
*17th C country house hotel set
in 11 acres of parkland and
gardens. Near Atherstone.*
Bedrooms: 117 double &
41 twin, 2 family rooms.
Bathrooms: 160 private.
Bed & breakfast: £72-£150
single, £85-£220 double.
Half board: £60-£90 daily.
Lunch available.
Evening meal 7pm (l.o.
10pm).
Parking for 100.
Credit: Access, Visa, Diners,
Amex.

MARKET HARBOROUGH

Leicestershire
Map ref 4C3

There have been markets
here since the early 13th
C, and the town was also
an important coaching
centre, with several
ancient hostelries. The
early 17th C grammar
school was once the
butter market.
*Tourist Information
Centre ☎ (0858) 462649
or 462699*

Angel Hotel M
COMMENDED

37 High Street, Market
Harborough, LE16 7NL
☎ (0858) 463123/462702
*300-year-old coaching inn.
Four poster rooms with jacuzzi.
Licensed bar and restaurant.
Special weekend breaks.*
Bedrooms: 11 single, 9 double
& 8 twin, 2 family rooms.
Bathrooms: 30 private.
Bed & breakfast: £41.50-
£46.50 single, £51.50-£56.50
double.
Half board: £55-£60 daily.
Lunch available.
Evening meal 7pm (l.o.
10pm).

Parking for 40.
Credit: Access, Visa, Diners,
Amex.

Dingley Lodge M

Harborough Road, Dingley,
Market Harborough, LE16 8PJ
☎ Dingley (085 885) 365
*Elegant, spacious country
house in its own grounds,
recently restored, commanding
extensive views. Home cooking,
comfortably furnished and en-
suite facilities.*
Bedrooms: 1 single, 3 double
& 2 twin, 1 family room.
Bathrooms: 7 private.
Bed & breakfast: from £22
single, from £33 double.
Parking for 15.

MARKFIELD

Leicestershire
Map ref 4C3

8m NW. Leicester

Field Head Hotel
COMMENDED

Markfield Lane, Markfield,
LE6 0PS
☎ (0530) 245454
Fax (0530) 243740
Telex 342296
Ⓒ Lansbury
*A new hotel on the A50, 1 mile
from junction 22 off the M1.
Originally an old farmhouse, the
hotel has been built in local stone.*
Bedrooms: 10 double &
17 twin, 1 family room.
Bathrooms: 28 private.
Bed & breakfast: £29-£76
single, £58-£88 double.
Half board: £42-£90 daily.
Lunch available.
Evening meal 7pm (l.o. 10pm).
Parking for 70.
Credit: Access, Visa, Diners,
Amex.

MATLOCK

Derbyshire
Map ref 4B2

The town lies beside the
narrow valley of the River
Derwent surrounded by
steep wooded hills. Good
centre for exploring
Derbyshire's best scenery.

Derwent House M

Knowleston Place, Matlock,
DE4 3BU
☎ (0629) 584681

Continued ▶

---

*Individual proprietors have supplied all
details of accommodation. Although we
do check for accuracy, we advise you to
confirm prices and other information at
the time of booking.*

MATLOCK
Continued

Charming 17th/18th C house situated close to park and the River Derwent. Well-known for our full English breakfasts.
Bedrooms: 2 single, 1 double & 1 twin, 1 family room.
Bathrooms: 1 private, 1 public.
Bed & breakfast: from £15 single, from £30 double.
Parking for 2.

Jackson Tor House M
76 Jackson Road, Matlock, DE4 3JQ
☎ (0629) 582348
Family-run hotel overlooking Matlock. Ideal for touring the national park, many historic houses and picturesque countryside.
Bedrooms: 10 single, 6 double & 10 twin, 1 family rooms.
Bathrooms: 4 private, 7 public; 1 private shower.
Bed & breakfast: £19-£32 single, £35-£60 double.
Half board: £25.50-£40 daily.
Evening meal 6pm (l.o. 5pm).
Parking for 25.

Parkfield Guest House M
115 Lime Tree Road, Matlock, DE4 3DU
☎ (0629) 57221
House is built of Derbyshire stone and overlooks the surrounding hills. All bedrooms are fully en-suite. A warm welcome.
Bedrooms: 1 double & 2 twin, 1 family room.
Bathrooms: 4 private, 1 public.
Bed & breakfast: £25-£29 single, £42-£46 double.
Half board: £31-£39 daily, £210-£260 weekly.
Parking for 12.

The Red House Hotel M
COMMENDED
Old Road, Darley Dale, Nr. Matlock, DE4 2ER
☎ Matlock (0629) 734854
Attractive country house situated on the edge of the beautiful Peak District National Park. Delightful gardens and panoramic views.
Bedrooms: 1 single, 6 double & 1 twin, 1 family room.
Bathrooms: 9 private.

Bed & breakfast: £45-£50 single, £70-£75 double.
Half board: £58-£62 daily, from £325 weekly.
Lunch available.
Evening meal 7.30pm (l.o. 9pm).
Parking for 20.
Credit: Access, Visa, Diners, Amex.

Riber Hall M
Matlock, DE4 5JU
☎ (0629) 582795
Elizabethan hotel in peaceful Derbyshire countryside. Antique four-poster beds in intimate surroundings, and whirlpool baths. Ancient walled garden and orchard. Conservatory.
Bedrooms: 11 double.
Bathrooms: 11 private, 1 public.
Bed & breakfast: £76-£90 single, £90-£134 double.
Lunch available.
Evening meal 7pm (l.o. 9.30pm).
Parking for 50.
Credit: Access, Visa, C.Bl., Diners, Amex.

Robertswood M
COMMENDED
Farley Hill, Matlock, DE4 3LL
☎ (0629) 55642
Spacious Victorian residence on the edge of Matlock, with panoramic views. Near Chatsworth. All bedrooms en-suite. Friendly, warm welcome.
Bedrooms: 4 double & 3 twin.
Bathrooms: 7 private.
Bed & breakfast: £25-£32 single, £45-£49 double.
Half board: £37-£44 daily, £250-£293 weekly.
Evening meal 7pm (l.o. midday).
Parking for 8.
Credit: Access, Visa.

Sheriff Lodge Hotel M
APPROVED
51 Dimple Road, Matlock, DE4 3JX
☎ (0629) 582973
Small family-run establishment with a comfortable and homely atmosphere. We pride ourselves on our varied and reasonably priced cuisine. Our customers say: "Best food in Matlock".

Bedrooms: 2 single, 7 double & 3 twin, 1 family room.
Bathrooms: 11 private; 2 private showers.
Bed & breakfast: £18-£25 single, £36-£45 double.
Half board: £30-£35 daily.
Lunch available.
Evening meal 6pm (l.o. 10pm).
Parking for 20.
Credit: Access, Visa.

Sycamore Guest House M
76 High Street, Town Head, Bonsall, Nr. Matlock, DE4 2AA
☎ Wirksworth (0629) 823903
Small family guesthouse on the edge of the Peak District National Park, central to most of Derbyshire's beauty spots and ideal for walking or touring holidays.
Bedrooms: 1 single, 3 double & 2 twin, 1 family room.
Bathrooms: 3 private, 1 public; 1 private shower.
Bed & breakfast: £16.50-£17 single, £33-£34 double.
Half board: £25.50-£26 daily.
Evening meal 6.30pm (l.o. 7.30pm).
Parking for 6.

Winstaff Guest House M
COMMENDED
Derwent Avenue, (Off Old English Road), Matlock, DE4 3LX
☎ (0629) 582593
In a pleasant, quiet and private cul-de-sac with a garden backing on to the River Derwent. Central for many tourist attractions.
Bedrooms: 4 double & 2 twin, 1 family room.
Bathrooms: 2 private, 2 public.
Bed & breakfast: £18-£22 single, £35-£40 double.
Half board: £27.50-£32 daily, £173-£202 weekly.
Evening meal 6.30pm (l.o. midday).
Parking for 6.

The national Crown scheme is explained in full on pages 536 – 539.

MATLOCK BATH
Derbyshire
Map ref 4B2

19th C spa town with many attractions including several caverns to visit, a lead mining museum and a family fun park. There are marvellous views over the surrounding countryside from the Heights of Abraham, to which a cable car gives access.
Tourist Information Centre ☎ (0629) 55082

Hodgkinsons Hotel M
COMMENDED
150 South Parade, Matlock Bath, DE4 3NR
☎ Matlock (0629) 582170
Georgian hotel, beautifully restored with original features. Open fires, sauna and hairdressing salon. Terraced garden with lovely views.
Bedrooms: 1 single, 5 double.
Bathrooms: 6 private.
Bed & breakfast: £40-£65 single, £50-£80 double.
Half board: £62-£87 daily.
Evening meal 7.30pm (l.o. 9.30pm).
Parking for 6.
Credit: Access, Amex.

Sunnybank Guest House M
COMMENDED
Clifton Road, Matlock Bath, DE4 3PW
☎ Matlock (0629) 584621
Comfortable, spacious Victorian house with views over peaceful surroundings, offering a high standard of accommodation. Near Chatsworth and the Derbyshire Dales.
Bedrooms: 1 single, 2 double & 3 twin.
Bathrooms: 3 private, 1 public.
Bed & breakfast: £21-£30 single, £34-£50 double.
Half board: £27-£41 daily, £176-£258 weekly.
Evening meal 7pm (l.o. 10am).
Credit: Access, Visa.

Temple Hotel M
COMMENDED
Temple Walk, Matlock Bath, DE4 3PG
☎ Matlock (0629) 583911
Fax: 0629 580851

The hotel nestles comfortably amid "Little Switzerland" scenery of picturesque Matlock Bath, overlooking the Vale of the River Derwent from a steep, wooded hillside. All bedrooms en-suite with colour TV.
Bedrooms: 1 single, 7 double & 3 twin, 3 family rooms.
Bathrooms: 14 private.
Bed & breakfast: £39-£46 single, £59-£65 double.
Half board: from £49 daily, from £322 weekly.
Lunch available.
Evening meal 6.30pm (l.o. 10pm).
Parking for 32.
Credit: Access, Visa, Diners, Amex.

MELTON MOWBRAY

Leicestershire
Map ref 4C3

Close to the attractive Vale of Belvoir and famous for its pork pies and Stilton cheese which are the subjects of special displays in the museum. It has a beautiful church with a tower 100 ft high.
Tourist Information Centre ☎ (0664) 69946

Amberley

4 Church Lane, Asfordby, Melton Mowbray, LE14 3RU
☎ (0664) 812314
Modern, ranch-style bungalow with 1 acre of lawns, floodlit gardens and river frontage with fishing. 3 miles west of Melton, tucked away behind a church.
Bedrooms: 1 single, 1 double.
Bathrooms: 1 public.
Bed & breakfast: £13-£16 single, £25-£30 double.
Parking for 6.

Sysonby Knoll Hotel M
COMMENDED

Asfordby Road, Melton Mowbray, LE13 0HP
☎ (0664) 63563
Family owned and run hotel, in its own grounds, offering a cosy bar and restaurant serving table d'hote and a la carte meals. Bar snacks available lunchtime and evening. Overlooks gardens and River Eye.
Bedrooms: 6 single, 11 double & 6 twin, 2 family rooms.

Bathrooms: 25 private, 2 public.
Bed & breakfast: £28-£38.50 single, £42-£49 double.
Lunch available.
Evening meal 7pm (l.o. 9pm).
Parking for 30.
Credit: Access, Visa.

MIDDLETON

Northamptonshire
Map ref 4C3

3m W. Corby

Valley View

3 Camsdale Walk, Middleton, Market Harborough, Leicestershire LE16 8YR
☎ Rockingham (0536) 770874
An elevated, stone built house with panoramic views of the Welland Valley. Within easy distance of Market Harborough and Corby.
Bedrooms: 1 double & 1 twin.
Bathrooms: 1 public.
Bed & breakfast: £12-£14 single, £24-£28 double.
Parking for 2.

MONSAL HEAD

Derbyshire
Map ref 4B2

3m NW. Bakewell

Cliffe House

Monsal Head, Bakewell, DE4 1NL
☎ Great Longstone (062 987) 376
Country house, decorated with care, with splendid views of Monsal Dale and an ideal base for exploring the Peak District. Traditional home cooking.
Bedrooms: 8 double, 2 family rooms.
Bathrooms: 10 private.
Bed & breakfast: £27-£30 single, £38-£44 double.
Half board: £29-£32 daily.
Evening meal 7.30pm (l.o. 10am).
Parking for 12.
Credit: Access, Visa.

Monsal Head Hotel M

Monsal Head, Bakewell, DE4 1NL
☎ Great Longstone (062 987) 250

An ideal centre for a holiday or weekend break in the centre of the Peak District National Park. All bedrooms enjoy excellent views of the countryside, some with a conservatory/balcony directly overlooking the Monsal Dale.
Bedrooms: 6 double & 1 twin, 1 family room.
Bathrooms: 6 private, 2 public.
Bed & breakfast: £29.25-£41.25 single, £39-£55 double.
Half board: £30.25-£38.25 daily, £257.50-£411.75 weekly.
Lunch available.
Evening meal 7pm (l.o. 9.30pm).
Parking for 12.
Credit: Access, Visa.

NEW MILLS

Derbyshire
Map ref 4B2

8m NW. Buxton

Sycamore Inn

Sycamore Road, Birchvale, Via Stockport, Cheshire SK12 5AB
☎ New Mills (0663) 742715 & 747568
Freehouse on the banks of the River Sett. Home-made food, traditional beers, extensive natural play area and barbecue gardens.
Bedrooms: 2 single, 2 double & 2 twin, 1 family room.
Bathrooms: 7 private.
Bed & breakfast: £30-£33 single, £42.50-£48.50 double.
Lunch available.
Evening meal 6.30pm (l.o. 10.30pm).
Parking for 50.
Credit: Access, Visa.

NEWARK

Nottinghamshire
Map ref 4C2

The town has many fine old houses and ancient inns near the large, cobbled market-place. Substantial ruins of the 12th C castle, where King John died, dominate the riverside walk and there are several interesting museums. Sherwood Forest is nearby.
Tourist Information Centre ☎ (0636) 78962

The Appleton Hotel
COMMENDED

73 Appletongate, Newark, NG24 1LN
☎ (0636) 71616

Homely, family-run hotel, 300 yards from the main railway station. Lunches and evening meals available by prior arrangement.
Bedrooms: 4 single, 2 double & 1 twin.
Bathrooms: 7 private.
Bed & breakfast: £28-£39 single, from £45 double.
Half board: from £38 daily.
Lunch available.
Evening meal 7pm (l.o. 7.30pm).
Parking for 7.
Credit: Access, Visa, C.Bl.

The Grange Hotel M
COMMENDED

73 London Road, Newark, NG24 1RZ
☎ (0636) 703399
Attractive red brick Victorian property in a quiet residential area, only a short walk from the historic town centre.
Bedrooms: 2 single, 10 double & 2 twin, 1 family room.
Bathrooms: 15 private.
Bed & breakfast: £39.50-£50 single, £52.50-£65 double.
Half board: £40-£50 daily.
Lunch available.
Evening meal 7pm (l.o. 9pm).
Parking for 9.
Credit: Access, Visa.

South Parade Hotel M

117 Balderton Gate, Newark, NG24 1RY
☎ (0636) 703008
Privately-owned hotel in ideal quiet location. Close to castle, river and market-place. 5 minutes' walk from town centre.
Bedrooms: 6 single, 6 double & 2 twin, 2 family rooms.
Bathrooms: 10 private, 3 public; 1 private shower.
Bed & breakfast: £41.50 single, £56 double.
Half board: £40-£50 daily.
Lunch available.
Evening meal 7pm (l.o. 8.30pm).
Parking for 12.
Credit: Access, Visa, Amex.

The Willow Tree Inn M
Listed

Front Street, Barnby-in-the-Willows, Newark, NG24 2SA
☎ (0636) 626613
Heavily beamed inn in a conservation village surrounded by historic places. Close to the Trent and Witham Fisheries, and Newark, off the A17 and A1.

Continued ▶

NEWARK
Continued

Bedrooms: 1 single, 4 double.
Bathrooms: 2 private,
1 public.
Bed & breakfast: from £16
single, from £25 double.
Lunch available.
Evening meal 7pm.
Parking for 50.
Credit: Access, Visa.

NEWINGTON

Nottinghamshire
Map ref 4C2

2km NE Bawtry

The Olde Malt House Private Guest House
COMMENDED

Newington, Near Bawtry,
Doncaster, DN10 6DJ
☎ Doncaster (0302) 710013
*Newly built high standard bed
and breakfast accommodation,
with the added facility of a
fitted kitchen. Ideally situated
for A1 (5 minutes), M1 and
M18. Major rail networks
north-south are in close
proximity.*
Bedrooms: 1 single, 2 double
& 1 twin, 1 family room.
Bathrooms: 2 private,
1 public; 1 private shower.
Bed & breakfast: £28-£30
single, £38-£40 double.
Half board: £34-£36 daily,
£150 weekly.
Evening meal 6pm (l.o.
midday).
Parking for 5.

NORTHAMPTON

Northamptonshire
Map ref 2C1

A bustling town and a
shoe manufacturing
centre, with excellent
shopping facilities,
several museums and
parks, a theatre and a
concert hall. Several old
churches include 1 of only
4 round churches in
Britain.
*Tourist Information
Centre* ☎ (0604) 22677

Aarandale Regent Hotel & Guest House M

6-8 Royal Terrace, Barrack
Road, Northampton,
NN1 3RF
☎ (0604) 31096

*Small and cosy, family-run
hotel/guesthouse within easy
walking distance of town centre,
bus and train stations. Evening
meals by arrangement only.*
Bedrooms: 4 single, 6 double
& 6 twin, 4 family rooms.
Bathrooms: 5 public.
Bed & breakfast: £18-£22
single, £32-£38 double.
Evening meal 7.30pm (l.o.
9.30pm).
Parking for 14.

Birchfields M
Listed APPROVED

17 Hester Street,
Northampton, NN2 6AP
☎ (0604) 28199
*A small friendly guesthouse off
the M1 exit 15.*
Bedrooms: 1 single, 1 double
& 4 twin.
Bathrooms: 2 public.
Bed & breakfast: £13-£14
single, £26-£28 double.
Half board: £14 daily.

Broomhill Hotel M
COMMENDED

Holdenby Road, Spratton,
Northampton, NN6 8LD
☎ Northampton
(0604) 845959
*A converted Victorian country
house with some splendid
views. As a welcomed guest
you will be offered relaxed, old
fashioned hospitality, while
chef will tempt you with his
interesting and varied menus. 6
miles north of Northampton.*
Bedrooms: 2 single, 3 double
& 7 twin.
Bathrooms: 12 private.
Bed & breakfast: £65-£70
single, £75-£80 double.
Lunch available.
Evening meal 7pm (l.o.
9.30pm).
Parking for 100.
Credit: Access, Visa, Diners,
Amex.

10 Church View
Wootton, Northampton,
NN4 0LJ
☎ (0604) 761626/767040
*Quiet, friendly, family-run
guesthouse, near the M1,
Castle Ashby and Billing
Aquadrome. Ideal for
Collingtree Golf Course and
Turners Musical Merry-go-
round. Lunches and evening
meals are served by prior
arrangement.*
Bedrooms: 1 single, 1 double
& 1 twin.
Bathrooms: 2 public.

Bed & breakfast: £17-£19
single, £34-£36 double.
Half board: £25-£27 daily.
Parking for 6.

Claremont Guest House
Listed

80 St. George's Avenue,
Northampton, NN2 6JF
☎ (0604) 718045
*Small family guesthouse facing
the old racecourse.*
Bedrooms: 6 single.
Bathrooms: 4 public.
Bed & breakfast: from £17.65
single, from £35.25 double.
Parking for 4.

The Coach House M
APPROVED

8-10 East Park Parade,
Northampton, NN1 4LA
☎ (0604) 250981
*Friendly hotel 1 mile north of
the town centre, overlooking a
park. Convenient for shops and
industrial areas.*
Bedrooms: 9 single, 13 double
& 5 twin, 3 family rooms.
Bathrooms: 21 private,
2 public; 7 private showers.
Bed & breakfast: £25-£50
single, £50-£65 double.
Half board: £32-£60 daily.
Lunch available.
Evening meal 7pm (l.o.
9.30pm).
Parking for 14.
Credit: Access, Visa, Diners,
Amex.

Four Seasons Hotel
APPROVED

16/17 East Park Parade,
Kettering Road,
Northampton, NN1 4LE
☎ (0604) 20810
*A private hotel close to
Northampton town centre,
providing a warm and friendly
atmosphere.*
Bedrooms: 13 single, 4 double
& 6 twin, 6 family rooms.
Bathrooms: 29 private
showers.
Bed & breakfast: £15-£25
single, £25-£35 double.
Evening meal 6pm (l.o.
8.45pm).
Parking for 8.
Credit: Access, Visa.

Grand Hotel M
COMMENDED

Gold Street, Northampton,
NN1 1RE
☎ (0604) 250511
Telex 311198 GRAND G

*Centrally located in a busy
market town with many
splendid tourist attractions to
see in the area. Easy access to
London and the south and
Birmingham and the north.*
Bedrooms: 40 single, 9 double
& 12 twin, 1 family room.
Bathrooms: 62 private.
Bed & breakfast: max. £52
single, max. £62 double.
Half board: max. £63 daily.
Lunch available.
Evening meal 6.30pm (l.o.
9.30pm).
Parking for 26.
Credit: Access, Visa, Diners,
Amex.

Holiday Inn Garden Court M

Bedford Road, Northampton,
NN4 0YF
☎ (0604) 22777
Holiday Inn
*A business and leisure hotel,
5 minutes' drive from both the
town centre and the M1,
junction 15.*
Bedrooms: 49 double &
56 twin.
Bathrooms: 105 private.
Bed & breakfast: £47.75-
£68.25 single, £56-£76.50
double.
Half board: £61-£81.50 daily.
Lunch available.
Evening meal 7pm (l.o.
10.15pm).
Parking for 120.
Credit: Access, Visa, Diners,
Amex.

Hollington Guest House M
Listed

22 Abington Grove,
Northampton, NN1 4QW
☎ (0604) 32584
*Comfortable guesthouse, close
to town centre and with easy
access to M1. TV and tea-
making facilities in all rooms.*
Bedrooms: 2 single, 2 double
& 1 twin, 2 family rooms.
Bathrooms: 2 public.
Bed & breakfast: from £16
single, from £25 double.
Evening meal 6pm (l.o. 7pm).
Parking for 6.

Lime Trees Hotel M
COMMENDED

8 Langham Place, Barrack
Road, Northampton,
NN2 6AA
☎ (0604) 32188
Fax (0604) 233012

Beautifully restored, family-run hotel with restaurant, set in a Georgian terrace, with easy access to the motorway.
Bedrooms: 9 single, 9 double & 2 twin, 1 family room.
Bathrooms: 19 private, 2 public.
Bed & breakfast: £33-£50 single, £45-£62 double.
Half board: £40-£65 daily.
Lunch available.
Evening meal 7pm (l.o. 9.30pm).
Parking for 24.
Credit: Access, Visa, Diners, Amex.

Northampton Moat House ♨
COMMENDED
Silver Street, Northampton, NN1 2TA
☎ (0604) 22441 Telex 311142
Queens Moat Houses
Modern town-centre hotel decorated to an executive standard. Banqueting facilities for 5 to 500 persons.
Bedrooms: 15 single, 47 double & 74 twin, 4 family rooms.
Bathrooms: 140 private.
Bed & breakfast: £71-£75 single, £89-£95 double.
Half board: £86-£90 daily.
Lunch available.
Evening meal 5pm (l.o. 10.30pm).
Parking for 200.
Credit: Access, Visa, Diners, Amex.

Plough Hotel
Bridge Street, Northampton, NN1 1PF
☎ (0604) 38401
A recently refurbished, impressive Victorian building restored to old fashioned charm of bygone ages. In the centre of Northampton.
Bedrooms: 15 single, 4 double & 7 twin, 1 family room.
Bathrooms: 19 private, 3 public.
Bed & breakfast: £24.50-£47 single, £34.50-£57 double.
Half board: £32-£55 daily.
Lunch available.
Evening meal 7pm (l.o. 9pm).
Parking for 100.
Credit: Access, Visa, Diners, Amex.

Poplars Hotel
Cross Street, Moulton, Nr. Northampton, NN3 1RZ
☎ (0604) 643983

Personal attention is given at this small country hotel in the heart of Northamptonshire. Within easy reach of many tourist attractions.
Bedrooms: 12 single, 4 double & 1 twin, 4 family rooms.
Bathrooms: 15 private, 2 public.
Bed & breakfast: £18-£34 single, £30-£45 double.
Half board: £28-£44 daily.
Evening meal 6.30pm (l.o. 6.30pm).
Parking for 21.
Credit: Access, Visa.

The Queen Eleanor Hotel ♨
COMMENDED
London Road, Wootton, Northampton, NN4 0JJ
☎ (0604) 762468
A popular hotel which takes its name from a cross erected by Edward I in loving memory of Queen Eleanor. Open plan bar and restaurant. Large garden, patio and children's play area. 1 mile off junction 15 of the M1, on the Northampton ring road.
Bedrooms: 4 double & 11 twin, 4 family rooms.
Bathrooms: 19 private.
Bed & breakfast: max. £55 single, max. £63 double.
Lunch available.
Evening meal 7pm (l.o. 10pm).
Parking for 120.
Credit: Access, Visa, Diners, Amex.

Stakis Country Court Hotel
100 Watering Lane, Collingtree, Northampton, NN4 0XW
☎ (0604) 700666
Stakis
A modern, 2 storey hotel built around a central landscaped courtyard. Extensive leisure facilities. Half board rate based on a minimum 2 night stay.
Bedrooms: 82 single, 54 double & 4 twin, 4 family rooms.
Bathrooms: 144 private.
Bed & breakfast: from £91 single, from £109 double.
Half board: from £46 daily.
Lunch available.
Evening meal 7pm (l.o. 10pm).
Parking for 219.
Credit: Access, Visa, C.Bl., Diners, Amex.

Swallow Hotel ♨
COMMENDED
Eagle Drive, Northampton, NN4 0HW
☎ (0604) 768700 Telex 31562
Swallow
A new hotel incorporating a leisure centre, in a rural setting overlooking a lake and golf-course. Easy access to the motorway.
Bedrooms: 50 single, 16 double & 44 twin, 12 family rooms.
Bathrooms: 122 private.
Bed & breakfast: £27.50-£91.50 single, £55-£109 double.
Lunch available.
Evening meal 7pm (l.o. 10.30pm).
Parking for 166.
Credit: Access, Visa, Diners, Amex.

NOTTINGHAM
Nottinghamshire
Map ref 4C2

Modern city with a wide range of industries including lace. Its castle is now a museum and art gallery with a statue of Robin Hood outside. Many attractions include "The Tales of Robin Hood", with 'flight to Sherwood' experience; the Lace Hall in a converted church; excellent shopping facilities, theatres, museums, Wollaton Hall and the National Water Sports Centre.
Tourist Information Centre ☎ (0602) 470661 or 823558

Cambridge Hotel ♨
APPROVED
63-65 Loughborough Road, West Bridgford, Nottingham, NG2 7LA
☎ (0602) 811036/815927
Friendly atmosphere, close to the city centre, cricket ground, water sports centre and university. Licensed bar and snooker room. All rooms with complimentary video and satellite TV.
Bedrooms: 12 single, 4 double & 4 twin.
Bathrooms: 11 private, 4 public; 3 private showers.
Bed & breakfast: £34-£47 single, £58-£64 double.
Half board: £40-£60 daily, £200-£300 weekly.

Evening meal 6pm (l.o. 9.30pm).
Parking for 30.
Credit: Access, Visa, Diners, Amex.

Clifton Hotel ♨
126 Nottingham Road, Long Eaton, Nottingham, NG10 2BZ
☎ Long Eaton (0602) 734277
Friendly, family-run hotel close to M1, exit 25. 10 minutes from Donington Racecourse, East Midlands Airport, Derby and Nottingham.
Bedrooms: 5 single, 1 double & 2 twin, 2 family rooms.
Bathrooms: 2 private, 2 public.
Bed & breakfast: £18-£28 single, £26-£33 double.
Half board: £24.50-£34.50 daily.
Evening meal 6.30pm (l.o. 5.30pm).
Parking for 25.

The Croft Hotel ♨
Listed APPROVED
6-8 North Road, West Bridgford, Nottingham, NG2 7NH
☎ (0602) 812744
Small, private hotel in a quiet residential area. Close to Trent Bridge, water sports centre and 1.5 miles from city centre.
Bedrooms: 8 single, 4 double & 2 twin, 2 family rooms.
Bathrooms: 5 public.
Bed & breakfast: from £18 single, from £30 double.
Evening meal 6pm (l.o. 8pm).
Parking for 12.

The Gallery Hotel
8-10 Radcliffe Road, West Bridgford, Nottingham, NG2 5FW
☎ (0602) 813651/811346
Close to Trent Bridge cricket ground, Nottingham Forest football ground and National Water Sports Centre and 20 minutes from the city centre.
Bedrooms: 4 single, 4 double & 4 twin, 3 family rooms.
Bathrooms: 4 public; 4 private showers.
Bed & breakfast: £21-£25 single, £34-£38 double.
Half board: £28-£33 daily.
Evening meal 6pm (l.o. 7pm).
Parking for 21.

George Hotel ♨

George Street, Nottingham,
NG1 3BP
☎ (0602) 475641
Telex 378150
ⓒⓇ Friendly
*City centre hotel with an
atmosphere of charm and
character. Although the hotel
has been extensively
modernised, its historic links
with the past have been
carefully retained.*
Bedrooms: 23 single,
20 double & 26 twin, 1 family
room.
Bathrooms: 70 private.
Bed & breakfast: £53.50-
£66.20 single, £66.75-£81.90
double.
Lunch available.
Evening meal 7pm (l.o.
9.15pm).
Credit: Access, Visa, Diners,
Amex.

Grantham Hotel ♨

24-26 Radcliffe Road, West
Bridgford, Nottingham,
NG2 5FW
☎ (0602) 811373
*A family-run hotel offering
modern accommodation in a
comfortable atmosphere.
Convenient for the centre of
Nottingham, Trent Bridge and
the National Water Sports
Centre.*
Bedrooms: 17 single, 2 double
& 5 twin.
Bathrooms: 8 private,
3 public.
Bed & breakfast: £20-£25
single, £37-£40 double.
Half board: £120-£150
weekly.
Parking for 8.
Credit: Access, Visa.

Greenwood Lodge ♨ COMMENDED

Third Avenue, Sherwood
Rise, Nottingham, NG7 6JH
☎ (0602) 621206
*1 mile from city centre. All
rooms en-suite with tea and
coffee facilities, trouser press,
TV, telephone. Car park.*
Bedrooms: 2 double & 2 twin.
Bathrooms: 4 private.
Bed & breakfast: £25-£27.50
single, £35-£38.50 double.

Evening meal 8pm.
Parking for 5.
Credit: Access, Visa.

Holiday Inn Garden Court ♨ COMMENDED

Castle Marina Park,
Nottingham, NG7 1GX
☎ (0602) 500600
ⓒⓇ Holiday Inn
*Situated on the edge of town.
Easily accessible from M1
junction 24. Bistro-style bar
and restaurant.*
Bedrooms: 86 double &
14 twin.
Bathrooms: 100 private.
Bed & breakfast: £47-£66
single, £54-£73 double.
Lunch available.
Evening meal 6.30pm (l.o.
10pm).
Parking for 120.
Credit: Access, Visa, C.Bl.,
Diners, Amex.

Lucieville Hotel ♨

349 Derby Road,
Nottingham, NG7 2DZ
☎ (0602) 787389
*Tudor style hotel close to the
city centre. Fresh flowers and
complimentary wine are in all
the bedrooms. Non-smokers
only, please.*
Bedrooms: 3 single, 3 double
& 2 twin.
Bathrooms: 8 private.
Bed & breakfast: £46-£59.50
single, £50-£75 double.
Lunch available.
Evening meal 7pm (l.o.
9.30pm).
Parking for 12.
Credit: Access, Visa.

The Milford Hotel ♨ APPROVED

Pavilion Road, West
Bridgford, Nottingham,
NG2 5FG
☎ (0602) 811464
*Family-run hotel. Close to the
River Trent, county cricket
ground, National Water Sports
Centre and the city centre.*
Bedrooms: 6 single, 2 double
& 5 twin, 1 family room.
Bathrooms: 4 public.
Bed & breakfast: £18-£20
single, £32-£36 double.
Half board: £24-£26 daily,
£154-£168 weekly.
Evening meal 6pm (l.o. 7pm).

Parking for 14.
Credit: Access, Visa, Diners,
Amex.

P & J Hotel ♨ APPROVED

277 Derby Road, Lenton,
Nottingham, NG7 2DP
☎ (0602) 783998
*3-storey red brick building on a
main road with a car park at
the rear. Half a mile from the
city centre and close to the
Queens Medical Hospital and
University. Direct access to
M1 junction 25.*
Bedrooms: 4 single, 2 double
& 1 twin, 11 family rooms.
Bathrooms: 9 private,
4 public; 2 private showers.
Bed & breakfast: £23-£33
single, £38-£46 double.
Evening meal 6pm (l.o. 8pm).
Parking for 10.
Credit: Access, Visa, Amex.

The Regency House Hotel ♨ COMMENDED

198 Derby Road,
Nottingham, NG7 1NJ
☎ (0602) 474520
*A complete refurbishment has
transformed this Regency
building into a stylish hotel.
500 yards from the city centre.*
Bedrooms: 4 single, 6 twin,
1 family room.
Bathrooms: 11 private.
Bed & breakfast: £25.50-
£27.95 single, £42-£46.90
double.
Half board: £32-£42.50 daily,
£230-£315 weekly.
Lunch available.
Parking for 11.
Credit: Access, Visa, Amex.

Rockaway Private Hotel & Restaurant ♨

Station Road, Beeston,
Nottingham, NG9 2AB
☎ (0602) 224570
*A family run hotel and
restaurant with the personal
touch. Ideal for Nottingham
tennis centre and Nottingham
University, also Boots and
GEC Plessey
Telecommunications.*
Bedrooms: 14 single, 7 double
& 5 twin.
Bathrooms: 19 private,
3 public.
Bed & breakfast: £26.50-
£33.60 single, £42.60-£55
double.

Half board: £33.75-£40.85
daily.
Lunch available.
Evening meal 6pm (l.o.
10pm).
Parking for 13.
Credit: Access, Visa.

St. Andrews Private Hotel ♨ APPROVED

310 Queens Road, Beeston,
Nottingham, NG9 1JA
☎ (0602) 254902
*Friendly, family-run
guesthouse with easy access to
Nottingham city centre, the
university, M1 and East
Midlands International
Airport. Convenient for
Sherwood Forest and
Derbyshire.*
Bedrooms: 4 single, 1 double
& 3 twin, 2 family rooms.
Bathrooms: 1 private,
4 public.
Bed & breakfast: £17.50-£26
single, £28-£36 double.
Half board: £25.50-£32.75
daily.
Evening meal 5.45pm (l.o.
7.30pm).
Parking for 6.

Stakis Nottingham Victoria Hotel ♨

Milton Street, Nottingham,
NG1 3PZ
☎ (0602) 419561 Telex 37401
ⓒⓇ Stakis
*Centrally situated within easy
walking distance of the
Theatre Royal, Nottingham's
many nightlife activities,
shopping centres and the castle.
Half board rate based on a
minimum 2 night stay.*
Bedrooms: 60 single,
67 double & 21 twin,
18 family rooms.
Bathrooms: 166 private.
Bed & breakfast: £79-£90
single, £103-£113 double.
Half board: from £40 daily.
Lunch available.
Evening meal 7pm (l.o.
9.45pm).
Parking for 18.
Credit: Access, Visa, Diners,
Amex.

Tudor Lodge Hotel ♨ APPROVED

400 Nuthall Road,
Nottingham, NG8 5DR
☎ (0602) 781730

Charming Tudor-style house in half an acre of cared for gardens. Cosy, informal atmosphere and friendly, helpful staff. 2.5 miles from M1 junction 26.
Bedrooms: 2 single, 3 double, 2 family rooms.
Bathrooms: 3 private, 2 public; 1 private shower.
Bed & breakfast: £25-£35 single, £35-£50 double.
Parking for 10.
Credit: Access, Visa, Diners, Amex.

OAKHAM

Leicestershire
Map ref 4C3

Pleasant former county town of Rutland has a fine 12th C Great Hall, part of its castle, housing a historic collection of horseshoes. An octagonal Butter Cross stands in the market-place and Rutland County Museum, Rutland Farm Park and Rutland Water are other attractions.
Tourist Information Centre ☎ (0572) 724329

Barnsdale Country Club M

🏆🏆🏆 COMMENDED
Stamford Road, Nr. Oakham, LE15 8AB
☎ (0572) 757901
Set in 60 acres overlooking Rutland Water, offering extensive leisure and sporting facilities and a gourmet restaurant. Self-catering lodges are also available.
Bedrooms: 14 single, 35 double & 8 twin, 2 family rooms.
Bathrooms: 53 private, 3 public.
Bed & breakfast: £58-£72 single, £75-£127 double.
Lunch available.
Evening meal 7pm (l.o. 9.45pm).
Parking for 170.
Credit: Access, Visa, C.Bl., Diners, Amex.

Barnsdale Lodge Hotel M

🏆🏆🏆🏆 COMMENDED
The Avenue, Exton, Nr. Oakham, LE15 8AH
☎ (0572) 724678

A country farmhouse hotel furnished in Edwardian style. On the side of Rutland Water, 2 miles from Oakham.
Bedrooms: 4 single, 5 double & 6 twin, 2 family rooms.
Bathrooms: 17 private.
Bed & breakfast: £46-£58 single, £66-£75 double.
Lunch available.
Evening meal 7pm (l.o. 9.45pm).
Parking for 107.
Credit: Access, Visa, C.Bl., Diners, Amex.

Boultons Country House Hotel M

🏆🏆🏆🏆 COMMENDED
4 Catmos Street, Oakham, LE15 6HW
☎ (0572) 722844
ⓒ Consort
In the former county of Rutland. Unspoilt surroundings with many attractions, including Rutland Water. County-style ambience, pub circa 1604 and intimate restaurant.
Bedrooms: 7 single, 12 double & 4 twin, 2 family rooms.
Bathrooms: 25 private.
Bed & breakfast: £37.50-£50 single, £55-£70 double.
Half board: £40-£55 daily, £225-£315 weekly.
Lunch available.
Evening meal 7pm (l.o. 9.30pm).
Parking for 15.
Credit: Access, Visa, Diners, Amex.

Normanton Park Hotel M

Normanton Park, South Shore, Rutland Water, LE15 8RP
☎ Stamford (0780) 720315
Family-run conversion of a Georgian coach house. Restaurant and coffee lounge open all year. Unique position on the south shore of Rutland Water, 6 miles from Oakham.
Bedrooms: 1 single, 5 double & 5 twin, 5 family rooms.
Bathrooms: 14 private, 1 public.
Bed & breakfast: £46-£50 single, £66-£72.50 double.
Lunch available.
Evening meal 7.30pm (l.o. 9.45pm).
Parking for 100.
Credit: Access, Visa, C.Bl., Diners, Amex.

White Lion Hotel

30 Melton Road, Oakham, LE15 5AR
☎ (0572) 724844
Grade II listed family-run public house at quiet end of Oakham, adjacent to BR station.
Bedrooms: 1 single, 1 double & 1 twin, 1 family room.
Bathrooms: 4 private.
Bed & breakfast: from £30 single, from £40 double.
Lunch available.
Evening meal 6pm (l.o. 9pm).
Parking for 20.

OUNDLE

Northamptonshire
Map ref 3A1

Historic town situated on the River Nene with narrow alleys and courtyards and many stone buildings, including a fine church and historic inns.
Tourist Information Centre ☎ (0832) 274333

Castle Farm Guest House M

Castle Farm, Fotheringhay, Peterborough, PE8 5HZ
☎ Cotterstock (083 26) 200
850-acre mixed farm. An early 19th C stone farmhouse in beautiful surroundings, with lawns running down to the River Nene and adjoining the Fotheringhay Castle site. 2 rooms can be adapted to family rooms. Packed lunches by arrangement.
Bedrooms: 1 single, 1 double & 2 twin, 2 family rooms.
Bathrooms: 5 private, 1 public.
Bed & breakfast: £22-£27.50 single, £33-£43 double.
Half board: £30.50-£36 daily, £213.50-£252 weekly.
Evening meal 7pm.
Parking for 12.

PEAK DISTRICT

See Aldwark, Ashbourne, Ashford-in-the-Water, Bakewell, Bamford, Baslow, Buxton, Castleton, Edale, Glossop, Hartington, Hathersage, Hayfield, Hope, Monsal Head, New Mills, Rowsley.

RADCLIFFE-ON-TRENT

Nottinghamshire
Map ref 4C2

5m E. Nottingham

Yew Trees Hotel

🏆🏆 APPROVED
16 Shelford Road, Radcliffe-on-Trent, Nottingham, NG12 2AG
☎ (0602) 333818
In a village location, close to the shops and to rail and bus services to Nottingham. Also conveniently placed for the National Water Sports Centre.
Bedrooms: 6 single, 1 twin, 1 family room.
Bathrooms: 3 private, 1 public.
Bed & breakfast: £15-£19 single, £29-£35 double.
Half board: £22-£26 daily.
Evening meal 6.30pm (l.o. 4pm).
Parking for 6.

RAGNALL

Nottinghamshire
Map ref 4C2

13m N. Newark-on-Trent

Ragnall House

🏆🏆 APPROVED
Ragnall, Newark, NG22 0UR
☎ Dunham-on-Trent (0777) 228575
Large listed Georgian family house in over an acre of grounds in a small village close to the River Trent. Good local inns and restaurants nearby.
Bedrooms: 1 single, 2 twin, 1 family room.
Bathrooms: 1 private, 1 public; 2 private showers.
Bed & breakfast: £11.50-£13 single, £23-£26 double.
Parking for 8.

> *National Crown ratings were correct at the time of going to press but are subject to change. Please check at the time of booking.*

REDMILE

Leicestershire
Map ref 4C2

8m. W. Grantham
Vale of Belvoir village,
overlooked by the hilltop
castle.

Redmile House Hotel
29 Main Street, Redmile,
Nottinghamshire NG13 0GA
☎ Bottesford (0949) 43086
A Grade II listed Georgian
farmhouse standing in its own
grounds in the centre of
Redmile village. Easy access to
Belvoir Castle. The double
room can be adapted to a
family room if required.
Bedrooms: 2 double & 2 twin,
1 family room.
Bathrooms: 3 private,
1 public.
Bed & breakfast: £16.50-
£18.50 single, £33-£37 double.
Half board: £25-£27 daily,
£161-£175 weekly.
Lunch available.
Evening meal 5.30pm (l.o.
6.30pm).
Parking for 20.

RETFORD

Nottinghamshire
Map ref 4C2

Market town on the River
Idle with a pleasant
market square and
Georgian houses. The
surrounding villages were
the homes and meeting
places of the early Pilgrim
Fathers.
Tourist Information
Centre ☎ (0777) 860780

Elms Hotel
👑👑👑👑 APPROVED
London Road, Retford,
DN22 7DX
☎ (0777) 708957
A 19th C house with extensive
gardens. All bedrooms en-suite
with TV, radio, telephone, tea
and coffee facilities. A la carte
dining, table d'hote menu, bar
meals.
Bedrooms: 1 single, 4 double
& 3 twin, 1 family room.
Bathrooms: 9 private.
Bed & breakfast: £31-£36
single, £41-£46 double.
Half board: £40-£60 daily,
£235-£300 weekly.
Lunch available.
Evening meal 7pm (l.o.
10pm).

Parking for 120.
Credit: Access, Visa, Diners,
Amex.

The Old Plough
👑👑 HIGHLY COMMENDED
Top Street, North Wheatley,
Retford, DN22 9DB
☎ Gainsborough
(0427) 880916
Listed Georgian dwelling
offering accommodation and
home cooked food in a small
village between Retford and
Gainsborough.
Bedrooms: 2 double & 1 twin.
Bathrooms: 3 private.
Bed & breakfast: £22 single,
£44 double.
Half board: £34 daily, £238
weekly.
Evening meal 8pm (l.o. 8pm).
Parking for 4.

West Retford Hotel M
24 North Road, Retford,
DN22 7XG
☎ (0777) 706333 Telex 56143
🅡 Rank
18th C country house located
in extensive grounds. Recently
refurbished and developed, the
hotel now offers an a la carte
restaurant and 3 bars. Ideal
base for touring Sherwood
Forest and the Dukeries.
Bedrooms: 9 double &
11 twin, 37 family rooms.
Bathrooms: 57 private.
Bed & breakfast: £41-£71
single, £62-£86 double.
Lunch available.
Evening meal 7pm (l.o.
10pm).
Parking for 100.
Credit: Access, Visa, Diners,
Amex.

RIPLEY

Derbyshire
Map ref 4B2

10m N. Derby

Hammersmith House Hotel M
👑👑👑
Butterley Lane,
Hammersmith, Ripley,
DE5 3RA
☎ (0773) 742574/745462
Large countryside house,
convenient for the Peak
District National Park and
many stately homes, with good
leisure facilities nearby.

Bedrooms: 2 single, 5 double
& 3 twin, 2 family rooms.
Bathrooms: 12 private,
1 public.
Bed & breakfast: £32-£35
single, £42-£45 double.
Half board: £40.50-£43.50
daily, £245-£305 weekly.
Evening meal 7pm (l.o. 8pm).
Parking for 40.
Credit: Access, Visa.

ROWSLEY

Derbyshire
Map ref 4B2

4m SE. Bakewell
Village at the meeting
point of the Rivers Wye
and Derwent, and on the
edge of the Haddon and
Chatsworth estates. 19th
C water-powered flour
mill, working and open to
visitors, with craft
workshops.

East Lodge Country House Hotel M
👑👑👑👑 COMMENDED
Rowsley, Matlock, DE4 2EF
☎ (0629) 734474
Small, tastefully furnished
country house hotel in 10 acres
of grounds, close to Chatsworth
House and Haddon Hall.
Bedrooms: 3 single, 6 double
& 6 twin.
Bathrooms: 15 private.
Bed & breakfast: £42-£48
single, £65-£78 double.
Half board: £47-£57 daily,
£297-£360 weekly.
Evening meal 7.30pm (l.o.
8.30pm).
Credit: Access, Visa, Amex.

Peacock Hotel M
👑👑👑👑👑 COMMENDED
Rowsley, Matlock, DE4 2EB
☎ Matlock (0629) 733518
Formerly the Dower House to
Haddon Hall (14th-15th C),
the hotel is furnished with
antiques from that era.
Bedrooms: 3 single, 7 double
& 7 twin, 3 family rooms.
Bathrooms: 15 private,
2 public.
Bed & breakfast: £85.20-
£95.20 single, £114.40-
£124.70 double.
Half board: £106.70-£116.70
daily, £746.90-£816.90
weekly.
Lunch available.

Evening meal 7pm (l.o.
9.30pm).
Parking for 50.
Credit: Access, Visa, Diners,
Amex.

SARACENS HEAD

Lincolnshire
Map ref 3A1

2m NW. Holbeach

Whaplode Manor
Saracens Head, Holbeach,
Spalding, PE12 8AZ
☎ Holbeach (0406) 22837
An 18th C Georgian manor
farmhouse in pleasant rural
surroundings, offering a
friendly atmosphere with home
cooking and comfortable
accommodation.
Bedrooms: 3 double & 1 twin,
1 family room.
Bathrooms: 2 private,
2 public; 1 private shower.
Bed & breakfast: from £15.50
single, from £30 double.
Half board: from £22 daily.
Evening meal 7.30pm (l.o
9pm).
Parking for 5.
Credit: Access, Visa.

SHELTON

Nottinghamshire
Map ref 4C2

10m NW. Grantham

Shelton Hall
👑👑👑 COMMENDED
Shelton, Newark, NG23 5JQ
☎ Whatton (0949) 50180
Peaceful country home with
mature grounds near the A1.
Within easy reach of
Nottingham, Grantham and
Newark.
Bedrooms: 1 double & 2 twin.
Bathrooms: 3 private.
Bed & breakfast: £30-£35
single, £50-£60 double.
Half board: £46.50-£60 daily.
Lunch available.
Evening meal 7pm (l.o. 9pm).
Parking for 8.

SHERWOOD FOREST

See Barnby Moor,
Kersall, Laneham,
Mansfield, Ragnall,
Retford, Worksop.

SIBSEY

Lincolnshire
Map ref 3A1

Northlands Post Office

Carrington Road,
Northlands, Sibsey,
PE22 QUA
☎ (0205) 750221
*Family-run guesthouse offering
home-cooked food and a high
standard of accommodation.
7 miles from Boston, on the
Grimsby road.*
Bedrooms: 1 double & 1 twin.
Bathrooms: 1 public.
Bed & breakfast: from £12
single, from £24 double.
Half board: from £16 daily,
from £112 weekly.
Evening meal 6pm (l.o. 8pm).
Parking for 6.

SKEGNESS

Lincolnshire
Map ref 4D2

Famous seaside resort
with 6 miles of sandy
beaches and bracing air.
Its attractions include
swimming pools, bowling
greens, gardens,
Natureland Marine Zoo,
golf-courses and a wide
range of entertainment at
the Embassy Centre. To
the south lies Gibraltar
Point, a large nature
reserve.
*Tourist Information
Centre* ☎ (0754) 764821

The Dovedale

118 Drummond Road,
Skegness, PE25 3EH
☎ (0754) 4656
*Private, detached hotel in a
quiet location yet close to all
amenities.*
Bedrooms: 1 single, 4 double
& 2 twin, 3 family rooms.
Bathrooms: 2 public.
Bed & breakfast: £20-£30
double.
Half board: £13.50-£18.50
daily, £70-£95 weekly.
Evening meal 5.30pm (l.o.
5.30pm).
Parking for 6.

Elmanton ♨

62 Scarborough Avenue,
Skegness, PE25 2TB
☎ (0754) 3616
*Located 50 yards from the
seafront and all amenities.*
Bedrooms: 1 single, 2 double
& 1 twin, 6 family rooms.

Bathrooms: 4 private,
2 public.
Bed & breakfast: £10-£15
single, £20-£30 double.
Half board: £14.50-£19.50
daily, £80-£95 weekly.
Evening meal 6pm.

Grosvenor House Hotel ♨

North Parade, Skegness,
PE25 2TE
☎ (0754) 763376
*The hotel is midway along the
seafront, near the bathing pool,
bowling greens, sun castle, and
the Embassy Conference
Centre.*
Bedrooms: 11 single,
11 double & 5 twin, 10 family
rooms.
Bathrooms: 20 private,
4 public.
Bed & breakfast: £20.75-
£24.50 single, £41.50-£49
double.
Half board: £28.50-£32.60
daily, £185.20-£212.50
weekly.
Lunch available.
Evening meal 6.30pm (l.o.
7.30pm).
Parking for 6.
Open April-October.
Credit: Access, Visa, Diners,
Amex.

Merrydale Guest House ♨

13 Glentworth Crescent,
Skegness, PE25 2TG
☎ (0754) 66485
*Family-run guesthouse with a
warm, friendly atmosphere and
home cooking. In a quiet, yet
central position.*
Bedrooms: 1 single, 6 double
& 2 twin, 2 family rooms.
Bathrooms: 3 public;
3 private showers.
Bed & breakfast: £10-£11
single, £20-£22 double.
Half board: £12-£13.50 daily,
£70-£85 weekly.
Evening meal 5.30pm.
Parking for 4.
Open January, March-
December.

Saxby Hotel ♨
💙 COMMENDED

12 Saxby Avenue, Skegness,
PE25 3LG
☎ (0754) 763905

*Family-run hotel on a corner in
a quiet residential area of
Skegness. 300 yards from
seafront.*
Bedrooms: 2 single, 7 double
& 1 twin, 4 family rooms.
Bathrooms: 4 private,
2 public.
Bed & breakfast: £15-£17
single, £30-£35 double.
Half board: £22.50-£25 daily,
£110-£140 weekly.
Evening meal 6pm (l.o. 6pm).
Parking for 10.
Credit: Access, Visa.

SLEAFORD

Lincolnshire
Map ref 3A1

Market town whose
parish church has one of
the oldest stone spires in
England and particularly
fine tracery round the
windows.
*Tourist Information
Centre* ☎ (0529) 414294

Cross Keys Hotel
💙💙💙 COMMENDED

4 Cross Key Yard, Eastgate,
Sleaford, NG34 7DH
☎ (0529) 305463 & 414495
*A small and friendly totally
renovated hotel, discreetly
positioned in the town centre at
the end of quiet, picturesque
mews.*
Bedrooms: 3 single, 2 double
& 5 twin, 2 family rooms.
Bathrooms: 6 private,
2 public.
Bed & breakfast: £23-£32
single, £34-£43 double.
Lunch available.
Evening meal 7pm (l.o. 8pm).
Parking for 8.
Credit: Access, Visa.

The Lincolnshire Oak Hotel ♨
💙💙💙 COMMENDED

East Road, Sleaford,
NG34 7EQ
☎ (0529) 413807
*Comfortable privately-run
hotel, with restaurant, function
and conference facilities for up
to 140 people. Just off the A17.*
Bedrooms: 5 single, 7 double
& 2 twin.
Bathrooms: 14 private.
Bed & breakfast: £35-£47
single, £45-£65 double.
Evening meal 7pm (l.o. 9pm).
Parking for 50.
Credit: Access, Visa, Amex.

The Mallards Hotel ♨
💙💙💙

6-8 Eastgate, Sleaford,
NG34 7DJ
☎ (0529) 303062
*Grade II listed hotel in the
centre of town, offering a good
restaurant, fine wines and
comfortable, relaxing rooms.*
Bedrooms: 4 single, 5 double
& 2 twin.
Bathrooms: 11 private.
Bed & breakfast: from £39
single, from £49 double.
Lunch available.
Evening meal 7pm (l.o. 9pm).
Parking for 7.
Credit: Access, Visa, Amex.

The Tally Ho Inn ♨

Aswarby, Nr. Sleaford,
NG34 8SA
☎ Culverthorpe (052 95) 205
*200-year-old inn carefully
converted from stables, offers
en-suite bedrooms, real ale, a
small restaurant and log fires
in winter.*
Bedrooms: 2 double & 4 twin.
Bathrooms: 6 private.
Bed & breakfast: £28-£30
single, £42-£48 double.
Half board: £38-£40 daily.
Lunch available.
Evening meal 7pm (l.o.
9.45pm).
Parking for 50.

SOUTH NORMANTON

Derbyshire
Map ref 4C2

Village near the
Nottinghamshire border
and close to Hardwick
Hall, Newstead Abbey
and the National
Tramway Museum at
Crich.

The Swallow Hotel ♨
💙💙💙💙

Carter Lane East, South
Normanton, DE55 2EH
☎ Ripley (0773) 812000
Telex 377264
Ⓒ Swallow
*A modern hotel on the borders
of the Derbyshire Peak
District, Sherwood Forest and
the Dukeries. Leisure facilities
include a spa bath and sunbeds
in addition to those shown in
the symbols.*
Bedrooms: 54 single,
60 double & 44 twin, 3 family
rooms.

Continued ▶

SOUTH NORMANTON
Continued

Bathrooms: 161 private.
Bed & breakfast: £80-£85 single, £98-£120 double.
Half board: from £100 daily.
Lunch available.
Evening meal 7pm (l.o. 10pm).
Parking for 280.
Credit: Access, Visa, Diners, Amex.

♿ ⚡ 📞 ⊡ ♦ 🅿 Ⓥ ✂ 🍴 📺 ⊘ ☕ 🍴 ⚲ ♻ 🏥 SP Ⓣ

SPALDING
Lincolnshire
Map ref 3A1

This Fenland town is famous for its bulbfields which attract visitors from all over the world. A spectacular Flower Parade takes place at the beginning of May each year and the tulips at Springfields show gardens are followed by displays of roses and bedding plants.
Tourist Information Centre ☎ *(0775) 725468*

Cley Hall Hotel M
✿✿✿ COMMENDED
22 High Street, Spalding, PE11 1TX
☎ (0775) 725157
Georgian hotel has river frontage with mature gardens, and a period restaurant, bars and bistro. 500 metres from town centre, 'O' gauge railway in garden.
Bedrooms: 4 single, 3 double & 4 twin.
Bathrooms: 11 private.
Bed & breakfast: £26-£46 single, £38-£49.50 double.
Half board: £35.95-£55.95 daily.
Lunch available.
Evening meal 7pm (l.o. 9.30pm).
Parking for 20.
Credit: Access, Visa, Diners, Amex.

♿ ⚡ 📞 ⊡ ♦ ⚡ Ⓥ 🅿 ⊙ 🍴 ☀ SP 🏥

The Red Lion Hotel M
✿✿ COMMENDED
Market Place, Spalding, PE11 1SU
☎ (0775) 722869
Sympathetically refurbished 18th C town centre hotel offering en-suite accommodation. Real food, real ales and value for money.

Bedrooms: 1 single, 7 double & 7 twin.
Bathrooms: 15 private.
Bed & breakfast: £26-£45 single, £38-£55 double.
Lunch available.
Evening meal 7pm (l.o. 9pm).
Credit: Access, Visa, Diners, Amex.

♿ ⚡ 📞 ⊡ ♦ ♦ Ⓥ 🅿 📺 ●
🌑 ⚲ 🍴 SP 🏥 Ⓣ

STAMFORD
Lincolnshire
Map ref 3A1

Exceptionally beautiful and historic town with many houses of architectural interest, several notable churches and other public buildings all in the local stone. Burghley House, built by William Cecil, is a magnificent Tudor mansion on the edge of the town.
Tourist Information Centre ☎ *(0780) 55611*

Bull & Swan
High Street, St. Martins, Stamford, PE9 2JL
☎ (0780) 63558
Old coaching house on the old A1 in Stamford, offering homely, warm accommodation with beams and open fires.
Bedrooms: 3 double & 1 twin, 3 family rooms.
Bathrooms: 4 private, 1 public.
Bed & breakfast: £27-£31 single, £38-£44 double.
Half board: £36-£40 daily.
Lunch available.
Evening meal 4.15pm (l.o. 10.15pm).
Parking for 16.
Credit: Access, Visa.

♿ ⊙ 📞 ⊡ ♦ Ⓥ ⊞ ⚲ 🍴
🍴 🏥 SP 🏥

THRAPSTON
Northamptonshire
Map ref 3A2

8m SW. Oundle

The 16th C. Woolpack Hotel M
✿✿✿
6 Kettering Road, Islip, Nr. Thrapston, NN14 3JU
☎ Thrapston (080 12) 2578
Overlooking the River Nene, this 16th C inn is in a quiet village.
Bedrooms: 1 double & 12 twin.
Bathrooms: 13 private.

Bed & breakfast: from £38 single, from £50 double.
Lunch available.
Evening meal 6.30pm (l.o. 9.15pm).
Parking for 50.
Credit: Access, Visa.

♿ ⚡ 📞 ⊙ ⊡ ♦ ⚡ ✂ Ⓦ
⚲ 🍴 🍴 SP 🏥

TOWCESTER
Northamptonshire
Map ref 2C1

Town built on the site of a Roman settlement. It has some interesting old buildings, including an inn featured in one of Dickens' novels. The racecourse lies alongside the A5 Watling Street.

Saracens Head Hotel M
219 Watling Street.
Towcester, NN12 7BX
☎ (0327) 50414
Traditional coaching inn, recently completely refurbished and rebuilt to a high standard, serving variety of food and drinks.
Bedrooms: 4 single, 10 double & 6 twin, 2 family rooms.
Bathrooms: 22 private, 2 public.
Bed & breakfast: £60-£65 single, £70-£90 double.
Lunch available.
Evening meal 6.45pm (l.o. 9.30pm).
Parking for 42.
Credit: Access, Visa, C.Bl., Diners, Amex.

♿ ⚡ 📞 ⊡ ♦ Ⓥ ✂ 🅿 📺
⊞ ⚲ 🍴 🍴 SP 🏥

UPPINGHAM
Leicestershire
Map ref 4C3

Quiet market town dominated by its famous public school which was founded in 1584. It has many stone houses and is surrounded by attractive countryside.

Crown Hotel M
✿✿✿✿
High Street East, Uppingham, Oakham, LE15 9PY
☎ (0572) 822302
17th C listed building near Rutland Water. Trout and coarse fishing are available nearby.
Bedrooms: 2 single, 3 double & 1 twin, 1 family room.
Bathrooms: 7 private.
Bed & breakfast: £36 single, £48 double.

Lunch available.
Evening meal 7pm (l.o. 9pm).
Parking for 20.
Credit: Access, Visa.

♿ ⚡ 📞 ⊡ ♦ Ⓥ ⚡ 🍴 ⊞ ⚲
🍴 🏥 🏥

Garden Hotel M
✿✿✿✿ COMMENDED
High Street West, Uppingham, Oakham, LE15 9QD
☎ (0572) 822352
Historic homely hotel with secluded walled garden. Restaurant open daily for all meals, specialising in traditional home-made British cuisine. Interesting, sensibly-priced wine list.
Bedrooms: 3 single, 4 double & 3 twin, 1 family room.
Bathrooms: 10 private, 1 public.
Bed & breakfast: £41 single, £52 double.
Half board: from £55 daily.
Lunch available.
Evening meal 7.30pm (l.o. 9pm).
Credit: Access, Visa, Amex.

♿ ⚡ ⊙ 📞 ♦ Ⓥ 🅿 📺
⊞ ⚲ 🍴 🏥 SP

Rutland House
✿✿
61 High Street East, Uppingham, Oakham, LE15 3PY
☎ (0572) 822497
Centrally located in ancient Uppingham, this small family-run hotel has bedrooms individually designed to complement its Victorian architecture. The aim is to offer stylish accommodation and value for money.
Bedrooms: 2 single, 1 double & 1 twin.
Bathrooms: 4 private.
Bed & breakfast: £27 single, £37 double.
Parking for 3.

♿ ⚡ ⊙ 📞 ⚡ ⋓ ♦ Ⓥ ⊞
⚲ ♻ 🏥

WEEDON
Northamptonshire
Map ref 2C1

Crossroads Hotel M
✿✿✿✿ COMMENDED
High Street, Weedon, Northampton, NN7 4PX
☎ (0327) 40354 Telex 312311
Ⓑ Best Western
Privately-owned hotel at the junction of the A5 and A45, 3 miles from M1 junction 16. Full conference and dining facilities in character surroundings. Facilities include 2 rooms for the physically disabled.

Bedrooms: 5 single, 18 double
& 20 twin, 5 family rooms.
Bathrooms: 48 private.
Bed & breakfast: £40-£75
single, £50-£90 double.
Half board: £50-£95 daily.
Lunch available.
Evening meal 6pm (l.o.
10pm).
Parking for 100.
Credit: Access, Visa, Diners,
Amex.

Globe Hotel ⚑
⚑ ⚑ ⚑ COMMENDED

High Street, Weedon,
Northampton, NN7 4QD
☎ (0327) 40336
*17th C countryside inn with a
Royal Charter. Old world
atmosphere and freehouse
hospitality with English
cooking.*
Bedrooms: 3 single, 5 double
& 5 twin, 2 family rooms.
Bathrooms: 15 private.
Bed & breakfast: £35-£45
single, £39.50-£55 double.
Half board: £32-£38 daily.
Lunch available.
Evening meal 11am (l.o.
10pm).
Parking for 40.
Credit: Access, Visa, Diners,
Amex.

WELLINGBOROUGH

Northamptonshire
Map ref 3A2

Manufacturing town,
mentioned in the
Domesday Book, with
some old buildings and
inns, in one of which
Cromwell stayed on his
way to Naseby. It has
attractive gardens in the
centre of the town and 2
interesting churches.
*Tourist Information
Centre* ☎ (0933) 228101

Columbia Hotel
19 Northampton Road,
Wellingborough, NN8 3HG
☎ (0933) 229333
*Family-run hotel offering a
friendly and personal service,
half a mile from centre of
thriving market town.*
Bedrooms: 7 single, 14 double
& 7 twin, 1 family room.
Bathrooms: 29 private.
Bed & breakfast: £30-£48
single, £45-£58 double.
Half board: £36.25-£58.75
daily.
Lunch available.

Evening meal 6.30pm (l.o.
9.30pm).
Parking for 18.
Credit: Access, Visa, Amex.

High View Hotel ⚑
⚑ ⚑ COMMENDED

156 Midland Road,
Wellingborough, NN8 1NG
☎ (0933) 278733
*Attractive Victorian building
with a pleasant garden. In a
quiet area near the town centre,
station and trading estates.*
Bedrooms: 6 single, 4 double
& 6 twin, 1 family room.
Bathrooms: 14 private,
1 public.
Bed & breakfast: £24-£44
single, £34-£50 double.
Lunch available.
Evening meal 6.30pm (l.o.
8.30pm).
Parking for 9.
Credit: Access, Visa, Diners,
Amex.

Oak House Private
Hotel ⚑
⚑ ⚑ ⚑ APPROVED

9 Broad Green,
Wellingborough, NN8 4LE
☎ (0933) 271133
*Small, homely hotel with a
comfortable atmosphere, on the
edge of the town centre.
Double-glazed. Enclosed car
park.*
Bedrooms: 5 single, 5 double
& 6 twin.
Bathrooms: 15 private;
1 private shower.
Bed & breakfast: £28-£32
single, from £42 double.
Half board: £29.50-£40.50
daily.
Evening meal 6.15pm (l.o.
midday).
Parking for 9.
Credit: Access, Visa.

WEST HADDON

Northamptonshire
Map ref 4C3

7m NE. Daventry

Pytchley Hotel ⚑
⚑ ⚑ ⚑ COMMENDED

High Street, West Haddon,
Northampton, NN6 7AP
☎ (0788) 510426
*Georgian building in centre of
village, offering English and
European cuisine. Close to
many large towns and places of
interest such as Althorp,
Holdenby and Silverstone.*

Bedrooms: 4 single, 3 double
& 7 twin, 3 family rooms.
Bathrooms: 17 private.
Bed & breakfast: £45-£50
single, £55-£65 double.
Lunch available.
Evening meal 7pm (l.o.
10.30pm).
Parking for 60.
Credit: Access, Visa, Diners,
Amex.

WOODHALL SPA

Lincolnshire
Map ref 4D2

Attractive town which was
formerly a spa. It has
excellent sporting
facilities with a
championship golf-course
and is surrounded by pine
woods.

Claremont Guest House
⚑ ⚑

9-11 Witham Road,
Woodhall Spa, LN10 6RW
☎ (0526) 52000
*Family-run guesthouse within
easy reach of the town's
sporting and leisure facilities.
We offer personal service and a
friendly atmosphere. Evening
meal by prior request only.*
Bedrooms: 2 single, 1 double
& 4 twin, 1 family room.
Bathrooms: 2 public.
Bed & breakfast: max. £17.50
single, max. £30 double.
Lunch available.
Parking for 5.

The Golf Hotel ⚑
The Broadway, Woodhall
Spa, LN10 6SG
☎ (0526) 53535 Telex 56448
Ⓒ Principal
*Set in acres of gardens, near
the famous Woodhall Spa golf-
course and a short drive from
historic city of Lincoln.
Completely refurbished.*
Bedrooms: 6 single, 17 double
& 27 twin.
Bathrooms: 50 private.
Bed & breakfast: from £67
single, from £89 double.
Half board: from £53.50
daily.
Lunch available.
Evening meal 7.30pm (l.o.
9.30pm).
Parking for 100.
Credit: Access, Visa, Diners,
Amex.

Oglee Guest House
⚑ ⚑ ⚑ APPROVED

16 Stanhope Avenue,
Woodhall Spa, LN10 6SP
☎ (0526) 53512
*Privately-run guesthouse in a
tree-lined avenue in this pretty,
wooded town. Off street
parking.*
Bedrooms: 1 double & 2 twin,
2 family rooms.
Bathrooms: 2 private,
2 public.
Bed & breakfast: £16-£22
single, £30-£36 double.
Half board: £24-£31 daily.
Evening meal 8pm.
Parking for 6.
Credit: Access, Visa.

WORKSOP

Nottinghamshire
Map ref 4C2

Market town close to the
Dukeries, where a
number of ducal families
had their estates, some of
which, like Clumber Park,
may be visited. The upper
room of the 14th C
gatehouse of the priory
housed the country's first
elementary school in
1628.
*Tourist Information
Centre* ☎ (0909) 501148

Clumber Park Hotel
Clumber Park, Worksop,
S80 3PA
☎ Mansfield (0623) 835333
Telex 378527
Ⓒ Lansbury
*Newly refurbished hotel
offering traditional comfort
and character. Adjacent to
Clumber Park, close to
Sherwood Forest and Rufford
Abbey. Easily accessible from
A1 via A614 towards
Nottingham.*
Bedrooms: 2 single, 21 double
& 24 twin, 1 family room.
Bathrooms: 48 private,
2 public.
Bed & breakfast: £32-£68
single, £64-£80 double.
Half board: £38-£45 daily.
Lunch available.
Evening meal 7pm (l.o.
10pm).
Parking for 240.
Credit: Access, Visa, C.Bl.,
Diners, Amex.

Lindrick Lodge Hotel
The Green, Carlton-in-
Lindrick, Worksop, S81 9AB
☎ (0909) 731649
*Small, family-run hotel in
pleasant surroundings, offering
a friendly service. Restaurant
with extensive wine list.*
Bedrooms: 2 single, 1 double
& 2 twin.
Bathrooms: 5 private.
Bed & breakfast: £40 single,
£50 double.
Evening meal 6pm (l.o.
10pm).
Parking for 25.
Credit: Access, Visa, Amex.
ॐ ℄ ⌨ ♥ ⬚ Ⓥ ◑ ▦ ☎
✕ ⋈

Sherwood Guest House M
☆☆ APPROVED
57 Carlton Road, Worksop,
S80 1PP
☎ (0909) 474209 & 478214
*In Robin Hood country, near
M1 and A1 and close to
station and town centre.
Comfortable rooms, recently
double glazed.*
Bedrooms: 1 single, 5 twin,
1 family room.
Bathrooms: 2 private,
2 public.
Bed & breakfast: £15-£17.50
single, £30-£35 double.
ॐ ♨ ⊕ ⌨ ♥ ⬚ 🛗 ☐ Ⓥ ✕
⌨ Ⓣ ▦ ⊿ ⋈ GAP

---

*Individual proprietors have supplied all
details of accommodation. Although we
do check for accuracy, we advise you to
confirm prices and other information at
the time of booking.*

Key to symbols

*Information about many of the services
and facilities at establishments listed in
this guide is given in the form of
symbols. The key to these symbols is
inside the back cover flap. You may find
it helpful to keep the flap open when
referring to the entry listings.*

THE CROWN IS YOUR SURE SIGN

OF WHERE TO STAY

HOTELS, GUESTHOUSES, INNS, B&Bs & FARMHOUSES

Throughout Britain, the tourist boards now inspect over 17,000 hotels, guesthouses, inns, B&Bs and farmhouses, every year, to help you find the ones that suit you best.

THE CLASSIFICATIONS: **'Listed'**, and then **ONE to FIVE CROWN,** tell you the range of facilities and services you can expect. The more Crowns, the wider the range.

THE GRADES: **APPROVED, COMMENDED and HIGHLY COMMENDED,** where they appear, indicate the quality standard provided. If no grade is shown, you can still expect a high standard of cleanliness.

Every classified place to stay has a Fire Certificate, where this is required under the Fire Precautions Act, and all carry Public Liability Insurance.

'Listed': Clean and comfortable accommodation, but the range of facilities and services may be limited.

ONE CROWN: Accommodation with additional facilities, including washbasins in all bedrooms, a lounge and use of a phone.

TWO CROWN: A wider range of facilities and services, including morning tea and calls, bedside lights, colour TV in lounge or bedrooms, assistance with luggage.

THREE CROWN: At least one-third of the bedrooms with ensuite WC and bath or shower, plus easy chair, full length mirror. Shoe cleaning facilities and hairdryers available. Hot evening meals available.

FOUR CROWN: At least three-quarters of the bedrooms with ensuite WC and bath/shower plus colour TV, radio and phone, 24-hour access and lounge service until midnight. Last orders for meals 8.30 pm or later.

FIVE CROWN: All bedrooms having WC, bath and shower ensuite, plus a wide range of facilities and services, including room service, all-night lounge service and laundry service. Restaurant open for breakfast, lunch and dinner.

Every Crown classified place to stay is likely to provide some of the facilities and services of a higher classification. More information available from any Tourist Information Centre.

We've checked them out before you check in!

ACCESSIBILITY IS THE KEY *to this region's success as a touring and holiday destination. Spliced by the M1, the M4 and the newly-completed M40, what was once a playground for Londoners is now for everyone. Vast tracks of woodland, undulating downs and miles of rivers and canals offer endless scope for leisure and pleasure pursuits. Beautiful Oxford (the city of dreaming spires), St. Albans (Roman Verulamium) and very Royal Windsor will appeal to seekers after history and heritage. And for everyone there are the myriad towns and villages with cosy pubs, quaint teashops and fine restaurants.*

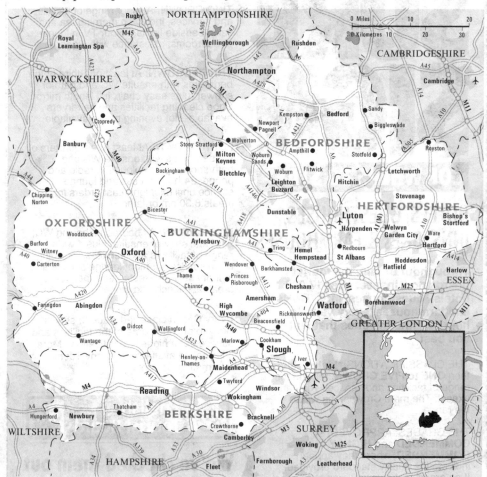

PLEASE REFER TO THE COLOUR MAPS AT THE BACK OF THIS GUIDE FOR ALL PLACES WITH ACCOMMODATION LISTINGS.

WHERE TO GO, WHAT TO SEE

Ashmolean Museum
Beaumont Street, Oxford,
Oxfordshire OX1 2PH
☎ Oxford (0865) 278000
Some of the greatest art and archaeological treasures in the country.

Beale Bird Park
The Child-Beale Wildlife Trust,
Church Farm, Lower Basildon,
Reading, Berkshire RG8 9NH
☎ Upper Basildon (0491) 671325
Established 35 years ago as the Child-Beale Wildlife Trust, park features wildfowl, pheasants, highland cattle, rare sheep, llamas, pets' corner. Narrow-gauge railway.

Bekonscot Model Village
Warwick Road, Beaconsfield,
Buckinghamshire HP9 2PZ
☎ Beaconsfield (0494) 672919
A complete 1930s model village, with zoo, cinema, minster, cricket match, 1,200 inhabitants, model railway.

Blenheim Palace
Woodstock, Oxfordshire
OX7 1PS
☎ Woodstock (0993) 811325
Birthplace of Sir Winston Churchill. Architecture by Vanburgh, park by Capability Brown. Bronzes, tapestries, furniture, paintings, adventure playground, butterfly house, plant centre, maze.

Bodleian Library
Broad Street, Oxford,
Oxfordshire OX1 3BG
☎ Oxford (0865) 277165
Early books and manuscript works. Guided tours of the Divinity School, Convocation House and Duke Humphrey's library. No children under 14 please.

Broughton Castle
Banbury, Oxfordshire
OX15 5EB
☎ Banbury (0295) 262624

Blenheim Palace — birthplace of Sir Winston Churchill

Medieval moated house built in 1300 and enlarged between 1550 — 1600. Home of Lord and Lady Saye and Sele and family home for 600 years. Civil War connections.

Chiltern Open Air Museum
Newland Park, Gorelands
Lane, Chalfont St. Giles,
Buckinghamshire HP8 4AD
☎ Chalfont St. Giles (024 07) 71117
Historic Chiltern buildings rescued from demolition and re-erected. Displays of farm machinery and tools.

Cotswold Wildlife Park
Bradwell Grove, Burford,
Oxfordshire OX8 4JW
☎ Burford (0993) 823006
Tropical house, aquarium, reptile house, butterfly/insect house, 200 acres of garden and woodland, many wild animals, brass rubbing centre, railway, shop.

Courage Shire Horse Centre
Cherry Garden Lane,
Maidenhead Thicket,
Maidenhead, Berkshire
SL6 3QD
☎ Littlewick Green (062 882) 4848

Home of Courage prize-winning shire horses. Display of harness and brasses, farrier's workshop, audio-visual, small animal/bird area, play area, tea room.

Didcot Railway Centre
Great Western Society, Didcot,
Oxfordshire OX11 7NJ
☎ Didcot (0235) 817200
Living museum re-creating the golden age of the Great Western Railway. Steam locomotives and trains, engine shed, small relics museum.

Hatfield House
Hatfield, Hertfordshire
AL9 5NQ
☎ Hatfield (0707) 262823
Jacobean house built in 1611 and old palace built in 1497. Famous paintings, fine furniture and possessions of Queen Elizabeth I. Extensive park and gardens.

The Herb Farm
Lea Meadow, Peppard Road,
Sonning Common, Reading,
Berkshire RG4 9NJ
☎ Kidmore End (0734) 724220
Herb garden including River of Thyme, Herb Wheel, formal garden and informal borders. Hundreds of herbs and scented plants. Restored 15th C barn.

Knebworth House, Gardens and Park
Knebworth, Hertfordshire
SG3 6PY
☎ Stevenage (0438) 812661
Tudor manor house, refashioned in 19th C by Bulwer-Lytton. Fine collection of manuscripts, portraits. Jacobean banqueting hall, adventure playground, gift shop.

Leighton Buzzard Railway
Page's Park Station, Billington Road, Leighton Buzzard, Bedfordshire LU7 8TN
☎ Leighton Buzzard (0525) 373888
Preserved industrial railway, with steam locomotives from India, French Cameroons. Diesel collection. 3-mile 2ft gauge railway with sharp bends and gradients.

Luton Hoo – The Wernher Collection
Luton, Bedfordshire LU1 3TQ
☎ Luton (0582) 22955
Historic house built in 1767, with paintings, tapestries and porcelain. Jewellery by Carl Faberge, mementoes of the Russian Imperial family.

Mapledurham House
Mapledurham, Reading, Berkshire RG4 7TR
☎ Reading (0734) 723350
Elizabethan mansion on banks of River Thames. Interesting collection of paintings and family portraits. Oak staircase, moulded ceilings, operational 15th C watermill.

Museum of St. Albans
Hatfield Road, St. Albans, Hertfordshire AL1 3RR
☎ St. Albans (0727) 56679
Purpose-built museum of 1898. Craft tools and workshops, local and natural history. Story of St. Albans from Roman times to present.

The Oxford Story
6 Broad Street, Oxford, Oxfordshire OX1 3AJ
☎ Oxford (0865) 728822
Heritage centre depicting 8 centuries of university history in

A 1929 Parnall Elf at the Shuttleworth Collection

sights, sounds, personalities and smells. Visitors are transported on moving desks.

Royalty and Empire Exhibition
Windsor and Eton Central Station, Thames Street, Windsor, Berkshire SL4 1PJ
☎ Windsor (0753) 857837
Restored GWR station built in 1897 for Queen Victoria's Diamond Jubilee. Theatre show "60 Glorious Years" with animated figures of the period.

Sheldonian Theatre
Broad Street, Oxford, Oxfordshire OX1 3AZ
☎ Oxford (0865) 277299
Built in 1663, one of Sir Christopher Wren's earliest works. Principal assembly hall for the university and venue for important ceremonies.

Shuttleworth Collection
Old Warden Aerodrome, Biggleswade, Bedfordshire SG18 9ER
☎ Northill (076 727) 288
Unique historic collection of genuine veteran aircraft from 1909 Bleriot to 1942 Spitfire, all in flying condition. Cars dating from 1898 Panhard.

Stratfield Saye House
Stratfield Saye, Reading, Berkshire RG7 2BT
☎ Basingstoke (0256) 882882

House built in 1630. Displays many personal possessions of the Iron Duke, including funeral hearse. Gardens and pleasure grounds.

The Swiss Garden
Biggleswade Road, Old Warden, Biggleswade, Bedfordshire
☎ Biggleswade (076 727) 666
Attractive garden dating from the 19th C and taking its name from the tiny Swiss thatched cottage in the centre.

University of Oxford Botanic Garden
Rose Lane, Oxford, Oxfordshire OX1 4AX
☎ Oxford (0865) 276920
Over 8,000 species of plant in garden and greenhouses, plus herbaceous borders, rock and bog gardens.

Waterperry Gardens
Waterperry, Wheatley, Oxfordshire OX9 1JZ
☎ Kingston Blount (0844) 339254
Ornamental gardens covering 6 acres of the 38-acre 18th C Waterperry House estate. Saxon village church, garden shop and tea shop.

Wellington Country Park
Riseley, Reading, Berkshire RG7 1SP
☎ Heckfield (0734) 326444
500-acre country park with

*National Dairy Museum.
Miniature steam railway, crazy
golf, children's farm and
playground, windsurfing, boating,
nature trails, deer park, fishing.*

Whipsnade Wild Animal Park
Dunstable, Bedfordshire
LU6 2LF
☎ Whipsnade (0582) 872171
*Over 2,000 animals (200
species) in 500-acre beautiful
parkland setting. Birds of prey,
children's zoo, steam railway,
discovery centre.*

Windsor Castle
Windsor, Berkshire SL4 1NT
☎ Windsor (0753) 868286
*Official residence of HM the
Queen and royal residence for
9 centuries. State apartments,
Queen Mary's dolls' house,
exhibition of the Queen's
presents, carriages.*

Windsor Safari Park
Winkfield Road, Windsor,
Berkshire SL4 4AY
☎ Windsor (0753) 830886
*African theme park with drive-
through game reserves and
"African Adventure". Safari
road trains and funicular railway
pass the elephant gardens,
seaworld and bird display.*

Woburn Abbey
Woburn, Bedfordshire
MK43 0TP
☎ Woburn (0525) 290666

*18th C Palladian mansion.
European and oriental porcelain,
fine English silver, French and
English furniture.*

Woodside Farm and Wild Fowl Park
Mancroft Road, Slip End,
Luton, Bedfordshire LU1 4DJ
☎ Luton (0582) 841044
*6-acre park with farm shop,
poultry centre, arts and crafts,
wildfowl collection, rare breeds
centre, blacksmith, children's
play area, coffee shop.*

MAKE A DATE FOR...

Milton Keynes Garden Show
Milton Keynes Bowl, Watling
Street, Milton Keynes,
Buckinghamshire
2 – 4 May

Newbury Spring Festival
Various venues, Newbury,
Berkshire
2 – 16 May

50th Royal Windsor Horse Show
Home Park, Windsor,
Berkshire
13 – 17 May

National Patchwork Championships
Hatfield House, Hatfield,
Hertfordshire
4 – 7 June

Horse racing – Royal Ascot
Ascot Racecourse, Ascot,
Berkshire
16 – 19 June

Henley Royal Regatta
Henley-on-Thames, Oxfordshire
1 – 5 July

Henley Festival of Music and the Arts
Henley-on-Thames, Oxfordshire
8 – 11 July

Reading Rock Festival
Littlejohn's Farm, Cow Lane,
Reading, Berkshire
28 – 30 August

National Carriage Driving Championships
Windsor Great Park, Windsor,
Berkshire
29 – 31 August

Blenheim Audi International Horse Trials
Blenheim Palace, Woodstock,
Oxfordshire
24 – 27 September

FIND OUT MORE

Further information about
holidays and attractions in the
Thames & Chilterns region is
available from:
Thames & Chilterns Tourist Board
The Mount House, Church
Green, Witney, Oxfordshire
OX8 6DZ
☎ (0993) 778800

These publications are available
free from the Thames &
Chilterns Tourist Board:
A Cottage in the Country
(Self-Catering Holidays)

Events in the Thames & Chilterns

*Historic Houses in the Thames
& Chilterns*

*Gardens in the Thames &
Chilterns*

Also available are:
*Where to Go in the Thames &
Chilterns* £1.50

*A Day Out of London Official
Tourist Map* £2.95

Welcome to Oxford 50p

Welcome to Henley 20p

Big cats at Whipsnade Wild Animal Park and Windsor Safari Park

Places to stay

ACCOMMODATION ENTRIES *in this regional section are listed in alphabetical order of place name, and then in alphabetical order of establishment.*

THE MAP REFERENCES *refer to the colour maps towards the end of the guide. The first figure is the map number; the letter and figure which follow indicate the grid reference on the map.*

THE SYMBOLS *at the end of each accommodation entry give information about services and facilities. A 'key' to these symbols is inside the back cover flap, which can be kept open for easy reference.*

ABINGDON
Oxfordshire
Map ref 2C1

6m S. Oxford
Attractive former county town on River Thames with many interesting buildings, including 17th C County Hall, now a museum, in the market-place and the remains of an abbey.
Tourist Information Centre ☎ *(0235) 522711*

Abingdon Lodge Hotel M
👑👑👑👑
Marcham Rd., Abingdon, OX14 1TZ
☎ (0235) 553456
Telex 837750
CR Consort
Modern hotel with restaurant and 7 function rooms. On the A34/A415 junction into Abingdon, 5 miles from Oxford.
Bedrooms: 32 double & 31 twin.
Bathrooms: 63 private.
Bed & breakfast: £45-£76 single, £58-£82 double.
Half board: £40-£86.50 daily, £280-£366 weekly.
Lunch available.
Evening meal 7pm (l.o. 10pm).
Parking for 85.
Credit: Access, Visa, Diners, Amex.
⏱️🍳📞📱📺🛗📻 ⬤ 🖥️ ⬛🍽️✖️ SP T

Crown and Thistle Hotel M
👑👑 COMMENDED
Bridge St., Abingdon, OX14 3HS
☎ (0235) 522556
Lovely old coaching inn, which is a listed building, with an attractive cobbled courtyard. Dating from around 1605, its name signifies the union of England and Scotland by James I. Close to the town centre and River Thames.
Bedrooms: 5 single, 9 double & 4 twin, 3 family rooms.
Bathrooms: 21 private.
Bed & breakfast: £45-£56 single, £73-£79 double.
Lunch available.
Evening meal 6pm (l.o. 10.30pm).
Parking for 36.
Credit: Access, Visa, Diners, Amex.
⏱️🍳📞⬤📱📺🛗 ⬤ 🖥️⬛🍽️✖️ SP 📻

Knowl Hotel
52 Stert St., Abingdon, OX14 3JU
☎ (0235) 554661
Recently refurbished hotel retaining many historic features, near town centre. Plenty of parking nearby. Large restaurant available for functions. Outside catering service. Conferences.
Bedrooms: 3 single, 7 double & 7 twin, 1 family room.
Bathrooms: 14 private, 2 public.
Bed & breakfast: £26-£40 single, £38-£50 double.
Half board: £32-£50 daily.
Lunch available.

Evening meal 6.30pm (l.o. 9pm).
Parking for 6.
Credit: Access, Visa.
⏱️🍳📞📱⬤📺 V ✖️ 📻 📺 🖥️⬛🍽️🛗 OAP 📻 SP 📻

Thame Lane House M
🏠
1 Thame Lane, Culham, Abingdon, OX14 3DS
☎ (0235) 524177
Large, comfortable house set in wooded gardens. Off the A415 by the European School, Culham. 16-cover licensed restaurant offering French cuisine.
Bedrooms: 2 single, 1 double & 1 twin, 1 family room.
Bathrooms: 1 private, 2 public.
Bed & breakfast: £25-£38 single, £40-£52 double.
Half board: £35-£58 daily.
Evening meal 7pm (l.o. 8.30pm).
Parking for 7.
Credit: Access, Visa.
⏱️3📱⬤ 📺 V 🖥️⬛ ❄️ ✖️ 📻

> *National Crown ratings were correct at the time of going to press but are subject to change. Please check at the time of booking.*

ASCOT
Berkshire
Map ref 2C2

Small country town famous for its racecourse which was founded by Queen Anne. The race meeting each June is attended by the Royal Family.

Brockenhurst Hotel M
👑👑👑 COMMENDED
Brockenhurst Rd., South Ascot, SL5 9HA
☎ (0344) 21912
Fax (0344) 873252
Elegant Edwardian house, situated near shops and station. Licensed restaurant, separate lounge and bar.
Bedrooms: 7 double, 3 family rooms.
Bathrooms: 10 private.
Bed & breakfast: £45-£85 single, £60-£100 double.
Half board: £55-£120 daily, £385-£770 weekly.
Lunch available.
Evening meal 6pm (l.o. 9.30pm).
Parking for 14.
Credit: Access, Visa, Diners, Amex.
⏱️📞⬤📱⬤ 📺 V 📻 🖥️ ⬛🍽️❄️✖️ 📻 ⬤ T

Ennis Lodge
Winkfield Rd., Ascot, SL5 7EX
☎ (0344) 21009

> *Half board prices shown are per person but in some cases may be based on double/twin occupancy.*

Situated in the centre of Ascot, this private guesthouse offers the businessman and visitors to the area easy access to airports, railway stations, Windsor, Bracknell and motorways. High quality rooms with all facilities.
Bedrooms: 4 twin.
Bathrooms: 2 private,
1 public.
Bed & breakfast: £28-£35 single, £32-£45 double.
Parking for 5.
🛇 ❏ ♥ ㉾ ♨ 🛏 ᴤᴘ

Highclere Hotel ⋒
☸☸☸ COMMENDED
Kings Rd., Sunninghill,
Ascot, SL5 9AD
☎ (0344) 25220
Fax (0344) 872528
Small Edwardian private hotel, 10 minutes from Windsor Castle and Wentworth.
Bedrooms: 1 single, 6 double & 4 twin.
Bathrooms: 11 private,
3 public.
Bed & breakfast: £38-£60 single, £48-£75 double.
Half board: £42-£53 daily.
Lunch available.
Evening meal 6pm (l.o.
9.30pm).
Parking for 14.
Credit: Access, Visa, Amex.
🛇 ♨ ☏ ⊙ ❏ ♥ Ⅵ ᴤ ⊡
▦ ᴧ ⊥ ⟡ ❖ 🛉 ⚲ ᴤᴘ
🈁

AYLESBURY
Buckinghamshire
Map ref 2C1

Historic county town in the Vale of Aylesbury. The cobbled market square has a Victorian clock tower and the 15th C King's Head Inn (National Trust). Interesting county museum and 13th C parish church.
Tourist Information Centre ☎ (0296) 382308

The Bell ⋒
Market Square, Aylesbury,
HP20 1TX
☎ (0296) 89835
A small comfortable inn in the market square.
Bedrooms: 6 single, 4 double & 7 twin.
Bathrooms: 17 private.
Bed & breakfast: from £60 single, from £65 double.
Lunch available.
Evening meal 7pm (l.o.
9.30pm).
Credit: Access, Visa, Diners, Amex.
🛇 ☏ ⊙ ❏ ♥ 🛉 Ⅵ ᴤ ▦
ᴧ 🛉 ⚲ ᴤᴘ ⊡

Five Bells Hotel
40 Main St., Weston Turville,
Aylesbury, HP22 5RW
☎ Aylesbury (0296) 613131
A country hotel within easy reach of the Chiltern Hills and many other places of historic interest. In village 3 miles south of Aylesbury.
Bedrooms: 5 single, 10 double & 3 twin.
Bathrooms: 18 private.
Bed & breakfast: £31-£51 single, £41-£61 double.
Half board: £42-£66 daily, £325-£455 weekly.
Lunch available.
Evening meal 7pm (l.o.
9.30pm).
Parking for 80.
Credit: Access, Visa, Diners, Amex.
🛇 ♨ ᴤ ☏ ⊙ ❏ ♥ 🛉 Ⅵ
ᴤ ▦ ᴧ ⊥ 🛉 ᴤᴘ

Hartwell House ⋒
☸☸☸☸ HIGHLY COMMENDED
Oxford Rd., Aylesbury,
HP17 8NL
☎ (0296) 747444
Telex 837108
🅖🅡 Small Luxury Hotels
2 miles from Aylesbury on A418 towards Oxford, Hartwell House is one of the most historic houses of Buckinghamshire.
Bedrooms: 5 single, 11 double & 15 twin, 1 family room.
Bathrooms: 32 private.
Bed & breakfast: £100.75-£118.25 single, £149-£320.50 double.
Lunch available.
Evening meal 7.30pm (l.o.
9.45pm).
Parking for 70.
Credit: Access, Visa, Diners, Amex.
🛇8 ᴤ ☏ ⊙ ❏ 🛉 Ⅵ ᴤ ◉
🈁 ▦ ⊥ 🛉 ⟡ ❖ 🛉 ⚲
⚲ ᴤᴘ 🈁 ⊡

BAMPTON
Oxfordshire
Map ref 2C1

*5m SW. Witney
Small market town, well known for its Spring Bank Holiday Monday Fete with Morris Dance Festival.*

Romany Inn ⋒
Listed
Bridge St., Bampton,
OX8 2HA
☎ Bampton Castle
(0993) 850237
Listed building dating from the 17th C. Lounge bar with separate dining room. Log fires in winter.
Bedrooms: 2 double & 4 twin.

Bathrooms: 3 private,
1 public.
Bed & breakfast: £17.50-£21 single, £25-£36 double.
Half board: £20.50-£30 daily, £120-£180 weekly.
Lunch available.
Evening meal 6.30pm (l.o.
10pm).
Parking for 3.
🛇 ᴤ ♥ 🛉 ᴤ ⊡ 🈁 🈁

BANBURY
Oxfordshire
Map ref 2C1

Famous for its cattle market, cakes and Nursery Rhyme Cross. Founded in Saxon times, it has some fine houses and interesting old inns. A good centre for touring Warwickshire and the Cotswolds.
Tourist Information Centre ☎ (0295) 259855

Banbury Moat House ⋒
☸☸☸☸ COMMENDED
Oxford Rd., Banbury,
OX16 9AH
☎ (0295) 259361
Telex 838967 BB MOAT
🅖🅡 Queens Moat Houses
An elegant Georgian building which has all modern facilities. Ideal for touring the Cotswolds, Stratford and Oxford.
Bedrooms: 15 single, 25 double & 7 twin, 2 family rooms.
Bathrooms: 49 private.
Bed & breakfast: £27-£69 single, £54-£79 double.
Half board: £39.25-£81.25 daily.
Lunch available.
Evening meal 7pm (l.o.
9.45pm).
Parking for 40.
Credit: Access, Visa, Diners, Amex.
🛇 ᴤ 🈁 ☏ ⊙ ❏ ♥ 🛉 Ⅵ
🛉 ᴤ ◉ ▦ ᴧ ⊥ ᴤᴘ 🈁 ⊡

Belmont Guest House
☸☸
34 Crouch St., Banbury,
OX16 9PR
☎ (0295) 262308
Family-run guesthouse approximately 200 yards from Banbury Cross. Away from the main road.
Bedrooms: 2 single, 2 double & 3 twin, 1 family room.
Bathrooms: 5 private,
1 public; 1 private shower.

Bed & breakfast: £18-£30 single, £28-£35 double.
Parking for 6.
Credit: Access, Visa.
🛇7 ᴤ ❏ ♥ Ⅵ ᴤ 🈁 ᴧ ᴥ
🈁 🈁

Calthorpe Lodge Guest House ⋒
☸
4 Calthorpe Rd., Banbury,
OX16 8HS
☎ (0295) 252325
Family-run period house near town centre.
Bedrooms: 3 single, 1 double & 1 twin.
Bathrooms: 4 private,
1 public.
Bed & breakfast: £25-£35 single, £35-£45 double.
Evening meal 6.30pm (l.o.
8pm).
Parking for 6.
Credit: Access, Visa.
🛇 ⊙ ❏ ♥ ㉾ 🛉 Ⅵ ◉ ▦
ᴧ 🈁

Cotswold Guest House
45 Oxford Rd., Banbury,
OX16 9AH
☎ (0295) 256414
Character Georgian house within walking distance of the town centre. Friendly staff always on hand for local information.
Bedrooms: 2 single, 3 family rooms.
Bathrooms: 1 private;
2 private showers.
Bed & breakfast: £16-£20 single, £32-£38 double.
Half board: £20-£25 daily, £120-£140 weekly.
Lunch available.
Evening meal 6pm (l.o. 8pm).
Parking for 6.
🛇2 ㉾ ❏ ♥ ㉾ 🛉 Ⅵ ᴤ
⊡ ◉ ▦ ᴧ ⊥ ⊡ᴀᴘ ⚲ ᴤᴘ 🈁

Kelvedon Guest House
☸
11 Broughton Rd., Banbury,
OX16 9QB
☎ (0295) 263028
Friendly, comfortable guesthouse, a few minutes from Banbury Cross.
Bedrooms: 2 twin, 2 family rooms.
Bathrooms: 3 private,
2 public.
Bed & breakfast: £18-£22 single, £28-£35 double.
Parking for 3.
🛇 ❏ ♥ ㉾ ᴤ ⊡ ▦ 🈁

La Madonette Country Guest House
☸☸ COMMENDED
North Newington, Nr.
Banbury, OX15 6AA
☎ Banbury (0295) 730212
Continued ▶

BANBURY

Continued

17th C miller's house set in beautiful countryside on edge of Cotswolds. Half a mile from Broughton Castle, close to Stratford-upon-Avon, Warwick and Oxford.
Bedrooms: 3 double & 3 twin.
Bathrooms: 6 private.
Bed & breakfast: £32-£37.50 single, £45-£55 double.
Parking for 20.
Credit: Access, Visa.
🛏 ♨ 📞 🍴 ⚘ Ⓥ 📶 📺 📶 🛗 🍴 ⟨⟩ ♿ ✽ ✗ 🏖 🏮

Prospect House Guest House M
☺☺☺ COMMENDED
70 Oxford Rd., Banbury, OX16 9AN
☎ (0295) 268749
Detached house with lovely grounds, in the most convenient area of town.
Bedrooms: 1 single, 6 double & 2 twin.
Bathrooms: 9 private.
Bed & breakfast: £30-£38 single, £40-£50 double.
Half board: £28.50-£43.50 daily.
Evening meal 7pm.
Parking for 10.
Credit: Access, Visa.
🛏 ♨ ® 📷 📶 ⚘ 🍴 📶 📺 🍴 ✽ ✗ 🏖 SP

Thatched House Hotel M
☺☺☺ APPROVED
Sulgrave, Banbury, OX17 2SE
☎ (029 576) 232 & 262
Fax (0295) 712335
A well-preserved 17th C thatched building in a cottage garden, directly opposite Sulgrave Manor, the ancestral home of George Washington.
Bedrooms: 3 single, 2 double & 2 twin.
Bathrooms: 5 private, 1 public.
Bed & breakfast: £28-£40 single, £60-£70 double.
Half board: £36-£60 daily.
Lunch available.
Evening meal 7.30pm (l.o. 9.30pm).
Parking for 14.
Credit: Access, Visa, Diners, Amex.
🛏 📶 🍴 📷 Ⓥ 🍴 📶 📷 🍴 🏖 ✽ 🏮 🏖 SP 📶 T

Treetops Guest House
☺
28 Dashwood Rd., Banbury, OX16 8HD
☎ (0295) 254444

Comfortable accommodation in an elegant Victorian town house, in a quiet location on the A361, 5 minutes' walk from town centre.
Bedrooms: 1 single, 1 twin, 3 family rooms.
Bathrooms: 2 public.
Bed & breakfast: £14-£16.50 single, £27-£28 double.
Parking for 2.
🛏 ♨ 📶 🍴 🏖 📺 📶 ✗ 🏮

Winston's
☺☺ COMMENDED
65 Oxford Rd., Banbury, OX16 9AJ
☎ (0295) 270790
Victorian private hotel 5 minutes from Banbury Cross and within easy reach of Shakespeare Country. Residents' bar. A real "home from home".
Bedrooms: 4 single, 2 twin, 2 family rooms.
Bathrooms: 7 private, 1 public.
Bed & breakfast: £32-£36 single, £44-£48 double.
Parking for 8.
Credit: Access, Visa, Diners, Amex.
🛏 📞 ® 📶 ⚘ 🍴 📶 🏖 ✗

Wroxton House Hotel M
☺☺☺☺
Wroxton St. Mary, Nr. Banbury, OX15 6QB
☎ (0295) 730777 Telex 83409
Ⓒ Best Western
Picturesque thatched hotel in lovely village 3 miles from Banbury. Candlelit restaurant specialising in fish and game dishes according to season.
Bedrooms: 5 single, 28 double & 4 twin.
Bathrooms: 37 private, 1 public.
Bed & breakfast: from £55 single, from £110 double.
Half board: from £75 daily.
Lunch available.
Evening meal 7.30pm (l.o. 9.30pm).
Parking for 75.
Credit: Access, Visa, C.Bl., Diners, Amex.
🛏 📶 📞 ® 📶 ⚘ 🍴 Ⓥ 📶 📺 ⦿ 🍴 🏖 🍴 ⟨⟩ 🍴 ✽ 🏖 SP 📶 T

> *We advise you to confirm your booking in writing.*

> *Please mention this guide when making a booking.*

BEDFORD

Bedfordshire
Map ref 2D1

Busy county town with interesting buildings and churches near the River Ouse which has pleasant riverside walks. Many associations with John Bunyan including Bunyan Meeting House, museum and statue. The Bedford Museum and Cecil Higgins Art Gallery are of interest.
Tourist Information Centre ☎ (0234) 215226

Barns Hotel & Restaurant M
Cardington Rd., Bedford, MK44 3SA
☎ (0234) 270044
Fax (0234) 273102
Ⓒ Lansbury
A new hotel developed from a 17th C manor house and adjacent to the River Great Ouse.
Bedrooms: 19 double & 28 twin, 2 family rooms.
Bathrooms: 49 private.
Bed & breakfast: £33-£75 single, £66-£87 double.
Half board: £46-£90 daily.
Lunch available.
Evening meal 7pm (l.o. 10pm).
Parking for 120.
Credit: Access, Visa, Diners, Amex.
🛏 📶 📞 📶 ⚘ 🍴 Ⓥ ✗ 🍴 ⦿ 🍴 🏖 🍴 ⟨⟩ 🏖 ✽ SP 📶 T

Bedford Moat House M
St. Mary's St., Bedford, MK42 0AR
☎ (0234) 355131
Telex 825243
Ⓒ Queens Moat Houses
Comfortable modern hotel on the banks of the River Great Ouse, in charming market town. An ideal base for tourists.
Bedrooms: 31 single, 15 double & 33 twin, 21 family rooms.
Bathrooms: 100 private.
Bed & breakfast: from £70 single, from £85 double.
Lunch available.
Evening meal 7pm (l.o. 9.45pm).
Parking for 75.
Credit: Access, Visa, Diners, Amex.
🛏 📶 ® 📶 ⚘ 🍴 Ⓥ ✗ 🍴 📺 ⦿ 🍴 📶 🏖 🍴 🏖 SP T

Bedford Oak House
☺☺☺
33 Shakespeare Rd., Bedford, MK40 2DX
☎ (0234) 266972
Mock Tudor house convenient for town centre and station. Basic and en-suite rooms with TV and hot drinks facility.
Bedrooms: 1 single, 9 double & 4 twin, 1 family room.
Bathrooms: 8 private, 2 public; 1 private shower.
Bed & breakfast: £21-£29 single, £30-£38 double.
Parking for 15.
Credit: Access, Visa, Amex.
🛏 📶 📶 📶 📶 📺 📶 🏖 🍴 ✗ 🏮

Clarendon House Hotel
☺☺
25-27 Ampthill Rd., Bedford, MK42 9JP
☎ (0234) 266054
Attractive Edwardian house hotel, on the A6 south of Bedford and with good access to M1, A1, Woburn Abbey and Bedford.
Bedrooms: 9 single, 2 double & 6 twin.
Bathrooms: 13 private, 2 public.
Bed & breakfast: £21.50-£33.50 single, £35.50-£43 double.
Half board: £30-£42.50 daily.
Evening meal 7pm (l.o. 8pm).
Parking for 15.
Credit: Access, Visa, Diners, Amex.
🛏 📶 📶 🍴 Ⓥ 📶 📺 📶

De Parys Hotel
De Parys Avenue, Bedford, MK40 2UA
☎ (0234) 352121 & 352793
Fax (0234) 353889
In a quiet tree-lined avenue, with its own gardens and overlooking Bedford School. Close to town centre and Bedford Park.
Bedrooms: 9 single, 6 double & 8 twin, 2 family rooms.
Bathrooms: 25 private, 4 public.
Bed & breakfast: £36-£62 single, £48-£77 double.
Half board: £289-£324 weekly.
Lunch available.
Evening meal 7pm (l.o. 9.30pm).
Parking for 36.
Credit: Access, Visa, Diners, Amex.
🛏 📶 📞 ® 📶 ⚘ 🍴 Ⓥ 🍴 📶 🏖 🍴 ⟨⟩ 🍴 ✽ 🏮 🏖 DAP SP T

No. 1 The Grange
☜☜☜ COMMENDED

Sunderland Hill, Ravensden,
MK44 2SH
☎ Bedford (0234) 771771
Elegant, spacious, family-run accommodation in rural surroundings. Two riding schools and Mosbray golf course nearby. Non-smokers please.
Bedrooms: 1 single, 1 double & 1 twin.
Bathrooms: 1 private, 2 public.
Bed & breakfast: max. £18 single, max. £32 double.
Half board: £28.50-£30.50 daily.
Evening meal 6.30pm (l.o. midday).
Parking for 10.

The Queens Head Hotel ℳ
☜☜☜☜ COMMENDED

2 Rushden Rd., Milton Ernest, Bedford, MK44 1RV
☎ (0234) 272822
Telex 94014159 FMCL G (Ref QH)
Restored country inn on the A6, 5 miles north of Bedford. Bars and restaurant open to non-residents.

Individual proprietors have supplied all details of accommodation. Although we do check for accuracy, we advise you to confirm prices and other information at the time of booking.

National Crown ratings were correct at the time of going to press but are subject to change. Please check at the time of booking.

The national Crown scheme is explained in full on pages 536 – 539.

Bedrooms: 1 single, 7 double & 5 twin.
Bathrooms: 13 private.
Bed & breakfast: £48-£55 single, £55-£70 double.
Lunch available.
Evening meal 7pm (l.o. 10pm).
Parking for 21.
Credit: Access, Visa, Amex.

BICESTER
Oxfordshire
Map ref 2C1

Market town with large army depot and well-known hunting centre with hunt established in the late 18th C. The ancient parish church displays work of many periods. Nearby is the Jacobean mansion of Rousham House with gardens landscaped by William Kent.

Bignell Park Hotel
Chesterton, Nr Bicester,
OX6 8UE
☎ (0869) 241444
Cotswold period house circa 1740, set in 2.5 acres with mature gardens, in rural Oxfordshire.
Bedrooms: 1 single, 4 double & 2 twin.
Bathrooms: 2 public.
Bed & breakfast: £30-£50 single, £44-£80 double.
Half board: £38-£66 daily.
Lunch available.
Evening meal 7pm (l.o. 9.30pm).
Parking for 18.
Credit: Access, Visa, Diners, Amex.

Littlebury Hotel
Kings End, Bicester,
OX6 7DR
☎ (0869) 252595
Family owned and run town centre hotel in quiet location with plenty of parking, offering fine food and hospitality.
Bedrooms: 8 single, 4 double & 16 twin, 9 family rooms.
Bathrooms: 33 private, 3 public.
Bed & breakfast: £33-£48.50 single, £48.50-£63.80 double.
Half board: £38-£61 daily.
Lunch available.
Evening meal 7pm (l.o. 10pm).
Parking for 52.
Credit: Access, Visa, Amex.

BISHOP'S STORTFORD
Hertfordshire
Map ref 2D1

8m N. Harlow
Fine old town on the River Stort with many interesting buildings, particularly Victorian, and an imposing parish church. The vicarage where Cecil Rhodes was born is now a museum.
Tourist Information Centre ☎ (0279) 655261

High Willows
Listed

91 Dunmow Rd., Bishop's Stortford, CM23 5HF
☎ (0279) 659780
Family-run guesthouse, within walking distance of town centre and railway station. Close to airport and motorway.
Bedrooms: 1 double & 2 twin, 2 family rooms.
Bathrooms: 1 private, 1 public.
Bed & breakfast: £20-£25 single, £34-£40 double.
Half board: £23-£31 daily, £161-£217 weekly.
Evening meal 7pm (l.o. midday).
Parking for 7.

BOREHAMWOOD
Hertfordshire
Map ref 2D1

Busy town beside the A1 Great North Road.
Tourist Information Centre ☎ 081-207 2277

Hartwood
36 Gables Avenue,
Borehamwood, WD6 4SP
☎ 081-207 6891
Detached family house.
Bedrooms: 1 single, 1 double.
Bathrooms: 1 private, 1 public.
Bed & breakfast: £14-£16 single, £33-£38 double.
Evening meal 7pm.

BRACKNELL
Berkshire
Map ref 2C2

Designated a New Town in 1949, the town has ancient origins. Set in heathlands, it is an excellent centre for golf and walking. South Hill Park, an 18th C mansion, houses an art centre.
Tourist Information Centre ☎ (0344) 423149

Hilton National ℳ
Bagshot Rd., Bracknell,
RG12 3QJ
☎ (0344) 424801
Telex 848058
Ⓡ Hilton
Well-situated in a thriving part of Berkshire, with comfortable facilities.
Bedrooms: 22 single, 95 double & 50 twin.
Bathrooms: 167 private.
Bed & breakfast: £110.50-£119.50 single, £128.50-£145 double.
Lunch available.
Evening meal 7pm (l.o. 9.45pm).
Parking for 250.
Credit: Access, Visa, C.Bl., Diners, Amex.

Stirrups Country House Hotel ℳ
☜☜☜☜ COMMENDED

Maidens Green, Nr Windsor, Bracknell, RG12 6LD
☎ Winkfield Row
(0344) 882284 Telex 882300
Privately owned hotel in Berkshire's racing heartland, situated between Windsor, Ascot and Bracknell.
Bedrooms: 1 single, 18 double & 4 twin, 1 family room.
Bathrooms: 24 private.
Bed & breakfast: £40-£85 single, £60-£100 double.
Half board: £55-£100 daily.
Lunch available.
Evening meal 7pm (l.o. 10pm).
Parking for 100.
Credit: Access, Visa, Diners, Amex.

The symbol Ⓡ and the name of a hotel group or consortium after a hotel address means that bookings can be made through a central reservations office. These are listed on page 540.

BUCKINGHAM

Buckinghamshire
Map ref 2C1

Interesting old market
town surrounded by rich
farmland. It has many
Georgian buildings,
including the Town Hall
and Old Jail and many old
almshouses and inns.
Stowe School nearby has
magnificent 18th C
landscaped gardens.

Buckingham Lodge Hotel M
登登登登

A421, Ring Road South,
Buckingham, MK18 1RY
☎ (0280) 822622
Fax (0280) 823074
*Opened in 1990, just outside
Buckingham and within easy
reach of Cotswolds, Blenheim,
Oxford, Stratford-upon-Avon
and Woburn.*
Bedrooms: 15 single,
15 double & 34 twin, 6 family
rooms.
Bathrooms: 70 private.
Bed & breakfast: £45-£76
single, £56-£86 double.
Half board: £44-£86 daily,
max. £480 weekly.
Lunch available.
Evening meal 7pm (l.o.
10pm).
Parking for 110.
Credit: Access, Visa.

Villiers Hotel M
登登登登

24 Castle St., Buckingham,
MK18 1BP
☎ (0280) 822444
Fax (0280) 822113
*Bedrooms are set around an
old coaching inn courtyard,
incorporating restaurant, bars
and shops.*
Bedrooms: 3 single, 15 double
& 16 twin, 4 family rooms.
Bathrooms: 38 private.
Bed & breakfast: max. £75
single, max. £89 double.
Half board: max. £89 daily,
max. £93 weekly.
Lunch available.
Evening meal 7pm (l.o.
10.30pm).
Parking for 36.
Credit: Access, Visa, Diners,
Amex.

*The symbols are
explained on the
flap inside the
back cover.*

BURFORD

Oxfordshire
Map ref 2B1

One of the most beautiful
Cotswold wool towns
with Georgian and Tudor
houses, many antique
shops and a picturesque
High Street sloping to the
River Windrush.
*Tourist Information
Centre* ☎ *(099 382) 3558*

Cotswold Gateway Hotel M
登登登登

Cheltenham Rd., Burford,
OX8 4HX
☎ (0993) 822695
*Privately-owned hotel at the
top of Burford Hill. Recently
refurbished.*
Bedrooms: 6 double & 5 twin,
5 family rooms.
Bathrooms: 16 private.
Bed & breakfast: £55-£65
single, £65-£85 double.
Half board: £70-£80 daily.
Lunch available.
Evening meal 7pm (l.o.
9.30pm).
Parking for 30.
Credit: Access, Visa, Diners,
Amex.

Elm Farm House M
登登登 COMMENDED

Meadow Lane, Fulbrook,
Burford, OX8 4BW
☎ (099 382) 3611
*Cotswold-stone house with
walled garden, in quiet village.*
Bedrooms: 1 single, 2 double
& 4 twin.
Bathrooms: 3 private,
1 public.
Bed & breakfast: £29.50-
£34.50 single, £41-£57 double.
Half board: £44.50-£49.50
daily, £304.50-£339.50 weekly.
Evening meal 7.30pm (l.o.
7.30pm).
Parking for 10.
Open February-December.
Credit: Access, Visa, Amex.

Golden Pheasant Hotel M
登登登登 COMMENDED

High St., Burford, OX8 4RJ
☎ (099 382) 3223 & 3417
Fax (099 382) 2621
*Beautifully restored 15th C
inn. Large open fireplaces,
traditional English and French
cuisine. Central for Oxford,
Stratford-upon-Avon, Bath and
the neighbouring Cotswold
villages.*

Bedrooms: 1 single, 5 double
& 4 twin, 2 family rooms.
Bathrooms: 12 private.
Bed & breakfast: £55-£60
single, £75-£85 double.
Lunch available.
Evening meal 7pm (l.o.
9.30pm).
Parking for 16.
Credit: Access, Visa, Amex.

The Inn for All Seasons M
登登登

The Barringtons, Burford,
OX8 4TN
☎ Windrush (045 14) 324
Fax (045 14) 375
*Located in the heart of the
Cotswolds, this former
coaching inn has been
preserved to retain the charm
of bygone days.*
Bedrooms: 5 double & 5 twin.
Bathrooms: 10 private.
Bed & breakfast: £39-£47
single, £65-£72 double.
Half board: £54-£62 daily,
£240-£260 weekly.
Lunch available.
Evening meal 7pm (l.o.
9.30pm).
Parking for 30.
Credit: Access, Visa.

CHINNOR

Oxfordshire
Map ref 2C1

4m SE. Thame

Plough and Harrow M
登登登 COMMENDED

Sydenham, Chinnor,
OX9 4LD
☎ Kingston Blount
(0844) 51367
*Traditional beer house
providing a full a la carte
menu, table d'hote and bar
food, and en-suite
accommodation.*
Bedrooms: 2 single, 2 double
& 3 twin.
Bathrooms: 7 private.
Bed & breakfast: £30-£55
single, £50-£65 double.
Lunch available.
Evening meal 7pm (l.o.
10pm).
Parking for 40.
Credit: Access, Visa, Diners,
Amex.

CHIPPING NORTON

Oxfordshire
Map ref 2C1

Old market town set high
in the Cotswolds and an
ideal touring centre. The
wide market-place
contains many 16th C and
17th C stone houses and
the Town Hall and Tudor
Guildhall.
*Tourist Information
Centre* ☎ *(0608) 644379.*

Market House M
登登 COMMENDED

4 Middle Row, Chipping
Norton, OX7 5NH
☎ (0608) 642781
*Pleasant rooms in town centre.
Own parking. Meals by
arrangement with
establishment's own restaurant.*
Bedrooms: 2 double & 1 twin.
Bathrooms: 3 private.
Bed & breakfast: £15-£22
single, from £35 double.
Half board: £25-£30 daily,
£150-£210 weekly.
Lunch available.
Evening meal 6pm (l.o.
10pm).
Parking for 3.
Credit: Access, Visa, Diners,
Amex.

Southcombe Guest House
登 APPROVED

Southcombe, Chipping
Norton, OX7 5JF
☎ (0608) 643068
*Well-decorated pebbledash
guesthouse set in 3.5 acres, at
the junction of the A44/A34,
2 miles south of Chipping
Norton.*
Bedrooms: 3 double & 2 twin,
1 family room.
Bathrooms: 2 private,
2 public.
Bed & breakfast: £18-£26
single, £32-£38 double.
Half board: £23-£27 daily.
Lunch available.
Evening meal 7pm (l.o. 6pm).
Parking for 10.

The White Hart M
High Street, Chipping
Norton, OX7 5AD
☎ (0608) 642572
Resort
*This handsome inn overlooks
the town's wide High Street.
Its Georgian facade is a local
landmark.*
Bedrooms: 2 single, 9 double
& 8 twin, 1 family room.
Bathrooms: 20 private.

Bed & breakfast: £22.50-£41 single, £45-£61 double. Lunch available. Evening meal 7pm (l.o. 9pm). Parking for 16. Credit: Access, Visa, C.Bl., Diners, Amex.

CHISLEHAMPTON

Oxfordshire
Map ref 2C1

Village close to Oxford near the site of the famous Civil War battle of Chalgrove Field. An obelisk marks the site.

The Coach and Horses M
COMMENDED

Stadhampton Rd., Chislehampton, OX9 7UX
☎ Stadhampton (0865) 890255
Picturesque 16th C listed coaching inn with beamed restaurant. Rooms with views of the countryside surround a landscaped and cobbled courtyard. One room has been thoughtfully designed for disabled guests.
Bedrooms: 5 double & 4 twin.
Bathrooms: 9 private.
Bed & breakfast: £39-£58 single, £54.50-£76 double.
Half board: £40.25-£72 daily, £300-£424 weekly.
Lunch available.
Evening meal 7pm (l.o. 10pm).
Parking for 30.
Credit: Access, Visa, Diners, Amex.

CHURCHILL

Oxfordshire
Map ref 2C1

The Forge House M
COMMENDED

Churchill, Nr. Chipping Norton, OX7 6NJ
☎ Kingham (0608) 658173
Relaxed accommodation in Cotswold-stone house and converted forge. Inglenook log fire. Four poster beds (one en-suite with jacuzzi). Personal service and advice on touring the Cotswolds and nearby places of interest.
Bedrooms: 3 double & 1 twin, 1 family room.
Bathrooms: 5 private.

Bed & breakfast: £26-£48 single, £42-£48 double.
Parking for 6.

CLANFIELD

Oxfordshire
Map ref 2C1

Pretty brookside village. Nearby lies the moated Friars Court, on the site of which once stood a building of the Knights Hospitallers.

Plough Hotel & Restaurant M
COMMENDED

Clanfield, Oxford, OX8 2RB
☎ (036 781) 222 & 494
Telex 437334 attention Plough
Elizabethan manor, dating from 1560, in the heart of the Cotswolds.
Bedrooms: 4 double & 2 twin.
Bathrooms: 6 private.
Bed & breakfast: £66-£85 single, £86-£105 double.
Half board: £87-£106 daily, £275-£335 weekly.
Lunch available.
Evening meal 7.30pm (l.o. 10pm).
Parking for 40.
Credit: Access, Visa, Diners, Amex.

CLIFTON HAMPDEN

Oxfordshire
Map ref 2C2

3m SE. Abingdon
Picturesque village on the River Thames with attractive timber-framed cottages. The thatched riverside inn 'The Barley Mow', featured in 'Three Men in a Boat', faces the village from across the river. Fine views of village from parish church.

The Barley Mow Hotel M

Clifton Hampden, Abingdon, OX14 3EH
☎ (086 730) 7847
Jerome K. Jerome described this pretty inn's distinctive 13th C black and white timbering and its charm in "Three Men in a Boat". It is tucked away on the backwaters of the River Thames.
Bedrooms: 2 single, 2 double.
Bathrooms: 1 private, 2 public.

Bed & breakfast: £36-£43 single, £56 double.
Lunch available.
Evening meal 7.30pm (l.o. 9.30pm).
Parking for 250.
Credit: Access, Visa, Diners, Amex.

CROWTHORNE

Berkshire
Map ref 2C2

Village which has grown up around Wellington and Broadmoor Hospital. The Devil's Highway Roman road passes through the village and 2 Roman milestones can still be seen.

Dial House Private Hotel M

62 Dukes Ride, Crowthorne, RG11 6DL
☎ (0344) 776941
Fax (0344) 777191
Small family-run hotel offering English and German cuisine and refreshment. Fully licensed. Close to Windsor, Bracknell, Ascot, Wokingham, Sandhurst and Camberley.
Bedrooms: 6 single, 4 double & 3 twin, 3 family rooms.
Bathrooms: 14 private, 1 public.
Bed & breakfast: £34-£60 single, £58-£79 double.
Half board: £47-£74 daily.
Lunch available.
Evening meal 7.30pm (l.o. 7.30pm).
Parking for 20.
Credit: Access, Visa.

DATCHET

Berkshire
Map ref 2D2

Boating and angling remain the town's chief attractions, with Black Potts being a favourite haunt of anglers. Datchet Mead is associated with a misadventure of Falstaff in the 'Merry Wives of Windsor'.

The Manor Hotel M

The Green, Datchet, SL3 9EA
☎ Slough (0753) 43442
Telex 41363
Calotels

Village hotel, 1 mile downstream from Windsor. Within easy reach of Heathrow Airport.
Bedrooms: 7 single, 12 double & 11 twin.
Bathrooms: 30 private.
Bed & breakfast: £35-£83 single, £70-£95 double.
Lunch available.
Evening meal 7.30pm (l.o. 10pm).
Parking for 20.
Credit: Access, Visa, Diners, Amex.

DEDDINGTON

Oxfordshire
Map ref 2C1

Attractive former market town with a large market square and many fine old buildings.

Holcombe Hotel & Restaurant M
COMMENDED

High St., Deddington, OX15 0SL
☎ (0869) 38274
Fax (0869) 37167
Best Western
300-year-old hotel in scenic Cotswold village on A4260 between Oxford and Banbury. Ideal for touring Stratford, Oxford, Blenheim and the Cotswolds.
Bedrooms: 2 single, 8 double & 6 twin, 1 family room.
Bathrooms: 17 private.
Bed & breakfast: £59-£68 single, £69.50-£85 double.
Half board: from £45 daily, from £310 weekly.
Lunch available.
Evening meal 7pm (l.o. 10.30pm).
Parking for 60.
Credit: Access, Visa, Amex.

Unicorn Hotel M

Market Place, Deddington, OX15 0SE
☎ (0869) 38266
Fax (0869) 38036
17th C Cotswold border coaching inn, 10 minutes from M40 junctions 10 and 11, on A4260 Banbury to Oxford road.
Bedrooms: 4 single, 3 double, 2 family rooms.
Bathrooms: 9 private.
Bed & breakfast: £30 single, £45 double.
Lunch available.

Continued ▶

305

DEDDINGTON
Continued

Evening meal 6.30pm (l.o. 9pm).
Parking for 31.
Credit: Access, Visa.

🖢 ⅃ ⌖ ⌂ ▯ ▯ V ▯
🪑 ❀ ☼ DAP ⦚ SP 🎏 T

DORCHESTER ON THAMES
Oxfordshire
Map ref 2C2

Ancient village set above the confluence of the River Thame with the Thames. It has a 12th C abbey with a beautiful stained glass and stone Jesse window and many other features of interest.

White Hart Hotel M
👑 👑 👑 👑 **COMMENDED**
High St., Dorchester-on-Thames, OX10 7HN
☎ Oxford (0865) 340074
Fax (0865) 341082
An ancient coaching inn tucked away in a quiet unspoilt village.
Bedrooms: 2 single, 9 double & 7 twin, 2 family rooms.
Bathrooms: 20 private.
Bed & breakfast: £66.50-£83 single, £87-£123 double.
Half board: £80-£93.50 daily.
Lunch available.
Evening meal 7pm (l.o. 9.30pm).
Parking for 25.
Credit: Access, Visa, Diners, Amex.

🖢 🖴 ⅃ ⌕ ⌂ ▯ ⌖ ▯ V
⧖ TV ▯ 🪑 ⌖ ☼ 🎏
SP T

DUNSTABLE
Bedfordshire
Map ref 2D1

Modern town with remains of a 12th C Augustinian priory in the parish church. The Dunstable Downs are famous for gliding and in the parkland of Whipsnade Zoo on the edge of the Downs many animals roam freely.
Tourist Information Centre ☎ (0582) 471012

Bellows Mill
👑 👑 👑 **COMMENDED**
Bellows Mill, Eaton Bray, Dunstable, LU6 1QZ
☎ (0525) 220548/220205

Delightful old water mill with converted stables. Tennis court, fly fishing, games room. All rooms en-suite with TV and telephone.
Bedrooms: 3 double & 2 twin.
Bathrooms: 5 private.
Bed & breakfast: £43.48-£45.50 single.
Half board: £39-£55.50 daily.
Lunch available.
Evening meal 7pm (l.o. 10pm).
Parking for 12.
Credit: Access, Visa.

🖢 🖴 ⅃ ⌕ ⌂ ▯ V ▯ ▥
🪑 ⌖ 🪑 ⌕ ⅃ ✓ ☼ ⌖ 🎏
🎏

The Highwayman Hotel M
👑 👑 👑
London Rd., Dunstable, LU6 3DX
☎ (0582) 601122 & 661999
Fax (0582) 603812
Hotel on A5, Luton Airport 8 miles away. Close to Woburn Abbey and Whipsnade Zoo.
Bedrooms: 24 single, 3 double & 11 twin.
Bathrooms: 38 private.
Bed & breakfast: £47.50-£55 single, £55-£65 double.
Lunch available.
Evening meal 7pm (l.o. 9pm).
Parking for 50.
Credit: Access, Visa, Diners, Amex.

🖢 🖴 ⅃ ⌕ ⌂ ▯ ⌖ ▯ V ◐
▥ 🪑 ⌖ ⅃ SP 🎏 T

ELSTREE
Hertfordshire
Map ref 2D1

Edgwarebury Hotel M
👑 👑 👑 👑 **COMMENDED**
Barnet Lane, Elstree, WD6 3RE
☎ 081-953 8227
Telex 918707
CR Lansbury
Large country house hotel set in 10 acres of landscaped gardens.
Bedrooms: 20 single, 17 double & 13 twin.
Bathrooms: 50 private.
Bed & breakfast: from £28 single, from £56 double.
Half board: from £40 daily.
Lunch available.
Evening meal 7pm (l.o. 10pm).
Parking for 120.
Credit: Access, Visa, Diners, Amex.

🖢 🖴 🕾 ⅃ ⌕ ⌂ ▯ ⌖ V
⧖ ◐ ▥ 🪑 ⌖ ⅃ ☼ ⌖ SP
🎏 T

EYNSHAM
Oxfordshire
Map ref 2C1

6m W. Oxford
Small market town has attractive 18th C Swinford Bridge with stone toll-house where tolls are levied on motorists. There are stone houses in the market square and an arcaded market hall.

All Views
👑 👑 **COMMENDED**
67 Old Witney Rd., On main A40, Eynsham, OX8 1PU
☎ Oxford (0865) 880891
7.5-acre sheep farm. 1991-built Cotswold stone chalet bungalow, adjacent A40 between Oxford and Witney. Designed with guests' comfort in mind. All rooms have full facilities.
Bedrooms: 1 single, 2 double & 1 twin.
Bathrooms: 4 private.
Bed & breakfast: £29.50-£34.50 single, £39.50-£46 double.
Parking for 30.

🖴 ⅃ ⌕ ⌂ ▯ ⌖ UL ▯ TV ▥
🪑 ❀ ☼ 🎏 ⅃ SP

FARINGDON
Oxfordshire
Map ref 2B2

Ancient stone-built market town in the Vale of the White Horse. The 17th C market hall stands on pillars and the 13th C church has some fine monuments. A great monastic tithe barn is nearby at Great Coxwell.
Tourist Information Centre ☎ (0367) 242191

The Crown Hotel M
Market Place, Faringdon, SN7 7HU
☎ (0367) 242744
16th C coaching inn with courtyard, log fires. Good buttery and bar food. Wedding reception, conference and banqueting services available.
Bedrooms: 2 single, 4 double & 5 twin, 1 family room.
Bathrooms: 8 private, 1 public.
Bed & breakfast: £32-£44 single, £37-£50 double.
Lunch available.
Evening meal 6pm (l.o. 10pm).
Parking for 20.
Credit: Access, Visa.

🖢 🖴 🕾 ⅃ ⌂ ▯ ⌖ ▯ V ▥ ▥
🪑 ⌖ SP 🎏 T

Faringdon Hotel M
👑 👑 👑
Market Place, Faringdon, SN7 7HL
☎ (0367) 20536
Comfortable and completely refurbished hotel situated in the market square.
Bedrooms: 6 single, 11 double & 2 twin, 3 family rooms.
Bathrooms: 22 private.
Bed & breakfast: from £43.50 single, from £53.50 double.
Half board: £54-£58 daily.
Evening meal 7pm (l.o. 9pm).
Parking for 5.
Credit: Access, Visa, Diners, Amex.

🖢 🖴 ⅃ ⌕ ⌂ ▯ ⌖ ▯ V
▥ ▥ 🪑 ⌖ ⅃ 🎏 T

Portwell Guest House M
👑 👑 👑
Market Place, Faringdon, SN7 7HU
☎ (0367) 240197
In the centre of the market-place of this country market town. Within easy reach of the Cotswolds.
Bedrooms: 1 single, 2 double & 2 twin, 2 family rooms.
Bathrooms: 7 private.
Bed & breakfast: £28-£30 single, £35-£36 double.
Half board: £33-£35 daily, £180-£200 weekly.
Evening meal 7pm (l.o. 8pm).
Parking for 3.

🖢 🖴 🖴 ⌂ ▯ ⌖ ▯ V ▥ ▥ TV ▥

Sudbury House Hotel and Conference Centre M
👑 👑 👑 👑 **COMMENDED**
56 London St., Faringdon, SN7 8AA
☎ (0367) 241272
A Grade II listed Georgian building, situated in peaceful surroundings midway between Oxford and Swindon.
Bedrooms: 39 double & 10 twin.
Bathrooms: 49 private.
Bed & breakfast: £35 single, £70 double.
Half board: £50 daily.
Lunch available.
Evening meal 7pm (l.o. 10.15pm).
Parking for 85.
Credit: Access, Visa, Diners, Amex.

🖢 🖴 ⅃ ⌕ ⌂ ▯ ⌖ ▯ V ✕
▥ ◐ ⊞ ▥ 🪑 ⌖ ⅃ ⌖ ☼ ✕
⧖ SP 🎏 T

White Horse Inn M
Listed **COMMENDED**
Woolstone, Nr. Faringdon, SN7 7QL
☎ Uffington (036 782) 726
Fax (036 782) 566

---

*16th C inn 10 miles from M4
and close to White Horse Hill.
Log fires, oak beams. Real
ales, a la carte restaurant and
bar snacks.*
Bedrooms: 2 double & 4 twin,
1 family room.
Bathrooms: 6 private.
Bed & breakfast: £40 single,
£60 double.
Half board: £35-£50 daily.
Lunch available.
Evening meal 7pm (l.o.
10pm).
Parking for 80.
Credit: Access, Visa, C.Bl.,
Diners, Amex.

2m S. Ampthill

Flitwick Manor M

Church Rd., Flitwick,
MK45 1AE
☎ (0525) 712242
Telex 823535 FM
*An English manor with log
fires, antiques, tranquillity. 40
minutes' drive from London.*
Bedrooms: 3 single, 10 double
& 2 twin.
Bathrooms: 15 private.
Bed & breakfast: £70-£135
single, £98-£190 double.
Lunch available.
Evening meal 7pm (l.o.
10.30pm).
Parking for 50.
Credit: Access, Visa, Amex.

On the London Road,
Gerrards Cross is
distinguished by its wide
gorse and beech tree
common.

Ethorpe Hotel M

Packhorse Rd., Gerrards
Cross, SL9 8HY
☎ (0753) 882039
*In its own pretty, landscaped
gardens, a splendid building
close to this delightful
Buckinghamshire town.*
Bedrooms: 4 single, 17 double
& 4 twin, 4 family rooms.
Bathrooms: 29 private.
Bed & breakfast: £72-£81
single, £88 double.
Lunch available.

Evening meal 6pm (l.o.
10.30pm).
Parking for 80.
Credit: Access, Visa, Diners,
Amex.

Riverside town on the
Oxfordshire/Berkshire
border, linked by an
attractive bridge to
Streatley with views to
the Goring Gap.

Miller of Mansfield

High St., Goring-on-Thames,
RG8 9AW
☎ (0491) 872829
Fax (0491) 874200
*Ivy-covered inn with Tudor
style exterior. Interior has
original beams, open fires and
comfortable bedrooms.*
Bedrooms: 3 single, 4 double
& 3 twin.
Bathrooms: 4 private,
2 public.
Bed & breakfast: £28-£40
single, £43-£56 double.
Lunch available.
Evening meal 7pm (l.o.
10pm).
Parking for 10.
Credit: Access, Visa.

Delightful country town
with many scenic walks
through surrounding
woods and fields.

The Laurels Guest House

APPROVED

22 Leyton Rd., Harpenden,
AL5 2HU
☎ (0582) 712226
*Modernised guesthouse
overlooking the common in
picturesque area. Close to
shops and amenities. 20
minutes to London.*
Bedrooms: 3 single, 2 double
& 2 twin, 3 family rooms.
Bathrooms: 2 public.
Bed & breakfast: £21-£23
single, £33-£36 double.
Parking for 3.

Milton Hotel M

25 Milton Rd., Harpenden,
AL5 5LA
☎ (0582) 762914
*Family-run hotel in quiet
residential area. Close to
mainline station, junction 9/10,
M1 and M25. Large car park.*
Bedrooms: 5 single, 2 double
& 1 twin.
Bathrooms: 3 private,
2 public.
Bed & breakfast: £21-£26
single, £33-£36 double.
Parking for 9.

Pleasant market town
greatly expanded since
the 1950s but with older
origins. The High Street
has pretty cottages and
18th C houses and the
Norman parish church
has a fine 14th C timber
spire. The Grand Union
Canal runs nearby.
*Tourist Information
Centre ☎ (0442) 64451*

Southville Private Hotel

Listed

9 Charles St., Hemel
Hempstead, HP1 1JH
☎ (0442) 251387
*Small, family-run hotel in a
quiet residential road. Within
walking distance of town
centre, bus and railway station.
Car park.*
Bedrooms: 10 single, 2 double
& 6 twin, 1 family room.
Bathrooms: 6 public.
Bed & breakfast: £18.50-£27
single, £33-£39 double.
Parking for 9.
Credit: Access, Visa.

The famous Thames
Regatta is held in this
prosperous and attractive
town at the beginning of
July each year. The town
has many Georgian
buildings and old
coaching inns and the
parish church has some
fine monuments.
*Tourist Information
Centre ☎ (0491) 578034*

The Flower Pot

Ferry Lane, Aston, Henley-
on-Thames, RG9 3DG
☎ (0491) 574721
*Comfortable accommodation,
good food and real ales in
secluded location near River
Thames.*
Bedrooms: 2 double & 2 twin.
Bathrooms: 2 private,
1 public.
Bed & breakfast: £36-£43
single, £45-£54 double.
Half board: £27-£65 daily,
£150-£360 weekly.
Lunch available.
Evening meal 7pm (l.o. 9pm).
Parking for 30.
Credit: Access, Visa.

Regency House Hotel M

COMMENDED

4 River Terrace, Henley-on-
Thames, RG9 1BG
☎ (0491) 571133
*Elegant riverside hotel
overlooking Henley Bridge and
the Regatta course beyond.
Well-appointed comfortable
rooms with pleasant river
views.*
Bedrooms: 1 single, 3 double
& 1 twin.
Bathrooms: 5 private.
Bed & breakfast: £47-£63
single, £55-£73 double.
Credit: Access, Visa, Amex.

---

*Individual proprietors have supplied all
details of accommodation. Although we
do check for accuracy, we advise you to
confirm prices and other information at
the time of booking.*

*The enquiry coupons at the back will
help you when contacting proprietors.*

Hertfordshire
Map ref 2D1

Old county town with attractive cottages and houses and fine public buildings. The remains of the ancient castle, childhood home of Elizabeth I, now form the Council offices and the grounds are open to the public.
Tourist Information Centre ☎ *(0992) 584322*

Hall House ⚊
👑👑👑 HIGHLY COMMENDED
Broad Oak End, (Off Bramfield Rd.), Hertford, SG14 2JA
☎ (0992) 582807
Tranquil, 15th C country house, rebuilt in woodland setting on the edge of Hertford town. Non-smokers only please.
Bedrooms: 3 double.
Bathrooms: 3 private, 1 public.
Bed & breakfast: £45 single, £60 double.
Half board: £63 daily.
Evening meal 6pm (l.o. 7.30pm).
Parking for 7.
Credit: Access, Visa.
⊚🖵♻🔕🔆🕅⊤🎹🄰
🔾❄🛩🚬🏮

Buckinghamshire
Map ref 2C2

Famous for furniture-making, historic examples of which feature in the museum. The 18th C Guildhall and the octagonal market house were designed by the Adam brothers. West Wycombe Park and Hughenden Manor (National Trust) are nearby.
Tourist Information Centre ☎ *(0494) 421892*

The Alexandra Hotel
Queen Alexandra Rd., High Wycombe, HP11 2JX
☎ (0494) 463494
Telex 837442 BEEKS G
New town centre hotel. Tastefully furnished bedrooms with an emphasis on quality. Conference facilities available. Easy access to several major motorways and tourist towns such as Windsor and Oxford.
Bedrooms: 2 single, 24 double & 2 twin, 1 family room.

Bathrooms: 29 private.
Bed & breakfast: £71.50-£75.50 single, £87-£91 double.
Evening meal 7pm (l.o. 8.30pm).
Parking for 30.
Credit: Access, Visa, Amex.
🔾♿🗝🕻⊚🖵♻🔕🔆🔕🔆
🎹🄰🛥🕅🛩🆂🄿

Belmont Guest House
9 & 11 Priory Avenue, High Wycombe, HP13 6SQ
☎ (0494) 27046
Victorian-style guesthouse within easy walking distance of the town and public transport. Centrally located for Oxfordshire, Berkshire and Buckinghamshire.
Bedrooms: 8 single, 1 double & 10 twin, 1 family room.
Bathrooms: 6 private, 3 public; 1 private shower.
Bed & breakfast: £25-£35 single, £35-£45 double.
Evening meal 6pm (l.o. 9pm).
Parking for 20.
Credit: Access, Visa, Diners, Amex.
🔾♿🖵♻🔕🔆🕅✂🎹🄰
🛥🛩🆂🄿⊤

The Chiltern Hotel
👑👑👑
181-183 West Wycombe Rd., High Wycombe, HP12 3AF
☎ (0494) 452597 & 436678
Popular hotel taking its name from the surrounding Chiltern Hills. Relaxed friendly atmosphere, selective menus, traditional beers. Group bookings welcome.
Bedrooms: 7 single, 1 double & 6 twin, 2 family rooms.
Bathrooms: 8 private, 3 public.
Bed & breakfast: £30-£40 single, £42-£55 double.
Half board: £35-£50 daily, £245-£350 weekly.
Lunch available.
Evening meal 6.30pm (l.o. 8pm).
Parking for 16.
Credit: Access, Visa.
🔾♿🗝🖵⊚🖵♻🔕🔆🕅✂
🛥⊤🎹🄰🛥🕅🛩❄

The symbols are explained on the flap inside the back cover.

Map references apply to the colour maps towards the end of this guide.

Hertfordshire
Map ref 2D1

Once a flourishing wool town. Full of interest, with many fine old buildings centred around the market square. These include the 17th C almshouses, old inns and the Victorian Corn Exchange.
Tourist Information Centre ☎ *(0462) 434738*

Firs Hotel ⚊
👑👑👑 **APPROVED**
83 Bedford Rd., Hitchin, SG5 2TY
☎ (0462) 422322
Fax (0462) 432051
Family-run establishment in welcoming surroundings, with own Italian restaurant. Convenient for visiting London, Luton Airport, Bedford and Stevenage.
Bedrooms: 16 single, 1 double & 11 twin, 2 family rooms.
Bathrooms: 24 private, 3 public.
Bed & breakfast: £31-£49 single, £48-£59 double.
Evening meal 7pm (l.o. 9.30pm).
Parking for 26.
Credit: Access, Visa, Diners, Amex.
🔾♿🕻🖵🔕🔆🕅⊤🎹🄰
🎹🄰🛥⊤🄰

Highbury Lodge Hotel
👑👑
Highbury Rd., Hitchin, SG4 9RW
☎ (0462) 432983
Small family-run hotel in residential area overlooking parkland.
Bedrooms: 4 single, 1 double & 3 twin, 1 family room.
Bathrooms: 6 private, 2 public.
Bed & breakfast: £28-£32 single, £40-£46 double.
Parking for 10.
Credit: Access, Visa.
🔾🖵♻🕅⊤🎹🄰🛥🄰

The Red Lion and Lodge Hotel ⚊
Listed COMMENDED
Kings Walden Rd., Great Offley, Nr. Hitchin, SG5 3DZ
☎ (0462) 76281 & 76792
16th C inn, set in Hertfordshire countryside, only 5 minutes' drive from Hitchin and Luton. Friendly and informal.
Bedrooms: 4 double & 1 twin.
Bathrooms: 5 private.
Bed & breakfast: £45-£55 single, £55-£65 double.

Half board: £55-£73 daily.
Evening meal 7pm (l.o. 9.30pm).
Parking for 10.
Credit: Access, Visa, Diners, Amex.
🔾♿🕻⊚🖵♻🔕🄲🔆🕅⚫
🎹🄰🛥❄🛩🕅🄰🆂🄿🏮

Berkshire
Map ref 2C2

Moor Farm
Ascot Rd., Holyport, SL6 2HY
☎ Maidenhead (0628) 33761
100-acre mixed farm. 700-year-old farmhouse, 4 miles from Windsor, 12 miles from Heathrow and 25 miles from central London. Close to M4 junction 8 and 9. No smoking in bedrooms please.
Bedrooms: 2 twin.
Bathrooms: 2 private.
Bed & breakfast: £34-£38 double.
Parking for 4.
🔾🔕🔆🕅🛥⊤🎹🄰🛥►❄
🛩🕅🏮

Oxfordshire
Map ref 2C1

Village with attractive timbered and thatched cottages, on the edge of Ot Moor. The Oxfordshire Way footpath passes close to the village.

Studley Priory Hotel ⚊
👑👑👑👑 **COMMENDED**
Horton-cum-Studley, OX9 1AZ
☎ Stanton St. John
(086 735) 203 & 254
Telex 262433
🄲🅁 Consort
A converted Elizabethan manor house in a rural setting, with a restaurant that specialises in English cooking. Half board price quoted is per person based on minimum 2 nights' stay.
Bedrooms: 9 single, 2 double & 5 twin, 2 family rooms.
Bathrooms: 18 private.
Bed & breakfast: £88-£150 single, £98-£190 double.
Half board: from £120 daily.
Lunch available.
Evening meal 7.30pm (l.o. 9.30pm).
Parking for 101.
Credit: Access, Visa, C.Bl., Diners, Amex.
🔾♿🛥🕻⊚🖵♻🔕🔆🕅⚫
🛥🎹🄰🛥⊤🔾❄🛩🕅🔕
🏮⊤

HUNGERFORD

Berkshire
Map ref 2C2

Attractive town on the Avon Canal and the River Kennet, famous for its fishing. It has a wide High Street and many antique shops. Nearby is the Tudor manor of Littlecote with its large Roman mosaic.

The Bear Hotel M
☗☗☗☗ COMMENDED
Charnham St., Hungerford, RG17 0EL
☎ (0488) 682512
Fax (0488) 684357
Ⓒ Resort
13th C coaching inn, traditionally furnished, with timber beams and open fires. 3 miles from junction 14 on the M4, ideally situated for the Cotswolds, Berkshire Downs and Newbury Races.
Bedrooms: 4 single, 28 double & 9 twin.
Bathrooms: 41 private.
Bed & breakfast: £32.50-£87.50 single, £65-£105 double.
Lunch available.
Evening meal 7.30pm (l.o. 9.30pm).
Parking for 60.
Credit: Access, Visa, Diners, Amex.
🖙🖥🛏📞🕮🗑🖏 Ⓥ
🖂◉🕮🛏🍴🏐 SP 🏵 🍸

Marshgate Cottage Hotel M
☗☗ COMMENDED
Marsh Lane, Hungerford, RG17 0QX
☎ (0488) 682307
Fax (0488) 685475
Family-run hotel ranged around south-facing walled courtyard, linked to 350-year-old thatched cottage. Overlooks marshland, trout streams and canal. Lovely walks, bird-watching. Important antiques centre. 1 hour from Heathrow. French, German and Scandinavian languages spoken.
Bedrooms: 1 single, 3 double & 3 twin, 2 family rooms.
Bathrooms: 7 private, 2 public.
Bed & breakfast: £25.50-£34.75 single, £35-£49 double.
Evening meal 7pm (l.o. 9pm).
Parking for 9.
Open February-December.
Credit: Access, Visa, Amex.
🖙5🖥🕮📞🕮🗑🖏 Ⓥ
🍴🖂🕮🛏🍴🏐🏵🏵🏵
🍸

The Three Swans Hotel
117 High St., Hungerford, RG17 0DL
☎ (0488) 682721
Fax (0488) 681708
Ⓒ Resort
Hotel in the centre of Hungerford dating back some 700 years. Recently refurbished, it now offers new bedrooms and a new brasserie-style restaurant.
Bedrooms: 4 single, 4 double & 5 twin, 1 family room.
Bathrooms: 4 public; 7 private showers.
Bed & breakfast: £22.50-£41 single, £45-£51 double.
Lunch available.
Evening meal 6.30pm (l.o. 9.30pm).
Parking for 40.
Credit: Access, Visa, Diners, Amex.
🖙🖥🖏🕮 CB Ⓥ 🏐 SP 🏵 🍸

HURLEY

Berkshire
Map ref 2C2

4m NW. Maidenhead

Ye Olde Bell Hotel M
Hurley, Nr. Maidenhead, SL6 5LX
☎ (0628) 825881
Fax (0628) 825939
Ⓒ Resort
Built in 1135, the hotel is reputed to be the oldest inn in England. Henley-on-Thames, Eton, Windsor and Ascot within 10 miles.
Bedrooms: 5 single, 22 double & 3 twin, 4 family rooms.
Bathrooms: 34 private.
Bed & breakfast: £32.50-£94.50 single, £65-£107 double.
Lunch available.
Evening meal 7.30pm (l.o. 9.30pm).
Parking for 150.
Credit: Access, Visa, Diners, Amex.
🖙🖥🖏📞🕮🗑🖏 🛊 Ⓥ
🍴◉🕮🛏🍴🏵🏵🏵 SP
🏵 🍸

Individual proprietors have supplied all details of accommodation. Although we do check for accuracy, we advise you to confirm prices and other information at the time of booking.

KINGHAM

Oxfordshire
Map ref 2B1

Small village set in beautiful scenery near the River Evenlode and the woodlands of Wychwood. Popular with ornithologists for the variety of rare birds which can be seen here.

The Mill House Hotel and Restaurant M
☗☗☗☗ COMMENDED
Kingham, OX7 6UH
☎ (0608) 658188
Fax (0608) 658492
Telex 849041 Sharet G TVH 003
Converted flour mill, bordered by the original mill stream. Cosy lounge bar with roaring log fire. Ideal for touring the beautiful Cotswolds.
Bedrooms: 11 double & 11 twin, 1 family room.
Bathrooms: 23 private.
Bed & breakfast: £46-£57 single, £72-£96 double.
Half board: £54-£65 daily, £378-£455 weekly.
Lunch available.
Evening meal 7pm (l.o. 9.30pm).
Parking for 60.
Credit: Access, Visa, Diners, Amex.
🖙5🖥🕮📞🕮🗑🖏 🛊 Ⓥ
🍴🕮🛏🍴🕛🏵🎣🏵🐾🦌
🏵 SP 🏵 🍸

KNOWL HILL

Berkshire
Map ref 2C2

3m NE. Twyford

Bird In Hand M
☗☗☗☗ COMMENDED
Bath Rd., Knowl Hill, Twyford, Nr. Reading, RG10 9UP
☎ (0628) 822781 & 826622
Extended 14th C coaching inn, 4 miles west of Maidenhead. 25 minutes' drive to Heathrow and 30 miles from London.
Bedrooms: 1 single, 2 double & 12 twin.
Bathrooms: 15 private.
Bed & breakfast: £50-£75 single, £70-£100 double.
Half board: £67.50-£92.50 daily, £500-£675 weekly.
Lunch available.
Evening meal 7pm (l.o. 10.30pm).
Parking for 80.
Credit: Access, Visa, Diners, Amex.
🖙🖥📞🕮🗑🖏 🛊 Ⓥ 🍴
🕮🛏🍴🏵🐾 DAP SP

LEIGHTON BUZZARD

Bedfordshire
Map ref 2C1

Large market town with many buildings of interest including a fine 15th C market cross, the 17th C Holly Lodge and a number of old inns. The Grand Union Canal is nearby and in Page's Park is a narrow gauge railway.

Hunt Hotel
☗☗☗ APPROVED
19 Church Rd., Leighton Buzzard, LU7 7LR
☎ (0525) 374692
Family-owned and run. Overlooking parkland but still close to town centre, M1 and London-to-Birmingham rail link.
Bedrooms: 5 single, 7 double & 1 twin, 2 family rooms.
Bathrooms: 12 private, 1 public.
Bed & breakfast: £25-£48 single, £46-£66 double.
Lunch available.
Evening meal 6.30pm (l.o. 10pm).
Parking for 24.
Credit: Access, Visa, C.Bl., Diners, Amex.
🖙📞🕮🗑🖏 🛊 Ⓥ 🍴◉
🕮🛏🍴 SP 🏵

LUTON

Bedfordshire
Map ref 2D1

Bedfordshire's largest town with its own airport, several industries and an excellent shopping centre. The town's history is depicted in the museum and art gallery in Wardown Park. Luton Hoo has a magnificent collection of treasures. *Tourist Information Centre* ☎ (0582) 401579 (Luton Airport) (0582) 405100

Ackworth Hotel
☗ APPROVED
36 Studley Rd., Luton, LU3 1BB
☎ (0582) 31614
Small family-run hotel within half mile of town centre and 4 miles from Luton International Airport.
Bedrooms: 5 twin, 3 family rooms.
Bathrooms: 8 private.

Continued ▶

LUTON
Continued

Bed & breakfast: from £30 single, from £40 double.
Half board: £28-£38 daily, £168-£228 weekly.
Evening meal 6pm (l.o. 7.30pm).
Parking for 10.

Arlington Hotel
137 New Bedford Rd., Luton, LU3 1LF
☎ (0582) 419614
Modern hotel within easy reach of town centre and airport. Opposite Wardown Park and close to many sports facilities including Bath Road swimming pool and Stockwood Park.
Bedrooms: 4 single, 10 double & 7 twin, 3 family rooms.
Bathrooms: 19 private, 2 public; 2 private showers.
Bed & breakfast: from £35.50 single, £43.50-£51.90 double.
Half board: from £44.45 daily, from £280 weekly.
Evening meal 6pm (l.o. 8pm).
Parking for 25.
Credit: Access, Visa, Diners, Amex.

The Red Lion Hotel M
Castle St., Luton, LU1 3AA
☎ (0582) 413881
Fax (0582) 23864
Lansbury
Town centre hotel, convenient for shopping facilities and local tourist attractions. 1 mile from Luton Airport.
Bedrooms: 9 single, 14 double & 13 twin, 2 family rooms.
Bathrooms: 38 private.
Bed & breakfast: max. £76 single, max. £88 double.
Half board: max. £90 daily.
Lunch available.
Evening meal 7pm (l.o. 10.30pm).
Parking for 48.
Credit: Access, Visa, Diners, Amex.

> *National Crown ratings were correct at the time of going to press but are subject to change. Please check at the time of booking.*

MAIDENHEAD
Berkshire
Map ref 2C2

Attractive town on the River Thames which is crossed by an elegant 18th C bridge and by Brunel's well-known railway bridge. It is a popular place for boating with delightful riverside walks. The Courage Shire Horse Centre is nearby.
Tourist Information Centre ☎ *(0628) 781110*

Brayfield Arms Hotel
Monkey Island Lane, Bray, Maidenhead, SL6 2EA
☎ Maidenhead (0628) 20004
Fax (0628) 21251
Small, family-run hotel with good bar facilities, a la carte restaurant with freshly cooked food and friendly atmosphere.
Bedrooms: 4 single, 6 double & 6 twin.
Bathrooms: 16 private.
Bed & breakfast: £50-£55 single, £55-£65 double.
Lunch available.
Evening meal 7pm (l.o. 10.30pm).
Credit: Access, Visa, Diners, Amex.

Chauntry House Hotel M

High St., Bray, Maidenhead, SL6 2AB
☎ (0628) 73991/2/3
Fax (0628) 773089
18th C former village gaol and workhouse, now a listed country house hotel in its own grounds. 15 minutes' drive from Heathrow Airport and 30 minutes' drive from London.
Bedrooms: 2 single, 6 double & 5 twin.
Bathrooms: 13 private.
Bed & breakfast: from £96 single, from £117 double.
Half board: from £114.95 daily.
Lunch available.
Evening meal 7.30pm (l.o. 9.30pm).
Parking for 20.
Credit: Access, Visa, Diners, Amex.

Clifton Guest House
21 Crauford Rise, Maidenhead, SL6 7LR
☎ (0628) 23572

Fully-licensed, family-run hotel near town centre. Convenient for Heathrow, Windsor Castle and the M4, M40 and M25 motorways.
Bedrooms: 3 single, 2 double & 5 twin, 2 family rooms.
Bathrooms: 5 private, 4 public.
Bed & breakfast: £24-£30 single, £37-£42 double.
Evening meal 6pm (l.o. 9.30pm).
Parking for 10.
Credit: Access, Visa.

Elva Lodge Hotel
Castle Hill, Maidenhead, SL6 4AD
☎ (0628) 22948 & 34883
Fax (0628) 38855
Located in central Maidenhead, close to the M4 and 20 minutes from Heathrow Airport.
Bedrooms: 12 single, 8 double & 4 twin, 3 family rooms.
Bathrooms: 10 private, 9 public; 8 private showers.
Bed & breakfast: £30-£55 single, £48-£65 double.
Half board: £40-£70 daily, £252-£441 weekly.
Lunch available.
Evening meal 6pm (l.o. 10.30pm).
Parking for 31.
Credit: Access, Visa, Diners, Amex.

Kingswood Hotel M
Boyn Hill Avenue, Maidenhead, SL6 4EN
☎ (0628) 33598
Fax (0628) 25516
Telex 847330 KINGS
Converted Victorian house in town centre, yet very quiet and convenient for Heathrow, Windsor Castle, Ascot Races and Henley Regatta.
Bedrooms: 4 single, 9 double & 1 twin, 1 family room.
Bathrooms: 15 private.
Bed & breakfast: £60-£65 single, £80-£95 double.
Lunch available.
Evening meal 7pm (l.o. 9.45pm).
Parking for 18.
Credit: Access, Visa, Diners, Amex.

Monkey Island Hotel M
COMMENDED
Bray-on-Thames, Maidenhead, SL6 2EE
☎ (0628) 23400
Beautiful island in the Thames Valley, approached by footbridge. Close to Windsor, Ascot, Henley and Oxford. 26 miles from London and 15 miles from Heathrow Airport.
Bedrooms: 2 single, 8 double & 13 twin, 2 family rooms.
Bathrooms: 25 private.
Bed & breakfast: £74.10-£91.50 single, £102-£122.50 double.
Half board: £97.75-£115.15 daily.
Lunch available.
Evening meal 7.30pm (l.o. 9.45pm).
Parking for 100.
Credit: Access, Visa, Diners, Amex.

Old Court Hotel
Bath Rd., Taplow, Maidenhead, SL6 0AH
☎ (0628) 71248 & 21440
Late Victorian with original mosaic, privately owned and managed, providing a homely, comfortable and friendly atmosphere.
Bedrooms: 11 single, 4 double & 4 twin, 5 family rooms.
Bathrooms: 3 private, 5 public; 1 private shower.
Bed & breakfast: £35-£50 single, £45-£56 double.
Half board: £44-£60 daily.
Evening meal 7pm (l.o. 9pm).
Parking for 40.
Credit: Access, Visa.

Thamesbrook Guest House
COMMENDED
18 Ray Park Avenue, Maidenhead, SL6 8DS
☎ (0628) 783855
In a quiet location near river, Boulters Lock and town centre. Spacious, well-decorated rooms. Pubs and restaurants nearby.
Bedrooms: 1 double & 2 twin, 1 family room.
Bathrooms: 1 private, 2 public.
Bed & breakfast: £20-£25 single, £32-£38 double.
Parking for 6.

MARLOW

Buckinghamshire
Map ref 2C2

Attractive Georgian town
on the River Thames,
famous for its 19th C
suspension bridge. The
High Street contains
many old houses and
there are connections
with writers including
Shelley and the poet T.S.
Eliot.

The Country House **M**
Bisham, Marlow, SL7 1RP
☎ (0628) 890606
Fax (0628) 890983
*Edwardian house in tranquil
grounds. 300-yard level walk
from Marlow Bridge and the
High Street.*
Bedrooms: 3 single, 3 double
& 1 twin, 1 family room.
Bathrooms: 8 private.
Bed & breakfast: from £64
single, from £78 double.
Parking for 10.
Credit: Access, Visa, Amex.

Danesfield House **M**
Medmenham, Marlow,
SL7 3ES
☎ Maidenhead
(0628) 891010 Telex 848078
Fax (0628) 890408
*Exclusive hotel set in 65 acres
of outstanding gardens
overlooking the River Thames
between Marlow and Henley.*
Bedrooms: 8 single, 63 double
& 22 twin.
Bathrooms: 92 private.
Bed & breakfast: £148-£240
single, £209.75-£267.25
double.
Half board: £125-£250 daily.
Lunch available.
Evening meal 6.30pm (l.o.
10pm).
Parking for 150.
Credit: Access, Visa, Diners,
Amex.

Holly Tree House **M**
COMMENDED
Burford Close, Marlow
Bottom, SL7 3NF
☎ (0628) 891110
*Detached house set in large
gardens with fine views over
the valley. Quiet yet convenient
location. Large car park. All
rooms fully en-suite.*
Bedrooms: 1 single, 2 double
& 1 twin.
Bathrooms: 4 private.

Bed & breakfast: £47.50-
£59.95 single, £59.95-£65.95
double.
Parking for 8.
Credit: Access, Visa, Amex.

MAULDEN

Bedfordshire
Map ref 2D1

Malletts **M**
COMMENDED
Great Farm, Silsoe Rd.,
Maulden, MK45 2AZ
☎ (0525) 402248
*Elegant Georgian country
house, built by Duke of
Bedford. Extensive health and
leisure facilities including hair
and beauty salons. Fully-
licensed French restaurant.
Close to Woburn, Milton
Keynes and Luton.*
Bedrooms: 1 single, 6 double
& 1 twin.
Bathrooms: 8 private.
Bed & breakfast: £59-£69
single, £85-£125 double.
Half board: £75-£85 daily,
£475-£575 weekly.
Lunch available.
Evening meal 7pm (l.o.
9.30pm).
Parking for 78.
Credit: Access, Visa, Diners,
Amex.

MILTON COMMON

Oxfordshire
Map ref 2C1

9m E. Oxford

Belfry Hotel **M**
COMMENDED
Milton Common, Oxford,
OX9 2JW
☎ Great Milton
(0844) 279381 Telex 837968
CB Inter
*Tudor-style country hotel,
privately owned. Well-placed
for touring. Indoor leisure
complex with swimming pool,
sauna, solarium, mini gym.*
Bedrooms: 11 single,
36 double & 30 twin.
Bathrooms: 77 private.
Bed & breakfast: £70-£87.50
single, £85-£105 double.
Lunch available.
Evening meal 7.30pm (l.o.
9.30pm).

---

*We advise you to
confirm your
booking in writing.*

Parking for 200.
Credit: Access, Visa, Diners,
Amex.

⊕ Display advertisement
appears on page 560.

MILTON KEYNES

Buckinghamshire
Map ref 2C1

Designated a New Town
in 1967, Milton Keynes
offers a wide range of
housing and is
abundantly planted with
trees. It has excellent
shopping facilities and 3
centres for leisure and
sporting activities. The
Open University is based
here.
*Tourist Information
Centre* **☎** *(0908) 691995*

Broughton Hotel **M**
COMMENDED
Broughton Village, Nr.
Milton Keynes, MK10 9AA
☎ (0908) 667726
Telex 826730 WELLCO 9
*On the outskirts of Milton
Keynes, conveniently located
for the M1 junction 14.*
Bedrooms: 1 single, 4 double
& 24 twin, 2 family rooms.
Bathrooms: 31 private.
Bed & breakfast: £67.50-£75
single, £70-£90 double.
Lunch available.
Evening meal 7pm (l.o.
9.30pm).
Parking for 58.
Credit: Access, Visa, Diners,
Amex.

Friendly Hotel **M**
Monks Way, Two Mile Ash,
Milton Keynes, MK8 8LY
☎ (0908) 561666
Telex 826152
CB Friendly
*New hotel close to the centre of
town and recreational areas.
Newly built indoor leisure
centre.*
Bedrooms: 15 double &
30 twin, 5 family rooms.
Bathrooms: 50 private.
Bed & breakfast: £56.75-
£69.45 single, £77.50-£92.65
double.
Lunch available.
Evening meal 7pm (l.o.
10pm).
Parking for 76.
Credit: Access, Visa, Diners,
Amex.

Kingfishers
Listed APPROVED
9 Rylstone Close, Heelands,
Milton Keynes, MK13 7QT
☎ (0908) 310231
*Large private home set in
quarter acre of grounds, close
to Milton Keynes city centre,
bus, coach and railway
stations.*
Bedrooms: 2 double & 1 twin.
Bathrooms: 2 private,
1 public.
Bed & breakfast: £20-£30
single, £35-£40 double.
Parking for 6.

NETTLEBED

Oxfordshire
Map ref 2C2

The White Hart Hotel
High St., Nettlebed,
RG9 5DD
☎ (0491) 641245
*Oak beamed 17th C coaching
inn with log fires and large
garden, conveniently placed for
Henley, Oxford and Reading.*
Bedrooms: 1 double & 5 twin.
Bathrooms: 6 private.
Bed & breakfast: £60-£85
double.
Lunch available.
Evening meal 6.30pm (l.o.
10pm).
Parking for 50.
Credit: Access, Visa.

NEWBURY

Berkshire
Map ref 2C2

Ancient town surrounded
by the Downs and on the
Kennet and Avon Canal. It
has many buildings of
interest, including the
17th C Cloth Hall, which
is now a museum. The
famous racecourse is
nearby.
*Tourist Information
Centre* **☎** *(0635) 30267*

The Bell at Boxford
Lambourn Rd., Newbury,
RG16 8DD
☎ Boxford (048 838) 721
Fax (048 838) 749
*Traditional inn with real ales,
food and extensive wine list. 4
miles from Newbury on the
Lambourn road. A la carte
restaurant.*
Bedrooms: 1 single, 8 double
& 1 twin.
Bathrooms: 10 private.
Continued ▶

NEWBURY

Continued

Bed & breakfast: £30-£56
single, £45-£68 double.
Half board: £35-£70 daily.
Lunch available.
Evening meal 7pm (l.o.
10pm).
Parking for 55.
Credit: Access, Visa, Diners,
Amex.

Elcot Park Resort Hotel M

Kintbury, Nr. Newbury,
RG16 8NJ
☎ Kintbury (0488) 58100
Fax (0488) 58288
Resort
*Elegant and peaceful 18th C
mansion, in beautiful park and
gardens laid out by the Royal
Gardener, Sir William Paxton.
Log fires, individually
decorated bedrooms and dinner
by candlelight.*
Bedrooms: 2 single, 62 double
& 6 twin, 5 family rooms.
Bathrooms: 75 private.
Bed & breakfast: £42.50-
£94.50 single, £85-£112
double.
Lunch available.
Evening meal 7.30pm (l.o.
9.30pm).
Parking for 138.
Credit: Access, Visa, Diners,
Amex.

Enborne Grange Hotel M

Enborne St., Wash Common,
Newbury, RG14 6RP
☎ (0635) 40046
*Delightful rural setting
overlooking South Downs.
Within easy reach of Newbury
and major tourist attractions.*
Bedrooms: 5 single, 18 double
& 2 twin, 1 family room.
Bathrooms: 26 private,
1 public.
Bed & breakfast: £50-£60
single, £70-£76 double.
Lunch available.
Evening meal 7.30pm (l.o.
9.30pm).
Parking for 80.
Credit: Access, Visa, Amex.

Foley Lodge Hotel M
COMMENDED

Stockcross, Newbury,
RG16 8JU
☎ (0635) 528770
Fax (0635) 528398

*A former Victorian hunting
lodge, carefully restored and
developed into a well-appointed
country house hotel.*
Bedrooms: 51 double &
14 twin, 4 family rooms.
Bathrooms: 69 private.
Bed & breakfast: £49-£101
single, £57-£123 double.
Half board: £49-£84 daily.
Lunch available.
Evening meal 7pm (l.o.
10pm).
Parking for 140.
Credit: Access, Visa, Diners,
Amex.

Hilton National Hotel M
COMMENDED

Pinchington Lane, Newbury,
RG14 7HL
☎ (0635) 529000
Fax (0635) 529337
Hilton
*New hotel, situated just off the
A34, offering traditional
standards of service. Stubbs
Restaurant and Piano Bar.*
Bedrooms: 73 double &
39 twin.
Bathrooms: 112 private.
Bed & breakfast: £52-£96.70
single, £104-£126.65 double.
Half board: £68-£117.10
daily.
Lunch available.
Evening meal 7pm (l.o.
10pm).
Parking for 160.
Credit: Access, Visa, Diners,
Amex.

The Limes Guest House

368 London Rd., Newbury,
RG13 2QH
☎ (0635) 33082
*Originally built in 1910 during
the Edwardian era, and
conveniently situated on the A4
between Newbury and
Thatcham.*
Bedrooms: 3 single, 3 double
& 3 twin.
Bathrooms: 9 private.
Bed & breakfast: £36-£40
single, £46-£50 double.
Half board: £52-£60 daily.
Evening meal 7.30pm (l.o.
9.30pm).
Parking for 10.
Credit: Access, Visa.

Nalderhill House
COMMENDED

Wickham Heath, Stockcross,
Newbury, RG16 8EU
☎ (0635) 41783

*Large Victorian country house
with exceptional views over
surrounding countryside.
Landscaped gardens and
grounds in peaceful setting. 4
miles to Newbury town centre.*
Bedrooms: 2 double & 3 twin.
Bathrooms: 3 private,
1 public.
Bed & breakfast: £30-£35
single, £35-£45 double.
Parking for 10.
Credit: Visa, Amex.

Regency Park Hotel M
COMMENDED

Bowling Green Rd.,
Thatcham, Nr. Newbury,
RG13 3RP
☎ Newbury (0635) 871555
Telex 847844 REGPRK
*Comfortable hotel that blends
architecturally with the former
family home constructed earlier
this century.*
Bedrooms: 5 single, 30 double
& 15 twin.
Bathrooms: 50 private.
Bed & breakfast: £54.25-
£100.50 single, £65.50-£119
double.
Half board: £39-£119 daily.
Lunch available.
Evening meal 6.30pm (l.o.
10.30pm).
Parking for 100.
Credit: Access, Visa, Diners,
Amex.

Stakis Newbury Hotel M
COMMENDED

Oxford Rd., Newbury,
RG16 8XY
☎ (0635) 247010
Stakis
*Modern hotel located off
junction 13 of M4. Leisure
club, restaurant, bar,
courtyard. Children's
programme weekends. Half
board rate based on a
minimum 2 night stay.*
Bedrooms: 58 double &
50 twin, 4 family rooms.
Bathrooms: 112 private.
Bed & breakfast: £89-£99
single, £112-£122 double.
Half board: from £33 daily.
Lunch available.
Evening meal 6.30pm (l.o.
10pm).
Parking for 150.
Credit: Access, Visa, Diners,
Amex.

The White Hart Inn

Hamstead Marshall,
Newbury, RG15 0HW
☎ Kintbury (0488) 58201
*Traditional rural inn with oak
beams and log fire.
Comfortable accommodation in
barn conversion.*
Bedrooms: 2 single, 2 twin,
2 family rooms.
Bathrooms: 6 private.
Bed & breakfast: £40-£45
single, £50-£55 double.
Lunch available.
Evening meal 7pm (l.o.
10pm).
Parking for 35.
Credit: Access, Visa, Diners,
Amex.

NEWPORT PAGNELL

Buckinghamshire
Map ref 2C1

The Coach House Hotel M
COMMENDED

London Rd., Newport
Pagnell, MK16 0JA
☎ (0908) 613688
Fax (0908) 617335
Lansbury
*New hotel built around a listed
Georgian property, off junction
14 of the M1. Ideally situated,
close to Milton Keynes.*
Bedrooms: 24 double &
25 twin.
Bathrooms: 49 private.
Bed & breakfast: £33-£87
single, £66-£99 double.
Half board: £46-£117 daily.
Lunch available.
Evening meal 7pm (l.o. 10pm).
Parking for 162.
Credit: Access, Visa, Diners,
Amex.

Swan Revived Hotel M
COMMENDED

High St., Newport Pagnell,
Milton Keynes, MK16 8AR
☎ (0908) 610565
Fax (0908) 210995
Telex 826801
*Famous coaching inn, where
guests can enjoy every modern
comfort. Perfect stopping place
for those travelling north or
south, or for exploring.*
Bedrooms: 20 single,
16 double & 3 twin, 2 family
rooms.
Bathrooms: 41 private.
Bed & breakfast: £27.50-£60
single, £45-£70 double.
Half board: £39-£46.50 daily.
Lunch available.
Evening meal 7.15pm (l.o.
10pm).

Parking for 18.
Credit: Access, Visa, Diners, Amex.

🐾 🔧 📷 📞 ⊡ 🖥 🅱 ♿ Ⅴ
🛏 ⬤ 🔱 🎢 📖 📻 🍴 ⚓ OAP SP
🕮 Ⓣ

OLD WINDSOR

Berkshire
Map ref 2D2

2m SE. Windsor

Union Inn M

COMMENDED

17 Crimp Hill, Old Windsor,
SL4 2QY
☎ (0753) 861955
Fax (0753) 831378
Freehouse hotel with 50-seat restaurant. Traditional beamed bar. Situated in open countryside.
Bedrooms: 4 single, 8 double.
Bathrooms: 12 private.
Bed & breakfast: £40-£51 single, £50-£65 double.
Lunch available.
Evening meal 7pm (l.o. 10pm).
Parking for 32.
Credit: Access, Visa, Amex.

🐾 📞 ⊡ ♻ Ⅴ 📖 🛏 ✕ 🍴
SP

OLNEY

Buckinghamshire
Map ref 2C1

The Four Pillars Restaurant and Hotel M

60 High St., Olney,
MK46 4BE
☎ Bedford (0234) 711563
Extensive a la carte menu. Restaurant caters for both English and Continental tastes.
Bedrooms: 2 single, 3 double & 2 twin.
Bathrooms: 7 private, 2 public.
Bed & breakfast: £31.50-£37.50 single, £47.50-£53.50 double.
Lunch available.
Evening meal 6pm (l.o. 10pm).
Parking for 12.
Credit: Access, Visa, Diners, Amex.

🐾 📷 ⊡ ♻ 🅱 Ⅴ ✕ 📻
📖 🛏 🍴 ❋ ✕ 🖼 OAP SP 🕮

The Mill House M

COMMENDED

Church St., Olney,
MK46 4AD
☎ Bedford (0234) 711381
Georgian country house in a large garden with a river flowing through. Beside historic church associated with poets Cowper and Newton. A Wolsey Lodge house.

Bedrooms: 1 double & 2 twin.
Bathrooms: 2 private,
1 public.
Bed & breakfast: from £23 single, from £46 double.
Half board: £38-£48 daily.
Parking for 3.

🅱 ♻ 🃏 Ⅴ 🅱 📻 📖 🛏 ⚓ ♫
❋ ✕ 🖼 🕮

The White House Guest House

APPROVED

10 High Street South, Olney,
Milton Keynes, MK46 4AA
☎ Bedford (0234) 711478
Country town guesthouse with family atmosphere, providing clean, warm, comfortable accommodation. Within easy reach of Bedford, Milton Keynes and Northampton.
Bedrooms: 2 single, 1 double & 4 twin, 1 family room.
Bathrooms: 1 public;
3 private showers.
Bed & breakfast: £24-£26 single, £37-£39 double.
Half board: £31-£33 daily, £186-£198 weekly.
Evening meal 6pm (l.o. 4pm).
Parking for 4.

🐾 📷 ♿ 🅱 🖥 Ⅴ 🛏 📻
⚓ ✕ 🖼

OXFORD

Oxfordshire
Map ref 2C1

Beautiful university town with many ancient colleges, some dating from the 13th C, and numerous buildings of historic and architectural interest. The Ashmolean Museum has outstanding collections. There are lovely gardens and meadows with punting on the Cherwell.
Tourist Information Centre ☎ *(0865) 726871*

Acorn Guest House

Listed APPROVED

260 Iffley Rd., Oxford,
OX4 1SE
☎ (0865) 247998
Situated mid-way between the centre of town and the ring-road and so convenient for local amenities and more distant attractions.
Bedrooms: 2 single, 1 twin, 3 family rooms.
Bathrooms: 2 public.
Bed & breakfast: £18-£24 single, £36-£40 double.
Parking for 5.
Credit: Access, Visa.

🐾 ⊡ ♻ 🅱 Ⅴ 📖 ⚓ ✕

The Athena Guest House M

Listed

253-255 Cowley Rd., Oxford,
OX4 1XQ
☎ (0865) 243124 & 243916
Large, comfortable Victorian guesthouse with colour TV in all rooms. Close to shops and restaurants. Easy transport to station and city centre. Ideal for small or large groups.
Bedrooms: 3 single, 6 twin, 3 family rooms.
Bathrooms: 1 private, 3 public; 2 private showers.
Bed & breakfast: £15-£18 single, £30-£45 double.
Parking for 7.

🐾 5 ⊡ ♻ 🅱 🛏 📻 📖 ⚓ ✕

Becket House

Listed

5 Becket St., Nr. Station, Oxford, OX1 1PP
☎ (0865) 724675
Friendly guesthouse convenient for rail and bus station, city centre and colleges. Simple clean accommodation.
Bedrooms: 4 single, 1 double & 3 twin, 1 family room.
Bathrooms: 3 public.
Bed & breakfast: £16-£20 single, £32-£40 double.
Credit: Access, Visa.

🐾 📷 ⊡ ♻ 🅱 Ⅴ 🛏 📻 📖
⚓ ✕

Bowood House Hotel M

238 Oxford Rd., Kidlington,
Oxford, OX5 1EB
☎ Oxford (0865) 842288
Completely modernised family-run hotel close to shops. On the A4260, 4 miles from city centre. Frequent bus service to Oxford.
Bedrooms: 7 single, 8 double & 4 twin, 3 family rooms.
Bathrooms: 20 private, 2 public.
Bed & breakfast: £25-£50 single, £55-£70 double.
Half board: £35-£45 daily.
Evening meal 6.30pm (l.o. 8.30pm).
Parking for 27.
Credit: Access, Visa.

🐾 📷 ♿ 📞 📷 ⊡ ♻ 🅱 Ⅴ
🛏 📖 ⚓ 🍴 ♿ ✕ 🖼 SP

Bravalla Guest House M

Listed COMMENDED

242 Iffley Rd., Oxford,
OX4 1SE
☎ (0865) 241326 & 250511
A small family-run guesthouse within half a mile of Magdalen College with its famous deer park. 1 mile from city centre.
Bedrooms: 3 double & 1 twin.
Bathrooms: 4 private, 2 public.

Bed & breakfast: £25-£40 single, £35-£42 double.
Parking for 4.
Credit: Access, Visa.

⊡ ♻ 🅱 Ⅴ 📖 ⚓ 🖼 OAP SP

Bronte Guest House M

☺☺

282 Iffley Rd., Oxford,
OX4 4AA
☎ (0865) 244594
Close to Iffley village and church, 1 mile from city centre. Bus stop outside, but easy walking distance to city centre and colleges.
Bedrooms: 2 double & 2 twin, 1 family room.
Bathrooms: 2 private, 1 public.
Bed & breakfast: £26-£38 double.
Parking for 5.

🐾 ⊡ ♻ 🅱 Ⅴ 🛏 📻 📖 ⚓
✕ 🚭

Casa Villa M

☺☺ APPROVED

388 Banbury Rd., Oxford,
OX2 7PW
☎ (0865) 512642
Detached guesthouse in north Oxford with front and back gardens. Friendly and pleasant service provided. Close to all amenities and easy access to M40.
Bedrooms: 3 single, 5 double & 1 twin, 2 family rooms.
Bathrooms: 6 private, 2 public.
Bed & breakfast: £25-£29.50 single, £40-£49 double.
Parking for 6.
Credit: Access, Visa, Amex.

🐾 📷 📷 ⊡ 🅱 🛏 📻 📖 ⚓
❋ ✕ 🚭 SP

Combermere House

Listed

11 Polstead Rd., Oxford,
OX2 6TW
☎ (0865) 56971
Family-run Victorian house in quiet tree-lined road in residential north Oxford, one mile from city centre and colleges.
Bedrooms: 5 single, 2 twin, 2 family rooms.
Bathrooms: 9 private.
Bed & breakfast: £25-£33 single, £38-£48 double.
Parking for 3.
Credit: Access, Visa.

🐾 📷 ⊡ ♻ 🅱 🖥 Ⅴ ✕ 📖
⚓ 🖼 Ⓣ

Conifer Lodge M

☺☺

159 Eynsham Rd., Botley,
Oxford, OX2 9NE
☎ (0865) 862280

Continued ▶

OXFORD
Continued

House on the outskirts of Oxford city, overlooking farmland and offering a warm, friendly welcome.
Bedrooms: 1 single, 2 twin, 1 family room.
Bathrooms: 4 private, 1 public.
Bed & breakfast: £16-£28 single, £30-£42 double.
Parking for 8.
Open April-December.

Cotswold House
COMMENDED
363 Banbury Rd., Oxford, OX2 7PL
☎ (0865) 310558
Well-situated elegant property offering a high standard of furnishings and facilities in each of its 6 rooms.
Bedrooms: 1 single, 2 double & 1 twin, 2 family rooms.
Bathrooms: 6 private.
Bed & breakfast: £30-£32 single, £45-£50 double.
Parking for 5.

Courtfield Private Hotel
367 Iffley Rd., Oxford, OX4 4DP
☎ (0865) 242991
Large individually designed house in tree-lined road. Modern, spacious bedrooms, most en-suite. Ample parking.
Bedrooms: 4 double & 1 twin, 1 family room.
Bathrooms: 4 private, 1 public.
Bed & breakfast: £25-£30 single, £36-£42 double.
Parking for 7.
Credit: Access, Visa, Amex.

Earlmont Guest House
322-324 Cowley Rd., Oxford, OX4 2AF
☎ (0865) 240236
Friendly, comfortable guesthouse within easy reach of city centre and ring road. Vegetarians catered for. Non-smoking rooms available.
Bedrooms: 3 single, 3 double & 4 twin, 2 family rooms.
Bathrooms: 1 private, 4 public; 2 private showers.
Bed & breakfast: £25-£40 single, £35-£45 double.
Parking for 11.
Credit: Access, Visa, Amex.

Gables
COMMENDED
6 Cumnor Hill, Oxford, OX2 9HA
☎ (0865) 862153
Modern house, 2 miles from city centre, but with a country atmosphere. Direct route from railway station. Within easy reach of beautiful Cotswolds.
Bedrooms: 1 single, 1 double & 2 twin, 1 family room.
Bathrooms: 4 private, 2 public.
Bed & breakfast: £18-£20 single, £37-£42 double.
Parking for 10.

Grapevines M
308 Banbury Rd., Oxford, OX2 7ED
☎ (0865) 54690
New hotel offering friendly and efficient service, close to excellent shopping facilities.
Bedrooms: 2 single, 1 double & 3 twin.
Bathrooms: 6 private.
Bed & breakfast: £32.50-£37.50 single, £47.50-£52.50 double.
Evening meal 6pm (l.o. 7.30pm).
Parking for 5.
Credit: Access, Visa.

Green Gables
COMMENDED
326 Abingdon Rd., Oxford, OX1 4TE
☎ (0865) 725870
Large house with gabled exterior, 1.25 miles from Oxford city centre. On A414, secluded by trees.
Bedrooms: 2 single, 2 double & 1 twin, 1 family room.
Bathrooms: 3 private, 1 public.
Bed & breakfast: £17-£34 single, £30-£42 double.
Parking for 6.
Credit: Visa.

Green Views M
95 Sunningwell Rd., Oxford, OX1 4SY
☎ (0865) 249603
Enjoying country views, located beside a lake and bowling green. Within walking distance of the centre of Oxford. Homely atmosphere.
Bedrooms: 4 single, 1 double & 2 twin.
Bathrooms: 1 private, 3 public.

Bed & breakfast: £16-£18 single, £32-£37 double.
Parking for 4.

Hollybush Guest House
Listed
530 Banbury Rd., Oxford, OX2 8EG
☎ (0865) 54886
Pretty Edwardian, family-run guesthouse on main road to city. Easy access to Blenheim Palace, Cotswolds, London and Stratford-upon-Avon.
Bedrooms: 1 single, 1 double & 2 twin.
Bathrooms: 1 private, 1 public.
Bed & breakfast: £18-£22 single, £34-£45 double.
Half board: £26-£32 daily.
Parking for 4.

Isis Guest House M
COMMENDED
45-53 Iffley Rd., Oxford, OX4 1ED
☎ (0865) 248894 & 242466
Modernised, Victorian, city centre guesthouse within walking distance of colleges and shops. Easy access to ring road.
Bedrooms: 9 single, 5 double & 21 twin, 2 family rooms.
Bathrooms: 14 private, 7 public.
Bed & breakfast: £19-£30 single, £38-£42 double.
Parking for 18.
Open July-September.
Credit: Access, Visa.

Linton Lodge Hotel M
9-13 Linton Rd., Oxford, OX2 6UJ
☎ (0865) 53461 Telex 837093
🅷 Hilton
Close to colleges and city centre, with library, restaurant, cosy bar, offering an English country house atmosphere. Pleasant gardens.
Bedrooms: 17 single, 18 double & 34 twin, 2 family rooms.
Bathrooms: 71 private.
Bed & breakfast: £40-£88 single, £70-£105 double.
Half board: £58-£116 daily, £370-£777 weekly.
Lunch available.
Evening meal 7pm (l.o. 9.30pm).
Parking for 40.
Credit: Access, Visa, Diners, Amex.

Lonsdale Guest House
Listed
312 Banbury Rd., Oxford, OX2 7ED
☎ (0865) 54872
Victorian house close to shops, launderette, swimming pool, squash and tennis courts. Beverages available.
Bedrooms: 2 single, 1 double & 5 twin, 1 family room.
Bathrooms: 1 public; 5 private showers.
Bed & breakfast: £20-£25 single, £35-£40 double.
Parking for 2.

Marlborough House (Private Hotel) M
Listed
321 Woodstock Rd., Oxford, OX2 7NY
☎ (0865) 311321
Fax (0865) 515329
Bed and breakfast accommodation, just 2 miles from Oxford city centre.
Bedrooms: 2 single, 1 double & 8 twin, 1 family room.
Bathrooms: 12 private, 1 public.
Bed & breakfast: from £50 single, from £60 double.
Parking for 6.
Credit: Access, Visa.

Mount Pleasant
APPROVED
76 London Rd., Headington, Oxford, OX3 9AJ
☎ (0865) 62749
A small, family-run hotel offering full facilities. Situated on the A40 and convenient for Oxford shopping, hospitals, colleges, visiting the Chilterns and the Cotswolds.
Bedrooms: 2 double & 5 twin, 1 family room.
Bathrooms: 8 private.
Bed & breakfast: £38-£50 single, £45-£65 double.
Half board: £45.50-£52.50 daily.
Lunch available.
Evening meal 6pm (l.o. 9.30pm).
Parking for 6.
Credit: Access, Visa, Diners, Amex.

Newton House
82-84 Abingdon Rd., Oxford, OX1 4PL
☎ (0865) 240561
Victorian house within walking distance of city centre.

Bedrooms: 2 double & 4 twin,
6 family rooms.
Bathrooms: 3 private,
3 public.
Bed & breakfast: £16-£30
single, £28-£40 double.
Parking for 8.
Credit: Access, Visa.

Norham Guest House
Listed

16 Norham Rd., Oxford,
OX2 6SF
☎ (0865) 515352
*Victorian house in conservation
area. 500 yards from university
parks and walking distance
from city centre.*
Bedrooms: 2 single, 1 double
& 3 twin, 2 family rooms.
Bathrooms: 2 public.
Bed & breakfast: £20 single,
£40-£45 double.
Parking for 4.

The Old Black Horse Hotel M
APPROVED

102 St. Clements, Oxford,
OX4 1AR
☎ (0865) 244691
*Former coaching inn with
private car park close to
Magdalen Bridge, short walk
to colleges, riverside walks and
city centre.*
Bedrooms: 1 single, 3 double
& 2 twin, 2 family rooms.
Bathrooms: 8 private,
1 public.
Bed & breakfast: £53-£66
single, from £79 double.
Lunch available.
Evening meal 7pm (l.o. 9pm).
Parking for 25.
Credit: Access, Visa.

Pine Castle Hotel M
COMMENDED

290 Iffley Rd., Oxford,
OX4 4AE
☎ (0865) 241497/727230
*Friendly guesthouse close to
the city and River Thames.*
Bedrooms: 1 single, 1 double
& 1 twin, 2 family rooms.
Bathrooms: 1 public;
1 private shower.
Bed & breakfast: £35-£40
double.
Evening meal 6pm (l.o. 6pm).
Parking for 4.
Credit: Access, Visa.

Pine Lodge Guest House
COMMENDED

201 Cumnor Hill, Oxford,
OX2 9PJ
☎ (0865) 862217
Fax (0865) 864468
*Large, detached house near
city bus route. Close to ring
road, convenient for
motorways.*
Bedrooms: 4 double & 1 twin,
1 family room.
Bathrooms: 6 private.
Bed & breakfast: £25-£48
single, £40-£55 double.
Parking for 20.
Credit: Access, Visa.

Portland House

338 Banbury Rd., Oxford,
OX2 7PR
☎ (0865) 52076 & 53796
*Light, spacious, Edwardian
character house. Few minutes'
walk to various restaurants,
sports facilities, river and
parks. Close to city centre.*
Bedrooms: 1 double & 3 twin,
1 family room.
Bathrooms: 3 public;
2 private showers.
Bed & breakfast: £19-£21
single, £32-£36 double.
Parking for 5.

The Priory Hotel M
COMMENDED

Church Way, Iffley, Oxford,
OX4 4DZ
☎ (0865) 749988
Fax (0865) 748525
*A country house hotel set in 3
acres of landscaped gardens,
within the city of Oxford.*
Bedrooms: 2 single, 38 double
& 4 twin, 5 family rooms.
Bathrooms: 49 private.
Bed & breakfast: £55-£90
single, £65-£120 double.
Half board: £50-£130 daily.
Lunch available.
Evening meal 7pm (l.o.
9.30pm).
Parking for 75.
Credit: Access, Visa, Amex.

River Hotel M

17 Botley Rd., Oxford,
OX2 0AA
☎ (0865) 243475
Fax (0865) 724306
*Dine overlooking the Thames,
in this riverside hotel.
Residents' bar. Within walking
distance of city and colleges.
Ample parking. Ideal for
business and tourist travellers.*

Bedrooms: 13 single, 8 double
& 1 twin, 2 family rooms.
Bathrooms: 18 private,
2 public; 2 private showers.
Bed & breakfast: £35-£50
single, £56-£62 double.
Half board: £40-£60 daily.
Evening meal 6.30pm (l.o.
8pm).
Parking for 25.
Credit: Access, Visa.

Tilbury Lodge Private Hotel

5 Tilbury Lane, Eynsham
Rd., Botley, Oxford,
OX2 9NB
☎ (0865) 862138
*Situated in a quiet country
lane, just 2 miles west of the
city centre. Ideal base for
touring the Cotswolds. Four
poster and jacuzzi available.*
Bedrooms: 2 single, 3 double
& 2 twin, 2 family rooms.
Bathrooms: 9 private.
Bed & breakfast: £30-£33
single, £51-£67 double.
Parking for 9.
Credit: Access, Visa.

Victoria Hotel M

180 Abingdon Rd., Oxford,
OX1 4RA
☎ (0865) 724536
*Victorian hotel completely
modernised. 10 minutes'
walking distance from city
centre.*
Bedrooms: 7 single, 3 double
& 1 twin, 2 family rooms.
Bathrooms: 14 private,
3 public.
Bed & breakfast: £37.50-
£52.50 single, £52.50-£65.50
double.
Lunch available.
Evening meal 7pm (l.o. 9pm).
Parking for 20.
Credit: Access, Visa.

The Westminster Guest House M

350 Iffley Rd., Oxford,
OX4 4AU
☎ (0865) 250924
*Semi-detached house, one and
a quarter miles from city
centre. Bus-stop immediately
outside the front door. Clean,
pleasant and comfortable
accommodation. TV lounge.*
Bedrooms: 1 single, 2 double
& 1 twin.

Bathrooms: 1 public;
1 private shower.
Bed & breakfast: £20-£22
single, £32-£36 double.
Parking for 3.

The White House M
Listed COMMENDED

315 Iffley Rd., Oxford,
OX4 4AG
☎ (0865) 244524
*Warm and friendly home to
share for visitors to Oxford
and surrounding areas.*
Bedrooms: 1 single, 3 double
& 1 twin, 3 family rooms.
Bathrooms: 2 public.
Bed & breakfast: £20-£28
single, £32-£38 double.
Evening meal 6pm (l.o. 8pm).
Parking for 7.

Willow Reaches Private Hotel M
COMMENDED

1 Wytham St., Oxford,
OX1 4SU
☎ (0865) 721545
Fax (0865) 251139
*A comfortable, small hotel in a
quiet location, 20 minutes' walk
from the city centre. Bridal
suite.*
Bedrooms: 4 single, 2 double
& 2 twin, 1 family room.
Bathrooms: 9 private,
1 public.
Bed & breakfast: £39-£42
single, £49.50-£52.50 double.
Half board: £54-£61 daily,
£378-£427 weekly.
Evening meal 7pm (l.o. 9pm).
Parking for 9.
Credit: Access, Diners,
Amex.

Windrush
Listed

11 Iffley Rd., Oxford,
OX4 1EA
☎ (0865) 247933
*Near Magdalen Bridge. Easy
walk to all places of interest,
Airport/London coaches, shops
and restaurants. Healthy
Eating Award. Non-smokers
preferred.*
Bedrooms: 1 single, 2 double
& 3 twin, 2 family rooms.
Bathrooms: 2 public.
Bed & breakfast: £17-£20
single, £28-£37 double.
Credit: Access, Visa.

---

*Please mention this
guide when making
a booking.*

PANGBOURNE

Berkshire
Map ref 2C2

A pretty stretch of river
where the Pang joins the
Thames with views of the
lock, weir and toll bridge.
Once the home of
Kenneth Grahame, author
of 'Wind in the Willows'.

The Copper Inn M
COMMENDED

Church Rd., Pangbourne-on-
Thames, RG8 7AR
☎ (0734) 842244
Fax (0734) 845542
Resort
*Elegantly restored Georgian
coaching inn with beautiful,
secluded garden. Emphasis on
warm welcome.*
Bedrooms: 2 single, 13 double
& 6 twin, 1 family room.
Bathrooms: 22 private.
Bed & breakfast: £32.50-
£87.50 single, £65-£105
double.
Lunch available.
Evening meal 7.30pm (l.o.
10pm).
Parking for 20.
Credit: Access, Visa, Diners,
Amex.

POTTERS BAR

Hertfordshire
Map ref 2D1

Lynden House M
Listed

24 Hanyards Lane, Cuffley,
Potters Bar, EN6 4AT
☎ (0707) 874556
*Spacious family home with
modern comfortable bedrooms,
in a quiet village location.
Close to A1, M1 and M25, 45
minutes from Central London
by train. Brochure available.
Non-smokers only please.*
Bedrooms: 1 single, 1 double
& 1 twin.
Bathrooms: 1 public.
Bed & breakfast: £18 single,
£32-£36 double.
Parking for 8.
Credit: Access, Visa.

---

*Half board prices shown are per person
but in some cases may be based on
double/twin occupancy.*

PRINCES RISBOROUGH

Buckinghamshire
Map ref 2C1

Old market town with
many 16th C cottages,
houses and a brick
Market House at its
centre.

Bernard Arms Hotel
APPROVED

Risborough Rd., Great
Kimble, Princes Risborough,
HP17 0XS
☎ Princes Risborough
(084 44) 6172/6173
*A small, friendly hotel, public
house and restaurant located in
the Chilterns and near the
Ridgeway Path, between
Princes Risborough and
Aylesbury (A4010).*
Bedrooms: 1 single, 2 double
& 1 twin, 1 family room.
Bathrooms: 1 public;
5 private showers.
Bed & breakfast: £35-£40
single, £45-£50 double.
Half board: £50-£55 daily.
Lunch available.
Evening meal 7pm (l.o.
10pm).
Parking for 40.
Credit: Access, Visa.

PUCKERIDGE

Hertfordshire
Map ref 2D1

Vintage Corner Hotel M
COMMENDED

Old Cambridge Rd.,
Puckeridge, SG11 1SA
☎ Ware (0920) 822722
Fax (0920) 822877
*Quiet modern hotel in
picturesque village of
Puckeridge, between junction
of A10 and A120. Attractive
restaurant.*
Bedrooms: 5 single, 24 double
& 19 twin.
Bathrooms: 48 private.
Bed & breakfast: £50-£75
single, £60-£85 double.
Lunch available.
Evening meal 7pm (l.o.
9.15pm).
Parking for 80.
Credit: Access, Visa, Diners,
Amex.

READING

Berkshire
Map ref 2C2

Busy, modern county
town with large shopping
centre and many leisure
and recreation facilities.
There are several
interesting museums and
the Duke of Wellington's
Stratfield Saye is nearby.
*Tourist Information
Centre* ☎ (0734) 566226

Abbey House Private Hotel M
COMMENDED

118 Connaught Rd., Reading,
RG3 2UF
☎ (0734) 590549
*Warm, friendly hotel run by
the proprietors. Close to town
centre. Reduced rates at
weekends.*
Bedrooms: 6 single, 4 double
& 10 twin.
Bathrooms: 11 private,
3 public; 1 private shower.
Bed & breakfast: £28-£43.50
single, £44-£54.50 double.
Evening meal 7pm (l.o.
8.30pm).
Parking for 14.
Credit: Access, Visa, Amex.

Aeron Private Hotel M
COMMENDED

191 Kentwood Hill, Tilehurst,
Reading, RG3 6JE
☎ (0734) 424119 & 427654
Fax (0734) 451953
*Small family-run hotel in
residential area, catering for
business people and
holidaymakers.*
Bedrooms: 13 single, 4 double
& 5 twin, 2 family rooms.
Bathrooms: 6 private,
6 public; 2 private showers.
Bed & breakfast: £30-£44
single, £46-£57 double.
Half board: from £38.50
daily.
Evening meal 6.30pm (l.o.
8.15pm).
Parking for 24.
Credit: Access, Visa, Amex.

Crescent Hotel
Listed

35 Coley Avenue, Reading,
RG1 6LL
☎ (0734) 507980
*Friendly, licensed hotel in the
centre of Reading, close to all
amenities.*
Bedrooms: 5 single, 4 double
& 7 twin.
Bathrooms: 5 public;
2 private showers.

Bed & breakfast: £18-£20
single, £25-£35 double.
Evening meal 6pm (l.o. 9pm).
Parking for 16.
Credit: Access, Visa.

Dittisham Guest House
Listed APPROVED

63 Tilehurst Rd., Reading,
RG3 2JL
☎ (0734) 569483
*Renovated Edwardian property
with garden, in a quiet, but
central location.*
Bedrooms: 4 single, 1 family
room.
Bathrooms: 3 private,
1 public.
Bed & breakfast: £19-£27.50
single, £25-£40 double.
Half board: £24-£33.50 daily.
Evening meal 6.30pm (l.o.
7.45pm).
Parking for 5.
Credit: Access, Visa.

George Hotel M
APPROVED

King St., Reading, RG1 2HE
☎ (0734) 573445
*A former coaching inn, on the
London to Bath run, dating
from the 15th C. Pretty
cobbled courtyard, well-
appointed bedrooms and 2
delightful restaurants.*
Bedrooms: 18 single,
13 double & 35 twin, 2 family
rooms.
Bathrooms: 68 private.
Bed & breakfast: £62-£67
single, £73 double.
Lunch available.
Evening meal 7pm (l.o.
10.30pm).
Credit: Access, Visa, Diners,
Amex.

Rainbow Corner Hotel M
COMMENDED

132-138 Caversham Rd.,
Reading, RG1 8AY
☎ (0734) 588140 & 581542
Fax (0734) 586500
*Family-run hotel, recently
refurbished. All rooms en-suite.
Bar and restaurant. 5 minutes
from the station and town
centre, 1 minute from the river.*
Bedrooms: 6 single, 12 double
& 3 twin, 1 family room.
Bathrooms: 22 private.
Bed & breakfast: £38-£63.95
single, £46-£84.90 double.
Half board: £49.95-£75.90
daily, £471.87-£515.97 weekly.
Lunch available.

Evening meal 7pm (l.o. 9.30pm).
Parking for 21.
Credit: Access, Visa, Diners, Amex.

Rainbow Travel Lodge

152 Caversham Rd., Reading, RG1 8AZ
☎ (0734) 588140
Recently refurbished small travel lodge, 5 minutes from station and town centre, 1 minute from the river.
Bedrooms: 1 single, 2 double & 5 twin.
Bathrooms: 8 private.
Bed & breakfast: £35-£38 single, £38-£44 double.
Half board: £46.95-£49.95 daily, £328.65-£349.65 weekly.
Parking for 2.
Credit: Access, Visa, Diners, Amex.

Ramada Hotel ♨

Oxford Rd., Reading, RG1 7RH
☎ (0734) 586222
Telex 847785
Hotel in town centre next to shopping area, within walking distance of the rail station and River Thames.
Bedrooms: 66 single, 10 double & 119 twin, 1 family room.
Bathrooms: 196 private.
Bed & breakfast: £45-£105 single, £60-£115 double.
Lunch available.
Evening meal 6pm (l.o. 11.30pm).
Parking for 75.
Credit: Access, Visa, C.Bl., Diners, Amex.

The Ship Hotel ♨
COMMENDED

4-8 Duke St., Reading, RG1 4RY
☎ (0734) 583455
Fax (0734) 504450
Best Western
In the town centre with easy access to major roads and the railway station.
Bedrooms: 9 single, 16 double & 4 twin, 1 family room.
Bathrooms: 30 private.
Bed & breakfast: £60-£75 single, £70-£85 double.
Half board: £74-£84 daily, £490-£560 weekly.
Lunch available.
Evening meal 7pm (l.o. 10pm).

Parking for 30.
Credit: Access, Visa, Diners, Amex.

Thameside Hotel ♨

148-150 Caversham Rd., Reading, RG1 8AZ
☎ (0734) 590135
Fax (0734) 502009
Hotel situated close to the river and town centre.
Bedrooms: 7 single, 3 double & 6 twin, 3 family rooms.
Bathrooms: 14 private, 2 public; 5 private showers.
Bed & breakfast: £30-£45 single, £45-£48 double.
Half board: £35-£40 daily.
Lunch available.
Evening meal 6pm (l.o. 8.30pm).
Parking for 15.
Credit: Access, Visa, Diners, Amex.

Warren Dene Hotel

1017 Oxford Rd., Tilehurst, Reading, RG3 6TL
☎ (0734) 422556
Elegant Victorian hotel on the outskirts of Reading. Period bar lounge and decor throughout. Most rooms fully en-suite. Family rooms available.
Bedrooms: 1 single, 5 double & 5 twin.
Bathrooms: 7 private, 2 public.
Bed & breakfast: £26-£38 single, £38-£45 double.
Evening meal (l.o. 9pm).
Parking for 12.

New Redbourn flanks Watling Street whilst the older part clusters around the pond and common.

The Aubrey Park Hotel ♨

Hemel Hempstead Rd., Redbourn, Nr. St. Albans, AL3 7AF
☎ (0582) 792105 Telex 82195
Park Hotels
An elegant, well-appointed, friendly hotel set in 6 acres of well-kept gardens and woodland. Only 25 miles north of London via the M1.
Bedrooms: 86 double & 31 twin, 2 family rooms.

Bathrooms: 119 private.
Bed & breakfast: £28-£93.25 single, £56-£110.50 double.
Half board: £38-£105 daily.
Lunch available.
Evening meal 7pm (l.o. 9.45pm).
Parking for 160.
Credit: Access, Visa, Diners, Amex.

Old town lying at the crossing of the Roman road Ermine Street and the Icknield Way. It has many interesting old houses and inns.

The Old Bull Inn
COMMENDED

High St., Royston, SG8 9AW
☎ (0763) 242003
Fax (0763) 241273
Traditional town centre coaching inn. Conference and banqueting facilities. Recently refurbished to a high standard.
Bedrooms: 8 single, 1 double & 1 twin, 1 family room.
Bathrooms: 11 private.
Bed & breakfast: £45-£55 single, £55-£69 double.
Lunch available.
Evening meal 7.30pm (l.o. 9.30pm).
Parking for 40.

As Verulamium this was one of the largest towns in Roman Britain and its remains can be seen in the museum. The Norman cathedral was built from Roman materials to commemorate Alban, the first British Christian martyr. The fortified clock tower is one of only two in Britain.
Tourist Information Centre ☎ (0727) 864511

The Apples Hotel ♨
COMMENDED

133 London Rd., St. Albans, AL1 1TA
☎ (0727) 44111
Family-run hotel in beautiful gardens within easy reach of city centre, station and major motorways. Heated swimming pool.

Bedrooms: 1 single, 6 double & 2 twin.
Bathrooms: 9 private.
Bed & breakfast: max. £50 single, max. £59 double.
Half board: max. £62 daily.
Evening meal 7.30pm (l.o. 9pm).
Parking for 10.
Credit: Access, Visa, Diners.

Ardmore House Hotel
COMMENDED

54 Lemsford Rd., St. Albans, AL1 3PP
☎ (0727) 59313 & (0727) 861411
Large, detached Edwardian house with garden, in conservation area, close to Clarence Park and within 5 minutes of city centre and railway station. Excellent base for visitors to London.
Bedrooms: 8 single, 7 double & 7 twin, 2 family rooms.
Bathrooms: 19 private; 2 private showers.
Bed & breakfast: £32.90-£44.65 single, £39.95-£49.35 double.
Evening meal 6pm (l.o. 8pm).
Parking for 34.
Credit: Access, Visa.

Grays Guest House

282 Hatfield Rd., St Albans, AL4 0DN
☎ (0727) 56535
Clean, comfortable Edwardian house. Personal friendly service. Easy access to London, A1, M25 and M1. Large car park.
Bedrooms: 5 single, 4 twin, 1 family room.
Bathrooms: 3 private, 2 public; 2 private showers.
Bed & breakfast: £21-£26 single, £33-£36 double.
Parking for 11.

Lake Holidays Hotel ♨
COMMENDED

234 London Rd., St. Albans, AL1 1JQ
☎ (0727) 40904 Telex 266020 CORAL P.G.
Consort
A family hotel, half a mile from the centre of the historic Roman city of Verulamium.
Bedrooms: 19 single, 5 double & 16 twin, 2 family rooms.
Bathrooms: 42 private.
Bed & breakfast: £53.50-£58.50 single, £69.50-£74.50 double.
Half board: £49.50-£74.50 daily.

Continued ▶

ST ALBANS

Continued

Lunch available.
Evening meal 7pm (l.o.
9.30pm).
Parking for 70.
Credit: Access, Visa, Diners,
Amex.

Newpark House Hotel M

North Orbital Rd., Nr.
London Colney Roundabout,
St. Albans, AL1 1EG
☎ Bowmansgreen
(0727) 24839
Fax (0727) 26700
*On A414 trunk road eastbound
to A1(M). Pebble-dash,
3-storey house, small
landscaped garden with patio
and fish pond.*
Bedrooms: 9 single, 4 twin.
Bathrooms: 5 public.
Bed & breakfast: £21-£25
single, £42-£50 double.
Parking for 30.
Credit: Access, Visa.

St. Michael's Manor Hotel M
COMMENDED

Fishpool St., St. Albans,
AL3 4RY
☎ (0727) 864444
Telex 917647 STMM
*16th C manor house in centre
of Roman Verulamium.*
Bedrooms: 11 single, 7 double
& 8 twin.
Bathrooms: 26 private.
Bed & breakfast: £64-£90
single, £80-£105 double.
Half board: from £58 daily.
Lunch available.
Evening meal 7pm (l.o.
9.30pm).
Parking for 70.
Credit: Access, Visa, Diners,
Amex.

Sopwell House Hotel and Country Club M
COMMENDED

Cottonmill Lane, Sopwell, St.
Albans, AL1 2HQ
☎ (0727) 864477
Telex 927823
Best Western
*Elegant Georgian country
house in rural surroundings
only 1 mile from the city
centre. Country Club opened in
1991. Weekend breaks
available.*
Bedrooms: 66 double &
18 twin.

Bathrooms: 84 private.
Bed & breakfast: £72.25-
£107.25 single, £89.75-£124.75
double.
Half board: £90.75-£125.75
daily, £560-£670 weekly.
Lunch available.
Evening meal 7.30pm (l.o.
9.30pm).
Parking for 175.
Credit: Access, Visa, Diners,
Amex.

SAUNDERTON

Buckinghamshire
Map ref 2C1

*1m SW. Princes
Risborough*
Small village close to the
Ridgeway long distance
footpath. The site of a
Roman villa is near the
church.

The Rose & Crown Inn M
COMMENDED

Wycombe Rd., Saunderton,
Nr. Princes Risborough,
HP17 9NP
☎ Princes Risborough
(084 44) 5299 & (084 44) 2241
Fax: (084 44) 3140
*Family-run, Georgian-style
country inn set in Chiltern
Hills. Log fires. 1 mile from
the village of Saunderton, half
a mile from Ridgeway Path.*
Bedrooms: 6 single, 10 double
& 1 twin.
Bathrooms: 14 private,
1 public.
Bed & breakfast: £40.50-£67
single, £71.25-£77 double.
Half board: £58-£92 daily.
Lunch available.
Evening meal 7pm (l.o.
9.30pm).
Parking for 40.
Credit: Access, Visa, Diners,
Amex.

SHIPTON-UNDER-WYCHWOOD

Oxfordshire
Map ref 2B1

Situated in the ancient
Forest of Wychwood with
many fine old houses and
an interesting parish
church. Nearby is Shipton
Court, a gabled
Elizabethan house set in
beautiful grounds that
include an ornamental
lake and a tree-lined
avenue approach.

Lamb Inn M

Shipton-under-Wychwood,
OX7 6DQ
☎ (0993) 830465
*Cotswold-stone inn on the edge
of an attractive village.*
Bedrooms: 3 double & 2 twin.
Bathrooms: 5 private.
Bed & breakfast: from £68
double.
Lunch available.
Evening meal 7pm (l.o.
9.30pm).
Parking for 25.
Credit: Access, Amex.

SILSOE

Bedfordshire
Map ref 2D1

The Old George Hotel

High St., Silsoe, MK45 4EP
☎ (0525) 60218
*Traditional inn with a large
restaurant open to the general
public. Two minutes' walk to
Wrest Park House. Gardens.
Dogs accepted by special
arrangement.*
Bedrooms: 2 single, 1 double
& 1 twin, 2 family rooms.
Bathrooms: 2 public.
Bed & breakfast: £28 single,
£48 double.
Lunch available.
Evening meal 6.30pm (l.o.
10pm).
Parking for 50.
Credit: Access, Visa.

---

*Individual proprietors have supplied all
details of accommodation. Although we
do check for accuracy, we advise you to
confirm prices and other information at
the time of booking.*

---

*Please mention this guide when making
a booking.*

SLOUGH

Berkshire
Map ref 2D2

A busy town with a large
trading estate, Slough is
an excellent centre for
recreation with many
open spaces. The ancient
village of Upton, now part
of Slough, has an
interesting Norman
church and Cliveden
House is nearby.

Colnbrook Lodge Guest House

Bath Rd., Colnbrook, Slough,
SL3 0NZ
☎ (0753) 685958
*Small family-run guesthouse
10 minutes from London
Heathrow Airport. Easy access
by bus to Windsor and
London. Evening meal
available.*
Bedrooms: 4 single, 1 double
& 3 twin.
Bathrooms: 2 private,
2 public.
Bed & breakfast: £28-£40
single, £30-£50 double.
Parking for 10.
Credit: Access, Visa.

Eton Lodge

26 Albert St., Slough,
SL1 2BU
☎ (0753) 20133
Fax (0753) 781831
*House within walking distance
of shops and entertainments.
Short drive to Windsor Castle,
river, safari park, M4 and
Heathrow. Ample private
parking.*
Bedrooms: 2 double & 3 twin,
1 family room.
Bathrooms: 6 private.
Bed & breakfast: £30-£36
single, £41-£47 double.
Parking for 10.
Credit: Access, Visa.

Highways Guest House M

95 London Rd., Langley,
Slough, SL3 7RS
☎ (0753) 24715 & 23022
*Comfortable accommodation
set in half an acre of pleasant
garden. Located on A4,
convenient for London,
Heathrow Airport and
Windsor.*
Bedrooms: 2 single, 2 double
& 4 twin, 2 family rooms.
Bathrooms: 2 public.

Bed & breakfast: £24-£27 single, £35-£40 double. Parking for 15.

[symbols]

Hertfordshire
Map ref 2D1

New Town with many well-planned modern buildings, a museum and leisure centre. Much of the old town still remains with old houses, cottages and inns. Nearby is the great house and park of Knebworth.
Tourist Information Centre ☎ (0438) 369441

Gate Hotel

1 Gates Way, Stevenage, SG1 3LJ
☎ (0438) 314126
Telex 825566
Set in Old Stevenage in centre of town close to shops, rail and bus station, yet in very quiet and scenic surroundings.
Bedrooms: 5 single, 20 double & 18 twin, 2 family rooms.
Bathrooms: 45 private.
Bed & breakfast: £35-£64 single, £45-£70 double.
Lunch available.
Evening meal 7pm (l.o. 10.30pm).
Parking for 35.
Credit: Access, Visa, C.Bl., Diners, Amex.

[symbols]

Oxfordshire
Map ref 2C2

4m NW. Henley-on-Thames
The fine manor house of Stonor Park has been a family home for over 800 years and its private chapel has been a centre of catholicism since Tudor times. The park is one of the most beautiful in southern England.

The Stonor Arms M
😀😀😀😀 COMMENDED

Stonor Village, RG9 6HE
☎ Turville Heath
(049 163) 345
Situated in the Stonor Valley, 4 miles from Henley-on-Thames on the B480.
Bedrooms: 4 double & 5 twin.
Bathrooms: 9 private.
Bed & breakfast: £82.50-£127.50 single, £92.50-£137.50 double.

Evening meal 7pm (l.o. 9.30pm).
Parking for 35.
Credit: Access, Visa.

[symbols]

Berkshire
Map ref 2C2

Pretty village on the River Thames, linked to Goring by an attractive bridge. It has Georgian houses and cottages and beautiful views over the countryside and the Goring Gap.

The Swan Diplomat M
😀😀😀😀 COMMENDED

Streatley-on-Thames, RG8 9HR
☎ Goring on Thames
(0491) 873737 Telex 848259
Beautifully situated on the banks of the River Thames, 1 hour's drive from Oxford, Windsor and London Heathrow.
Bedrooms: 9 single, 25 double & 11 twin, 1 family room.
Bathrooms: 46 private.
Bed & breakfast: £97.75-£105.75 single, £127.50-£214.50 double.
Half board: £112.25-£130.75 daily.
Lunch available.
Evening meal 7.30pm (l.o. 9.30pm).
Parking for 145.
Credit: Access, Visa, Diners, Amex.

[symbols]

Bedfordshire
Map ref 2D1

The Anchor Hotel M

Great North Rd., Tempsford, Sandy, SG19 2AS
☎ (0767) 40233 & 40822
Fax (0767) 41123
Inn built in 1831 as a country mansion. Bounded by the River Ouse, with its own moorings and coarse fishing from hotel's river bank. 11 acres of grounds and a garden play area for children.
Bedrooms: 2 single, 7 double & 1 twin.
Bathrooms: 8 private, 1 public.
Bed & breakfast: £39-£45 single, £58 double.
Lunch available.
Evening meal 6.30pm (l.o. 10pm).

Parking for 150.
Credit: Access, Visa, Diners, Amex.

[symbols]

Oxfordshire
Map ref 2C1

Historic market town on the River Thame. The wide, unspoilt High Street has many styles of architecture with medieval timber-framed cottages, Georgian houses and some famous inns.
Tourist Information Centre ☎ (084 421) 2834

Meadowsweet

32 Bridge Rd., Ickford, Aylesbury, Buckinghamshire HP18 9HX
☎ (0844) 338877
Located 6 miles from Thame, 12 miles from Oxford and 2 miles M40 in beautiful Buckinghamshire countryside. Home-made produce served.
Bedrooms: 1 single, 3 double.
Bathrooms: 1 public.
Bed & breakfast: £17.50 single, £30 double.
Half board: £24 daily, £168 weekly.
Evening meal 7pm (l.o. 8.30pm).
Parking for 2.

[symbols]

Peacock Hotel and Restaurant M
😀😀😀😀 COMMENDED

Henton, Nr. Chinnor
☎ Kingston Blount
(0844) 53519
Fax (0844) 53891
Charming thatched country hotel set at the foot of the Chilterns. Full a la carte candlelit restaurant. Four poster beds, executive room with spa bath and the Chiltern Suite.
Bedrooms: 3 single, 15 double & 1 twin.
Bathrooms: 19 private.
Bed & breakfast: £50-£75 single, £68-£95 double.
Lunch available.
Evening meal 6pm (l.o. 10.30pm).
Parking for 60.
Credit: Access, Visa, Amex.

[symbols]

The Spread Eagle Hotel M
😀😀😀😀 COMMENDED

Cornmarket, Thame, OX9 2BW
☎ (084 421) 3661
Telex 83343
Converted 17th C coaching inn, in centre of small country market town. Fothergills Restaurant features a choice of menus. Banqueting and conference facilities. Good base for touring the Thames Valley.
Bedrooms: 5 single, 23 double & 4 twin, 1 family room.
Bathrooms: 33 private.
Bed & breakfast: £71.35-£92.35 single, £81.85-£134.35 double.
Half board: £88.10-£108.70 daily, £616.10-£760.90 weekly.
Lunch available.
Evening meal 7pm (l.o. 10pm).
Parking for 80.
Credit: Access, Visa, Diners, Amex.

[symbols]

Hertfordshire
Map ref 2C1

Pleasant town near lovely countryside and woods. Tring has a fine church with a large 14th C tower. Tring Park houses the Rothschild Zoological Collection, now part of the Natural History Museum. The Tring Reservoirs National Nature Reserve is nearby.

The Rose & Crown M
😀😀😀😀 COMMENDED

High St., Tring, HP23 5AH
☎ (044 282) 4071
Fax (0442) 890735
CR Lansbury
An attractive Tudor-style hotel in the centre of a market town.
Bedrooms: 10 single, 12 double & 4 twin, 1 family room.
Bathrooms: 27 private.
Bed & breakfast: £35-£76 single, £70-£88 double.
Half board: £46-£90 daily.
Lunch available.
Evening meal 7pm (l.o. 10pm).
Parking for 50.
Credit: Access, Visa, Diners, Amex.

[symbols]

TRING

Continued

The Royal Hotel M
♛♛♛
Tring, HP23 5QR
☎ (044 282) 7616 & 8588
Fax (0442) 890383
On the famous Ridgeway Path, close to the pretty village of Aldbury.
Bedrooms: 2 single, 8 double & 7 twin, 3 family rooms.
Bathrooms: 15 private, 1 public.
Bed & breakfast: £30-£50 single, £40-£60 double.
Lunch available.
Evening meal 7.30pm (l.o. 9pm).
Parking for 50.
Credit: Access, Visa, Diners, Amex.

TURVEY

Bedfordshire
Map ref 2D1

Ancient village, mainly rebuilt of local stone in the 19th C. Both the bridge over the River Ouse and the church date from the 13th C.

The Laws Hotel
♛♛ APPROVED
Turvey, Bedford, MK43 8DB
☎ Turvey (023 064) 213/655
Telex 825711
Small country house hotel with a restaurant and large gardens. Central for Bedford, Northampton and Milton Keynes.
Bedrooms: 2 single, 6 double & 2 twin, 1 family room.
Bathrooms: 11 private.
Bed & breakfast: £42-£44 single, £55-£70 double.
Lunch available.
Evening meal 7.30pm (l.o. 9.30pm).
Parking for 50.
Credit: Access, Visa, Amex.

National Crown ratings were correct at the time of going to press but are subject to change. Please check at the time of booking.

WADDESDON

Buckinghamshire
Map ref 2C1

The first point-to-point steeplechase in England was run in 1835 from Waddesdon Windmill to a field just below Aylesbury Church, and is vividly described in Fowler's "Echoes of Old Country Life". The present manor house was built by Baron Ferdinand de Rothschild at the end of the 19th C in the style of a French chateau.

The Five Arrows
High St., Waddesdon, HP18 0JE
☎ Aylesbury (0296) 651727
Pleasant hotel close to Waddesdon Manor, Blenheim Palace, the Cotswolds and Claydon House. Traditional Sunday lunch served.
Bedrooms: 2 single, 2 double & 3 twin.
Bathrooms: 7 private.
Bed & breakfast: from £37.50 single, from £50 double.
Half board: £54-£85 daily.
Lunch available.
Evening meal 7.15pm (l.o. 9.30pm).
Parking for 15.
Credit: Access, Visa.

WALLINGFORD

Oxfordshire
Map ref 2C2

Site of an ancient ford over the River Thames, now crossed by a 900-ft-long bridge. The town has many timber-framed and Georgian buildings, Gainsborough portraits in the 17th C Town Hall and a few remains of a Norman Castle.
Tourist Information Centre ☎ *(0491) 35351 ext 3810*

The Shillingford Bridge Hotel M
♛♛♛
Shillingford, Wallingford, OX10 8LZ
☎ Warborough (086 732) 8567
Fax (086 732) 8636
Telex 837763
CR Forestdale
On one of the loveliest reaches of the River Thames, with a quarter-mile stretch of river frontage. 11 miles from Oxford and Henley-on-Thames.

Bedrooms: 13 single, 15 double & 3 twin, 2 family rooms.
Bathrooms: 33 private.
Bed & breakfast: £45-£63.50 single, £60-£85 double.
Half board: £49.50-£85 daily.
Lunch available.
Evening meal 7.30pm (l.o. 10pm).
Parking for 120.
Credit: Access, Visa, Diners, Amex.

WANTAGE

Oxfordshire
Map ref 2C2

Market town in the Vale of the White Horse where King Alfred was born. His statue stands in the town square.

The Bear Hotel M
Market Place, Wantage, OX12 8AB
☎ (023 57) 66366
Telex 41363
CR Calotels
16th C coaching inn with character, overlooking square in historic market town.
Bedrooms: 8 single, 9 double & 17 twin, 3 family rooms.
Bathrooms: 37 private.
Bed & breakfast: £29-£66 single, £58-£80 double.
Lunch available.
Evening meal 7pm (l.o. 9.30pm).
Credit: Access, Visa, Diners, Amex.

WARE

Hertfordshire
Map ref 2D1

Interesting riverside town with picturesque summer-houses lining the tow-path of the River Lea. The town has many timber-framed and Georgian houses and the famous Great Bed of Ware is now in the Victoria and Albert Museum.

Briggens House Hotel M
♛♛♛♛
Briggens Park, Stansted Rd., (A414), Stansted Abbotts, Nr. Ware, SG12 8LD
☎ Roydon (0279) 792416
Telex 817906
CR Queens Moat Houses

Country house hotel, set in 80 acres of beautiful parkland, with own golf-course, tennis and swimming.
Bedrooms: 15 single, 35 double & 4 twin.
Bathrooms: 54 private.
Bed & breakfast: from £77.50 single, from £95 double.
Lunch available.
Evening meal 7.30pm (l.o. 10pm).
Parking for 100.
Credit: Access, Visa, Diners, Amex.

Hanbury Manor M
♛♛♛♛ HIGHLY COMMENDED
Thundridge, Nr. Ware, SG12 0SD
☎ Ware (0920) 487722
CR Small Luxury Hotels
Superbly located 25 miles north of London en route to Cambridge. A unique country house resort offering extensive leisure facilities, 18-hole golf course designed by Jack Nicklaus II, creche, and three dining rooms under the guidance of Albert Roux.
Bedrooms: 1 single, 33 double & 49 twin, 15 family rooms.
Bathrooms: 98 private.
Bed & breakfast: £135-£315 single, £145-£325 double.
Half board: £67.50-£177.50 daily.
Lunch available.
Evening meal 6.30pm (l.o. 10.30pm).
Parking for 200.
Credit: Access, Visa, Diners, Amex.

WATFORD

Hertfordshire
Map ref 2D1

Large town with many industries but with some old buildings, particularly around St. Mary's Church which contains some fine monuments. The grounds of Cassiobury Park, once the home of the Earls of Essex, form a public park and golf-course.

Spiders Web Hotel M
♛♛♛ APPROVED
Watford by-Pass (A41), Watford, WD2 8HQ
☎ 081-950 6211
Telex 935213

Close to M1 junction 5 and M25 and 30 minutes to London. Bedrooms have 24 hour in-house movie facility, hair-dryer and trouser press. Full leisure complex.
Bedrooms: 7 single, 45 double & 108 twin, 10 family rooms.
Bathrooms: 170 private.
Bed & breakfast: max. £80 single, max. £90 double.
Lunch available.
Evening meal 7pm (l.o. 9.30pm).
Parking for 500.
Credit: Access, Visa, C.Bl., Diners, Amex.

WATLINGTON

Oxfordshire
Map ref 2C2

Interesting former market town on the Icknield Way with narrow streets and many old half-timbered houses. The gabled Town Hall was built in the 17th C and the church of St. Leonard has a painting by a pupil of Carracci.

The Well House Restaurant and Hotel M
COMMENDED
34-40 High St., Watlington, OX9 5PY
☎ (049 161) 3333
Fax (049 161) 2025
Integrated period house and cottage plus 15th C restaurant in the High Street of small historic country town. 30 minutes from Heathrow.
Bedrooms: 1 single, 5 double & 4 twin.
Bathrooms: 10 private.
Bed & breakfast: from £40 single, £60-£70 double.
Half board: £38-£58 daily, £228-£348 weekly.
Lunch available.
Evening meal 7.30pm (l.o. 9.30pm).
Parking for 15.
Credit: Access, Visa, C.Bl., Diners, Amex.

WELWYN

Hertfordshire
Map ref 2D1

5m S. Stevenage

Clock Hotel
Link Rd., Welwyn, AL6 9XA
☎ (043 871) 6911
Fax (043 871) 4065
Friendly
By the picturesque Welwyn village, and 45 minutes from London.
Bedrooms: 79 double & 18 twin, 1 family room.
Bathrooms: 98 private.
Bed & breakfast: £59.25-£71.95 single, £77.50-£92.65 double.
Lunch available.
Evening meal 7pm (l.o. 9.45pm).
Parking for 150.
Credit: Access, Visa, Diners, Amex.

Tewin Bury Farmhouse M
Tewin Bury Farm, Nr. Welwyn, AL6 0JB
☎ Welwyn (043 871) 7793
Fax (0438) 840440
400-acre arable farm. Delightful historic farmhouse by the River Mimram in peaceful countryside. Ideally located for London, Cambridge and Hatfield House. Near M1 and M25.
Bedrooms: 3 single, 3 double & 5 twin, 5 family rooms.
Bathrooms: 16 private.
Bed & breakfast: £30-£54 single, £46-£54 double.
Half board: £30-£64 daily, £210-£315 weekly.
Lunch available.
Evening meal 6pm (l.o. 10pm).
Parking for 40.
Credit: Access, Visa, Amex.

WESTON-ON-THE-GREEN

Oxfordshire
Map ref 2C1

9m N. Oxford
Pretty village with stocks on the village green and thatched cottages. The church of St. Mary's has an attractive setting and a fine tower dating from the 12th C.

Weston Manor Hotel M
Weston-on-the-Green, OX6 8QL
☎ Bletchington (0869) 50621
Telex 83409
Best Western
16 C country house hotel in magnificent grounds. Well-appointed bedrooms, Baronial Hall restaurant. Short break weekend rates available.
Bedrooms: 22 double & 15 twin, 2 family rooms.
Bathrooms: 39 private.
Bed & breakfast: £80-£85 single, £100-£115 double.
Half board: £60-£65 daily, £325-£350 weekly.
Lunch available.
Evening meal 7.30pm (l.o. 9.30pm).
Parking for 100.
Credit: Access, Visa, Diners, Amex.

WINDSOR

Berkshire
Map ref 2D2

Town dominated by the spectacular castle, the home of the Royal Family for over 900 years. Parts are open to the public. There are many attractions including the Great Park, Eton, Windsor Safari Park and trips on the river.
Tourist Information Centre ☎ (0753) 852010

Alma House
Listed
56 Alma Rd., Windsor, SL4 3HA
☎ (0753) 862983 & 855620
An elegant Victorian house within 5 minutes' walk of Windsor Castle, town centre, river and parks. Heathrow Airport 11 miles.
Bedrooms: 1 single, 2 double, 1 family room.

Bathrooms: 1 public; 2 private showers.
Bed & breakfast: £20-£25 single, £32-£38 double.
Parking for 3.

Clarence Hotel
APPROVED
9 Clarence Rd., Windsor, SL4 5AE
☎ (0753) 864436
Fax (0753) 857060
Recently refurbished hotel run by the owner. Close to shopping centre, Windsor Castle and Eton College.
Bedrooms: 2 single, 4 double & 9 twin, 6 family rooms.
Bathrooms: 21 private, 1 public.
Bed & breakfast: £33-£35 single, £49-£51 double.
Parking for 2.
Credit: Access, Visa, Diners, Amex.

Dorset Private Hotel
COMMENDED
4 Dorset Rd., Windsor, SL4 3BA
☎ (0753) 852669
Gracious Victorian residence in the heart of Royal Windsor, within walking distance of Windsor Castle, River Thames and Eton College.
Bedrooms: 5 twin.
Bathrooms: 5 private.
Bed & breakfast: max. £55 single, max. £67 double.
Parking for 7.
Credit: Access, Visa, Diners, Amex.

Eton Guest House
Listed
122-123 Eton High St., Eton, Windsor, SL4 6AN
☎ (0753) 861033
Located in the middle of Eton High Street, 5 minutes' walk from Windsor Castle, Eton College and the River Thames.
Bedrooms: 4 single, 5 double & 6 twin, 3 family rooms.
Bathrooms: 4 private, 3 public; 1 private shower.
Bed & breakfast: £21-£23 single, £31-£37 double.
Half board: £19.50-£22 daily, £136.50-£154 weekly.
Evening meal 5.30pm (l.o. 7.30pm).
Parking for 12.

Half board prices shown are per person but in some cases may be based on double/twin occupancy.

Map references apply to the colour maps towards the end of this guide.

WINDSOR

Continued

Fairlight Lodge Royal Windsor Hotel M
◇◇◇ COMMENDED
41 Frances Rd., Windsor,
SL4 3AQ
☎ (0753) 861207
Comfortable Victorian property, once the mayoral residence, quietly situated, but close to River Thames, castle and town centre.
Bedrooms: 2 single, 3 double & 2 twin, 3 family rooms.
Bathrooms: 10 private.
Bed & breakfast: £34-£40 single, £51-£60 double.
Half board: £40-£50 daily, £250-£310 weekly.
Evening meal 7.30pm (l.o. 9.30pm).
Parking for 10.
Credit: Access, Visa, Amex.
➤ ➠ ⌂ ♥ ᵻ Ⓥ ⌐ ⓣⓥ ▥
ᵃ ⍭ ⋈ ⊞

Holiday Inn - Slough/Windsor M
◇◇◇◇
Ditton Rd., Langley, Slough,
SL3 8PT
☎ (0753) 544244
Telex 848646
Ⓖ Holiday Inn
Close to M4 and M25, with easy access to London and Heathrow Airport. Well-appointed bedrooms, restaurant, leisure club. Ideally located for visiting many local attractions.
Bedrooms: 245 double & 103 twin, 4 family rooms.
Bathrooms: 352 private.
Bed & breakfast: from £37 single, from £74 double.
Half board: from £47 daily, from £250 weekly.
Lunch available.
Evening meal 7pm (l.o. 11pm).
Parking for 402.
Credit: Access, Visa, Diners, Amex.
➤ ♨ ℓ ⍟ ⌂ ♥ ᵻ Ⓥ ⍓
⌐ ⍨ ▥ ᵃ ⍭ ⓣ ⍒ ✿ ✈
⌸ ℘ ▸ ✿ ᴳᴬᴾ ◈ ˢᴾ ⊤

Melrose House
◇◇ COMMENDED
53 Frances Rd., Windsor,
SL4 3AQ
☎ (0753) 865328
Elegant Victorian detached residence, in the heart of Windsor. 5 minutes' walk from the castle.
Bedrooms: 4 double & 3 twin, 2 family rooms.
Bathrooms: 9 private.

Bed & breakfast: £28-£30 single, £38-£42 double.
Parking for 9.
➤ ➠ ⌂ ♥ ᵻ ᵁᴸ ⍓ ⌐ ⓣⓥ ◐
▥ ᵃ ⍭ ⊞

Oakley Court Hotel M
◇◇◇◇◇
Windsor Rd., Water Oakley,
Nr. Windsor, SL4 5UR
☎ Maidenhead (0628) 74141
Telex 849958
Ⓖ Queens Moat Houses
Victorian mansion on the banks of the River Thames in 35 acres of landscaped gardens. 5 minutes' drive from Windsor, 15 minutes from London Heathrow.
Bedrooms: 31 double & 61 twin.
Bathrooms: 92 private.
Bed & breakfast: £116.75-£234.75 single, £145.50-£244.50 double.
Half board: £203.50-£302.50 daily.
Lunch available.
Evening meal 7.30pm (l.o. 10pm).
Parking for 120.
Credit: Access, Visa, C.Bl., Diners, Amex.
➤ ♨ ♨ ℓ ⍟ ⌂ ♥ Ⓥ ⍓
◐ ▥ ⍨ ᵃ ⍭ ⍒ ✈ ▸ ✿ ✈
◈ ˢᴾ ⊞ ⊤

Royal Adelaide Hotel M
◇◇◇◇
Kings Rd., Windsor,
SL4 2AG
☎ (0753) 863916
Fax (0753) 830682
Hotel is close to town centre overlooking Long Walk and within walking distance of tourist attractions in Windsor.
Bedrooms: 22 single, 13 double & 4 twin, 2 family rooms.
Bathrooms: 41 private.
Bed & breakfast: £40-£65 single, £50-£80 double.
Half board: £45-£80 daily.
Lunch available.
Evening meal 7pm (l.o. 9.30pm).
Parking for 20.
Credit: Access, Visa, Diners, Amex.
➤ ♨ ℓ ⍟ ⌂ ♥ ᵻ Ⓥ ⍓
◐ ▥ ᵃ ⍭ ⍒ ✈ ᴳᴬᴾ ◈ ˢᴾ ⍭
⊤

Runnymede Hotel M
◇◇◇◇◇ COMMENDED
Windsor Rd., Egham, Surrey
TW20 0AG
☎ Egham (0784) 436171 &
Fax (0784) 436340
Telex 934900
Modern hotel on the A308, off the M25 junction 13, overlooking the Thames at Bell-Weir Lock. Leisure centre opening in autumn 1992.

Bedrooms: 48 single, 21 double & 24 twin, 32 family rooms.
Bathrooms: 125 private.
Bed & breakfast: £112-£128 single, £137-£166 double.
Half board: from £132 daily.
Lunch available.
Evening meal 7pm (l.o. 9.45pm).
Parking for 250.
Credit: Access, Visa, Diners, Amex.
➤ ℓ ⍟ ⌂ ♥ ᵻ Ⓥ ⍓ ⌐
ⓣⓥ ◐ ⍭ ▥ ᵃ ⍒ ✈ ✿ ◈ ◈
ˢᴾ ⍭ ⊤

Ye Harte and Garter Hotel M
◇◇◇
High St., Windsor, SL4 1LR
☎ (0753) 863426
Situated directly opposite Windsor Castle and a short walk from the river and shops. A period building of character. Beautiful ballroom for functions.
Bedrooms: 16 single, 16 double & 10 twin, 8 family rooms.
Bathrooms: 43 private, 2 public.
Bed & breakfast: £54-£71 single, £83-£89 double.
Lunch available.
Evening meal 6pm (l.o. 10.30pm).
Credit: Access, Visa, Diners, Amex.
➤ ℓ ⍟ ⌂ ♥ ᵻ Ⓥ ⍓ ⌐
◐ ⍭ ▥ ᵃ ⍒ ✈ ⍒ ˢᴾ ⍭

WITNEY

Oxfordshire
Map ref 2C1

Town famous for its blanket-making and mentioned in the Domesday Book. The market-place contains the Butter Cross, a medieval meeting place, and there is a green with merchants' houses.
Tourist Information Centre ☎ (0993) 775802

The Court Inn M
◇◇
43 Bridge St., Witney,
OX8 6DA
☎ (0993) 703228
Historic inn with modern amenities. Centrally heated bedrooms, lounge bar and games room. Personal service.
Bedrooms: 3 single, 2 double & 3 twin, 2 family rooms.
Bathrooms: 5 private, 1 public; 1 private shower.
Bed & breakfast: £17-£27 single, £32-£38 double.
Half board: £21-£32 daily.
Lunch available.

Evening meal 7pm (l.o. 9pm).
Parking for 12.
Credit: Access, Visa.
➤ ⍟ ⌂ ♥ ᵻ ▥ ᵃ ⍒ ⌧ ⍒
ˢᴾ ⍭

Crofters Guest House
◇◇ COMMENDED
29 Oxford Hill, Witney,
OX8 6JU
☎ (0993) 778165
Within 10 minutes' walk of Witney, providing a comfortable and homely atmosphere. Convenient for Oxford, Stratford-upon-Avon and the Cotswolds.
Bedrooms: 1 double & 1 twin, 3 family rooms.
Bathrooms: 2 private, 1 public; 1 private shower.
Bed & breakfast: £16-£22 single, £30-£40 double.
Parking for 6.
➤ ♨ ⌂ ♥ ᵻ ᵁᴸ Ⓥ ⓣⓥ ▥ ᵃ
⍒ ✿ ⌧ ⍭

Greystones Lodge Hotel
◇◇ COMMENDED
34 Tower Hill, Witney,
OX8 5ES
☎ (0993) 771898
Quiet, comfortable private hotel set in three-quarters of an acre of pleasant garden. Conveniently located for visiting Oxford and the Cotswolds.
Bedrooms: 4 single, 3 double & 4 twin, 1 family room.
Bathrooms: 1 private, 1 public; 10 private showers.
Bed & breakfast: £22.90-£28 single, £36.95-£42 double.
Half board: £28-£31.50 daily.
Evening meal 7pm (l.o. 7.30pm).
Parking for 20.
Credit: Visa, Diners, Amex.
➤ ♨ ⌂ Ⓥ ⌐ ⓣⓥ ▥ ᵃ
⍒ ✿ ⍭

The Marlborough Hotel
◇◇
28 Market Square, Witney,
OX8 7BB
☎ (0993) 776353
Situated in the town centre. Ideal for touring the Cotswolds, Oxford City and Woodstock (Blenheim Palace).
Bedrooms: 8 single, 12 double & 3 twin.
Bathrooms: 23 private.
Bed & breakfast: £47-£55 single, £57-£65 double.
Lunch available.
Evening meal 7pm (l.o. 9.30pm).
Parking for 18.
Credit: Access, Visa, Diners.
➤ ♨ ℓ ⌂ ♥ ᵻ Ⓥ ⍓ ⌐
▥ ᵃ ⍭ ⍒ ˢᴾ ⍭

The Witney Lodge Hotel M

Ducklington Lane, Witney, OX8 7TJ
☎ (0993) 779777 Telex 83459
Built in traditional Cotswold style, just outside the historic blanket-making town of Witney at A40/A415 junction, offering old world charm with modern facilities.
Bedrooms: 35 double & 28 twin, 7 family rooms.
Bathrooms: 70 private.
Bed & breakfast: £45-£72 single, £50-£82 double.
Half board: £50-£82 daily, £280-£480 weekly.
Lunch available.
Evening meal 7pm (l.o. 10pm).
Parking for 160.
Credit: Access, Visa, C.Bl., Diners, Amex.
➳ ⅏ 🖼 📞 ⓡ 🖵 ♥ ⓘ Ⓥ ⅄ ⅊ ● 🖿 ⌷ 🍽 🎿 ♨ ✈ ⅮⒶ🄵 ⅀ SP T

Pleasant town which grew up around the silk trade and has some half-timbered and Georgian houses.

Cantley House M
COMMENDED

Milton Rd., Wokingham, RG11 5QG
☎ (0734) 789912
Fax (0734) 774294
Traditional Victorian house built in 1880. Owned by Marquis of Ormonde. In rural location, 5 minutes from M4 junction 10.
Bedrooms: 14 single, 11 double & 3 twin, 1 family room.
Bathrooms: 29 private.
Bed & breakfast: £52-£64 single, £62-£78 double.
Half board: from £41 daily.
Lunch available.
Evening meal 7.30pm (l.o. 10pm).
Parking for 70.
Credit: Access, Visa, Diners, Amex.
➳ ⅏ 🖼 📞 ⓡ 🖵 ♥ ⓘ Ⓥ ⅊ ● 🖿 ⌷ 🍽 🅿 ⅊ ♨ SP 🏠 T

Stakis Wokingham St. Annes Manor Hotel M

London Rd., Wokingham, RG11 1SF
☎ (0734) 772550
Telex 847342
Ⓖ Stakis

Extended country manor house in 25 acres of parkland. 2 minutes from the M4, 10 minutes from the M3. Extensive indoor and outdoor leisure facilities. Half board rate based on a minimum 2 night stay.
Bedrooms: 6 single, 30 double & 60 twin, 34 family rooms.
Bathrooms: 130 private.
Bed & breakfast: £114-£124 single, £140-£150 double.
Half board: from £53 daily.
Lunch available.
Evening meal 7pm (l.o. 9.45pm).
Parking for 200.
Credit: Access, Visa, C.Bl., Diners, Amex.
➳ ⅏ ⅏ 📞 ⓡ 🖵 ♥ ⓘ Ⓥ ⅄ 🖿 ⅀ ● 🖿 ⌷ 🍽 ⅊ ♨ 🏠 🅿 ⅊ ♨ ⅮⒶ🄵 ⅀ SP 🏠

Roman Room Ristorante Italiano Hotel

42 Church St., Wolverton, Milton Keynes, MK12 5JN
☎ (0908) 318020 & (0908) 568793 after 6pm
Italian and continental restaurant, also English cooking. Weekly rates available. Parking.
Bedrooms: 1 single, 1 double & 6 twin, 1 family room.
Bathrooms: 5 private, 1 public.
Bed & breakfast: £23-£30 single, £35-£45 double.
Half board: £28.50-£35.50 daily.
Evening meal 7pm (l.o. 10pm).
Parking for 10.
Credit: Access, Visa.
➳ 🖵 ♥ ⓘ Ⓥ ⅄ 🖿 ⅊ 🍽 ✈ 🏠 ⅮⒶ🄵 ⅀

Chiltern Chase Lodge Hotel M

Goring Rd., Woodcote, Nr. Reading, Berkshire RG8 0SD
☎ Checkendon (0491) 680775
Country hotel with oak-beamed restaurant. Overlooking the village green, it is a pleasant venue for wedding receptions, parties and functions.

Bedrooms: 3 single, 1 double & 1 twin.
Bathrooms: 2 public.
Bed & breakfast: from £19.50 single, from £36.20 double.
Half board: from £25 daily.
Lunch available.
Evening meal 6.30pm (l.o. 9pm).
Parking for 20.
Credit: Access, Visa.
➳ ♥ ⓘ Ⓥ 🖿 ⓣⓥ 🖿 ⌷ 🍽 🏠

Small country town clustered around the park gates of Blenheim Palace, the superb 18th C home of the Duke of Marlborough. The town has well-known inns and an interesting museum. Sir Winston Churchill was born and buried nearby.

Feathers Hotel M

Market St., Woodstock, OX7 1SX
☎ (0993) 812291
Fax (0993) 813158
A small hotel filled with antiques and chintz, with restaurant and a typical English bar.
Bedrooms: 1 single, 6 double & 7 twin, 3 family rooms.
Bathrooms: 17 private.
Bed & breakfast: £75-£95 single, £90-£145 double.
Lunch available.
Evening meal 7.30pm (l.o. 9.45pm).
Credit: Access, Visa, Diners, Amex.
➳ 📞 ⓡ 🖵 ♥ ⓘ Ⓥ 🖿 🖿 ⌷ 🍽 ☀ 🏠 ⅀ SP 🏠 T

Merrydown Private Guest House
COMMENDED

37 Brook Hill, Woodstock, OX7 1JE
☎ (0993) 811835
Detached house in quiet, secluded position overlooking Glyme Valley in Woodstock. Short walk from town centre and Blenheim Palace.
Bedrooms: 2 double.
Bathrooms: 2 private.
Bed & breakfast: £15-£30 single, £28-£30 double.
Parking for 2.
🖵 🖵 ♥ Ⓤ Ⓥ 🖿 ⓣⓥ 🖿 ⌷ 🏠 SP

Punch Bowl Inn M
Listed

12 Oxford St., Woodstock, OX7 1TR
☎ (0993) 811218
Family-run pub in the centre of Woodstock. Close to Blenheim Palace main entrance. A good touring centre for Oxford and the Cotswolds.
Bedrooms: 3 single, 4 double & 1 twin, 2 family rooms.
Bathrooms: 3 private, 2 public.
Bed & breakfast: £29-£34 single, £39-£44 double.
Lunch available.
Evening meal 6.30pm (l.o. 9.30pm).
Parking for 20.
Credit: Access, Visa.
➳ ⅏ 🖵 ♥ ⓘ Ⓥ 🖿 ⌷ ♨ 🏠

Vickers Hotel and Restaurant
Listed

Market Place, Woodstock, OX7 1SY
☎ (0993) 811212
Fax (0993) 811030
16th C hotel and restaurant in the centre of Woodstock. English food cooked in the old fashioned way. Individually decorated rooms.
Bedrooms: 6 double.
Bathrooms: 6 private.
Bed & breakfast: £35-£55 single, £45-£75 double.
Lunch available.
Evening meal 6pm (l.o. 10.30pm).
Credit: Access, Visa, Diners, Amex.
➳ ⅏ 📞 ⓡ 🖵 ♥ ⓘ Ⓥ 🖿 🖿 ⌷ 🍽 ⅀ SP

Please mention this guide when making a booking.

Use a coupon

When requesting further information from advertisers in this guide, you may find it helpful to use the advertisement enquiry coupons which can be found towards the end of the guide. These should be cut out and mailed direct to the companies in which you are interested. Do remember to include your name and address.

THE CROWN IS YOUR SURE SIGN OF WHERE TO STAY

HOTELS, GUESTHOUSES, INNS, B&Bs & FARMHOUSES

Throughout Britain, the tourist boards now inspect over 17,000 hotels, guesthouses, inns, B&Bs and farmhouses, every year, to help you find the ones that suit you best.

THE CLASSIFICATIONS: '**Listed**', and then **ONE to FIVE CROWN,** tell you the range of facilities and services you can expect. The more Crowns, the wider the range.

THE GRADES: **APPROVED, COMMENDED and HIGHLY COMMENDED,** where they appear, indicate the quality standard provided. If no grade is shown, you can still expect a high standard of cleanliness.

Every classified place to stay has a Fire Certificate, where this is required under the Fire Precautions Act, and all carry Public Liability Insurance.

'**Listed**': Clean and comfortable accommodation, but the range of facilities and services may be limited.

ONE CROWN: Accommodation with additional facilities, including washbasins in all bedrooms, a lounge and use of a phone.

TWO CROWN: A wider range of facilities and services, including morning tea and calls, bedside lights, colour TV in lounge or bedrooms, assistance with luggage.

THREE CROWN: At least one-third of the bedrooms with ensuite WC and bath or shower, plus easy chair, full length mirror. Shoe cleaning facilities and hairdryers available. Hot evening meals available.

FOUR CROWN: At least three-quarters of the bedrooms with ensuite WC and bath/shower plus colour TV, radio and phone, 24-hour access and lounge service until midnight. Last orders for meals 8.30 pm or later.

FIVE CROWN: All bedrooms having WC, bath and shower ensuite, plus a wide range of facilities and services, including room service, all-night lounge service and laundry service. Restaurant open for breakfast, lunch and dinner.

Every Crown classified place to stay is likely to provide some of the facilities and services of a higher classification. More information available from any Tourist Information Centre.

We've checked them out before you check in!

TIMELESS NATURAL BEAUTY *sums up the region of East Anglia, stretching from the outskirts of London in the south to the lonely Wash in the north. If touring is your pleasure, East Anglia is for you. Twist and turn down the country lanes, stopping awhile in the old market towns or the pretty villages with their*

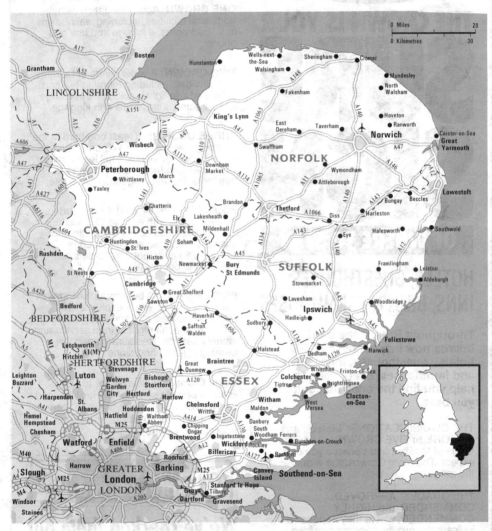

PLEASE REFER TO THE COLOUR MAPS AT THE BACK OF THIS GUIDE FOR ALL PLACES WITH ACCOMMODATION LISTINGS.

half-timbered houses or to admire the splendid churches. Explore the sprawling Fens, the reedy Norfolk Broads, the sandy heaths of Breckland, the estuaries of Essex, the long, sunny coastline. And then search out the rich history of the cities and towns — Norwich, Colchester, Cambridge, Bury St. Edmunds, to name but a few.

WHERE TO GO, WHAT TO SEE

100th Bomb Group Memorial Museum
Common Road, Dickleburgh, Diss, Norfolk
☎ Diss (0379) 740708
Museum housed in original World War II control tower. History of the 100th Bomb Group plus 8th Air Force exhibits. Visitor centre.

Boat World
Harbour Road, Oulton Broad, Suffolk NR32 3LZ
☎ Lowestoft (0502) 574441
Exhibits ranging from ocean cruising yachts to boarding boats for the RNLI. Exhibits on east coast rescues, boat building and the Broads hire fleets.

The Bygone Village
Fleggburgh, Great Yarmouth, Norfolk NR29 3AF
☎ Fleggburgh (0493) 369770
Re-created turn-of-century village in 40 acres. Craft cottages, railway, glass blowing, pets' paddock, steam engines, bygone collection.

Cambridge and County Folk Museum
2 – 3 Castle Street, Cambridge, Cambridgeshire CB3 0AQ
☎ Cambridge (0223) 355159
16th C former farmhouse, an inn from 17th C to 1934. Wide variety of objects relating to everyday life of people of Cambridge.

Coalhouse Fort
Princess Margaret Road, East Tilbury, Grays, Essex RM18 8PB
☎ Grays (0375) 844203
Victorian Thames defence fortress. Thameside Aviation Museum, military vehicles, artillery displays, rifle range and park.

Cockley Cley Iceni Village and Museums
Cockley Cley, Nr. Swaffham, Norfolk PE37 8AG
☎ Swaffham (0760) 721339
Authentic reconstruction of Iceni village on original site. Saxon church, medieval cottage and East Anglian Museum.

Colchester Zoo
Maldon Road, Stanway, Colchester, Essex CO3 5SL
☎ Colchester (0206) 331292
150 species of animals, reptile house/aquarium, 40 acres of gardens, lakes, 11th C church, picnic area. Mini railway, amusement arcade, play areas.

East Anglia Transport Museum
Chapel Road, Carlton Colville, Lowestoft, Suffolk NR33 8BL
☎ Lowestoft (0502) 518459
Transport museum with the emphasis on movement. Working trams, trolley buses, steam roller and 1916 Thornycroft lorry, all in 1930s street scene.

Elton Hall
Elton, Nr. Peterborough, Cambridgeshire PE8 6SH
☎ Oundle (0832) 280223
Historic house and gardens. Fine collection of paintings, furniture, books, Henry VIII's prayer book. Shop.

Gainsborough's House
46 Gainsborough Street, Sudbury, Suffolk CO10 6EU
☎ Sudbury (0787) 72958
Birthplace of Thomas Gainsborough. Elegant townhouse with paintings, print workshop, designer crafts gallery. Garden.

The reconstructed Iceni village at Cockley Cley

Hedingham Castle
Castle Hedingham, Halstead,
Essex CO9 3DJ
☎ Hedingham (0787) 60261
*Norman castle built in 1140,
with four storeys.*

John Webb's Windmill
Thaxted, Nr. Dunmow, Essex
CM6 2PY
☎ Thaxted (0371) 830366
*Four floors of mill can be
explored. Main machinery is
intact and on view. Rural
museum.*

Kings College Chapel
Kings College, Cambridge,
Cambridgeshire CB2 1ST
☎ Cambridge (0223) 350411
*Exhibition in pictures, works of
art and models, showing how
and why the chapel was built.*

Letheringsett Watermill
Riverside Road, Letheringsett,
Holt, Norfolk NR25 7YD
☎ Holt (0263) 713153
*Historic working watermill with
iron waterwheel and main
gearing restored. Vintage Ruston
Hornsby oil engine.*

Mangapps Farm Railway Museum
Southminster Road, Burnham-
on-Crouch, Essex CM0 8QQ
☎ Maldon (0621) 784898
*Large collection of railway
relics, restored station,
locomotives, coaches and
wagons. Working railway line,
farm bygones, animals.*

Minsmere Nature Reserve
Westleton, Saxmundham,
Suffolk IP17 3BY
☎ Westleton (072 873) 281
*Two walks, 2 miles long, with
hides on coastal lagoon and reed
bed. Shop.*

Mole Hall Wildlife Park
Widdington, Saffron Walden,
Essex CB11 3SS
☎ Saffron Walden (0799) 40400
*Otters, chimps, guanaco, lemurs,
wallabies, deer, owls, waterfowl,*

*etc. Butterfly pavilion. Attractive
gardens, picnic and play areas,
pets' corner.*

Mountfitchet Castle and Norman Village
Stansted, Essex CM24 8SP
☎ Bishops Stortford (0279)
813237
*Reconstructed Norman motte
and bailey castle and village of
Domesday period. Grand hall,
church, prison, siege tower,
weapons.*

The National Horseracing Museum
99 High Street, Newmarket,
Suffolk CB8 8JL
☎ Newmarket (0638) 667333
*5 permanent galleries telling the
great story of the development
of horseracing. British sporting
art.*

Norfolk's Dried Flower Centre
Neatishead, Norfolk NR12 8YH
☎ Wroxham (0603) 783588
*Growers and suppliers of quality
dried flowers and arrangements.
Workshop open for advice and
help.*

Norwich Cathedral
62 The Close, Norwich,
Norfolk NR1 4CH
☎ Norwich (0603) 626290
*Norman cathedral of 1096.
14th C roof bosses depicting
bible scenes from Adam and
Eve to Resurrection. Cloisters,
cathedral close. Shop and
buffet.*

Pensthorpe Waterfowl Park and Nature Reserve
Pensthorpe, Fakenham,
Norfolk NR21 0LN
☎ Fakenham (0328) 851465
*Large waterfowl and wildfowl
collection. Information centre,
conservation shop, adventure
play area, walks and nature
trails.*

Peterborough Museum and Art Gallery
Priestgate, Peterborough,
Cambridgeshire PE1 1LF
☎ Peterborough (0733)
343329
*Local history, geology,
archaeology, natural history,
folk life, industry, militaria,
costume, period shop. Victorian
rooms and art.*

Pleasure Beach
South Beach Parade, Great
Yarmouth, Norfolk NR30 3EH
☎ Great Yarmouth (0493)
844585
*Rollercoaster, looping star, log
flume, magic carpet, monorail,
big wheel, galloping horses,
rapido express and the condor.*

Pleasurewood Hills American Theme Park
Corton Road, Lowestoft,
Suffolk NR32 5DZ
☎ Lowestoft (0502) 513626
*Tempest chair lift, cine 180,
railway, pirate ship, fort,
Aladdin's cave, parrot shows,
rollercoaster, waveswinger,
haunted castle, star ride
Enterprise.*

Sacrewell Farm and Country Centre
Sacrewell, Thornhaugh,
Peterborough, Cambridgeshire
PE8 6HJ
☎ Stamford (0780) 782222
*500-acre farm, with working
watermill, gardens, shrubberies,
nature and general interest
trails. 18th C buildings, displays
of farm, rural and domestic
bygones.*

Stained Glass Museum
The Cathedral, Ely,
Cambridgeshire CB7 4DN
☎ Ely (0353) 667735
*Examples of stained glass from
the 13th C to present day.
Models of modern workshop.*

Thetford Forest Park
Forestry Commission, Santon
Downham, Brandon, Suffolk
IP27 0TJ
☎ Thetford (0842) 810271
*Working forest, and a place for
relaxation and recreation.*

West Stow Country Park and Anglo-Saxon Village
Icklingham Road, West Stow, Bury St. Edmunds, Suffolk IP28 6HE
☎ Culford (0284) 728718
Reconstructions of 5 Anglo-Saxon buildings, another in process of reconstruction. Displays of excavation plans and finds.

Wicken Fen Nature Reserve
Lode Lane, Wicken, Ely, Cambridgeshire CB7 5XP
☎ Ely (0353) 720274
Last remaining undrained portion of East Anglia's Great Level, rich in plant and invertebrate life. Working windpump.

Wildfowl and Wetlands Centre
100 Bank, Welney, Wisbech, Cambridgeshire PE14 9TN
☎ Ely (0353) 860711
Wetland nature reserve of 900 acres, attracting large numbers of ducks and swans in winter and waders in spring and summer. Range of wild plants, butterflies and insects.

Wildfowl and Wetlands Centre

MAKE A DATE FOR...

Mildenhall Air Fête
RAF Mildenhall, Bury St. Edmunds, Suffolk
23 – 24 May*

Suffolk Show
Suffolk Showground, Ipswich, Suffolk
27 – 28 May

Aldeburgh Festival of Music and the Arts
Snape Maltings Concert Hall, Aldeburgh, Suffolk
12 – 28 June

Royal Norfolk Show
The Showground, Dereham, Norwich, Norfolk
1 – 2 July

Duxford Classic Fighter Display
Duxford Airfield, Duxford, Cambridgeshire
4 – 5 July

Cambridge Festival
Various venues, Cambridge, Cambridgeshire
11 – 25 July

East of England Agricultural Show
East of England Showground, Peterborough, Cambridgeshire
21 – 23 July

Sandringham Flower Show
Sandringham House, Sandringham, Norfolk
29 July

Thames Sailing Barge Race
Seafront, Southend-on-Sea, Essex
29 August

Duxford '92 Flying Day
Duxford Airfield, Duxford, Cambridgeshire
13 September

* Provisional dates only

FIND OUT MORE

Further information about holidays and attractions in the East Anglia region is available from:
East Anglia Tourist Board
Toppesfield Hall, Hadleigh, Suffolk IP7 5DN
☎ (0473) 822922

These publications are available free from the East Anglia Tourist Board:

Bed & Breakfast Touring Map for the East of England

East Anglia, the Real England

Also available are (prices include postage and packing):

East Anglia Guide £3.20

East Anglia Leisure Map £3.20

Gardens to Visit in East Anglia £1

Places to stay

ACCOMMODATION ENTRIES *in this regional section are listed in alphabetical order of place name, and then in alphabetical order of establishment.*

THE MAP REFERENCES *refer to the colour maps towards the end of the guide. The first figure is the map number; the letter and figure which follow indicate the grid reference on the map.*

THE SYMBOLS *at the end of each accommodation entry give information about services and facilities. A 'key' to these symbols is inside the back cover flap, which can be kept open for easy reference.*

ACLE

Norfolk
Map ref 3C1

8m W. Great Yarmouth
Market town has church
with 11th C round tower
and font dating from
1410.

East Norwich Inn
♛♛♛
Old Rd., Acle, NR13 3QN
☎ Great Yarmouth
(0493) 751112
*Family-run inn, in the heart of
the Broads, 10 miles from
Great Yarmouth off the A47.*
Bedrooms: 4 double & 2 twin,
3 family rooms.
Bathrooms: 9 private.
Bed & breakfast: £24.50-£26
single, £32-£35 double.
Lunch available.
Evening meal 7pm (l.o.
10pm).
Parking for 35.
Credit: Access, Visa.

**Mannings Hotel,
Restaurant and Country
Club**
♛♛♛ APPROVED
South Walsham Rd., Acle,
Norwich, NR13 3ES
☎ Great Yarmouth
(0493) 750377
*Standing in 4 acres in
Broadlands midway between
Great Yarmouth and Norwich.
On B1140 half a mile from
Acle.*
Bedrooms: 1 single, 5 double
& 3 twin, 1 family room.
Bathrooms: 10 private.

Bed & breakfast: from £30
single, from £35 double.
Half board: from £39 daily.
Lunch available.
Evening meal 7pm (l.o.
10pm).
Parking for 40.
Credit: Access, Visa, Amex.

ALCONBURY

Cambridgeshire
Map ref 3A2

4m NW. Huntingdon

**Alconbury House
Hotel** ♛
♛♛♛
Alconbury Weston,
Huntingdon, PE17 5JG
☎ (0480) 890807
*Charming "bijou" hotel and
restaurant offering something
for everyone. Real food, fresh
flowers, pot pourri, real log
fires and more.*
Bedrooms: 14 single, 4 double
& 7 twin, 1 family room.
Bathrooms: 26 private.
Bed & breakfast: £25-£45
single, £40-£55 double.
Half board: £33-£58 daily,
£261-£348 weekly.
Lunch available.
Evening meal 7pm (l.o.
9.30pm).
Parking for 60.
Credit: Access, Visa, Diners,
Amex.

ALDEBURGH

Suffolk
Map ref 3C2

6m SE. Saxmundham
A prosperous port in the
16th C, now famous for
the Aldeburgh Music
Festival held annually in
June. The 16th C Moot
Hall, now a museum, is a
timber-framed building
once used as an open
market.

Uplands Hotel ♛
♛♛♛
Victoria Rd., Aldeburgh,
IP15 5DX
☎ (0728) 452420 &
(0728) 452156
*Country house hotel with an
emphasis on comfort, courtesy
and cleanliness. Restaurant
overlooks the gardens.*
Bedrooms: 4 single, 5 double
& 9 twin, 2 family rooms.
Bathrooms: 17 private,
1 public.
Bed & breakfast: £26-£45
single, £57-£60 double.
Half board: £39-£45 daily.
Evening meal 7pm (l.o.
8.30pm).
Parking for 20.
Credit: Access, Visa, Diners,
Amex.

Wentworth Hotel ♛
♛♛♛ COMMENDED
Wentworth Rd., Aldeburgh,
IP15 5BB
☎ (0728) 452312 & 453357
Ⓒ️ Consort

---

*Privately owned and run
country house hotel facing the
sea. Two lounges, cosy bar and
log fires.*
Bedrooms: 7 single, 10 double
& 14 twin.
Bathrooms: 30 private,
1 public.
Bed & breakfast: £38-£54
single, £79-£110 double.
Lunch available.
Evening meal 7pm (l.o. 9pm).
Parking for 16.
Credit: Access, Visa, Diners,
Amex.

White Lion Hotel ♛
♛♛♛♛
Market Cross Place,
Aldeburgh, IP15 5BJ
☎ (0728) 452720
Telex 94017152
*Imposing hotel standing
directly on the seafront of
totally unspoilt fishing town of
great charm, famous for
classical music concerts.*
Bedrooms: 2 single, 21 double
& 14 twin, 1 family room.
Bathrooms: 38 private.
Bed & breakfast: £55-£70
single, £70-£90 double.
Half board: £43-£60 daily,
£291-£410 weekly.
Lunch available.
Evening meal 7pm (l.o. 9pm).
Parking for 15.
Credit: Access, Visa, Diners,
Amex.

> *We advise you to
> confirm your
> booking in writing.*

ATTLEBOROUGH
Norfolk
Map ref 3B1

Market town, mostly destroyed in 1559 by fire, now a cider-making centre. Church with fine Norman tower.

Earles ▲
APPROVED
Stow Bedon House, Stow Bedon, Attleborough, NR17 1BX
☎ Caston (095 383) 284
Country house hotel with certain country club facilities free to guests. Secluded situation in Breckland. Just off the B1075 Thetford to Watton road.
Bedrooms: 1 single, 4 double & 1 twin.
Bathrooms: 5 private, 1 public.
Bed & breakfast: £40-£55 single, £70-£100 double.
Half board: £48-£68 daily, £225-£400 weekly.
Lunch available.
Evening meal 7pm (l.o. 9.30pm).
Parking for 25.
Open January.
Credit: Access, Visa.

AYLSHAM
Norfolk
Map ref 3B1

12m N. Norwich
Small town on the River Bure with an attractive market-place, interesting church and several fine houses. Nearby is Blickling Hall (National Trust). Trains may be boarded here at the terminal of the Bure Valley Railway (narrow gauge steam railway) which runs on 9 miles of the Old Great Eastern trackbed, between Wroxham and Aylsham.

The Aylsham Motel
APPROVED
Norwich Rd., Aylsham, NR11 6JH
☎ (0263) 734851
New privately-owned purpose-built motel, with all en-suite, in peaceful surroundings. Restaurant and bar, ample parking.
Bedrooms: 2 double & 11 twin, 1 family room.
Bathrooms: 14 private.

Bed & breakfast: from £33.50 single, from £46.50 double.
Lunch available.
Evening meal 7pm (l.o. 9.30pm).
Parking for 100.
Credit: Access, Visa.

BACTON-ON-SEA
Norfolk
Map ref 3C1

5m NE. North Walsham

Seacroft Guest House
APPROVED
Beach Rd., Bacton-on-Sea, Norwich, NR12 OHS
☎ Walcott (0692) 650302
Large Victorian house close to shops and beach. Home cooking and personal supervision. Off B1159 via Seacroft caravan park.
Bedrooms: 2 single, 3 double & 2 twin, 2 family rooms.
Bathrooms: 2 private, 3 public.
Bed & breakfast: £14.50-£20 single, £28-£40 double.
Half board: £25-£30 daily, £160-£200 weekly.
Evening meal 6pm (l.o. 8pm).
Parking for 15.
Open March-November.
Credit: Access, Visa.

BADLEY
Suffolk
Map ref 3B2

2m SE. Stowmarket

The Mill House
Badley, Ipswich, IP6 8RR
☎ Needham Market
(0449) 720154
Comfortable 16th C Suffolk longhouse, centrally situated 1.5 miles from Needham Market on B1113. En-suite rooms, licensed.
Bedrooms: 1 double & 1 twin, 1 family room.
Bathrooms: 3 private.
Bed & breakfast: from £35 double.
Half board: from £26 daily.
Evening meal 7pm.
Parking for 6.

Please mention this guide when making a booking.

BARNHAM BROOM
Norfolk
Map ref 3B1

4m N. Wymondham

Barnham Broom Hotel, Conference & Leisure Centre ▲
Barnham Broom, Norwich, NR9 4DD
☎ (060 545) 393
Telex 975711
Ⓑ Best Western
In 120 acres of beautiful countryside, with a relaxed and friendly atmosphere. Excellent sports facilities, 2 18 hole golf-courses. Large conference complex.
Bedrooms: 1 single, 7 double & 38 twin, 6 family rooms.
Bathrooms: 52 private.
Bed & breakfast: £59.50-£62 single, £79.50-£80 double.
Half board: £71-£72 daily.
Lunch available.
Evening meal 7.30pm (l.o. 9.30pm).
Parking for 200.
Credit: Access, Visa, Diners, Amex.

BASILDON
Essex
Map ref 3B3

One of the New Towns planned after World War II. It overlooks the estuary of the River Thames and is set in undulating countryside. The main feature is the town square with a traffic-free pedestrian concourse.

The Chichester Hotel
COMMENDED
Old London Rd., Wickford, Basildon, SS11 8UE
☎ (0268) 560555
A picturesque family-run hotel with restaurant, dinner-dance restaurant and functions complex. Surrounded by farmland in the Basildon, Chelmsford, Southend triangle.
Bedrooms: 17 single, 9 double & 8 twin.
Bathrooms: 34 private.
Bed & breakfast: £49-£55 single, £61-£65 double.
Lunch available.
Evening meal 7pm (l.o. 9.30pm).

Parking for 41.
Credit: Access, Visa, Diners, Amex.

BATTLESBRIDGE
Essex
Map ref 3B3

2m E. Wickford

The Cottages Guest House
Listed COMMENDED
The Cottages, Beeches Rd., Battlesbridge, SS11 8TJ
☎ Southend (0702) 232105
Rural cottage, close to Southend, Chelmsford and Basildon. Good views. Half a mile from Battlesbridge Antique Centre. Extensive parking. Bridal room.
Bedrooms: 1 single, 2 double & 2 twin.
Bathrooms: 1 public.
Bed & breakfast: from £15 single, £25-£40 double.
Half board: £21.50-£25 daily.
Evening meal 6.30pm (l.o. 8pm).
Parking for 14.

BECCLES
Suffolk
Map ref 3C1

8m W. Lowestoft
Fire destroyed the town in the 16th C and it was rebuilt in Georgian red brick. The River Waveney, on which the town stands, is popular with boating enthusiasts and has an annual regatta. Home of Beccles and District Museum and the William Clowes Printing Museum.

The Swan
Loddon Rd., Gillingham, Beccles, NR34 0LD
☎ (0502) 712055
Modern motel offering chalet-type accommodation in 5 acres of grounds. Close to Norfolk Broads and historic town of Beccles.
Bedrooms: 10 double & 1 twin, 3 family rooms.
Bathrooms: 14 private.
Bed & breakfast: £30-£32 single, £40-£60 double.
Lunch available.
Evening meal 6pm (l.o. 10.30pm).

Continued ▶

BECCLES

Continued

Parking for 50.
Credit: Access, Visa.

BIRCHANGER

Essex
Map ref 2D1

2m NE. Bishop's Stortford
Lying east of River Stort, the village is strung out along a winding road running up a hillside. Much restored small church with Norman nave and 2 12th C doorways.

The Cottage
🏳 COMMENDED

71 Birchanger Lane, Birchanger, Bishop's Stortford, Hertfordshire CM23 5QA
☎ Bishop's Stortford, (0279) 812349
17th C house with panelled rooms and inglenook fireplaces. Large garden. Quiet rural setting yet close to Stansted Airport and M11 junction 8.
Bedrooms: 2 single, 3 double & 4 twin, 1 family room.
Bathrooms: 8 private, 1 public.
Bed & breakfast: £25-£32 single, £45 double.
Half board: £33-£43 daily.
Evening meal 6.30pm (l.o 9am).
Parking for 10.
Credit: Access, Visa.

The symbol ℂℝ and the name of a hotel group or consortium after a hotel address means that bookings can be made through a central reservations office. These are listed on page 540.

The national Crown scheme is explained in full on pages 536 – 539.

BLAKENEY

Norfolk
Map ref 3B1

5m NW. Holt
Picturesque village on the north coast of Norfolk and a former port and fishing village. The 15th C red bricked Guildhall stands on a brick-vaulted undercroft. Marshy creeks extend towards Blakeney Point (National Trust) and are a paradise for naturalists, with trips to the reserve and to see the seals from Blakeney Quay.

Blakeney Hotel 🅼
🏳🏳🏳🏳🏳 COMMENDED

Quayside, Blakeney, Nr. Holt, NR25 7NE
☎ Cley (0263) 740797
Traditional, privately-owned, friendly hotel overlooking National Trust harbour. Relax, sail, walk, play golf or bird-watch.
Bedrooms: 8 single, 18 double & 22 twin, 4 family rooms.
Bathrooms: 52 private.
Bed & breakfast: £43-£68 single, £86-£176 double.
Half board: £51-£80 daily, £345-£469 weekly.
Lunch available.
Evening meal 7pm (l.o. 9.30pm).
Parking for 75.
Credit: Access, Visa, Diners, Amex.

Flintstones Guest House 🅼
Listed COMMENDED

Wiveton, Holt, NR25 7TL
☎ Cley (0263) 740337
Attractive licensed guesthouse in picturesque rural surroundings near village green. 1 mile from Cley and Blakeney with good sailing and bird-watching. All rooms with private facilities. Non-smokers only please.
Bedrooms: 2 double, 3 family rooms.
Bathrooms: 5 private.
Bed & breakfast: £16.50-£18 single, £25-£28 double.
Half board: max. £22 daily.
Evening meal 7pm (l.o. 5pm).
Parking for 5.

BRAINTREE

Essex
Map ref 3B2

11m NE. Chelmsford
On the old Roman road from St. Albans to Colchester. The Heritage Centre in the Town Hall describes Braintree's former international importance in wool, silk and engineering, the Working Silk Museum houses England's last hand loom silk weaving mill. St. Michael's parish church includes some Roman bricks and Braintree market was first chartered in 1199. 6 miles to the north-east is Gosfield Hall, a Tudor courtyard house.

The Old House 🅼
🏳🏳

11 Bradford St., Braintree, CM7 6AS
☎ (0376) 550457
16th C timber-framed house with a Jacobean panelled bar and dining room. Large inglenook giving a warm, homely atmosphere.
Bedrooms: 4 double & 1 twin, 1 family room.
Bathrooms: 3 private, 1 public.
Bed & breakfast: £22.50-£36 single, £35.25-£42 double.
Half board: £28.05-£43.05 daily.
Evening meal 6pm (l.o. 8pm).
Parking for 7.
Credit: Visa.

The White Hart 🅼
🏳🏳🏳🏳

Bocking End, Braintree, CM7 6AB
☎ (0376) 21401 Telex 988835
ℂℝ Lansbury
Town centre hotel, created around an original 15th C coaching inn.
Bedrooms: 5 single, 7 double & 17 twin, 4 family rooms.
Bathrooms: 33 private.
Bed & breakfast: £24-£63 single, £48-£75 double.
Half board: £37-£66 daily.
Lunch available.
Evening meal 6pm (l.o. 10.30pm).
Parking for 51.
Credit: Access, Visa, Diners, Amex.

BRENTWOOD

Essex
Map ref 2D2

11m SW. Chelmsford
The town grew up in the late 12th C and then developed as a staging post, being strategically placed close to the London to Chelmsford road. Deer roam by the lakes in the 428 acre park at South Weald, part of Brentwood's attractive Green Belt. Cater Museum is 5 miles to the east.
Tourist Information Centre ☎ (0277) 200601

Brentwood Moat House 🅼
🏳🏳🏳🏳 COMMENDED

London Rd., Brentwood, CM14 4NR
☎ (0277) 225252
Telex 995182
ℂℝ Queens Moat Houses
Original Tudor building dating back to 1512. Hunting lodge owned by Catherine of Aragon.
Bedrooms: 16 double & 17 twin, 5 family rooms.
Bathrooms: 38 private.
Bed & breakfast: £85-£89 single, £97-£99.50 double.
Half board: £123-£137 daily.
Lunch available.
Evening meal 7.15pm (l.o. 10.15pm).
Parking for 120.
Credit: Access, Visa, Diners, Amex.

Individual proprietors have supplied all details of accommodation. Although we do check for accuracy, we advise you to confirm prices and other information at the time of booking.

The symbols are explained on the flap inside the back cover.

BUNGAY

Suffolk
Map ref 3C1

14m SE. Wymondham
Market town and yachting
centre on the River
Waveney with the
remains of a great 12th C
castle. In the market-
place stands the Butter
Cross, rebuilt in 1689
after being largely
destroyed by fire. The
town's major industries
since the 18th C have
been printing and leather
working. Nearby at
Earsham is the Otter
Trust.

Dove Restaurant

Wortwell, Nr. Harleston,
Norfolk IP20 0EN
☎ (098 686) 315
*A former railway hotel, now
established restaurant offering
accommodation. On the
Norfolk/Suffolk border. Good
centre for the Waveney Valley.*
Bedrooms: 2 double & 1 twin.
Bathrooms: 2 private,
1 public.
Bed & breakfast: £15-£17.50
single, £25-£30 double.
Lunch available.
Evening meal 7pm (l.o.
9.30pm).
Parking for 15.
Credit: Access, Visa.
⑤ ♡ ▮ Ⓥ ⅄ ⑰ ▥ ♨ ☎
Ⓤ ▸ ⁂ 🛏

BUNWELL

Norfolk
Map ref 3B1

5m SE. Attleborough

Bunwell Manor Hotel ᛗ
⚘⚘ APPROVED

Bunwell St., Bunwell, Nr.
Norwich, NR16 1QU
☎ (0953) 788304
*Tudor country manor house in
its own grounds. Comfortable
rooms, friendly service and
interesting menus. Situated in
Bunwell Street, 12 miles south
of Norwich. Children and dogs
welcome.*
Bedrooms: 1 single, 6 double
& 2 twin, 1 family room.
Bathrooms: 10 private.
Bed & breakfast: £40-£44
single, £55-£60 double.
Half board: £35 daily.
Lunch available.
Evening meal 7pm (l.o.
9.30pm).
Parking for 25.
Credit: Access, Visa.
⑤ ♨ ℄ ▭ ♡ ▮ Ⓥ ⅋ ▥
♨ ☎ ⁂ 🛏 ☬ ⚙ 🛏 🆃

BURNHAM MARKET

Norfolk
Map ref 3B1

Has a broad green,
surrounded by Georgian
houses and cottages, and
a particularly interesting
church with a gallery of
sculptures around the
tower battlements.

The Hoste Arms ᛗ
⚘⚘⚘ COMMENDED

The Green, Burnham Market,
King's Lynn, PE31 8HD
☎ (0328) 738257
*Magnificent old coaching inn,
in Norfolk's most beautiful
village. Probably the finest
bedrooms on the North Norfolk
coast. 2 dining rooms with
fresh local produce, mainly
fish. Home of Nelson.*
Bedrooms: 4 single, 4 double
& 3 twin, 1 family room.
Bathrooms: 12 private.
Bed & breakfast: from £36
single, from £60 double.
Half board: £46-£52 daily,
from £250 weekly.
Lunch available.
Evening meal 6.30pm.
Parking for 35.
⑤ ♨ ℄ ▭ ♡ ♨ ▮ ⅄ ⅋
▥ ☎ ⁂ Ⓤ ⚙ 🛏 🛏 ⚘ SP 🛏

BURNHAM-ON-CROUCH

Essex
Map ref 3B3

9m SE. Maldon
Popular yachting and
boatbuilding centre with 5
yacht clubs. The town lies
on the north bank of the
Crouch, 6 miles from the
sea. The High Street
contains a mixture of
Georgian and Victorian
architecture.

Ye Olde White Harte
⚘⚘

The Quay, Burnham-on-
Crouch, CM0 8AS
☎ Maldon (0621) 782106
*20th C and 17th C building
overlooking Crouch Estuary
and Essex Marshes.
Comfortably appointed, with
old world atmosphere in both
bars and restaurant.*
Bedrooms: 3 double & 6 twin,
2 family rooms.
Bathrooms: 11 private,
1 public.

*We advise you to
confirm your
booking in writing.*

Bed & breakfast: £19-£35
single, £35-£60 double.
Half board: from £27 daily.
Lunch available.
Evening meal 7.30pm (l.o.
9pm).
Parking for 15.
⑤ ⑧ ▭ ▮ ⃝ Ⓥ ⅋ ⑰ ▭ ☎
🛏

BURY ST. EDMUNDS

Suffolk
Map ref 3B2

Ancient market and
cathedral town which
takes its name from the
martyred Saxon King, St.
Edmund. Bury St.
Edmunds has many fine
buildings including the
Athenaeum and Moyses
Hall, reputed to be the
oldest Norman house in
the county.
*Tourist Information
Centre* ☎ (0284) 764667

Bradfield House Restaurant and Hotel
⚘⚘⚘⚘ COMMENDED

Bradfield Combust, Bury St.
Edmunds, IP30 0LR
☎ Sicklesmere (0284) 86301
& 868196
*17th C timber framed house set
in mature grounds with
Victorian herb garden.
Relaxed atmosphere.
Restaurant noted for high
standard of country cuisine.
4 miles south of Bury St.
Edmunds towards Lavenham.*
Bedrooms: 1 single, 2 double
& 1 twin.
Bathrooms: 4 private.
Bed & breakfast: £35-£40
single, £45-£70 double.
Half board: £47.50-£52.50
daily, £308-£339 weekly.
Evening meal 7pm (l.o.
9.30pm).
Parking for 14.
Credit: Access, Visa.
⑤ ♨ ℄ ⑧ ▭ ♡ ▮ Ⓥ ⅋
▥ ☎ ♨ ⁂ 🛏 🛏 ⚘ SP 🛏

Butterfly Hotel ᛗ

A45 Bury East Exit, Moreton
Hall, Bury St. Edmunds,
IP32 7BW
☎ (0284) 760884
Telex 818360
*Modern building with rustic
style and decor, around open
central courtyard. Special
weekend rates available.*
Bedrooms: 23 single,
15 double & 12 twin.
Bathrooms: 50 private.
Bed & breakfast: £60-£65
single, £65-£70 double.

Half board: £70-£75 daily.
Lunch available.
Evening meal 7pm (l.o.
10pm).
Parking for 70.
Credit: Access, Visa, Diners,
Amex.
⑤ ♨ ℄ ▭ ♡ ▮ Ⓥ ⅄
⅋ ◉ 🛏 ▭ ☎ ⁂ 🛏 SP 🆃

The Chantry Hotel

8 Sparhawk St., Bury St.
Edmunds, IP33 1RY
☎ (0284) 767427
*Georgian hotel in town centre,
near the Abbey Gardens,
cathedral and Theatre Royal.
Special weekend breaks
available.*
Bedrooms: 4 single, 6 double
& 5 twin, 2 family rooms.
Bathrooms: 17 private,
1 public.
Bed & breakfast: £33-£42
single, £44-£49 double.
Half board: £28-£57 daily.
Evening meal 7.30pm (l.o
6.45pm).
Parking for 16.
Credit: Access, Visa.
⑤ ♨ ℄ ▭ ♡ ▮ Ⓥ ⅋
🛏 ☎ 🛏 SP 🛏 🆃

Dunston Guest House/Hotel ᛗ
⚘⚘⚘

8 Springfield Rd., Bury St.
Edmunds, IP33 3AN
☎ (0284) 767981
*Attractive Victorian
guesthouse/hotel providing high
standard accommodation,
quietly situated half a mile
from town centre. Licensed.
Sun lounge, garden and car
park. Groups welcome.*
Bedrooms: 6 single, 3 double
& 4 twin, 4 family rooms.
Bathrooms: 9 private,
4 public.
Bed & breakfast: £18-£27.50
single, £32-£40 double.
Half board: £28-£37.50 daily.
Evening meal 6pm.
Parking for 12.
⑤ ♨ ▭ ♡ ♨ ▮ Ⓥ ⅋ ⑰
🛏 ☎ ♨ ⚙ ⁂ ⅄

Grange Hotel ᛗ
⚘⚘⚘ APPROVED

Barton Rd., Thurston, Bury
St. Edmunds, IP31 3PQ
☎ Pakenham (0359) 31260
*Family-owned country house
hotel with chef/proprietor.*
Bedrooms: 2 single, 7 double
& 5 twin, 1 family room.
Bathrooms: 11 private,
2 public; 2 private showers.
Bed & breakfast: £27-£46
single, £41-£59 double.
Lunch available.

Continued ▶

BURY ST. EDMUNDS
Continued

Evening meal 7pm (l.o.
9.30pm).
Parking for 80.
Credit: Access, Visa.

⛎ ✆ 📺 ❄ ☎ Ⓥ ⊟ ⛁ ⬦
🍴 ❄ ✗ ⌨ SP

Hamling House Hotel M
⚜⚜⚜⚜ **COMMENDED**

Bull Rd., Pakenham, Bury St.
Edmunds, IP31 2LW
☎ (0359) 30934
*Delightful frequently re-visited
Alpine-style country house
hotel in picturesque village of
Pakenham, near historic Bury
St. Edmunds. Tranquil
gardens.*
Bedrooms: 1 single, 2 double
& 3 twin, 1 family room.
Bathrooms: 7 private.
Bed & breakfast: £45-£48
single, £55-£60 double.
Half board: £38-£48 daily.
Lunch available.
Evening meal 7pm (l.o.
8.30pm).
Parking for 10.
Credit: Access, Visa, Diners,
Amex.

⛎ ⛁ ⚙ ✆ Ⓡ ☐ ❄ ⫟ Ⓥ
⊟ 📺 ⬛ ⛁ ❄ ✻ SP Ⓣ

High Green House M
⚜⚜⚜ **COMMENDED**

Nowton, Bury St. Edmunds,
IP29 2LZ
☎ Sicklesmere (028 486) 293
*Modernised Tudor house with
a garden, ample parking and
views of the surrounding
countryside. Home produce.
Colour TV all rooms.*
Bedrooms: 1 single, 1 double
& 2 twin, 1 family room.
Bathrooms: 5 private.
Bed & breakfast: £16 single,
£32 double.
Half board: £32 daily,
max. £224 weekly.
Evening meal 7.30pm (l.o.
8pm).
Parking for 6.

⛎ ⛁ ⚙ ✆ Ⓡ ☐ ❄ ⫟ Ⓥ ⊟ 📺
📖 ⬛ ⛁ ⚘ ❄ ⌨ DAP SP 🔲

---

*The symbols are
explained on the
flap inside the
back cover.*

---

*Map references
apply to the colour
maps towards the
end of this guide.*

CAMBRIDGE
Cambridgeshire
Map ref 2D1

*A most important and
beautiful city on the River
Cam with 31 colleges
forming one of the oldest
universities in the world.
Numerous museums,
good shopping centre,
restaurants, theatres,
cinema and fine
bookshops.
Tourist Information
Centre ☎ (0223) 322640*

All Seasons Guest
House
Listed

219-221 Chesterton Rd.,
Cambridge, CB1 1AN
☎ (0223) 353386
*Detached Georgian house with
large rear garden, within
walking distance of the city
centre.*
Bedrooms: 3 single, 1 double
& 2 twin, 3 family rooms.
Bathrooms: 3 public.
Bed & breakfast: £13-£13.50
single, £26-£27 double.
Half board: £18-£19 daily.
Evening meal 6pm (l.o. 2pm).
Parking for 4.

⛎ ⛁ ☐ ⫟ Ⓥ 📖 ⬛ ⛁
DAP

Antwerp Guest House M
⚜⚜

36 Brookfields, Mill Rd.,
Cambridge, CB1 3NW
☎ (0223) 247690
*On A1134 ring road between
Addenbrookes Hospital and
Cambridge Airport. Near the
city's amenities, and bus and
railway stations. Pleasant
gardens.*
Bedrooms: 2 double & 5 twin,
1 family room.
Bathrooms: 2 private,
2 public.
Bed & breakfast: £21.15-
£25.85 single, £28.20-£32.90
double.
Half board: £28.20-£32.90
daily.
Lunch available.
Evening meal 6.30pm (l.o.
4pm).
Parking for 8.

⛎2 ⛁ ☐ ❄ ⫟ Ⓥ ⊟ 📺 📖
⬛ ⫟ ✗ ✻ SP

Arundel House Hotel M
⚜⚜⚜ **COMMENDED**

53 Chesterton Rd.,
Cambridge, CB4 3AN
☎ (0223) 67701
*Friendly, privately-owned 19th
C terraced hotel. Beautiful
location overlooking the River
Cam and open parkland, near
the city centre and colleges.*

Bedrooms: 33 single,
24 double & 25 twin, 6 family
rooms.
Bathrooms: 79 private,
8 public.
Bed & breakfast: £28-£53
single, £41.50-£72 double.
Lunch available.
Evening meal 6.30pm (l.o.
9.30pm).
Parking for 70.
Credit: Access, Visa, Diners,
Amex.

⛎ ⛁ ✆ Ⓡ ☐ ❄ ⫟ Ⓥ ⫟
⊟ ⬤ 📖 ⬛ ⛁ ⫟ ✗ ⌨ SP Ⓣ

Ashtrees Guest House
Listed **APPROVED**

128 Perne Rd., Cambridge,
CB1 3RR
☎ (0223) 411233
*Comfort and an enjoyable stay
is the priority. Individually
decorated rooms to a high
standard. Home cooking.*
Bedrooms: 2 single, 2 double
& 1 twin, 2 family rooms.
Bathrooms: 1 private,
1 public.
Bed & breakfast: from £17
single, from £30 double.
Half board: £22-£24 daily.
Evening meal 6.30pm (l.o.
7.30pm).
Parking for 6.
Credit: Access, Visa.

⛎ ⛁ ☐ ❄ Ⓤ ⫟ ⛁ 📖 ✗ ⌨

Assisi Guest House

193 Cherry Hinton Rd.,
Cambridge, CB1 4BX
☎ (0223) 246648 & 211466
*Warm, welcoming, family-run
guesthouse, ideally situated for
the city, colleges and
Addenbrookes Hospital. All
modern facilities.*
Bedrooms: 6 single, 2 double
& 1 twin, 1 family room.
Bathrooms: 7 private,
2 public.
Bed & breakfast: £18-£26
single, £32-£36.44 double.
Parking for 17.
Credit: Access, Visa, Amex.

⛎ ⛁ ☐ Ⓤ ⫟ Ⓥ ⫟ ⊟ 📺
📖 ⬛ ✗ DAP SP 🔲

Bon Accord House M
⚜⚜

20 St. Margarets Square,
Cambridge, CB1 4AP
☎ (0223) 246568 & 411188
*Quietly but conveniently
situated, south of the
fascinating historic centre of
Cambridge. Non-smokers only
please.*
Bedrooms: 7 single, 1 twin,
1 family room.
Bathrooms: 1 private,
3 public.

Bed & breakfast: £18.50-£30
single, £31-£46 double.
Parking for 14.
Credit: Access, Visa.

⛎ Ⓡ ☐ ❄ Ⓤ ⫟ ⛁ Ⓥ ⫟ ✗
📖 ⬛ ✗

Brooklands Guest
House

95 Cherry Hinton Rd.,
Cambridge, CB1 4BS
☎ (0223) 242035
*A small, friendly family-run
guesthouse. Well decorated,
with satellite TV, jacuzzi bath
and four-poster bed.*
Bedrooms: 3 double.
Bathrooms: 3 private,
1 public.
Bed & breakfast: £37-£40
double.
Half board: £53-£56 daily.
Lunch available.
Evening meal 6.30pm (l.o.
7.30pm).
Parking for 3.

⛎ ⛁ ☐ ❄ Ⓤ ⫟ ⛁ Ⓥ
✗ ⊟ 📺 Ⓥ 📖 ⬛ ⛁ ❄

Cambridgeshire Moat
House M
⚜⚜⚜ **COMMENDED**

Bar Hill, Cambridge,
CB3 8EU
☎ Crafts Hill (0954) 780555
Telex 817141
Ⓒ® Queens Moat Houses
*Modern hotel with extensive
leisure and conference facilities
including 18-hole golf course,
indoor swimming pool and
leisure centre.*
Bedrooms: 8 double &
92 twin.
Bathrooms: 100 private.
Bed & breakfast: £51.50-
£71.50 single, £78-£88.90
double.
Half board: from £49.50
daily.
Evening meal 7pm (l.o.
10pm).
Parking for 200.
Credit: Access, Visa, Diners,
Amex.

⛎ ⛁ ✆ Ⓡ ☐ ❄ ⫟ Ⓥ ⊟
⬤ 📖 ⬛ ⛁ Ⓣ ⌨ ✗ ♪ ▶ ❄
SP Ⓣ

Centennial Hotel M
⚜⚜⚜ **APPROVED**

63-71 Hills Rd., Cambridge,
CB2 1PG
☎ (0223) 314652
Telex 817019
*Modernised family-run hotel
opposite the botanical gardens.
Central, near entertainment
and colleges. Fully licensed bar
and restaurant. Parking.*
Bedrooms: 7 single, 20 double
& 12 twin, 2 family rooms.
Bathrooms: 41 private,
1 public.

Bed & breakfast: £50-£58 single, £65-£73 double.
Half board: £63-£71 daily.
Lunch available.
Evening meal 6.30pm (l.o. 9.30pm).
Parking for 32.
Credit: Access, Visa, Diners, Amex.

Cristinas
罒罒

47 St. Andrews Rd., Cambridge, CB1 1DL
☎ (0223) 65855 & 327700
Small family-run business in quiet location, a short walk from city centre and colleges.
Bedrooms: 3 double & 2 twin, 1 family room.
Bathrooms: 4 private, 2 public.
Bed & breakfast: £22-£24 single, £34-£40 double.
Parking for 8.

De Freville House
COMMENDED

166 Chesterton Rd., Cambridge, CB4 1DA
☎ (0223) 354993
Family-run Victorian house retaining its original character. 15 minutes' walk from city centre and colleges. Non-smoking house.
Bedrooms: 2 single, 4 double & 2 twin.
Bathrooms: 3 private, 2 public; 2 private showers.
Bed & breakfast: £15-£18 single, £28-£34 double.

Dresden Villa Guest House

34 Cherry Hinton Rd., Cambridge, CB1 4AA
☎ (0223) 247539
Friendly family guesthouse near the railway station, within easy reach of the city centre. Free tea and coffee. TV in all rooms.
Bedrooms: 2 single, 3 double & 2 twin, 2 family rooms.
Bathrooms: 5 private, 2 public; 1 private shower.
Bed & breakfast: £20-£22 single, £34-£38 double.
Half board: £28-£30 daily, £196-£210 weekly.
Evening meal 7pm (l.o. 8pm).
Parking for 8.

Fairways Guest House
罒罒罒

141-143 Cherry Hinton Rd., Cambridge, CB1 4BX
☎ (0223) 246063
Charming Victorian house offering a friendly atmosphere and featuring locked car parking at night. Near Addenbrookes Hospital and 1 mile from the city centre and golf-course. Fully licensed bar-lounge with bar meals.
Bedrooms: 4 single, 4 double & 4 twin, 2 family rooms.
Bathrooms: 8 private, 3 public.
Bed & breakfast: £19.50-£26 single, £33-£39 double.
Evening meal 6pm (l.o. 9pm).
Parking for 20.
Credit: Visa.

Garden House Hotel M
罒罒罒罒

Granta Place, off Mill Lane, Cambridge, CB2 1RT
☎ (0223) 63421 Telex 81463
Ⓖ Queens Moat Houses
Modern hotel in riverside gardens close to the city centre, shops, principal colleges and museums.
Bedrooms: 28 double & 83 twin, 7 family rooms.
Bathrooms: 118 private.
Bed & breakfast: £77-£128 single, £108-£154 double.
Half board: £72.95-£146.95 daily.
Lunch available.
Evening meal 7pm (l.o. 9.45pm).
Parking for 180.
Credit: Access, Visa, Diners, Amex.

Holiday Inn, Cambridge

Downing St., Cambridge, CB2 3DT
☎ (0223) 464466
Ⓗ Holiday Inn
Fully air conditioned modern hotel, with residents' pool, conference and banqueting facilities for up to 150 delegates and free parking, in the heart of historic Cambridge.
Bedrooms: 87 double & 112 twin.
Bathrooms: 199 private.
Bed & breakfast: £48-£100 single, £96-£130 double.
Half board: £60-£120 daily, £420-£840 weekly.
Lunch available.
Evening meal 7pm (l.o. 10pm).

Parking for 60.
Credit: Access, Visa, C.Bl., Diners, Amex.

Kirkwood House
Listed COMMENDED

172 Chesterton Rd., Cambridge, CB4 1DA
☎ (0223) 313874
Edwardian family house which is maintained to a high standard. Close to river and city centre.
Bedrooms: 1 single, 2 double & 2 twin.
Bathrooms: 2 private, 1 public.
Bed & breakfast: £18-£22 single, £34-£42 double.
Parking for 4.
Open February-December.

L'Aquila Guest House
APPROVED

12 Rock Rd., Off Cherry Hinton Rd., Cambridge, CB1 4UF
☎ (0223) 245432
Comfortable family-run guesthouse. Convenient for the station and about 20 minutes' walk from the city centre. All rooms with private facilities.
Bedrooms: 1 single, 2 double.
Bathrooms: 3 private, 1 public.
Bed & breakfast: £20-£22 single, £32-£34 double.
Parking for 2.

Lensfield Hotel M
罒罒 APPROVED

53 Lensfield Rd., Cambridge, CB2 1EN
☎ (0223) 355017
Telex 818183
A family-run central hotel with ample parking.
Bedrooms: 7 single, 11 double & 10 twin, 4 family rooms.
Bathrooms: 28 private, 4 public; 4 private showers.
Bed & breakfast: £32-£42 single, £55-£62 double.
Half board: £39-£69 daily.
Evening meal 6.30pm (l.o. 9pm).
Parking for 6.
Credit: Access, Visa, Amex.

Regent Hotel
罒罒

41 Regent St., Cambridge, CB2 1AB
☎ (0223) 351470

Small family-run hotel offering personal service, in a convenient, central location.
Bedrooms: 5 single, 11 double & 9 twin, 1 family room.
Bathrooms: 26 private.
Bed & breakfast: £50-£55 single, £67.50-£72 double.
Half board: £70-£75 daily, £490-£525 weekly.
Lunch available.
Evening meal 6.30pm (l.o. 9pm).
Parking for 2.
Credit: Access, Visa, Diners, Amex.

Rosswill Guest House
罒罒

17-19 Chesterton Rd., Cambridge, CB4 3AL
☎ (0223) 67871
Overlooking Jesus Green and River Cam, within 10 minutes' walk of King's College and city centre.
Bedrooms: 4 single, 3 double & 3 twin, 3 family rooms.
Bathrooms: 4 private, 2 public; 1 private shower.
Bed & breakfast: £19-£20 single, £32-£42 double.
Parking for 11.

Sorrento Hotel M
罒罒罒 APPROVED

190-196 Cherry Hinton Rd., Cambridge, CB1 4AN
☎ (0223) 243533
Small family hotel in a quiet residential area. Close to town centre, with personal service and English/French/Italian cooking.
Bedrooms: 4 single, 11 double & 5 twin, 2 family rooms.
Bathrooms: 19 private, 1 public; 3 private showers.
Bed & breakfast: £36-£46 single, £51-£56 double.
Half board: £47-£52 daily.
Evening meal 6.30pm (l.o. 8.30pm).
Parking for 25.
Credit: Access, Visa.

Southampton House M
Listed

7 Elizabeth Way, Cambridge, CB4 1DE
☎ (0223) 357780
Victorian property with friendly atmosphere, only 8 minutes' walk along riverside to city centre, colleges and new shopping mall.
Bedrooms: 1 single, 1 double & 1 twin, 3 family rooms.

Continued ▶

CAMBRIDGE
Continued

Bathrooms: 1 private,
2 public; 2 private showers.
Bed & breakfast: £17-£22
single, £28-£38 double.
Parking for 8.

CAMPSEA ASH

Suffolk
Map ref 3C2

2m E. Wickham Market

The Old Rectory M

Campsea Ash, Woodbridge,
IP13 0PU
☎ Wickham Market
(0728) 746524
*Large, family country house in
mature grounds offering
comfortable accommodation
with food and wine under the
owner's supervision.*
Bedrooms: 1 single, 3 double
& 2 twin.
Bathrooms: 6 private.
Bed & breakfast: from £30
single, from £45 double.
Half board: from £36 daily,
from £226 weekly.
Evening meal 7.50pm (l.o.
9pm).
Parking for 15.
Credit: Access, Visa, Diners,
Amex.

CAWSTON

Norfolk
Map ref 3B1

4m SW. Aylsham
Village with one of the
finest churches in the
country. St. Agnes, built
in the Perpendicular style,
was much patronised by
Michael de la Pole, Earl of
Suffolk (1414), and has a
magnificent hammer-
beam roof and numerous
carved angels.

Grey Gables Country House Hotel M

Norwich Rd., Cawston, Nr.
Norwich, NR10 4EY
☎ (0603) 871259
*Former rectory in pleasant,
rural setting, 10 miles from
Norwich, coast and Broads.
Wine cellar, emphasis on food.
Comfortably furnished with
many antiques.*
Bedrooms: 2 single, 3 double
& 1 twin, 1 family room.

Bathrooms: 5 private,
1 public.
Bed & breakfast: £34-£43
single, £44-£54 double.
Half board: £29-£42 daily,
£192-£216 weekly.
Evening meal 7pm (l.o. 9pm).
Parking for 15.
Credit: Access, Visa.

CHATTERIS

Cambridgeshire
Map ref 3A2

7m S. March

Cross Keys M
APPROVED

16 Market Hill, Chatteris,
PE16 6BA
☎ (035 43) 3036 & 2644
*Elizabethan coaching inn built
around 1540, Grade II listed.
A la carte menu and bar meals
available. Friendly atmosphere,
oak-beamed lounge with open
log fires.*
Bedrooms: 1 double & 5 twin,
1 family room.
Bathrooms: 5 private,
1 public.
Bed & breakfast: £21-£35
single, £32.50-£45 double.
Lunch available.
Evening meal 7pm (l.o.
10pm).
Parking for 10.
Credit: Access, Visa, Diners,
Amex.

CHEDISTON

Suffolk
Map ref 3C2

3m W. Halesworth

Saskiavill M

Chediston, Halesworth,
IP19 0AR
☎ (0986) 873067
*Travelling west from
Halesworth on the B1123, turn
right after 2 miles at the
signpost for Chediston Green.
After crossing the hump-
backed bridge over the stream,
Saskiavill is the fourth
property on the left.*
Bedrooms: 2 double & 2 twin,
1 family room.
Bathrooms: 3 private,
2 public.
Bed & breakfast: £14-£16
single, £28-£32 double.

Half board: £17-£19 daily,
£101-£115 weekly.
Evening meal 6.30pm.
Parking for 8.

CHELMSFORD

Essex
Map ref 3B3

The county town of
Essex, originally a Roman
settlement,
Caesaromagus, thought
to have been destroyed
by Boudicca. Situated in
the heart of heavily
cultivated farmland and
with an important
livestock market. Growth
of the town's industry can
be traced in the excellent
museum in Oaklands
Park. 15th C parish
church has been
Chelmsford Cathedral
since 1914.
*Tourist Information
Centre ☎ (0245) 283400*

Beechcroft Private Hotel

211 New London Rd.,
Chelmsford, CM2 0AJ
☎ (0245) 352462
*Central hotel offering clean
and comfortable
accommodation with friendly
service. Under family
ownership and management.*
Bedrooms: 12 single, 3 double
& 3 twin, 2 family rooms.
Bathrooms: 8 private,
5 public.
Bed & breakfast: £25.75-
£32.95 single, £41.65-£52.30
double.
Parking for 15.
Credit: Access, Visa.

Boswell House Hotel

118 Springfield Rd.,
Chelmsford, CM2 6LF
☎ (0245) 287587
*Victorian town house in central
location, offering high-standard
accommodation in friendly and
informal surroundings. Homely
atmosphere and home cooking.*
Bedrooms: 5 single, 6 double,
2 family rooms.
Bathrooms: 13 private.
Bed & breakfast: £35-£42
single, £52-£58 double.
Half board: £44-£51 daily,
£308-£357 weekly.
Lunch available.
Evening meal 7pm (l.o.
8.30pm).

Parking for 15.
Credit: Access, Visa, Diners,
Amex.

The Chelmer Hotel

2-4 Hamlet Rd., Chelmsford,
CM2 0EU
☎ (0245) 353360 & 261751
*Friendly and homely
atmosphere. Close to all
amenities and priding itself as
the most economic hotel in
Chelmsford.*
Bedrooms: 2 single, 2 double
& 5 twin, 2 family rooms.
Bathrooms: 2 public.
Bed & breakfast: £18-£20
single, £30-£36 double.
Parking for 2.

Miami Motel M
APPROVED

Princes Rd., Chelmsford,
CM2 9AJ
☎ (0245) 264848 & 269603
Telex 995430
*Family-run hotel, 1 mile from
town centre.*
Bedrooms: 28 single,
19 double & 10 twin.
Bathrooms: 57 private.
Bed & breakfast: £50-£65
single, £70-£80 double.
Lunch available.
Evening meal 6.30pm (l.o.
10pm).
Parking for 80.
Credit: Access, Visa, Diners,
Amex.

South Lodge Hotel M
APPROVED

196 New London Rd.,
Chelmsford, CM2 0AR
☎ (0245) 264564 Telex 99452
*Pleasantly situated hotel with
garden. Convenient for A12 to
East Coast or London. Close
to town centre and cricket
ground.*
Bedrooms: 21 single, 8 double
& 10 twin, 2 family rooms.
Bathrooms: 41 private.
Bed & breakfast: £55-£62.50
single, £60-£77.50 double.
Lunch available.
Evening meal 6.30pm (l.o.
9.30pm).
Parking for 50.
Credit: Access, Visa, Diners,
Amex.

> *The symbols are
> explained on the
> flap inside the
> back cover.*

CLACTON-ON-SEA

Essex
Map ref 3B3

Developed in the 1870s into a popular holiday resort with pier, pavilion, funfair, theatres and traditional amusements. The Martello Towers on the seafront were built like many others in the early 19th C to defend Britain against Napoleon.
Tourist Information Centre ☎ (0255) 423400

Chudleigh Hotel
COMMENDED

Agate Rd., Marine Parade West, Clacton-on-Sea, CO15 1RA
☎ (0255) 425407
Licensed private hotel with resident proprietors, 200 metres from central seafront gardens and near the pier and main shops. Forecourt parking. Fluent Italian and French spoken. Winner of hygiene award.
Bedrooms: 3 single, 4 double & 1 twin, 4 family rooms.
Bathrooms: 11 private, 1 public.
Bed & breakfast: £25-£27.50 single, £45-£50 double.
Half board: £34.50-£35 daily, £180-£195 weekly.
Evening meal 6.15pm (l.o. 6.45pm).
Parking for 6.
Credit: Access, Visa, Diners, Amex.

Sandrock Hotel

1 Penfold Rd., Marine Parade West, Clacton-on-Sea, CO15 1JN
☎ (0255) 428215
Small, exclusive, family-owned hotel just off the seafront, close to shopping centre and pier. Free parking.
Bedrooms: 4 double & 2 twin, 1 family room.
Bathrooms: 7 private, 1 public.
Bed & breakfast: £25.50-£26.50 single, £45-£47 double.
Half board: £30.50-£32.50 daily, £165-£175 weekly.
Lunch available.
Evening meal 6.30pm (l.o. 8pm).
Parking for 5.
Credit: Access, Visa.

CLARE

Suffolk
Map ref 3B2

7m NW. Sudbury
Attractive village with many of the houses displaying pargetting work and the site of a castle first mentioned in 1090. Clare Country Park occupies the site of the castle bailey and old railway station. Ancient House Museum in the 15th C priest's house contains local bygones.

Bell Hotel ♨
COMMENDED

Market Hill, Clare, CO10 8NN
☎ (0787) 277741
Ⓜ Minotels
16th C posting house with beamed restaurant and wine bar. Within easy reach of ports. 60 miles from London.
Bedrooms: 1 single, 14 double & 3 twin, 2 family rooms.
Bathrooms: 20 private, 1 public.
Bed & breakfast: £49-£55 single, £60-£99.95 double.
Half board: £45-£70 daily.
Lunch available.
Evening meal 7pm (l.o. 9.30pm).
Parking for 16.
Credit: Access, Visa, Diners, Amex.

The Plough Inn ♨

Hundon, Nr Clare, Sudbury, CO10 8DT
☎ (044 086) 789
Delightfully-situated traditional country inn, ideally placed for Cambridge, Bury St Edmunds, Lavenham, etc, and the picture-postcard villages of Suffolk and north Essex.
Bedrooms: 4 double & 3 twin, 1 family room.
Bathrooms: 8 private.
Bed & breakfast: £39.50-£50 single, £55-£67.50 double.
Lunch available.
Evening meal 7pm (l.o. 9.30pm).
Parking for 50.
Credit: Access, Visa, Amex.

Please check prices and other details at the time of booking.

COGGESHALL

Essex
Map ref 3B2

5m E. Braintree
The National Trust property 'Paycocke's' is at Coggeshall. It is a 16th century half-timbered merchant's house featuring a richly-carved interior.

White Heather Guest House

19 Colchester Rd., Coggeshall, Nr Colchester, CO6 1RP
☎ (0376) 563004
On the edge of Coggeshall, offering overnight accommodation and breakfast.
Bedrooms: 3 single, 2 double & 1 twin.
Bathrooms: 2 private, 3 public.
Bed & breakfast: £20-£25 single, £40-£45 double.
Parking for 8.

COLCHESTER

Essex
Map ref 3B2

Britain's oldest recorded town standing on the River Colne and famous for its oysters. Numerous historic buildings, ancient remains and museums. Plenty of parks and gardens, extensive shopping centre, theatre and zoo.
Tourist Information Centre ☎ (0206) 712920

Colchester Mill Hotel
COMMENDED

East St., Colchester, CO1 2TS
☎ (0206) 865022
Telex 988785
Weddings, functions and conferences catered for. Conservatory garden restaurant offers good food.
Bedrooms: 26 single, 25 double & 6 twin, 3 family rooms.
Bathrooms: 60 private.
Bed & breakfast: £42-£82 double.
Lunch available.
Evening meal 7pm (l.o. 10pm).
Parking for 200.
Credit: Access, Visa, Diners, Amex.

The Globe Hotel

71 North Station Rd., Colchester, CO1 1RQ
☎ (0206) 573881
Victorian pub/hotel, built in 1850, close to all local amenities.
Bedrooms: 2 single, 3 double & 3 twin, 4 family rooms.
Bathrooms: 12 private.
Bed & breakfast: £25-£30 single, £45-£60 double.
Half board: £30-£40 daily, £180-£250 weekly.
Evening meal 6pm (l.o. 8pm).
Parking for 20.
Credit: Access, Visa, Diners, Amex.

King's Ford Park Hotel ♨
APPROVED

Layer Rd., Colchester, CO2 0HS
☎ (0206) 34301
Telex 987562 G
Privately-owned 18th C manor house in 18 acres. Offering peace and tranquillity, yet within 2 miles of the town centre.
Bedrooms: 1 single, 8 double & 3 twin, 1 family room.
Bathrooms: 13 private, 1 public.
Bed & breakfast: £63-£69 single, £79-£85 double.
Lunch available.
Evening meal 7pm (l.o. 9.30pm).
Parking for 100.
Credit: Access, Visa, Diners, Amex.

Peveril Hotel ♨

51 North Hill, Colchester, CO1 1PY
☎ (0206) 574001
Friendly, family-run hotel with fine restaurant and bar. All rooms have colour TV, alarm clock, tea and coffee facilities.
Bedrooms: 6 single, 5 double & 4 twin, 2 family rooms.
Bathrooms: 3 public.
Bed & breakfast: £22-£26 single, £33-£38 double.
Half board: £25-£36 daily, £150-£200 weekly.
Lunch available.

Continued ▶

The national Crown scheme is explained in full on pages 536 – 539.

COLCHESTER

Continued

Evening meal 7pm (l.o. 10pm).
Parking for 4.
Credit: Access, Visa.

Scheregate Hotel M
APPROVED

36 Osborne St., Colchester, CO2 7DB
☎ (0206) 573034
Interesting 15th C building, centrally situated, providing accommodation at moderate prices.
Bedrooms: 14 single, 11 twin, 1 family room.
Bathrooms: 1 private, 4 public.
Bed & breakfast: £12.50-£17 single, £25-£44 double.
Parking for 30.

Wellesley Court Private Hotel
Listed APPROVED

15 Wellesley Rd., Colchester, CO3 3HE
☎ (0206) 766880
Family-run hotel in a quiet cul-de-sac, 5 minutes' walk from town centre. All rooms have colour TV.
Bedrooms: 1 double & 9 twin, 3 family rooms.
Bathrooms: 3 private, 3 public.
Bed & breakfast: £20.50-£29 single, £34-£39 double.
Parking for 16.
Credit: Access, Visa.

Wivenhoe Park Hotel, Restaurant and Conference Centre M
≡≡≡

Wivenhoe Park, Colchester, CO4 3SQ
☎ (0206) 863666
Georgian mansion in 200 acres of parkland on the outskirts of Colchester.
Bedrooms: 38 single, 10 double & 14 twin.
Bathrooms: 47 private, 2 public.
Bed & breakfast: £31.40-£66.20 single, £75.40-£87.20 double.
Lunch available.
Evening meal 7pm (l.o. 9pm).
Parking for 80.
Credit: Access, Visa.

COLTISHALL

Norfolk
Map ref 3C1

8m NE. Norwich
On the River Bure, with an RAF station nearby. The village is attractive with many pleasant 18th C brick houses and a thatched church.

The Norfolk Mead Hotel M
≡≡≡≡

The Mead, Coltishall, Norwich, NR12 7DN
☎ Norwich (0603) 737531
Beautiful Georgian country house set in 12 acres of parkland, gardens with river frontage. Boating, birdlife, fishing, outdoor swimming pool and restaurant.
Bedrooms: 5 double & 3 twin, 2 family rooms.
Bathrooms: 10 private.
Bed & breakfast: £49-£59 single, £65-£85 double.
Half board: £63-£73 daily, £285-£375 weekly.
Evening meal 7pm (l.o. 9pm).
Parking for 50.
Credit: Access, Visa, Diners, Amex.

CROMER

Norfolk
Map ref 3B1

Once a small fishing village and now famous for its fishing boats that still work off the beach and offer freshly caught crabs. A delightful resort with excellent bathing on sandy beaches fringed by cliffs. The narrow streets of old Cromer encircle the church of SS. Peter and Paul which has a splendid tower. The town boasts a fine pier, theatre, museum and a lifeboat station.

The Bath House
≡≡≡

The Promenade, Cromer, NR27 9HE
☎ (0263) 514260
Enjoy a stay at this fine old Regency inn, situated right on the promenade and only paces from the beach.
Bedrooms: 1 single, 3 double & 3 twin.
Bathrooms: 7 private.
Bed & breakfast: £24.50-£26.50 single, £49-£53 double.

Half board: £32-£34 daily, from £185 weekly.
Lunch available.
Evening meal 6.30pm (l.o. 9pm).
Parking for 7.
Open March-December.
Credit: Access, Visa, Amex.

Cliftonville Hotel M
≡≡≡

Runton Rd., Cromer, NR27 9AS
☎ (0263) 512543
Victorian hotel on the West Cliff facing the sea and gardens. Central heating. Ideal for touring historic north Norfolk and Norfolk Broads.
Bedrooms: 14 single, 12 double & 14 twin, 4 family rooms.
Bathrooms: 26 private, 7 public; 1 private shower.
Bed & breakfast: £25-£40 single, £48-£68 double.
Half board: £35-£44 daily, £237-£306 weekly.
Lunch available.
Evening meal 7.15pm (l.o. 9pm).
Parking for 22.
Credit: Access, Visa, Diners, Amex.

Red Lion Hotel
≡≡≡ COMMENDED

Brook St., Cromer, NR27 9HD
☎ (0263) 514964
Charming Victorian hotel by the sea. Caring for the comfort and convenience of patrons, who reciprocate by returning year after year with their friends.
Bedrooms: 1 single, 5 double & 5 twin, 1 family room.
Bathrooms: 12 private.
Bed & breakfast: £35-£36 single, £70-£72 double.
Half board: £42-£44 daily, £294-£308 weekly.
Lunch available.
Evening meal 7pm (l.o. 9.30pm).
Parking for 12.
Credit: Access, Visa, Amex.

Half board prices shown are per person but in some cases may be based on double/twin occupancy.

CROSTWICK

Norfolk
Map ref 3C1

5m NE. Norwich

Old Rectory
≡≡≡≡

North Walsham Rd., Crostwick, Norwich, NR12 7BG
☎ (0603) 738513
Old Victorian rectory set amidst 2.5 acres of mature trees. Well placed for the Broads and Norwich. Homely accommodation.
Bedrooms: 3 double & 10 twin.
Bathrooms: 13 private.
Bed & breakfast: £26-£30 single, £37.50-£40 double.
Half board: £32-£40 daily.
Evening meal 6.30pm (l.o. 1pm).
Parking for 15.
Credit: Access, Visa.

DEREHAM

Norfolk
Map ref 3B1

16m W. Norwich
East Dereham is famous for its associations with the poet William Cowper and also Bishop Bonner, chaplain to Cardinal Wolsey. His home is now an archaeological museum. Around the charming market-place are many notable buildings.

The King's Head Hotel M
≡≡≡≡

Norwich St., East Dereham, NR19 1AD
☎ (0362) 693842
A modernised 17th C hotel within easy reach of Norwich, the coastal resorts and Norfolk Broads.
Bedrooms: 8 single, 4 double & 2 twin, 1 family room.
Bathrooms: 12 private, 2 public.
Bed & breakfast: £34-£37 single, £46-£50 double.
Lunch available.
Evening meal 7pm (l.o. 9.30pm).
Parking for 22.
Credit: Access, Visa, Diners, Amex.

DISS

Norfolk
Map ref 3B2

An old market town built around 3 sides of the Mere, a placid water of 6 acres and beside the village green. Although modernised, some interesting Tudor, Georgian and Victorian buildings around the market-place remain. St Mary's Church has a fine knapped flint chancel.

Salisbury House M
⬛⬛⬛ COMMENDED
Victoria Rd., Diss, IP22 3JG
☎ (0379) 644738
Country house hotel set in an acre of grounds, with well-appointed en-suite bedrooms and restaurant offering interesting cuisine and wines.
Bedrooms: 3 double.
Bathrooms: 3 private.
Bed & breakfast: £38-£45 single, £55-£66 double.
Lunch available.
Evening meal 7.30pm (l.o. 9pm).
Parking for 11.
Credit: Access, Visa.
[symbols]

DOWNHAM MARKET

Norfolk
Map ref 3B1

10m S. *King's Lynn*
Market town above the surrounding Fens on the River Ouse. Oxburgh Hall (National Trust) is 8 miles east, a magnificent 15th C moated dwelling owned by one family, the Bedingfields, for almost 500 years.

Castle Hotel M
⬛⬛⬛ APPROVED
High St., Downham Market, PE38 9HF
☎ (0366) 384311
Telex 817787
17th C coaching inn in centre of town. Restaurant, bar, lounge, conference rooms and function room (max. 80 persons). Four poster room with jacuzzi. Vegetarian menu in restaurant.
Bedrooms: 1 single, 5 double & 5 twin.
Bathrooms: 9 private, 1 public.
Bed & breakfast: max. £36 single, max. £45 double.
Half board: max. £46.90 daily, max. £206.50 weekly.

Lunch available.
Evening meal 5.30pm (l.o. 10pm).
Parking for 27.
Credit: Access, Visa, Diners, Amex.
[symbols]

The Crown Hotel M
⬛
Bridge St., Downham Market, PE38 9DH
☎ (0366) 382322
17th C coaching inn under the personal supervision of the owners, offering English cooking and real ale. Ample car parking.
Bedrooms: 1 single, 5 double & 4 twin.
Bathrooms: 7 private, 2 public.
Bed & breakfast: £26-£34 single, £36-£44 double.
Half board: £34-£48 daily.
Lunch available.
Evening meal 6pm (l.o. 10pm).
Parking for 30.
Credit: Access, Visa, Diners, Amex.
[symbols]

ELY

Cambridgeshire
Map ref 3A2

14m NE. Cambridge
Until the 17th C when the Fens were drained, Ely was an island. The cathedral, completed in 1189, dominates the surrounding area. One particular feature is the central octagonal tower with a fan-vaulted timber roof and wooden lantern. Also has a local history museum and stained glass museum.
Tourist Information Centre ☎ (0353) 662062

Nyton Hotel M
⬛⬛⬛ APPROVED
7 Barton Rd., Ely, CB7 4HZ
☎ (0353) 662459
In a quiet, residential area overlooking Fenland countryside and adjoining golf-course. Close to city centre and cathedral.
Bedrooms: 4 single, 4 double & 3 twin, 2 family rooms.
Bathrooms: 13 private.
Bed & breakfast: £34-£39 single, £54-£58 double.
Half board: £43-£54 daily, £280-£360 weekly.
Lunch available.
Evening meal 6.30pm (l.o. 9pm).

Parking for 25.
Credit: Access, Visa, Diners, Amex.
[symbols]

EPPING

Essex
Map ref 2D1

Epping retains its identity as a small market town despite its nearness to London. Epping Forest covers 2000 acres and at Chingford Queen Elizabeth I's Hunting Lodge houses a display on the forest's history and wildlife.

Uplands M
Listed APPROVED
181a Lindsey St., Epping, CM16 6RF
☎ (0378) 73733
Private house with rural views. Close to M25, M11 for Stansted Airport and Central Line underground for London. Pay phone available.
Bedrooms: 2 single, 2 family rooms.
Bathrooms: 2 public.
Bed & breakfast: from £16 single, from £32 double.
Parking for 6.
[symbols]

FELIXSTOWE

Suffolk
Map ref 3C2

11m SE. Ipswich
Seaside resort that developed at the end of the 19th C. Lying in a gently curving bay with a 2-mile-long beach and backed by a wide promenade of lawns and floral gardens. Ferry links to the continent.
Tourist Information Centre ☎ (0394) 276770

Dolphin Hotel M
⬛
41 Beach Station Rd., Felixstowe, IP11 8BY
☎ (0394) 282261
Private hotel, 5 minutes from beach and passenger terminal, 10 minutes from town centre.
Bedrooms: 3 single, 2 double & 2 twin, 1 family room.
Bathrooms: 2 private, 2 public.
Bed & breakfast: £19-£26 single, £28-£38 double.
Lunch available.

Evening meal 7pm (l.o. 9.30pm).
Parking for 24.
Credit: Access, Visa.
[symbols]

Fludyer Arms Hotel M
Listed APPROVED
Undercliff Rd. East, Felixstowe, IP11 7LU
☎ (0394) 283279
Closest hotel to the sea in Felixstowe. Two fully licensed bars and family room overlooking the sea. All rooms have superb sea views. Colour TV. Specialises in home-cooked food, with children's and vegetarian menus available.
Bedrooms: 2 single, 4 double & 2 twin, 1 family room.
Bathrooms: 4 private, 2 public.
Bed & breakfast: £18-£26 single, £32-£40 double.
Lunch available.
Evening meal 7pm (l.o. 9pm).
Parking for 14.
Credit: Access, Visa.
[symbols]

Iddlesleigh Private Hotel
Listed
11 Constable Rd., Felixstowe, IP11 7HL
☎ (0394) 670546
Private house with conservatory leading to indoor heated pool. Close to sea, shops and many local places of interest.
Bedrooms: 2 single, 1 double & 1 twin.
Bathrooms: 2 public.
Bed & breakfast: £14-£17.50 single, £28-£35 double.
Half board: £21-£25 daily, £92-£120 weekly.
Evening meal 5pm (l.o. 6pm).
Parking for 4.
[symbols]

Orwell Moat House
⬛⬛⬛
Hamilton Rd., Felixstowe, IP11 7DX
☎ (0394) 285511
Telex 987676
⬛ Queens Moat Houses
Old Victorian railway hotel.
Bedrooms: 7 single, 12 double & 34 twin, 5 family rooms.
Bathrooms: 58 private.
Bed & breakfast: from £25 single, from £50 double.
Half board: from £42.50 daily, from £280 weekly.
Lunch available.
Evening meal 7pm (l.o. 9.45pm).

Continued ▶

FELIXSTOWE

Continued

Parking for 215.
Credit: Access, Visa, Diners, Amex.

Waverley Hotel M

Wolsey Gardens, Felixstowe, IP11 7DF
☎ (0394) 282811
Telex 987568 WAVELY.G
Privately-owned recently refurbished Victorian town centre hotel, high on the clifftop, overlooking the promenade and the North Sea. Half board price based on a minimum 2 night stay.
Bedrooms: 5 single, 8 double & 6 twin, 1 family room.
Bathrooms: 20 private.
Bed & breakfast: £44.50-£50.45 single, £55.95-£73.15 double.
Half board: £32 daily, £224 weekly.
Lunch available.
Evening meal 7pm (l.o. 10.30pm).
Parking for 26.
Credit: Access, Visa, Diners, Amex.

FORDHAM

Cambridgeshire
Map ref 3B2

5m N. Newmarket

Inglenook Guest House
😃😃 APPROVED

42 Carter St., Fordham, Ely, CB7 5NG
☎ Newmarket (0638) 720387
250-year-old house with purpose-built annexe and 4 en-suite bedrooms. In the centre of the village, convenient for all amenities.
Bedrooms: 4 twin.
Bathrooms: 4 private, 1 public.
Bed & breakfast: £16-£18.50 single, £25-£29.50 double.
Parking for 7.

FRAMLINGHAM

Suffolk
Map ref 3C2

9m N. Woodbridge
Pleasant old market town with an interesting church, impressive castle and some attractive houses round Market Hill. The town's history can be traced at the Lanman Museum.

Birch Drive

Long Green, Bedfield, Woodbridge, IP13 7JD
☎ Worlingworth (072 876) 396
Detached house, set back from road in attractive setting with natural pond and garden. Five miles from Framlingham.
Bedrooms: 2 single, 1 double & 1 twin.
Bathrooms: 2 public.
Bed & breakfast: £10-£13 single, £20-£26 double.
Half board: £15-£19.50 daily, £98-£129 weekly.
Evening meal 7pm (l.o. midday).
Parking for 5.

FRESSINGFIELD

Suffolk
Map ref 3B2

4m S. Harleston

Chippenhall Hall

Fressingfield, Eye, IP21 5TD
☎ (037 986) 8180 & 733
Listed Tudor manor house, heavily beamed and with inglenook fireplaces, in 7 acres, one mile outside Fressingfield on B1116 to Framlingham.
Bedrooms: 3 double.
Bathrooms: 3 private.
Bed & breakfast: £36-£42 single, £46-£52 double.
Half board: £39-£46 daily, £245-£290 weekly.
Evening meal 7.30pm (l.o. 7.30pm).
Parking for 12.
Credit: Access, Visa, Amex.

FRINTON-ON-SEA

Essex
Map ref 3C2

5m NE. Clacton-on-Sea
Sedate town that developed as a resort at the end of the 19th C and still retains an air of Victorian gentility. Fine sandy beaches, good fishing and golf.

Maplin Hotel M
😃😃😃😃 APPROVED

The Esplanade, Frinton-on-Sea, CO13 9EL
☎ (0255) 673832
Overlooking the famous greensward and sea, a small family hotel in a bow-windowed building.
Bedrooms: 2 single, 7 twin, 2 family rooms.
Bathrooms: 9 private, 1 public.
Bed & breakfast: £40-£80 single, £80-£90 double.
Lunch available.
Evening meal 7pm (l.o. 9pm).
Parking for 12.
Open February-December.
Credit: Access, Visa, Diners, Amex.

Uplands Guest House
😃😃

41 Hadleigh Rd., Frinton-on-Sea, CO13 9HQ
☎ (0255) 674889
Relax in a friendly atmosphere, with home cooking and personal service. Lounge with colour TV and residents' bar. 3 minutes to sea, shops and Crescent Gardens. Ample car parking. No smoking in bedrooms.
Bedrooms: 3 single, 2 double & 2 twin, 1 family room.
Bathrooms: 2 private, 2 public; 1 private shower.
Bed & breakfast: £20-£25 single, £40-£50 double.
Half board: £30.50-£35.50 daily.
Evening meal 6.30pm (l.o. 10am).
Parking for 6.

GARBOLDISHAM

Norfolk
Map ref 3B2

7m W. Diss

Ingleneuk Lodge M
😃😃😃 COMMENDED

Hopton Rd., Garboldisham, Diss, IP22 2RQ
☎ (095 381) 541

Modern bungalow in quiet wooded countryside. South facing patio and riverside walk. Central for touring. On B1111, 1 mile south of village.
Bedrooms: 3 single, 4 double & 2 twin, 2 family rooms.
Bathrooms: 10 private, 1 public.
Bed & breakfast: £20-£29 single, £32.50-£45 double.
Half board: £29-£41.75 daily, £189-£232 weekly.
Evening meal 6.30pm (l.o. 1pm).
Parking for 20.
Credit: Access, Visa, Amex.

GISLINGHAM

Suffolk
Map ref 3B2

The Old Guildhall M
😃😃😃 COMMENDED

Mill St., Gislingham, Nr. Eye, IP23 8JT
☎ Mellis (037 978) 3361
15th C Guildhall in attractive grounds, retaining many historic features. Tranquil Suffolk village within 5 miles of Diss.
Bedrooms: 1 double & 2 twin.
Bathrooms: 3 private.
Bed & breakfast: £40 single, £50 double.
Half board: £35 daily, £200 weekly.
Evening meal 7pm (l.o. 9pm).
Parking for 5.
Open February-December.

GISSING

Norfolk
Map ref 3B2

4m NE. Diss

The Old Rectory
😃😃😃 COMMENDED

Rectory Lane, Gissing, Diss, IP22 3XB
☎ Tivetshall (037 977) 575
Elegant Victorian house in 3 acres, peaceful, comfortable, tastefully decorated and furnished. Every effort has been made to ensure a memorable stay. Indoor pool.
Bedrooms: 1 double & 1 twin, 1 family room.
Bathrooms: 3 private.
Bed & breakfast: £32-£36 single, £44-£48 double.
Half board: £38-£40 daily, £252-£266 weekly.

Individual proprietors have supplied all details of accommodation. Although we do check for accuracy, we advise you to confirm prices and other information at the time of booking.

Evening meal 7.45pm (l.o. 7.45pm).
Parking for 6.

GORLESTON-ON-SEA

Norfolk
Map ref 3C1

A well-frequented seaside resort separated from Great Yarmouth by the River Yare. The long, sandy beach is backed by cliffs and there is a pavilion and a swimming pool. Fishing and sailing are popular.

Squirrel's Nest

71 Avondale Rd., Gorleston-on-Sea, Great Yarmouth, NR31 6DJ
☎ (0493) 662746
Friendly, family-run hotel, one minute from sea and all amenities. Most rooms with sea view. From A12 turn right at second traffic lights past hospital, left at Marine Parade.
Bedrooms: 1 single, 5 double & 2 twin, 1 family room.
Bathrooms: 9 private, 1 public.
Bed & breakfast: £25-£35 single, £50-£70 double.
Half board: £40-£55 daily, £195-£220 weekly.
Lunch available.
Evening meal 5.30pm (l.o. 9.30pm).
Parking for 5.
Credit: Access, Visa, Amex.

GREAT BADDOW

Essex
Map ref 3B3

2m S. Chelmsford

Pontlands Park Country Hotel and Restaurant ⚠
HIGHLY COMMENDED
West Hanningfield Rd., Great Baddow, Chelmsford, CM2 8HR
☎ (0245) 76444 Telex 995256
Victorian mansion, now a small country hotel and restaurant. Health and leisure centre, sauna, solarium, jacuzzi, covered swimming pool, garden coffee shop.
Bedrooms: 2 single, 13 double & 2 twin.
Bathrooms: 17 private.

Bed & breakfast: £79-£83 single, max. £115 double.
Half board: £99-£103 daily.
Lunch available.
Evening meal 7pm (l.o. 10pm).
Parking for 70.
Credit: Access, Visa, Diners, Amex.

GREAT BIRCHAM

Norfolk
Map ref 3B1

3m S. Docking

King's Head Hotel ⚠
APPROVED
Great Bircham, King's Lynn, PE31 6RJ
☎ Syderstone (048 523) 265
Family-run country hotel with 3 bars, restaurant and beer garden. Near Sandringham, King's Lynn and the coast.
Bedrooms: 2 double & 3 twin.
Bathrooms: 5 private.
Bed & breakfast: £43-£45 single, £50-£58 double.
Lunch available.
Evening meal 7pm (l.o. 10pm).
Parking for 80.
Credit: Access, Visa, Amex.
⊕ Display advertisement appears on page 358.

GREAT DUNMOW

Essex
Map ref 3B2

9m E. Bishop's Stortford
On the main Roman road from Bishop's Stortford to Braintree. The artist Sir George Beaumont, co-founder of the National Gallery, lived here. Doctor's Pond, near the square, was where the first lifeboat was tested in 1785. Home of the Dunmow Flitch trials held every 4 years on Whit Monday.
Tourist Information Centre ☎ (0371) 874533

Starr Restaurant

Market Place, Great Dunmow, CM6 1AX
☎ (0371) 874321
15th C coaching inn offering many original features. Traditional English/French cooking using only fresh produce.

Bedrooms: 8 double.
Bathrooms: 8 private.
Bed & breakfast: max. £60 single, £85-£110 double.
Half board: £61.50-£86 daily.
Lunch available.
Evening meal 7pm (l.o. 9.30pm).
Parking for 28.
Credit: Access, Visa, Amex.

Winston's Hotel

3-5 North St., Great Dunmow, CM6 1AZ
☎ (0371) 872576 & (0371) 872274
Owner-run hotel with a relaxed atmosphere for the travelling executive. Situated in the town centre, 4 miles from new Stansted Airport terminal. Gymnasium and sauna.
Bedrooms: 9 single, 1 double & 1 twin.
Bathrooms: 11 private.
Bed & breakfast: £40-£50 single, £60-£70 double.
Evening meal 7pm (l.o. 8pm).
Parking for 9.
Credit: Access, Visa, Amex.

GREAT RYBURGH

Norfolk
Map ref 3B1

3m SE. Fakenham

The Boar Inn ⚠
Listed **APPROVED**
Great Ryburgh, Nr. Fakenham, NR21 0DX
☎ (032 878) 212
Village inn opposite Saxon church. Beamed dining room and bar with inglenook. Log fire in winter.
Bedrooms: 1 single, 1 double & 2 twin.
Bathrooms: 1 public.
Bed & breakfast: £21-£22.50 single, £33-£35.75 double.
Lunch available.
Evening meal 7pm (l.o. 9.30pm).
Parking for 20.
Credit: Access, Visa.

National Crown ratings were correct at the time of going to press but are subject to change. Please check at the time of booking.

GREAT WITCHINGHAM

Norfolk
Map ref 3B1

2m S. Reepham
Home of the Norfolk Wildlife Park which has the world's largest collection of British and European mammals and specialises in breeding endangered species.

Lenwade House Hotel

Great Witchingham, Norwich, NR9 5QP
☎ (0603) 872288
A Tudor-style, country house hotel in 18 acres of woodlands and gardens with a river frontage. Facilities include a jacuzzi.
Bedrooms: 2 single, 15 double & 15 twin, 3 family rooms.
Bathrooms: 35 private.
Bed & breakfast: £45-£65 single, £60-£75 double.
Half board: £59-£79 daily.
Lunch available.
Evening meal 7pm (l.o. 10pm).
Parking for 40.
Credit: Access, Visa, C.Bl., Diners, Amex.

GREAT YARMOUTH

Norfolk
Map ref 3C1

One of Britain's major seaside resorts with 5 miles of seafront and every possible amenity including an award winning leisure complex offering a huge variety of all-weather sports and entertainment facilities. Busy harbour and fishing centre. Interesting area around the quay with a number of museums. Maritime museum on seafront, Sea Life Centre opened in summer 1990.
Tourist Information Centre ☎ (0493) 846345 or (accommodation) 846344

Ambassador Hotel ⚠

64 Wellesley Rd., Great Yarmouth, NR30 1EX
☎ (0493) 855120
Continued ▶

A recently modernised and refurbished family hotel, with personal service and an informal atmosphere, 200 yards to the seafront and within walking distance of the town centre.
Bedrooms: 15 single, 9 double & 7 twin, 5 family rooms.
Bathrooms: 36 private, 2 public.
Bed & breakfast: from £28 single, from £45 double.
Half board: from £37 daily, from £250 weekly.
Evening meal 5.30pm (l.o. 9pm).
Credit: Access, Visa.

Bouverie House
Listed

105 North Denes Rd., Great Yarmouth, NR30 4LN
☎ (0493) 844716
Small family-run guesthouse. Home cooking with fresh produce purchased daily. Public gardens at front. Ample free parking within 25 yards.
Bedrooms: 1 single, 2 double, 2 family rooms.
Bathrooms: 1 public.
Bed & breakfast: £11-£15 single, £22-£30 double.
Half board: £15-£19 daily, £78-£95 weekly.
Evening meal 5.30pm (l.o. 5.30pm).
Credit: Access, Visa.

Burlington Hotel M

North Drive, Great Yarmouth, NR30 1EG
☎ (0493) 844568
Views of the sea and sandy beach. Facilities include a pool, solarium and sauna. A family-run hotel priding itself on good food.
Bedrooms: 2 single, 4 double & 12 twin, 10 family rooms.
Bathrooms: 26 private, 1 public.
Bed & breakfast: £27-£50 single, £38-£62 double.
Half board: £26-£40 daily, £145-£220 weekly.
Lunch available.
Evening meal 6pm (l.o. 8pm).
Parking for 40.
Open February-December.
Credit: Access, Visa, Amex.

Clover Court
15 Princes Rd., Great Yarmouth, NR30 2DG
☎ (0493) 842175
Some bedrooms with sea views, all rooms with own private toilet and shower. Refurbished bar/lounge. City and Guilds catering.
Bedrooms: 1 single, 3 double & 1 twin, 7 family rooms.
Bathrooms: 10 private, 1 public; 1 private shower.
Half board: £12-£18 daily, £80-£125 weekly.
Evening meal 5pm (l.o. 5pm).
Open April-October.

Furzedown Private Hotel
APPROVED

19-20 North Drive, Great Yarmouth, NR30 4EW
☎ (0493) 844138
Hotel overlooking the sea. Centrally heated throughout. Established over 30 years.
Bedrooms: 3 single, 9 double & 7 twin, 7 family rooms.
Bathrooms: 13 private, 4 public.
Bed & breakfast: £19.50-£28.50 single, £39-£57 double.
Half board: £25.50-£37.50 daily, £140-£185 weekly.
Lunch available.
Evening meal 6pm (l.o. 7pm).
Parking for 25.
Credit: Access, Visa.

Gladstone House
Listed

92 St. Peters Rd., Great Yarmouth, NR30 3AU
☎ (0493) 843181
Good position for holiday or overnight stop. Close to all local amenities. Small car park available.
Bedrooms: 2 single, 7 double & 1 twin, 1 family room.
Bathrooms: 2 public.
Bed & breakfast: max. £15 single, max. £25 double.
Half board: max. £18 daily.
Evening meal 6.30pm (l.o. 7.30pm).
Parking for 6.

Palm Court Hotel M

North Drive, Great Yarmouth, NR30 1EF
☎ (0493) 844568
Sea views, heated indoor pool, sauna, solarium, lift and car park, in a resort with sandy beaches and crammed with history.

Bedrooms: 6 single, 12 double & 21 twin, 8 family rooms.
Bathrooms: 35 private, 5 public.
Bed & breakfast: £27-£50 single, £38-£62 double.
Half board: £36-£40 daily, £145-£220 weekly.
Lunch available.
Evening meal 6pm (l.o. 9pm).
Parking for 40.
Open March-December.
Credit: Access, Visa, Amex.

Ryecroft
91 North Denes Rd., Great Yarmouth, NR30 4LW
☎ (0493) 844015
Small family-run business with a friendly and relaxed atmosphere at all times.
Bedrooms: 1 single, 4 double & 2 twin, 3 family rooms.
Bathrooms: 2 public.
Bed & breakfast: £12.50-£14 single, £25-£28 double.
Half board: £16-£18 daily, £85-£98 weekly.
Evening meal 5.30pm (l.o. 5.30pm).
Parking for 10.

Spindrift Private Hotel M
APPROVED

36 Wellesley Rd., Great Yarmouth, NR30 1EU
☎ (0493) 858674
Attractively situated small private hotel, close to all amenities and with Beach Coach Station and car park at rear. Front bedrooms have sea views.
Bedrooms: 2 single, 3 double & 1 twin, 2 family rooms.
Bathrooms: 4 private, 1 public.
Bed & breakfast: £16-£19 single, £26-£36 double.
Half board: £17.50-£22.50 daily, £105-£120 weekly.
Evening meal 5.15pm (l.o. 1pm).

Star Hotel

24 Hall Quay, Great Yarmouth, NR30 1HG
☎ (0493) 842294
Telex 975080
Queens Moat Houses
16th C building overlooking river in this popular seaside resort. Bars, restaurant/carvery, open fire in lounge.

Bedrooms: 5 single, 14 double & 17 twin, 4 family rooms.
Bathrooms: 40 private.
Bed & breakfast: £45-£50 single, £62-£65 double.
Half board: from £37.50 daily.
Lunch available.
Evening meal 7pm (l.o. 9.45pm).
Parking for 22.
Credit: Access, Visa, Diners, Amex.

Stratford Private Hotel
62 Apsley Rd., Great Yarmouth, NR30 2HG
☎ (0493) 855121
Delightfully situated near Britannia Pier and Regent Road. Personally supervised by proprietors. Home cooking. Reduced rates for OAPs.
Bedrooms: 5 double & 1 twin, 5 family rooms.
Bathrooms: 2 public; 2 private showers.
Bed & breakfast: £13.50-£14.50 single, £26-£29 double.
Half board: £17-£18 daily, £100-£110 weekly.
Evening meal 5.50pm (l.o. 6pm).
Parking for 4.

8m W. Ipswich
Former wool town, lying on a tributary of the River Stour. The church of St. Mary stands among a remarkable cluster of medieval buildings.
Tourist Information Centre ☎ (0473) 822922

Gables Hotel M
COMMENDED

Angel St., Hadleigh, IP7 5EY
☎ (0473) 827169
15th C timbered hall residence in historic market town, recently converted to private hotel offering all modern amenities.
Bedrooms: 1 single, 2 double & 1 twin.
Bathrooms: 2 private, 2 public.
Bed & breakfast: £20-£40 single, £40-£60 double.
Half board: £37.50-£57.50 daily, £242.50-£362.50 weekly.
Evening meal 7pm (l.o. 9pm).
Parking for 6.

Odds and Ends House M
🛏🛏

131 High St., Hadleigh,
Ipswich, IP7 5EG
☎ (0473) 822032
*Comfortable house within
walking distance of shops,
restaurant and swimming pool.
Ground floor rooms with
wheelchair facilities available
in recently converted garden
annexe.*
Bedrooms: 4 single, 2 double
& 4 twin.
Bathrooms: 5 private,
2 public.
Bed & breakfast: £18-£32
single, £32-£40 double.
Half board: £28-£42 daily.
Lunch available.
Evening meal 7pm (l.o. 5pm).
Parking for 2.
Credit: Access, Visa.

HARLOW
Essex
Map ref 2D1

Although one of the New
Towns, it was planned so
that it could develop
alongside the existing old
town. It has a museum of
local history and a Nature
Reserve with nature trails
and study centre.

Churchgate Manor Hotel M
🛏🛏🛏

Churchgate St., Old Harlow,
Harlow, CM17 0JT
☎ (0279) 420246
Telex 818289
Best Western
*Spacious hotel in secluded
grounds with large indoor
leisure complex and swimming
pool. Close to M11, M25 and
Stansted Airport. 16th C
restaurant and bars. Extensive
conference facilities for up to
200 persons. Special value
weekend breaks.*
Bedrooms: 22 single,
24 double & 24 twin,
15 family rooms.
Bathrooms: 85 private.
Bed & breakfast: £56-£79
single, £85-£95 double.
Lunch available.
Evening meal 7pm (l.o.
9.45pm).
Parking for 120.
Credit: Access, Visa, Diners,
Amex.

HARWICH
Essex
Map ref 3C2

*16m E. Colchester
A port where the Rivers
Orwell and Stour
converge and enter the
North Sea. The old town
still has a medieval
atmosphere with its
narrow streets. To the
south is the seaside
resort of Dovercourt with
long sandy beaches.
Tourist Information
Centre ☎ (0255) 506139*

The Pier at Harwich M
🛏🛏🛏 COMMENDED

The Quay, Harwich,
CO12 3HH
☎ (0255) 241212
*Victorian building on the
quayside in old Harwich,
overlooking the twin estuaries
of the Stour and Orwell rivers.*
Bedrooms: 6 double.
Bathrooms: 6 private.
Bed & breakfast: £45-£60
single, £62.50-£72.50 double.
Lunch available.
Evening meal 6pm (l.o.
9.30pm).
Parking for 10.
Credit: Access, Visa.

HEACHAM
Norfolk
Map ref 3B1

*2m S. Hunstanton
The portrait of a Red
Indian princess who
married John Rolfe of
Heacham Hall in 1614
appears on the village
sign. Caley Mill is the
centre of lavender
growing.*

Saint Annes Guest House
🛏🛏 COMMENDED

53 Neville Rd., Heacham,
King's Lynn, PE31 7HB
☎ (0485) 70021
*Large 19th C house, close to
North Norfolk coast.*
Bedrooms: 4 double & 2 twin,
1 family room.
Bathrooms: 2 private,
2 public.
Bed & breakfast: £14-£17
single, £28-£34 double.
Half board: £21-£24 daily,
£147-£168 weekly.
Evening meal 6pm (l.o. 7pm).
Parking for 3.

HEVINGHAM
Norfolk
Map ref 3B1

Marsham Arms Hotel M
🛏🛏🛏 COMMENDED

Holt Rd., Hevingham,
Norwich, NR10 5NP
☎ (060 548) 268
*Old established freehouse and
restaurant with 8 self-
contained study bedrooms.
5 miles from Norwich airport
on the B1149.*
Bedrooms: 2 double & 6 twin.
Bathrooms: 8 private.
Bed & breakfast: £35-£40
single, £45-£55 double.
Lunch available.
Evening meal 6pm (l.o.
10pm).
Parking for 100.
Credit: Access, Visa, Amex.

HEYDON
Norfolk
Map ref 3B1

*3m N. Reepham
Small village of great
charm with one of the
county's prettiest greens.*

Cropton Hall Hotel M
Listed APPROVED

Saxthorpe, NR11 6RX
☎ (026 387) 869
*Jacobean country hotel in own
quiet surroundings, in
conservation area of great
natural beauty.*
Bedrooms: 1 single, 4 double
& 3 twin.
Bathrooms: 8 private.
Bed & breakfast: £14.95-
£20.50 single, £29.90-£45
double.
Half board: £19.95-£29.50
daily, £129.95-£189.95
weekly.
Evening meal 7pm (l.o.
9.30pm).
Parking for 20.
Credit: Access, Visa, Diners,
Amex.

---

*National Crown
ratings were correct
at the time of going
to press but are
subject to change.
Please check at the
time of booking.*

HOLT
Norfolk
Map ref 3B1

*10m W. Cromer
Much of the town centre
was destroyed by fire in
1708 but has since been
restored. The famous
Gresham's School
founded by Sir Thomas
Gresham is sited here.*

Glavenside Guest House M
Listed

Letheringsett, Nr Holt,
Norfolk NR25 7AR
☎ Holt (0263) 713181
*River Glaven flows through 4
acre grounds to the sea at
Blakeney, 5 miles away. Rock
and water gardens. Good base
for many places of interest.
Cooking facilities. Entrance
doors open 24 hours all year.
Renovated historic building.*
Bedrooms: 1 single, 3 double,
2 family rooms.
Bathrooms: 4 public.
Bed & breakfast: £10-£17
single, £20-£34 double.
Parking for 8.

Lawns Hotel M
🛏🛏🛏 COMMENDED

Station Rd., Holt, NR25 6BS
☎ (0263) 713390
*Elegant Georgian hotel with
charming rooms. Family-run to
a high standard. Emphasis on
fine cuisine and hospitality.
Short stroll from the town.*
Bedrooms: 2 single, 5 double
& 2 twin, 2 family rooms.
Bathrooms: 11 private, 1 public.
Bed & breakfast: £33-£50
single, £55 double.
Half board: £45.50-£51 daily,
£280-£300 weekly.
Lunch available.
Evening meal 7pm (l.o.
8.30pm).
Parking for 12.
Credit: Access, Visa, Amex.

HORNDON-ON-THE-HILL
Essex
Map ref 3B3

5m SW. Basildon

Hill House
Listed COMMENDED

High Rd., Horndon-on-the-
Hill, SS17 8LD
☎ Stanford Le Hope
(0375) 642463

Continued ▶

HORNDON-ON-THE-HILL

Continued

Georgian house with individually styled bedrooms, in centre of village.
Bedrooms: 7 double & 3 twin.
Bathrooms: 10 private.
Bed & breakfast: £45-£65 double.
Lunch available.
Evening meal 7.30pm (l.o. 9.45pm).
Parking for 10.
Credit: Access, Visa.

HORNING

Norfolk
Map ref 3C1

3m E. Hoveton
Riverside village and well-known Broadland centre. Occasional glimpses of the river can be caught between picturesque thatched cottages.

Petersfield House Hotel M

COMMENDED
Lower St., Horning, Norwich, NR12 8PF
☎ (0692) 630741
Set slightly back from the banks of the River Bure, the hotel occupies one of the choicest positions on the Broads.
Bedrooms: 3 single, 9 double & 5 twin, 1 family room.
Bathrooms: 18 private.
Bed & breakfast: £57-£63 single, £72-£82 double.
Half board: from £50 daily, from £350 weekly.
Lunch available.
Evening meal 7.30pm (l.o. 9.30pm).
Parking for 25.
Credit: Access, Visa, Diners, Amex.

HORSFORD

Norfolk
Map ref 3B1

5m NW. Norwich

Becklands

105 Holt Rd., Horsford, Norwich, NR10 3AB
☎ (0603) 898582 & 898020
Quietly located modern house overlooking open countryside. 5 miles north of Norwich. Central for the Broads and coastal areas.

Bedrooms: 8 single, 2 double & 1 twin.
Bathrooms: 4 public.
Bed & breakfast: £14-£16 single, £28-£32 double.
Parking for 30.

HUNSTANTON

Norfolk
Map ref 3B1

14m NE. King's Lynn
Seaside resort which faces the Wash. The shingle and sand beach is backed by striped cliffs and many unusual fossils can be found here. The town, sometimes known as Hunstanton St. Edmund, is predominantly Victorian. Kingdom of the Sea Centre on the southern promenade and Oasis family leisure centre with indoor and outdoor pools.
Tourist Information Centre ☎ (0485) 532610

Le Strange Arms Hotel M

Golf Course Rd., Old Hunstanton, Hunstanton, PE36 6JJ
☎ (0485) 534411
Telex 817403 LESTRA-G
Consort
Fine country house by the sea. Large grounds with own private beach and lovely views over the sea and coastline.
Bedrooms: 3 single, 17 double & 15 twin, 3 family rooms.
Bathrooms: 38 private.
Bed & breakfast: £45-£60 single, £60-£75 double.
Half board: £42.50-£50 daily.
Lunch available.
Evening meal 7pm (l.o. 9pm).
Parking for 100.
Credit: Access, Visa, Diners, Amex.

Sunningdale Hotel

3-5 Avenue Rd., Hunstanton, PE36 5BW
☎ (0485) 532562
Small hotel close to beach, town centre and all local amenities. Excellent base for touring north Norfolk.
Bedrooms: 2 single, 4 double & 5 twin.
Bathrooms: 11 private.
Bed & breakfast: from £24 single, from £40 double.

Half board: from £30 daily.
Evening meal 6pm (l.o. 8pm).
Credit: Access, Visa.

HUNTINGDON

Cambridgeshire
Map ref 3A2

15m NW. Cambridge
Attractive, interesting town which abounds in associations with the Cromwell family. The town is connected to Godmanchester by a beautiful 14th C bridge over the great River Ouse.
Tourist Information Centre ☎ (0480) 425831

Brecklyn Guest House

9 Euston St., Huntingdon, PE18 6QR
☎ (0480) 455564
Homely accommodation near town centre, Cromwell's birthplace and other historic buildings. Fishing, bowls, river cruising, cathedrals at Peterborough, Ely. 1 hour from London. 3 rooms with hot and cold water.
Bedrooms: 2 single, 1 twin, 1 family room.
Bathrooms: 1 public.
Bed & breakfast: £13 single, £26 double.

Redwing Lodge

Great North Rd., Sawtry, Huntingdon
☎ Ramsey (0487) 832778
Fax (0480) 496197
Purpose-built motel off southbound carriageway of A1. Happy Eater restaurant on site.
Bedrooms: 37 family rooms.
Bathrooms: 37 private.
Bed & breakfast: from £24 single, from £29.50 double.
Lunch available.
Parking for 46.
Credit: Access, Visa, Amex.

Tollbar Lodge

Great North Rd., Sawtry, Huntingdon, PE17 5YY
☎ (0487) 832569
Fax (0480) 496197
One mile south of Sawtry on A1. Happy Eater restaurant on site.
Bedrooms: 39 family rooms.
Bathrooms: 39 private.
Bed & breakfast: from £24 single, from £29.50 double.

Parking for 45.
Credit: Access, Visa, Diners, Amex.

IPSWICH

Suffolk
Map ref 3B2

Interesting county town and major port on the River Orwell. Birthplace of Cardinal Wolsey. Christchurch Mansion, set in a fine park, contains a good collection of furniture and pictures, with works by Gainsborough, Constable and Munnings.
Tourist Information Centre ☎ (0473) 258070

Anglesea Hotel M

COMMENDED
10 Oban St., Ipswich, IP1 3PH
☎ (0473) 255630
Victorian house, now tastefully refurbished as a small hotel, in quiet conservation area. Within easy walking distance of town centre. Bar meals always available; one hour's notice required for full 3-course meal.
Bedrooms: 1 single, 3 twin, 3 family rooms.
Bathrooms: 7 private.
Bed & breakfast: £32-£39 single, £42-£49 double.
Evening meal 6.30pm (l.o. 9pm).
Parking for 9.
Credit: Access, Visa, Amex.

Belstead Brook Hotel M

Belstead Rd., Ipswich, IP2 9HB
☎ (0473) 684241
Telex 987674
Best Western
Part Tudor country house, oak panelled restaurant, open fires; willow lined gardens where peacocks stroll. Four-poster suite. Modern accommodation includes garden suites with whirlpool baths and executive suites with therapeutic air baths.
Bedrooms: 5 single, 41 double, 4 family rooms.
Bathrooms: 50 private.
Bed & breakfast: £76.50-£87 single, £93.50-£114 double.
Lunch available.
Evening meal 7.30pm (l.o. 9.30pm).
Parking for 100.

Credit: Access, Visa, Diners, Amex.

Carlton Hotel

Berners St., Ipswich,
IP1 3LN
☎ (0473) 254955 & 211145
Town centre hotel with a friendly atmosphere, home cooking and personal service.
Bedrooms: 8 single, 6 double & 5 twin, 1 family room.
Bathrooms: 16 private, 4 public.
Bed & breakfast: £30-£38 single, £40-£48 double.
Evening meal 6pm (l.o. 9pm).
Parking for 14.
Credit: Access, Visa, Amex.

⊙ Display advertisement appears on page 358.

Chequers Hotel

Listed | **APPROVED**
7-9 Ancaster Rd., Ipswich,
IP2 9AG
☎ (0473) 602385
Family-run hotel, close to Ipswich station. Ample parking. Colour TV all rooms, some private facilities available. Licensed. Tea/coffee facilities.
Bedrooms: 6 single, 3 double & 4 twin, 3 family rooms.
Bathrooms: 1 private, 3 public; 2 private showers.
Bed & breakfast: £18-£26 single, £29-£45 double.
Half board: £26.50 daily.
Evening meal 7pm (l.o. 8pm).
Parking for 20.

The Gables of Park Road M

17 Park Rd., Ipswich,
IP1 3SX
☎ (0473) 54252
Distinguished Victorian hotel with beautiful quiet garden, adjacent historic Christchurch Park in preservation area. Evening meals available.
Bedrooms: 7 single, 3 double & 1 twin, 1 family room.
Bathrooms: 1 private, 2 public.
Bed & breakfast: £25-£35 single, £35-£45 double.
Evening meal 6.30pm (l.o. 6.30pm).
Parking for 10.
Credit: Visa.

Novotel M

Greyfriars Rd., Ipswich,
IP1 1UP
☎ (0473) 232400
Telex 987684
Ⓝ Novotel
Town centre situation, access from A12/A45. 2 minutes from mainline station. All bedrooms have king-size bed and couch, radio, TV. Conference facilities. Restaurant, bar. Weekend breaks.
Bedrooms: 94 double, 6 family rooms.
Bathrooms: 100 private.
Bed & breakfast: £40-£65 single, £47.50-£72.50 double.
Lunch available.
Evening meal 6pm (l.o. 11.55pm).
Parking for 50.
Credit: Access, Visa, Diners, Amex.

Portman Hotel

8 Crescent Rd., Ipswich,
IP1 2EX
☎ (0473) 255314 & 251273
Comfortable, welcoming, family hotel, catering for the individual as well as for groups. Disabled guests are welcome as the proprietor is a state registered nurse.
Bedrooms: 6 single, 1 double & 4 twin, 1 family room.
Bathrooms: 1 private, 2 public; 2 private showers.
Bed & breakfast: £20-£26 single, £28-£36 double.
Lunch available.
Evening meal 6.30pm (l.o. 2.30pm).
Parking for 12.

Queenscliffe House Hotel

Queenscliffe Rd., Ipswich,
IP2 9AS
☎ (0473) 690293
Elegant Victorian house close to the station and town centre, in quiet wooded area, not on main road. 5 minutes to the A12 and A45.
Bedrooms: 4 single, 1 double & 3 twin, 2 family rooms.
Bathrooms: 8 private, 3 public; 1 private shower.
Bed & breakfast: £30-£35 single, £40-£50 double.
Half board: £30-£45 daily.
Evening meal 7pm (l.o. 8pm).
Parking for 12.
Credit: Access, Visa.

Tamarisk House

Sandy Lane, Barham,
Ipswich, IP6 0PB
☎ (0473) 831825
5 miles from Ipswich and close to A45 Bury St. Edmunds. Village house with beams and inglenook. Gipping Valley walks and fishing. Local pub and easy car parking.
Bedrooms: 2 double, 1 family room.
Bathrooms: 2 public.
Bed & breakfast: max. £20 single, max. £30 double.
Parking for 10.

The Waverley Hotel

19 Willoughby Rd., Ipswich,
IP2 8AW
☎ (0473) 601239
Friendly family-run licensed hotel. 100 yards from station, close to town centre. All rooms have TV and tea-making facilities. Evening meals available.
Bedrooms: 1 single, 2 double & 2 twin, 1 family room.
Bathrooms: 1 private, 1 public; 3 private showers.
Bed & breakfast: £22.50-£30 single, £34.50-£36 double.
Half board: £29.25-£36.75 daily.
Evening meal 7pm (l.o. 8pm).
Parking for 5.
Credit: Access, Visa.

Westerfield House Hotel

Humber Doucy Lane,
Ipswich, IP4 3QG
☎ (0473) 231344
Charming Georgian house with extensive grounds and four-poster suites. Delightful à la carte restaurant. Tennis courts, outdoor pool, ample parking.
Bedrooms: 4 double & 22 twin, 4 family rooms.
Bathrooms: 30 private.
Bed & breakfast: from £59.50 single, from £69.50 double.
Lunch available.
Evening meal 7pm (l.o. 9pm).
Parking for 100.
Credit: Access, Visa, Amex.

The enquiry coupons at the back will help you when contacting proprietors.

Norfolk
Map ref 3B1

Combines the attractions of a busy town, port and agricultural centre. Many outstanding buildings. The Guildhall and Town Hall are both built of flint in a striking chequer design. The Customs House was built in 1683.
Tourist Information Centre ☎ *(0553) 763044*

The Beeches

APPROVED
2 Guanock Terrace, King's Lynn, PE30 5QT
☎ (0553) 766577
Detached Victorian house, all rooms with TV, tea/coffee facilities and most en-suite. Full English breakfast and 3-course evening meal with coffee.
Bedrooms: 1 single, 2 double & 3 twin, 1 family room.
Bathrooms: 4 private, 1 public.
Bed & breakfast: £18-£23 single, £25-£34 double.
Half board: £24.50-£29.50 daily, £140-£200 weekly.
Evening meal 6.30pm (l.o. 7.30pm).
Parking for 3.

Butterfly Hotel M

A10-147 Roundabout,
Hardwick Narrows, King's Lynn, PE30 4NB
☎ (0553) 771707
Telex 818313
Modern building with rustic style and decor, set around an open central courtyard. Special weekend rates available.
Bedrooms: 25 single, 15 double & 10 twin.
Bathrooms: 50 private.
Bed & breakfast: £60-£65 single, £65-£70 double.
Half board: £70-£75 daily.
Lunch available.
Evening meal 7pm (l.o. 10pm).
Parking for 70.
Credit: Access, Visa, Diners, Amex.

Globe Hotel M

Tuesday Market Place,
King's Lynn, PE30 1EZ
☎ (0553) 772617

Continued ▶

KING'S LYNN

Continued

The original Globe existed around 1645, although it was probably built long before. The adjacent Tuesday Market Place was once a venue for public hangings. Centrally located, near the River Ouse.
Bedrooms: 11 single, 10 double & 17 twin, 2 family rooms.
Bathrooms: 40 private.
Bed & breakfast: £44-£53 single, £62 double.
Evening meal 6pm (l.o. 10pm).
Parking for 23.
Credit: Access, Visa, Diners, Amex.

The Grange Hotel
COMMENDED
Willow Park, South Wooton Lane, King's Lynn, PE30 3BP
☎ (0553) 673777 & 671222
Impressive Edwardian hotel set in its own grounds offers spacious, en-suite bedrooms. Ideal for weekend breaks. Resident proprietors.
Bedrooms: 1 single, 7 double & 2 twin.
Bathrooms: 10 private.
Bed & breakfast: from £39.50 single, from £53 double.
Half board: from £36 daily.
Lunch available.
Evening meal 7pm (l.o. 8.30pm).
Parking for 15.
Credit: Access, Visa, Amex.

Havana Guest House
117 Gaywood Rd., King's Lynn, PE30 2PU
☎ (0553) 772331
Comfortable bedrooms with colour co-ordinated soft furnishings. Ground floor en-suites. Ample private parking. 10 minutes' walk to town centre and an hour's drive to four cathedral cities.
Bedrooms: 1 single, 3 double & 2 twin, 1 family room.
Bathrooms: 2 private, 1 public.
Bed & breakfast: from £15 single, £25-£30 double.
Parking for 8.

We advise you to confirm your booking in writing.

Knights Hill Hotel
COMMENDED
Knights Hill Village, South Wootton, King's Lynn, PE30 3HQ
☎ (0553) 675566
Telex 818118 Knight G
Best Western
Sympathetically restored farm offering a choice of accommodation styles, 2 restaurants, a country pub and an extensive health club.
Bedrooms: 8 single, 30 double & 12 twin.
Bathrooms: 50 private.
Bed & breakfast: £71-£83.50 single, £89-£101 double.
Half board: £60-£66 daily.
Lunch available.
Evening meal 6.30pm (l.o. 10pm).
Parking for 300.
Credit: Access, Visa, Diners, Amex.

Maranatha Guest House
115 Gaywood Rd., Gaywood, King's Lynn, PE30 2PU
☎ (0553) 774596
Large carrstone and brick residence with gardens front and rear. 10 minutes' walk from the town centre. Direct road to Sandringham and the coast.
Bedrooms: 2 single, 2 double & 2 twin.
Bathrooms: 1 private, 2 public.
Bed & breakfast: £12-£15 single, from £20 double.
Evening meal 6pm (l.o. 6pm).
Parking for 6.

Oakwood House Hotel
Tottenhill, King's Lynn, PE33 0RH
☎ (0553) 810256
Mainly 18th C building on the A10 4 miles south of King's Lynn, with easy access to most parts of Suffolk, Cambridgeshire and Lincolnshire. All rooms are on the ground or first floors.
Bedrooms: 2 single, 6 double & 2 twin.
Bathrooms: 8 private, 1 public.
Bed & breakfast: £21-£38 single, £46-£48 double.
Half board: £227 weekly.

Evening meal 7.30pm (l.o. 8.30pm).
Parking for 30.
Credit: Access, Visa.

Red Cat Hotel and Restaurant
North Wootton, King's Lynn, PE30 3QH
☎ (0553) 631244
Traditional, friendly, country hotel, minutes from King's Lynn, golf-course, Royal Sandringham Estate, Norfolk coast and bird reserves.
Bedrooms: 4 single, 2 double & 1 twin, 1 family room.
Bathrooms: 7 private, 1 public.
Bed & breakfast: max. £33 single, max. £47 double.
Half board: max. £40 daily, max. £180 weekly.
Lunch available.
Evening meal 7pm (l.o. 9pm).
Parking for 51.
Credit: Access, Visa.

Sixty-One
61 King George V Avenue, King's Lynn, PE30 2QE
☎ (0553) 774485
Quiet locality near college and sports centre, easy walking access to town centre. Considerate attention from resident owner.
Bedrooms: 1 single, 2 twin.
Bathrooms: 1 public.
Bed & breakfast: £12-£15 single, £22-£24 double.
Parking for 3.

The Tudor Rose
APPROVED
St. Nicholas St., Off Tuesday Market Place, King's Lynn, PE30 1LR
☎ (0553) 762824
Owner-run, friendly, historic town centre hotel. 15th C beamed restaurant offering local fish, seafood, steaks and game. Real ale bars.
Bedrooms: 5 single, 7 double & 2 twin.
Bathrooms: 11 private, 3 public.
Bed & breakfast: £30-£40 single, £45-£50 double.
Half board: £32-£49 daily, £200-£220 weekly.
Lunch available.

Please mention this guide when making a booking.

Evening meal 6.30pm (l.o. 8.30pm).
Credit: Access, Visa, Diners, Amex.

LAVENHAM

Suffolk
Map ref 3B2

6m NE. Sudbury
A former prosperous wool town of timber-framed buildings with the cathedral-like church and its tall tower. The market-place is 13th C and the Guildhall now houses a museum.

Angel Hotel
COMMENDED
Market Place, Lavenham, CO10 9QZ
☎ Sudbury (0787) 247388
Family-run 15th C inn overlooking famous Guildhall. All rooms en-suite. Freshly cooked local food, menu changing daily.
Bedrooms: 1 single, 4 double & 1 twin, 1 family room.
Bathrooms: 7 private.
Bed & breakfast: £25-£35 single, £45-£60 double.
Half board: £35-£45 daily, £220-£330 weekly.
Lunch available.
Evening meal 6.45pm (l.o. 9.15pm).
Parking for 5.

The Great House Restaurant and Hotel
Listed
Market Place, Lavenham, CO10 9QZ
☎ Sudbury (0787) 247431
Famous and historic house with covered outside courtyard, dating from the 15th C. Quietly and ideally located, full of warmth and oak furniture for a relaxing stay. French gourmet cuisine.
Bedrooms: 4 family rooms.
Bathrooms: 4 private.
Bed & breakfast: £50-£60 single, £68-£88 double.
Half board: max. £64.95 daily.
Lunch available.
Evening meal 7pm (l.o. 10.30pm).
Parking for 10.
Open February-December.
Credit: Access, Visa.

LEISTON

Suffolk
Map ref 3C2

4m E. Saxmundham
Busy industrial town near
the coast. The abbey
sited here in 1363 was for
hundreds of years used
as a farm until it was
restored in 1918.

White Horse Hotel M
♛♛♛

Station Rd., Leiston,
IP16 4HD
☎ (0728) 830694
*18th C Georgian hotel with a
relaxed and informal
atmosphere, only 2 miles from
the sea, in the heart of bird-
watching country.*
Bedrooms: 4 single, 5 double
& 3 twin, 1 family room.
Bathrooms: 11 private,
3 public.
Bed & breakfast: £29.50-£35
single, £46-£55 double.
Lunch available.
Evening meal 7.30pm (l.o.
10pm).
Parking for 16.
Credit: Access, Visa.
⌔ ⌷ ▢ ⌾ ▨ Ⓥ ✕ ≓ ⊟
⌑ ⏃ ✿ ⋈ [DAP] ⊠ [SP] [T]

LITTLE BARNEY

Norfolk
Map ref 3B1

The Old Brick Kilns M
♛♛♛ COMMENDED

Little Barney, Fakenham,
NR21 ONL
☎ Thursford (0328) 878305
*Converted cottages in rural
setting. Turn right off A148
Fakenham/Holt road. 200
yards on right to Barney, left
into Little Barney, house at
end of lane.*
Bedrooms: 1 single, 1 double
& 1 twin.
Bathrooms: 3 private.
Bed & breakfast: £19 single,
£38 double.
Half board: £31.50 daily,
£207.20 weekly.
Evening meal 6pm (l.o.
10am).
Parking for 8.
⌔ ⌀ ▢ ⌾ ⓘ ▨ Ⓥ ≓ ⊙ ⊟
⌑ ⏃ ⋒ ✿ ⋈ ⋇

---

*The symbols are explained on the flap
inside the back cover.*

---

*Map references apply to the colour maps
towards the end of this guide.*

LONG MELFORD

Suffolk
Map ref 3B2

3m N. Sudbury
One of Suffolk's loveliest
villages, remarkable for
the length of its main
street. Holy Trinity
Church is considered to
be the finest village
church in England. The
National Trust own the
Elizabethan Melford Hall
and nearby Kentwell Hall
is also open to the public.

Black Lion Hotel M
♛♛♛♛ COMMENDED

The Green, Long Melford,
Sudbury, CO10 9DN
☎ (0787) 312356
*A restored 17th C coaching inn
overlooking the village green.*
Bedrooms: 1 single, 6 double
& 2 twin.
Bathrooms: 9 private.
Bed & breakfast: £40-£55
single, £60-£80 double.
Half board: £45-£65 daily.
Lunch available.
Evening meal 7pm (l.o.
9.30pm).
Parking for 8.
Credit: Access, Visa.
⌔ ⌸ ⌀ ▢ ⌾ ⓘ Ⓥ ≓
⊟ ⌑ ⏃ ⋈ ⋒

LOUGHTON

Essex
Map ref 2D1

St. Olaves Hotel
107 High Rd., Loughton,
IG10 4JB
☎ 081-508 1699
*Small, friendly family-run
hotel. 5 minutes' walk to
Central Line station, 25
minutes to London, 5 minutes'
walk to Epping Forest. 30
minutes to Stansted Airport.*
Bedrooms: 2 single, 2 double
& 2 twin, 2 family rooms.
Bathrooms: 3 public;
3 private showers.
Bed & breakfast: £27-£46
single, £37-£56 double.
Parking for 8.
Credit: Access, Visa.
⌔ ⌸ ▢ ⌾ ⓘ ▨ Ⓥ ≓ ◉ ⊟
⌑ ⏃ ✕ ⋈

LOWESTOFT

Suffolk
Map ref 3C1

Seaside town with wide
sandy beaches. Important
fishing port with
picturesque fishing
quarter and also the site
of the first recorded
lighthouse in England.
Home of the famous
Lowestoft porcelain and
birthplace of Benjamin
Britten. Several museums
with a maritime flavour.
*Tourist Information
Centre* ☎ *(0502) 523000*

Amity Guest House M
♛♛♛

396 London Rd. South,
Lowestoft, NR33 0BQ
☎ (0502) 572586
*Comfortable, friendly, family-
run guesthouse, with home
cooking. Close to beaches and
park.*
Bedrooms: 3 single, 3 double
& 3 twin, 3 family rooms.
Bathrooms: 6 private,
2 public.
Bed & breakfast: £17-£25
single, £32-£36 double.
Half board: £24-£32 daily.
Evening meal 6pm (l.o. 2pm).
Credit: Access, Visa, Amex.
⌔ ⌸ ⌀ ⌾ ⓘ ▨ Ⓥ ≓ ⓉⓋ ⊟
⌑ ⌂ ▲ ⋈

Fairways Guest
House M
♛♛♛ APPROVED

398 London Rd. South,
Lowestoft, NR33 0BQ
☎ (0502) 572659
*Spacious, well furnished and
comfortable guesthouse with
personal service. Easy access to
Suffolk Heritage Coast.*
Bedrooms: 2 single, 1 twin,
4 family rooms.
Bathrooms: 3 private,
2 public.
Bed & breakfast: £15-£22
single, £30-£36 double.
Evening meal 6pm (l.o.
7.50pm).
Parking for 4.
Credit: Access, Visa, Amex.
⌔ ⌸ ▢ ⌾ ⓘ ▨ Ⓥ ≓ ⓉⓋ ⊟
⌑ [DAP] ⋇ [SP]

Foxlea House M
♛♛♛ APPROVED

298 London Rd. South,
Lowestoft, NR33 0BG
☎ (0502) 569753
*Owner-run, friendly
guesthouse, boasting high
standards of accommodation,
service and food. Close to
beach and shops.*
Bedrooms: 2 single, 1 double
& 1 twin.

Bathrooms: 1 public.
Bed & breakfast: £15-£20
single, £30 double.
⌔ ⊙ ▢ ⌾ ⌁ ⌸ ▧ Ⓥ ≓ ⊟ ⌑
⋈ ⋇ [DAP] ⋇ [SP] [T]

Rockville House M
♛♛♛ COMMENDED

6 Pakefield Rd., Lowestoft,
NR33 0HS
☎ (0502) 581011
*Quietly situated in south
Lowestoft near Suffolk
Heritage Coast. Private beach
hut. All bedrooms have colour
TV. Lounge with open fire.*
Bedrooms: 3 single, 3 double
& 1 twin, 1 family room.
Bathrooms: 3 private,
2 public.
Bed & breakfast: £18.40-
£32.50 single, £31.70-£41.75
double.
Half board: £25.10-£41.75
daily.
Evening meal 6pm (l.o.
10am).
Credit: Access, Visa.
⌔ ⊙ ▢ ⌾ ⌁ Ⓥ ≓ ⊟ ⌑
⋈ ⋇ [DAP] ⋇ [SP] [T]

MAXEY

Cambridgeshire
Map ref 3A1

7m NW. Peterborough

Abbey House M
♛♛♛

West End Rd., Maxey, Nr.
Peterborough, PE6 9EJ
☎ Market Deeping
(0778) 344642
*Close to historic Stamford.
Ideal for touring the eastern
shires with their abundance of
abbeys, cathedrals, stately
homes and attractive villages.
Evening meal by arrangement.*
Bedrooms: 2 single, 3 double
& 3 twin.
Bathrooms: 5 private,
1 public.
Bed & breakfast: £16-£25
single, £28-£41 double.
Parking for 12.
⌔⑥ ⌸ ⌀ ▢ ⌾ ⌁ Ⓥ ≓ ⓉⓋ
⊟ ⌑ ⏃ ✕ ⋈ ⋒

---

*The enquiry
coupons at the
back will help you
when contacting
proprietors.*

---

*Please check prices
and other details at
the time of booking.*

MILDENHALL
Suffolk
Map ref 3B2

8m NE. Newmarket
Town that has grown considerably in size in the last 20 years but still manages to retain a pleasant small country town centre. The church of St. Mary and St. Andrew is the largest in Suffolk and over the porch is the Pervis Chamber, which was also used as a schoolroom in the Middle Ages. Mildenhall and District museum deals with local history, particularly RAF Mildenhall and the Mildenhall Treasure.

Riverside Hotel M
✺✺✺✺
Mill St., Mildenhall, IP28 7DP
☎ (0638) 717274
Ⓖ Best Western
Grade II Regency-style manor house in picturesque riverside setting. Recently refurbished to a high standard. Bridge weekends.
Bedrooms: 4 single, 9 double & 5 twin, 3 family rooms.
Bathrooms: 17 private, 2 public.
Bed & breakfast: £46-£53 single, £65-£78 double.
Lunch available.
Evening meal 6.30pm (l.o. 9pm).
Parking for 50.
Credit: Access, Visa, Diners, Amex.
⚒ ♨ 🛏 📞 ⓞ ▢ ♦ ⓘ Ⓥ
⊨ 🖼 ▦ ♨ ⛽ ✲ ❧ SP
🈺 Ⓣ

MUNDESLEY-ON-SEA
Norfolk
Map ref 3C1

4m NE. North Walsham
Small seaside resort with a superb sandy beach and excellent bathing. Nearby is a smock-mill still with cap and sails.

Manor Hotel
Coast Rd., Mundesley-on-Sea, NR11 8BG
☎ (0263) 720309
Family-run hotel on North Norfolk cliffs, with a friendly, efficient atmosphere. Restaurant, 2 bars, outdoor swimming pool (summer only).
Bedrooms: 14 double & 12 twin, 2 family rooms.

Bathrooms: 23 private, 2 public.
Bed & breakfast: £25-£28.50 single, £42-£48 double.
Half board: £140-£180 weekly.
Lunch available.
Evening meal 7pm (l.o. 8.50pm).
Parking for 30.
⚒ ⓑ ♦ ⓘ Ⓥ ⊨ ♨ ▦ ▤
🍴 🛋 ⚒ ✲ ⛽ SP

Overcliff Lodge
✺✺
46 Cromer Rd., Mundesley-on-Sea, NR11 8DB
☎ (0263) 720016
Popular licensed family-run guesthouse offering home cooking and family atmosphere. Ideal for touring Broadland and North Norfolk.
Bedrooms: 2 single, 3 double & 2 twin.
Bathrooms: 3 private, 1 public.
Bed & breakfast: £13-£14 single, £26-£34 double.
Half board: £21-£25 daily, £140-£160 weekly.
Evening meal 6.30pm (l.o. 8.30pm).
Parking for 17.
⚒ ♨ ⓘ Ⓥ ⊨ ♨ ▦ ♨ 🍴
▶ 🖼 ⛽ SP

NEEDHAM MARKET
Suffolk
Map ref 3B2

3m SE. Stowmarket
Interesting town on the Ipswich to Bury St. Edmunds road containing Georgian houses in the High Street, the Friends' Meeting House, the 17th C timber-framed grammar school and the 'Bull Inn' with carved corner-post.

The Annex
Listed COMMENDED
17 High St., Needham Market, Ipswich, IP6 8AL
☎ (0449) 720687
Close to all local amenities and recreational facilities. Family suites available if required. Payphone for guests' use. Private car park.
Bedrooms: 1 single, 2 double & 1 twin.
Bathrooms: 2 public.
Bed & breakfast: £14-£18 single, £28 double.
Parking for 4.
⚒ 5 ♨ ▢ ♦ ⓤ ⓘ Ⓥ ✈ 🖼

Please mention this guide when making a booking.

NEWMARKET
Suffolk
Map ref 3B2

Centre of the English horse-racing world and the headquarters of the Jockey Club and National Stud. Racecourse and horse sales. The National Horse Racing Museum traces the history and development of the Sport of Kings.

Bedford Lodge Hotel M
✺✺✺
Bury Rd., Newmarket, CB8 7BX
☎ (0638) 663175
Ⓖ Best Western
Georgian hunting lodge in secluded gardens. Bedrooms with private bath or shower, restaurant and homely lounge bar.
Bedrooms: 6 single, 40 double & 14 twin, 3 family rooms.
Bathrooms: 63 private.
Bed & breakfast: £55-£70 single, £70-£100 double.
Lunch available.
Evening meal 7pm (l.o. 9.30pm).
Parking for 90.
Credit: Access, Visa, Diners, Amex.
⚒ ♨ ♨ ⓞ ▢ ♦ ⓘ Ⓥ ⊨
♨ ◐ 🈺 ▦ ▤ 🛋 ⚒ ✲ ✈ ❧
SP 🈺 Ⓣ

NORFOLK BROADS

See Acle, Bungay, Coltishall, Crostwick, Gorleston-on-Sea, Great Yarmouth, Horning, Lowestoft, North Walsham, Norwich, South Walsham, Stalham, Wroxham.

NORTH WALSHAM
Norfolk
Map ref 3C1

14m N. Norwich
Weekly market has been held here for 700 years. 1 mile south of town is a cross commemorating the Peasants' Revolt of 1381. Nelson attended the local Paston Grammar School, founded in 1606 and still flourishing.

Beechwood Hotel M
✺✺✺ COMMENDED
20 Cromer Rd., North Walsham, NR28 0HD
☎ (0692) 403231

In its own gardens with many roses, shrubs, large trees, extensive lawns and numerous rhododendrons.
Bedrooms: 1 single, 2 double & 3 twin, 5 family rooms.
Bathrooms: 7 private, 2 public.
Bed & breakfast: £21-£24 single, £42-£48 double.
Half board: £31-£34 daily, £139-£199 weekly.
Evening meal 7pm (l.o. 7.30pm).
Parking for 11.
⚒ 5 ♨ ♨ ♦ ♨ Ⓥ ▦ ▤ ♨ ♣ ✲
🖼 SP Ⓣ

NORWICH
Norfolk
Map ref 3C1

Beautiful cathedral city and county town on the River Wensum with many fine museums and medieval churches. Norman castle, Guildhall and interesting medieval streets. Good shopping centre and market. *Tourist Information Centre* ☎ *(0603) 666071 or (accommodation) 761082*

The Abbey Hotel
Listed APPROVED
16 Stracey Rd., Thorpe Rd., Norwich, NR1 1EZ
☎ (0603) 612915
Private hotel, offering warm and friendly service. Close to city centre and only 5 minutes' walk from railway station.
Bedrooms: 5 single, 1 double & 2 twin, 1 family room.
Bathrooms: 1 public.
Bed & breakfast: £15-£16 single, £30-£32 double.
⚒ 2 ♨ ⓤ ⓘ Ⓥ ⊨ ♨ ▦ ▤
✈ ⒼⒶⓅ

The Almond Tree Hotel and Restaurant M
✺✺✺✺
441 Dereham Rd., Costessey, Norwich, NR5 0SG
☎ (0603) 748798 & 749114
On the main A47 Dereham Road at Costessey, the hotel is easily located. Convenient for the commercial and industrial estates and the picturesque county towns and villages of East Anglia.
Bedrooms: 1 double & 5 twin.
Bathrooms: 6 private.
Bed & breakfast: £41.75-£42.95 single, £55.50-£57.90 double.
Lunch available.

Evening meal 7pm (l.o.
9.45pm).
Parking for 22.
Credit: Access, Visa, Amex.

Annesley Hotel M
COMMENDED
6-8 Newmarket Rd.,
Norwich, NR2 2LA
☎ (0603) 624553
*Georgian building in its own
grounds in a residential area of
Norwich, five minutes' walk
from the city centre.*
Bedrooms: 6 single, 7 double
& 3 twin, 2 family rooms.
Bathrooms: 14 private,
4 public.
Bed & breakfast: from £45
single, from £55 double.
Evening meal 7pm (l.o. 9pm).
Parking for 20.
Credit: Access, Visa, Diners,
Amex.

Aspland Hotel M
Listed
6 Aspland Rd., off Riverside
Rd., Norwich, NR1 1SH
☎ (0603) 628999
*In quiet cul-de-sac off
Riverside Road, 5 minutes
from railway station, 10
minutes from cathedral and
city centre.*
Bedrooms: 1 single, 1 double
& 4 twin, 1 family room.
Bathrooms: 4 private,
1 public.
Bed & breakfast: £15-£25
single, £27-£35 double.
Parking for 5.
Credit: Access, Visa.

Beeches Hotel,
Victorian Gardens M
APPROVED
4-6 Earlham Rd., Norwich,
NR2 3DB
☎ (0603) 621167
*Welcoming hotel, set in large,
wooded gardens. Tastefully
restored to form an oasis in the
historic heart of Norwich.*
Bedrooms: 14 single,
10 double & 3 twin, 3 family
rooms.
Bathrooms: 18 private,
2 public.
Bed & breakfast: £37-£45
single, £45-£65 double.
Half board: £30-£55 daily,
£210-£385 weekly.
Evening meal 6pm (l.o. 7pm).
Parking for 30.
Credit: Access, Visa.

Hotel Belmonte and
Belmonte Restaurant
60-62 Prince of Wales Rd.,
Norwich, NR1 1LT
☎ (0603) 622533
*Accommodation with 100
seater restaurant and bar. Live
music Friday and Saturday
with nightclub open Thursday,
Friday and Saturday nights.*
Bedrooms: 3 single, 4 double
& 2 twin.
Bathrooms: 9 private.
Bed & breakfast: £35-£40
single, £50-£55 double.
Half board: £48-£55 daily,
£288-£330 weekly.
Lunch available.
Evening meal 7pm (l.o.
11pm).
Credit: Access, Visa, Amex.

Butterfield Hotel M
4 Stracey Rd., Norwich,
NR1 1EZ
☎ (0603) 624041
*Family hotel with friendly
atmosphere. Close to city,
railway and coach stations.
Fully-licensed, bar and lounge.
Rooms with private facilities
and colour TV.*
Bedrooms: 4 single, 3 double
& 3 twin, 2 family rooms.
Bathrooms: 4 private,
2 public.
Bed & breakfast: £15-£20
single, £30-£39 double.
Half board: £21-£26 daily,
£140-£175 weekly.
Evening meal 6pm (l.o. 7pm).

Caistor Hall Hotel M
Caistor St. Edmund,
Norwich, NR14 8QN
☎ (0603) 624406
Telex 975247 CHACOM G
*Set in tranquil 30-acre gardens
less than 3 miles from the
cathedral city of Norwich.*
Bedrooms: 1 single, 9 double
& 5 twin, 3 family rooms.
Bathrooms: 18 private.
Bed & breakfast: £35-£65
single, £50-£80 double.
Half board: £48-£83 daily,
£300-£550 weekly.
Lunch available.
Evening meal 7pm (l.o.
9.30pm).
Parking for 250.
Credit: Access, Visa.

Conifers Hotel M
APPROVED
162 Dereham Rd., Norwich,
NR2 3AH
☎ (0603) 628737
*Yorkstone-clad Victorian house
close to city centre and local
amenities.*
Bedrooms: 4 single, 1 double
& 2 twin, 1 family room.
Bathrooms: 1 private,
3 public.
Bed & breakfast: £15-£17
single, £30-£34 double.
Parking for 4.

The Corner House
62 Earlham Rd., Norwich,
NR2 3DF
☎ (0603) 627928
*Large Victorian house with
friendly atmosphere, 10
minutes from city centre. TV,
coffee/tea facilities in all
bedrooms, plus residents'
lounge area. Car parking.*
Bedrooms: 3 double.
Bathrooms: 2 private;
1 private shower.
Bed & breakfast: £20-£25
single, £30-£35 double.
Parking for 4.

Crofters Hotel M
2 Earlham Rd., Norwich,
NR2 3DA
☎ (0603) 613287 & 620169
*Commercial and family hotel
in own secluded grounds.
Central location near main
business and shopping area.*
Bedrooms: 2 single, 4 double
& 4 twin, 5 family rooms.
Bathrooms: 10 private,
1 public.
Bed & breakfast: £22.50-£31
single, £36-£44 double.
Half board: £26-£39 daily.
Evening meal 6pm (l.o. 7pm).
Parking for 30.

Cumberland Hotel M
APPROVED
212-216 Thorpe Rd.,
Norwich, NR1 1TJ
☎ (0603) 34550 & 34560
*Close to city centre in elevated
position with ample private
parking. Independently-run
hotel offering personal and
friendly service.*
Bedrooms: 12 single, 9 double
& 4 twin, 5 family rooms.
Bathrooms: 17 private,
3 public.

Bed & breakfast: £26-£45
single, £38-£55 double.
Lunch available.
Evening meal 6.30pm (l.o.
10.30pm).
Parking for 63.
Credit: Access, Visa, Amex.

Earlham Guest House
COMMENDED
147 Earlham Rd., Norwich,
NR2 3RG
☎ (0603) 54169
*Elegant Victorian residence
ideally situated for city centre
and university and near good,
reasonably priced eating
places.*
Bedrooms: 2 single, 3 double
& 2 twin.
Bathrooms: 1 private,
2 public.
Bed & breakfast: £16-£18
single, £29-£35 double.

Edmar Lodge
APPROVED
64 Earlham Rd., Norwich,
NR2 3DF
☎ (0603) 615599
*Comfortable accommodation
with all facilities. English
breakfast. 10 minutes' walk
from city centre. Keys
provided.*
Bedrooms: 2 single, 1 double
& 1 twin, 1 family room.
Bathrooms: 2 private,
1 public; 1 private shower.
Bed & breakfast: £15-£20
single, £25-£35 double.
Parking for 6.

Elm Farm Chalet
Hotel M
St. Faiths, Norwich,
NR10 3HH
☎ Norwich (0603) 898366
*Accommodation in chalets and
farmhouse, in rural
surroundings 4 miles north of
Norwich. Ideal base for touring
Norfolk and Suffolk.*
Bedrooms: 8 single, 8 double
& 2 twin, 1 family room.
Bathrooms: 19 private,
2 public.
Bed & breakfast: £25.50-
£33.75 single, £43.25-£50.50
double.
Half board: £35.50-£43.50
daily, £242.50-£300 weekly.
Lunch available.

Continued ▶

Evening meal 6.30pm (l.o. 8pm).
Parking for 20.
Credit: Access, Visa, Amex.

Friendly Hotel M
COMMENDED
2 Barnard Rd., Bowthorpe, Norwich, NR5 9JB
☎ (0603) 741161
Telex 975557
Friendly
A new hotel on the A47, 4 miles west of Norwich city centre. Function facilities for 4 to 260 people.
Bedrooms: 33 double & 33 twin, 14 family rooms.
Bathrooms: 80 private.
Bed & breakfast: £56.75-£69.45 single, £77.50-£92.65 double.
Lunch available.
Evening meal 6.30pm (l.o. 10pm).
Parking for 100.
Credit: Access, Visa, Diners, Amex.

Fuchsias Guest House
Listed APPROVED
139 Earlham Rd., Norwich, NR2 3RG
☎ (0603) 51410
Friendly family-run Victorian guesthouse, convenient for city centre and university. On good bus routes.
Bedrooms: 1 single, 2 double & 2 twin, 1 family room.
Bathrooms: 1 private, 2 public.
Bed & breakfast: £16-£18 single, £28-£36 double.

Garden House Hotel M
APPROVED
Salhouse Rd., Rackheath, Norwich, NR13 6AA
☎ Norwich (0603) 720007
Family-owned hotel with lovely gardens. Ideally located for the Broads and 5 miles north of Norwich. Renowned restaurant.
Bedrooms: 2 single, 4 double & 2 twin.
Bathrooms: 6 private, 1 public.
Bed & breakfast: £19.95-£35 single, £45 double.
Half board: £30.95-£33.50 daily, £195 weekly.
Lunch available.

Evening meal 7pm (l.o. 9.30pm).
Parking for 30.
Credit: Access, Visa.

The Georgian House Hotel M
APPROVED
32-34 Unthank Rd., Norwich, NR2 2RB
☎ (0603) 615655
Hotel comprises 2 old, connected Georgian houses, with an a la carte menu and a bar. 5 minutes' walk from the city centre.
Bedrooms: 10 single, 10 double & 5 twin, 2 family rooms.
Bathrooms: 27 private.
Bed & breakfast: £39.50 single, £53 double.
Half board: £33-£46 daily, £203-£255.50 weekly.
Evening meal 6.30pm (l.o. 7.30pm).
Parking for 40.
Credit: Access, Visa, Diners, Amex.

Georgian Hotel and Leisure Club
Listed APPROVED
Salhouse Rd., Rackheath, Norwich NR13 6LA
☎ (0603) 721092
Leisure hotel in country setting within easy reach of the city centre. Facilities include squash, swimming, snooker, gymnasium, solarium, sauna.
Bedrooms: 1 single, 13 double & 4 twin, 2 family rooms.
Bathrooms: 20 private, 4 public.
Bed & breakfast: £25-£29 single, £33-£39 double.
Half board: £33-£36 daily.
Lunch available.
Evening meal 6pm (l.o. 9pm).
Parking for 74.
Credit: Access, Visa.

Heathcote Hotel M
19-23 Unthank Rd., Norwich, NR2 2PA
☎ (0603) 625639
Long established, friendly hotel close to the city centre. Licensed restaurant and cocktail bar.
Bedrooms: 9 single, 9 double & 7 twin, 2 family rooms.
Bathrooms: 15 private, 4 public.
Bed & breakfast: £29-£37 single, £45-£55 double.

Evening meal 6.30pm (l.o. 7.30pm).
Parking for 20.
Credit: Access, Visa.

Marlborough House Hotel
22 Stracey Rd., Norwich, NR1 1EZ
☎ (0603) 628005
Small family-run hotel near shopping centre and station. 15 minutes from city centre. Full central heating, licensed bar. All bedrooms have colour TV, tea and coffee making facilities. Double and family rooms have en-suites. Car park available.
Bedrooms: 4 single, 3 double & 2 twin, 2 family rooms.
Bathrooms: 6 private, 1 public.
Bed & breakfast: £16.50-£27.50 single, £38.50-£41 double.
Half board: £22.50-£33.50 daily, £157.50-£192.50 weekly.
Lunch available.
Evening meal 5.30pm (l.o. 4.30pm).
Parking for 8.

Hotel Nelson M
COMMENDED
Prince of Wales Rd., Norwich, NR1 1DX
☎ (0603) 760260
Telex 975203
Best Western
Modern, purpose-built hotel on the riverside close to the railway station and city centre. Easy access to the Broads and coast.
Bedrooms: 26 single, 45 double & 50 twin.
Bathrooms: 121 private.
Bed & breakfast: £73-£80 single, £85-£90 double.
Half board: £45-£50 daily.
Lunch available.
Evening meal 6.45pm (l.o. 9.45pm).
Parking for 128.
Credit: Access, Visa, Diners, Amex.

Hotel Norwich M
COMMENDED
121-131 Boundary Rd., Norwich, NR3 2BA
☎ (0603) 787260
Telex 975337
Best Western

Modern hotel conveniently located on the ring road, with easy access to the city centre, countryside, coastlines and Norfolk Broads. New leisure centre.
Bedrooms: 19 single, 23 double & 51 twin, 15 family rooms.
Bathrooms: 108 private.
Bed & breakfast: from £60.75 single, £71-£74 double.
Half board: from £37.75 daily, from £205 weekly.
Lunch available.
Evening meal 7pm (l.o. 10pm).
Parking for 221.
Credit: Access, Visa, Diners, Amex.

Norwich Ambassador Hotel M
Norwich Airport, Cromer Rd., Norwich, NR6 6JA
☎ (0603) 410544
Newly-built hotel in quiet location 5 minutes from city centre. Modern facilities including leisure area and landscaped garden.
Bedrooms: 4 single, 80 double & 20 twin, 4 family rooms.
Bathrooms: 108 private.
Bed & breakfast: £50-£63 single, £60-£75 double.
Half board: £37-£50 daily.
Lunch available.
Evening meal 7pm (l.o. 10.30pm).
Parking for 320.
Credit: Access, Visa, C.Bl., Diners, Amex.

The Old Rectory
COMMENDED
103 Yarmouth Rd., Norwich, NR7 0HF
☎ (0603) 39357
Fine, well-equipped Georgian residence, in a tranquil setting overlooking Yare Valley. Favoured by businessmen, honeymooners and the discerning public.
Bedrooms: 5 double.
Bathrooms: 5 private.
Bed & breakfast: £47.20-£51.70 single, £69-£78.10 double.
Lunch available.
Evening meal 6pm (l.o. 10pm).
Parking for 22.
Credit: Access, Visa, Diners, Amex.

Station Hotel M
♦♦♦

5-7 Riverside Rd., Norwich,
NR1 1SQ
☎ (0603) 622556 & 611064
*Candlelit restaurant, fresh food
and friendly staff. Facing the
yacht station, 1 minute from
railway station, 5 minutes from
city centre and shops. Closed
Christmas week.*
Bedrooms: 6 single, 7 double
& 7 twin.
Bathrooms: 13 private,
2 public.
Bed & breakfast: £23-£34
single, £30-£46 double.
Lunch available.
Evening meal 6pm (l.o.
9.30pm).
Parking for 12.
Credit: Access, Visa.
♿ ♨ ♦ ⓤ ▢ ♥ ⓘ 🛏
📺 ⬤ ▥ ♨ ✕ ⒹⒶⒻ ⚲ ⓢⓟ ⓣ

Wedgewood House M
♦♦♦

42 St. Stephens Rd.,
Norwich, NR1 3RE
☎ (0603) 625730
*Family-run hotel close to coach
station. Walking distance to
shops and places of interest.
Parking.*
Bedrooms: 2 single, 4 double
& 3 twin, 2 family rooms.
Bathrooms: 8 private,
1 public.
Bed & breakfast: from £17
single, from £35 double.
Half board: from £26 daily.
Evening meal 6.30pm (l.o.
7.30pm).
Parking for 7.
Credit: Access, Visa, Amex.
♿ ▢ ♥ ⓤ ▣ ♥ ✕ 🛏 ♨
✕ ⒹⒶⒻ ⓢⓟ ⓣ

ORFORD

Suffolk
Map ref 3C2

*9m E. Woodbridge
Once a thriving port, now
a quiet village of brick
and timber buildings,
famous for its castle.
Orford comes to life
during the summer when
boats tie up at the quay.*

The Crown and Castle Hotel M
♦♦♦ COMMENDED

Orford, Nr. Woodbridge,
IP12 2LJ
☎ (0394) 450205
*Fine old timbered coaching
house, opposite the castle.*
Bedrooms: 3 single, 6 double
& 11 twin.

Bathrooms: 11 private,
2 public.
Bed & breakfast: £35-£48
single, £55-£65 double.
Half board: £47.50-£57.50
daily.
Lunch available.
Evening meal 7pm (l.o.
8.45pm).
Parking for 20.
Credit: Access, Visa, C.Bl.,
Diners, Amex.
♿ ♨ ♦ ⓤ ▢ ♥ ⓘ 🛏
📺 ▥ ♨ ✕ ❀ ⚲ ♨ ⓢⓟ ⓣ

PETERBOROUGH

Cambridgeshire
Map ref 3A1

*Prosperous and rapidly
expanding cathedral city
on the edge of the Fens
on the River Nene.
Catherine of Aragon is
buried in the cathedral.
City Museum and Art
Gallery. Ferry Meadows
Country Park has
numerous leisure
facilities.
Tourist Information
Centre ☎ (0733) 317336*

Aaron Park Hotel and Lancaster House

109 & 112 Park Rd.,
Peterborough, PE1 2TR
☎ (0733) 64849
*Family owned and run, just
5 minutes' walk from the
Queensgate shopping centre.*
Bedrooms: 9 single, 3 double
& 3 twin, 2 family rooms.
Bathrooms: 4 private,
3 public; 4 private showers.
Bed & breakfast: £25-£41
single, £45-£49 double.
Half board: £31-£47 daily.
Evening meal 6.30pm (l.o.
7pm).
Parking for 15.
Credit: Access, Visa, Amex.
♿ ♨ ▢ ♥ ⓘ ⓥ 🛏 📺 ▥
♨ ⓣ ⓢⓟ ⓣ

The Bell Inn M
♦♦♦♦ COMMENDED

Great North Rd., Stilton,
Peterborough, PE7 3RA
☎ (0733) 241066
*Old coaching inn, restored as a
hotel including conference and
banqueting facilities. Off A1,
just south of Norman Cross
roundabout.*
Bedrooms: 2 single, 14 double
& 2 twin, 1 family room.
Bathrooms: 19 private.
Bed & breakfast: £55-£60
single, £65-£70 double.
Lunch available.
Evening meal 7pm (l.o.
9.30pm).

Parking for 30.
Credit: Access, Visa, Diners,
Amex.
♿5 ♨ ♥ ⓤ ▢ ♥ ⓘ ⓥ
🛏 ⬤ ▥ ♨ ✕ ✕ ♨ ⓢⓟ ⓑ

Butterfly Hotel M
♦♦♦

Thorpe Meadows, Off
Longthorpe Parkway,
Peterborough, PE3 6GA
☎ (0733) 64240 Telex 818360
*By the water's edge at Thorpe
Meadows, this modern hotel
maintains all the traditional
values of design and comfort.
Special weekend rates
available.*
Bedrooms: 33 single,
18 double & 15 twin, 4 family
rooms.
Bathrooms: 70 private.
Bed & breakfast: £60-£65
single, £65-£70 double.
Half board: £70-£75 daily.
Lunch available.
Evening meal 7pm (l.o.
10pm).
Parking for 80.
Credit: Access, Visa, Diners,
Amex.
♿ ♨ ♦ ⓡ ▢ ♥ ⓘ ⓥ ✕
⬤ ▥ ♨ ✕ ⅋ ✕ ⓢⓟ ⓣ

Chesterton Priory
♦♦♦ COMMENDED

Chesterton, Peterborough,
PE7 3UB
☎ (0733) 390678
*Fine Victorian country house in
2 acres of secluded grounds.
Close to the A1, East of
England Showground and
Peterborough Business Park.
Conference facilities for 20.*
Bedrooms: 1 single, 5 double
& 2 twin.
Bathrooms: 8 private.
Bed & breakfast: £41-£49
single, £56-£65 double.
Half board: £49.50-£64 daily.
Evening meal 6pm (l.o. 9pm).
Parking for 20.
Credit: Access, Visa.
♿7 ♨ ♥ ⓡ ▢ ♥ ⓘ ⓥ
✕ 🛏 ▥ ♨ ✕ ✦ ❀ ✕
ⓢⓟ ⓑ

Dalwhinnie Lodge Hotel
♦♦ APPROVED

31-35 Burghley Rd.,
Peterborough, PE1 2QA
☎ (0733) 65968
*Licensed family-run hotel with
home cooking, 5 minutes from
city centre, bus and train
station. High standard
maintained and a warm
welcome always guaranteed.*
Bedrooms: 6 single, 6 twin,
5 family rooms.
Bathrooms: 2 private,
3 public; 4 private showers.

Bed & breakfast: £25.85-
£36.42 single, £41.13-£52.87
double.
Half board: £32.88-£59.90
daily.
Evening meal 6pm (l.o.
midday).
Parking for 14.
Credit: Visa, Amex.
♿ ♨ ♥ ⓡ ▢ ♥ ⓘ ⓥ ✕
🛏 📺 ⬤ ▥ ♨ ⓘ

The Lodge Hotel

130 Lincoln Rd.,
Peterborough, PE1 2NR
☎ (0733) 341489
*Friendly licensed hotel and
restaurant offering good
facilities. Within easy walking
distance of city centre, bus and
railway stations.*
Bedrooms: 5 single, 2 double
& 2 twin.
Bathrooms: 9 private,
1 public.
Bed & breakfast: £43-£48
single, £54-£60 double.
Evening meal 6pm (l.o.
9.30pm).
Parking for 9.
Credit: Access, Visa, Amex.
♿5 ▢ ♥ ♥ ⓘ ⓥ 🛏 ▥ ♨
✕ ♨ ⓢⓟ

Swallow Hotel M
♦♦♦♦

Lynch Wood, Peterborough
Business Park, Peterborough,
PE2 0GB
☎ (0733) 371111 Telex 32422
Swallow G
Ⓖ Swallow
*New hotel a minute from
A1/A605 junction on the edge
of Nene Country Park and
opposite East of England
showground. In picturesque
village of Alwalton. Large
leisure complex.*
Bedrooms: 2 single,
116 double & 38 twin,
7 family rooms.
Bathrooms: 163 private.
Bed & breakfast: max. £91.50
single, max. £109 double.
Lunch available.
Evening meal 7pm (l.o.
10.30pm).
Parking for 250.
Credit: Access, Visa, Diners,
Amex.
♿ ♨ ♥ ⓡ ▢ ♥ ⓘ ⓥ ✕
🛏 ♨ ▣ ♨ ✕ ⓘ ✦ ✕ 🛏
Ⓤ ❀ ⚲ ⓢⓟ ♨ ⓣ

---

*National Crown
ratings were correct
at the time of going
to press but are
subject to change.
Please check at the
time of booking.*

RAMSEY

Cambridgeshire
Map ref 3A2

10m SE. Peterborough

George Hotel ♨
♨♨♨ COMMENDED

63 High St., Ramsey,
Huntingdon, PE17 1AA
☎ (0487) 815264
Ⓡ Minotels
*16th C coaching inn with
modern furnishings, in a
country town with good views.
Access to golf-course.*
Bedrooms: 3 single, 4 double
& 4 twin.
Bathrooms: 11 private.
Bed & breakfast: £42-£45
single, £60-£65 double.
Half board: £45-£57 daily.
Lunch available.
Evening meal 7pm (l.o.
9.30pm).
Parking for 40.
Credit: Access, Visa, Diners,
Amex.

SAFFRON WALDEN

Essex
Map ref 2D1

12m N. Bishop's Stortford
Takes its name from the
saffron crocus once
grown around the town.
The church of St. Mary is
most impressive with
large, superb carvings,
magnificent roofs and
brasses. A town maze
can be seen on the
common. 2 miles south-
west is Audley End, a
magnificent Jacobean
mansion owned by
English Heritage.
*Tourist Information
Centre* ☎ (0799) 24282

Cricketers Arms ♨
♨♨♨ COMMENDED

Rickling Green, Saffron
Walden, CB11 3YG
☎ (079 988) 322 & 595
*Large village inn facing the
green and cricket pitch. Two
bars, patio and restaurant. In
tranquil setting just off the
B1383 at Quendon.*
Bedrooms: 5 double, 2 family
rooms.
Bathrooms: 7 private.
Bed & breakfast: £40-£60
single, £45-£105 double.
Half board: £32.50-£72.50
daily.
Lunch available.
Evening meal 6.30pm (l.o.
10pm).

Parking for 40.
Credit: Access, Visa, Amex.

Queens Head Inn
♨♨♨

High St., Littlebury, Saffron
Walden, CB11 4TD
☎ (0799) 22251
*Friendly, family-run freehouse
and hotel close to Audley End.
All rooms en-suite. Tastefully
refurbished. Delightful menu.*
Bedrooms: 2 single, 2 double
& 1 twin, 1 family room.
Bathrooms: 6 private.
Bed & breakfast: £30.30-£35
single, £39.10-£45 double.
Half board: £30-£35 daily,
£200-£245 weekly.
Lunch available.
Evening meal 7pm (l.o. 9pm).
Parking for 30.
Credit: Access, Visa.

Saffron Hotel ♨
♨♨♨

10-18 High St., Saffron
Walden, CB10 1AY
☎ (0799) 22676 Telex 81653
*16th C hotel in market town.
South of Cambridge, close to
Duxford Air Museum and
Stansted Airport.*
Bedrooms: 5 single, 10 double
& 4 twin, 2 family rooms.
Bathrooms: 16 private,
2 public; 2 private showers.
Bed & breakfast: £28-£45
single, £50-£75 double.
Half board: £40-£58 daily.
Lunch available.
Evening meal 6.30pm (l.o.
9.30pm).
Parking for 8.
Credit: Access, Visa, Diners,
Amex.

ST IVES

Cambridgeshire
Map ref 3A2

5m E. Huntingdon
Picturesque market town
with a narrow 6-arched
bridge spanning the River
Ouse on which stands a
bridge chapel. There are
numerous Georgian and
Victorian buildings and
the Norris Museum has a
good local collection.

The Dolphin Hotel ♨
♨♨♨♨ APPROVED

Bridgefoot, London Rd.,
St. Ives, PE17 4EP
☎ (0480) 66966

*Friendly hotel taking pride in
its cuisine and service.
Panoramic views over the River
Ouse. Located near town
centre.*
Bedrooms: 6 double &
14 twin, 2 family rooms.
Bathrooms: 22 private.
Bed & breakfast: from £55
single, from £70 double.
Lunch available.
Evening meal 7pm (l.o.
10pm).
Parking for 100.
Credit: Access, Visa, Diners,
Amex.

The Golden Lion Hotel
Market Hill, St. Ives,
PE17 4AL
☎ (0480) 492100
*Former 16th C coaching inn,
fully licensed, modernised and
refurnished. Near river and
medieval chapeled bridge.*
Bedrooms: 8 single, 8 double
& 2 twin, 3 family rooms.
Bathrooms: 17 private,
2 public.
Bed & breakfast: £26-£36
single, from £42 double.
Lunch available.
Evening meal 7pm (l.o.
10pm).
Parking for 3.
Credit: Access, Visa.

St. Ives Motel ♨
♨♨♨

London Rd., St. Ives,
PE17 4EX
☎ (0480) 63857
*Modern, comfortable
accommodation with its own
garden, 1 mile from town.
Completely refurbished in
1989. Restaurant meals and
bar snacks served every day.
Friendly, personal service.*
Bedrooms: 5 double & 9 twin,
2 family rooms.
Bathrooms: 16 private.
Bed & breakfast: £41-£47.50
single, £43-£50 double.
Lunch available.
Evening meal 7.15pm (l.o.
9.30pm).
Parking for 80.
Credit: Access, Visa, Diners,
Amex.

Slepe Hall Hotel ♨
♨♨♨

Ramsey Rd., St. Ives,
PE17 4RB
☎ (0480) 63122

*Former Victorian girls' school
converted in 1966. Now a
Grade II listed building, 5
minutes' walk from the Great
River Ouse and historic town
centre. Extensive bar and
restaurant menus.*
Bedrooms: 2 single, 4 double
& 9 twin, 1 family room.
Bathrooms: 16 private.
Bed & breakfast: from £56
single, from £65 double.
Half board: from £69 daily.
Lunch available.
Evening meal 7pm (l.o.
9.45pm).
Parking for 70.
Credit: Access, Visa, Diners,
Amex.

The Willow Guest
House & Tea Room
45 High St., Hemingford
Grey, St, Ives, PE18 9BJ
☎ (0480) 494748
*Large private house in the
centre of village just 1.5 miles
from St Ives. Colour TV in all
bedrooms.*
Bedrooms: 2 single, 2 double,
1 family room.
Bathrooms: 5 private.
Bed & breakfast: from £20
single, from £35 double.
Half board: £29.50-£32 daily.
Parking for 7.

ST NEOTS

Cambridgeshire
Map ref 2D2

8m SW. Huntingdon
Pleasant market town on
the River Ouse with a
large square which grew
up around a 10th C
priory. There are many
interesting buildings and
St. Mary's is one of the
largest medieval
churches in the county.

Abbotsley Golf Hotel
♨♨♨ APPROVED

Eynesbury Hardwicke, St.
Neots, PE19 4XN
☎ (0480) 74000
*125-acre mixed farm.
Charming country hotel amidst
its own delightful golf course.
Offers good golf, good food,
good accommodation and good
times.*
Bedrooms: 2 single, 16 twin.
Bathrooms: 18 private.
Bed & breakfast: £40-£50
single, £60-£70 double.
Lunch available.
Evening meal 7pm (l.o.
9.15pm).

Parking for 100.
Credit: Access, Visa.

Old Falcon Hotel

Market Square, St. Neots,
PE19 2AW
☎ Huntingdon (0480) 72749
*Old coaching inn situated in
town centre. Bar and
restaurant open to non-
residents, conference and
banqueting facilities available.*
Bedrooms: 6 single, 1 double
& 1 twin.
Bathrooms: 7 private,
1 public.
Bed & breakfast: £35-£40
single, £40-£45 double.
Lunch available.
Evening meal 7pm (l.o.
9.30pm).
Credit: Access, Visa, Diners,
Amex.

SCARNING
Norfolk
Map ref 3B1

2m W. East Dereham

Scarning Dale

Dale Rd., Scarning, East
Dereham, NR19 2QN
☎ (036 287) 269
*17th C house set in 25 acres of
pretty Norfolk countryside, just
off A47. Indoor heated pool.*
Bedrooms: 2 single, 2 double
& 1 twin.
Bathrooms: 2 private,
1 public.
Bed & breakfast: from £30
single, from £56 double.
Half board: from £45 daily.
Lunch available.
Evening meal 7.30pm (l.o.
9pm).
Parking for 8.

SHERINGHAM
Norfolk
Map ref 3B1

Holiday resort with
Victorian and Edwardian
hotels and a sand and
shingle beach where the
fishing boats are hauled
up. The North Norfolk
Railway operates from
Sheringham Station
during the summer. Other
attractions include,
museums, theatre and
Splash Fun Pool.

The Beacon Hotel M

1 Nelson Rd., Sheringham,
NR26 8BT
☎ (0263) 822019
*A small, quiet, peaceful hotel
by the sea, with accent on
cleanliness, comfort and
English food.*
Bedrooms: 2 single, 3 double
& 2 twin.
Bathrooms: 3 private,
2 public.
Half board: max. £29 daily,
max. £182 weekly.
Evening meal 7pm (l.o. 7pm).
Parking for 5.
Open May-September.
Credit: Access, Visa.

Beeston Hills Lodge

64 Cliff Rd., Sheringham,
NR26 8BJ
☎ (0263) 825936
*Family-run Edwardian lodge
ideally situated with sea views
and next to hills, putting green
and cliff walks. Near the
beach.*
Bedrooms: 1 double & 2 twin,
1 family room.
Bathrooms: 1 public;
1 private shower.
Bed & breakfast: £12.50-
£18.50 single, £25-£37 double.
Parking for 5.

SOUTH WALSHAM
Norfolk
Map ref 3C1

3m NW. Acle
Village famous for having
2 churches in adjoining
churchyards. South
Walsham Broad consists
of an inner and outer
section, the former being
private. Alongside, the
Fairhaven Garden Trust
has woodland and water-
gardens open to the
public.

**South Walsham Hall
Hotel M**

South Walsham, Norwich,
NR13 6DQ
☎ (060 549) 378
Telex UNIEX 97394
*Small country house hotel
situated between Great
Yarmouth and Norwich, on the
B1140.*
Bedrooms: 1 single, 7 double
& 21 twin.
Bathrooms: 26 private,
1 public.
Bed & breakfast: £40-£70
single, £60-£120 double.
Half board: £40-£55 daily,
£245-£350 weekly.
Lunch available.
Evening meal 7pm (l.o.
10pm).
Parking for 100.
Credit: Access, Visa, Diners,
Amex.

> *Half board prices
> shown are per
> person but in some
> cases may be based
> on double/twin
> occupancy.*

SOUTHEND-ON-SEA
Essex
Map ref 3B3

On the Thames Estuary
and the nearest seaside
resort to London. Famous
for its pier and unique
pier trains. Other
attractions include Peter
Pan's Playground, a
marine activity centre for
watersports, excellent
fishing facilities, indoor
swimming pools and
indoor rollerskating.
*Tourist Information
Centre* ☎ *(0702) 355122
or 355120*

Anchorage Guest House
Listed

32 Manor Rd., Westcliff-on-
Sea, Southend-on-Sea,
SS0 7SS
☎ (0702) 347873
*Small, friendly, family-run
guesthouse, close to seafront,
local shops and station.*
Bedrooms: 1 single, 2 double,
2 family rooms.
Bathrooms: 1 public.
Bed & breakfast: £12.50-£15
single, £25-£28 double.
Evening meal 6pm (l.o.
8.30pm).
Parking for 3.

Balmoral Hotel
APPROVED

34-36 Valkyrie Rd.,
Southend-on-Sea, SS0 8BU
☎ (0702) 342947
*Family-run hotel 500 yards
from the seafront and Westcliff
station. Close to the centre of
Southend and A13.*
Bedrooms: 11 single, 7 double
& 4 twin.
Bathrooms: 22 private.
Bed & breakfast: £37.50-£41
single, £52-£59 double.
Half board: £35-£46.50 daily.
Continued ▶

Use a coupon

*When enquiring about accommodation you
may find it helpful to use the booking
enquiry coupons which can be found towards
the end of the guide. These should be cut out
and mailed direct to the establishments in
which you are interested. Do remember to
include your name and address.*

SOUTHEND-ON-SEA

Continued

Lunch available.
Evening meal 6.30pm (l.o. 8.30pm).
Parking for 18.
Credit: Access, Visa.

Cliffview Guesthouse

Listed APPROVED

8 Clifftown Parade,
Southend-on-Sea, SS1 1DP
☎ 0702 (331 645)
Within a conservation area, 5 minutes' walk from seafront, town centre and main railway lines.
Bedrooms: 6 single, 5 double & 3 twin, 3 family rooms.
Bathrooms: 2 public; 3 private showers.
Bed & breakfast: £18-£20 single, £30-£40 double.
Parking for 6.
Credit: Access, Visa, Amex.

Ilfracombe House Hotel ♨

Wilson Rd., Southend-on-Sea, SS1 1HQ
☎ (0702) 351000
Totally refurbished Victorian house in a conservation area adjacent to cliff gardens, sea, town centre and main rail links.
Bedrooms: 5 single, 4 double & 3 twin, 1 family room.
Bathrooms: 13 private.
Bed & breakfast: £30-£38 single, £40-£48 double.
Half board: £39.80-£47.80 daily, £300 weekly.
Lunch available.
Evening meal 6.30pm (l.o. 7.30pm).
Credit: Access, Visa, Diners, Amex.

Malvern Lodge Guest House

Listed

29 Seaforth Rd., Southend-on-Sea, SS0 7SN
☎ (0702) 345692
Small guesthouse under direct supervision of proprietors. Opposite station and near seafront.
Bedrooms: 4 single, 2 double & 2 twin, 1 family room.
Bathrooms: 3 public.
Bed & breakfast: £12-£14 single, £24-£28 double.
Parking for 4.

Prittlewell Hotel

Listed

350 Victoria Avenue,
Southend-on-Sea, SS2 6NA
☎ (0702) 466924
On main A127 road into Southend. Half a mile from town centre and close to park, football stadium and all amenities. Lounge, licensed bar.
Bedrooms: 5 single, 4 double & 2 twin, 1 family room.
Bathrooms: 3 private, 2 public; 1 private shower.
Bed & breakfast: £19-£23 single, £38-£46 double.
Half board: £24-£30 daily, £150-£190 weekly.
Evening meal 6pm (l.o. 6.30pm).

Roslin Hotel ♨

COMMENDED

Thorpe Esplanade, Thorpe Bay, Southend-on-Sea, SS1 3BG
☎ (0702) 586375 Telex 99262
Hotel overlooking the Thames Estuary in residential Thorpe. Within easy reach of Southend and 45 minutes from London.
Bedrooms: 9 single, 14 double & 17 twin, 4 family rooms.
Bathrooms: 44 private.
Bed & breakfast: £38-£50 single, £60-£65 double.
Half board: £40-£50 daily, £255-£280 weekly.
Lunch available.
Evening meal 6.30pm (l.o. 10pm).
Parking for 34.
Credit: Access, Visa, Diners, Amex.

Terrace Hotel

8 Royal Terrace, Southend-on-Sea, SS1 1DY
☎ (0702) 348143
Friendly licensed hotel in a quiet Regency terrace, overlooking the pier, estuary and gardens. Close to the High Street, shops and railway stations. Noted for cleanliness.
Bedrooms: 3 single, 1 double & 3 twin, 2 family rooms.
Bathrooms: 3 private, 2 public.
Bed & breakfast: max. £18.50 single, max. £35 double.
Lunch available.

SOUTHWOLD

Suffolk
Map ref 3C2

8m E. Halesworth
Pleasant and attractive seaside town with a triangular market square and spacious greens around which stand flint, brick and colour-washed cottages. The parish church of St. Edmund is one of the greatest churches in Suffolk.

Dunburgh Guest House

28 North Parade, Southwold, IP18 6LT
☎ (0502) 723253
Elegant Victorian house overlooking the sea. All bedrooms have sea views. Comfortable and relaxed atmosphere. Home cooking.
Bedrooms: 2 double & 1 twin.
Bathrooms: 1 private, 2 public.
Bed & breakfast: £20-£21 single, £36-£44 double.
Half board: £26-£30 daily.
Evening meal 7pm (l.o. 7pm).

Mrs. R.D. Hemsley

28 Field Stile Rd.,
Southwold, IP18 6LD
☎ (0502) 723588
Comfortable accommodation near beach and town centre. Pets welcome.
Bedrooms: 1 single, 1 double & 1 twin.
Bathrooms: 1 public.
Bed & breakfast: £20 single, £32 double.
Half board: £30-£35 daily, £210-£245 weekly.
Lunch available.
Evening meal 6.30pm (l.o. 9.30pm).

SPROUGHTON

Suffolk
Map ref 3B2

Finjaro

Valley Farm Drive, Hadleigh Rd., Sproughton, Ipswich, IP8 3EL
☎ Hintlesham (047 387) 581
New chalet bungalow in private road. One mile from A12, A45, A1071. Turn right at Post House Hotel traffic lights, over the roundabout, second turning on the left.
Bedrooms: 2 double & 1 twin, 1 family room.

Bathrooms: 1 private, 1 public.
Bed & breakfast: £16-£18 single, £28-£32 double.
Half board: £20-£22 daily, £95-£120 weekly.
Evening meal 7pm (l.o. 8pm).
Parking for 6.

STALHAM

Norfolk
Map ref 3C1

7m SE. North Walsham
Lies on the edge of the Broads.

Kingfisher Hotel ♨

COMMENDED

High St., Stalham, Norwich, NR12 9AN
☎ (0692) 81974
Modern, licensed hotel with a friendly atmosphere, ideal for touring the Norfolk countryside. Children welcome.
Bedrooms: 2 single, 9 double & 3 twin, 3 family rooms.
Bathrooms: 17 private.
Bed & breakfast: £35-£36 single, £44-£55 double.
Half board: £31-£40 daily.
Lunch available.
Evening meal 7pm (l.o. 9.30pm).
Parking for 45.
Credit: Access, Visa.

STOKE HOLY CROSS

Norfolk
Map ref 3C1

4m S. Norwich

Salamanca Farm ♨

Stoke Holy Cross, Nr. Norwich, NR14 8QJ
☎ Framingham Earl (050 86) 2322
175-acre mixed/dairy farm. Victorian house offering full English breakfast. Set in beautiful undulating country, 4 miles from Norwich.
Bedrooms: 3 double & 1 twin.
Bathrooms: 1 private, 2 public.
Bed & breakfast: £15-£17 single, £28-£34 double.
Parking for 8.

Please check prices and other details at the time of booking.

STOKE-BY-NAYLAND

Suffolk
Map ref 3B2

5m SW. Hadleigh
Picturesque village with a fine group of half-timbered cottages near the church of St. Mary, the tower of which was one of Constable's favourite subjects. In School Street are the Guildhall and the Maltings, both 16th C timber-framed buildings.

The Angel Inn M
COMMENDED
Polstead Rd., Stoke-by-Nayland, Colchester, Essex CO6 4SA
☎ Nayland (0206) 263245 & (0206) 263246
Beautifully restored freehouse and restaurant in the historic village of Stoke-by-Nayland, in the heart of Constable Country.
Bedrooms: 1 single, 4 double & 1 twin.
Bathrooms: 6 private.
Bed & breakfast: £38.50 single, £51.25 double.
Lunch available.
Evening meal 6.30pm (l.o. 9pm).
Parking for 25.
Credit: Access, Visa, Diners, Amex.

SUDBURY

Suffolk
Map ref 3B2

3m NW. Colchester
Former important cloth and market town on the River Stour. Birthplace of Thomas Gainsborough whose home is now an art gallery and museum. The Corn Exchange is an excellent example of early Victorian civic building.

Old Bull and Trivets
Church St., Ballingdon, Sudbury, CO10 6BL
☎ (0787) 74120
16th C guesthouse and restaurant of character and charm. Within 10 minutes' walk of town centre. Ideal centre for touring.
Bedrooms: 1 single, 3 double & 1 twin, 4 family rooms.
Bathrooms: 6 private; 3 private showers.

Bed & breakfast: £21-£34 single, £34-£46 double.
Half board: £24-£46 daily.
Evening meal 3pm (l.o. 10pm).
Parking for 20.
Credit: Access, Visa, Diners, Amex.

SWAFFHAM

Norfolk
Map ref 3B1

14m SE. King's Lynn
Busy market town with a triangular market-place, a domed rotunda built in 1783 and a number of Georgian houses. The 15th C church possesses a large library of ancient books.

Corfield House M
COMMENDED
Sporle, Swaffham, PE32 2EA
☎ Swaffham (0760) 23636
Country guesthouse with comfortable, well-fitted rooms, 1 on ground floor. Personal service. Peaceful surroundings. Well placed for touring north Norfolk.
Bedrooms: 1 single, 2 double & 2 twin.
Bathrooms: 5 private.
Bed & breakfast: £18.50 single, £33-£37 double.
Half board: £26.50-£28.50 daily, £170-£185 weekly.
Evening meal 7.30pm (l.o. 6pm).
Parking for 5.
Open April-December.
Credit: Access, Visa.

THAXTED

Essex
Map ref 3B2

6m SE. Saffron Walden
Small town rich in outstanding buildings and dominated by its hilltop medieval church. The magnificent Guildhall was built by the Cutlers' Guild in the late 14th C. A windmill built in 1804 has been restored and houses a rural museum.

The Four Seasons Hotel
COMMENDED
Walden Rd., Thaxted, CM6 2RE
☎ (0371) 830129

Small, comfortable country hotel run by resident proprietors, with well-appointed accommodation and friendly atmosphere.
Bedrooms: 3 single, 4 double & 2 twin.
Bathrooms: 9 private.
Bed & breakfast: £55-£60 single, £65-£75 double.
Lunch available.
Evening meal 7pm (l.o. 9.30pm).
Parking for 100.
Credit: Access, Visa, Amex.

The Swan Hotel
COMMENDED
Bullring, Thaxted, CM6 2DL
☎ (0371) 830321
A high standard inn offering lively village bar and attractive en-suite accommodation, some with jacuzzi. Weekend rates available.
Bedrooms: 5 single, 8 double & 7 twin.
Bathrooms: 20 private.
Bed & breakfast: £55 single, £65-£75 double.
Lunch available.
Evening meal 5pm (l.o. 10pm).
Parking for 33.
Credit: Access, Visa, Diners, Amex.

THETFORD

Norfolk
Map ref 3B2

12m N. Bury St. Edmunds
Small, medieval market town with numerous reminders of its long history: the ruins of the 12th C priory, Iron Age earthworks at Castle Hill and a Norman castle mound. Timber-framed Ancient House is now a museum.
Tourist Information Centre ☎ *(0842) 752599*

The Historical Thomas Paine Hotel M
APPROVED
White Hart St., Thetford, IP24 1AA
☎ (0842) 755631 Telex 58298
Attention T.P.H.
Ⓒ Best Western
Historic Georgian hotel and restaurant, on the Norfolk/Suffolk border. An ideal touring base.
Bedrooms: 4 single, 7 double & 3 twin.

Bathrooms: 13 private; 1 private shower.
Bed & breakfast: £46-£52 single, £58-£65 double.
Lunch available.
Evening meal 7pm (l.o. 9.30pm).
Parking for 30.
Credit: Access, Visa, Diners, Amex.

TITCHWELL

Norfolk
Map ref 3B1

5m E. Hunstanton

Briarfields
Main St., Titchwell, King's Lynn, PE31 8BB
☎ Brancaster (0485) 210742
Small country hotel within a recent barn conversion, offering a high standard of accommodation and service.
Bedrooms: 11 double & 4 twin.
Bathrooms: 15 private.
Bed & breakfast: from £27.50 single, £50-£60 double.
Half board: £34.95-£39.95 daily, £244.65-£279.65 weekly.
Lunch available.
Evening meal 7pm (l.o. 8.30pm).
Parking for 40.

WALTHAM ABBEY

Essex
Map ref 2D1

King Harold rebuilt the church in 1060 and it is believed he was buried here after the Battle of Hastings. Henry II founded a priory, 300 years later, which became Waltham Abbey. Henry VIII suppressed the Abbey and it was demolished, except for the nave and great gateway.

Swallow Hotel M
COMMENDED
Old Shire Lane, Waltham Abbey, EN9 3LX
☎ Lea Valley (0992) 717170
Telex 916596
Ⓒ Swallow
Traditionally built new property at junction 26 of the M25. 2 restaurants, cocktail bar, residents' lounge and leisure club.

Continued ▶

WALTHAM ABBEY

Continued

Bedrooms: 78 single,
18 double & 57 twin, 10 family
rooms.
Bathrooms: 163 private.
Bed & breakfast: £55-£90
single, £65-£99 double.
Half board: £49.50-£68.25
daily.
Lunch available.
Evening meal 5.30pm (l.o.
11pm).
Parking for 240.
Credit: Access, Visa, Diners,
Amex.

WELLS-NEXT-THE-SEA

Norfolk
Map ref 3B1

9m N. Fakenham
Seaside resort and small
port on the north coast. The
Buttlands is a large tree-
lined green surrounded by
Georgian houses and from
here narrow streets lead to
the quay.

The Cobblers Guest House

Standard Rd., Wells-next-
the-Sea, NR23 1JU
☎ Fakenham (0328) 710155
& 711092
*In a quiet setting within a large
walled garden. All rooms with
washbasins, TVs, tea/coffee
facilities (some en-suite). Fully
licensed, guest lounges.*
Bedrooms: 4 double & 1 twin.
Bathrooms: 2 private,
2 public.
Bed & breakfast: £15-£17
single, £29-£31 double.
Half board: £22.95-£24.95
daily.
Evening meal 6.30pm (l.o.
7pm).
Parking for 8.

Crown Hotel ℳ

The Buttlands, Wells-next-
the-Sea, NR23 1EX
☎ Fakenham (0328) 710209
Ⓒ Minotels
*Famous old coaching inn set
amongst Norfolk's finest
coastal scenery.*
Bedrooms: 1 single, 6 double
& 4 twin, 4 family rooms.
Bathrooms: 10 private,
1 public.
Bed & breakfast: £43-£50
single, £54-£62 double.

Lunch available.
Evening meal 7.30pm (l.o.
9.30pm).
Parking for 10.
Credit: Access, Visa, Diners,
Amex.

Scarborough House
COMMENDED

Clubbs Lane, Wells-next-the-
Sea, NR23 1DP
☎ Fakenham (0328) 710309
& 711661
*Spacious licensed Victorian
manse with private parking. 2
lounges, family rooms, garden
and bar, restaurant, four-
posters, log fires. Dogs welcome.*
Bedrooms: 3 double & 3 twin,
2 family rooms.
Bathrooms: 4 private,
2 public.
Bed & breakfast: £23-£26
single, £36-£50 double.
Half board: £28.95-£36.95
daily, £190-£250 weekly.
Evening meal 7.30pm (l.o.
9pm).
Parking for 10.
Credit: Access, Visa, Amex.

The Well House

Standard Rd., Wells-next-the-
Sea, NR23 1JY
☎ Fakenham (0328) 710443
*16th C manor house and
gentleman's residence with old
world charm, now a small
family-run guesthouse
overlooking salt marshes.
Adjacent to quay, 1 mile from
the sea, ideal for birdwatching.*
Bedrooms: 2 double & 1 twin,
1 family room.
Bathrooms: 4 private.
Bed & breakfast: £17-£18
double.
Parking for 4.

WISBECH

Cambridgeshire
Map ref 3A1

12m SW. King's Lynn
The town is the centre of
the agricultural and
flower-growing industries
of Fenland. Peckover
House (National Trust) is
an important example of
domestic architecture.
*Tourist Information
Centre* ☎ *(0945) 583263*

Crown Lodge Country Hotel ℳ
COMMENDED

Downham Rd., Outwell,
Wisbech, PE14 8SE
☎ (0945) 773391

*A warm welcome awaits you at
this small hotel, which offers a
relaxed, friendly atmosphere
supported by super leisure
facilities.*
Bedrooms: 6 double.
Bathrooms: 6 private.
Bed & breakfast: £31-£35
single, £37-£45 double.
Lunch available.
Evening meal 6pm (l.o.
9.45pm).
Parking for 50.
Credit: Access, Visa, Diners.

White Lion Hotel

5 South Brink, Wisbech,
PE13 1JD
☎ (0945) 584813
Ⓒ Consort
*Family hotel with friendly
service, in the town centre by
the river and on the main road
to the coast.*
Bedrooms: 4 single, 9 double
& 4 twin, 1 family room.
Bathrooms: 16 private,
1 public.
Bed & breakfast: from £35
single, from £45 double.
Half board: from £65 daily,
from £380 weekly.
Lunch available.
Evening meal 7pm (l.o.
9.30pm).
Parking for 25.
Credit: Access, Visa, Diners,
Amex.

WITHAM

Essex
Map ref 3B3

9m NE. Chelmsford
Delightful town whose
history goes back to the
time of King Alfred. The
High Street contains 16th
C houses and the Spread
Eagle, a famous Essex
inn. The 14th C church is
near the site of an ancient
defensive mound.

Rivenhall Resort Hotel ℳ
COMMENDED

Rivenhall End, Witham,
CM9 3BH
☎ (0376) 516969 Telex 99414
Ⓒ Resort
*Purpose-built single storey
hotel situated on the A12
between Colchester and
Chelmsford, convenient for the
port of Maldon.*
Bedrooms: 12 single,
29 double & 11 twin, 3 family
rooms.
Bathrooms: 55 private.

Bed & breakfast: £28.50-
£68.50 single, £57-£87 double.
Lunch available.
Evening meal 7pm (l.o.
9.30pm).
Parking for 150.
Credit: Access, Visa, Diners,
Amex.

White Hart Hotel

Newland St., Witham,
CM8 2AF
☎ (0376) 512245
*A 14th C former coaching inn
of historic interest, operating a
restaurant 7 days per week.
Function room, 2 bars.*
Bedrooms: 5 single, 5 double
& 7 twin, 1 family room.
Bathrooms: 18 private.
Bed & breakfast: from £38.50
single, from £50.50 double.
Half board: £47.65-£58 daily.
Lunch available.
Evening meal 6pm (l.o. 9pm).
Parking for 45.
Credit: Access, Visa, Amex.

WROXHAM

Norfolk
Map ref 3C1

7m NE. Norwich
Yachting centre on the
River Bure which houses
the headquarters of the
Norfolk Broads Yacht
Club. The church of St.
Mary has a famous
doorway and the manor
house nearby dates back
to 1623.

The Broads Hotel ℳ

Station Rd., Wroxham,
Norwich, NR12 8UR
☎ (0603) 782869
*A family hotel in the heart of
Broadland, 2 minutes from
shops, boat hire and fishing. An
ideal touring base for the coast
and the city of Norwich.*
Bedrooms: 7 single, 18 double
& 4 twin, 1 family room.
Bathrooms: 27 private,
1 public; 1 private shower.
Bed & breakfast: from £35
single, £45-£55 double.
Half board: from £43 daily,
from £258 weekly.
Lunch available.
Evening meal 7pm (l.o.
9.30pm).
Parking for 40.
Credit: Access, Visa, Diners,
Amex.

WYMONDHAM

Norfolk
Map ref 3B1

9m SW. Norwich
Busy market town with a charming octagonal market cross. In 1615 a great fire destroyed most of its buildings but the Green Dragon Inn, now one of the oldest in the country, survived.

Abbey Hotel M
😋😋😋
10 Church St., Wymondham,
NR18 0PH
☎ (0953) 602148
Telex 975711
Hotel in a quiet street. Noted for good value and home cooking. Central for touring Norfolk. Extensive sports and leisure facilities available at the nearby Barnham Broom Hotel, Conference and Leisure Centre.
Bedrooms: 3 single, 13 double & 9 twin, 1 family room.
Bathrooms: 26 private.
Bed & breakfast: £45-£48 single, £65-£70 double.
Half board: £57.50-£58 daily.

Lunch available.
Evening meal 7.30pm (l.o. 9.30pm).
Parking for 3.
Credit: Access, Visa, Diners, Amex.

Cobweb Cottage
Listed APPROVED
Queens St., Spooner Row,
Nr. Wymondham,
NR18 9JU
☎ (0953) 604070
Delightful old world cottage in quiet location 2.5 miles from Wymondham, 15 minutes from Norwich, central for touring Norfolk. Homely accommodation and cooking. Smoking in lounge and gardens only.
Bedrooms: 2 single, 2 double & 1 twin.
Bathrooms: 3 public.
Bed & breakfast: £15-£17 single, £30-£34 double.
Half board: £23-£26 daily.
Evening meal 7pm (l.o. 8.30pm).
Parking for 6.
Credit: Access, Visa.

Key to symbols

Information about many of the services and facilities at establishments listed in this guide is given in the form of symbols. The key to these symbols is inside the back cover flap. You may find it helpful to keep the flap open when referring to the entry listings.

Follow the Country Code

🌢 *Enjoy the countryside and respect its life and work*
🌢 *Guard against all risk of fire* 🌢 *Fasten all gates*
🌢 *Keep your dogs under close control* 🌢 *Keep to public paths across farmland* 🌢 *Use gates and stiles to cross fences, hedges and walls* 🌢 *Leave livestock, crops and machinery alone* 🌢 *Take your litter home*
🌢 *Help to keep all water clean* 🌢 *Protect wildlife, plants and trees* 🌢 *Take special care on country roads*
🌢 *Make no unnecessary noise*

IPSWICH

THE CARLTON HOTEL has 20 comfortable bedrooms (4 on ground floor) — most have private bathrooms. All have direct dial telephones, colour TV, tea and coffee making facilities. The hotel is licensed, with ample car parking and situated in the town centre. Personal attention is our speciality. We are pleased to accept Access, Visa and American Express.

Carlton Hotel, Berners Street, Ipswich, Suffolk IP1 3LN.
☎ (0473) 254955/211145

Hamilton Hotel

156 Chesterton Road, Cambridge, Cambridgeshire.
Tel: Cambridge (0223) 65664 – reservations & enquiries
Fax: (0223) 314866

Member of Cambridge Hotels & Guest House Association. AA Listed.

Hamilton Hotel is situated approximately one mile from the city centre and is close to the River Cam. There are 15 comfortable bedrooms. All rooms have tea/coffee making facilities, colour TV, telephone, most with en-suite facilities. Our tariff includes a variety of breakfasts including the full traditional English. Our licensed bar offers a wide selection of snacks and bar meals.

King's Head Hotel

Gt. Bircham, King's Lynn, Norfolk PE31 6RJ
Tel: Syderstone (048 523) 265
(On B1153)

👑👑 **APPROVED**

Country hotel and restaurant, situated close to Sandringham, King's Lynn and the coast.

Five en suite bedrooms, tea/coffee making facilities and colour TV.

Wine and Dine in the lodge restaurant, food especially prepared by the proprietor. English and Continental Cuisine. Fresh Norfolk Seafood and produce, a la carte available lunchtime and evening, traditional Sunday lunch. Bar meals. Garden. Car park.

Use a coupon

When requesting further information from advertisers in this guide, you may find it helpful to use the advertisement enquiry coupons which can be found towards the end of the guide. These should be cut out and mailed direct to the companies in which you are interested. Do remember to include your name and address.

THE CROWN IS YOUR SURE SIGN

OF WHERE TO STAY

HOTELS, GUESTHOUSES, INNS, B&Bs & FARMHOUSES

Throughout Britain, the tourist boards now inspect over 17,000 hotels, guesthouses, inns, B&Bs and farmhouses, every year, to help you find the ones that suit you best.

THE CLASSIFICATIONS: **'Listed'**, and then **ONE to FIVE CROWN,** tell you the range of facilities and services you can expect. The more Crowns, the wider the range.

THE GRADES: **APPROVED, COMMENDED and HIGHLY COMMENDED,** where they appear, indicate the quality standard provided. If no grade is shown, you can still expect a high standard of cleanliness.

Every classified place to stay has a Fire Certificate, where this is required under the Fire Precautions Act, and all carry Public Liability Insurance.

'Listed': Clean and comfortable accommodation, but the range of facilities and services may be limited.

ONE CROWN: Accommodation with additional facilities, including washbasins in all bedrooms, a lounge and use of a phone.

TWO CROWN: A wider range of facilities and services, including morning tea and calls, bedside lights, colour TV in lounge or bedrooms, assistance with luggage.

THREE CROWN: At least one-third of the bedrooms with ensuite WC and bath or shower, plus easy chair, full length mirror. Shoe cleaning facilities and hairdryers available. Hot evening meals available.

FOUR CROWN: At least three-quarters of the bedrooms with ensuite WC and bath/shower plus colour TV, radio and phone, 24-hour access and lounge service until midnight. Last orders for meals 8.30 pm or later.

FIVE CROWN: All bedrooms having WC, bath and shower ensuite, plus a wide range of facilities and services, including room service, all-night lounge service and laundry service. Restaurant open for breakfast, lunch and dinner.

Every Crown classified place to stay is likely to provide some of the facilities and services of a higher classification. More information available from any Tourist Information Centre.

We've checked them out before you check in!

WHY IS THIS ENGLAND'S *most popular holiday region? Probably because there's something for everyone. Whether you're looking for sun, sea, sand and surf or great walking and touring country or are on the heritage and history trail, the West Country will not disappoint. It's unique in having two holiday coastlines: 650 miles, peppered with quaint fishing harbours,*

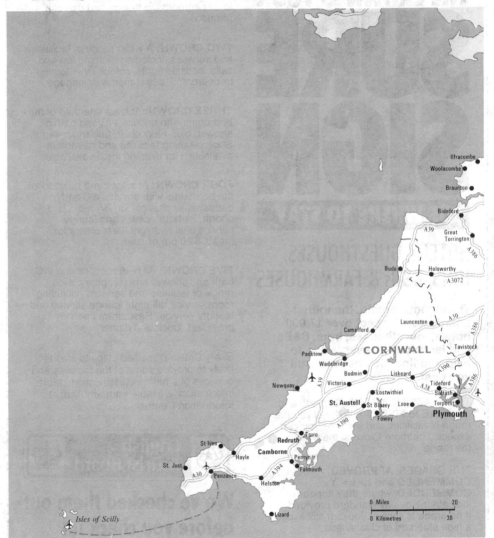

PLEASE REFER TO THE COLOUR MAPS AT THE BACK OF THIS GUIDE FOR

picturesque villages and sophisticated resorts. There's spectacular scenery, from soaring cliffs to plunging gorges, from colourful caves to the emptiness of the moors and hills. And there's plenty of history to be savoured, from the Roman heritage of Bath to the ancient sites of early man across Wiltshire.

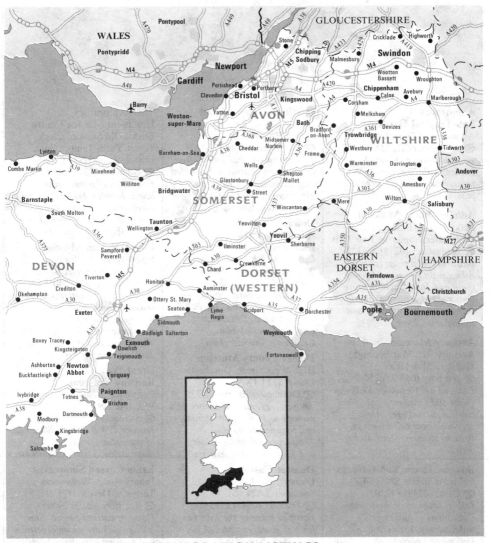

ALL PLACES WITH ACCOMMODATION LISTINGS.

WHERE TO GO, WHAT TO SEE

The Exploratory Hands-on Science Centre

Abbotsbury Sub-Tropical Gardens
Abbotsbury, Dorset
☎ Abbotsbury (0305) 871387
English Heritage Grade I garden, with 20 acres of exotic trees, shrubs and herbaceous plants.

Admiral Blake Museum
Blake House, Blake Street, Bridgwater, Somerset TA6 3NB
☎ Bridgwater (0278) 456127
Battle of Sedgemoor relics, Admiral Blake room, shipping room and John Chubb Picture Gallery. Video films of Battle of Sedgemoor, River Parrot and sailing ship "Irene".

Avebury Museum
Avebury, Nr. Marlborough, Wiltshire SN8 1RF
☎ Avebury (067 23) 250
Founded by Alexander Keiller in 1930s and containing one of the most important prehistoric archaeological collections in Britain. Remains from Avebury area.

Bowood House and Gardens
Calne, Wiltshire SN11 0LZ
☎ Calne (0249) 812102
18th C house by Robert Adam. Collections of paintings, watercolours, Victoriana, Indiana and porcelain. Landscaped park with lake, terraces, waterfall, grottos.

Dartington Crystal Ltd
Linden Close, Torrington, Devon EX38 7AN
☎ Torrington (0805) 23797
Manufacture of hand-made lead crystal table glassware by skilled craftsmen. Glass Centre and glassware exhibition. Glass blowers hand-blowing glassware.

Dobwalls Family Adventure Park
Dobwalls, Nr. Liskeard, Cornwall PL14 6HD
☎ Liskeard (0579) 20325
Forest railroad: 2 miles of scenically dramatic miniature railway based on the American railroad scene. Edwardian countryside exhibition. Children's Adventureland.

Dorset County Museum
High West Street, Dorchester, Dorset DT1 1XA
☎ Dorchester (0305) 262735
Archaeology, natural history and geology of Dorset. Local history and bygones displays. Temporary exhibition gallery and Thomas Hardy material.

Dunster Castle
Dunster, Nr. Minehead, Somerset TA24 6SL
☎ Dunster (0643) 821314
Fortified home of the Luttrells for 600 years, remodelled 100 years ago. Fine 17th C staircase and plaster ceilings. Terrace garden with rare shrubs.

The Exploratory Hands-on Science Centre
Bristol Old Station, Clock Tower Yard, Temple Gate, Bristol, Avon BS1 6QU
☎ Bristol (0272) 252008
Exhibition of lights, lenses, lasers, bubbles, bridges, illusions, gyroscopes and much more, all housed in Brunel's original engine shed and drawing office.

Fleet Air Arm Museum
Royal Naval Air Station, Yeovilton, Somerset BA22 8HT
☎ Ilchester (0935) 840565
Over 50 historic aircraft, displays and equipment, including Concorde prototype. Falklands campaign, Kamikaze, RNAS 1914 – 1918, The Wrens and Harrier Jump Jet Story exhibitions.

Great Western Railway Museum
Faringdon Road, Swindon, Wiltshire SN1 5BJ
☎ Swindon (0793) 526161
Historic GWR locos, wide range of nameplates, models, illustrations, posters and tickets.

Kents Cavern Showcaves
Ilsham Road, Wellswood, Torquay, Devon TQ1 2JF
☎ Torquay (0803) 294059
Home of earliest people. Story-telling tours are an unforgettable and exciting experience in an extensive and beautiful underground world.

Killerton House
Broadclyst, Nr. Exeter, Devon
EX5 3LE
☎ Exeter (0392) 881345
*18th C house built for the
Acland family, now houses
collection of costumes shown in
various room settings. 15 acres
of hillside garden with rare trees
and shrubs.*

Land's End
Sennen, Penzance, Cornwall
TR19 7AA
☎ Sennen (0736) 871501
*Spectacular cliffs with
breathtaking vistas. Superb,
multi-sensory Last Labyrinth
Show, hotel, art gallery,
exhibitions and much more.*

Longleat House
Warminster, Wiltshire
BA12 7NN
☎ Warminster (0985) 844551
*Great Elizabethan house with
lived-in atmosphere. Important
libraries and Italian ceilings.
Safari Park.*

Lyme Regis Experience
Marine Parade, Lyme Regis,
Dorset DT7 3JH
☎ Lyme Regis (0297) 443039
*Historical tableaux and multiple
projector audio-visual depicting
the history of Lyme from the
salt-boiling monks of 774 AD to
the present day.*

Morwellham Quay
and Open Air Museum
Morwellham Quay, Nr.
Tavistock, Devon PL19 8JL
☎ Tavistock (0822) 832766
*Riverside tramway takes visitors
underground into a copper mine.
Blacksmith's and cooper's
workshop, 19th C cottage, water
wheels, shire horse carriage
rides.*

Parnham House
Beaminster, Dorset DT8 3NA
☎ Beaminster (0308) 862204
*Tudor manor house with
additions and embellishments by*

Parnham House — home of The School for Craftsmen in Wood

*John Nash in 1810. Home of
John Makepeace and his famous
furniture-making workshops.
14 acres of gardens.*

Plymouth Dome
The Hoe, Plymouth, Devon
PL1 2NZ
☎ Plymouth (0752) 668000
*New purpose-built visitor
interpretation centre showing the
history of Plymouth and its
people from Stone Age
beginning to satellite technology.*

Priston Mill
Priston Mill Farm, Priston,
Nr. Bath, Avon BA2 9EQ
☎ Bath (0225) 423894
*Domesday water mill, tithe barn,
nature trail, farm animals, cow
milking. Play areas, trailer
rides. Machinery driven by 21ft
water wheel.*

Roman Baths Museum
Pump Room, Abbey Church
Yard, Bath, Avon BA1 1LZ
☎ Bath (0225) 461111
*Roman baths and temple
precinct, hot springs and Roman
monuments. Jewellery, coins,
votive offerings from the sacred
spring.*

Salisbury Cathedral
The Close, Salisbury, Wiltshire
SP1 2FF
☎ Salisbury (0722) 28726
Gothic cathedral consecrated in

*1258. Famous spire rising to
record height of 404 feet was
added in 14th C. Ancient clock
mechanism dates from 1386.
Magna Carta.*

The Timewalk
Brewers Quay, Hope Square,
Weymouth, Dorset DT4 8TR
☎ Weymouth (0305) 777622
*Timewalk through history of
Weymouth from the Black
Death to World War II.*

Tintagel Castle
Tintagel, Cornwall PL34 0AA
☎ Camelford (0840) 770328
*Medieval ruined castle on wild,
windswept coast. Famous for
associations with Arthurian
legend. Built largely in 13th C
by Richard, Earl of Cornwall,
and used as a prison in 14th C.*

Trelissick Garden
Feock, Nr. Truro, Cornwall
TR3 6QL
☎ Truro (0872) 862090
*Large garden, lovely at all
seasons. Superb views of* ▶

▶ *estuary and Falmouth harbour. Woodland walks beside the River Fal.*

The Tropical Bird Gardens

Rode, Nr. Bath, Somerset
BA3 6QW
☎ Frome (0373) 830326
Hundreds of exotic birds in lovely natural surroundings. 17 acres of woodland, gardens and lakes with children's play areas, pets' corner, steam railway, clematis collection.

Tropicana Pleasure Beach

Marine Parade, Weston-super-Mare, Avon BS23 1BE
☎ Weston-super-Mare (0934) 626581
Heated surf pool with water chutes. Play equipment for children of all ages. Toddlers' pool. Fountains.

Wookey Hole Caves and Mill

Wookey Hole, Wells, Somerset
BA5 1BB
☎ Wells (0749) 672243
The most spectacular caves in Britain. Working Victorian paper mill. "Fairground by Night" exhibition. Edwardian Penny Pier Arcade. Archaeological museum. Mirror maze.

MAKE A DATE FOR...

Golf — Benson and Hedges International Open

St. Mellion Golf and Country Club, St. Mellion, Saltash, Cornwall
6 — 10 May

Badminton Horse Trials

Badminton, Avon
7 — 10 May

Helston Furry Dance

Various venues, Helston, Cornwall
8 May

Devon County Show

Westpoint Showground, Clyst St. Mary, Nr. Exeter, Devon
21 — 23 May

Bath International Festival

Various venues, Bath, Avon
22 May — 7 June

Royal Bath and West Show

Royal Bath and West Showground, Shepton Mallet, Somerset
27 — 30 May

Tolpuddle Martyrs Rally

Village Centre, Tolpuddle, Dorset
19 July

Sidmouth International Festival of Folk Art

Various venues, Sidmouth, Devon
31 July — 7 August

Salisbury Festival

Various venues, Salisbury, Wiltshire
5 — 19 September

Bridgwater Guy Fawkes Carnival

Town Centre, Bridgwater, Somerset
5 November

FIND OUT MORE

Further information about holidays and attractions in the West Country is available from:
West Country Tourist Board
60 St David's Hill, Exeter
EX4 4SY
☎ (0392) 76351

These publications are available free from the West Country Tourist Board:

England's West Country — Holidays '92

Bed and Breakfast Touring Map for the West Country '92

West Country Holiday Homes '92

Activity and Leisure Holidays '92

Also available is:

Where to Stay in the West Country 1992 £2.50

Bridgwater Guy Fawkes Carnival — 5 November

Places to stay

ACCOMMODATION ENTRIES *in this regional section are listed in alphabetical order of place name, and then in alphabetical order of establishment.*

THE MAP REFERENCES *refer to the colour maps towards the end of the guide. The first figure is the map number; the letter and figure which follow indicate the grid reference on the map.*

THE SYMBOLS *at the end of each accommodation entry give information about services and facilities. A 'key' to these symbols is inside the back cover flap, which can be kept open for easy reference.*

AMESBURY

Wiltshire
Map ref 2B2

7m N. Salisbury
Standing on the banks of the River Avon, this is the nearest town to Stonehenge on Salisbury Plain. The area is rich in prehistoric sites.
Tourist Information Centre ☎ *(0980) 622833*

George Hotel
High St., Amesbury,
SP4 7ET
☎ (0980) 622108
A traditional town centre hotel offering food and accommodation suiting commercial and tourist clientele. A stone's throw from Stonehenge.
Bedrooms: 14 single, 9 double & 5 twin, 3 family rooms.
Bathrooms: 10 private, 6 public; 1 private shower.
Bed & breakfast: £25-£35 single, £40-£55 double.
Half board: £30-£35 daily.
Lunch available.
Evening meal 7pm (l.o. 9.30pm).
Parking for 84.
Credit: Access, Visa, Diners, Amex.
🛏 ® ♿ Ⅵ 🍴 🧺 🔖 🏥

ASHBURTON

Devon
Map ref 1C2

Formerly a thriving wool centre and important as one of Dartmoor's 4 stannary towns. Today's busy market town retains many period buildings and an atmosphere of medieval times. Ancient tradition is maintained in the annual ale-tasting and bread-weighing ceremony. Good centre for exploring Dartmoor or the south Devon coast.

The Old Coffee House
Listed
27-29 West St., Ashburton,
TQ13 7DT
☎ (0364) 52539
Charming 16th C listed property on fringe of Dartmoor. Licensed restaurant with good guest facilities. Cosy lounge. A non-smoking establishment.
Bedrooms: 1 double & 2 twin.
Bathrooms: 2 public.
Bed & breakfast: £18 single, £28 double.
Half board: £25 daily.
Lunch available.
Evening meal 5.50pm (l.o. 7pm).
🛏 ♿ Ⅵ ✂ 🔖 📺 🧺
🍴 ✕ 🔖 🏥

BADMINTON

Avon
Map ref 2B2

5m E. Chipping Sodbury
Small village close to Badminton House, a 17th to 18th C Palladian mansion which has been the seat of the Dukes of Beaufort for centuries. The 3-day Badminton Horse Trials are held in the Great Park every May.

Bodkin House Hotel
🏵 🏵 🏵 COMMENDED
A46, Bath to Stroud Rd.,
Badminton, GL9 1AF
☎ Didmarton (045 423) 310 & 422
Beautifully restored 17th C Cotswold coaching inn, providing large, well-appointed en-suite bedrooms. Renowned for its good food.
Bedrooms: 5 double & 2 twin, 1 family room.
Bathrooms: 8 private.
Bed & breakfast: £35-£45 single, £50-£60 double.
Lunch available.
Evening meal 7pm (l.o. 10pm).
Parking for 35.
Credit: Access, Visa, Diners, Amex.
🛏 🔖 ♿ ® 🍴 ♿ Ⅵ 🧺
🖥 🍴 ✿ 🔖 🔖 🏥

Petty France Hotel ♨
🏵 🏵 🏵 COMMENDED
A46, Dunkirk, Badminton,
GL9 1AF
☎ Didmarton (045 423) 361 & Fax (045 423) 768
℗ Consort

Informal country house atmosphere on the edge of the Cotswolds, good walking, many sights to visit, convenient Bath, Bristol.
Bedrooms: 2 single, 12 double & 5 twin, 1 family room.
Bathrooms: 20 private.
Bed & breakfast: £59-£80 single, £75-£95 double.
Half board: £75-£125 daily.
Lunch available.
Evening meal 7.30pm (l.o. 10pm).
Parking for 51.
Credit: Access, Visa, Diners, Amex.
🛏 🧺 🔖 ♿ 🔖 🍴 ♿ Ⅵ
🖥 🧺 🍴 🔖 🔖 🏥
🏥 📺

BAMPTON

Devon
Map ref 1D1

6m N. Tiverton
Riverside market town, famous for its fair each October.

Bridge House Hotel
24 Luke St., Bampton,
Tiverton, EX16 9NF
☎ (0398) 331298
Approximately 250 years old, built of local stone. Specialising in sporting breaks. Fly fishing, riding and clay pigeon shooting. Weekend and midweek breaks.
Bedrooms: 2 single, 2 double & 1 twin, 2 family rooms.
Bathrooms: 4 private, 1 public.
Bed & breakfast: £35-£39 double.
Half board: £27-£35 daily, from £203 weekly.
Continued ▶

Individual proprietors have supplied all details of accommodation. Although we do check for accuracy, we advise you to confirm prices and other information at the time of booking.

BAMPTON

Continued

Lunch available.
Evening meal 6pm (l.o. 10pm).
Credit: Access, Visa.

Courtyard Hotel & Restaurant M
19, Fore St., Bampton, Tiverton, EX16 9ND
☎ (0398) 331536
Comfortable small hotel and restaurant on the edge of Exmoor. Within easy reach of both coasts.
Bedrooms: 1 single, 3 double & 1 twin, 1 family room.
Bathrooms: 3 private, 1 public.
Bed & breakfast: from £15 single, £30-£35 double.
Half board: £21-£30 daily.
Lunch available.
Evening meal 7pm (l.o. 9.30pm).
Parking for 40.
Credit: Access, Visa, Diners, Amex.

The Swan
Bampton, Tiverton, EX16 9NG
☎ (0398) 31257
Family-run 15th C hotel with friendly atmosphere and good food and wine. On the edge of Exmoor.
Bedrooms: 1 single, 3 double & 1 twin, 1 family room.
Bathrooms: 2 private, 1 public.
Bed & breakfast: £14.50-£18.50 single, £29-£37 double.
Half board: £23.50-£27.50 daily, £154.50-£182.50 weekly.
Lunch available.
Evening meal 6pm (l.o. 10pm).
Credit: Access, Visa, Diners.

The symbols are explained on the flap inside the back cover.

Map references apply to the colour maps towards the end of this guide.

BARNSTAPLE

Devon
Map ref 1C1

At the head of the Taw Estuary, once a ship-building and textile town, now an important agricultural centre with attractive areas of period building, a modern civic centre and riverside leisure centre. Attractions include Queen Anne's Walk, a charming colonnaded arcade, Pannier Market and Cattle Market, open on Fridays, and the Athenaeum which houses a library.
Tourist Information Centre ☎ (0271) 47177

Downrew House Hotel M
COMMENDED
Bishop's Tawton, Barnstaple, EX32 0DY
☎ Barnstaple (0271) 42497 & 46673 & Fax (0271) 23947
Queen Anne country house in glorious setting. Gourmet cuisine, own golf, heated pool, tennis, croquet. Ideal for coast and countryside.
Bedrooms: 4 double & 6 twin, 2 family rooms.
Bathrooms: 12 private, 1 public.
Half board: £68.50-£84 daily.
Lunch available.
Evening meal 7pm (l.o. 9.30pm).
Parking for 15.
Credit: Access, Visa.

Home Park Farm Accommodation
COMMENDED
Lower Blakewell, Muddiford, Barnstaple, EX31 4ET
☎ Barnstaple (0271) 42955
70-acre sheep farm. Set in Devonshire countryside, very quiet and peaceful, with outdoor children's play area. Take the A39 Lynton road out of Barnstaple, fork left on to the B3230, turn off main road towards fisheries, continue to end.
Bedrooms: 3 family rooms.
Bathrooms: 3 private.
Bed & breakfast: £15-£20 single, £25-£30 double.
Half board: £18.50-£21.50 daily, £120-£130 weekly.

Evening meal 6pm (l.o. 6pm).
Parking for 4.
Open June-August.

Yeo Dale Hotel M
APPROVED
Pilton Bridge, Barnstaple, EX31 1PG
☎ (0271) 42954
Family-run hotel located minutes from town centre and overlooking park. Ideal touring base for North Devon.
Bedrooms: 3 single, 1 double & 3 twin, 3 family rooms.
Bathrooms: 5 private, 3 public.
Bed & breakfast: £15-£26 single, £31-£46 double.
Half board: £22.50-£33.50 daily, £157.50-£234.50 weekly.
Evening meal 7pm (l.o. 7.30pm).
Credit: Access, Visa, Amex.

BATH

Avon
Map ref 2B2

Georgian spa city encircled by hills beside the River Avon. Important Roman site with impressive reconstructed baths, uncovered in 19th C. Bath Abbey built over Norman abbey on site of monastery where first king of England was crowned (AD 973). Fine architecture in mellow local stone. Pump Room, art gallery and other museums.
Tourist Information Centre ☎ (0225) 462831

Arden Hotel M
COMMENDED
73 Great Pulteney St., Bath, BA2 4DL
☎ (0225) 466601 & Fax (0225) 465548
Small personal family-run hotel, situated in Bath's famous Great Pulteney Street. Elegantly restored and refurbished in 1990 to offer the quietness and restfulness of a Georgian town house.
Bedrooms: 1 single, 3 double & 3 twin, 3 family rooms.
Bathrooms: 10 private.
Bed & breakfast: £45-£70 single, £60-£80 double.
Lunch available.

Evening meal 7.30pm (l.o. 10.30pm).
Parking for 3.
Credit: Access, Visa.

Arosa
Listed
124 Lower Oldfield Pk., Bath, BA2 3HS
☎ (0225) 425778
Family-owned and run house within easy walking distance of Bath city centre.
Bedrooms: 1 family room.
Bathrooms: 1 public.
Bed & breakfast: £14-£18 single, £28-£32 double.
Parking for 4.

Ashley Villa Hotel M
26 Newbridge Rd., Bath, BA1 3JZ
☎ (0225) 421683
Comfortably furnished licensed hotel with relaxing informal atmosphere, close to city centre. All rooms en-suite. Swimming pool.
Bedrooms: 2 single, 7 double & 2 twin, 3 family rooms.
Bathrooms: 14 private.
Bed & breakfast: £35-£39 single, £49-£59 double.
Half board: £43-£47 daily.
Evening meal 6pm (l.o. 9pm).
Parking for 10.
Credit: Access, Visa.

Astor House
14 Oldfield Rd., Bath, BA2 3ND
☎ (0225) 429134
Lovely Victorian house with comfortable, spacious rooms and large secluded garden. Peaceful, elegant atmosphere.
Bedrooms: 3 double & 4 twin.
Bathrooms: 2 public.
Bed & breakfast: £28-£32 double.
Parking for 4.
Open April-October.

Audley House
HIGHLY COMMENDED
Park Gdns., Bath, BA1 2XP
☎ (0225) 333110 & Fax (0225) 482879
Fine listed residence in a secluded acre of lawns and mature trees, close to the city centre. Non-smokers only please.
Bedrooms: 2 double & 1 twin.
Bathrooms: 3 private.

Bed & breakfast: max. £40 single, max. £40 double.
Half board: £46-£56 daily.
Evening meal 7.30pm (l.o. 8pm).
Parking for 7.
Credit: Access, Visa.

Avon Hotel M
APPROVED

9 Bathwick St., Bath, BA2 6NX
☎ (0225) 446176/422226 & Fax (0225) 447452
Beautifully restored and refurbished early Georgian hotel (1750), half a mile level walk to Roman Baths, shops, etc. Large floodlit car park.
Bedrooms: 2 single, 4 double & 3 twin, 3 family rooms.
Bathrooms: 12 private.
Bed & breakfast: £29.50-£35 single, £29.75-£58 double.
Parking for 20.
Credit: Access, Visa, Diners, Amex.

Bailbrook Lodge Hotel M
COMMENDED

35/37 London Road West, Bath, BA1 7HZ
☎ (0225) 859090
Georgian house with splendid views overlooking the Avon Valley, near M4 and on the outskirts of Bath.
Bedrooms: 8 double & 5 twin.
Bathrooms: 13 private.
Bed & breakfast: £30-£40 single, £45-£60 double.
Half board: £35-£52.50 daily.
Lunch available.
Evening meal 7pm (l.o. 9pm).
Parking for 20.
Credit: Access, Visa, Diners, Amex.

Bath Lodge Hotel & Restaurant
COMMENDED

Norton St. Philip, Bath, BA3 6NH
☎ Limpley Stoke (0225) 723737 & Fax (0225) 723193
Small castle with four-poster beds and private balconies, overlooking natural waterfalled stream and gardens with adjacent forestry beyond. On the A36 south of Bath.
Bedrooms: 3 double, 1 family room.
Bathrooms: 4 private.
Bed & breakfast: £55-£80 single, £80-£100 double.
Lunch available.

Evening meal 7pm (l.o. 10pm).
Parking for 20.
Credit: Access, Visa, Amex.

The Bath Tasburgh M
COMMENDED

Warminster Rd., Bathampton, Bath, BA2 6SH
☎ (0225) 425096/463842
Spacious, elegant Victorian house/hotel with beautiful views and canal frontage, set in lovely grounds with easy access to tourist attractions. En-suite rooms. Parking.
Bedrooms: 1 single, 5 double & 3 twin, 4 family rooms.
Bathrooms: 10 private, 1 public.
Bed & breakfast: £31-£42 single, £43-£58 double.
Parking for 15.
Credit: Access, Visa, Diners, Amex.

Berni Royal Hotel M

Manvers St., Bath, BA1 1JP
☎ (0225) 463134
Georgian in appearance, an attractive Victorian building in a central position, close to all services. Royal prefix given as a reminder of Queen Victoria's visit to Bath.
Bedrooms: 6 single, 13 double & 7 twin, 4 family rooms.
Bathrooms: 30 private.
Bed & breakfast: £56-£66 single, £73 double.
Lunch available.
Evening meal 6pm (l.o. 10.30pm).
Credit: Access, Visa, Diners, Amex.

Bloomfield House M
COMMENDED

146 Bloomfield Rd., Bath, BA2 2AS
☎ (0225) 420105
Fine Regency country house with superb views over the city, offering antique furniture, silk curtains and a warm welcome.
Bedrooms: 1 single, 3 double & 1 twin.
Bathrooms: 5 private.
Bed & breakfast: £20-£35 single, £35-£55 double.
Parking for 9.
Credit: Access, Visa.

Brompton House Hotel M
COMMENDED

St. John's Rd., Bathwick, Bath, BA2 6PT
☎ (0225) 420972/448423
Elegant Georgian rectory in beautiful secluded gardens. 5 minutes' level walk to city centre. Car park.
Bedrooms: 2 single, 7 double & 2 twin, 1 family room.
Bathrooms: 12 private.
Bed & breakfast: £27-£37 single, £47-£57 double.
Parking for 12.
Credit: Access, Visa.

⚑ Display advertisement appears on page 447.

Cedar Lodge

13 Lambridge, London Rd., Bath, BA1 6BJ
☎ (0225) 423468
Conveniently situated for the city centre or countryside, this beautiful detached Georgian house offers period elegance, combined with home comfort. Individually designed bedrooms.
Bedrooms: 2 double, 1 family room.
Bathrooms: 1 public; 1 private shower.
Bed & breakfast: £32-£45 double.
Evening meal 7.30pm (l.o. 11am).
Parking for 7.

Circus Mansions

36 Brock St., Bath, BA1 2LJ
☎ (0225) 336462
Georgian house with original entrance hall and staircase, 2 double bedrooms with private bath/WC. Central heating in rooms. Located in the Circus.
Bedrooms: 1 single, 2 double & 1 twin, 1 family room.
Bathrooms: 5 private.
Bed & breakfast: max. £25 single, max. £44 double.

Combe Grove Manor Hotel and Country Club M
HIGHLY COMMENDED

Monkton Combe, Bath, BA2 7HS
☎ Bath (0225) 834644 & Fax (0225) 834961

Beautiful manor house recently refurbished to the highest standards. 2 miles from centre of Bath with excellent sports facilities.
Bedrooms: 9 single, 19 double & 11 twin, 2 family rooms.
Bathrooms: 41 private.
Bed & breakfast: £80-£110 single, £95-£130 double.
Lunch available.
Evening meal 7pm (l.o. 9.30pm).
Parking for 200.
Credit: Access, Visa, Diners, Amex.

Cranleigh M

159 Newbridge Hill, Bath, BA1 3PX
☎ (0225) 310197
B&B in non-smoking, spacious Victorian house. Comfortable, thoughtfully equipped rooms, some en-suite, all with colour TV. Generous breakfasts. Parking.
Bedrooms: 1 single, 2 double & 2 twin, 3 family rooms.
Bathrooms: 3 private, 2 public.
Bed & breakfast: £22-£35 single, £36-£50 double.
Parking for 5.

Dorian House

One Upper Oldfield Park, Bath, BA2 3JX
☎ (0225) 426336
Guesthouse in exclusive district, just 10 minutes' stroll to city. All rooms en-suite, telephone, hair-dryer, etc.
Bedrooms: 1 single, 2 double & 2 twin, 2 family rooms.
Bathrooms: 7 private.
Bed & breakfast: £33-£39 single, £44-£62 double.
Parking for 9.
Credit: Access, Visa, Diners, Amex.

Dorset Villa Guest House M
COMMENDED

14 Newbridge Rd., Bath, BA1 3JX
☎ (0225) 425975
Small friendly relaxed establishment, recently refurbished, 1 mile from city centre and with own car park.
Bedrooms: 5 double & 1 twin, 1 family room.
Bathrooms: 5 private, 1 public.

Continued ▶

BATH
Continued

Bed & breakfast: £26-£33 single, £36-£43 double. **Half board:** £28-£31.50 daily, £119-£178 weekly. Evening meal 7pm (l.o. 9pm). Parking for 6. Credit: Access, Visa.

Dukes Hotel M
👑👑👑 COMMENDED
Great Pulteney St., Bath, BA2 4DN
☎ (0225) 463512
Telex 449227
Elegantly refurbished Georgian town house hotel. Centrally located. Full restaurant and bar. Personal service and welcome from resident proprietor and staff.
Bedrooms: 4 single, 10 double & 3 twin, 4 family rooms. Bathrooms: 21 private.
Bed & breakfast: £50-£65 single, £60-£95 double. Lunch available. Evening meal 6.45pm (l.o. 8.30pm).
Credit: Access, Visa, Amex.

Edgar Hotel
👑👑 APPROVED
64 Gt. Pulteney St., Bath, BA2 4DN
☎ (0225) 420619
Small private hotel, proprietor-run, in Great Pulteney Street which leads to centre of Bath. Roman remains approximately 600 yards away.
Bedrooms: 2 single, 9 double & 4 twin, 1 family room. Bathrooms: 16 private.
Bed & breakfast: £25-£30 single, £35-£50 double.

🔄 Display advertisement appears on page 448.

Forres Guest House
👑👑
172 Newbridge Rd., Lower Weston, Bath, BA1 3LE
☎ (0225) 427698
Edwardian family guesthouse with friendly, informative hosts, who are ex-teachers and love Bath. River Avon and Cotswold Way close by. Traditional and vegetarian breakfasts. Colour TV in all rooms.
Bedrooms: 2 double & 2 twin, 1 family room.

Bathrooms: 5 private, 1 public.
Bed & breakfast: £28-£36 double. Parking for 5. Open April-October.

Gainsborough Hotel M
👑👑👑
Weston La., Bath, BA1 4AB
☎ (0225) 311380
Small country house hotel in quiet, secluded garden near Victoria Park. The abbey and Roman Baths are 1.25 miles away.
Bedrooms: 2 single, 8 double & 4 twin, 2 family rooms. Bathrooms: 16 private.
Bed & breakfast: £35-£40 single, £55-£70 double. Evening meal 7pm (l.o. 8.30pm). Parking for 18.
Credit: Access, Visa, Amex.

Haute Combe
👑👑👑
176 Newbridge Rd., Bath, BA1 3LE
☎ (0225) 420061
Sunny, south-facing 19th C property, close to park-and-ride scheme for city attractions yet away from the crowds.
Bedrooms: 1 single, 5 double, 2 family rooms. Bathrooms: 5 private, 1 public; 1 private shower.
Bed & breakfast: £18-£28 single, £28-£44 double. **Half board:** £28-£38 daily. Evening meal 8pm (l.o. 6pm). Parking for 8.
Credit: Access, Visa, Amex.

Highways House
👑👑
143 Wells Rd., Bath, BA2 3AL
☎ (0225) 421238
Elegant Victorian family home with resident proprietors. 10 minutes' walk to Bath city centre. Full English breakfast served.
Bedrooms: 1 single, 3 double & 3 twin. Bathrooms: 6 private, 1 public.
Bed & breakfast: £33-£38 single, £48-£56 double. Parking for 8.

Hilton National
👑👑👑👑 COMMENDED
Walcot St., Bath, BA1 5BJ
☎ (0225) 463411
Telex 449519
CR Hilton
Modern hotel overlooking the River Avon and Pulteney Bridge, close to the abbey and the Roman Baths. Central location within walking distance of the sights of the city.
Bedrooms: 28 single, 63 double & 53 twin, 6 family rooms. Bathrooms: 150 private.
Bed & breakfast: £58-£76 single, £106-£116 double. **Half board:** £70-£88 daily. Lunch available. Evening meal 7pm (l.o. 9.30pm). Parking for 15.
Credit: Access, Visa, Diners, Amex.

Holly Lodge
👑👑 HIGHLY COMMENDED
8 Upper Oldfield Pk., Bath, BA2 3JZ
☎ (0225) 424042/339187 & Fax (0225) 481138
Elegant Victorian house set in its own grounds, enjoying magnificent views of the city.
Bedrooms: 1 single, 3 double & 2 twin. Bathrooms: 6 private.
Bed & breakfast: £40-£50 single, £60-£65 double. Parking for 8.
Credit: Access, Visa, Diners.

Jay Court
122 Walcot St., Bath, BA1 5BG
☎ (0225) 448838
Hotel apartments in central Bath, attractively furnished, serviced daily, cleaned, beds made, washing-up undertaken. Entrance hall, 2 double bedrooms, living/dining room, bathroom and kitchen. Prices quoted are per apartment, and do not include breakfast/evening meal. Telephone for colour brochure.
Bedrooms: 3 double & 3 twin. Bathrooms: 6 private.
Apartments (sleep 4): from £75 daily, from £355 weekly, per apartment.
Credit: Access, Visa, Amex.

Kennard Hotel M
👑👑👑 COMMENDED
11 Henrietta St., Bath, BA2 6LL
☎ (0225) 310472 & (0225) 330159
Converted Georgian house in quiet street. A few minutes' level walk to city centre, abbey, Roman Baths, Pump Rooms and Henrietta Park.
Bedrooms: 2 single, 6 double & 3 twin, 2 family rooms. Bathrooms: 10 private, 2 public.
Bed & breakfast: £25-£35 single, £38-£58 double.
Credit: Access, Visa, Amex.

Laura Place Hotel M
👑👑 COMMENDED
3 Laura Pl., Great Pulteney St., Bath, BA2 4BH
☎ (0225) 463815
18th C town house, centrally located in Georgian square. 2 minutes from Roman Baths, Pump Rooms and abbey.
Bedrooms: 1 single, 4 double & 3 twin, 1 family room. Bathrooms: 7 private, 1 public.
Bed & breakfast: £25-£50 single, £45-£80 double. Parking for 10. Open March-December.
Credit: Access, Visa, Amex.

Leighton House M
👑👑👑 COMMENDED
139 Wells Rd., Bath, BA2 3AL
☎ (0225) 314769
An elegant and spacious Victorian guesthouse set in gardens with own car park. 10 minutes' walk from city centre. Evening meals available by arrangement.
Bedrooms: 3 double & 2 twin, 2 family rooms. Bathrooms: 7 private.
Bed & breakfast: £42-£46 single, £52-£56 double. **Half board:** £41-£61 daily, £273-£287 weekly. Evening meal 7pm (l.o. 5pm). Parking for 7.
Credit: Access, Visa.

Limpley Stoke Hotel ⋒
⚜⚜⚜ APPROVED

Lower Limpley Stoke, Bath,
BA3 6HZ
☎ (0225) 723333 & Fax
(0225) 722406
ℂℝ Consort
*Delightfully situated in the
noted valley of the River Avon.
Bordered by the counties of
Somerset, Wiltshire and Avon.
4 miles south of Bath on
A36/B3108.*
Bedrooms: 12 double &
36 twin, 7 family rooms.
Bathrooms: 55 private.
Bed & breakfast: £60-£67.50
single, £70-£80 double.
Half board: £49-£55 daily,
£315-£355 weekly.
Evening meal 7pm (l.o.
8.45pm).
Parking for 60.
Credit: Access, Visa, Diners,
Amex.

The Manor House
⚜⚜ COMMENDED

Mill La., Monkton Combe,
Bath, BA2 7HD
☎ Bath (0225) 723128 -
*Restful, rambling 16th century
manor in rural valley 2 miles
from Bath. Area of
Outstanding Natural Beauty
beside a wooded Site of Special
Scientific Interest. Inglenook
fires, Victorian conservatory,
breakfasts served until noon.*
Bedrooms: 1 double & 1 twin,
1 family room.
Bathrooms: 1 private,
1 public.
Bed & breakfast: £20 single,
£36-£45 double.
Parking for 6.

Millers Hotel ⋒
⚜⚜

69 Great Pulteney St., Bath,
BA2 4DL
☎ (0225) 465798
*Centrally situated in Bath and
close to all attractions and
amenities. Some bedrooms
have colour TV. Some
unrestricted parking.*
Bedrooms: 4 single, 3 double
& 4 twin, 3 family rooms.
Bathrooms: 5 private,
3 public.
Bed & breakfast: £25-£38
single, £38-£52 double.
Lunch available.

Newbridge House
⚜⚜ HIGHLY COMMENDED

35 Kelston Rd., Bath,
BA1 3QH
☎ (0225) 446676
*Palatial country house set in its
own grounds overlooking the
Avon Valley and the new Bath
Marina and restaurant.*
Bedrooms: 2 single, 10 double
& 1 twin.
Bathrooms: 13 private.
Bed & breakfast: £38 single,
£58 double.
Parking for 15.
Credit: Access, Visa, Diners,
Amex.

North Parade Hotel ⋒
⚜⚜ APPROVED

10 North Parade, Bath,
BA2 4AL
☎ (0225) 463384 & Fax
(0225) 442322
*Georgian building in the city
centre overlooking Parade
Gardens. Run by resident
family to ensure personal
service.*
Bedrooms: 9 single, 5 double
& 4 twin.
Bathrooms: 12 private,
2 public.
Bed & breakfast: £25.75-£43
single, £55.70-£86 double.
Half board: £34.95-£52.20
daily.
Evening meal 6.30pm (l.o.
9pm).
Credit: Access, Visa, Diners,
Amex.

Oakleigh House ⋒
⚜⚜ COMMENDED

19 Upper Oldfield Pk., Bath,
BA2 3JX
☎ (0225) 315698
*Your comfort is assured at this
tastefully modernised Victorian
home, quietly situated only 10
minutes from the city centre.*
Bedrooms: 3 double & 1 twin.
Bathrooms: 4 private.
Bed & breakfast: £30-£45
single, £40-£52 double.
Parking for 4.
Credit: Access, Visa.

---

*Please mention this
guide when making
a booking.*

---

*The symbols are explained on the flap
inside the back cover.*

Old Mill Hotel &
Restaurant ⋒
⚜⚜⚜ APPROVED

Tollbridge Rd., Bath,
BA1 7DE
☎ (0225) 858476 & Fax
(0225) 852600
*Riverside hotel with
breathtaking views, 2 miles
from centre of Bath. Unique
water wheel restaurant with a
rotating floor. Most rooms with
river views.*
Bedrooms: 2 single, 5 double
& 5 twin, 5 family rooms.
Bathrooms: 17 private.
Bed & breakfast: £35-£38
single, £45-£55 double.
Half board: £32.50-£40 daily.
Lunch available.
Evening meal 7.30pm (l.o.
9.30pm).
Parking for 35.
Credit: Access, Visa, Diners,
Amex.

⊕ Display advertisements
appear on page 447 and page
557.

The Old School
House ⋒
⚜⚜ COMMENDED

Church St., Bathford, Bath,
BA1 7RR
☎ Bath (0225) 859593
*Pretty Victorian schoolhouse of
Bath stone in peaceful
conservation area. Views and
fine walks overlooking Avon
Valley. 3 miles to Bath centre.
All rooms have full private
facilities. Dinners, licensed.
Non-smoking.*
Bedrooms: 4 double.
Bathrooms: 4 private.
Bed & breakfast: £40 single,
£54-£60 double.
Half board: £44.50-£57.50
daily, £275-£350 weekly.
Evening meal 7pm (l.o. 7pm).
Parking for 6.
Credit: Access, Visa.

Paradise House Hotel
⚜⚜

86-88 Holloway, Bath,
BA2 4PX
☎ (0225) 317723 & Fax
(0225) 482005
*Lovely Bath stone house in
very quiet cul-de-sac within 4
minutes' walk of city. Superb
views from rear.*
Bedrooms: 4 double & 4 twin,
1 family room.
Bathrooms: 7 private,
1 public.

Bed & breakfast: £37-£58
single, £44-£65 double.
Parking for 5.
Credit: Access, Visa, Amex.

The Plaine ⋒
⚜⚜⚜

Norton St. Philip, Bath,
BA3 6LE
☎ Faulkland (0373) 834723
& Fax (0373) 834723
*In the heart of a conservation
village, facing the famous
George Inn, one time
headquarters of the Duke of
Monmouth. 6 miles south of
Georgian Bath in unspoilt
countryside. Peaceful walks.
Non-smoking house.*
Bedrooms: 3 double.
Bathrooms: 3 private.
Bed & breakfast: £35-£39
single, £39-£48 double.
Parking for 4.
Credit: Access, Visa, C.Bl.,
Diners, Amex.

Pratt's Hotel ⋒
⚜⚜⚜

South Pde., Bath, BA2 4AB
☎ (0225) 460441 & Fax
(0225) 448807
Telex 444827PRAHOT G
ℂℝ Forestdale
*Georgian hotel with all
comforts in the centre of
historic Bath, "the city of
flowers".*
Bedrooms: 11 single,
13 double & 17 twin, 5 family
rooms.
Bathrooms: 46 private.
Bed & breakfast: from £62.50
single, from £77.50 double.
Lunch available.
Evening meal 7pm (l.o.
9.30pm).
Credit: Access, Visa, Diners,
Amex.

Priory Hotel &
Restaurant ⋒

Weston Rd., Bath, BA1 2XT
☎ (0225) 331922 & Fax
(0225) 44612
*Country house style hotel in a
quiet suburb of Bath.
Renowned restaurant,
beautifully appointed rooms
and glorious garden.*
Bedrooms: 3 single, 6 double
& 12 twin.
Bathrooms: 21 private.
Bed & breakfast: £95-£110
single, £125-£180 double.
Half board: £120-£145 daily.
Lunch available.

Continued ▶

BATH

Continued

Evening meal 7.15pm (l.o. 9.30pm).
Parking for 26.
Credit: Access, Visa, Diners, Amex.

Queensberry Hotel M

Russel St., Bath, BA1 2QF
☎ (0225) 447928
Fax (0225) 446065
Telex 445628
Occupying 3 fine period houses in the heart of Georgian Bath. A haven of tranquillity in the midst of the city.
Bedrooms: 13 double & 11 twin.
Bathrooms: 24 private.
Bed & breakfast: £79-£120 single, £79-£135 double.
Credit: Access, Visa, Amex.

Royal Crescent Hotel M
HIGHLY COMMENDED

16 Royal Crescent, Bath, BA1 2LS
☎ (0225) 319090
Telex 444251
Queens Moat Houses
Elegant Georgian townhouse in the heart of Bath. Individually designed bedrooms and suites. Extensive wine list.
Bedrooms: 3 single, 14 double & 14 twin, 13 family rooms.
Bathrooms: 44 private.
Bed & breakfast: from £110 single, £145-£205 double.
Half board: £103-£132.50 daily.
Lunch available.
Evening meal 7pm (l.o. 9.30pm).
Parking for 16.
Credit: Access, Visa, Diners, Amex.

Hotel Saint Clair
APPROVED

1 Crescent Gdns., Upper Bristol Rd., Bath, BA1 2NA
☎ (0225) 425543
Small family hotel 5 minutes' walk from city, 2 minutes from Royal Crescent. Large public car park 1 minute away. One night stays welcome.
Bedrooms: 3 single, 4 double & 2 twin, 1 family room.

Bathrooms: 2 private, 2 public.
Bed & breakfast: £20-£25 single, £34-£38 double.
Credit: Access, Visa.

Siena Hotel M

25 Pulteney Rd., Bath, BA2 4EZ
☎ (0225) 425495
Fine Victorian building overlooking Bath Abbey, a few minutes' level walk from centre. Refurnished to provide spacious well-appointed en-suite rooms.
Bedrooms: 3 single, 5 double & 3 twin, 3 family rooms.
Bathrooms: 14 private.
Bed & breakfast: from £25 single, from £40 double.
Evening meal 6pm (l.o. 8pm).
Parking for 12.
Credit: Access, Visa.

Underhill Lodge
COMMENDED

Warminster Rd., Bathampton, Bath, BA2 6XQ
☎ (0225) 464992
Distinctive, secluded, licensed property with delightful valley views. Offering high standard accommodation. 1.5 miles from Bath along A36 Warminster Road.
Bedrooms: 1 single, 2 double & 1 twin.
Bathrooms: 4 private.
Bed & breakfast: £35-£42 single, £50-£58 double.
Evening meal 7.30pm (l.o. 7.30pm).
Parking for 10.
Credit: Access, Visa.

Villa Magdala Hotel
Listed

Henrietta Rd., Bath, BA2 6LX
☎ (0225) 466329
Quietly situated villa, overlooking Henrietta Park. Close to the city centre and Roman Baths. All rooms en-suite. Car parking.
Bedrooms: 11 double & 4 twin, 4 family rooms.
Bathrooms: 17 private.
Bed & breakfast: max. £41 single, £56-£70 double.
Parking for 15.
Credit: Access, Visa.

Wellsgate
COMMENDED

131 Wells Rd., Bath, BA2 3AN
☎ (0225) 310688
Peaceful Victorian elegance, large colourful gardens and panoramic views. Full or vegetarian breakfasts with home-made jams. Close to city centre. Garages and private parking.
Bedrooms: 2 double & 1 twin.
Bathrooms: 3 private.
Bed & breakfast: £20-£27 single, £30-£38 double.
Half board: £30-£35 daily, £180-£245 weekly.
Evening meal 6pm.
Parking for 5.

Wentworth House Hotel M
COMMENDED

106 Bloomfield Rd., Bath, BA2 2AP
☎ (0225) 339193
Fine Victorian house in three-quarters of an acre of secluded grounds with swimming pool, large car park, lawns and gardens. In a quiet residential area.
Bedrooms: 3 single, 9 double & 6 twin, 2 family rooms.
Bathrooms: 16 private, 1 public.
Bed & breakfast: £23-£38 single, £40-£55 double.
Half board: £35-£50 daily.
Evening meal 7pm (l.o. 6.30pm).
Parking for 20.
Credit: Access, Visa.

Williams Guest House M

81 Wells Rd., Bath, BA2 3AN
☎ (0225) 312179
Victorian house providing friendly atmosphere, close to city. Personal tours provided by proprietor in his taxi. Non-smokers only, please.
Bedrooms: 1 twin.
Bathrooms: 1 private.
Bed & breakfast: £20-£25 single, £35-£40 double.
Parking for 9.

BATHAMPTON
Avon
Map ref 2B2

Orchard House Hotel M
COMMENDED

Warminster Rd., Bathampton, Bath, BA2 6XG
☎ Bath (0225) 466115

Minotels
A comfortable hotel, 2 miles from Bath city centre. All bedrooms en-suite, sauna and solarium. Car park.
Bedrooms: 9 double, 3 family rooms.
Bathrooms: 12 private, 4 public.
Bed & breakfast: £37-£39 single, £47-£49 double.
Evening meal 6.30pm (l.o. 8pm).
Parking for 16.
Credit: Access, Visa, Diners, Amex.

BATHEASTON
Avon
Map ref 2B2

Suburb north-east of Bath.

Fern Cottage Hotel M
COMMENDED

9 Northend, Batheaston, Bath, BA1 7EE
☎ Bath (0225) 858190
Charming Grade II listed 18th C hotel with original gas-lit bar and restaurant. Rural and quiet yet only minutes from centre of Bath.
Bedrooms: 4 double & 2 twin.
Bathrooms: 6 private, 1 public.
Bed & breakfast: £29-£39 single, £45-£65 double.
Half board: £39-£50 daily.
Evening meal 7.30pm (l.o. 9pm).
Parking for 8.

BEAMINSTER
Dorset
Map ref 2A3

Old country town of mellow local stone set amid hills and rural vales.

Bridge House Hotel M
APPROVED

Prout Bridge, Beaminster, DT8 3AY
☎ (0308) 862200
Minotels
Attractive 13th C building with beautiful walled garden. Rooms have all modern facilities. Restaurant serves fresh, local produce cooked to order.
Bedrooms: 1 single, 8 double & 4 twin, 1 family room.
Bathrooms: 14 private.
Bed & breakfast: £32.50-£51 single, £59-£80 double.
Half board: £49.50-£60 daily, £299-£362 weekly.

Lunch available.
Evening meal 7pm (l.o. 9pm).
Parking for 22.
Credit: Access, Visa, Amex.

≌ ⚮ ✆ Ⓑ ☐ ♥ ⓘ Ⓥ ⌯
▥ ▰ ▼ ♿ ✿ ☐ SP ⊞ Ⓣ

BEER

Devon
Map ref 1D2

Formerly noted for lace-
making and smuggling,
this picturesque fishing
village lies close to some
of Devon's most striking
cliff scenery at Beer
Head. Smugglers' caves.
Quarries to west of village
were worked in Roman
times.

Anchor Inn
Fore St., Beer, EX12 3ET
☎ Seaton (0297) 20386
*Overlooking the sea.
Traditional country hospitality
with a la carte restaurant
specialising in local sea food.
Cliff top gardens. Winter
breaks available.*
Bedrooms: 6 double & 2 twin,
1 family room.
Bathrooms: 4 private,
3 public.
Bed & breakfast: £30-£35
single, £45-£60 double.
Lunch available.
Evening meal 7pm (l.o.
9.30pm).
Credit: Access, Visa.

≌ ☐ ♥ ⓘ Ⓥ ⌯ ⓣ ▥ ✕
▰ SP

BERE FERRERS

Devon
Map ref 1C2

7m S. Tavistock

Lanterna Hotel
≌
Bere Ferrers, Yelverton,
PL20 7JL
☎ Tavistock (0822) 840380
*Small quiet private hotel set in
a quaint old rural village on
the banks of the River Tavy.*
Bedrooms: 2 double & 2 twin,
1 family room.
Bathrooms: 3 private,
1 public.
Bed & breakfast: £15.50-£19
single, £31-£38 double.
Half board: £20.50-£24 daily,
£123-£144 weekly.
Lunch available.
Evening meal 6.30pm (l.o.
9pm).
Parking for 8.
Credit: Access, Visa.

≌ Ⓑ ♥ ⓘ Ⓥ ⌯ ⓣ ▥ ▰
✕ ▰

BERRYNARBOR

Devon
Map ref 1C1

Small village set in a
wooded valley, close to
Exmoor and to the wild
North Devon coast.

Langleigh House
≌ APPROVED
The Village, Berrynarbor,
Ilfracombe, EX34 9SG
☎ Combe Martin
(0271) 883410
*Friendly family-run guesthouse
providing all home-cooked
food, in the beautiful North
Devon village of Berrynarbor.*
Bedrooms: 1 single, 3 double
& 1 twin, 1 family room.
Bathrooms: 4 private,
1 public.
Bed & breakfast: £14-£15
single, £28-£30 double.
Half board: £20.50-£21.50
daily, £138-£144 weekly.
Evening meal 6.30pm (l.o.
midday).
Parking for 6.

≌ ♥ Ⓤ ⓘ Ⓥ ⌯ ⓣ ▥ ▰
✿ ▰

BICKLEIGH

Devon
Map ref 1D2

Pretty village of thatched
cottages where a 5-
arched bridge crosses the
River Exe. Other features
include Bickleigh Castle
with its imposing
gatehouse and Norman
chapel and a craft centre
based on a working mill
and farm.

Bickleigh Cottage
Country Hotel
≌ ≌
Bickleigh, Tiverton,
EX16 8RJ
☎ (088 45) 230
Ⓒ Minotels
*On the river bank in a famous
Devon beauty spot, offering
comfort and family
atmosphere. An ideal touring
centre.*
Bedrooms: 1 single, 4 double
& 4 twin.
Bathrooms: 7 private,
2 public.
Bed & breakfast: £19.50
single, £21.50 double.
Half board: £31 daily.
Evening meal 7pm (l.o. 5pm).
Parking for 12.
Open April-October.
Credit: Access, Visa.

▰ ♥ ⌯ ⓣ ▰ ✿ ✕ ▰ ▰
Ⓣ

BIDEFORD

Devon
Map ref 1C1

Once the home port of Sir
Richard Grenville, this
handsome town with its
17th C merchants'
houses flourished as a
shipbuilding and cloth
town, later dealing in
Newfoundland cod and
American tobacco. The
mile-long quay is still
busy with light shipping
as well as pleasure craft.
The bridge of 24 arches
was built about 1460.
Charles Kingsley stayed
here while writing
Westward Ho!

Durrant House Hotel
≌ ≌ ≌ ≌
Heywood Rd., Northam,
Bideford, EX39 3QB
☎ (0237) 472361 Telex 46740
Ⓒ Consort
*Originally a Georgian
residence, now a hotel offering
modern facilities including an
outdoor swimming pool.
Halfway between Bideford and
Westward Ho! 10% reduction
for weekly stays. 3 suites
available.*
Bedrooms: 11 double &
110 twin, 17 family rooms.
Bathrooms: 138 private.
Bed & breakfast: £46.75-£56
single, £71.50-£81 double.
Half board: £41.25-£46.75
daily.
Lunch available.
Evening meal 7.30pm (l.o.
9.30pm).
Parking for 201.
Credit: Access, Visa, Diners,
Amex.

≌ ✆ Ⓑ ☐ ♥ ⓘ Ⓥ ⌯ ●
⊞ ▥ ▼ ⧖ ⓤ Ⓤ ▶ ✿ Ⓖ
▰ SP ⊞ Ⓣ

The Mount Hotel ⋈
≌ ≌ ≌ APPROVED
North Down Rd., Bideford,
EX39 3LP
☎ (0237) 473748
*Small, family-run hotel over
200 years old, with character
and charm. Peaceful garden.
Short walk to town centre and
quay. Ideal base for touring
North Devon and Tarka
country.*
Bedrooms: 2 single, 4 double
& 1 twin, 1 family room.
Bathrooms: 5 private,
1 public.
Bed & breakfast: £18.50-£25
single, £31-£41 double.
Half board: £24.50-£33.50
daily, £170-£223.50 weekly.

Evening meal 6.30pm (l.o.
5.50pm).
Parking for 4.
Credit: Access, Visa.

≌ 5 ♥ ⓘ Ⓥ ⌖ ⌯ ⓣ ▥ ▰
▼ ✕ ▰ Ⓖ ⧖ SP ⊞

Riversford Hotel ⋈
≌ ≌ ≌ ≌ APPROVED
Limers La., Bideford,
EX39 2RG
☎ (0237) 474239/470381 &
Fax (0237) 421661
Ⓒ Inter
*Peace and tranquillity in
gardens beside the River
Torridge. Candlelit restaurant,
English cooking. Close to
sandy beaches and well placed
for touring. Take the A386
from Bideford to Northam for
a mile, turn right into Limers
Lane.*
Bedrooms: 2 single, 7 double
& 5 twin, 2 family rooms.
Bathrooms: 14 private,
2 public.
Bed & breakfast: £27-£55
single, £36-£43 double.
Half board: £46-£62 daily,
£248-£350 weekly.
Lunch available.
Evening meal 7pm (l.o. 9pm).
Parking for 22.
Credit: Access, Visa, Diners,
Amex.

≌ ⚮ ✆ Ⓑ ☐ ♥ ⓘ Ⓥ ⌯
ⓣ ● ▥ ▰ ⧖ ⓤ Ⓤ ▶ ✿
⒈ SP ⊞

Sunset Hotel ⋈
≌ ≌ ≌ APPROVED
Landcross, Bideford,
EX39 5JA
☎ (0237) 472962
*Small, elegant country hotel in
peaceful, picturesque location
1.5 miles from town,
specialising in home cooking.
Delightful en-suite bedrooms
with beverages and colour TVs.
Non-smoking establishment.*
Bedrooms: 1 single, 1 double
& 1 twin, 2 family rooms.
Bathrooms: 3 private,
1 public; 1 private shower.
Bed & breakfast: £20-£25
single, £37-£46 double.
Half board: £28-£34 daily,
£119-£220 weekly.
Lunch available.
Evening meal 7pm (l.o. 7pm).
Parking for 10.
Open February-November.
Credit: Access, Visa.

≌ ☐ ♥ ⓘ Ⓥ ⌖ ⌯ ⓣ ▥
▰ ✿ ⓤ Ⓤ ▶ ✿ Ⓖ SP

Yeoldon Country House
Hotel & Restaurant ⋈
≌ ≌ ≌ COMMENDED
Durrant La., Northam,
Bideford, EX39 2RL
☎ (0237) 474400

Continued ▶

BIDEFORD

Continued

Victorian country house, now an impressive comfortable hotel. English and continental cooking and an interesting wine list. Hospitable owners, friendly and efficient staff.
Bedrooms: 4 double & 4 twin, 2 family rooms.
Bathrooms: 10 private.
Bed & breakfast: £36.25-£49.25 single, £72.50-£79.75 double.
Half board: £53.20-£58.50 daily, £267.75-£294 weekly.
Lunch available.
Evening meal 7pm (l.o. 9pm).
Parking for 20.
Credit: Access, Visa, C.Bl., Diners, Amex.
⌕ ♨ 📞 ▭ ⇆ ♿ ⓘ Ⓥ
⌣ ⇌ ● ▥ ▱ Ⓣ ♨ Ս ⛳
✏ ❀ ⦿ SP Ⓣ
ⒶⒹ Display advertisement appears on page 449.

BIGBURY
Devon
Map ref 1C3

3m S. Modbury

Trebles Cottage Hotel
♔♔♔
Kingston, Kingsbridge, TQ7 4PT
☎ Bigbury-on-Sea (0548) 810268 & 558222
Attractive 1801 cottage in large secluded grounds on village edge. High standard of food and comfort. Homely atmosphere.
Bedrooms: 3 double & 2 twin.
Bathrooms: 5 private.
Bed & breakfast: £35-£40 single, £45-£48 double.
Half board: £25-£28 daily.
Evening meal 7.15pm (l.o. 6pm).
Parking for 10.
Credit: Visa.
⦿ ▭ ⇆ ⓘ Ⓥ ⇌ ▥ ▱ ❀
⛳ ❧ SP

BIGBURY-ON-SEA
Devon
Map ref 1C3

Small resort on Bigbury Bay at the mouth of the River Avon. Wide sands, rugged cliffs. Burgh Island can be reached on foot at low tide.

Henley Hotel
♔♔♔ COMMENDED
Folly Hill, Bigbury-on-Sea, Kingsbridge, TQ7 4AR
☎ (0548) 810240 & Fax (0548) 810331

Ⓖ Minotels
Small comfortable hotel on the edge of the sea. Spectacular views from most rooms. Rural coastal village. Non-smokers only please.
Bedrooms: 1 single, 2 double & 2 twin, 2 family rooms.
Bathrooms: 7 private.
Bed & breakfast: £21.50-£25.50 single, £43-£51 double.
Half board: £35-£38 daily, £225-£242.50 weekly.
Lunch available.
Evening meal 6.30pm (l.o. 8pm).
Parking for 10.
Credit: Access, Visa, Amex.
⌕ ♨ 📞 ▭ ♿ ⓘ Ⓥ ⌣
⇌ ▥ ♨ Ⓣ ▱ ❀ ♨ DAP ❧
SP Ⓣ

BODMIN
Cornwall
Map ref 1B2

County town south-west of Bodmin Moor with a ruined Augustinian priory and beautiful church, containing the casket said to have held relics of St. Petroc, to whom the church is dedicated, Prior Vyvyan's tomb of local slate and a fine Norman font. Interesting buildings include Tudor Guildhall, classic Assize Courts and Victorian County Gaol. Nearby are Lanhydrock House and Pencarrow House.

Mount Pleasant Farm Hotel Ⓜ
♔♔
Mount Village, Bodmin, PL30 4EX
☎ Cardinham (020 882) 342
17th C farmhouse in the heart of Cornish countryside. Ideally positioned for exploring Cornwall. Half an hour's drive from north and south coast and 5 miles from Bodmin.
Bedrooms: 1 single, 3 double & 2 twin, 1 family room.
Bathrooms: 6 private, 1 public.
Bed & breakfast: £14-£15 single, £34-£36 double.
Half board: £22-£24 daily, £139-£154 weekly.
Evening meal 7pm (l.o. 4pm).
Parking for 10.
Open April-October.
⌕ ♿ ⓘ Ⓥ ⇌ Ⓣ ▥ ▱ ❀
⛳ ▱

Please check prices and other details at the time of booking.

Tredethy Country Hotel Ⓜ
♔♔♔
Helland Bridge, Bodmin, PL30 4QS
☎ St. Mabyn (020 884) 262/364/325
Gracious living with spacious rooms, log fires in winter and absolute peace and quiet in beautiful surroundings. From Bodmin take the Launceston road, then the Helland turn off, to Helland Bridge. Tredethy is up the hill over the bridge.
Bedrooms: 1 single, 7 double & 3 twin.
Bathrooms: 11 private.
Bed & breakfast: £28-£40 single, £44-£68 double.
Half board: £32-£45 daily, £190-£260 weekly.
Evening meal 7pm (l.o. 8.30pm).
Parking for 30.
Credit: Access, Visa, Diners, Amex.
⌕ ♨ ▭ ♿ ⓘ Ⓥ ⌣ ⇌
Ⓣ ● ▥ ▱ ⇌ Ⓣ Ս ⛳ ❀
⛳ ▱ SP ▱ Ⓣ

Westberry Hotel
Rhind St., Bodmin, PL31 2EL
☎ (0208) 72772/72736
Comfortable hotel in North Cornish town, an ideal base for touring both coasts.
Bedrooms: 3 single, 9 double & 6 twin, 2 family rooms.
Bathrooms: 16 private, 2 public.
Bed & breakfast: £24-£40 single, £34-£45 double.
Half board: £35-£51 daily, £170-£190 weekly.
Lunch available.
Evening meal 7pm (l.o. 9pm).
Parking for 30.
Credit: Access, Visa, Diners.
⌕ ♨ ♿ ▭ ♿ ⓘ Ⓥ ⇌ Ⓣ
▥ ▱ Ⓣ ⛳ ❧ ● SP Ⓣ

BOLVENTOR
Cornwall
Map ref 1C2

9m NE. Bodmin

Jamaica Inn
Bolventor, Launceston, PL15 7TS
☎ Pipers Pool (056 686) 250
World famous coaching house on Bodmin Moor. Potters Museum of Curiosity and Dame Daphne du Maurier Memorial Room to visit.
Bedrooms: 4 double & 2 twin.
Bathrooms: 6 private.
Bed & breakfast: £29.50-£40 single, £49-£70 double.
Lunch available.

Evening meal 6pm (l.o. 10pm).
Parking for 200.
Credit: Access, Visa.
⌕ ♨ ▭ ♿ ⓘ Ⓥ ▥ ⛳ ❧
▱ ▱

BOSCASTLE
Cornwall
Map ref 1B2

Small, unspoilt village in Valency Valley, steeply built at meeting of 2 rivers. Active as a port until onset of railway era and tourism, its dramatic natural harbour affords rare shelter on this wild coast. Attractions include spectacular blow-hole, Celtic field strips, part-Norman church. 2 miles east, St. Juliot Church was restored by Thomas Hardy (1872).

Bottreaux House Hotel Ⓜ
♔♔♔ COMMENDED
Boscastle, PL35 0BG
☎ (084 05) 231
Character Georgian house with panoramic views overlooking unspoilt harbour village. Specialising in comfort and cuisine. On B3266 Camelford to Boscastle road.
Bedrooms: 5 double & 2 twin.
Bathrooms: 7 private.
Bed & breakfast: £26-£28 single, £46-£50 double.
Evening meal 7.30pm (l.o. 9.30pm).
Parking for 10.
Open February-November.
Credit: Access, Visa.
⌕ 10 ♨ ▭ ♿ ⓘ Ⓥ ⌣ ⇌
▥ ▱ ▱ ❧ SP ▱ Ⓣ

Forrabury House Ⓜ
♔♔
Forrabury Common, Boscastle, PL35 0DJ
☎ (084 05) 469
The former rectory to Forrabury Church. Offers bed and breakfast, full board or half board accommodation. Various diets catered for on request.
Bedrooms: 2 double & 1 twin, 1 family room.
Bathrooms: 3 private, 1 public; 1 private shower.
Bed & breakfast: £12-£15 single, £24-£30 double.
Half board: £19.50-£22.50 daily, £132.50-£152.50 weekly.
Lunch available.

Evening meal 6.30pm (l.o. 10am).
Parking for 5.

📞5 🖤 📺 🛋 📺 ◉ 🛏 ▲
🏷 🐾 SP 🏠

Melbourne House ⚘
☺☺☺ COMMENDED

New Rd., Boscastle, PL35 0DH
☎ (0840) 250650
Victorian house in National Trust harbour village offering tranquillity, comfort and food. Ideally situated for coastal walks, beaches and touring.
Bedrooms: 1 single, 3 double & 2 twin.
Bathrooms: 3 private, 2 public.
Bed & breakfast: £12-£17 single, £24-£34 double.
Half board: £20.50-£25.50 daily, £129-£164 weekly.
Evening meal 7pm (l.o. 6pm).
Parking for 8.
Credit: Access, Visa.

🖤🖳 📺 🛏 🛋 ▲ 🍴 ∪
✿ 🏃 🏠 OAP 🐾 SP

The Old Coach House ⚘
☺☺☺

Tintagel Rd., Boscastle, PL35 0AS
☎ (0840) 250398
Relax in beautiful 300-year-old former coach-house. All en-suite with colour TV. Licensed. Friendly and helpful service.
Bedrooms: 1 single, 3 double & 1 twin, 1 family room.
Bathrooms: 6 private.
Bed & breakfast: £15-£22 single, £30-£44 double.
Lunch available.
Evening meal 7pm (l.o. 6pm).
Parking for 6.
Open March-November.
Credit: Access, Visa, Amex.

📞6 👟 ◉ 🖳 🖤 🛏 📺 🖤 ✂ 🛋
🛏 ▲ ᕕ ∪ 🏃 🏠 SP 🏠 T

Tanglewood Guest House
☺☺

Fore St., Boscastle, PL35 0AX
☎ (0840) 250333
Friendly guesthouse in centre of village conservation area, near Harbour Cliffs protected by the National Trust.
Bedrooms: 1 single, 1 double.
Bathrooms: 1 public.
Bed & breakfast: £10-£12 single, £28-£30 double.
Parking for 2.

📞10 ◉ 🖳 🖤 🖳 🖤 🛏 📺
🛋 ✿ 🏃 🏠

Tolcarne Hotel ⚘
☺☺☺ COMMENDED

Tintagel Rd., Boscastle, PL35 0AS
☎ (0840) 250654
Delightful house of character in own grounds with lovely views near lovely coastal paths along the dramatic Cornish coastline. Home cooking, including vegetarian and special diets. Warm welcome.
Bedrooms: 1 single, 4 double & 3 twin, 1 family room.
Bathrooms: 8 private, 2 public.
Bed & breakfast: £16-£21 single, £32-£38 double.
Half board: £23.50-£26.50 daily, £158-£167 weekly.
Evening meal 7pm (l.o. 5.30pm).
Parking for 15.
Open April-October.
Credit: Access, Visa, Amex.

📞🖳 📺 🛏 📺 🛋 ▲
∪ 🏃 ✿ SP

Standing by the river just east of Dartmoor National Park, this old town has good moorland views. Its church, with a 14th C tower, holds one of Devon's finest medieval rood screens.

Dolphin Hotel

Station Rd., Bovey Tracey, TQ13 9AL
☎ (0626) 832413
Formerly a coaching house, has recently been completely refurbished and now offers a high standard of accommodation and food.
Bedrooms: 1 single, 3 double & 4 twin.
Bathrooms: 8 private.
Bed & breakfast: from £30 single, from £50 double.
Half board: £28.50-£33.50 daily.
Lunch available.
Evening meal 6.30pm (l.o. 9.30pm).
Parking for 50.
Credit: Access, Visa.

📞🖤 ◉ 🖳 🖤 🛏 🖤 🛋 ▲
🍴 ∪ 🏃 🏠 🏠

Huddled steeply beside the river, the old stone buildings of this former cloth-weaving town reflect continuing prosperity from the Middle Ages. There is a tiny Anglo-Saxon church, part of a monastery sacked by Danes. The part-14th C bridge carries a medieval chapel, later used as a gaol. Nearby are Westwood Manor, Great Chalfield Manor and one of England's largest tithe barns at Barton Farm.
Tourist Information Centre ☎ (022 16) 5797

Bradford Old Windmill ⚘

4 Masons La., Bradford-on-Avon, BA15 1QN
☎ (0225) 866842
Circular tower of converted windmill standing high above the Cotswold-stone town of Bradford-on-Avon. Peaceful situation close to Bath. Non-smokers only please.
Bedrooms: 1 single, 1 double & 1 twin, 1 family room.
Bathrooms: 3 private, 1 public.
Bed & breakfast: £25-£35 single, £39-£59 double.
Half board: £40-£65 daily.
Evening meal 8pm (l.o. 10am).
Parking for 4.

📞6 ◉ 🖳 🖤 🖳 🖤 🛏
▲ 🏃 🏠 OAP 🐾 SP 🏠

Burghope Manor
☺☺ COMMENDED

Winsley, Bradford-on-Avon, BA15 2LA
☎ Bath (0225) 723557 & Fax (0225) 723113 Telex 444337
ACTBUS G.HERITAGE
Historic 13th C manor house in its own grounds on the edge of the village of Winsley. 5.5 miles from Bath, 1.5 miles from Bradford-on-Avon. Delightful country pubs and restaurants within easy walking and driving distance.
Bedrooms: 3 twin.
Bathrooms: 3 private.
Bed & breakfast: £45-£55 single, £60-£70 double.
Evening meal 7.45pm (l.o. 8pm).
Parking for 24.

Credit: Access, Visa, Diners, Amex.

📞10 ◉ 🖳 🖤 🖳 🛉 🖤 🛏
📺 🛋 ▲ 🍴 ᕕ ∪ 🍴 ✂ ✿
🏃 🐾 SP 🏠 T

Leigh Park Hotel ⚘
☺☺☺☺ COMMENDED

Bradford-on-Avon, BA15 2RA
☎ (022 16) 4885 & Fax (022 16) 2315
ⒸⓇ Consort
Quiet and relaxing hotel set in 4 acres with a vineyard in its grounds. Personal attention from the owners. Facilities include a snooker room.
Bedrooms: 4 single, 8 double & 5 twin, 3 family rooms.
Bathrooms: 20 private, 1 public.
Bed & breakfast: £72-£78 single, £80-£90 double.
Half board: from £98 daily, from £686 weekly.
Lunch available.
Evening meal 7pm (l.o. 8.30pm).
Parking for 62.
Credit: Access, Visa, Diners, Amex.

📞 👟 🖽 📞 🖳 🖤 🛉 🖤
🛏 🛋 ▲ 🍴 🛉 ᕕ 🏃 ✿
🏃 🏠

Northover House

163 Bath Rd., Bradford-on-Avon, BA15 1SW
☎ (022 16) 7542
Detached house built in Bath stone, with attractive gardens. Bedrooms with TV, tea and coffee facilities.
Bedrooms: 3 double.
Bathrooms: 1 private, 1 public.
Bed & breakfast: £20-£25 single, £34-£40 double.
Parking for 6.

📞🖳 🖤 🖳 🖤 ✂ 🛏 🖤
▲ 🏃 🏠 OAP

Priory Steps ⚘

Newtown, Bradford-on-Avon, BA15 1NQ
☎ (022 16) 2230
17th C house in delightful location, with fine views over the Avon Valley. Comfortable and well-appointed accommodation.
Bedrooms: 3 double & 2 twin.
Bathrooms: 5 private.
Bed & breakfast: £38-£42 single, £54-£58 double.
Half board: £41-£44 daily.
Evening meal 7.30pm (l.o. 7.30pm).
Parking for 7.
Credit: Access, Visa.

👟 ◉ 🖳 🖤 🛉 🖤 🛏 🛋 ▲
🍴 🏃 🏠 T

Half board prices shown are per person but in some cases may be based on double/twin occupancy.

BRADFORD-ON-AVON

Continued

Widbrook Grange M
COMMENDED
Trowbridge Rd., Bradford-on-Avon, BA15 1UH
☎ (022 16) 4750 & 3173
19th C Bath-stone house with own grounds, in open countryside on the outskirts of the town. Horse riding and golf nearby.
Bedrooms: 1 single, 5 double & 4 twin, 2 family rooms.
Bathrooms: 11 private, 1 public.
Bed & breakfast: £43-£49 single, £55-£75 double.
Parking for 55.
Credit: Access, Visa, Amex.

BRANSCOMBE

Devon
Map ref 1D2

5m E. Sidmouth
Scattered village of unusual character. Houses of cob and thatch are sited irregularly on the steep wooded slopes of a combe, which widens towards the sea. Much of Branscombe Estate is National Trust property.

Three Horseshoes M
Branscombe, Seaton, EX12 3BR
☎ (029 780) 251
Family-run inn with beams, brasses, log fires. Short distance from several seaside resorts. Beautiful countryside with excellent walks.
Bedrooms: 2 single, 7 double & 2 twin, 1 family room.
Bathrooms: 5 private, 2 public.
Bed & breakfast: £15.50-£19 single, £31-£38 double.
Half board: from £22.50 daily, from £150 weekly.
Evening meal 6pm (l.o. 10pm).
Parking for 102.
Credit: Access, Visa, Diners, Amex.

The national Crown scheme is explained in full on pages 536 – 539.

BRENT KNOLL

Somerset
Map ref 1D1

2m NE. Burnham-on-Sea
Village sheltering beneath the south-west slopes of Brent Knoll, at the summit of which is an Iron Age fort (National Trust). There are wide views over levels toward the sea. Among notable features in the church is a series of fine carvings on 3 medieval bench ends. Easy access to the M5 between Bristol and Exeter and to seaside places on the Somerset/Avon coast.

Shrub Farm Country House Hotel M
COMMENDED
Burton Row, Brent Knoll, Highbridge, TA9 4BX
☎ (0278) 760479 & Fax (0278) 760513
Warm and friendly 500-year-old farmhouse nestling in 3.5 acres of own grounds. All rooms en-suite and attractively decorated. Restaurant offers table d'hote, a la carte, cream teas, bar snacks and Sunday lunches.
Bedrooms: 1 single, 6 double & 2 twin, 1 family room.
Bathrooms: 10 private.
Bed & breakfast: £35-£45 single, £45-£55 double.
Half board: £35-£50 daily.
Lunch available.
Evening meal 7pm (l.o. 9.30pm).
Parking for 20.
Credit: Access, Visa.

BRIDESTOWE

Devon
Map ref 1C2

6m SW. Okehampton
Small Dartmoor village with a much restored 15th C church, and Great Links Tor rising to the south-east.

Fox & Hounds Hotel
Bridestowe, Okehampton, EX20 4HF
☎ Lydford (082 282) 206
Small family-run hotel offering home cooking, situated on the edge of Dartmoor.
Bedrooms: 2 single, 2 double & 2 twin, 2 family rooms.
Bathrooms: 6 private, 8 public.

Bed & breakfast: £20-£22 single, £38-£40 double.
Half board: £27-£30 daily, £180-£190 weekly.
Lunch available.
Evening meal 6pm (l.o. 10pm).
Parking for 60.
Credit: Access, Visa.

BRIDGWATER

Somerset
Map ref 1D1

Originally major medieval port on the River Parrett, now small industrial town with mostly 19th C or modern architecture. Georgian Castle Street leads to West Quay and site of 13th C castle razed to the ground by Cromwell. Birthplace of Cromwellian admiral Robert Blake is now a museum. Arts centre and theatre, lido.

Apple Tree Inn
COMMENDED
Keenthorne, Nether Stowey, Bridgwater, TA5 1HZ
☎ (0278) 733238
Small family hotel easily located on the main A39, surrounded by rolling Quantock Hills. Large car park and gardens. Well known restaurant. In Nether Stowey, some 8 miles west of Bridgwater.
Bedrooms: 3 single, 6 double & 4 twin, 2 family rooms.
Bathrooms: 15 private.
Bed & breakfast: £37-£40 single, £50-£55 double.
Half board: £56-£60 daily, £265-£350 weekly.
Lunch available.
Evening meal 6.30pm (l.o. 9.30pm).
Parking for 60.
Credit: Access, Visa, Amex.

Friarn Court Hotel M
37 St. Mary St., Bridgwater
☎ (0278) 452859
Fax (0278) 452988
Comfortable small hotel with restaurant and cosy bar, ideal base for business or pleasure. Inexpensive weekend break rates. Colour brochure.
Bedrooms: 1 single, 4 double & 7 twin.
Bathrooms: 10 private, 1 public.
Bed & breakfast: £40-£69.50 single, £40-£69.50 double.

Lunch available.
Evening meal 7.30pm (l.o. 9.30pm).
Parking for 14.
Credit: Access, Visa, Diners, Amex.

Quantock View House
APPROVED
Bridgwater Rd., North Petherton, Bridgwater, TA6 6PR
☎ (0278) 663309
Comfortable, family-run guesthouse in central Somerset. En-suite facilities available. Free-range eggs. Only 200 yards from M5 junction 24.
Bedrooms: 2 double & 1 twin, 1 family room.
Bathrooms: 1 private, 1 public; 1 private shower.
Bed & breakfast: £12-£15 single, £24-£30 double.
Half board: £18-£21 daily, £120-£140 weekly.
Evening meal 6.30pm (l.o. 3pm).
Parking for 5.

Walnut Tree Inn M
COMMENDED
North Petherton, Bridgwater, TA6 6QA
☎ (0278) 662255 & Fax (0278) 663946
CR Best Western
18th C coaching inn on A38, 1 mile from M5 exit 24. A welcome stopover for businessmen and tourists.
Bedrooms: 2 single, 17 double & 7 twin, 2 family rooms.
Bathrooms: 28 private.
Bed & breakfast: £47-£79 single, £67-£99 double.
Lunch available.
Evening meal 7pm (l.o. 10pm).
Parking for 74.
Credit: Access, Visa, Diners, Amex.

---

*The symbol **CR** and the name of a hotel group or consortium after a hotel address means that bookings can be made through a central reservations office. These are listed on page 540.*

Dorset
Map ref 2A3

Market town and chief
producer of nets and
ropes just inland of
dramatic Dorset coast.
Ropes once made for
hangman's noose as well
as for shipping and
fishing boats. Old, broad
streets built for drying
and twisting, long back
gardens for rope-walks.
Grand arcaded Town Hall
and Georgian buildings,
traditional inns. Local
history museum has
Roman relics. Charles II
stopped here on his flight
to France.
*Tourist Information
Centre* ☎ *(0308) 24901*

Bridport Arms Hotel ⋔
⌓⌓ APPROVED
West Bay, Bridport,
DT6 4EN
☎ (0308) 22994
*16th C thatched hotel on
beach. Restaurant specialising
in local sea food.*
Bedrooms: 3 single, 4 double
& 3 twin, 3 family rooms.
Bathrooms: 6 private,
3 public.
Bed & breakfast: £21.50-
£29.50 single, £40-£55 double.
Half board: £32-£38 daily,
£200-£250 weekly.
Lunch available.
Evening meal 7pm (l.o. 9pm).
Parking for 14.
Credit: Access, Visa.
🛌 ♥ ∅ ⊟ 🆃📺 ▥ ♨ 𝕀 SP
🖾

Britmead House
Hotel ⋔
⌓⌓ COMMENDED
154 West Bay Rd., Bridport,
DT6 4EG
☎ (0308) 22941
*Elegant, detached, tastefully
decorated house, renowned for
hospitality, comfort and meals.
10 minutes' walk to harbour
and beaches.*
Bedrooms: 4 double & 2 twin,
1 family room.
Bathrooms: 5 private,
1 public.
Bed & breakfast: £20.40-£29
single, £31.50-£44 double.
Half board: £25.95-£33 daily,
£174.65-£217 weekly.
Evening meal 7pm (l.o. 5pm).
Parking for 8.
Credit: Access, Visa, C.Bl.,
Diners, Amex.
🛌⌓♨ ⊡ 🔲 ♨ 𝕀 ⊻ ⤒ ♨
▥ ♨ ▶ ❋ ⱶ ᴳᴬᴾ SP 🆃

Durbeyfield Guest House
West Bay, Bridport, DT6 4EL
☎ (0308) 23307
*Family-run guesthouse, amidst
charming hills and coastal
scenery. 2 minutes from beach,
harbour and golf-course. Good
home cooking.*
Bedrooms: 2 single, 3 double
& 2 twin, 2 family rooms.
Bathrooms: 2 public.
Bed & breakfast: £14-£17.50
single, £28-£35 double.
Half board: £23.50-£27 daily.
Evening meal 6.30pm (l.o.
midday).
Parking for 10.
🛌⌓♨ 𝕀 ♨ 📺 ▥ ♨ ᴳᴬᴾ
SP 🖾

Haddon House Hotel ⋔
⌓⌓⌓
West Bay, Bridport,
DT6 4EL
☎ (0308) 23626 &
(0308) 25323
*Country house hotel, situated
300 yards from picturesque
harbour and coast, renowned
for cuisine. Well situated for
touring Dorset, Devon and
Somerset.*
Bedrooms: 2 single, 6 double
& 3 twin, 2 family rooms.
Bathrooms: 13 private.
Bed & breakfast: £39.50-£45
single, £52-£60 double.
Half board: £210-£265
weekly.
Lunch available.
Evening meal 7pm (l.o.
8.30pm).
Parking for 44.
Credit: Access, Visa, Diners,
Amex.
🛌⌓♨ ⦿ ⊡ ♨ 𝕀 ⊻ ♨
▥ ♨ 𝕀 ⱶ ❋ SP 🆃

---

*Individual
proprietors have
supplied all details
of accommodation.
Although we do
check for accuracy,
we advise you to
confirm prices and
other information
at the time of
booking.*

*The enquiry
coupons at the
back will help you
when contacting
proprietors.*

Avon
Map ref 2A2

Important since Saxon
times, today a university
town and major port. City
grew around medieval
river docks, now the
Floating Harbour, then
busy with fish, trade, sea
warfare and exploration
(Cabot sailed for
Newfoundland 1497).
Merchant Venturers
founded here 1552. Fine
old churches and
cathedral; Georgian
theatre and Exchange;
wide views of Avon
Gorge from Brunel's
Clifton Bridge.
*Tourist Information
Centre* ☎ *(0272) 260767*

Alandale Hotel
⌓⌓
Tyndalls Park Rd., Bristol,
BS8 1PG
☎ (0272) 735407
*Formerly a Victorian
gentleman's residence, now an
elegant, warm and comfortable
hotel with personal service.
Close to city centre.*
Bedrooms: 8 single, 6 double
& 3 twin.
Bathrooms: 17 private.
Bed & breakfast: £27-£38
single, £40-£50 double.
Parking for 10.
Credit: Access, Visa.
🛌⌓♨ ⦿ 🔲 ♨ 𝕀 ▥ ♨ 🖾

Alcove Guest House
⌓
508/510 Fishponds Rd.,
Bristol, BS16 3DT
☎ (0272) 653886 & 652436
*Clean and comfortable
accommodation with personal
service. Noted for its food.*
Bedrooms: 1 single, 3 double
& 3 twin, 2 family rooms.
Bathrooms: 2 private,
4 public.
Bed & breakfast: £18-£25
single, £30-£36 double.
Parking for 9.
🛌⌓♨ 🔲 ♨ 𝕀 ▥ ♨ 𝕀

Arches Hotel
⌓ APPROVED
132 Cotham Brow, Cotham,
Bristol, BS6 6AE
☎ (0272) 247398
*Small friendly private hotel
close to central stations and
100 yards from main A38.
Option of traditional or
vegetarian breakfast.*
Bedrooms: 5 single, 3 double,
3 family rooms.
Bathrooms: 2 public.

Bed & breakfast: £20.50-
£23.50 single, £36-£42 double.
Credit: Access, Visa.
🛌⌓♨ ⊔ 𝕌 ⊻ ♨ ▥
♨ ✕ 🖾

Berkeley Square
Hotel ⋔
⌓⌓⌓⌓ COMMENDED
15 Berkeley Square, Clifton,
Bristol, BS1 1HB
☎ (0272) 254000 & Fax
(0272) 252970
*Elegant hotel opened in 1990
on a fine Georgian square in
the heart of Bristol.
Continental bar and
restaurant.*
Bedrooms: 25 single,
12 double & 6 twin.
Bathrooms: 43 private.
Bed & breakfast: £66-£76
single, from £89 double.
Lunch available.
Evening meal 6pm (l.o.
10.30pm).
Parking for 6.
Credit: Access, Visa, Diners,
Amex.
🛌⌓♨ ⦿ ⊡ ♨ 𝕀 ⊻
▥ ⦿ 𝕀 ▥ ♨ 𝕀 ❋ ♨
🖾 🆃

Bristol Hilton ⋔
⌓⌓⌓⌓ COMMENDED
Redcliffe Way, Bristol,
BS1 6NJ
☎ (0272) 260041
Telex 449240
Ⓗ Hilton
*City centre hotel, recently
refurbished. New Galleria Bar
and Kiln Restaurant. Located
very near Temple Meads
railway station. Half board
rate refers to a weekend break.*
Bedrooms: 7 single, 98 double
& 96 twin.
Bathrooms: 201 private.
Bed & breakfast: £115-£135
single, £140-£160 double.
Half board: from £70 daily.
Lunch available.
Evening meal 7pm (l.o.
10.30pm).
Parking for 150.
Credit: Access, Visa, Diners,
Amex.
🛌⌓♨ ⦿ ⊡ ♨ 𝕀 ⊻
▥ ⦿ 𝕀 ▥ ♨ 𝕀 ⱶ ♨ 🔳
♨ SP 🖾

Camden Hotel
⌓⌓
129 Coronation Rd.,
Southville, Bristol, BS3 1RE
☎ (0272) 231062
*Small friendly hotel, only a few
minutes from city centre. Close
to theatres, exhibition centre,
museums and Bristol dockland.*
Bedrooms: 3 single, 1 double
& 1 twin, 5 family rooms.
Bathrooms: 2 private,
2 public.

Continued ▶

BRISTOL
Continued

Bed & breakfast: £16.50 single, £29-£33 double.
Half board: £21.50 daily.
Evening meal 6pm (l.o. 7pm).
Parking for 4.
🛇 🖵 🕏 🖩 ☎ 🔌 🏌

Clifton Hotel M
⌂⌂⌂

St. Paul's Rd., Clifton,
Bristol, BS8 1LX
☎ (0272) 736882 & Fax
(0272) 741082 Telex 449075
Located in an attractive and convenient area. Adventurous food and pleasant atmosphere in Racks Wine Bar and Restaurant. Shops and attractions nearby.
Bedrooms: 26 single,
12 double & 21 twin, 4 family rooms.
Bathrooms: 44 private,
6 public; 1 private shower.
Bed & breakfast: £27-£44 single, £44-£64 double.
Lunch available.
Evening meal 6.30pm (l.o. 10pm).
Parking for 12.
Credit: Access, Visa, Diners, Amex.
🛇 🕏 🕭 📞 🖭 🖵 🕏 🕯 🖩 🔌 ⚡
🌑 🎇 🖩 🕭 🞈 SP 🎒 🖵

Courtlands Hotel
⌂⌂⌂ COMMENDED

1 Redland Court Rd.,
Redland, Bristol, BS6 7EE
☎ (0272) 424432 & Fax
(0272) 232432
Family-run hotel, north of the city centre, overlooking Redland Grove and offering quiet discreet service.
Bedrooms: 11 single, 4 double & 3 twin, 5 family rooms.
Bathrooms: 17 private,
2 public.
Bed & breakfast: £24-£38 single, £44-£50 double.
Half board: £30-£33 daily.
Lunch available.
Evening meal 7pm (l.o. 8pm).
Parking for 12.
Credit: Access, Visa.
🛇 🕏 📞 📟 🖵 🕏 🖭 ⚡
🖱 🖃 🖩 🕭 🏌 🞈 🌼 ✕ 🎒
🖵

Downs View Guest House
⌂

38 Upper Belgrave Rd.,
Clifton, Bristol, BS8 2XN
☎ (0272) 737046
Victorian guesthouse near Bristol Zoo, Clifton Suspension Bridge and overlooking Durham Downs. Close to shops and buses.

Bedrooms: 5 single, 6 double & 3 twin, 2 family rooms.
Bathrooms: 4 private,
2 public.
Bed & breakfast: £22-£30 single, £35-£45 double.
🕏 2 🖊 🖵 🕏 🖩 🖭 🖃 🔌 🛋
🎒

Rockleaze House
Listed

91 Gloucester Rd. North,
Filton, Bristol, BS12 7PT
☎ (0272) 692536
A Victorian house between the M4/M5 interchange and Bristol Centre. Equally appealing to the business person and tourist.
Bedrooms: 4 single, 1 double & 1 twin, 1 family room.
Bathrooms: 2 public.
Bed & breakfast: £17-£18 single, £28.50-£31 double.
Parking for 4.
🛇 🖵 🕏 🖩 🖭 🖩 🛋

Rodney Hotel M
⌂⌂⌂ COMMENDED

4 Rodney Pl., Clifton, Bristol,
BS8 4HY
☎ (0272) 735422
Telex 449075
Georgian mansion located in Clifton village near suspension bridge. Restaurant and bar with garden service in summer.
Bedrooms: 14 single,
14 double & 3 twin.
Bathrooms: 31 private.
Bed & breakfast: £56-£68 single, £87 double.
Lunch available.
Evening meal 7pm (l.o. 10pm).
Credit: Access, Visa, Diners, Amex.
🛇 🕏 📞 📟 🖵 🕏 🖩 🖭 ⚡
🌑 🖩 🛋 🏌 🖱 SP 🎒 🖵

Rowan Lodge Hotel
⌂ APPROVED

41 Gloucester Road North,
Filton Park, Bristol, BS7 0SN
☎ (0272) 312170
Small family-run hotel in residential area. On A38 with access to M4, M5 and M32 and to the city.
Bedrooms: 1 single, 1 double & 2 twin, 2 family rooms.
Bathrooms: 2 private,
2 public.
Bed & breakfast: £18-£30 single, £30-£40 double.
Half board: £21.50-£36.50 daily, £140-£210 weekly.
Evening meal 6.30pm (l.o. 5.30pm).
Parking for 7.
🛇 🖵 🕏 🖩 🖟 🖭 🛋 ✕

Towns Talk & Bristol Airport Motel
⌂⌂⌂

A38 Bridgwater Rd.,
Bedminster Down, Bristol,
BS13 7AD
☎ (0275) 392441
Fax (0272) 393362
Motel halfway between Bristol city centre and the airport. Busy night club, free for residents. Good restaurant with extensive menu.
Bedrooms: 10 single,
12 double & 10 twin, 4 family rooms.
Bathrooms: 36 private.
Bed & breakfast: £35-£45 single, £45-£65 double.
Half board: £45-£65 daily.
Evening meal 7pm (l.o. 10.30pm).
Parking for 700.
Credit: Access, Visa.
🛇 🖊 🕏 🖵 🕏 🖭 🖃 🔌 🌑
🖩 🏌 SP 🖵

Unicorn Hotel M
Prince St., Bristol, BS1 4QF
☎ (0272) 230333 Telex 44315
🄌 Rank
Modern hotel overlooking quay and close to city centre. Special weekend rates. Restaurant, lounge bar and waterfront tavern.
Bedrooms: 123 single,
43 double & 76 twin, 2 family rooms.
Bathrooms: 244 private.
Bed & breakfast: £63.50-£77.95 single, £92-£96.90 double.
Lunch available.
Evening meal 6.30pm (l.o. 10pm).
Parking for 400.
Credit: Access, Visa, C.Bl., Diners, Amex.
🛇 📞 📟 🖵 🕏 🖭 ✕ 🔌
🌑 🎇 🖩 🛋 🏌 SP 🖵

Washington Hotel M
⌂

11-15 St. Paul's Rd., Bristol,
BS8 1LX
☎ (0272) 733980
Telex 449075
Newly converted rooms, close to the shopping centre, suspension bridge and zoo.
Bedrooms: 19 single,
10 double & 12 twin, 5 family rooms.
Bathrooms: 35 private,
5 public.
Bed & breakfast: £26-£42 single, £43-£56 double.
Parking for 20.
Credit: Access, Visa, Diners, Amex.
🛇 🖊 📞 📟 🖵 🕏 ✕ 🔌 🖭
🖩 🛋 SP

BRIXHAM
Devon
Map ref 1D2

Famous for its trawling fleet in the 19th C, a steeply-built fishing port overlooking the harbour and fish market. A statue of William of Orange recalls his landing here before deposing James II. There is an aquarium and museum. Good cliff views and walks.
Tourist Information Centre ☎ (0803) 852861

Fairwinds
New Rd., Brixham,
TQ5 8DA
☎ (0803) 853564
First class guesthouse. Good centre for touring. Evening meal optional. Ground and first floor rooms.
Bedrooms: 3 double, 3 family rooms.
Bathrooms: 1 public.
Half board: £18-£22 daily, from £125 weekly.
Evening meal 5.45pm (l.o. 6.45pm).
Parking for 9.
Open April-October.
🛇 🖊 🖩 🖭 🖃 🖭 🌑 🖩
GAP

Harbour Side Guest House
Listed

65 Berry Head Rd., Brixham,
TQ5 9AA
☎ (0803) 858899
Overlooking the outer harbour and marina, opposite the lifeboat station and close to Breakwater Beach. Within walking distance of town.
Bedrooms: 1 single, 2 double, 2 family rooms.
Bathrooms: 1 private,
1 public.
Bed & breakfast: £14-£18 single, £26-£32 double.
Half board: £20-£25 daily.
Evening meal 6pm (l.o. 8pm).
🛇 🖊 🖵 🕏 🖩 🖟 🖃 📺 🌑

Mimosa Cottage
Listed

75 New Rd., Brixham,
TQ5 8NL
☎ (0803) 855719
Spacious centrally heated Georgian guesthouse only a short walk from town and seafront. Situated on left side of main approach road (A3022) just before town centre.
Bedrooms: 1 single, 2 double & 1 twin.
Bathrooms: 1 private,
1 public; 1 private shower.

Bed & breakfast: £14-£15 single, £25-£30 double.
Parking for 3.

[symbols]

Richmond House Hotel

APPROVED

Higher Manor Rd., Brixham,
TQ5 8HA
☎ (0803) 882391
*Detached Victorian house with
Laura Ashley interior, sun trap
garden and adjacent car park.
En-suite available. Convenient
for shops and harbour, yet
quiet location. First left after
Golden Lion.*
Bedrooms: 2 single, 1 double
& 1 twin, 4 family rooms.
Bathrooms: 2 private,
3 public.
Bed & breakfast: from £17.25
single, from £30.50 double.
Parking for 5.
Open February-November.
Credit: Access, Visa.

[symbols]

Woodlands Guest House M

COMMENDED

Parkham Rd., Brixham,
TQ5 9BU
☎ (0803) 852040
*Set on a hill overlooking
Brixham town and harbour,
beautiful rooms, all en-suite.
Expect quality and service.
Non-smokers only please.*
Bedrooms: 1 single, 3 double,
1 family room.
Bathrooms: 5 private.
Bed & breakfast: £17.50-
£18.50 single, £34-£37 double.
Parking for 4.
Open April-October.
Credit: Access, Visa.

[symbols]

BROAD CHALKE

Wiltshire
Map ref 2B3

5m SW. Wilton
Delightful River Ebble
Valley village with a 13th
C church displaying a
notable porch and central
tower.

The Queens Head Inn

Broad Chalke, Salisbury,
SP5 5EN
☎ (0722) 780344
*15th C building with stone
walls and old beams. Set in the
beautiful Chalke Valley, 8
miles from Salisbury.*
Bedrooms: 3 double & 1 twin.
Bathrooms: 4 private.

Bed & breakfast: £30 single,
£45 double.
Evening meal 7pm (l.o.
9.30pm).
Parking for 40.
Credit: Access, Visa.

[symbols]

BUCKFAST

Devon
Map ref 1C2

Situated on the south-
east edge of Dartmoor,
this village is visited for
its handsome 20th C
abbey which occupies the
site of a Cistercian
monastery. The main part
was built from 1906-32 by
untrained Benedictine
monks, one member only
having served a short
apprenticeship as a
stonemason. The chapel
which was added in the
1960s is particularly fine.

Furzeleigh Mill Country Hotel M

Dartbridge, Buckfast,
TQ11 0JP
☎ Buckfastleigh
(0364) 43476
*Detached 16th C former mill
with sunny south-facing aspect,
lovely gardens, views, within
Dartmoor National Park, close
to famous Buckfast Abbey.
Ideal touring centre for moor
and coastline. Noted for good
food, hospitality and comfort.*
Bedrooms: 3 single, 7 double
& 4 twin, 1 family room.
Bathrooms: 12 private,
2 public.
Bed & breakfast: £24-£28.50
single, £32-£45.50 double.
Half board: £24.75-£39.75
daily, £159.50-£199.50
weekly.
Lunch available.
Evening meal 6.45pm (l.o.
8.30pm).
Parking for 32.
Credit: Access, Visa.

[symbols]

---

*National Crown
ratings were correct
at the time of going
to press but are
subject to change.
Please check at the
time of booking.*

BUCKFASTLEIGH

Devon
Map ref 1C2

Small manufacturing and
market town just south of
Buckfast Abbey on the
fringe of Dartmoor.
Return trips can be taken
by steam train on a
reopened line along the
beautiful Dart Valley.

Royal Oak House M

APPROVED

59 Jordan St., Buckfastleigh,
TQ11 0AX
☎ (0364) 43611
*Small family-run guesthouse on
the edge of Dartmoor, with
spacious rooms and full
breakfast menu.*
Bedrooms: 5 double & 1 twin,
1 family room.
Bathrooms: 2 private,
2 public.
Bed & breakfast: £15-£20
single, £24-£35 double.
Lunch available.
Open March-November.

[symbols]

BUCKLAND MONACHORUM

Devon
Map ref 1C2

4m S. Tavistock
Village just north of
Buckland Abbey, home of
Sir Francis Drake.
Founded by Cistercians,
the building is of unique
interest through its
conversion into a country
home by Sir Richard
Grenville. Much of the
interior and the nearby
medieval tithe barn now
serve as a museum of
Drake and Grenville
mementoes, including
Drake's drum. Beautiful
gardens.

Uppaton House M

APPROVED

Coppicetown Rd., Buckland
Monachorum, Yelverton,
PL20 7LL
☎ (0822) 853226
*19th C house set in 2.5 acres of
gardens on the edge of
Dartmoor. Good views.
Excellent base for touring.*
Bedrooms: 2 single, 2 double
& 2 twin, 2 family rooms.
Bathrooms: 4 private,
3 public.
Bed & breakfast: £12-£15.50
single, £24-£31 double.

Half board: £18.50-£22 daily,
£125.50-£150 weekly.
Evening meal 6pm (l.o. 8pm).
Parking for 10.

[symbols]

BUDE

Cornwall
Map ref 1C2

Sandy resort on dramatic
Atlantic coast. High cliffs
give spectacular sea and
inland views. Georgian
cottages beside canal
basin, otherwise 19th and
20th C development.
Golf-course, cricket pitch,
folly, surfing, coarse-
fishing and boating.
Mother-town Stratton
was base of Royalist Sir
Bevil Grenville and
birthplace of his famous
retainer, the 'Cornish
Giant', Anthony Payne.
*Tourist Information
Centre* ☎ *(0288) 354240*

Bude Haven Hotel

COMMENDED

Flexbury Ave., Bude,
EX23 8NS
☎ (0288) 352305
*Edwardian family hotel with
comfortable, relaxing
atmosphere and friendly
service, in a quiet, residential
area. Convenient for beach,
town, and golf-course.*
Bedrooms: 2 single, 5 double
& 4 twin, 2 family rooms.
Bathrooms: 13 private.
Bed & breakfast: £20-£21
single, £40-£42 double.
Half board: £27-£29 daily,
£170-£186 weekly.
Evening meal 6.30pm (l.o.
7.30pm).
Parking for 8.
Credit: Access, Visa, Amex.

[symbols]

Camelot Hotel

COMMENDED

Downs View, Bude,
EX23 8RE
☎ (0288) 352361 & Fax
(0288) 355470
*Comfortable family-run hotel
situated close to the famous
Crooklets Beach and
overlooking a championship
golf-course.*
Bedrooms: 2 single, 5 double
& 11 twin, 3 family rooms.
Bathrooms: 21 private.
Bed & breakfast: £24-£28
single, £48-£56 double.
Half board: £34-£38 daily,
£195-£240 weekly.

Continued ▶

BUDE

Continued

Evening meal 7pm (l.o. 8.30pm).
Parking for 18.
Credit: Access, Visa, Amex.

Cliff Hotel ⚲
COMMENDED
Crooklets Beach, Bude, EX23 8NG
☎ (0288) 353110
Indoor pool and spa, solarium, putting, tennis court. 5 acres of land, near National Trust cliffs, 200 yards from the beach. Chef/proprietor.
Bedrooms: 2 single, 3 double & 1 twin, 9 family rooms.
Bathrooms: 15 private.
Bed & breakfast: £20-£26 single, £38-£50 double.
Half board: £23-£31 daily, £165-£200 weekly.
Lunch available.
Evening meal 6.30pm (l.o. 7.30pm).
Parking for 15.
Open April-October.

Edgcumbe Hotel ⚲
19 Summerleaze Cres., Bude, EX23 8HJ
☎ (0288) 353846
Homely and friendly hotel where comfort and hospitality are assured. Beautiful views over sea and harbour.
Bedrooms: 3 single, 3 double & 4 twin, 5 family rooms.
Bathrooms: 8 private, 2 public; 1 private shower.
Bed & breakfast: £16-£21.50 single, £32-£43 double.
Half board: £24.50-£30 daily, £145.25-£177 weekly.
Lunch available.
Evening meal 6.30pm (l.o. 7.30pm).
Parking for 7.
Credit: Access, Visa, Amex.

Florida Hotel ⚲
Summerleaze Cres., Bude, EX23 8HJ
☎ (0288) 352451
Superb location overlooking beach, downs and town. 5 choice menu, buffet Saturdays. Colour TV, radio, tea and coffee facilities in all rooms.
Bedrooms: 2 single, 10 double & 3 twin, 4 family rooms.
Bathrooms: 12 private, 3 public; 2 private showers.
Bed & breakfast: £18.75-£22 single, £37.50-£44 double.

Half board: £29-£32.50 daily, £175.50-£212 weekly.
Lunch available.
Evening meal 6.30pm (l.o. 7.30pm).
Parking for 10.
Open April-October.
Credit: Access, Visa.

Grosvenor Hotel
Summerleaze Cres., Bude, EX23 8HH
☎ (0288) 352062
Family hotel with views of beach and river. English and international food served. Golfing holidays arranged. Children and dogs welcome.
Bedrooms: 1 single, 3 double & 4 twin, 5 family rooms.
Bathrooms: 12 private, 1 public.
Bed & breakfast: £17-£19.50 single, £34-£40 double.
Half board: £29.50-£31 daily, £175-£195 weekly.
Lunch available.
Evening meal 7pm (l.o. 8.30pm).
Parking for 5.
Open April-November.

Meva-Gwin Hotel ⚲
APPROVED
Upton, Bude, EX23 0LY
☎ (0288) 352347
On Marine Drive between Bude and Widemouth Bay. Coastal and rural views from all rooms, friendly atmosphere, traditional English cooking.
Bedrooms: 2 single, 4 double & 1 twin, 5 family rooms.
Bathrooms: 11 private, 1 public.
Bed & breakfast: £14-£20 single, £34-£40 double.
Half board: £23.95-£27.95 daily, £126-£160 weekly.
Lunch available.
Evening meal 6.30pm (l.o. 6.30pm).
Parking for 44.
Open April-October.

The symbols are explained on the flap inside the back cover.

Map references apply to the colour maps towards the end of this guide.

Hotel Penarvor ⚲
Crooklets Beach, Bude, EX23 8NE
☎ (0288) 352036 & Fax (0288) 355027
Family-run hotel, 50 yards from surf beach and with panoramic views of coast and countryside. 200 yards from golf-course.
Bedrooms: 1 single, 9 double & 6 twin.
Bathrooms: 16 private.
Bed & breakfast: £20-£26 single, £40-£52 double.
Half board: £30-£36 daily, £195-£220 weekly.
Lunch available.
Evening meal 6.30pm (l.o. 8.30pm).
Parking for 20.
Open March-October.
Credit: Access, Visa, Amex.

Pencarrol Guest House
APPROVED
21 Downs View, Bude, EX23 8RF
☎ (0288) 352478
Early Edwardian Cornish stone and brick built house occupying south facing corner site. Sea views and overlooking golf-course.
Bedrooms: 1 single, 4 double & 2 twin, 1 family room.
Bathrooms: 2 private, 2 public.
Bed & breakfast: £12.50-£17 single, £25-£34 double.
Half board: £19-£23.50 daily, £114-£141 weekly.
Evening meal 6.30pm (l.o. 5pm).
Parking for 1.
Open January-November.

Trelawny Hotel
Marine Dr., Widemouth Bay, Bude, EX23 0AH
☎ (0288) 361328
Premier hotel fronting Atlantic surf-swept beach, 3 miles south of Bude. Breathtaking coastal/headland views. Surf equipment for hire. Bar.
Bedrooms: 2 single, 5 double & 2 twin, 3 family rooms.
Bathrooms: 12 private.
Bed & breakfast: £20 single, £40 double.
Half board: £28 daily, £168-£189 weekly.
Evening meal 7pm (l.o. 9pm).
Parking for 20.
Open April-October.
Credit: Access, Visa.

BURBAGE

Wiltshire
Map ref 2B2

4m E. Pewsey
Village close to Savernake Forest, famous as a habitat for deer. Close by are the remains of Wolf Hall mansion, where a great banquet in honour of Jane Seymour took place in 1536.

The Old Vicarage ⚲
COMMENDED
Burbage, Marlborough, SN8 3AG
☎ (0672) 810495
Victorian country house in 2-acre garden, offering peace and comfort. Within easy reach of Bath, Salisbury, Oxford and Windsor.
Bedrooms: 1 single, 1 double & 1 twin.
Bathrooms: 3 private.
Bed & breakfast: from £32 single, from £55 double.
Lunch available.
Evening meal 8pm (l.o. 6pm).
Parking for 10.
Open February-December.
Credit: Access, Visa.

BURNHAM-ON-SEA

Somerset
Map ref 1D1

Small resort with extensive sands near the National Nature Reserve on Bridgwater Bay. The resort grew in place of an intended spa to be funded from lighthouse tolls. The lighthouse is now one of the town's attractions, as is the 15th C church whose white marble altar, made by Grinling Gibbons to Inigo Jones' design, was salvaged from James II's Whitehall Chapel.
Tourist Information Centre ☎ *(0278) 787852*

The Queen's Hotel ⚲
APPROVED
Pier St., Burnham-on-Sea, TA8 1BT
☎ (0278) 783045
Delightfully situated on the seafront. Built in 1850 and completely renovated to a high standard, offering friendly personal service. Satellite TV in all rooms.

Bedrooms: 2 single, 12 double & 2 twin, 1 family room.
Bathrooms: 17 private,
4 public.
Bed & breakfast: £30-£40 single, £48-£60 double.
Half board: £42.50-£50 daily.
Lunch available.
Evening meal 6.30pm (l.o. 9pm).
Parking for 20.
Credit: Access, Visa.

Royal Clarence Hotel ♏

31 The Esplanade, Burnham-on-Sea, TA8 1BQ
☎ (0278) 783138
Ⓜ Minotels
*Seafront coaching inn,
providing comfortable
accommodation and
specialising in traditional ales.
Good base for touring
Somerset.*
Bedrooms: 3 single, 6 double & 6 twin, 2 family rooms.
Bathrooms: 14 private;
3 private showers.
Bed & breakfast: £28 single, £43 double.
Half board: £38 daily, £196 weekly.
Lunch available.
Evening meal 7pm (l.o. 8.30pm).
Parking for 20.

Shalimar Guest House
APPROVED

174 Berrow Rd., Burnham-on-Sea, TA8 2JE
☎ (0278) 785898
*Large bungalow on coast road
close to town, golf-course and
beach. Offering high standard
accommodation with homely
atmosphere and food.*
Bedrooms: 1 double & 1 twin, 2 family rooms.
Bathrooms: 3 private,
1 public.
Bed & breakfast: £15.50-£17.95 single, £25-£27 double.
Half board: £18.75-£19.95 daily, £118-£125 weekly.
Evening meal 5pm (l.o. 7pm).
Parking for 5.

Prosperity from wool in the 15th C endowed this ancient market town with a fine church in the Perpendicular style. To the east are chalk downlands and at Oldbury Castle, an Iron Age fort, a 17th C white horse is carved into the hillside.

Chilvester Hill House
COMMENDED

Calne, SN11 0LP
☎ (0249) 813981 & 815785 &
Fax (0249) 814217
*Professional family accepting
guests in their spacious
Victorian house. Weekly rates
on application.*
Bedrooms: 1 double & 2 twin.
Bathrooms: 3 private,
1 public.
Bed & breakfast: £40-£50 single, £60-£75 double.
Half board: £48-£72 daily.
Evening meal 8pm (l.o. 10am).
Parking for 6.
Credit: Access, Visa, Diners, Amex.

Hayle Farm Hotel & Restaurant

Quemerford, Calne,
SN11 8UJ
☎ (0249) 813275
*A small country house hotel
with en-suite accommodation,
good cuisine and grounds of 4
acres. Situated on A4 between
Calne and Marlborough. Near
Avebury.*
Bedrooms: 3 single, 2 double & 2 twin.
Bathrooms: 7 private.
Bed & breakfast: £36.50-£39 single, £46-£49 double.
Half board: £28-£40 daily.
Lunch available.
Evening meal 7pm (l.o. 9.30pm).
Parking for 100.
Credit: Access, Visa.

3m NW. Bridgwater
Quantock Hills village with Brymore House, birthplace of John Pym, a leading statesman in the reign of Charles I, lying to the west. 3 fine old 16th C houses are close by.

Swang Farm

Cannington, Bridgwater,
TA5 2NJ
☎ Spaxton (0278) 67478
*600-acre mixed farm.
Comfortable accommodation in
caring relaxed atmosphere of
large farmhouse with beautiful
outlook. Heated pool. Good
base for walking/driving in the
West Country.*
Bedrooms: 3 double & 1 twin.
Bathrooms: 4 private.
Bed & breakfast: £20-£30 single, £40-£50 double.
Parking for 12.

Overlooking St. Ives Bay and with fine beaches.

Endsleigh Guest House
Listed APPROVED

St. Ives Rd., Carbis Bay, St. Ives, TR26 2SF
☎ Penzance (0736) 795777
*Family-run guesthouse with
large dining room and 2
lounges. Near buses, beaches
and golf-course, 1 mile from
St. Ives town.*
Bedrooms: 1 single, 5 double & 1 twin, 3 family rooms.
Bathrooms: 2 public.
Bed & breakfast: £10-£12 single, £20-£24 double.
Half board: £13-£15 daily, £83-£95 weekly.
Evening meal 6.30pm (l.o. 4pm).
Parking for 10.

Hotel Rotorua

Trencrom La., Carbis Bay,
St. Ives, TR26 2TD
☎ Penzance (0736) 795419
*Modern private hotel in quiet
wooded lane near many
sporting activities and beaches.*
Bedrooms: 1 single, 1 double & 1 twin, 10 family rooms.
Bathrooms: 13 private,
1 public.
Bed & breakfast: £17-£23 single, £34-£46 double.

Half board: £23.50-£29.50 daily, £164.50-£206.50 weekly.
Lunch available.
Evening meal 7pm (l.o. 5.30pm).
Parking for 10.
Open April-October.

St. Kew Hotel

St. Ives Rd., Carbis Bay,
St. Ives, TR26 2RT
☎ Penzance (0736) 795918
*Family-run licensed hotel
overlooking Carbis Bay. En-
suite rooms with sea views.
Friendly service. Ideal touring
base. Pets by arrangement.*
Bedrooms: 1 single, 4 double & 1 twin, 2 family rooms.
Bathrooms: 5 private,
1 public; 1 private shower.
Bed & breakfast: £13-£18 single, £30-£46 double.
Half board: £21-£31 daily, £140-£217 weekly.
Evening meal 6.30pm (l.o. 7pm).
Parking for 7.

George Hotel
COMMENDED

Market Pl., Castle Cary,
BA7 7AH
☎ (0963) 50761
*15th C thatched coaching inn
with en-suite rooms, 2 bars and
panelled dining room.
Centrally located for many
attractions.*
Bedrooms: 4 single, 6 double & 6 twin.
Bathrooms: 16 private.
Bed & breakfast: £42-£46 single, £57-£65 double.
Half board: £45-£62 daily.
Lunch available.
Evening meal 7pm (l.o. 9.30pm).
Parking for 10.
Credit: Access, Visa.

Individual proprietors have supplied all details of accommodation. Although we do check for accuracy, we advise you to confirm prices and other information at the time of booking.

The enquiry coupons at the back will help you when contacting proprietors.

CASTLE COMBE

Wiltshire
Map ref 2B2

One of England's prettiest villages, in a steep woodland valley by a brook. The handsome Perpendicular church recalls the village's prosperous times as a cloth-weaving centre. No trace remains of the original castle, but the 13th C effigy of its founder Walter de Dunstanville lies in the church.

Manor House M
HIGHLY COMMENDED
Castle Combe, Chippenham, SN14 7HR
☎ (0249) 782206 & Fax (0249) 782159 Telex 449931
Country house dating from 14th C. Exquisite setting in one of England's prettiest villages in the southern Cotswolds. 12 miles from Bath.
Bedrooms: 16 double & 16 twin, 4 family rooms.
Bathrooms: 36 private.
Bed & breakfast: £100-£250 double.
Half board: £85-£160 daily.
Lunch available.
Evening meal 7.30pm (l.o. 9pm).
Parking for 100.
Credit: Access, Visa, Diners, Amex.
⑤ ⚒ ⛴ ✆ ⊙ ◻ ✿ ⓘ Ⓥ ⊣ ⓣ ⚙ ⚵ ℛ ↗ ♪ ▶ ❀ ⦸ SP ℝ Ⓣ

CHAGFORD

Devon
Map ref 1C2

Handsome stone houses, some from the Middle Ages, grace this former stannary town on northern Dartmoor. Since the last century it has been a popular centre for walking expeditions and for tours of the antiquities on the rugged moor. There is a splendid 15th C granite church, said to be haunted by the poet Godolphin.

Easton Court Hotel M
COMMENDED
Easton Cross, Chagford, TQ13 8JL
☎ (0647) 433469
Small, quiet, 15th C hotel on the edge of Dartmoor. "Brideshead Revisited" was written in the library.

Bedrooms: 5 double & 2 twin.
Bathrooms: 7 private.
Bed & breakfast: £42-£48 single, £72-£78 double.
Half board: £47-£55 daily, £294-£315 weekly.
Evening meal 7.30pm (l.o. 8.30pm).
Parking for 15.
Open February-December.
Credit: Access, Visa, Amex.
⑤ ⚒ ⛴ ✆ ⊙ ◻ ✿ ⓘ Ⓥ ⊣ ⓣ ⚙ ▥ ⚵ ♪ ⛴ ▶ ✿ ❀ ⦸ SP ℝ Ⓣ

Three Crowns Hotel M
APPROVED
High St., Chagford, TQ13 8AJ
☎ (0647) 433444 & Fax (0647) 433117
13th C hotel of character in picturesque village within Dartmoor National Park. Varied cuisine. Function room.
Bedrooms: 1 single, 8 double & 6 twin, 2 family rooms.
Bathrooms: 17 private, 3 public.
Bed & breakfast: £25-£35 single, £50-£60 double.
Half board: £40-£50 daily, £200-£220 weekly.
Lunch available.
Evening meal 7pm (l.o. 9.30pm).
Parking for 21.
Credit: Access, Visa, C.Bl., Diners, Amex.
⑤ ✿ ▯ ◻ ✿ ⓘ Ⓥ ⊣ ⓣ ▥ ⚵ ⛴ ⚒ ⚙ Ⓤ ▶ ✓ ⦸ SP ℝ ℝ

CHARD

Somerset
Map ref 1D2

Market town in hilly countryside. The wide main street has some handsome buildings, among them the Guildhall, court house and almshouses. Modern light industry and dairy produce have replaced 19th C lace making which came at decline of cloth trade after 600 years.
Tourist Information Centre ☎ *(0460) 67463*

Lordleaze Hotel
COMMENDED
Lordleaze Lane, Off Forton Rd., Chard, TA20 2HW
☎ (0460) 61066 & Fax (0460) 66468
Attractive country hotel, 1 mile from Chard. Old world bar, lovely restaurant, log fires in winter, charming bedrooms. Ideal for coast and countryside.
Bedrooms: 1 single, 9 double & 1 twin, 1 family room.

Bathrooms: 12 private.
Bed & breakfast: £32-£35 single, £50-£55 double.
Half board: £45-£48 daily, £270-£288 weekly.
Lunch available.
Evening meal 7pm (l.o. 9.30pm).
Parking for 50.
Credit: Access, Visa, Amex.
⑤ ⚒ ✆ ⊙ ◻ ✿ ⓘ Ⓥ ⊣ ⦿ ◻ ⚒ ⛴ ⚙ DAP ⦸ SP Ⓣ

CHARMOUTH

Dorset
Map ref 1D2

Set back from the fossil-rich cliffs, a small coastal town where Charles II came to the Queen's Armes when seeking escape to France. Just south at low tide, the sandy beach rewards fossil-hunters; at Black Ven in 1811 a fossilised ichthyosaurus (now in London's Natural History Museum) was found.

Fernhill Hotel
⚜⚜⚜
Charmouth, Bridport, DT6 6BX
☎ (0297) 60492 & Fax (0297) 60492
Hotel and bungalows standing in 14 acres of most beautiful Dorset countryside, only a mile from the beach.
Bedrooms: 3 single, 8 double & 2 twin, 2 family rooms.
Bathrooms: 6 public; 4 private showers.
Bed & breakfast: £25-£32 single, £50-£60 double.
Lunch available.
Evening meal 7.30pm (l.o. 8.45pm).
Parking for 100.
Credit: Access, Visa.
⑤ ⊙ ◻ ✿ ⓘ Ⓥ ⊣ ⓣ ▥ ⚵ ⛴ ⚙ ⚒ ⛴ ▶ ✿ ⦸ SP Ⓣ

Hensleigh M
COMMENDED
Lower Sea La., Charmouth, Bridport, DT6 6LW
☎ (0297) 60830
Comfortable, well-equipped, family-run hotel. Friendly atmosphere. Home cooking using local produce. Quiet position, 300 metres from sea and coastal walks.
Bedrooms: 2 single, 3 double & 3 twin, 2 family rooms.
Bathrooms: 10 private.
Bed & breakfast: £19.25-£21.45 single, £38.50-£42.90 double.
Half board: £28.50-£30.70 daily, £189-£204 weekly.

Lunch available.
Evening meal 6.45pm (l.o. 7.30pm).
Parking for 15.
Open February-November.
⑤ ⚒ ⛴ ✿ ⓘ Ⓥ ⊣ ▥ ⚵ SP

Newlands House
COMMENDED
Stonebarrow La., Charmouth, DT6 6RA
☎ (0297) 60212
16th C former farmhouse of character, comfortably furnished with an ambience of quiet relaxation. Set in 2 acres of old gardens and orchards at foot of National Trust Golden Cap Estate. Noted for food. Smoking permitted in bar lounge only.
Bedrooms: 3 single, 4 double & 3 twin, 2 family rooms.
Bathrooms: 11 private, 1 public.
Bed & breakfast: £19.60-£22.25 single, £39.20-£44.25 double.
Half board: £29.50-£32.15 daily, £185.90-£202.60 weekly.
Evening meal 7pm (l.o. midday).
Parking for 15.
Open March-October.
⑤ 6 ◻ ✿ ⓘ Ⓥ ⅏ ⊣ ⓣ ▥ ⚒ ✿ ⚵ SP

Queen's Armes Hotel M
⚜⚜⚜
The Street, Charmouth, Bridport, DT6 6QF
☎ (0297) 60339
Reputed to be the sixth oldest inn in England and where King Charles II stayed. Old oak beams, walls with original stone fireplaces, medieval paintings.
Bedrooms: 3 single, 5 double & 3 twin.
Bathrooms: 11 private.
Bed & breakfast: £25-£28 single, £50-£56 double.
Half board: £35-£42 daily, £220-£260 weekly.
Evening meal 6.30pm (l.o. 8pm).
Parking for 15.
Open February-October.
Credit: Access, Visa.
⑤ 5 ⚒ ⛴ ◻ ✿ ⓘ Ⓥ ⊣ ⓣ ▥ ⚒ ✿ ⚵ SP ℝ

Thatch Lodge Hotel M
⚜⚜⚜
The Street, Charmouth, DT6 6PQ
☎ (0297) 60407 & Fax (0297) 60407
Charming 15th C cottage with bar and interesting continental and English cooking using local produce when possible.

Bedrooms: 4 double & 2 twin,
1 family room.
Bathrooms: 6 private,
1 public.
Bed & breakfast: £25-£32
single, £36-£48 double.
Half board: £28-£34 daily,
£177-£215 weekly.
Lunch available.
Evening meal 7pm (l.o. 9pm).
Parking for 15.
Credit: Access, Visa.

The White House M
COMMENDED
2 Hillside, The Street,
Charmouth, DT6 6PJ
☎ (0297) 60411
Listed Georgian house with
many original period features
including Georgian windows
and bow doors. Furnished in
keeping with the period.
Bedrooms: 1 single, 4 double
& 2 twin.
Bathrooms: 6 private;
1 private shower.
Bed & breakfast: £46-£48.50
single, £72-£77 double.
Half board: £53-£55 daily.
Lunch available.
Evening meal 7pm (l.o.
9.15pm).
Parking for 15.
Open March-November.
Credit: Access, Visa.

CHEDDAR
Somerset
Map ref 1D1

Large village at foot of
Mendips just south of the
spectacular Cheddar
Gorge. Close by are
Roman and Saxon sites
and famous show caves.
Traditional Cheddar
cheese is still made here.

Gordons Hotel
Cliff St., Cheddar, BS27 3PT
☎ (0934) 742497
Once a farmhouse, now a
comfortable hotel with
considerable charm and
character. Heated outdoor
swimming pool. Steak house
restaurant.
Bedrooms: 2 single, 8 double
& 1 twin, 2 family rooms.
Bathrooms: 5 private,
2 public; 3 private showers.
Bed & breakfast: £18.50-£30
single, £35-£45 double.
Half board: from £27.50
daily, from £160 weekly.
Lunch available.
Evening meal 6pm (l.o. 9pm).

Parking for 10.
Open February-December.
Credit: Access, Visa, Diners.

Market Cross Hotel
The Cross, Church St.,
Cheddar, BS27 3RA
☎ (0934) 742264
Privately-owned listed Regency
hotel, 5 minutes' walk from the
famous Cheddar Gorge, caves
and Mendip Hills. Wells,
Glastonbury, Bristol and Bath
are within easy reach.
Bedrooms: 1 single, 2 double
& 1 twin, 2 family rooms.
Bathrooms: 2 private,
1 public.
Bed & breakfast: £16.50-
£17.50 single, £32-£39 double.
Half board: £25-£30 daily.
Evening meal 7pm (l.o. 8pm).
Parking for 8.
Credit: Access, Visa.

Tor Farm M
Listed COMMENDED
Nyland, Cheddar, BS27 3UP
☎ (0934) 743710 &
(0934) 742549
33-acre mixed farm. On A371
between Cheddar and Draycott
(take the road signposted
Nyland). Quiet and peaceful
on Somerset Levels. Private
fishing. Ideally situated for
visiting Cheddar, Bath,
Wookey Hole, Glastonbury,
Wells and coast.
Bedrooms: 1 single, 5 double
& 2 twin, 1 family room.
Bathrooms: 3 private,
2 public; 2 private showers.
Bed & breakfast: from £15.50
single, £26-£34 double.
Evening meal 7pm (l.o. 4pm).
Parking for 10.
Credit: Access, Visa.

Winston Manor Hotel M
APPROVED
Bristol Road, Churchill,
Bristol, Avon BS19 5NL
☎ (0934) 852348
Attractive, privately owned
hotel offering warm welcome,
on edge of Mendips,
conveniently situated 5 miles
south of Bristol Airport and 5
miles north of Cheddar.
Bedrooms: 6 single, 6 double
& 2 twin, 1 family room.
Bathrooms: 14 private.
Bed & breakfast: from £43.50
single, from £59 double.
Half board: from £43 daily,
from £225 weekly.

Lunch available.
Evening meal 7pm (l.o.
9.45pm).
Parking for 50.
Credit: Access, Visa, Amex.

CHETNOLE
Dorset
Map ref 2A3

Foys
COMMENDED
Chetnole, Sherborne,
DT9 6PD
☎ Yetminster (0935) 872686
19th C country house set in
quiet rural location, large
beautiful garden with views.
On edge of small village.
Bedrooms: 1 double & 1 twin.
Bathrooms: 1 public.
Bed & breakfast: £29-£40
double.
Evening meal 7pm (l.o. 7pm).
Parking for 4.

CHEW STOKE
Avon
Map ref 2A2

Attractive village in the
Mendip Hills with an
interesting Tudor rectory
and the remains of a
Roman villa. To the south
is the Chew Valley
reservoir with its
extensive leisure
facilities.

Orchard House
COMMENDED
Bristol Rd., Chew Stoke,
Bristol, BS18 8UB
☎ Chew Magna
(0272) 333143
Comfortable accommodation in
a carefully modernised
Georgian house and coach
house annexe. Home cooking
using local produce.
Bedrooms: 1 single, 2 double
& 3 twin, 1 family room.
Bathrooms: 2 private,
2 public.
Bed & breakfast: from £16
single, from £32 double.
Half board: from £23.50
daily.
Evening meal 6.30pm (l.o.
10am).
Parking for 9.

> *Please mention this*
> *guide when making*
> *a booking.*

CHIDEOCK
Dorset
Map ref 1D2

Village of creamy
sandstone thatched
cottages sheltering in
valley near the dramatic
Dorset coast. The church
holds an interesting
processional cross in
mother-of-pearl and the
manor house close by is
associated with the richly-
decorated Victorian
Roman Catholic church.
Seatown's pebble beach
is flanked by limestone
cliffs.

Chideock House Hotel M
Chideock, Bridport,
DT6 6JN
☎ (0297) 89242
15th C thatched house in
Chideock village. Situated on
the A35, 3 miles west of
Bridport and less than 1 mile
from the sea.
Bedrooms: 1 single, 3 double
& 3 twin, 2 family rooms.
Bathrooms: 6 private,
1 public.
Bed & breakfast: £30-£35
single, £48-£50 double.
Half board: from £45 daily,
£463-£510 weekly.
Evening meal 7pm (l.o.
9.30pm).
Parking for 20.
Credit: Access, Visa.

CHILLINGTON
Devon
Map ref 1D3

4m E. Kingsbridge

White House Hotel M
COMMENDED
Chillington, Kingsbridge,
TQ7 2JX
☎ (0548) 580580
Georgian country house,
between Salcombe and
Dartmouth, 2 miles from the
sea at Torcross. Sandy
beaches, sailing, golf and cliff
walks all within easy reach.
Bedrooms: 4 double & 3 twin,
1 family room.
Bathrooms: 6 private,
1 public.
Bed & breakfast: £50-£79
double.
Half board: £33.75-£47.90
daily, £197.75-£292.25 weekly.
Lunch available.

Continued ▶

CHILLINGTON
Continued

Evening meal 7pm (l.o. 8.05pm).
Parking for 8.
Open April-October.
🛏⛵📵☎💷♿📺🍴♨🚫🅿️

CHIPPENHAM
Wiltshire
Map ref 2B2

12m NE. Bath
Ancient market town with modern industry, retaining a large cattle market and some half-timbered houses. Notable early buildings include the medieval Town Hall and the gabled 15th C Yelde Hall, now a local history museum, which has a wooden turret. On the outskirts Hardenhuish has a charming hilltop church by the Georgian architect John Wood of Bath.
Tourist Information Centre ☎ (0249) 657733

Stanton Manor Hotel & Restaurant
Stanton St.Quintin, Chippenham, SN14 6DQ
☎ Malmesbury (0666) 837552 & Fax (0666) 887022
Set in delightful gardens and woodland, yet just off the M4 (junction 17) 4 miles north of Chippenham. A warm welcome awaits at this elegant hotel.
Bedrooms: 4 double & 1 twin.
Bathrooms: 5 private.
Bed & breakfast: from £64 single, from £78 double.
Lunch available.
Evening meal 7pm (l.o. 9.30pm).
Parking for 40.
Credit: Access, Visa, Amex.
🛏⛵📵☎💷♿📺🍴

CHOLDERTON
Wiltshire
Map ref 2B2

5m E. Amesbury

Park House Guest House & Motel
▲▲▲ APPROVED
Cholderton, Salisbury, SP4 0EG
☎ (0980) 64256

17th C former coaching inn built of brick and flint with slate roof. 5 miles east of Stonehenge, 10 miles north of Salisbury and 9 miles west of Andover.
Bedrooms: 5 single, 9 double & 7 twin, 2 family rooms.
Bathrooms: 10 private, 3 public.
Bed & breakfast: £17-£27.50 single, £34-£38.50 double.
Half board: £21-£34.50 daily.
Evening meal 7pm (l.o. 8.30pm).
Parking for 30.
🛏⛵📵☎💷♿📺🍴

CHUDLEIGH KNIGHTON
Devon
Map ref 1D2

Tynedale Guest House ▲
▲▲
Chudleigh Knighton, Newton Abbot, TQ13 0ET
☎ Chudleigh (0626) 852317
Former rectory with large garden, in the centre of a quiet village. Ideal touring centre, minutes from A38. Personal attention assured.
Bedrooms: 1 single, 1 double & 1 twin, 2 family rooms.
Bathrooms: 3 private, 3 public.
Bed & breakfast: £17-£20 single, £32-£36 double.
Parking for 6.
🛏⛵📵☎💷♿📺🍴

CLEVEDON
Avon
Map ref 1D1

Handsome Victorian resort on shingly shores of Severn Estuary. Seafront entertainments and pier, golf links with ruined folly, part-Norman clifftop church. Tennyson and Thackeray stayed at the splendid Clevedon Court just to the east. Basically medieval with later additions, the manor and its fine chapel window overlook terraces with rare plants. Walk-round craft centre nearby.

Walton Park Hotel ▲
1 Wellington Ter., Clevedon, BS21 7BL
☎ (0272) 874253 & Fax (0272) 343577

Spacious, bright hotel set in 2 acres of gardens and overlooking the Severn Estuary. Exceptionally quiet location, yet only 2 miles from M5 junction 20.
Bedrooms: 12 single, 7 double & 18 twin, 1 family room.
Bathrooms: 38 private.
Bed & breakfast: £32-£55 single, £64-£69.50 double.
Half board: £45-£52.50 daily, from £315 weekly.
Lunch available.
Evening meal 7.30pm (l.o. 9pm).
Parking for 40.
Credit: Access, Visa, Diners, Amex.
🛏⛵☎💷♿📺🍴

CLOVELLY
Devon
Map ref 1C1

Clinging to wild wooded cliffs, fishing village with steep cobbled street zigzagging, or cut in steps, to harbour. Carrying sleds stand beside whitewashed flower-decked cottages. Charles Kingsley's father was rector of the church with its Norman porch, set high up near the Hamlyn family's Clovelly Court.

Foxdown Manor ▲
Horn's Cross, Parkham, Bideford, EX39 5PJ
☎ Horn's Cross (0237) 451325/451642
Small family-run country house hotel set in 17 acres of woodland and gardens, six miles east of Clovelly. The standard of accommodation will appeal to discerning guests.
Bedrooms: 1 single, 4 double & 2 twin, 1 family room.
Bathrooms: 8 private, 1 public.
Bed & breakfast: £40-£57 single, £68-£101 double.
Half board: £58-£76 daily, £333-£423 weekly.
Lunch available.
Evening meal 7.15pm (l.o. 9pm).
Parking for 30.
Credit: Access, Visa.
🛏⛵☎💷♿📺🍴

New Inn Hotel ▲
High St., Clovelly, Bideford, EX39 5TQ
☎ (0237) 431636

Traditional inn situated in unique privately owned village - cobbled streets, no vehicles allowed. Fresh fish and local produce in restaurant.
Bedrooms: 3 single, 9 double & 5 twin, 3 family rooms.
Bathrooms: 5 private, 2 public; 4 private showers.
Bed & breakfast: from £19.75 single, £39.50-£50 double.
Half board: £31-£36.50 daily.
Lunch available.
Evening meal 6.30pm (l.o. 9pm).
Parking for 220.
Credit: Access, Visa, C.Bl., Diners, Amex.
🛏⛵☎💷♿📺🍴

Red Lion Hotel ▲
The Quay, Clovelly, Bideford, EX39 5TF
☎ (0237) 431237
18th C quayside inn in one of the world's unique villages.
Bedrooms: 8 double & 3 twin, 1 family room.
Bathrooms: 12 private.
Bed & breakfast: £32 single, £51 double.
Half board: £42-£45 daily.
Lunch available.
Evening meal 6.30pm (l.o. 9pm).
Parking for 12.
Credit: Access, Visa.
🛏⛵☎💷♿📺🍴

COLYTON
Devon
Map ref 1D2

Surrounded by fertile farmland, this small riverside town was an early Saxon settlement. Medieval prosperity from the wool trade built the grand church tower with its octagonal lantern and the church's fine west window.

Swallows Eaves ▲
▲▲▲ COMMENDED
Colyford, Colyton, EX13 6QJ
☎ Colyton (0297) 53184
Attractive award-winning hotel for discerning guests, in an area of outstanding natural beauty. Quality rooms and interesting food. Attractive breaks - third day free.
Bedrooms: 4 double & 4 twin.
Bathrooms: 8 private.
Bed & breakfast: £25-£30 single, £50-£60 double.
Half board: £38.50-£44.50 daily, £238-£280 weekly.
Lunch available.
Evening meal 7pm (l.o. 8pm).

Parking for 10.
Credit: Amex.

White Cottage Hotel
COMMENDED

Dolphin St., Colyton,
EX13 6NA
☎ (0297) 52401
*Small privately run 15th C
hotel - still giving old fashioned
standards of personal service
and food.*
Bedrooms: 1 single, 2 double
& 2 twin, 1 family room.
Bathrooms: 6 private.
Bed & breakfast: £30.90-
£35.90 single, £51.90-£54.90
double.
Half board: £39.90-£44.90
daily.
Lunch available.
Evening meal 7.15pm (l.o.
9pm).
Parking for 20.
Credit: Access, Visa.

COMBE MARTIN

Devon
Map ref 1C1

Seaside village spreading
along its valley to a rocky
beach. Silver was mined
here in the Middle Ages,
market gardening yields
today's produce. An
unusual sight is the Pack
of Cards pub, while the
church with its gargoyles
is noted for panel
paintings on the 15th C
rood screen.

Saffron House Hotel M
APPROVED

King St., Combe Martin,
EX34 0BX
☎ (0271) 883521
*17th C hotel set in own
grounds close to beaches and
Exmoor. Well-appointed en-
suite rooms. Heated pool.
Children and pets very
welcome. Ideal touring centre.*
Bedrooms: 4 double & 1 twin,
5 family rooms.
Bathrooms: 6 private,
2 public; 2 private showers.
Bed & breakfast: £15.50-
£18.50 single, £31-£37 double.
Half board: £23.50-£26.50
daily, £145-£165 weekly.
Evening meal 6.30pm.
Parking for 10.
Credit: Access, Visa.

CONSTANTINE BAY

Cornwall
Map ref 1B2

3m W. Padstow
Wide sands backed with
tall dunes looking toward
lighthouse on Trevose
Head. Beautiful sand-
dune golf-course has the
ruined chapel of St.
Constantine whose font
can be seen in St. Merryn
Church just inland.

Treglos Hotel M
COMMENDED

Constantine Bay, Padstow,
PL28 8JH
☎ Padstow (0841) 520727
Telex 45795 WSTTLX G
TGS
Ⓒ Consort
*Overlooking sea and golf-
course. Varied English/French
food and hospitality in quiet
country surroundings. Under
personal supervision of owners.*
Bedrooms: 8 single, 3 double
& 29 twin, 4 family rooms.
Bathrooms: 44 private,
1 public.
Half board: £47.50-£60.50
daily, £269.50-£395 weekly.
Lunch available.
Evening meal 7.45pm (l.o.
9.30pm).
Parking for 60.
Open March-November.
Credit: Access, Visa.

CORSHAM

Wiltshire
Map ref 2B2

Growing town with old
centre showing Flemish
influence, legacy of
former prosperity from
weaving. The church,
restored last century,
retains Norman features.
The Elizabethan Corsham
Court, with additions by
Capability Brown, has
fine furniture and an
outstanding collection of
paintings.

Methuen Arms Hotel M

2 High St, Corsham,
SN13 0HB
☎ (0249) 714867 & Fax
(0249) 712004
*14th C origins, charming stone-
walled restaurant, 2 bars,
skittle alley. Conveniently
placed for Bath, Stonehenge
and the Cotswolds.*

Bedrooms: 6 single, 11 double
& 7 twin, 1 family room.
Bathrooms: 24 private,
1 public; 1 private shower.
Bed & breakfast: £43-£49
single, £61-£68 double.
Half board: £50-£70 daily.
Lunch available.
Evening meal 7pm (l.o.
10pm).
Parking for 106.
Credit: Access, Visa.

Rudloe Park Hotel &
Restaurant M
COMMENDED

Leafy La., Corsham,
SN13 0PA
☎ Bath (0225) 810555 & Fax
(0225) 811412
*An old country house set in 4
acres of lawns and gardens,
with beautiful views down the
valley to Bath. No smoking in
the restaurant.*
Bedrooms: 8 double & 2 twin,
1 family room.
Bathrooms: 11 private.
Bed & breakfast: £55-£60
single, £80-£90 double.
Half board: £57-£62 daily.
Lunch available.
Evening meal 7pm (l.o.
10pm).
Parking for 70.
Credit: Access, Visa, C.Bl.,
Diners, Amex.

CRANTOCK

Cornwall
Map ref 1B2

2m SW. Newquay
Pretty village of thatched
cottages and seaside
bungalows. Village
stocks, once used against
smugglers, are in the
churchyard and the pub
has a smugglers' hideout.

Crantock Bay Hotel M

Crantock, Newquay,
TR8 5SE
☎ (0637) 830229 & Fax
(0637) 831111
Ⓒ Minotels
*Long established family hotel
on headland, with grounds
leading directly on to beach.
National Trust land nearby.
Wonderful walking country.*
Bedrooms: 9 single, 9 double
& 18 twin.
Bathrooms: 36 private,
1 public.
Bed & breakfast: £26-£39
single, £52-£78 double.
Half board: £35-£49 daily.

Lunch available.
Evening meal 7pm (l.o.
8.30pm).
Parking for 36.
Open March-November.
Credit: Access, Visa, Diners,
Amex.

CREDITON

Devon
Map ref 1D2

Ancient town in fertile
valley, once prosperous
from wool, now active in
cider-making. Said to be
the birthplace of St.
Boniface. The 13th C
Chapter House, the
church governors'
meeting place, holds a
collection of armour from
the Civil War.

Coombe House Country
Hotel M
APPROVED

Coleford, Crediton,
EX17 5BY
☎ Copplestone (0363) 84487
*Country hotel in beautiful,
relaxed setting. Ideal for
touring. Heated pool, tennis
court. 5 acres of ground. A la
carte restaurant.*
Bedrooms: 2 single, 3 double
& 3 twin, 3 family rooms.
Bathrooms: 10 private,
2 public.
Bed & breakfast: £28 single,
£48-£58 double.
Half board: £41-£43 daily,
from £231 weekly.
Lunch available.
Evening meal 7.30pm (l.o.
9.30pm).
Parking for 90.
Credit: Access, Visa, Amex.

---

*Individual
proprietors have
supplied all details
of accommodation.
Although we do
check for accuracy,
we advise you to
confirm prices and
other information
at the time of
booking.*

383

CREWKERNE

Somerset
Map ref 1D2

This charming little market town on the Dorset border nestles in undulating farmland and orchards in a conservation area. Built of local sandstone with Roman and Saxon origins. Dominated by the magnificent St. Bartholomew's Church dating from the 15th C. All set amidst peaceful countryside, thatched cottages, stately homes and romantic legends. St. Bartholomew's Fair is held in September.

Broadview ⚠
🎖🎖🎖 HIGHLY COMMENDED

43 East St., Crewkerne, TA18 7AG
☎ (0460) 73424
Secluded colonial-style bungalow, traditionally furnished. Friendly relaxing atmosphere. In an acre of landscaped grounds, featuring a water garden. Lovely views and comfortable individually furnished en-suite/private rooms. Quality home-cooking.
Bedrooms: 1 double & 2 twin.
Bathrooms: 3 private.
Bed & breakfast: £23-£25 single, max. £33 double.
Half board: max. £25 daily, max. £175 weekly.
Evening meal 6.30pm (l.o. midday).
Parking for 6.

CRICKLADE

Wiltshire
Map ref 2B2

Standing on the upper Thames, an old town and former Anglo-Saxon settlement. The Roman road from Cirencester passes through and canals pass to north and south. The church, its lofty Tudor tower dominating the town, has work of varying periods from the 12th C to 1930.

Upper Chelworth Farm Hotel
🎖🎖🎖 COMMENDED

Cricklade, Swindon, SN6 6HD
☎ Swindon (0793) 750440

Situated 1 mile from the Cotswold Water Parks. Large garden with fish pool and bird aviaries.
Bedrooms: 3 single, 2 double & 1 twin, 1 family room.
Bathrooms: 6 private, 1 public.
Bed & breakfast: £30-£40 single, £38-£55 double.
Half board: £42-£70 daily, £180-£215 weekly.
Lunch available.
Evening meal 5pm (l.o. 7pm).
Parking for 12.
Credit: Access, Visa.

CROYDE

Devon
Map ref 1C1

7m SW. Ilfracombe
Pretty village with thatched cottages near Croyde Bay. To the south stretch Saunton Sands and their dunelands Braunton Burrows with interesting flowers and plants, nature reserve and golf-course. Cliff walks and bird-watching at Baggy Point, west of the village.

Croyde Bay House Hotel
🎖🎖🎖 COMMENDED

Moor Lane, Croyde, Braunton, EX33 1PA
☎ (0271) 890270
Unique position overlooking bay, with the highest tides reaching the hotel's garden wall. All rooms with beautiful views, en-suite, tea making facilities.
Bedrooms: 3 double & 2 twin, 2 family rooms.
Bathrooms: 7 private, 1 public.
Bed & breakfast: £30-£40 single, £60-£79 double.
Half board: £35-£48.50 daily, £257.50-£291 weekly.
Evening meal 7.15pm (l.o. 8pm).
Parking for 7.
Open March-November.
Credit: Access, Visa.

Moorsands House Hotel
🎖🎖🎖 APPROVED

Moor Lane, Croyde Bay, Braunton, EX33 1NP
☎ (0271) 890781
Hotel with sea views, 5 minutes from beach. All rooms with en-suite shower and WC, TV and tea-making facilities. Excellent menu, wine list, bar.

Bedrooms: 4 double & 2 twin, 2 family rooms.
Bathrooms: 8 private.
Bed & breakfast: £20-£23 single, £34-£40 double.
Half board: £25.50-£31.50 daily, £164-£206 weekly.
Evening meal 7pm (l.o. 6pm).
Parking for 8.
Open April-October.
Credit: Access, Visa.

CULLOMPTON

Devon
Map ref 1D2

Market town on former coaching routes, with pleasant tree-shaded cobbled pavements and some handsome 17th C houses. Earlier prosperity from the wool industry is reflected in the grandness of the church with its fan-vaulted aisle built by a wool-stapler in 1526.

Rullands
🎖🎖🎖 COMMENDED

Rull La., Cullompton, EX15 1NQ
☎ (0884) 33356
14th C country house amid beautiful Devon countryside. Within easy reach of all country pursuits, the M5 and the historic town of Tiverton.
Bedrooms: 2 single, 2 double.
Bathrooms: 3 private; 1 private shower.
Bed & breakfast: £22.50-£27.50 single, £42.50-£47.50 double.
Half board: £32.50-£40 daily.
Lunch available.
Evening meal 7.15pm (l.o. 9.30pm).
Parking for 20.
Credit: Access, Visa.

DARTMOOR

See Ashburton, Bovey Tracey, Bridestowe, Buckfastleigh, Buckland Monachorum, Chagford, Haytor, Horrabridge, Lustleigh, Lydford, Mary Tavy, Moretonhampstead, Okehampton, Tavistock, Two Bridges, Widecombe-in-the-Moor, Yelverton.

We advise you to confirm your booking in writing.

DARTMOUTH

Devon
Map ref 1D3

Ancient port, now a resort, on wooded slopes above natural harbour at mouth of Dart. Has fine period buildings, notably town houses near Quay and Butterwalk of 1635. The church is richly-furnished and the harbour castle ruin recalls earlier importance when Crusader fleets assembled here. Royal Naval College, grandly built in 1905, dominates from hill. Carnival, June; Regatta, August.
Tourist Information Centre ☎ (0803) 834224

The Captains House
🎖🎖🎖 COMMENDED

18 Clarence St., Dartmouth, TQ6 9NW
☎ (0803) 832133
18th C listed house. Tasteful decor and personal service. Close to river and shops.
Bedrooms: 1 single, 3 double & 1 twin.
Bathrooms: 5 private.
Bed & breakfast: £22-£25 single, £32-£40 double.
Credit: Amex.

Eastdown House
🎖🎖🎖 COMMENDED

Eastdown, Blackawton, Totnes, TQ9 7AP
☎ (080 421) 372
Spacious 18th C Georgian house 6 miles from Dartmouth in splendid rural setting. Friendly atmosphere and en-suite facilities.
Bedrooms: 2 double & 1 twin.
Bathrooms: 3 private.
Bed & breakfast: £28-£32 double.
Evening meal 7pm (l.o. 9.30pm).
Parking for 4.

Royal Castle Hotel ⚠
🎖🎖🎖 COMMENDED

11 The Quay, Dartmouth, TQ6 9PS
☎ (0803) 833033 & Fax (0803) 835445
Historic 17th C quayside coaching inn with resident proprietors, offering traditional style food and service. Open fires, comfortable bedrooms.
Bedrooms: 4 single, 10 double & 7 twin, 4 family rooms.
Bathrooms: 25 private.

Bed & breakfast: £37-£48 single, £62-£98 double.
Half board: £36-£62 daily, £216-£350 weekly.
Lunch available.
Evening meal 6.45pm (l.o. 9.45pm).
Parking for 3.
Credit: Access, Visa.

Stoke Lodge Hotel M
♛♛♛♛ COMMENDED
Cinders La., Stoke Fleming, Dartmouth, TQ6 0RA
☎ (0803) 770523
Country house hotel with sea and village views. Heated indoor and outdoor swimming pools and leisure facilities, including all-weather tennis court.
Bedrooms: 3 single, 8 double & 8 twin, 5 family rooms.
Bathrooms: 24 private.
Bed & breakfast: £36-£42.50 single, £57-£70 double.
Half board: £37.50-£44 daily, £255.50-£299 weekly.
Lunch available.
Evening meal 7pm (l.o. 9pm).
Parking for 50.

Sunnybanks Guest House
♛♛♛ APPROVED
1 Vicarage Hill, Dartmouth, TQ6 9EW
☎ (0803) 832766
If you are looking for high standards of cleanliness, en-suite rooms, full breakfast, countryside views and garaging facilities nearby for your car, this is the place.
Bedrooms: 1 single, 6 double & 2 twin, 1 family room.
Bathrooms: 4 private, 1 public; 5 private showers.
Bed & breakfast: £16-£17.50 single, £32-£44 double.
Half board: £26-£32 daily, £180-£290 weekly.
Evening meal 6pm (l.o. 8pm).
Parking for 3.

Victoria Hotel M
27-29 Victoria Rd., Dartmouth, TQ6 9RT
☎ Dartmouth (0803) 832572 & 832116
Freehouse family-run hotel in town centre, with friendly personal service. Family lounge, 2 bars, restaurant serving local fish and home-made dishes.
Bedrooms: 2 single, 3 double & 3 twin, 2 family rooms.

Bathrooms: 4 private, 2 public.
Bed & breakfast: £18-£22.50 single, £36-£54 double.
Half board: £25-£35 daily, £175-£210 weekly.
Lunch available.
Evening meal 7pm (l.o. 9.30pm).
Credit: Access, Visa.

DAWLISH
Devon
Map ref 1D2

Small resort, developed in Regency and Victorian periods beside Dawlish Water which runs down from the Haldon Hills. Town centre has ornamental riverside gardens with black swans. One of British Rail's most scenic stretches was built by Brunel alongside jagged red cliffs between the sands and the town.
Tourist Information Centre ☎ (0626) 863589

Brockington House M
♛♛♛ COMMENDED
139 Exeter Rd., Dawlish, EX7 0AN
☎ (0626) 863588
Licensed guesthouse on coast road (A379). 5 minutes' walk from sea. Town centre approximately three-quarters of a mile away.
Bedrooms: 1 single, 8 double & 1 twin.
Bathrooms: 6 private, 1 public.
Bed & breakfast: £17-£18.50 single, £34-£41 double.
Half board: £26-£29.50 daily, £170-£190 weekly.
Evening meal 7pm (l.o. 5pm).
Parking for 10.
Credit: Access, Visa, Amex.

Langstone Cliff Hotel M
♛♛♛
Dawlish Warren, Dawlish, EX7 0NA
☎ (0626) 865155 & Fax (0626) 867166
Consort
Family-owned hotel set in 19 acres of grounds, overlooking the sea. Extensive leisure and conference facilities.
Bedrooms: 10 single, 10 double & 10 twin, 34 family rooms.
Bathrooms: 64 private, 3 public.
Bed & breakfast: £42-£50 single, £72-£90 double.

Half board: £41-£54 daily, from £280 weekly.
Lunch available.
Evening meal 7pm (l.o. 9pm).
Parking for 200.
Credit: Access, Visa, Diners, Amex.

Radfords Country Hotel M
♛♛♛ COMMENDED
Lower Dawlish Water, Dawlish, EX7 0QN
☎ (0626) 863322
Highly specialised family hotel near the sea. Service, entertainment and safety standards for children of all ages.
Bedrooms: 37 family rooms.
Bathrooms: 37 private.
Bed & breakfast: £20-£30 single, £40-£60 double.
Half board: £30-£45 daily, £190-£295 weekly.
Evening meal 6pm (l.o. 7pm).
Parking for 52.
Open March-November.
Credit: Access, Visa.

DEVIZES
Wiltshire
Map ref 2B2

Standing on the Kennet and Avon Canal, old market town near the Vale of Pewsey. Rebuilt Norman castle, good 18th C buildings and old inns. All 3 churches are of interest, notably St. John's with 12th C work and Norman tower. Museum of Wiltshire's archaeology and natural history reflects wealth of prehistoric sites on Salisbury Plain and at other locations nearby.
Tourist Information Centre ☎ (0380) 729408

Black Swan Hotel
♛♛♛
Market Pl., Devizes, SN10 1JQ
☎ (0380) 723259
Historic 18th C coaching inn.
Bedrooms: 1 single, 5 double & 4 twin.
Bathrooms: 10 private.
Bed & breakfast: £35-£40 single, £52-£57 double.
Half board: £40-£50 daily.
Lunch available.
Evening meal 7pm (l.o. 9pm).
Parking for 12.
Credit: Access, Visa.

The Castle Hotel M
♛♛♛♛
New Park St., Devizes, SN10 1DS
☎ (0380) 729300 & Fax (0380) 729155
Well-appointed accommodation in family-run environment. A la carte restaurant and popular bar. All rooms en-suite.
Bedrooms: 6 single, 5 double & 7 twin, 1 family room.
Bathrooms: 19 private.
Bed & breakfast: £40-£45 single, £55-£60 double.
Half board: £37.50-£55 daily.
Lunch available.
Evening meal 6.30pm (l.o. 10pm).
Parking for 4.
Credit: Access, Visa, Diners, Amex.

Long Street Guest House
♛♛
27 Long St., Devizes, SN10 1NW
☎ (0380) 724245
300 yards from town centre. Panelled dining room. Spacious bedrooms, 3 with a lot of character.
Bedrooms: 1 single, 3 double & 3 twin.
Bathrooms: 6 private, 1 public.
Bed & breakfast: £17-£20 single, £30-£40 double.
Parking for 7.

Pinecroft
♛♛ APPROVED
Potterne Rd., Devizes, SN10 5DA
☎ (0380) 721433
Comfortable Georgian family house with spacious rooms and exquisite garden. Only 3 minutes' walk from town centre.
Bedrooms: 2 double & 2 twin, 1 family room.
Bathrooms: 4 private, 1 public.
Bed & breakfast: £18-£23 single, £32-£36 double.
Parking for 6.
Credit: Access, Visa, Amex.

Rathlin
♛♛♛ COMMENDED
Wick Lane, Devizes, SN10 5DP
☎ (0380) 721999

Continued ▶

DEVIZES

Continued

Elegant period charm, all rooms en-suite and individually furnished. Quiet location close to town centre. Tranquil gardens. Ample parking.
Bedrooms: 2 double & 2 twin.
Bathrooms: 4 private,
1 public.
Bed & breakfast: £20 single,
£34 double.
Evening meal 6pm (l.o. 7.30pm).
Parking for 5.

ॐ ᗌ ᗆ ᖸ ▥ █ ✓ ⬚ ▥
⬛ ✗ ▦ ⊡ ᔕᔿ ▦ Ⓣ

DITTISHAM

Devon
Map ref 1D2

Old village with thatched cottages close to the Dart Estuary. The church is noted for its 15th C carved stone and attractive painted stone pulpit. A ferry crosses to Greenway where Sir Walter Raleigh's half-brother Sir Humphrey Gilbert was born.

The Red Lion Inn M
APPROVED

Dittisham, Dartmouth,
TQ6 0ES
☎ (080 422) 235
Fax (080 422) 443
Commanding position in centre of attractive village, with magnificent views of River Dart and the moors. Terrace and garden, newly-opened restaurant.
Bedrooms: 2 double & 2 twin.
Bathrooms: 2 private,
1 public.
Bed & breakfast: £17.50-£22.50 single, £33-£42 double.
Lunch available.
Evening meal 7pm (l.o. 9.30pm).
Parking for 14.
Credit: Access, Visa.

ॐ ᗌ ᖵ ᖸ ▥ █ ⬛ ▦ ᔕᔿ ▦

The symbols are explained on the flap inside the back cover.

Map references apply to the colour maps towards the end of this guide.

DORCHESTER

Dorset
Map ref 2B3

Busy medieval county town (cloth and ale-producing centre) destroyed by fires in 17th and 18th C. Cromwellian stronghold and scene of Judge Jeffrey's Bloody Assize (his High Street lodging is now a restaurant) after Monmouth Rebellion of 1685. Tolpuddle Martyrs were tried in Shire Hall. Museum has Roman and earlier exhibits and Hardy relics.
Tourist Information Centre ☎ *(0305) 267992*

Hadley Lodge
APPROVED

Main Rd., Winterbourne Abbas, Dorchester,
DT2 9LW
☎ Martinstown (030 589) 558
Large modernised country house, providing comfortable accommodation, 5 miles west of Dorchester. Convenient for touring west Dorset. Home-cooked food.
Bedrooms: 1 double & 2 twin, 2 family rooms.
Bathrooms: 2 private,
1 public.
Bed & breakfast: £14-£17 single, £28-£34 double.
Half board: £21-£24 daily,
£147-£168 weekly.
Evening meal 7pm (l.o. 7pm).
Parking for 6.
Open April-October.

ॐ ᗌ ᗆ ᖸ ▥ ⬚ �𝕋𝕍 ▥ █ ᔋ ✿
✗ ▦ ▦

Wessex Royale Hotel

32 High West St.,
Dorchester, DT1 1UP
☎ (0305) 262660
Fax (0305) 251941
Georgian town centre hotel, recently refurbished to a high standard, with extensive restaurant, bar and function facilities.
Bedrooms: 3 single, 14 double & 4 twin, 1 family room.
Bathrooms: 22 private.
Bed & breakfast: £25-£45 single, £39.50-£59.50 double.
Half board: £35-£55 daily,
£210-£330 weekly.
Lunch available.
Evening meal 6pm (l.o. 11.30pm).
Parking for 5.
Credit: Access, Visa, C.Bl., Diners, Amex.

ॐ ⬚ ᖵ ⓐ ᗐ ⬚ ᔋ ᖲ ᖸ ▥ ✓
⬤ █ ⬛ ᔋ ✗ ⊡ ᔕᔿ ▦ Ⓣ

DULVERTON

Somerset
Map ref 1D1

Set among woods and hills of south-west Exmoor, a busy riverside town with a 13th C church. The Rivers Barle and Exe are rich in salmon and trout. The Exmoor National Park Headquarters at Dulverton Information Centre are open throughout the year.

Carnarvon Arms Hotel M
🏰🏰🏰

Brushford, Dulverton,
TA22 9AE
☎ (0398) 23302 & Fax (0398) 24022
Privately-owned country hotel overlooking the picturesque Barle Valley, on the edge of Exmoor National Park. Closed most of February.
Bedrooms: 6 single, 4 double & 14 twin, 2 family rooms.
Bathrooms: 22 private,
1 public.
Bed & breakfast: £38-£48 single, £80-£100 double.
Half board: £45-£55 daily,
£315-£385 weekly.
Lunch available.
Evening meal 7.30pm (l.o. 9.30pm).
Parking for 100.
Credit: Access, Visa.

ॐ ᗊ ᖵ ᗐ ⬚ ⓘ ▥ ✓ ⬚
▥ ⬛ ᔋ ᖰ ᖲ ৬ Ⓤ ◡ ✿
▦ ᔋ ᔕᔿ

Exton House Hotel M
🏰🏰🏰 COMMENDED

Exton, Dulverton, TA22 9JT
☎ Winsford (064 385) 365
Former rectory in a delightful rural setting on the side of the Exe Valley. Turn off A396 at Bridgetown and we are half a mile on right.
Bedrooms: 1 single, 2 double & 2 twin, 1 family room.
Bathrooms: 4 private,
1 public.
Bed & breakfast: £20-£32.50 single, £40-£55 double.
Half board: £27.50-£35 daily,
£183-£233 weekly.
Evening meal 7.30pm (l.o. 2pm).
Parking for 6.
Credit: Access, Visa.

ॐ ᗊ ᗐ ⬚ ⓘ ▥ ✓ ⬚ ▥
⬛ ✿ ▦ ᔋ ᔕᔿ

DUNSTER

Somerset
Map ref 1D1

Ancient town with views of Exmoor and the Quantocks, whose historic hilltop castle has been continuously occupied since it was begun in 1070. Medieval prosperity from cloth built the octagonal Yarn Market, late 16th C, and the church with its broad wagon roof. A riverside mill, packhorse bridge and 18th C hilltop folly occupy other interesting corners in the town.

Bilbrook Lawns Hotel M
🏰🏰🏰 APPROVED

Bilbrook, Minehead,
TA24 6HE
☎ Washford (0984) 40331
Detached Georgian country house hotel set in extensive lawned gardens bordered by a stream.
Bedrooms: 4 double & 3 twin.
Bathrooms: 4 private,
1 public.
Bed & breakfast: £21.50-£25 single, £33-£44 double.
Half board: £27-£35.50 daily,
£150-£185 weekly.
Lunch available.
Evening meal 7.30pm (l.o. 7.30pm).
Parking for 8.
Open March-October, December.
Credit: Amex.

ॐ ᗊ ᗐ ⓘ ▥ ⬚ ▥ █ ⬛ ᔋ
ᖰ ✿ ▦ ᔋ ᔕᔿ

Exmoor House Hotel M
🏰🏰🏰 COMMENDED

12 West Street, Dunster,
TA24 6SN
☎ (0643) 821268
Near Dunster Castle, Exmoor, Brendons, Quantocks and coast. Farm fresh food, interesting wines, lounges and restaurant. Home comforts. Non-smokers only please.
Bedrooms: 4 double & 3 twin.
Bathrooms: 7 private.
Bed & breakfast: £30.50-£33 single, £45-£50 double.
Half board: £37-£41 daily,
£224-£245 weekly.
Evening meal 7.30pm (l.o. 7pm).
Open February-November.
Credit: Access, Visa, Diners, Amex.

ᔋ ⬚ ⬚ ᗊ ᗌ ⓘ ▥ ✓ ⬚ 𝕋𝕍
⬤ █ ⬛ Ⓤ ᖰ ✗ ▦ ᔕᔿ ▦ Ⓣ

Langtry Country House Hotel M
COMMENDED
Washford, Watchet,
TA23 0NT
☎ (0984) 40484
*In 4 acres of gardens and
paddocks in secluded position
close to Exmoor and the coast.
Panoramic views of the
Quantocks. Edwardian
licensed restaurant and bar.*
Bedrooms: 4 double & 2 twin,
1 family room.
Bathrooms: 7 private.
Bed & breakfast: £42-£50
double.
Half board: £33-£37 daily,
£225-£240 weekly.
Evening meal 7pm (l.o. 9pm).
Parking for 12.
Credit: Access, Visa.

Yarn Market Hotel M
25 High St., Dunster,
TA24 8SL
☎ (0643) 821425
*Central and accessible hotel in
quaint English village, an ideal
location from which to explore
the Exmoor National Park.*
Bedrooms: 1 single, 1 double
& 1 twin, 1 family room.
Bathrooms: 4 private.
Bed & breakfast: £20-£27.50
single, £40-£55 double.
Half board: £26-£35 daily,
£187-£215 weekly.
Lunch available.
Evening meal 6pm (l.o. 8pm).
Parking for 6.
Credit: Visa, Amex.

EGGESFORD
Devon
Map ref 1C2

2m S. Chulmleigh
Quiet village among
rolling hills and on the
west side of the River
Taw. Close by is
Eggesford Forest.

Fox and Hounds, Eggesford House Hotel M
Eggesford, Chulmleigh,
EX18 7JZ
☎ Chulmleigh (0769) 80345
*Country house hotel offering
peace and tranquillity. Set in
some 30 acres of woodland.
Fishing for trout, salmon and
sea trout on the River Taw.
New 9-hole par 3 golf course in
hotel grounds.*

Bedrooms: 3 single, 6 double
& 10 twin, 1 family room.
Bathrooms: 20 private,
1 public.
Bed & breakfast: £33.50-
£43.50 single, £67-£87 double.
Half board: £43.50-£50.50
daily, £230-£300 weekly.
Lunch available.
Evening meal 6pm (l.o. 9pm).
Parking for 109.
Credit: Access, Visa.

EVERSHOT
Dorset
Map ref 2A3

Set in hilly country at
source of the River
Frome, a small village
with a sophisticated, bow-
fronted High Street of
raised pavements. The
church has an unusual
spire.

The Acorn Inn Hotel M
COMMENDED
28 Fore St., Evershot,
Dorchester, DT2 0JW
☎ (0935) 83228
*Hardy's historic 16th C
country inn with beamed bars,
log fires and candlelit
restaurants (one non-smoking).
1.5 miles off A37 Yeovil to
Dorchester road.*
Bedrooms: 5 double & 1 twin,
2 family rooms.
Bathrooms: 8 private,
1 public.
Bed & breakfast: £34-£55
single, £52-£90 double.
Half board: £80-£170 daily,
£231-£350 weekly.
Lunch available.
Evening meal 6.30pm (l.o.
9.45pm).
Parking for 40.
Credit: Access, Visa.

Rectory House M
COMMENDED
Fore St., Evershot, DT2 0JW
☎ (093 583) 273
*Lovely 18th C rectory in
picturesque village.*
Bedrooms: 4 double & 2 twin.
Bathrooms: 6 private.
Bed & breakfast: from £40
single, max. £60 double.
Half board: max. £45 daily,
max. £250 weekly.
Evening meal 6.30pm (l.o.
7.30pm).
Parking for 8.
Credit: Access, Visa.

EXETER
Devon
Map ref 1D2

University city rebuilt after
the 1940s around its
venerable cathedral.
Suffered Danish raids
under Anglo-Saxons but
repulsed William I until
1068. Attractions include
early Norman towers
preserved in 13th C
cathedral with fine west
front; notable waterfront
buildings; Maritime
Museum; Guildhall;
Cathedral library;
Rougemont House
Museum of Costume and
Lace; Royal Albert
Memorial Museum;
Northcott Theatre.
*Tourist Information
Centre ☎ (0392) 265297*

Braeside Guest House
21 New North Rd., Exeter,
EX4 4HF
☎ (0392) 56875
*In city centre, 5 minutes' walk
from stations, bus depot and
High Street.*
Bedrooms: 2 single, 2 double
& 2 twin, 1 family room.
Bathrooms: 2 public;
2 private showers.
Bed & breakfast: £15-£16
single, £26-£30 double.
Half board: £20-£22 daily,
£135-£140 weekly.
Evening meal 7pm (l.o. 5pm).

Clock Tower Hotel M
16 New North Rd., Exeter,
EX4 4HF
☎ (0392) 52493 & Fax
(0392) 218445
*Homely accommodation in the
city centre. Coach and railway
stations within 10 minutes'
walk. All modern facilities. En-
suite facilities.*
Bedrooms: 3 single, 7 double
& 3 twin, 3 family rooms.
Bathrooms: 8 private,
3 public.
Bed & breakfast: £14-£19
single, £24-£34 double.
Half board: £17-£22 daily,
£94-£119 weekly.
Evening meal 6pm (l.o. 4pm).
Credit: Access, Visa.

Countess Wear Lodge M
398 Topsham Rd., Exeter,
EX2 6HE
☎ Topsham (039 287) 5441
Telex 42551 EXMOAT
Queens Moat Houses

*Modern hotel close to the city
centre and the M5 junction 30.
Well-placed for touring the
West Country.*
Bedrooms: 12 single, 9 double
& 22 twin, 1 family room.
Bathrooms: 44 private.
Bed & breakfast: £54.50-£60
single, £70-£77.50 double.
Lunch available.
Evening meal 7pm (l.o.
9.45pm).
Parking for 120.
Credit: Access, Visa, Diners,
Amex.

Ebford House Hotel M
COMMENDED
Exmouth Rd., Ebford, Exeter,
EX3 0QH
☎ (0392) 877658
Minotels
*Beautiful Georgian country
house surrounded by lovely
gardens, fine views. Warm
welcome, delicious food and
wine. 5 minutes from M5 and
airport.*
Bedrooms: 4 single, 10 double
& 4 twin.
Bathrooms: 18 private.
Bed & breakfast: £48-£55
single, £60-£82 double.
Half board: £59-£69 daily.
Lunch available.
Evening meal 6.30pm (l.o.
9.30pm).
Parking for 46.
Credit: Access, Visa, Amex.

Fairwinds Hotel M
COMMENDED
Kennford, Exeter, EX6 7UD
☎ (0392) 832911
*Unique little hotel in beautiful
rural surroundings. High
standard of cleanliness and
service with a varied menu.
Non-smoking restaurant and
bar.*
Bedrooms: 2 single, 5 double
& 1 twin.
Bathrooms: 6 private;
2 private showers.
Bed & breakfast: £25-£44
single, £49-£54 double.
Half board: £34-£42 daily,
£192-£215 weekly.
Evening meal 6.30pm (l.o.
8pm).
Parking for 9.
Credit: Access, Visa.

Hotel Gledhills
♛♛

32 Alphington Rd., Exeter,
EX2 8HN
☎ (0392) 71439 &
(0392) 30469
*Comfortable, friendly, licensed,
family-run hotel, conveniently
located close to city centre,
Plaza Leisure Complex,
attractive coast and
countryside. Closed at
Christmas.*
Bedrooms: 6 single, 2 double,
4 family rooms.
Bathrooms: 7 private,
1 public; 2 private showers.
Bed & breakfast: £18-£25
single, £39-£41 double.
Half board: £22-£29 daily.
Evening meal 6.30pm (l.o.
7pm).
Parking for 11.
Credit: Access, Visa, Amex.
🕹 🐦 🖵 ♥ 🛗 📋 ☑ 🖃 📺 ▥
🖾 ✈ 🐎

Globe Hotel

Fore St., Topsham, Exeter,
EX3 0HR
☎ (0392) 873471
*Family-run old coaching inn in
the centre of the old part of
Topsham.*
Bedrooms: 1 single, 7 double
& 6 twin.
Bathrooms: 14 private.
Bed & breakfast: £32-£35
single, £42-£50 double.
Lunch available.
Evening meal 7pm (l.o.
9.30pm).
Parking for 14.
Credit: Access, Visa, Amex.
🕹 🏄 🐦 📞 ☺ 🖵 ♥ 🛗 ☑
▥ 🖾 🍽 🐎 🐎

Great Western Hotel M
♛♛♛

Station Approach, St.
David's, Exeter, EX4 4NU
☎ (0392) 74039
*Hotel has easy access to
railway station. Bar,
restaurant, lounge, conference
room and car park.*
Bedrooms: 23 single, 6 double
& 10 twin, 1 family room.
Bathrooms: 31 private,
5 public.
Bed & breakfast: £26-£40
single, £38-£48 double.
Lunch available.
Evening meal 7pm (l.o.
9.30pm).
Parking for 30.
Credit: Access, Visa, Diners,
Amex.
🕹 📞 ☺ 🖵 ♥ 🛗 📋 ☑ 🖃 📺
▥ 🖾 🍽 🗗 SP

The Lord Haldon
Hotel M

Dunchideock, Exeter,
EX6 7YF
☎ (0392) 832483 & Fax
(0392) 833765
*Family-run, historic former
mansion within own grounds,
offering panoramic views. 5
miles south-west of Exeter and
well placed for Dartmoor and
coast.*
Bedrooms: 2 single, 10 double
& 4 twin, 3 family rooms.
Bathrooms: 19 private,
1 public.
Bed & breakfast: from £27.25
single, from £54.50 double.
Half board: from £39.75
daily, from £245 weekly.
Lunch available.
Evening meal 7pm (l.o.
10pm).
Parking for 80.
Credit: Access, Visa.
🕹 🐦 📞 ☺ 🖵 ♥ 🛗 📋 ▥ 🖃
📺 🌑 🖾 🍽 🕐 ☼ ♨ SP
🗗 📋

Raffles Hotel
♛♛♛ COMMENDED

11 Blackall Rd., Exeter,
EX4 4HD
☎ (0392) 70200
*Restored spacious Victorian
house, furnished and decorated
to period. Close to city centre,
university and theatres.*
Bedrooms: 2 single, 2 double
& 2 twin, 1 family room.
Bathrooms: 7 private.
Bed & breakfast: £24-£26
single, £34-£36 double.
Half board: £25-£34 daily.
Evening meal 7pm (l.o.
midday).
Parking for 2.
Credit: Access, Visa.
🕹 🐦 📞 ☺ 🖵 ♥ 🛗 📋 ▥ 🖃 📺 ▥
🖾 🍽 DAP ♨ SP 🗗

Royal Clarence Hotel M

Cathedral Yard, Exeter,
EX1 1HD
☎ (0392) 58464 Telex 42551
Ⓠ Queens Moat Houses
*Overlooking the cathedral and
grounds in the centre of Exeter,
this Georgian building is
steeped in English history. The
restaurant combines a bar and
carvery.*
Bedrooms: 17 single,
20 double & 19 twin.
Bathrooms: 56 private.
Bed & breakfast: £60-£75
single, £75-£90 double.
Half board: £49.50-£55 daily.
Lunch available.
Evening meal 7pm (l.o.
9.30pm).
Parking for 10.

Credit: Access, Visa, C.Bl.,
Diners, Amex.
🕹 🐦 📞 ☺ 🖵 ▥ 🛗 ♥ 📋 ☑ ▥
🖃 🌑 🍽 🐦 🍽 🍴 🛗 DAP ✂
SP 🗗 📋

St. Andrews Hotel M
♛♛♛

28 Alphington Rd., Exeter,
EX2 8HN
☎ (0392) 76784
*Established family-run
Victorian house with modern
hotel amenities. Relaxed
atmosphere and a warm
welcome.*
Bedrooms: 4 single, 8 double
& 3 twin, 2 family rooms.
Bathrooms: 17 private,
2 public.
Bed & breakfast: £39-£48.50
single, £59.50-£70 double.
Evening meal 7pm (l.o.
8.15pm).
Parking for 20.
Credit: Access, Visa, Amex.
🕹 🏄 📞 ☺ 🖵 ♥ 📋 ☑ 🖃
▥ 🖾 🍽 🛗 🗗 📋

*See Combe Martin,
Dulverton, Dunster,
Lynmouth, Lynton,
Porlock, Simonsbath,
Wheddon Cross,
Withypool, Woody Bay.*

Developed as a seaside
resort in George III's
reign, set against the
woods of the Exe Estuary
and red cliffs of Orcombe
Point. Extensive sands,
small harbour, chapel and
almshouses, a model
railway and A la Ronde, a
16-sided house.

Balcombe House
Hotel M
♛♛♛

Stevenstone Rd., Exmouth,
EX8 2EP
☎ (0395) 266349
*Comfortable, quiet, small but
spacious hotel set in half an
acre walled garden. Personal
attention with wide choice of
menus. Ample parking.*
Bedrooms: 1 single, 4 double
& 3 twin, 4 family rooms.
Bathrooms: 12 private.
Bed & breakfast: £22.75-
£28.60 single, £45.50-£52
double.
Half board: £32.75-£39.25
daily, £202-£230.50 weekly.
Lunch available.

Evening meal 7pm (l.o. 6pm).
Parking for 15.
Open April-October.
🕹 10 🐦 ☺ 🖵 ♥ 🛗 ✂ 🖃
▥ 🖾 👁 ❅ ✈ 🗗 SP

Ben Wyvis Guest House

31 Morton Rd., Exmouth,
EX8 1BA
☎ (0395) 263798
*In level position, 150 yards
from seafront and central for
all amenities.*
Bedrooms: 1 double & 2 twin,
1 family room.
Bathrooms: 1 private,
1 public.
Bed & breakfast: max. £12.50
single, max. £25 double.
Half board: max. £17.50
daily, max. £98 weekly.
Evening meal 6pm (l.o.
6.30pm).
Parking for 3.
🕹 🖵 ♥ ▥ 📋 ☑ 🖃 📺 ▥
DAP

Devoncourt Hotel M

16 Douglas Ave., Exmouth,
EX8 2EX
☎ (0395) 272277 & Fax
(0395) 269315
*Standing in four acres of
beautiful subtropical gardens,
sloping gently towards the sea,
overlooking the sandy beaches.
Leisure area with indoor and
outdoor heated swimming pool,
restaurant and carvery.*
Bedrooms: 1 single, 9 double
& 5 twin, 33 family rooms.
Bathrooms: 48 private.
Bed & breakfast: £38-£53
single, £76-£106 double.
Half board: £48.95-£63.95
daily, £342.65-£447.65
weekly.
Lunch available.
Evening meal 7pm (l.o.
9.30pm).
Parking for 54.
Credit: Access, Visa, Diners,
Amex.
🕹 📞 ☺ 🖵 ♥ 🛗 📋 ☑ 🖃
🌑 🍽 🖾 🐦 ⚡ 🍴 🍷 ♪
🕐 ► ❅ ✈ 🗗 ♨ SP 📋

The Kerans Hotel M
♛♛♛ COMMENDED

Esplanade, Exmouth,
EX8 1DS
☎ (0395) 275275
*Seaview rooms with mini-bar,
direct-dial telephone, colour
TV, tea-making and en-suite
facilities. Easy access by road
or rail.*
Bedrooms: 2 single, 3 double
& 1 twin, 1 family room.
Bathrooms: 6 private,
1 public.
Bed & breakfast: £29-£32
single, £48-£52 double.
Half board: £33-£35 daily,
£165-£175 weekly.

Evening meal 6.30pm (l.o. midday).
Parking for 5.
Credit: Access, Visa, Amex.
⌖5 \ ⌂ ⚲ ⚙ ⓥ ⇥ ⓣⓥ ●
▥ ▴ ⋇ Ⓓ ⒮ ⓣ

Pendennis Guest House
⚘⚘
84 St. Andrews Rd.,
Exmouth, EX8 1AS
☎ (0395) 271458
Large, comfortable family guesthouse with TV and bar lounges. Come and go as you please. Only 200 yards from the beach.
Bedrooms: 2 single, 2 double, 3 family rooms.
Bathrooms: 2 public.
Bed & breakfast: £13-£14 single, £26-£28 double.
Half board: £18.50-£19.50 daily.
Evening meal 6.30pm (l.o. 3pm).
Parking for 3.
Open January-November.
⌖ ⚙ ⇥ ⓣⓥ ▥ ▴ ⋇ ✗ ⋇ ⒮

Royal Beacon Hotel ₥
⚘⚘⚘⚘ COMMENDED
The Beacon, Exmouth, EX8 2AF
☎ (0395) 264886 & 265269 &
Fax (0395) 268890
Ⓖ Best Western
South facing with magnificent sea views. Various diets catered for by arrangement.
Bedrooms: 7 double & 10 twin, 3 family rooms.
Bathrooms: 20 private, 4 public.
Bed & breakfast: £42-£45.70 single, £72.60-£78.40 double.
Half board: £53.20-£56.80 daily, £346.30-£372.40 weekly.
Lunch available.
Evening meal 6.30pm (l.o. 11.30pm).
Parking for 30.
Credit: Access, Visa, C.Bl., Diners, Amex.
⌖ ⚙ \ Ⓓ ⌂ ⚙ ⓥ ✗ ⇥ ⓣⓥ ▥ ▴ ⒯ ● Ü ▸ ❅ Ⓓ ⓝ ⒮ ⌗ ⓣ

The Swallows
⚘⚘⚘ COMMENDED
11 Carlton Hill, Exmouth, EX8 2AJ
☎ (0395) 263937
Recently opened guesthouse only 300 yards from seafront, pleasantly converted to modern standards and providing comfortable accommodation.
Bedrooms: 1 single, 2 double & 2 twin, 1 family room.
Bathrooms: 5 private, 1 public.

Bed & breakfast: £15-£24 single, £32-£38 double.
Half board: £23-£32 daily, £155-£217 weekly.
Evening meal 6.30pm.
Parking for 4.
⌖ ⌂ ⚙ ⓊⓁ ⓥ ⇥ ▥ ▴ ✗ ⋇ ⒮

FALFIELD
Avon
Map ref 2B2
4m NE. Thornbury

The Park Hotel
⚘⚘⚘
Falfield, Wotton-under-Edge, Gloucestershire, GL12 8DR
☎ (0454) 260550
Country house with a large garden situated just off A38, 1 mile south of junction 14 on M5.
Bedrooms: 3 single, 2 double & 2 twin, 3 family rooms.
Bathrooms: 7 private, 1 public.
Bed & breakfast: £35-£45 single, £45-£55 double.
Lunch available.
Evening meal 7pm (l.o. 10pm).
Parking for 100.
Credit: Access, Visa, Diners, Amex.
⌖ \ Ⓓ ⌂ ⚙ ⚙ ⓥ ⇥ ▥ ▴ ⒯ ❅ ⋇ Ⓓ ⓝ ⒮ ⓣ

FALMOUTH
Cornwall
Map ref 1B3

Busy port and fishing harbour, popular resort on the balmy Cornish Riviera. Henry VIII's Pendennis Castle faces St. Mawes Castle across the broad natural harbour and yacht basin Carrick Roads, which receives 7 rivers.
Tourist Information Centre ☎ (0326) 312300

Hotel Anacapri ₥
⚘⚘⚘ COMMENDED
Gyllyngvase Rd., Sea Front, Falmouth, TR11 4DJ
☎ (0326) 311454
Attractive hotel in a beautiful spot overlooking Falmouth Bay, offering pretty bedrooms, comfort, personal service and panoramic views. Bar.
Bedrooms: 1 single, 6 double & 7 twin, 2 family rooms.
Bathrooms: 16 private.
Bed & breakfast: from £27.03 single, from £47 double.
Half board: £29.38-£32.90 daily, £205.63-£230.30 weekly.

Evening meal 6.30pm (l.o. 7.30pm).
Parking for 16.
Credit: Access, Visa, Diners, Amex.
⌖ ⌂ ⚙ ⚙ ⓥ ⇥ ▥ ● ▥ ▴ ⋇ ⒮ ⓣ

Bradgate Guest House
⚘⚘ APPROVED
4 Florence Pl., Falmouth, TR11 3NJ
☎ (0326) 314108
Small family-run guesthouse within easy reach of beaches and town facilities. Home comforts provided.
Bedrooms: 2 single, 2 double & 1 twin, 2 family rooms.
Bathrooms: 1 private, 2 public.
Bed & breakfast: £13.50-£14.50 single, £27-£30.50 double.
Half board: £21-£25 daily, £132.30-£163.10 weekly.
Evening meal 6.30pm (l.o. 4pm).
Parking for 5.
Open March-December.
⌖ ⚙ ⚙ ⓊⓁ ⚙ ⓥ ✗ ⇥ ⓣⓥ ▴ ⋇ ⒮ ⌗

Braemar Guest House
9 Avenue Rd., Falmouth, TR11 4AZ
☎ (0326) 313418
Small family-run guesthouse close to town and main beaches. A warm welcome assured.
Bedrooms: 1 single, 3 double & 2 twin, 2 family rooms.
Bathrooms: 2 private, 2 public.
Bed & breakfast: £14-£16 single, £28-£32 double.
Half board: £21-£23 daily, £120-£140 weekly.
Evening meal 6pm (l.o. 5pm).
Parking for 8.
⌖ ⌂ ⚙ ⚙ ⓥ ⇥ ⓣⓥ ▥ ⋇ ⓝ

Broadmead Hotel ₥
⚘⚘⚘ COMMENDED
Kimberley Park Rd., Falmouth, TR11 2DD
☎ (0326) 315704
Small hotel, tastefully decorated and furnished, with traditional English cooking. Overlooking Kimberley Park, near the centre of Falmouth. Private car park.
Bedrooms: 3 single, 6 double & 3 twin.
Bathrooms: 10 private, 1 public; 1 private shower.
Bed & breakfast: £20-£23 single, £46-£52 double.
Half board: £31-£34 daily, £186-£204 weekly.
Lunch available.

Evening meal 7pm (l.o. 8pm).
Parking for 8.
Credit: Access, Visa.
⌖ ⚙ ⚙ \ Ⓓ ⚙ ⚙ ⚙ ⓥ
✗ ⇥ ⓣⓥ ▥ ▴ ▵ Ⓓ ⒮ ⓣ

Croft Hotel ₥
⚘⚘⚘ COMMENDED
4-6 Gyllyngvase Hill, Falmouth, TR11 4DN
☎ (0326) 312814
All rooms en-suite, colour TV, telephone and tea/coffee facilities. Indoor pool 86F.
Bedrooms: 4 single, 7 double & 4 twin, 10 family rooms.
Bathrooms: 25 private.
Bed & breakfast: £25-£27 single, £50-£54 double.
Half board: £32-£35 daily, £185-£240 weekly.
Lunch available.
Evening meal 6.30pm (l.o. 7.15pm).
Parking for 30.
Open January-November.
Credit: Access, Visa.
⌖2 ⚙ \ Ⓓ ⌂ ⚙ ⚙ ⓥ ✗
⇥ ▥ ▴ ⒯ Ⓓ ⒮ Ⓓ ⓣ

Green Lawns Hotel ₥
⚘⚘⚘ COMMENDED
Western Ter., Falmouth, TR11 4QJ
☎ (0326) 312734 Telex 45169
Privately-run hotel specialising in comfort and cuisine. Leisure complex attached.
Bedrooms: 5 single, 17 double & 9 twin, 9 family rooms.
Bathrooms: 40 private.
Bed & breakfast: £48-£65 single, £60-£90 double.
Half board: £46-£81 daily, £320-£420 weekly.
Lunch available.
Evening meal 6.45pm (l.o. 10pm).
Parking for 60.
Credit: Access, Visa, C.Bl., Diners, Amex.
⌖ ⚙ ⚙ \ Ⓓ ⌂ ⚙ ⚙ ⓥ
⇥ ● ▥ ▴ ⒯ ▵ Ⓓ ⓝ ⌗
♫ Ü ▸ ❅ ⒮ ⌗ ⓣ

Grove Hotel
Grove Pl., Falmouth, TR11 4AU
☎ (0326) 319577
Owner-managed, homely harbourside hotel. Level walk to coaches, railway, town and quays. Public car and dinghy parks opposite.
Bedrooms: 2 single, 5 double & 5 twin, 3 family rooms.
Bathrooms: 8 private, 3 public.
Bed & breakfast: £18-£21.50 single, £36-£43 double.
Half board: £27-£30.50 daily, from £178 weekly.

Continued ▶

FALMOUTH

Continued

Evening meal 7pm (l.o. 9pm).
Open February-November.
Credit: Access, Visa.

Gyllyngdune Manor Hotel ⚔
APPROVED

Melvill Rd., Falmouth,
TR11 4AR
☎ (0326) 312978
*Old Georgian manor house
situated in 2 acres of beautiful
gardens. 10 minutes' walk from
town centre, 2 minutes' walk
from beach overlooking
Falmouth Bay.*
Bedrooms: 3 single, 12 double
& 11 twin, 4 family rooms.
Bathrooms: 30 private,
1 public.
Bed & breakfast: £38-£46
single, £76-£92 double.
Half board: £51-£59 daily,
£329-£385 weekly.
Lunch available.
Evening meal 7pm (l.o. 9pm).
Parking for 24.
Open February-December.
Credit: Access, Visa, Diners,
Amex.

Maenheere Hotel ⚔

3 Grove Pl., Falmouth,
TR11 4AU
☎ (0326) 312009
*In a magnificent harbourside
position with level approach to
town centre, beaches and
stations. Launderette and beer
garden. Fully licensed bar and
lunchtime and evening meals.*
Bedrooms: 9 single, 2 double
& 1 twin, 6 family rooms.
Bathrooms: 10 private,
3 public.
Bed & breakfast: £24.50-
£27.50 single, £39.50-£44
double.
Lunch available.
Evening meal 7pm (l.o.
9.30pm).
Credit: Access, Visa.

Park Grove Hotel ⚔

Kimberley Park Rd.,
Falmouth, TR11 2DD
☎ (0326) 313276
*Small hotel, centrally located,
overlooking the beautiful
Kimberley Park. Supervised by
resident proprietors.*

Bedrooms: 3 single, 5 double
& 5 twin, 4 family rooms.
Bathrooms: 15 private,
1 public.
Bed & breakfast: £25-£26
single, £50-£52 double.
Half board: £28-£31 daily,
£175-£195 weekly.
Evening meal 6.30pm (l.o.
7pm).
Parking for 20.
Open March-November.
Credit: Access, Visa.

Pendower Hotel
APPROVED

Sea View Rd., Falmouth,
TR11 4EF
☎ (0326) 312108
*Set in a large garden, ideally
situated between the town and
beaches. Own sauna and
heated, outdoor swimming
pool.*
Bedrooms: 8 single, 8 double
& 5 twin, 9 family rooms.
Bathrooms: 21 private,
3 public.
Bed & breakfast: £23-£28
single, £46-£56 double.
Half board: £33-£39 daily,
£231-£273 weekly.
Evening meal 7pm (l.o. 7pm).
Parking for 30.
Open March-November.
Credit: Access, Visa.

Penmere Manor Hotel ⚔

Mongleath Rd., Falmouth,
TR11 4PN
☎ (0326) 211411 Telex 45608
PMHTL
*Georgian country house with
modern extensions overlooking
Falmouth Bay. Leisure
facilities include indoor and
outdoor pools, jacuzzi, spa,
sauna, solarium, snooker,
games tables, croquet, chess,
table tennis and darts. Well-
appointed bedrooms. Closed at
Christmas only.*
Bedrooms: 10 single, 8 double
& 6 twin, 15 family rooms.
Bathrooms: 39 private.
Bed & breakfast: £52-£58
single, £77.50-£115 double.
Half board: £354.50-£500
weekly.
Lunch available.
Evening meal 7pm (l.o. 9pm).
Parking for 50.
Credit: Access, Visa, Diners,
Amex.

St. Michaels of Falmouth ⚔
COMMENDED

Seafront, Gyllyngvase Beach,
Falmouth, TR11 4NB
☎ (0326) 312707 & Fax
(0326) 319147 Telex 45540
CR Consort
*"Hotel for all seasons", in prize
winning gardens, adjoining the
beach. Heated indoor
swimming pool, sauna and
jacuzzi. Magnificent sea views.*
Bedrooms: 15 single,
20 double & 25 twin,
15 family rooms.
Bathrooms: 75 private.
Bed & breakfast: £35-£55
single, £70-£90 double.
Half board: £49-£69 daily,
£254-£450 weekly.
Lunch available.
Evening meal 7pm (l.o.
10pm).
Parking for 100.
Credit: Access, Visa, Diners,
Amex.

Telford

47 Melvill Rd., Falmouth,
TR11 4DG
☎ (0326) 314581
*Convenient for town, beaches
and gardens. Offers modern,
comfortable accommodation
with a friendly welcome to
guests and traditional English
cooking.*
Bedrooms: 1 single, 3 double
& 1 twin, 1 family room.
Bathrooms: 4 private,
1 public.
Bed & breakfast: £12-£14
single, £24-£28 double.
Half board: £16.50-£18.50
daily, £98-£119 weekly.
Evening meal 6pm (l.o. 5pm).
Parking for 6.
Open March-October.

Tresillian House Hotel ⚔
COMMENDED

3 Stracey Rd., Falmouth,
TR11 4DW
☎ (0326) 312425/311139
*Family-run hotel in a quiet
area, close to safe beaches,
town and harbours. Traditional
cuisine.*
Bedrooms: 1 single, 4 double
& 3 twin, 4 family rooms.
Bathrooms: 12 private.
Bed & breakfast: £19.90-
£22.50 single, £39.80-£45
double.
Half board: £22.50-£27.25
daily, £150-£172.50 weekly.
Lunch available.

Evening meal 6.30pm (l.o.
7.30pm).
Parking for 8.
Open March-October.

FARMBOROUGH

Avon
Map ref 2B2

4m NW. Radstock

The Streets Hotel
COMMENDED

The Street, Farmborough,
Bath, BA3 1AR
☎ Timsbury (0761) 71452
Telex 44830 SHF ACCENT
G
*In picturesque village of
Farmborough, 7 miles from
Bath and 10 miles from
Bristol, off the A39.*
Bedrooms: 1 single, 4 double
& 3 twin.
Bathrooms: 8 private.
Bed & breakfast: £42-£48
single, £50-£58 double.
Half board: £55.80-£61.80
daily.
Evening meal 7.30pm (l.o.
8.50pm).
Parking for 8.
Credit: Access, Visa, Amex.

FONTHILL GIFFORD

Wiltshire
Map ref 2B3

7m NE. Shaftesbury

Beckford Arms ⚔

Fonthill Gifford, Tisbury,
SP3 6PX
☎ Tisbury (0747) 870385 &
Fax (0747) 51496
*Tastefully refurbished,
comfortable 18th C inn,
between Tisbury and Hindon in
area of outstanding beauty. 2
miles A303, convenient for
Salisbury.*
Bedrooms: 2 single, 4 double
& 1 twin.
Bathrooms: 5 private;
2 private showers.
Bed & breakfast: £25-£27.50
single, £45-£49.50 double.
Half board: £30-£35 daily,
from £192.50 weekly.
Lunch available.
Evening meal 7pm (l.o.
10pm).
Parking for 42.
Credit: Access, Visa.

FOWEY

Cornwall
Map ref 1C3

Set on steep slopes at the mouth of the Fowey River, important clayport and fishing town. Ruined forts guarding the shore recall days of 'Fowey Gallants' who ruled local seas. The handsome, lofty church rises above the town and nearby Place House, rebuilt in the 19th C, was refuge for 15th C townsfolk in French raids. Ferries to Polruan and Bodinnick; Regatta, August.
Tourist Information Centre ☎ (0726) 833616

Ashley House Hotel ♨

14 The Esplanade, Fowey, PL23 1HY
☎ (0726) 832310
Centrally situated in a pleasant part of Fowey. Personal service, charming bar with log fire, garden. Excellent base for touring Cornwall, with opportunities for walking, fishing and sailing.
Bedrooms: 1 single, 4 double & 1 twin.
Bathrooms: 4 private, 2 public.
Bed & breakfast: £20-£30 double.
Evening meal 7pm (l.o. 7pm).
Open April-October.
ॐ 🖵 ♥ Ⓥ 🖃 ⓉⓋ 🌠 🛏 🛒

Carnethic House Hotel ♨
🏳🏳🏳 COMMENDED
Lambs Barn, Fowey, PL23 1HQ
☎ (0726) 833336
Regency house in 1.5 acres of mature gardens. Heated pool. Home cooking with local fish a speciality. Informal atmosphere.
Bedrooms: 1 single, 4 double & 1 twin, 2 family rooms.
Bathrooms: 5 private, 2 public; 2 private showers.
Bed & breakfast: £28-£35 single, £40-£52 double.
Half board: £32-£38 daily, £200-£250 weekly.
Lunch available.
Evening meal 7.30pm (l.o. 8.30pm).
Parking for 20.
Open February-November.
Credit: Access, Visa, Diners, Amex.
ॐ 🛎 🖻 🖵 ♥ 🎄 🗡 ⋎ Ⓥ
⊙ ⑩ ▣ 🍽 🎄 ♨ ♗ Ⓤ ⏃
✤ 🛏 🆂🅿 🛒 Ⓣ

Cormorant Hotel
🏳🏳🏳 COMMENDED
Golant, Fowey, PL23 1LL
☎ (0726) 833426
Small, attractive, family-run hotel with panoramic views of the Fowey estuary. Noted for its hospitality and food. Indoor heated swimming pool with removable roof giving the best of both worlds.
Bedrooms: 4 double & 7 twin.
Bathrooms: 11 private.
Bed & breakfast: £38-£48 single, £76-£86 double.
Half board: £50-£60 daily.
Lunch available.
Evening meal 7pm (l.o. 8.30pm).
Parking for 15.
Credit: Access, Visa, Amex.
ॐ 🛎 🗲 🖻 🖵 ♥ 📷 🖃
⑩ ▣ 🍽 🛒

Fowey Hall ♨
4 Hanson Dr., Fowey, PL23 1ET
☎ (0726) 833104/832321
A magnificent country house standing in lovely grounds and overlooking the River Fowey and estuary. A warm welcome awaits.
Bedrooms: 11 single, 24 twin, 5 family rooms.
Bathrooms: 18 public.
Bed & breakfast: £15-£22 single, £25-£40 double.
Half board: £19.50-£30 daily, £130-£220 weekly.
Lunch available.
Evening meal 7pm.
Parking for 60.
ॐ ♥ ⓊⓀ 🖻 ▣ Ⓥ 🖃 ⓉⓋ ⑩ 🛎
⏃ 🎄 ✤ 🗡 🛏 ♗ Ⓣ

Fowey Hotel
Esplanade, Fowey, PL23 1HX
☎ (0726) 832551/2/3 & Fax (0726) 832125
Superb views over the Fowey estuary can be enjoyed from the sun terrace and public rooms of this hotel.
Bedrooms: 7 single, 11 double & 9 twin, 3 family rooms.
Bathrooms: 26 private, 4 public.
Bed & breakfast: £36-£44 single, £67-£80 double.
Half board: £46-£54 daily, £298-£344 weekly.
Lunch available.
Evening meal 7pm (l.o. 9pm).
Parking for 24.
Credit: Access, Visa, Diners, Amex.
ॐ 🗲 🖻 🖵 ♥ 🛎 ▣ Ⓥ 🖃 ⑩
⏃ ⑩ ▣ 🍽 ⏃ 🎄 ✤ 🆓 ♗ 🆂🅿
🛒 Ⓣ

Marina Hotel ♨
🏳🏳🏳 COMMENDED
Esplanade, Fowey, PL23 1HY
☎ (0726) 833315

Privately-run, comfortably appointed Georgian hotel of character with balcony rooms, in quiet situation. Own moorings, waterside garden and restaurant.
Bedrooms: 6 double & 5 twin.
Bathrooms: 11 private.
Bed & breakfast: £50-£72 double.
Half board: £36-£50 daily, £250-£325 weekly.
Lunch available.
Evening meal 7pm (l.o. 8.30pm).
Open March-October.
Credit: Access, Visa, Diners, Amex.
ॐ 🛎 🗲 🖻 🖵 ♥ ▣ Ⓥ 🖃
⑩ ⑩ 🛎 🍽 🛏 ♗ 🆂🅿 🛒

The Old Ferry Inn ♨
🏳🏳 COMMENDED
Bodinnick-By-Fowey, PL23 1LX
☎ Polruan (0726) 870237
Comfortably furnished and with harbour views from lounge and most bedrooms. Sailing and cliff walks nearby. Food includes local fish.
Bedrooms: 4 double & 7 twin, 1 family room.
Bathrooms: 8 private, 2 public.
Bed & breakfast: £30.50-£40 single, £60-£80 double.
Half board: £46.50-£56 daily, £320-£343 weekly.
Lunch available.
Evening meal 7.30pm (l.o. 8.15pm).
Parking for 14.
Open March-October.
Credit: Visa.
ॐ 🖻 ♥ 🛎 Ⓥ 🖃 ⓉⓋ 🛏 🛒
Ⓣ

Old Quay House Hotel
Fore St., Fowey, PL23 1AQ
☎ (0726) 833302
Family-run hotel on water's edge with private quay and mooring. Home cooking.
Bedrooms: 2 single, 7 double & 3 twin, 1 family room.
Bathrooms: 9 private, 1 public; 2 private showers.
Bed & breakfast: max. £24.50 single, £41-£49 double.
Half board: £32.50-£36.50 daily, £217-£245.50 weekly.
Lunch available.
Evening meal 7pm (l.o. 8.30pm).
Credit: Access, Visa.
ॐ 🛎 🖵 ♥ 🛎 Ⓥ 🖃 ⓉⓋ 🆂🅿
🛒

The Wheelhouse
60 Esplanade, Fowey, PL23 1JA
☎ (0726) 832452
Delightful family-run Victorian licensed guesthouse. Sea and harbour views, home cooking.

Bedrooms: 1 single, 3 double & 2 twin, 1 family room.
Bathrooms: 2 public.
Bed & breakfast: £15-£17.50 single, £30-£35 double.
Half board: £25-£27.50 daily, £160-£177.50 weekly.
Evening meal 7.30pm (l.o. midday).
Open March-October.
Ⓑ ♥ 🛎 Ⓥ 🖃 ⓉⓋ ⑩ 🗡 🛒

FROME

Somerset
Map ref 2B2

Old market town with modern light industry, its medieval centre watered by the River Frome. Above Cheap Street with its flagstones and watercourse is the church showing work of varying periods. Interesting buildings include 18th C wool merchants' houses. Local history museum.

Fourwinds Guest House
🏳🏳🏳 COMMENDED
19 Bath Rd., Frome, BA11 2HJ
☎ (0373) 62618
Chalet bungalow with some bedrooms on ground floor. TV and tea making facilities. Licensed, good food.
Bedrooms: 1 single, 3 double & 1 twin, 1 family room.
Bathrooms: 4 private, 2 public.
Bed & breakfast: £18-£22 single, £32-£38 double.
Half board: £26-£30 daily.
Evening meal 6pm (l.o. 7pm).
Parking for 10.
ॐ 🛎 🖵 ♥ 🛎 Ⓥ ⋎ ⓉⓋ ⑩
🛎 ♗ 🗡 🛒 ♥

Keyford Elms Hotel and Restaurant ♨
🏳🏳🏳
92 Locks Hill, Frome, BA11 1NG
☎ (0373) 63321
18th C rectory in its own grounds on outskirts of Frome, near Longleat and Bath.
Bedrooms: 1 double & 2 twin, 5 family rooms.
Bathrooms: 3 private, 2 public.
Bed & breakfast: £19-£30 single, £30-£45 double.
Half board: from £25.50 daily, from £164.50 weekly.
Lunch available.
Evening meal 7.30pm (l.o. 10pm).
Parking for 30.
Credit: Access, Visa.
ॐ 🛎 🖵 ♥ 🛎 Ⓥ 🖃 ⑩ 🛎
⏃ ✤ 🗡 🛏 🆂🅿 🛒

FROME
Continued

Mendip Lodge Hotel Μ
☆☆☆ COMMENDED
Bath Rd., Frome, BA11 2HP
☎ (0373) 63223 & Fax
(0373) 63990 Telex 44832
CR Best Western
Set in 3.5 acres overlooking Mendip Hills, near Bath, Wells and Longleat.
Bedrooms: 6 single, 10 double & 12 twin, 12 family rooms.
Bathrooms: 40 private.
Bed & breakfast: £55-£62.50 single, £70-£77 double.
Half board: £45-£55 daily.
Lunch available.
Evening meal 7pm (l.o. 9.30pm).
Parking for 70.
Credit: Access, Visa, Diners, Amex.
☽ ♨ ☎ ⊡ ⌷ ♥ ⋔ ▦ Ⓥ ⌿
◑ ▥ ☎ ♆ ⌖ ☆ ❀ ↖ SP Ⓣ

GLASTONBURY
Somerset
Map ref 2A2

Old market town associated with Joseph of Arimathea and the birth of English Christianity. Built around its once-glorious 7th C abbey, whose medieval remains are said to be the site of King Arthur's burial, it prospered from wool until the 19th C. Glastonbury Tor is its ancient tower gives panoramic views over flat country rich in remains of Celtic lake communities.

Berewall Farm Country Guest House
☆☆☆ APPROVED
Cinnamon La., Glastonbury, BA6 8LL
☎ (0458) 31451
32-acre grazing farm. Comfortable farmhouse offering a homely welcome to all. Ponies are available for riding.
Bedrooms: 2 single, 2 double & 2 twin, 3 family rooms.
Bathrooms: 9 private.
Bed & breakfast: £21-£23 single, £37-£40 double.
Half board: £175-£185 weekly.
Evening meal 6.30pm (l.o. 7.30pm).
Parking for 12.
☽ ♨ ⌷ ♥ ⋔ ▦ ⊞ Ⓥ ⌖
♆ ♞ ♐ ℧ ❀ ✻ ⤧ ⩔ SP

George & Pilgrims Hotel Μ
1 High St., Glastonbury, BA6 9DP
☎ (0458) 31146
CR Resort
Some historic bedrooms have massive four-poster beds and are furnished with a predominance of antiques. Home-cooked food from local produce. Extensive wine list.
Bedrooms: 1 single, 7 double & 5 twin, 1 family room.
Bathrooms: 14 private.
Bed & breakfast: £22.50-£46 single, £45-£61 double.
Lunch available.
Evening meal 7pm (l.o. 10.30pm).
Parking for 6.
Credit: Access, Visa, Diners, Amex.
☽ ⚶ ⛁ ☎ ⊡ ♥ ⋔ ⋔ ▥
♆ ⌖ SP ⟁ Ⓣ

Number Three Restaurant and Hotel Μ
☆☆☆ COMMENDED
3 Magdalene St., Glastonbury, BA6 9EW
☎ (0458) 32129
Elegant listed Georgian house. Its beautiful garden, floodlit at night, adjoins the abbey ruins.
Bedrooms: 3 double & 2 twin, 1 family room.
Bathrooms: 6 private.
Bed & breakfast: £50 single, £70-£80 double.
Half board: £61-£76 daily.
Evening meal 7pm (l.o. 9.30pm).
Parking for 8.
Open February-December.
Credit: Access, Visa.
☽ ♨ ⌷ ☎ ⌷ ♥ ⋔ Ⓥ
✂ ⌿ ▥ ☎ ♐ ✻ ⤧ ⟁ ⟁

GRAMPOUND
Cornwall
Map ref 1B3

6m SW. St. Austell

Perran House Μ
☆☆
Fore St., Grampound, Truro, TR2 4RS
☎ St. Austell (0726) 882066
Family-run guesthouse between St. Austell and Truro, offering personal service. Central for touring.
Bedrooms: 1 single, 3 double & 1 twin.
Bathrooms: 3 private, 1 public.
Bed & breakfast: £12-£14 single, £24-£33 double.
Parking for 6.
Credit: Access, Visa.
☽ ⊡ ⌷ ♥ UK ⋔ Ⓥ ⌿ ▥
♆ ⤧ ⟁ ⟁ Ⓣ

GREINTON
Somerset
Map ref 1D1

5m W. Street

Greylake Motel & Licensed Restaurant Μ
☆☆☆
Greinton, Bridgwater, TA7 9BP
☎ Ashcott (0458) 210383
Delightful 16th C motel with beams and inglenooks, offering 20th C facilities. On the A361 and an ideal touring centre for Somerset.
Bedrooms: 3 single, 2 double & 3 twin.
Bathrooms: 5 private, 1 public.
Bed & breakfast: from £17.50 single, from £39.50 double.
Half board: from £26.75 daily.
Lunch available.
Evening meal 7pm (l.o. 9pm).
Parking for 24.
Credit: Access, Visa, Diners, Amex.
☽ ♨ ⊡ ⌷ ♥ ⋔ Ⓥ ⌿ ⓉⓋ
▥ ☎ ♐ ⌖ ᴅᴀᴘ SP Ⓣ

GUNNISLAKE
Cornwall
Map ref 1C2

Steep roadside village with late Georgian houses built when tin mining flourished here. One of the ancient entries into Cornwall, the 14th C 'New Bridge' still spans the Tamar.

Hingston House Country Hotel Μ
☆☆☆ COMMENDED
St. Anns Chapel, Gunnislake, PL18 9HB
☎ Tavistock (0822) 832468
Beautiful country house overlooking Tamar Valley. Cotehele House and St. Mellion golf-course nearby. Central for exploring Devon and Cornwall.
Bedrooms: 1 single, 6 double & 2 twin, 1 family room.
Bathrooms: 8 private, 1 public.
Bed & breakfast: £24-£29.50 single, £40-£49 double.
Half board: £32.50-£37 daily, £126-£192 weekly.
Lunch available.
Evening meal 7.30pm (l.o. 8.30pm).
Parking for 10.
Credit: Access, Visa.
☽ ⊡ ⌷ ♥ ⋔ Ⓥ ✂ ⌿ ⓉⓋ
▥ ☎ ♐ ⓟ ✻ ⤧ ⩔ SP ⟁

HARTLAND
Devon
Map ref 1C1

4m W. Clovelly
Hamlet on high, wild country near Hartland Point. Just west, the parish church tower makes a magnificent landmark; the light, unrestored interior holds one of Devon's finest rood screens. There are spectacular cliffs around Hartland Point and the lighthouse.

Hartland Quay Hotel
☆☆
Hartland, Bideford, EX39 6DU
☎ (0237) 441218
Small family-run hotel overlooking the rugged Atlantic coastline. Coastal walks. Important geological area.
Bedrooms: 2 single, 6 double & 6 twin, 2 family rooms.
Bathrooms: 8 private, 3 public.
Bed & breakfast: £16.50-£18 single, £33-£36 double.
Half board: £22-£25 daily, £140-£160 weekly.
Lunch available.
Evening meal 7pm (l.o. 9pm).
Parking for 100.
Open March-October.
Credit: Access, Visa.
☽ ♥ ⋔ Ⓥ ⌿ ⓉⓋ ⟲

HAYTOR
Devon
Map ref 1D2

5m N. Ashburton
Rugged moorland with dramatic craggy rock formation on the eastern edge of Dartmoor National Park. Granite from local quarries was used for the British Museum, the National Gallery and London Bridge. Near the village of Haytor Vale is a nature reserve with many species of trees and birds.

The Bel Alp House Country Hotel Μ
☆☆☆ HIGHLY COMMENDED
Haytor, Bovey Tracey, Newton Abbot, TQ13 9XX
☎ (0364) 661217 & Fax (0364) 661292
A small elegant country house hotel on the edge of Dartmoor in one of the most spectacular settings in the West Country. Comfort and personal service.

Bedrooms: 4 double & 5 twin.
Bathrooms: 9 private.
Bed & breakfast: £69-£84
single, £126-£144 double.
Half board: £87-£111 daily,
£588-£735 weekly.
Lunch available.
Evening meal 7.30pm (l.o.
8.30pm).
Parking for 20.
Open March-November.
Credit: Access, Visa.

Moorland Hotel M
APPROVED
Haytor, Newton Abbot,
TQ13 9XT
☎ (0364) 661407
*Set in delightful grounds below
Haytor Rock. Superb views of
open moorland and coast from
all hotel rooms and self-
catering apartments.*
Bedrooms: 2 single, 11 double
& 8 twin, 2 family rooms.
Bathrooms: 23 private.
Bed & breakfast: from £32
single, from £64 double.
Half board: from £45 daily,
from £285 weekly.
Lunch available.
Evening meal 7.30pm (l.o.
9.30pm).
Parking for 50.

HELSTON
Cornwall
Map ref 1B3

Handsome town with
steep, curving main street
and narrow alleys. In
medieval times it was a
major port and one of
Cornwall's 4 stannary
towns. Most buildings
date from Regency and
Victorian periods, with
19th C Town Hall and
classically-styled church.
The famous May dance,
the Furry, is thought to
have pre-Christian
origins. A museum of
local history occupies the
old Butter Market.

Gwealdues Hotel
Falmouth Rd., Helston,
TR13 8JX
☎ (0326) 572808 & Fax
(0326) 561388
*Fully licensed modern hotel
with en-suite rooms and central
heating. Bar meals and a la
carte restaurant available.
Swimming pool. Large
banqueting room.*

Bedrooms: 1 single, 5 double
& 3 twin, 3 family rooms.
Bathrooms: 9 private,
2 public.
Bed & breakfast: £25-£30
single, £30-£40 double.
Half board: £20-£25 daily,
£140-£175 weekly.
Lunch available.
Evening meal 7.30pm (l.o.
10pm).
Parking for 60.
Credit: Access, Visa.

Nansloe Manor Country Hotel
Meneage Rd., Helston,
TR13 0SB
☎ (0326) 574691
*Formerly a small manor house,
more recently converted to a
comfortable hotel. Set in own
4.5 acre grounds on the south
side of Helston. Well situated
for touring, golf and beaches.*
Bedrooms: 5 double & 2 twin.
Bathrooms: 7 private.
Bed & breakfast: £36-£48
single, £60-£84 double.
Lunch available.
Evening meal 7pm (l.o.
9.30pm).
Parking for 40.
Credit: Access, Visa, Amex.

HEMYOCK
Devon
Map ref 1D2

5m S. Wellington

Orchard Lea
Culmstock Rd., Hemyock,
EX15 3RN
☎ (0823) 680057
*Small guesthouse with
panoramic views. Good touring
centre, offering peace and
quiet. On B3391, 6 miles from
M5 junction 27.*
Bedrooms: 1 double & 1 twin.
Bathrooms: 1 public.
Half board: £12.50-£16 daily,
£80-£110 weekly.
Evening meal 7pm (l.o.
8.30pm).
Parking for 3.
Open April-October.

---

*The enquiry
coupons at the
back will help you
when contacting
proprietors.*

HIGH BICKINGTON
Devon
Map ref 1C1

Village whose church is
noted for the fine carving
of its late-medieval
bench-ends. Numbering
about 70, they form North
Devon's largest
collection.

Seckington House
COMMENDED
High Bickington,
Umberleigh, EX37 9BT
☎ (0769) 60494
*Previously a farmhouse,
Seckington House is one mile
south west of the village of
High Bickington.*
Bedrooms: 1 double & 2 twin.
Bathrooms: 2 public.
Bed & breakfast: £24 double.
Half board: £19 daily, £126
weekly.
Evening meal 6.30pm (l.o.
10am).
Parking for 4.
Open April-October.

HONITON
Devon
Map ref 1D2

Old coaching town in
undulating farmland.
Formerly famous for lace-
making, it is now an
antiques trade centre and
market town. Small
museum.

The Belfry Country Hotel M
COMMENDED
Yarcombe, Honiton,
EX14 9BD
☎ Upottery (040 486) 234 &
588
CR Minotels
*Attractively converted old
school building. Family-run
hotel with friendly atmosphere,
set in beautiful countryside and
within easy reach of coast.*
Bedrooms: 3 double & 2 twin,
1 family room.
Bathrooms: 6 private.
Bed & breakfast: £39-£42
single, £59-£63.50 double.
Half board: £45.45-£47.70
daily, £243-£260 weekly.
Lunch available.
Evening meal 7.30pm (l.o.
9pm).
Parking for 10.
Credit: Access, Visa, Diners,
Amex.

Greyhound Inn M
Fenny Bridges, Honiton,
EX14 0BJ
☎ Honiton (0404) 850380
*17th C thatched, cottage-style
inn, heavily beamed. Former
coaching inn retaining original
charming character, now
offering every modern amenity.*
Bedrooms: 9 double & 1 twin.
Bathrooms: 10 private.
Bed & breakfast: from £38
single, from £52 double.
Lunch available.
Evening meal 6pm (l.o.
10pm).
Parking for 80.
Credit: Access, Visa, Diners,
Amex.

Honiton Motel M
APPROVED
Turks Head Corner, Exeter
Rd., Honiton, EX14 8PQ
☎ (0404) 43440/45400
*Ideal midway point from
Cornwall to the north for a 1
night stop or touring base.
Friendly atmosphere.*
Bedrooms: 4 double & 9 twin,
2 family rooms.
Bathrooms: 15 private.
Bed & breakfast: £26-£30
single, £44-£50 double.
Half board: from £33.50
daily, from £210 weekly.
Lunch available.
Evening meal 7pm (l.o. 9pm).
Parking for 150.
Credit: Access, Visa.

HORRABRIDGE
Devon
Map ref 1C2

*4m SE. Tavistock
Beside the River
Walkham at the south-
west edge of Dartmoor.*

Overcombe Hotel M
COMMENDED
Horrabridge, Yelverton,
PL20 7RN
☎ Yelverton (0822) 853501
*Situated in west Dartmoor,
between Plymouth and
Tavistock. Ideal for walking
and touring. Friendly
comfortable hotel offering
personal service.*
Bedrooms: 1 single, 5 double
& 3 twin, 2 family rooms.
Bathrooms: 10 private,
3 public.
Bed & breakfast: £19-£24
single, £38-£43 double.
Half board: £29.75-£34.75
daily, £182-£202 weekly.

Continued ▶

WEST COUNTRY

HORRABRIDGE
Continued

Lunch available.
Evening meal 7.30pm (l.o. 7.15pm).
Parking for 12.
Credit: Access, Visa.

ILFRACOMBE

Devon
Map ref 1C1

Seaside resort of Victorian grandeur set on hillside between cliffs with sandy coves. Earlier a small port and fishing town. On a rock at the mouth of the harbour stands an 18th C lighthouse, built over a medieval chapel. There are fine formal gardens and 2 working mills, restored and open to the public. Museum, donkey rides. Chambercombe Manor, interesting and charming old house, nearby.
Tourist Information Centre ☎ (0271) 863001

Arlington Hotel
Sommers Cres., Ilfracombe, EX34 9DT
☎ (0271) 862252
Comprehensively equipped bedrooms (including satellite colour TV), sauna, solarium, heated outdoor pool. Entertainment nightly at sister hotel nearby.
Bedrooms: 1 single, 16 double & 4 twin, 9 family rooms.
Bathrooms: 30 private.
Bed & breakfast: £20-£35 single, £50-£76 double.
Half board: £25-£38 daily, £189-£245 weekly.
Evening meal 7pm (l.o. 8.30pm).
Parking for 29.
Credit: Access, Visa, Amex.

Capstone Hotel & Restaurant
St. James Pl., Ilfracombe, EX34 9BJ
☎ (0271) 863540
Family-run hotel with restaurant on ground floor. Close to harbour and all amenities. Local seafood a speciality.

Bedrooms: 1 single, 7 double & 1 twin, 3 family rooms.
Bathrooms: 12 private, 2 public.
Bed & breakfast: £15-£19.75 single, £28-£38 double.
Half board: £20-£27.50 daily, £140-£180 weekly.
Lunch available.
Evening meal 6pm (l.o. 10pm).
Open April-October.
Credit: Access, Visa, Amex.

Cliffe (Hydro) Hotel M
APPROVED
Hillsborough Rd., Ilfracombe, EX34 9NP
☎ (0271) 863606 & 866500
Magnificent views over the harbour and sea. Good food, and a indoor leisure centre. Open daily.
Bedrooms: 5 single, 15 double & 15 twin, 2 family rooms.
Bathrooms: 33 private, 3 public.
Bed & breakfast: £35-£45 single, £60-£75 double.
Half board: £45-£60 daily, £225-£255 weekly.
Lunch available.
Evening meal 7pm (l.o. 8.30pm).
Parking for 6.
Credit: Access, Visa.

Cresta Hotel
Torrs Pk., Ilfracombe, EX34 8AY
☎ (0271) 863742
Hotel stands in its own grounds on the level to the main seafront and principal places of interest.
Bedrooms: 6 single, 8 double & 6 twin, 11 family rooms.
Bathrooms: 17 private, 5 public.
Bed & breakfast: £17.50-£20 single, £35-£40 double.
Half board: £23.50-£26 daily, £164.50-£182 weekly.
Evening meal 6pm (l.o. 6.30pm).
Parking for 34.
Open April-October.
Credit: Access, Visa.

Elmfield Hotel
Torrs Pk., Ilfracombe, EX34 8AZ
☎ (0271) 863377
In quiet position close to town, with 1 acre of gardens. Adjacent to the famous Torrs Walks.

Bedrooms: 1 single, 11 double & 2 twin.
Bathrooms: 13 private, 1 public.
Bed & breakfast: £33 single, £66 double.
Half board: £36 daily, £210 weekly.
Lunch available.
Evening meal 7pm (l.o. 7.30pm).
Parking for 15.
Open April-October.
Credit: Access, Visa.

The Ilfracombe Carlton Hotel M
COMMENDED
Runnacleave Rd., Ilfracombe, EX34 8AR
☎ (0271) 862446 & Fax (0271) 865379
Consort
Comfortable, friendly hotel with bars, dancing, buttery and 24-hour service. Central location adjacent to beach and seafront.
Bedrooms: 5 single, 20 double & 20 twin, 5 family rooms.
Bathrooms: 40 private, 5 public.
Bed & breakfast: £25-£27.50 single, £45-£50 double.
Half board: £35.50-£38 daily, £185-£195 weekly.
Lunch available.
Evening meal 7pm (l.o. 8.30pm).
Parking for 25.
Credit: Access, Visa, Amex.

Lympstone Private Hotel
Cross Pk., Ilfracombe, EX34 8BJ
☎ (0271) 863038
Homely, family-run hotel in a quiet cul-de-sac, virtually on the seafront. Near shops and Torrs Walks. Resident proprietors for 18 years.
Bedrooms: 3 single, 7 double & 1 twin, 4 family rooms.
Bathrooms: 10 private, 2 public.
Bed & breakfast: £14-£17 single, £28-£34 double.
Parking for 6.
Open March-October.

Strathmore Hotel
57 St. Brannocks Rd., Ilfracombe, EX34 8EQ
☎ (0271) 862248

Small, friendly hotel close to Bicclescombe Park and all amenities, providing service and hospitality.
Bedrooms: 1 single, 4 double & 1 twin, 3 family rooms.
Bathrooms: 7 private, 2 public.
Bed & breakfast: £13-£17 single, £26-£34 double.
Half board: £19.50-£23.50 daily, £123-£145.50 weekly.
Evening meal 6.30pm (l.o. 5pm).
Parking for 7.
Credit: Access, Visa, Diners, Amex.

The Torrs Hotel M
APPROVED
Torrs Pk., Ilfracombe, EX34 8AY
☎ (0271) 862334
Victorian mansion with fine views, beside the Torrs Coastal Walk (National Trust). Close to the seafront and town centre.
Bedrooms: 1 single, 5 double & 3 twin, 5 family rooms.
Bathrooms: 14 private, 2 public.
Bed & breakfast: £19.50-£22 single, £39-£44 double.
Half board: £25.50-£28 daily, £178.50-£196 weekly.
Evening meal 6.30pm (l.o. 7.30pm).
Parking for 14.
Open March-October.
Credit: Access, Visa, Diners, Amex.

Trimstone Manor Hotel M
Trimstone, Ilfracombe, EX34 8NR
☎ (0271) 62841
English country manor in 54 acres. Indoor leisure centre and complete outdoor activities. 2 miles from Woolacombe sands.
Bedrooms: 1 single, 7 double & 5 twin, 5 family rooms.
Bathrooms: 18 private.
Half board: £160-£190 weekly.
Lunch available.
Evening meal 7pm (l.o. 8.30pm).
Parking for 52.
Credit: Access, Visa, Amex.

Westwell Hall Hotel

APPROVED

Torrs Pk., Ilfracombe,
EX34 8AZ
☎ (0271) 862792
*Elegant early Victorian house
set in 2 acres of mature
gardens, adjacent to National
Trust walks. Overlooking the
sea and town in quiet location.*
Bedrooms: 1 single, 4 double
& 3 twin, 2 family rooms.
Bathrooms: 10 private.
Bed & breakfast: £20-£22
single, £40-£44 double.
Half board: £25-£33 daily,
£175-£195 weekly.
Evening meal 7pm (l.o. 8pm).
Parking for 12.
Credit: Access, Visa.

ILLOGAN

Cornwall
Map ref 1B3

2m NW. Redruth

Aviary Court Hotel

COMMENDED

Marys Well, Illogan, Redruth,
TR16 4QZ
☎ Portreath (0209) 842256
*Charming country house hotel
set in over 2 acres of secluded
gardens. Portreath 5 minutes
by car or a 20 minute
woodland walk.*
Bedrooms: 4 double & 1 twin,
1 family room.
Bathrooms: 6 private.
Bed & breakfast: £35.75-
£41.25 single, £51.75-£57.25
double.
Half board: £36.65-£39.40
daily, £219.75-£236.25 weekly.
Evening meal 7pm (l.o. 8.45pm).
Parking for 25.
Credit: Diners, Amex.

ILMINSTER

Somerset
Map ref 1D2

Former wool town with
modern industry, set in
undulating, pastoral
country. Fine market
square of mellow ham
stone and Elizabethan
school house. The 15th C
church has a handsome
tower and a lofty, light
interior with some notable
brass memorials. Just
north is an arts centre with
theatre and art gallery.

Bay House

Bay Hill, Ilminster, TA19 0AT
☎ (0460) 52120

*Family-run country guesthouse
overlooking rural market town.
Large gardens with
magnificent views of the
Blackdown Hills. Good touring
centre.*
Bedrooms: 1 single, 2 double
& 3 twin, 2 family rooms.
Bathrooms: 2 public.
Bed & breakfast: £18-£20
single, £30-£33 double.
Half board: £23.50-£28 daily,
£137.50-£165 weekly.
Evening meal 6.30pm (l.o.
10am).
Parking for 10.

Shrubbery Hotel M

APPROVED

Ilminster, TA19 9AR
☎ (0460) 52108
Fax (0460) 53660
Consort
*Victorian gentleman's
residence, converted into
modernised country house
hotel, built of local ham stone
and with terraced lawns. Ideal
touring centre.*
Bedrooms: 1 single, 4 double
& 6 twin, 2 family rooms.
Bathrooms: 13 private.
Bed & breakfast: £35-£60
single, £50-£100 double.
Half board: £280-£320
weekly.
Lunch available.
Evening meal 7.30pm (l.o.
9.30pm).
Parking for 100.
Credit: Access, Visa, C.Bl.,
Diners, Amex.

INSTOW

Devon
Map ref 1C1

Popular sailing centre on
the Torridge Estuary,
between Bideford and
Barnstaple, headquarters
of the British Jousting
Centre. Tapeley Park
House, standing in Italian
gardens, has fine 18th C
plasterwork ceilings and
collections of china and
furniture.

Anchorage Hotel

The Quay, Instow, Bideford,
EX39 4HX
☎ (0271) 860655/860475
*Beautifully situated on Instow
quay overlooking water. Quiet
location but near many
outstanding places of interest.
Specialists in golfing holidays.*
Bedrooms: 7 double & 8 twin,
2 family rooms.

Bathrooms: 17 private.
Bed & breakfast: £20-£23.50
single, £40-£47 double.
Half board: £30.70-£33.75
daily, £202.50-£214.80
weekly.
Evening meal 7pm (l.o.
8.30pm).
Parking for 17.
Open February-December.
Credit: Access, Visa.

The Commodore Hotel M

COMMENDED

Marine Pde., Instow,
EX39 4JN
☎ (0271) 860347
Fax (0271) 861233
*Situated in its own grounds
overlooking the Torridge and
Taw Estuaries, minutes from
north Devon link road.
Privately owned and managed.*
Bedrooms: 1 single, 8 double
& 8 twin, 3 family rooms.
Bathrooms: 20 private.
Bed & breakfast: £50-£56
single, £79-£90 double.
Half board: £45-£52 daily,
£298-£350 weekly.
Lunch available.
Evening meal 7pm (l.o.
9.15pm).
Parking for 150.
Credit: Access, Visa, Amex.

ISLES OF SCILLY

Cornwall
Map ref 1A3

Tiny, rocky islands
grouped around main
island of St. Mary's. Fish
and spring flowers
marketed; fields have tall
windbreaks of pittisporum
and escallonia set against
vivid blue seas and silver
sands. Tresco's tropical
gardens have a collection
of ships' figureheads.
Hugh Town on St. Mary's,
with its busy harbour, is
the only town. Romantic
history of shipwrecks,
kelping and smuggling.
*Tourist Information
Centre ☎ (0720) 22536*

Brantwood Hotel M

COMMENDED

Rocky Hill, St. Mary's, Isles
of Scilly, TR21 0NW
☎ Scillonia (0720) 22531 &
Fax (0720) 22301 Telex 45117
HELSTON G

*Centrally situated, with own
large garden, offering personal
service. Accent on food,
furnishings and service.*
Bedrooms: 4 double.
Bathrooms: 4 private.
Bed & breakfast: £33-£38
single, £66-£76 double.
Open June-September.
Credit: Access, Visa, Amex.

Carnwethers Country House

COMMENDED

Pelistry Bay, St. Mary's, Isles
of Scilly, TR21 0NX
☎ Scillonia (0720) 22415
*Family-run hotel in peaceful
gardens close to secluded
beaches, coastal walks and
nature trails. Library and
videos on marine and
Scillonian subjects. Outdoor
heated pool and croquet lawn.*
Bedrooms: 1 single, 4 double
& 3 twin, 2 family rooms.
Bathrooms: 9 private,
2 public; 1 private shower.
Half board: £30-£46 daily.
Evening meal 6.30pm (l.o.
6.30pm).
Parking for 3.
Open April-October.

Covean Cottage

St. Agnes, Isles of Scilly,
TR22 0PL
☎ Scillonia (0720) 22620
*Small cosy cottage guesthouse
with sea views. Friendly
atmosphere and personal
attention assured. Ideal get
away from it all holiday. En-
suite facilities available.*
Bedrooms: 2 double & 1 twin.
Bathrooms: 2 private,
1 public.
Bed & breakfast: £14-£19
single.
Half board: £22-£27 daily.
Lunch available.
Evening meal 6pm (l.o. 7pm).
Open January-November.

Fairlawn

Listed COMMENDED

McFarlands Down, St.
Mary's, Isles of Scilly,
TR21 0NS
☎ Scillonia (0720) 22942
*Modern detached chalet
bungalow, with attractive
lawned garden, close to
beautiful coast. Friendly
atmosphere, freshly-prepared
food. Non-smokers only,
please.*

Continued ▶

Bedrooms: 1 twin, 1 family room.
Bathrooms: 1 private, 1 public.
Half board: £27.80-£29.80 daily, £194.60-£208.60 weekly.
Evening meal 6pm (l.o. 6pm).
Open April-October.

Harbourside Hotel
COMMENDED
The Quay, St. Mary's, Isles of Scilly, TR21 0HV
☎ (0720) 22352
A new small hotel situated right on St. Mary's Quay. Every room has a view of the sea.
Bedrooms: 5 double & 4 twin, 3 family rooms.
Bathrooms: 12 private.
Bed & breakfast: £31-£38.50 single, £62-£77 double.
Half board: £43.45-£49.50 daily.
Evening meal 6.30pm (l.o. 9pm).

Hell Bay Hotel M
COMMENDED
Bryher, Isles of Scilly, TR23 0PR
☎ Scillonia (0720) 22947
Fax (0720) 23004
Only hotel on beautiful and still unspoilt peaceful island. All rooms are garden suites with private lounge and TV. Safe sandy beaches, coastal walks, boat trips and fishing expeditions. Windsurfing.
Bedrooms: 5 double & 5 twin, 4 family rooms.
Bathrooms: 14 private.
Half board: £49-£64 daily, £275-£427 weekly.
Lunch available.
Evening meal 7.15pm (l.o. 8.45pm).
Open March-October.
Credit: Access, Visa.

Star Castle Hotel M
COMMENDED
The Garrison, St. Mary's, Isles of Scilly, TR21 0JA
☎ Scillonia (0720) 22317
An Elizabethan castle in 4.5 acres of tropical gardens. Tennis, indoor heated pool, garden apartments, castle rooms, family rooms.
Bedrooms: 2 single, 5 double & 12 twin, 5 family rooms.
Bathrooms: 24 private, 1 public.

Half board: £46-£60 daily.
Evening meal 6.45pm (l.o. 8pm).
Open March-October.

Tregarthen's Hotel M
St. Mary's, Isles of Scilly, TR21 0PP
☎ Scillonia (0720) 22540
Ⓡ Best Western
Century-old hotel, overlooking the harbour and off islands. Close to shops, beaches and quay.
Bedrooms: 7 single, 7 double & 14 twin, 5 family rooms.
Bathrooms: 25 private, 2 public.
Half board: £52-£68 daily.
Lunch available.
Evening meal 7pm (l.o. 8pm).
Open March-October.
Credit: Access, Visa, Diners, Amex.

KENTON
Devon
Map ref 1D2

Devon Arms Hotel M
Kenton, Exeter, EX6 8LD
☎ (0626) 890213
Old coaching house situated on the A379 midway between Dawlish and Exeter.
Bedrooms: 2 twin, 4 family rooms.
Bathrooms: 2 public; 3 private showers.
Bed & breakfast: £17-£25 single, £30-£40 double.
Half board: £20-£35 daily, £110-£195 weekly.
Lunch available.
Evening meal 6.30pm (l.o. 9.30pm).
Parking for 20.
Credit: Access, Visa.

KEYNSHAM
Avon
Map ref 2B2

Busy town on the River Avon between Bath and Bristol.

Grasmere Court Hotel
22-24 Bath Rd., Keynsham, Bristol, BS18 1SN
☎ Bristol (0272) 862662
Well-appointed hotel with high standard of decor and accommodation. Private facilities. Situated on A4 between Bath and Bristol.

Bedrooms: 3 single, 7 double & 3 twin, 3 family rooms.
Bathrooms: 16 private.
Bed & breakfast: £35-£54 single, £46-£65 double.
Evening meal 6.30pm (l.o. 7.30pm).
Parking for 18.
Credit: Access, Visa.

KINGSBRIDGE
Devon
Map ref 1C3

Formerly important as a port, now a market town overlooking head of beautiful, wooded estuary winding deep into rural countryside. Summer art exhibitions; William Cookworthy Museum.
Tourist Information Centre ☎ *(0548) 853195*

Ashleigh House
COMMENDED
Ashleigh Rd., Kingsbridge, TQ7 1HB
☎ (0548) 852893
Spacious accommodation, furnished to high standard, overlooking countryside but near town and quay. Sun and TV lounges and choice of menu.
Bedrooms: 1 single, 4 double & 2 twin, 1 family room.
Bathrooms: 3 private, 2 public.
Bed & breakfast: £14.50-£15.50 single, £29-£31 double.
Half board: £22-£23 daily, £146.50-£153 weekly.
Evening meal 6.45pm (l.o. 4pm).
Parking for 6.
Open April-October.
Credit: Access, Visa.

Buckland-Tout-Saints Hotel
Kingsbridge, TQ7 2DS
☎ (0548) 853055
Fax (0548) 856261
Ⓡ Small Luxury Hotels
Elegance with simplicity is the principle on which we operate. Individually decorated bedrooms, comfortable lounges with fresh flowers and pot-pourri. A peaceful oasis 2.5 miles north-east of Kingsbridge off A381.
Bedrooms: 1 single, 7 double & 4 twin.
Bathrooms: 12 private.
Bed & breakfast: £85-£95 single, £105-£140 double.
Lunch available.

Evening meal 7.30pm (l.o. 9.30pm).
Parking for 22.
Open February-December.
Credit: Access, Visa, C.Bl., Diners, Amex.

Crabshell Motor Lodge M
Embankment Rd., Kingsbridge, TQ7 1JZ
☎ (0548) 853301
On water's edge of Salcombe Estuary. Boat moorings. Waterside bar/restaurant with extensive seafood menu. Rooms with private balcony, colour TV, kitchenette, refrigerator.
Bedrooms: 2 double & 17 twin, 5 family rooms.
Bathrooms: 24 private.
Bed & breakfast: £37.50 single, £49.50-£52 double.
Half board: £36.25-£37.50 daily.
Lunch available.
Evening meal 6.30pm (l.o. 9.30pm).
Parking for 33.
Credit: Access, Visa.

KINGSKERSWELL
Devon
Map ref 1D2

The Barn Owl Inn M
COMMENDED
Aller Mills, Kingskerswell, Newton Abbot, TQ12 5AN
☎ (0803) 872130/872968
16th C farmhouse inn offering a high standard of accommodation, all rooms en-suite with colour TV, tea-making and telephone. 3 bars, log fires, a la carte restaurant.
Bedrooms: 1 single, 5 double.
Bathrooms: 6 private.
Bed & breakfast: £47.50 single, £60-£75 double.
Half board: £55-£60 daily.
Lunch available.
Evening meal 7pm (l.o. 9.30pm).
Parking for 60.
Credit: Access, Visa.

The enquiry coupons at the back will help you when contacting proprietors.

KINGSTEIGNTON

Devon
Map ref 1D2

4m NE. Newton Abbot

Passage House Hotel M
🌑🌑🌑 COMMENDED
Hackney La., Kingsteignton,
Newton Abbot, TQ12 3QH
☎ Newton Abbot
(0626) 55515 & Fax
(0626) 63336
*This modern hotel offers a high
standard of comfort and
service. Leave A380 for the
A381 and follow the racecourse
signs.*
Bedrooms: 10 single,
10 double & 10 twin, 9 family
rooms.
Bathrooms: 39 private.
Bed & breakfast: £59-£69
single, £85-£95 double.
Half board: £47 daily.
Lunch available.
Evening meal 7pm (l.o.
9.30pm).
Parking for 200.
Credit: Access, Visa, Diners,
Amex.
🛏🍴📞🖥🕯💷 V ⅒
🌱 ◉ 🎿 🖥 ⅏ 🍴🔁▶
❄ 🐾 SP T

KNOWSTONE

Devon
Map ref 1D1

7m E. South Molton

Knowstone Court Country House Hotel & Restaurant M
🌑🌑🌑 COMMENDED
Knowstone, South Molton,
EX36 4RW
☎ Anstey Mills (039 84) 457
& 511 & Fax (039 84) 457
*Elegant Victorian rectory
situated on the edge of small
Devonshire village of thatched
cottages and 13th C church.*
Bedrooms: 1 single, 5 double
& 2 twin.
Bathrooms: 8 private.
Bed & breakfast: £42-£45
single, £60-£66 double.
Half board: £38-£45 daily.
Lunch available.
Evening meal 7pm (l.o. 9pm).
Parking for 14.
Credit: Access, Visa, Amex.
🛏📞🖥🕯💷 V ⅒🍴🖥
⅏ 🍴❄ 🐾 🐾 SP 🏨

---

*The national Crown
scheme is explained
in full on pages
536 – 539.*

LAND'S END

Cornwall
Map ref 1A3

The Old Manor Hotel
🌑🌑 APPROVED
Sennen, Land's End,
TR19 7AD
☎ (0736) 871280
*On A30, 1 mile from Land's
End, very easy to find, near
superb beach. Built of hand-
dressed granite for the squire.*
Bedrooms: 4 double & 1 twin,
3 family rooms.
Bathrooms: 4 private,
2 public; 1 private shower.
Bed & breakfast: £14-£26
single, £32-£44 double.
Half board: £21.50-£33.50
daily, £136.50-£213.50
weekly.
Lunch available.
Evening meal 6.30pm (l.o.
7.30pm).
Parking for 52.
Credit: Access, Visa, Amex.
🛏🍴📞🖥🕯💷 V 🖥 📺
⅏ 🕯 ◡ ❄ 🐾 SP 🏨

Sennen Cove Hotel M
🌑🌑
Marias La., Sennen Cove,
Penzance, TR19 7BZ
☎ (0736) 871275
*Hotel overlooking Sennen Cove
and Cape Cornwall.
Magnificent views of sea from
all rooms. Situated on cliffside.*
Bedrooms: 1 single, 5 double
& 3 twin, 1 family room.
Bathrooms: 4 private,
2 public.
Bed & breakfast: £17-£20
single, £34-£50 double.
Half board: £27-£30 daily,
£155-£183 weekly.
Evening meal 7pm (l.o.
7.30pm).
Parking for 10.
Open March-November.
Credit: Access, Visa.
🛏🖥🕯💷 V 🖥 📺 ◉ ⅏
⅏ 🐾 ❄ 🐾 🐾 SP

The State House M
🌑🌑
Land's End, Sennen,
Penzance, TR19 7AA
☎ (0736) 871844
*Situated on Land's End.
Britain's most visited
landmark.*
Bedrooms: 1 single, 15 double
& 18 twin.
Bathrooms: 34 private.
Bed & breakfast: £34.50-£60
single, £49-£100 double.
Half board: £38.50-£74 daily.
Lunch available.
Evening meal 7pm (l.o.
9.30pm).

Parking for 2.
Credit: Access, Visa, Amex.
🛏🐾📞🖥🕯💷 V ◉
⅏ ⅏ 🍴🔁 ⅂ ◡ ▶ 🐾 SP
T

LAUNCESTON

Cornwall
Map ref 1C2

Medieval 'Gateway to
Cornwall', county town
until 1838, founded by the
Normans under their
hilltop castle near the
original monastic
settlement. Today's hilly
market town, overlooked
by its castle ruin, has a
handsome square with
Georgian houses and an
elaborately-carved granite
church.
*Tourist Information
Centre ☎ (0566) 772321*

Country Friends Restaurant
St Leonards House, Polson,
Launceston, PL15 9QR
☎ (0566) 774479
*400-year-old Devon longhouse
with stone fireplaces, exposed
beams and wood burners.
Cordon Bleu cuisine. Riding
holidays available. Ideal
touring area.*
Bedrooms: 2 twin, 2 family
rooms.
Bathrooms: 1 public;
3 private showers.
Bed & breakfast: £15-£17
single, £30-£34 double.
Half board: £27-£29 daily.
Evening meal 7.30pm (l.o.
9.30pm).
Parking for 10.
Credit: Access, Visa.
🛏3🖥🕯💷 V 🖥 📺 ⅏ ◡ ⅂
▶ ❄ 🐾

Glencoe Villa
🌑🌑 APPROVED
13 Race Hill, Launceston,
PL15 9BB
☎ (0566) 773012 & 775819
*Large 3-storey, hilltop
Victorian-type house with
superb views across Tamar
Valley. 4 minutes from town
centre.*
Bedrooms: 2 single, 2 double
& 1 twin, 3 family rooms.
Bathrooms: 3 private,
2 public.
Bed & breakfast: £15-£22
single, £27-£32 double.
Evening meal 7pm (l.o.
9.30pm).
Parking for 6.
Credit: Access, Visa.
🛏🐾🖥🕯💷 V ⅒🖥
⅏ 🐾 ❄ 🐾

Trethorne Leisure Farm M
Kennards House,
Launceston, PL15 8QE
☎ (0566) 86324
*400-acre dairy farm. Leisure
farm where you can milk a
cow, ride a pony and watch
chicks hatch. Home-cooked
food. Homely, relaxed
atmosphere. Golf driving range
on farm.*
Bedrooms: 3 double, 3 family
rooms.
Bathrooms: 5 private,
1 public; 1 private shower.
Bed & breakfast: £14-£15
single, £28-£30 double.
Half board: £20-£21 daily,
£140-£147 weekly.
Evening meal 7pm (l.o. 7pm).
Parking for 12.
🛏🐾 U 🕯💷 V 🖥 📺 ⅏ ⅏
🍴🐾 ⅂ ❄ 🐾

LIFTON

Devon
Map ref 1C2

Village in Lyd Valley,
noted for salmon and
trout fishing.

Arundell Arms Hotel M
🌑🌑🌑 COMMENDED
Lifton, PL16 0AA
☎ (0566) 784666 & Fax
(0566) 84494
🅒🅑 Best Western
*Famous sporting hotel on
Devon/Cornwall border, near
moors and coast. Fly fishing
courses, also own salmon and
trout fishing and shooting.
Restaurant has French-trained
chef.*
Bedrooms: 10 single, 7 double
& 12 twin.
Bathrooms: 29 private.
Bed & breakfast: £35.75-£56
single, £67.50-£88 double.
Half board: £52.75-£77.50
daily, £346.50-£516 weekly.
Lunch available.
Evening meal 7.30pm (l.o.
9pm).
Parking for 80.
Credit: Access, Visa, Diners,
Amex.
🛏🐾📞◉🖥🕯💷 V ⅒
🖥 ⅏ ⅏ 🍴🕯 ◡ ⅂ ▶ ⅂
❄ 🐾 🐾 SP T

The Thatched Cottage Country Hotel & Restaurant
🌑🌑🌑 COMMENDED
Sprytown, Lifton, PL16 0AY
☎ (0566) 84224
*16th C thatched cottage with
well-appointed en-suite rooms,
set in 2.5 acres of gardens.
Licensed restaurant. 100 yards
from A30 trunk road.*

Continued ▶

LIFTON
Continued

Bedrooms: 1 double & 1 twin,
2 family rooms.
Bathrooms: 4 private.
Bed & breakfast: from £29.50
single, from £59 double.
Lunch available.
Evening meal 7.30pm (l.o.
9.30pm).
Parking for 10.
Credit: Access, Visa, Amex.

LISKEARD
Cornwall
Map ref 1C2

Former stannary town
with a livestock market
and light industry,
situated at the head of a
valley running to the
Riviera coast. Handsome
Georgian and Victorian
residences and a fine
Victorian Guildhall reflect
the prosperity of the
mining boom. The large
church has an early 20th
C tower and a Norman
font.

Country Castle Hall M
APPROVED
Liskeard, PL14 4EB
☎ (0579) 342694 & 342691
100 years old, with French-
style tower, standing in 2.5
acres overlooking the Looe
Valley and 1 mile from
Liskeard centre.
Bedrooms: 4 single, 3 double
& 2 twin, 1 family room.
Bathrooms: 10 private,
1 public.
Bed & breakfast: from £38
single, £53-£64 double.
Half board: £52-£54 daily.
Lunch available.
Evening meal 7pm (l.o.
8.30pm).
Parking for 50.
Open January-October,
December.
Credit: Access, Visa.

Elnor Guest House
1 Russell St., Liskeard,
PL14 4BP
☎ (0579) 42472
Home-from-home with friendly
family atmosphere in 100-year-
old town house between the
station and market town.
Bedrooms: 2 single, 4 double
& 2 twin, 1 family room.
Bathrooms: 4 private,
2 public.

Bed & breakfast: £14-£17
single, £28-£34 double.
Half board: £23-£26 daily,
£154-£175 weekly.
Evening meal 6pm (l.o. 6pm).
Parking for 6.

Lord Eliot Hotel
Castle St., Liskeard,
PL14 3AU
☎ (0579) 42717
Fully-licensed residential hotel
on A38. Modern bedrooms all
en-suite, dining room open to
non-residents.
Bedrooms: 2 single, 6 double
& 7 twin, 1 family room.
Bathrooms: 15 private,
3 public.
Bed & breakfast: £34.08-
£42.30 single, £54.05-£61.10
double.
Lunch available.
Evening meal 7pm (l.o.
9.45pm).
Parking for 80.
Credit: Access, Visa, Diners,
Amex.

THE LIZARD
Cornwall
Map ref 1B3

Ending in England's most
southerly point, a treeless
peninsula with rugged,
many-coloured cliffs and
deep shaded valleys
facing the Helford River.
Kynance Cove famous for
serpentine cliffs, lovely
sands.

Housel Bay Hotel M
COMMENDED
Housel Cove, The Lizard,
Helston, TR12 7PG
☎ (0326) 290417
Clifftop position near
England's most southerly point
overlooking the Atlantic
Ocean. Safe sandy beach,
coastal walks and breathtaking
views.
Bedrooms: 4 single, 12 double
& 7 twin.
Bathrooms: 23 private.
Bed & breakfast: from £25
single, £50-£90 double.
Half board: £40-£60 daily,
£245-£345 weekly.
Lunch available.
Evening meal 7.30pm (l.o.
9pm).
Parking for 34.
Open February-December.
Credit: Access, Visa, Amex.

LONG SUTTON
Somerset
Map ref 2A3

Good touring base, close
to the Sedgemoor
wetlands with their flora
and fauna. Between
Somerton, ancient capital
of Wessex, and Langport,
an old inland port on the
River Parrett.

The Devonshire Arms Hotel
COMMENDED
Long Sutton, Langport,
TA10 9LP
☎ (0458) 241271
Built as a hunting lodge by the
Duke of Devonshire in 1787.
Bedrooms: 5 double & 1 twin,
1 family room.
Bathrooms: 6 private,
1 public; 1 private shower.
Bed & breakfast: £28.50-£35
single, £35-£55 double.
Half board: from £35 daily.
Lunch available.
Evening meal 7pm (l.o.
11pm).
Parking for 20.
Credit: Access, Visa, Amex.

LOOE
Cornwall
Map ref 1C2

Small resort developed
around former fishing and
smuggling ports
occupying the deep
estuary of the East and
West Looe Rivers.
Narrow winding streets,
with old inns; museums
and art gallery are
housed in interesting old
buildings. West Looe has
a medieval seamen's
chapel restored with
timbers from a captured
Spanish ship. Shark
fishing centre, boat trips;
busy harbour.

Allhays Country House Hotel M
COMMENDED
Talland Bay, Looe, PL13 2JB
☎ Polperro (0503) 72434 &
Fax (0503) 72929
Family-owned hotel in
extensive gardens overlooking
sea. Fresh fish, local and
home-grown products served in
garden room restaurant.
Bedrooms: 4 double & 3 twin.
Bathrooms: 4 private,
1 public; 3 private showers.
Bed & breakfast: £52-£72
double.

Half board: £38.50-£48.50
daily, £245-£308 weekly.
Evening meal 7pm (l.o. 9pm).
Parking for 14.
Credit: Access, Visa.

Commonwood Manor Hotel M
St. Martins Rd., Looe,
PL13 1LP
☎ (050 36) 2929
Spacious and relaxing country
house hotel. Set in 3 acre
estate overlooking the River
Looe valley and countryside
beyond, yet only 10 minutes'
walk to harbour and town.
Bedrooms: 7 double & 2 twin,
1 family room.
Bathrooms: 10 private,
2 public.
Bed & breakfast: £31-£38
single, £58-£66 double.
Lunch available.
Evening meal 7pm (l.o. 8pm).
Parking for 20.
Open March-October.
Credit: Access, Visa, Amex.

Coombe Farm M
COMMENDED
Widegates, Looe, PL13 1QN
☎ Widegates (050 34) 223
10-acre smallholding.
Delightful country house in
lovely grounds with superb
views to the sea. Log fires,
candlelit dining. Games room.
Near glorious walks and
beaches.
Bedrooms: 1 single, 2 double
& 1 twin, 4 family rooms.
Bathrooms: 1 private,
2 public.
Bed & breakfast: from £16.50
single, from £33 double.
Half board: from £26.50
daily, from £177 weekly.
Evening meal 7pm (l.o. 7pm).
Parking for 12.
Open March-October.

Deganwy Hotel
Station Rd., East Looe,
PL13 1HL
☎ (050 36) 2984
Small family hotel facing Looe
River, within 5 minutes' walk
of the town and beach.
Bedrooms: 2 single, 4 double
& 1 twin, 3 family rooms.
Bathrooms: 2 private,
2 public.
Bed & breakfast: £11-£15
single, £22-£30 double.
Half board: £18-£25 daily.

Evening meal 6.30pm (l.o.
10am).
Open March-October.
♒ ▭ ♥ 🏄 ♒ 🖶 TV ▦ ♨ ♒ ☒
SP

Fieldhead Hotel ♨
♒♒♒ COMMENDED
Portuan Rd., Hannafore,
West Looe, PL13 2DR
☎ (050 36) 2689
*Turn-of-the-century house set
in lovely gardens in quiet area,
with panoramic views of the
sea and bay.*
Bedrooms: 1 single, 7 double
& 3 twin, 2 family rooms.
Bathrooms: 13 private.
Bed & breakfast: £33-£36
single, £54-£64 double.
Half board: £39-£44 daily,
£230-£270 weekly.
Lunch available.
Evening meal 6.30pm (l.o.
8.30pm).
Parking for 15.
Open February-November.
Credit: Access, Visa, Amex.
♒5 🖫 ♒ ☎ 🖶 ♒ ♥ V
🏄 TV ▦ ♨ 🍴 ♣ ✺ U ✿
🔀 DAP SP 🏄

Klymiarven Hotel ♨
♒♒♒ COMMENDED
Barbican Hill, East Looe,
PL13 1BB
☎ (050 36) 2333
*Country house hotel
overlooking Looe, with
magnificent harbour views,
offering seclusion even at the
height of the season.*
Bedrooms: 1 single, 6 double
& 3 twin, 4 family rooms.
Bathrooms: 14 private.
Bed & breakfast: £25-£36
single, £50-£72 double.
Half board: £36-£47 daily,
£220-£295 weekly.
Lunch available.
Evening meal 7pm (l.o.
8.30pm).
Parking for 16.
Open February-December.
Credit: Access, Visa.
♒ ♒ ♒ ☎ 🖶 ♒ ♥ V ♒
TV ♨ 🍴 ♣ ♨ ✿ 🔀 SP 🏠

The Panorama Hotel ♨
♒♒♒
Hannafore Rd., Looe,
PL13 2DE
☎ (0503) 262123
*Family hotel, varied food,
friendly atmosphere.
Magnificent setting overlooking
miles of beautiful coastline.*
Bedrooms: 2 single, 4 double
& 1 twin, 3 family rooms.
Bathrooms: 10 private,
1 public.
Bed & breakfast: £20-£30
single, £40-£60 double.
Half board: £28-£38 daily,
£168-£228 weekly.

Evening meal 6.30pm (l.o.
10pm).
Parking for 8.
Open March-October.
Credit: Access, Visa.
♒ 🖫 🖶 ♒ ♥ ♒ V ♒
TV ▦ ♨ 🍴 🔀 🐾 DAP 🐾 SP

Pixies Holt ♨
♒♒
Shutta, Looe, PL13 1JD
☎ (0503) 62726
*Built in 1878 for a ship's
captain, with views across the
two rivers. Only 10 minutes'
walk to the fishing port of
Looe.*
Bedrooms: 1 single, 4 double
& 1 twin, 1 family room.
Bathrooms: 4 private,
1 public.
Bed & breakfast: £16.40-
£20.50 single, £32.80-£41
double.
Parking for 8.
Open March-October.
Credit: Access, Visa, Amex.
♒10 🖫 ♒ 🖶 ♥ 🏄 ♒ TV
▦ ♨ ✿ 🔀 🏠 SP T

St. John's Court Hotel
East Cliff, East Looe,
PL13 1DE
☎ (050 36) 2301
*Small family-run hotel with sea
and harbour views, 2 minutes
from town, harbour and sandy
beach.*
Bedrooms: 2 single, 5 double
& 1 twin, 3 family rooms.
Bathrooms: 5 private,
2 public.
Bed & breakfast: £14-£18
single, £28-£36 double.
Half board: £22-£26 daily,
£157-£182 weekly.
Evening meal 7pm (l.o. 1pm).
Parking for 5.
Open March-October.
Credit: Access, Visa, Amex.
♒ ♒ TV ♥ 🏄 V ▦ ♨ 🏄
SP

Hotel Trevanion
Hannafore Rd., Looe,
PL13 2DE
☎ (050 36) 2003
*Family-run hotel with
panoramic views over the
harbour, beach and coastline.
En-suite rooms and
comfortable bar.*
Bedrooms: 3 single, 7 double
& 1 twin, 3 family rooms.
Bathrooms: 7 private,
4 public.
Bed & breakfast: £17-£21
single, £31-£42 double.
Half board: £23-£28.50 daily,
£144-£180 weekly.
Evening meal 6.30pm (l.o.
6.30pm).
Open April-October.
Credit: Access, Visa.
♒ ▭ ♥ 🏄 V ♒ TV 🍴 🐾
SP

Cornwall
Map ref 1B2

*Tourist Information
Centre* ☎ *(0208) 872207*

Restormel Lodge
Hotel ♨
♒♒♒ COMMENDED
19 Castle Hill, Lostwithiel,
PL22 0DD
☎ Bodmin (0208) 872223
*Set in the beautiful Fowey
Valley. Warm, spacious well-
equipped bedrooms.
Imaginative menus of delicious
food and friendly, efficient
service.*
Bedrooms: 2 single, 15 double
& 12 twin, 3 family rooms.
Bathrooms: 32 private.
Bed & breakfast: £41.50-£44
single, £51-£62 double.
Half board: £35-£45 daily,
£251-£270 weekly.
Lunch available.
Evening meal 7pm (l.o.
9.30pm).
Parking for 45.
Credit: Access, Visa, Diners,
Amex.
♒ 🖫 ♒ ☎ 🖶 ♒ ♥ V ♒
▦ ♨ 🍴 ♣ ✿ 🐾 SP T

Devon
Map ref 1D2

Riverside village of pretty
thatched cottages
gathered around its 15th
C church with fine carved
screen. The traditional
Mayday festival has
dancing round the
maypole. Just west is a
well-known beauty spot,
Lustleigh Cleave, where
wild Dartmoor is
breached by the River
Bovey which flows
through a deep valley of
boulders and trees.

Eastwrey Barton
Hotel ♨
♒♒♒ COMMENDED
Lustleigh, Newton Abbot,
TQ13 9SN
☎ (064 77) 338
*Well-appointed 17th C country
house hotel. Peaceful, relaxing
and renowned for good food
and personal service.*
Bedrooms: 3 double & 3 twin.
Bathrooms: 6 private.
Bed & breakfast: £29 single,
£58 double.
Half board: £42 daily, £280
weekly.
Evening meal 7.30pm (l.o.
7.30pm).

Parking for 20.
Open March-October.
Credit: Access, Visa.
♒12 🖶 ♒ ♒ ♥ V ♒ ▦ ♨
🍴 ✿ 🏄 SP

Devon
Map ref 1C2

Former important tin
mining town, a small
village on edge of West
Dartmoor. Remains of
Norman castle where all
falling foul of tinners'
notorious 'Lydford Law'
were incarcerated. Bridge
crosses River Lyd where
it rushes through a mile-
long gorge of boulders
and trees over pools,
rocks and waterfall.

Lydford House Hotel ♨
♒♒♒
Lydford, Okehampton,
EX20 4AU
☎ (082 282) 347
Ⓜ Minotels
*Family-run country house
hotel, peacefully set in own
grounds on edge of Dartmoor.
Superb touring centre. Own
riding stables.*
Bedrooms: 3 single, 4 double
& 2 twin, 4 family rooms.
Bathrooms: 11 private,
2 public.
Bed & breakfast: max. £28.50
single, max. £57 double.
Half board: max. £40 daily,
£236-£252 weekly.
Lunch available.
Evening meal 7pm (l.o. 8pm).
Parking for 30.
Credit: Access, Visa, Amex.
♒5 🖫 ♒ ☎ 🖶 ♒ ♥ V
🔀 ♒ ▦ ♨ 🍴 U ♣ ✿
DAP SP 🏠 T

Moor View Hotel ♨
♒♒♒ APPROVED
Vale Down, Lydford,
Okehampton, EX20 4BB
☎ (082 282) 220
*Victorian country house hotel,
dining room and tea garden set
in over 1.5 acres of land. Large
rooms with lovely views over
the moors.*
Bedrooms: 3 double, 1 family
room.
Bathrooms: 4 private.
Bed & breakfast: £33 single,
£44 double.
Half board: £46 daily.
Lunch available.
Evening meal 7.30pm (l.o.
9pm).
Parking for 15.
Credit: Access, Visa.
♒2 🖶 ♒ ♒ ♥ 🏄 V 🔀 ♒ TV
▦ ♨ 🍴 U ♣ ✿ 🏄 DAP
SP 🏠

LYME REGIS

Dorset
Map ref 1D2

Pretty, historic fishing town and resort set against the fossil-rich cliffs of Lyme Bay. In medieval times it was an important port and cloth centre. The Cobb, a massive stone breakwater, shelters the ancient harbour which is still lively with boats.
Tourist Information Centre ☎ *(0297) 442138*

Hotel Buena Vista M
🍴🍴 APPROVED
Pound St., Lyme Regis, DT7 3HZ
☎ (0297) 442494
🅖 Inter
Regency house with a country house atmosphere in an unrivalled position overlooking the bay. Close to the town and beaches.
Bedrooms: 3 single, 9 double & 4 twin, 1 family room.
Bathrooms: 17 private.
Bed & breakfast: £34-£38 single, £60-£88 double.
Half board: £39-£53 daily, £234-£318 weekly.
Evening meal 7pm (l.o. 8pm).
Parking for 20.
Credit: Access, Visa, Diners, Amex.
🛇 ♨ 🔌 🖵 🌣 🖵 Ⓥ ✕ 🖵 🛋 🅿 🌣 SP T

Kersbrook Hotel M
🍴🍴🍴 COMMENDED
Pound Rd., Lyme Regis, DT7 3HX
☎ (0297) 442596/442576
Thatched, 18th C listed hotel in its own picturesque gardens, set high above Lyme Bay and with unique views of the bay.
Bedrooms: 2 single, 7 double & 3 twin.
Bathrooms: 10 private.
Bed & breakfast: £45-£60 single, £60-£80 double.
Half board: £48-£56 daily.
Lunch available.
Evening meal 7.30pm (l.o. 9pm).
Parking for 16.
Open February-November.
Credit: Access, Visa.
🛇 ♨ 🖵 Ⓣ 🌣 SP 🕮 🖵 Ⓥ 🖵 🛋 🅿 🌣 SP 🕮 🖵

Orchard Country Hotel
Rousdon, Lyme Regis, DT7 3XW
☎ (0297) 442972
Established, friendly hotel set in mature walled garden. Just over 2 miles from Lyme Regis, in lush East Devon.

Bedrooms: 3 single, 5 double & 6 twin.
Bathrooms: 14 private.
Bed & breakfast: £30-£35 single, £54-£62 double.
Half board: £37-£43 daily, £198-£235 weekly.
Evening meal 7.30pm (l.o. 8.15pm).
Parking for 25.
Open April-October.
Credit: Access, Visa.
🛇8 ♨ 🖵 🌣 Ⓥ 🖵 Ⓣ 🕮 🛋 🕮 ♿ Ⓤ 🅿 🌣 🕮 SP

Pitt White Wholefood Guest House
Mill La., Uplyme, Lyme Regis, DT7 3TZ
☎ (0297) 442094
Peaceful Victorian house in secluded woodland gardens near the sea. Friendly and informal atmosphere. Vegetarian cooking our speciality.
Bedrooms: 1 single, 3 double & 1 twin, 3 family rooms.
Bathrooms: 3 private, 1 public; 1 private shower.
Half board: £19.50-£25 daily, £123-£158 weekly.
Evening meal 7pm.
Parking for 10.
🛇8 ♨ 🖵 Ⓤ 🖵 Ⓥ ✕ 🖵 Ⓣ 🕮 🛋 Ⓣ Ⓤ ♩ 🅿 🌣 🕮 ⌑P 🕮 ⟊ SP 🕮

St. Michaels Hotel M
🍴🍴 APPROVED
Pound St., Lyme Regis, DT7 3HZ
☎ (0297) 442503
An elegant Georgian house with all the charm and atmosphere of a bygone age.
Bedrooms: 2 single, 6 double & 4 twin, 1 family room.
Bathrooms: 13 private.
Bed & breakfast: £28-£36 single, £56-£72 double.
Half board: £36-£38 daily, £198-£249 weekly.
Evening meal 6.30pm (l.o. 7.30pm).
Parking for 13.
Credit: Access, Visa.
🛇8 ♨ 🖵 🌣 Ⓥ ✕ 🖵 🕮 🛋 Ⓣ 🚻 SP

White House
🍴🍴 COMMENDED
47 Silver St., Lyme Regis, DT7 3HR
☎ (0297) 443420
Fine views of Dorset coastline from rear of this 18th C guesthouse. A short walk from beach, gardens and shops.
Bedrooms: 5 double & 2 twin.
Bathrooms: 7 private.

Bed & breakfast: £35-£38 double.
Parking for 6.
Open April-October.
🛇10 ⑩ 🖵 🌣 🛋 🖵 🕮 🚻 SP 🕮

LYNMOUTH

Devon
Map ref 1C1

Resort set beneath lofty, bracken-covered cliffs and pinewood gorges where 2 rivers meet, cascade and flow between boulders to the town. Lynton, set on cliffs above, can be reached by water-operated cliff railway from the Victorian esplanade. Valley of the Rocks, to the west, gives dramatic walks.

Bath Hotel M
🍴🍴🍴 APPROVED
Lynmouth, EX35 6EL
☎ Lynton (0598) 52238
Friendly, family-run hotel by picturesque Lynmouth Harbour. Ideal centre for exploring Exmoor National Park.
Bedrooms: 1 single, 10 double & 11 twin, 2 family rooms.
Bathrooms: 24 private.
Bed & breakfast: £30-£40 single, £52-£74 double.
Half board: £38.50-£50 daily, £230-£300 weekly.
Lunch available.
Evening meal 7pm (l.o. 8.30pm).
Parking for 17.
Open March-October.
Credit: Access, Visa, Diners, Amex.
🛇 ☎ ⑩ 🖵 🌣 🛋 Ⓥ 🕮 🛋 🚻 🕮 ⌑P SP T

East Lyn House M
🍴🍴🍴 COMMENDED
17 Watersmeet Rd., Lynmouth, EX35 6EP
☎ Lynton (0598) 52540
Riverside hotel in central position with a large sun terrace. Overlooking the East Lyn River and village. Spectacular valley views.
Bedrooms: 6 double & 2 twin.
Bathrooms: 5 private; 3 private showers.
Bed & breakfast: £20-£22 single, £40-£44 double.
Half board: £30-£32 daily, £200-£220 weekly.
Evening meal 6.30pm (l.o. 8.30pm).
Parking for 12.
Credit: Access, Visa.
🛇8 ⑩ 🖵 🌣 🛋 Ⓥ 🖵 🕮 🛋 🚻 ⌑P ⟊ SP

The Heatherville
🍴🍴 COMMENDED
3 Tors Park., Lynmouth, EX35 6NB
☎ (0598) 52327
Country house hotel in secluded part of valley, 3 minutes from harbour. Friendly hotel run on home-from-home basis.
Bedrooms: 6 double & 2 twin, 1 family room.
Bathrooms: 5 private, 2 public.
Bed & breakfast: £40-£44 double.
Half board: £30-£32 daily, £188-£202 weekly.
Evening meal 7pm (l.o. 7pm).
Parking for 9.
Open April-October.
🛇7 🌣 🛋 Ⓥ 🖵 Ⓣ 🕮 🚻 ⌑P SP

Rock House Hotel
🍴🍴 APPROVED
Lynmouth, EX35 6EN
☎ Lynton (0598) 53508
Set in a unique and unrivalled position, perched on the water's edge overlooking picturesque harbour and River Lyn.
Bedrooms: 3 double & 2 twin, 1 family room.
Bathrooms: 4 private, 1 public.
Bed & breakfast: £24-£31 single, £48-£62 double.
Half board: £36-£43 daily, £215-£260 weekly.
Lunch available.
Evening meal 7pm (l.o. 9pm).
Parking for 6.
Open February-December.
Credit: Access, Visa, Diners, Amex.
🛇 ♨ 🖵 🌣 🛋 Ⓥ 🖵 Ⓣ 🕮 🚻 SP

LYNTON

Devon
Map ref 1C1

Hilltop resort on Exmoor coast linked to its seaside twin, Lynmouth, by a water-operated cliff railway which descends from the town hall. Spectacular surroundings of moorland cliffs with steep chasms of conifer and rocks through which rivers cascade.

Alford House Hotel M
🍴🍴🍴 COMMENDED
Alford Ter., Lynton, EX35 6AT
☎ (0598) 52359

*Beautifully situated with
superb coastal views.
Delightful en-suite rooms, some
with four-poster beds. Warm
welcome and home cooking.*
Bedrooms: 1 single, 6 double
& 1 twin.
Bathrooms: 7 private,
1 public.
Bed & breakfast: £19-£25
single, £40-£50 double.
Half board: £30-£34 daily,
£175-£195 weekly.
Evening meal 7.30pm (l.o.
7pm).
Credit: Access, Visa.
🏄9 ♨ 🖨 🛏 ✿ 🛆 ☎ V ✗ 🛏
TV ▥ ♨ ✕ 🛏 DAP ⚡ SP T

Gordon House Hotel ♙
♛♛ COMMENDED

31 Lee Rd., Lynton,
EX35 6BS
☎ (0598) 53203
*Attractive Victorian
gentleman's residence
sympathetically restored.
Charming hotel with warm
friendly atmosphere amd
reputation for good food.*
Bedrooms: 5 double & 1 twin,
1 family room.
Bathrooms: 7 private,
1 public.
Bed & breakfast: £19.60-
£24.50 single, £35-£43 double.
Half board: £27.75-£29.75
daily.
Evening meal 7pm (l.o.
5.30pm).
Parking for 7.
Open March-November.
Credit: Access, Visa.
🏄5 ♨ ☎ 🖨 ✿ 🛆 V 🛏 TV
▥ 🛆 ✕ 🛏 DAP SP 🏠

Ingleside Hotel ♙
♛♛♛

Lynton, EX35 6HW
☎ (0598) 52223
*Family-run hotel with high
standards in elevated position
overlooking village. Ideal
centre for exploring Exmoor.*
Bedrooms: 4 double & 1 twin,
2 family rooms.
Bathrooms: 7 private.
Bed & breakfast: £23-£26
single, £42-£48 double.
Half board: £33-£37 daily,
£224-£252 weekly.
Evening meal 7pm (l.o. 6pm).
Parking for 10.
Open March-October.
Credit: Access, Visa.
🏄5 ♨ ☎ 🖨 ✿ 🛆 V 🛏 ▥
🛆 ✿ ✕ 🛏 DAP SP T

North Cliff Hotel ♙
♛♛♛

North Walk, Lynton,
EX35 6HJ
☎ (0598) 52357

---

*Family-run hotel of character
with secluded grounds. All
rooms overlook Lynmouth Bay
and Watersmeet Valley. Ample
parking on forecourt.*
Bedrooms: 2 single, 9 double
& 2 twin, 2 family rooms.
Bathrooms: 12 private,
3 public.
Bed & breakfast: £20-£24
single, £40-£48 double.
Half board: £29-£33 daily,
£185-£205 weekly.
Lunch available.
Evening meal 7pm (l.o. 6pm).
Parking for 15.
Open February-November.
🏄 ♨ ☎ 🖨 ✿ 🛆 TV ▥ 🛆 ♣
🛏 SP 🏠 T

Rockvale Hotel
♛♛♛

Lee Road, Lynton,
EX35 6HW
☎ (0598) 52279/53343
*Centrally, yet quietly located
hotel with extensive views.
Offering pretty en-suite rooms,
bar, choice of menu and large
level car park.*
Bedrooms: 1 single, 4 double
& 1 twin, 2 family rooms.
Bathrooms: 6 private,
2 public.
Bed & breakfast: £22-£31
single, £44-£51 double.
Half board: £35-£38 daily.
Lunch available.
Evening meal 7pm (l.o. 7pm).
Parking for 10.
Open February-October.
Credit: Access, Visa.
🏄4 ♨ ☎ ✿ 🛆 ✿ 🛏 ▥
🛆 ✿ 🛏 SP

St. Vincent Licensed
Guest House
♛♛♛

Castle Hill, Lynton,
EX35 6AJ
☎ (0598) 52244
*Charming, detached period
guesthouse beside Exmoor
museum in centre of Lynton.
Residents' lounge with colour
TV, bar and a small cottage
tea garden.*
Bedrooms: 1 single, 1 double
& 2 twin, 2 family rooms.
Bathrooms: 2 private,
1 public.
Bed & breakfast: £13-£16.50
single, £26-£33 double.
Half board: £21-£25 daily,
£140-£166 weekly.
Evening meal 6.30pm (l.o.
4pm).
Parking for 4.
Open April-October.
🏄 ✿ 🛆 🛏 TV ✕ 🛏 🏠

Sandrock Hotel ♙
♛♛♛ COMMENDED

Longmead, Lynton,
EX35 6DH
☎ (0598) 53307
*Comfortable family-run hotel,
quietly situated near local
beauty spots. Bowls green and
tennis courts.*
Bedrooms: 2 single, 4 double
& 3 twin.
Bathrooms: 7 private,
1 public.
Bed & breakfast: £18.50-
£22.50 single, £24-£39 double.
Half board: £29-£34 daily,
£195.50-£224 weekly.
Evening meal 7pm (l.o. 8pm).
Parking for 9.
Open February-November.
Credit: Access, Visa, Amex.
🏄 ☎ ✿ 🛆 🛆 V 🛆 🛏 ▥
🛆 ♣ 🛏 SP T

Sylvia House Hotel ♙
♛♛♛

Lydiate Lane, Lynton,
EX16 6HE
☎ (0598) 52391
*Delightful Georgian hotel in
the very heart of England's
romantic Little Switzerland.
Offering hospitality of a
bygone age and elegance at
moderate terms.*
Bedrooms: 2 single, 5 double
& 1 twin.
Bathrooms: 6 private,
1 public.
Bed & breakfast: £13-£18
single, £30-£36 double.
Half board: £24.50-£29 daily,
£150-£170 weekly.
Evening meal 7pm (l.o.
10am).
🏄 ♨ ☎ 🖨 ✿ 🛆 V ✗ 🛏
TV ▥ 🛆 ☎ DAP ⚡ SP

Top of the World
1 Woodland View, Lynbridge,
Lynton, EX35 6BE
☎ Lynton (0598) 53693
*Charming Victorian house on
high ground, with glorious
views across the West Lyn
Valley. Three-quarters of a
mile from Lynton.*
Bedrooms: 1 double & 1 twin.
Bathrooms: 1 public.
Bed & breakfast: £27 double.
Half board: £21 daily.
Evening meal 6.45pm (l.o.
5pm).
Parking for 2.
Open January-October.
🏄 UL 🛆 V 🛏 TV ▥ 🛆 ✿
🛏

Valley House Hotel
♛♛ APPROVED

Lynbridge Rd., Lynton,
EX35 6BD
☎ (0598) 52285

---

*Victorian house nestling
against rockface overlooking
West Lyn River and
Lynmouth. Ideal for
naturalists. Magnificent views.
Peaceful yet centrally located.*
Bedrooms: 3 double, 2 family
rooms.
Bathrooms: 5 private,
1 public.
Bed & breakfast: £40-£60
double.
Half board: £32-£42 daily.
Lunch available.
Evening meal 7.15pm (l.o.
9pm).
Parking for 8.
Credit: Access, Visa, Diners,
Amex.
🏄 🛆 🛏 🛆 V ✗ 🛏 TV ▥
🛆 ♨ ✿ ✕ 🛏 ⚡ SP T

Woodlands Hotel
♛♛♛ COMMENDED

Lynbridge, Lynton,
EX35 6AX
☎ (0598) 52324
*A detached Victorian house set
on high ground, run by resident
proprietors. Comfortably
furnished. Sorry, no children or
pets.*
Bedrooms: 1 single, 3 double
& 2 twin.
Bathrooms: 5 private,
2 public.
Bed & breakfast: £27-£30
single, £54-£60 double.
Half board: £36-£39 daily,
£234 weekly.
Evening meal 7.15pm (l.o.
6pm).
Parking for 8.
Open March-October.
Credit: Access, Visa.
☎ 🛆 🛏 🛆 V 🛏 ▥ 🛆 🎵
✿ ✕ T

MALMESBURY

Wiltshire
Map ref 2B2

Overlooking the River
Avon, an old town
dominated by its great
church, once a
Benedictine abbey. The
surviving Norman nave
and porch are noted for
fine sculptures, 12th C
arches and musicians'
gallery.
*Tourist Information
Centre* ☎ *(0666) 823748*

Crudwell Court Hotel ♙
♛♛♛♛ COMMENDED

Crudwell, Malmesbury,
SN16 9EP
☎ (066 67) 355 & 7194/5
Continued ▶

MALMESBURY

Continued

17th C vicarage, comfortably furnished with heated swimming pool and 3 acres of grounds. Panelled restaurant open to non-residents.
Bedrooms: 1 single, 14 double.
Bathrooms: 15 private.
Bed & breakfast: £85-£110 double.
Half board: £60-£75 daily.
Lunch available.
Evening meal 7pm (l.o. 9.30pm).
Parking for 16.
Credit: Access, Visa, Diners, Amex.
⏳ ♨ ☎ 🅿 ♥ î 🆅 🗐 🎠
🖼 🍴 ⚲ ► ☼ 🌣 SP 🎠 T

Mayfield House Hotel ⋒
♨♨♨

Crudwell, Malmesbury, SN16 9EW
☎ (066 67) 409 & 7198
In own grounds with walled garden, 4 miles north of Malmesbury. Convenient for many stately homes, Cotswolds and spa towns of Bath and Cheltenham.
Bedrooms: 4 single, 8 double & 7 twin, 1 family room.
Bathrooms: 20 private.
Bed & breakfast: £45-£55 single, £58-£68 double.
Evening meal 7pm (l.o. 9.30pm).
Parking for 50.
Credit: Access, Visa, Amex.
⏳ ♨ ☎ 🅿 ♥ î 🆅 🗐
TV 🗐 ⚲ 🍴 ☼ SP 🎠 T

Whatley Manor ⋒
♨♨♨

Easton Grey, Malmesbury, SN16 0RB
☎ (0666) 822888
Telex 449380 WHOTEL
Cotswold manor house in extensive grounds, between Bath and the Cotswolds.
Bedrooms: 13 double & 13 twin, 3 family rooms.
Bathrooms: 29 private.
Bed & breakfast: £79-£89 single, £105-£125 double.
Lunch available.
Evening meal 7.30pm (l.o. 9pm).
Parking for 60.
Credit: Access, Visa, Diners, Amex.
⏳ ♨ ☎ 🅿 ♥ î 🆅
🖼 ◉ 🗐 ⚲ 🍴 🏌 ♨ ♟ ✎
♪ ☼ 🌣 SP 🎠 T

Half board prices shown are per person but in some cases may be based on double/twin occupancy.

MARAZION

Cornwall
Map ref 1B3

Old town sloping to Mount's Bay with views of St. Michael's Mount and a causeway to the island revealed at low tide. In medieval times it catered for pilgrims. The Mount is crowned by a 15th C castle built around the former Benedictine monastery of 1044.

Chymorvah Tolgarrick Hotel ⋒
♨♨♨ COMMENDED

Marazion, TR17 0DQ
☎ Penzance (0736) 710497
Family-run hotel and tea garden overlooking St. Michael's Mount and Mount's Bay. Spacious grounds with own access to beach.
Bedrooms: 1 single, 5 double & 1 twin, 2 family rooms.
Bathrooms: 9 private, 1 public.
Bed & breakfast: £18-£26 single, £36-£52 double.
Half board: £25-£33.50 daily, £170-£216 weekly.
Lunch available.
Evening meal 6.30pm (l.o. 2.30pm).
Parking for 9.
Credit: Access, Visa, Amex.
⏳5 ♨ 🗐 ☎ ♥ 🅿 ♥ UL î
🆅 🍴 🗐 ⚲ ♨ ☼ ♨ ☼ DAP SP
🎠
⊙ Display advertisement appears on page 447.

Cutty Sark Marazion Hotel

The Square, Marazion, Penzance, TR17 0AP
☎ Penzance (0736) 710334
Family-run comfortable old inn, specialising in seafood and real home cooking. The nearest hotel to St Michael's Mount.
Bedrooms: 1 single, 5 double & 4 twin, 2 family rooms.
Bathrooms: 7 private, 1 public; 5 private showers.
Bed & breakfast: £15-£20 single, £26-£44 double.
Lunch available.
Evening meal 7pm (l.o. 9.30pm).
Parking for 20.
Credit: Access, Visa.
⏳ 🗐 ☼ î 🆅 🍴 TV ⚲ ♨
🎠 SP

MARLBOROUGH

Wiltshire
Map ref 2B2

Important market town, in a river valley cutting through chalk downlands. The broad main street, with colonnaded shops on one side, shows a medley of building styles, mainly from the Georgian period. Lanes wind away on either side and a church stands at each end.

Merlin Hotel

36/39 High St., Marlborough, SN8 1LW
☎ (0672) 512151 & (0672) 55966
Early Georgian classical style hotel in the High Street. Ample car parking adjacent. Attractive wine bar and licensed restaurant.
Bedrooms: 4 single, 4 double & 6 twin, 1 family room.
Bathrooms: 13 private, 2 public.
Bed & breakfast: £35-£40 single, £45-£50 double.
Half board: £40-£45 daily.
Lunch available.
Evening meal 7pm (l.o. 9.30pm).
Credit: Access, Visa.
⏳ ♥ 🗐 ♥ 🆅 🗐 ⚲ DAP 🎠

MARY TAVY

Devon
Map ref 1C2

4m NE. Tavistock
Moorland village spread over former mining area near the River Tavy. Wheal Friendship worked from late 18th C until 1925, the engine house of Wheal Betsy is preserved by the National Trust. Remains of other mining villages can be seen on the surrounding craggy moors.

Moorland Hall ⋒
♨♨♨ COMMENDED

Bentor Rd., Mary Tavy, Tavistock, PL19 9PY
☎ (0822) 810466/810661
A Victorian country house hotel, parts of which are 200 years old, set amid beautiful gardens and paddocks. Direct access on to Dartmoor, near Devon and Cornish beaches.
Bedrooms: 3 double & 4 twin, 1 family room.

Bathrooms: 8 private, 1 public.
Bed & breakfast: from £32 single, £50-£57 double.
Half board: £38-£42 daily, from £250 weekly.
Evening meal 6.30pm (l.o. 8pm).
Parking for 20.
Credit: Access, Visa.
⏳ ♨ 🗐 🅿 ♥ î 🆅 🗐 ⚲
⚲ 🍴 ⊙ ☼ 🎠 ☼

MAWGAN PORTH

Cornwall
Map ref 1B2

4m NE. Newquay
Holiday village occupying a steep valley on the popular coastal route to Newquay. Golden sands, rugged cliffs and coves. Nearby Bedruthan Steps offers exhilarating cliff walks and views. The chapel of a Carmelite nunnery, once the home of the Arundells, may be visited.

White Lodge Hotel

Mawgan Porth, Newquay, TR8 4BN
☎ St. Mawgan (0637) 860512 & 860244
Situated in own grounds 100 yards from beach. Sea and cliff views from most bedrooms, the dining room and bar. Open at Christmas and New Year.
Bedrooms: 1 single, 8 double, 6 family rooms.
Bathrooms: 10 private, 2 public.
Bed & breakfast: £19-£20 single, £38-£40 double.
Half board: £25.50-£26.50 daily, £150-£180 weekly.
Lunch available.
Evening meal 6pm (l.o. 8pm).
Parking for 18.
Open March-November.
Credit: Access, Visa, Amex.
⏳ ♨ 🗐 🅿 ♥ î 🆅 🗐 TV
🗐 ⚲ ♨ ☼ ► ☼ ♨ SP T

MAWNAN SMITH

Cornwall
Map ref 1B3

4m S. Falmouth

Budock Vean Golf & Country House Hotel ⋒
♨♨♨♨ COMMENDED

Mawnan Smith, Falmouth, TR11 5LG
☎ Falmouth (0326) 250288
Telex 45266
Country house hotel set in sub-tropical grounds with own golf course. Facilities free to guests.

Bedrooms: 10 single, 10 double & 36 twin, 2 family rooms.
Bathrooms: 58 private.
Half board: £57.20-£88.50 daily, £350-£511 weekly.
Evening meal 7.30pm (l.o. 9pm).
Parking for 100.
Open March-December.
Credit: Access, Visa, Diners, Amex.

Small industrial town standing on the banks of the River Avon. Old weavers' cottages and Regency houses are grouped around the attractive church which has traces of Norman work. The 18th C Round House, once used for dyeing fleeces, is now a craft centre.
Tourist Information Centre ☎ *(0225) 707424*

Beechfield House 🏚
COMMENDED
Beanacre, Melksham, SN12 7PU
☎ (0225) 703700
Built in 1878 of mellow Bath stone in ornate architectural style of Victorian era. Set in 8 acres of gardens. Sympathetically restored into a fine small country house.
Bedrooms: 7 double & 17 twin.
Bathrooms: 24 private.
Bed & breakfast: from £88.50 single, from £117 double.
Lunch available.
Evening meal 7pm (l.o. 9.30pm).
Parking for 30.
Credit: Access, Visa, Diners, Amex.

Longhope Guest House
9 Beanacre Rd., Melksham, SN12 8AG
☎ (0225) 706737
Situated in its own grounds on the A350 Melksham - Chippenham road. Half a mile from Melksham town centre, 10 miles from M4 junction 17.
Bedrooms: 2 single, 1 double & 3 twin, 2 family rooms.
Bathrooms: 6 private, 1 public; 1 private shower.

Bed & breakfast: £18 single, max. £33 double.
Half board: max. £24 daily, max. £142 weekly.
Evening meal 6.30pm (l.o. 7pm).
Parking for 12.

Shaw Country Hotel 🏚
COMMENDED
Bath Rd., Shaw, Melksham, SN12 8EF
☎ (0225) 702836 & Fax (0225) 790275
400-year-old farmhouse in own grounds, 9 miles from Bath. Licensed bar and restaurant, with table d'hote and a la carte menus.
Bedrooms: 3 single, 7 double & 3 twin.
Bathrooms: 13 private.
Bed & breakfast: £40-£48 single.
Half board: £59-£78 daily.
Lunch available.
Evening meal 7pm (l.o. 9.30pm).
Parking for 20.
Credit: Access, Visa, Amex.

Small town with a grand Perpendicular church surrounded by Georgian houses, with old inns and a 15th C chantry house. On the chalk downs overlooking the town is an Iron Age fort.
Tourist Information Centre ☎ *(0747) 860341*

The Beeches
Chetcombe Rd., Mere, BA12 6AU
☎ (0747) 860687
Comfortable old toll house with interesting carved stairway and gallery. Standing in a beautiful garden at entrance to an early English village.
Bedrooms: 1 double & 1 twin, 1 family room.
Bathrooms: 1 public; 2 private showers.
Bed & breakfast: £16-£18 single, £28-£35 double.
Half board: £25-£27 daily, £147-£160 weekly.
Evening meal 6pm (l.o. 10pm).
Parking for 6.

Chetcombe House Hotel
COMMENDED
Chetcombe Rd., Mere, BA12 6AZ
☎ (0747) 860219
Country house hotel set in 1 acre of mature gardens, close to Stourhead House and Garden. Ideal touring centre. Home-cooked local produce a speciality.
Bedrooms: 1 single, 2 double & 2 twin.
Bathrooms: 5 private.
Bed & breakfast: £27-£29 single, £46-£48 double.
Half board: £33-£39 daily, £210-£245 weekly.
Lunch available.
Evening meal 7pm (l.o. 5pm).
Parking for 10.
Credit: Access, Visa, Amex.

Talbot Hotel
APPROVED
The Square, Mere, BA12 6DR
☎ (0747) 860427
16th C coaching inn with interesting features, ideally situated for visits to Stourhead, Longleat, Stonehenge, Salisbury, Bath, Sherborne and Cheddar.
Bedrooms: 2 single, 3 double & 1 twin, 1 family room.
Bathrooms: 6 private, 1 public.
Bed & breakfast: £32.50 single, £53 double.
Half board: from £175 weekly.
Lunch available.
Evening meal 7pm (l.o. 9.30pm).
Parking for 20.
Credit: Access, Visa, Amex.

Individual proprietors have supplied all details of accommodation. Although we do check for accuracy, we advise you to confirm prices and other information at the time of booking.

Small fishing town, a favourite with holidaymakers. Earlier prosperity came from pilchard fisheries, boat-building and smuggling. By the harbour are fish cellars, some converted, and a local history museum is housed in an old boat-building shed on the north quay. Handsome Methodist chapel; shark fishing, sailing.

Mevagissey House 🏚
COMMENDED
Vicarage Hill, Mevagissey, PL26 6SZ
☎ (0726) 842427
Georgian country house in a woodland setting on a hillside, set in 4 acres. Elegant, spacious rooms, many facilities, licensed bar, home cooking.
Bedrooms: 3 double & 1 twin, 2 family rooms.
Bathrooms: 4 private, 1 public.
Bed & breakfast: £22-£27 single, £34-£44 double.
Half board: £29-£34 daily, £203-£224 weekly.
Evening meal 7.30pm (l.o. 5pm).
Parking for 12.
Open March-October.
Credit: Access, Visa.

Seapoint House Hotel 🏚
COMMENDED
Battery Ter., Mevagissey, PL26 6QS
☎ (0726) 842684
Family-run hotel with beautiful views overlooking the bay and harbour. All bedrooms with en-suite facilities, colour TV and hot drinks.
Bedrooms: 1 single, 6 double & 1 twin, 2 family rooms.
Bathrooms: 10 private.
Bed & breakfast: £25-£30 single, £50-£60 double.
Half board: £35-£40 daily, £210-£240 weekly.
Evening meal 7pm (l.o. 7pm).
Parking for 10.
Open March-October.
Credit: Access, Visa.

The enquiry coupons at the back will help you when contacting proprietors.

MEVAGISSEY

Continued

Sharks Fin Hotel
APPROVED

The Quay, Mevagissey,
PL26 6QU
☎ (0726) 843241
*Historic building situated on
the quay, tastefully converted
into a hotel.*
Bedrooms: 2 single, 6 double
& 1 twin, 2 family rooms.
Bathrooms: 4 private,
1 public; 7 private showers.
Bed & breakfast: £16.50-£21
single, £33-£55 double.
Lunch available.
Evening meal 5.45pm (l.o.
9.45pm).
Open March-November.
Credit: Access, Visa, Diners,
Amex.

Steep House ⋔
⋓⋓⋓

Portmellon Cove,
Mevagissey, St. Austell,
PL26 2PH
☎ (0726) 843732 Telex 45526
YOULDEN
*Good cooking, residential
licence, outdoor covered pool.
Well-equipped bedrooms.
Winter breaks available.
Wonderful views.*
Bedrooms: 6 double & 1 twin.
Bathrooms: 1 private,
2 public; 1 private shower.
Bed & breakfast: £27-£40
double.
Half board: £22-£29 daily.
Lunch available.
Evening meal 8pm (l.o.
7.30pm).
Parking for 10.
Credit: Access, Visa, Amex.

Tremarne Hotel ⋔
⋓⋓⋓ **APPROVED**

Polkirt, Mevagissey, St.
Austell, PL26 6UY
☎ (0726) 842213
*In a quiet secluded area with
views of sea and country.
Within easy reach of
Mevagissey harbour and
Portmellon bathing beach.*
Bedrooms: 8 double & 4 twin,
2 family rooms.
Bathrooms: 14 private,
1 public.
Bed & breakfast: £24.50-£28
single, £41-£48 double.
Half board: £28-£35 daily,
£182-£224 weekly.
Evening meal 7pm (l.o. 8pm).

Parking for 14.
Open March-November.
Credit: Access, Visa, Amex.

Trevalsa Court Hotel ⋔
⋓⋓⋓ **APPROVED**

Polstreath Hill, St. Austell,
St. Austell, PL26 6TH
☎ (0726) 842468
*Clifftop position with superb
sea views and access to beach
in peaceful surroundings. Ideal
for touring. Ample car parking.
Accent on fresh food,
vegetarian/special diets.
Ground floor room ideal for
semi-disabled persons.*
Bedrooms: 1 single, 4 double
& 3 twin, 2 family rooms.
Bathrooms: 10 private.
Bed & breakfast: £24-£28
single, £48-£68 double.
Half board: £34-£43 daily,
£238-£301 weekly.
Lunch available.
Evening meal 6.30pm (l.o.
8pm).
Parking for 40.
Open February-November.
Credit: Access, Visa.

MILTON DAMEREL

Devon
Map ref 1C2

*5m NE. Holsworthy
Tiny village beside the
Rivers Waldon and
Torridge, within easy
reach of the charming
market town of Great
Torrington.*

Woodford Bridge
Hotel ⋔

Milton Damerel, Holsworthy,
EX22 7LL
☎ (040 926) 481
Fax (040 926) 328
*Pretty, thatched coaching inn
retaining many original
features. A la carte and
carvery restaurants. Indoor
pool and sports facilities. On
A388 between Holsworthy and
Bideford.*
Bedrooms: 1 single, 9 double
& 2 twin.
Bathrooms: 12 private.
Bed & breakfast: £45-£65
single, £70-£90 double.
Lunch available.
Evening meal 7pm (l.o. 9pm).
Parking for 100.
Credit: Access, Visa, Diners,
Amex.

MINEHEAD

Somerset
Map ref 1D1

Victorian resort with
spreading sands
developed around old,
steeply-built fishing port
on the coast below
Exmoor. Former
fishermen's cottages
stand beside the 17th C
harbour; cobbled streets
of thatched cottages
climb the hill in steps to
the church. Boat trips,
steam railway. Hobby
Horse festival on 1 May.
*Tourist Information
Centre* ☎ *(0643) 702624*

Beach Hotel
The Avenue, Minehead,
TA24 5AP
☎ (0643) 2193
*Situated on the promenade,
hotel extends a warm welcome,
with high standard service,
English cooking, comfortable
accommodation and a relaxing
atmosphere.*
Bedrooms: 6 single, 10 double
& 30 twin, 4 family rooms.
Bathrooms: 50 private.
Bed & breakfast: from £25
single, from £45 double.
Half board: from £32 daily.
Lunch available.
Evening meal 6.30pm (l.o.
8.45pm).
Parking for 30.
Credit: Access, Visa, Diners,
Amex.

Beaconwood Hotel ⋔
⋓⋓⋓⋓ **APPROVED**

Church Rd., North Hill,
Minehead, TA24 5SB
☎ (0643) 702032
*Quiet, comfortable and
relaxing family-run hotel in 2
acres of terraced garden.
Unimpaired views of Exmoor
and the sea.*
Bedrooms: 3 double & 8 twin,
2 family rooms.
Bathrooms: 13 private,
2 public.
Bed & breakfast: £29.50-£35
single, £44-£55 double.
Half board: £34-£39.50 daily,
£220-£255 weekly.
Lunch available.
Evening meal 6.30pm (l.o.
8pm).
Parking for 30.
Credit: Access, Visa.

Marston Lodge Hotel
⋓⋓⋓ **COMMENDED**

St. Michaels Rd., North Hill,
Minehead, TA24 5JP
☎ (0643) 702510
*Set in lovely gardens with
superb sea and moorland views,
we offer relaxation and
comfort.*
Bedrooms: 2 single, 6 double
& 2 twin, 2 family rooms.
Bathrooms: 12 private.
Bed & breakfast: £22-£25
single, £44-£50 double.
Half board: £31.50-£35 daily,
£189-£206 weekly.
Lunch available.
Evening meal 7pm (l.o.
7.30pm).
Parking for 9.
Open February-December.
Credit: Access, Visa.

Mayfair Hotel
⋓⋓⋓

25 The Avenue, Minehead,
TA24 5AY
☎ (0643) 702719/702052
*Dutch/English family-run,
conveniently situated on level, 3
minutes shops and sea. Home
cooking. Decorated to high
standard.*
Bedrooms: 3 single, 4 double
& 1 twin, 8 family rooms.
Bathrooms: 16 private.
Bed & breakfast: £23-£25
single, £42-£46 double.
Half board: £30-£33 daily,
£150-£165 weekly.
Lunch available.
Evening meal 6.30pm (l.o.
9.30pm).
Parking for 14.
Open March-November.

Mentone Hotel ⋔
⋓⋓⋓ **APPROVED**

The Parks, Minehead,
TA24 8BS
☎ (0643) 705229
*Quiet, comfortable and near
shops. All rooms have radio,
TV, tea/coffee; most have
private facilities.*
Bedrooms: 2 single, 4 double
& 3 twin.
Bathrooms: 7 private,
1 public.
Bed & breakfast: £17-£20
single, £34-£40 double.
Half board: £23-£26 daily,
£155-£176 weekly.
Evening meal 6.45pm (l.o.
6.45pm).
Parking for 9.
Open April-October.

York House Inn
😊😊😊

48 The Ave., Minehead,
TA24 5AN
☎ (0643) 705151
*200 yards from the seafront, 5
minutes to 18-hole golf-course
with reduced rates for guests.
Fully licensed.*
Bedrooms: 6 single, 7 double
& 6 twin, 1 family room.
Bathrooms: 16 private.
Bed & breakfast: £21-£23
single, £42-£46 double.
Lunch available.
Evening meal 6pm (l.o. 9pm).
Parking for 12.
Credit: Access, Visa, Diners,
Amex.
🖐5 🕻 📠 🛏 📺 ▥ 🖙 🛠 🛏
🅣

MORETON-HAMPSTEAD
Devon
Map ref 1C2

Small market town with a
row of 17th C
almshouses standing on
the Exeter road.
Surrounding moorland is
scattered with ancient
farmhouses, prehistoric
sites.

Cookshayes Country Guest House M
😊😊😊 COMMENDED

33 Court St.,
Moretonhampstead,
TQ13 8LG
☎ (0647) 40374
*Licensed guesthouse on edge of
Dartmoor. Ornamental
gardens with ample parking.
Traditionally furnished. Accent
on food and comfort.*
Bedrooms: 1 single, 4 double
& 2 twin, 1 family room.
Bathrooms: 6 private,
2 public.
Bed & breakfast: £18 single,
£31-£39 double.
Half board: £26-£30 daily,
£175-£203 weekly.
Evening meal 7pm (l.o. 5pm).
Parking for 15.
Open March-October.
Credit: Access, Visa.
🖐7 🎇 🛏 📠 🛏 📠 ▾ 🖐
▥ ⌨ ❄ 🛠 🅐🅟 🆂🅟 🅣

Gate House
😊😊

North Bovey, Newton Abbot,
TQ13 8RB
☎ (0647) 40479
*15th C thatched house in a
beautiful Dartmoor village.
Offering peace, seclusion and
comfort. Traditional or
vegetarian cooking. Closed at
Christmas.*

Bedrooms: 2 double & 1 twin.
Bathrooms: 3 private.
Bed & breakfast: £43 double.
Half board: £32.50 daily,
£227.50 weekly.
Evening meal 7.30pm.
Parking for 4.
🖐 🖵 🖐 🛠 📠 🛏 📻 ● ▥ ⌨
🍴 🕻 ▾ ❄ 🛠 🛏 🅣

White Hart Hotel M
😊😊😊 COMMENDED

The Square,
Moretonhampstead,
TQ13 8NF
☎ (0647) 40406 & Fax
(0647) 40565
Ⓜ Minotels
*Historic inn in centre of
moorland town. Antiques, log
fires, rural bar. A la carte
restaurant and bar meals.*
Bedrooms: 1 single, 9 double
& 6 twin, 4 family rooms.
Bathrooms: 20 private,
1 public.
Bed & breakfast: £37-£40
single, £57.50-£60 double.
Lunch available.
Evening meal 6pm (l.o.
8.30pm).
Parking for 12.
Credit: Access, Visa, Diners,
Amex.
🕻 🅑 🖵 ⌨ 📠 ▤ 🛏 ▥
🛏 🍴 🌾 🆂🅟 🛠 🅣

MORTEHOE
Devon
Map ref 1C1

Old coastal village with
small, basically Norman
church. Wild cliffs, inland
combes; sand and surf at
Woolacombe.

The Cleeve House M
😊😊😊 COMMENDED

Mortehoe, Woolacombe,
EX34 7ED
☎ Woolacombe
(0271) 870719
*Home cooking, a warm
welcome, peace and tranquillity
in surroundings that will please
the discerning guest.*
Bedrooms: 4 double & 1 twin.
Bathrooms: 5 private,
1 public.
Bed & breakfast: £20-£22
single, £38-£44 double.
Half board: £27-£36 daily,
£183.75-£227 weekly.
Evening meal 7.30pm (l.o.
5pm).
Parking for 9.
Open March-November.
🖐10 🛏 📺 ▥ 🖐 📠 ▥ 🛏
🕻 ▾ ❄ 🛠 🆂🅟

Gull Rock
😊😊😊

Mortehoe, Woolacombe,
EX34 7EA
☎ Woolacombe
(0271) 870534
*Attractive detached Edwardian
house quietly set amidst
National Trust land with
spectacular walks, scenic walks,
sandy beaches and secluded
coves.*
Bedrooms: 1 single, 2 double
& 1 twin, 3 family rooms.
Bathrooms: 7 private.
Bed & breakfast: £20-£25
single, £35-£37 double.
Half board: £40-£45 daily,
£130-£140 weekly.
Evening meal 7pm (l.o. 7pm).
Parking for 6.
Open March-October.
🖐 ❄ 📠 ▥ 🖐 📠 📺 ▥ 🛏
🍴 🛠 🅐🅟 🆂🅟

Lundy House Hotel M
😊😊😊

Chapel Hill, Mortehoe,
Woolacombe, EX34 7DZ
☎ Woolacombe
(0271) 870372
*Magnificently situated on
coastal path with spectacular
sea views. Traditional home
cooking, licensed bar/lounge.
Pets welcome. Bargain breaks.*
Bedrooms: 2 single, 3 double,
5 family rooms.
Bathrooms: 6 private,
1 public.
Bed & breakfast: £16-£19
single, £32-£44 double.
Half board: £24.50-£30.50
daily, £162-£202 weekly.
Lunch available.
Evening meal 7.30pm (l.o.
4pm).
Parking for 10.
Open February-October.
🖐6 🅑 ▥ 🖐 📠 ▥ 🛏 📠 🕻
❄ 🛠 🅐🅟 🆂🅟

Sunnycliffe Hotel M
😊😊😊 COMMENDED

Mortehoe, Woolacombe,
EX34 7EB
☎ Woolacombe
(0271) 870597
*Small, select hotel beautifully
situated above sandy cove
overlooking beach. Traditional
English food cooked by
qualified chef/proprietor.
Sorry, no children or pets.*
Bedrooms: 6 double & 2 twin.
Bathrooms: 8 private,
2 public.
Bed & breakfast: £25-£31
single, £46-£58 double.
Half board: £36-£42 daily,
£194-£250 weekly.

Evening meal 7pm (l.o. 7pm).
Parking for 11.
Open February-November.
🎇 📠 🖵 🖐 📠 ▥ 🖐 🛠 🛏 ▥
🛏 ❄ 🛠 🛠 🆂🅟

MOUSEHOLE
Cornwall
Map ref 1A3

2m S. Penzance
Old fishing port
completely rebuilt after
destruction in the 16th C
by Spanish raiders.
Twisting lanes and
granite cottages with
luxuriant gardens rise
steeply from the harbour;
just south is a private bird
sanctuary.

Carn Du Hotel
😊😊😊

Raginnis Hill, Mousehole,
Penzance, TR19 6SS
☎ Penzance (0736) 731233
*An elegant Victorian house in
an elevated position above
Mousehole. Cosy lounge,
delightful cocktail bar and
licensed restaurant specialising
in seafood and local vegetables.
Terraced gardens.*
Bedrooms: 1 single, 3 double
& 3 twin.
Bathrooms: 7 private.
Bed & breakfast: £23-£28
single, £46-£56 double.
Half board: £33-£40 daily,
£230-£270 weekly.
Lunch available.
Evening meal 7pm (l.o.
8.30pm).
Parking for 12.
Open January, March-
December.
Credit: Access, Visa, Amex.
🖐 📠 🖵 🖐 📠 ▥ 🖐 📺 ▥
🛏 🛠 🛠 🆂🅟

Lobster Pot M
😊😊😊 APPROVED

Mousehole, Penzance,
TR19 6QX
☎ Penzance (0736) 731251
*Perched on the harbour's edge,
this unique hotel and
restaurant offers a standard of
comfort and cuisine out of the
ordinary.*
Bedrooms: 2 single, 12 double
& 6 twin, 5 family rooms.
Bathrooms: 22 private,
1 public.
Bed & breakfast: £26-£40
single, £52-£100 double.
Half board: £35.50-£60 daily,
£247-£420 weekly.
Lunch available.

Continued ▶

---

*Map references apply to the colour maps
towards the end of this guide.*

MOUSEHOLE
Continued

Evening meal 7.30pm (l.o. 9.45pm).
Open March-January.
Credit: Access, Visa, Amex.

🛏 ♿ 🕯 ⏰ 🍴 🅿 📺 🍷 ▦ ⚓
📺 🅰 ⛟ 🐕 SP ▦

🔵 Display advertisement appears on page 449.

MULLION
Cornwall
Map ref 1B3

Small holiday village with a golf-course, set back from the coast. The church has a serpentine tower of 1500, carved roof and beautiful medieval bench-ends. Beyond Mullion Cove, with its tiny harbour, wild untouched cliffs stretch south-eastward toward Lizard Point.

Mullion Cove Hotel 🅜
🏆🏆🏆 APPROVED

Mullion Cove, Mullion, TR12 7EP
☎ (0326) 240328
Beautiful late Victorian hotel overlooking Mullion Cove and harbour. Warm and friendly atmosphere.
Bedrooms: 9 single, 13 double & 9 twin, 4 family rooms.
Bathrooms: 21 private, 6 public.
Bed & breakfast: £25.50-£28.75 single, £51-£75 double.
Half board: £40-£52 daily, £261-£340 weekly.
Lunch available.
Evening meal 7pm (l.o. 8.30pm).
Parking for 50.
Open March-November.
Credit: Access, Visa, Diners.

🛏 ♿ 🅿 🕯 🅥 ⚓ 📺 ⛟
🍴 🐾 ⚲ ⏰ 🅿 ❄ 🐕 DAP 🍴
SP ▦

NETHER STOWEY
Somerset
Map ref 1D1

6m W. Bridgwater
Winding village below east slopes of Quantocks with attractive old cottages of varying periods. A Victorian clock tower stands at its centre, where a village road climbs the hill beside a small stream.

Castle of Comfort Hotel
Dodington, Nether Stowey, Bridgwater, TA5 1LE
☎ Holford (027 874) 264
Licensed 16th C hotel and restaurant in Quantock Hills. Ideal for walking and touring, within easy reach of M5.
Bedrooms: 1 single, 3 double & 1 twin, 1 family room.
Bathrooms: 2 private, 1 public.
Bed & breakfast: £22-£36 single, £32-£54 double.
Half board: £28-£46 daily, £189-£276 weekly.
Lunch available.
Evening meal 7.30pm (l.o. 9.30pm).
Parking for 12.
Credit: Access, Visa, Amex.

🛏 ♿ 🅿 🕯 ⏰ ❄ 🐕 📺
▦ 🅰 ⚲ 🐕 SP ▦

NEWLYN
Cornwall
Map ref 1A3

1m S. Penzance
Cornwall's main fishing port, with a busy harbour and solid grey houses. By the harbour is the handsome building of the deep-sea fishermen's mission. The Passmore Edwards Gallery (known as the Newlyn Art Gallery), which exhibits local work, was built for the 19th C artists' colony which later moved to St. Ives.

Panorama Private Hotel
🏆🏆

Chywoone Hill, Newlyn, Penzance, TR18 5AR
☎ (0736) 68498
Panoramic views of Mount's Bay from nearly all rooms. Modern house and amenities. Friendly atmosphere and personal attention.

Bedrooms: 2 single, 5 double & 1 twin.
Bathrooms: 4 private, 1 public.
Bed & breakfast: £17-£22 single, £34-£44 double.
Half board: £28-£33 daily, £187-£225 weekly.
Evening meal 7pm (l.o. 4pm).
Parking for 12.
Credit: Access, Visa, Diners, Amex.

🛏3 ♿ 🅿 🕯 ⏰ 🅥 ⚓ 📺
🔵 ▦ 🅰 ⚲ 🍴 🅿 ❄ 🐕 SP

NEWQUAY
Cornwall
Map ref 1B2

Popular resort spread over dramatic cliffs around its old fishing port. Many beaches with abundant sands, caves and rock pools; excellent surf. Pilots' gigs are still raced from the harbour and on the landward stands the Huer's House of whitewashed stone, surviving from pilchard-fishing days.
Tourist Information Centre ☎ *(0637) 871345*

Alicia Guest House
136 Henver Rd., Newquay, TR3 3EQ
☎ (0637) 874328
Comfortable family-run guesthouse near beaches and facilities. Traditional home cooking and relaxed, friendly atmosphere.
Bedrooms: 2 double, 3 family rooms.
Bathrooms: 2 private, 2 public.
Bed & breakfast: £15-£21 single.
Half board: £22-£35 daily, £80-£112 weekly.
Evening meal 6.30pm.
Parking for 9.
Open March-October.

🛏 ♿ 🅿 ⛟ 🅥 ⚓ 📺 🅰 🐕
⛟ DAP SP

Aloha Hotel
🏆🏆

122/124 Henver Rd., Newquay, TR3 3EQ
☎ (0637) 878366
Friendly, comfortable family-run hotel with home cooking. Well situated for beaches, touring Cornwall and for Newquay nightlife.
Bedrooms: 3 single, 5 double, 6 family rooms.
Bathrooms: 6 private, 2 public; 4 private showers.
Bed & breakfast: £12-£19 single, £24-£38 double.

Half board: £16-£27 daily, £95-£160 weekly.
Evening meal 6.30pm (l.o. 10am).
Parking for 14.
Open February-December.
Credit: Access, Visa.

🛏 ♿ 🅿 🅿 🕯 🍴 🅨 🐕 📺
▦ 🅰 ⚲ 🐕 SP

Atlantic Hotel
🏆🏆🏆🏆🏆 COMMENDED

Newquay, TR7 1EN
☎ (0637) 872244
Set on own headland in 10+ acres. Sea views from all sides and all bedrooms. Totally refurbished since 1987.
Bedrooms: 14 single, 33 double & 11 twin, 22 family rooms.
Bathrooms: 80 private, 6 public.
Bed & breakfast: £49.35-£55.23 single, £91.66-£103.40 double.
Half board: £52.88-£58.75 daily, £199.75-£229.13 weekly.
Lunch available.
Evening meal 7pm (l.o. 9pm).
Parking for 150.
Credit: Access, Visa.

🛏 ♿ 🅿 🕯 ⏰ 🅥 🍴
⚓ 📺 ♿ ✠ ▦ 🅰 🍴 🛏 ♿
🔵 🔳 🐾 ⚲ 🅿 🍴 ❄ 🐕 🐕
SP ▦ 🆃

Bon-A-Cord
19 Carminow Way, Newquay, TR7 3AY
☎ (0637) 876557
Guesthouse with a warm, welcoming and friendly atmosphere. Good food, close to beaches.
Bedrooms: 1 single, 3 double & 1 twin, 3 family rooms.
Bathrooms: 1 public; 4 private showers.
Bed & breakfast: £12-£15 single, £24-£30 double.
Half board: £16-£20 daily, £90-£120 weekly.
Evening meal 6pm (l.o. 6.30pm).
Parking for 5.
Open March-October.

🛏 ⏰ 🅥 ⚓ 📺 ▦ 🍴 🐕 DAP

Bon Ami Hotel
🏆🏆 APPROVED

Trenance La., Newquay, TR7 2HX
☎ (0637) 874009
Family-run, detached hotel with residential licence, situated in Trenance Gardens. Most rooms have view of boating lake and gardens. All rooms have heating and private shower and toilet en-suite. Midweek bookings accepted.

Bedrooms: 2 single, 6 double & 1 twin.
Bathrooms: 9 private, 1 public.
Bed & breakfast: £15-£20 single, £30-£40 double.
Half board: £22-£27 daily, £125-£155 weekly.
Evening meal 6.30pm (l.o. 8pm).
Parking for 9.
Open April-October.
📺❒♦🛄🅥🍴📺▦⚓ ♨☐ 🅓🅐🅟 🆂🅿

Brakespear Hotel
44-46 Edgecumbe Ave., Newquay, TR7 2NJ
☎ (0637) 874771
Hotel for the family run by a family. Good decor throughout. Close to all amenities, 3 minutes from railway station, gardens, bowling green.
Bedrooms: 2 single, 2 double & 3 twin, 3 family rooms.
Bathrooms: 2 private, 3 public; 4 private showers.
Bed & breakfast: £14-£16 single, £28-£32 double.
Half board: £20-£24 daily, £128-£138 weekly.
Evening meal 6pm (l.o. 6pm).
Parking for 7.
Open January-November.
📺❒🅑♦🛄🅥🍴📺🅓🅐🅟 🆂🅿

Hotel California M
Pentire Cres., Newquay, TR7 1PU
☎ (0637) 879292 & Fax (0637) 875611
Indoor and outdoor pools, sauna, solarium, gym, snooker, American 10-pin bowling centre, nightclub, tennis, squash. Magnificent views and good food.
Bedrooms: 7 single, 33 double & 1 twin, 32 family rooms.
Bathrooms: 73 private.
Bed & breakfast: £25-£30 single, £50-£60 double.
Half board: £30-£35 daily, £120-£255 weekly.
Lunch available.
Evening meal 7pm (l.o. 8.45pm).
Parking for 50.
Credit: Access, Visa.
📺❒🅑♦📞🅑🍴🅓🅕♠🅥 🍴🔭🅿☐▶♨🆂🅿

Charlton House Hotel M
☸☸☸ APPROVED
6 Hilgrove Rd., Newquay, TR7 2QY
☎ (0637) 873392

Please mention this guide when making a booking.

Family hotel close to beaches and within easy walking distance of zoo, leisure gardens and shops. Tea and coffee facilities, TV in all rooms. Heated outdoor swimming pool.
Bedrooms: 3 single, 15 double & 6 twin, 4 family rooms.
Bathrooms: 15 private, 3 public.
Bed & breakfast: £14-£19.50 single, £28-£39 double.
Half board: £16.50-£25 daily, £109-£165 weekly.
Evening meal 6.30pm (l.o. 7pm).
Parking for 15.
Open April-October.
Credit: Access, Visa.
📺❒🛄♦🍴🅥🍴📺 ♠⚓🔭🅴🅓🅐🅟♨🆂🅿

Claremont House
Listed COMMENDED
35 Trebarwith Cres., Newquay, TR7 1DX
☎ (0637) 875383
Close to Towan Beach, the coach station, shops and coastal footpath. Some rooms with sea views, some with en-suite facilities. Full central heating.
Bedrooms: 1 single, 2 double & 1 twin, 3 family rooms.
Bathrooms: 1 private, 1 public.
Bed & breakfast: £18-£22 single, £36-£44 double.
Half board: £25-£29 daily, £130-£168 weekly.
Lunch available.
Evening meal 6.30pm (l.o. 7pm).
📺❒🅑♦🍴🅥🍴📺🛄 ⚓🔭🅴🅓🅐🅟♨🆂🅿

Coranne Guest House
25 Hilgrove Rd., Newquay, TR7 2QZ
☎ (0637) 873864
Bungalow guesthouse standing in its own grounds. Close to all amenities.
Bedrooms: 1 single, 2 double & 1 twin, 3 family rooms.
Bathrooms: 1 public.
Bed & breakfast: £15-£19 single, £29-£38 double.
Half board: £19-£27 daily, £108-£150 weekly.
Evening meal 6.15pm.
Parking for 10.
📺❒3🛄♦🍴📺🛄▦♨🆂🅿

Corisande Manor Hotel M
☸☸☸
Riverside Ave., Pentire, Newquay, TR7 1PL
☎ (0637) 872042

South facing with 3 acres of peaceful grounds. Private foreshore, rowing boats and solarium. Same ownership since 1968.
Bedrooms: 5 single, 8 double & 3 twin, 3 family rooms.
Bathrooms: 16 private, 7 public.
Bed & breakfast: £18-£24 single, £36-£48 double.
Half board: £25-£33.50 daily, £135-£190 weekly.
Lunch available.
Evening meal 7pm (l.o. 7.30pm).
Parking for 19.
Open May-October.
Credit: Access, Visa.
📺3🛄🅑☐♦🍴🅥🍴🛄 ⚓♠🌢🅴🆂🅿▦🆃

Cornish Coast Hotel
Tower Rd., Newquay, TR7 1LU
☎ (0637) 872773
Family hotel, close to harbour, shops and beaches. Overlooking golf-courses and Fistral Bay. Warm friendly welcome assured. No restrictions.
Bedrooms: 3 single, 11 double & 4 twin, 6 family rooms.
Bathrooms: 17 private, 3 public.
Bed & breakfast: £16-£29 single, £32-£58 double.
Half board: £19-£30 daily, £115-£180 weekly.
Evening meal 6.30pm (l.o. 7pm).
Parking for 35.
Open June-September.
📺5🛄🅑☐♦🍴🅓🅐🅟

Euro Hotel M
☸☸☸ APPROVED
9 Esplanade Rd., Pentire, Newquay, TR7 1PS
☎ (0637) 873333 & Fax (0637) 878717
Seafront family hotel. All rooms en-suite with direct-dial telephone, satellite TV, baby listening. Creche, games rooms, heated pool, sauna, solarium, jacuzzi.
Bedrooms: 7 single, 22 double & 10 twin, 39 family rooms.
Bathrooms: 76 private, 2 public.
Half board: £25-£48 daily, £149-£289 weekly.
Lunch available.
Evening meal 7pm (l.o. 8.30pm).
Parking for 32.
Credit: Access, Visa, Amex.
📺❒📞☐♦🍴🅥📺🛄 🅴🍴🔭🅓♠⚓🔭🍴 ♨🆂🅿🆃

Great Western Hotel
☸☸☸
Cliff Rd., Newquay, TR7 2PT
☎ (0637) 872010
Clifftop hotel above Great Western and Tolcarne beaches and close to town centre. Many rooms with sea views. En-suite bathrooms throughout. Heated indoor pool.
Bedrooms: 7 single, 28 double & 16 twin, 21 family rooms.
Bathrooms: 72 private, 1 public.
Bed & breakfast: £28-£42 single, £51-£78 double.
Half board: £35-£47 daily, £156-£242 weekly.
Lunch available.
Evening meal 6pm (l.o. 9pm).
Parking for 20.
Credit: Access, Visa, Diners, Amex.
📺❒🅑☐♦🍴🅥🍴🅴 🛄⚓🍴🔭🅰🔭♨🆂🆃

Kilbirnie Hotel
☸☸☸
Narrowcliff, Newquay, TR7 2RS
☎ (0637) 875155
🅒🅑 Consort
Centrally situated, overlooking beaches. Good accommodation, cuisine and service. Heated indoor and outdoor swimming pools. Lift to all floors.
Bedrooms: 10 single, 32 double & 19 twin, 11 family rooms.
Bathrooms: 72 private.
Bed & breakfast: £26-£38 single, £52-£76 double.
Half board: £30-£42 daily, £182-£260 weekly.
Lunch available.
Evening meal 7.30pm (l.o. 8.30pm).
Parking for 70.
Credit: Access, Visa.
📺❒♦📞☐♦🍴🅥🍴 ⬤🅴🍴⚓🔭♠🔭🅴 🅰🆂🅿

Philema Hotel M
☸☸☸
1 Esplanade Rd., Pentire, Newquay, TR7 1PY
☎ (0637) 872571
Recently refurbished family home with friendly, informal atmosphere overlooking Fistral Beach and golf-course. New leisure complex and apartments also available.
Bedrooms: 4 single, 8 double & 4 twin, 15 family rooms.
Bathrooms: 26 private, 4 public.
Bed & breakfast: £22-£28 single, £44-£56 double.
Half board: £26.50-£33 daily, £133-£225 weekly.

Continued ▶

Evening meal 6.30pm (l.o. 7.30pm).
Parking for 31.
Open February-November.
Credit: Access, Visa.

The Quies Hotel M
APPROVED
84 Mount Wise, Newquay, TR7 2BS
☎ (0637) 872924
Family-run hotel overlooking Newquay Bay, well situated for all the town's amenities. Ideal base for touring beautiful Cornwall.
Bedrooms: 1 single, 5 double & 1 twin, 3 family rooms.
Bathrooms: 8 private, 1 public.
Bed & breakfast: £15.50-£24 single, £31-£48 double.
Half board: £22-£30.50 daily, £125-£176.50 weekly.
Lunch available.
Evening meal 6.30pm (l.o. 7.30pm).
Parking for 12.
Open March-December.
Credit: Access, Visa.

Rolling Waves Hotel
Alexandra Rd., Porth, Newquay, TR7 3NB
☎ (0637) 873236
Home from home in ideal location overlooking beautiful, sandy beach and headland of Porth. 2 miles to all Newquay amenities.
Bedrooms: 1 single, 7 double & 1 twin, 1 family room.
Bathrooms: 6 private, 1 public.
Bed & breakfast: £15.95-£22.50 single, £30-£45 double.
Half board: £19.95-£29.95 daily, £138-£185 weekly.
Evening meal 6.30pm.
Parking for 10.
Credit: Access, Visa.

Trebarwith Hotel
Trebarwith Cres., Newquay, TR7 1BZ
☎ (0637) 872288
On the sea edge with 350 feet of private sea frontage, in a central position away from traffic noise.
Bedrooms: 3 single, 20 double & 12 twin, 6 family rooms.
Bathrooms: 41 private.

Half board: £25-£41 daily, £170-£290 weekly.
Lunch available.
Evening meal 7.15pm (l.o. 8.30pm).
Parking for 40.
Open March-October.
Credit: Access, Visa.

Tregarn Hotel M
Pentire Cres., Newquay, TR7 1PX
☎ (0637) 874292
Family hotel with facilities for all weathers. Entertainment most nights. Few minutes' walk to Fistral Beach and the River Gannel estuary.
Bedrooms: 6 single, 13 double & 7 twin, 16 family rooms.
Bathrooms: 34 private, 5 public.
Bed & breakfast: £17-£35 single, £34-£70 double.
Half board: £25-£45 daily, £160-£270 weekly.
Lunch available.
Evening meal 6.30pm (l.o. 7.30pm).
Parking for 50.
Open March-December.
Credit: Access, Visa.

Trevone Hotel M
APPROVED
Mount Wise, Newquay, TR7 2BP
☎ (0637) 873039
Run by the Chegwin family for 68 years. Delicious home-cooked food in plenty. Evening entertainment in season. Interesting landscape and perennial garden with stream and pond. Central for touring Cornwall.
Bedrooms: 7 single, 13 double & 9 twin, 3 family rooms.
Bathrooms: 27 private, 3 public; 1 private shower.
Bed & breakfast: £14-£21.50 single, £28-£42 double.
Half board: £18-£27 daily, £120-£165 weekly.
Evening meal 7pm (l.o. 7.30pm).
Parking for 24.
Open April-October.

Westward Ho! Hotel
26 Headland Rd., Newquay, TR7 1HN
☎ (0637) 873069
Magnificently situated in its own grounds and commanding one of the most spectacular views to be found in Newquay. Indoor heated swimming pool.

Bedrooms: 5 single, 16 double & 6 twin, 5 family rooms.
Bathrooms: 20 private, 6 public; 1 private shower.
Bed & breakfast: £20-£30 single, £40-£60 double.
Half board: £25-£40 daily, £190-£208 weekly.
Lunch available.
Evening meal 6.45pm (l.o. 6.45pm).
Parking for 32.
Open April-October.
Credit: Access, Visa.

Wheal Treasure Hotel
72 Edgcumbe Ave., Newquay, TR7 2NN
☎ (0637) 874136
Lovely old house set in own gardens adjacent to Trenance Valley Gardens, bowling green, tennis courts and zoo.
Bedrooms: 6 double & 1 twin, 5 family rooms.
Bathrooms: 11 private, 2 public; 1 private shower.
Bed & breakfast: £16-£19 single, £32-£38 double.
Half board: £20-£28 daily, £140-£170 weekly.
Evening meal 6.15pm (l.o. 5.15pm).
Parking for 10.
Open May-October.

Whipsiderry Hotel M
COMMENDED
Trevelgue Rd., Porth, Newquay, TR7 3LY
☎ (0637) 874777
Set in own grounds overlooking Porth Beach and Newquay Bay. Badger watch from hotel.
Bedrooms: 2 single, 11 double & 2 twin, 5 family rooms.
Bathrooms: 20 private, 2 public.
Bed & breakfast: £18.50-£26 single, £34-£49.50 double.
Half board: £24-£38 daily, £155.50-£230 weekly.
Evening meal 6.30pm (l.o. 8pm).
Parking for 30.
Open April-October.

Windsor Hotel M
APPROVED
Mount Wise, Newquay, TR7 2AY
☎ (0637) 875188
A hotel for all the family, with indoor and outdoor swimming pools, jacuzzi, sauna, solarium, gym, putting, squash court. Secluded suntrap gardens.
Bedrooms: 3 single, 18 double & 7 twin, 15 family rooms.

Bathrooms: 43 private, 2 public.
Bed & breakfast: £20-£40 single, £40-£65 double.
Half board: £25-£46 daily, £175-£265 weekly.
Lunch available.
Evening meal 7.15pm (l.o. 8.30pm).
Parking for 70.
Open February-December.
Credit: Access, Visa, Amex.

Windward Hotel
COMMENDED
Alexandra Rd., Porth, Newquay, TR7 3NB
☎ (0637) 873185
Newly designed and extended hotel on coastal road to Padstow, overlooking Porth Bay. 1.5 miles north of Newquay.
Bedrooms: 11 double, 3 family rooms.
Bathrooms: 14 private.
Bed & breakfast: £29-£42 double.
Half board: £25-£34 daily, £160-£218 weekly.
Evening meal 6.30pm (l.o. 6.30pm).
Parking for 14.
Credit: Access, Visa.

NEWTON ABBOT
Devon
Map ref 1D2

Lively market town at the head of the Teign Estuary, a centre for the clay mining district of Dartmoor. A former railway town, it is well-placed for moorland or seaside excursions. Interesting old houses nearby include Bradley Manor dating from the 15th C and Forde House, visited by Charles I and William of Orange.
Tourist Information Centre ☎ (0626) 67494

Hazelwood Hotel
APPROVED
33a Torquay Rd., Newton Abbot, TQ12 2LW
☎ Newton Abbot (0626) 66130
Attractive, turn of the century building in quiet residential location, 5 minutes' walk from town centre, rail and coach stations. Own garden. Licensed restaurant, residents' lounge, car park.
Bedrooms: 3 double & 4 twin.

Bathrooms: 4 private,
2 public; 1 private shower.
Bed & breakfast: £30-£35
single, £44-£49 double.
Half board: £39.50-£44.50
daily.
Lunch available.
Evening meal 7pm (l.o. 8pm).
Parking for 6.
Credit: Access, Visa.
🛇 🕯 📞 ⬛ 🖵 🕁 🛈 Ⓥ 📺
🔺 ⌇

The Rendezvous Hotel
Listed APPROVED

41 Wolborough St., Newton
Abbot, TQ12 1JQ
☎ (0626) 53211
Fax (0626) 335388
Family-run hotel, once a
coaching inn, near clock tower
and convenient for sea and
moors. Non-residents welcome.
Bedrooms: 2 single, 2 double
& 4 twin, 2 family rooms.
Bathrooms: 4 private,
2 public.
Bed & breakfast: £14.95-
£24.95 single, £24.95-£39.95
double.
Evening meal 8pm (l.o.
10pm).
Credit: Access, Visa.
🛇 🕯 🖵 🛈 ◑ 📺 🔺 ✕ ᴅᴀᴘ
SP 🏕

6m NE. Okehampton

Kayden House Hotel
APPROVED

High St., North Tawton,
EX20 2HF
☎ (0837) 82242
Comfortable, homely
atmosphere. Ideally situated in
central Devon for visiting
countryside and beaches.
Bedrooms: 2 single, 2 double
& 2 twin, 1 family room.
Bathrooms: 5 private,
2 public.
Bed & breakfast: £17-£22
single, £30-£38 double.
Lunch available.
Evening meal 7pm (l.o.
9.30pm).
Credit: Access, Visa.
🛇 🖵 🕁 🛈 Ⓥ 📺 🖩 🔺
♻ 🏕

National Crown
ratings were correct
at the time of going
to press but are
subject to change.
Please check at the
time of booking.

Busy market town near
the high tors of northern
Dartmoor. The Victorian
church, with William
Morris windows and a
15th C tower, stands on
the site of a Saxon
church. A Norman castle
ruin overlooks the river to
the west of the town.
Museum of Dartmoor
Life.

Heathfield House M
COMMENDED

Okehampton, EX20 1EW
☎ (0837) 54211
Friendly country guesthouse
specialising in the personal
touch and walking holidays on
remote areas of northern
Dartmoor. Non-smokers
preferred.
Bedrooms: 1 single, 1 double
& 1 twin, 1 family room.
Bathrooms: 3 private;
1 private shower.
Bed & breakfast: £18-£21
single, £36-£42 double.
Half board: £30-£35 daily,
from £200 weekly.
Lunch available.
Evening meal 7pm (l.o. 9pm).
Parking for 8.
Open January-November.
Credit: Access, Visa.
🛇 ⬛ 🖵 🕁 🛈 Ⓥ ✕ 📺
🖩 🔺 ⟲ ▶ 🏕 SP

Former wool town with
modern light industry set
in countryside on the
River Otter. The
Cromwellian commander,
FairFax, made his
headquarters here briefly
during the Civil War. The
interesting church, dating
from the 14th C, is built to
cathedral plan. Rolling of
tar barrels custom on
Bonfire Night.

Fluxton Farm Hotel M
⚜⚜⚜

Ottery St. Mary, EX11 1RJ
☎ (0404) 812818
Spacious hotel in former
farmhouse with comfortable
bedrooms and sitting rooms.
Local fresh home-cooked food
served in candlelit dining room.
Log fires in season. Trout
fishing in the River Otter.
Bedrooms: 3 single, 3 double
& 4 twin, 2 family rooms.

Bathrooms: 10 private,
1 public.
Bed & breakfast: £21-£25
single, £42-£50 double.
Half board: £27.50-£32 daily,
£180-£210 weekly.
Evening meal 6.50pm (l.o.
6pm).
Parking for 20.
Open February-December.
🛇 5 ⬛ 🕁 Ⓥ ✕ 🔺 📺 🖩 🔺
❄ 🚲 ♻ SP 🏕

Stafford Hotel
⚜⚜⚜ APPROVED

5 Cornhill, Ottery St. Mary,
EX11 1DW
☎ (0404) 812025
Family-run hotel offering
personal service in a relaxed
and homely atmosphere. All
meals cooked to order by our
Italian chef, Shaun!
Bedrooms: 1 single, 3 double
& 2 twin, 1 family room.
Bathrooms: 7 private.
Bed & breakfast: £29.50-
£34.50 single, £30.50-£49.50
double.
Half board: £35-£45 daily,
£145-£245 weekly.
Lunch available.
Evening meal 6pm (l.o.
10.30pm).
Credit: Access, Visa, Amex.
🛇 🕯 📞 🖵 🕁 🛈 Ⓥ 🔺 📺
🖩 🔺 ⌇ ᴅᴀᴘ ♻ SP 🏕

Venn Ottery Barton
Country House M
⚜⚜⚜

Venn Ottery, Ottery St.
Mary, EX11 1RZ
☎ Ottery St. Mary
(0404) 812733
Comfortable, family-run,
licensed 16th C country hotel
with full central heating.
Friendly welcome, ideal for
touring and walks.
Bedrooms: 2 single, 4 double
& 7 twin, 3 family rooms.
Bathrooms: 11 private,
3 public.
Bed & breakfast: £20.50-
£26.50 single, £37-£49 double.
Half board: £32-£40 daily,
£189-£245 weekly.
Evening meal 7pm (l.o.
7.30pm).
Parking for 16.
Credit: Access, Visa.
🛇 🕯 🕁 🛈 Ⓥ ✕ 🔺 📺 🖩
🔺 ♞ ❄ 🚲 ♻ SP 🏕

Half board prices
shown are per
person but in some
cases may be based
on double/twin
occupancy.

Old town encircling its
harbour on the Camel
Estuary. The fine 15th C
church overlooking the
town has notable bench-
ends and a carved font.
There are fine houses
such as the 15th C Abbey
House on North Quay and
Raleigh's Court House on
South Quay. Tall cliffs
and golden sands along
the coast and ferry to
Rock. Famous 'Obby
'Oss Festival on May Day.

The Cross House
Church St., Padstow,
PL28 8BG
☎ (0841) 532391
Peaceful Grade II listed
building in old part of
Padstow, 300 yards from
harbour. Small restaurant and
pretty garden overlooking
estuary.
Bedrooms: 1 single, 4 double
& 1 twin, 1 family room.
Bathrooms: 2 private,
2 public.
Bed & breakfast: £20-£25
single, £40-£50 double.
Lunch available.
Evening meal 6pm (l.o.
midnight).
🛇 🕁 🛈 Ⓥ 🔺 📺 🖩 🔺 ✕
ᴅᴀᴘ ♻ SP 🏕

The Dower House
Private Hotel M
⚜⚜⚜ COMMENDED

Fentonluna La., Padstow,
PL28 8BA
☎ (0841) 532317
Listed 19th C dower house,
with views over Padstow,
estuary and bird gardens. Few
minutes from harbour.
Bedrooms: 1 single, 2 double
& 2 twin, 3 family rooms.
Bathrooms: 5 private,
1 public.
Bed & breakfast: £23-£30
single, £34-£52 double.
Half board: £28-£37 daily,
£186-£243 weekly.
Evening meal 7pm (l.o.
6.30pm).
Parking for 9.
Open March-December.
🛇 🕁 🛈 Ⓥ 🔺 📺 🖩 🔺
⌇ ♞ 🚲 SP 🏕

Green Waves Hotel
⚜⚜⚜

Trevone, Padstow,
PL28 8RD
☎ Padstow (0841) 520114
Continued ▶

PADSTOW

Continued

Long established, small, family-run hotel in quiet cul-de-sac. Set in well-kept garden facing south to the sea. All rooms have colour TV and tea making facilities. Half-size snooker table available.
Bedrooms: 2 single, 9 double & 6 twin, 3 family rooms.
Bathrooms: 15 private, 4 public.
Bed & breakfast: £17.50-£22.50 single, £35-£45 double.
Half board: £24.50-£29.50 daily, £138-£167 weekly.
Evening meal 7pm (l.o. 7pm).
Parking for 17.
Open April-September.

Newlands Hotel M

Main Rd., Trevone Bay, Padstow, PL28 8QX
☎ (0841) 520469
Friendly licensed hotel close to a fine sandy beach and coastal walks. 2 miles from Padstow.
Bedrooms: 1 single, 6 double & 3 twin.
Bathrooms: 9 private, 2 public.
Bed & breakfast: £18.50-£21 single, £40-£46 double.
Half board: £24-£30 daily, £160-£175 weekly.
Evening meal 6.30pm (l.o. 4.30pm).
Parking for 15.

Old Custom House Inn
COMMENDED

South Quay, Padstow, PL28 8BL
☎ Padstow, (0841) 532359
Comfortable quayside inn in the small fishing port of Padstow. Personally run by Mr and Mrs Allen.
Bedrooms: 1 single, 16 double & 6 twin, 2 family rooms.
Bathrooms: 25 private.
Bed & breakfast: £45-£67.50 single, £62-£90 double.
Lunch available.
Evening meal 7pm (l.o. 9pm).
Open March-December.
Credit: Access, Visa, Diners, Amex.

Old Mill Country House

Little Petherick, Padstow
☎ Rumford (0841) 540388
16th C listed corn mill with waterwheel. In own gardens by stream in country village. Retains original character, period furnishings.

Bedrooms: 4 double & 2 twin.
Bathrooms: 5 private, 1 public.
Bed & breakfast: £28-£45 single, £40-£50 double.
Half board: £29.25-£36.25 daily, £207-£242 weekly.
Evening meal 7pm (l.o. 6pm).
Parking for 15.
Open March-November.

Old Ship Hotel

Mill Square, Padstow, PL28 8AE
☎ (0841) 532357
Popular fully licensed family hotel in own grounds. Grade II listed building close to harbour, beaches and coastal path.
Bedrooms: 2 single, 2 double & 2 twin, 6 family rooms.
Bathrooms: 6 private; 6 private showers.
Bed & breakfast: £19-£31 single, £38-£52 double.
Lunch available.
Evening meal 6pm (l.o. 9.30pm).
Parking for 20.
Credit: Access, Visa.

St. Petroc's House Hotel

4 New St, Padstow, PL28 8EA
☎ (0841) 532700
Fifth oldest building in Padstow. Renovated traditionally. Very friendly and centrally situated. English cooking.
Bedrooms: 2 single, 3 double & 3 twin, 3 family rooms.
Bathrooms: 8 private, 1 public.
Bed & breakfast: £30-£40 single, £50-£80 double.
Half board: £35-£50 daily, £189-£294 weekly.
Evening meal 6.30pm (l.o. 10pm).
Open March-December.
Credit: Access, Visa.

Woodlands Country House Hotel
COMMENDED

Treator, Padstow, PL28 8RU
☎ (0841) 532426
Delightful country house in rural setting near beaches and golf-course, offering picturesque walks, modern amenities and choice of cuisine.
Bedrooms: 5 double & 1 twin, 3 family rooms.
Bathrooms: 9 private.

Bed & breakfast: £20-£25 single, £40-£50 double.
Half board: £30-£35 daily, £180-£185 weekly.
Evening meal 6.30pm (l.o. 5pm).
Parking for 15.

PAIGNTON

Devon
Map ref 1D2

Lively seaside resort with a pretty harbour on Torbay. Bronze Age and Saxon sites are occupied by the 15th C church, which has a Norman door and font.
Tourist Information Centre ☎ *(0803) 558383*

Balmar Hotel

16 Leighon Rd., Paignton, TQ3 2BQ
☎ (0803) 557535
Licensed hotel providing full English breakfast and optional evening meal.
Bedrooms: 1 single, 3 double, 5 family rooms.
Bathrooms: 3 private, 1 public; 1 private shower.
Bed & breakfast: £12-£15 single, £24-£30 double.
Half board: £15-£18 daily, £88-£110 weekly.
Evening meal 6pm (l.o. 6pm).
Open April-September.

Bay Cottage Guest House
Listed APPROVED

4 Beach Rd., Paignton, TQ4 6AY
☎ (0803) 525729
Delightful clean and comfortable guesthouse, close to seafront. Home cooking. Torbay in Bloom award winner.
Bedrooms: 3 single, 6 double & 1 twin, 1 family room.
Bathrooms: 2 private, 3 public.
Bed & breakfast: £13-£16 single, £26-£32 double.
Half board: £17-£19 daily, £110-£120 weekly.
Evening meal 6pm (l.o. 4pm).

Danethorpe Hotel
APPROVED

23 St. Andrews Rd., Roundham, Paignton, TQ4 6HA
☎ (0803) 551251

Small, detached licensed hotel, close to all amenities. All rooms with colour TV, tea/coffee facilities, hairdryer and clock radio.
Bedrooms: 2 single, 6 double & 1 twin, 1 family room.
Bathrooms: 4 private, 2 public.
Bed & breakfast: £15.50-£18 single, £31-£36 double.
Half board: £23-£25 daily, £138-£155 weekly.
Lunch available.
Evening meal 6pm (l.o. 6pm).
Parking for 12.
Credit: Access, Visa, Amex.

Marina House Hotel
COMMENDED

Alta Vista Rd., Goodrington Sands, Paignton, TQ4 6BZ
☎ (0803) 525548
Family-owned Victorian country-style hotel in its own grounds overlooking Goodrington Sands and in a quiet location. Ideal base for touring.
Bedrooms: 1 single, 11 double & 4 twin, 2 family rooms.
Bathrooms: 18 private.
Bed & breakfast: £19.60-£23.65 single, £39.20-£47.30 double.
Half board: £27.60-£31.65 daily, £165.50-£190 weekly.
Evening meal 6.30pm (l.o. 7.30pm).
Parking for 18.
Open March-October.
Credit: Access, Visa.

Marine Hotel

Seafront, Paignton, TQ4 6AP
☎ (0803) 559778
Situated in the heart of Paignton on the level and right on the seafront, with panoramic views from all the public rooms and most bedrooms.
Bedrooms: 6 single, 3 double & 11 twin, 8 family rooms.
Bathrooms: 13 private, 4 public.
Bed & breakfast: £15-£18 single, £30-£36 double.
Half board: £19-£23 daily, £138-£155 weekly.
Lunch available.
Evening meal 6pm (l.o. 6pm).
Parking for 20.
Open February-December.
Credit: Access, Visa.

Newholme Guest House
Listed

119 Torquay Rd., Paignton, TQ3 2SF
☎ (0803) 558289

Conveniently situated near beach, park, shops and all amenities. Open all year including Christmas (special rates).
Bedrooms: 2 double & 1 twin, 3 family rooms.
Bathrooms: 1 public.
Bed & breakfast: £10-£12 single, from £24 double.
Half board: £15-£17 daily, £80-£95 weekly.
Evening meal 6pm (l.o. 4pm).

Preston Sands Hotel ⚘
🏅🏅 COMMENDED

10/12 Marine Pde, Sea Front, Preston, Paignton, TQ3 2NU
☎ (0803) 558718
Hotel is situated 15 yards from the water's edge. All bedrooms are en-suite with radio, TV and coffee/tea making facilities.
Bedrooms: 1 single, 17 double & 8 twin.
Bathrooms: 24 private, 3 public.
Bed & breakfast: £18-£25 single, £36-£50 double.
Half board: £25-£33 daily, £140-£219 weekly.
Lunch available.
Evening meal 6pm (l.o. 7pm).
Parking for 24.
Credit: Amex.

Redcliffe Hotel
🏅🏅🏅

Marine Dr., Paignton, TQ3 2NL
☎ (0803) 526397
Fax (0803) 528030
Choice location in 4 acres of grounds directly adjoining the beach. Games room and an outdoor swimming pool.
Bedrooms: 12 single, 19 double & 23 twin, 5 family rooms.
Bathrooms: 58 private, 1 public.
Bed & breakfast: £38-£48 single, £76-£96 double.
Half board: £44-£56 daily, £280-£350 weekly.
Evening meal 7pm (l.o. 8.30pm).
Parking for 100.
Credit: Access, Visa.

Hotel Retreat
43 Marine Dr., Paignton, TQ3 2NS
☎ (0803) 550596
Small private hotel in own grounds. On the level opposite sandy Preston beach. Suitable for all ages.

Bedrooms: 1 single, 4 double & 2 twin, 3 family rooms.
Bathrooms: 5 private, 3 public; 1 private shower.
Bed & breakfast: £16-£20 single, £32-£40 double.
Half board: £24-£30 daily, £145-£185 weekly.
Evening meal 6.45pm (l.o. 6pm).
Parking for 14.
Open April-October.
Credit: Access, Visa.

Silversea Guest House
🏠

14 Norman Rd., Paignton, TQ3 2BE
☎ (0803) 556331
Small friendly guesthouse in a level position, adjacent to seafront, and short walk to town, rail and bus stations.
Bedrooms: 1 single, 1 double & 1 twin, 2 family rooms.
Bathrooms: 2 public.
Bed & breakfast: £11-£13 single, £22-£26 double.
Half board: £16-£18 daily, £90-£108 weekly.
Evening meal 6pm (l.o. midday).
Open March-October.

South Sands Hotel
🏅🏅🏅 APPROVED

12 Alta Vista Rd., Goodrington, Paignton, TQ4 6BZ
☎ (0803) 557231
Friendly family hotel, licensed and offering warm hospitality. Wonderful location adjacent beaches. Easy walk to town and all amenities.
Bedrooms: 2 single, 3 double, 14 family rooms.
Bathrooms: 18 private, 1 public.
Bed & breakfast: £18-£25 single, £36-£50 double.
Half board: £23-£33 daily, £140-£180 weekly.
Evening meal 6pm (l.o. 7pm).
Parking for 17.
Credit: Access, Visa.

Southlawn Guest House ⚘
68 Upper Manor Rd., Preston, Paignton, TQ3 2TJ
☎ (0803) 551305
Licensed bungalow-style guesthouse convenient for beaches and other attractions. Situated in one of the quieter residential areas. Sauna, sunbed.

Bedrooms: 3 single, 4 double & 1 twin, 2 family rooms.
Bathrooms: 2 public; 3 private showers.
Bed & breakfast: £13-£15 single, £26-£30 double.
Half board: £17-£19 daily, £115-£130 weekly.
Evening meal 6pm (l.o. midday).
Parking for 8.
Open April-October.
Credit: Access, Visa.

Summerhill Hotel ⚘
🏅🏅🏅

Braeside Rd., Goodrington Sands, Paignton, TQ4 6BX
☎ (0803) 558101
Comfortable hotel with spacious suntrap gardens. Adjacent to sandy beach and park. Close to harbour, leisure centre and water theme park.
Bedrooms: 3 single, 9 double & 8 twin, 5 family rooms.
Bathrooms: 24 private, 1 public.
Bed & breakfast: £18-£26.50 single, £35-£48.50 double.
Half board: £23-£29 daily, £150-£183 weekly.
Lunch available.
Evening meal 6.30pm (l.o. 7pm).
Parking for 25.
Open March-October.

Sunhill Hotel ⚘
🏅🏅🏅

Alta Vista Rd., Goodrington Sands, Paignton, TQ4 6DA
☎ (0803) 557532
Fax (0803) 663850
🆑 Inter
With access on to Goodrington beach this quiet, spacious comfortable hotel enjoys spectacular views over Torbay.
Bedrooms: 6 single, 14 double & 8 twin, 1 family room.
Bathrooms: 29 private.
Bed & breakfast: £27-£36 single, £54-£72 double.
Half board: £37-£46 daily, £230-£290 weekly.
Lunch available.
Evening meal 7pm (l.o. 8pm).
Parking for 30.
Credit: Access, Visa, Amex.

Sunny Bank Private Hotel
2 Cleveland Rd., Paignton, TQ4 6EN
☎ (0803) 525540

Family-run licensed hotel 150 yards from 3 beaches and harbour in select area. Friendly service and access at all times. Choice of menu.
Bedrooms: 3 single, 4 double & 1 twin, 4 family rooms.
Bathrooms: 2 private, 2 public; 4 private showers.
Bed & breakfast: £13-£17.50 single, £26-£35 double.
Half board: £18-£22.50 daily, £92-£130 weekly.
Lunch available.
Evening meal 6pm (l.o. 4pm).
Parking for 8.
Credit: Access, Visa.

Torbay Court Hotel
🏅🏅 APPROVED

Steartfield Rd., Paignton, TQ3 2BG
☎ (0803) 663332
Situated in a quiet, secluded position. A few yards' walk on the level to the seafront. Close to park and amenities.
Bedrooms: 9 single, 14 double & 29 twin, 4 family rooms.
Bathrooms: 56 private.
Bed & breakfast: £12-£15 single.
Half board: £17-£22.50 daily, £117.20-£157 weekly.
Evening meal 6pm (l.o. 6.30pm).
Parking for 16.
Open April-October.

Torbay Sands Hotel
16 Marine Pde., Preston, Paignton, TQ3 2NU
☎ (0803) 525568
Only 15 yards from beach and with some of the finest views over Torbay from the public rooms.
Bedrooms: 2 single, 7 double & 4 twin, 4 family rooms.
Bathrooms: 11 private, 2 public.
Bed & breakfast: £13.50-£16 single, £27-£32 double.
Half board: £18.50-£21.50 daily, £90-£105 weekly.
Evening meal 6pm (l.o. 6pm).
Parking for 6.
Credit: Access, Visa.

Wynncroft Hotel ⚘
🏅🏅 COMMENDED

2 Elmsleigh Pk., Paignton, TQ4 5AT
☎ (0803) 525728
Centrally situated hotel in ideal level situation, where comfort, friendliness and food are a priority.

Continued ▶

PAIGNTON
Continued

Bedrooms: 6 double & 3 twin,
2 family rooms.
Bathrooms: 8 private,
1 public; 3 private showers.
Bed & breakfast: £23-£29
single, £44-£50 double.
Half board: £29-£35 daily,
£174-£210 weekly.
Lunch available.
Evening meal 6pm (l.o. 7pm).
Parking for 8.
Open January-November.
Credit: Access, Visa.
🛇🕉️📞🛈 Ⓥ 🖿 📺 ▥ ⌂
✖3 ᴅᴀᴘ 🆂🅿️

PATCHWAY
Avon
Map ref 2A2

6m N. Bristol

Stakis Leisure Lodge
M5 Junction 16, Patchway,
Bristol, BS12 4JF
☎ (0454) 201144
Telex 445774
Ⓡ Stakis
*New hotel with extensive
leisure facilities. Adjacent to
M5 junction 16 and 1 mile
from M4 junction 20. Half
board rate based on a
minimum 2 night stay.*
Bedrooms: 37 double &
73 twin, 2 family rooms.
Bathrooms: 112 private.
Bed & breakfast: £91-£101
single, £116-£126 double.
Half board: from £33 daily.
Lunch available.
Evening meal 6pm (l.o.
10pm).
Parking for 130.
Credit: Access, Visa, Diners,
Amex.
🛇🕉️📞🚗🛈🖢 🛈 Ⓥ ⚡
◑▥ ᴅᴀ🔥🛈 🆂️❄️ ᴅᴀᴘ
🆂🅿️ Ⓣ

---

*National Crown
ratings were correct
at the time of going
to press but are
subject to change.
Please check at the
time of booking.*

---

*Half board prices
shown are per
person but in some
cases may be based
on double/twin
occupancy.*

PENZANCE
Cornwall
Map ref 1B3

Granite-built resort and
fishing port on Mount's
Bay, with mainly Victorian
promenade and some
fine Regency terraces.
Former prosperity came
from tin trade, pilchard
fishing and smuggling.
Grand Georgian-style
church by harbour.
Georgian Egyptian
building at head of
Chapel Street and the
municipal Morrab
Gardens.
*Tourist Information
Centre ☎ (0736) 62207*

Alexandra Hotel ♨
😁😁😁 **APPROVED**

Alexandra Ter., Seafront,
Penzance, TR18 4NX
☎ (0736) 62644 & 66333
Telex 934999 TX LINK G
*Family-run licensed hotel on
seafront with friendly relaxed
atmosphere. Large car park,
superb sea-views. Open all
year.*
Bedrooms: 4 single, 10 double
& 6 twin, 12 family rooms.
Bathrooms: 29 private,
2 public.
Bed & breakfast: from £22
single, from £44 double.
Half board: from £31 daily,
from £186 weekly.
Lunch available.
Evening meal 7pm (l.o.
8.30pm).
Parking for 21.
Credit: Access, Visa, Amex.
🛇🕉️Ⓒ🚗🛈🕉️ Ⓥ 🖿 ▥
⌂🍴 ᴅᴀᴘ 🚭 🆂🅿️ Ⓣ

Ashton Family Guest
House ♨
Listed **APPROVED**

14 Mennaye Rd., Penzance,
TR18 4NG
☎ (0736) 62546
*Friendly family guesthouse. All
rooms have hot and cold water,
colour TV and tea making
facilities. Children and pets
welcome.*
Bedrooms: 1 single, 1 double
& 2 twin, 2 family rooms.
Bathrooms: 1 private,
2 public.
Bed & breakfast: £12-£13
single, £24-£26 double.
Half board: £18.50-£19.50
daily, £125.50-£129.50
weekly.
Evening meal 6pm (l.o. 5pm).
🛇🚗🛈🕉️ ᵁᴸ 🛈 🖿 📺 ▥ 🚭
ᴅᴀᴘ 🚭 🆂🅿️

Cliff Hotel
1 Penrose Ter., Penzance,
TR18 2HH
☎ (0736) 68888 & 63524
*Superb panoramic views.
Conveniently situated for rail,
heliport and coaches. Run by
the same family for over 65
years.*
Bedrooms: 8 single, 5 double
& 2 twin, 1 family room.
Bathrooms: 3 private,
3 public; 1 private shower.
Bed & breakfast: £17-£21
single, £34-£50 double.
Half board: £31-£35 daily,
£205.10-£230.30 weekly.
Evening meal 6.30pm (l.o.
7pm).
Parking for 11.
Credit: Access, Visa, C.Bl.,
Diners, Amex.
🛇🕉️🛈 Ⓥ 🖿 📺 ⌂ 🆂🅿️ 🔥
Ⓣ

Estoril Hotel ♨
😁😁😁 **APPROVED**

46 Morrab Rd., Penzance,
TR18 4EX
☎ (0736) 62468 & 67471
*Victorian house carefully
modernised to give comfortable
accommodation together with
personal service.*
Bedrooms: 1 single, 4 double
& 4 twin, 1 family room.
Bathrooms: 10 private.
Bed & breakfast: £22-£26
single, £44-£52 double.
Half board: £30-£37 daily,
£210-£245 weekly.
Lunch available.
Evening meal 6.45pm (l.o.
7.30pm).
Parking for 4.
Open February-November.
Credit: Access, Visa.
🛇🕉️📞Ⓒ🚗🛈 Ⓥ 🖿
◑▥ᴅᴀ🔥 🆂🅿️ Ⓣ

Garswood Guest House
Alexandra Rd., Penzance,
TR18 4LX
☎ (0736) 62551
*Family-run guesthouse close to
promenade. All rooms are
bright, spacious and have tea
and coffee facilities and colour
TV.*
Bedrooms: 1 single, 2 double
& 1 twin, 2 family rooms.
Bathrooms: 2 public.
Bed & breakfast: £11.50-
£12.50 single, £23-£25 double.
Half board: £17-£18.50 daily,
£115-£125 weekly.
Evening meal 6.30pm (l.o.
7pm).
🛇🚗🕉️🛈 Ⓥ 🔥 ᴅᴀᴘ

Glencree Guesthouse ♨
😁😁

19 Penare Rd., Penzance,
TR18 3AJ
☎ (0736) 64775

*Homely accommodation with
personal service. All rooms
have colour TV, free tea and
coffee facilities. En-suite rooms
available. Children welcome.*
Bedrooms: 1 single, 2 double
& 1 twin, 2 family rooms.
Bathrooms: 2 private,
2 public.
Bed & breakfast: £12.50-£14
single, £25-£28 double.
Half board: £17.50-£19 daily,
£115.50-£126 weekly.
Lunch available.
Evening meal 6pm (l.o.
6.30pm).
🛇🕉️🚗🛈 🛈 Ⓥ 🖿 ▥
ᴅᴀᴘ 🆂🅿️

Glendower Guest House
5 Mennaye Rd., Penzance,
TR18 4NG
☎ (0736) 65991
*Homely, comfortable
guesthouse, tastefully furnished
with en-suite rooms, TV and
tea/coffee making facilities.
Close to promenade, buses and
town centre.*
Bedrooms: 2 double & 1 twin,
1 family room.
Bathrooms: 2 public.
Bed & breakfast: from £11
single, from £22 double.
Half board: from £17 daily,
from £119 weekly.
Evening meal 7pm (l.o. 7pm).
🛇🕉️ᵁᴸ 🛈 Ⓥ 🖿 📺 ▥ ⌂
🔥 ᴅᴀᴘ

Harbour Lights
Listed

3 Lannoweth Rd., Penzance,
TR18 3AB
☎ (0736) 61813
*Quietly situated off main A30
close to rail and coach station.
Warm welcome on arrival.
Many rooms have sea views.*
Bedrooms: 2 single, 1 double,
2 family rooms.
Bathrooms: 1 public.
Bed & breakfast: £13-£15
single, £26-£30 double.
🛇🚗🕉️🛈 🛈 Ⓥ ▥ 🔥 ᴅᴀᴘ
🆂🅿️

Pendennis Hotel
😁😁

Alexandra Road, Penzance,
TR18 4LZ
☎ (0736) 63823
*A small family-run hotel close
to sea and town centre.*
Bedrooms: 2 double, 5 family
rooms.
Bathrooms: 4 private,
2 public.
Bed & breakfast: £11-£14
single, £22-£28 double.
Half board: £16.50-£19.50
daily.

Evening meal 6pm (l.o. 6.30pm).
Credit: Access, Visa.

Penmorvah Hotel M
Alexandra Rd., Penzance, TR18 4LZ
☎ (0736) 63711 & (0736) 60100
350 yards from promenade in tree-lined avenue. Easy reach of town centre, ideal location for touring.
Bedrooms: 2 single, 2 double & 2 twin, 4 family rooms.
Bathrooms: 10 private.
Bed & breakfast: £15-£22 single, £30-£44 double.
Half board: £22-£30 daily, £145-£195 weekly.
Evening meal 6.30pm (l.o. 6pm).
Credit: Access, Visa, Amex.

The Queens Hotel
APPROVED
The Promenade, Penzance, TR18 4HG
☎ (0736) 62371
Victorian hotel with superb views across Mount's Bay. Strollers brasserie, bar, restaurant, exciting atmosphere.
Bedrooms: 15 single, 20 double & 27 twin, 9 family rooms.
Bathrooms: 71 private.
Bed & breakfast: £33-£48 single, £55-£65 double.
Half board: £35-£60 daily, £245-£420 weekly.
Lunch available.
Evening meal 7pm (l.o. 8.45pm).
Parking for 100.
Credit: Access, Visa, Diners, Amex.

Scillonia Guest House
5 Penrose Ter., Penzance, TR18 2HQ
☎ (0736) 67964
Small Cornish family guesthouse with emphasis on cleanliness and a good breakfast. Close to rail, coach and ferry terminals. Sea views.
Bedrooms: 1 single, 2 double, 3 family rooms.
Bathrooms: 2 public.
Bed & breakfast: £12.50-£13.50 single, £25-£27 double.
Open January-November.

Sea & Horses Hotel M
APPROVED
Alexandra Ter., Sea Front, Penzance, TR18 4NX
☎ (0736) 61961
Hotel in quiet terrace overlooking seafront, with uninterrupted views over Mount's Bay. Accent on cleanliness, friendliness and food.
Bedrooms: 2 single, 2 double & 3 twin, 4 family rooms.
Bathrooms: 8 private; 3 private showers.
Bed & breakfast: £19.50-£22 single, £36-£44 double.
Half board: £27.50-£31.50 daily, £186.50-£212.50 weekly.
Evening meal 7pm (l.o. 6pm).
Parking for 12.
Open February-November.
Credit: Access, Visa.

Tarbert Hotel M
COMMENDED
11 Clarence St., Penzance, TR18 2NU
☎ (0736) 63758
Ⓖ Minotels
Georgian listed building, featuring exposed granite walls and open fires. In conservation area near town centre, parks and promenade.
Bedrooms: 2 single, 6 double & 4 twin.
Bathrooms: 12 private, 1 public.
Bed & breakfast: £27-£30 single, £48-£60 double.
Half board: £36.25-£43 daily, £216-£261 weekly.
Evening meal 7pm (l.o. 8.30pm).
Parking for 5.
Open January-November.
Credit: Access, Visa, Diners, Amex.

Torwood House Hotel M
Alexandra Road, Penzance, TR18 1DF
☎ (0736) 60063
Recently refurbished Victorian house run by professional hoteliers. Good food, nice surroundings, a home from home.
Bedrooms: 3 double, 3 family rooms.
Bathrooms: 5 private, 1 public.
Bed & breakfast: £10.50-£20.50 single, £21-£41 double.
Half board: £20.50-£30.50 daily, £129-£192 weekly.
Evening meal 6pm (l.o. 7.30pm).

Parking for 5.
Credit: Access, Visa, Diners, Amex.

Tremont Hotel M
Alexandra Rd., Penzance, TR18 4LZ
☎ (0736) 62614
Family-run hotel with home cooking and friendly service. Ideal position in town with easy car parking. Send for colour brochure.
Bedrooms: 3 single, 2 double & 3 twin, 1 family room.
Bathrooms: 6 private, 1 public.
Bed & breakfast: £11-£12 single, £26-£30 double.
Half board: £20-£22 daily, £134-£147 weekly.
Evening meal 6.30pm (l.o. 5.30pm).

Trenant Private Hotel M
Alexandra Rd., Penzance, TR18 4LX
☎ (0736) 62005
Small, comfortable, friendly hotel with a charming Victorian atmosphere. Pleasantly situated in a tree-lined avenue adjoining the promenade. Just 10 minutes' walk from the town centre.
Bedrooms: 3 single, 2 double & 2 twin, 3 family rooms.
Bathrooms: 4 private, 2 public.
Bed & breakfast: £14-£16 single, £28-£40 double.
Half board: £21-£28 daily, £135-£180 weekly.
Evening meal 6.30pm (l.o. 10am).

Union Hotel M
Chapel St., Penzance, TR18 4AE
☎ (0736) 62319
16th C hotel, reputedly the oldest in Penzance. Privately run. Historic dining room and theatre. Intimate restaurant and 2 interesting bars.
Bedrooms: 3 single, 10 double & 11 twin, 4 family rooms.
Bathrooms: 25 private, 2 public.
Bed & breakfast: £19.95-£29.95 single, £34-£54 double.
Half board: £25-£37.95 daily, £157-£239 weekly.
Lunch available.
Evening meal 6pm (l.o. 8.30pm).

Parking for 20.
Credit: Access, Visa, Diners, Amex.

Warwick House Hotel M
APPROVED
17 Regent Ter., Penzance, TR18 4DW
☎ (0736) 63881
Family-run hotel near the sea, station and heliport. Tastefully decorated rooms, most with sea views. Some rooms with showers.
Bedrooms: 1 single, 2 double & 2 twin, 1 family room.
Bathrooms: 2 private, 1 public; 1 private shower.
Bed & breakfast: £16 single, £32-£36 double.
Evening meal 6.30pm (l.o. 6.30pm).
Parking for 10.
Open February-October.

PERRANPORTH

Cornwall
Map ref 1B2

Small seaside resort developed around a former mining village. Today's attractions include exciting surf, rocks, caves and extensive sand dunes.

Beach Dunes Hotel
APPROVED
Ramoth Way, Perranporth, TR6 0BY
☎ (0872) 572263 & Fax (0872) 573824
In the dunes overlooking Perran Beach and adjoining golf-course. Access to beach.
Bedrooms: 2 single, 5 double & 1 twin, 2 family rooms.
Bathrooms: 6 private, 1 public.
Bed & breakfast: £20.50-£25.50 single, £41-£51 double.
Half board: £28.50-£35 daily, £180-£225 weekly.
Evening meal 6.30pm (l.o. 7.30pm).
Parking for 15.
Open March-October.
Credit: Access, Visa, Amex.

Hillside Lodge Hotel
4 St. Michaels Rd., Perranporth, TR6 0HG
☎ Truro (0872) 572319

Continued ▶

PERRANPORTH
Continued

*Quiet licensed hotel with
secluded garden close to beach
and shops. Varied menus.
Caring and friendly
atmosphere. Under owner's
personal supervision.*
Bedrooms: 2 single, 3 double
& 2 twin, 4 family rooms.
Bathrooms: 5 private,
3 public.
Bed & breakfast: £14.50-
£18.50 single, £29-£37 double.
Half board: £21.50-£25.50
daily, £143.50-£171.50
weekly.
Evening meal 6pm (l.o. 6pm).
Parking for 11.
Open February-October.

Perrancourt Private Hotel
27 Tywarnhayle Rd.,
Perranporth, TR6 0DX
☎ (0872) 572151
*Comfortable, stone-built,
family-run hotel in quiet
position overlooking village and
sand dunes. Good touring
centre for Cornwall.*
Bedrooms: 1 single, 4 double
& 1 twin, 5 family rooms.
Bathrooms: 5 private,
2 public.
Bed & breakfast: £13.50-
£18.50 single, £27-£37 double.
Half board: £18-£23.50 daily,
£120-£160 weekly.
Evening meal 6.30pm (l.o.
6.30pm).
Parking for 7.
Open March-November.

Tides Reach Hotel
Ponsmere Rd., Perranporth,
TR6 0BW
☎ (0872) 572188
*Charming detached hotel,
centrally situated in level
position just yards from large
sandy beach and convenient for
local shops.*
Bedrooms: 2 single, 5 double,
3 family rooms.
Bathrooms: 5 private,
1 public.
Bed & breakfast: £15-£19
single, £30-£38 double.
Half board: £21.50-£25.50
daily.
Evening meal 6.30pm (l.o.
6.30pm).
Parking for 10.
Open March-October.
Credit: Access, Visa.

PIDDLETRENTHIDE
Dorset
Map ref 2B3

Old Bakehouse Hotel & Restaurant M
Piddletrenthide, Dorchester,
DT2 7QR
☎ (030 04) 305
*Country hotel in Hardy's
Wessex. All bedrooms en-suite,
colour TV. Swimming pool.
Restaurant.*
Bedrooms: 2 single, 6 double
& 2 twin.
Bathrooms: 10 private.
Bed & breakfast: £28.50
single, £50-£57 double.
Half board: £40-£43.50 daily,
£255-£285 weekly.
Lunch available.
Evening meal 7pm (l.o. 9pm).
Parking for 16.
Open February-December.
Credit: Access, Visa.

The Poachers Inn M
COMMENDED
Piddletrenthide, Dorchester,
DT2 7QX
☎ (030 04) 358
*16th C inn with riverside
garden, in beautiful Piddle
Valley. Swimming pool. All
rooms en-suite, colour TV, tea-
making facilities, telephone.
Brochure available.*
Bedrooms: 1 single, 5 double
& 2 twin, 3 family rooms.
Bathrooms: 11 private.
Bed & breakfast: £29 single,
£42 double.
Half board: £32 daily, £200
weekly.
Lunch available.
Evening meal 6pm (l.o.
10pm).
Parking for 30.

---

*Individual
proprietors have
supplied all details
of accommodation.
Although we do
check for accuracy,
we advise you to
confirm prices and
other information
at the time of
booking.*

PILTON
Somerset
Map ref 2A2

3m SW. Shepton Mallet
Old village of stone
houses, encircled by hills.
A manor house stands
near the church, which
shows a harmony of
architectural styles dating
from Norman times, and
is now the centre of the
flourishing Pilton Manor
Vineyard.

Long House Hotel
APPROVED
Mount Pleasant, Pilton,
BA4 4BP
☎ (074 989) 701
*Unusual 18th C house in quiet
picturesque Somerset village
just off the A361. Home
cooking, wholefoods. Licensed.*
Bedrooms: 1 single, 2 double
& 2 twin, 1 family room.
Bathrooms: 5 private,
1 public.
Bed & breakfast: £16.50-£25
single, £33-£38 double.
Half board: £26.50-£35 daily.
Lunch available.
Evening meal 7.30pm.
Parking for 8.
Credit: Access, Visa, Amex.

PLYMOUTH
Devon
Map ref 1C2

Devon's largest city,
major port and naval
base, shopping and
tourist centre. Rebuilt
after bombing of the
1940s behind old harbour
area, the Barbican. Old
merchants' houses and
inns, customs houses,
Prysten House in
Barbican and ambitious
architecture in modern
centre, with aquarium,
museum and art gallery,
The Dome - a new
heritage centre on the
Hoe. Superb coastal
views over Plymouth
Sound from the Hoe.
*Tourist Information
Centre* ☎ *(0752) 264849*

Alexander Hotel
Greenbank Road, Plymouth,
PL4 8NL
☎ (0752) 663247/225536
*Friendly family-run hotel with
well-furnished, spacious rooms,
5 with private showers. Ideal
central location for business
and holidays.*

Bedrooms: 2 single, 1 double
& 2 twin, 2 family rooms.
Bathrooms: 1 public;
5 private showers.
Bed & breakfast: £13-£17
single, £26-£30 double.
Half board: £20-£24 daily.
Lunch available.
Evening meal 6pm (l.o. 6pm).
Parking for 8.
Credit: Access, Visa.

Barley Guest House
26 Lipson Rd., Lipson,
Plymouth, PL4 8PW
☎ (0752) 663466
*Warm and friendly guesthouse
offering spacious
accommodation. Close to all
amenities.*
Bedrooms: 2 single, 1 double
& 2 twin, 2 family rooms.
Bathrooms: 2 public;
1 private shower.
Bed & breakfast: £13-£15
single, £26-£30 double.
Half board: £20-£22 daily.
Lunch available.
Evening meal 6pm (l.o. 8pm).
Parking for 3.

Boringdon Hall Hotel M
Colebrook, Plympton,
Plymouth, PL7 4DP
☎ (0752) 344455
*Grade I Tudor mansion hotel
in 12 acres of landscaped
grounds. Offering four-poster
accommodation, Admirals
carvery, gallery restaurant,
bars and leisure facilities.*
Bedrooms: 20 double &
19 twin, 1 family room.
Bathrooms: 40 private.
Bed & breakfast: £65.50-
£67.50 single, £86-£110
double.
Lunch available.
Evening meal 7pm (l.o.
10pm).
Parking for 250.
Credit: Access, Visa, C.Bl.,
Diners, Amex.

Bowling Green Hotel M
9-10 Osborne Place, Lockyer
St., The Hoe, Plymouth,
PL1 2PU
☎ (0752) 667485
*Rebuilt Victorian property with
views of Dartmoor.
Overlooking Sir Francis
Drake's bowling green on
beautiful Plymouth Hoe.*
Bedrooms: 1 single, 6 double
& 2 twin, 3 family rooms.
Bathrooms: 8 private;
4 private showers.

Bed & breakfast: £25-£32 single, £34-£44 double.
Parking for 4.
Credit: Access, Visa.
⌂ ☎ ⊙ ⌨ □ ⓤ Ⓥ ⌧ TV
◖ ▥ ♨ DAP SP T

Brittany Guest House

28 Athenaeum St., Plymouth, PL1 2RQ
☎ (0752) 262247
2 minutes' walk from Hoe Promenade and close to all amenities. Spacious rooms, some en-suite.
Bedrooms: 1 single, 2 double & 4 twin, 2 family rooms.
Bathrooms: 2 private, 2 public.
Bed & breakfast: £13-£17 single, £26-£40 double.
Parking for 5.
Credit: Access, Visa.
⌂3 ♨ □ ♥ ⓤ ▮ ▥ ♨ ⌧
DAP SP

Caledonia Guest House

27 Athenaeum St., Plymouth, PL1 2RQ
☎ (0752) 229052
Comfortable guesthouse 2 minutes from Hoe and town centre.
Bedrooms: 1 single, 3 double & 3 twin, 2 family rooms.
Bathrooms: 3 private, 2 public.
Bed & breakfast: £13-£15 single, £26-£34 double.
Parking for 5.
⌂ ♨ □ ♥ ⓤ □ ♨ ⌧ DAP

Churston Hotel

♨♨
1 Apsley Rd., Plymouth, PL4 6PJ
☎ (0752) 664850 & Fax (0752) 664850
Small family-run hotel in residential area with unrestricted parking. Convenient for railway station, city centre and Central Park. Arrive guests - depart friends.
Bedrooms: 4 single, 3 twin, 1 family room.
Bathrooms: 2 private, 2 public.
Bed & breakfast: £14-£16 single, £28-£32 double.
Half board: £21.50-£23.50 daily, £150-£160 weekly.
Evening meal 6pm (l.o. 6pm).
Parking for 3.
⌂ ♨ □ ♥ ▮ Ⓥ ⌧ ⌧ TV
▥ ♨ ⓣ ⌧ DAP SP

Corner Guest House

98 Devonport Rd., Stoke, Plymouth, PL3 4DS
☎ (0752) 561908
Situated on the main bus route, close to the Tamar Ferry and the city centre. Moderate terms.

Bedrooms: 3 single, 2 double & 2 twin, 2 family rooms.
Bathrooms: 2 public.
Bed & breakfast: £11-£12 single, £21-£23 double.
Parking for 1.
⌂ Ⓜ ♨ □ ⓤ ⌧ ♨ ⌧ ✕
SP

Drake's View Hotel

33 Grand Pde., West Hoe, Plymouth, PL1 3DQ
☎ (0752) 221500
Friendly family hotel with patio and garden with beautiful views of the sea. Completely refurbished to a high standard.
Bedrooms: 5 double & 2 twin, 2 family rooms.
Bathrooms: 9 private.
Bed & breakfast: £38 single, £50 double.
Half board: £35 daily.
Evening meal 5pm (l.o. 7pm).
Credit: Access, Visa.
⌂ ⊙ □ ♥ ▮ Ⓥ ⌧ ⌧ TV
▥ ♨ ⓣ ✕ ⓢ SP ▦

Duke of Cornwall Hotel M

♨♨♨♨ COMMENDED
Millbay Rd., Plymouth, PL1 3LG
☎ (0752) 266256 & Fax (0752) 600062
Ⓡ Best Western
Within walking distance of Theatre Royal and city centre main shopping area, the Barbican, the Hoe and directly opposite Pavilions Conference and Leisure Centre.
Bedrooms: 17 single, 14 double & 31 twin, 7 family rooms.
Bathrooms: 69 private.
Bed & breakfast: £55-£65 single, £65-£90 double.
Half board: £45-£75 daily, £315-£500 weekly.
Lunch available.
Evening meal 7pm (l.o. 9.30pm).
Parking for 45.
Credit: Access, Visa, Diners, Amex.
⌂ ♨ ⌨ ⊙ □ ♥ ▮ Ⓥ ⌧
◖ ⌧ ▥ ♨ ⓣ DAP ⓢ SP ▦
ⓣ

Furzehill Hotel

♨♨
43 Furzehill Rd., Mutley, Plymouth, PL4 7JZ
☎ (0752) 662625 & Fax (0725) 662625
Small family hotel on bus route to city centre, coach and railway station. Close to city shopping centre, the Hoe, Barbican, theatre, restaurants and other amenities.
Bedrooms: 2 single, 3 double & 3 twin, 2 family rooms.
Bathrooms: 2 public;
4 private showers.

Bed & breakfast: £13.50 single, £26 double.
Half board: £20.25 daily, £127.57 weekly.
Evening meal 6pm (l.o. 8pm).
Parking for 4.
Credit: Access, Visa.
⌂ ♨ ⊙ □ ♥ ▮ Ⓥ ⌧ ⌧
TV ▥ ♨ ⓣ ✕ DAP SP ⓣ

Grand Hotel M

♨♨♨♨ COMMENDED
Elliott St., The Hoe, Plymouth, PL1 2PT
☎ (0752) 661195
Fax (0752) 600653
Telex 45359
Built in 1879, the hotel retains many of its original architectural details and combines sea views with quiet Victorian elegance. Weekend breaks available on a bed and breakfast basis, with or without dinner.
Bedrooms: 35 double & 38 twin, 4 family rooms.
Bathrooms: 77 private.
Bed & breakfast: £60-£90 single, £70-£120 double.
Half board: £74.50-£104.50 daily.
Evening meal 7pm (l.o. 10pm).
Parking for 70.
Credit: Access, Visa, C.Bl., Diners, Amex.
⌂ ⌧ ⊙ □ ♥ ▮ Ⓥ ⌧ ⌧
◖ ▣ ▥ ♨ ⓣ ✕ SP ▦ ⓣ

Lamplighter Hotel

♨♨ APPROVED
103 Citadel Rd., The Hoe, Plymouth, PL1 2RN
☎ (0752) 663855
Small friendly hotel on Plymouth Hoe, 5 minutes' walk from the city centre.
Bedrooms: 6 double & 2 twin, 1 family room.
Bathrooms: 7 private, 1 public; 2 private showers.
Bed & breakfast: £18-£20 single, £30-£35 double.
Parking for 4.
Credit: Access, Visa.
⌂ □ ♥ ⓤ Ⓥ ⌧ TV ▥ ♨
♨ ✕ ▦

Langdon Court Hotel & Restaurant M

♨♨♨ APPROVED
Down Thomas, Plymouth, PL9 0DY
☎ (0752) 862358 & Fax (0752) 863428
Elizabethan manor house in 7 acres of garden and woodland, yet only 6 miles from Plymouth city centre.
Bedrooms: 3 single, 3 double & 4 twin, 3 family rooms.
Bathrooms: 13 private.
Bed & breakfast: £28-£44 single, £52-£64 double.

Half board: £41-£59 daily.
Lunch available.
Evening meal 7.30pm (l.o. 9pm).
Parking for 100.
Credit: Access, Visa, Diners, Amex.
⌂ ⊙ □ ♥ ▮ Ⓥ ⌧ ♨ ⓣ
❋ ⌧ SP ▦ ⓣ

Loma Loma M

Listed APPROVED
227 Citadel Rd., The Hoe, Plymouth, PL1 2NG
☎ (0752) 661859
Close to historic Barbican, Hoe, bus station and ferry terminal. Only 5 minutes' walk to main shopping centre. Supervised by the proprietors.
Bedrooms: 1 single, 2 double & 2 twin, 1 family room.
Bathrooms: 1 public; 4 private showers.
Bed & breakfast: £14-£15 single, £25-£26 double.
Open April-October.
⌂ ♨ □ ⓤ TV ▥ ♨

Novotel Plymouth M

Marsh Mills Roundabout, 270 Plymouth Rd., Plymouth, PL6 8NH
☎ (0752) 221422 Telex 45711 NOVPLYG
Ⓡ Novotel
Ideally situated at the entrance to Plymouth on the A38. Easy access to and from Devon and Cornwall.
Bedrooms: 25 single, 25 double & 25 twin, 25 family rooms.
Bathrooms: 100 private.
Bed & breakfast: £32-£58 single, £44-£70 double.
Half board: £34-£42 daily.
Lunch available.
Evening meal 5pm (l.o. 11.30pm).
Parking for 150.
Credit: Access, Visa, C.Bl., Diners, Amex.
⌂ ♨ ⌧ ⊙ □ ♥ ▮ Ⓥ ⌧
⌧ ◖ ▣ ▥ ♨ ⓣ ⓑ ⓧ ⓤ
❋ ♨ SP ⓣ

Olivers Hotel and Restaurant M

♨♨♨ COMMENDED
33 Sutherland Rd., Mutley, Plymouth, PL4 6BN
☎ (0752) 663923
Hotel and restaurant situated in a quiet residential area. En-suite rooms include trouser press, hair-dryer and telephone.
Bedrooms: 2 single, 2 double & 1 twin, 1 family room.
Bathrooms: 4 private, 1 public.
Bed & breakfast: £19-£29 single, £44 double.
Evening meal 6pm (l.o. 7.30pm).

Continued ▶

PLYMOUTH

Continued

Parking for 2.
Credit: Access, Visa, C.Bl., Diners, Amex.

Phantele Guest House

176 Devonport Rd., Stoke, Plymouth, PL1 5RD
☎ (0752) 561506
Small family-run guesthouse about 2 miles from city centre. Convenient base for touring. Close to continental and Torpoint ferries.
Bedrooms: 2 single, 2 twin, 2 family rooms.
Bathrooms: 2 private, 2 public.
Bed & breakfast: £12-£13.50 single, £23-£31 double.
Half board: £16.50-£20.50 daily, £103.90-£123 weekly.
Evening meal 6pm (l.o. 5pm).

Plymouth Moat House ⚜
COMMENDED
Armada Way, Plymouth, PL1 2HJ
☎ (0752) 662866 & Fax (0752) 673816 Telex 45637
Queens Moat Houses
Situated on historic Plymouth Hoe in the heart of the city, a short walk from the shopping centre and the Barbican.
Bedrooms: 44 single, 37 double & 76 twin, 76 family rooms.
Bathrooms: 201 private.
Bed & breakfast: £47.25-£90 single, £73.35-£106 double.
Half board: £47.25-£142 daily.
Lunch available.
Evening meal 7pm (l.o. 10.30pm).
Parking for 175.
Credit: Access, Visa, Diners, Amex.

Rosaland Hotel ⚜
APPROVED
32 Houndiscombe Rd., Plymouth, PL4 6HQ
☎ (0752) 664749
Close to centre, station, Hoe and Barbican. Fully refurbished. En-suite available. Satellite TV in all rooms. You're assured of a warm welcome.
Bedrooms: 4 single, 2 double & 1 twin, 2 family rooms.

Bathrooms: 1 private, 2 public; 4 private showers.
Bed & breakfast: from £15 single, from £28 double.
Half board: from £21 daily, from £140 weekly.
Evening meal 6pm (l.o. 6pm).
Parking for 3.
Credit: Access, Visa.

St. Lawrence of St. James Guest House
16 St. James Place West, The Hoe, Plymouth P11 3AT
☎ (0752) 671901
Family-run guesthouse in a quiet location but a short walk from Barbican, city centre and bus station. Close to the Hoe, Pavilions and ferry port. Open all year. Pay phone and satellite TV.
Bedrooms: 1 single, 2 double & 2 twin, 1 family room.
Bathrooms: 2 private, 2 public; 2 private showers.
Bed & breakfast: £15-£17 single, £26-£30 double.
Half board: £22-£22.50 daily, max. £157.50 weekly.
Evening meal 6pm (l.o. 7.30pm).

St. Malo Guest House ⚜
19 Garden Cres., West Hoe, Plymouth, PL1 3DA
☎ (0752) 222961
Small family-run guesthouse, close to seafront and Brittany ferries. Attractive flat sun roof with views of Plymouth sound.
Bedrooms: 2 double & 2 twin, 3 family rooms.
Bathrooms: 2 public; 1 private shower.
Bed & breakfast: £13-£15 single, £25-£27 double.
Half board: £19.50-£21.50 daily.
Evening meal 6pm (l.o. 7.30pm).

Squires Guest House
7 St. James Place East, The Hoe, Plymouth, PL1 3AS
☎ (0752) 261459
A charming Victorian house converted to a high standard with modern facilities, within easy walking distance of the Hoe, city centre, Barbican, new Pavilion complex and bus station.
Bedrooms: 2 single, 2 double & 1 twin, 3 family rooms.
Bathrooms: 1 private, 1 public; 5 private showers.

Bed & breakfast: £14-£16 single, £26-£30 double.
Parking for 4.

Victoria Court Hotel ⚜⚜⚜
COMMENDED
62/64 North Road East, Plymouth, PL4 6AL
☎ Plymouth (0752) 668133
Elegant and tasteful surroundings mixed with good old fashioned service provide for a memorable stay in this convenient and centrally located Victorian hotel.
Bedrooms: 2 single, 4 double & 4 twin, 4 family rooms.
Bathrooms: 7 private, 2 public.
Bed & breakfast: £20-£35 single, £35-£50 double.
Half board: £30-£47.50 daily.
Evening meal 6.30pm (l.o. 8pm).
Parking for 6.
Credit: Access, Visa.

Wiltun Hotel ⚜
39 Grand Pde., West Hoe, Plymouth, PL1 3DQ
☎ (0752) 667072
Licensed family-run hotel. Overlooking Plymouth Sound and Drakes Island. Close to Hoe, Barbican, city centre, ferryport and Millbay Marina.
Bedrooms: 1 single, 3 double & 3 twin, 2 family rooms.
Bathrooms: 3 public.
Bed & breakfast: £15-£17.50 single, £30-£35 double.
Half board: £22.50-£25 daily, £140-£160 weekly.
Evening meal 6pm (l.o. 6pm).
Credit: Access, Visa.

POLBATHIC

Cornwall
Map ref 1C2

6m W. Torpoint

The Old Mill House ⚜⚜
APPROVED
Polbathic, Torpoint, PL11 3HA
☎ St Germans (0503) 30596
A 250-year-old mill overlooking the River Lynher, fully licensed and close to many popular attractions.
Bedrooms: 2 single, 4 double & 1 twin, 3 family rooms.
Bathrooms: 3 public.
Bed & breakfast: £12.50-£14 single, £25-£28 double.
Half board: £20-£25 daily, £150-£165 weekly.

Lunch available.
Evening meal 6pm (l.o. 7pm).
Parking for 12.

POLPERRO

Cornwall
Map ref 1C3

Picturesque fishing village clinging to steep valley slopes about its harbour. A river splashes past cottages and narrow lanes twist between. The harbour mouth, guarded by jagged rocks, is closed by heavy timbers during storms.

Claremont Hotel ⚜
APPROVED
Polperro, PL13 2RG
☎ (0503) 72241
Family-run hotel in historic fishing village. Continental atmosphere and French cuisine for a relaxing holiday.
Bedrooms: 1 single, 6 double & 2 twin, 2 family rooms.
Bathrooms: 10 private, 1 public.
Bed & breakfast: £18-£29 single, £37-£55 double.
Half board: £29-£38 daily, £170-£250 weekly.
Lunch available.
Evening meal 7.30pm (l.o. 8.30pm).
Parking for 16.
Credit: Access, Visa, Amex.

Crumplehorn Inn, Mill and Restaurant.
Polperro, Looe, PL13 2RJ
☎ (0503) 72348
16th C watermill and coaching house converted to comfortable bed and breakfast and self-catering accommodation. Local ales. Fresh fish and seafood restaurant.
Bedrooms: 2 single, 5 double & 3 twin, 4 family rooms.
Bathrooms: 14 private.
Bed & breakfast: £23-£28 single, £36-£54 double.
Half board: £36-£43 daily.
Lunch available.
Evening meal 6.30pm (l.o. 10pm).
Parking for 30.
Credit: Access, Visa, Amex.

Penryn House Hotel ⚜
The Coombes, Polperro, PL13 2RQ
☎ (0503) 72157

Elegant Victorian hotel in heart of village. Excellent romantic getaway or Cornish touring base. Varied menu, fireside bar.
Bedrooms: 1 single, 10 double & 2 twin.
Bathrooms: 10 private, 2 public.
Bed & breakfast: £18.15-£21 single, £33.50-£43 double.
Half board: £26.25-£31.50 daily, £175-£215 weekly.
Lunch available.
Evening meal 7.30pm (l.o. 9.30pm).
Parking for 14.
Credit: Access, Visa.

POLZEATH

Cornwall
Map ref 1B2

Small resort on Padstow Bay and the widening Camel Estuary, with excellent sands and bathing. Pentire Head (National Trust), a notable viewpoint, lies to the north.

Seascape Hotel M

Polzeath, PL27 6SX
☎ Trebetherick (0208) 863638
Catering exclusively for adults, renowned for food and a high degree of comfort with magnificent sea views. Honeymoon and Christmas specials.
Bedrooms: 1 single, 11 double & 3 twin.
Bathrooms: 15 private.
Bed & breakfast: £21-£22 single, £50-£52 double.
Half board: £33-£36 daily, £200-£240 weekly.
Evening meal 7pm (l.o. 6pm).
Parking for 18.
Open March-October, December.
Credit: Access, Visa.

The White Heron

Polzeath, Wadebridge, PL27 6TJ
☎ Trebetherick (0208) 863623
Family-run licensed restaurant with accommodation, 500 yards from famous sandy surfing beaches. Cliff walks with breathtaking scenery.
Bedrooms: 2 double & 1 twin, 2 family rooms.
Bathrooms: 1 private, 2 public.

Bed & breakfast: £18-£27.50 double.
Evening meal 6.30pm (l.o. 10.30pm).
Parking for 10.
Credit: Access, Visa.

PORLOCK

Somerset
Map ref 1D1

Village set between steep Exmoor hills and the sea at the head of beautiful Porlock Vale. The narrow street shows a medley of building styles. South westward is Porlock Weir with its old houses and tiny harbour and further along the wooded shingle shore at Culbone is England's smallest medieval church.

Anchor & Ship Hotel M
COMMENDED

Porlock Harbour, Exmoor, Minehead, TA24 8PB
☎ (0643) 862636 & Fax (0643) 862843
Attractive, comfortable hotel, 10 yards from the water's edge of small, picturesque harbour amid Exmoor's magnificent scenery and coastline.
Bedrooms: 6 single, 8 double & 9 twin, 3 family rooms.
Bathrooms: 20 private, 3 public.
Bed & breakfast: £39-£49 single, £60.50-£102.50 double.
Half board: £55-£74.50 daily, £315-£432 weekly.
Lunch available.
Evening meal 7pm (l.o. 9.15pm).
Parking for 30.
Credit: Access, Visa, Amex.

Doverhay Place M

Porlock, Minehead, TA24 8EX
☎ (0643) 862398
Telex 667047
Charming country house set in spacious attractive gardens, on outskirts of Porlock village. Renowned for good food.
Bedrooms: 8 single, 12 twin, 8 family rooms.
Bathrooms: 8 public.
Bed & breakfast: £13.25-£20.25 single, £22-£36 double.
Half board: £20.25-£28.25 daily, £130-£220 weekly.
Lunch available.
Evening meal 7pm.
Parking for 30.

Myrtle Cottage M

High St., Porlock, TA24 8PU
☎ (0643) 862978
Charming 16th C thatched cottage situated in picturesque village centre, overlooking Porlock Bay. Ideal base for walking and exploring Exmoor.
Bedrooms: 2 double & 1 twin.
Bathrooms: 1 public.
Bed & breakfast: from £14.50 single, from £29 double.
Half board: from £25 daily, from £165 weekly.
Evening meal 7.30pm (l.o. 7.30pm).
Parking for 4.

The Oaks Hotel M
COMMENDED

Porlock, Minehead, TA24 8ES
☎ (0643) 862265
Edwardian gentleman's residence commanding spectacular views of coast, countryside and village. Specialising in fresh local produce with traditional English and French style cooking. Open log fires throughout the year.
Bedrooms: 2 single, 4 double & 3 twin, 2 family rooms.
Bathrooms: 11 private.
Bed & breakfast: from £40 single, from £65 double.
Half board: from £47.50 daily, from £295 weekly.
Evening meal 7pm (l.o. 8.30pm).
Parking for 11.
Credit: Amex.

Porlock Vale House
COMMENDED

Porlock Weir, Minehead, TA24 8NY
☎ (0643) 862338
Edwardian country house, set in 24 beautiful acres with moor and sea views. Sailing from Porlock Weir. En-suite accommodation.
Bedrooms: 9 double & 5 twin.
Bathrooms: 11 private, 1 public.
Bed & breakfast: £40-£50 double.
Half board: from £32.50 daily, £195-£250 weekly.
Evening meal 6.30pm (l.o. 8.30pm).
Parking for 12.
Credit: Access, Visa.

PORT GAVERNE

Cornwall
Map ref 1B2

5m N. Wadebridge
Hamlet in cove adjoining Port Isaac, on the dramatic North Cornish coast. Peaceful haven for sunbathing and safe swimming.

Headlands Hotel M
APPROVED

Port Gaverne, Port Isaac, PL29 3SH
☎ Bodmin (0208) 880260
On clifftop overlooking Port Gaverne Cove, with breathtaking sea views. Comfortable bedrooms. Renowned for cuisine and hospitality.
Bedrooms: 5 double & 5 twin, 1 family room.
Bathrooms: 11 private.
Bed & breakfast: £29-£37.50 single, £58-£75 double.
Half board: £40-£48.50 daily, £240-£290 weekly.
Lunch available.
Evening meal 7pm (l.o. 10pm).
Parking for 35.
Credit: Access, Visa, Diners, Amex.

Port Gaverne Hotel M
COMMENDED

Port Gaverne, Port Isaac, PL29 3SQ
☎ Bodmin (0208) 880244 & Fax (0208) 880151
17th C Cornish coastal inn, gently and comfortably restored. Located in a sheltered cove in an area of unusual natural beauty.
Bedrooms: 2 single, 10 double & 3 twin, 4 family rooms.
Bathrooms: 19 private.
Bed & breakfast: £36-£44 single, £72-£88 double.
Half board: £52.50-£62.50 daily, £275-£357 weekly.
Lunch available.
Evening meal 7pm (l.o. 9.30pm).
Parking for 22.
Open February-December.
Credit: Access, Visa, Diners, Amex.

Please check prices and other details at the time of booking.

PORT ISAAC
Cornwall
Map ref 1B2

Old fishing port of whitewashed cottages, twisting stairways and narrow alleys. A stream splashes down through the centre to the harbour. Nearby stands a 19th C folly, Doyden Castle, with a magnificent view of the coast.

The Castle Rock Hotel M
APPROVED
4 New Rd, Port Isaac, PL29 3SB
☎ Bodmin (0208) 880300
Superbly situated overlooking Atlantic and Port Isaac Bay. Most rooms have sea view. High standard of comfort and cuisine. Spring, autumn and Christmas/New Year breaks. Brochure available.
Bedrooms: 3 single, 8 double & 5 twin, 1 family room.
Bathrooms: 15 private, 1 public.
Bed & breakfast: £24-£30 single, £48-£60 double.
Half board: £35-£40 daily, £215-£250 weekly.
Lunch available.
Evening meal 7pm (l.o. 8.30pm).
Parking for 20.
Open March-December.
Credit: Access, Visa.

Cornish Arms
Pendoggett, St. Kew, PL30 3HH
☎ Bodmin (0208) 880263
Delightful 16th C coaching inn, surrounded by unspoilt countryside. Noted for food. Charming, spacious bedrooms. Special breaks available.
Bedrooms: 4 double & 3 twin.
Bathrooms: 5 private, 1 public.
Bed & breakfast: £36-£43 single, £47-£70 double.
Half board: £34.95-£50 daily.
Lunch available.
Evening meal 7.15pm (l.o. 9.30pm).
Parking for 40.
Credit: Access, Visa, C.Bl., Diners, Amex.

Fairholme
COMMENDED
30 Trewetha La., Port Isaac, PL29 3RW
☎ (0208) 880397

Homely guesthouse in higher part of quaint fishing village. Personal attention and home cooking.
Bedrooms: 3 double & 1 twin, 2 family rooms.
Bathrooms: 1 private, 2 public; 1 private shower.
Bed & breakfast: £14-£17.50 single, £28-£35 double.
Half board: £21.50-£25 daily, £145-£171.50 weekly.
Evening meal 6.30pm (l.o. 10.30am).
Parking for 8.
Open April-October.
Credit: Access, Visa.

Old School Hotel M
Fore St, Port Isaac, PL29 3RB
☎ (0208) 880721
Converted Victorian school in clifftop position overlooking historic fishing village. Surrounded by National Trust property on North Cornwall Heritage Coast. 2 half-tester beds.
Bedrooms: 5 double & 4 twin, 4 family rooms.
Bathrooms: 13 private, 1 public.
Bed & breakfast: £17-£24 single, £34-£61 double.
Half board: £27-£34 daily, £189-£238 weekly.
Lunch available.
Evening meal 6.30pm (l.o. 9.30pm).
Parking for 28.
Credit: Access, Visa.

Slipway Hotel M
Harbour Front, Port Isaac, PL29 3RH
☎ Bodmin (0208) 880264
16th C hotel, all rooms different in decor, many with low doors and beams. Overlooking harbour. Restaurant famous for its fine fresh fish, shellfish and local produce.
Bedrooms: 2 single, 5 double & 2 twin, 1 family room.
Bathrooms: 5 private, 2 public.
Bed & breakfast: £20-£22 single, £40-£56 double.
Lunch available.
Evening meal 7pm (l.o. 9.30pm).
Parking for 9.
Open January, March-December.
Credit: Access, Visa, Amex.

PORTHLEVEN
Cornwall
Map ref 1B3

Old fishing port with handsome Victorian buildings overlooking Mount's Bay. An extensive, shingly beach reaches south-east towards the Loe Bar, where the pebbles make a lake on the landward side.

Harbour Inn
COMMENDED
Commercial Rd., Porthleven, Helston, TR13 9JD
☎ Helston (0326) 573876
150-year-old inn on harbour edge. Restaurant open 7 days per week. Most bedrooms en-suite, many with harbour views.
Bedrooms: 1 single, 6 double & 2 twin, 1 family room.
Bathrooms: 8 private, 1 public.
Bed & breakfast: £31.50 single, £54 double.
Lunch available.
Evening meal 6.30pm (l.o. 9.30pm).
Parking for 10.
Credit: Access, Visa, Amex.

PORTLAND
Dorset
Map ref 2B3

Joined by a narrow isthmus to the coast, a stony promontory sloping from the lofty landward side to a lighthouse on Portland Bill at its southern tip. Villages are built of the white limestone for which the 'isle' is famous.

Alexandria Hotel
APPROVED
71 Wakeham, Easton, Portland, DT5 1HW
☎ (0305) 822270 & 820108
Well-equipped hotel with comfortable bedrooms and a la carte Italian restaurant. All food cooked to order by Giovanni himself. Warm, intimate and friendly atmosphere.
Bedrooms: 6 single, 4 double & 4 twin, 2 family rooms.
Bathrooms: 10 private, 3 public; 4 private showers.
Bed & breakfast: £20-£30 single, £32-£45 double.
Half board: £30-£35 daily, £180-£220 weekly.
Lunch available.

Evening meal 7pm (l.o. 9.30pm).
Parking for 18.
Credit: Access, Visa, Amex.

Portland Heights Hotel
Yeates Corner, Portland, DT5 2EN
☎ (0305) 821361
Best Western
Modern hotel situated on the summit of Portland. Enjoy spectacular sea views in comfortable surroundings. Excellent leisure facilities.
Bedrooms: 1 single, 21 double & 40 twin, 4 family rooms.
Bathrooms: 66 private.
Bed & breakfast: £59.50-£69 single, £78-£88 double.
Half board: £46-£56 daily.
Lunch available.
Evening meal 7pm (l.o. 9.30pm).
Parking for 250.
Credit: Access, Visa, Diners, Amex.

PORTLOE
Cornwall
Map ref 1B3

6m SW. Mevagissey
Old fishing village and small resort where majestic cliffs rise from Veryan Bay. Unspoilt National Trust coast stretches south-westward to Nare Head.

Lugger Hotel M
COMMENDED
Portloe, Truro, TR2 5RD
☎ Truro (0872) 501322 & Fax (0872) 501691
17th C smugglers' inn, at the water's edge in a quiet, picturesque cove, where fishing boats moor alongside.
Bedrooms: 3 single, 8 double & 8 twin.
Bathrooms: 19 private.
Half board: £55-£60 daily, £280-£385 weekly.
Lunch available.
Evening meal 7pm (l.o. 9pm).
Parking for 25.
Open February-December.
Credit: Access, Visa, Diners, Amex.

We advise you to confirm your booking in writing.

PORTSCATHO

Cornwall
Map ref 1B3

Coastal village spreading along low cliffs of Gerrans Bay on the eastern side of the Roseland Peninsula. Seaside buildings show a variety of styles from late Georgian houses to small, interestingly-designed modern blocks.

Gerrans Bay Hotel M
ᵂᵂᵂ COMMENDED

Gerrans, Portscatho, TR2 5ED
☎ (0872) 580338
Set in superb countryside, near sandy beaches. Home-cooked food and personal service. Complimentary golf and bowls. Adequate parking facilities.
Bedrooms: 2 single, 5 double & 5 twin, 2 family rooms.
Bathrooms: 12 private; 2 private showers.
Bed & breakfast: £26-£28.25 single, £52-£56.50 double.
Half board: £37.25-£41.25 daily, £240-£255 weekly.
Lunch available.
Evening meal 7.30pm (l.o. 8pm).
Parking for 16.
Open April-October, December.
Credit: Access, Visa, Amex.

Roseland House Hotel

Rosevine, Portscatho, Truro, TR2 5EW
☎ (0872) 580644
Centrally-heated bedrooms with magnificent sea views over the bay. Path to secluded, private beach with coastal walks. Peaceful and quiet.
Bedrooms: 2 single, 9 double & 5 twin, 2 family rooms.
Bathrooms: 18 private.
Bed & breakfast: £28-£35 single, £56-£70 double.
Half board: £40-£50 daily, £245-£320 weekly.
Evening meal 7.30pm (l.o. 8pm).
Parking for 23.
Open March-November, December.

Rosevine Hotel M

Portscatho, Truro, TR2 5EW
☎ (0872) 580230 & 580206
Peaceful Georgian country house hotel with delightful gardens, overlooking safe, sandy beach. Good food. Complimentary golf and tennis.
Bedrooms: 1 single, 5 double & 7 twin, 2 family rooms.
Bathrooms: 11 private, 2 public; 2 private showers.
Bed & breakfast: £23-£39 single, £46-£78 double.
Half board: £38-£63 daily, £252.70-£418 weekly.
Lunch available.
Evening meal 7.15pm (l.o. 8.30pm).
Parking for 40.
Open April-October.
Credit: Access, Visa.

PORTWRINKLE

Cornwall
Map ref 1C2

6m W. Torpoint
Situated in Whitsand Bay, this relatively unspoilt resort was once an industrious pilchard fishing village. The old pilchard cellars and tiny harbour are said to date from the Middle Ages. There are also two easily accessible sandy beaches, rock pools and a golf-course.

Whitsand Bay Hotel M

Portwrinkle, Torpoint, PL11 3BU
☎ St. Germans (0503) 30276
Spectacularly sited country mansion with sea views and 18-hole golf-course, indoor heated pools and leisure complex. Self-catering units also available.
Bedrooms: 6 single, 8 double & 6 twin, 16 family rooms.
Bathrooms: 30 private, 3 public.
Bed & breakfast: £15-£24.50 single, £30-£53 double.
Lunch available.
Evening meal 7.30pm (l.o. 8.30pm).
Parking for 50.
Open March-December.

RADSTOCK

Avon
Map ref 2B2

Thriving small town ideally situated for touring the Mendip Hills.

The Bell Hotel

Market Pl., Radstock, Bath, BA3 3AE
☎ (0761) 36218
Family-run ensuring personal attention, professional chef. Large, comfortable rooms. Close to Bath, Downside Abbey, Cheddar Gorge and Wookey Hole caves.
Bedrooms: 1 single, 2 double & 2 twin, 1 family room.
Bathrooms: 5 private.
Bed & breakfast: from £26.50 single, from £36.50 double.
Half board: from £32.50 daily.
Lunch available.
Evening meal 7pm (l.o. 10pm).
Parking for 2.
Credit: Access, Visa.

The Rookery
ᵂᵂᵂ APPROVED

Wells Rd., Radstock, Bath, BA3 3RS
☎ (0761) 32626
Homely, family-run guesthouse with licensed restaurant situated between Bath and Wells. Ideal for touring the West Country.
Bedrooms: 1 single, 2 double & 2 twin, 3 family rooms.
Bathrooms: 8 private, 1 public.
Bed & breakfast: £18-£30 single, £38-£55 double.
Lunch available.
Evening meal 7pm (l.o. 8.30pm).
Parking for 10.
Credit: Access, Visa.

RANGEWORTHY

Avon
Map ref 2B2

Rangeworthy Court Hotel M
ᵂᵂᵂᵂ APPROVED

Wotton Rd., Rangeworthy, Bristol, BS17 5ND
☎ Bristol (0454) 228347 & Fax (0454) 228945
ᴄʀ Inter
17th C country manor house with relaxing, peaceful atmosphere and popular restaurant. Less than 20 minutes from the M4, M5 and Bristol.

Bedrooms: 5 single, 8 double & 1 twin, 2 family rooms.
Bathrooms: 16 private.
Bed & breakfast: £48-£54 single, £66-£72 double.
Half board: from £40 daily, from £273 weekly.
Lunch available.
Evening meal 7pm (l.o. 9pm).
Parking for 60.
Credit: Access, Visa, Diners, Amex.

ROCK

Cornwall
Map ref 1B2

6m NW. Wadebridge
Small resort and boating centre beside the abundant sands of the Camel Estuary. A fine golf-course stretches northward along the shore to Brea Hill, thought to be the site of a Roman settlement. Passenger ferry service from Padstow.

Gleneglos Hotel M
ᵂᵂᵂ APPROVED

Trewint La., Rock, Wadebridge, PL27 6LU
☎ Trebetherick (0208) 862369
Small country-style hotel. Family-run, with home-prepared meals. Within five minutes' drive of 3 beaches, golf, walking and pony trekking.
Bedrooms: 3 double & 1 twin, 2 family rooms.
Bathrooms: 5 private, 1 public.
Bed & breakfast: max. £19 single, max. £25 double.
Half board: max. £45 daily, £145-£188 weekly.
Evening meal 6.30pm (l.o. 9.30pm).
Parking for 24.
Open February-December.
Credit: Access, Visa.

Roskarnon House Hotel M
ᵂᵂᵂ

Rock, Wadebridge, PL27 6LD
☎ Trebetherick (020 886) 2785
Edwardian house in an acre of lawned gardens, facing south and overlooking Camel Estuary. 20 yards from the beach and 50 yards from the golf-course.

Continued ▶

National Crown ratings were correct at the time of going to press but are subject to change. Please check at the time of booking.

ROCK
Continued

Bedrooms: 2 single, 7 double & 5 twin, 1 family room.
Bathrooms: 6 private,
4 public; 3 private showers.
Bed & breakfast: from £20 single, £40-£65 double.
Half board: £25-£40 daily, £175-£330 weekly.
Lunch available.
Evening meal 7pm (l.o. 8.30pm).
Parking for 12.
Open March-October.
🐕 👶 🏠 Ⓥ ⌀ 📺 👶 🎯 Ű
✒ ❄ 🎪 DAP SP 🏠

Silvermead
Rock, Wadebridge,
PL27 6LB
☎ Bodmin (0208) 862425
Off main road affording superb estuary views. Sailing club and windsurfing. 150 yards from beach and adjacent to St. Enodoc 36-hole golf-course. Residential licence.
Bedrooms: 2 single, 2 double & 2 twin, 2 family rooms.
Bathrooms: 4 private,
1 public.
Bed & breakfast: £15-£30 single, £25-£40 double.
Half board: £20-£35 daily, £133-£200 weekly.
Evening meal 6pm (l.o. 8pm).
Parking for 8.
🐕 👶 🏠 🖀 Ⓥ ⌀ 📺 🏠 ▭ ▸
❄ 🎪 DAP SP 🏠

RUANHIGHLANES
Cornwall
Map ref 1B3

11m SE. Truro
Village at the northern end of the Roseland Peninsula.

The Hundred House Hotel 🏠
☕☕☕ COMMENDED
Ruan Highlanes, Truro,
TR2 5JR
☎ (0872) 501336
Charming small hotel set in beautiful countryside, 1.5 miles from sandy beaches. Home cooking, log fires, personal service from resident owners.
Bedrooms: 2 single, 4 double & 4 twin.
Bathrooms: 10 private.
Bed & breakfast: £27-£32.50 single, £54-£65 double.
Half board: £35-£44 daily, £224-£280 weekly.
Evening meal 7.30pm (l.o. 5pm).

Parking for 15.
Open March-October.
Credit: Access, Visa.
🐕6 👶 🏠 🖀 ⌀ Ⓥ ✂ ▭ 🛏
▭ ❄ 🎪 SP 🏠

ST AGNES
Cornwall
Map ref 1B3

Small town in a once-rich mining area on the north coast. Miners' terraced cottages and granite houses slope to the church. Some interesting old mine workings remain, but the chief attraction must be the magnificent coastal scenery and superb walks. St. Agnes Beacon (National Trust) offers one of Cornwall's most extensive views.

Penkerris 🏠
☕
Penwinnick Rd., St. Agnes,
TR5 0PA
☎ (087 255) 2262
Enchanting Edwardian residence in own grounds, just inside St. Agnes on B3277 road. Large lawn for relaxation. Walking distance from magnificent cliffs and beach.
Bedrooms: 1 single, 4 double & 1 twin, 1 family room.
Bathrooms: 2 private,
3 public.
Bed & breakfast: £12-£20 single, £22-£30 double.
Half board: £16.50-£21.50 daily, £105-£125 weekly.
Lunch available.
Evening meal 6.30pm (l.o. 10am).
Parking for 8.
Credit: Access, Visa.
🐕 ⓔ 🏠 ⌀ 🖀 Ⓥ ▭ 📺 ▭
❄ 🎪 DAP SP 🏠 Ⓣ

Rose-in-Vale Country House Hotel 🏠
☕☕☕ COMMENDED
Mithian, St. Agnes, TR5 0QD
☎ St. Agnes (087 255) 2202
Georgian country house of character, with extensive grounds, set in own secluded wooded valley. Peaceful, relaxed atmosphere. Four-poster master bedroom. Special breaks available.
Bedrooms: 2 single, 8 double & 4 twin, 3 family rooms.
Bathrooms: 17 private.
Bed & breakfast: £28-£36 single, £50.50-£76 double.
Half board: £30.25-£43 daily, £211.75-£301 weekly.
Lunch available.

Evening meal 7pm (l.o. 8pm).
Parking for 40.
Open March-October.
Credit: Access, Visa.
🐕 👶 🏠 📞 🖀 ⌀ ⓔ Ⓥ ▭
📺 ▭ 🛏 🎯 👶 🍴 ❄ 🎪 SP
🏠 Ⓣ

Rosemundy House Hotel 🏠
Rosemundy, St. Agnes,
TR5 0UF
☎ (087 255) 2101
Family-run country house hotel in lovely grounds near sea, offering tranquillity, attractive bar, a 45-foot pool and a games room.
Bedrooms: 6 single, 18 double & 9 twin, 11 family rooms.
Bathrooms: 44 private.
Bed & breakfast: £21-£34 single, £42-£68 double.
Half board: £25-£38 daily, £140-£230 weekly.
Lunch available.
Evening meal 7pm (l.o. 8pm).
Parking for 40.
Open March-October.
🐕 👶 🏠 ⌀ 🖀 Ⓥ ✂ ▭ 📺
🛏 🍴 🎯 👶 ❄ 🎪 SP 🏠 Ⓣ

Sunholme Hotel
Goonvrea Rd., St. Agnes,
TR5 0NW
☎ (087 255) 2318
Comfortable country house in extensive grounds with magnificent country and coastal views. Traditional cuisine and personal service.
Bedrooms: 1 single, 2 double & 1 twin, 6 family rooms.
Bathrooms: 10 private,
1 public.
Bed & breakfast: £25-£28 single, £50-£56 double.
Half board: £35-£38 daily, £195-£215 weekly.
Evening meal 7pm (l.o. 9pm).
Parking for 15.
Open February-December.
Credit: Access, Visa.
🐕 👶 🏠 🖀 ⌀ Ⓥ ✂ ▭ 📺
🛏 🍴 ❄ 🎪 🔌 SP

Tregarthen Country Cottage Hotel 🏠
☕☕☕ COMMENDED
Mount Hawke, Truro,
TR4 8BW
☎ Porthtowan (0209) 890399
Small, tastefully furnished hotel in pleasant rural surroundings. Lovely bedrooms with private facilities. 2 miles from the North Cornish coast.
Bedrooms: 6 double & 3 twin.
Bathrooms: 9 private.
Bed & breakfast: £25 single, £50 double.
Half board: £35 daily, £180 weekly.

Evening meal 6.30pm (l.o. 7.30pm).
Parking for 12.
🐕 🖀 Ⓥ ▭ 📺 🛏 ▭ 🍴 Ű
❄ 🎯 👶 🔌 SP

ST AUSTELL
Cornwall
Map ref 1B3

Cornwall's china-clay town, on a slope between the clay district's spoil-cones and the clay ports and bathing beaches on St. Austell Bay. The traffic-free centre has a fine church of Pentewan stone and an Italianate Town and Market Hall, still a busy market-place.

Boscundle Manor 🏠
☕☕☕ HIGHLY COMMENDED
Tregrehan, St. Austell,
PL25 3RL
☎ Par (072 681) 3557 & Fax (072 681) 4997
Lovely 18th C house in secluded grounds, furnished with many antiques and run like a private country house. 2 miles north-east of St. Austell.
Bedrooms: 2 single, 4 double & 5 twin.
Bathrooms: 11 private.
Bed & breakfast: £65-£80 single, £110 double.
Half board: £75-£100 daily, £450-£510 weekly.
Evening meal 7.30pm (l.o. 8.30pm).
Parking for 15.
Open April-October.
Credit: Access, Visa.
🐕 📞 ⓔ 🏠 ⌀ 🖀 Ⓥ ▭ 🛏
🛏 🍴 🎯 👶 ❄ 🎪 SP 🏠 Ⓣ

Pen-Star Guest House
☕☕ APPROVED
20 Cromwell Rd., St. Austell,
PL25 4PS
☎ (0726) 61367
Guest accommodation offers homely and friendly atmosphere, lounge with colour TV. Licensed.
Bedrooms: 2 single, 4 family rooms.
Bathrooms: 2 public.
Bed & breakfast: from £19 single, from £36 double.
Half board: from £27 daily, from £182 weekly.
Evening meal 6pm (l.o. 4.30pm).
Parking for 8.
Credit: Access, Visa, Amex.
🐕 🖀 ⌀ Ⓥ ▭ 📺 🛏 🛏 🍴
DAP SP

Selwood House Hotel ⋀
⛢⛢⛢ APPROVED
60 Alexandra Rd., St.
Austell, PL25 4QN
☎ (0726) 65707
*Detached, family-run hotel,
centrally situated for holidays
and business, in the beautiful
St. Austell Bay.*
Bedrooms: 3 single, 4 double
& 2 twin, 2 family rooms.
Bathrooms: 11 private.
Bed & breakfast: £31-£35
single, £59-£66 double.
Half board: £39-£44 daily,
£270-£305 weekly.
Evening meal 6.30pm (l.o.
7pm).
Parking for 13.
Credit: Access, Visa, Diners,
Amex.

The Wheal Lodge
91 Sea Rd., Carlyon Bay, St.
Austell, PL25 3SH
☎ Par (072 681) 5543
*Adjoining the coastal path in a
beautiful area directly above
the sea. Good Cornish food
and a sincere Cornish welcome.*
Bedrooms: 1 single, 2 double
& 1 twin, 2 family rooms.
Bathrooms: 6 private.
Bed & breakfast: £35-£40
single, £60-£70 double.
Half board: £52.50-£65 daily,
£239-£259 weekly.
Lunch available.
Parking for 20.

Winchmore
72 Alexandra Rd., St.
Austell, PL25 4QN
☎ (0726) 74585
*Homely family-run guesthouse
close to recreation centre, rail
and bus stations. Only 1.5
miles from picturesque
Charlestown harbour.*
Bedrooms: 1 single, 2 double
& 1 twin, 2 family rooms.
Bathrooms: 1 public.
Bed & breakfast: £11-£12.50
single, £22-£25 double.
Half board: £15.50-£17 daily,
£105-£115.50 weekly.
Evening meal 5.45pm (l.o.
10pm).
Parking for 4.

> *Half board prices
> shown are per
> person but in some
> cases may be based
> on double/twin
> occupancy.*

ST IVES
Cornwall
Map ref 1B3

Old fishing port, artists'
colony and holiday town
with good surfing beach.
Fishermen's cottages,
granite fish cellars, a
sandy harbour and
magnificent headlands
typify a charm that has
survived since the 19th C
pilchard boom.
*Tourist Information
Centre ☎ (0736) 796297*

Anchorage
⛢⛢ COMMENDED
5 Bunkers Hill, St. Ives,
TR26 1LJ
☎ Penzance (0736) 797135
*18th C fisherman's cottage
guest house with exceptional
decor. Short walk to beach.
Full of old world charm.*
Bedrooms: 1 single, 3 double
& 1 twin, 1 family room.
Bathrooms: 3 private,
1 public; 1 private shower.
Bed & breakfast: £15-£17
single, £32-£38 double.

Bella Vista Guest House
Listed
St. Ives Rd., Carbis Bay, St.
Ives, TR26 2SF
☎ Penzance (0736) 796063
*Located 1 mile from town and
700 yards from beach where
activities include surfing and
sailing. Pony trekking, golf,
fishing, beautiful cliff and
country walks all nearby.*
Bedrooms: 2 single, 1 double,
2 family rooms.
Bathrooms: 1 public.
Bed & breakfast: £13-£17
single, £26-£34 double.
Half board: £20-£24 daily,
£140-£168 weekly.
Evening meal 6pm (l.o. 3pm).
Parking for 5.
Open April-October.

Blue Hayes Guest House
⛢⛢⛢
Trelyon Ave., St. Ives,
TR26 2AD
☎ Penzance (0736) 797129
*Comfortable detached
guesthouse with panoramic sea
views over St. Ives Bay and a
quiet, colourful garden. Warm
and friendly atmosphere.*
Bedrooms: 2 single, 5 double,
2 family rooms.
Bathrooms: 5 private,
2 public.

Bed & breakfast: £25.85-
£28.85 single, £47.20-£57.65
double.
Half board: £34.45-£39.60
daily, £198-£225 weekly.
Evening meal 6.30pm.
Parking for 10.
Open March-October.
Credit: Access, Visa.

Dean Court Hotel
⛢⛢⛢
Trelyon Ave., St. Ives,
TR26 2AD
☎ Penzance (0736) 796023
*Hotel, situated in its own
grounds, overlooks
Porthminster beach and St.
Ives harbour. Ample free
parking.*
Bedrooms: 1 single, 9 double
& 2 twin.
Bathrooms: 12 private.
Bed & breakfast: £24-£31
single, £48-£62 double.
Half board: £30-£38 daily,
£175-£215 weekly.
Evening meal 6.30pm (l.o.
6pm).
Parking for 12.
Open April-October.

Derwent Guest House
⛢⛢
6 Sea View Ter., St. Ives,
TR26 2DH
☎ Penzance (0736) 797505
*Delightfully situated with
superb views over St. Ives bay
and harbour. Near town,
beaches, bus and railway
station.*
Bedrooms: 1 single, 2 double
& 1 twin, 2 family rooms.
Bathrooms: 1 private,
2 public.
Bed & breakfast: £11-£15
single, £22-£30 double.
Half board: £16-£20 daily,
£105-£135 weekly.
Evening meal 6pm (l.o. 6pm).
Parking for 5.

Garrack Hotel ⋀
⛢⛢⛢ COMMENDED
Higher Ayr, St. Ives,
TR26 3AA
☎ Penzance (0736) 796199 &
Fax (0736) 798955
*Family-managed hotel with
superb sea views. Quiet
location. Ample free parking.
Heated indoor pool, sauna,
solarium.*
Bedrooms: 6 single, 7 double
& 5 twin, 3 family rooms.
Bathrooms: 15 private,
5 public.
Bed & breakfast: £26.50-£46
single, £53-£92 double.

Half board: £41-£60.50 daily,
£259-£395.50 weekly.
Lunch available.
Evening meal 7pm (l.o.
8.30pm).
Parking for 30.
Credit: Access, Visa, Diners,
Amex.

Glentworth
⛢⛢
Carthew Ter., St. Ives,
TR26 1EB
☎ (0736) 797892
*Family guesthouse with lounge
bar, ocean views, parking.
Located in a quiet terrace, 5
minutes from beach and town.*
Bedrooms: 1 single, 1 double,
4 family rooms.
Bathrooms: 1 private,
2 public.
Bed & breakfast: £12-£15
single, £24-£30 double.
Half board: £18.50-£21.50
daily, £129.50-£150 weekly.
Evening meal 6.30pm (l.o.
7pm).
Parking for 5.
Open April-October.

Hobblers Restaurant &
Guesthouse ⋀
Wharf Rd., St. Ives,
TR26 1LG
☎ (0736) 796439
*17th C pilot's house situated
directly on harbour front.
Three guest bedrooms over
licensed old world fresh fish
restaurant.*
Bedrooms: 1 single, 1 double
& 1 twin.
Bathrooms: 1 public.
Bed & breakfast: £15 single,
£30 double.
Evening meal 6pm (l.o.
10pm).
Open April-October.
Credit: Access, Visa, Diners,
Amex.

Longships Hotel
⛢⛢⛢ APPROVED
Talland Rd., St. Ives,
TR26 2DF
☎ Penzance (0736) 798180
*Overlooking St. Ives Bay,
minutes by foot from town
centre and beaches. Most
rooms have sea view.*
Bedrooms: 3 single, 8 double
& 4 twin, 9 family rooms.
Bathrooms: 24 private.
Bed & breakfast: £17.50-
£25.50 single, £35-£51 double.
Half board: £21.50-£32 daily,
£149.50-£203 weekly.

Continued ▶

ST IVES
Continued

Lunch available.
Evening meal 6pm (l.o. 7pm).
Parking for 18.
Credit: Access, Visa.

The Nook Hotel
≌≌

St. Ives, TR26 1EQ
☎ Penzance (0736) 795913
Family hotel in secluded gardens, near cliffpath, beaches and harbour. Children's play area and car park. Traditional home cooking.
Bedrooms: 3 single, 5 double & 2 twin, 3 family rooms.
Bathrooms: 6 private, 3 public.
Bed & breakfast: £15-£22 single, £30-£44 double.
Half board: £22-£29 daily, £164-£200 weekly.
Evening meal 6.30pm (l.o. 7pm).
Parking for 15.
Open April-October.

Ocean Breezes Private Hotel
≌≌

Barnoon, St. Ives, TR26 1JD
☎ Penzance (0736) 795587
Granite built hotel overlooking Porthmeor beach. 2 minutes' walk from the town centre.
Bedrooms: 5 single, 5 double & 5 twin, 5 family rooms.
Bathrooms: 6 private, 3 public; 3 private showers.
Bed & breakfast: £20-£29 single, £40-£58 double.
Half board: £28.25-£37.25 daily, £166-£224.50 weekly.
Lunch available.
Evening meal 6pm (l.o. 9.30pm).
Parking for 4.
Credit: Access, Visa, Diners, Amex.

Old Vicarage Hotel
≌≌≌ COMMENDED

Parc-an-Creet, St. Ives, TR26 2ET
☎ Penzance (0736) 796124
Well converted Victorian rectory with great character and charm in wooded grounds off the B3306. Just over half a mile from town centre and beaches.
Bedrooms: 2 single, 3 double, 3 family rooms.
Bathrooms: 4 private, 3 public; 2 private showers.

Bed & breakfast: £17.60-£20 single, £31.20-£44 double.
Evening meal 6.45pm (l.o. 6.45pm).
Parking for 15.
Open March-October.
Credit: Access, Visa.

Pondarosa Hotel
≌≌ COMMENDED

10 Porthminster Ter., St. Ives, TR26 2DQ
☎ Penzance (0736) 795875
Charming Victorian house with well-appointed, comfortable accommodation in quiet location yet convenient for town and beaches. Interesting garden and conservatory.
Bedrooms: 1 single, 2 double & 1 twin, 4 family rooms.
Bathrooms: 2 private, 2 public; 3 private showers.
Bed & breakfast: £15-£18 single, £33-£40 double.
Half board: £24-£28 daily, £150-£180 weekly.
Lunch available.
Evening meal 6.30pm (l.o. 6.30pm).
Parking for 10.

Porthminster Hotel ⋀
≌≌≌

The Terrace, St. Ives, TR26 2BN
☎ Penzance (0736) 795221
ⒼⓇ Best Western
Established family hotel overlooking Porthminster Beach, with magnificent views of bay from most bedrooms and public rooms.
Bedrooms: 5 single, 15 double & 18 twin, 11 family rooms.
Bathrooms: 49 private.
Bed & breakfast: £45-£51 single, £90-£102 double.
Half board: £56-£62 daily, £392-£434 weekly.
Lunch available.
Evening meal 7.15pm (l.o. 8.30pm).
Parking for 38.
Credit: Access, Visa, C.Bl., Diners, Amex.

Primavera Private Hotel
≌≌

14 Draycott Ter., St. Ives, TR26 2EF
☎ Penzance (0736) 795595
Small friendly hotel overlooking Porthminster Beach, with warm, personal and efficient service. Carefully prepared food and special dietary needs catered for.

Bedrooms: 2 single, 1 double, 2 family rooms.
Bathrooms: 2 private, 1 public.
Bed & breakfast: £14-£18 single, £28-£40 double.
Lunch available.
Evening meal (l.o. 9pm).
Open June-September.

Hotel Saint Eia
≌≌≌ COMMENDED

Trelyon Ave., St. Ives, TR26 2AA
☎ Penzance (0736) 795531 & Fax (0736) 793591
Privately owned family hotel within 10 minutes' walk of St. Ives town centre and overlooking Porthminster Beach.
Bedrooms: 1 single, 8 double & 5 twin, 4 family rooms.
Bathrooms: 6 private, 2 public; 7 private showers.
Bed & breakfast: £21-£25 single, £46-£60 double.
Lunch available.
Evening meal 6pm (l.o. 9pm).
Parking for 20.
Credit: Access, Visa.

Seagulls Guest House
≌≌

4 Godrevy Ter., St. Ives, TR26 1JA
☎ Penzance (0736) 797273
Panoramic sea views overlooking island and beaches. Superior rooms with private facilities. Reputation for comfort and hospitality. Free private parking.
Bedrooms: 1 single, 3 double, 1 family room.
Bathrooms: 3 private, 1 public; 1 private shower.
Bed & breakfast: £14-£16 single, £28-£32 double.
Parking for 10.
Open January-November.

Individual proprietors have supplied all details of accommodation. Although we do check for accuracy, we advise you to confirm prices and other information at the time of booking.

ST JUST-IN-PENWITH
Cornwall
Map ref 1A3

4m N. Land's End
Coastal parish of craggy moorland scattered with engine houses and chimney stacks of disused mines. The old mining town of St. Just has handsome 19th C granite buildings. North of the town are the dramatic ruined tin mines at Botallack and, at Boscaswell, the Geevor Tin Mine Museum.

Bosavern House ⋀
≌≌ APPROVED

St Just-in-Penwith, Penzance, TR19 7RD
☎ (0736) 788301
Cornish guesthouse, 300 years old, set in a walled garden with sea and moorland views. Log fires, home cooking and friendly atmosphere.
Bedrooms: 1 single, 3 double & 2 twin, 4 family rooms.
Bathrooms: 5 private, 2 public.
Bed & breakfast: from £12 single, from £24 double.
Half board: from £19.50 daily.
Evening meal 7pm (l.o. 10am).
Parking for 15.
Open March-October.

ST JUST-IN-ROSELAND
Cornwall
Map ref 1B3

Parish overlooking Carrick Roads on the Roseland Peninsula. The riverside church of St. Just has a beautiful setting under a steep slope of tall trees and sub-tropical shrubs.

Rose Da Mar Hotel
≌≌≌ COMMENDED

St. Just-in-Roseland, Truro, TR2 5JB
☎ St. Mawes (0326) 270450
A small, well-appointed private hotel with superb river and country views. Situated in an area of outstanding natural beauty.
Bedrooms: 2 single, 2 double & 2 twin, 2 family rooms.
Bathrooms: 5 private, 2 public.

Bed & breakfast: £25 single, £43.30-£55.50 double.
Half board: £35.65-£41.75 daily, £243.35-£284.95 weekly.
Evening meal 7.30pm (l.o. 6pm).
Parking for 9.
Open March-October.
⚗ ✿ 🅿 🛏 📺 ⅲ 🎿 Ⓣ

ST KEYNE
Cornwall
Map ref 1C2

2m S. Liskeard

The Old Rectory Country House Hotel
❦❦❦ COMMENDED
St. Keyne, Liskeard, PL14 4RL
☎ (0579) 42617
Peacefully secluded, elegant old rectory with mature gardens. On the B3254 Liskeard to Looe road. Closed at Christmas.
Bedrooms: 1 single, 5 double & 2 twin.
Bathrooms: 7 private, 1 public.
Bed & breakfast: £24-£30 single, £55-£60 double.
Half board: £36-£39 daily.
Evening meal 7pm (l.o. 8pm).
Parking for 30.
Credit: Access, Visa.
⚗ 🅿 🖥 ✿ 🅿 🛏 ⅲ 🎿 🍴 🍷 ✿ 🐾 🅂🄿 🎏

ST MAWES
Cornwall
Map ref 1B3

Small resort and yachting centre in a pretty estuary setting on the Roseland Peninsula. Enclosed by fields and woods of the Percuil River, it is said to be the warmest winter resort in Britain.

The Idle Rocks Hotel M
❦❦❦ COMMENDED
Harbourside, St. Mawes, Truro, TR2 5AN
☎ (0326) 270771 & Fax (0326) 270062
Hotel at the water's edge overlooking yachting harbour, well known for locally-caught fish. Tranquillity and relaxed atmosphere.
Bedrooms: 2 single, 13 double & 2 twin, 6 family rooms.
Bathrooms: 23 private.
Bed & breakfast: £20-£50 single, £40-£100 double.
Half board: £40-£68 daily, £238-£413 weekly.
Lunch available.

Evening meal 7.15pm (l.o. 9.15pm).
Credit: Access, Visa, Amex.
🖥 ⚗ 📞 ☎ 🅿 ✿ 🅿 Ⓥ 🎿 🛏 ⅲ ⚗ 🍴 🎏 ✿ 🅂🄿 Ⓣ

ST MAWGAN
Cornwall
Map ref 1B2

Pretty village on wooded slopes in the Vale of Lanherne. At its centre, an old stone bridge is overlooked by the church with its lofty buttressed tower. Among the ancient stone crosses in the churchyard is a 15th C lantern cross with carved figures.

Dalswinton Country House Hotel
❦❦❦
St. Mawgan, Newquay, TR8 4EZ
☎ (0637) 860385
Small, licensed hotel with log fires, in lovely rural setting with scenic views down wooded valley to sea.
Bedrooms: 4 double & 2 twin, 3 family rooms.
Bathrooms: 9 private.
Bed & breakfast: £14-£21.50 single, £28-£43 double.
Half board: £22.50-£29.50 daily, £137-£195 weekly.
Lunch available.
Evening meal 6.30pm (l.o. 7.30pm).
Parking for 14.
Credit: Access, Visa.
🖥 ⚗ 🅿 🖥 ✿ Ⓥ 🛏 📺 ⅲ 🅿 🍴 ✿ 🐾 ∪ ❄ 🄿 🐾 🅂🄿 Ⓣ

SALCOMBE
Devon
Map ref 1C3

Sheltered yachting resort of whitewashed houses and narrow streets in a balmy setting on the Kingsbridge Estuary. Palm, myrtle and other Mediterranean plants flourish. There are sandy bays and creeks for boating.

Devon Tor Private Hotel
Devon Rd., Salcombe, TQ8 8HJ
☎ (0548) 843106
Small, non-smoking, family-run hotel with magnificent views over Salcombe Estuary and beaches. Home-cooking, friendly personal service and quality accommodation.

Bedrooms: 2 single, 2 double & 2 twin, 1 family room.
Bathrooms: 4 private, 1 public.
Bed & breakfast: £20-£22 single, £40-£50 double.
Half board: £30-£35 daily, £185-£235 weekly.
Evening meal 6.30pm (l.o. 4pm).
Parking for 5.
Open January-November.
🐾9 ⚗ ✿ Ⓥ 🎿 🛏 📺 ⅲ 🅿 🐾 🎏 🅂🄿

Lyndhurst Hotel M
❦❦❦
Bonaventure Rd., Salcombe, TQ8 8BG
☎ (0548) 842481
Friendly hotel enjoying an atmosphere of informality. Magnificent views. Traditional menus. Resident proprietors. Non-smokers only please.
Bedrooms: 5 double & 2 twin, 1 family room.
Bathrooms: 8 private.
Bed & breakfast: £18.50-£23 single, £37-£46 double.
Half board: £28.50-£34 daily, £169.50-£238 weekly.
Evening meal 7pm (l.o. 4.30pm).
Parking for 4.
Open January-October.
🐾7 🖥 🅿 ✿ 🅿 Ⓥ 🎿 🛏 ● ⅲ 🅿 🐾 🎏 🅂🄿 🎏 Ⓣ

Torre View Hotel M
❦❦❦ COMMENDED
Devon Rd., Salcombe, TQ8 8HJ
☎ (0548) 842633
Large detached residence commanding extensive views of the estuary and sea.
Bedrooms: 5 double & 1 twin, 2 family rooms.
Bathrooms: 5 private.
Bed & breakfast: £25-£30 single, £43-£51 double.
Half board: £32-£36 daily, £200-£225 weekly.
Evening meal 7pm (l.o. 6pm).
Parking for 5.
Open February-October.
Credit: Access, Visa.
🖥 ✿ 🅿 🛏 📺 ⅲ 🅿 ∪ 🄿 🐾 🎏 🅂🄿

Woodgrange Hotel
❦❦❦
Devon Rd., Salcombe, TQ8 8HJ
☎ (0548) 842439/842006
🄒🄱 Minotels
Small Victorian hotel overlooking the beautiful Salcombe estuary, set in its own south facing grounds.
Bedrooms: 2 single, 3 double & 3 twin, 1 family room.
Bathrooms: 9 private.

Bed & breakfast: £24-£26 single, £48-£52 double.
Half board: £36-£38 daily, £225-£232 weekly.
Evening meal 7pm (l.o. 8.30pm).
Parking for 12.
Open April-October.
Credit: Access, Visa, Diners, Amex.
🖥 📞 🅿 🖥 ✿ 🅿 Ⓥ 🛏 ⅲ 🅿 🍴 🎏 🅂🄿

SALISBURY
Wiltshire
Map ref 2B3

Beautiful city and ancient regional capital set amid water meadows on the medieval plain. Buildings of all periods are dominated by the stately cathedral whose spire is the tallest in England. Built between 1220 and 1258, the cathedral is one of the purest examples of Early English architecture.
Tourist Information Centre ☎ *(0722) 334956*

Byways House M
❦❦❦
31 Fowlers Rd., Salisbury, SP1 2QP
☎ (0722) 328364 & Fax (0722) 322146
Attractive family-run Victorian house with cathedral view, in quiet area of city centre. Car park. Bedrooms en-suite with colour TV. Traditional English breakfast and evening meal.
Bedrooms: 4 single, 7 double & 7 twin, 5 family rooms.
Bathrooms: 19 private, 1 public.
Bed & breakfast: £17-£25 single, £31-£37 double.
Half board: £23.50-£27 daily.
Evening meal 6pm (l.o. 7pm).
Parking for 15.
Credit: Access, Visa.
🖥 ⚗ 🅿 🅿 ✿ 🅿 Ⓥ 🎿 🛏 ⅲ 🅿 🍴 👥 🐾 ❄ 🄳🄰🄵 🐾 🅂🄿 🎏 Ⓣ

The Coach and Horses
❦❦ APPROVED
39 Winchester St., Salisbury, SP1 1HG
☎ (0722) 336254 & Fax (0722) 414319
Salisbury's oldest coaching inn, recently refurbished and now offering comfort and varied cuisine. Only non-smoking accommodation available.
Bedrooms: 2 double.
Bathrooms: 2 private.
Bed & breakfast: £39.50-£42.50 single, £49.50-£52.50 double.

Continued ▶

SALISBURY

Continued

Lunch available.
Evening meal (l.o. 10pm).
Credit: Access, Visa.

County Hotel M
Bridge St., Salisbury,
SP1 2ND
☎ (0722) 20229
Over 100 years old, built of mellow Salisbury stone, a Victorian listed building reputedly with its own ghost. Overlooking the river and close to the shops.
Bedrooms: 3 single, 15 double & 10 twin, 3 family rooms.
Bathrooms: 31 private.
Bed & breakfast: £55-£65 single, £73 double.
Lunch available.
Evening meal 6pm (l.o. 10pm).
Parking for 31.
Credit: Access, Visa, C.Bl., Diners, Amex.

Cranston Guest House
5 Wain-a-Long Rd.,
Salisbury, SP1 1LJ
☎ (0722) 336776
Large detached town house covered in Virginia Creeper. 10 minutes' walk from town centre and cathedral.
Bedrooms: 2 single, 1 double & 2 twin, 1 family room.
Bathrooms: 4 private, 1 public.
Bed & breakfast: £15-£16 single, £30-£32 double.
Evening meal 6pm.
Parking for 3.
Open April-October.

Glen Lyn Guest House
6 Bellamy La., Milford Hill,
Salisbury, SP1 2SP
☎ (0722) 327880
Elegant Victorian house, situated in quiet lane within short walk of city centre. Easy parking. Non-smokers only please.
Bedrooms: 1 single, 4 double & 3 twin, 1 family room.
Bathrooms: 4 private, 2 public.
Bed & breakfast: £18-£24 single, £32-£40 double.
Parking for 7.

Holmhurst Guest House
Downton Rd., Salisbury,
SP2 8AR
☎ (0722) 323164
Pleasant town house, a short walk from Salisbury Cathedral. Riverside and country walks. Easy access to coastal resorts.
Bedrooms: 1 single, 3 double & 3 twin, 1 family room.
Bathrooms: 5 private, 1 public.
Bed & breakfast: £16-£24 single, £28-£32 double.
Parking for 8.
Open April-October.

Leena's Guest House
50 Castle Rd., Salisbury,
SP1 3RL
☎ (0722) 335419
Attractive Edwardian house with friendly atmosphere, close to riverside walks and park. Modern facilities include en-suite and ground-floor rooms.
Bedrooms: 1 single, 2 double & 2 twin, 1 family room.
Bathrooms: 3 private, 1 public; 1 private shower.
Bed & breakfast: from £16 single, from £27 double.
Parking for 7.

The New Inn at Salisbury M
41/43 New Street, Salisbury,
SP1 2PH
☎ (0722) 327679 & 326662
15th C inn of character near the cathedral. Beautifully restored rooms with private facilities, all exclusively for non-smokers.
Bedrooms: 4 double & 2 twin.
Bathrooms: 6 private.
Bed & breakfast: £25-£35 single, £45-£65 double.
Lunch available.
Evening meal 6pm (l.o. 10pm).
Parking for 3.
Credit: Access, Visa, Diners, Amex.

Old Bell Inn M
2 Saint Ann St., Salisbury,
SP1 2DN
☎ (0722) 327958
Telex 411485
Delightful period inn with restaurant, in the shadow of the soaring spire of Salisbury Cathedral.
Bedrooms: 5 double & 2 twin.
Bathrooms: 7 private.

Bed & breakfast: £50-£55 single, £55-£60 double.
Evening meal 7pm (l.o. 9.30pm).
Parking for 11.
Credit: Access, Visa, Diners, Amex.

Old Mill Hotel
APPROVED
Town Path, Harnham,
Salisbury, SP2 8EU
☎ (0722) 327517
This former mill is peacefully located on the River Nadder, surrounded by the water meadows with views of Salisbury Cathedral. The restaurant, dating from 1135, specialises in traditional English fare. An ideal touring centre for the south of England.
Bedrooms: 2 single, 5 double & 1 twin, 3 family rooms.
Bathrooms: 11 private.
Bed & breakfast: £30-£45 single, £60-£80 double.
Lunch available.
Evening meal 6.30pm (l.o. 9.45pm).
Parking for 16.
Credit: Access, Visa, Amex.

Red Lion Hotel
Milford St., Salisbury,
SP1 2AN
☎ (0722) 323334 & Fax
(0722) 25756 Telex 477674
Best Western
Originally a coaching inn, now a city centre hotel with all modern facilities. Ideal for business or pleasure.
Bedrooms: 11 single, 18 double & 23 twin, 4 family rooms.
Bathrooms: 56 private.
Bed & breakfast: £56-£66 single, £86-£96 double.
Half board: £51-£66 daily, £357-£462 weekly.
Lunch available.
Evening meal 7pm (l.o. 9.30pm).
Parking for 21.
Credit: Access, Visa, Diners, Amex.

Richburn Guest House
APPROVED
23 & 25 Estcourt Rd.,
Salisbury, SP1 3AP
☎ (0722) 325189
Large, tastefully renovated Victorian house with homely family atmosphere. All modern amenities and large car park. Close to city centre and parks.

Bedrooms: 1 single, 5 double & 2 twin, 2 family rooms.
Bathrooms: 2 private, 2 public.
Bed & breakfast: £15-£17 single, £24-£36 double.
Parking for 12.

Rokeby Guest House
3 Wain-a-Long Rd.,
Salisbury, SP1 1LJ
☎ (0722) 329800
Warm, welcoming, elegant Edwardian guesthouse of "upstairs, downstairs" type with family hospitality, set in landscaped grounds. Only a ten minute stroll from city centre but situated quietly just off main A30 London road. Open at Christmas for special 3-night full board package.
Bedrooms: 1 single, 1 double & 2 twin, 2 family rooms.
Bathrooms: 4 public.
Bed & breakfast: £18-£20 single, £28-£30 double.
Parking for 6.

Rose & Crown Hotel M
Harnham Rd., Salisbury,
SP2 8JF
☎ (0722) 327908 Telex 47224
ROSCRN G
Queens Moat Houses
13th C inn on the banks of the River Avon, in the shadow of Salisbury Cathedral. 3 rooms are suitable for disabled guests.
Bedrooms: 7 double & 12 twin, 9 family rooms.
Bathrooms: 28 private.
Bed & breakfast: £70.50-£98.50 single, £101-£140 double.
Lunch available.
Evening meal 7pm (l.o. 9.30pm).
Parking for 50.
Credit: Access, Visa, C.Bl., Diners, Amex.

The Trafalgar Hotel
APPROVED
33 Milford St., Salisbury,
SP1 2AP
☎ (0722) 338686 & Fax
(0722) 414496
Resort
Charming 14th C hotel offering good facilities and cuisine at an acceptable price.
Bedrooms: 4 single, 7 double & 5 twin.
Bathrooms: 16 private.
Bed & breakfast: £22.50-£46 single, £45-£61 double.
Lunch available.

Evening meal 7pm (l.o. 9.30pm).
Credit: Access, Visa, Diners, Amex.

♿ ♨ ☎ ⊕ ☐ ♥ 🛉 Ⅴ ● ♨ ► ✕ 🎬 SP 🏚 Ⓣ

Victoria Lodge Guest House ᴍ

♔♔♔ **APPROVED**

61 Castle Rd., Salisbury, SP1 3RH
☎ (0722) 20586 & Fax (0722) 414507
Warm, comfortable guesthouse set away from main street, within easy walking distance of city centre.
Bedrooms: 2 single, 6 double & 5 twin, 2 family rooms.
Bathrooms: 14 private, 2 public.
Bed & breakfast: £20-£25 single, £30-£40 double.
Evening meal 6pm (l.o. 9pm).
Parking for 30.

♿ ♨ ⊕ ☐ ♥ 🛉 Ⅴ ◄ �📺 ● 🕮 ♨ 🛉 ► ❄ Ⓣ

White Horse Hotel ᴍ

♔♔♔

38 Castle St., Salisbury, SP1 1BN
☎ (0722) 327844 & Fax (0722) 327844
Hotel of Victorian origin in heart of historic city of Salisbury. Offering a warm welcome and comfortable stay.
Bedrooms: 2 single, 9 double & 3 twin, 1 family room.
Bathrooms: 9 private, 2 public.
Bed & breakfast: £25-£35 single, £40-£55 double.
Lunch available.
Evening meal 7pm (l.o. 9.30pm).
Parking for 16.
Credit: Access, Visa, Diners.

♿ ☎ ⊕ ☐ ♥ 🛉 Ⅴ ◄ 🕮 ♨ 🛉 ✕ DAP SP 🏚 Ⓣ

SALISBURY PLAIN

See Amesbury, Salisbury, Warminster, Winterbourne Stoke.

The symbols are explained on the flap inside the back cover.

Map references apply to the colour maps towards the end of this guide.

SAUNTON

Devon
Map ref 1C1

Houses situated on a minor road at the end of Braunton Burrows, part of which is a nature reserve, important to botanists and ornithologists. Nearby is a fine golf-course and a 3 mile beach, Saunton Sands.

Preston House Hotel ᴍ

♔♔♔ **COMMENDED**

Saunton, Braunton, EX33 1LG
☎ Croyde (0271) 890472 & Fax (0271) 890555
Edwardian country house hotel, beautifully furnished, with sea view. Lovingly prepared country-fresh food.
Bedrooms: 2 single, 6 double & 7 twin.
Bathrooms: 15 private, 1 public.
Bed & breakfast: £28.50-£51 single, £57-£82 double.
Lunch available.
Evening meal 7pm (l.o. 8.30pm).
Parking for 20.
Credit: Access, Visa.

♨ ☎ ☐ ♥ 🛉 Ⅴ ◄ 📺 🕮 ♨ 🛉 ♥ ⌚ ► ❄ ✕ ⚓

SEATON

Devon
Map ref 1D2

Small resort lying near the mouth of the River Axe. A mile-long beach extends to the dramatic cliffs of Beer Head. Annual arts and drama festival.
Tourist Information Centre ☎ (0297) 21660 or 21689

Beach End Guest House ᴍ

♔♔ **COMMENDED**

8 Trevelyan Rd., Seaton, EX12 2NL
☎ (0297) 23388
Nearest guesthouse to beach. All rooms have sea views. English cooking our speciality. Morning tea/evening beverages included.
Bedrooms: 1 single, 3 double & 1 twin, 1 family room.
Bathrooms: 2 public.
Bed & breakfast: max. £15 single, max. £30 double.

Half board: max. £23.50 daily, max. £156 weekly.
Evening meal 7pm (l.o. 3pm).
Parking for 8.
Open February-October.

♿ ☐ 🛉 Ⅴ ◄ 📺 ✕ 🎬 ⚓

Beaumont

Castle Hill, Seaton, EX12 2QW
☎ (0297) 20832
Attractive and spacious seafront guesthouse offering comfort, personal attention and home cooking.
Bedrooms: 1 single, 5 family rooms.
Bathrooms: 3 private, 1 public; 1 private shower.
Bed & breakfast: £13-£15 single, £25-£30 double.
Half board: £22-£24 daily, £148-£160 weekly.
Evening meal 7.30pm (l.o. 7.30pm).
Parking for 7.

♿ ♨ ☐ ♥ 🛉 🛉 Ⅴ ● 🕮 ♨ 🎬 SP

SEMINGTON

Wiltshire
Map ref 2B2

2m S. Melksham

Somerset Arms

♔♔ **APPROVED**

High St., Semington, Trowbridge, BA14 6JR
☎ (0380) 870328/870067
300-year-old coaching inn, 100 yards from Kennet and Avon Canal.
Bedrooms: 1 single, 7 double & 1 twin, 2 family rooms.
Bathrooms: 8 private, 1 public.
Bed & breakfast: £25-£35 single, £40-£50 double.
Half board: £33-£40 daily.
Lunch available.
Evening meal 6pm (l.o. 10.30pm).
Parking for 50.
Credit: Access, Visa, Diners, Amex.

♿ ♨ ☎ ⊕ ☐ ♥ 🛉 Ⅴ ⚒ ◄ 📺 ● 🕮 ♨ 🛉 🛉 ⌚ DAP SP

SENNEN

Cornwall
Map ref 1A3

The last village before Land's End. Magnificent beach at Sennen Cove.

The Old Success Inn ᴍ

♔♔♔

Sennen Cove, Land's End, Penzance, TR19 7DG
☎ Penzance (0736) 871232

Refurbished inn nestles in one of Cornwall's most beautiful bays, within yards of the superb Whitesands Beach.
Bedrooms: 1 single, 8 double & 2 twin.
Bathrooms: 9 private, 1 public.
Bed & breakfast: £20-£27 single, £40-£54 double.
Half board: £28-£35 daily.
Lunch available.
Evening meal 7pm (l.o. 9pm).
Parking for 20.
Credit: Visa.

♿ ♨ ☐ ♥ 🛉 ◄ 📺 🕮 🛉 ✕ ⚓ SP Ⓣ

Sunny Bank Hotel

Sea View Hill, Sennen, Land's End, TR19 7AR
☎ (0736) 871278
Comfortable detached house in large gardens. 5 minutes from Sennen Cove beach. Close to Land's End and Minack Theatre.
Bedrooms: 2 single, 5 double & 2 twin, 2 family rooms.
Bathrooms: 2 public; 2 private showers.
Bed & breakfast: £13-£15 single, £26-£34 double.
Half board: £19-£23 daily, £120-£144 weekly.
Evening meal 6.30pm (l.o. 8pm).
Parking for 20.
Open January-November.

♿ ♨ Ⅴ ◄ 📺 🕮 ❄ 🎬 SP

SHALDON

Devon
Map ref 1D2

Pretty resort facing Teignmouth from the south bank of the Teign Estuary. Regency houses harmonise with others of later periods; there are old cottages and narrow lanes. On the Ness, a sandstone promontory nearby, a tunnel built in the 19th C leads to a beach revealed at low tide.

Glenside Hotel ᴍ

♔♔♔ **COMMENDED**

Ringmore Rd., Shaldon, TQ14 0EP
☎ (0626) 872448
Old world cottage-style hotel by the riverside. Licensed and family-run, with home cooking. Easy walking. Car park.
Bedrooms: 2 single, 5 double & 3 twin.
Bathrooms: 7 private, 1 public.
Bed & breakfast: £17.50-£22 single, £35-£44 double.

Continued ▶

SHALDON
Continued

Half board: £26.50-£31 daily,
£166.50-£190.50 weekly.
Evening meal 6.30pm (l.o.
6.30pm).
Parking for 10.
Open January-October,
December.
ゝ♋♥🛏 ☎ Ⅴ ⊨ 🏧 ▨
SP

Ness House Hotel
Marine Parade, Shaldon,
TQ14 0HP
☎ (0626) 873480 & (0626)
873486
*Overlooking Teign estuary.
Elegant restaurant and
comfortable bars. Most rooms
have balconies overlooking the
sea.*
Bedrooms: 1 single, 8 double
& 1 twin, 2 family rooms.
Bathrooms: 12 private.
Bed & breakfast: £30-£45
single, £55-£70 double.
Lunch available.
Evening meal 7pm (l.o.
10pm).
Parking for 20.
Credit: Access, Visa, Amex.
ゝ♋ ℂ 📞 🛏 Ⅴ ⊨ 🏧
🍽 ► ✗ 🅟 SP 🏛

SHEPTON MALLET
Somerset
Map ref 2A2

Important, stone-built
market town beneath the
south-west slopes of the
Mendips. Thriving rural
industries include glove
and shoe making,
dairying and cider
making; the remains of a
medieval 'shambles' in
the square date from the
town's prosperity as a
wool centre.

Bowlish House
👑👑👑 COMMENDED
Coombe Lane, Shepton
Mallet, BA4 5JD
☎ (0749) 342022
*Restaurant with
accommodation in a listed
Georgian house, on the Wells
road outside Shepton Mallet.*
Bedrooms: 3 double & 1 twin.
Bathrooms: 4 private.
Bed & breakfast: from £48
single, £48-£55 double.
Half board: from £43.50
daily.
Evening meal 7pm (l.o.
9.30pm).
Parking for 10.
Credit: Access, Visa.
ゝ⊙♫⊡♥🛏 Ⅴ ⊨ 🏧 ▪
🍽 ♻ ❊ 🅟 🏛

Pecking Mill Inn and Hotel
👑👑👑
A371, Evercreech, Shepton
Mallet, BA4 6PG
☎ (0749) 830336/830006
*16th C inn with oak-beamed
restaurant and open log fire.
Old world atmosphere with all
modern amenities.*
Bedrooms: 1 single, 5 double.
Bathrooms: 6 private.
Bed & breakfast: £33 single,
£44 double.
Lunch available.
Evening meal 7pm (l.o.
10pm).
Parking for 23.
Credit: Access, Visa, Diners,
Amex.
ゝ ℂ ⊙ ⊡ ♥ 🛏 Ⅴ ⊨ 🏧
▪ 🍽 ✗ 🅟 🏛

Thatched Cottage Inn ⋒
👑👑👑
63-67 Charlton Rd., Shepton
Mallet, BA4 5QF
☎ (0749) 342058 & Fax
(0749) 343265
*On A361 Frome to Shepton
Mallet, superior country inn
offering accommodation,
relaxed and informal lounge
bar and restaurant.*
Bedrooms: 6 double & 2 twin.
Bathrooms: 8 private.
Bed & breakfast: £45-£55
single, £75-£85 double.
Lunch available.
Evening meal 6.30pm (l.o.
9.30pm).
Parking for 40.
Credit: Access, Visa.
ゝ ℂ ⊙ ⊡ ♥ 🛏 Ⅴ ⅍ 🏧
⊙ 🏧 ▪ 🍽 ✗ 🅟 SP 🏛 T

SHERBORNE
Dorset
Map ref 2B3

Historic town of
hamstone, a business
and market centre for a
wide area and a
developing cultural centre
with a range of activities.
The home of Dorset
Opera. In Anglo-Saxon
times it was a cathedral
city and until the
Dissolution there was a
monastery here.
*Tourist Information
Centre* ☎ *(0935) 815341*

Britannia Inn
👑👑
Westbury, Sherborne,
DT9 3EH
☎ (093 581) 3300
*Originally the Lord Digby
School for Girls, built in 1743,
now a listed building.*

Bedrooms: 1 single, 1 double
& 3 twin, 2 family rooms.
Bathrooms: 1 private,
3 public.
Bed & breakfast: £17.50-
£18.50 single, £32-£36 double.
Evening meal 7pm (l.o. 9pm).
Parking for 13.
Credit: Access, Visa.
ゝ♋ ⊡ Ⅴ 🏧 🍽 🅟 🏛

Quinns
👑👑👑 COMMENDED
Marston Rd., Sherborne,
DT9 4BL
☎ (0935) 815008
*Delightful accommodation in
modern house. All rooms en-
suite, television, tea/coffee
making facilities. Spacious
lounge. Dinners by
arrangement. Car park.*
Bedrooms: 1 single, 1 double
& 1 twin.
Bathrooms: 3 private.
Bed & breakfast: £20-£25
single, £40-£48 double.
Parking for 4.
ゝ8 ⊡ ♥ 🛏 Ⅰ Ⅴ ⊨ 🏧 ▪
✗ 🅟 SP

SHIPHAM
Somerset
Map ref 1D1

3m N. Cheddar
Peaceful village on the
slopes of the Mendip
Hills, once a centre for
calamine mining.

Daneswood House Hotel ⋒
👑👑👑 COMMENDED
Chuck Hill, Shipham,
Winscombe, Avon BS25 1RD
☎ (093 484) 3145 & Fax
(093 484) 3824
*Country house hotel situated
deep in the Mendip Hills in
quiet elevated woodland
setting. Emphasis on fine wines
and food.*
Bedrooms: 9 double & 3 twin.
Bathrooms: 12 private.
Bed & breakfast: £57.50-£75
single, £65-£115 double.
Half board: £75-£105 daily.
Lunch available.
Evening meal 7pm (l.o.
9.30pm).
Parking for 30.
Credit: Access, Visa, Diners,
Amex.
ゝ♋ ℂ ⊙ ⊡ ♥ Ⅴ 🛏 ◉
🏧 ▪ 🍽 ❊ 🏧 SP 🏛

Penscot Farm House Hotel ⋒
Shipham, Winscombe,
BS25 1TW
☎ Winscombe
(093 484) 2659
ⓒⓡ Minotels

Cosy old world atmosphere
with log fires in winter, oak
beams and English-style food.
Situated in Mendip foothills
with lovely views and walks.
Bedrooms: 3 single, 6 double
& 5 twin, 3 family rooms.
Bathrooms: 12 private,
3 public.
Bed & breakfast: £25.50-
£29.50 single, £40-£46.50
double.
Half board: £28-£31.50 daily,
£171.50-£205 weekly.
Lunch available.
Evening meal 7pm (l.o. 9pm).
Parking for 40.
Open January-November.
Credit: Access, Visa, C.Bl.,
Diners, Amex.
ゝ♋♋ ℂ ⊙ ♥ 🛏 Ⅴ 🛏
⅍ 🅣 ◉ 🏧 ▪ 🍽 ♓ ❊ SP
🏛 T

SIDBURY
Devon
Map ref 1D2

3m N. Sidmouth
Small, rural village set in
the deep valley of the
River Sid. Thatched or
slate-roofed cottages are
gathered around the
Norman church which has
an Anglo-Saxon crypt.
The countryside with its
old farmhouses is
beautiful and the coast
lies 3 miles to the south.

Orchardside Hotel and Restaurant
Cotford Rd., Sidbury,
Sidmouth, EX10 0SQ
☎ (039 57) 351
*Lovely small country hotel and
restaurant, set in 1 acre of
garden and surrounded by
outstanding countryside on
A375 Honiton to Sidmouth
road.*
Bedrooms: 2 double & 2 twin,
1 family room.
Bathrooms: 3 private,
1 public.
Bed & breakfast: £16-£18
single, £32-£36 double.
Half board: £25-£26.50 daily,
£154-£165 weekly.
Lunch available.
Evening meal 6.30pm (l.o.
8.30pm).
Parking for 20.
Credit: Access, Visa.
ゝ2♋⊡♥🛏 Ⅴ 🏧 ▪ ♿
❊ ✗ 🅟 ⓖⓐⓟ SP

Sid Valley Country Hotel ⋒
👑👑👑 COMMENDED
Sidbury, Sidmouth, EX10 0QJ
☎ (039 57) 274 & 587
Telex 932905 LARCH G

Totally renovated 17th C building, set in 5-acre gardens/pastureland. Heated pool. Trout stream, riding, golfing, shooting. Idyllic views. Dine in style with choice of 50 wines.
Bedrooms: 4 double & 3 twin, 1 family room.
Bathrooms: 8 private.
Bed & breakfast: £39.20-£44.35 single, £58.40-£68.70 double.
Half board: £43.80-£49.45 daily, £272.40-£305.45 weekly.
Evening meal 7pm (l.o. 8.30pm).
Parking for 13.
Open February-October.
Credit: Access, Visa.

SIDMOUTH
Devon
Map ref 1D2

13m E. Exeter
Charming resort set amid lofty red cliffs where the River Sid meets the sea. The wealth of ornate Regency and Victorian villas recalls the time when this was one of the south coast's most exclusive resorts. Museum; August International Festival of Folk Arts.

Canterbury Guest House

Salcombe Rd., Sidmouth, EX10 8PR
☎ (0395) 513373
Old house of charm and character overlooking River Sid. Close to shops, seafront and National Trust parkland.
Bedrooms: 3 double & 2 twin, 3 family rooms.
Bathrooms: 7 private, 1 public.
Bed & breakfast: £16-£19.50 single, £32-£39 double.
Half board: £22-£25.50 daily, £152-£172 weekly.
Evening meal 6pm (l.o. 4.30pm).
Parking for 6.
Open March-December.

Devoran Hotel
COMMENDED
Esplanade, Sidmouth, EX10 8AU
☎ (0395) 513151

Family-owned hotel overlooking beach, very close to town centre and amenities. Relaxed, happy atmosphere, with home-cooked food.
Bedrooms: 4 single, 8 double & 6 twin, 5 family rooms.
Bathrooms: 21 private, 3 public; 2 private showers.
Bed & breakfast: £26-£32 single, £52-£64 double.
Half board: £32-£40 daily, £190-£240 weekly.
Evening meal 6.45pm (l.o. 7.30pm).
Parking for 4.
Open March-November.

Fortfield Hotel M

Sidmouth, EX10 8NU
☎ (0395) 512403 & Fax (0395) 512403
Country house style hotel overlooking sea, with solarium and leisure centre. Privately-owned and family managed. Elegant decor and friendly atmosphere.
Bedrooms: 5 single, 9 double & 31 twin, 10 family rooms.
Bathrooms: 55 private, 3 public.
Bed & breakfast: £34-£58 single, £68-£116 double.
Half board: £39-£63 daily, £259-£427 weekly.
Lunch available.
Evening meal 7pm (l.o. 8.30pm).
Parking for 60.
Credit: Access, Visa, Diners, Amex.

Groveside Guest House M
APPROVED
Vicarage Rd., Sidmouth, EX10 8UQ
☎ (0395) 513406
Family-run detached guesthouse, comfortably furnished and close to all amenities.
Bedrooms: 1 single, 3 double & 2 twin, 2 family rooms.
Bathrooms: 3 private, 2 public.
Bed & breakfast: £12-£16 single, £24-£32 double.
Half board: £18.50-£23 daily, £128-£160 weekly.
Evening meal 6pm (l.o. 4.30pm).
Parking for 7.
Open March-November.

Mount Pleasant Hotel

Salcombe Rd., Sidmouth, EX10 8JA
☎ (0395) 514694 & Fax (0395) 514694
Early Georgian residence in a quiet situation, close to all amenities, with a pleasant outlook and large garden. All rooms en-suite, ample car parking.
Bedrooms: 2 single, 6 double & 6 twin, 2 family rooms.
Bathrooms: 15 private; 1 private shower.
Bed & breakfast: £25-£28 single, £48-£52 double.
Half board: £32-£39 daily, £220-£255 weekly.
Lunch available.
Evening meal 7pm (l.o. 8pm).
Parking for 21.
Open April-October.

Hotel Riviera M
HIGHLY COMMENDED
The Esplanade, Sidmouth, EX10 8AY
☎ (0395) 515201 Telex 42551
Exonia G. Riviera
An attractive hotel offering old fashioned hospitality with modern amenities, superbly situated at the centre of the Esplanade overlooking Lyme Bay.
Bedrooms: 13 single, 6 double & 15 twin.
Bathrooms: 32 private, 1 public.
Bed & breakfast: £42-£63 single, £84-£126 double.
Half board: £48-£69 daily, £336-£483 weekly.
Lunch available.
Evening meal 7pm (l.o. 9pm).
Parking for 21.
Credit: Access, Visa, Diners, Amex.

Royal Glen Hotel

Glen Rd., Sidmouth, EX10 8RW
☎ (0395) 513221/578124/5
In its own grounds 1 minute from the seafront, this hotel was once the residence of Queen Victoria. All public rooms have sea views.
Bedrooms: 9 single, 4 double & 17 twin, 4 family rooms.
Bathrooms: 32 private, 2 public.
Bed & breakfast: £21-£46.50 single, £48-£93 double.
Half board: £30-£51.50 daily, £185-£350.50 weekly.
Lunch available.

Evening meal 7pm (l.o. 8.30pm).
Parking for 24.
Credit: Access, Visa, Amex.

Royal York & Faulkner Hotel M
APPROVED
Esplanade, Sidmouth, EX10 8AZ
☎ (0395) 513043/513184 & Fax (0395) 577472
Tastefully modernised Regency hotel, in centre of Esplanade, overlooking sea. All amenities. Leisure complex. Indoor short mat bowls. Reduced golf fees.
Bedrooms: 22 single, 10 double & 30 twin, 7 family rooms.
Bathrooms: 68 private, 4 public.
Bed & breakfast: £20-£27.50 single, £40-£55 double.
Half board: £25-£48.50 daily, £170-£320 weekly.
Lunch available.
Evening meal 7.15pm (l.o. 8.30pm).
Parking for 10.
Open February-December.
Credit: Access, Visa.

Ryton Guest House

52-54 Winslade Rd., Sidmouth, EX10 9EX
☎ (0395) 513981
The aim here is to make your holiday as happy as possible, with hospitality second to none and home cooking.
Bedrooms: 2 single, 3 double & 1 twin, 3 family rooms.
Bathrooms: 1 private, 3 public.
Bed & breakfast: £13-£18 single, £24-£33 double.
Half board: £18-£24 daily, £125-£155 weekly.
Evening meal 6.30pm (l.o. 4pm).
Parking for 8.

Salcombe Hill House Hotel M

Beatlands Rd., Sidmouth, EX10 8JQ
☎ (0395) 514697 & 514398
Set in lovely grounds, quiet, yet close to all Sidmouth's amenities. Outdoor heated swimming pool. Ample parking. Mini-breaks available.

Continued ▶

SIDMOUTH

Continued

Bedrooms: 6 single, 6 double
& 14 twin, 5 family rooms.
Bathrooms: 31 private,
2 public.
Bed & breakfast: £24-£38
single, £48-£76 double.
Half board: £35-£52 daily,
£205-£330 weekly.
Lunch available.
Evening meal 7.15pm (l.o.
8.30pm).
Parking for 40.
Open March-October.
Credit: Access, Visa, Diners.

Sidmount Hotel M
☺☺☺ APPROVED

Station Rd., Sidmouth,
EX10 8XJ
☎ (0395) 513432
*Imposing Georgian property,
built 1825, on an elevated site
with views from Salcombe Hill
to Peak Hill and the sea.*
Bedrooms: 6 double & 7 twin,
2 family rooms.
Bathrooms: 15 private.
Bed & breakfast: £22.30-
£34.60 single, £44.60-£58.90
double.
Half board: £25.10-£35.80
daily, £147-£220 weekly.
Lunch available.
Evening meal 6.30pm (l.o.
7pm).
Parking for 17.
Open March-November.

Westcliff Hotel M

Manor Rd., Sidmouth,
EX10 8RU
☎ (0395) 513252 & Fax
(0395) 578203
*Family-run hotel set in 2 acres
of lovely grounds overlooking
the sea. Outdoor heated pool
and games room. International
menu.*
Bedrooms: 8 single, 5 double
& 16 twin, 11 family rooms.
Bathrooms: 40 private.
Bed & breakfast: £34.25-
£58.03 single, £68.50-£113.41
double.
Half board: £43-£70.73 daily,
£287-£450.80 weekly.
Lunch available.
Evening meal 7.30pm (l.o.
8.30pm).
Parking for 50.
Open March-November.
Credit: Access, Visa.

Woodlands Hotel M
☺☺☺ APPROVED

Cotmaton Cross, Sidmouth,
EX10 8HG
☎ (0395) 513120/513166
*Family-owned Regency
country house, set in award-
winning gardens and offering
complete relaxation. Near sea
and shops.*
Bedrooms: 8 single, 1 double
& 13 twin, 1 family room.
Bathrooms: 18 private,
3 public.
Bed & breakfast: £18-£29.75
single, £36-£59.50 double.
Half board: £23-£35.75 daily,
£161-£250.25 weekly.
Lunch available.
Evening meal 7pm (l.o. 8pm).
Parking for 23.
Credit: Access, Visa.

SIMONSBATH

Somerset
Map ref 1C1

7m SE. Lynton
Village beside the
beautiful River Barle,
deep in Exmoor. From the
Middle Ages until the 19th
C this was stag-hunting
country.

Emmetts Grange Farm
Guest House M
☺☺☺ COMMENDED

Simonsbath, Minehead,
TA24 7LD
☎ Exford (064 383) 282
*1200-acre hill stock farm.
Attractive country house in a
lovely, quiet position 2.5 miles
out of Simonsbath on the South
Molton road. Specialises in
country cooking.*
Bedrooms: 1 single, 1 double
& 2 twin.
Bathrooms: 2 private,
1 public.
Bed & breakfast: £19-£22
single, £38-£44 double.
Half board: £31-£34 daily,
£190-£210 weekly.
Evening meal 8pm (l.o. 6pm).
Parking for 6.
Open March-October.

---

*National Crown
ratings were correct
at the time of going
to press but are
subject to change.
Please check at the
time of booking.*

SOMERTON

Somerset
Map ref 2A3

Old market town,
important in Saxon times,
situated at a gap in the
hills south-east of
Sedgemoor. Attractive
red-roofed stone houses
surround the 17th C
octagonal market cross
and among other
handsome buildings are
the Town Hall and
almshouses of about the
same period.

The Unicorn at
Somerton M

West St., Somerton,
TA11 7PR
☎ (0458) 72101
*Traditional English inn, serving
home-cooked food and real
ales, in comfortable
atmospheric surroundings.
Personal attention by the
owners.*
Bedrooms: 1 single, 3 double
& 3 twin.
Bathrooms: 6 private,
2 public.
Bed & breakfast: £22-£30
single, £32-£36 double.
Lunch available.
Evening meal 7pm (l.o.
10pm).
Parking for 45.
Credit: Access, Visa, Diners,
Amex.

SOUTH MOLTON

Devon
Map ref 1C1

Busy market town at the
mouth of the Yeo Valley
near southern Exmoor.
Wool, mining and
coaching brought
prosperity between the
Middle Ages and the 19th
C and the fine square
with Georgian buildings, a
Guildhall and Assembly
Rooms reflects this
former affluence.

West Down

Whitechapel, South Molton,
EX36 3EQ
☎ Bishops Nympton
(076 97) 373
*On the edge of Exmoor, only
15 miles from North Devon
coast, and set in 30 acres.*
Bedrooms: 3 double & 1 twin,
1 family room.
Bathrooms: 5 private,
2 public.
Bed & breakfast: £18.50-
£19.50 single, £37-£39 double.

Half board: £25.50-£26.50
daily, £150-£160 weekly.
Lunch available.
Evening meal 7pm.
Parking for 10.

SOUTH PETHERTON

Somerset
Map ref 1D2

5m E. Ilminster
Small town with a
restored 15th C house,
King Ina's Palace. The
Roman Fosse Way
crosses the River Parrett
to the east by way of an
old bridge on which there
are 2 curious carved
figures.

Oaklands
☺☺☺ COMMENDED

8 Palmer St., South Petherton,
TA13 5DB
☎ (0460) 41998/40272
*Grade II listed Georgian house
in secluded garden with heated
outdoor swimming pool. TV in
bedrooms on request. Guide
dogs accepted.*
Bedrooms: 3 double & 1 twin,
1 family room.
Bathrooms: 5 private,
1 public.
Bed & breakfast: £40-£60
single, £50-£75 double.
Half board: £60-£80 daily.
Evening meal 7pm (l.o.
9.30pm).
Parking for 12.
Open February-December.
Credit: Access, Visa.

SOUTH ZEAL

Devon
Map ref 1C2

4m E. Okehampton
Small village following its
13th C plan. A medieval
chapel, rebuilt in the 18th
C, occupies the market-
place. Spoil heaps near
the village recall former
copper mining days.

Poltimore M
☺☺☺ APPROVED

South Zeal, Okehampton,
EX20 2PD
☎ Okehampton
(0837) 840209
*Thatched Devon longhouse
delightfully located on edge of
Dartmoor with panoramic
views. Ideal base for walking
or touring. Home cooking.*

Bedrooms: 2 single, 3 double & 2 twin.
Bathrooms: 4 private, 1 public.
Bed & breakfast: £16-£22 single, £32-£48 double.
Half board: £25-£34 daily, £160-£210 weekly.
Evening meal 7pm (l.o. 5pm).
Parking for 15.
Credit: Access, Visa, Amex.
❦10 🖵 ❦ 🛗 Ⅴ 🛏 📺 ▥ ⌷ ❋ 🗚 ﹋ SP T

SPREYTON
Devon
Map ref 1C2

7m E. Okehampton

Downhayes
⬛⬛ COMMENDED
Spreyton, Crediton, Devon. EX17 5AR
☎ Bow (0363) 82378
Very comfortable guesthouse, noted for its food. Situated in lovely countryside between Dartmoor and Exmoor. Ideal for exploring Devon.
Bedrooms: 3 double.
Bathrooms: 2 private, 1 public.
Bed & breakfast: £26.25-£32 single, £37-£45 double.
Half board: £31-£44.50 daily, £195.50-£280 weekly.
Evening meal 7.30pm (l.o. 9pm).
Parking for 6.
Credit: Visa.
❦12 ⌷ ⌷ Ⅴ ❦ 🛗 Ⅴ 🛏 📺 ▥ ⌷ ♣ ❋ 🗚 ﹋

STOKE GABRIEL
Devon
Map ref 1D2

Fishing village on a sheltered creek near the head of the Dart Estuary. Old houses and cobble stones enhance views of water and boats; there is an old water-mill and a spreading yew tree more than 1000 years old leans in the churchyard.

The Red Slipper
⬛⬛⬛ COMMENDED
Stoke Gabriel, TQ9 6RU
☎ (080 428) 315
English home-cooked food and well-appointed accommodation in a beautiful village on the River Dart.
Bedrooms: 1 double & 2 twin, 1 family room.
Bathrooms: 3 private; 1 private shower.
Bed & breakfast: £35.50-£42 double.

Half board: £31-£34 daily, £115-£136.50 weekly.
Lunch available.
Evening meal 7.30pm (l.o. 8.30pm).
Parking for 6.
Open March-October.
❦ ⌷ ⌷ ⌷ 🛗 Ⅴ 🛏 📺 ▥ ⌷ ⌷ ❋ 🗚

SWINDON
Wiltshire
Map ref 2B2

Wiltshire's industrial and commercial centre, an important railway town in the 19th C, situated just north of the Marlborough Downs. The original market town occupies the slopes of Swindon Hill and the railway village created in the mid-19th C has been preserved. Railway museum, art gallery, theatre and leisure centre.
Tourist Information Centre ☎ (0793) 530328

Blunsdon House Hotel M
⬛⬛⬛⬛
Blunsdon, Swindon, SN2 4AD
☎ (0793) 721701 & Fax (0793) 444491 Telex 444491 - BHHG
Ⓡ Best Western
A beautiful, 20-mile view across the vale of Cricklade to the Cotswolds. Leisure club now open. Special weekend breaks available.
Bedrooms: 9 single, 51 double & 18 twin, 10 family rooms.
Bathrooms: 88 private.
Bed & breakfast: £90-£97.50 single, £100-£107.50 double.
Half board: £103-£115 daily.
Lunch available.
Evening meal 7pm (l.o. 10.30pm).
Parking for 300.
Credit: Access, Visa, C.Bl., Diners, Amex.
❦ ﹋ ⌷ ☎ ⌷ ❦ 🛗 Ⅴ 🛏 ◑ ▥ ⌷ ♣ ⌷ ❋ ♠ 🗚 🌂 ❋ 🗚 ﹋ SP T
🔷 Display advertisement appears on page 324.

Fairview Guest House
52 Swindon Rd., Wootton Bassett, Swindon, SN4 8EU
☎ Swindon (0793) 852283
Detached guesthouse in town close to the M4 junction 16 (1.25 miles) and an easy 5 mile drive from Swindon.
Bedrooms: 3 single, 3 double & 4 twin, 2 family rooms.

Bathrooms: 2 private, 4 public; 3 private showers.
Bed & breakfast: £18.40-£32 single, £35-£45 double.
Half board: £26.30 daily.
Evening meal 6.30pm (l.o. 2.30pm).
Parking for 17.
❦ ﹋ ⌷ 🖵 ❦ 🛗 ⌷ Ⅴ 🛏 📺 ▥ ⌷ ⌷ OAP 🌂 SP T

Moormead Country Hotel M
Listed COMMENDED
Moormead Rd., Wroughton, Swindon, SN4 9BY
☎ (0793) 814744 & Fax (0793) 814119
Privately-owned hotel, recently refurbished throughout to a high standard. Full a la carte menu. Ideal touring base.
Bedrooms: 6 single, 4 double & 26 twin.
Bathrooms: 36 private.
Bed & breakfast: £30-£80 single, £50-£90 double.
Half board: £55-£97 daily.
Lunch available.
Evening meal 7pm (l.o. 9.30pm).
Parking for 60.
Credit: Access, Visa, Amex.
❦ ⌷ ☎ 🖵 ❦ 🛗 Ⅴ 🛏 ◑ ▥ ⌷ 🍽 ❋ 🗚 SP T

Relian Guest House
⬛⬛
151-153 County Rd., Swindon, SN1 2EB
☎ (0793) 521416
Quiet house adjacent to Swindon Town Football Club and near town centre. Close to bus and rail stations. Free car parking.
Bedrooms: 4 single, 1 double & 2 twin, 1 family room.
Bathrooms: 2 public; 4 private showers.
Bed & breakfast: from £19 single.
Parking for 7.
❦2 ⌷ ❦ UL 🛗 🛏 📺 ▥ 🗚

The School House Hotel & Restaurant M
⬛⬛⬛⬛ COMMENDED
Hook St., Hook, Swindon, SN4 8EF
☎ (0793) 851198 & Fax (0793) 851025 Telex 449703
Small but charming country house hotel in a converted 1860 school house. Combining modern facilities and Victorian decor. Rural but close to M4 and Swindon.
Bedrooms: 2 single, 5 double & 2 twin, 1 family room.
Bathrooms: 10 private.
Bed & breakfast: £74 single, £82.50 double.

Half board: £61.25-£94 daily.
Lunch available.
Evening meal 6pm (l.o. 10pm).
Parking for 40.
Credit: Access, Visa, Diners, Amex.
❦ ﹋ ⌷ ☎ 🖵 ❦ 🛗 Ⅴ 🛏 📺 ◑ ▥ ⌷ ♣ 🌂 ❋ 🗚 OAP 🌂 SP 🏵 T

South Marston Country Club
South Marston, Swindon, SN3 4SL
☎ (0793) 827777
Telex 444634
Ideally situated for exploring the Cotswolds, the hotel offers an extensive range of sports and leisure facilities.
Bedrooms: 2 double & 38 twin.
Bathrooms: 40 private.
Bed & breakfast: £27.50-£75 single, £55-£85 double.
Evening meal 7pm (l.o. 9.45pm).
Parking for 150.
Credit: Access, Visa, Diners, Amex.
❦ ﹋ ⌷ ☎ 🖵 ❦ 🛗 Ⅴ 🛏 📺 ◑ ▥ ⌷ ♣ 🌂 ♠ ⌷ ♣ 🗚 🏵 ❋ 🌂 SP T

Waite Meads House Private Hotel
⬛⬛⬛
2 High St., Purton, Swindon, SN5 9AA
☎ (0793) 771972
5 minutes from junction 16 M4, on the edge of the Cotswolds.
Bedrooms: 5 single, 4 double & 5 twin, 1 family room.
Bathrooms: 15 private.
Bed & breakfast: £28-£48 single, £36-£60 double.
Evening meal 6.30pm (l.o. 7.30pm).
Parking for 12.
Credit: Access, Visa.
❦ ﹋ ⌷ ☎ 🖵 🛗 Ⅴ 🛏 📺 ▥ ⌷ 🗚 OAP SP

TALLAND BAY

Cornwall
Map ref 1C3

Small, rocky bay sheltered by bracken-covered cliffs between Polperro and Looe. The old church with its carved bench-ends is set into a hillside, high over the sea.

Talland Bay Hotel M

COMMENDED

Talland Bay, Looe, PL13 2JB
☎ Polperro (0503) 72667
16th C Cornish country house with antique furniture, mentioned in the Domesday Book. Rural situation with 2 acres of gardens overlooking bay. Seafood specialities and fine wines.
Bedrooms: 4 single, 4 double & 11 twin, 3 family rooms.
Bathrooms: 22 private.
Half board: £45-£85 daily, £310-£595 weekly.
Lunch available.
Evening meal 7pm (l.o. 9pm).
Parking for 20.
Credit: Access, Visa, Diners, Amex.

TAUNTON

Somerset
Map ref 1D1

County town, well-known for its public schools, sheltered by gentle hill-ranges on the River Tone. Medieval prosperity from wool has continued in marketing and manufacturing and the town retains many fine period buildings.
Tourist Information Centre ☎ *(0823) 274785*

The Blorenge Guest House

57 Staplegrove Rd., Taunton, TA1 1DG
☎ (0823) 283005
Large Victorian house with 3 original four-poster beds, licensed bar, swimming pool. 5 minutes' walk to town centre and railway station.
Bedrooms: 3 single, 3 double & 3 twin, 2 family rooms.
Bathrooms: 3 private, 3 public; 3 private showers.
Bed & breakfast: £12.50-£15 single, £26-£30 double.

Half board: £20.50-£23.50 daily, from £130 weekly.
Evening meal 6pm (l.o. 6pm).
Parking for 10.
Credit: Visa.

Castle Hotel M

HIGHLY COMMENDED

Castle Green, Taunton, TA1 1NF
☎ (0823) 272671 Telex 46488
With its own fascinating Norman garden, ideally situated for exploring the West Country. Accent on food and wine.
Bedrooms: 14 single, 11 double & 10 twin.
Bathrooms: 35 private.
Bed & breakfast: from £75 single, £99-£180 double.
Half board: from £97.50 daily.
Lunch available.
Evening meal 7.30pm (l.o. 9pm).
Parking for 40.
Credit: Access, Visa, Diners, Amex.

Falcon Hotel M

APPROVED

Henlade, Taunton, TA3 5DH
☎ (0823) 442502
Family-owned country house hotel in own grounds only one mile east of M5 (junction 25). Informal atmosphere, comfortable and well equipped.
Bedrooms: 3 single, 4 double & 3 twin, 1 family room.
Bathrooms: 11 private.
Bed & breakfast: £27.50-£45 single, £45-£55 double.
Half board: £35-£40 daily.
Lunch available.
Evening meal 7pm (l.o. 9.30pm).
Parking for 25.
Credit: Access, Visa, Amex.

Forde House

COMMENDED

9 Upper High St., Taunton, TA1 3PX
☎ (0823) 279042
Peaceful location in the centre of town, close to all amenities, including public park and golf course. Warm welcome guaranteed.
Bedrooms: 1 single, 2 double & 2 twin.
Bathrooms: 5 private.

Bed & breakfast: £22-£25 single, £44-£46 double.
Parking for 5.

Higher Dipford Farm

COMMENDED

Dipford, Trull, Taunton, TA3 7NU
☎ Taunton (0823) 275770
120-acre dairy farm. Old Somerset longhouse with inglenook fireplaces. Real farmhouse fare using own produce from the dairy. Fresh salmon a speciality. Friendly atmosphere.
Bedrooms: 2 double & 1 twin, 2 family rooms.
Bathrooms: 5 private.
Bed & breakfast: £30-£32 single, £50-£56 double.
Half board: £40-£45 daily, £259-£273 weekly.
Evening meal 7pm (l.o. 10pm).
Parking for 12.

The Jays Nest

Meare Green, Stoke St. Gregory, Taunton, TA3 6HZ
☎ Taunton (0823) 490250
Detached country hotel in peaceful setting in West Sedgemoor, ideal for walking and wildlife, central for coast, Mendips, Quantocks and Exmoor. Wholefoods, fresh garden vegetables, traditional home cooking.
Bedrooms: 3 double & 2 twin, 1 family room.
Bathrooms: 3 private, 1 public.
Bed & breakfast: £18-£25 single, £36-£45 double.
Half board: £27-£35 daily, £178-£200 weekly.
Lunch available.
Evening meal 6pm (l.o. 10pm).
Parking for 18.
Credit: Amex.

Meryan House Hotel

COMMENDED

Bishops Hull, Taunton, TA1 5EG
☎ (0823) 337445
Delightful 17th C period residence with beams and inglenooks, in peaceful surroundings near Taunton. Personal attention assured at all times.
Bedrooms: 1 single, 9 double & 2 twin.
Bathrooms: 12 private.

Bed & breakfast: £36-£40 single, £40-£50 double.
Lunch available.
Evening meal 7.30pm (l.o. 8pm).
Parking for 17.
Credit: Access, Visa.

Roughmoor Cottage Guest House

COMMENDED

Silk Mills Rd., Bishops Hull, Taunton, TA1 5AA
☎ (0823) 331931
Large modern detached property set in 1.25 acres of landscaped garden including new tennis court. Heated indoor swimming pool and table tennis room. 1.5 miles from Taunton centre.
Bedrooms: 1 double & 1 twin, 1 family room.
Bathrooms: 3 private.
Bed & breakfast: £20.50-£21.50 single, £34-£36 double.
Half board: £30-£31 daily, £189 weekly.
Lunch available.
Evening meal 6.30pm (l.o. 5pm).
Parking for 9.

TAVISTOCK

Devon
Map ref 1C2

Old market town beside the River Tavy on the western edge of Dartmoor. Developed around its 10th C abbey, of which some fragments remain, it became a stannary town in 1305 when tin-streaming thrived on the moors. Tavistock Goose Fair, October.

The Horn of Plenty M

Gulworthy, Tavistock, PL19 8JD
☎ (0822) 832528
Country house hotel and gourmet restaurant with extensive, beautiful views of the Tamar Valley and moors beyond. Just off the A390 between Tavistock and Gunnislake.
Bedrooms: 4 double & 3 twin.
Bathrooms: 7 private.
Bed & breakfast: £51-£58 single, £71-£78 double.
Lunch available.

Evening meal 7pm (l.o. 9.30pm).
Parking for 25.
Credit: Access, Visa, Amex.

▨10 ⌂ ☎ ⏍ ⏸ ⏷ ♦ 𝖎 ▽
⤬ ◻ ▦ ⌷ ♦ ⏍ ✿ ⌸ SP T

The Old Coach House Hotel

▨▨▨

Ottery, Tavistock, PL19 8NS
☎ (0822) 617515
19th C coach house with lovely walled garden, set amid rolling farmland, yet only 5 minutes from Tavistock and Dartmoor. Ideal for touring or relaxing.
Bedrooms: 1 single, 1 double & 1 twin.
Bathrooms: 3 private.
Bed & breakfast: £19-£27 single, £38-£54 double.
Half board: £27-£35 daily, £160-£210 weekly.
Lunch available.
Evening meal 6.30pm (l.o. 9pm).
Parking for 6.

▨10 ⌂ ♦ ⏷ ⓊⓁ 𝖎 ◻ ▦ TV ▥
◻ ⏍ ✿ ⌸ ⌷ DAP ❧ SP

TEIGNMOUTH

Devon
Map ref 1D2

Set on the north bank of the beautiful Teign Estuary, busy fishing and shipbuilding port handling timber and locally-quarried ball-clay. A bridge crosses to the pretty town of Shaldon and there are good views of the estuary from here.
Tourist Information Centre ☎ (0626) 779769

Belvedere Hotel

▨▨▨

Barnpark Rd., Teignmouth, TQ14 8PJ
☎ (0626) 774561
Family-run early Victorian vicarage with sea views from many rooms. Close to sea and shops.
Bedrooms: 1 single, 7 double & 3 twin, 2 family rooms.
Bathrooms: 12 private, 1 public.
Bed & breakfast: £20.50-£23 single, £41-£46 double.
Half board: £25.50-£28 daily, £161.50-£175 weekly.
Lunch available.
Evening meal 6.30pm (l.o. 7.30pm).
Parking for 11.
Credit: Access, Visa.

▨ ♦ ⌷ ♦ 𝖎 ▽ ▦ TV ▥
◻ ⏍ ⌖ ✿ ⤬ ⌸ DAP ❧ SP T

London Hotel ♨

▨▨▨▨ APPROVED

Bank St., Teignmouth, TQ14 8AW
☎ (0626) 776336 & Fax (0626) 778457
Situated in town centre with easy access to beaches and moors. Families catered for. Leisure facilities including indoor swimming pool.
Bedrooms: 1 single, 14 double & 7 twin, 8 family rooms.
Bathrooms: 30 private, 4 public.
Bed & breakfast: £24-£35 single, £48-£60 double.
Half board: £28-£45 daily.
Lunch available.
Evening meal 6pm (l.o. 10pm).
Parking for 10.
Credit: Access, Visa, Diners, Amex.

▨ ⌸ ☎ ⏍ ⌷ ♦ 𝖎 ▽ ▥
● ⏢ ▥ ⏍ ⏍ ⌖ ⌅ ⌀ ⌸ ➴
▶ ⌸ DAP ❧ SP T

Rathlin House Hotel

▨▨

Upper Hermosa Rd., Teignmouth, TQ14 9JW
☎ (0626) 774473
Friendly family hotel with homely atmosphere and tastefully furnished for your holiday relaxation. Home cooking.
Bedrooms: 1 single, 3 double & 2 twin, 4 family rooms.
Bathrooms: 4 private, 2 public.
Bed & breakfast: £13-£16 single, £26-£32 double.
Half board: £18-£24 daily, £100-£160 weekly.
Evening meal 6.30pm (l.o. 5.30pm).
Parking for 14.
Open March-October.

▨ ♦ ✿ ♦ 𝖎 ▽ ▥ TV ▶ DAP
SP

The symbol CR and the name of a hotel group or consortium after a hotel address means that bookings can be made through a central reservations office. These are listed on page 540.

Please mention this guide when making a booking.

THURLESTONE

Devon
Map ref 1C3

Small resort of thatched cottages standing above coastal cliffs near the winding estuary of Devon's Avon. The village has a fine golf-course and a good beach.

Heron House Hotel ♨

▨▨▨▨ APPROVED

Thurlestone Sands, Kingsbridge, TQ7 3JY
☎ Kingsbridge (0548) 561308 & 561600
Superbly located at the edge of the sea, overlooking Thurlestone Rock and Bigbury Bay.
Bedrooms: 10 double & 5 twin, 3 family rooms.
Bathrooms: 18 private.
Bed & breakfast: £40-£65 single, £80-£130 double.
Half board: £48-£73 daily, £295-£436 weekly.
Evening meal 7.50pm (l.o. 8.50pm).
Parking for 50.
Open February-December.
Credit: Access, Visa.

▨ ♦ ⏍ ⌷ ♦ 𝖎 ▽ ▦
◻ ⏍ ⌖ ✺ ⌀ ▶ ✿ ⌸ ❧
SP T

TIMSBURY

Avon
Map ref 2B2

3m N. Midsomer Norton

Old Malt House Hotel ♨

▨▨▨ APPROVED

Radford, Timsbury, Bath, BA3 1QF
☎ (0761) 70106
CR Minotels
Family-run hotel and restaurant, in lovely countryside. Tastefully converted and furnished, including antiques. Ideal for touring Bath, Wells and Mendip Hills.
Bedrooms: 2 single, 4 double & 2 twin, 2 family rooms.
Bathrooms: 10 private.
Bed & breakfast: £31-£33 single, £52-£56 double.
Half board: £39-£47.50 daily, from £243.25 weekly.
Evening meal 7pm (l.o. 8.30pm).
Parking for 26.
Credit: Access, Visa, Diners, Amex.

▨3 ⌷ ☎ ⌷ ♦ 𝖎 ▽ ▥ ▦ ♦
⏍ ✿ ⤬ ⌸ SP ⏩ T

TINTAGEL

Cornwall
Map ref 1B2

Coastal village near the legendary home of King Arthur. A lofty headland with the ruin of a Norman castle and traces of a Celtic monastery still visible in the turf.

Bosayne Guest House

Atlantic Rd., Tintagel, PL34 0DE
☎ Camelford (0840) 770514
Spacious, comfortable, family-run guesthouse situated in an historic beauty spot, offering a warm welcome and personal service.
Bedrooms: 2 single, 3 double & 2 twin, 3 family rooms.
Bathrooms: 1 private, 2 public.
Bed & breakfast: £12-£14 single, £24-£28 double.
Half board: £18-£20 daily.
Evening meal 6.30pm (l.o. 8.30pm).
Parking for 8.

▨ ♦ ⌷ ♦ 𝖎 ⓊⓁ 𝖎 ▽ ▥ TV
▦ ◻ ⏍ ⌖ DAP ❧

Bossiney House Hotel ♨

▨▨▨ APPROVED

Tintagel, PL34 0AX
☎ Camelford (0840) 770240 & Fax (0840) 770501
Family-run hotel set in 2.5 acres of garden. Close to castle and overlooking the beautiful north Cornwall coast.
Bedrooms: 10 double & 7 twin, 3 family rooms.
Bathrooms: 17 private, 1 public.
Bed & breakfast: £25.50-£28 double.
Half board: £35-£38.50 daily, £234-£258 weekly.
Lunch available.
Evening meal 7pm (l.o. 10pm).
Parking for 30.
Open March-October.
Credit: Access, Visa, Diners, Amex.

▨ ♦ ⌷ ♦ 𝖎 ▽ ▥ TV ▦ ◻
⏍ ⌖ ⌀ ⌖ ✺ DAP ❧ SP T

Castle Villa

▨▨ COMMENDED

Molesworth St., Tintagel, PL34 0BZ
☎ Camelford (0840) 770373
Over 150 years old, Castle Villa is within easy walking distance of the 11th C church, post office and King Arthur's castle.
Bedrooms: 1 single, 2 double & 1 twin, 1 family room.
Bathrooms: 2 public.

Continued ▶

TINTAGEL

Continued

Bed & breakfast: £11.50-
£13.50 single, £23-£27 double.
Half board: £21-£23.50 daily,
£132.30-£148 weekly.
Evening meal 7pm (l.o.
10am).
Parking for 6.
Credit: Access, Visa.
🛇 📥 📞 🛉 📖 Ⅴ ⅄ 🖙 📺
▥ ▲ 🄺 ᴅᴀᴘ ⅏ SP

King Arthur's Castle Hotel

😑😑 APPROVED

Atlanta Rd., Tintagel,
PL34 0DQ
☎ Camelford (0840) 770202
& Fax (0840) 770978
*Located in one of the most
spectacular parts of Cornwall,
standing on very high and
rugged coastline which
commands majestic views.
Overlooks the ruins of Tintagel
Castle, the home of King
Arthur.*
Bedrooms: 12 single,
14 double & 18 twin, 6 family
rooms.
Bathrooms: 50 private,
12 public.
Bed & breakfast: from £25.85
single, from £50 double.
Half board: from £35 daily,
from £222 weekly.
Lunch available.
Evening meal 7pm (l.o.
10pm).
Parking for 106.
Open April-October.
Credit: Access, Visa.
🛇 📞 📥 🛉 📖 Ⅴ ⅄ 🖙 📺
● 📧 ▥ ▲ 🍴 🛆 ᵱ Ʊ
♪ ✳ ✕ ᴅᴀᴘ 🄺
🖐 Display advertisement
appears on page 448.

Old Malt House

😑😑 COMMENDED

Fore St., Tintagel, PL34 0DA
☎ Camelford (0840) 770461
*14th C property with
interesting features, situated in
village centre very close to the
old post office and castle.*
Bedrooms: 1 single, 5 double
& 1 twin, 1 family room.
Bathrooms: 3 private,
2 public.
Bed & breakfast: £13.50-
£14.50 single, £27-£29 double.
Half board: £21-£24 daily.
Lunch available.
Evening meal 5pm (l.o. 9pm).
Parking for 12.
Open March-October.
🛇 📥 📞 🛉 📖 ⅄ 📺 ▥ ▲
🄺

Pengenna Hotel

😑😑 COMMENDED

Fore St., Tintagel, PL34 0DD
☎ Camelford (0840) 770223
*Nearest hotel to King Arthur's
Castle. Enjoy the Pengenna
experience. Teas, luncheons
and dinners served in our
beautiful gardens. Snug bar
and old world restaurant.*
Bedrooms: 4 double & 1 twin.
Bathrooms: 2 private,
4 public.
Bed & breakfast: £32-£40
double.
Half board: £23-£27 daily.
Lunch available.
Evening meal 6pm (l.o.
9.30pm).
Parking for 10.
Open April-November.
Credit: Access, Visa.
🛇 📥 📞 🛉 📖 Ⅴ 🖙 📺 ✕
SP

Polkerr Guest House ⋒

😑😑😑 COMMENDED

Tintagel, PL34 0BY
☎ Camelford (0840) 770382
*Period country house, quality
accommodation. Home
cooking, close to village. Ideal
for touring and bathing.*
Bedrooms: 1 single, 4 double
& 1 twin, 1 family room.
Bathrooms: 5 private,
1 public.
Bed & breakfast: £12-£14
single, £24-£30 double.
Half board: £18.50-£21.50
daily.
Evening meal 6.30pm (l.o.
5.30pm).
Parking for 9.
🛇 📥 📞 🛉 Ⓤ Ⅴ 🖙 📺 ▥
▲ 🛆 ✳ ✕ 🄺 🄺

Tintagel Arms Hotel & Zorba's Tavern

😑😑 COMMENDED

Fore Street, Tintagel,
PL34 0DB
☎ (0840) 770780
*Main street position close to
Old Post Office and King
Arthur's Castle.*
Bedrooms: 7 double.
Bathrooms: 7 private.
Bed & breakfast: £40-£50
double.
Lunch available.
Evening meal 6pm (l.o.
10pm).
Parking for 10.
Credit: Access, Visa.
🄺 📥 📞 🛉 📖 Ⅴ ▥ ▲ ✕
🄺

---

*The symbols are
explained on the
flap inside the
back cover.*

Trebrea Lodge ⋒

😑😑😑 COMMENDED

Trenale, Tintagel, PL34 0HR
☎ Camelford (0840) 770410
*Grand old Cornish house set in
4 acres facing the sea. Friendly
and informal atmosphere.*
Bedrooms: 1 single, 3 double
& 3 twin.
Bathrooms: 7 private.
Bed & breakfast: £38-£50
single, £55-£80 double.
Half board: £42-£55 daily,
£270-£350 weekly.
Evening meal 8pm (l.o. 8pm).
Parking for 7.
Credit: Access, Visa, Amex.
🛇 📞 📥 📞 🛉 📖 ⅄ 🖙
▥ ▲ 🍴 Ʊ ✳ 🄺 🄺

Trewarmett Lodge Hotel and Restaurant

😑😑 COMMENDED

Trewarmett, Tintagel,
PL34 0ET
☎ Camelford (0840) 770460
*Converted from village pub to
family-run hotel and
restaurant, providing
comfortable, homely
accommodation and personal
service. Situated in a beautiful
area.*
Bedrooms: 1 single, 3 double
& 1 twin, 1 family room.
Bathrooms: 1 private,
2 public.
Bed & breakfast: £16.95-£19
single, £33-£40 double.
Half board: £27-£29.50 daily,
£149-£163 weekly.
Lunch available.
Evening meal 6.30pm (l.o.
9pm).
Parking for 10.
Open March-November.
Credit: Access, Visa.
🛇 📥 🛉 📖 Ⅴ ⅄ 🖙 📺 ▥ ▲
✳ 🄺 ᴅᴀᴘ SP 🄺 🅣

Willapark Manor Hotel ⋒

Bossiney, Tintagel,
PL34 0BA
☎ Camelford (0840) 770782
*Character house in 14 acres of
garden and woodland,
overlooking sea. Private access
to coast path and beach.
Friendly, informal atmosphere.*
Bedrooms: 2 single, 7 double
& 1 twin, 2 family rooms.
Bathrooms: 11 private,
1 public.
Bed & breakfast: £22-£24
single, £44-£48 double.
Half board: £31.50-£35 daily,
£183-£198 weekly.
Lunch available.
Evening meal 6.30pm (l.o.
7.30pm).
Parking for 20.
🛇 📥 🄺 📥 📞 🛉 Ⅴ 🖙 📺
▲ 🍴 ✳ 🄺 ᴅᴀᴘ ⅏ SP

TIVERTON

Devon
Map ref 1D2

Busy market and textile
town, settled since the
9th C, at the meeting of 2
rivers below southern
Exmoor. Town houses,
Tudor almshouses and
parts of the fine church
were built by wealthy
cloth merchants; a
medieval castle is
incorporated into a
private house and the
original building of
Blundells School is
preserved by the National
Trust.
*Tourist Information
Centre ☎ (0884) 255827*

Angel Guest House

😑😑

13 St. Peter St., Tiverton,
EX16 6NU
☎ (0884) 253392
*Licensed Georgian guesthouse
close to centre and facilities of
this historic town. Separate bar
and comfortable residents'
lounge.*
Bedrooms: 1 single, 2 double
& 1 twin, 2 family rooms.
Bathrooms: 2 public.
Bed & breakfast: £12-£13
single, £24-£26 double.
Half board: £19-£20 daily,
£125-£135 weekly.
Evening meal 6.30pm (l.o.
7pm).
Parking for 3.
🛇 📞 Ⅴ 🖙 📺 ▥ ▲ ✕
🄺 🄺

Bridge Guest House

😑😑 COMMENDED

23 Angel Hill, Tiverton,
EX16 6PE
☎ (0884) 252804
*Attractive Victorian town
house on a bank of the River
Exe, with pretty riverside tea
garden. Licensed dining room
with home-cooking.*
Bedrooms: 5 single, 2 double
& 1 twin, 2 family rooms.
Bathrooms: 4 private,
2 public.
Bed & breakfast: £16-£17.50
single, £35-£38 double.
Half board: £24-£26 daily.
Evening meal 6.30pm (l.o.
7pm).
Parking for 7.
🛇 📥 📞 📞 🛉 Ⅴ 🖙 📺 ▥
▲ ♪ 🄺 ᴅᴀᴘ SP 🄺

Tiverton Hotel ⋒

😑😑😑 COMMENDED

Blundells Rd., Tiverton,
EX16 4DB
☎ (0884) 256120 Telex 42551
EXONIAG

Modern, comfortable hotel on edge of the town in heart of beautiful River Exe Valley. Ideal base for touring West Country.
Bedrooms: 15 double & 15 twin, 45 family rooms.
Bathrooms: 75 private.
Bed & breakfast: £33-£46 single, £54-£80 double.
Lunch available.
Evening meal 6.30pm (l.o. 9.15pm).
Parking for 130.
Credit: Access, Visa, Diners, Amex.
🛇 🕭 🎧 ⌂ 🖳 🕯 📺 ⅄
🛌 ⬤ 🛎 🍴 🗲 👂 🐾 SP T
⊙ Display advertisement appears on page 449.

Display advertisement appears on page 449.

TORCROSS

Devon
Map ref 1D3

3m N. Start Point

Torcross Apartment Hotel M
♛♛♛

Torcross, Kingsbridge, TQ7 2TQ
☎ Kingsbridge (0548) 580206
At the water's edge on Slapton Sands, beautifully-appointed apartments, some ground floor. Superb sea views. Waterside restaurant and village inn serving fresh local fish.
Bedrooms: 6 twin.
Bathrooms: 6 private.
Bed & breakfast: £40-£60 double.
Lunch available.
Evening meal 7pm (l.o. 9.30pm).
Parking for 25.
Open March-November.
🛇 🕭 🖳 🕯 📺 🎧 📺 🏠 ▱
🗜 SP 🎦 T

TORMARTON

Avon
Map ref 2B2

3m SE. Chipping Sodbury

Compass Inn M
♛♛♛ COMMENDED

Tormarton, Badminton, GL9 1JB
☎ Badminton (0454) 218242 & 218577
Fax (0454) 218741
⊙ Inter
Traditional Cotswold stone inn with log fires and modern bedrooms. Hot and cold buffet and a la carte restaurant.
Bedrooms: 2 single, 11 double & 13 twin, 6 family rooms.
Bathrooms: 32 private.

Bed & breakfast: £49.95-£64.95 single, £65.50-£79.50 double.
Half board: from £48.50 daily.
Lunch available.
Evening meal 6.30pm (l.o. 10pm).
Parking for 100.
Credit: Access, Visa, Diners, Amex.
🛇 🕭 🎧 ⌂ 🖳 🕯 🖳 ⅄
🖳 🏠 🍴 🌟 SP T

TORQUAY

Devon
Map ref 1D2

Devon's grandest resort, developed from a fishing village. Smart apartments and terraces rise from the seafront and Marine Drive along the headland gives views of beaches and colourful cliffs.
Tourist Information Centre ☎ (0803) 297428

Abbey Lawn Hotel M
♛♛♛♛ COMMENDED

Scarborough Rd., Torquay, TQ2 5UQ
☎ (0803) 295791 & 299199 & Fax (0803) 291460
Telex 299670 HOLTEL G
Central yet secluded location enjoying sea views. Upgraded and completely refurbished throughout. New indoor swimming pool and leisure facilities.
Bedrooms: 9 single, 20 double & 24 twin, 11 family rooms.
Bathrooms: 56 private.
Bed & breakfast: £35-£60 single, £60-£140 double.
Lunch available.
Evening meal 7pm (l.o. 8.30pm).
Parking for 40.
Credit: Access, Visa, Diners, Amex.
🛇 🕭 🎧 ⌂ 🖳 🕯 🖳 ⅄ ▱
⬤ 🎫 🖳 🏠 🛎 🗜 🗲 🔦 🔯 ▨
🅿 🕐 🏃 🎿 🐾 DAP 🏸 SP 🎦
T

Ansteys Lea Hotel M
♛♛♛

Babbacombe Rd., Wellswood, Torquay, TQ1 2QJ
☎ (0803) 294843
Gracious Victorian hotel, set in own landscaped gardens, three-quarters of a mile from Torquay harbour and 10 minutes' walk from beach.
Bedrooms: 4 single, 8 double & 3 twin, 6 family rooms.
Bathrooms: 21 private.
Bed & breakfast: £20-£27 single, £40-£54 double.

Half board: £26-£33 daily, £151-£224 weekly.
Lunch available.
Evening meal 6.30pm (l.o. 8pm).
Parking for 18.
Open February-November.
Credit: Access, Visa.
🛇 🕭 🖳 🕯 🖳 🕯 🔯 ▱
🖳 🏠 🛎 🗜 🌟 🔦 DAP 🏸 SP T

Bahamas Hotel
♛♛

17 Avenue Rd., Torquay, TQ2 5LB
☎ (0803) 296005
Family hotel with emphasis on food and service. 5 minutes from the sea and English Riviera centre. All en-suite rooms.
Bedrooms: 1 single, 3 double & 6 twin, 2 family rooms.
Bathrooms: 12 private.
Bed & breakfast: £19-£22 single, £38-£44 double.
Half board: £25-£28 daily, £169-£189 weekly.
Evening meal 6pm (l.o. 6pm).
Parking for 14.
Credit: Access, Visa.
🛇 🕭 🖳 🕯 🕯 🖳 📺 ▱
🍴 🏸 SP

Hotel Balmoral M
♛♛♛

Meadfoot Sea Rd., Torquay, TQ1 2LQ
☎ (0803) 293381
Uniquely situated, licensed hotel in own grounds overlooking Meadfoot beach, within easy reach of Torquay harbour and shops.
Bedrooms: 3 single, 11 double & 4 twin, 6 family rooms.
Bathrooms: 24 private.
Bed & breakfast: from £22 single, from £44 double.
Half board: from £28.50 daily, from £168 weekly.
Lunch available.
Evening meal 6.45pm (l.o. 8.30pm).
Parking for 18.
Credit: Access, Visa, Amex.
🛇 🕭 🎧 ⌂ 🖳 🕯 🖳 ▱
🖳 🏠 🍴 🗜 🔦 SP T

Barn Hayes Country Hotel M
♛♛♛ COMMENDED

Brim Hill, Maidencombe, Torquay, TQ1 4TR
☎ (0803) 327980
Country hotel in unique Devon coastal hamlet overlooking Lyme Bay. Family suites in delightful gardens with swimming pool.
Bedrooms: 3 single, 4 double & 1 twin, 5 family rooms.
Bathrooms: 8 private, 2 public.

Bed & breakfast: £21-£24 single, £38-£44 double.
Half board: £29-£32 daily, £196-£217 weekly.
Lunch available.
Evening meal 6.30pm (l.o. 7.30pm).
Parking for 15.
Open February-December.
Credit: Access, Visa.
🛇 ⌂ 🕯 🖳 🖳 📺 🖳
🍴 🗜 🔦 🌟 🔯 🛌 🏸 SP

Beau Vista Guest House
♛

14 Ash Hill Rd., Torquay, TQ1 3HZ
☎ (0803) 297202
Centrally situated in quiet road near town centre, entertainment and coach station. Sea views and ample parking.
Bedrooms: 4 family rooms.
Bathrooms: 2 private, 1 public.
Bed & breakfast: £20-£36 double.
Half board: £14-£22 daily, £85-£120 weekly.
Evening meal 6pm (l.o. 6pm).
Parking for 4.
🛇 🕭 UL 🕯 🖳 ⅄ ▱
🛫 🔯 DAP SP

Beauly Guest House M
♛ COMMENDED

503 Babbacombe Rd., Torquay, TQ1 1HL
☎ (0803) 296993
Warm hospitality, providing quality and value. 600 yards from harbour and amenities. Short breaks welcome.
Bedrooms: 2 twin, 3 family rooms.
Bathrooms: 5 private.
Bed & breakfast: £15-£20 single, £30-£40 double.
🛇 🕭 🎧 🖳 🕯 UL 🕯 🖳
📺 🖳 🏠 DAP 🏸 SP

Belmont Hotel M
♛♛♛

66 Belgrave Rd., Torquay, TQ2 5HY
☎ (0803) 295028
Fully refurbished, family-run hotel, central for all amenities, conference and leisure facilities. Our reputation is your guarantee.
Bedrooms: 2 single, 3 double & 4 twin, 4 family rooms.
Bathrooms: 9 private, 1 public.
Bed & breakfast: £12-£20 single, £24-£40 double.
Half board: £18.50-£27 daily, £98-£165 weekly.
Evening meal 6pm (l.o. 5pm).
Parking for 4.
Credit: Access, Visa.
🛇 🕭 🎧 ⌂ 🖳 🕯 UL 🕯 🖳
🖳 📺 🏠 DAP 🏸 SP

The Berberry Hotel
🏵🏵🏵 COMMENDED
64 Bampfylde Rd., Torquay,
TQ1 5AY
☎ (0803) 297494
*Delightful, detached family-run
hotel with chef/proprietor. In
level position close to seafront
and conference centre.*
Bedrooms: 1 single, 5 double
& 2 twin, 2 family rooms.
Bathrooms: 10 private.
Bed & breakfast: £19-£24
single, £38-£48 double.
Half board: £29 daily,
£164.50-£196 weekly.
Evening meal 6pm (l.o. 7pm).
Parking for 11.
Open January-November.
Credit: Access, Visa.
🛇8🕭🛆🖵♦🛈🖼🖵📺🆚🛆
🍴🗙 ᴼᴬᴾ SP T

Bowden Close Hotel ᴹ
🏵🏵🏵
Teignmouth Rd.,
Maidencombe, Torquay,
TQ1 4TJ
☎ (0803) 328029
*Licensed Victorian country
house hotel in tranquil setting,
with panoramic sea/coastal
views. Family-run. Varied
menus. Large car park.*
Bedrooms: 3 single, 11 double
& 5 twin.
Bathrooms: 15 private,
1 public.
Bed & breakfast: £20.50-£23
single, £41-£46 double.
Half board: £27.50-£33 daily,
£178.50-£210 weekly.
Lunch available.
Evening meal 6.30pm (l.o.
8pm).
Parking for 32.
Credit: Access, Visa, Amex.
🛇♦🛆🖵♦🛈🆚🖵📺🖽
🛆🍴🕸 SP T

Braddon Hall Hotel
🏵🏵
70 Braddons Hill Road East,
Torquay, TQ1 1HF
☎ (0803) 293908
*Delightful detached hotel of
character and charm, close to
harbour. Friendly relaxed
atmosphere, varied menus.*
Bedrooms: 1 single, 9 double
& 1 twin, 1 family room.
Bathrooms: 12 private,
1 public.
Bed & breakfast: £18-£20
single, £36-£40 double.
Half board: £23-£25 daily,
£145-£170 weekly.

Evening meal 6.30pm (l.o.
6.30pm).
Parking for 9.
Credit: Access, Visa.
🛇5🖽🛆🖵♦🛈🆚🖼🖽
🛆🍴🗙 ᴼᴬᴾ 🕸 SP 🎞

Brocklehurst Hotel
🏵🏵🏵
Rathmore Rd., Torquay,
TQ2 6NZ
☎ (0803) 292735
*Situated in parkland, a few
minutes' level walk from
seafront, English Riviera
Conference Centre and
gardens. French/German
spoken.*
Bedrooms: 1 single, 3 double
& 3 twin, 3 family rooms.
Bathrooms: 7 private,
2 public.
Bed & breakfast: £13-£18
single, £26-£40 double.
Half board: £20-£29 daily,
£140-£213 weekly.
Evening meal 6.30pm (l.o.
7pm).
Parking for 9.
Open March-November.
Credit: Access, Visa.
🛇🖽🛆🖵♦🛈🆚🖼📺
🖽🛆🍴🖽 ᴼᴬᴾ SP

Bute Court Hotel ᴹ
🏵🏵🏵 COMMENDED
Belgrave Rd., Torquay,
TQ2 5HQ
☎ (0803) 213055
Ⓜ Minotels
*Family-run hotel overlooking
Torbay and adjoining English
Riviera Centre. Large lounges
and bar. 5-course choice menu.*
Bedrooms: 10 single,
13 double & 14 twin, 11 family
rooms.
Bathrooms: 44 private,
4 public.
Bed & breakfast: £19-£33
single, £36-£58 double.
Half board: £24-£38 daily,
£160-£235 weekly.
Lunch available.
Evening meal 6.30pm (l.o.
8pm).
Parking for 38.
Credit: Access, Visa, C.Bl.,
Diners, Amex.
🛇🛆🕭🛈🖵♦🛈🆚🖽
📺🎞🖼🛆🍴🛆🕭🔍
🕸🕸 SP 🖽 🎞

Chester Court Hotel
30 Cleveland Rd., Torquay,
TQ2 5BE
☎ (0803) 294565
*Small family-run hotel. Ample
parking, colour TVs, free baby
sitting. Level walk to English
Rivera Centre and seafront.*
Bedrooms: 3 single, 3 double
& 1 twin, 4 family rooms.
Bathrooms: 8 private,
2 public.

Bed & breakfast: £13-£17
single, £24-£32 double.
Half board: £17-£21 daily,
£99-£126 weekly.
Evening meal 6pm (l.o.
6.30pm).
Parking for 11.
🛇🛆🖵♦🛈🆚🖼
🖽🛆🕸🗙 ᴼᴬᴾ SP T

Chesterfield Hotel
🏵🏵
62 Belgrave Rd., Torquay,
TQ2 5HY
☎ (0803) 292318
*Family-run hotel in the centre
of Torquay 500 yards from
beach, gardens and town
centre. 300 yards from
conference/leisure centre.*
Bedrooms: 4 double & 2 twin,
4 family rooms.
Bathrooms: 7 private,
2 public.
Bed & breakfast: £12-£19
single, £22-£38 double.
Half board: £18-£25 daily,
£95-£165 weekly.
Evening meal 6pm (l.o. 4pm).
Parking for 3.
Credit: Access, Visa.
🛇🛆🕭🖵♦🛈🆚📺
🔵🖽🛆🕭 ᴼᴬᴾ SP

Claver Guest House
119 Abbey Rd., Torquay,
TQ2 5NP
☎ (0803) 297118
*A warm welcome awaits you.
Close to beach, harbour and all
entertainments. Home-cooked
food – you'll never leave the
table hungry!*
Bedrooms: 2 single, 2 double
& 1 twin, 3 family rooms.
Bathrooms: 2 public.
Bed & breakfast: £12.50-£15
single, £25-£30 double.
Half board: £18.50-£21 daily,
£110-£129.50 weekly.
Evening meal 6pm (l.o. 6pm).
Parking for 4.
🛇🛆🖵🛈🆚🖼📺🖽🗙
ᴼᴬᴾ SP

Clovelly Guest House
🏵
91 Avenue Rd., Torquay,
TQ2 5LH
☎ (0803) 292286
*Semi-detached property of
Victorian construction, on level
main road to beach.*
Bedrooms: 1 single, 2 double
& 1 twin, 2 family rooms.
Bathrooms: 1 public;
1 private shower.
Bed & breakfast: £10-£12
single, £20-£24 double.
Half board: £15.50-£18.50
daily, £105-£126 weekly.
Evening meal 6pm (l.o. 7pm).
Parking for 4.
Credit: Visa.
🛇🖽🖵♦🖵🆚🛈🆚🖼📺
🖽🛆 ᴼᴬᴾ 🕸 SP T

Colindale Hotel
20 Rathmore Rd., Chelston,
Torquay, TQ2 6NY
☎ Chelston (0803) 293947
*Lovely, quiet position, opposite
park and 300 yards level walk
to main beach. Good food.*
Bedrooms: 1 single, 3 double,
4 family rooms.
Bathrooms: 2 private,
2 public.
Bed & breakfast: £13-£15
single, £26-£34 double.
Half board: £19-£24 daily,
£123-£151 weekly.
Evening meal 6.30pm.
Parking for 6.
Open March-November.
🛇5♦🛈🆚🖼📺🗙🖽 ᴼᴬᴾ

County Hotel
52/54 Belgrave Rd., Torquay,
TQ2 5HS
☎ (0803) 294452
*Family hotel with a friendly
atmosphere and home cooking,
500 yards from beach, town
centre and railway station.*
Bedrooms: 4 single, 7 double
& 11 twin, 5 family rooms.
Bathrooms: 18 private,
3 public; 1 private shower.
Bed & breakfast: £15-£18
single, £30-£36 double.
Half board: £21-£25 daily,
£120-£145 weekly.
Lunch available.
Evening meal 6.30pm.
Parking for 7.
Credit: Access, Visa, Amex.
🛇🛆🕭🕭🕭🖵♦🛈🆚🔍
🖽📺🖽🖽 ᴼᴬᴾ 🕸 SP T

Craig Court Hotel
🏵🏵 APPROVED
10 Ash Hill Rd., Torquay,
TQ1 3HZ
☎ (0803) 294400
*Small hotel situated a short
distance from the town centre
and the harbour. Quiet location
with a lovely garden and choice
of menus.*
Bedrooms: 2 single, 4 double
& 2 twin, 2 family rooms.
Bathrooms: 5 private,
3 public.
Bed & breakfast: £15-£21
single, £30-£42 double.
Half board: £20.50-£28 daily,
£143.50-£182 weekly.
Evening meal 6pm (l.o. 9am).
Parking for 10.
Open April-October.
🛇🛆♦🛈🆚🖽📺🛆🗙
🖽 SP 🖽

Cranmore Guest House
🏵🏵🏵 APPROVED
89 Avenue Rd., Torquay,
TQ2 5LH
☎ (0803) 298488

Friendly, family-run, small hotel offering home cooking. No restrictions, close to all amenities.
Bedrooms: 2 single, 3 double & 1 twin, 2 family rooms.
Bathrooms: 4 private, 1 public.
Bed & breakfast: £11-£13 single, £22-£30 double.
Half board: £16.50-£20.50 daily, £115.50-£143.50 weekly.
Evening meal 6pm (l.o. 6.30pm).
Parking for 4.
Credit: Access, Visa, Amex.

Crofton House Hotel

Croft Rd, Torquay, TQ2 5TZ
☎ (0803) 293761
Elegant Edwardian hotel set in sun trap gardens with swimming pool. Superb level location. Jacuzzi, sauna, solarium, entertainment.
Bedrooms: 3 single, 16 double & 9 twin, 11 family rooms.
Bathrooms: 33 private, 2 public.
Bed & breakfast: £25-£35 single, £46-£70 double.
Half board: £27-£39 daily, £155-£240 weekly.
Lunch available.
Evening meal 6.45pm (l.o. 8pm).
Parking for 13.
Credit: Access, Visa.

Ellington Court Hotel
[APPROVED]

St. Lukes Rd. South, Torquay, TQ2 5NZ
☎ (0803) 294957 & Fax (0803) 201383
Licensed hotel in own grounds with sea views. Centrally situated and convenient for beach, shops, harbour, and leisure centre.
Bedrooms: 6 double & 2 twin, 4 family rooms.
Bathrooms: 12 private, 2 public.
Bed & breakfast: £20-£25 single, £40-£50 double.
Half board: £55-£65 daily, £150-£190 weekly.
Evening meal 6pm (l.o. 7pm).
Parking for 12.

Everglades Hotel
[APPROVED]

32 St. Marychurch Rd., Torquay, TQ1 3HY
☎ (0803) 295389

Detached hotel with own secluded garden, south-facing and within easy reach of beaches and main shopping area.
Bedrooms: 1 single, 5 double & 1 twin, 4 family rooms.
Bathrooms: 11 private.
Bed & breakfast: £18.50-£21.50 single, £37-£43 double.
Half board: £26-£29 daily, £175-£196 weekly.
Lunch available.
Evening meal 6pm (l.o. 8.30pm).
Parking for 11.
Credit: Access, Amex.

Exmouth View Hotel

St. Albans Rd., Babbacombe, Torquay, TQ1 3LJ
☎ (0803) 327307/329967
Private family-run hotel 50 yards from seafront, offering dancing, entertainment and a friendly atmosphere. Close to all amenities.
Bedrooms: 6 single, 13 double & 5 twin, 6 family rooms.
Bathrooms: 19 private, 2 public.
Bed & breakfast: £13-£26.50 single, £26-£53 double.
Half board: £15.90-£31 daily, £101.50-£210 weekly.
Evening meal 6.30pm.
Parking for 24.
Credit: Access, Visa.

Fairmount House Hotel
[COMMENDED]

Herbert Rd., Chelston, Torquay, TQ2 6RW
☎ (0803) 605446
Small hotel offering real home cooking and high quality accommodation. Peaceful setting near Cockington village. Dogs welcome.
Bedrooms: 2 single, 3 double & 1 twin, 2 family rooms.
Bathrooms: 8 private, 2 public.
Bed & breakfast: £23.50-£26.50 single, £47-£53 double.
Half board: £34-£37 daily, £225-£246 weekly.
Lunch available.
Evening meal 6.30pm (l.o. 7.30pm).
Parking for 8.
Open March-October.
Credit: Access, Visa, Amex.

Hotel Fiesta

50 St. Marychurch Rd., Torquay, TQ1 3JE
☎ (0803) 292388

Elegant Georgian hotel in its own spacious grounds, within easy reach of the town, beaches and entertainment.
Bedrooms: 1 single, 4 double & 1 twin, 3 family rooms.
Bathrooms: 3 private, 3 public.
Bed & breakfast: £13-£16 single, £26-£32 double.
Half board: £18-£21 daily, £98-£118 weekly.
Evening meal 6pm (l.o. 6pm).
Parking for 10.
Open April-October.
Credit: Access, Visa.

Hotel Fluela
[APPROVED]

15/17 Hatfield Rd., Torquay, TQ1 3BW
☎ (0803) 297512
Detached family-run hotel with friendly atmosphere and home-cooked food. Centrally located with private car park.
Bedrooms: 9 double & 1 twin, 3 family rooms.
Bathrooms: 13 private, 1 public.
Bed & breakfast: £34-£45 double.
Half board: £125-£187 weekly.
Evening meal 6.30pm (l.o. 7.30pm).
Parking for 18.
Credit: Access, Visa.

Frognel Hall

Higher Woodfield Rd., Torquay, TQ1 2LD
☎ (0803) 298339
Beautiful listed mansion in 2 acres of secluded grounds, offering a country house setting right in the heart of Torquay. Careful refurbishment, together with the addition of leisure facilities, have enhanced Frognel.
Bedrooms: 3 single, 8 double & 7 twin, 10 family rooms.
Bathrooms: 26 private, 1 public.
Bed & breakfast: £17.50-£26.50 single.
Half board: £25-£35 daily, £115-£185 weekly.
Lunch available.
Evening meal 7pm (l.o. 7.30pm).
Parking for 20.
Open March-November, December.
Credit: Access, Visa.

Gleneagles Hotel ♏
[APPROVED]

Asheldon Rd., Wellswood, Torquay, TQ1 2QS
☎ (0803) 293637/297011 & Fax (0803) 295106
Modern hotel overlooking Ansteys Cove. There is a path through the grounds to the beach. Pool, jacuzzi, solarium and entertainment provided.
Bedrooms: 8 single, 21 double & 9 twin, 6 family rooms.
Bathrooms: 44 private.
Bed & breakfast: £26.67-£38.97 single, £53.34-£77.94 double.
Half board: £35.90-£46.15 daily, £215.40-£271.80 weekly.
Evening meal 7pm (l.o. 8.30pm).
Parking for 40.
Credit: Access, Visa, Diners, Amex.

⊕ Display advertisement appears on page 448.

Hantwell Guest House
[Listed]

487 Babbacombe Rd., Torquay, TQ1 1HL
☎ (0803) 293990
A warm welcome awaits you. 700 yards from harbour and all amenities. Cleanliness assured. Food and hygiene certificate.
Bedrooms: 1 single, 4 family rooms.
Bathrooms: 1 public.
Bed & breakfast: £13-£16 single, £26-£32 double.
Half board: £18-£21 daily, £85-£130 weekly.
Evening meal 6pm (l.o. 6pm).

Hylton Court Hotel

109 Abbey Rd., Torquay, TQ2 5NP
☎ (0803) 294464/298643
Centrally situated, within walking distance of beach and shopping centre. Friendly and informal atmosphere. Ample parking.
Bedrooms: 4 single, 13 double & 9 twin, 2 family rooms.
Bathrooms: 11 private, 5 public.
Bed & breakfast: from £15 single, from £30 double.
Half board: from £20 daily, from £140 weekly.
Evening meal 6pm (l.o. 7pm).
Parking for 30.
Credit: Visa.

Jesmond Dene Hotel
⚜⚜

85 Abbey Rd., Torquay,
TQ2 5NN
☎ (0803) 293062
Friendly family hotel with personal service and no restrictions. Ideally central for seafront, shops and entertainments.
Bedrooms: 4 single, 4 double, 3 family rooms.
Bathrooms: 2 public.
Bed & breakfast: £12-£15 single, £24-£30 double.
Half board: £16.50-£19.50 daily, £82-£100 weekly.
Evening meal 6pm (l.o. 9am).
Parking for 3.

Kistor Hotel
⚜⚜⚜⚜

Belgrave Rd., Torquay,
TQ2 5HF
☎ (0803) 212632 & Fax
(0803) 293219
Located 120 metres from seafront between marina and conference centre. Free use of indoor pool, spa pool and sauna.
Bedrooms: 6 single, 25 double & 14 twin, 14 family rooms.
Bathrooms: 59 private.
Bed & breakfast: £29-£39.90 single, £58-£79.80 double.
Half board: £35.50-£46.50 daily, £279-£296 weekly.
Lunch available.
Evening meal 7pm (l.o. 8.30pm).
Parking for 45.
Credit: Access, Visa, Diners, Amex.

Lincombe Hall Hotel
Meadfoot Rd., Torquay,
TQ1 2JX
☎ Torquay (0803) 213361 &
Fax (0803) 211485
A delightful Georgian house built in 1822, set in over 4 acres of gardens and with all facilities. Various diets available including diabetic and vegetarian.
Bedrooms: 1 single, 23 double & 10 twin, 9 family rooms.
Bathrooms: 43 private.
Bed & breakfast: £30.45-£40 single, £60.90-£80 double.
Half board: £40.95-£48.30 daily, £205.80-£287.80 weekly.
Lunch available.

Evening meal 7pm (l.o. 8.30pm).
Parking for 60.
Credit: Access, Visa, Diners, Amex.

Lindon House Hotel
⚜⚜ **APPROVED**

97 Braddons Hill Road East,
Torquay, TQ1 1HF
☎ (0803) 292074 & Fax
(0803) 292074
Relax in the homely atmosphere of this small licensed hotel, near harbour and seafront. Good home cooking. Short breaks available.
Bedrooms: 4 double & 2 twin, 1 family room.
Bathrooms: 2 public.
Bed & breakfast: £15.50-£19.50 single, £27-£35 double.
Half board: £20.50-£24.50 daily, £133-£160 weekly.
Lunch available.
Evening meal 6.30pm (l.o. 7pm).
Credit: Access, Visa.

Livermead Cliff Hotel ⋏
⚜⚜⚜⚜ **COMMENDED**

Sea Front, Torquay,
TQ2 6RQ
☎ (0803) 299666 & Fax
(0803) 294496
Ⓖ Best Western
Situated at the water's edge in a secluded garden, with magnificent views over Torbay. Family owned and run. 950 yards from English Riviera Centre, 1 mile from town centre and shops. Ample parking.
Bedrooms: 12 single, 8 double & 22 twin, 22 family rooms.
Bathrooms: 64 private, 1 public.
Bed & breakfast: £32-£52.50 single, £60-£99 double.
Half board: £38.50-£63 daily, £259-£399 weekly.
Lunch available.
Evening meal 7pm (l.o. 8.30pm).
Parking for 77.
Credit: Access, Visa, Diners, Amex.

Manor House Hotel
Old Mill Rd., Seaway Lane,
Torquay, TQ2 6PS
☎ (0803) 605164 & Fax
(0803) 606841 Telex 94017169

Licensed hotel with good facilities, including a games room, heated indoor swimming pool and sauna, mini-bar, satellite television, snooker room.
Bedrooms: 1 single, 12 double & 4 twin, 7 family rooms.
Bathrooms: 24 private, 2 public.
Bed & breakfast: £28.50-£54 single, £57-£90 double.
Half board: £40-£55 daily, £231-£320 weekly.
Lunch available.
Evening meal 7pm (l.o. 9.30pm).
Parking for 40.
Credit: Access, Visa, C.Bl., Diners, Amex.

Maple Lodge
⚜⚜ **COMMENDED**

36 Ash Hill Rd., Torquay,
TQ1 3JD
☎ (0803) 297391
Detached guesthouse with beautiful views. Relaxed atmosphere, home cooking, en-suite and shower rooms. Centrally situated for town and beaches.
Bedrooms: 1 single, 3 double & 1 twin, 2 family rooms.
Bathrooms: 1 private, 1 public; 2 private showers.
Bed & breakfast: from £12.50 single, from £25 double.
Half board: from £17 daily.
Evening meal 6pm (l.o. 10am).
Parking for 5.
Open April-October.

Millbrook House Hotel
⚜⚜⚜ **COMMENDED**

Old Mill Rd., Chelston,
Torquay, TQ2 6AP
☎ (0803) 297394
Small, elegant hotel noted for comfort and food. Level walk to seafront, Abbey Gardens. Cellar bar, games room, mini-gym.
Bedrooms: 2 single, 4 double & 3 twin.
Bathrooms: 8 private; 1 private shower.
Bed & breakfast: £17.50-£19.50 single, £35-£45 double.
Half board: £26-£32 daily, from £175 weekly.
Evening meal 7pm (l.o. 8pm).
Parking for 12.
Credit: Access, Visa.

Mount Edgcombe Hotel
23 Avenue Rd., Torquay,
TQ2 5LB
☎ (0803) 292310
Detached, family-run hotel, providing good food, bar, TV lounge. Level walk to seafront, gardens, theatre and shops.
Bedrooms: 1 single, 8 double & 1 twin, 4 family rooms.
Bathrooms: 6 private, 2 public.
Bed & breakfast: £15-£19 single, £30-£38 double.
Half board: £22-£26 daily, £147-£175 weekly.
Evening meal 6.45pm (l.o. 7.15pm).
Parking for 12.
Credit: Access, Visa.

New Sefton Hotel
⚜⚜⚜

Babbacombe Downs Rd.,
Babbacombe, Torquay,
TQ1 3LH
☎ (0803) 328728/326591
Level location offering superb panoramic seaviews. Ideal for bowls, tennis, golf, fishing and local attractions. Games room. Short mat indoor bowling (by arrangement).
Bedrooms: 11 single, 11 double & 15 twin, 10 family rooms.
Bathrooms: 47 private.
Bed & breakfast: £35-£42 single, £70-£84 double.
Half board: £44-£51 daily, £301-£350 weekly.
Lunch available.
Evening meal 6.30pm (l.o. 9pm).
Parking for 47.
Credit: Access, Visa, Amex.

Norcliffe Hotel
⚜⚜⚜

Sea Front, Babbacombe
Downs, Torquay, TQ1 3LF
☎ (0803) 328456
Traditional family hotel in a seafront corner position, close to beaches, shops and golf-course.
Bedrooms: 3 single, 7 double & 6 twin, 4 family rooms.
Bathrooms: 19 private, 2 public.
Bed & breakfast: £15-£25 single, £30-£50 double.
Half board: £24-£34 daily, £168-£238 weekly.
Lunch available.
Evening meal 6.30pm (l.o. 7.30pm).
Parking for 16.
Credit: Visa.

Olivia Court Hotel
❦❦❦

Braddons Hill Rd., Torquay,
TQ1 1HD
☎ (0803) 292595
*Quiet villa in a select part of
Torquay and within easy
walking distance of harbour
and all entertainments.
Vegetarian cooking and special
diets.*
Bedrooms: 1 single, 8 double
& 5 twin, 2 family rooms.
Bathrooms: 9 private,
2 public.
Bed & breakfast: £17.50-
£21.50 single, £35-£43 double.
Half board: £25.50-£29.50
daily, £151-£180 weekly.
Evening meal 6.30pm (l.o.
7pm).
Parking for 4.
Open February-December.
Credit: Access, Visa, Amex.

Osborne Hotel ⋒
❦❦❦❦ COMMENDED

Hesketh Cres., Meadfoot
Beach, Torquay, TQ1 2LL
☎ (0803) 213311
Fax (0803) 296788
*Magnificent Regency crescent
set in over 5 acres of private
gardens sweeping down to
Meadfoot Beach. Indoor and
outdoor pool. Acclaimed
restaurant.*
Bedrooms: 10 double &
11 twin, 2 family rooms.
Bathrooms: 23 private.
Bed & breakfast: £54-£67
single, £108-£134 double.
Half board: £61-£81 daily,
£363-£488 weekly.
Lunch available.
Evening meal 7pm (l.o.
10pm).
Parking for 75.
Credit: Access, Visa.

Penney's Folley Hotel
Listed APPROVED

20 Vicarage Rd., Chelston,
Torquay, TQ2 6HX
☎ (0803) 607503
*Semi-detatched Victorian hotel
with old world restaurant.
Overlooking church and village
green. TV in bedrooms on
request and room service.*
Bedrooms: 2 single, 4 double
& 1 twin, 3 family rooms.
Bathrooms: 6 private,
1 public.
Bed & breakfast: £15 single,
£30-£35 double.
Half board: £20-£25 daily,
£126-£140 weekly.

Evening meal 6.30pm (l.o.
7.30pm).
Parking for 8.

Red House Hotel ⋒
❦❦❦ COMMENDED

Rousdown Rd., Torquay,
TQ2 6PB
☎ (0803) 607811
*Newly-built hotel with free use
of keep-fit facilities, heated
indoor pool, sauna, spa bath.
Self-catering apartments
adjoining.*
Bedrooms: 1 single, 4 double
& 2 twin, 3 family rooms.
Bathrooms: 10 private.
Bed & breakfast: £22.45-£43
single, £35.80-£61 double.
Half board: £25-£35 daily,
£157.50-£228 weekly.
Evening meal 6.30pm (l.o.
8pm).
Parking for 12.
Credit: Access, Visa.

Sandhurst Hotel
❦❦

8 Manor Rd., Babbacombe,
Torquay, TQ1 3XJ
☎ (0803) 329722
*Situated close to the sea and
within easy reach of all
amenities.*
Bedrooms: 1 single, 9 double
& 3 twin, 3 family rooms.
Bathrooms: 12 private,
4 public.
Bed & breakfast: £14-£17
single, £28-£34 double.
Half board: £18-£21 daily,
£112-£126 weekly.
Evening meal 6pm (l.o. 6pm).
Parking for 20.
Open May-October.

Sevens Hotel ⋒
❦❦

27 Morgan Ave., Torquay,
TQ2 5RR
☎ (0803) 293523
*On a quiet avenue central to all
attractions. Large bar and
games room.*
Bedrooms: 3 single, 6 double
& 2 twin, 3 family rooms.
Bathrooms: 4 private,
3 public.
Bed & breakfast: £14.35-
£17.45 single, £26.65-£32.80
double.
Half board: £17.45-£20.50
daily, £112.75-£138.37
weekly.
Evening meal 6pm (l.o. 6pm).
Parking for 10.

Shedden Hall Hotel ⋒
❦❦❦

Shedden Hill, Torquay,
TQ2 5TY
☎ (0803) 292964
*Family-run hotel with
magnificent views of Torquay
and seafront. Town, theatre
and leisure centre all within
easy walking distance.*
Bedrooms: 1 single, 14 double
& 8 twin, 4 family rooms.
Bathrooms: 25 private,
1 public.
Bed & breakfast: £21-£36
single, £46-£56 double.
Half board: £29-£44 daily,
£209-£246 weekly.
Lunch available.
Evening meal 6.30pm (l.o.
8pm).
Parking for 30.
Credit: Access, Visa, Diners,
Amex.

Shirley Hotel ⋒
❦❦❦

Braddons Hill Rd. East,
Torquay, TQ1 1HF
☎ Torquay (0803) 293016
*Friendly family-run licensed
hotel close to harbour, shops
and entertainment. Swimming
pool, jacuzzi and sauna.*
Bedrooms: 2 single, 8 double
& 2 twin, 2 family rooms.
Bathrooms: 11 private,
2 public; 1 private showers.
Bed & breakfast: £14-£20
single, £28-£44 double.
Half board: £20.50-£26.50
daily, £136-£190 weekly.
Lunch available.
Evening meal 6pm (l.o. 4pm).
Parking for 6.
Credit: Access, Visa.

The Skerries Hotel
❦❦

25 Morgan Ave., Torquay,
TQ2 5RR
☎ (0803) 293618
*Small family hotel with
resident proprietors. Close to a
small park and only a short
walk from the town and beach.*
Bedrooms: 2 single, 5 double
& 2 twin, 3 family rooms.
Bathrooms: 3 private,
2 public.
Bed & breakfast: £12-£16
single, £24-£30 double.
Half board: £17-£20 daily,
£110-£129.50 weekly.
Evening meal 6pm (l.o.
10am).
Parking for 7.

Sunleigh Hotel
❦❦❦

Livermead Hill, Torquay,
TQ2 6QY
☎ (0803) 607137
*Standing in own grounds
overlooking bay, 3 minutes
from Livermead beach. Short
walk to Cockington Village
and central for touring.*
Bedrooms: 2 single, 11 double
& 6 twin, 3 family rooms.
Bathrooms: 20 private,
1 public.
Bed & breakfast: £20-£25.50
single, £40-£51 double.
Half board: £24-£29.50 daily,
£153-£197 weekly.
Evening meal 6pm (l.o. 7pm).
Parking for 17.
Open March-November.

Templestowe Hotel ⋒
❦❦❦

2-6 Tor Church Rd.,
Torquay, TQ2 5UU
☎ (0803) 299499
*Family-owned hotel in central
position offering traditional
English food with choice of
menu. Personal service and
friendly atmosphere.*
Bedrooms: 18 single,
19 double & 22 twin,
28 family rooms.
Bathrooms: 87 private,
2 public.
Bed & breakfast: £27-£43
single, £54-£86 double.
Half board: £30.25-£46.20
daily, £189-£290 weekly.
Evening meal 7pm (l.o.
8.30pm).
Parking for 50.
Credit: Access, Visa.

Torbay Rise Hotel
❦❦

Old Mill Rd., Torquay,
TQ2 6HL
☎ (0803) 605541
*Licensed hotel in own grounds,
close to beaches and shops.
Some rooms have sea views.*
Bedrooms: 2 single, 10 double
& 1 twin, 2 family rooms.
Bathrooms: 14 private,
1 public.
Bed & breakfast: £17-£23
single, £32-£44 double.
Half board: £21-£27 daily,
£142-£184 weekly.
Evening meal 6.30pm (l.o.
midday).
Parking for 10.
Open April-October.
Credit: Access, Visa.

437

Torquays Travellers Rest

19 Torquay Rd.,
Kingskerswell, Newton
Abbot, TQ12 5HH
☎ (0803) 873143
*Large modern detached
guesthouse on A380 on the
outskirts of Torquay. In-room
facilities. Good food. Pub
adjacent.*
Bedrooms: 1 single, 7 double
& 2 twin, 3 family rooms.
Bathrooms: 3 public.
Bed & breakfast: £12-£14
single, £24-£28 double.
Evening meal 6pm (l.o. 7pm).
Parking for 12.
Credit: Access, Visa.

Tower Hall Hotel

Solsbro Rd., Torquay,
TQ2 6PF
☎ (0803) 605292
*Licensed hotel with relaxed,
welcoming atmosphere, set in
peaceful area yet close to
beach and leisure/conference
centre.*
Bedrooms: 3 single, 6 double
& 3 twin, 3 family rooms.
Bathrooms: 1 private,
3 public; 3 private showers.
Bed & breakfast: £12.50-
£16.50 single, £25-£33 double.
Half board: £20-£24 daily,
£135-£160 weekly.
Evening meal 6.30pm (l.o.
7.30pm).
Parking for 10.

Treander Guest House

10 Morgan Av., Torquay,
TQ2 5RS
☎ (0803) 296906
*Ideally situated for all
amenities. Open all year. Free
car park. Tea making facilities
in all bedrooms. Colour TV.
Comfort given high priority.*
Bedrooms: 1 single, 1 double
& 1 twin, 3 family rooms.
Bathrooms: 2 public.
Bed & breakfast: £11.50-
£13.50 single, £23-£27 double.
Half board: £15.50-£20.50
daily, £92-£102 weekly.
Evening meal 6pm (l.o.
6.30pm).
Parking for 4.

Trees Hotel

Bronshill Rd., Torquay,
TQ1 3HA
☎ (0803) 326073

---

*Secluded small hotel with
licensed bar, Devonshire
cooking and relaxing gardens
with ample parking. Non-
smokers only please.*
Bedrooms: 1 single, 3 double
& 1 twin, 2 family rooms.
Bathrooms: 6 private,
1 public.
Bed & breakfast: £15-£22
single, £30-£44 double.
Half board: £18-£56 daily,
£126-£186 weekly.
Evening meal 6pm (l.o. 1pm).
Parking for 8.
Credit: Visa.

Westwood Hotel M
☞☞☞ APPROVED
111 Abbey Rd., Torquay,
TQ2 5NP
☎ (0803) 293818
*A lovely detached licensed
hotel, with parking and
secluded garden. Situated in
town centre with easy access to
all amenities.*
Bedrooms: 2 single, 12 double
& 8 twin, 4 family rooms.
Bathrooms: 26 private.
Bed & breakfast: £15-£18
single, £28-£32 double.
Half board: £20-£25 daily,
£135-£165 weekly.
Evening meal 6pm (l.o. 7pm).
Parking for 12.
Credit: Access.

Perched high above the
River Torridge, with a
charming market square,
Georgian Town Hall and a
museum. The famous
Dartington Crystal
Factory, Rosemoor
Gardens and Plough Arts
Centre are all located in
the town.

Beaford House Hotel

Beaford, Winkleigh,
EX19 8AB
☎ (080 53) 305 & 330
*Beautiful country hotel
overlooking the River Torridge
and 5 miles SE of Torrington.
Home cooked meals and
friendly warm atmosphere.
Ideal for a peaceful break.
Heated pool, tennis, golf and
riding.*
Bedrooms: 4 double & 1 twin,
4 family rooms.
Bathrooms: 7 private,
2 public.
Bed & breakfast: £21-£26
single, £42-£52 double.

Half board: £30-£36 daily,
from £130 weekly.
Lunch available.
Evening meal 7pm (l.o.
7.30pm).
Parking for 40.

Old market town steeply
built near the head of the
Dart Estuary. Remains of
medieval gateways, a
noble church, 16th C
Guildhall and medley of
period houses recall
former wealth from cloth
and shipping, continued
in rural and water
industries.
*Tourist Information
Centre ☎ (0803) 863168*

Lyssers
☞☞☞ COMMENDED
4 Chapel La., Bridgetown,
Totnes, TQ9 5AF
☎ (0803) 866513
Fax (0803) 865156
*Converted barn with a wealth
of beams. Central for town.
High level of personal service.
Well known for sea food.*
Bedrooms: 1 single, 3 double
& 2 twin, 1 family room.
Bathrooms: 5 private,
1 public.
Bed & breakfast: £25-£30
single, £40-£45 double.
Half board: £30-£55 daily.
Evening meal 6.30pm (l.o.
9pm).
Parking for 18.
Credit: Access, Visa.

The Old Forge at Totnes M
☞☞ COMMENDED
Seymour Place, Totnes,
TQ9 5AY
☎ (0803) 862174
*All modern comforts in a
delightful 600-year-old stone
building, with beautiful walled
garden, cobbled driveway and
fully operational smithy
workshop. Weekly and off-
season discount.*
Bedrooms: 3 double & 2 twin,
5 family rooms.
Bathrooms: 6 private,
1 public.
Bed & breakfast: from £30
single, £35-£50 double.
Parking for 10.
Credit: Access, Visa.

Royal Seven Stars Hotel M
☞☞☞ APPROVED
The Plains, Totnes,
TQ9 5DD
☎ (0803) 862125 & 863241 &
Fax (0803) 867925
*Old coaching inn in the centre
of Totnes, near River Dart.
Short drive to coast and
Dartmoor. Brochures available
on request.*
Bedrooms: 1 single, 11 double
& 3 twin, 1 family room.
Bathrooms: 12 private,
4 public.
Bed & breakfast: £39-£49
single, £50-£70 double.
Half board: £40-£50 daily,
£240-£300 weekly.
Lunch available.
Evening meal 7pm (l.o.
9.30pm).
Parking for 20.
Credit: Access, Visa, Diners.

Sea Trout Inn
☞☞☞ COMMENDED
Staverton, Totnes, TQ9 6PA
☎ (080 426) 274
*Delightful beamed country inn,
in attractive village by the
River Dart, offering food and
friendly atmosphere. Good base
for walking and touring
Dartmoor and South Devon.*
Bedrooms: 6 double & 3 twin,
1 family room.
Bathrooms: 10 private.
Bed & breakfast: £36-£40
single, £43-£52 double.
Half board: £34-£38 daily,
£230-£250 weekly.
Lunch available.
Evening meal 7pm (l.o. 10pm).
Parking for 50.
Credit: Access, Visa.

Coimbatore Hotel
☞☞ APPROVED
West View, Trevone Bay,
Padstow, PL28 8RD
☎ Padstow (0841) 520390
*Private hotel standing in
spacious, enclosed garden, 150
yards from beach. Home
cooking stylishly presented.
Comfortable family rooms and
lounges. Bar snack lunches
available.*
Bedrooms: 2 single, 3 double
& 2 twin, 3 family rooms.
Bathrooms: 10 private.
Bed & breakfast: £17.50
single, £35 double.
Half board: £27 daily, £189
weekly.

Evening meal 6.30pm (l.o. 6.30pm).
Parking for 12.
Credit: Access, Visa.
🛏 ♨ ♥ 🛆 📺 🖃 📺 🖼 ♨
SP

Trevone Bay Hotel
♨♨ COMMENDED

Trevone Bay, Padstow,
PL28 8QS
☎ (0841) 520243
Hotel to suit all ages, with panoramic views, coastal walks and a sandy beach nearby. Home cooking, choice of menu, 3 lounges and a bar.
Bedrooms: 3 single, 4 double & 3 twin, 3 family rooms.
Bathrooms: 13 private.
Bed & breakfast: £20-£27 single, £36-£50 double.
Half board: £25-£34 daily, £145-£190 weekly.
Lunch available.
Evening meal 7pm (l.o. 7.30pm).
Parking for 12.
Open April-October.
Credit: Access, Visa.
🛏 ♥ 🛆 📺 🖃 📺 🖼 SP

TREYARNON BAY
Cornwall
Map ref 1B2

4m W. Padstow

Waterbeach Hotel M
♨♨♨ APPROVED

Treyarnon Bay, Padstow,
PL28 8JW
☎ (0841) 520292
Designed to take advantage of the sunshine and views across the Atlantic. Accommodates 30 people in comfort.
Bedrooms: 4 single, 4 double & 5 twin, 7 family rooms.
Bathrooms: 14 private, 2 public.
Half board: £31-£39 daily, £199-£260 weekly.
Evening meal 7.30pm (l.o. 8.15pm).
Parking for 25.
Open March-October.
Credit: Access, Visa, Amex.
🛏 ♨ ♥ ☏ 🖵 ♥ 🛆 📺 📺 🔠 🛆 ♿ ♨ ♣ ✳ ⚓ T

TROON
Cornwall
Map ref 1B3

Sea View Farm
♨

Croft Mitchell, Troon,
Camborne, TR14 9JH
☎ Praze (0209) 831260
Family-run guesthouse, 1 mile past the village of Troon. Many major resorts within easy reach.

Bedrooms: 3 double & 1 twin, 2 family rooms.
Bathrooms: 3 public.
Bed & breakfast: £12-£15 single, £24-£30 double.
Half board: £20-£23 daily, £131-£146 weekly.
Evening meal 6pm (l.o. 7pm).
Parking for 8.
Open January-November.
🛏 ♥ UL 🛆 📺 🛆 ⚓ 🖼 OAP SP

TROWBRIDGE
Wiltshire
Map ref 2B2

Wiltshire's administrative centre, a handsome market and manufacturing town with a wealth of merchants' houses and other Georgian buildings.
Tourist Information Centre ☎ *(0225) 777054*

Brookfield House
♨♨ COMMENDED

Vaggs Hill, Southwick,
Trowbridge, BA14 9NA
☎ (0373) 830615
120-acre dairy farm. Barn converted in 1989, in completely rural location on boundary between Somerset and Wiltshire. South-facing aspects. Farm is 100 yards away.
Bedrooms: 2 double & 1 twin.
Bathrooms: 2 public.
Bed & breakfast: £12-£20 single, £28-£36 double.
Parking for 10.
🛏 🖵 🛆 UL 🖃 ♥ 📺 ● 🔠 🛆 ♺ ♣ ✳ ⚓ SP

Hilbury Court Hotel
♨♨♨

Hilperton Rd., Trowbridge,
BA14 7JW
☎ (0225) 752949
Set in its own grounds, and conveniently situated for business people and tourists alike.
Bedrooms: 3 single, 2 double & 7 twin, 1 family room.
Bathrooms: 7 private, 1 public; 3 private showers.
Bed & breakfast: £34-£42 single, £46-£56 double.
Half board: £45-£53 daily, £315-£371 weekly.
Evening meal 6.30pm (l.o. 6.30pm).
Parking for 20.
Credit: Access, Visa.
🛏 ♥ ☏ 🖵 ♥ 🛆 📺 🖃 📺 🔠 🛆 ♣ ✳ ⚓ 🖼

Old Manor Hotel
♨♨♨

Trowle, Trowbridge,
BA14 9BL
☎ (0225) 777393 & Fax
(0225) 765443
Quiet hotel set around old manor house with most rooms on ground floor. Antiques, pine, distinctive beds, en-suite rooms. Licensed residents' restaurant. Parking.
Bedrooms: 1 single, 8 double & 5 twin.
Bathrooms: 14 private.
Bed & breakfast: £40-£44 single, £52-£56 double.
Lunch available.
Evening meal 6.30pm (l.o. 8pm).
Parking for 20.
Credit: Access, Visa, Diners, Amex.
🛏 ♨ 🖫 ☏ ☏ 🖵 🛆 🛆 V 🖃 🛆 ♣ 🛆 ✳ ⚓ SP 🖼 T

TRURO
Cornwall
Map ref 1B3

Cornwall's administrative centre and cathedral city, set at the head of Truro River on the Fal Estuary. A medieval stannary town, it handled mineral ore from West Cornwall; fine Georgian buildings recall its heyday as a society haunt in the second mining boom.
Tourist Information Centre ☎ *(0872) 74555*

The Bay Tree Guest House
28 Ferris Town, Truro,
TR1 3JM
☎ (0872) 40274
Georgian house, within minutes' level walk of the city centre, near railway station. Beautifully decorated, with friendly and warm atmosphere awaiting.
Bedrooms: 2 single, 2 double.
Bathrooms: 2 public.
Bed & breakfast: £15 single, £30 double.
Half board: £23.50 daily.
Evening meal available.
🛏 ♨ 🖵 ♥ UL V ✂ 🛆 ⚓ 🖼

Marcorrie Hotel M
20 Falmouth Rd., Truro,
TR1 2HX
☎ (0872) 77374 & Fax
(0872) 41666
Family-run hotel close to the city centre. Ideal for business or holiday, central for touring Cornwall.

Bedrooms: 3 single, 3 double & 2 twin, 4 family rooms.
Bathrooms: 8 private, 1 public; 2 private showers.
Bed & breakfast: £18-£30 single, £35-£40 double.
Half board: £25-£38 daily, £175-£252 weekly.
Evening meal 7pm (l.o. 5pm).
Parking for 16.
Credit: Access, Visa, Amex.
🛏 ♨ ♥ 🖵 ♥ 🛆 V 🖃 📺 🔠 🛆 ✳ ⚓ 🖼 T

Rock Cottage Guest House
♨♨♨ COMMENDED

Blackwater, Truro, TR4 8EU
☎ Truro (0872) 560252
18th C beamed cottage, old world charm. Haven for non-smokers. Warm, friendly hospitality, personal service. Informal atmosphere. Farmland views.
Bedrooms: 2 double & 1 twin.
Bathrooms: 3 private.
Bed & breakfast: £20-£40 single, £34-£40 double.
Half board: £28-£48 daily.
Lunch available.
Evening meal 6pm (l.o. 3pm).
Parking for 4.
🛏 ♥ UL 🛆 ✂ ♥ 📺 🔠 🛆 ♺ ✳ ⚓ OAP SP

TWO BRIDGES
Devon
Map ref 1C2

8m E. Tavistock
Dartmoor hamlet on the banks of the West Dart River, at the heart of the moor.

Prince Hall Hotel M
♨♨♨♨ COMMENDED

Two Bridges, Yelverton,
PL20 6SA
☎ (082 289) 403/404 & Fax
(082 289) 676
Small friendly country house hotel set in the heart of Dartmoor. French owner/chef. Ideal for walking, riding and fishing.
Bedrooms: 1 single, 2 double & 3 twin, 2 family rooms.
Bathrooms: 8 private.
Bed & breakfast: £29.50-£34.50 single, £55-£69 double.
Half board: £42.50-£44.50 daily, £262.50-£276.50 weekly.
Evening meal 7.30pm (l.o. 8.30pm).
Parking for 15.
Credit: Access, Visa, Diners, Amex.
🛏 🖫 ♥ 🖵 🛆 V 🖃 🔠 🛆 ♺ ♣ ➤ ♣ ⚓ SP 🖼

439

TWO BRIDGES
Continued

Two Bridges Hotel ♨
♔♔♔ APPROVED
Two Bridges, Yelverton,
PL20 6SW
☎ (082 289) 581 & Fax
(082 289) 575
℗ Consort
18th C inn fronting river, with log fires, good food, wine and ales. Ideal for walking, riding, fishing and golf. In middle of Dartmoor.
Bedrooms: 1 single, 13 double & 8 twin, 2 family rooms.
Bathrooms: 20 private,
4 public.
Bed & breakfast: £23.50-£40 single, £40-£80 double.
Half board: £35.50-£52 daily.
Lunch available.
Evening meal 6pm (l.o 9pm).
Parking for 120.
Credit: Access, Visa, Diners, Amex.

WADEBRIDGE
Cornwall
Map ref 1B2

Old market town with Cornwall's finest medieval bridge, spanning the Camel at its highest navigable point. Twice-widened, the bridge is said to have been built on woolpacks sunk in the unstable sands of the river bed.

Hendra Country Guest House ♨
♔♔♔ COMMENDED
St. Kew Highway,
Wadebridge, Bodmin,
PL30 3EQ
☎ St. Mabyn (020 884) 343
Quiet secluded guesthouse in rural tranquillity, 2.5 miles north east of Wadebridge, half a mile from A39. Varied menu. Open all year.
Bedrooms: 1 single, 2 double & 1 twin, 1 family room.
Bathrooms: 4 private;
1 private shower.
Bed & breakfast: £17-£22.50 single, £34-£45 double.
Half board: £29.50-£35 daily, £193-£228 weekly.
Evening meal 7.30pm (l.o 6pm).
Parking for 8.

WARMINSTER
Wiltshire
Map ref 2B2

Attractive stone-built town high up to the west of Salisbury Plain. A market town, it originally thrived on cloth and wheat. Many prehistoric camps and barrows nearby, along with Longleat House and Safari Park.
Tourist Information Centre ☎ (0985) 218548

Old Bell Hotel ♨
♔♔♔
Market Pl., Warminster,
BA12 9AN
☎ (0985) 216611 & Fax
(0985) 217111
14th C inn with comfortable accommodation, close to Longleat, Stonehenge, Bath and Salisbury. Home-made bar snacks, cold table and restaurant.
Bedrooms: 3 single, 11 double & 4 twin, 2 family rooms.
Bathrooms: 14 private,
2 public.
Bed & breakfast: £39-£48 single, £54-£62 double.
Lunch available.
Evening meal 6pm (l.o. 10.30pm).
Parking for 20.
Credit: Access, Visa, Diners, Amex.

WATERGATE BAY
Cornwall
Map ref 1B2

Beautiful long board-riders' beach backed by tall cliffs, north-west of Newquay. A small holiday village nestles in a steep river valley making a cleft in the cliffs.

Tregurrian Hotel ♨
♔♔♔
Watergate Bay, Newquay,
TR8 4AB
☎ St. Mawgan (0637) 860280
On coast road between Newquay and Padstow, just 100 yards from golden sandy beach in an area reputed to have some of the finest beaches and coastline in Europe.
Bedrooms: 4 single, 11 double & 4 twin, 8 family rooms.
Bathrooms: 22 private,
2 public.
Bed & breakfast: £18-£30 single, £36-£56 double.

Half board: £26-£36 daily, £124-£222 weekly.
Lunch available.
Evening meal 6.45pm (l.o. 7.30pm).
Parking for 25.
Open April-October.
Credit: Access, Visa.

Watergate Bay Hotel ♨
♔♔♔
Watergate Bay, Newquay,
TR9 6DU
☎ St. Mawgan (0637) 860543
Family hotel beside own sandy beach with indoor and outdoor facilities and entertainments for all ages. All-weather sports hall.
Bedrooms: 8 single,
24 double, 25 family rooms.
Bathrooms: 53 private,
4 public.
Half board: £28-£40 daily, £140-£320 weekly.
Lunch available.
Evening meal 7pm (l.o. 8.30pm).
Parking for 80.
Open March-November.
Credit: Access, Visa.

WELLS
Somerset
Map ref 2A2

Small city set beneath the southern slopes of the Mendips, dominated by its magnificent cathedral. Built between 1180 and 1424, the cathedral is preserved in much of its original glory and with its ancient precincts forms one of our loveliest and most unified groups of medieval buildings.
Tourist Information Centre ☎ (0749) 72552

Ancient Gate House Hotel & Rugantino Restaurant ♨
20 Sadler St., Wells,
BA5 2RR
☎ (0749) 72029
14th C gatehouse overlooking cathedral. Interesting hotel with Italian restaurant, friendly atmosphere. 1 mile from Wells Golf Club.
Bedrooms: 5 double & 3 twin, 1 family room.
Bathrooms: 6 private,
1 public.
Bed & breakfast: £35-£40 single, £45-£50 double.

Half board: £36.50-£45.50 daily.
Lunch available.
Evening meal 7pm (l.o. 10.30pm).
Credit: Access, Visa, Diners, Amex.

Bekynton House
♔♔ APPROVED
7 St. Thomas St., Wells,
BA5 2UU
☎ (0749) 672222
Well-appointed, family-run guesthouse close to cathedral, Bishop's Palace. All bedrooms with colour TV, some en-suite. Non-smokers only please.
Bedrooms: 1 single, 4 double & 2 twin, 2 family rooms.
Bathrooms: 3 private,
3 public.
Bed & breakfast: £19-£25 single, £34-£42 double.
Parking for 7.
Credit: Access, Visa.

Charlton House Hotel ♨
♔♔♔ COMMENDED
Charlton Rd., Shepton Mallet,
BA4 4PR
☎ (0749) 342008
17th C country house hotel, in 7 acres of gardens with river.
Bedrooms: 2 single, 12 double & 3 twin, 2 family rooms.
Bathrooms: 19 private,
2 public.
Bed & breakfast: £65-£105 single, £95-£125 double.
Lunch available.
Evening meal 7pm (l.o. 9.30pm).
Parking for 50.
Credit: Access, Visa, Diners, Amex.

Tor Guest House
20 Tor St., Wells, BA5 2US
☎ (0749) 672322
Historic, sympathetically restored 17th C building in delightful grounds overlooking the cathedral. Attractive, comfortable, warm bedrooms. 3 minutes' walk to town centre.
Bedrooms: 1 single, 2 double & 2 twin, 1 family rooms.
Bathrooms: 2 private,
2 public.
Bed & breakfast: £16-£25 single, £32-£42 double.
Half board: £30-£35 daily, £200-£220 weekly.
Lunch available.

Evening meal 6.30pm (l.o.
10am).
Parking for 11.

Worth House Hotel ⋀
☺☺☺ APPROVED
Worth, Wells, BA5 1LW
☎ (0749) 72041
*Imposing house, parts of which
are 400 years old, set in quiet
valley with uninterrupted views
of Mendip Hills.*
Bedrooms: 1 single, 2 double
& 3 twin, 2 family rooms.
Bathrooms: 8 private.
Bed & breakfast: £28-£35
single, £56-£70 double.
Half board: £42-£50 daily,
£252-£300 weekly.
Lunch available.
Evening meal 7pm (l.o.
8.30pm).
Parking for 20.
Credit: Access, Visa.

3m NW. Abbotsbury

Manor Hotel ⋀
☺☺☺☺ COMMENDED
West Bexington, Dorchester,
DT2 9DF
☎ Burton Bradstock
(0308) 897616 & (0308) 897785
*16th C manor house, 500 yards
from Chesil Beach. Panoramic
views from most bedrooms.
3 real ales and character cellar
bar.*
Bedrooms: 2 single, 8 double
& 3 twin, 1 family room.
Bathrooms: 13 private.
Bed & breakfast: £39.50-£45
single, £65-£75 double.
Half board: £49-£59 daily,
£301-£325 weekly.
Lunch available.
Evening meal 7pm (l.o.
10pm).
Parking for 20.
Credit: Access, Visa, Amex.

Four Acres Hotel ⋀
☺☺☺☺ APPROVED
West Coker, Yeovil,
BA22 9AJ
☎ (093 586) 2555 & Fax
(093 586) 3929 Telex 46666
☺ Consort
*Charming, comfortable,
elegantly furnished Victorian
house with modern extension,
in its own grounds and gardens
in a quiet village outside
Yeovil.*
Bedrooms: 8 single, 12 double
& 4 twin.
Bathrooms: 24 private.
Bed & breakfast: £45-£64
single, £55-£75 double.
Half board: £57-£76 daily,
£350-£495 weekly.
Lunch available.
Evening meal 7pm (l.o.
9.45pm).
Parking for 45.
Credit: Access, Visa, Diners,
Amex.

4m NW. Braunton

The Long House
☺☺☺ COMMENDED
The Square, West Down,
EX34 8NF
☎ (0271) 863242
*Country cottage hotel in a tiny
North Devon village. 4
enchanting en-suite bedrooms.
Inspired home cooking and
intriguing wines.*
Bedrooms: 3 double & 1 twin.
Bathrooms: 4 private.
Bed & breakfast: max. £47
double.
Half board: max. £35 daily,
max. £227.50 weekly.
Lunch available.
Evening meal 7.30pm (l.o.
8.15pm).
Parking for 6.
Open March-November.
Credit: Access.

Large, friendly resort
developed in the 19th C.
Traditional seaside
attractions include
theatres and a dance hall.
The museum shows a
Victorian seaside gallery
and has Iron Age finds
from a hill fort on
Worlebury Hill in Weston
Woods.
*Tourist Information
Centre* ☎ (0934) 626838

Arosfa Hotel
☺☺☺
Lower Church Rd., Weston-
super-Mare, BS23 2AG
☎ (0934) 419523 & Fax
(0934) 636084
☺ Consort
*Recently refurbished hotel with
3 lounges, bars, dining room
and comfortable bedrooms.
Situated on level ground 100
yards from the town centre and
seafront.*
Bedrooms: 15 single,
12 double & 15 twin, 5 family
rooms.
Bathrooms: 45 private,
1 public.
Bed & breakfast: £40-£45
single, £55-£60 double.
Half board: from £238
weekly.
Lunch available.
Evening meal 7pm (l.o.
8.30pm).
Parking for 6.
Credit: Access, Visa, Diners,
Amex.

Bay Hotel
Seafront, 60 Knightstone
Rd., Weston-super-Mare,
BS23 2BE
☎ (0934) 624137
*Small comfortable hotel with
relaxed friendly atmosphere,
ideally located on the seafront
with magnificent sea views and
close to all amenities.*
Bedrooms: 2 single, 3 double
& 4 twin.
Bathrooms: 9 private.
Bed & breakfast: £27-£30
single, £49-£54 double.
Half board: £34.50-£37 daily,
£205.30-£220 weekly.
Lunch available.
Evening meal 6.30pm (l.o.
7.30pm).
Parking for 8.
Credit: Access, Visa, Amex.

Baymead Hotel
☺☺
19/23 Longton Grove Rd.,
Weston-super-Mare,
BS23 1LS
☎ (0934) 622951
*Central, level and quiet
location, 500 yards from
seafront. Privately owned by
Cutler family since 1965.
Comfortable en-suite rooms
with TV, tea/coffee making.*
Bedrooms: 10 single, 6 double
& 14 twin, 3 family rooms.
Bathrooms: 30 private,
3 public.
Bed & breakfast: £15-£22
single, £30-£40 double.
Half board: £20-£26 daily,
£123-£160 weekly.
Evening meal 6.15pm (l.o.
6.45pm).

Beachlands Hotel ⋀
☺☺☺☺ APPROVED
17 Uphill Rd. North.,
Weston-super-Mare,
BS23 4NG
☎ (0934) 621401 &
(0934) 621966
*On the level, overlooking
Weston Golf Course and 300
yards from beach. Individually
designed bedrooms.*
Bedrooms: 6 single, 2 double
& 5 twin, 5 family rooms.
Bathrooms: 18 private,
1 public.
Bed & breakfast: £28.50-
£33.50 single, £57-£67 double.
Half board: £38.75-£43.75
daily, £224.50-£259.50 weekly.
Lunch available.
Evening meal 6.45pm (l.o.
8.30pm).
Parking for 15.
Credit: Access, Visa, Diners,
Amex.

Berni Royal Hotel ⋀
South Parade, Weston-super-
Mare, BS23 1JN
☎ (0934) 623601 & Fax
(0934) 415135
*One of Weston's oldest hotels,
built in 1810. Yards from the
high street, with views over
large lawns and seafront. Well
appointed, with an air of
Georgian elegance. Ground
floor beautifully refurbished
recently.*
Bedrooms: 11 single,
22 double & 4 twin.
Bathrooms: 37 private.
Bed & breakfast: £51-£62
single, £73 double.
Lunch available.

Continued ▶

Evening meal 6pm (l.o. 10.30pm).
Parking for 150.
Credit: Access, Visa, Diners, Amex.

Braeside Guest House M
COMMENDED
2 Victoria Pk., Weston-super-Mare, BS23 2HZ
☎ (0934) 626642
Delightful, family-run hotel, ideally situated near seafront. Price includes colour TV and tea/coffee making facilities.
Bedrooms: 1 single, 5 double & 1 twin, 2 family rooms.
Bathrooms: 9 private.
Bed & breakfast: £20.50-£22.50 single, £41-£45 double.
Half board: £28-£30 daily, £168-£189 weekly.
Lunch available.
Evening meal 6.30pm (l.o. 6pm).

Commodore Hotel M
COMMENDED
Sand Bay, Kewstoke, Weston-super-Mare, BS22 9UZ
☎ (0934) 415778
Fax (0934) 636438
Traditional hotel facilities with popular restaurant, lounge bar and buffet services. Situated in unspoilt bay close to major resort amenities.
Bedrooms: 3 single, 11 double & 2 twin, 2 family rooms.
Bathrooms: 16 private, 3 public.
Bed & breakfast: £46.25-£50 single, £60-£65 double.
Half board: £41-£61 daily, £248-£344 weekly.
Lunch available.
Evening meal 6.30pm (l.o. 9.30pm).
Parking for 80.
Credit: Access, Visa, Diners, Amex.

Crescent Hotel
9/11 Claremont Cres., Weston-super-Mare, BS23 2EE
☎ (0934) 621212
Family owned and managed hotel, patio for guests' use overlooking Weston Bay. Lift to all floors. Fully licensed.

Bedrooms: 6 single, 10 double & 15 twin, 2 family rooms.
Bathrooms: 26 private, 2 public.
Bed & breakfast: £21.60-£23.60 single, £43.20-£47.20 double.
Half board: £26-£28 daily, £136.25-£163 weekly.
Evening meal 6.30pm (l.o. 6.30pm).
Open May-September.
Credit: Access, Visa.

Daunceys Hotel
APPROVED
11/14 Claremont Cres., Weston-super-Mare, BS23 2EE
☎ (0934) 621144
Family-run hotel, directly overlooking the sea. Garden for guests' enjoyment. Two lifts to all floors. Fully licensed.
Bedrooms: 17 single, 11 double & 17 twin, 5 family rooms.
Bathrooms: 47 private, 3 public.
Bed & breakfast: £28.50-£29.50 single, £57-£59 double.
Half board: £35.50-£36 daily, £194-£220 weekly.
Lunch available.
Evening meal 6.30pm (l.o. 6.45pm).
Credit: Access, Visa.

Dorville Hotel
Madeira Rd., Weston-super-Mare, BS23 3EX
☎ (0934) 621522 & 621139
Free house, friendly family hotel. Period rooms. Quiet position overlooking the sea. 2 bars, terrace lounge. Established over 60 years.
Bedrooms: 10 single, 21 double & 8 twin, 2 family rooms.
Bathrooms: 27 private, 6 public.
Bed & breakfast: £21-£26.50 single, £42-£48 double.
Half board: £25.95-£28.50 daily, £129.95-£169.50 weekly.
Lunch available.
Evening meal 6pm (l.o. 7.30pm).
Parking for 14.
Open April-November.

Four Seasons Guest House
103 Locking Rd., Weston-super-Mare, BS23 3EW
☎ (0934) 631124

All ages are welcome at this friendly, family-run guesthouse only 10 minutes' level walk from beach and shops. "Bring your own wine" scheme with evening meals.
Bedrooms: 1 single, 2 double, 4 family rooms.
Bathrooms: 2 public.
Bed & breakfast: £10.50-£12 single, £21-£24 double.
Half board: £16.50-£18 daily, £105-£110 weekly.
Evening meal 6pm (l.o. 6pm).
Parking for 3.

Moorlands M
APPROVED
Hutton, Weston-super-Mare, BS24 9QH
☎ Bleadon (0934) 812283
Family-run 18th C house in mature landscaped grounds. Caring, traditional cooking. Log fires. Pony rides for children.
Bedrooms: 2 single, 2 double, 4 family rooms.
Bathrooms: 4 private, 2 public.
Bed & breakfast: £16-£17 single, £32-£34 double.
Half board: £24-£25 daily, £144-£150 weekly.
Evening meal 6.30pm (l.o. 5pm).
Parking for 8.
Credit: Amex.

Newton House
COMMENDED
79 Locking Rd., Weston-super-Mare, BS23 3DW
☎ (0934) 629331
Friendly, licensed accommodation. En-suites available, satellite TV and tea facilities in all rooms. Some four-poster beds. Car park.
Bedrooms: 2 single, 2 double, 4 family rooms.
Bathrooms: 5 private, 1 public.
Bed & breakfast: £15.50-£18 single, £31-£36 double.
Half board: £22-£25.50 daily.
Lunch available.
Evening meal 6pm (l.o. 2pm).
Parking for 9.
Credit: Access, Visa, Diners, Amex.

Royal Pier Hotel
Birnbeck Rd., Weston-super-Mare, BS23 2EJ
☎ (0934) 626644
Best Western

Situated on the water's edge overlooking Weston Bay. Refurbished throughout to high standards, complementing food and service. Free parking.
Bedrooms: 5 single, 8 double & 21 twin, 6 family rooms.
Bathrooms: 38 private, 3 public.
Bed & breakfast: £48-£64 single, £69-£75 double.
Half board: £48-£58 daily, £265-£295 weekly.
Lunch available.
Evening meal 7pm (l.o. 9.15pm).
Parking for 70.
Credit: Access, Visa, Diners, Amex.

Rozel Hotel M
Madeira Cove, Weston-super-Mare, BS23 2BU
☎ (0934) 415268 & Fax (0934) 415268
Inter
Elegant Victorian building sympathetically modernised, offering well-furnished lounges, fully-equipped bedrooms and a friendly relaxed atmosphere.
Bedrooms: 8 single, 12 double & 10 twin, 14 family rooms.
Bathrooms: 44 private, 2 public.
Bed & breakfast: £47-£58 single, £70-£90 double.
Half board: £55-£60 daily.
Lunch available.
Evening meal 7pm (l.o. 8.30pm).
Parking for 70.
Credit: Access, Visa, Diners, Amex.

Saxonia
APPROVED
95 Locking Rd., Weston-super-Mare, BS23 3EW
☎ (0934) 633856
Friendly family-run licensed guesthouse near beach, 15 minutes from Tropicana Leisure Centre. En-suite rooms. Shower, hair-dryer and colour TV in all rooms. Stair-lift.
Bedrooms: 2 single, 2 double & 1 twin, 3 family rooms.
Bathrooms: 5 private; 3 private showers.
Bed & breakfast: £14.50-£20 single, £19-£40 double.
Half board: £21-£27 daily.

Evening meal 6.30pm (l.o.
midday).
Parking for 4.
Credit: Access, Visa.

Tralee Hotel M

32/34 Birnbeck Rd., Weston-
super-Mare, BS23 2BX
☎ (0934) 626707
*Detached, licensed, seafront
hotel with views across Weston
Bay. Lift available. Easy level
walk to all main amenities.*
Bedrooms: 8 single, 14 double
& 11 twin, 4 family rooms.
Bathrooms: 12 private,
4 public.
Bed & breakfast: £13.50-
£16.50 single, £25-£32 double.
Half board: £17.50-£21.50
daily, £105-£120 weekly.
Lunch available.
Evening meal 6pm (l.o. 6pm).
Parking for 11.
Open April-October.

Weston Bay Hotel

2 Clevedon Rd., Weston-
super-Mare, BS23 1DG
☎ (0934) 628903
*Centrally located on seafront
opposite Tropicana leisure
complex and overlooking the
sea. A warm welcome awaits in
this family-run hotel.*
Bedrooms: 1 single, 2 double
& 1 twin, 3 family rooms.
Bathrooms: 6 private,
1 public.
Bed & breakfast: from £15
single, from £30 double.
Half board: from £20 daily,
from £120 weekly.
Parking for 12.
Open April-October.

WESTWARD HO!

Devon
Map ref 1C1

Small resort, whose name
comes from the title of
Charles Kingsley's
famous novel, on
Barnstaple Bay, close to
the Taw and Torridge
Estuary. There are good
sands and a notable golf-
course - one of the oldest
in Britain.

Buckleigh Lodge

135 Bay View Rd., Westward
Ho!, Bideford, EX39 1BJ
☎ Bideford (0237) 475988

*Fine late Victorian house in
own grounds, with magnificent
views over the bay and close to
a large, safe sandy beach.*
Bedrooms: 1 single, 2 double
& 2 twin, 1 family room.
Bathrooms: 3 private,
2 public.
Bed & breakfast: £14.50-£17
single, £29-£34 double.
Half board: £21.50-£24 daily.
Evening meal 7pm (l.o. 5pm).
Parking for 7.

Culloden House Hotel

Fosketh Hill, Westward Ho!,
Bideford, EX39 1JA
☎ Bideford (0237) 479421
*Carefully converted Victorian
house with sea views. Golf-
course nearby.*
Bedrooms: 7 twin, 2 family
rooms.
Bathrooms: 7 private,
1 public.
Bed & breakfast: £22-£32
single, £44-£50 double.
Half board: £35-£47 daily,
£250-£325 weekly.
Lunch available.
Evening meal 7.30pm (l.o.
9.30pm).
Parking for 9.
Open March-October.
Credit: Access, Visa, Diners,
Amex.

WEYMOUTH

Dorset
Map ref 2B3

Ancient port and one of
the south's earliest
resorts. Curving beside a
long, sandy beach, the
elegant Georgian
esplanade is graced with
a statue of George III and
a cheerful Victorian
Jubilee clock tower.
*Tourist Information
Centre ☎ (0305) 772444*

Cumberland Hotel

95 Esplanade, Weymouth,
DT4 7BA
☎ (0305) 785644
*Centre of Weymouth Bay,
close to all amenities, rail and
bus stations.*
Bedrooms: 6 double & 1 twin,
5 family rooms.
Bathrooms: 12 private.
Bed & breakfast: £22.50-£25
single, £38-£45 double.
Half board: £25-£28 daily,
£138-£168 weekly.

Evening meal 6pm (l.o.
6.30pm).
Parking for 2.

Double Delight Licensed Hotel

87 Dorchester Rd.,
Weymouth, DT4 7JY
☎ (0305) 782113/834018
*Licensed hotel near seafront
and centre. Offering English
bed and breakfast and Chinese
evening meals. Non-residents
welcome.*
Bedrooms: 4 double & 1 twin,
2 family rooms.
Bathrooms: 3 public.
Bed & breakfast: £20-£25
single, £30-£35 double.
Evening meal 6pm (l.o.
10.30pm).
Open April-October.

Florian Guest House

59 Abbotsbury Rd.,
Westham, Weymouth,
DT4 0AQ
☎ (0305) 773836
*Semi-detached guesthouse on
main road leading to seafront
and town.*
Bedrooms: 1 single, 3 double
& 2 twin.
Bathrooms: 6 private.
Bed & breakfast: £15-£17
single, £30-£34 double.
Half board: £19-£21 daily,
£95-£130 weekly.
Evening meal 5.45pm (l.o.
4.30pm).
Parking for 7.

Hazeldene Guest House

Listed

16 Abbotsbury Rd.,
Weymouth, DT4 0AE
☎ (0305) 782579
*Small, comfortable guesthouse,
catering for 20 people. Short
walk to main amenities of
Weymouth.*
Bedrooms: 1 single, 2 double
& 1 twin, 4 family rooms.
Bathrooms: 3 public.
Bed & breakfast: £13-£15
single, £26-£30 double.
Half board: £16-£18 daily,
£85-£132 weekly.
Evening meal 6pm (l.o. 2pm).
Parking for 8.

Kings Acre Hotel

140 The Esplanade,
Weymouth, DT4 7NH
☎ (0305) 782534

*Comfortable, seafront hotel
with superb views. Ideally
situated, close to all amenities.*
Bedrooms: 1 single, 5 double
& 1 twin, 6 family rooms.
Bathrooms: 5 private,
2 public; 1 private shower.
Bed & breakfast: £16-£25
single, £30-£38 double.
Half board: £20-£30 daily,
£115-£169 weekly.
Evening meal 6pm (l.o. 3pm).
Parking for 9.
Open January-November.
Credit: Access, Visa.

Moonfleet Manor M

Fleet Rd., Weymouth,
DT3 4ED
☎ (0305) 786948 & Fax
(0305) 774395
*Family activity holiday hotel in
open countryside overlooking
English Channel. Facilities
usually associated with a
country club, including 4 rink
bowls hall.*
Bedrooms: 3 single, 19 double
& 6 twin, 9 family rooms.
Bathrooms: 37 private.
Bed & breakfast: £34-£44
single, £68-£74 double.
Half board: £38-£48 daily,
£240-£285 weekly.
Lunch available.
Evening meal 7pm (l.o.
9.30pm).
Parking for 200.
Credit: Access, Visa, Diners,
Amex.

Newbridge House

Listed **APPROVED**

7 Commercial Rd.,
Weymouth, DT4 7DW
☎ (0305) 787010
*Terrace-type guesthouse
situated overlooking Radipole
Lake and bird sanctuary.
Convenient for esplanade,
railway and coach station.*
Bedrooms: 2 single, 2 double
& 2 twin.
Bathrooms: 1 public.
Bed & breakfast: £12-£15
single, £24-£28 double.
Half board: £18.50-£21.50
daily.
Evening meal 6pm (l.o. 7pm).

*The national Crown
scheme is explained
in full on pages
536 — 539.*

WEYMOUTH

Continued

Rosslare
♛♛

145 Dorchester Rd.,
Weymouth, DT4 7LE
☎ (0305) 785913
*Small, licensed, friendly
guesthouse situated on the
main Dorchester road leading
into Weymouth.*
Bedrooms: 1 single, 2 twin,
4 family rooms.
Bathrooms: 4 private,
1 public.
Bed & breakfast: £13-£17
single, £26-£34 double.
Half board: £18-£22 daily,
£95-£120 weekly.
Evening meal 6pm (l.o. 5pm).
Parking for 5.
Credit: Access, Visa.
⌂ ▯ ♥ ⚓ ▤ V ⌷ ⊓ ▥ 🍴
✕ 🐾 ▨ DAP ⚲ SP

Sunningdale Hotel M
♛♛♛

52 Preston Rd., Weymouth,
DT3 6QD
☎ Preston (Dorset)
(0305) 832179
*Country-style family hotel with
a relaxed and comfortable
atmosphere, set in 2 acres of
gardens. 1.5 miles from town
centre.*
Bedrooms: 1 single, 7 double
& 4 twin, 8 family rooms.
Bathrooms: 10 private,
3 public; 3 private showers.
Bed & breakfast: £19.30-
£24.30 single, £38.60-£48.60
double.
Half board: £24.90-£31 daily,
£155-£193 weekly.
Lunch available.
Evening meal 6pm (l.o. 7pm).
Open April-October.
Credit: Access, Visa.
⌂ ▦ ⚲ V ⌷ ⊓ ⊓ ▥
🍴 ♣ ⚲ ✺ SP

Westwey Hotel
♛♛♛ COMMENDED

62 Abbotsbury Rd.,
Weymouth, DT4 0BJ
☎ (0305) 784564
*Comfortable hotel situated
close to town and beach.*
Bedrooms: 1 single, 5 double
& 2 twin, 3 family rooms.
Bathrooms: 8 private,
2 public.
Bed & breakfast: £15.50-
£17.50 single, £31-£35 double.
Half board: £20.50-£22.50
daily, £117-£140 weekly.
Evening meal 6pm (l.o.
6.30pm).
Parking for 10.
⌂ 1 ⊙ ▯ ⚲ ▦ V ⊓ ⊓ ▥
⌷ 🍴 ✕ DAP ⚲ SP

WHEDDON CROSS

Somerset
Map ref 1D1

*5m SW. Dunster
Crossroads hamlet in the
heart of Exmoor National
Park.*

Exmoor House M
♛♛♛ COMMENDED

Wheddon Cross, Minehead,
TA24 7DU
☎ Timberscombe
(0643) 841432
*Spacious, comfortable
guesthouse in Exmoor National
Park. Perfect centre for
touring and walking. Personal
attention guaranteed.*
Bedrooms: 4 double & 2 twin,
2 family rooms.
Bathrooms: 6 private,
2 public; 1 private shower.
Bed & breakfast: from £16.50
single, from £33 double.
Half board: from £24.50
daily, from £155 weekly.
Evening meal 7pm (l.o.
5.30pm).
Parking for 9.
Open March-November.
Credit: Access, Visa.
⌂ ⚲ 1 V ⌷ ⊓ ▥ ⌷ ✕
▨ SP

WIDECOMBE-IN-
THE-MOOR

Devon
Map ref 1C2

Old village in pastoral
country under the high
tors of East Dartmoor.
The 'Cathedral of the
Moor' stands near a tiny
square, once used for
archery practice, which
has a 16th C Church
House among other old
buildings.

Sheena Tower
♛♛

Widecombe-in-the-Moor,
Newton Abbot, TQ13 7TE
☎ (036 42) 381
*Comfortable moorland
guesthouse overlooking
Widecombe village, offering a
relaxed holiday in picturesque
surroundings. Well placed for
discovering Dartmoor.*
Bedrooms: 1 single, 2 double
& 1 twin, 2 family rooms.
Bathrooms: 1 private,
2 public.
Bed & breakfast: £12-£14
single, £24-£28 double.
Half board: £18-£20 daily.

Evening meal 7pm (l.o.
midday).
Parking for 10.
Open February-October.
⌂ ⚲ ♥ ⌷ ▦ ⊓ ▥ ⌷ ✺
▨

WINCANTON

Somerset
Map ref 2B3

Thriving market town,
rising from the rich
pastures of Blackmoor
Vale near the Dorset
border, with many
attractive 18th C stone
buildings. Steeplechase
racecourse.
*Tourist Information
Centre ☎ (0963) 34063*

Holbrook Country
House Hotel M

Holbrook, Wincanton,
BA9 8BS
☎ (0963) 32377
*Delightful country house in 15
acres of peaceful countryside, 2
hours from London. Ideal base
for touring Somerset and
Dorset. Reliable, friendly
service. Same personal family
ownership since 1946.*
Bedrooms: 5 single, 6 double
& 5 twin, 3 family rooms.
Bathrooms: 16 private,
4 public.
Bed & breakfast: £30-£39.50
single, £60-£72 double.
Half board: £47-£50 daily,
from £310 weekly.
Lunch available.
Evening meal 7.30pm (l.o.
8.30pm).
Parking for 34.
Credit: Access, Visa, Amex.
⌂ ⚲ ⊙ ♥ 1 V ⌷ ⊓ ▥
⌷ 🍴 ♣ ⚲ 🐾 ✺ ▨ ▨
SP 🎱

WINTERBOURNE

Avon
Map ref 2B2

6m NE. Bristol

The Grange Resort
Hotel M

Northwoods, Winterbourne,
Bristol, BS17 1RP
☎ (0454) 777333 & Fax
(0454) 777447
🅖🅡 Resort
*Recently refurbished hotel in a
peaceful rural setting. 10 miles
north of Bristol and 20 minutes
from Bath. All bedrooms en-
suite. Facilities include health
and leisure club.*
Bedrooms: 4 single, 44 double
& 4 twin.
Bathrooms: 52 private.

Bed & breakfast: £32.50-
£84.50 single, £65-£102
double.
Lunch available.
Evening meal 7pm (l.o.
9.30pm).
Parking for 100.
Credit: Access, Visa, Diners,
Amex.
⌂ ⚲ ⌕ ⊙ ▯ ⚲ 1 V ✕
⌷ ● ▥ ⌷ 🍴 ⚲ ✺ ⚲ ♣
SP 🎱

WINTERBOURNE
STOKE

Wiltshire
Map ref 2B2

5m W. Amesbury

Scotland Lodge M
♛♛ APPROVED

Winterbourne Stoke,
Salisbury, SP3 4TF
☎ Shrewton (0980) 620943 &
Mobile (0860) 272599
*Historic, comfortable country
house with private bathrooms.
Helpful service. Ideal touring
base. French and some German
spoken. Also self-contained
unit.*
Bedrooms: 1 double & 2 twin.
Bathrooms: 3 private.
Bed & breakfast: £20-£25
single, £35-£42 double.
Parking for 5.
⌂ ▯ ⚲ ⓤ V ⌷ ▥ ⌷ ✺
✕ ▨ ▨

WITHERIDGE

Devon
Map ref 1D2

9m W. Tiverton

Thelbridge Cross Inn M
♛♛♛ COMMENDED

Thelbridge, Witheridge,
EX17 4SQ
☎ Tiverton (0884) 860316
*Charming 17th C inn situated
on the B3042 between
Witheridge and Chawleigh.
Enviable reputation for home-
cooked cuisine, warmth and
hospitality.*
Bedrooms: 5 double & 2 twin,
1 family room.
Bathrooms: 8 private.
Bed & breakfast: £28-£35
single, £52-£65 double.
Half board: £38-£45 daily,
£245-£280 weekly.
Lunch available.
Evening meal 7pm (l.o.
9.30pm).
Parking for 50.
Credit: Access, Visa.
⌂ ⚲ ⌕ ⊙ ▯ ⚲ 1 V ⊓
▥ 🍴 ⚲ ✕ ▨ SP

WITHYPOOL

Somerset
Map ref 1D1

Pretty village high on
Exmoor near the beautiful
River Barle. On Winsford
Hill (National Trust) are
Bronze Age barrows
known as the
Wambarrows.

Westerclose Country House
COMMENDED

Withypool, Minehead,
TA24 7QR
☎ Exford (0643) 83302
*Surrounded by beautiful
unspoilt countryside, above the
River Barle. Offering a high
standard of food, comfort and
service. Wonderful moorland
views. Follow hotel signs once
in Withypool.*
Bedrooms: 2 single, 3 double
& 4 twin, 1 family room.
Bathrooms: 10 private.
Bed & breakfast: £28-£30
single, £58-£68 double.
Half board: £50-£52 daily,
£320-£327 weekly.
Lunch available.
Evening meal 7.30pm (l.o.
9.30pm).
Parking for 15.
Credit: Access, Visa, Amex.

WOODY BAY

Devon
Map ref 1C1

3m W. Lynton
Rocky bay backed by
dramatic cliffs thick with
oak woods on the
western Exmoor coast.
To the west over
Martinhoe Hill the River
Heddon reaches the sea
through a steep wooded
valley.

Woody Bay Hotel M
COMMENDED

Woody Bay, Parracombe,
EX31 4QX
☎ Parracombe (059 83) 264
*Nestling in the woods with
magnificent views over
National Trust woodland and
the Exmoor coastline. Very
quiet. Ideal for walking.*
Bedrooms: 1 single, 8 double
& 4 twin, 1 family room.
Bathrooms: 13 private,
1 public.
Bed & breakfast: £26-£38
single, £46-£82 double.
Half board: £38-£50 daily,
£245-£350 weekly.
Lunch available.

Evening meal 7.15pm (l.o.
8.30pm).
Parking for 15.
Open February-December.
Credit: Access, Visa.

WOOKEY

Somerset
Map ref 2A2

2m W. Wells
Small village below the
southern slopes of the
Mendips, near the River
Axe. 1 mile or so north-
east, the river runs
through spectacular
limestone caverns at
Wookey Hole.

Fenny Castle House M
COMMENDED

Fenny Castle, Wookey, Wells,
BA5 1NN
☎ (0749) 72265
*Riverside setting overlooking
moat and bailey castle.
Country house in 60 acres on
boundary of levels. Restaurant,
delightful accommodation.*
Bedrooms: 1 single, 3 double
& 2 twin.
Bathrooms: 6 private.
Bed & breakfast: £27.50-£30
single, £55-£60 double.
Half board: £42.50-£46 daily,
£250-£275 weekly.
Lunch available.
Evening meal 6pm (l.o. 9pm).
Parking for 60.
Credit: Access, Visa.

WOOLACOMBE

Devon
Map ref 1C1

Between Morte Point and
Baggy Point,
Woolacombe and
Mortehoe offer 3 miles of
the finest sand and surf
on this outstanding
coastline. Much of the
area is owned by the
National Trust.

Byways Hotel
COMMENDED

The Esplanade, Woolacombe,
EX34 7DJ
☎ (0271) 870511
*Small family-run hotel, good
food plus every comfort.
Superb views to sea and moors.
Direct access to beach.*
Bedrooms: 1 single, 3 double
& 2 twin, 1 family room.
Bathrooms: 6 private;
1 private shower.

Bed & breakfast: £16-£20.50
single, £32-£41 double.
Half board: £21.50-£26 daily,
£131-£155 weekly.
Evening meal 7pm (l.o.
7.30pm).
Parking for 7.
Open April-October.
Credit: Access, Visa.

Camberley

Beach Rd., Woolacombe,
EX34 7AA
☎ (0271) 870231
*Small family hotel overlooking
the sea and countryside. Well-
appointed rooms with en-suite
facilities, colour TV, tea and
coffee making. Licensed bar.
Off-road parking.*
Bedrooms: 3 double, 3 family
rooms.
Bathrooms: 6 private.
Bed & breakfast: £30-£40
double.
Half board: £22-27 daily,
£125-£170 weekly.
Evening meal 6.30pm (l.o.
5.30pm).
Parking for 6.

Crossways Hotel

The Esplanade,
Woolacombe, EX34 7DJ
☎ (0271) 870395
*Friendly, family-run hotel in
quiet seafront position
overlooking Combesgate beach
and valley. All rooms recently
refurbished.*
Bedrooms: 1 single, 3 double,
5 family rooms.
Bathrooms: 5 private,
1 public; 2 private showers.
Bed & breakfast: £15.50-
£21.50 single, £31-£43 double.
Half board: £21.25-£27 daily,
£147.50-£186 weekly.
Lunch available.
Evening meal 6.30pm (l.o.
6.30pm).
Parking for 10.
Open March-October.

Headlands Hotel M

Beach Rd., Woolacombe,
EX34 7BT
☎ (0271) 870320
*Well-appointed hotel renowned
for comfort, service and fine
menu, with fabulous views of
National Trust countryside and
Woolacombe Bay.*
Bedrooms: 1 single, 7 double
& 3 twin, 3 family rooms.

Bathrooms: 10 private,
2 public.
Bed & breakfast: £20-£30
single, £40-£60 double.
Half board: £25-£35 daily,
£150-£210 weekly.
Evening meal 7pm (l.o. 8pm).
Parking for 16.
Open March-October.
Credit: Access, Visa.

Little Beach Hotel M
COMMENDED

The Esplanade, Woolacombe,
EX34 7DJ
☎ (0271) 870398
*Elegant family-run hotel by the
sea, offering spectacular views
over 3 miles of golden sands
and National Trust coastline.*
Bedrooms: 2 single, 7 double
& 1 twin.
Bathrooms: 8 private,
1 public.
Bed & breakfast: £25.50-
£28.50 single, £44-£69.50
double.
Half board: £31.25-£43 daily,
£205-£270 weekly.
Evening meal 7.15pm (l.o.
8pm).
Parking for 8.
Open March-October.
Credit: Access, Visa.

Pebbles Hotel and Restaurant M
COMMENDED

Combesgate Beach,
Mortehoe, Woolacombe,
EX34 7EA
☎ Woolacombe
(0271) 870426
*Hotel with integral restaurants,
adjoining National Trust land.
Spectacular views of sea and
coast. Direct access to beach.*
Bedrooms: 1 single, 7 double
& 1 twin, 3 family rooms.
Bathrooms: 11 private,
1 public.
Bed & breakfast: £20-£24
single, £40-£48 double.
Half board: £30-£34 daily,
£173-£231 weekly.
Lunch available.
Evening meal 7pm (l.o.
9.30pm).
Parking for 31.
Open February-December.
Credit: Access, Visa.

Springside Country House

Mullacott Rd., Woolacombe,
EX34 7HF
☎ (0271) 870452

Continued ▶

WOOLACOMBE
Continued

All bedrooms overlook open countryside or the sea. Ideal centre for touring, midway between Woolacombe and Ilfracombe.
Bedrooms: 1 single, 4 double, 3 family rooms.
Bathrooms: 6 private, 1 public.
Bed & breakfast: £29-£36 double.
Evening meal 6.30pm (l.o. 4pm).
Parking for 12.
Open April-October.

Watersmeet Hotel
ꕥꕥꕥꕥ **COMMENDED**

Mortehoe, Woolacombe, EX34 7EB
☎ (0271) 870333 & Fax (0271) 870890
Attractive waterside hotel with lovely garden and own access to sandy beach. Reputation for comfort and cuisine.
Bedrooms: 4 single, 10 double & 7 twin, 3 family rooms.
Bathrooms: 24 private.
Half board: £42-£70 daily, £282-£470 weekly.
Lunch available.
Evening meal 7pm (l.o. 8.30pm).
Parking for 50.
Open February-November.
Credit: Access, Visa, Diners, Amex.

> *Half board prices shown are per person but in some cases may be based on double/twin occupancy.*

Woolacombe Bay Hotel M
ꕥꕥꕥꕥꕥ

Woolacombe, EX34 7BN
☎ Woolacombe, (0271) 870388 Telex 46761
Ⓒ Best Western
Gracious hotel in 6 acres of gardens leading to the sea. With heated pools, squash, tennis, solarium, sauna, pitch and putt, short-mat bowling. Self-catering also available.
Bedrooms: 1 single, 24 double & 10 twin, 24 family rooms.
Bathrooms: 59 private.
Half board: £51-£103 daily, £284-£594 weekly.
Evening meal 7.30pm (l.o. 9.30pm).
Parking for 70.
Open February-December.
Credit: Access, Visa, Diners, Amex.

YELVERTON
Devon
Map ref 1C2

Village on the edge of Dartmoor, where ponies wander over the flat common. Buckland Abbey is 2 miles southwest, while Burrator Reservoir is 2 miles to the east.

Blowiscombe Barton M
ꕥꕥꕥ **COMMENDED**

Milton Combe, Yelverton, PL20 6HR
☎ Yelverton (0822) 854853
Modernised farmhouse surrounded by rolling farmland, yet only 800 yards from village pub and national park. Heated swimming pool. 8 miles from Plymouth centre.
Bedrooms: 4 double & 1 twin.

Bathrooms: 4 private, 1 public.
Bed & breakfast: £16-£19 single, £30-£34 double.
Half board: £23-£25 daily.
Evening meal 6.30pm (l.o. 8.30pm).
Parking for 6.

Greenwell Farm
ꕥꕥ

Meavy, Yelverton, PL20 6PY
☎ (0822) 853563
220-acre beef, sheep & hill farm. Fresh country air, breathtaking views and country cuisine set the scene at Greenwell. This busy family farm welcomes you to share the countryside.
Bedrooms: 1 double & 1 twin, 1 family room.
Bathrooms: 3 private.
Bed & breakfast: £34-£40 double.
Half board: £26.50-£30.50 daily.
Evening meal 6pm (l.o. midday).
Parking for 8.

Moorland Links Hotel M
ꕥꕥꕥꕥ **COMMENDED**

Yelverton, PL20 6DA
☎ (0822) 852245 Telex 45616 MORLNK
Ⓒ Forestdale
Comfortable hotel set high on Dartmoor with breathtaking views of the Tamar Valley, yet within a few miles of Plymouth.
Bedrooms: 3 single, 18 double & 9 twin.
Bathrooms: 30 private.
Bed & breakfast: £62.50-£95 single, £77.50-£100 double.
Evening meal 7.30pm (l.o. 10pm).

Parking for 120.
Credit: Access, Visa, Diners, Amex.

Rosemont Hotel
ꕥꕥ **COMMENDED**

Greenmont Ter., Yelverton, PL20 6DR
☎ (0822) 852175
Small, friendly, family-run hotel in quiet village on edge of Dartmoor. An ideal spot for touring West Country. Quality food.
Bedrooms: 2 single, 1 double & 2 twin, 3 family rooms.
Bathrooms: 3 public.
Bed & breakfast: £16 single, £32-£40 double.
Half board: £28.50-£32.50 daily, £183.50-£207.50 weekly.
Lunch available.
Evening meal 6.30pm (l.o. 6.30pm).
Parking for 9.

Waverley Guest House M
ꕥꕥ **APPROVED**

5 Greenbank Ter., Yelverton, PL20 6DR
☎ (0822) 854617
Family-run guesthouse on edge of Dartmoor, 9 miles from Plymouth and 6 miles from Tavistock. Children and pets welcome.
Bedrooms: 2 single, 2 twin, 1 family room.
Bathrooms: 1 public; 5 private showers.
Bed & breakfast: £15-£16 single, £30-£32 double.
Half board: £23-£24 daily, £161-£168 weekly.
Evening meal 6pm (l.o. 9am).
Parking for 3.

Key to symbols

Information about many of the services and facilities at establishments listed in this guide is given in the form of symbols. The key to these symbols is inside the back cover flap. You may find it helpful to keep the flap open when referring to the entry listings.

Use a coupon

When requesting further information from advertisers in this guide, you may find it helpful to use the advertisement enquiry coupons which can be found towards the end of the guide. These should be cut out and mailed direct to the companies in which you are interested. Do remember to include your name and address.

SOUTH OF ENGLAND

A PROSPEROUS FARMING AND COMMERCIAL AREA *both today and in times past, taking in Hampshire, the Isle of Wight and the eastern part of Dorset. On the coast or inland, there's plenty to interest and excite. Beach buffs will head for "Queen of the Coast" Bournemouth which takes pride in catering for the young, the old and the "in-betweens" alike. Sea salts will target Portsmouth, with its splendid naval heritage area, and Poole, with its great natural harbour. Those with a "green" tinge will seek out the New Forest and the Purbecks. And just a short hop over the Solent is the ever-delightful playground of the Isle of Wight.*

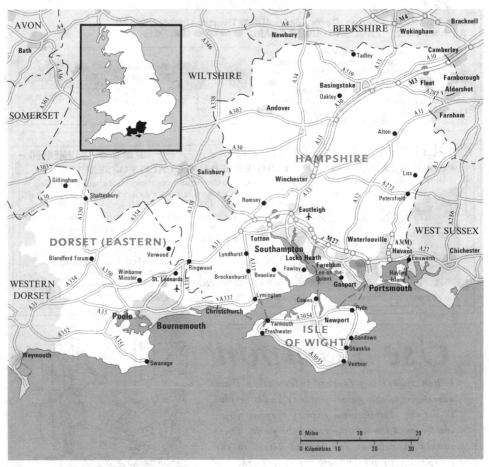

PLEASE REFER TO THE COLOUR MAPS AT THE BACK OF THIS GUIDE FOR ALL PLACES WITH ACCOMMODATION LISTINGS.

WHERE TO GO, WHAT TO SEE

Jane Austen's House
Chawton, Alton, Hampshire
GU34 1SD
☎ Alton (0420) 83262
*The house in which Jane Austen
and her family lived from
1809–1817, containing
numerous exhibits from their
lifetime. Pleasant garden
suitable for picnics.*

Barton Manor Vineyard and Gardens
Whippingham, East Cowes, Isle
of Wight PO32 6LB
☎ Isle of Wight (0983) 292835
*20 acres of beautiful gardens.
5-acre vineyard and superb
estate vinery, with display of
winemaking equipment. Water
garden, woodland walks, scented
garden.*

Beaulieu Palace House
Beaulieu, Hampshire SO42 7ZN
☎ Beaulieu (0590) 612345
*The home of Lord and Lady
Montagu, the house has been in
the family since it was acquired
in 1538 following the dissolution
of the monasteries by Henry
VIII. National Motor Museum,
monastic life exhibition, shops.*

Blackgang Chine Theme Park
Blackgang Chine, Ventnor, Isle
of Wight PO38 2HN
☎ Isle of Wight (0983) 730330
*Theme park with water and
clifftop gardens. Dinosaur park,
Frontierland, model village,
maze, Nurseryland.*

Breamore House
Breamore, Hampshire SP6 2DF
☎ Downton (0725) 22233
*Elizabethan manor house dating
from 1583, with fine collection of
works of art, furniture, tapestries,
needlework and paintings,
mainly 17th and 18th C Dutch
School.*

Broadlands
Romsey, Hampshire SO51 9ZD
☎ Romsey (0794) 517888

Beaulieu Palace House — home of Lord and Lady Montagu

*Home of the late Lord
Mountbatten. Magnificent
18th C house and contents.
Superb views across River Test.
Mountbatten exhibition and
audio-visual presentation.*

Carisbrooke Castle
Newport, Isle of Wight
PO30 1XY
☎ Isle of Wight (0983) 522107
*Splendid Norman castle, where
Charles I was imprisoned. The
Governors' Lodge houses the
county museum. Wheelhouse
with wheel operated by donkeys.*

Corfe Castle
Wareham, Dorset
☎ Corfe Castle (0929) 480921
*Ruins of former royal castle
besieged and "slighted" in 1646.*

The D Day Museum
Clarence Esplanade,
Portsmouth, Hampshire
PO5 3PA
☎ Portsmouth (0705) 827261
*Incorporates Overlord
embroidery which depicts Allied
invasion of Normandy. Displays
of D Day action and some of the
vehicles that took part.*

The Dorset Heavy Horse Centre
Grains Hill, Edmondsham,
Verwood, Wimborne, Dorset
BH21 5RJ
☎ Verwood (0202) 824040
*Shire, Pecheron and Suffolk
horses. Old farm wagons and
implements. Parades of
horses. Demonstrations of
plaiting and harnessing. Pets'
corner.*

The Hillier Gardens and Arboretum
Jermyns Lane, Ampfield, Nr.
Romsey, Hampshire SO51 0QA
☎ Braishfield (0794) 68787
*The largest collection of trees
and shrubs of its kind in the
British Isles, planted within an
attractive landscape of over 160
acres.*

HMS Victory
HM Naval Base, Portsmouth,
Hampshire PO1 3PZ
☎ Portsmouth (0705) 839766
*Lord Nelson's flagship at
Trafalgar. His cabin, the cockpit
where he died. Tours of the gun
decks.*

Keepers with Snow Leopard cubs at Marwell Zoological Park

HMS Warrior
Victory Gate, HM Naval Base,
Portsmouth, Hampshire
PO1 3QX
☎ Portsmouth (0705) 291379
*The world's first iron battleship.
Four decks completely restored
to show life in the Victorian
navy of 1860. Cabins,
wardroom, engine and cannon.*

Isle of Wight Steam Railway
Railway Station, Havenstreet,
Isle of Wight PO33 4DS
☎ Isle of Wight (0983) 882204
*Steam train rides in original Isle
of Wight carriages, behind
locomotives between 75 and 115
years old. Museum of island
railwayana.*

Isle of Wight Wax Museum
High Street, Brading, Isle of
Wight PO36 0DQ
☎ Isle of Wight (0983) 407286
*Cameos of island history with
authentic costumes, wax figures,
period furniture and harmonious
settings, displayed in the ancient
rectory mansion.*

Kingston Lacy
Wimborne, Dorset BH21 4EA
☎ Wimborne (0202) 883402
*Historic house recently restored
by the National Trust. Fine
collection of paintings. Garden
and park.*

Marwell Zoological Park
Colden Common, Winchester,
Hampshire SO21 1JH
☎ Owslebury (0962) 777406
*Large zoo breeding endangered
species. Over 800 animals
including big cats, giraffes, deer,
zebras, monkeys, hippos and
birds.*

Mary Rose Ship Hall and Exhibition
HM Naval Base, Portsmouth,
Hampshire PO1 3PZ
☎ Portsmouth (0705) 812931
*Reconstruction and conservation
of Henry VIII's warship, and
exhibition of the ship's treasures.*

Museum of Army Flying
Middle Wallop, Stockbridge,
Hampshire SO20 8DY
☎ Andover (0264) 384421
*Purpose-built museum on edge
of airfield tells the story of 100
years of army flying. Exciting
and unique collection of aircraft.*

New Forest Butterfly Farm
Longdown, Ashurst,
Nr. Southampton, Hampshire
SO4 4UH
☎ Ashurst (0703) 292166
*Large indoor tropical garden
housing numerous exotic free-
flying butterflies and moths from
all over the world. Other insects
and dragonfly ponds.*

The New Forest Owl Sanctuary
Crow Lane, Crow, Ringwood,
Hampshire BH24 3EA
☎ Ringwood (0425) 476487
*Sanctuary for barn owls destined
to be released into the wild.
Incubation room, hospital unit
and 100 aviaries.*

Osborne House
East Cowes, Isle of Wight
PO32 6JY
☎ Isle of Wight (0983) 200022
*Queen Victoria's royal and state
apartments. Swiss cottage and
museum. Royal nurseries.*

Paultons Park
Ower, Romsey, Hampshire
SO51 6AL
☎ Southampton (0703) 814442
*140 acres of parkland with exotic
birds, gardens, lake, waterwheel,
Kids' Kingdom, railway,
animated shows, bumper boats,
Romany museum, pets' corner.*

Romany Folklore Museum and Workshop
Limesend Yard, High Street,
Selborne, Hampshire
GU34 3JW
☎ Selborne (042 050) 486
*Displays of all aspects of Romany
life. Full-size living caravans and
tents. Complete wagon builder's
workshop (60 years old).*

Royal Corps of Signals Museum
Blandford Camp, Blandford,
Dorset DT11 8RH
☎ Blandford (0258) 482248
*History of army communications
from Crimean War to Falklands
campaign. Vehicles, uniforms,
medals and badges.*

Royal Marines Museum
Southsea, Hampshire PO4 9PX
☎ Southsea (0705) 819385

Children love meeting Percy, the Paultons Owl!

History of Royal Marines from 1664 to present day. Dynamic Falklands audio-visual and chilled Arctic display. New history gallery featuring a talking head of Hannah Snell.

The Tank Museum
Bovington Camp, Wareham, Dorset BH20 6JG
☎ Bindon Abbey (0929) 403463
Largest and most comprehensive museum collection of armoured fighting vehicles in the world. Over 240 vehicles, supporting displays and video theatres.

Ventnor Botanic Garden
Undercliff Drive, Ventnor, Isle of Wight PO38 1UL
☎ Isle of Wight (0983) 855397
22 acres of garden containing some 10,000 plants. Rare and exotic trees, shrubs, alpines, perennials, succulents and conifers. Temperate house.

MAKE A DATE FOR...

International Air Show
Army Air Corps Centre, Middle Wallop, Hampshire
9 − 10 May

Bournemouth Music Festival
Winter Gardens Theatre, Exeter Road, Bournemouth, Dorset
20 June − 4 July

Isle of Wight Tennyson Centenary Festival 1992
Quay Arts Centre, Sea Street, Newport, Isle of Wight
20 June − 31 July

New Forest and Hampshire County Show
New Park, Brockenhurst, Hampshire
28 − 30 July

Cowes Week
Cowes, Isle of Wight
1 − 9 August

Portsmouth and Southsea Show
Southsea Common, Portsmouth, Hampshire
7 − 9 August

Hampshire County Show
Royal Victoria Country Park, Netley Abbey, Hampshire
14 − 16 August

Great Dorset Steam Fair
Tarrant Hinton, Blandford Forum, Dorset
2 − 6 September

Southampton International Boat Show
Mayflower Park, Southampton, Hampshire
11 − 19 September

FIND OUT MORE

Further information about holidays and attractions in the South of England region is available from:
Southern Tourist Board
40 Chamberlayne Road, Eastleigh, Hampshire SO5 5JH
☎ (0703) 620006

These publications are available free from the Southern Tourist Board (please telephone (0703) 620555):

Southern England Holidays '92 − a guide to the region and its accommodation

Take a Break − value for money breaks

The Isle of Wight Guide

Places to stay

ACCOMMODATION ENTRIES *in this regional section are listed in alphabetical order of place name, and then in alphabetical order of establishment.*

THE MAP REFERENCES *refer to the colour maps towards the end of the guide. The first figure is the map number; the letter and figure which follow indicate the grid reference on the map.*

THE SYMBOLS *at the end of each accommodation entry give information about services and facilities. A 'key' to these symbols is inside the back cover flap, which can be kept open for easy reference.*

ALTON

Hampshire
Map ref 2C2

10m SE. Basingstoke
Pleasant old market town standing on the Pilgrim's Way, with some attractive Georgian buildings. The parish church still bears the scars of bullet marks, evidence of a bitter struggle between the Roundheads and the Royalists.

The Grange Hotel & Restaurant M
♔♔♔

17 London Road,
Holybourne, Alton,
GU34 4EG
☎ (0420) 86565
Fax (0420) 541346
Privately-run country house hotel, set in 2 acres, with a restaurant and bar open to non-residents.
Bedrooms: 11 single,
10 double & 11 twin, 2 family rooms.
Bathrooms: 34 private.
Bed & breakfast: £46-£61 single, £61-£71 double.
Half board: £56-£71 daily.
Lunch available.
Evening meal 7pm (l.o. 9pm).
Parking for 60.
Credit: Access, Visa, Diners, Amex.
❄🕯🚲📻☎🛏👤♿ Ⓥ✂
🛎📺🏧🅿🍴👣🧍❄ SP

Half board prices shown are per person but in some cases may be based on double/twin occupancy.

AMPFIELD

Hampshire
Map ref 2C3

Village 3 miles east of Romsey. The Hillier Garden and Arboretum lies three quarters of a mile west off the A31 along Jermyns Lane.

Potters Heron Hotel M
♔♔♔♔ **COMMENDED**

Ampfield, Nr. Romsey,
SO51 9ZF
☎ Southampton
(0703) 266611 Telex 47459
Ⓒ Lansbury
Thatched building in rural surroundings. Recently completely refurbished. Well placed for Winchester, New Forest and Test Valley.
Bedrooms: 37 double &
23 twin.
Bathrooms: 60 private.
Bed & breakfast: from £30 single, from £60 double.
Half board: from £42 daily.
Lunch available.
Evening meal 7pm (l.o. 10pm).
Parking for 200.
Credit: Access, Visa, Diners, Amex.
❄🕯🚲☎📻🛏👤 Ⓥ
🛎🅿💷🏧🍴👣♿🧍🐕
✱✎ SP 📱

ANDOVER

Hampshire
Map ref 2C2

13m NW. Winchester
Town that achieved importance from the wool trade and now has much modern development. A good centre for visiting places of interest.
Tourist Information Centre ☎ (0264) 24320

Amberley Hotel M
♔♔

70 Weyhill Road, Andover,
SP10 3NP
☎ (0264) 352224
Telex 477055
Small, comfortably furnished hotel, with attractive restaurant open to non-residents. Private meetings, luncheons and wedding receptions can be booked.
Bedrooms: 6 single, 3 double & 5 twin, 3 family rooms.
Bathrooms: 9 private,
2 public.
Bed & breakfast: £23-£34 single, £36-£45 double.
Half board: £26-£54 daily.
Lunch available.
Evening meal 6.45pm (l.o. 9.15pm).
Parking for 16.
Credit: Access, Visa, Diners, Amex.
❄🕯☎📻🛏👤🏧📺🍴
🛎🍴🧍

Amport Inn M
♔♔♔

Amport, Nr. Andover,
SP11 8AE
☎ (0264) 710371

Friendly inn in attractive Hampshire village, with racecourses, riding and fishing nearby. Businessmen welcome weekdays. Breakaway weekends available. Sauna and indoor pool.
Bedrooms: 3 double & 4 twin, 2 family rooms.
Bathrooms: 9 private,
1 public.
Bed & breakfast: £40-£50 single, £50-£60 double.
Lunch available.
Evening meal 7.30pm (l.o. 10pm).
Parking for 54.
Credit: Access, Visa.
❄🕯☎📻👤 Ⓥ🏧📺
🛎🍴💷🏧🅿♿🧍🐕 SP
📱

Ashley Court Hotel M
♔♔♔♔ **COMMENDED**

Micheldever Road, Andover,
SP11 6LA
☎ (0264) 357344
Fax (0264) 356755
Ⓒ Consort
Half a mile from town centre, quietly set in nearly 4 acres of grounds. Friendly atmosphere, good restaurant, conference and banqueting facilities.
Bedrooms: 10 single,
12 double & 13 twin.
Bathrooms: 35 private.
Bed & breakfast: £50-£70 single, £50-£96 double.
Half board: £40-£85 daily, £280-£500 weekly.
Lunch available.
Evening meal 7pm (l.o. 9.30pm).
Parking for 80.
Credit: Access, Visa, Amex.
❄🕯☎📻👤 Ⓥ🏧
📺🛎🍴♿✱🐕 SP
📱

BARTON ON SEA

Hampshire
Map ref 2B3

Seaside village with views
of the Isle of Wight.
Within easy driving
distance of the New
Forest.

Cliff House Hotel & Restaurant ▲
☖☖☖☖ COMMENDED

Marine Drive West, Barton
on Sea, New Milton,
BH25 7QL
☎ New Milton (0425) 619333
& Fax (0425) 612462
*Fully licensed clifftop hotel
with beautiful furnishings,
restaurant, bar and lounge,
overlooking Christchurch Bay.
Chef/proprietor.*
Bedrooms: 2 single, 5 double
& 2 twin.
Bathrooms: 9 private,
1 public.
Bed & breakfast: £44-£50
single, £68-£85 double.
Half board: £49.50-£65.50
daily, £321-£425 weekly.
Lunch available.
Evening meal 7pm (l.o. 9pm).
Parking for 50.
Credit: Access, Visa, Diners,
Amex.
▷10 ♨ ♦ ⊡ ♡ ⋒ ⓥ
⋎ ⋒ ▥ ▱ ↑ ✿ ☓ ⋒ ⅃
⑤Ⓟ

Eureka Guest House ▲
☖☖ COMMENDED

Christchurch Road, Barton on
Sea, New Milton, BH25 6QQ
☎ New Milton (0425) 610289
*An attractive, well-appointed,
comfortable, friendly
guesthouse offering home
cooking and ample parking.
Close to cliffs, beaches and
New Forest.*
Bedrooms: 1 single, 5 double.
Bathrooms: 5 private,
1 public.
Bed & breakfast: £15-£18
single, £30-£36 double.
Half board: £22-£25 daily.
Evening meal 7pm (l.o. 5pm).
Parking for 8.
▷ ♨ ⊡ ♡ ⓤ ⓥ ▥
▱ ☓ ⋒ ⑤Ⓟ

Laurel Lodge

48 Western Avenue, Barton
on Sea, New Milton,
BH25 7PZ
☎ New Milton (0425) 618309
*Need pampering? Small,
welcoming establishment with
home cooking. Many local
beaches, cliff top walks. 3 miles
from New Forest. Lots to do -
or just relax.*
Bedrooms: 2 double & 1 twin,
1 family room.

Bathrooms: 1 private,
2 public.
Bed & breakfast: £16-£18
single, £26-£33 double.
Half board: £20.50-£24 daily,
£130-£150 weekly.
Lunch available.
Evening meal 6.30pm.
Parking for 4.
▷ ♨ ⊡ ♡ ⓤ ⋒ ⓥ ⋒ ▣
▥ ▱ ⋒ ⋒ Ⓓ ☓ ⑤Ⓟ

The Old Coastguard Hotel ▲
☖☖

53 Marine Drive East,
Barton on Sea, BH25 7DX
☎ New Milton (0425) 612987
*Peaceful clifftop hotel close to
the New Forest, with English
cooking and personal service in
a friendly atmosphere. Some
ground floor rooms.*
Bedrooms: 4 double & 3 twin.
Bathrooms: 5 private,
1 public.
Bed & breakfast: £37-£43
double.
Half board: £26.50-£29.50
daily, £180-£200 weekly.
Evening meal 7pm (l.o. 6pm).
Parking for 10.
Credit: Access, Visa.
▷12 ♨ ⋒ ⋒ ⋒ ⓥ ⋒ ▣
▥ ▱ ✿ ⋒

BASINGSTOKE

Hampshire
Map ref 2C2

Rapidly developing
commercial and industrial
centre. The town is
surrounded by charming
villages and places to
visit.
*Tourist Information
Centre* ☎ *(0256) 817618*

The Carroll's Guest House

104 Gershwin Road,
Brighton Hill, Basingstoke,
RG22 4HJ
☎ (0256) 55153
*Small, homely guesthouse
offering home cooking.*
Bedrooms: 1 single, 2 twin.
Bathrooms: 1 public.
Bed & breakfast: £17-£20
single, £30-£34 double.
Half board: £20-£25 daily,
£120-£150 weekly.
Evening meal 6pm (l.o.
6.30p).
Parking for 4.
▷ ♨ ⊡ ⋒ ♡ ⓤ ⋎ ⋒ ⋒
▥ ▱ ☓ ⋒ ⋒ Ⓓ

---

*Please check prices
and other details at
the time of booking.*

The Centrecourt Hotel & Tennis Centre ▲
☖☖☖☖ COMMENDED

Centre Drive, Chineham,
Basingstoke, RG24 0FY
☎ (0256) 816664
*Hotel is complemented by a
superb, purpose-built tennis
centre, including 6 indoor and
5 outdoor tennis courts, indoor
heated pool, spa bath, steam
room, sauna and gym. Half
board price based on weekend
break.*
Bedrooms: 24 double &
26 twin.
Bathrooms: 50 private.
Bed & breakfast: £97-£110
single, £110-£123 double.
Half board: £49.50-£56 daily.
Lunch available.
Evening meal 6.30pm (l.o.
10pm).
Parking for 123.
Credit: Access, Visa, Diners,
Amex.
▷ ♦ ⊡ ⋒ ⋒ ⓥ ⋎ ⋒ ⋒
● ⊛ ▥ ▱ ↑ ⋒ ⋒ ⋒ Ⓓ
⋒ ⑤Ⓟ Ⓣ

Fernbank Guest House ▲
Listed COMMENDED

4 Fairfields Road,
Basingstoke, RG21 3DR
☎ (0256) 21191
*Situated in a quiet residential
area, close to restaurants and
sports facilities. Tastefully
decorated to a high standard,
this hotel has optional en-suite
rooms.*
Bedrooms: 11 single, 4 double
& 2 twin, 2 family rooms.
Bathrooms: 9 private,
4 public.
Bed & breakfast: £22-£37
single, £38-£44 double.
Parking for 18.
Credit: Access, Visa.
▷ ♨ ⊡ ⋒ ♡ ⓤ ⓥ ⋎ ▥
▱ ☓

Hilton Lodge Hotel ▲
☖☖☖☖☖ COMMENDED

Old Common Road,
Blackdam, Basingstoke,
RG21 3PR
☎ (0256) 460460
Telex 859038
Ⓒ Hilton
*Modern hotel with conference
and leisure facilities.*
Bedrooms: 6 single, 71 double
& 48 twin, 19 family rooms.
Bathrooms: 144 private.
Bed & breakfast: £106-£126
single, £124-£144 double.
Half board: £124-£144 daily.
Lunch available.
Evening meal 7pm (l.o.
10pm).
Parking for 100.

Credit: Access, Visa, Diners,
Amex.
▷ ♨ ♦ ⊡ ⋒ ♡ ⋒ ⋒ ⓥ ⋎
⋒ ● ▥ ▱ ↑ ⋒ ⋒ ⋒ ⋒
⑤Ⓟ Ⓣ

Hilton National ▲

Aldermaston Roundabout,
Ringway North, Basingstoke,
RG24 9NV
☎ (0256) 20212 Telex 858223
Ⓒ Hilton
*Extensively refurbished modern
hotel with comfortable new
restaurant, piano bar and
eating house. Executive suites
with jacuzzis. New leisure
centre includes indoor heated
pool, gymnasium and sauna.*
Bedrooms: 27 single,
73 double & 16 twin, 18 family
rooms.
Bathrooms: 134 private.
Bed & breakfast: £102-£108
single, £125-£142 double.
Lunch available.
Evening meal 7pm (l.o.
9.45pm).
Parking for 150.
Credit: Access, Visa, Diners,
Amex.
▷ ♨ ♦ ⊡ ⋒ ♡ ⋒ ⓥ ⋎
⋒ ● ⋒ ⊛ ▥ ▱ ↑ ⋒ ⋒
⋒ ✿ ⑤Ⓟ Ⓣ

BLANDFORD FORUM

Dorset
Map ref 2B3

Almost completely
destroyed by fire in 1731,
the town was rebuilt in a
handsome Georgian
style. The church is large
and grand and the town is
the hub of a rich farming
area.
*Tourist Information
Centre* ☎ *(0258) 451989*

Anvil Hotel & Restaurant ▲
☖☖☖☖ COMMENDED

Salisbury Road, Pimperne,
Blandford Forum, DT11 8UQ
☎ (0258) 453431 & 480182
*16th C thatched fully licensed
hotel and restaurant in the
heart of Dorset. Beamed, a la
carte restaurant with log fire
and flagstone floor.*
Bedrooms: 1 single, 5 double
& 2 twin, 1 family room.
Bathrooms: 9 private.
Bed & breakfast: £40 single,
£60 double.
Lunch available.
Evening meal 7pm (l.o.
9.45pm).
Parking for 25.
Credit: Access, Visa, Diners,
Amex.
▷ ♦ ⋒ ⊡ ♡ ⋒ ⓥ ⋒ ▥
↑ ✔ ✿ ⑤Ⓟ ⋒

BLANDFORD FORUM

Continued

Crown Hotel

☆☆☆ **COMMENDED**

1 West Street, Blandford
Forum, DT11 7AJ
☎ (0258) 456626
Fax (0258) 451084
Telex 418292
Ⓒ Consort
*An original Georgian coaching
hotel built in 1756, overlooking
watermeadows on the southern
edge of town.*
Bedrooms: 12 single, 6 double
& 10 twin, 1 family room.
Bathrooms: 29 private.
Bed & breakfast: £58 single,
£68 double.
Lunch available.
Evening meal 7.15pm (l.o.
9.15pm).
Parking for 69.
Credit: Access, Visa, Diners,
Amex.

Fairfield House ▲

☆☆☆

Church Road, Pimperne,
Blandford Forum, DT11 8UB
☎ (0258) 456756
*Distinctive, Grade II, Georgian
house set in a peaceful village.
Easy access to the
coast/countryside and historic
heritage of Dorset. Stable for
own horse or riding school
lessons and hacks available.
Clay shooting and golfing
arranged on request.
Residential and restaurant
licence.*
Bedrooms: 1 single, 1 double
& 2 twin, 1 family room.
Bathrooms: 5 private.
Bed & breakfast: £28-£33
single, £45-£55 double.
Half board: £33-£38 daily.
Evening meal 7pm (l.o. 6pm).
Parking for 10.
Credit: Access, Visa, Amex.

La Belle Alliance ▲

☆☆ **COMMENDED**

Whitecliff Mill Street,
Blandford Forum, DT11 7BP
☎ (0258) 452842
Fax (0258) 480054
*Comfortable and elegant small
hotel with emphasis on quality,
cuisine and service.*
Bedrooms: 2 double & 2 twin,
1 family room.
Bathrooms: 5 private.
Bed & breakfast: £40-£50
single, £55-£70 double.
Half board: £45-£55 daily.

Evening meal 7pm (l.o.
10pm).
Parking for 13.
Open February-December.
Credit: Access, Visa, Amex.

BOURNEMOUTH

**Dorset
Map ref 2B3**

Seaside town set among
the pines with a mild
climate, sandy beaches
and fine coastal views.
The town has wide
streets with excellent
shops, a pier, a pavilion,
museums and conference
centre.
*Tourist Information
Centre* ☎ (0202) 789789

Albrightleigh Guest House ▲

☆☆☆

4 Burnaby Road,
Westbourne, Bournemouth,
BH4 8JF
☎ (0202) 764054
*Comfortable and friendly
family-run guesthouse with
views across Alum Chine and
sea. Within minutes' walk of
the beach.*
Bedrooms: 4 double & 1 twin,
2 family rooms.
Bathrooms: 7 private,
2 public.
Bed & breakfast: £14-£18
single, £28-£36 double.
Half board: £19-£23 daily,
£114-£140 weekly.
Evening meal 6pm (l.o. 6pm).
Parking for 5.
Credit: Access, Visa.

Alum Bay Hotel ▲

19 Burnaby Road, Alum
Chine, Bournemouth,
BH4 8JF
☎ (0202) 761034
*Family-run hotel which offers
every comfort, with home-
cooked food, nicely furnished
public rooms and cosy bar.*
Bedrooms: 1 single, 5 double
& 3 twin, 3 family rooms.
Bathrooms: 7 private,
1 public.
Bed & breakfast: £17-£23
single, £30-£42 double.
Half board: £21.50-£27 daily,
£129-£162 weekly.
Evening meal 6pm (l.o. 6pm).
Parking for 10.
Credit: Access, Visa.

Amarillo Hotel

☆

52 Frances Road, Knyveton
Gardens, Bournemouth,
BH1 3SA
☎ (0202) 553884
*Small family hotel in quiet
position overlooking gardens.
Near beach, shopping centre
and railway station.*
Bedrooms: 1 single, 4 double,
1 family room.
Bathrooms: 2 public.
Bed & breakfast: £13-£16
single, £26-£32 double.
Half board: £18-£21 daily,
£115-£125 weekly.
Evening meal 6pm (l.o. 7pm).
Parking for 5.

Arlington Hotel ▲

☆☆☆

Exeter Park Road, Lower
Gardens, Bournemouth,
BH2 5BD
☎ (0202) 552879 & 553012
*Family-run hotel overlooking
Bournemouth pine gardens.
100 metres traffic-free, level
walk to square, beach, shops
and Bournemouth International
Centre.*
Bedrooms: 3 single, 11 double
& 8 twin, 6 family rooms.
Bathrooms: 28 private,
1 public.
Half board: £32.50-£37 daily,
£198-£239.50 weekly.
Lunch available.
Evening meal 6.30pm (l.o.
8pm).
Parking for 24.
Credit: Access, Visa.

Avon Royal Hotel ▲

☆☆☆

45 Christchurch Road,
Bournemouth, BH1 3PA
☎ (0202) 292800
Fax (0202) 299198
*Hotel with lounge bar
overlooking an acre of garden.
High standard restaurant
offering a varied menu. Family
and ground floor rooms
available.*
Bedrooms: 3 single, 10 double
& 6 twin, 4 family rooms.
Bathrooms: 14 private,
4 public.
Bed & breakfast: £16-£20
single, £32-£40 double.
Half board: £22-£26 daily,
£140-£180 weekly.
Lunch available.

Evening meal 6.30pm (l.o.
7.30pm).
Parking for 24.
Credit: Access, Visa.

Avonwood Hotel ▲

20 Owls Road, Boscombe,
Bournemouth, BH5 1AF
☎ (0202) 394704
*A friendly, family-run hotel,
with a relaxed atmosphere and
home cooking. 4 minutes' walk
from beaches and shops.*
Bedrooms: 3 single, 10 double
& 3 twin; 4 family rooms.
Bathrooms: 10 private,
4 public.
Bed & breakfast: £15-£22
single, £30-£44 double.
Half board: £21-£28 daily,
£140-£175 weekly.
Evening meal 6pm (l.o. 4pm).
Parking for 16.
Credit: Access, Visa.

Balmoral Hotel ▲

☆☆ **APPROVED**

11-13 Kerley Road, West
Cliff, Bournemouth,
BH2 5DW
☎ (0202) 551186 & 290037
*Traditional family hotel in a
fine clifftop position
overlooking the sea.*
Bedrooms: 8 single, 10 double
& 8 twin, 6 family rooms.
Bathrooms: 25 private,
3 public; 4 private showers.
Bed & breakfast: £17.50-£25
single, £35-£50 double.
Half board: £25-£32.50 daily,
£145-£195 weekly.
Evening meal 6.30pm (l.o.
7.30pm).
Parking for 40.
Credit: Access, Visa, Diners,
Amex.

Bay View Hotel ▲

☆☆☆ **COMMENDED**

Southbourne Overcliff Drive,
Bournemouth, BH6 3QB
☎ (0202) 429315
*Clifftop location on more
relaxing side of Bournemouth,
close to Christchurch. Safe
bathing and clifftop walks.
Close to level and crown green
bowls.*
Bedrooms: 2 single, 9 double
& 3 twin.
Bathrooms: 12 private,
1 public.
Bed & breakfast: £13-£22
single, £26-£44 double.
Half board: £19-£28 daily,
£120-£195 weekly.

Evening meal 6.30pm (l.o.
7.30pm).
Parking for 12.
🛏10 ⌂ ▯ ↻ ▯ V ⊯ ▥
🍴 ✕ ▥ OAP ↘ SP

Bella Vista Hotel ♏
Listed APPROVED
5 Studland Road, Alum
Chine, Bournemouth,
BH4 8HZ
☎ (0202) 763591
*Small family hotel, close to sea
and situated in beautiful Alum
Chine. All home cooking by
Gwen and Wallace. Full board
on Sundays.*
Bedrooms: 2 single, 5 double
& 2 twin, 4 family rooms.
Bathrooms: 9 private,
2 public.
Bed & breakfast: £17-£19
single, £34-£38 double.
Half board: £23-£25 daily,
£160-£180 weekly.
Evening meal 6pm (l.o. 7pm).
Parking for 8.
Open April-October.
🛏 ↻ ▯ V ⊯ ▥ ▥ 🔔 ▥
T

Bonnington Hotel ♏
APPROVED
44 Tregonwell Road,
Bournemouth, BH2 5NT
☎ (0202) 553621
*Friendly hotel in central
Bournemouth, a short stroll
from beach, conference centre
and shops. Choice of menu.
Cocktail bar.*
Bedrooms: 10 double &
6 twin, 4 family rooms.
Bathrooms: 16 private,
2 public.
Bed & breakfast: £40-£54
double.
Half board: £25-£31 daily,
£160-£205 weekly.
Evening meal 6.15pm (l.o.
6.45pm).
Parking for 16.
Open March-December.
Credit: Access, Visa.
🛏 ▯ ↻ ▯ V ⊯ ▥ ▥ ▵
▥ SP

Cadogan Hotel ♏
COMMENDED
8 Poole Road, Bournemouth,
BH2 5QU
☎ (0202) 763006
Fax (0202) 766168
*Set in spacious grounds close
to the town centre, convenient
for shopping and entertainment
and a few minutes' walk to the
beach through Durley Chine.*
Bedrooms: 12 single,
20 double & 21 twin, 3 family
rooms.
Bathrooms: 56 private.
Bed & breakfast: £27-£35
single, £54-£60 double.

Half board: £32-£43 daily,
£145-£235 weekly.
Lunch available.
Evening meal 6.30pm (l.o.
8.45pm).
Parking for 60.
Credit: Access, Visa, Diners,
Amex.
🛏 ▵ ▱ ↻ ▯ ▯ ↻ ▯ V
▵ TV ◐ ▯ ▥ ▵ 🍴 🔔 ✳
OAP ↘ SP T

Carisbrooke Hotel ♏
⛫⛫⛫⛫
42 Tregonwell Road,
Bournemouth, BH2 5NT
☎ (0202) 290432
*Modern family hotel in
excellent central location,
adjacent to Winter Gardens
and near sea and Bournemouth
International Centre.*
Bedrooms: 3 single, 6 double
& 5 twin, 8 family rooms.
Bathrooms: 19 private,
2 public.
Bed & breakfast: £20-£30
single, £40-£58 double.
Half board: £26-£35 daily,
£155-£199 weekly.
Evening meal 6.30pm (l.o.
7pm).
Parking for 19.
Credit: Access, Visa, Amex.
🛏 ▵ ▱ ↻ ▯ V ⊯ TV ▥
▵ 🍴 OAP ↘ SP T

Carlton Hotel ♏
East Overcliff, Bournemouth,
BH1 3DN
☎ (0202) 552011 Telex 41244
*Independently-owned hotel,
with superb sea views, health
club, outdoor swimming pool.
Award-winning cuisine.*
Bedrooms: 11 single,
21 double & 25 twin, 7 family
rooms.
Bathrooms: 64 private.
Bed & breakfast: £79.50-£120
single, £130-£185 double.
Half board: £79 daily, £475
weekly.
Lunch available.
Evening meal 7pm (l.o.
10pm).
Parking for 165.
Credit: Access, Visa, C.Bl.,
Diners, Amex.
🛏 ▵ ▱ ↻ ▯ ◐ ▯ ▯ V ⊯
◐ ▯ ▥ ▵ 🍴 ▵ 🔔 ✲ ✳
✕ ↘ SP ▥ T

Chequers Hotel ♏
⛫⛫⛫ **APPROVED**
West Cliff Road, West Cliff,
Bournemouth, BH2 5EX
☎ (0202) 553900
*Delightful, comfortable, family-
run hotel renowned for food.
Sea, shops, International
Centre within easy walking
distance.*
Bedrooms: 2 single, 15 double
& 1 twin, 6 family rooms.

Bathrooms: 20 private,
1 public.
Bed & breakfast: £18-£30
single, £36-£60 double.
Half board: £20-£34 daily,
£130-£225 weekly.
Evening meal 6.30pm (l.o.
10pm).
Parking for 27.
Open February-December.
Credit: Access, Visa.
🛏 ▵ ▱ ↻ ▯ V ⊯ TV
▥ ▵ 🔔 OAP ↘ SP T

Chine Hotel ♏
⛫⛫⛫⛫ **APPROVED**
Boscombe Spa Road,
Boscombe, Bournemouth,
BH5 1AX
☎ (0202) 396234
Fax (0202) 391737
*Faces due south overlooking
the sea, with panoramic views
of the whole of Poole Bay and
Boscombe Chine gardens.*
Bedrooms: 9 single, 29 double
& 44 twin, 15 family rooms.
Bathrooms: 97 private.
Bed & breakfast: £40-£50
single, £80-£100 double.
Half board: £56-£65 daily,
£330-£390 weekly.
Lunch available.
Evening meal 7pm (l.o.
8.30pm).
Parking for 45.
Credit: Access, Visa, Diners,
Amex.

Chinebeach Hotel ♏
14 Studland Road, Alum
Chine, Bournemouth,
BH4 8JA
☎ (0202) 767015 & 761218
*Family-run hotel with wide
range of facilities, in beautiful
summer location. Reasonable
prices, popular with all ages.*
Bedrooms: 2 single, 7 double
& 4 twin, 10 family rooms.
Bathrooms: 17 private,
2 public.
Bed & breakfast: £11-£21
single, £22-£42 double.
Half board: £16-£27 daily,
£107-£177 weekly.
Evening meal 6pm (l.o. 3pm).
Parking for 10.
Credit: Access, Visa.
🛏 ▵ ↻ ▯ V ✂
⊯ TV ◐ ▥ ▵ ▵ 🔔 ✕
OAP ↘ SP T

The Cintra Hotel
10-12 Florence Road,
Boscombe, Bournemouth,
BH5 1HF
☎ (0202) 396103

*Family-run south facing hotel
only 5 minutes' walk from
sandy beaches. Pier, shopping
centre and entertainment
nearby. Five-course evening
meal and full English
breakfast. Coaches welcome.*
Bedrooms: 11 single, 8 double
& 8 twin, 12 family rooms.
Bathrooms: 9 private,
8 public.
Bed & breakfast: £14-£18.50
single, £28-£36 double.
Half board: £19-£25.50 daily,
£90-£160 weekly.
Evening meal 6pm (l.o.
10am).
Parking for 14.
🛏 ▵ ▯ ↻ ▯ V ⊯ TV ▵
🍴 ▵ OAP ↘ SP T

Clematis Guest House
5 Westby Road, Boscombe,
Bournemouth, BH5 1HA
☎ (0202) 394791
*Small, comfortable, family-run
guesthouse, 5 minutes from
beach, offering fresh food and
choice of menu.*
Bedrooms: 2 single, 3 double,
3 family rooms.
Bathrooms: 2 public.
Bed & breakfast: £11-£15
single, £22-£30 double.
Half board: £15-£19 daily,
£112-£120 weekly.
Evening meal 6pm (l.o. 6pm).
Parking for 8.
🛏 ▵ ↻ ▯ ⊯ TV ▥ ▵ OAP

Cliff End Hotel ♏
⛫⛫⛫ **APPROVED**
Manor Road, East Cliff,
Bournemouth, BH1 3EX
☎ (0202) 309711 Telex 41141
RJL
⊕ Consort
*On the beautiful East Cliff, the
hotel has all the amenities for
an enjoyable, well-deserved
break. "A hotel for all
seasons".*
Bedrooms: 4 single, 12 double
& 8 twin, 16 family rooms.
Bathrooms: 40 private.
Bed & breakfast: £25-£33.50
single, £50-£67 double.
Half board: £30-£40 daily,
£168-£252 weekly.
Lunch available.
Evening meal 7pm (l.o.
8.30pm).
Parking for 40.
Credit: Access, Visa, Amex.
🛏 ▵ ↻ ▯ ▯ ↻ ▯ V ▵
◐ ▯ ▥ ▵ 🍴 ▵ ✳ ♗ OAP
SP ▥ T

Cliffeside Hotel ♏
⛫⛫⛫
East Overcliff Drive,
Bournemouth, BH1 3AQ
☎ (0202) 555724
Telex 418297 (C.H.)
Continued ▶

BOURNEMOUTH

Continued

On East Cliff with views to the Isle of Wight and the Purbeck Hills. Within easy reach of the town centre.
Bedrooms: 10 single, 20 double & 21 twin, 10 family rooms.
Bathrooms: 61 private.
Bed & breakfast: £35-£49 single, £70-£98 double.
Half board: £35-£52 daily, £224-£329 weekly.
Lunch available.
Evening meal 6.45pm (l.o. 8.30pm).
Parking for 50.
Credit: Access, Visa.

The Connaught Hotel 🅼
COMMENDED
West Hill Road, West Cliff, Bournemouth, BH2 5PH
☎ (0202) 298020
Refurbished hotel centrally situated in an acre of grounds. Restaurant, 3 bars, ballroom, indoor leisure centre with all facilities.
Bedrooms: 11 single, 25 double & 12 twin, 12 family rooms.
Bathrooms: 60 private.
Bed & breakfast: £56-£70 single, £90-£105 double.
Half board: £68-£88 daily, £296-£378 weekly.
Lunch available.
Evening meal 6.30pm (l.o. 10pm).
Parking for 50.
Credit: Access, Visa, Diners, Amex.

The Cottage 🅼
COMMENDED
12 Southern Road, Southbourne, Bournemouth, BH6 3SR
☎ (0202) 422764
Character family-run hotel noted for home-prepared fresh cooking and tastefully furnished accommodation. No smoking in dining room and bedrooms.
Bedrooms: 1 single, 1 double & 2 twin, 3 family rooms.
Bathrooms: 4 private, 2 public; 1 private shower.
Bed & breakfast: £13.50-£17.50 single, £27-£35 double.
Half board: £19.50-£23.50 daily, £128-£154 weekly.
Evening meal 6pm (l.o. 6pm).
Parking for 8.

The County Hotel
Westover Road, Bournemouth, BH1 2BT
☎ (0202) 552385
Comfortable and friendly hotel in the heart of Bournemouth, only 2 minutes' walk from beaches, theatres, cinemas and shops. Bar lunches.
Bedrooms: 5 single, 15 double & 19 twin, 12 family rooms.
Bathrooms: 46 private, 5 public.
Bed & breakfast: £20-£40 single, £40-£60 double.
Half board: £26-£45 daily, £160-£219 weekly.
Evening meal 6.30pm (l.o. 8pm).
Credit: Access, Visa, Amex.

Craiglea Hotel 🅼
75 Sea Road, Boscombe, Bournemouth, BH5 1BG
☎ (0202) 395910
Small friendly hotel 120 yards from pier and beach. Comfortable bar lounge.
Bedrooms: 2 single, 4 double & 2 twin, 2 family rooms.
Bathrooms: 7 private, 1 public.
Bed & breakfast: £11-£20 single, £22-£44 double.
Half board: £17.50-£26.50 daily, £80-£140 weekly.
Evening meal 6pm.
Parking for 5.

Cransley Hotel
11 Knyveton Road, East Cliff, Bournemouth, BH1 3QG
☎ (0202) 290067
Set in delightful grounds in pine-clad road. Close to East Cliff and all amenities. High standards and personal attention assured.
Bedrooms: 1 single, 5 double & 4 twin, 2 family rooms.
Bathrooms: 9 private, 1 public; 1 private shower.
Bed & breakfast: £14-£24 single, £28-£52 double.
Half board: £20-£30 daily, £100-£149 weekly.
Evening meal 6pm (l.o. 6pm).
Parking for 10.
Open April-November.
Credit: Access, Visa.

Crosbie Hall Hotel
21 Florence Road, Boscombe, Bournemouth, BH5 1HJ
☎ (0202) 394714

Delightful character hotel offering comfort, cleanliness, food, friendly atmosphere and excellent value. Near beach, gardens, shops and transport.
Bedrooms: 3 single, 5 double & 2 twin, 7 family rooms.
Bathrooms: 12 private, 2 public.
Bed & breakfast: £15-£24 single, £30-£48 double.
Half board: £22-£30 daily, £119-£184 weekly.
Evening meal 6pm (l.o. 6.15pm).
Parking for 14.
Open January-October.

Cumberland Hotel 🅼
East Overcliff Drive, Bournemouth, BH1 3AF
☎ (0202) 290722
Telex 418297 CuH
Modern hotel with all rooms en-suite, offering a high standard of personal service, entertainment and amenities for businessmen and holidaymakers alike.
Bedrooms: 12 single, 32 double & 52 twin, 6 family rooms.
Bathrooms: 102 private, 1 public.
Half board: £36-£55 daily, £245-£360 weekly.
Lunch available.
Evening meal 7pm (l.o. 8.30pm).
Parking for 50.
Credit: Access, Visa.

Dorset Rivers Hotel 🅼
APPROVED
17 Drummond Road, Boscombe, Bournemouth, BH1 4DP
☎ (0202) 396550
Small hotel run by chef/proprietor close to Boscombe Gardens. Easy walk to sea and new shopping centre.
Bedrooms: 2 single, 2 double & 2 twin, 2 family rooms.
Bathrooms: 4 private, 1 public; 1 private shower.
Bed & breakfast: £14.50-£21.50 single, £29-£43 double.
Half board: £20-£27 daily, £105-£150 weekly.
Evening meal 6pm (l.o. 2pm).
Parking for 3.

Durley Hall Hotel 🅼
7 Durley Chine Road, Bournemouth, BH2 5JS
☎ (0202) 766886
🆑 Consort
Set in secluded gardens, minutes from town centre and beach, offering exceptional facilites. Indoor leisure complex, outdoor pool, hairdresser and beautician.
Bedrooms: 12 single, 28 double & 20 twin, 21 family rooms.
Bathrooms: 81 private.
Bed & breakfast: £40-£60 single, £80-£120 double.
Half board: £55.50-£75.50 daily, £262-£428 weekly.
Lunch available.
Evening meal 7pm (l.o. 8.45pm).
Parking for 150.
Credit: Access, Visa, Diners, Amex.

East Anglia Hotel 🅼
APPROVED
6 Poole Road, Bournemouth, BH2 5QX
☎ (0202) 765163
Fax (0202) 752949
Ideally situated for town centre, beach and Bournemouth International Centre. Fully modernised hotel offering every comfort plus solarium, free jacuzzi, sauna and mini-gym.
Bedrooms: 17 single, 16 double & 22 twin, 18 family rooms.
Bathrooms: 73 private.
Bed & breakfast: £38-£42.50 single, £70-£85 double.
Half board: £44-£51.50 daily, £280-£325.50 weekly.
Lunch available.
Evening meal 6.30pm (l.o. 8.30pm).
Parking for 60.
Credit: Access, Visa, Diners, Amex.

Egerton House Hotel
Listed
385 Holdenhurst Road, Queens Park, Bournemouth, BH8 9AN
☎ (0202) 394024
Tastefully appointed, family-run hotel, near Bournemouth and Boscombe town centre and West Cliff Promenade. Convenient for public transport.
Bedrooms: 2 single, 3 double & 2 twin, 2 family rooms.

Bathrooms: 1 private,
2 public.
Bed & breakfast: £14-£16
single, £28-£32 double.
Half board: £16-£19 daily,
£90-£110 weekly.
Lunch available.
Evening meal 6pm (l.o. 6pm).
Parking for 8.
 ♿ 🛁 🖳 🖁 🏃 ✠ 📺 ▥
🛄 ✕ SP

Elstead Hotel M
🏵🏵🏵🏵 COMMENDED

Knyveton Road,
Bournemouth, BH1 3QP
☎ (0202) 293071
*Set in a pleasant garden, with
ample parking, offering a
friendly atmosphere and
personal service.*
Bedrooms: 8 single, 18 double
& 22 twin, 3 family rooms.
Bathrooms: 50 private,
2 public.
Bed & breakfast: £26.50-£30
single, from £53 double.
Half board: £40-£42 daily,
£258-£272 weekly.
Lunch available.
Evening meal 7pm (l.o.
8.30pm).
Parking for 46.
Open April-October.
Credit: Access, Visa.
 ♿ 🖳 🖁 🏃 🖁 ▥ ✠ 🏃
🟥 🖩 ▥ 🛄 ♦ ★ 🌢 SP ⊤

Fircroft Hotel M
🏵🏵🏵 APPROVED

Owls Road, Bournemouth,
BH5 1AE
☎ (0202) 309771
Fax (0202) 302542
*Long-established family hotel,
close to sea and comprehensive
shopping. Free entry to hotel-
owned sports and leisure club
between 9am and 6pm.*
Bedrooms: 6 single, 16 double
& 12 twin, 15 family rooms.
Bathrooms: 49 private.
Bed & breakfast: £22.50-
£26.50 single, £45-£53 double.
Half board: £29-£33 daily,
£140-£207 weekly.
Lunch available.
Evening meal 6.30pm (l.o.
8pm).
Parking for 50.
Credit: Access, Visa, Amex.
 ♿ 🖳 ☎ 🖳 🖁 ▥ 🟥
📺 🖩 ▥ 🛄 ♦ ★ 🌢 🔲
★ DAP 🌢 SP ⊤

The Five Ways Hotel M
🏵🏵🏵 APPROVED

23 Argyll Road, Boscombe,
Bournemouth, BH5 1EB
☎ (0202) 301509 & 304971
*Near beach and shopping
parade, especially suitable for
family holidays. All rooms en-
suite. 5% discount for
pensioners, off season.*

Bedrooms: 4 single, 5 double
& 2 twin, 4 family rooms.
Bathrooms: 15 private.
Bed & breakfast: £18-£21
single, £36-£42 double.
Half board: £23-£26.50 daily,
£127.50-£162.50 weekly.
Lunch available.
Evening meal 6pm (l.o.
10am).
Parking for 10.
Open February-December.
Credit: Access, Visa.
 ♿ 🖳 ☎ 🖳 🖁 ▥ 🟥 ✠ 📺
🖩 🛄 🖁 ⊤ DAP 🌢 SP

The Garthlyn Hotel M
🏵🏵🏵 COMMENDED

6 Sandbourne Road, Alum
Chine, Westbourne,
Bournemouth, BH4 8JH
☎ (0202) 761016
*Hotel of character with lovely
gardens. Good quality beds,
home cooking and comforts. 4
minutes' walk to beaches (hut
available).*
Bedrooms: 6 double & 1 twin,
3 family rooms.
Bathrooms: 9 private,
1 public.
Bed & breakfast: £22.50-£30
single, £40-£55 double.
Half board: £30-£37.50 daily,
£170-£200 weekly.
Evening meal 6pm (l.o. 8pm).
Parking for 9.
 ♿4 📺 🖳 🖁 ▥ ✠ 🟥 📺 🖁
🖩 🛄 ♦ ★ ❉ ✕ DAP 🌢 SP

Golden Sands Hotel M
🏵🏵🏵 APPROVED

83 Alumhurst Road, Alum
Chine, Bournemouth,
BH4 8HR
☎ (0202) 763832
*Small, well-run hotel, where
comfort and good home cooked
food are the priorities.
Personal service with homely
atmosphere.*
Bedrooms: 6 double & 3 twin,
1 family room.
Bathrooms: 10 private.
Bed & breakfast: £19-£25
single, £38-£50 double.
Half board: £27-£32 daily,
£143-£190 weekly.
Evening meal 6pm (l.o. 4pm).
Parking for 10.
Open February-December.
 ♿4 📺 🖳 🖁 ✠ 🟥 📺 🖩 ▥
🛄 DAP 🌢 SP

Grindley House Hotel
22 St. Catherine's Road,
Southbourne, Bournemouth,
BH6 4AB
☎ (0202) 421243

---

*The national Crown
scheme is explained
in full on pages
536 – 539.*

---

*Small, family-run, comfortable
hotel with beautiful sea views,
spacious accommodation and
home cooking. Home-from-
home atmosphere. Peaceful
area of Bournemouth within
easy reach of town centre,
Christchurch and riverside
activities.*
Bedrooms: 2 single, 3 double
& 1 twin, 2 family rooms.
Bathrooms: 3 private,
3 public.
Bed & breakfast: £14-£16.50
single, £24-£29 double.
Half board: £19-£21.50 daily,
£119-£135 weekly.
Evening meal 6pm (l.o.
6.30pm).
Parking for 6.
 ♿ 🖳 🖁 ▥ 🟥 📺
SP

Hartford Court Hotel M
🏵🏵🏵 COMMENDED

48 Christchurch Road,
Bournemouth, BH1 3PE
☎ (0202) 551712 & 293682
*Recently extended hotel with
additional bedrooms and
tastefully refurbished public
areas. Large car park. Close to
sea and town centre.*
Bedrooms: 9 single, 23 double
& 4 twin, 4 family rooms.
Bathrooms: 32 private,
1 public.
Bed & breakfast: £23-£27
single, £37-£50 double.
Half board: £24.50-£33 daily,
£135-£205 weekly.
Evening meal 6pm (l.o.
7.30pm).
Parking for 36.
Credit: Access, Visa, Diners,
Amex.
 ♿10 ♿ 🖳 ☎ 🖳 🖁 ▥
🟥 📺 🖩 🛄 ♦ ★ 🌢 🔲 SP

Hawthorns Hotel M
🏵🏵🏵 COMMENDED

Westerham Road/Alumhurst
Road, Westbourne,
Bournemouth, BH4 8EY
☎ (0202) 760220
*Small, friendly hotel, recently
refurbished. Close to Alum
Chine, beaches and
Westbourne shopping arcades.*
Bedrooms: 2 single, 3 double
& 2 twin, 2 family rooms.
Bathrooms: 9 private,
1 public.
Bed & breakfast: £15-£20
single, £30-£40 double.
Half board: £20-£25 daily,
£120-£160 weekly.
Evening meal 6pm (l.o.
7.30pm).
Parking for 6.
Credit: Access, Visa.
 ♿ 🖳 ☎ 🖳 🖁 ▥ 🟥 ✠ 🟥 📺
🖩 🛄 ✕ DAP 🌢 SP

The Hermitage Hotel
🏵🏵🏵🏵 COMMENDED

Exeter Road, Bournemouth,
BH2 5AH
☎ (0202) 557363
Fax (0202) 559173
*On the seafront overlooking the
pier, the hotel is within minutes
of the town centre and
Bournemouth International
Centre.*
Bedrooms: 24 single,
43 double, 4 family rooms.
Bathrooms: 71 private.
Bed & breakfast: £41-£52.50
single, £82-£100 double.
Half board: £48.50-£57.50
daily.
Lunch available.
Evening meal 6.45pm (l.o.
8.45pm).
Parking for 60.
Credit: Access, Visa, Diners,
Amex.
 ♿ 🖳 🖌 ☎ 🖳 🖁 ▥ ✠
🟥 📺 🖩 🛄 ♦ ★ 🌢 ★ 🔲
🌢 SP 🔲 ⊤

Highclere Private
Hotel M
🏵🏵🏵 APPROVED

15 Burnaby Road, Alum
Chine, Bournemouth,
BH4 8JF
☎ (0202) 761350
*Small family hotel with ample
parking, garden, playroom,
solarium and some bedrooms
with sea views. Children very
welcome at reduced tariff.*
Bedrooms: 3 double & 1 twin,
5 family rooms.
Bathrooms: 9 private.
Bed & breakfast: £21.50-
£23.50 single, £43-£27.50
double.
Half board: £24-£27.50 daily,
£145-£164 weekly.
Evening meal 6pm (l.o.
5.30pm).
Parking for 7.
Open April-October.
Credit: Access, Visa, Amex.
 ♿3 🖳 ☎ 🖳 🖁 ▥ 🟥 📺
🖩 DAP SP ⊤

Hilde's Guest House
211 Holdenhurst Road,
Bournemouth, BH8 8DE
☎ (0202) 555171
*Comfortable, small guesthouse
with a homely atmosphere,
close to coach and railway
stations, superb shopping centre
and magnificent beaches.*
Bedrooms: 2 single, 4 double
& 2 twin, 1 family room.
Bathrooms: 2 public.
Bed & breakfast: £14-£20
single, £26-£30 double.
Continued ▶

459

BOURNEMOUTH
Continued

Half board: £18-£20 daily, £120-£140 weekly.
Evening meal 6pm (l.o. 6.30pm).
Parking for 8.

Hinton Firs ⋔
COMMENDED
Manor Road, East Cliff, Bournemouth, BH1 3HB
☎ (0202) 555409
Fax (0202) 299607
Friendly family hotel set among pines in the heart of the East Cliff, with 4 sunny lounges facing sheltered garden and pool.
Bedrooms: 12 single, 13 double & 13 twin, 14 family rooms.
Bathrooms: 52 private, 1 public.
Bed & breakfast: £33-£50 single, £66-£96 double.
Half board: £38-£55 daily, £266-£330 weekly.
Lunch available.
Evening meal 7pm (l.o. 8.30pm).
Parking for 40.
Credit: Access, Visa.

The Hollies Guest House
19 Norwich Avenue, Bournemouth, BH2 5TG
☎ (0202) 551394
Town centre guesthouse, with TV lounge, dining room with separate tables, hot and cold water and shaver points in all bedrooms. Free car parking.
Bedrooms: 1 single, 4 double, 2 family rooms.
Bathrooms: 2 public.
Bed & breakfast: £12.50-£15 single, £24-£28 double.
Parking for 7.
Open February-November.

Kingsley Guest House ⋔
Listed
38 St. Michaels Road, Bournemouth, BH2 5DY
☎ (0202) 295210
Family-run guesthouse, 5 minutes from beach, town centre and Bournemouth International Centre. Home cooking.
Bedrooms: 1 single, 2 double & 1 twin, 1 family room.
Bathrooms: 1 private, 1 public.
Bed & breakfast: £10-£15 single, £20-£40 double.

Half board: £17-£26 daily, £110-£150 weekly.
Evening meal 6pm (l.o. 6.30pm).

Lynmouth Private Hotel
Listed
3 Hamilton Road, Boscombe, Bournemouth, BH1 4EQ
☎ (0202) 393131
Small family-run hotel, ideally situated for sea and shops, with comfortable rooms. Price reductions for pensioners.
Bedrooms: 1 single, 1 double & 1 twin, 3 family rooms.
Bathrooms: 1 private, 1 public; 1 private shower.
Bed & breakfast: £14-£15 single, £27-£29 double.
Half board: £18-£20 daily, £125-£130 weekly.
Evening meal 6pm.
Parking for 5.

Marsham Court Hotel ⋔
APPROVED
Russell-Cotes Road, East Cliff, Bournemouth, BH1 3AB
☎ (0202) 552111
Fax (0202) 294744
Overlooking bay in quiet central situation with sun terraces, outdoor swimming pool. Edwardian bar and summer entertainment. Free accommodation for children. Snooker. Parking.
Bedrooms: 10 single, 21 double & 44 twin, 11 family rooms.
Bathrooms: 86 private.
Bed & breakfast: £53-£63 single, £86-£96 double.
Half board: £50-£55 daily, £322-£357 weekly.
Lunch available.
Evening meal 7pm (l.o. 9pm).
Parking for 100.
Credit: Access, Visa, Diners, Amex.

Mayfield Private Hotel
⊕⊕
46 Frances Road, Bournemouth, BH1 3SA
☎ (0202) 551839
Overlooking public gardens with tennis, bowling, putting greens. Central for sea, shops and main rail/coach stations. Some rooms with shower or toilet/shower. Licensed.
Bedrooms: 1 single, 4 double & 2 twin, 1 family room.

Bathrooms: 4 private, 2 public; 3 private showers.
Bed & breakfast: £13-£16 single, £26-£32 double.
Half board: £18-£21 daily, £97-£120 weekly.
Evening meal 6pm.
Parking for 5.
Open January-November.

Hotel Mon Bijou
47 Manor Road, East Cliff, Bournemouth, BH1 3EU
☎ (0202) 551389
An enchanting hotel of character personally maintained by proprietors. Exquisitely furnished. Well-appointed bedrooms with trouser press, hairdryer, video. French cuisine.
Bedrooms: 5 double & 2 twin.
Bathrooms: 7 private.
Bed & breakfast: £28-£33 single, £48-£65 double.
Half board: £33-£40 daily, £190-£250 weekly.
Evening meal 7pm (l.o. 8pm).
Parking for 8.
Credit: Access, Visa, Amex.

Norfolk Royale Hotel ⋔
HIGHLY COMMENDED
Richmond Hill, Bournemouth, BH2 6EN
☎ (0202) 551521
Telex 418474
In the heart of Bournemouth amidst wonderful shops and a wide range of entertainment and within walking distance of beaches.
Bedrooms: 9 single, 46 double & 32 twin, 8 family rooms.
Bathrooms: 95 private.
Bed & breakfast: £56-£103.50 single, £82-£142 double.
Half board: £57-£65 daily.
Lunch available.
Evening meal 7pm (l.o. 11pm).
Parking for 88.
Credit: Access, Visa, C.Bl., Diners, Amex.

Norland Private Hotel ⋔
⊕⊕
6 Westby Road, Boscombe, Bournemouth, BH5 1HD
☎ (0202) 396729
Comfortable, family hotel with residential licence, English food and attentive service at all times. Children and senior citizens at reduced rates.
Bedrooms: 1 single, 5 double, 3 family rooms.
Bathrooms: 3 private, 2 public.

Bed & breakfast: £13-£17 single, £26-£38 double.
Half board: £18-£22 daily, £105-£130 weekly.
Evening meal 6pm (l.o. 4pm).
Parking for 7.

Palace Court Hotel ⋔
COMMENDED
Westover Road, Bournemouth, BH1 2BZ
☎ (0202) 557681
Fax (0202) 554918
Telex 418451
Modern, centrally-located hotel with garage parking. Most rooms with sea views and balconies. Leisure complex and pool, a choice of restaurants with nightspot.
Bedrooms: 9 single, 56 double & 27 twin, 15 family rooms.
Bathrooms: 107 private.
Bed & breakfast: £60-£65 single, £95-£190 double.
Half board: £57.50-£110 daily, £315-£770 weekly.
Lunch available.
Evening meal 7pm (l.o. 9pm).
Parking for 200.
Credit: Access, Visa, Diners, Amex.

Hotel Piccadilly ⋔
⊕⊕⊕
Bath Road, Bournemouth, BH1 2NN
☎ (0202) 552559 & 556420
Central location with food served in attractive Fountains restaurant. Stylish bedrooms recently refurbished providing every convenience. Car parking facilities.
Bedrooms: 5 single, 24 double & 14 twin, 2 family rooms.
Bathrooms: 45 private.
Bed & breakfast: £39-£45 single, £57-£69 double.
Half board: £36-£40 daily, £225-£275 weekly.
Lunch available.
Evening meal 6.30pm (l.o. 9pm).
Parking for 36.
Credit: Access, Visa, Diners, Amex.

Queen's Hotel ⋔
⊕⊕⊕
Meyrick Road, East Cliff, Bournemouth, BH1 3DL
☎ (0202) 554415
Telex 418297
Modern, family-run hotel near the beach, ideal for family holidays, with facilities for business conventions.

Bedrooms: 9 single, 47 double & 46 twin, 8 family rooms.
Bathrooms: 110 private.
Half board: £36-£55 daily, £240-£350 weekly.
Lunch available.
Evening meal 7pm (l.o. 9pm).
Parking for 80.
Credit: Access, Visa.

Riviera Hotel M
APPROVED
12-16 Burnaby Road, Alum Chine, Bournemouth, BH4 8JF
☎ (0202) 763653 Telex 41363
Ⓡ Calotels
Family hotel occupying unique position overlooking Alum Chine with uninterrupted views of the Isle of Wight.
Bedrooms: 6 single, 22 double & 20 twin, 30 family rooms.
Bathrooms: 78 private.
Bed & breakfast: £25-£50 single, £50-£100 double.
Half board: £30-£50 daily, £210-£350 weekly.
Lunch available.
Evening meal 7pm (l.o. 8.30pm).
Parking for 80.
Credit: Access, Visa.

Hotel Riviera
APPROVED
Westcliff Gardens, Bournemouth, BH2 5HL
☎ (0202) 552845
On the West Cliff of Bournemouth overlooking the sea, with a garden which has direct access to the clifftop.
Bedrooms: 7 single, 13 double & 10 twin, 4 family rooms.
Bathrooms: 34 private.
Bed & breakfast: £24-£30 single, £48-£60 double.
Half board: £30-£36 daily, £180-£230 weekly.
Lunch available.
Evening meal 6.30pm (l.o. 7.15pm).
Parking for 24.
Open April-October.
Credit: Access, Visa.

Rivoli Hotel
95 St. Michael's Road, West Cliff, Bournemouth, BH2 5DS
☎ (0202) 290292
Detached building situated on Bournemouth's West Cliff, 150 yards from clifftop walk, with access to beach and pier without crossing road.

Bedrooms: 6 single, 5 double & 3 twin, 4 family rooms.
Bathrooms: 10 private, 2 public.
Bed & breakfast: £18-£23.50 single, £36-£47 double.
Half board: £24-£30 daily, £145-£180 weekly.
Evening meal 6.30pm (l.o. 7pm).
Parking for 14.
Open February-December.
Credit: Access, Visa.

Royal Exeter Hotel M
APPROVED
Exeter Road, Bournemouth, BH2 5AG
☎ (0202) 290566 & 290567
Within walking distance of the beach and town centre. The original holiday home of Bournemouth, built 1810.
Bedrooms: 6 single, 17 double & 3 twin, 10 family rooms.
Bathrooms: 36 private.
Bed & breakfast: £48-£55 single, £64 double.
Lunch available.
Evening meal 6pm (l.o. 10pm).
Parking for 65.
Credit: Access, Visa, Diners, Amex.

San Remo Hotel
7 Durley Road, Bournemouth, BH2 5JQ
☎ (0202) 290558
Ideally situated, facing south, completely detached, with ample parking, a homely atmosphere and varied menu. Ground floor bedrooms.
Bedrooms: 2 single, 7 double & 3 twin, 6 family rooms.
Bathrooms: 14 private, 2 public.
Bed & breakfast: £17-£22 single, £19.50-£24.50 double.
Half board: £22-£27 daily, £122-£199 weekly.
Evening meal 6pm (l.o. 6.30pm).
Parking for 20.
Open March-October.

The Savoy Hotel
APPROVED
West Hill Road, West Cliff, Bournemouth, BH2 5EJ
☎ (0202) 294241
Fax (0202) 398367
Elegant Victorian hotel in large grounds on Bournemouth's fashionable West Cliff. Beach and town centre only a stroll away.

Bedrooms: 20 single, 31 double & 30 twin, 10 family rooms.
Bathrooms: 91 private.
Bed & breakfast: £37.50-£53.50 single, £92.50-£114 double.
Half board: £49-£57 daily.
Lunch available.
Evening meal 7pm (l.o. 8.30pm).
Parking for 70.
Credit: Access, Visa, Diners, Amex.

Seabreeze Hotel M
32 St. Catherines Road, Southbourne, Bournemouth, BH6 4AB
☎ (0202) 433888
Located opposite beach with glorious sea views and easy access to Bournemouth and Christchurch. Peaceful, small hotel with family atmosphere. Generous home cooking. Children half price. Vegetarians welcome.
Bedrooms: 1 single, 1 double & 2 twin, 4 family rooms.
Bathrooms: 6 private, 1 public.
Bed & breakfast: £14-£20 single, £28-£32 double.
Evening meal 6pm (l.o. 4pm).
Parking for 8.

Seaway Wavecrest Lodge
30 St. Catherines Road, Southbourne, Bournemouth, BH6 4AB
☎ (0202) 423636
Delightfully situated overlooking sea, yet within easy reach of Christchurch and Bournemouth.
Bedrooms: 1 single, 2 double & 2 twin, 4 family rooms.
Bathrooms: 8 private, 1 public.
Bed & breakfast: £14.50-£16 single, £27-£31 double.
Half board: £20-£22 daily, £125-£135 weekly.
Evening meal 6.15pm (l.o. 10am).
Parking for 9.
Open February-November.

Southernhay Hotel M
COMMENDED
42 Alum Chine Road, Westbourne, Bournemouth, BH4 8DX
☎ (0202) 761251
You are sure of a warm welcome. Own keys. Full English breakfast.

Bedrooms: 1 single, 3 double & 2 twin, 1 family room.
Bathrooms: 6 private, 2 public.
Bed & breakfast: £16-£20 single, £35-£44 double.
Parking for 10.
Credit: Access, Visa.

Sun Court Hotel M
APPROVED
West Hill Road, West Cliff, Bournemouth, BH2 5PH
☎ (0202) 551343
A modern hotel 5 minutes' walk from all amenities, offering high standards of cleanliness and comfort. Bar lunches.
Bedrooms: 5 single, 14 double & 13 twin, 4 family rooms.
Bathrooms: 36 private.
Bed & breakfast: £29.25-£38.50 single, £58.50-£77 double.
Half board: £34.75-£44.50 daily, £137-£266 weekly.
Lunch available.
Evening meal 7pm (l.o. 8.30pm).
Parking for 52.
Credit: Access, Visa, Diners, Amex.

Suncliff Hotel M
East Overcliff Drive, Bournemouth, BH1 3AG
☎ (0202) 291711 Telex 41363
Ⓡ Calotels
Overlooking Bournemouth Bay with uninterrupted views of the Purbeck Hills and Isle of Wight.
Bedrooms: 13 single, 28 double & 25 twin, 29 family rooms.
Bathrooms: 95 private.
Bed & breakfast: £29-£57 single, £58-£114 double.
Half board: £30-£65 daily, £210-£455 weekly.
Lunch available.
Evening meal 7pm (l.o. 8.30pm).
Parking for 60.
Credit: Access, Visa, Diners, Amex.

The Swallow Highcliff
COMMENDED
St. Michael's Road, West Cliff, Bournemouth, BH2 5DU
☎ (0202) 557702
Telex 417153
Ⓡ Swallow

Continued ▶

461

SOUTH OF ENGLAND

BOURNEMOUTH
Continued

Clifftop position, close to main shopping area and car parking. Bar, brasserie and nightclub within grounds and children's playrooms indoors and out.
Bedrooms: 13 single, 55 double & 54 twin, 35 family rooms.
Bathrooms: 157 private.
Bed & breakfast: from £85 single, from £120 double.
Lunch available.
Evening meal 7pm (l.o. 9pm).
Parking for 130.
Credit: Access, Visa, Diners, Amex.

Taurus Park Hotel
16 Knyveton Road, Bournemouth, BH1 3QN
☎ (0202) 557374
Modern establishment, pleasantly and conveniently situated on the East Cliff, within easy reach of both coach and train stations.
Bedrooms: 5 single, 24 double & 10 twin, 7 family rooms.
Bathrooms: 33 private, 8 public.
Bed & breakfast: £15.50-£22 single, £31-£44 double.
Half board: £18-£26 daily, £106-£178.50 weekly.
Evening meal 6.30pm (l.o. 7.30pm).
Parking for 20.

Tralee Hotel M
West Hill Road, West Cliff, Bournemouth, BH2 5EQ
☎ (0202) 556246
Leisure and entertainment facilities for all the family. Cliff top position close to town centre, shops, shows and leisure centre.
Bedrooms: 2 single, 29 double & 29 twin, 30 family rooms.
Bathrooms: 90 private, 2 public.
Bed & breakfast: £32.25-£44.50 single, £64.50-£89 double.
Half board: £37.25-£49.50 daily, £260.75-£329.50 weekly.
Lunch available.
Evening meal 6.45pm (l.o. 8pm).
Parking for 40.
Credit: Access, Visa, C.Bl., Diners, Amex.

Trent Private Hotel M
12 Studland Road, Westbourne, Bournemouth, BH4 8JA
☎ (0202) 761088
In Alum Chine, with steps from the garden to within 300 yards of the beach. Sea views from some bedrooms. Half board price based on a double room.
Bedrooms: 5 double & 2 twin, 3 family rooms.
Bathrooms: 9 private, 1 public; 1 private shower.
Bed & breakfast: £22-£25 single, £40-£50 double.
Half board: £23-£25 daily, £140-£170 weekly.
Evening meal 6.15pm (l.o. 6.30pm).
Parking for 10.
Credit: Access, Visa.

Trouville Hotel M
Priory Road, West Cliff, Bournemouth, BH2 5DH
☎ (0202) 552262 & Fax (0202) 294810
Centrally situated, recently refurbished hotel. Within easy walking distance of the beach and town centre amenities.
Bedrooms: 9 single, 27 double & 29 twin, 14 family rooms.
Bathrooms: 79 private, 1 public.
Half board: £35-£49.50 daily, £245-£340 weekly.
Evening meal 7pm (l.o. 8.30pm).
Parking for 76.
Credit: Access, Visa.

Ullswater Hotel M
Westcliff Gardens, Bournemouth, BH2 5HW
☎ (0202) 555181
On the West Cliff, a few minutes from the town centre and shops, 150 yards from the clifftop and path to beach.
Bedrooms: 8 single, 14 double & 13 twin, 7 family rooms.
Bathrooms: 42 private.
Bed & breakfast: £23-£30 single, £46-£60 double.
Half board: £23.50-£35 daily, £154-£220 weekly.
Lunch available.
Evening meal 7pm (l.o. 8pm).
Parking for 10.
Credit: Access, Visa, Amex.

Wessex Hotel M
�*COMMENDED*
West Cliff Road, Bournemouth, BH2 5EU
☎ (0202) 551911
Ⓖ Forestdale
Close to beach and shops, with good parking facilities, themed bars, leisure facilities and seasonal entertainment.
Bedrooms: 14 single, 31 double & 28 twin, 11 family rooms.
Bathrooms: 84 private.
Bed & breakfast: from £57.50 single, from £77.50 double.
Lunch available.
Evening meal 6.30pm (l.o. 9.15pm).
Parking for 200.
Credit: Access, Visa, Diners, Amex.

West Leigh Hotel M
26 West Hill Road, West Cliff, Bournemouth, BH2 5PG
☎ (0202) 296989
Facilities of sauna, jacuzzi, solarium, mini gym and indoor pool are unusual for this size of hotel. Lunch served on Sundays.
Bedrooms: 2 single, 15 double & 11 twin.
Bathrooms: 27 private, 2 public.
Bed & breakfast: £25-£35 single, £45-£63 double.
Half board: £31-£37 daily, £180-£230 weekly.
Evening meal 6.30pm (l.o. 7.30pm).
Parking for 27.
Credit: Access, Visa, Diners, Amex.

Whitehall Hotel
Exeter Park Road, Bournemouth, BH2 5AX
☎ (0202) 554682
Fax (0202) 554682
Adjacent to Bournemouth International Centre, with private footpath into central gardens and traffic-free access to shops and beach.
Bedrooms: 13 single, 17 double & 14 twin, 5 family rooms.
Bathrooms: 44 private, 4 public.
Bed & breakfast: £26-£27 single, £52-£54 double.
Half board: £36-£37 daily, £179-£233 weekly.
Evening meal 6.30pm (l.o. 8pm).

Parking for 25.
Open March-November.
Credit: Access, Visa, Diners, Amex.

Winter Dene Hotel
11 Durley Road South, West Cliff, Bournemouth, BH2 5JH
☎ (0202) 554150
Family-run hotel in own grounds, central for beach, shops and Bournemouth International Centre. All rooms en-suite with TV and tea/coffee-making facilities. Parking.
Bedrooms: 4 single, 4 double, 7 family rooms.
Bathrooms: 15 private, 1 public.
Bed & breakfast: £21-£26.50 single, £42-£53 double.
Half board: £26.50-£32 daily, £161-£200 weekly.
Evening meal 6pm.
Parking for 12.
Open March-December.

Winterbourne Hotel M
Priory Road, Bournemouth, BH2 5DJ
☎ (0202) 296366
Fax (0202) 780073
Ⓖ Inter
Enjoying a prime position with magnificent sea view, the hotel is within 500 metres of Bournemouth International Centre, shops, theatres and beach.
Bedrooms: 6 single, 13 double & 10 twin, 12 family rooms.
Bathrooms: 41 private.
Bed & breakfast: £34-£45 single, £60-£81 double.
Half board: £41-£47 daily, £160-£290 weekly.
Lunch available.
Evening meal 6.30pm (l.o. 8pm).
Parking for 34.
Credit: Access, Visa, Amex.

Wood Lodge Hotel M
10 Manor Road, East Cliff, Bournemouth, BH1 3EY
☎ (0202) 290891
Pleasant and comfortable house of character in delightful surroundings, 300 yards from the East Overcliff Drive. Ideally situated for enjoying Bournemouth's many excellent facilities.

462

Bedrooms: 2 single, 5 double & 3 twin, 5 family rooms.
Bathrooms: 14 private, 1 public.
Bed & breakfast: £23.75-£29.50 single, £47.50-£59 double.
Half board: £29-£36 daily, £180-£214 weekly.
Evening meal 6.30pm (l.o. 7pm).
Parking for 12.
Open April-October.
Credit: Access, Visa.

Woodcroft Tower Hotel M
APPROVED

Gervis Road, East Cliff, Bournemouth, BH1 3DE
☎ (0202) 558202
CR Consort
Secluded hotel facing south in an acre of well laid out garden, within a few minutes' walk of shops, entertainments and seafront.
Bedrooms: 3 single, 16 double & 12 twin, 9 family rooms.
Bathrooms: 38 private, 5 public.
Bed & breakfast: £30-£40 single, £50-£60 double.
Half board: £34-£45 daily, £199-£240 weekly.
Evening meal 7pm (l.o. 8.30pm).
Parking for 40.
Credit: Access, Visa.

Wychcote Hotel M

2 Somerville Road, West Cliff, Bournemouth, BH2 5LH
☎ (0202) 557898
Small, well-appointed, private hotel standing in its own gardens. Quiet but near to all facilities. Varied food.
Bedrooms: 1 single, 6 double & 4 twin, 1 family room.
Bathrooms: 8 private, 2 public.
Bed & breakfast: £17.50-£25 single, £35-£50 double.
Half board: £25-£29.50 daily, £130-£195 weekly.
Evening meal 6.15pm.
Parking for 15.
Open February-December.
Credit: Access, Visa.

Please mention this guide when making a booking.

BRAMSHAW

Hampshire
Map ref 2C3

5m NW. Lyndhurst
On the northern fringe of the New Forest, hidden among the trees. At Nomansland, so called as it was originally the squatters who built it, red-brick houses sit back from the village green with its cricket pitch.

Bramble Hill Hotel M
Bramshaw, Nr. Lyndhurst, SO43 7JG
☎ Southampton (0703) 813165
In the quiet part of the New Forest. Own livery stables for guests' horses and 2 golf-courses nearby in Bramshaw.
Bedrooms: 1 single, 8 double & 2 twin, 2 family rooms.
Bathrooms: 9 private, 3 public.
Bed & breakfast: £35-£55 single, £70-£90 double.
Half board: £45-£70 daily, £285-£350 weekly.
Lunch available.
Evening meal 7pm (l.o. 9.30pm).
Parking for 70.
Open April-December.
Credit: Access, Visa.

BROCKENHURST

Hampshire
Map ref 2C3

Attractive village with thatched cottages and a ford in its main street. Well placed for visiting the New Forest.

Balmer Lawn Hotel M
Lyndhurst Road, Brockenhurst, SO42 7ZB
☎ Lymington (0590) 23116
Telex 47457
CR Hilton
Set in the heart of the New Forest, offering peaceful surroundings and a whole range of sporting relaxations. Newly refurbished and with a new leisure complex which includes an indoor heated pool.
Bedrooms: 13 single, 22 double & 18 twin, 5 family rooms.
Bathrooms: 58 private.
Bed & breakfast: £55-£85 single, £85-£115 double.
Lunch available.
Evening meal 7pm (l.o. 9.30pm).
Parking for 80.

Credit: Access, Visa, C.Bl., Diners, Amex.

Careys Manor Hotel M
COMMENDED

Brockenhurst, New Forest, SO42 7RH
☎ Lymington (0590) 23551 & Fax (0590) 22799
Attractive old manor. Most rooms overlooking lovely gardens. Large indoor pool complex. Log fires. Bargain breaks all year. Renowned restaurant.
Bedrooms: 3 single, 53 double & 23 twin.
Bathrooms: 79 private.
Bed & breakfast: £73.90-£79.90 single, £99.90-£127.90 double.
Half board: £57-£70 daily, £299-£390 weekly.
Lunch available.
Evening meal 7pm (l.o. 10pm).
Parking for 200.
Credit: Access, Visa, Diners, Amex.

Cloud Hotel M
APPROVED

Meerut Road, Brockenhurst, SO42 7TW
☎ Lymington (0590) 22165 & 22254
A quiet country hotel overlooking the New Forest, with forest views, home-from-home cooking and comforts. Lunch on Sundays. 4 nights for the price of 3.
Bedrooms: 8 single, 3 double & 4 twin, 4 family rooms.
Bathrooms: 5 public.
Bed & breakfast: £33-£42 single, £66-£84 double.
Half board: £47-£52 daily, £235-£250 weekly.
Evening meal 7pm (l.o. 8pm).
Parking for 21.

The Cottage Hotel & Restaurant M
COMMENDED

Sway Road, Brockenhurst, SO42 7SH
☎ Lymington (0590) 22296
Old-world cottage with oak beams and log fire in winter. Morning coffee, lunches, cream teas, and dinners by candlelight.
Bedrooms: 1 single, 4 double & 1 twin.
Bathrooms: 6 private.

Bed & breakfast: £38-£40 single, £58-£64 double.
Half board: £41-£44 daily, £265-£275 weekly.
Lunch available.
Evening meal 7pm (l.o. 9.50pm).
Parking for 10.
Credit: Access, Visa.

Forest Park Hotel M

Rhinefield Road, Brockenhurst, SO42 7ZG
☎ Lymington (0590) 22844
Telex 47572 FORTPK G
CR Forestdale
Comfortable English country house in own south facing grounds, peacefully set in the New Forest.
Bedrooms: 2 single, 23 double & 8 twin, 5 family rooms.
Bathrooms: 38 private, 4 public.
Bed & breakfast: from £62.50 single, from £77.50 double.
Lunch available.
Evening meal 7.30pm (l.o. 10pm).
Parking for 50.
Credit: Access, Visa, Diners, Amex.

New Park Manor Hotel M
COMMENDED

Lyndhurst Road, Brockenhurst, New Forest, SO42 7QH
☎ Lymington (0590) 23467
Former Royal Hunting Lodge set in New Forest parkland. Leisure facilities include own horse riding stables and outdoor heated swimming pool.
Bedrooms: 1 single, 18 double & 4 twin, 4 family rooms.
Bathrooms: 27 private.
Bed & breakfast: from £62 single, £104-£124 double.
Half board: £65-£78 daily.
Lunch available.
Evening meal 7pm (l.o. 9.30pm).
Parking for 40.
Credit: Access, Visa, Diners, Amex.

Thatched Cottage Hotel
16 Brookley Road, Brockenhurst, SO42 7RR
☎ Lymington (0590) 23090 & Fax (0590) 23479
Continued ▶

BROCKENHURST
Continued

Charming country cottage hotel built in 1627 with large, beautiful garden. Convenient for golf, swimming, horseriding. Some bedrooms with four-poster beds and log fires. Mountain bikes for hire.
Bedrooms: 4 double & 1 twin.
Bathrooms: 5 private.
Bed & breakfast: from £30 single, £45-£80 double.
Half board: £45-£80 daily.
Lunch available.
Evening meal 7.30pm (l.o. 9.30pm).
Parking for 9.
Open March-December.
Credit: Access, Visa.
🐕10 🛁 📠 🖲 🍴 🕯 🖺 Ⅴ 🗲 🖾 📖 ⚓ 🍴 ∪ ❋ 🎪 SP 🎣 Ⓣ

The Watersplash Hotel M
🏆🏆🏆 APPROVED
The Rise, Brockenhurst, SO42 7ZP
☎ Lymington (0590) 22344
Quiet, Victorian country house hotel set in beautiful gardens, renowned for good food, service and accommodation.
Bedrooms: 3 single, 9 double & 8 twin, 3 family rooms.
Bathrooms: 23 private.
Bed & breakfast: £49-£59 single, £60-£80 double.
Half board: £49-£59 daily, £250-£270 weekly.
Lunch available.
Evening meal 7pm (l.o. 8pm).
Parking for 33.
Credit: Access, Visa.
🐕 🛁 🖾 🕯 🖲 🖵 🕯 Ⅴ 🖾 🖺 📖 ⚓ 🍴 🕯 🔥 ∪ ❋ 📵 🎣 SP

BURLEY
Hampshire
Map ref 2B3

5m SE. Ringwood
Attractive centre from which to explore the south-west part of the New Forest. There is an ancient earthwork on Castle Hill nearby, which also offers good views.

Burley Manor Hotel M
🏆
Burley, Nr.Ringwood, BH24 4BS
☎ (042 53) 3522 Telex 41565 BURMAN/G
Ⓒ Forestdale
Beautiful country manor house hotel set in 54 acres of parkland in the heart of the New Forest.

Bedrooms: 21 double & 8 twin, 1 family room.
Bathrooms: 30 private.
Bed & breakfast: from £62.50 single, £77.50-£87.50 double.
Lunch available.
Evening meal 7pm (l.o. 10pm).
Parking for 100.
Credit: Access, Visa, Diners, Amex.
🐕 🛁 🖾 🕯 🖲 🖵 🕯 Ⅴ 🗲 🖾 📖 ⚓ 🍴 ⤳ ∪ 🐾 ❋ 🖾 SP 📖 Ⓣ

CADNAM
Hampshire
Map ref 2C3

Village with numerous attractive cottages and an inn, close to the start of the M27.

The Old Well Restaurant
Copythorne, Nr. Cadnam, SO4 2PE
☎ Southampton (0703) 812321 & 812700
Family-owned business for over 30 years. Spacious accommodation and friendly service, with good access to New Forest and Southampton ferries.
Bedrooms: 3 double & 1 twin, 2 family rooms.
Bathrooms: 3 private, 1 public.
Bed & breakfast: £20-£25 single, £35-£45 double.
Lunch available.
Evening meal 7pm (l.o. 10pm).
Parking for 50.
Credit: Access, Visa.
🐕 🖵 🕯 📖 ⚓ 🍴 🕱 🖾

CHRISTCHURCH
Dorset
Map ref 2B3

Tranquil town lying between the Avon and Stour just before they converge and flow into Christchurch Harbour. A fine 11th C church and the remains of a Norman castle and house can be seen.
Tourist Information Centre ☎ (0202) 471780

Belvedere Hotel M
🏆
59 Barrack Road, Christchurch, BH23 1PD
☎ (0202) 485978

Large, Victorian, detached house ideally situated for beaches, yachting, fishing and golfing. Excellent scenery in the New Forest for walking and picnicking.
Bedrooms: 2 single, 3 double & 2 twin, 2 family rooms.
Bathrooms: 4 public.
Bed & breakfast: £17-£18 single, £34-£36 double.
Lunch available.
Evening meal 6pm (l.o. 4pm).
Parking for 13.
🐕 🛁 🖾 🍴 🕯 ∪ 🖵 🖺 Ⅴ 🖾 SP 🖾 Ⓣ 🐾 SP

The Old Vicarage Hotel M
🏆🏆🏆
Lyndhurst Road, Hinton, Christchurch, BH23 7DU
☎ Highcliffe (0425) 277006
Tastefully refurbished Victorian house in extensive grounds. Centrally situated for Bournemouth, New Forest, coast and all sporting activities.
Bedrooms: 4 double & 3 twin.
Bathrooms: 7 private.
Bed & breakfast: £41.25-£51.25 single, £57.20-£67.20 double.
Half board: £33.50-£43.50 daily.
Evening meal 6.30pm (l.o. 8.30pm).
Parking for 20.
Credit: Access, Visa.
🐕 🛁 🖵 🕯 Ⅴ 🖾 🖺 ⚓ 🍴 ❋ 🎪 🖾 SP

Tyrrells Ford Hotel M
🏆🏆🏆 COMMENDED
Avon, Nr. Christchurch, BH23 7BH
☎ Bransgore (0425) 72646 & Fax (0425) 72262
Charming 18th C country house in 10 acres of garden. Minstrels' gallery, lounge, panelled restaurant. Warm welcome assured.
Bedrooms: 4 single, 7 double & 5 twin.
Bathrooms: 16 private.
Bed & breakfast: £45-£60 single, £60-£90 double.
Half board: £35-£50 daily.
Lunch available.
Evening meal 7.30pm (l.o. 9.30pm).
Parking for 60.
Credit: Access, Visa.
🐕 🕯 🖲 🖵 🕯 Ⅴ 🖾 🖺 ⚓ 🍴 ❋ 🎪 📵 🎣 SP 📖

CORFE CASTLE
Dorset
Map ref 2B3

One of the most spectacular ruined castles in Britain. Norman in origin, the castle was a Royalist stronghold during the Civil War and held out until 1645. The village had a considerable marble-carving industry in the Middle Ages.

Mortons House Hotel M
🏆🏆🏆 COMMENDED
East Street, Corfe Castle, BH20 5EE
☎ (0929) 480988
Attractive Elizabethan manor house with castle views. Walled gardens, coastal and country pursuits, suites and four-poster bed. Licensed gourmet restaurant.
Bedrooms: 13 double & 3 twin, 1 family room.
Bathrooms: 17 private.
Bed & breakfast: from £52 single, from £80 double.
Half board: from £62.50 daily.
Lunch available.
Evening meal 7.30pm (l.o. 9.30pm).
Parking for 35.
Credit: Access, Visa.
🐕 🛁 🖾 🕯 🖲 🖵 🕯 🕯 Ⅴ 🗲 🖾 📖 ⚓ 🍴 ❋ 📵 SP

DROXFORD
Hampshire
Map ref 2C3

Village with numerous Georgian buildings. Izaak Walton was a frequent visitor to the 18th C rectory now owned by the National Trust.

The Coach House Motel M
Listed
Brookbridge, Droxford, SO3 1QT
☎ (0489) 877812
Modern motel accommodation in area of outstanding beauty, surrounded by leisure facilities and adjacent to pub/restaurant.
Bedrooms: 2 single, 6 double.
Bathrooms: 8 private.
Bed & breakfast: £27.50-£37.50 single, £37.50-£45 double.
Parking for 12.
Credit: Access, Visa, Diners, Amex.
🐕 🛁 🖵 🕯 🖾 📖 ⚓ 🍴 ∪ ⤒ 🎪 📖

The symbols are explained on the flap inside the back cover.

EASTLEIGH

**Hampshire
Map ref 2C3**

Town developed around the railway engineering works built there in 1889. The borough stretches from Southampton Water to the Test Valley in the north. Yachting centres at Hamble and Bursledon.
Tourist Information Centre ☎ *(0703) 641261*

Homeleigh ⋀

184 Southampton Road, Eastleigh, SO5 5QW
☎ (0703) 616480
Comfortable guesthouse, quarter of a mile to airport and junction 5, M27 to Portsmouth ferries. 5 minutes' walk mainline railway station, shops and restaurants.
Bedrooms: 3 single, 1 double & 2 twin.
Bathrooms: 1 public.
Bed & breakfast: £13-£16 single, £26-£32 double.
Half board: £21-£24 daily, £147-£168 weekly.
Credit: Access, Visa.
⚒ 🜂 🛁 🖳 🕁 Ⓤ ⛗ ✕ 🏠
ᴰᴬᴾ

Twyford Lodge Guest House ⋀

104-106 Twyford Road, Eastleigh, SO5 4HN
☎ (0703) 612245
Friendly, family-run guesthouse, convenient for mainline station and airport. Residents' bar.
Bedrooms: 3 single, 2 double & 6 twin, 4 family rooms.
Bathrooms: 1 private, 3 public; 1 private shower.
Bed & breakfast: £17-£27 single, £34-£38 double.
Half board: from £22 daily.
Evening meal 6pm (l.o. 7pm).
Parking for 14.
⚒ 🛁 🖳 🌢 🚗 📺 ⛟ ✕ 🏠

EMSWORTH

**Hampshire
Map ref 2C3**

Old port, now a yachting centre, set between 2 small creeks on Chichester Harbour. Yachtbuilding is the chief industry. There are some good Georgian buildings and 2 tide-mills.

The Brookfield Hotel ⋀
🥂🥂🥂🥂 **COMMENDED**

Havant Road, Emsworth, PO10 7LF
☎ (0243) 373363
Fax (0243) 376342
Privately owned and run country house hotel between the old fishing village of Emsworth and Havant on the A27.
Bedrooms: 7 single, 22 double & 12 twin.
Bathrooms: 41 private.
Bed & breakfast: max. £55 single, max. £68 double.
Half board: max. £67 daily.
Lunch available.
Evening meal 7pm (l.o. 9.30pm).
Parking for 80.
Credit: Access, Visa, Diners, Amex.
⚒ 🛁 🖳 🌢 ☏ 🖳 ⛟ 🛡 Ⓥ
⛟ 🍽 🛁 🍷 ✦ ✕ 🆂🅿

Merry Hall Hotel ⋀
🥂🥂🥂

73 Horndean Road, Emsworth, PO10 7PU
☎ (0243) 372424
Well-appointed family-run hotel offering friendly service, with spacious lounge overlooking large attractive garden. Well situated for touring southern England.
Bedrooms: 3 single, 3 double & 3 twin, 1 family room.
Bathrooms: 7 private; 3 private showers.
Bed & breakfast: £24-£32 single, £48-£52 double.
Lunch available.
Evening meal 6pm (l.o. 9pm).
Parking for 12.
Credit: Access, Visa.
⚒ 🛁 ☏ 🖳 🕁 🛡 Ⓥ ⛟ 📺
⊙ 🍽 🛁 🍷 🐾 ✦ ✕ ᴰᴬᴾ 🆂🅿

FAREHAM

**Hampshire
Map ref 2C3**

Lies on a quiet backwater of Portsmouth Harbour. The High Street is lined with fine Georgian buildings.
Tourist Information Centre ☎ *(0329) 221342*

Acton Lodge Hotel ⋀
🥂🥂🥂 **COMMENDED**

225A West Street, Fareham, PO16 0ET
☎ (0329) 231200
Fax (0329) 822429
Small commercial hotel and restaurant, ideally situated on A27 close to railway station, main street and shops. Car park at rear.
Bedrooms: 3 twin, 2 family rooms.
Bathrooms: 5 private.
Bed & breakfast: £30-£47 single, £47-£58 double.
Half board: £39.95-£54.95 daily, £250-£300 weekly.
Evening meal 7pm (l.o. 9.30pm).
Parking for 12.
Credit: Access, Visa, Amex.
⚒ 🛁 ☏ 🖳 🕁 🛡 Ⓥ 📺
⊙ 🍽 🛁 🍷 ♥ 🆂🅿 🅃

Avenue House Hotel ⋀
🥂🥂 **COMMENDED**

22 The Avenue, Fareham, PO14 1NS
☎ (0329) 232175
Comfortable, small hotel, with charm and character, set in mature gardens. 5 minutes' walk to town centre, railway station and restaurants.
Bedrooms: 3 single, 5 double & 2 twin, 3 family rooms.
Bathrooms: 13 private.
Bed & breakfast: £32-£43 single, £42-£53 double.
Parking for 13.
Credit: Access, Visa, Amex.
⚒ 🛁 🖳 ☏ 🖳 🖳 🕁 🛡 Ⓥ
⛟ 🍽 🛁 🍷 🐾 ♥ ✕ 🆂🅿 🅃

Carrick House Hotel ⋀
Listed

11-13 East Street, Fareham, PO16 0BW
☎ (0329) 234678
Georgian listed building offering historical interest and a warm welcome. Car parking space available immediately opposite.
Bedrooms: 4 single, 1 double & 2 twin, 1 family room.
Bathrooms: 2 public.
Bed & breakfast: £17.50-£25 single, £35-£50 double.

Half board: £22.50-£32.50 daily.
Evening meal 6pm (l.o. 8pm).
⚒ 🛁 🖳 🖳 🕁 🛡 Ⓥ 📺
⊙ 🛁 ✕ 🏠

Mrs. P.R. Hobbs
Listed

22 Pennine Walk, Fareham, PO14 1QQ
☎ (0329) 286875
Old world lounge, kitchen, diner and lovely garden for summer. High standard of cleanliness.
Bedrooms: 2 single, 1 double.
Bathrooms: 1 private, 2 public.
Bed & breakfast: £10-£12 single, £20-£24 double.
Parking for 2.
⚒🜂 🜂 🛁 🖳 Ⓤ ⛗ 📺 ⛶
🛁 ✕ 🏠 ᴰᴬᴾ

Red Lion Hotel ⋀
🥂🥂🥂🥂 **COMMENDED**

East Street, Fareham, PO16 0BP
☎ (0329) 822640 Telex 86204
ⒸⓇ Lansbury
Restored coaching inn, close to Portsmouth and Southampton.
Bedrooms: 17 single, 18 double & 7 twin, 2 family rooms.
Bathrooms: 44 private, 1 public.
Bed & breakfast: from £26 single, from £52 double.
Half board: from £38 daily.
Lunch available.
Evening meal 7pm (l.o. 10pm).
Parking for 136.
Credit: Access, Visa, Diners, Amex.
⚒ 🛁 🖳 ☏ 🖳 🕁 🛡 Ⓥ
⛟ 📺 ⊙ ⛗ 🛁 🍷 🖐 🆂🅿
🏠 🅃

The Roundabout Hotel
🥂🥂 **APPROVED**

Wallington Shore Road, Fareham, PO16 8SB
☎ (0329) 822542
Fax (0329) 234533
Family-run hotel with stimulating and friendly atmosphere, specialising in traditional home cooking. Easy access to south coast towns via M27.
Bedrooms: 5 single, 7 double & 3 twin, 2 family rooms.
Bathrooms: 13 private, 1 public.
Bed & breakfast: £25-£40 single, £30-£50 double.
Lunch available.
Evening meal 6pm (l.o. 10pm).

Continued ▶

National Crown ratings were correct at the time of going to press but are subject to change. Please check at the time of booking.

Map references apply to the colour maps towards the end of this guide.

FAREHAM

Continued

Parking for 42.
Credit: Access, Visa, Diners, Amex.

≳ ⌞ ⊡ ⌂ 🛉 ⎓ V ⊨ ▦ ⌸
🍴 ⍉ SP T

FARNBOROUGH

Hampshire
Map ref 2C2

Home of the Royal Aircraft Establishment and the site of the biennial International Air Show. St. Michael's Abbey was built by the Empress Eugenie, wife of Napoleon III of France and together with their son they are buried in the crypt.
Tourist Information Centre ☎ *(0252) 513838*

Alexandra Hotel M
⚘⚘⚘ COMMENDED

144 Alexandra Road, Farnborough, GU14 6RP
☎ (0252) 541050
Ⓒ Minotels
Well-appointed, comfortable hotel, managed by proprietors and family, with emphasis on cleanliness and service.
Bedrooms: 5 single, 1 double & 6 twin.
Bathrooms: 12 private, 1 public.
Bed & breakfast: £50 single, £61 double.
Half board: from £60 daily.
Evening meal 7pm (l.o. 9pm).
Parking for 10.
Credit: Access, Visa, Diners, Amex.

≳ ⌞ ⊡ ⌂ 🛉 V ⊨ ⊤ ▦
▱ ❈ ⍢ T

The Falcon Hotel
⚘⚘⚘

68 Farnborough Road, Farnborough, GU14 6TH
☎ (0252) 545378
Fax (0252) 522539
Recently upgraded hotel on the A325 opposite Farnborough's aerospace centre. 3 miles from M3 junction 4, 2 miles from Aldershot garrison town.
Bedrooms: 8 single, 14 double & 6 twin, 2 family rooms.
Bathrooms: 30 private.
Bed & breakfast: £65 single, £75 double.
Half board: £77.50 daily.
Lunch available.
Evening meal 7pm (l.o. 9.30pm).
Parking for 30.
Credit: Access, Visa.

≳ ⌂ ▦ ⌞ ⊡ ⌂ 🛉 V
⊨ ● ▦ ▱ 🍴 ⍢ ⍢ SP T

FERNDOWN

Dorset
Map ref 2B3

Sharing the attractions of Bournemouth, of which it is now a part, and well placed for exploring the New Forest.

Coach House Inn
⚘⚘⚘ APPROVED

Tricketts Cross, Ferndown, BH22 9NW
☎ (0202) 861222
Fax (0202) 894130
Ⓒ Consort
Set in beautiful wooded surroundings, close to the New Forest and 6 miles from Bournemouth with its golden beaches. Half board price based on a minimum 2 night stay.
Bedrooms: 22 double & 22 twin.
Bathrooms: 44 private.
Bed & breakfast: £48-£53 single, £68-£73 double.
Half board: £38.50-£43 daily.
Lunch available.
Evening meal 7pm (l.o. 9.30pm).
Parking for 118.
Credit: Access, Visa, Diners, Amex.

≳ ⌂ ⌞ ⊡ ⌂ 🛉 V ⊨
⊤ ▦ ▱ 🍴 ⌖ SP T

FORDINGBRIDGE

Hampshire
Map ref 2B3

On the north-west edge of the New Forest. A medieval bridge crosses the Avon at this point and gave the town its name. A good centre for walking, exploring and fishing.

Ashburn Hotel & Restaurant M
⚘⚘⚘ COMMENDED

Damerham Road (B3078), Fordingbridge, SP6 1JP
☎ (0425) 652060
Ⓒ Minotels
Comfortable, family-run country house hotel, renowned for food and friendly atmosphere. Delightful garden with outdoor heated swimming pool.
Bedrooms: 5 single, 9 double & 7 twin, 2 family rooms.
Bathrooms: 23 private.
Bed & breakfast: £39.50 single, £70 double.
Half board: £266.50 weekly.
Lunch available.
Evening meal 7.30pm (l.o. 9.30pm).

Parking for 60.
Credit: Access, Visa.

≳ ⌂ ⌞ ⊡ ⊡ 🛉 🛈 V ⍢
⊨ ⊤ ▦ ▱ 🍴 ⍫ ⋃ ❈ ❉ ⍢
SP T

The Old Post Office

Purlieu Lane, Godshill, Fordingbridge, SP6 2LW
☎ (0425) 653719
On the edge of the New Forest and ideal for touring.
Bedrooms: 1 double & 2 twin.
Bathrooms: 1 public.
Bed & breakfast: £11 single, £22 double.
Half board: £17 daily, £80 weekly.
Evening meal 6pm (l.o. 9pm).
Parking for 4.

≳ UL 🛈 V ⊨ ⊤ ▱ ✕ 🅟

GILLINGHAM

Dorset
Map ref 2B3

Stock Hill House Hotel & Restaurant M
⚘⚘⚘ HIGHLY COMMENDED

Stock Hill, Wyke, Gillingham, SP8 5NR
☎ (0747) 823626
Family-run country house hotel and restaurant in peaceful 10 acres of wildest north Dorset.
Bedrooms: 2 single, 3 double & 3 twin.
Bathrooms: 8 private.
Half board: £75-£85 daily.
Lunch available.
Evening meal 7.30pm (l.o. 8.45pm).
Parking for 40.
Credit: Access, Visa.

≳ 7 🅐 ⌞ ⊡ ⊡ 🛈 V ⍢ ▱
▦ ▱ 🍴 ❈ ✕ 🅟 ⍢ GAP SP 🅟

HAVANT

Hampshire
Map ref 2C3

Once a market town famous for making parchment. Nearby at Leigh Park extensive early 19th C landscape gardens and parklands are open to the public. Right in the centre of the town stands the interesting 13th C church of St. Faith.
Tourist Information Centre ☎ *(0705) 480024*

Bear Hotel M
⚘⚘⚘

East Street, Havant, PO9 1AA
☎ (0705) 486501
Fax (0705) 470551
Telex 869136
Ⓒ Lansbury

Hotel in a town centre location, close to shops, A27/M27, bus and rail station, Chichester and Portsmouth.
Bedrooms: 14 single, 19 double & 9 twin.
Bathrooms: 42 private.
Bed & breakfast: from £28 single, from £56 double.
Half board: from £40 daily.
Lunch available.
Evening meal 7pm (l.o. 10pm).
Parking for 150.
Credit: Access, Visa, Diners, Amex.

≳ ⌞ ⊡ ⌂ 🛉 🛈 V ⊨ ●
▦ ▱ 🍴 ⍢ SP 🅟 T

Holland Guest House M

33 Bedhampton Hill, Havant, PO9 3JN
☎ (0705) 475913
Fax (0705) 470134
Comfortable, friendly guesthouse, ideal for touring, continental ferry port, business and the sea.
Bedrooms: 3 single, 1 double, 1 family room.
Bathrooms: 1 private, 1 public.
Bed & breakfast: £15-£20 single, £27-£32 double.
Evening meal 5pm (l.o. 6.45pm).
Parking for 6.

≳ UL 🛈 V ⍢ ⊨ ⊤ ▦ ▱
✕ 🅟

The Old Mill Guest House M
⚘⚘

Mill Lane, Bedhampton, Havant, PO9 3JH
☎ (0705) 454948
Georgian house in large grounds by a lake abundant in wildlife. Modernised, comfortable retreat. John Keats rested here.
Bedrooms: 1 double & 3 twin, 1 family room.
Bathrooms: 5 private.
Bed & breakfast: £25 single, £39 double.
Parking for 10.

≳ ⊡ UL 🛈 V ⊨ ⊤ ▦ ▱
⍫ ❈ 🅟 🅟

The symbols are explained on the flap inside the back cover.

Map references apply to the colour maps towards the end of this guide.

HAYLING ISLAND

Hampshire
Map ref 2C3

Small, flat island of
historic interest,
surrounded by natural
harbours and with fine
sandy beaches, linked to
the mainland by a road.
Tourist Information
Centre ☎ (0705) 467111

Cockle Warren Cottage Hotel M
36 Seafront, Hayling Island,
PO11 9HL
☎ (0705) 464961
*Lovely farmhouse-style hotel
with hens and ducks. French
and English country cooking.
Home-made bread. Four-
poster and Victorian beds.
Heated swimming pool. Log
fires in winter.*
Bedrooms: 4 double & 1 twin.
Bathrooms: 5 private.
Bed & breakfast: £30-£45
single, £48-£68 double.
Evening meal 8pm (l.o. 4pm).
Parking for 9.
Credit: Access, Visa.

Newtown House Hotel M
Manor Road, Hayling Island,
PO11 0QR
☎ (0705) 466131
Fax (0705) 461366
*Set in own grounds, a quarter
of a mile from seafront. Indoor
leisure complex with heated
pool, gym and jacuzzi. Tennis.*
Bedrooms: 10 single,
11 double & 4 twin, 3 family
rooms.
Bathrooms: 26 private,
2 public.
Bed & breakfast: £35-£46.50
single, £55-£67.50 double.
Half board: max. £42 daily.
Lunch available.
Evening meal 7pm (l.o.
9.30pm).
Parking for 45.
Credit: Access, Visa, Diners,
Amex.

The Rook Hollow Licensed Hotel M
COMMENDED
84 Church Road, Hayling
Island, PO11 0NX
☎ (0705) 467080 & 469620
*Very comfortable, pretty hotel.
Relax in a friendly atmosphere
with Wendy and Pam as your
hosts.*

Bedrooms: 1 single, 2 double
& 4 twin.
Bathrooms: 3 private,
1 public.
Bed & breakfast: £20-£34
single, £34-£50 double.
Half board: £28-£38 daily.
Lunch available.
Evening meal 6pm (l.o. 9pm).
Parking for 9.
Credit: Access, Visa, Diners.

HEDGE END

Hampshire
Map ref 2C3

5m E. Southampton
Busy residential and
shopping suburb 2 miles
west of Botley.

Copper Beeches House Hotel M
Listed
72 Lower Northam Road,
Hedge End, Nr.
Southampton, SO3 4FT
☎ Botley (0489) 787447
*Nicely furnished
accommodation with happy
atmosphere. In centre of
thriving country town, 3
minutes from M27 junction 7
or 8.*
Bedrooms: 5 single, 4 double,
1 family room.
Bathrooms: 2 private,
2 public.
Bed & breakfast: £18.50-
£27.50 single, £34-£37.50
double.
Evening meal 6pm (l.o. 9pm).
Parking for 16.

HOOK

Hampshire
Map ref 2C2

Astride the A30 some 6
miles east of
Basingstoke.

Oaklea Guest House M
London Road, Hook, Nr.
Basingstoke, RG27 9LA
☎ (0256) 762673
*Fine Victorian house in walled
garden, ideally situated for
tourists and business people
alike - 35 minutes from
Heathrow and 1 hour from
Waterloo.*
Bedrooms: 6 single, 1 double
& 2 twin, 1 family room.
Bathrooms: 4 private,
3 public.
Bed & breakfast: £23-£36
single, £32-£47 double.

Half board: £33.25-£46.25
daily, £232.75-£323.75
weekly.
Evening meal 7pm (l.o.
midday).
Parking for 12.

Raven Hotel M
Station Road, Hook, Nr.
Basingstoke, RG27 9HS
☎ (0256) 762541
Telex 858901
CR Lansbury
*In Hook village, convenient for
Basingstoke and Hampshire
countryside.*
Bedrooms: 2 single, 21 double
& 15 twin.
Bathrooms: 38 private.
Bed & breakfast: from £24
single, from £48 double.
Half board: from £36 daily.
Lunch available.
Evening meal 7pm (l.o.
10pm).
Parking for 100.
Credit: Access, Visa, Diners,
Amex.

HORNDEAN

Hampshire
Map ref 2C3

8m NE. Portsmouth

The Ship & Bell Hotel M
COMMENDED
6 London Road, Horndean,
Portsmouth, PO8 0BZ
☎ Portsmouth (0705) 592107
*Former 17th C coaching inn
with plenty of character, on the
A3. Site of the original Gales
Brewery.*
Bedrooms: 8 double & 5 twin.
Bathrooms: 13 private.
Bed & breakfast: from £35
single, from £45 double.
Half board: from £40 daily.
Lunch available.
Evening meal 6pm (l.o.
9.30pm).
Parking for 20.
Credit: Access, Visa.

ISLE OF WIGHT-ALVERSTONE

Isle of Wight
Map ref 2C3

The Grange Country Guest House M
COMMENDED
Alverstone, Nr. Sandown,
PO36 0EZ
☎ (0983) 403729
*A family-run guesthouse set in
the peaceful surroundings of
Alverstone, below the downs
and yet only 2 miles from
sandy beaches.*
Bedrooms: 1 single, 2 double
& 3 twin, 1 family room.
Bathrooms: 7 private.
Bed & breakfast: £18.50-
£20.50 single, £37-£41 double.
Half board: £31-£34 daily,
£163-£187 weekly.
Evening meal 6.30pm (l.o.
7.30pm).
Parking for 6.
Open February-November.

ISLE OF WIGHT-BONCHURCH

Isle of Wight
Map ref 2C3

1m NE. Ventnor
Sheltered suburb at the
foot of St. Boniface
Down.

The Lake Hotel M
APPROVED
Shore Road, Bonchurch,
Ventnor, PO38 1RF
☎ (0983) 852613
*Charming country house hotel
set in 2 acres of beautiful
gardens, in secluded situation
400 metres from beach.*
Bedrooms: 2 single, 8 double
& 4 twin, 7 family rooms.
Bathrooms: 19 private,
5 public.
Bed & breakfast: £16-£18
single, £44-£54 double.
Half board: £22-£27 daily,
£149-£175 weekly.
Evening meal 6.30pm (l.o.
7pm).
Parking for 20.
Open March-October.

*The symbol **CR** and the name of a hotel
group or consortium after a hotel address
means that bookings can be made through
a central reservations office. These are
listed on page 540.*

ISLE OF WIGHT-CHALE

Isle of Wight
Map ref 2C3

Village overlooking Chale Bay and near Blackgang Chine which has a children's maze, a water garden and a museum displaying many objects from shipwrecks.

Clarendon Hotel & Wight Mouse Inn M
COMMENDED

Chale, PO38 2HA
☎ (0983) 730431
17th C coaching hotel overlooking Freshwater Bay and the Needles. Children most welcome. 5 real ales, 365 whiskies and live entertainment nightly, all year round.
Bedrooms: 1 single, 4 double & 1 twin, 7 family rooms.
Bathrooms: 9 private, 3 public.
Bed & breakfast: £23-£26 single, £46-£52 double.
Half board: £32-£35 daily, £175-£195 weekly.
Lunch available.
Evening meal 7pm (l.o. 10pm).
Parking for 200.
Credit: Access.

ISLE OF WIGHT-COLWELL BAY

Isle of Wight
Map ref 2C3

2-mile curving stretch of sand.

Ontario Private Hotel M

Colwell Common Road, Colwell Bay, Freshwater, PO39 0DD
☎ (0983) 753237
Four minutes from beach, offering accommodation of a high standard with licensed bar, choice of menu. Children and pets welcome.
Bedrooms: 1 single, 2 double & 1 twin, 3 family rooms.
Bathrooms: 3 private, 2 public; 2 private showers.
Bed & breakfast: £17-£19 single, £34-£38 double.
Half board: £23-£25.50 daily, £149-£165 weekly.
Evening meal 6.30pm (l.o. 7pm).
Parking for 9.

ISLE OF WIGHT-COWES

Isle of Wight
Map ref 2C3

Regular ferry and hovercraft services cross the Solent to Cowes. The town is the headquarters of the Royal Yacht Squadron and Cowes Week is held every August.

Padmore House Hotel M
APPROVED

Beatrice Avenue, Whippingham, East Cowes, PO32 6LP
☎ (0983) 293210
Beautifully situated in tranquil surroundings overlooking the Medina Valley. 1 mile from Osborne House and close to ferries and hydrofoil.
Bedrooms: 3 single, 3 double & 3 twin.
Bathrooms: 9 private, 1 public.
Bed & breakfast: £35-£48 single, £70-£75 double.
Half board: £48-£61 daily, £225-£270 weekly.
Lunch available.
Evening meal 7.30pm (l.o. 9.30pm).
Parking for 30.
Credit: Access, Visa, Diners, Amex.

ISLE OF WIGHT-FRESHWATER

Isle of Wight
Map ref 2C3

This part of the island is associated with Tennyson, who lived in the village for 30 years. A monument on Tennyson's Down commemorates the poet.

Albion Hotel M
COMMENDED

Freshwater Bay, PO40 9RA
☎ (0983) 753631
On the water's edge with fine views of the English Channel and surrounding countryside. Most rooms have sea views and balconies.
Bedrooms: 9 single, 10 double & 21 twin, 3 family rooms.
Bathrooms: 43 private, 3 public.
Bed & breakfast: £20-£33 single, £31.50-£52 double.
Half board: £29-£44 daily, £203-£308 weekly.
Lunch available.

Evening meal 7pm (l.o. 9pm).
Parking for 75.
Credit: Access, Visa, Diners, Amex.

Farringford Hotel M
COMMENDED

Bedbury Lane, Freshwater, PO40 9PE
☎ (0983) 752500 & 752700
Telex 417165
Set in 33-acre grounds, offers traditional hotel service and also self-catering suites, the best of both worlds. 9-hole golf-course available.
Bedrooms: 3 single, 2 double & 7 twin, 7 family rooms.
Bathrooms: 19 private.
Bed & breakfast: £22-£40 single, £44-£80 double.
Half board: £35-£55 daily, £210-£333 weekly.
Lunch available.
Evening meal 7.30pm (l.o. 9.30pm).
Parking for 152.
Credit: Access, Visa, Diners, Amex.

Royal Standard Hotel M

School Green Road, Freshwater, PO40 9AJ
☎ (0983) 753227
Small, family-run hotel, serving comprehensive bar meals. Freehouse with 2 bars, restaurant, function room.
Bedrooms: 3 single, 3 double & 1 twin, 3 family rooms.
Bathrooms: 8 private; 2 private showers.
Bed & breakfast: £20-£25 single, £40-£50 double.
Lunch available.
Evening meal 6pm (l.o. 10pm).
Parking for 5.

Individual proprietors have supplied all details of accommodation. Although we do check for accuracy, we advise you to confirm prices and other information at the time of booking.

ISLE OF WIGHT-RYDE

Isle of Wight
Map ref 2C3

The island's chief entry port, connected to Portsmouth by ferries and hovercraft. 7 miles of sandy beaches with a half-mile pier, esplanade and gardens.

Biskra House Beach Hotel & Restaurant M

17 St. Thomas Street, Ryde, PO33 2DL
☎ (0983) 67913
Small, select, privately-run hotel overlooking the Solent. All rooms en-suite and equipped to a high standard.
Bedrooms: 8 double & 1 twin.
Bathrooms: 9 private, 1 public.
Bed & breakfast: £29.50-£31.50 single, £38-£47.50 double.
Lunch available.
Evening meal 7pm (l.o. 10.30pm).
Parking for 12.
Credit: Access, Visa.

Brantoria Guest House M

44 St. Thomas Street, Ryde, PO33 2DL
☎ (0983) 62724
1 minute from the beach, with car park opposite. Close to ferry and public transport.
Bedrooms: 2 double & 2 twin, 1 family room.
Bathrooms: 1 public.
Bed & breakfast: from £12.50 single, from £25 double.
Half board: from £19 daily, from £107 weekly.
Evening meal 6pm.

Dean House Hotel M

2 Dover Street, Ryde, PO33 2AQ
☎ (0983) 62535
Comfortable, privately-run hotel, open all year. Overlooking the Solent, 2 minutes' walk to hovercraft, bus and train terminals, close to town centre. Weekend packages available. Opposite ice rink, bowling and marina.
Bedrooms: 2 single, 5 double & 3 twin, 4 family rooms.
Bathrooms: 7 private, 2 public.
Bed & breakfast: £22-£32 single, £40-£50 double.
Half board: £30-£42 daily.

Lunch available.
Evening meal 6.30pm (l.o. 9.45pm).
Parking for 12.
Credit: Access, Visa, Diners, Amex.

The Grosvenor Guest House M
🏆🏆

37 Nelson Street, Ryde, PO33 2EY
☎ (0983) 62392
Homely accommodation with good home cooking and own keys. Close to shops, beach and Esplanade.
Bedrooms: 1 single, 2 double & 1 twin, 2 family rooms.
Bathrooms: 2 public.
Bed & breakfast: £10.50-£11.50 single, £21-£23 double.
Half board: £15-£16 daily, £100-£105 weekly.
Evening meal 6pm (l.o. 7pm).

Royal Esplanade Hotel M
🏆🏆🏆

16 The Esplanade, Ryde, PO33 2ED
☎ (0983) 62549
Hotel of charm and character, with superb views of the Solent. Patio garden with palms surrounding the heated swimming pool.
Bedrooms: 9 single, 25 double & 21 twin, 20 family rooms.
Bathrooms: 60 private, 10 public.
Bed & breakfast: £20-£30 single, £40-£60 double.
Half board: £25-£35.50 daily, £120-£210 weekly.
Evening meal 6.30pm (l.o. 8.45pm).
Parking for 7.
Credit: Access, Visa, Amex.

Hotel Ryde Castle
🏆🏆🏆🏆 APPROVED

Esplanade, Ryde, PO33 1JA
☎ (0983) 63755 Telex 869466 TARAS-G
Best Western
16th C castle, built by Henry VIII to defend Spithead, overlooking Serpentine. Beautifully furnished and well-appointed rooms. Renowned for fresh cuisine.
Bedrooms: 6 single, 6 double & 3 twin, 2 family rooms.
Bathrooms: 17 private.
Bed & breakfast: £50-£95 single, £70-£123 double.

Half board: £62.50-£107.50 daily, £276.50-£752.50 weekly.
Lunch available.
Evening meal 7pm (l.o. 10pm).
Parking for 75.
Credit: Access, Visa, Diners, Amex.

Yelf's Hotel M
🏆🏆🏆

Union Street, Ryde, PO33 2LG
☎ (0983) 64062 & Fax (0983) 63937
Once an important coaching house, the hotel has become a popular base for holidaymakers seeking the island's many attractions.
Bedrooms: 5 single, 5 double & 9 twin, 2 family rooms.
Bathrooms: 21 private.
Bed & breakfast: £30-£50 single, £50-£65 double.
Half board: £25-£45 daily, £175-£245 weekly.
Lunch available.
Evening meal 7pm (l.o. 9pm).
Credit: Access, Visa, Diners, Amex.

ISLE OF WIGHT- SANDOWN
Isle of Wight
Map ref 2C3

The 6-mile sweep of Sandown Bay is one of the island's finest stretches, with excellent sands. The pier has a pavilion and sun terrace; the esplanade has amusements, bars, eating-places and gardens.
Tourist Information Centre ☎ (0983) 403886

Farnborough House M
48 Victoria Road, Sandown, PO36 8AL
☎ (0983) 406541
Small family guesthouse, offering a pleasant, homely atmosphere. In the centre of Sandown, close to beaches and amenities.
Bedrooms: 1 double & 1 twin, 1 family room.
Bathrooms: 1 public.
Bed & breakfast: £11-£12.50 single, £22-£25 double.
Half board: £15-£16.50 daily, £98-£104 weekly.
Parking for 2.

Montrene Hotel M
🏆🏆🏆 COMMENDED

Avenue Road, Sandown, PO36 8BN
☎ (0983) 403722
Well situated standing in its own grounds within 100 yards of the beach. Leisure complex with indoor heated pool.
Bedrooms: 5 single, 13 double & 7 twin, 18 family rooms.
Bathrooms: 40 private, 2 public.
Bed & breakfast: £23-£28 single, £46-£56 double.
Half board: £31-£37 daily, £217-£259 weekly.
Lunch available.
Evening meal 6pm (l.o. 7pm).
Parking for 39.
Credit: Access, Visa.

Sandringham Hotel M
Esplanade, Sandown, PO36 8AH
☎ (0983) 403448
Large modern hotel on the seafront, with the water's edge just 50 yards from the door.
Bedrooms: 25 single, 10 double & 18 twin, 77 family rooms.
Bathrooms: 106 private, 4 public.
Bed & breakfast: £22-£39 single, £44-£78 double.
Half board: £27-£41 daily, £151-£246 weekly.
Evening meal 6.30pm (l.o. 9.30pm).
Parking for 9.

ISLE OF WIGHT- SANDOWN LAKE
Isle of Wight
Map ref 2C3

Halfway between Sandown and Shanklin, with its own beach and shopping centre.

Haytor Lodge M
🏆🏆 APPROVED

16 Cliff Path, Lake, Sandown, PO36 8PL
☎ (0983) 402969
Superior guesthouse situated on famous cliff path overlooking Sandown Bay. Large garden with seats for guests, large lounge and dining room.
Bedrooms: 2 single, 1 twin, 5 family rooms.
Bathrooms: 6 private, 1 public.
Bed & breakfast: £11-£15 single, £26-£32 double.

Half board: £16-£20 daily, £97-£119 weekly.
Evening meal 6pm.
Parking for 10.
Open January-November.

ISLE OF WIGHT- SEAVIEW
Isle of Wight
Map ref 2C3

Has a sandy beach and is very much a family resort. Good prawn and lobster fishing.

Northbank Hotel
Circular Road, Seaview, PO34 5ET
☎ (0983) 612227
A family hotel by the sea. In a splendid position on Seaview waterfront, with magnificent views of the Solent.
Bedrooms: 8 single, 6 double & 4 twin, 2 family rooms.
Bathrooms: 5 public.
Bed & breakfast: £25-£30 single, £50-£60 double.
Half board: £40-£45 daily, £220-£300 weekly.
Lunch available.
Evening meal 7pm (l.o. 9pm).
Parking for 18.
Open April-October.

Seaview Hotel M
🏆🏆🏆🏆

High Street, Seaview, PO34 5EX
☎ (0983) 612711
Small, professionally-run, family hotel next to sea, with well-known and exceptionally busy restaurant specialising in local fish.
Bedrooms: 4 double & 12 twin.
Bathrooms: 16 private, 2 public.
Bed & breakfast: from £43.50 single, from £65 double.
Half board: from £45 daily.
Lunch available.
Evening meal 7pm (l.o. 10pm).
Parking for 14.
Credit: Access, Visa, Amex.

Half board prices shown are per person but in some cases may be based on double/twin occupancy.

Set on a cliff with gentle
slopes leading down to
the beach, esplanade and
marine gardens. The
picturesque, old thatched
village nestles at the end
of the wooded chine.
*Tourist Information
Centre ☎ (0983) 862942*

Alverstone Manor Hotel ♠
♛♛♛ COMMENDED
32 Luccombe Road, Shanklin,
PO37 6RR
☎ (0983) 862586
*In its own grounds overlooking
Sandown/Shanklin Bay.
Within easy reach of Old
Village, town and beach.
2 acres of gardens with heated
swimming pool, lawn tennis
court and putting green.*
Bedrooms: 1 single, 3 double
& 1 twin, 7 family rooms.
Bathrooms: 11 private,
3 public.
Bed & breakfast: £23-£27
single, £46-£54 double.
Half board: £29-£33 daily,
£203-£231 weekly.
Evening meal 6.30pm (l.o.
7.30pm).
Parking for 15.
Open March-October.

Apse Manor Country House ♠
♛♛♛ COMMENDED
Apse Manor Road, Shanklin,
PO37 7PN
☎ (0983) 866651
*Recently restored 16th C
manor house in a lovely
country setting, 1.5 miles from
Shanklin. Ideal for a relaxing
holiday in beautiful
surroundings.*
Bedrooms: 4 double & 2 twin,
1 family room.
Bathrooms: 7 private.
Bed & breakfast: £50-£54
double.
Half board: £33-£35 daily,
£210-£225 weekly.
Evening meal 7pm (l.o.
7.15pm).
Parking for 12.

Brunswick Hotel ♠
♛♛♛♛ COMMENDED
Queens Road, Shanklin,
PO37 6AN
☎ (0983) 863245

*Well-situated hotel offering all
modern amenities. Fresh local
produce used when available.
Commands a fine position.*
Bedrooms: 2 single, 11 double
& 11 twin, 10 family rooms.
Bathrooms: 34 private,
1 public.
Bed & breakfast: from £28
single, from £56 double.
Half board: from £35 daily.
Evening meal 7pm (l.o. 8pm).
Parking for 25.
Open March-November.
Credit: Access, Visa.

The Carlton Hotel ♠
♛♛♛
9 Park Road, Shanklin,
PO37 6AY
☎ (0983) 862517
*Small family-run licensed hotel
with beautiful sea views. All
rooms en-suite with colour TV
and tea/coffee making
facilities. Home cooking.*
Bedrooms: 2 single, 6 double
& 3 twin, 2 family rooms.
Bathrooms: 13 private.
Bed & breakfast: £20-£24
single, £40-£48 double.
Half board: £24-£28 daily,
£160-£190 weekly.
Evening meal 6.30pm (l.o.
6.30pm).
Parking for 10.
Credit: Access, Visa.

Cliff Tops Hotel ♠
♛♛♛ COMMENDED
Park Road, Shanklin,
PO37 6BB
☎ (0983) 863262
*A modern, fully licensed hotel
facing the sea, close to beach
and town, with spacious public
rooms and all year round tariff
package. 2 bars, 2 restaurants
and full leisure facilities
including indoor pool, bowls,
saunas, steam rooms, spa bath,
gymnasium and sun beds.*
Bedrooms: 6 single, 16 double
& 12 twin, 54 family rooms.
Bathrooms: 88 private.
Bed & breakfast: £65.50-£75
single, £94-£110 double.
Half board: £300-£375
weekly.
Lunch available.
Evening meal 6.45pm (l.o.
10pm).
Parking for 40.
Credit: Access, Visa, Diners,
Amex.

The Crescent Hotel ♠
♛♛
21 Hope Road, Shanklin,
PO37 6EA
☎ (0983) 863140
*Small, comfortable, licensed
hotel. Two minutes from cliff
walks and beach, close to town
and evening entertainment.
Home cooking.*
Bedrooms: 2 single, 7 double
& 1 twin, 3 family rooms.
Bathrooms: 5 private,
3 public.
Bed & breakfast: £15-£20
single, £30-£40 double.
Half board: £20-£25 daily,
£120-£150 weekly.
Evening meal 6.15pm.
Parking for 10.
Open April-October.
Credit: Visa.

Culham Lodge Hotel ♠
♛♛♛
31 Landguard Manor Road,
Shanklin, PO37 7HZ
☎ (0983) 862880
*Charming hotel in beautiful
tree-lined road, with heated
swimming pool, solarium,
conservatory, home cooking
and personal service.*
Bedrooms: 1 single, 6 double
& 3 twin.
Bathrooms: 8 private,
2 public.
Bed & breakfast: £13-£14.50
single, £26-£29 double.
Half board: £20-£21.50 daily,
£125-£140 weekly.
Evening meal 6pm (l.o. 4pm).
Parking for 8.
Open April-October.

Keats Green Hotel ♠
♛♛♛
3 Queens Road, Shanklin,
PO37 6AN
☎ (0983) 862742
*Ideally situated on Keats
Green Park overlooking the
sea. 5 minutes' walk to the
beach, town centre and Old
Village.*
Bedrooms: 4 single, 15 double
& 13 twin, 3 family rooms.
Bathrooms: 34 private,
2 public.
Half board: £145-£220
weekly.
Lunch available.
Evening meal 6.45pm (l.o.
5.45pm).
Parking for 32.
Open March-October.
Credit: Access, Visa.

Luccombe Hall Hotel ♠
♛♛♛
Luccombe Road, Shanklin,
PO37 6RL
☎ (0983) 862719 & 864590
Telex 869441 UTNK G Ref
LH1
*In secluded gardens on clifftop
overlooking bay, with
swimming pools, squash and
grass tennis courts. Ideal for
relaxed holidays.*
Bedrooms: 3 single, 7 double
& 8 twin, 12 family rooms.
Bathrooms: 30 private,
2 public.
Bed & breakfast: £28-£34
single, £56-£68 double.
Half board: £39-£50 daily,
£212-£300 weekly.
Lunch available.
Evening meal 6.45pm (l.o.
8.30pm).
Parking for 26.
Credit: Access, Visa.

Melbourne-Ardenlea Hotel ♠
♛♛♛♛
4-6 Queens Road, Shanklin,
PO37 6AP
☎ (0983) 862283
*Family-run hotel, providing
service and courtesy in pleasant
surroundings.*
Bedrooms: 9 single, 12 double
& 19 twin, 12 family rooms.
Bathrooms: 52 private,
2 public.
Bed & breakfast: £21-£36
single, £42-£72 double.
Half board: £26-£41 daily,
£182-£287 weekly.
Lunch available.
Evening meal 6.30pm (l.o.
8pm).
Parking for 30.
Open March-October.
Credit: Access, Visa.

Monteagle Hotel ♠
♛♛♛
Priory Road, Shanklin,
PO37 6RJ
☎ (0983) 862854
*Spacious and well-appointed
hotel, standing in its own
grounds with swimming pool.
Good standard of service and
food.*
Bedrooms: 2 single, 12 double
& 10 twin, 14 family rooms.
Bathrooms: 35 private,
2 public; 1 private shower.
Bed & breakfast: £22-£28
single, £44-£56 double.
Half board: £26-£32 daily,
£140-£200 weekly.

Lunch available.
Evening meal 6.30pm (l.o. 7pm).
Parking for 30.
Open March-November.
Credit: Access, Visa.

Osborne House Hotel M
COMMENDED
Esplanade, Shanklin,
PO37 6BN
☎ (0983) 862501
Tastefully modernised Victorian residence, 25 yards from the sea, where bookings are accepted on a daily basis. Dining room is non-smoking.
Bedrooms: 1 single, 9 double & 2 twin.
Bathrooms: 12 private, 2 public.
Bed & breakfast: from £33 single, from £66 double.
Evening meal 7pm (l.o. 8pm).
Open January-October.
Credit: Access, Visa.

Queensmead Hotel M
12 Queens Road, Shanklin,
PO37 6AN
☎ (0983) 862342
Sea views, spacious public rooms, heated swimming pool, solarium and choice of menu.
Bedrooms: 2 single, 13 double & 10 twin, 6 family rooms.
Bathrooms: 29 private, 2 public.
Bed & breakfast: £26-£33 single.
Half board: £28-£35 daily, £174-£230 weekly.
Lunch available.
Evening meal 6.30pm (l.o. 6.30pm).
Parking for 20.
Open March-October, December.
Credit: Access, Visa.

St. Leonards Hotel M
22 Queens Road, Shanklin,
PO37 6AW
☎ (0983) 862121
A 3-storey family hotel, pleasantly situated, set back from road, with flower bordered lawn and parking facilities. Close to all amenities.
Bedrooms: 1 double & 1 twin, 5 family rooms.
Bathrooms: 4 private, 2 public.

Bed & breakfast: £15.80-£19.25 single, £31.60-£38.50 double.
Half board: £20.80-£24.25 daily, £128-£150 weekly.
Evening meal 6pm.
Parking for 7.
Credit: Access, Visa.

The Shanklin Hotel M
Clarendon Road, Shanklin,
PO37 6DP
☎ (0983) 862286
Live entertainment and dancing nightly. Fabulous "Starlite" ballroom, bars. En-suite sea view rooms with colour TV.
Bedrooms: 11 single, 6 double & 28 twin, 35 family rooms.
Bathrooms: 70 private, 6 public.
Bed & breakfast: £27-£35 single, £50-£60 double.
Half board: £28-£33 daily, £147-£196 weekly.
Evening meal 6.30pm (l.o. 7.30pm).
Parking for 101.
Open March-November.

Shanklin Manor House Hotel M
Old Village, Shanklin,
PO37 6QX
☎ (0983) 862777
Majestic manor house in 4.5 acres of beautiful gardens in the famous Old Village. A few minutes' walk from town, theatre and beach.
Bedrooms: 5 single, 17 double & 10 twin, 6 family rooms.
Bathrooms: 38 private, 1 public.
Bed & breakfast: £31.50-£40 single, £29.50-£36 double.
Half board: £37-£46 daily, £235-£280 weekly.
Evening meal 7pm (l.o. 8pm).
Parking for 50.
Open February-November.

Woodlands Private Hotel M
30 Littlestairs Road,
Shanklin, PO37 6HS
☎ (0983) 862646
Small, licensed, family hotel, close to cliff walk and beach, in quiet area handy for buses.
Bedrooms: 1 single, 7 double, 3 family rooms.
Bathrooms: 2 public.
Bed & breakfast: £12 single, £24-£30 double.

Half board: £15 daily, £105 weekly.
Evening meal 6pm (l.o. 6pm).
Parking for 4.

ISLE OF WIGHT-TOTLAND BAY
Isle of Wight
Map ref 2C3

On the Freshwater Peninsula. It is possible to walk from here around to Alum Bay.

The Nodes Country Hotel M
Alum Bay Old Road, Totland Bay, PO39 0HZ
☎ (0983) 752859
Country house hotel in extensive grounds with glorious countryside and coastal views. Only 10 minutes' walk from safe, sandy beaches.
Bedrooms: 1 single, 4 double & 2 twin, 4 family rooms.
Bathrooms: 9 private, 2 public.
Bed & breakfast: £18-£24 single, £36-£48 double.
Half board: £26.50-£34.50 daily, £175-£225 weekly.
Evening meal 6.30pm (l.o. 3pm).
Parking for 15.

Osborne House M
Granville Road, Totland Bay, PO39 0AX
☎ (0983) 752989
Small family-run guesthouse. Comfortable accommodation, some rooms with private shower. Varied menu and home cooking.
Bedrooms: 3 double, 1 family room.
Bathrooms: 1 public; 2 private showers.
Bed & breakfast: £13-£14 single, £26-£28 double.
Half board: £16.50-£18 daily, £105-£120 weekly.
Evening meal 6pm (l.o. 7pm).
Parking for 4.
Open February-November.
Credit: Access, Visa.

Westgrange Country Hotel M
Alum Bay Old Road, Totland Bay, PO39 0HZ
☎ (0983) 752227

In magnificent rural setting close to sea, with secluded grounds. Ideal for a quiet country holiday.
Bedrooms: 1 single, 2 double & 2 twin, 8 family rooms.
Bathrooms: 9 private, 3 public.
Bed & breakfast: £22.50-£26.50 single, £45-£53 double.
Half board: £32.50-£36.50 daily, £173.50-£214.50 weekly.
Lunch available.
Evening meal 6.30pm (l.o. 7pm).
Parking for 18.
Open March-October.
Credit: Access, Visa.

ISLE OF WIGHT-VENTNOR
Isle of Wight
Map ref 2C3

Town lies at the bottom of an 800-ft hill and has a reputation as a winter holiday and health resort due to its mild climate. There is a pier, small esplanade and Winter Gardens.

Burlington Hotel M
COMMENDED
Bellevue Road, Ventnor,
PO38 1DB
☎ (0983) 852113
Friendly family-run hotel with heated swimming pool, commanding wonderful sea views. Central, yet affords peace and quiet.
Bedrooms: 3 single, 6 double & 9 twin, 5 family rooms.
Bathrooms: 23 private, 1 public.
Bed & breakfast: £20-£28 single, £40-£56 double.
Half board: £28.50-£35 daily, £200-£245 weekly.
Evening meal 6.30pm (l.o. 8pm).
Parking for 20.
Open March-October.
Credit: Access, Visa.

Hillside Hotel M
COMMENDED
Mitchell Avenue, Ventnor,
PO38 1DR
☎ (0983) 852271
Ventnor's only thatched hotel, built in 1801, in its own 2 acres of beautifully wooded grounds overlooking the sea.
Bedrooms: 1 single, 7 double & 2 twin, 1 family room.

Continued ▶

SOUTH OF ENGLAND

Bathrooms: 11 private.
Bed & breakfast: £17.50-
£18.50 single, £35-£37 double.
Half board: £25-£27 daily,
£175-£189 weekly.
Evening meal 6.30pm (l.o.
7pm).
Parking for 15.
Credit: Access, Visa, Amex.

The Lawyers Rest Country House Hotel M
COMMENDED
Undercliff Drive, St.
Lawrence, Ventnor,
PO38 1XF
☎ (0983) 852610
*Early Victorian house in
picturesque coastal village.
Superb views across suntrap
terraced gardens to the sea.
Elegant but informal.*
Bedrooms: 1 single, 5 double
& 2 twin.
Bathrooms: 8 private,
1 public.
Bed & breakfast: £38.20
single, £65.80-£76.40 double.
Half board: £38.78-£44.06
daily, £244.30-£277.58 weekly.
Lunch available.
Evening meal 7pm (l.o. 7pm).
Parking for 12.
Open January-October,
December.
Credit: Access, Visa, Amex.

Hotel Pelham M
Alma Road, Ventnor,
PO38 1JU
☎ (0983) 852252
*Family hotel, 50 yards from
beach, with beautiful sea views
from most rooms.*
Bedrooms: 2 single, 2 double,
6 family rooms.
Bathrooms: 3 private,
2 public.
Bed & breakfast: £12-£16
single, £24-£32 double.
Half board: £18-£22 daily,
£110-£149 weekly.
Evening meal 6pm (l.o. 6pm).
Parking for 2.

Hotel Picardie M
APPROVED
The Esplanade, Ventnor,
PO38 1JX
☎ (0983) 852647

*An informal, family-run
seafront hotel, mainly non-
smoking. Stairlift to first floor.
Relaxed atmosphere and home
cooking.*
Bedrooms: 5 double & 2 twin,
3 family rooms.
Bathrooms: 10 private,
1 public.
Bed & breakfast: £15.40
single, £30.80 double.
Half board: £22.40 daily,
£148 weekly.
Evening meal 6.30pm (l.o.
4pm).
Open March-October.
Credit: Access, Visa.

The Ventnor Towers Hotel M
COMMENDED
Madeira Road, Ventnor,
PO38 1QT
☎ (0983) 852277
Telex 8951182 GECOMS
Consort
*Family-run hotel with
extensive leisure facilities, in
own grounds overlooking the
sea. Comfortable rooms with
beautiful views. 5-course table
d'hote and a la carte menus.*
Bedrooms: 3 single, 12 double
& 8 twin, 4 family rooms.
Bathrooms: 27 private.
Bed & breakfast: £29-£35
single, £58-£70 double.
Half board: £39-£45 daily.
Lunch available.
Evening meal 7pm (l.o.
8.30pm).
Parking for 41.
Credit: Access, Visa, Diners,
Amex.

LINWOOD
Hampshire
Map ref 2B3

*4m NE. Ringwood
An area of New Forest
farms with camp sites.*

High Corner Inn M
COMMENDED
Linwood, Nr. Ringwood,
BH24 3QY
☎ Ringwood (0425) 473973
& Fax (0425) 480015
*Situated down a drovers' track,
in 7 secluded acres in the heart
of the New Forest, 4 miles
north-east of Ringwood.*
Bedrooms: 3 double & 3 twin,
2 family rooms.
Bathrooms: 8 private.
Bed & breakfast: £41.50-
£45.50 single, £59.50-£66
double.

Half board: £38.50-£41.75
daily.
Lunch available.
Evening meal 7pm (l.o.
10pm).
Parking for 203.
Credit: Access, Visa, Diners,
Amex.

LONGHAM
Dorset
Map ref 2B3

*5m N. Bournemouth
Astride the A348 Poole to
Ringwood road and on
the north bank of the
River Stour. The river
floods its banks in this
area when the weather is
severe.*

Bridge House Hotel M
COMMENDED
2 Ringwood Road, Longham,
Wimborne, BH22 9AN
☎ Bournemouth
(0202) 578828 & Fax (0202)
572620 Telex 48484
*Mediterranean-style hotel and
restaurant.*
Bedrooms: 4 single, 23 double
& 10 twin.
Bathrooms: 37 private.
Bed & breakfast: £52-£53
single, £75-£90 double.
Half board: £50-£65 daily,
£300-£400 weekly.
Lunch available.
Evening meal 7pm (l.o.
10pm).
Parking for 200.
Credit: Access, Visa, Amex.

LYMINGTON
Hampshire
Map ref 2C3

Small, pleasant town with
bright cottages and
attractive Georgian
houses, lying on the edge
of the New Forest with a
ferry service to the Isle of
Wight. A sheltered
harbour makes it a busy
yachting centre.

Albany House M
Highfield, Lymington,
SO41 9GB
☎ (0590) 671900
*Elegant Regency house in
Georgian market town, with
charming English walled
garden and views of Isle of
Wight and Solent.*

Bedrooms: 2 single, 1 double
& 1 twin, 1 family room.
Bathrooms: 3 private,
1 public.
Bed & breakfast: £18.50-£24
single, £32-£48 double.
Half board: £25.50-£36 daily,
£178.50-£234.50 weekly.
Evening meal 7pm (l.o. 7pm).
Parking for 5.

Passford House Hotel M
COMMENDED
Mount Pleasant Lane,
Lymington, SO41 8LS
☎ (0590) 682398
Fax (0590) 683494
*Charming country house on the
edge of the New Forest, with
spacious lounges, well-
appointed accommodation and
a recently added leisure centre.*
Bedrooms: 5 single, 18 double
& 27 twin, 6 family rooms.
Bathrooms: 56 private,
1 public.
Bed & breakfast: from £75
single, from £107 double.
Half board: from £71.50
daily.
Lunch available.
Evening meal 7pm (l.o. 9pm).
Parking for 84.
Credit: Access, Visa, Amex.

Westover Hall Hotel M
Park Lane, Milford-on-Sea,
SO41 0PT
☎ Lymington (0590) 643044
& Fax (0590) 44490
*All rooms en-suite, with
telephone, TV and radio.
Renowned restaurant with
affordable wine list. Privately
owned and run by Mrs P.
Roth.*
Bedrooms: 2 single, 6 double
& 5 twin.
Bathrooms: 13 private.
Bed & breakfast: £38-£48
single, £70-£110 double.
Half board: £47-£67 daily,
£300-£450 weekly.
Lunch available.
Evening meal 7.30pm.
Parking for 40.
Credit: Access, Visa, Diners,
Amex.

*The symbols are
explained on the
flap inside the
back cover.*

LYNDHURST

Hampshire
Map ref 2C3

The 'capital' of the New
Forest, surrounded by
attractive woodland
scenery and delightful
villages. The town is
dominated by the
Victorian Gothic-style
church where the original
Alice in Wonderland is
buried.
*Tourist Information
Centre* ☎ (0703) 282269

The Bell Inn Hotel M
👑👑👑👑

Bramshaw Golf Club, Brook,
Lyndhurst, SO43 7HE
☎ Southampton
(0703) 812214
*Built in 1782, a listed building,
this country inn is located in
the New Forest, 1 mile from
access point 1 on M27.
Southampton 12 miles,
Salisbury 15 miles,
Bournemouth 18 miles. Own
two 18-hole golf-courses.*
Bedrooms: 3 single, 7 double
& 12 twin.
Bathrooms: 22 private.
Bed & breakfast: £53.50-£60
single, £76-£85 double.
Half board: £63-£72 daily.
Lunch available.
Evening meal 7.30pm (l.o.
9.30pm).
Parking for 170.
Credit: Access, Visa, Diners,
Amex.
🛏️🍴📞📺🖥️🛎️☎ V ⚒
🖬 🛢️🅿️ ⏸️ ☀️ 🔗 SP 🖾
T

Knightwood Lodge M
👑👑👑

Southampton Road,
Lyndhurst, SO43 7BU
☎ (0703) 282502
Fax (0703) 283730
*On the edge of Lyndhurst
overlooking the New Forest.
Indoor health centre.*
Bedrooms: 2 single, 7 double
& 2 twin, 1 family room.
Bathrooms: 12 private,
1 public.
Bed & breakfast: £26.50-£34
single, £40-£50 double.
Half board: £36.50-£44.50
daily.
Evening meal 6.30pm (l.o.
8.30pm).
Parking for 10.
Credit: Access, Visa, Diners,
Amex.
🛏️5 🍴🖥️📞🛎️🛢️ V 🖬
🖬🛢️🚲🔗 SP 🖾 T

Lyndhurst Park Hotel M
👑👑👑👑

High Street, Lyndhurst,
SO43 7NL
☎ (0703) 283923
Telex 477802 FODALE G
🅖 Forestdale
*Elegant Georgian mansion,
with comfortable interior, set in
own grounds in "capital" of
New Forest.*
Bedrooms: 5 single, 29 double
& 22 twin, 3 family rooms.
Bathrooms: 59 private.
Bed & breakfast: from £62.50
single, from £77.50 double.
Lunch available.
Evening meal 7pm (l.o.
10pm).
Parking for 100.
Credit: Access, Visa, Diners,
Amex.
🛏️🍴📞📺🖥️🛎️🛢️ V ⚒
🖬 ⓞ🔗🛢️☀️🛎️🅿️🚲☀️
🚶♿☀️ 🔗 SP 🖾 T

The New Forest Inn

Emery Down, Lyndhurst,
SO43 7DY
☎ (0703) 282329
*New Forest country inn set in
woodlands, offering a warm
welcome and good food.*
Bedrooms: 4 double.
Bathrooms: 4 private.
Bed & breakfast: £25-£30
single, £50-£60 double.
Lunch available.
Evening meal 6pm (l.o.
9.30pm).
Parking for 25.
Credit: Access, Visa.
🛏️🍴📺🛎️ V 🖬📺🖥️🛢️
🛎️♿☀️ 🖾

Ormonde House Hotel M
👑👑👑 APPROVED

Southampton Road,
Lyndhurst, SO43 7BT
☎ (0703) 282806
*Hotel set in own grounds with
an open forest outlook. Town
centre within easy reach. Ideal
for touring.*
Bedrooms: 2 single, 6 double
& 4 twin.
Bathrooms: 12 private.
Bed & breakfast: £25-£30
single, £40-£54 double.
Half board: £30-£37 daily,
£190-£233 weekly.
Parking for 16.
Credit: Access, Visa.
🛏️🍴📞📺🖥️UL🖬🖥️🛢️
♿ 🖾 DAP SP T

South View Hotel M
Listed APPROVED

Gosport Lane, Lyndhurst,
SO43 7BL
☎ (0703) 282224

*Comfortable rooms close to the
town centre, in the heart of the
New Forest. Some with private
bathrooms.*
Bedrooms: 3 double & 3 twin,
1 family room.
Bathrooms: 3 private,
2 public.
Bed & breakfast: £22-£28
single, £36-£42 double.
Parking for 10.
🛏️🍴UL🛢️🖥️📺🖥️🛢️🖾
DAP

Whitemoor House Hotel M
👑👑 COMMENDED

Southampton Road,
Lyndhurst, SO43 7BU
☎ (0703) 282186
*Comfortable hotel with an open
outlook to the forest. Within
easy reach of Southampton,
Beaulieu and the coast.*
Bedrooms: 3 double & 1 twin,
1 family room.
Bathrooms: 5 private,
1 public.
Bed & breakfast: £25-£30
single, £40-£44 double.
Evening meal 6.30pm.
Parking for 10.
Credit: Access, Visa.
🛏️🍴🖥️ V ⚒🖬📺🖥️
🛢️ ♿☀️ 🖾

MIDDLE WALLOP

Hampshire
Map ref 2C2

On the main Salisbury to
Andover road and
between Over Wallop and
Nether Wallop. The Army
Air Corps (Museum) and
Training Centre is 2 miles
north-east.

Fifehead Manor M
👑👑👑👑

Middle Wallop, Stockbridge,
SO20 8EG
☎ Andover (0264) 781565 &
Fax (0264) 781400
*Comfortable manor house, part
of which dates from the 11th
C. Located close to the famous
River Test.*
Bedrooms: 6 single, 6 double
& 4 twin.
Bathrooms: 16 private.
Bed & breakfast: £50-£55
single, £70-£95 double.
Half board: £75-£80 daily,
£525-£560 weekly.
Lunch available.
Evening meal 7.30pm (l.o.
9.30pm).
Parking for 50.
Credit: Access, Visa, Diners,
Amex.
🛏️🍴📞📱 V 🖬🖥️🛢️
🍴♿☀️🖾 SP 🖾 T

MILFORD-ON-SEA

Hampshire
Map ref 2C3

Victorian seaside resort
with shingle beach and
good bathing, set in
pleasant countryside and
looking out over the Isle
of Wight. Nearby is Hurst
Castle, built by Henry VIII.

Compton Hotel M
👑👑

59 Keyhaven Road, Milford-
on-Sea, Lymington,
SO41 0QX
☎ Lymington (0590) 643117
*Small, private hotel with en-
suite rooms and TV. Outdoor
heated swimming pool. English
and vegetarian cooking.
Licensed.*
Bedrooms: 2 single, 3 double
& 1 twin, 1 family room.
Bathrooms: 4 private,
1 public.
Bed & breakfast: £17-£20
single, £34-£36 double.
Half board: £24-£26 daily,
£160-£165 weekly.
Evening meal 6.30pm (l.o.
6.30pm).
Parking for 8.
🛏️🍴📞📺🛎️ V ⚒🖬📺
🖥️🛢️🍴♿🛎️ DAP 🖾 SP

South Lawn Hotel M
👑👑👑 COMMENDED

Lymington Road, Milford-on-
Sea, Lymington, SO41 0RF
☎ Lymington (0590) 643911
& Fax (0590) 644820
*Attractive country house in
peaceful surroundings, where
chef/proprietor ensures that
food, comfort and personal
service predominate.*
Bedrooms: 6 double &
18 twin.
Bathrooms: 24 private.
Bed & breakfast: max. £47.50
single, max. £90 double.
Half board: max. £58.25
daily, max. £377 weekly.
Evening meal 7pm (l.o.
8.30pm).
Parking for 50.
Credit: Access, Visa.
🛏️7🍴📞🖥️📱 V 🖬🖥️
🛢️♿☀️🚶🖾 SP

---

*National Crown
ratings were correct
at the time of going
to press but are
subject to change.
Please check at the
time of booking.*

NETLEY ABBEY

Hampshire
Map ref 2C3

*4m SE. Southampton
Romantic ruin, set in
green lawns against a
background of trees on
the east bank of
Southampton Water. The
abbey was built in the
13th C by Cistercian
monks from Beaulieu.*

La Casa Blanca M
♨♨

48 Victoria Road, Netley
Abbey, SO3 5DQ
☎ Southampton
(0703) 453718
*Small, pleasantly situated
licensed hotel. Friendly
welcome, well-equipped
bedrooms and home cooking.*
Bedrooms: 4 single, 2 double
& 3 twin, 1 family room.
Bathrooms: 1 private,
3 public.
Bed & breakfast: £21 single,
£34 double.
Half board: £23-£27 daily.
Evening meal 6.30pm (l.o.
9.30pm).
Parking for 3.
Credit: Access, Visa.
ち ♨ ℄ �ⓑ ◻ ♥ ⓘ Ⓥ ⊨
⛻ ⛾ ▨ ♨ ☒ SP

NEW FOREST

*See Barton on Sea,
Bramshaw, Brockenhurst,
Burley, Cadnam,
Fordingbridge, Linwood,
Lymington, Lyndhurst,
Milford-on-Sea,
Ringwood, Sway,
Woodlands.*

NORTH WALTHAM

Hampshire
Map ref 2C2

Wheatsheaf Hotel M
♨♨♨

North Waltham, Nr.
Basingstoke, RG25 2BB
☎ Basingstoke (0256) 398282
Telex 859775
Ⓖ Lansbury
*Rural hotel, well placed for
Basingstoke and the
Hampshire countryside.*
Bedrooms: 3 single,
25 double.
Bathrooms: 28 private.
Bed & breakfast: from £26
single, from £52 double.
Half board: from £38 daily.
Lunch available.
Evening meal 7pm (l.o.
10.30pm).
Parking for 70.

Credit: Access, Visa, Diners,
Amex.
ち ♨ ♨ ℄ ⓑ ◻ ♥ ⊨ Ⓥ
⛾ ♨ ▣ ● ▥ ▨ ♨ ⓣ 🏐 SP 🏠
Ⓣ

PETERSFIELD

Hampshire
Map ref 2C3

*Grew prosperous from
the wool trade and was
famous as a coaching
centre. Its attractive
market square is
dominated by a statue of
William III. Close by are
Petersfield Heath with
numerous ancient
barrows and Butser Hill
with magnificent views.*
*Tourist Information
Centre ☎ (0730) 68829*

Langrish House M
♨♨♨ COMMENDED

Langrish, Petersfield,
GU32 1RN
☎ Petersfield (0730) 66941
*Delightful old English manor
house with panoramic views set
in 13 acres of beautiful
countryside. Idyllic country
walks and three golf-courses
nearby.*
Bedrooms: 6 single, 6 double
& 6 twin.
Bathrooms: 18 private.
Bed & breakfast: £45-£55
single, £59-£70 double.
Half board: £57-£74 daily.
Evening meal 7.30pm (l.o.
9.30pm).
Parking for 50.
Credit: Access, Visa, Diners,
Amex.
ち ♨ ℄ ◻ ▣ ⓘ Ⓥ ⛻ ⊨
⛾ ▥ ▣ ♨ Ⓣ ♥ ✱ ⒹⒶⓅ SP
🏠 Ⓣ

POOLE

Dorset
Map ref 2B3

*Tremendous natural
harbour makes Poole a
superb boating centre.
The harbour area is
crowded with historic
buildings including the
15th C Town Cellars
housing a maritime
museum.*
*Tourist Information
Centre ☎ (0202) 673322*

Arndale Court Hotel
62-66 Wimborne Road,
Poole, BH15 2BY
☎ (0202) 683746
*Completely refurbished hotel,
close to quay, town, British
Rail and ferry terminal. All
rooms en-suite.*

Bedrooms: 5 single, 7 double
& 4 twin, 16 family rooms.
Bathrooms: 32 private.
Bed & breakfast: £35-£45
single, £45-£57 double.
Half board: £32-£58 daily.
Evening meal 7pm (l.o. 9pm).
Parking for 32.
Credit: Access, Visa, Diners,
Amex.
ち ♨ ℄ ◻ ▣ ♥ ⓘ Ⓥ ⊨
▥ ▣ ♨ ▤ SP Ⓣ

Dolphin Hotel M
High Street, Poole,
BH15 1DU
☎ (0202) 673612
Telex 417205
*In the town centre, close to
coach and railway stations.*
Bedrooms: 35 single,
19 double & 12 twin.
Bathrooms: 66 private.
Bed & breakfast: from £57.50
single, from £69.50 double.
Lunch available.
Evening meal 6pm (l.o.
10.30pm).
Parking for 60.
Credit: Access, Visa, Diners,
Amex.
ち ♨ ℄ ◻ ▣ ♥ ⓘ Ⓥ ●
⛻ ▥ ▣ ♨ ♨ SP Ⓣ

Harmony Hotel M
♨♨

19 St. Peter's Road,
Parkstone, Poole, BH14 0NZ
☎ (0202) 747510
*The hotel offers friendly service
in peaceful, residential area
close to all local amenities and
is ideally placed as a touring
centre.*
Bedrooms: 4 double & 4 twin,
3 family rooms.
Bathrooms: 8 private,
1 public; 1 private shower.
Bed & breakfast: £23-£30
single, £41-£50 double.
Evening meal 7pm (l.o.
8.30pm).
Parking for 14.
Credit: Access, Visa.
ち3 ♨ ℄ ◻ ♥ Ⓥ ⊨ ● ▥
▣ ♨ ▤ ⒹⒶⓅ SP

The Inn in the Park M
♨♨

26 Pinewood Road,
Branksome Park, Poole,
BH13 6JS
☎ Bournemouth
(0202) 761318
*Small, friendly, family-owned
pub with sun terrace, log fire
and easy access to the beach.*
Bedrooms: 3 double & 1 twin,
1 family room.
Bathrooms: 5 private.
Bed & breakfast: £29-£35
single, £43-£52 double.
Lunch available.

Evening meal 7pm (l.o.
9.30pm).
Parking for 15.
Credit: Access, Visa.
ち ◻ ♥ ▥ ♨ ▣ ▤ ♨

Mansion House Hotel M
♨♨♨♨ COMMENDED

11 Thames Street, Poole,
BH15 1JN
☎ (0202) 685666
*Close to quay in the historic
part of old town, with well-
appointed bedrooms.*
Bedrooms: 9 single, 13 double
& 6 twin.
Bathrooms: 28 private.
Bed & breakfast: £70-£75
single, £100-£115 double.
Half board: £80-£85 daily,
£480-£510 weekly.
Lunch available.
Evening meal 7.30pm (l.o.
10pm).
Parking for 40.
Credit: Access, Visa, C.Bl.,
Diners, Amex.
ち ♨ ℄ ◻ ▣ ⓘ Ⓥ ⊨ ●
▥ ▣ ♨ ♨ SP 🏠 Ⓣ

Norfolk Lodge Hotel M
♨♨♨ COMMENDED

1 Flaghead Road, Canford
Cliffs, Poole, BH13 7JL
☎ (0202) 708614
*Small hotel, beautifully
positioned in Canford Cliffs
and close to beach. Large bar,
attractive restaurant and
adequate parking space.*
Bedrooms: 1 single, 4 double
& 6 twin, 7 family rooms.
Bathrooms: 16 private,
2 public; 2 private showers.
Bed & breakfast: £35-£40
single, £52-£56 double.
Half board: £35-£49 daily,
£165-£250 weekly.
Lunch available.
Evening meal 6.30pm (l.o.
8.30pm).
Parking for 16.
Credit: Access, Visa, Amex.
ち ♨ ℄ ◻ ▣ ⓘ Ⓥ ⛻
⊨ ▥ ▣ ♨ ✱ ⒹⒶⓅ ♨ SP

The Rosemount Hotel
167 Bournemouth Road,
Lower Parkstone, Poole,
BH14 9HT
☎ (0202) 732138
*Small family-run hotel on main
road between Poole and
Bournemouth. Offering varied
food, cleanliness and friendly
service.*
Bedrooms: 4 double & 2 twin,
2 family rooms.
Bathrooms: 2 public;
2 private showers.
Bed & breakfast: £15-£17
single, £30-£35 double.
Half board: £19.50-£21.50
daily, £120-£130 weekly.

Evening meal 6pm (l.o.
8.30pm).
Parking for 6.

POOLE-SANDBANKS

Dorset
Map ref 2B3

Lies to the east of Poole.
Boats can be hired from
here for exploring all the
inlets and islands in Poole
Harbour, and a car ferry
operates to Shell Bay.

Harbour Heights Hotel M
COMMENDED
73 Haven Road, Sandbanks,
Poole, BH13 7LW
☎ (0202) 707272
Fax (0202) 708594
*Modern, family-owned hotel
with panoramic views
overlooking Poole Harbour.
Midway between Poole and
Bournemouth and close to
beach.*
Bedrooms: 11 single,
25 double & 12 twin.
Bathrooms: 48 private,
1 public.
Bed & breakfast: £47-£50
single, £80-£85 double.
Half board: £62-£67 daily,
£350-£400 weekly.
Lunch available.
Evening meal 7pm (l.o.
9.30pm).
Parking for 84.
Credit: Access, Visa, Diners,
Amex.

Haven Hotel M
COMMENDED
Banks Road, Sandbanks,
Poole, BH13 7QL
☎ Bournemouth
(0202) 707333 & Fax (0202)
708796
*Standing on the very edge of
the sea overlooking the
entrance to Poole Yacht
Harbour and Purbeck Hills.*
Bedrooms: 18 single,
27 double & 45 twin, 6 family
rooms.
Bathrooms: 96 private.
Bed & breakfast: £51-£90
single, £102-£158 double.
Half board: £66.50-£89 daily,
£399-£520 weekly.
Lunch available.
Evening meal 7pm (l.o. 9pm).
Parking for 200.

Credit: Access, Visa, Diners,
Amex.

Sandbanks Hotel M
COMMENDED
Banks Road, Sandbanks,
Poole, BH13 7PS
☎ Bournemouth
(0202) 707377 & Fax (0202)
708855
*On a sand peninsula right on
the water's edge with views of
the sea and Poole Harbour.*
Bedrooms: 16 single,
17 double & 47 twin, 25 family
rooms.
Bathrooms: 105 private.
Bed & breakfast: £45-£55
single, £90-£110 double.
Half board: £60-£70 daily,
£360-£420 weekly.
Lunch available.
Evening meal 7pm (l.o.
8.30pm).
Parking for 200.
Credit: Access, Visa, Diners,
Amex.

PORTSMOUTH & SOUTHSEA

Hampshire
Map ref 2C3

There have been
connections with the
Navy since early times
and the first dock was
built in 1194. HMS
Victory, Nelson's flagship,
is here and Charles
Dickens' former home is
open to the public.
Neighbouring Southsea
has a promenade with
magnificent views of
Spithead.
*Tourist Information
Centre* ☎ (0705) 826722

Abbey Lodge Guest House M
APPROVED
30 Waverley Road, Southsea,
PO5 2PW
☎ (0705) 828285
*Friendly, family-run
guesthouse, ideal for seafront,
ferries and attractions.
Satellite TV in all rooms.
Home cooking a speciality.
Route maps sent. Fax and
computer available.*
Bedrooms: 3 single, 3 double
& 1 twin, 2 family rooms.
Bathrooms: 3 public.

Bed & breakfast: £11-£15
single, £22-£30 double.
Half board: £18-£22 daily.
Evening meal 6.30pm.

April House M
7 Malvern Road, Southsea,
PO5 2LZ
☎ (0705) 814824
*Clean, comfortable guesthouse,
close to Rock Gardens,
Pyramid centre, beach and all
facilities. All rooms have colour
TV and electric kettle.*
Bedrooms: 2 single, 3 double
& 2 twin, 2 family rooms.
Bathrooms: 2 public;
1 private shower.
Bed & breakfast: £14-£17
single, £28-£34 double.
Parking for 4.
Open May-October.

Aquarius Court Hotel M
34 St. Ronans Road,
Southsea, PO4 0PT
☎ (0705) 822872
*Small, family-run hotel,
5 minutes from seafront.
Unrestricted car parking in
drive and road. No restrictions.*
Bedrooms: 2 single, 2 double
& 4 twin, 4 family rooms.
Bathrooms: 2 public.
Bed & breakfast: £13.50-
£14.50 single, £27-£29 double.
Half board: £19-£20.50 daily,
£120-£127 weekly.
Lunch available.
Evening meal 6pm (l.o. 4pm).
Parking for 4.
Credit: Access, Visa.

Arcade Hotel M
Winston Churchill Avenue,
Portsmouth, PO1 2LX
☎ (0705) 821992
Telex 869429
*Newly built modern city centre
hotel. Within walking distance
of shopping centre, main
railway station and Guildhall.*
Bedrooms: 4 single, 36 double
& 77 twin, 27 family rooms.
Bathrooms: 144 private.
Bed & breakfast: £25-£46
single, £35-£57 double.
Half board: from £37.75
daily.
Lunch available.
Evening meal 6.30pm (l.o.
9.45pm).
Parking for 50.
Credit: Access, Visa, Diners,
Amex.

The Ashburton Hotel M
25 Ashburton Road,
Southsea, PO5 3JS
☎ (0705) 871187
Fax (0705) 871177
*Comfortable family-run hotel
with private car parking.
Central position, 10 minutes
from ferry terminal. Early
breakfasts catered for.*
Bedrooms: 2 single, 4 double
& 1 twin.
Bathrooms: 7 private.
Bed & breakfast: £23-£33
single, £37-£47 double.
Half board: £26.50-£41 daily,
£175-£275 weekly.
Evening meal 7pm (l.o.
10.30pm).
Parking for 3.
Credit: Access, Visa.

Averano Guest House M
Listed
65 Granada Road, Southsea,
PO4 0RQ
☎ (0705) 820079
*One minute to seafront, buses
and coaches, children's sporting
facilities, South Parade Pier,
canoe lake and nightclubs.*
Bedrooms: 2 single, 5 double
& 2 twin, 2 family rooms.
Bathrooms: 3 public.
Bed & breakfast: £12-£15
single, £24-£30 double.
Parking for 11.

The Dolphins Hotel & Snobbs Cocktail Bar & Restaurant M
10-11 Western Parade,
Southsea, PO5 3JF
☎ (0705) 823823 & 820833
*On the seafront, overlooking
the common. Near to Mary
Rose, HMS Victory, HMS
Warrior and ferry terminals.
Attractive bar and restaurant
with a la carte and table d'hote
menus.*
Bedrooms: 5 single, 12 double
& 2 twin, 14 family rooms.
Bathrooms: 20 private,
7 public; 2 private showers.
Bed & breakfast: £22-£30
single, £38-£45 double.
Half board: £32-£42 daily,
£196-£230 weekly.
Evening meal 7.30pm (l.o.
9.45pm).
Credit: Access, Visa, Diners,
Amex.

PORTSMOUTH & SOUTHSEA

Continued

Gainsborough House
🏵🏵 COMMENDED

9 Malvern Road, Southsea,
PO5 2LZ
☎ (0705) 822604
Long established guesthouse, a few minutes from seafront and wihin easy reach of continental ferry port and local attractions.
Bedrooms: 2 single, 2 double & 2 twin, 1 family room.
Bathrooms: 2 public.
Bed & breakfast: £13.50-£14.50 single, £27-£29 double.

Granada House Hotel M
🏵🏵 APPROVED

29 Granada Road, Southsea,
PO4 0RD
☎ (0705) 861575
The hotel offers spacious bedrooms and English or continental breakfast.
Bedrooms: 1 single, 2 double & 2 twin, 2 family rooms.
Bathrooms: 5 private, 2 public.
Bed & breakfast: £12.50-£17.50 single, £28-£38 double.
Half board: from £21 daily, £100-£160 weekly.
Evening meal 6pm (l.o. 8pm).
Parking for 10.

Hamilton House M
🏵 COMMENDED

95 Victoria Road North,
Southsea, PO5 1PS
☎ (0705) 823502
Delightful family-run guesthouse, 5 minutes by car to ferry terminals and tourist attractions. Some en-suite rooms available. Breakfast served from 6am.
Bedrooms: 1 single, 2 double & 3 twin, 2 family rooms.
Bathrooms: 3 private, 2 public.
Bed & breakfast: £13-£15 single, £26-£30 double.
Half board: £18-£20 daily, £120-£135 weekly.
Evening meal 6pm.

Hilton National M

Eastern Road, Farlington,
Portsmouth, PO6 1UN
☎ (0705) 219111 Telex 86598
☞ Hilton
New lodge-style hotel with 120-cover restaurant, conference and leisure facilities.

Bedrooms: 55 double & 45 twin, 22 family rooms.
Bathrooms: 122 private.
Bed & breakfast: £50-£115 single, £60-£137 double.
Half board: £61.95-£126.95 daily.
Lunch available.
Evening meal 7pm (l.o. 10.30pm).
Parking for 250.
Credit: Access, Visa, Diners, Amex.

Holiday Inn Portsmouth M
🏵🏵🏵🏵 COMMENDED

North Harbour, Portsmouth,
PO6 4SH
☎ Cosham (0705) 383151
Telex 86611
☞ Holiday Inn
North of city centre, close to M27 and A3. Children under 19 stay free when sharing parents' room. Indoor pool, squash, gym.
Bedrooms: 94 double, 76 family rooms.
Bathrooms: 170 private.
Bed & breakfast: £35-£95 single, £70-£117 double.
Half board: £45-£110 daily.
Lunch available.
Evening meal 6.30pm (l.o. 11pm).
Parking for 200.
Credit: Access, Visa, C.Bl., Diners, Amex.

Lamorna Guest House
Listed

23 Victoria Road South,
Southsea, PO5 2BX
☎ (0705) 811157
Small guesthouse on three floors. Clean and comfortable, centrally heated accommodation. Under 10 minutes by car from ferry terminal.
Bedrooms: 1 single, 2 double, 2 family rooms.
Bathrooms: 1 public.
Bed & breakfast: £13-£14.50 single, £24-£27 double.
Half board: £19-£21 daily.
Evening meal 6.30pm (l.o. 6.30pm).

Mayville Hotel

4 Waverley Road, Southsea,
PO5 2PN
☎ (0705) 732461

Established hotel within easy reach of seafront and shops. Ample enclosed car parking. Pets welcome. 10 minutes from ferry terminals and naval heritage museums.
Bedrooms: 7 single, 4 double & 3 twin, 4 family rooms.
Bathrooms: 18 private, 1 public.
Bed & breakfast: £22.50-£23.50 single, £41-£42 double.
Half board: £30-£31 daily, £163.50-£170 weekly.
Evening meal 6.30pm (l.o. 7pm).
Parking for 21.
Credit: Access, Visa.

Newleaze Guest House M
Listed

11 St. Edward's Road,
Southsea, PO5 3DH
☎ (0705) 832735
Small friendly establishment with home cooking, giving good value for money. Within easy reach of continental ferry port.
Bedrooms: 2 single, 2 double & 2 twin, 1 family room.
Bathrooms: 1 public; 1 private shower.
Bed & breakfast: £13-£15 single, £24-£30 double.
Half board: £16.50-£20 daily, £96-£118 weekly.
Evening meal 6pm.
Credit: Access, Visa.

Oakdale Guest House M
🏵🏵

71 St. Ronans Road,
Southsea, PO4 0PP
☎ (0705) 737358
Small, comfortable guesthouse in ideal area for seafront, shops, historic ships, ferries and rail terminals.
Bedrooms: 2 double, 4 family rooms.
Bathrooms: 6 private.
Bed & breakfast: £15-£17 single, £30-£34 double.
Half board: £20-£22 daily, from £135 weekly.
Evening meal 6pm.
Credit: Access, Visa.

Oakleigh Guest House M
🏵🏵

48 Festing Grove, Southsea,
PO4 9QD
☎ (0705) 812276

Family-run guesthouse, offering personal service. Children and OAPs are welcome. Colour TV, hot and cold water.
Bedrooms: 2 single, 2 double & 1 twin, 2 family rooms.
Bathrooms: 1 public.
Bed & breakfast: £12 single, £24 double.
Half board: £16 daily, £105 weekly.
Evening meal 6pm (l.o. 4pm).

The Queen's Hotel M
🏵🏵🏵🏵

Clarence Parade, Southsea,
PO5 3LJ
☎ (0705) 822466
Fax (0705) 821901
☞ Consort
Completely refurbished Edwardian-style hotel in prime position on Southsea's seafront. Within easy reach of historic landmarks and the ferry terminals. Breathtaking views of Solent and Isle of Wight.
Bedrooms: 12 single, 22 double & 30 twin, 6 family rooms.
Bathrooms: 70 private.
Bed & breakfast: £55-£65 single, £80-£100 double.
Half board: £52.50-£77.50 daily, £346.50-£375 weekly.
Lunch available.
Evening meal 7.30pm (l.o. 9.30pm).
Parking for 100.
Credit: Access, Visa, Diners, Amex.

St. David's Guest House M
🏵🏵 COMMENDED

19 St. David's Road,
Southsea, PO5 1QH
☎ (0705) 826858
Small, family-run guesthouse close to shops, restaurants and theatre, convenient for seafront and continental ferry.
Bedrooms: 1 double & 3 twin, 2 family rooms.
Bathrooms: 2 public.
Bed & breakfast: £14-£18 single, £24-£28 double.

St. Margarets Hotel M
🏵🏵🏵 COMMENDED

3 Craneswater Gate,
Southsea, PO4 0NZ
☎ (0705) 820097

*Family-run licensed hotel with
3 of the bedrooms on ground
floor. Near the canoe lake,
seafront, Portsmouth Naval
Heritage and ferryport.*
Bedrooms: 4 single, 4 double
& 3 twin, 3 family rooms.
Bathrooms: 8 private,
2 public.
Bed & breakfast: £22-£28
single, £36-£40 double.
Half board: £30-£36 daily,
£190-£240 weekly.
Evening meal 6pm (l.o. 6pm).
Parking for 4.
Credit: Access, Visa.

Salisbury Hotel M
⚜⚜⚜
57-59 Festing Road,
Southsea, PO4 0NQ
☎ (0705) 823606 & 828147 &
Fax (0705) 820955
*Two minutes' walk from the
sea, in an attractive area of
Southsea. The licensed
restaurant overlooks a
delightful garden, available for
residents' use and barbecue
parties.*
Bedrooms: 6 single, 7 double
& 5 twin, 6 family rooms.
Bathrooms: 10 private,
2 public; 8 private showers.
Bed & breakfast: £20-£36
single, £36-£52 double.
Half board: £29-£46 daily,
£160-£230 weekly.
Lunch available.
Evening meal 6.30pm (l.o.
9pm).
Parking for 20.
Credit: Access, Visa, Amex.

The Sandringham Hotel M
⚜⚜⚜
Osborne Road/Clarence
Parade, Southsea, PO5 3LR
☎ (0705) 826969 & 822914 &
Fax (0705) 822330
*Impressive hotel with private
facilities and sea views from
most bedrooms. 100 seat
restaurant, function/conference
room for 120 complete with bar
and dance floor, elegant wine
house. Large free car park
opposite hotel.*
Bedrooms: 10 single,
14 double & 10 twin,
11 family rooms.
Bathrooms: 45 private,
2 public.
Bed & breakfast: £30-£38
single, £44-£50 double.
Half board: £38-£48 daily,
£180-£220 weekly.
Lunch available.

Evening meal 7pm (l.o.
9.30pm).
Credit: Access, Visa, Diners,
Amex.

Saville Hotel
38-39 Clarence Parade,
Southsea, P05 2EU
☎ (0705) 812526 & 822491
Telex 86626 MYNEWS G
*Owner-managed private hotel,
close to seafront and floral
parklands. Passenger lift. Live
music/dancing in season.*
Bedrooms: 9 single, 9 double
& 16 twin, 11 family rooms.
Bathrooms: 21 private,
8 public; 1 private shower.
Bed & breakfast: £23.50-£34
single, £37.60-£47 double.
Half board: £30-£40.50 daily,
£152.75-£164.50 weekly.
Evening meal 6.30pm (l.o.
6.30pm).
Parking for 4.
Credit: Access, Visa, Diners,
Amex.

The Shropshire Court Guest House M
⚜⚜
33 Granada Road, Southsea,
PO4 0RD
☎ (0705) 731043
*Family-run guesthouse close to
sea, ferry port and all
amenities. Immaculate
accommodation and friendly,
informal atmosphere. Early
breakfast available.*
Bedrooms: 2 single, 2 double
& 3 twin, 2 family rooms.
Bathrooms: 3 public.
Bed & breakfast: £15-£16
single, £30-£32 double.
Parking for 7.

Turret Hotel
Clarence Parade, Southsea,
PO5 2HZ
☎ (0705) 291810
*On Southsea seafront opposite
the new Pyramids Centre and
the Lady's Mile. Most unusual
building with turret and
marvellous views.*
Bedrooms: 4 single, 7 double
& 2 twin.
Bathrooms: 7 private,
3 public.
Bed & breakfast: £20-£30
single, £40-£50 double.
Credit: Access, Visa, Amex.

Victoria Court Hotel M
⚜⚜⚜
29 Victoria Road North,
Southsea, PO5 1PL
☎ (0705) 820305
*Extensively modernised,
Victorian residence, on a direct
route to Southsea. Close to
seafront, ferries and both main
shopping centres.*
Bedrooms: 2 double & 2 twin,
4 family rooms.
Bathrooms: 8 private,
1 public.
Bed & breakfast: £25 single,
£33 double.
Half board: £25.50 daily,
£162 weekly.
Evening meal 7pm (l.o.
8.30pm).
Credit: Access, Visa.

Waverley Park Lodge Guest House
⚜
99 Waverley Road, Southsea,
PO5 2PL
☎ (0705) 730402
*Comfortable guesthouse with
family rooms for overnight
accommodation. Easy reach of
ferryport, arrangement for
early breakfast. Chef/owner.*
Bedrooms: 1 single, 2 double
& 1 twin, 2 family rooms.
Bathrooms: 1 public.
Bed & breakfast: £13-£15
single, £25-£26 double.
Half board: £21-£23 daily.
Evening meal 6pm (l.o. 6pm).
Credit: Access, Visa.

Westfield Hall Hotel M
⚜⚜⚜
65 Festing Road, Southsea,
PO4 0NQ
☎ (0705) 826971
Fax (0705) 870200
*A small exclusive hotel
situated in its own grounds,
with large car park 3 minutes
from Southsea's seafront,
promenade and canoe lake.*
Bedrooms: 2 single, 6 double
& 3 twin, 4 family rooms.
Bathrooms: 14 private,
2 public.
Bed & breakfast: £22-£36
single, £42-£50 double.
Half board: £32-£46 daily,
£62-£70 weekly.
Evening meal 6.30pm (l.o.
6.30pm).
Parking for 17.
Credit: Access, Visa, Diners,
Amex.

The White House Hotel
⚜⚜⚜
26 South Parade, Southsea,
PO5 2JF
☎ (0705) 823709 & 829145
*A small, exclusive hotel in a
fine position on the seafront,
with residents' bar.*
Bedrooms: 3 single, 5 double,
5 family rooms.
Bathrooms: 13 private.
Bed & breakfast: £16-£25
single, £32-£42 double.
Half board: £25-£34 daily.
Lunch available.
Evening meal 5.45pm (l.o.
6.30pm).
Credit: Access, Visa.

RINGWOOD

Hampshire
Map ref 2B3

Market town by the River
Avon comprising old
cottages, many of them
thatched. Although just
outside the New Forest,
there is heath and
woodland nearby and it is
a good centre for horse-
riding and walking.

Moortown Lodge Hotel & Restaurant M
⚜⚜⚜ COMMENDED
244 Christchurch Road,
Ringwood, BH24 3AS
☎ (0425) 471404
*Charming Georgian hotel
which originally formed part of
the Gladstone family estate.
Chef/proprietor. Freshly-
cooked food. Situated at edge
of New Forest, one mile from
town centre on B3347.*
Bedrooms: 1 single, 2 double
& 2 twin, 1 family room.
Bathrooms: 5 private,
1 public.
Bed & breakfast: £29-£42
single, £52-£60 double.
Half board: £33-£56 daily,
£215-£338 weekly.
Evening meal 7pm (l.o.
8.30pm).
Parking for 7.
Credit: Access, Visa.

*National Crown
ratings were correct
at the time of going
to press but are
subject to change.
Please check at the
time of booking.*

ROMSEY

Hampshire
Map ref 2C3

Town grew up around the important abbey and lies on the banks of the River Test, famous for trout and salmon. Broadlands House, home of the late Lord Mountbatten, is open to the public.
Tourist Information Centre ☎ *(0794) 512987*

New Forest Heathlands Hotel at the Vine Inn M
😊😊😊😊

Romsey Road, Ower, Nr. Romsey, Southampton, SO51 6ZJ
☎ Southampton (0703) 814333 & Fax (0703) 812123 Telex 8954665 VBSTLX REF QUA
Traditional hotel, set in 2 acres of gardens, built on to a 16th C inn. Near junction 2 of M27. Open to non-residents.
Bedrooms: 2 single, 25 double & 19 twin, 6 family rooms.
Bathrooms: 52 private.
Bed & breakfast: £63-£77 single, £77-£92 double.
Half board: £80-£88 daily.
Lunch available.
Evening meal 7pm (l.o. 9.30pm).
Parking for 130.
Credit: Access, Visa, Diners, Amex.
🏥 🛆 🕭 🏮 🖵 🐧 🛢 Ⓥ 🏱
🖶 ● 🎞 🛆 🍴 🖰 🖐 ✓
❄ ♦ SP 🏕 T

Country Accommodation, The Old Post Office M
😊😊 COMMENDED

New Road, Michelmersh, Nr. Romsey, SO51 0NL
☎ Romsey (0794) 68739
In pretty village location, interesting conversion from old forge, bakery and post office. All ground floor rooms, some beamed. On-site parking.
Bedrooms: 1 double & 2 twin, 1 family room.
Bathrooms: 4 private.
Bed & breakfast: £25 single, £30 double.
Parking for 10.
🏥 🛆 🖵 🖰 UL Ⓥ 🖶 TV 🎞
🖐 🏮 🏕

Wessex Guest House
Listed

5 Palmerston Street, Romsey, SO51 8GF
☎ (0794) 512038

---

200 yards from Broadlands Park, home of the late Lord Mountbatten, now open to the public.
Bedrooms: 1 single, 4 double & 1 twin, 2 family rooms.
Bathrooms: 3 public.
Bed & breakfast: £15-£16 single, £30-£32.50 double.
🏥 🛆 🖵 UL 🎞 🖐 🏕

ST LEONARDS

Dorset
Map ref 2B3

St. Leonards Hotel M
Ringwood Road, St. Leonards, Nr. Ringwood, Hampshire BH24 2NP
☎ Ringwood (0425) 471220 Telex 418215
CR Lansbury
Rural hotel set in attractive grounds, convenient for New Forest and Bournemouth.
Bedrooms: 15 double & 16 twin, 2 family rooms.
Bathrooms: 33 private.
Bed & breakfast: from £28 single, from £56 double.
Half board: from £40 daily.
Lunch available.
Evening meal 7pm (l.o. 10pm).
Parking for 250.
Credit: Access, Visa, Diners, Amex.
🏥 🛆 🕭 🕻 🕮 🖵 🖰 🐧 Ⓥ
✓ 🖶 ● 🎞 🛆 🍴 🖰 🏮 🛢
❄ ♦ SP T

SARISBURY GREEN

Hampshire
Map ref 2C3

5m NW. Fareham Village astride the A27.

Dormy House Hotel M
😊😊😊 COMMENDED

21 Barnes Lane, Sarisbury-Warsash, Southampton, SO3 6DA
☎ Locks Heath (0489) 572626
Victorian house near Hamble River marinas between Southampton and Portsmouth. Family-run by qualified chef, offering accommodation and food at reasonable cost.
Bedrooms: 2 single, 4 double & 3 twin, 1 family room.
Bathrooms: 8 private, 1 public.
Bed & breakfast: £23.50-£36.50 single, £45.80-£49.50 double.
Half board: £33.45-£46.45 daily.

Evening meal 6.30pm (l.o. midday).
Parking for 14.
🏥 🛆 🖵 🖰 UL 🛢 Ⓥ 🖶 TV
🎞 🛆 🖐 🏕

SHAFTESBURY

Dorset
Map ref 2B3

Hilltop town with a long history. The ancient and cobbled Gold Hill is one of the most attractive in Dorset. There is an excellent small museum containing a collection of buttons for which the town is famous.

The Coppleridge M
😊😊😊😊 COMMENDED

Elm Hill, Motcombe, Shaftesbury, SP7 9HW
☎ (0747) 51980
A converted 18th C farmhouse set in 15 acres of meadow, woodland and gardens, overlooking beautiful Blackmoor Vale. Large car park and tennis courts available.
Bedrooms: 6 double & 4 twin.
Bathrooms: 10 private.
Bed & breakfast: £30-£35 single, £55-£60 double.
Lunch available.
Evening meal 7pm (l.o. 10.30pm).
Parking for 100.
Credit: Access, Visa, Amex.
🏥 🛆 🕻 🕮 🖵 🖰 🐧 🖶 TV
🎞 🛆 🍴 🏮 🛢 🖰 🖐 ❄
🖐

Grove House Hotel M
Ludwell, Shaftesbury, SP7 9ND
☎ Donhead (0747) 828365
Small, quiet private hotel in rural area, within easy reach of many places of interest. Varied cuisine and warm hospitality.
Bedrooms: 1 single, 4 double & 5 twin, 1 family room.
Bathrooms: 11 private, 1 public.
Bed & breakfast: £24-£26 single, £48-£52 double.
Half board: £38-£42 daily, £234-£248 weekly.
Lunch available.
Evening meal 7pm (l.o. 7.30pm).
Parking for 12.
Open February-November.
Credit: Access, Visa.
🏥5 🕮 🖵 🖰 🛢 Ⓥ 🖐 🖶 🎞
🛆 🍴 🏮 🏕 SP

Please mention this guide when making a booking.

Mitre Inn
23 High Street, Shaftesbury, SP7 8JE
☎ (0747) 52488
An old inn, modernised, with panoramic views of North Dorset and the Blackmoor Vale.
Bedrooms: 1 single, 2 double & 1 twin, 1 family room.
Bathrooms: 2 public.
Bed & breakfast: from £25 single, £37-£39 double.
Half board: £35-£50 daily, from £210 weekly.
Lunch available.
Evening meal 6.30pm (l.o. 10pm).
🏥5 🖵 🖰 🛢 Ⓥ 🖐 🖶 TV 🎞
🛆 🍴 🏮 🏕 SP

Royal Chase Hotel
Royal Chase Roundabout, Shaftesbury, SP7 8DB
☎ (0747) 53355 & Fax (0747) 51969 Telex 418414
CR Best Western
Rural country town hotel with new indoor swimming pool/leisure complex. Choice of restaurants and standard or added quality bedrooms. Half board price based on a minimum 2 nights stay.
Bedrooms: 3 single, 12 double & 12 twin, 8 family rooms.
Bathrooms: 35 private.
Bed & breakfast: £60-£75 single, £70.50-£110 double.
Half board: £53-£60 daily, £318-£360 weekly.
Lunch available.
Evening meal 6pm (l.o. 9.45pm).
Parking for 100.
Credit: Access, Visa, Diners, Amex.
🏥 🛆 🛒 🕻 🖵 🖰 🛢 Ⓥ
🖶 ● 🎞 🛆 🍴 🖰 🖰 ❄ 🖐
SP 🏕 T

The Sunridge Hotel M
Bleke Street, Shaftesbury, SP7 8AW
☎ (0747) 53130
A warm and friendly, family-run hotel with a relaxed atmosphere, offering swimming pool and sauna and good food.
Bedrooms: 4 double & 3 twin, 3 family rooms.
Bathrooms: 10 private.
Bed & breakfast: max. £35 single, max. £49.50 double.
Half board: max. £225 weekly.
Lunch available.
Evening meal 7pm (l.o. 9pm).
Parking for 12.
Credit: Access, Visa.
🏥 🛆 🖵 🖰 🛢 Ⓥ 🖶 🎞 🛆
🍴 🖰 🖰 🖐 GAP SP 🏕

Hampshire
Map ref 2C3

One of Britain's leading
seaports with a long
history, and now
developed as a major
container port. In the 18th
C it became a fashionable
resort with the assembly
rooms and theatre. The
old Guildhall is now a
museum and the Wool
House a maritime
museum. Sections of the
medieval wall can still be
seen.
*Tourist Information
Centre* ☎ *(0703) 832615*

Amsterdam Hotel M
Listed
36-38 Hill Lane,
Southampton, SO1 5AY
☎ (0703) 228612
*Comfortable, licensed hotel,
with a friendly atmosphere,
offering good value for money.*
Bedrooms: 6 single, 3 double
& 4 twin, 2 family rooms.
Bathrooms: 2 private,
3 public.
Bed & breakfast: £16-£32
single, £32-£42 double.
Half board: £21-£44 daily,
£135-£308 weekly.
Evening meal 7pm (l.o. 9pm).
Parking for 10.
Credit: Access, Visa.

Anglesea Road Hotel M
30-34 Anglesea Road,
Shirley, Southampton,
SO1 5QH
☎ (0703) 789297
Fax (0703) 702807
*Close to hospitals, buses, shops
and railway. Facilities include
games room, fully licensed bar
and restaurant, bowling green,
conference room.*
Bedrooms: 6 single, 8 double
& 2 twin, 1 family room.
Bathrooms: 10 private,
3 public.
Bed & breakfast: £23-£38
single, £36-£49 double.
Evening meal 6.30pm (l.o.
8.15pm).
Parking for 56.
Credit: Access, Visa, Amex.

Ashelee Lodge M
Listed
36 Atherley Road, Shirley,
Southampton, SO1 5DQ
☎ (0703) 222095

*Homely guesthouse, garden
with pool. Near station, M27
and Sealink ferryport. Good
touring base for New Forest,
Salisbury, Winchester, etc.
Evening meal by arrangement.*
Bedrooms: 2 single, 1 double
& 1 twin.
Bathrooms: 1 public.
Bed & breakfast: £12.50
single, £25 double.
Evening meal 6pm.
Parking for 2.

Banister House Hotel M
☜☜
Banister Road, Southampton,
SO1 2JJ
☎ (0703) 221279
*Friendly welcome in this
family-run hotel which is
central and in a residential
area.*
Bedrooms: 11 single, 6 double
& 5 twin, 2 family rooms.
Bathrooms: 8 private,
6 public; 7 private showers.
Bed & breakfast: £21.50-
£26.50 single, £30-£35 double.
Half board: £21.50-£33 daily.
Evening meal 6.30pm (l.o.
8pm).
Parking for 14.
Credit: Access, Visa, Amex.

Botley Park Hotel & Country Club M
☜☜☜☜☜ COMMENDED
Winchester Road, Boorley
Green, Botley, SO3 2UA
☎ (0489) 780888
Fax (0489) 789242
Ⓡ Rank
*Purpose-designed to cater for
the evolving leisure and
business demands of the 1990s.
Few minutes' drive from M27,
60 minutes from London, 50
minutes to Heathrow Airport.
Amenities available at the hotel
or locally include golf, sauna,
solaria, gymnasium, jacuzzi
and indoor heated pool.
Conference facilities for up to
250.*
Bedrooms: 41 double &
56 twin, 3 family rooms.
Bathrooms: 100 private.
Bed & breakfast: £57-£87
single, £67-£102 double.
Lunch available.
Evening meal 7pm (l.o.
9.45pm).
Parking for 250.
Credit: Access, Visa, Diners,
Amex.

Cedar Lodge
Listed APPROVED
100 Cedar Road, Portswood,
Southampton, SO2 1AH
☎ (0703) 226761
*Small guesthouse, with friendly
service and easy access to
Southampton centre and
university.*
Bedrooms: 1 single, 2 twin,
1 family room.
Bathrooms: 1 public.
Bed & breakfast: £13 single,
£26 double.
Half board: £20 daily, £130-
£140 weekly.
Evening meal 7pm (l.o.
7.30pm).

Eaton Court Hotel
☜☜☜
32 Hill Lane, Southampton,
SO1 5AY
☎ (0703) 223081
*A small, owner-run hotel for
business and leisure stays,
providing all the amenities
guests now expect.*
Bedrooms: 7 single, 6 double
& 2 twin.
Bathrooms: 5 private,
2 public.
Bed & breakfast: £20-£28
single, £32-£40 double.
Evening meal 7pm (l.o. 8pm).
Parking for 12.
Credit: Access, Visa.

Edgecombe House Hotel M
188 Regents Park Road,
Shirley, Southampton,
SO1 3NY
☎ (0703) 773760
*Comfortable and friendly,
family-run hotel, within easy reach of the New
Forest and Southampton city
centre.*
Bedrooms: 6 single, 3 double
& 3 twin, 1 family room.
Bathrooms: 5 private,
3 public.
Bed & breakfast: £23-£35
single, £40-£48 double.
Evening meal 7pm (l.o. 1pm).
Parking for 12.
Credit: Access, Visa, Amex.

Elizabeth House Hotel M
☜☜☜
43-44 The Avenue,
Southampton, SO1 2SX
☎ (0703) 224327

*On Southampton's main access
route to and from the North.
Close to city centre, airport,
docks, university, common and
motorways. Special weekend
rate, £21 per person per night.*
Bedrooms: 11 single,
11 double & 2 twin.
Bathrooms: 20 private,
2 public.
Bed & breakfast: £35-£45
single, max. £57 double.
Lunch available.
Evening meal 6pm (l.o. 9pm).
Parking for 20.
Credit: Access, Visa, Diners,
Amex.

Hilton National
Bracken Place, Chilworth,
Southampton, SO2 3UB
☎ (0703) 702700 Telex 47594
Ⓗ Hilton
*Overlooking open countryside,
near the village of Chilworth.
Close to main intersections of
the M27 and A33.*
Bedrooms: 135 twin.
Bathrooms: 135 private.
Bed & breakfast: £55-£100
single, £110-£150 double.
Lunch available.
Evening meal 7pm (l.o.
10pm).
Parking for 230.
Credit: Access, Visa, Diners,
Amex.

Hunters Lodge Hotel
☜☜☜ COMMENDED
25 Landguard Road, Shirley,
Southampton, SO1 5DL
☎ (0703) 227919
Fax (0703) 230913
*Friendly, family hotel, aiming
to give a good service to all
guests, 2 minutes' walk from
central Southampton.*
Bedrooms: 9 single, 4 double
& 2 twin, 2 family rooms.
Bathrooms: 7 private,
2 public; 3 private showers.
Bed & breakfast: £23.50-
£33.49 single, £44.06-£52.29
double.
Half board: £31.73-£41.72
daily, £158.65-£208.60 weekly.
Evening meal 6.30pm (l.o.
6.30pm).
Parking for 19.
Credit: Access, Visa, Amex.

La Valle Guest House
Listed
111 Millbrook Road East,
Freemantle, Southampton,
SO1 0HP
☎ (0703) 227821

Continued ▶

SOUTHAMPTON
Continued

Close to city centre, bus and railway stations. All rooms have central heating and colour TV.
Bedrooms: 1 single, 1 double & 1 twin, 2 family rooms.
Bathrooms: 2 public.
Bed & breakfast: £10 single, £20 double.
Parking for 6.

Landguard Lodge
COMMENDED
21 Landguard Road, Shirley, Southampton, SO1 5DL
☎ (0703) 636904
Cosy, comfortable, well-run establishment, recently refurbished and with a good standard of facilities, in a quiet, central location.
Bedrooms: 10 single, 1 double & 1 twin, 1 family room.
Bathrooms: 4 private, 3 public.
Bed & breakfast: £15-£20 single, £30-£35 double.
Parking for 6.
Credit: Access, Visa, Amex.

The Lodge
APPROVED
No. 1 Winn Road, The Avenue, Southampton, SO2 1EH
☎ (0703) 557537
Family-run private hotel in quiet surroundings, close to city centre, station and docks. The aim is to please.
Bedrooms: 8 single, 1 double & 4 twin, 1 family room.
Bathrooms: 6 private, 3 public.
Bed & breakfast: £20.95-£29.95 single, £34-£40 double.
Half board: £28.45-£38.45 daily.
Evening meal 7pm (l.o. 9pm).
Parking for 10.
Credit: Access, Visa.

Madison House M
APPROVED
137 Hill Lane, Southampton, SO1 5AF
☎ (0703) 333374
Spacious Victorian house, offering good standards with many facilities. All bedrooms have TV and independent heating controls. Very friendly service.
Bedrooms: 2 single, 3 double & 2 twin, 2 family rooms.
Bathrooms: 3 private, 2 public.

Bed & breakfast: £14.50-£16 single, £27-£32 double.
Parking for 6.

The Mayfair Guest House
11 Landguard Road, Shirley, Southampton, SO1 5DL
☎ (0703) 229861
Family-run business with an accent on food and personal service.
Bedrooms: 7 single, 1 twin, 2 family rooms.
Bathrooms: 2 public.
Bed & breakfast: £14.50-£15 single, £29-£30 double.
Evening meal 6pm (l.o. 6pm).
Parking for 6.

Nirvana Hotel M
APPROVED
386 Winchester Road, Bassett, Southampton, SO1 7DH
☎ (0703) 790087 & 790993
Smaller establishment offering personal and friendly service. Comfortably furnished bedrooms with colour TV, most with telephones. Cosy Tudor bar and restaurant open 4 days per week. Hot bar snacks available at weekends. Special weekend rates.
Bedrooms: 10 single, 5 double & 3 twin, 1 family room.
Bathrooms: 8 private, 3 public.
Bed & breakfast: £27-£40 single, £43-£50 double.
Half board: £39.50-£40.50 daily, £249-£255 weekly.
Lunch available.
Evening meal 7pm (l.o. 8.45pm).
Parking for 21.
Credit: Access.

Northlands Hotel M
Northlands Road, Southampton, SO9 3ZW
☎ (0703) 333871
Fax (0703) 230360
Family-run hotel with friendly atmosphere, in quiet location opposite County Cricket Ground, 10 minutes from city centre and docks and on major bus routes.
Bedrooms: 8 single, 4 double & 6 twin, 1 family room.
Bathrooms: 7 private, 3 public.
Bed & breakfast: £34-£42 single, £46-£54 double.
Half board: £44-£52 daily.

Lunch available.
Evening meal 6.30pm (l.o. 9pm).
Parking for 22.
Credit: Access, Visa.

Novotel Southampton M
1 West Quay Road, Southampton, SO1 0RA
☎ (0703) 330550
Telex 477641
Novotel
New city centre hotel, 5 minutes' walk from railway station. Easy access from M3, M27 and docks. Conference and banqueting facilities for 500. Indoor leisure centre with a heated indoor swimming pool, sauna, exercise area.
Bedrooms: 121 double.
Bathrooms: 121 private.
Bed & breakfast: from £66.50 single, from £75.50 double.
Lunch available.
Evening meal 6pm (l.o. 11.30pm).
Parking for 200.
Credit: Access, Visa, Diners, Amex.

Ophir Villa
7-9 Roberts Road, Hill Lane, Southampton, SO1 5DF
☎ (0703) 226876
We welcome you to this family-run establishment located in quiet, central position, close to city centre, docks and station.
Bedrooms: 9 single, 2 double, 5 family rooms.
Bathrooms: 13 private, 2 public.
Bed & breakfast: £20-£25 single, £40-£48 double.
Half board: £30-£35 daily.
Evening meal 6.30pm (l.o. 2pm).
Parking for 16.

Rosida Garden Hotel M
APPROVED
25-27 Hill Lane, Southampton, SO1 5AB
☎ (0703) 228501
Friendly owner-managed city centre hotel, convenient for station, docks, hospitals, airport and university. Heated outdoor swimming pool and garden.
Bedrooms: 14 single, 6 double & 4 twin, 4 family rooms.
Bathrooms: 28 private.
Bed & breakfast: £45-£48 single, £62-£72 double.

Half board: £55-£59 daily, £349-£372 weekly.
Evening meal 6.30pm (l.o. 8pm).
Parking for 30.
Credit: Access, Visa, Diners, Amex.

St. John's Guest House
329 Portswood Road, Southampton, SO2 1LD
☎ (0703) 559790
Small, traditional, personally-run establishment, close to airport, university and railway station.
Bedrooms: 1 single, 2 double & 1 twin, 1 family room.
Bathrooms: 1 public.
Bed & breakfast: £13-£15 single, £23-£25 double.
Parking for 5.

Southampton Moat House M
COMMENDED
Highfield Lane, Portswood, Southampton, SO9 1YQ
☎ (0703) 559555 Telex 47186
Queens Moat Houses
Modern hotel with high standard a la carte restaurant, bar and 4 separate conference rooms. All public rooms and bedrooms underwent major refurbishment during 1990-91.
Bedrooms: 14 single, 14 double & 29 twin, 9 family rooms.
Bathrooms: 66 private.
Bed & breakfast: from £66 single, from £92 double.
Half board: from £81 daily.
Lunch available.
Evening meal 7pm (l.o. 10pm).
Parking for 100.
Credit: Access, Visa, C.Bl., Diners, Amex.

Southampton Park Hotel M
Cumberland Place, Southampton, SO9 4NY
☎ (0703) 223467 Telex 47439 SOTNPK G
Forestdale
Comfortable, traditional city centre hotel, pleasantly furnished, with indoor leisure facilities. Opposite Watts Park, near shops, entertainment, coach and rail stations.
Bedrooms: 31 single, 21 double & 17 twin, 2 family rooms.

Bathrooms: 71 private.
Bed & breakfast: from £69
single, from £87.50 double.
Lunch available.
Evening meal 7pm (l.o.
10pm).
Parking for 9.
Credit: Access, Visa, Diners,
Amex.

Wessex Hotel M
☆☆☆ COMMENDED

Northlands Road,
Southampton, SO1 2LH
☎ (0703) 631744
Fax (0703) 639243
*In quiet location by Hampshire
cricket ground, near city
centre, docks and central
railway station. Large sun
terrace with barbecue facilities
available.*
Bedrooms: 15 single, 9 double
& 8 twin, 2 family rooms.
Bathrooms: 34 private.
Bed & breakfast: max. £44
single, max. £57.50 double.
Half board: max. £54 daily.
Lunch available.
Evening meal 6.30pm (l.o.
8.30pm).
Parking for 28.
Credit: Access, Visa, Amex.

STOCKBRIDGE

Hampshire
Map ref 2C2

Set in the Test Valley
which has some of the
best fishing in England.
The wide main street has
houses of all styles,
mainly Tudor and
Georgian.

Carbery Guest House M
☆☆☆ COMMENDED

Salisbury Hill, Stockbridge,
SO20 6EZ
☎ Andover (0264) 810771
*Fine old Georgian house in an
acre of landscaped gardens and
lawns, overlooking the River
Test. Games and swimming
facilities, riding and fishing can
be arranged. Ideal for touring
the South Coast and the New
Forest.*
Bedrooms: 4 single, 3 double
& 3 twin, 1 family room.
Bathrooms: 8 private,
1 public.
Bed & breakfast: £18.80-
£26.65 single, £37.60-£43.48
double.

Half board: £28.20-£35.97
daily, £197-£245 weekly.
Evening meal 7pm (l.o. 6pm).
Parking for 12.

Grosvenor Hotel M
☆☆☆ COMMENDED

High Street, Stockbridge,
SO20 6EU
☎ Andover (0264) 810606
Telex 477677
CR Lansbury
*Country town hotel in Test
Valley, within easy reach of
Romsey, Salisbury and
Winchester. Enclosed garden.*
Bedrooms: 4 single, 14 double
& 7 twin.
Bathrooms: 25 private.
Bed & breakfast: from £28
single, from £56 double.
Half board: from £40 daily.
Lunch available.
Evening meal 7.30pm (l.o.
9.45pm).
Parking for 60.
Credit: Access, Visa, Diners,
Amex.

STUBBINGTON

Hampshire
Map ref 2C3

Crofton Manor Hotel

Titchfield Road,
Stubbington, Fareham
PO14 2EB
☎ (0329) 667341
Fax (0329) 668401
*Run as a country house hotel
with conference, function and
catering facilities.*
Bedrooms: 2 single, 3 double
& 2 twin.
Bathrooms: 3 private,
2 public.
Bed & breakfast: £15-£35
single, £20-£50 double.
Lunch available.
Evening meal 7pm (l.o.
10pm).
Parking for 200.
Credit: Access, Visa, Diners,
Amex.

⊛ Display advertisement
appears on page 485.

---

*National Crown
ratings were correct
at the time of going
to press but are
subject to change.
Please check at the
time of booking.*

STUDLAND

Dorset
Map ref 2B3

On a beautiful stretch of
coast and good for
walking, with a National
Nature Reserve to the
north. The Norman
church is the finest in the
country, with superb
rounded arches and
vaulting. Brownsea
Island, where the first
scout camp was held, lies
in Poole Harbour but
within the parish
boundary.

Knoll House Hotel
☆☆☆

Studland, Nr. Swanage,
BH19 3AH
☎ (092 944) 251
Fax (092 944) 423
*Independent country hotel in
National Trust Reserve. Access
to 3-mile beach from 100-acre
grounds. Many facilities.
Weekly rates are for full
board.*
Bedrooms: 29 single, 20 twin,
30 family rooms.
Bathrooms: 56 private,
10 public.
Half board: £51-£77 daily,
£356-£540 weekly.
Lunch available.
Evening meal 7.30pm (l.o.
8.15pm).
Parking for 100.
Open April-October.

The Manor House Hotel M
☆☆☆ COMMENDED

Beach Road, Studland, Nr.
Swanage, BH19 3AU
☎ (092 944) 288
*18th C manor house in
secluded gardens overlooking
the sea and safe, sandy
beaches. Oak-panelled bar and
dining room. Tennis courts.*
Bedrooms: 6 double & 6 twin,
6 family rooms.
Bathrooms: 18 private,
1 public.
Half board: £46-£57 daily,
£270-£333 weekly.
Lunch available.
Evening meal 7pm (l.o.
8.30pm).
Parking for 40.
Open February-December.
Credit: Access, Visa.

STURMINSTER NEWTON

Dorset
Map ref 2B3

Every Monday this small
town holds a livestock
market. One of the
bridges over the River
Stour is a fine medieval
example and bears a
plaque declaring that
anyone 'injuring' it will be
deported.

The Old Bridge Cottage Restaurant
Listed COMMENDED

The Bridge, Sturminster
Newton, DT10 2BS
☎ (0258) 72689
*Attractive 17th C cottage
restaurant in the heart of the
Blackmore Vale, overlooking
the famous medieval bridge
and working mill.*
Bedrooms: 1 double & 2 twin.
Bathrooms: 1 private,
1 public.
Bed & breakfast: £18-£26
single, £38-£42 double.
Half board: from £28 daily.
Lunch available.
Evening meal 6pm (l.o.
9.30pm).
Parking for 8.
Credit: Access, Visa.

SWANAGE

Dorset
Map ref 2B3

Began life as an Anglo-
Saxon port, then a
quarrying centre of
Purbeck marble. Now the
safe, sandy beach set in a
sweeping bay and flanked
by downs is good walking
country, making it an
ideal resort.
*Tourist Information
Centre* ☎ (0929) 422885

Horseshoe House Hotel M
☆☆

9 Cliff Avenue, Swanage,
BH19 1LX
☎ (0929) 422194
*Elegant family-run hotel,
4 minutes from beach, offering
cuisine and comfort of a good
standard.*
Bedrooms: 2 single, 2 double
& 1 twin, 3 family rooms.
Bathrooms: 4 private,
1 public; 2 private showers.
Bed & breakfast: £18-£20
single, £36-£40 double.

Continued ▶

SWANAGE

Continued

Half board: £24-£26 daily, £140-£150 weekly.
Evening meal 6pm (l.o. 4pm).
Parking for 5.
Open April-October.

Ingleside Guest House M

16 Park Road, Swanage, BH19 2AD
☎ (0929) 423005
Family-run guesthouse just 2 minutes' walk from sea and beach.
Bedrooms: 1 single, 4 double & 1 twin, 1 family room.
Bathrooms: 1 public; 2 private showers.
Bed & breakfast: £12-£16 single, £24-£32 double.
Half board: £19-£23 daily, £119-£143 weekly.
Evening meal 6.30pm (l.o. 4.30pm).
Credit: Access, Visa.

Methodist Guild Holidays, Highcliffe
APPROVED
4 Highcliffe Road, Swanage, BH19 1LW
☎ (0929) 424806
Set on clifftop overlooking sea, Swanage Bay and Ballard Downs, with private steps to sandy beach and safe bathing.
Bedrooms: 6 single, 10 double & 6 twin, 12 family rooms.
Bathrooms: 11 public.
Half board: from £150 weekly.
Lunch available.
Evening meal 6.45pm.
Parking for 12.

The Oxford Hotel M
COMMENDED
3-5 Park Road, Swanage, BH19 2AA
☎ (0929) 422247
100 yards from town centre and beaches. Basic or en-suite available. Ideal centre for the Purbecks. Friendly family atmosphere. Resident proprietors.
Bedrooms: 2 single, 6 double & 2 twin, 4 family rooms.
Bathrooms: 7 private, 2 public.
Bed & breakfast: £18.50-£20.50 single, £37-£41 double.
Half board: £27-£29 daily, £180-£195 weekly.

Evening meal 6.30pm (l.o. 4pm).
Open March-October.

The Pines Hotel M
COMMENDED
Burlington Road, Swanage, BH19 1LT
☎ (0929) 425211
Fax (0929) 422075
Telex 418297
Family-run hotel set amid the Purbeck countryside at quiet end of Swanage Bay. Own access to beach.
Bedrooms: 4 single, 10 double & 11 twin, 24 family rooms.
Bathrooms: 49 private, 1 public.
Bed & breakfast: £37-£42 single, £74-£84 double.
Half board: £42-£54 daily, £301-£325 weekly.
Lunch available.
Evening meal 7.30pm (l.o. 9pm).
Parking for 60.
Credit: Access, Visa.

Sandringham Hotel M
COMMENDED
20 Durlston Road, Swanage, BH19 2HX
☎ (0929) 423076
In a quiet residential area overlooking sea, 5 minutes from town, beach, downs and country park.
Bedrooms: 2 single, 3 double & 1 twin, 5 family rooms.
Bathrooms: 11 private, 1 public.
Bed & breakfast: £21.50-£25.50 single, £43-£51 double.
Evening meal 6.30pm (l.o. 6.30pm).
Parking for 10.
Open March-December.

SWAY

Hampshire
Map ref 2C3

Small village on the south-western edge of the New Forest. It is noted for its 220-ft tower, Peterson's Folly, built in the 1870s by a retired Indian judge to demonstrate the value of concrete as a building material.

String of Horses M

Mead End, Sway, Lymington, SO41 6EH
☎ Lymington (0590) 682631

Unique, secluded hotel set in 4 acres, in the New Forest. Well-appointed bedrooms and fantasy bathrooms with spa baths.
Bedrooms: 6 double.
Bathrooms: 6 private.
Bed & breakfast: £52.50-£55 single, £65-£95 double.
Half board: £50-£65 daily, £315-£409.50 weekly.
Lunch available.
Evening meal 7.30pm (l.o. 9pm).
Parking for 12.
Credit: Access, Visa, Amex.

The Tower M
COMMENDED
Barrows Lane, Sway, Nr. Lymington, SO41 6DE
☎ (0590) 682117
Fax (0590) 683785
220 feet high tower in 1.5 acres of garden, set in farmland between the Solent and New Forest.
Bedrooms: 2 double & 2 twin.
Bathrooms: 4 private, 1 public.
Bed & breakfast: £98 double.
Parking for 5.
Open April-October.
Credit: Access, Visa, Diners, Amex.

White Rose Hotel M
APPROVED
Village Centre, Sway, Nr. Lymington, SO41 6BA
☎ Lymington (0590) 682754
Family-run country house hotel with 6 acres of grounds, in small village on edge of New Forest.
Bedrooms: 2 single, 5 double & 2 twin, 2 family rooms.
Bathrooms: 9 private, 2 public.
Bed & breakfast: £37-£45 single, £58-£74 double.
Half board: £39-£55 daily, £154-£336 weekly.
Lunch available.
Evening meal 7pm (l.o. 8.45pm).
Parking for 50.
Credit: Access, Visa, Amex.

WAREHAM

Dorset
Map ref 2B3

This site has been occupied since pre-Roman times and has a turbulent history. In 1762 fire destroyed much of the town, so the buildings now are mostly Georgian.

Kemps Country House Hotel M
COMMENDED
East Stoke, Wareham, BH20 6AL
☎ Bindon Abbey
(0929) 462563
Victorian rectory set in spacious grounds overlooking the Purbeck Hills. 2 miles west of Wareham on the A352.
Bedrooms: 1 single, 8 double & 2 twin, 4 family rooms.
Bathrooms: 14 private, 1 public.
Bed & breakfast: £55-£69 single, £82-£110 double.
Half board: £57-£83 daily, £290-£581 weekly.
Lunch available.
Evening meal 7pm (l.o. 10pm).
Parking for 36.
Credit: Access, Visa, Diners, Amex.

The Priory Hotel M
HIGHLY COMMENDED
Church Green, Wareham, BH20 4ND
☎ (0929) 552772 & 551666
Telex 41143 PRIORYG
Former Priory of Lady St. Mary (dating from early 16th C) standing in 4.5 acres of beautifully landscaped gardens on the banks of the River Frome.
Bedrooms: 3 single, 12 double & 4 twin.
Bathrooms: 19 private.
Bed & breakfast: £60-£95 single, £75-£175 double.
Half board: £60-£110 daily.
Lunch available.
Evening meal 7.30pm (l.o. 10pm).
Parking for 20.
Credit: Access, Visa, Diners, Amex.

Half board prices shown are per person but in some cases may be based on double/twin occupancy.

Springfield Country Hotel M

COMMENDED

Grange Road, Stoborough, Wareham, BH20 5AL
☎ (0929) 552177
Fax (0929) 551862
Secluded country hotel in beautiful grounds, providing food in a true English setting.
Bedrooms: 4 single, 16 double & 6 twin, 6 family rooms.
Bathrooms: 32 private.
Bed & breakfast: £58-£63 single, £96-£104 double.
Half board: £61-£67 daily, £315-£428 weekly.
Lunch available.
Evening meal 7pm (l.o. 9.30pm).
Parking for 150.
Credit: Access, Visa, Amex.

Worgret Manor Hotel M

Worgret Road, Wareham, BH20 6AB
☎ (0929) 552957
Comfortable, family-run hotel, offering service in a relaxed and friendly manner.
Bedrooms: 5 double & 5 twin.
Bathrooms: 5 private, 2 public.
Bed & breakfast: £30-£36 single, £44-£50 double.
Lunch available.
Evening meal 7pm (l.o. 10pm).
Parking for 40.
Credit: Access, Visa.

WEST LULWORTH

Dorset
Map ref 2B3

Well-known for Lulworth Cove, the almost landlocked circular bay of chalk and limestone cliffs.

Bishop's Cottage Hotel M

APPROVED

West Lulworth, Wareham, BH20 5RQ
☎ (092 941) 261 & 404
Comfortable family hotel overlooking Lulworth Cove, ideal for walking. Outdoor heated swimming pool. 11 rooms have TV and direct-dial telephone.
Bedrooms: 3 single, 12 double & 5 twin, 5 family rooms.
Bathrooms: 17 private, 4 public.

Bed & breakfast: £18-£25 single, £38-£50 double.
Half board: £27-£34 daily, £187-£225 weekly.
Lunch available.
Evening meal 7pm (l.o. 10pm).
Credit: Access, Visa.

Gatton House Hotel M

West Lulworth, Wareham, BH20 5RU
☎ (092 941) 252
Small country house hotel commanding stunningly beautiful views across West Lulworth village to the Purbecks beyond. Within walking distance of Lulworth Cove.
Bedrooms: 6 double & 1 twin, 1 family room.
Bathrooms: 8 private.
Bed & breakfast: £26-£30 single, £50-£56 double.
Half board: £38.50-£42.50 daily, £252-£277.50 weekly.
Evening meal 7pm (l.o. 6.30pm).
Parking for 12.
Open March-December.
Credit: Access, Visa.

Lulworth Cove Hotel

West Lulworth, Nr. Wareham, BH20 5RQ
☎ (092 941) 333
Fax (092 941) 534
Hotel and pub specialising in home-made food, carvery and local seafood. Spectacular views of Lulworth Cove from many bedrooms.
Bedrooms: 10 double & 2 twin, 2 family rooms.
Bathrooms: 6 private, 1 public; 7 private showers.
Bed & breakfast: £20-£25 single, £40-£50 double.
Half board: £27-£32 daily, £162-£192 weekly.
Lunch available.
Evening meal 6.30pm (l.o. 9.30pm).
Parking for 11.
Credit: Access, Visa, Diners, Amex.

Shirley Hotel M

COMMENDED

West Lulworth, Wareham, BH20 5RL
☎ (092 941) 358
Homely, modern hotel close to Lulworth Cove and coastal footpath. Ideal for walking or touring. Friendly relaxed atmosphere.

Bedrooms: 5 single, 8 double & 4 twin, 2 family rooms.
Bathrooms: 19 private.
Bed & breakfast: £18-£25 single, £36-£50 double.
Half board: £27-£33.50 daily, £189-£213.50 weekly.
Evening meal 6pm (l.o. 9pm).
Parking for 22.
Open March-October.
Credit: Access, Visa.

WIMBORNE MINSTER

Dorset
Map ref 2B3

Market town centred on the twin-towered Minster Church of St. Cuthberga which gave the town the second part of its name. Good touring base for the surrounding countryside, depicted in the writings of Thomas Hardy.
Tourist Information Centre ☎ (0202) 886116

Beechleas Hotel

17 Poole Road, Wimborne Minster, BH21 1QA
☎ (0202) 841684
Georgian building, beautifully restored, with large double bedrooms, lounge, dining room, conservatory, attractive garden, own car park.
Bedrooms: 5 double & 2 twin.
Bathrooms: 7 private.
Bed & breakfast: £51-£68 single, £65-£85 double.
Half board: £45-£55 daily.
Evening meal 7pm (l.o. 9.30pm).
Parking for 8.
Open February-December.
Credit: Access, Visa.

Northill House M

COMMENDED

Horton, Wimborne, BH21 7HL
☎ Witchampton (0258) 840407
A mid-Victorian former farmhouse, modernised to provide comfortable bedrooms. Log fires and cooking using fresh produce.
Bedrooms: 5 double & 3 twin, 1 family room.
Bathrooms: 9 private.
Bed & breakfast: £32 single, £58 double.
Half board: £41.50-£44.50 daily, £261.45-£280.35 weekly.
Evening meal 7.30pm (l.o. 6.30pm).

Parking for 12.
Open February-December.
Credit: Access, Visa, Amex.

WINCHESTER

Hampshire
Map ref 2C3

King Alfred the Great made Winchester the capital of Saxon England. A magnificent Norman cathedral, with one of the longest naves in Europe, dominates the city. Home of Winchester College founded in 1382.
Tourist Information Centre ☎ (0962) 840500

Mrs. A.S. Baird M

Listed COMMENDED

Rutland House, 11 Park Road, Winchester, SO22 6AA
☎ (0962) 860196
A personal and warm welcome is assured in this fine Edwardian residence, surrounded by peaceful gardens with marvellous views. Ideally situated. Some facilities for disabled guests. French spoken. No smoking.
Bedrooms: 1 single, 1 double & 2 twin.
Bathrooms: 1 private, 2 public.
Bed & breakfast: £18.50-£25 single, £37-£43 double.
Half board: £29-£35.50 daily, from £196 weekly.
Evening meal 6.45pm (l.o. 5pm).
Parking for 4.

Cathedral View

COMMENDED

9A Magdalen Hill, Winchester, SO23 8HJ
☎ (0962) 863802
Edwardian guesthouse with views across historic city and cathedral. 5 minutes' walk from city centre. En-suite facilities, TV, parking.
Bedrooms: 3 double, 2 family rooms.
Bathrooms: 5 private.
Bed & breakfast: £27-£30 single, £36-£44 double.
Evening meal (l.o. midday).
Parking for 4.

We advise you to confirm your booking in writing.

WINCHESTER
Continued

Chantry Mead Hotel ♨
⚜⚜⚜⚜ COMMENDED
Bereweeke Road, Winchester,
SO22 6AJ
☎ (0962) 844166
Fax (0962) 852767
*Friendly, family-run hotel with
beautiful gardens, in quiet rural
area 15 minutes' walk from
city centre. Spacious car park.*
Bedrooms: 3 single, 4 double
& 8 twin, 1 family room.
Bathrooms: 14 private,
2 public.
Bed & breakfast: £20-£50
single, £35-£70 double.
Lunch available.
Evening meal 7pm (l.o.
9.30pm).
Parking for 22.
Credit: Access, Visa, Amex.

Harestock Lodge
Hotel ♨
⚜⚜
Harestock Road, Winchester,
SO22 6NX
☎ (0962) 881870
*Privately-run country house
hotel set in secluded gardens
on the edge of historic
Winchester.*
Bedrooms: 3 single, 7 double
& 5 twin, 5 family rooms.
Bathrooms: 9 private,
1 public; 11 private showers.
Bed & breakfast: £35.50-£40
single, £44-£53 double.
Half board: from £30 daily,
from £192 weekly.
Lunch available.
Evening meal 6.30pm (l.o.
9.30pm).
Parking for 22.
Credit: Access, Visa, Amex.

Lainston House ♨
⚜⚜⚜⚜⚜ COMMENDED
Sparsholt, Winchester,
SO21 2LT
☎ (0962) 863588
Fax (0962) 72672
Telex 477375
*Magnificent, Georgian, listed
17th C country house set in 63
acres of parkland. Recently
completely refurbished and
noted for its food and service.*
Bedrooms: 7 single, 10 double
& 14 twin, 1 family room.
Bathrooms: 32 private.
Bed & breakfast: from
£102.50 single, from £130
double.
Half board: from £152.50
daily.
Lunch available.

Evening meal 7pm (l.o.
10pm).
Parking for 96.
Credit: Access, Visa, C.Bl.,
Diners, Amex.

Marwell Resort Hotel ♨
⚜⚜⚜⚜ COMMENDED
Marwell Zoological Park,
Colden Common, Winchester,
SO21 1JY
☎ Owslebury (0962) 777681
& Fax (0962) 777625
Ⓡ Resort
*Newly-built hotel in colonial
style, with restaurant, coffee
shop, indoor health and leisure
club, heated pool, sauna,
jacuzzi and exercise
equipment.*
Bedrooms: 24 double,
36 family rooms.
Bathrooms: 60 private.
Bed & breakfast: £28.50-
£79.50 single, £57-£97 double.
Lunch available.
Evening meal 7pm (l.o.
9.30pm).
Parking for 120.
Credit: Access, Visa, C.Bl.,
Diners, Amex.

Portland House Hotel ♨
⚜⚜ COMMENDED
63 Tower Street, Winchester,
SO23 8TA
☎ (0962) 865195
*Quietly situated, family-run
establishment, close to city
centre and convenient for the
station and theatre.*
Bedrooms: 1 double & 3 twin,
1 family room.
Bathrooms: 5 private.
Bed & breakfast: £30-£35
single, £40-£50 double.

The Rising Sun
14 Bridge Street, Winchester,
SO23 8HL
☎ (0962) 862564
*Bed and breakfast in 15th C
inn with Courage ale and
home-cooked food. Close to
city centre.*
Bedrooms: 1 double & 2 twin.
Bathrooms: 1 public.
Bed & breakfast: max. £30
double.
Evening meal (l.o. 10pm).

---

*Please check prices
and other details at
the time of booking.*

The Royal Hotel ♨
⚜⚜⚜⚜ COMMENDED
St. Peter Street, Winchester,
SO23 8BS
☎ (0962) 840840
Telex 477071 ROYAL G
Ⓡ Best Western
*This old traditional hotel
retains its original charm and
has been refurbished to give its
guests 20th C comfort.*
Bedrooms: 52 double &
22 twin, 1 family room.
Bathrooms: 75 private.
Half board: £46-£49 daily.
Lunch available.
Evening meal 7pm (l.o.
10pm).
Parking for 60.
Credit: Access, Visa, Diners,
Amex.

Sparsholt College ♨
Listed
Sparsholt, Winchester,
SO21 2NF
☎ Sparsholt (096 272) 441
*En-suite accommodation in
attractive rural grounds. 4
miles from Winchester. Ideal
touring base for groups and
individuals. Licensed bars.*
Bedrooms: 306 single,
1 double & 4 twin.
Bathrooms: 222 private,
20 public.
Bed & breakfast: £19-£22
single, £34-£39 double.
Half board: £28-£31.50 daily.
Lunch available.
Evening meal 5pm (l.o. 7pm).
Parking for 200.
Open April-May, July-
September.
Credit: Access, Visa, C.Bl.,
Diners, Amex.

Stratton House ♨
Listed
Stratton Road, St. Giles Hill,
Winchester, SO23 8JQ
☎ (0962) 863919 & 864529 &
Fax (0962) 842095
*A lovely old Victorian house
with an acre of grounds, in an
elevated position on St. Giles
Hill.*
Bedrooms: 1 single, 2 double
& 1 twin, 2 family rooms.
Bathrooms: 1 private,
3 public; 2 private showers.
Bed & breakfast: £18.50-£20
single, £37-£40 double.
Half board: £24.50-£27 daily,
£165-£180 weekly.
Evening meal 6pm (l.o. 4pm).
Parking for 8.

Winchester Moat
House ♨
⚜⚜⚜⚜ COMMENDED
Worthy Lane, Winchester,
SO23 7AB
☎ (0962) 868102
Fax (0962) 840862
Telex 47383
Ⓡ Queens Moat Houses
*New hotel with good leisure
facilities, peacefully situated in
England's ancient capital.
Convenient for touring south
coast and New Forest.*
Bedrooms: 38 double &
34 twin.
Bathrooms: 72 private.
Bed & breakfast: £45-£50
single, £70-£80 double.
Half board: £45-£47.50 daily,
£270-£285 weekly.
Lunch available.
Evening meal 7pm (l.o.
9.30pm).
Parking for 110.
Credit: Access, Visa, Diners,
Amex.

WOODLANDS
Hampshire
Map ref 2C3

Scattered village on the
edge of the New Forest
west of Southampton.

Busketts Lawn Hotel ♨
⚜⚜⚜ APPROVED
174 Woodlands Road,
Woodlands, Nr.
Southampton, SO4 2GL
☎ Ashurst (0703) 292272 &
292077 & Fax (0703) 292487
*Delightful country house hotel
in quiet forest surroundings,
8 miles west of Southampton.
Heated swimming pool.*
Bedrooms: 4 single, 5 double
& 3 twin, 2 family rooms.
Bathrooms: 14 private.
Bed & breakfast: £33.50-£47
single, £50-£67 double.
Half board: £37.75-£46.25
daily, £224-£250 weekly.
Lunch available.
Evening meal 7pm (l.o.
8.30pm).
Parking for 50.
Credit: Access, Visa, Diners,
Amex.

---

*The enquiry
coupons at the
back will help you
when contacting
proprietors.*

Use a coupon

When requesting further information from advertisers in this guide, you may find it helpful to use the advertisement enquiry coupons which can be found towards the end of the guide. These should be cut out and mailed direct to the companies in which you are interested. Do remember to include your name and address.

SOUTH EAST ENGLAND

NOT KNOWN AS THE "GARDEN OF ENGLAND" FOR NOTHING.

From the fruit orchards and hopfields of Kent and the vineyards of Sussex to the treasure trove of gardens open to the public at historic houses and stately homes, the region is a veritable feast of crops and colour. On the coast there's a difficult choice to make: will it be bustling Brighton, Edwardian Eastbourne or historic Hastings? Perhaps somewhere quieter, like Littlehampton or Broadstairs. When inland, linger in the leafy lanes, explore historic Canterbury, Arundel and Tunbridge Wells, wander on the wild Romney Marsh or walk the paths across the downs.

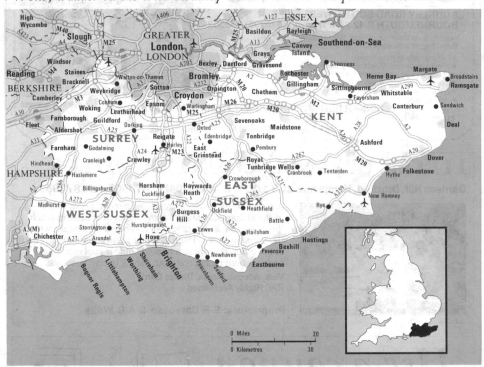

PLEASE REFER TO THE COLOUR MAPS AT THE BACK OF THIS GUIDE FOR ALL PLACES WITH ACCOMMODATION LISTINGS.

WHERE TO GO, WHAT TO SEE

Apuldram Roses
Apuldram Lane, Dell Quay,
Apuldram, Chichester,
W. Sussex PO20 7EF
☎ Chichester (0243) 785769
*Specialist rose nursery with 250
clearly labelled varieties.*

Archbishop's Palace
Old Palace Gardens, Mill
Street, Maidstone, Kent
☎ Maidstone (0622) 754497
*Old palace of historic and
architectural interest, undergoing
refurbishment and due to re-open
as a Heritage Centre in May
1992.*

Arundel Castle
Arundel, W. Sussex BN18 9AB
☎ Arundel (0903) 883136
*Impressive Norman stronghold
in extensive grounds, much
restored in 18th/19th C. 11th C
keep, barons' hall, armoury,
chapel. Paintings by Van Dyck
and Gainsborough.*

Bedgebury National Pinetum
Nr. Goudhurst, Kent TN17 2SL
☎ Goudhurst (0580) 211044
*The Forestry Commission's
superb collection of specimen
conifers, in 150 acres with lake
and streams. Rhododendrons and
azaleas. Visitor Centre.*

The Bluebell Railway
– Living Museum
Sheffield Park Station, Sheffield
Park, Nr. Uckfield, E. Sussex
TN22 3QL
☎ Newick (082 572) 2370
*5½ miles of standard gauge
track from Sheffield Park to
Horsted Keynes and extension,
with Victorian stations. Large
collection of steam engines,
museum.*

Buckleys Yesterday's World
90 High Street, Battle,
E. Sussex TN33 0AQ
☎ Battle (042 46) 4269
*Over 30,000 exhibits in a
Wealden hall house recall
shopping and domestic life from*

The impressive Norman stronghold of Arundel Castle

*1850 to 1950. Post Office,
toyshop, grocer's, chemist,
stationer's, draper's.*

Charleston Farmhouse
Firle, Lewes, E. Sussex
BN8 6LL
☎ Ripe (0323) 811265
*17th – 18th C farmhouse, home
of Vanessa and Clive Bell and
Duncan Grant. House and
contents decorated by the artists.
Newly restored garden room.
Traditional flint-walled garden.*

Chichester Cathedral
West Street, Chichester,
W. Sussex PO19 1PX
☎ Chichester (0243) 782595
*Mainly Norman architecture.
Detached bell tower. Chagall
window. Sutherland painting.
Font by John Skelton.
Tapestries by Piper and Ursula
Benker-Schirmer. Carvings.*

Chichester Harbour
Water Tours
9 Cawley Road, Chichester,
W. Sussex PO19 1UZ
☎ Chichester (0243) 786418
Sightseeing trips on the

*"Wingate" from Itchenor
around the attractive Chichester
Harbour – an area of
outstanding natural beauty and
noted wildlife reserve. Full
commentary.*

Denmans Garden
Fontwell, Nr. Arundel,
W. Sussex BN18 0SU
☎ Eastgate (0243) 542808
*Walled, gravel and water
gardens, natural layout of trees,
climbers and wall shrubs for
all-year interest. Glass areas.
School of Garden Design.*

Eastbourne Pier
Grand Parade, Eastbourne,
E. Sussex BN21 3EL
☎ Eastbourne (0323) 410466
*Family amusement arcade,
public bar, children's play area,
discotheque, resident
entertainment in summer season,
shops.*

Great Dixter House
and Gardens
Northiam, Rye, E. Sussex
TN31 6PH
☎ Northiam (0797) 253160 ▶

▶ *Fine example of 15th C manor house with antique furniture and needlework. Unique great hall restored by Lutyens, who also designed the garden — topiary, meadow garden, flower beds.*

Guildford Boat House River Trips

Millbrook, Guildford, Surrey GU1 3XJ
☎ Guildford (0483) 504494
Regular trips from Guildford to St. Catherines Lock and Farncombe along River Wey. Cruising restaurant, Edwardian-style electric launch, narrow boat. Rowing boats and canoes.

Headcorn Flower Centre and Vineyard

Grigg Lane, Headcorn, Kent TN27 9LX
☎ Headcorn (0622) 890250
14-acre vineyard with vineyard trail. 7 acres of flower houses with chrysanthemums, orchids and lilies. 6-acre reservoir.

The Historic Dockyard

Chatham, Kent ME4 4TE
☎ Medway (0634) 812551
Historic 18th C 80-acre dockyard, now a living museum. Former HMS Gannet undergoing restoration. Sail and colour loft, ordnance mews, "Wooden Walls" gallery.

Horton Park Farm

Horton Lane, Epsom, Surrey KT19 8PT
☎ Epsom (0372) 743984
Rare breeds livestock farm. Angora goats and rabbits. Spinning and weaving at Sheep Shop.

Howletts Zoo Park

Bekesbourne, Canterbury, Kent CT4 5EL
☎ Canterbury (0227) 721286
55-acre parkland with large gorilla and tiger collection and many other animals.

Iden Croft Herbs

Frittenden Road, Staplehurst, Kent TN12 0DH
☎ Staplehurst (0580) 891432
Large herb farm with walled

Depth Charge — Britain's first 4-channel water ride at Thorpe Park

garden and variety of aromatic gardens, demonstrating the beauty and use of herbs. Thyme rockery of special interest.

Manor Farm Craft Centre

Wood Lane, Seale, Farnham, Surrey GU10 1HR
☎ Runfold (025 18) 3661
Visitors can watch glass blowing, wood turning, knitting and work on jewellery and Tiffany stained glass.

The Old Needlemakers

West Street, Lewes, E. Sussex BN7 2NZ
☎ Lewes (0273) 471582
Converted 19th C candle factory housing craft workshops. Candle makers, stained glass, leather crafts and other specialist shops.

Powell Cotton Museum

Quex House and Gardens, Quex Park, Birchington, Kent CT7 0BH
☎ Thanet (0843) 42168
Regency house with period furniture. Museum with ethnograhic collections, diorama of African and Asian animals, weapons, archaeology, Chinese porcelain.

The Royal Horticultural Society's Garden

Wisley, Woking, Surrey GU23 6QB
☎ Guildford (0483) 224234
World-famous RHS garden covering 250 acres of vegetable, fruit and ornamental gardens. Trial grounds, glasshouses, rock garden, ponds, rose gardens, model and specialist gardens.

Smarts Amusement Park
Seafront, Littlehampton,
W. Sussex BN17 5LL
☎ Littlehampton (0903) 721200
*Large indoor and outdoor
amusement park for all ages.
Many rides including dodgems,
Waltzer and Cyclone Roller
Coaster, waterslides, sandy
beaches, river.*

Smugglers Adventure
St. Clement's Caves, West Hill,
Hastings, E. Sussex TN34 3HY
☎ Hastings (0424) 422964
*One acre of caves housing the
largest smuggling exhibition in
the country. Museum, audio-
visual show and 50 life-size
figures with dramatic sound and
lighting effects.*

Thorpe Park
Staines Road, Chertsey, Surrey
KT16 8PN
☎ Chertsey (0932) 562633
*One of Europe's leading family
leisure parks. Magic mill,
water-buses, Phantom Fantasia,
Treasure Island, Thunder River,
Carousel Kingdom.*

The Westcott Gallery
4 Guildford Road, Westcott,
Nr. Dorking, Surrey RH4 3NR
☎ Dorking (0306) 76261
*Gallery with 19th and 20th C
paintings and work of
contemporary Surrey artists. At
least 3 main exhibitions per year.*

Whitbread Hop Farm
Beltring, Paddock Wood,
Tonbridge, Kent TN12 6PY
☎ Maidstone (0622) 872068
*Hop farm with large complex of
Victorian oasts, museum of hop
farming, rural crafts, adventure
playground, Whitbread shire
horses and mini zoo.*

The Wildfowl and Wetlands Centre
Mill Road, Arundel, W. Sussex
BN18 9PB
☎ Arundel (0903) 883355
*Wildfowl and Wetlands Trust's
reserve in 60 acres of
watermeadows. Tame swans,
ducks, geese and many wild
birds. Film theatre and visitor
centre with gallery.*

MAKE A DATE FOR...

Holiday on Ice '92
Brighton Centre, Kings Road,
Brighton, E. Sussex
3 – 26 January

European Clown Convention
Various venues, Bognor Regis,
W. Sussex
20 – 22 March

Easter Egg Hunt
Leeds Castle, Maidstone, Kent
18 – 20 April

Rochester Chimney Sweeps Festival
Various venues, Rochester,
Kent
1 – 4 May

Brighton International Festival
Various venues, Brighton,
E. Sussex
1 – 24 May

English Hop Festival
Various venues, Kent
5 – 6 September

Pilkington Glass Ladies' Tennis Championship
Devonshire Park, College
Road, Eastbourne, E. Sussex
15 – 20 June

Claremont Landscape Garden Fête
Claremont, Esher, Surrey
15 – 19 July

Showjumping – Silk Cut Derby
All England Jumping Course,
Hickstead, W. Sussex
27 – 30 August

Canterbury Festival
Various venues, Canterbury,
Kent
10 – 24 October

FIND OUT MORE

Further information about
holidays and attractions in the
South East England region is
available from:
South East England Tourist Board
The Old Brew House, Warwick
Park, Tunbridge Wells, Kent
TN2 5TU
☎ (0892) 540766

These publications are available
free from the South East
England Tourist Board:

*South East England
Accommodation Guide*

Holiday Selector

Take a Break 1991/92

Diary of Events

Places to Visit Open in Winter

Also available are the following
(prices include postage and
packing):

*Hundreds of Places to Visit in
the South East* £2.25

*Leisure Map for South East
England* £3.30

European Clown Convention – 20 – 22 March

Places to stay

ACCOMMODATION ENTRIES *in this regional section are listed in alphabetical order of place name, and then in alphabetical order of establishment.*

THE MAP REFERENCES *refer to the colour maps towards the end of the guide. The first figure is the map number; the letter and figure which follow indicate the grid reference on the map.*

THE SYMBOLS *at the end of each accommodation entry give information about services and facilities. A 'key' to these symbols is inside the back cover flap, which can be kept open for easy reference.*

AMBERLEY

W. Sussex
Map ref 2D3

Amberley Castle Country House Hotel & Restaurant ᴍ
Amberley, Nr. Arundel,
BN18 9ND
☎ Bury (West Sussex)
(0798) 831992
Fax (0798) 831998
Independent country house hotel and restaurant offering creative and traditionally-inspired cuisine. Historic medieval castle in 12 acres. Rural Weald and Downland setting.
Bedrooms: 11 double & 1 twin.
Bathrooms: 12 private.
Bed & breakfast: £100-£175 single, £130-£225 double.
Half board: from £130 daily.
Lunch available.
Evening meal 6.30pm (l.o. 10pm).
Parking for 54.
Credit: Access, Visa, Diners, Amex.

> *Half board prices shown are per person but in some cases may be based on double/twin occupancy.*

> *The symbols are explained on the flap inside the back cover.*

ARDINGLY

W. Sussex
Map ref 2D3

4m N. Haywards Heath
Famous for the South of England Agricultural Showground and public school. Nearby is Wakehurst Place (National Trust), the gardens of which are administered by the Royal Botanic Gardens, Kew.

Ardingly Inn ᴍ
Street Lane, Ardingly,
RH17 6UA
☎ (0444) 892214
Village inn located in Sussex Weald adjacent to South of England Showground. Close to M23. Gatwick 11 miles. Local attractions include Wakehurst Place and Bluebell Railway.
Bedrooms: 3 double & 3 twin.
Bathrooms: 3 private, 1 public.
Bed & breakfast: £35.75-£55 double.
Lunch available.
Evening meal 6pm (l.o. 10pm).
Parking for 12.
Credit: Access, Visa, Diners, Amex.

ARUNDEL

W. Sussex
Map ref 2D3

Pleasant town on the River Arun, dominated by Arundel Castle, home of the Dukes of Norfolk. There are many 18th C houses and the Toy and Military Museum, Wildfowl Trust Reserve and Heritage Centre.
Tourist Information Centre ☎ *(0903) 882268*

Arundel Park Hotel
≋≋≋≋ APPROVED
Station Approach, Arundel,
BN18 9JL
☎ (0903) 882588
Refurbished to high standard, three bedrooms on ground floor. Pleasant lounge bar, informal restaurant serving home-cooked food to suit all tastes. Central for travel to many places of interest. Two minutes from main line railway station.
Bedrooms: 1 single, 9 double & 2 twin.
Bathrooms: 12 private.
Bed & breakfast: £38-£40 single, £48-£60 double.
Lunch available.
Evening meal 7pm (l.o. 9pm).
Parking for 60.
Credit: Access, Visa.

Avisford Park Hotel ᴍ
≋≋≋≋≋ COMMENDED
Yapton La., Walberton,
Arundel, BN18 0LS
☎ Yapton (0243) 551215
Telex 86137

Georgian manor style house in 62 acres of parkland between Arundel and Chichester. All rooms with views of the grounds.
Bedrooms: 28 single, 44 double & 26 twin, 2 family rooms.
Bathrooms: 100 private.
Bed & breakfast: £70-£85 single, £106-£140 double.
Lunch available.
Evening meal 7.30pm (l.o. 9.30pm).
Parking for 200.
Credit: Access, Visa, Diners, Amex.

Bridge House ᴍ
≋≋≋
18 Queen St., Arundel,
BN18 9JG
☎ (0903) 882779 & 882142
In the centre of town, with views of castle, river and downs. Ideal centre for exploring beautiful Sussex. 3 double en-suite bedrooms in 16th C cottage annexe.
Bedrooms: 2 single, 4 double & 2 twin, 6 family rooms.
Bathrooms: 7 private, 3 public.
Bed & breakfast: £16-£28 single, £30-£40 double.
Half board: £23-£38 daily, £158-£180 weekly.
Evening meal 6pm (l.o. 8pm).
Parking for 10.
Credit: Access, Visa.

Burpham Country Hotel M
♔♔♔

Burpham, Nr. Arundel,
BN18 9RJ
☎ (0903) 882160
In one of the most peaceful and unspoilt villages in West Sussex, with superb downland views. Ideal for walking holidays.
Bedrooms: 1 single, 5 double & 4 twin.
Bathrooms: 10 private.
Bed & breakfast: from £38 single, £60-£68 double.
Half board: £42.75-£46.75 daily.
Lunch available.
Evening meal 7pm (l.o. 8pm).
Parking for 12.
Credit: Access, Visa.

Norfolk Arms Hotel M
♔♔♔

High St., Arundel,
BN18 9AD
☎ (0903) 882101
Telex 878436 NORFOK G
Ⓖ Forestdale
Charming 18th C Georgian coaching inn set under the battlements of Arundel Castle.
Bedrooms: 4 single, 17 double & 13 twin.
Bathrooms: 34 private, 2 public.
Bed & breakfast: from £52.50 single, £72.50-£82.50 double.
Lunch available.
Evening meal 7pm (l.o. 10pm).
Parking for 29.
Credit: Access, Visa, Diners, Amex.

Swan Hotel M
♔♔♔

High St., Arundel,
BN18 9AG
☎ (0903) 882314
A small, centrally located, privately-run hotel. Our emphasis is on fresh produce, well cooked and attractively served in comfortable surroundings.
Bedrooms: 2 single, 4 double & 6 twin, 1 family room.
Bathrooms: 13 private.
Bed & breakfast: max. £47 single, max. £60 double.
Half board: £40-£57 daily.
Lunch available.

Please mention this guide when making a booking.

Evening meal 7pm (l.o. 9.30pm).
Credit: Access, Visa, Diners, Amex.

ASHFORD
Kent
Map ref 3B4

13m SW. Canterbury
Once a market centre for the farmers of the Weald of Kent and Romney Marsh. The town centre has a number of Tudor and Georgian houses.
Tourist Information Centre ☎ (0233) 629165

Croft Hotel M
♔♔♔ APPROVED

Canterbury Rd., Kennington,
Ashford, TN25 4DU
☎ (0233) 622140
Fax (0233) 622140
Old, country-type house situated in a peaceful, rural area on the outskirts of the town.
Bedrooms: 8 single, 6 double & 11 twin, 3 family rooms.
Bathrooms: 28 private.
Bed & breakfast: £35-£45 single, £46-£56 double.
Evening meal 6.30pm (l.o. 8pm).
Parking for 32.
Credit: Access, Visa, C.Bl.

Quantock House
♔♔ COMMENDED

Quantock Drive, Ashford,
TN24 8QH
☎ Ashford (0233) 638921
Small family-run establishment within easy walking distance of town centre and all its facilities but located within a quiet residential area.
Bedrooms: 1 single, 1 double & 1 twin.
Bathrooms: 3 private.
Bed & breakfast: £16-£18 single, £27-£32 double.
Half board: £23-£25 daily, £161-£175 weekly.
Evening meal 6pm (l.o. 7.30pm).
Parking for 3.

Warren Cottages
Listed APPROVED

136 The Street,
Willesborough, Ashford,
Kent. TN25 0NB
☎ (0233) 621905

300-year-old guesthouse with oak beams, open fireplaces and a cosy atmosphere. On old coaching route with easy access to M20 and a short drive from many places of interest.
Bedrooms: 2 single, 2 double.
Bathrooms: 1 private, 1 public.
Bed & breakfast: £25-£38 single, £45-£50 double.
Half board: £34-£39 daily, £238-£273 weekly.
Lunch available.
Evening meal 6.30pm (l.o. 9.30pm).
Parking for 7.
Credit: Access, Visa.

ASHINGTON
W. Sussex
Map ref 2D3

4m NW. Steyning

Mill House Hotel M
♔♔♔ COMMENDED

Mill Lane, Ashington,
RH20 3BZ
☎ (0903) 892426
Fax (0903) 892855
A 1740 period house with some additions and a pretty garden, set in a quiet country lane. Large double lounge with log fires in winter.
Bedrooms: 4 single, 5 double & 1 twin.
Bathrooms: 9 private, 1 public.
Bed & breakfast: £44.80-£52.50 single, £73.80-£84.40 double.
Half board: £55.45-£65.45 daily, from £294 weekly.
Lunch available.
Evening meal 7pm (l.o. 9.45pm).
Parking for 10.
Credit: Access, Visa, Diners, Amex.

BAGSHOT
Surrey
Map ref 2C2

Once a staging town. The heath was famous for its highwaymen. Nearby is the Royal Military Academy at Sandhurst.

Little Melrose
Westwood Rd., Windlesham,
Bagshot
☎ Ascot (0344) 872692
100-year-old bungalow, modernised to a high standard, situated in one acre in residential road just off A30.
Bedrooms: 3 double & 2 twin.

Bathrooms: 1 private, 1 public.
Bed & breakfast: from £20 single, from £40 double.
Half board: from £32 daily, from £200 weekly.
Evening meal 7pm (l.o. 8pm).
Parking for 4.

BATTLE
E. Sussex
Map ref 3B4

Built on the site of the Battle of Hastings, when William defeated Harold II and so became the Conqueror in 1066. This thriving town contains many old buildings, including the impressive abbey ruins. The museum deals with history from the Neolithic age and has a fine collection relating to the Sussex iron industry.
Tourist Information Centre ☎ (042 46) 3721

George Hotel M
♔♔♔

23 High Street, Battle,
TN33 0EA
☎ (042 46) 4466
Fax (042 46) 4853
Ⓖ Resort
Traditional coaching inn (1699), in a delightful setting in historic Battle. Traditional cuisine.
Bedrooms: 3 single, 8 double & 7 twin, 4 family rooms.
Bathrooms: 22 private.
Bed & breakfast: £22.50-£41 single, £45-£56 double.
Lunch available.
Evening meal 7pm (l.o. 9.30pm).
Parking for 30.
Credit: Access, Visa, Diners, Amex.

The Old Deanery M
Upper Lake, Battle,
E. Sussex TN33 0AQ
☎ (042 46) 4409
Elizabethan deanery set beside Battle Abbey and ancient Norman church. Unique historical atmosphere. Residence of the deans since 13th century. 4-poster and jacuzzi suites. Private gardens on battlefield. Town centre location in area of outstanding natural beauty.
Bedrooms: 1 single, 3 double & 1 twin, 1 family room.
Continued ▶

BATTLE
Continued

Bathrooms: 6 private,
1 public.
Bed & breakfast: £25-£35
single, £30-£70 double.
Parking for 20.

Powdermills Country House Hotel M

Powdermill Lane, Battle,
TN33 0SP
☎ (042 46) 5511
Fax (042 46) 4540
*Comfortable and spacious
listed Georgian country house
hotel in 150 acres of timbered
parkland. Trout and coarse
fishing lakes. In "1066"
country adjacent to Battle
Abbey.*
Bedrooms: 2 single, 6 double
& 5 twin, 1 family room.
Bathrooms: 14 private.
Bed & breakfast: £40-£45
single, £55-£95 double.
Half board: £45-£55 daily,
£255-£355 weekly.
Lunch available.
Evening meal 9.30pm (l.o.
9.30pm).
Parking for 34.
Credit: Access, Visa.

BENENDEN
Kent
Map ref 3B4

3m SE. Cranbrook
Set on a high ridge, with a
big tree-lined village
green where cricket is
played on summer
weekends. Tile-hung
cottages and a white
weatherboarded post
office mingle with 19th C
houses and a sandstone
church.

Crit Hall
Listed **HIGHLY COMMENDED**
Cranbrook Rd., Benenden,
TN17 4EU
☎ Cranbrook (0580) 240609
Fax (0580) 241743
*Elegant Georgian country
house, near Sissinghurst, with
panoramic views. Imaginative
dinners. Licensed. Many
National Trust properties and
gardens nearby.*
Bedrooms: 3 twin.
Bathrooms: 3 private.
Bed & breakfast: £22-£25
single, £37-£40 double.

Half board: £34-£37 daily.
Evening meal 7.30pm (l.o.
8pm).
Parking for 6.
Open February-November.

BEXHILL-ON-SEA
E. Sussex
Map ref 3B4

Popular seaside resort
with a gently shelving
beach of shingle and firm
sand at low tide. A
feature is the De la Warr
Pavilion, containing a
theatre, ballroom,
banqueting suite,
restaurant and sun
terrace. East of the town,
at Little Gally Hill, a
submerged forest can be
seen at low tide, a land
bridge which linked
Britain to the continent
10,000 years ago.
*Tourist Information
Centre* ☎ (0424) 212023

Bedford Lodge Hotel M

Cantelupe Road, Bexhill-on-
Sea, TN40 1PR
☎ (0424) 730097
*Imposing family-run Victorian
building in quiet residential
area close to promenade and
town. Wholesome cooking.
Easy parking.*
Bedrooms: 4 single, 1 double
& 1 twin, 1 family room.
Bathrooms: 3 private,
2 public.
Bed & breakfast: £18-£23
single, £36-£45 double.
Half board: £26-£31 daily,
£155-£190 weekly.
Lunch available.
Evening meal 6pm (l.o.
7.30pm).
Parking for 1.
Credit: Access, Visa.

Buenos Aires
Listed
24 Albany Rd., Bexhill-on-
Sea, TN40 1BZ
☎ (0424) 212269
*Well-established guesthouse
adjacent to seafront, theatre
and town centre, offering
comfortable accommodation
and a friendly atmosphere.*
Bedrooms: 1 double & 1 twin,
2 family rooms.
Bathrooms: 1 public.
Bed & breakfast: £16 single,
£28-£30 double.

Half board: £20.50-£22.50
daily, £138.50-£152 weekly.
Evening meal 6pm (l.o.
midday).

Cooden Resort Hotel M

Cooden Beach, Bexhill-on-
Sea, TN39 4TT
☎ Cooden (042 43) 2281
Fax (042 43) 6142
CR Resort
*Beautifully situated on the
beach, providing an ideal
centre for exploring "1066"
country. Golf facilities
available, with discounts for
guests, and a health and leisure
club is on site.*
Bedrooms: 9 single, 15 double
& 11 twin, 5 family rooms.
Bathrooms: 40 private,
1 public.
Bed & breakfast: £32.50-
£69.50 single, £65-£92 double.
Lunch available.
Evening meal 7pm (l.o.
9.30pm).
Parking for 100.
Credit: Access, Visa, Diners,
Amex.

The Granville Hotel M
APPROVED
Sea Road, Bexhill-on-Sea,
TN40 1EE
☎ Bexhill (0424) 215437
*Splendid, modernised, family-
owned Victorian hotel, in quiet
situation close to town centre
and beach. Reduced rates at
weekends.*
Bedrooms: 2 single, 14 double
& 33 twin, 1 family room.
Bathrooms: 50 private.
Bed & breakfast: £34.75-
£49.75 single, £69.50 double.
Half board: £47.75-£62.75
daily, £268.50-£328.50
weekly.
Lunch available.
Evening meal 6pm (l.o. 9pm).
Credit: Access, Visa, Diners,
Amex.

Northern Hotel M
COMMENDED
72-82 Sea Rd., Bexhill-on-Sea,
TN40 1JN
☎ (0424) 212836
*Terrace of 6 large Edwardian
town houses in quiet seaside
resort. Convenient as touring
base for "1066" country.*
Bedrooms: 9 single, 4 double
& 6 twin, 1 family room.
Bathrooms: 20 private,
3 public.

Bed & breakfast: £33-£36
single, £56-£62 double.
Half board: £42-£46 daily,
£264.60-£289.80 weekly.
Lunch available.
Evening meal 5.45pm (l.o.
8pm).
Credit: Access, Visa.

Park Lodge Hotel M
COMMENDED
16 Egerton Rd., Bexhill-on-
Sea, TN39 3HH
☎ (0424) 216547
*Comfortable Victorian hotel in
quiet position adjacent to
seafront and close to all
amenities. Renowned for home-
cooked food.*
Bedrooms: 2 single, 3 double
& 3 twin, 2 family rooms.
Bathrooms: 6 private,
1 public; 2 private showers.
Bed & breakfast: £17-£28
single, £35-£42 double.
Half board: £24-£31 daily,
£160-£170 weekly.
Evening meal 6pm (l.o. 7pm).
Credit: Access, Visa.

Selsdon House
COMMENDED
23 Jameson Rd., Bexhill-on-
Sea, TN40 1EG
☎ (0424) 221191
*Family-run guesthouse close to
sea, station, shops and buses.
Most bedrooms are on the first
floor.*
Bedrooms: 1 single, 2 double,
2 family rooms.
Bathrooms: 1 private,
2 public.
Bed & breakfast: £15-£16
single, £30-£38 double.
Half board: £21-£26 daily,
£127-£161 weekly.
Evening meal 6pm (l.o. 3pm).
Parking for 2.

---

*Half board prices
shown are per
person but in some
cases may be based
on double/twin
occupancy.*

---

*The national Crown
scheme is explained
in full on pages
536 - 539.*

BIDDENDEN

Kent
Map ref 3B4

Perfect village with black and white houses, a tithe barn and a pond. Part of the village is grouped around a green with a village sign depicting the famous Biddenden Maids. It was an important centre of the Flemish weaving industry, hence the beautiful Old Cloth Hall.

Birchley M
🏅 HIGHLY COMMENDED

Fosten Green Lane, Biddenden, Nr Ashford, TN27 8DZ
☎ Biddenden (0580) 291413
Peacefully secluded 1632 beamed house in 6-acre garden, log fires, panelled lounge, carved inglenook fireplace in dining room. Convenient for most Kent attractions. Non-smokers only please.
Bedrooms: 1 double & 2 twin.
Bathrooms: 3 private.
Bed & breakfast: £30-£50 single, £40-£60 double.
Parking for 8.
Credit: Access, Visa.
⌖5🖵🖵Ⓤ🛈🎔ⓉⅢ🗕 🕾🖰✿✕🛄🎱Ⓣ

BOGNOR REGIS

W. Sussex
Map ref 2D3

5 miles of firm, flat sand have made the town a popular family resort. Well supplied with gardens, children's activities in Hotham Park and the Bognor Regis Centre for entertainment.
Tourist Information Centre ☎ (0243) 823140

Beachcroft Hotel M
🏅🏅🏅 APPROVED

Clyde Rd., Felpham, Bognor Regis, PO22 7AH
☎ (0243) 827142
Family-run hotel in beachside location, with south-facing garden and indoor heated pool. Weekly dancing. Table d'hote and a la carte menus.
Bedrooms: 8 single, 6 double & 16 twin, 5 family rooms.
Bathrooms: 35 private.
Bed & breakfast: £30 single, £48-£59 double.
Half board: £34-£39.50 daily, £210-£248 weekly.
Lunch available.

Evening meal 7pm (l.o. 9pm).
Parking for 40.
Open January-November.
Credit: Access, Visa, Amex.
⌖1🖰📞🖵✿🛈 ⒱🚭Ⓣ Ⅲ🗕🕾✕🎱 SP

Black Mill House Hotel M
🏅🏅🏅 APPROVED

Princess Ave., Bognor Regis, PO21 2QU
☎ Bognor Regis (0243) 821945/865596
Fax (0243) 821316
Quiet situation, 300 yards from sea and Marine Gardens. Picnic lunches and afternoon teas. Enclosed garden. Special offers for children.
Bedrooms: 9 single, 5 double & 6 twin, 6 family rooms.
Bathrooms: 18 private, 5 public.
Bed & breakfast: £27-£38.50 single, £46-£68 double.
Half board: £32-£48 daily, £168-£267 weekly.
Lunch available.
Evening meal 7pm (l.o. 8pm).
Parking for 13.
Credit: Access, Visa, Diners, Amex.
⌖🖰📞🖵✿🛈 ⒱✂ 🚭Ⓣ Ⅲ🗕🕾✿🎱🛄🎱 SP Ⓣ

Homestead Private Hotel
🏅🏅

90 Aldwick Rd., Bognor Regis, PO21 2PD
☎ (0243) 823443
Family-run hotel with friendly, relaxed atmosphere, 200 yards from the beach, convenient for shops, entertainment and outdoor recreation.
Bedrooms: 2 single, 2 double & 2 twin, 2 family rooms.
Bathrooms: 1 private, 1 public; 1 private shower.
Bed & breakfast: £12-£13 single, £24-£26 double.
Half board: £16.50-£17.50 daily, from £106.50 weekly.
Evening meal 6pm (l.o. 7pm).
Parking for 12.
Credit: Access, Visa.
⌖🖰🛈 ⒱🚭Ⓣ Ⅲ🗕 OAP

Ramla Guest House

72 Victoria Drive, Bognor Regis, PO21 2TA
☎ (0243) 827340
Comfortable family-run guesthouse in quiet road, close to sea, town centre and railway station. Restaurant licence pending. Parking facilities.
Bedrooms: 1 single, 2 double & 1 twin, 2 family rooms.
Bathrooms: 1 public.

Bed & breakfast: £12.50-£16 double.
Half board: £17.50-£21.50 daily.
Evening meal 5.30pm (l.o. 9.30pm).
Parking for 3.
⌖🖰✿🚭🎔Ⅲ🗕🛄 🚭 OAP 🐾

Steyne House (Private Hotel)

10, West Street, Bognor Regis PO21 1UF
☎ (0243) 828476
Family-run private hotel 200 yards from the sea and town centre, overlooking picturesque gardens. All rooms have TV and tea/coffee-making facilities.
Bedrooms: 3 single, 1 double & 1 twin, 2 family rooms.
Bathrooms: 1 public; 1 private shower.
Bed & breakfast: £11.50-£17 single, £23-£34 double.
Half board: £18-£23 daily, £126-£161 weekly.
Evening meal 6pm.
Parking for 2.
⌖🖵✿🛈 ⒱🚭Ⓣ Ⅲ🗕 OAP 🐾 SP

BOLNEY

W. Sussex
Map ref 2D3

Hickstead Resort Hotel M

Jobs Lane, Bolney, RH17 5PA
☎ Burgess Hill (0444) 248023
Fax 0444 245280
🆑 Resort
Just off the A23, midway between Gatwick and Brighton. Fully refurbished bedrooms, bar, restaurants, banqueting/conference facilities and health club.
Bedrooms: 49 family rooms.
Bathrooms: 49 private.
Bed & breakfast: £28.50-£69.50 single, £57-£92 double.
Lunch available.
Evening meal 7pm (l.o. 9.15pm).
Parking for 100.
Credit: Access, Visa, Diners, Amex.
⌖🖰📞⏍🖵✿🛈 ⒱✂ 🚭🍽Ⅲ🗕🕾🛄✿🎱 ▶ ✿🐾 SP Ⓣ

BRAMLEY

Surrey
Map ref 2D2

3m S. Guildford

Pinkerton

Gosden Common, Bramley, Nr Guildford, GU5 0AQ
☎ Guildford (0483) 898889
Pretty, old cottage beside cricket common. Large lounge with television. Plenty of parking in drive. One bedroom and bathroom upstairs. TV. Tea and coffee making facilities in bedroom.
Bedrooms: 1 twin.
Bathrooms: 1 private.
Bed & breakfast: £30-£35 double.
⌖✿Ⓤ Ⓣ Ⅲ🗕🕾✕🎱

BRENCHLEY

Kent
Map ref 3B4

6m NE. Tunbridge Wells
In the centre of this village is a small green, around which stand half-timbered, tile-hung and weatherboarded houses.

Bull Inn at Brenchley M
🏅🏅 COMMENDED

High Street, Brenchley, TN12 7NQ
☎ (089 272) 2701
Victorian village inn set in the heart of the Weald of Kent. Comfortable accommodation with traditional English ales and home-cooked food.
Bedrooms: 1 single, 2 double & 1 twin.
Bathrooms: 4 private.
Bed & breakfast: £25-£40 single, £30-£50 double.
Half board: £32-£55 daily, £200-£350 weekly.
Lunch available.
Evening meal 6pm (l.o. 9.30pm).
Parking for 10.
Credit: Access, Visa.
⌖🖰⏍🖵✿🛈 ⒱🚭Ⓣ ◐Ⅲ🗕🛄🍽Ü✍✿✕🎱 SP 🎱

> *We advise you to confirm your booking in writing.*

Individual proprietors have supplied all details of accommodation. Although we do check for accuracy, we advise you to confirm prices and other information at the time of booking.

BRIGHTON & HOVE

E. Sussex
Map ref 2D3

First and largest seaside resort in the south-east. Attractions include the Dome, Royal Pavilion, Theatre Royal, Volks Railway, Sea Life Centre, Palace Pier, Stanmer Park, Marina, Conference and Exhibition Centre and 'The Lanes'.
Neighbouring Hove is a resort in its own right with interesting Museum of Art and King Alfred's Leisure Centre.
Tourist Information Centre ☎ (0273) 23755; for Hove (0273) 775400 or 746100

Aannabelles Olde English Lodging House ⋈

9 Charles Street, Brighton, E.Sussex BN2 1TG
☎ (0273) 605845/677419
Fax (0273) 62170
Established in 1790 in the heart of Brighton. Still retaining the charm of yesteryear but with all modern facilities. Restaurant.
Bedrooms: 2 single, 2 double & 1 twin.
Bathrooms: 5 private.
Bed & breakfast: £29.50 single, £59-£69.50 double.
Evening meal 6.30pm.
Parking for 15.
Credit: Access, Visa, C.Bl., Diners, Amex.

Adelaide Hotel ⋈

51 Regency Sq., Brighton, BN1 2FF
☎ (0273) 205286
Fax (0273) 220904
Small, quiet and informal hotel. Convenient for all amenities, seafront and conference centre. Midweek and weekend breaks.
Bedrooms: 3 single, 7 double & 1 twin, 1 family room.
Bathrooms: 12 private, 1 public.
Bed & breakfast: £36-£60 single, £55-£72 double.
Half board: £48.50-£72.50 daily.
Evening meal 6.30pm (l.o. 8.30pm).
Credit: Access, Visa, Diners, Amex.

Albany Hotel

St. Catherine's Ter., Kingsway, Hove, BN3 2RR
☎ (0273) 773807
Situated on Kingsway, Grade II historic building. Sea view from front bedrooms. 1 mile west of Brighton West Pier.
Bedrooms: 1 single, 5 double & 2 twin, 1 family room.
Bathrooms: 9 private.
Bed & breakfast: £21-£27 single, £29.50-£37.50 double.
Half board: £21-£32 daily.
Evening meal 6.30pm (l.o. 5pm).

The Alexandra Hotel ⋈

42 Brunswick Ter., Hove, Brighton, BN3 1HA
☎ Brighton (0273) 202722
Telex 877579 ALEXBR G
Grade I listed Regency hotel on Hove seafront, combining the elegance of a bygone era with modern amenities.
Bedrooms: 22 single, 16 double & 19 twin, 4 family rooms.
Bathrooms: 61 private.
Bed & breakfast: from £69.50 single, from £86 double.
Lunch available.
Evening meal 6.30pm (l.o. 9.30pm).
Credit: Access, Visa, Diners, Amex.

Allendale Hotel ⋈

3, New Steine, Brighton, BN2 1PB
☎ Brighton (0273) 675436/672994
Fax (0273) 602603
Regency hotel, offering every facility for a comfortable, enjoyable and stress-free stay. Privately run, overlooking garden square and sea.
Bedrooms: 5 single, 1 double & 2 twin, 5 family rooms.
Bathrooms: 6 private, 2 public; 2 private showers.
Bed & breakfast: £27-£30 single, £38-£64 double.
Half board: £29-£42 daily, £190-£270 weekly.
Credit: Access, Visa, Diners, Amex.

Ambassador Hotel ⋈
APPROVED

22 New Steine, Marine Pde., Brighton, BN2 1PD
☎ (0273) 676869

Family-run, licensed hotel overlooking sea, near conference centres. All rooms en-suite. Telephone, radio, tea/coffee facilities and colour TV.
Bedrooms: 3 single, 2 double, 4 family rooms.
Bathrooms: 9 private.
Bed & breakfast: £23-£30 single, £40-£54 double.
Credit: Access, Visa, Diners, Amex.

Amblecliff Hotel

35 Upper Rock Gdns., Brighton, BN2 1QF
☎ (0273) 676945
Close to seafront, all entertainments and conference centre.
Bedrooms: 3 single, 6 double & 2 twin.
Bathrooms: 7 private, 2 public.
Bed & breakfast: £17-£30 single, £34-£49 double.
Evening meal 6pm (l.o. 6pm).
Parking for 3.
Credit: Access, Visa, Amex.

Aquarium Guest House

13 Madeira Pl., Brighton, BN1 1TN
☎ (0273) 605761
Small guesthouse close to seafront, shops, theatre and all amenities.
Bedrooms: 4 double & 4 twin.
Bathrooms: 2 public.
Bed & breakfast: £12-£18 single, £14-£20 double.

Arlanda Hotel ⋈
COMMENDED

20 New Steine, Brighton, BN2 1PD
☎ Brighton (0273) 699300
Family-run, licensed hotel in garden square, with sea views. 2 minutes from town centre and 100 metres from sea.
Bedrooms: 4 single, 3 double & 3 twin, 2 family rooms.
Bathrooms: 12 private.
Bed & breakfast: £28-£32 single, £46-£62 double.
Lunch available.
Credit: Access, Visa, Diners, Amex.

The national Crown scheme is explained in full on pages 536 – 539.

Ascott House Hotel ⋈

21 New Steine, Marine Pde., Brighton, BN2 1PD
☎ (0273) 688085
Central hotel in seafront garden square, close to the Royal Pavilion, Lanes, Palace Pier, aquarium and conference centre.
Bedrooms: 4 single, 8 family rooms.
Bathrooms: 9 private, 2 public; 2 private showers.
Bed & breakfast: £25-£35 single, £48-£66 double.
Credit: Access, Visa, Diners, Amex.

Brighton Hotel

145 Kings Road, Brighton, BN1 2PQ
☎ (0273) 820555
Fax (0273) 821555
Overlooking seafront, some rooms offering four-poster or water beds and jacuzzi. All rooms en-suite. Licensed bar, restaurant, health club.
Bedrooms: 15 single, 33 double & 4 twin.
Bathrooms: 52 private.
Bed & breakfast: £35-£40 single, £48-£75 double.
Evening meal 6.30pm (l.o. 9.30pm).
Parking for 14.
Credit: Access, Visa, Diners, Amex.

Cavalaire House

34 Upper Rock Gdns., Brighton, BN2 1QF
☎ (0273) 696899
Close to all amenities, offering rooms with or without private facilities. Book 7 nights and get 1 night free.
Bedrooms: 1 single, 3 double & 3 twin, 2 family rooms.
Bathrooms: 3 private, 1 public; 3 private showers.
Bed & breakfast: £17-£18 single, £28-£42 double.

Chatsworth Hotel

9 Salisbury Rd., Hove, BN3 3AB
☎ (0273) 737360
Long established, well-appointed, comfortable hotel in quiet position close to sea, shops and buses. Accent on food.
Bedrooms: 5 single, 1 twin, 3 family rooms.
Bathrooms: 3 public.
Bed & breakfast: £18-£20 single, £34-£36 double.

Half board: £23-£25 daily, £119-£126 weekly.
Evening meal 6.30pm (l.o. 7pm).

Chester Court Hotel
7 Charlotte Street, Brighton, BN2 1AG
☎ (0273) 621750
Small period hotel refurbished to high standard with comfort in mind, close to seafront with all amenities at hand.
Bedrooms: 4 single, 4 double & 2 twin, 1 family room.
Bathrooms: 2 public; 7 private showers.
Bed & breakfast: £16-£18 single, £32-£36 double.
Open February-December.

Colson House
17 Upper Rock Gdns., Brighton, BN2 1QE
☎ (0273) 694922
Listed Regency hotel with original features throughout, sympathetically restored. Adjacent to the sea, close to all entertainments and conference centre.
Bedrooms: 1 single, 3 double & 3 twin.
Bathrooms: 7 private.
Bed & breakfast: from £18 single, £32-£45 double.
Half board: £26-£32.50 daily.
Lunch available.
Evening meal 6pm (l.o. 6.30pm).
Credit: Access, Visa.

Cornerways Hotel
18-20 Caburn Road, Hove, BN3 6EF
☎ (0273) 731882 & (0273) 24766 (Guests)
An Edwardian house on the A27 with easy access and parking. Personal service from the proprietors and home cooking. 15 minutes' walk from seafront.
Bedrooms: 3 single, 3 double & 2 twin, 2 family rooms.
Bathrooms: 1 private, 3 public.
Bed & breakfast: £15-£16 single, £30-£32 double.
Half board: £22-£23 daily.
Evening meal 6.30pm (l.o. 2pm).

Cosmopolitan Hotel ♠
☻☻☻
31 New Steine, Marine Pde., Brighton, BN2 1PB
☎ (0273) 682461
Fax (0273) 622311

In a commanding position in seafront square, overlooking the beach and Palace Pier. Central for shopping, entertainments and conference centres.
Bedrooms: 10 single, 3 double & 3 twin, 11 family rooms.
Bathrooms: 19 private, 3 public.
Bed & breakfast: £18-£28 single, £34-£52 double.
Credit: Access, Visa, Diners, Amex.

Cranleigh Guest House
22-23 Terminus Rd., Brighton, BN1 3PD
☎ (0273) 27971
Clean and comfortable with a friendly atmosphere, the nearest guesthouse to Brighton railway station.
Bedrooms: 2 single, 2 double & 3 twin, 2 family rooms.
Bathrooms: 3 public.
Bed & breakfast: max. £15 single, max. £28 double.

Fyfield House
☻☻ APPROVED
26 New Steine, Brighton, BN2 1PD
☎ (0273) 602770
Friendly, family-run hotel, with a home-from-home atmosphere. Anna and Peter ensure a nice stay.
Bedrooms: 4 single, 3 double & 1 twin, 1 family room.
Bathrooms: 4 private, 1 public; 1 private shower.
Bed & breakfast: £14-£23 single, £30-£45 double.
Credit: Access, Visa, Diners, Amex.

Hove Excelsior Hotel
☻☻☻☻ COMMENDED
205-209 Kingsway, Hove, BN3 4FD
☎ (0273) 773991
Family-run hotel overlooking Hove seafront and tennis courts. Fully licensed bars and restaurant.
Bedrooms: 18 double & 34 twin, 6 family rooms.
Bathrooms: 58 private.
Bed & breakfast: £30-£75 single, £45-£75 double.
Half board: £38-£75 daily, from £225 weekly.
Lunch available.
Evening meal 6.30pm (l.o. 10pm).
Parking for 25.

Credit: Access, Visa, C.Bl., Diners, Amex.

Kempton House Hotel ♠
☻☻☻
33-34 Marine Parade., Brighton, BN2 1TR
☎ (0273) 570248
Recently refurbished seafront hotel overlooking beach and Palace Pier. En-suite sea view rooms. Licensed bar.
Bedrooms: 6 double & 2 twin, 4 family rooms.
Bathrooms: 12 private.
Bed & breakfast: £30-£40 single, £44-£52 double.
Half board: £32-£36 daily, £203-£231 weekly.
Evening meal 6pm.
Credit: Access, Visa, Diners, Amex.

Kennedy Palace Hotel
11-12 Marine Pde., Brighton, BN2 1TL
☎ (0273) 604928 & 697595
Seafront position overlooking Aquarium and Palace Pier. Close to pavilion and Lanes. Licensed bar and restaurant. Some rooms with seaviews.
Bedrooms: 4 single, 6 double & 4 twin, 3 family rooms.
Bathrooms: 17 private, 2 public.
Bed & breakfast: £27-£30 single, £40-£45 double.
Half board: £26-£33 daily, £165-£215 weekly.
Lunch available.
Evening meal 6pm (l.o. 10pm).
Credit: Access, Visa, C.Bl., Amex.

Kimberley Hotel ♠
☻☻ APPROVED
17 Atlingworth St., Brighton, BN2 1PL
☎ (0273) 603504
Family-run hotel, 2 minutes from seafront and central for amusements, shopping, marina and conference centre. Licensed residents' bar.
Bedrooms: 3 single, 3 double & 5 twin, 4 family rooms.
Bathrooms: 1 private, 2 public; 13 private showers.
Bed & breakfast: £18-£22 single, £34-£40 double.
Open January-October.
Credit: Access, Visa, Amex.

Lawns Hotel ♠
☻☻☻
Kingsway, Hove, Brighton, BN3 2GT
☎ (0273) 736277
Seafront hotel. 10 minutes' walk from centre. We cater for conferences, seminars, functions, exhibitions/ workshops and coach parties.
Bedrooms: 6 single, 17 double & 3 twin, 15 family rooms.
Bathrooms: 41 private.
Bed & breakfast: £35-£48 single, £45-£58 double.
Half board: £33-£58.50 daily, £210-£400 weekly.
Lunch available.
Evening meal 6.30pm (l.o. 8.30pm).
Credit: Access, Visa, Diners, Amex.

Marina House Hotel ♠
☻☻
8 Charlotte St., Marine Parade, Brighton, BN2 1AG
☎ (0273) 605349/679484
Fax (0273) 605349
Cosy, well-maintained elegant hotel, offering a warm welcome, cleanliness, comfort and hospitality. English breakfast, licensed restaurant. Central for Palace Pier, conferences and exhibitions, adjacent to the sea and a few minutes from the Marina, Royal Pavilion and all amenities. Flexible breakfast, check-in and check-out times.
Bedrooms: 3 single, 7 double.
Bathrooms: 7 private, 1 public.
Bed & breakfast: £12.50-£21 single, £25-£39 double.
Half board: £21.50-£30 daily, £135-£183 weekly.
Lunch available.
Evening meal 6.30pm (l.o. 5pm).
Credit: Access, Visa, Diners, Amex.

Melford Hall Hotel ♠
41 Marine Parade, Brighton, BN2 1PE
☎ (0273) 681435
Listed building well positioned on seafront and within easy walking distance of all the entertainment that Brighton has to offer. Many rooms with sea views.
Bedrooms: 4 single, 10 double & 5 twin, 1 family room.
Bathrooms: 16 private, 2 public.
Bed & breakfast: £20-£25 single, £40-£50 double.
Continued ▶

BRIGHTON & HOVE
Continued

Parking for 12.
Credit: Access, Visa, Diners,
Amex.

Oak Hotel M
West Street, Brighton,
BN1 2DX
☎ (0273) 220033
*Brand new hotel in the heart of
the town, close to the seafront,
adjoining the Brighton
Conference Centre and the
famous Lanes. Within walking
distance of Brighton station.*
Bedrooms: 2 single, 56 double
& 80 twin.
Bathrooms: 138 private.
Bed & breakfast: £35-£37
single, £49.50-£52.50 double.
Half board: £34-£44 daily,
£195-£309.75 weekly.
Lunch available.
Evening meal 6.30pm (l.o.
10pm).
Credit: Access, Visa, Diners,
Amex.

Old Ship Hotel M
King's Rd., Brighton,
BN1 1NR
☎ (0273) 29001 Telex 877101
OLSHIP
*Old world character hotel on
Brighton's seafront. Noted
restaurant. Refurbishment
programme now completed.
Sea view and executive rooms
available.*
Bedrooms: 11 single,
85 double & 53 twin, 3 family
rooms.
Bathrooms: 152 private.
Bed & breakfast: £55-£95
single, £70-£120 double.
Half board: £55-£60 daily.
Lunch available.
Evening meal 7pm (l.o. 9pm).
Parking for 60.
Credit: Access, Visa, C.Bl.,
Diners, Amex.

Paskins Hotel M
☆☆☆ APPROVED
19 Charlotte St., Brighton,
BN2 1AG
☎ (0273) 601203
*Small family-run licensed hotel
centrally located in town
centre. Most rooms with en-
suite facilities, some four-poster
beds.*
Bedrooms: 7 single, 8 double
& 3 twin, 1 family room.
Bathrooms: 16 private,
1 public.

Bed & breakfast: £19-£30
single, £30-£55 double.
Half board: £28.95-£39.95
daily, £180-£250 weekly.
Evening meal 7pm (l.o. 9am).
Credit: Access, Visa, Diners,
Amex.

Pier View M
☆☆ APPROVED
28 New Steine, Brighton,
BN2 1PD
☎ (0273) 605310
*Smart, friendly, family-run
hotel with a real pier view.
Near town centre, shops and
many places of interest.*
Bedrooms: 3 single, 3 double
& 1 twin, 3 family rooms.
Bathrooms: 8 private,
2 public.
Bed & breakfast: £20-£30
single, £44-£52 double.
Credit: Access, Visa, Amex.

Portland House Hotel M
55-56 Regency Sq., Brighton,
BN1 2FF
☎ (0273) 820464
*Regency building in seafront
square. Minutes away from
conference centre, shops and
historic Lanes.*
Bedrooms: 10 single, 6 double
& 6 twin, 2 family rooms.
Bathrooms: 24 private.
Bed & breakfast: £30-£40
single, £50-£80 double.
Half board: £37-£52 daily,
£210-£330 weekly.
Lunch available.
Evening meal 6pm (l.o. 6pm).
Open February-December.
Credit: Access, Visa, Diners,
Amex.

Preston Resort Hotel M
216 Preston Rd., Brighton,
BN1 6UU
☎ (0273) 507853
Fax (0273) 540039
⊕ Resort
*Fully-refurbished bedrooms,
newly-built restaurant, bar and
health club. On main A23 into
Brighton, close to Preston Park.*
Bedrooms: 5 single, 18 double
& 10 twin, 1 family room.
Bathrooms: 34 private.
Bed & breakfast: £28.50-
£59.50 single, £57-£82 double.
Lunch available.
Evening meal 7pm (l.o.
9.45pm).
Parking for 60.
Credit: Access, Visa, Diners,
Amex.

Prince Regent Hotel
29 Regency Square, Brighton,
BN1 2FH
☎ (0273) 29962
Fax (0273) 748162
*Mid-terrace mansion, whose
elegant decor retains all the
splendour of the Regency
period. Two antique four-poster
beds and ground-floor jacuzzi.
Balcony room with spectacular
sea view.*
Bedrooms: 3 single, 13 double
& 4 twin.
Bathrooms: 20 private.
Bed & breakfast: from £30
single, £50-£80 double.
Credit: Access, Visa, Diners.

Princes Marine Hotel M
☆☆☆☆ APPROVED
153 Kingsway, Hove,
BN3 2WE
☎ Brighton (0273) 207660
*Commanding seafront hotel in
Hove, only minutes from
Brighton Centre. Opposite
beach and leisure centre, with
waterslides and pools.
Restaurant, bar, games room.*
Bedrooms: 8 single, 8 double
& 29 twin, 3 family rooms.
Bathrooms: 48 private.
Bed & breakfast: £30-£45
single, £50-£60 double.
Half board: £32-£38 daily,
£200-£240 weekly.
Lunch available.
Evening meal 6pm (l.o. 9pm).
Parking for 21.
Credit: Access, Visa, Diners,
Amex.

Queens Hotel
Kings Rd., Brighton,
BN1 1NS
☎ (0273) 21222 Telex 877414
*Central seafront hotel with
well-appointed en-suite
bedrooms. Seaview restaurant.
Health and leisure club.
Excellent conference and
banqueting facilities.*
Bedrooms: 2 single, 39 double
& 37 twin, 12 family rooms.
Bathrooms: 90 private.
Bed & breakfast: £80-£85
single, £90-£95 double.
Lunch available.
Evening meal 7pm (l.o.
10pm).
Parking for 16.
Credit: Access, Visa, C.Bl.,
Diners, Amex.

Queensbury Hotel
☆☆
58, Regency Square,
Brighton, BN1 2GB
☎ (0273) 25558
Fax (0273) 24800
*Family-run bed and breakfast,
close to the beach, shopping,
entertainment and exhibition/
conference centres, but just far
enough away to avoid the
traffic noise.*
Bedrooms: 1 single, 7 double
& 4 twin, 4 family rooms.
Bathrooms: 6 private,
3 public; 9 private showers.
Bed & breakfast: £25-£38
single, £40-£60 double.
Credit: Access, Visa.

Royal Albion Hotel M
35, Old Steine, Brighton,
BN1 1NT
☎ (0273) 29202 Telex 878277
⊕ Park Hotels
*Regency-style seafront hotel,
totally refurbished.
Magnificent sea views from
restaurant and lounge. Midway
between the Brighton
Conference Centre and the
Marina.*
Bedrooms: 28 single,
40 double & 90 twin.
Bathrooms: 158 private.
Bed & breakfast: £35-£95
single, £70-£120 double.
Half board: £45-£109 daily,
£315-£763 weekly.
Lunch available.
Evening meal 7.30pm (l.o.
9.15pm).
Credit: Access, Visa, Diners,
Amex.

Ryford Hotel M
6-7 New Steine, Brighton,
BN2 1PB
☎ (0273) 681576
*Family hotel in one of the
finest positions on the seafront.
Close to Palace Pier, Brighton
Centre and main shopping
amenities. Brochure on request.*
Bedrooms: 7 single, 6 double
& 7 twin, 7 family rooms.
Bathrooms: 7 public.
Bed & breakfast: £17-£25
single, £34-£40 double.
Open April-October.

Sackville Hotel M
☆☆☆☆ COMMENDED
189 Kingsway, Hove,
BN3 4GU
☎ (0273) 736292
Telex 877830

Seafront hotel. Some rooms have sea views and balcony. Oak-panelled bar, and restaurant offering comprehensive menus complemented by extensive wine list.
Bedrooms: 13 single, 23 double & 7 twin, 2 family rooms.
Bathrooms: 45 private.
Bed & breakfast: from £60 single, from £70 double.
Half board: from £35 daily, from £245 weekly.
Lunch available.
Evening meal 7.30pm (l.o. 10pm).
Parking for 23.
Credit: Access, Visa, Diners, Amex.
ら 舟 ℄ ⊙ ♫ ⇨ 🛈 ⅴ ⅟ 🗲
🛏 ● 🎦 ▦ ◢ 🍽 ⚲ SP 🆃

St. Catherines Lodge Hotel ⋔
♨♨♨♨
Kingsway, Hove, BN3 2RZ
☎ Brighton (0273) 778181
Telex 877073
🆉 Inter
Well-established seafront hotel. Restaurant specialises in traditional English dishes. Four-poster honeymoon rooms. Attractive cocktail bar, games rooms, garden, and easy parking. Situated opposite King Alfred sports and leisure centre, water-slides, tenpin bowling and gym.
Bedrooms: 11 single, 23 double & 12 twin, 4 family rooms.
Bathrooms: 40 private, 5 public.
Bed & breakfast: from £36 single, from £60 double.
Half board: from £40 daily, from £240 weekly.
Lunch available.
Evening meal 7pm (l.o. 9pm).
Parking for 4.
Credit: Access, Visa, Diners, Amex.
ら 🖫 ℄ ⊙ ♫ 🛈 ⅴ ⅟
🛏 ● 🎦 ▦ ◢ 🍽 ⚲ 🗡 🕱 DAP
SP 🆃

Hotel Seafield ⋔
♨♨♨
23 Seafield Rd., Hove, BN3 2TP
☎ (0273) 735912
Family-run hotel with home-cooked food, close to the seafront and main shopping centre. Free street parking in addition to private parking. Free video film shows every evening.
Bedrooms: 1 single, 4 double & 3 twin, 2 family rooms.
Bathrooms: 8 private, 3 public.

Bed & breakfast: £16-£30 single, £40-£50 double.
Evening meal 6pm (l.o. 5pm).
Parking for 7.
Open July-October.
ら 🖫 ⊙ ♫ ⇨ ⅴ ⅟ 🛏 🆃
● 🎦 ▦ ◢ DAP SP 🆃

Seaholme Hotel
10-11 Seafield Rd., Hove, BN3 2TN
☎ (0273) 731066
This friendly hotel has been built up by the Coleman family over the past 17 years. Courtesy bus available for parties.
Bedrooms: 9 single, 6 double & 12 twin, 5 family rooms.
Bathrooms: 23 private, 2 public.
Bed & breakfast: £16-£26 single, £33-£41 double.
Half board: £21-£27 daily, from £130 weekly.
Lunch available.
Evening meal 6pm (l.o. 8pm).
Parking for 13.
Credit: Access, Visa.
ら 🖫 ⊙ ♫ ⇨ ⅴ
🛏 ● 🎦 ◢ 🍽 🕱 SP

Shalimar Hotel
23 Broad St., Marine Pde., Brighton, BN2 1TJ
☎ (0273) 605316 & 694314
In central Brighton, beautifully decorated Victorian style house with cast iron balcony, overlooking the Palace Pier and seafront. Most rooms have private shower, WC and bidet.
Bedrooms: 1 single, 3 double & 1 twin, 4 family rooms.
Bathrooms: 5 private, 2 public; 2 private showers.
Bed & breakfast: £20-£30 single, £35-£55 double.
Half board: £35-£42.50 daily, £245-£297.50 weekly.
Credit: Access, Visa, Diners, Amex.
ら12 🖫 ℄ ⊙ ♫ ⇨ 🛈 ⅴ
▦ 🗡 🕱 SP 🆃

Sheridan Hotel ⋔
♨♨
64 Kings Road, Brighton E.Sussex BN1 1NA
☎ Brighton (0273) 23221
Telex 877659
Elegant Victorian building on Brighton seafront, very close to Conference Centre, shops and all amenities. Fish a speciality in our up-market restaurant.
Bedrooms: 6 single, 20 double & 27 twin, 4 family rooms.
Bathrooms: 57 private.
Half board: £43-£48 daily.
Lunch available.
Evening meal 7pm (l.o. 10pm).

Credit: Access, Visa, C.Bl., Diners, Amex.
ら 🖫 ℄ ⊙ ♫ ⇨ 🛈 ⅴ ⅟
🛏 📺 ● 🎦 ◢ 🍽 ⚲ DAP 🕱
SP 🕮 🆃

Southdene Guest House
12 Madeira Pl., Brighton, BN2 1TN
☎ (0273) 683195
Friendly guesthouse 2 minutes from Palace Pier. Access to rooms all day. Resident proprietor.
Bedrooms: 1 single, 3 double & 2 twin.
Bathrooms: 2 public.
Bed & breakfast: £12-£13 single, £22-£24 double.
ら ⊙ ♫ ⇨ ⅶ ◢ 🗡 🕱

Terrace Hotel
28-29 Brunswick Ter., Hove, BN3 1HJ
☎ (0273) 820080
Fax (0273) 205200
Situated on Hove seafront, offering carvery restaurant, licensed bar and health club. All rooms en-suite with many overlooking seafront.
Bedrooms: 13 single, 19 double & 4 twin, 6 family rooms.
Bathrooms: 42 private.
Bed & breakfast: £35-£40 single, £48-£75 double.
Lunch available.
Evening meal 6.30pm (l.o. 10pm).
Credit: Access, Visa, Diners, Amex.
ら 🖫 ℄ ⊙ ♫ ⇨ ⅴ 🛏 ⅟
● 🖂 🎦 ▦ ◢ 🍽 🖬 🗡 DAP
SP 🕮 🆃

The Twenty One Hotel
21 Charlotte St., Marine Pde., Brighton, BN2 1AG
☎ (0273) 686450
Early Victorian townhouse with elegantly furnished bedrooms. Exquisite Victorian room features an 1830s four-poster. Garden suite also available.
Bedrooms: 4 double & 2 twin.
Bathrooms: 5 private, 1 public.
Bed & breakfast: £35-£50 single, £46-£68 double.
Half board: £37.50-£57 daily.
Credit: Access, Visa, Amex.
ら12 🖫 ℄ ⊙ ♫ ⇨ ⅴ 🛏
▦ ◢ 🗡 🕱 ⚲ SP 🆃

Wellington Hotel ⋔
♨♨♨
27 Waterloo Street, Hove, BN3 1AN
☎ Brighton (0273) 23171

Small, centrally-situated friendly hotel with individually decorated bedrooms. Bed, breakfast and evening dinner throughout the year. Licensed bar, conservatory lounge.
Bedrooms: 3 single, 3 double & 2 twin, 3 family rooms.
Bathrooms: 10 private; 1 private shower.
Bed & breakfast: £20-£27.50 single, £40-£55 double.
Half board: £28-£35 daily, £175-£190 weekly.
Evening meal 6pm (l.o. 6.30pm).
Credit: Access, Visa, Amex.
ら 🖫 🖀 ℄ ⊙ ♫ ⇨ ⅴ 🛏
📺 ▦ ◢ DAP 🕱 SP 🆃

Whitehaven Hotel ⋔
♨♨♨♨
34 Wilbury Rd., Hove, BN3 3JP
☎ (0273) 778355
Fax (0273) 731177
Elegant family-managed hotel with garden and easy parking, on quiet wide road near sea and shops. All bedrooms extensively equipped and with en-suite facilities.
Bedrooms: 6 single, 5 double & 4 twin, 2 family rooms.
Bathrooms: 17 private.
Bed & breakfast: £52.50-£55 single, £70-£75 double.
Lunch available.
Evening meal 7pm (l.o. 9.30pm).
Credit: Access, Visa, C.Bl., Diners, Amex.
ら8 🖫 ℄ ⊙ ♫ ⇨ 🛈 ⅴ
⅟ 🛏 ▦ ◢ 🍽 ⚲ 🗡 🕱 DAP
SP 🆃

⬛⬛⬛ BROADSTAIRS ⬛⬛⬛
Kent
Map ref 3C3

Popular seaside resort with numerous sandy bays. Charles Dickens spent his summers at Bleak House (now a museum) where he wrote parts of David Copperfield. The Dickens Festival is held in June, when many people wear Dickensian costume.
Tourist Information Centre ☎ *(0843) 68399*

The Bay Tree Hotel
♨♨♨
12 Eastern Espl., Broadstairs, CT10 1DR
☎ (0843) 62502
Continued ▶

Please mention this guide when making a booking.

BROADSTAIRS

Continued

A beautiful building overlooking the sea, close to Bleak House and the town made famous by Charles Dickens. Residential parking. Function licence for 1-20 people.
Bedrooms: 1 single, 4 double & 6 twin.
Bathrooms: 11 private, 1 public.
Bed & breakfast: £18.50-£20 single, £37-£40 double.
Half board: £26.50-£30 daily, £156-£170 weekly.
Evening meal 6pm.
Parking for 12.
Credit: Access.

Castlemere Hotel M
COMMENDED
Western Espl., Broadstairs, CT10 1TD
☎ Thanet (0843) 61566
Fax (0843) 866379
Located at the quiet end of the Western Esplanade, in its own garden, on a cliff overlooking the English Channel.
Bedrooms: 17 single, 7 double & 11 twin, 2 family rooms.
Bathrooms: 30 private, 2 public.
Bed & breakfast: £35-£38.50 single, £66-£77 double.
Half board: £47.75-£51.25 daily, £311.50-£332.50 weekly.
Lunch available.
Evening meal 7pm (l.o. 8pm).
Parking for 27.
Credit: Access, Visa.

Royal Albion Hotel and Marchesi Restaurant M
COMMENDED
Albion St., Broadstairs, CT10 1LU
☎ Thanet (0843) 68071
Telex 965761
CR Consort
The hotel, overlooking Viking Bay with its old Tudor jetty, has 2 restaurants, bar, and ample car parking.
Bedrooms: 3 single, 7 double & 7 twin, 3 family rooms.
Bathrooms: 19 private.
Bed & breakfast: £60-£65 single, £72-£75 double.
Half board: £51-£55 daily, £295-£300 weekly.
Lunch available.
Evening meal 6.30pm (l.o. 9.30pm).

Parking for 20.
Credit: Access, Visa, Diners, Amex.

Velindre Hotel M
10 Western Espl., Broadstairs, CT10 1JG
☎ Thanet (0843) 61485
On top of cliffs, overlooking the sea with fine panoramic views. Indoor heated swimming pool and leisure centre.
Bedrooms: 4 single, 5 double & 2 twin, 2 family rooms.
Bathrooms: 1 private, 1 public; 12 private showers.
Bed & breakfast: £21.46-£23.50 single, £42.92-£47 double.
Half board: £27.46-£33 daily, £192.22-£231 weekly.
Lunch available.
Evening meal 7pm (l.o. 8pm).
Parking for 6.
Credit: Access, Visa, Diners, Amex.

Westfield Lodge
Granville Avenue, Broadstairs, CT10 1PX
☎ Thanet (0843) 62615
Painting holidays with tuition from April to end September in addition to normal holidays.
Bedrooms: 4 family rooms.
Bathrooms: 1 public.
Bed & breakfast: £11.75-£12.50 single, £23.50-£25 double.
Half board: £16.75-£18.25 daily, £105-£115 weekly.
Evening meal 6pm (l.o. 6pm).

The White House Hotel M
59 Kingsgate Ave., Kingsgate, Broadstairs, CT10 3LW
☎ Thanet (0843) 63315
A small licensed hotel close to beautiful sandy Botany Bay and golf-course. Ideal for cliff walks, fishing and bathing.
Bedrooms: 1 single, 3 double & 3 twin, 1 family room.
Bathrooms: 4 private, 1 public.
Bed & breakfast: £19.60-£24.85 single, £35.20-£45.70 double.
Half board: £25.30-£30.55 daily, £149.10-£170.80 weekly.

Evening meal 6.30pm (l.o. 6pm).
Parking for 9.
Credit: Access, Visa.

CAMBERLEY

Surrey
Map ref 2C2

Well-known for the Royal Staff College and the nearby Royal Military Academy, Sandhurst, where part of the National Army Museum is open to the public.

Burwood House Hotel M
15 London Rd., Camberley, GU15 3UQ
☎ (0276) 685686
On main A30 2 miles from M3, 12 miles from Windsor and 25 minutes from Heathrow.
Bedrooms: 8 single, 7 double & 2 twin, 2 family rooms.
Bathrooms: 19 private.
Bed & breakfast: £35-£55 single, £45-£65 double.
Half board: £35.95-£67.95 daily, £285.65-£420.65 weekly.
Evening meal 7pm (l.o. 8.30pm).
Parking for 14.
Credit: Access, Visa, Diners, Amex.

CANTERBURY

Kent
Map ref 3B3

Birthplace of English Christianity and a place of pilgrimage since the martyrdom of Thomas Becket in 1170. Seat of the Primate of All England and the site of Canterbury Cathedral. Not to be missed are St. Augustine's Abbey, St. Martin's (the oldest church in England), Royal Museum and Old Weaver's House and the exciting new Pilgrim's Way attraction.
Tourist Information Centre ☎ (0227) 766567

Abba Hotel M
Station Rd West, Canterbury, CT2 8AN
☎ (0227) 464771
Fax (0233) 720758

A pleasant Victorian hotel within easy reach of the city centre. Quiet location near the West Gate, close to the railway station with easy access to London and the Kent coast.
Bedrooms: 5 single, 3 double & 6 twin, 5 family rooms.
Bathrooms: 3 private, 4 public; 1 private shower.
Bed & breakfast: £20-£24 single, £30-£40 double.
Half board: £26-£30 daily, £175-£200 weekly.
Lunch available.
Evening meal 6.30pm (l.o. 9.30pm).
Parking for 7.

Alexandra House M
Listed
1 Roper Rd., Canterbury, CT2 7EH
☎ Canterbury (0227) 767011
Small family-run guesthouse close to city centre, cathedral, university, Canterbury West station and Marlowe Theatre.
Bedrooms: 3 single, 2 double & 1 twin, 3 family rooms.
Bathrooms: 2 public; 4 private showers.
Bed & breakfast: £17-£21 single, £30-£40 double.
Parking for 6.

Anns Hotel M
Listed
63 London Rd., Canterbury, CT2 8JZ
☎ (0227) 768767
Comfortable Victorian guesthouse close to the city centre, where the family proprietors offer comfort and friendly service.
Bedrooms: 6 double & 9 twin, 4 family rooms.
Bathrooms: 11 private, 2 public; 1 private shower.
Bed & breakfast: £18-£24 single, £34-£44 double.
Parking for 20.
Credit: Access, Visa, C.Bl., Diners, Amex.

Canterbury Hotel M
COMMENDED
71 New Dover Rd., Canterbury, CT1 3DZ
☎ (0227) 450551
Telex 965809 FB CH
Pleasant hotel, 10 minutes from city centre, providing high standards of personal service and comfort.
Bedrooms: 5 single, 5 double & 13 twin, 4 family rooms.
Bathrooms: 27 private.

Bed & breakfast: from £40 single, from £58 double.
Half board: from £49 daily.
Lunch available.
Evening meal 7pm (l.o. 10pm).
Parking for 45.
Credit: Access, Visa, Diners, Amex.

Castle Court Guest House **M**
Listed

8 Castle St., Canterbury, CT1 2QF
☎ (0227) 463441
Friendly family-run guesthouse in listed Georgian building, close to cathedral, parks and restaurants, bus/railway station. Full English breakfast.
Bedrooms: 4 single, 5 double & 3 twin.
Bathrooms: 2 public.
Bed & breakfast: £15-£20 single, £30-£34 double.
Parking for 2.
Credit: Access, Visa.

Cathedral Gate Hotel **M**
Listed APPROVED

36 Burgate, Canterbury, CT1 2HA
☎ (0227) 464381
Fax (0227) 462800
Central position at main entrance to the cathedral. Car parking nearby. Baby listening service. Old world charm at reasonable prices. English breakfast extra.
Bedrooms: 6 single, 7 double & 8 twin, 4 family rooms.
Bathrooms: 12 private, 3 public; 2 private showers.
Bed & breakfast: £22-£42.50 single, £40-£64 double.
Evening meal 7pm (l.o. 9pm).
Parking for 12.
Credit: Access, Visa, Diners, Amex.

Clare-Ellen Guest House **M**
COMMENDED

9 Victoria Rd., Wincheap, Canterbury, CT1 3SG
☎ (0227) 760205
Victorian house with large elegant rooms. 10 minutes' walk to city centre. 5 minutes to station. Car park and garage available.
Bedrooms: 1 single, 2 double & 1 twin, 1 family room.
Bathrooms: 3 public.

Bed & breakfast: £15-£19 single, £30-£36 double.
Parking for 8.

Ebury Hotel **M**
COMMENDED

New Dover Rd., Canterbury, CT1 3DX
☎ (0227) 768433 Fax (0227) 459187
Family-run, Victorian hotel just outside city centre. Licensed restaurant, large public rooms and bedrooms. Heated indoor pool and spa.
Bedrooms: 2 single, 6 double & 3 twin, 4 family rooms.
Bathrooms: 15 private.
Bed & breakfast: £39-£41 single, £57.50-£62.50 double.
Half board: £33.75-£53 daily, £215-£250 weekly.
Evening meal 7pm (l.o. 8.30pm).
Parking for 21.
Credit: Access, Visa, Amex.

Ersham Lodge Hotel **M**

12 New Dover Rd., Canterbury, CT1 3AP
☎ (0227) 463174 Fax (0227) 455482
Tudor-style house close to city centre. Friendly atmosphere. Elegant public rooms and patio, comfortable well furnished bedrooms. Bar.
Bedrooms: 1 single, 3 double & 8 twin, 2 family rooms.
Bathrooms: 11 private, 1 public; 2 private showers.
Bed & breakfast: £29-£37 single, £39-£56 double.
Parking for 12.
Credit: Access, Visa, Amex.

Falstaff Hotel

St. Dunstans St. Canterbury, CT2 8AF
☎ (0227) 462138 Telex 96394
CR Lansbury
A former coaching inn dating back to the 15th C, in the heart of the town close to Westgate Towers.
Bedrooms: 9 single, 11 double & 3 twin, 1 family room.
Bathrooms: 24 private.
Bed & breakfast: from £31 single, from £62 double.
Half board: from £43 daily.
Lunch available.
Evening meal 7pm (l.o. 9.45pm).
Parking for 50.
Credit: Access, Visa, Diners, Amex.

Guildford Lodge Guest House

42 Nunnery Fields, Canterbury, CT1 3JT
☎ (0227) 462284
Small family-run guesthouse close to city centre, Canterbury East station and the cricket ground. Colour TV in all rooms. Coach parties welcome.
Bedrooms: 8 single, 4 double & 6 twin, 3 family rooms.
Bathrooms: 4 private, 3 public.
Bed & breakfast: £12-£18 single, £30-£38 double.
Half board: £16-£18 daily, £100-£130 weekly.
Lunch available.
Evening meal 6pm (l.o. 5pm).
Parking for 8.
Credit: Amex.

Highfield Hotel

Summer Hill, Harbledown, Canterbury, CT2 8NH
☎ Canterbury (0227) 462772
Victorian house in an acre of garden, 1 mile from city centre off the main London Road into Canterbury.
Bedrooms: 2 single, 3 double & 3 twin.
Bathrooms: 3 private, 2 public.
Bed & breakfast: £24-£28 single, £34-£52 double.
Parking for 12.
Credit: Access, Visa.

Leura Guest House **M**
Listed APPROVED

77 Sturry Rd., Canterbury, CT1 1BU
☎ (0227) 453959
Family-run guesthouse 10 minutes away from the city centre, cathedral and Kings School. Near the stadium, sports centre and swimming pool. Full breakfast, clean accommodation.
Bedrooms: 2 single, 1 double & 1 twin, 2 family rooms.
Bathrooms: 1 private, 1 public.
Bed & breakfast: £17-£18 single, £33-£40 double.
Half board: £24-£25 daily, £150-£166 weekly.
Evening meal 6.30pm (l.o. 10am).
Parking for 3.

Lindens Guest House
Listed COMMENDED

38b St. Dunstans St., Canterbury, CT2 8BY
☎ (0227) 462339

Victorian house offering high standard of service and cleanliness, 5 minutes' walk from city centre. Full English breakfast. Private car park at rear.
Bedrooms: 1 single, 1 double & 1 twin.
Bathrooms: 2 public.
Bed & breakfast: £12-£16 single, £24-£30 double.
Parking for 4.

Magnolia House **M**
COMMENDED

36 St. Dunstans Ter., Canterbury, CT2 8AX
☎ (0227) 765121
Georgian house in attractive city street. Close to university, gardens, river and city centre. Very quiet house within a walled garden, ideal for guests to relax in.
Bedrooms: 2 single, 3 double & 1 twin.
Bathrooms: 6 private.
Bed & breakfast: £28-£32 single, £42-£50 double.
Parking for 4.
Credit: Access, Visa, Amex.

Millers Arms Inn **M**
APPROVED

Mill Lane, Canterbury., CT21 2AA
☎ Canterbury (0227) 456057
Near the site of an old riverside mill in the historic and beautiful city of Canterbury. Fine food and hospitality, as experienced by pilgrims and visitors of all kinds for more than 1,000 years.
Bedrooms: 3 single, 5 double & 3 twin, 1 family room.
Bathrooms: 11 private, 1 public.
Bed & breakfast: £25-£30 single, £38-£50 double.
Lunch available.
Credit: Access, Visa, Diners, Amex.

Moors Head Hotel

Station Approach, Adisham, Nr. Canterbury, CT3 3JE
☎ Nonington (0304) 840935
Friendly guesthouse with licensed bar, bed and breakfast, restaurant facilities. Near station, motor racing, fishing and golf. 5 miles from Canterbury.
Bedrooms: 1 single, 3 double & 2 twin, 1 family room.
Bathrooms: 2 public.
Bed & breakfast: £23-£35 single, £33-£45 double.

Continued ▶

CANTERBURY

Continued

Lunch available.
Evening meal 6pm (l.o. 11pm).
Parking for 30.
♨ ♋ ✕ ♨ ♿ Ⓥ ✂ ℡ ▥ ♨
♩ ♦ ✝ ✿ ✕ ⓭ ⅏ ⎵ ℻

The Old Coach House ♔
[♛♛♛ APPROVED]
Dover Road, (A2) Barham,
Canterbury, CT4 6SA
☎ (0227) 831218 Fax (0227) 831932
On A2 midway between Canterbury and Dover. French spoken. Convenient for ferries and Lydden Circuit. Brasserie and a la carte French restaurant.
Bedrooms: 2 double & 3 twin.
Bathrooms: 5 private.
Bed & breakfast: £38.75-£40.75 single, £47.50-£51.50 double.
Half board: £48.75-£55 daily.
Lunch available.
Evening meal 7pm (l.o. 9pm).
Parking for 80.
Credit: Access, Diners.
♨ ☐ ♨ ⅁ Ⓥ ✂ ℡ ▥ ⎵
♩ Ⓤ ✿ ✕ ℻

Pointers Hotel ♔
[♛♛♛ COMMENDED]
1 London Rd., Canterbury,
CT2 8LR
☎ (0227) 456846
Family-run Georgian hotel close to city centre, cathedral and university.
Bedrooms: 2 single, 8 double & 2 twin, 2 family rooms.
Bathrooms: 8 private,
2 public; 2 private showers.
Bed & breakfast: £30-£38 single, £42-£54 double.
Half board: £23.50-£50 daily, £203-£252 weekly.
Evening meal 7.30pm (l.o. 8.30pm).
Parking for 10.
Credit: Access, Visa, Diners, Amex.
♨ ☐ ℡ ♨ ⅏ ✂ ◐ ▥
⎵ ▸ ⅏ ℻

St. Stephens Guest House ♔
100 St. Stephens Rd.,
Canterbury, CT2 7JL
☎ (0227) 767644
Mock-Tudor house set in attractive garden within easy walking distance of the city centre and cathedral. Colour TV in rooms. Car park.
Bedrooms: 3 single, 6 double & 1 twin.
Bathrooms: 1 private,
2 public.

Bed & breakfast: £15.40-£26 single, £30.80-£36 double.
Half board: £21.40-£32 daily.
Evening meal 7pm (l.o. 11am).
Parking for 8.
Credit: Access, Visa, Amex.
♨ ⅁ Ⓤ ⅏ Ⓥ ✂ ℡ ▥ ⎵
✿ ✕

Slatters Hotel
[♛♛♛♛]
St. Margaret St., Canterbury,
CT1 2TR
☎ (0227) 463271
Fax (0227) 764117
⅏ Queens Moat Houses
Comfortable, modern accommodation in ancient building, part Tudor, part Queen Anne with Roman remains. 200 yards from cathedral.
Bedrooms: 8 single, 9 double & 9 twin, 5 family rooms.
Bathrooms: 28 private,
1 public.
Bed & breakfast: £59-£66 single, £69-£76 double.
Half board: £39-£45 daily.
Lunch available.
Evening meal 6.30pm (l.o. 9.15pm).
Parking for 18.
Credit: Access, Visa, Diners, Amex.
♨ ℡ ⅁ ☐ ♨ ⅏ ▮ Ⓥ ◐ ⊞
▥ ⎵ ▸ ✕ ⅏ ℻ ⊤

Thanington Hotel ♔
[♛♛ COMMENDED]
140 Wincheap, Canterbury,
CT1 3RY
☎ (0227) 453227
Bed and breakfast in style, bedrooms with all facilities. 5 minutes' walk to city centre. Private car parking. Colour brochure available.
Bedrooms: 5 double & 3 twin,
2 family rooms.
Bathrooms: 10 private.
Bed & breakfast: £38-£45 single, £55-£63 double.
Parking for 12.
Credit: Access, Visa.
♨ ℡ ⅁ ☐ ♨ ⅏ Ⓤ ✂ ℡
▥ ⎵ ✕ ℻ ⅏ ℻

Tudor House
6 Best Lane., Canterbury,
CT1 2JB
☎ Canterbury (0227) 65650
A comfortable family-run bed and breakfast establishment in the town centre. Near cathedral. Boats available for hire.
Bedrooms: 1 single, 1 double,
1 family room.
Bathrooms: 2 public.

Bed & breakfast: £15-£18 single, £28-£34 double.
Parking for 1.
♨ ⅉ10 ☐ ♨ ⅏ ⅏ Ⓥ ▥ ✕
✕ ℻

Victoria Hotel ♔
[♛♛♛ APPROVED]
59 London Rd., Canterbury,
CT2 8JY
☎ (0227) 459333
10 minutes' walk or 3 minutes' drive from the city centre, offering personal service in a friendly, informal atmosphere.
Bedrooms: 10 single, 6 double & 14 twin, 4 family rooms.
Bathrooms: 34 private.
Bed & breakfast: £44-£56 single, £73 double.
Lunch available.
Evening meal 6pm (l.o. 10.30pm).
Parking for 50.
Credit: Access, Visa, Diners, Amex.
♨ ♨ ℡ ⅁ ☐ ♨ ▮ Ⓥ ✂
◐ ▥ ⎵ ♩ ✿ ✕ ⅏ ℻

The White House ♔
[♛♛]
6, St.Peters Lane,
Canterbury, CT1 2BP
☎ Canterbury (0227) 761836
Regency house situated within the city walls next to the Marlowe Theatre. Superior family-run accommodation with all rooms en-suite.
Bedrooms: 1 double & 1 twin,
1 family room.
Bathrooms: 3 private.
Bed & breakfast: £25-£30 single, £35-£40 double.
♨ ☐ ♨ ⅏ Ⓤ Ⓥ ✂ ♨ ◐ ▥
⎵ ✕ ℻ ⅏ ℻ ⅏ ℻

Yorke Lodge ♔
[♛♛ COMMENDED]
50 London Rd., Canterbury,
CT2 8LF
☎ (0227) 451243
Fax (0227) 451243
Spacious, elegant Victorian house, close to city centre. Relax and enjoy a special bed and breakfast.
Bedrooms: 1 single, 1 double & 1 twin, 3 family rooms.
Bathrooms: 6 private.
Bed & breakfast: £18-£30 single, £35-£45 double.
Parking for 6.
Credit: Access, Visa, Amex.
♨ ℡ ⅁ ☐ ♨ ⅏ Ⓤ Ⓥ ✂ ♨
℡ ▥ ⎵ ♩ ✕ ⅏ ℻ ⊤

CHARLWOOD

Surrey
Map ref 2D2

*5m S. Reigate
Small old village with ancient church, near Gatwick Airport. Close by are Gatwick Zoo and Aviaries.*

Stanhill Court Hotel ♔
[♛♛♛♛ APPROVED]
Stanhill Rd., Charlwood, Nr.
Horley, RH6 0EP
☎ (0293) 862166
Telex 878322
Fax (0293) 862773
Victorian country house run as hotel/reception centre with country club facilities. 35-acre grounds with clay shooting, fishing ponds, native pasture, ancient woodland, open-air theatre, Victorian walled garden. Billiard room. Courtesy transport and term car parking for Gatwick.
Bedrooms: 1 single, 5 double & 3 twin, 2 family rooms.
Bathrooms: 10 private.
Bed & breakfast: £52.95-£75.95 single, £55.90-£112.90 double.
Half board: £42.90-£71.35 daily.
Lunch available.
Evening meal 7pm (l.o. 10.30pm).
Parking for 75.
Credit: Access, Visa, Diners, Amex.
♨ ♨ ℡ ⅁ ☐ ♨ ⅏ ▮ Ⓥ
℡ ▥ ⎵ ♩ ♨ Ⓤ ♩ ✎ ✿
✕ ⅏ ℻ ⊤

CHATHAM

Kent
Map ref 3B3

One of the Medway Towns. Famous for its naval depots and dockyards in which many famous ships were built, notably Nelson's 'Victory'.

Holmwood Hotel
158, Maidstone Road,
Chatham, ME4 6EN
☎ Medway (0634) 842849
Quiet converted 1900s house with large established terraced garden with lawns and crazy paving. Under personal supervision. Most rooms en-suite. Facilities for the less severely disabled.
Bedrooms: 9 single, 4 twin.
Bathrooms: 8 private,
1 public; 4 private showers.
Bed & breakfast: £22-£25 single, £36-£40 double.
Lunch available.

Map references apply to the colour maps towards the end of this guide.

Evening meal 6pm (l.o. 9pm).
Parking for 15.
Credit: Access, Visa.

Credit: Access, Visa, Diners,
Amex.

Unique "medieval manor" in 23 acres of idyllic parkland by the beach. Well-appointed bedrooms.
Bedrooms: 2 single,
11 double.
Bathrooms: 13 private.
Bed & breakfast: £65-£85 single, £95-£180 double.
Half board: £90-£120 daily.
Lunch available.
Evening meal 7.30pm (l.o. 10pm).
Parking for 50.
Credit: Access, Visa, Diners, Amex.

Set in 27 acres of gardens and woodland, a choice location for both business and pleasure. On the A3, 1 mile from the M25.
Bedrooms: 88 double &
46 twin, 18 family rooms.
Bathrooms: 152 private.
Bed & breakfast: £52-£101 single, £102-£150 double.
Half board: £65-£85 daily.
Lunch available.
Evening meal 7pm (l.o. 10pm).
Parking for 200.
Credit: Access, Visa, Diners, Amex.

CHICHESTER

W. Sussex
Map ref 2C3

The county town of West Sussex with a beautiful Norman cathedral lying beneath the South Downs. Noted for its Georgian architecture but also has modern buildings like the Festival Theatre. Surrounded by places of interest, including Fishbourne Roman Palace and Weald and Downland Open-Air Museum.
Tourist Information Centre ☎ (0243) 775888

Ship Hotel M

North St., Chichester,
PO19 1NH
☎ Chichester (0243) 782028
Fax (0243) 774254
18th C Georgian hotel in the city centre. Festival Theatre and cathedral 400 yards from hotel. Extensively refurbished in period style.
Bedrooms: 12 single,
12 double & 9 twin, 4 family rooms.
Bathrooms: 33 private.
Bed & breakfast: £44-£84 single, £88-£168 double.
Half board: £55-£106 daily, £350-£700 weekly.
Lunch available.
Evening meal 7.30pm (l.o. 9.30pm).
Parking for 38.
Credit: Access, Visa, Diners.

Crouchers Bottom Country Hotel M
COMMENDED

Birdham Road, Apuldram,
Chichester PO20 7EH
☎ Chichester (0243) 784995
Fax (0243) 539797
Quiet small country hotel, close to Chichester Harbour and only 2 miles south of Chichester. Log fire in lounge. New garden restaurant opened 1991.
Bedrooms: 3 double & 3 twin.
Bathrooms: 6 private.
Bed & breakfast: £46-£51 single, £58-£85 double.
Half board: £45-£60 daily.
Evening meal 6.30pm (l.o. 9pm).
Parking for 8.
Credit: Access, Visa.

Suffolk House Hotel
COMMENDED

3 East Row, Chichester,
PO19 1PD
☎ (0243) 778899 & 778924
Fax (0243) 787282
Conveniently situated in the heart of the city, perfect venue for all social and business occasions. Ideal base for visiting a variety of commercial and historical interests.
Bedrooms: 4 single, 5 double & 1 twin, 1 family room.
Bathrooms: 11 private.
Bed & breakfast: £56.50-£60 single, £79-£84 double.
Evening meal 6.30pm (l.o. 9.30pm).
Parking for 6.
Credit: Access, Visa, Amex.

The Inglenook Hotel & Restaurant M
COMMENDED

255 Pagham Rd., Nyetimber,
Pagham, PO21 3QB
☎ (0243) 262495 & 265411 &
Fax (0243) 262668
Family-run business, with oak beams and log fires, 1 mile from the sea. Large gardens, pleasant bar, and restaurant with seafood specialities.
Bedrooms: 1 single, 11 double & 6 twin, 2 family rooms.
Bathrooms: 20 private.
Bed & breakfast: £47.50-£60 single, £70-£150 double.
Half board: £55-£67.50 daily, £210-£250 weekly.
Lunch available.
Evening meal 6pm (l.o. 10pm).
Parking for 38.

CLIMPING

W. Sussex
Map ref 2D3

Village, 1 mile from the sea on the Arun Estuary, with attractive 12th/13th C church.

Bailiffscourt Hotel M

Climping, BN17 5RW
☎ Littlehampton
(0903) 723511 Telex 877870
BLFSCT G

COBHAM

Kent
Map ref 3B3

4m SE. Gravesend

Ye Olde Leather Bottle M
APPROVED

The Street, Cobham, Nr. Gravesend, DA12 3BZ
☎ Meopham (0474) 814327
Built in 1629, this residential inn is famous for its character and charm, history and associations with Charles Dickens and, most importantly, its splendid hospitality.
Bedrooms: 2 single, 4 double & 1 twin.
Bathrooms: 2 private,
2 public.
Bed & breakfast: £37-£43 single, £54-£72 double.
Lunch available.
Evening meal 7pm (l.o. 10pm).
Parking for 52.
Credit: Access, Visa, Diners, Amex.

COBHAM

Surrey
Map ref 2D2

Village in 2 parts, Street Cobham on the A3 Portsmouth Road and Church Cobham with the restored Norman church of St. Andrew and a 19th C mill.

Hilton National M

Seven Hills Road South,
Cobham, KT11 1EW
☎ (0932) 864471
Telex 929196
⊕ Hilton

COPTHORNE

W. Sussex
Map ref 2D2

3m NE. Crawley
Residential village on the Surrey/West Sussex border, near Crawley and within easy reach of Gatwick Airport.

The Copthorne London Gatwick M
COMMENDED

Copthorne Rd., Copthorne,
RH10 3PG
☎ (0342) 714971 Telex 95500
Country house hotel, in over 100 acres of Sussex countryside, within easy reach of Gatwick Airport. Courtesy bus service. Squash club on site.
Bedrooms: 136 double & 75 twin, 16 family rooms.
Bathrooms: 227 private.
Bed & breakfast: £106.95-£126.95 single, £116.95-£207.95 double.
Half board: £121.95-£141.95 daily.
Lunch available.
Evening meal 7pm (l.o. 9.30pm).
Parking for 300.
Credit: Access, Visa, C.Bl., Diners, Amex.

The national Crown scheme is explained in full on pages 536 – 539.

We advise you to confirm your booking in writing.

CRANBROOK

Kent
Map ref 3B4

Old town, a centre for the weaving industry in the 15th C. The 72-ft-high Union Mill is a 3-storeyed windmill, still in working order.

Hartley Mount Hotel M

😊😊😊😊 COMMENDED

Hartley Rd., Cranbrook, TN17 3QX
☎ (0580) 712230 & 713099
Fax 0580 712588
Edwardian country house hotel with licensed restaurant on the A229. Set in 2-acre garden with glorious views of the Weald. Resident proprietors.
Bedrooms: 1 single, 2 double & 1 twin, 1 family room.
Bathrooms: 5 private.
Bed & breakfast: £50-£55 single, £70-£98 double.
Lunch available.
Evening meal 8pm (l.o. 9.30pm).
Parking for 22.
Credit: Access, Visa.

🛇 🖭 📞 🖵 🕏 🕹 Ⓥ 🕱
🛏 🎟 🛋 🍽 🐾 🕭 ☀ 🗙
🏮 SP Ⓣ

CRAWLEY

W. Sussex
Map ref 2D2

One of the first New Towns built after World War II, but it also has some old buildings. Set in magnificent wooded countryside.

Gatwick Manor Hotel M

😊😊😊 APPROVED

London Rd., Lowfield Heath (Gatwick), Crawley, RH10 2ST
☎ (0293) 26301 & 35251
Telex 87529 Fax (0293) 513077
Modern, comfortable accommodation in the old world garden setting of a 13th C manor house which also incorporates a 15th C great hall and a 16th C tithe barn. Situated halfway between London and Brighton, with easy access to Gatwick Airport.
Bedrooms: 7 double & 20 twin, 3 family rooms.
Bathrooms: 30 private.
Bed & breakfast: from £73 single, from £81 double.
Lunch available.
Evening meal 6pm (l.o. 10.30pm).

Parking for 250.
Credit: Access, Visa, Diners, Amex.

🛇 🖭 📞 🖵 🕏 Ⓥ 🕭 🗙
Ⓣ Ⓥ 🎟 🛋 🍽 🕹 ☀ 🗙 SP
🏮

Little Foxes Guest House

😊😊 COMMENDED

Ifield Rd., Ifield Wood, Crawley, RH11 0JY
☎ (0293) 552430
Bungalow in 5 acres of grounds. 10 minutes from Gatwick Airport. 14 days' parking, courtesy transport and breakfast included in price.
Bedrooms: 1 single, 7 double & 3 twin, 2 family rooms.
Bathrooms: 13 private.
Bed & breakfast: £48-£55 single, £59-£69 double.
Parking for 50.
Credit: Access, Visa, Amex.

🛇 🖭 🖵 🕏 Ⓤ ● 🎟 🛋 ∪
☀ 🐾 🗙 Ⓣ

CROWBOROUGH

E. Sussex
Map ref 2D2

Pleasant, residential town standing on the highest ridge of the Ashdown Forest.

Winston Manor Hotel

Beacon Rd., Crowborough, TN6 1AD
☎ (0892) 652772 Fax (0892) 665537
On A26 road, 7 miles from Tunbridge Wells. Ideal for conferences, wedding receptions, private parties. Short or long stay. Leisure complex including indoor pool and coffee shop.
Bedrooms: 10 single, 29 double & 8 twin, 3 family rooms.
Bathrooms: 50 private.
Bed & breakfast: £35-£61.50 single, £60-£88 double.
Half board: from £50 daily.
Lunch available.
Evening meal 7.30pm (l.o. 9.30pm).
Parking for 120.
Credit: Access, Visa, Diners, Amex.

🛇 📞 🖵 🕏 🕹 Ⓥ 🕭 ● 🖃
🎟 🛋 🍽 🕏 🐾 🕭 🕭 SP 🏮
Ⓣ

CUCKFIELD

W. Sussex
Map ref 2D3

The High Street is lined with Elizabethan and Georgian shops, inns and houses and was once part of the London to Brighton coach road. Nearby Nymans (National Trust) is a 30-acre garden with fine topiary work.

Hilton Park Hotel M

😊😊😊😊

Cuckfield, Nr. Haywards Heath, RH17 5EG
☎ Haywards Heath (0444) 455555
Quiet country house hotel in own 3 acre grounds with panoramic views of South Downs.
Bedrooms: 2 single, 3 double & 3 twin, 4 family rooms.
Bathrooms: 10 private, 3 public.
Bed & breakfast: £48-£52 single, £66-£72 double.
Half board: £45-£68 daily.
Lunch available.
Evening meal 7pm (l.o. 8pm).
Parking for 52.
Credit: Access, Visa, Diners, Amex.

🛇 🖭 📞 🖭 🕏 🕹 🍴 🗙 🖃
Ⓥ 🎟 🛋 🍽 ☀ 🐾 🕭 SP
Ⓣ

Kings Head

😊😊

South St., Cuckfield, RH17 5JY
☎ Haywards Heath (0444) 454006
Busy family inn offering "real ale, real food (no chips) with real people". Jeremys restaurant available Tuesday - Friday.
Bedrooms: 2 double & 5 twin, 2 family rooms.
Bathrooms: 8 private, 1 public.
Bed & breakfast: £42 single, £55 double.
Half board: £47-£67 daily.
Evening meal 7pm (l.o. 10pm).
Parking for 7.
Credit: Access, Visa, Diners, Amex.

🛇 📞 🖵 🕏 🍴 Ⓥ 🎟 🛋 🕭
SP 🏮

DEAL

Kent
Map ref 3C4

Coastal town and popular holiday resort. Deal Castle was built by Henry VIII as a fort and the museum is devoted to finds excavated in the area. Also the Time-ball Tower Museum. Angling available from both beach and pier.
Tourist Information Centre ☎ (0304) 369576

Beachbrow Hotel

Beach St., Deal, CT14 6HY
☎ (0304) 374338 & 373159
Listed Georgian building of historic interest, overlooking pier and beach. Interesting nautical paintings and prints. Ideal for holiday breaks and for golfers.
Bedrooms: 7 single, 9 double & 6 twin, 3 family rooms.
Bathrooms: 6 private, 5 public; 2 private showers.
Bed & breakfast: £18-£28 single, £28-£42 double.
Half board: £27.50-£37.50 daily, £165-£225 weekly.
Evening meal 7pm (l.o. 9pm).
Credit: Access, Visa, Diners, Amex.

🛇 🖵 🍴 Ⓥ 🗙 🖃 Ⓣ 🍴 ᴅᴀᴘ
SP 🏮

Camden Cottage Guest House

Listed

47 Kingsdown Road, Walmer, Deal, CT14 8BL
☎ (0304) 361906
Delightful family-run guesthouse, a minute's walk from the beach and close to the village of Kingsdown.
Bedrooms: 2 single, 1 double & 1 twin.
Bathrooms: 2 public.
Bed & breakfast: £20 single, £40 double.
Half board: £28 daily, £196 weekly.
Lunch available.
Evening meal 6pm (l.o. 9pm).
Parking for 3.
Credit: Access, Visa.

🛇 🔏 Ⓤ 🍴 🖃 Ⓣ 🎟 🛋 🗙
🏮 ᴅᴀᴘ

Cannongate Guest House

Listed APPROVED

26 Gilford Rd., Deal, CT14 7DJ
☎ (0304) 375238
The house is situated in historic Deal and is only 2 minutes from the castle, shops, sea and boats.

Individual proprietors have supplied all details of accommodation. Although we do check for accuracy, we advise you to confirm prices and other information at the time of booking.

Bedrooms: 1 single, 2 double & 1 twin, 1 family room.
Bathrooms: 2 public.
Bed & breakfast: £12.50 single, £25 double.
Half board: £19.50 daily, £130 weekly.
Evening meal 6pm (l.o. 11am).
Parking for 1.
🕭🖵♿ⓊⓁ 📱 Ⓥ 💤 ⓉⓋ 🎗 ♨ 🚗 🐾 SP

Finglesham Grange M
🏅🏅🏅 COMMENDED
Finglesham, Nr. Deal,
CT14 0NQ
☎ Sandwich (0304) 611314
Georgian country house in 4.5 acres of secluded grounds situated outside village just 4 miles from Deal and Sandwich.
Bedrooms: 1 double & 2 twin.
Bathrooms: 3 private.
Bed & breakfast: £20-£25 single, £40 double.
Half board: £27-£30 daily.
Evening meal 7pm (l.o. 5pm).
Parking for 5.
ⓊⓁ 📱 🎗 ♨ ⓉⓋ 🚗 ❄ 🐾 🎋

Guildford House Hotel M
49 Beach St., Deal,
CT14 6HY
☎ (0304) 375015
Family-run seafront hotel with private bar, close to shopping centre, golf-courses and local historic sights.
Bedrooms: 2 single, 7 twin, 2 family rooms.
Bathrooms: 1 public; 7 private showers.
Bed & breakfast: £18-£24 single, £36-£46 double.
Half board: £23-£27 daily, £150-£175 weekly.
Lunch available.
Evening meal 7pm (l.o. 9pm).
Credit: Access, Visa.
🕭🖵♿ 📱 Ⓥ ♨ ⓉⓋ 🚗 ⏃ 🎋 🐾 SP 🎋

Hardicot Guest House M
🏅🏅 COMMENDED
Kingsdown Rd., Walmer,
Deal, CT14 8AW
☎ (0304) 373867
Large, quiet, detached Victorian house with Channel views and secluded garden. Ideal for sea fishing, cliff walks and golfing.
Bedrooms: 1 double & 1 twin, 1 family room.
Bathrooms: 1 public; 1 private shower.
Bed & breakfast: £17-£20 single, £34-£40 double.
Parking for 3.
🕭5♿ ⓊⓁ 📱 Ⓥ ♨ ⓉⓋ 🎗 🚗 ❄ 🐾 🎋

Sutherland House Private Hotel M
🏅🏅 COMMENDED
186 London Rd., Deal,
CT14 9PT
☎ Deal (0304) 362853
Semi-detached Edwardian house, retaining its character and with decor of the period, in a quiet residential area on the A258 Deal - Sandwich road. Licensed restaurant. Golf nearby.
Bedrooms: 2 double & 5 twin, 1 family room.
Bathrooms: 2 private; 4 private showers.
Bed & breakfast: £26.95-£36 single, £39 double.
Half board: £33.50-£41 daily.
Evening meal 7.30pm (l.o. 3pm).
Parking for 17.
Credit: Access, Visa, Diners, Amex.
🕭3♿🖵♨ 📱 Ⓥ 🎗 ♨ 🎗 🚗 🏋 ❄ 🎋 SP

DORKING
Surrey
Map ref 2D2

Ancient market town and a good centre for walking, delightfully set between Box Hill and the Downs.

Torridon Guest House
Longfield Road, Dorking,
RH4 3DF
☎ (0306) 883724
Fax (0306) 880759
Chalet bungalow in quiet location with garden adjacent to extensive woodland. 10 minutes' walk to town and bus route.
Bedrooms: 1 double & 1 twin.
Bathrooms: 1 public; 1 private shower.
Bed & breakfast: £20 single, £30-£36 double.
Half board: £21-£29 daily.
Evening meal 7pm (l.o. 9pm).
Parking for 4.
🕭🖵❄♿🖵♨ ⓊⓁ 📱 Ⓥ 🎗 ⓉⓋ 🎗 🚗 ❄ 🎋

Half board prices shown are per person but in some cases may be based on double/twin occupancy.

Please check prices and other details at the time of booking.

DOVER
Kent
Map ref 3C4

Once a Cinque Port, now the busiest passenger port in the world. Still a historic town and seaside resort beside the famous White Cliffs. Numerous buildings trace the town's history from the new 'White Cliffs Experience' attraction to the Roman Painted House and lighthouse, Saxon church, Norman castle, 13th C Maison Dieu and adjacent Victorian "Old Town Gaol".
Tourist Information Centre ☎ *(0304) 205108*

Ardmore Private Hotel M
🏅🏅
18 Castle Hill Rd., Dover,
CT16 1QW
☎ (0304) 205895
Situated in the lee of Dover Castle. Near sports complex and ruins of Saxon church. Views of harbour and town.
Bedrooms: 2 double & 1 twin, 1 family room.
Bathrooms: 4 private.
Bed & breakfast: £26-£45 double.
Parking for 1.
🕭🖵♿ⓊⓁ Ⓥ 🎗 ♨ 🎗 🎋 SP 🎋

Beaufort House
🏅🏅 APPROVED
18 East Cliff, Dover,
CT16 1LU
☎ (0304) 216444
Fax (0304) 211100
Listed Regency building on Marine Parade below the castle. 150 yards from ferry terminals with exciting harbour views.
Bedrooms: 3 single, 8 double & 9 twin, 6 family rooms.
Bathrooms: 26 private, 2 public.
Bed & breakfast: £29-£38 single, £35-£52 double.
Evening meal 6.30pm (l.o. 9.30pm).
Parking for 25.
Credit: Access, Visa, C.Bl.
🕭♿📞🖵♨ 📱 Ⓥ 🎗 ⓉⓋ ♨ ♨ 🚗 🏋 ℂ SP 🎋 🎋

Conifers Guest House M
🏅🏅
241 Folkestone Rd., Dover,
CT17 9LL
☎ (0304) 205609

Small family-run guesthouse, 5 minutes from seafront and docks. Reduced rates for children sharing parents' bedroom. Early breakfast available.
Bedrooms: 1 single, 1 twin, 4 family rooms.
Bathrooms: 1 private, 2 public.
Bed & breakfast: £13-£16 single, £24-£30 double.
Half board: £22-£25 daily.
Evening meal 7pm (l.o. 6pm).
Parking for 5.
🕭3🖵♿ⓊⓁ 🎗 ⓉⓋ 🎗 🚗 ❄ 🎋

Dell Guest House
🏅🏅
233 Folkestone Rd., Dover,
CT17 9SL
☎ (0304) 202422
Victorian house with modern facilities. Convenient for Dover Priory railway station, docks and hoverport. Ideal overnight stay for the continental traveller.
Bedrooms: 2 single, 1 double & 1 twin, 2 family rooms.
Bathrooms: 2 public.
Bed & breakfast: £15-£17 single, £24-£28 double.
Parking for 6.
🕭🖵♿ⓊⓁ 🎗 ♨ 🚗 ❄ 🎋 SP

Dover Moat House M
🏅🏅🏅 COMMENDED
Townwall St., Dover,
CT16 1SZ
☎ (0304) 203270 Telex 96458
ⒼⒹ Queens Moat Houses
Close to ferry and hovercraft terminals, within easy reach of town centre, seafront, castle and heritage centre.
Bedrooms: 17 single, 30 double & 32 twin.
Bathrooms: 79 private.
Bed & breakfast: £80.70-£89 single, £99.40-£109 double.
Lunch available.
Evening meal 7pm (l.o. 9.15pm).
Parking for 8.
Credit: Access, Visa, Diners, Amex.
🕭♿📞⌖🖵♨ 📱 Ⓥ 🎗 ♨ ● 🎗 🚗 🏋 & ℂ SP Ⓣ

Elmo Guest House M
🏅🏅
120 Folkestone Rd., Dover,
CT17 9SP
☎ (0304) 206236
Conveniently situated for ferries and Hoverport terminals and within easy reach of the town centre and railway station; overnight stops our speciality.
Bedrooms: 1 single, 2 double, 2 family rooms.
Continued ▶

DOVER
Continued

Bathrooms: 2 public.
Bed & breakfast: £14-£16
single, £24-£26 double.
Half board: £30-£34 daily.
Evening meal 6.30pm (l.o.
9pm).
Parking for 8.

Gateway Hovertel M
♛♛

Snargate St., Dover,
CT16 9BZ
☎ (0304) 205479
*Town motel blended with
century-old hotel, close to
Hoverport, shops, restaurants,
heritage centre and both ferry
terminals. Stay 2 days and
save £10.*
Bedrooms: 1 single, 7 double
& 12 twin, 7 family rooms.
Bathrooms: 27 private.
Bed & breakfast: £25-£30
single, £40-£45 double.
Evening meal 5pm (l.o. 7pm).
Parking for 28.
Credit: Access, Visa.

Gordon Guest House M
♛

23 Castle St., Dover,
CT16 1PT
☎ (0304) 201894
*A friendly welcome at this
family guesthouse, near ferries,
shops and restaurants. Budget
breaks in low season.*
Bedrooms: 2 double & 2 twin,
2 family rooms.
Bathrooms: 2 public;
4 private showers.
Bed & breakfast: £16-£26
single, £24-£34 double.

Gordon House Hotel

30-32 East Cliff, Dover,
CT16 1LU
☎ (0304) 204459
*Under the "White Cliffs of
Dover" the hotel overlooks the
harbour and is just 2 minutes
from the car ferry and
Hoverport terminals. Well
placed for cliff walks and
visiting the castle and town.*
Bedrooms: 8 single, 7 double
& 4 twin, 2 family rooms.
Bathrooms: 10 private,
4 public.
Bed & breakfast: £18-£25
single, £32-£40 double.
Lunch available.
Evening meal 7pm (l.o. 9pm).
Parking for 5.

Loddington House
Hotel M

14 East Cliff, Dover,
CT16 1LX
☎ (0304) 201947
*Small family-run Regency-
style hotel with panoramic
views over harbour and
Channel, 200 yards from ferry
terminal.*
Bedrooms: 1 single, 2 double
& 2 twin, 1 family room.
Bathrooms: 4 private,
1 public.
Bed & breakfast: £25-£28
single, £40-£50 double.
Evening meal 7.30pm (l.o.
8.30pm).

Longfield Guest House

203 Folkestone Rd., Dover,
CT17 9SL
☎ (0304) 204716
*Large detached guesthouse
close to station and docks.
Suitable for ferry travellers.
Residents' lounge bar with
snacks available. Car park and
garage.*
Bedrooms: 5 single, 1 double
& 2 twin, 2 family rooms.
Bathrooms: 2 public.
Bed & breakfast: £14-£16
single, £26-£29 double.
Evening meal 6pm (l.o. 9pm).
Parking for 9.
Open January-November.

Maison Dieu Guest
House

Listed APPROVED

89 Maison Dieu Road,
Dover, CT16 1RU
☎ (0304) 204033
*Owner's home where guests are
warmly welcome. Close to town
centre, rail and bus terminals
and 5 minutes from all docks.*
Bedrooms: 2 single, 1 double
& 1 twin, 3 family rooms.
Bathrooms: 2 public.
Bed & breakfast: £18 single,
£24-£30 double.
Half board: £18-£24 daily.
Evening meal 6pm (l.o.
8.30pm).
Parking for 7.
Credit: Access, Visa.

Mildmay Hotel M
♛♛♛

Folkestone Rd., Dover,
CT17 9SF
☎ (0304) 204278
*On the A20 Dover to London
road, 2 minutes from the town
centre and close to car ferry,
hoverport terminals and Dover
Priory railway station.*

Bedrooms: 2 single, 6 double
& 10 twin, 4 family rooms.
Bathrooms: 22 private.
Bed & breakfast: £32-£40
single, £40-£50 double.
Lunch available.
Evening meal 7pm (l.o. 9pm).
Parking for 32.
Open February-December.
Credit: Access, Visa, Diners,
Amex.

The Norman Guest
House

Listed

75 Folkestone Rd., Dover,
CT17 9RZ
☎ (0304) 207803
*Opposite Dover Priory railway
station and close to shops,
ferries, hovercraft ports and all
amenities.*
Bedrooms: 1 single, 2 double
& 2 twin, 3 family rooms.
Bathrooms: 2 public.
Bed & breakfast: £10-£13
single, £20-£26 double.
Evening meal 7.30pm (l.o.
8.30pm).
Parking for 6.

Pennyfarthing
♛♛♛

109 Maison Dieu Rd., Dover,
CT16 1RT
☎ (0304) 205563
*2 minutes from ferry and
hovercraft. Close to centre of
town, restaurants and long-
term parking. Ideal for
overnight or short stays.*
Bedrooms: 1 single, 2 double
& 1 twin, 2 family rooms.
Bathrooms: 4 private;
2 private showers.
Bed & breakfast: £16-£18
single, £28-£35 double.
Parking for 6.

St. Brelades Guest
House M

♛♛ APPROVED

80-82 Buckland Ave., Dover,
CT16 2NW
☎ (0304) 206126
*Attractive, friendly guesthouse
minutes from docks. Full
breakfast service from 7.00am
to 9.00 am. Residents' bar and
evening meals available. Secure
off-street parking.*
Bedrooms: 1 single, 2 double
& 1 twin, 4 family rooms.
Bathrooms: 2 public;
2 private showers.
Bed & breakfast: £12-£19
single, £24-£34 double.
Half board: £18.50-£27.50
daily.

Evening meal 6pm (l.o. 8pm).
Parking for 7.
Credit: Access, Visa.

St. Margaret's Hotel
♛♛♛

Reach Rd., St. Margarets-at-
Cliffe, Nr. Dover, CT15 6AE
☎ (0304) 853262
*Just 5 minutes from the end of
the A2. Take A258 and follow
signs to St.Margaret's. Hotel
has health club, 2 indoor pools,
restaurant. Just 10 minutes
away from the mainline station,
ferryport and hoverport.*
Bedrooms: 12 double &
8 twin, 4 family rooms.
Bathrooms: 24 private.
Bed & breakfast: £36-£38
single, £48-£58 double.
Lunch available.
Evening meal 7pm (l.o.
9.30pm).
Parking for 100.
Credit: Access, Visa.

St. Martins Guest
House M

♛♛

17 Castle Hill Rd., Dover,
CT16 1QW
☎ (0304) 205938
*Situated in the lee of Dover
Castle, rear of sports complex
and ruins of Saxon church,
with views of harbour and
town.*
Bedrooms: 1 single, 4 double
& 3 twin, 1 family room.
Bathrooms: 1 public;
7 private showers.
Bed & breakfast: £20-£25
single, £20-£40 double.
Parking for 1.
Credit: Access.

Sharon Guest House

100-102 Folkestone Rd.,
Dover, CT17 9SP
☎ (0304) 204373
*Christian family-run
guesthouse convenient for
docks, railway station and
town centre. Established 1966.*
Bedrooms: 2 single, 3 double
& 3 twin, 3 family rooms.
Bathrooms: 2 public.
Bed & breakfast: £10-£13
single, £20-£26 double.
Parking for 10.

Tower Guest House

♛♛ COMMENDED

98 Priory Hill, Dover,
CT17 0AD
☎ (0304) 208212

Converted water tower in quiet surroundings. Most rooms with private bathrooms. 6 minutes' drive to docks. Lock-up garages available.
Bedrooms: 1 double & 2 twin, 2 family rooms.
Bathrooms: 3 private, 1 public.
Bed & breakfast: £28-£35 double.
Parking for 2.

Walletts Court Hotel and Restaurant M
😔😔😔 **COMMENDED**
West-Cliffe, St. Margaret's at Cliffe, Dover, CT15 6EW
☎ (0304) 852424
Restored 17th C manor and barn with inglenook fireplaces. Ideal for history enthusiasts. In rural setting, 3 miles from Dover. Saturday evening gourmet dinners, non-residents welcome; open as a restaurant Tuesday to Saturday for dinner only.
Bedrooms: 2 double & 3 twin, 2 family rooms.
Bathrooms: 7 private.
Bed & breakfast: £37-£50 single, £45-£60 double.
Half board: £40-£47.50 daily.
Evening meal 7pm (l.o. 9pm).
Parking for 10.
Credit: Access, Visa.

White Cliffs Hotel M
😔😔😔😔
Marine Parade (Sea Front), Dover, CT17 9BP
☎ (0304) 203633 Telex 0304 965422 Fax (0304) 216320
Traditional English hotel on the seafront, close to all departure points for the continent. Pleasant, friendly staff. Special breaks available, terms on request.
Bedrooms: 9 single, 18 double & 23 twin, 5 family rooms.
Bathrooms: 55 private, 4 public.
Bed & breakfast: £45-£50 single, £72-£75 double.
Lunch available.
Evening meal 7pm (l.o. 9.30pm).
Parking for 25.
Credit: Access, Visa, C.Bl., Diners, Amex.

Please mention this guide when making a booking.

Whitmore Guest House
Listed **APPROVED**
261 Folkestone Rd., Dover, CT17 9LL
☎ (0304) 203080
Small well-established family guesthouse, close to railway station, town centre, docks and hoverport. En-suite rooms also available.
Bedrooms: 1 double & 1 twin, 2 family rooms.
Bathrooms: 1 private, 1 public.
Bed & breakfast: £15-£20 single, £24-£30 double.
Half board: £22-£27 daily, £140-£180 weekly.
Parking for 4.

EAST DEAN
E. Sussex
Map ref 2D3

4m W. Eastbourne
Pretty village on a green near Friston Forest and Birling Gap.

Birling Gap Hotel M
😔😔😔😔 **APPROVED**
East Dean, Eastbourne, BN20 0AB
☎ Eastbourne (0323) 423197
Fax (0323) 423030
Magnificent Seven Sisters clifftop position, with views of country, sea, beach, superb downland walks. Old world "Thatched Bar" and "Oak Room Restaurant". Coffee shop and games room, function and conference suite.
Bedrooms: 1 single, 4 double & 2 twin, 2 family rooms.
Bathrooms: 9 private, 1 public.
Bed & breakfast: £20-£30 single, £30-£50 double.
Half board: £22-£35 daily, £130-£220 weekly.
Lunch available.
Evening meal 6pm (l.o. 9.30pm).
Parking for 100.
Credit: Access, Visa, Diners, Amex.

National Crown ratings were correct at the time of going to press but are subject to change. Please check at the time of booking.

EAST HORSLEY
Surrey
Map ref 2D2

6m SW. Leatherhead
Village on the A246 road but surrounded by wooded countryside. North Downs are nearby to the south.

Thatchers Resort Hotel M
Epsom Rd., East Horsley, KT24 6TB
☎ (048 65) 4291
Fax (048 65) 4222
Ⓡ Resort
Fine Tudor-style hotel, refurbished 1984, in delightful Surrey countryside. Ideal setting for conferences, weddings and weekend breaks.
Bedrooms: 7 single, 28 double & 11 twin, 13 family rooms.
Bathrooms: 59 private.
Bed & breakfast: £32.50-£87.50 single, £65-£105 double.
Lunch available.
Evening meal 7.30pm (l.o. 9.30pm).
Parking for 100.
Credit: Access, Visa, Diners, Amex.

EASTBOURNE
E. Sussex
Map ref 3B4

One of the finest, most elegant resorts on the south-east coast and beautifully situated beside Beachy Head. Long promenade, plenty of gardens, several theatres, Towner Art Gallery, Lifeboat Museum and the Redoubt, housing the Sussex Combined Services Museum and Aquarium.
Tourist Information Centre ☎ (0323) 411400

Adrian House M
😔😔😔
24 Selwyn Rd., Eastbourne, BN21 2LR
☎ (0323) 20372
Small, family-run private hotel in quiet area. Ample private parking.
Bedrooms: 2 single, 3 double & 3 twin, 2 family rooms.
Bathrooms: 5 private, 2 public.
Bed & breakfast: £13 single, £26-£30 double.

Half board: £19-£21 daily, £105-£125 weekly.
Evening meal 6pm (l.o. 6pm).
Parking for 10.

Bay Lodge Hotel M
😔😔😔
61-62 Royal Pde., Eastbourne, BN22 7AQ
☎ (0323) 32515 Fax (0323) 35009
Small seafront hotel opposite Redoubt Gardens, close to bowling greens, sailing clubs and entertainments. Large sun-lounge.
Bedrooms: 3 single, 5 double & 4 twin.
Bathrooms: 8 private, 2 public.
Bed & breakfast: £15-£25 single, £30-£45 double.
Half board: £23-£34 daily, £168-£191 weekly.
Evening meal 6pm (l.o. 6pm).
Open March-October.
Credit: Access, Visa.

Beach Haven Hotel
😔😔😔 **COMMENDED**
61, Pevensey Road, Eastbourne, BN21 3HS
☎ Eastbourne (0323) 26195
High standard of food, comfort and cleanliness complement pleasant surroundings throughout.
Bedrooms: 5 single, 2 double & 2 twin.
Bathrooms: 3 private, 1 public.
Bed & breakfast: £15-£17.50 single, £30-£35 double.
Half board: £17.50-£22.50 daily, £122.50-£140 weekly.
Evening meal 6pm (l.o. 6.30pm).

Bracken Guest House
😔😔 **APPROVED**
3 Hampden Ter., Latimer Rd., Eastbourne, BN22 7BL
☎ (0323) 25779
Friendly, comfortable family-run guesthouse, serving traditional English food. Close to seafront, town centre and entertainment.
Bedrooms: 1 single, 1 double & 1 twin, 2 family rooms.
Bathrooms: 1 private, 1 public.
Bed & breakfast: £13.50-£16 single, £27-£32 double.
Half board: £16.50-£19.50 daily, £89-£103 weekly.
Evening meal 6pm.

Cherry Tree Hotel M

⚘⚘⚘ COMMENDED

15 Silverdale Rd., Eastbourne,
BN20 7AJ
☎ (0323) 22406
*Small hotel and restaurant. All
bedrooms en-suite with colour
TV, telephone, tea/coffee
making. A la carte, table
d'hote restaurant.*
Bedrooms: 2 single, 3 double
& 3 twin, 2 family rooms.
Bathrooms: 10 private.
Bed & breakfast: £20-£26
single, £40-£52 double.
Half board: £29-£35 daily.
Evening meal 6pm (l.o. 9pm).
Credit: Access, Visa.
♿7 ♨ ↋ ☐ ♦ ⓘ Ⅴ ⋈ ⅢⅢ
🛏 ℐ Ⅺ ⽥ ⛷ SP

Downland Hotel M

⚘⚘⚘

37 Lewes Rd., Eastbourne,
BN21 2BU
☎ (0323) 32689
Ⓒ Minotels
*Elegant Edwardian residence
beautifully converted to provide
every modern comfort.
Attentive service, award-
winning restaurant. Temporary
membership of nearby sports
and leisure complex.*
Bedrooms: 2 single, 8 double
& 1 twin, 4 family rooms.
Bathrooms: 15 private.
Bed & breakfast: £27.50-
£37.50 single, £55-£75 double.
Half board: £195-£275
weekly.
Evening meal 7pm (l.o. 9pm).
Parking for 10.
Open February-December.
Credit: Access, Visa, Diners,
Amex.
♿ ♨ ↋ ⑤ ☐ ♦ ⓘ Ⅴ ⋈
Ⓣ ⅢⅢ 🛏 ℐ ⴼ Ⅺ ⽥ SP

Edelweiss Private Hotel M

⚘⚘

10-12 Elms Ave., Eastbourne,
BN21 3DN
☎ Eastbourne (0323) 32071
*A fun family-run hotel within
easy walking distance of the
seafront, pier, shops, theatres,
coach and railway stations.*
Bedrooms: 3 single, 6 double
& 5 twin, 1 family room.
Bathrooms: 3 public.
Bed & breakfast: £12.85-
£14.50 single, £25.70-£29
double.
Half board: £16.25-£17.50
daily, £89.25-£112 weekly.
Evening meal 6pm (l.o. 7pm).
Credit: Access, Visa.
♿ ♨ ☐ ♦ ⓘ Ⅴ ⋈ Ⓣ ⅢⅢ
🛏 ℐ Ⅺ ⽥ SP ⽥

Far End Private Hotel

⚘⚘⚘

139 Royal Pde., Eastbourne,
BN22 7LH
☎ (0323) 25666
*Family hotel on seafront in a
level position close to all
amenities, and with car park.*
Bedrooms: 2 single, 5 double
& 3 twin.
Bathrooms: 4 private,
2 public.
Bed & breakfast: £16-£17
single, £32-£40 double.
Half board: £22-£26 daily,
£133-£176 weekly.
Evening meal 6pm (l.o. 6pm).
Parking for 8.
Open April-October.
☐ ♦ Ⅴ ⋈ Ⓣ ⅢⅢ 🛏 ℐ ⽥
⛷ SP

Flamingo Hotel M

⚘⚘⚘

20 Enys Rd., Eastbourne,
BN21 2DN
☎ (0323) 21654
*Peaceful, well-furnished, period
hotel in tree-lined road in
pleasant part of town. Bargain
breaks available.*
Bedrooms: 2 single, 4 double
& 3 twin, 2 family rooms.
Bathrooms: 11 private.
Bed & breakfast: from £19.50
single, from £39 double.
Half board: from £27 daily,
from £162 weekly.
Evening meal 6.30pm.
Credit: Access, Visa.
♿⑤ ♨ ☐ ♦ Ⅴ ⋈ ⅢⅢ 🛏
Ⅺ ⽥ ⛷ SP

Gladwyn Hotel M

⚘⚘ APPROVED

16 Blackwater Rd.,
Eastbourne, BN21 4JD
☎ (0323) 33142
*Private hotel overlooking
Devonshire Park. Close to sea,
shops and theatres. Residential
licence. TV and tea/coffee
making facilites in all
bedrooms, most en-suite.*
Bedrooms: 1 single, 4 double
& 5 twin, 2 family rooms.
Bathrooms: 8 private,
1 public; 2 private showers.
Bed & breakfast: £15.75-
£18.75 single, £31.50-£37.50
double.
Half board: £20.75-£23.75
daily.
Evening meal 6.30pm.
♿ ♨ ☐ ♦ Ⅴ ⋈ Ⓣ ⽥ ⽥
⛷ SP Ⓣ

Langham Hotel M

⚘⚘⚘ COMMENDED

Royal Pde., Eastbourne,
BN22 7AH
☎ Eastbourne (0323) 31451

*Seafront hotel with modern
accommodation. 2 bars, one
overlooking the sea with sun
terrace. Varied menus with
mostly fresh food, some from
our own farm.*
Bedrooms: 21 single,
12 double & 49 twin, 5 family
rooms.
Bathrooms: 87 private,
1 public.
Bed & breakfast: £33-£37
single, £58-£66 double.
Half board: from £29 daily.
Lunch available.
Evening meal 6.30pm (l.o.
7.30pm).
Parking for 3.
Open March-November.
Credit: Access, Visa.
♿ ♨ ↋ ☐ ♦ ⓘ Ⅴ ⋈
⋈ Ⓣ ● ⑤ ⅢⅢ 🛏 ℐ ⽥ SP
Ⓣ

Lansdowne Hotel M

⚘⚘⚘⚘

King Edward's Pde.,
Eastbourne, BN21 4EE
☎ Eastbourne (0323) 25174
Telex 878624
Ⓒⓑ Best Western
*Privately owned and run hotel
in premier seafront position
with bar, spacious lounges and
elegant public areas. Theatres,
shops and sporting facilities
nearby.*
Bedrooms: 41 single,
21 double & 62 twin, 6 family
rooms.
Bathrooms: 130 private,
4 public.
Bed & breakfast: £47-£62
single, £76-£96 double.
Half board: £45-£66.50 daily,
£286-£465 weekly.
Lunch available.
Evening meal 6.30pm (l.o.
8.30pm).
Parking for 22.
Credit: Access, Visa, Diners,
Amex.
♿ ↋ ⑤ ☐ ♦ ⓘ Ⅴ ⋈ ⽥
Ⓣ ● ⅢⅢ 🛏 ℐ ⴲ ↺ ⽥
⛷ SP Ⓣ

Mansion Hotel

⚘⚘⚘

Grand Pde., Eastbourne,
BN21 3YS
☎ (0323) 27411
Ⓒⓑ Friendly
*Elegant Victorian building,
modernised to high standard,
sits proudly on the seafront,
central for all Eastbourne's
amenities.*
Bedrooms: 37 single,
28 double & 51 twin, 6 family
rooms.
Bathrooms: 79 private,
15 public.
Bed & breakfast: £53.50-
£66.20 single, £66.75-£81.90
double.
Lunch available.

Evening meal 6.30pm (l.o.
8.30pm).
Credit: Access, Visa, Diners,
Amex.
♿ ♨ ↋ ☐ ♦ ⋈ ⓘ Ⅴ ⋈
Ⓣ Ⅴ ⽥ ⅢⅢ 🛏 ℐ Ⅺ ⛷ SP
Ⓣ

Merrywood

⚘⚘

15 Cambridge Rd.,
Eastbourne, BN22 7BS
☎ (0323) 25116
*Small, family-run guesthouse
noted for its comfort and food,
close to shops and all
amenities. No smoking in
public rooms.*
Bedrooms: 1 single, 3 double
& 3 twin, 1 family room.
Bathrooms: 2 public.
Bed & breakfast: £14.50-£15
single, £29-£33 double.
Half board: £21-£23 daily,
£105-£120 weekly.
Lunch available.
Evening meal 6pm (l.o. 6pm).
♿⑤ ♨ ☐ ♦ Ⅴ ⋈ Ⓤ Ⅴ ⋈ Ⓣ ⅢⅢ
Ⅺ ⽥ ⽥ SP

Oakwood Hotel M

⚘⚘ APPROVED

28 Jevington Gdns.,
Eastbourne, BN21 4HN
☎ Eastbourne (0323) 21900
*Small licensed hotel
accommodating 26 guests in a
friendly, homely atmosphere.
English dishes served in
pleasant surroundings.*
Bedrooms: 6 single, 5 double
& 3 twin, 1 family room.
Bathrooms: 4 private,
3 public.
Bed & breakfast: £18-£25
single, £35-£48 double.
Half board: £24-£32 daily,
£135-£168 weekly.
Evening meal 6pm (l.o.
6.30pm).
♿ ♨ ♦ ⓘ Ⅴ ⋈ Ⓣ 🛏 ℐ
⽥ ⽥ ⛷ SP

Princes Hotel M

⚘⚘⚘⚘ APPROVED

Lascelles Terrace,
Eastbourne, BN21 4BL
☎ (0323) 22056 Fax (0323)
27469
Ⓒⓑ Inter
*Friendly family hotel, ideal
centre for exploring the many
historic monuments and beauty
spots of Sussex.*
Bedrooms: 16 single,
10 double & 17 twin, 2 family
rooms.
Bathrooms: 45 private,
2 public.
Bed & breakfast: £25-£45
single, £50-£90 double.
Half board: £35-£55 daily,
£260-£350 weekly.
Lunch available.
Evening meal 6.45pm (l.o.
8.30pm).

Credit: Access, Visa, Diners, Amex.

⬥ ⬥ ⬥ ⬥ ⬥ ⬥ ⬥ ⬥ ⬥
⬥ ⬥ ⬥ ⬥ ⬥ ⬥ ⬥ ⬥ SP
⬥ ⬥

Rockville Hotel
⬥⬥

20-22 Bourne St., Eastbourne, BN21 3ER
☎ (0323) 38488
Comfortable family-run hotel close to sea and shops with home cooking, licensed bar and TV lounge. Some en-suite bedrooms with TV.
Bedrooms: 3 single, 6 double & 2 twin, 2 family rooms.
Bathrooms: 3 private, 4 public.
Bed & breakfast: from £13 single, £26-£34 double.
Half board: £19.50-£23.50 daily, £136.50-£164.50 weekly.
Evening meal 6pm (l.o. 6pm).
⬥3 ⬥ ⬥ ⬥ ⬥ ⬥ DAP ⬥ SP

Royal Hotel

8-9 Marine Pde., Eastbourne, BN21 3DX
☎ (0323) 24027
Seafront hotel near shops, theatres, restaurants. Majority of rooms face the sea, all with TV and tea making facilities. Central heating.
Bedrooms: 2 single, 8 double & 3 twin.
Bathrooms: 1 private, 2 public; 5 private showers.
Bed & breakfast: £13-£20 single, £26-£36 double.
Evening meal 6pm (l.o. midday).
Open February-December.
⬥ ⬥ ⬥ ⬥ ⬥ ⬥ ⬥ ⬥ DAP
SP

Sovereign View Guest House
⬥⬥

93 Royal Pde., Eastbourne, BN22 7AE
☎ (0323) 21657
Comfortable guesthouse with some en-suite rooms, on seafront close to amenities. Traditional cooking, own keys, colour TV and unrestricted parking.
Bedrooms: 4 double & 3 twin.
Bathrooms: 2 private, 2 public.
Bed & breakfast: £15-£17 single, £30-£34 double.
Half board: £22-£24 daily, £120-£142 weekly.
Evening meal 6pm (l.o. 4pm).
Open April-September.
⬥12 ⬥ ⬥ ⬥ ⬥ ⬥ ⬥ DAP
⬥

Stratford Hotel and Restaurant
59 Cavendish Pl., Eastbourne, BN21 3RL
☎ (0323) 24051 & 26391
Ideally situated near promenade, coaches and shopping centre. Licensed, centrally heated throughout. Ground floor and family rooms available. Tea making facilities and colour TV in all rooms. Most rooms with modern en-suite.
Bedrooms: 2 single, 4 double & 4 twin, 4 family rooms.
Bathrooms: 12 private, 2 public.
Bed & breakfast: £17-£20 single, £34-£40 double.
Half board: £25-£27 daily, £105-£130 weekly.
Evening meal 6pm (l.o. 6pm).
Credit: Access, Visa, Diners.
⬥1 ⬥ ⬥ ⬥ ⬥ ⬥ ⬥ ⬥
⬥ ⬥ ⬥ DAP ⬥ SP ⬥

Sunnydene Guest House
60 Ceylon Pl., Eastbourne, BN22 8AB
☎ (0323) 642274
Homely atmosphere. Colour television lounge. Twin and double bedrooms all with tea-making, central heating. Varied menu.
Bedrooms: 2 double & 2 twin, 1 family room.
Bathrooms: 2 public.
Bed & breakfast: £20-£30 double.
Half board: £15-£20 daily, £105-£130 weekly.
Evening meal 6pm (l.o. 6pm).
Open April-October.
⬥5 ⬥ UL ⬥ ⬥ ⬥ ⬥ DAP ⬥

The Wish Tower ⓜ
King Edward's Pde., Eastbourne, BN21 4EB
☎ (0323) 22676
ⓒⓡ Principal
Elegant seaside hotel within easy reach of all attractions. Most rooms have sea views. Refurbished public rooms invite total relaxation.
Bedrooms: 25 single, 11 double & 28 twin, 3 family rooms.
Bathrooms: 59 private, 4 public; 6 private showers.
Bed & breakfast: from £72 single, from £94 double.
Half board: from £54 daily.
Lunch available.
Evening meal 7pm (l.o. 8.45pm).
Credit: Access, Visa, Diners, Amex.
⬥ ⬥ ⬥ ⬥ ⬥ ⬥ ⬥ ⬥ ⬥
⬥ ⬥ ⬥ ⬥ ⬥ ⬥ ⬥ ⬥ SP
⬥

York House Hotel ⓜ
⬥⬥⬥

14-22 Royal Pde., Eastbourne, BN22 7AP
☎ (0323) 412918
ⓒⓡ Consort
Exceptional sea-views and bar lunches on the terrace of the Verandah Bar. 5-course dinner, followed by dancing in the Lancaster Room. An early dip in the heated indoor pool.
Bedrooms: 30 single, 23 double & 42 twin, 8 family rooms.
Bathrooms: 93 private, 7 public.
Bed & breakfast: £30-£35 single, £60-£70 double.
Half board: £37-£42 daily, £159-£252 weekly.
Lunch available.
Evening meal 6.30pm (l.o. 7.30pm).
Credit: Access, Visa.
⬥ ⬥ ⬥ ⬥ ⬥ ⬥ ⬥ ⬥
⬥ ⬥ ⬥ ⬥ ⬥ ⬥ ⬥ ⬥ SP
⬥

EPSOM

Surrey
Map ref 2D2

Horse races have been held on the slopes of Epsom Downs for centuries. The racecourse is the home of the world-famous Derby. Many famous old homes are here, among them the 17th C Waterloo House.

Angleside Guest House
Listed

27 Ashley Rd., Epsom, KT18 5BD
☎ (0372) 724303
Owner-run establishment midway between Gatwick and Heathrow Airports, close to the High Street, downs and racecourse.
Bedrooms: 1 single, 2 double & 3 twin, 2 family rooms.
Bathrooms: 1 public; 3 private showers.
Bed & breakfast: £18-£22.50 single, £36-£40 double.
Parking for 8.
⬥ ⬥ ⬥ ⬥ ⬥ ⬥ ⬥ ⬥ ⬥

Epsom Downs Hotel ⓜ
⬥⬥⬥ COMMENDED

9 Longdown Rd., Epsom, KT17 3PT
☎ Epsom (037 27) 40643/21639 & 45199/45190 Fax (037 27) 23259

Serving Epsom and Gatwick in quiet suburban environment. 10 minutes from junction 8 of the M25 for Gatwick. 5 minutes from Chessington World of Adventures.
Bedrooms: 9 single, 4 double & 4 twin.
Bathrooms: 14 private; 3 private showers.
Bed & breakfast: £35-£63 single, £47-£72 double.
Lunch available.
Evening meal 6.30pm (l.o. 9.30pm).
Parking for 16.
Credit: Access, Visa, Diners, Amex.
⬥ ⬥ ⬥ ⬥ ⬥ ⬥ ⬥ ⬥ ⬥
⬥ ⬥ ⬥ ⬥ ⬥ ⬥ ⬥ SP

Heathside Hotel ⓜ
⬥⬥⬥⬥

A217-Brighton Rd., Burgh Heath, Tadworth, KT20 6BW
☎ Burgh Heath (0737) 353355
Modern, new extension with conference/leisure facilities, pool, conservatory, and restaurant open for breakfast, lunch and dinner. Close to M25, Gatwick, Epsom Downs racing.
Bedrooms: 2 single, 18 double & 21 twin, 32 family rooms.
Bathrooms: 73 private.
Bed & breakfast: from £23 single, from £41 double.
Half board: from £38 daily.
Lunch available.
Evening meal 6pm (l.o. 10pm).
Parking for 140.
Credit: Access, Visa, Diners, Amex.
⬥ ⬥ ⬥ ⬥ ⬥ ⬥ ⬥ ⬥ ⬥
⬥ ⬥ ⬥ ⬥ ⬥ ⬥ ⬥ ⬥ SP
⬥

White House Hotel
⬥⬥⬥ COMMENDED

Downs Hill Rd., Epsom, KT18 5HW
☎ (037 27) 22472
Charming, spacious, traditional mansion converted into a modern hotel. Epsom town and station only minutes away with regular train services to London.
Bedrooms: 9 single, 2 double & 3 twin, 1 family room.
Bathrooms: 7 private, 1 public; 6 private showers.
Bed & breakfast: £39.50-£52.50 single, £59.50-£65.50 double.
Evening meal 7pm (l.o. 8.45pm).
Parking for 15.
Credit: Access, Visa.
⬥ ⬥ ⬥ ⬥ ⬥ ⬥ ⬥ ⬥ ⬥
⬥ ⬥ ⬥ ⬥ ⬥

ESHER

Surrey
Map ref 2D2

Residential town beside the River Mole. Claremont, a mansion built for Clive of India in 1772, lies to the south. It is set in fine gardens laid out by Capability Brown and administered separately by the National Trust.

Haven Hotel M

Portsmouth Rd., Esher, KT10 9AR
☎ 081-398 0023
Inter
Licensed hotel and restaurant half a mile from Esher station, 20 minutes to Waterloo. Wooded setting with easy access to M3/4/25.
Bedrooms: 6 single, 6 double & 4 twin, 4 family rooms.
Bathrooms: 20 private, 1 public.
Bed & breakfast: £42-£65 single, £53-£75 double.
Half board: £36.50-£75 daily.
Lunch available.
Evening meal 7pm (l.o. 8.30pm).
Parking for 20.
Credit: Access, Visa, Diners, Amex.

EWELL

Surrey
Map ref 2D2

Nonsuch Palace, begun by Henry VII, has long since disappeared but the fine park remains and is open to the public.

Nonsuch Park Hotel

355-357 London Rd., Ewell, KT17 2DE
☎ 081-393 0771
Small family-owned hotel offering every amenity in a relaxed friendly atmosphere. Close to London, yet near countryside and several places of historic interest.
Bedrooms: 2 single, 4 double & 3 twin, 2 family rooms.
Bathrooms: 4 private, 2 public; 3 private showers.
Bed & breakfast: £34.50-£45 single, £50-£55 double.
Half board: £39.50-£45 daily.

Evening meal 6.30pm (l.o. 8.30pm).
Parking for 9.
Credit: Access, Visa.

FARNHAM

Surrey
Map ref 2C2

Town noted for its Georgian houses. Willmer House (now a museum) has a facade of cut and moulded brick with fine carving and panelling in the interior. The 12th C castle has been occupied by Bishops of both Winchester and Guildford.
Tourist Information Centre ☎ (0252) 715109

The Bishop's Table Hotel M
COMMENDED
27 West St., Farnham, GU9 7DR
☎ (0252) 715545 & 710222 &
Fax (0252) 733494
Telex 94016743 BISH G
Best Western
An 18th C inn, once used as a training school for clergy, well situated for exploring Surrey and Hampshire.
Bedrooms: 8 single, 8 double & 2 twin.
Bathrooms: 16 private, 1 public.
Bed & breakfast: £67-£81 single, £87-£90 double.
Half board: £83-£105.50 daily.
Lunch available.
Evening meal 7pm (l.o. 9.45pm).
Credit: Access, Visa, Diners, Amex.

Eldon Hotel
APPROVED
43 Frensham Rd., Lower Bourne, Farnham, GU10 3PZ
☎ Frensham (025 125) 2745 & 4559
Small, quiet, family-run, country hotel with fully equipped gymnasium, two squash courts, solarium and pool tables. Near all local amenities, swimming pool, countryside and local town.
Bedrooms: 4 single, 2 double & 8 twin.
Bathrooms: 12 private, 1 public.
Bed & breakfast: £30-£45 single, £40-£60 double.
Half board: £35-£65 daily.

Evening meal 7pm (l.o. 10pm).
Parking for 80.
Credit: Access, Visa, Amex.

FAVERSHAM

Kent
Map ref 3B3

Historic town, once a port, dating back to prehistoric times. Abbey Street has more than 50 listed buildings. Roman and Anglo-Saxon finds and other exhibits can be seen in a museum in the Maison Dieu at Ospringe. Fleur de Lis Heritage Centre.
Tourist Information Centre ☎ (0795) 534542

Garden Hotel & Restaurant
HIGHLY COMMENDED
167-169 The Street, Boughton Under Blean, Nr. Faversham, ME13 9BH
☎ Canterbury (0227) 751411
Telex 965358
In village just off the A2 between Faversham and Canterbury. English/French food. Conference facilities. Weddings and private parties catered for.
Bedrooms: 1 single, 2 double & 7 twin.
Bathrooms: 10 private.
Bed & breakfast: £55 single, £75 double.
Half board: £75 daily.
Lunch available.
Evening meal 7pm (l.o. 9.30pm).
Parking for 20.
Credit: Access, Visa, C.Bl., Diners, Amex.

FAWKHAM

Kent
Map ref 2D2

10m NE. Sevenoaks Village with small, pretty church set amongst trees. Nearby is the famous motor-racing circuit of Brands Hatch.

Brandshatch Place M
COMMENDED
Fawkham Green, Nr. Sevenoaks, DA3 8NQ
☎ Ash Green (0474) 872239

Redbrick Georgian country house built by Duke of Norfolk in 1806, surrounded by 12 acres of parkland and garden. Elegant decor.
Bedrooms: 2 single, 20 double & 7 twin.
Bathrooms: 29 private.
Bed & breakfast: from £82.50 single, from £105 double.
Lunch available.
Evening meal 7pm (l.o. 9.30pm).
Parking for 60.
Credit: Access, Visa, Diners, Amex.

FOLKESTONE

Kent
Map ref 3C4

Popular resort and important cross-channel port. The town has a fine promenade, the Leas, from where orchestral concerts and other entertainments are presented. Horse-racing at Westenhanger.
Tourist Information Centre ☎ (0303) 58594

Abbey House Hotel M

5-6 Westbourne Gdns., Folkestone, CT20 2JA
☎ (0303) 55514
Friendly Edwardian hotel, fully licensed, close to sea, promenade and bandstand. All rooms with TV, tea making and some en-suite. Unrestricted street parking.
Bedrooms: 3 single, 2 double & 5 twin, 4 family rooms.
Bathrooms: 2 private, 2 public.
Bed & breakfast: £16-£17 single, £30-£42 double.
Half board: £24.50-£25.50 daily, £155-£161 weekly.
Lunch available.
Evening meal 6.30pm (l.o. 9.30pm).
Credit: Access.

Augusta Hotel M

4 Augusta Gdns., Folkestone, CT20 2RR
☎ (0303) 850952
Small, licensed hotel in central position, close to sea and Leas. Spacious patio with access to private gardens. An elegant Victorian building with style (but no lift).
Bedrooms: 3 single, 1 double & 1 twin, 3 family rooms.

Bathrooms: 8 private,
1 public.
Bed & breakfast: £24-£27
single, £51-£53 double.
Half board: £34-£37 daily,
£220-£240 weekly.
Lunch available.
Evening meal 6pm (l.o.
7.45pm).
Credit: Access, Visa, Diners,
Amex.

Banque Hotel M
COMMENDED
4 Castle Hill Ave.,
Folkestone, CT20 2QT
☎ (0303) 53797
*Small hotel near seafront and
shops. All rooms en-suite with
colour TV, telephone, radio,
tea/coffee facilities and room
service. Car park.*
Bedrooms: 3 single, 2 double
& 5 twin, 2 family rooms.
Bathrooms: 12 private.
Bed & breakfast: £25 single,
£50 double.
Parking for 4.
Credit: Access, Visa, Diners,
Amex.

Belmonte Private Hotel
COMMENDED
30 Castle Hill Ave.,
Folkestone, CT20 2RE
☎ (0303) 254470 Fax (0303)
250568
*Small, family-run, private
licensed hotel which specialises
in providing clean and
comfortable accommodation in
a friendly atmosphere. Accent
on cooking.*
Bedrooms: 3 single, 3 double
& 2 twin, 1 family room.
Bathrooms: 5 private,
2 public.
Bed & breakfast: £22-£26
single, £44-£48 double.
Half board: £38-£42 daily,
£228-£252 weekly.
Lunch available.
Evening meal 7pm (l.o. 4pm).
Parking for 4.

Cliff View
10, Seagrove Road, East Cliff,
Folkestone, CT19 6AY
☎ Folkestone (0303) 53629
*Warm and welcoming on the
East Cliff with lovely views.
Tennis and golf/putting course
10 minutes away. On doorstep
of Little Switzerland.*
Bedrooms: 1 single, 1 double,
1 family room.

Bathrooms: 1 public.
Bed & breakfast: £12-£14
single, £24-£28 double.

Harbourside M
14, Wear Bay Road,
Folkestone, CT19 6AT
☎ Folkestone (0303) 56528
*Well-appointed en-suite
accommodation. Spectacular
views, warm hospitality and
value for money. Licensed and
fully geared for your comfort.*
Bedrooms: 3 double.
Bathrooms: 3 private.
Bed & breakfast: £18-£25
single, £35-£45 double.
Credit: Amex.

Horseshoe Private Hotel
29 Westbourne Gdns.,
Folkestone, CT20 2HY
☎ (0303) 43433
*Friendly private hotel in
residential West End close to
the Leas. All rooms are
attractive and welcoming.
Home cooking. Ample parking.*
Bedrooms: 3 single, 3 double
& 3 twin, 1 family room.
Bathrooms: 4 private,
2 public.
Bed & breakfast: £17-£21
single, £34-£42 double.
Half board: £24-£28 daily,
£112-£145 weekly.
Evening meal 6.30pm (l.o.
4.30pm).
Parking for 1.

Langhorne Garden Hotel M
10-12 Langhorne Gdns.,
Folkestone, CT20 2EA
☎ Folkestone (0303) 57233
*Situated in a quiet residential
part of the town, close to the
Leas and sea, a few minutes by
car from the station and ferry
terminal.*
Bedrooms: 3 single, 5 double
& 20 twin, 2 family rooms.
Bathrooms: 23 private,
2 public.
Bed & breakfast: £22-£25
single, £40-£45 double.
Half board: £27-£30 daily,
£160-£185 weekly.
Lunch available.
Evening meal 6.30pm (l.o.
7.30pm).
Credit: Access, Visa, Diners,
Amex.

Lister Guest House
COMMENDED
Sandgate Esplanade,
Folkestone, CT20 3DX
☎ (0303) 48617
*Small select seafront
guesthouse. No smoking.
Private parking. On A259.
Good access for touring Kent
and Continent.*
Bedrooms: 1 double & 2 twin.
Bathrooms: 1 public.
Bed & breakfast: £15-£20
single, £25-£30 double.
Parking for 4.
Open January-November.

Normandie Guest House
39 Cheriton Rd., Folkestone,
CT20 1DD
☎ (0303) 56233
*Central, near all local
amenities, with parking nearby.
Early breakfast served.
Convenient for the harbour and
trips to the continent.*
Bedrooms: 1 single, 1 double
& 2 twin, 2 family rooms.
Bathrooms: 1 public.
Bed & breakfast: £13-£15
single, £26-£30 double.

Sunny Lodge Guest House M
Listed APPROVED
85 Cheriton Rd., Folkestone,
CT20 2QL
☎ (0303) 251498
*Warm welcome and a
comfortable stay offered at this
conveniently situated
guesthouse. Near all amenities.
Junction 13 of M20 for town.*
Bedrooms: 2 single, 3 double
& 1 twin, 2 family rooms.
Bathrooms: 2 public.
Bed & breakfast: £14-£16
single, £25-£27 double.
Parking for 4.

GATWICK AIRPORT
Map ref 2D2

*See also Charlwood,
Copthorne, Crawley,
Horley, Horsham, Redhill,
Reigate.*

London Gatwick Airport Hilton M
COMMENDED
Gatwick Airport - London,
W. Sussex RH6 0LL
☎ (0293) 518080
Telex 877021
CR Hilton

*The only hotel linked by direct,
covered walkway to Gatwick's
south terminal and rapid
transit system to the north
terminal.*
Bedrooms: 193 double &
340 twin, 17 family rooms.
Bathrooms: 550 private.
Bed & breakfast: £100-£150
single, £100-£160 double.
Lunch available.
Evening meal 6pm (l.o.
11pm).
Credit: Access, Visa, C.Bl.,
Diners, Amex.

Gatwick Sterling Hotel M
COMMENDED
Gatwick Airport, Crawley,
W. Sussex RH6 0PH
☎ (0293) 567070 Telex 87202
STELGW
*Opened autumn 1990,
connected by covered walkway
to North Terminal. Impressive
atrium with 3 restaurants.
Leisure club with pool.*
Bedrooms: 2 single,
267 double & 205 twin.
Bathrooms: 474 private.
Bed & breakfast: £74-£129
single, £93-£148 double.
Half board: £91-£143 daily.
Lunch available.
Evening meal 6pm (l.o.
11pm).
Parking for 110.
Credit: Access, Visa, C.Bl.,
Diners, Amex.

GILLINGHAM
Kent
Map ref 3B3

The largest Medway
Town, it merges into its
neighbour Chatham.
*Tourist Information
Centre* ☎ *(Farthing
Corner) (0634) 360323*

Oast Manor Hotel M
COMMENDED
Star Lane, Off Hempstead
Road, Hempstead,
Gillingham, ME7 3NN
☎ Medway
(0634) 376615/379586
*In quiet, beautiful Hempstead
Valley countryside but only
5 minutes' journey from
Gillingham Business Park,
A2 and M2.*
Bedrooms: 3 single, 6 double
& 1 twin.
Bathrooms: 9 private,
1 public.

Continued ▶

GILLINGHAM
Continued

Bed & breakfast: £40-£70 single, £70-£85 double.
Lunch available.
Evening meal 7pm (l.o. 10pm).
Parking for 38.
Credit: Access, Visa, Amex.

GODSTONE
Surrey
Map ref 2D2

Most attractive village, set in a gap of the chalk North Downs. The green has a cricket pitch and a small pond.

The Godstone Hotel M
The Green, Godstone, RH9 8DT
☎ (0883) 742461
400-year-old Elizabethan building with exposed beams. Now a small family hotel with a friendly, homely atmosphere.
Bedrooms: 5 double & 2 twin, 1 family room.
Bathrooms: 8 private.
Bed & breakfast: from £35 single, from £48 double.
Lunch available.
Evening meal 7pm (l.o. 10pm).
Parking for 40.
Credit: Access, Visa, Diners, Amex.

GOODWOOD
W. Sussex
Map ref 2C3

Goodwood House, an 18th C mansion standing in lovely parkland, houses an impressive art collection. The racecourse lies high on the Downs. Nearby is an excellent 18-hole golf-course.

Goodwood Park Hotel, Golf and Country Club M
HIGHLY COMMENDED
Goodwood, Nr. Chichester, PO18 0QB
☎ Chichester (0243) 775537
Telex 869173
Adjacent to Goodwood House, the hotel has been tastefully developed and retains the original character of its 1786 forebear. Swimming pool and golf course.

Bedrooms: 7 single, 38 double & 41 twin, 3 family rooms.
Bathrooms: 89 private.
Bed & breakfast: £55-£100 single, £85-£140 double.
Half board: £51-£61 daily, £315-£385 weekly.
Lunch available.
Evening meal 7pm (l.o. 9.30pm).
Parking for 250.
Credit: Access, Visa, Diners, Amex.

GRAVESEND
Kent
Map ref 3B3

Industrial riverside town where the Thames pilots are based. The statue of the Red Indian princess, Pocahontas, stands by St. George's church.
Tourist Information Centre ☎ (0474) 337600

The Clarendon Royal Hotel M
Royal Pier Rd., Gravesend, DA12 2BE
☎ (0474) 363151
A Lord Clarendon once owned this hotel. It was built in the days of James II, who is said to have stayed here. The hotel overlooks the river and is 1 mile from the town centre.
Bedrooms: 5 single, 5 double & 10 twin, 4 family rooms.
Bathrooms: 14 private, 3 public.
Bed & breakfast: £51-£62 single, £56-£67 double.
Lunch available.
Evening meal 6pm (l.o. 10.30pm).
Parking for 140.
Credit: Access, Visa, Diners, Amex.

Tollgate Motel
Watling St., Tollgate, Gravesend, DA13 9RA
☎ (0474) 357655
Telex 966227
At the junction of A227 and A2 London/Dover road, with the M20/M25 motorway links only 7 miles away. London 33 miles, Dover 50 miles, Dartford Tunnel 7 miles. Ideally situated to suit the needs of both tourist and businessman.
Bedrooms: 2 single, 58 double & 54 twin.

Bathrooms: 114 private.
Bed & breakfast: £57.75-£64.35 single, £70.95-£85 double.
Lunch available.
Evening meal 6pm (l.o. 10.30pm).
Parking for 200.
Credit: Access, Visa, Diners, Amex.

GUILDFORD
Surrey
Map ref 2D2

Bustling town with many historic monuments, one of which is the Guildhall clock jutting out over the old High Street. The modern cathedral occupies a commanding position on Stag Hill.
Tourist Information Centre ☎ (0483) 444007

Atkinsons Guest House
129 Stoke Rd., Guildford, GU1 1ET
☎ Guildford (0483) 38260
Small comfortable guesthouse close to park, town centre and convenient for public transport and all local amenities.
Bedrooms: 1 single, 2 twin, 1 family room.
Bathrooms: 2 private, 1 public.
Bed & breakfast: £19-£27 single, £33-£38 double.
Parking for 3.

Badenweiler M
Listed APPROVED
35 Poplar Road, Shalford, Guildford GU4 8DH
☎ (0483) 506037
South of Guildford on A281. Continental cooking. Ample parking. Children under 10 half price. Non-smokers only please.
Bedrooms: 1 single, 1 double & 1 twin, 1 family room.
Bathrooms: 2 public.
Bed & breakfast: £17-£20 single, £30-£35 double.
Half board: £20-£26 daily, from £100 weekly.
Evening meal 7pm (l.o. 9.30pm).
Parking for 6.

Blanes Court Hotel
Albury Rd., Guildford, GU1 2BT
☎ (0483) 573171

Bed and breakfast accommodation, mostly en-suite rooms, all with colour TV, tea/coffee facilities. Garden lounge, cosy bar serving snacks. In a quiet area within easy walking distance of town and country.
Bedrooms: 8 single, 5 double & 4 twin, 2 family rooms.
Bathrooms: 13 private, 1 public.
Bed & breakfast: £30-£35 single, £50-£60 double.
Parking for 20.
Credit: Access, Visa, Amex.

The Bramley Grange Hotel
Horsham Rd., Bramley, Guildford, GU5 0BL
☎ (0483) 893434/898703
Telex 859948 BRAMGH
Best Western
Victorian hotel set in 7 acres of grounds, just 5 minutes' drive from Guildford.
Bedrooms: 5 single, 35 double & 5 twin, 2 family rooms.
Bathrooms: 47 private.
Bed & breakfast: £97.50-£110 single, £110-£120 double.
Lunch available.
Evening meal 7.30pm (l.o. 10pm).
Parking for 65.
Credit: Access, Visa, Amex.

Carlton Hotel
London Rd., Guildford, GU1 2AF
☎ (0483) 576539 & 575158
Within 3 minutes' walk of London Road station on the London to Guildford line via Cobham. 2 minutes' walk from the High Street and main thoroughfare.
Bedrooms: 12 single, 6 double & 7 twin, 10 family rooms.
Bathrooms: 19 private, 5 public.
Bed & breakfast: £26-£36 single, £40-£46 double.
Evening meal 6.30pm (l.o. 8.30pm).
Parking for 50.
Credit: Access, Visa, Amex.

Crawford House Hotel
73 Farnham Rd., Guildford, GU2 5PF
☎ (0483) 579299
Very close to mainline station, well-appointed rooms with en-suite facilities. Ample car parking. Courteous service. Good breakfast.

Bedrooms: 7 single, 3 double
& 4 twin.
Bathrooms: 6 private,
2 public; 5 private showers.
Bed & breakfast: £23.50-£35
single, £40-£45 double.
Parking for 22.
Credit: Access, Visa.

Devon House

11, Waterden Road,
Guildford, GU1 2AN
☎ Guildford (0483) 67927
*Charming newly furnished
Victorian house only 5 minutes
from town centre and
2 minutes from London Road
station.*
Bedrooms: 1 twin, 1 family
room.
Bathrooms: 2 public.
Bed & breakfast: £20-£22
single, £35-£38 double.

Quinns Hotel

78 Epsom Rd., Guildford,
GU1 2BX
☎ (0483) 60422
Fax (0483) 578551
Telex 859754 MHANCO
*Built in 1893 as a private
house for the Wheat family,
and used from 1944-53 as the
rectory for Holy Trinity
Church.*
Bedrooms: 3 single, 3 double
& 3 twin, 2 family rooms.
Bathrooms: 3 private,
4 public; 8 private showers.
Bed & breakfast: £38-£48
single, £68-£80 double.
Half board: £54-£60.50 daily,
£365-£480 weekly.
Evening meal 6.20pm (l.o.
4pm).
Parking for 15.
Credit: Access, Visa, Diners,
Amex.

Weybrook House

113 Stoke Road, Guildford,
GU1 1ET
☎ Guildford (0483) 302394
*Easy access to town centre, bus
and rail stations, park and
leisure facilities. Heathrow and
Gatwick half an hour (airport
car service).*
Bedrooms: 1 single, 1 double,
1 family room.
Bathrooms: 2 public.
Bed & breakfast: £18-£20
single, £28-£34 double.
Half board: £19-£25 daily.
Evening meal 7pm (l.o.
10am).

Parking for 3.
Credit: Access, Visa, Diners,
Amex.

HAILSHAM

E. Sussex
Map ref 2D3

An important market town
since Norman times and
still one of the largest
markets in Sussex. 2
miles west, at Upper
Dicker, is Michelham
Priory, an Augustinian
house founded in 1229.
*Tourist Information
Centre ☎ (0323) 840604*

Boship Farm Hotel M

Lower Dicker, Hailsham,
BN27 4AT
☎ (0323) 844826
Telex 878400 BOSFAR G
Ⓖ Forestdale
*17th C oak-beamed farmhouse,
sympathetically converted into
a comfortable hotel with the
addition of bedroom wings,
conference suite and leisure
facilities.*
Bedrooms: 35 double &
9 twin, 2 family rooms.
Bathrooms: 46 private.
Bed & breakfast: £57.50-
£77.50 single, £77.50-£100
double.
Lunch available.
Evening meal 7pm (l.o.
10pm).
Parking for 100.
Credit: Access, Visa, Diners,
Amex.

HARTFIELD

E. Sussex
Map ref 2D2

Pleasant village in
Ashdown Forest, the
setting for A. A. Milne's
'Winnie the Pooh' stories.

Bolebroke Watermill M

Edenbridge Rd., Hartfield,
TN7 4JP
☎ Hartfield (0892) 770425
*6.5-acre smallholding.
Watermill (1086) and miller's
barn with Honeymooners'
Hayloft in romantic, secluded
woodland. Accommodation of
great rustic charm set around
mill machinery. Regret, some
very steep stairs!*
Bedrooms: 4 double.
Bathrooms: 4 private.

Bed & breakfast: £40-£50
single, £45-£55 double.
Half board: £34.50-£62 daily.
Evening meal 7pm (l.o.
10am).
Parking for 16.
Open March-November.
Credit: Access, Visa, Amex.

HASLEMERE

Surrey
Map ref 2C2

Town set in hilly, wooded
countryside, much of it in
the keeping of the
National Trust. Its
outstanding attractions
are the Dolmetsch
Workshops, the
educational museum and
the annual music festival.

Lythe Hill Hotel M

Petworth Rd., Haslemere,
GU27 3BQ
☎ (0428) 651251
*Hotel forms a hamlet of
beautifully restored historic
buildings in 14 acres of
parkland in the Surrey hills.
French and English restaurant,
tennis, croquet. One hour from
London.*
Bedrooms: 6 single, 19 double
& 5 twin, 10 family rooms.
Bathrooms: 40 private.
Bed & breakfast: £81.50-
£91.50 single, £100-£165
double.
Half board: £98-£108 daily.
Lunch available.
Evening meal 7.15pm (l.o.
9.30pm).
Parking for 150.
Credit: Access, Visa, Amex.

---

*National Crown
ratings were correct
at the time of going
to press but are
subject to change.
Please check at the
time of booking.*

---

*Half board prices
shown are per
person but in some
cases may be based
on double/twin
occupancy.*

HASTINGS

E. Sussex
Map ref 3B4

Ancient town which
became famous as the
base from which William
the Conqueror set out to
fight the Battle of
Hastings. Later became
one of the Cinque Ports,
now a leading resort.
Fishermen's museum and
Hastings Embroidery
inspired by the Bayeux
Tapestry and the new
Sealife Centre.
*Tourist Information
Centre ☎ (0424) 718888*

Ashburnham Lodge

APPROVED
62, London Road, St.
Leonards-on-Sea, Hastings,
TN37 6AS
☎ Hastings
(0424) 438575/716891
*The hotel provides a high
standard of service at a price
that most people can afford.
Also caters for the disabled.*
Bedrooms: 4 single, 8 double
& 7 twin, 2 family rooms.
Bathrooms: 21 private.
Bed & breakfast: £34.65-
£39.65 single, £49.34-£52.34
double.
Half board: £34.67-£49.65
daily, £190-£230 weekly.
Lunch available.
Evening meal 7pm (l.o. 9pm).
Parking for 7.
Credit: Access, Visa, Amex.

Beechwood Hotel

59 Baldslow Rd., Hastings,
TN34 2EY
☎ (0424) 420078
*Late Victorian building with
panoramic views of sea, castle
and park, in quiet residential
area. 1 mile from station and
beach.*
Bedrooms: 5 single, 2 double
& 3 twin.
Bathrooms: 3 private,
1 public.
Bed & breakfast: £13-£28
single, £24-£40 double.
Half board: £20-£35 daily,
£120-£210 weekly.
Lunch available.
Evening meal 6pm (l.o.
10pm).
Parking for 6.

Burlington Hotel
APPROVED

2 Robertson Ter., Hastings,
TN34 1JE
☎ (0424) 722303
*Prime seafront position. All
amenities easily accessible. Tea
and coffee making facilities
and colour TV in all rooms.
Relaxing atmosphere.*
Bedrooms: 3 single, 10 double
& 2 twin, 1 family room.
Bathrooms: 10 private,
2 public.
Bed & breakfast: £18.70-£24
single, £35-£45 double.
Half board: £27-£32 daily,
£175-£210 weekly.
Evening meal 6.30pm (l.o.
9pm).
Credit: Access, Visa, Diners,
Amex.

Eagle House Hotel M

12 Pevensey Rd., St.
Leonards-on-Sea, Hastings,
TN38 0JZ
☎ (0424) 430535 & 441273
*Large Victorian residence in its
own grounds. Well placed for
visiting "1066" country.*
Bedrooms: 18 double &
4 twin.
Bathrooms: 19 private,
2 public.
Bed & breakfast: £32-£33
single, £38-£45 double.
Half board: £33.95-£47.95
daily.
Lunch available.
Evening meal 6.30pm (l.o.
8.30pm).
Parking for 14.
Credit: Access, Visa, Diners,
Amex.

Grand Hotel

Grand Pde., St. Leonards-on-
Sea, Hastings, TN38 0DD
☎ (0424) 428510
*Family-run seafront hotel,
close to all amenities. Fully
licensed with international
cooking. Unrestricted parking.
Radio-room call/baby listening
in all rooms. Reductions for
children. French spoken.*
Bedrooms: 4 single, 7 double
& 7 twin, 2 family rooms.
Bathrooms: 8 private,
3 public.
Bed & breakfast: £12.50-£50
single, £25-£100 double.

Half board: £17.50-£65 daily,
£122.50-£340 weekly.
Lunch available.
Evening meal 6pm (l.o. 7pm).

Marina House

1 Sturdee Pl., Hastings,
TN34 3AJ
☎ (0424) 424834
*Small, friendly, family
guesthouse on the seafront with
sea views from 3 bedrooms and
dining room.*
Bedrooms: 1 single, 3 double
& 2 twin.
Bathrooms: 1 public.
Bed & breakfast: £10-£12
single, £20-£24 double.
Evening meal 5pm (l.o.
5.30pm).
Open January-November.

Mayfair Hotel

9 Eversfield Place, St.
Leonards-on-Sea, Hastings,
TN37 6BY
☎ Hastings (0424) 434061
*Family-owned and run hotel,
situated on the seafront,
several rooms are en-suite and
face the sea. Close to town
centre.*
Bedrooms: 2 single, 2 double
& 2 twin, 2 family rooms.
Bathrooms: 4 private,
1 public; 4 private showers.
Bed & breakfast: £14-£18
single, £28-£40 double.
Evening meal 6pm (l.o. 7pm).

Parkside House
HIGHLY COMMENDED

59 Lower Park Rd., Hastings,
TN34 2LD
☎ (0424) 433096
*2-storey Victorian house
opposite Alexandra Park. 10
minutes' walk to town centre
and beaches. Quiet location.
No parking restrictions.*
Bedrooms: 1 single, 1 double
& 1 twin, 1 family room.
Bathrooms: 2 private,
1 public; 1 private shower.
Bed & breakfast: £18-£32
single, £32-£40 double.
Half board: £23-£27 daily,
£155-£180 weekly.
Evening meal 6pm (l.o.
midday).

Ridge Guest House

361 The Ridge, Hastings,
TN34 2RD
☎ (0424) 754240
*Newly converted guesthouse
with restaurant on the B2093
road, half a mile from
Conquest Hospital.*
Bedrooms: 1 single, 5 double
& 4 twin, 1 family room.
Bathrooms: 11 private.
Bed & breakfast: £16-£18
single, £26-£30 double.
Half board: £20-£23 daily,
from £105 weekly.
Evening meal 6pm (l.o.
9.30pm).
Parking for 32.
Credit: Access, Amex.

Rutland Guest House

17 Grosvenor Cres., St.
Leonards-on-Sea, Hastings
☎ Hastings
(0424) 432620/714720
*Seafront, family-run
guesthouse, close to amenities.
Adequate parking nearby.
Railway station within 5
minutes. Collection from train/
coach station arranged.*
Bedrooms: 5 single, 3 double
& 1 twin, 3 family rooms.
Bathrooms: 2 public.
Bed & breakfast: £12-£18
single, £24-£36 double.

Tudor
COMMENDED

191 Bexhill Rd., St. Leonards-
on-Sea, Hastings, TN38 8BG
☎ (0424) 424485
*Small, high standard
guesthouse offering personal
service. All rooms have colour
TV. Parking on premises.*
Bedrooms: 1 double & 1 twin.
Bathrooms: 1 public.
Bed & breakfast: £13-£15
single, £24-£28 double.
Half board: £17-£19 daily,
£112-£119 weekly.
Evening meal 6pm (l.o. 4pm).
Parking for 3.

---

*The enquiry
coupons at the
back will help you
when contacting
proprietors.*

---

*Village in 3 parts: Gill's
Green, Highgate and the
Moor. There is a
colonnaded shopping
centre, large village
green, church and inn
which is associated with
the Hawkhurst smuggling
gang.*

Tudor Court Hotel M

Rye Rd., Hawkhurst,
TN18 5DA
☎ (0580) 752312
Telex 957565
Ⓡ Best Western
*Picturesque country house
hotel superbly located in the
Weald of Kent, on A268 Rye
road. Ideally placed for visiting
Kent and Sussex beauty spots
and Camber Sands.*
Bedrooms: 5 single, 6 double
& 7 twin.
Bathrooms: 18 private.
Bed & breakfast: from £52
single, £82-£87 double.
Half board: £54-£65 daily,
£309-£324.50 weekly.
Lunch available.
Evening meal 7.30pm (l.o.
9.15pm).
Parking for 53.
Credit: Access, Visa, Diners,
Amex.

Woodham Hall Hotel M
APPROVED

Rye Rd., Hawkhurst,
TN18 5DA
☎ (0580) 753428
*Country house on the edge of
the village, in interesting,
historical surroundings.
Personal, friendly service.
Tennis, snooker and putting
available. Ideal for holiday or
business.*
Bedrooms: 1 single, 1 double
& 2 twin, 2 family rooms.
Bathrooms: 5 private;
1 private shower.
Bed & breakfast: £24-£35
single, £35-£45 double.
Evening meal 7pm (l.o. 6pm).
Parking for 30.
Credit: Access, Visa, Diners,
Amex.

---

*Half board prices shown are per person
but in some cases may be based on
double/twin occupancy.*

HENFIELD

W. Sussex
Map ref 2D3

7m N. Shoreham-by-Sea
In flat or gently sloping
countryside with views to
the Downs. Early English
church with a fine
Perpendicular tower.

Tottington Manor Hotel
COMMENDED
Edburton, Nr. Henfield,
BN5 9LJ
☎ Steyning (0903) 815757
Fax (0903) 879331
*16th C country manor house
with log fires and oak beams,
set in its own grounds at the
foot of the South Downs.*
Bedrooms: 5 double & 1 twin.
Bathrooms: 6 private.
Bed & breakfast: £40-£44
single, £62-£70 double.
Half board: £55-£75 daily,
£350-£400 weekly.
Lunch available.
Evening meal 7pm (l.o.
9.15pm).
Parking for 80.
Credit: Access, Visa, Diners,
Amex.

HERSTMONCEUX

E. Sussex
Map ref 3B4

4m E. Hailsham
Pleasant village noted for
its woodcrafts but
dominated by the
beautiful 15th C
Herstmonceux Castle (not
open to visitors).

Cleavers Lyng ⋒
Church Rd., Herstmonceux,
Nr. Hailsham, BN27 1QJ
☎ (0323) 833131
*Picturesque, 16th C country
hotel in 1-acre gardens. Oak
beams and inglenook fireplace.*
Bedrooms: 2 single, 2 double
& 4 twin.
Bathrooms: 4 public.
Bed & breakfast: £17.25-
£18.50 single, £34.50-£37
double.
Half board: £26.20-£28.45
daily, £177.50-£182.50
weekly.
Lunch available.
Evening meal 7pm (l.o.
7.30pm).
Parking for 16.

The Horse Shoe Inn ⋒
Windmill Hill.,
Herstmonceux, BN27 4RU
☎ (0323) 833265 Fax (0323)
832001
Resort
*Elizabethan-style half-timbered
hotel, with 15 en-suite
bedrooms, in peaceful setting
close to station. Good
sightseeing. Golf nearby.
Friendly service in
bar/restaurant.*
Bedrooms: 15 double.
Bathrooms: 15 private.
Bed & breakfast: £22.50-£41
single, £45-£51 double.
Lunch available.
Evening meal 7pm (l.o.
10pm).
Parking for 100.
Credit: Access, Visa, Diners,
Amex.

White Friars Hotel ⋒
Boreham Street,
Herstmonceux, Nr.
Hailsham, BN27 4SE
☎ (0323) 832355
Fax (0323) 833882
Best Western
*17th C country house hotel
overlooking Sussex Weald, in 4
acres of gardens. Beamed
lounges, log fires, cheerful
staff. Varied and interesting
menu.*
Bedrooms: 5 single, 7 double
& 6 twin, 2 family rooms.
Bathrooms: 20 private.
Bed & breakfast: £40-£60
single, £60-£90 double.
Half board: £50-£90 daily.
Lunch available.
Evening meal 7pm (l.o.
9.30pm).
Parking for 80.
Credit: Access, Visa, Diners,
Amex.

HORLEY

Surrey
Map ref 2D2

Town on the London to
Brighton road, just north
of Gatwick Airport, with
an ancient parish church
and 15th C inn.

Chalet Guest House ⋒
COMMENDED
77 Massetts Road, Horley,
Surey, RH6 7EB
☎ (0293) 821666
*Family-run modern
guesthouse. Convenient for
Gatwick Airport, motorways,
railway station, local bus,
shops, pubs and restaurants.*

Bedrooms: 3 single, 1 double
& 2 twin.
Bathrooms: 5 private,
1 public.
Bed & breakfast: £22-£28
single, £38-£44 double.
Parking for 14.
Credit: Access, Visa.

Cottage Guest House ⋒
Listed
33 Massetts Road, Horley,
Surrey. RH6 7DQ
☎ (0293) 775341/783812
*Small friendly pretty cottage in
pleasant residential area, five
minutes from Gatwick, short
walk to town centre,
restaurants, pubs and Horley
station.*
Bedrooms: 1 single, 2 double
& 1 twin, 1 family room.
Bathrooms: 1 private,
1 public.
Bed & breakfast: £25-£35
single, £35-£43 double.
Parking for 8.
Credit: Access, Visa.

Felcourt Guest House ⋒
Listed APPROVED
79 Massetts Rd., Horley,
RH6 7EB
☎ (0293) 782651/776255
*1 mile from Gatwick, ideal for
travellers. En-suite rooms
available, tea/coffee facilities,
central heating. Long term
parking available, £10 per
week.*
Bedrooms: 2 single, 1 double,
2 family rooms.
Bathrooms: 2 private,
1 public.
Bed & breakfast: £18-£25
single, £28-£38 double.
Parking for 12.

Gainsborough Lodge ⋒
COMMENDED
39 Massetts Rd., Horley,
RH6 7DT
☎ (0293) 783982
*Extended Edwardian house set
in attractive garden. Five
minutes' walk from Horley
station and town centre. Five
minutes' drive from Gatwick
Airport.*
Bedrooms: 3 single, 2 double
& 5 twin, 2 family rooms.
Bathrooms: 12 private.
Bed & breakfast: £32.50-
£36.50 single, £38.50-£46.50
double.
Parking for 16.
Credit: Access, Visa.

Gatwick Moat House
Longbridge Roundabout,
Gatwick, Horley, RH6 0AB
☎ (0293) 785599
Telex 877138
Queens Moat Houses
*All bedrooms are air
conditioned and double-glazed
for comfort, with in-house
movies, direct-dial telephone
and tea and coffee making
facilities. Courtesy bus service
for Gatwick Airport and rail
terminal.*
Bedrooms: 56 double &
58 twin, 8 family rooms.
Bathrooms: 122 private.
Bed & breakfast: £65.85-
£80.05 single, £75-£104.20
double.
Half board: £78-£93 daily.
Lunch available.
Evening meal 3pm (l.o.
10.30pm).
Parking for 150.
Credit: Access, Visa, C.Bl.,
Diners, Amex.

The Lawn Guest House
Listed COMMENDED
30 Massetts Rd., Horley,
RH6 7DE
☎ (0293) 775751
*Ideal for travellers using
Gatwick. Pleasantly situated.
Few minutes' walk to town
centre, pubs and restaurants.
Good base for London and the
South Coast.*
Bedrooms: 2 double & 5 twin.
Bathrooms: 3 private,
2 public.
Bed & breakfast: £24-£31
single, £35-£42 double.
Parking for 7.
Credit: Access, Visa.

Massetts Lodge
COMMENDED
28, Massetts Road, Horley,
RH6 7DE
☎ Crawley (0293) 782738
*Victorian guesthouse 5 minutes
from Gatwick (away from
flightpath). Central heating,
long term car parking and
English breakfast.*
Bedrooms: 1 single, 3 double
& 1 twin, 3 family rooms.
Bathrooms: 5 private,
2 public.
Bed & breakfast: £23-£33
single, £35-£41 double.
Half board: £22-£40 daily,
£154-£280 weekly.
Evening meal 6pm (l.o.
7.45pm).
Parking for 9.
Credit: Access, Visa, Amex.

HORLEY
Continued

Masslink House
70 Massetts Road, Horley,
RH6 7ED
☎ Horley (0293) 785798
*Comfortable Victorian family
house, close to Gatwick
Airport, caters for holiday
travellers and London visitors.
Holiday parking available.*
Bedrooms: 1 single, 2 double
& 3 twin, 1 family room.
Bathrooms: 1 private,
2 public.
Bed & breakfast: £23-£25
single, £32-£42 double.
Parking for 13.

Melville Lodge Guest House ♨
15, Brighton Road, Horley,
Nr. Gatwick, RH6 7HH
☎ (0293) 784951
*Detached Edwardian house
built in early 1900. 5 minutes'
drive to Gatwick Airport. 10
minutes' walk to town centre
and railway station. Full
cooked breakfast available.*
Bedrooms: 1 single, 2 double
& 2 twin, 1 family room.
Bathrooms: 3 private,
2 public.
Bed & breakfast: £20-£25
single, £35-£40 double.
Parking for 6.
Credit: Access, Visa.

Rosemead Guest House ♨
Listed COMMENDED
19 Church Rd., Horley,
RH6 7EY
☎ (0293) 784965
*Small guesthouse 5 minutes
from Gatwick Airport,
providing English breakfast
after 7.30 am. Continental
before. Car parking. French
spoken.*
Bedrooms: 2 single, 1 double
& 1 twin, 2 family rooms.
Bathrooms: 2 public.
Bed & breakfast: £18-£21
single, £32-£35 double.
Parking for 8.
Credit: Access, Visa.

Skylane Hotel
Brighton Rd., Horley,
RH6 8QG
☎ (0293) 786971
Telex 878143

*Airport hotel with en-suite
rooms, attractive prices. Good
restaurant. Friendly service,
with courtesy coach to/from
Gatwick.*
Bedrooms: 1 single, 9 double
& 44 twin, 5 family rooms.
Bathrooms: 59 private.
Bed & breakfast: £42.95-
£45.45 single, £53-£62.70
double.
Half board: £54.95-£62.95
daily.
Lunch available.
Evening meal 7pm (l.o.
9.45pm).
Parking for 150.
Credit: Access, Visa, Diners,
Amex.

Springwood Guest House
58 Massetts Road, Horley,
RH6 7DS
☎ Horley (0293) 775998
*Elegant detached Victorian
house in pleasant residential
road close to Gatwick Airport.
Long-term car parking, with
transport.*
Bedrooms: 2 single, 2 double
& 3 twin, 1 family room.
Bathrooms: 2 public.
Bed & breakfast: £18-£22
single, £30-£34 double.
Parking for 10.

Valetta ♨
Massetts Road, Horley,
RH6 7DJ
☎ (0293) 783388
*Warm, welcoming, family-run
guesthouse, convenient for
Gatwick Airport and M23
(junction 9). Full English
breakfast after 7.30 am.*
Bedrooms: 2 single, 1 double
& 1 twin, 1 family room.
Bathrooms: 2 public.
Bed & breakfast: from £21
single, from £32 double.
Parking for 6.

Vulcan Lodge Guest House ♨
COMMENDED
27 Massetts Rd., Horley, Nr.
Gatwick, RH6 7DQ
☎ (0293) 771522
*Picturesque, comfortable house
featuring exposed beams, 5
minutes from Gatwick Airport.
Local restaurants, shops, pubs
and trains within easy walking
distance.*
Bedrooms: 2 single, 1 double
& 1 twin.
Bathrooms: 3 private,
1 public.

Bed & breakfast: £22-£29.50
single, £38-£40 double.
Parking for 8.

Yew Tree
Listed
31 Massetts Rd., Horley,
RH6 7DQ
☎ (0293) 785855
*Tudor-style house with half an
acre of garden. 3 minutes by
taxi from Gatwick Airport and
3 minutes' walk from town
centre.*
Bedrooms: 2 single, 2 double
& 1 twin, 1 family room.
Bathrooms: 1 public;
1 private shower.
Bed & breakfast: £15-£20
single, £30-£35 double.
Parking for 10.
Credit: Access.

HORSHAM
W. Sussex
Map ref 2D2

Busy town with much
modern development but
still retaining its old
character. The museum in
Causeway House is
devoted chiefly to local
history and the
agricultural life of the
country.
*Tourist Information
Centre ☎ (0403) 211661*

Brookfield Farm Hotel ♨
APPROVED
Winterpit Lane, Plummers
Plain, Horsham, RH13 6LY
☎ Lower Beeding
(0403) 891645/891568
*250-acre mixed farm. In
beautiful countryside in a
central position, ideal for
touring. Convenient for
Gatwick Airport. Lift service
and long term car parking
available. Family-run. A warm
welcome assured.*
Bedrooms: 7 single,
10 double.
Bathrooms: 16 private,
1 public; 1 private shower.
Bed & breakfast: £30-£35
single, £35-£55 double.
Lunch available.
Evening meal 6.50pm (l.o.
9.50pm).
Parking for 100.
Credit: Access, Visa, Amex.

Cisswood House Restaurant and Hotel ♨
COMMENDED
Sandy Gate Lane, Lower
Beeding, Horsham,
RH13 6NF
☎ Lower Beeding (0403)
891216 & Fax (0403) 891621
*Country house restaurant with
well-appointed bedrooms,
family-run by the
chef/proprietor and his wife.
Convenient for Gatwick
Airport, Crawley and
Horsham. 3 conference rooms.*
Bedrooms: 7 single, 22 double
& 5 twin.
Bathrooms: 34 private.
Bed & breakfast: £65-£75
single, £82.50-£130 double.
Half board: from £85 daily.
Lunch available.
Evening meal 7pm (l.o.
9.15pm).
Parking for 65.
Credit: Access, Visa, Diners,
Amex.

Horsham Wimblehurst Hotel
6 Wimblehurst Rd., Horsham,
RH12 2ED
☎ (0403) 62319 & 62774
Fax (0403) 211212
*Family-run hotel, 8 minutes
from town centre and station
(London 1 hour). 8 miles from
Gatwick. Taxi service
available.*
Bedrooms: 1 single, 5 double
& 5 twin, 3 family rooms.
Bathrooms: 12 private,
2 public; 2 private showers.
Bed & breakfast: £34.99-
£39.99 single, £39.99-£49.99
double.
Half board: £44.99-£49.99
daily.
Evening meal 6pm (l.o.
6.45pm).
Parking for 14.
Credit: Access, Visa.

Westlands
COMMENDED
Brighton Road, Monksgate,
Horsham, RH13 6JD
☎ Lower Beeding
(0403) 891383
*Elegant large Victorian house,
situated in Sussex countryside.
Close to village pubs, Gatwick,
coast and places of interest.*
Bedrooms: 1 single, 1 double
& 1 twin, 1 family room.
Bathrooms: 1 private,
2 public.
Bed & breakfast: max. £27.50
single, £38.50-£42.50 double.
Parking for 8.

Ye Olde King's Head Hotel

Listed

Carfax, Horsham,
RH12 1EG
☎ (0403) 53126
*15th C coaching inn situated in
town centre, 20 minutes from
Gatwick and M23. Convenient
for coast and surrounding
countryside.*
Bedrooms: 15 single,
20 double & 5 twin, 2 family
rooms.
Bathrooms: 41 private,
1 public; 1 private shower.
Bed & breakfast: £30-£65
single, £45-£80 double.
Lunch available.
Evening meal 7pm (l.o.
9.45pm).
Parking for 40.
Credit: Access, Visa, Diners,
Amex.

LEWES

E. Sussex
Map ref 2D3

Historic county town with
Norman castle. The steep
High Street has mainly
Georgian buildings. There
is a folk museum at Anne
of Cleves House and the
archaeological museum is
in Barbican House.
*Tourist Information
Centre* ☎ *(0273) 483448*

Berkeley House Hotel M

🏰🏰 **COMMENDED**

2 Albion Street, Lewes,
BN7 2ND
☎ Lewes (0273) 476057
*Elegant Georgian townhouse.
Quiet, conservation area
location in town centre. South-
facing roof terrace. Licensed,
candlelit no-smoking
restaurant.*
Bedrooms: 3 single, 2 double
& 1 twin, 1 family room.
Bathrooms: 2 private,
3 public.
Bed & breakfast: £26.50-
£36.75 single, £35-£55.50
double.
Half board: £28.25-£47.50
daily, £188-£304 weekly.
Evening meal 7.30pm (l.o.
8pm).
Credit: Access, Visa, Amex.

HOVE

See Brighton & Hove.

LEATHERHEAD

Surrey
Map ref 2D2

Old county town in the
Green Belt, with the
modern Thorndike
Theatre.

Preston Cross Hotel & Country Club M

🏰🏰🏰🏰 **COMMENDED**

Rectory Lane, Little
Bookham, Leatherhead,
KT23 4DY
☎ (0372) 456642
Fax (0372) 457456
*Just off the A246 Leatherhead
to Guildford road, comfortable,
friendly hotel set in 4 acres of
landscaped gardens. Ideal for
visiting London and the South
Coast.*
Bedrooms: 4 single, 3 double
& 13 twin, 3 family rooms.
Bathrooms: 23 private.
Bed & breakfast: £55-£70
single, £70-£85 double.
Half board: £70-£85 daily.
Lunch available.
Evening meal 7.30pm (l.o.
10pm).
Parking for 200.
Credit: Access, Visa, Diners,
Amex.

LITTLEHAMPTON

W. Sussex
Map ref 2D3

8m W. Worthing
Ancient port at the mouth
of the River Arun, now a
popular holiday resort,
offering flat, sandy
beaches, sailing, fishing
and boat trips. The
Sussex Downs are a
short walk inland.

Bracken Lodge Guest House M

🏰🏰🏰 **COMMENDED**

43 Church Street,
Littlehampton, BN17 5PU
☎ Littlehampton
(0903) 723174
*Warm welcome and first class
service. Close to beach, town,
golf-courses and swimming
centre. Attractive home and
gardens.*
Bedrooms: 1 single, 1 double
& 1 twin, 1 family room.
Bathrooms: 4 private.
Bed & breakfast: £27.50-£30
single, £45-£48 double.

Half board: £38.50-£41 daily.
Evening meal 7pm (l.o.
5.30pm).
Parking for 6.
Credit: Access, Visa.

Colbern Hotel M

🏰🏰🏰

South Terrace, Seafront,
Littlehampton, BN17 5LQ
☎ (0903) 714270
Telex 934999 TXLINK G
MBX 219996530.
*Friendly family-run hotel with
lounge and balcony overlooking
the Greens and sea. River,
leisure facilities and town are
nearby.*
Bedrooms: 2 single, 4 double
& 3 twin.
Bathrooms: 9 private,
1 public.
Bed & breakfast: £20-£25
single, £40-£50 double.
Half board: £28.50-£34.50
daily, £182-£210 weekly.
Evening meal 6.30pm (l.o.
8pm).
Credit: Access, Visa, Diners,
Amex.

MAIDSTONE

Kent
Map ref 3B3

Busy county town of Kent
on the River Medway has
many interesting features
and is an excellent centre
for excursions. Museum
of carriages, Chillington
Manor House Museum
and Art Gallery,
Archbishop's Palace,
Allington Castle, Mote
Park.
*Tourist Information
Centre* ☎ *(0622) 673581*

Boxley House Hotel M

🏰🏰🏰🏰 **COMMENDED**

The Street, Boxley, Nr.
Maidstone, ME14 3DZ
☎ (0622) 692269 Fax (0622)
683536
*Comfortable, quiet, Georgian
country house hotel set in 17
acres of beautiful parkland,
nestling at the foot of the
North Downs.*
Bedrooms: 5 single, 6 double
& 4 twin, 3 family rooms.
Bathrooms: 18 private.
Bed & breakfast: £49-£54
single, £75-£85 double.
Lunch available.
Evening meal 7pm (l.o.
9.15pm).

Parking for 200.
Credit: Access, Visa, Diners,
Amex.

Grangemoor Hotel M

🏰🏰🏰 **COMMENDED**

St. Michael's Rd., Maidstone,
ME16 8BS
☎ (0622) 677623 Fax (0622)
678246
*One hour from London and the
Kent coast, in a quiet position
on the edge of town. The hotel
has rear gardens, restaurant
and bar.*
Bedrooms: 10 single,
10 double & 12 twin, 4 family
rooms.
Bathrooms: 33 private,
3 public.
Bed & breakfast: £30-£50
single, £42-£60 double.
Half board: £42-£62 daily.
Lunch available.
Evening meal 6.30pm (l.o.
10pm).
Parking for 60.
Credit: Access, Visa.

Mark House Hotel

7 St. Michaels Rd.,
Maidstone, ME16 8BS
☎ (0622) 676586
*Converted and modernised
Victorian house. Licensed
restaurant, residents'
bar/lounge. Close to town
centre. Quiet and comfortable.*
Bedrooms: 16 single, 2 double
& 2 twin.
Bathrooms: 3 public.
Bed & breakfast: £17-£28
single, £28-£38 double.
Half board: £25-£38 daily.
Evening meal 7pm (l.o. 9pm).
Parking for 40.
Credit: Access, Visa.

Rock House Hotel

🏰🏰 **COMMENDED**

102 Tonbridge Rd.,
Maidstone, ME16 8SL
☎ (0622) 751616
*Family-run guesthouse close to
town centre. Convenient for
London, Gatwick and Channel
ports. French and Spanish
spoken.*
Bedrooms: 3 single, 4 double
& 3 twin, 2 family rooms.
Bathrooms: 2 public;
7 private showers.
Bed & breakfast: £26-£33
single, £39-£42 double.
Parking for 7.
Credit: Access, Visa.

MAIDSTONE

Continued

Russell Hotel M

Listed APPROVED

136 Boxley Rd., Maidstone,
ME14 2AH
☎ (0622) 692221
ⒸⓇ Inter
*Converted convent school a few
minutes from Maidstone and
1.5 miles from the M20. Set in
secluded grounds with ample
parking.*
Bedrooms: 17 single,
14 double & 7 twin, 4 family
rooms.
Bathrooms: 42 private.
Bed & breakfast: £49.50-£60
single, £75-£85 double.
Half board: from £59.45
daily.
Lunch available.
Evening meal 7pm (l.o. 9pm).
Parking for 100.
Credit: Access, Visa, Diners,
Amex.

Stakis Country Court Hotel M

Bearsted Road, Whavering,
Maidstone, ME14 5AA
☎ (0622) 34322 Telex 965689
Fax (0622) 34600
ⒸⓇ Stakis
*Large bedrooms, superb leisure
club, five conference rooms.
Just off junction 7 on the M20.
Half board rate based on a
minimum 2 night stay.*
Bedrooms: 62 double &
82 twin.
Bathrooms: 144 private.
Bed & breakfast: from £97
single, from £119 double.
Half board: from £46 daily.
Lunch available.
Evening meal 7pm (l.o.
9.30pm).
Credit: Access, Visa, C.Bl.,
Diners, Amex.

Willington Court M

COMMENDED

Willington St., Maidstone,
ME15 8JW
☎ (0622) 38885
*17th C Tudor-style house,
traditionally furnished.
Antiques, four-poster bed.
Adjacent to Mote Park and
near Leeds Castle.*
Bedrooms: 1 single, 1 double
& 1 twin, 1 family room.
Bathrooms: 1 private,
1 public.

Bed & breakfast: from £15
single, £30-£40 double.
Parking for 6.

MARGATE

Kent
Map ref 3C3

Oldest and most famous
resort in Kent. Many
Regency and Victorian
buildings survive from the
town's early days. There
are 9 miles of sandy
beach. 'Dreamland' is a
20-acre amusement park
and the Winter Gardens
offers concert hall
entertainment.
*Tourist Information
Centre* ☎ *(0843) 220241*

Ambassador Hotel

63-73 Norfolk Rd.,
Cliftonville, Margate,
CT9 2HX
☎ (0843) 292113
*Centrally located for all
holiday amenities and shops.*
Bedrooms: 9 single, 35 double
& 27 twin, 5 family rooms.
Bathrooms: 43 private,
6 public.
Bed & breakfast: from £24.75
single, from £49.50 double.
Half board: from £32 daily,
from £140 weekly.
Evening meal 6pm (l.o.
6.30pm).
Open February-December.

Ashbourne House

WWW

16 Surrey Rd., Cliftonville,
Margate, CT9 2LA
☎ (0843) 227112
*Three-storey terraced building.
Verandah to one bedroom.*
Bedrooms: 1 single, 5 double
& 2 twin, 2 family rooms.
Bathrooms: 1 private,
2 public.
Bed & breakfast: £12 single,
£24 double.
Half board: £18 daily, £88-
£93 weekly.
Evening meal 6pm (l.o. 6pm).
Open April-October.

Braemar Private Hotel M

Listed

1 Stanley Rd., Cliftonville,
Margate, CT9 2DL
☎ Thanet (0843) 224198
*Small hotel with a big warm
welcome, within easy reach of
all amenities.*

Bedrooms: 2 single, 3 twin,
6 family rooms.
Bathrooms: 2 public.
Bed & breakfast: £10-£12
single, £20-£24 double.
Half board: £14-£16 daily,
£85-£92 weekly.
Evening meal 6pm.

Bridge Hotel M

WWWW

13-15 St. Mildreds Road.,
Westgate, Margate, CT8 8RE
☎ Thanet (0843) 31023
Fax (0843) 35564
*Totally rebuilt and refurbished
100-year-old establishment
upgraded to international
standards. Hotel and public
house complete with coffee
shop/restaurant.*
Bedrooms: 3 single, 10 double
& 1 twin, 4 family rooms.
Bathrooms: 18 private.
Bed & breakfast: £37.60-
£41.50 single, £52.88-£58.50
double.
Half board: £47.10-£51 daily.
Lunch available.
Evening meal 7pm (l.o.
9.45pm).
Parking for 8.
Credit: Access, Visa.

Brierdene Hotel

Listed

17/21 Warwick Road,
Cliftonville, Margate,
CT9 2JU
☎ (0843) 220937
*Comfortable hotel in prime
position between beaches, shops
and bowls complexes. Live
entertainment, coach tours and
lots more!*
Bedrooms: 5 single, 10 double
& 6 twin, 11 family rooms.
Bathrooms: 6 private,
6 public.
Bed & breakfast: £17.50-£20
single, £34-£44 double.
Half board: £22-£25 daily,
£115-£135 weekly.
Lunch available.
Evening meal 6pm (l.o.
6.30pm).

Charrington Hotel

WW

98 Grosvenor Place Margate,
CT9 1UY
☎ (0843) 221162
*3 minutes from sea and town
centre.*
Bedrooms: 2 single, 4 double
& 1 twin, 2 family rooms.
Bathrooms: 1 public;
4 private showers.

Bed & breakfast: £14-£16
single.
Half board: £19-£21 daily.
Evening meal 8pm (l.o.
10.30pm).

Clintons

WWW COMMENDED

9, Dalby Square, Cliftonville,
CT9 2ER
☎ Thanet
(0843) 290598/299550
*Set in illuminated garden
square, this elegant hotel offers
comfortable en-suite bedrooms,
spacious lounge, licensed
restaurant, saunas, jacuzzi,
gymnasium and solarium.*
Bedrooms: 5 double & 5 twin,
3 family rooms.
Bathrooms: 13 private,
4 public.
Bed & breakfast: £22-£28
single, £32-£38 double.
Half board: £21-£24 daily.
Evening meal 6pm (l.o. 8pm).
Parking for 6.
Credit: Access, Visa, Diners.

Edgewater Private Hotel

99 Sea Rd., Westgate-on-Sea,
Margate, CT8 8QE
☎ (0843) 31933
*Family hotel on seafront with
licensed bar, TV lounge, indoor
swimming pool, car parking,
pool room.*
Bedrooms: 1 single, 3 double
& 2 twin, 6 family rooms.
Bathrooms: 12 private.
Bed & breakfast: £22-£26
single, £38-£44 double.
Half board: £28-£32 daily,
£164.50-£176.25 weekly.
Lunch available.
Parking for 14.
Credit: Visa.

The Greswolde Hotel

WWW

20 Surrey Rd, Margate,
CT9 2LA
☎ (0843) 223956
*Elegant Victorian hotel
retaining much of its original
character, 100 yards from
promenade and championship
bowling greens. Ideal for
touring and golf.*
Bedrooms: 2 double & 2 twin,
2 family rooms.
Bathrooms: 6 private.
Bed & breakfast: £19 single,
£31 double.
Credit: Access, Visa.

Ivyside Hotel ⋒
😊😊😊😊

25 Sea Rd., Westgate-on-Sea,
Margate, CT8 8SB
☎ Thanet (0843) 31082
*Seafront hotel offering special
weekend and midweek breaks
with excellent reductions.
Facilities for families and
conferences.*
Bedrooms: 8 single, 7 double
& 15 twin, 35 family rooms.
Bathrooms: 63 private,
3 public.
Bed & breakfast: £23-£36
single, £46-£72 double.
Half board: £30-£43 daily,
£210-£301 weekly.
Lunch available.
Evening meal 6.30pm (l.o.
8.30pm).
Parking for 25.
Credit: Access, Visa.
🛇 🖕 🍴 ⊡ 🖵 🖊 ⅋ 🖭 📺
● 🏃 🛋 🍴 🛆 🌸 🗠 ☂ 🐾
⅄ ☼ 🛏 ⅀ SP

Lonsdale Court Hotel ⋒
😊😊😊 APPROVED

51-61 Norfolk Rd.,
Cliftonville, Margate,
CT9 2HX
☎ Thanet (0843) 221053
*Family hotel close to sea and
shops. Nightly entertainment
including bands, discos in
season. Sports hall and leisure
facilities including badminton,
indoor bowls, sauna, solarium
and a heated indoor pool.*
Bedrooms: 10 single,
17 double & 12 twin,
25 family rooms.
Bathrooms: 64 private,
1 public.
Bed & breakfast: £30-£35
single, £50-£60 double.
Lunch available.
Evening meal 7pm (l.o.
8.30pm).
Credit: Access, Visa.
🛇 🖕 🍴 ⊡ 🖵 🖊 ⅋ 🖭 📺
● 🖃 🛋 🍴 🛆 🗠 ☂ 🐾
☼ 🛏 OAP ⅀ SP ⊤

Raymonde Hotel ⋒
Listed

1-7 Ethelbert Rd.,
Cliftonville, Margate,
CT9 1SH
☎ Thanet (0843) 223991
*Privately-owned family hotel
under the supervision of
proprietress. Aim is to provide
a good standard of food,
service and hygiene. Family
entertainment most evenings.*
Bedrooms: 7 single, 9 double
& 9 twin, 5 family rooms.
Bathrooms: 10 private,
4 public.
Bed & breakfast: £17-£25
single, £33-£48 double.

Half board: £24-£32 daily,
£130-£175 weekly.
Lunch available.
Evening meal 6pm.
🛇 🖕 ⊡ 🖵 ⅋ ⊡ 🖭 ⅋ 📺 ⅊
🖃 🛋 🍴 🛆 ☼ OAP ⅀ SP

Riverdale Hotel ⋒
😊😊😊

40-46 Sweyn Rd.,
Cliftonville, Margate,
CT9 2DF
☎ Thanet (0843) 223628
*Close to sandy beaches,
promenade, shops and
traditional seaside amenities.
Versatile and imaginative
cuisine. In-house entertainment
some nights.*
Bedrooms: 7 single, 12 double
& 8 twin, 7 family rooms.
Bathrooms: 18 private,
4 public.
Bed & breakfast: £19.50-
£27.50 single, £39-£44 double.
Half board: £26-£34 daily,
£132-£175 weekly.
Lunch available.
Evening meal 6pm (l.o.
6.30pm).
Open March-December.
Credit: Access, Visa, Diners,
Amex.
🛇 🖕 ⊡ 🖵 ⅋ ⅋ 🖭 🖊 ●
🖃 🛋 🛏 OAP ⅀ SP ⊤

Seabrook Guest House

35 Canterbury Rd.,
Westbrook, Margate,
CT9 5AW
☎ Thanet (0843) 297854
*Friendly guesthouse close to
beach, station and shops.
Comfortable accommodation,
home cooking with varied
menu, own keys, and personal
attention at all times.*
Bedrooms: 2 single, 3 double
& 1 twin, 2 family rooms.
Bathrooms: 1 public.
Bed & breakfast: £12-£15
single, £24-£30 double.
Half board: £18-£21 daily,
£110-£125 weekly.
Evening meal 6pm (l.o. 6pm).
🛇2 🖕 ⅋ 🖭 🖊 📺 ● 🖃 🛏
OAP ⅀ SP

Seacroft Hotel

28-29 Dalby Sq., Cliftonville,
Margate, CT9 2EP
☎ (0843) 225475
*Close to all amenities and
entertainments and overlooking
well-kept illuminated gardens.
Free parking around the
square.*
Bedrooms: 2 single, 12 double
& 7 twin, 4 family rooms.
Bathrooms: 3 public;
2 private showers.
Half board: £75-£95 weekly.
Evening meal 6pm (l.o.
6.30pm).
🛇 🖕 ⅋ 🖵 ⅋ 🖭 🖊 📺 ⅊
🛏 OAP ⅀ SP

Smithy's Aparthotel ⋒
c/o Lonsdale Court Hotel,
Norfolk Rd., Cliftonville,
Margate, CT9 2HX
☎ Thanet (0843) 221053
*Seafront holiday centre. Choice
of self-catering or hotel
amenities. Weekly
entertainment in season. Multi-
purpose sports and badminton
hall. Indoor heated swimming
pool, solarium and sauna in
sister hotel.*
Bedrooms: 25 family rooms.
Bathrooms: 25 private.
Bed & breakfast: £25-£35
single, £40-£50 double.
Lunch available.
Evening meal 6.30pm (l.o.
9.30pm).
Parking for 25.
🛇 🖕 ⊡ 🖵 ⅋ 🖭 🖊 📺
⅊ 🖃 🛋 🍴 🛆 🗠 🛏 OAP ⅀
SP ⊤

Waterside Private Hotel
61 Sea Rd., Westgate-on-Sea,
Margate, CT8 8QG
☎ Thanet (0843) 32194
*Waterside family hotel for a
peaceful holiday, overlooking
Westgate Bay. No yellow lines,
no VAT.*
Bedrooms: 3 double & 2 twin,
7 family rooms.
Bathrooms: 2 public;
3 private showers.
Bed & breakfast: max. £14
single, max. £28 double.
Half board: max. £18 daily,
max. £110 weekly.
Evening meal 6pm.
Parking for 10.
Open April-October.
🛇 🖕 🍴 🖵 ⅋ 🖭 📺 ● 🛋
🛏 🖽 OAP ⅀ 🖾

Westbrook Bay House ⋒
😊😊 COMMENDED

12 Royal Esplanade,
Westbrook, Margate,
CT9 5DW
☎ Thanet (0843) 292700
*Family-run guesthouse situated
on the seafront.*
Bedrooms: 2 single, 2 double
& 2 twin, 4 family rooms.
Bathrooms: 3 private,
2 public; 2 private showers.
Bed & breakfast: £15-£16.50
single, £30-£33 double.
Half board: £19.50-£21 daily.
Evening meal 6pm (l.o. 4pm).
🛇 ⊡ 🖵 ⅋ 🖭 🖊 📺 🖃
🛏 OAP ⅀ SP

White Lodge Guest House ⋒
😊😊 COMMENDED

12, Domneva Road,
Westgate-on-Sea, Margate,
CT8 8PE
☎ Thanet (0843) 31828

*Beautifully appointed late
Victorian detached house. 100
yards from sandy beach and
with fine sea views. Secluded
rear garden.*
Bedrooms: 1 single, 3 double
& 1 twin, 2 family rooms.
Bathrooms: 5 private,
2 public.
Bed & breakfast: £16.50-£22
single, £33-£39.50 double.
Half board: £23-£28.50 daily,
£150-£184 weekly.
Lunch available.
Evening meal 6pm (l.o. 8pm).
Parking for 3.
🛇 🖕 🖵 ⅋ 🖭 🖊 ⅋ 📺
🖃 🛋 🛏 🖽 OAP SP ⊤

> MAYFIELD

E. Sussex
Map ref 2D3

8m S. Tunbridge Wells
On a ridge offering wide
views of the Sussex
Weald. Fire swept
through the village in
1389, thus the oldest
houses in the main street
date from the 15th C.

Rose and Crown Inn
😊😊😊 COMMENDED

Fletching Street, Mayfield,
TN20 6TE
☎ Mayfield (0435) 872200
*Charming character inn dated
1546, with unspoilt oak-
beamed bars and real log fires.
Delightfully quaint beamed
bedrooms. Pretty garden.*
Bedrooms: 3 double.
Bathrooms: 3 private.
Bed & breakfast: £38-£44.50
single, £48-£61 double.
Half board: £35-£40 daily.
Lunch available.
Evening meal 7pm (l.o.
9.30pm).
Parking for 15.
🛇7 ⊡ 🖵 ⅋ 🖭 🖊 📺 🖃 🛋
🍴 🗠 ☼ 🛏 🖽 ⅀ SP 🖾

MIDHURST

W. Sussex
Map ref 2C3

On the outskirts of the
town are the remains of
Cowdray Park, a
substantial 16th C
fortified mansion. There is
a museum and the public
can watch the famous
Cowdray Park polo.

Park House Hotel ⋒
😊😊😊😊 COMMENDED

Bepton, Nr. Midhurst,
GU29 0JB
☎ (073 081) 2880 & 3543
Continued ▶

MIDHURST
Continued

A beautifully situated country house hotel, equipped to give maximum comfort, with the atmosphere and amenities of an English country home.
Bedrooms: 2 single, 2 double & 7 twin.
Bathrooms: 11 private, 1 public.
Bed & breakfast: £46-£48.30 single, £80.50-£84.50 double.
Half board: £59.80-£62.70 daily, £315-£350 weekly.
Lunch available.
Evening meal 8pm (l.o. 9pm).
Parking for 22.
Credit: Access, Visa.
⛵ 🏃 ℃ 🔞 💷 🥚 🍴 Ⓥ 📠
📺 ▥ ♨ 🔧 ⚘ ✿ 🐾

Southdown's Hotel and Country Restaurant ♨
🏰🏰🏰🏰 **COMMENDED**
Trotton, Rogate, Nr. Petersfield, Hampshire GU31 5JN
☎ Rogate (0730) 821521
Fax (0730) 821790
Country hotel set in its own gardens with full leisure facilities. Ideal for a peaceful rest away from it all. 3 miles west of Midhurst.
Bedrooms: 13 double & 7 twin, 2 family rooms.
Bathrooms: 22 private.
Bed & breakfast: £50-£60 single, £65-£90 double.
Half board: £40-£50 daily.
Lunch available.
Evening meal 7.30pm (l.o. 10pm).
Parking for 70.
Credit: Access, Visa, Amex.
⛵ 🏃 🐎 ℃ 🔞 🥚 💷 🚗 Ⓥ
✂ 📠 ▥ ♨ 🍴 👜 ⚘ 🎿 🔧
🔄 ♩ ➤ ✎ 🚶 🐾 🐕 🐴 SP 🐎
T

MINSTER-IN-SHEPPEY
Kent
Map ref 3B3

Perched on a hilltop from which 5 major waterways can be seen. One of its main features is the twin church of St. Mary and St. Sexburga.

Beach Hotel ♨
Seaside Avenue, Minster, Sheppey, ME12 2NA
☎ (0795) 872364
Ideally situated with seaviews, cliff walks. 2 miles from Sheerness. Good food. Licensed bars. En-suite motel accommodation. Ample car parking.

Bedrooms: 4 single, 1 double & 25 twin.
Bathrooms: 30 private, 1 public.
Bed & breakfast: £20-£25 single, £27.50-£35 double.
Half board: £25-£30 daily, £120-£180 weekly.
Lunch available.
Evening meal 6.30pm (l.o. 9pm).
Credit: Access.
⛵ 🏃 🐎 ♨ ℃ Ⓥ 📠 📺 ▥ ♨
🍴 👜 🐎 🔧 ✿ 🐾 SP T

NEW ROMNEY
Kent
Map ref 3B4

Capital of Romney Marsh. Now 1 mile from the sea, it was one of the original Cinque Ports. Romney, Hythe and Dymchurch Railway's main station is here.

Broadacre Hotel ♨
🏰🏰🏰 **APPROVED**
North St., New Romney, TN28 8DR
☎ (0679) 62381
Small 16th C family-run hotel offering a warm, friendly welcome and personal attention. Intimate restaurants, lounge bar and family garden.
Bedrooms: 3 single, 4 double & 1 twin, 1 family room.
Bathrooms: 9 private.
Bed & breakfast: £30-£40 single, £40-£55 double.
Half board: £29-£55 daily, from £190 weekly.
Lunch available.
Evening meal 7pm (l.o. 9pm).
Parking for 9.
Credit: Access, Visa, Diners, Amex.
⛵ 🏃 🔞 💷 ▥ 🚗 🍴 ✿ SP 📠
📠 📺 ▥ 👜 🍴 ✿ SP ✂

NEWHAVEN
E. Sussex
Map ref 2D3

Town has the terminal of a car-ferry service to Dieppe in France.

The Old Volunteer Guest House
1 South Rd., Newhaven, BN9 9QL
☎ (0273) 515204
This guesthouse was formerly a public house for 100 years. 5 minutes from railway and cross-Channel boat to Dieppe.
Bedrooms: 4 single, 6 double & 3 twin, 4 family rooms.
Bathrooms: 3 private, 3 public; 1 private shower.

Bed & breakfast: £18.50-£33 single, £30-£48 double.
Credit: Access, Visa, Diners, Amex.
⛵ 🏃 📠 ▥ 💷 🔞 ◑ ▥ ♨

OCKLEY
Surrey
Map ref 2D2

Village by the Roman road Stane Street. In 851 King Ethelwulf defeated the Danes in battle on Ockley Green. Behind the village is Leith Hill with its outstanding views.

Gatton Manor Hotel, Golf and Country Club
🏰🏰🏰 **APPROVED**
Ockley, Nr. Dorking, RH5 5PQ
☎ Oakwoodhill (030 679) 555 & 556
200-acre estate with championship length golf-course. Hotel, a la carte restaurants, conference suites, bowls, fishing.
Bedrooms: 2 double & 8 twin.
Bathrooms: 10 private, 2 public.
Bed & breakfast: £55-£65 single, £90 double.
Half board: £50-£65 daily.
Lunch available.
Evening meal 7pm (l.o. 9.30pm).
Parking for 150.
Credit: Access, Visa.
⛵ 🏃 ℃ 🔞 💷 🔧 Ⓥ 🔄 📠
📺 ▥ 👜 🍴 ♩ ♒ ➤ ✎ ✿
🐴 🐎 SP

PEACEHAVEN
E. Sussex
Map ref 2D3

1m W. Newhaven
Development started in 1915 when it was to have been called Anzac-on-Sea. A monument on the cliff marks the spot where the Greenwich Meridian leaves Britain.
Tourist Information Centre ☎ (0273) 582668.

The Brighton Motel ♨
🏰🏰🏰 **APPROVED**
1 South Coast Rd., Peacehaven, BN10 8SY
☎ (0273) 583736
Cliff-top motel with fully licensed restaurant and free house bar. Disabled guests catered for.
Bedrooms: 16 double & 9 twin, 3 family rooms.
Bathrooms: 28 private.

Bed & breakfast: £36-£55 single, £45-£55 double.
Half board: £30-£40 daily, £210 weekly.
Lunch available.
Evening meal 7pm (l.o. 9.30pm).
Parking for 50.
Credit: Access, Visa, C.Bl., Diners, Amex.
⛵ 🏃 ℃ 🔞 📠 🔧 🥚 Ⓥ ▥
🐴 T

PENSHURST
Kent
Map ref 2D2

Village in a hilly wooded setting with Penshurst Place, the ancestral home of the Sidney family since 1552, standing in delightful grounds with a formal Tudor garden.

Swale Cottage
Listed **COMMENDED**
Old Swaylands Lane, Off Poundsbridge Lane, Penshurst, Nr. Tonbridge, TN11 8AH
☎ Penshurst (0892) 870738
Charmingly converted Grade II listed barn in idyllically tranquil wooded valley. Three attractively furnished en-suite rooms. Close to Penshurst Place, Hever, and Chartwell. Gatwick is 30 minutes' drive. Near A26, off the B2176.
Bedrooms: 2 double & 1 twin.
Bathrooms: 3 private.
Bed & breakfast: £26-£28 single, £40-£44 double.
Parking for 7.
⛵ 🏃10 🐎 🔞 💷 Ⓥ 📠 📺
▥ 👜 ✿ 🐕 🐴 SP 🐎

PETWORTH
W. Sussex
Map ref 2D3

Town dominated by Petworth House, the great 17th C mansion, set in 2000 acres of parkland laid out by Capability Brown. The house contains wood-carvings by Grinling Gibbons.

Melrose
The Street, Graffham, Petworth, GU28 0QB
☎ Graffham (079 86) 541
Detached private house with panoramic views in centre of picturesque Downland village midway between Petworth and Midhurst. Ideal base for touring and rambling.
Bedrooms: 1 single, 2 double.
Bathrooms: 1 public.

Bed & breakfast: £17 single,
£28 double.
Half board: £21-£24 daily.
Parking for 4.

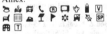

PULBOROUGH

W. Sussex
Map ref 2D3

Here is Parham, an
Elizabethan mansion with
unusually tall, mullioned
windows and a long
gallery measuring 158 ft.
The house and the
surrounding park and
garden can be visited. In
the grounds stands the
church of St. Peter.

Chequers Hotel ₥
≝≝≝

Church Pl., Pulborough,
RH20 1AD
☎ (0798) 872486 & (0798)
872486 Fax (0798) 872715
ⓒⓡ Minotels
*Queen Anne hotel in picturesque
village, overlooking the South
Downs. Licensed restaurant,
coffee shop. Bedrooms with all
facilities, some on ground floor
and some four-posters. New
garden conservatory.*
Bedrooms: 1 single, 5 double
& 2 twin, 3 family rooms.
Bathrooms: 11 private.
Bed & breakfast: £40-£45
single, £60-£70 double.
Half board: £35-£80 daily,
£245-£315 weekly.
Lunch available.
Evening meal 7.30pm (l.o.
8.30pm).
Parking for 14.
Credit: Access, Visa, Diners,
Amex.

White Horse Inn ₥
≝≝≝ COMMENDED

The Street, Sutton, Nr.
Pulborough, RH20 1PS
☎ Sutton (079 87) 221
Fax (079 87) 291
*Pretty Georgian village inn
close to South Downs Way.
Roman villa one mile. Garden,
log fires.*
Bedrooms: 2 double & 2 twin.
Bathrooms: 4 private.
Bed & breakfast: £38 single,
£48 double.
Half board: £36-£50 daily,
£176-£237 weekly.
Lunch available.
Evening meal 7pm (l.o.
9.45pm).
Parking for 12.
Credit: Access, Visa.

RAMSGATE

Kent
Map ref 3C3

Popular holiday resort
with good sandy beaches.
At Pegwell Bay is the
replica of a Viking
longship. Terminal for
car-ferry service to
Dunkirk.
*Tourist Information
Centre ☎ (0843) 591086*

Arundel

46 Westcliff Rd., Ramsgate,
CT11 9NT
☎ Thanet (0843) 593652
*Warm, friendly, family-run
hotel, 5 minutes' walk from
ferries, shops and beaches.
Home cooking. Mini-breaks
available.*
Bedrooms: 1 single, 3 double,
4 family rooms.
Bathrooms: 3 public.
Bed & breakfast: £12-£14
single, £22-£24 double.
Half board: £13.50-£15.50
daily, £79-£84 weekly.
Evening meal 5.30pm (l.o.
6pm).
Parking for 6.

Belvidere Guest House

26 Augusta Rd., Ramsgate,
CT11 8JS
☎ Thanet (0843) 588809
*Friendly family-run guesthouse
on East Cliff, minutes from
beach, ferry terminal and
shops.*
Bedrooms: 2 double, 3 family
rooms.
Bathrooms: 1 public.
Bed & breakfast: £11-£15
single, £20-£24 double.
Half board: £15-£20 daily,
£98-£119 weekly.
Evening meal 6pm (l.o. 8pm).
Parking for 12.

Channel View

14 Nelson Crescent,
Ramsgate, CT11 9JF
☎ Thanet (0843) 591717
*Grade II Regency building
some 200 years old overlooking
harbour and marina.
Completely refurbished in
1989.*
Bedrooms: 3 single, 2 double
& 3 twin, 1 family room.
Bathrooms: 3 private,
2 public; 1 private shower.
Bed & breakfast: from £12
single, from £24 double.

Eastwood Guest House

28, Augusta Road, Ramsgate,
CT11 8JS
☎ Thanet (0843) 591505
*Comfortable homely
guesthouse with sea views, on
east side of Ramsgate harbour.*
Bedrooms: 4 double, 3 family
rooms.
Bathrooms: 3 public.
Bed & breakfast: £12.50-£15
single, £22-£25 double.
Half board: £16.50-£19.50
daily, £95-£115 weekly.
Evening meal 6.30pm (l.o.
8pm).
Parking for 14.

Goodwin View Hotel ₥
≝≝

19 Wellington Cres.,
Ramsgate, CT11 8JD
☎ Thanet (0843) 591419
*Seafront licensed hotel in
Grade II listed historic
building overlooking harbour
and beach. Bookings made for
ferry-users. Terminal and town
within walking distance.*
Bedrooms: 5 single, 2 double
& 4 twin, 2 family rooms.
Bathrooms: 3 private,
3 public.
Bed & breakfast: £16.50-£25
single, £30-£42.50 double.
Half board: £22.50-£33.25
daily, £141.50-£204 weekly.
Evening meal 6pm.

Marina Resort Hotel ₥
≝≝≝≝

Harbour Parade, Ramsgate,
CT11 8LJ
☎ (0843) 588276 Fax (0843)
586866
ⓒⓡ Resort
*Thanet's newest hotel,
overlooking attractive marina,
offers health club, a la carte
menu, all bedrooms with TV
and en-suite facilities.*
Bedrooms: 4 single, 15 double
& 35 twin, 5 family rooms.
Bathrooms: 59 private.
Bed & breakfast: £28.50-
£72.50 single, £57-£95 double.
Lunch available.
Evening meal 7pm (l.o.
9.30pm).
Credit: Access, Visa, Diners,
Amex.

Ravensmere Guest
House

3 Albion Rd., Ramsgate,
CT11 8DJ
☎ Thanet (0843) 592915

Small family-run house with
comfortable and friendly
atmosphere. Good home-
cooked food. Close to all
amenities. Own keys. Ample
parking.
Bedrooms: 4 double, 2 family
rooms.
Bathrooms: 1 public.
Bed & breakfast: from £11
single, from £22 double.
Half board: from £14 daily.
Evening meal 6.30pm (l.o.
7.30pm).

Shirley's Hotel ₥
≝≝

8 Nelson Cres., Ramsgate,
CT11 9JF
☎ Thanet (0843) 584198
*Overlooking Ramsgate harbour
and Sally Line ferry terminal.
2 minutes from town centre. All
rooms have colour TV and
some are en-suite.*
Bedrooms: 3 single, 2 double
& 5 twin, 2 family rooms.
Bathrooms: 3 private,
2 public.
Bed & breakfast: £13-£15
single, £25-£35 double.

Tancliff Private Hotel ₥
≝≝≝

20 Wellington Cres., East
Cliff, Ramsgate, CT11 8JD
☎ Thanet (0843) 593016
*In a clifftop Regency crescent,
overlooking sands and harbour
and close to town centre and
ferry terminal.*
Bedrooms: 3 single, 3 double
& 2 twin, 2 family rooms.
Bathrooms: 6 private,
1 public; 4 private showers.
Bed & breakfast: £18-£30
single, £36-£40 double.
Half board: £25-£37 daily,
£150-£210 weekly.
Evening meal 6pm (l.o.
midday).

REDHILL

Surrey
Map ref 2D2

Part of the borough of
Reigate and now the
commercial centre.
Gatwick Airport is 3 miles
to the south.

Ashleigh House Hotel
Listed APPROVED

39 Redstone Hill, Redhill,
RH1 4BG
☎ (0737) 764763

Continued ▶

REDHILL

Continued

Friendly family-run early Edwardian house, 500 yards from railway station, London 30 minutes, Gatwick Airport 15 minutes.
Bedrooms: 3 single, 2 double & 3 twin, 1 family room.
Bathrooms: 1 private, 2 public; 2 private showers.
Bed & breakfast: £27 single, £40-£48 double.
Parking for 9.

Hunters Lodge Hotel

Nutfield Rd., Redhill, RH1 4ED
☎ (0737) 773139
On the A25 between Redhill and Nutfield. Two Victorian mansions dating back to 1850. Recently tastefully renovated.
Bedrooms: 5 single, 13 double & 7 twin.
Bathrooms: 25 private.
Bed & breakfast: from £60 single, from £71 double.
Half board: £45.75-£70 daily.
Evening meal 7pm (l.o. 9.45pm).
Parking for 50.
Credit: Access, Visa, Diners, Amex.

Nutfield Priory ♠
COMMENDED
Nutfield, Redhill, RH1 4EN
☎ (0737) 822066
Built in 1872 for Joshua Fielden MP, set in 40 acres of Surrey countryside with unsurpassed views. Large ornate building of towers, elaborate carvings, stonework cloisters and stained glass windows.
Bedrooms: 7 single, 31 double & 13 twin.
Bathrooms: 51 private.
Bed & breakfast: from £85 single, from £113 double.
Lunch available.
Evening meal 7pm (l.o. 10pm).
Parking for 150.
Credit: Access, Visa, Diners, Amex.

> *Map references apply to the colour maps towards the end of this guide.*

REIGATE

Surrey
Map ref 2D2

Old town on the edge of the North Downs with modern developments. Just outside the town on Reigate Heath stands an old windmill, which has been converted into a church.

Beechwood House
39 Hatchlands Rd., Redhill, RH1 6AP
☎ (0737) 761444 & 764277
Victorian house with easy access to all amenities and Gatwick Airport. 10 minutes' walk from mainline station (Victoria 30 minutes).
Bedrooms: 2 single, 1 double & 3 twin, 1 family room.
Bathrooms: 2 public.
Bed & breakfast: £30-£35 single, £40-£45 double.
Parking for 9.

Bridge House Hotel & Restaurant
Reigate Hill, Reigate, RH2 9RP
☎ (0737) 246801
Telex 268810 Fax (0737) 223756
Most rooms have own balcony with views over South Downs. 2 minutes from junction 8 on M25. 15 minutes from Gatwick and 35 minutes from Heathrow.
Bedrooms: 8 single, 6 double & 23 twin, 3 family rooms.
Bathrooms: 40 private.
Bed & breakfast: £40-£60 single, £50-£90 double.
Lunch available.
Evening meal 7.30pm (l.o. 10pm).
Parking for 150.
Credit: Access, Visa, Diners, Amex.

Cranleigh Hotel ♠
APPROVED
41 West St., Reigate, RH2 9BL
☎ (0737) 223417 Fax (0737) 223734
Ⓜ Minotels
Close to town centre and railway station, on the main road to the south-west, within a short distance of Gatwick Airport and easy reach of the centre of London. 1 mile from M25.
Bedrooms: 2 single, 3 double & 3 twin, 2 family rooms.

Bathrooms: 8 private, 2 public.
Bed & breakfast: £42-£60 single, £60-£75 double.
Evening meal 7.30pm (l.o. 8pm).
Parking for 6.
Credit: Access, Visa, C.Bl., Diners, Amex.

Prince of Wales Hotel
2 Holmesdale Rd., Reigate, RH2 0BQ
☎ Reigate (073 72) 43122
Public house at the bottom of Reigate Hill next door to the station. 5 minutes from M25 motorway.
Bedrooms: 1 single, 4 twin, 1 family room.
Bathrooms: 1 private, 4 public.
Bed & breakfast: from £25 single, from £45 double.
Half board: from £30 daily, from £175 weekly.
Lunch available.
Evening meal 6pm (l.o. 8pm).
Parking for 20.

ROBERTSBRIDGE

E. Sussex
Map ref 3B4

Small town in well-wooded country near the River Rother, with a number of old timber and boarded houses. An important local industry is the making of Gray-Nicolls cricket bats.

Parsonage Farm
Salehurst, Robertsbridge, TN32 5PJ
☎ (0580) 880446
300-acre mixed and hops farm. 15th C farmhouse with beams and panelling. Relaxed atmosphere. Within easy reach of South Coast resorts and many places of historic interest and natural beauty.
Bedrooms: 1 single, 1 twin, 1 family room.
Bathrooms: 1 public.
Bed & breakfast: £13 single, £26 double.
Half board: max. £20 daily, max. £130 weekly.
Evening meal 6.30pm.
Parking for 20.
Open January-August, November-December.

ROCHESTER

Kent
Map ref 3B3

Ancient cathedral city on the River Medway. Has many places of interest connected with Charles Dickens (who lived nearby) including the fascinating Dickens Centre. Also massive castle overlooking the river and Guildhall Museum.
Tourist Information Centre ☎ (0634) 843666

Belmont Guest House
18/19 New Road, Rochester, ME1 1BG
☎ Medway (0634) 812262
Proprietor is always available and ready to assist in making guests welcome. Excellent views to front and rear of guesthouse, in a nice area. Evening meals by arrangement only.
Bedrooms: 10 single, 5 double & 1 twin.
Bathrooms: 4 public.
Bed & breakfast: £13-£15 single, £20-£26 double.
Parking for 6.

Medway Manor Hotel
16 New Rd., Rochester, ME1 1BG
☎ Medway (0634) 847985
Family-run hotel with historic and scenic views, convenient for London and south east coast. Leisure facilities available.
Bedrooms: 5 single, 25 double & 9 twin, 3 family rooms.
Bathrooms: 31 private, 5 public.
Bed & breakfast: £35-£85 single, £45-£120 double.
Half board: £42-£105 daily, £294-£735 weekly.
Lunch available.
Evening meal 6.30pm (l.o. 9.30pm).
Parking for 50.
Credit: Access, Visa, Diners, Amex.

> *The national Crown scheme is explained in full on pages 536–539.*

> *The symbols are explained on the flap inside the back cover.*

ROMNEY MARSH

Kent
Map ref 3B4

Chatswood Lodge Guest House

37, High Street, Lydd,
Romney Marsh
☎ Lydd (0679) 20410
*Attractive detached house with
secluded large gardens,
offering peaceful and homely
surroundings. Within easy
reach of sea and local
amenities.*
Bedrooms: 1 double & 2 twin,
1 family room.
Bathrooms: 1 public.
Bed & breakfast: £13.50-
£16.50 single, £26-£30 double.
Half board: £20-£22 daily,
£120-£135 weekly.
Evening meal 6.30pm (l.o.
7.30pm).
Parking for 8.

RUSTINGTON

W. Sussex
Map ref 2D3

1m E. Littlehampton
Village with thatched
cottages and a medieval
church.

Mayday Hotel M
COMMENDED

12 Broadmark Lane,
Rustington, BN16 2HH
☎ (0903) 771198
*In own gardens 400 yards from
the beach yet ideally placed for
exploring the countryside with
its many attractions. Under the
personal supervision of the
proprietors, a warm welcome
assured.*
Bedrooms: 2 single, 3 double
& 4 twin, 1 family room.
Bathrooms: 6 private,
2 public.
Bed & breakfast: £24-£32.70
single, £53-£61.81 double.
Half board: £27-£40.87 daily,
£210.48-£231.93 weekly.
Evening meal 7pm (l.o.
7.50pm).
Parking for 12.
Credit: Access, Visa.

---

*Half board prices
shown are per
person but in some
cases may be based
on double/twin
occupancy.*

RYE

E. Sussex
Map ref 3B4

Cobbled, hilly streets and
fine old buildings make
Rye, once a Cinque Port,
a most picturesque town.
Noted for its church with
ancient clock, potteries
and antique shops, and
the Ypres Tower
Museum.
*Tourist Information
Centre* ☎ (0797) 226696

Aviemore Guest House M

28/30 Fishmarket Road, Rye,
TN31 7LP
☎ (0797) 223052
*Owner-run, friendly guesthouse
offering a warm welcome and
hearty breakfast. Overlooking
"Town Salts" and the River
Rother. 2 minutes from town
centre.*
Bedrooms: 1 single, 3 double
& 3 twin, 1 family room.
Bathrooms: 4 private,
2 public.
Bed & breakfast: £15-£20
single, £28-£36 double.
Half board: £19-£24 daily,
£124-£149 weekly.
Evening meal 6pm (l.o.
10pm).
Credit: Access, Visa, Amex.

Broomhill Lodge Hotel M
COMMENDED

Rye Foreign, Rye,
TN31 7UN
☎ Iden (079 78) 421
*Early 19th C country house
hotel set in 2 acres of gardens
with superb views over Sussex
countryside. 1.5 miles north-
west of Rye.*
Bedrooms: 2 single, 7 double
& 3 twin.
Bathrooms: 12 private.
Bed & breakfast: £40 single,
£64-£75 double.
Half board: £44-£55 daily,
£275-£360 weekly.
Evening meal 7.30pm (l.o.
9.30pm).
Parking for 12.
Credit: Access, Visa, Amex.

Cinque Ports Lodge M

93 Lydd Road, Camber,
TN31 7RS
☎ Rye (0797) 226017

---

*Modern, friendly hotel situated
100 yards from sandy beach.
Ancient Rye short ride away.
Health club, swimming pools
adjacent.*
Bedrooms: 5 double & 2 twin,
1 family room.
Bathrooms: 8 private.
Bed & breakfast: £25-£38
single, £40-£55 double.
Half board: £30-£37 daily,
£180-£220 weekly.
Lunch available.
Evening meal 6.50pm (l.o.
8.50pm).
Parking for 10.
Credit: Access, Visa.

Flackley Ash Hotel & Restaurant M
APPROVED

London Rd., Peasmarsh,
Rye, TN31 6YH
☎ Peasmarsh (079 721) 651
& Fax (079 721) 510
Telex 957210 RLTG
Best Western
*Georgian country house hotel
in 5 acres. Swimming pool and
leisure centre. Fresh fish, well-
stocked cellar. Half board rate
based on a minimum 2 night
stay.*
Bedrooms: 20 double &
10 twin, 2 family rooms.
Bathrooms: 32 private.
Bed & breakfast: £59-£63
single, £89 double.
Half board: £48-£55 daily,
£300-£339 weekly.
Lunch available.
Evening meal 7pm (l.o.
9.30pm).
Parking for 60.
Credit: Access, Visa, Diners,
Amex.

Green Hedges M

Rye Hill, Rye, E.Sussex
TN31 7NH
☎ Rye (0797) 222185
*Large Edwardian country
house in a private road. 1.5
acres of landscaped gardens
with heated swimming pool.
Within 10 minutes' walk of
town centre. Ample parking.*
Bedrooms: 2 double & 1 twin.
Bathrooms: 3 private,
1 public.
Bed & breakfast: £45-£50
double.

Holloway House M
COMMENDED

High St., Rye, TN31 7JF
☎ Rye (0797) 224748
*Creeper-covered Tudor
building in heart of
conservation area. Heavily
beamed, Caern stone fireplaces,
oak panelling, antique beds and
furnishings. Hearty breakfasts.*
Bedrooms: 4 double & 1 twin,
2 family rooms.
Bathrooms: 7 private.
Bed & breakfast: £35-£70
single, £50-£70 double.
Half board: £40-£50 daily,
£245-£305 weekly.
Lunch available.
Evening meal 6pm (l.o. 9pm).
Credit: Access, Visa.

The Hope Anchor Hotel

Watchbell St., Rye,
TN31 7HA
☎ (0797) 222216
*17th C hotel at the end of
cobbled street with magnificent
views of surrounding
countryside. Restaurant
specialises in local fish and
fresh vegetables.*
Bedrooms: 1 single, 7 double
& 5 twin, 1 family room.
Bathrooms: 10 private,
3 public.
Bed & breakfast: £34-£38
single, £49.20-£56.50 double.
Half board: £32.80-£37.75
daily.
Lunch available.
Evening meal 7pm (l.o. 9pm).
Credit: Access, Visa.

Jeake's House M
COMMENDED

Mermaid St., Rye, TN31 7ET
☎ (0797) 222828 Fax (0797)
225758
*Recapture the past in this
historic building, in a
cobblestoned street at the heart
of the old town. Honeymoon
suite available.*
Bedrooms: 1 single, 7 double
& 1 twin, 3 family rooms.
Bathrooms: 10 private,
2 public.
Bed & breakfast: £21 single,
£38-£50 double.
Credit: Access, Visa, Amex.

Old Borough Arms

The Strand, Rye, TN31 7DB
☎ (0797) 222128
Continued ▶

RYE

Continued

The inn is built into the Old Wall of Rye and has a fully licensed restaurant for 30 people.
Bedrooms: 2 single, 5 double, 2 family rooms.
Bathrooms: 9 private.
Bed & breakfast: £20-£30 single, £36-£50 double.
Lunch available.
Evening meal 7pm (l.o. 8.45pm).
Parking for 4.
Credit: Access, Visa.
🐕 👶 🖵 💆 🖊 📺 🏛 🚪 SP 🏠

The Old Vicarage Hotel M
👑👑👑 COMMENDED
15 East St., Rye, TN31 7JY
☎ (0797) 225131
Family-run Georgian hotel and restaurant in conservation area. Spacious rooms and elegant restaurant with panoramic views over Romney Marsh.
Bedrooms: 2 double, 2 family rooms.
Bathrooms: 4 private.
Bed & breakfast: £42-£49 single, £62-£72 double.
Half board: £41-£46 daily, £259-£280 weekly.
Evening meal 7pm (l.o. 9pm).
Open February-December.
Credit: Access, Visa, Diners.
🐕 👶 🖵 ☎ 💆 🐾 💆 V 🖊
🏛 🍴 👶 🚪 SP 🏠

Playden Cottage Guesthouse M
👑👑👑 COMMENDED
Military Rd., Rye, TN31 7NY
☎ (0797) 222234
Large character cottage, said to be "Grebe" from E.F.Benson's Mapp and Lucia novels. Personal service in a comfortable family home. Own gardens, rural aspect.
Bedrooms: 1 double & 2 twin.
Bathrooms: 3 private, 1 public.
Bed & breakfast: £30-£50 single, £40-£50 double.
Parking for 7.
🐕12 🖵 U 🖊 💆 V 🖊 📺 🏛
🚪 ❋ ✕ 🏠 SP 🏠

Strand House M
👑👑 COMMENDED
Winchelsea, Nr. Rye, TN36 4JT
☎ Rye (0797) 226276
Fine old 15th C house with oak beams and inglenook fireplaces. Located just off A259. 10% discount for weekly terms except in high season.

Bedrooms: 8 double & 1 twin, 1 family room.
Bathrooms: 8 private, 1 public.
Bed & breakfast: £20-£32 single, £28-£42 double.
Parking for 15.
🐕8 👶 🖵 💆 🐾 V 🖊 🏛 🚪
🍴 ❋ 🏠 SP 🏠

Top o'The Hill at Rye M
👑👑
Rye Hill, Rye, TN31 7NH
☎ (0797) 223284
Small friendly inn offering traditional food and accommodation. Central for touring Kent and Sussex with Channel ports nearby.
Bedrooms: 3 double & 2 twin, 1 family room.
Bathrooms: 6 private.
Bed & breakfast: from £17 single, from £32 double.
Lunch available.
Evening meal 7pm (l.o. 9.30pm).
Parking for 32.
Credit: Access, Visa.
🐕 👶 🖵 💆 ☎ V 📺 🖊 🏛 🚪
🍴 👶 🚪 🏠 SP 🏠

RYE FOREIGN
E. Sussex
Map ref 3B4

Village set behind the ancient town and port of Rye.

Rumpels Motel M
Rye Road, Rye Foreign, Nr. Rye, TN31 7SY
☎ Peasmarsh (079 721) 494 & 495
Set in 3 acres of grounds surrounded by beautiful Sussex countryside. Main building is over 200 years old. Pets' corner, craft shop.
Bedrooms: 7 double & 2 twin, 4 family rooms.
Bathrooms: 13 private, 1 public.
Bed & breakfast: £20-£30 single, £32.50-£42.50 double.
Half board: £50-£55 daily, £170-£180 weekly.
Lunch available.
Evening meal 7pm (l.o. 10.30pm).
Parking for 54.
Credit: Access, Visa, Diners, Amex.
🐕 👶 🖵 ☎ 🖵 💆 🐾 V 🖊 🏛
🚪 🍴 👶 🐾 ❋ 🚪 SP 🏠

The enquiry coupons at the back will help you when contacting proprietors.

SANDWICH
Kent
Map ref 3C3

Delightful old market town, once a Cinque Port, now 2 miles from the sea. Many interesting old buildings including the 16th C Barbican and the Guildhall which contains the town's treasures. Several excellent golf-courses.

Bell Hotel M
👑👑👑👑 APPROVED
The Quay, Sandwich, CT13 9EF
☎ (0304) 613388
Fax (0304) 615308
Originally 16th C riverside inn within heart of conservation area. Fully modernised in traditional manner.
Bedrooms: 8 single, 6 double & 14 twin, 1 family room.
Bathrooms: 29 private.
Bed & breakfast: £60-£65 single, £85-£115 double.
Half board: £56.50-£72 daily, £298-£385 weekly.
Lunch available.
Evening meal 7pm (l.o. 9.30pm).
Parking for 8.
Credit: Access, Visa, Amex.
🐕 ☎ 🖵 🖵 💆 V 🖊 🖊
🍴 🏛 🚪 🍴 U 🖊 📠 🐾 SP
🏠 T

SARRE
Kent
Map ref 3C3

Crown Inn (The Cherry Brandy House) M
👑👑👑
Sarre, Nr. Birchington, CT7 0LF
☎ Thanet (0843) 47808
Fax (0843) 47914
An ideal centre for exploring Canterbury, Thanet and east Kent. Our unique liqueur has been available here since 1650.
Bedrooms: 9 double & 2 twin, 1 family room.
Bathrooms: 12 private.
Bed & breakfast: max. £43.50 single, max. £56.50 double.
Lunch available.
Evening meal 7pm (l.o. 9.30pm).
Parking for 27.
Credit: Access, Visa, Diners, Amex.
🐕 👶 🖵 💆 ☎ 🖵 💆 V
🖊 📺 🏛 🚪 🍴 👶 ❋ 🏠 🐾
SP 🏠 T

SEAFORD
E. Sussex
Map ref 2D3

The town was a bustling port until 1579 when the course of the River Ouse was diverted. The downlands around the town make good walking country, with fine views of the Seven Sisters cliffs.
Tourist Information Centre ☎ (0323) 897426

Clearview Hotel
36-38 Claremont Rd., Seaford, BN25 2BD
☎ (0323) 890138
Easily reached from main A259 Eastbourne to Brighton road and only 100 metres from railway and town centre. Evening meals available. Special rates for weekend breaks.
Bedrooms: 2 single, 5 double & 2 twin, 3 family rooms.
Bathrooms: 11 private.
Bed & breakfast: £23.50-£28.20 single, £35-£41.20 double.
Lunch available.
Evening meal 7pm (l.o. 10pm).
Credit: Access, Visa, Diners, Amex.
🐕 ☎ 🖵 🖵 💆 🖊 V 🖊 🖊
🚪 🍴 🏠 📠 🐾 SP T

SEDLESCOMBE
E. Sussex
Map ref 3B4

3m NE. Battle
Pretty village with a long, wide green on which stands a water pump under a gable-roofed shelter. Nearby is the Pestalozzi Children's Village.

The Brickwall Hotel
👑👑👑👑 APPROVED
Sedlescombe, Nr. Battle, TN33 0QA
☎ (0424) 870253
16th C manor house set amidst 3 acres of gardens, on quiet village green.
Bedrooms: 3 single, 7 double & 13 twin, 2 family rooms.
Bathrooms: 25 private.
Bed & breakfast: £45-£47 single, £58-£60 double.
Half board: £260-£300 weekly.
Lunch available.
Evening meal 7pm (l.o. 9pm).
Parking for 33.

Credit: Access, Visa, Diners, Amex.

[symbols]

SEVENOAKS

Kent
Map ref 2D2

Set in pleasant wooded country, with a distinctive character and charm. Nearby is Knole (National Trust), home of the Sackville family and one of the largest houses in England, set in a vast deer park.
Tourist Information Centre ☎ *(0732) 450305*

Holmesdale House
High Street., Brasted, Sevenoaks, TN16 1HS
☎ Westerham (0959) 64834
Large Victorian (and part 17th C) house on the A25 opposite The Bull Inn at Brasted, between Sevenoaks and Westerham.
Bedrooms: 2 single, 1 double & 1 twin, 2 family rooms.
Bathrooms: 2 private, 1 public; 1 private shower.
Bed & breakfast: £16-£20 single, £36-£40 double.
Parking for 6.
[symbols]

Moorings Hotel ⋀
⌂⌂⌂
97 Hitchen Hatch Lane, Sevenoaks, TN13 3BE
☎ (0732) 452589
Friendly family hotel offering high standard accommodation for tourists and business travellers. Near British Rail station for fast trains to London.
Bedrooms: 5 single, 3 double & 12 twin, 2 family rooms.
Bathrooms: 18 private, 2 public; 1 private shower.
Bed & breakfast: £30-£45 single, £40-£60 double.
Half board: £40-£55 daily.
Evening meal 7pm (l.o. 9pm).
Parking for 22.
Credit: Access, Visa.
[symbols]

Stone Ridge ⋀
Listed
168 Maidstone Road, Borough Green, Sevenoaks, TN15 8JD
☎ Borough Green
(0732) 882053

Comfortable Edwardian country house with friendly atmosphere in beautiful surroundings. Convenient for famous Kentish places, motorways and London. Non-smokers preferred.
Bedrooms: 1 twin, 1 family room.
Bathrooms: 1 private, 2 public.
Bed & breakfast: £15-£25 single, £28-£38 double.
Half board: £18-£30 daily, £108-£180 weekly.
Evening meal 6pm (l.o. midday).
Parking for 4.
Credit: Access, Visa.
[symbols]

SHEPPERTON

Surrey
Map ref 2D2

Made famous by its connections with the British film industry, this town by the Thames retains an air of detachment from London, despite being only 10 miles from the centre of the capital.

Warren Lodge Hotel
⌂⌂⌂
Church Sq., Shepperton, TW17 9JZ
☎ Walton-on-Thames (0932) 242972 & Fax (0932) 253883 Telex 923981
300-year-old hotel standing in a delightful, shady garden by the river, just off the main road. A mulberry tree from Hampton Court was planted here by Cardinal Wolsey.
Bedrooms: 22 single, 19 double & 6 twin, 5 family rooms.
Bathrooms: 49 private; 3 private showers.
Bed & breakfast: £60-£85 single, £85-£100 double.
Lunch available.
Evening meal 7pm (l.o. 10pm).
Parking for 16.
Credit: Access, Visa, Diners, Amex.
[symbols]

> *Half board prices shown are per person but in some cases may be based on double/twin occupancy.*

SHOREHAM-BY-SEA

W. Sussex
Map ref 2D3

Popular seaside resort and an ancient town. The harbour provides a safe yacht anchorage and the River Adur some excellent fishing. The Marlipins Museum contains a wide variety of local history exhibits.

Old Erringham Hall ⋀
Listed **COMMENDED**
Steyning Rd., Shoreham-by-Sea, BN43 5FD
☎ Brighton (0273) 452755 & 464649
Mentioned in Domesday Book of 1086. Downland setting with magnificent views. Four-poster bed in oak-panelled room. Five minutes north of Shoreham on A283 Steyning Road. After large roundabout second turn right up private road.
Bedrooms: 3 double.
Bathrooms: 1 public; 1 private shower.
Bed & breakfast: max. £30 single, £38-£45 double.
Half board: max. £42 daily.
Lunch available.
Evening meal 6.30pm (l.o. 9pm).
Parking for 50.
[symbols]

SITTINGBOURNE

Kent
Map ref 3B3

The town's position and its ample supply of water make it an ideal site for the paper-making industry. Delightful villages and orchards lie round about.

Beaumont Guest House
74 London Rd., Sittingbourne, ME10 1NS
☎ (0795) 472536
Friendly, family-run establishment in a convenient location close to Canterbury and Maidstone. Sheerness ferry terminal only 20 minutes away. Easy access to M2 and M20.
Bedrooms: 2 single, 2 double & 3 twin, 2 family rooms.
Bathrooms: 2 public; 8 private showers.
Bed & breakfast: £20-£40 single, £37-£50 double.
Parking for 9.
[symbols]

Coniston Hotel
70 London Rd., Sittingbourne, ME10 1NT
☎ (0795) 472131
Fax (0795) 28056
In the "Garden of England" on the London-Dover road, set in 2 acres surrounded by flower gardens. Central for touring.
Bedrooms: 19 single, 19 double & 23 twin, 4 family rooms.
Bathrooms: 57 private, 4 public.
Bed & breakfast: £40-£55 single, £50-£70 double.
Half board: £37-£67 daily.
Lunch available.
Evening meal 7pm (l.o. 10pm).
Parking for 120.
Credit: Access, Visa, Diners, Amex.
[symbols]

Hempstead House
⌂⌂⌂ **COMMENDED**
London Road, Bapchild, Sittingbourne, ME9 9PP
☎ Sittingbourne
(0795) 428020
Exclusive country house situated on main A2 between Canterbury and London, offering comfortable accommodation and friendly hospitality.
Bedrooms: 1 double, 1 family room.
Bathrooms: 2 private.
Bed & breakfast: £45-£50 single, £50-£56 double.
Half board: £60-£65 daily.
Evening meal 7pm (l.o. 9pm).
Parking for 10.
[symbols]

STAINES

Surrey
Map ref 2D2

Ever since Roman days Staines has been a river crossing of the Thames on the route to the West from London.

Stanwell Hall Hotel
171 Town La., Stanwell, Staines, TW19 7PW
☎ Ashford (Middlesex) (0784) 252292
Ⓒ Consort
Victorian country house set in own garden, close to Heathrow Airport, M25, M40, M4 and M3.
Bedrooms: 8 single, 4 double & 5 twin, 1 family room.
Continued ▶

STAINES

Continued

Bathrooms: 18 private.
Bed & breakfast: £75-£85 single, £95-£150 double.
Lunch available.
Evening meal 7pm (l.o. 9.30pm).
Parking for 30.
Credit: Access, Visa, Diners, Amex.

STEYNING

W. Sussex
Map ref 2D3

This village has an interesting jumble of building styles. Half a mile to the east is Bramber Castle, a ruin now in the care of the National Trust.

Nash Country Hotel

COMMENDED

Horsham Rd., Steyning, BN4 3AA
☎ (0903) 814988
Country house, circa 1240, with modern additions, overlooking South Downs. Views from all rooms. Wildfowl lake and vineyard.
Bedrooms: 1 single, 1 double & 2 twin.
Bathrooms: 1 private, 1 public.
Bed & breakfast: £25-£30 single, £45 double.
Evening meal 6.30pm (l.o. 8.30pm).
Parking for 20.

TENTERDEN

Kent
Map ref 3B4

Most attractive market town with a broad main street full of 16th C houses and shops. The tower of the 15th C parish church is the finest in Kent.

Collina House Hotel

5 East Hill, Tenterden, TN30 6RL
☎ (058 06) 4852
Edwardian house overlooking orchards and garden, within walking distance of picturesque town. Swiss-trained proprietors offering both English and continental cooking.
Bedrooms: 3 single, 4 double & 2 twin, 2 family rooms.

Bathrooms: 11 private.
Bed & breakfast: £25-£28 single, £34-£38 double.
Half board: £35-£38 daily, £210-£220 weekly.
Evening meal 7pm (l.o. 9.30pm).
Parking for 16.
Credit: Access, Visa, Diners, Amex.

Little Silver Country Hotel M

COMMENDED

Ashford Rd., St. Michaels, Tenterden, TN30 6SP
☎ (0233) 850321
Quality accommodation in Tudor-style hotel. Honeymoon and brass bedded rooms, all en-suite. Attractive gardens. Full a la carte menu available. Personal service, delightful atmosphere.
Bedrooms: 5 double & 3 twin, 2 family rooms.
Bathrooms: 10 private.
Bed & breakfast: £50-£70 single, £65-£95 double.
Half board: £62-£86 daily, £390-£541.80 weekly.
Lunch available.
Evening meal 6.30pm (l.o. 10pm).
Parking for 50.
Credit: Access, Visa, Amex.

Woolpack Hotel

26 High St., Tenterden, TN30 6AP
☎ (058 06) 2934
Delightful 15th C coaching inn with creaking boards, lovely ship beams and secret passages. Log fires in the inglenook fireplaces. Beer garden.
Bedrooms: 1 single, 2 double & 2 twin.
Bathrooms: 1 public.
Bed & breakfast: £18-£22 single, £36-£42 double.
Half board: £25-£32 daily.
Lunch available.
Evening meal 6pm (l.o. 9pm).
Parking for 28.

Half board prices shown are per person but in some cases may be based on double/twin occupancy.

TUNBRIDGE WELLS

Kent
Map ref 2D2

This 'Royal' town became famous as a spa in the 17th C and much of its charm is retained, as in the Pantiles, a delightful shaded walk lined with elegant shops. Also a brand new heritage attraction 'A Day at the Wells'. Rich in parks and gardens and a good centre for walks.
Tourist Information Centre ☎ *(0892) 515675*

Clarken Guest House

61, Frant Road, Tunbridge Wells, TN2 5LH
☎ Tunbridge Wells, (0892) 533397
Large Victorian detached house on A267 main Eastbourne/Hastings road. 5 minutes from mainline station to London. 5 minutes to Pantiles. French spoken.
Bedrooms: 2 single, 6 twin, 2 family rooms.
Bathrooms: 3 private, 2 public.
Bed & breakfast: £16-£24 single, £32-£44 double.
Parking for 7.

Danehurst M

COMMENDED

41 Lower Green Rd., Rusthall, Tunbridge Wells, TN4 8TW
☎ (0892) 527739
Be treated as a privileged guest in our home, where we concentrate on high standards and attention to detail.
Bedrooms: 1 single, 2 double & 2 twin, 1 family room.
Bathrooms: 4 private, 1 public.
Bed & breakfast: £25-£39.50 single, £36-£48 double.
Half board: £43.98-£58.48 daily, £307.86-£409.36 weekly.
Evening meal 7.30pm (l.o. 8.30pm).
Parking for 5.
Credit: Access, Visa.

Hotel Kingswood M

COMMENDED

Pembury Rd., Tunbridge Wells, TN27 9BB
☎ (0892) 535736/511269
Fax (0892) 513321

Comfortable Tudor-style country house hotel, conveniently situated in secluded grounds on A264. Near town centre. Licensed.
Bedrooms: 3 single, 4 double & 5 twin, 3 family rooms.
Bathrooms: 15 private.
Bed & breakfast: £46-£56 single, £62-£72 double.
Half board: £58-£68 daily, £366-£430 weekly.
Evening meal 7pm (l.o. 8.30pm).
Parking for 30.
Credit: Access, Visa, Diners, Amex.

Pembury Resort Hotel M

COMMENDED

8 Tonbridge Rd., Pembury, Tunbridge Wells, TN2 4BR
☎ (0892) 823567
Fax (0892) 823931
Ⓡ Resort
Newly built hotel, close to the town of Tunbridge Wells. Attractive health and leisure club, elegant restaurant, extensive conference and banqueting facilities. Off main A21 trunk road at Pembury.
Bedrooms: 31 double & 49 twin.
Bathrooms: 80 private.
Bed & breakfast: £30-£76 single, £60-£86 double.
Half board: £42-£88 daily.
Lunch available.
Evening meal 7.30pm (l.o. 9.30pm).
Parking for 128.
Credit: Access, Visa, Diners, Amex.

Periquito Hotel M

COMMENDED

84 Mount Ephraim, Tunbridge Wells, TN4 8BU
☎ (0892) 542911
Fax (0892) 537541
Listed Regency building overlooking common. Fully refurbished in 1991 with bright welcoming decor that enhances original features. 15 minutes' drive from the M25 junction 5.
Bedrooms: 26 single, 32 double & 5 twin, 13 family rooms.
Bathrooms: 76 private.
Bed & breakfast: £53-£65 single, £58.50-£73 double.
Lunch available.
Evening meal 7pm (l.o. 10pm).
Parking for 40.

Credit: Access, Visa, Diners, Amex.

Royal Wells Inn M
✿✿✿ COMMENDED

Mount Ephraim, Tunbridge Wells, TN4 8BE
☎ (0892) 511188 Fax (0892) 511908
Family hotel, totally refurbished. All rooms have private bathroom. New conservatory restaurant serving quality food.
Bedrooms: 5 single, 12 double & 6 twin.
Bathrooms: 23 private.
Bed & breakfast: £60-£65 single, £75-£85 double.
Half board: £55-£80 daily.
Lunch available.
Evening meal 7.30pm (l.o. 9.30pm).
Parking for 25.
Credit: Access, Visa, Diners, Amex.

Russell Hotel M
✿✿✿ COMMENDED

80 London Rd., Tunbridge Wells, TN1 1DZ
☎ (0892) 544833
Fax (0892) 515846
Telex 95177
CR Inter
Large Victorian house facing common, only minutes from town centre. Totally refurbished to highest modern standards.
Bedrooms: 2 single, 11 double & 10 twin, 3 family rooms.
Bathrooms: 26 private.
Bed & breakfast: £62-£68 single, £76-£80 double.
Half board: £77.50-£83.50 daily.
Lunch available.
Evening meal 7pm (l.o. 9.30pm).
Parking for 20.
Credit: Access, Visa, Diners, Amex.

Southview Guest House

21 Rusthall Road, Rusthall, Tunbridge Wells, TN4 8RD
☎ Tunbridge Wells, (0892) 520174
Approximately 1 mile from town overlooking Rusthall Common. Good bus service.
Lounge shared with residential guests. Homely atmosphere.
Bedrooms: 6 single, 3 double, 1 family room.
Bathrooms: 1 public; 1 private shower.

Bed & breakfast: £12-£13 single, £24-£26 double.
Half board: £14-£15 daily, £98-£105 weekly.
Lunch available.
Evening meal 7pm (l.o. 3pm).

The Spa Hotel M
✿✿✿ COMMENDED

Mount Ephraim, Tunbridge Wells, TN4 8XJ
☎ Tunbridge Wells (0892) 520331 & Fax (0892) 510575 Telex 957188
Built in 1766 and opened as a hotel in 1880. Located on the A264 East Grinstead road. Privately owned, with extensive leisure and sporting facilities. Weekend breaks available.
Bedrooms: 23 single, 14 double & 34 twin, 5 family rooms.
Bathrooms: 76 private.
Bed & breakfast: £76.50-£81.50 single, £99-£112 double.
Half board: £96.50-£101.50 daily, £392-£441 weekly.
Lunch available.
Evening meal 7pm (l.o. 9.30pm).
Parking for 120.
Credit: Access, Visa, Diners, Amex.

Swan Hotel M
✿✿✿ COMMENDED

The Pantiles, Tunbridge Wells, TN2 5TD
☎ Tunbridge Wells (0892) 527590/541450
Fax (0892) 541465
Opposite bandstand and Heritage Centre on Pantiles. Bar snacks available all day in Pantiles Cafe Bar. Weddings and meetings catered for.
Bedrooms: 3 single, 9 double & 5 twin.
Bathrooms: 17 private.
Bed & breakfast: £55-£67.50 single, £80.50-£110 double.
Lunch available.
Evening meal 6.30pm (l.o. 9pm).
Parking for 18.
Credit: Access, Visa, C.Bl., Diners, Amex.

Warwick Grange Hotel M
✿✿

67 Warwick Park, Tunbridge Wells, TN2 5EJ
☎ (0892) 525486
Fax (0892) 537044

Small friendly hotel near Pantiles, next to Nevill Cricket Ground and close to shops. Set in lovely gardens.
Bedrooms: 3 single, 5 double & 3 twin, 1 family room.
Bathrooms: 4 private, 3 public.
Bed & breakfast: £23-£32 single, £38-£44 double.
Parking for 4.
Credit: Access, Visa.

UCKFIELD

E. Sussex
Map ref 2D3

Once a medieval market town and centre of the iron industry, Uckfield is now a busy country town on the edge of the Ashdown Forest.

Buxted Park M
✿✿✿✿ HIGHLY COMMENDED

Buxted, Uckfield, TN22 4AY
☎ (082 581) 2711
Fax (082 581) 2770
Country house hotel in 32 acres of parkland. 43 bedrooms and suites with private facilities, health club, cinema, swimming pool and fishing.
Bedrooms: 2 single, 30 double & 11 twin.
Bathrooms: 43 private.
Bed & breakfast: £70-£75 single, £83-£145 double.
Lunch available.
Evening meal 7pm (l.o. 9.30pm).
Parking for 60.
Credit: Access, Visa, Amex.

Halland Forge Hotel & Restaurant M
✿✿✿ COMMENDED

Halland, Nr. Lewes, BN8 6PW
☎ (0825) 840456
Fax (0825) 84773
CR Inter
Attractive hotel with fully licensed restaurant and coffee shop. Facilities for meetings and functions. Garden and woodland walks. Ideal touring centre, 4 miles from Uckfield.
Bedrooms: 11 double & 7 twin, 2 family rooms.
Bathrooms: 20 private.
Bed & breakfast: £49.75-£54 single, £68-£73.35 double.
Half board: £65.25-£69.50 daily, £248-£273 weekly.
Lunch available.
Evening meal 7pm (l.o. 9.30pm).

Parking for 70.
Credit: Access, Visa, Diners, Amex.

Hooke Hall M
✿✿✿ COMMENDED

250 High St., Uckfield, TN22 1EN
☎ (0825) 761578
Fax (0825) 768025
Elegant Queen Anne town house, recently completely refurbished, with individual comfortably designed rooms equipped to a high standard.
Bedrooms: 3 double & 3 twin.
Bathrooms: 6 private.
Bed & breakfast: £35-£70 single, £60-£100 double.
Half board: £45-£75 daily.
Evening meal 7.30pm (l.o. 9pm).
Parking for 7.
Credit: Access, Visa.

WALTON-ON-THAMES

Surrey
Map ref 2D2

Busy town beside the Thames, retaining a distinctive atmosphere despite being only 12 miles from central London. Close to Hampton Court Palace, Sandown Park Race Course and Claremont Landscape Garden, Esher.
Tourist Information Centre ☎ (0932) 228844

Ashley Park Hotel
✿✿✿

Ashley Park Rd., Walton-on-Thames, KT12 1JR
☎ (0932) 220196
Close to Walton station (B.R.) with frequent services to central London. Easy reach of Heathrow Airport. A la carte restaurant, conference facilities, car park and garden.
Bedrooms: 5 single, 10 double & 12 twin, 1 family room.
Bathrooms: 28 private.
Bed & breakfast: £50-£65 single, £60-£80 double.
Lunch available.
Evening meal 7pm (l.o. 9.30pm).
Parking for 60.
Credit: Access, Visa, Diners, Amex.

WATERINGBURY

Kent
Map ref 3B4

5m SW. Maidstone
On the River Medway
which provides excellent
coarse fishing.

Wateringbury Hotel
❀❀❀❀

Tonbridge Rd.,
Wateringbury, Maidstone,
ME18 5NS
☎ Maidstone (0622) 812632
Telex 96265
CR Lansbury
*Recently refurbished hotel in
village location, overlooking
river and farmland.*
Bedrooms: 34 double &
5 twin, 1 family room.
Bathrooms: 40 private.
Bed & breakfast: from £26
single, from £52 double.
Half board: from £38 daily.
Lunch available.
Evening meal 7pm (l.o.
10pm).
Parking for 60.
Credit: Access, Visa, Diners,
Amex.
⮽ ♨ ➠ ℄ ☏ ⌨ ♫ ☖ î Ⓥ
✂ ⧖ ◉ 🎟 ♨ ♨ î ☕ ✿ ❄
✈ ♨ ↘ SP T

WEST MALLING

Kent
Map ref 3B3

Became prominent in
Norman times when an
abbey was established
here.

Scott House
37 High St., West Malling,
ME19 6QH
☎ (0732) 841380/870025
*Georgian town house furnished
to a high standard. A family
home from which is run an
antique business as well as bed
and breakfast. No smoking.*
Bedrooms: 1 double & 2 twin.
Bathrooms: 3 private.
Bed & breakfast: £39 single,
£50 double.
Credit: Access, Visa.
☏ ⌨ ♨ UL ♨ ⧖ 🎟 ✈ ♨
🏠

---

*National Crown
ratings were correct
at the time of going
to press but are
subject to change.
Please check at the
time of booking.*

WESTERHAM

Kent
Map ref 2D2

This small country town
near the Kent/Surrey
border sits in the wooded
slopes of the glorious
North Downs. Made
famous as the birthplace
of General Wolfe and
close to Churchill's house
at Chartwell.

The Kings Arms
Hotel M
❀❀❀❀ COMMENDED

Market Sq., Westerham,
TN16 1AN
☎ (0959) 62990 Fax (0959)
61240
*200-year-old coaching inn
combining tradition with
comfort. Close to Gatwick
Airport, M25 and various
places of interest.*
Bedrooms: 2 single, 9 double
& 6 twin, 1 family room.
Bathrooms: 17 private.
Bed & breakfast: £60-£65
single, £75-£90 double.
Half board: £48.50-£63.50
daily.
Lunch available.
Evening meal 7pm (l.o.
10pm).
Parking for 36.
Credit: Access, Visa, Diners,
Amex.
⮽ ♨ ℄ ☏ ⌨ ♫ î Ⓥ ⧖
🎟 ♨ î ❄ ✈ SP 🏠 T

WEYBRIDGE

Surrey
Map ref 2D2

Old town on the site
where, according to
tradition, Julius Caesar
crossed the Thames in
55BC. Now a large
suburb with luxurious
houses and a famous golf
club.

Kingston Guest House
15 Heath Rd., Weybridge,
KT13 8TE
☎ (0932) 856191
*Edwardian house within easy
walking distance of shops and
mainline station. Centrally
situated for London, Heathrow
Airport, Hampton Court and
Windsor Castle. Non-smokers
only please.*
Bedrooms: 2 twin, 1 family
room.
Bathrooms: 1 public;
3 private showers.
Bed & breakfast: £28-£38
single, £38-£48 double.
Parking for 2.
⮽10 ♨ UL ✂ 🎟 ♨ ✈ ♨

Oatlands Park Hotel M
❀❀❀❀ COMMENDED

Oatlands Dr., Weybridge,
KT13 9HB
☎ (0932) 847242
Telex 915123
*Country house hotel in its own
grounds, with easy access from
Central London, Heathrow,
and the M25 orbital motorway.
Special weekend rates
available on request.*
Bedrooms: 28 single,
45 double & 54 twin, 4 family
rooms.
Bathrooms: 117 private,
10 public.
Bed & breakfast: £97-£108
single, £128-£143 double.
Half board: £113-£124 daily.
Lunch available.
Evening meal 7pm (l.o.
10pm).
Parking for 100.
Credit: Access, Visa, Diners,
Amex.
⮽ ♨ ➠ ℄ ☏ ⌨ ♫ î Ⓥ
♨ ⧖ ◉ 🎟 ♨ î ☕ ♀ ➤
❄ ↘ SP 🏠 T

WHITSTABLE

Kent
Map ref 3B3

Seaside resort and
yachting centre on Kent's
north shore. The beach is
shingle and there are the
usual seaside amenities
and entertainments.
*Tourist Information
Centre ☎ (0227) 275482*

Windyridge Guest
House M
❀❀❀

Wraik Hill, Whitstable,
CT5 3BY
☎ (0227) 263506
*Directions: on leaving the M2
continue on the A299
(signposted Whitstable and
Ramsgate) to the first
roundabout. Complete the
roundabout thus coming back
on oneself for a further 100
yards and then turn left into
Wraik Lane.*
Bedrooms: 3 single, 3 double
& 1 twin, 1 family room.
Bathrooms: 3 private,
1 public; 1 private shower.
Bed & breakfast: £16.50-
£19.50 single, £30.50-£38.50
double.
Half board: £25-£27 daily,
£160-£175 weekly.
Evening meal 6pm (l.o.
10am).
Parking for 7.
⮽5 ♨ ☏ ♨ î Ⓥ ✂ ♨ TV
🎟 ♨ î ❄ ✈ ♨ ↘ SP 🏠

WILMINGTON

E. Sussex
Map ref 2D3

6m NW. Eastbourne
The Long Man of
Wilmington, a great figure
cut out of the turf of
Windover Hill, overlooks
the village. Its origin is a
mystery. Wilmington
Priory houses an
interesting agricultural
museum.

Crossways Restaurant &
Hotel
Wilmington, Nr. Polegate,
BN26 5SG
☎ Polegate (0323) 482455
*Georgian-style hotel and
restaurant, run by chef/
proprietor, in 2 acres of
grounds. Directly opposite the
Long Man of Wilmington and
Wilmington Priory.*
Bedrooms: 2 single, 3 double
& 2 twin.
Bathrooms: 7 private,
1 public.
Bed & breakfast: £26-£34
single, £55-£59 double.
Evening meal 7.30pm (l.o.
9pm).
Parking for 25.
Credit: Access, Visa.
℄ ♨ ♨ î Ⓥ 🎟 ♨ ❄ ✈
♨ SP 🏠

WOKING

Surrey
Map ref 2D2

One of the largest towns
in Surrey, which
developed with the
coming of the railway in
the 1830s. Old Woking
was a market town in the
17th C and still retains
several interesting
buildings.

The Dutch
Woodham Rd., Woking,
GU21 4EQ
☎ (0483) 724255
*Small peaceful private hotel,
ideally situated for touring
Surrey and for business visits
to Woking. 27 minutes from
London.*
Bedrooms: 1 double & 2 twin,
1 family room.
Bathrooms: 4 private.
Bed & breakfast: £50-£52
single, £67-£69 double.
Half board: £62-£64 daily.
Evening meal 7pm (l.o. 8pm).
Parking for 6.
⮽1 ☏ ♨ ♨ UL 🎟 ♨ ❄
SP T

WORTHING

W. Sussex
Map ref 2D3

Largest town in West Sussex, a popular seaside resort with extensive sand and shingle beaches. Seafishing is excellent here. The museum contains finds from Cissbury Ring.
Tourist Information Centre ☎ *(0903) 210022*

Ardington Hotel
Steyne Gdns., Worthing, BN11 3DZ
☎ (0903) 30451
Family-owned and managed hotel overlooking Steyne Gardens adjacent to seafront. Near town centre, entertainments, national bowling greens. Comfortable bar/lounge and restaurant.
Bedrooms: 25 single, 15 double & 11 twin, 4 family rooms.
Bathrooms: 53 private, 1 public.
Bed & breakfast: £35-£55 single, £65-£77 double.
Half board: £42.50-£65 daily.
Lunch available.
Evening meal 7pm (l.o. 8.30pm).
Credit: Access, Visa, Diners, Amex.
⑃ ♨ ＼ ⑧ 口 ⇄ ⑪ ⊬ ⇔
● ⎙ ♨ ￤ ⏰ ⑤⑫

Beach Hotel M
Marine Pde., Worthing, BN11 3QJ
☎ (0903) 34001 Fax (0903) 34567
Privately-owned hotel overlooking sea, away from town but within easy walking distance of shops. Many places of interest nearby.
Bedrooms: 52 single, 25 twin, 7 family rooms.
Bathrooms: 84 private.
Bed & breakfast: £51-£59.25 single, £76.50-£86.50 double.
Half board: £61.50-£69.75 daily.
Lunch available.
Evening meal 7pm (l.o. 8.45pm).
Parking for 50.
Credit: Access, Visa, Diners, Amex.
⑃♨ ＼ ⑧口⇄ ￤ Ⓥ ⇔ ●
⊞ ⎙ ♨ ⏰ ⑤⑫⑫ ⑤⑫ ⑫

Blair House
♛♛♛
11 St. Georges Rd., Worthing, BN11 2DS
☎ (0903) 34071

Under the supervison of the chef/proprietor. Close to the town centre and amenities, 2 minutes from the sea. All en-suite rooms.
Bedrooms: 1 single, 3 double & 2 twin, 1 family room.
Bathrooms: 6 private, 1 public; 1 private shower.
Bed & breakfast: £18-£20 single, £35-£40 double.
Half board: £25.50-£27.50 daily, £178-£192 weekly.
Evening meal 6.30pm.
Parking for 4.
Credit: Access, Visa.
⑃口⇄ ￤ Ⓥ ⇄ ⎙ ⏰ ☓
⑤⑫ ⑤⑫

Bonchurch Hotel M
♛♛ COMMENDED
1 Winchester Rd., Worthing, BN11 4DJ
☎ (0903) 202492
"Home from home". Pleasant house on A259, close to all amenities, shops, museum and downs.
Bedrooms: 3 single, 2 double & 2 twin.
Bathrooms: 3 private, 1 public.
Bed & breakfast: £14-£17 single, £28-£34 double.
Half board: £22.50-£25.50 daily, £140-£160 weekly.
Evening meal 6.15pm (l.o. 4pm).
Parking for 4.
⑃④⇄ 口⇄ ⎕ ￤ ⇄ ⑫⑫
☓ ⑤⑫ ⑤⑫

The Burlington Hotel M
♛♛♛♛ APPROVED
Marine Pde., Worthing, BN11 3QL
☎ (0903) 211222
Fax (0903) 209561
Well-appointed, recently refurbished hotel overlooking sea and gardens. Within 10 minutes' walk of town centre.
Bedrooms: 11 single, 7 double & 10 twin, 2 family rooms.
Bathrooms: 30 private.
Bed & breakfast: £43 single, £65.50 double.
Half board: £44-£54.25 daily, £257.50-£317 weekly.
Lunch available.
Evening meal 7pm (l.o. 8.45pm).
Credit: Access, Visa, Amex.
⑃♨ ＼ ⑧口⇄ ￤ Ⓥ ⇄
● ⊞ ⎙ ♨ ⏰ ☓ ⑤⑫ ⑫ ⑫

Cavendish Hotel
♛♛♛♛ COMMENDED
115-116 Marine Parade, Worthing, BN11 3QG
☎ Worthing (0903) 36767
Fax 0903 823840

Fully licensed seafront hotel. Open to non-residents. Specialising in food and wine. Most rooms en-suite.
Bedrooms: 7 single, 6 double & 4 twin.
Bathrooms: 13 private, 1 public.
Bed & breakfast: £24.75-£39 single, £45-£65 double.
Half board: £34.75-£49 daily, max. £245 weekly.
Lunch available.
Evening meal 7pm (l.o. 9pm).
Parking for 4.
Credit: C.Bl.
⑃① ♨ ＼ ⑧口⇄ ￤ Ⓥ ⇄
⑫ ● ⎙ ♨ ⏰ ☓ ⑤⑫ ⑤⑫ ⑫

Chapman's Hotel
27 Railway Approach, Worthing, BN11 1UR
☎ (0903) 30690 Fax (0903) 204266
Centrally located in Worthing immediately opposite main railway station.
Bedrooms: 2 double & 16 twin.
Bathrooms: 18 private.
Bed & breakfast: from £29 single, from £50 double.
Half board: from £44 daily.
Lunch available.
Evening meal 6pm (l.o. 9.30pm).
Parking for 6.
Credit: Access, Visa, Diners, Amex.
⑃ ＼ ⑧口⇄ ￤ Ⓥ ⊬ ⇄
⎙ ♨ ⏰ ☓ ☓ ⑤⑫

Delmar Hotel
♛♛♛
1-2 New Parade, Worthing, BN11 2BQ
☎ (0903) 211834
Family-run licensed hotel, extensively refurbished overlooking sea and gardens. In quiet situation, convenient for all local amenities and town.
Bedrooms: 6 single, 4 double & 2 twin, 1 family room.
Bathrooms: 10 private, 1 public.
Bed & breakfast: £22.33-£24.68 single, £40-£55 double.
Half board: £34.59-£37.60 daily, £217.92-£236.88 weekly.
Evening meal 6.30pm (l.o. 4.30pm).
Parking for 5.
Credit: Access, Visa.
⑃♨ ♨ ＼ ⑧口⇄ ￤ ⊬
⇄ ⑫ ⎙ ♨ ❄ ☓ ⇄ ⑤⑫

Granville Hotel M
74-76 Marine Parade, Worthing, BN11 3QB
☎ (0903) 39464

Listed Georgian building facing the sea and immediately adjacent to shopping precincts. Two multi-storey car parks within 200 yards. Cellar bar and restaurant.
Bedrooms: 2 single, 16 double & 4 twin.
Bathrooms: 22 private.
Bed & breakfast: £37-£39 single, £58-£60 double.
Half board: £65-£69 daily, £272-£282 weekly.
Lunch available.
Evening meal 6pm (l.o. 9pm).
Parking for 4.
Credit: Visa, Diners, Amex.
⑃♨ ＼ ⑧口⇄ ￤ Ⓥ ⇄ ●
⊞ ⎙ ♨ ⏰ ☓ ⑤⑫ ⑤⑫ ⑫
⑫

Heene House Hotel M
♛♛♛
140 Heene Rd., Worthing, BN11 4PJ
☎ Worthing (0903) 33213 & 210804
An imposing detached Edwardian property in a conservation area, set in pretty gardens.
Bedrooms: 2 single, 7 double & 4 twin, 2 family rooms.
Bathrooms: 11 private, 2 public.
Bed & breakfast: £22-£33.50 single, £37-£52 double.
Half board: £29.41-£40.91 daily, £157.20-£263.50 weekly.
Lunch available.
Evening meal 7pm (l.o. 8.30pm).
Parking for 7.
Credit: Access, Visa, Diners, Amex.
⑃♨ ＼ ⑧口⇄ ￤ Ⓥ ⇄
⎙ ♨ ⏰ ❄ ☓ ⑤⑫ ⑫

Kingsway Hotel M
117-119 Marine Parade, Worthing, BN11 3QQ
☎ (0903) 37542
Fax (0903) 204173
Central seafront hotel near shops and entertainments. South facing, double-glazed. Carvery restaurant. Comfortable bar and lounges. Lift and car park.
Bedrooms: 13 single, 6 double & 8 twin, 1 family room.
Bathrooms: 28 private, 1 public.
Bed & breakfast: £43.50-£55 single, £57.40-£65 double.
Half board: £36.65-£51.25 daily, £250.25-£360 weekly.
Lunch available.
Evening meal 7pm (l.o. 9pm).
Parking for 12.
Credit: Access, Visa, Amex.
⑃ ＼ ⑧口⇄ ￤ Ⓥ ⊬ ⇄
● ⊞ ⎙ ♨ ⏰ ☓ ⇄ ☓
⑤⑫ ⑫ ⑫

WORTHING
Continued

Moorings Hotel M
COMMENDED
4 Selden Rd., Worthing,
BN11 2LL
☎ (0903) 208882
*Victorian house, tastefully
renovated and retaining many
original features. Close to the
beach, Beach House Park,
Aquarena, children's
playground and town centre.*
Bedrooms: 1 single, 3 double
& 2 twin, 2 family rooms.
Bathrooms: 8 private.
Bed & breakfast: £20-£22
single, £40-£44 double.
Half board: £28-£30 daily,
£176-£184 weekly.
Evening meal 7pm.
Parking for 5.
Credit: Access, Visa.
⌖ ⑧ ☐ ✿ ⓘ Ⓥ ⊣ ▥ ▵
Ⅰ ✕ ⋈ ⬚ SP T

Rosedale Guest House
12 Bath Rd., Worthing,
BN11 3NU
☎ (0903) 33181
*Family-run guesthouse offering
warm, comfortable rooms.
Home cooking and full English
breakfast. Ideally situated for
seafront and Worthing town
centre.*
Bedrooms: 1 single, 1 double
& 2 twin, 1 family room.

Bathrooms: 1 private,
2 public.
Bed & breakfast: £15-£17
single, £30-£35 double.
Half board: £22.50-£25 daily,
£157.50-£175 weekly.
Evening meal 6pm (l.o. 6pm).
⌖ ⑧ ☐ ✿ ⓤ ▥ ⬚ SP

Windsor House Hotel M
COMMENDED
14-20 Windsor Rd., Worthing,
BN11 2LX
☎ (0903) 39655
*Close to amenities, but away
from main road traffic noise.
Open for coffee, lunch, teas.
Carvery restaurant and car
park. Service with a smile.*
Bedrooms: 1 single, 11 double
& 12 twin, 6 family rooms.
Bathrooms: 30 private,
1 public.
Bed & breakfast: from £42.50
single, from £63 double.
Half board: from £42 daily,
from £236 weekly.
Lunch available.
Evening meal 6pm (l.o. 9pm).
Parking for 18.
Credit: Access, Visa.
⌖ ⌓ ☎ ⌨ ☐ ✿ ⓘ Ⓥ ⊣
▥ ▵ ⒶⅠ ✕ ⬚ ⬚ SP T

Woodlands Guest House
COMMENDED
20-22 Warwick Gdns.,
Worthing, BN11 1PF
☎ (0903) 33557 &
(0831) 248412

*Family-run guesthouse
providing home-cooked food
and friendly service. All
bedrooms are well-appointed
and comfortably furnished.*
Bedrooms: 3 single, 3 double
& 3 twin, 3 family rooms.
Bathrooms: 6 private,
2 public.
Bed & breakfast: £16-£21
single, £29-£39 double.
Half board: £21-£27 daily,
£125-£165 weekly.
Evening meal 6pm (l.o. 5pm).
Parking for 8.
⌖ ☐ ✿ Ⓥ ⓘ ⊁ ⊣ ▥
▵ ⒶⅡ ⬚ SP

WROTHAM
Kent
Map ref 3B3

Below Wrotham Hill close
to the North Downs Way,
the village has an
impressive 14th C church
and several interesting
old buildings, some
dating from Elizabethan
times.

The Bull Hotel M
APPROVED
Bull La., Wrotham, Nr.
Sevenoaks, TN15 7RF
☎ Borough Green
(0732) 885522

*Privately-run 14th C coaching
inn, in secluded historic village
close to M20 and M25. Half
an hour from Gatwick and
London.*
Bedrooms: 1 single, 3 double
& 5 twin, 1 family room.
Bathrooms: 6 private,
1 public.
Bed & breakfast: from £35
single, max. £56 double.
Lunch available.
Evening meal 7pm (l.o.
10pm).
Parking for 50.
Credit: Access, Visa, C.Bl.,
Diners, Amex.
⌖ ⌨ ☐ ✿ ⓘ Ⓥ ⊣ ▥
▵ Ⅰ ⋈ ⬚

Hilltop Hotel
Labour-in-Vain Road,
Stanstead, Nr. Sevenoaks,
TN15 7NW
☎ (0732) 822696 & 822481
*Between West Kingsdown and
Wrotham on the A20. Access
to M25, M26 and M20. Set
amid unrivalled scenery.*
Bedrooms: 2 single, 3 double
& 4 twin, 1 family room.
Bathrooms: 3 private,
1 public; 2 private showers.
Bed & breakfast: from £28
single, £40-£45 double.
Lunch available.
Parking for 40.
Credit: Visa.
⌖ ⌨ ☐ ✿ ⓘ ⊣ ▥ ▵ ▵
Ⅰ ⚲ ✿

Use a coupon

*When requesting further information from
advertisers in this guide, you may find it helpful
to use the advertisement enquiry coupons which
can be found towards the end of the guide. These
should be cut out and mailed direct to the
companies in which you are interested. Do
remember to include your name and address.*

General advice and information

BEFORE SENTENCE IS PASSED MY CLIENT WISHES TO POINT OUT THAT HIS HOLIDAY IS BOOKED FOR AUGUST

MAKING A BOOKING

When enquiring about accommodation, as well as checking prices and other details you will need to state your requirements clearly and precisely – for example:

1. Arrival and departure dates with acceptable alternatives if appropriate.
2. The accommodation you need. For example: double room with twin beds, private bath and WC.
3. The terms you want. For example: room only; bed & breakfast; bed, breakfast and evening meal (half board); bed, breakfast, lunch and evening meal (full board).
4. If you will have children with you give their ages, state whether you would like them to share your room or have an adjacent room and mention any special requirements such as a cot.
5. Tell the management about any particular requirements such as a ground floor room or special diet.

Misunderstandings can occur very easily over the telephone so we recommend that all bookings should be confirmed in writing if time permits.

When first enquiring in writing about a reservation you may find it helpful to use the booking enquiry coupons (pages 541 – 547) which can be cut out and mailed to the establishment(s) of your choice. Remember to include your name and address and please enclose a stamped and addressed envelope or an international reply coupon if writing from outside Britain.

DEPOSITS AND ADVANCE PAYMENTS

For reservations made weeks or months ahead a deposit is usually payable and the amount will vary according to the length of booking, time of year, number in party and so on. The deposit will be deducted from the total bill at the end of your stay.

More and more establishments, particularly larger hotels in big towns, now require payment for the room on arrival if a prior reservation has not been made – especially if you arrive late and/or with little luggage. Regrettably this practice has become necessary because of the number of guests who have left without paying their bills.

If you are asked to pay on arrival it may be advisable to see your room first to ensure that it meets your requirements.

CREDIT CARD PAYMENTS

Where payments for accommodation are made by credit card, proprietors may charge a higher rate than for payment by cash or cheque. The difference is to cover the percentage paid by the proprietor to the credit card company. Not all proprietors make this additional charge but if you intend to pay by credit card it is worth asking whether it would be cheaper to pay by cash or cheque.

CANCELLATIONS

When you accept offered accommodation, on the telephone or in writing, you are entering into a legally binding contract with the proprietor of the establishment. This means that if you cancel a reservation, fail to take up the accommodation or leave prematurely the proprietor may be entitled to compensation if the accommodation cannot be relet for all or a good part of the booked period. If a deposit has been paid it is likely to be forfeited and an additional payment may be demanded.

However, no such claim can be made by the proprietor until after the booked period, during which time every effort should be made to relet the accommodation. Any circumstances which might lead to repudiation of a contract may also need to be taken into account and, in the case of a dispute, legal advice should be sought by both parties.

It is therefore in your own interests to advise the management immediately if you have to change your travel plans, cancel a booking or leave prematurely.

INSURANCE

Travel and holiday insurance protection policies are available quite cheaply and will safeguard you in the event of your having to cancel or curtail your holiday. Your insurance company or travel agent can advise you further on this. Some hotels also offer insurance schemes.

BY THE WAY, I SHALL BE ARRIVING AFTER SUNSET

ARRIVING LATE

If you will be arriving late in the evening it is advisable to say so at the time of booking; if you are delayed on your way, a telephone call to inform the management that you will be late might help to avoid problems on arrival.

SERVICE CHARGES AND TIPPING

Many establishments now levy a service charge automatically and if so this fact must be stated clearly in the offer of accommodation at the time of booking. If the offer is then accepted by you the service charge becomes part of the contract.

At establishments where a service charge of this kind is made there is no need for you to give tips to the staff unless some particular or exceptional service has been rendered. In the case of meals the usual amount is 10% of the total bill.

TELEPHONE CALL CHARGES

There is no restriction on the charges that can be made by hotels for telephone calls made through their switchboard or via direct-dial telephones in bedrooms. Unit charges are frequently considerably higher than British Telecom's standard charges. Hoteliers claim that they need to charge higher rates to defray the cost of providing the service.

Although it is a condition of a national Crown rating that a hotel's unit charges are displayed alongside telephones, it is not always easy to see how these compare with the standard charges. Before using a hotel telephone for long-distance calls within Britain or overseas, you may wish to ask how the charges compare.

SECURITY OF VALUABLES

Property of value may be deposited for safe-keeping with the proprietor or manager of the establishment who should give you a receipt and who will then generally be liable for the value of the property in the case of loss. For your peace of mind we advise you to adopt this procedure. In establishments which do not accept articles for safe custody, you are advised to keep valuables under your personal supervision.

You may find that proprietors of some establishments disclaim, by notice, liability for property brought on to their premises by a guest; however, if a guest engages overnight accommodation in a hotel the proprietor is only permitted to restrict his liability to the minimum imposed upon him under the Hotel Proprietors Act, 1956. Under this Act, a proprietor of a hotel is liable for the value of the loss or damage to any property (other than a motor car or its contents) of a guest who has engaged overnight accommodation, but if the proprietor has a notice in the form prescribed by that Act, liability is limited to the sum of £50 in respect of one article and a total of £100 in the case of any one guest.

These limits do not apply, however, if you have deposited the property with the proprietor for safe-keeping or if the property is lost through the default, neglect or wilful act of the proprietor or his staff.

To be effective, any notice intended to disclaim or restrict liability must be prominently displayed in the reception area of, or in the main entrance to, the premises.

CODE OF CONDUCT

All establishments appearing in this guide have agreed to observe the following Code of Conduct:
1. To ensure high standards of courtesy and cleanliness; catering and service appropriate to the type of establishment.
2. To describe fairly to all visitors and prospective visitors the amenities, facilities and services provided by the establishment, whether by advertisement, brochure, word of mouth or any other means. To allow visitors to see accommodation, if requested, before booking.
3. To make clear to visitors exactly what is included in all prices quoted for accommodation, meals and ▶

▶ refreshments, including service charges, taxes and other surcharges. Details of charges, if any, for heating or for additional services or facilities available should also be made clear. If applicable the establishment should comply with the provisions of the Hotel Industry's Voluntary Code of Booking Practice.

4. To adhere to, and not to exceed, prices current at time of occupation for accommodation or other services.

5. To advise visitors at the time of booking, and subsequently of any change, if the accommodation offered is in an unconnected annexe, or similar, or by boarding out, and to indicate the location of such accommodation and any difference in comfort and amenities from accommodation in the main establishment.

6. To give each visitor, on request, details of payments due and a receipt if required.

7. To deal promptly and courteously with all enquiries, requests, reservations, correspondence and complaints from visitors.

8. To allow an English Tourist Board representative reasonable access to the establishment, on request, to confirm that the Tourist Board Code of Conduct is being observed.

COMMENTS AND COMPLAINTS

Accommodation establishments have a number of legal and statutory responsibilities to their customers in areas such as the provision of information on prices, the provision of adequate fire precautions and the safeguarding of valuables. Like other businesses, they must also meet the requirements of the Trade Descriptions Acts 1968 and 1972 when describing and offering accommodation and facilities. All establishments appearing in this guide have declared that they fulfil all applicable statutory obligations.

The establishment descriptions and other details appearing in this guide have been provided by proprietors and they have paid for their entries to appear.

The English Tourist Board cannot guarantee the accuracy of the information in this guide and accepts no responsibility for any error or misrepresentation. All liability for loss, disappointment, negligence or other damage caused by reliance on the information contained in this guide, or in the event of bankruptcy or liquidation or cessation of trade of any company, individual or firm mentioned, is hereby excluded. Prices and other details should always be carefully checked at the time of booking.

We naturally hope that you will not have any cause for complaint but problems do inevitably occur from time to time. If you are dissatisfied, make your complaint to the management at the time of the incident. This gives the management an opportunity to take action at once to investigate and to put things right without delay. The longer a complaint is left the more difficult it is to deal with effectively.

In certain circumstances the English Tourist Board may look into complaints. However, the Board has no statutory control over establishments or their methods of operation and cannot become involved in legal or contractual matters.

We find it very helpful to receive comments about establishments in 'Where to Stay' and suggestions on how to improve the guide. We would like to hear from you. Our address is on page 584.

FOR HIS HOLIDAY READING GEORGE IS TAKING THE TRADE DESCRIPTIONS ACT

About the guide entries

I SAID IT WAS REMOTE, DIDN'T I?

make this as clear as possible and provide a basis for comparison we have adopted a standardised approach.

For example, we show:

1. Bed and breakfast. Price for overnight accommodation with breakfast — single room and double room.

The double room price is for two people. If a double room is occupied by one person there is normally a reduction in the quoted tariff, but some establishments may charge the full rate.

2. Half board. Price for room, breakfast and evening meal, per person per day and per person per week.

A number of establishments do not quote or offer an inclusive room and breakfast rate in their published tariff. In such cases the minimum charge for breakfast has been added to the room charge to arrive at a combined price.

Some establishments provide a continental breakfast only for the room and breakfast tariff and make an extra charge if a full English breakfast is ordered. Establishments which provide a continental breakfast only are indicated by the symbol CB.

IM SURE THEY'LL UNDERSTAND IF YOU ASK FOR THE CONTINENTAL BREAKFAST IN ENGLISH

PHRASE BOOK

There is a statutory requirement for establishments which have at least four bedrooms, or eight beds, to display overnight accommodation charges in the reception area or at the entrance. This is to ensure that prospective guests can obtain ▶

LOCATIONS

Establishments are listed in this guide under the name of the place where they are situated or, in the case of isolated spots in the countryside, under the nearest village or town. City, town and village names are listed alphabetically within each regional section together with the county name. For smaller places an indication of their location is also given. For example '5m N. Anytown' means 5 miles North of Anytown.

Map references are given against each colour name. These refer to the colour maps, starting on page 561. The first figure is the map number; the letter and figure which follow indicate the grid reference on the map. Some entries were included just before the guide went to press and therefore may not appear on the maps.

ADDRESSES

The county names are not normally repeated in the entries for each establishment but you should ensure that you use the full postal address and postcode when writing.

TELEPHONE NUMBERS

The telephone number, exchange name (where this differs from the name of the town under which the establishment is listed) and STD code (in brackets) are given immediately below the establishment address in the listings pages of this guide. The STD code applies to calls made anywhere in the UK except for local calls.

PRICES

The prices appearing in this publication will serve as a general guide, but we strongly advise you to check them at the time of booking. This information was supplied to us by proprietors in the summer of 1991 and changes may have occurred since the guide went to press. Prices are shown in pounds sterling and include Value Added Tax if applicable.

Some, but not all, establishments include a service charge in their standard tariff so this should also be checked at the time of booking.

There are many different ways of quoting prices for accommodation and in order to

▶ adequate information about prices before taking up accommodation. When you arrive it is in your own interests to check prices and what they include.

A reduced price is often quoted for children, especially when sharing a room with their parents. Some establishments, however, charge the full price when a child occupies a room which might otherwise have been let at the full rate to an adult.

The upper age limit for reductions for children may vary according to the establishment and should therefore be checked at the time of booking.

Prices often vary according to the time of year and may be substantially lower outside the peak holiday weeks. Many hotels and other establishments offer special 'package' rates (for example, fully inclusive weekend rates) particularly in the autumn, winter and spring.

Further details of bargain packages can be obtained from the establishments themselves or from the English Tourist Board and England's Regional Tourist Boards. Your local travel agent may also have information about these packages and can help you make bookings.

BATHROOMS

Each accommodation entry shows the number of private bathrooms available, the number of public bathrooms and the number of private showers. The term 'private bathroom' means a bath and/or shower plus a WC ensuite with the bedroom; 'private shower' means a shower ensuite with the bedroom but no WC.

Public bathrooms are normally equipped with a bath and sometimes also a shower attachment. Some establishments, however, have showers only. If the availability of a bath is an important factor, this should be checked before booking.

MEALS

The starting time for the serving of evening meals and the last order time (l.o.) is shown in each entry. At some smaller establishments you may be asked at breakfast time or midday whether you will require a meal that evening. So, the last order time for an evening meal could be, say, 9.30am or 1.30pm. The abbreviation 24hr. means that a meal of some kind is always available.

Although the accommodation prices shown in each entry are for bed and breakfast and/or half board, many establishments offer luncheon facilities and this is indicated by the words 'Lunch available'.

OPENING PERIODS

Except where an opening period is shown (e.g. Open March – October), the establishment should be open throughout the year.

SYMBOLS

Information about many of the services and facilities available at establishments is given at the end of each entry in the form of symbols. The key to these symbols can be found inside the back cover flap. You may find it helpful to fold out the flap when referring to the entries.

ALCOHOLIC DRINKS

Alcoholic drinks are available at all types of accommodation listed in this guide unless the symbol ⓤⓛ appears. However, the licence to serve drinks may be restricted, for example to diners only, so you may wish to check this when enquiring about accommodation.

SMOKING

Many establishments offer facilities for non-smokers, ranging from no-smoking bedrooms and lounges to a no-smoking area of the restaurant/dining room. Some establishments prefer not to accommodate smokers and in such cases the establishment description makes this clear.

DOGS

Many establishments will accept guests with dogs but we advise you to confirm this at the time of booking when you should also enquire about any extra charges and any restrictions on movement within the establishment. Some establishments will not accept dogs in any circumstances and these are marked with the symbol ✖.

Visitors from overseas should not bring pets of any kind into Britain unless they are prepared for the animals to go into lengthy quarantine. Owing to the continuing threat of rabies, penalties for ignoring the regulations are extremely severe.

CREDIT CARDS

Indicated immediately above the line of symbols at the end of each accommodation entry are credit/charge cards that are accepted by the establishment. However, you are advised to check this at the time you make a booking if you intend to pay by this method. The abbreviations are:

Access – Access/Eurocard/ Mastercard
Visa – Visa/Barclaycard/ Trustcard
C.Bl – Carte Blanche
Diners – Diners
Amex – American Express

CONFERENCES AND GROUPS

Establishments which can cater for conferences of 10 persons or more have been marked with the symbol ♟. Rates are often negotiable and the price may be affected by a number of factors such as the time of year, number of people and any special requirements stipulated by the organiser.

Holidays for physically disabled people

Many of the accommodation establishments listed in this guide show the ♿ symbol to indicate that they may be suitable for physically disabled guests.

The minimum requirements laid down by the Tourist Board for such establishments are as follows:

At least one entrance must have no steps or be equipped with a ramp whose gradient does not exceed 1:12. The entrance door must have a clear opening width of at least 80cm.

Where provided, the following accommodation must either be on the ground floor or accessible by lift (NB where access to a specified area involves step(s), a ramp with a gradient of no more than 1:12 must be provided): – Reception; Restaurant/Dining Room; Lounge; Bar; TV Lounge; public WC; and at least one bedroom served either by a private bath/ shower and WC ensuite or by public facilities on the same floor.

A lift giving access to any of the above must have at least 80cm clear gate opening width; the lift must be at least 140cm deep and 110cm wide.

Doors giving access to any of the above areas (including bath/WC facilities) must have at least 75cm clear opening width.

In bedrooms, private or public bathrooms and WCs used by disabled people, there must be a clear space immediately adjacent to the bed, bath or WC with a width of at least 75cm. In bedrooms, there must be a turning space of 120cm × 120cm (in bathrooms and WCs:

110cm × 70cm) clear of the line of the doorswing.

Please check the suitability of the establishment at the time of booking and ensure that the management is fully aware of any special requirements.

ACCESSIBLE

When travelling, look for the new 'Tourism for All' – Accessible stickers. They indicate those places that have been visited by Holiday Care Service and which are likely to meet the needs of wheelchair users.

Holiday Care Service is a national charity providing information and support on holidays for people who are elderly or disabled, with low income or who are lone

parents. It can be contacted at: 2 Old Bank Chambers, Station Road, Horley, Surrey RH6 9HW. Tel: (0293) 774535 Fax: (0293) 784647 Minicom: (0293) 776943 24-hour Answering Service.

NATIONAL SCHEME FOR BRITAIN

The Tourist Boards are intending to introduce a national scheme that will identify those places to stay that meet the needs of three categories of wheelchair users:

► **Category 1:**
Accessible to an independent wheelchair user.

► **Category 2:**
Accessible to a wheelchair user with assistance.

► **Category 3:**
Accessible to a wheelchair user able to walk a few paces and up 3 steps.

At the time of going to press details have yet to be finalised but it is likely that new symbols, indicating the three categories of accessibility, will begin to be displayed on premises during 1992 and appear in the 1993 editions of our 'Where to Stay' guides.

National Crown Scheme

The national Crown scheme was introduced in 1986 and is now the largest accommodation rating scheme in Britain, with over 17,000 hotels, motels, guesthouses, inns, B&Bs and farmhouses offering you the reassurance of a national Crown rating.

Wherever you see the Crown sign displayed you can be confident that the facilities and services at the establishment have been inspected and found to meet National Tourist Board minimum standards for the rating. And every rated establishment is re-inspected each year to check the facilities and services.

To help you find accommodation that offers even higher standards than those required for a simple Crown rating, the Tourist Boards have introduced three levels of quality grading, using the terms APPROVED, COMMENDED and HIGHLY COMMENDED.

Establishments that apply for a quality grading are subject to a more rigorous inspection, which takes into account such important aspects as warmth of welcome, atmosphere and efficiency of service as well as the quality of furnishings, fitments and equipment.

The quality gradings apply to all the Crown bands. So, for example, a Listed or One Crown B&B or guesthouse could be Highly Commended if its facilities and services, although relatively limited in range, are provided to an exceptionally high quality standard.

The national Crown ratings that appear in the accommodation entries in this 'Where to Stay' guide were correct at the time of going to press.

Entries which do not bear a Crown rating may have applied for inspection but had not been inspected at the time of going to press.

What follows is a guide to the facilities and services you will find at accommodation establishments with national Crown ratings from Listed to Five Crown. Further information is available from the English Tourist Board (address on page 584), from one of the 12 Regional Tourist Boards or from any Tourist Information Centre.

LISTED

Establishments displaying the LISTED sign meet the National Tourist Board minimum standards. They fulfil their statutory obligations, including the requirements of the Fire Precautions Act 1971 (if applicable), the Price Display Orders 1977 and 1979 (if applicable) and have public liability insurance.

Buildings, fixtures, furnishings, fittings and decor are maintained in sound and clean condition. In addition, you can expect:

Bedrooms to have...
- ▶ Internal lock, bolt or equivalent on bedroom door.
- ▶ Reasonable free space for movement and for easy access to beds, doors and drawers.
- ▶ Minimum recommended floor areas, excluding private bath or shower

areas, of: 60 sq.ft. single bedrooms, 90 sq.ft. double bedrooms, 110 sq.ft. twin bedded rooms. Family rooms: 30 sq.ft. plus 60 sq.ft. for each double bed plus 40 sq.ft. for each adult single bed plus 20 sq.ft. for each cot.
▶ Minimum bed sizes (except for children's beds) of 6′ × 2′6″ for single beds and 6′ × 4′ for double beds.
▶ Mattresses in sound condition and either spring interior, foam or similar quality.
▶ Clean bedding and in sufficient quantity, with bed linen changed for every new guest and at least once a week. Bed linen other than nylon available on request.
▶ Beds made daily and the bedrooms cleaned daily.
▶ Clean hand towel for every new guest and bath towels available on request. Fresh soap provided for each new letting.
▶ Adequate ventilation, at least one external window and opaque curtains or blinds on all windows.
▶ Minimum lighting levels of 100 watts in single bedrooms and 150 watts in double bedrooms. Switches for room light by the door and bed or alternatively a separate bedside light. All bulbs, unless decorative, covered or with shades.
▶ Carpet or bedside rugs or mats.
▶ A wardrobe or clothes hanging space (with four hangers per person).
▶ Dressing table or equivalent with mirror adjacent, bedside table or equivalent, adequate drawer space, one chair or equivalent, waste paper container, ashtray (where smoking permitted), one drinking tumbler per guest, a 13 amp socket or adaptor, electric razor point (or adaptor available).
▶ Adequate heating available at no extra charge.

Bathrooms to have...
▶ Bath or shower, wash handbasin and mirror (if any bedrooms without a wash handbasin), soap.
▶ Adequate heating and ventilation.
▶ Hot water available at all reasonable times.
▶ No extra charge for baths or showers.
▶ There will be at least one bathroom available at all reasonable times for every 10 resident guests (or one for every 15 guests if wash handbasin in every bedroom).
LISTED establishments also provide at least one WC, adequately ventilated, for every 10 resident guests and there will be a sanitary disposal bin and toilet paper in each WC.
    Additional benefits of a LISTED establishment include...
▶ Provision of cooked breakfast (unless continental breakfast only advertised) in a dining/breakfast room (unless meals are served only in bedrooms).
▶ Public areas well lit for safety and comfort, adequately heated (according to season) and cleaned daily.
▶ Furthermore, you will be informed, when booking, if access to the establishment is restricted during the day.

ONE CROWN

Accommodation displaying the single CROWN will provide all the minimum standard facilities and services of a Listed establishment plus several additional comforts and conveniences.
    For instance, you can expect both single and double beds in a ONE CROWN establishment to be larger — and nylon bed linen will not be used.
    There will be a washbasin, with hot and cold running

water at all reasonable times, either in the bedroom or in a private bathroom and there will be a mirror with light adjacent to or above the washbasin.
    You will enjoy the comfort of at least one chair or equivalent per guest, with a minimum of two in family rooms. You will have access to your bedroom at all times.
    At least one bathroom, with bath or shower, will be provided for every 10 resident guests — and at least one bathroom for the sole use of guests. There will be at least one WC for every 8 resident guests. Access to the bathrooms and WCs from bedrooms will not be through such areas as reception and lounge.
    You will find a lounge or foyer area with an adequate number of easy chairs and you will have access at all reasonable times. A cooked breakfast will be available.
    There will be a reception facility (or bell to call for attention), you will have use of a telephone and tourist information will be available.

TWO CROWN

With every additional Crown, you can expect additional facilities.
    For instance, TWO CROWN establishments meet all the requirements of Listed and One Crown ratings and offer several additional comforts and services.
    The dining/breakfast room will be separate from the lounge unless meals are served only in the bedrooms. You can enjoy early morning tea/coffee in your bedroom — served on request unless there are beverage-making facilities in the bedroom. You may order a hot beverage in the evening, again available on request unless there are facilities in the bedroom.
    There may be alarm clocks in bedrooms or else you can ▶

▶ request an early morning call. If there is no TV in your room, you can be sure there will be a colour TV in the lounge, always provided that the establishment is in a signal reception area.

Double beds will have bedside lights or a single bedhead light, will have access from both sides and there will be a bedside table or equivalent for each person. Single beds will have a bedside or bedhead light. You will also find an electric razor point near a mirror and light.

You can request assistance with your luggage when you check in and check out.

THREE CROWN

Are you particular about having your own bath or shower with WC ensuite? The chances are you can arrange this at a THREE CROWN establishment because at least 33% of the bedrooms will have these facilities.

You will find an easy chair in your bedroom (there will be an additional chair if you have booked a twin or double room). There will also be a full-length mirror, luggage stand and fixed heating with automatic and individual control.

Tea/coffee-making facilities will be provided in the bedrooms on request (unless 24-hour room service is offered). Resident guests can also obtain a hot evening meal while, for early departures in the morning, a continental breakfast will be provided on request.

Should you need any assistance, you can talk to the staff or proprietor who will be available throughout the day.

You can also request a hairdryer, iron and ironing board and you will find shoe-cleaning facilities provided. A public telephone will be available unless there are direct-dial telephones in all the bedrooms.

You will have access to the establishment and to your bedroom at all times.

FOUR CROWN

If Three Crown facilities are not enough, why not book into a FOUR CROWN establishment and enjoy even more?

For instance, 75% of all bedrooms will have a private bath or shower and WC ensuite. You can relax in your room and watch colour TV or listen to the radio − and your room telephone will enable you to make external calls.

If dining in, you will be able to invite non-resident guests (providing they are pre-booked) and you will be offered a selection of wines and a choice of dishes for each course; last orders will be 20.30hrs or later.

You'll be able to call room service for continental breakfast, drinks and light snacks between 07.00 and 23.00hrs while lounge service of drinks and snacks will be available until midnight.

If the establishment has four or more floors, a passenger lift will ease the upward journey.

Writing tables will be available if comparable facilities are not available in bedrooms and additional facilities like laundry service, message-taking, newspapers and toiletries will be available on request.

You will find reception staff on duty during the day and evening while the proprietor and/or staff will be on site and on call 24 hours a day.

FIVE CROWN

If you are checking into an establishment displaying FIVE CROWNS, you can expect the most of everything. Every facility of establishments up to the Four Crown rating will be there to enjoy − plus a few more.

Every bedroom, for instance, will have private bath, fixed shower attachment and WC ensuite. A bathrobe and/or bathsheet and toiletries will be on hand.

There will be a writing table or equivalent with seat and the direct-dial telephone will be capable of being used at both writing table and bed.

If your clothes need pressing, you can summon a valet and also avail yourself of the 24-hour return service for laundry and dry cleaning (except at weekends).

Room service of hot meals is assured from breakfast time to midnight while hot and cold snacks and drinks will be available at any time. If you

decide to take breakfast in the restaurant, you can be served at the table and will be offered a choice of hot and cold dishes.

You will benefit from an all-night lounge service, there will be a night porter on duty and a shoe-cleaning service.

The restaurant will be open for breakfast, lunch and dinner and it will offer a wide selection of wines and dishes, with last orders for dinner at 21.00hrs or later.

Additionally, according to the nature of the establishment, you may find extra features, such as a cocktail bar, shop, hairdresser's, leisure facilities, business services, etc.

Key to symbols

Information about many of the services and facilities at establishments listed in this guide is given in the form of symbols. The key to these symbols is inside the back cover flap. You may find it helpful to keep the flap open when referring to the entry listings.

Central Reservations Offices

Some of the accommodation establishments in this guide are members of hotel groups or consortia which maintain a central reservations office. These entries are identified with the symbol **CR**, and the name of the group or consortium, appearing after the establishment's address and telephone number.

Bookings or enquiries can be made direct to the establishment or to the central reservations office.

BEST WESTERN
Best Western Hotels, Vine House, 143 London Road, Kingston upon Thames, Surrey KT2 6NA
☎ 081-541 0033 Telex 8814912 Fax 081-546 1638

CALOTELS
Calotels, 3rd Floor Suite, Hampshire House, Bourne Avenue, Bournemouth, Dorset BH2 6DP
☎ Bournemouth (0202) 297888 Telex 41363 CALTEL-G Fax (0202) 299182

CONSORT
Consort Hotels, Ryedale Building, Piccadilly, York, YO1 1PN
☎ York (0904) 643151 Telex 57515 Fax (0904) 611320

FORESTDALE
Forestdale Hotels, Central Sales Office, Lyndhurst Park Hotel, High Street, Lyndhurst, Hampshire SO43 7NL
☎ 0800 378640 (calls are free) Fax (0703) 283019

FRIENDLY
Friendly Hotels, Ryedale Building, Piccadilly, York, YO1 1PN
☎ 0800 591910 (calls are free) Telex 57515 (Attn Friendly) Fax (0904) 611320 (Attn Friendly)

HILTON
Hilton UK, P.O. Box 137, Millbuck House, Clarendon Road, Watford, Hertfordshire WD1 1DN
☎ 071-734 6000 Telex 897618 Fax (0923) 815594

HOLIDAY INN
Holiday Inn Worldwide Reservation, 10 – 12 New College Parade, Finchley Road, London NW3 5EP
☎ 071-722 7755 Telex 27574 Fax 071-722 5483

INTER
Inter Hotels, 2 Cromwell Park, Chipping Norton, Oxfordshire OX7 5SR
☎ (0608) 642211 Telex 83604 Fax (0608) 642264

LANSBURY
Lansbury Hotels, Whitbread House, Park Street West, Luton, Bedfordshire LU1 3BG
☎ Luton (0582) 400158 Telex 826259 Fax (0582) 400024

MINOTELS
Minotels, 5 King's Road, Cleveleys, Lancashire FY5 1BY
☎ Blackpool (0253) 866266 Telex 67596 MARCON-G Fax (0253) 866251

NOVOTEL
Resinter Reservations, Novotel Hotel, 1 Shortlands, London W6 8DR
☎ 071-724 1000 Telex 24361 Fax 081-748 9116

PARK HOTELS
Park Hotels, 26 – 33 Queens Gardens, Hyde Park, London W2 3BD
☎ 071-224 8888 Telex 24442 Fax 071-724 5820

PRINCIPAL
Principal Hotels, Principal House, 11 Ripon Road, Harrogate, N. Yorkshire HG1 2JA
☎ 0800 454454 (calls are free) Telex 57643 PRINHG Fax (0423) 500086

QUEENS MOAT HOUSES
Queens Moat Houses, 9 – 17 Eastern Road, Romford, Essex RM1 3NG
☎ 0800 289330 (calls are free) Telex 929751 Fax (0708) 761033

RANK
Rank Hotels, 1 Thameside Centre, Kew Bridge Road, Brentford, Middlesex TW8 0HF
☎ 081-569 7120 Telex 267270 Fax 081-569 7109

RESORT
Resort Hotels, Resort House, Edward Street, Brighton, E. Sussex BN1 2HW
☎ 0345 313213 (calls charged at local rate) Telex 877247 Fax (0273) 606675

SMALL LUXURY HOTELS
Small Luxury Hotels, 21 Blades Court, Deodar Road, London SW15 2NU
☎ 0800 282124 (calls are free) Telex 269264 Fax 081-877 9477

STAKIS
Stakis Hotels, West Mains Road, East Kilbride, Glasgow G74 1PQ
☎ East Kilbride (035 52) 49235 Telex 778704 Fax (035 52) 45305

SWALLOW
Swallow Hotels, P.O. Box 8, Seaburn Terrace, Seaburn, Sunderland, SR6 8BB
☎ 091-529 4666 Telex 53168 Fax 091-529 5062

Booking coupons

✂

▶ Please complete this coupon and mail it direct to the establishment in which you are interested. Do not send it to the English Tourist Board. Remember to enclose a stamped addressed envelope (or international reply coupon).

▶ Tick as appropriate and complete the reverse side if you are interested in making a booking.

▶ ☐ **Please send me a brochure or further information, and details of prices charged.**

▶ ☐ **Please advise me, as soon as possible, if accommodation is available as detailed overleaf.**

My name is: _____ (BLOCK CAPITALS)

Address: _____

_____

_____

Telephone number: _____ Date: _____

**WHERE TO STAY 1992
HOTELS & GUESTHOUSES**

English Tourist Board

✂

▶ Please complete this coupon and mail it direct to the establishment in which you are interested. Do not send it to the English Tourist Board. Remember to enclose a stamped addressed envelope (or international reply coupon).

▶ Tick as appropriate and complete the reverse side if you are interested in making a booking.

▶ ☐ **Please send me a brochure or further information, and details of prices charged.**

▶ ☐ **Please advise me, as soon as possible, if accommodation is available as detailed overleaf.**

My name is: _____ (BLOCK CAPITALS)

Address: _____

_____

_____

Telephone number: _____ Date: _____

**WHERE TO STAY 1992
HOTELS & GUESTHOUSES**

English Tourist Board

Booking coupons

✂ ─ ─ ─ ─ ─ ─ ─ ─ ─ ─

▶ **Please complete this side if you are interested in making a booking.**

I am interested in booking accommodation for:

_____ adults and _____ children (ages: _____)

<small>(Please give the number of people and the ages of any children)</small>

From (date of arrival): _____ To (date of departure): _____

or alternatively from: _____ to: _____

Accommodation required: _____

_____

_____

Meals required: _____

Other/special requirements: _____

▶ **Please enclose a stamped addressed envelope (or international reply coupon).**
▶ **Please read the information on pages 530 − 534 before confirming any booking.**

✂ ─ ─ ─ ─ ─ ─ ─ ─ ─ ─

▶ **Please complete this side if you are interested in making a booking.**

I am interested in booking accommodation for:

_____ adults and _____ children (ages: _____)

<small>(Please give the number of people and the ages of any children)</small>

From (date of arrival): _____ To (date of departure): _____

or alternatively from: _____ to: _____

Accommodation required: _____

_____

_____

Meals required: _____

Other/special requirements: _____

▶ **Please enclose a stamped addressed envelope (or international reply coupon).**
▶ **Please read the information on pages 530 − 534 before confirming any booking.**

Booking coupons

▶ Please complete this coupon and mail it direct to the establishment in which you are interested. Do not send it to the English Tourist Board. Remember to enclose a stamped addressed envelope (or international reply coupon).

▶ Tick as appropriate and complete the reverse side if you are interested in making a booking.

▶ ☐ **Please send me a brochure or further information, and details of prices charged.**

▶ ☐ **Please advise me, as soon as possible, if accommodation is available as detailed overleaf.**

My name is: _____ (BLOCK CAPITALS)

Address: _____

_____

_____

Telephone number: _____ Date: _____

WHERE TO STAY 1992
HOTELS & GUESTHOUSES

English Tourist Board

✂

▶ Please complete this coupon and mail it direct to the establishment in which you are interested. Do not send it to the English Tourist Board. Remember to enclose a stamped addressed envelope (or international reply coupon).

▶ Tick as appropriate and complete the reverse side if you are interested in making a booking.

▶ ☐ **Please send me a brochure or further information, and details of prices charged.**

▶ ☐ **Please advise me, as soon as possible, if accommodation is available as detailed overleaf.**

My name is: _____ (BLOCK CAPITALS)

Address: _____

_____

_____

Telephone number: _____ Date: _____

WHERE TO STAY 1992
HOTELS & GUESTHOUSES

English Tourist Board

Booking coupons

✂ —

▶ **Please complete this side if you are interested in making a booking.**

I am interested in booking accommodation for:

      adults and   children (ages:)

(Please give the number of people and the ages of any children)

From (date of arrival):   To (date of departure):

or alternatively from: to:

Accommodation required:

\
\

Meals required:

Other/special requirements:

▶ **Please enclose a stamped addressed envelope (or international reply coupon).**
▶ **Please read the information on pages 530 – 534 before confirming any booking.**

✂ —

▶ **Please complete this side if you are interested in making a booking.**

I am interested in booking accommodation for:

      adults and   children (ages:)

(Please give the number of people and the ages of any children)

From (date of arrival):   To (date of departure):

or alternatively from: to:

Accommodation required:

\
\

Meals required:

Other/special requirements:

▶ **Please enclose a stamped addressed envelope (or international reply coupon).**
▶ **Please read the information on pages 530 – 534 before confirming any booking.**

Booking coupons

✂

▶ Please complete this coupon and mail it direct to the establishment in which you are interested. Do not send it to the English Tourist Board. Remember to enclose a stamped addressed envelope (or international reply coupon).

▶ Tick as appropriate and complete the reverse side if you are interested in making a booking.

▶ ☐ **Please send me a brochure or further information, and details of prices charged.**

▶ ☐ **Please advise me, as soon as possible, if accommodation is available as detailed overleaf.**

My name is: _____ (BLOCK CAPITALS)

Address: _____

_____

_____

Telephone number: _____ Date: _____

WHERE TO STAY 1992
HOTELS & GUESTHOUSES

English Tourist Board

✂

▶ Please complete this coupon and mail it direct to the establishment in which you are interested. Do not send it to the English Tourist Board. Remember to enclose a stamped addressed envelope (or international reply coupon).

▶ Tick as appropriate and complete the reverse side if you are interested in making a booking.

▶ ☐ **Please send me a brochure or further information, and details of prices charged.**

▶ ☐ **Please advise me, as soon as possible, if accommodation is available as detailed overleaf.**

My name is: _____ (BLOCK CAPITALS)

Address: _____

_____

_____

Telephone number: _____ Date: _____

WHERE TO STAY 1992
HOTELS & GUESTHOUSES

English Tourist Board

Booking coupons

✂

▶ **Please complete this side if you are interested in making a booking.**

I am interested in booking accommodation for:

_____ adults and _____ children (ages: _____)

<small>(Please give the number of people and the ages of any children)</small>

From (date of arrival): _____   To (date of departure): _____

or alternatively from: _____   to: _____

Accommodation required: _____

_____

_____

Meals required: _____

Other/special requirements: _____

▶ **Please enclose a stamped addressed envelope (or international reply coupon).**
▶ **Please read the information on pages 530 – 534 before confirming any booking.**

✂

▶ **Please complete this side if you are interested in making a booking.**

I am interested in booking accommodation for:

_____ adults and _____ children (ages: _____)

<small>(Please give the number of people and the ages of any children)</small>

From (date of arrival): _____   To (date of departure): _____

or alternatively from: _____   to: _____

Accommodation required: _____

_____

_____

Meals required: _____

Other/special requirements: _____

▶ **Please enclose a stamped addressed envelope (or international reply coupon).**
▶ **Please read the information on pages 530 – 534 before confirming any booking.**

Booking coupons

▶ Please complete this coupon and mail it direct to the establishment in which you are interested. Do not send it to the English Tourist Board. Remember to enclose a stamped addressed envelope (or international reply coupon).

▶ Tick as appropriate and complete the reverse side if you are interested in making a booking.

▶ ☐ **Please send me a brochure or further information, and details of prices charged.**

▶ ☐ **Please advise me, as soon as possible, if accommodation is available as detailed overleaf.**

My name is: (BLOCK CAPITALS)

Address: _____

_____

_____

Telephone number: _____ Date: _____

**WHERE TO STAY 1992
HOTELS & GUESTHOUSES**

English Tourist Board

▶ Please complete this coupon and mail it direct to the establishment in which you are interested. Do not send it to the English Tourist Board. Remember to enclose a stamped addressed envelope (or international reply coupon).

▶ Tick as appropriate and complete the reverse side if you are interested in making a booking.

▶ ☐ **Please send me a brochure or further information, and details of prices charged.**

▶ ☐ **Please advise me, as soon as possible, if accommodation is available as detailed overleaf.**

My name is: (BLOCK CAPITALS)

Address: _____

_____

_____

Telephone number: _____ Date: _____

**WHERE TO STAY 1992
HOTELS & GUESTHOUSES**

English Tourist Board

Booking coupons

✂

▶ **Please complete this side if you are interested in making a booking.**

I am interested in booking accommodation for:

      adults and   children (ages:)

(Please give the number of people and the ages of any children)

From (date of arrival):   To (date of departure):

or alternatively from: to:

Accommodation required:

Meals required:

Other/special requirements:

▶ **Please enclose a stamped addressed envelope (or international reply coupon).**
▶ **Please read the information on pages 530 − 534 before confirming any booking.**

✂

▶ **Please complete this side if you are interested in making a booking.**

I am interested in booking accommodation for:

      adults and   children (ages:)

(Please give the number of people and the ages of any children)

From (date of arrival):   To (date of departure):

or alternatively from: to:

Accommodation required:

Meals required:

Other/special requirements:

▶ **Please enclose a stamped addressed envelope (or international reply coupon).**
▶ **Please read the information on pages 530 − 534 before confirming any booking.**

Advertisement coupons

▶ Please complete this coupon and mail it direct to the advertiser from whom you would like to receive further information. Do not send it to the English Tourist Board.

To (advertiser's name): _____

Please send me a brochure or further information on the following, as advertised by you in the English Tourist Board's **WHERE TO STAY 1992** Guide:

_____

_____

My name and address are on the reverse.

▶ Please complete this coupon and mail it direct to the advertiser from whom you would like to receive further information. Do not send it to the English Tourist Board.

To (advertiser's name): _____

Please send me a brochure or further information on the following, as advertised by you in the English Tourist Board's **WHERE TO STAY 1992** Guide:

_____

_____

My name and address are on the reverse.

▶ Please complete this coupon and mail it direct to the advertiser from whom you would like to receive further information. Do not send it to the English Tourist Board.

To (advertiser's name): _____

Please send me a brochure or further information on the following, as advertised by you in the English Tourist Board's **WHERE TO STAY 1992** Guide:

_____

_____

My name and address are on the reverse.

Advertisement coupons

✂ ---

From (name): _____ (BLOCK CAPITALS)

Address: _____

_____

_____

_____ Postcode: _____

Telephone Exchange: _____ STD Code: _____ No: _____

Date: _____

✂ ---

From (name): _____ (BLOCK CAPITALS)

Address: _____

_____

_____

_____ Postcode: _____

Telephone Exchange: _____ STD Code: _____ No: _____

Date: _____

✂ ---

From (name): _____ (BLOCK CAPITALS)

Address: _____

_____

_____

_____ Postcode: _____

Telephone Exchange: _____ STD Code: _____ No: _____

Date: _____

Advertisement coupons

Advertisement coupons

✂ --

From (name): _____ (BLOCK CAPITALS)

Address: _____

_____

_____

Postcode: _____

Telephone Exchange: _____ STD Code: _____ No: _____

Date: _____

✂ --

From (name): _____ (BLOCK CAPITALS)

Address: _____

_____

_____

Postcode: _____

Telephone Exchange: _____ STD Code: _____ No: _____

Date: _____

✂ --

From (name): _____ (BLOCK CAPITALS)

Address: _____

_____

_____

Postcode: _____

Telephone Exchange: _____ STD Code: _____ No: _____

Date: _____

Advertisement coupons

✂

► Please complete this coupon and mail it direct to the advertiser from whom you would like to receive further information. Do not send it to the English Tourist Board.

To (advertiser's name): _____

Please send me a brochure or further information on the following, as advertised by you in the English Tourist Board's **WHERE TO STAY 1992** Guide:

_____

_____

My name and address are on the reverse.

✂

► Please complete this coupon and mail it direct to the advertiser from whom you would like to receive further information. Do not send it to the English Tourist Board.

To (advertiser's name): _____

Please send me a brochure or further information on the following, as advertised by you in the English Tourist Board's **WHERE TO STAY 1992** Guide:

_____

_____

My name and address are on the reverse.

✂

► Please complete this coupon and mail it direct to the advertiser from whom you would like to receive further information. Do not send it to the English Tourist Board.

To (advertiser's name): _____

Please send me a brochure or further information on the following, as advertised by you in the English Tourist Board's **WHERE TO STAY 1992** Guide:

_____

_____

My name and address are on the reverse.

Advertisement coupons

✂ -

From (name): _____ (BLOCK CAPITALS)

Address: _____

_____

_____

Postcode: _____

Telephone Exchange: _____ STD Code: _____ No: _____

Date: _____

✂ -

From (name): _____ (BLOCK CAPITALS)

Address: _____

_____

_____

Postcode: _____

Telephone Exchange: _____ STD Code: _____ No: _____

Date: _____

✂ -

From (name): _____ (BLOCK CAPITALS)

Address: _____

_____

_____

Postcode: _____

Telephone Exchange: _____ STD Code: _____ No: _____

Date: _____

MILEAGE CHART

The distances between towns on the mileage chart are given to the nearest mile, and are measured along the normal AA recommended routes. It should be noted that AA recommended routes do not necessarily follow the shortest distances between places but are based on the quickest travelling time, making maximum use of motorways or dual-carriageway roads.

Map locations: Inverness, Aberdeen, Fort William, Perth, Glasgow, Edinburgh, Stranraer, Carlisle, Newcastle upon Tyne, Middlesbrough, Kendal, York, Preston, Leeds, Hull, Liverpool, Manchester, Lincoln, Holyhead, Sheffield, Stoke on Trent, Nottingham, Norwich, Birmingham, Aberystwyth, Northampton, Cambridge, Carmarthen, Gloucester, Colchester, Oxford, LONDON, Cardiff, Bristol, Guildford, Maidstone, Dover, Barnstaple, Taunton, Southampton, Brighton, Exeter, Dorchester, Plymouth, Penzance.

The towns are numbered as follows:

1 Aberdeen · 2 Aberystwyth · 3 Barnstaple · 4 Birmingham · 5 Brighton · 6 Bristol · 7 Cambridge · 8 Cardiff · 9 Carlisle · 10 Carmarthen · 11 Colchester · 12 Dorchester · 13 Dover · 14 Edinburgh · 15 Exeter · 16 Fort William · 17 Glasgow · 18 Gloucester · 19 Guildford · 20 Holyhead · 21 Hull · 22 Inverness · 23 Kendal · 24 Leeds · 25 Lincoln · 26 Liverpool · 27 Maidstone · 28 Manchester · 29 Middlesbrough · 30 Newcastle · 31 Norwich · 32 Nottingham · 33 Oxford · 34 Penzance · 35 Perth · 36 Plymouth · 37 Sheffield · 38 Southampton · 39 Stranraer · 40 Taunton · 41 York · 42 LONDON

No. Place	1	2	3	4	5	6	7	8	9	10	11	12	13	14	15	16	17	18	19	20	21	22	23	24	25	26	27	28	29	30	31	32	33	34	35	36	37	38	39	40	41
2 Aberystwyth	468																																								
3 Barnstaple	605	222																																							
4 Birmingham	431	122	178																																						
5 Brighton	611	290	206	185																																					
6 Bristol	515	132	100	88	170																																				
7 Cambridge	473	218	269	101	121	172																																			
8 Cardiff	534	116	138	108	205	47	207																																		
9 Carlisle	232	235	372	198	378	282	260	302																																	
10 Carmarthen	521	48	200	170	268	110	270	68	288																																
11 Colchester	526	288	292	171	112	195	47	230	313	293																															
12 Dorchester	597	214	95	170	118	62	182	129	364	192	208																														
13 Dover	631	323	278	206	78	210	122	245	398	308	113	206																													
14 Edinburgh	126	335	472	298	478	381	343	401	99	388	396	463	466																												
15 Exeter	588	206	40	162	172	84	252	121	355	183	275	54	250	455																											
16 Fort William	159	445	581	407	587	491	470	511	209	498	522	573	608	133	565																										
17 Glasgow	146	334	471	297	477	381	359	401	98	387	412	463	497	46	454	102																									
18 Gloucester	480	110	126	54	157	36	124	66	247	128	172	118	198	347	110	457	346																								
19 Guildford	568	226	176	143	45	106	92	141	335	204	103	98	101	435	148	545	434	102																							
20 Holyhead	462	106	327	153	333	237	249	205	229	154	319	319	353	328	310	438	328	202	290																						
21 Hull	360	228	322	135	283	231	144	251	173	314	196	313	266	231	305	382	272	197	241	222																					
22 Inverness	106	493	630	456	636	540	518	560	257	546	571	622	656	157	613	65	172	505	593	487	431																				
23 Kendal	284	190	327	153	333	237	253	257	51	243	318	319	353	151	310	260	150	202	290	184	165	309																			
24 Leeds	336	174	310	115	264	220	149	240	123	226	201	302	271	206	294	333	222	185	221	167	61	381	72																		
25 Lincoln	397	198	272	94	216	182	95	202	185	264	148	265	218	268	256	394	284	147	175	205	48	442	177	73																	
26 Liverpool	358	111	275	101	281	185	217	205	125	159	267	267	302	225	259	334	224	150	238	104	130	383	80	75	142																
27 Maidstone	593	285	234	168	50	166	85	201	361	264	76	162	45	428	206	570	460	154	57	316	228	619	316	233	180	264															
28 Manchester	352	131	263	89	269	172	161	192	119	184	214	254	289	219	246	329	218	138	226	124	99	377	74	44	85	35	251														
29 Middlesbrough	277	244	359	172	321	268	200	288	96	296	253	350	323	147	342	281	195	234	278	237	87	308	85	63	125	145	285	114													
30 Newcastle	237	273	388	202	350	298	230	318	57	338	353	108	372	241	152	264	308	267	142	268	100	93	154	175	315	144	39														
31 Norwich	498	280	330	163	168	233	63	269	286	331	58	244	170	369	313	495	385	187	160	306	152	543	278	174	104	243	132	186	226	255											
32 Nottingham	403	160	236	54	196	146	87	165	190	228	140	228	217	273	219	400	289	111	153	176	93	448	163	73	35	109	179	70	130	160	119										
33 Oxford	497	159	171	62	110	74	101	109	264	172	124	117	130	364	154	473	363	50	67	219	189	522	219	169	124	167	106	155	226	143	102										
34 Penzance	701	318	111	275	287	196	365	234	468	296	388	168	364	568	112	678	567	222	262	423	418	726	423	406	368	371	320	359	455	485	426	332	267								
35 Perth	87	381	518	344	524	428	406	447	145	434	459	510	544	42	501	103	59	393	481	375	276	114	197	269	330	271	506	265	193	153	431	336	410	614							
36 Plymouth	630	247	59	203	215	125	293	162	397	225	317	97	293	496	45	606	496	151	191	352	346	655	352	335	297	300	249	287	383	413	355	261	196	78	543						
37 Sheffield	377	163	272	86	234	182	124	202	164	264	176	264	256	373	263	148	192	157	67	422	122	35	48	77	217	37	104	134	149	44	140	369	310	297							
38 Southampton	575	226	143	129	64	78	132	141	343	203	158	55	156	442	109	552	442	101	48	298	256	600	297	237	215	246	112	233	294	323	194	169	67	224	488	152	207				
39 Stranraer	240	343	479	305	485	389	368	409	107	395	420	471	506	132	463	188	85	354	443	336	280	265	158	231	292	232	468	227	203	161	393	298	371	575	153	504	271	450			
40 Taunton	556	173	51	130	157	51	220	89	323	151	243	46	229	423	34	533	422	77	127	278	273	581	278	261	223	226	185	214	310	340	281	187	127	147	469	75	224	94	430		
41 York	323	201	316	129	277	225	157	245	117	253	210	307	280	193	299	327	216	191	235	194	37	375	90	24	81	102	242	71	50	87	182	87	183	412	263	340	61	250	225	267	
42 LONDON	546	237	217	120	60	120	61	155	313	217	61	130	80	413	200	522	412	105	30	268	218	571	268	199	145	216	38	204	256	285	115	131	57	313	459	241	169	80	420	168	242

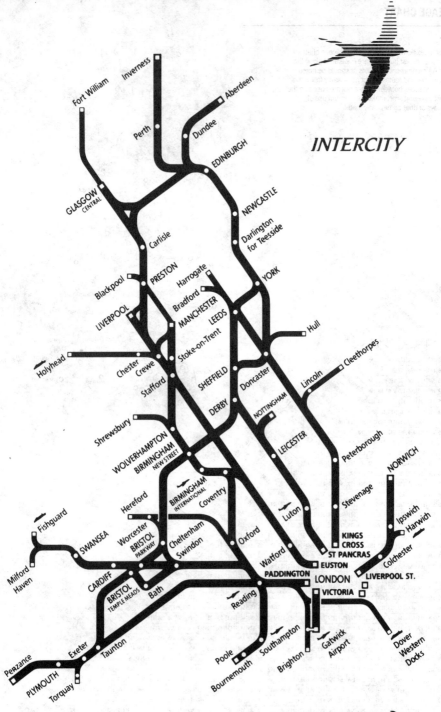

INTERCITY

© British Railways Board 1990/91

TLB/91/0908

Whatever your interest

Make the most of your holiday with these inexpensive guides. Each one is either produced or officially endorsed by the English Tourist Board.

They're authoritative, high-quality publications that bring together the best of England for the holiday visitor. Whether you're looking for exciting things to do, new places to go or simply somewhere to stay, you'll find these easy-to-use handbooks are full of bright ideas and well-informed suggestions.

They cover many different kinds of holidays and activities from all parts of the country – with something to appeal to everyone in the family. Packed with details, addresses and up-to-the-minute information, they make holiday planning almost as much fun as the holiday itself!

ETB HOLIDAY GUIDES – THE FUN WAY
TO PLAN YOUR HOLIDAY

ve've a guide for you!

Vhere to Stay
3est-selling England guides to: *Hotels & Guesthouses; Bed & 3reakfast, Farmhouses, Inns & Hostels; Self-Catering Holiday Homes*. Also in the *Where to Stay* series: *Camping & Caravan Parks in Britain*. With descriptions of towns, comprehensive indexes, maps and features on the English regions.

Stay On A Farm
In association with the Farm Holiday Bureau UK and Charles Letts). Official guide to early 1,000 farms in membership of the Farm Holiday Bureau. All inspected and approved by the national Tourist boards. B&B, half-board, self-catering. Enjoy the countryside from the unique hospitality of a working farm.

The Countryside Directory
(In association with Sphere and The Royal Agricultural Society of England). From farming museums to pick your own fruit and vegetable farms, agricultural shows to afternoon teas — whatever you need to know about countryside activities.

Let's Do It
(In association with Charles Letts). Hundreds of ideas for holidays and breaks in England. Discover new interests or improve existing skills — from action and sport, study courses, special interests, holidays afloat and children's holidays.

Holidays Afloat
Your official guide to boating and watersports around Britain. (In association with

Burlington and the British Marine Industries Federation). Whatever catches your imagination — whether a relaxing cruise or a course in powerboat handling — *Holidays Afloat* contains all the information you need to plan and enjoy your holiday or short break. Details of hundreds of holiday companies and informative features. Fully illustrated, maps, glossaries, etc.

Family Leisure Guides
(In association with Charles Letts). Essential guides for anyone wanting to combine a favourite sport with a weekend break or short holiday for all the family: *Horse Racing; Golf; Birdwatching; Horse Riding*. Fully illustrated with details of leisure attractions around each Course.

Please send me the following publications (please tick):

Where to Stay: Hotels & Guesthouses £9.50 Ref. CM962 ☐

Where to Stay: Bed & Breakfast, Farmhouses, Inns & Hostels £7.99 Ref. CM963 ☐

Where to Stay: Self-Catering Holiday Homes £5.99 Ref. CM964 ☐

Where to Stay: Camping & Caravan Parks in Britain £6.50 Ref. CM965 ☐

Stay On A Farm £6.99 Ref. CM532 ☐

The Countryside Directory £8.50 Ref. CM282 ☐

Let's Do It £4.75 Ref. CM362 ☐

Holidays Afloat £5.99 Ref. CM302 ☐

Golf (Family Leisure Guide) £10.99 Ref. CM333 ☐

Horse Racing (Family Leisure Guide) £10.99 Ref. CM382 ☐

Birdwatching (Family Leisure Guide) £10.99 Ref. CM025 ☐

Horse Riding (Family Leisure Guide) £10.99 Ref. CM143 ☐

This offer is open to readers living in Great Britain including Northern Ireland and remains open until 31st December 1993. All prices include VAT (where applicable) and postage and packing. All publications will normally be despatched within 28 days of receipt of order and remittance unless an item is out of stock in which case a full refund will be given. If more than one item is ordered, they will be despatched in separate packs. If you are not entirely satisfied, please return the item to: English Tourist Board Publications, Dept. D, 24 Grosvenor Gardens, London SW1W 0ET within seven days in the condition in which it was received, with a covering letter and your money will be refunded in full. We cannot be held responsible for returned items lost in transit. All publication prices valid up until December 31st 1992. Thereafter you will be informed of any price increases for 1993 publications.

All prices inclusive of VAT, Postage & Packing. Prices based upon 1992 editions and valid until 31st December 1992. Thereafter 1993 editions will be despatched. You will be advised of any price increases when you place your order.

Name (Mr/Mrs/Ms) _____ Initials _____
(Block capitals please)

Address _____
(Block capitals please)
_____ Postcode: _____

I enclose a crossed cheque/P.O. (not cash). Value £ _____ made payable to the ENGLISH TOURIST BOARD. Please write your name and address on back of cheque and send to Dept. D, English Tourist Board, 24 Grosvenor Gardens, London SW1W 0ET.

I wish to pay by Visa/Access/Mastercard/Eurocard (delete as necessary)

My number is ☐☐☐☐ ☐☐☐☐ ☐☐☐☐ ☐☐☐☐   Expiry date _____

Signature: _____   Date: _____

Please tick this box if you do not wish to receive any further information from ETB or other organisations ☐

Card holders may order direct by telephoning 071-824 8266 (24 hour service)
Please quote reference number

COLOUR MAPS

PLACES WITH ACCOMMODATION *listed in this guide are shown in black on the maps which follow.*

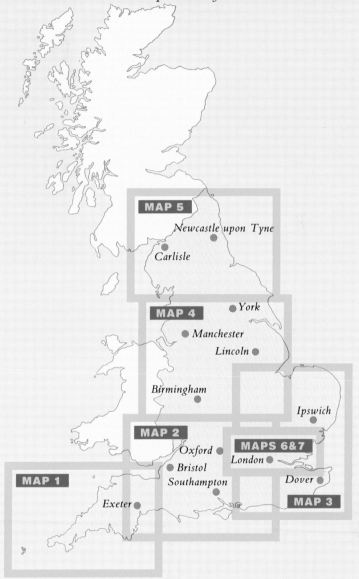

MAP 5

Newcastle upon Tyne

Carlisle

MAP 4

York

Manchester

Lincoln

Birmingham

MAP 2

MAPS 6&7

Oxford

Ipswich

Bristol

London

Southampton

MAP 1

Dover

MAP 3

Exeter

Map 1

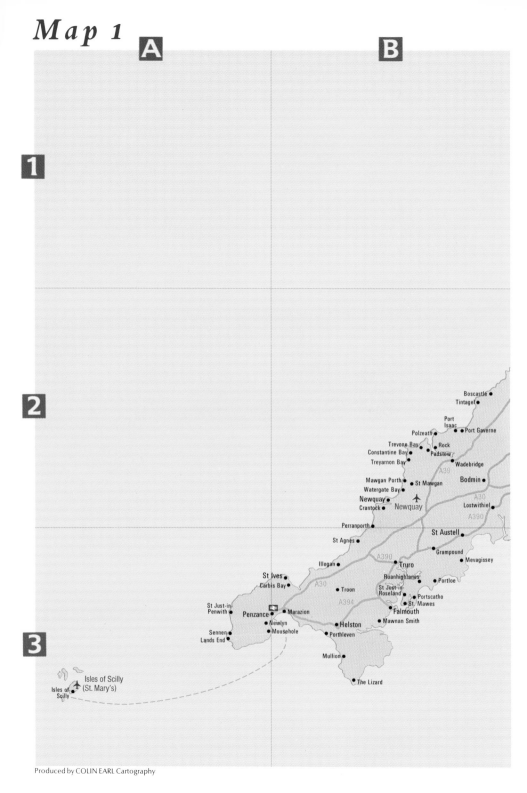

A B

1

2

Boscastle
Tintagel
Port
Isaac
Polzeath ● Port Gaverne
Trevone Bay ● Rock
Constantine Bay ● Padstow
Treyarnon Bay
Wadebridge
A39
Mawgan Porth ● St Mawgan
Bodmin
Watergate Bay
A30
Newquay
Newquay
Lostwithiel
Crantock
A390
Perranporth
St Austell
St Agnes
Grampound
Illogan
Mevagissey
A390
Truro
St Ives
Ruanhighlanes
Portloe
Carbis Bay
A30
Troon
St Just-in-
Roseland
Portscatho
St Just-in-
A394
St. Mawes
Penwith
Penzance ● Marazion
Falmouth
Newlyn
Helston
Mawnan Smith
Sennen
Mousehole
Lands End
Porthleven

3

Mullion

Isles of Scilly
(St. Mary's)
Isles of
Scilly

The Lizard

Produced by COLIN EARL Cartography

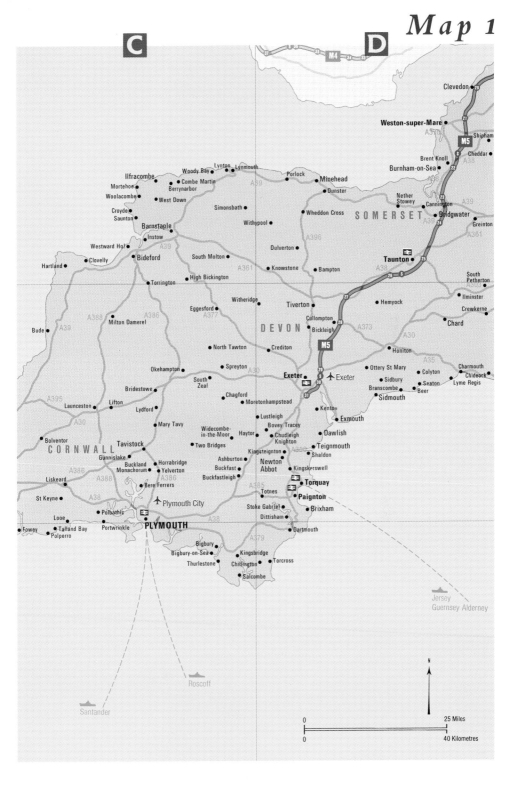

Map 1

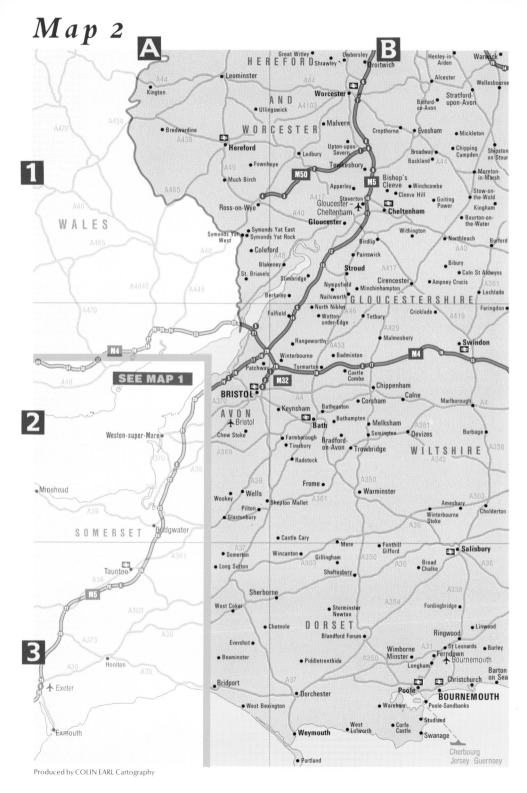

Map 2

A   **B**

Great Witley • Ombersley
HEREFORD   Shrawley   Droitwich   Henley-in-Arden   Warwick

• Leominster   Alcester   • Wellesbourne

AND   Bidford-on-Avon   Stratford-upon-Avon

WORCESTER   A4103   Worcester

• Ullingswick   Cropthorne   Evesham   • Mickleton

WORCESTER   • Malvern   Broadway   Chipping Campden   Shipston on Stour

• Bredwardine   • Hereford   • Ledbury   Upton-upon-Severn   Buckland   A44   Moreton-in-Marsh

A438   • Fownhope   Tewkesbury   Bishop's Cleeve   Winchcombe   Stow-on-the-Wold

M50   Cleeve Hill   Guiting Power   Kingham

• Much Birch   Apperley   Staverton   Cheltenham   • Bourton-on-the-Water

A465   Ross-on-Wye   Gloucester – Cheltenham   Withington   • Northleach   Burford

Gloucester   Birdlip   A40

Symonds Yat East   Painswick   • Bibury   Coln St Aldwyns

Symonds Yat West   Symonds Yat Rock   Stroud   Ampney Crucis   Lechlade

• Coleford   Cirencester   Faringdon

Blakeney   Nympsfield   Minchinhampton   GLOUCESTERSHIRE

St. Briavels   Slimbridge   Nailsworth   Cricklade   A419

Berkeley   North Nibley   Tetbury

Falfield   Wotton-under-Edge   Malmesbury   Swindon

Rangeworthy   A433   Badminton   A4

Winterbourne   Tormarton   Castle Combe   M4

Patchway   Chippenham   Marlborough   A4

M32   A4   Corsham   Calne

BRISTOL   Keynsham   Batheaston

AVON   Bath   Bathampton   Melksham   A361   Burbage

• Bristol   Chew Stoke   Farmborough   Semington   Devizes

Timsbury   Bradford-on-Avon   Trowbridge   WILTSHIRE   A342   A338

• Radstock

Weston-super-Mare   Frome   Warminster

A368   Amesbury   A303   Cholderton

Wookey   Wells   Winterbourne Stoke   A36

Minehead   Pilton   Shepton Mallet   A361

Glastonbury   Castle Cary   Mere   Fonthill Gifford   Salisbury

SOMERSET   Bridgwater   Somerton   Wincanton   Broad Chalke

• Long Sutton   Gillingham   A30   A36

Taunton   Shaftesbury   A338

M5   Sherborne   Fordingbridge

West Coker   Sturminster Newton   Ringwood   • Linwood

Chetnole   DORSET   St Leonards   Burley

Honiton   Evershot   Blandford Forum   Wimborne Minster   Ferndown   Bournemouth   Barton on Sea

Exeter   Beaminster   Piddletrenthide   A350   Longham   Poole-Sandbanks

Bridport   A37   Poole   Christchurch

Dorchester   BOURNEMOUTH

Exmouth   West Bexington   Wareham   Studland

Weymouth   West Lulworth   Corfe Castle   Swanage

Portland   Cherbourg   Jersey Guernsey

WALES

A470   A438   A44   A49   A40   A465   A48   A449   A417   A429   A46   A38   A37   A39   A303   A354   A31

SEE MAP 1

Produced by COLIN EARL Cartography

1   **2**   **3**

Map 2

C D

M40 M1 NORTHAMPTON

Daventry · Weedon · Flore · Castle Ashby · St Neots · Cambridge ✈ Cambridge
Farthingstone · Towcester · Turvey · Bedford · M11
Blakesley · Olney · Newport Pagnell · Tempsford
Oxhill · BEDFORDSHIRE · Royston · Saffron Walden
Banbury · Wolverton · Maulden · Silsoe · A10 · London Stansted
Buckingham · Milton Keynes · Flitwick · Hitchin · ✈ Stansted
Deddington · Chipping Norton · BUCKINGHAMSHIRE · Leighton Buzzard · Stevenage · Bishop's Stortford · HERTFORDSHIRE
Churchill · Weston-on-the-Green · Bicester · Dunstable · LUTON · Puckeridge · Harlow
Shipton-under-Wychwood · Woodstock · Waddesdon · A1(M) · Welwyn · Luton · Hertford · Ware
OXFORDSHIRE · Aylesbury · Tring · Harpenden · Waltham Abbey · Epping
Witney · Eynsham · Horton cum Studley · Thame · Hemel Hempstead · Redbourn · M10 · St Albans · Potters Bar · Loughton
Oxford ⊞ · Princes Risborough · Borehamwood · M25 · Brentwood
Bampton · Clanfield · Milton Common · Saunderton · Chinnor · High Wycombe · Watford · M1 · Elstree
Abingdon · Clifton Hampden · Watlington · Gerrards Cross · GREATER
Wantage · Dorchester on Thames · M40 · A12
BERKSHIRE · Stonor · Marlow · LONDON · London City
Wallingford · Nettlebed · Hurley · Maidenhead · See maps 6 and 7 · ✈ London City
Streatley · Woodcote · Henley-on-Thames · Slough · LONDON
Goring on Thames · Knowl Hill · Holyport · Datchet · London Heathrow · M20
Pangbourne · READING ⊞ · A329(M) · M4 · Windsor · Old Windsor · Staines · M26
Hungerford · Newbury · Wokingham · Bracknell · Ascot · Shepperton · Faversham
Crowthorne · Bagshot · M3 · Weybridge · Walton-on-Thames · Esher · Ewell
Camberley · Woking · Cobham · Epsom · Westerham
Basingstoke · Hook · Farnborough · Leatherhead · M25 · Sevenoaks
Andover · North Waltham · Guildford · Farnham · East Horsley · Godstone · A21
M3 · Dorking · Reigate · Redhill · Penshurst
Middle Wallop · Alton · Bramley · Gatwick Airport · M23 · Tunbridge Wells
Stockbridge · SURREY · Ockley · Horley · Copthorne · Hartfield
Haslemere · Charlwood · London Gatwick · Crawley
Winchester · WEST · Horsham · Crowborough · A26
HAMPSHIRE · Petersfield · Midhurst · Petworth · Ardingly · Mayfield
Ampfield · SUSSEX · Bolney · Cuckfield · Uckfield
Romsey · Eastleigh · Southampton · Droxford · Pulborough · Henfield · A22
Bramshaw · Cadnam · Horndean · Ashington · Amberley · Steyning · Lewes · Hailsham
SOUTHAMPTON ⊞ · Hedge End · A3(M) · Goodwood · Shoreham-by-Sea · Wilmington
Woodlands · Lyndhurst · Salisbury Green · Havant · Arundel · Worthing · BRIGHTON & HOVE · Newhaven
Netley Abbey · M27 · Fareham · Emsworth · Chichester · Rustington · Peacehaven · East Dean
Brockenhurst · Stubbington · Hayling Island · Climping · Littlehampton · Seaford
Sway · PORTSMOUTH & SOUTHSEA · Bognor Regis
Lymington · Cowes · Ryde · Seaview
Milford-on-Sea · Colwell Bay · Freshwater · Alverstone · Sandown
Totland · Freshwater · ISLE OF WIGHT · Sandown Lake · Shanklin
Chale · Bonchurch · Ventnor

Cherbourg Le Havre Caen St. Malo · Dieppe

N

0 · 25 Miles
0 · 40 Kilometres

Jersey Guernsey

Map 3

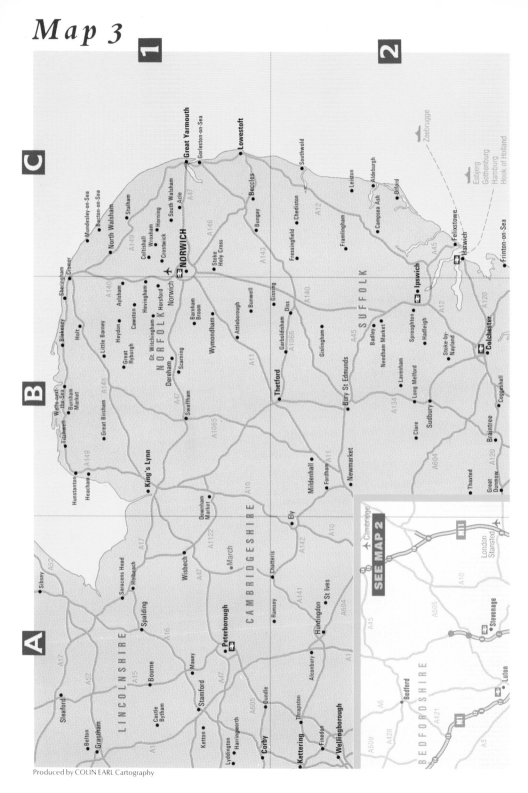

Produced by COLIN EARL Cartography

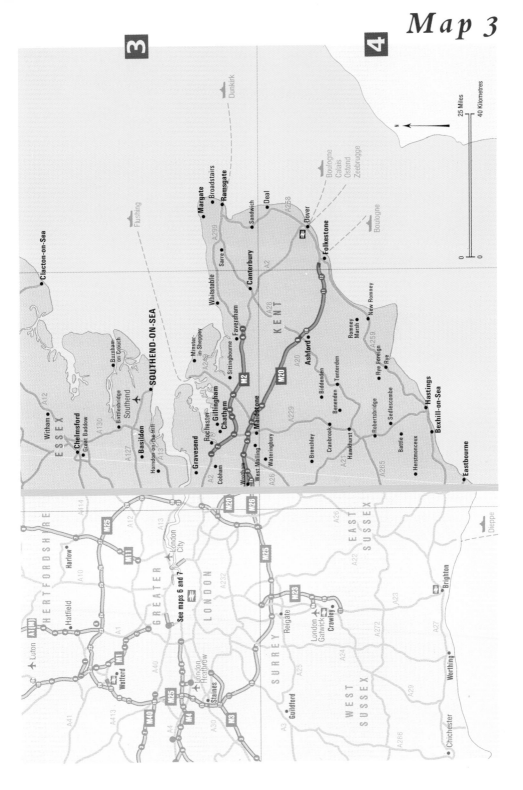

Map 3

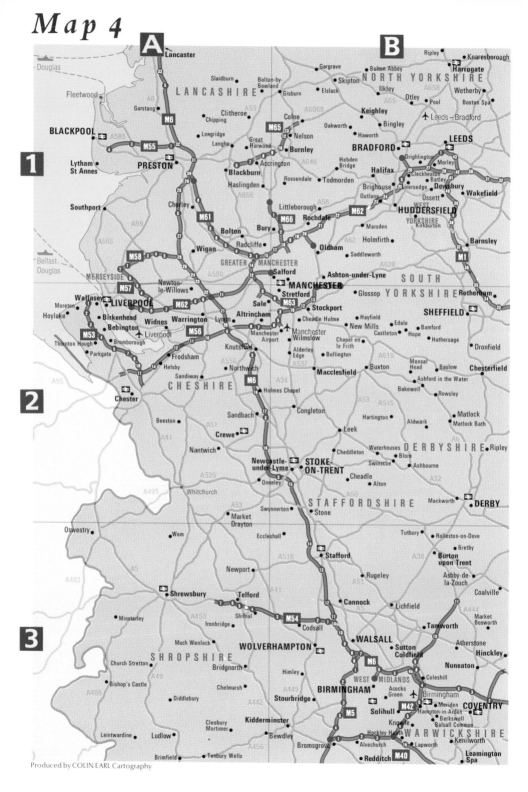

Map 4

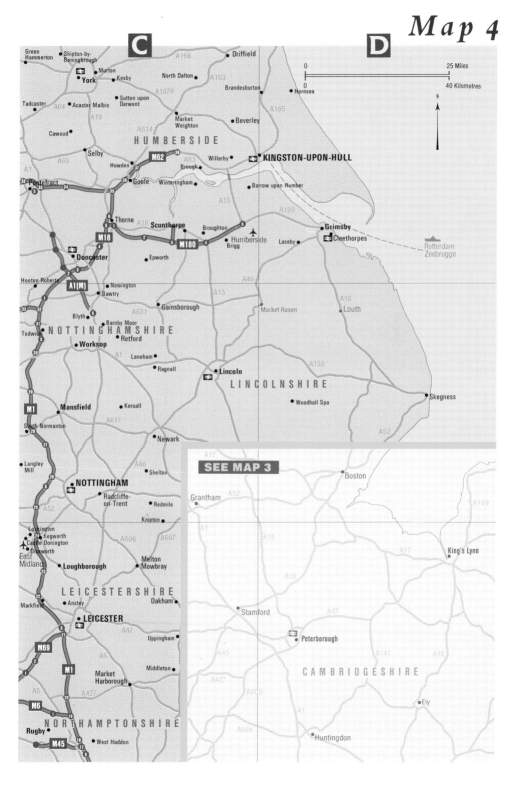

Map 4

Map 5

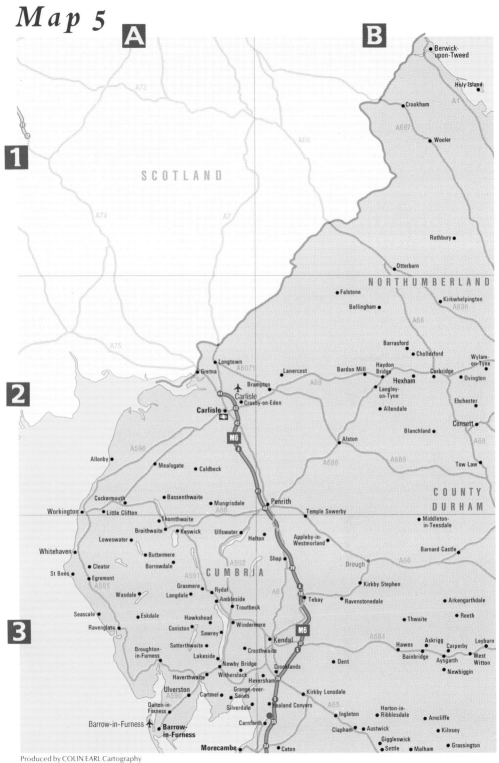

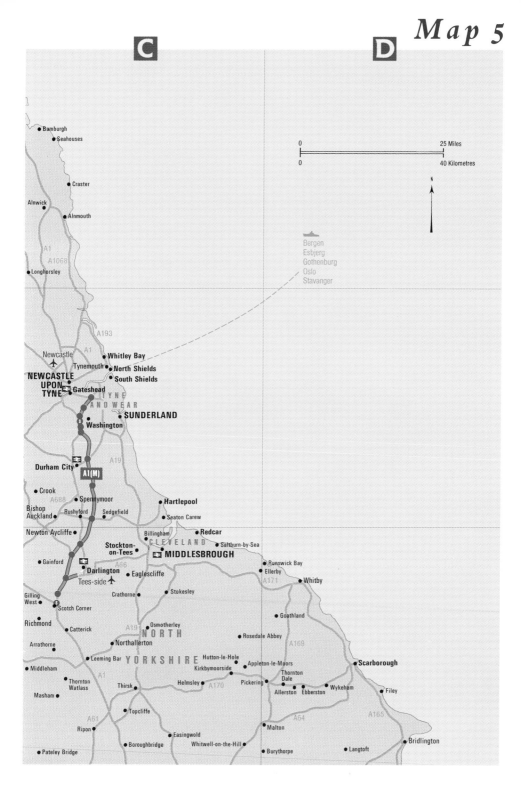

Map 5

C D

0   25 Miles
0   40 Kilometres

N

Bergen
Esbjerg
Gothenburg
Oslo
Stavanger

• Bamburgh
• Seahouses
• Craster
Alnwick •
• Alnmouth
A1
A1068
• Longhorsley

A193
A1
Newcastle ✈ • Whitley Bay
Tynemouth • • North Shields
NEWCASTLE • South Shields
UPON
TYNE • Gateshead
TYNE
AND WEAR
• SUNDERLAND
• Washington

Durham City • ⊞
A1(M) A19
• Crook
A688 • Spennymoor
Bishop Rushyford • • Sedgefield
Auckland • Hartlepool
Newton Aycliffe • • Seaton Carew
• Gainford Billingham • • Redcar
Stockton- CLEVELAND • Saltburn-by-Sea
on-Tees
⊞ ⊟ MIDDLESBROUGH
• Darlington Eaglescliffe • • Runswick Bay
Tees-side ✈ A66 Ellerby •
Gilling Crathorne • • Stokesley A171 • Whitby
West •
Scotch Corner • • Goathland
Richmond • • Catterick
Arrathorne • A19 Osmotherley • • Rosedale Abbey
NORTH A169
• Middleham Northallerton •
• Leeming Bar YORKSHIRE Hutton-le-Hole •
• Scarborough
• Thornton Kirkbymoorside • Appleton-le-Moors •
Watlass Thornton
Masham • Thirsk • Helmsley • Dale
A1 Pickering • • Wykeham • Filey
A170 Allerston • Ebberston •
A61
• Topcliffe
Ripon • A64 A165
• Malton • Bridlington
• Pateley Bridge Easingwold • • Langtoft
Boroughbridge • Whitwell-on-the-Hill • • Burythorpe

Map 6

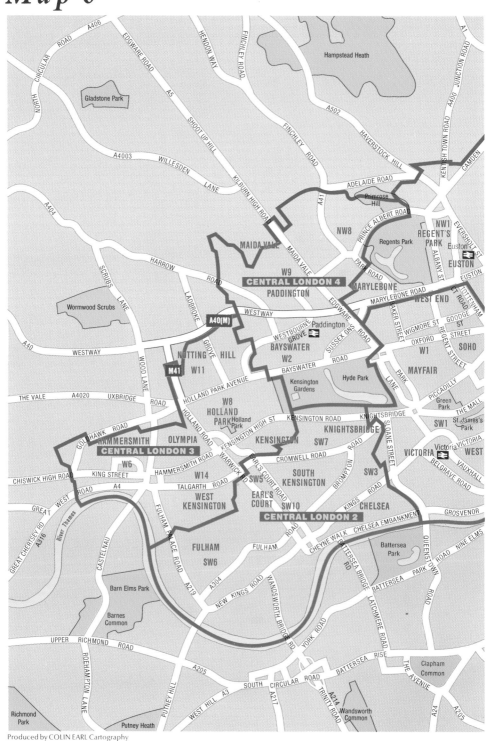

Map 6

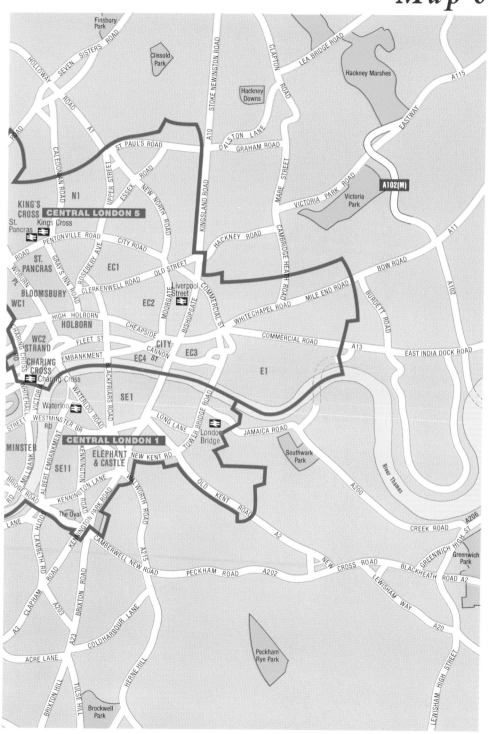

Map 7

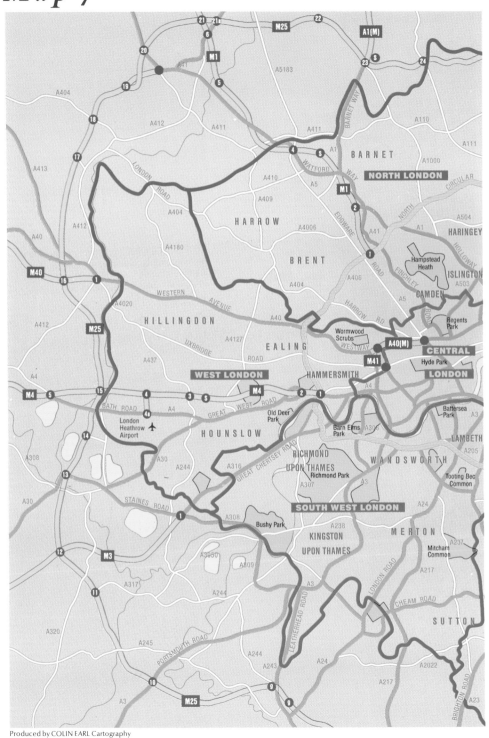

Map 7

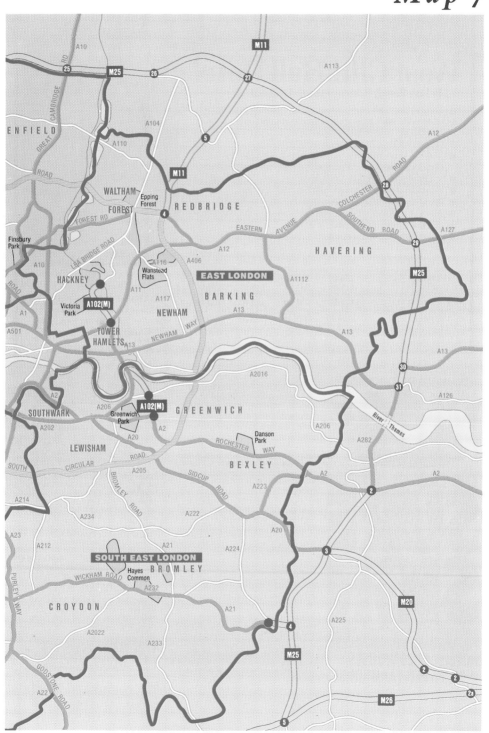

THE CROWN IS YOUR SURE SIGN
OF WHERE TO STAY
HOTELS, GUESTHOUSES, INNS, B&Bs & FARMHOUSES

Throughout Britain, the tourist boards now inspect over 17,000 hotels, guesthouses, inns, B&Bs and farmhouses, every year, to help you find the ones that suit you best.

THE CLASSIFICATIONS: 'Listed', and then ONE to FIVE CROWN, tell you the range of facilities and services you can expect. The more Crowns, the wider the range.

THE GRADES: APPROVED, COMMENDED and HIGHLY COMMENDED, where they appear, indicate the quality standard provided. If no grade is shown, you can still expect a high standard of cleanliness.

Every classified place to stay has a Fire Certificate, where this is required under the Fire Precautions Act, and all carry Public Liability Insurance.

'Listed': Clean and comfortable accommodation, but the range of facilities and services may be limited.

ONE CROWN: Accommodation with additional facilities, including washbasins in all bedrooms, a lounge and use of a phone.

TWO CROWN: A wider range of facilities and services, including morning tea and calls, bedside lights, colour TV in lounge or bedrooms, assistance with luggage.

THREE CROWN: At least one-third of the bedrooms with ensuite WC and bath or shower, plus easy chair, full length mirror. Shoe cleaning facilities and hairdryers available. Hot evening meals available.

FOUR CROWN: At least three-quarters of the bedrooms with ensuite WC and bath/shower plus colour TV, radio and phone, 24-hour access and lounge service until midnight. Last orders for meals 8.30 pm or later.

FIVE CROWN: All bedrooms having WC, bath and shower ensuite, plus a wide range of facilities and services, including room service, all-night lounge service and laundry service. Restaurant open for breakfast, lunch and dinner.

Every Crown classified place to stay is likely to provide some of the facilities and services of a higher classification. More information available from any Tourist Information Centre.

We've checked them out before you check in!

Town index

THE FOLLOWING cities, towns and villages all have accommodation listed in this guide. If the place where you wish to stay is not shown, the colour maps (starting on page 561) will help you to find somewhere suitable in the same area.

Check the maps

The place you wish to visit may not have accommodation entirely suited to your needs, but there could be somewhere ideal quite close by. Check the colour maps towards the end of this guide to identify nearby towns and villages with accommodation listed in the guide, and then use the town index to find page numbers.

Use a coupon

When enquiring about accommodation you may find it helpful to use the booking enquiry coupons which can be found towards the end of the guide. These should be cut out and mailed direct to the establishments in which you are interested. Do remember to include your name and address.

Follow the Country Code

🍀 *Enjoy the countryside and respect its life and work*
🍀 *Guard against all risk of fire* 🍀 *Fasten all gates*
🍀 *Keep your dogs under close control* 🍀 *Keep to*
public paths across farmland 🍀 *Use gates and stiles*
to cross fences, hedges and walls 🍀 *Leave livestock,*
crops and machinery alone 🍀 *Take your litter home*
🍀 *Help to keep all water clean* 🍀 *Protect wildlife,*
plants and trees 🍀 *Take special care on country roads*
🍀 *Make no unnecessary noise*

I'M LOOKING FOR STATUS SYMBOLS

WHERE TO STAY

Key to symbols

Information about many of the services
and facilities at establishments listed in
this guide is given in the form of
symbols. The key to these symbols is
inside the back cover flap. You may find
it helpful to keep the flap open when
referring to the entry listings.

Index to advertisers

YOU CAN OBTAIN *further information from any display advertiser in this guide by completing an advertisement enquiry coupon. You will find these coupons on pages 549 – 553.*

Where to Stay in England

Published by: English Tourist Board, Thames Tower, Black's Road, Hammersmith, London W6 9EL. *Internal Reference Number:* ETB/15/92 AS/1329/45M/91

Managing Editor: Sally Marshall *Compilation, Design & Production:* Guide Associates, Croydon *Colour Photography (covers and pages 1 − 5 and 10 − 12):* Glyn Williams, Syndication International *Illustrations:* Susie Louis *Cartoons:* Hector Breeze *Cartography:* Colin Earl Cartography, Alton *Typesetting:* Spottiswoode Ballantyne Printers Ltd, Colchester, and Guide Associates, Croydon *Printing & Binding:* Bemrose Security & Promotional Printing, Derby *Advertisement Sales:* Madison Bell Ltd, 3 St. Peter's Street, Islington Green, London N1 8JD. Telephone: 071-359 7737.

The information contained in this guide has been published in good faith on the basis of information submitted to the English Tourist Board by the proprietors of the premises listed, who have paid for their entries to appear. The English Tourist Board cannot guarantee the accuracy of the information in this guide and accepts no responsibility for any error or misrepresentation. All liability for loss, disappointment, negligence or other damage caused by reliance on the information contained in this guide, or in the event of bankruptcy, or liquidation, or cessation of trade of any company, individual or firm mentioned, is hereby excluded.

The English Tourist Board
The Board is a statutory body created by the Development of Tourism Act 1969 to develop and market England's tourism. Its main objectives are to provide a welcome for people visiting England; to encourage people living in England to take their holidays there; and to encourage the provision and improvement of tourist amenities and facilities in England. The Board has a statutory duty to advise the Government on tourism matters relating to England and, with Government approval and support, administers the national classification & grading schemes for tourist accommodation in England.